D1370719

Department of Economic
and Social Affairs
Statistics Division

Département des affaires
économiques et sociales
Division de statistique

Statistical Yearbook

Fifty-first issue

Data available as of March 2007

Annuaire statistique

Cinquante et unième édition

Données disponibles en mars 2007

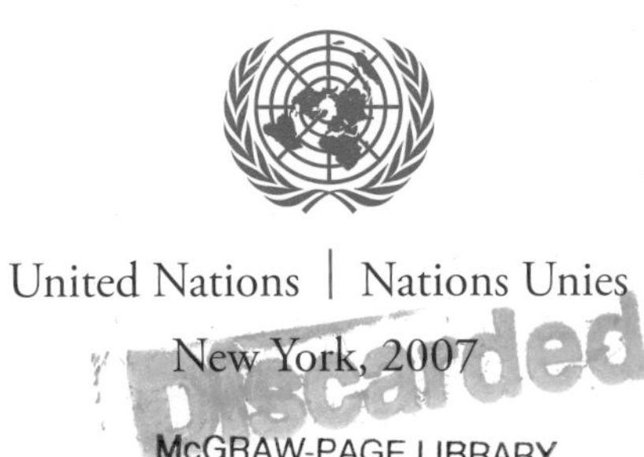

United Nations | Nations Unies

New York, 2007

Discarded
McGRAW-PAGE LIBRARY
RANDOLPH-MACON COLLEGE
ASHLAND, VIRGINIA 23005

Department of Economic and Social Affairs

The Department of Economic and Social Affairs of the United Nations Secretariat is a vital interface between global policies in the economic, social and environmental spheres and national action. The Department works in three main interlinked areas: (i) it compiles, generates and analyses a wide range of economic, social and environmental data and information on which States Members of the United Nations draw to review common problems and to take stock of policy options; (ii) it facilitates the negotiations of Member States in many intergovernmental bodies on joint courses of action to address ongoing or emerging global challenges; and (iii) it advises interested Governments on the ways and means of translating policy frameworks developed in United Nations conferences and summits into programmes at the country level and, through technical assistance, helps build national capacities.

Note

The designations employed and the presentation of the material in this publication do not imply the expression of any opinion whatsoever on the part of the Secretariat of the United Nations concerning the legal status of any country, city or area, or of its authorities, or concerning the delimitation of its frontiers or boundaries.

In general, statistics contained in the present publication are those available to the United Nations Secretariat up to March 2007 and refer to 2006 or earlier. They therefore reflect the country nomenclature currently in use.

The term "country" as used in the text of this publication also refers, as appropriate, to territories or areas.

The designations "developed" and "developing" which appear in some tables are intended for statistical convenience and do not necessarily express a judgement about the stage reached by a particular country or area in the development process.

Symbols of United Nations documents are composed of capital letters combined with figures.

ST/ESA/STAT/SER.S/27

UNITED NATIONS PUBLICATION
Sales No. E/F.07.XVII.1

ISBN 978-92-1-061228-9
ISSN 0082-8459

Copyright © United Nations 2007
All rights reserved

Département des affaires économiques et sociales

Le Département des affaires économiques et sociales du Secrétariat de l'Organisation des Nations Unies assure le lien essentiel entre les politiques adoptées au plan international dans les domaines économique, social et écologique et les mesures prises au plan national. Il mène ses activités dans trois grands domaines interdépendants : i) il compile, produit et analyse une grande variété de données et d'informations économiques, sociales et écologiques dont les États Membres de l'ONU tirent parti pour examiner les problèmes communs et faire le point sur les possibilités d'action; ii) il facilite les négociations que les États Membres mènent dans un grand nombre d'organes intergouvernementaux sur les moyens d'action à employer conjointement pour faire face aux problèmes mondiaux existants ou naissants; et iii) il aide les gouvernements intéressés à traduire les orientations politiques établies lors des conférences et sommets de l'ONU en programmes nationaux et contribue à renforcer les capacités des pays en leur apportant une assistance technique.

Note

Les appellations employées dans la présente publication et la présentation des données qui y figurent n'impliquent, de la part du Secrétariat de l'Organisation des Nations Unies, aucune prise de position quant au statut juridique des pays, territoires, villes ou zones, ou de leurs autorités, ni quant au tracé de leurs frontières ou limites.

En règle générale, les statistiques contenues dans la présente publication sont celles dont disposait le Secrétariat de l'Organisation des Nations Unies jusqu'à mars 2007 et portent sur la période finissant en 2006. Elles reflètent donc la nomenclature des pays en vigueur à l'époque.

Le terme « pays », tel qu'il est utilisé ci-après, peut également désigner des territoires ou des zones.

Les appellations « développées » et « en développement » qui figurent dans certains tableaux sont employées à des fins exclusivement statistiques et n'expriment pas nécessairement un jugement quant au niveau de développement atteint par tel pays ou telle région.

Les cotes des documents de l'Organisation des Nations Unies se composent de lettres majuscules et de chiffres.

ST/ESA/STAT/SER.S/27

PUBLICATION DES NATIONS UNIES
Numéro de vente : E/F.07.XVII.1

ISBN 978-92-1-061228-9
ISSN 0082-8459

Copyright © Nations Unies 2007
Tous droits réservés

Preface

This is the fifty-first issue of the United Nations *Statistical Yearbook*, prepared by the Statistics Division of the Department of Economic and Social Affairs. Ever since the compilation of data for the *Statistical Yearbook* series was initiated in 1948, it has consistently provided a wide range of internationally available statistics on social and economic conditions and activities at the national, regional and world levels.

The tables include series covering from one to ten years, depending upon data availability and space constraints. The ten-year tables generally cover the years 1995 to 2004 or 1996 to 2005. For the most part, the statistics presented are those which were available to the Statistics Division as of March 2007.

The *Yearbook* tables are based on data which have been compiled by the Statistics Division mainly from official national and international sources as these are more authoritative and comprehensive, more generally available as time series and more comparable among countries than other sources. These sources include the United Nations Statistics Division in the fields of national accounts, industry, energy, transport and international trade, the United Nations Statistics Division and Population Division in the field of demographic statistics, and over 20 offices of the United Nations system and international organizations in other specialized fields. In some cases, official sources have been supplemented by other sources and estimates, where these have been subjected to professional scrutiny and debate and are consistent with other independent sources.

The United Nations agencies and other international, national and specialized organizations which furnished data are listed under "Statistical sources and references" at the end of the *Yearbook*. Acknowledgement is gratefully made for their generous and valuable cooperation in continually providing data.

The 69 tables of the *Yearbook* are organized in four parts. The first part presents key world and regional aggregates and totals. In the other three parts, the subject matter is generally presented by countries or areas, with world and regional aggregates shown in some cases only. Parts two, three and four cover, respectively, population and social topics, national economic activity and international economic relations. Each chapter ends with brief technical notes on statistical sources and methods for the tables it includes.

The three annexes contain information on country and area nomenclature and the conversion coefficients and factors used in the various tables, and list those tables which were added to or omitted from the last issue of the *Yearbook*.

* * *

The *Statistical Yearbook* is prepared by the Statistical Dissemination Section, Statistical Services Branch of the Statistics Division, Department of Economic and Social

Préface

La présente édition de *l'Annuaire statistique* des Nations Unies est la cinquante et unième, préparée par la Division de statistique du Département des affaires économiques et sociales. Depuis son instauration en 1948 comme outil de compilation des données statistiques internationales, l'*Annuaire statistique* s'efforce de constamment diffuser un large éventail de statistiques disponibles sur les activités et conditions économiques et sociales, aux niveaux national, régional et mondial.

Les tableaux présentent des séries qui couvrent d'un à dix ans, en fonction de la disponibilité des données et des contraintes d'espace. Les tableaux décennaux couvrent généralement les années 1995 à 2004 ou 1996 à 2005. La majeure partie des statistiques présentées ici sont celles dont disposait la Division de statistique en mars 2007.

Les tableaux de l'*Annuaire* sont construits essentiellement à partir des données compilées par la Division de statistique et provenant de sources officielles, nationales et internationales; c'est en effet la meilleure source si l'on veut des données fiables, complètes et comparables, et si l'on a besoin de séries chronologiques. Ces sources sont: la Division de statistique du Secrétariat de l'Organisation des Nations Unies pour ce qui concerne la comptabilité nationale, l' industrie, l'énergie, les transports et le commerce extérieur, la Division de statistique et la Division de la population du Secrétariat de l'Organisation des Nations Unies pour les statistiques démographiques; et plus de 20 bureaux du système des Nations Unies et d'organisations internationales pour les autres domaines spécialisés. Dans quelques cas, les données officielles sont complétées par des informations et des estimations provenant d'autres sources qui ont été examinées par des spécialistes et confirmées par des sources indépendantes.

Les institutions spécialisées des Nations Unies et les autres organisations internationales, nationales et spécialisées qui ont fourni des données sont énumérées dans la section "Sources statistiques et références" figurant à la fin de l'ouvrage. Les auteurs de l'*Annuaire statistique* les remercient de leur précieuse et généreuse collaboration.

Les 69 tableaux de l'*Annuaire* sont regroupés en quatre parties. La première partie présente les principaux agrégats et totaux aux niveaux mondial et régional. Dans les trios parties suivantes, les thèmes sont généralement présentés par pays ou régions. Les agrégats mondiaux ou régionaux ne son indiqués que dans certains cas seulement. Les trois parties autres sont consacrées à la population et aux questions sociales (deuxième partie), à l'activité économique nationale (troisième partie) et aux relations économiques internationales (quatrième partie). Chaque chapitre termine par une brève note technique sur les sources et les méthodes statistiques utilisées pour les tableaux présentés.

Affairs of the United Nations Secretariat. The programme manager is Mary Jane Holupka and the chief editor is Jacob Assa. They are assisted by Anna Marie Scherning and David Carter. Maria Jakosalem and Thataw Batun also contributed to the production of this *Yearbook*. Bogdan Dragovic developed the software.

Comments on the present *Yearbook* and its future evolution are welcome. They may be sent via e-mail to statistics@un.org or to the United Nations Statistics Division, Statistical Dissemination Section, New York, NY 10017, USA.

Les trois annexes donnent des renseignements sur la nomenclature des pays et des zones, ainsi que sur les coefficients et facteurs de conversion employés dans les différents tableaux. Une liste des tableaux ajoutés et supprimés depuis la dernière édition de l'*Annuaire* y est également disponible.

* * *

L'*Annuaire statistique* est préparé par la Section de la diffusion des statistiques, Service des statistiques de services de la Division de statistique, Département des affaires économiques et sociales du Secrétariat de l'Organisation des Nations Unies. La responsable du programme est Mary Jane Holupka, et le rédacteur en chef est Jacob Assa. Ils sont secondés par Anna Marie Scherning et David Carter. Maria Jakosalem et Thataw Batun contribuent également à la publication de cet *Annuaire.* Bogdan Dragovic est chargé des logiciels.

Les observations sur la présente édition de l'*Annuaire* et les suggestions de modification pour l'avenir seront reçues avec intérêt. Elles peuvent être envoyées par message électronique à statistics@un.org, ou adressées à la Division de statistique des Nations Unies, Section de la Diffusion Statistique, New York, N.Y. 10017 (États-Unis d'Amérique).

Contents

Table des matières

Contents (*continued*)

Part Three. Economic activity

Table des matières (*suite*)

Troisième partie. Activité économique

Contents (*continued*)

Table des matières (*suite*)

Contents (*continued*)

Part Four. International economic relations

Table des matières (*suite*)

Quatrième partie. Relations économiques internationales

** Asterisks preceding table names identify tables that were presented in previous issues of the *Statistical Yearbook* which are not contained in the present issue. These tables will be updated in future issues of the *Yearbook* when new data become available.

** Ce symbole indique les tableaux publiés dans les éditions précédentes de l'Annuaire statistique mais qui n'ont pas été repris dans la présente édition. Ces tableaux seront actualisés dans les futures livraisons de l'Annuaire à mesure que des données nouvelles deviendront disponibles.

Explanatory notes

In general, the statistics presented in the present publication are based on information available to the Statistics Division of the United Nations Secretariat as of March 2007.

Units of measurement

The metric system of weights and measures has been employed throughout the *Statistical Yearbook*. For conversion coefficients and factors, see annex II.

Symbols and conventions used in the tables

.	A point is used to indicate decimals.
-	A hyphen between years, e.g., 1998-1999, indicates the full period involved, including the beginning and end years.
/	A slash between years indicates a financial year, school year or crop year, e.g., 1998/99.
...	Data not available or not applicable.
*	Provisional or estimated figure.
#	Marked break in series.
^0	Not zero but less than half of the unit used.

Details and percentages in the tables do not necessarily add to totals because of rounding.

Notes explicatives

En général, les statistiques qui figurent dans la présente publication sont fondées sur les informations dont disposait la Division de statistique du Secrétariat de l'ONU au mars 2007.

Unités de mesure

Le système métrique de poids et mesures a été utilisé dans tout l'*Annuaire statistique*. On trouvera à l'annexe II les coefficients et facteurs de conversion.

Signes et conventions employés dans les tableaux

.	Les décimales sont précédées d'un point.
-	Un tiret entre des années, par exemple "1998-1999", indique que la période est embrassée dans sa totalité, y compris la première et la dernière année.
/	Une barre oblique entre des années renvoie à un exercice financier, à une année scolaire ou à une campagne agricole, par exemple "1998/99".
...	Données non disponibles ou non applicables.
*	Chiffre provisoire ou estimatif.
#	Discontinuité notable dans la série.
^0	Non nul mais inférieur à la moitié de l'unité employée.

Les chiffres étant arrondis, les totaux ne correspondent pas toujours à la somme exacte des éléments ou pourcentages figurant dans les tableaux.

Introduction

This is the fifty-first issue of the United Nations *Statistical Yearbook*, prepared by the Statistics Division, Department of Economic and Social Affairs, of the United Nations Secretariat. The tables include series covering from one to ten years, depending upon data availability and space constraints. The ten-year tables generally cover the years 1995 to 2004 or 1996 to 2005. For the most part, the statistics presented are those which were available to the Statistics Division as of March 2007.

Objective and content of the Statistical Yearbook

The main purpose of the *Statistical Yearbook* is to provide in a single volume a comprehensive compilation of internationally available statistics on social and economic conditions and activities, at world, regional and national levels, covering a ten-year period to the extent possible.

Most of the statistics presented in the *Yearbook* are extracted from more detailed, specialized databases prepared by the Statistics Division and by many other international statistical services. Thus, while the specialized databases concentrate on monitoring topics and trends in particular social and economic fields, the *Statistical Yearbook* tables aim to provide data for a more comprehensive, overall description of social and economic structures, conditions, changes and activities. The objective has been to collect, systematize, coordinate and present in a consistent way the most essential components of comparable statistical information which can give a broad picture of social and economic processes.

The content of the *Statistical Yearbook* is planned to serve a general readership. The *Yearbook* endeavours to provide information for various bodies of the United Nations system as well as for other international organizations, governments and non-governmental organizations, national statistical, economic and social policy bodies, scientific and educational institutions, libraries and the public. Data published in the *Statistical Yearbook* may also be of interest to companies and enterprises and to agencies engaged in market research. The *Statistical Yearbook* thus provides information on a wide range of social and economic issues which are of concern in the United Nations system and among the governments and peoples of the world. A particular value of the *Yearbook* is that it facilitates meaningful analysis of issues by systematizing and coordinating the data across many fields and shedding light on such interrelated issues as:

- General economic growth and related economic conditions;
- Progress towards the Millennium Development Goals;
- Population and urbanization, and their growth and impact;

Introduction

La présente édition est la cinquante et unième de *l'Annuaire statistique* des Nations Unies, établi par la Division de statistique du Département des affaires économiques et sociales du Secrétariat de l'Organisation des Nations Unies. Les tableaux présentent des séries qui couvrent d'un à dix ans, en fonction de la disponibilité des données et des contraintes d'espace. Les tableaux décennaux couvrent généralement les années 1995 à 2004 ou 1996 à 2005. La majeure partie des statistiques présentées ici sont celles dont disposait la Division de Statistique au mars 2007.

Objectif et contenu de l'Annuaire statistique

Le principal objectif de *l'Annuaire statistique* est de fournir en un seul volume un inventaire complet de statistiques internationales concernant la situation et les activités sociales et économiques aux niveaux mondial, régional et national, sur une période s'étalant, dans la mesure du possible, sur dix ans.

La plupart des données qui figurent dans l'*Annuaire statistique* proviennent de bases de données spécialisées davantage détaillées, préparées par la Division de statistique et par bien d'autres services statistiques internationaux. Tandis que les bases de données spécialisées se concentrent sur le suivi de domaines socioéconomiques particuliers, les données de l'*Annuaire* sont présentées de telle sorte qu'elles fournissent une description globale et exhaustive des structures, conditions, transformations et activités socioéconomiques. On a cherché à recueillir, systématiser, coordonner et présenter de manière cohérente les principales informations statistiques comparables, de manière à dresser un tableau général des processus socioéconomiques.

Le contenu de l'*Annuaire statistique* a été élaboré en vue d'un lectorat large. Les renseignements fournis devraient ainsi pouvoir être utilisés par les divers organismes du système des Nations Unies, mais aussi par d'autres organisations internationales, les gouvernements et les organisations non gouvernementales, les organismes nationaux de statistique et de politique économique et sociale, les institutions scientifiques et les établissements d'enseignement, les bibliothèques et les particuliers. Les données publiées dans l'*Annuaire* peuvent également intéresser les sociétés et entreprises, et les organismes spécialisés dans les études de marché. L'*Annuaire* présente des informations sur un large éventail de questions socioéconomiques liées aux préoccupations actuelles du système des Nations Unies, des gouvernements et des peuples du monde entier. Une qualité particulière de l'*Annuaire* est de faciliter une analyse approfondie de ces questions en systématisant et en articulant les données d'un domaine/secteur à l'autre, et en apportant un éclairage sur des sujets interdépendants, tels que :

- Employment, inflation and wages;
- Energy production and consumption and the development of new energy sources;
- Expansion of trade;
- Supply of food and alleviation of hunger;
- The financial situation of countries and external payments and receipts;
- Education, training and eradication of illiteracy;
- Improvement in general living conditions;
- Pollution and protection of the environment;
- Assistance provided to developing countries for social and economic development purposes.

Organization of the Yearbook

The 69 tables of the *Yearbook* are grouped into four broad parts:

- Part One: World and Region Summary (chapter I, tables 1-7);
- Part Two: Population and Social Statistics (chapters II-V: tables 8-15);
- Part Three: Economic Activity (chapters VI-XV: tables 16-57);
- Part Four: International Economic Relations (chapters XVI-XX: tables 58-69).

The more aggregated information shown in part one provides an overall picture of development at the world and region levels. More specific and detailed information for analysis concerning individual countries or areas is presented in the other three parts. Each of these parts is divided into chapters, by topic, and each chapter ends with a section on "Technical notes", which provides brief descriptions of major statistical concepts, definitions and classifications required for interpretation and analysis of the data. Information on the methodology used for the computation of the figures can be found in the publications on methodology of the United Nations and its agencies, listed in the section "Statistical sources and references" at the end of the *Yearbook*.

Part One, World and Region Summary, comprises seven tables highlighting the principal trends in the world as well as in each of the regions and in the major economic and social sectors. It contains global totals of important aggregate statistics needed for the analysis of economic growth, the structure of the world economy, major changes in world population and expansion of external merchandise trade. The global totals are, as a rule, subdivided into major geographical areas.

Part Two, Population and Social Statistics, comprises eight tables which contain more detailed statistical series on population, as well as education, nutrition, and communication.

Of the 42 tables in Part Three, Economic Activity, 26 provide data on national accounts, index numbers of industrial

- La croissance économique générale, et les conditions économiques qui lui sont liées;
- Les progrès accomplis dans la réalisation des Objectifs du Millénaire pour le Développement;
- La population et l'urbanisation, leur croissance et leur impact;
- L'emploi, l'inflation et les salaires;
- La production et la consommation d'énergie et le développement de nouvelles sources d'énergie;
- L'expansion des échanges;
- L'approvisionnement alimentaire et la lutte contre la faim;
- La situation financière, les paiements et recettes extérieurs des pays;
- L'éducation, la formation et l'élimination de l'analphabétisme;
- L'amélioration des conditions de vie;
- La pollution et la protection de l'environnement;
- L'assistance aux pays en développement à des fins socioéconomiques.

Présentation de l'Annuaire

Les 69 tableaux de l'*Annuaire* sont groupés en quatre parties:

- La première partie : Aperçu mondial et régional (chapitre I, tableaux 1 à 7);
- La deuxième partie : Statistiques démographiques et sociales (chapitres II à V, tableaux 8 à 15);
- La troisième partie : Activité économique (chapitres VI à XV, tableaux 16 à 57);
- La quatrième partie : Relations économiques internationales (chapitres XVI à XX, tableaux 58 à 69).

Les valeurs les plus agrégées qui figurent dans la première partie donnent un tableau global du développement à l'échelon mondial et régional, tandis que les trois autres parties contiennent des renseignements plus précis et détaillés qui se prêtent mieux à une analyse par pays ou par zones. Chacune de ces trois parties est divisée en chapitres portant sur des sujets donnés, et chaque chapitre comprend une section intitulée "Notes techniques" où l'on trouve une brève description des principales notions, définitions et classifications statistiques nécessaires pour interpréter et analyser les données. Les méthodes de calcul utilisées sont décrites dans les publications se référant à la méthodologie des Nations Unies et de leurs organismes, énumérées à la fin de l'*Annuaire* dans la section "Sources et références statistiques".

La première partie, intitulée "Aperçu mondial et régional", comprend sept tableaux présentant les principales tendances dans le monde et dans les régions ainsi que dans les principaux secteurs économiques et sociaux. Elle fournit des chiffres mon-

production, interest rates, labour force, wages and prices, transport, energy, environment and science and technology; 16 tables provide data on production in the major branches of the economy (using, in general, the International Standard Industrial Classification, ISIC), namely agriculture, hunting, forestry and fishing, and manufacturing. Consumption data are combined with the production data in tables on specific commodities, where feasible.

Part Four, International Economic Relations, comprises 12 tables on international merchandise trade, balance of payments, international tourism, international finance and development assistance.

An index (in English only) is provided at the end of the *Yearbook*.

Annexes and regional groupings of countries or areas

The annexes to the *Statistical Yearbook,* and the section "Explanatory notes" preceding the Introduction, provide additional essential information on the *Yearbook's* contents and presentation of data.

Annex I provides information on countries or areas covered in the *Yearbook* tables and on their arrangement in geographical regions and economic or other groupings. The geographical groupings shown in the *Yearbook* are generally based on continental regions unless otherwise indicated. However, strict consistency in this regard is impossible. A wide range of classifications is used for different purposes in the various international agencies and other sources of statistics for the *Yearbook*. These classifications vary in response to administrative and analytical requirements.

Similarly, there is no common agreement in the United Nations system concerning the terms "developed" and "developing" when referring to the stage of development reached by any given country or area, and its corresponding classification in one or the other grouping. The *Yearbook* thus refers more generally to "developed" or "developing" regions on the basis of conventional practice. Following this practice, "developed" regions or areas comprise Canada and the United States in Northern America, Japan in Asia, Australia and New Zealand in Oceania, and Europe, while all of Africa and the remainder of the Americas, Asia and Oceania comprise the "developing regions". These designations are intended for statistical convenience and do not necessarily express a judgement about the stage reached by a particular country or area in the development process.

Annex II provides detailed information on conversion coefficients and factors used in various tables, and annex III provides a list of tables added and omitted in the present edition of the *Yearbook*. Tables for which a sufficient amount of new data is not available are not being published in this

diaux pour les principaux agrégats statistiques nécessaires pour analyser la croissance économique, la structure de l'économie mondiale, les principaux changements dans la population mondiale et l'expansion du commerce extérieur de marchandises. En règle générale, les chiffres mondiaux sont répartis par grandes régions géographiques.

La deuxième partie, intitulée "Population et statistiques sociales", comporte huit tableaux où figurent des séries plus détaillées concernant la population, l'éducation, la nutrition, et la communication.

La troisième partie, intitulée "Activité économique", comporte 42 tableaux, 26 qui présentent des statistiques concernant les comptes nationaux, les nombres indices relatifs à la production industrielle, les taux d'intérêt, la population active, les prix et les salaires, le transport, l'énergie, l'environnement, et la science et technologie; et 16 qui présentent des données sur la production des principales branches d'activité économique (en utilisant en général la *Classification internationale type, par industrie, de toutes les branches d'activité économique*): agriculture, chasse, sylviculture et pêche, et industries manufacturières. Les tableaux traitant de certains produits de base associent autant que possible les données relatives à la consommation aux valeurs concernant la production.

La quatrième partie, intitulée "Relations économiques internationales", comprend 12 tableaux relatifs au commerce international de marchandises, aux balances des paiements, au tourisme international, aux finances internationales, et à l'aide au développement.

Un index (en anglais seulement) figure à la fin de l'*Annuaire*.

Annexes et groupements régionaux des pays et zones

Les annexes à l'*Annuaire statistique,* et la section intitulée "Notes explicatives" qui précède l'introduction, offrent d'importantes informations complémentaires quant à la teneur et à la présentation des données figurant dans le présent ouvrage.

L'annexe I donne des renseignements sur les pays ou zones couverts par les tableaux de l'*Annuaire* et sur leur regroupement en régions géographiques et groupements économiques ou autres. Sauf indication contraire, les groupements géographiques figurant dans l'*Annuaire* sont généralement fondés sur les régions continentales, mais une présentation absolument systématique est impossible à cet égard car les diverses institutions internationales et autres sources de statistiques employées pour la confection de l'*Annuaire* emploient, selon l'objet de l'exercice, des classifications fort différentes en réponse à diverses exigences d'ordre administratif ou analytique.

Il n'existe pas non plus dans le système des Nations Unies de définition commune des termes "développé" et "en développement" pour décrire le niveau atteint en la matière

Yearbook. Their titles nevertheless are still listed in the table of contents since it is planned that they will be published in a later issue as new data are compiled by the collecting agency.

Data comparability, quality and relevance

The major challenge continuously facing the *Statistical Yearbook* is to present series which are as nearly comparable across countries as the available statistics permit. Considerable efforts have already been made among the international suppliers of data and by the staff of the *Statistical Yearbook* to ensure the compatibility of various series by coordinating time periods, base years, prices chosen for valuation, and so on. This is indispensable in relating various bodies of data to each other and in facilitating analysis across different sectors. Thus, for example, relating data on short-term interest rates to those on prices makes it possible to arrive at a general understanding about the inflation environment, and relating a country's data on tourism expenditure in other countries to those on its per capita GDP provides a gauge on that country's wealth status. In general, the data presented reflect the methodological recommendations of the United Nations Statistical Commission issued in various United Nations publications, and of other international bodies concerned with statistics. Publications containing these recommendations and guidelines are listed in the section "Statistical sources and references" at the end of the *Yearbook*. The use of international recommendations not only promotes international comparability of the data but also ensures a degree of compatibility regarding the underlying concepts, definitions and classifications relating to different series. However, much work remains to be done in this area and, for this reason, some tables can serve only as a first source of data, which require further adjustment before being used for more in-depth analytical studies. While on the whole, a significant degree of comparability has been achieved in international statistics, there will remain some limitations, for a variety of reasons.

One common cause of non-comparability of economic data is different valuations of statistical aggregates such as national income, wages and salaries, output of industries and so forth. Conversion of these and similar series originally expressed in national prices into a common currency, for example into United States dollars, through the use of exchange rates, is not always satisfactory owing to frequent wide fluctuations in market rates and differences between official rates and rates which would be indicated by unofficial markets or purchasing power parities. The use of different kinds of sources for obtaining data is another cause of incomparability. This is true, for example, in the case of employment

par un pays ou une zone donnés ni pour les classifier dans l'un ou l'autre de ces groupes. Ainsi, dans l'*Annuaire*, on s'en remet à l'usage pour qualifier les régions de "développées" ou "en développement". Selon cet usage, les régions ou zones développées sont le Canada et les Etats-Unis dans l'Amérique septentrionale, le Japon dans l'Asie, l'Australie et la Nouvelle-Zélande dans l'Océanie, et l'Europe, alors que toute l'Afrique et le reste des Amériques, l'Asie et l'Océanie constituent les régions en développement. Ces appellations sont utilisées pour plus de commodité dans la présentation des statistiques et n'impliquent pas nécessairement un jugement quant au stade de développement auquel est parvenu tel pays ou telle zone.

L'annexe II fournit des renseignements sur les coefficients et facteurs de conversion employés dans les différents tableaux, et l'annexe III contient la liste de tableaux qui ont été ajoutés ou omis dans la présente édition de l'*Annuaire*. Les tableaux pour lesquels on ne dispose pas d'une quantité suffisante des données nouvelles, n'ont pas été publiés dans cet *Annuaire*. Comme ils seront repris dans une prochaine édition à mesure que des données nouvelles seront dépouillées par l'office statistique d'origine, ses titres figurent toujours dans la table des matières.

Comparabilité, qualité et pertinence des statistiques

Le défi majeur auquel l'*Annuaire Statistique* fait continuellement face est de présenter des séries aussi comparables entre les pays que la disponibilité des statistiques le permettent. Les sources internationales de données et les auteurs de l'*Annuaire* ont réalisé des efforts considérables pour faire en sorte que diverses séries soient compatibles, en harmonisant les périodes de référence, les années de base, les prix utilisés pour les évaluations, etc. Cette démarche est indispensable si l'on veut rapprocher divers ensembles de données, et faciliter l'analyse intersectorielle de l'économie. Ainsi, lier les données concernant les taux d'intérêt à court terme à celles des prix permet d'arriver à une compréhension globale de l'environnement de l'inflation; lier les données de dépenses touristiques d'un pays dans d'autres pays à celles de son PIB par tête fournit un indicateur de la richesse de ce pays. De façon générale, les données sont présentées selon les recommandations méthodologiques formulées par la Commission de statistique des Nations Unies, et par les autres entités internationales impliquées dans les statistiques. Les titres des publications contenant ces recommandations et leurs lignes directrices figurent à la fin de l'*Annuaire*, dans la section "Sources et références statistiques". Le respect des recommandations internationales tend non seulement à promouvoir la comparabilité internationale des données, mais elle assure également une certaine comparabilité entre

and unemployment, where data are obtained from different sources, namely household and labour force sample surveys, establishment censuses or surveys, official estimates, social insurance statistics and employment office statistics, which are not fully comparable in many cases. Non-comparability of data may also result from differences in the institutional patterns of countries. Certain variations in social and economic organization and institutions may have an impact on the comparability of the data even if the underlying concepts and definitions are identical. These and other causes of non-comparability of the data are briefly explained in the technical notes to each chapter.

A further set of challenges relate to timeliness, quality and relevance of the data contained in the *Yearbook*. Users generally demand the most up-to-date statistics. However, due to the different development stages of statistical capacity in different countries, data for the most recent years may only be available for a small number of countries. For a global print publication, therefore, a balance has to be struck between presenting the most updated information and satisfactory country coverage. Of course the UN Statistics Division's website offers greater flexibility in presenting continuously updated information and is therefore a useful complement to the annual print publication. Furthermore, as most of the information presented in this *Yearbook* is collected through specialized United Nations agencies and partners, the timeliness is continuously enhanced by improving the communication and data flow between countries and the specialized agencies on the one hand, and between the UN Statistics Division and the specialized agencies on the other. The development of new XML-based data transfer protocols will address this issue and is expected to make international data flows more efficient in the future.

Data quality at the international level is a function of the data quality at the national level. The UN Statistics Division in close cooperation with its partners in the UN agencies and the international statistical system continues to support countries' efforts to improve both the coverage and the quality of their data. Metadata, as for example reflected in the footnotes and technical notes of this publication, are an important service to the user to allow an informed assessment of the quality of the data. Given the wide variety of sources for the *Yearbook*, there is of course an equally wide variety of data formats and accompanying metadata. An important challenge for the UN Statistics Division and its partners for the future is to work further towards the standardization, or at least harmonization, of metadata.

The final challenge relates to maintaining the relevance of the series included in the *Yearbook*. As new policy concerns enter the developmental debate, the UN Statistics Division

les concepts, les définitions et classifications utilisés. Mais comme il reste encore beaucoup à faire dans ce domaine, les données présentées dans certains tableaux n'ont qu'une valeur indicative, et nécessiteront des ajustements plus poussés avant de pouvoir servir à des analyses approfondies. Bien que l'on soit parvenu, dans l'ensemble, à un degré de comparabilité appréciable en matière de statistiques internationales, diverses raisons expliquent que subsistent encore de nombreuses limitations.

Une cause commune de non comparabilité des données économiques réside dans la diversité des méthodes d'évaluation employées pour comptabiliser des agrégats tels que le revenu national, les salaires et traitements, la production des différentes branches d'activité industrielle, etc. Il n'est pas toujours satisfaisant de ramener la valeur des séries de ce type—exprimée à l'origine en prix nationaux—à une monnaie commune (par exemple le dollar des États-Unis) car les taux de change du marché connaissent fréquemment de fortes fluctuations, et parce que les taux officiels ne coïncident pas avec ceux des marchés officieux ni avec les parités réelles de pouvoir d'achat. Le recours à des sources diverses pour la collecte des données est un autre facteur qui limite la comparabilité. C'est le cas, par exemple, des données d'emploi et de chômage, obtenues par des moyens aussi peu comparables que les sondages, le dépouillement des registres d'assurances sociales et les enquêtes auprès des entreprises. Dans certains cas, les données ne sont pas comparables en raison de différences entre les structures institutionnelles des pays. Des changements dans l'organisation et les institutions économiques et sociales peuvent affecter la comparabilité des données, même si les concepts et définitions sont fondamentalement identiques. Ces causes, et d'autres, de non comparabilité des données sont brièvement expliquées dans les notes techniques de chaque chapitre.

Un autre ensemble de défis à relever concerne la fraîcheur, la qualité et la pertinence des données présentées dans l'*Annuaire*. Les utilisateurs exigent généralement des données les plus récentes possibles. Toutefois, selon le niveau de développement de la capacité statistique des pays, les données pour les dernières années peuvent n'être disponibles que pour un nombre limité de pays. Dans le cadre d'une publication mondiale, un équilibre doit être trouvé entre la présentation de l'information la plus récente et une couverture géographique satisfaisante. Bien entendu, le site Internet de la Division de statistique des Nations Unies offre une plus grande flexibilité, puisqu'il propose une information actualisée au fil de l'eau, et constitue ainsi un complément utile à la publication papier annuelle. Par ailleurs, étant donné que la plupart des informations présentées dans cet *Annuaire* sont collectées parmi les agences spécialisées des Nations Unies

will need to introduce new series that describe concerns that have gained prominence as well as to prune outdated data and continue to update the recurrent *Yearbook* series that still address those issues which are most pertinent. Often choosing the appropriate moment when the statistical information on new topics has matured sufficiently so as to be able to disseminate meaningful global data can be challenging. Furthermore, a balance has to continuously be found between the ever-increasing amount of information available for dissemination and the space limitations of the print version of the *Statistical Yearbook*. International comparability, data availability and data quality will remain the key criteria to guide the UN Statistics Division in its selection.

Needless to say, more can always be done to improve the *Statistical Yearbook*'s scope, coverage, design, metadata and timeliness. The *Yearbook* team continually strives to improve upon each of these aspects and to make its publication as responsive as possible to its users' needs and expectations, while at the same time focusing on a manageable body of data and metadata. Since data disseminated in digital form have clear advantages over those in print, as much of the *Yearbook* information as possible will continue to be included in the Statistics Division's online databases. Still, the *Statistical Yearbook* will continue to claim its rightful place among the products of the Statistics Division as a useful, compact resource for a general understanding of the global social and economic situation.

et autres partenaires, la fraîcheur des données est continuellement améliorée, grâce à une meilleure communication et un meilleur échange de données entre les pays et les agences spécialisées d'une part, et entre la Division de statistique des Nations Unies et les agences spécialisées d'autre part. Le développement de nouveaux protocoles de transfert de données basés sur le langage XML devrait contribuer à rendre, à l'avenir, les échanges de données internationales encore plus efficaces.

La qualité des données au niveau international est fonction de la qualité des données au niveau national. La Division de statistique des Nations Unies, en étroite collaboration avec ses partenaires dans les agences de l'ONU et dans le système statistique international, continue de soutenir les efforts des pays pour améliorer à la fois la couverture et la qualité de leurs données. Des métadonnées, comme l'illustrent les notes de bas de page et les notes techniques de cette publication, constituent un important service fourni à l'utilisateur pour lui permettre d'évaluer de manière avisée la qualité des données. Etant donné la grande variété des sources de *l'Annuaire*, il y a bien entendu une non moins grande variété de formats de données et de métadonnées associées. Un important défi que la Division de statistique des Nations Unies et ses partenaires doivent relever dans le futur est d'aboutir à la standardisation, ou au moins l'harmonisation, des métadonnées.

Le dernier défi concerne la constance de la pertinence des séries présentées dans *l'Annuaire*. Au fur et à mesure que de nouvelles préoccupations politiques pénètrent le débat lié au développement, la Division de statistique des Nations Unies doit introduire dans l'*Annuaire* de nouvelles séries qui leur sont liées, et, ce faisant, effectuer une coupe sombre parmi les données qui lui semblent dépassées, tout en s'assurant de continuer à actualiser les séries récurrentes de qui paraissent encore pertinentes. Souvent, choisir le moment idoine auquel les données statistiques sur de nouveaux thèmes sont suffisamment matures pour qu'elles puissent, au niveau mondial, être diffusées sans hésitation, est un défi en soi. Par ailleurs, un équilibre doit continuellement être trouvé entre le volume toujours croissant d'informations disponibles à la diffusion, et les contraintes d'espace de la version papier de l'*Annuaire statistique*. La comparabilité internationale, la disponibilité des données et leur qualité devront rester le principal critère à considérer par la Division de statistique des Nations Unies dans sa sélection.

Inutile de dire qu'il est toujours possible d'améliorer l'*Annuaire statistique* en ce qui concerne son champ, sa couverture, sa conception générale, ses métadonnées et sa mise à jour. L'équipe en charge de l'*Annuaire* s'évertue en permanence à améliorer chacun de ces aspects, et de faire en

sorte que cette publication réponde au plus près aux besoins et aux attentes de ses utilisateurs, sans toutefois oublier de mettre l'accent sur un corpus gérable de données et de métadonnées. Puisqu'il est avéré que les données diffusées de manière digitale ont des avantages comparés à celles diffusées sur papier, autant d'informations de l'*Annuaire* que possible continueront d'être inclues dans les bases de données électroniques de la Division de statistique. L'*Annuaire statistique* garde toujours une place de choix parmi les produits de la Division de statistique comme une ressource compact et utile pour une compréhension général de la situation sociale et économique globale.

Part One

World and region summary

Première partie

Aperçu mondial et régional

Chapter I World and region summary (tables 1-7)

This part of the *Statistical Yearbook* presents selected aggregate series on principal economic and social topics for the world as a whole and for the major regions. The topics include population and surface area, agricultural and industrial production, external trade, government financial reserves, and energy production and consumption. More detailed data on individual countries and areas are provided in the subsequent parts of the present *Yearbook*. These comprise Part Two: Population and Social Statistics; Part Three: Economic Activity; and Part Four: International Economic Relations.

Regional totals between series may be incomparable owing to differences in definitions of regions and lack of data for particular regional components. General information on regional groupings is provided in annex I of the *Yearbook*. Supplementary information on regional groupings used in specific series is provided, as necessary, in table footnotes and in the technical notes at the end of chapter I.

Chapitre I Aperçu mondial et régional (tableaux 1 à 7)

Cette partie de l'*Annuaire statistique* présente, pour le monde entier et ses principales subdivisions, un choix d'agrégats ayant trait à des questions économiques et sociales essentielles: population et superficie, production agricole et industrielle, commerce extérieur, réserves financières publiques, et la production et la consommation d'énergie. Des statistiques plus détaillées pour divers pays ou zones figurent dans les parties ultérieures de l'*Annuaire*, c'est-à-dire dans les deuxième, troisième et quatrième parties intitulées respectivement: population et statistiques sociales, activités économiques et relations économiques internationales.

Les totaux régionaux peuvent être incomparables entre les séries en raison de différences dans la définition des régions et de l'absence de données sur tel ou tel élément régional. A l'annexe I de l'*Annuaire*, on trouvera des renseignements généraux sur les groupements régionaux. Des informations complémentaires sur les groupements régionaux pour certaines séries bien précises sont fournies, lorsqu'il y a lieu, dans les notes figurant au bas des tableaux et dans les notes techniques à la fin du chapitre I.

1 World statistics: selected series

Population, production, external trade and finance

Statistiques mondiales : séries principales

Population, production, commerce extérieur et finances

Series Séries	Unit or base Unité ou base	1996	1997	1998	1999	2000	2001	2002	2003	2004	2005
Population — Population											
World population[1] Population mondiale[1]	million	5 802	5 883	5 964	6 045	6 124	6 203	6 281	6 359	6 389	6 465
Output / production — Production											
Gross domestic product — Produit intérieur brut											
GDP at current prices PIB aux prix courants	billion US $ milliard $ E.U.	30 292	30 152	29 907	31 018	31 850	31 640	32 930	37 019	41 610	44 923
GDP per capita PIB par habitant	US $ $ E.U.	5 222	5 126	5 015	5 132	5 201	5 101	5 243	5 822	6 465	6 896
GDP real rates of growth Taux de l'accroissement réels	%	3.3	3.6	2.4	3.3	4.2	1.7	1.9	2.8	4.0	3.5
Agriculture, forestry and fishing production — Production agricole, forestière et de la pêche											
Index numbers — Indices											
All commodities Tous produits	1999-01 = 100	91.4	93.6	95.1	98.2	100.1	101.6	103.2	106.3	110.7	111.3
Food Produits alimentaires	1999-01 = 100	90.9	93.1	95.0	98.3	100.2	101.6	103.4	106.5	110.5	111.1
Quantities — Quantités											
Cereals Céréales	million t.	2 072	2 095	2 083	2 085	2 060	2 107	2 028	2 090	2 282	2 265
Meat Viande	million t.	147	152	157	160	161	163	168	172	175	179
Roundwood Bois rond	million m3	3 234	3 305	3 224	3 293	3 358	3 271	3 299	3 368	3 423	3 503
Fish production Production halieutique	million t.	129	131	128	138	143	143	146	147	156	158
Industrial production — Production industrielle											
Index numbers[2] — Indices[2]											
All commodities Tous produits	1995 = 100	103.1	108.4	110.5	115.3	123.9	121.5	122.0	126.3	134.3	141.4
Mining Mines	1995 = 100	103.1	105.1	106.0	103.8	107.4	106.6	104.4	109.2	110.9	111.9
Manufacturing Manufactures	1995 = 100	103.0	109.0	111.2	116.9	126.4	123.5	124.0	128.4	137.5	145.7
Quantities — Quantités											
Coal[3] Houille [3]	million t.	3 792	3 804	3 640	3 266	3 294	3 475	3 525	3 836	4 212	4 509
Lignite and brown coal[3] Lignite et charbon brun[3]	million t.	945	930	901	1 263	1 292	1 328	1 332	1 350	1 358	1 384
Crude petroleum[3] Pétrole brut[3]	million t.	3 147	3 249	3 289	3 205	3 331	3 327	3 295	3 432	3 550	3 609
Natural gas[3] Gaz naturel[3]	petajoules pétajoules	106 352	106 098	108 347	110 800	115 093	116 222	118 880	122 745	127 574	130 128
Electricity[3,4] Electricité[3,4]	billion kWh milliard kWh	13 803	14 084	14 399	14 823	15 454	15 541	16 171	16 772	17 554	18 335
Fertilizers[5] Engrais[5]	million t.	...	...	...	...	...	...	150	156	163	163

Series Séries	Unit or base Unité ou base	1996	1997	1998	1999	2000	2001	2002	2003	2004	2005
Sugar, raw Sucre, brut	million t.	125	125	126	135	130	131	142	148	147	141
Woodpulp Pâte de bois	million t.	157	163	160	164	172	166	168	171	176	174
Sawnwood Sciages	million m3	387	394	379	389	386	380	394	400	420	428
External trade — Commerce extérieur											
Value — Valeur											
Import, c.i.f. Importations c.a.f.	billion US$ milliard $E.-U.	5 111	5 287	5 243	5 459	6 156	5 935	6 149	7 167	8 745	9 905
Exports, f.o.b. Exportations f.o.b.	billion US$ milliard $E.-U.	5 042	5 231	5 165	5 353	5 983	5 752	6 026	7 006	8 515	9 668
Volume: index of exports — Volume : indice des exportations											
All commodities Tous produits	2000 = 100	72	80	83	88	100	99	103	109	121	132
Manufactures Produits manufacturés	2000 = 100	71	80	82	89	100	101	103	112	116	...
Unit value: index of exports[6] — Valeur unitaure : indice des exportations[6]											
All commodities Tous produits	2000 = 100	117	110	104	102	100	97	97	107	117	121
Manufactures Produits manufacturés	2000 = 100	118	110	108	103	100	98	98	104	111	...
Finance — Finances											
Internatonal reserves minus gold, billion SDR[7] — Réserves internationals moins l'or, milliard de DTS[7]											
All countries Tous les pays	billion SDR milliard DTS	1 145.8	1 265.5	1 248.6	1 371.4	1 552.2	1 707.7	1 857.5	2 122.8	2 490.1	2 969.7
Position in IMF Disponibilité au FMI	billion SDR milliard DTS	38.0	47.1	60.6	54.8	47.4	56.9	66.1	66.5	55.8	28.6
Foreign exchange Devises	billion SDR milliard DTS	1 089.2	1 197.9	1 167.6	1 298.1	1 486.3	1 631.3	1 771.7	2 036.2	2 413.9	2 921.0
SDR (special drawing rights) DTS (droits de triage spéc.)	billion SDR milliard DTS	18.5	20.5	20.4	18.5	18.5	19.6	19.7	19.9	20.3	20.1

Source

Databases of the Food and Agriculture Organization of the United Nations (FAO), Rome; the International Monetary Fund (IMF), Washington, D.C.; and the United Nations Statistics Division, New York.

Notes

1 Mid-year estimates (as of August 2007).
2 Excluding China and the countries of the former USSR (except Russian Federation and Ukraine).
3 As of September 2007.
4 Electricity generated by establishments for public or private use.
5 Year beginning 1 July.
6 Indices computed in US dollars.
7 End of period.

Source

Les bases de données de l'Organisation des Nations Unies pour l'alimentation et l'agriculture (FAO), Rome ; du Fonds Monétaire International (FMI), Washington, D.C. ; et de la Division de statistique de l'Organisation de Nations Unies, New York.

Notes

1 Estimations au milieu de l'année (dès août 2007).
2 Non compris la Chine et les pays de l'ancienne URSS (sauf la Fédération de Russie et Ukraine).
3 Dès septembre 2007.
4 L'électricité produite par des entreprises d'utilisation publique ou privée.
5 L'année commençant le 1er juillet.
6 Indice calculé en dollars des Etats-Unis.
7 Fin de la période.

Population, rate of increase, birth and death rates, surface area and density

Population, taux d'accroissement, taux de natalité, taux de mortalité, superficie et densité

Major areas and regions Grandes régions	Mid-year population estimates (millions) Estimations de population au milieu de l'année (millions) 1950	1960	1970	1980	1990	2000	2004	Annual rate of increase Taux d'accroissement annuel % 2000 - 2005	Crude birth rate Taux bruts de natalité (p.1,000) 2000 - 2005	Crude death rate Taux bruts de mortalité (p.1,000) 2000 - 2005	Surface area (km²) Superficie (km²) (000) 2004	Density[1] Densité[1] 2004
World Monde	**2 520**	**3 024**	**3 697**	**4 442**	**5 280**	**6 086**	**6 389**	**1.2**	**21**	**9**	**136 127**	**47**
Africa Afrique	224	282	364	479	636	812	887	2.2	38	15	30 312	29
Eastern Africa Afrique orientale	65	82	109	146	198	256	281	2.4	41	17	6 361	44
Middle Africa Afrique centrale	26	32	41	54	73	96	107	2.6	46	20	6 613	16
Northern Africa Afrique du Nord	53	67	86	112	144	175	188	1.7	26	7	8 525	22
Southern Africa Afrique australe	16	20	26	33	42	52	54	0.7	24	17	2 675	20
Western Africa Afrique occidentale	64	80	102	134	178	234	258	2.4	42	18	6 138	42
Northern America[2] Amérique septentrionale[2]	172	204	232	256	283	315	328	1.0	14	8	21 776	15
Latin America and the Caribbean Amérique latine et Caraïbes	167	219	285	362	444	523	554	1.4	22	6	20 546	27
Caribbean Caraïbes	17	20	25	29	34	38	39	0.9	20	8	234	166
Central America Amérique centrale	37	50	68	91	113	136	145	1.6	24	5	2 480	58
South America Amérique du sud	113	148	192	242	297	349	370	1.4	21	6	17 832	21
Asia[3] Asie[3]	1 396	1 699	2 140	2 630	3 169	3 676	3 860	1.2	20	8	31 880	121
Eastern Asia Asie orientale	671	792	987	1 178	1 350	1 479	1 516	0.6	13	7	11 763	129
South-central Asia Asie centrale et du Sud	496	617	780	978	1 226	1 485	1 586	1.6	26	9	10 791	147
South-eastern Asia Asie du Sud-Est	178	223	286	358	440	519	548	1.4	21	7	4 495	122
Western Asia Asie occidentale	51	67	88	116	154	193	210	2.1	26	6	4 831	43
Europe[3] Europe[3]	547	604	656	692	721	728	729	0.0	10	12	23 049	32
Eastern Europe Europe orientale	220	254	276	295	311	305	299	-0.5	10	14	18 814	16
Northern Europe Europe septentrionale	77	81	86	89	92	94	96	0.3	11	10	1 810	53
Southern Europe Europe méridionale	109	118	127	138	143	146	149	0.4	10	10	1 317	113
Western Europe Europe occidentale	141	152	166	170	176	184	186	0.2	10	10	1 108	167

2 Population, rate of increase, birth and death rates, surface area and density (*continued*)
Population, taux d'accroissement, taux de natalité, taux de mortalité, superficie et densité (*suite*)

Major areas and regions Grandes régions	Mid-year population estimates (millions) Estimations de population au milieu de l'année (millions)							Annual rate of increase Taux d'accroissement annuel %	Crude birth rate Taux bruts de natalité (p.1,000)	Crude death rate Taux bruts de mortalité (p.1,000)	Surface area (km²) Superficie (km²) (000)	Density[1] Densité[1]
	1950	1960	1970	1980	1990	2000	2004	2000 - 2005			2004	2004
Oceania[2] Océanie[2]	13	16	20	23	27	31	33	1.3	17	7	8 564	4
Australia and New Zealand Australie et Nouvelle-Zélande	10	13	16	18	20	23	24	1.1	13	7	8 012	3
Melanesia Mélanésie	2	3	3	4	6	7	8	2.0	31	10	541	14
Micronesia Micronésie	0	0	0	0	0	1	1	1.9	26	5	3	167
Polynesia Polynésie	0	0	0	1	1	1	1	1.2	24	5	8	75

Source

United Nations Statistics Division, New York, "Demographic Yearbook 2004" and the demographic statistics database.

Notes

1 Population per square kilometre of surface area. Figures are merely the quotients of population divided by surface area and are not to be considered either as reflecting density in the urban sense or as indicating the supporting power of a territory's land and resources.

2 Hawaii, a state of the United States of America, is included in Northern America rather than Oceania.

3 The European portion of Turkey is included in Western Asia rather than Europe.

Source

Organisation des Nations Unies, Division de statistique, New York, "Annuaire démographique 2004" et la base de données pour les statistiques démographiques.

Notes

1 Nombre d'habitants au kilomètre carré. Il s'agit simplement du quotient du chiffre de la population divisé par celui de la superficie: il ne faut pas y voir d'indication de la densité au sens urbain du terme ni de l'effectif de population que les terres et les ressources du territoire sont capables de nourrir.

2 Hawaii, un Etat des Etats-Unis d'Amérique, est comprise en Amérique septentrionale plutôt qu'en Océanie.

3 La partie européenne de la Turquie est comprise en Asie Occidentale plutôt qu'en Europe.

3 Index numbers of total agricultural and food production

1999 – 2001 = 100

Indices de la production agricole totale et de la production alimentaire

1999 – 2001 = 100

Region — Région	1996	1997	1998	1999	2000	2001	2002	2003	2004	2005
World — Monde										
Total agricultural production — Production agricole totale	**91.4**	**93.6**	**95.1**	**98.2**	**100.1**	**101.6**	**103.2**	**106.3**	**110.7**	**111.3**
Food production — Production alimentaire	**90.9**	**93.1**	**95.0**	**98.3**	**100.2**	**101.6**	**103.4**	**106.5**	**110.5**	**111.1**
Africa — Afrique										
Total agricultural production — Production agricole totale	92.7	91.7	95.7	98.9	99.7	101.5	103.2	107.7	109.2	110.2
Food production — Production alimentaire	92.2	91.0	95.3	98.8	99.8	101.4	103.5	108.5	109.6	110.6
America, North — Amérique du Nord										
Total agricultural production — Production agricole totale	94.0	97.1	97.6	99.8	101.4	98.8	97.6	100.8	107.4	106.7
Food production — Production alimentaire	93.4	96.5	98.1	99.9	101.7	98.4	97.8	101.0	106.9	106.0
America, South — Amérique du Sud										
Total agricultural production — Production agricole totale	87.0	90.0	91.8	97.4	99.5	103.1	107.0	112.6	117.5	120.2
Food production — Production alimentaire	86.7	90.2	91.7	97.6	99.4	102.9	106.7	113.0	116.7	119.6
Asia — Asie										
Total agricultural production — Production agricole totale	87.9	91.0	93.7	97.2	100.1	102.7	105.2	109.6	113.5	115.3
Food production — Production alimentaire	87.1	90.1	93.4	97.2	100.1	102.7	105.4	109.8	113.2	115.2
Europe — Europe										
Total agricultural production — Production agricole totale	100.8	101.0	98.7	100.1	100.1	99.8	101.5	98.3	104.6	101.1
Food production — Production alimentaire	100.8	101.0	98.7	100.1	100.1	99.8	101.6	98.4	104.8	101.2
Oceania — Océanie										
Total agricultural production — Production agricole totale	90.9	91.7	95.7	98.6	99.1	102.3	89.9	100.0	99.2	101.1
Food production — Production alimentaire	90.6	90.8	95.2	98.4	98.6	103.0	91.6	103.2	101.0	103.4

Source

Food and Agriculture Organization of the United Nations (FAO), Rome, FAOSTAT data, last accessed October 2006, http://faostat.fao.org.

Source

Organisation des Nations Unies pour l'alimentation et l'agriculture (FAO), Rome, données FAOSTAT, dernier accès octobre 2006, http://faostat.fao.org.

4 Index numbers of per capita agricultural and food production

1999 – 2001 = 100

Indices de la production agricole et de la production alimentaire par habitant

1999 – 2001 = 100

Region — Région	1996	1997	1998	1999	2000	2001	2002	2003	2004	2005
World — Monde										
Per capita agricultural production — Production agricole par habitant	**96.4**	**97.4**	**97.6**	**99.5**	**100.1**	**100.4**	**100.7**	**102.4**	**105.4**	**104.7**
Per capita food production — Production alimentaire par habitant	**95.9**	**96.9**	**97.5**	**99.5**	**100.2**	**100.3**	**100.8**	**102.6**	**105.2**	**104.5**
Africa — Afrique										
Per capita agricultural production — Production agricole par habitant	101.8	98.3	100.2	101.1	99.7	99.2	98.7	100.8	99.9	98.7
Per capita food production — Production alimentaire par habitant	101.2	97.5	99.8	101.1	99.8	99.1	99.0	101.5	100.3	99.1
America, North — Amérique du Nord										
Per capita agricultural production — Production agricole par habitant	98.1	100.3	99.7	100.8	101.4	97.8	95.6	97.7	103.1	101.4
Per capita food production — Production alimentaire par habitant	97.4	99.6	100.2	101.0	101.7	97.4	95.8	97.9	102.7	100.8
America, South — Amérique du Sud										
Per capita agricultural production — Production agricole par habitant	92.3	94.1	94.5	98.9	99.5	101.6	104.1	107.9	111.2	112.2
Per capita food production — Production alimentaire par habitant	92.0	94.3	94.5	99.1	99.4	101.5	103.7	108.3	110.4	111.7
Asia — Asie										
Per capita agricultural production — Production agricole par habitant	92.9	94.9	96.3	98.5	100.1	101.4	102.5	105.4	107.9	108.3
Per capita food production — Production alimentaire par habitant	92.1	93.9	96.0	98.5	100.1	101.4	102.7	105.7	107.6	108.2
Europe — Europe										
Per capita agricultural production — Production agricole par habitant	100.8	101.0	98.6	100.1	100.1	99.8	101.6	98.5	105.0	101.5
Per capita food production — Production alimentaire par habitant	100.8	101.0	98.6	100.1	100.1	99.9	101.7	98.6	105.1	101.6
Oceania — Océanie										
Per capita agricultural production — Production agricole par habitant	96.1	95.6	98.3	99.9	99.1	101.0	87.6	96.3	94.4	95.1
Per capita food production — Production alimentaire par habitant	95.7	94.7	97.8	99.7	98.6	101.7	89.3	99.4	96.1	97.3

Source

Food and Agriculture Organization of the United Nations (FAO), Rome, FAOSTAT data, last accessed October 2006, http://faostat.fao.org.

Source

Organisation des Nations Unies pour l'alimentation et l'agriculture (FAO), Rome, données FAOSTAT, dernier accès octobre 2006, http://faostat.fao.org.

5 Index numbers of industrial production

1995 = 100

Indices de la production industrielle

1995 = 100

Region and industry [ISIC Rev. 3] Région et industrie [CITI Rév. 3]	Weight (%) Pond. (%)	1999	2000	2001	2002	2003	2004	2005
World — Monde								
Total industry [CDE] — Total, industrie [CDE]	100.0	115.3	123.9	121.5	122.0	126.3	134.3	141.4
Total mining [C] — Total, industries extractives [C]	7.4	103.8	107.4	106.6	104.4	109.2	110.9	111.9
Coal — Houille	0.7	100.3	99.7	101.6	102.3	104.2	107.8	112.5
Crude petroleum and natural gas Pétrole brut et gaz naturel	5.0	101.4	105.2	104.0	100.5	106.2	107.6	108.4
Metal ores — Minerais métalliques	0.7	117.5	123.3	121.8	122.8	125.8	127.6	126.7
Total manufacturing [D] Total, industries manufacturières [D]	82.6	116.9	126.4	123.5	124.0	128.4	137.5	145.7
Food, beverages, tobacco Industries alimentaires, boissons, tabac	10.3	104.9	106.4	107.1	108.4	109.7	111.6	114.2
Textiles — Textiles	2.4	96.1	97.1	92.0	89.9	86.9	86.8	84.6
Wearing apparel, leather and footwear Articles d'habillement, cuir et chaussures	2.7	85.1	83.4	77.1	70.1	66.4	64.9	60.8
Wood and wood products — Bois et articles en bois	1.9	104.8	106.5	101.1	102.5	102.9	107.6	108.3
Paper, printing, publishing and recorded media Papier, imprimerie, édition et supports enregistré	7.1	106.8	108.1	104.5	104.0	102.8	104.6	105.2
Chemicals and related products Produits chimiques et alliés	14.0	113.5	116.8	116.4	120.1	122.7	127.0	130.2
Non-metallic mineral products Produits minéraux non métalliques	3.4	103.3	105.8	104.2	103.7	104.3	106.9	108.5
Basic metals — Métallurgie de base	4.7	103.4	108.8	106.0	107.6	110.1	114.5	114.6
Fabricated metal products Fabrications d'ouvrages en métaux	11.7	104.1	110.9	107.0	104.7	104.7	111.5	116.8
Office and related electrical products Machines de bureau et autres appareils élect.	12.7	174.5	222.0	214.2	213.3	239.3	278.9	318.9
Transport equipment — Equipement de transports	8.0	120.6	124.4	124.8	129.5	133.0	141.6	148.9
Electricity, gas, water [E] — Electricité, gaz et eau [E]	10.0	111.2	115.1	115.9	118.8	121.9	124.7	128.2
Developed regions[1] — Régions développées[1]								
Total industry [CDE] — Total, industrie [CDE]	100.0	115.7	124.2	121.4	120.9	124.3	131.3	137.9
Total mining [C] — Total, industries extractives [C]	4.6	100.7	102.0	101.8	100.9	100.4	99.7	98.2
Coal — Houille	0.6	93.2	90.7	91.0	89.1	87.4	88.3	87.8
Crude petroleum and natural gas Pétrole brut et gaz naturel	2.7	100.2	102.4	102.6	101.2	100.3	98.9	95.7
Metal ores — Minerais métalliques	0.4	100.5	102.7	99.4	96.7	94.2	93.2	95.9
Total manufacturing [D] Total, industries manufacturières [D]	84.9	117.3	126.9	123.6	122.8	126.5	134.5	142.1
Food, beverages, tobacco Industries alimentaires, boissons, tabac	9.5	103.7	104.7	105.4	106.3	106.7	107.3	108.7
Textiles — Textiles	1.8	94.5	93.9	88.2	84.3	80.4	77.4	74.0
Wearing apparel, leather and footwear Articles d'habillement, cuir et chaussures	2.4	82.4	78.0	71.1	62.4	57.8	54.3	50.2
Wood and wood products — Bois et articles en bois	2.0	106.7	108.3	102.5	103.9	103.7	108.3	109.6
Paper, printing, publishing and recorded media Papier, imprimerie, édition et supports enregistré	8.1	106.9	108.1	104.5	103.7	102.1	103.7	104.0
Chemicals and related products Produits chimiques et alliés	13.7	111.6	114.5	114.1	118.0	119.3	122.0	123.3
Non-metallic mineral products Produits minéraux non métalliques	3.2	101.6	104.1	101.7	99.3	99.0	100.9	101.1
Basic metals — Métallurgie de base	4.7	100.6	106.1	102.6	103.0	103.7	107.0	105.8
Fabricated metal products Fabrications d'ouvrages en métaux	12.7	104.7	110.5	106.3	103.1	102.6	108.3	114.0
Office and related electrical products Machines de bureau et autres appareils élect.	14.0	175.1	222.4	214.6	209.2	234.1	270.3	308.9

Region and industry [ISIC Rev. 3] Région et industrie [CITI Rév. 3]	Weight (%) Pond. (%)	1999	2000	2001	2002	2003	2004	2005
Transport equipment — Equipement de transports	8.7	120.2	122.3	121.7	125.2	126.9	133.1	137.6
Electricity, gas, water [E] — Electricité, gaz et eau [E]	10.5	108.6	112.0	112.6	114.8	117.4	119.5	122.2
Developing economies[2] — Economies en développement[2]								
Total industry [CDE] — Total, industrie [CDE]	100.0	114.0	122.7	121.9	126.3	134.2	146.1	155.2
Total mining [C] — Total, industries extractives [C]	18.3	106.8	112.9	111.5	108.0	118.0	122.1	125.6
Coal — Houille	1.2	113.4	116.3	121.4	127.0	135.5	144.2	158.4
Crude petroleum and natural gas Pétrole brut et gaz naturel	14.3	102.2	107.3	105.1	100.0	110.6	114.1	118.0
Metal ores — Minerais métalliques	1.7	134.7	144.2	144.5	149.2	157.8	162.5	157.9
Total manufacturing [D] Total, industries manufacturières [D]	73.7	114.7	124.3	123.3	129.3	137.0	151.4	162.1
Food, beverages, tobacco Industries alimentaires, boissons, tabac	13.3	108.3	111.0	112.1	114.3	118.1	123.6	129.8
Textiles — Textiles	4.8	98.5	102.0	97.8	98.5	97.0	101.1	100.8
Wearing apparel, leather and footwear Articles d'habillement, cuir et chaussures	3.6	92.5	97.9	93.3	91.0	89.3	93.6	89.5
Wood and wood products — Bois et articles en bois	1.5	94.4	96.3	93.5	94.6	98.5	103.3	101.3
Paper, printing, publishing and recorded media Papier, imprimerie, édition et supports enregistré	3.2	105.8	108.2	104.3	106.6	109.5	114.1	117.2
Chemicals and related products Produits chimiques et alliés	15.0	120.5	124.9	124.7	127.7	134.8	145.0	155.0
Non-metallic mineral products Produits minéraux non métalliques	4.2	108.6	111.3	111.9	117.1	120.6	125.0	131.2
Basic metals — Métallurgie de base	4.7	114.2	119.6	119.4	125.7	135.6	144.1	149.3
Fabricated metal products Fabrications d'ouvrages en métaux	7.9	100.3	113.9	111.6	115.0	118.4	132.0	134.4
Office and related electrical products Machines de bureau et autres appareils élect.	7.3	170.3	218.3	211.1	244.7	278.5	344.9	395.9
Transport equipment — Equipement de transports	5.2	123.0	138.4	145.5	158.0	173.5	198.4	224.0
Electricity, gas, water [E] — Electricité, gaz et eau [E]	8.0	124.5	131.3	133.2	139.5	145.9	152.0	159.4
Northern America[3] — Amérique septentrionale[3]								
Total industry [CDE] — Total, industrie [CDE]	100.0	133.8	148.8	145.1	145.1	152.8	167.1	183.4
Total mining [C] — Total, industries extractives [C]	6.6	98.6	100.9	101.4	98.6	99.6	100.5	99.5
Coal — Houille	0.6	104.4	103.1	108.6	102.7	98.3	102.3	101.7
Crude petroleum and natural gas Pétrole brut et gaz naturel	4.8	95.7	98.9	99.6	97.2	98.2	97.9	96.2
Metal ores — Minerais métalliques	0.6	99.0	101.7	94.1	88.6	84.1	83.7	86.3
Total manufacturing [D] Total, industries manufacturières [D]	81.6	140.5	158.3	153.8	153.4	162.5	179.8	199.4
Food, beverages, tobacco Industries alimentaires, boissons, tabac	8.1	104.1	105.9	106.4	107.5	107.5	109.2	111.8
Textiles — Textiles	1.6	104.0	103.0	93.0	91.8	87.3	84.6	82.6
Wearing apparel, leather and footwear Articles d'habillement, cuir et chaussures	2.1	87.9	85.5	73.2	61.3	56.8	54.4	52.6
Wood and wood products — Bois et articles en bois	2.9	117.9	118.1	110.8	115.6	114.5	121.7	124.4
Paper, printing, publishing and recorded media Papier, imprimerie, édition et supports enregistré	9.1	108.2	108.9	103.0	101.3	97.7	98.9	100.2
Chemicals and related products Produits chimiques et alliés	14.2	113.3	115.0	111.9	118.3	118.3	123.0	124.1
Non-metallic mineral products Produits minéraux non métalliques	2.0	118.4	119.3	115.9	116.2	116.9	122.7	124.8
Basic metals — Métallurgie de base	3.5	109.7	107.7	98.6	100.0	97.5	102.6	100.7
Fabricated metal products Fabrications d'ouvrages en métaux	12.1	111.6	117.6	107.1	103.3	102.0	109.9	114.1
Office and related electrical products Machines de bureau et autres appareils élect.	13.7	278.1	378.2	379.8	370.1	428.1	510.3	614.4
Transport equipment — Equipement de transports	9.5	127.8	122.9	117.4	122.4	124.7	129.4	135.9
Electricity, gas, water [E] — Electricité, gaz et eau [E]	11.8	107.5	110.2	109.5	113.4	115.6	116.8	120.2

Region and industry [ISIC Rev. 3] Région et industrie [CITI Rév. 3]	Weight (%) Pond. (%)	1999	2000	2001	2002	2003	2004	2005
Latin America and the Caribbean — Amérique latine et Caraïbes								
Total industry [CDE] — Total, industrie [CDE]	100.0	113.2	119.0	118.4	119.1	121.7	130.0	133.9
Total mining [C] — Total, industries extractives [C]	10.2	126.5	135.5	136.5	133.9	137.4	143.4	147.6
Coal — Houille	0.3	111.1	106.2	96.1	97.1	99.3	101.8	111.3
Crude petroleum and natural gas Pétrole brut et gaz naturel	5.6	115.7	120.5	121.4	117.4	116.2	120.6	125.5
Metal ores — Minerais métalliques	2.7	141.0	147.1	147.0	144.6	157.5	167.0	169.1
Total manufacturing [D] Total, industries manufacturières [D]	81.2	110.6	116.1	115.6	116.4	118.4	127.6	131.4
Food, beverages, tobacco Industries alimentaires, boissons, tabac	18.4	110.5	111.5	113.9	114.7	115.9	123.1	127.4
Textiles — Textiles	3.3	90.8	96.2	89.4	85.5	87.2	96.1	96.2
Wearing apparel, leather and footwear Articles d'habillement, cuir et chaussures	3.4	92.6	97.7	89.8	86.2	83.9	87.9	87.1
Wood and wood products — Bois et articles en bois	2.0	107.1	110.5	107.3	112.1	116.9	125.0	120.6
Paper, printing, publishing and recorded media Papier, imprimerie, édition et supports enregistré	3.7	107.9	111.9	108.2	110.2	113.4	119.8	125.4
Chemicals and related products Produits chimiques et alliés	19.5	115.0	117.8	115.7	115.0	117.5	124.8	128.7
Non-metallic mineral products Produits minéraux non métalliques	4.0	111.3	114.4	112.5	113.2	113.1	119.2	124.4
Basic metals — Métallurgie de base	4.1	115.3	118.7	116.6	120.5	130.8	142.1	144.4
Fabricated metal products Fabrications d'ouvrages en métaux	8.8	102.1	111.6	112.4	113.0	113.6	126.8	127.4
Office and related electrical products Machines de bureau et autres appareils élect.	4.9	119.8	135.0	135.2	129.3	127.3	138.3	146.6
Transport equipment — Equipement de transports	5.5	125.2	146.4	152.3	162.1	166.7	187.6	197.3
Electricity, gas, water [E] — Electricité, gaz et eau [E]	8.6	122.2	126.9	123.6	128.0	133.9	136.8	140.8
Asia — Asie								
Total industry [CDE] — Total, industrie [CDE]	100.0	105.0	111.9	107.0	108.6	113.8	121.1	125.7
Total mining [C] — Total, industries extractives [C]	7.9	102.4	106.9	104.5	101.3	109.8	111.6	113.5
Coal — Houille	0.7	110.4	113.6	121.0	124.5	133.6	142.7	156.5
Crude petroleum and natural gas Pétrole brut et gaz naturel	5.8	99.9	104.9	101.3	95.5	106.0	108.0	110.8
Metal ores — Minerais métalliques	0.3	140.9	157.8	157.8	186.1	169.5	159.9	109.6
Total manufacturing [D] Total, industries manufacturières [D]	82.8	104.2	111.4	105.5	107.4	112.4	120.5	125.2
Food, beverages, tobacco Industries alimentaires, boissons, tabac	10.3	100.5	102.1	101.7	102.5	105.1	105.0	107.2
Textiles — Textiles	2.8	93.6	94.0	90.1	89.4	86.0	86.8	85.7
Wearing apparel, leather and footwear Articles d'habillement, cuir et chaussures	2.9	79.0	75.7	69.1	63.4	60.1	58.5	53.5
Wood and wood products — Bois et articles en bois	1.2	76.9	75.1	69.2	64.8	64.8	64.9	64.2
Paper, printing, publishing and recorded media Papier, imprimerie, édition et supports enregistré	5.7	100.6	100.1	97.6	97.0	96.6	96.8	97.3
Chemicals and related products Produits chimiques et alliés	13.1	109.6	112.2	112.0	113.6	117.9	122.4	126.9
Non-metallic mineral products Produits minéraux non métalliques	3.7	91.7	93.4	89.9	89.1	89.4	89.0	89.6
Basic metals — Métallurgie de base	5.9	95.8	104.0	101.8	104.5	109.0	113.0	114.9
Fabricated metal products Fabrications d'ouvrages en métaux	9.0	91.5	99.0	91.4	87.9	90.6	99.2	102.0
Office and related electrical products Machines de bureau et autres appareils élect.	16.4	128.0	154.5	134.9	144.2	162.5	189.3	201.6
Transport equipment — Equipement de transports	7.3	106.0	111.2	112.8	121.3	126.0	138.4	149.4
Electricity, gas, water [E] — Electricité, gaz et eau [E]	9.3	114.9	120.5	122.4	125.6	129.0	134.5	140.2

Region and industry [ISIC Rev. 3] Région et industrie [CITI Rév. 3]	Weight (%) Pond. (%)	1999	2000	2001	2002	2003	2004	2005
Asia excluding Israel and Japan — Asie à l'exception de l'Israël et du Japon								
Total industry [CDE] — Total, industrie [CDE]	100.0	115.3	126.8	125.6	133.0	144.4	159.6	172.7
Total mining [C] — Total, industries extractives [C]	19.1	102.1	107.2	104.4	100.3	109.8	112.1	113.9
Coal — Houille	1.8	114.4	119.0	126.9	133.3	143.1	153.0	168.1
Crude petroleum and natural gas Pétrole brut et gaz naturel	15.7	99.9	104.9	101.3	95.4	105.9	107.9	110.6
Metal ores — Minerais métalliques	0.7	142.8	160.8	161.0	190.2	173.1	163.2	110.5
Total manufacturing [D] Total, industries manufacturières [D]	73.2	117.5	130.9	129.5	139.9	152.2	171.5	187.9
Food, beverages, tobacco Industries alimentaires, boissons, tabac	11.0	104.0	108.7	109.2	113.8	121.5	125.2	134.1
Textiles — Textiles	5.6	101.4	104.4	101.2	104.1	101.4	103.9	103.7
Wearing apparel, leather and footwear Articles d'habillement, cuir et chaussures	3.7	87.3	93.6	90.4	88.7	88.6	94.0	86.4
Wood and wood products — Bois et articles en bois	1.2	81.7	82.3	78.7	76.8	79.8	81.1	81.3
Paper, printing, publishing and recorded media Papier, imprimerie, édition et supports enregistré	3.1	102.7	103.5	98.7	101.4	103.5	106.0	106.2
Chemicals and related products Produits chimiques et alliés	13.6	125.9	132.5	133.6	140.0	151.3	165.2	180.7
Non-metallic mineral products Produits minéraux non métalliques	4.3	104.0	108.2	110.2	117.7	123.6	127.0	132.2
Basic metals — Métallurgie de base	5.4	112.5	119.2	120.6	128.1	137.0	145.4	152.3
Fabricated metal products Fabrications d'ouvrages en métaux	7.9	97.4	114.9	110.4	115.9	121.9	136.4	140.2
Office and related electrical products Machines de bureau et autres appareils élect.	9.0	182.1	238.2	229.4	272.2	314.4	394.1	455.0
Transport equipment — Equipement de transports	5.4	121.7	133.4	141.7	156.5	180.6	209.1	247.2
Electricity, gas, water [E] — Electricité, gaz et eau [E]	7.7	126.9	136.2	141.4	149.1	155.9	164.4	173.9
Europe — Europe								
Total industry [CDE] — Total, industrie [CDE]	100.0	110.3	116.2	116.7	116.0	117.1	120.7	122.3
Total mining [C] — Total, industries extractives [C]	5.1	100.4	100.4	99.5	100.4	100.1	100.3	97.3
Coal — Houille	1.1	80.1	76.2	73.0	70.7	70.1	69.4	67.1
Crude petroleum and natural gas Pétrole brut et gaz naturel	3.1	106.0	105.7	106.2	108.0	107.4	107.5	103.2
Metal ores — Minerais métalliques	0.2	93.5	98.8	97.9	104.6	108.2	110.9	110.6
Total manufacturing [D] Total, industries manufacturières [D]	85.0	111.0	117.5	117.9	116.9	117.9	121.8	123.7
Food, beverages, tobacco Industries alimentaires, boissons, tabac	10.4	105.6	106.8	108.5	111.2	112.4	113.8	115.9
Textiles — Textiles	2.5	94.1	95.8	92.5	88.3	85.5	82.6	78.5
Wearing apparel, leather and footwear Articles d'habillement, cuir et chaussures	2.7	84.3	81.5	79.6	72.3	68.1	64.2	58.4
Wood and wood products — Bois et articles en bois	1.9	106.9	112.6	108.7	108.6	110.3	115.3	116.3
Paper, printing, publishing and recorded media Papier, imprimerie, édition et supports enregistré	7.4	111.4	114.7	112.4	113.0	113.3	116.6	116.1
Chemicals and related products Produits chimiques et alliés	13.9	115.1	120.8	122.9	127.3	130.1	133.1	135.8
Non-metallic mineral products Produits minéraux non métalliques	4.2	103.3	107.7	107.7	105.5	106.1	109.5	109.8
Basic metals — Métallurgie de base	4.6	102.0	110.4	110.0	108.7	109.2	113.0	111.3
Fabricated metal products Fabrications d'ouvrages en métaux	15.5	106.4	112.9	114.6	113.2	112.9	117.9	120.7
Office and related electrical products Machines de bureau et autres appareils élect.	9.7	126.2	145.7	143.4	133.9	136.5	145.4	152.1
Transport equipment — Equipement de transports	8.1	127.1	135.0	137.6	137.1	140.1	147.2	150.5
Electricity, gas, water [E] — Electricité, gaz et eau [E]	9.8	109.2	113.1	115.3	116.4	119.6	121.6	123.5

5 Index numbers of industrial production — 1995 = 100 (*continued*)
Indices de la production industrielle — 1995 = 100 (*suite*)

Region and industry [ISIC Rev. 3] Région et industrie [CITI Rév. 3]	Weight (%) Pond. (%)	1999	2000	2001	2002	2003	2004	2005
Oceania — Océanie								
Total industry [CDE] — Total, industrie [CDE]	100.0	108.1	111.2	113.9	115.6	119.2	119.2	120.3
Total mining [C] — Total, industries extractives [C]	18.3	109.6	121.0	123.6	124.2	124.7	121.2	126.9
Coal — Houille	4.2	116.6	126.5	134.3	142.5	144.6	148.5	157.1
Crude petroleum and natural gas Pétrole brut et gaz naturel	6.0	94.9	116.4	119.4	114.3	109.3	97.5	96.4
Metal ores — Minerais métalliques	6.7	122.8	131.6	134.3	131.4	135.3	137.0	144.1
Total manufacturing [D] Total, industries manufacturières [D]	69.4	108.2	109.6	112.1	114.1	118.7	119.7	119.3
Food, beverages, tobacco Industries alimentaires, boissons, tabac	15.0	114.3	116.0	120.7	120.6	123.8	123.9	124.9
Textiles — Textiles	1.9	95.3	92.9	86.2	77.7	73.0	68.3	58.0
Wearing apparel, leather and footwear Articles d'habillement, cuir et chaussures	2.2	95.2	92.8	86.0	77.6	72.8	68.1	58.0
Wood and wood products — Bois et articles en bois	2.8	96.1	105.0	104.1	106.7	111.2	111.4	112.4
Paper, printing, publishing and recorded media Papier, imprimerie, édition et supports enregistré	7.3	103.5	107.3	109.9	113.4	113.8	115.9	115.7
Chemicals and related products Produits chimiques et alliés	10.0	109.8	113.4	116.5	117.1	123.6	117.5	118.0
Non-metallic mineral products Produits minéraux non métalliques	3.7	103.8	109.9	111.8	118.3	128.5	133.3	140.2
Basic metals — Métallurgie de base	8.5	106.7	103.2	102.9	110.5	114.5	115.3	112.3
Fabricated metal products Fabrications d'ouvrages en métaux	5.6	108.2	108.1	111.2	115.5	121.6	126.3	125.9
Office and related electrical products Machines de bureau et autres appareils élect.	4.8	111.7	111.2	116.8	117.5	125.3	131.7	132.9
Transport equipment — Equipement de transports	5.8	12.0	111.5	116.9	117.5	125.5	131.9	133.0
Electricity, gas, water [E] — Electricité, gaz et eau [E]	12.3	105.3	105.9	109.5	111.1	114.1	113.2	116.3

Source

United Nations Statistics Division, New York, the index numbers of industrial production database.

Notes

1 Northern America (Canada and the United States), Europe, Australia, Israel, Japan, New Zealand and South Africa.
2 Latin America and the Caribbean, Africa (excluding South Africa), Asia (excluding Israel and Japan), Oceania (excluding Australia and New Zealand).
3 Canada and the United States.

Source

Organisation des Nations Unies, Division de statistique, New York, la base de données pour les indices de la production industrielle.

Notes

1 Amérique septentrionale (le Canada et les Etats-Unis), Europe, l'Australie, l'Israël, la Nouvelle-Zélande et l'Afrique du Sud.
2 Amérique latine et Caraïbes, Afrique (non compris l'Afrique du Sud), Asie (non compris l'Israël et le Japon), Océanie (non compris l'Australie et la Nouvelle-Zélande).
3 Le Canada et les Etats-Unis.

Production, trade and consumption of commercial energy

Thousand metric tons of oil equivalent and kilograms per capita

Production, commerce et consommation d'énergie commerciale

Milliers de tonnes d'équivalent pétrole et kilogrammes par habitant

Region	Year Année	Primary energy production – Production d'énergie primaire: Total Totale	Solids Solides	Liquids Liquides	Gas Gaz	Electricity Electricité	Changes in stocks Variations des stocks	Imports Importations	Export Exportation
World	**1998**	**8 591 944**	**2 232 978**	**3 710 585**	**2 206 363**	**442 018**	**54 327**	**3 428 721**	**3 502 22**
	1999	**8 487 463**	**2 138 637**	**3 631 984**	**2 266 080**	**450 762**	**-58 083**	**3 470 347**	**3 510 66**
	2000	**8 716 291**	**2 156 360**	**3 768 554**	**2 328 615**	**462 762**	**-70 153**	**3 698 153**	**3 725 61**
	2001	**8 840 425**	**2 261 788**	**3 762 810**	**2 355 050**	**460 777**	**66 749**	**3 769 815**	**3 763 07**
	2002	**8 898 696**	**2 286 135**	**3 711 561**	**2 429 897**	**471 103**	**10 703**	**3 817 511**	**3 760 929**
	2003	**9 270 367**	**2 440 337**	**3 868 171**	**2 491 562**	**470 296**	**13 635**	**3 979 729**	**3 962 615**
	2004	**9 693 989**	**2 630 696**	**4 015 758**	**2 551 949**	**495 586**	**21 476**	**4 260 226**	**4 241 05**
Africa	1998	650 993	129 124	410 577	104 120	7 172	15 211	76 044	397 69
	1999	652 065	129 638	402 679	112 158	7 589	9 653	77 864	419 749
	2000	674 757	127 657	420 220	119 043	7 836	-341	80 545	446 884
	2001	674 540	126 992	420 460	119 292	7 795	1 166	83 197	446 86
	2002	678 236	125 065	415 578	128 902	8 691	125	85 356	442 12
	2003	714 629	129 579	441 351	135 209	8 489	807	85 358	472 16
	2004	751 813	131 753	468 548	142 512	9 000	-1 219	90 831	500 40
America, North	1998	2 193 767	613 238	732 226	718 191	130 112	36 771	757 055	404 085
	1999	2 072 642	510 235	707 906	718 566	135 935	-8 820	776 414	387 67
	2000	2 080 368	494 073	717 002	732 045	137 248	-56 705	830 179	412 905
	2001	2 095 993	519 145	719 520	728 416	128 912	66 501	862 400	413 53
	2002	2 099 269	498 017	727 060	735 919	138 273	-20 616	842 863	418 57
	2003	2 082 350	481 383	738 323	725 882	136 762	-6 251	891 600	437 81
	2004	2 094 218	500 585	734 668	718 209	140 756	-3	948 384	455 448
America, South	1998	520 478	31 830	357 375	86 688	44 585	373	90 560	259 838
	1999	516 370	30 907	351 101	90 008	44 354	-5 135	83 375	246 44
	2000	520 551	35 754	355 696	82 064	47 037	-108	83 713	253 834
	2001	521 974	38 257	351 518	87 239	44 960	1 750	85 179	255 890
	2002	508 196	37 834	337 895	85 658	46 809	13 140	83 078	241 910
	2003	509 848	41 177	330 949	88 746	48 975	5 442	80 880	239 564
	2004	541 292	43 782	348 692	98 286	50 534	-353	90 335	264 028
Asia	1998	3 002 793	932 627	1 531 335	444 828	94 003	447	1 116 489	1 344 899
	1999	3 033 478	953 561	1 501 322	485 295	93 300	-35 088	1 165 172	1 346 784
	2000	3 187 193	981 171	1 576 316	533 921	95 785	-15 433	1 261 109	1 434 050
	2001	3 260 032	1 048 245	1 557 184	555 138	99 465	-4 204	1 261 086	1 440 063
	2002	3 284 596	1 096 594	1 493 483	594 004	100 514	6 302	1 305 924	1 383 735
	2003	3 577 698	1 249 318	1 596 696	630 643	101 042	6 445	1 365 715	1 492 812
	2004	3 867 965	1 413 205	1 679 509	661 751	113 501	10 716	1 512 575	1 617 917
Europe	1998	1 992 707	370 794	641 323	818 312	162 279	957	1 357 174	959 973
	1999	1 992 632	366 348	636 524	824 071	165 688	-13 259	1 331 450	968 329
	2000	2 013 656	359 813	658 858	824 134	170 852	7 575	1 408 472	1 022 318
	2001	2 035 124	359 615	672 966	826 621	175 921	-3 997	1 442 707	1 044 044
	2002	2 072 777	353 275	700 679	846 004	172 819	10 118	1 463 684	1 105 688
	2003	2 132 967	363 136	726 782	871 925	171 124	7 317	1 519 348	1 152 412
	2004	2 178 756	358 023	751 446	891 718	177 569	11 197	1 580 807	1 230 988
Oceania	1998	231 205	155 365	37 750	34 222	3 868	569	31 399	135 738
	1999	220 277	147 948	32 452	35 982	3 895	-5 434	36 072	141 689
	2000	239 766	157 893	40 461	37 407	4 006	-5 142	34 134	155 624
	2001	252 763	169 534	41 162	38 344	3 724	5 534	35 247	162 680
	2002	255 622	175 350	36 866	39 410	3 996	1 634	36 606	168 896
	2003	252 874	175 745	34 070	39 157	3 904	-125	36 828	167 849
	2004	259 945	183 349	32 897	39 473	4 226	1 138	37 292	172 275

Source

United Nations Statistics Division, New York, the energy statistics database, last accessed January 2007.

Production, trade and consumption of commercial energy—Thousand metric tons of oil equivalent and kilograms per capita (*continued*)

Production, commerce et consommation d'énergie commerciale—Milliers de tonnes d'équivalent pétrole et kilogrammes par habitant (*suite*)

Bunkers - Soutes			Consumption - Consommation							
Air Avion	Sea Maritime	Unallocated Nondistribué	Per capita Par habitant	Total Totale	Solids Solides	Liquids Liquides	Gas Gaz	Electricity Electricité	Year Année	Région
99 374	**136 661**	**260 664**	**1 323**	**7 967 413**	**2 251 635**	**3 094 998**	**2 178 772**	**442 009**	**1998**	**Monde**
106 628	**145 663**	**207 977**	**1 317**	**8 044 958**	**2 190 249**	**3 142 560**	**2 261 130**	**451 019**	**1999**	
110 904	**148 387**	**247 579**	**1 334**	**8 252 112**	**2 266 017**	**3 177 168**	**2 346 137**	**462 789**	**2000**	
108 713	**140 648**	**248 407**	**1 322**	**8 282 648**	**2 276 747**	**3 213 417**	**2 330 768**	**461 716**	**2001**	
110 729	**144 751**	**197 996**	**1 339**	**8 491 098**	**2 331 600**	**3 250 154**	**2 436 870**	**472 475**	**2002**	
112 082	**144 810**	**273 681**	**1 365**	**8 743 273**	**2 502 646**	**3 273 756**	**2 496 258**	**470 613**	**2003**	
121 792	**157 851**	**274 361**	**1 408**	**9 137 677**	**2 700 142**	**3 397 340**	**2 544 627**	**495 569**	**2004**	
4 152	7 029	48 495	340	254 457	92 546	99 763	55 075	7 073	1998	Afrique
4 476	8 160	15 801	354	272 091	95 831	112 287	56 107	7 866	1999	
5 117	7 548	24 327	344	271 765	95 352	113 474	55 081	7 857	2000	
4 690	7 419	20 807	342	276 789	96 059	114 661	57 869	8 200	2001	
4 538	6 517	19 777	351	290 514	92 953	121 705	66 886	8 970	2002	
4 488	7 482	20 079	348	294 970	96 731	122 113	67 610	8 516	2003	
4 480	6 483	18 623	360	313 875	103 909	131 325	69 586	9 054	2004	
22 061	27 532	16 245	5 221	2 444 128	555 765	1 058 413	699 740	130 211	1998	Amérique du Nord
23 541	31 390	5 381	5 093	2 409 889	469 072	1 086 405	718 420	135 992	1999	
23 653	33 591	4 630	5 204	2 492 473	491 580	1 101 205	762 510	137 179	2000	
21 695	24 640	17 793	4 907	2 414 232	479 328	1 103 797	702 278	128 830	2001	
21 137	28 089	2 302	4 999	2 492 640	484 740	1 115 925	753 444	138 531	2002	
20 609	23 835	19 395	4 921	2 478 545	488 603	1 128 608	724 677	136 657	2003	
20 989	29 334	17 465	4 942	2 519 370	497 307	1 161 956	719 362	140 744	2004	
2 402	3 607	20 507	968	324 310	23 994	169 112	86 612	44 590	1998	Amérique du Sud
2 202	4 487	24 833	961	326 918	23 566	170 035	88 976	44 341	1999	
1 953	5 128	23 773	926	319 684	23 625	167 210	81 925	46 923	2000	
1 915	5 633	18 586	917	323 380	22 216	169 684	86 599	44 881	2001	
1 898	5 749	8 621	894	319 956	21 050	166 954	85 276	46 676	2002	
2 118	5 538	17 362	884	320 705	22 027	161 067	88 784	48 827	2003	
2 763	5 886	17 397	929	341 907	22 996	171 143	97 226	50 543	2004	
25 141	52 435	145 694	711	2 550 667	1 050 437	950 527	455 059	94 645	1998	Asie
24 840	57 171	133 414	734	2 671 528	1 100 861	980 975	495 874	93 818	1999	
26 287	55 248	169 732	755	2 778 417	1 142 143	1 010 310	529 272	96 692	2000	
27 761	54 713	171 909	760	2 830 875	1 170 878	1 015 616	544 027	100 354	2001	
31 201	55 218	153 543	785	2 960 521	1 228 612	1 040 500	590 023	101 386	2002	
31 358	58 435	190 648	831	3 163 716	1 375 605	1 059 888	626 955	101 268	2003	
36 745	63 293	195 282	898	3 456 588	1 558 697	1 131 144	653 242	113 506	2004	
42 572	44 937	36 686	2 647	2 264 757	476 516	768 716	857 903	161 622	1998	Europe
48 434	43 288	34 031	2 620	2 243 260	456 687	745 534	875 932	165 107	1999	
50 768	45 653	31 198	2 639	2 264 617	469 049	735 200	890 235	170 133	2000	
49 256	47 128	26 961	2 701	2 314 438	465 593	761 683	911 435	175 726	2001	
49 116	48 037	16 305	2 695	2 307 196	461 010	761 566	911 705	172 915	2002	
50 473	48 453	28 280	2 763	2 365 380	476 829	757 867	959 243	171 441	2003	
53 581	51 700	27 342	2 770	2 384 755	473 443	757 797	976 020	177 496	2004	
3 046	1 121	-6 963	4 365	129 094	52 377	48 467	24 383	3 868	1998	Océanie
3 136	1 168	-5 483	4 050	121 272	44 232	47 323	25 822	3 895	1999	
3 125	1 218	-6 082	4 125	125 156	44 268	49 769	27 113	4 006	2000	
3 396	1 117	-7 649	3 994	122 932	42 673	47 976	28 560	3 724	2001	
2 839	1 141	-2 552	3 848	120 270	43 234	43 505	29 536	3 996	2002	
3 038	1 068	-2 083	3 751	119 956	42 852	44 213	28 988	3 904	2003	
3 232	1 157	-1 747	3 727	121 182	43 790	43 976	29 190	4 226	2004	

Source

Organisation des Nations Unies, Division de statistique, New York, la base de données pour les statistiques énergétiques, dernier accès janvier 2007.

Total imports and exports: index numbers

Volume and unit value indices and terms of trade (2000 = 100)

Exportations et importations totales : indices

Indices du volume et de la valeur unitaire et termes de l'échange (2000 = 100)

Region	1997	1998	1999	2001	2002	2003	2004	2005	Région
Total									**Total**
Exports : Volume[1]	**80**	**83**	**88**	**99**	**103**	**109**	**121**	**132**	**Exp.: Volume[1]**
Exports : Unit value indices US $[2]	**110**	**104**	**102**	**97**	**97**	**107**	**117**	**121**	**Exp.: Indices de la val. unit. en $ E.U.[2]**
Imports : Volume[1]	**79**	**84**	**90**	**100**	**104**	**111**	**124**	**132**	**Imp.: Volume[1]**
Imports : Unit value indices US $[2]	**107**	**101**	**99**	**96**	**96**	**104**	**114**	**121**	**Imp.: Indices de la val. unit. en $ E.U.[2]**
Developed economies[3]									Economies développées[3]
Exports : Volume[1]	83	87	90	99	102	104	112	117	Exp.: Volume[1]
Exports : Unit value indices US $[2]	110	107	104	98	99	111	122	127	Exp.: Indices de la val. unit. en $ E.U.[2]
Imports : Volume[1]	78	85	91	100	102	108	117	124	Imp.: Volume[1]
Imports : Unit value indices US $[2]	108	102	100	96	97	107	116	123	Imp.: Indices de la val. unit. en $ E.U.[2]
Terms of trade[4]	101	104	104	101	102	104	104	103	Termes de l'échange[4]
North America									Amérique du Nord
Exports : Volume[1]	85	87	89	94	92	93	98	104	Exp.: Volume[1]
Exports : Unit value indices US $[2]	102	99	100	99	97	101	106	112	Exp.: Indices de la val. unit. en $ E.U.[2]
Imports : Volume[1]	74	82	91	96	100	105	116	123	Imp.: Volume[1]
Imports : Unit value indices US $[2]	99	93	94	97	95	98	103	111	Imp.: Indices de la val. unit. en $ E.U.[2]
Terms of trade[4]	102	106	106	102	102	103	103	101	Termes de l'échange[4]
Europe									Europe
Exports : Volume[1]	80	86	90	103	106	109	118	123	Exp.: Volume[1]
Exports : Unit value indices US $[2]	116	113	107	98	101	118	130	134	Exp.: Indices de la val. unit. en $ E.U.[2]
Imports : Volume[1]	78	86	91	101	104	108	118	124	Imp.: Volume[1]
Imports : Unit value indices US $[2]	114	110	104	97	99	115	127	132	Imp.: Indices de la val. unit. en $ E.U.[2]
Terms of trade[4]	102	103	103	100	102	103	102	102	Termes de l'échange[4]
Asia and the Pacific									Asie et le Pacifique
Exports : Volume[1]	90	89	91	91	96	99	108	106	Exp.: Volume[1]
Exports : Unit value indices US $[2]	99	92	96	94	91	98	108	115	Exp.: Indices de la val. unit. en $ E.U.[2]
Imports : Volume[1]	87	83	91	103	102	109	117	119	Imp.: Volume[1]
Imports : Unit value indices US $[2]	104	92	93	88	88	94	104	113	Imp.: Indices de la val. unit. en $ E.U.[2]
Terms of trade[4]	95	100	103	107	103	105	104	101	Termes de l'échange[4]
Africa									Afrique
Exports : Volume[1]	80	77	83	100	100	107	127	159	Exp.: Volume[1]
Exports : Unit value indices US $[2,5]	102	93	95	93	95	110	122	124	Exp.: Indices de la val. unit. en $ E.U.[2,5]
Northern Africa									Afrique du Nord
Exports : Volume	87	85	82	102	99	122	153	203	Exp.: Volume
Exports : Unit value indices US $	82	74	87	90	93	95	99	100	Exp.: Indices de la val. unit. en $ E.U.
Sub-Saharan Africa									Afrique subsaharienne
Exports : Volume	76	73	84	100	102	99	110	130	Exp.: Volume
Exports : Unit value indices US $	113	106	101	95	97	121	143	151	Exp.: Indices de la val. unit. en $ E.U.
Latin America and the Carib.									Amér. latine et Caraïbes
Exports : Volume[1]	77	86	91	102	102	105	119	134	Exp.: Volume[1]
Exports : Unit value indices US $[2]	103	91	92	94	95	101	109	117	Exp.: Indices de la val. unit. en $ E.U.[2]
Imports : Volume[1]	74	86	88	99	100	103	111	111	Imp.: Volume[1]
Imports : Unit value indices US $[2]	115	105	98	99	91	92	104	122	Imp.: Indices de la val. unit. en $ E.U.[2]
Terms of trade[4]	90	87	94	95	104	110	105	96	Termes de l'échange[4]
Latin America									Amérique latine
Exports : Volume[1]	76	86	91	102	102	104	119	134	Exp.: Volume[1]
Exports : Unit value indices US $[2]	103	91	92	94	95	101	109	117	Exp.: Indices de la val. unit. en $ E.U.[2]

7 Total imports and exports: index numbers—Volume and unit value indices and terms of trade (2000 = 100) *(continued)*

Exportations et importations totales : indices—Indices du volume et de la valeur unitaire et termes de l'échange (2000 = 100) *(suite)*

Region	1997	1998	1999	2001	2002	2003	2004	2005	Région
Western Asia									Asie occidentale
Exports : Volume[1]	68	61	76	96	101	116	136	166	Exp.: Volume[1]
Exports : Unit value indices US $[2]	109	106	102	97	96	103	115	124	Exp.: Indices de la val. unit. en $ E.U.[2]
Imports : Volume[1]	84	85	89	97	106	116	136	155	Imp.: Volume[1]
Imports : Unit value indices US $[2]	105	101	96	99	99	106	118	127	Imp.: Indices de la val. unit. en $ E.U.[2]
Terms of trade[4]	104	105	106	98	97	97	98	97	Termes de l'échange[4]
Other Asia									Autre Asie
Exports : Volume[1]	71	76	83	99	114	132	160	186	Exp.: Volume[1]
Exports : Unit value indices US $[2]	112	100	99	94	90	93	98	102	Exp.: Indices de la val. unit. en $ E.U.[2]
Imports : Volume[1]	88	80	84	98	110	128	156	172	Imp.: Volume[1]
Imports : Unit value indices US $[2]	100	90	94	95	93	96	104	110	Imp.: Indices de la val. unit. en $ E.U.[2]
Terms of trade[4]	112	111	105	98	97	96	95	92	Termes de l'échange[4]
Eastern Asia									Asie orientale
Exports : Volume[1]	72	78	84	101	118	145	179	213	Exp.: Volume[1]
Exports : Unit value indices US $[2]	110	98	97	94	91	92	98	100	Exp.: Indices de la val. unit. en $ E.U.[2]
Imports : Volume[1]	78	72	82	101	117	143	173	188	Imp.: Volume[1]
Imports : Unit value indices US $[2]	104	93	92	92	89	93	101	107	Imp.: Indices de la val. unit. en $ E.U.[2]
Terms of trade[4]	106	105	105	102	102	99	96	93	Termes de l'échange[4]
Southern Asia									Asie australe
Exports : Volume[1]	67	65	80	101	118	124	142	178	Exp.: Volume[1]
Exports : Unit value indices US $[2]	117	109	103	94	92	103	114	117	Exp.: Indices de la val. unit. en $ E.U.[2]
Imports : Volume[1]	86	95	94	106	111	131	137	208	Imp.: Volume[1]
Imports : Unit value indices US $[2]	101	90	96	96	102	108	136	118	Imp.: Indices de la val. unit. en $ E.U.[2]
Terms of trade[4]	115	121	107	98	90	95	84	99	Termes de l'échange[4]
South-eastern Asia									Asie du Sud-Est
Exports : Volume[1]	69	75	83	96	106	112	135	145	Exp.: Volume[1]
Exports : Unit value indices US $[2]	117	101	102	94	90	92	96	102	Exp.: Indices de la val. unit. en $ E.U.[2]
Imports : Volume[1]	90	77	83	95	101	105	127	135	Imp.: Volume[1]
Imports : Unit value indices US $[2]	114	98	97	97	95	98	104	114	Imp.: Indices de la val. unit. en $ E.U.[2]
Terms of trade[4]	102	103	104	97	94	94	93	89	Termes de l'échange[4]

Source

United Nations Statistics Division, New York, trade statistics database.

Source

Organisation des Nations Unies, Division de statistique, New York, la base de données pour les statistiques du commerce extérieur.

Notes

1 Volume indices are derived from value data and unit value indices. They are base-period weighted.

2 Regional aggregates are current-period weighted.

3 This classification is intended for statistical convenience and does not, necessarily, express a judgement about the stage reached by a particular country in the development process.

4 Unit value index of exports divided by unit value index of imports.

5 Improved estimates as of February 2005.

Notes

1 Les indices du volume sont calculés à partir des chiffres de la valeur et des indices de valeur unitaire. Ils sont à coéfficients de pondération correspondant à la périod en base.

2 Les totaux régionaux sont à coéfficients de pondération correspondant à la période en cours.

3 Cette classification est utilisée pour plus de commodité dans la presentation des statistique et n'implique pas nécessairement un jugement quant au stage de développement auquel est parvenu un pays donné.

4 Indices de la valeur unitaire des exportations divisé par l'indice de la valeur unitaire des importations.

5 Estimations améliorées jusqu'en février 2005.

Technical notes: tables 1-7

Table 1: The series of world aggregates on population, output, production, external trade and finance have been compiled from statistical publications and databases of the United Nations and the specialized agencies and other institutions. The sources should be consulted for detailed information on compilation and coverage.

Table 2 presents estimates of population size, rates of population increase, crude birth and death rates, surface area and population density for the world and regions. Unless otherwise specified, all figures are estimates of the order of magnitude and are subject to a substantial margin of error.

The population estimates and rates presented in this table were prepared by the Population Division of the United Nations Secretariat and published in *World Population Prospects: The 2006 Revision.*

The average annual percentage rates of population growth were calculated by the Population Division of the United Nations Secretariat, using an exponential rate of increase formula.

Crude birth and crude death rates are expressed in terms of the average annual number of births and deaths respectively, per 1,000 mid-year population. These rates are estimated.

Surface area totals were obtained by summing the figures for the individual countries or areas.

Density is the number of persons in the 2004 total population per square kilometre of total surface area.

The scheme of regionalization used for the purpose of making these estimates is presented in annex I. Although some continental totals are given, and all can be derived, the basic scheme presents macro regions that are so drawn as to obtain greater homogeneity in sizes of population, types of demographic circumstances and accuracy of demographic statistics.

Tables 3-4: The index numbers in table 3 refer to agricultural production, which is defined to include both crop and livestock products. Seeds and feed are excluded. The index numbers of food refer to commodities which are considered edible and contain nutrients. Coffee, tea and other inedible commodities are excluded.

The index numbers of total agricultural and food production in table 3 are calculated by the Laspeyres formula with the base year period 1999-2001. The latter is provided in order to diminish the impact of annual fluctuations in agricultural output during base years on the indices for the period. Production quantities of each commodity are weighted by 1999-2001 average national producer prices and summed for each year. The index numbers are based on production data for a calendar year.

Index numbers for the world and regions are computed in a similar way to the country index numbers except that in-

Notes techniques : tableaux 1 à 7

Tableau 1: Les séries d'agrégats mondiaux sur la population, la production, le commerce extérieur et les finances ont été établies à partir de publications statistiques et bases de données des Nations Unies et les institutions spécialisées et autres organismes. On doit se référer aux sources pour tous renseignements détaillés sur les méthodes de calcul et la portée des statistiques.

Le *Tableau 2* présente les estimations mondiales et régionales de la population, des taux d'accroissement de la population, des taux bruts de natalité et de mortalité, de la superficie et de la densité de population. Sauf indication contraire, tous les chiffres sont des estimations de l'ordre de grandeur et comportent une assez grande marge d'erreur.

Les estimations de la population et tous les taux présentés dans ce tableau ont été établis par la Division de la population du Secrétariat des Nations Unies et publiés dans "*World Population Prospects: The 2006 Révision*".

Les pourcentages annuels moyens de l'accroissement de la population ont été calculés par la Division de la population du Secrétariat des Nations Unies, sur la base d'une formule de taux d'accroissement exponentiel.

Les taux bruts de natalité et de mortalité sont exprimés, respectivement, sur la base du nombre annuel moyen de naissances et de décès par tranche de 1.000 habitants au milieu de l'année. Ces taux sont estimatifs.

On a déterminé les superficies totales en additionnant les chiffres correspondant aux différents pays ou régions.

La densité est le nombre de personnes de la population totale de 2004 par kilomètre carré de la superficie totale.

Le schéma de régionalisation utilisé aux fins de l'établissement de ces estimations est présenté dans l'annexe I. Bien que les totaux de certains continents soient donnés et que tous puissent être déterminés, le schéma de base présente les grandes régions qui sont établies de manière à obtenir une plus grande homogénéité en ce qui concerne l'ampleur des populations, les types de conditions démographiques et la précision des statistiques démographiques.

Tableaux 3-4: Les indices du tableau 3 se rapportent à la production agricole, qui est définie comme comprenant à la fois les produits de l'agriculture et de l'élevage. Les semences et les aliments pour les animaux sont exclus de cette définition. Les indices de la production alimentaire se rapportent aux produits considérés comme comestibles et contenant des éléments nutritifs. Le café, le thé et les produits non comestibles sont exclus.

Les indices de la production agricole et de la production alimentaire présentés au tableau 3 sont calculés selon la formule de Laspeyres avec les années 1999-2001 comme période de référence, cela afin de limiter l'incidence, sur les indices corres-

stead of using different commodity prices for each country group, "international commodity prices" derived from the Gheary-Khamis formula are used for all country groupings. This method assigns a single "price" to each commodity.

The indexes in table 4 are calculated as a ratio between the index numbers of total agricultural and food production in table 3 described above and the corresponding index numbers of population.

For further information on the series presented in these tables, see the FAO *Statistical Yearbook* and http://faostat.fao.org.

Table 5: The index numbers of industrial production are classified according to tabulation categories, divisions and combinations of divisions of the International Standard Industrial Classification of All Economic Activities, Revision 3, (ISIC Rev. 3) for mining (category C), manufacturing (category D), and electricity, gas and water (category E).

The indices indicate trends in value added at constant prices. The measure of value added used is the national accounts concept, which is defined as gross output less the cost of materials, supplies, fuel and electricity consumed and services received.

Each series is compiled using the Laspeyres formula, that is, the indices are base-weighted arithmetic means. The weight base year is 1995 and value added, generally at factor cost, is used in weighting.

For most countries the estimates of value added used as weights are derived from the results of national industrial censuses or similar inquiries relating to 1995. These data, in national currency, are adjusted to the ISIC where necessary and are subsequently converted into US dollars.

Within each of the ISIC categories (tabulation categories, divisions and combinations of divisions) shown in the tables, the indices for the country aggregations (regions or economic groupings) are calculated directly from the country data. The indices for the World, however, are calculated from the aggregated indices for the groupings of developed and developing countries.

China and the countries of the former USSR (except Russian Federation and Ukraine) are excluded from their respective regions.

Table 6: For a description of the series in table 6, see the technical notes to chapter XIII.

Table 7: For a description of the series in table 7, see the technical notes to chapter XVI. The composition of the regions is presented in table 58.

pondant à la période considérée, des fluctuations annuelles de la production agricole enregistrée pendant les années de référence. Les chiffres de production de chaque produit sont pondérés par les prix nationaux moyens à la production pour la période 1999-2001 et additionnés pour chaque année. Les indices sont fondés sur les données de production de l'année civile.

Les indices pour le monde et les régions sont calculés de la même façon que les indices par pays, mais au lieu d'appliquer des prix différents aux produits de base pour chaque groupe de pays, on a utilisé des "prix internationaux" établis d'après la formule de Gheary-Khamis pour tous les groupes de pays. Cette méthode attribue un seul "prix" à chaque produit de base.

Les indices du tableau 4 sont calculés comme ratio entre les indices de la production alimentaire et de la production agricole totale du tableau 3 décrits ci-dessus et les indices de population correspondants.

Pour tout renseignement complémentaire sur les séries présentées dans ces tableaux, voir l'*Annuaire Statistique de la FAO* et http://faostat.fao.org.

Tableau 5: Les indices de la production industrielle sont classés selon les catégories de classement, les divisions ou des combinaisons des divisions de la Classification Internationale type, par industrie, de toutes les branches d'activité économique, Révision 3 (CITI Rev. 3) qui concernent les industries extractives (la catégorie C) et les industries manufacturières (la catégorie D), ainsi que l'électricité, le gaz et l'eau (la catégorie E).

Ces indices représentent les tendances de la valeur ajoutée aux prix constants. La mesure utilisée pour la valeur ajoutée correspond à celle qui est appliquée aux fins de la comptabilité nationale, c'est-à-dire égale à la valeur de la production brute diminuée des coûts des matériaux, des fournitures, de la consommation de carburant et d'électricité ainsi que des services reçus.

Chaque série a été établie au moyen de la formule de Laspeyres, ce qui signifie que les indices sont des moyennes arithmétiques affectées de coefficients de pondération. L'année de base de pondération est l'année 1995 et on utilise généralement pour la pondération la valeur ajoutée au coût des facteurs.

Pour la plupart des pays, les estimations de la valeur ajoutée qui sont utilisées comme coefficients de pondération sont tirées des résultats des recensements industriels nationaux ou enquêtes analogues concernant l'année 1995. Ces données, en monnaie nationale, sont ajustées s'il y a lieu aux normes de la CITI et ultérieurement converties en dollars des Etats-Unis.

A l'intérieur de chacune des subdivisions de la CITI (catégories de classement, divisions et combinaisons des divisions) indiquées dans les tableaux, les indices relatifs aux assemblages de pays (régions géographiques ou groupements économiques) sont calculés directement à partir des données des pays.

Toutefois, les indices concernant le *Monde* sont calculés à partir des indices agrégés applicables aux groupements de pays développés et de pays en développement.

La Chine et les pays de l'ancienne URSS (sauf la Fédération de Russie et Ukraine) sont exclus de leurs régions respectives.

Tableau 6: On trouvera une description de la série de statistiques du tableau 6 dans les notes techniques du chapitre XIII.

Tableau 7: On trouvera une description de la série de statistiques du tableau 7 dans les notes techniques du chapitre XVI. La composition des régions est présentée au tableau 58.

Part Two

Population and social statistics

Deuxième partie

Population et statistiques sociales

Chapter II	Population and human settlements (tables 8 and 9)
Chapter III	Education (tables 10 and 11)
Chapter IV	Nutrition (table 12)
Chapter V	Communication (tables 13-15)

Chapitre II	Population et établissements humains (tableaux 8 et 9)
Chapitre III	Éducation (tableaux 10 et 11)
Chapitre IV	Nutrition (tableau 12)
Chapitre V	Communication (tableaux 13 à 15)

Part Two of the *Yearbook* presents statistical series on a wide range of population and social topics for all countries or areas of the world for which data have been made available. The topics include population and population growth, surface area and density; education; food supply; telephones and Internet users.

La deuxième partie de l'*Annuaire* présente, pour tous les pays ou zones du monde pour lesquels des données sont disponibles, des séries statistiques concernant une large gamme de questions démographiques et sociales: population et croissance démographique, superficie et densité; éducation; disponibilités alimentaires; téléphones et usagers d'Internet.

Population by sex, rate of population increase, surface area and density

Population selon le sexe, taux d'accroissement de la population, superficie et densité

Country or area Pays ou zone	Latest census Dernier recensement Date	 Both sexes Les deux sexes	 Men Hommes	 Women Femmes	Mid-year estimates (thousands) Estimations au milieu de l'année (milliers) 2000	 2004	Annual rate of increase Taux d'accroissement annuel % 2000-2004	Surface area Superficie (km²) 2004	Density Densité 2004&
Africa Afrique									
Algeria[1] Algérie[1]	25 VI 1998	29 100 867	14 698 589	14 402 278	30 416	32 364	1.6	2 381 741	14
Angola[2,3] Angola[2,3]	15 XII 1970	5 646 166	2 943 974	2 702 192	...	...	...	1 246 700	...
Benin Bénin	11 II 2002	6 769 914[1]	3 284 119[1]	3 485 795[1]	6 169[3]	...	...	112 622	...
Botswana[3] Botswana[3]	17 VIII 2001	*1 680 863	*813 488	*867 375	1 653	1 711	0.9	581 730	3
Burkina Faso[3] Burkina Faso[3]	10 XII 1996	10 312 609	4 970 882	5 341 727	11 347	12 496	2.4	274 000	46
Burundi[3] Burundi[3]	16 VIII 1990	5 139 073	2 473 599	2 665 474	...	...	...	27 834	...
Cameroon[3] Cameroun[3]	10 IV 1987	10 493 655	...	...	...	...	...	475 442	...
Cape Verde[3] Cap-Vert[3]	16 VI 2000	436 863	211 479	225 384	435	...	...	4 033	...
Central African Rep.[3] Rép. centrafricaine[3]	8 XII 2003	3 151 072	1 569 446	1 581 626	...	...	...	622 984	...
Chad[3,4] Tchad[3,4]	8 IV 1993	6 279 931	...	...	...	...	...	1 284 000	...
Comoros[3,5] Comores[3,5]	1 IX 2003	575 660	...	...	...	...	...	2 235	...
Congo[3] Congo[3]	6 VI 1996	*2 600 000	...	...	2 893	...	...	342 000	...
Côte d'Ivoire[3] Côte d'Ivoire[3]	21 XI 1998	15 366 672	7 844 621	7 522 050	16 402	18 546	3.1	322 463	58
Dem. Rep. of the Congo[3] Rép. dém. du Congo[3]	1 VII 1984	29 916 800	14 543 800	15 373 000	...	...	...	2 344 858	...
Djibouti[3] Djibouti[3]	11 XII 1960	81 200	...	...	...	...	...	23 200	...
Egypt[3] Egypte[3]	19 XI 1996	59 312 914	30 351 390	28 961 524	63 976	71 223	2.7	1 001 449	71
Equatorial Guinea[3,6] Guinée équatoriale[3,6]	1 II 2002	1 014 999	501 387	513 612	...	...	...	28 051	...
Eritrea[3] Erythrée[3]	9 V 1984	2 748 304	1 374 452	1 373 852	...	...	...	117 600	...
Ethiopia[3] Ethiopie[3]	11 X 1994	53 477 265	26 910 698	26 566 567	63 495	71 066	2.8	1 104 300	64
Gabon[3] Gabon[3]	1 XII 2003	*1 269 000	...	...	1 206	...	...	267 668	...
Gambia[3] Gambie[3]	15 IV 2003	*1 364 507	*676 726	*687 781	1 393	...	...	11 295	...
Ghana[3] Ghana[3]	26 III 2000	18 912 079	9 357 382	9 554 697	*18 412	...	...	238 533	...
Guinea[3] Guinée[3]	1 XII 1996	*7 156 406	*3 497 979	*3 658 427	...	...	...	245 857	...
Guinea-Bissau[3] Guinée-Bissau[3]	1 XII 1991	983 367	476 210	507 157	...	1 296	...	36 125	36
Kenya[3] Kenya[3]	24 VIII 1999	28 686 607	14 205 589	14 481 018	30 150	34 191	3.1	580 367	59

Country or area Pays ou zone	Latest census — Dernier recensement Date	Both sexes Les deux sexes	Men Hommes	Women Femmes	Mid-year estimates (thousands) — Estimations au milieu de l'année (milliers) 2000	2004	Annual rate of increase — Taux d'accroissement annuel % 2000-2004	Surface area — Superficie (km²) 2004	Density — Densité 2004&
Lesotho Lesotho	14 IV 1996	1 960 069[1]	964 346[1]	995 723[1]	2 144[3]	...	...	30 355	...
Liberia[3] Libéria[3]	1 II 1984	2 101 628	1 063 127	1 038 501	...	...	...	111 369	...
Libyan Arab Jamah.[3,7] Jamah. arabe libyenne[3,7]	11 VIII 1995	4 404 986	2 236 943	2 168 043	5 125	...	...	1 759 540	...
Madagascar[3] Madagascar[3]	1 VIII 1993	12 238 914	6 088 116	6 150 798	15 085	17 206	3.3	587 041	29
Malawi[3,8] Malawi[3,8]	1 IX 1998	9 933 868	4 867 563	5 066 305	10 475	*11 938	3.3	118 484	101
Mali[1] Mali[1]	1 IV 1998	9 790 492	4 847 436	4 943 056	10 243	...	...	1 240 192	...
Mauritania[3] Mauritanie[3]	1 XI 2000	2 548 157	1 240 414	1 307 743	2 645	...	...	1 025 520	...
Mauritius[1] Maurice[1]	2 VII 2000	1 178 848	583 756	595 092	1 187	1 233	1.0	2 040	605
Morocco[3] Maroc[3]	1 IX 2004	29 680 069	14 640 662	15 039 407	28 705	30 540	1.5	446 550	68
Mozambique[3,9,10] Mozambique[3,9,10]	1 VIII 1997	16 099 246	7 714 306	8 384 940	17 691	...	...	801 590	...
Namibia[3,11] Namibie[3,11]	27 VIII 2001	1 830 330	887 721	942 572	*1 817	...	...	824 292	...
Niger Niger	20 V 2001	*10 790 352[3]	*5 380 287[3]	*5 410 065[3]	10 493[1]	11 857[1]	3.1[1]	1 267 000	9
Nigeria[3,8] Nigéria[3,8]	26 XI 1991	88 992 220	44 529 608	44 462 612	115 224	...	...	923 768	...
Réunion Réunion	8 III 1999	706 180[1]	347 076[1]	359 104[1]	722[3]	769[3]	1.6	2 510	306
Rwanda[1] Rwanda[1]	16 VIII 2002	8 128 553	3 879 448	4 249 105	...	...	...	26 338	...
Saint Helena ex. dep.[3] Sainte-Hélène sans dép.[3]	8 III 1998	5 157	2 612	2 545	...	...	...	122	...
Ascension[1] Ascension[1]	8 III 1998	712	458	254	...	...	...	88	...
Tristan da Cunha[3] Tristan da Cunha[3]	31 XII 1988	296	139	157	...	...	...	98	...
Sao Tome and Principe Sao Tomé-et-Principe	25 VIII 2001	137 599[1]	68 236[1]	69 363[1]	135[3]	146[3]	1.9	964	152
Senegal[1] Sénégal[1]	8 XII 2002	*9 956 202	*4 886 485	*5 069 717	9 427	10 564	2.8	196 722	54
Seychelles[12] Seychelles[12]	26 VIII 2002	81 755[1]	40 751[1]	41 004[1]	81[3]	82[3]	0.4	455	181
Sierra Leone[3] Sierra Leone[3]	4 XII 2004	*4 963 298	*2 412 860	*2 550 438	4 944	...	...	71 740	...
Somalia[3] Somalie[3]	15 II 1987	7 114 431	3 741 664	3 372 767	...	...	...	637 657	...
South Africa[3,10,13] Afrique du Sud[3,10,13]	10 X 2001	*44 819 778	*21 434 041	*23 385 737	43 686	46 587	1.6	1 221 037	38
Sudan[3] Soudan[3]	15 IV 1993	24 940 683	12 518 638	12 422 045	31 081	*34 512	2.6	2 505 813	14
Swaziland[3] Swaziland[3]	11 V 1997	929 718	440 154	489 564	...	...	...	17 364	...
Togo[3] Togo[3]	22 XI 1981	2 719 567	1 325 641	1 393 926	4 629	5 090	2.4	56 785	90
Tunisia[3] Tunisie[3]	28 IV 2004	9 932 400	...	...	9 564	*9 941	1.0	163 610	61

Country or area / Pays ou zone	Latest census / Dernier recensement: Date	Latest census: Both sexes / Les deux sexes	Latest census: Men / Hommes	Latest census: Women / Femmes	Mid-year estimates (thousands) / Estimations au milieu de l'année (milliers): 2000	Mid-year estimates: 2004	Annual rate of increase / Taux d'accroissement annuel %: 2000-2004	Surface area / Superficie (km²): 2004	Density / Densité: 2004&
Uganda[3] Ouganda[3]	12 IX 2002	24 442 084	11 929 803	12 512 281	22 972	…	…	241 038	…
United Rep. of Tanzania[3] Rép.-Unie de Tanzanie[3]	24 VIII 2002	*34 443 603	*16 829 861	*17 613 742	…	…	…	945 087	…
Western Sahara[3,14] Sahara occidental[3,14]	31 XII 1970	76 425	43 981	32 444	…	…	…	266 000	…
Zambia[3] Zambie[3]	25 X 2000	9 885 591	4 946 298	4 939 293	9 337	11 090	4.3	752 618	15
Zimbabwe[3] Zimbabwe[3]	17 VIII 2002	11 631 657	…	…	…	…	…	390 757	…
America, North Amérique du Nord									
Anguilla[3] Anguilla[3]	9 V 2001	11 430	5 628	5 802	11	13	2.7	91	138
Antigua and Barbuda[3] Antigua-et-Barbuda[3]	28 V 2001	77 426	37 002	40 424	72	81	2.9	442	184
Aruba[1] Aruba[1]	14 X 2000	90 508	43 435	47 073	91	98	1.8	180	543
Bahamas[3] Bahamas[3]	1 V 2000	303 611	147 715	155 896	*303	…	…	13 878	…
Barbados[3] Barbade[3]	1 V 2000	250 010	119 926	130 084	269	272	0.3	430	634
Belize[3] Belize[3]	12 V 2000	240 204	121 278	118 926	250	283	3.1	22 966	12
Bermuda[1,15] Bermudes[1,15]	20 V 2000	62 059	29 802	32 257	63	*63	0.0	53	1 189
British Virgin Islands[3] Iles Vierges britanniques[3]	21 V 2001	20 647	10 627	10 020	…	22	…	151	147
Canada[1,16,17] Canada[1,16,17]	15 V 2001	30 007 095	14 706 850	15 300 245	30 689	31 974	1.0	9 970 610	3
Cayman Islands Iles Caïmanes	10 X 1999	39 410[3]	…	…	40[1]	…	…	264	…
Costa Rica[1] Costa Rica[1]	26 VI 2000	3 810 179	1 902 614	1 907 565	3 486	*4 248	4.9	51 100	83
Cuba Cuba	6 IX 2002	11 177 743[1]	5 597 233[1]	5 580 510[1]	11 130[3]	11 236[3]	0.2	110 861	101
Dominica[3,18] Dominique[3,18]	12 V 2001	69 625	35 073	34 552	72	71	0.0	751	95
Dominican Republic Rép. dominicaine	20 X 2002	8 562 541[1]	4 265 215[1]	4 297 326[1]	8 552[3]	8 870[3]	0.9	48 671	182
El Salvador[3] El Salvador[3]	27 IX 1992	5 118 599	2 485 613	2 632 986	6 276	*6 757	1.8	21 041	321
Greenland[1,19] Groenland[1,19]	1 VII 2000	56 124	29 989	26 135	56	57	0.3	2 175 600	…
Grenada[3,20] Grenade[3,20]	25 V 2001	102 632	50 481	52 151	101	…	…	344	…
Guadeloupe[1,21] Guadeloupe[1,21]	8 III 1999	422 222	203 146	219 076	428	*445	1.0	1 705	261
Guatemala[10] Guatemala[10]	24 XI 2002	11 237 196[1]	…	…	11 385[3]	*12 390	2.1	108 889	114
Haiti[1] Haïti[1]	11 I 2003	8 373 750	…	…	7 959	…	…	27 750	…
Honduras[3] Honduras[3]	28 VII 2001	*6 071 200	*3 000 530	*3 070 670	6 369	*7 028	2.5	112 088	63
Jamaica[1] Jamaïque[1]	10 IX 2001	2 607 632	1 283 547	1 324 085	2 589	2 615	0.2	10 991	238

Country or area / Pays ou zone	Latest census / Dernier recensement: Date	Both sexes / Les deux sexes	Men / Hommes	Women / Femmes	Mid-year estimates (thousands) / Estimations au milieu de l'année (milliers): 2000	2004	Annual rate of increase / Taux d'accroissement annuel %: 2000-2004	Surface area / Superficie (km²): 2004	Density / Densité: 2004&
Martinique[1] Martinique[1]	8 III 1999	381 325	180 910	200 415	385	*394	0.6	1 102	357
Mexico[1] Mexique[1]	14 II 2000	97 483 412	47 592 253	49 891 159	100 569	105 350	1.2	1 958 201	54
Montserrat[3] Montserrat[3]	12 V 2001	4 491	2 418	2 073	*5	...	...	102	...
Netherlands Antilles[1,22] Antilles néerlandaises[1,22]	29 I 2001	175 653	82 521	93 132	179	183	0.5	800	229
Nicaragua[1] Nicaragua[1]	25 IV 1995	4 357 099	2 147 105	2 209 994	4 957	5 375	2.0	130 000	41
Panama[3] Panama[3]	14 V 2000	2 839 177	1 432 566	1 406 611	2 856	*3 172	2.6	75 517	42
Puerto Rico[1,23] Porto Rico[1,23]	1 IV 2000	3 808 610	1 833 577	1 975 033	3 818	3 895	0.5	8 875	439
Saint Kitts and Nevis[3] Saint-Kitts-et-Nevis[3]	14 V 2001	45 841	22 784	23 057	40	...	...	261	...
Saint Lucia[3] Sainte-Lucie[3]	22 V 2001	157 164	76 741	80 423	156	*162	1.0	539	301
Saint Pierre and Miquelon[3] Saint-Pierre-et-Miquelon[3]	8 III 1999	6 316	3 147	3 169	...	...	...	242	...
St. Vincent-Grenadines[3,24] St. Vincent-Grenadines[3,24]	14 V 2001	*109 202	...	...	112	...	...	388	...
Trinidad and Tobago[3] Trinité-et-Tobago[3]	15 V 2000	1 262 366	633 051	629 315	1 290	...	...	5 130	...
Turks and Caicos Islands Iles Turques et Caïques	20 VIII 2001	19 886[3]	9 896[3]	9 990[3]	18[1]	27[1]	9.9	948	29
United States[1,25] Etats-Unis[1,25]	1 IV 2000	281 421 906	138 053 563	143 368 343	282 193	293 623	1.0	9 629 091	30
United States Virgin Is.[1,23] Iles Vierges américaines[1,23]	1 IV 2000	108 612	51 864	56 748	109	...	...	347	...
America, South Amérique du Sud									
Argentina[3] Argentine[3]	18 XI 2001	36 260 130	17 659 072	18 601 058	36 784	38 226	1.0	2 780 400	14
Bolivia[3] Bolivie[3]	5 IX 2001	8 280 184	4 130 342	4 149 842	8 428	9 227	2.3	1 098 581	8
Brazil[26] Brésil[26]	1 VIII 2000	169 799 170[1]	83 576 015[1]	86 223 155[1]	167 724[3]	*181 586[3]	2.0	8 514 877	21
Chile[3] Chili[3]	24 IV 2002	15 116 435	7 447 695	7 668 740	15 398	16 093	1.1	756 096	21
Colombia[3] Colombie[3]	24 X 1993	33 109 840	16 296 539	16 813 301	42 299	45 295	1.7	1 138 914	40
Ecuador[3,27] Equateur[3,27]	25 XI 2001	12 156 608	6 018 353	6 138 255	12 299	13 027	1.4	283 561	46
Falkland Is. (Malvinas)[3,28,29] Iles Falkland (Malvinas)[3,28,29]	8 IV 2001	2 913	1 598	1 315	...	...	...	12 173	...
French Guiana[1] Guyane française[1]	8 III 1999	156 790	78 963	77 827	164	*187	3.3	90 000	2
Guyana[3] Guyana[3]	15 IX 2002	751 223	376 034	375 189	742	...	...	214 969	...
Paraguay[3] Paraguay[3]	28 VIII 2002	5 163 198	2 603 242	2 559 956	...	...	...	406 752	...
Peru[3,10,30,31] Pérou[3,10,30,31]	18 VII 2005	*26 152 265	*13 061 026	*13 091 239	25 939	27 547	1.5	1 285 216	21
Suriname[32,33] Suriname[32,33]	2 VIII 2004	492 829[3]	247 846[3]	244 618[3]	464[1]	487[1]	1.2	163 820	3

Population by sex, rate of population increase, surface area and density (*continued*)
Population selon le sexe, taux d'accroissement de la population, superficie et densité (*suite*)

Country or area Pays ou zone	Latest census Dernier recensement Date	 Both sexes Les deux sexes	 Men Hommes	 Women Femmes	Mid-year estimates (thousands) Estimations au milieu de l'année (milliers) 2000	 2004	Annual rate of increase Taux d'accroissement annuel % 2000-2004	Surface area Superficie (km²) 2004	Density Densité 2004&
Uruguay[3,10] Uruguay[3,10]	22 V 1996	3 163 763	1 532 288	1 631 475	3 301	3 302	0.0	175 016	19
Venezuela (Bolivarian Rep. of)[3,30] Venezuela (Rép. bolivar. du)[3,30]	30 X 2001	23 054 210	11 402 869	11 651 341	24 311	26 127	1.8	912 050	29
Asia **Asie**									
Afghanistan[3,34] Afghanistan[3,34]	23 VI 1979	13 051 358	6 712 377	6 338 981	21 770	...	...	652 090	...
Armenia[35] Arménie[35]	10 X 2001	3 002 594[3]	1 407 220[3]	1 595 374[3]	3 221[1]	3 214[1]	-0.1	29 800	108
Azerbaijan Azerbaïdjan	27 I 1999	7 953 438[1]	3 883 155[1]	4 070 283[1]	8 049[3]	8 306[3]	0.8	86 600	96
Bahrain[3] Bahreïn[3]	7 IV 2001	650 604	373 649	276 955	638	707	2.6	694	1 019
Bangladesh[3] Bangladesh[3]	22 I 2001	*123 151 246	*62 735 988	*60 415 258	...	...	...	143 998	...
Bhutan[3] Bhoutan[3]	30 V 2005	672 425	364 482	307 943	678	...	...	47 000	...
Brunei Darussalam[3] Brunéi Darussalam[3]	21 VIII 2001	*332 844	*168 974	*163 870	325	360	2.6	5 765	62
Cambodia[3,36] Cambodge[3,36]	3 III 1998	11 437 656	5 511 408	5 926 248	12 688	13 091	0.8	181 035	72
China[37,38,39,40] Chine[37,38,39,40]	1 XI 2000	1 242 612 226[1]	640 275 969[1]	602 336 257[1]	1 262 645[3]	1 296 075[3]	0.7	9 596 961	135
China, Hong Kong SAR[1,41] Chine, Hong Kong RAS[1,41]	14 III 2001	6 708 389	3 285 344	3 423 045	6 665	6 883	0.8	1 099	6 263
China, Macao SAR[1] Chine, Macao RAS[1]	23 VIII 2001	435 235	208 865	226 370	431	457	1.5	26	17 574
Cyprus[1,42] Chypre[1,42]	1 X 2001	689 565	338 497	351 068	694	737	1.5	9 251	80
Georgia Géorgie	17 I 2002	4 371 535[1]	2 061 753[1]	2 309 782[1]	4 418[3]	4 318[3]	-0.6	69 700	62
India[3,43,44] Inde[3,43,44]	1 III 2001	1 028 610 328	532 156 772	496 453 556	1 016 320	1 085 600	1.6	3 287 263	330
Indonesia[45] Indonésie[45]	30 VI 2000	206 264 595[3]	103 417 180[3]	102 847 415[3]	...	217 077[1]	...	1 904 569	114
Iran (Islamic Rep. of)[1,46] Iran (Rép. islamique d')[1,46]	23 X 1996	60 055 488	30 515 159	29 540 329	63 664	67 477	1.5	1 648 195	41
Iraq[3,47] Iraq[3,47]	16 X 1997	19 184 543	9 536 570	9 647 973	23 577	...	...	438 317	...
Israel[1,48] Israël[1,48]	4 XI 1995	5 548 523	2 738 175	2 810 348	6 289	6 809	2.0	22 145	307
Japan[3,49] Japon[3,49]	1 X 2000	126 925 843	62 110 764	64 815 079	126 843	127 670	0.2	377 873	338
Jordan[3,50,51] Jordanie[3,50,51]	1 X 2004	5 100 981	2 628 717	2 472 264	4 857	5 350	2.4	89 342	60
Kazakhstan Kazakhstan	26 II 1999	14 953 126[1]	7 201 785[1]	7 751 341[1]	14 884[3]	15 013[3]	0.2	2 724 900	6
Korea, Dem. P. R.[3] Corée, R. p. dém. de[3]	31 XII 1993	21 213 378	10 329 699	10 883 679	22 963	23 612	0.7	120 538	196
Korea, Republic of[3,52] Corée, République de[3,52]	1 XI 2000	46 136 101	23 158 582	22 977 519	47 008	48 082	0.6	99 538	483
Kuwait[3] Koweït[3]	20 IV 1995	1 575 570	913 402	662 168	2 138	2 391	2.8	17 818	134
Kyrgyzstan Kirghizistan	24 III 1999	4 822 938[1]	2 380 465[1]	2 442 473[1]	4 915[3]	5 093[3]	0.9	199 900	25

Country or area / Pays ou zone	Latest census / Dernier recensement: Date	Both sexes / Les deux sexes	Men / Hommes	Women / Femmes	Mid-year estimates (thousands) / Estimations au milieu de l'année (milliers): 2000	2004	Annual rate of increase / Taux d'accroissement annuel %: 2000-2004	Surface area / Superficie (km²): 2004	Density / Densité: 2004[&]
Lao People's Dem. Rep.[3,53] Rép. dém. pop. lao[3,53]	1 III 1995	4 574 848	2 260 986	2 313 862	5 218	5 836	2.8	236 800	25
Lebanon[54,55] Liban[54,55]	15 X 1970	2 126 325	1 080 015	1 046 310	...	...	...	10 400	...
Malaysia[56,57] Malaisie[56,57]	5 VII 2000	23 274 690[1]	11 853 432[1]	11 421 258[1]	23 495[3]	25 581[3]	2.1	329 847	78
Maldives[3] Maldives[3]	31 III 2000	270 101	137 200	132 901	271	289	1.6	298	971
Mongolia[3] Mongolie[3]	5 I 2000	2 373 493	1 177 981	1 195 512	2 407	...	...	1 564 116	...
Myanmar[3] Myanmar[3]	31 III 1983	35 307 913	17 518 255	17 789 658	...	...	...	676 578	...
Nepal[1,58] Népal[1,58]	22 VI 2001	23 151 423	11 563 921	11 587 502	*22 904	...	...	147 181	...
Occupied Palestinian Terr.[3,59] Terr. palestinien occupé[3,59]	9 XII 1997	2 601 669	1 322 264	1 279 405	3 149	3 638	3.6	6 020	604
Oman[3] Oman[3]	7 XII 2003	2 340 815	1 313 239	1 027 576	2 401	2 416	0.1	309 500	8
Pakistan[3,60] Pakistan[3,60]	2 III 1998	130 579 571	67 840 137	62 739 434	137 510	150 468	2.3	796 095	189
Philippines[1] Philippines[1]	1 V 2000	76 504 077	38 524 267	37 979 810	76 348	82 664	2.0	300 000	276
Qatar[3] Qatar[3]	16 III 2004	744 029	496 382	247 647	617	756	5.1	11 000	69
Saudi Arabia[3] Arabie saoudite[3]	15 IX 2004	22 678 262	12 557 240	10 121 022	20 379	22 529	2.5	2 149 690	10
Singapore[3,61] Singapour[3,61]	30 VI 2000	4 017 700	2 061 800	1 955 900	4 018	4 240	1.3	683	6 208
Sri Lanka[3,62] Sri Lanka[3,62]	17 VII 2001	*16 864 544	*8 343 964	*8 520 580	19 359	19 462	0.1	65 610	297
Syrian Arab Republic[3,63] Rép. arabe syrienne[3,63]	3 IX 1994	13 782 315	7 048 906	6 733 409	16 320	17 980	2.4	185 180	97
Tajikistan[3] Tadjikistan[3]	20 I 2000	*6 127 000	*3 082 000	*3 045 000	6 188	...	...	143 100	...
Thailand[1] Thaïlande[1]	1 IV 2000	60 617 200	29 850 100	30 767 100	61 770	64 177	1.0	513 115	125
Timor-Leste[3] Timor-Leste[3]	11 VII 2004	*924 642	*467 757	*456 885	...	...	...	14 874	...
Turkey[3] Turquie[3]	22 X 2000	67 803 927	34 346 735	33 457 192	67 420	71 152	1.3	783 562	91
Turkmenistan[3] Turkménistan[3]	10 I 1995	4 483 251	2 225 331	2 257 920	...	...	...	488 100	...
United Arab Emirates[3,64] Emirats arabes unis[3,64]	17 XII 1995	2 411 041	1 606 804	804 237	...	...	...	83 600	...
Uzbekistan Ouzbékistan	12 I 1989	19 810 077[1]	9 784 156[1]	10 025 921[1]	24 650[3]	...	...	447 400	...
Viet Nam[3] Viet Nam[3]	1 IV 1999	76 323 173	37 469 117	38 854 056	77 686	82 032	1.4	331 689	247
Yemen[3] Yémen[3]	16 XII 1994	14 587 807	7 473 540	7 114 267	18 261	...	...	527 968	...
Europe **Europe**									
Albania[3] Albanie[3]	1 IV 2001	*3 069 275	*1 530 443	*1 538 832	3 061	3 127	0.5	28 748	109
Andorra[19] Andorre[19]	1 VII 2000	66 089[3]	34 344[3]	31 745[3]	66[1]	75[1]	3.1	468	160

Population by sex, rate of population increase, surface area and density (*continued*)
Population selon le sexe, taux d'accroissement de la population, superficie et densité (*suite*)

Country or area / Pays ou zone	Latest census / Dernier recensement: Date	Both sexes / Les deux sexes	Men / Hommes	Women / Femmes	Mid-year estimates (thousands) / Estimations au milieu de l'année (milliers): 2000	2004	Annual rate of increase / Taux d'accroissement annuel %: 2000-2004	Surface area / Superficie (km²): 2004	Density / Densité: 2004[&]
Austria[1] / Autriche[1]	15 V 2001	8 032 926	3 889 189	4 143 737	8 012	8 175	0.5	83 858	97
Belarus / Bélarus	16 II 1999	10 045 237[1]	4 717 621[1]	5 327 616[1]	10 005[3]	9 825[3]	-0.5	207 600	47
Belgium[1] / Belgique[1]	1 X 2001	10 296 350	5 035 446	5 260 904	10 251	10 421	0.4	30 528	341
Bosnia and Herzegovina / Bosnie-Herzégovine	31 III 1991	4 377 033[1]	2 183 795[1]	2 193 238[1]	3 781[3]	*3 842[3]	0.4	51 197	75
Bulgaria[3] / Bulgarie[3]	1 III 2001	7 928 901	3 862 465	4 066 436	8 170	*7 781	-1.2	110 912	70
Channel Is.: Guernsey / Iles Anglo-Norm.: Guernesey	29 IV 2001	59 807[1]	29 138[1]	30 669[1]	60[3]	60[3]	0.0	78	774
Channel Is.: Jersey / Iles Anglo-Norm.: Jersey	11 III 2001	87 186[1]	42 485[1]	44 701[1]	…	88[3]	…	116	755
Croatia[1] / Croatie[1]	31 III 2001	4 437 460	2 135 900	2 301 560	4 381	4 439	0.3	56 538	79
Czech Republic[1] / République tchèque[1]	1 III 2001	10 230 060	4 982 071	5 247 989	10 273	10 207	-0.2	78 866	129
Denmark[1,19,65] / Danemark[1,19,65]	1 I 2001	5 349 212	2 644 319	2 704 893	5 337	5 401	0.3	43 094	125
Estonia / Estonie	31 III 2000	1 370 052[1]	631 851[1]	738 201[1]	1 370[3]	1 349[3]	-0.4	45 100	30
Faeroe Islands[1,19] / Iles Féroé[1,19]	1 VII 2002	47 350	…	…	…	…	…	1 399	…
Finland[1,19] / Finlande[1,19]	31 XII 2000	5 181 115	2 529 341	2 651 774	5 176	5 228	0.2	338 145	15
France[1,66] / France[1,66]	8 III 1999	58 520 688	28 419 419	30 101 269	58 970	*60 381	0.6	551 500	109
Germany[67,68,69] / Allemagne[67,68,69]		82 491 000[70]	40 330 000[70]	42 161 000[70]	82 188[1]	82 501[1]	0.1	357 022	231
Gibraltar[3,71] / Gibraltar[3,71]	12 XI 2001	27 495	13 644	13 851	27	29	1.4	6	4 784
Greece[3,72,73] / Grèce[3,72,73]	18 III 2001	10 964 020	5 431 816	5 532 204	10 917	11 062	0.3	131 957	84
Holy See *[3,19,74] / Saint-Siège *[3,19,74]	1 VII 2000	798	529	269	…	…	…	…	…
Hungary[3] / Hongrie[3]	1 II 2001	10 198 315	4 850 650	5 347 665	10 024	10 107	0.2	93 032	109
Iceland[1,19] / Islande[1,19]	1 VII 2000	281 154	140 718	140 436	281	*292	1.0	103 000	3
Ireland[3,75] / Irlande[3,75]	28 IV 2002	3 917 203	1 946 164	1 971 039	3 787	4 044	1.6	70 273	58
Isle of Man[1] / Ile de Man[1]	29 IV 2001	76 315	37 372	38 943	75	78	0.9	572	136
Italy / Italie	21 X 2001	57 110 144[3]	27 617 335[3]	29 492 809[3]	56 942[1]	58 175[1]	0.5	301 318	193
Latvia / Lettonie	31 III 2000	2 377 383[1]	1 094 964[1]	1 282 419[1]	2 373[3]	2 313[3]	-0.6	64 600	36
Liechtenstein[3] / Liechtenstein[3]	5 XII 2000	33 307	16 420	16 887	33	34	1.3	160	215
Lithuania[1] / Lituanie[1]	6 IV 2001	3 483 972	1 629 148	1 854 824	3 500	3 436	-0.5	65 300	53
Luxembourg[1] / Luxembourg[1]	15 II 2001	439 539	216 541	222 998	436	453	1.0	2 586	175
Malta[1,76] / Malte[1,76]	26 XI 1995	378 132	186 836	191 296	390	401	0.7	316	1 270

Country or area / Pays ou zone	Latest census / Dernier recensement: Date	Both sexes / Les deux sexes	Men / Hommes	Women / Femmes	Mid-year estimates (thousands) / Estimations au milieu de l'année (milliers): 2000	2004	Annual rate of increase / Taux d'accroissement annuel %: 2000-2004	Surface area / Superficie (km²): 2004	Density / Densité: 2004&
Monaco[1] / Monaco[1]	21 VI 2000	32 020	15 544	16 476	...	...	...	2	...
Netherlands[1] / Pays-Bas[1]	1 I 2002	16 105 285	7 971 967	8 133 318	15 926	16 282	0.6	41 528	392
Norway[1,19,77] / Norvège[1,19,77]	3 XI 1990	4 520 947	2 240 281	2 280 666	4 491	4 592	0.6	385 155	12
Poland[3,78,79,80] / Pologne[3,78,79,80]	20 V 2002	38 230 080	18 516 403	19 713 677	38 256	38 180	0.0	312 685	122
Portugal[3,81] / Portugal[3,81]	12 III 2001	*10 148 259	*4 862 699	*5 285 560	10 226	10 502	0.7	91 982	114
Republic of Moldova[82] / République de Moldova[82]	5 X 2004	*3 388 071[3]	*1 632 519[3]	*1 755 549[3]	3 639[1]	3 604[1]	-0.2	33 851	106
Romania[1] / Roumanie[1]	18 III 2002	21 680 974	10 568 741	11 112 233	22 435	*21 684	-0.9	238 391	91
Russian Federation[83] / Fédération de Russie[83]	9 X 2002	*145 537 200[3]	*67 805 700[3]	*77 731 500[3]	146 597[1]	143 821[1]	-0.5	17 098 242	8
San Marino[3,19] / Saint-Marin[3,19]	1 VII 2000	26 941	13 185	13 756	27	29	2.2	61	482
Serbia and Montenegro[1,84,85,86] / Serbie-et-Monténégro[1,84,85,86]	31 III 2002	8 065 676	3 925 805	4 139 871	10 634	*8 147	...	102 173	...
Slovakia[1] / Slovaquie[1]	25 V 2001	5 379 455	2 612 515	2 766 940	5 401	*5 382	-0.1	49 033	110
Slovenia[1] / Slovénie[1]	31 III 2002	*1 964 036	*958 576	*1 005 460	1 990	1 997	0.1	20 256	99
Spain[87] / Espagne[87]	1 XI 2001	40 847 371[3]	20 012 882[3]	20 834 489[3]	40 264[1]	42 692[1]	1.5	505 992	84
Svalbard and Jan Mayen Is.[3,88] / Svalbard et îles Jan Mayen[3,88]	1 XI 1960	3 431	2 545	886	...	...	...	62 422	...
Sweden[1,19] / Suède[1,19]	1 VII 2000	8 872 110	4 386 436	4 485 674	8 872	8 994	0.3	449 964	20
Switzerland[1] / Suisse[1]	5 XII 2000	7 204 055	3 519 698	3 684 357	7 184	*7 390	0.7	41 284	179
TFYR of Macedonia / L'ex-R.y. Macédoine	1 XI 2002	2 022 547[1]	1 015 377[1]	1 007 170[1]	2 024[3]	2 033[3]	0.1	25 713	79
Ukraine[1] / Ukraine[1]	5 XII 2001	48 457 102	22 441 344	26 015 758	49 176	47 271	-1.0	603 700	78
United Kingdom[3,89,90] / Royaume-Uni[3,89,90]	29 IV 2001	58 789 187	28 579 867	30 209 320	58 886	59 835	0.4	242 900	246
Oceania / Océanie									
American Samoa[1,23] / Samoa américaines[1,23]	1 IV 2000	57 291	29 264	28 027	58	64	2.6	199	322
Australia[10] / Australie[10]	7 VIII 2001	18 972 350[3]	9 362 021[3]	9 610 329[3]	19 153[1]	20 111[1]	1.2	7 741 220	3
Cook Islands[3,91] / Iles Cook[3,91]	1 XII 2001	18 027	9 303	8 724	18	20	3.0	236	86
Fiji[3] / Fidji[3]	25 VIII 1996	775 077	393 931	381 146	...	...	...	18 274	...
French Polynesia[3,92] / Polynésie française[3,92]	7 XI 2002	245 516	...	...	231	251	2.0	4 000	63
Guam[1,23] / Guam[1,23]	1 IV 2000	154 805	79 181	75 624	...	166	...	549	303
Kiribati[3,93] / Kiribati[3,93]	7 XI 2000	*84 494	*41 646	*42 848	...	...	...	726	...
Marshall Islands[3] / Iles Marshall[3]	1 VI 1999	50 848	26 034	24 814	53	...	...	181	...

8 Population by sex, rate of population increase, surface area and density (*continued*)
Population selon le sexe, taux d'accroissement de la population, superficie et densité (*suite*)

Country or area / Pays ou zone	Latest census / Dernier recensement: Date	Both sexes / Les deux sexes	Men / Hommes	Women / Femmes	Mid-year estimates (thousands) / Estimations au milieu de l'année (milliers): 2000	2004	Annual rate of increase / Taux d'accroissement annuel %: 2000-2004	Surface area / Superficie (km²): 2004	Density / Densité: 2004&
Micronesia (Fed. States of)[1] Micronésie (Etats féd. de)[1]	1 IV 2000	107 008	54 191	52 817	119	...	...	702	...
Nauru[3] Nauru[3]	17 IV 1992	9 919	5 079	4 840	12	...	...	21	...
New Caledonia[3,94] Nouvelle-Calédonie[3,94]	31 VIII 2004	*230 789	*116 485	*114 304	213	230	1.9	18 575	12
New Zealand[1,95] Nouvelle-Zélande[1,95]	6 III 2001	3 820 749	1 863 309	1 957 440	3 858	*4 061	1.3	270 534	15
Niue[3] Nioué[3]	7 IX 2001	1 788	897	891	...	...	...	260	...
Norfolk Island[3] Ile Norfolk[3]	7 VIII 2001	2 601	1 257	1 344	...	...	...	36	...
Northern Mariana Islands[3] Iles Mariannes du Nord[3]	1 IV 2000	69 221	31 984	37 237	72	...	...	464	...
Palau[3] Palaos[3]	15 IV 2000	19 129	...	...	19	...	...	459	...
Papua New Guinea[3,96] Papouasie-Nvl-Guinée[3,96]	9 VII 2000	5 190 786	2 691 744	2 499 042	5 100	...	...	462 840	...
Pitcairn[3] Pitcairn[3]	31 XII 1991	66	...	...	...	...	...	5	...
Samoa[3] Samoa[3]	5 XI 2001	176 710	92 050	84 660	171	...	...	2 831	...
Solomon Islands[3,97] Iles Salomon[3,97]	21 XI 1999	409 042	211 381	197 661	...	...	...	28 896	...
Tokelau[3] Tokélaou[3]	11 X 2001	1 537	761	776	...	...	...	12	...
Tonga[3,98] Tonga[3,98]	30 XI 1996	97 784	49 615	48 169	100	...	...	747	...
Tuvalu[3] Tuvalu[3]	1 XI 2002	9 561	4 729	4 832	...	...	...	26	...
Vanuatu[1] Vanuatu[1]	16 XI 1999	186 678	95 682	90 996	...	...	...	12 189	...
Wallis and Futuna Islands[3] Iles Wallis et Futuna[3]	22 VII 2003	14 944	7 494	7 450	...	...	...	200	...

Source

United Nations Statistics Division, New York, "Demographic Yearbook 2004" and the demographic statistics database.

Source

Organisation des Nations Unies, Division de statistique, New York, "Annuaire démographique 2004" et la base de données pour les statistiques démographiques.

Notes

& Population per square kilometre of surface area in 2004. Figures are merely the quotients of population divided by surface area and are not to be considered either as reflecting density in the urban sense or as indicating the supporting power of a territory's land and resources.

1 De jure population.
2 Including the enclave of Cabinda.
3 De facto population.
4 Census results have been adjusted for under-enumeration, estimated at 1.4 per cent.
5 Census results, excluding Mayotte.
6 Comprising Bioko (which includes Pagalu) and Rio Muni (which includes Corisco and Elobeys).
7 For Libyan nationals only.
8 Data for estimates refer to national projections.

Notes

& Nombre d'habitants au kilomètre carré en 2004. Il s'agit simplement du quotient du chiffre de la population divisé par celui de la superficie: il ne faut pas y voir d'indication de la densité au sens urbain du terme ni de l'effectif de population que les terres et les ressources du territoire sont capables de nourrir.

1 Population de droit.
2 Y compris l'enclave de Cabinda.
3 Population de fait.
4 Les résultats du recensement ont été ajustés pour compenser les lacunes du dénombrement, estimées à 1,4 p. 100.
5 Les résultats du recensement, non compris Mayotte.
6 Comprend Bioko (qui comprend Pagalu) et Rio Muni (qui comprend Corisco et Elobeys).
7 Pour les nationaux libyens seulement.
8 Les données se réfèrent aux projections nationales.

9 Census results have been adjusted for under-enumeration, estimated at 5.1 per cent.

10 Mid-year estimates have been adjusted for under-enumeration, at latest census.

11 The number of males and / or females excludes persons whose sex is not stated.

12 Data exclude adjustment for under-enumeration, estimated at 2.4 per cent.

13 Data refer to estimated population after considering HIV.

14 Comprising the Northern Region (former Saguia el Hamra) and Southern Region (former Rio de Oro).

15 Excluding the institutional population.

16 For 2004, updated postcensal estimates.

17 For 2000, final intercensal estimates.

18 Census data excluding the institutional population.

19 Population statistics are compiled from registers.

20 Including Carriacou and other dependencies in the Grenadines.

21 Including dependencies: Marie-Galante, la Désirade, les Saintes, Petite-Terre, St. Barthélemy and French part of St. Martin.

22 Comprising Bonaire, Curaçao, Saba, St. Eustatius and Dutch part of St. Martin.

23 Including armed forces stationed in the area.

24 Including Bequia and other islands in the Grenadines.

25 Excluding armed forces overseas and civilian citizens absent from country for an extended period of time.

26 Data include persons in remote areas, military personnel outside the country, merchant seamen at sea, civilian seasonal workers outside the country, and other civilians outside the country, and exclude nomads, foreign military, civilian aliens temporarily in the country, transients on ships and Indian jungle population.

27 Excluding nomadic Indian tribes.

28 A dispute exists between the governments of Argentina and the United Kingdom of Great Britain and Northern Ireland concerning sovereignty over the Falkland Islands (Malvinas).

29 Excluding dependencies, of which South Georgia (area 3 755 km2) had an estimated population of 499 in 1964 (494 males, 5 females). The other dependencies namely, the South Sandwich group (surface area 337 km2) and a number of smaller islands, are presumed to be uninhabited.

30 Excluding Indian jungle population.

31 The population for the year 2005 corresponds to the population enumerated in the census conducted between 18 July and 20 August 2005. The total population is 27 219 264 inhabitants.

32 The previous census was conducted only 16 months earlier (on 31 March 2003) but it was repeated because all of its data were destroyed in a fire before they could be fully processed, analyzed, and reported.

33 Figures for male and female population do not add up to the figure for total population, because they exclude 1009 persons of unknown sex.

34 Census results, excluding nomad population.

35 The methodology used for calculating the number of the de facto and de jure population in the 2001 census data differs as follows from the methodology used in previous censuses: the duration that defines a person as being ' temporary present ' or ' temporary absent ' is now ' under one year '. The previously applied definition was for 6 months.

36 Excluding foreign diplomatic personnel and their dependants.

9 Les résultats du recensement ont été ajustés pour compenser les lacunes du dénombrement, estimées à 5,1 p. 100.

10 Les estimations au milieu de l'année tiennent compte d'un ajustement destiné à compenser les lacunes du dénombrement lors du dernier recensement.

11 Il n'est pas tenu compte dans le nombre d'hommes et de femmes des personnes dont le sexe n'est pas indiqué.

12 Les données n'ont pas été ajustées pour compenser les lacunes du dénombrement, estimées à 2,4 p. 100.

13 Les données portent sur la population estimée après prise en compte du VIH.

14 Comprend la région septentrionale (ancien Saguia-el-Hamra) et la région méridionale (ancien Rio de Oro).

15 Non compris la population dans les institutions.

16 Pour 2004, estimations post censitaires mises à jour.

17 Pour 2000, estimations inter censitaires finales.

18 Les données de recensement non compris la population dans les institutions.

19 Les statistiques de la population sont compilées à partir des registres.

20 Y compris Carriacou et les autres dépendances du groupe des îles Grenadines.

21 Y compris les dépendances: Marie-Galante, la Désirade, les Saintes, Petite-Terre, Saint-Barthélemy et la partie française de Saint-Martin.

22 Comprend Bonaire, Curaçao, Saba, Saint-Eustache et la partie néerlandaise de Saint-Martin.

23 Y compris les militaires en garnison sur le territoire.

24 Y compris Bequia et des autres îles dans les Grenadines.

25 Non compris les militaires à l'étranger, et les civils hors du pays pendant une période prolongée.

26 Y compris les personnes dans des régions éloignées, le personnel militaire en dehors du pays, les marins marchands, les ouvriers saisonniers civils de couture en dehors du pays, et autres civils en dehors du pays, et non compris les nomades, les militaires étrangers, les étrangers civils temporairement dans le pays, les transiteurs sur des bateaux et les Indiens de la jungle.

27 Non compris les tribus d'Indiens nomades.

28 La souveraineté sur les îles Falkland (Malvinas) fait l'objet d'un différend entre le Gouvernement argentin et le Gouvernement du Royaume-Uni de Grande-Bretagne et d'Irlande du Nord.

29 Non compris les dépendances, parmi lesquelles figure la Géorgie du Sud (3 755 km2) avec une population estimée à 499 personnes en 1964 (494 du sexe masculin et 5 du sexe féminin). Les autres dépendances, c'est-à-dire le groupe des Sandwich de Sud (superficie: 337 km2) et certaines petites-îles, sont présumées inhabitées.

30 Non compris les Indiens de la jungle.

31 La population pour 2005 correspond à la population dénombrée lors du recensement réalisé entre le 18 juillet et le 20 août 2005. La population totale compte 27 219 264 habitants.

32 Le recensement précédent a eu lieu seulement 16 mois auparavant (le 31 mars 2003), mais a dû être refait parce que toutes les données ont été détruites dans un incendie avant que l'on n'ait pu les traiter et les analyser.

33 Les chiffres relatifs à la population masculine et féminine ne correspondent pas au chiffre de la population totale, parce que l'on en a exclu 1 009 personnes de sexe inconnu.

34 Les résultats du recensement, non compris les nomades.

35 La méthode utilisée pour dénombrer la population présente et la population légale dans le contexte du recensement de 2001 diffère de celle qui a été appliquée lors des recensements antérieurs en ce que la durée considérée pour définir la ' présence temporaire ' ou ' l'absence temporaire ' était dorénavant fixée à ' moins d'un an ' alors qu'elle était de 6 mois auparavant.

36 Non compris le personnel diplomatique étranger et les membres de leur famille les accompagnants.

37 Estimates for 2000 have been adjusted on the basis of the Population Census of 2000.

38 For the civilian population of 31 provinces, municipalities and autonomous regions.

39 Estimates for 2004 have been estimated on the basis of the annual National Sample Surveys on Population Changes.

40 For statistical purposes, the data for China do not include those for the Hong Kong Special Administrative Region (Hong Kong SAR), Macao Special Administrative Region (Macao SAR) and Taiwan Province of China.

41 Data refer to Hong Kong resident population at the census moment, which covers usual residents and mobile residents. Usual residents refer to two categories of people: (1) Hong Kong permanent residents who had stayed in Hong Kong for at least three months during the six months before or for at least three months during the six months after the census moment, regardless of whether they were in Hong Kong or not at the census moment; and (2) Hong Kong non-permanent residents who were in Hong Kong at the census moment. Mobile Residents are Hong Kong permanent residents who had stayed in Hong Kong for at least one month but less than three months during the six months before or for at least one month but less than three months during the six months after the census moment, regardless of whether they were in Hong Kong or not at the census moment.

42 Data include all population irrespective of citizenship, who at the time of the census have resided in the country or intended to reside for a period of at least one year. It does not distinguish between those present or absent at the time of census. Data refer to government-controlled areas.

43 Census data exclude Mao-Maram, Paomata and Purul sub-divisions of Senapati district of Manipur. The population of Manipur including the estimated population of the three sub-divisions of Senapati district is 2,291,125 (Males 1,161,173 and females 1,129,952).

44 Including data for the Indian-held part of Jammu and Kashmir, the final status of which has not yet been determined.

45 Census data include an estimated population of 459 557 persons in urban and 1 857 659 persons in rural areas that were not directly enumerated, and a population of 566 403 persons in urban and 1 717 578 persons in rural areas that decline the participation. Also included are 421 399 non permanent residents (the homeless, the crew of ships carrying national flags, boat/floating house people, remote located tribesmen and refugees).

46 Estimates relate to the Iranian Year which begins on 21 March and ends on 20 March of the following year.

47 For the 1997 population census, data exclude population in three autonomous provinces in the north of the country.

48 Including data for East Jerusalem and Israeli residents in certain other territories under occupation by Israeli military forces since June 1967.

49 Excluding diplomatic personnel outside the country and foreign military and civilian personnel and their dependants stationed in the area.

50 Excluding data for Jordanian territory under occupation since June 1967 by Israeli military forces. Excluding foreigners, including registered Palestinian refugees.

51 Census results have not been adjusted for under-enumeration, estimated at 3.6 per cent.

52 Including diplomats and their families abroad, but excluding foreign diplomats, foreign military personnel, and their families in the country.

53 From year 2000-2004, calculated base on Population census 1995 structure and growth rate at year 2000.

54 Sample survey, de facto.

37 Les estimations pour 2000 ont été ajustées à partir des résultats du recensement de la population de 2000.

38 Pour la population civile seulement de 31 provinces, municipalités et régions autonomes.

39 Les estimations pour 2004 ont été estimées sur la base de l'enquête annuelle "National Sample Survey on Population Changes".

40 Pour la présentation des statistiques, les données pour la Chine ne comprennent pas la Région Administrative Spéciale de Hong Kong (Hong Kong RAS), la Région Administrative Spéciale de Macao (Macao RAS) et la province de Taiwan.

41 Les données se rapportent à la population résidente à Hong Kong au moment du recensement. Cette population est composée des résidants habituels et des résidants mobiles. La population résidente est partagée en deux catégories: (1) les résidents permanents qui ont habité à Hong Kong au moins trois mois pendant les six mois précédents ou les six mois suivants le recensement; (2) les habitants non-permanents de Hong Kong qui étaient à Hong Kong au moment du recensement. La population mobile se rapporte aux résidents permanents de Hong Kong qui ont habité à Hong Kong pendant les six mois après le recensement pour une période comprise entre un mois et trois mois, indépendamment du fait qu'ils étaient à Hong Kong au moment du recensement au pays.

42 Les chiffres comprennent toute la population, quelle que soit la nationalité, qui à l'époque de recensement avait résidé dans le pays, ou avait l'intention de résider, pendant une période de au moins un an. Il n'y a pas de distinction entre les personnes présentes ou absentes au moment du recensement. Les données se rapportent aux zones contrôlées par le Gouvernement.

43 Les données de recensement non compris les subdivisions Mao-Maram Paomata et Purul du district de Senapati dans l'État du Manipur. Cet État compte 2 291 125 habitants (1 161 173 hommes et 1 129 952 femmes), y compris la population estimative des trois subdivisions du district de Senapati.

44 Y compris les données pour la partie du Jammu et du Cachemire occupée par l'Inde dont le statut définitif n'a pas encore été déterminé.

45 Les données du recensement, y compris l'estimation de 459 557 personnes dans les zones urbaines et de 1 857 659 personnes dans les zones rurales qui n'ont pas été énumérées directement, aussi que 566 403 personnes qui n'ont pas répondu dans les zones urbaines et de 1 717 578 personnes dans les zones rurales. Y compris 421 399 résidants non permanents (les sans abri, l'équipage des bateaux portant le drapeau national, les habitants des embarcations ou des maisons flottantes, les habitants des tribus isolées et les réfugiés).

46 Les estimations concernent l'année iranienne, qui commence le 21 mars et se termine le 20 mars de l'année suivante.

47 Pour le recensement de 1997, la population des trois provinces autonomes dans le nord du pays est exclue.

48 Y compris les données pour Jérusalem-Est et les résidents israéliens dans certains autres territoires occupés depuis 1967 par les forces armées israéliennes.

49 Non compris le personnel diplomatique hors du pays ni les militaires et agents civils étrangers en poste sur le territoire et les membres de leur famille les accompagnants.

50 Non compris les données pour le territoire jordanien occupé depuis juin 1967 par les forces armées israéliennes. Non compris les étrangers, mais y compris les réfugiés de Palestine enregistrés.

51 Les résultats du recensement n'ont pas été ajustés pour compenser les lacunes du dénombrement, estimées à 3.6 p. 100.

52 Y compris le personnel diplomatique et les membres de leurs familles à l'étranger, mais sans tenir compte du personnel diplomatique et militaire étranger et des membres de leurs familles.

53 Pour les années 2000 à 2004, on a pris pour base la structure issue du recensement de population de 1995 et le taux de croissance de 2000.

54 Enquête par sondage, population de fait.

55 Excluding Palestinian refugees in camps.

56 Census results have been adjusted for under-enumeration.

57 Excluding Malaysian citizens and permanent residents who were away or intended to be away from the country for more than six months Excluding Malaysian military, naval and diplomatic personnel and their families outside the country, and tourists, businessman who intended to be in Malaysia for less than six months.

58 Data including estimated population from household listing from Village Development Committees and Wards which could not be enumerated at the time of census.

59 Total population does not include the Palestinian population living in those parts of Jerusalem governorate which were annexed by Israel in 1967, amounting to 210,209 persons. Likewise, the result does not include the estimates of not enumerated population based on the findings of the post enumeration study, i.e. 83,805 persons.

60 Excluding data for the Pakistan-held part of Jammu and Kashmir, the final status of which has not yet been determined.

61 Census results, excluding transients afloat and non-locally domiciled military and civilian services personnel and their dependants and visitors.

62 The Population and Housing Census 2001 did not cover the whole area of the country due to the security problems; the Census was complete in 18 districts only; in three districts it was not possible to conduct it; and in four districts it was partially conducted.

63 Including Palestinian refugees.

64 Comprising 7 sheikdoms of Abu Dhabi, Dubai, Sharjah, Ajaman, Umm al Qaiwain, Ras al Khaimah and Fujairah, and the area lying within the modified Riyadh line as announced in October 1955.

65 Excluding the Faeroe Islands and Greenland.

66 Excluding Overseas Departments, namely French Guiana, Guadeloupe, Martinique and Réunion, shown separately. De jure population but excluding diplomatic personnel outside country and including members of alien armed forces not living in military camps and foreign diplomatic personnel not living in embassies or consulates.

67 Data of the micro census - a 1% household sample survey - refer to a single reference week in spring (usually last week in April).

68 Excluding homeless persons.

69 Excluding foreign military personnel and foreign diplomatic and consular personnel and their family members in the country.

70 Sample survey, de jure.

71 Excluding families of military personnel, visitors and transients.

72 Mid-year population excludes armed forces stationed outside the country, but includes alien armed forces stationed in the area.

73 Census data including armed forces stationed outside the country, but excluding alien armed forces stationed in the area.

74 Data refer to the Vatican City State.

75 Estimates refer to 15th of April.

76 Including foreigners residing in Malta for 12 months before the census date and excluding foreign diplomatic personnel.

77 Including residents temporarily outside the country.

78 Surface area includes inland waters as well as part of internal waters.

79 Average year data for 2000 contain revised data according to the final results of population census 2002.

55 Non compris les réfugiés de Palestine dans les camps.

56 Les résultats du recensement ont été ajustés pour compenser les lacunes du dénombrement.

57 Non compris les citoyens Malaisiens et les résidents permanents qui étaient ou qui ont prévu d'être hors du pays pour six mois ou plus. Non compris le personnel militaire Malaisien, le personnel naval ou diplomatique et leurs familles hors du pays, et les touristes et les hommes d'affaires qui avaient l'intention de rester en Malaisie moins de six mois.

58 Les données incluent la population estimée par les listes des ménages des comités de développement des villages et des circonscriptions qui n'ont pas pu être énumérée au moment du recensement.

59 Les données relatives à la population totale ne comprennent pas la population palestinienne -équivalent à 210 209 personnes - habitant dans les territoires du gouvernorat de Jérusalem qui ont été annexés par Israël en 1967 Egalement, les données ne tiennent pas compte des estimations de la population calculée sur la base des résultats de l'enquête post censitaire, équivalent à 83 805 personnes.

60 Non compris les données pour le Jammu et Cachemire occupée par le Pakistan dont le statut définitif n'a pas encore été déterminé.

61 Les résultats du recensement, non compris les personnes de passage à bord de navires ni les militaires et agents civils non-résidents et les membres de leur famille les accompagnants et visiteurs.

62 Le recensement de la population et de l'habitat en 2001 n' pas couvert la totalité du pays pour des problèmes de sécurité ; le recensement à été complété seulement en 18 districts ; dans 3 districts ça n'a pas été possible de conduire le recensement et dans 4 districts il a été partialement conduit.

63 Y compris les réfugiés de Palestine.

64 Comprend les sept cheikhats d'Abou Dhabi, Dabai, Ghârdja, Adjmân, Oumm-al-Quiwaïn, Ras al Khaîma et Foudjaïra, ainsi que la zone délimitée par la ligne de Riad modifiée comme il a été annoncé en octobre 1955.

65 Non compris les îles Féroé et Groenland.

66 Non compris les départements d'outre-mer, c'est-à-dire la Guyane française, la Guadeloupe, la Martinique et la Réunion, qui font l'objet de rubriques distinctes. Population de droit, non compris le personnel diplomatique hors du pays et y compris les militaires étrangers ne vivant pas dans des camps militaires et le personnel diplomatique étranger ne vivant pas dans les ambassades ou les consulats.

67 Les données du micro recensement (enquête sur les ménages, réalisée sur un échantillon de 1 %) concernent une seule semaine de référence au printemps (habituellement la dernière semaine d'avril).

68 Non compris les personnes sans domicile fixe.

69 Non compris le personnel militaire étranger, le personnel diplomatique et consulaire étranger et les membres de leur famille se trouvant dans le pays.

70 Enquête par sondage, Population de droit.

71 Non compris les familles des militaires, ni les visiteurs et transients.

72 Les estimations au milieu de l'année non compris les militaires en garnison hors du pays, mais y compris les militaires étrangers en garnison sur le territoire.

73 Les données de recensement y compris les militaires hors du pays, mais non compris les militaires étrangers en garnison sur le territoire.

74 Les données se réfèrent à la Cité du Vatican.

75 Les estimations se rapportent au 15 avril.

76 Y compris les étrangers habitant à Malte pour 12 mois avant le recensement et le personnel diplomatique étrangers.

77 Y compris les nationaux se trouvant temporairement hors du pays.

78 Superficie comprends les eaux intérieures et une partie des eaux situées en deçà de la ligne de base de la mer.

79 Les données annuelles moyennes pour 2000 comportent des données révisées en fonction des résultats du recensement de 2002.

80 Excluding civilian aliens within country, but including civilian nationals temporarily outside country.

81 Including the Azores and Madeira Islands.

82 Data do not include information for Transnistria and the municipality of Bender.

83 Estimates were updated taking into account the results of the 2002 All-Russian population census.

84 For 2004, without data for Kosovo and Metohia.

85 For 2000, estimates of Kosovo and Metohia computed on the basis of natural increases from year 1997.

86 The census figure for Serbia and Montenegro consists of the final results of the population census held in the Republic of Serbia in 2002 (which was not carried out on the territory of Kosovo and Metohia) and the final results of the 2003 Census for the Republic of Montenegro.

87 Including the Balearic and Canary Islands, and Alhucemas, Ceuta, Chafarinas, Melilla and Penon de Vélez de la Gomera.

88 Inhabited only during the winter season. Census data are for total population while estimates refer to Norwegian population only. Included also in the de jure population of Norway.

89 Excluding Channel Islands and Isle of Man, shown separately.

90 Population estimate for 2000 were revised in light of the local studies.

91 Excluding Niue, shown separately, which is part of Cook Islands, but because of remoteness is administered separately.

92 Comprising Austral, Gambier, Marquesas, Rapa, Society and Tuamotu Islands.

93 Including Christmas, Fanning, Ocean and Washington Islands.

94 Including the islands of Huon, Chesterfield, Loyalty, Walpole and Belep Archipelago.

95 Including Campbell and Kermadec Islands (population 20 in 1961, surface area 148 km2) as well as Antipodes, Auckland, Bounty, Snares, Solander and Three Kings island, all of which are uninhabited.

96 Comprising eastern part of New Guinea, the Bismarck Archipelago, Bougainville and Buka of Solomon Islands group and about 600 smaller islands.

97 Comprising the Solomon Islands group (except Bougainville and Buka which are included with Papua New Guinea shown separately), Ontong, Java, Rennel and Santa Cruz Islands.

98 Data for estimates based on the results of the 1996 population census not necessarily mid-year estimated.

80 Non compris les civils étrangers dans le pays, mais y compris les civils nationaux temporairement hors du pays.

81 Y compris les Açores et Madère.

82 Les données ne tiennent pas compte de l'information sur la Transnistria et la municipalité de Bender.

83 Les estimations ont été calculées compte tenu des résultats du recensement de la population de la Fédération de Russie de 2002.

84 Pour 2004, sans les données pour le Kosovo and Metohie.

85 Pour 2000, les estimations pour le Kosovo et la Metohia ont été calculées sur la base des incréments naturels depuis 1997.

86 Le total pour la Serbie-et-Monténégro se consiste des résultats finals de recensement da la population de la République de Serbie du 2002 (qui n'a été pas conduit pour le territoire de Kosovo et Metohie) et les résultats finals de recensement de la population de la République de Monténégro du 2003.

87 Y compris les Baléares et les Canaries, Al Hoceima, Ceuta, les îles Zaffarines, Melilla et Penon de Vélez de la Gomera.

88 N'est habitée pendant la saison d'hiver. Les données de recensement se rapportent à la population totale, mais les estimations ne concernent que la population norvégienne, comprise également dans la population de droit de la Norvège.

89 Non compris les îles Anglo-Normandes et l'île de Man, qui font l'objet de rubriques distinctes.

90 Les estimations de la population pour l'année 2000 ont été révisées en fonction d'études locales.

91 Non compris Nioué, qui fait l'objet d'une rubrique distincte et qui fait partie des îles Cook, mais qui, en raison de son éloignement, est administrée séparément.

92 Comprend les îles Australes, Gambier, Marquises, Rapa, de la Societé et Tuamotou.

93 Y compris les îles Christmas, Fanning, Océan et Washington.

94 Y compris les îles Huon, Chesterfield, Loyauté et Walpole, et l'archipel Belep.

95 Y compris les îles Campbell et Kermadec (20 habitants en 1961, superficie: 148 km2) ainsi que les îles Antipodes, Auckland, Bounty, Snares, Solander et Three Kings, qui sont toutes inhabitées.

96 Comprend l'est de la Nouvelle-Guinée, l'archipel Bismarck, Bougainville et Buka (ces deux dernières du groupe des Salomon) et environ 600 îlots.

97 Comprend les îles Salomon (à l'exception de Bougainville et de Buka dont la population est comprise dans celle de Papouasie-Nouvelle Guinée qui font l'objet d'une rubrique distincte), ainsi que les îles Ontong, Java, Rennel et Santa Cruz.

98 Les estimations d'après les résultats du recensement de la population de 1996, pas nécessairement des estimations en milieu d'année.

Population in urban and rural areas, rates of growth and largest urban agglomeration population

Population urbaine, population rurale, taux d'accroissement et population de l'agglomération urbaine la plus peuplée

Region, country or area Région, pays ou zone	Year Année	Population estimates and projections / Estimations de la population et projections Rural % Rurale %	Urban % Urbaine %	Annual growth rate (%)[1] / Taux d'accroissement annuel (%)[1] Rural population Population rurale	Urban population Population urbaine	Population of largest urban agglomeration with 750,000 inhabitants or more in 2005 / Population de l'agglomération urbaine la plus peuplée avec 750,000 habitants ou plus en 2005 Number (000s) Nombre (000s)	% of urban % de urbaine	% of total % de totale
World	**2005**	**51.3**	**48.7**	**0.3**	**2.0**	**...**	**...**	**...**
Monde	**2010**	**49.2**	**50.8**	**0.2**	**1.9**	**...**	**...**	**...**
Africa	**2005**	**61.7**	**38.3**	**1.4**	**3.2**	**...**	**...**	**...**
Afrique	**2010**	**59.5**	**40.5**	**1.3**	**3.2**	**...**	**...**	**...**
Algeria	2005	36.7	63.3	-0.3	2.5	3 200	15.4	9.7
Algérie	2010	33.5	66.5	-0.3	2.3	3 576	15.2	10.1
Angola	2005	46.7	53.3	1.4	4.0	2 766	32.5	17.4
Angola	2010	43.4	56.6	1.2	3.7	3 303	31.9	18.0
Benin	2005	59.9	40.1	2.3	4.0	...	...	...
Bénin	2010	57.9	42.1	1.9	3.8	...	...	...
Botswana	2005	42.6	57.4	-2.3	0.9	...	...	...
Botswana	2010	38.8	61.2	-2.3	0.6	...	...	...
Burkina Faso	2005	81.7	18.3	2.4	5.1	926	38.3	7.0
Burkina Faso	2010	79.7	20.3	2.2	5.2	1 170	37.5	7.6
Burundi	2005	90.0	10.0	3.4	6.8	...	...	...
Burundi	2010	88.4	11.6	2.7	6.1	...	...	...
Cameroon	2005	45.4	54.6	-0.4	3.1	1 761	19.8	10.8
Cameroun	2010	41.1	58.9	-0.5	2.7	2 076	19.9	11.7
Cape Verde	2005	42.7	57.3	0.5	3.5	...	...	...
Cap-Vert	2010	39.0	61.0	0.3	3.1	...	...	...
Central African Rep.	2005	62.0	38.0	1.1	1.9	...	...	...
Rép. centrafricaine	2010	61.1	38.9	0.9	2.1	...	...	...
Chad	2005	74.7	25.3	2.0	4.4	888	36.0	9.1
Tchad	2010	72.4	27.6	2.0	4.8	1 097	35.7	9.9
Comoros	2005	63.0	37.0	1.5	4.3	...	...	...
Comores	2010	59.6	40.4	1.1	4.0	...	...	...
Congo	2005	39.8	60.2	1.9	3.6	1 173	48.7	29.3
Congo	2010	37.9	62.1	2.1	3.9	1 390	48.3	30.0
Côte d'Ivoire	2005	55.0	45.0	0.9	2.7	3 577	43.8	19.7
Côte d'Ivoire	2010	52.8	47.2	0.7	2.8	4 032	43.2	20.4
Dem. Rep. of the Congo	2005	67.9	32.1	2.1	4.9	6 049	32.7	10.5
Rép. dém. du Congo	2010	64.8	35.2	1.9	4.8	7 526	31.8	11.2
Djibouti	2005	13.9	86.1	-1.5	2.1	...	...	...
Djibouti	2010	11.9	88.1	-1.0	1.9	...	...	...
Egypt	2005	57.2	42.8	1.5	2.3	11 128	35.1	15.0
Egypte	2010	56.3	43.7	1.1	2.4	12 041	34.0	14.8
Equatorial Guinea	2005	61.1	38.9	2.0	2.6	...	...	...
Guinée équatoriale	2010	60.3	39.7	1.7	2.9	...	...	...
Eritrea	2005	80.6	19.4	2.5	5.2	...	...	...
Erythrée	2010	78.4	21.6	1.9	5.0	...	...	...
Ethiopia	2005	84.0	16.0	2.0	4.0	2 893	23.4	3.7
Ethiopie	2010	82.7	17.4	1.8	4.1	3 407	22.6	3.9
Gabon	2005	16.4	83.6	-1.6	2.2	...	...	...
Gabon	2010	14.0	86.0	-1.1	1.8	...	...	...
Gambia	2005	46.1	53.9	0.4	3.9	...	...	...
Gambie	2010	41.9	58.1	0.2	3.3	...	...	...

Region, country or area Région, pays ou zone	Year Année	Population estimates and projections / Estimations de la population et projections Rural % Rurale %	Urban % Urbaine %	Annual growth rate (%)[1] / Taux d'accroissement annuel (%)[1] Rural population Population rurale	Urban population Population urbaine	Population of largest urban agglomeration with 750,000 inhabitants or more in 2005 / Population de l'agglomération urbaine la plus peuplée avec 750,000 habitants ou plus en 2005 Number (000s) Nombre (000s)	% of urban % de urbaine	% of total % de totale
Ghana Ghana	2005	52.2	47.8	0.4	3.4	1 981	18.7	9.0
	2010	48.5	51.5	0.2	3.1	2 321	18.5	9.5
Guinea Guinée	2005	67.0	33.0	1.5	3.6	1 425	46.0	15.2
	2010	64.7	35.3	1.6	4.0	1 669	45.1	15.9
Guinea-Bissau Guinée-Bissau	2005	70.4	29.6	2.8	3.2	...	...	...
	2010	70.0	30.0	2.7	3.7	...	...	...
Kenya Kenya	2005	79.3	20.7	2.2	3.9	2 773	39.0	8.1
	2010	77.8	22.2	2.0	4.2	3 326	38.5	8.5
Lesotho Lesotho	2005	81.3	18.7	-0.6	1.1	...	...	...
	2010	79.9	20.1	-0.8	1.6	...	...	...
Liberia Libéria	2005	41.9	58.1	1.2	4.1	936	49.0	28.5
	2010	38.5	61.5	1.1	3.9	1 129	48.3	29.7
Libyan Arab Jamah. Jamah. arabe libyenne	2005	15.2	84.8	-0.1	2.2	2 098	42.2	35.8
	2010	13.7	86.3	0.0	2.0	2 326	41.9	36.1
Madagascar Madagascar	2005	73.2	26.8	2.2	3.5	1 585	31.8	8.5
	2010	71.8	28.2	1.8	3.7	1 853	31.1	8.8
Malawi Malawi	2005	82.8	17.2	1.6	4.7	...	...	...
	2010	80.5	19.5	1.5	4.7	...	...	...
Mali Mali	2005	69.5	30.5	2.0	4.7	1 368	33.2	10.1
	2010	66.7	33.3	2.0	4.8	1 700	32.7	10.9
Mauritania Mauritanie	2005	59.6	40.4	2.4	3.3	...	...	...
	2010	58.6	41.4	1.9	3.3	...	...	...
Mauritius[2] Maurice[2]	2005	57.6	42.4	0.7	1.1	...	...	...
	2010	57.2	42.8	0.3	1.3	...	...	...
Morocco Maroc	2005	41.3	58.7	-0.2	2.5	3 138	17.0	10.0
	2010	38.1	61.9	-0.3	2.3	3 294	15.7	9.7
Mozambique Mozambique	2005	65.5	34.5	0.5	3.9	1 320	19.3	6.7
	2010	61.6	38.4	0.4	3.6	1 586	19.1	7.3
Namibia Namibie	2005	64.9	35.1	0.0	2.6	...	...	...
	2010	62.0	38.0	0.0	2.6	...	...	...
Niger Niger	2005	83.2	16.8	3.0	4.4	850	36.2	6.1
	2010	82.2	17.8	2.8	4.8	1 049	35.9	6.4
Nigeria Nigéria	2005	51.8	48.2	0.5	3.7	10 886	17.2	8.3
	2010	47.8	52.2	0.3	3.3	13 717	18.0	9.4
Réunion Réunion	2005	7.6	92.4	-3.5	1.7	...	...	...
	2010	6.0	94.0	-2.6	1.3	...	...	...
Rwanda Rwanda	2005	80.7	19.3	1.1	6.5	779	44.6	8.6
	2010	76.1	23.9	0.8	5.8	1 146	47.3	11.3
Saint Helena[3] Sainte-Hélène[3]	2005	61.1	38.9	1.0	1.5	...	...	...
	2010	60.5	39.5	0.5	1.8	...	...	...
Sao Tome and Principe Sao Tomé-et-Principe	2005	42.0	58.0	0.1	3.5	...	...	...
	2010	37.8	62.2	-0.1	3.1	...	...	...
Senegal Sénégal	2005	58.4	41.6	1.8	2.9	2 159	44.6	18.5
	2010	57.1	42.9	1.5	3.0	2 478	44.2	18.9
Seychelles Seychelles	2005	47.1	52.9	-0.2	1.8	...	...	...
	2010	44.7	55.3	-0.5	1.9	...	...	...
Sierra Leone Sierra Leone	2005	59.3	40.7	0.8	3.8	799	35.6	14.5
	2010	55.6	44.4	0.9	4.0	924	33.9	15.1
Somalia Somalie	2005	64.8	35.2	2.4	4.3	1 320	45.6	16.0
	2010	62.5	37.5	1.8	4.0	1 545	43.0	16.1

Region, country or area Région, pays ou zone	Year Année	Population estimates and projections / Estimations de la population et projections: Rural % Rurale %	Urban % Urbaine %	Annual growth rate (%)[1] / Taux d'accroissement annuel (%)[1]: Rural population Population rurale	Urban population Population urbaine	Population of largest urban agglomeration with 750,000 inhabitants or more in 2005 / Population de l'agglomération urbaine la plus peuplée avec 750,000 habitants ou plus en 2005: Number (000s) Nombre (000s)	% of urban % de urbaine	% of total % de totale
South Africa Afrique du Sud	2005	40.7	59.3	-1.1	1.0	3 254	11.6	6.9
	2010	38.3	61.7	-1.3	0.8	3 574	12.1	7.5
Sudan Soudan	2005	59.2	40.8	0.5	4.2	4 518	30.6	12.5
	2010	54.8	45.2	0.2	3.5	5 178	28.4	12.9
Swaziland Swaziland	2005	75.9	24.1	-0.8	0.7	...	...	...
	2010	74.5	25.5	-0.9	1.2	...	...	...
Togo Togo	2005	59.9	40.1	1.3	4.3	1 337	54.3	21.8
	2010	56.3	43.7	1.0	4.0	1 639	53.7	23.5
Tunisia Tunisie	2005	34.7	65.3	-0.1	1.6	...	...	...
	2010	32.8	67.2	-0.3	1.5	...	...	...
Uganda Ouganda	2005	87.4	12.6	3.5	4.8	1 319	36.4	4.6
	2010	86.7	13.3	3.6	5.5	1 612	34.9	4.7
United Rep. of Tanzania Rép.-Unie de Tanzanie	2005	75.8	24.2	1.2	3.5	2 676	28.8	7.0
	2010	73.6	26.4	1.0	3.5	3 260	29.5	7.8
Western Sahara Sahara occidental	2005	8.4	91.6	3.6	4.7	...	...	...
	2010	8.0	92.0	3.0	4.1	...	...	...
Zambia Zambie	2005	65.0	35.0	1.4	2.1	1 260	30.8	10.8
	2010	64.3	35.7	1.4	2.5	1 408	31.1	11.1
Zimbabwe Zimbabwe	2005	64.1	35.9	-0.2	1.9	1 515	32.5	11.6
	2010	61.7	38.3	-0.3	1.9	1 650	32.2	12.3
America, North Amérique du Nord	**2005**	**19.3**	**80.7**	**-0.6**	**1.3**	**...**	**...**	**...**
	2010	**17.9**	**82.2**	**-0.7**	**1.2**	**...**	**...**	**...**
Anguilla Anguilla	2005	0.0	100.0	0.0	1.4	...	...	...
	2010	0.0	100.0	0.0	1.3	...	...	...
Antigua and Barbuda Antigua-et-Barbuda	2005	60.9	39.1	0.4	2.5	...	...	...
	2010	58.4	41.6	0.0	2.6	...	...	...
Aruba Aruba	2005	53.4	46.6	0.7	0.9	...	...	...
	2010	53.1	46.9	0.3	0.8	...	...	...
Bahamas Bahamas	2005	9.6	90.4	-1.1	1.5	...	...	...
	2010	8.5	91.5	-0.6	1.3	...	...	...
Barbados Barbade	2005	47.3	52.7	-1.1	1.3	...	...	...
	2010	44.3	55.7	-1.2	1.3	...	...	...
Belize Belize	2005	51.7	48.3	1.4	2.3	...	...	...
	2010	50.6	49.4	0.9	2.3	...	...	...
Bermuda Bermudes	2005	0.0	100.0	0.0	0.3	...	...	...
	2010	0.0	100.0	0.0	0.2	...	...	...
British Virgin Islands Iles Vierges britanniques	2005	39.5	60.5	-0.5	2.1	...	...	...
	2010	36.4	63.6	-0.7	1.8	...	...	...
Canada Canada	2005	19.9	80.1	0.3	1.0	5 312	20.5	16.5
	2010	19.3	80.7	0.0	1.0	5 737	21.1	17.0
Cayman Islands Iles Caïmanes	2005	0.0	100.0	0.0	1.5	...	...	...
	2010	0.0	100.0	0.0	0.9	...	...	...
Costa Rica Costa Rica	2005	38.3	61.7	0.1	2.3	1 217	45.6	28.1
	2010	35.7	64.3	-0.2	2.1	1 374	45.8	29.5
Cuba Cuba	2005	24.5	75.5	0.8	0.0	2 189	25.7	19.4
	2010	25.2	74.8	0.2	0.1	2 159	25.4	19.0
Dominica Dominique	2005	27.1	72.9	-0.3	1.5	...	...	...
	2010	25.4	74.6	-0.6	1.4	...	...	...
Dominican Republic Rép. dominicaine	2005	33.2	66.8	-1.0	2.4	2 022	34.1	22.7
	2010	29.5	70.5	-1.0	2.1	2 240	33.4	23.5

9 Population in urban and rural areas, rates of growth and largest urban agglomeration population (*continued*)
Population urbaine, population rurale, taux d'accroissement et population de l'agglomération urbaine la plus peuplée (*suite*)

Region, country or area Région, pays ou zone	Year Année	Population estimates and projections / Estimations de la population et projections: Rural % Rurale %	Urban % Urbaine %	Annual growth rate (%)[1] / Taux d'accroissement annuel (%)[1]: Rural population Population rurale	Urban population Population urbaine	Population of largest urban agglomeration with 750,000 inhabitants or more in 2005 / Population de l'agglomération urbaine la plus peuplée avec 750,000 habitants ou plus en 2005: Number (000s) Nombre (000s)	% of urban % de urbaine	% of total % de totale
El Salvador El Salvador	2005	40.2	59.8	0.8	2.1	1 517	36.9	22.0
	2010	38.7	61.3	0.5	2.0	1 662	36.3	22.3
Greenland Groenland	2005	17.1	82.9	-1.4	0.6	...	...	...
	2010	15.7	84.3	-1.3	0.5	...	...	...
Grenada Grenade	2005	69.4	30.6	1.3	1.7	...	...	...
	2010	69.0	31.0	1.1	2.2	...	...	...
Guadeloupe Guadeloupe	2005	0.2	99.8	-8.2	0.6	...	...	...
	2010	0.2	99.8	-6.0	0.4	...	...	...
Guatemala Guatemala	2005	52.8	47.2	1.5	3.4	984	16.6	7.8
	2010	50.5	49.5	1.2	3.2	1 103	15.7	7.8
Haiti Haïti	2005	61.2	38.8	0.3	3.0	2 129	64.4	25.0
	2010	57.9	42.1	0.1	2.8	2 460	64.0	26.9
Honduras Honduras	2005	53.5	46.5	1.2	3.1	927	27.7	12.9
	2010	51.2	48.8	0.8	2.9	1 075	27.5	13.4
Jamaica Jamaïque	2005	46.9	53.1	-0.3	1.0	...	...	...
	2010	45.3	54.7	-0.6	1.0	...	...	...
Martinique Martinique	2005	2.1	97.9	-0.8	0.3	...	...	...
	2010	2.0	98.0	-1.0	0.2	...	...	...
Mexico Mexique	2005	24.0	76.0	0.0	1.5	19 411	23.9	18.1
	2010	22.7	77.3	-0.2	1.4	20 688	23.6	18.3
Montserrat Montserrat	2005	86.5	13.5	1.0	2.2	...	...	...
	2010	85.7	14.3	0.6	2.3	...	...	...
Netherlands Antilles Antilles néerlandaises	2005	29.6	70.4	-0.4	1.0	...	...	...
	2010	28.3	71.7	-0.7	1.0	...	...	...
Nicaragua Nicaragua	2005	41.0	59.0	1.1	2.6	1 165	36.0	21.2
	2010	39.1	60.9	0.7	2.5	1 312	35.5	21.6
Panama Panama	2005	29.2	70.8	-1.3	2.7	1 216	53.1	37.6
	2010	25.2	74.8	-1.2	2.3	1 379	52.5	39.3
Puerto Rico Porto Rico	2005	2.4	97.6	-12.7	0.8	2 605	67.5	65.9
	2010	1.2	98.8	-9.3	0.6	2 758	68.8	67.9
Saint Kitts and Nevis Saint-Kitts-et-Nevis	2005	67.8	32.2	1.0	1.2	...	...	...
	2010	67.6	32.4	0.7	1.7	...	...	...
Saint Lucia Sainte-Lucie	2005	72.4	27.6	0.7	1.1	...	...	...
	2010	72.0	28.0	0.5	1.5	...	...	...
Saint Pierre and Miquelon Saint-Pierre-et-Miquelon	2005	11.0	89.0	0.7	1.3	...	...	...
	2010	10.7	89.3	0.3	1.1	...	...	...
St. Vincent-Grenadines St. Vincent-Grenadines	2005	54.1	45.9	-0.2	1.3	...	...	...
	2010	52.2	47.8	-0.5	1.3	...	...	...
Trinidad and Tobago Trinité-et-Tobago	2005	87.8	12.2	-0.1	2.8	...	...	...
	2010	86.1	13.9	-0.2	2.8	...	...	...
Turks and Caicos Islands Iles Turques et Caïques	2005	55.9	44.1	1.0	1.9	...	...	...
	2010	54.8	45.2	0.5	1.8	...	...	...
United States Etats-Unis	2005	19.2	80.8	-0.7	1.3	18 718	7.8	6.3
	2010	17.7	82.3	-0.8	1.2	19 388	7.5	6.2
United States Virgin Is. Iles Vierges américaines	2005	5.8	94.2	-4.1	0.2	...	...	...
	2010	4.7	95.3	-3.4	0.0	...	...	...
America, South Amérique du Sud	**2005**	**18.4**	**81.6**	**-0.8**	**1.7**	**...**	**...**	**...**
	2010	**16.5**	**83.5**	**-0.7**	**1.5**	**...**	**...**	**...**
Argentina Argentine	2005	9.9	90.1	-0.7	1.2	12 550	36.0	32.4
	2010	9.1	90.9	-0.7	1.1	13 067	35.3	32.1

Population in urban and rural areas, rates of growth and largest urban agglomeration population (*continued*)
Population urbaine, population rurale, taux d'accroissement et population de l'agglomération urbaine la plus peuplée (*suite*)

Region, country or area Région, pays ou zone	Year Année	Rural % Rurale %	Urban % Urbaine %	Annual growth rate (%)[1] / Taux d'accroissement annuel (%)[1]: Rural population Population rurale	Urban population Population urbaine	Population of largest urban agglomeration with 750,000 inhabitants or more in 2005 / Population de l'agglomération urbaine la plus peuplée avec 750,000 habitants ou plus en 2005: Number (000s) Nombre (000s)	% of urban % de urbaine	% of total % de totale
Bolivia Bolivie	2005	35.8	64.2	0.4	2.5	1 527	25.9	16.6
	2010	33.5	66.5	0.2	2.2	1 692	25.3	16.9
Brazil Brésil	2005	15.8	84.2	-1.9	1.8	18 333	7.3	9.8
	2010	13.5	86.5	-1.7	1.5	19 582	7.1	9.9
Chile Chili	2005	12.4	87.6	-1.3	1.3	5 683	...	34.9
	2010	11.0	89.0	-1.2	1.1	5 982	...	34.9
Colombia Colombie	2005	27.3	72.7	0.3	1.8	7 747	23.4	17.0
	2010	25.8	74.2	0.0	1.7	8 416	23.2	17.2
Ecuador Equateur	2005	37.2	62.8	0.1	2.2	2 387	28.7	18.0
	2010	34.8	65.2	-0.1	2.0	2 709	29.3	19.1
Falkland Is. (Malvinas) Iles Falkland (Malvinas)	2005	9.8	90.2	-5.8	1.2	...	...	...
	2010	7.1	92.9	-4.6	0.9	...	...	...
French Guiana Guyane française	2005	24.4	75.6	1.6	2.4	...	...	...
	2010	23.7	76.4	1.2	2.3	...	...	...
Guyana Guyana	2005	71.8	28.2	-0.1	0.2	...	...	...
	2010	71.5	28.5	-0.5	0.4	...	...	...
Paraguay Paraguay	2005	41.5	58.5	0.7	3.2	1 858	51.6	30.2
	2010	38.5	61.5	0.5	2.9	2 264	53.5	32.9
Peru Pérou	2005	27.4	72.6	0.6	1.7	7 186	35.4	25.7
	2010	26.3	73.7	0.4	1.7	7 590	34.3	25.2
Suriname Suriname	2005	26.1	73.9	-0.8	1.0	...	...	...
	2010	24.4	75.6	-1.0	0.9	...	...	...
Uruguay Uruguay	2005	8.0	92.0	-0.8	0.8	1 264	39.7	36.5
	2010	7.5	92.5	-0.9	0.7	1 260	38.1	35.2
Venezuela (Bolivarian Republic of) Venezuela (Rép. Bolivar. du)	2005	6.6	93.4	-3.5	2.0	2 913	11.7	10.9
	2010	5.1	94.9	-2.7	1.7	2 988	10.8	10.3
Asia Asie	**2005**	**60.2**	**39.8**	**0.2**	**2.4**	**...**	**...**	**...**
	2010	**57.5**	**42.5**	**0.0**	**2.3**	**...**	**...**	**...**
Afghanistan Afghanistan	2005	77.1	22.9	3.0	5.1	2 994	43.8	10.0
	2010	75.2	24.8	2.4	4.7	3 753	42.5	10.5
Armenia Arménie	2005	35.9	64.1	0.0	-0.3	1 103	57.1	36.6
	2010	36.3	63.7	-0.3	0.0	1 102	58.0	37.0
Azerbaijan Azerbaïdjan	2005	48.5	51.5	0.6	0.9	1 856	42.9	22.1
	2010	48.1	51.9	0.4	1.1	1 910	42.1	21.9
Bahrain Bahreïn	2005	3.5	96.5	-5.5	1.9	...	...	...
	2010	2.4	97.6	-4.1	1.6	...	...	...
Bangladesh Bangladesh	2005	74.9	25.1	1.2	3.5	12 430	35.0	8.8
	2010	72.7	27.3	0.9	3.4	14 625	34.6	9.4
Bhutan Bhoutan	2005	88.9	11.1	1.8	5.1	...	...	...
	2010	87.2	12.8	1.7	5.0	...	...	...
Brunei Darussalam Brunéi Darussalam	2005	26.5	73.5	0.4	2.6	...	...	...
	2010	24.3	75.7	0.2	2.3	...	...	...
Cambodia Cambodge	2005	80.3	19.7	1.2	4.9	1 364	49.2	9.7
	2010	77.2	22.8	1.0	4.6	1 664	47.0	10.7
China[4] Chine[4]	2005	59.6	40.4	-1.0	2.7	14 503	2.7	1.1
	2010	55.1	44.9	-1.1	2.4	15 790	2.6	1.2
China, Hong Kong SAR Chine, Hong Kong RAS	2005	0.0	100.0	0.0	1.0	7 041	100.0	100.0
	2010	0.0	100.0	0.0	0.9	7 416	100.0	100.0
China, Macao SAR Chine, Macao RAS	2005	0.0	100.0	0.0	0.7	...	...	...
	2010	0.0	100.0	0.0	0.7	...	...	...

Region, country or area / Région, pays ou zone	Year / Année	Population estimates and projections / Estimations de la population et projections: Rural % / Rurale %	Urban % / Urbaine %	Annual growth rate (%)[1] / Taux d'accroissement annuel (%)[1]: Rural population / Population rurale	Urban population / Population urbaine	Population of largest urban agglomeration with 750,000 inhabitants or more in 2005 / Population de l'agglomération urbaine la plus peuplée avec 750,000 habitants ou plus en 2005: Number (000s) / Nombre (000s)	% of urban / % de urbaine	% of total / % de totale
Cyprus Chypre	2005	30.7	69.3	0.4	1.3	...	...	...
	2010	29.7	70.3	0.2	1.4	...	...	...
Georgia Géorgie	2005	47.8	52.2	-1.0	-0.6	1 047	44.8	23.4
	2010	47.3	52.7	-1.0	-0.1	1 024	45.2	23.8
India Inde	2005	71.3	28.7	1.0	2.3	18 196	5.7	1.6
	2010	69.9	30.1	0.7	2.5	20 036	5.6	1.7
Indonesia Indonésie	2005	51.9	48.1	-1.1	3.3	13 215	12.3	5.9
	2010	46.3	53.7	-1.3	2.6	15 206	12.0	6.5
Iran (Islamic Rep. of) Iran (Rép. islamique d')	2005	33.1	66.9	-0.3	2.1	7 314	15.7	10.5
	2010	30.5	69.5	-0.2	2.1	7 807	15.1	10.5
Iraq Iraq	2005	33.1	66.9	2.6	2.3	5 904	30.6	20.5
	2010	33.4	66.6	2.1	2.4	6 593	30.4	20.3
Israel Israël	2005	8.4	91.6	1.4	1.7	3 012	48.9	44.8
	2010	8.3	91.7	0.9	1.4	3 256	48.5	44.5
Japan Japon	2005	34.2	65.8	-0.5	0.4	35 197	41.8	27.5
	2010	33.2	66.8	-0.9	0.3	35 467	41.3	27.6
Jordan Jordanie	2005	17.7	82.3	0.2	2.5	...	27.5	22.7
	2010	16.1	83.9	0.0	2.2	...	27.5	23.1
Kazakhstan Kazakhstan	2005	42.7	57.3	-0.7	0.4	1 156	13.6	7.8
	2010	41.4	58.6	-0.7	0.7	1 164	13.4	7.9
Korea, Dem. P. R. Corée, R. p. dém. de	2005	38.4	61.6	-0.6	0.9	3 351	24.2	14.9
	2010	36.6	63.4	-0.8	1.0	3 439	23.7	15.0
Korea, Republic of Corée, République de	2005	19.2	80.8	-0.9	0.6	9 645	25.0	20.2
	2010	18.1	81.9	-1.1	0.5	9 554	24.0	19.7
Kuwait Koweït	2005	1.7	98.3	1.4	2.5	1 810	68.5	67.4
	2010	1.6	98.4	0.9	2.1	2 099	70.0	68.9
Kyrgyzstan Kirghizistan	2005	64.2	35.8	0.9	1.6	798	42.3	15.2
	2010	63.4	36.6	0.5	1.8	841	41.2	15.1
Lao People's Dem. Rep. Rép. dém. pop. lao	2005	79.4	20.6	1.7	4.0	...	...	...
	2010	77.4	22.6	1.4	4.0	...	...	...
Lebanon Liban	2005	13.4	86.6	0.1	1.2	1 777	57.4	49.7
	2010	12.8	87.2	-0.1	1.1	1 941	59.0	51.5
Malaysia Malaisie	2005	32.7	67.3	-1.3	2.9	1 405	8.2	5.5
	2010	28.2	71.8	-1.3	2.4	1 534	7.8	5.6
Maldives Maldives	2005	70.4	29.6	1.7	4.0	...	...	...
	2010	68.0	32.1	1.4	3.9	...	...	...
Mongolia Mongolie	2005	43.3	56.7	0.9	1.5	863	57.5	32.6
	2010	42.5	57.5	0.6	1.7	932	57.6	33.1
Myanmar Myanmar	2005	69.4	30.6	-0.1	2.9	4 107	26.5	8.1
	2010	66.1	33.9	-0.3	2.7	4 635	25.9	8.8
Nepal Népal	2005	84.2	15.8	1.3	4.8	815	19.1	3.0
	2010	81.8	18.2	1.1	4.6	1 028	18.9	3.4
Occupied Palestinian Terr. Terr. palestinien occupé	2005	28.4	71.6	2.8	3.3	...	...	...
	2010	27.9	72.1	2.3	3.1	...	...	...
Oman Oman	2005	28.5	71.5	2.0	2.2	...	...	...
	2010	28.3	71.7	1.6	2.2	...	...	...
Pakistan Pakistan	2005	65.2	34.9	1.4	3.3	11 608	21.1	7.4
	2010	63.0	37.0	1.1	3.3	13 252	20.4	7.6
Philippines Philippines	2005	37.3	62.7	-0.5	2.8	10 686	20.5	12.9
	2010	33.6	66.4	-0.5	2.4	11 799	19.7	13.1

Population in urban and rural areas, rates of growth and largest urban agglomeration population (*continued*)
Population urbaine, population rurale, taux d'accroissement et population de l'agglomération urbaine la plus peuplée (*suite*)

Region, country or area Région, pays ou zone	Year Année	Population estimates and projections / Estimations de la population et projections: Rural % Rurale %	Urban % Urbaine %	Annual growth rate (%)[1] / Taux d'accroissement annuel (%)[1]: Rural population Population rurale	Urban population Population urbaine	Population of largest urban agglomeration with 750,000 inhabitants or more in 2005 / Population de l'agglomération urbaine la plus peuplée avec 750,000 habitants ou plus en 2005: Number (000s) Nombre (000s)	% of urban % de urbaine	% of total % de totale
Qatar Qatar	2005	4.6	95.4	0.0	2.0	...	...	...
	2010	4.2	95.8	-0.1	1.7	...	...	...
Saudi Arabia Arabie saoudite	2005	19.0	81.0	1.2	2.6	4 193	21.1	17.1
	2010	17.9	82.1	0.9	2.4	4 863	21.4	17.6
Singapore Singapour	2005	0.0	100.0	0.0	1.2	4 326	100.0	100.0
	2010	0.0	100.0	0.0	1.0	4 590	100.0	100.0
Sri Lanka Sri Lanka	2005	84.9	15.1	0.8	0.8	...	...	...
	2010	84.9	15.1	0.5	1.4	...	...	...
Syrian Arab Republic Rép. arabe syrienne	2005	49.4	50.6	1.9	2.8	2 272	26.1	11.9
	2010	48.3	51.7	1.4	2.7	2 559	25.6	11.9
Tajikistan Tadjikistan	2005	75.3	24.7	1.6	1.1	...	...	...
	2010	75.8	24.2	1.6	2.0	...	...	...
Thailand Thaïlande	2005	67.7	32.3	0.3	1.8	6 593	31.8	10.3
	2010	66.0	34.0	0.0	1.9	6 963	30.7	10.4
Timor-Leste Timor-Leste	2005	73.5	26.5	4.9	7.0	...	...	...
	2010	71.3	28.7	2.8	5.2	...	...	...
Turkey Turquie	2005	32.7	67.3	-0.2	2.0	9 712	19.7	13.3
	2010	30.4	69.6	-0.4	1.8	10 546	19.4	13.5
Turkmenistan Turkménistan	2005	53.8	46.2	0.6	2.1	...	...	...
	2010	51.9	48.1	0.2	2.3	...	...	...
United Arab Emirates Emirats arabes unis	2005	23.3	76.7	2.1	2.3	1 330	38.6	29.6
	2010	23.1	76.9	1.6	2.2	1 537	39.7	30.5
Uzbekistan Ouzbékistan	2005	63.3	36.7	1.4	1.6	2 181	22.4	8.2
	2010	63.1	36.9	1.1	2.0	2 284	21.6	8.0
Viet Nam Viet Nam	2005	73.6	26.4	0.6	3.0	5 065	22.8	6.0
	2010	71.2	28.8	0.4	3.0	5 698	22.0	6.4
Yemen Yémen	2005	72.7	27.3	2.5	4.6	1 801	31.5	8.6
	2010	70.6	29.4	2.3	4.6	2 339	32.5	9.5
Europe Europe	**2005**	**27.8**	**72.2**	**-0.6**	**0.1**	**...**	**...**	**...**
	2010	**27.1**	**72.9**	**-0.9**	**0.1**	**...**	**...**	**...**
Albania Albanie	2005	54.6	45.4	-0.9	2.1	...	...	...
	2010	50.9	49.1	-0.8	2.1	...	...	...
Andorra Andorre	2005	9.4	90.6	3.3	-0.2	...	...	...
	2010	11.0	89.0	2.0	-0.3	...	...	...
Austria Autriche	2005	34.0	66.0	-0.2	0.3	2 260	41.8	27.6
	2010	33.4	66.6	-0.6	0.4	2 352	42.8	28.5
Belarus Bélarus	2005	27.8	72.2	-2.3	0.1	1 778	25.2	18.2
	2010	25.4	74.6	-2.3	0.0	1 875	26.5	19.8
Belgium Belgique	2005	2.8	97.2	-0.7	0.2	1 012	10.0	9.7
	2010	2.7	97.3	-0.8	0.1	1 050	10.3	10.0
Bosnia and Herzegovina Bosnie-Herzégovine	2005	54.3	45.7	-0.9	1.4	...	...	...
	2010	51.4	48.6	-1.5	1.1	...	...	...
Bulgaria Bulgarie	2005	30.0	70.0	-1.6	-0.4	1 093	20.2	14.1
	2010	28.7	71.3	-1.9	-0.4	1 063	20.0	14.3
Channel Islands Iles Anglo-Normandes	2005	69.5	30.5	0.3	0.5	...	...	...
	2010	69.2	30.8	0.1	0.8	...	...	...
Croatia Croatie	2005	43.5	56.5	-0.7	0.4	...	...	...
	2010	42.2	57.8	-1.2	0.2	...	...	...
Czech Republic République tchèque	2005	26.5	73.5	-0.1	-0.1	1 171	15.6	11.5
	2010	26.5	73.5	-0.6	0.0	1 183	15.8	11.6

Region, country or area Région, pays ou zone	Year Année	Rural % Rurale %	Urban % Urbaine %	Annual growth rate (%)[1] / Taux d'accroissement annuel (%)[1]: Rural population Population rurale	Urban population Population urbaine	Population of largest urban agglomeration with 750,000 inhabitants or more in 2005 / Population de l'agglomération urbaine la plus peuplée avec 750,000 habitants ou plus en 2005: Number (000s) Nombre (000s)	% of urban % de urbaine	% of total % de totale
Denmark Danemark	2005	14.4	85.6	-0.6	0.4	1 088	23.4	20.0
	2010	13.8	86.2	-0.8	0.4	1 094	23.0	19.9
Estonia Estonie	2005	30.9	69.1	-0.5	-0.2	...	...	...
	2010	30.7	69.3	-0.8	0.0	...	...	...
Faeroe Islands Iles Féroé	2005	61.2	38.8	0.3	1.2	...	...	...
	2010	60.1	39.9	0.1	1.4	...	...	...
Finland Finlande	2005	38.9	61.1	-0.1	0.4	1 091	34.0	20.8
	2010	38.4	61.6	-0.4	0.5	1 120	34.2	21.1
France France	2005	23.3	76.7	-0.6	0.6	9 820	21.2	16.2
	2010	22.2	77.8	-0.8	0.6	9 856	20.6	16.0
Germany Allemagne	2005	24.8	75.2	-0.3	0.1	3 389	5.5	4.1
	2010	24.4	75.6	-0.6	0.1	3 389	5.4	4.1
Gibraltar Gibraltar	2005	0.0	100.0	0.0	0.1	...	...	...
	2010	0.0	100.0	0.0	0.0	...	...	...
Greece Grèce	2005	41.0	59.0	-0.2	0.4	3 230	49.2	29.0
	2010	40.3	59.7	-0.6	0.5	3 248	48.6	29.0
Holy See[5] Saint-Siège[5]	2005	0.0	100.0	0.0	0.1	...	...	...
	2010	0.0	100.0	0.0	0.0	...	...	...
Hungary Hongrie	2005	33.7	66.3	-1.5	0.3	1 693	25.3	16.8
	2010	31.7	68.3	-1.6	0.3	1 664	24.4	16.7
Iceland Islande	2005	7.2	92.8	-0.4	0.9	...	...	...
	2010	6.8	93.2	-0.5	0.8	...	...	...
Ireland Irlande	2005	39.5	60.5	0.5	1.8	1 037	41.4	25.0
	2010	38.0	62.0	0.1	1.7	1 107	40.4	25.0
Isle of Man Ile de Man	2005	48.2	51.8	-0.2	0.0	...	...	...
	2010	47.9	52.1	-0.4	0.2	...	...	...
Italy Italie	2005	32.4	67.6	-0.4	0.2	3 348	8.5	5.8
	2010	31.6	68.4	-0.8	0.2	3 332	8.4	5.7
Latvia Lettonie	2005	32.2	67.8	-0.7	-0.4	...	...	...
	2010	31.8	68.2	-1.0	-0.3	...	...	...
Liechtenstein Liechtenstein	2005	85.4	14.6	0.9	0.6	...	...	...
	2010	85.6	14.4	0.7	1.2	...	...	...
Lithuania Lituanie	2005	33.4	66.6	-0.4	-0.5	...	...	...
	2010	33.6	66.4	-0.7	-0.3	...	...	...
Luxembourg Luxembourg	2005	17.2	82.8	1.9	1.1	...	...	...
	2010	17.8	82.2	1.3	1.1	...	...	...
Malta Malte	2005	4.7	95.3	-5.4	0.7	...	...	...
	2010	3.5	96.5	-4.3	0.6	...	...	...
Monaco Monaco	2005	0.0	100.0	0.0	1.2	...	...	...
	2010	0.0	100.0	0.0	1.1	...	...	...
Netherlands Pays-Bas	2005	19.8	80.2	-2.5	1.0	1 101	8.8	7.0
	2010	17.1	82.9	-2.3	0.8	1 118	8.5	7.1
Norway Norvège	2005	22.6[6]	77.4[6]	0.0[6]	0.6[6]	802[6]	22.4[6]	17.4
	2010	22.1[6]	77.9[6]	-0.2[6]	0.6[6]	825[6]	22.4[6]	17.4
Poland Pologne	2005	38.0	62.1	-0.5	0.2	1 680	7.0	4.4
	2010	37.2	62.8	-0.8	0.3	1 686	7.0	4.4
Portugal Portugal	2005	42.4	57.6	-1.1	1.5	2 761	45.7	26.3
	2010	39.3	60.7	-1.3	1.2	2 890	44.4	27.0
Republic of Moldova République de Moldova	2005	53.3	46.7	-0.7	0.3	...	...	...
	2010	52.0	48.0	-1.0	0.6	...	...	...

Region, country or area Région, pays ou zone	Year Année	Population estimates and projections / Estimations de la population et projections: Rural % Rurale %	Urban % Urbaine %	Annual growth rate (%)[1] / Taux d'accroissement annuel (%)[1]: Rural population Population rurale	Urban population Population urbaine	Population of largest urban agglomeration with 750,000 inhabitants or more in 2005 / Population de l'agglomération urbaine la plus peuplée avec 750,000 habitants ou plus en 2005: Number (000s) Nombre (000s)	% of urban % de urbaine	% of total % de totale
Romania Roumanie	2005	46.3	53.7	-0.8	0.0	1 934	16.6	8.9
	2010	45.4	54.6	-1.1	0.1	1 941	16.7	9.1
Russian Federation Fédération de Russie	2005	27.0	73.0	-0.1	-0.6	10 654	10.2	7.4
	2010	27.4	72.6	-0.5	-0.5	10 967	10.8	7.8
San Marino Saint-Marin	2005	2.8	97.2	-15.2	1.0	...	...	...
	2010	1.3	98.7	-12.4	0.6	...	...	...
Serbia and Montenegro Serbie-et-Monténégro	2005	47.8	52.2	-0.5	0.4	1 106	20.2	10.5
	2010	46.6	53.4	-0.9	0.5	1 094	19.6	10.4
Slovakia Slovaquie	2005	43.8	56.2	-0.3	0.2	...	...	...
	2010	43.2	56.8	-0.6	0.4	...	...	...
Slovenia Slovénie	2005	49.0	51.0	-0.4	0.2	...	...	...
	2010	48.1	51.9	-0.8	0.4	...	...	...
Spain Espagne	2005	23.3	76.7	-0.2	0.6	5 608	17.0	13.0
	2010	22.6	77.4	-0.6	0.4	5 977	17.6	13.6
Sweden Suède	2005	15.8	84.2	-0.2	0.4	1 708	22.4	18.9
	2010	15.5	84.5	-0.4	0.4	1 745	22.5	19.0
Switzerland Suisse	2005	24.8	75.2	-1.4	0.6	1 144	21.0	15.8
	2010	23.0	77.0	-1.5	0.5	1 183	21.0	16.2
TFYR of Macedonia L'ex-R.y. Macédoine	2005	31.1	68.9	-2.2	1.1	...	...	...
	2010	27.7	72.3	-2.1	0.9	...	...	...
Ukraine Ukraine	2005	32.2	67.8	-1.7	-0.7	2 672	8.5	5.7
	2010	31.1	68.9	-1.9	-0.7	2 738	9.0	6.2
United Kingdom Royaume-Uni	2005	10.3	89.7	-0.5	0.4	8 505	15.9	14.3
	2010	9.9	90.1	-0.7	0.4	8 607	15.8	14.2
Oceania Océanie	**2005**	**29.2**	**70.8**	**0.9**	**1.3**	**...**	**...**	**...**
	2010	**28.8**	**71.2**	**0.7**	**1.2**	**...**	**...**	**...**
American Samoa Samoa américaines	2005	8.7	91.3	-2.4	2.3	...	...	...
	2010	7.0	93.0	-1.7	2.0	...	...	...
Australia[7] Australie[7]	2005	11.8	88.2	-0.6	1.2	4 331	24.4	21.5
	2010	10.9	89.1	-0.6	1.1	4 540	24.0	21.4
Cook Islands Iles Cook	2005	29.6	70.4	-2.8	0.6	...	...	...
	2010	26.2	73.8	-2.7	0.3	...	...	...
Fiji Fidji	2005	49.2	50.8	-0.4	1.7	...	...	...
	2010	46.6	53.4	-0.6	1.5	...	...	...
French Polynesia Polynésie française	2005	48.3	51.7	1.4	1.3	...	...	...
	2010	48.4	51.6	0.9	1.5	...	...	...
Guam Guam	2005	6.0	94.0	-1.0	1.6	...	...	...
	2010	5.3	94.7	-0.9	1.4	...	...	...
Kiribati Kiribati	2005	52.6	47.4	0.2	3.5	...	...	...
	2010	48.5	51.5	0.0	3.1	...	...	...
Marshall Islands Iles Marshall	2005	33.3	66.7	2.4	3.5	...	...	...
	2010	32.2	67.8	1.8	3.2	...	...	...
Micronesia (Fed. States of) Micronésie (Etats féd. de)	2005	77.7	22.3	0.5	0.9	...	...	...
	2010	77.3	22.7	0.2	1.2	...	...	...
Nauru Nauru	2005	0.0	100.0	0.0	1.2	...	...	...
	2010	0.0	100.0	0.0	1.0	...	...	...
New Caledonia Nouvelle-Calédonie	2005	36.3	63.7	0.6	2.2	...	...	...
	2010	34.5	65.5	0.3	2.0	...	...	...
New Zealand Nouvelle-Zélande	2005	13.8	86.2	-0.1	0.8	1 148	33.1	28.5
	2010	13.2	86.8	-0.3	0.8	1 208	33.4	29.0

Region, country or area Région, pays ou zone	Year Année	Population estimates and projections / Estimations de la population et projections: Rural % Rurale %	Urban % Urbaine %	Annual growth rate (%)[1] / Taux d'accroissement annuel (%)[1]: Rural population Population rurale	Urban population Population urbaine	Population of largest urban agglomeration with 750,000 inhabitants or more in 2005 / Population de l'agglomération urbaine la plus peuplée avec 750,000 habitants ou plus en 2005: Number (000s) Nombre (000s)	% of urban % de urbaine	% of total % de totale
Niue Nioué	2005	63.3	36.7	0.0	2.7	...	...	...
	2010	60.1	39.9	-0.2	2.5	...	...	...
Northern Mariana Islands Iles Mariannes du Nord	2005	5.5	94.5	-1.0	2.5	...	...	...
	2010	4.7	95.3	-1.3	1.6	...	...	...
Palau Palaos	2005	30.4	69.6	0.3	0.7	...	...	...
	2010	29.9	70.1	0.0	0.7	...	...	...
Papua New Guinea Papouasie-Nouvelle-Guinée	2005	86.6	13.4	1.7	2.7	...	...	...
	2010	86.0	14.0	1.4	3.1	...	...	...
Pitcairn Pitcairn	2005	100.0	0.0	0.3	0.0	...	...	...
	2010	100.0	0.0	0.0	0.0	...	...	...
Samoa Samoa	2005	77.6	22.4	0.2	1.3	...	...	...
	2010	76.6	23.4	-0.3	1.4	...	...	...
Solomon Islands Iles Salomon	2005	83.0	17.0	2.0	4.1	...	...	...
	2010	81.4	18.6	1.6	4.1	...	...	...
Tokelau Tokélaou	2005	100.0	0.0	1.2	0.0	...	...	...
	2010	100.0	0.0	1.0	0.0	...	...	...
Tonga Tonga	2005	76.0	24.0	-0.2	1.3	...	...	...
	2010	74.7	25.3	-0.5	1.6	...	...	...
Tuvalu Tuvalu	2005	51.9	48.1	-0.5	1.4	...	...	...
	2010	49.6	50.4	-0.6	1.4	...	...	...
Vanuatu Vanuatu	2005	76.5	23.5	1.3	3.6	...	...	...
	2010	74.4	25.6	1.0	3.6	...	...	...
Wallis and Futuna Islands Iles Wallis et Futuna	2005	100.0	0.0	1.5	0.0	...	...	...
	2010	100.0	0.0	1.5	0.0	...	...	...

Source

United Nations Population Division, New York, "World Urbanization Prospects: The 2005 Revision" (Pop/DB/WUP/Rev. 2005/1/F6, 7, 9, 10, 12, 13); data set in digital form.

Notes

1 Annual rates of growth calculated for the periods 2005-2010 and 2010-2015.
2 Including Agalega, Rodrigues and Saint Brandon.
3 Including Ascension and Tristan da Cunha.
4 For statistical purposes, the data for China do not include those for the Hong Kong Special Administrative Region (Hong Kong SAR) and Macao Special Administrative Region (Macao SAR).
5 Data refer to the Vatican City State.
6 Including Svalbard and Jan Mayen Islands.
7 Including Christmas Island, Cocos (Keeling) Islands and Norfolk Island.

Source

Organisation des Nations Unies, Division de la population, New York, "World Urbanization Prospects : The 2005 Revision", (Pop/DB/WUP/Rev. 2005/1/F6, 7, 9, 10, 12, 13); données sous la forme numérique.

Notes

1 Ces taux d'accroissement annuel ont été calculés pour les périodes 2005 à 2010 et 2010 à 2015.
2 Y compris Agalega, Rodrigues et Saint Brandon.
3 Y compris Ascension et Tristan da Cunha.
4 Pour la présentation des statistiques, les données pour la Chine ne comprennent pas la Région Administrative Spéciale de Hong Kong (Hong Kong RAS) et la Région Administrative Spéciale de Macao (Macao RAS).
5 Les données se réfèrent à la Cité du Vatican.
6 Y compris îles Svalbard et Jan Mayen.
7 Y compris les îles Christmas, Cocos (Keeling) et Norfolk.

Technical notes: tables 8 and 9

Table 8 is based on detailed data on population and its growth and distribution published in the United Nations *Demographic Yearbook*. Only official national population estimates reported to the United Nations Statistics Division are included in this table. For a comprehensive description of methods of evaluation and the limitations of the data, consult the *Demographic Yearbook*.

Unless otherwise indicated, figures refer to de facto (present-in-area) population for the present territory; surface area estimates include inland waters.

Table 9: The statistics on population in urban and rural areas, rates of growth and largest urban agglomeration population of each country or area are estimates and projections published by the Population Division of the Department of Economic and Social Affairs of the United Nations Secretariat in the *World Urbanization Prospects: The 2005 Revision*. Because of national differences in the specific characteristics that distinguish urban from rural areas, there are no internationally agreed definitions of urban and rural. In most countries, the distinction is mainly based on size of locality. For the latest available census definition of urban areas in a particular country or area, reference should be made to the *Demographic Yearbook*.

An urban agglomeration comprises the city or town proper and also the suburban fringe or thickly settled territory lying outside, but adjacent to, its boundaries. The largest urban agglomerations refer to those inhabited by 750,000 people or more.

Annual rates of change in urban and rural population are computed as average annual percentage changes using mid-year population estimates.

Notes techniques : tableaux 8 et 9

Le *tableau 8* est fondé sur des données détaillées sur la population, sa croissance et sa distribution, publiées dans l'*Annuaire démographique* des Nations Unies. Le tableau inclut seulement des estimations officielles de la population qui ont été envoyées à la Division de Statistique des Nations Unies. Pour une description complète des méthodes d'évaluation et une indication des limites des données, voir l'*Annuaire démographique*.

Sauf indication contraire, les chiffres se rapportent à la population effectivement présente sur le territoire tel qu'il est actuellement défini; les estimations de superficie comprennent les étendues d'eau intérieures.

Le *tableau 9:* Les statistiques sur la population urbaine, la population rurale, les taux d'accroissement et population de l'agglomération urbaine la plus peuplée de chaque pays ou zone sont des estimations et projections publiées par la Division de la population du Département des affaires économiques et sociales du Secrétariat des Nations Unies dans « *World Urbanization Prospects: The 2005 Revision*. » Il n'existe pas de définition reconnue à l'échelle internationale des zones urbaines et rurales parce que les caractéristiques retenues pour distinguer ces deux types de zone diffèrent d'un pays à un autre. Dans la plupart des pays, cette distinction est essentiellement une fonction de la taille des agglomérations. Pour la définition la plus récente des zones urbaines utilisée dans une région ou un pays donné, se reporter à l'*Annuaire démographique*.

L'agglomération urbaine comprend la ville proprement dite et ses faubourgs ou banlieues, et tout territoire à forte densité de population situé à sa périphérie. Les agglomérations urbaines les plus peuplées se rapportent à celles habitées par 750 000 personnes ou plus.

Les taux annuels de variation des populations urbaines et rurales se calculent sur la base de la variation annuelle moyenne en pourcentage déterminée à partir des estimations de la population au milieu de l'année.

10

Education at the primary, secondary and tertiary levels

Number of students enrolled and percentage female

Enseignement primaire, secondaire et supérieur

Nombre d'étudiants inscrits et étudiantes féminines en pourcentage

Country or area Pays ou zone	Year[t] Année[t]	Primary education Enseignement primaire		Secondary education Enseignement secondaire		Tertiary education Enseignement supérieur	
		Total	% F	Total	% F	Total	% F
Afghanistan Afghanistan	2000	749 360	0.0	...	...	...	...
	2001	773 623	0.0	362 415	0.0	...	...
	2002	2 667 629	30.2	...	...	...	...
	2003	3 781 015	34.8	406 895[1]	24.4[1]	26 211[1]	20.4[1]
	2004	4 430 142	29.1	594 306	16.3	27 648	20.4
	2005	4 318 819	35.7	651 453	23.4	...	...
Albania Albanie	2000	283 249	48.3	363 689	48.7	40 125	59.9
	2001	274 233	48.6	377 198	48.7	40 859	61.4
	2002	263 603	47.8	382 779[1]	47.2[1]	42 160	62.0
	2003	252 829	48.1	396 139	48.3	43 600	62.3
	2004	250 487	48.2	397 056	47.9	53 014	62.1
Algeria Algérie	2000	4 843 313	46.8	...	...	...	...
	2001	4 720 950	46.8	...	...	549 009[1]	...
	2002	4 691 870	47.0	3 424 208[1]	50.1[1]	624 788[1]	...
	2003	4 612 574	47.0	3 548 484	50.5	682 775[1]	...
	2004	4 507 703	47.0	3 677 107	50.7	716 452	51.0
	2005	4 361 744	47.0	3 755 821[1]	50.7[1]	755 463	56.9
Andorra Andorre	2002	4 108	47.4	3 132	50.3	267	49.8
	2003	4 142	47.2	3 194	50.2	306	48.7
	2004	4 264	47.1	3 250	49.9	331	48.6
	2005	4 085	46.9	3 737	50.3	342	50.9
Angola Angola	2000	...	...	354 984	45.3	...	...
	2001	...	...	413 695	44.2	...	...
	2002	...	...	...	...	12 566	39.9[2]
	2003	...	...	...	...	48 184	...
	2004	...	...	...	...	37 547	...
	2005	...	...	...	...	48 184	...
Anguilla Anguilla	2000	1 539	50.3	1 099[1]	50.7[1]	...	...
	2001	1 489	48.9	1 096	51.0	...	...
	2002	1 427	49.0	1 073[1]	51.4[1]	...	...
	2003	1 447	49.7	1 100[1]	50.7[1]	12	100.0
	2004	1 433	50.0	1 076	51.1	21	81.0
	2005	1 449	50.8	1 024	50.5	33	75.8
Antigua and Barbuda Antigua-et-Barbuda	2000	13 025	62.0	5 276	50.2	...	...
Argentina Argentine	2000	4 898 224	49.1	3 832 258	50.9	1 766 933[1]	60.3[1]
	2001	4 900 225	49.1	3 953 677	50.8	1 918 708	59.2
	2002	4 914 441	49.2	3 976 213	50.7	2 026 735	59.3
	2003	4 674 869	49.0	3 499 181	50.9	2 101 437	59.7
	2004	4 685 532	49.0	3 516 365	50.9	2 127 113	58.0
Armenia Arménie	2000	166 849[1]	48.8[1]	389 642[1]	49.3[1]	62 794	53.7
	2001	155 423	48.7	384 165	50.8	68 704	54.6
	2002	143 815	48.5	377 716	50.8	75 474	53.7
	2003	134 664	48.3	364 995	49.8	73 603	53.7
	2004	...	...	392 575	49.7	79 321	55.5
	2005	125 149	48.2	365 400	49.6	86 629	55.5
Aruba Aruba	2000	9 263	48.6	6 178	50.5	1 578	60.6
	2001	9 436	48.6	6 428	51.1	1 628	60.6
	2002	9 840	48.2	6 757	51.5	1 592	60.4
	2003	9 897	48.0	6 869	51.6	1 672	59.3
	2004	10 185	47.9	6 973	50.6	1 704	60.2
	2005	10 250	48.3	7 116	50.7	2 106	59.8

Country or area Pays ou zone	Year[t] Année[t]	Primary education Enseignement primaire Total	%F	Secondary education Enseignement secondaire Total	%F	Tertiary education Enseignement supérieur Total	%F
Australia Australie	2000	1 905 951	48.6	2 589 474	48.9	845 132	54.3
	2001	1 914 395	48.6	2 499 676	48.4	868 689	54.2
	2002	1 933 765	48.6	2 513 670	48.0	1 012 210	54.0
	2003	1 931 817	48.6	2 568 791	48.1	1 005 977	54.1
	2004	1 934 549	48.6	2 492 235	47.8	1 002 998	54.2
	2005	1 934 941	48.6	2 491 457	47.6	1 015 060	54.5
Austria Autriche	2000	392 407	48.4	748 659	47.7	261 229	51.0
	2001	392 339	48.5	749 135	47.7	264 669	51.8
	2002	386 484	48.5	755 581	47.5	223 735	52.7
	2003	379 920	48.6	764 426	47.5	229 802	53.0
	2004	372 963	48.7	770 391	47.4	238 522	53.3
	2005	362 822	48.7	781 292	47.5	244 410	53.7
Azerbaijan Azerbaïdjan	2000	700 136	48.9	945 393	48.9	117 077	40.0
	2001	693 760	48.2	1 020 131	48.0	120 693	41.6
	2002	668 902	48.1	1 040 175	48.1	121 475	44.2
	2003	635 652	47.7	1 094 387	47.9	121 156	44.7
	2004	607 007	47.8	1 085 632	48.0	122 770	46.0
	2005	568 097	47.7	1 069 980	47.9	128 634	46.7
Bahamas Bahamas	2000[1]	33 645	48.8	27 095	48.5	...	...
	2001[1]	33 995	49.2	27 760	48.4	...	...
	2002	34 153	49.5	31 713	51.0	...	...
	2003[1]	34 579	49.4	29 985	50.3	...	...
	2004[1]	36 070	49.2	30 857	49.6	...	...
	2005	37 050	49.1	32 089	49.7	...	...
Bahrain Bahreïn	2000	77 720	48.9	61 058	50.6	...	...
	2001	79 407	48.9	62 221	51.0	...	...
	2002	81 057	48.7	64 439	50.7	...	...
	2003	81 887	48.9	67 160	50.2	19 079	61.9
	2004	82 708	48.9	69 638	49.9	18 524[1]	63.1[1]
	2005	83 299	48.7	71 645	50.0	18 841	67.8
Bangladesh Bangladesh	2000	17 667 985	48.9	10 329 065	49.7	726 701	32.3
	2001	17 659 220	49.1	10 690 742	50.9	878 537	33.8
	2002	17 561 828	49.7	11 024 326	51.3	855 339	32.0
	2003	17 462 973	49.3	11 051 234	51.3	877 335	32.0
	2004	17 953 300	49.6	10 354 760	49.6	821 364	31.6
	2005	...	...	...	...	911 600	33.5
Barbados Barbade	2000	24 475	48.9	21 016	50.3	8 074	72.3
	2001	24 225	49.1	20 866	49.4	7 979	70.7
	2002	23 394	49.2	20 872	49.4	...	...
	2003	23 074	48.9	20 947	49.7	...	...
	2004	22 327	48.9	21 300	49.7	...	...
	2005	22 249	49.2	21 418	49.4	...	...
Belarus Bélarus	2000	599 732	48.4	1 001 757	49.8	411 861	56.1
	2001	560 931	48.4	992 394	49.9	437 995	56.2
	2002	511 863	48.3	982 230	49.7	463 544	56.8
	2003	437 005	48.3	997 760	49.6	488 650	57.1
	2004	403 841	47.8	969 768	49.1	507 360	57.1
	2005	379 577	47.8	928 488	49.1	528 508	56.8
Belgium Belgique	2000	773 742	48.6	1 057 536	51.2	355 748	52.3
	2001	771 889	48.6	1 125 256	51.4	359 265	52.8
	2002	767 787	48.7	1 149 329	51.6	366 982	53.1
	2003	761 730	48.7	1 181 327	51.3	374 532	53.3
	2004	747 111	48.8	805 778	48.0	386 110	53.8
	2005	738 580	48.8	814 539	48.0	389 547	54.4

Country or area Pays ou zone	Year[t] Année[t]	Primary education Enseignement primaire Total	%F	Secondary education Enseignement secondaire Total	%F	Tertiary education Enseignement supérieur Total	%F
Belize Belize	2000	44 788	48.3	23 235	50.9	...	...
	2001	45 246	48.5	24 395	50.8	...	...
	2002[1]	46 999	48.3	25 604	50.3	...	...
	2003	47 187	48.8	27 880[1]	50.6[1]	527	64.9[2]
	2004	48 996	48.7	31 224	50.3	722	70.2
	2005	50 389	48.4	31 377[1]	49.7[1]	...	...
Benin Bénin	2000	932 424	40.2	229 228	31.2	18 753	19.8
	2001	1 054 936	40.6	256 744[1]	31.8[1]	19 758[1]	19.8[1]
	2002	1 152 798	41.3	287 292[1]	31.8[1]	...	...
	2003	1 233 214	41.9	312 427[2]	31.5[2]	...	...
	2004	1 319 648	42.8	344 890	31.7	...	...
	2005	1 318 140	43.6	435 449[1]	35.4[1]	...	...
Bermuda Bermudes	2001	4 959	49.6	4 566	51.1	1 942	55.0
	2002	4 910	50.3	4 565	51.5	1 960[1]	55.1[1]
	2003	4 879	50.1	4 660	52.4	...	...
	2004	4 810	50.7	4 803	53.1	...	...
	2005	4 760	50.4	4 756	52.4	...	...
Bhutan Bhoutan	2000	85 092	46.1	23 301	44.7	1 837[1]	33.8[1]
	2001	88 204	46.8	26 311	45.5	1 893[1]	33.8[1]
	2002[1]	91 390	47.4	29 194	45.4	...	...
	2005	99 458	48.7	42 144	47.1	...	...
Bolivia Bolivie	2000	1 492 023	48.7	876 841[1]	48.2[1]	278 763	...
	2001	1 501 040	48.8	926 190	48.3	301 984	...
	2002	1 544 430	48.8	996 577[1]	48.3[1]	311 015	...
	2003	1 531 996	48.9	1 048 881	48.4	337 914	...
	2004[1]	1 541 559	49.0	...	...	346 056	...
Botswana Botswana	2000	324 283	49.7	162 663[1]	51.1[1]	6 332	42.4
	2001	329 451	49.6	163 354	51.0	7 651	47.0
	2002	330 835	49.4	166 000	51.2	8 372	44.8
	2003	330 376	49.5	166 915	51.4	...	...
	2004	328 692	49.3	169 727[1]	51.0[1]	10 197	46.4
	2005	330 888	49.2	165 377[1]	50.9[1]	10 950	49.8
Brazil Brésil	2000	20 211 506	47.7	26 096 870	51.6	2 781 328	56.2
	2001	19 727 684	47.8	26 441 248	51.6	3 125 745	56.1
	2002	19 380 387	47.7	26 789 210	51.6	3 582 105	56.5
	2003	18 919 122	47.7	24 592 569	51.7	3 994 422	56.4
	2004	18 968 584	47.2	25 127 503	51.6	4 275 027	56.3
British Virgin Islands Iles Vierges britanniques	2000	2 783	49.8	1 543[1]	50.3[1]	750[1]	72.0[1]
	2001	2 775	49.7[1]	1 562	51.0	669	63.2
	2002	2 811	49.0	1 593	50.5	758	69.0
	2003	2 780	47.9	1 633	53.7	1 025[1]	71.7[1]
	2004	2 824	48.2	1 707	52.1	1 136	69.5
	2005	2 898	48.2	1 882	54.2	1 200[1]	68.8[1]
Brunei Darussalam Brunéi Darussalam	2000	44 981	47.5	35 209	49.9	3 984	64.8
	2001	44 487	47.6	36 986	49.6	4 479	63.2
	2002	44 882	47.9	38 692	49.2	4 513[1]	63.9[1]
	2003	46 242	48.1	40 022	49.3	4 546	64.7
	2004	46 382	47.9	42 167	49.0	4 917	66.0
	2005	46 012	47.9	43 900	48.8	5 023	66.5
Bulgaria Bulgarie	2000	392 876	48.1	696 073	48.1	261 321	57.3
	2001	374 361	48.1	695 474	48.2	247 006	56.3
	2002	349 616	48.2	693 289	48.1	228 394	54.0
	2003	333 016	48.2	707 251	48.1	230 513	52.8
	2004	314 221	48.3	704 678	47.7	228 468	52.5
	2005	290 017	48.4	685 640	47.7	237 909	52.1

Country or area Pays ou zone	Year[t] Année[t]	Primary education Enseignement primaire Total	 % F	Secondary education Enseignement secondaire Total	 % F	Tertiary education Enseignement supérieur Total	 % F
Burkina Faso	2000	852 160	40.8	189 689	39.0	...	...
Burkina Faso	2001	901 321	41.3	199 278	39.2	12 322	25.4[1]
	2002	956 721[1]	41.7[1]	204 847[1]	39.2[1]	15 535	25.4
	2003	1 012 150	42.1	236 914	39.9	18 200	22.4
	2004	1 139 512	43.2	265 508[1]	40.4[1]	18 868[1]	22.4[1]
	2005	1 270 837	43.7	295 412	40.7	27 942	30.7
Burundi	2000	710 364[2]	44.5[2]	...	...	6 132	26.8
Burundi	2001	750 699	44.4	...	...	6 289	27.2
	2002	817 223	44.0	...	...	10 546	30.4
	2003	894 859	44.6	129 204	43.5	11 915[1]	31.9[1]
	2004	968 488	45.4	152 251	43.0	15 706	27.7
	2005	1 036 859	46.2	173 717[1]	42.6[1]	16 889[1]	27.7[1]
Cambodia	2000	2 248 109	45.8	351 357	34.9	22 108	25.1
Cambodge	2001	2 431 142	46.3	396 876	35.6	25 416	27.3
	2002	2 728 698	46.5	475 637	37.0	32 010	28.8
	2003	2 772 113	46.8	560 197	38.4	43 210	28.8[1]
	2004	2 762 882	47.0	631 508[1]	40.2[1]	45 370	31.3
	2005	2 695 372	47.2	...	...	56 810	31.5
Cameroon	2000	2 237 083	45.7	699 669	...	65 697[1]	...
Cameroun	2001	2 689 052	46.2	848 216	44.1	68 495	...
	2002	2 741 627[2]	45.9[2]	932 201[1]	42.5[1]	77 707	38.8[1]
	2003	2 798 523	45.7	1 019 958[2]	40.8[1]	81 318	38.8[1]
	2004	2 979 011	45.8	1 160 957	40.9[2]	83 903[2]	38.8[1]
	2005[2]	3 000 781	45.7	1 197 505	44.2	99 864	39.5
Canada	2000	2 456 436	48.8	2 621 457	48.6	1 212 161	56.0
Canada	2002	2 460 943[1]	48.6[1]	2 709 025[1]	48.6[1]	1 254 833	56.4
	2004[1]	2 389 188	48.6	2 999 244	48.1	1 326 711	56.4
Cape Verde	2000	91 636	49.0	...	...	801	51.1[1]
Cap-Vert	2001	90 640	49.0	45 954	50.9[1]	718	51.1[2]
	2002	89 809	48.9	48 055	50.9	1 810	51.0
	2003	87 841	48.7	49 522	52.0	2 215	52.9
	2004	85 138	48.6	49 790	52.2	3 036	52.6
	2005	82 952	48.5	51 672	51.7	3 910	51.0
Cayman Islands	2000	3 435	50.0	2 342	49.2	380[1]	73.7[1]
Iles Caïmanes	2001	3 549	49.0	2 337	48.4	390	74.6
	2002	3 579	49.4	2 341	50.4	...	...
	2004	3 361	48.5	2 701	50.8	...	...
	2005	3 240	48.4	2 824	47.8	...	...
Central African Rep.	2000	...	...	...	...	6 323	16.2
Rép. centrafricaine	2001	458 585[2]	40.9[2]	70 162[1]	...	...	...
	2002	410 562[2]	40.4[2]	71 893[1]	...	...	...
	2003	414 537	41.0	...	...	...	...
	2004	363 158	40.2	...	...	6 384	...
	2005[1]	367 983	40.2	...	...	6 270	...
Chad	2000	913 547	37.8	137 269	22.1	5 901	15.0
Tchad	2001	984 224	38.7	142 031[1]	22.1[1]	6 106[1]	15.0[1]
	2002	1 085 247	39.1	184 996	24.9	...	...
	2003	1 164 093	39.7	212 632[1]	24.3[1]	7 397	10.2
	2004	1 271 985	39.5	227 856	24.8	10 081	12.5
	2005	1 262 393	40.1	236 754[1]	24.8[1]	10 468[1]	12.5[1]
Chile	2000	1 798 515	48.5	1 391 283	49.7	452 177	47.2
Chili	2002	1 753 952	48.5	1 496 937	49.6	521 609	47.5
	2003	1 713 538	48.5	1 557 120	49.5	567 114	47.8
	2004	1 755 997	47.9	1 594 966	49.5	580 815	48.0
	2005	1 720 951	48.0	1 630 099	49.5	663 694	48.1

Country or area Pays ou zone	Year[t] Année[t]	Primary education Enseignement primaire Total	%F	Secondary education Enseignement secondaire Total	%F	Tertiary education Enseignement supérieur Total	%F
China[3] Chine[3]	2000	...	...	81 487 960	...	7 364 111	...
	2001	130 132 548	47.6	86 516 712	46.8[1]	9 398 581	...
	2002	125 756 891	47.3	90 722 795	...	12 143 723	...
	2003	121 662 360	47.2	95 624 760	46.8	15 186 217	43.8
	2004	120 998 605	47.2	98 762 802	47.5	19 417 044	43.8[1]
	2005	112 739 964	47.0[1]	100 631 925	47.5[1]	21 335 646	46.6
China, Hong Kong SAR Chine, Hong Kong RAS	2000	491 851	48.2	...	...	...	...
	2001	498 175	48.1	490 039	48.5	...	...
	2002	497 376	48.1	488 537	48.5	...	...
	2003	487 465	48.1	487 218	48.8	146 039[2]	50.3[2]
	2004	472 863	48.1	492 779	48.9	147 724	51.2
	2005	451 171	48.0	498 354	48.9	152 294	51.0
China, Macao SAR Chine, Macao RAS	2000	47 262	47.3	35 367	50.5	7 471	52.0
	2001	45 663	47.2	38 943	50.2	13 996	44.6
	2002	44 368	47.0	42 017	50.2	20 420	36.9
	2003	41 917	46.8	44 425	50.2	26 272	36.5
	2004	39 872	46.7	46 509	49.6	24 815	40.5
	2005	37 401	46.8	46 539	49.4	23 420	42.8
Colombia Colombie	2000	5 221 018	48.9	3 568 889	51.5	934 085	51.6
	2001	5 131 463	48.8	3 377 954	51.6	977 243	51.8
	2002	5 193 055	48.8	3 723 348	51.6	989 745	51.5
	2003[1]	5 207 149	48.7	3 788 991	51.6	986 680	51.5
	2004	5 259 033	48.7	4 050 525	51.6	1 112 574	51.3
	2005	5 298 257	48.5	4 297 228	51.6	1 223 594	51.3
Comoros Comores	2000	93 421	45.4[1]	28 122[1]	44.5[1]	714	41.9[1]
	2001[1]	98 564	44.8	...	...	...	...
	2002	104 274	44.3	33 874	45.3	...	...
	2003	104 274	44.3	38 272	44.9	1 707	43.2
	2004	103 809	46.2	42 919	42.5	1 779[1]	43.2[1]
	2005[1]	106 700	46.2	43 349	42.5	...	...
Congo Congo	2000	418 707	47.8	172 980	41.0	15 629	23.8
	2001	500 921	48.2	...	...	13 403	11.9
	2002	525 093	48.3	194 101[1]	42.3[1]	12 164	15.8
	2003	509 507	48.2	204 096	40.5	12 456[1]	15.8[1]
	2004	584 370	48.1	235 294[1]	45.5[1]	...	...
	2005	597 304	47.9	...	...	...	...
Cook Islands Iles Cook	2000	2 379	47.3	1 704	50.6	...	...
	2001	2 402	46.5	1 804	50.4	...	...
	2002	2 388	46.9	1 881	49.0	...	...
	2003	2 254	47.2	1 891	48.7	...	...
	2004[1]	2 265	47.2	1 901	48.6	...	...
Costa Rica Costa Rica	2000	551 465	48.1	255 643	50.8	61 654	53.4
	2001	552 302	48.5	280 341	50.5	79 182	52.7
	2002	545 509	48.1	288 965	50.5	77 283	52.4
	2003	541 494[1]	48.1[1]	305 940	50.5[1]	79 499[1]	52.3[1]
	2004	558 084	48.3	339 763	50.0	108 765	54.3
	2005	542 087	48.3	347 244	50.0	110 717[1]	54.3[1]
Côte d'Ivoire Côte d'Ivoire	2000	1 943 501	42.7	619 969[1]	35.1[1]	...	...
	2001	2 046 861	43.2	663 636[1]	35.5[1]	...	...
	2002	2 116 223	42.3	736 649[1]	35.6[1]	...	...
	2003[2]	2 046 165	44.2	...	...	...	...
Croatia Croatie	2000	199 084	48.5	410 407	49.4	96 798	52.7
	2001	195 638	48.5	405 164	49.4	104 168	52.5
	2002	193 179	48.6	401 921	49.4	112 537	52.5
	2003	192 004	48.6	399 845	49.3	121 722	53.2

Country or area Pays ou zone	Year[t] Année[t]	Primary education Enseignement primaire Total	 % F	Secondary education Enseignement secondaire Total	 % F	Tertiary education Enseignement supérieur Total	 % F
Cuba Cuba	2000	1 045 578	47.7	789 927	49.9	158 674	53.5
	2001	1 006 888	47.7	836 642	50.0	178 021	52.1
	2002	971 542	47.8	895 742	48.5	191 262	54.4
	2003	925 335	47.7	938 047	48.3	235 997	56.2
	2004	906 293	47.7	932 338	49.1	396 516	62.3[1]
	2005	895 045	47.8	937 493	49.1	471 858	62.1[2]
Cyprus Chypre	2000	63 952	48.5	63 054	49.8	10 414	57.1
	2001	63 637	48.5	64 065	49.1	11 934	58.0
	2002	63 717	48.6	63 871	49.0	13 927	54.8
	2003	62 868	48.6	64 711	48.9	18 272	49.5
	2004	61 731	48.8	64 534	49.2	20 849	47.9
	2005	61 247	48.7	64 293	49.2	20 078	52.0
Czech Republic République tchèque	2000	644 956	48.6	957 763	49.3	253 695	49.8
	2001	630 680	48.4	1 004 130	49.6	260 044	50.1
	2002	603 843	48.4	998 608	49.5	284 485	51.2
	2003	566 581	48.3	1 000 493	49.5	287 001	50.7
	2004	534 366	48.3	982 208	49.1	318 858	51.2
	2005	502 831	48.3	975 284	49.2	336 307	52.6
Dem. Rep. of the Congo Rép. dém. du Congo	2000 [1]	...	...	1 253 046	34.3	...	...
	2002	5 455 391	43.9	1 612 840	36.7	...	...
	2003 [1]	5 589 634	43.9	1 655 023	36.7	...	...
Denmark Danemark	2000	384 197	48.6	426 149	50.1	189 162	56.9
	2001	395 870	48.7	441 523	50.1	192 022	56.4
	2002	415 205	48.7	434 517	50.0	196 204	57.4
	2003	417 506[1]	48.7[1]	446 863	50.1	201 746	57.9
	2004	419 806	48.7	449 750	49.8	217 130	57.9
	2005	414 103	48.7	464 952	49.5	232 255	57.4
Djibouti Djibouti	2000	38 191	41.9	15 812	39.3	190	46.8
	2001	42 692	42.8	18 808	38.1	496	41.7
	2002	44 321	42.9	20 516	37.9	728	44.5
	2003	46 564[1]	43.3[1]	23 496[1]	39.3[1]	906	40.9
	2004	48 713	43.8	26 549	40.4	1 134	44.8
	2005	50 651	44.6	30 142	39.5	1 696	41.7
Dominica Dominique	2000	11 774	48.3	7 429	52.8	...	...
	2001	11 430	48.3	7 456	52.2	...	...
	2002	10 984	48.0	7 500	52.1	...	...
	2003	10 460	48.3	7 724	51.7	...	...
	2004	9 872	48.3	7 477	50.4	...	...
	2005	9 441	48.7	7 476	50.0	...	...
Dominican Republic Rép. dominicaine	2000	1 363 609	48.4	653 558	54.8	...	...
	2001 [1]	1 403 848	49.4	752 488	54.3	...	...
	2002	1 399 844	49.4	757 790	54.3	...	...
	2003	1 374 624	49.4[1]	752 096[1]	54.4[1]	286 954	61.3
	2004	1 281 885	47.8	782 690	54.3	293 565[1]	61.3[1]
	2005	1 289 745	47.9	808 352	53.9	...	...
Ecuador Equateur	2000	1 925 420	49.0	917 245	49.7	...	...
	2001	1 955 060	49.1	936 406	49.7	...	...
	2002	1 982 636	49.1	966 362	49.4	...	...
	2003	1 987 465	49.1	972 777	49.6	...	...
	2004	1 989 665	49.0	996 535	49.3	...	...
	2005 [1]	2 000 297	49.0	999 713	49.2	...	...
Egypt Egypte	2000 [1]	7 947 488	46.9	8 028 170	47.1	...	...
	2001 [1]	7 856 340	47.2	8 323 597	47.3	...	...
	2002 [1]	7 855 433	47.4	8 360 316	47.1	...	...
	2003	7 874 308[1]	47.6[1]	8 384 065[1]	47.3[1]	2 153 865	...
	2004 [1]	7 928 380	47.9	8 329 822	47.4	2 512 399	...
	2005	9 563 627	47.3	8 177 320	47.0	2 594 186[1]	...

Country or area Pays ou zone	Year[t] Année[t]	Primary education Enseignement primaire Total	% F	Secondary education Enseignement secondaire Total	% F	Tertiary education Enseignement supérieur Total	% F
El Salvador El Salvador	2000	949 077	48.0	420 959	49.2	114 675	54.3
	2001	967 748	48.1	435 571	49.5	109 946	54.2
	2002	987 676	47.8	461 215	49.6	113 366	54.2
	2003	1 016 098	48.2	488 515	49.9	116 521	53.9
	2004	1 045 485	48.2	520 332	49.9	120 264	54.4
	2005	1 045 484	48.2	524 202	50.0	122 431	54.7
Equatorial Guinea Guinée équatoriale	2000	73 307	48.8[1]	20 679[1]	37.6[1]	1 003	30.3
	2001	78 477	48.8	19 809	...	...	...
	2002	78 390	47.6	21 173[1]	36.4[1]	...	...
	2003	73 771	49.2	...	...	...	...
	2005	75 809	48.7	...	...	...	...
Eritrea Erythrée	2000	295 941	44.9	135 209	41.1	4 135	14.3
	2001	298 691	45.0	142 124	41.6	5 505	13.4
	2002	330 278	44.3	152 723	39.3	5 507	13.4
	2003	359 299	44.4	161 273	39.2	5 755[1]	13.3[1]
	2004	374 997	44.2	194 124	36.1	4 612	13.1
	2005	377 512	44.4	216 944	37.2	...	...
Estonia Estonie	2000	123 406	47.9	116 465	49.9	53 613	58.5
	2001	117 289	47.7	118 980	49.5	57 778	60.1
	2002	108 637	47.8	123 269	49.4	60 648	61.5
	2003	100 171	47.7	123 074	49.7	63 625	61.5
	2004	92 098	47.9	124 382	49.4	65 659	61.8
	2005	85 539	47.9	124 493	49.1	67 760	61.5
Ethiopia Ethiopie	2000	4 873 683	40.0	2 167 595	37.9	67 732	21.7
	2001	5 453 405	41.6	2 692 881	37.9	87 431	21.4
	2002	5 813 817	42.5	3 133 357	37.5	101 829	26.4
	2003	6 017 305	43.1	3 463 586	37.0	147 954	25.2
	2004	6 489 947	44.5	3 920 467	37.9	172 111	25.2
	2005	8 019 287	46.0	4 488 907	39.1	191 165	24.4
Fiji Fidji	2000	114 710	48.0	97 840	50.7	...	...
	2001	115 312	48.3	96 431	50.3	...	...
	2002	114 267	48.6	97 696	50.4	...	...
	2003	113 432	48.3	99 210	50.3	12 779[1]	53.2[1]
	2004	113 449	48.0	102 023	50.1	12 783	53.1
	2005[1]	113 643	48.0	101 741	50.1	12 717	53.1
Finland Finlande	2000	388 063	48.8	490 454	51.1	270 185	53.7
	2001	392 150	48.8	493 187	51.4	279 628	53.9
	2002	393 267	48.9	492 757	51.6	283 805	54.1
	2003	392 741	48.8	496 834	51.4	291 664	53.5
	2004	387 934	48.8	425 966	50.0	299 888	53.4
	2005	381 785	48.9	430 596	50.0	305 996	53.6
France France	2000	3 884 560	48.6	5 928 745	48.9	2 015 344	54.2
	2001	3 837 902	48.6	5 876 047	49.0	2 031 743	54.1
	2002	3 807 739	48.6	5 851 530	49.0	2 029 179	54.8
	2003	3 791 555	48.6	5 859 127	49.1	2 119 149	55.0
	2004	3 783 197	48.6	5 826 848	49.0	2 160 300	55.0
	2005	4 015 490	48.5	6 036 192	49.0	2 187 383	55.2
Gabon Gabon	2000[1]	266 221	49.6	89 572	46.3	...	...
	2001	265 714	49.6	100 718[1]	...	...	...
	2002	281 871	49.5	105 191[1]	...	...	...
	2003	279 816	49.5	...	...	...	...
	2004[1]	281 371	49.4	...	...	...	...
Gambia Gambie	2000	154 664	45.9	53 351	40.5	...	...
	2001	156 839	47.6	56 755	41.4	...	...
	2002	170 922	49.6	75 339[1]	42.9[1]	...	...
	2003	174 984	49.5	74 140[1]	45.3[1]	...	...
	2004	174 836	51.1	84 768	45.1	1 530	19.2

Country or area / Pays ou zone	Year[t] / Année[t]	Primary education / Enseignement primaire: Total	% F	Secondary education / Enseignement secondaire: Total	% F	Tertiary education / Enseignement supérieur: Total	% F
Georgia / Géorgie	2000	298 352	48.7	441 149	48.8	137 046	49.2
	2001	276 389	48.8	444 974	49.1	140 627	49.0
	2002	254 030	48.7	447 381	49.0	149 142	49.8
	2003	238 371	48.3	450 345	48.9	155 453	48.8
	2004	362 582	48.3	319 766	48.7	155 058	50.5
	2005	337 071	48.5	315 428	49.2	174 255	50.4
Germany / Allemagne	2000	3 655 859	48.5	8 307 277	48.4	...	...
	2001	3 519 051	48.5	8 387 525	48.4	...	...
	2002	3 373 176	48.5	8 465 150	48.3	...	...
	2003	3 303 737	48.6	8 446 559	48.3	...	...
	2004	3 305 386	48.6	8 381 930	48.2	...	...
	2005	3 306 136	48.7	8 267 636	48.2	...	...
Ghana / Ghana	2000	2 560 886	47.2	1 056 616	44.0	54 658	25.0
	2001	2 477 990	47.4	1 029 258	44.7	64 098	28.5
	2002	2 586 434	47.5	1 107 247[1]	44.9[1]	68 389	27.8
	2003	2 519 272	48.4	1 170 764[1]	45.0[1]	70 293	31.8
	2004	2 678 912	47.4	1 276 670	44.5	69 968	31.5
	2005	2 929 536	47.9	1 350 410[1]	45.0[1]	119 559	34.9
Gibraltar / Gibraltar	2000	2 366	48.0	1 471	48.1	...	...
	2001	2 377	48.0	1 550	49.1	...	...
Greece / Grèce	2000	645 313	48.4	738 744	49.4	422 317	50.0
	2001	636 460	48.4	743 462	49.1	478 205	51.1
	2002	646 343	48.3	...	...	529 233	51.2
	2003	652 052	48.4	713 850	48.5	561 468	51.0
	2004	657 492	48.2	695 838	48.3	597 007	51.7
	2005	650 242	48.5	715 537	47.7	646 587	51.1
Grenada / Grenade	2000	16 178	48.7	...	...	...	...
	2001	15 974	48.4	...	...	...	...
	2002	17 378	48.3	14 467	52.9	...	...
	2003	16 598	49.6	14 860	48.9	...	...
	2004	15 819	48.6	13 660	51.4	...	...
	2005	16 072[1]	48.7[1]	13 675[2]	50.1[2]	...	...
Guatemala / Guatemala	2000	1 909 389	46.8	503 884	46.9	...	...
	2001	1 971 539	47.0	547 913	47.1	...	...
	2002	2 075 694	47.2	608 420	47.0	111 739	43.0
	2003[1]	2 178 200	47.4	653 492	47.2	114 764	43.0
	2004	2 280 706	47.5	698 561	47.4	...	...
	2005	2 345 301	47.6	754 496	47.6	...	...
Guinea / Guinée	2000	790 497	39.8	203 087[1]	26.7[1]	...	...
	2001	853 623	41.1	240 567[1]	28.1[1]	...	...
	2002	997 645	42.1	279 173[1]	29.1[1]	...	...
	2003	1 073 458	42.7	310 482[1]	31.0[1]	16 858[1]	15.6[1]
	2004	1 147 388	43.3	348 780	31.3	17 218	15.6
	2005	1 206 743	44.1	423 479[1]	33.4[1]	23 788	18.6
Guinea-Bissau / Guinée-Bissau	2000	150 041	40.2	25 736	35.4	463	15.6
	2001[1]	155 033	40.2	26 543	35.5	473	15.6
Guyana / Guyana	2000	108 909	48.6	69 589[1]	50.0[1]	...	...
	2001	109 292	48.9	72 028	50.3	...	...
	2002[1]	109 012	48.8	69 259	50.3	...	...
	2003	110 828	49.0	64 954	...	4 848	...
	2004	114 637[1]	48.7[1]	68 979[1]	50.8[1]	6 933	65.3
	2005	116 756	49.0	70 615	50.0	7 278	67.6

Country or area Pays ou zone	Year[t] Année[t]	Primary education Enseignement primaire Total	%F	Secondary education Enseignement secondaire Total	%F	Tertiary education Enseignement supérieur Total	%F
Honduras Honduras	2000	1 094 792	49.6	...	...	90 620	56.1
	2001 [1]	1 115 579	49.6	...	...	96 612	56.1
	2002 [1]	...	...	...	...	110 489	58.6
	2003	...	...	...	...	119 877	58.6
	2004	1 257 358	49.0	554 810	54.6	122 874[1]	58.6[1]
	2005 [1]	1 268 150	49.0	565 535	54.6	...	...
Hungary Hongrie	2000	500 946	48.4	1 001 855	49.1	307 071	53.9
	2001	489 768	48.4	1 007 476	49.1	330 549	54.8
	2002	477 865	48.4	1 013 471	49.1	354 386	55.3
	2003	464 013	48.5	1 029 979	49.0	390 453	56.7
	2004	446 610	48.4	963 242	48.7	422 177	57.3
	2005	430 561	48.3	960 215	48.7	436 012	58.4
Iceland Islande	2000	31 282	48.3	32 133	50.7	9 667	61.9
	2001	31 786	48.5	32 186	50.4	10 184	62.7
	2002	31 465	48.6	33 486	50.3	11 584	63.2
	2003	31 470	48.4	34 587	50.4	13 347	63.7
	2004	30 984	48.4	32 700	49.5	14 710	64.5
	2005 [1]	30 879	48.4	32 888	49.5	15 529	64.5
India Inde	2000	113 612 541	43.6	71 030 515	39.6	9 404 460	37.8
	2001	113 826 978	43.8	72 392 727	39.8	9 834 046	38.7
	2002	115 194 579	44.2	76 215 685	40.7	10 576 653	39.1
	2003	125 568 597	46.8	81 050 129	42.6	11 295 041	38.4
	2004	136 193 772[1]	46.8[1]	83 858 267	42.8	11 852 936	38.2
	2005	140 012 901[1]	47.1[1]	89 461 794	42.9	11 777 296	39.4
Indonesia Indonésie	2000 [1]	28 201 934	48.3	14 263 912	48.1	...	...
	2001	28 690 131	48.6	14 828 085	48.8	3 017 887	42.8
	2002	28 926 377	48.6	15 140 713	49.0	3 175 833	45.9
	2003	29 050 834	48.7	15 872 535	49.0	3 441 429	43.9
	2004	29 142 093	48.7	16 353 933	49.1	3 551 092	43.8
	2005	29 149 746	48.3[1]	15 993 187	49.0[1]	3 640 270[1]	43.8[1]
Iran (Islamic Rep. of) Iran (Rép. islamique d')	2000	8 287 537	47.5	9 954 767	47.3	1 404 880	45.3
	2001	7 968 437	47.6	9 933 471	47.3	1 569 776	47.4
	2002	7 513 015	47.8	9 916 372	47.5	1 566 509	49.1
	2003	7 028 924	47.9	10 024 105	47.2	1 714 433	50.7
	2004	7 306 634	51.1	10 312 561	47.1	1 954 920	51.4
	2005	7 307 056	53.7	9 942 201	47.2	2 126 274	51.0
Iraq Iraq	2000	3 639 362	44.0	1 224 253	37.0	288 670	34.1
	2001	4 031 346	44.1	1 257 106	36.6	...	...
	2002	4 135 761	44.5	1 294 395[1]	36.6[1]	317 993[1]	34.0[1]
	2003	4 280 602	44.5	1 477 616	40.5	...	...
	2004	4 334 609	44.3	1 706 234	38.9	412 545	36.2
	2005 [1]	4 430 267	44.3	1 751 164	38.9	424 908	36.2
Ireland Irlande	2000	449 638	48.5	338 247	50.6	160 611	54.1
	2001	443 617	48.5	328 424	50.8	166 600	54.7
	2002	445 947	48.5	323 043	51.0	176 296	55.1
	2003	447 618	48.5	320 620	50.9	181 557	55.7
	2004	450 413	48.5	320 560	50.7	188 315	55.2
	2005	454 060	48.5	317 337	51.0	186 561	54.9
Israel Israël	2000	738 610	48.5	587 663	48.8	255 891	57.3
	2001	748 580	48.7	594 210	48.6	270 979	56.7
	2002	760 346	48.7	606 141	48.5	299 716	56.5
	2003	769 856	48.6	603 321	48.3	301 326	55.7
	2004	775 021	48.8	607 224	48.8	301 227	55.8
	2005	784 663	48.9	610 341	48.7	310 937	56.0

Country or area Pays ou zone	Year[t] Année[t]	Primary education Enseignement primaire Total	 % F	Secondary education Enseignement secondaire Total	 % F	Tertiary education Enseignement supérieur Total	 % F
Italy Italie	2000	2 836 333	48.6	4 404 331	...	1 770 002	55.5
	2001	2 810 337	48.5	4 473 362	48.1	1 812 325	56.0
	2002	2 789 880	48.1	4 515 802	47.8	1 854 200	56.2
	2003	2 778 877	48.4	4 528 300	48.5[1]	1 913 352	56.2
	2004	2 768 386	48.4	4 505 699	48.5	1 986 497	56.2
	2005	2 771 247	48.3	4 507 408	48.4	2 014 998	56.6
Jamaica Jamaïque	2000	326 847	49.2	228 764	50.6	35 995	65.0
	2001	328 496	48.9	227 703	50.5[1]	42 502	66.8[1]
	2002	329 762	48.9	228 316	50.4	45 394	68.8
	2003	325 302	48.9	229 701	50.1	45 770[1]	69.9[1]
	2004	331 286	48.9	245 533	49.9	...	...
	2005	326 411	48.8	246 332	50.1	...	...
Japan Japon	2000	7 528 907	48.8	8 782 114	49.1	3 982 069	44.9
	2001	7 394 582	48.8	8 605 812	49.0	3 972 468	44.9
	2002	7 325 866	48.8	8 394 050	49.0	3 966 667	45.1
	2003	7 268 928	48.8	8 131 217	48.9	3 984 400	45.6
	2004	7 257 223	48.8	7 894 456	48.9	4 031 604	45.8
	2005	7 231 854	48.8	7 710 439	48.8	4 038 302	45.9
Jordan Jordanie	2000	723 508	48.8	583 535	49.5[1]	142 190	51.4
	2002	766 093	48.8	606 615	49.4	162 688	48.9
	2003	786 154	48.9	613 120	49.3	186 189	51.1
	2004	799 888	48.9	615 731	49.2	214 106	51.2
	2005	804 904	48.9	625 682	49.2	217 823	50.3
Kazakhstan Kazakhstan	2000	1 208 320	49.3	2 002 880	49.6	370 321	54.0
	2001	1 190 069	48.8	2 031 675	48.6	445 651	54.2
	2002	1 158 299	48.8	2 019 821	48.7	519 815	55.2
	2003	1 120 005	48.9	2 067 168	49.2	603 072	56.6
	2004	1 079 598	48.8	2 090 152	48.6	664 449	57.4
	2005	1 023 974	48.8	2 039 911	48.5	753 181	58.1
Kenya Kenya	2000	5 034 858	49.4	1 908 703	48.5	89 016	35.1
	2001	...	...	...	...	94 629	34.8
	2002	4 903 529	48.4	2 063 409	48.7	98 115[1]	34.8[1]
	2003	5 811 381	48.5	2 197 336	50.4	...	...
	2004	5 926 078	48.3	2 419 856[1]	48.1[1]	102 798	37.5
	2005	6 075 706	48.7	2 464 042[1]	48.6[1]	...	...
Kiribati Kiribati	2000	14 566	47.7	11 638	61.1	...	...
	2001	15 693	49.1	10 586	56.7	...	...
	2002	14 809	48.7	10 334	52.5	...	...
	2003	15 798	48.3	11 372	52.9	...	...
	2004	15 611	49.6	11 581	52.8	...	...
	2005	16 132	49.4	11 331	51.7	...	...
Korea, Republic of Corée, République de	2000	3 945 977	47.2	4 176 780	47.9	2 837 880	35.2
	2001	4 030 413	47.0	3 958 702	47.8	3 003 498	35.6
	2002	4 099 649	46.9	3 768 040	47.7	3 129 899	36.0
	2003	4 148 432	46.9	3 661 759	47.5	3 210 142	36.4
	2004	4 185 330	47.0	3 645 617	47.4	3 223 431	36.6
	2005	4 125 423	47.1	3 692 513	47.2	3 224 875	36.8
Kuwait Koweït	2000	140 182	48.9	239 997	49.5	...	...
	2001	141 419	48.9	243 757[1]	50.0[1]	34 779[1]	63.3[1]
	2002	148 712	48.6	243 468[1]	49.8[1]	36 982	63.3
	2003	154 056	49.0	260 695	49.7	37 153	64.5
	2004	158 271	49.0	267 114	49.9	36 866[1]	64.3[1]
	2005	202 826	48.5	248 895	49.7	38 630	70.2

Country or area Pays ou zone	Year[t] Année[t]	Primary education Enseignement primaire		Secondary education Enseignement secondaire		Tertiary education Enseignement supérieur	
		Total	% F	Total	% F	Total	% F
Kyrgyzstan Kirghizistan	2000	465 596	48.8	659 451	50.2	160 684	50.1
	2001	458 660	48.6	683 832	49.5	190 508	50.8
	2002	453 357	48.7	689 036	49.6	209 245	53.0
	2003	449 399	48.9	739 259	49.7	201 128	54.1
	2004	444 417	49.0	732 618	49.6	205 224	54.0
	2005	434 155	48.7	721 205	49.5	220 460	55.3
Lao People's Dem. Rep. Rép. dém. pop. lao	2000	831 521	45.2	264 586	40.5	14 149	33.9
	2001	828 113	45.4	288 389	41.0	16 745	36.5
	2002	852 857	45.5	320 275	41.4	23 018[2]	35.6[2]
	2003	875 300	45.6	353 362	41.9	28 117	35.8
	2004	884 629	45.9	379 579	42.2	33 760	38.0
	2005	890 821	46.0	393 856	42.5	47 424	41.2
Latvia Lettonie	2000	134 919	48.4	266 498	49.7	91 237	63.4
	2001	125 634	48.6	274 193	49.3	102 783	61.8
	2002	113 923	48.4	278 230	49.1	110 500	61.5
	2003	103 359	48.2	276 072	48.8	118 944	61.7
	2004	92 453	48.1	275 586	48.8	127 656	62.3
	2005	84 369	47.9	271 631	49.0	130 706	63.2
Lebanon Liban	2000	384 539	47.9	383 217	51.4	116 014	51.7
	2001	453 986	48.2	322 136	51.7	134 018	51.9
	2002	452 050	48.1	336 170	51.5	142 951	52.9
	2003	449 311	48.2	350 211	51.3	144 050	54.0
	2004	453 578	48.2	359 062	51.4	154 635	52.3
	2005	452 607	48.2	362 366	51.5	165 730	52.8
Lesotho Lesotho	2000	410 745	50.6	74 313	56.8	4 470[1]	61.8[1]
	2001	415 007	50.2	79 266	56.0	4 976	63.5
	2002	418 668	50.1	82 258	56.1	5 005	58.0
	2003	429 522	50.0	84 318	56.0	6 108	61.3
	2004	427 009	49.7	89 468	55.9	...	...
	2005	422 278	49.6	94 460	55.8	7 918	56.9
Liberia Libéria	2000	496 253	41.9	135 509	41.7	44 107	42.8
Libyan Arab Jamah. Jamah. arabe libyenne	2000	794 293[1]	48.5[1]	...	...	290 060	48.6
	2001	766 087	49.2	...	...	324 603[1]	50.2[1]
	2002	750 204	48.8	824 538	50.5	359 146	51.4
	2003	739 028	48.0	797 992[1]	50.5[1]	375 028[1]	51.4[1]
	2004	745 428	48.0	...	...	...	...
	2005	713 902	48.4	701 536	53.3[1]	...	...
Liechtenstein Liechtenstein	2003	2 218	49.8	3 255	45.0	440	27.0
	2004	2 266	49.8	3 273	45.2	532	26.7
Lithuania Lituanie	2000	218 181	48.7	421 120	48.9	121 904	60.0
	2001	211 650	48.5	433 054	48.8	135 923	59.8
	2002	197 463	48.6	442 830	48.6	148 788	60.5
	2003	183 542	48.5	447 952	48.5	167 606	60.0
	2004	170 216	48.6	431 303	48.8	182 656	60.0
	2005	158 105	48.6	423 706	48.8	195 405	60.1
Luxembourg Luxembourg	2000	32 458	49.2	32 996	50.2	2 437	51.7[1]
	2001	33 266	48.7	33 606	50.4	2 533	53.1
	2002	33 966	48.6	34 038	50.4	2 965	52.8[1]
	2003	34 081	48.7	34 716	50.2	3 077	53.3
	2004	34 603	48.7	35 208	50.2	3 042[1]	52.9[1]
	2005	35 016	48.8	35 946	50.4	...	...

Country or area Pays ou zone	Year[t] Année[t]	Primary education Enseignement primaire Total	% F	Secondary education Enseignement secondaire Total	% F	Tertiary education Enseignement supérieur Total	% F
Madagascar Madagascar	2000	2 208 321	49.0	...	...	32 156	46.2
	2001	2 307 500	49.0	...	...	31 386	45.5
	2002	2 407 644	49.0	...	...	32 593	45.4
	2003	2 856 480	48.9	...	...	37 252[1]	46.3[1]
	2004	3 366 470	48.9	...	...	42 143	47.3
	2005	3 597 731	48.9	...	...	44 948	47.0
Malawi Malawi	2000	2 694 645	48.9	486 786	42.8	...	...
	2001	2 845 836	48.9	518 251	43.6	...	...
	2002	2 846 589	48.9	517 690[1]	43.6[1]	...	...
	2003	...	...	...	...	4 565	29.2
	2004	2 841 640	50.3	505 303	44.6	5 089	35.3
	2005	2 867 993	50.2	515 462	44.8	...	...
Malaysia Malaisie	2000	3 025 977	48.7	2 205 426	51.2	549 205	51.0
	2001	3 033 019	48.7	2 246 874	51.1	557 118	54.3
	2002	3 009 009	48.7	2 300 062	51.3	632 309	55.1
	2003	3 056 266	48.6	2 518 642	51.9	725 865	57.2
	2004	3 159 376	48.6	2 583 993	51.9	731 077	55.4
Maldives Maldives	2000	73 522	48.6	20 010	51.3	...	...
	2001	71 054	48.4	24 607	51.0	...	...
	2002	68 242	48.1	25 365	52.6	...	...
	2003	66 169	47.8	28 612	51.6	73	69.9
	2004	63 300	47.6	28 878[1]	51.9[1]	73[1]	69.9[1]
	2005	57 873	47.8	...	...	...	...
Mali Mali	2000	1 016 575	42.0	257 833[1]	35.2[1]	19 751	32.0
	2001	1 127 360	41.7	...	...	21 861	33.0
	2002	1 227 267	42.3	...	...	22 632	33.0
	2003	1 294 672	42.7	349 615	34.6	25 516[1]	31.5[1]
	2004	1 396 791	43.1	388 418	36.7	28 578	34.6
	2005	1 505 903	43.4	429 716	37.5[1]	32 609	31.5[1]
Malta Malte	2000	34 261	48.6	36 081	48.7	6 315	53.3
	2001	33 530	48.4	36 243	47.9	7 422	54.8
	2002	32 717	48.2	36 478	48.4	7 259	56.9
	2003	31 710	48.1	37 556	48.4	8 946	57.0
	2004	31 064	48.2	41 723	46.8	7 867	55.9
	2005	29 114	47.0	38 961	49.3	9 441	56.3
Marshall Islands Iles Marshall	2000[1]	8 300	47.6	...	...	...	...
	2001[1]	8 530	47.1	...	...	888	56.4
	2002	8 757	47.0	6 353	49.5	903	56.5
	2003[1]	8 907	47.0	6 460	49.5	919	56.5
	2004	8 250	47.5	5 846	49.8	...	...
	2005[1]	8 393	47.5	5 901	49.8	...	...
Mauritania Mauritanie	2000	355 822	48.4	65 606	41.7	...	...
	2001	360 677	48.2	76 658	42.9	9 033	16.8
	2002	375 695	48.8	78 730	43.1	8 173	21.3
	2003	394 401	49.2	84 407	44.4	8 941	21.4[2]
	2004	434 181	49.4	88 926	45.3	9 292	23.7
	2005	443 615	50.0	92 796	45.9	8 758	24.5
Mauritius Maurice	2000	135 237	49.2	105 432	48.5[1]	8 256	45.0
	2001	134 085	49.3	107 846	48.8	12 469	56.9
	2002	132 432	49.4	111 766	49.4	12 602	55.8
	2003	129 616	49.4	118 234	49.2	16 764	57.9
	2004	126 226	49.3	122 556	49.0	17 781	57.6
	2005	123 562	49.2	127 891[1]	49.1[1]	16 852	55.3

Country or area Pays ou zone	Year[t] Année[t]	Primary education Enseignement primaire Total	% F	Secondary education Enseignement secondaire Total	% F	Tertiary education Enseignement supérieur Total	% F
Mexico Mexique	2000	14 765 603	48.7	9 094 103	50.2	1 962 763	48.7
	2001	14 792 528	48.8	9 357 144	50.5	2 047 895	49.0
	2002	14 843 381	48.8	9 692 976	50.9	2 147 075	49.3
	2003	14 857 191	48.8	10 188 185	51.5	2 236 791	49.6
	2004	14 781 327	48.8	10 403 853	51.2	2 322 781	50.0
	2005	14 700 005	48.8	10 564 404	51.2	2 384 858	50.3
Micronesia (Fed. States of) Micronésie (Etats féd. de)	2000[1]	...	...	...	...	1 539	...
	2004	19 105	48.3	13 506	48.8	...	...
	2005	18 793	48.1	13 634	49.3	...	...
Monaco Monaco	2000	2 008	48.5	2 929	50.9	...	...
	2001	1 985	48.9	2 971	48.4	...	...
	2004	1 831	...	3 078	...	...	...
Mongolia Mongolie	2000	253 441	50.2	225 848	54.7	74 025	63.8
	2001	250 436	50.1	258 265	54.4	84 970	63.2
	2002	241 258	50.0	282 089	53.9	90 275	63.2
	2003	238 676	49.6	312 774	53.1	98 031	62.4
	2004	235 730	49.4	333 193	52.5	108 738	61.8
	2005	251 205	49.5	339 249	52.4	123 824	61.4
Montserrat Montserrat	2000	383	43.9	284	48.6	...	...
	2001	413	44.8	297	47.5	...	...
	2002	456	45.2	301	48.2	...	...
	2003[1]	465	45.2	285	49.5	...	...
	2004	468	44.7	284	48.9	...	...
	2005	509	46.2	298	49.3	...	...
Morocco Maroc	2000	3 669 605	44.8	1 541 100	43.7	276 375	42.3
	2001	3 842 000	45.6	1 608 279[1]	43.8[1]	310 258	43.7
	2002	4 029 112	46.2	1 685 063[1]	44.0[1]	315 343[1]	43.7[1]
	2003	4 101 157	46.4	1 758 057	44.5	335 755	44.9
	2004	4 070 182	46.5	1 879 483	44.8	343 599	45.7
	2005	4 022 600	46.4	1 952 456[1]	45.1[1]	366 879	45.1
Mozambique Mozambique	2000	2 543 820	43.0	123 810	38.4	11 619	...
	2001	2 829 787	43.5	142 553	38.8	...	...
	2002	3 023 321	44.1	180 531	39.6	...	...
	2003	...	...	...	...	17 225	32.2
	2004	3 569 473	45.3	243 428	41.1	22 256	31.6
	2005	3 942 829	45.7	305 877	40.8	28 298	33.1
Myanmar Myanmar	2000	4 857 955	49.3	2 268 402	51.2	550 705[1]	...
	2001	4 781 543	49.3	2 301 919	48.4	553 456	63.4[1]
	2002	4 778 851	49.6	2 372 593	48.1	555 060[1]	...
	2003	4 889 325	49.7	2 382 608	48.1	...	...
	2004	4 932 646	49.7	2 544 437	48.0	...	...
	2005	4 948 198	49.9	2 589 312	49.1	...	...
Namibia Namibie	2000	389 434	50.0	124 196	52.8	...	...
	2001	397 459	50.0	135 943	53.1	13 339	45.6
	2002	404 783	50.1	138 099	52.7	11 030	57.9
	2003	408 912	49.9	140 976	52.9	11 788	53.2
	2004	403 412	50.0	153 641	49.7	12 197	53.2
	2005	404 198	49.8	148 104	53.1	...	...
Nauru Nauru	2000	1 589	53.5	662	54.4	...	...
	2001	1 618	48.6	636	49.2	...	...
	2002	1 324	49.8	573	53.6	...	...
	2003	1 375	46.8	645	50.4	...	...
	2004[1]	1 375	46.8	645	50.4	...	...

Education at the primary, secondary and tertiary levels—Number of students enrolled and percentage female (*continued*)
Enseignement primaire, secondaire et supérieur—Nombre d'étudiants inscrits et étudiantes féminines en pourcentage (*suite*)

Country or area Pays ou zone	Year[t] Année[t]	Primary education Enseignement primaire Total	 % F	Secondary education Enseignement secondaire Total	 % F	Tertiary education Enseignement supérieur Total	 % F
Nepal Népal	2000	3 780 314	42.6	1 348 212	40.1	94 401	27.5
	2001	3 623 150	44.1	1 501 503	40.2	103 290	20.7[1]
	2002	3 853 618	44.8	1 690 198	41.0	119 670	20.6
	2003	3 928 684	45.4	1 822 063	41.9	124 817	24.1
	2004	4 025 692	45.4	...	...	147 123	27.6
	2005	4 030 045	46.3	2 054 165	44.7[1]	...	...
Netherlands Pays-Bas	2000	1 278 581	48.3	1 379 253	47.9	487 649	50.0
	2001	1 282 041	48.3	1 402 928	48.1	504 042	50.5
	2002	1 287 069	48.3	1 397 939	48.2	516 769	50.7
	2003	1 290 625	48.2	1 415 170	48.6	526 767	51.0
	2004	1 283 014	48.2	1 396 696	48.5	543 396	50.9
	2005	1 277 990	48.2	1 410 249	48.4	564 983	51.0
Netherlands Antilles Antilles néerlandaises	2000	24 911	48.4	14 418	52.4	2 561	55.5
	2001	23 650	45.9	14 652	52.6	2 433	57.7
	2002	22 924	49.2	15 093	52.2	2 285	59.7
	2003[1]	22 667	49.2	15 268	52.1	...	...
New Zealand Nouvelle-Zélande	2000	359 555	48.6	443 882	50.3	171 962	58.8
	2001	355 532	48.4	456 155	...	177 634	58.6
	2002	361 866	48.4[1]	482 959	51.6	185 099	58.8
	2003	356 442	48.5	503 706	51.3	195 511	58.6
	2004	353 062	48.5	503 241	50.3	243 425	58.4
	2005	352 845	48.5	526 152	50.2	239 983	58.7
Nicaragua Nicaragua	2000	838 437	49.4	333 210	53.4	...	...
	2001	868 070	49.3	353 724	53.5	96 479[1]	52.2[1]
	2002	923 391	48.9	382 951	53.3	100 363	52.2
	2003	927 217	48.7	412 343[1]	52.7[1]	103 577[1]	52.1[1]
	2004	941 957	48.6	416 405	52.7	...	...
	2005	945 089	48.4	437 853	52.7	...	...
Niger Niger	2000	579 486	39.3	106 182[1]	38.7[1]	...	...
	2001	656 589	39.6	108 033[1]	38.9[1]	...	...
	2002	760 987	39.8	112 033	38.5	...	...
	2003	857 592	40.1	126 137	38.9	8 596[1]	27.4[1]
	2004	980 033	40.3	158 343	38.5	8 774	27.4
	2005	1 064 056	40.8	181 641	39.1	10 799	29.6
Nigeria Nigéria	2000[1]	18 802 361	43.8	...	...	...	...
	2003[1]	20 936 749	44.4	...	...	1 234 219	34.6
	2004	21 110 003	44.7	6 316 302	43.7	1 289 656	34.6
	2005	22 267 407	44.9	6 397 581	44.6	...	...
Niue Nioué	2000	250	46.0[1]	260[1]	51.9[1]	...	...
	2001	234	45.7	242	49.6	...	...
	2002	251	...	240	...	...	...
	2004	184	51.1	209	50.7	...	...
	2005	178	50.6	206	48.1	...	...
Norway Norvège	2000	419 805	48.7	371 659	49.4	190 943	58.4
	2001	426 475	48.7	369 943	49.3	190 054	59.2
	2002	429 445	48.7	373 015	49.3	197 064	59.6
	2003	432 618	48.6	385 009	49.3	212 395	59.7
	2004	432 345	48.7	400 159	49.5	213 845	59.6
	2005	429 652	48.7	403 026	48.9	213 940	59.6
Occupied Palestinian Terr. Terr. palestinien occupé	2000	388 163	48.9	477 378	50.1	71 207	46.5
	2001	398 978	49.0	510 214	50.6	80 543	47.4
	2002	402 370	49.0	544 935	50.3	88 930	47.9
	2003	401 372	49.0	582 736	50.2	104 567	49.5
	2004	388 948	48.9	628 495	50.1	121 928	49.5
	2005	387 138	48.8	685 585	50.3	127 214[1]	49.5[1]

Education at the primary, secondary and tertiary levels — Number of students enrolled and percentage female (*continued*)
Enseignement primaire, secondaire et supérieur — Nombre d'étudiants inscrits et étudiantes féminines en pourcentage (*suite*)

Country or area Pays ou zone	Year[t] Année[t]	Primary education Enseignement primaire Total	 % F	Secondary education Enseignement secondaire Total	 % F	Tertiary education Enseignement supérieur Total	 % F
Oman Oman	2000	315 976	48.0	242 533	49.1	...	...
	2001	316 889	48.2	254 496	48.9	...	...
	2002	316 633	48.3	266 923	48.6	36 204[1]	41.0[1]
	2003	314 064	48.5	279 302	48.1	36 826	41.5
	2004	306 210	48.6	286 413	47.9	41 578	51.8
	2005	297 120	48.8	292 783	47.7	48 483	50.8
Pakistan Pakistan	2000	13 987 198[2]	39.1[1]	...	...	...	...
	2001[2]	14 204 954	39.1	6 548 857	39.4	...	...
	2002	14 489 107[2]	39.1[2]	6 396 378[1]	40.4[1]	385 506[1]	43.2[1]
	2003	15 093 960	40.6	6 485 293	41.1	401 056	43.2
	2004	16 207 286	40.8	7 271 999	40.8	520 666	42.7
	2005	17 257 947	41.8	7 244 911	41.1	782 621	45.1
Palau Palaos	2000	1 942	47.7	1 901	47.9	597[1]	69.0[1]
	2001	1 897[1]	...	1 898[1]	48.2[1]	480	63.5
	2002[1]	...	...	...	...	484	63.4
	2003[1]	1 809	43.6	2 465	52.2	...	...
	2004	1 855	48.0	2 273	50.4	...	...
	2005[1]	1 918	48.0	2 269	50.0	...	...
Panama Panama	2000	400 408	48.2	234 153	50.5	118 502	62.1
	2001	408 249	48.2	244 097	50.8	117 864	62.4
	2002	419 904	48.2	251 228	50.7	117 601	62.1
	2003	424 500[1]	48.2[1]	253 012[1]	50.7[1]	130 026	60.6
	2004	429 837	48.3	253 900	50.8	128 558	61.6
	2005	430 152	48.2	256 224	50.8	126 242	61.2
Papua New Guinea Papouasie-Nvl-Guinée	2000	647 804	45.1	156 144	40.9	...	...
	2001	628 358	45.2	170 271	40.3	...	...
	2002	660 425	44.8	184 651	40.8	...	...
	2003[1]	680 786	45.0	190 321	41.0	...	...
Paraguay Paraguay	2000	966 476[1]	48.2[1]	459 260	50.1	83 088	56.9
	2001	966 548[1]	48.2[1]	497 935	49.8	96 598	57.2
	2002	962 661	48.2	519 930	49.7[1]	146 892[1]	57.6[1]
	2003	935 722	48.3	510 881	49.6	143 913[1]	57.2[1]
	2004	930 918	48.4	526 001	49.7	149 120[1]	56.6[1]
Peru Pérou	2000	4 338 080	49.0	2 374 178	47.5	...	...
	2001	4 317 368	49.1	2 484 775	47.5	823 995[1]	48.8[1]
	2002	4 283 046	49.1	2 539 682	47.5	831 345[1]	51.1[1]
	2003	4 200 489	49.0	2 605 247	49.4	839 584[1]	51.1[1]
	2004	4 133 386	49.0	2 661 880	49.6	896 501[1]	50.0[1]
	2005	4 077 361	49.1	2 691 311	49.6	909 315[1]	50.0[1]
Philippines Philippines	2001	12 759 918	48.9	5 386 434	51.3	2 432 002	...
	2002	12 826 218	48.7	5 816 699	51.4	2 467 267	55.6
	2003	12 970 635	48.6	6 069 063	51.5	2 427 211	55.3
	2004	13 017 973	48.5	6 308 792	51.6	2 420 997	55.2
	2005	13 083 744	48.6	6 352 482	51.7	2 402 649	54.2
Poland Pologne	2000	3 318 722	48.4	3 988 001	48.4	1 579 571	57.5
	2001	3 221 253	48.5	3 973 962	48.3	1 774 985	58.0
	2002	3 105 262	48.5	3 949 993	48.1	1 906 268	57.9
	2003	2 983 070	48.6	3 895 167	47.8	1 983 360	57.8
	2004	2 855 692	48.6	3 480 054	49.1	2 044 298	57.6
	2005	2 723 661	48.6	3 444 903	48.6	2 118 081	57.5
Portugal Portugal	2000	810 996	47.7	831 193	50.6	373 745	56.5
	2001	801 545	48.4	813 172	50.3	387 703	57.0
	2002	769 910	47.8	797 065	...	396 601	57.0
	2003	767 872	47.5	766 172	51.0	400 831	56.6
	2004	758 476	47.5	665 213	51.4	395 063	56.1
	2005	752 739	47.6	669 529	51.2	380 937	55.7

Education at the primary, secondary and tertiary levels — Number of students enrolled and percentage female (*continued*)
Enseignement primaire, secondaire et supérieur — Nombre d'étudiants inscrits et étudiantes féminines en pourcentage (*suite*)

Country or area / Pays ou zone	Year[t] / Année[t]	Primary education / Enseignement primaire: Total	% F	Secondary education / Enseignement secondaire: Total	% F	Tertiary education / Enseignement supérieur: Total	% F
Qatar / Qatar	2000	61 067	48.2	47 413	49.1	...	...
	2001	62 465	48.8	46 931	50.1	7 808	73.2
	2002	64 255	47.9	49 042	49.7	7 831	72.5
	2003	66 473	48.3	51 888	49.5	7 826	72.8
	2004	65 351	48.5	53 953	48.9	9 287	71.4
	2005	69 991	48.7	55 705	49.4	9 760	68.0
Republic of Moldova / République de Moldova	2000	252 193	48.7	413 910	49.8	103 944	56.3
	2001	238 713	48.9	413 418	49.9	102 825	55.7
	2002	227 470	48.7	413 916	49.9	107 731	56.6
	2003	215 442	48.7	410 590	50.0	114 238	56.4
	2004	201 650	48.6	399 812	50.1	126 885	57.1
	2005	184 159	48.5	382 577	49.9	118 528	59.1
Romania / Roumanie	2000	1 189 058	48.5	2 225 691	49.4	452 621	51.8
	2001	1 090 172	48.3	2 248 802	49.3	533 152	53.5
	2002	1 028 697	48.3	2 254 849	49.4	582 221	54.4
	2003	990 807	48.3	2 218 124	49.4	643 911	54.3
	2004	1 005 533	48.3	2 154 734	49.3	685 718	54.8
	2005	970 295	48.4	2 089 646	49.2	738 806	54.6
Russian Federation / Fédération de Russie	2001	5 702 348	48.6	...	...	...	...
	2002	5 554 607	48.6	15 340 411[1]	49.0[1]	...	...
	2003	5 416 925	48.7	14 521 818	48.9	8 115 305[1]	56.8[1]
	2004	5 329 613	48.7	13 558 904	48.8	8 622 097[1]	57.0[1]
	2005	5 308 605	48.8	12 433 155	48.7	9 019 556[1]	57.0[1]
Rwanda / Rwanda	2000	1 431 657	49.6	129 620	49.1	11 628[1]	33.7[1]
	2001	1 475 572	50.0	163 576	49.6	12 802	33.7
	2002	1 534 510	50.3	...	...	15 940	34.1
	2003	1 636 563	50.5	189 153	47.5	20 393	36.8
	2004	1 752 588	50.8	203 551	47.7	25 233	39.1
	2005[1]	1 723 997	50.8	203 822	47.6	26 378	39.0
Saint Kitts and Nevis / Saint-Kitts-et-Nevis	2000	6 922	48.6	3 708[1]	51.1[1]	...	...
	2001	6 717	49.9	3 931[1]	48.2[1]	...	...
	2002	6 440	49.3	4 240	50.9	...	...
	2003	6 401	49.0	4 098	52.6	...	...
	2004	6 394	50.2	3 903[1]	52.0[1]	...	...
	2005	6 350	49.8	3 939[1]	50.7[1]	...	...
Saint Lucia / Sainte-Lucie	2000	25 347	49.3	12 530	57.2	...	...
	2001	25 481	48.7	12 738	56.5	...	...
	2002	24 954	48.9	12 743	56.9	...	...
	2003	24 573	48.4	14 110[1]	53.1[1]	2 051[1]	67.7[1]
	2004	23 821	48.3	14 209	52.6	2 285	77.8
	2005	23 573	48.6	13 786	54.3	2 197	73.8
St. Vincent-Grenadines / St. Vincent-Grenadines	2000	19 183	48.2	9 679[1]	56.9[1]	...	...
	2001	19 052	48.3	9 756	53.6[1]	...	...
	2002	18 130	48.4	9 920	52.4	...	...
	2003	18 629	48.7	9 624	52.0	...	...
	2004	17 536	48.4	10 398	51.5[1]	...	...
	2005	17 858	47.0	9 780	55.2	...	...
Samoa / Samoa	2000	28 026	48.1	21 681	50.4	1 182	44.3
	2001	29 203	48.1	22 185	50.4	1 179[1]	44.4[1]
	2002	30 164	47.9	22 941	50.3	...	...
	2003	31 059	47.8	23 427	50.7	...	...
	2004	31 175	48.0	23 764	50.6	...	...
	2005[1]	31 596	47.9	24 242	50.7	...	...
San Marino / Saint-Marin	2000	1 249	48.0	988	49.3	942	57.9
	2004	1 445	...	...	...	...	...

Country or area Pays ou zone	Year[t] Année[t]	Primary education Enseignement primaire Total	 % F	Secondary education Enseignement secondaire Total	 % F	Tertiary education Enseignement supérieur Total	 % F
Sao Tome and Principe Sao Tomé-et-Principe	2001 [1]	27 795	47.9	...	...	...	...
	2002 [1]	28 780	48.3	7 367	45.4	...	...
	2003	29 347	48.5	6 753	53.5	...	...
	2004	29 784	48.7	7 423	50.5	...	...
	2005	30 468	48.6	8 091	51.1	...	...
Saudi Arabia Arabie saoudite	2000	...	...	...	...	404 094	55.9
	2001 [1]	...	...	...	...	432 348	54.9
	2002 [1]	...	...	...	...	444 800	58.8
	2003	3 172 281[1]	49.2[1]	2 576 946[1]	48.1[1]	525 344	58.2
	2004	3 225 893	49.2	2 684 708	48.2	573 732	58.7
	2005	3 263 648	49.1	2 732 249	48.1	603 671	58.1
Senegal Sénégal	2000	1 107 712	46.0	249 547	39.2	...	...
	2001	1 159 721	46.5	260 738	39.5	...	...
	2002	1 197 081	47.1	289 263	39.9	...	...
	2003	1 287 093	47.5	309 959	40.6	50 375[1]	...
	2004	1 382 749	48.3	360 016	41.6	52 282	...
	2005	1 444 163	48.6	405 899	42.5	59 127[2]	...
Serbia and Montenegro Serbie-et-Monténégro	2000	389 314	48.7	784 526	49.4	233 043	53.0
	2001	379 575	48.8	761 408	49.3	208 689	53.7
Seychelles Seychelles	2000	10 025	49.3	7 742	50.6	...	...
	2001	9 782	49.0	7 514	50.7	...	...
	2002	9 623	48.8	7 525	49.9	...	...
	2003	9 477	48.6	7 551	50.2	...	...
	2004	8 906	48.8	7 406	50.7	...	...
	2005	9 204	48.3	7 520	48.2	...	...
Sierra Leone Sierra Leone	2000	442 915	...	...	...	...	...
	2001	554 308	41.6	155 567	41.6[1]	8 795	28.8
	2002 [1]	...	...	...	...	9 041	28.8
	2004	1 158 399	42.2	203 797	39.3	...	...
	2005	1 291 355	45.0	213 839	42.8	...	...
Singapore Singapour	2000	305 705	...	200 209	...	...	...
	2001	302 566	...	211 457	...	...	...
	2002	302 501	...	219 378	...	...	...
	2003	299 939	...	230 985	...	...	...
	2004	296 419	...	238 215	...	...	...
	2005	290 261	...	241 964	...	...	...
Slovakia Slovaquie	2000	309 399	48.5	671 670	49.4	135 914	50.4
	2001	300 189	48.7	663 555	49.3	143 909	51.3
	2002	284 312	48.7	666 238	49.2	152 182	52.1
	2003	270 004	48.5	669 578	49.1	158 089	53.1
	2004	254 906	48.5	673 712	49.3	164 667	54.1
	2005	242 459	48.5	662 659	49.2	181 419	55.3
Slovenia Slovénie	2000	86 850	49.2	218 251	49.6	83 816	56.1
	2001	86 388	48.5	224 747	49.3	91 494	56.1
	2002	86 021	48.5	220 804	48.9	99 214	57.5
	2003	87 085	48.5	217 587	48.6	101 458	56.2
	2004	93 371	48.6	187 817	48.8	104 396	56.9
	2005	93 156	48.4	181 299	48.7	112 228	57.8
Solomon Islands Iles Salomon	2000	57 364	46.1	13 527	42.1	...	...
	2001	64 986[1]	46.5[1]	16 480	43.0	...	...
	2002	66 480	46.5	21 700	42.9	...	...
	2003 [1]	68 146	46.5	21 885	42.8	...	...
	2004 [1]	70 906	46.8	22 157	43.5	...	...
	2005	72 670	46.8	22 487	43.5	...	...

Education at the primary, secondary and tertiary levels—Number of students enrolled and percentage female (*continued*)
Enseignement primaire, secondaire et supérieur—Nombre d'étudiants inscrits et étudiantes féminines en pourcentage (*suite*)

Country or area Pays ou zone	Year[t] Année[t]	Primary education Enseignement primaire Total	% F	Secondary education Enseignement secondaire Total	% F	Tertiary education Enseignement supérieur Total	% F
South Africa Afrique du Sud	2000	7 444 802	48.6	4 141 946	52.4	644 763	55.3
	2001	7 413 415	48.9	4 250 400	52.2	658 588	53.5
	2002	7 465 728	48.9	4 353 817	51.7	675 160	53.7
	2003	7 470 476	48.8	4 446 841	51.5	717 793	53.8
	2004	7 444 142	48.7	4 593 492	51.5	744 489	54.2
	2005	...	...	...	...	735 073	54.6
Spain Espagne	2000	2 539 995	48.4	3 245 950	50.2	1 828 987	52.9
	2001	2 505 203	48.4	3 183 282	50.0	1 833 527	52.5
	2002	2 490 744	48.3	3 106 777	50.2	1 832 760	53.1
	2003	2 488 319	48.3	3 052 662	50.0	1 840 607	53.1
	2004	2 497 513	48.4	3 048 188	50.2	1 839 903	53.8
	2005	2 484 903	48.3	3 107 816	50.1	1 809 353	53.7
Sri Lanka[1] Sri Lanka[1]	2002	1 764 300	48.9	2 344 960	50.7	...	...
	2003	1 702 035	49.0	2 320 093	50.6	...	...
	2004	1 612 318	...	2 332 326	49.4	...	...
Sudan Soudan	2000	2 566 503	45.1	979 514	...	204 114[1]	47.2[1]
	2001	2 799 783	45.0	1 151 554	48.2	...	...
	2002	2 889 062	45.1	1 172 732	47.8	...	...
	2003	3 028 127	45.5	1 278 633	47.1	...	...
	2004	3 208 186	45.5	1 393 778	47.1	...	...
	2005	3 278 090	45.6	1 369 735	47.5	...	...
Suriname Suriname	2001	64 852	48.9	41 874	53.1	...	...
	2002	64 023	48.7	42 253	57.2	5 186	62.0
	2003[1]	64 659	48.7	41 000	56.3	...	...
	2005	65 527	48.3	45 818	55.8	...	...
Swaziland Swaziland	2000	213 986	48.4	60 253	50.2	4 738	48.5
	2001	212 063	48.6	61 277	50.8	4 761[1]	...
	2002	209 037	48.1	62 676	50.4	5 193	54.6
	2003	208 444	48.5	62 401	50.2	5 369[1]	54.4[1]
	2004	218 352	48.1	67 696	49.1	6 594	52.4
	2005	214 054[1]	48.1[1]	67 849[1]	49.0[1]	5 897	52.0
Sweden Suède	2000	775 706	49.3	933 669	54.6	346 878	58.2
	2001	786 027	49.3	928 424	54.4	358 020	59.1
	2002	785 774	49.4	934 608	53.5	382 851	59.5
	2003	774 888	49.4	917 978	52.9	414 657	59.6
	2004	690 758	48.6	711 798	49.5	429 623	59.6
	2005	658 461	48.7	735 494	48.6	426 723	59.6
Switzerland Suisse	2000	538 372	48.6	549 369	47.0	156 879	42.6
	2001	537 744	48.6	553 618	47.2	163 373	42.7
	2002	536 423	48.6	550 317	47.2	170 085	43.3
	2003	535 577	48.6	555 505	47.3	185 965	44.2
	2004	532 092	48.5	563 701	47.2	195 947	44.9
	2005	524 222	48.6	574 783	47.3	199 696	46.0
Syrian Arab Republic Rép. arabe syrienne	2000	2 774 922	47.0	1 069 040	46.9	...	...
	2001	2 835 023	47.2	1 124 752	46.4	...	...
	2002	2 904 569	47.2	1 182 424	46.6	...	...
	2003	2 149 493	47.5	2 119 690	47.1	...	...
	2004	2 192 764	47.6	2 249 116	47.2	...	...
	2005	2 252 145	47.8	2 389 383	47.4	...	...
Tajikistan Tadjikistan	2000	691 891	47.4	795 380	45.6	79 978	25.2
	2001	680 100	47.4	847 445	44.8	78 540	23.9
	2002	684 542	48.1	899 236	44.5	85 171	24.5
	2003	694 930	48.0	948 341	44.8	97 466	25.0
	2004	690 270	48.0	973 673	45.1	108 456	24.8
	2005	693 078	48.2	984 410	44.8	119 317	25.9

Country or area Pays ou zone	Year[t] Année[t]	Primary education Enseignement primaire Total	% F	Secondary education Enseignement secondaire Total	% F	Tertiary education Enseignement supérieur Total	% F
Thailand Thaïlande	2000	6 100 647	48.3	...	...	1 900 272	54.1
	2001	6 023 714	48.4	4 072 108	48.5[1]	2 095 694	52.6
	2002	6 056 420	48.3	4 150 184[1]	49.2[1]	2 155 334	52.1
	2003[1]	5 997 390	48.3	4 128 232	49.2	2 205 581	52.9
	2004	6 054 517	48.4	4 253 380	50.9	2 251 453	53.7
	2005	5 974 615	48.1	4 533 173	50.5[1]	2 359 127	52.4
TFYR of Macedonia L'ex-R.y. Macédoine	2000	126 606	48.4	221 961	47.8	36 922	55.0
	2001	123 661	48.5	222 081	47.9	40 246	55.8
	2002	121 109	48.8	218 834	48.0	44 710	55.2
	2003	116 635	48.4	218 649	48.1	45 624	56.2
	2004	113 362	48.4	215 760	48.0	46 637	57.0
	2005	110 149	48.3	214 005	48.0	49 364	56.7
Timor-Leste Timor-Leste	2001	188 900	...	40 350[1]	...	...	...
	2002	183 626	...	46 680	...	6 349[2]	52.9[2]
	2003	183 800	...	...	...	...	...
	2004	183 483	47.1	73 005	48.1	...	...
	2005	177 970	46.9	74 822	48.7	...	...
Togo Togo	2000	914 919	43.8	260 877[1]	30.5[1]	15 171	16.9
	2001	945 103	44.3	...	...	18 455[1]	16.9[1]
	2002	977 534	44.9	...	...	...	...
	2003	975 063	45.2	353 781[1]	32.3[1]	...	...
	2004	984 846	45.6	375 385	33.2	...	...
	2005	996 707	45.9	399 038[1]	33.7[1]	...	...
Tokelau Tokélaou	2000	247	48.2	180	49.4	...	...
	2001	266	46.2	202	55.9	...	...
	2002	266	45.9	202	55.9	...	...
	2003	227	50.2	191	47.6	...	...
	2004[1]	243	57.2	175	45.1	...	...
Tonga Tonga	2000	16 697	46.6	14 524	49.4	526	60.5[1]
	2001	17 033	47.2	14 127	49.2	453	60.5[1]
	2002	17 105	47.1	14 567	49.8	600	60.5[1]
	2003	17 891	46.9	15 743	...	668	60.5
	2004	17 113	46.9	14 032	49.2[1]	657[1]	59.8[1]
	2005[1]	16 940	47.0	...	...	...	...
Trinidad and Tobago Trinité-et-Tobago	2000	168 532	49.1	113 142[1]	51.7[1]	7 737	59.3
	2001	155 366	48.8	114 567[1]	51.3[1]	8 614	60.0
	2002	141 427[2]	49.1[2]	108 778[1]	51.8[1]	9 867	58.9
	2003	141 036	48.6	107 880[1]	51.4[1]	12 316	61.1
	2004	137 313[2]	48.5[2]	105 381[2]	51.1[2]	16 751	55.4
	2005	129 703[2]	48.6[2]	97 080[2]	50.4[2]	16 920[1]	55.6[1]
Tunisia Tunisie	2000	1 413 795	47.4	1 104 095[1]	50.3[1]	180 044	...
	2001	1 373 904	47.6	1 143 082	50.2	207 388	48.1[1]
	2002	1 325 707	47.6	1 169 368	49.9	226 102	53.9
	2003	1 277 124	47.7	1 148 523	50.8	263 414	54.9
	2004	1 228 347	47.7	1 210 012	...	291 842	56.5
	2005	1 184 301	47.7	1 239 468	51.1	311 569	57.2
Turkey Turquie	2000[1]	7 850 103	46.7	...	...	1 588 367	39.6
	2001	8 014 733[1]	47.0[1]	5 271 056[1]	42.0[1]	1 607 388	40.8
	2002	8 210 961[1]	47.2[1]	5 500 246[1]	42.5[1]	1 677 936	41.4
	2003	7 904 361[1]	47.5[1]	5 742 070[1]	42.0[1]	1 918 483	42.3
	2004	7 872 546[1]	47.6[1]	5 330 923[1]	42.0[1]	1 972 662	41.4
	2005	7 947 603[1]	47.7[1]	5 075 720[1]	44.2[1]	2 106 351	41.9

Country or area Pays ou zone	Year[t] Année[t]	Primary education Enseignement primaire Total	% F	Secondary education Enseignement secondaire Total	% F	Tertiary education Enseignement supérieur Total	% F
Turks and Caicos Islands Iles Turques et Caïques	2000	2 018	47.7	1 218	55.3	...	...
	2001	2 176	49.2	1 339[1]	52.7[1]	...	...
	2002	2 137	48.9	1 411[1]	49.8[1]	...	...
	2003	1 810	48.8	1 395[1]	49.2[1]	...	...
	2004	2 117	50.9	1 516	48.9	...	...
	2005	2 220	51.1	1 686[1]	47.8[1]	...	...
Tuvalu Tuvalu	2000	1 517	48.1	...	...	...	...
	2001	1 427	50.2	912	46.2	...	...
	2002	1 283	51.1	...	...	...	...
	2003	1 344	50.5	...	...	...	...
	2004	1 404	49.9	...	...	...	...
Uganda Ouganda	2000	6 559 013	48.2	546 977	43.4	55 767	33.8
	2001	6 900 916	48.9	570 520[1]	43.3[1]	62 586	34.5
	2002	7 354 153	49.4	687 613[1]	44.5[1]	71 544[1]	34.5[1]
	2003	7 633 314	49.3	716 736[1]	44.6[1]	74 090[1]	34.5[1]
	2004	7 377 292	49.4	732 792	44.4	88 360	38.4
	2005	7 223 879	49.6	760 337[1]	44.5[1]	...	...
Ukraine Ukraine	2000	2 078 699	48.6	5 204 485	49.1	1 811 538	52.6
	2001	2 065 348	48.7	5 123 602	48.6[2]	1 950 755	53.1
	2002	2 047 085	48.7	4 982 947	48.9	2 134 676	53.4[2]
	2003	1 960 512	48.7	4 824 077	48.7	2 296 221	53.8[2]
	2004	1 850 734	48.6	4 445 974	48.5[2]	2 465 074	53.9[2]
	2005	1 945 715	48.6	4 042 827	46.8	2 604 875	54.1
United Arab Emirates Emirats arabes unis	2000	273 144	47.9	210 002	50.0	43 459[1]	68.5[1]
	2001	280 248	48.0	220 134	49.6	58 656[1]	66.6[1]
	2002	285 744	48.1	226 407	49.9	63 419[1]	66.4[1]
	2003	248 370	48.3	273 491	49.4	68 182[1]	66.3[1]
	2004	254 602	48.3	279 496	49.1	...	...
	2005	262 807	48.5	284 978	48.9	...	...
United Kingdom Royaume-Uni	2000	4 631 623	48.8	5 304 140	49.2	2 024 138	53.9
	2001	4 596 110	48.8	5 366 439	49.1	2 067 349	54.5
	2002	4 536 143	48.8	5 507 398	49.1	2 240 680	55.2
	2003	4 488 162	48.8	5 530 597	49.6	2 287 833	55.9
	2004	4 685 733	48.8	5 699 526	49.4	2 247 441	57.0
	2005	4 634 991	48.7	5 747 422	49.3	2 287 541	57.2
United Rep. of Tanzania Rép.-Unie de Tanzanie	2000	4 382 410	49.5	...	...	...	...
	2001	4 881 588	49.3	...	...	21 960	13.3
	2002	5 981 338	49.0	...	...	26 505[1]	23.5[1]
	2003	6 562 772	48.7	...	...	31 049	30.7
	2004	7 083 063	48.8	...	...	42 948	29.2
	2005	7 541 208	48.9	...	...	51 080[1]	32.4[1]
United States Etats-Unis	2000	24 973 176	48.4	22 593 562	49.0	13 202 880	55.8
	2001	25 297 600	48.7	23 087 042	49.0	13 595 580	55.9
	2002	24 855 480	49.0	23 196 310	48.5	15 927 987	56.3
	2003	24 848 518	48.9	23 854 458	48.7	16 611 711	56.6
	2004	24 559 494	48.1	24 185 786	49.2	16 900 471	57.1
	2005	24 454 602	48.5	24 431 934	49.2	17 272 044	57.2
Uruguay Uruguay	2000	360 834	48.5	303 883	52.2	97 641[1]	64.0[1]
	2001	359 557	48.4	315 968	52.2	96 857[1]	63.7[1]
	2002	364 858	48.4	332 175	52.0	98 520[1]	65.3[1]
	2003	365 423	48.4	343 617	52.5	101 298[1]	66.3[1]
	2004	366 205	48.3	339 057	52.6	103 431[1]	66.2[1]

Education at the primary, secondary and tertiary levels—Number of students enrolled and percentage female (*continued*)
Enseignement primaire, secondaire et supérieur—Nombre d'étudiants inscrits et étudiantes féminines en pourcentage (*suite*)

Country or area Pays ou zone	Year[t] Année[t]	Primary education Enseignement primaire Total	% F	Secondary education Enseignement secondaire Total	% F	Tertiary education Enseignement supérieur Total	% F
Uzbekistan Ouzbékistan	2002[1]	2 562 594	49.0	4 100 961	48.6	380 623	43.9
	2003	2 513 342	49.0	4 160 903	48.6	393 910	43.9
	2004[1]	2 440 603	49.0	4 234 948	48.5	407 582	43.9
Vanuatu Vanuatu	2000	35 674	47.6	10 446	51.8	656	...
	2001	36 482	47.9	10 934	46.2	675	...
	2002	37 470	48.0	12 313	47.0	895	35.4[1]
	2003	39 388	48.1	12 800	44.0	914	36.2
	2004	38 960	47.8	13 837	44.7	955[1]	36.1[1]
	2005[1]	39 341	47.8	...	...	...	...
Venezuela (Bolivarian Republic of) Venezuela (République bolivarienne du)	2000	3 327 797	48.5	1 543 425	53.6	668 109	58.6
	2001	3 423 480	48.5	1 677 807	53.0	...	...
	2002	3 506 780	48.5	1 811 127	52.8	927 835	51.4[1]
	2003	3 449 984	48.4	1 866 114	52.5	983 217[1]	51.0[1]
	2004	3 453 379	48.4	1 953 506	52.3	1 049 780[2]	...
	2005	3 449 290	48.4	2 028 388	52.1	...	...
Viet Nam Viet Nam	2000	10 063 025	47.7	7 926 126	47.0	732 187	41.6
	2001	9 751 434	47.7	8 318 192	47.1	749 253	42.1
	2002	9 336 913	47.5	8 783 340	47.4	784 675	42.8
	2003	8 841 004	47.5	9 265 801	47.4	829 459	43.0
	2004	8 350 191	47.3	9 588 698	48.0	1 328 485[1]	40.9[1]
	2005	7 773 484	47.5	9 939 319	48.6	1 354 543	40.9
Yemen Yémen	2000[1]	2 463 540	37.6	1 150 869	28.3	173 130	20.8
	2001	2 643 579	37.6	1 249 016[1]	28.3[1]	...	...
	2002	2 783 371	38.8	...	...	...	...
	2003	2 950 403	39.8	1 373 362	30.1	...	...
	2004	3 107 801	40.5	1 446 369	31.2	192 071	26.2
	2005	3 219 554	41.6	1 455 216	32.1	201 043	26.1
Zambia Zambie	2000	1 589 544	48.1	276 301	44.5	24 553[1]	31.6[1]
	2001	1 625 647	48.2	304 132	43.4	...	...
	2002	1 731 579	48.1	351 442	45.2	...	...
	2004	2 251 357	48.7	363 613	44.1	...	...
	2005	2 565 419	48.4	408 971[1]	44.8[1]	...	...
Zimbabwe Zimbabwe	2000	2 460 669	49.1	844 183	46.8	48 894[1]	37.4[1]
	2001	2 534 796	49.2	866 171	47.0	59 582[1]	36.7[1]
	2002	2 399 250	49.4	828 456	46.9	60 221[1]	40.8[1]
	2003	2 361 588	49.5	758 229	47.5	55 689[1]	38.8[1]

Source

United Nations Educational, Scientific and Cultural Organization (UNESCO) Institute for Statistics, Montreal, the UNESCO Institute for Statistics (UIS) database, May 2007.

Notes

t Data relate to the calendar year in which the academic year ends.

1 UIS estimation.
2 National estimation.
3 For statistical purposes, the data for China do not include those for the Hong Kong Special Administrative Region (Hong Kong SAR) and Macao Special Administrative Region (Macao SAR).

Source

L'Institut de statistique de l'Organisation des Nations Unies pour l'éducation, la science et la culture (UNESCO), Montréal, la base de données de l'institut de statistique de l'UNESCO (ISU), mai 2007.

Notes

t Les données se réfèrent à l'année civile durant laquelle l'année scolaire se termine.

1 Estimation de l'ISU.
2 Estimation nationale.
3 Pour la présentation des statistiques, les données pour la Chine ne comprennent pas la Région Administrative Spéciale de Hong Kong (Hong Kong RAS) et la Région Administrative Spéciale de Macao (Macao RAS).

11 Public expenditure on education: percentage of GNI and government expenditure

Dépenses publiques afférentes à l'éducation : pourcentage par rapport au RNB et aux dépenses du gouvernement

Country or area	As % of Gross National Income (GNI) En % du Revenu National Brut (RNB)				As % of total government expenditure En % des dépenses totales du gouvernement			
Pays ou zone	2002	2003	2004	2005	2002	2003	2004	2005
Albania[1] Albanie[1]	2.8	...	...	...	8.4	...	...	...
Antigua and Barbuda Antigua-et-Barbuda	4.0	...	...	...	...	...	...	...
Argentina Argentine	4.3	3.8	4.0	...	13.8	12.0	13.1	...
Aruba Aruba	...	...	...	...	15.6	...	13.8	15.4
Australia Australie	5.0	4.9	4.9	...	...	...	...	...
Austria Autriche	5.8	5.6	5.5	...	...	10.8	10.8	...
Azerbaijan Azerbaïdjan	3.4	3.5	3.7[1]	2.8	20.7	19.2	...	19.6
Bangladesh Bangladesh	2.2	2.3	2.1	2.4	15.8	15.5	14.8	14.2
Barbados Barbade	7.3	7.8	7.5	7.2	16.7	17.3	16.7	16.4
Belarus Bélarus	...	5.8[1]	5.7	6.0	...	...	13.0	11.3
Belgium Belgique	6.1	6.1	6.0	...	...	11.8	12.2	...
Belize Belize	6.1[1]	5.7	5.9	...	20.0[1]	18.1	...	...
Benin Bénin	3.2[1]	...	4.4	3.5[1]	...	...	17.1	14.1[1]
Bolivia Bolivie	6.4	6.6	...	...	19.7	18.1	...	...
Botswana Botswana	...	...	...	11.0	...	...	...	21.5
Brazil Brésil	4.3	...	4.5	...	10.9	...	...	...
British Virgin Islands Iles Vierges britanniques	...	...	...	...	...	...	17.8	12.4
Bulgaria Bulgarie	3.6	4.4	...	...	...	...	...	...
Burkina Faso Burkina Faso	...	...	...	4.7	...	...	...	16.6
Burundi Burundi	4.0	4.9[1]	5.3	5.2	13.0	...	17.3	17.7
Cambodia Cambodge	1.9	2.0[1]	2.0	...	...	...	...	...
Cameroon Cameroun	3.4[1]	3.7	3.6	1.8[2]	14.5[1]	17.3	17.2	8.6[2]
Canada Canada	5.4	...	...	...	...	...	...	...
Cape Verde Cap-Vert	8.1	7.8[1]	7.2	7.2	17.0	...	20.7	25.4
Chad Tchad	...	2.1	1.9	2.5	...	...	7.7	10.1
Chile Chili	4.4	4.3	4.0	3.8	18.7	19.1	18.5	...
China, Hong Kong SAR Chine, Hong Kong RAS	3.9	4.3	4.5	4.1	21.9	23.3	23.3	23.0

Country or area Pays ou zone	As % of Gross National Income (GNI) En % du Revenu National Brut (RNB)				As % of total government expenditure En % des dépenses totales du gouvernement			
	2002	2003	2004	2005	2002	2003	2004	2005
China, Macao SAR Chine, Macao RAS	...	...	...	...	16.1	...	14.0	...
Colombia Colombie	5.3	5.4[1]	5.2	5.0	15.6	...	11.7	11.1
Comoros Comores	3.9	...	...	...	24.1	...	...	...
Congo Congo	4.4[1]	3.7	3.3	2.8	9.4[1]	9.9	9.0	8.1
Costa Rica Costa Rica	5.2	5.3[1]	5.1	...	22.4	...	18.5	...
Croatia Croatie	4.6	4.9	...	...	10.0	10.0	...	...
Cuba Cuba	...	...	...	...	18.7	...	19.4	16.6
Cyprus Chypre	6.4	7.6	6.5	...	15.0	16.2	14.4	...
Czech Republic République tchèque	4.6	4.8	4.7	...	...	9.5	10.0	...
Denmark Danemark	8.7	8.5	8.6	...	...	15.1	15.3	...
Djibouti Djibouti	...	...	5.5	7.1	...	...	20.5	27.3
Dominican Republic Rép. dominicaine	2.4	2.5[1]	1.2	1.9	12.4	...	6.3	9.7
El Salvador El Salvador	2.9	2.8	...	2.8	20.0	...	...	...
Equatorial Guinea Guinée équatoriale	...	...	...	...	4.0	4.0[1]	...	...
Eritrea Erythrée	4.1	4.1[1]	3.8	5.4	...	...	...	...
Estonia Estonie	6.0	6.0	5.6	...	15.5	15.4	14.9	...
Ethiopia[1] Ethiopie[1]	3.8	...	...	...	...	...	...	...
Fiji Fidji	6.3	6.4[1]	6.4	...	20.0	...	...	...
Finland Finlande	6.4	6.6	6.6	...	12.7	12.8	12.8	...
France France	5.5	5.9	5.8	...	...	11.0	10.9	...
Gambia Gambie	3.0	2.4[1]	2.1[1]	...	8.9	...	...	...
Georgia Géorgie	2.2	2.2[1]	2.8	...	11.8	...	13.1	...
Germany Allemagne	4.7	4.7	4.6	...	...	9.7	9.8	...
Ghana Ghana	...	...	...	5.5	...	...	...	...
Greece Grèce	3.9	4.0	4.3	...	7.9	8.0	8.5	...
Grenada Grenade	...	6.0	...	...	...	12.9	...	...
Guinea Guinée	...	...	2.2	2.1	...	...	...	...
Guyana Guyana	9.1	7.5[1]	5.8	9.1	18.4	...	12.0	14.5
Hungary Hongrie	5.6	6.3	5.9	...	10.3	11.9	11.1	...

Public expenditure on education: percentage of GNI and government expenditure *(continued)*
Dépenses publiques afférentes à l'èducation : pourcentage par rapport au RNB et aux dépenses du gouvernement *(suite)*

Country or area Pays ou zone	As % of Gross National Income (GNI) En % du Revenu National Brut (RNB) 2002	2003	2004	2005	As % of total government expenditure En % des dépenses totales du gouvernement 2002	2003	2004	2005
Iceland Islande	7.8[1]	8.3	8.3	...	16.5[1]	16.8	16.6	...
India Inde	...	3.7	3.8	...	...	10.7	...	...
Indonesia Indonésie	1.1	1.0	...	...	9.0[1]	...	...	...
Iran (Islamic Rep. of) Iran (Rép. islamique d')	4.9	4.8	4.7	4.7	21.7	17.7	17.9	22.8
Ireland Irlande	5.3	5.4	5.6	...	12.8	13.2	14.0	...
Israel Israël	7.8	7.5	7.1	...	13.7	13.7	...	...
Italy Italie	4.8	4.9	4.7	...	9.2	9.5	9.6	...
Jamaica Jamaïque	6.4	5.2	4.7	5.6	12.3	9.5	...	8.8
Japan Japon	3.5	3.6	3.5	...	10.6	9.7	9.8	...
Kazakhstan Kazakhstan	3.2	3.2[1]	2.4	2.5	...	...	...	...
Kenya Kenya	6.2[1]	6.5	6.8	...	...	22.1	29.2	...
Kiribati[1] Kiribati[1]	9.1	...	...	...	...	...	...	...
Korea, Republic of Corée, République de	4.5	4.6	4.6	...	15.5	15.0	16.5	...
Kuwait Koweït	5.7	6.0	5.3	4.5	14.8	...	13.6	12.7
Kyrgyzstan Kirghizistan	4.6	4.6[1]	...	...	...	...	...	...
Lao People's Dem. Rep. Rép. dém. pop. lao	2.8	2.4[1]	2.4	2.5	10.6	11.0[1]	10.8	11.7
Latvia Lettonie	5.7	5.3	...	...	16.1	15.4	...	...
Lebanon Liban	2.7	2.8[1]	2.7	2.7	12.3	...	12.7	11.0
Lesotho Lesotho	...	...	...	10.8	...	...	...	29.8
Lithuania Lituanie	5.9	5.3	5.4	...	17.1	15.7	15.6	...
Madagascar Madagascar	...	...	3.4[1]	3.2	...	...	18.2[1]	25.3
Malawi Malawi	...	5.9	...	...	...	...	...	...
Malaysia Malaisie	8.7	8.4	6.6	...	20.3	28.0	25.2	...
Maldives Maldives	8.6[1]	8.6	7.6[1]	7.5	...	...	...	15.0
Mali Mali	3.6	4.3	4.5	4.5	13.3	16.8	16.9	14.8
Malta Malte	4.5	...	...	...	10.1	...	...	...
Marshall Islands Iles Marshall	6.8	9.2	9.5[1]	...	...	15.8	...	...
Mauritania Mauritanie	3.2	3.5	2.9[1]	2.4	...	...	...	8.3
Mauritius Maurice	3.3	4.7	4.7	4.5	...	...	15.7	14.3

Public expenditure on education: percentage of GNI and government expenditure *(continued)*

Dépenses publiques afférentes à l'èducation : pourcentage par rapport au RNB et aux dépenses du gouvernement *(suite)*

Country or area Pays ou zone	As % of Gross National Income (GNI) En % du Revenu National Brut (RNB)				As % of total government expenditure En % des dépenses totales du gouvernement			
	2002	2003	2004	2005	2002	2003	2004	2005
Mexico Mexique	5.4	5.9	5.5	...	...	23.8	25.6	...
Mongolia Mongolie	9.0	7.4[1]	5.4	...	...	...	...	...
Morocco Maroc	6.6	6.5[1]	6.4	6.8	26.4	...	27.8	27.2
Mozambique Mozambique	...	...	3.9	...	...	...	19.5	...
Namibia Namibie	7.5[1]	6.8	...	...	...	...	...	...
Nepal Népal	3.4	3.4	...	...	13.9	14.9	...	...
Netherlands Pays-Bas	5.2	5.4	5.5	...	...	10.8	11.2	...
New Zealand Nouvelle-Zélande	7.1	7.1	7.2	7.0	16.2	20.9	...	...
Nicaragua Nicaragua	3.3	3.3[1]	...	...	15.0	...	...	...
Niger Niger	2.4[1]	...	2.3	...	...	...	...	...
Niue Nioué	...	...	...	...	10.1	...	...	...
Norway Norvège	7.6	7.6	7.7	...	16.1	15.7	16.6	...
Oman Oman	4.5	4.1	4.3	...	22.6	21.3	24.2	24.2
Pakistan Pakistan	...	2.0[1]	2.0	2.4	...	...	6.4	10.9
Palau[1] Palaos[1]	9.8	...	...	...	...	...	...	...
Panama Panama	4.5	4.7[1]	4.1[1]	...	7.7	...	8.9[1]	...
Paraguay Paraguay	4.4	4.3	...	...	11.4	10.8	...	...
Peru Pérou	3.1	2.9	3.0	2.6	17.1	...	17.0	13.7
Philippines Philippines	3.0	3.0	2.5	...	17.8	17.2	16.4	...
Poland Pologne	5.5	5.7	5.7	...	12.3	12.6	12.7	...
Portugal Portugal	5.9	6.0	5.8	...	...	12.2	11.5	...
Republic of Moldova République de Moldova	4.6	4.4[1]	...	3.8	21.4	...	...	21.1
Romania Roumanie	3.6	3.5	...	...	...	...	...	...
Russian Federation Fédération de Russie	3.9[1]	3.8	3.6[1]	...	10.7[1]	12.3	12.9[1]	...
Rwanda Rwanda	...	...	...	3.9	...	...	...	12.2
Saint Kitts and Nevis Saint-Kitts-et-Nevis	3.7	5.0	5.0[1]	10.8	7.9[1]	12.7	...	...
Saint Lucia Sainte-Lucie	8.4[1]	5.4[1]	5.1	6.2	...	...	15.6	16.9
St. Vincent-Grenadines St. Vincent-Grenadines	10.4	11.7[1]	11.7	8.7	20.3	...	20.5	16.1
Samoa[1] Samoa[1]	4.5	...	...	...	13.7	...	...	...

Public expenditure on education: percentage of GNI and government expenditure (*continued*)

Dépenses publiques afférentes à l'èducation : pourcentage par rapport au RNB et aux dépenses du gouvernement (*suite*)

Country or area	As % of Gross National Income (GNI) En % du Revenu National Brut (RNB)				As % of total government expenditure En % des dépenses totales du gouvernement			
Pays ou zone	2002	2003	2004	2005	2002	2003	2004	2005
Saudi Arabia Arabie saoudite	7.7	7.2	6.7	...	26.9	28.5	27.6	...
Senegal Sénégal	3.7	...	4.1	5.5	...	...	...	18.9
Seychelles Seychelles	5.8	5.7	5.7[1]	...	...	...	...	...
Sierra Leone[1] Sierra Leone[1]	4.9	4.7	4.3	3.9	...	...	...	...
Slovakia Slovaquie	4.4	4.4	4.3	...	9.9	11.0	10.8	...
Slovenia Slovénie	6.0	6.1	6.0	...	12.5	12.6	...	...
South Africa Afrique du Sud	5.4	5.2	5.5	5.5	18.5	18.5	18.1	17.9
Spain Espagne	4.3	4.4	4.3	...	...	11.2	11.0	...
Swaziland Swaziland	5.0	7.0	6.2	...	...	...	...	...
Sweden Suède	7.7	7.5	7.3	...	...	12.8	12.9	...
Switzerland Suisse	5.6	5.6	5.6	...	...	13.0	...	...
Tajikistan Tadjikistan	2.9	2.6	2.9	3.6	17.8	16.3	16.9	18.0
Thailand Thaïlande	...	...	4.3	4.3	...	...	26.8	25.0
TFYR of Macedonia L'ex-R.y. Macédoine	3.5	...	...	...	15.6	...	...	...
Togo Togo	2.7	...	...	...	13.6	...	...	...
Tokelau Tokélaou	...	...	...	...	10.7	14.5	...	...
Tonga Tonga	4.8	5.2	4.9	...	13.1	13.5	...	...
Trinidad and Tobago[1] Trinité-et-Tobago[1]	4.5	...	...	...	...	...	...	...
Tunisia Tunisie	6.7	7.8	7.8	7.6	...	...	...	20.8
Turkey Turquie	3.6	3.8	...	...	...	...	...	...
Turks and Caicos Islands Iles Turques et Caïques	...	...	...	...	16.5	...	...	11.8
Uganda[1] Ouganda[1]	...	...	5.3	...	...	...	18.3	...
Ukraine Ukraine	5.5	5.7	5.4	6.5	20.3	19.8	18.1	18.9
United Arab Emirates Emirats arabes unis	2.0[2]	1.8[2]	1.6[2]	...	23.5[2]	24.9[2]	25.0[2]	27.4[1]
United Kingdom Royaume-Uni	5.3	5.4	5.3	...	11.5[1]	12.7	12.1	...
United States Etats-Unis	5.6	5.8	5.9	...	...	15.2	15.3	...
Uruguay Uruguay	2.6	2.3	2.7	...	9.6	7.9	...	...
Vanuatu Vanuatu	9.3	10.0	...	...	...	...	...	...
Zambia Zambie	...	...	3.1	2.2	...	...	14.8	...

Source

United Nations Educational, Scientific and Cultural Organization (UNESCO) Institute for Statistics, Montreal, the UNESCO Institute for Statistics (UIS) database, May 2007.

Notes

1 UIS estimation.
2 National estimation.

Source

L'Institut de statistique de l'Organisation des Nations Unies pour l'éducation, la science et la culture (UNESCO), Montréal, la base de données de l'institut de statistique de l'UNESCO (ISU), mai 2007.

Notes

1 Estimation de l'ISU.
2 Estimation nationale.

Technical notes: tables 10 and 11

Detailed data and explanatory notes on education can be found on the UNESCO Institute for Statistics web site www.uis.unesco.org. Brief notes which pertain to the statistical information shown in tables 10 and 11 are given below.

Table 10: The definitions and classifications applied by UNESCO are those set out in the *Revised Recommendation concerning the International Standardization of Education Statistics* (1978) and the 1976 and 1997 versions of the *International Standard Classification of Education* (ISCED). Data are presented in table 10 according to the terminology of the ISCED-97.

According to the ISCED, these educational levels are defined as follows:

- Primary education (ISCED level 1): Programmes normally designed on a unit or project basis to give pupils a sound basic education in reading, writing and mathematics along with an elementary understanding of other subjects such as history, geography, natural science, social science, art and music. Religious instruction may also be featured. It is sometimes called elementary education.
- Secondary education (ISCED levels 2 and 3): Lower secondary education (ISCED 2) is generally designed to continue the basic programmes of the primary level but the teaching is typically more subject-focused, requiring more specialized teachers for each subject area. The end of this level often coincides with the end of compulsory education. In upper secondary education (ISCED 3), the final stage of secondary education in most countries, education is often organized even more along subject lines and teachers typically need a higher or more subject-specific qualification than at ISCED level 2.
- Tertiary education (ISCED levels 5 and 6): Programmes with an educational content more advanced than what is offered at ISCED levels 3 and 4. The first stage of tertiary education, ISCED level 5, covers level 5A, composed of largely theoretically based programmes intended to provide sufficient qualifications for gaining entry to advanced research programmes and professions with high skill requirements; and level 5B, where programmes are generally more practical, technical and/or occupationally specific. The second stage of tertiary education, ISCED level 6, comprises programmes devoted to advanced study and original research, and leading to the award of an advanced research qualification.

The ISCED-97 also introduced a new category or level between upper secondary and tertiary education called post-secondary non-tertiary education (ISCED level 4). This level includes programmes that lie between the upper-secondary

Notes techniques : tableaux 10 et 11

On trouvera des données détaillées et des notes explicatives sur l'éducation sur le site Web de l'Institut de statistique de l'UNESCO www.uis.unesco.org. Ci-après figurent des notes sommaires, relatives aux principaux éléments d'information statistique figurant dans les tableaux 10 et 11.

Tableau 10: Les définitions et classifications appliquées par l'UNESCO sont tirées de la *Recommandation révisée concernant la normalisation internationale des statistiques de l'éducation* (1978) et des versions de 1976 et de 1997 de la *Classification internationale type de l'éducation* (CITE). La terminologie utilisée dans le tableau 10 est celle de la CITE-1997.

Dans la CITE, les niveaux d'enseignement sont définis comme suit:

- Enseignement primaire (niveau 1 de la CITE): Programmes s'articulant normalement autour d'une unité ou d'un projet visant à donner aux élèves un solide enseignement de base en lecture, en écriture et en mathématiques et des connaissances élémentaires dans d'autres matières telles que l'histoire, la géographie, les sciences naturelles, les sciences sociales, le dessin et la musique. Dans certains cas, une instruction religieuse est aussi considérée. Appelé parfois enseignement élémentaire.
- Enseignement secondaire (niveaux 2 et 3 de la CITE): Le premier cycle de l'enseignement secondaire (CITE 2) est généralement destiné à compléter les programmes de base de l'enseignement primaire mais dont l'enseignement est généralement plus orienté vers les matières enseignées faisant appel à des enseignants plus spécialisés. La fin de ce niveau coïncide souvent avec celle de la scolarité obligatoire. Dans le deuxième cycle de l'enseignement secondaire (CITE 3), étape finale de l'enseignement secondaire dans plusieurs pays, l'enseignement est souvent organisé en une plus grande spécialisation et les enseignants doivent souvent être plus qualifiés ou spécialisés qu'au niveau 2 de la CITE.
- Enseignement supérieur (niveaux 5 et 6 de la CITE): Programmes dont le contenu est plus avancé que celui offert aux niveaux 3 et 4 de la CITE. Le premier cycle de l'enseignement supérieur, niveau 5 de la CITE, couvre le niveau 5A, composé de programmes fondés dans une large mesure sur la théorie et destinés à offrir des qualifications suffisantes pour être admis à suivre des programmes de recherche de pointe ou à exercer une profession exigeant de hautes compétences; et le niveau 5B, dont les programmes sont dans une large mesure d'ordre pratique, technique et/ou spécifiquement professionnel. Le deuxième cycle de l'enseignement supérieur, niveau 6 de la CITE, comprend des programmes consacrés à des

and tertiary levels of education from an international point of view, even though they might clearly be considered as upper-secondary or tertiary programmes in a national context. They are often not significantly more advanced than programmes at ISCED 3 (upper secondary) but they serve to broaden the knowledge of participants who have already completed a programme at level 3. The students are usually older than those at level 3. ISCED 4 programmes typically last between six months and two years.

Table 11: Public expenditure on education consists of current and capital expenditures on education by local, regional and national governments, including municipalities. Household contributions are excluded. Current expenditure on education includes expenditure for goods and services consumed within the current year and which would need to be renewed if needed the following year. It includes expenditure on: staff salaries and benefits; contracted or purchased services; other resources including books and teaching materials; welfare services; and other current expenditure such as subsidies to students and households, furniture and equipment, minor repairs, fuel, telecommunications, travel, insurance and rents. Capital expenditure on education includes expenditure for assets that last longer than one year. It includes expenditure for construction, renovation and major repairs of buildings and the purchase of heavy equipment or vehicles.

études approfondies et à des travaux de recherche originaux, et conduisant à l'obtention d'un titre de chercheur hautement qualifié.

La CITE de 1997 a également introduit une nouvelle catégorie (ou nouveau niveau) entre l'enseignement secondaire et l'enseignement supérieur, appelée enseignement postsecondaire non supérieur (niveau 4 de la CITE). À ce niveau se trouvent des programmes qui, du point de vue des établissements, sont intermédiaires entre le deuxième cycle du secondaire et le premier cycle du supérieur, encore qu'il serait tout à fait possible de les considérer, dans le contexte national, comme appartenant au deuxième cycle du secondaire ou au supérieur. Ils ne sont souvent pas beaucoup plus avancés que des programmes du niveau 3 de la CITE (deuxième cycle du secondaire) mais servent à élargir les connaissances de ceux qui les suivent et qui ont déjà achevé un programme de niveau 3. Les étudiants y sont généralement plus âgés que ceux du niveau 3. Pour la plupart, ces programmes du niveau 4 de la CITE ont une durée comprise entre six mois et deux ans.

Tableau 11: Les données relatives aux dépenses publiques afférentes à l'éducation se rapportent aux dépenses courantes et en capital de l'éducation engagées par l'administration au niveau local, régional, national/central, y inclus les municipalités. Les contributions des ménages sont exclues. Les dépenses ordinaires (ou courantes) en éducation se réfèrent aux dépenses couvrant les biens et les services consommés dans l'année en cours et qui doivent être renouvelées périodiquement. Elles comprennent les dépenses en: salaires et avantages du personnel, services achetés ou assurés sous contrat, l'achat d'autres ressources y compris les manuels scolaires et du matériel pour l'enseignement, les services sociaux et d'autres dépenses de fonctionnement telles que les subventions aux étudiants et aux ménages, les fournitures et l'équipement, les réparations légères, les combustibles, les télécommunications, les voyages, les assurances et les loyers. Dépenses en capital pour l'éducation se réfèrent aux dépenses qui couvrent l'achat de biens d'une durée supérieure à une année. Elles peuvent comprendre les dépenses de construction, de rénovation et de grosses réparations de bâtiments, ainsi que l'achat d'équipements ou véhicules.

12 Food supply
Kilocalories per capita per day

Disponibilités alimentaires
Kilocalories par habitant par jour

Country or area — Pays ou zone	1990	1995	1998	1999	2000	2001	2002	2003	2004	2005
Albania — Albanie	2 656	3 048	2 886	2 914	2 912	2 912	2 926	2 952	3 004	3 075
Algeria — Algérie	2 923	2 797	2 923	2 940	2 935	2 951	2 999	3 114	3 272	3 439
Angola — Angola	1 861	1 815	1 902	1 981	2 084	2 195	2 306	2 420	2 543	2 672
Antigua and Barbuda — Antigua-et-Barbuda	2 324	1 859	1 635	1 570	1 509	1 477	1 480	1 507	1 437	1 491
Argentina — Argentine	2 956	3 367	3 278	3 276	3 214	3 173	3 117	3 113	2 964	2 854
Armenia — Arménie	...	2 244	2 125	2 087	2 029	2 006	2 028	2 131	2 234	2 321
Australia — Australie	3 044	3 454	3 460	3 389	3 351	3 259	3 202	3 136	3 110	3 101
Austria — Autriche	3 558	3 546	3 681	3 731	3 759	3 746	3 740	3 701	3 723	3 715
Azerbaijan — Azerbaïdjan	...	2 109	2 177	2 267	2 384	2 506	2 633	2 736	2 823	2 903
Bahamas — Bahamas	2 540	2 045	1 774	1 689	1 610	1 537	1 614	1 693	1 778	1 788
Bahrain — Bahreïn	2 621	2 756	2 637	2 657	2 796	2 818	2 887	2 945	2 976	2 986
Bangladesh — Bangladesh	2 037	1 913	2 024	2 082	2 133	2 170	2 186	2 194	2 193	2 194
Barbados — Barbade	3 177	2 979	2 841	2 997	2 947	2 971	2 993	2 892	2 757	2 695
Belarus — Bélarus	...	3 003	2 594	2 466	2 596	2 720	2 767	2 787	2 829	2 769
Belgium — Belgique	...	...	...	...	4 318	4 107	3 927	3 839	3 760	3 676
Belgium-Luxembourg — Belgique-Luxembourg	3 174	3 361	3 226	3 229	...	...	...	...	...	...
Belize — Belize	2 731	3 145	2 955	2 823	2 811	2 767	2 914	2 990	2 906	2 837
Benin — Bénin	2 232	2 195	2 249	2 253	2 257	2 277	2 343	2 433	2 521	2 592
Bhutan — Bhoutan	2 223	2 855	2 954	2 811	2 674	2 544	2 420	2 419	2 543	2 569
Bolivia — Bolivie	2 175	2 368	2 351	2 337	2 349	2 358	2 325	2 327	2 298	2 263
Bosnia and Herzegovina — Bosnie-Herzégovine	...	2 705	2 951	2 949	2 968	3 087	3 178	3 296	3 468	3 649
Botswana — Botswana	2 389	2 258	2 092	2 036	2 008	2 001	2 006	1 968	1 918	1 862
Brazil — Brésil	2 804	2 943	2 984	3 021	2 998	3 078	3 110	3 173	3 222	3 275
Brunei Darussalam — Brunéi Darussalam	2 991	3 675	3 527	3 670	3 495	3 336	3 178	3 028	2 896	2 783
Bulgaria — Bulgarie	3 402	2 811	2 808	2 686	2 585	2 478	2 607	2 683	2 749	2 750
Burkina Faso — Burkina Faso	2 471	2 575	2 487	2 474	2 489	2 505	2 520	2 519	2 489	2 467
Burundi — Burundi	2 006	1 793	1 726	1 712	1 715	1 723	1 732	1 721	1 722	1 691
Cambodia — Cambodge	1 881	1 930	2 019	2 102	2 170	2 249	2 286	2 344	2 421	2 501
Cameroon — Cameroun	2 100	2 032	2 099	2 080	2 138	2 209	2 260	2 310	2 381	2 440
Canada — Canada	3 084	3 307	3 452	3 550	3 586	3 565	3 577	3 578	3 607	3 608
Cape Verde — Cap-Vert	4 539	4 268	4 173	3 976	3 790	3 602	3 420	3 260	3 103	2 954
Central African Rep. — Rép. centrafricaine	1 954	1 854	1 976	1 952	1 976	1 995	1 970	1 875	1 971	2 040
Chad — Tchad	1 707	1 775	1 887	1 924	1 917	1 935	1 921	1 901	1 859	1 828
Chile — Chili	2 622	2 903	2 936	2 876	2 881	2 884	2 910	2 987	3 036	3 033
China[1] — Chine[1]	2 706	2 840	2 924	2 919	2 908	2 902	2 904	2 916	2 946	3 009
Colombia — Colombie	2 618	2 715	2 719	2 732	2 732	2 755	2 759	2 767	2 794	2 796
Comoros — Comores	2 065	2 223	1 968	1 905	1 886	1 907	1 933	1 987	2 018	2 076
Congo — Congo	2 319	2 095	2 149	2 227	2 289	2 333	2 323	2 291	2 274	2 258
Cook Islands — Iles Cook	2 532	3 164	3 002	2 861	2 729	2 576	2 457	2 436	2 508	2 587
Costa Rica — Costa Rica	2 673	2 867	2 895	2 993	2 984	2 974	2 957	2 880	2 819	2 762
Côte d'Ivoire — Côte d'Ivoire	2 375	1 942	2 051	2 156	2 148	2 120	2 191	2 222	2 237	2 293
Croatia — Croatie	...	2 458	2 518	2 547	2 633	2 701	2 782	2 897	2 894	2 907
Cuba — Cuba	2 850	2 269	2 618	2 757	2 905	3 051	3 194	3 317	3 445	3 472
Cyprus — Chypre	3 155	3 071	3 350	3 335	3 320	3 342	3 370	3 330	3 262	3 105
Czech Republic — République tchèque	...	3 191	3 268	3 213	3 201	3 179	3 213	3 296	3 335	3 332
Dem. Rep. of the Congo — Rép. dém. du Congo	2 229	1 829	1 661	1 627	1 590	1 555	1 515	1 466	1 411	1 367
Denmark — Danemark	3 217	3 291	3 357	3 432	3 428	3 422	3 454	3 498	3 489	3 470
Djibouti — Djibouti	1 887	2 325	2 589	2 719	2 751	2 669	2 670	2 782	2 928	3 080
Dominica — Dominique	3 075	3 702	3 371	3 357	3 343	3 506	3 406	3 247	3 182	3 094

Country or area — Pays ou zone	1990	1995	1998	1999	2000	2001	2002	2003	2004	2005
Dominican Republic — Rép. dominicaine	2 277	2 293	2 346	2 263	2 334	2 343	2 360	2 386	2 414	2 457
Ecuador — Equateur	2 477	2 677	2 677	2 710	2 709	2 724	2 720	2 749	2 732	2 738
Egypt — Egypte	3 207	3 373	3 432	3 425	3 478	3 498	3 453	3 404	3 313	3 250
El Salvador — El Salvador	2 570	2 543	2 530	2 494	2 544	2 555	2 596	2 639	2 683	2 726
Equatorial Guinea — Guinée équatoriale	2 014	1 565	1 585	1 673	1 668	1 767	1 851	1 953	2 051	2 062
Eritrea — Erythrée	...	1 207	1 401	1 474	1 535	1 490	1 417	1 348	1 283	1 238
Estonia — Estonie	...	3 833	3 613	3 444	3 543	3 585	3 604	3 469	3 302	3 409
Ethiopia — Ethiopie	...	1 565	1 672	1 700	1 730	1 761	1 777	1 801	1 823	1 846
Faeroe Islands — Iles Féroé	2 617	3 056	3 534	3 675	3 851	4 039	3 853	3 732	3 556	3 504
Falkland Is. (Malvinas) — Iles Falkland (Malvinas)	2 174	1 785	1 536	1 519	1 464	1 387	1 321	1 316	1 284	1 264
Fiji — Fidji	2 634	2 776	3 093	3 133	3 250	3 334	3 474	3 600	3 760	3 935
Finland — Finlande	3 057	2 907	3 079	3 167	3 158	3 134	3 183	3 196	3 200	3 228
France — France	3 654	3 605	3 615	3 646	3 659	3 652	3 659	3 608	3 599	3 569
French Guiana — Guyane française	2 435	2 114	1 820	1 727	1 634	1 563	1 490	1 423	1 355	1 292
French Polynesia — Polynésie française	3 091	3 953	3 772	3 588	3 422	3 259	3 105	2 961	3 072	3 159
Gabon — Gabon	2 558	2 537	2 697	2 740	2 775	2 784	2 788	2 823	2 859	2 893
Gambia — Gambie	2 511	2 153	2 178	2 146	2 112	2 103	2 139	2 198	2 296	2 400
Georgia — Géorgie	...	2 342	2 201	2 179	2 246	2 326	2 446	2 573	2 705	2 843
Germany — Allemagne	3 480	3 354	3 380	3 449	3 490	3 521	3 536	3 573	3 607	3 589
Ghana — Ghana	2 241	2 698	2 709	2 719	2 761	2 823	2 927	3 057	3 211	3 362
Greece — Grèce	3 360	3 406	3 367	3 415	3 459	3 436	3 478	3 455	3 591	3 695
Grenada — Grenade	2 685	2 582	2 585	2 571	2 518	2 530	2 509	2 468	2 446	2 425
Guam — Guam	2 649	2 189	2 270	2 159	2 054	1 954	1 859	1 765	1 679	1 597
Guatemala — Guatemala	2 304	2 261	2 189	2 185	2 212	2 227	2 285	2 282	2 294	2 298
Guinea — Guinée	2 233	2 423	2 434	2 453	2 463	2 513	2 534	2 573	2 595	2 612
Guinea-Bissau — Guinée-Bissau	2 194	1 986	1 902	1 999	2 036	1 936	1 862	1 822	1 879	1 902
Guyana — Guyana	2 478	2 589	2 673	2 694	2 651	2 581	2 594	2 526	2 655	2 784
Haiti — Haïti	1 794	1 859	1 955	1 995	1 994	2 003	1 965	1 913	1 896	1 863
Honduras — Honduras	2 211	2 353	2 444	2 515	2 568	2 661	2 703	2 748	2 774	2 752
Hungary — Hongrie	3 838	3 248	3 245	3 258	3 259	3 284	3 300	3 281	3 404	3 438
Iceland — Islande	3 109	3 044	3 053	3 132	3 173	3 222	3 244	3 291	3 305	3 245
India — Inde	2 427	2 399	2 461	2 461	2 468	2 473	2 470	2 491	2 516	2 529
Indonesia — Indonésie	2 731	2 866	2 839	2 877	2 904	2 927	2 948	2 959	2 952	2 972
Iran (Islamic Rep. of) — Iran (Rép. islamique d')	3 117	3 166	3 266	3 240	3 284	3 333	3 343	3 378	3 412	3 425
Ireland — Irlande	3 751	3 616	3 568	3 677	3 635	3 621	3 627	3 586	3 503	3 503
Israel — Israël	3 276	3 156	3 407	3 472	3 575	3 639	3 685	3 742	3 789	3 831
Italy — Italie	3 601	3 545	3 663	3 675	3 689	3 690	3 663	3 708	3 746	3 754
Jamaica — Jamaïque	2 620	3 220	2 911	2 992	3 098	3 027	3 025	3 078	3 234	3 382
Japan — Japon	2 891	2 826	2 792	2 798	2 801	2 805	2 806	2 807	2 816	2 838
Jordan — Jordanie	2 971	2 777	2 509	2 496	2 582	2 715	2 854	2 989	3 138	3 299
Kazakhstan — Kazakhstan	...	3 320	2 856	2 746	2 743	2 790	2 895	2 954	2 995	3 027
Kenya — Kenya	2 074	2 117	2 064	2 066	2 059	2 062	2 026	1 990	1 988	1 974
Kiribati — Kiribati	2 643	2 827	2 851	2 890	2 794	2 731	2 689	2 712	2 765	2 818
Korea, Dem. P. R. — Corée, R. p. dém. de	2 645	2 345	2 094	2 089	2 070	2 120	2 156	2 213	2 302	2 419
Korea, Republic of — Corée, République de	2 956	3 000	2 971	2 994	2 994	3 021	3 019	3 015	3 021	3 040
Kuwait — Koweït	2 232	2 236	2 573	2 703	2 724	2 848	2 989	3 144	3 288	3 420
Kyrgyzstan — Kirghizistan	...	2 462	2 823	2 947	3 036	3 051	3 047	3 034	3 007	3 027
Lao People's Dem. Rep. — Rép. dém. pop. lao	2 231	2 332	2 516	2 644	2 767	2 887	3 028	3 153	3 313	3 481
Latvia — Lettonie	...	2 998	3 258	3 339	3 257	3 099	3 038	3 028	2 961	2 875
Lebanon — Liban	3 007	2 863	2 895	2 816	2 747	2 834	2 862	2 797	2 857	2 916
Lesotho — Lesotho	2 321	1 808	1 556	1 480	1 408	1 339	1 274	1 211	1 152	1 096
Liberia — Libéria	2 340	1 832	2 069	1 982	1 884	1 929	1 917	1 900	1 997	2 078
Libyan Arab Jamah. — Jamah. arabe libyenne	3 450	3 118	3 240	3 262	3 220	3 152	3 047	3 005	2 939	2 885

Country or area — Pays ou zone	1990	1995	1998	1999	2000	2001	2002	2003	2004	2005
Lithuania — Lituanie	...	3 117	3 342	3 282	3 346	3 338	3 379	3 399	3 468	3 530
Madagascar — Madagascar	2 201	2 082	2 101	2 129	2 133	2 116	2 077	2 049	2 042	2 046
Malawi — Malawi	1 972	2 093	2 262	2 328	2 362	2 368	2 355	2 281	2 298	2 231
Malaysia — Malaisie	2 718	2 741	2 684	2 699	2 755	2 771	2 763	2 828	2 934	3 035
Maldives — Maldives	2 680	2 421	2 391	2 551	2 662	2 807	2 943	3 047	3 183	3 327
Mali — Mali	2 349	2 824	2 771	2 794	2 799	2 818	2 813	2 777	2 750	2 766
Malta — Malte	3 111	3 045	3 391	3 429	3 451	3 466	3 546	3 727	3 915	3 762
Martinique — Martinique	3 145	2 491	2 091	1 997	1 899	1 808	1 722	1 638	1 559	1 485
Mauritania — Mauritanie	2 711	3 471	3 337	3 184	3 032	2 888	2 753	2 616	2 490	2 395
Mauritius — Maurice	2 981	3 000	3 049	3 005	3 088	3 100	3 040	2 976	2 970	2 945
Mexico — Mexique	3 240	3 110	3 116	3 114	3 167	3 202	3 196	3 248	3 244	3 252
Mongolia — Mongolie	2 076	1 935	2 127	2 122	2 045	1 945	1 855	1 809	1 859	1 954
Morocco — Maroc	3 166	3 153	3 211	3 134	3 127	3 211	3 293	3 386	3 401	3 492
Mozambique — Mozambique	1 818	1 906	2 105	2 102	2 090	2 121	2 225	2 256	2 258	2 288
Myanmar — Myanmar	2 559	3 099	2 969	2 989	3 079	3 085	3 199	3 345	3 498	3 619
Namibia — Namibie	2 001	1 565	1 651	1 735	1 802	1 850	1 898	1 936	1 971	1 996
Nepal — Népal	2 358	2 185	2 223	2 253	2 288	2 337	2 386	2 431	2 469	2 503
Netherlands — Pays-Bas	3 529	3 506	3 446	3 427	3 477	3 551	3 537	3 564	3 525	3 479
New Caledonia — Nouvelle-Calédonie	2 987	3 805	3 820	3 640	3 774	3 640	3 460	3 293	3 134	2 984
New Zealand — Nouvelle-Zélande	3 343	3 202	3 197	3 225	3 261	3 274	3 286	3 302	3 342	3 397
Nicaragua — Nicaragua	2 222	2 010	2 187	2 303	2 276	2 364	2 370	2 417	2 487	2 542
Niger — Niger	2 122	2 085	2 153	2 193	2 216	2 218	2 197	2 166	2 121	2 061
Nigeria — Nigéria	2 428	2 540	2 565	2 551	2 533	2 530	2 543	2 591	2 662	2 733
Norway — Norvège	3 140	3 161	3 257	3 243	3 289	3 312	3 338	3 364	3 401	3 449
Oman — Oman	2 347	2 361	2 578	2 650	2 580	2 460	2 475	2 427	2 548	2 677
Pakistan — Pakistan	2 345	2 443	2 480	2 478	2 443	2 417	2 396	2 391	2 395	2 422
Palau — Palaos	1 860	2 365	2 746	2 873	3 006	3 144	3 305	3 461	3 634	3 815
Panama — Panama	2 427	2 268	2 317	2 335	2 343	2 336	2 394	2 495	2 574	2 627
Papua New Guinea — Papouasie-Nvl-Guinée	2 234	2 247	2 246	2 191	2 192	2 167	2 175	2 163	2 155	2 185
Paraguay — Paraguay	2 499	2 911	2 920	2 900	2 890	2 893	2 890	2 802	2 691	2 563
Peru — Pérou	1 836	2 157	2 400	2 401	2 518	2 579	2 542	2 522	2 591	2 583
Philippines — Philippines	2 300	2 338	2 349	2 377	2 406	2 428	2 457	2 473	2 475	2 478
Poland — Pologne	3 485	3 408	3 500	3 521	3 565	3 495	3 568	3 538	3 574	3 503
Portugal — Portugal	3 334	3 483	3 580	3 649	3 679	3 749	3 686	3 678	3 634	3 639
Qatar — Qatar	4 117	3 690	4 152	4 077	3 920	3 823	3 711	3 596	3 521	3 546
Republic of Moldova — République de Moldova	...	3 074	3 070	3 005	3 004	3 011	3 122	3 055	3 132	3 295
Réunion — Réunion	2 573	2 021	1 712	1 628	1 549	1 473	1 399	1 331	1 266	1 205
Romania — Roumanie	3 170	3 364	3 468	3 424	3 440	3 539	3 636	3 759	3 934	4 137
Russian Federation — Fédération de Russie	...	2 947	2 737	2 866	2 949	3 030	3 113	3 272	3 275	3 363
Rwanda — Rwanda	1 854	1 945	1 829	1 839	1 875	1 924	1 966	1 983	1 984	1 936
Saint Kitts and Nevis — Saint-Kitts-et-Nevis	2 508	3 229	3 735	3 956	4 172	4 382	4 612	4 849	5 104	4 861
Saint Lucia — Sainte-Lucie	2 919	2 716	2 823	2 826	2 798	2 677	2 557	2 504	2 473	2 494
Saint Vincent-Grenadines — Saint Vincent-Grenadines	2 386	2 641	2 837	2 706	2 612	2 720	2 784	2 761	2 635	2 620
Samoa — Samoa	2 751	3 046	3 103	2 985	2 953	2 963	3 106	3 264	3 424	3 592
Sao Tome and Principe — Sao Tomé-et-Principe	2 454	3 120	3 263	3 235	3 226	3 384	3 492	3 352	3 382	3 418
Saudi Arabia — Arabie saoudite	2 922	3 130	3 065	3 222	3 283	3 160	3 217	3 257	3 356	3 527
Senegal — Sénégal	2 352	2 141	2 124	2 183	2 223	2 293	2 324	2 387	2 452	2 513
Seychelles — Seychelles	2 353	2 305	2 516	2 433	2 311	2 340	2 323	2 438	2 438	2 547
Sierra Leone — Sierra Leone	2 116	2 067	2 046	1 944	1 876	1 902	1 907	1 887	1 870	1 874
Singapore — Singapour	3 434	3 702	3 520	3 481	3 569	3 593	3 542	3 564	3 536	3 410
Slovakia — Slovaquie	...	2 989	3 054	3 025	2 926	2 822	2 776	2 771	2 719	2 592
Slovenia — Slovénie	...	2 937	2 838	2 862	2 723	2 593	2 466	2 495	2 623	2 756
Solomon Islands — Iles Salomon	2 185	2 039	2 096	2 099	2 171	2 222	2 218	2 212	2 121	2 056

Country or area — Pays ou zone	1990	1995	1998	1999	2000	2001	2002	2003	2004	2005
South Africa — Afrique du Sud	2 724	2 665	2 678	2 706	2 713	2 759	2 778	2 845	2 902	2 933
Spain — Espagne	3 194	3 409	3 454	3 443	3 366	3 285	3 221	3 209	3 211	3 169
Sri Lanka — Sri Lanka	2 307	2 356	2 455	2 498	2 557	2 517	2 457	2 481	2 528	2 559
Sudan — Soudan	2 051	2 173	2 051	2 004	1 982	1 979	2 038	2 143	2 235	2 351
Suriname — Suriname	2 545	2 828	2 687	2 641	2 625	2 646	2 682	2 767	2 866	2 973
Swaziland — Swaziland	2 373	1 942	2 091	2 174	2 155	2 045	1 943	1 843	1 751	1 664
Sweden — Suède	3 007	3 086	3 134	3 119	3 131	3 131	3 173	3 227	3 173	3 132
Switzerland — Suisse	3 175	3 030	2 984	2 969	3 095	3 183	3 222	3 260	3 196	3 085
Syrian Arab Republic — Rép. arabe syrienne	2 891	2 896	2 940	2 970	2 905	2 957	3 033	3 015	3 051	3 058
Tajikistan — Tadjikistan	...	2 071	1 802	1 714	1 649	1 654	1 667	1 749	1 839	1 909
Thailand — Thaïlande	2 353	2 710	2 709	2 750	2 780	2 793	2 699	2 567	2 445	2 329
TFYR of Macedonia — L'ex-R.y. Macédoine	...	2 570	2 725	2 826	2 737	2 729	2 763	2 831	2 866	2 955
Timor-Leste — Timor-Leste	2 171	2 118	1 939	2 040	1 940	1 886	1 970	1 874	1 782	1 705
Togo — Togo	2 287	2 077	2 069	2 041	2 019	2 012	2 032	2 061	2 095	2 123
Tokelau — Tokélaou	1 822	1 467	1 279	1 226	1 189	1 135	1 158	1 211	1 203	1 224
Tonga — Tonga	2 703	2 826	2 824	2 692	2 558	2 447	2 330	2 280	2 259	2 156
Trinidad and Tobago — Trinité-et-Tobago	2 594	2 356	2 469	2 596	2 529	2 585	2 660	2 726	2 852	2 946
Tunisia — Tunisie	3 000	3 030	3 050	3 009	3 046	3 066	3 083	3 147	3 272	3 408
Turkey — Turquie	3 653	3 538	3 567	3 547	3 518	3 458	3 435	3 421	3 415	3 416
Turkmenistan — Turkménistan	...	2 570	2 557	2 647	2 743	2 840	2 952	3 055	3 143	3 217
Tuvalu — Tuvalu	1 928	2 116	2 492	2 612	2 734	2 870	3 012	3 168	3 325	3 493
Uganda — Ouganda	2 362	2 097	2 142	2 204	2 246	2 268	2 287	2 300	2 319	2 333
Ukraine — Ukraine	...	3 167	2 906	2 882	2 946	3 050	3 101	3 138	3 157	3 289
United Arab Emirates — Emirats arabes unis	2 961	2 829	2 440	2 326	2 210	2 108	2 097	2 013	1 936	1 902
United Kingdom — Royaume-Uni	3 174	3 326	3 355	3 374	3 378	3 377	3 372	3 383	3 401	3 446
United Rep. of Tanzania — Rép.-Unie de Tanzanie	2 175	2 263	2 241	2 255	2 253	2 237	2 211	2 175	2 192	2 230
United States — Etats-Unis	3 576	3 686	3 765	3 804	3 815	3 822	3 795	3 781	3 734	3 691
Uruguay — Uruguay	2 657	2 617	2 620	2 656	2 781	2 924	3 073	3 233	3 400	3 576
Uzbekistan — Ouzbékistan	...	2 628	2 364	2 315	2 281	2 270	2 260	2 245	2 227	2 201
Vanuatu — Vanuatu	2 478	2 252	2 261	2 205	2 136	2 072	2 042	2 033	2 031	2 025
Venezuela (Boliv. Rep. of) — Venezuela (Rép. boliv. du)	2 486	2 431	2 391	2 440	2 473	2 467	2 420	2 392	2 377	2 417
Viet Nam — Viet Nam	2 113	2 376	2 377	2 409	2 454	2 518	2 600	2 697	2 791	2 892
Yemen — Yémen	1 950	2 070	2 112	2 120	2 114	2 095	2 050	1 998	1 956	1 926
Zambia — Zambie	2 020	1 912	1 757	1 769	1 753	1 782	1 754	1 764	1 716	1 642
Zimbabwe — Zimbabwe	2 030	1 965	2 067	2 137	2 179	2 076	2 039	1 949	1 866	1 794

Source

Food and Agriculture Organization of the United Nations (FAO), Rome, FAOSTAT Nutrition database, last accessed July 2007.

Source

Organisation des Nations Unies pour l'alimentation et l'agriculture (FAO), Rome, les données alimentaires de FAOSTAT, dernier accès juillet 2007.

Notes

1 For statistical purposes, the data for China do not include those for the Hong Kong Special Administrative Region (Hong Kong SAR), Macao Special Administrative Region (Macao SAR) and Taiwan Province of China.

Notes

1 Pour la présentation des statistiques, les données pour la Chine ne comprennent pas la Région Administrative Spéciale de Hong Kong (Hong Kong RAS), la Région Administrative Spéciale de Macao (Macao RAS) et la province de Taiwan.

Technical notes: table 12

Estimates on food supply are published by the Food and Agriculture Organization of the United Nations in *Food Balance Sheets* and on its Web site http://faostat.fao.org, where the data give estimates of per capita food supplies per day in terms of caloric value. Per capita supplies in terms of product weight are derived from the total supplies available for human consumption (i.e. "Food") by dividing the quantities of food by the total population actually partaking of the food supplies during the reference period, i.e. the present in-area (de facto) population within the present geographical boundaries of the country. In other words, nationals living abroad during the reference period are excluded, but foreigners living in the country are included. Adjustments are made wherever possible for part-time presence or absence, such as temporary migrants, tourists and refugees supported by special schemes (if it has not been possible to allow for the amounts provided by such schemes under imports). In almost all cases, the population figures used are the mid-year estimates published by the United Nations Population Division.

Per capita supply figures represent only the average supply available for the population as a whole and do not necessarily indicate what is actually consumed by individuals. Even if they are taken as an approximation of per capita consumption, it is important to bear in mind that there could be considerable variation in consumption between individuals.

Notes techniques : tableau 12

Les estimations sur les disponibilités alimentaires sont publiées par l'Organisation des Nations Unies pour l'alimentation et l'agriculture dans les *Bilans alimentaires* et sur le site Web http://faostat.fao.org où les données donnent des estimations des disponibilités alimentaires par habitant par jour en calories. Les disponibilités par habitant exprimées en poids du produit sont calculées à partir des disponibilités totales pour la consommation humaine (c'est-à-dire "Alimentation humaine") en divisant ce chiffre par la population totale qui a effectivement eu accès aux approvisionnements alimentaires durant la période de référence, c'est-à-dire par la population présente (de facto) dans les limites géographiques actuelles du pays. En d'autres termes, les ressortissants du pays vivant à l'étranger durant la période de référence sont exclus, mais les étrangers vivant dans le pays sont inclus. Des ajustements ont été opérés chaque fois que possible pour tenir compte des présences ou des absences de durée limitée, comme dans le cas des immigrants/émigrants temporaires, des touristes et des réfugiés bénéficiant de programmes alimentaires spéciaux (s'il n'a pas été possible de tenir compte des vivres fournis à ce titre à travers les importations). Dans la plupart des cas, les données démographiques utilisées sont les estimations au milieu de l'année publiées par la Division de la population des Nations Unies.

Les disponibilités alimentaires par habitant ne représentent donc que les disponibilités moyennes pour l'ensemble de la population et n'indiquent pas nécessairement la consommation effective des individus. Même si elles sont considérées comme une estimation approximative de la consommation par habitant, il importe de ne pas oublier que la consommation peut varier beaucoup selon les individus.

13 Cellular mobile telephone subscribers

Number and per 100 inhabitants

Abonnés au téléphone mobile

Nombre et pour 100 habitants

Country or area	1998	1999	2000	2001	2002	2003	2004	2005	Pays ou zone
Afghanistan									Afghanistan
Number	0	0	0	0	25 000	200 000	600 000	1 200 000	Nombre
Per 100 inhabitants	0	0	0	0	0	1	2	4	Pour 100 habitants
Albania									Albanie
Number	5 600	11 008	29 791	392 650	851 000	1 100 000	1 259 590	...	Nombre
Per 100 inhabitants	0	0	1	13	28	36	39	...	Pour 100 habitants
Algeria									Algérie
Number	18 000	72 000	86 000	100 000	450 244	1 446 927	4 882 414	13 661 355	Nombre
Per 100 inhabitants	0	0	0	0	1	5	15	42	Pour 100 habitants
American Samoa									Samoa américaines
Number	1 500	1 800	1 992	2 156	2 036	2 100	2 250	...	Nombre
Per 100 inhabitants	3	3	3	4	3	3	4	...	Pour 100 habitants
Andorra									Andorre
Number	14 117	20 600	23 543	29 429	32 790	51 893	62 600	64 560	Nombre
Per 100 inhabitants	21	31	36	45	49	78	87	96	Pour 100 habitants
Angola									Angola
Number	9 820	24 000	25 806	75 000	140 000	350 000	740 000	1 094 115	Nombre
Per 100 inhabitants	0	0	0	1	1	2	5	10	Pour 100 habitants
Anguilla									Anguilla
Number	787	*1 475	2 163	1 773	2 974	8 844	13 101	20 995	Nombre
Antigua and Barbuda+									Antigua-et-Barbuda+
Number	*1 500	8 500	22 000	25 000[1]	38 205	...	54 000	86 000	Nombre
Per 100 inhabitants	2	11	29	32	49	...	67	106	Pour 100 habitants
Argentina+									Argentine+
Number	2 670 862	3 848 869	6 487 950	6 741 791	6 566 740[2]	7 842 233	13 512 383	22 100 000	Nombre
Per 100 inhabitants	7	11	18	18	18	21	35	57	Pour 100 habitants
Armenia									Arménie
Number	7 831	8 161	17 486	25 504	71 349	114 379	203 309	320 000	Nombre
Per 100 inhabitants	0	0	1	1	2	4	7	11	Pour 100 habitants
Aruba									Aruba
Number	5 380	12 000	15 000	53 000	61 800	69 952	98 389	108 200	Nombre
Per 100 inhabitants	6	13	16	57	65	72	100	135	Pour 100 habitants
Australia+									Australie+
Number	4 918 000	6 315 000	8 562 000	11 132 000	12 575 000	14 347 000	16 480 000	18 420 000	Nombre
Per 100 inhabitants	26	33	45	57	65	72	83	91	Pour 100 habitants
Austria									Autriche
Number	2 292 900	4 250 393	6 117 000	6 541 000	6 736 000	7 094 502[3]	7 989 955	8 160 000	Nombre
Per 100 inhabitants	29	53	76	81	83	89	97	106	Pour 100 habitants
Azerbaijan									Azerbaïdjan
Number	65 000	370 000	420 400	730 000	794 000	1 057 000	1 456 523	2 242 000	Nombre
Per 100 inhabitants	1	5	5	9	10	13	17	27	Pour 100 habitants
Bahamas									Bahamas
Number	8 072	15 911	31 524	60 555	121 759	116 267	186 007	227 800	Nombre
Per 100 inhabitants	3	5	10	20	39	39	58	71	Pour 100 habitants
Bahrain									Bahreïn
Number	92 063	133 468	205 727	299 587	388 990	443 109	649 764	748 703[4]	Nombre
Per 100 inhabitants	14	20	31	44	56	63	91	103	Pour 100 habitants
Bangladesh+									Bangladesh+
Number	75 000	149 000	279 000	520 000[2]	1 075 000	1 365 000	2 781 560	9 000 000	Nombre
Per 100 inhabitants	0	0	0	0	1	1	2	6	Pour 100 habitants
Barbados+									Barbade+
Number	12 000	20 309	28 467	53 111	97 193	140 000	200 138	206 190	Nombre
Per 100 inhabitants	5	8	11	20	36	52	74	77	Pour 100 habitants

Cellular mobile telephone subscribers — Number and per 100 inhabitants (*continued*)
Abonnés au téléphone mobile — Nombre et pour 100 habitants (*suite*)

Country or area	1998	1999	2000	2001	2002	2003	2004	2005	Pays ou zone
Belarus									Bélarus
Number	12 155	23 457	49 353	138 329	462 630	1 118 000	2 239 287	4 097 997	Nombre
Per 100 inhabitants	0	0	0	1	5	11	23	42	Pour 100 habitants
Belgium									Belgique
Number	1 756 287	3 186 602	5 629 000	7 697 000	8 101 777[2]	8 605 834	9 131 705	9 460 000	Nombre
Per 100 inhabitants	17	31	55	75	78	83	87	90	Pour 100 habitants
Belize+									Belize+
Number	3 535	6 591	16 812	39 155	51 729	60 403	91 663	93 089	Nombre
Per 100 inhabitants	2	3	7	15	20	23	35	44	Pour 100 habitants
Benin									Bénin
Number	6 286	7 269	55 476	125 000[2]	218 770	236 175	386 680	750 000	Nombre
Per 100 inhabitants	0	0	1	2	3	3	5	10	Pour 100 habitants
Bermuda+									Bermudes+
Number	12 572[1]	12 800	13 000	13 333	*30 000	40 000	49 000	...	Nombre
Per 100 inhabitants	20	20	21	21	47	63	77	...	Pour 100 habitants
Bhutan									Bhoutan
Number	0	0	0	0	0	7 998	19 138	37 842	Nombre
Per 100 inhabitants	0	0	0	0	0	1	2	5	Pour 100 habitants
Bolivia									Bolivie
Number	239 272	420 344	582 620	779 917	1 023 333	1 278 844	1 800 789	2 421 402	Nombre
Per 100 inhabitants	3	5	7	9	12	14	20	26	Pour 100 habitants
Bosnia and Herzegovina									Bosnie-Herzégovine
Number	25 181	52 607	93 386	444 711	748 780	1 074 790	1 407 441	1 594 367	Nombre
Per 100 inhabitants	1	1	2	12	20	28	36	41	Pour 100 habitants
Botswana[5]+									Botswana[5]+
Number	15 190	92 000	200 000	316 000	435 000	522 840	563 782	823 070	Nombre
Per 100 inhabitants	1	6	14	20	26	30	32	47	Pour 100 habitants
Brazil									Brésil
Number	7 368 218	15 032 698	23 188 171	28 745 769	34 880 964	46 373 266	65 605 000	86 210 000	Nombre
Per 100 inhabitants	4	9	13	16	20	26	36	46	Pour 100 habitants
British Virgin Islands+									Iles Vierges britanniques+
Number	...	...	...	...	8 000	...	...	...	Nombre
Brunei Darussalam									Brunéi Darussalam
Number	49 129	66 000	95 000	143 000	153 640	177 370	202 450	232 900	Nombre
Per 100 inhabitants	16	21	29	42	45	51	57	62	Pour 100 habitants
Bulgaria									Bulgarie
Number	127 000	350 000	738 000	1 550 000	2 597 548	3 500 869	4 729 731	6 244 693	Nombre
Per 100 inhabitants	2	4	9	20	33	45	61	81	Pour 100 habitants
Burkina Faso									Burkina Faso
Number	2 730	5 036	25 245	76 000[6]	113 000[6]	227 000[6]	398 000[6]	572 200[6]	Nombre
Per 100 inhabitants	0	0	0	1	1	2	3	5	Pour 100 habitants
Burundi									Burundi
Number	620	800	16 320	33 416[2]	52 000	64 000	100 560	153 000	Nombre
Per 100 inhabitants	0	0	0	0	1	1	1	2	Pour 100 habitants
Cambodia									Cambodge
Number	61 345	89 117	130 547	223 458	380 000	498 388	861 500	1 062 000	Nombre
Per 100 inhabitants	1	1	1	2	3	4	6	8	Pour 100 habitants
Cameroon									Cameroun
Number	5 000	6 000	103 279	417 295	701 507	1 077 000	1 536 594	2 179 035	Nombre
Per 100 inhabitants	0	0	1	3	4	7	9	14	Pour 100 habitants
Canada									Canada
Number	5 346 000	6 911 038	8 727 000	10 649 000	11 872 000	13 228 000	14 984 396	16 600 000	Nombre
Per 100 inhabitants	18	23	28	34	38	42	47	53	Pour 100 habitants
Cape Verde									Cap-Vert
Number	1 020	8 068	19 729	31 507	42 949	53 342	65 780	81 721	Nombre
Per 100 inhabitants	0	2	5	7	10	12	14	17	Pour 100 habitants
Cayman Islands+									Iles Caïmanes+
Number	5 170	8 410	10 700	17 000	...	21 040	33 800	...	Nombre

Country or area	1998	1999	2000	2001	2002	2003	2004	2005	Pays ou zone
Central African Rep.									Rép. centrafricaine
Number	1 633	4 162	4 967	11 000	12 600	40 000	60 000	100 000	Nombre
Per 100 inhabitants	0	0	0	0	0	1	2	2	Pour 100 habitants
Chad									Tchad
Number	0	0	5 500	22 000	34 200[3]	65 000	123 000	210 000	Nombre
Per 100 inhabitants	0	0	0	0	0	1	1	2	Pour 100 habitants
Chile									Chili
Number	964 248	2 260 687	3 401 525	5 271 565	6 445 698[2]	7 520 280	9 566 581	10 569 572	Nombre
Per 100 inhabitants	7	15	22	33	41	49	62	68	Pour 100 habitants
China[7]									Chine[7]
Number	23 863 000	43 296 000	85 260 000	144 820 000	206 005 000	269 953 000	334 824 000	393 428 000	Nombre
Per 100 inhabitants	2	3	7	11	16	21	26	30	Pour 100 habitants
China, Hong Kong SAR+									Chine, Hong Kong RAS+
Number	3 174 369	4 275 048	5 447 346	5 776 360	6 395 725	7 349 202	8 213 959	8 693 368	Nombre
Per 100 inhabitants	49	65	82	86	94	108	119	123	Pour 100 habitants
China, Macao SAR									Chine, Macao RAS
Number	82 114	118 101	141 052	194 475	276 138	364 031	432 450	532 758	Nombre
Per 100 inhabitants	19	27	33	45	63	81	93	116	Pour 100 habitants
Colombia									Colombie
Number	1 800 229	1 966 535	2 256 801	3 265 261	4 596 594	6 186 206	10 400 578	21 849 993	Nombre
Per 100 inhabitants	4	5	5	8	11	14	23	48	Pour 100 habitants
Comoros									Comores
Number	0	0	0	0	0	2 000	9 375	16 065	Nombre
Per 100 inhabitants	0	0	0	0	0	0	1	2	Pour 100 habitants
Congo									Congo
Number	3 390	5 000	70 000	150 000	221 800[3]	330 000	383 653	490 000	Nombre
Per 100 inhabitants	0	0	2	5	7	9	10	12	Pour 100 habitants
Cook Islands+									Iles Cook+
Number	285	506	552	942[1]	1 499	3 384	3 650	4 004	Nombre
Costa Rica									Costa Rica
Number	108 770	138 178	211 614	326 944	502 478	778 299	923 084	1 101 035	Nombre
Per 100 inhabitants	3	4	6	8	13	19	22	25	Pour 100 habitants
Côte d'Ivoire									Côte d'Ivoire
Number	91 212	257 134	472 952	728 545	1 027 058	1 280 696	1 674 332	2 349 439	Nombre
Per 100 inhabitants	1	2	3	4	6	8	10	13	Pour 100 habitants
Croatia									Croatie
Number	182 500	295 000	1 033 000	*1 755 000	2 340 000	2 537 300	2 835 500	2 983 900	Nombre
Per 100 inhabitants	4	7	23	40	54	58	64	80	Pour 100 habitants
Cuba									Cuba
Number	4 056	5 136	6 536	8 579	17 851	35 356	75 797	135 534	Nombre
Per 100 inhabitants	0	0	0	0	0	0	1	1	Pour 100 habitants
Cyprus									Chypre
Number	116 429	151 649	218 324	314 355	417 933	551 752	640 515	718 842	Nombre
Per 100 inhabitants	18	23	32	46	58	77	79	86	Pour 100 habitants
Czech Republic									République tchèque
Number	965 476	1 944 553	4 346 009	6 947 151	8 610 177	9 708 683	10 782 567	11 775 878	Nombre
Per 100 inhabitants	9	19	42	68	84	95	106	115	Pour 100 habitants
Dem. Rep. of the Congo									Rép. dém. du Congo
Number	10 000	12 000	15 000	150 000	560 000	973 252	1 990 722	2 746 094	Nombre
Per 100 inhabitants	0	0	0	0	1	2	4	5	Pour 100 habitants
Denmark									Danemark
Number	1 931 101	2 628 585	3 363 552	3 960 165	4 477 752	4 767 277	5 167 998	5 469 345	Nombre
Per 100 inhabitants	36	49	63	74	83	88	95	100	Pour 100 habitants
Djibouti									Djibouti
Number	220	280	230	3 000	15 000	23 000	34 482	44 053	Nombre
Per 100 inhabitants	0	0	0	0	2	3	5	6	Pour 100 habitants
Dominica+									Dominique+
Number	650	*800	*1 200	7 710	12 173	23 786	41 838	…	Nombre
Per 100 inhabitants	1	1	2	11	17	33	59	…	Pour 100 habitants

Country or area	1998	1999	2000	2001	2002	2003	2004	2005	Pays ou zone
Dominican Republic									Rép. dominicaine
Number	209 384	424 434	705 431	1 270 082	1 700 609	2 122 543	2 534 063	3 623 289	Nombre
Per 100 inhabitants	3	5	9	16	20	24	29	41	Pour 100 habitants
Ecuador									Equateur
Number	242 812	383 185	482 213	859 152	1 560 861	2 398 161	3 544 174	6 246 332	Nombre
Per 100 inhabitants	2	3	4	7	12	18	27	47	Pour 100 habitants
Egypt+									Egypte+
Number	90 786	480 974	1 359 900	2 793 800	4 494 700	5 797 530	7 643 060	13 629 602	Nombre
Per 100 inhabitants	0	1	2	4	7	8	11	18	Pour 100 habitants
El Salvador									El Salvador
Number	137 114	511 365	743 628	857 782	888 818	1 149 790	1 832 579	2 411 753	Nombre
Per 100 inhabitants	2	8	12	13	14	17	28	35	Pour 100 habitants
Equatorial Guinea									Guinée équatoriale
Number	297	600	5 000	15 000	32 000	41 500	61 900	96 900	Nombre
Per 100 inhabitants	0	0	1	3	6	8	12	19	Pour 100 habitants
Eritrea									Erythrée
Number	0	0	0	0	0	0	20 000	40 438	Nombre
Per 100 inhabitants	0	0	0	0	0	0	0	1	Pour 100 habitants
Estonia									Estonie
Number	247 000	387 000	557 000	651 200	881 000	1 050 241	1 255 731	1 445 300	Nombre
Per 100 inhabitants	17	27	39	46	65	78	94	109	Pour 100 habitants
Ethiopia+									Ethiopie+
Number	0	6 740	17 757	27 500	50 369	97 827	178 000	410 630	Nombre
Per 100 inhabitants	0	0	0	0	0	0	0	1	Pour 100 habitants
Faeroe Islands									Iles Féroé
Number	6 516	10 761	16 971	24 487	34 737	38 026	41 298	42 533	Nombre
Per 100 inhabitants	15	24	37	53	75	82	88	89	Pour 100 habitants
Falkland Is. (Malvinas)									Iles Falkland (Malvinas)
Number	0	0	0	0	0	0	0	766[8]	Nombre
Fiji									Fidji
Number	8 000	23 380	55 057	80 933	89 900	109 882	142 190	176 651	Nombre
Per 100 inhabitants	1	3	7	10	11	13	17	24	Pour 100 habitants
Finland									Finlande
Number	2 845 985	3 273 433	3 728 625	4 175 587	4 516 772	4 747 126	4 988 000	5 270 000	Nombre
Per 100 inhabitants	55	63	72	80	87	91	96	100	Pour 100 habitants
France									France
Number	11 210 100	21 433 500	29 052 360	36 997 400	38 585 300	41 683 100	44 551 800	48 099 000	Nombre
Per 100 inhabitants	19	37	49	62	65	70	74	80	Pour 100 habitants
French Guiana									Guyane française
Number	4 000	18 000	39 830	75 320	87 300	92 000	98 000	...	Nombre
Per 100 inhabitants	3	11	24	45	50	51	54	...	Pour 100 habitants
French Polynesia									Polynésie française
Number	11 060	21 929	39 900	67 300	52 250	60 100	72 525	87 000	Nombre
Per 100 inhabitants	5	10	17	28	21	24	29	34	Pour 100 habitants
Gabon									Gabon
Number	9 694	8 891	120 000	150 000	279 289	300 000	489 367	649 807	Nombre
Per 100 inhabitants	1	1	10	12	21	22	36	47	Pour 100 habitants
Gambia+									Gambie+
Number	5 048	5 307	*5 600	55 085	100 000	149 300	175 000	247 478	Nombre
Per 100 inhabitants	0	0	0	4	8	11	12	16	Pour 100 habitants
Georgia									Géorgie
Number	60 000	133 243	194 741	301 327	503 619	711 224	840 600	1 459 180	Nombre
Per 100 inhabitants	1	3	4	6	11	16	19	33	Pour 100 habitants
Germany									Allemagne
Number	13 913 000	23 446 000	48 202 000	56 126 000	59 128 000	64 800 000	71 300 000	79 200 000	Nombre
Per 100 inhabitants	17	29	59	68	72	79	86	96	Pour 100 habitants
Ghana									Ghana
Number	41 753	70 026	130 045	243 797	386 775	795 529	1 695 000	2 842 444	Nombre
Per 100 inhabitants	0	0	1	1	2	4	8	13	Pour 100 habitants

Country or area	1998	1999	2000	2001	2002	2003	2004	2005	Pays ou zone
Greece									Grèce
Number	2 047 000	3 904 000	5 932 403	7 963 742	9 314 260	8 936 202	9 305 738	10 042 633	Nombre
Per 100 inhabitants	19	37	56	75	85	78	84	92	Pour 100 habitants
Greenland									Groenland
Number	8 899	13 521	15 977	16 747	19 924	27 400	32 200	...	Nombre
Per 100 inhabitants	16	24	29	30	35	48	...	...	Pour 100 habitants
Grenada									Grenade
Number	1 410	2 010	4 300	6 410	7 550	42 290	43 310	46 860	Nombre
Per 100 inhabitants	1	2	4	6	7	41	42	46	Pour 100 habitants
Guadeloupe[9]									Guadeloupe[9]
Number	14 227	88 080	169 840	292 520	299 100	289 400	314 700	...	Nombre
Per 100 inhabitants	3	21	40	68	69	66	71	...	Pour 100 habitants
Guam									Guam
Number	12 837[2]	20 000	27 200	32 600	70 500	79 800	98 000	...	Nombre
Per 100 inhabitants	9	13	18	21	44	49	59	...	Pour 100 habitants
Guatemala									Guatemala
Number	111 445	337 800	856 831	1 146 441	1 577 085	2 034 776	3 168 256	4 510 067	Nombre
Per 100 inhabitants	1	3	8	10	13	17	25	36	Pour 100 habitants
Guernsey									Guernesey
Number	11 665	15 320	21 885	31 539	36 580	41 530	43 824	...	Nombre
Per 100 inhabitants	19	25	35	56	65	74	79	...	Pour 100 habitants
Guinea									Guinée
Number	21 567	25 182	42 112	55 670	90 772	111 500	154 900	189 000	Nombre
Per 100 inhabitants	0	0	1	1	1	1	2	2	Pour 100 habitants
Guinea-Bissau									Guinée-Bissau
Number	0	0	0	0	0	1 275	41 664	67 000	Nombre
Per 100 inhabitants	0	0	0	0	0	0	3	7	Pour 100 habitants
Guyana[9]									Guyana[9]
Number	1 454	2 815	39 830	75 320	79 400	137 955	171 656	281 368	Nombre
Per 100 inhabitants	0	0	5	10	11	18	23	37	Pour 100 habitants
Haiti									Haïti
Number	10 000	25 000	55 000	91 500	140 000	320 000	400 000	...	Nombre
Per 100 inhabitants	0	0	1	1	2	4	5	...	Pour 100 habitants
Honduras									Honduras
Number	34 896	78 588	155 271	237 629	326 508	379 362	707 201	1 281 462	Nombre
Per 100 inhabitants	1	1	2	4	5	6	10	18	Pour 100 habitants
Hungary									Hongrie
Number	1 070 154	1 628 153	3 076 279	4 967 430	6 886 111	7 944 586	8 727 188[10]	9 320 000	Nombre
Per 100 inhabitants	11	16	30	49	68	79	86	92	Pour 100 habitants
Iceland									Islande
Number	104 280	172 614	214 896	248 131	260 438[2]	279 670	290 068	304 001	Nombre
Per 100 inhabitants	38	62	76	86	90	97	99	103	Pour 100 habitants
India+									Inde+
Number	1 195 400	1 884 311	3 577 095	6 431 520	12 687 637	26 154 405	47 300 000	90 000 000	Nombre
Per 100 inhabitants	0	0	0	1	1	2	4	8	Pour 100 habitants
Indonesia									Indonésie
Number	1 065 820	2 220 969	3 669 327	6 520 947	11 700 000	18 495 251	30 336 607	46 909 972	Nombre
Per 100 inhabitants	1	1	2	3	6	9	14	21	Pour 100 habitants
Iran (Islamic Rep. of)+									Iran (Rép. islamique d')+
Number	389 974	490 478	962 595	2 087 353	2 279 143	3 449 876	4 271 028	7 222 538[11]	Nombre
Per 100 inhabitants	1	1	2	3	3	5	6	10	Pour 100 habitants
Iraq+									Iraq+
Number	0	0	0	0	20 000	80 000	574 000	...	Nombre
Per 100 inhabitants	0	0	0	0	0	0	2	...	Pour 100 habitants
Ireland+									Irlande+
Number	946 000	1 677 000	2 461 000	2 970 000	3 000 000	3 500 000	3 860 000	4 270 000	Nombre
Per 100 inhabitants	26	45	65	77	76	88	95	103	Pour 100 habitants

Country or area	1998	1999	2000	2001	2002	2003	2004	2005	Pays ou zone
Israel									Israël
Number	2 147 000	2 880 000	4 400 000	5 900 000	6 334 000	6 618 367	7 221 955	7 757 000	Nombre
Per 100 inhabitants	36	47	70	85	95	98	105	112	Pour 100 habitants
Italy									Italie
Number	20 489 000	30 296 000	42 246 000	51 246 000	54 200 000[3]	56 770 000[12]	62 750 000	72 200 000	Nombre
Per 100 inhabitants	36	53	74	88	96	98	108	124	Pour 100 habitants
Jamaica+									Jamaïque+
Number	78 624	144 388	366 952	*635 000	1 187 295	1 600 000	2 200 000	2 700 000	Nombre
Per 100 inhabitants	3	6	14	23	47	60	75	106	Pour 100 habitants
Japan[13]+									Japon[13]+
Number	47 307 592	56 845 594	66 784 374	74 819 158	81 118 324	86 655 000	91 474 000	96 484 000[5]	Nombre
Per 100 inhabitants	37	45	53	59	64	68	72	75	Pour 100 habitants
Jersey									Jersey
Number	18 225	24 636	44 742	61 417	...	81 200	83 900	...	Nombre
Per 100 inhabitants	21	29	52	70	...	92	95	...	Pour 100 habitants
Jordan									Jordanie
Number	82 429	118 417	388 949	865 627	1 219 597	1 325 313	1 624 110	...	Nombre
Per 100 inhabitants	2	2	8	17	23	24	29	...	Pour 100 habitants
Kazakhstan									Kazakhstan
Number	29 700	49 500	197 300	582 000	1 027 000	1 330 730	2 758 940	4 955 200	Nombre
Per 100 inhabitants	0	0	1	4	7	9	19	33	Pour 100 habitants
Kenya+									Kenya+
Number	10 756	23 757	127 404[5]	600 000	1 187 122[5]	1 590 785	2 546 157	4 611 970	Nombre
Per 100 inhabitants	0	0	0	2	4	5	8	13	Pour 100 habitants
Kiribati									Kiribati
Number	22	200	300	395	495	526	615	...	Nombre
Per 100 inhabitants	0	0	0	0	1	1	1	...	Pour 100 habitants
Korea, Republic of									Corée, République de
Number	14 018 612	23 442 724	26 816 398	29 045 596	32 342 493	33 591 758	36 586 052	38 342 323	Nombre
Per 100 inhabitants	31	51	58	61	68	70	76	79	Pour 100 habitants
Kuwait									Koweït
Number	250 000	300 000	476 000	877 920	1 227 000	1 420 000	2 000 000	2 379 811	Nombre
Per 100 inhabitants	12	14	22	39	52	57	78	89	Pour 100 habitants
Kyrgyzstan									Kirghizistan
Number	1 350	2 574	9 000	27 000	53 084	138 279	263 375	541 652	Nombre
Per 100 inhabitants	0	0	0	1	1	3	6	10	Pour 100 habitants
Lao People's Dem. Rep.									Rép. dém. pop. lao
Number	6 453	12 078	12 681	29 545	55 160	112 275	204 191	638 202	Nombre
Per 100 inhabitants	0	0	0	1	1	2	4	11	Pour 100 habitants
Latvia									Lettonie
Number	167 460	274 344	401 272	656 835	917 196	1 219 550	1 536 712	1 871 602	Nombre
Per 100 inhabitants	7	11	17	28	39	53	67	81	Pour 100 habitants
Lebanon[2]									Liban[2]
Number	505 300	627 000	743 000	766 754	775 104	820 000	888 000	990 000	Nombre
Per 100 inhabitants	16	19	23	23	23	23	25	28	Pour 100 habitants
Lesotho+									Lesotho+
Number	9 831	12 000	21 600	57 000	96 843	101 474	159 000	245 052	Nombre
Per 100 inhabitants	1	1	1	3	8	7	11	14	Pour 100 habitants
Liberia									Libéria
Number	0	0	1 500	2 000	...	47 250[2]	94 370	160 000	Nombre
Per 100 inhabitants	0	0	0	0	...	1	3	5	Pour 100 habitants
Libyan Arab Jamah.									Jamah. arabe libyenne
Number	20 000	30 000	40 000	50 000	70 000	127 000	234 800	...	Nombre
Per 100 inhabitants	0	1	1	1	1	2	4	...	Pour 100 habitants
Liechtenstein[2]									Liechtenstein[2]
Number	7 500	9 000	10 000	11 000	11 402	25 000	25 500	27 503	Nombre
Per 100 inhabitants	23	28	30	33	34	73	74	79	Pour 100 habitants

Cellular mobile telephone subscribers — Number and per 100 inhabitants (*continued*)
Abonnés au téléphone mobile — Nombre et pour 100 habitants (*suite*)

Country or area	1998	1999	2000	2001	2002	2003	2004	2005	Pays ou zone
Lithuania									Lituanie
Number	267 615	332 000	524 000	1 017 999	1 645 568	2 169 866	3 421 538	4 353 447	Nombre
Per 100 inhabitants	7	9	14	29	47	63	99	127	Pour 100 habitants
Luxembourg									Luxembourg
Number	130 500	209 190	303 274	409 064	473 000[2]	539 000	646 000	719 950	Nombre
Per 100 inhabitants	31	48	69	93	106	119	141	155	Pour 100 habitants
Madagascar									Madagascar
Number	12 784	35 752	63 094	147 500	163 010	283 666	333 888	510 269	Nombre
Per 100 inhabitants	0	0	0	1	1	2	2	3	Pour 100 habitants
Malawi									Malawi
Number	10 500	22 500	49 000	55 730	86 047	135 114	222 135	429 305	Nombre
Per 100 inhabitants	0	0	0	1	1	1	2	3	Pour 100 habitants
Malaysia									Malaisie
Number	2 200 000	2 990 000	5 121 748	7 385 240	9 053 000	11 124 112	14 611 902	19 545 000	Nombre
Per 100 inhabitants	10	14	22	31	37	44	57	75	Pour 100 habitants
Maldives									Maldives
Number	1 610	2 930	7 640	18 890	41 900	66 470	113 250	202 070	Nombre
Per 100 inhabitants	1	1	3	7	15	23	35	...	Pour 100 habitants
Mali									Mali
Number	4 473	6 387	10 398	45 340	52 639	244 930	400 000	869 576	Nombre
Per 100 inhabitants	0	0	0	0	1	2	4	8	Pour 100 habitants
Malta									Malte
Number	22 531	37 541	114 444	239 416	276 859	289 992	306 067	323 980	Nombre
Per 100 inhabitants	6	10	29	61	70	73	77	81	Pour 100 habitants
Marshall Islands									Iles Marshall
Number	345	443	447	489	552	598	644	...	Nombre
Per 100 inhabitants	1	1	1	1	1	1	1	...	Pour 100 habitants
Martinique									Martinique
Number	55 000	102 000	162 080	286 120	298 300	277 800	295 400	...	Nombre
Per 100 inhabitants	15	27	42	74	77	71	75	...	Pour 100 habitants
Mauritania									Mauritanie
Number	0	0	15 300	110 463	247 238	350 954	522 400	745 615	Nombre
Per 100 inhabitants	0	0	1	4	9	13	18	24	Pour 100 habitants
Mauritius									Maurice
Number	60 448	102 119	180 000	272 416	348 137	462 405	547 745	656 828	Nombre
Per 100 inhabitants	5	9	15	23	29	38	44	53	Pour 100 habitants
Mayotte									Mayotte
Number	0	0	0	0	20 300	33 200	48 100	...	Nombre
Per 100 inhabitants	0	0	0	0	13	20	29	...	Pour 100 habitants
Mexico									Mexique
Number	3 349 475	7 731 635	14 077 880	21 757 559	25 928 266	30 097 700	38 451 135	47 140 950	Nombre
Per 100 inhabitants	4	8	14	22	26	29	37	44	Pour 100 habitants
Micronesia (Fed. States of)									Micronésie (Etats féd. de)
Number	0	0	0	0	100	5 869	12 782	14 094	Nombre
Per 100 inhabitants	0	0	0	0	0	5	12	13	Pour 100 habitants
Monaco									Monaco
Number	11 470	13 080	13 930	14 300	14 870	15 080	15 750	17 190	Nombre
Per 100 inhabitants	35	40	42	42	44	44	45	49	Pour 100 habitants
Mongolia									Mongolie
Number	9 032	34 562	154 600	195 000	216 000	319 000	428 695	557 207	Nombre
Per 100 inhabitants	0	1	7	8	9	13	16	21	Pour 100 habitants
Montserrat									Montserrat
Number	250	300	489	1 200	1 500	1 800	2 180	...	Nombre
Morocco[14]									Maroc[14]
Number	116 645	369 174	2 342 000	4 771 739	6 198 670	7 359 870	9 336 878	12 392 805	Nombre
Per 100 inhabitants	0	1	8	17	21	25	31	41	Pour 100 habitants
Mozambique									Mozambique
Number	6 725	12 243	51 065	152 652	254 759	435 757	708 000	1 220 000	Nombre
Per 100 inhabitants	0	0	0	1	1	2	4	8	Pour 100 habitants

Country or area	1998	1999	2000	2001	2002	2003	2004	2005	Pays ou zone
Myanmar									Myanmar
Number	8 516	11 389	13 397	22 671	47 982	66 517	92 452	183 434	Nombre
Per 100 inhabitants	0	0	0	0	0	0	0	0	Pour 100 habitants
Namibia+									Namibie+
Number	19 500	30 000	82 000	106 600	150 000[5]	223 671	286 095	495 000	Nombre
Per 100 inhabitants	1	2	5	6	8	12	14	24	Pour 100 habitants
Nauru[2]									Nauru[2]
Number	850	1 000	1 200	1 500	...	...	...	...	Nombre
Nepal+									Népal+
Number[2]	0	5 500	10 226	17 286[1]	21 881	81 867	116 778	248 820	Nombre[2]
Per 100 inhabitants	0	0	0	0	0	0	0	1	Pour 100 habitants
Netherlands									Pays-Bas
Number	3 351 000	6 745 460	10 755 000	12 200 000	12 100 000	13 200 000	14 800 000	15 834 000	Nombre
Per 100 inhabitants	21	43	67	76	75	81	91	97	Pour 100 habitants
Netherlands Antilles									Antilles néerlandaises
Number	16 000	30 000	...	...	...	200 000	200 000	...	Nombre
Per 100 inhabitants	8	14	...	...	...	90	90	...	Pour 100 habitants
New Caledonia									Nouvelle-Calédonie
Number	13 040	25 450	49 948	67 917	80 000	97 113	116 443	134 265	Nombre
Per 100 inhabitants	6	12	23	31	36	42	50	57	Pour 100 habitants
New Zealand+									Nouvelle-Zélande+
Number	790 000	1 395 000	1 542 000	2 288 000	2 449 000	2 599 000	3 027 000	3 530 000	Nombre
Per 100 inhabitants	21	36	40	59	62	66	76	88	Pour 100 habitants
Nicaragua									Nicaragua
Number	18 310	44 229	90 294	164 509	237 248	466 706	738 624	1 119 379	Nombre
Per 100 inhabitants	0	1	2	3	5	8	13	19	Pour 100 habitants
Niger									Niger
Number	1 349	2 192	2 056	2 126	35 142	59 307	148 276	299 899	Nombre
Per 100 inhabitants	0	0	0	0	0	0	1	2	Pour 100 habitants
Nigeria									Nigéria
Number	20 000	25 000	30 000	*400 000	1 607 931	3 149 473	9 147 209	18 587 000[15]	Nombre
Per 100 inhabitants	0	0	0	0	1	3	7	14	Pour 100 habitants
Niue									Nioué
Number	...	380	410	400	490	600	650	...	Nombre
Northern Mariana Islands									Iles Mariannes du Nord
Number	...	2 905[16]	3 000	13 200	17 137	18 619	20 474	...	Nombre
Per 100 inhabitants	...	4	4	19	23	24	27	...	Pour 100 habitants
Norway									Norvège
Number	2 072 000	2 664 000	3 224 000	3 593 000	3 790 000[2]	4 060 829	4 524 750	4 754 453	Nombre
Per 100 inhabitants	47	59	72	79	83	89	98	103	Pour 100 habitants
Occupied Palestinian Terr.[17]									Terr. palestinien occupé[17]
Number	100 000	117 000	175 941	300 000	320 000	480 000	974 345	1 094 640	Nombre
Per 100 inhabitants	3	4	6	9	9	13	26	30	Pour 100 habitants
Oman									Oman
Number	98 000	121 000	162 000	323 000	463 000	594 000	806 280	1 333 225	Nombre
Per 100 inhabitants	4	5	7	13	19	24	32	52	Pour 100 habitants
Pakistan+									Pakistan+
Number	196 096	265 614	306 493	742 606	1 698 536	2 404 400	5 022 908	12 771 203	Nombre
Per 100 inhabitants	0	0	0	1	1	2	3	8	Pour 100 habitants
Panama									Panama
Number	85 883	232 888	410 401	475 141	525 845	692 406	1 259 948	1 351 924	Nombre
Per 100 inhabitants	3	8	14	16	17	22	40	52	Pour 100 habitants
Papua New Guinea									Papouasie-Nvl-Guinée
Number	5 558	7 059	8 560	10 700	15 000	17 500	22 000	26 000	Nombre
Per 100 inhabitants	0	0	0	0	0	0	1	1	Pour 100 habitants
Paraguay									Paraguay
Number	231 520	435 611	820 810	1 150 000	1 667 018	1 770 345	1 749 048	1 887 000	Nombre
Per 100 inhabitants	4	8	15	20	29	30	29	31	Pour 100 habitants

Cellular mobile telephone subscribers — Number and per 100 inhabitants *(continued)*
Abonnés au téléphone mobile — Nombre et pour 100 habitants *(suite)*

Country or area	1998	1999	2000	2001	2002	2003	2004	2005	Pays ou zone
Peru									Pérou
Number	742 642	1 013 314	1 273 857	1 793 284	2 306 944	2 930 343	4 092 558	5 583 356	Nombre
Per 100 inhabitants	3	4	5	7	9	11	15	20	Pour 100 habitants
Philippines									Philippines
Number	1 733 652	2 849 980	6 454 359	12 159 163	15 383 001	22 509 560	32 935 875	34 778 995	Nombre
Per 100 inhabitants	2	4	8	16	19	28	40	41	Pour 100 habitants
Poland									Pologne
Number	1 928 042	3 956 500	6 747 000	10 004 661	*13 898 471	*17 401 222	23 096 065	29 166 391	Nombre
Per 100 inhabitants	5	10	17	26	36	45	60	76	Pour 100 habitants
Portugal									Portugal
Number	3 074 633	4 671 458	6 664 951	7 977 537	8 670 000	10 030 472	10 362 120	11 447 670	Nombre
Per 100 inhabitants	31	47	67	77	83	96	98	109	Pour 100 habitants
Puerto Rico[18]									Porto Rico[18]
Number	580 000	813 800	926 448	1 128 736	1 800 000	1 860 000	2 682 000	...	Nombre
Per 100 inhabitants	15	22	24	29	47	48	69	...	Pour 100 habitants
Qatar									Qatar
Number	65 756	84 365	120 856	177 929	266 703	376 535	490 333	716 763	Nombre
Per 100 inhabitants	12	15	20	28	40	53	66	92	Pour 100 habitants
Republic of Moldova									République de Moldova
Number	7 000	18 000	139 000	225 000	338 225	475 942	787 000	1 089 800	Nombre
Per 100 inhabitants	0	0	3	5	8	11	18	26	Pour 100 habitants
Réunion									Réunion
Number	50 300	111 000	276 100	421 100	454 600	521 500	579 200	...	Nombre
Per 100 inhabitants	7	16	40	58	61	69	76	...	Pour 100 habitants
Romania									Roumanie
Number	643 000	1 355 500	2 499 000	3 845 116	5 110 591	7 039 898	10 215 388	13 354 138	Nombre
Per 100 inhabitants	3	6	11	17	23	32	47	62	Pour 100 habitants
Russian Federation									Fédération de Russie
Number	747 160	1 370 630	3 263 200	7 750 499	17 608 756	36 135 135	73 722 222	120 000 000	Nombre
Per 100 inhabitants	1	1	2	5	12	25	51	84	Pour 100 habitants
Rwanda									Rwanda
Number	5 000	11 000	39 000	65 000	82 391[3]	130 720	138 728	290 000	Nombre
Per 100 inhabitants	0	0	1	1	1	2	2	3	Pour 100 habitants
Saint Kitts and Nevis+									Saint-Kitts-et-Nevis+
Number	440	700	1 200	*2 100	5 000	...	10 000	...	Nombre
Per 100 inhabitants	1	2	3	5	12	...	24	...	Pour 100 habitants
Saint Lucia*+									Sainte-Lucie*+
Number	1 900	2 300	2 500	2 700	14 310	...	93 000	105 660	Nombre
Per 100 inhabitants	1	2	2	2	9	...	58	66	Pour 100 habitants
Saint Vincent-Grenadines+									Saint Vincent-Grenadines+
Number	750	1 420	2 361	7 492	9 982	62 911	72 000	70 620	Nombre
Per 100 inhabitants	1	1	2	7	9	53	60	59	Pour 100 habitants
Samoa									Samoa
Number	1 480	2 432	2 500	2 500	2 700	10 500	16 000	24 000	Nombre
Per 100 inhabitants	1	1	1	1	2	6	9	13	Pour 100 habitants
San Marino									Saint-Marin
Number	4 980	9 580	14 503	15 854	16 759	16 900	17 085	17 150	Nombre
Sao Tome and Principe									Sao Tomé-et-Principe
Number	0	0	0	0	1 980	4 819	7 745	12 000	Nombre
Per 100 inhabitants	0	0	0	0	1	3	5	8	Pour 100 habitants
Saudi Arabia									Arabie saoudite
Number	627 321	836 628	1 375 881	2 528 640	5 007 965	7 238 224	9 175 764	13 300 000	Nombre
Per 100 inhabitants	3	4	6	11	22	31	38	58	Pour 100 habitants
Senegal									Sénégal
Number	27 487	87 879	250 251	301 811	553 449	782 423	1 121 314	1 730 106	Nombre
Per 100 inhabitants	0	1	3	3	5	8	11	15	Pour 100 habitants
Serbia and Montenegro*									Serbie-et-Monténégro*
Number	240 000	605 697	1 303 609	1 997 809	2 750 397	3 634 613	4 729 629	5 229 000	Nombre
Per 100 inhabitants	2	6	12	19	34	45	58	64	Pour 100 habitants

Cellular mobile telephone subscribers — Number and per 100 inhabitants (*continued*)
Abonnés au téléphone mobile — Nombre et pour 100 habitants (*suite*)

Country or area	1998	1999	2000	2001	2002	2003	2004	2005	Pays ou zone
Seychelles+									Seychelles+
Number	5 190	16 316	25 961	36 683	44 731	49 229	54 369	57 003	Nombre
Per 100 inhabitants	7	21	34	47	57	62	68	71	Pour 100 habitants
Sierra Leone									Sierra Leone
Number	0	0	11 940	26 895	67 000	113 214[2]	...	...	Nombre
Per 100 inhabitants	0	0	0	1	1	2	...	...	Pour 100 habitants
Singapore+									Singapour+
Number	1 094 700	1 630 800	2 747 400	2 991 600	3 313 000	3 577 000	3 997 000	4 384 600	Nombre
Per 100 inhabitants	28	41	68	72	80	86	96	101	Pour 100 habitants
Slovakia									Slovaquie
Number	465 364	664 072	1 243 736	2 147 331	2 923 383	3 678 774	4 275 164	4 540 374	Nombre
Per 100 inhabitants	9	12	23	40	54	68	79	84	Pour 100 habitants
Slovenia									Slovénie
Number	161 606	631 411	1 215 601	1 470 085	1 667 234	1 739 146	1 848 637	1 759 232	Nombre
Per 100 inhabitants	8	32	61	74	84	87	93	89	Pour 100 habitants
Solomon Islands+									Iles Salomon+
Number	702	1 093	1 151	967	999	1 060	3 000	6 000	Nombre
Per 100 inhabitants	0	0	0	0	0	0	1	1	Pour 100 habitants
Somalia									Somalie
Number	0	0	80 000	85 000	100 000	200 000	500 000	500 000	Nombre
Per 100 inhabitants	0	0	1	1	1	3	6	6	Pour 100 habitants
South Africa+									Afrique du Sud+
Number	3 337 000	5 188 000	8 339 000	10 787 000	13 702 000	16 860 000	20 839 000	33 959 958	Nombre
Per 100 inhabitants	8	12	18	23	29	36	44	72	Pour 100 habitants
Spain									Espagne
Number	6 437 444	15 003 708	24 265 059	29 655 729	33 530 997	37 219 839	38 646 796	41 327 911	Nombre
Per 100 inhabitants	16	37	60	72	82	87	89	100	Pour 100 habitants
Sri Lanka									Sri Lanka
Number	174 202	256 655	430 202	667 662	931 580	1 393 403	2 213 553	3 361 775	Nombre
Per 100 inhabitants	1	1	2	4	5	7	11	16	Pour 100 habitants
Sudan									Soudan
Number	8 600	13 000	23 000	103 846	190 778	527 233	1 048 558	1 827 940	Nombre
Per 100 inhabitants	0	0	0	0	1	2	3	5	Pour 100 habitants
Suriname									Suriname
Number	6 007	17 500	41 048	87 000	108 363	168 522	212 819	232 785	Nombre
Per 100 inhabitants	1	4	9	20	25	38	48	52	Pour 100 habitants
Swaziland+									Swaziland+
Number	4 700	14 000	33 000	55 000	68 000	85 000[5]	145 000	200 000	Nombre
Per 100 inhabitants	0	1	3	5	7	8	13	19	Pour 100 habitants
Sweden									Suède
Number	4 109 000	5 126 000	6 372 300	7 178 000	7 949 000	8 801 000	9 775 000[19]	8 436 500	Nombre
Per 100 inhabitants	46	58	72	81	89	98	108	101	Pour 100 habitants
Switzerland									Suisse
Number	1 698 565	3 057 509	4 638 519	5 275 791	5 736 303	6 189 000	6 275 000	6 834 000	Nombre
Per 100 inhabitants	24	43	64	73	79	84	85	92	Pour 100 habitants
Syrian Arab Republic									Rép. arabe syrienne
Number	0	4 000	30 000	200 000	400 000	1 185 000	2 345 000	2 950 000	Nombre
Per 100 inhabitants	0	0	0	1	2	7	13	15	Pour 100 habitants
Tajikistan									Tadjikistan
Number	420	625	1 160	1 630	13 200	47 617	135 000	265 000	Nombre
Per 100 inhabitants	0	0	0	0	0	1	2	4	Pour 100 habitants
Thailand+									Thaïlande+
Number	1 976 960	2 339 400	3 056 000	7 550 000	10 171 550	21 828 180	27 378 660	31 136 540	Nombre
Per 100 inhabitants	3	4	5	12	16	35	43	48	Pour 100 habitants
TFYR of Macedonia									L'ex-R.y. Macédoine
Number	30 087	48 733	115 748	223 275	365 346	776 000	985 600	1 261 328	Nombre
Per 100 inhabitants	2	2	6	11	18	38	49	62	Pour 100 habitants

13 Cellular mobile telephone subscribers — Number and per 100 inhabitants (*continued*)
Abonnés au téléphone mobile — Nombre et pour 100 habitants (*suite*)

Country or area	1998	1999	2000	2001	2002	2003	2004	2005	Pays ou zone
Togo									Togo
Number	7 500	17 000	50 000	95 000	170 000	243 613	332 565	435 979	Nombre
Per 100 inhabitants	0	0	1	2	3	5	7	9	Pour 100 habitants
Tonga[2]									Tonga[2]
Number	130	140	180	240	3 350	11 200	16 400	29 870	Nombre
Per 100 inhabitants	0	0	0	0	3	11	16	30	Pour 100 habitants
Trinidad and Tobago+									Trinité-et-Tobago+
Number	26 307	38 659	161 860	256 106	262 772	336 352	651 189	800 000	Nombre
Per 100 inhabitants	2	3	13	20	20	26	50	61	Pour 100 habitants
Tunisia									Tunisie
Number	38 998	55 258	119 165	389 208	574 334	1 917 530	3 735 695	5 680 726	Nombre
Per 100 inhabitants	0	1	1	4	6	19	37	56	Pour 100 habitants
Turkey									Turquie
Number	3 506 127	8 121 517	16 133 405	19 572 897	23 323 118	27 887 535	34 707 549	43 608 965	Nombre
Per 100 inhabitants	5	12	24	28	33	39	48	60	Pour 100 habitants
Turkmenistan									Turkménistan
Number	3 000	4 000	7 500	8 173	8 173	9 187	50 100	...	Nombre
Per 100 inhabitants	0	0	0	0	0	0	1	...	Pour 100 habitants
Turks and Caicos Islands									Iles Turques et Caïques
Number	...	...	...	...	9 052	19 361	25 085	...	Nombre
Tuvalu									Tuvalu
Number	0	0	0	0	0	500	1 300	...	Nombre
Uganda+									Ouganda+
Number	30 000	56 358	126 913	283 520	393 310	776 169	1 165 035[10]	1 525 125	Nombre
Per 100 inhabitants	0	0	1	1	2	3	4	5	Pour 100 habitants
Ukraine									Ukraine
Number	115 500	216 567	818 524	2 224 600	3 692 700	6 498 423	13 735 000	17 214 280	Nombre
Per 100 inhabitants	0	0	2	5	8	14	29	37	Pour 100 habitants
United Arab Emirates									Emirats arabes unis
Number	493 278	832 267	1 428 115	1 909 303	2 428 071	2 972 331	3 683 117	4 534 480	Nombre
Per 100 inhabitants	17	27	44	55	65	74	86	101	Pour 100 habitants
United Kingdom+									Royaume-Uni+
Number	14 878 000	27 185 000	43 452 000	46 283 000	49 228 000	54 400 000	61 091 000	65 500 000	Nombre
Per 100 inhabitants	25	46	73	77	83	91	101	112	Pour 100 habitants
United Rep. of Tanzania									Rép.-Unie de Tanzanie
Number	37 940	50 950	110 518	275 560	606 859	1 942 000	1 942 000	3 389 787	Nombre
Per 100 inhabitants	0	0	0	1	2	5	5	9	Pour 100 habitants
United States									Etats-Unis
Number	69 209 321	86 047 003	109 478 031	128 374 512	140 766 842	158 721 981	182 400 000	201 558 330	Nombre
Per 100 inhabitants	25	31	39	45	49	55	63	72	Pour 100 habitants
United States Virgin Is.*									Iles Vierges américaines*
Number	25 000	30 000	35 000	41 000	...	49 300	64 200	...	Nombre
Per 100 inhabitants	23	28	32	38	...	45	58	...	Pour 100 habitants
Uruguay									Uruguay
Number	151 341	319 131	410 787	519 991	513 528	497 530	600 000	1 154 922	Nombre
Per 100 inhabitants	5	10	13	16	16	15	19	36	Pour 100 habitants
Uzbekistan									Ouzbékistan
Number	26 826	40 389	53 128	128 012	186 900	320 815	544 100	720 000	Nombre
Per 100 inhabitants	0	0	0	1	1	1	2	3	Pour 100 habitants
Vanuatu									Vanuatu
Number	220	300	365	350	4 900	7 800	10 504	12 692	Nombre
Per 100 inhabitants	0	0	0	0	2	4	5	6	Pour 100 habitants
Venezuela (Bolivarian Rep. of)									Venezuela (Rép. bol. du)
Number	2 009 757	3 784 735	5 447 172	6 472 584	6 541 894	7 015 121	8 420 980	12 495 721	Nombre
Per 100 inhabitants	9	16	23	26	26	27	32	47	Pour 100 habitants
Viet Nam									Viet Nam
Number	222 700	328 671	788 559	1 251 195	1 902 388	2 742 000	4 960 000	9 593 200	Nombre
Per 100 inhabitants	0	0	1	2	2	3	6	11	Pour 100 habitants

Cellular mobile telephone subscribers — Number and per 100 inhabitants (*continued*)

Abonnés au téléphone mobile — Nombre et pour 100 habitants (*suite*)

Country or area	1998	1999	2000	2001	2002	2003	2004	2005	Pays ou zone
Yemen									Yémen
Number	16 146	27 677	32 000	152 000	411 083	700 000	1 072 000	2 000 000	Nombre
Per 100 inhabitants	0	0	0	1	2	3	5	10	Pour 100 habitants
Zambia+									Zambie+
Number	8 260	28 190	98 853	121 200	139 092	241 000	464 354	946 558	Nombre
Per 100 inhabitants	0	0	1	1	1	2	4	8	Pour 100 habitants
Zimbabwe+									Zimbabwe+
Number	19 000	174 000	266 441	314 002	338 779	363 651	423 606	699 000	Nombre
Per 100 inhabitants	0	2	2	3	3	3	4	6	Pour 100 habitants

Source

International Telecommunication Union (ITU), Geneva, the ITU database.

Notes

+ The data shown generally relate to the fiscal year used in each country, unless indicated otherwise. Countries whose reference periods coincide with the calendar year ending 31 December are not listed.

  Year beginning 22 March: Iran (Islamic Republic).

  Year beginning 1 April: Antigua and Barbuda, Barbados, Belize, Bermuda, Botswana, British Virgin Islands, Cayman Islands, China - Hong Kong, Cook Islands, Dominica, Gambia, India, Ireland, Israel (prior to 1986), Jamaica, Japan, Lesotho, Seychelles, Singapore (beginning 1983), Solomon Islands, South Africa, St. Helena, St. Kitts and Nevis, St. Lucia, St. Vincent and the Grenadines, Swaziland, Trinidad and Tobago, United Kingdom, and Zambia.

  Year ending 30 June: Australia, Bangladesh, Egypt, Ethiopia, Iraq, Kenya, New Zealand (beginning 2000; prior to 2000, year ending 1 April), Pakistan, Uganda, and Zimbabwe.

  Year ending 15 July: Nepal.

  Year ending 30 September: Argentina (beginning 1991), Namibia (beginning 1993), and Thailand.

1 Data refer to 31 December.
2 ITU estimate.
3 September.
4 August.
5 December.
6 Including Celtel subscribers.
7 For statistical purposes, the data for China do not include those for the Hong Kong Special Administrative Region (Hong Kong SAR), Macao Special Administrative Region (Macao SAR) and Taiwan Province of China.
8 GSM mobile was launched on 12 December 2005
9 Active mobile subscribers
10 November.
11 October.
12 30 June.
13 Including Personal Handyphone System.
14 Including Western Sahara.
15 July.
16 As of 31 March 2000.
17 Users use Israel cellular network.
18 Data refer to the Puerto Rico Telephone Authority.
19 June.

Source

Union internationale des télécommunications (UIT), Genève, la base de données de l'UIT.

Notes

+ Sauf indication contraire, les données indiquées concernent généralement l'exercice budgétaire utilisé dans chaque pays. Les pays ou territoires dont la période de référence coïncide avec l'année civile se terminant le 31 décembre ne sont pas répertoriés ci-dessous.

  Exercice commençant le 22 mars : Iran (République islamique d').

  Exercice commençant le 1er avril : Afrique du Sud, Antigua-et-Barbuda, Barbade, Belize, Bermudes, Botswana, Chine-Hong Kong, Dominique, Gambie, Îles Caïmanes, Îles Cook, Îles Salomon, Îles Vierges britanniques, Inde, Irlande, Israël (antérieur à 1986), Jamaïque, Japon, Lesotho, Royaume-Uni, Saint-Kitts-et-Nevis, Saint-Vincent-et-les Grenadines, Sainte-Hélène, Sainte-Lucie, Seychelles, Singapour (à partir de 1983), Swaziland, Trinité-et-Tobago et Zambie.

  Exercice se terminant le 30 juin : Australie, Bangladesh, Égypte, Éthiopie, Iraq, Kenya, Nouvelle-Zélande (à partir de 2000; avant 2000, exercice se terminant le1er avril), Ouganda, Pakistan et Zimbabwe.

  Exercice se terminant le 15 juillet : Népal.

  Exercice se terminant le 30 septembre : Argentine (à partir de 1991), Namibie (à partir de 1993), et Thaïlande.

1 Les données se réfèrent au31 décembre.
2 Estimation de l'UIT.
3 Septembre.
4 Août.
5 Décembre.
6 Y compris les abonnés au Celtel.
7 Pour la présentation des statistiques, les données pour la Chine ne comprennent pas la Région Administrative Spéciale de Hong Kong (Hong Kong RAS), la Région Administrative Spéciale de Macao (Macao RAS) et la province de Taiwan.
8 Le service de téléphonie mobile GSM a été lancé le 12 décembre 2005.
9 Nombre d'abonnés actifs de la téléphonie mobile.
10 Novembre.
11 Octobre.
12 30 juin.
13 Y compris "Personal Handyphone System".
14 Y compris les données de Sahara occidental.
15 Juillet.
16 Dès le 31 mars 2000.
17 Les abonnés utilisent le réseau israélien de téléphonie mobile.
18 Les données se réfèrent à "Puerto Rico Telephone Authority".
19 Juin.

14

Telephones

Main telephone lines in operation and lines per 100 inhabitants

Téléphones

Nombre de lignes téléphoniques en service et lignes pour 100 habitants

Country or area	1998	1999	2000	2001	2002	2003	2004	2005	Pays ou zone
Afghanistan									Afghanistan
Number (thousands)	*29	*29	*29	29	*33	*37	*50	*100	Nombre (en miliers)
Per 100 inhabitants	0.1	0.1	0.1	0.1	0.1	0.1	0.2	0.3	Pour 100 habitants
Albania									Albanie
Number (thousands)	116	140	153	197	220	255	275	...	Nombre (en miliers)
Per 100 inhabitants	3.7	4.5	4.9	6.4	7.1	8.3	8.6	...	Pour 100 habitants
Algeria									Algérie
Number (thousands)	1 477	1 600	1 761	1 880	1 950	2 147	2 487[1]	2 572[1]	Nombre (en miliers)
Per 100 inhabitants	5.0	5.3	5.8	6.1	6.2	6.7	7.7[1]	7.8[1]	Pour 100 habitants
American Samoa									Samoa américaines
Number (thousands)	10	10	*10	*13	14	11	10	...	Nombre (en miliers)
Per 100 inhabitants	18.5	18.2	17.9	21.5	23.6	17.6	18.2	...	Pour 100 habitants
Andorra									Andorre
Number (thousands)	33	34	34	35[2]	35[2]	35[2]	35	35	Nombre (en miliers)
Per 100 inhabitants	43.9	44.7	43.9	43.2	42.6	41.8	52.3	52.8	Pour 100 habitants
Angola									Angola
Number (thousands)	65[3]	67[3]	65	77	80	85	94	94[4]	Nombre (en miliers)
Per 100 inhabitants	0.5	0.5	0.5	0.6	0.6	0.6	0.7	0.6	Pour 100 habitants
Anguilla									Anguilla
Number (thousands)	6	6[5]	6	6	...	5	6	6	Nombre (en miliers)
Per 100 inhabitants	50.7	52.8	54.9	54.3	...	46.1	47.2	45.2	Pour 100 habitants
Antigua and Barbuda+									Antigua-et-Barbuda+
Number (thousands)	34	37	38	37[6]	38	38	38	...	Nombre (en miliers)
Per 100 inhabitants	46.0	48.5	50.1	48.0	48.4	47.7	47.2	...	Pour 100 habitants
Argentina+									Argentine+
Number (thousands)	7 095[7]	7 223[7]	7 894[7]	8 131[7]	7 709[7]	8 606	8 700	8 800	Nombre (en miliers)
Per 100 inhabitants	19.7	19.8	21.5	21.9	20.5	22.7	22.8	22.8	Pour 100 habitants
Armenia									Arménie
Number (thousands)	557	544	533	531	543	564	582	...	Nombre (en miliers)
Per 100 inhabitants	17.8	17.6	17.3	17.3	17.8	18.6	19.2	...	Pour 100 habitants
Aruba									Aruba
Number (thousands)	35	37	*38	37	...	...	...	...	Nombre (en miliers)
Per 100 inhabitants	39.1	40.3	41.4	39.7	...	...	...	...	Pour 100 habitants
Australia+									Australie+
Number (thousands)	9 540	9 760	10 350	10 485	10 905	10 965	11 660	11 460	Nombre (en miliers)
Per 100 inhabitants	51.0	51.6	54.0	54.0	55.5	55.2	58.6	56.9	Pour 100 habitants
Austria									Autriche
Number (thousands)[8]	4 008	3 939	3 997	3 997	3 883	3 877	3 821	3 739	Nombre (en miliers)[8]
Per 100 inhabitants	50.2	49.3	49.9	49.6	47.9	47.7	46.2	45.3	Pour 100 habitants
Azerbaijan									Azerbaïdjan
Number (thousands)	680	730	801	865	924	941	1 025	1 091	Nombre (en miliers)
Per 100 inhabitants	8.5	9.0	9.8	10.5	11.2	11.3	12.3	13.0	Pour 100 habitants
Bahamas									Bahamas
Number (thousands)	106	111	114	123	127	132	140	...	Nombre (en miliers)
Per 100 inhabitants	36.2	37.4	37.9	40.3	40.8	41.9	43.9	...	Pour 100 habitants
Bahrain									Bahreïn
Number (thousands)	158	165	171	174	175	186	192	197[9]	Nombre (en miliers)
Per 100 inhabitants	24.6	25.2	25.4	25.4	25.2	26.3	26.8	27.0	Pour 100 habitants
Bangladesh+									Bangladesh+
Number (thousands)	413	433	491	565	606	742	831	1 070	Nombre (en miliers)
Per 100 inhabitants	0.3	0.3	0.4	0.4	0.5	0.5	0.6	0.8	Pour 100 habitants
Barbados+									Barbade+
Number (thousands)[10]	113	115	*124	129	133	134	136	135	Nombre (en miliers)[10]
Per 100 inhabitants	42.4	43.0	46.3	48.1	49.4	49.7	50.1	50.1	Pour 100 habitants

Country or area	1998	1999	2000	2001	2002	2003	2004	2005	Pays ou zone
Belarus									Bélarus
Number (thousands)	2 490	2 638	2 752	2 862	2 967	3 071	3 176	3 284	Nombre (en miliers)
Per 100 inhabitants	24.6	26.2	27.4	28.7	29.9	31.1	32.4	33.7	Pour 100 habitants
Belgium									Belgique
Number (thousands)[8]	4 857	5 009	5 036	5 132	4 932	4 875	4 801	...	Nombre (en miliers)[8]
Per 100 inhabitants	47.5	48.9	49.1	49.8	47.6	46.9	46.0	...	Pour 100 habitants
Belize+									Belize+
Number (thousands)	32	36	36	35	31	33	34	33	Nombre (en miliers)
Per 100 inhabitants	14.3	15.4	14.9	13.7	12.1	12.8	12.9	12.3	Pour 100 habitants
Benin									Bénin
Number (thousands)	38	44	52	59	63	67	73	76	Nombre (en miliers)
Per 100 inhabitants	0.6	0.7	0.8	0.9	0.9	0.9	1.0	1.0	Pour 100 habitants
Bermuda+									Bermudes+
Number (thousands)	54	55	56	56	*56	...	...	...	Nombre (en miliers)
Per 100 inhabitants	86.2	87.8	89.2	88.9	88.3	...	...	...	Pour 100 habitants
Bhutan									Bhoutan
Number (thousands)	10	12	14	18	20	25	30	33	Nombre (en miliers)
Per 100 inhabitants	1.6	1.8	2.2	2.6	2.8	3.4	3.9	4.0	Pour 100 habitants
Bolivia									Bolivie
Number (thousands)	452	503	511	524	591	610	625	646	Nombre (en miliers)
Per 100 inhabitants	5.7	6.2	6.1	6.2	6.8	6.9	6.9	7.0	Pour 100 habitants
Bosnia and Herzegovina									Bosnie-Herzégovine
Number (thousands)	333	368	780[11]	847[11]	903[11]	938[11]	952[11]	969[11]	Nombre (en miliers)
Per 100 inhabitants	9.1	9.6	20.6	22.3	23.7	24.5	24.6	24.8	Pour 100 habitants
Botswana+									Botswana+
Number (thousands)	102	124	136	143	142	132	136	132	Nombre (en miliers)
Per 100 inhabitants	6.5	7.7	8.3	8.5	8.3	7.4	7.7	7.5	Pour 100 habitants
Brazil									Brésil
Number (thousands)[12]	19 987	24 985	30 926	37 431	38 811	39 205	39 579	39 853	Nombre (en miliers)[12]
Per 100 inhabitants	11.8	14.6	17.8	21.2	21.7	21.6	21.5	21.39	Pour 100 habitants
British Virgin Islands+									Iles Vierges britanniques+
Number (thousands)	*10	*10	*10	*11	12[13]	...	...	...	Nombre (en miliers)
Per 100 inhabitants	50.7	50.6	50.7	50.3	55.3	...	...	...	Pour 100 habitants
Brunei Darussalam									Brunéi Darussalam
Number (thousands)	78	79	*81	*88	81	82	83	84	Nombre (en miliers)
Per 100 inhabitants	24.7	24.6	24.2	25.9	23.6	23.4	23.2	22.4	Pour 100 habitants
Bulgaria									Bulgarie
Number (thousands)	2 758	2 833	2 882	2 887	2 872	2 818	2 727	2 483	Nombre (en miliers)
Per 100 inhabitants	33.1	34.2	35.4	36.6	36.6	36.1	35.1	32.1	Pour 100 habitants
Burkina Faso									Burkina Faso
Number (thousands)	41	47	53	58	62	65	81	97	Nombre (en miliers)
Per 100 inhabitants	0.4	0.4	0.5	0.5	0.5	0.5	0.6	0.7	Pour 100 habitants
Burundi									Burundi
Number (thousands)	18	19	*20	*21	22	24	28	...	Nombre (en miliers)
Per 100 inhabitants	0.3	0.3	0.3	0.3	0.3	0.3	0.4	...	Pour 100 habitants
Cambodia									Cambodge
Number (thousands)[14]	24	28	31	33	35	36	...	...	Nombre (en miliers)[14]
Per 100 inhabitants	0.2	0.2	0.2	0.2	0.3	0.3	...	...	Pour 100 habitants
Cameroon									Cameroun
Number (thousands)	94	95	*95	*106	111	95	99	100	Nombre (en miliers)
Per 100 inhabitants	0.7	0.6	0.6	0.7	0.7	0.6	0.6	0.6	Pour 100 habitants
Canada									Canada
Number (thousands)	19 294	20 380	20 840	21 126	20 622	20 612	20 610	18 276	Nombre (en miliers)
Per 100 inhabitants	63.8	66.8	67.7	67.9	65.5	64.9	64.3	56.6	Pour 100 habitants
Cape Verde									Cap-Vert
Number (thousands)	40	47	55	64	70	72	73	71	Nombre (en miliers)
Per 100 inhabitants	9.6	10.9	12.6	14.5	15.6	15.6	15.7	14.1	Pour 100 habitants

Telephones — Main telephone lines in operation and lines per 100 inhabitants (*continued*)
Téléphones — Nombre de lignes téléphoniques en service et lignes pour 100 habitants (*suite*)

Country or area	1998	1999	2000	2001	2002	2003	2004	2005	Pays ou zone
Cayman Islands+									Iles Caïmanes+
Number (thousands)	28	32	35	38	...	...	...	...	Nombre (en miliers)
Per 100 inhabitants	74.7	82.0	88.2	92.9	...	...	...	...	Pour 100 habitants
Central African Rep.									Rép. centrafricaine
Number (thousands)	10	10	9	9	9	10	10	10	Nombre (en miliers)
Per 100 inhabitants	0.3	0.3	0.3	0.2	0.2	0.2	0.3	0.2	Pour 100 habitants
Chad									Tchad
Number (thousands)	9	10	10[5]	11[5]	12	12	13	13	Nombre (en miliers)
Per 100 inhabitants	0.1	0.1	0.1	0.1	0.2	0.2	0.1	0.1	Pour 100 habitants
Chile									Chili
Number (thousands)	3 047	3 109	3 303	3 478	3 467	3 251	3 318	3 436	Nombre (en miliers)
Per 100 inhabitants	20.6	20.7	21.7	22.6	23.0	21.3	21.5	22.0	Pour 100 habitants
China[15]									Chine[15]
Number (thousands)	87 421	108 716	144 829	180 368	214 222	262 747	311 756	350 433	Nombre (en miliers)
Per 100 inhabitants	7.0	8.6	11.2	13.7	16.7	20.3	24.0	26.6	Pour 100 habitants
China, Hong Kong SAR+									Chine, Hong Kong RAS+
Number (thousands)	3 729	3 869	3 926	3 898	3 832	3 806	3 763	3 795	Nombre (en miliers)
Per 100 inhabitants	57.0	58.6	58.9	58.0	56.5	55.9	54.4	53.9	Pour 100 habitants
China, Macao SAR									Chine, Macao RAS
Number (thousands)	174	178	177	176	176	175	174	174	Nombre (en miliers)
Per 100 inhabitants	40.9	41.5	40.9	40.4	39.9	38.9	37.4	37.9	Pour 100 habitants
Colombia									Colombie
Number (thousands)	6 367	6 665	7 193	7 372[16]	7 766	7 848	7 589	7 679	Nombre (en miliers)
Per 100 inhabitants	15.6	16.0	17.0	17.2	17.9	17.9	16.7	16.8	Pour 100 habitants
Comoros									Comores
Number (thousands)	6	7	7	9	10	13	15	17	Nombre (en miliers)
Per 100 inhabitants	0.9	1.0	1.0	1.2	1.3	1.7	1.9	2.1	Pour 100 habitants
Congo									Congo
Number (thousands)	22[5]	22[5]	22[5]	22	22	7	14	...	Nombre (en miliers)
Per 100 inhabitants	0.8	0.8	0.7	0.7	0.7	0.2	0.4	...	Pour 100 habitants
Cook Islands+									Iles Cook+
Number (thousands)	5	5	6	6[6]	6	7	6[5]	7	Nombre (en miliers)
Per 100 inhabitants	28.1	29.4	31.0	32.8	33.5	35.7	33.0	36.5	Pour 100 habitants
Costa Rica									Costa Rica
Number (thousands)	742	803	899	945	1 038	1 159	1 343	1 389	Nombre (en miliers)
Per 100 inhabitants	20.9	22.4	23.5	23.7	25.8	27.8	31.6	32.1	Pour 100 habitants
Côte d'Ivoire									Côte d'Ivoire
Number (thousands)	170	219	264	294	325	238	258	259	Nombre (en miliers)
Per 100 inhabitants	1.2	1.5	1.8	1.8	2.0	1.4	1.5	1.4	Pour 100 habitants
Croatia									Croatie
Number (thousands)	1 558	1 634	1 721	*1 781	1 825	1 871	1 888	1 890	Nombre (en miliers)
Per 100 inhabitants	34.8	36.5	38.5	40.7	41.7	42.8	42.7	41.5	Pour 100 habitants
Cuba									Cuba
Number (thousands)	388	434	489	574	666	724	768	856	Nombre (en miliers)
Per 100 inhabitants	3.5	3.9	4.4	5.1	5.9	6.4	6.8	7.5	Pour 100 habitants
Cyprus									Chypre
Number (thousands)	405	424	440	435	427	424[8]	418	420	Nombre (en miliers)
Per 100 inhabitants	61.4	63.4	64.8	63.1	59.8	59.0	51.8	50.3	Pour 100 habitants
Czech Republic									République tchèque
Number (thousands)	3 741	3 806	3 872	3 861	3 675	3 626	3 428	3 217	Nombre (en miliers)
Per 100 inhabitants	36.3	37.0	37.7	37.8	36.0	35.5	33.6	31.5	Pour 100 habitants
Dem. Rep. of the Congo									Rép. dém. du Congo
Number (thousands)*	9	10	10	10	10	10	11	11	Nombre (en miliers)*
Per 100 inhabitants^	0.0	0.0	0.0	0.0	0.0	0.0	0.0	0.0	Pour 100 habitants^
Denmark									Danemark
Number (thousands)[8]	3 496	3 638	3 835	3 865	3 701	3 615	3 492	3 350	Nombre (en miliers)[8]
Per 100 inhabitants	66.0	68.5	72.0	72.2	68.9	67.0	64.5	61.7	Pour 100 habitants

Country or area	1998	1999	2000	2001	2002	2003	2004	2005	Pays ou zone
Djibouti									Djibouti
Number (thousands)	8	9	10	10	10	10	11	11	Nombre (en miliers)
Per 100 inhabitants	1.3	1.4	1.5	1.5	1.5	1.5	1.6	1.6	Pour 100 habitants
Dominica+									Dominique+
Number (thousands)	20	21	*23	23[17]	24	22	21	...	Nombre (en miliers)
Per 100 inhabitants	28.0	29.8	31.7	32.5	33.2	31.5	29.4	...	Pour 100 habitants
Dominican Republic									Rép. dominicaine
Number (thousands)	772	827	894	955	909	909	936	896	Nombre (en miliers)
Per 100 inhabitants	9.9	10.5	11.2	11.8	10.6	10.5	10.6	10.1	Pour 100 habitants
Ecuador									Equateur
Number (thousands)	991	1 130	1 224	1 336	1 426	1 549	1 616	1 701	Nombre (en miliers)
Per 100 inhabitants	8.1	9.1	9.7	10.4	11.0	11.8	12.2	12.9	Pour 100 habitants
Egypt+									Egypte+
Number (thousands)	3 972[18]	4 686[18]	5 484[18]	6 695	7 736	8 736	9 464	10 396	Nombre (en miliers)
Per 100 inhabitants	6.5	7.5	8.6	10.4	11.5	12.7	13.5	14.0	Pour 100 habitants
El Salvador									El Salvador
Number (thousands)	387	495	625	650	668	753	888	971	Nombre (en miliers)
Per 100 inhabitants	6.4	8.0	10.0	10.2	10.3	11.3	13.4	14.1	Pour 100 habitants
Equatorial Guinea									Guinée équatoriale
Number (thousands) *	6	6	6	7	9	10	11	10	Nombre (en miliers)*
Per 100 inhabitants	1.3	1.3	1.3	1.5	1.7	1.8	2.1	2.0	Pour 100 habitants
Eritrea									Erythrée
Number (thousands)	24	27	31	31	36	38	39	38	Nombre (en miliers)
Per 100 inhabitants	0.7	0.8	0.8	0.8	0.9	0.9	0.9	0.9	Pour 100 habitants
Estonia									Estonie
Number (thousands)	499	515	523	506	475	461	444	442	Nombre (en miliers)
Per 100 inhabitants	34.4	35.7	36.3	35.4	35.1	34.1	33.3	33.3	Pour 100 habitants
Ethiopia+									Ethiopie+
Number (thousands)	164	194	232	284	354	435	484	610	Nombre (en miliers)
Per 100 inhabitants	0.3	0.3	0.4	0.4	0.5	0.6	0.7	0.8	Pour 100 habitants
Faeroe Islands									Iles Féroé
Number (thousands)	24	25	25	23	24	24	24	24	Nombre (en miliers)
Per 100 inhabitants	54.4	55.7	55.4	51.4	52.0	51.0	49.8	...	Pour 100 habitants
Falkland Is. (Malvinas)									Iles Falkland (Malvinas)
Number (thousands)	2	2	2	2	2	3	3	3	Nombre (en miliers)
Per 100 inhabitants	93.2	96.1	98.6	99.0	98.5	104.0	103.1	...	Pour 100 habitants
Fiji									Fidji
Number (thousands)	77	82	86[5]	92	98	102	105	110	Nombre (en miliers)
Per 100 inhabitants	9.7	10.1	10.7	11.3	11.9	12.4	...	...	Pour 100 habitants
Finland									Finlande
Number (thousands)[19]	2 841	2 850	2 849	2 806	2 726	2 568	2 368	2 120	Nombre (en miliers)[19]
Per 100 inhabitants	55.1	55.2	55.0	54.0	52.3	49.2	45.4	40.4	Pour 100 habitants
France									France
Number (thousands)[8]	34 099	33 888	33 987	34 084	34 124	33 913	33 703	33 697	Nombre (en miliers)[8]
Per 100 inhabitants	58.4	57.8	57.7	57.4	57.2	56.4	56.0	59.0	Pour 100 habitants
French Guiana									Guyane française
Number (thousands)	46	49	50[5]	51[5]	...	...	...	...	Nombre (en miliers)
Per 100 inhabitants	30.5	31.3	30.7	30.2	...	...	...	...	Pour 100 habitants
French Polynesia									Polynésie française
Number (thousands)	53	52	54[5]	53	53	54	53	53	Nombre (en miliers)
Per 100 inhabitants	23.3	22.8	22.7	22.1	21.7	21.4	21.5	20.9	Pour 100 habitants
Gabon									Gabon
Number (thousands)	39	38	39	37	32	38	39	39	Nombre (en miliers)
Per 100 inhabitants	3.3	3.2	3.2	3.0	2.5	2.9	2.9	2.8	Pour 100 habitants
Gambia+									Gambie+
Number (thousands)[20]	26	29	*33	35	38	...	...	44	Nombre (en miliers)[20]
Per 100 inhabitants	2.2	2.4	2.6	2.7	2.9	...	...	2.9	Pour 100 habitants

Country or area	1998	1999	2000	2001	2002	2003	2004	2005	Pays ou zone
Georgia									Géorgie
Number (thousands)	629	672	509	569	640	667	683	...	Nombre (en miliers)
Per 100 inhabitants	13.0	14.1	10.8	12.2	13.9	14.6	15.1	...	Pour 100 habitants
Germany									Allemagne
Number (thousands)[21]	46 530	48 210	50 220	52 330	53 670	54 233	54 574	55 046	Nombre (en miliers)[21]
Per 100 inhabitants	56.7	58.7	61.1	63.5	65.0	65.7	66.1	66.6	Pour 100 habitants
Ghana									Ghana
Number (thousands)	133	161	213	245	275	291	313	322	Nombre (en miliers)
Per 100 inhabitants	0.7	0.8	1.1	1.2	1.3	1.4	1.5	1.5	Pour 100 habitants
Greece									Grèce
Number (thousands)[8]	5 536	5 611	5 659	5 608	6 294	6 300	6 349	6 303	Nombre (en miliers)[8]
Per 100 inhabitants	52.2	52.8	53.6	52.9	57.1	55.0	57.2	56.7	Pour 100 habitants
Greenland									Groenland
Number (thousands)	25	26	26	26	25	...	...	...	Nombre (en miliers)
Per 100 inhabitants	44.6	45.7	46.8	46.7	44.7	...	...	...	Pour 100 habitants
Grenada									Grenade
Number (thousands)	27	29	31	33	34	33	33	...	Nombre (en miliers)
Per 100 inhabitants	27.2	29.0	30.9	32.2	32.9	32.0	32.0	...	Pour 100 habitants
Guadeloupe									Guadeloupe
Number (thousands)	197	201	205	210[5]	...	...	...	...	Nombre (en miliers)
Per 100 inhabitants	47.1	47.6	48.0	48.7	...	...	...	...	Pour 100 habitants
Guam									Guam
Number (thousands)	75[22]	78[22]	74[22]	80	...	...	...	...	Nombre (en miliers)
Per 100 inhabitants	50.0	50.9	48.0	50.9	...	...	...	...	Pour 100 habitants
Guatemala									Guatemala
Number (thousands)	517	611	677	756	846	944	1 132	1 248	Nombre (en miliers)
Per 100 inhabitants	4.8	5.5	5.9	6.5	7.1	7.7	8.9	9.9	Pour 100 habitants
Guernsey									Guernesey
Number (thousands)[8]	48	51	53	55	56	55	55	...	Nombre (en miliers)[8]
Per 100 inhabitants	77.6	81.2	84.7	97.7	99.5	99.4	98.8	...	Pour 100 habitants
Guinea									Guinée
Number (thousands)	15	21	24	25	26	26	26	...	Nombre (en miliers)
Per 100 inhabitants	0.2	0.3	0.3	0.3	0.3	0.3	0.3	...	Pour 100 habitants
Guinea-Bissau									Guinée-Bissau
Number (thousands)	8	6	11	10	11	11	...	...	Nombre (en miliers)
Per 100 inhabitants	0.7	0.5	0.9	0.8	0.9	0.8	...	...	Pour 100 habitants
Guyana									Guyana
Number (thousands)	60	64	*68	80	80	92	103	110	Nombre (en miliers)
Per 100 inhabitants	8.1	8.6	9.2	10.7	10.8	12.3	13.7	14.7	Pour 100 habitants
Haiti									Haïti
Number (thousands)[5]	65	70	73	80	130	140	140	...	Nombre (en miliers)[5]
Per 100 inhabitants	0.8	0.9	0.9	1.0	1.6	1.8	1.7	...	Pour 100 habitants
Honduras									Honduras
Number (thousands)	249	279	299	310	322	334	390	494	Nombre (en miliers)
Per 100 inhabitants	4.0	4.4	4.8	4.7	4.9	4.9	5.6	6.9	Pour 100 habitants
Hungary									Hongrie
Number (thousands)	3 423	3 726	3 798	3 742	3 669	3 603	3 564	3 356	Nombre (en miliers)
Per 100 inhabitants	33.6	36.7	37.2	36.8	36.2	35.6	35.3	33.2	Pour 100 habitants
Iceland									Islande
Number (thousands)[8]	174	185	196	197	188	193	190	194	Nombre (en miliers)[8]
Per 100 inhabitants	63.1	66.4	69.9	68.5	65.3	66.6	65.0	65.9	Pour 100 habitants
India+									Inde+
Number (thousands)	21 594	26 511	32 436	38 536	41 420[23]	42 000	43 960[24]	49 750	Nombre (en miliers)
Per 100 inhabitants	2.2	2.7	3.2	3.8	4.0	4.0	4.1	4.5	Pour 100 habitants
Indonesia									Indonésie
Number (thousands)	5 572	6 080	6 663	7 219	7 750[25]	8 058	9 992	12 772	Nombre (en miliers)
Per 100 inhabitants	2.7	3.0	3.2	3.5	3.7	3.7	4.5	5.7	Pour 100 habitants

Country or area	1998	1999	2000	2001	2002	2003	2004	2005	Pays ou zone
Iran (Islamic Rep. of)+									Iran (Rép. islamique d')+
Number (thousands)	7 355	8 371	9 486	10 897	12 888	15 341	16 342	18 986	Nombre (en milliers)
Per 100 inhabitants	11.9	13.3	14.9	16.9	19.7	23.1	23.4	27.3	Pour 100 habitants
Iraq+									Iraq+
Number (thousands)	650	*675	*675	675	1 128[26]	1 183[26]	*1 034	...	Nombre (en milliers)
Per 100 inhabitants	3.0	3.0	2.9	2.9	4.7	4.7	4.0	...	Pour 100 habitants
Ireland+									Irlande+
Number (thousands)[8]	1 633	1 737	1 832	1 860	1 975	1 955	2 015	2 052	Nombre (en milliers)[8]
Per 100 inhabitants	44.1	46.4	48.4	48.5	50.2	49.1	49.8	49.0	Pour 100 habitants
Israel									Israël
Number (thousands)	2 807	2 878	2 974	3 033	3 006	2 913	2 896	2 936	Nombre (en milliers)
Per 100 inhabitants	46.9	47.1	47.4	46.6	45.3	43.1	42.2	42.6	Pour 100 habitants
Italy									Italie
Number (thousands)[8]	25 986	26 502	27 153	27 353[27]	27 142	26 596[28]	25 957[28]	25 049	Nombre (en milliers)[8]
Per 100 inhabitants	45.3	46.2	47.4	47.1	48.1	45.9	44.8	43.1	Pour 100 habitants
Jamaica+									Jamaïque+
Number (thousands)	463	487	494	*511	433	459	391	342	Nombre (en milliers)
Per 100 inhabitants	18.0	18.9	19.0	19.6	16.5	17.4	14.6	12.9	Pour 100 habitants
Japan+									Japon+
Number (thousands)	62 413	62 054	61 957	61 326	60 772	60 219	59 608	58 053[17]	Nombre (en milliers)
Per 100 inhabitants	49.4	49.0	48.8	48.2	47.7	47.2	46.6	45.9	Pour 100 habitants
Jersey									Jersey
Number (thousands)	69	70	73	74	...	...	...	...	Nombre (en milliers)
Per 100 inhabitants	79.9	81.5	84.1	84.8	...	...	...	...	Pour 100 habitants
Jordan									Jordanie
Number (thousands)	511	565	620	660	675	623	638	...	Nombre (en milliers)
Per 100 inhabitants	10.7	11.5	12.3	12.7	12.7	11.4	11.4	...	Pour 100 habitants
Kazakhstan									Kazakhstan
Number (thousands)	1 775	1 760	1 834	1 940	2 082	2 228	2 500	...	Nombre (en milliers)
Per 100 inhabitants	11.6	11.6	12.2	13.0	14.0	15.0	16.8	...	Pour 100 habitants
Kenya+									Kenya+
Number (thousands)	288	*290	292	309	321	328	299	282	Nombre (en milliers)
Per 100 inhabitants	1.0	1.0	1.0	1.0	1.0	1.0	0.9	0.8	Pour 100 habitants
Kiribati									Kiribati
Number (thousands)	3	3	3[5]	4	4	...	...	...	Nombre (en milliers)
Per 100 inhabitants	3.4	3.7	4.0	4.2	5.1	...	...	...	Pour 100 habitants
Korea, Dem. P. R.									Corée, R. p. dém. de
Number (thousands) *	500	500	500	860	916	980	...	...	Nombre (en milliers)*
Per 100 inhabitants	2.3	2.3	2.3	3.9	4.1	4.4	...	...	Pour 100 habitants
Korea, Republic of									Corée, République de
Number (thousands)[19]	20 089	25 619	25 863	25 775	25 735	25 128	23 568	23 745	Nombre (en milliers)[19]
Per 100 inhabitants	44.2	56.1	56.2	54.4	54.0	52.5	49.0	49.2	Pour 100 habitants
Kuwait									Koweït
Number (thousands)	427	456	467	472	482	487	497	510	Nombre (en milliers)
Per 100 inhabitants	21.1	21.6	21.3	20.8	20.4	19.6	19.5	19.0	Pour 100 habitants
Kyrgyzstan									Kirghizistan
Number (thousands)	368	371	376	388	395	396	416	438	Nombre (en milliers)
Per 100 inhabitants	7.8	7.6	7.7	7.8	7.9	7.9	8.2	8.3	Pour 100 habitants
Lao People's Dem. Rep.									Rép. dém. pop. lao
Number (thousands)	28	35	41	53	62	70	75	75	Nombre (en milliers)
Per 100 inhabitants	0.6	0.7	0.8	1.0	1.1	1.2	1.3	1.3	Pour 100 habitants
Latvia									Lettonie
Number (thousands)	742	732[29]	735[29]	722	701	654	650	731	Nombre (en milliers)
Per 100 inhabitants	30.2	30.0	30.3	30.7	30.1	28.2	28.5	31.7	Pour 100 habitants
Lebanon									Liban
Number (thousands)	566[5]	571[5]	576	626	679	700	630	990	Nombre (en milliers)
Per 100 inhabitants	17.7	17.6	17.5	18.7	19.9	20.0	17.7	27.7	Pour 100 habitants

Telephones — Main telephone lines in operation and lines per 100 inhabitants (*continued*)
Téléphones — Nombre de lignes téléphoniques en service et lignes pour 100 habitants (*suite*)

Country or area	1998	1999	2000	2001	2002	2003	2004	2005	Pays ou zone
Lesotho+									Lesotho+
Number (thousands)	21	*22	*22	21[17]	29[17]	35[17]	37[17]	48[17]	Nombre (en miliers)
Per 100 inhabitants	1.2	1.2	1.2	1.2	1.6	2.0	2.1	2.7	Pour 100 habitants
Liberia[30]									Libéria[30]
Number (thousands)*	7	7	7	7	7	...	...	...	Nombre (en miliers)*
Per 100 inhabitants	0.2	0.2	0.2	0.2	0.2	...	...	...	Pour 100 habitants
Libyan Arab Jamah.									Jamah. arabe libyenne
Number (thousands)	500	*550	*605	*660	*720	*750	...	...	Nombre (en miliers)
Per 100 inhabitants	9.1	10.1	10.8	11.8	13.0	13.6	...	...	Pour 100 habitants
Liechtenstein									Liechtenstein
Number (thousands)	20	20	20	20	20	20	20	20	Nombre (en miliers)
Per 100 inhabitants	61.7	60.9	61.1	60.0	58.8	58.0	57.7	57.5	Pour 100 habitants
Lithuania									Lituanie
Number (thousands)[20,31]	1 113	1 153	1 188	1 152	936	824	820	756	Nombre (en miliers)[20,31]
Per 100 inhabitants	30.1	31.2	32.2	33.0	26.9	23.9	23.8	23.4	Pour 100 habitants
Luxembourg									Luxembourg
Number (thousands)[32]	255	252	249	257	249	245	245	245	Nombre (en miliers)[32]
Per 100 inhabitants	59.8	58.2	56.8	58.4	55.7	54.3	53.4	52.6	Pour 100 habitants
Madagascar									Madagascar
Number (thousands)	47	50	55	58	59	60	59	67	Nombre (en miliers)
Per 100 inhabitants	0.3	0.3	0.3	0.4	0.3	0.3	0.3	0.4	Pour 100 habitants
Malawi									Malawi
Number (thousands)	37	42	46	55	73	85	93	103	Nombre (en miliers)
Per 100 inhabitants	0.4	0.4	0.4	0.5	0.7	0.8	0.8	0.8	Pour 100 habitants
Malaysia									Malaisie
Number (thousands)	4 384	4 431	4 634	4 710	4 670	4 572	4 446	4 366	Nombre (en miliers)
Per 100 inhabitants	20.2	20.3	19.9	19.7	19.0	18.2	17.4	16.8	Pour 100 habitants
Maldives									Maldives
Number (thousands)	20	22	24	27	29	30	32	32	Nombre (en miliers)
Per 100 inhabitants	7.7	8.4	9.0	9.9	10.2	10.5	9.6	...	Pour 100 habitants
Mali									Mali
Number (thousands)	27	34	39	51	57	61	75	75	Nombre (en miliers)
Per 100 inhabitants	0.3	0.3	0.4	0.5	0.5	0.6	0.7	0.7	Pour 100 habitants
Malta									Malte
Number (thousands)	192	198	204	208	207	208	207	202	Nombre (en miliers)
Per 100 inhabitants	49.9	51.2	52.4	53.0	52.3	52.1	51.6	50.4	Pour 100 habitants
Marshall Islands									Iles Marshall
Number (thousands)	4	4	4	4	4	4	...	...	Nombre (en miliers)
Per 100 inhabitants	7.5	7.6	7.7	8.0	8.2	8.3	...	...	Pour 100 habitants
Martinique									Martinique
Number (thousands)	172	172	172[5]	172[5]	...	...	...	...	Nombre (en miliers)
Per 100 inhabitants	45.4	45.1	44.7	44.5	...	...	...	...	Pour 100 habitants
Mauritania									Mauritanie
Number (thousands)	15	17	19	25	32	38	39	41	Nombre (en miliers)
Per 100 inhabitants	0.6	0.7	0.7	1.0	1.2	1.4	1.3	1.3	Pour 100 habitants
Mauritius									Maurice
Number (thousands)	245	257	281	307	327	348	354	357	Nombre (en miliers)
Per 100 inhabitants	21.2	21.9	23.5	25.6	27.0	28.5	28.7	28.8	Pour 100 habitants
Mayotte									Mayotte
Number (thousands)	12	10	10	*10	*10	...	...	...	Nombre (en miliers)
Per 100 inhabitants	8.9	6.8	6.8	6.5	6.2	...	...	...	Pour 100 habitants
Mexico									Mexique
Number (thousands)[33]	9 927	10 927	12 332	13 774	14 975	16 330	18 073[18]	19 512	Nombre (en miliers)[33]
Per 100 inhabitants	10.4	11.2	12.5	13.9	14.9	16.0	17.2	18.2	Pour 100 habitants
Micronesia (Fed. States of)									Micronésie (Etats féd. de)
Number (thousands)	9	10[5]	10[5]	10	10	11	12	12	Nombre (en miliers)
Per 100 inhabitants	8.5	9.2	9.0	9.4	9.4	10.3	10.8	11.2	Pour 100 habitants

Country or area	1998	1999	2000	2001	2002	2003	2004	2005	Pays ou zone
Mongolia									Mongolie
Number (thousands)	103	103	118	124	128	138	146	156	Nombre (en miliers)
Per 100 inhabitants	4.5	4.4	5.0	5.2	5.3	5.6	5.6	5.9	Pour 100 habitants
Montserrat									Montserrat
Number (thousands)[34]	*3	*3	3	...	...	...	...	...	Nombre (en miliers)[34]
Per 100 inhabitants	95.7	74.3	70.3	...	...	...	...	...	Pour 100 habitants
Morocco[35]									Maroc[35]
Number (thousands)	1 393	1 471	1 425	1 191	1 127	1 219	1 309	1 341	Nombre (en miliers)
Per 100 inhabitants	5.1	5.3	5.0	4.2	3.9	4.1	4.4	4.4	Pour 100 habitants
Mozambique									Mozambique
Number (thousands)	75	78	86	89	84	78	70	70	Nombre (en miliers)
Per 100 inhabitants	0.5	0.5	0.5	0.5	0.5	0.4	0.4	0.4	Pour 100 habitants
Myanmar									Myanmar
Number (thousands)	229	249	271	295	342	363	425	476	Nombre (en miliers)
Per 100 inhabitants	0.5	0.6	0.5	0.6	0.7	0.7	0.8	...	Pour 100 habitants
Namibia+									Namibie+
Number (thousands)	106	108	110	117	121	127	128	139	Nombre (en miliers)
Per 100 inhabitants	6.3	6.2	6.2	6.4	6.5	6.6	6.4	6.8	Pour 100 habitants
Nauru									Nauru
Number (thousands)	2	2[5]	2[5]	2	...	...	...	...	Nombre (en miliers)
Per 100 inhabitants	15.0	15.5	15.7	16.0	...	...	...	...	Pour 100 habitants
Nepal+									Népal+
Number (thousands)	208	253	267	298[6]	328	372	418	449	Nombre (en miliers)
Per 100 inhabitants	1.0	1.2	1.2	1.3	1.4	1.6	1.7	1.7	Pour 100 habitants
Netherlands									Pays-Bas
Number (thousands)[8]	9 337	9 613	9 889	8 158	8 026[5]	7 846	7 861	7 600	Nombre (en miliers)[8]
Per 100 inhabitants	59.2	60.6	61.9	50.7	49.6	48.2	48.4	46.6	Pour 100 habitants
Netherlands Antilles									Antilles néerlandaises
Number (thousands) *	78	79	80	81	...	...	...	...	Nombre (en miliers)*
Per 100 inhabitants	36.6	36.8	37.2	37.2	...	...	...	...	Pour 100 habitants
New Caledonia									Nouvelle-Calédonie
Number (thousands)	49	51	51	51	52	52	53	55	Nombre (en miliers)
Per 100 inhabitants	24.0	24.1	23.8	23.1	23.2	22.7	23.0	23.3	Pour 100 habitants
New Zealand+									Nouvelle-Zélande+
Number (thousands)	1 809	1 833	1 831	1 823	1 765	1 798	1 801	1 729	Nombre (en miliers)
Per 100 inhabitants	47.4	47.8	47.5	47.0	44.8	45.6	45.1	42.9	Pour 100 habitants
Nicaragua									Nicaragua
Number (thousands)	141	150	164	158	172	205	214	221	Nombre (en miliers)
Per 100 inhabitants	3.0	3.0	3.2	3.0	3.3	3.7	3.8	...	Pour 100 habitants
Niger									Niger
Number (thousands)	18	19[5]	20	22	22	23	24	24	Nombre (en miliers)
Per 100 inhabitants	0.2	0.2	0.2	0.2	0.2	0.2	0.2	0.2	Pour 100 habitants
Nigeria									Nigéria
Number (thousands)	439	473	553	600	702	889	1 028	1 223	Nombre (en miliers)
Per 100 inhabitants	0.4	0.4	0.5	0.5	0.6	0.7	0.8	0.9	Pour 100 habitants
Niue									Nioué
Number (thousands)	1[5]	1[5]	1[5]	1	1	1	1	1	Nombre (en miliers)
Per 100 inhabitants	42.0	49.7	56.5	60.8	55.9	53.0	53.0	...	Pour 100 habitants
Northern Mariana Islands									Iles Mariannes du Nord
Number (thousands)	21	21	21	...	...	...	...	...	Nombre (en miliers)
Per 100 inhabitants	32.8	31.6	30.9	...	...	...	...	...	Pour 100 habitants
Norway									Norvège
Number (thousands)	2 475	2 446	2 401	2 338	2 402	2 236	2 180	2 129	Nombre (en miliers)
Per 100 inhabitants	55.7	54.6	53.3	51.7	52.8	48.9	47.4	46.1	Pour 100 habitants
Occupied Palestinian Terr.									Terr. palestinien occupé
Number (thousands)	167	222	272	292	302	316	357	349	Nombre (en miliers)
Per 100 inhabitants	5.8	7.4	8.6	8.9	8.7	8.7	9.7	9.4	Pour 100 habitants

Telephones — Main telephone lines in operation and lines per 100 inhabitants (*continued*)
Téléphones — Nombre de lignes téléphoniques en service et lignes pour 100 habitants (*suite*)

Country or area	1998	1999	2000	2001	2002	2003	2004	2005	Pays ou zone
Oman									Oman
Number (thousands)	220	220	222	231	228	236	243	265	Nombre (en miliers)
Per 100 inhabitants	9.3	9.2	9.1	9.3	9.1	9.4	9.6	10.3	Pour 100 habitants
Pakistan+									Pakistan+
Number (thousands)	2 661	2 874	3 053	3 252	3 655	4 047	4 502	5 278	Nombre (en miliers)
Per 100 inhabitants	2.0	2.1	2.2	2.3	2.5	2.7	3.0	3.4	Pour 100 habitants
Panama									Panama
Number (thousands)	419	462	429	382	387	381	410	440	Nombre (en miliers)
Per 100 inhabitants	15.1	16.4	15.1	13.2	12.9	12.2	12.9	13.6	Pour 100 habitants
Papua New Guinea									Papouasie-Nvl-Guinée
Number (thousands)	57	60	65	62	62	62	62	...	Nombre (en miliers)
Per 100 inhabitants	1.2	1.2	1.3	1.2	1.1	1.1	1.1	...	Pour 100 habitants
Paraguay									Paraguay
Number (thousands)	261	268	283	289[36]	273	281	303	320	Nombre (en miliers)
Per 100 inhabitants	5.0	5.0	5.1	5.1	4.7	4.7	5.0	5.2	Pour 100 habitants
Peru									Pérou
Number (thousands)	1 555	1 688	1 717	1 571	1 657	1 839	2 050	2 251	Nombre (en miliers)
Per 100 inhabitants	6.3	6.7	6.7	6.0	6.2	6.7	7.4	8.0	Pour 100 habitants
Philippines									Philippines
Number (thousands)	2 492[19]	2 892[19]	3 061	3 315	3 311	3 340	3 437	3 367	Nombre (en miliers)
Per 100 inhabitants	3.4	3.9	4.0	4.2	4.2	4.1	4.2	4.0	Pour 100 habitants
Poland									Pologne
Number (thousands)[8]	8 812	10 175	10 946	11 400	11 860	*12 292	12 553	11 836	Nombre (en miliers)[8]
Per 100 inhabitants	22.8	26.3	28.3	29.5	30.7	31.9	32.6	30.6	Pour 100 habitants
Portugal									Portugal
Number (thousands)	4 117	4 230	4 321	4 385	4 351	4 281	4 238	4 234	Nombre (en miliers)
Per 100 inhabitants	41.3	42.3	43.1	42.4	41.8	40.9	40.3	40.3	Pour 100 habitants
Puerto Rico[37]									Porto Rico[37]
Number (thousands)[38]	1 262	1 295	1 299	1 288	1 276	1 213[18]	1 112[18]	...	Nombre (en miliers)[38]
Per 100 inhabitants	33.6	34.3	34.1	33.6	33.1	31.3	28.5	...	Pour 100 habitants
Qatar									Qatar
Number (thousands)	151	155	160	167	177	185	191	205	Nombre (en miliers)
Per 100 inhabitants	27.4	26.8	26.4	26.2	26.3	26.1	25.7	26.4	Pour 100 habitants
Republic of Moldova									République de Moldova
Number (thousands)	657	555	584	639	719	791	863	929	Nombre (en miliers)
Per 100 inhabitants	15.3	12.9	13.7	15.0	16.9	18.7	20.3	22.1	Pour 100 habitants
Réunion									Réunion
Number (thousands)	243	268	280[5]	300[5]	...	...	...	...	Nombre (en miliers)
Per 100 inhabitants	35.6	38.0	40.1	41.0	...	...	...	...	Pour 100 habitants
Romania									Roumanie
Number (thousands)	3 599	3 740	3 899	4 116	4 215	4 332	4 389	4 391	Nombre (en miliers)
Per 100 inhabitants	16.0	16.7	17.4	18.4	19.3	20.0	20.3	20.2	Pour 100 habitants
Russian Federation									Fédération de Russie
Number (thousands)	29 246	30 949	32 070	33 278	35 500	36 100	38 500[24]	40 100[24]	Nombre (en miliers)
Per 100 inhabitants	19.8	21.0	21.9	22.8	24.4	25.0	26.8	27.9	Pour 100 habitants
Rwanda									Rwanda
Number (thousands)	11	13	18	22	25	26	23	...	Nombre (en miliers)
Per 100 inhabitants	0.2	0.2	0.2	0.3	0.3	0.3	0.3	...	Pour 100 habitants
Saint Helena+									Sainte-Hélène+
Number (thousands)	2	2	2	2[6]	2	2	2	2	Nombre (en miliers)
Per 100 inhabitants	38.7	40.7	41.7	43.4	44.1	44.9	46.0	45.6	Pour 100 habitants
Saint Kitts and Nevis+									Saint-Kitts-et-Nevis+
Number (thousands)	18	20	*22	*23	24	...	25	...	Nombre (en miliers)
Per 100 inhabitants	45.7	49.8	54.2	55.2	57.1	...	59.3	...	Pour 100 habitants
Saint Lucia+									Sainte-Lucie+
Number (thousands)	40	44	*49	50	51	...	...	...	Nombre (en miliers)
Per 100 inhabitants	26.6	29.0	31.7	32.1	32.6	...	...	...	Pour 100 habitants

14 Telephones—Main telephone lines in operation and lines per 100 inhabitants (*continued*)
Téléphones—Nombre de lignes téléphoniques en service et lignes pour 100 habitants (*suite*)

Country or area	1998	1999	2000	2001	2002	2003	2004	2005	Pays ou zone
Saint Vincent-Grenadines+									Saint Vincent-Grenadines+
Number (thousands)	21	24	25	26	27	21	19	23	Nombre (en miliers)
Per 100 inhabitants	18.8	20.9	22.0	22.7	23.4	17.8	15.7	18.9	Pour 100 habitants
Samoa									Samoa
Number (thousands)	8	9[5]	9[5]	10	12	13	...	...	Nombre (en miliers)
Per 100 inhabitants	4.9	4.9	4.8	5.4	6.5	7.3	...	...	Pour 100 habitants
San Marino									Saint-Marin
Number (thousands)	19	20	20	21	21	21	21	21	Nombre (en miliers)
Per 100 inhabitants	77.3	76.0	75.2	75.9	76.3	76.6	76.9	77.2	Pour 100 habitants
Sao Tome and Principe									Sao Tomé-et-Principe
Number (thousands)	4	5	5	5	6	7	7	...	Nombre (en miliers)
Per 100 inhabitants	3.2	3.3	3.3	3.8	4.4	4.7	4.6	...	Pour 100 habitants
Saudi Arabia									Arabie saoudite
Number (thousands)	2 167	2 706	2 965	3 233	3 318	3 503	3 695	3 800	Nombre (en miliers)
Per 100 inhabitants	10.7	13.0	13.8	14.6	14.6	15.0	15.4	15.5	Pour 100 habitants
Senegal									Sénégal
Number (thousands)	140	166	206	237	225	229	245	267	Nombre (en miliers)
Per 100 inhabitants	1.6	1.8	2.2	2.4	2.2	2.2	2.4	2.3	Pour 100 habitants
Serbia and Montenegro									Serbie-et-Monténégro
Number (thousands)	2 319	2 281	2 406	2 444	2 493	2 612	2 685	...	Nombre (en miliers)
Per 100 inhabitants	21.8	21.4	22.6	22.9	30.7	32.1	32.9	...	Pour 100 habitants
Seychelles+									Seychelles+
Number (thousands)	19	20	21	21	21	21	21	21	Nombre (en miliers)
Per 100 inhabitants	24.5	25.6	26.7	27.3	27.1	26.8	26.6	26.5	Pour 100 habitants
Sierra Leone									Sierra Leone
Number (thousands)	17	18	19	23	24	...	...	...	Nombre (en miliers)
Per 100 inhabitants	0.4	0.4	0.4	0.5	0.5	...	...	...	Pour 100 habitants
Singapore+									Singapour+
Number (thousands)	1 778	1 877	1 946	1 948	1 927	1 890	1 857	1 844	Nombre (en miliers)
Per 100 inhabitants	45.3	47.5	48.4	47.1	46.3	45.3	44.4	43.5	Pour 100 habitants
Slovakia									Slovaquie
Number (thousands)	1 539	1 655	1 698	1 556	1 403	1 295	1 250	1 197	Nombre (en miliers)
Per 100 inhabitants	28.5	30.7	31.4	28.9	26.1	24.1	23.2	22.2	Pour 100 habitants
Slovenia									Slovénie
Number (thousands)[39]	723	758	785	802	808	812	811	816	Nombre (en miliers)[39]
Per 100 inhabitants	36.3	38.1	39.5	40.2	40.5	40.7	41.3	41.5	Pour 100 habitants
Solomon Islands+									Iles Salomon+
Number (thousands)[40]	8	8	8[41]	7[41]	7[41]	6[41]	7	7	Nombre (en miliers)[40]
Per 100 inhabitants	2.0	2.0	1.8	1.7	1.5	1.3	1.4	1.5	Pour 100 habitants
Somalia									Somalie
Number (thousands) *	23	24	25	35	35	100	100	100	Nombre (en miliers)*
Per 100 inhabitants	0.3	0.4	0.4	0.5	0.5	1.3	1.3	1.2	Pour 100 habitants
South Africa+									Afrique du Sud+
Number (thousands)	5 075	5 493	4 962	4 924	4 844	4 821	4 850	4 729	Nombre (en miliers)
Per 100 inhabitants	11.4	12.2	10.9	10.7	10.4	10.3	10.3	10.0	Pour 100 habitants
Spain									Espagne
Number (thousands)	16 289	16 480	17 104	17 531	17 641	17 759	17 934	18 322	Nombre (en miliers)
Per 100 inhabitants	40.9	41.0	42.2	42.6	42.9	41.6	41.5	42.9	Pour 100 habitants
Sri Lanka									Sri Lanka
Number (thousands)	524	672	767	827	883	939	993	1 244	Nombre (en miliers)
Per 100 inhabitants	2.9	3.7	4.2	4.4	4.7	4.9	5.1	6.0	Pour 100 habitants
Sudan									Soudan
Number (thousands)	162	251	387	448	672	937	1 029	670	Nombre (en miliers)
Per 100 inhabitants	0.6	0.8	1.2	1.4	2.0	2.8	3.0	1.8	Pour 100 habitants
Suriname									Suriname
Number (thousands)	67	71	75	77	79	80	82	81	Nombre (en miliers)
Per 100 inhabitants	15.8	16.5	17.4	17.7	17.9	18.0	18.3	18.0	Pour 100 habitants

Country or area	1998	1999	2000	2001	2002	2003	2004	2005	Pays ou zone
Swaziland+									Swaziland+
Number (thousands)	29	31	32	34	35	46	45	35	Nombre (en miliers)
Per 100 inhabitants	3.0	3.2	3.2	3.3	3.4	4.4	4.1	3.4	Pour 100 habitants
Sweden									Suède
Number (thousands)[8]	6 389	6 519	6 728	6 717	6 579	6 543	6 447	...	Nombre (en miliers)[8]
Per 100 inhabitants	72.2	73.6	75.8	75.4	73.6	72.9	71.5	...	Pour 100 habitants
Switzerland									Suisse
Number (thousands)[8]	4 884	5 066	5 236	5 383[42]	5 388	5 323	5 253	5 146	Nombre (en miliers)[8]
Per 100 inhabitants	68.4	70.6	72.6	74.3	74.0	72.3	71.0	68.7	Pour 100 habitants
Syrian Arab Republic									Rép. arabe syrienne
Number (thousands)	1 477	1 600	1 675	1 817	2 099	2 414	2 660	2 903	Nombre (en miliers)
Per 100 inhabitants	9.5	9.9	10.3	10.9	12.3	13.8	14.6	15.2	Pour 100 habitants
Tajikistan									Tadjikistan
Number (thousands)	221	213	219	227	238	245	...	...	Nombre (en miliers)
Per 100 inhabitants	3.7	3.5	3.6	3.7	3.7	3.7	...	...	Pour 100 habitants
Thailand+									Thaïlande+
Number (thousands)	5 038	5 216	5 591	6 049	6 557	6 632	6 812	7 035	Nombre (en miliers)
Per 100 inhabitants	8.4	8.6	9.1	9.8	10.5	10.5	10.7	11.0	Pour 100 habitants
TFYR of Macedonia									L'ex-R.y. Macédoine
Number (thousands)	439	471	507	539	560	525	537	533	Nombre (en miliers)
Per 100 inhabitants	22.0	23.5	25.2	26.7	27.7	25.9	26.4	26.2	Pour 100 habitants
Togo									Togo
Number (thousands)	31	38	43	48	51	61	66	63[43]	Nombre (en miliers)
Per 100 inhabitants	0.7	0.8	0.9	1.0	1.0	1.2	1.3	1.0	Pour 100 habitants
Tonga									Tonga
Number (thousands)	9	9	10[5]	11	11	...	...	...	Nombre (en miliers)
Per 100 inhabitants	8.7	9.3	9.8	10.9	11.3	...	...	...	Pour 100 habitants
Trinidad and Tobago+									Trinité-et-Tobago+
Number (thousands)	264	279	317	312	318	319	322	323	Nombre (en miliers)
Per 100 inhabitants	20.6	21.6	24.5	24.0	24.4	24.5	24.7	24.8	Pour 100 habitants
Tunisia									Tunisie
Number (thousands)	752	850	955	1 056	1 149	1 164	1 204	1 257	Nombre (en miliers)
Per 100 inhabitants	8.1	9.0	10.0	10.9	11.7	11.8	12.1	12.5	Pour 100 habitants
Turkey									Turquie
Number (thousands)	16 807	17 912	18 395	18 904	18 890	18 917	19 125	18 978	Nombre (en miliers)
Per 100 inhabitants	25.5	26.7	27.0	27.3	26.9	26.5	26.5	25.9	Pour 100 habitants
Turkmenistan									Turkménistan
Number (thousands)	354	359	364	388	374	376	...	...	Nombre (en miliers)
Per 100 inhabitants	8.2	8.2	8.2	8.0	7.7	7.7	...	...	Pour 100 habitants
Turks and Caicos Islands									Iles Turques et Caïques
Per 100 inhabitants	13.8	15.4	17.5	18.4	16.3	15.6	14.8	...	Pour 100 habitants
Tuvalu									Tuvalu
Number (thousands)	1	1	*1	1	1	1	1	1	Nombre (en miliers)
Per 100 inhabitants	6.4	6.7	7.0	6.8	6.9	7.0	6.8	...	Pour 100 habitants
Uganda+									Ouganda+
Number (thousands)	57	57[44]	62	56	55	61	72	101	Nombre (en miliers)
Per 100 inhabitants	0.2	0.2	0.3	0.2	0.2	0.2	0.3	0.3	Pour 100 habitants
Ukraine									Ukraine
Number (thousands)	9 698	10 074	10 417	10 670	10 833	11 110	12 142	...	Nombre (en miliers)
Per 100 inhabitants	19.3	20.3	21.2	22.0	22.6	23.4	25.8	...	Pour 100 habitants
United Arab Emirates									Emirats arabes unis
Number (thousands)	915	975	1 020	1 053	1 094	1 136	1 188	1 237	Nombre (en miliers)
Per 100 inhabitants	32.3	32.2	31.4	30.2	29.1	28.1	27.7	27.5	Pour 100 habitants
United Kingdom+									Royaume-Uni+
Number (thousands)[8]	32 829	34 021	35 228	34 579	34 184	33 550	33 700	31 796	Nombre (en miliers)[8]
Per 100 inhabitants	55.4	57.2	58.9	57.6	57.9	56.4	56.4	53.3	Pour 100 habitants

Telephones—Main telephone lines in operation and lines per 100 inhabitants (*continued*)
Téléphones—Nombre de lignes téléphoniques en service et lignes pour 100 habitants (*suite*)

Country or area	1998	1999	2000	2001	2002	2003	2004	2005	Pays ou zone
United Rep. of Tanzania									Rép.-Unie de Tanzanie
Number (thousands)	122	150	174	178	162	147	148	154	Nombre (en miliers)
Per 100 inhabitants	0.4	0.4	0.5	0.5	0.4	0.4	0.4	0.4	Pour 100 habitants
United States									Etats-Unis
Number (thousands)[45]	179 850	189 502	192 513	191 697	189 390	183 042	177 947	175 350	Nombre (en miliers)[45]
Per 100 inhabitants	65.2	67.9	68.4	67.2	65.8	62.9	60.6	...	Pour 100 habitants
United States Virgin Is.									Iles Vierges américaines
Number (thousands)	65	67	68	*69	69	70	71	...	Nombre (en miliers)
Per 100 inhabitants	60.3	62.3	62.9	63.5	63.1	63.0	63.9	...	Pour 100 habitants
Uruguay									Uruguay
Number (thousands)	824	897	929	951	947	938	1 000	1 006	Nombre (en miliers)
Per 100 inhabitants	25.9	28.1	29.0	29.6	29.4	29.0	30.9	31.0	Pour 100 habitants
Uzbekistan									Ouzbékistan
Number (thousands)	1 537	1 599	1 655	1 663	1 681	1 717	...	...	Nombre (en miliers)
Per 100 inhabitants	6.4	6.6	6.7	6.7	6.6	6.7	...	...	Pour 100 habitants
Vanuatu									Vanuatu
Number (thousands)	5	*6	7	7	7	7	7	7	Nombre (en miliers)
Per 100 inhabitants	2.8	2.9	3.5	3.4	3.3	3.1	3.2	...	Pour 100 habitants
Venezuela (Bolivarian Rep. of)									Venezuela (Rép. bolivar. du)
Number (thousands)	2 592	2 551	2 536	2 705	2 842	2 956	3 346	3 606	Nombre (en miliers)
Per 100 inhabitants	11.2	10.8	10.5	10.9	11.3	11.5	12.8	13.5	Pour 100 habitants
Viet Nam									Viet Nam
Number (thousands)	1 744	2 106	2 543	3 050	3 929	4 402	10 125	15 845	Nombre (en miliers)
Per 100 inhabitants	2.3	2.7	3.2	3.8	4.9	5.4	12.2	18.8	Pour 100 habitants
Yemen									Yémen
Number (thousands)	250	284	347	423	542	685	798	...	Nombre (en miliers)
Per 100 inhabitants	1.5	1.6	1.9	2.2	2.8	3.4	3.8	...	Pour 100 habitants
Zambia+									Zambie+
Number (thousands)	78	83	83	86	88	88	92	95	Nombre (en miliers)
Per 100 inhabitants	0.8	0.8	0.8	0.8	0.8	0.8	0.8	0.8	Pour 100 habitants
Zimbabwe+									Zimbabwe+
Number (thousands)	237	239	249	254	288	301	317	328	Nombre (en miliers)
Per 100 inhabitants	2.1	2.1	2.2	2.2	2.5	2.6	2.7	2.8	Pour 100 habitants

Source

International Telecommunication Union (ITU), Geneva, the ITU database.

Notes

\+ The data shown generally relate to the fiscal year used in each country, unless indicated otherwise. Countries whose reference periods coincide with the calendar year ending 31 December are not listed.
Year beginning 22 March: Iran (Islamic Republic).
Year beginning 1 April: Antigua and Barbuda, Barbados, Belize, Bermuda, Botswana, British Virgin Islands, Cayman Islands, China - Hong Kong, Cook Islands, Dominica, Gambia, India, Ireland, Israel (prior to 1986), Jamaica, Japan, Lesotho, Seychelles, Singapore (beginning 1983), Solomon Islands, South Africa, St. Helena, St. Kitts and Nevis, St. Lucia, St. Vincent and the Grenadines, Swaziland, Trinidad and Tobago, United Kingdom, and Zambia.
Year ending 30 June: Australia, Bangladesh, Egypt, Ethiopia, Iraq, Kenya, New Zealand (beginning 2000; prior to 2000, year ending 1 April), Pakistan, Uganda, and Zimbabwe.
Year ending 15 July: Nepal.
Year ending 30 September: Argentina (beginning 1991), Namibia (beginning 1993), and Thailand.

1 Since 2004: "Autorité de Régulation de la Poste et des Télécommunications (ARPT)".

2 Analogic lines + XDSI lines.

Source

Union internationale des télécommunications (UIT), Genève, la base de données de l'UIT.

Notes

\+ Sauf indication contraire, les données indiquées concernent généralement l'exercice budgétaire utilisé dans chaque pays. Les pays ou territoires dont la période de référence coïncide avec l'année civile se terminant le 31 décembre ne sont pas répertoriés ci-dessous.
Exercice commençant le 22 mars : Iran (République islamique d').
Exercice commençant le 1er avril : Afrique du Sud, Antigua-et-Barbuda, Barbade, Belize, Bermudes, Botswana, Chine-Hong Kong, Dominique, Gambie, Îles Caïmanes, Îles Cook, Îles Salomon, Îles Vierges britanniques, Inde, Irlande, Israël (antérieur à 1986), Jamaïque, Japon, Lesotho, Royaume-Uni, Saint-Kitts-et-Nevis, Saint-Vincent-et-les Grenadines, Sainte-Hélène, Sainte-Lucie, Seychelles, Singapour (à partir de 1983), Swaziland, Trinité-et-Tobago et Zambie.
Exercice se terminant le 30 juin : Australie, Bangladesh, Égypte, Éthiopie, Iraq, Kenya, Nouvelle-Zélande (à partir de 2000; avant 2000, exercice se terminant le 1er avril), Ouganda, Pakistan et Zimbabwe.
Exercice se terminant le 15 juillet : Népal.
Exercice se terminant le 30 septembre : Argentine (à partir de 1991), Namibie (à partir de 1993), et Thaïlande.

1 A partir de 2004: Autorité de Régulation de la Poste et des Télécommunications (ARPT).

2 Lignes analogiques et "XDSI".

3 Data refer to Angola Telecom.
4 First semester.
5 ITU estimate.
6 As of 31 December.
7 1994-2002 only refers to "Telefónica de Argentina S.A. y Telecom Argentina S.A." From 2002 all licensees are included (352 in 2003).
8 Including ISDN channels.
9 August.
10 Prior to 2002, data refer to BET and Bartel. Beginning 2002, data refer to Cable and Wireless.
11 Including ISDN equivalents.
12 Conventional telephony terminals in service.
13 Caribbean Telecommunications Union.
14 WLL lines included.
15 For statistical purposes, the data for China do not include those for the Hong Kong Special Administrative Region (Hong Kong SAR), Macao Special Administrative Region (Macao SAR) and Taiwan Province of China.
16 Ministry of Communication estimate.
17 December.
18 June.
19 Telephone subscribers (Finland: from 1996 the basis for the compilation of the statistics changed).
20 Excluding public call offices.
21 Telephone channels including ISDN and own consumption, excluding public payphones.
22 US Federal Communications Commission's Statistics of Communications Common Carriers.
23 Subscriber lines.
24 October.
25 September. Telkom.
26 Central Organisation for Statistics & IT.
27 September.
28 Data refer to Telecom Italia Wireline.
29 Lattelekom.
30 Data after 1990 may not be directly comparable to earlier years due to civil uprising.
31 Without ISDN channels.
32 Including digital lines.
33 Lines in service.
34 Decrease due to the reduction of population since the volcanic crisis in 1995.
35 Including Western Sahara.
36 Decrease in lines available in the public sector.
37 Data refer to the Puerto Rico Telephone Authority.
38 Switched access lines.
39 Including ISDN subscribers.
40 Billable lines.
41 The number of fixed lines declined due to civil war.
42 SWISSCOM at September 2001.
43 Drop results from the termination of contract for clients that had not paid.
44 Including data from MTN.
45 Data up to 1980 refer to main stations reported by FCC. From 1981, data refer to "Local Loops".

3 Les données se réfèrent à "Angola Telecom".
4 Premier trimestre.
5 Estimation de l'UIT.
6 Dès le 31 décembre.
7 Les chiffres de 1994-2002 ne concernent que "Telefónica de Argentina S.A. y Telecom Argentina S.A." À partir de 2002 tous les détenteurs de licence sont compris (352 en 2003).
8 RNIS inclus.
9 Août.
10 Avant 2002, les données se réfèrent au "BET" et "Bartel". A partir de 2002 les données se réfèrent au "Cable and Wireless".
11 Y compris les équivalents du RNIS.
12 Terminaux de téléphonie conventionnelle en service.
13 "Caribbean Telecommunications Union".
14 Y compris les lignes "WLL".
15 Pour la présentation des statistiques, les données pour la Chine ne comprennent pas la Région Administrative Spéciale de Hong Kong (Hong Kong RAS), la Région Administrative Spéciale de Macao (Macao RAS) et la province de Taiwan.
16 Estimation du ministère de communication.
17 Décembre.
18 Juin.
19 Abonnés au téléphone. (Finlande : à compter de 1996, la base de calcul des statistiques à changé).
20 Cabines publiques exclues.
21 Voies téléphoniques, y compris RNIS et consommation personnelle, excluant les téléphones publics payants.
22 "US Federal Communications Commission's Statistics of Communications Common Carriers".
23 Lignes d'abonnés au téléphone.
24 Octobre.
25 Septembre. Telkom.
26 "Central Organisation for Statistics & IT".
27 Septembre.
28 Les données se réfèrent au "Telecom Italia Wireline".
29 Lattelekom.
30 Les données datant d'après et d'avant 1990 peuvent ne pas être directement comparables en raison de la révolte civile.
31 Sans RNIS.
32 Y compris lignes digitales.
33 Lignes en service.
34 Baisse due à la diminution de la population depuis l'éruption volcanique de 1995.
35 Y compris les données de Sahara occidental.
36 Diminution des lignes disponibles dans le secteur publique.
37 Les données se réfèrent à "Puerto Rico Telephone Authority".
38 Lignes d'accès déviées.
39 Y compris les abonnés au ISDN.
40 Lignes payables.
41 Le nombre de lignes fixes a diminué en raison de la guerre civile.
42 SWISSCOM: Septembre 2001.
43 2005 : la diminution est due à la résiliation des contrats de clients dont le compte était en souffrance.
44 Y compris les données du "MTN".
45 Les données pour 1980 se réfèrent aux stations principales. Dès 1981, les données se réfèrent aux "Local Loops".

15

Internet users

Estimated number and number per 100 inhabitants

Usagers d'Internet

Nombre estimatif et nombre pour 100 habitants

Country or area	1998	1999	2000	2001	2002	2003	2004	2005	Pays ou zone
Afghanistan									Afghanistan
Number	...	...	...	1 000	1 000	20 000	25 000	30 000	Nombre
Per 100 inhabitants	...	...	...	^0	^0	^0	^0	1	Pour 100 habitants
Albania									Albanie
Number	2 000	2 500	3 500	10 000	12 000	30 000	75 000	188 000	Nombre
Per 100 inhabitants	^0	^0	^0	^0	^0	1	2	6	Pour 100 habitants
Algeria									Algérie
Number	6 000	60 000	150 000	200 000	500 000	700 000	1 500 000	1 920 000	Nombre
Per 100 inhabitants	^0	^0	^0	1	2	2	5	6	Pour 100 habitants
Andorra									Andorre
Number	4 500	5 000	7 000	...	...	10 049	20 724	21 922	Nombre
Per 100 inhabitants	7	8	11	...	...	15	31	33	Pour 100 habitants
Angola									Angola
Number	2 500	10 000	15 000	20 000	41 000	...	75 000	85 000	Nombre
Per 100 inhabitants	^0	^0	^0	^0	^0	...	1	1	Pour 100 habitants
Anguilla									Anguilla
Number	...	...	2 500	3 000	...	3 700	3 300	3 750	Nombre
Antigua and Barbuda									Antigua-et-Barbuda
Number	3 000	4 000	5 000	7 000	10 000	14 000	20 000	29 000	Nombre
Per 100 inhabitants	4	5	7	9	13	18	25	36	Pour 100 habitants
Argentina+									Argentine+
Number	300 000	1 200 000	2 600 000	3 650 000	4 100 000	4 530 000	6 153 603	6 863 466	Nombre
Per 100 inhabitants	1	3	7	10	11	12	16	18	Pour 100 habitants
Armenia									Arménie
Number	4 000	30 000	40 000	50 000	60 000	140 000	150 000	161 000	Nombre
Per 100 inhabitants	^0	1	1	2	2	5	5	5	Pour 100 habitants
Aruba									Aruba
Number	...	4 000	14 000	24 000	24 000	24 000	24 000	24 000	Nombre
Per 100 inhabitants	...	4	15	26	25	25	24	24	Pour 100 habitants
Australia+									Australie+
Number	4 200 000	5 600 000	6 600 000	7 700 000	10 500 000	11 300 000	13 000 000	14 190 000	Nombre
Per 100 inhabitants	22	30	34	40	53	57	65	70	Pour 100 habitants
Austria									Autriche
Number[1]	1 230 000	1 840 000	2 700 000	3 150 000	3 340 000	3 730 000	3 900 000	4 000 000	Nombre[1]
Per 100 inhabitants	15	23	34	39	41	46	48	49	Pour 100 habitants
Azerbaijan									Azerbaïdjan
Number	3 000	8 000	12 000	25 000	300 000	350 000	408 000	678 800	Nombre
Per 100 inhabitants	^0	^0	^0	^0	4	4	5	8	Pour 100 habitants
Bahamas									Bahamas
Number	6 908	11 307	13 130	16 923	60 000[2]	84 000	93 000	103 000	Nombre
Per 100 inhabitants	2	4	4	6	19	27	29	32	Pour 100 habitants
Bahrain									Bahreïn
Number	20 000	30 000	40 000	100 000	122 794	150 000	152 721	155 000	Nombre
Per 100 inhabitants	3	5	6	15	18	21	21	21	Pour 100 habitants
Bangladesh									Bangladesh
Number	5 000	50 000	100 000	186 000	204 000	243 000	300 000	370 000	Nombre
Per 100 inhabitants^	0	0	0	0	0	0	0	0	Pour 100 habitants^
Barbados[3]									Barbade[3]
Number	5 000	6 000	10 000	15 000	30 000[4]	100 000	150 000	160 000	Nombre
Per 100 inhabitants	2	2	4	6	11	37	55	59	Pour 100 habitants
Belarus									Bélarus
Number	7 500	50 000	187 036	430 263	891 227	1 607 048	2 461 093	3 394 421	Nombre
Per 100 inhabitants	^0	^0	2	4	9	16	25	35	Pour 100 habitants

Internet users — Estimated number and number per 100 inhabitants (*continued*)
Usagers d'Internet — Nombre estimatif et nombre pour 100 habitants (*suite*)

Country or area	1998	1999	2000	2001	2002	2003	2004	2005	Pays ou zone
Belgium									Belgique
Number	800 000	1 400 000	3 000 000	3 200 000	3 400 000	4 000 000	4 200 000	4 800 000	Nombre
Per 100 inhabitants	8	14	29	31	33	38	40	46	Pour 100 habitants
Belize+									Belize+
Number	5 000	10 000	15 000	...	...	...	16 000	26 000	Nombre
Per 100 inhabitants	2	4	6	...	...	...	6	10	Pour 100 habitants
Benin									Bénin
Number	3 000	10 000	15 000	25 000	50 000	70 000	100 000	425 000	Nombre
Per 100 inhabitants	^0	^0	^0	^0	1	1	1	6	Pour 100 habitants
Bermuda+									Bermudes+
Number	20 000	25 000	27 000	30 000	...	36 000	39 000	42 000	Nombre
Per 100 inhabitants	32	40	43	48	...	57	61	65	Pour 100 habitants
Bhutan									Bhoutan
Number	...	750	2 250	5 000	10 000	15 000	20 000	25 000	Nombre
Per 100 inhabitants	...	^0	^0	1	1	2	3	3	Pour 100 habitants
Bolivia									Bolivie
Number	50 000[4]	80 000[4]	120 000[4]	180 000[4]	270 000[4]	310 000	400 000	480 000	Nombre
Per 100 inhabitants	1	1	1	2	3	4	4	5	Pour 100 habitants
Bosnia and Herzegovina									Bosnie-Herzégovine
Number	5 000	7 000	40 000	45 000	100 000	150 000[4]	585 000	806 421	Nombre
Per 100 inhabitants	^0	^0	1	1	3	4	15	21	Pour 100 habitants
Botswana+									Botswana+
Number	10 000	19 000	50 000	60 000	60 000	60 000	60 000	60 000	Nombre
Per 100 inhabitants	1	1	3	4	3	3	3	3	Pour 100 habitants
Brazil									Brésil
Number[4]	2 500 000	3 500 000	5 000 000	8 000 000	14 300 000	18 000 000	22 000 000	32 129 971	Nombre[4]
Per 100 inhabitants	1	2	3	5	8	10	12	17	Pour 100 habitants
British Virgin Islands									Iles Vierges britanniques
Number	...	...	...	...	4 000	...	...	...	Nombre
Brunei Darussalam									Brunéi Darussalam
Number	20 000	25 000	30 000	44 039	53 386	69 662	107 799	134 953	Nombre
Per 100 inhabitants	6	8	9	13	16	20	30	36	Pour 100 habitants
Bulgaria									Bulgarie
Number	150 000	234 600	430 000	605 000	630 000	932 000	1 234 000	1 591 705	Nombre
Per 100 inhabitants	2	3	5	8	8	12	16	21	Pour 100 habitants
Burkina Faso									Burkina Faso
Number	5 000	7 000	9 000	19 000	25 000	48 000	53 200	64 600	Nombre
Per 100 inhabitants^	0	0	0	0	0	0	0	0	Pour 100 habitants^
Burundi									Burundi
Number	1 000	2 500	5 000	7 000	8 000	14 000	25 000	40 000	Nombre
Per 100 inhabitants	^0	^0	^0	^0	^0	^0	^0	1	Pour 100 habitants
Cambodia									Cambodge
Number	2 000	4 000	6 000	10 000	30 000	35 000	41 000	44 000	Nombre
Per 100 inhabitants^	0	0	0	0	0	0	0	0	Pour 100 habitants^
Cameroon									Cameroun
Number	2 000	20 000	40 000	45 000	60 000	100 000	170 000	250 000	Nombre
Per 100 inhabitants	^0	^0	^0	^0	^0	1	1	2	Pour 100 habitants
Canada									Canada
Number	7 500 000	11 000 000	12 971 000[5]	14 000 000[6]	15 200 000[4]	17 600 000	20 000 000	22 000 000	Nombre
Per 100 inhabitants	25	36	42	45	48	55	62	68	Pour 100 habitants
Cape Verde									Cap-Vert
Number	2 000	5 000	8 000	12 000	16 000	20 000	25 000	29 000	Nombre
Per 100 inhabitants	^0	1	2	3	4	4	5	6	Pour 100 habitants
Central African Rep.									Rép. centrafricaine
Number	1 000	1 500	2 000	3 000	5 000	6 000	9 000	11 000	Nombre
Per 100 inhabitants^	0	0	0	0	0	0	0	0	Pour 100 habitants^

Country or area	1998	1999	2000	2001	2002	2003	2004	2005	Pays ou zone
Chad									Tchad
Number	335	1 000	3 000	4 000	15 000	30 000	35 000	40 000	Nombre
Per 100 inhabitants^	0	0	0	0	0	0	0	0	Pour 100 habitants^
Chile									Chili
Number	250 000	625 000	2 537 308	3 102 200	3 575 000	4 000 000	4 300 000	4 510 928	Nombre
Per 100 inhabitants	2	4	17	20	24	26	28	29	Pour 100 habitants
China[7]									Chine[7]
Number	2 100 000	8 900 000	22 500 000	33 700 000	59 100 000	79 500 000	94 000 000	111 000 000	Nombre
Per 100 inhabitants	^0	1	2	3	5	6	7	8	Pour 100 habitants
China, Hong Kong SAR+									Chine, Hong Kong RAS+
Number	947 000[4]	1 400 000[4]	1 855 200[8]	2 601 300[8]	2 918 800[8]	3 212 800[8]	3 479 700[8]	3 526 200[8]	Nombre
Per 100 inhabitants	14	21	28	39	43	47	50	50	Pour 100 habitants
China, Macao SAR									Chine, Macao RAS
Number	30 000	40 000	60 000	101 000	115 000	120 000	150 000	170 000	Nombre
Per 100 inhabitants	7	9	14	23	26	27	32	37	Pour 100 habitants
Colombia									Colombie
Number	433 000	664 000	878 000	1 154 000	2 000 113	3 084 232[9]	3 865 860	4 738 544	Nombre
Per 100 inhabitants	1	2	2	3	5	7	9	10	Pour 100 habitants
Comoros									Comores
Number	200	800	1 500	2 500	3 200	5 000	8 000	20 000	Nombre
Per 100 inhabitants	^0	^0	^0	^0	^0	1	1	3	Pour 100 habitants
Congo									Congo
Number	100	500	800	1 000	5 000	15 000	36 000	50 000	Nombre
Per 100 inhabitants	^0	^0	^0	^0	^0	^0	1	1	Pour 100 habitants
Cook Islands[4]									Iles Cook[4]
Number	...	2 300	2 750	3 200	3 600	4 200	4 500	5 000	Nombre
Costa Rica									Costa Rica
Number	100 000	150 000	228 000	384 000	815 745	850 000	885 000	922 500	Nombre
Per 100 inhabitants	3	4	6	10	20	20	21	21	Pour 100 habitants
Côte d'Ivoire									Côte d'Ivoire
Number	10 000	20 000	40 000	70 000	90 000	140 000	160 000	200 000	Nombre
Per 100 inhabitants	^0	^0	^0	^0	1	1	1	1	Pour 100 habitants
Croatia									Croatie
Number	150 000	200 000	299 380	518 000	789 000	1 014 000	1 375 300	1 472 400	Nombre
Per 100 inhabitants	3	4	7	12	18	23	31	32	Pour 100 habitants
Cuba									Cuba
Number	25 000[10]	34 800[10]	60 000[10]	120 000[10]	160 000[10]	98 000[11]	150 000[11]	190 000[11]	Nombre
Per 100 inhabitants	^0	^0	1	1	1	1	1	2	Pour 100 habitants
Cyprus									Chypre
Number	68 000	88 000	120 000	150 000	210 000	250 000	298 000	326 000	Nombre
Per 100 inhabitants	10	13	18	22	29	35	37	39	Pour 100 habitants
Czech Republic									République tchèque
Number	400 000	700 000	1 000 000	1 500 000	2 600 180	2 395 000[12]	2 576 000[12]	2 758 000[12]	Nombre
Per 100 inhabitants	4	7	10	15	25	23	25	27	Pour 100 habitants
Dem. Rep. of the Congo									Rép. dém. du Congo
Number	200	500	3 000	6 000	50 000	75 000	112 500	140 625	Nombre
Per 100 inhabitants^	0	0	0	0	0	0	0	0	Pour 100 habitants^
Denmark									Danemark
Number	1 200 000[4]	1 626 000[13]	2 090 000[13]	2 300 000[4]	2 390 500	2 481 000[4,14]	2 725 000[4,14]	2 854 000[4,14]	Nombre
Per 100 inhabitants	23	31	39	43	44	46	50	53	Pour 100 habitants
Djibouti									Djibouti
Number	650	750	1 400	3 300	4 500	6 500	9 000	10 000	Nombre
Per 100 inhabitants	^0	^0	^0	1	1	1	1	1	Pour 100 habitants
Dominica									Dominique
Number	2 000	2 000	6 000	9 000	12 500	16 000	20 500	26 000	Nombre
Per 100 inhabitants	3	3	8	13	17	22	29	...	Pour 100 habitants

Internet users — Estimated number and number per 100 inhabitants (*continued*)
Usagers d'Internet — Nombre estimatif et nombre pour 100 habitants (*suite*)

Country or area	1998	1999	2000	2001	2002	2003	2004	2005	Pays ou zone
Dominican Republic									Rép. dominicaine
Number	20 000	96 000	327 118	397 333[15]	500 000	650 000	800 000	1 500 000	Nombre
Per 100 inhabitants	^0	1	4	5	6	7	9	17	Pour 100 habitants
Ecuador									Equateur
Number	15 000	100 000	180 000	333 000	537 881	569 727	624 579	968 000	Nombre
Per 100 inhabitants	^0	1	1	3	4	4	5	7	Pour 100 habitants
Egypt									Egypte
Number	100 000[9]	200 000[9]	450 000	600 000	1 900 000	3 000 000	3 900 000	5 100 000	Nombre
Per 100 inhabitants	^0	^0	1	1	3	4	6	7	Pour 100 habitants
El Salvador									El Salvador
Number	25 000	50 000	70 000	150 000	300 000	550 000	587 475	637 000	Nombre
Per 100 inhabitants	^0	1	1	2	5	8	9	9	Pour 100 habitants
Equatorial Guinea									Guinée équatoriale
Number	470	500	700	900	1 800	3 000	5 000	7 000	Nombre
Per 100 inhabitants	^0	^0	^0	^0	^0	1	1	1	Pour 100 habitants
Eritrea									Erythrée
Number	300	900	5 000	6 000	9 000	30 000	50 000	80 000	Nombre
Per 100 inhabitants	^0	^0	^0	^0	^0	1	1	2	Pour 100 habitants
Estonia									Estonie
Number	150 000	200 000	391 600	429 656	444 000	600 000	670 000	690 000	Nombre
Per 100 inhabitants	10	14	27	30	33	44	50	52	Pour 100 habitants
Ethiopia+									Ethiopie+
Number	6 000	8 000	10 000	25 000	50 000	75 000	113 000	164 000	Nombre
Per 100 inhabitants^	0	0	0	0	0	0	0	0	Pour 100 habitants^
Faeroe Islands									Iles Féroé
Number	5 000	10 000	15 000	20 000	25 000	28 000	32 000	33 000	Nombre
Per 100 inhabitants	11	22	33	44	54	60	68	70	Pour 100 habitants
Falkland Is. (Malvinas)									Iles Falkland (Malvinas)
Number	...	1 600	1 700	1 900	1 900	1 900	2 000	2 500	Nombre
Per 100 inhabitants	...	22	33	44	53	59	66	...	Pour 100 habitants
Fiji									Fidji
Number	5 000	7 500	12 000	15 000	50 000	55 000	61 000	70 000	Nombre
Per 100 inhabitants	1	1	1	2	6	7	7	8	Pour 100 habitants
Finland									Finlande
Number[16]	1 311 000	1 667 000	1 927 000	2 235 320	2 529 000	2 560 000	2 680 000	2 800 000[17]	Nombre[16]
Per 100 inhabitants	25	32	37	43	49	49	51	53	Pour 100 habitants
France									France
Number[18]	3 704 000	5 370 000	8 460 000	15 653 000	18 057 000	21 765 000	23 732 000	26 154 000	Nombre[18]
Per 100 inhabitants	6	9	14	26	30	36	39	43	Pour 100 habitants
French Guiana									Guyane française
Number	1 500	2 000	16 000	20 000	25 000	31 000	38 000	42 000	Nombre
Per 100 inhabitants	1	1	10	12	14	17	21	22	Pour 100 habitants
French Polynesia									Polynésie française
Number	3 000	8 000	15 000	15 000	20 000	35 000	45 000	55 000	Nombre
Per 100 inhabitants	1	3	6	6	8	14	18	21	Pour 100 habitants
Gabon									Gabon
Number	2 000	3 000	15 000	17 000	25 000	35 000	40 000	67 000	Nombre
Per 100 inhabitants	^0	^0	1	1	2	3	3	5	Pour 100 habitants
Gambia+									Gambie+
Number	2 500	9 000	12 000	18 000	25 000	35 000	49 000	57 978	Nombre
Per 100 inhabitants	^0	1	1	1	2	3	3	4	Pour 100 habitants
Georgia									Géorgie
Number	5 000	20 000	23 000	46 500	73 500	117 020	175 600	271 420	Nombre
Per 100 inhabitants	^0	^0	^0	1	2	3	4	6	Pour 100 habitants
Germany									Allemagne
Number	8 100 000	17 100 000	24 800 000	26 000 000	28 000 000	33 000 000	35 200 000	37 500 000	Nombre
Per 100 inhabitants	10	21	30	32	34	40	43	43	Pour 100 habitants

Country or area	1998	1999	2000	2001	2002	2003	2004	2005	Pays ou zone
Ghana									Ghana
Number	6 000	20 000	30 000	40 000	170 000	250 000	368 000	401 310	Nombre
Per 100 inhabitants	^0	^0	^0	^0	1	1	2	2	Pour 100 habitants
Greece									Grèce
Number	350 000	750 000	1 000 000	915 347	1 485 281	1 718 435	1 955 000	2 001 000	Nombre
Per 100 inhabitants	3	7	9	9	13	15	18	18	Pour 100 habitants
Greenland									Groenland
Number	8 187	12 102	17 841	20 000	25 000	31 000	38 000	...	Nombre
Per 100 inhabitants	15	22	32	36	44	54	...	...	Pour 100 habitants
Grenada									Grenade
Number	1 500	2 500	4 113	5 200	15 000	19 000	...	...	Nombre
Per 100 inhabitants	1	2	4	5	15	19	...	...	Pour 100 habitants
Guadeloupe									Guadeloupe
Number	2 000	7 000	25 000	40 000	50 000	63 000	79 000	85 000	Nombre
Per 100 inhabitants	^0	2	6	9	11	14	18	19	Pour 100 habitants
Guam									Guam
Number	6 800	13 000	25 000	40 000	50 000	55 000	60 000	65 000	Nombre
Per 100 inhabitants	5	9	16	25	31	34	36	38	Pour 100 habitants
Guatemala									Guatemala
Number	50 000	65 000	80 000	200 000	400 000	550 000	760 000	1 000 000	Nombre
Per 100 inhabitants	^0	1	1	2	3	4	6	8	Pour 100 habitants
Guinea									Guinée
Number	500	5 000	8 000	15 000	35 000	40 000	46 000	50 000	Nombre
Per 100 inhabitants	^0	^0	^0	^0	^0	1	1	1	Pour 100 habitants
Guinea-Bissau									Guinée-Bissau
Number	300	1 500	3 000	4 000	14 000	19 000	26 000	31 000	Nombre
Per 100 inhabitants	^0	^0	^0	^0	1	1	2	2	Pour 100 habitants
Guyana									Guyana
Number	2 000	30 000	50 000	100 000	125 000	140 000	145 000	160 000	Nombre
Per 100 inhabitants	^0	4	7	13	17	19	19	21	Pour 100 habitants
Haiti									Haïti
Number	2 000	6 000	20 000	30 000	80 000	150 000	500 000	600 000	Nombre
Per 100 inhabitants	^0	^0	^0	^0	1	2	6	7	Pour 100 habitants
Honduras									Honduras
Number	18 000	35 000	75 000	90 000	168 560	185 510	222 273	260 000	Nombre
Per 100 inhabitants	^0	1	1	1	3	3	3	4	Pour 100 habitants
Hungary									Hongrie
Number	400 000	600 000	715 000	1 480 000	1 600 000	2 400 000	2 700 000	3 000 000	Nombre
Per 100 inhabitants	4	6	7	15	16	24	27	30	Pour 100 habitants
Iceland									Islande
Number	100 000	115 000	125 000	140 000	150 000	166 000	167 830	182 981	Nombre
Per 100 inhabitants	36	41	44	49	52	57	57	62	Pour 100 habitants
India+									Inde+
Number	1 400 000	2 800 000	5 500 000	7 000 000	16 580 000	18 481 044[19]	35 000 000	60 000 000	Nombre
Per 100 inhabitants	^0	^0	1	1	2	2	3	5	Pour 100 habitants
Indonesia									Indonésie
Number	510 000	900 000	1 900 000	4 200 000	4 500 000	8 080 534	11 226 143	16 000 000	Nombre
Per 100 inhabitants	^0	^0	1	2	2	4	5	7	Pour 100 habitants
Iran (Islamic Rep. of)									Iran (Rép. islamique d')
Number	65 000	250 000	625 000	1 005 000	3 168 000	4 800 000	6 600 000	7 600 000	Nombre
Per 100 inhabitants	^0	^0	1	2	5	7	9	11	Pour 100 habitants
Iraq									Iraq
Number	...	...	...	12 500	25 000	30 000	36 000	...	Nombre
Per 100 inhabitants^	...	...	...	0	0	0	0	...	Pour 100 habitants^
Ireland+									Irlande+
Number	300 000[4]	410 000[12]	679 000[12]	895 000[12]	1 102 000[12]	1 260 000[12]	1 198 000[12]	1 400 000[20]	Nombre
Per 100 inhabitants	8	11	18	23	28	32	30	34	Pour 100 habitants

Country or area	1998	1999	2000	2001	2002	2003	2004	2005	Pays ou zone
Israel+									Israël+
Number	600 000	800 000	1 270 000	1 079 419	1 125 201	1 264 530	1 496 625	1 685 879	Nombre
Per 100 inhabitants	10	13	20	17	17	19	22	24	Pour 100 habitants
Italy									Italie
Number	2 600 000	8 200 000	13 200 000	15 600 000	19 800 000	22 880 000	27 170 000	28 000 000[9]	Nombre
Per 100 inhabitants	5	14	23	27	35	40	47	48	Pour 100 habitants
Jamaica									Jamaïque
Number	50 000	60 000	80 000	100 000	600 000	800 000	1 067 000	1 232 258	Nombre
Per 100 inhabitants	2	2	3	4	23	30	40	46	Pour 100 habitants
Japan									Japon
Number	16 940 000[21]	27 060 000[21]	38 000 000[21]	48 900 000[21]	59 220 000[21]	61 640 000[21]	79 480 000[21]	85 290 000[22]	Nombre
Per 100 inhabitants	13	21	30	38	46	48	62	67	Pour 100 habitants
Jordan									Jordanie
Number	60 816	120 000	127 317	234 000	307 469	444 039	629 524	719 830	Nombre
Per 100 inhabitants	1	2	3	5	6	8	11	13	Pour 100 habitants
Kazakhstan									Kazakhstan
Number	20 000	70 000	100 000	150 000	250 000	300 000	400 000	609 200	Nombre
Per 100 inhabitants	^0	^0	1	1	2	2	3	4	Pour 100 habitants
Kenya+									Kenya+
Number	15 000	35 000	100 000	200 000	400 000	1 000 000	1 054 920	1 111 000	Nombre
Per 100 inhabitants	^0	^0	^0	1	1	3	3	3	Pour 100 habitants
Kiribati									Kiribati
Number	500	1 000	1 500	2 000	2 000	2 000	2 000	2 000	Nombre
Per 100 inhabitants	1	1	2	2	2	2	2	2	Pour 100 habitants
Korea, Republic of									Corée, République de
Number	3 103 000	10 860 000	19 040 000	24 380 000	26 270 000	29 220 000	31 580 000	33 010 000	Nombre
Per 100 inhabitants	7	24	41	51	55	61	66	68	Pour 100 habitants
Kuwait									Koweït
Number	60 000	100 000	150 000	200 000	250 000	567 000	600 000	700 000	Nombre
Per 100 inhabitants	3	5	7	9	11	23	24	26	Pour 100 habitants
Kyrgyzstan									Kirghizistan
Number	3 500	10 000	51 600	150 600	152 000	200 000	263 000	280 000	Nombre
Per 100 inhabitants	^0	^0	1	3	3	4	5	5	Pour 100 habitants
Lao People's Dem. Rep.									Rép. dém. pop. lao
Number	500	2 000	6 000	10 000	15 000	19 000	20 900	25 000	Nombre
Per 100 inhabitants^	0	0	0	0	0	0	0	0	Pour 100 habitants^
Latvia									Lettonie
Number	80 000	105 000	150 000	170 000	310 000	560 000	810 000	1 030 000	Nombre
Per 100 inhabitants	3	4	6	7	13	24	35	45	Pour 100 habitants
Lebanon									Liban
Number	100 000	200 000	300 000	260 000	400 000	500 000	600 000	700 000	Nombre
Per 100 inhabitants	3	6	9	8	12	14	17	20	Pour 100 habitants
Lesotho									Lesotho
Number	200	1 000	4 000	5 000	21 000	30 000	43 000	51 480	Nombre
Per 100 inhabitants	^0	^0	^0	^0	1	2	2	3	Pour 100 habitants
Liberia									Libéria
Number	100	300	500	1 000	...	...	...	...	Nombre
Per 100 inhabitants^	0	0	0	0	...	...	...	...	Pour 100 habitants^
Libyan Arab Jamah.									Jamah. arabe libyenne
Number	...	7 000	10 000	20 000	125 000	160 000	205 000	232 044	Nombre
Per 100 inhabitants	...	^0	^0	^0	2	3	4	4	Pour 100 habitants
Liechtenstein									Liechtenstein
Number	...	...	12 000	15 000	20 000	20 000	22 000	22 000	Nombre
Per 100 inhabitants	...	...	37	45	59	58	64	63	Pour 100 habitants
Lithuania									Lituanie
Number	70 000	103 000	225 000	250 000	500 000	695 700	767 000	882 906	Nombre
Per 100 inhabitants	2	3	6	7	14	20	22	26	Pour 100 habitants

15 Internet users—Estimated number and number per 100 inhabitants (*continued*)
Usagers d'Internet—Nombre estimatif et nombre pour 100 habitants (*suite*)

Country or area	1998	1999	2000	2001	2002	2003	2004	2005	Pays ou zone
Luxembourg									Luxembourg
Number	50 000[4]	75 000[4]	100 000[4]	160 000[23]	165 000[12]	170 000[4]	270 810[4]	315 000[4]	Nombre
Per 100 inhabitants	12	17	23	36	37	38	59	68	Pour 100 habitants
Madagascar									Madagascar
Number	9 000	25 000	30 000	35 000	55 000	70 500	90 000	100 000	Nombre
Per 100 inhabitants	^0	^0	^0	^0	^0	^0	^0	1	Pour 100 habitants
Malawi									Malawi
Number	2 000	10 000	15 000	20 000	27 000	36 000	46 140	52 500	Nombre
Per 100 inhabitants^	0	0	0	0	0	0	0	0	Pour 100 habitants^
Malaysia									Malaisie
Number	1 500 000	2 800 000	4 977 000	6 346 650	7 842 000	8 643 000	9 879 000	11 016 000	Nombre
Per 100 inhabitants	7	13	21	27	32	35	39	42	Pour 100 habitants
Maldives									Maldives
Number	1 500	3 000	6 000	10 000	15 000	17 000	19 000	20 087	Nombre
Per 100 inhabitants	1	1	2	4	5	6	6	...	Pour 100 habitants
Mali									Mali
Number	2 000	6 277	15 000	20 000	25 000	35 000	50 000	60 000	Nombre
Per 100 inhabitants	^0	^0	^0	^0	^0	^0	^0	1	Pour 100 habitants
Malta									Malte
Number	25 000	30 000	51 000	70 000	80 410	96 022	111 634	127 247	Nombre
Per 100 inhabitants	7	8	13	18	20	24	28	32	Pour 100 habitants
Marshall Islands									Iles Marshall
Number	...	500	800	900	1 250	1 400	2 000	2 200	Nombre
Per 100 inhabitants	...	1	2	2	2	3	4	...	Pour 100 habitants
Martinique									Martinique
Number	2 000	5 000	30 000	40 000	60 000	80 000	110 000	130 000	Nombre
Per 100 inhabitants	1	1	8	10	15	20	28	33	Pour 100 habitants
Mauritania									Mauritanie
Number	1 000	3 000	5 000	7 000	10 000	12 000	14 000	20 000	Nombre
Per 100 inhabitants	^0	^0	^0	^0	^0	^0	^0	1	Pour 100 habitants
Mauritius									Maurice
Number	30 000	55 000	87 000	106 000	125 000[23]	150 000	240 000	300 000	Nombre
Per 100 inhabitants	3	5	7	9	10	12	19	24	Pour 100 habitants
Mayotte									Mayotte
Number	...	...	1 800	...	...	...	...	...	Nombre
Per 100 inhabitants	...	...	1	...	...	...	...	...	Pour 100 habitants
Mexico									Mexique
Number	1 222 379	1 822 198	5 058 000	7 410 124	10 764 715	12 218 830	14 036 475	18 091 789	Nombre
Per 100 inhabitants	1	2	5	7	11	12	13	17	Pour 100 habitants
Micronesia (Fed. States of)									Micronésie (Etats féd. de)
Number	2 000	3 000	4 000	5 000	6 000	10 000	12 000	14 000	Nombre
Per 100 inhabitants	2	3	4	5	6	9	11	13	Pour 100 habitants
Monaco									Monaco
Number	...	...	13 500	15 000	15 500	16 000	17 000	18 000	Nombre
Per 100 inhabitants	...	...	40	44	45	46	49	51	Pour 100 habitants
Mongolia									Mongolie
Number	3 400	12 000	30 000	40 000	50 000	142 800	200 000	268 300	Nombre
Per 100 inhabitants	^0	1	1	2	2	6	8	10	Pour 100 habitants
Morocco[24]									Maroc[24]
Number	40 000	50 000	200 000	400 000	700 000	1 000 000	3 500 000[25]	4 600 000	Nombre
Per 100 inhabitants	^0	^0	1	1	2	3	12	15	Pour 100 habitants
Mozambique									Mozambique
Number	3 500	10 000	20 000	30 000	50 000	83 000	138 000	178 000	Nombre
Per 100 inhabitants	^0	^0	^0	^0	^0	^0	1	1	Pour 100 habitants
Myanmar									Myanmar
Number	...	70	...	136	202	11 474	11 682	31 540	Nombre
Per 100 inhabitants^	...	0	...	0	0	0	0	0	Pour 100 habitants^

Internet users — Estimated number and number per 100 inhabitants (*continued*)

Usagers d'Internet — Nombre estimatif et nombre pour 100 habitants (*suite*)

Country or area	1998	1999	2000	2001	2002	2003	2004	2005	Pays ou zone
Namibia+									Namibie+
Number	5 000	6 000	30 000	45 000	50 000	65 000	75 000	80 563	Nombre
Per 100 inhabitants	^0	^0	2	2	3	3	4	4	Pour 100 habitants
Nauru									Nauru
Number	...	...	...	300	...	...	...	...	Nombre
Nepal									Népal
Number	15 000	35 000	50 000	60 000[26]	80 000	100 000	120 000	225 000	Nombre
Per 100 inhabitants	^0	^0	^0	^0	^0	^0	^0	1	Pour 100 habitants^
Netherlands									Pays-Bas
Number	3 500 000	6 200 000	7 000 000	7 900 000	8 200 000	8 500 000	10 000 000	12 060 000[27]	Nombre
Per 100 inhabitants	22	39	44	49	51	52	62	74	Pour 100 habitants
Netherlands Antilles									Antilles néerlandaises
Number	...	2 000	...	...	...	...	...	...	Nombre
Per 100 inhabitants	...	1	...	...	...	...	...	...	Pour 100 habitants
New Caledonia									Nouvelle-Calédonie
Number	4 000	12 000	30 000	40 000	50 000	60 000	70 000	76 000	Nombre
Per 100 inhabitants	2	6	14	18	22	26	30	32	Pour 100 habitants
New Zealand+									Nouvelle-Zélande+
Number	750 000	1 113 000	1 515 000	1 762 000	1 908 000	2 110 000	2 350 000[4]	2 754 000	Nombre
Per 100 inhabitants	20	29	39	45	48	53	59	68	Pour 100 habitants
Nicaragua									Nicaragua
Number	15 000	25 000	50 000	75 000	90 000	100 000	125 000	140 000	Nombre
Per 100 inhabitants	^0	1	1	1	2	2	2	2	Pour 100 habitants
Niger									Niger
Number	300	3 000	4 000	12 000	15 000	19 000	24 000	29 000	Nombre
Per 100 inhabitants^	0	0	0	0	0	0	0	0	Pour 100 habitants^
Nigeria									Nigéria
Number	30 000	50 000	80 000	115 000	420 000	750 000	1 769 661	5 000 000	Nombre
Per 100 inhabitants	^0	^0	^0	^0	^0	1	1	4	Pour 100 habitants
Niue									Nioué
Number	...	300	500	600	700	750	800	850	Nombre
Norway									Norvège
Number	1 000 000[4]	1 100 000[28]	1 200 000[28]	1 319 400[28]	1 398 600[28]	1 583 300[28]	1 792 000[28]	2 702 000[28]	Nombre
Per 100 inhabitants	22	25	27	29	31	35	39	58	Pour 100 habitants
Occupied Palestinian Terr.									Terr. palestinien occupé
Number	...	...	35 000	60 000	105 000	145 000	160 000	243 000	Nombre
Per 100 inhabitants	...	...	1	2	3	4	4	7	Pour 100 habitants
Oman									Oman
Number	20 000	50 000	90 000	120 000	180 000	210 000	245 000	285 000	Nombre
Per 100 inhabitants	1	2	4	5	7	8	10	11	Pour 100 habitants
Pakistan									Pakistan
Number	61 900	80 000	300 000	500 000	1 000 000	8 000 000	10 000 000	10 500 000	Nombre
Per 100 inhabitants	^0	^0	^0	^0	1	5	7	7	Pour 100 habitants
Panama									Panama
Number	43 375	61 700	107 455	121 425	144 963	173 085	196 548	206 200	Nombre
Per 100 inhabitants	2	2	4	4	5	6	6	6	Pour 100 habitants
Papua New Guinea									Papouasie-Nvl-Guinée
Number	12 000	35 000	45 000	50 000	75 000	80 000	90 000	105 000	Nombre
Per 100 inhabitants	^0	1	1	1	1	2	2	2	Pour 100 habitants
Paraguay									Paraguay
Number	10 000	20 000	40 000	60 000	100 000	120 000	200 000	200 000	Nombre
Per 100 inhabitants	^0	^0	1	1	2	2	3	3	Pour 100 habitants
Peru									Pérou
Number	300 000[4]	500 000[4]	800 000[4]	2 000 000	2 400 000	2 850 000	3 220 000[4]	4 600 000[4]	Nombre
Per 100 inhabitants	1	2	3	8	9	10	12	16	Pour 100 habitants

Country or area	1998	1999	2000	2001	2002	2003	2004	2005	Pays ou zone
Philippines									Philippines
Number	823 000	1 090 000	1 540 000	2 000 000	3 500 000	4 000 000	4 400 000	4 614 759	Nombre
Per 100 inhabitants	1	1	2	3	4	5	5	5	Pour 100 habitants
Poland									Pologne
Number	1 581 000	2 100 000	2 800 000	3 800 000	8 880 000	8 970 000[4]	9 000 000	10 000 000	Nombre
Per 100 inhabitants	4	5	7	10	23	23	23	26	Pour 100 habitants
Portugal									Portugal
Number	1 000 000	1 500 000	1 680 200[4]	1 860 400[4]	2 267 200[4]	2 674 000	2 575 727	2 856 116[27]	Nombre
Per 100 inhabitants	10	15	17	18	22	26	24	27	Pour 100 habitants
Puerto Rico[29]									Porto Rico[29]
Number	100 000	200 000	400 000	600 000	677 000	764 000	862 000	915 618	Nombre
Per 100 inhabitants	3	5	11	16	18	20	22	23	Pour 100 habitants
Qatar									Qatar
Number	20 000	24 000	30 000	40 000	70 000	140 760	165 000	219 000	Nombre
Per 100 inhabitants	4	4	5	6	10	20	22	28	Pour 100 habitants
Republic of Moldova									République de Moldova
Number	11 000	25 000	52 600	60 000	150 000	288 000	406 000	550 000	Nombre
Per 100 inhabitants	^0	1	1	1	4	7	10	13	Pour 100 habitants
Réunion									Réunion
Number[30]	9 000	10 000	100 000	120 000	150 000	180 000	200 000	220 000	Nombre[30]
Per 100 inhabitants	1	1	14	16	20	24	26	28	Pour 100 habitants
Romania									Roumanie
Number	500 000	600 000	800 000	1 000 000	2 200 000	4 000 000	4 500 000	4 772 971	Nombre
Per 100 inhabitants	2	3	4	4	10	18	21	22	Pour 100 habitants
Russian Federation									Fédération de Russie
Number	1 200 000	1 500 000	2 900 000	4 300 000	6 000 000	12 000 000	18 500 000	21 800 000	Nombre
Per 100 inhabitants	1	1	2	3	4	8	13	15	Pour 100 habitants
Rwanda									Rwanda
Number	800	5 000	5 000	20 000	25 000	31 000	38 000	50 000	Nombre
Per 100 inhabitants	^0	^0	^0	^0	^0	^0	^0	1	Pour 100 habitants
Saint Helena									Sainte-Hélène
Number	79	300	300	400[26]	500	600	700	750	Nombre
Saint Kitts and Nevis									Saint-Kitts-et-Nevis
Number	1 500	2 000	2 700	3 600	10 000	...	...	...	Nombre
Per 100 inhabitants	4	5	7	9	24	...	...	...	Pour 100 habitants
Saint Lucia									Sainte-Lucie
Number	2 000	3 000	8 000	13 000	...	34 000	55 000	...	Nombre
Per 100 inhabitants	1	2	5	8	...	21	34	...	Pour 100 habitants
Saint Vincent-Grenadines									St. Vincent-Grenadines
Number	2 000	3 000	3 500	5 500	6 000	7 000	8 000	10 000	Nombre
Per 100 inhabitants	2	3	3	5	5	6	7	8	Pour 100 habitants
Samoa									Samoa
Number	400	500	1 000	3 000	4 000	5 000	5 500	6 000	Nombre
Per 100 inhabitants	^0	^0	1	2	2	3	3	3	Pour 100 habitants
San Marino									Saint-Marin
Number	370	11 360	13 150	13 850	14 340	14 481	15 000	15 200	Nombre
Per 100 inhabitants	5	9	11	12	13	13	20	...	Pour 100 habitants
Sao Tome and Principe									Sao Tomé-et-Principe
Number	400	500	6 500	9 000	11 000	15 000	20 000	23 000	Nombre
Per 100 inhabitants	^0	^0	5	6	8	10	13	15	Pour 100 habitants
Saudi Arabia									Arabie saoudite
Number	20 000	100 000	460 000	1 000 000	1 400 000	1 800 000	2 360 000	3 000 000	Nombre
Per 100 inhabitants	^0	^0	2	5	6	8	10	12	Pour 100 habitants
Senegal									Sénégal
Number	7 500	30 000	40 000	100 000	105 000	225 000	482 000	540 000	Nombre
Per 100 inhabitants	^0	^0	^0	1	1	2	5	5	Pour 100 habitants

Internet users — Estimated number and number per 100 inhabitants (*continued*)
Usagers d'Internet — Nombre estimatif et nombre pour 100 habitants (*suite*)

Country or area	1998	1999	2000	2001	2002	2003	2004	2005	Pays ou zone
Serbia and Montenegro									Serbie-et-Monténégro
Number	65 000	80 000	400 000	600 000	640 000	847 000	1 517 015	...	Nombre
Per 100 inhabitants	1	1	4	6	8	10	19	...	Pour 100 habitants
Seychelles									Seychelles
Number	2 000	5 000	6 000[4]	9 000[26]	11 736	12 000	20 000	21 000	Nombre
Per 100 inhabitants	3	7	8	12	15	15	25	26	Pour 100 habitants
Sierra Leone									Sierra Leone
Number	600	2 000	5 000	7 000	8 000	9 000	10 000	...	Nombre
Per 100 inhabitants^	0	0	0	0	0	0	0	...	Pour 100 habitants^
Singapore+									Singapour+
Number[4]	750 000	950 000	1 300 000	1 700 000	2 100 000	2 135 034	2 421 782	1 731 585[12]	Nombre[4]
Per 100 inhabitants	19	24	32	41	50	51	58	40	Pour 100 habitants
Slovakia									Slovaquie
Number	144 539	292 359	507 029	674 039	862 833	1 375 809	1 652 214	1 905 150	Nombre
Per 100 inhabitants	3	5	9	13	16	26	31	35	Pour 100 habitants
Slovenia									Slovénie
Number	200 000	250 000	300 000	600 000	750 000	800 000	950 000	1 090 000	Nombre
Per 100 inhabitants	10	13	15	30	38	40	48	55	Pour 100 habitants
Solomon Islands									Iles Salomon
Number	2 000	2 000	2 000	2 000	2 200	2 500	3 000	4 000	Nombre
Per 100 inhabitants	1	^0	^0	^0	^0	1	1	1	Pour 100 habitants
Somalia									Somalie
Number	500	1 000	15 000	6 000	9 000	30 000	86 000	90 000	Nombre
Per 100 inhabitants	^0	^0	^0	^0	^0	^0	1	1	Pour 100 habitants
South Africa+									Afrique du Sud+
Number	1 266 000	1 820 000	2 400 000	2 890 000	3 100 000	3 325 000	3 566 000	5 100 000	Nombre
Per 100 inhabitants	3	4	5	6	7	7	8	11	Pour 100 habitants
Spain									Espagne
Number[31]	1 733 000	2 830 000	5 486 000	7 388 000	7 856 000	15 300 000	15 140 000	17 233 000	Nombre[31]
Per 100 inhabitants	4	7	14	18	19	36	35	40	Pour 100 habitants
Sri Lanka									Sri Lanka
Number	55 000	65 000	121 500	150 000	200 000	280 000	280 000	350 000	Nombre
Per 100 inhabitants	^0	^0	1	1	1	1	1	2	Pour 100 habitants
Sudan									Soudan
Number	2 000	5 000	30 000	150 000	300 000	937 000	1 140 000	2 800 000	Nombre
Per 100 inhabitants	^0	^0	^0	^0	1	3	3	8	Pour 100 habitants
Suriname									Suriname
Number	7 587	8 715	11 709	14 520	20 000	23 000	30 000	32 000	Nombre
Per 100 inhabitants	2	2	3	3	5	5	7	7	Pour 100 habitants
Swaziland									Swaziland
Number	1 000[32]	5 000[32]	10 000[32]	14 000[32]	20 000[32]	27 000[32]	36 000[32]	41 569	Nombre
Per 100 inhabitants	^0	1	1	1	2	3	3	4	Pour 100 habitants
Sweden									Suède
Number	2 961 000	3 666 000	4 048 000	4 600 000	5 125 000	5 655 000	6 800 000[27]	6 890 000[27]	Nombre
Per 100 inhabitants	33	41	46	52	57	63	75	76	Pour 100 habitants
Switzerland									Suisse
Number	939 000	1 473 000	2 096 000	2 800 000	3 000 000	3 300 000	3 500 000	3 800 000	Nombre
Per 100 inhabitants	13	21	29	39	41	45	47	51	Pour 100 habitants
Syrian Arab Republic									Rép. arabe syrienne
Number	10 000	20 000	30 000	60 000	365 000	610 000	800 000	1 100 000	Nombre
Per 100 inhabitants	^0	^0	^0	^0	2	3	4	6	Pour 100 habitants
Tajikistan									Tadjikistan
Number	...	2 000	3 000	3 200	3 500	4 120	5 000	19 521	Nombre
Per 100 inhabitants^	...	0	0	0	0	0	0	0	Pour 100 habitants^
Thailand+									Thaïlande+
Number	500 000	1 300 000	2 300 000	3 536 019	4 800 000	6 030 000[33]	6 971 502	7 284 200	Nombre
Per 100 inhabitants	1	2	4	6	8	10	11	11	Pour 100 habitants

Country or area	1998	1999	2000	2001	2002	2003	2004	2005	Pays ou zone
TFYR of Macedonia									L'ex-R.y. Macédoine
Number	20 000	30 000	50 000	70 000	100 000	126 000	159 000	159 889	Nombre
Per 100 inhabitants	1	2	2	3	5	6	8	8	Pour 100 habitants
Togo									Togo
Number	15 000	30 000	100 000	150 000	200 000	210 000	221 000	300 000	Nombre
Per 100 inhabitants	^0	1	2	3	4	4	4	6	Pour 100 habitants
Tonga									Tonga
Number	750	1 000	2 400	2 800	2 900	3 000	3 000	3 000	Nombre
Per 100 inhabitants	1	1	2	3	3	3	3	3	Pour 100 habitants
Trinidad and Tobago									Trinité-et-Tobago
Number	35 000	75 000	100 000	120 000[19]	138 000[19]	153 000	160 000	163 000	Nombre
Per 100 inhabitants	3	6	8	9	11	12	12	12	Pour 100 habitants
Tunisia									Tunisie
Number	10 000	150 000	260 000	410 000	505 500	630 000	835 000	953 770	Nombre
Per 100 inhabitants	^0	2	3	4	5	6	8	9	Pour 100 habitants
Turkey									Turquie
Number	450 000	1 500 000	2 500 000	3 500 000	4 300 000	6 000 000	10 220 000	11 204 340	Nombre
Per 100 inhabitants	1	2	4	5	6	8	14	15	Pour 100 habitants
Turkmenistan									Turkménistan
Number	...	2 000	6 000	8 000	14 000	20 000[4]	36 000	48 299	Nombre
Per 100 inhabitants	...	^0	^0	^0	^0	^0	1	1	Pour 100 habitants
Tuvalu									Tuvalu
Number	...	...	500	1 000	1 250	1 500	1 600	1 700	Nombre
Per 100 inhabitants	...	...	1	2	3	3	...	...	Pour 100 habitants
Uganda									Ouganda
Number	15 000	25 000	40 000	60 000	100 000	125 000	200 000	500 000	Nombre
Per 100 inhabitants	^0	^0	^0	^0	^0	^0	1	2	Pour 100 habitants
Ukraine									Ukraine
Number	150 000	200 000	350 000	600 000	900 000	2 500 000	3 750 000	4 560 000	Nombre
Per 100 inhabitants	^0	^0	1	1	2	5	8	10	Pour 100 habitants
United Arab Emirates									Emirats arabes unis
Number	200 000	458 000	765 000	896 826	1 016 796	1 110 207	1 185 000	1 321 693	Nombre
Per 100 inhabitants	7	15	24	26	27	27	28	29	Pour 100 habitants
United Kingdom+									Royaume-Uni+
Number	8 000 000[4]	12 500 000[4]	15 800 000[34]	19 800 000[34]	25 000 000[34]	26 025 000[34]	28 094 000[34]	32 076 000[34]	Nombre
Per 100 inhabitants	14	21	26	33	42	44	47	54	Pour 100 habitants
United Rep. of Tanzania									Rép.-Unie de Tanzanie
Number	3 000	25 000	40 000	60 000	80 000	250 000	333 000	384 323	Nombre
Per 100 inhabitants	^0	^0	^0	^0	^0	1	1	1	Pour 100 habitants
United States									Etats-Unis
Number[4]	84 587 000	102 000 000	124 000 000	142 823 000	159 000 000	161 632 400	185 000 000	197 800 000	Nombre[4]
Per 100 inhabitants	31	37	44	50	55	56	63	66	Pour 100 habitants
United States Virgin Is.									Iles Vierges américaines
Number	10 000	12 000	15 000	20 000	30 000	30 000	30 000	30 000	Nombre
Per 100 inhabitants	9	11	14	18	27	27	27	27	Pour 100 habitants
Uruguay									Uruguay
Number	230 000	330 000	350 000	370 000	380 000	530 000	567 175	668 000	Nombre
Per 100 inhabitants	7	10	11	12	12	16	17	21	Pour 100 habitants
Uzbekistan									Ouzbékistan
Number	5 000	7 500	120 000	150 000	275 000	492 000	675 000	880 000	Nombre
Per 100 inhabitants	^0	^0	^0	1	1	2	3	3	Pour 100 habitants
Vanuatu									Vanuatu
Number	500	1 000	4 000	5 500	7 000	7 500	7 500	7 500	Nombre
Per 100 inhabitants	^0	1	2	3	3	4	3	3	Pour 100 habitants
Venezuela (Bolivarian Rep. of)									Venezuela (Rép. boliv. du)
Number	325 000	680 000	820 000	1 153 000	1 244 000	1 934 791	2 207 136	3 354 921	Nombre
Per 100 inhabitants	1	3	3	5	5	8	8	13	Pour 100 habitants

Internet users — Estimated number and number per 100 inhabitants (*continued*)
Usagers d'Internet — Nombre estimatif et nombre pour 100 habitants (*suite*)

Country or area	1998	1999	2000	2001	2002	2003	2004	2005	Pays ou zone
Viet Nam									Viet Nam
Number	10 000	100 000	200 000	1 009 544	1 500 000	3 098 007	6 345 049	10 710 980	Nombre
Per 100 inhabitants	^0	^0	^0	1	2	4	8	13	Pour 100 habitants
Yemen									Yémen
Number	4 000	10 000	15 000	17 000	100 000	120 000	180 000	220 454	Nombre
Per 100 inhabitants	^0	^0	^0	^0	1	1	1	1	Pour 100 habitants
Zambia+									Zambie+
Number	3 000	15 000	20 000	25 000	52 420[19]	110 000	231 000	334 751	Nombre
Per 100 inhabitants	^0	^0	^0	^0	^0	1	2	3	Pour 100 habitants
Zimbabwe+									Zimbabwe+
Number[4]	10 000	20 000	50 000	100 000	500 000	800 000	820 000	1 000 000	Nombre[4]
Per 100 inhabitants	^0	^0	^0	1	4	7	7	8	Pour 100 habitants

Source

International Telecommunication Union (ITU), Geneva, the ITU database.

Notes

\+ Note: The data shown generally relate to the fiscal year used in each country, unless indicated otherwise. Countries whose reference periods coincide with the calendar year ending 31 December are not listed.

Year beginning 22 March: Iran (Islamic Republic).

Year beginning 1 April: Antigua and Barbuda, Barbados, Belize, Bermuda, Botswana, British Virgin Islands, Cayman Islands, China - Hong Kong, Cook Islands, Dominica, Gambia, India, Ireland, Israel (prior to 1986), Jamaica, Japan, Lesotho, Seychelles, Singapore (beginning 1983), Solomon Islands, South Africa, St. Helena, St. Kitts and Nevis, St. Lucia, St. Vincent and the Grenadines, Swaziland, Trinidad and Tobago, United Kingdom, and Zambia.

Year ending 30 June: Australia, Bangladesh, Egypt, Ethiopia, Iraq, Kenya, New Zealand (beginning 2000; prior to 2000, year ending 1 April), Pakistan, Uganda, and Zimbabwe.

Year ending 15 July: Nepal.

Year ending 30 September: Argentina (beginning 1991), Namibia (beginning 1993), and Thailand.

1 Regular users of the Internet, age 14+.

2 ITU estimate based on 3 times the number of subscribers.

3 Prior to 2002, data refer to BET and Bartel. Beginning 2002, data refer to Cable and Wireless.

4 ITU estimate.

5 Population age 15+ using in last year.

6 Population age 18+ using in last week.

7 For statistical purposes, the data for China do not include those for the Hong Kong Special Administrative Region (Hong Kong SAR), Macao Special Administrative Region (Macao SAR) and Taiwan Province of China.

8 Population age 10+ who accessed Internet in previous year.

9 June.

10 Including those who used only international email.

11 Only persons who use Internet (not just email).

12 Age 15+.

Source

Union internationale des télécommunications (UIT), Genève, la base de données de l'UIT.

Notes

\+ Note: Sauf indication contraire, les données indiquées concernent généralement l'exercice budgétaire utilisé dans chaque pays. Les pays ou territoires dont la période de référence coïncide avec l'année civile se terminant le 31 décembre ne sont pas répertoriés ci-dessous.

Exercice commençant le 22 mars : Iran (République islamique d').

Exercice commençant le 1er avril : Afrique du Sud, Antigua-et-Barbuda, Barbade, Belize, Bermudes, Botswana, Chine-Hong Kong, Dominique, Gambie, Îles Caïmanes, Îles Cook, Îles Salomon, Îles Vierges britanniques, Inde, Irlande, Israël (antérieur à 1986), Jamaïque, Japon, Lesotho, Royaume-Uni, Saint-Kitts-et-Nevis, Saint-Vincent-et-les Grenadines, Sainte-Hélène, Sainte-Lucie, Seychelles, Singapour (à partir de 1983), Swaziland, Trinité-et-Tobago et Zambie.

Exercice se terminant le 30 juin : Australie, Bangladesh, Égypte, Éthiopie, Iraq, Kenya, Nouvelle-Zélande (à partir de 2000; avant 2000, exercice se terminant le 1er avril), Ouganda, Pakistan et Zimbabwe.

Exercice se terminant le 15 juillet : Népal.

Exercice se terminant le 30 septembre : Argentine (à partir de 1991), Namibie (à partir de 1993), et Thaïlande.

1 Utilisateurs réguliers de l'Internet âgés de plus de 14 ans.

2 Estimation de l'UIT basée sur le nombre d'abonnés multiplié par 3.

3 Avant 2002, les données se réfèrent au "BET" et "Bartel". A partir de 2002 les données se réfèrent au "Cable and Wireless".

4 Estimation de l'UIT.

5 Population âgée de plus de 15 ans utilisant au cours de l'année écoulée.

6 Population âgée de plus de 18 ans utilisant au cours de la dernière semaine.

7 Pour la présentation des statistiques, les données pour la Chine ne comprennent pas la Région Administrative Spéciale de Hong Kong (Hong Kong RAS), la Région Administrative Spéciale de Macao (Macao RAS) et la province de Taiwan.

8 Population âgée de plus de 10 ans s'étant branchée sur l'Internet au cours de l'année écoulée.

9 Juin.

10 Y compris ceux qui n'ont utilisé que des services internationaux de messagerie électronique.

11 Exclusivement les utilisateurs d'Internet (mais non seulement du courrier électronique).

12 Population âgée de plus de 15 ans.

13 e-Mail users.

14 Age 15-74 using at least once in the last week

15 As of 30 September.

16 Has used at least one other Internet application besides e-mail in last 3 months. Age 15+.

17 Persons aged 15 to 74 years.

18 1996-98, 18+; 1999-00, 15+ using in the last year; from 2001, 11+, using in the last month.

19 December.

20 Those who used Internet in the last 3 months.

21 PC-based only.

22 Including users accessing internet through cellphones, PHS and game console.

23 Age 12+.

24 Including Western Sahara.

25 Including users who went on the internet at least once, no matter the location.

26 Data refer to 31 December.

27 Persons aged 16 to 74 years.

28 Norsk Gallup.

29 Data refer to the Puerto Rico Telephone Authority.

30 France Télécom only.

31 At November of year indicated. Age 14+.

32 Note: The data shown generally relate to the fiscal year used in each country, unless indicated otherwise. Countries whose reference periods coincide with the calendar year ending 31 December are not listed. Year beginning 22 March: Iran (Islamic Republic).Year beginning 1 April: Antigua and Barbuda, Barbados, Belize, Bermuda, British Virgin Islands, Cayman Islands, China - Hong Kong SAR, Cook Islands, Dominica, Gambia, India, Ireland, Jamaica, Japan, Lesotho, Seychelles, Singapore (beginning 1983), Solomon Islands, South Africa, St. Helena, St. Kitts and Nevis, St. Lucia, St. Vincent and the Grenadines, Swaziland, Trinidad and Tobago, United Kingdom, and Zambia.Year ending 30 June: Australia, Bangladesh, Egypt (prior to 2000), Ethiopia, Iraq, Kenya, New Zealand (beginning 2000; prior to 2000, year ending 1 April), Pakistan, Uganda, and Zimbabwe.Year ending 15 July: Nepal.Year ending 30 September: Argentina, Namibia (beginning 1993), and Thailand.

33 Age 6+.

34 Adult (age 16+) population using the internet in the last 3 months.

13 Utilisateurs de courrier électronique.

14 Personnes de 15 à 74 ans l'ayant utilisé au moins une fois au cours de la semaine précédente.

15 Au 30 septembre.

16 A utilisé au moins une application Internet autre que le courrier électronique au cours des trois derniers mois. Population âgée de plus de 15 ans.

17 Personnes âgées de 15 à 74 ans.

18 1996 à 1998, population âgée de plus de 18 ans; 1999 à 2000, 15+ ayant utilisé l'Internet au cours de la dernière année; à partir de 2001, population âgée de plus de 11 ans ayant utilisé l'Internet au cours du dernier mois.

19 Décembre.

20 Personnes ayant utilisé Internet au cours des trois derniers mois.

21 Pour ordinateurs personnels seulement.

22 Comprend les utilisateurs qui naviguent sur Internet au moyen de téléphones mobiles, de téléphones PHS et de consoles de jeux.

23 Population âgée de plus de 12 ans.

24 Y compris les données de Sahara occidental.

25 Y compris les usagers ayant accédé à l'Internet une fois au moins quel que soit le lieu.

26 Les données se réfèrent au 31 décembre.

27 Personnes âgées de 16 à 74 ans.

28 Norsk Gallup.

29 Les données se réfèrent à "Puerto Rico Telephone Authority".

30 France Télécom seulement.

31 En november de l'année indiquée. Population agée de plus de 14 ans.

32 Note: sauf indication contraire, les données indiquées concernent généralement l'exercice budgétaire utilisé dans chaque pays. Les pays ou territoires dont la période de référence coïncide avec l'année civile se terminant le 31 décembre ne sont pas répertoriés ci-dessous. Exercice commençant le 22 mars : Iran (République islamique d'). Exercice commençant le 1er avril : Afrique du Sud, Antigua-et-Barbuda, Barbade, Belize, Bermudes, Chine - Hong Kong RAS, Dominique, Gambie, Îles Caïmanes, Îles Cook, Îles Salomon, Îles Vierges britanniques, Inde, Irlande, Jamaïque, Japon, Lesotho, Royaume-Uni, Saint-Kitts-et-Nevis, Saint-Vincent-et-les Grenadines, Sainte-Hélène, Sainte-Lucie, Seychelles, Singapour (à partir de 1983), Swaziland, Trinité-et-Tobago et Zambie.Exercice se terminant le 30 juin : Australie, Bangladesh, Égypte (antérieur à 2000), Éthiopie, Iraq, Kenya, Nouvelle-Zélande (à partir de 2000; avant 2000, exercice se terminant le 1er avril), Ouganda, Pakistan et Zimbabwe.Exercice se terminant le 15 juillet : Népal.Exercice se terminant le 30 septembre : Argentine, Namibie (à partir de 1993), et Thaïlande.

33 Population âgée de plus de 6 ans.

34 Population agée de plus de 16 ans utilisant au cours des trois derniers mois.

Technical notes: tables 13-15

The statistics included in *Tables 13-15* were obtained from the statistics database (see www.itu.int) and the *Yearbook of Statistics, Telecommunication Services* of the International Telecommunication Union.

Table 13: The number of mobile cellular telephone subscribers (as well as the number of subscribers per 100 inhabitants) refers to users of portable telephones subscribing to an automatic public mobile telephone service using cellular technology which provides access to the Public Switched Telephone Network (PSTN). The number of subscribers per 100 inhabitants is calculated by dividing the number of subscribers by the population and multiplying by 100.

Table 14: This table shows the number of main (fixed) lines in operation and the main lines in operation per 100 inhabitants for the years indicated. Main telephone lines refer to the telephone lines connecting a customer's equipment to the Public Switched Telephone Network (PSTN) and which have a dedicated port on a telephone exchange. Note that in most countries, main lines also include public telephones. The number of main telephone lines per 100 inhabitants is calculated by dividing the number of main lines by the population and multiplying by 100.

Table 15: The estimated number of Internet users is measured in a growing number of countries through regular surveys. In situations where surveys are not available, an estimate can be derived based on the number of subscribers. The number of users per 100 inhabitants is calculated by dividing the number of users by the population and multiplying by 100.

Notes techniques : tableaux 13 à 15

Les données présentées dans les *Tableaux 13 à 15* proviennent de la base de données (voir www.itu.int) et *l'Annuaire statistique, Services de télécommunications* de l'Union internationale des télécommunications.

Tableau 13: Les abonnés mobiles (et les abonnés mobiles pour 100 habitants) désignent les utilisateurs de téléphones portatifs abonnés à un service automatique public de téléphones mobiles ayant accès au Réseau de téléphone public connecté (RTPC). Le nombre d'abonnés pour 100 habitants se calcule en divisant le nombre d'abonnés par la population et en multipliant par 100.

Tableau 14: Ce tableau indique le nombre de lignes principales (fixes) en service et les lignes principales en service pour 100 habitants pour les années indiquées. Les lignes principales sont des lignes téléphoniques qui relient l'équipement terminal de l'abonné au Réseau de téléphone public connecté (RTPC) et qui possèdent un accès individualisé aux équipements d'un central téléphonique. Pour la plupart des pays, le nombre de lignes principales en service indiqué comprend également les lignes publiques. Le nombre de lignes principales pour 100 habitants se calcule en divisant le nombre de lignes principales par la population et en multipliant par 100.

Tableau 15: Le nombre d'utilisateurs d'internet est recensé à l'aide d'enquêtes standards dans un nombre croissant de pays. Quand les enquêtes ne sont pas disponibles, il est estimé grâce au nombre d'abonnés. Le nombre d'utilisateurs pour 100 habitants est calculé en divisant le nombre d'utilisateurs par le nombre d'habitants, multiplié par 100.

Part Three

Economic activity

Troisième partie

Activité économique

Chapter VI	National accounts and industrial production (tables 16-22)
Chapter VII	Financial statistics (tables 23 and 24)
Chapter VIII	Labour force (table 25 and 26)
Chapter IX	Wages and prices (tables 27-29)
Chapter X	Agriculture (tables 30-35)
Chapter XI	Manufacturing (tables 36-45)
Chapter XII	Transport equipment and transportation services (tables 46-49)
Chapter XIII	Energy (tables 50 and 51)
Chapter XIV	Environment (tables 52-55)
Chapter XV	Science and technology (tables 56 and 57)

Part Three of the *Yearbook* presents statistical series on production and consumption for a wide range of economic activities, and other basic series on major economic topics, for all countries or areas of the world for which data are available. Included are basic tables on national accounts, finance, labour force, wages and prices, a wide range of agricultural, mined and manufactured commodities, transport, energy, environment and research and development personnel and expenditure.

International economic topics such as external trade are covered in Part Four.

Chapitre VI	Comptabilités nationales et production industrielle (tableaux 16 à 22)
Chapitre VII	Statistiques financières (tableaux 23 et 24)
Chapitre VIII	Main-d'œuvre (tableaux 25 et 26)
Chapitre IX	Salaires et prix (tableaux 27 à 29)
Chapitre X	Agriculture (tableaux 30 à 35)
Chapitre XI	Industries manufacturières (tableaux 36 à 45)
Chapitre XII	Matériel de transport et services de transports (tableaux 46 à 49)
Chapitre XIII	Energie (tableaux 50 et 51)
Chapitre XIV	Environnement (tableaux 52 à 55)
Chapitre XV	Science et technologie (tableaux 56 et 57)

La troisième partie de l'*Annuaire* présente, pour une large gamme d'activités économiques, des séries statistiques sur la production et la consommation, et, pour tous les pays ou zones du monde pour lesquels des données sont disponibles, d'autres séries fondamentales ayant trait à des questions économiques importantes. Y figurent des tableaux de base consacrés à la comptabilité nationale, aux finances, à la main-d'œuvre, aux salaires et aux prix, à un large éventail de produits agricoles, miniers et manufacturés, aux transports, à l'énergie, à l'environnement, au personnel employé à des travaux de recherche et développement et dépenses de recherche et développement.

Les questions économiques internationales comme le commerce extérieur sont traitées dans la quatrième partie.

16 Gross domestic product and gross domestic product per capita

In millions of US dollars at current and constant 1990 prices; per capita US dollars; real rates of growth

Produit intérieur brut et produit intérieur brut par habitant

En millions de dollars E.U. aux prix courants et constants de 1990 ; par habitant en dollars E.U. ; taux de croissance réels

Country or area	1999	2000	2001	2002	2003	2004	2005	Pays ou zone
World								**Monde**
GDP at current prices	**30 852 912**	**31 678 619**	**31 462 473**	**32 717 346**	**36 756 087**	**41 278 164**	**44 475 204**	**PIB aux prix courants**
GDP per capita	**5 130**	**5 210**	**5 110**	**5 240**	**5 820**	**6 460**	**6 880**	**PIB par habitant**
GDP at constant prices	**27 738 931**	**28 893 679**	**29 382 464**	**29 953 781**	**30 780 742**	**32 019 643**	**33 118 350**	**PIB aux prix constants**
Growth rates	**3.3**	**4.2**	**1.7**	**1.9**	**2.8**	**4.0**	**3.4**	**Taux de croissance**
Afghanistan								**Afghanistan**
GDP at current prices	3 016	2 963	2 221	4 411	4 585	5 319	6 504	PIB aux prix courants
GDP per capita	131	125	90	170	168	186	218	PIB par habitant
GDP at constant prices	3 824	2 539	2 300	2 983	3 537	3 820	4 346	PIB aux prix constants
Growth rates	-5.9	-33.6	-9.4	29.7	18.6	8.0	13.8	Taux de croissance
Albania								**Albanie**
GDP at current prices	3 490	3 709	4 114	4 505	5 859	7 549	8 538	PIB aux prix courants
GDP per capita	1 139	1 211	1 342	1 464	1 894	2 426	2 728	PIB par habitant
GDP at constant prices	2 294	2 444	2 618	2 731	2 886	3 079	3 264	PIB aux prix constants
Growth rates	13.3	6.5	7.1	4.3	5.7	6.7	6.0	Taux de croissance
Algeria								**Algérie**
GDP at current prices	48 641	54 790	55 181	56 948	68 017	85 021	102 257	PIB aux prix courants
GDP per capita	1 620	1 799	1 785	1 815	2 134	2 628	3 112	PIB par habitant
GDP at constant prices	71 560	73 277	75 183	78 265	83 983	88 350	93 033	PIB aux prix constants
Growth rates	3.2	2.4	2.6	4.1	7.3	5.2	5.3	Taux de croissance
Andorra								**Andorre**
GDP at current prices	1 436	1 360	1 538	1 809	2 378	2 786	3 091	PIB aux prix courants
GDP per capita	21 782	20 624	23 263	27 253	35 675	41 621	46 029	PIB par habitant
GDP at constant prices	1 540	1 618	1 833	1 981	2 111	2 175	2 332	PIB aux prix constants
Growth rates	2.1	5.0	13.3	8.1	6.6	3.0	7.2	Taux de croissance
Angola								**Angola**
GDP at current prices	6 153	9 130	8 936	10 960	13 825	19 498	28 853	PIB aux prix courants
GDP per capita	456	660	629	750	919	1 259	1 810	PIB par habitant
GDP at constant prices	10 779	11 104	11 453	13 097	13 549	15 067	17 277	PIB aux prix constants
Growth rates	3.2	3.0	3.1	14.4	3.4	11.2	14.7	Taux de croissance
Anguilla								**Anguilla**
GDP at current prices	106	108	110	113	118	146	157	PIB aux prix courants
GDP per capita	9 600	9 617	9 646	9 733	9 960	12 191	12 840	PIB par habitant
GDP at constant prices	84	85	88	86	88	100	103	PIB aux prix constants
Growth rates	3.7	1.3	2.6	-1.4	2.2	12.7	3.5	Taux de croissance
Antigua and Barbuda								**Antigua-et-Barbuda**
GDP at current prices	652	665	697	715	754	818	856	PIB aux prix courants
GDP per capita	8 664	8 698	8 984	9 087	9 478	10 165	10 507	PIB par habitant
GDP at constant prices	527	534	546	560	589	632	651	PIB aux prix constants
Growth rates	4.1	1.5	2.2	2.5	5.2	7.2	3.0	Taux de croissance
Argentina								**Argentine**
GDP at current prices	283 665	284 346	268 831	102 042	129 596	153 129	183 310	PIB aux prix courants
GDP per capita	7 771	7 707	7 212	2 711	3 410	3 991	4 731	PIB par habitant
GDP at constant prices	213 187	211 505	202 180	180 153	196 074	213 778	233 440	PIB aux prix constants
Growth rates	-3.4	-0.8	-4.4	-10.9	8.8	9.0	9.2	Taux de croissance
Armenia								**Arménie**
GDP at current prices	1 845	1 912	2 118	2 376	2 807	3 555	4 868	PIB aux prix courants
GDP per capita	595	620	691	779	924	1 175	1 614	PIB par habitant
GDP at constant prices	1 382	1 463	1 604	1 815	2 069	2 278	2 596	PIB aux prix constants
Growth rates	3.3	5.9	9.6	13.2	14.0	10.1	13.9	Taux de croissance
Aruba								**Aruba**
GDP at current prices	1 723	1 859	1 899	1 911	2 011	2 134	2 258	PIB aux prix courants
GDP per capita	18 970	20 182	20 294	20 088	20 785	21 725	22 696	PIB par habitant
GDP at constant prices	1 357	1 408	1 397	1 362	1 383	1 431	1 477	PIB aux prix constants
Growth rates	1.1	3.7	-0.7	-2.5	1.5	3.5	3.2	Taux de croissance

16

Gross domestic product and gross domestic product per capita—In millions of US dollars at current and constant 1990 prices; per capita US dollars; real rates of growth (*continued*)

Produit intérieur brut et produit intérieur brut par habitant—En millions de dollars E.U. aux prix courants et constants de 1990 ; par habitant en dollars E.U. ; taux de croissance réels (*suite*)

Country or area	1999	2000	2001	2002	2003	2004	2005	Pays ou zone
Australia								**Australie**
GDP at current prices	416 241	399 658	380 556	425 304	543 643	655 652	709 446	PIB aux prix courants
GDP per capita	22 086	20 956	19 725	21 797	27 557	32 877	35 199	PIB par habitant
GDP at constant prices	433 063	441 459	458 112	472 981	491 809	503 258	516 846	PIB aux prix constants
Growth rates	4.0	1.9	3.8	3.2	4.0	2.3	2.7	Taux de croissance
Austria								**Autriche**
GDP at current prices	213 104	193 838	193 178	207 696	256 162	294 324	306 065	PIB aux prix courants
GDP per capita	26 341	23 942	23 821	25 553	31 432	36 020	37 373	PIB par habitant
GDP at constant prices	205 368	212 261	214 025	216 088	219 122	224 471	228 514	PIB aux prix constants
Growth rates	3.3	3.4	0.8	1.0	1.4	2.4	1.8	Taux de croissance
Azerbaijan								**Azerbaïdjan**
GDP at current prices	4 581	5 273	5 708	6 236	7 276	8 680	12 561	PIB aux prix courants
GDP per capita	567	647	696	756	876	1 039	1 493	PIB par habitant
GDP at constant prices	3 775	4 195	4 608	5 095	5 664	6 239	7 755	PIB aux prix constants
Growth rates	7.4	11.1	9.9	10.6	11.2	10.2	24.3	Taux de croissance
Bahamas								**Bahamas**
GDP at current prices	4 704	5 004	5 131	5 389	5 503	5 661	5 870	PIB aux prix courants
GDP per capita	15 835	16 599	16 781	17 378	17 499	17 759	18 168	PIB par habitant
GDP at constant prices	3 829	3 902	3 934	4 023	4 081	4 155	4 268	PIB aux prix constants
Growth rates	4.0	1.9	0.8	2.3	1.4	1.8	2.7	Taux de croissance
Bahrain								**Bahreïn**
GDP at current prices	6 620	7 971	7 928	8 447	9 699	11 013	13 348	PIB aux prix courants
GDP per capita	10 076	11 861	11 576	12 137	13 741	15 386	18 370	PIB par habitant
GDP at constant prices	6 643	6 998	7 321	7 702	8 253	8 702	9 317	PIB aux prix constants
Growth rates	4.3	5.3	4.6	5.2	7.2	5.4	7.1	Taux de croissance
Bangladesh								**Bangladesh**
GDP at current prices	48 301	48 626	48 955	51 924	57 261	61 916	64 058	PIB aux prix courants
GDP per capita	382	377	372	387	419	445	452	PIB par habitant
GDP at constant prices	48 841	51 416	53 687	56 508	60 052	63 280	66 760	PIB aux prix constants
Growth rates	5.9	5.3	4.4	5.3	6.3	5.4	5.5	Taux de croissance
Barbados								**Barbade**
GDP at current prices	2 478	2 559	2 554	2 476	2 695	2 816	2 996	PIB aux prix courants
GDP per capita	9 338	9 616	9 573	9 256	10 048	10 474	11 116	PIB par habitant
GDP at constant prices	1 907	1 950	1 899	1 908	1 946	2 018	2 081	PIB aux prix constants
Growth rates	0.5	2.3	-2.6	0.5	2.0	3.7	3.1	Taux de croissance
Belarus								**Bélarus**
GDP at current prices	12 138	10 418	12 355	14 595	17 825	23 142	29 566	PIB aux prix courants
GDP per capita	1 204	1 039	1 239	1 471	1 807	2 359	3 031	PIB par habitant
GDP at constant prices	15 761	16 673	17 461	18 336	19 618	21 860	23 877	PIB aux prix constants
Growth rates	3.4	5.8	4.7	5.0	7.0	11.4	9.2	Taux de croissance
Belgium								**Belgique**
GDP at current prices	253 810	231 933	231 661	251 826	309 900	357 712	370 815	PIB aux prix courants
GDP per capita	24 705	22 509	22 423	24 316	29 859	34 396	35 590	PIB par habitant
GDP at constant prices	240 893	250 202	252 824	256 624	258 971	265 678	268 992	PIB aux prix constants
Growth rates	3.1	3.9	1.0	1.5	0.9	2.6	1.2	Taux de croissance
Belize								**Belize**
GDP at current prices	732	832	869	927	981	1 036	1 105	PIB aux prix courants
GDP per capita	3 094	3 436	3 505	3 657	3 789	3 918	4 097	PIB par habitant
GDP at constant prices	572	615	643	673	735	769	793	PIB aux prix constants
Growth rates	6.1	7.5	4.6	4.7	9.2	4.6	3.1	Taux de croissance
Benin								**Bénin**
GDP at current prices	2 489	2 359	2 499	2 808	3 557	4 060	4 378	PIB aux prix courants
GDP per capita	356	328	337	366	449	496	519	PIB par habitant
GDP at constant prices	2 738	2 871	3 051	3 186	3 309	3 421	3 541	PIB aux prix constants
Growth rates	5.3	4.9	6.2	4.4	3.9	3.4	3.5	Taux de croissance
Bermuda								**Bermudes**
GDP at current prices	3 326	3 522	3 661	3 960	4 288	4 505	4 090	PIB aux prix courants
GDP per capita	53 146	56 026	57 978	62 438	67 324	70 452	63 731	PIB par habitant
GDP at constant prices	2 558	2 645	2 658	2 811	2 935	2 983	3 058	PIB aux prix constants
Growth rates	3.5	3.4	0.5	5.8	4.4	1.6	2.5	Taux de croissance

16 Gross domestic product and gross domestic product per capita—In millions of US dollars at current and constant 1990 prices; per capita US dollars; real rates of growth (*continued*)

Produit intérieur brut et produit intérieur brut par habitant—En millions de dollars E.U. aux prix courants et constants de 1990 ; par habitant en dollars E.U. ; taux de croissance réels (*suite*)

Country or area	1999	2000	2001	2002	2003	2004	2005	Pays ou zone
Bhutan								**Bhoutan**
GDP at current prices	409	447	493	539	613	708	917	PIB aux prix courants
GDP per capita	216	231	249	266	296	334	424	PIB par habitant
GDP at constant prices	454	497	540	578	618	671	730	PIB aux prix constants
Growth rates	7.8	9.5	8.6	7.1	6.8	8.7	8.8	Taux de croissance
Bolivia								**Bolivie**
GDP at current prices	8 285	8 398	8 142	7 924	8 089	8 773	9 728	PIB aux prix courants
GDP per capita	1 017	1 010	959	915	916	974	1 059	PIB par habitant
GDP at constant prices	6 874	7 047	7 165	7 340	7 544	7 814	8 026	PIB aux prix constants
Growth rates	0.4	2.5	1.7	2.4	2.8	3.6	2.7	Taux de croissance
Bosnia and Herzegovina								**Bosnie-Herzégovine**
GDP at current prices	4 686	4 527	4 795	5 606	7 100	8 569	9 132	PIB aux prix courants
GDP per capita	1 250	1 177	1 229	1 430	1 812	2 192	2 337	PIB par habitant
GDP at constant prices	19 406	20 457	21 035	21 377	21 504	21 706	22 868	PIB aux prix constants
Growth rates	9.5	5.4	2.8	1.6	0.6	0.9	5.4	Taux de croissance
Botswana								**Botswana**
GDP at current prices	4 654	4 889	4 903	5 045	7 341	8 498	8 850	PIB aux prix courants
GDP per capita	2 682	2 787	2 777	2 849	4 144	4 804	5 014	PIB par habitant
GDP at constant prices	5 417	5 774	6 265	6 406	6 834	7 288	7 568	PIB aux prix constants
Growth rates	4.1	6.6	8.5	2.2	6.7	6.6	3.8	Taux de croissance
Brazil								**Brésil**
GDP at current prices	536 633	601 732	508 433	460 838	505 732	603 948	799 413	PIB aux prix courants
GDP per capita	3 132	3 461	2 883	2 576	2 788	3 284	4 289	PIB par habitant
GDP at constant prices	544 906	568 668	576 132	587 233	590 433	619 578	639 715	PIB aux prix constants
Growth rates	0.8	4.4	1.3	1.9	0.5	4.9	3.3	Taux de croissance
British Virgin Islands								**Iles Vierges britanniques**
GDP at current prices	673	784	839	813	782	873	972	PIB aux prix courants
GDP per capita	33 416	38 203	40 207	38 385	36 425	40 147	44 150	PIB par habitant
GDP at constant prices	201	229	237	229	213	235	257	PIB aux prix constants
Growth rates	9.6	13.7	3.8	-3.5	-7.2	10.5	9.2	Taux de croissance
Brunei Darussalam								**Brunéi Darussalam**
GDP at current prices	4 215	4 316	4 176	4 273	4 773	5 530	6 280	PIB aux prix courants
GDP per capita	12 945	12 944	12 231	12 229	13 350	15 122	16 800	PIB par habitant
GDP at constant prices	4 016	4 129	4 254	4 375	4 542	4 620	4 758	PIB aux prix constants
Growth rates	2.6	2.8	3.0	2.8	3.8	1.7	3.0	Taux de croissance
Bulgaria								**Bulgarie**
GDP at current prices	12 955	12 600	13 599	15 568	19 938	24 131	26 419	PIB aux prix courants
GDP per capita	1 609	1 576	1 712	1 974	2 545	3 102	3 420	PIB par habitant
GDP at constant prices	16 506	17 396	18 104	18 989	19 834	20 938	22 188	PIB aux prix constants
Growth rates	2.3	5.4	4.1	4.9	4.5	5.6	6.0	Taux de croissance
Burkina Faso								**Burkina Faso**
GDP at current prices	2 979	2 415	2 635	3 006	4 028	4 945	5 397	PIB aux prix courants
GDP per capita	272	214	226	250	324	386	408	PIB par habitant
GDP at constant prices	5 186	4 932	5 232	5 473	5 905	6 295	6 665	PIB aux prix constants
Growth rates	3.7	-4.9	6.1	4.6	7.9	6.6	5.9	Taux de croissance
Burundi								**Burundi**
GDP at current prices	810	711	664	630	597	681	845	PIB aux prix courants
GDP per capita	127	110	100	92	85	94	112	PIB par habitant
GDP at constant prices	979	970	991	1 035	1 023	1 068	1 121	PIB aux prix constants
Growth rates	-1.0	-0.9	2.1	4.5	-1.2	4.4	5.0	Taux de croissance
Cambodia								**Cambodge**
GDP at current prices	3 521	3 668	3 794	4 088	4 357	4 888	5 397	PIB aux prix courants
GDP per capita	282	288	292	308	322	354	384	PIB par habitant
GDP at constant prices	3 030	3 285	3 466	3 647	3 905	4 205	4 498	PIB aux prix constants
Growth rates	12.6	8.4	5.5	5.2	7.0	7.7	7.0	Taux de croissance
Cameroon								**Cameroun**
GDP at current prices	10 022	9 287	9 633	10 880	13 723	15 806	16 823	PIB aux prix courants
GDP per capita	689	625	636	704	871	986	1 031	PIB par habitant
GDP at constant prices	16 853	17 621	18 417	19 155	19 959	20 980	21 805	PIB aux prix constants
Growth rates	4.3	4.6	4.5	4.0	4.2	5.1	3.9	Taux de croissance

Gross domestic product and gross domestic product per capita—In millions of US dollars at current and constant 1990 prices; per capita US dollars; real rates of growth (*continued*)

Produit intérieur brut et produit intérieur brut par habitant—En millions de dollars E.U. aux prix courants et constants de 1990 ; par habitant en dollars E.U. ; taux de croissance réels (*suite*)

Country or area	1999	2000	2001	2002	2003	2004	2005	Pays ou zone
Canada								**Canada**
GDP at current prices	651 202	714 453	705 069	724 304	854 711	976 742	1 131 760	PIB aux prix courants
GDP per capita	21 420	23 280	22 749	23 132	27 017	30 563	35 073	PIB par habitant
GDP at constant prices	727 687	765 903	779 428	803 348	819 381	843 380	881 977	PIB aux prix constants
Growth rates	5.6	5.3	1.8	3.1	2.0	2.9	4.6	Taux de croissance
Cape Verde								**Cap-Vert**
GDP at current prices	597	539	563	621	814	930	1 038	PIB aux prix courants
GDP per capita	1 356	1 197	1 220	1 315	1 683	1 877	2 048	PIB par habitant
GDP at constant prices	553	593	630	663	694	724	770	PIB aux prix constants
Growth rates	11.9	7.3	6.1	5.3	4.7	4.4	6.3	Taux de croissance
Cayman Islands								**Iles Caïmanes**
GDP at current prices	1 266	1 323	1 357	1 415	1 468	1 533	1 593	PIB aux prix courants
GDP per capita	32 949	33 319	33 168	33 658	34 044	34 756	35 381	PIB par habitant
GDP at constant prices	1 320	1 333	1 340	1 364	1 391	1 415	1 435	PIB aux prix constants
Growth rates	3.5	1.0	0.6	1.7	2.0	1.7	1.4	Taux de croissance
Central African Rep.								**Rép. centrafricaine**
GDP at current prices	987	906	928	984	1 126	1 246	1 325	PIB aux prix courants
GDP per capita	266	240	242	253	286	313	328	PIB par habitant
GDP at constant prices	1 482	1 489	1 535	1 541	1 472	1 491	1 524	PIB aux prix constants
Growth rates	3.6	0.5	3.1	0.4	-4.5	1.3	2.2	Taux de croissance
Chad								**Tchad**
GDP at current prices	1 486	1 386	1 700	1 977	2 727	4 399	4 942	PIB aux prix courants
GDP per capita	187	169	200	224	299	466	507	PIB par habitant
GDP at constant prices	2 149	2 147	2 368	2 567	2 965	3 950	4 254	PIB aux prix constants
Growth rates	-0.1	-0.1	10.3	8.4	15.5	33.2	7.7	Taux de croissance
Chile								**Chili**
GDP at current prices	72 996	75 196	68 569	67 266	73 370	94 125	111 339	PIB aux prix courants
GDP per capita	4 795	4 879	4 396	4 264	4 600	5 838	6 833	PIB par habitant
GDP at constant prices	59 617	62 292	64 397	65 803	68 259	72 395	76 644	PIB aux prix constants
Growth rates	-0.8	4.5	3.4	2.2	3.7	6.1	5.9	Taux de croissance
China								**Chine**
GDP at current prices	998 678	1 079 191	1 191 157	1 303 590	1 470 699	1 720 401	1 981 648	PIB aux prix courants
GDP per capita	804	862	945	1 027	1 151	1 339	1 533	PIB par habitant
GDP at constant prices	952 414	1 032 417	1 118 108	1 219 856	1 341 841	1 477 367	1 623 627	PIB aux prix constants
Growth rates	7.6	8.4	8.3	9.1	10.0	10.1	9.9	Taux de croissance
China, Hong Kong SAR								**Chine, Hong Kong RAS**
GDP at current prices	163 287	168 754	166 541	163 710	158 364	165 743	172 649	PIB aux prix courants
GDP per capita	24 925	25 426	24 778	24 063	23 005	23 804	24 521	PIB par habitant
GDP at constant prices	108 728	119 565	120 327	122 539	126 386	136 785	143 124	PIB aux prix constants
Growth rates	4.0	10.0	0.6	1.8	3.1	8.2	4.6	Taux de croissance
China, Macao SAR								**Chine, Macao RAS**
GDP at current prices	5 917	6 102	6 187	6 824	7 925	10 359	10 992	PIB aux prix courants
GDP per capita	13 492	13 757	13 819	15 122	17 443	22 657	23 887	PIB par habitant
GDP at constant prices	4 017	4 248	4 371	4 813	5 494	7 066	7 242	PIB aux prix constants
Growth rates	-2.4	5.7	2.9	10.1	14.2	28.6	2.5	Taux de croissance
Colombia								**Colombie**
GDP at current prices	86 301	83 766	81 995	81 243	80 348	98 281	121 877	PIB aux prix courants
GDP per capita	2 084	1 989	1 915	1 866	1 817	2 188	2 673	PIB par habitant
GDP at constant prices	60 253	62 016	62 928	64 145	66 779	69 459	72 238	PIB aux prix constants
Growth rates	-4.2	2.9	1.5	1.9	4.1	4.0	4.0	Taux de croissance
Comoros								**Comores**
GDP at current prices	223	204	220	247	318	368	380	PIB aux prix courants
GDP per capita	327	292	306	335	419	474	477	PIB par habitant
GDP at constant prices	275	282	288	295	301	307	316	PIB aux prix constants
Growth rates	1.9	2.4	2.3	2.3	2.1	1.9	2.8	Taux de croissance
Congo								**Congo**
GDP at current prices	2 354[1]	3 220[1]	2 794[1]	3 018	3 481	4 137	5 528	PIB aux prix courants
GDP per capita	707[1]	937[1]	788[1]	825	924	1 065	1 382	PIB par habitant
GDP at constant prices	3 012[1]	3 259[1]	3 377[1]	3 559	3 587	3 731	4 073	PIB aux prix constants
Growth rates	-3.0	8.2	3.6	5.4	0.8	4.0	9.2	Taux de croissance

16

Gross domestic product and gross domestic product per capita—In millions of US dollars at current and constant 1990 prices; per capita US dollars; real rates of growth (*continued*)

Produit intérieur brut et produit intérieur brut par habitant—En millions de dollars E.U. aux prix courants et constants de 1990 ; par habitant en dollars E.U. ; taux de croissance réels (*suite*)

Country or area	1999	2000	2001	2002	2003	2004	2005	Pays ou zone
Cook Islands								**Iles Cook**
GDP at current prices	81	81	86	102	143	173	183	PIB aux prix courants
GDP per capita	4 229	4 291	4 651	5 548	7 828	9 594	10 201	PIB par habitant
GDP at constant prices	68	78	81	84	90	95	94	PIB aux prix constants
Growth rates	2.7	13.9	4.9	2.6	8.0	5.6	-1.0	Taux de croissance
Costa Rica								**Costa Rica**
GDP at current prices	15 796	15 947	16 403	16 844	17 514	18 557	19 818	PIB aux prix courants
GDP per capita	4 114	4 059	4 086	4 111	4 194	4 363	4 580	PIB par habitant
GDP at constant prices	11 828	12 041	12 171	12 523	13 324	13 876	14 449	PIB aux prix constants
Growth rates	8.2	1.8	1.1	2.9	6.4	4.1	4.1	Taux de croissance
Côte d'Ivoire								**Côte d'Ivoire**
GDP at current prices	12 561	10 682	10 735	11 692	14 255	16 064	16 785	PIB aux prix courants
GDP per capita	767	638	630	674	810	899	925	PIB par habitant
GDP at constant prices	15 571	15 156	15 156	15 154	15 152	15 421	15 495	PIB aux prix constants
Growth rates	1.9	-2.7	0.0	0.0	0.0	1.8	0.5	Taux de croissance
Croatia								**Croatie**
GDP at current prices	19 906	18 428	19 861	22 798	28 801	34 309	36 947	PIB aux prix courants
GDP per capita	4 393	4 090	4 415	5 060	6 369	7 557	8 118	PIB par habitant
GDP at constant prices	20 643	21 232	22 176	23 332	24 329	25 253	26 152	PIB aux prix constants
Growth rates	-0.9	2.9	4.4	5.2	4.3	3.8	3.6	Taux de croissance
Cuba								**Cuba**
GDP at current prices	30 299	32 685	33 820	36 089	38 625	41 065	46 932	PIB aux prix courants
GDP per capita	2 734	2 938	3 030	3 224	3 443	3 652	4 165	PIB par habitant
GDP at constant prices	25 234	26 777	27 580	28 077	29 143	30 717	34 356	PIB aux prix constants
Growth rates	6.3	6.1	3.0	1.8	3.8	5.4	11.8	Taux de croissance
Cyprus								**Chypre**
GDP at current prices	9 603	9 124	9 491	10 431	13 211	15 561	16 723	PIB aux prix courants
GDP per capita	13 991	13 155	13 534	14 700	18 333	21 111	22 432	PIB par habitant
GDP at constant prices	8 537	8 967	9 337	9 532	9 717	10 087	10 478	PIB aux prix constants
Growth rates	4.8	5.0	4.1	2.1	1.9	3.8	3.9	Taux de croissance
Czech Republic								**République tchèque**
GDP at current prices	59 051	55 703	60 871	73 756	90 602	107 694	122 345	PIB aux prix courants
GDP per capita	5 744	5 425	5 935	7 198	8 850	10 528	11 972	PIB par habitant
GDP at constant prices	36 512	37 933	38 934	39 514	40 782	42 695	45 236	PIB aux prix constants
Growth rates	1.2	3.9	2.6	1.5	3.2	4.7	6.0	Taux de croissance
Dem. Rep. of the Congo								**Rép. dém. du Congo**
GDP at current prices	5 525[1]	5 256[1]	5 270[1]	5 548	5 634	6 507	7 212	PIB aux prix courants
GDP per capita	113[1]	105[1]	103[1]	105	104	117	125	PIB par habitant
GDP at constant prices	5 550[1]	5 167[1]	5 059[1]	5 234	5 532	5 909	6 300	PIB aux prix constants
Growth rates	-4.2	-6.9	-2.1	3.5	5.7	6.8	6.6	Taux de croissance
Denmark								**Danemark**
GDP at current prices	173 944	160 082	160 476	173 881	213 909	244 917	258 718	PIB aux prix courants
GDP per capita	32 708	29 980	29 940	32 325	39 634	45 236	47 641	PIB par habitant
GDP at constant prices	169 546	175 528	176 766	177 589	178 820	182 165	187 727	PIB aux prix constants
Growth rates	2.6	3.5	0.7	0.5	0.7	1.9	3.1	Taux de croissance
Djibouti								**Djibouti**
GDP at current prices	536	553	573	592	625	664	705	PIB aux prix courants
GDP per capita	773	774	782	790	817	852	889	PIB par habitant
GDP at constant prices	513	516	526	540	559	575	593	PIB aux prix constants
Growth rates	2.2	0.7	1.9	2.6	3.5	3.0	3.2	Taux de croissance
Dominica								**Dominique**
GDP at current prices	268	269	262	252	258	271	283	PIB aux prix courants
GDP per capita	3 457	3 457	3 353	3 223	3 297	3 451	3 580	PIB par habitant
GDP at constant prices	198	199	192	184	188	201	206	PIB aux prix constants
Growth rates	0.8	0.5	-3.8	-4.0	2.2	6.8	2.6	Taux de croissance
Dominican Republic								**Rép. dominicaine**
GDP at current prices	17 378	19 772	21 605	21 625	16 325	18 452	29 101	PIB aux prix courants
GDP per capita	2 134	2 392	2 576	2 540	1 889	2 104	3 272	PIB par habitant
GDP at constant prices	12 268	13 266	13 748	14 356	14 088	14 363	15 696	PIB aux prix constants
Growth rates	8.1	8.1	3.6	4.4	-1.9	2.0	9.3	Taux de croissance

Gross domestic product and gross domestic product per capita—In millions of US dollars at current and constant 1990 prices; per capita US dollars; real rates of growth (*continued*)

Produit intérieur brut et produit intérieur brut par habitant—En millions de dollars E.U. aux prix courants et constants de 1990 ; par habitant en dollars E.U. ; taux de croissance réels (*suite*)

Country or area	1999	2000	2001	2002	2003	2004	2005	Pays ou zone
Ecuador								**Equateur**
GDP at current prices	16 674	15 934	21 250	24 899	28 691	32 964	33 062	PIB aux prix courants
GDP per capita	1 375	1 295	1 702	1 966	2 232	2 528	2 499	PIB par habitant
GDP at constant prices	13 557	13 937	14 681	15 304	15 860	17 073	17 188	PIB aux prix constants
Growth rates	-6.3	2.8	5.3	4.2	3.6	7.6	0.7	Taux de croissance
Egypt								**Egypte**
GDP at current prices	95 668	99 601	94 438	90 064	77 109	84 019	101 406	PIB aux prix courants
GDP per capita	1 449	1 480	1 377	1 288	1 082	1 157	1 370	PIB par habitant
GDP at constant prices	60 663	62 801	64 801	67 478	70 258	73 747	77 434	PIB aux prix constants
Growth rates	5.4	3.5	3.2	4.1	4.1	5.0	5.0	Taux de croissance
El Salvador								**El Salvador**
GDP at current prices	12 465	13 134	13 813	14 312	14 941	15 824	16 980	PIB aux prix courants
GDP per capita	2 024	2 091	2 157	2 194	2 249	2 340	2 468	PIB par habitant
GDP at constant prices	7 372	7 531	7 660	7 831	7 973	8 095	8 266	PIB aux prix constants
Growth rates	3.4	2.2	1.7	2.2	1.8	1.5	2.1	Taux de croissance
Equatorial Guinea								**Guinée équatoriale**
GDP at current prices	738	1 216	1 777	2 186	2 976	4 523	5 651	PIB aux prix courants
GDP per capita	1 684	2 709	3 867	4 649	6 185	9 189	11 222	PIB par habitant
GDP at constant prices	772	873	1 465	1 760	2 000	2 480	2 633	PIB aux prix constants
Growth rates	23.2	13.1	67.8	20.2	13.6	24.1	6.2	Taux de croissance
Eritrea								**Erythrée**
GDP at current prices	726	634	671	623	742	933	1 077	PIB aux prix courants
GDP per capita	212	178	181	161	183	220	245	PIB par habitant
GDP at constant prices	1 443	1 254	1 369	1 378	1 420	1 445	1 457	PIB aux prix constants
Growth rates	0.0	-13.1	9.2	0.7	3.0	1.8	0.8	Taux de croissance
Estonia								**Estonie**
GDP at current prices	5 571	5 477	5 977	7 038	9 190	11 234	12 762	PIB aux prix courants
GDP per capita	4 043	4 007	4 405	5 220	6 852	8 414	9 598	PIB par habitant
GDP at constant prices	4 699	5 068	5 396	5 787	6 174	6 656	7 214	PIB aux prix constants
Growth rates	0.3	7.9	6.5	7.2	6.7	7.8	8.4	Taux de croissance
Ethiopia								**Ethiopie**
GDP at current prices	6 145	6 473	6 410	6 041	6 623	8 013	9 297	PIB aux prix courants
GDP per capita	92	94	91	84	90	106	120	PIB par habitant
GDP at constant prices	10 953	11 539	12 429	12 628	12 092	13 479	14 468	PIB aux prix constants
Growth rates	6.0	5.4	7.7	1.6	-4.2	11.5	7.3	Taux de croissance
Fiji								**Fidji**
GDP at current prices	1 942	1 686	1 662	1 843	2 309	2 728	2 998	PIB aux prix courants
GDP per capita	2 420	2 080	2 030	2 231	2 770	3 244	3 536	PIB par habitant
GDP at constant prices	1 716	1 687	1 720	1 775	1 793	1 888	1 901	PIB aux prix constants
Growth rates	8.8	-1.7	2.0	3.2	1.0	5.3	0.7	Taux de croissance
Finland								**Finlande**
GDP at current prices	128 874	120 563	122 122	132 561	162 304	185 909	193 155	PIB aux prix courants
GDP per capita	24 957	23 290	23 528	25 466	31 090	35 511	36 798	PIB par habitant
GDP at constant prices	158 064	165 932	167 639	171 332	175 505	181 858	185 653	PIB aux prix constants
Growth rates	3.4	5.0	1.0	2.2	2.4	3.6	2.1	Taux de croissance
France[2]								**France**[2]
GDP at current prices	1 455 813	1 327 962	1 339 741	1 457 393	1 799 946	2 059 960	2 126 578	PIB aux prix courants
GDP per capita	23 967	21 776	21 877	23 695	29 134	33 197	34 128	PIB par habitant
GDP at constant prices	1 466 301	1 525 309	1 553 596	1 569 556	1 586 623	1 623 420	1 642 660	PIB aux prix constants
Growth rates	3.2	4.0	1.9	1.0	1.1	2.3	1.2	Taux de croissance
French Polynesia								**Polynésie française**
GDP at current prices	3 531	3 242	3 224	3 564	4 471	5 144	5 388	PIB aux prix courants
GDP per capita	15 218	13 732	13 416	14 577	17 984	20 358	20 998	PIB par habitant
GDP at constant prices	3 550	3 692	3 741	3 904	4 059	4 203	4 347	PIB aux prix constants
Growth rates	4.0	4.0	1.3	4.4	4.0	3.5	3.4	Taux de croissance
Gabon								**Gabon**
GDP at current prices	4 614	5 019	4 589	4 800	5 926	7 063	7 919	PIB aux prix courants
GDP per capita	3 707	3 945	3 538	3 637	4 418	5 184	5 723	PIB par habitant
GDP at constant prices	6 370	6 247	6 371	6 351	6 476	6 577	6 711	PIB aux prix constants
Growth rates	-11.3	-1.9	2.0	-0.3	2.0	1.6	2.0	Taux de croissance

16 **Gross domestic product and gross domestic product per capita**—In millions of US dollars at current and constant 1990 prices; per capita US dollars; real rates of growth *(continued)*

Produit intérieur brut et produit intérieur brut par habitant—En millions de dollars E.U. aux prix courants et constants de 1990 ; par habitant en dollars E.U. ; taux de croissance réels *(suite)*

Country or area	1999	2000	2001	2002	2003	2004	2005	Pays ou zone
Gambia								**Gambie**
GDP at current prices	432	421	418	370	366	415	480	PIB aux prix courants
GDP per capita	339	320	308	265	255	281	316	PIB par habitant
GDP at constant prices	449	474	501	485	517	560	586	PIB aux prix constants
Growth rates	6.4	5.5	5.8	-3.2	6.7	8.3	4.6	Taux de croissance
Georgia								**Géorgie**
GDP at current prices	2 800	3 044	3 207	3 396	3 991	5 202	6 490	PIB aux prix courants
GDP per capita	586	645	687	736	874	1 151	1 450	PIB par habitant
GDP at constant prices	3 123	3 180	3 332	3 516	3 904	4 149	4 537	PIB aux prix constants
Growth rates	2.9	1.8	4.8	5.5	11.1	6.3	9.3	Taux de croissance
Germany								**Allemagne**
GDP at current prices	2 143 556	1 900 220	1 890 954	2 018 744	2 441 667	2 751 113	2 794 856	PIB aux prix courants
GDP per capita	26 056	23 076	22 941	24 467	29 566	33 288	33 800	PIB par habitant
GDP at constant prices	2 036 740	2 102 116	2 128 182	2 129 443	2 125 449	2 160 134	2 180 945	PIB aux prix constants
Growth rates	2.0	3.2	1.2	0.1	-0.2	1.6	1.0	Taux de croissance
Ghana								**Ghana**
GDP at current prices	7 710	4 978	5 309	6 160	7 624	8 620	10 393	PIB aux prix courants
GDP per capita	397	251	261	297	359	398	470	PIB par habitant
GDP at constant prices	9 138	9 480	9 876	10 325	10 867	11 437	12 102	PIB aux prix constants
Growth rates	4.4	3.7	4.2	4.5	5.2	5.2	5.8	Taux de croissance
Greece								**Grèce**
GDP at current prices	128 401	115 997	119 108	135 035	175 549	209 119	225 201	PIB aux prix courants
GDP per capita	11 750	10 569	10 813	12 223	15 851	18 842	20 252	PIB par habitant
GDP at constant prices	103 673	108 315	113 824	118 182	123 799	129 589	134 329	PIB aux prix constants
Growth rates	3.4	4.5	5.1	3.8	4.8	4.7	3.7	Taux de croissance
Grenada								**Grenade**
GDP at current prices	380	410	395	408	444	437	454	PIB aux prix courants
GDP per capita	3 748	4 031	3 886	4 003	4 354	4 274	4 415	PIB par habitant
GDP at constant prices	296	317	301	306	329	315	318	PIB aux prix constants
Growth rates	7.0	7.0	-4.9	1.5	7.5	-4.1	0.9	Taux de croissance
Guatemala								**Guatemala**
GDP at current prices	18 318	19 289	20 980	23 304	24 884	27 276	31 923	PIB aux prix courants
GDP per capita	1 679	1 727	1 835	1 990	2 074	2 219	2 534	PIB par habitant
GDP at constant prices	11 052	11 451	11 718	11 982	12 237	12 573	12 971	PIB aux prix constants
Growth rates	4.1	3.6	2.3	2.2	2.1	2.7	3.2	Taux de croissance
Guinea								**Guinée**
GDP at current prices	3 621	3 134	3 044	3 044	3 446	3 788	3 058	PIB aux prix courants
GDP per capita	438	372	353	346	383	412	325	PIB par habitant
GDP at constant prices	4 123	4 200	4 367	4 550	4 606	4 732	4 872	PIB aux prix constants
Growth rates	4.7	1.9	4.0	4.2	1.2	2.7	3.0	Taux de croissance
Guinea-Bissau								**Guinée-Bissau**
GDP at current prices	225	215	199	204	239	281	298	PIB aux prix courants
GDP per capita	169	158	142	141	160	182	188	PIB par habitant
GDP at constant prices	246	265	265	246	248	258	264	PIB aux prix constants
Growth rates	7.8	7.5	0.2	-7.2	0.6	4.3	2.3	Taux de croissance
Guyana								**Guyana**
GDP at current prices	695	713	712	726	743	788	786	PIB aux prix courants
GDP per capita	937	958	955	971	992	1 051	1 046	PIB par habitant
GDP at constant prices	648	639	653	660	656	666	647	PIB aux prix constants
Growth rates	3.0	-1.4	2.2	1.1	-0.6	1.5	-2.8	Taux de croissance
Haiti								**Haïti**
GDP at current prices	3 922	3 515	3 365	3 077	2 708	3 501	3 884	PIB aux prix courants
GDP per capita	501	443	418	377	327	416	455	PIB par habitant
GDP at constant prices	2 334	2 354	2 329	2 316	2 328	2 240	2 273	PIB aux prix constants
Growth rates	2.3	0.9	-1.0	-0.5	0.5	-3.8	1.5	Taux de croissance
Honduras								**Honduras**
GDP at current prices	5 424	6 025	6 400	6 580	6 945	7 536	8 374	PIB aux prix courants
GDP per capita	866	938	972	977	1 008	1 069	1 162	PIB par habitant
GDP at constant prices	3 984	4 213	4 323	4 440	4 594	4 825	5 026	PIB aux prix constants
Growth rates	-1.9	5.7	2.6	2.7	3.5	5.0	4.2	Taux de croissance

16 Gross domestic product and gross domestic product per capita—In millions of US dollars at current and constant 1990 prices; per capita US dollars; real rates of growth (*continued*)

Produit intérieur brut et produit intérieur brut par habitant—En millions de dollars E.U. aux prix courants et constants de 1990 ; par habitant en dollars E.U. ; taux de croissance réels (*suite*)

Country or area	1999	2000	2001	2002	2003	2004	2005	Pays ou zone
Hungary								**Hongrie**
GDP at current prices	48 409	47 035	52 322	65 592	83 148	100 764	109 239	PIB aux prix courants
GDP per capita	4 723	4 600	5 129	6 446	8 192	9 953	10 818	PIB par habitant
GDP at constant prices	37 352	39 296	40 998	42 562	44 002	46 298	48 203	PIB aux prix constants
Growth rates	4.2	5.2	4.3	3.8	3.4	5.2	4.1	Taux de croissance
Iceland								**Islande**
GDP at current prices	8 689	8 628	7 851	8 723	10 792	13 061	15 814	PIB aux prix courants
GDP per capita	31 198	30 675	27 644	30 427	37 300	44 735	53 687	PIB par habitant
GDP at constant prices	7 817	8 141	8 451	8 362	8 615	9 323	9 839	PIB aux prix constants
Growth rates	4.3	4.1	3.8	-1.0	3.0	8.2	5.5	Taux de croissance
India								**Inde**
GDP at current prices	449 846	464 937	481 491	506 749	592 493	688 803	800 783	PIB aux prix courants
GDP per capita	448	455	464	481	553	634	726	PIB par habitant
GDP at constant prices	530 968	551 900	580 205	604 075	656 065	702 558	763 549	PIB aux prix constants
Growth rates	7.1	3.9	5.1	4.1	8.6	7.1	8.7	Taux de croissance
Indonesia								**Indonésie**
GDP at current prices	153 820	165 021	164 146	200 111	237 416	253 022	281 276	PIB aux prix courants
GDP per capita	745	789	775	932	1 092	1 150	1 263	PIB par habitant
GDP at constant prices	181 158	190 072	197 349	205 985	215 701	226 595	239 276	PIB aux prix constants
Growth rates	0.8	4.9	3.8	4.4	4.7	5.1	5.6	Taux de croissance
Iran (Islamic Rep. of)								**Iran (Rép. islamique d')**
GDP at current prices	112 757[3]	112 695[3]	122 173[3]	141 266	147 020	179 521	216 713	PIB aux prix courants
GDP per capita	1 717[3]	1 698[3]	1 824[3]	2 090	2 157	2 609	3 117	PIB par habitant
GDP at constant prices	142 156[3]	150 591[3]	158 697[3]	171 118	184 864	196 889	208 470	PIB aux prix constants
Growth rates	2.7	5.9	5.4	7.8	8.0	6.5	5.9	Taux de croissance
Iraq								**Iraq**
GDP at current prices	14 834	20 969	17 575	17 437	10 621	27 366	33 379	PIB aux prix courants
GDP per capita	609	836	681	657	389	975	1 159	PIB par habitant
GDP at constant prices	33 776	32 555	33 864	31 940	17 804	26 083	26 761	PIB aux prix constants
Growth rates	24.3	-3.6	4.0	-5.7	-44.3	46.5	2.6	Taux de croissance
Ireland								**Irlande**
GDP at current prices	96 537	96 166	104 799	122 832	156 988	184 459	201 763	PIB aux prix courants
GDP per capita	25 748	25 298	27 128	31 233	39 182	45 214	48 642	PIB par habitant
GDP at constant prices	87 198	95 235	101 121	107 304	112 074	117 087	122 735	PIB aux prix constants
Growth rates	10.7	9.2	6.2	6.1	4.4	4.5	4.8	Taux de croissance
Israel								**Israël**
GDP at current prices	108 863	121 023	118 877	108 923	114 976	122 389	129 648	PIB aux prix courants
GDP per capita	18 292	19 891	19 123	17 163	17 758	18 542	19 280	PIB par habitant
GDP at constant prices	90 710	98 139	97 822	96 403	97 663	102 232	107 232	PIB aux prix constants
Growth rates	2.5	8.2	-0.3	-1.5	1.3	4.7	4.9	Taux de croissance
Italy								**Italie**
GDP at current prices	1 200 787	1 097 343	1 117 348	1 218 977	1 507 113	1 724 523	1 762 475	PIB aux prix courants
GDP per capita	20 834	19 013	19 332	21 060	26 002	29 716	30 339	PIB par habitant
GDP at constant prices	1 281 010	1 326 895	1 350 718	1 355 337	1 355 841	1 370 285	1 369 797	PIB aux prix constants
Growth rates	1.9	3.6	1.8	0.3	0.0	1.1	0.0	Taux de croissance
Jamaica								**Jamaïque**
GDP at current prices	7 738	7 889	8 116	8 471	8 190	8 825	10 063	PIB aux prix courants
GDP per capita	3 014	3 052	3 121	3 240	3 117	3 344	3 796	PIB par habitant
GDP at constant prices	4 508	4 540	4 609	4 660	4 765	4 810	4 844	PIB aux prix constants
Growth rates	1.0	0.7	1.5	1.1	2.3	0.9	0.7	Taux de croissance
Japan								**Japon**
GDP at current prices	4 347 650	4 649 615	4 087 724	3 904 826	4 231 250	4 584 885	4 558 950	PIB aux prix courants
GDP per capita	34 299	36 601	32 113	30 620	33 125	35 841	35 593	PIB par habitant
GDP at constant prices	3 276 646	3 372 945	3 385 923	3 390 451	3 450 683	3 530 123	3 622 775	PIB aux prix constants
Growth rates	-0.2	2.9	0.4	0.1	1.8	2.3	2.6	Taux de croissance
Jordan								**Jordanie**
GDP at current prices	8 150	8 461	8 976	9 561	10 161	11 515	12 535	PIB aux prix courants
GDP per capita	1 683	1 702	1 756	1 817	1 877	2 071	2 198	PIB par habitant
GDP at constant prices	6 112	6 371	6 707	7 090	7 378	7 946	8 343	PIB aux prix constants
Growth rates	3.4	4.3	5.3	5.7	4.1	7.7	5.0	Taux de croissance

16 **Gross domestic product and gross domestic product per capita**—In millions of US dollars at current and constant 1990 prices; per capita US dollars; real rates of growth (*continued*)

Produit intérieur brut et produit intérieur brut par habitant—En millions de dollars E.U. aux prix courants et constants de 1990 ; par habitant en dollars E.U. ; taux de croissance réels (*suite*)

Country or area	1999	2000	2001	2002	2003	2004	2005	Pays ou zone
Kazakhstan								**Kazakhstan**
GDP at current prices	16 871	18 292	22 153	24 637	30 834	43 152	56 088	PIB aux prix courants
GDP per capita	1 113	1 217	1 483	1 655	2 076	2 908	3 783	PIB par habitant
GDP at constant prices	18 748	20 594	23 384	25 664	28 058	30 748	33 638	PIB aux prix constants
Growth rates	2.7	9.8	13.5	9.8	9.3	9.6	9.4	Taux de croissance
Kenya								**Kenya**
GDP at current prices	12 896	12 705	13 059	13 191	15 036	16 088	19 184	PIB aux prix courants
GDP per capita	430	414	416	412	459	481	560	PIB par habitant
GDP at constant prices	13 283	13 363	13 948	14 003	14 391	15 015	15 727	PIB aux prix constants
Growth rates	2.3	0.6	4.4	0.4	2.8	4.3	4.7	Taux de croissance
Kiribati								**Kiribati**
GDP at current prices	51	47	47	50	57	66	72	PIB aux prix courants
GDP per capita	583	526	510	535	601	680	721	PIB par habitant
GDP at constant prices	30	30	29	29	29	32	34	PIB aux prix constants
Growth rates	-8.6	2.1	-5.4	-0.2	2.3	8.9	5.6	Taux de croissance
Korea, Dem. P. R.								**Corée, R. p. dém. de**
GDP at current prices	10 280	10 608	11 022	10 910	11 051	11 168	12 260	PIB aux prix courants
GDP per capita	452	462	476	468	471	473	517	PIB par habitant
GDP at constant prices	11 390	11 538	11 960	12 105	12 320	12 320	12 430	PIB aux prix constants
Growth rates	6.2	1.3	3.7	1.2	1.8	0.0	0.9	Taux de croissance
Korea, Republic of								**Corée, République de**
GDP at current prices	445 401	511 659	481 894	546 935	608 146	680 492	787 627	PIB aux prix courants
GDP per capita	9 582	10 938	10 244	11 572	12 813	14 283	16 472	PIB par habitant
GDP at constant prices	438 726	475 957	494 217	528 666	545 039	570 817	593 433	PIB aux prix constants
Growth rates	9.5	8.5	3.8	7.0	3.1	4.7	4.0	Taux de croissance
Kuwait								**Koweït**
GDP at current prices	30 123	37 718	34 890	38 119	46 200	55 718	74 214	PIB aux prix courants
GDP per capita	14 348	16 916	14 908	15 636	18 298	21 377	27 621	PIB par habitant
GDP at constant prices	28 025	29 338	29 552	31 062	35 221	37 403	38 602	PIB aux prix constants
Growth rates	-4.9	4.7	0.7	5.1	13.4	6.2	3.2	Taux de croissance
Kyrgyzstan								**Kirghizistan**
GDP at current prices	1 250	1 370	1 527	1 606	1 922	2 212	2 441	PIB aux prix courants
GDP per capita	256	277	304	316	374	425	464	PIB par habitant
GDP at constant prices	1 647	1 737	1 829	1 829	1 957	2 095	2 082	PIB aux prix constants
Growth rates	3.7	5.4	5.3	0.0	7.0	7.0	-0.6	Taux de croissance
Lao People's Dem. Rep.								**Rép. dém. pop. lao**
GDP at current prices	1 454	1 733	1 754	1 830	2 130	2 512	2 872	PIB aux prix courants
GDP per capita	282	328	325	331	376	434	485	PIB par habitant
GDP at constant prices	1 505	1 593	1 685	1 784	1 887	2 017	2 165	PIB aux prix constants
Growth rates	7.3	5.8	5.8	5.9	5.8	6.9	7.3	Taux de croissance
Latvia								**Lettonie**
GDP at current prices	7 219	7 726	8 231	9 203	11 055	13 597	15 244	PIB aux prix courants
GDP per capita	3 019	3 256	3 492	3 929	4 744	5 865	6 608	PIB par habitant
GDP at constant prices	5 268	5 631	6 082	6 474	6 941	7 534	8 219	PIB aux prix constants
Growth rates	3.3	6.9	8.0	6.4	7.2	8.5	9.1	Taux de croissance
Lebanon								**Liban**
GDP at current prices	17 009	16 679	17 065	18 462	19 396	20 856	21 184	PIB aux prix courants
GDP per capita	5 057	4 909	4 970	5 322	5 535	5 891	5 923	PIB par habitant
GDP at constant prices	5 627	5 627	5 831	5 754	5 927	6 223	6 285	PIB aux prix constants
Growth rates	1.0	0.0	3.6	-1.3	3.0	5.0	1.0	Taux de croissance
Lesotho								**Lesotho**
GDP at current prices	911	859	763	699	1 077	1 324	1 335	PIB aux prix courants
GDP per capita	513	481	425	389	598	737	744	PIB par habitant
GDP at constant prices	854	865	893	924	955	974	968	PIB aux prix constants
Growth rates	0.2	1.3	3.2	3.5	3.3	2.0	-0.7	Taux de croissance
Liberia								**Libéria**
GDP at current prices	442	561	543	559	435	492	561	PIB aux prix courants
GDP per capita	152	183	172	174	135	152	171	PIB par habitant
GDP at constant prices	392	481	495	513	352	361	391	PIB aux prix constants
Growth rates	22.9	22.6	2.9	3.7	-31.3	2.4	8.5	Taux de croissance

Gross domestic product and gross domestic product per capita—In millions of US dollars at current and constant 1990 prices; per capita US dollars; real rates of growth (*continued*)

Produit intérieur brut et produit intérieur brut par habitant—En millions de dollars E.U. aux prix courants et constants de 1990 ; par habitant en dollars E.U. ; taux de croissance réels (*suite*)

Country or area	1999	2000	2001	2002	2003	2004	2005	Pays ou zone
Libyan Arab Jamah.								**Jamah. arabe libyenne**
GDP at current prices	30 483	34 265	28 420	19 131	23 273	28 025	37 173	PIB aux prix courants
GDP per capita	5 859	6 457	5 252	3 466	4 135	4 882	6 351	PIB par habitant
GDP at constant prices	34 540	35 348	35 529	35 443	42 280	44 135	46 022	PIB aux prix constants
Growth rates	0.7	2.3	0.5	-0.2	19.3	4.4	4.3	Taux de croissance
Liechtenstein								**Liechtenstein**
GDP at current prices	2 664	2 484	2 492	2 689	3 071	3 413	3 482	PIB aux prix courants
GDP per capita	81 980	75 583	75 020	80 123	90 627	99 767	100 860	PIB par habitant
GDP at constant prices	2 414	2 491	2 472	2 449	2 402	2 452	2 497	PIB aux prix constants
Growth rates	10.4	3.2	-0.7	-0.9	-1.9	2.1	1.9	Taux de croissance
Lithuania								**Lituanie**
GDP at current prices	10 840	11 462	12 141	14 128	18 548	22 456	24 864	PIB aux prix courants
GDP per capita	3 078	3 275	3 488	4 075	5 369	6 521	7 247	PIB par habitant
GDP at constant prices	6 691	7 002	7 453	7 957	8 792	9 406	10 064	PIB aux prix constants
Growth rates	-1.7	4.7	6.4	6.8	10.5	7.0	7.0	Taux de croissance
Luxembourg								**Luxembourg**
GDP at current prices	21 187	20 270	20 199	22 614	28 987	33 594	36 468	PIB aux prix courants
GDP per capita	49 364	46 573	45 778	50 568	63 974	73 189	78 442	PIB par habitant
GDP at constant prices	19 097	20 709	21 231	22 003	22 451	23 405	24 350	PIB aux prix constants
Growth rates	8.4	8.4	2.5	3.6	2.0	4.2	4.0	Taux de croissance
Madagascar								**Madagascar**
GDP at current prices	3 721	3 878	4 530	4 397	5 473	4 364	4 950	PIB aux prix courants
GDP per capita	237	239	272	256	311	241	266	PIB par habitant
GDP at constant prices	3 492	3 657	3 877	3 386	3 715	3 911	4 162	PIB aux prix constants
Growth rates	4.7	4.7	6.0	-12.7	9.7	5.3	6.4	Taux de croissance
Malawi								**Malawi**
GDP at current prices	1 776	1 744	1 717	1 935	1 764	1 903	2 140	PIB aux prix courants
GDP per capita	158	151	146	160	143	151	166	PIB par habitant
GDP at constant prices	3 023	3 071	2 923	3 001	3 183	3 346	3 409	PIB aux prix constants
Growth rates	1.3	1.6	-4.8	2.7	6.1	5.1	1.9	Taux de croissance
Malaysia								**Malaisie**
GDP at current prices	79 148	90 320	88 001	95 266	103 952	118 318	130 770	PIB aux prix courants
GDP per capita	3 520	3 927	3 746	3 974	4 254	4 753	5 159	PIB par habitant
GDP at constant prices	80 351	87 469	87 747	91 567	96 526	103 420	108 912	PIB aux prix constants
Growth rates	6.1	8.9	0.3	4.4	5.4	7.1	5.3	Taux de croissance
Maldives								**Maldives**
GDP at current prices	589	624	625	641	691	753	770	PIB aux prix courants
GDP per capita	2 086	2 151	2 098	2 096	2 204	2 345	2 338	PIB par habitant
GDP at constant prices	426	445	460	488	533	584	583	PIB aux prix constants
Growth rates	7.8	4.4	3.3	6.1	9.2	9.6	-0.2	Taux de croissance
Mali								**Mali**
GDP at current prices	2 954	2 670	3 032	3 304	4 291	4 831	5 181	PIB aux prix courants
GDP per capita	261	229	253	267	337	368	383	PIB par habitant
GDP at constant prices	3 594	3 709	4 158	4 330	4 653	4 754	5 061	PIB aux prix constants
Growth rates	6.7	3.2	12.1	4.2	7.4	2.2	6.4	Taux de croissance
Malta								**Malte**
GDP at current prices	3 881	3 793	3 771	4 031	4 753	5 304	5 573	PIB aux prix courants
GDP per capita	9 966	9 682	9 570	10 178	11 943	13 265	13 877	PIB par habitant
GDP at constant prices	3 860	4 054	4 064	4 108	4 020	4 030	4 217	PIB aux prix constants
Growth rates	4.7	5.0	0.2	1.1	-2.1	0.2	4.7	Taux de croissance
Marshall Islands								**Iles Marshall**
GDP at current prices	95	99	99	105	105	108	111	PIB aux prix courants
GDP per capita	1 856	1 896	1 855	1 896	1 826	1 811	1 791	PIB par habitant
GDP at constant prices	60	59	58	61	62	63	63	PIB aux prix constants
Growth rates	0.8	-2.0	-1.5	4.0	2.0	1.5	0.8	Taux de croissance
Mauritania								**Mauritanie**
GDP at current prices	964	928	967	983	1 180	1 351	1 672	PIB aux prix courants
GDP per capita	375	351	355	350	408	453	545	PIB par habitant
GDP at constant prices	1 528	1 601	1 670	1 708	1 818	1 942	2 048	PIB aux prix constants
Growth rates	5.6	4.8	4.3	2.3	6.4	6.9	5.4	Taux de croissance

Gross domestic product and gross domestic product per capita—In millions of US dollars at current and constant 1990 prices; per capita US dollars; real rates of growth (*continued*)

Produit intérieur brut et produit intérieur brut par habitant—En millions de dollars E.U. aux prix courants et constants de 1990 ; par habitant en dollars E.U. ; taux de croissance réels (*suite*)

Country or area	1999	2000	2001	2002	2003	2004	2005	Pays ou zone
Mauritius								**Maurice**
GDP at current prices	4 266	4 552	4 539	4 744	5 634	6 317	6 288	PIB aux prix courants
GDP per capita	3 634	3 839	3 790	3 922	4 613	5 123	5 052	PIB par habitant
GDP at constant prices	3 985	4 350	4 579	4 658	4 854	5 074	5 228	PIB aux prix constants
Growth rates	2.9	9.2	5.3	1.7	4.2	4.5	3.0	Taux de croissance
Mexico								**Mexique**
GDP at current prices	480 600	580 792	621 866	648 629	638 797	683 069	768 437	PIB aux prix courants
GDP per capita	4 873	5 803	6 125	6 301	6 122	6 462	7 180	PIB par habitant
GDP at constant prices	346 767	369 622	369 501	372 354	377 530	393 240	404 412	PIB aux prix constants
Growth rates	3.8	6.6	0.0	0.8	1.4	4.2	2.8	Taux de croissance
Micronesia (Fed. States of)								**Micronésie (Etats féd. de)**
GDP at current prices	198	214	217	223	232	228	239	PIB aux prix courants
GDP per capita	1 852	1 998	2 022	2 067	2 134	2 081	2 168	PIB par habitant
GDP at constant prices	154	163	163	168	175	169	171	PIB aux prix constants
Growth rates	-3.8	5.7	0.2	2.9	4.3	-3.5	1.4	Taux de croissance
Monaco								**Monaco**
GDP at current prices	791	727	738	808	1 005	1 157	1 203	PIB aux prix courants
GDP per capita	23 967	21 776	21 877	23 695	29 134	33 197	34 128	PIB par habitant
GDP at constant prices	797	835	856	871	886	912	929	PIB aux prix constants
Growth rates	4.0	4.8	2.5	1.7	1.7	3.0	1.9	Taux de croissance
Mongolia								**Mongolie**
GDP at current prices	906	946	1 016	1 118	1 274	1 612	1 867	PIB aux prix courants
GDP per capita	366	379	403	438	493	617	706	PIB par habitant
GDP at constant prices	1 236	1 249	1 262	1 313	1 386	1 535	1 642	PIB aux prix constants
Growth rates	3.2	1.1	1.0	4.0	5.6	10.7	7.0	Taux de croissance
Montenegro								**Monténégro**
GDP at current prices	837	942	1 114	1 225	1 571	1 906	2 042	PIB aux prix courants
GDP per capita	1 346	1 538	1 812	1 985	2 541	3 072	3 310	PIB par habitant
GDP at constant prices	1 407	1 450	1 421	1 446	1 480	1 535	1 598	PIB aux prix constants
Growth rates	-8.3	3.1	-2.0	1.7	2.4	3.7	4.1	Taux de croissance
Montserrat								**Montserrat**
GDP at current prices	35	35	35	38	38	41	42	PIB aux prix courants
GDP per capita	7 325	8 920	9 964	10 848	9 951	9 793	9 449	PIB par habitant
GDP at constant prices	40	38	36	37	37	38	38	PIB aux prix constants
Growth rates	-9.1	-3.5	-7.0	3.2	-0.7	4.6	-0.7	Taux de croissance
Morocco								**Maroc**
GDP at current prices	35 249	33 335	33 901	36 094	43 813	50 031	51 461	PIB aux prix courants
GDP per capita	1 212	1 129	1 131	1 186	1 418	1 596	1 617	PIB par habitant
GDP at constant prices	31 930	32 235	34 265	35 358	37 311	38 894	39 356	PIB aux prix constants
Growth rates	-0.1	1.0	6.3	3.2	5.5	4.2	1.2	Taux de croissance
Mozambique								**Mozambique**
GDP at current prices	4 064	3 832	3 697	4 092	4 789	5 912	6 682	PIB aux prix courants
GDP per capita	232	214	202	219	251	304	338	PIB par habitant
GDP at constant prices	4 425	4 511	5 102	5 518	5 955	6 401	6 894	PIB aux prix constants
Growth rates	7.5	1.9	13.1	8.2	7.9	7.5	7.7	Taux de croissance
Myanmar								**Myanmar**
GDP at current prices	6 576	7 275	7 634	10 369	10 000	10 062	10 938	PIB aux prix courants
GDP per capita	140	152	158	212	202	201	217	PIB par habitant
GDP at constant prices	9 084	10 333	11 505	12 888	14 672	15 406	16 099	PIB aux prix constants
Growth rates	10.9	13.7	11.3	12.0	13.8	5.0	4.5	Taux de croissance
Namibia								**Namibie**
GDP at current prices	3 386	3 414	3 216	3 122	4 473	5 713	6 130	PIB aux prix courants
GDP per capita	1 827	1 802	1 666	1 593	2 252	2 843	3 018	PIB par habitant
GDP at constant prices	3 421	3 540	3 625	3 867	4 001	4 239	4 389	PIB aux prix constants
Growth rates	3.4	3.5	2.4	6.7	3.5	5.9	3.5	Taux de croissance
Nauru								**Nauru**
GDP at current prices	34	33	31	36	44	52	55	PIB aux prix courants
GDP per capita	2 836	2 702	2 518	2 784	3 357	3 874	4 068	PIB par habitant
GDP at constant prices	30	30	30	30	30	30	30	PIB aux prix constants
Growth rates	-1.9	-0.1	0.6	0.8	0.0	0.0	0.0	Taux de croissance

16

Gross domestic product and gross domestic product per capita—In millions of US dollars at current and constant 1990 prices; per capita US dollars; real rates of growth (*continued*)

Produit intérieur brut et produit intérieur brut par habitant—En millions de dollars E.U. aux prix courants et constants de 1990 ; par habitant en dollars E.U. ; taux de croissance réels (*suite*)

Country or area	1999	2000	2001	2002	2003	2004	2005	Pays ou zone
Nepal								**Népal**
GDP at current prices	5 012	5 338	5 487	5 429	5 998	6 727	7 412	PIB aux prix courants
GDP per capita	210	218	220	213	230	253	273	PIB par habitant
GDP at constant prices	5 407	5 738	6 061	6 025	6 229	6 438	6 600	PIB aux prix constants
Growth rates	4.5	6.1	5.6	-0.6	3.4	3.4	2.5	Taux de croissance
Netherlands								**Pays-Bas**
GDP at current prices	415 595	386 510	400 651	437 827	537 619	606 734	624 187	PIB aux prix courants
GDP per capita	26 282	24 313	25 069	27 252	33 293	37 392	38 296	PIB par habitant
GDP at constant prices	395 685	409 401	415 243	415 561	415 009	422 126	426 912	PIB aux prix constants
Growth rates	4.0	3.5	1.4	0.1	-0.1	1.7	1.1	Taux de croissance
Netherlands Antilles								**Antilles néerlandaises**
GDP at current prices	2 736	2 798	2 884	2 905	3 002	3 081	3 204	PIB aux prix courants
GDP per capita	15 476	15 931	16 406	16 417	16 787	17 032	17 540	PIB par habitant
GDP at constant prices	2 282	2 221	2 249	2 256	2 288	2 313	2 334	PIB aux prix constants
Growth rates	-1.8	-2.7	1.3	0.3	1.4	1.1	0.9	Taux de croissance
New Caledonia								**Nouvelle-Calédonie**
GDP at current prices	3 325	3 003	2 982	3 233	3 939	4 326	4 341	PIB aux prix courants
GDP per capita	15 765	13 949	13 574	14 431	17 250	18 598	18 328	PIB par habitant
GDP at constant prices	2 916	2 978	2 976	3 022	3 040	3 008	3 013	PIB aux prix constants
Growth rates	0.9	2.1	-0.1	1.6	0.6	-1.1	0.2	Taux de croissance
New Zealand								**Nouvelle-Zélande**
GDP at current prices	58 052	52 673	52 496	60 520	80 846	98 469	109 607	PIB aux prix courants
GDP per capita	15 340	13 795	13 609	15 515	20 488	24 683	27 209	PIB par habitant
GDP at constant prices	56 858	58 076	60 366	63 182	65 431	67 845	69 233	PIB aux prix constants
Growth rates	5.3	2.1	3.9	4.7	3.6	3.7	2.0	Taux de croissance
Nicaragua								**Nicaragua**
GDP at current prices	3 743	3 907	4 125	4 026	4 102	4 496	4 910	PIB aux prix courants
GDP per capita	770	788	815	780	779	836	895	PIB par habitant
GDP at constant prices	4 824	5 022	5 171	5 210	5 341	5 616	5 840	PIB aux prix constants
Growth rates	7.0	4.1	3.0	0.8	2.5	5.1	4.0	Taux de croissance
Niger								**Niger**
GDP at current prices	1 913	1 666	1 814	2 065	2 523	2 792	3 245	PIB aux prix courants
GDP per capita	168	141	149	164	193	207	232	PIB par habitant
GDP at constant prices	3 208	3 126	3 358	3 538	3 671	3 649	3 909	PIB aux prix constants
Growth rates	1.0	-2.6	7.4	5.3	3.8	-0.6	7.1	Taux de croissance
Nigeria								**Nigéria**
GDP at current prices	51 983	67 359	63 429	66 218	78 441	87 845	113 461	PIB aux prix courants
GDP per capita	453	573	527	538	623	683	863	PIB par habitant
GDP at constant prices	48 904	51 296	53 716	56 204	61 581	65 633	69 720	PIB aux prix constants
Growth rates	1.2	4.9	4.7	4.6	9.6	6.6	6.2	Taux de croissance
Norway								**Norvège**
GDP at current prices	158 099	166 905	169 739	190 277	222 697	254 706	295 513	PIB aux prix courants
GDP per capita	35 332	37 072	37 486	41 798	48 673	55 396	63 960	PIB par habitant
GDP at constant prices	162 736	167 353	171 915	173 817	175 778	181 189	185 281	PIB aux prix constants
Growth rates	2.1	2.8	2.7	1.1	1.1	3.1	2.3	Taux de croissance
Occupied Palestinian Terr.								**Terr. palestinien occupé**
GDP at current prices	4 179	4 116	3 816	3 484	3 921	4 068	4 179	PIB aux prix courants
GDP per capita	1 374	1 307	1 171	1 035	1 128	1 134	1 129	PIB par habitant
GDP at constant prices	3 455	3 263	3 054	2 940	3 189	3 253	3 412	PIB aux prix constants
Growth rates	8.8	-5.6	-6.4	-3.8	8.5	2.0	4.9	Taux de croissance
Oman								**Oman**
GDP at current prices	15 710	19 868	19 949	20 325	21 784	24 778	30 269	PIB aux prix courants
GDP per capita	6 539	8 136	8 072	8 154	8 676	9 779	11 792	PIB par habitant
GDP at constant prices	17 389	18 343	19 720	20 226	20 632	21 795	22 627	PIB aux prix constants
Growth rates	-0.2	5.5	7.5	2.6	2.0	5.6	3.8	Taux de croissance
Pakistan								**Pakistan**
GDP at current prices	70 598	70 709	67 219	73 701	83 510	94 969	110 017	PIB aux prix courants
GDP per capita	507	496	461	495	550	614	697	PIB par habitant
GDP at constant prices	72 861	74 842	76 234	78 688	82 584	87 856	94 695	PIB aux prix constants
Growth rates	4.3	2.7	1.9	3.2	5.0	6.4	7.8	Taux de croissance

16 Gross domestic product and gross domestic product per capita—In millions of US dollars at current and constant 1990 prices; per capita US dollars; real rates of growth (*continued*)

Produit intérieur brut et produit intérieur brut par habitant—En millions de dollars E.U. aux prix courants et constants de 1990 ; par habitant en dollars E.U. ; taux de croissance réels (*suite*)

Country or area	1999	2000	2001	2002	2003	2004	2005	Pays ou zone
Palau								**Palaos**
GDP at current prices	113	117	121	115	117	120	123	PIB aux prix courants
GDP per capita	5 970	6 076	6 194	5 849	5 909	6 029	6 150	PIB par habitant
GDP at constant prices	79	79	83	83	85	86	88	PIB aux prix constants
Growth rates	-5.4	0.3	4.5	1.1	1.5	2.0	2.0	Taux de croissance
Panama								**Panama**
GDP at current prices	11 456	11 621	11 808	12 272	12 933	14 204	15 241	PIB aux prix courants
GDP per capita	3 959	3 939	3 927	4 007	4 146	4 473	4 716	PIB par habitant
GDP at constant prices	9 694	9 957	10 014	10 237	10 668	11 474	12 105	PIB aux prix constants
Growth rates	3.9	2.7	0.6	2.2	4.2	7.6	5.5	Taux de croissance
Papua New Guinea								**Papouasie-Nvl-Guinée**
GDP at current prices	3 706	3 864	3 470	3 434	4 169	4 935	5 330	PIB aux prix courants
GDP per capita	716	729	640	620	737	855	905	PIB par habitant
GDP at constant prices	5 708	5 708	5 862	5 981	6 143	6 296	6 473	PIB aux prix constants
Growth rates	10.1	0.0	2.7	2.0	2.7	2.5	2.8	Taux de croissance
Paraguay								**Paraguay**
GDP at current prices	7 301	7 095	6 446	5 092	5 552	6 950	7 684	PIB aux prix courants
GDP per capita	1 368	1 297	1 150	887	945	1 155	1 248	PIB par habitant
GDP at constant prices	6 055	5 853	5 973	5 970	6 200	6 456	6 630	PIB aux prix constants
Growth rates	-1.5	-3.3	2.1	0.0	3.8	4.1	2.7	Taux de croissance
Peru								**Pérou**
GDP at current prices	51 393	53 131	53 699	56 554	60 800	68 634	76 607	PIB aux prix courants
GDP per capita	2 013	2 047	2 037	2 113	2 238	2 490	2 739	PIB par habitant
GDP at constant prices	42 196	43 430	43 510	45 659	47 468	49 751	52 487	PIB aux prix constants
Growth rates	0.9	2.9	0.2	4.9	4.0	4.8	5.5	Taux de croissance
Philippines								**Philippines**
GDP at current prices	76 157	75 031	71 216	76 814	79 202	86 123	97 653	PIB aux prix courants
GDP per capita	1 025	990	922	976	988	1 055	1 176	PIB par habitant
GDP at constant prices	56 453	59 115	60 873	63 581	66 445	70 449	74 061	PIB aux prix constants
Growth rates	3.4	4.7	3.0	4.4	4.5	6.0	5.1	Taux de croissance
Poland								**Pologne**
GDP at current prices	164 482	166 561	185 787	191 448	209 541	241 592	290 006	PIB aux prix courants
GDP per capita	4 255	4 310	4 809	4 958	5 430	6 265	7 527	PIB par habitant
GDP at constant prices	86 904	90 338	91 256	92 507	96 067	101 199	104 481	PIB aux prix constants
Growth rates	4.1	4.0	1.0	1.4	3.8	5.3	3.2	Taux de croissance
Portugal								**Portugal**
GDP at current prices	121 659	112 650	115 711	127 461	155 212	177 595	183 300	PIB aux prix courants
GDP per capita	11 955	11 017	11 260	12 338	14 944	17 009	17 466	PIB par habitant
GDP at constant prices	96 296	100 076	102 093	102 872	101 720	102 922	103 307	PIB aux prix constants
Growth rates	3.9	3.9	2.0	0.8	-1.1	1.2	0.4	Taux de croissance
Puerto Rico								**Porto Rico**
GDP at current prices	61 702	69 208	71 306	74 362	78 947	82 033	86 882	PIB aux prix courants
GDP per capita	16 198	18 047	18 472	19 142	20 198	20 863	21 970	PIB par habitant
GDP at constant prices	47 429	50 424	50 720	50 877	52 517	52 660	53 788	PIB aux prix constants
Growth rates	3.3	6.3	0.6	0.3	3.2	0.3	2.1	Taux de croissance
Qatar								**Qatar**
GDP at current prices	12 393	17 760	17 741	19 707	23 701	31 591	42 113	PIB aux prix courants
GDP per capita	21 390	29 290	27 615	28 715	32 324	40 662	51 809	PIB par habitant
GDP at constant prices	12 204	13 097	13 923	14 945	15 820	17 584	18 723	PIB aux prix constants
Growth rates	3.2	7.3	6.3	7.3	5.9	11.2	6.5	Taux de croissance
Republic of Moldova								**République de Moldova**
GDP at current prices	1 172	1 288	1 481	1 662	1 981	2 598	2 917	PIB aux prix courants
GDP per capita	273	301	348	392	468	616	694	PIB par habitant
GDP at constant prices	1 352	1 380	1 465	1 579	1 684	1 808	1 936	PIB aux prix constants
Growth rates	-3.4	2.1	6.1	7.8	6.6	7.4	7.1	Taux de croissance
Romania								**Roumanie**
GDP at current prices	35 592	37 025	40 181	45 825	59 507	75 489	98 566	PIB aux prix courants
GDP per capita	1 602	1 674	1 824	2 088	2 722	3 464	4 540	PIB par habitant
GDP at constant prices	31 558	32 236	34 088	35 834	37 706	40 891	42 555	PIB aux prix constants
Growth rates	-1.2	2.1	5.7	5.1	5.2	8.4	4.1	Taux de croissance

16 **Gross domestic product and gross domestic product per capita**—In millions of US dollars at current and constant 1990 prices; per capita US dollars; real rates of growth (*continued*)

Produit intérieur brut et produit intérieur brut par habitant—En millions de dollars E.U. aux prix courants et constants de 1990 ; par habitant en dollars E.U. ; taux de croissance réels (*suite*)

Country or area	1999	2000	2001	2002	2003	2004	2005	Pays ou zone
Russian Federation								**Fédération de Russie**
GDP at current prices	195 908	259 718	306 618	345 488	431 488	590 287	765 968	PIB aux prix courants
GDP per capita	1 332	1 772	2 100	2 377	2 984	4 102	5 349	PIB par habitant
GDP at constant prices	347 963	382 917	402 412	421 501	452 475	484 798	515 883	PIB aux prix constants
Growth rates	6.4	10.0	5.1	4.7	7.3	7.1	6.4	Taux de croissance
Rwanda								**Rwanda**
GDP at current prices	1 875	1 732	1 654	1 669	1 684	1 823	2 118	PIB aux prix courants
GDP per capita	250	216	197	194	192	205	234	PIB par habitant
GDP at constant prices	2 490	2 646	2 822	3 086	3 107	3 227	3 389	PIB aux prix constants
Growth rates	6.5	6.3	6.7	9.3	0.7	3.8	5.0	Taux de croissance
Saint Kitts and Nevis								**Saint-Kitts-et-Nevis**
GDP at current prices	305	329	342	351	365	405	453	PIB aux prix courants
GDP per capita	7 584	8 138	8 399	8 522	8 761	9 588	10 612	PIB par habitant
GDP at constant prices	229	239	244	246	248	264	275	PIB aux prix constants
Growth rates	3.5	4.5	2.0	1.0	0.6	6.6	4.1	Taux de croissance
Saint Lucia								**Sainte-Lucie**
GDP at current prices	692	707	685	703	739	787	851	PIB aux prix courants
GDP per capita	4 518	4 575	4 403	4 483	4 669	4 934	5 292	PIB par habitant
GDP at constant prices	538	530	503	511	527	561	590	PIB aux prix constants
Growth rates	2.5	-1.4	-5.1	1.6	3.2	6.3	5.1	Taux de croissance
St. Vincent-Grenadines								**St. Vincent-Grenadines**
GDP at current prices	330	335	346	365	380	408	428	PIB aux prix courants
GDP per capita	2 861	2 891	2 965	3 117	3 223	3 443	3 596	PIB par habitant
GDP at constant prices	312	318	321	333	346	363	376	PIB aux prix constants
Growth rates	4.2	1.8	1.0	3.7	4.1	4.9	3.6	Taux de croissance
Samoa								**Samoa**
GDP at current prices	230	231	240	262	319	375	406	PIB aux prix courants
GDP per capita	1 307	1 301	1 339	1 450	1 748	2 040	2 196	PIB par habitant
GDP at constant prices	238	254	269	273	282	292	300	PIB aux prix constants
Growth rates	1.3	6.8	6.1	1.3	3.5	3.5	2.5	Taux de croissance
San Marino								**Saint-Marin**
GDP at current prices	853	774	815	880	1 123	1 287	1 315	PIB aux prix courants
GDP per capita	31 952	28 708	29 975	32 087	40 616	46 148	46 781	PIB par habitant
GDP at constant prices	1 197	1 223	1 291	1 295	1 345	1 372	1 372	PIB aux prix constants
Growth rates	9.0	2.2	5.5	0.3	3.9	2.0	0.0	Taux de croissance
Sao Tome and Principe								**Sao Tomé-et-Principe**
GDP at current prices	47	46	48	54	59	64	73	PIB aux prix courants
GDP per capita	343	332	334	367	396	421	464	PIB par habitant
GDP at constant prices	67	69	72	75	78	82	85	PIB aux prix constants
Growth rates	2.5	3.0	4.0	4.1	4.5	4.5	3.2	Taux de croissance
Saudi Arabia								**Arabie saoudite**
GDP at current prices	160 957	188 442	183 012	188 551	214 573	250 558	314 021	PIB aux prix courants
GDP per capita	7 706	8 771	8 285	8 305	9 199	10 462	12 779	PIB par habitant
GDP at constant prices	130 331	136 671	137 419	137 595	148 134	155 886	165 276	PIB aux prix constants
Growth rates	-0.8	4.9	0.5	0.1	7.7	5.2	6.0	Taux de croissance
Senegal								**Sénégal**
GDP at current prices	4 751	4 374	4 611	4 982	6 410	7 617	8 274	PIB aux prix courants
GDP per capita	471	423	435	459	576	669	710	PIB par habitant
GDP at constant prices	7 525	7 943	8 388	8 858	8 956	9 538	10 110	PIB aux prix constants
Growth rates	5.0	5.6	5.6	5.6	1.1	6.5	6.0	Taux de croissance
Serbia								**Serbie**
GDP at current prices	9 378	8 068	10 624	14 254	19 024	22 440	24 207	PIB aux prix courants
GDP per capita	1 207	1 053	1 373	1 901	2 543	3 007	3 244	PIB par habitant
GDP at constant prices	20 460	21 521	22 615	23 638	24 213	26 475	28 141	PIB aux prix constants
Growth rates	-22.8	5.2	5.1	4.5	2.4	9.3	6.3	Taux de croissance
Seychelles								**Seychelles**
GDP at current prices	622	618	618	699	703	703	699	PIB aux prix courants
GDP per capita	8 106	8 008	7 944	8 912	8 883	8 799	8 668	PIB par habitant
GDP at constant prices	565	564	552	559	523	513	499	PIB aux prix constants
Growth rates	1.9	-0.1	-2.2	1.3	-6.3	-2.0	-2.7	Taux de croissance

Gross domestic product and gross domestic product per capita—In millions of US dollars at current and constant 1990 prices; per capita US dollars; real rates of growth *(continued)*

Produit intérieur brut et produit intérieur brut par habitant—En millions de dollars E.U. aux prix courants et constants de 1990 ; par habitant en dollars E.U. ; taux de croissance réels *(suite)*

Country or area	1999	2000	2001	2002	2003	2004	2005	Pays ou zone
Sierra Leone								**Sierra Leone**
GDP at current prices	669	636	884	1 033	1 073	1 071	1 162	PIB aux prix courants
GDP per capita	153	141	189	211	210	201	210	PIB par habitant
GDP at constant prices	593	615	727	927	1 012	1 087	1 169	PIB aux prix constants
Growth rates	-8.1	3.8	18.2	27.4	9.2	7.4	7.5	Taux de croissance
Singapore								**Singapour**
GDP at current prices	82 611	92 717	85 612	88 468	92 727	107 502	116 775	PIB aux prix courants
GDP per capita	21 056	23 079	20 897	21 251	21 974	25 161	26 997	PIB par habitant
GDP at constant prices	70 321	77 374	75 607	78 664	80 971	88 029	93 645	PIB aux prix constants
Growth rates	7.2	10.0	-2.3	4.0	2.9	8.7	6.4	Taux de croissance
Slovakia								**Slovaquie**
GDP at current prices	20 407	20 291	20 884	24 239	32 665	41 092	46 417	PIB aux prix courants
GDP per capita	3 781	3 757	3 866	4 487	6 047	7 607	8 594	PIB par habitant
GDP at constant prices	17 510	17 867	18 543	19 399	20 265	21 379	22 688	PIB aux prix constants
Growth rates	1.5	2.0	3.8	4.6	4.5	5.5	6.1	Taux de croissance
Slovenia								**Slovénie**
GDP at current prices	21 317	19 098	19 616	22 121	27 749	32 494	34 030	PIB aux prix courants
GDP per capita	10 836	9 710	9 974	11 246	14 106	16 518	17 302	PIB par habitant
GDP at constant prices	20 037	20 817	21 374	22 085	22 643	23 906	24 831	PIB aux prix constants
Growth rates	5.6	3.9	2.7	3.3	2.5	5.6	3.9	Taux de croissance
Solomon Islands								**Iles Salomon**
GDP at current prices	380	338	335	274	256	276	299	PIB aux prix courants
GDP per capita	933	808	778	619	564	592	626	PIB par habitant
GDP at constant prices	272	234	214	209	220	232	242	PIB aux prix constants
Growth rates	-0.2	-14.2	-8.2	-2.7	5.6	5.5	4.0	Taux de croissance
Somalia								**Somalie**
GDP at current prices	2 070	2 070	1 974	2 056	2 100	2 213	2 182	PIB aux prix courants
GDP per capita	304	295	273	276	272	278	265	PIB par habitant
GDP at constant prices	734	759	786	813	831	854	878	PIB aux prix constants
Growth rates	3.5	3.5	3.5	3.5	2.1	2.8	2.8	Taux de croissance
South Africa								**Afrique du Sud**
GDP at current prices	133 184	132 878	118 479	110 882	166 169	214 663	238 825	PIB aux prix courants
GDP per capita	2 958	2 913	2 569	2 381	3 542	4 547	5 035	PIB par habitant
GDP at constant prices	128 807	134 158	137 828	142 913	147 166	153 744	160 346	PIB aux prix constants
Growth rates	2.4	4.2	2.7	3.7	3.0	4.5	4.3	Taux de croissance
Spain								**Espagne**
GDP at current prices	617 906	580 673	608 354	686 104	880 948	1 039 673	1 124 612	PIB aux prix courants
GDP per capita	15 283	14 261	14 796	16 489	20 903	24 379	26 115	PIB par habitant
GDP at constant prices	653 461	686 411	710 739	729 789	751 670	774 931	801 485	PIB aux prix constants
Growth rates	4.7	5.0	3.5	2.7	3.0	3.1	3.4	Taux de croissance
Sri Lanka								**Sri Lanka**
GDP at current prices	16 114	16 717	16 046	16 861	18 600	20 341	23 927	PIB aux prix courants
GDP per capita	820	842	801	834	912	989	1 154	PIB par habitant
GDP at constant prices	12 908	13 680	13 493	14 035	14 860	15 666	16 638	PIB aux prix constants
Growth rates	4.3	6.0	-1.4	4.0	5.9	5.4	6.2	Taux de croissance
Sudan								**Soudan**
GDP at current prices	9 697	11 549	13 028	14 718	16 108	19 040	24 667	PIB aux prix courants
GDP per capita	301	351	388	430	462	536	681	PIB par habitant
GDP at constant prices	20 630	22 335	23 762	25 295	26 838	28 761	31 065	PIB aux prix constants
Growth rates	6.0	8.3	6.4	6.5	6.1	7.2	8.0	Taux de croissance
Suriname								**Suriname**
GDP at current prices	757	775	665	955	1 122	1 285	1 503	PIB aux prix courants
GDP per capita	1 759	1 785	1 519	2 166	2 529	2 879	3 346	PIB par habitant
GDP at constant prices	489	498	520	531	560	603	634	PIB aux prix constants
Growth rates	-1.4	1.9	4.6	2.1	5.4	7.8	5.1	Taux de croissance
Swaziland								**Swaziland**
GDP at current prices	1 377	1 388	1 260	1 192	1 904	2 396	2 588	PIB aux prix courants
GDP per capita	1 359	1 356	1 223	1 153	1 840	2 317	2 507	PIB par habitant
GDP at constant prices	1 161	1 185	1 205	1 238	1 268	1 296	1 325	PIB aux prix constants
Growth rates	3.5	2.1	1.7	2.8	2.4	2.2	2.2	Taux de croissance

16 Gross domestic product and gross domestic product per capita—In millions of US dollars at current and constant 1990 prices; per capita US dollars; real rates of growth *(continued)*

Produit intérieur brut et produit intérieur brut par habitant—En millions de dollars E.U. aux prix courants et constants de 1990 ; par habitant en dollars E.U. ; taux de croissance réels *(suite)*

Country or area	1999	2000	2001	2002	2003	2004	2005	Pays ou zone
Sweden								**Suède**
GDP at current prices	253 722	242 003	221 543	243 563	304 145	350 145	357 683	PIB aux prix courants
GDP per capita	28 621	27 261	24 890	27 265	33 905	38 871	39 561	PIB par habitant
GDP at constant prices	285 674	298 053	301 238	307 252	312 454	324 155	332 912	PIB aux prix constants
Growth rates	4.5	4.3	1.1	2.0	1.7	3.7	2.7	Taux de croissance
Switzerland								**Suisse**
GDP at current prices	264 882	246 044	250 345	276 225	322 699	358 611	365 887	PIB aux prix courants
GDP per capita	37 101	34 328	34 815	38 312	44 659	49 534	50 451	PIB par habitant
GDP at constant prices	252 594	261 715	264 441	265 250	264 522	269 985	275 020	PIB aux prix constants
Growth rates	1.3	3.6	1.0	0.3	-0.3	2.1	1.9	Taux de croissance
Syrian Arab Republic								**Rép. arabe syrienne**
GDP at current prices	17 806	19 651	21 174	21 659	20 724	23 318	25 812	PIB aux prix courants
GDP per capita	1 087	1 169	1 228	1 225	1 143	1 255	1 355	PIB par habitant
GDP at constant prices	19 576	19 693	20 702	21 926	22 170	22 623	23 416	PIB aux prix constants
Growth rates	-3.6	0.6	5.1	5.9	1.1	2.0	3.5	Taux de croissance
Tajikistan								**Tadjikistan**
GDP at current prices	1 087	870	1 066	1 218	1 554	2 073	2 342	PIB aux prix courants
GDP per capita	179	141	171	193	244	322	360	PIB par habitant
GDP at constant prices	1 008	1 092	1 203	1 318	1 452	1 606	1 726	PIB aux prix constants
Growth rates	3.7	8.3	10.2	9.5	10.2	10.6	7.5	Taux de croissance
Thailand								**Thaïlande**
GDP at current prices	122 630	122 725	115 536	126 877	142 920	161 688	176 602	PIB aux prix courants
GDP per capita	2 015	1 998	1 863	2 027	2 263	2 539	2 749	PIB par habitant
GDP at constant prices	126 044	132 031	134 892	142 065	152 057	161 440	168 638	PIB aux prix constants
Growth rates	4.4	4.8	2.2	5.3	7.0	6.2	4.5	Taux de croissance
TFYR of Macedonia								**L'ex-R.y. Macédoine**
GDP at current prices	3 673	3 587	3 437	3 791	4 630	5 369	5 651	PIB aux prix courants
GDP per capita	1 835	1 785	1 705	1 875	2 285	2 644	2 778	PIB par habitant
GDP at constant prices	4 029	4 213	4 022	4 057	4 171	4 244	4 405	PIB aux prix constants
Growth rates	4.3	4.5	-4.5	0.9	2.8	1.8	3.8	Taux de croissance
Timor-Leste								**Timor-Leste**
GDP at current prices	270	316	368	343	336	339	354	PIB aux prix courants
GDP per capita	370	438	498	443	406	382	374	PIB par habitant
GDP at constant prices	162	184	215	200	188	192	198	PIB aux prix constants
Growth rates	-35.5	13.7	16.5	-6.7	-6.2	1.8	3.2	Taux de croissance
Togo								**Togo**
GDP at current prices	1 576	1 329	1 328	1 476	1 759	2 061	2 187	PIB aux prix courants
GDP per capita	304	248	240	260	301	344	356	PIB par habitant
GDP at constant prices	2 037	2 022	2 018	2 101	2 158	2 223	2 262	PIB aux prix constants
Growth rates	2.5	-0.8	-0.2	4.1	2.7	3.0	1.8	Taux de croissance
Tonga								**Tonga**
GDP at current prices	153	148	130	142	163	189	214	PIB aux prix courants
GDP per capita	1 532	1 481	1 290	1 404	1 603	1 850	2 089	PIB par habitant
GDP at constant prices	153	161	164	169	174	176	181	PIB aux prix constants
Growth rates	2.3	5.3	1.8	3.2	2.7	1.3	2.5	Taux de croissance
Trinidad and Tobago								**Trinité-et-Tobago**
GDP at current prices	6 809	8 154	8 825	9 008	10 691	12 319	14 763	PIB aux prix courants
GDP per capita	5 318	6 347	6 846	6 966	8 241	9 467	11 311	PIB par habitant
GDP at constant prices	7 311	7 815	8 446	8 786	9 963	10 611	11 322	PIB aux prix constants
Growth rates	8.0	6.9	8.1	4.0	13.4	6.5	6.7	Taux de croissance
Tunisia								**Tunisie**
GDP at current prices	20 799	19 444	19 969	21 016	24 955	28 134	29 049	PIB aux prix courants
GDP per capita	2 200	2 033	2 064	2 149	2 524	2 815	2 875	PIB par habitant
GDP at constant prices	18 689	19 566	20 516	20 861	22 020	23 307	24 461	PIB aux prix constants
Growth rates	6.1	4.7	4.9	1.7	5.6	5.8	5.0	Taux de croissance
Turkey								**Turquie**
GDP at current prices	184 858	199 264	145 573	184 162	239 700	301 999	362 614	PIB aux prix courants
GDP per capita	2 753	2 920	2 101	2 621	3 364	4 182	4 954	PIB par habitant
GDP at constant prices	199 474	214 154	198 103	213 835	226 226	246 431	264 618	PIB aux prix constants
Growth rates	-4.7	7.4	-7.5	7.9	5.8	8.9	7.4	Taux de croissance

Gross domestic product and gross domestic product per capita—In millions of US dollars at current and constant 1990 prices; per capita US dollars; real rates of growth (*continued*)

Produit intérieur brut et produit intérieur brut par habitant—En millions de dollars E.U. aux prix courants et constants de 1990 ; par habitant en dollars E.U. ; taux de croissance réels (*suite*)

Country or area	1999	2000	2001	2002	2003	2004	2005	Pays ou zone
Turkmenistan								**Turkménistan**
GDP at current prices	3 857	4 157[1]	4 442[1]	4 531[1]	4 774[1]	5 145[1]	5 826[1]	PIB aux prix courants
GDP per capita	868	923[1]	973[1]	979[1]	1 016[1]	1 079[1]	1 205[1]	PIB par habitant
GDP at constant prices	2 287	2 413[1]	2 517[1]	2 524[1]	2 606[1]	2 737[1]	2 999[1]	PIB aux prix constants
Growth rates	16.5	5.5	4.3	0.3	3.3	5.0	9.6	Taux de croissance
Turks and Caicos Islands								**Iles Turques et Caïques**
GDP at current prices	295	319	359	367	410	486	570	PIB aux prix courants
GDP per capita	16 067	16 463	17 316	16 502	17 235	19 288	21 694	PIB par habitant
GDP at constant prices	238	249	267	270	295	329	375	PIB aux prix constants
Growth rates	8.7	4.9	7.0	1.2	9.3	11.4	13.9	Taux de croissance
Tuvalu								**Tuvalu**
GDP at current prices	14	12	13	15	18	23	26	PIB aux prix courants
GDP per capita	1 362	1 204	1 253	1 421	1 780	2 209	2 516	PIB par habitant
GDP at constant prices	14	12	14	15	15	16	17	PIB aux prix constants
Growth rates	2.4	-12.8	13.2	5.5	2.0	6.9	4.8	Taux de croissance
Uganda								**Ouganda**
GDP at current prices	6 017	5 734	5 784	6 015	6 435	7 820	9 115	PIB aux prix courants
GDP per capita	255	236	230	232	240	281	316	PIB par habitant
GDP at constant prices	6 853	7 152	7 614	7 974	8 473	8 954	9 452	PIB aux prix constants
Growth rates	6.5	4.4	6.4	4.7	6.3	5.7	5.6	Taux de croissance
Ukraine								**Ukraine**
GDP at current prices	31 581	31 262	38 009	42 393	50 133	64 881	81 669	PIB aux prix courants
GDP per capita	636	636	783	883	1 055	1 381	1 757	PIB par habitant
GDP at constant prices	36 799	38 967	42 565	44 799	49 098	55 062	56 515	PIB aux prix constants
Growth rates	-0.2	5.9	9.2	5.2	9.6	12.1	2.6	Taux de croissance
United Arab Emirates								**Emirats arabes unis**
GDP at current prices	55 193	70 522	69 546	74 959	88 536	104 204	133 757	PIB aux prix courants
GDP per capita	18 154	21 719	19 939	19 956	21 962	24 322	29 751	PIB par habitant
GDP at constant prices	50 886	57 135	59 114	60 173	67 325	72 312	76 349	PIB aux prix constants
Growth rates	4.4	12.3	3.5	1.8	11.9	7.4	5.6	Taux de croissance
United Kingdom								**Royaume-Uni**
GDP at current prices	1 464 975	1 442 777	1 434 896	1 571 372	1 805 663	2 132 156	2 198 796	PIB aux prix courants
GDP per capita	25 057	24 592	24 372	26 598	30 459	35 847	36 851	PIB par habitant
GDP at constant prices	1 211 405	1 260 273	1 288 302	1 314 059	1 347 149	1 389 268	1 414 606	PIB aux prix constants
Growth rates	3.0	4.0	2.2	2.0	2.5	3.1	1.8	Taux de croissance
United Rep. of Tanzania								**Rép.-Unie de Tanzanie**
GDP at current prices	8 638	9 093	9 453	9 772	10 297	11 351	12 586	PIB aux prix courants
GDP per capita	261	269	274	277	287	310	337	PIB par habitant
GDP at constant prices	6 465	6 795	7 219	7 742	8 292	8 848	9 465	PIB aux prix constants
Growth rates	3.5	5.1	6.2	7.2	7.1	6.7	7.0	Taux de croissance
United States								**Etats-Unis**
GDP at current prices	9 216 200	9 764 800	10 075 900	10 417 600	10 918 500	11 679 200	12 455 800	PIB aux prix courants
GDP per capita	32 767	34 364	35 107	35 945	37 313	39 536	41 768	PIB par habitant
GDP at constant prices	7 684 781	7 968 520	8 028 989	8 158 495	8 380 215	8 734 868	9 016 159	PIB aux prix constants
Growth rates	4.5	3.7	0.8	1.6	2.7	4.2	3.2	Taux de croissance
Uruguay								**Uruguay**
GDP at current prices	20 913	20 086	18 561	12 277	11 191	13 216	16 792	PIB aux prix courants
GDP per capita	6 306	6 011	5 514	3 620	3 277	3 842	4 849	PIB par habitant
GDP at constant prices	11 507	11 341	10 961	9 735	9 972	11 159	11 871	PIB aux prix constants
Growth rates	-2.4	-1.4	-3.3	-11.2	2.4	11.9	6.4	Taux de croissance
Uzbekistan								**Ouzbékistan**
GDP at current prices	17 081	13 759	9 312[1]	9 877	10 155	12 016	12 381	PIB aux prix courants
GDP per capita	701	557	371[1]	388	393	458	466	PIB par habitant
GDP at constant prices	13 913	14 469	15 087[1]	15 726	16 426	17 698	18 583	PIB aux prix constants
Growth rates	4.4	4.0	4.3[1]	4.2	4.5	7.7	5.0	Taux de croissance
Vanuatu								**Vanuatu**
GDP at current prices	251	245	234	235	276	311	329	PIB aux prix courants
GDP per capita	1 337	1 277	1 199	1 180	1 359	1 501	1 556	PIB par habitant
GDP at constant prices	217	223	216	206	211	217	223	PIB aux prix constants
Growth rates	-3.2	2.7	-2.7	-4.9	2.4	3.0	2.8	Taux de croissance

16 Gross domestic product and gross domestic product per capita—In millions of US dollars at current and constant 1990 prices; per capita US dollars; real rates of growth *(continued)*

Produit intérieur brut et produit intérieur brut par habitant—En millions de dollars E.U. aux prix courants et constants de 1990 ; par habitant en dollars E.U. ; taux de croissance réels *(suite)*

Country or area	1999	2000	2001	2002	2003	2004	2005	Pays ou zone
Venezuela (Bolivarian Rep. of)								**Venezuela (Rép. bolivar. du)**
GDP at current prices	97 974	117 148	122 910	92 889	83 522	109 764	132 373	PIB aux prix courants
GDP per capita	4 090	4 798	4 939	3 664	3 235	4 176	4 949	PIB par habitant
GDP at constant prices	55 774	57 831	59 794	54 498	50 293	59 272	64 802	PIB aux prix constants
Growth rates	-6.0	3.7	3.4	-8.9	-7.7	17.9	9.3	Taux de croissance
Viet Nam								**Viet Nam**
GDP at current prices	28 684	31 173	32 685	35 064	39 553	45 724	53 153	PIB aux prix courants
GDP per capita	370	396	410	434	482	550	631	PIB par habitant
GDP at constant prices	12 579	13 433	14 359	15 376	16 505	17 791	19 290	PIB aux prix constants
Growth rates	4.8	6.8	6.9	7.1	7.3	7.8	8.4	Taux de croissance
Yemen								**Yémen**
GDP at current prices	7 660	9 652	9 987	10 787	11 870	13 811	15 508	PIB aux prix courants
GDP per capita	441	538	540	565	602	679	739	PIB par habitant
GDP at constant prices	6 579	7 046	7 397	7 655	7 944	8 252	8 562	PIB aux prix constants
Growth rates	4.8	7.1	5.0	3.5	3.8	3.9	3.8	Taux de croissance
Zambia								**Zambie**
GDP at current prices	3 132	3 239	3 637	3 697	4 305	5 440	7 315	PIB aux prix courants
GDP per capita	299	303	333	333	381	474	627	PIB par habitant
GDP at constant prices	3 864	4 002	4 198	4 336	4 523	4 803	5 050	PIB aux prix constants
Growth rates	2.2	3.6	4.9	3.3	4.3	6.2	5.1	Taux de croissance
Zimbabwe								**Zimbabwe**
GDP at current prices	5 964	5 628[1]	5 609[1]	5 427[1]	5 000[1]	3 071	2 198	PIB aux prix courants
GDP per capita	478	447[1]	442[1]	424[1]	389[1]	237	169	PIB par habitant
GDP at constant prices	10 035	9 267[1]	9 018[1]	8 576[1]	7 743[1]	7 796	7 243	PIB aux prix constants
Growth rates	-3.6	-7.6	-2.7	-4.9	-9.7	0.7	-7.1	Taux de croissance

Source

United Nations Statistics Division, New York, the national accounts database.

Source

Organisation des Nations Unies, Division de statistique, New York, la base de données sur les comptes nationaux.

Notes

1 Price-adjusted rates of exchange (PARE) are used for selected years for conversion to US dollars due to large distortions in the dollar levels of per capita GDP with the use of IMF market exchange rates.

2 Including Guadeloupe, Martinique, Réunion and French Guiana.

3 Weighted rates of exchange were used for the period 1985-2001.

Notes

1 Pour certaines années, on utilise les Taux de change corrigés des prix (TCCP) pour effectuer la conversion en dollars des États-Unis, en raison des aberrations importantes relevées dans les niveaux du PNB exprimés en dollars après conversion à l'aide des taux de change du marché communiqués par le FMI.

2 Y compris Guadeloupe, Martinique, Réunion et Guyane française.

3 Pour la période 1985 à 2001, on a utilisé des taux de change pondérés.

17 Gross domestic product by type of expenditure at current prices

Percentage distribution

Dépenses imputées au produit intérieur brut aux prix courants

Répartition en pourcentage

Country or area Pays ou zone	Year Année	GDP at current prices (mil. nat.cur.) PIB aux prix courants (millions monnaie nat.)	% of Gross domestic product – en % du Produit intérieur brut Household final consumption expenditure Consom. finale des ménages	Govt. final consumption expenditure Consom. finale des admin. publiques	Gross fixed capital formation Formation brute de capital fixe	Changes in inventories Variation des stocks	Exports of goods and services Exportations de biens et services	Imports of goods and services Importations de biens et services
Afghanistan+	2002	182 862	101.5	7.9	12.3	...	58.4	80.0
Afghanistan+	2003	217 898	96.4	8.0	12.7	...	48.5	65.6
Albania[1]	2002	631 338	64.6[2]	11.6	47.4	0.8	19.3	43.7
Albanie[1]	2003	714 049	63.3[2]	11.2	51.4	1.8	19.8	43.8
	2004	775 864	...	...	...	...	21.2	42.9
Algeria	2001	4 260 811	43.4	14.7	22.7	4.8	36.4	21.8
Algérie	2002	4 537 691	43.8	15.4	24.5	6.4	35.4	25.5
	2003	5 264 187	40.4	14.8	24.0	6.3	38.2	23.8
Angola	1988	239 640	45.5	32.9	14.6	0.0	32.8	25.8
Angola	1989	278 866	48.2	28.9	11.2	0.9	33.8	23.1
	1990	308 062	44.7	28.5	11.1	0.6	38.9	23.8
Anguilla	2001	297	80.0	17.9	32.5	...	67.2	97.7
Anguilla	2002	305	80.3	17.9	28.0	...	62.4	88.6
	2003	318	82.5	17.8	29.6	...	64.0	93.9
Antigua and Barbuda	1984	468	69.8	18.5	23.6	0.0	73.7	85.6
Antigua-et-Barbuda	1985	541	71.5	18.3	28.0	0.0	75.7	93.5
	1986	642	69.7	18.9	36.1	0.0	75.2	99.9
Argentina[1]	2003	375 909	63.2	11.4	15.1[4]	...	25.0	14.2
Argentine[1]	2004	447 643	62.8	11.1	19.2[4]	...	25.3	18.2
	2005	532 268[3]	61.3	11.9	21.5[4]	...	24.6	19.1
Armenia[1]	2003	1 624 643	83.3[2]	10.2	23.0	1.3[5]	32.2	50.0
Arménie[1]	2004	1 896 442	84.0[2]	10.7	22.7	1.3[5]	27.4	42.5
	2005	2 228 028	77.7[2]	11.2	27.9	0.5[5]	27.0	40.0
Aruba[1]	2000	3 327	50.0	22.0	23.7	0.9	74.4	71.0
Aruba[1]	2001	3 399	50.4	23.7	21.9	0.6	72.6	69.1
	2002	3 421	52.6	26.3	22.4	0.9	69.3	71.5
Australia+[1]	2002	782 798	59.0	18.1	24.8	0.4	19.1	21.4
Australie+[1]	2003	838 251	58.8	17.9	25.3	0.7	17.3	20.0
	2004	891 524	58.6	18.3	25.5	0.2	18.4	21.2
Austria[1]	2003	226 968	56.6	18.1	21.4	0.4	48.4	44.8
Autriche[1]	2004	237 039	55.7	17.8	21.0	0.4	51.0	46.1
	2005	246 113	55.5	17.7	20.8	0.4	53.2	47.8
Azerbaijan[1]	2003	35 732 500	60.0[2]	12.4	52.9	0.3[5]	42.0	65.5
Azerbaïdjan[1]	2004	42 651 000	55.8[2]	12.9	57.7	0.3[5]	48.8	72.7
	2005	59 377 500	40.1[2]	9.8	45.7[4]	...	62.9	56.4
Bahamas[1]	2003	5 503	68.5[6]	14.3	29.3	2.7	44.0	55.4
Bahamas[1]	2004	5 661[3]	68.8[6]	14.6	29.4	2.8	46.8	59.4
	2005	5 869[3]	67.8[6]	14.9	29.8	3.0	49.1	61.7
Bahrain	2002	3 176	45.2	18.5	17.3	4.3	81.2	66.6
Bahreïn	2003	3 647	43.0	18.4	19.7	1.8	81.1	64.0
	2004	4 141	42.0	17.0	21.6	1.1	82.4	64.2
Bangladesh+[1]	2002	3 005 801	76.0	5.3	23.4	...	14.2	20.0
Bangladesh+[1]	2003	3 329 731	74.9	5.5	24.0	...	15.5	20.8
	2004	3 684 757	74.2	5.6	24.4	...	15.4	22.6
Barbados	2002	4 952	64.1	24.6	16.9	-0.3	50.1	55.3
Barbade	2003	5 390	65.7	23.2	16.9	-0.1	50.7	56.3
	2004	5 632	70.7	21.3	19.2	0.2	49.4	60.8
Belarus[1]	2002	26 138 300	59.5[2]	21.0	22.0	0.2	63.6	67.4
Bélarus[1]	2003	36 564 800	57.1[2]	21.4	25.4	1.2	65.2	69.1
	2004	49 991 800	53.7[2]	20.6	27.1	3.3	67.9	74.3

Country or area / Pays ou zone	Year / Année	GDP at current prices (mil. nat.cur.) / PIB aux prix courants (millions monnaie nat.)	% of Gross domestic product – en % du Produit intérieur brut: Household final consumption expenditure / Consom. finale des ménages	Govt. final consumption expenditure / Consom. finale des admin. publiques	Gross fixed capital formation / Formation brute de capital fixe	Changes in inventories / Variation des stocks	Exports of goods and services / Exportations de biens et services	Imports of goods and services / Importations de biens et services
Belgium[1] Belgique[1]	2002	261 124	54.1[2]	22.3	19.5	-0.3	83.7	79.2
	2003	269 546	54.5[2]	22.8	18.9	0.1	81.5	77.7
	2004	283 752	54.0[2]	22.6	18.5	1.9	83.7	80.8
Belize[1] Belize[1]	1998	1 258	67.3	17.4	21.3	3.1	52.9	62.1
	1999	1 377	65.1	17.1	26.5	3.0	51.3	63.2
	2000	1 514	68.4	15.3	31.0	3.2	48.8	66.7
Benin Bénin	2003	2 067 463	77.2	12.6	19.5	0.8	21.0	31.1
	2004	2 144 700	75.9	12.1	19.4	1.3	20.0	28.6
	2005	2 309 092	76.2	11.9	19.3	-0.3	21.4	28.4
Bermuda+[1] Bermudes+[1]	2000	3 378	51.5[2]	10.9	19.5	0.6[5]	47.3	34.4
	2001	3 539	50.2[2]	...	...	...	1.4[7]	20.4[8]
	2002	3 715	49.3[2]	...	...	...	1.5[7]	20.1[8]
Bhutan Bhoutan	1998	16 337	57.1	20.2	37.9	0.3	31.5	47.0
	1999	19 123	52.6	22.3	42.5	0.6	29.9	47.9
	2000	21 698	52.2	20.4	43.5	0.2	29.8	46.1
Bolivia Bolivie	2002	56 818	73.6	15.9	15.7	0.9	21.6	27.6
	2003	61 959	71.0	16.5	12.9	0.5	25.5	26.3
	2004	69 626	68.2	15.2	12.6	-0.3	30.7	26.4
Botswana+[1] Botswana+[1]	2002	31 922	29.2[2]	33.1	24.3	1.9	48.8	36.8
	2003	36 338	28.4[2]	33.5	24.0	5.5	44.4	34.9
	2004	39 881	28.8[2]	34.3	24.0	6.0	39.8	32.2
Brazil[1] Brésil[1]	2002	1 346 028	58.0	20.1	18.3	1.4	15.5	13.4
	2003	1 556 182	56.7	19.9	17.8	2.0	16.4	12.8
	2004	1 766 621	55.2	18.8	19.6	1.7	18.0	13.4
British Virgin Islands[1] Iles Vierges britanniques[1]	2003	782[3,9]	38.2[2]	9.6	24.0	-1.4	107.5	78.0
	2004	873[3,9]	37.7[2]	9.4	24.1	-1.5	108.2	77.9
	2005	972[3,9]	37.1[2]	9.3	24.0	-1.5	108.8	77.7
Brunei Darussalam Brunéi Darussalam	1982	9 126	5.5	10.0	12.4	0.0[10]	89.3	17.2
	1983	8 124	9.5	11.4	9.9	0.0[10]	88.3	19.0
	1984	8 069	-5.6	31.1	6.5	0.0[10]	84.5	16.5
Bulgaria[1] Bulgarie[1]	2002	32 335	68.8[2]	18.0	18.3	1.5[5]	53.1	59.8
	2003	34 547	68.8[2]	19.0	19.4	2.4[5]	53.6	63.0
	2004	38 008	68.1[2]	18.7	20.9	2.6[5]	58.4	68.7
Burkina Faso Burkina Faso	1991	811 676	76.2	14.7	21.8	1.4	11.4	25.4
	1992	812 590	76.2	14.4	21.3	-0.2	9.7	21.4
	1993	832 349	77.2	14.4	20.4	0.8	9.7	22.5
Burundi Burundi	1990	196 656	83.0	19.5	16.4	-0.6	8.0	26.2
	1991	211 898	83.9	17.0	18.1	-0.5	10.0	28.5
	1992	226 384	82.9	15.6	21.1	0.4	9.0	29.0
Cambodia[1] Cambodge[1]	2002	15 994 247	82.4[2]	5.7	20.5	-0.3	57.8	65.9
	2003	17 310 521	78.9[2]	5.6	21.4	3.8	58.6	67.8
	2004	19 629 567	78.6[2]	4.9	23.6	2.1	64.7	75.8
Cameroon+[1] Cameroun+[1]	1996	4 793 080	...	...	13.1	-0.2	24.7	17.4
	1997	5 370 580	...	...	12.8	0.1	24.0	19.0
	1998	5 744 000	...	...	13.5	-0.1	24.0	20.4
Canada[1] Canada[1]	2002	1 136 664	56.3[2]	19.6	19.8	-0.1	41.9	37.5
	2003	1 197 494	56.0[2]	19.7	19.9	0.6	38.4	34.5
	2004	1 270 760	55.4[2]	19.5	20.4	0.6	38.6	34.4
Cape Verde Cap-Vert	2001	69 380	88.2	17.3	31.7	0.0	18.9	56.0
	2002	72 758	88.5	18.4	35.9	-0.1	20.9	63.7
	2003	79 527	86.5	20.1	31.1	-0.1	14.6	52.1
Cayman Islands Iles Caïmanes	1989	474	65.0	14.1	23.2	...	60.1	68.8
	1990	590	62.5	14.2	21.4	...	64.1	58.5
	1991	616	62.5	15.1	21.8	...	58.9	52.8

Gross domestic product by type of expenditure at current prices — Percentage distribution (*continued*)
Dépenses imputées au produit intérieur brut aux prix courants — Répartition en pourcentage (*suite*)

Country or area Pays ou zone	Year Année	GDP at current prices (mil. nat.cur.) PIB aux prix courants (millions monnaie nat.)	% of Gross domestic product – en % du Produit intérieur brut Household final consumption expenditure Consom. finale des ménages	Govt. final consumption expenditure Consom. finale des admin. publiques	Gross fixed capital formation Formation brute de capital fixe	Changes in inventories Variation des stocks	Exports of goods and services Exportations de biens et services	Imports of goods and services Importations de biens et services
Central African Rep. Rép. centrafricaine	1986	388 647	82.1	15.6	12.9	-0.1	18.2	28.6
	1987	360 942	80.6	17.5	12.9	-0.2	17.8	28.6
	1988	376 748	80.7	16.1	9.8	0.7	17.7	25.1
Chad Tchad	1999	915 000	28.5	16.8	14.0	-2.6	18.1	40.7
	2000	928 000	24.6	17.6	15.5	2.2	18.1	44.9
	2001	1 088 000	24.5	17.3	38.7	2.1	16.9	62.0
Chile[1] Chili[1]	2003	50 954 390	61.5[2]	12.4	21.1	0.8	36.6	32.5
	2004	57 905 728	57.8[2]	12.0	20.2	1.1	40.8	31.9
	2005	64 549 137	...	11.6	22.1	0.9	41.8	33.6
China[1,11] Chine[1,11]	2002	12 033 269	40.6	11.6	34.8	0.3	25.1	22.8
	2003	13 582 276	38.8	10.9	37.8	0.2	29.6	27.6
	2004	15 987 834	36.9	10.3	39.0	0.3	34.0	31.4
China, Hong Kong SAR[1] Chine, Hong Kong RAS[1]	2002	1 276 757	58.6[2]	10.3	22.4	0.4	149.6	141.3
	2003	1 233 143	58.3[2]	10.6	21.2	0.7	171.2	162.0
	2004	1 290 808	59.1[2]	9.9	21.6	0.4	189.7	180.8
China, Macao SAR[1] Chine, Macao RAS[1]	2002	54 819	36.9[2]	11.5	10.6	0.4	104.3	63.7
	2003	63 566	32.5[2]	10.7	14.1	0.5	103.3	61.2
	2004	83 103	27.4[2]	8.5	16.2	0.7	105.0	57.9
Colombia[1] Colombie[1]	2000	174 896 258	63.0[2]	21.2	12.6	1.1[5]	21.5	19.4
	2001	188 558 786	65.4[2]	20.8	13.6	0.6[5]	20.4	20.8
	2002	203 451 400	66.5[2]	19.6	14.5	0.7[5]	19.4	20.7
Comoros Comores	1989	63 397	77.8	27.6	14.4	4.6	14.9	39.3
	1990	66 370	79.7	25.7	12.2	8.0	11.7	37.3
	1991	69 248	80.9	25.3	12.3	4.0	15.5	38.0
Congo Congo	1987	690 523	56.6[2]	20.6	20.9	-1.1	41.7	38.6
	1988	658 964	60.1[2]	21.1	19.6	-1.0	40.6	40.4
	1989	773 524	52.8	18.7	16.4	-0.5	47.6	35.0
Cook Islands Iles Cook	2003	246	...	...	...	...	76.1	65.7
	2004	258	...	...	...	...	68.0	61.3
	2005	260	...	...	...	...	76.8	62.2
Costa Rica[1] Costa Rica[1]	2003	6 982 288	66.8	14.5	19.2	1.5	46.7	48.5
	2004	8 126 742	66.1	14.2	18.6	4.2	46.3	49.5
	2005	9 468 594	66.0	13.9	19.2	5.1	49.0	53.1
Côte d'Ivoire Côte d'Ivoire	1998	7 457 508	65.1[2]	13.7	14.3	0.6	41.3	34.9
	1999	7 734 000	63.2[2]	14.6	14.5	-1.3	39.7	30.8
	2000	7 605 000	67.2[2]	15.5	12.3	-1.0	39.8	33.8
Croatia[1] Croatie[1]	2002	179 390	59.9[2]	21.0	24.6	3.8	45.4	54.7
	2003	193 067	58.7[2]	20.6	27.5	2.9	47.1	56.8
	2004	207 082	58.1[2]	19.9	27.6	2.6	47.5	55.7
Cuba[1] Cuba[1]	2002	36 089	54.3	38.7	8.5	0.0	10.7	12.3
	2003	38 625	54.3	38.4	7.6	0.3	12.0	12.7
	2004	41 065	51.2	41.2	7.9	0.3	13.7	14.2
Cyprus[1] Chypre[1]	2003	6 815	62.9[2]	19.9	17.8	-0.4	47.3	47.5
	2004	7 255	64.5[2]	18.4	19.1	1.2	47.4	50.6
	2005	*7 740	65.1[2]	18.1	19.2	1.4	47.1	50.9
Czech Republic[1] République tchèque[1]	2003	2 555 783	51.5[2]	23.6	26.8	0.3[5]	62.2	64.4
	2004	2 767 717	50.2[2]	22.5	26.9	0.9[5]	71.2	71.7
	2005	2 931 071	49.1[2]	22.4	26.4	0.0[5]	72.8	70.7
Dem. Rep. of the Congo Rép. dém. du Congo	1987	326 946	77.1	22.4	20.3	5.3	63.2	88.2
	1988	622 822	...	37.2	19.0	3.7	81.0	...
	1989	2 146 811	...	14.4	13.4	3.2	46.5	...
Denmark[1] Danemark[1]	2003	1 409 162	47.9[2]	26.3	19.5	0.2[5]	45.0	39.0
	2004	1 467 310	48.4[2]	26.5	19.8	0.4[5]	45.2	40.3
	2005	1 551 510	48.5[2]	25.9	20.6	0.3[5]	48.6	43.9

Country or area / Pays ou zone	Year / Année	GDP at current prices (mil. nat.cur.) / PIB aux prix courants (millions monnaie nat.)	% of Gross domestic product – en % du Produit intérieur brut: Household final consumption expenditure / Consom. finale des ménages	Govt. final consumption expenditure / Consom. finale des admin. publiques	Gross fixed capital formation / Formation brute de capital fixe	Changes in inventories / Variation des stocks	Exports of goods and services / Exportations de biens et services	Imports of goods and services / Importations de biens et services
Djibouti Djibouti	1996	88 233	64.6	33.6	19.3	-0.9	40.3	56.8
	1997	87 289	59.3	34.7	21.4	0.2	42.2	57.8
	1998	88 461	67.3	29.0	23.2	0.2	43.4	63.0
Dominica Dominique	2000	732	62.6	21.9	27.5	0.0	53.3	67.5
	2001	713	64.7	21.3	25.1	0.0	45.9	63.1
	2002	685	69.6	21.5	22.0	...	46.3	59.4
Dominican Republic[1] Rép. dominicaine[1]	1994	179 130	76.8	4.6	17.9	3.4	37.4	40.2
	1995	209 646	78.6	4.3	16.1	3.3	34.5	36.7
	1996	232 993	81.4	4.7	17.3	3.6	18.1	25.1
Ecuador[1] Equateur[1]	2002	24 899[12]	69.3	10.8	23.3	3.2	24.7	31.2
	2003	28 691[12]	69.2	11.5	21.2	0.2	25.0	27.1
	2004	32 964[12]	67.4	11.3	21.1	1.4	26.9	28.2
Egypt+[1] Egypte+[1]	2002	405 256	74.2[2]	12.2	16.4	0.7	19.5	23.0
	2003	451 154	71.3[2]	11.6	17.2	1.0	21.8	22.8
	2004	510 750	72.1[2]	11.1	15.5	0.7	28.8	28.3
El Salvador El Salvador	2002	14 312	88.1	10.5	16.4	-0.3	26.4	41.1
	2003	14 941	88.9	10.8	16.7	0.0	26.7	43.0
	2004	15 824	90.9	10.5	15.6	0.0	27.2	44.2
Equatorial Guinea Guinée équatoriale	1989	42 256	54.3	22.2	19.6	0.0	40.4	36.6
	1990	44 349	53.2	15.3	34.6	-3.1	59.7	59.7
	1991	46 429	75.9	14.4	18.4	-2.3	28.4	34.7
Estonia[1] Estonie[1]	2002	116 915	58.4[2]	19.2	28.7	3.1[5]	74.3	81.4
	2003	127 334	58.1[2]	19.4	28.9	3.1[5]	74.3	81.9
	2004	141 493	56.0[2]	19.0	28.4	2.8[5]	78.4	86.1
Ethiopia+ Ethiopie+	1997	41 465	79.2	10.9	19.1	...	16.2	23.3
	1998	44 896	78.4	14.2	19.0	...	16.2	26.4
	1999	48 949	81.4	16.0	20.8	...	14.5	30.2
Fiji Fidji	1999	3 662	54.0	16.6	13.8	1.1	60.4	64.2
	2000	3 505	59.0	18.1	11.5	1.1	59.7	67.2
	2001	3 836	57.0	17.1	13.5	1.0	55.7	60.7
Finland[1] Finlande[1]	2003	143 807	52.3[2]	22.2	18.3	0.5	36.9	30.7
	2004	149 725	51.9[2]	22.5	18.8	0.5	37.8	32.4
	2005	155 320	52.4[2]	22.5	19.2	1.1	38.7	35.2
France[1] France[1]	2003	1 594 814	56.4[2]	23.7	18.8	0.0[5]	25.6	24.6
	2004	1 659 020	56.6[2]	23.7	19.2	0.3[5]	25.7	25.5
	2005	1 710 024	57.1[2]	23.7	19.7	0.5[5]	26.1	27.1
French Guiana Guyane française	1990	6 526	64.4	35.0	47.8	-0.2	67.3	114.3
	1991	7 404	60.1	34.4	40.5	1.5	81.1	117.6
	1992	7 976	58.9	34.2	30.8	1.5	65.4	90.8
French Polynesia Polynésie française	1991	305 211	63.9	39.3	18.4	-0.2	9.3	30.7
	1992	314 265	63.9	47.8	16.7	0.0	8.3	27.4
	1993	329 266	61.5	38.3	16.2	-0.2	10.5	26.4
Gabon Gabon	1987	1 020 600	48.6	23.7	26.7[4]	...	41.3	40.3
	1988	1 013 600	48.1	21.8	36.2[4]	...	37.3	43.4
	1989	1 168 066	48.4	18.4	23.3[4]	...	50.3	40.3
Gambia+ Gambie+	1991	2 920	83.7	13.0	18.2[13]	...	45.3[14]	60.1[15]
	1992	3 078	81.2	13.2	22.4[13]	...	45.2[14]	61.9[15]
	1993	3 243	78.1	15.1	27.1[13]	...	36.6[14]	56.9[15]
Georgia[1] Géorgie[1]	2002	7 457	77.8[2]	9.8	24.5	1.0[5]	29.2	42.4
	2003	8 564	72.2[2]	9.2	26.4	1.0[5]	31.8	46.4
	2004	9 970	72.3[2]	14.7	28.5	0.8[5]	31.1	47.5
Germany[1] Allemagne[1]	2003	2 163 400	59.5[2]	19.2	17.8	-0.5[5]	35.7	31.7
	2004	2 215 650	59.2[2]	18.6	17.4	-0.2[5]	38.0	33.1
	2005	2 247 400	59.3[2]	18.6	17.1	0.1[5]	40.1	35.1

Country or area / Pays ou zone	Year / Année	GDP at current prices (mil. nat.cur.) / PIB aux prix courants (millions monnaie nat.)	% of Gross domestic product – en % du Produit intérieur brut: Household final consumption expenditure / Consom. finale des ménages	Govt. final consumption expenditure / Consom. finale des admin. publiques	Gross fixed capital formation / Formation brute de capital fixe	Changes in inventories / Variation des stocks	Exports of goods and services / Exportations de biens et services	Imports of goods and services / Importations de biens et services
Ghana / Ghana	1994	5 205 200	73.7	13.7	22.6	1.4[16]	22.5	33.9
	1995	7 752 600	76.2	12.1	21.1	-1.1[16]	24.5	32.8
	1996	11 339 200	76.1	12.0	20.6	0.9[16]	24.9	34.5
Greece[1] / Grèce[1]	2003	155 543	67.7[2]	16.6	25.3	0.0	19.6	29.2
	2004	168 417	67.1[2]	16.6	25.2	0.0	20.8	29.7
	2005	181 088	67.1[2]	16.4	23.7	0.1	20.8	28.0
Grenada / Grenade	1990	541	64.9	20.5	38.9	3.1	44.4	71.8
	1991	567	69.2	18.8	40.0	3.7	45.4	77.1
	1992	578	66.5	19.9	32.4	2.1	38.6	59.4
Guadeloupe / Guadeloupe	1990	15 201	92.8	30.8	33.9	1.1	4.9	63.5
	1991	16 415	87.3	31.0	33.0	1.0	6.1	58.4
	1992	17 972	84.1	29.3	27.8	1.3	4.5	47.0
Guatemala / Guatemala	2003	197 599	86.6	7.3	14.3	4.5	16.7	29.4
	2004	216 749	88.1	6.4	14.5	5.3	16.8	31.1
	2005	243 699	89.2	5.9	15.0	4.2	15.6	29.9
Guinea-Bissau / Guinée-Bissau	1990	510 094	100.9	11.4	13.8	0.9	12.0	39.0
	1991	854 985	100.6	12.6	10.4	0.9	13.4	38.0
	1992	1 530 010	111.1	10.7	26.5[4]	...	8.2	56.5
Guyana / Guyana	1999	123 665	43.8	24.2	38.5[4]	...	-10.1[17]	...
	2000	130 013	49.9	27.5	38.5[4]	...	...	...
	2001	133 403	55.5	22.9	38.5[4]	...	...	...
Haiti+ / Haïti+	1997	51 578	...	...	12.5	...	11.5	27.1
	1998	59 055	...	...	12.9	...	13.2	28.6
	1999	66 425	...	...	13.1	...	13.3	28.2
Honduras / Honduras	1998	70 438	67.0	10.1	28.2	2.7	46.1	54.1
	1999	77 095	68.8	11.3	29.8	4.8	41.3	56.0
	2000	87 523	70.0	12.0	27.2	4.6	42.3	56.1
Hungary[1] / Hongrie[1]	2003	18 650 746	55.3[2]	24.6	22.3	2.2	61.7	66.1
	2004	20 429 456	54.4[2]	23.8	22.7	2.7	64.3	67.9
	2005	21 802 261	54.9[2]	23.6	23.2	0.5	66.4	68.5
Iceland[1] / Islande[1]	2003	827 863	57.6[2]	25.8	19.9	-0.2	34.9	38.0
	2004	916 765	57.4[2]	24.9	23.5	-0.1	34.6	40.2
	2005	995 991	60.2[2]	24.7	28.7	-0.1	31.5	45.0
India+ / Inde+	2001	22 719 840	65.4	12.5	22.1	0.1	12.8	13.7
	2002	24 633 240	64.3	11.8	22.2	0.4	14.4	15.4
	2003	27 600 250	63.8	11.3	22.7	0.3	14.8	16.1
Indonesia[1] / Indonésie[1]	2003	2 013 674 600	68.1	8.1	19.5	6.1	30.5	23.1
	2004	2 273 141 500	67.4	8.4	21.7	1.5	32.1	27.4
	2005	2 729 708 200	65.4	8.2	22.0	0.3	33.5	29.2
Iran (Islamic Rep. of)+[1] / Iran (Rép. Islamique d')+[1]	2002	975 717 770	51.2[2]	12.7	23.4[4]	...	24.9	22.6
	2003	1 204 665 350	50.5[2]	12.8	22.3[4]	...	25.7	22.7
	2004	1 546 390 280	...	12.9	21.3[4]	...	26.9	24.3
Iraq / Iraq	1998	4 570 100	79.0	7.9	3.8[4]	...	...	...
	1999	6 809 790	61.0	6.4	3.9[4]	...	...	...
	2000	7 398 604	59.7	6.2	7.3[4]	...	...	...
Ireland[1] / Irlande[1]	2002	130 515	45.1[2]	15.0	22.3	0.5[5]	93.3	76.3
	2003	139 097	45.3[2]	15.3	23.0	0.9[5]	83.7	67.6
	2004	148 556	44.5[2]	15.7	24.4	0.5[5]	83.1	67.8
Israel[1] / Israël[1]	2002	516 058	56.2[2]	29.6	17.8	0.1	35.6	39.3
	2003	523 618	56.3[2]	28.7	17.2	-0.8	37.1	38.5
	2004	548 544	56.5[2]	27.3	16.9	-0.2	42.0	42.5
Italy[1] / Italie[1]	2003	1 335 354	59.1[2]	19.7	20.4	0.3[5]	24.6	24.0
	2004	1 388 870	58.6[2]	19.8	20.6	0.2[5]	25.3	24.6
	2005	1 417 241	58.9[2]	20.3	20.6	0.3[5]	26.3	26.4

Country or area Pays ou zone	Year Année	GDP at current prices (mil. nat.cur.) PIB aux prix courants (millions monnaie nat.)	% of Gross domestic product – en % du Produit intérieur brut Household final consumption expenditure Consom. finale des ménages	Govt. final consumption expenditure Consom. finale des admin. publiques	Gross fixed capital formation Formation brute de capital fixe	Changes in inventories Variation des stocks	Exports of goods and services Exportations de biens et services	Imports of goods and services Importations de biens et services
Jamaica Jamaïque	2002	410 133	72.2	16.0	31.6	0.2	36.1	56.1
	2003	472 906	72.5	15.5	29.7	0.2	40.6	58.5
	2004	540 086	71.4	14.5	31.4	0.1	40.9	58.2
Japan[1] Japon[1]	2002	489 618 400	57.7[2]	18.0	23.3	-0.3	11.4	10.1
	2003	490 543 500	57.4[2]	18.0	22.9	0.1	12.0	10.4
	2004	496 050 500	57.4[2]	18.0	22.9	-0.2	13.4	11.4
Jordan Jordanie	2001	6 364	81.1[2]	22.9	19.4	1.6	42.1	67.1
	2002	6 779	78.2[2]	22.7	19.0	1.2	44.8	65.9
	2003	7 204	78.3[2]	23.2	20.6	0.2	45.0	67.3
Kazakhstan[1] Kazakhstan[1]	2002	3 776 277	54.6[2]	11.6	24.0	3.3	47.0	47.0
	2003	4 611 975	54.5[2]	11.3	23.0	2.7	48.4	43.0
	2004	5 870 134	53.5[2]	11.6	25.1	1.2	52.2	43.5
Kenya[1] Kenya[1]	2002	1 038 764	78.5	16.7	17.1	-0.8	24.3	31.4
	2003	1 141 780	76.1	17.8	15.7	1.7	24.6	31.6
	2004	1 273 716	74.9	17.0	16.3	1.9	28.0	37.2
Korea, Republic of[1] Corée, République de[1]	2003	724 675 000	53.7[2]	13.3	29.9	0.0[5]	37.9	35.6
	2004	779 380 500	51.5[2]	13.5	29.5	0.8[5]	44.0	39.7
	2005	806 621 900	52.6[2]	14.1	29.3	0.8[5]	42.5	40.0
Kuwait Koweït	2002	11 585	49.6	25.3	15.8	1.3	44.6	36.6
	2003	13 768	43.3	23.8	13.5	1.1	54.0	35.7
	2004	16 420	37.8	21.0	13.1	1.1	60.2	33.2
Kyrgyzstan[1] Kirghizistan[1]	2001	73 883	64.8[2]	17.5	16.8	1.2[5]	36.7	37.0
	2002	75 367	67.5[2]	18.6	16.3	1.3[5]	39.6	43.3
	2003	83 872	77.9[2]	16.8	13.6	-1.8[5]	38.7	45.3
Latvia[1] Lettonie[1]	2003	6 393	62.4[2]	21.4	24.4	4.3[5]	42.1	54.6
	2004	7 421	63.0[2]	19.6	27.5	5.6[5]	44.0	59.7
	2005	8 937	62.4[2]	17.7	29.8	4.4[5]	48.1	62.4
Lebanon[1] Liban[1]	2000	25 143 000	...	...	21.0	-0.6	13.6	37.1
	2001	25 726 000	...	...	20.7	2.4	15.1	41.0
	2002	27 832 000	...	...	19.7	-1.3	15.9	36.1
Lesotho[1] Lesotho[1]	1999	5 565	102.8[2]	21.3	47.6	1.0	24.4	94.8
	2000	5 986	101.1[2]	19.1	44.4	-2.3	29.7	92.1
	2001	6 478	101.7[2]	18.2	43.1	-2.6	39.3	99.6
Liberia Libéria	1987	1 090	65.5	13.2	11.1	0.6[18]	40.2	32.7
	1988	1 158	63.3	11.8	10.0	0.3[18]	39.0	27.8
	1989	1 194	55.0	11.9	8.1	0.3[18]	43.7	23.1
Libyan Arab Jamah. Jamah. arabe libyenne	1983	8 805	39.2	32.7	25.1	-1.1	42.1	38.0
	1984	8 013	38.6	33.6	25.3	0.5	41.4	39.4
	1985	8 277	37.6	31.7	19.7	0.4	37.4	26.7
Lithuania[1] Lituanie[1]	2002	51 948	64.4[2]	19.4	20.3	1.6[5]	52.8	58.6
	2003	56 772	64.6[2]	18.4	21.2	1.7[5]	51.3	57.2
	2004	62 440	65.1[2]	17.9	21.8	2.4[5]	52.3	59.4
Luxembourg[1] Luxembourg[1]	2003	25 684	41.0[2]	16.5	21.1	0.2[5]	134.5	113.3
	2004	27 056	40.9[2]	16.9	20.5	-0.1[5]	148.6	126.9
	2005	29 324	39.7[2]	16.6	20.3	1.1[5]	158.1	135.8
Madagascar Madagascar	1990	4 601 600	86.0[19]	8.0	17.0	...	15.9	26.9
	1991	4 906 400	92.2[19]	8.6	8.2	...	17.3	26.2
	1992	5 584 500	90.0[19]	8.2	11.6	...	15.6	25.3
Malawi Malawi	1994	10 319	74.4[20]	28.3	12.0	...	31.8	40.7
	1995	20 923	30.4[20]	21.9	11.9	...	32.2	38.2
	1996	33 918	56.1[20]	17.5	11.2	...	15.5	27.1
Malaysia Malaisie	2002	362 012	44.1[2]	13.7	23.1	0.9	114.6	96.4
	2003	395 017	43.6[2]	13.9	22.0	-0.5	113.4	92.5
	2004	449 609	42.9[2]	13.2	20.4	2.2	121.2	99.9

Gross domestic product by type of expenditure at current prices — Percentage distribution (*continued*)
Dépenses imputées au produit intérieur brut aux prix courants — Répartition en pourcentage (*suite*)

Country or area Pays ou zone	Year Année	GDP at current prices (mil. nat.cur.) PIB aux prix courants (millions monnaie nat.)	% of Gross domestic product – en % du Produit intérieur brut Household final consumption expenditure Consom. finale des ménages	Govt. final consumption expenditure Consom. finale des admin. publiques	Gross fixed capital formation Formation brute de capital fixe	Changes in inventories Variation des stocks	Exports of goods and services Exportations de biens et services	Imports of goods and services Importations de biens et services
Maldives[1] Maldives[1]	2002	8 200	30.5	23.2	25.5	0.0	86.5	65.6
	2003	8 841	28.9	21.9	27.2	0.0	87.7	65.7
	2004	9 640	27.5	24.9	36.1	0.0	94.8	83.3
Mali Mali	1990	683 300	79.0	15.2	20.0	2.2	17.3	33.7
	1991	691 400	85.1	15.3	20.0	-2.4	17.5	35.5
	1992	737 400	82.2	14.2	17.6	2.7	17.8	34.6
Malta[1] Malte[1]	2002	1 748	62.6[2]	21.5	15.5	-0.8[5]	85.4	84.3
	2003	1 793	62.7[2]	22.0	20.1	-0.6[5]	80.7	85.0
	2004	1 828	63.1[2]	22.5	20.8	1.1[5]	75.8	83.4
Martinique Martinique	1990	19 320	83.6	29.7	26.7	1.9	8.4	50.3
	1991	20 787	84.0	28.8	25.6	1.4	7.4	47.1
	1992	22 093	84.3	28.7	23.6	-0.9	6.8	42.5
Mauritania Mauritanie	1986	59 715	85.4	14.3	22.7	1.5	55.4	79.4
	1987	67 216	82.6	13.6	20.8	1.7	48.3	67.0
	1988	72 635	79.6	14.2	17.0	1.4	49.1	61.3
Mauritius[1] Maurice[1]	2003	156 523	61.4	14.2	22.7	0.3	56.7	55.4
	2004	174 501	63.5	14.3	21.8	2.7	54.5	56.9
	2005	187 245	68.3	14.6	21.4	2.0	57.7	63.9
Mexico[1] Mexique[1]	2002	6 263 137	69.1[2]	12.1	19.3	1.4	26.8	28.7
	2003	6 891 992	68.7[2]	12.4	18.9	1.6	27.8	29.5
	2004	7 709 096	68.1[2]	11.9	19.6	2.4	29.6	31.6
Mongolia Mongolie	2002	1 240 787	77.9[2]	18.3	29.1	3.1[5]	63.4	84.7
	2003	1 461 169	70.6[2]	16.8	34.1	3.9[5]	65.5	85.1
	2004	1 910 881	62.6[2]	16.4	32.3	4.3[5]	75.1	87.2
Montserrat Montserrat	1984	94	96.4	20.6	23.7	2.7	13.6	56.9
	1985	100	96.3	20.3	24.7	1.5	11.7	54.4
	1986	114	89.5	18.7	33.0	2.8	10.1	53.9
Morocco Maroc	2002	397 782	60.5	20.1	22.9	-0.2	28.9	32.2
	2003	419 485	59.1	21.0	24.0	0.1	27.9	32.1
	2004	443 673	60.4	21.0	24.6	0.5	28.7	35.1
Mozambique[1] Mozambique[1]	2002	96 883 500	62.2[2]	11.2	21.1	8.8	23.9	27.2
	2003	113 902 500	67.9[2]	12.5	26.3	1.2	25.4	33.2
	2004	133 510 400	65.7[2]	12.5	21.2	1.4	33.8	34.7
Myanmar+ Myanmar+	1996	791 980	...	...	14.9	-2.7	0.7	1.5
	1997	1 109 554	...	...	13.5	-0.9	0.6	1.3
	1998	1 559 996	...	...	11.8	-0.7	0.5	1.0
Namibia[1] Namibie[1]	2002	32 908	55.6[2]	26.4	21.2	-1.4	49.6	51.6
	2003	33 840	55.5[2]	26.5	29.2	0.7	51.4	55.0
	2004	36 901	52.1[2]	24.5	25.2	0.3	46.3	45.0
Nepal+ Népal+	2003	456 675	77.9	10.2	19.1	7.0	16.0	30.1
	2004	495 589	77.5	10.2	19.2	8.0	16.8	31.7
	2005	529 003	77.7	10.1	19.3	6.8	16.4	30.2
Netherlands[1] Pays-Bas[1]	2003	476 349	49.7[2]	24.4	19.1	0.0[5]	63.3	56.3
	2004	488 642	48.9[2]	24.3	19.4	0.2[5]	67.1	59.9
	2005	501 921	48.6[2]	24.0	19.5	...	71.2	63.0
Netherlands Antilles[1] Antilles néerlandaises[1]	2001	5 162	53.8[2]	21.6	25.8	0.6	82.8	84.6
	2002	5 199	55.3[2]	20.9	25.4	0.1	80.3	81.9
	2003	5 368	55.8[2]	21.4	23.6	0.1	82.9	83.8
New Caledonia Nouvelle-Calédonie	1990	250 427	57.3	32.6[21]	24.4	-1.1	22.0	35.4
	1991	272 235	53.8	32.8[21]	23.9	1.3	20.1	32.2
	1992	281 427	56.7	33.7[21]	23.7	0.1	16.8	31.4
New Zealand+[1] Nouvelle-Zélande+[1]	2002	130 856	58.6[2]	17.5	21.2	0.6[5]	32.4	30.6
	2003	139 225	58.7[2]	17.5	22.6	0.8[5]	29.1	28.8
	2004	148 558	58.9[2]	17.8	23.5	1.1[5]	29.0	30.1

Country or area / Pays ou zone	Year / Année	GDP at current prices (mil. nat.cur.) / PIB aux prix courants (millions monnaie nat.)	% of Gross domestic product – en % du Produit intérieur brut: Household final consumption expenditure / Consom. finale des ménages	Govt. final consumption expenditure / Consom. finale des admin. publiques	Gross fixed capital formation / Formation brute de capital fixe	Changes in inventories / Variation des stocks	Exports of goods and services / Exportations de biens et services	Imports of goods and services / Importations de biens et services
Nicaragua[1] / Nicaragua[1]	2002	57 099	78.7[2]	15.5	28.7	3.5	22.6	49.0
	2003	62 458	78.9[2]	16.0	27.7	3.7	24.1	50.4
	2004	70 271	80.2[2]	15.2	30.0	3.8	25.0	54.1
Niger / Niger	2003	1 466 267	77.6	16.1	15.1	1.8	16.5	27.0
	2004	1 474 910	78.2	18.4	16.5	-1.8	16.8	28.0
	2005	1 711 461	75.0	17.0	16.7	2.7	18.4	29.8
Nigeria+ / Nigéria+	1999	3 320 311	59.3	7.6	5.3	0.0	49.7	21.9
	2000	4 980 943	49.1	5.2	5.4	0.0	58.9	18.6
	2001	5 639 863	60.3	4.9	7.0	0.0	55.4	27.5
Norway[1] / Norvège[1]	2003	1 576 745	45.7[2]	22.5	17.5	0.9	40.4	27.0
	2004	1 716 933	44.3[2]	21.6	18.0	1.9	42.7	28.5
	2005	1 903 841	41.8[2]	20.4	18.7	1.9	45.3	28.1
Occupied Palestinian Terr.[1] / Terr. palestinien occupé[1]	2001	3 816	94.6[2]	32.8	24.9	0.6	12.1	64.9
	2002	3 484	96.7[2]	34.7	17.9	0.6	11.0	60.8
	2003	3 921	102.1[2]	27.2	23.5	0.2	9.6	62.6
Oman[1] / Oman[1]	2001	7 670	43.9	22.3	12.7	0.0	57.3	36.1
	2002	7 807	44.1	23.1	12.7	0.1	57.1	36.8
	2003	*8 343	43.8	22.2	15.7[4]	...	55.9	37.5
Pakistan+[1] / Pakistan+[1]	2003	4 822 842	73.6	8.9	15.3	1.7	16.9	16.3
	2004	5 532 663	73.3	8.4	15.6	1.7	16.0	14.9
	2005	6 547 590	80.0	7.8	15.3	1.6	15.3	19.9
Panama[1] / Panama[1]	2001	11 808	61.6	13.9	15.2	2.4	72.7	65.9
	2002	12 272	64.3	14.8	13.6	2.2	67.5	62.3
	2003	12 862	60.5	14.3	17.2	1.9	64.0	58.0
Papua New Guinea[1] / Papouasie-Nvl-Guinée[1]	2000	10 750	60.1	16.2	20.0	1.3	43.9	41.5
	2001	11 758	71.9	15.5	20.2	1.6	42.3	51.5
	2002	13 375	73.9	14.4	18.3	1.5	38.8	46.9
Paraguay / Paraguay	1993	11 991 719	81.3	6.7	22.0[22]	0.9[23]	36.9	47.9
	1994	14 960 131	88.4	6.8	22.5[22]	0.9[23]	34.2	52.8
	1995	17 699 000	85.3	7.2	23.1[22]	0.9[23]	35.0	51.2
Peru[1] / Pérou[1]	2002	198 871	71.9	10.2	17.7	1.1	16.5	17.4
	2003	211 492	70.8	10.4	17.8	1.0	17.7	17.7
	2004	234 261	68.7	10.1	18.0	0.5	20.9	18.3
Philippines / Philippines	2002	3 963 872	69.4	11.5	17.6	0.1	50.2	50.7
	2003	4 293 026	69.6	11.1	16.7	0.0	49.5	51.5
	2004	4 826 343	69.3	10.2	16.5	0.6	50.6	50.0
Poland[1] / Pologne[1]	2002	781 112	66.4[2]	18.1	19.0	-0.1	29.6	33.0
	2003	814 922	66.0[2]	17.6	18.4	0.5	34.4	36.9
	2004	883 656	64.9[2]	16.9	18.2	1.8	39.1	40.9
Portugal[1] / Portugal[1]	2003	137 523	63.9[2]	20.1	22.5	0.3[5]	28.0	34.8
	2004	143 029	64.5[2]	20.5	22.3	0.6[5]	28.5	36.5
	2005	147 395	65.5[2]	21.1	21.6	0.7[5]	28.5	37.4
Puerto Rico+ / Porto Rico+	2000	69 208	54.3[2]	11.2	16.9	0.7	77.6	60.6
	2001	71 306	54.0[2]	11.7	15.9	0.4	75.9	57.9
	2002	74 362	54.0[2]	12.1	15.3	0.4	82.0	63.8
Qatar[1] / Qatar[1]	2000	64 646	15.2	19.7	19.5	0.7	67.3	22.3
	2001	64 579	15.5	19.8	22.5	0.8	65.1	23.7
	2002	65 088	15.8	20.0	22.2	0.7	65.6	24.2
Republic of Moldova[1] / République de Moldova[1]	2003	27 619	90.6[2]	19.7	18.6	4.6	53.3	86.7
	2004	32 032	89.0[2]	14.9	21.2	5.2	51.2	81.5
	2005	36 755	92.9[2]	15.5	24.4	5.4	53.1	91.3
Réunion / Réunion	1992	33 787	76.1	28.4	28.6	2.1	3.4	38.6
	1993	33 711	76.4	28.6	25.7	-0.4	3.1	36.2
	1994	35 266	78.0	28.9	28.1	0.1	2.9	38.0

Country or area / Pays ou zone	Year / Année	GDP at current prices (mil. nat.cur.) / PIB aux prix courants (millions monnaie nat.)	% of Gross domestic product – en % du Produit intérieur brut: Household final consumption expenditure / Consom. finale des ménages	Govt. final consumption expenditure / Consom. finale des admin. publiques	Gross fixed capital formation / Formation brute de capital fixe	Changes in inventories / Variation des stocks	Exports of goods and services / Exportations de biens et services	Imports of goods and services / Importations de biens et services
Romania[1] Roumanie[1]	2003	1 975 648 100	66.0[2]	19.6	21.4	0.4[5]	34.7	42.2
	2004	2 463 716 500[24]	67.8[2]	18.9	21.6	0.7[5]	35.9	45.0
	2005	*2 871 862 500	68.1[2]	19.6	23.1	-0.4[5]	33.0	43.4
Russian Federation[1] Fédération de Russie[1]	2003	13 243 240	50.5[2]	17.6	18.2	2.6[5]	35.2	23.8
	2004	17 008 388	48.9[2]	16.5	18.0	2.7[5]	34.4	22.0
	2005	21 664 978	48.0[2]	16.0	17.9	2.9[5]	35.2	21.4
Rwanda Rwanda	2000	681 455	90.2	8.9	18.0	...	6.3	23.4
	2001	732 276	90.4	9.5	17.4	...	8.7	26.1
	2002	784 000	91.5	9.5	17.9	...	7.1	24.6
Saint Kitts and Nevis Saint-Kitts-et-Nevis	2001	932	51.4	20.6	53.7[4]	...	44.3	70.0
	2002	958	62.3	19.0	47.7[4]	...	43.2	72.2
	2003	997	61.2	17.7	47.1[4]	...	44.6	70.5
Saint Lucia Sainte-Lucie	2001	1 766	55.8	27.7	26.0	...	54.4	64.0
	2002	1 827	56.2	26.9	22.8	...	46.3	52.2
	2003	1 866	67.3	24.5	21.9	...	55.4	69.1
Saint Vincent-Grenadines Saint Vincent-Grenadines	2002	986	59.8	20.5	29.7	...	48.8	58.8
	2003	1 025	65.2	19.7	33.3	...	45.6	63.6
	2004	1 101[3]	66.9	19.7	34.9	...	45.2[3]	66.8[3]
San Marino Saint-Marin	1997	1 279 857	...	...	38.4	3.2	234.2	238.3
	1998	1 400 841	...	...	37.0	4.9	202.0	203.8
	1999	1 551 010	...	...	41.4	5.3	197.1	200.0
Sao Tome and Principe Sao Tomé-et-Principe	1986	2 478	76.1	30.3	13.6	0.9	0.0	50.8
	1987	3 003	63.1	24.8	15.4	1.1	0.0	43.1
	1988	4 221	71.8	21.2	15.7	0.0	0.0	66.8
Saudi Arabia+ Arabie saoudite+	2002	707 067	36.8	26.1	18.1	1.6	41.2	23.8
	2003	*804 648	33.6	24.6	18.4	1.4	46.1	24.1
	2004	*939 591	30.1	23.2	17.4	1.6	52.7	24.9
Senegal Sénégal	1998	2 746 000	75.5	11.8	17.7	2.1	29.9	37.0
	1999	2 925 000	74.3	12.7	19.6	1.1	30.4	38.0
	2000	3 114 000	72.9	14.0	17.3	5.6	29.7	39.6
Serbia Serbie	2001	708 423	81.3[2]	27.0	9.2	5.3	25.4	48.3
	2002	919 231	74.0[2]	31.4	13.1	2.1	25.9	46.4
	2003	1 095 402	75.4[2]	31.7	14.1	0.7	23.5	45.3
Serbia and Montenegro Serbie-et-Monténégro	1998	148 370	70.7[2]	28.2	11.6	-1.1[5]	23.4	32.8
	#1999[25]	191 099	68.0[2]	28.9	12.6	-0.5[5]	11.2	20.3
	2000[25]	381 661	70.5[2]	28.3	15.4	-6.6[5]	9.2	16.8
Seychelles Seychelles	1998	3 201	50.0	31.2	34.0	0.6	-15.8[17]	...
	1999	3 330	45.3	27.8	41.5	1.8	-16.4[17]	...
	2000	3 424	39.4	27.1	35.7	0.5	-2.6[17]	...
Sierra Leone+ Sierra Leone+	1988	43 947	86.7	7.5	12.7	0.8	14.5[26]	22.3
	1989	82 837	84.7	6.6	13.5	0.5	19.7[26]	25.1
	1990	150 175	77.9	10.4	10.1	1.8	25.4[26]	25.7
Singapore Singapour	2003	161 547	46.0	11.8	24.1	-8.5	213.5	185.3
	2004	181 704	43.6	10.7	23.8	-4.4	230.4	202.8
	2005	194 360	41.9	10.6	21.8	-3.2	243.0	213.1
Slovakia[1] Slovaquie[1]	2002	1 111 484	57.9[2]	20.3	29.0[4]	1.6	70.9	78.1
	2003	1 212 665	56.7[2]	20.5	25.0	-0.4[5]	76.5	78.4
	2004	1 355 114	56.8[2]	20.0	23.9	1.9[5]	75.2	77.9
Slovenia[1] Slovénie[1]	2001	4 761 815	56.3[2]	20.5	24.5	-0.6[5]	57.6	58.3
	2002	5 314 494	54.6[2]	20.2	23.3	0.4[5]	57.6	56.1
	2003	5 747 168	54.4[2]	20.3	23.9	1.4[5]	56.5	56.5
Solomon Islands Iles Salomon	1986	253	63.1	33.3	25.2	1.0	52.6	75.2[27]
	1987	293	63.1	36.3	20.4	2.7	55.9	78.4[27]
	1988	367	68.6	31.4	30.0	2.7	52.4	85.0[27]

17 Gross domestic product by type of expenditure at current prices — Percentage distribution (*continued*)
Dépenses imputées au produit intérieur brut aux prix courants — Répartition en pourcentage (*suite*)

Country or area Pays ou zone	Year Année	GDP at current prices (mil. nat.cur.) PIB aux prix courants (millions monnaie nat.)	% of Gross domestic product - en % du Produit intérieur brut Household final consumption expenditure Consom. finale des ménages	Govt. final consumption expenditure Consom. finale des admin. publiques	Gross fixed capital formation Formation brute de capital fixe	Changes in inventories Variation des stocks	Exports of goods and services Exportations de biens et services	Imports of goods and services Importations de biens et services
Somalia Somalie	1985	87 290	90.5[19]	10.6[28]	8.9[28]	2.9[23]	4.2[7]	17.0[29]
	1986	118 781	89.1[19]	9.7[28]	16.8[28]	1.0[23]	5.8[7]	22.4[29]
	1987	169 608	88.8[19]	11.1[28]	16.8[28]	4.8[23]	5.9[7]	27.2[29]
South Africa[1] Afrique du Sud[1]	2002	1 168 778	61.8	18.4	15.0	1.0	32.7	29.1
	2003	1 257 026	62.5	19.3	15.8	1.1	27.9	26.0
	2004	1 386 658	62.8	19.7	16.1	1.4	26.6	27.3
Spain[1] Espagne[1]	2003	780 550	57.4[2]	17.4	27.1	0.4	26.4	28.6
	2004	837 316	57.7[2]	17.8	27.9	0.4	25.9	29.7
	2005	904 323	57.7[2]	17.8	29.4	0.3	25.4	30.6
Sri Lanka[1] Sri Lanka[1]	2002	1 612 987	71.5	12.7	20.4	1.7	35.4	42.0
	2003	1 795 259	71.8	12.3	20.3	1.3	35.2	41.3
	2004	2 058 396	72.2	12.8	21.7	1.8	35.9	44.8
Sudan+ Soudan+	1994	5 522 838	84.1	4.6	9.4	6.8	4.6	9.5
	#1996	10 330 678	81.9	7.5	12.3	9.6	8.0	19.2
	1997	16 769 372	85.6	5.4	12.2	5.7	10.2	19.2
Suriname Suriname	2002	2 240 127[30]	...	27.0	81.8[4]	...	42.0	50.8
	2003	2 918 132[30]	...	31.8	77.7[4]	...	49.3	58.8
	2004	3 513 565[30]	...	14.6	92.3[4]	...	60.7	67.7
Swaziland+[1] Swaziland+[1]	2001	10 846	68.3	18.4	24.6	...	92.1	103.4
	2002	12 560	72.1	16.4	19.8	...	86.3	94.7
	2003	14 401	76.2	14.8	18.0	...	77.8	86.9
Sweden[1] Suède[1]	2003	2 459 413	48.9[2]	28.1	16.0	0.4[5]	43.5	36.9
	2004	2 573 176	48.2[2]	27.4	16.1	0.1[5]	46.0	37.8
	2005	2 672 998	48.0[2]	27.2	17.0	0.1[5]	48.6	40.9
Switzerland[1] Suisse[1]	2002	430 527	60.2[2]	11.7	21.6	0.1[5]	43.7	37.3
	2003	434 562	60.5[2]	11.9	20.7	0.3[5]	43.4	36.9
	2004	445 931	60.4[2]	11.9	20.9	-0.6[5]	46.2	38.9
Syrian Arab Republic Rép. arabe syrienne	2002	1 016 519	59.5	12.3	20.3	...	39.8	31.9
	2003	1 067 265	60.3	13.5	22.8	...	32.4	29.5
	2004	1 203 509	63.5	14.0	21.0	...	35.1	33.5
Tajikistan[1] Tadjikistan[1]	2000	1 807	73.2[2]	8.5	9.4	2.2	85.1	74.9
	2001	2 529	74.9[2]	9.5	9.2	7.4	67.3	69.3
	2002	3 366	74.0[2]	9.1	10.8	7.2	66.2	65.4
Thailand Thaïlande	2002	5 450 643	57.2	11.1	22.8	1.0	64.2	57.5
	2003	5 928 975	57.2	10.7	24.0	0.9	65.6	58.8
	2004	6 503 488	56.7	11.1	25.9	1.2	70.5	65.8
TFYR of Macedonia[1] L'ex-R.y. Macédoine[1]	2002	243 970	77.1[2]	22.4	16.6	4.0	38.0	58.2
	2003	251 486	76.3[2]	20.7	16.7	3.2	37.9	54.8
	2004	265 257	77.9[2]	20.8	17.8	3.7	40.2	60.5
Timor-Leste Timor-Leste	2000	393[12]	52.1	43.3	31.7	3.2	21.2	51.6
Togo Togo	1984	304 800	66.0	14.0	21.2	-1.5	51.9	51.6
	1985	332 500	66.0	14.2	22.9	5.2	48.3	56.7
	1986	363 600	69.0	14.4	23.8	5.3	35.6	48.2
Tonga+ Tonga+	2002	312	110.9[2]	15.7	19.2	1.0	18.9	66.3
	2003	349	111.7[2]	14.3	18.1	0.9	20.3	65.0
	2004	372	109.9[2]	14.0	16.7	0.8	21.2	62.6
Trinidad and Tobago[1] Trinité-et-Tobago[1]	2002	56 290	61.6	13.6	18.8	0.5	50.3	44.7
	2003	67 302	54.1	13.3	16.4	1.3	54.8	39.8
	2004	76 892	51.5	13.8	15.6	1.2	59.8	42.0
Tunisia[1] Tunisie[1]	2003	32 202	63.1	15.7	23.4	1.7	43.8	47.7
	2004	35 148	63.1	15.4	22.7	1.7	46.8	49.7
	2005	37 311	63.6	15.5	22.5	-0.3	48.8	50.1

Country or area Pays ou zone	Year Année	GDP at current prices (mil. nat.cur.) PIB aux prix courants (millions monnaie nat.)	% of Gross domestic product – en % du Produit intérieur brut					
			Household final consumption expenditure Consom. finale des ménages	Govt. final consumption expenditure Consom. finale des admin. publiques	Gross fixed capital formation Formation brute de capital fixe	Changes in inventories Variation des stocks	Exports of goods and services Exportations de biens et services	Imports of goods and services Importations de biens et services
Turkey Turquie	2003	359 763	66.6	13.6	15.5	7.3	27.4	30.7
	2004	430 511	66.1	13.2	17.8	7.9	28.9	34.7
	2005	487 202	67.4	13.1	19.6	5.2	27.4	34.0
Turkmenistan[1] Turkménistan[1]	2000	25 648 000	70.8[2]	...	...	...	...	...
	2001	35 118 973	70.8[2]	...	...	...	...	...
	2002	45 239 913	70.8[2]	...	...	...	...	...
Turks and Caicos Islands[1] Iles Turques et Caïques[1]	2003	410	35.4	15.9	25.0[4]	...	69.7	46.0
	2004	486	31.1	20.5	31.0[4]	...	68.0	50.6
	2005	570	38.2	17.1	39.0[4]	...	64.8	59.2
Tuvalu Tuvalu	1996	16[31]	...	...	67.6[4]	...	...	...
	1997	18[31]	...	...	51.2[4]	...	...	...
	1998	21[31]	...	...	54.9[4]	...	...	...
Uganda Ouganda	2001	10 154 503	80.5	14.3	19.3	0.4	11.9	25.6
	2002	10 812 390	79.9	14.9	20.2	0.4	11.6	26.5
	2003	12 637 469	79.4	13.6	21.6	0.4	13.0	27.4
Ukraine[1] Ukraine[1]	2003	267 344	56.4[2]	19.0	20.6	1.4[5]	57.8	55.2
	2004	345 113	53.8[2]	17.6	22.5	-1.4[5]	61.2	53.7
	2005	418 529	58.2[2]	19.5	21.1	0.7[5]	51.9	51.4
United Arab Emirates Emirats arabes unis	1990	124 008	38.6	16.3	19.4	1.0	65.4	40.8
	1991	124 500	41.4	16.9	20.7	1.1	67.6	47.7
	1992	128 400	45.5	17.8	23.2	1.2	69.1	56.8
United Kingdom[1] Royaume-Uni[1]	2003	1 105 919	65.6[2]	21.0	15.9	0.4[5]	25.5	28.3
	2004	1 164 541	65.3[2]	21.2	16.3	0.5[5]	25.2	28.6
	2005	1 209 334	65.3[2]	21.8	16.6	0.2[5]	26.1	30.0
United Rep. of Tanzania[1] Rép.-Unie de Tanzanie[1]	2001	8 284 690	83.5	6.2	16.8	0.2	15.5	23.7
	2002	9 445 482	79.4	6.3	18.9	0.2	16.1	22.3
	2003	10 692 420	82.0	6.5	18.5	0.2	17.8	26.7
United States[1] Etats-Unis[1]	2002	10 417 600	70.6[2]	15.4	17.9	0.1	9.7	13.7
	2003	10 918 500	70.6[2]	15.9	18.0	0.2	9.6	14.2
	2004	11 679 200	70.3[2]	15.8	18.7	0.5	10.1	15.4
Uruguay Uruguay	2003	315 678	74.6[2]	11.4	9.4	3.2[32]	26.1	24.6
	2004	379 353	73.7[2]	10.8	11.3	1.8[32]	30.9	28.5
	2005	411 042	73.5[2]	11.2	12.9	0.3[32]	29.8	27.6
Uzbekistan[1] Ouzbékistan[1]	1999	2 128 660	62.1[2]	20.6	27.2	-10.1	0.1[17]	...
	2000	3 255 600	61.9[2]	18.7	24.0	-4.4	-0.2[17]	...
	2001	4 868 400	61.6[2]	18.4	25.7	-5.5	-0.3[17]	...
Vanuatu Vanuatu	1993	23 779	49.2	28.4	25.5	2.3	45.3	53.8
	1994	24 961	49.2	27.7	26.5	2.3	47.3	57.2
	1995	27 255	46.9	25.4	29.8	2.1	44.2	53.6
Venezuela (Bolivarian Rep. of)[1] Venezuela (Rép. bolivarienne du)[1]	2001	88 946 000	54.9[2]	14.2	24.0	3.5[5]	22.7	19.4
	2002	107 840 000	53.5[2]	13.0	21.9	-0.8[5]	30.4	18.1
	2003	134 217 000	54.7[2]	12.9	15.6	0.0[5]	33.8	17.0
Viet Nam[1] Viet Nam[1]	2001	481 295 000	64.9	6.3	29.2	2.0	-2.3[17]	...
	2002	535 762 000	65.1	6.2	31.1	2.1	-5.2[17]	...
	2003	605 586 000	64.9	6.9	33.0	2.1	-7.6[17]	...
Yemen[1] Yémen[1]	2002	1 894 497	66.4	15.0	19.6	-0.2	36.7	37.4
	2003	2 177 463	64.0	14.3	22.3	0.9	36.2	37.6
	2004	2 551 994	64.9	13.5	19.5	-0.5	36.8	34.2
Zambia Zambie	2001	13 132 693	69.9	12.8	18.7	1.4	26.9	29.7
	2002	16 260 430	69.4	13.0	21.6	1.3	23.7	29.0
	2003	20 377 051	66.6	14.6	24.8	1.3	20.6	28.0
Zimbabwe Zimbabwe	2002	1 698 180	107.4[2]	9.5	5.5	-14.3	5.5	9.2
	2003	5 518 757	112.6[2]	11.0	3.2	-16.2	1.5	3.3
	2004	15 563 920	114.6[2]	32.8	2.7	1.8	61.4	84.1

Source

United Nations Statistics Division, New York, national accounts database.

Notes

+ The national accounts data generally relate to the fiscal year used in each country, unless indicated otherwise. Countries whose reference periods coincide with the calendar year ending 31 December are not listed below.
  - Year beginning 21 March: Afghanistan, Iran (Islamic Republic).
  - Year beginning 1 April: Bermuda, India, Myanmar, New Zealand, Nigeria.
  - Year beginning 1 July: Australia, Bangladesh, Cameroon, Gambia, Pakistan, Puerto Rico, Saudi Arabia, Sierra Leone, Sudan.
  - Year ending 30 June: Botswana, Egypt, Swaziland, Tonga.
  - Year ending 7 July: Ethiopia.
  - Year ending 15 July: Nepal.
  - Year ending 30 September: Haiti.

1 Data compiled in accordance with the concepts and definitions of the System of National Accounts 1993 (1993 SNA).
2 Including "Non-profit institutions serving households" (NPISHs) final consumption expenditure.
3 Preliminary data.
4 Gross capital formation.
5 Including acquisitions less disposals of valuables.
6 Derived from available data.
7 Exports of goods only.
8 Imports of goods only.
9 At producers' prices.
10 Land improvement is not included.
11 For statistical purposes, the data for China do not include those for the Hong Kong Special Administrative Region (Hong Kong SAR), Macao Special Administrative Region (Macao SAR) and Taiwan Province of China.
12 Data in US dollars.
13 The estimates refer to central government capital formation only.
14 Includes net travel and tourism income.
15 Includes net freight and insurance.
16 Cocoa is valued at cost to the Ghana Cocoa Marketing Board. Stocks of other export commodities, including minerals, are valued at export prices.
17 Net exports.
18 Data in 1980 includes only increase in iron ore stocks. Beginning 1981, it includes increase in iron ore and rubber stocks.
19 Obtained as a residual.
20 Including changes in inventories.
21 Including education and health.
22 Includes communications equipment.
23 Includes livestock only.
24 Semi-final data.
25 Beginning 1999, data for Kosovo and Metohia are excluded.
26 Includes an upward adjustment for the estimated value of diamonds smuggled out of the country.
27 Valued f.o.b.
28 Includes the value of technical assistance from abroad.
29 Refers to imports of goods and non-factor services.
30 Excludes the informal sector.
31 GDP at market prices.
32 Refers to increase in stocks of wool and livestock in the private sector, and to stocks held by the public sector.

Source

Organisation des Nations Unies, Division de statistique, New York, la base de données sur les comptes nationaux.

Notes

+ Sauf indication contraire, les données sur les comptes nationaux concernent généralement l'exercice budgétaire utilisé dans chaque pays. Les pays où territoires dont la période de référence coïncide avec l'année civile se terminant le 31 décembre ne sont pas répertoriés ci-dessous.
  - Exercice commençant le 21 mars: Afghanistan, Iran (République islamique d').
  - Exercice commençant le 1er avril: Bermudes, Inde, Myanmar, Nigéria, Nouvelle-Zélande.
  - Exercice commençant le 1er juillet: Arabie saoudite, Australie, Bangladesh, Cameroun, Gambie, Pakistan, Porto Rico, Sierra Leone, Soudan.
  - Exercice se terminant le 30 juin: Botswana, Égypte, Swaziland, Tonga.
  - Exercice se terminant le 7 juillet: Éthiopie.
  - Exercice se terminant le 15 juillet: Népal.
  - Exercice se terminant le 30 septembre: Haïti.

1 Données compilées selon les concepts et définitions du Système de comptabilité nationale de 1993 (SCN 1993).
2 Y compris la consommation finale des institutions sans but lucratif au service des ménages.
3 Données préliminaires.
4 Formation brute de capital.
5 Y compris les acquisitions moins cessions d'objets de valeur.
6 Calculés à partir des données disponibles.
7 Exportations de biens uniquement.
8 Importations de biens uniquement.
9 Aux prix à la production.
10 L'amélioration des terres n'est pas comprise.
11 Pour la présentation des statistiques, les données pour la Chine ne comprennent pas la Région Administrative Spéciale de Hong Kong (Hong Kong RAS), la Région Administrative Spéciale de Macao (Macao RAS) et la province de Taiwan.
12 Les données sont exprimées en dollars des États-Unis.
13 Les chiffres ne concernent que la formation de capital des administrations centrales.
14 Comprend les recettes nettes des voyages et du tourisme.
15 Comprend les montants nets du fret et de l'assurance.
16 Le cacao est valorisé au prix coûtant du "Ghana Cocoa Marketing Board". Les stocks des autres produits d'exportation, minéraux compris, sont valorisés au prix à l'exportation.
17 Exportations nettes.
18 Ne comprend que l'accroissement des stocks de minerai de fer. À partir de 1981, comprend l'accroissement des stocks de minerai de fer et de caoutchouc.
19 Obtenu comme valeur résiduelle.
20 Y compris les variations des stocks.
21 Y compris l'éducation et la santé.
22 Y compris les matériels de communication.
23 Ne comprend que le bétail.
24 Données demi-finales.
25 A compter de 1999, non compris les données de Kosovo et Metohia.
26 Compris un ajustement en hausse rendant compte de la valeur estimative des diamants sortis du pays en fraude.
27 Valeur f.o.b.
28 Compris la valeur de l'assistance technique étrangère.
29 Concerne les importations de biens et de services autres que les services des facteurs.
30 Non compris le secteur informel.
31 PIB aux prix du marché.
32 Concerne les accroissements de stocks de laine et de bétail dans le secteur privé, et les stocks dans le secteur public.

18

Value added by industries at current prices
Percentage distribution

Valeur ajoutée par branche d'activité aux prix courants
Répartition en pourcentage

Country or area Pays ou zone	Year Année	Value added, Gross (mil. nat.cur) Valeur ajoutée, brute (mil. mon. nat.)	% of Value added – % de la valeur ajoutée: Agriculture, hunting, forestry and fishing Agriculture, chasse, sylviculture et pêche	Mining and quarrying Activités extractives	Manufacturing Activités de fabrication	Electricity, gas and water supply Electricité, gaz et eau	Construction Construction	Wholesale, retail trade, restaurants and hotels Commerce, restaurants, hôtels	Transport, storage & communication Transports, entrepôts, communications	Other activities Autres activités
Afghanistan+ Afghanistan+	2002	180 292	49.8	0.1	15.1	0.0	4.8	10.1	9.6	10.4
	2003	220 393	48.5	0.2	15.1	0.4	5.5	9.2	11.3	9.7
Albania[1] Albanie[1]	2002	582 873	23.6	0.7	4.6	1.5	11.9	23.5	10.4	23.9
	2003	652 423	23.3	0.6	5.0	2.7	13.3	21.4	10.7	22.9
	2004	704 477	21.9	8.7[2,3]	...	...	14.7	54.6[4]	...	...
Algeria Algérie	2001	4 075 738	10.1	36.5	6.3	1.3	7.9	12.9	8.3	16.8
	2002	4 284 371	9.7	35.5	6.2	1.3	8.6	13.2	8.5	16.9
	2003	4 991 489	10.2	38.5	5.6	1.2	8.0	12.3	8.3	15.9
Andorra Andorre	2002	1 785	0.7	...	4.6	1.4	10.2	36.4	2.7	43.9
	2003	1 968	0.6	...	5.0	1.3	10.7	37.6	3.6	41.2
	2004	2 098	0.6	...	5.1	1.2	11.3	38.8	3.2	39.8
Angola Angola	1988	236 682	16.0	27.1	8.3	0.2	4.1	11.7[5]	3.5	29.1[5]
	1989	276 075	19.3	29.7	6.2	0.2	3.3	11.4[5]	3.0	27.1[5]
	1990	305 831	18.0	32.9	5.0	0.1	2.9	10.7[5]	3.2	27.0[5]
Anguilla Anguilla	2001	273[6]	2.3	0.8	1.2	3.9	11.5	33.5	13.1	33.7
	2002	267[6]	2.7	0.8	1.3	5.5	10.8	31.3	14.2	33.4
	2003	282[6]	2.6	1.0	1.4	4.9	10.5	31.9	13.5	34.2
Antigua and Barbuda Antigua-et-Barbuda	1986	567[6]	4.3	1.7	3.8	3.5	8.9	23.6	15.6	38.5
	1987	649[6]	4.5	2.2	3.5	3.5	11.3	24.1	15.6	35.3
	1988	776[6]	4.1	2.2	3.1	4.0	12.7	23.7	14.3	35.9
Argentina[1] Argentine[1]	2003	353 374[7]	11.0	5.8	23.9	1.7	3.3	14.0	8.5	31.8
	2004	414 039[7]	10.4	5.7	24.1	1.7	4.2	14.1	9.0	30.9
	2005	493 155[7]	9.4	5.8	23.2	1.7	4.9	14.3	9.0	31.7
Armenia[1] Arménie[1]	2003	1 495 269	23.4	...	21.2	...	17.1	12.4	6.4	19.6
	2004	1 757 689	24.5	...	20.8	...	16.7	12.6	6.4	19.0
	2005	2 063 119	20.4	...	20.5	...	23.3	11.8	6.0	18.0
Aruba[1] Aruba[1]	2000	3 231	0.4[8]	...	3.8[9]	6.2[9]	6.0	24.4	9.0	50.3
	2001	3 308	0.4[8]	...	3.3[9]	7.0[9]	5.4	23.6	9.3	51.0
	2002	3 333	0.4[8]	...	3.3[9]	6.9[9]	4.7	22.4	9.2	53.1
Australia+[1] Australie+[1]	2002	712 091	3.3	5.0	12.6	2.5	6.4	14.2	7.9	48.1
	2003	762 850	3.5	4.5	12.7	2.5	6.7	14.2	7.8	48.0
	2004	815 073	3.3	5.3	12.4	2.4	6.8	14.1	7.9	47.6
Austria[1] Autriche[1]	2002	198 688	2.0	0.4	19.9	2.4	7.4	17.5	7.5	42.9
	2003	204 285	1.9	0.4	19.4	2.6	7.7	17.4	7.4	43.2
	2004	212 586	1.9	0.4	19.9	2.4	7.5	17.6	7.2	43.0
Azerbaijan[1] Azerbaïdjan[1]	2003	32 983 800[10]	13.5	29.8	9.4	1.2	12.2	8.2	10.8	15.6
	2004	39 572 400[10]	11.8	31.3	8.9	1.1	13.4	8.3	10.3	15.7
	2005	54 820 500[10]	10.0	42.7	7.8	0.9	10.9	7.5	8.7	12.1
Bahamas[1] Bahamas[1]	2002	5 388[7]	2.7	1.0	4.6	3.2	7.4	22.2	9.2	49.6
	2003	5 624[7]	2.7	1.0	4.4	3.3	7.2	22.0	9.3	50.0
	2004	5 799[7]	2.1	1.0	4.5	3.3	6.8	22.3	8.8	51.3
Bahrain Bahreïn	2002	3 459	0.6	22.7	10.8	1.3	3.9	10.3	7.2	43.3
	2003	3 972	0.6	22.9	10.2	1.2	3.5	9.7	6.6	45.2
	2004	4 583	0.4	21.3	9.6	1.1	3.3	11.0	6.6	46.7

Country or area / Pays ou zone	Year / Année	Value added, Gross (mil. nat.cur) / Valeur ajoutée, brute (mil. mon. nat.)	Agriculture, hunting, forestry and fishing / Agriculture, chasse, sylviculture et pêche	Mining and quarrying / Activités extractives	Manufacturing / Activités de fabrication	Electricity, gas and water supply / Electricité, gaz et eau	Construction / Construction	Wholesale, retail trade, restaurants and hotels / Commerce, restaurants, hôtels	Transport, storage & communication / Transports, entrepôts, communications	Other activities / Autres activités
			% of Value added – % de la valeur ajoutée							
Bangladesh+[1] Bangladesh+[1]	2002	2 898 729	21.8	1.1	15.8	1.4	7.9	14.2	10.7	27.1
	2003	3 194 631	21.0	1.1	16.1	1.4	7.9	14.5	10.8	27.1
	2004	3 546 638	20.0	1.1	16.6	1.4	8.2	14.8	10.7	27.1
Barbados Barbade	2002	4 066[6]	3.8	0.7	6.5	3.4	5.6	28.4	7.3	44.4
	2003	4 335[6]	4.5	0.7	6.8	3.3	5.4	28.9	6.7	43.9
	2004	4 600[6]	3.6	0.8	6.9	3.1	5.6	28.9	6.9	44.2
Belarus[1] Bélarus[1]	2002	22 860 700	11.6	...	29.9	...	6.7	12.4	11.9	27.7
	2003	31 442 100	10.0	...	31.1	...	7.1	12.5	11.2	28.0
	2004	43 455 600	10.2	...	33.0	...	7.4	11.8	11.1	26.5
Belgium[1] Belgique[1]	2001	235 464	1.4	0.1	18.5	2.6	5.0	13.4	6.9	52.2
	2002	242 077	1.2	0.1	18.2	2.5	4.8	13.8	6.8	52.5
	2003	249 943	1.3	0.1	17.4	2.3	4.8	13.8	6.9	53.3
Belize[1] Belize[1]	1998	1 051[10,11]	19.1	0.6	13.2	3.4	5.7	18.9	10.4	37.9
	1999	1 154[10,11]	19.7	0.6	13.0	3.4	6.5	20.8	11.0	36.1
	2000	1 311[10,11]	17.2	0.7	13.1	3.3	7.1	21.6	9.9	29.8
Benin Bénin	2003	1 865 555	35.6	0.3	9.2	1.4	4.4	18.8	8.6	21.8
	2004	1 925 676	35.9	0.3	8.7	1.3	4.5	18.4	8.5	22.4
	2005	2 077 523	36.2	0.3	8.9	1.4	4.5	18.4	8.4	22.0
Bermuda+[1] Bermudes+[1]	2002	3 991	0.8	...	2.1	2.1	5.3[8]	14.6	6.9	68.3
	2003	4 300	0.8	...	1.7	1.9	5.7[8]	13.7	6.3	69.9
	2004	4 547	0.8	...	1.7	1.8	6.0[8]	13.7	5.9	70.0
Bhutan Bhoutan	1998	16 537[6]	36.6	1.6	9.8	11.7	10.2	7.0	8.3	14.8
	1999	18 957[6]	35.0	1.7	9.3	12.2	11.1	6.8	8.6	15.2
	2000	21 654[6]	35.9	1.6	8.0	11.6	12.5	6.8	8.6	15.0
Bolivia Bolivie	2001	48 407	14.7	7.0	14.8	3.3	3.1	11.5	12.8	34.1
	2002	50 805	14.5	7.2	14.7	3.2	3.5	11.5	13.3	33.4
	2003	54 742	15.2	8.5	14.6	3.3	2.6	11.4	13.7	32.7
Bosnia and Herzegovina[1] Bosnie-Herzégovine[1]	2002	9 442	12.1	2.3	12.3	6.3	5.1	15.5	11.1	35.3
	2003	10 005	10.6	2.4	12.6	7.2	4.8	16.5	11.2	34.7
	2004	11 104	11.5	2.5	12.3	7.3	4.7	17.2	10.9	33.6
Botswana+[1] Botswana+[1]	2002	30 881	2.6	36.4	4.5	2.4	5.6	11.8	3.7	32.9
	2003	34 733	2.5	36.4	4.5	2.7	5.7	12.0	3.7	32.6
	2004	37 517	2.5	36.1	4.3	2.8	5.6	12.0	3.7	33.0
Brazil[1] Brésil[1]	2002	1 199 145[10]	8.7	3.4	23.3	3.6	8.0	7.7[5]	5.3	46.2[5]
	2003	1 395 604[10]	9.9	3.9	24.2	3.4	7.2	7.7[5]	5.6	43.4[5]
	2004	1 581 501[10]	10.1	4.2	24.1	3.4	7.3	7.8[5]	5.2	42.6[5]
British Virgin Islands[1] Iles Vierges britanniques[1]	2003	805	1.1[12]	0.0	3.4	2.0	6.1	26.7	11.1	49.6
	2004	896	1.0[12]	0.0	3.0	2.0	4.9	27.6	11.4	50.0
	2005	1 002	0.9[12]	0.0	2.7	2.0	6.0	27.1	11.2	49.9
Brunei Darussalam Brunéi Darussalam	1996	7 886	2.5	34.7[2]	...	1.0	5.8	11.9	4.8	39.3
	1997	8 268	2.6	33.6[2]	...	1.0	6.2	12.1	4.9	39.6
	1998	8 331	2.8	31.6[2]	...	1.1	6.5	12.6	5.1	40.4
Bulgaria[1] Bulgarie[1]	2002	28 526	12.1	1.4	17.4	5.7	4.5	9.4	13.8	35.6
	2003	30 227	11.6	1.5	18.2	5.5	4.5	9.3	13.8	35.7
	2004	32 942	10.9	1.6	18.7	4.8	4.8	9.6	14.0	35.6
Burkina Faso Burkina Faso	1991	780 492	33.8	0.9	14.2	0.9	5.7	1.7	4.1	1.6
	1992	782 551	32.7	0.9	15.3	1.1	5.7	1.6	4.2	1.6
	1993	808 487	33.9	0.8	14.7	1.3	5.6	1.7	4.4	1.5

Country or area Pays ou zone	Year Année	Value added, Gross (mil. nat.cur) Valeur ajoutée, brute (mil. mon. nat.)	% of Value added – % de la valeur ajoutée							
			Agriculture, hunting, forestry and fishing Agriculture, chasse, sylviculture et pêche	Mining and quarrying Activités extractives	Manufacturing Activités de fabrication	Electricity, gas and water supply Electricité, gaz et eau	Construction Construction	Wholesale, retail trade, restaurants and hotels Commerce, restaurants, hôtels	Transport, storage & communication Transports, entrepôts, communications	Other activities Autres activités
Burundi Burundi	1988	149 067	48.9	1.0[3]	16.5	...	2.9	12.9	2.6	15.2
	1989	175 627	47.0	1.2[3]	18.5	...	3.3	10.8	3.3	16.0
	1990	192 050	52.4	0.8[3]	16.8	...	3.4	4.9	3.1	18.5
Cambodia[1] Cambodge[1]	2002	15 090 963	34.2	0.3	19.6	0.6	6.1	15.9	7.2	16.2
	2003	16 399 945	35.1	0.3	20.5	0.6	6.4	14.5	7.1	15.5
	2004	18 527 496	32.9	0.3	21.5	0.6	6.7	15.3	7.4	15.2
Cameroon+[1] Cameroun+[1]	1996	4 467 110	22.0	5.5	21.3	0.9	3.2	21.0	5.2	20.9
	1997	5 013 530	23.6	5.6	21.3	0.8	2.1	19.9	5.8	20.8
	1998	5 362 130	23.6	5.6	21.3	0.8	2.1	19.9	5.8	20.8
Canada[1] Canada[1]	2000	999 926	2.3	6.1	19.2	2.9	5.0	13.3	7.0	44.2
	2001	1 032 186	2.2	5.8	17.9	2.9	5.3	13.6	7.2	45.1
	2002	1 069 702	2.2	5.0	17.6	2.9	5.4	13.8	7.1	46.0
Cape Verde Cap-Vert	2001	64 273	12.4	1.0	4.5	1.4	8.0	22.1	24.9	25.8
	2002	67 055	11.3	1.8	4.8	0.6	8.8	23.8	22.5	26.4
	2003	73 361	11.0	1.8	4.5	1.4	8.3	23.8	23.5	25.8
Cayman Islands Iles Caïmanes	1989	473	0.4	0.6	1.9	3.2	11.0	24.5	11.0	47.6
	1990	580	0.3	0.3	1.6	3.1	9.7	24.5	10.9	49.8
	1991	605	0.3	0.3	1.5	3.1	9.1	22.8	10.7	52.1
Central African Rep. Rép. centrafricaine	1983	243 350	40.8	2.5	7.8[13]	0.5	2.1	21.2[5]	4.2	20.8[5]
	1984	268 725	40.7	2.8	8.1[13]	0.9	2.7	21.7[5]	4.3	18.8[5]
	1985	308 549	42.4	2.5	7.5[13]	0.8	2.6	22.0[5]	4.2	17.9[5]
Chad Tchad	1999	875 000[6]	38.6	...	12.9	0.7[14]	1.7	22.4	3.3	17.7
	2000	889 000[6]	38.9	...	11.8	0.7[14]	1.7	22.3	3.4	18.8
	2001	1 045 000[6]	37.1	...	13.7	0.7[14]	1.6	23.0	3.4	17.9
Chile[1] Chili[1]	2003	48 286 099[7]	5.6	9.1	19.0	3.2	8.3	9.8	7.6	37.3
	2004	54 657 456[7]	5.6	14.2	18.0	3.0	7.9	8.7	7.2	35.3
	2005	60 654 404[7]	5.4	17.0	17.1	3.0	8.3	8.6	6.9	33.8
China[1,15] Chine[1,15]	2002	12 033 269	13.4	38.2[2,3]	...	...	5.8	7.0	5.3	17.6
	2003	13 582 276	12.5	39.1[2,3]	...	...	6.0	6.8	4.9	17.2
	2004	15 987 834	13.0	39.3[2,3]	...	...	6.0	6.3	4.8	...
China, Hong Kong SAR[1] Chine, Hong Kong RAS[1]	2002	1 234 949	0.1[16]	0.0	4.2	3.2	4.2	25.1[17]	9.9	53.4[17]
	2003	1 202 908	0.1[16]	0.0	3.7	3.2	3.7	25.7[17]	9.8	53.8[17]
	2004	1 245 621	0.1[16]	0.0	3.6	3.2	3.2	27.0[17]	10.1	52.8[17]
China, Macao SAR[1] Chine, Macao RAS[1]	2001	42 509	...	0.0	7.9	3.0	2.2	11.2	6.5	69.3
	2002	45 989	...	0.0	6.9	2.6	2.6	12.0	6.5	69.4
	2003	51 064	...	0.0	6.1	2.6	3.9	11.5	5.3	70.6
Colombia[1] Colombie[1]	2000	168 124 471	13.5	6.4	15.2	3.7	3.8	11.0	7.4	38.9
	2001	180 184 781	13.0	5.2	15.1	4.5	3.7	11.1	8.1	39.3
	2002	194 052 700	12.7	5.2	15.1	4.4	4.1	11.0	8.1	39.3
Comoros Comores	1989	64 731	40.0	...	3.9	0.8	3.4	25.1	3.9	22.8
	1990	67 992	40.4	...	4.1	0.9	3.1	25.1	4.1	22.3
	1991	71 113	40.8	...	4.2	0.9	2.7	25.1	4.2	22.1
Congo Congo	1987	678 106	12.2	22.9	8.8	1.6	3.2	15.1	10.5	25.8
	1988	643 830	14.2	17.1	8.8	2.0	2.7	16.7	11.3	27.2
	1989	757 088	13.3	28.6	7.2	1.9	1.8	14.7	9.3	23.3
Cook Islands Iles Cook	2003	252	14.9	...	3.4	1.5	3.5	36.7	13.1	26.8
	2004	264	13.3	...	3.5	1.6	4.4	37.7	13.2	26.8
	2005	266	12.5	...	3.6	1.8	2.9	39.6	13.4	26.2

Value added by industries at current prices — Percentage distribution (*continued*)
Valeur ajoutée par branche d'activité aux prix courants — Répartition en pourcentage (*suite*)

Country or area Pays ou zone	Year Année	Value added, Gross (mil. nat.cur) Valeur ajoutée, brute (mil. mon. nat.)	% of Value added – % de la valeur ajoutée							
			Agriculture, hunting, forestry and fishing Agriculture, chasse, sylviculture et pêche	Mining and quarrying Activités extractives	Manufacturing Activités de fabrication	Electricity, gas and water supply Electricité, gaz et eau	Construction Construction	Wholesale, retail trade, restaurants and hotels Commerce, restaurants, hôtels	Transport, storage & communication Transports, entrepôts, communications	Other activities Autres activités
Costa Rica[1] Costa Rica[1]	2003	6 607 896	8.4	0.1	20.3	2.6	4.4	18.3	9.1	36.7
	2004	7 682 813	8.3	0.1	20.8	2.8	4.5	18.6	9.2	35.7
	2005	8 958 898	8.6	0.1	21.0	2.9	4.5	18.8	9.1	34.9
Côte d'Ivoire Côte d'Ivoire	1998	6 984 000	25.6	0.6	21.9	1.6	2.3	20.4	6.0	21.3
	1999	7 449 000	23.2	0.3	22.2	2.0	3.5	21.9	5.7	21.1
	2000	7 323 000	24.8	0.3	22.4	1.6	2.9	19.0	5.5	23.2
Croatia[1] Croatie[1]	2002	152 038	8.6	0.8	19.5	2.8	5.6	15.5	10.4	36.8
	2003	165 630	8.0	...	22.4[3,8]	...	6.5	15.7	10.7	36.7
	2004	178 365	7.9	...	22.2[3,8]	...	6.6	15.5	10.9	36.9
Cuba[1] Cuba[1]	2002	35 770	5.6	1.5	14.4	1.6	4.8	24.1	8.5	39.5
	2003	38 255	5.4	1.5	13.4	1.6	4.7	24.3	8.3	40.9
	2004	40 670	5.1	1.4	12.9	1.4	4.9	23.2	8.2	42.7
Cyprus[1] Chypre[1]	2003	6 440	3.5	0.3	9.6	2.3	7.8	20.0	8.2	48.3
	2004	6 863	3.1	0.3	9.5	2.2	8.2	20.1	8.4	48.1
	2005	7 302	3.0	0.3	9.2	2.2	8.6	19.6	8.3	48.7
Czech Republic[1] République tchèque[1]	2003	2 367 098	3.0	1.2	25.3	3.9	7.0	14.4	11.4	33.8
	2004	2 530 927	3.3	1.2	25.9	4.0	6.9	14.5	10.9	33.4
	2005	2 666 174	3.0	1.2	25.6	4.3	6.6	14.7	10.7	33.8
Denmark[1] Danemark[1]	2002	1 175 635	2.2	2.6	15.8	2.0	5.1	13.7	8.1	50.5
	2003	1 210 554	2.0	2.4	15.0	2.2	5.2	13.6	8.5	51.2
	2004	1 255 240	1.9	2.9	13.6	2.0	5.5	13.4	8.8	51.8
Djibouti Djibouti	1996	76 435	3.5[12]	0.2	2.8	6.8[14]	5.7	15.9	21.7	43.4
	1997	75 964	3.6[12]	0.2	2.8	6.6[14]	6.0	16.1	23.1	41.6
	1998	78 263	3.6[12]	0.2	2.7	5.3[14]	6.4	16.4	26.0	39.4
Dominica Dominique	2000	676[6]	16.6	0.7	8.1	5.1	7.4	13.3	15.7	31.5
	2001	657[6]	15.7	0.7	7.2	5.5	7.5	13.5	14.8	33.6
	2002	627[6]	16.9	0.6	7.2	4.9	6.5	13.6	12.8	35.4
Dominican Republic[1] Rép. dominicaine[1]	1994	165 808	10.8	1.1	20.2	1.4	7.7	16.4	9.8	32.6
	1995	193 436	10.1	1.3	19.6	1.7	7.7	17.3	9.0	33.3
	1996	228 022	8.9	1.0	19.3	1.8	7.3	20.4	8.8	32.5
Ecuador[1] Equateur[1]	2002	22 859[7]	9.0	12.6[18]	8.3	2.7	8.9	17.8	12.9	27.9
	2003	26 596[7]	8.2	13.6[18]	7.5	2.5	8.1	16.2	13.1	30.9
	2004	30 620[7]	7.5	17.5[18]	6.0	2.0	8.5	15.1	12.0	31.4
Egypt+[1] Egypte+[1]	2002	428 151	13.1	9.5	16.6[19]	1.8	4.2	17.3	8.0	29.5
	2003	475 035	13.7	10.1	16.1[19]	2.0	4.4	16.5	8.5	28.6
	2004	534 427	14.6	11.9	17.6	1.8	3.6	13.6	8.8	28.2
El Salvador El Salvador	2002	13 925[20]	8.7	0.5	23.8	1.8	4.9	19.7	9.2	31.3
	2003	14 466[20]	8.7	0.5	23.7	1.8	5.0	19.5	9.3	31.4
	2004	15 318[20]	9.1	0.5	23.1	1.7	4.3	19.7	10.1	31.4
Equatorial Guinea Guinée équatoriale	1989	40 948	56.1	...	1.3	3.1	3.7	8.8	2.0	25.0
	1990	42 765	53.6	...	1.3	3.4	3.8	7.6	2.2	28.0
	1991	43 932	53.1	...	1.4	3.1	3.0	7.6	1.9	30.0
Estonia[1] Estonie[1]	2002	103 557	4.7	0.9	17.4	2.9	6.4	14.4	14.5	38.9
	2003	112 763	4.2	1.0	17.9	3.0	6.4	14.4	14.4	38.7
	2004	125 661	4.3	0.9	18.4	2.9	6.7	14.3	14.0	38.6
Ethiopia incl. Eritrea Ethiopie y comp. Erythrée	1990	11 436[6]	41.1	0.2	11.1	1.5	3.6	9.6[5]	7.2	25.7[5]
	1991	12 295[6]	41.0	0.3	10.3	1.5	3.2	9.4[5]	7.1	27.3[5]
	1992	12 544[6]	50.3	0.3	9.1	1.3	2.8	10.2[5]	5.4	20.6[5]

Country or area Pays ou zone	Year Année	Value added, Gross (mil. nat.cur) Valeur ajoutée, brute (mil. mon. nat.)	% of Value added – % de la valeur ajoutée Agriculture, hunting, forestry and fishing Agriculture, chasse, sylviculture et pêche	Mining and quarrying Activités extractives	Manufacturing Activités de fabrication	Electricity, gas and water supply Electricité, gaz et eau	Construction Construction	Wholesale, retail trade, restaurants and hotels Commerce, restaurants, hôtels	Transport, storage & communication Transports, entrepôts, communications	Other activities Autres activités
Fiji Fidji	2002	3 592	14.8	0.9	14.4	2.8	4.0	16.2	16.0	30.8
	2003	3 789	14.4	1.0	13.5	2.8	4.3	16.5	16.8	30.8
	2004	4 130	14.0	1.1	14.5	2.7	4.1	19.1	15.3	29.1
Finland[1] Finlande[1]	2002	122 594	3.5	0.3	23.3	2.1	5.3	12.0	10.8	42.8
	2003	124 433	3.4	0.3	22.7	2.3	5.3	12.0	10.9	43.2
	2004	129 929	3.1	0.3	22.1	2.4	5.4	12.2	10.8	43.7
France[1] France[1]	2003	1 434 812	2.5	0.2	14.1	1.7	5.3	13.4	6.4	56.6
	2004	1 489 308	2.5	0.2	13.8	1.7	5.6	13.1	6.3	56.9
	2005	1 531 273	2.2	0.2	13.3	1.7	5.8	12.9	6.4	57.6
French Guiana Guyane française	1990	6 454	10.1	7.6	...	0.7	12.8	13.5	7.7	47.5
	1991	7 385	7.4	7.6	...	0.5	12.1	13.1	12.3	47.0
	1992	8 052	7.2	9.0	...	0.6	10.8	11.9	11.4	49.1
French Polynesia Polynésie française	1991	305 211	4.1	...	7.5[21]	1.8[21]	5.7	...	...	29.3
	1992	314 265	3.8	...	7.5[21]	2.1[21]	5.9	...	...	29.5
	1993	329 266	3.9	...	6.7[21]	2.1[21]	5.7	...	...	29.0
Gabon Gabon	1987	986 000	10.9	28.4	7.1[22]	2.7	7.2	9.2	8.1	26.5
	1988	965 700	11.2	22.6	7.3[22]	3.0	5.2	14.4	9.1	27.3
	1989	1 128 400	10.4	32.3	5.7[22]	2.5	5.5	12.4	8.2	23.1
Gambia+ Gambie+	1991	2 962	22.3	0.0	5.5	0.9	4.4	39.1	10.9	17.0
	1992	3 100	18.4	0.0	5.7	1.0	4.7	41.7	11.2	17.4
	1993	3 296	20.2	0.0	5.1	1.0	4.5	38.3	12.5	18.4
Georgia[1] Géorgie[1]	2002	6 961[10]	20.6	0.7	13.7	4.5	5.5	16.9	15.2	24.0
	2003	8 042[10]	20.6	0.9	13.9	4.0	6.8	17.2	14.8	22.8
	2004	9 135[10]	17.8	0.9	14.2	3.5	6.8	17.3	14.9	25.5
Germany[1] Allemagne[1]	2002	1 935 030	1.1	0.2	22.4	1.8	4.6	12.5	5.7	51.7
	2003	1 949 040	1.1	0.2	22.3	2.0	4.3	12.4	5.6	52.2
	2004	2 003 180	1.1	0.2	22.7	2.0	4.1	12.4	5.6	51.8
Ghana Ghana	1994	4 686 000	42.0	6.3	10.1	3.0	8.3	6.4	4.8	18.2
	1995	7 040 200	42.7	5.3	10.3	2.9	8.3	6.5	4.3	18.8
	1996	10 067 000	43.9	5.3	9.7	3.0	8.5	6.5	4.2	17.9
Greece[1] Grèce[1]	2002	125 913	7.1	...	11.6	...	8.3	20.8	8.7	42.4
	2003	137 421[11]	...	...	11.4	1.8	8.8	21.2	8.6	42.6
	2004	149 771[11]	5.7	0.6	11.1	1.8	8.5	21.7	9.7	43.5
Grenada Grenade	1989	393[11]	18.7	0.4	5.3	2.9	10.3	18.8	13.9	34.4
	1990	440	16.2	0.4	5.1	3.0	10.1	18.7	13.7	32.8
	1991	463	14.9	0.4	5.3	3.1	10.4	19.5	14.3	32.1
Guadeloupe Guadeloupe	1990	15 036	6.7	5.4[2]	...	1.0	7.4	18.3	5.9	55.2
	1991	16 278	7.3	6.1[2]	...	1.4	7.0	16.5	6.0	55.5
	1992	17 968	6.7	6.9[2]	...	1.7	6.5	16.2	7.9	54.1
Guinea-Bissau Guinée-Bissau	1989	358 875	44.6	7.9[2,3]	...	...	9.7	25.7	3.6	8.5
	1990	510 094	44.6	8.2[2,3]	...	...	10.0	25.7	3.7	7.8
	1991	854 985	44.7	8.5[2,3]	...	...	8.4	25.8	3.9	8.7
Guyana Guyana	1999	105 095[6]	41.2[12]	15.4	3.5[3]	...	4.5[23]	4.1[5]	6.8	24.5[5]
	2000	108 087[6]	36.1[12]	15.9	3.2[3]	...	4.9[23]	4.4[5]	7.8	27.7[5]
	2001	112 218[6]	35.4[12]	15.7	3.2[3]	...	5.0[23]	4.4[5]	8.6	27.8[5]
Honduras Honduras	1998	60 068[6]	19.1	1.8	18.6	5.1	5.1	12.3	5.0	33.0
	1999	65 881[6]	15.9	2.0	19.6	4.9	5.9	12.7	5.2	33.8
	2000	75 924[6]	15.0	2.0	19.8	4.8	5.7	12.8	5.2	34.7

Country or area Pays ou zone	Year Année	Value added, Gross (mil. nat.cur) Valeur ajoutée, brute (mil. mon. nat.)	% of Value added – % de la valeur ajoutée Agriculture, hunting, forestry and fishing Agriculture, chasse, sylviculture et pêche	Mining and quarrying Activités extractives	Manufacturing Activités de fabrication	Electricity, gas and water supply Electricité, gaz et eau	Construction Construction	Wholesale, retail trade, restaurants and hotels Commerce, restaurants, hôtels	Transport, storage & communication Transports, entrepôts, communications	Other activities Autres activités
Hungary[1] Hongrie[1]	2002	14 619 417	3.7	0.2	21.8	3.0	5.3	13.2	8.2	44.6
	2003	15 944 731	3.3	0.2	22.3	3.0	4.9	12.9	8.0	45.3
	2004	17 372 489	3.9	0.2	22.5	3.1	5.0	12.6	8.1	44.6
Iceland[1] Islande[1]	2002	681 228	8.9	0.1	13.3	3.6	7.0	12.1	8.2	46.7
	2003	697 710	7.4	0.1	12.6	3.6	7.9	12.5	7.4	48.5
	2004	764 446	6.7	0.1	12.8	3.7	8.3	12.7	7.1	48.6
India+ Inde+	2001	20 814 740[6]	24.5	2.3	15.4	2.1	6.0	14.5	7.6	27.6
	2002	22 548 880[6]	22.5	2.8	15.6	2.2	6.2	14.8	7.7	28.3
	2003	25 197 850[6]	22.8	2.5	15.6	2.1	6.2	14.9	8.0	27.8
Indonesia[1] Indonésie[1]	2003	2 013 674 600[24]	15.2	8.3	28.3	1.0	6.2	16.6	5.9	23.6
	2004	2 273 141 500[24]	14.6	8.6	28.1	1.0	6.3	16.2	6.3	24.2
	2005	2 729 708 200[24]	13.4	10.4	28.1	0.9	6.4	15.8	6.6	23.4
Iran (Islamic Rep.of)+[1] Iran (République islamique d')+[1]	2002	960 603 380	11.1	17.6[25]	14.9	2.0	4.9	14.1	7.1[11]	28.4
	2003	1 183 021 940	11.0	18.0[25]	15.2	2.6	4.0	13.6	7.0[11]	28.6
	2004	1 514 189 600	10.2	20.9[25]	15.5	2.6	3.7	13.4	6.6	26.9
Iraq Iraq	2001	41 494 367[26]	6.9	74.3	1.5	0.2	1.2	6.5	6.3	3.2
	2002	41 242 664[26]	8.5	70.4	1.5	0.2	1.6	6.4	7.9	3.5
	2003	29 894 476[26]	8.3	68.1	1.0	0.2	0.7	6.5	7.6	7.4
Ireland[1] Irlande[1]	2002	117 792[27]	2.6	0.4	32.2	1.0	7.7	12.0	5.3	38.8
	2003	124 317[27]	2.5	0.4	28.4	1.0	8.3	13.2	5.5	40.7
	2004	131 777	2.5	0.4	27.0	1.1	9.0	12.6	5.4	42.0
Israel[1] Israël[1]	2002	469 890	1.8	...	14.7[8]	2.0	5.1	9.8	6.9	59.6
	2003	460 952	1.7	...	14.6[8]	2.3	5.3	10.2	7.4	58.5
	2004	489 551	1.8	...	14.9[8]	2.2	4.8	10.6	7.2	58.5
Italy[1] Italie[1]	2003	1 203 740	2.5	0.4	19.0	2.0	5.6	15.7	7.6	47.0
	2004	1 249 158	2.5	0.4	19.0	2.0	5.9	15.5	7.7	47.1
	2005	1 272 762	2.3	0.4	18.4	2.0	6.0	15.4	7.8	47.7
Jamaica Jamaïque	2002	397 716[7]	5.7	3.9	13.0	3.4	9.7	24.4[28]	12.8	27.0
	2003	462 930[7]	5.2	4.4	12.8	3.4	9.5	24.3[28]	12.2	28.2
	2004	523 112[7]	5.2	4.4	12.9	3.6	10.2	25.0[28]	11.9	26.8
Japan[1] Japon[1]	2002	512 410 900	1.6	0.1	19.8	2.6	6.5	13.2[5]	6.7	49.4[5]
	2003	512 100 000	1.6	0.1	20.1	2.5	6.5	12.9[5]	6.7	49.7[5]
	2004	514 832 800	1.6	0.1	20.2	2.5	6.2	13.0[5]	6.8	49.6[5]
Jordan Jordanie	2001	5 593	2.2	3.1	14.6	2.5	4.1	11.8	16.2	45.3
	2002	6 034	2.5	3.1	15.8	2.6	4.2	11.1	15.5	45.2
	2003	6 493	2.7	3.0	16.1	2.5	4.1	10.7	15.6	45.3
Kazakhstan[1] Kazakhstan[1]	2002	3 560 198[26]	8.5	12.9	15.4	3.0	6.7	13.6	12.3	27.6
	2003	4 370 285[26]	8.3	12.8	15.0	2.9	6.3	13.2	13.1	28.4
	2004	5 626 811[26]	7.4	14.2	13.9	2.5	6.3	13.9	12.3	29.5
Kenya[1] Kenya[1]	2002	931 377[26]	28.5	0.5	11.0	2.2	3.5	11.3	11.2	31.7
	2003	1 026 307[26]	27.9	0.6	10.7	2.3	3.6	11.1	11.1	32.8
	2004	1 147 432[26]	26.9	0.6	11.0	2.0	4.0	12.4	11.4	31.7
Korea, Republic of[1] Corée, République de[1]	2003	639 761 892[7]	3.8	0.3	26.4	2.7	9.6	10.3	7.5	39.4
	2004	694 317 500[7]	3.8	0.3	28.6	2.4	9.3	9.8	7.3	38.4
	2005	718 031 700[7]	3.3	0.3	28.4	2.4	9.2	9.8	7.2	39.2
Kuwait Koweït	2002	11 983	0.5	36.9	7.6	2.3	2.6	7.9	5.0	37.3
	2003	14 184	0.5	41.0	7.6	2.1	2.3	7.5	4.8	34.2
	2004	16 960	0.4	46.2	7.8	1.8	2.1	6.8	4.2	30.7

Country or area Pays ou zone	Year Année	Value added, Gross (mil. nat.cur) Valeur ajoutée, brute (mil. mon. nat.)	% of Value added – % de la valeur ajoutée: Agriculture, hunting, forestry and fishing Agriculture, chasse, sylviculture et pêche	Mining and quarrying Activités extractives	Manufacturing Activités de fabrication	Electricity, gas and water supply Electricité, gaz et eau	Construction Construction	Wholesale, retail trade, restaurants and hotels Commerce, restaurants, hôtels	Transport, storage & communication Transports, entrepôts, communications	Other activities Autres activités
Kyrgyzstan[1] Kirghizistan[1]	2001	69 044	37.0	0.5	18.9	5.3	4.0	13.9	4.5	15.9
	2002	69 452	37.3	0.5	14.2	4.7	3.7	16.7	5.5	17.3
	2003	76 846	36.7	0.5	14.5	3.9	3.2	18.2	5.9	17.2
Lao People's Dem. Republic Rép. dém. pop. lao	1999	10 253 626	53.7	0.5	17.0	2.4	2.7	11.8	5.8	6.1
	2000	13 565 564	52.5	0.5	17.0	3.1	2.3	11.7	5.9	7.0
	2001	15 563 971	51.2	0.5	17.9	2.9	2.4	11.8	6.0	7.3
Latvia[1] Lettonie[1]	2003	5 716	4.1	0.3	13.3	3.1	5.6	19.3	15.3	38.9
	2004	6 662	4.4	0.3	13.2	3.0	5.8	20.5	15.3	37.5
	2005	7 934	4.1	0.3	12.8	2.6	6.3	22.1	15.5	36.2
Lebanon[1] Liban[1]	2000	25 142 000[24]	6.4	...	12.0[8]	0.9	8.0	19.9[5]	6.5	46.3[5]
	2001	25 726 000[24]	6.0	...	12.3[8]	1.2	8.2	19.7[5]	6.7	46.0[5]
	2002	27 832 000[24]	5.8	...	11.7[8]	1.0	7.7	21.8[5]	6.5	45.5[5]
Lesotho[1] Lesotho[1]	1999	5 182[26]	16.9	0.1	15.9	6.2	17.9	9.5	3.5	29.8
	2000	5 637[26]	17.8	0.1	16.1	5.6	17.5	10.1	3.4	29.3
	2001	6 078[26]	18.0	0.1	16.8	5.7	17.3	10.3	3.5	28.3
Liberia Libéria	1987	1 009	37.8	10.4	7.2	1.9	3.2	6.0	7.5	26.0
	1988	1 080	38.2	10.7	7.4	1.7	2.7	5.9	7.3	26.1
	1989	1 119	36.7	10.9	7.3	1.7	2.4	5.7	7.1	28.3
Libyan Arab Jamah. Jamah. arabe libyenne	1983	8 482	3.0	48.8	3.2	0.9	10.4	6.1	4.6	23.0
	1984	7 681	3.4	40.9	3.9	1.2	11.1	7.9	5.3	26.4
	1985	8 050	3.5	41.6	4.5	1.3	11.4	7.0	5.0	25.8
Lithuania[1] Lituanie[1]	2002	46 154	7.0	0.6	18.8	4.1	6.3	19.1	13.4	30.7
	2003	50 794	6.4	0.6	19.4	4.7	7.1	19.0	13.4	29.4
	2004	56 033	5.9	0.5	20.5	4.4	7.2	19.5	12.8	29.2
Luxembourg[1] Luxembourg[1]	2002	21 623	0.6	0.1	10.3	1.3	6.6	12.1	10.2	58.8
	2003	23 101	0.6	0.1	9.7	1.4	6.3	11.9	9.7	60.3
	2004	24 043	0.6	0.1	9.4	1.3	5.9	12.2	9.7	60.9
Madagascar Madagascar	1983	1 187 400	44.2	15.6	...	...	...	30.4	...	9.7
	1984	1 323 100	43.9	16.2	...	...	...	30.3	...	9.7
	1985	1 500 600	43.5	16.9	...	...	...	30.1	...	9.5
Malawi Malawi	1984	1 322	37.4[29]	...	18.6	1.8	2.0	6.8	4.9	28.6
	1985	1 540	34.7[29]	...	17.5	1.5	2.2	12.8	4.8	26.4
	1986	1 694	34.5[29]	...	20.3	1.2	2.0	11.5	3.5	27.1
Malaysia Malaisie	2002	378 987	8.7	9.0	29.2	3.2	3.8	13.4	6.6	26.0
	2003	412 233	9.2	10.0	29.8	3.1	3.7	12.8	6.5	25.0
	2004	467 570	9.1	12.1	30.2	2.9	3.3	12.5	6.4	23.5
Mali Mali	1990	655 600	47.8	1.6	8.1[30]	3.8[31]	...	18.8	4.9	15.1
	1991	662 500	46.1	1.7	6.9[30]	4.3[31]	...	20.2	5.0	15.9
	1992	707 000	47.2	1.5	7.0[30]	4.4[31]	...	19.3	5.0	15.6
Malta[1] Malte[1]	2002	1 515[10]	2.7	0.3	20.8	2.0	4.7	18.9	10.4	43.9
	2003	1 569[10]	2.5	0.3	20.6	1.5	4.7	19.0	9.9	46.0
	2004	1 572[10]	2.7	0.4	19.1	0.9	4.8	19.0	9.9	48.3
Marshall Islands Iles Marshall	1999	94	8.8	0.3	3.4	2.4	11.3	18.3	5.9	49.6
	2000	97	10.0	0.3	4.6	3.2	11.1	17.6	5.4	47.9
	2001	98	10.5	0.3	4.6	3.5	11.5	17.2	5.1	47.3
Martinique Martinique	1990	18 835	5.7	7.9[2]	...	2.5	4.9	18.9	6.2	53.9
	1991	20 377	5.7	7.8[2]	...	2.4	5.3	18.9	6.3	53.6
	1992	21 869	5.1	8.1[2]	...	2.2	5.2	18.4	6.5	54.5

Country or area / Pays ou zone	Year / Année	Value added, Gross (mil. nat.cur) / Valeur ajoutée, brute (mil. mon. nat.)	% of Value added - % de la valeur ajoutée: Agriculture, hunting, forestry and fishing / Agriculture, chasse, sylviculture et pêche	Mining and quarrying / Activités extractives	Manufacturing / Activités de fabrication	Electricity, gas and water supply / Electricité, gaz et eau	Construction / Construction	Wholesale, retail trade, restaurants and hotels / Commerce, restaurants, hôtels	Transport, storage & communication / Transports, entrepôts, communications	Other activities / Autres activités
Mauritania / Mauritanie	1987	60 302[6]	32.3	8.3	12.1	...	6.3	13.0	5.1	22.8
	1988	65 069[6]	32.4	7.7	13.0	...	6.3	13.2	5.1	22.3
	1989	75 486[6]	34.2	10.4	10.3	...	6.4	...	4.9	14.5
Mauritius[1] / Maurice[1]	2003	144 091	6.0	0.1	20.6	2.4	5.7	17.1	12.9	35.4
	2004	159 213	5.9	0.1	20.0	2.3	5.5	17.8	12.5	35.9
	2005	172 310	5.3	0.1	18.8	2.0	5.3	18.6	12.7	37.2
Mexico[1] / Mexique[1]	2002	5 819 424	3.8	1.3[32]	18.4[32]	1.4	5.0	19.7	10.5	39.9
	2003	6 320 583	3.8	1.3[32]	17.8[32]	1.3	5.2	20.1	10.2	40.4
	2004	7 042 434	3.8	1.4[32]	17.8[32]	1.3	5.4	20.6	10.3	39.3
Mongolia / Mongolie	2002	1 090 174[6]	23.5	11.5	5.3	5.1	2.7	17.0	16.8	18.1
	2003	1 304 189[6]	22.5	14.2	5.4	4.4	3.4	16.1	15.6	18.3
	2004	1 706 593[6]	23.4	21.4	4.4	4.0	2.7	13.5	14.2	16.4
Montserrat / Montserrat	1985	90[6]	4.8	1.3	5.7	3.7	7.9	18.0	11.5	47.2
	1986	103[6]	4.3	1.4	5.6	3.7	11.3	18.7	11.6	43.4
	1987	118[6]	4.1	1.3	5.7	3.2	11.5	22.1	11.1	41.0
Morocco / Maroc	2002	388 315	16.5	1.9[9]	17.2	7.0[14,18]	5.0	14.2	7.4	30.9
	2003	412 208	17.0	1.6[9]	17.0	6.8[14,18]	5.0	14.0	7.2	31.5
	2004	434 614	16.2	1.7[9]	16.8	7.4[14,18]	5.1	14.2	7.2	31.4
Mozambique[1] / Mozambique[1]	2002	97 447 500	22.2	0.3	12.0	3.7	7.9	26.0	11.3	16.7
	2003	114 031 700	22.1	0.3	12.6	4.4	8.1	23.8	12.5	16.2
	2004	133 245 000	21.2	0.9	13.5	5.3	7.0	23.3	13.9	14.9
Myanmar+ / Myanmar+	1996	791 980	60.1	0.6	7.1	0.3[33]	2.4	22.6[5]	3.5	3.4[5,34]
	1997	1 109 554	59.4	0.6	7.1	0.1[33]	2.4	23.2[5]	3.9	3.1[5,34]
	1998	1 559 996	59.1	0.5	7.2	0.1[33]	2.4	23.9[5]	4.0	2.7[5,34]
Namibia[1] / Namibie[1]	2002	30 106[26]	10.9	15.2	11.0	2.8	2.4	13.3	6.9	37.5
	2003	31 616[26]	11.3	9.4	12.2	3.2	3.3	14.7	7.5	38.4
	2004	33 962[26]	9.8	11.3	13.3	3.4	3.3	14.1	7.4	37.4
Nepal+ / Népal+	2003	437 546[6]	39.1	0.5	7.8	2.5	10.3	10.1	8.8	21.0
	2004	474 129[6]	38.7	0.5	7.7	2.4	10.3	10.4	9.2	20.8
	2005	504 101[6]	38.3	0.5	7.8	2.4	10.5	9.8	9.4	21.2
Netherlands[1] / Pays-Bas[1]	2002	414 374	2.3	2.4	14.3	1.7	5.7	15.8	7.4	50.4
	2003	425 093	2.3	2.4	14.0	1.8	5.6	15.2	7.4	51.2
	2004	435 184	2.1	2.7	14.0	1.6	5.7	15.0	7.5	51.5
Netherlands Antilles[1] / Antilles néerlandaises[1]	2001	4 883[26]	0.7	...	5.7[8]	4.3	3.9	16.2	9.6	59.6
	2002	4 860[26]	0.7	...	5.8[8]	3.9	4.3	18.6	9.0	57.7
	2003	5 024[26]	0.7	...	5.3[8]	4.0	4.1	18.9	8.6	58.4
New Caledonia / Nouvelle-Calédonie	1994	306 748	1.9	7.4	6.6	1.5	6.0	23.0[5]	6.3	47.4[5]
	1995	329 296	1.8	8.7	6.0	1.5	5.7	22.2[5]	6.3	47.7[5]
	1996	335 482	1.7	8.5	5.7	1.6	5.0	22.8[5]	6.7	47.8[5]
New Zealand+[1] / Nouvelle-Zélande+[1]	1999	105 341	7.0	1.1	16.0	2.8	4.6	15.0	7.7	45.7
	2000	111 314	8.6	1.2	16.3	2.5	4.3	14.7	7.4	44.8
	2001	120 072	9.1	1.2	16.0	2.5	4.4	15.3	7.2	44.3
Nicaragua[1] / Nicaragua[1]	2002	53 028	19.5	1.0	15.6	3.5	7.5	17.2	4.6	31.2
	2003	57 844	19.1	0.9	15.5	3.4	7.6	17.1	4.6	31.8
	2004	65 268	19.2	1.0	15.6	3.4	7.8	17.1	4.7	31.3
Niger / Niger	2003	1 379 713	44.5	2.2	6.6	1.4	2.6	14.1	6.6	22.1
	2004	1 377 052	40.8	2.2	6.8	1.3	2.9	14.7	7.3	24.0
	2005	1 599 875	44.3	2.4	6.1	1.2	2.7	13.5	7.1	22.7

Country or area / Pays ou zone	Year / Année	Value added, Gross (mil. nat.cur) / Valeur ajoutée, brute (mil. mon. nat.)	% of Value added – % de la valeur ajoutée: Agriculture, hunting, forestry and fishing / Agriculture, chasse, sylviculture et pêche	Mining and quarrying / Activités extractives	Manufacturing / Activités de fabrication	Electricity, gas and water supply / Electricité, gaz et eau	Construction / Construction	Wholesale, retail trade, restaurants and hotels / Commerce, restaurants, hôtels	Transport, storage & communication / Transports, entrepôts, communications	Other activities / Autres activités
Nigeria+ Nigéria+	2003	9 913 518	32.6	41.6	4.7	0.2	1.2	11.3	2.5	5.9
	2004	11 411 067	34.2	37.3	3.1	0.2	1.5	13.3	3.4	7.0
	2005	14 610 881	32.5	38.9	2.8	0.2	1.5	13.5	2.9	7.7
Norway[1] Norvège[1]	2001	1 377 414	1.8	22.6	10.8	2.2	4.1	10.3	9.1	39.0
	2002	1 369 980	1.7	19.4	10.8	2.5	4.5	10.7	9.1	41.3
	2003	1 427 267	1.5	19.6	10.8	2.7	4.4	10.3	8.8	42.0
Occupied Palestinian Terr.[1] Terr. palestinien occupé[1]	2001	3 284	10.3	0.7	14.2	2.1	4.7	11.2	7.8	49.0
	2002	3 070	11.2	0.6	13.3	1.9	3.9	12.3	8.2	48.7
	2003	3 494	10.8	0.3	11.7	2.0	5.7	12.8	7.0	49.8
Oman[1] Oman[1]	2001	7 819[7]	2.0	42.0	8.2	1.0	2.0	12.0	6.4	26.3
	2002	7 974[7]	2.0	41.2	7.6	1.0	2.1	12.4	6.7	27.0
	2003	8 510[7,11]	1.9	38.0	8.1	1.3	2.3	12.4	6.8	26.7
Pakistan+[1] Pakistan+[1]	2003	4 481 412	23.6	1.9	16.2	2.7	2.3	17.5	13.6	22.2
	2004	5 142 610	22.3	2.1	17.6	2.9	2.3	17.9	13.6	21.2
	2005	6 129 676	21.6	2.0	18.2	2.5	2.3	18.1	14.7	20.5
Palau[1] Palaos[1]	1999	111	4.1	0.2	1.5	3.1	7.4	31.7	8.9	43.3
	2000	115	4.1	0.2	1.5	3.1	7.6	31.3	9.0	43.3
	2001	118	4.0	0.2	1.5	3.2	7.8	31.1	9.2	43.1
Panama[1] Panama[1]	2001	11 530	7.5	0.7	9.0	2.8	4.0	16.7	14.0	45.4
	2002	11 870	7.5	0.8	8.2	2.9	3.6	16.0	14.4	46.6
	2003	12 411	7.5	1.0	7.4	2.9	4.8	15.0	14.8	46.5
Papua New Guinea[1] Papouasie-Nvl-Guinée[1]	2000	10 258[10]	32.2	24.0	10.0	1.4	4.4	8.8	4.3	16.5
	2001	11 226[10]	31.9	21.4	11.4	1.5	6.1	9.6	5.0	14.7
	2002	12 803[10]	34.6	16.8	11.1	1.5	7.6	11.3	4.9	13.7
Paraguay Paraguay	1993	11 991 719	24.5	0.4	16.5	3.4	5.9	30.4[5,35]	3.9	15.0[5]
	1994	14 960 131	23.7	0.4	15.7	3.9	6.0	30.5[5,35]	3.9	15.9[5]
	1995	17 699 000	24.8	0.3	15.7	4.3	6.0	29.5[5,35]	3.7	15.8[5]
Peru[1] Pérou[1]	2002	181 981	7.8	5.9	16.1	2.4	5.9	19.3	8.5	33.9
	2003	192 856	7.6	6.6	15.6	2.5	6.0	19.0	8.7	34.1
	2004	212 877	7.3	8.6	15.9	2.4	6.0	18.5	8.6	32.7
Philippines Philippines	2002	3 963 873	15.1	0.8	23.1	3.1	4.8	15.9	7.0	30.1
	2003	4 293 026	14.7	1.0	23.4	3.2	4.4	15.9	7.3	30.1
	2004	4 826 343	15.2	1.1	23.1	3.2	4.4	16.0	7.6	29.3
Poland[1] Pologne[1]	2002	682 861[27]	3.1	2.3	17.5	3.9	6.6	22.0	7.8	36.8
	2003	708 606[27]	3.0	2.2	18.3	4.0	6.0	20.9	7.8	37.8
	2004	771 386[27]	2.9	2.8	20.2	3.6	5.5	20.7	7.7	36.6
Portugal[1] Portugal[1]	2001	112 817	3.6	0.4	16.7	2.4	7.8	17.6	6.8	44.7
	2002	117 751	3.3	0.4	16.4	2.5	7.6	17.6	6.8	45.4
	2003	119 429	3.4	0.4	15.8	2.5	6.7	17.5	7.0	46.7
Puerto Rico+ Porto Rico+	2000	68 491	0.5	0.1	42.4	2.3	2.5[36]	13.2	4.6	34.4
	2001	70 975	0.3	0.1	43.0	2.3	2.5[36]	12.8	4.7	34.3
	2002	74 297	0.3	0.1	42.1	2.4	2.3[36]	12.6	4.5	35.7
Qatar[1] Qatar[1]	2000	65 707	0.4	59.5	5.3	1.2	3.5	5.7	3.1	21.3
	2001	65 776	0.4	56.0	5.9	1.5	4.5	6.0	3.4	22.4
	2002	66 410	0.4	56.5	5.9	1.5	4.1	5.9	3.4	22.3
Republic of Moldova[1] République de Moldova[1]	2003	24 170	20.9	0.3	17.6	2.2	3.4	13.4	12.3	29.9
	2004	28 247	19.9	0.4	16.5	2.5	3.9	13.1	13.4	30.3
	2005	31 467	16.7	0.5	16.9	2.5	4.1	13.6	14.1	31.7

Value added by industries at current prices — Percentage distribution (*continued*)
Valeur ajoutée par branche d'activité aux prix courants — Répartition en pourcentage (*suite*)

Country or area Pays ou zone	Year Année	Value added, Gross (mil. nat.cur) Valeur ajoutée, brute (mil. mon. nat.)	% of Value added – % de la valeur ajoutée: Agriculture, hunting, forestry and fishing Agriculture, chasse, sylviculture et pêche	Mining and quarrying Activités extractives	Manufacturing Activités de fabrication	Electricity, gas and water supply Electricité, gaz et eau	Construction Construction	Wholesale, retail trade, restaurants and hotels Commerce, restaurants, hôtels	Transport, storage & communication Transports, entrepôts, communications	Other activities Autres activités
Réunion Réunion	1990	27 417	4.0	9.1[2]	...	4.7	5.9	20.5	4.0	51.7
	1991	30 371	3.7	9.1[2]	...	4.1	7.1	19.9	4.6	51.5
	1992	32 832	3.5	9.0[2]	...	4.1	6.8	20.0	4.5	50.1
Romania[1] Roumanie[1]	2003	1 754 018 400	13.0	1.6	23.4	3.2	6.5	11.7	11.0	29.5
	2004	2 195 764 500	14.3	28.2[2,3]	...	...	6.7	12.3	10.8	27.6
	2005	2 529 844 300	10.1	27.7[2,3]	...	...	7.3	54.9[37]	...	...
Russian Federation[1] Fédération de Russie[1]	2003	11 866 341	6.7	6.6	16.7	3.6	6.0	22.6	10.6	27.2
	2004	15 102 894	6.0	9.5	17.5	3.5	5.5	21.6	11.1	25.3
	2005	19 027 469	5.4	10.5	17.4	3.4	5.7	21.6	10.2	25.7
Rwanda Rwanda	2000	680 822	40.7	0.3	10.0	0.6	8.9	10.4	7.3	22.0
	2001	731 919	41.4	0.5	9.9	0.5	8.5	10.2	7.5	21.5
	2002	794 978	43.1	0.5	9.5	0.4	8.1	10.0	7.5	20.9
Saint Kitts and Nevis Saint-Kitts-et-Nevis	2001	845	2.9	0.3	9.8	1.9	16.6	16.6	13.0	38.9
	2002	857	3.1	0.4	8.7	2.6	16.0	16.4	13.0	39.8
	2003	877	2.8	0.3	8.7	2.7	14.8	18.3	12.7	39.7
Saint Lucia Sainte-Lucie	2001	1 630	6.3	0.4	4.5	5.4	7.7	22.9	19.1	28.9
	2002	1 651	5.9	0.4	4.4	5.1	7.1	22.5	19.7	29.9
	2003	1 701	4.9	0.4	4.6	5.0	6.7	23.6	19.9	30.0
St. Vincent-Grenadines St. Vincent-Grenadines	2002	869	9.3	0.2	6.3	5.8	10.7	19.2	18.6	30.0
	2003	909	8.3	0.2	5.5	6.2	11.1	19.4	19.1[11]	30.4
	2004	978	7.8	0.2	5.2	6.0	12.0	20.1	18.9	29.7
Samoa Samoa	2001	846	14.7	...	15.8	4.6	6.4	20.8	11.6	26.0
	2002	898	14.5	...	15.1	4.7	6.0	21.9	11.7	26.1
	2003	953	12.9	...	16.3	4.5	5.9	21.6	12.1	26.7
Sao Tome and Principe Sao Tomé-et-Principe	1986	2 259	29.2	...	2.3	0.3	3.4	19.4	5.3	40.1
	1987	2 797	31.5	...	1.3	1.4	3.8	17.1	5.6	39.2
	1988	3 800	32.1	...	1.7	1.0	4.2	18.8	4.1	38.1
Saudi Arabia+ Arabie saoudite+	2002	714 395	5.1	33.2	10.2	1.3	6.3	7.2	4.5	32.3
	2003	811 805	4.5	36.2	10.6	1.2	5.4	6.6	4.1	30.9
	2004	946 703	3.9	41.9	10.0	1.1	5.4	6.1	3.8	27.7
Senegal Sénégal	1998	2 746 000[11]	17.9	1.0	12.3	2.3	4.0	27.5	11.1	23.1
	1999	2 925 000[11]	18.6	1.1	12.1	2.2	4.4	27.0	11.3	22.6
	2000	3 114 000[11]	19.4	1.1	12.0	2.2	4.3	25.7	11.9	22.4
Serbia Serbie	2001	619 623	22.4	1.5	25.1	1.5	3.6	9.5	8.3	28.0
	2002	771 492	17.0	1.9	21.5	4.1	3.9	10.4	9.2	31.9
	2003	908 196	14.4	1.9	18.6	4.6	4.6	11.0	8.9	36.1
Serbia and Montenegro[38] Serbie-et-Monténégro[38]	2000	358 753	21.1	3.6	22.1	2.5	3.9	11.9	7.1	27.8
	2001	702 402	20.9	4.0	21.8	2.6	3.7	11.1	7.8	28.0
	2002	857 966	16.3	4.3	19.5	4.2	3.8	9.5	9.1	33.3
Seychelles Seychelles	1999	3 179[11]	3.2	...	15.8[8,30]	2.4	10.2	8.3	32.8	21.7
	2000	3 274[11]	3.0	...	20.6[8,30]	1.5	9.1	9.9	33.8	22.6
	2001	3 278[11]	3.1	...	20.0[8,30]	1.9	9.4	10.7	33.0	23.3
Sierra Leone+ Sierra Leone+	1988	42 364	39.3	6.3	7.7	0.3	2.6	20.9	10.5	12.3
	1989	81 921	37.3	7.0	7.1	0.2	1.9	25.0	10.8	10.6
	1990	148 652	35.3	9.5	8.7	0.1	1.3	20.3	8.9	15.9
Singapore Singapour	2003	151 457[10]	0.1[39]	...	25.5	1.8	4.6	17.1	12.7	43.5
	2004	170 627[10]	0.1[39]	...	28.0	1.7	4.0	17.4	12.6	40.4
	2005	183 325[10]	0.1[39]	...	28.4	1.6	3.8	17.7	12.6	39.9

Country or area Pays ou zone	Year Année	Value added, Gross (mil. nat.cur) Valeur ajoutée, brute (mil. mon. nat.)	% of Value added – % de la valeur ajoutée							
			Agriculture, hunting, forestry and fishing Agriculture, chasse, sylviculture et pêche	Mining and quarrying Activités extractives	Manufacturing Activités de fabrication	Electricity, gas and water supply Electricité, gaz et eau	Construction Construction	Wholesale, retail trade, restaurants and hotels Commerce, restaurants, hôtels	Transport, storage & communication Transports, entrepôts, communications	Other activities Autres activités
Slovakia[1] Slovaquie[1]	2002	1 002 053	4.4	0.7	21.8	3.3	5.3	15.4	11.4	37.7
	2003	1 103 653	4.0	0.6	20.8	5.1	5.3	15.0	10.8	38.4
	2004	1 226 220	3.9	0.5	21.0	5.0	5.6	15.1	10.7	38.2
Slovenia[1] Slovénie[1]	2001	4 237 439	2.9	0.6	26.9	3.0	5.9	13.8	7.0	40.1
	2002	4 728 867	3.1	0.5	26.3	3.1	5.6	13.6	6.9	40.9
	2003	5 108 742	2.6	0.5	26.7	2.9	5.7	13.9	7.1	40.6
Solomon Islands Iles Salomon	1984	199	53.5	-0.2	3.6	0.9	3.8	10.6	5.2	22.6
	1985	213	50.4	-0.7	3.8	1.0	4.2	10.4	5.1	25.8
	1986	224	48.3	-1.2	4.5	1.2	5.1	8.4	5.8	27.9
Somalia Somalie	1985	84 050[6]	66.1	0.3	4.9	0.1	2.2	10.1	6.7	9.5
	1986	112 584[6]	62.5	0.4	5.5	0.2	2.7	10.3	7.3	11.1
	1987	163 175[6]	64.9	0.3	5.1	-0.5	2.9	10.7	6.8	9.8
South Africa[1] Afrique du Sud[1]	2002	1 063 880	4.2	8.7	19.7	2.4	2.3	13.5	9.4	39.9
	2003	1 141 132	3.6	7.4	19.4	2.5	2.4	13.8	9.7	41.3
	2004	1 242 864	3.1	7.0	19.1	2.4	2.3	14.1	9.8	42.2
Spain[1] Espagne[1]	2002	661 540	3.9	0.3	17.4	1.9	9.4	18.4	7.5	41.2
	2003	704 676	3.7	0.3	16.9	1.9	10.0	18.3	7.4	41.5
	2004	753 313	3.5	0.3	16.3	1.8	10.8	18.6	7.4	41.4
Sri Lanka[1] Sri Lanka[1]	2002	1 441 072[6]	16.6	1.4	19.8	2.2	6.6	19.9	12.3	21.2
	2003	1 615 228[6]	15.1	1.6	20.0	2.6	6.6	19.3	12.4	22.4
	2004	1 839 809[6]	14.6	1.6	19.9	2.6	6.6	19.6	12.8	22.3
Sudan+ Soudan+	1994	4 440 648	40.5	6.5[2]	...	0.7	3.8	46.6[40]	...	1.9
	#1996	9 015 824	37.1	9.6[2]	...	0.9	5.0	44.4[40]	...	3.0
	1997	15 865 432	40.5	9.1[2]	...	0.8	6.9	39.8[40]	...	2.8
Suriname Suriname	2002	2 381 346	7.3	7.5	14.4	6.0	2.6	10.2	7.7	30.1
	2003	3 079 194	7.0	7.3	13.7	5.8	2.6	13.0	7.8	27.6
	2004	3 773 875	5.8	9.5	14.5	5.1	3.2	12.2	8.1	25.9
Swaziland+[1] Swaziland+[1]	2001	7 987[11]	13.2	0.4	33.9	1.4	5.7	8.6	4.8	22.2
	2002	8 854	...	0.5	33.7	1.4	5.7	8.9	4.9	22.0
	2003	9 564	...	0.5	34.2	1.4	5.6	9.0	4.8	22.8
Sweden[1] Suède[1]	2001	2 003 290	1.9	0.2	20.6	2.7	4.4	12.1	8.2	49.9
	2002	2 074 721	1.8	0.2	20.2	2.6	4.4	12.0	8.2	50.5
	2003	2 151 248	1.8	0.3	19.7	2.8	4.3	12.1	8.2	50.9
Switzerland[1] Suisse[1]	2001	425 688	1.4	0.2	19.2	2.6	5.4	15.6	5.9	49.8
	2002	435 734	1.3	0.2	18.8	2.4	5.4	15.4	6.2	50.3
	2003	438 507	1.2	0.2	18.5	2.3	5.5	15.3	6.3	50.8
Syrian Arab Republic Rép. arabe syrienne	2002	1 016 519	25.0	19.1	6.0	1.1	3.1	17.6	13.3	15.0
	2003	1 067 265	24.8	19.1	4.0	1.2	3.7	16.7	14.1	16.4
	2004	1 203 509	23.0	20.6	3.1	0.7	2.8	18.2	14.1	17.5
Tajikistan[1] Tadjikistan[1]	2000	1 662	29.4	...	26.0[3,8]	...	3.7	20.1	5.3	15.6
	2001	2 302	29.1	...	24.9[3,8]	...	4.5	21.1	4.3	16.0
	2002	3 045	29.1	...	24.4[3,8]	...	4.2	22.3	4.1	15.9
Thailand Thaïlande	2002	4 863 087	10.6	2.4	31.9	3.3	3.2	20.3	9.1	19.2
	2003	5 247 586	11.6	2.5	33.5	3.3	3.2	18.7	8.5	18.8
	2004	5 809 683	11.3	2.6	33.8	3.3	3.2	18.7	8.4	18.7
TFYR of Macedonia[1] L'ex-R.y. Macédoine[1]	2002	202 752	12.1	0.5	18.7	4.5	5.9	15.5	10.2	32.6
	2003	218 766	13.1	0.5	18.1	5.4	6.2	15.1	9.6	32.1
	2004	232 877	12.9	0.4	17.0	4.8	6.3	17.3	8.9	32.4

Country or area Pays ou zone	Year Année	Value added, Gross (mil. nat.cur) Valeur ajoutée, brute (mil. mon. nat.)	% of Value added – % de la valeur ajoutée							
			Agriculture, hunting, forestry and fishing Agriculture, chasse, sylviculture et pêche	Mining and quarrying Activités extractives	Manufacturing Activités de fabrication	Electricity, gas and water supply Electricité, gaz et eau	Construction Construction	Wholesale, retail trade, restaurants and hotels Commerce, restaurants, hôtels	Transport, storage & communication Transports, entrepôts, communications	Other activities Autres activités
Timor-Leste Timor-Leste	1996	368	30.4	1.0[41]	3.0	0.7[14]	19.9	9.7	9.9	25.4
	1997	342	33.7	1.0[41]	3.1	0.7[14]	18.1	9.1	9.7	24.6
	1998	127	41.1	0.6[41]	2.8	0.8[14]	10.6	7.2	12.0	24.9
Togo Togo	1980	223 479	28.5	9.8	7.4	1.8	6.2	20.6	6.9	5.7
	1981	242 311	28.6	9.3	6.7	1.7	4.5	21.8	7.1	6.2
Tonga+ Tonga+	2002	265	27.5	0.4	4.5	1.9	9.1	15.1	7.5	34.0
	2003	293	29.0	0.3	4.4	1.7	8.5	15.7	7.5	32.8
	2004	315	27.3	0.3	4.4	1.9	7.9	17.5	6.7	34.0
Trinidad and Tobago[1] Trinité-et-Tobago[1]	2002	58 477[7]	1.1	15.6	15.2	1.4	6.9	18.2	9.4	28.1
	2003	73 225[7]	0.8	22.5	17.0	1.2	7.0	15.7	7.5	25.0
	2004	82 715[7]	0.6	24.3	16.5	1.1	7.4	15.2	6.7	24.2
Tunisia[1] Tunisie[1]	2003	28 254[6]	13.8	3.2	20.4	1.6[14]	6.1	17.2	10.0	19.3
	2004	30 889[6]	14.4	3.8	20.1	1.7[14]	6.0	17.0	10.4	18.7
	2005	33 180[6]	13.1	...	19.7	1.5[14]	5.9	17.3	11.2	3.3
Turkey Turquie	1995	7 748 669 629	15.7	1.3	22.6	2.5	5.5	20.5	12.7	19.3
	1996	15 022 756 536	16.6	1.2	20.8	2.7	5.7	20.1	12.9	19.9
	1997	29 235 581 842[11]	15.0	1.2	21.3	2.5	5.9	20.7	13.8	20.9
Turkmenistan[1] Turkménistan[1]	1999	20 056 000	24.8	...	31.4[3,8]	...	12.2	4.1	6.7	20.8
	2000	25 648 000	22.9	...	35.0[3,8]	...	6.8	3.5	6.6	25.1
	2001	33 863 000	24.7	...	36.6[3,8]	...	5.7	4.2	5.4	23.5
Turks and Caicos Islands[1] Iles Turques et Caïques[1]	2003	376	1.4	0.7	3.0	4.2	8.2	36.9	10.3	35.3
	2004	448	1.4	0.8	2.5	4.5	10.3	34.3	10.5	35.7
	2005	521	1.3	1.0	2.4	4.1	12.3	33.9	9.9	35.1
Tuvalu Tuvalu	2000	25	17.3	0.8	3.2	4.5	4.6	12.6	10.0	47.0
	2001	27	17.4	0.7	3.3	4.9	4.4	12.3	10.5	46.4
	2002	29	15.9	0.8	3.5	5.0	4.8	12.9	11.9	45.3
Uganda Ouganda	2001	9 312 930	33.6	0.8	9.9	1.4	9.2	14.2	5.7	25.2
	2002	9 892 243	31.1	0.8	9.7	1.4	9.9	14.1	6.3	26.7
	2003	11 597 319	33.6	0.7	8.7	1.3	10.0	14.2	6.9	24.6
Ukraine[1] Ukraine[1]	2003	244 497	11.9	4.4	20.3	5.0	4.2	13.6	14.4	26.1
	2004	318 321	11.7	3.9	20.1	3.9	4.5	13.6	13.4	28.7
	2005	375 275	10.8	4.2	19.7	3.7	4.5	12.9	13.6	30.6
United Arab Emirates Emirats arabes unis	1988	90 137[6]	1.8	33.2	9.1	2.3	9.8	11.3	5.6	26.8
	1989	104 730[6]	1.8	37.3	8.3	2.1	9.1	10.2	5.4	25.7
	1990	127 737[6]	1.6	45.4	7.2	1.8	7.8	8.8	4.6	22.7
United Kingdom[1] Royaume-Uni[1]	2002	972 003[26]	0.9	2.3	15.2	1.7	5.6	15.0	7.7	51.5
	2003	1 027 654[26]	1.0	2.2	14.2	1.7	5.9	15.0	7.6	52.4
	2004	1 082 793[26]	0.9	2.8	14.3	1.5	6.2	15.0	7.2	52.1
United Rep. of Tanzania[1] Rép.-Unie de Tanzanie[1]	2001	7 792 480[6]	43.7	1.5	7.2[30]	1.6	5.2	11.9	4.6	24.0
	2002	8 868 717[6]	43.8	1.7	7.2[30]	1.6	5.3	11.7	4.6	24.1
	2003	9 993 889[6]	44.2	1.9	7.1[30]	1.6	5.5	11.5	4.5	23.6
United States[1] Etats-Unis[1]	2002	9 693 200[6,11,42]	...	1.1	15.2	2.1	5.0	16.7	6.7	59.8
	2003	10 163 700[6,11,42]	...	1.4	14.6	2.2	4.9	16.5	6.6	60.1
	2004	10 869 800[6,11,42]	...	1.6	14.2	2.2	5.1	16.5	6.6	60.0
Uruguay Uruguay	2003	330 582[7]	12.4	0.2	17.7	4.7	3.3	11.4	9.2	41.0
	2004	390 482[7]	11.6	0.2	20.7	4.5	3.4	12.6	9.3	37.7
	2005	415 171[7]	9.2	0.2	21.9	4.9	3.8	13.0	9.5	37.6

Country or area / Pays ou zone	Year / Année	Value added, Gross (mil. nat.cur) / Valeur ajoutée, brute (mil. mon. nat.)	Agriculture, hunting, forestry and fishing / Agriculture, chasse, sylviculture et pêche	Mining and quarrying / Activités extractives	Manufacturing / Activités de fabrication	Electricity, gas and water supply / Electricité, gaz et eau	Construction / Construction	Wholesale, retail trade, restaurants and hotels / Commerce, restaurants, hôtels	Transport, storage & communication / Transports, entrepôts, communications	Other activities / Autres activités
			% of Value added – % de la valeur ajoutée							
Uzbekistan[1] Ouzbékistan[1]	2000	2 788 137	34.9	...	15.8[3,8]	...	7.0	10.9	9.3	22.2
	2002	6 565 515	34.2	...	16.7[3,8]	...	5.6	11.3	...	22.9
	2003	8 369 111	33.3	...	17.6[3,8]	...	5.2	10.9	...	23.3
Vanuatu Vanuatu	1999	34 016[7]	15.5	...	4.4	1.9	2.9	38.3	11.0	26.1
	2000	35 284[7]	14.9	...	4.2	1.7	3.0	38.0	11.6	26.7
	2001	35 712[7]	14.3	...	3.8	1.9	3.0	37.8	12.6	26.5
Venezuela (Bol. Rep. of)[1] Venezuela (Rép. bolivarienne du)[1]	2001	84 997 600	4.4	14.7	17.8	2.4	10.0	10.1	6.8	33.7
	2002	103 987 700	4.0	19.5	17.0	2.4	9.5	9.4	6.5	31.7
	2003	130 498 000	4.4	24.1	17.6	2.1	6.4	10.1	6.4	28.9
Viet Nam[1] Viet Nam[1]	2001	481 295 000	23.2	9.2	19.8	3.3	5.8	17.3	4.0	17.3
	2002	535 762 000	23.0	8.6	20.6	3.4	5.9	17.3	3.9	17.2
	2003	605 586 000	21.8	9.4	20.8	3.8	5.9	16.9	3.7	17.6
Yemen[1] Yémen[1]	2002	1 906 732	13.9	29.6	5.6	0.9	4.8	12.9	12.3	19.9
	2003	2 186 536	13.6	30.0	5.7	0.9	5.3	13.3	11.7	19.5
	2004	2 558 740	12.9	31.1	5.6	0.9	6.2	13.4	11.2	18.6
Yugoslavia, SFR Yougoslavie, Rfs	1988	14 645	11.2	2.7	40.3	2.2	6.2	7.6	11.1	18.6
	1989	224 684	11.3	2.4	41.4	1.7	6.4	6.6	10.5	19.7
	1990	966 420	12.9	2.5	31.2	1.7	7.9	8.5	12.3	23.1
Zambia Zambie	2001	12 384 595	20.8	4.2	10.4	3.6	5.9	21.4	6.9	26.7
	2002	15 487 658	21.0	3.7	10.9	3.2	6.9	22.0	6.8	25.5
	2003	19 538 931	21.7	2.9	11.3	3.1	7.8	22.4	5.5	25.3
Zimbabwe Zimbabwe	2002	1 652 756	18.1	0.7	7.4	1.5[14]	0.8	8.2	10.4	53.0
	2003	5 129 106	15.7	0.6	11.6	1.4[14]	0.8	9.0	8.1	52.9
	2004	12 879 575[11]	13.1	7.0	...	2.9[14]	0.9	15.0	8.0	32.2

Source

United Nations Statistics Division, New York, national accounts database.

Notes

+ The national accounts data generally relate to the fiscal year used in each country, unless indicated otherwise. Countries whose reference periods coincide with the calendar year ending 31 December are not listed below.
  - Year beginning 21 March: Afghanistan, Iran (Islamic Republic).
  - Year beginning 1 April: Bermuda, India, Myanmar, New Zealand, Nigeria.
  - Year beginning 1 July: Australia, Bangladesh, Cameroon, Gambia, Pakistan, Puerto Rico, Saudi Arabia, Sierra Leone, Sudan.
  - Year ending 30 June: Botswana, Egypt, Swaziland, Tonga.
  - Year ending 7 July: Ethiopia.
  - Year ending 15 July: Nepal.
  - Year ending 30 September: Haiti.

1 Data compiled in accordance with the concepts and definitions of the System of National Accounts 1993 (1993 SNA).
2 Including "Manufacturing".
3 Including "Electricity, gas and water".
4 Data refers to other services.

Source

Organisation des Nations Unies, Division de statistique, New York, la base de données sur les comptes nationaux.

Notes

+ Sauf indication contraire, les données sur les comptes nationaux concernent généralement l'exercice budgétaire utilisé dans chaque pays. Les pays où territoires dont la période de référence coïncide avec l'année civile se terminant le 31 décembre ne sont pas répertoriés ci-dessous.
  - Exercice commençant le 21 mars: Afghanistan, Iran (République islamique d').
  - Exercice commençant le 1er avril: Bermudes, Inde, Myanmar, Nigéria, Nouvelle-Zélande.
  - Exercice commençant le 1er juillet: Arabie saoudite, Australie, Bangladesh, Cameroun, Gambie, Pakistan, Porto Rico, Sierra Leone, Soudan.
  - Exercice se terminant le 30 juin: Botswana, Égypte, Swaziland, Tonga.
  - Exercice se terminant le 7 juillet: Éthiopie.
  - Exercice se terminant le 15 juillet: Népal.
  - Exercice se terminant le 30 septembre: Haïti.

1 Données compilées selon les concepts et définitions du Système de comptabilité nationale de 1993 (SCN 1993).
2 Y compris "les industries manufacturières".
3 Y compris "l'électricité, le gaz et l'eau".
4 Les données concernent les autres services.

5 Restaurants and hotels are included in "Other activities".
6 Value added at factor cost.
7 At producers' prices. Includes Financial intermediation services indirectly measured (FISIM).
8 Including mining and quarrying.
9 Oil refining included in "Electricity, gas and water".
10 Excluding Financial intermediation services indirectly measured (FISIM).
11 Including statistical discrepancy.
12 Excluding hunting.
13 Includes diamond cutting.
14 Excluding gas.
15 For statistical purposes, the data for China do not include those for the Hong Kong Special Administrative Region (Hong Kong SAR) and Macao Special Administrative Region (Macao SAR).
16 Agriculture and fishing only.
17 Repair of motor vehicles, motorcycles and personal and households goods are included in "Other Activities".
18 Including petroleum refining.
19 Including non-petroleum mining activities.
20 At producers' prices. Includes Financial intermediation services indirectly measured (FISIM).
21 Includes manufacturing of energy-generating products.
22 Including repair services.
23 Including engineering and sewage services.
24 Refers to gross domestic product.
25 Including oil production.
26 Including Financial intermediation services indirectly measured (FISIM).
27 Financial intermediation services indirectly measured (FISIM) is distributed to uses.
28 Excluding repair of motor vehicles, motorcycles and personal and household goods.
29 Includes all non-monetary output.
30 Including handicrafts.
31 Including construction.
32 Basic petroleum manufacturing is included in mining and quarrying.
33 Electricity only. Gas and water are included in "Other activities".
34 Including gas and water supply.
35 Includes Financial intermediation, except insurance and pension funding.
36 Contract construction only.
37 Data refers to all Service industries, including Trade, Transport and telecommunications, Public Administration, and Other services.
38 As from 1999: excluding Kosovo and Metohia.
39 Including quarrying.
40 Includes Transport, storage and communications; Financial intermediation, real estate, renting and business activities; and Education, health and social work; other community, social and personal services, and Private households with employed persons.
41 Refers to non-oil and gas mining only, excludes Quarrying.
42 Taxes less subsidies are included in the data for each of the industries.
43 Includes crude petroleum production.
44 Value added by industries is at factor cost and net of consumption of fixed capital.

5 Restaurants et hôtels sont inclus dans "autres activités".
6 Valeur ajoutée au coût des facteurs.
7 Aux prix à la production. Y compris les Services d'intermédiation financière mesurés indirectement (SIFMI).
8 Y compris les industries extractives.
9 Le raffinage du pétrole y compris dans "l'électricité, le gaz et l'eau".
10 Non compris les Services d'intermédiation financière mesurés indirectement (SIFMI).
11 Y compris une divergence statistique.
12 Non compris le chasse.
13 Y compris la taille de diamant.
14 Non compris le gaz.
15 Pour la présentation des statistiques, les données pour la Chine ne comprennent pas la Région Administrative Spéciale de Hong Kong (Hong Kong RAS) et la Région Administrative Spéciale de Macao (Macao RAS).
16 Agriculture et la pêche seulement.
17 Les réparations de véhicules à moteur, de motocycles et d'articles personnels et ménagers sont incluses dans "autres activités".
18 Y compris le raffinage du pétrole.
19 Y compris les activités de l'extraction du non-pétrole.
20 Aux prix à la production. Y compris les Services d'intermédiation financière mesurés indirectement (SIFMI).
21 Y compris la fabrication de produits producteurs d'énergie.
22 Y compris les services de réparation.
23 Y compris génie civil et services d'égouts.
24 Concerné le produit intérieur brut.
25 Y compris la production de pétrole.
26 Y compris les Services d'intermédiation financière mesurés indirectement (SIFMI).
27 Services d'intermédiation financière mesurés indirectement (SIFMI) est distribué à ses utilisations.
28 Non compris les réparations de véhicules à moteur, de motocycles et d'articles personnels et ménagers.
29 Y compris l'ensemble de la production non monétaire.
30 Y compris l'artisanat.
31 Y compris la construction.
32 Les industries extractives y compris fabrication de produits pétroliers de base.
33 Seulement électricité. Le gaz et l'eau sont inclus dans les "autres activités".
34 Y compris le gaz et l'eau.
35 Y compris l'intermédiation financière sauf les assurances et la caisse des pensions.
36 Construction sous contrat seulement.
37 Les données concernent l'ensemble des branches de services, dont le Commerce, les Transports et télécommunications, l'Administration publique, et les Autres services.
38 A partir de 1999: non compris Kosovo et Metohia.
39 Y compris les carrières.
40 Comprend Transports, entreposage et communications ; Intermédiation financière, activités immobilières, de location et commerciales ; Éducation, santé et action sociale ; Autres services communautaires, sociaux et individuels, et Ménages privés comptant des salariés.
41 Activités extractives hormis pétrole et gaz, non compris les carrières.
42 Les impôts, moins les subventions, sont inclus dans les données sur chaque industrie.
43 Y compris la production de pétrole brut.
44 La valeur ajoutée par les industries est calculée au coût des facteurs, après déduction de la consommation de capital fixe.

Relationships among the principal national accounting aggregates

As a percentage of GDP

Relations entre les principaux agrégats de la comptabilité nationale

En pourcentage du PIB

Country or area Pays ou zone	Year Année	GDP at current prices (mil.nat.cur.) PIB aux prix courants (millions monnaie nat.)	As a percentage of GDP — En pourcentage du PIB					
			Plus: Compensation of employees and property income from/to the rest of the world, net Plus : Rémuneration des salariés et revenus de la propriété du/au reste du monde, net	Equals: Gross national income Égale : Revenu national brut	Plus: Net current transfers from/ to the rest of the world Plus : Transfers courants du/au reste du monde, net	Equals: Gross national disposable income Égale : Revenu national disponible brut	Less: Final consumption expenditure Moins : Dépense de consommation finale	Equals: Gross savings Égale : Épargne brut
Algeria	2001	4 260 811	-2.9[1]	97.1	2.5	99.6	58.0	41.6
Algérie	2002	4 537 691	-3.8[1]	96.2	3.0	99.2	59.2	39.9
	2003	5 264 187	-3.6[1]	96.4	3.5	99.9	55.1	44.8
Angola	1988	239 640	-11.1	88.9	-1.9	87.0	78.4	8.6
Angola	1989	278 866	-10.5	89.5	-1.6	87.9	77.1	10.8
	1990	308 062	-12.4	87.6	-4.2	83.4	73.2	10.2
Anguilla	2001	297	-3.2	96.8	1.1	98.0	98.0	0.0
Anguilla	2002	305	-4.7	95.3	0.1	95.5	98.2	-2.7
	2003	318	-4.7	95.3	-0.1	95.3	100.3	-5.0
Argentina[2]	2003	375 909	-6.0	94.0	0.4	94.4	74.6	19.7[3]
Argentine[2]	2004	447 643	-5.9	94.1	0.5	94.6	73.9	20.6[3]
	2005	532 268	-3.5	96.5	0.4	96.9	73.2	23.7[3]
Armenia[2]	2001	1 175 877	-0.1	99.9	8.3	108.2	104.8	3.4
Arménie[2]	2002	1 362 472	-0.5	99.5	7.5	107.1	99.1	8.0
	2003	1 624 643	-1.1	98.9	8.0	106.9	93.5	13.4
Aruba[2]	2000	3 327	-4.7	95.3	-1.7	93.5	72.0	21.5
Aruba[2]	2001	3 399	-6.6	93.4	2.7	96.1	74.1	22.1
	2002	3 421	...	...	...	...	78.9	...
Australia+[2]	2002	782 798	-2.9	97.1	0.0	97.1	77.1	20.0
Australie+[2]	2003	838 251	-2.8	97.2	0.0	97.1	76.8	20.4
	2004	891 524	-3.5	96.7	0.0	96.7	76.9	19.8
Austria[2]	2003	226 968	-1.1	98.9	-1.0	97.9	74.7	23.2
Autriche[2]	2004	237 039	-1.2	98.8	-1.0	97.8	73.5	24.2
	2005	246 113	-1.2	98.8	-1.1	97.6	73.3	24.4
Azerbaijan[2]	2003	35 732 500	-6.1	93.9	11.7	105.7	72.4	33.3
Azerbaïdjan[2]	2004	42 651 000	-8.2	91.9	10.4	102.4	68.7	33.7
	2005	59 377 500	...	...	...	...	49.8	...
Bahamas[2]	2003	5 503	-2.0[1]	98.0	0.9	98.9	82.8[5]	16.1
Bahamas[2]	2004	*5 661	-1.6[1]	98.4	4.4	102.8	83.4[5]	19.5
	2005	5 869[4]	-0.8[1]	99.2	1.5	100.6	82.7[5]	17.9
Bahrain	2002	3 176	-5.2[1]	93.8	-10.1	83.5	63.7	...
Bahreïn	2003	3 647	-5.1[1]	93.7	-11.2	83.8	61.4	...
	2004	4 141	-5.2[1]	94.8	-10.2	84.6	59.0	...
Bangladesh+[2]	2002	3 005 801	5.5	105.5	0.7	106.2	81.4	24.9
Bangladesh+[2]	2003	3 329 731	5.3	105.3	0.6	105.9	80.5	25.4
	2004	3 684 757	5.7	105.7	0.6	106.3	79.8	26.5
Barbados	2002	4 952	-4.3	95.7	3.5	99.1	88.7	10.5
Barbade	2003	5 390	-4.0	96.0	3.4	99.5	88.8	10.6
	2004	5 632	-3.8	96.2	3.5	99.7	92.0	7.7
Belarus[2]	2002	26 138 300[6]	0.1	100.1	1.2	101.3	80.5	20.7
Bélarus[2]	2003	36 564 800[6]	-0.2	99.8	1.1	100.9	78.5	22.4
	2004	49 991 800[6]	-0.1	99.9	1.2	101.2	74.3	26.8
Belgium[2]	2002	261 124	2.4	102.4	-1.0	101.4	76.4	25.0
Belgique[2]	2003	269 546	1.9	101.9	-1.2	100.7	77.2	23.4
	2004	283 752	1.4	101.4	-1.3	100.1	76.6	23.5
Belize[2]	1998	1 258	...	94.9	...	100.2	84.8	...
Belize[2]	1999	1 377	...	95.1	...	...	82.3	...
	2000	1 514	...	...	...	...	83.7	...

Country or area Pays ou zone	Year Année	GDP at current prices (mil.nat.cur.) PIB aux prix courants (millions monnaie nat.)	As a percentage of GDP — En pourcentage du PIB					
			Plus: Compensation of employees and property income from/to the rest of the world, net Plus : Rémuneration des salariés et revenus de la propriété du/au reste du monde, net	Equals: Gross national income Égale : Revenu national brut	Plus: Net current transfers from/ to the rest of the world Plus : Transfers courants du/au reste du monde, net	Equals: Gross national disposable income Égale : Revenu national disponible brut	Less: Final consumption expenditure Moins : Dépense de consommation finale	Equals: Gross savings Égale : Épargne brut
Benin	1989	479 200	...	99.2	11.1	110.2	94.4	12.6
Bénin	1990	502 300	...	...	...	...	93.6	...
	1991	535 500	...	...	...	...	94.6	...
Bermuda+[2]	2000	3 378	4.9	104.9	...	...	72.4	...
Bermudes+[2]	2001	3 539	7.0	107.0	...	...	...	...
	2002	3 715	2.8	102.8	...	...	...	...
Bhutan	1998	16 337	-14.2	94.1	4.2	99.0	77.3	36.6
Bhoutan	1999	19 123	-16.1	83.9	4.5	88.4	75.0	...
	2000	21 698	-15.9	84.1	5.8	89.8	72.6	...
Bolivia	2000	51 884	-2.7	97.3	2.4	99.7	91.2	8.5
Bolivie	2001	53 010	-2.6	97.4	4.1	101.5	91.6	9.9
	2002	55 933	-2.6	97.4	3.7	101.1	90.2	10.8
Botswana+[2]	2000	24 943	-6.0	94.0	0.0	94.0	61.6	32.4
Botswana+[2]	2001	28 671	-5.0	95.0	-0.2	94.9	59.9	34.9
	2002	32 000	-4.2	95.8	-0.1	95.7	62.1	33.6
Brazil[2]	2002	1 346 028	-3.9	96.1	0.5	96.7	78.2	18.5
Brésil[2]	2003	1 556 182	-3.5	96.5	0.6	97.0	76.6	20.4
	2004	1 766 621	-3.3	96.7	0.5	97.2	74.0	23.2
British Virgin Islands[2]	2003	782[4,7]	-6.9	93.1	5.1	98.2	47.8	50.4
Iles Vierges britanniques[2]	2004	873[4,7]	-6.4	93.7	5.0	98.7	47.1	51.8
	2005	972[4,7]	-5.9	94.1	5.2	99.4	46.3	53.1
Bulgaria[2]	2002	32 335	-1.7	98.3	3.4	101.7	86.8	14.9
Bulgarie[2]	2003	34 547	-3.2	96.8	3.5	100.3	87.7	12.5
	2004	38 008	-1.8	98.2	4.6	102.8	86.8	16.0
Burkina Faso	1991	811 676	0.3	100.3	1.5	...	90.9	...
Burkina Faso	1992	812 590	0.2	100.2	1.9	...	90.6	...
	1993	832 349	-0.1	99.9	1.9	...	91.6	...
Burundi	1990	196 656	...	98.0	...	...	102.5	...
Burundi	1991	211 898	...	99.0	...	...	100.9	...
	1992	226 384	...	98.7	...	...	98.5	...
Cambodia	1994	6 201 001	...	92.1	...	...	104.7	...
Cambodge	1995	7 542 711	...	95.1	...	...	95.6	...
	1996	8 324 792	...	93.6	...	...	95.5	...
Cameroon+[2]	1996	4 793 080	...	95.7	0.3	95.9	79.8	16.1
Cameroun+[2]	1997	5 370 580	...	...	...	...	82.0	...
	1998	5 744 000	...	...	...	...	82.9	...
Canada[2]	2002	1 136 664	-2.4	97.6	0.1	97.7	76.0	21.7
Canada[2]	2003	1 197 494	-2.3	97.7	0.0	97.8	75.7	22.1
	2004	1 270 760	-2.1	97.9	0.0	97.9	74.9	23.1
Cape Verde	1993	29 078	...	...	...	...	106.8	...
Cap-Vert	1994	33 497	...	...	...	...	104.5	...
	1995	37 705	...	...	...	...	109.1	...
Cayman Islands	1989	474	-10.8	89.2	...	92.0	79.3	12.7
Iles Caïmanes	1990	590	-10.3	89.7	...	92.2	76.8	15.4
	1991	616	-9.4	90.6	...	93.0	77.6	15.4
Chile[2]	2003	50 954 390	-6.2	93.8	0.9	94.6	73.9	20.7
Chili[2]	2004	57 905 728	-8.4	91.6	1.2	92.8	69.8	23.0
	2005	64 549 137	-9.2	90.8	1.5	92.4	68.7	23.6
China[2,8]	2002	12 033 269	-1.0	86.4	...	...	...	...
Chine[2,8]	2003	13 582 276	-0.5	86.0	...	...	...	...
	2004	15 987 834	-0.2	85.4	...	...	...	...

Country or area Pays ou zone	Year Année	GDP at current prices (mil.nat.cur.) PIB aux prix courants (millions monnaie nat.)	As a percentage of GDP — En pourcentage du PIB Plus: Compensation of employees and property income from/to the rest of the world, net Plus : Rémuneration des salariés et revenus de la propriété du/au reste du monde, net	Equals: Gross national income Égale : Revenu national brut	Plus: Net current transfers from/ to the rest of the world Plus : Transfers courants du/au reste du monde, net	Equals: Gross national disposable income Égale : Revenu national disponible brut	Less: Final consumption expenditure Moins : Dépense de consommation finale	Equals: Gross savings Égale : Épargne brut
China, Hong Kong SAR[2] Chine, Hong Kong RAS[2]	2002	1 276 757	0.4	100.4	-1.2	99.3	68.9	30.4
	2003	1 233 143	2.3	102.3	-1.2	101.2	68.8	32.3
	2004	1 290 808	2.1	102.1	-1.2	100.9	69.0	31.9
Colombia[2] Colombie[2]	2000	174 896 000	-2.7	97.3	2.1	99.3	84.2	15.1
	2001	188 559 000	-3.2	96.8	2.4	99.2	86.2	13.0
	2002	203 451 400	-3.5	96.5	3.7	100.2	86.1	14.1
Comoros Comores	1989	63 397	...	100.7	...	...	...	...
	1990	66 370	...	99.8	12.3	112.1	105.5	6.7
	1991	69 248	...	99.6	...	...	...	...
Congo Congo	1986	640 407	-6.5	93.5	-1.3	92.2	84.4	7.8
	1987	690 523	-11.1	88.9	-1.6	87.3	77.2	10.2
	1988	658 964	-13.7	86.3	-1.8	84.5	81.2	3.3
Costa Rica[2] Costa Rica[2]	2003	6 982 288	-4.1	95.9	1.2	97.1	81.2	15.9
	2004	8 126 742	-4.2	95.8	1.1	96.9	80.3	16.7
	2005	9 468 594	-4.1	95.9	1.4	97.3	79.8	17.4
Côte d'Ivoire Côte d'Ivoire	1998	7 457 508	-5.7	94.3	-3.1	91.2	78.7	12.4
	1999	7 734 000	-6.9	92.1	-2.7	89.1	77.8	11.3
	2000	7 605 000	-5.7	94.3	-3.5	90.8	82.7	8.1
Cuba[2] Cuba[2]	2001	29 557	4.6	...	...	...	...	...
	2002	30 680	1.8	...	...	...	...	...
	2003	32 337	-0.9	...	...	...	...	...
Cyprus[2] Chypre[2]	2002	6 370	...	95.9	...	...	...	...
	2003	6 815	...	97.7	...	...	...	...
	2004	7 255	...	95.9	...	...	...	...
Czech Republic[2] République tchèque[2]	2003	2 555 783	-4.5	95.5	0.6	96.1	75.1	21.0
	2004	2 767 717	-4.9	95.1	0.1	95.2	72.7	22.6
	2005	2 931 071	...	...	...	...	71.5	...
Dem. Rep. of the Congo Rép. dém. du Congo	1983	59 134	...	95.7	...	...	76.9	...
	1984	99 723	...	88.5	...	...	49.5	...
	1985	147 263	...	97.2	...	...	59.4	...
Denmark[2] Danemark[2]	2003	1 409 162	-0.7	99.3	-2.2	97.2	74.3	22.9
	2004	1 467 310	-0.3	99.7	-2.3	97.4	74.9	22.5
	2005	1 551 510	0.2	100.2	-2.0	98.1	74.4	23.8
Djibouti Djibouti	1996	88 233	1.0[1]	100.0	9.4	109.4	97.3	12.1
	1997	87 289	1.2[1]	99.9	8.3	108.2	94.2	14.0
	1998	88 461	1.2[1]	99.9	8.3	108.3	96.4	11.8
Dominica Dominique	1989	423	...	101.0	...	...	92.0	...
	1990	452	...	101.1	...	...	84.4	...
	1991	479	...	101.0	...	...	91.4	...
Dominican Republic[2] Rép. dominicaine[2]	1994	179 130	-2.2	97.8	6.7	104.5	81.4	23.1
	1995	209 646	-2.3	97.7	6.2	103.9	82.9	21.0
	1996	243 973	-5.4	94.6	6.1	100.7	82.2	18.5
Ecuador[2] Equateur[2]	2002	24 899	-5.1	92.6	6.6	99.2	80.0	21.4
	2003	28 691	-5.0	89.8	6.2	96.0	80.8	22.6
	2004	32 964	...	...	...	...	78.7	...
Egypt+[2] Egypte+[2]	2001	375 203	-0.2	102.3	3.5	105.8	86.9	18.8
	2002	405 256	-0.9	101.3	4.1	105.5	86.4	19.1
	2003	451 154	-0.7	101.6	3.9	105.5	82.9	22.6
El Salvador El Salvador	2002	14 312	-2.3	97.7	14.1	111.9	98.6	13.3
	2003	14 941	-2.7	97.3	14.2	111.4	99.7	11.8
	2004	15 824	-3.1	96.9	16.2	113.1	101.4	11.7

Country or area Pays ou zone	Year Année	GDP at current prices (mil.nat.cur.) PIB aux prix courants (millions monnaie nat.)	As a percentage of GDP — En pourcentage du PIB Plus: Compensation of employees and property income from/to the rest of the world, net Plus : Rémuneration des salariés et revenus de la propriété du/au reste du monde, net	Equals: Gross national income Égale : Revenu national brut	Plus: Net current transfers from/to the rest of the world Plus : Transfers courants du/au reste du monde, net	Equals: Gross national disposable income Égale : Revenu national disponible brut	Less: Final consumption expenditure Moins : Dépense de consommation finale	Equals: Gross savings Égale : Épargne brut
Estonia[2] Estonie[2]	2002	116 915	-4.6	95.4	1.6	97.0	77.6	19.4
	2003	127 334	-5.8	94.2	1.4	95.6	77.4	18.2
	2004	141 493	-6.5	93.5	1.5	95.0	75.0	20.0
Ethiopia+ Ethiopie+	1997	41 465	-0.5[9]	99.5	7.0	106.5	...	7.0
	1998	44 896	-0.4[9]	99.6	8.3	107.9	...	8.3
	1999	48 949	-0.4[9]	99.6	7.6	107.2	...	7.6
Fiji Fidji	1999	3 662	-4.1[5]	95.9[5]	2.8	98.6[5]	70.6	28.1[5]
	2000	3 505	-1.3[5]	98.7[5]	2.2	100.9[5]	77.1	23.8[5]
	2001	3 836	-4.2[5]	95.8[5]	5.3	101.1[5]	74.1	27.0[5]
Finland[2] Finlande[2]	2003	143 807	-1.4	98.6	-1.0	97.6	74.5	23.1
	2004	149 725	-0.4	99.6	-1.0	98.7	74.4	24.3
	2005	155 320	-0.1	99.9	-1.1	98.8	74.9	23.9
France[2] France[2]	2003	1 594 814	0.6	100.6	-1.4	99.2	80.2	19.1
	2004	1 659 020	0.6	100.6	-1.5	99.1	80.3	18.8
	2005	1 710 025	0.5	100.5	-1.6	98.9	80.8	18.1
French Guiana Guyane française	1990	6 526	-1.9[1]	98.1	36.3	134.4	99.4	35.0
	1991	7 404	-5.8[1]	94.2	35.9	130.1	94.5	35.6
	1992	7 976	-6.9[1]	93.1	36.4	129.6	93.1	36.4
Gabon Gabon	1987	1 020 600	-6.2[1]	93.8	-4.2	89.7	72.4	17.3
	1988	1 013 600	-7.4[1]	92.6	-7.6	85.0	69.9	15.1
	1989	1 168 066	-8.6[1]	91.4	-6.1	85.3	66.8	18.5
Gambia+ Gambie+	1991	2 920	...	98.3	...	115.7	96.7	19.0
	1992	3 078	...	98.7	...	114.1	94.4	19.7
	1993	3 243	...	98.5	...	114.4	93.3	21.1
Georgia[2] Géorgie[2]	2002	7 457	1.0	101.0	6.4	107.4	87.6	19.8
	2003	8 564	0.8	100.8	4.6	105.4	81.4	24.0
	2004	9 970	1.8	101.8	7.9	109.7	87.0	22.7
Germany[2] Allemagne[2]	2003	2 163 400	-0.7	99.3	-1.2	98.0	78.7	19.3
	2004	2 215 650	0.0	100.0	-1.2	98.8	77.9	20.9
	2005	2 247 400	0.2	100.2	-1.2	98.9	77.8	21.1
Ghana Ghana	1994	5 205 200	...	98.0	...	...	...	...
	1995	7 752 600	...	98.0	...	...	...	...
	1996	11 339 200	...	98.1	...	...	...	...
Greece[2] Grèce[2]	2003	155 543	-1.1	98.9	0.6	99.6	84.3	15.2
	2004	168 417	-0.8	99.2	0.1	99.4	83.7	15.7
	2005	181 088	-1.8	98.2	-0.1	98.1	83.5	14.6
Grenada Grenade	1984	275	...	98.9	...	...	99.1	...
	1985	311	...	98.9	...	...	99.0	...
	1986	350	...	99.2	...	...	97.7	...
Guadeloupe Guadeloupe	1990	15 201	-2.5[1]	97.5	37.3	134.8	123.6	11.2
	1991	16 415	-3.4[1]	96.6	35.4	132.0	118.3	13.7
	1992	17 972	-3.0[1]	97.0	36.6	133.6	113.4	20.2
Guatemala Guatemala	2003	197 599	-1.4[1]	98.6	9.9	108.5	93.8	14.6
	2004	216 749	-1.3[1]	98.7	11.0	109.7	94.5	15.2
	2005	243 699	-1.2[1]	98.8	10.9	109.8	95.1	14.7
Guinea-Bissau Guinée-Bissau	1986	46 973	-1.7[1]	98.3	2.9	101.3	102.8	-1.5
	1987	92 375	-0.5[1]	99.5	4.1	103.6	100.8	2.8
	1988	171 949	...	...	...	...	...	...
Guyana Guyana	1999	123 665	...	90.1	...	...	68.0	...
	2000	130 013	...	93.8	...	...	77.4	...
	2001	133 403	...	92.8	...	...	78.3	...

Relationships among the principal national accounting aggregates—As a percentage of GDP (*continued*)
Relations entre les principaux agrégats de la comptabilité nationale—En pourcentage du PIB (*suite*)

Country or area Pays ou zone	Year Année	GDP at current prices (mil.nat.cur.) PIB aux prix courants (millions monnaie nat.)	As a percentage of GDP — En pourcentage du PIB Plus: Compensation of employees and property income from/to the rest of the world, net Plus : Rémunération des salariés et revenus de la propriété du/au reste du monde, net	Equals: Gross national income Égale : Revenu national brut	Plus: Net current transfers from/ to the rest of the world Plus : Transfers courants du/au reste du monde, net	Equals: Gross national disposable income Égale : Revenu national disponible brut	Less: Final consumption expenditure Moins : Dépense de consommation finale	Equals: Gross savings Égale : Épargne brut
Haiti+ Haïti+	1995	35 207	...	98.7	22.8	121.5	108.1	13.4
	1996	43 234	...	99.6	17.1	116.7	104.9	11.8
	1997	51 789	...	99.6	14.1	113.7	103.7	10.0
Honduras Honduras	1998	70 438	...	95.9	9.3	105.2	77.1	28.1
	1999	77 095	...	96.9	13.6	110.5	80.1	30.4
	2000	87 523	...	97.0	12.5	109.6	82.0	27.6
Hungary[2] Hongrie[2]	2003	18 650 746	-4.9	95.1	...	...	79.9	...
	2004	20 429 456	-5.6	94.4	...	...	78.2	...
	2005	21 802 261	...	...	...	...	78.5	...
Iceland[2] Islande[2]	2003	827 863	-1.7	98.3	-0.1	98.2	83.4	14.8
	2004	916 765	-3.5	96.5	-0.1	96.4	82.3	14.1
	2005	995 991	-2.8	97.2	-0.2	97.0	84.9	12.1
India+ Inde+	2001	22 719 840	-0.7	99.3	3.2	102.5	77.9	23.4
	2002	24 633 240	-0.5	99.5	3.2	102.7	76.1	26.1
	2003	27 600 250	-0.5	99.5	3.8	103.3	75.1	28.1
Indonesia Indonésie	2001	1 467 660 000	...	95.8	...	...	74.0	...
	2002	1 610 570 000	...	96.6	...	...	77.8	...
	2003	1 786 690 000	...	95.5	...	...	78.5	...
Iran (Islamic Rep. of)+[2] Iran (Rép. islamique d')+[2]	2001	680 506 217	0.1	100.1	0.0	100.1	61.7	38.3
	2002	935 828 854	-0.2	99.8	0.0	99.8	57.6	42.2
	2003	1 126 947 103	0.1	100.1	0.0	100.1	57.3	42.8
Iraq Iraq	1989	21 026	...	96.7	...	95.9	81.9	14.0
	1990	23 297	...	96.7	...	96.5	76.8	19.6
	1991	19 940	...	96.7	...	97.4	83.5	13.9
Ireland[2] Irlande[2]	2002	130 515	-17.5	82.5	-0.5	82.0	60.1	21.9
	2003	139 097	-15.4	84.6	-0.6	84.0	60.6	23.4
	2004	148 556	-15.4	84.6	-0.8	83.8	60.1	23.7
Israel[2] Israël[2]	2002	516 058	-3.7	96.3	6.2	102.5	85.8	16.7
	2003	523 618	-3.5	96.5	5.5	102.1	85.0	17.1
	2004	548 544	-3.4	96.6	5.1	101.7	83.9	17.8
Italy[2] Italie[2]	2003	1 335 354	-0.8	99.2	-0.6	98.5	78.8	19.8
	2004	1 388 870	-0.6	99.4	-0.6	98.8	78.5	20.3
	2005	1 417 241	-0.3	99.7	-0.7	99.0	79.1	19.8
Jamaica Jamaïque	2002	410 133	-7.0	93.0	11.3	104.2	88.2	16.0
	2003	472 906	-6.0	94.0	13.0	107.0	88.0	19.0
	2004	540 086	-5.1	94.9	13.5	108.4	85.9	22.5
Japan[2] Japon[2]	2002	489 618 400	1.7	101.7	-0.1	101.6	75.7	25.3
	2003	490 543 500	1.7	101.7	-0.1	101.6	75.4	25.6
	2004	496 050 500	1.9	101.9	-0.1	101.8	75.4	25.5
Jordan Jordanie	2001	6 364	2.1	102.1	22.9	125.0	104.0	21.0
	2002	6 779	1.2	101.2	23.7	124.8	100.9	23.9
	2003	7 204	1.2	101.2	30.6	131.8	101.5	30.3
Kazakhstan[2] Kazakhstan[2]	2002	3 776 277	-4.6	95.4	0.5	95.9	66.2	29.7
	2003	4 611 975	-5.7	94.3	-0.5	93.8	65.7	28.1
	2004	5 870 134	-6.4	93.6	-1.1	92.4	65.1	27.3
Kenya[2] Kenya[2]	2002	1 038 764	-1.1	98.9	4.8	103.7	95.1	8.6
	2003	1 141 780	-0.6	99.4	5.4	104.8	93.8	11.0
	2004	1 273 716	-0.6	99.4	5.2	104.6	92.0	12.6
Korea, Republic of[2] Corée, République de[2]	2003	724 675 000	0.1	100.1	-0.5	99.6	67.0	32.6
	2004	779 380 500	0.2	100.2	-0.4	99.9	65.0	34.8
	2005	806 621 900	-0.1	99.9	-0.3	99.6	66.7	32.8

			As a percentage of GDP — En pourcentage du PIB					
Country or area Pays ou zone	Year Année	GDP at current prices (mil.nat.cur.) PIB aux prix courants (millions monnaie nat.)	Plus: Compensation of employees and property income from/to the rest of the world, net Plus : Rémuneration des salariés et revenus de la propriété du/au reste du monde, net	Equals: Gross national income Égale : Revenu national brut	Plus: Net current transfers from/ to the rest of the world Plus : Transfers courants du/au reste du monde, net	Equals: Gross national disposable income Égale : Revenu national disponible brut	Less: Final consumption expenditure Moins : Dépense de consommation finale	Equals: Gross savings Égale : Épargne brut
Kuwait Koweït	1999	9 170	17.0[9]	117.0	-6.7	110.3	78.9	31.4
	2000	11 510	17.9[9]	118.4	-5.2	113.2	63.3	49.8
	2001	10 700	14.0[9]	114.0	-6.0	108.1	69.9	38.2
Kyrgyzstan[2] Kirghizistan[2]	2001	73 883	-4.2	95.8	3.4	99.1	82.3	16.8
	2002	75 367	-3.7	96.3	7.3	103.5	86.2	17.4
	2003	83 872	-3.1	96.9	5.5	102.4	94.7	7.6
Latvia[2] Lettonie[2]	2003	6 393	-0.2	99.8	4.7	104.5	83.8	20.7
	2004	7 421	-2.2	97.9	4.9	102.7	82.5	20.2
	2005	8 937	-1.9	98.6	3.2	101.8	80.1	21.7
Lebanon[2] Liban[2]	2000	25 143 000	3.3	103.3	10.2	113.5	103.2	10.3
	2001	25 726 000	1.2	101.2	10.2	111.4	102.9	8.5
	2002	27 832 000	-1.1	98.9	11.2	110.2	101.9	8.3
Lesotho[2] Lesotho[2]	1999	5 565	25.0[1]	126.8	17.9	144.8	122.4	22.4
	2000	5 980	25.5[1]	125.5	17.5	142.9	120.4	22.5
	2001	6 478	23.4[1]	123.4	20.3	143.7	119.8	23.8
Liberia Libéria	1987	1 090	...	83.2	...	...	...	...
	1988	1 158	...	84.2	...	...	...	...
	1989	1 194	...	84.9	...	...	...	...
Libyan Arab Jamah. Jamah. arabe libyenne	1983	8 805	-6.9[9]	91.0	-0.2	90.9	72.0	18.9
	1984	8 013	-4.6[9]	92.7	-0.3	92.4	72.2	20.2
	1985	8 277	-2.9[9]	96.7	-0.2	96.5	69.2	27.3
Liechtenstein[2] Liechtenstein[2]	2001	4 205	...	89.9	...	...	...	...
	2002	4 191	...	88.3	...	...	...	...
	*2003	4 135	...	85.6	...	...	...	...
Lithuania[2] Lituanie[2]	2002	51 948	-1.1	98.9	1.6	100.6	83.8	16.8
	2003	56 772	-2.5	97.5	1.6	99.1	82.9	16.1
	2004	62 440	-2.6	97.4	1.8	99.2	83.0	16.2
Luxembourg[2] Luxembourg[2]	2002	24 028	-13.6	86.4	...	...	58.2	...
	2003	25 684	-18.9	81.1	...	...	57.5	...
	2004	27 056	-14.0	86.0	...	...	57.8	...
Madagascar — Madagascar	1980	689 800	...	99.9	...	...	...	...
Malawi Malawi	1994	11 209	-3.6	96.4	9.2	105.6	...	...
	1995	20 246	-3.1	96.9	9.6	105.0	...	...
	1996	23 993	-1.8	98.2	3.4	101.6	...	...
Malaysia Malaisie	2002	362 012	-6.9[1]	93.1	-2.9	90.2	57.7	32.4
	2003	395 017	-5.7[1]	94.3	-2.4	91.9	57.5	34.4
	2004	449 609	-5.5[1]	94.5	-3.3	91.3	56.1	35.2
Maldives[2] Maldives[2]	2002	8 200	-5.7[1]	94.3	-5.7	88.6	53.7	35.0
	2003	8 841	-5.1[1]	94.9	-6.4	88.5	50.8	37.7
	2004	9 640	-4.5[1]	95.5	-6.7	88.8	52.4	36.4
Mali Mali	1990	683 300	-1.2[1]	98.8	11.5	110.3	94.3	16.1
	1991	691 400	-1.3[1]	98.7	13.0	111.9	100.4	11.5
	1992	737 400	-1.2[1]	98.8	11.4	110.2	96.4	13.8
Malta[2] Malte[2]	2002	1 748	0.2[1]	100.2	...	...	...	...
	2003	1 793	-0.6	99.4	...	...	...	...
	2004	1 828	-1.3	98.5	...	...	...	...
Martinique Martinique	1990	19 320	-4.2[1]	95.8	33.7	...	113.3	...
	1991	20 787	-4.4[1]	95.6	30.7	...	112.8	...
	1992	22 093	-3.9[1]	96.1	33.4	...	113.1	...
Mauritania Mauritanie	1987	67 216	-5.1	94.9	8.1	103.0	96.2	6.7
	1988	72 635	-5.6	94.4	7.9	102.3	93.7	8.5
	1989	83 520	-3.6	96.4	9.0	105.4	...	...

Country or area / Pays ou zone	Year / Année	GDP at current prices (mil.nat.cur.) / PIB aux prix courants (millions monnaie nat.)	As a percentage of GDP — En pourcentage du PIB: Plus: Compensation of employees and property income from/to the rest of the world, net / Plus : Rémuneration des salariés et revenus de la propriété du/au reste du monde, net	Equals: Gross national income / Égale : Revenu national brut	Plus: Net current transfers from/ to the rest of the world / Plus : Transfers courants du/au reste du monde, net	Equals: Gross national disposable income / Égale : Revenu national disponible brut	Less: Final consumption expenditure / Moins : Dépense de consommation finale	Equals: Gross savings / Égale : Épargne brut
Mauritius[2] Maurice[2]	2003	156 523	-0.5	99.5	0.9	100.4	75.7	24.7
	2004	174 501	-0.2	99.8	0.8	100.6	77.9	22.7
	2005	187 245	0.1	100.1	1.1	101.2	82.8	18.3
Mexico[2] Mexique[2]	2002	6 263 137	-1.8	98.2	1.6	99.8	81.2	18.5
	2003	6 891 992	-1.8	98.2	2.2	100.3	81.1	19.2
	2004	7 709 096	-1.5	98.5	2.5	101.0	80.0	21.0
Mongolia Mongolie	2002	1 240 787	5.4	105.4	...	...	...	...
	2003	1 461 169	4.9	104.9	...	...	...	...
	2004	1 910 881	8.4	108.4	...	...	...	...
Morocco Maroc	2002	397 782	-1.8[1]	...	9.2	107.4	80.6	26.8
	2003	419 485	-1.6[1]	...	9.4	107.8	80.1	27.7
	2004	443 673	-1.1[1]	...	9.7	108.6	81.4	27.3
Mozambique[2] Mozambique[2]	2002	96 883 500	-14.4	85.6	15.3	100.9	73.4	27.5
	2003	113 902 500	-3.4	96.6	4.6	101.2	80.4	20.8
	2004	133 510 400	-4.9	95.1	5.2	100.3	78.2	22.0
Myanmar+ Myanmar+	1996	791 980	0.0[1]	100.0	...	100.0	88.5	11.4
	1997	1 109 554	0.0[1]	100.0	...	100.0	88.1	11.9
	1998	1 559 996	0.0[1]	100.0	...	100.0	89.4	10.6
Namibia[2] Namibie[2]	2002	32 908	1.1	101.1	8.8	109.9	82.0	27.9
	2003	33 840	5.1	105.1	10.2	115.4	82.0	33.3
	2004	36 901	1.3	101.3	11.7	113.0	76.6	36.3
Nepal+ Népal+	2003	456 675	3.5[1]	103.5	0.4[10]	104.0	88.0	16.0
	2004	495 589	2.6[1]	102.6	0.4[10]	103.0	87.6	15.4
	2005	529 003	2.0[1]	102.0	0.5[10]	102.4	87.7	14.7
Netherlands[2] Pays-Bas[2]	2003	476 349	0.2	100.2	-1.3	98.9	74.0	24.9
	2004	488 642	0.2	100.2	-1.4	98.8	73.2	25.7
	2005	501 921	0.9	100.9	-1.5	99.3	72.6	26.8
Netherlands Antilles[2] Antilles néerlandaises[2]	2001	5 162	0.7	100.7	0.3	101.0	75.3	25.6
	2002	5 198	0.0	100.0	3.8	103.9	76.3	27.6
	2003	5 368	-0.2	99.8	3.9	103.6	77.2	26.5
New Zealand+[2] Nouvelle-Zélande+[2]	2002	130 856	-5.4	94.6	0.1	94.7	76.1	18.6
	2003	139 225	-5.3	94.7	0.3	95.0	76.2	18.8
	2004	148 558	-6.7	93.3	0.3	93.6	76.7	16.9
Nicaragua[2] Nicaragua[2]	2002	57 099	-5.0[1]	95.0	11.5	106.5	94.2	12.3
	2003	62 458	-4.6[1]	95.4	12.6	107.9	94.9	13.1
	2004	70 271	-4.4[1]	95.6	13.6	109.2	95.4	13.8
Niger Niger	2003	1 466 267	-1.0	99.0	3.7	102.7	93.7	9.0
	2004	1 474 910	-0.5	99.5	3.0	102.5	96.5	6.0
	2005	1 711 461	-0.4	99.6	3.2	102.8	92.0	10.8
Nigeria+ Nigéria+	1992	549 809	-11.7	88.3	2.3	90.6	77.2	13.4
	1993	701 473	-10.5	89.5	2.5	92.0	80.6	11.5
	1994	914 334	-7.2	92.8	1.2	94.0	85.5	8.5
Norway[2] Norvège[2]	2003	1 576 745	0.9	100.9	-1.3	99.5	68.1	31.4
	2004	1 716 933	0.4	100.4	-1.0	99.4	65.9	33.5
	2005	1 903 841	0.6	100.6	-1.1	99.5	62.1	37.3
Occupied Palestinian Terr.[2] Terr. palestinien occupé[2]	2001	3 816	8.6	108.6	24.6	133.2	127.4	5.8
	2002	3 484	6.4	106.4	30.6	137.0	131.4	5.5
	2003	3 921	7.2	107.2	36.2	143.5	129.3	14.1
Oman[2] Oman[2]	2001	7 670	-3.6	96.4	-7.5	88.9	66.2	22.7
	2002	7 807	-3.9	96.1	-7.7	88.4	67.2	21.3
	2003	8 343	-4.2	*95.8	-7.5	88.3	66.0	22.3

Country or area Pays ou zone	Year Année	GDP at current prices (mil.nat.cur.) PIB aux prix courants (millions monnaie nat.)	As a percentage of GDP — En pourcentage du PIB Plus: Compensation of employees and property income from/to the rest of the world, net Plus : Rémuneration des salariés et revenus de la propriété du/au reste du monde, net	Equals: Gross national income Égale : Revenu national brut	Plus: Net current transfers from/to the rest of the world Plus : Transfers courants du/au reste du monde, net	Equals: Gross national disposable income Égale : Revenu national disponible brut	Less: Final consumption expenditure Moins : Dépense de consommation finale	Equals: Gross savings Égale : Épargne brut
Pakistan+[2] Pakistan+[2]	2003	4 822 842	...	103.1	...	...	82.5	...
	2004	5 532 663	...	102.2	...	...	81.6	...
	2005	6 547 590	...	101.9	...	...	87.8	...
Panama[2] Panama[2]	2001	11 808	-7.7	92.3	1.4	93.6	75.6	18.1[11]
	2002	12 272	-4.6	95.4	1.4	96.8	79.1	17.7[11]
	2003	12 862	-8.1	91.9	1.4	93.2	74.9	18.3[11]
Papua New Guinea[2] Papouasie-Nvl-Guinée[2]	2000	10 750	-3.6	90.5[12]	2.3	92.8	76.3	16.5
	2001	11 758	-3.5	89.7[12]	0.4	90.1	87.4	2.7
	2002	13 375	-3.0	90.2[12]	0.7	90.8	88.3	2.5
Paraguay Paraguay	1993	11 991 719	...	100.4	...	100.4	88.0	12.4
	1994	14 960 131	...	100.5	...	100.5	95.2	5.3
	1995	17 699 000	...	100.9	...	100.9	92.5	8.4
Peru Pérou	1996	148 278	...	97.3	...	...	80.6	...
	1997	172 389	...	97.5	...	...	78.7	...
	1998	183 179	...	97.7	...	...	80.9	...
Philippines Philippines	2002	3 963 872	6.4	106.4	1.1	107.6	80.9	26.6
	2003	4 293 026	7.0	107.0	1.2	108.1	80.7	27.4
	2004	4 826 343	7.1	107.1	1.0	108.1	79.5	28.6
Poland[2] Pologne[2]	2002	781 112	-1.0	99.0	1.7	100.7	84.5	16.2
	2003	814 922	-1.7	98.3	2.0	100.3	83.6	16.7
	2004	883 656	...	...	...	...	81.8	...
Portugal[2] Portugal[2]	2003	137 523	-1.2	98.8	1.5	100.3	84.0	16.3
	2004	143 029	-1.2	98.8	1.4	100.2	85.1	15.1
	2005	147 395	-1.6	98.4	1.0	99.4	86.5	12.9
Puerto Rico+ Porto Rico+	2000	69 208	-36.8	63.2	12.5	75.7	65.5	3.6
	2001	71 306	-37.5	62.5	13.4	75.9	65.7	4.4
	2002	74 362	-36.9	63.1	13.4	76.5	66.1	3.0
Republic of Moldova[2] République de Moldova[2]	2002	22 556	10.0	110.0	9.3	119.3	103.3	16.0
	2003	27 619	11.7	111.7	15.3	127.0	110.3	16.7
	2004	32 032	13.7	113.7	14.0	127.7	104.0	23.8
Réunion Réunion	1990	28 374	-2.5[1]	97.5	44.3	141.7	108.1	33.6
	1991	31 339	0.1[1]	100.7	42.7	143.4	103.5	39.9
	1992	33 787	-1.5[1]	98.4	43.6	142.1	104.5	37.6
Romania[2] Roumanie[2]	2003	1 975 648 100	-2.3	97.7	5.0	102.7	85.7	17.1
	2004	2 463 716 500[13]	-4.2	95.8	...	...	86.7	...
	2005	*2 871 862 500	-2.9	97.1	...	...	87.7	...
Russian Federation[2] Fédération de Russie[2]	2003	13 243 240[14]	-3.0	97.0	-0.1	96.9	68.1	28.7
	2004	17 008 388[14]	-2.2	97.8	-0.1	97.7	65.3	32.3
	2005	21 664 978[14]	-2.4	97.6	-0.1	97.5	63.9	33.6
Rwanda Rwanda	1987	171 430	-1.6	98.4	2.5	100.9	93.5	7.4
	1988	177 920	-2.0	98.0	2.9	100.9	93.6	7.3
	1989	190 220	-1.2	98.8	2.4	101.3	95.4	5.9
Saint Kitts and Nevis Saint-Kitts-et-Nevis	2003	978	-12.1	87.9	5.1	93.0	79.5	13.6
	2004	1 078	-9.7	90.3	4.6	94.8	72.7	22.2
	2005	1 158	-7.8	92.2	4.8	97.0	70.2	26.8
Saint Lucia Sainte-Lucie	2001	1 506	-7.5	109.7	2.5	112.2	98.0	14.1
	2002	1 524	-7.5	112.3	2.3	114.6	99.7	14.9
	2003	1 566	-8.3	110.9	2.3	113.2	109.4	3.8
Saint Vincent-Grenadines Saint Vincent-Grenadines	2002	986	-4.0	95.2	3.3	98.5	80.3	18.3
	2003	1 025	-5.3	93.8	3.4	97.2	84.9	12.3
	2004	1 101	-5.9	92.9	3.5	96.4	86.6	9.8

Country or area Pays ou zone	Year Année	GDP at current prices (mil.nat.cur.) PIB aux prix courants (millions monnaie nat.)	As a percentage of GDP — En pourcentage du PIB Plus: Compensation of employees and property income from/to the rest of the world, net Plus : Rémuneration des salariés et revenus de la propriété du/au reste du monde, net	Equals: Gross national income Égale : Revenu national brut	Plus: Net current transfers from/ to the rest of the world Plus : Transfers courants du/au reste du monde, net	Equals: Gross national disposable income Égale : Revenu national disponible brut	Less: Final consumption expenditure Moins : Dépense de consommation finale	Equals: Gross savings Égale : Épargne brut
San Marino Saint-Marin	1997	1 279 857	...	92.2	...	76.4	...	...
	1998	1 400 841	...	90.9	...	74.2	...	...
	1999	1 551 010	...	89.3	...	73.7	...	...
Saudi Arabia+ Arabie saoudite+	2001	686 296	1.0	101.0	-11.7	89.3	65.3	24.0
	2002	707 067	0.7	100.7	-11.8	88.9	62.9	26.0
	2003	*804 648	0.3	100.3	-9.3	91.1	58.2	32.9
Senegal Sénégal	2002	3 717 639	-7.5	92.5	6.9	99.4	93.2	6.2
	2003	3 960 841	-9.3	90.7	7.0	97.7	91.2	6.5
	2004	4 198 473	-10.2	89.8	6.5	96.3	92.0	4.3
Seychelles Seychelles	1998	3 201	...	97.2	...	...	81.2	...
	1999	3 330	...	97.3	...	...	73.1	...
	2000	3 424	...	96.3	...	...	66.4	...
Sierra Leone+ Sierra Leone+	1988	43 947	-0.9[1]	100.9	0.6	101.5	94.3	7.3
	1989	82 837	-0.8[1]	100.8	0.5	101.3	91.3	10.0
	1990	150 175	-5.0[1]	95.0	0.7	95.7	88.4	7.3
Singapore Singapour	2003	161 547	-2.9	97.1	-1.2	95.9	57.8	39.7
	2004	181 704	-2.1	97.9	-1.1	96.9	54.2	43.9
	2005	194 360	-0.5	99.5	-1.0	98.5	52.6	47.1
Slovakia[2] Slovaquie[2]	2002	1 098 658	-0.1	99.9	0.0	99.8	77.8	22.1
	2003	1 201 196	-0.1	99.9	1.1	101.0	76.4	24.6
	2004	1 325 486	-1.0	99.0	0.3	99.3	76.1	23.3
Slovenia[2] Slovénie[2]	1992	1 017 965	-0.7[1]	...	...	...	...	...
	1993	1 435 095	-0.4	...	...	...	...	...
Solomon Islands Iles Salomon	1984	222	-3.2[1]	94.2	...	100.8	78.2	22.6
	1985	237	-2.3[1]	95.0	...	101.0	91.6	9.4
	1986	253	-2.0[1]	92.6	...	115.7	94.8	20.9
Somalia Somalie	1985	87 290	...	97.8	10.1	107.9	101.1	6.8
	1986	118 781	...	96.3	14.2	110.5	98.8	11.7
	1987	169 608	...	96.8	21.3	118.0	99.9	18.2
South Africa[2] Afrique du Sud[2]	2002	1 168 778	-2.5	97.5	-0.5	97.0	80.2	16.7
	2003	1 257 026	-2.8	97.2	-0.5	96.7	81.8	15.6
	2004	1 386 658	-2.0	98.0	-0.7	97.3	82.5	14.1
Spain[2] Espagne[2]	2003	780 550	-1.4	98.6	-0.4	98.1	74.8	23.4
	2004	837 316	-1.6	98.4	-0.5	97.9	75.5	22.4
	2005	904 323	-1.6	98.4	-0.6	97.8	75.5	22.3
Sri Lanka[2] Sri Lanka[2]	2002	1 612 987	-1.5	98.5	6.5	105.0	84.1	20.5
	2003	1 795 259	-0.9	99.1	6.5	105.6	84.2	21.1
	2004	2 058 396	-1.0	99.0	6.6	105.6	85.1	20.1
Sudan+ Soudan+	1991	421 819	...	85.5	...	104.0	86.0	18.0
	1992	948 448	...	99.7	...	102.2	88.2	14.0
	1993	1 881 289	...	99.8	...	100.6	88.3	12.3
Suriname Suriname	2002	2 240 127	-4.5	95.5	-0.9	94.5	...	...
	2003	2 918 132	-4.4	95.6	-0.5	95.1	...	...
	2004	3 513 565	-4.9	95.1	1.0	96.1	...	...
Swaziland+[2] Swaziland+[2]	2001	10 846	...	104.2	2.7	106.9	86.7	20.2
	2002	12 560	...	100.5	6.1	106.5	88.6	17.9
	2003	14 401	...	103.5	6.2	109.6	91.0	18.6
Sweden[2] Suède[2]	2003	2 459 413	0.9	100.9	-0.9	100.0	77.0	23.0
	2004	2 573 176	-0.2	99.8	-1.4	98.4	75.6	22.8
	2005	2 672 998	-0.3	99.7	-1.5	98.2	75.2	23.0
Switzerland[2] Suisse[2]	2002	430 527	3.5	103.5	-2.4	101.2	71.9	29.0
	2003	434 562	7.9	107.9	-2.3	105.6	72.5	32.9
	2004	445 931	8.3	108.3	...	...	72.3	...

Country or area Pays ou zone	Year Année	GDP at current prices (mil.nat.cur.) PIB aux prix courants (millions monnaie nat.)	Plus: Compensation of employees and property income from/to the rest of the world, net Plus : Rémunération des salariés et revenus de la propriété du/au reste du monde, net	Equals: Gross national income Égale : Revenu national brut	Plus: Net current transfers from/ to the rest of the world Plus : Transfers courants du/au reste du monde, net	Equals: Gross national disposable income Égale : Revenu national disponible brut	Less: Final consumption expenditure Moins : Dépense de consommation finale	Equals: Gross savings Égale : Épargne brut
			As a percentage of GDP — En pourcentage du PIB					
Syrian Arab Republic Rép. arabe syrienne	2001	974 008	...	89.6	0.8	90.3	71.2	19.1
	2002	1 016 519	...	91.2	0.7	92.0	71.6	20.4
	2003	1 067 265	...	90.5	1.1	91.7	72.9	18.7
Thailand Thaïlande	2002	5 450 643	-1.6	98.4	0.5	98.9	68.3	30.5
	2003	5 928 975	-1.9	98.1	0.7	98.8	67.9	30.9
	2004	6 503 488	-1.9	98.1	1.3	99.4	67.8	31.6
TFYR of Macedonia[2] L'ex-R.y. Macédoine[2]	2001	233 841	...	98.8	...	...	94.8	...
	2002	243 970	...	99.2	...	...	99.5	...
	2003	251 486	...	99.3	...	...	97.0	...
Togo Togo	1984	304 800	...	...	...	...	80.0	...
	1985	332 500	...	...	...	...	80.2	...
	1986	363 600	...	...	...	...	83.4	...
Tonga+ Tonga+	2002	312	2.9	102.9	40.1	142.9	126.6	16.3
	2003	349	2.3	102.3	35.0	137.2	126.1	11.2
	2004	372	1.1	101.1	36.6	137.6	123.9	13.7
Trinidad and Tobago[2] Trinité-et-Tobago[2]	2002	56 290	-5.3[1]	94.7	0.6	95.3	75.2	20.1
	2003	67 302	-6.3[1]	93.7	0.5	94.2	67.4	26.9
	2004	76 892	-3.6[1]	96.4	0.4	96.8	65.4	31.4
Tunisia[2] Tunisie[2]	2002	29 924	-4.5	95.5	5.3	100.7	78.6	22.1
	2003	32 202	-4.1	95.9	5.1	101.0	78.8	22.2
	2004	35 148	-4.4	95.6	5.3	101.0	78.5	22.4
Turkey Turquie	2003	359 763	-0.9	99.1	0.0	99.1	80.2	18.9
	2004	430 511	-0.4	99.6	0.0	99.6	79.3	20.3
	2005	487 202	-0.2	99.8	...	...	80.5	...
Ukraine[2] Ukraine[2]	2002	225 810	-1.4	98.6	4.6	103.2	75.4	27.7
	2003	267 344	-1.2	98.8	4.4	103.2	75.4	27.8
	2004	345 113	-1.0	99.0	4.0	103.0	71.3	31.7
United Arab Emirates Emirats arabes unis	1988	87 106	0.3	100.3	-1.2	99.1	65.8	33.3
	1989	100 976	0.4	100.4	-0.7	99.7	61.7	38.0
	1990	124 008	-1.0	99.0	-8.9	90.1	54.9	35.1
United Kingdom[2] Royaume-Uni[2]	2003	1 105 919	2.1	102.1	-0.7	101.4	86.5	14.8
	2004	1 164 541	2.2	102.2	-0.9	101.3	86.5	14.8
	2005	1 209 334	2.2	102.2	-0.9	101.2	87.1	14.2
United Rep. of Tanzania[2] Rép.-Unie de Tanzanie[2]	2000	7 277 800	-0.9[1]	99.0	4.6	101.1	90.0	11.0
	2001	8 284 690	-0.9[1]	99.0	4.2	100.9	89.7	11.2
	2002	9 374 560	-0.9[1]	98.9	4.3	100.3	86.4	13.9
United States[2] Etats-Unis[2]	2002	10 417 600	0.3	100.5	-0.6	99.9	86.0	13.9
	2003	10 918 500	0.6	100.2	-0.7	99.5	86.5	13.1
	2004	11 679 200	0.5	99.8	-0.7	99.1	86.1	13.0
Uruguay Uruguay	2003	315 678	-4.5[1]	95.5	0.7	96.2	85.9	10.3
	2004	379 353	-4.4[1]	95.6	0.8	96.4	84.6	11.8
	2005	411 042	-3.5[1]	96.5	0.7	97.2	84.6	12.5
Vanuatu Vanuatu	1996	28 227	...	91.1	...	...	...	...
	1997	29 477	...	91.7	...	...	...	...
	1998	29 545	...	93.5	...	...	...	...
Venezuela (Bolivarian Rep. of)[2] Venezuela (Rép. bolivarienne du)[2]	2001	88 945 600	-1.7	98.3	-0.1	98.2	69.1	29.1
	2002	107 840 200	-3.0	97.0	-0.2	96.9	66.5	30.3
	2003	134 217 000	-2.9	97.1	0.0	97.1	67.6	29.5
Yemen[2] Yémen[2]	2002	1 894 497	-7.0	93.0	11.8	104.8	81.4	23.5
	2003	2 177 463	-8.1	91.9	11.0	103.0	78.3	24.7
	2004	2 551 994	-8.4	91.6	9.9	101.5	78.4	23.1

Country or area Pays ou zone	Year Année	GDP at current prices (mil.nat.cur.) PIB aux prix courants (millions monnaie nat.)	As a percentage of GDP — En pourcentage du PIB Plus: Compensation of employees and property income from/to the rest of the world, net Plus : Rémuneration des salariés et revenus de la propriété du/au reste du monde, net	Equals: Gross national income Égale : Revenu national brut	Plus: Net current transfers from/ to the rest of the world Plus : Transfers courants du/au reste du monde, net	Equals: Gross national disposable income Égale : Revenu national disponible brut	Less: Final consumption expenditure Moins : Dépense de consommation finale	Equals: Gross savings Égale : Épargne brut
Zambia Zambie	1986	12 963	-18.1	81.9	-1.2	80.7	77.4	3.3
	1987	19 778	-11.4[1]	88.6	0.5	89.1	82.0	7.1
	1988	27 725	-14.2[1]	85.8	1.0	86.9	79.8	7.1
Zimbabwe Zimbabwe	2001	709 214	...	98.3	...	...	...	...
	2002	1 698 180	...	99.5	...	...	...	...
	2003	5 518 757	...	99.9	...	...	...	...

Source

United Nations Statistics Division, New York, national accounts database.

Notes

+ The national accounts data generally relate to the fiscal year used in each country, unless indicated otherwise. Countries whose reference periods coincide with the calendar year ending 31 December are not listed below.
  - Year beginning 21 March: Afghanistan, Iran (Islamic Republic).
  - Year beginning 1 April: Bermuda, India, Myanmar, New Zealand, Nigeria.
  - Year beginning 1 July: Australia, Bangladesh, Cameroon, Gambia, Pakistan, Puerto Rico, Saudi Arabia, Sierra Leone, Sudan.
  - Year ending 30 June: Botswana, Egypt, Swaziland, Tonga.
  - Year ending 7 July: Ethiopia.
  - Year ending 15 July: Nepal.
  - Year ending 30 September: Haiti.

1 Property income - from and to the rest of the world, net.
2 Data compiled in accordance with the concepts and definitions of the System of National Accounts 1993 (1993 SNA).
3 Including acquisitions less disposals of valuables.
4 Preliminary data.
5 Derived from available data.
6 Beginning 2000, re-denomination of Belarusian roubles at 1 to 1000.
7 At producers' prices.
8 For statistical purposes, the data for China do not include those for the Hong Kong Special Administrative Region (Hong Kong SAR), Macao Special Administrative Region (Macao SAR) and Taiwan Province of China.
9 Compensation of employees - from and to the rest of the world, net.
10 Excludes official grants.
11 Includes capital transfers.
12 Net national income.
13 Semi-final data.
14 Re-denomination of Russian rubles at 1 to 1000.

Source

Organisation des Nations Unies, Division de statistique, New York, la base de données sur les comptes nationaux.

Notes

+ Sauf indication contraire, les données sur les comptes nationaux concernent généralement l'exercice budgétaire utilisé dans chaque pays. Les pays où territoires dont la période de référence coïncide avec l'année civile se terminant le 31 décembre ne sont pas répertoriés ci-dessous.
  - Exercice commençant le 21 mars: Afghanistan, Iran (République islamique d').
  - Exercice commençant le 1er avril: Bermudes, Inde, Myanmar, Nigéria, Nouvelle-Zélande.
  - Exercice commençant le 1er juillet: Arabie saoudite, Australie, Bangladesh, Cameroun, Gambie, Pakistan, Porto Rico, Sierra Leone, Soudan.
  - Exercice se terminant le 30 juin: Botswana, Égypte, Swaziland, Tonga.
  - Exercice se terminant le 7 juillet: Éthiopie.
  - Exercice se terminant le 15 juillet: Népal.
  - Exercice se terminant le 30 septembre: Haïti.

1 Revenus de la propriété - du et au reste du monde, net.
2 Données compilées selon les concepts et définitions du Système de la comptabilité nationale de 1993 (SCN 1993).
3 Y compris les acquisitions moins cessions d'objets de valeur.
4 Données préliminaires.
5 Calculés à partir des données disponibles.
6 A partir de 2000, instauration du nouveau rouble bélarussien par division par 1000 du rouble bélarussien ancien.
7 Aux prix à la production.
8 Pour la présentation des statistiques, les données pour la Chine ne comprennent pas la Région Administrative Spéciale de Hong Kong (Hong Kong RAS), la Région Administrative Spéciale de Macao (Macao RAS) et la province de Taiwan.
9 Rémunération des salariés - du et au reste du monde, net.
10 Non compris les dons officiels.
11 Y compris les transferts de capitaux.
12 Revenu national net.
13 Données demi-finales.
14 Instauration du nouveau rouble russe par division par 1000 du rouble russe ancien.

Government final consumption expenditure by function at current prices

Percentage distribution by divisions of Classification of the Functions of Government (COFOG)

Consommation finale des administrations publiques par fonction aux prix courants

Répartition en pourcentage par divisions de la Classification des fonctions des administrations publiques (COFOG)

Country or area Pays ou zone	Year Année	Total (mil. nat. curr.) Totale (millions monnaie nat.)	Divisions of the Classification of the Functions of Government (COFOG) t Divisions de la Classification des fonctions des administrations publiques (COFOG) t									
			Div. 01 (%)	Div. 02 (%)	Div. 03 (%)	Div. 04 (%)	Div. 05 (%)	Div. 06 (%)	Div. 07 (%)	Div. 08 (%)	Div. 09 (%)	Div. 10 (%)
Anguilla Anguilla	1999	64	42.2	...	9.4	7.8	...	3.1	15.6	...	17.2	1.6
	2000	58	41.4	...	10.3	8.6	...	1.7	15.5	...	19.0	3.4
	2001	62	38.7	...	11.3	8.1	...	1.6	16.1	...	19.4	3.2
Antigua and Barbuda Antigua-et-Barbuda	1984	67[1]	22.8	2.2	11.4	22.5	...	6.7	9.7	0.5	15.8	8.4
	1985	81[1]	25.1	2.2	11.4	20.9	...	7.7	11.5	0.6	14.0	6.6
	1986	108[1]	26.1	2.3	11.6	21.2	...	6.4	10.0	0.5	14.7	7.2
Argentina Argentine	1996	43 617	10.8	4.5	3.2	6.0	0.2	2.1	8.4	...	5.9[2]	43.2
	1997	45 156	9.4	4.4	3.1	5.9	0.2	2.1	7.1	...	6.0[2]	42.0
	1998	46 463	9.5	4.2	3.0	5.8	0.2	2.0	6.6	...	6.0[2]	41.0
Armenia[3] Arménie[3]	2001	84 669[4]	85.6[5]	...	...	2.9	...	3.8	...	2.0	...	0.8
	2002	84 958[4]	82.8[5]	...	...	3.5	...	3.6	...	3.2	...	1.0
	2003	101 859[4]	85.3[5]	...	...	3.7	...	4.2	...	3.2	...	1.1
Australia+[3] Australie+[3]	2000	125 264	9.1	8.3	7.0	7.1	0.0	1.2	26.0	3.0	17.4	8.8
	2001	132 301	7.3	8.4	7.0	8.3	0.1	1.2	26.7	2.7	17.5	8.6
	2002	141 564	6.1	8.8	7.3	8.1	0.3	1.3	27.0	2.5	17.9	9.2
Austria[3] Autriche[3]	2002	40 173	15.2	4.7	7.4	9.6	1.0	0.5	27.6	2.6	27.6	3.7
	2003	41 479	14.7	4.8	7.5	9.9	1.1	0.5	27.9	2.5	27.6	3.5
	2004	42 412	14.1	4.8	7.4	9.9	1.1	0.5	28.7	2.6	27.2	3.7
Azerbaijan[3] Azerbaïdjan[3]	2002	3 759 900	26.7	19.0	2.5	2.0[6]	...	0.0	13.3[7]	2.5	29.1	4.8
	2003	4 426 700	29.1	15.4	2.0	2.3[6]	...	-0.1	17.6[7]	3.5	28.2	2.0
	2004	5 502 200	29.7	15.8	1.7	0.5[6]	...	0.0	17.7[7]	3.4	28.9	2.2
Bahamas[3] Bahamas[3]	1993	408	17.4	4.2	14.5	15.9	...	...	18.6	1.5[8]	24.0	4.2
	1994	511	20.2	3.7	13.3	17.2	...	...	18.0	1.6[8]	23.1	3.5
	1995	484	18.4	3.9	14.5	17.6	...	...	18.0	1.9[8]	22.1	3.9
Bangladesh+[3] Bangladesh+[3]	1998	88 546	15.3	24.3	13.0	1.1	...	2.5	10.3	0.4	17.1	1.0
	1999	92 450	12.9	24.0	13.4	1.1	...	3.2	12.3	0.5	16.6	1.4
	2000	105 351	12.9	22.0	12.9	1.2	...	3.0	12.0	0.6	16.5	1.4
Belarus[3] Bélarus[3]	2002	1 948 700	72.3	...	...	22.3	...	...	...	...	...	0.6
	2003	2 918 400	74.1	...	...	20.5	...	...	...	...	...	0.6
	2004	4 203 500	69.9	...	...	25.1	...	...	...	...	...	0.5
Belgium[3] Belgique[3]	2001	55 090	12.3	5.7	6.8	9.2	1.1	0.2	29.1	1.8	27.5	6.3
	2002	58 244	12.2	5.3	7.1	9.1	1.0	0.2	28.4	2.6	27.3	6.7
	2003	61 336	12.0	5.1	7.0	8.9	1.0	0.2	29.6	2.6	26.9	6.8
Belize Belize	1989	229	12.7	4.3	5.3	40.3	...	6.3	7.9	1.4	16.5	0.7
	1990	279	12.7	3.4	7.9	37.5	...	6.7	6.8	2.6	15.3	3.3
	1991	321	16.6	3.4	7.0	32.6	...	6.1	6.6	2.4	16.8	4.0
Bermuda+ Bermudes+	1985	138	36.9	2.0	...	27.1	...	6.0	3.7	2.9	21.3	3.6
	1986	141	34.4	2.1	...	28.3	...	6.4	3.9	2.9	22.2	3.8
	1987	157	34.0	2.3	...	30.1	...	6.2	3.8	2.9	21.5	3.8
Bolivia Bolivie	1991	2 310	74.7	0.0	...	4.2	...	0.1	0.0	0.1	7.7	1.9
	1992	2 833	76.2	...	...	3.0	...	0.1	0.0	0.2	8.1	1.9
	1993	3 270	75.9	...	...	2.5	...	0.2	0.0	0.2	9.0	2.4
Botswana+[3] Botswana+[3]	2000	7 525	44.0[9]	...	...	11.2	...	6.2	6.5	2.4	26.4	3.4
	2001	8 742	43.7[9]	...	...	11.0	...	5.2	6.8	2.4	27.4	3.5
	2002	10 553	45.3[9]	...	...	10.8	...	4.3	6.3	2.5	27.4	3.4
Brazil[3] Brésil[3]	2001	230 741	73.3	...	...	...	...	...	11.2	...	15.5	...
	2002	270 965	71.6	...	...	...	...	...	11.8	...	16.6	...
	2003	309 631	70.7	...	...	...	...	...	12.0	...	17.3	...

20 Government final consumption expenditure by function at current prices — Percentage distribution by divisions of Classification of the Functions of Government (COFOG) *(continued)*

Consommation finale des administrations publiques par fonction aux prix courants — Répartition en pourcentage par divisions de la Classification des fonctions des administrations publiques (COFOG) *(suite)*

		Total (mil. nat. curr.)	Divisions of the Classification of the Functions of Government (COFOG) † Divisions de la Classification des fonctions des administrations publiques (COFOG) †									
Country or area Pays ou zone	Year Année	Totale (millions monnaie nat.)	Div. 01 (%)	Div. 02 (%)	Div. 03 (%)	Div. 04 (%)	Div. 05 (%)	Div. 06 (%)	Div. 07 (%)	Div. 08 (%)	Div. 09 (%)	Div. 10 (%)
British Virgin Islands Iles Vierges britanniques	1985	17[1]	23.3	...	10.8	20.7	...	4.1	14.9	0.8	23.6	1.8
	1986	19[1]	21.8	...	11.4	22.1	...	4.4	14.5	0.7	22.7	2.4
	1987	21[1]	23.3	...	11.0	20.2	...	5.5	15.8	0.5	21.1	2.6
Brunei Darussalam Brunéi Darussalam	1982	914	22.9	41.4	5.5	5.0	...	0.7	5.0	4.8	14.2	0.2
	1983	922	24.6	35.3	6.0	5.5	...	0.7	5.7	5.7	15.2	0.2
	1984	2 512	69.3	12.8	2.7	2.5	...	0.4	2.6	2.3	6.5	0.1
Burkina Faso Burkina Faso	1982	38 198[1]	8.2	28.3	8.7	9.9	...	0.3	10.0	2.4	16.6	...
	1983	38 864[1]	8.1	28.7	9.1	10.5	...	0.4	10.5	2.5	18.3	...
	1984	38 760[1]	7.3	30.4	8.7	10.8	...	0.2	10.3	2.5	19.0	...
Cameroon+ Cameroun+	1986	476 700	30.6	12.0	...	10.6	...	6.0	5.7	2.1	19.1	0.7
	1987	391 000	28.3	14.7	...	7.3	...	5.0	6.1	2.3	21.6	0.8
	1988	378 400	35.5	12.4	...	6.2	...	4.9	6.0	2.2	21.5	0.9
Cayman Islands Iles Caïmanes	1989	74[10]	31.1	...	14.9	20.3	...	1.4	13.5	...	13.5	4.1
	1990	94[10]	26.6	...	14.9	19.1	...	1.1	16.0	...	14.9	4.3
	1991	103[10]	27.2	...	14.6	20.4	...	1.9	14.6	...	14.6	5.8
Chad Tchad	1996	42 080[11]	1.5[12]	24.6	4.6[13]	7.2[14]	5.3[15]	1.1[16]	5.7[17]	...	22.8	27.0[18]
	1997	40 078[11]	1.0[12]	26.6	9.5[13]	6.6[14]	5.2[15]	1.1[16]	6.9[17]	...	23.6	20.7[18]
	2001	60 157[11]	...	20.2	8.4[13]	5.9[14]	5.2[15]	1.0[16]	6.3[17]	...	25.0	28.0[18]
China, Macao SAR[3] Chine, Macao RAS[3]	2002	6 323	18.7	...	28.8	11.4	0.1	0.7	15.6	4.1	11.9	8.7
	2003	6 830	19.6	...	27.7	12.0	0.2	0.7	15.7	3.9	11.4	9.0
	2004	7 093	19.8	...	27.9	11.7	0.2	0.6	15.2	3.7	11.6	9.3
Colombia Colombie	1992	3 965 104	29.5	10.8	...	16.6	...	0.6	7.7	0.8	24.8	8.9
	1993	5 108 076	28.5	10.2	...	16.2	...	0.6	11.0	0.9	24.0	8.2
	1994	7 652 736	36.2	9.8	...	8.5	...	0.4	14.3	0.9	21.0	8.6
Cook Islands[19] Iles Cook[19]	2003	81	19.3	...	5.2	39.3	...	9.2	11.7	0.9	14.4	...
	2004	84	17.8	...	4.7	41.2	...	9.7	11.2	0.8	14.6	...
	2005	86	23.3	...	4.8	31.4	...	10.6	13.2	1.0	15.8	...
Costa Rica[3] Costa Rica[3]	2002	898 115	34.3	...	...	...	...	...	33.0	...	32.7	...
	2003	1 011 166	32.1	...	...	...	...	...	34.1	...	33.9	...
	2004	1 150 736	32.0	...	...	...	...	...	34.3	...	33.7	...
Côte d'Ivoire Côte d'Ivoire	1996	983 370	73.5	...	...	...	...	...	6.2	...	20.3	...
	1997	1 029 358	69.3	...	...	...	...	...	19.7	...	11.0	...
	1998	1 018 653	68.3	...	...	...	...	...	19.9	...	11.8	...
Croatia[3] Croatie[3]	1996	30 973	6.2	25.1	12.0	15.0	...	8.4	0.5	1.3	11.6	14.2
	1997	34 395	6.3	20.3	12.1	15.7	...	6.0	0.5	1.6	11.8	18.8
	1998	41 390	8.2	17.8	10.3	15.6	...	6.3	2.0	1.4	11.3	19.4
Cyprus[3] Chypre[3]	2002	1 169	21.5	18.7	8.5	10.6	...	6.2	11.0	0.9	20.9	1.7
	2003	1 357	22.4	14.2	8.8	10.5	...	6.6	12.0	0.9	21.8	2.9
	2004	1 336	23.3	10.3	9.6	7.4	0.1	8.2	12.7	1.7	24.5	2.2
Czech Republic[3] République tchèque[3]	2002	555 198	12.6	7.8	9.6	14.6	2.2	1.1	26.8	2.6	19.2	3.5
	2003	605 895	11.4	9.1	9.7	15.3	2.7	1.1	25.9	2.8	18.3	3.8
	2004	621 895	11.5	6.6	9.8	15.7	3.6	1.2	26.9	2.6	18.2	3.9
Denmark[3] Danemark[3]	2002	360 212	7.1	5.8	3.4	7.4	1.5	0.5	24.7	4.5	23.2	22.0
	2003	371 118	6.8	5.9	3.4	7.2	1.4	0.6	25.0	4.5	23.1	22.1
	2004	388 318	6.6	5.9	3.4	7.3	1.4	0.6	24.9	4.4	23.5	21.9
Dominican Republic[3] Rép. dominicaine[3]	1994	8 265	66.3	...	2.7	...	...	...	12.8	...	18.1	...
	1995	9 115	61.2	...	2.7	...	...	...	12.6	...	23.4	...
	1996	10 843	61.1	...	2.3	...	...	...	12.5	...	24.1	...
Ecuador Equateur	1990	777 131[20]	13.0	14.5	7.0	13.9	...	4.4	4.8	0.2	27.5	6.1
	1991	1 009 000[20]	13.0	15.0	7.1	14.9	...	5.0	4.6	0.3	27.8	6.2
	1992	1 498 000[20]	12.8	15.9	7.3	16.1	...	4.3	3.9	0.2	26.8	7.8

20 Government final consumption expenditure by function at current prices — Percentage distribution by divisions of Classification of the Functions of Government (COFOG) *(continued)*

Consommation finale des administrations publiques par fonction aux prix courants — Répartition en pourcentage par divisions de la Classification des fonctions des administrations publiques (COFOG) *(suite)*

Country or area Pays ou zone	Year Année	Total (mil. nat. curr.) Totale (millions monnaie nat.)	Divisions of the Classification of the Functions of Government (COFOG) † Divisions de la Classification des fonctions des administrations publiques (COFOG) †									
			Div. 01 (%)	Div. 02 (%)	Div. 03 (%)	Div. 04 (%)	Div. 05 (%)	Div. 06 (%)	Div. 07 (%)	Div. 08 (%)	Div. 09 (%)	Div. 10 (%)
Estonia[3] Estonie[3]	1995	10 350	11.2	4.5	11.2	11.4	...	5.2	17.7	5.8	27.8	3.9
	1996	12 632	11.0	4.6	11.7	11.0	...	4.2	17.3	5.6	27.8	4.1
	#2003	24 643	11.8	6.5	11.8	8.1	2.5	1.2	18.7	5.9	28.3	5.2
Fiji Fidji	2000	561	18.9	12.2	9.3	16.4	...	1.0	14.7	...	27.1	0.4
	2001	566	20.4	12.0	10.0	19.4	...	1.0	12.8	...	23.9	0.5
	2002	572	16.1	9.8	10.0	18.3	...	1.3	14.3	...	29.4	0.6
Finland[3] Finlande[3]	2002	30 282	10.4	5.9	5.3	10.4	0.8	1.1	25.3	3.2	20.9	16.7
	2003	31 673	10.6	6.2	5.4	9.8	0.9	1.0	25.5	3.1	20.7	16.8
	2004	33 247	10.4	6.2	5.1	10.0	0.8	1.0	25.9	3.0	20.5	17.2
France[3] France[3]	2002	362 175	12.4	8.9	4.4	3.5	0.8	4.0	27.4	3.6	22.0	13.0
	2003	377 441	11.3	8.9	4.5	3.5	0.9	4.1	28.9	3.7	21.9	12.3
	2004	394 448	10.4	9.2	4.5	3.9	0.9	4.3	29.2	3.8	21.5	12.3
Gambia+ Gambie+	1989	659[1]	23.3	...	...	25.2	...	3.6	6.3	...	10.3[21]	0.1
	1990	819[1]	22.0	...	...	18.6	...	3.0	6.4	...	12.9[21]	0.1
	1991	804[1]	22.2	...	...	24.1	...	3.8	5.7	...	12.6[21]	0.1
Georgia[3] Géorgie[3]	#1993	1 213	...	1.9	8.2	30.3	...	...	0.6	0.2	5.7	0.5
	1994	119 012	...	5.4	10.1	63.6	...	...	3.2	1.2	4.8	9.0
	#1995	295	...	12.9	45.8	5.8	...	...	6.1	6.4	10.2	12.5
Germany[3] Allemagne[3]	2002	412 280	12.6	6.3	8.5	2.1	0.4	1.4	32.3	2.2	18.4	15.8
	2003	415 450	12.4	6.2	8.4	2.1	0.4	1.4	32.8	2.2	18.0	16.2
	2004	412 760	12.6	6.2	8.5	2.2	0.4	1.4	31.9	2.2	18.0	16.7
Greece[3] Grèce[3]	2002	25 114	18.9	24.5	9.2	3.3	...	0.8	17.3	1.7	19.9	4.4
	2003	25 482	18.8	22.1	9.4	0.8	...	0.8	18.3	1.8	23.5	4.5
	2004	27 789	24.8	17.7	9.7	1.3	...	1.0	17.6	1.6	23.1	3.3
Guinea-Bissau Guinée-Bissau	1986	6 423	44.0	...	...	22.7	...	...	11.8	...	18.4	0.9
	1987	10 776	44.0	...	...	22.7	...	...	11.8	...	18.4	1.2
Honduras Honduras	1995	3 495	27.8	9.5	...	...	...	...	20.5	...	39.1	...
	1996	4 556	26.0	8.2	...	...	...	...	27.6	...	36.7	...
	1997	5 377	31.0	7.3	...	...	...	...	24.9	...	35.2	...
Hungary Hongrie	1993	1 013 524	15.1	12.8	7.3	8.0	...	6.0	14.4	4.0	20.4	8.7
	1994	1 145 444	17.1	6.2	8.0	9.4	...	6.3	15.7	3.6	21.4	9.3
	2004[3]	4 861 291	17.5	4.7	9.6	4.9	0.7	1.7	25.0	4.3	23.5	8.0
Iceland[3] Islande[3]	2002	202 135	7.4	...	5.3	8.3	...	3.3	30.3	5.2	20.6	8.2
	2003	213 502	7.5	...	5.4	8.5	...	3.4	30.8	5.3	21.0	8.3
	2004	228 287	7.6	...	5.5	8.6	...	3.4	31.0	5.3	21.2	8.4
India+ Inde+	2000	2 093 410	24.9[22]	29.8	...	15.9	...	1.9	6.5	0.6	16.5	3.3
	2001	2 229 700	23.9[22]	30.6	...	15.9	...	1.6	6.1	1.0	16.6	3.1
	2002	2 257 670	30.8[22]	31.0	...	9.1	...	2.3	6.2	0.7	16.1	3.3
Iran (Islamic Rep. of)+[3] Iran (Rép. islamique d')+[3]	2001	96 739 000	7.8	19.7	6.7	14.6	0.9	2.5	6.7	3.0	12.3	21.3
	2002	122 291 839	8.9	19.1	4.4	24.7	0.8	3.3	5.1	2.3	5.8	16.9
	2003	145 671 800	13.0	20.7	7.9	12.7	0.1	1.1	7.9	2.9	7.6	16.9
Ireland[3] Irlande[3]	2002	19 637	9.4	3.6	8.0	11.0	...	4.9	38.6	1.8	16.4	6.2
	2003	21 223	9.3	3.6	7.9	11.0	...	3.1	39.9	1.7	17.2	6.3
	2004	23 267	9.3	3.6	7.9	11.0	...	3.1	39.9	1.7	17.2	6.3
Israel[3] Israël[3]	2002	152 954	6.9	32.5	5.6	3.4	2.5	1.1	17.2	2.3	23.6	5.0
	2003	150 071	6.9	31.4	5.7	3.6	2.4	1.1	18.0	2.4	23.3	5.1
	2004	150 009	6.9	29.9	6.1	3.8	2.4	1.1	18.1	2.3	24.3	5.2
Italy[3] Italie[3]	2002	238 921	12.3	5.7	9.8	6.7	1.4	1.3	32.6	2.2	23.8	...
	2003	253 035	12.6	6.5	9.7	6.7	1.5	1.3	31.7	2.1	23.8	4.0
	2004	260 063	11.9	6.3	9.0	6.9	1.6	1.4	33.6	2.2	23.1	4.0
Japan[3,23] Japon[3,23]	2001	86 985 900	8.8	4.8	6.5	12.1	6.3	1.4	35.7	0.4	19.8	4.2
	2002	87 536 300	9.0	4.8	6.5	12.4	6.4	1.4	35.5	0.4	19.5	4.1
	2003	88 002 000	9.3	4.8	6.4	12.1	6.5	1.4	36.0	0.4	19.1	4.0

20 Government final consumption expenditure by function at current prices — Percentage distribution by divisions of Classification of the Functions of Government (COFOG) (*continued*)

Consommation finale des administrations publiques par fonction aux prix courants — Répartition en pourcentage par divisions de la Classification des fonctions des administrations publiques (COFOG) (*suite*)

Country or area Pays ou zone	Year Année	Total (mil. nat. curr.) Totale (millions monnaie nat.)	Divisions of the Classification of the Functions of Government (COFOG) † Divisions de la Classification des fonctions des administrations publiques (COFOG) † Div. 01 (%)	Div. 02 (%)	Div. 03 (%)	Div. 04 (%)	Div. 05 (%)	Div. 06 (%)	Div. 07 (%)	Div. 08 (%)	Div. 09 (%)	Div. 10 (%)
Jordan Jordanie	1993	939	53.6[9]	...	...	...	...	...	10.2	6.4	21.9	1.0
	1994	986	59.3[9]	...	...	...	...	...	8.2	6.0	20.4	1.0
	1995	1 111	60.0[9]	...	...	...	...	...	8.3	5.6	21.3	0.9
Kazakhstan[3] Kazakhstan[3]	2002	434 999	11.7	8.0	17.8	12.6	...	2.6	15.2	3.5	25.1	3.4
	2003	519 195	11.8	7.8	17.6	12.6	...	2.3	15.7	4.3	24.6	3.4
	2004	681 787	13.0	7.5	17.4	12.2	...	2.3	16.2	4.3	23.7	3.5
Kenya Kenya	2001	8 437	25.4	10.8	...	...	...	...	9.9	...	42.6	11.3
	2002	9 217	25.4	10.8	...	...	...	...	9.9	...	42.6	11.3
	2003	9 773	27.6	10.4	...	...	...	...	9.9	...	41.4	10.7
Korea, Republic of[3] Corée, République de[3]	2002	88 512 200	13.9	17.4	9.6	12.7	1.5	0.7	17.1	1.3	21.6	4.2
	2003	96 203 200	13.8	17.3	9.4	11.8	1.5	0.6	16.8	1.3	22.7	4.7
	2004	105 516 900	13.8	17.5	9.1	12.4	1.5	0.6	16.7	1.3	22.5	4.8
Kuwait Koweït	1999	2 463	...	51.9	...	4.5	...	3.2	10.2	4.3	22.0	3.8
	2000	2 485	...	52.4	...	4.3	...	3.2	9.6	4.3	22.5	3.7
	2001	2 528	...	53.6	...	4.5	...	2.8	9.6	4.5	21.1	3.7
Kyrgyzstan[3] Kirghizistan[3]	2001	12 912	39.9	7.3	2.2	5.5	0.4	1.9	12.6	2.3	20.9	6.2
	2002	14 033	34.4	10.5	4.1	6.2	0.5	2.1	12.6	2.0	22.1	4.8
	2003	14 116	29.4	10.8	4.4	7.0	0.4	1.7	12.5	3.0	25.1	4.9
Latvia[3] Lettonie[3]	2002	1 208	...	3.1	...	...	...	...	16.0	6.0	24.4	3.0
	2003	1 371	...	3.3	...	...	...	...	15.7	5.2	24.1	2.9
	2004	1 451	...	3.8	...	...	...	...	16.7	5.4	24.5	3.0
Lesotho[3] Lesotho[3]	1999	1 188	25.6	...	19.1	4.7	...	10.7	13.1	...	6.1	...
	2000	1 144	27.7	...	20.2	5.5	...	11.6	13.2	...	8.1	...
	2001	1 176	27.4	...	20.6	6.7	...	11.8	14.0	...	7.7	...
Libyan Arab Jamah. Jamah. arabe libyenne	1980	2 351	68.8	...	...	7.7	...	1.2	7.4	0.9	11.5	2.3
Lithuania[3] Lituanie[3]	2003	10 388	6.1	7.6	10.9	11.2	2.5	3.1	16.8	4.3	30.7	6.9
	2004	11 100	10.3	7.1	10.2	8.2	1.6	1.2	21.2	3.3	29.3	7.6
Luxembourg[3] Luxembourg[3]	2003	4 228	16.0	1.5	5.6	10.6	3.3	1.5	24.2	4.1	24.2	9.1
	2004	4 580	15.9	1.4	5.5	9.9	3.2	1.5	25.1	4.1	24.1	9.3
	2005	5 004	17.6	1.4	5.4	9.5	3.1	1.4	25.1	3.9	23.0	9.6
Malaysia Malaisie	2001	42 265	15.4	17.1	7.8	11.8	...	...	11.4	...	31.2	5.4[24]
	2002	50 015	13.9	18.5	8.7	10.5	...	...	11.7	...	31.1	5.7[24]
	2003	54 913	13.4	19.5	8.8	10.0	...	...	12.0	...	30.3	5.9[24]
Maldives Maldives	1984	103	30.4	15.6	...	13.9	...	5.8	7.9	...	14.6	6.8
	1985	121	29.9	15.0	...	11.8	...	8.0	7.9	...	14.5	5.6
	1986	139	32.3	16.3	...	5.6	...	7.8	8.3	...	16.2	5.3
Malta[3] Malte[3]	2002	376	12.2	3.7	8.2	16.5	3.2	0.5	23.4	1.6	23.9	6.6
	2003	396	11.4	4.0	8.3	16.7	3.5	0.5	23.5	1.5	24.0	6.8
	2004	412	11.4	4.1	8.3	16.5	3.4	0.5	23.5	1.5	23.8	6.8
Mauritius[3] Maurice[3]	2002	19 855	22.6	1.4	13.5	11.7	...	6.0	15.8	1.9	24.8	2.3
	2003	22 272	22.1	1.3	13.3	11.4	...	5.9	15.6	2.3	25.8	2.4
	2004	25 031	23.0	1.2	13.3	10.6	...	5.9	16.7	1.9	24.9	2.4
Mexico[3] Mexique[3]	2000	612 621	13.2	...	15.4	7.6	...	...	21.2	5.1	35.9	1.6
	2001	683 377	11.7	...	15.4	7.4	...	...	21.6	5.2	37.1	1.6
	2002	758 495	11.6	...	16.0	7.5	...	...	21.2	5.1	36.9	1.6
Montserrat Montserrat	1983	18	15.1	0.4	10.9	27.0	...	0.8	17.4	1.4	17.7	9.2
	1984	19	19.6	0.3	10.5	27.2	...	-0.2	15.9	0.6	19.3	6.6
	1985	20	18.7	0.3	11.3	24.5	...	0.9	15.3	1.7	22.4	4.8
Nepal+ Népal+	1986	5 065	14.7	11.7	9.7	23.1	...	2.5	8.0	6.0	23.9	0.7
	1987	5 797	16.9	13.1	8.1	34.6	...	3.2	8.7	0.8	27.5	0.5
	1988	6 895	15.2	7.5	11.0	37.0	...	3.9	3.8	1.6	24.0	1.7

20 Government final consumption expenditure by function at current prices — Percentage distribution by divisions of Classification of the Functions of Government (COFOG) (*continued*)

Consommation finale des administrations publiques par fonction aux prix courants — Répartition en pourcentage par divisions de la Classification des fonctions des administrations publiques (COFOG) (*suite*)

Country or area Pays ou zone	Year Année	Total (mil. nat. curr.) Totale (millions monnaie nat.)	Divisions of the Classification of the Functions of Government (COFOG) t Divisions de la Classification des fonctions des administrations publiques (COFOG) t Div. 01 (%)	Div. 02 (%)	Div. 03 (%)	Div. 04 (%)	Div. 05 (%)	Div. 06 (%)	Div. 07 (%)	Div. 08 (%)	Div. 09 (%)	Div. 10 (%)
Netherlands[3] Pays-Bas[3]	2002	110 246	9.3	6.4	6.4	12.1	1.6	2.2	17.2	4.2	18.3	22.2
	2003	116 018	9.4	6.2	6.6	12.1	1.7	2.0	17.6	4.1	18.3	22.2
	2004	118 512	9.2	5.9	6.9	11.4	1.6	2.0	18.2	4.0	18.6	22.1
Netherlands Antilles[3] Antilles néerlandaises[3]	2001	1 114	13.7	-0.2	12.9	2.9	4.7	10.4	14.6	1.5	15.2	24.3
	2002	1 088	13.8	...	13.7	2.7	4.3	8.7	15.1	1.5	15.5	24.7
	2003	1 146	14.0	...	14.7	2.7	4.3	9.2	14.8	1.5	15.0	23.9
New Zealand+ Nouvelle-Zélande+	1992	12 658	22.5	8.0	9.7	5.8	...	...	20.1	...	26.3	7.7
	1993	12 692	22.3	8.2	10.2	5.6	...	...	19.9	...	26.3	7.4
	1994	12 682	22.9	7.3	10.3	5.9	...	...	20.1	...	26.1	7.5
Nicaragua[3] Nicaragua[3]	1998	5 218	21.0	4.8	9.4	28.7	1.4	...	12.7	0.5	17.1	3.0
	1999	7 061	18.7	4.1	8.5	30.8	1.4	...	14.3	0.5	15.3	4.5
	2000	8 428	20.0	4.3	8.6	33.3	1.2	...	12.2	0.4	15.4	3.3
Norway[3] Norvège[3]	2002	338 429	9.6	8.9	4.6	8.1	0.7	0.4	29.5	2.8	22.1	13.4
	2003	354 305	8.9	8.5	4.4	7.6	0.7	0.4	30.3	2.7	22.8	13.7
	2004	370 769	8.6	8.2	4.3	7.5	0.8	0.3	30.2	2.7	22.6	14.8
Oman[3] Oman[3]	2000	1 580	10.5	29.3[25]	11.6	7.7	...	5.4	10.1	2.8	21.4	1.2
	2001	1 712	10.7	33.2[25]	11.3	6.8	...	4.6	9.4	2.5	20.5	1.1
	2002	1 800	10.8	32.6[25]	12.0	5.9	...	4.7	9.5	2.5	20.8	1.0
Pakistan+[3] Pakistan+[3]	2003	466 014	34.7	...	7.4	21.3	0.0	2.2	4.1	0.4	15.3	13.3
	2004	468 701	47.3	...	10.3	7.1	0.6	1.0	4.3	0.3	11.7	16.7
	2005	520 144	43.8	...	9.8	12.6	0.6	1.2	4.8	0.5	10.2	16.0
Panama[3] Panama[3]	2001	1 646	19.8	...	15.9	6.5	0.3	0.5	7.8	0.9	25.9	22.2
	2002	1 819	24.5	...	14.4	6.2	0.3	0.5	6.4	0.9	23.7	23.2
	2003	1 845	18.3	...	18.2	6.0	0.2	0.4	7.2	0.9	24.6	24.1
Peru Pérou	1986	43[26]	56.6	...	...	5.7	...	0.2	9.2	1.3	25.0	2.1
	1987	94[26]	55.5	...	...	5.3	...	0.2	7.1	1.8	27.3	2.9
	1988	475[26]	54.1	...	...	6.7	...	0.2	7.6	2.5	26.1	2.7
Poland[3] Pologne[3]	2003	153 623	14.1	5.4	8.3	6.5	1.2	4.4	20.5	3.2	27.7	8.9
	2004	165 120	14.2	4.7	6.9	6.3	1.1	4.4	21.2	3.4	28.6	9.1
Portugal[3] Portugal[3]	2002	27 144	8.2	6.6	8.9	8.1	1.8	1.4	28.1	2.3	30.3	4.5
	2003	27 267	7.3	6.6	9.0	9.2	2.1	2.1	25.9	2.4	30.9	4.7
	2004	29 561	7.9	6.4	8.6	10.2	2.4	2.7	25.3	2.6	29.7	4.1
Republic of Moldova[3] République de Moldova[3]	2003	5 435	30.5[5]	...	...	8.2[27]	...	1.1	23.0	...	31.2	1.4
	2004	4 774	35.9[5]	...	...	11.9[27]	...	1.6	3.8	...	37.8	2.0
	2005	5 712	36.8[5]	...	...	10.8[27]	...	1.9	3.6	...	38.5	2.1
Romania Roumanie	1993	2 473 200	36.5[9]	...	...	11.7	...	...	22.3	4.7	22.6	2.1
	1994	6 851 800	39.0[9]	...	...	8.4	...	...	28.6	4.6	19.4	2.2
	1995	9 877 000	37.3[9]	...	...	14.5	...	...	19.0	5.5	21.4	2.3
Russian Federation[3] Fédération de Russie[3]	2003	2 330 573	53.2[5]	...	...	1.7[28]	...	2.9	22.7	2.9	15.1	...
	2004	2 801 545	51.9[5]	...	...	1.6[28]	...	3.0	23.4	2.9	15.6	...
	2005	3 457 997	53.9[5]	...	...	1.5[28]	...	3.1	21.4	2.9	15.7	...
Saint Vincent-Grenadines Saint Vincent-Grenadines	2002	202	9.9	...	11.9	22.8	...	1.5	18.8	...	25.7	7.9
	2003	202	10.9	...	11.9	21.8	...	1.5	18.3	...	25.2	7.9
	2004	217[29]	11.1	...	12.0	24.9	...	1.4	17.5	...	25.3	8.3
San Marino Saint-Marin	1997	354 322	18.9	0.3	4.8	9.5	...	7.2	19.5	6.2	17.4	16.2
	1998	377 657	19.6	0.3	5.1	9.6	...	7.9	17.3	6.3	17.6	16.1
	1999	423 728	17.0	0.3	5.0	8.9	...	7.4	20.7	6.5	16.8	17.4
Saudi Arabia+ Arabie saoudite+	1999	154 094	19.8	27.4	...	3.4	...	4.7	11.0	2.9[30]	29.4	0.4
	2000	183 804	18.0	27.9	...	4.7	...	5.3	11.7	3.0[30]	27.0	0.5
	2001	188 695	18.4	27.4	...	4.9	...	5.5	11.8	3.0[30]	26.4	0.5

Government final consumption expenditure by function at current prices—Percentage distribution by divisions of Classification of the Functions of Government (COFOG) *(continued)*

Consommation finale des administrations publiques par fonction aux prix courants—Répartition en pourcentage par divisions de la Classification des fonctions des administrations publiques (COFOG) *(suite)*

Country or area / Pays ou zone	Year / Année	Total (mil. nat. curr.) / Totale (millions monnaie nat.)	Divisions of the Classification of the Functions of Government (COFOG) ‡ / Divisions de la Classification des fonctions des administrations publiques (COFOG) ‡ Div. 01 (%)	Div. 02 (%)	Div. 03 (%)	Div. 04 (%)	Div. 05 (%)	Div. 06 (%)	Div. 07 (%)	Div. 08 (%)	Div. 09 (%)	Div. 10 (%)
Senegal / Sénégal	1994	258 400	8.8	14.6	8.1	4.1	...	...	5.8	1.3	31.4	...
	1995	278 500	8.8	14.6	7.3	3.8	...	...	5.7	1.2	30.2	...
	1996	289 100	9.0	15.4	8.0	3.9	...	...	5.6	1.2	30.1	...
Seychelles / Seychelles	1989	475	9.4	11.5	4.9	17.1	...	2.1	11.8	3.1	29.7	2.6
	1990	544	9.5	10.2	5.1	18.3	...	2.6	12.8	5.9	29.2	3.5
	1991	558	10.3	11.0	5.7	17.0	...	2.4	13.7	5.7	26.4	5.2
Sierra Leone+ / Sierra Leone+	1988	3 883[31]	18.5	7.2	...	28.0	...	0.8	5.9	...	13.2	1.0
	1989	7 620[31]	14.4	7.3	...	45.9	...	1.4	5.0	...	10.2	1.4
	1990	32 337[31]	11.9	5.6	...	27.9	...	1.0	2.1	0.0	6.2	0.6
Slovakia[3] / Slovaquie[3]	2003	247 687	10.8	8.1	8.9	15.0	3.0	3.4	10.3	3.0	17.5	20.2
	2004	269 023	10.4	8.8	9.5	15.4	3.1	2.8	10.4	2.6	14.8	22.2
Slovenia[3] / Slovénie[3]	1991	65 845	35.5	7.6	...	...	...	...	25.6	3.0	21.0	7.3
	1992	213 669	34.1	7.6	...	...	...	...	28.6	2.9	19.8	7.0
	1993	297 449	40.5	...	...	...	...	...	28.8	4.4	24.3	2.0
Spain / Espagne	1993	10 700 500[32]	8.4	9.6	11.8	7.5	...	3.4	24.7	3.2	22.2	5.3
	1994	10 963 200[32]	8.0	8.7	11.9	7.4	...	3.5	25.8	3.2	22.3	4.9
	1995	11 647 100[32]	8.3	9.0	12.5	7.4	...	3.7	24.1	3.2	22.9	4.8
Sri Lanka[3] / Sri Lanka[3]	2002	204 510	23.6	22.4	...	9.4	...	0.1	10.2	3.0	13.7	17.6
	2003	221 620	24.8	22.0	...	9.2	...	0.1	12.7	0.6	13.1	17.4
	2004	264 069	21.6	21.3	...	7.5	...	0.1	12.8	1.9	14.7	20.1
Sudan+ / Soudan+	1981	720	25.2[22]	18.6	...	12.4[33]	...	0.1	9.7	3.2	30.9	...
	1982	854	27.7[22]	19.0	...	14.4[33]	...	0.0	8.6	2.6	27.7	...
	1983	1 113	32.4[22]	22.5	...	14.4[33]	...	-0.2	5.1	2.2	23.7	...
Sweden[3] / Suède[3]	2002	658 154	9.1	6.8	4.9	6.4	0.2	0.6	24.2	2.7	23.6	21.7
	2003	691 692	9.2	6.5	4.9	6.3	0.2	0.6	24.4	2.7	23.5	21.8
	2004	704 845	8.7	6.2	4.8	6.1	0.2	0.6	24.4	2.7	24.6	21.9
Thailand / Thaïlande	2002	603 891	23.4	25.2[34]	...	2.7	...	2.3[21]	11.4	...	34.2	0.8
	2003	635 251	23.9	26.1[34]	...	1.4	...	2.1[21]	10.1	...	35.4	0.9
	2004	721 314	25.6	25.1[34]	...	1.8	...	2.1[21]	9.8	...	34.5	1.0
TFYR of Macedonia[3] / L'ex-R.y. Macédoine[3]	1991	199	37.6	...	...	...	...	2.5	21.8	3.8	27.1	6.7
	1992	2 302	38.3	...	...	...	...	1.2	28.9	3.0	23.4	4.7
	1993	12 472	42.6	...	...	...	...	0.4	24.3	3.4	23.5	5.5
Tonga+ / Tonga+	1985	21	20.7	4.2	7.0	31.9	...	...	12.2	...	13.6	1.9
	1986	27	22.7	3.7	7.1	29.0	...	...	11.9	...	13.8	1.9
	1987	32	26.9	3.4	6.9	26.3	...	...	10.3	...	13.1	1.9
Trinidad and Tobago[3] / Trinité-et-Tobago[3]	2002	7 652	23.2	...	20.2	14.6	...	8.6	9.8	...	23.1	0.5
	2003	8 956	21.1	...	19.8	16.8	...	7.3	10.0	...	24.5	0.5
	2004	10 653	21.0	...	19.2	18.0	...	7.7	9.0	...	24.6	0.5
Ukraine[3] / Ukraine[3]	2003	50 830	11.4	7.9	10.4	8.3	0.9	1.7	18.2	2.9	26.0	12.3
	2004	60 610	11.3	8.0	11.0	6.0	0.7	1.7	19.0	2.7	26.7	12.8
	2005	81 746	13.1	6.1	11.6	5.2	0.5	2.4	17.7	3.1	29.7	10.6
United Kingdom[3] / Royaume-Uni[3]	2002	210 967	5.3	12.4	10.7	6.5	2.6	2.0	30.0	2.1	17.8	10.6
	2003	231 777	6.0	12.4	10.6	6.5	2.5	1.8	30.1	1.9	17.2	11.0
	2004	246 810	6.0	11.8	10.5	5.9	2.4	2.1	31.5	1.7	17.0	11.1
United Rep. of Tanzania[35] / Rép.-Unie de Tanzanie[35]	1992	225 639[1]	17.5	8.5	8.5	16.5	...	0.4	5.9	2.5	7.7	0.7
	1993	336 855[1]	21.5	6.8	6.8	22.6	...	0.5	5.7	2.0	7.5	0.2
	1994	408 440[1]	21.1	4.9	7.5	22.9	...	0.6	7.2	2.1	7.6	0.2
United States[3] / Etats-Unis[3]	2002	1 608 365	9.6	23.3	13.0	12.1	...	0.5	4.8	1.4	30.8	4.6
	2003	1 731 704	9.4	25.0	12.9	11.7	...	0.5	4.6	1.5	29.8	4.6
	2004	1 844 627	9.6	26.3	12.9	11.6	...	0.4	4.2	1.5	28.8	4.6

20 Government final consumption expenditure by function at current prices — Percentage distribution by divisions of Classification of the Functions of Government (COFOG) *(continued)*

Consommation finale des administrations publiques par fonction aux prix courants — Répartition en pourcentage par divisions de la Classification des fonctions des administrations publiques (COFOG) *(suite)*

Country or area Pays ou zone	Year Année	Total (mil. nat. curr.) Totale (millions monnaie nat.)	Divisions of the Classification of the Functions of Government (COFOG) ŧ Divisions de la Classification des fonctions des administrations publiques (COFOG) ŧ									
			Div. 01 (%)	Div. 02 (%)	Div. 03 (%)	Div. 04 (%)	Div. 05 (%)	Div. 06 (%)	Div. 07 (%)	Div. 08 (%)	Div. 09 (%)	Div. 10 (%)
Vanuatu Vanuatu	1991	4 693	20.5	8.4	...	22.6	...	18.5[36]	10.3	...	19.8	...
	1992	5 112	22.6	8.7	...	21.2	...	16.1[36]	10.1	...	21.2	...
	1993	5 194	27.1	9.2	...	20.1	...	13.9[36]	9.7	...	20.0	...
Venezuela (Bolivarian Rep. of)[3] Venezuela (Rép. bolivarienne du)[3]	2001	12 663 400	13.5	7.2	6.3	4.4	0.5	3.2	14.3	1.2	41.8	7.6
	2002	14 027 200	11.9	5.2	6.1	6.4	0.5	2.9	14.9	1.1	43.2	7.8
	2003	17 288 000	13.8	4.7	6.0	6.7	0.4	3.4	14.5	1.2	42.1	7.2
Zimbabwe Zimbabwe	1989	5 568[37]	6.2	15.7	5.9	14.1	...	1.2	8.1	1.4	28.1	2.6
	1990	7 425[37]	28.1	13.1	4.9	20.8	...	1.6	6.5	2.0	19.9	3.1
	1991	7 788[37]	16.7	14.3	6.1	23.0	...	1.7	7.4	2.8	26.7	4.1

Source

United Nations Statistics Division, New York, national accounts database.

Notes

ŧ COFOG Divisions:
- Div. 01: General public services
- Div. 02: Defence
- Div. 03: Public order and safety
- Div. 04: Economic affairs
- Div. 05: Environmental protection
- Div. 06: Housing and community amenities
- Div. 07: Health
- Div. 08: Recreation, culture and religion
- Div. 09: Education
- Div. 10: Social protection

\+ The national accounts data generally relate to the fiscal year used in each country, unless indicated otherwise. Countries whose reference periods coincide with the calendar year ending 31 December are not listed below.
- Year beginning 21 March: Afghanistan, Iran (Islamic Republic).
- Year beginning 1 April: Bermuda, India, Myanmar, New Zealand, Nigeria.
- Year beginning 1 July: Australia, Bangladesh, Cameroon, Gambia, Pakistan, Puerto Rico, Saudi Arabia, Sierra Leone, Sudan.
- Year ending 30 June: Botswana, Egypt, Swaziland, Tonga.
- Year ending 7 July: Ethiopia.
- Year ending 15 July: Nepal.
- Year ending 30 September: Haiti.

1 Central government estimates only.
2 Including expenditure on culture.
3 Data compiled in accordance with the concepts and definitions of the System of National Accounts 1993 (1993 SNA).
4 Data refer only to collective government consumption expenditure (excludes individual consumption).
5 Including "Defence".
6 Including maintenance and servicing of roads and units servicing agriculture.
7 Including social security.
8 Including housing and community amenities.
9 Including defence and public order and safety.

Source

Organisation des Nations Unies, Division de statistique, New York, la base de données sur les comptes nationaux.

Notes

ŧ Divisions de la COFOG:
- Div. 01: Services généraux des administrations publiques
- Div. 02: Défense
- Div. 03: Ordre et sécurité publics
- Div. 04: Affaires économiques
- Div. 05: Protection de l'environnement
- Div. 06: Logements et équipements collectifs
- Div. 07: Santé
- Div. 08: Loisirs, culture et culte
- Div. 09: Enseignement
- Div. 10: Protection sociale

\+ Sauf indication contraire, les données sur les comptes nationaux concernent généralement l'exercice budgétaire utilisé dans chaque pays. Les pays où territoires dont la période de référence coïncide avec l'année civile se terminant le 31 décembre ne sont pas répertoriés ci-dessous.
- Exercice commençant le 21 mars: Afghanistan, Iran (République islamique d').
- Exercice commençant le 1er avril: Bermudes, Inde, Myanmar, Nigéria, Nouvelle-Zélande.
- Exercice commençant le 1er juillet: Arabie saoudite, Australie, Bangladesh, Cameroun, Gambie, Pakistan, Porto Rico, Sierra Leone, Soudan.
- Exercice se terminant le 30 juin: Botswana, Égypte, Swaziland, Tonga.
- Exercice se terminant le 7 juillet: Éthiopie.
- Exercice se terminant le 15 juillet: Népal.
- Exercice se terminant le 30 septembre: Haïti.

1 Administration centrale seulement.
2 Y compris dépenses de culture.
3 Données compilées selon les concepts et définitions du Système de comptabilité nationale de 1993 (SCN 1993).
4 Les données ne concernent que les dépenses de consommation collective des administrations publiques (à l'exclusion de la consommation individuelle).
5 Y compris "Défense".
6 Les données concernent l'entretien et le service des routes et les unités assurant des services agricoles.
7 Y compris sécurité sociale.
8 Y compris logement et équipements collectifs.
9 Y compris ordre et sécurité publics.

20 Government final consumption expenditure by function at current prices — Percentage distribution by divisions of Classification of the Functions of Government (COFOG) (*continued*)

Consommation finale des administrations publiques par fonction aux prix courants — Répartition en pourcentage par divisions de la Classification des fonctions des administrations publiques (COFOG) (*suite*)

10 Total government current expenditure only.
11 Excludes Office of the President, Ministries of Justice, Foreign Affairs, Information, among others.
12 Refers to inter-ministerial expenses only.
13 Refers to the Ministry of the Interior.
14 Refers to the Ministry of Finance and Planning.
15 Refers to the Ministry of Agriculture, Livestock Development and Environmental Protection.
16 Refers to the Ministry of Equipment, Transport and Telecommunication.
17 Refers to the Ministry of Health, Public Services and Social Affairs.
18 Twinning projects in the health sector.
19 General government expenditure data refer to fiscal year beginning 30 June.
20 Including compensation of employees and intermediate consumption of the following departmental enterprises: electricity, gas and steam, water works and supply and medical and other health services.
21 Including recreational, cultural and religion.
22 Including "Public order and safety".
23 General government expenditure data refer to fiscal year beginning 1 April.
24 Including housing and community amenities and recreation, culture and religion.
25 Data refer to defence affairs and services.
26 Figures in thousands.
27 Includes agriculture, transport, and other branches of the economy.
28 Data refer to agriculture, geology, exploration, hydrometerorology, transport, and communication.
29 Preliminary data.
30 Data refer to other community and social services.
31 Central government estimates only; including development expenditure.
32 Data in pesetas.
33 Including other functions.
34 Including justice and police.
35 General government expenditure data refer to fiscal year beginning 1 July.
36 Including "Social protection".
37 Central and local government estimates only.

10 Dépenses publiques courants seulement.
11 Non compris notamment le Cabinet du Président, et les Ministères de la justice, des affaires étrangères et de l'information.
12 Ne concerne que les dépenses interministérielles.
13 Concerne le Ministère de l'intérieur.
14 Concerne le Ministère des finances et de la planification.
15 Concerne le Ministère de l'agriculture, du développement de l'élevage et de la protection de l'environnement.
16 Concerne le Ministère de l'équipement, des transports et des télécommunications.
17 Concerne le Ministère de la santé, des services publics et des affaires sociales.
18 Projets jumelés dans le secteur de la santé.
19 Les données relatives aux dépenses générales de l'État portent sur l'année budgétaire commençant le 30 juin.
20 Y compris la rémunération des employés et la consommation intermédiaire des entreprises suivantes : électricité, gaz et vapeur, approvisionnement en eau, services médicaux et autres services sanitaires.
21 Y compris loisirs, affaires culturelles et religieuses.
22 Y compris "Ordre et sécurité publics".
23 Les données relatives aux dépenses générales de l'État portent sur l'année budgétaire commençant le 1e avril.
24 Y compris logement et équipements collectifs et loisirs, culture et religieuses
25 Les données se réfèrent aux affaires et services de la défense.
26 Données en milliers.
27 Y compris l'agriculture, les transports, et d'autres branches d'activité.
28 Les données concernent l'agriculture, la géologie, l'exploration, l'hydrométéorologie, les transports et les communications.
29 Données préliminaires.
30 Les données concernent les autres services collectifs et sociaux.
31 Administration centrale seulement; y compris dépenses de développement.
32 Les données sont exprimées en pesetas.
33 Y compris les autres fonctions.
34 Y compris justice et police.
35 Les données relatives aux dépenses générales de l'État portent sur l'année budgétaire commençant le 1e juillet.
36 Y compris "protection sociale".
37 Administration centrale et locale seulement.

21 Household consumption expenditure by purpose at current prices

Percentage distribution by divisions of the Classification of Individual Consumption according to Purpose (COICOP)

Dépenses de consommation des ménages par fonction aux prix courants

Répartition en pourcentage par divisions de la Nomenclature des fonctions de la consommation individuelle (COICOP)

Country or area Pays ou zone	Year Année	Total (mil. nat. curr.) Totale (millions monn. nat.)	Divisions of the Classification of Individual Consumption according to Purpose (COICOP) † Divisions de la Nomenclature des functions de la consommation individuelle (COICOP) †									
			Div. 01 + 02 (%)	Div. 03 (%)	Div. 04 (%)	Div. 05 (%)	Div. 06 (%)	Div. 07 + 08 (%)	Div. 09 (%)	Div. 10 (%)	Div. 11 (%)	Div. 12 (%)
Andorra Andorre	2001	710	22.6[1]	8.6	16.5	4.5	3.6	21.9[2]	4.4	1.0	8.1	8.7
	2002	767	21.7[1]	8.6	16.9	4.6	3.9	22.3[2]	4.9	1.0	7.2	9.0
	2003	804	21.1[1]	7.2	17.1	4.6	4.1	24.3[2]	4.8	1.1	6.6	9.1
Australia+[3] Australie+[3]	2002	462 095	15.2	3.9	19.5	5.6	4.9	14.8	12.0	3.3	7.4	13.3
	2003	493 287	15.0	3.8	19.3	5.7	5.0	14.7	12.0	3.3	7.7	13.4
	2004	522 551	14.9	3.8	19.3	5.6	5.2	14.7	11.8	3.5	7.6	13.6
Austria[3] Autriche[3]	2002	125 549	13.8	7.1	19.1	8.4	3.2	14.7	11.9	0.6	11.9	9.2
	2003	129 595	13.7	6.9	19.1	8.3	3.3	14.9	11.7	0.6	12.1	9.4
	2004	134 113	13.4	6.7	18.9	8.2	3.2	15.1	11.7	0.7	12.2	9.8
Azerbaijan[3] Azerbaïdjan[3]	2003	21 150 000	78.6	5.8	1.3	1.7	1.8	6.2	0.3	3.3	0.4	0.6
	2004	23 488 300	78.6	5.8	1.3	1.7	1.8	6.2	0.3	3.3	0.4	0.6
	2005	23 942 800	77.0	5.7	1.3	1.7	1.8	6.1	0.3	3.2	0.4	0.6
Belarus[3] Bélarus[3]	2002	15 113 800[4]	55.7	9.3	8.8	4.7	2.3	9.4	2.3	1.1	2.4	4.0
	2003	20 331 800[4]	52.7	8.3	11.7	4.2	2.2	11.0	2.9	1.3	2.1	3.6
	#2004	26 130 200[4]	51.5	7.9	12.3	4.4	2.2	11.0	3.4	1.3	2.5	3.5
Belgium[3] Belgique[3]	2001	132 573	16.6	5.5	23.6	5.7	4.0	16.6	10.0	0.6	5.4	12.0
	2002	134 617	17.3	5.6	23.6	5.8	4.4	16.6	9.4	0.6	5.5	11.3
	2003	140 223	17.5	5.4	23.5	5.7	4.5	16.5	9.1	0.6	5.3	11.9
Bolivia Bolivie	1994	21 444	34.7[5]	6.7	...	...	...	...	...	...	9.2	...
	1995	24 440	34.4[5]	6.5	...	...	...	...	...	...	9.5	...
	1996	28 200	35.7[5]	6.5	...	...	...	...	...	...	9.8	...
Botswana+[3] Botswana+[3]	1999	6 619	43.3	5.4	12.2	4.1	2.3	7.9	...	6.8	1.1	...
	2000	7 469	42.7	5.1	13.4	3.7	2.4	7.2	...	7.0	1.0	...
	2001	8 281	41.1	3.8	14.0	...	2.6	7.4	...	8.2	1.0	...
British Virgin Islands[3] Iles Vierges britanniques[3]	1997	231	16.5	10.4	19.5	6.9	1.7	13.0	2.2	1.3	7.8	21.2
	1998	253	16.2	9.5	20.6	6.7	2.0	12.6	1.6	1.2	7.5	22.1
	1999	280	15.7	10.0	20.7	6.4	2.5	11.8	2.9	1.1	6.1	22.9
Bulgaria[3] Bulgarie[3]	2002	23 548	28.6	3.6	22.7	3.2	3.9	21.2	4.5	1.1	8.5	2.6
	2003	25 153	27.5	3.5	22.4	3.4	4.0	22.1	4.7	1.0	8.7	2.8
	2004	27 631	28.4	3.7	21.0	3.4	4.1	22.3	4.7	1.0	8.7	2.8
Canada[3] Canada[3]	2002	627 482	14.0	5.2	23.4	6.6	4.1	17.4	10.7	1.3	7.5	9.8
	2003	653 257	14.1	5.1	23.7	6.7	4.2	17.0	10.6	1.3	7.3	9.9
	2004	684 537	14.1	5.1	23.6	6.8	4.3	16.8	10.6	1.4	7.3	10.1
Cape Verde Cap-Vert	1986	13 406	61.2	2.7	14.1	7.2	0.5	...	...	...	...	...
	1987	15 134	60.4	2.9	13.6	7.2	0.6	...	...	...	...	...
	1988	17 848	62.6	2.5	13.5	6.9	0.5	...	...	...	...	...
China, Hong Kong SAR[3] Chine, Hong Kong RAS[3]	2002	667 437	14.2	13.2[6]	22.5[7]	12.2	4.8	10.5	6.8[8]	2.6	...	13.2[9]
	2003	644 808	14.3	12.8[6]	23.2[7]	12.8	4.9	10.1	6.2[8]	2.8	...	13.1[9]
	2004	694 474	13.8	14.0[6]	21.2[7]	12.9	5.1	10.2	6.7[8]	2.6	...	13.4[9]
China, Macao SAR[3] Chine, Macao RAS[3]	2002	16 834	13.9	5.0	20.2	2.8	3.6	14.3	13.6	4.5	15.7	6.4
	2003	17 525	14.2	4.5	19.6	2.9	3.6	15.7	13.2	4.4	15.6	6.4
	2004	19 245	14.2	4.7	18.4	2.9	3.4	16.6	13.2	4.4	16.4	5.8
Colombia[3] Colombie[3]	2000	109 956 800	33.5	5.3	17.1	5.5	3.9	13.1	4.6	5.3	6.1	5.6
	2001	123 164 800	33.5	5.2	16.4	5.2	4.5	13.8	4.7	5.3	6.1	5.3
	2002	134 765 600	34.0	4.8	16.3	5.2	4.7	14.1	4.5	5.0	6.1	5.4
Côte d'Ivoire Côte d'Ivoire	1996	4 015 059	51.5	5.3	7.3	3.9	0.4	9.9	1.8	0.2	2.7	16.9
	1997	4 276 928	50.4	5.3	7.3	4.1	0.5	10.1	1.9	0.2	2.6	17.6
	1998	4 768 663	50.6	5.5	7.3	4.0	0.5	9.5	1.7	0.3	1.9	18.6

21

Household consumption expenditure by purpose in current prices—Percentage distribution by divisions of the Classification of Individual Consumption according to Purpose (COICOP) *(continued)*

Dépenses de consommation des ménages par fonction aux prix courants—Répartition en pourcentage par divisions de la Nomenclature des fonctions de la consommation individuelle (COICOP) *(suite)*

Country or area Pays ou zone	Year Année	Total (mil. nat. curr.) Totale (millions monn. nat.)	Divisions of the Classification of Individual Consumption according to Purpose (COICOP) † Divisions de la Nomenclature des functions de la consommation individuelle (COICOP) †									
			Div. 01 + 02 (%)	Div. 03 (%)	Div. 04 (%)	Div. 05 (%)	Div. 06 (%)	Div. 07 + 08 (%)	Div. 09 (%)	Div. 10 (%)	Div. 11 (%)	Div. 12 (%)
Croatia[3]	1999	94 101	27.0	7.3	19.7	9.3	2.6	14.6	5.2	2.7	7.5	4.3
Croatie[3]	2000	107 866	25.2	8.7	18.7	8.3	2.6	15.2	5.1	2.5	8.4	5.1
	2001	120 709	27.5	6.9	17.7	9.8	2.2	14.8	5.0	2.5	8.2	5.5
Cyprus[3]	2001	5 071	21.4	6.8	12.5	6.5	3.6	16.1	7.8	2.6	13.9	8.9
Chypre[3]	2002	5 101	21.9	6.9	12.8	6.7	3.6	16.5	8.0	2.7	12.7	8.1
	2003	5 222	21.8	7.0	12.8	6.7	3.8	16.5	8.0	2.9	12.6	8.0
Czech Republic[3]	2002	1 264 794	26.1	5.3	22.6	5.4	1.7	13.1	11.8	0.5	6.6	6.8
République tchèque[3]	2003	1 347 779	26.0	5.1	22.0	5.4	1.7	13.9	11.7	0.6	6.4	7.1
	2004	1 425 720	25.7	5.0	21.8	5.2	1.6	14.2	11.8	0.6	6.8	7.3
Denmark[3]	2002	643 124	16.5	4.9	27.4	5.9	2.6	13.8	10.8	0.8	4.9	12.4
Danemark[3]	2003	664 457	16.3	4.9	27.5	5.9	2.6	13.2	11.0	0.8	4.8	12.9
	2004	698 166	15.6	4.9	27.1	6.0	2.6	14.7	10.9	0.8	4.7	12.7
Dominican Republic[3]	1994	137 616	33.3	4.1	20.6	6.4	5.2	14.2	2.1	2.5	5.6	5.9
Rép. dominicaine[3]	1995	164 689	34.1	4.0	20.3	6.2	5.2	13.5	2.0	2.2	6.9	5.6
	1996	189 675	32.0	3.4	20.1	6.5	5.0	14.1	3.1	2.2	8.8	4.8
Ecuador	1991	8 432 000	38.9	9.9	5.3[10]	7.4	4.2	...	...	...	4.2	17.5
Equateur	1992	13 147 000	38.7	9.5	5.1[10]	7.2	4.5	...	...	...	4.4	18.3
	1993	19 374 000	37.8	9.2	5.2[10]	6.6	4.6	...	...	...	4.4	18.6
Estonia[3]	2002	72 160	30.6	6.0	22.8	4.8	2.1	13.9	6.7	1.2	5.3	6.4
Estonie[3]	2003	77 203	29.6	6.1	22.2	5.2	2.5	14.3	6.8	1.3	5.5	6.5
	2004	83 644	30.3	5.9	21.9	5.0	2.6	14.6	6.6	1.0	5.6	6.4
Fiji	1989	1 197	30.9	8.6	12.4	8.6	2.0	...	...	...	...	...
Fidji	1990	1 277	31.6	8.2	13.1	7.8	2.0	...	...	...	...	...
	1991	1 405	31.2	7.9	13.2	7.9	2.0	...	...	...	...	...
Finland[3]	2002	69 332	18.5	4.6	25.2	4.8	3.9	15.4	11.0	0.5	6.4	9.7
Finlande[3]	2003	72 226	18.4	4.7	25.5	4.9	4.0	16.1	11.0	0.4	6.4	8.5
	2004	74 485	17.7	4.8	25.6	5.2	4.1	16.0	11.3	0.4	6.3	8.5
France[3]	2003	889 899	17.7	5.1	23.5	6.0	3.3	17.1	9.3	0.6	6.3	11.1
France[3]	2004	925 316	17.4	5.0	23.8	5.9	3.4	17.3	9.3	0.7	6.2	11.0
	2005	962 183	16.9	4.8	24.5	5.8	3.5	17.5	9.2	0.7	6.1	11.1
Germany[3]	2002	1 201 140	15.3	5.7	23.5	7.4	4.4	16.6	9.7	0.7	5.5	11.4
Allemagne[3]	2003	1 217 660	15.3	5.5	23.8	7.2	4.4	16.4	9.5	0.7	5.3	11.9
	2004	1 244 080	15.3	5.4	23.8	7.1	4.7	16.6	9.4	0.7	5.2	11.8
Greece[3]	2002	102 999	20.4	10.3	15.6	6.4	5.7	10.9	5.8	1.7	17.2	6.0
Grèce[3]	2003	110 353	20.0	10.1	15.6	6.3	5.9	10.8	5.8	1.7	17.6	6.1
	#2004	118 642	19.6	10.1	15.4	6.2	6.0	10.9	6.0	1.6	18.4	5.9
Honduras	1984	4 742	44.6[5]	9.1	22.5	8.3	7.0	...	...	...	...	...
Honduras	1985	5 033	44.6[5]	9.1	22.5	8.3	7.0	...	...	...	...	...
	1986	5 421	44.5[5]	9.1	22.5	8.3	7.0	...	...	...	...	...
Hungary[3]	2002	9 331 920	27.0	4.4	18.2	6.7	3.7	19.9	7.7	1.2	4.9	6.4
Hongrie[3]	2003	10 387 255	26.5	4.2	18.6	6.7	3.7	20.1	7.8	1.3	4.7	6.4
	2004	10 994 981	25.9	4.0	19.5	7.4	3.7	20.1	7.9	1.2	5.1	5.2
Iceland[3]	2003	443 359	18.7	5.1	18.6	6.5	3.4	18.3	12.6	1.3	8.6	6.9
Islande[3]	2004	484 270	18.0	4.9	18.8	6.6	3.3	19.5	12.5	1.3	8.2	6.9
	2005	542 913	16.4	4.7	19.7	6.7	3.2	21.1	12.3	1.2	8.0	6.8
India+	2001	14 887 810	45.7	4.1	11.5	2.9	7.7	14.4	1.3	2.1	1.4	8.9
Inde+	2002	15 851 320	43.2	4.4	11.8	2.9	8.1	15.1	1.3	2.0	1.4	9.8
	2003	17 658 490	42.6	4.4	11.4	2.9	8.3	15.5	1.3	2.1	1.5	10.0
Iran (Islamic Rep. of)+[3]	2001	321 298 460	30.8[5]	7.9	30.1	6.9	6.0	10.2[11]	3.4	...	...	4.8
Iran (Rép. Islamique d')+[3]	2002	414 570 615	30.5[5]	7.6	30.3	6.6	6.4	10.9[11]	3.4	...	...	4.3
	2003	497 482 810	31.6[5]	8.1	29.8	6.7	6.0	10.1[11]	3.3	...	...	4.4

21 **Household consumption expenditure by purpose in current prices**—Percentage distribution by divisions of the Classification of Individual Consumption according to Purpose (COICOP) (*continued*)

Dépenses de consommation des ménages par fonction aux prix courants—Répartition en pourcentage par divisions de la Nomenclature des fonctions de la consommation individuelle (COICOP) (*suite*)

Country or area Pays ou zone	Year Année	Total (mil. nat. curr.) Totale (millions monn. nat.)	Divisions of the Classification of Individual Consumption according to Purpose (COICOP) † Divisions de la Nomenclature des functions de la consommation individuelle (COICOP) †									
			Div. 01 + 02 (%)	Div. 03 (%)	Div. 04 (%)	Div. 05 (%)	Div. 06 (%)	Div. 07 + 08 (%)	Div. 09 (%)	Div. 10 (%)	Div. 11 (%)	Div. 12 (%)
Ireland[3] Irlande[3]	2002	56 172	16.4	6.1	20.0	7.2	3.2	12.9	7.0	1.2	14.6	11.4
	2003	59 911	15.7	5.4	20.6	7.3	3.4	13.1	6.9	1.3	14.5	11.8
	2004	62 735	14.9	4.8	20.7	7.1	3.5	14.0	7.3	1.3	14.2	12.3
Israel[3] Israël[3]	2002	282 119	19.6	3.4	28.9	9.4	4.2	13.2	5.6	3.3	5.4	6.9
	2003	287 454	20.5	3.3	28.6	9.2	4.2	13.2	5.7	3.3	5.2	6.8
	2004	302 732	19.9	3.2	27.8	9.4	4.3	14.1	5.9	3.2	5.6	6.7
Italy[3] Italie[3]	2003	798 455	17.7	8.5	19.5	7.8	3.3	16.2	7.0	0.9	9.7	9.3
	2004	825 257	17.5	8.2	20.2	7.8	3.2	16.3	7.2	0.9	9.7	9.0
	2005	843 508	17.5	7.8	20.7	7.7	3.2	16.4	7.1	0.8	9.7	9.2
Jamaica Jamaïque	1986	8 497	52.6	5.4	15.2	6.8	3.2	...	2.8	0.2	16.1	10.0
	1987	9 849	52.1	6.0	14.5	6.9	3.4	...	2.7	0.2	16.2	10.7
	1988	11 388	49.6	5.8	13.1	6.8	3.5	...	2.5	0.2	13.6	10.6
Japan[3] Japon[3]	2002	274 254 400	18.7	4.1	24.0	4.0	4.0	13.4	11.3	2.2	7.6	10.7
	2003	273 358 300	18.4	3.9	24.3	3.9	4.2	13.7	11.3	2.2	7.6	10.6
	2004	276 273 700	18.3	3.7	24.4	3.8	4.2	13.9	11.3	2.2	7.5	10.7
Jordan Jordanie	#1984	1 375	39.6[5]	6.1	6.7	5.1	4.2[12]	...	2.9	3.4	...	...
	1985	1 415	38.5[5]	5.7	6.5	4.8	4.1[12]	...	2.9	3.4	...	...
	1986	1 238	38.8[5]	5.6	6.5	4.9	4.1[12]	...	3.0	3.4	...	...
Kenya[3] Kenya[3]	2002	814 919	45.2[5]	4.9	7.8	...	...	...	...	...	...	...
	2003	868 547	45.8[5]	4.9	7.7	...	...	...	...	...	...	...
	2004	954 649	45.8[5]	4.1	7.8	...	...	...	...	...	...	...
Korea, Republic of[3] Corée, République de[3]	2003	376 221 300	17.5	4.4	16.9	4.2	4.5	16.8	7.8	5.9	7.7	14.4
	2004	386 499 300	18.0	4.3	17.2	4.1	4.8	16.6	7.3	6.1	7.6	14.0
	2005	406 890 900	18.1	4.3	17.2	4.1	5.0	16.7	7.3	6.1	7.4	13.9
Kyrgyzstan[3] Kirghizistan[3]	2001	45 932	49.9	14.4	7.7	3.1	1.6	15.7	1.6	2.0	1.5	2.4
	2002	48 681	53.8	11.8	8.4	3.4	1.4	11.9	1.5	2.6	1.3	3.8
	2003	63 352	54.0	12.9	11.2	3.1	1.7	9.6	1.7	2.1	1.0	2.6
Latvia[3] Lettonie[3]	2002	3 517	32.6	7.6	21.5	3.1	4.6	12.8	7.4	1.8	4.7	3.8
	2003	3 906	31.0	7.1	21.4	3.4	4.6	13.8	7.8	2.8	4.1	4.1
	2004	4 538	29.4	6.9	21.4	3.4	4.9	15.2	8.3	2.3	4.1	4.0
Lebanon[3]—Liban[3]	1997	20 158 200	27.1	6.0	15.1	6.4	7.8	13.4[11]	1.2	10.8	2.8	0.7
Lithuania[3] Lituanie[3]	2002	34 218	35.0	6.0	16.9	5.0	4.6	16.9	6.5	0.6	3.2	5.2
	2003	37 354	35.2	5.8	15.2	5.1	4.3	18.0	7.0	0.7	3.3	5.4
	2004	41 187	35.4	6.6	14.1	5.2	4.1	17.7	7.0	0.8	3.6	5.6
Luxembourg[3] Luxembourg[3]	2002	11 329	20.8	4.5	21.4	8.2	1.4	18.8	8.1	0.3	7.4	9.1
	2003	11 806	20.9	4.2	21.4	8.1	1.4	18.9	8.0	0.4	7.2	9.5
	2004	12 527	21.4	3.9	21.0	8.0	1.4	20.0	8.1	0.3	6.8	9.0
Malaysia Malaisie	2001	167 125	28.7	2.9	22.7	6.3	2.1	19.2[11]	5.8	...	6.4	6.0
	2002	176 886	29.4	2.4	22.2	5.8	2.2	20.0[11]	5.9	...	6.3	5.9
	2003	184 239	29.5	2.3	22.1	5.6	2.1	20.8[11]	5.7	...	6.1	5.7
Malta[3] Malte[3]	2002	1 274	22.2	6.0	8.9	9.2	2.4	18.5	10.8	1.3	14.1	6.6
	2003	1 309	22.2	6.3	9.0	9.5	2.4	18.0	10.6	1.2	14.1	6.5
	2004	1 341	21.8	6.3	8.9	9.2	2.7	18.4	11.0	1.3	13.3	6.9
Mexico[3] Mexique[3]	2002	4 357 960	26.7	3.4	13.1	8.4	4.6	18.5	2.8	3.8	7.7	11.1
	2003	4 771 881	26.9	3.2	13.4	8.0	4.8	18.5	2.7	3.9	7.4	11.3
	2004	5 297 265	26.9	3.1	13.4	7.9	4.7	19.0	2.8	3.9	7.2	11.2
Namibia[3] Namibie[3]	2002	19 086	39.7[5]	6.4	13.6	...	...	...	...	...	...	...
	2003	19 915	38.2[5]	6.6	14.0	...	...	...	...	...	...	...
	2004	20 406	37.1[5]	6.6	14.9	...	...	...	...	...	...	...

21 Household consumption expenditure by purpose in current prices — Percentage distribution by divisions of the Classification of Individual Consumption according to Purpose (COICOP) *(continued)*

Dépenses de consommation des ménages par fonction aux prix courants — Répartition en pourcentage par divisions de la Nomenclature des fonctions de la consommation individuelle (COICOP) *(suite)*

Country or area — Pays ou zone	Year — Année	Total (mil. nat. curr.) — Totale (millions monn. nat.)	Divisions of the Classification of Individual Consumption according to Purpose (COICOP) ‡ — Divisions de la Nomenclature des functions de la consommation individuelle (COICOP) ‡ Div. 01 + 02 (%)	Div. 03 (%)	Div. 04 (%)	Div. 05 (%)	Div. 06 (%)	Div. 07 + 08 (%)	Div. 09 (%)	Div. 10 (%)	Div. 11 (%)	Div. 12 (%)
Netherlands[3]	2001	206 656	14.3	6.1	20.8	7.4	4.2	15.7	11.2	0.5	5.8	14.1
Pays-Bas[3]	2002	215 059	14.3	6.0	20.7	7.2	4.5	16.1	11.1	0.5	5.8	13.8
	2003	217 987	14.3	5.6	21.4	6.8	4.7	16.0	10.7	0.6	5.6	14.4
New Zealand[+3]	2002	78 883	17.1	4.6	18.9	10.6	...	13.8[13]	...	...	7.5[14]	11.1[15]
Nouvelle-Zélande[+3]	2003	83 821	17.1	4.6	18.7	10.7	...	13.9[13]	...	...	7.5[14]	11.0[15]
	2004	89 264	16.9	4.6	18.4	10.9	...	14.1[13]	...	...	7.6[14]	10.9[15]
Nicaragua[3]	1998	29 759	42.8	4.9	13.2	5.4	8.2	12.4	2.8	1.2	6.9	2.2
Nicaragua[3]	1999	34 144	42.0	5.0	13.3	5.5	8.1	13.1	2.8	1.2	6.8	2.2
	2000	38 906	40.8	4.8	14.6	5.4	8.2	13.5	2.8	1.4	6.4	2.2
Norway[3]	2001	616 231	19.4	5.9	20.7	6.4	2.9	17.5	13.2	0.6	6.4	7.1
Norvège[3]	2002	643 229	19.1	5.8	21.2	6.4	2.9	17.4	13.2	0.6	6.3	7.2
	2003	677 082	18.8	5.6	21.5	6.3	3.0	17.0	13.3	0.5	6.1	7.9
Panama[3] — Panama[3]	1996	5 824	24.6	5.7	24.2	4.9	4.3	14.5	5.1	1.6	4.0	11.2
Peru	1986	254 987[16]	...	9.3	1.8	12.4	3.9	...	...	...	...	...
Pérou	1987	497 603[16]	...	10.1	1.4	12.5	4.4	...	...	...	...	...
	1988	3 214 245[16]	...	11.6	0.8	13.6	4.6	...	...	...	...	...
Philippines	2002	2 750 994	49.4	2.7	4.8[17]	13.8	...	6.6	...	...	...	22.7
Philippines	2003	2 988 240	48.8	2.6	4.9[17]	13.4	...	7.1	...	...	...	23.2
	2004	3 344 220	48.6	2.5	4.7[17]	12.7	...	8.3	...	...	...	23.2
Poland[3]	2001	486 504[18]	27.9	4.6	23.8	4.4	4.4	13.6	7.3	1.6	3.1	9.3
Pologne[3]	2002	510 817[18]	26.8	4.5	24.6	4.5	4.7	13.7	7.0	1.7	3.0	9.4
	2003	530 033[18]	26.0	4.4	24.8	4.5	4.7	13.8	7.2	1.7	2.9	10.0
Portugal[3]	2001	83 020	20.6	7.7	13.0	7.2	4.8	17.9	6.3	1.2	10.5	10.7
Portugal[3]	2002	86 555	20.5	7.9	13.3	7.3	4.9	17.3	6.5	1.2	10.6	10.5
	2003	88 866	20.7	7.9	13.5	7.1	4.9	16.5	6.6	1.2	10.8	10.7
Puerto Rico[+]	2000	37 765	18.6	6.9	15.7	6.2	13.4	14.8	4.2	3.1	4.4	11.5
Porto Rico[+]	2001	36 599	19.1	7.2	17.2	6.1	14.1	15.9	4.1	3.3	4.6	12.2
	2002	38 222	19.5	7.1	17.8	5.9	14.0	15.6	4.2	3.2	4.5	12.2
Republic of Moldova[3]	1993	728	49.4	6.5	6.0	5.7	8.6	4.2	1.7	12.5	3.5	1.9
République de Moldova[3]	1996	5 243	42.9	6.6	5.0	2.9	9.9	9.3	1.4	12.6	2.2	7.2
Saudi Arabia[+]	1996	206 336	34.6[5]	7.8	14.7	9.2	0.9	17.9[11]	2.1	...	...	7.2
Arabie saoudite[+]	1997	206 185	34.7[5]	7.7	14.7	9.1	0.9	17.8[11]	2.1	...	...	7.0
	1998	198 574	37.3[5]	8.2	15.7	9.7	1.0	18.9[11]	2.2	...	...	7.2
Sierra Leone[+]	1984	3 970	...	4.0	15.1	3.3	1.0	...	...	...	...	...
Sierra Leone[+]	1985	6 199	...	3.1	15.0	2.7	0.9	...	...	...	...	...
	1986	15 972	...	2.8	14.1	2.2	1.1	...	...	...	...	...
Singapore	2003	69 869	10.8	3.7	17.3	6.7	5.9	20.9	11.5	2.7	8.1	12.5
Singapour	2004	75 140	10.6	3.7	16.1	6.5	6.7	21.2	11.8	2.6	8.3	12.6
	2005	78 061	10.6	3.7	15.9	6.7	7.1	20.2	11.7	2.6	8.6	13.0
Slovakia[3]	2002	633 660	27.6	4.2	22.8	5.3	2.6	13.2	9.1	0.8	8.0	6.3
Slovaquie[3]	2003	671 909	26.8	3.7	26.5	4.6	2.3	13.2	8.3	0.9	7.5	6.2
	2004	736 689	25.2	3.4	27.7	4.9	2.7	13.2	8.2	1.0	7.2	6.5
South Africa[3]	2002	722 091	26.6[5]	5.4	12.4	7.9	8.6	16.4[13]	4.4	3.1	3.0	12.3[15]
Afrique du Sud[3]	2003	785 632	26.9[5]	5.4	12.7	7.9	9.0	16.4[13]	4.3	3.1	3.1	11.3[15]
	2004	870 411	26.3[5]	5.7	12.7	7.8	8.9	16.7[13]	4.2	3.1	3.1	11.5[15]
Spain[3]	2002	445 491	17.9	6.0	15.8	5.5	3.4	14.3	9.2	1.6	18.1	8.5
Espagne[3]	2003	469 762	17.7	5.7	16.1	5.5	3.5	14.2	9.3	1.5	18.3	8.3
	2004	504 471	17.3	5.5	16.0	5.3	3.5	14.7	9.3	1.5	18.6	8.3
Sri Lanka[3]	2001	972 964	50.6	9.5	7.9	4.5	1.6	16.9	2.0	1.5	1.2	4.3
Sri Lanka[3]	2002	1 086 243	51.8	9.1	7.8	4.7	1.8	16.4	2.0	1.5	1.4	3.4
	2003	1 210 457	48.6	10.3	10.0	4.3	1.3	17.5[11]	3.5	...	...	4.5

21 Household consumption expenditure by purpose in current prices

Household consumption expenditure by purpose in current prices— Percentage distribution by divisions of the Classification of Individual Consumption according to Purpose (COICOP) (*continued*)

Dépenses de consommation des ménages par fonction aux prix courants— Répartition en pourcentage par divisions de la Nomenclature des fonctions de la consommation individuelle (COICOP) (*suite*)

Country or area Pays ou zone	Year Année	Total (mil. nat. curr.) Totale (millions monn. nat.)	Divisions of the Classification of Individual Consumption according to Purpose (COICOP) † Divisions de la Nomenclature des functions de la consommation individuelle (COICOP) †									
			Div. 01 + 02 (%)	Div. 03 (%)	Div. 04 (%)	Div. 05 (%)	Div. 06 (%)	Div. 07 + 08 (%)	Div. 09 (%)	Div. 10 (%)	Div. 11 (%)	Div. 12 (%)
Sudan Soudan	1981	5 386	62.8	5.6	15.8	4.6	5.2	...	...	...	...	...
	1982	7 897	60.4	7.5	15.3	5.6	5.3	...	...	...	...	...
	1983	9 385	64.7	5.3	15.2	5.5	4.1	...	...	...	...	...
Sweden[3] Suède[3]	2002	1 104 453	16.8	5.3	28.7	4.9	2.7	16.5	12.0	0.1	5.2	7.8
	2003	1 146 604	16.5	5.2	29.4	5.0	2.7	16.5	12.0	0.1	5.0	7.6
	2004	1 179 298	16.2	5.3	29.2	5.0	2.8	16.5	12.0	0.1	5.1	7.9
Switzerland[3] Suisse[3]	2002	251 021	14.5	4.2	23.6	4.7	14.3	10.3	8.6	0.5	7.6	11.7
	2003	254 468	14.8	4.0	23.5	4.6	14.7	10.2	8.6	0.5	7.4	11.8
	2004	260 548	14.7	3.9	23.6	4.6	14.9	10.2	8.5	0.5	7.4	11.7
Thailand Thaïlande	2002	3 316 645	30.0	10.0	8.3	6.5	6.5	15.7	6.6	1.0	9.1	6.2
	2003	3 583 547	30.7	9.3	8.1	6.5	6.5	16.7	6.5	1.0	8.3	6.4
	2004	3 906 833	30.5	8.5	7.9	6.5	6.5	17.2	6.8	1.0	8.7	6.5
Ukraine[3] Ukraine[3]	1997	50 617	...	...	7.4[19]	...	1.1[20]	4.9	0.2[21]	0.8	...	...
	1998	58 323	...	...	8.0[19]	...	0.9[20]	5.2	0.2[21]	1.3	...	...
	1999	71 310	...	...	7.2[19]	...	0.8[20]	5.9	0.2[21]	1.3	...	...
United Kingdom[3] Royaume-Uni[3]	2003	685 606	13.1	6.0	18.6	6.3	1.7	17.4	12.6	1.4	11.4	11.5
	2004	719 476	12.8	6.1	18.8	6.4	1.7	17.3	12.7	1.4	11.4	11.4
	2005	745 925	12.7	6.0	19.1	6.3	1.8	17.3	12.6	1.4	11.6	11.3
United States[3] Etats-Unis[3]	2002	7 355 900	9.2	4.8	17.6	4.9	18.3	13.5	9.1	2.6	6.0	14.1
	2003	7 710 400	9.1	4.7	17.5	4.8	18.8	13.4	9.0	2.6	6.1	14.1
	2004	8 214 200	9.1	4.6	17.3	4.8	19.0	13.2	9.0	2.6	6.2	14.2
Vanuatu Vanuatu	1987	8 198	47.6[5]	5.2	7.5	2.7	...	...	...	...	...	...
	1988	9 562	46.6[5]	5.5	7.4	2.7	...	...	...	...	...	...
	1989	10 545	46.0[5]	4.9	7.9	2.8	...	...	...	...	...	...
Venezuela (Bolivarian Rep. of)[3] Venezuela (Rép. bolivar. du)[3]	2001	47 751 600	29.2[22]	5.9	13.2	7.8	6.1	16.0	4.6	4.3	8.6	4.3
	2002	56 181 300	30.4[22]	4.8	13.5	7.5	6.1	15.5	4.4	4.5	9.0	4.4
	2003	71 735 000	32.5[22]	4.4	12.1	7.5	6.3	15.3	4.4	4.0	9.3	4.2
Zimbabwe Zimbabwe	1985	3 842	25.4[5]	11.6	17.1	7.8	4.2	...	1.4	5.2	9.0	7.1[15]
	1986	4 464	23.3[5]	10.7	15.7	11.8	5.3	...	0.6	5.3	9.0	7.4[15]
	1987	4 324	20.4[5]	10.3	15.4	12.9	7.1	...	0.6	6.0	8.7	7.9[15]

Source

United Nations Statistics Division, New York, national accounts database.

Notes

† COICOP Divisions:

- Div. 01+ 02: Food, beverages, tobacco and narcotics
- Div. 03: Clothing and footwear
- Div. 04: Housing, water, electricity, gas and other fuels
- Div. 05: Furnishings, household equipment and routine household maintenance
- Div. 06: Health
- Div. 07 + 08: Transport and communication
- Div. 09: Recreation and culture
- Div. 10: Education
- Div. 11: Restaurants and hotels
- Div. 12: Miscellaneous goods and services

+ The national accounts data generally relate to the fiscal year used in each country, unless indicated otherwise. Countries whose reference periods coincide with the calendar year ending 31 December are not listed below.

Source

Organisation des Nations Unies, Division de statistique, New York, base de données sur les comptes nationaux.

Notes

† Divisions de la COICOP:

- Div. 01 + 02: Alimentation, boissons, tabac et stupéfiants
- Div. 03: Articles d'habillement et chaussures
- Div. 04: Logement, eau, gaz, électricité et autres combustibles
- Div. 05: Meubles, articles de ménage et entretien courant de l'habitation
- Div. 06: Santé
- Div. 07 + 08: Transports et communication
- Div. 09: Loisirs et culture
- Div. 10: Enseignement
- Div. 11: Restaurants et hôtels
- Div. 12: Biens et services divers

+ Sauf indication contraire, les données sur les comptes nationaux concernent généralement l'exercice budgétaire utilisé dans chaque pays. Les pays où territoires dont la période de référence coïncide avec l'année civile se terminant le 31 décembre ne sont pas répertoriés ci-dessous.

Household consumption expenditure by purpose in current prices—Percentage distribution by divisions of the Classification of Individual Consumption according to Purpose (COICOP) (*continued*)

Dépenses de consommation des ménages par fonction aux prix courants—Répartition en pourcentage par divisions de la Nomenclature des fonctions de la consommation individuelle (COICOP) (*suite*)

- Year beginning 21 March: Afghanistan, Iran (Islamic Republic).
- Year beginning 1 April: Bermuda, India, Myanmar, New Zealand, Nigeria.
- Year beginning 1 July: Australia, Bangladesh, Cameroon, Gambia, Pakistan, Puerto Rico, Saudi Arabia, Sierra Leone, Sudan.
- Year ending 30 June: Botswana, Egypt, Swaziland, Tonga.
- Year ending 7 July: Ethiopia.
- Year ending 15 July: Nepal.
- Year ending 30 September: Haiti.

1 Alcoholic beverages, tobacco and narcotics only.
2 Communications only.
3 Data compiled in accordance with the concepts and definitions of the System of National Accounts 1993 (1993 SNA).
4 Beginning 2000, re-denomination of Belarusian roubles at 1 to 1000.
5 Food and non-alcoholic beverages only.
6 Including personal effects.
7 Including housing maintenance charges.
8 Including hotel expenditures.
9 Including restaurant expenditure.
10 Including transport and communication.
11 Transport only.
12 Including personal care.
13 Excluding communication which is included in "Miscellaneous goods and services".
14 Including expenditure on alcohol consumed in chartered clubs, taverns and hotels and restaurants.
15 Including communication.
16 Thousands.
17 Refers to water, electricity, gas and other fuels only.
18 Final consumption expenditure of resident households in the economic territory and the rest of the world.
19 Data refers to housing and communal services only.
20 Includes recreational, cultural and sporting activities, and social security.
21 Refers to culture, art, and mass media.
22 Excluding narcotics.

- Exercice commençant le 21 mars: Afghanistan, Iran (République islamique d').
- Exercice commençant le 1er avril: Bermudes, Inde, Myanmar, Nigéria, Nouvelle-Zélande.
- Exercice commençant le 1er juillet: Arabie saoudite, Australie, Bangladesh, Cameroun, Gambie, Pakistan, Porto Rico, Sierra Leone, Soudan.
- Exercice se terminant le 30 juin: Botswana, Égypte, Swaziland, Tonga.
- Exercice se terminant le 7 juillet: Éthiopie.
- Exercice se terminant le 15 juillet: Népal.
- Exercice se terminant le 30 septembre: Haïti.

1 Boissons alcoolisées, tabac et stupéfiants seulement.
2 Les communications seulement.
3 Données compilées selon les concepts et définitions du Système de comptabilité nationale de 1993 (SCN 1993).
4 A partir de 2000, instauration du nouveau rouble bélarussien par division par 1000 du rouble bélarussien ancien.
5 Alimentation et boissons non alcoolisées seulement.
6 Y compris effets personnels.
7 Y compris coût d'entretien du logement.
8 Y compris les dépenses d'hôtel.
9 Y compris les dépenses de restauration.
10 Y compris transports et communications.
11 Transports seulement.
12 Y compris les soins personnels.
13 À l'exclusion des communications, déjà incluses dans la rubrique "autres".
14 Y compris les dépenses consacrées à l'alcool consommé dans les clubs, les bars, les hôtels et restaurants.
15 Y compris communications.
16 En milliers.
17 Données provenant exclusivement l'eau, l'électricité, le gaz et les autres combustibles seulement.
18 Dépenses de consommation finale des ménages résidant dans le territoire économique et le reste du monde.
19 Les données concernent le logement et les services collectifs.
20 Y compris loisirs, affaires culturelles et sportives, et la sécurité sociale.
21 Concerne la culture, les arts et les médias.
22 À l'exclusion des stupéfiants.

22 Index numbers of industrial production

1995 = 100

Indices de la production industrielle

1995 = 100

Country or area and industry [ISIC Rev. 3] Pays ou zone et industrie [CITI Rév. 3]	1998	1999	2000	2001	2002	2003	2004	2005
Africa — Afrique								
Algeria — Algérie								
Total industry [CDE] Total, industrie [CDE]	95.7	96.0	97.3	97.0	98.1	99.3	99.7	101.1
Total mining [C] Total, industries extractives [C]	87.3	93.0	98.2	95.3	102.3	103.0	91.0	91.7
Total manufacturing [D] Total, industries manufacturières [D]	89.7	88.3	86.8	86.0	84.5	81.7	79.7	77.5
Food, beverages and tobacco — Aliments, boissons et tabac	107.1	105.5	96.1	84.0	68.0	53.9	45.5	39.0
Textiles, wearing apparel, leather, footwear Textiles, habillement, cuir et chaussures	69.5	51.0	45.7	41.3	43.6	43.0	39.0	38.8
Chemicals, petroleum, rubber and plastic products Prod. chimiques, pétroliers, caoutch. et plast.	99.7	103.8	104.8	108.8	106.0	104.3	93.6	93.6
Basic metals — Métaux de base	62.9	75.1	72.2	77.9	85.9	105.1	105.0	110.2
Metal products — Produits métalliques	64.7	72.0	74.5	85.5	82.6	79.0	87.2	82.9
Electricity [E] Electricité [E]	118.0	126.4	129.4	135.9	141.8	151.1	159.8	175.0
Burkina Faso — Burkina Faso								
Total industry [CDE] Total, industrie [CDE]	136.7	116.8	127.0	128.4	135.0	139.0	...	...
Cameroon[1] — Cameroun[1]								
Total industry [DE] Total, industrie [DE]	121.1	128.4	130.1	129.6	133.4	136.8	144.2	...
Total manufacturing [D] Total, industries manufacturières [D]	121.1	120.4	113.2	131.8	131.7	136.5	144.5	...
Electricity, gas and water [E] Electricité, gaz et eau [E]	121.0	127.0	128.3	118.1	133.2	139.9	147.1	...
Côte d'Ivoire — Côte d'Ivoire								
Total industry [CDE] Total, industrie [CDE]	138.8	143.2	132.0	126.5	121.0	114.8	118.4	127.1
Total mining [C] Total, industries extractives [C]	165.5	169.5	146.5	99.1	177.8	309.5	320.3	354.8
Total manufacturing [D] Total, industries manufacturières [D]	139.5	139.6	126.9	121.5	107.0	93.0	95.4	102.3
Food, beverages and tobacco — Aliments, boissons et tabac	127.1	139.5	133.0	130.2	108.9	...	...	...
Textiles and wearing apparel — Textiles et habillement	164.0	157.6	106.4	92.8	70.2	...	...	...
Chemicals, petroleum, rubber and plastic products Prod. chimiques, pétroliers, caoutch. et plast.	137.8	129.0	121.9	120.9	126.5	...	...	...
Metal products — Produits métalliques	112.8	106.5	89.5	76.2	83.4	...	...	...
Electricity and water [E] Electricité et eau [E]	134.7	157.0	156.5	159.7	172.5	165.0	172.8	183.2
Egypt[2] — Egypte[2]								
Total industry [CDE] Total, industrie [CDE]	127.2	134.6	132.8	138.2	146.6	180.6	198.2	...
Total mining [C] Total, industries extractives [C]	99.3	143.8	148.7	168.1	185.6	299.7	363.1	...
Total manufacturing [D] Total, industries manufacturières [D]	144.7	133.8	127.3	125.2	132.8	125.6	133.5	146.6
Food, beverages and tobacco — Aliments, boissons et tabac	147.1	153.1	170.5	127.1	126.3	109.7	110.1	108.4
Textiles and wearing apparel — Textiles et habillement	113.8	111.8	100.1	92.8	93.3	97.2	83.8	101.4
Chemicals, petroleum, rubber and plastic products Prod. chimiques, pétroliers, caoutch. et plast.	97.8	121.2	106.6	125.6	130.2	152.4	144.8	171.4
Basic metals — Métaux de base	139.0	156.3	164.2	146.5	167.0	232.8	183.0	152.8
Metal products — Produits métalliques	236.8	173.3	163.0	143.7	154.2	136.4	139.0	138.6
Electricity, gas and water [E] Electricité, gaz et eau [E]	117.3	127.1	137.4	151.6	181.9	197.1	212.2	...

Country or area and industry [ISIC Rev. 3] Pays ou zone et industrie [CITI Rév. 3]	1998	1999	2000	2001	2002	2003	2004	2005
Ethiopia[2] — Ethiopie[2]								
Total industry [CDE] Total, industrie [CDE]	107.2	116.1	120.9	126.2	128.7	131.5	139.4	147.0
Total mining [C] Total, industries extractives [C]	115.2	105.3	117.2	118.0	133.6	143.4	154.9	167.2
Total manufacturing [D] Total, industries manufacturières [D]	105.0	118.4	122.7	128.9	126.6	127.5	134.4	141.1
Electricity [E] Electricité [E]	111.0	112.8	117.3	121.2	132.9	138.6	148.3	157.2
Gabon — Gabon								
Total industry [DE] Total, industrie [DE]	118.4	121.8	114.1	127.5	133.1	131.0	133.8	142.3
Total manufacturing [D] Total, industries manufacturières [D]	115.8	121.7	110.5	125.3	129.1	120.8	122.4	137.9
Food, beverages and tobacco — Aliments, boissons et tabac	111.0	105.1	114.1	128.3	120.2	115.0	112.8	...
Chemicals and petroleum products Produits chimiques et pétroliers	131.8	141.0	110.7	119.6	150.9	121.0	127.1	...
Electricity and water [E] Electricité et eau [E]	121.8	121.8	118.5	130.3	138.2	143.8	148.1	157.6
Ghana — Ghana								
Total industry [CDE][3] Total, industrie [CDE][3]	103.3	109.3	110.9	138.3	138.4	138.0	...	...
Total mining [C] Total, industries extractives [C]	140.8	158.8	153.8	154.9	147.7	154.9	146.7	156.4
Total manufacturing [D] Total, industries manufacturières [D]	94.3	98.4	101.7	136.7	139.6	141.0	...	...
Food, beverages and tobacco — Aliments, boissons et tabac	107.6	101.4	102.0	156.4	190.9	197.7	...	...
Textiles, wearing apparel, leather, footwear Textiles, habillement, cuir et chaussures	102.0	102.2	102.6	105.5	109.5	123.0	...	...
Chemicals, petroleum, rubber and plastic products Prod. chimiques, pétroliers, caoutch. et plast.	90.3	97.5	106.0	100.8	106.9	110.2	...	...
Basic metals — Métaux de base	114.1	133.1	133.2	92.1	76.7	84.5	...	...
Metal products — Produits métalliques	121.8	119.7	119.8	117.7	96.1	97.9	...	...
Electricity [E] Electricité [E]	115.9	119.6	117.8	128.1	118.9	96.2	98.5	...
Kenya — Kenya								
Total industry [CD][3] Total, industrie [CD][3]	120.9	108.5	106.7	108.0	108.7	110.4	118.3	125.0
Total mining [C] Total, industries extractives [C]	110.6	122.3	110.6	138.2	114.3	121.0	152.4	172.6
Total manufacturing [D] Total, industries manufacturières [D]	121.2	108.2	106.6	107.3	108.6	110.1	117.5	123.9
Food, beverages and tobacco — Aliments, boissons et tabac	99.6	97.2	95.5	95.3	99.4	100.5	111.7	116.2
Textiles, wearing apparel, leather, footwear Textiles, habillement, cuir et chaussures	89.4	87.7	89.9	91.8	101.3	96.2	87.4	94.8
Chemicals, petroleum, rubber and plastic products Prod. chimiques, pétroliers, caoutch. et plast.	121.5	125.8	133.2	144.2	144.3	167.5	178.7	191.0
Metal products — Produits métalliques	100.1	95.1	84.5	84.9	97.8	98.9	133.4	124.6
Madagascar — Madagascar								
Total industry [CDE] Total, industrie [CDE]	123.9	129.0	147.8	158.9	129.4	165.4	171.5	192.6
Total mining [C] Total, industries extractives [C]	124.8	75.2	109.2	108.6	74.0	87.6	91.3	105.1
Total manufacturing [D] Total, industries manufacturières [D]	124.5	131.0	148.3	160.9	124.9	166.7	173.0	192.5
Food, beverages and tobacco — Aliments, boissons et tabac	107.6	131.8	139.1	150.6	132.2	160.1	163.8	190.1
Textiles, wearing apparel, leather, footwear Textiles, habillement, cuir et chaussures	97.8	112.6	109.0	130.5	78.6	100.1	102.0	126.6
Chemicals, petroleum, rubber and plastic products Prod. chimiques, pétroliers, caoutch. et plast.	146.7	145.9	163.8	184.2	114.3	195.4	203.4	176.9

Country or area and industry [ISIC Rev. 3] Pays ou zone et industrie [CITI Rév. 3]	1998	1999	2000	2001	2002	2003	2004	2005
Metal products — Produits métalliques	129.7	133.5	113.1	126.8	105.2	124.1	121.2	172.1
Electricity, gas and water [E] Electricité, gaz et eau [E]	121.1	129.7	152.4	159.0	158.0	177.0	182.5	217.8
Malawi — Malawi								
Total industry [DE] Total, industrie [DE]	99.4	90.4	91.2	81.8	81.9	79.7	85.9	140.6
Total manufacturing [D] Total, industries manufacturières [D]	94.4	81.2	80.2	68.1	68.2	66.1	71.9	80.4
Food, beverages and tobacco — Aliments, boissons et tabac	65.1	50.0	48.5	43.4	41.4	34.3	47.7	43.3
Textiles, wearing apparel, leather, footwear Textiles, habillement, cuir et chaussures	181.8	222.5	137.3	111.9	60.7	60.9	92.2	102.1
Electricity and water [E] Electricité et eau [E]	120.3	118.7	128.1	131.6	137.7	134.7	142.7	155.3
Mali — Mali								
Total industry [DE] Total, industrie [DE]	140.2	133.4	145.5	160.1	188.4	202.5	218.7	238.1
Food, beverages and tobacco — Aliments, boissons et tabac	104.3	98.7	106.1	106.7	110.1	110.6	101.1	129.8
Wearing apparel — Habillement	146.9	128.0	111.6	96.3	182.2	133.5	169.1	158.6
Chemicals and chemical products — Produits chimiques	101.2	91.3	83.8	70.2	71.4	68.5	65.6	58.8
Mauritius — Maurice								
Total industry [CDE] Total, industrie [CDE]	118.6	121.8	132.9	139.8	136.8	136.1	135.3	126.5
Total mining [C] Total, industries extractives [C]	113.5	116.9	120.4	113.4	57.8	58.3	58.6	56.5
Total manufacturing [D] Total, industries manufacturières [D]	119.7	122.4	132.9	139.2	136.1	134.1	132.7	122.4
Food, beverages and tobacco — Aliments, boissons et tabac	113.7	108.5	121.3	127.8	129.1	134.8	144.4	141.6
Textiles, wearing apparel, leather, footwear Textiles, habillement, cuir et chaussures	121.9	129.3	137.1	142.8	133.1	124.3	111.7	96.0
Chemicals, petroleum, rubber and plastic products Prod. chimiques, pétroliers, caoutch. et plast.	114.0	120.9	130.3	130.9	133.1	162.5	142.1	119.3
Basic metals — Métaux de base	118.2	124.1	130.3	137.6	161.8	145.9	146.6	150.4
Metal products — Produits métalliques	119.1	124.8	130.2	131.8	130.4	162.5	221.5	111.4
Electricity, gas and water [E] Electricité, gaz et eau [E]	128.5	139.6	171.9	190.3	193.2	209.0	217.5	227.2
Morocco — Maroc								
Total industry [CDE][3] Total, industrie [CDE][3]	110.6	111.8	114.6	119.7	123.8	128.1	133.1	139.7
Total mining [C][4] Total, industries extractives [C][4]	109.8	107.5	103.8	106.3	109.0	104.3	112.7	120.1
Total manufacturing [D][5] Total, industries manufacturières [D][5]	110.2	112.7	116.6	120.4	124.0	128.3	132.2	135.6
Food, beverages and tobacco — Aliments, boissons et tabac	112.4	114.6	120.6	130.0	131.6	136.5	146.3	149.6
Textiles, wearing apparel, leather, footwear Textiles, habillement, cuir et chaussures	110.7	109.2	110.5	109.1	108.9	105.8	105.1	103.2
Chemicals, petroleum, rubber and plastic products Prod. chimiques, pétroliers, caoutch. et plast.	109.5	116.5	118.1	123.3	127.8	126.0	133.2	136.8
Basic metals — Métaux de base	109.3	122.0	122.2	130.8	152.1	170.5	168.4	192.5
Metal products — Produits métalliques	103.0	109.6	114.9	120.1	123.3	130.4	133.4	135.4
Electricity [E] Electricité [E]	112.6	109.7	111.1	126.6	135.8	147.6	156.7	183.8
Senegal — Sénégal								
Total industry [CDE] Total, industrie [CDE]	102.9	104.4	99.7	100.5	125.6	130.7	145.8	148.4
Total mining [C] Total, industries extractives [C]	104.5	122.4	123.7	107.8	120.0	154.6	140.3	119.6
Total manufacturing [D][3] Total, industries manufacturières [D][3]	100.1	99.6	91.7	90.0	123.9	121.3	142.7	143.9
Food, beverages and tobacco — Aliments, boissons et tabac	95.2	96.5	93.7	77.4	94.6	102.4	129.7	139.1
Textiles — Textiles	101.0	82.2	79.2	98.9	50.2	70.9	56.9	52.6

Country or area and industry [ISIC Rev. 3] Pays ou zone et industrie [CITI Rév. 3]	1998	1999	2000	2001	2002	2003	2004	2005
Chemicals, petroleum, rubber and plastic products Prod. chimiques, pétroliers, caoutch. et plast.	108.5	79.5	101.3	84.6	124.0	115.8	117.1	106.0
Metal products — Produits métalliques	92.2	89.7	91.4	43.8	75.1	76.6	76.5	69.2
Electricity and water [E] Electricité et eau [E]	113.0	116.1	121.3	137.2	133.4	157.6	159.3	194.2
South Africa — Afrique du Sud								
Total industry [CDE][3] Total, industrie [CDE][3]	102.8	101.8	104.5	106.7	110.8	111.1	116.3	118.7
Total mining [C] Total, industries extractives [C]	99.2	97.2	95.8	97.1	97.9	101.9	107.8	107.0
Total manufacturing [D] Total, industries manufacturières [D]	102.8	102.2	106.0	109.0	113.9	111.8	116.6	120.7
Food and beverages — Aliments et boissons	103.1	101.8	99.0	104.0	101.0	102.9	110.7	117.5
Textiles, wearing apparel, leather, footwear Textiles, habillement, cuir et chaussures	89.9	89.4	87.2	84.5	90.2	83.6	87.3	85.3
Chemicals, petroleum, rubber and plastic products Prod. chimiques, pétroliers, caoutch. et plast.	102.4	105.6	106.8	110.9	120.2	113.9	118.2	122.1
Basic metals — Métaux de base	112.3	114.8	135.2	134.0	140.5	143.4	148.9	143.5
Metal products — Produits métalliques	100.5	99.0	106.4	113.1	120.6	117.0	120.5	396.9
Electricity [E] Electricité [E]	110.0	108.8	112.9	112.5	118.2	125.4	131.0	131.2
Swaziland — Swaziland								
Total industry [CDE][3] Total, industrie [CDE][3]	114.1	109.7	109.6	110.7	127.4	132.4	139.2	...
Total mining [C] Total, industries extractives [C]	99.6	85.6	65.9	52.8	59.0	46.8	51.4	...
Total manufacturing [D] Total, industries manufacturières [D]	114.0	109.0	110.1	111.1	128.0	133.5	141.1	...
Electricity, gas and water [E] Electricité, gaz et eau [E]	120.4	126.4	117.9	124.4	142.0	145.4	141.9	...
Tunisia — Tunisie								
Total industry [CDE] Total, industrie [CDE]	114.6	120.7	128.3	136.0	135.8	135.6	142.1	143.5
Total mining [C] Total, industries extractives [C]	109.8	112.9	109.6	106.1	106.9	101.8	106.1	107.6
Total manufacturing [D] Total, industries manufacturières [D]	115.9	122.5	133.2	144.1	143.0	143.5	150.5	151.2
Food, beverages and tobacco — Aliments, boissons et tabac	117.9	132.7	143.4	144.1	152.2	156.1	166.0	164.0
Textiles, wearing apparel, leather, footwear Textiles, habillement, cuir et chaussures	114.6	117.8	133.0	147.7	144.1	136.6	135.8	128.8
Chemicals, petroleum, rubber and plastic products Prod. chimiques, pétroliers, caoutch. et plast.	108.1	108.3	112.1	113.0	116.1	114.4	113.2	107.6
Basic metals — Métaux de base	100.3	119.6	124.5	118.5	96.2	78.6	64.8	73.8
Metal products — Produits métalliques	129.9	141.3	153.7	169.9	172.1	181.6	201.1	224.0
Electricity and water [E] Electricité et eau [E]	114.5	124.7	131.7	140.3	146.7	154.1	161.7	168.8
Uganda — Ouganda								
Total manufacturing [D] Total, industries manufacturières [D]	153.5	165.1	164.4	195.0	200.8	208.5	232.4	...
Food, beverages and tobacco — Aliments, boissons et tabac	138.8	148.5	82.2	147.1	159.6	172.2	185.1	...
Textiles, wearing apparel, leather, footwear Textiles, habillement, cuir et chaussures	148.2	155.9	121.1	87.6	110.5	105.8	103.3	...
Chemicals, rubber and plastic prod. Prod. chimiques, caoutchouc et plastiques	174.8	192.1	199.1	227.0	200.5	224.5	228.5	...
Basic metals — Métaux de base	280.7	319.3	286.8	307.3	523.8	456.8	574.2	...
Metal products — Produits métalliques	81.9	73.1	65.6	58.3	103.9	64.0	108.1	...
United Rep. of Tanzania — Rép.-Unie de Tanzanie								
Total manufacturing [D] Total, industries manufacturières [D]	115.4	119.2	137.0	142.6	163.8	185.5	200.0	214.7
Food, beverages and tobacco — Aliments, boissons et tabac	139.8	130.5	156.4	167.2	173.6	221.9	222.3	254.7

Country or area and industry [ISIC Rev. 3] Pays ou zone et industrie [CITI Rév. 3]	1998	1999	2000	2001	2002	2003	2004	2005
Textiles, leather and footwear — Textiles, cuir et chaussures	104.6	106.0	185.4	241.9	341.6	836.6	1 799.0	4 653.0
Chemicals, rubber and plastic prod. Prod. chimiques, caoutchouc et plastiques	80.0	86.6	138.1	127.6	112.1	206.3	226.8	272.6
Basic metals — Métaux de base	81.3	16.7	127.0	134.9	178.9	209.7	206.8	210.8
Metal products — Produits métalliques	122.3	132.1	120.3	113.5	102.1	117.1	95.9	98.9
Zambia — Zambie								
Total industry [CDE] Total, industrie [CDE]	103.8	91.0	93.3	98.1	96.7	105.5	114.7	124.4
Total mining [C] Total, industries extractives [C]	129.5	92.8	96.1	109.5	107.1	121.8	141.9	161.8
Total manufacturing [D] Total, industries manufacturières [D]	82.0	87.5	95.4	91.9	92.9	100.6	106.2	110.5
Food, beverages and tobacco — Aliments, boissons et tabac	52.2	57.2	57.6	64.8	70.3	74.5	78.9	81.7
Textiles and wearing apparel — Textiles et habillement	166.5	185.0	189.1	128.6	136.6	140.9	138.3	134.3
Chemicals, petroleum, rubber and plastic products Prod. chimiques, pétroliers, caoutch. et plast.	115.6	123.1	173.7	118.0	128.2	138.3	147.7	152.4
Basic metals — Métaux de base	74.3	77.5	80.8	45.7	47.7	54.9	56.6	55.4
Metal products — Produits métalliques	69.5	57.9	64.4	61.4	45.7	54.2	56.8	61.1
Electricity and water [E] Electricité et eau [E]	93.5	94.6	96.1	110.9	102.7	102.6	99.5	105.7
Zimbabwe — Zimbabwe								
Total industry [CDE][3] Total, industrie [CDE][3]	109.9	103.2	96.6	87.8	79.7	72.6	...	...
Total mining [C] Total, industries extractives [C]	108.6	103.4	95.0	81.7	83.5	83.0	...	...
Total manufacturing [D] Total, industries manufacturières [D]	112.0	103.7	97.4	88.6	76.1	69.3	61.0	...
Food, beverages and tobacco — Aliments, boissons et tabac	111.8	101.6	108.8	90.2	71.5	63.2	56.8	...
Textiles, wearing apparel, leather, footwear Textiles, habillement, cuir et chaussures	137.7	148.3	132.2	130.0	103.3	73.4	85.1	...
Chemicals, petroleum, rubber and plastic products Prod. chimiques, pétroliers, caoutch. et plast.	120.0	107.0	75.5	75.4	78.6	67.5	66.4	...
Basic metals and metal products Métaux de base et produits métalliques	81.1	78.7	76.7	68.4	59.5	62.4	48.3	...
Electricity [E] Electricité [E]	87.3	94.6	93.2	104.5	112.7	115.5	127.1	...
America, North · Amérique du Nord								
Barbados — Barbade								
Total industry [CDE] Total, industrie [CDE]	112.1	112.9	111.1	104.3	104.8	104.0	106.0	...
Total mining [C] Total, industries extractives [C]	126.8	155.4	122.6	102.8	86.8	81.8	78.6	...
Total manufacturing [D] Total, industries manufacturières [D]	109.1	107.2	106.5	98.3	98.8	97.8	99.3	...
Food, beverages and tobacco — Aliments, boissons et tabac	114.5	112.7	109.8	106.7	109.0	108.8	109.0	...
Wearing apparel — Habillement	69.2	65.0	69.9	44.1	32.9	30.8	32.2	...
Chemicals and petroleum products Produits chimiques et pétroliers	105.3	104.7	83.8	78.7	75.5	72.8	91.9	...
Metal products — Produits métalliques	87.5	80.8	78.9	54.9	53.7	47.0	51.9	...
Electricity and gas [E] Electricité et gaz [E]	117.3	123.6	123.5	128.0	130.2	133.7	136.8	...
Belize — Belize								
Total industry [DE] Total, industrie [DE]	105.0	105.0	120.0	120.2	115.7	...	...	...
Total manufacturing [D] Total, industries manufacturières [D]	101.8	107.2	125.4	125.2	119.6	...	...	...
Food, beverages and tobacco — Aliments, boissons et tabac	102.4	107.0	124.8	125.3	119.6	...	...	...
Wearing apparel — Habillement	108.6	108.4	89.1	76.3	59.9	...	...	...
Chemicals and chemical products — Produits chimiques	80.1	94.8	87.5	89.2	102.2	...	...	...
Metal products — Produits métalliques	54.6	46.3	40.2	31.0	29.4	...	...	...

Country or area and industry [ISIC Rev. 3] Pays ou zone et industrie [CITI Rév. 3]	1998	1999	2000	2001	2002	2003	2004	2005
Electricity and water [E] Electricité et eau [E]	122.3	93.1	91.4	93.3	94.6	...	...	...
Canada — Canada								
Total industry [CDE] Total, industrie [CDE]	109.9	116.1	125.9	121.2	123.3	124.0	126.4	128.0
Total mining [C] Total, industries extractives [C]	105.7	105.5	108.8	108.9	111.5	117.4	121.1	121.9
Total manufacturing [D] Total, industries manufacturières [D]	113.0	121.8	135.0	128.6	129.7	129.0	131.3	132.5
Food, beverages and tobacco — Aliments, boissons et tabac	105.2	104.8	109.0	114.6	114.1	112.5	114.8	116.6
Textiles, wearing apparel, leather, footwear Textiles, habillement, cuir et chaussures	106.2	104.0	120.0	114.6	110.6	102.1	95.6	86.5
Chemicals, petroleum, rubber and plastic products Prod. chimiques, pétroliers, caoutch. et plast.	101.8	106.4	117.8	119.7	125.8	128.2	131.6	131.2
Basic metals — Métaux de base	116.3	120.5	130.5	127.8	133.7	129.5	131.5	135.2
Metal products — Produits métalliques	116.5	134.4	155.3	135.5	130.0	130.9	134.0	137.5
Electricity, gas and water [E] Electricité, gaz et eau [E]	99.6	100.9	101.4	99.0	105.8	107.6	108.4	113.2
Costa Rica — Costa Rica								
Total industry [DE][3] Total, industrie [DE][3]	120.1	146.3	143.9	133.6	138.5	149.9	153.7	171.7
Total manufacturing [D] Total, industries manufacturières [D]	120.5	150.3	145.9	132.7	137.1	148.7	154.0	172.3
Food, beverages and tobacco — Aliments, boissons et tabac	115.9	118.7	117.3	112.7	110.1	112.2	111.3	110.9
Textiles, wearing apparel, leather, footwear Textiles, habillement, cuir et chaussures	91.5	83.1	74.1	67.0	65.8	63.5	66.1	65.9
Chemicals, petroleum, rubber and plastic products Prod. chimiques, pétroliers, caoutch. et plast.	100.1	100.6	103.4	106.1	115.8	119.9	120.2	126.3
Metal products — Produits métalliques	113.8	112.1	108.4	98.9	106.4	106.2	110.3	114.7
Electricity and water [E] Electricité et eau [E]	117.7	125.0	133.0	138.5	145.8	154.4	160.6	168.3
Cuba — Cuba								
Total industry [CDE] Total, industrie [CDE]	111.4	118.7	125.0	125.7	121.1	117.2	118.2	...
Total mining [C] Total, industries extractives [C]	121.8	163.7	191.9	194.8	227.9	235.6	218.0	...
Total manufacturing [D] Total, industries manufacturières [D]	113.4	116.7	122.7	125.5	117.3	120.8	121.6	...
Food, beverages and tobacco — Aliments, boissons et tabac	116.5	127.1	127.4	137.2	130.6	123.3	...	...
Textiles, wearing apparel, leather, footwear Textiles, habillement, cuir et chaussures	122.5	132.8	115.9	118.3	88.2	87.3	...	...
Chemicals, petroleum, rubber and plastic products Prod. chimiques, pétroliers, caoutch. et plast.	94.6	94.4	115.6	113.5	94.9	103.4	...	...
Basic metals — Métaux de base	149.9	147.8	155.9	160.4	155.6	145.8	...	...
Metal products — Produits métalliques	110.1	136.8	102.7	114.4	103.3	96.8	...	...
Electricity and water [E] Electricité et eau [E]	113.4	116.3	120.5	122.7	125.9	126.8	125.6	...
Dominican Republic — Rép. dominicaine								
Total industry [CDE] Total, industrie [CDE]	115.5	121.9	131.6	130.8	136.0	132.5	130.5	136.6
Total mining [C] Total, industries extractives [C]	88.8	87.4	99.0	83.6	81.3	88.4	91.7	90.2
Total manufacturing [D] Total, industries manufacturières [D]	117.1	124.2	133.6	131.8	137.1	133.4	134.3	141.5
Electricity and water [E] Electricité et eau [E]	138.2	149.4	159.8	189.2	203.9	186.7	150.1	157.0
El Salvador — El Salvador								
Total industry [CDE] Total, industrie [CDE]	117.5	121.7	126.4	131.7	135.6	138.8	139.5	141.7
Total mining [C] Total, industries extractives [C]	113.2	113.7	108.4	121.1	127.7	132.9	110.9	114.6

Country or area and industry [ISIC Rev. 3] Pays ou zone et industrie [CITI Rév. 3]	1998	1999	2000	2001	2002	2003	2004	2005
Total manufacturing [D] Total, industries manufacturières [D]	117.2	121.5	126.5	131.6	135.4	138.5	139.7	141.7
Food and beverages — Aliments et boissons	111.4	114.3	118.0	123.0	123.9	125.0	142.7	145.7
Textiles, wearing apparel, leather, footwear Textiles, habillement, cuir et chaussures	108.4	111.7	113.7	106.4	107.6	112.7	114.8	116.2
Chemicals, petroleum, rubber and plastic products Prod. chimiques, pétroliers, caoutch. et plast.	114.4	124.2	121.7	127.3	130.3	131.8	128.5	133.5
Basic metals and metal products Métaux de base et produits métalliques	129.9	132.3	135.3	139.4	142.9	145.2	153.2	161.1
Electricity [E] Electricité [E]	156.8	160.2	146.0	155.9	167.3	174.9	177.2	186.9
Haiti[6] — Haïti[6]								
Total industry [DE][3] Total, industrie [DE][3]	112.2	115.2	120.8	114.8	116.6	122.6	124.5	130.9
Total manufacturing [D] Total, industries manufacturières [D]	107.4	110.9	118.2	120.9	122.9	128.1	130.1	137.7
Food, beverages and tobacco — Aliments, boissons et tabac	112.0	149.8	173.4	179.8	182.5	183.4	187.1	205.4
Chemicals and chemical products — Produits chimiques	101.7	101.9	104.7	108.3	110.9	126.9	125.4	132.1
Electricity [E] Electricité [E]	130.7	132.0	130.8	91.0	92.2	101.3	102.9	104.5
Honduras — Honduras								
Total industry [CDE] Total, industrie [CDE]	117.1	120.3	127.5	132.0	137.4	143.8	149.4	158.8
Total mining [C] Total, industries extractives [C]	116.7	122.9	125.0	124.0	129.2	133.3	130.2	135.4
Total manufacturing [D] Total, industries manufacturières [D]	114.8	117.8	124.3	130.8	135.7	140.7	146.4	153.9
Food, beverages and tobacco — Aliments, boissons et tabac	162.9	180.0	195.9	213.5	228.9	244.1	259.5	278.2
Textiles, wearing apparel, leather, footwear Textiles, habillement, cuir et chaussures	193.6	221.4	246.3	271.7	289.4	306.9	328.2	348.8
Chemicals, petroleum, rubber and plastic products Prod. chimiques, pétroliers, caoutch. et plast.	151.2	169.5	186.1	199.3	212.8	228.2	247.2	264.0
Basic metals — Métaux de base	143.7	155.9	174.8	194.0	208.3	224.6	243.4	263.7
Metal products — Produits métalliques	153.4	174.4	193.1	211.8	227.4	244.9	264.7	284.1
Electricity, gas and water [E] Electricité, gaz et eau [E]	130.2	132.9	147.0	144.3	152.3	167.8	178.5	201.3
Mexico — Mexique								
Total industry [CDE][7] Total, industrie [CDE][7]	128.0	134.0	142.0	137.2	137.0	136.7	142.4	144.7
Total mining [C] Total, industries extractives [C]	116.0	113.6	117.9	119.6	120.1	124.5	128.9	130.4
Total manufacturing [D] Total, industries manufacturières [D]	130.8	136.4	145.8	140.2	139.3	137.5	143.0	144.8
Food, beverages and tobacco — Aliments, boissons et tabac	113.7	118.3	122.9	125.8	128.2	130.4	134.8	137.6
Textiles and wearing apparel — Textiles et habillement	132.6	136.9	144.2	131.9	124.2	115.7	119.1	115.9
Chemicals, petroleum, rubber and plastic products Prod. chimiques, pétroliers, caoutch. et plast.	120.7	123.5	127.6	122.7	122.3	124.2	128.1	130.0
Basic metals — Métaux de base	137.3	137.8	141.9	131.8	133.5	139.0	148.5	149.5
Metal products — Produits métalliques	162.4	173.6	197.2	183.6	179.8	171.1	179.9	182.1
Electricity [E] Electricité [E]	112.1	129.8	133.7	136.7	138.1	140.2	144.1	146.2
Panama — Panama								
Total industry [CDE][3] Total, industrie [CDE][3]	111.0	112.0	111.6	105.1	108.8	110.6	113.9	116.6
Total mining [C] Total, industries extractives [C]	179.2	214.6	190.6	184.7	215.9	269.6	301.7	303.8
Total manufacturing [D] Total, industries manufacturières [D]	109.9	105.3	100.0	93.4	94.7	96.0	96.6	98.7
Food, beverages and tobacco — Aliments, boissons et tabac	119.7	111.8	108.3	106.9	106.9	108.4	109.6	113.5
Textiles, wearing apparel, leather, footwear Textiles, habillement, cuir et chaussures	80.4	68.9	62.1	56.1	47.0	35.0	29.8	25.7

Country or area and industry [ISIC Rev. 3] Pays ou zone et industrie [CITI Rév. 3]	1998	1999	2000	2001	2002	2003	2004	2005
Chemicals, petroleum, rubber and plastic products Prod. chimiques, pétroliers, caoutch. et plast.	96.9	88.3	84.5	74.2	76.2	76.4	69.5	70.4
Basic metals — Métaux de base	124.3	177.1	135.6	55.1	69.9	70.6	77.0	71.9
Metal products — Produits métalliques	117.1	113.0	120.4	111.0	70.3	67.1	71.7	76.7
Electricity and water [E] Electricité et eau [E]	112.4	126.0	137.7	131.3	140.1	142.2	151.5	155.6
Trinidad and Tobago — Trinité-et-Tobago								
Total industry [DE] Total, industrie [DE]	125.3	139.0	146.4	157.6	187.7	205.5	218.0	240.1
Total manufacturing [D][3] Total, industries manufacturières [D][3]	125.8	140.1	148.7	162.2	193.3	213.7	226.9	250.5
Food, beverages and tobacco — Aliments, boissons et tabac	174.0	183.3	234.2	267.4	222.4	227.5	269.3	322.5
Textiles, leather and footwear — Textiles, cuir et chaussures	180.8	364.1	458.0	434.1	447.1	724.8	847.8	1 000.0
Chemicals and petroleum products Produits chimiques et pétroliers	175.6	236.6	270.6	264.1	361.5	477.1	568.7	796.9
Metal products — Produits métalliques	154.3	154.4	155.5	172.2	208.8	264.4	455.2	550.7
Electricity [E] Electricité [E]	120.1	127.1	121.5	106.4	125.9	114.4	119.5	125.3
United States — Etats-Unis								
Total industry [CDE] Total, industrie [CDE]	118.3	123.8	129.2	124.6	124.7	125.4	130.5	134.9
Total mining [C] Total, industries extractives [C]	101.9	96.9	99.1	100.1	95.8	95.6	95.3	93.3
Total manufacturing [D] Total, industries manufacturières [D]	120.9	127.3	133.2	127.6	127.7	128.5	134.6	140.0
Food, beverages and tobacco — Aliments, boissons et tabac	104.8	104.0	105.5	105.4	106.7	106.9	108.6	111.2
Textiles, wearing apparel, leather, footwear Textiles, habillement, cuir et chaussures	96.4	94.1	91.0	79.2	71.6	67.4	65.2	63.8
Chemicals, petroleum, rubber and plastic products Prod. chimiques, pétroliers, caoutch. et plast.	112.0	113.8	114.8	111.4	117.8	117.7	122.4	123.7
Basic metals — Métaux de base	108.6	108.3	104.8	94.8	95.7	93.4	98.9	96.3
Metal products — Produits métalliques	152.8	183.3	224.0	220.5	216.9	240.8	278.6	324.6
Electricity and gas [E] Electricité et gaz [E]	105.5	108.6	111.7	111.2	114.7	117.0	118.2	121.3
America, South · Amérique du Sud								
Argentina — Argentine								
Total manufacturing [D] Total, industries manufacturières [D]	115.9	103.8	101.8	90.4	81.6	95.8	109.3	119.4
Food, beverages and tobacco — Aliments, boissons et tabac	107.3	107.2	103.5	94.5	90.0	101.5	112.4	120.1
Textiles, wearing apparel, leather, footwear Textiles, habillement, cuir et chaussures	98.7	78.2	78.2	67.1	56.1	76.6	85.7	94.4
Chemicals, petroleum, rubber and plastic products Prod. chimiques, pétroliers, caoutch. et plast.	117.1	111.4	112.2	102.8	98.4	109.9	117.9	125.4
Basic metals — Métaux de base	129.5	99.7	103.4	97.5	103.2	114.8	126.3	135.3
Metal products — Produits métalliques	120.0	91.6	88.4	73.2	58.7	75.7	96.2	110.0
Bolivia — Bolivie								
Total industry [CDE][3] Total, industrie [CDE][3]	109.8	104.6	104.1	102.2	102.6	104.7	103.6	...
Total mining [C] Total, industries extractives [C]	106.7	95.1	93.6	90.5	90.7	91.4	85.5	...
Total manufacturing [D] Total, industries manufacturières [D]	112.0	113.4	113.8	113.0	113.3	117.0	121.1	...
Food, beverages and tobacco — Aliments, boissons et tabac	111.8	114.9	119.7	122.5	126.2	128.7	129.7	...
Textiles, wearing apparel, leather, footwear Textiles, habillement, cuir et chaussures	103.5	92.9	95.7	81.9	77.5	86.5	87.8	...
Chemicals, petroleum, rubber and plastic products Prod. chimiques, pétroliers, caoutch. et plast.	123.5	122.0	113.3	110.8	111.5	118.2	138.9	...
Basic metals — Métaux de base	84.7	87.1	90.5	79.1	82.4	89.2	90.0	...
Metal products — Produits métalliques	95.0	88.2	75.6	69.7	60.4	48.9	51.3	...
Electricity, gas and water [E] Electricité, gaz et eau [E]	126.2	131.6	135.6	136.5	141.7	143.8	148.0	...

Country or area and industry [ISIC Rev. 3] Pays ou zone et industrie [CITI Rév. 3]	1998	1999	2000	2001	2002	2003	2004	2005
Brazil — Brésil								
Total industry [CD] Total, industrie [CD]	103.4	102.9	109.6	111.3	114.4	114.4	124.0	127.8
Total mining [C] Total, industries extractives [C]	131.4	142.5	159.4	164.9	196.1	205.3	214.1	235.9
Total manufacturing [D] Total, industries manufacturières [D]	101.3	99.7	105.8	107.2	107.8	107.5	116.7	119.9
Food, beverages and tobacco — Aliments, boissons et tabac	106.3	108.7	106.6	110.8	108.9	106.5	111.8	113.9
Textiles, wearing apparel, leather, footwear Textiles, habillement, cuir et chaussures	85.1	84.4	89.5	83.6	85.0	78.1	82.8	80.1
Chemicals, petroleum, rubber and plastic products Prod. chimiques, pétroliers, caoutch. et plast.	111.8	112.7	114.2	112.6	111.0	109.6	114.9	116.5
Basic metals and metal products Métaux de base et produits métalliques	104.9	103.5	113.2	113.4	117.5	124.6	128.7	126.2
Metal products — Produits métalliques	96.7	94.0	108.1	117.2	124.4	128.9	147.1	151.7
Chile — Chili								
Total industry [CDE][3] Total, industrie [CDE][3]	118.8	124.9	130.1	132.2	132.9	140.6	152.8	158.2
Total mining [C] Total, industries extractives [C]	142.5	164.6	173.7	176.4	170.2	181.3	199.6	197.9
Total manufacturing [D] Total, industries manufacturières [D]	109.0	108.7	112.3	113.6	116.5	122.5	132.3	139.8
Food, beverages and tobacco — Aliments, boissons et tabac	100.2	101.6	104.5	108.3	111.4	115.0	123.5	130.4
Textiles, wearing apparel, leather, footwear Textiles, habillement, cuir et chaussures	77.6	68.7	67.2	59.3	56.2	61.8	69.2	68.4
Chemicals, petroleum, rubber and plastic products Prod. chimiques, pétroliers, caoutch. et plast.	124.2	131.1	144.8	153.5	160.0	165.9	176.2	198.1
Basic metals — Métaux de base	119.9	123.5	92.3	96.5	95.6	111.1	140.9	150.6
Metal products — Produits métalliques	107.6	99.3	104.7	106.6	100.4	100.7	107.0	116.6
Electricity [E] Electricité [E]	129.9	141.5	147.4	153.7	157.7	168.4	181.9	192.0
Colombia — Colombie								
Total manufacturing [D] Total, industries manufacturières [D]	98.2	85.0	93.2	94.3	95.0	97.7	104.5	108.4
Food, beverages and tobacco — Aliments, boissons et tabac	102.2	93.2	92.7	94.3	99.3	99.0	104.2	104.5
Textiles, wearing apparel, leather, footwear Textiles, habillement, cuir et chaussures	119.0	102.7	120.6	117.0	107.7	112.0	119.2	113.6
Chemicals, petroleum, rubber and plastic products Prod. chimiques, pétroliers, caoutch. et plast.	94.6	86.0	93.1	89.7	92.0	96.1	103.8	106.2
Basic metals — Métaux de base	97.9	93.3	123.7	118.0	124.4	160.3	185.0	205.1
Metal products — Produits métalliques	91.4	66.6	75.1	83.7	84.6	82.8	98.1	113.0
Ecuador — Equateur								
Total manufacturing [D] Total, industries manufacturières [D]	105.2	100.0	114.9	127.6	130.9	...	...	...
Food, beverages and tobacco — Aliments, boissons et tabac	105.9	104.5	107.7	119.6	123.4	...	...	...
Textiles, leather and footwear — Textiles, cuir et chaussures	101.3	95.8	114.7	118.0	119.5	...	...	...
Chemicals, petroleum, rubber and plastic products Prod. chimiques, pétroliers, caoutch. et plast.	106.8	97.0	107.4	112.5	116.4	...	...	...
Basic metals — Métaux de base	102.7	95.5	127.1	129.6	132.8	...	...	...
Metal products — Produits métalliques	101.6	67.1	97.0	151.8	153.6	...	...	...
Paraguay — Paraguay								
Total manufacturing [D] Total, industries manufacturières [D]	98.6	98.6	99.6	101.0	97.8	97.2	...	...
Food, beverages and tobacco — Aliments, boissons et tabac	106.6	110.0	112.5	114.2	117.9	117.2	...	...
Textiles, wearing apparel, leather, footwear Textiles, habillement, cuir et chaussures	88.3	84.9	92.3	99.1	82.4	87.1	...	...
Chemicals, petroleum, rubber and plastic products Prod. chimiques, pétroliers, caoutch. et plast.	72.0	68.6	64.2	67.3	63.3	60.7	...	...
Basic metals — Métaux de base	86.3	82.5	83.2	79.9	84.2	88.7	...	...
Metal products — Produits métalliques	99.1	99.1	99.1	99.1	99.1	95.5	...	...

Country or area and industry [ISIC Rev. 3] Pays ou zone et industrie [CITI Rév. 3]	1998	1999	2000	2001	2002	2003	2004	2005
Peru — Pérou								
Total industry [CDE] Total, industrie [CDE]	108.8	109.9	113.1	113.4	119.2	123.8	130.3	138.5
Total mining [C] Total, industries extractives [C]	118.9	134.5	137.7	151.3	169.5	178.6	187.9	203.3
Total manufacturing [D] Total, industries manufacturières [D]	103.1	102.4	108.3	109.1	115.5	119.2	128.1	136.3
Food, beverages and tobacco — Aliments, boissons et tabac	99.0	112.4	122.0	118.9	123.0	123.8	131.6	139.2
Textiles, wearing apparel, leather, footwear Textiles, habillement, cuir et chaussures	99.9	97.2	110.1	104.6	117.1	127.1	142.9	147.5
Chemicals, petroleum, rubber and plastic products Prod. chimiques, pétroliers, caoutch. et plast.	114.1	114.3	118.6	122.9	128.1	129.7	137.0	151.8
Basic metals — Métaux de base	121.4	121.9	128.1	132.7	129.1	132.9	135.3	135.2
Metal products — Produits métalliques	91.7	75.6	83.4	82.2	78.8	81.3	84.1	90.9
Electricity [E] Electricité [E]	126.7	130.5	134.6	136.9	144.3	150.4	157.3	165.7
Suriname — Suriname								
Total industry [CDE] Total, industrie [CDE]	106.7	99.0	...	...	...	...	...	...
Total mining [C] Total, industries extractives [C]	127.4	134.9	134.0	141.5	143.4	145.3	143.4	142.5
Total manufacturing [D] Total, industries manufacturières [D]	86.5	79.3	...	...	...	...	...	...
Electricity and water [E] Electricité et eau [E]	109.2	94.3	92.0	90.8	98.9	98.9	116.1	113.8
Uruguay — Uruguay								
Total manufacturing [D] Total, industries manufacturières [D]	125.0	122.6	127.5	129.6	136.7	147.2	178.7	199.3
Food, beverages and tobacco — Aliments, boissons et tabac	123.3	122.4	115.8	108.1	108.1	110.4	132.0	153.7
Textiles, wearing apparel, leather, footwear Textiles, habillement, cuir et chaussures	89.4	64.3	65.0	53.4	41.5	48.7	59.4	65.3
Chemicals, petroleum, rubber and plastic products Prod. chimiques, pétroliers, caoutch. et plast.	113.6	102.9	111.3	102.1	97.2	112.2	138.1	140.0
Basic metals — Métaux de base	111.5	105.2	101.0	99.7	99.7	120.3	152.8	170.6
Metal products — Produits métalliques	115.8	92.5	111.9	85.5	41.1	40.3	55.7	75.2
Venezuela (Bolivarian Republic of) — Venezuela (République bolivarienne du)								
Total industry [CDE] Total, industrie [CDE]	98.6	89.4	94.2	97.8	87.2	81.7	99.9	108.5
Total mining [C] Total, industries extractives [C]	101.3	89.0	102.6	105.4	110.0	100.6	112.5	111.1
Total manufacturing [D] Total, industries manufacturières [D]	99.8	86.8	92.4	95.9	79.8	72.7	93.7	104.4
Electricity [E] Electricité [E]	110.3	109.8	114.8	120.7	123.7	124.7	134.0	144.6
Asia · Asie								
Armenia — Arménie								
Total industry [CDE] Total, industrie [CDE]	100.2	105.5	112.3	118.3	135.6	156.1	159.8	171.9
Total mining [C] Total, industries extractives [C]	143.1	166.3	207.4	248.3	297.0	332.3	367.2	350.3
Total manufacturing [D] Total, industries manufacturières [D]	97.1	107.3	114.7	125.7	157.5	187.7	186.6	205.1
Food, beverages and tobacco — Aliments, boissons et tabac	101.4	112.1	117.0	123.7	138.0	203.0	216.9	234.2
Textiles, wearing apparel, leather, footwear Textiles, habillement, cuir et chaussures	117.5	75.1	73.0	84.4	84.6	108.9	211.3	153.6
Chemicals, petroleum, rubber and plastic products Prod. chimiques, pétroliers, caoutch. et plast.	93.0	101.5	115.3	97.9	83.1	81.3	103.3	156.6
Basic metals — Métaux de base	184.7	151.3	318.0	460.1	566.8	670.5	584.0	777.3
Metal products — Produits métalliques	68.2	74.4	88.1	120.2	102.4	131.1	93.8	89.8
Electricity and gas [E] Electricité et gaz [E]	105.7	100.0	102.6	95.1	81.4	83.4	95.1	108.2

Country or area and industry [ISIC Rev. 3] Pays ou zone et industrie [CITI Rév. 3]	1998	1999	2000	2001	2002	2003	2004	2005
Azerbaijan — Azerbaïdjan								
Total industry [CDE] Total, industrie [CDE]	95.6	99.1	105.9	111.3	115.3	122.4	129.3	172.7
Total mining [C] Total, industries extractives [C]	121.2	145.3	146.9	155.5	159.4	161.6	165.4	234.0
Total manufacturing [D] Total, industries manufacturières [D]	80.1	72.8	84.0	86.3	91.1	107.2	118.1	137.0
Electricity, gas and water [E] Electricité, gaz et eau [E]	103.6	104.7	107.9	108.6	113.7	132.3	135.3	141.8
Bangladesh[2] — Bangladesh[2]								
Total industry [CDE] Total, industrie [CDE]	112.5	121.4	131.5	140.9	147.6	157.2	164.8	168.4
Total mining [C] Total, industries extractives [C]	113.5	114.6	134.5	150.8	158.4	170.1	180.9	182.8
Total manufacturing [D] Total, industries manufacturières [D]	120.0	123.8	132.8	139.9	146.2	155.8	162.8	168.9
Food, beverages and tobacco — Aliments, boissons et tabac	99.4	98.0	105.2	108.3	125.2	129.6	133.4	145.2
Textiles, wearing apparel, leather, footwear Textiles, habillement, cuir et chaussures	122.8	127.7	132.3	141.9	149.0	156.0	166.5	184.5
Chemicals, petroleum, rubber and plastic products Prod. chimiques, pétroliers, caoutch. et plast.	104.4	98.2	103.5	112.7	113.5	133.9	134.9	141.5
Basic metals — Métaux de base	105.1	89.3	93.0	103.0	107.9	111.7	114.2	128.8
Metal products — Produits métalliques	151.9	116.6	117.5	117.3	123.9	120.4	126.1	155.5
Electricity [E] Electricité [E]	118.8	127.3	135.8	149.8	160.5	170.2	184.1	185.0
China, Hong Kong SAR — Chine, Hong Kong RAS								
Total industry [DE][3] Total, industrie [DE][3]	90.2	84.7	85.1	82.4	76.3	71.1	73.4	75.3
Total manufacturing [D] Total, industries manufacturières [D]	87.2	81.7	81.2	77.7	70.0	63.6	65.5	67.1
Food, beverages and tobacco — Aliments, boissons et tabac	89.7	88.2	85.5	84.0	90.9	80.4	85.0	86.0
Textiles and wearing apparel — Textiles et habillement	86.2	84.1	86.9	86.7	80.8	77.9	76.3	72.5
Chemicals and other non-metallic mineral products Prod. chimiques et minéraux non-métalliques	88.1	74.9	64.1	59.1	48.9	49.6	48.7	49.6
Basic metals and metal products Métaux de base et produits métalliques	84.0	80.0	79.2	72.5	56.0	44.5	49.5	54.6
Electricity and gas [E] Electricité et gaz [E]	111.9	106.8	113.4	117.0	122.7	126.4	131.3	135.4
China, Macao SAR[8] — Chine, Macao RAS[8]								
Total industry [CDE] Total, industrie [CDE]	100.9	101.2	112.6	106.2	106.0	108.2	114.7	...
Total mining [C] Total, industries extractives [C]	99.3	75.0	36.0	71.9	80.9	101.1	118.9	...
Total manufacturing [D] Total, industries manufacturières [D]	97.9	98.8	113.2	103.6	100.9	101.4	105.0	...
Electricity and gas [E] Electricité et gaz [E]	110.1	109.1	112.6	115.1	122.8	129.8	143.4	...
Cyprus — Chypre								
Total industry [CDE] Total, industrie [CDE]	99.4	100.9	105.4	105.1	105.2	104.3	106.2	106.4
Total mining [C] Total, industries extractives [C]	121.1	130.2	135.3	129.0	143.6	144.8	146.1	152.4
Total manufacturing [D] Total, industries manufacturières [D]	95.4	96.3	100.1	98.2	95.8	92.7	94.0	92.8
Food, beverages and tobacco — Aliments, boissons et tabac	94.5	98.1	102.0	100.8	96.9	98.7	96.8	97.2
Textiles, wearing apparel, leather, footwear Textiles, habillement, cuir et chaussures	81.7	76.0	70.1	67.2	55.3	39.8	34.1	30.3
Chemicals, petroleum, rubber and plastic products Prod. chimiques, pétroliers, caoutch. et plast.	101.7	101.8	102.6	105.7	107.0	101.5	94.7	87.5
Metal products — Produits métalliques	103.2	109.2	117.4	120.6	132.2	121.7	127.4	124.6
Electricity, gas and water [E] Electricité, gaz et eau [E]	116.0	123.5	131.7	141.6	153.6	165.1	170.4	179.7

Country or area and industry [ISIC Rev. 3] Pays ou zone et industrie [CITI Rév. 3]	1998	1999	2000	2001	2002	2003	2004	2005
Georgia — Géorgie								
Total industry [CDE] Total, industrie [CDE]	...	...	137.1	130.2	139.3	159.9	173.7	...
Total mining [C] Total, industries extractives [C]	...	...	203.0	217.0	205.7	324.4	282.2	...
Total manufacturing [D] Total, industries manufacturières [D]	...	...	139.4	136.3	162.5	191.1	219.6	...
Electricity, gas and water [E] Electricité, gaz et eau [E]	...	...	123.9	110.8	103.3	106.7	109.6	...
India[9] — Inde[9]								
Total industry [CDE] Total, industrie [CDE]	117.8	125.6	131.9	135.4	143.2	153.3	165.6	179.4
Total mining [C] Total, industries extractives [C]	104.1	105.1	108.1	109.5	115.9	122.0	127.1	128.5
Total manufacturing [D] Total, industries manufacturières [D]	119.5	128.0	134.9	138.7	147.1	158.0	171.8	187.9
Food, beverages and tobacco — Aliments, boissons et tabac	113.3	118.9	125.8	124.6	140.8	142.6	147.6	162.3
Textiles, wearing apparel, leather, footwear Textiles, habillement, cuir et chaussures	109.7	117.0	123.9	123.9	126.0	127.1	137.6	143.9
Chemicals, petroleum, rubber and plastic products Prod. chimiques, pétroliers, caoutch. et plast.	125.2	134.8	146.4	154.3	160.4	172.7	192.7	206.7
Basic metals — Métaux de base	106.8	112.1	114.2	119.1	130.1	142.0	150.0	173.1
Metal products — Produits métalliques	125.2	137.7	145.2	145.1	156.2	178.3	199.8	220.5
Electricity [E] Electricité [E]	118.0	126.6	131.7	135.7	140.1	147.1	154.7	162.7
Indonesia — Indonésie								
Total industry [CDE][3] Total, industrie [CDE][3]	97.6	95.1	108.2	111.5	115.8	130.1	139.6	152.3
Total mining [C] Total, industries extractives [C]	103.8	96.9	117.7	124.6	137.9	148.4	163.2	185.5
Total manufacturing [D] Total, industries manufacturières [D]	86.7	88.3	91.5	90.5	84.2	104.0	107.4	108.9
Food, beverages and tobacco — Aliments, boissons et tabac	93.5	87.3	85.4	83.7	80.1	91.0	95.4	115.5
Textiles, wearing apparel, leather, footwear Textiles, habillement, cuir et chaussures	84.0	89.2	90.0	83.0	79.7	80.4	86.5	76.2
Chemicals, petroleum, rubber and plastic products Prod. chimiques, pétroliers, caoutch. et plast.	104.3	109.6	106.7	102.3	91.8	99.8	121.6	205.2
Basic metals — Métaux de base	81.1	89.3	109.3	111.6	98.1	77.2	82.2	80.0
Metal products — Produits métalliques	50.5	59.4	95.3	110.1	99.5	106.3	123.6	131.4
Electricity [E] Electricité [E]	147.6	167.5	185.2	187.2	183.8	184.2	186.2	188.3
Iran (Islamic Rep. of) — Iran (Rép. islamique d')								
Total manufacturing [D] Total, industries manufacturières [D]	130.3	135.8	141.2	146.6	152.1	157.5	162.9	168.4
Food and beverages — Aliments et boissons	123.5	131.7	139.3	133.8	159.4	176.5	182.6	202.8
Textiles, wearing apparel, leather, footwear Textiles, habillement, cuir et chaussures	104.9	102.0	97.7	98.9	105.6	100.4	99.0	99.7
Chemicals, rubber and plastic prod. Prod. chimiques, caoutchouc et plastiques	115.2	124.4	129.6	137.6	147.5	165.5	182.5	200.5
Metal products — Produits métalliques	154.2	173.3	187.1	212.2	339.0	490.7	593.2	861.0
Israel — Israël								
Total industry [CD] Total, industrie [CD]	110.3	111.9	123.0	117.0	114.7	114.4	122.2	126.8
Total mining [C] Total, industries extractives [C]	109.2	108.2	105.7	107.8	116.2	112.8	109.6	112.0
Total manufacturing [D] Total, industries manufacturières [D]	110.3	112.0	123.6	117.3	114.7	114.5	122.7	127.5
Food, beverages and tobacco — Aliments, boissons et tabac	103.9	105.3	105.4	104.3	102.8	100.4	102.1	102.7
Textiles — Textiles	97.7	102.3	96.6	88.4	84.5	81.5	81.8	82.2
Chemicals, petroleum, rubber and plastic products Prod. chimiques, pétroliers, caoutch. et plast.	119.1	118.0	122.1	128.0	145.3	153.5	169.4	179.6

Country or area and industry [ISIC Rev. 3] Pays ou zone et industrie [CITI Rév. 3]	1998	1999	2000	2001	2002	2003	2004	2005
Basic metals — Métaux de base	101.1	100.6	102.6	95.3	86.6	77.0	83.0	84.8
Metal products — Produits métalliques	106.7	104.3	114.4	108.7	106.1	104.3	108.5	112.8
Japan — Japon								
Total industry [CDE] Total, industrie [CDE]	99.0	99.9	105.5	98.7	97.6	100.6	106.0	106.6
Total mining [C] Total, industries extractives [C]	86.4	86.1	85.8	85.5	80.3	81.9	81.9	85.0
Total manufacturing [D] Total, industries manufacturières [D]	98.5	99.3	105.2	98.0	96.8	99.9	105.4	105.8
Food, beverages and tobacco — Aliments, boissons et tabac	97.8	98.6	99.0	98.2	97.1	97.3	95.4	94.5
Textiles, wearing apparel, leather, footwear Textiles, habillement, cuir et chaussures	82.4	77.1	70.9	63.9	56.7	52.1	48.4	44.9
Chemicals, petroleum, rubber and plastic products Prod. chimiques, pétroliers, caoutch. et plast.	100.5	103.1	104.2	103.4	102.9	104.5	105.2	105.3
Basic metals — Métaux de base	92.0	91.5	100.1	97.0	98.5	102.0	104.8	105.5
Metal products — Produits métalliques	102.7	105.7	117.5	104.7	105.8	112.7	124.2	127.1
Electricity and gas [E] Electricité et gaz [E]	106.8	108.2	111.5	111.7	112.6	114.2	118.1	122.6
Jordan — Jordanie								
Total industry [CDE] Total, industrie [CDE]	102.1	102.5	109.6	122.5	129.9	118.8	133.0	146.7
Total mining [C] Total, industries extractives [C]	99.4	106.6	108.4	110.9	119.0	116.5	112.1	110.7
Total manufacturing [D] Total, industries manufacturières [D]	104.1	102.0	110.0	125.0	132.3	119.5	136.0	151.8
Food, beverages and tobacco — Aliments, boissons et tabac	107.7	119.0	140.5	166.4	199.4	201.9	227.1	266.6
Textiles, wearing apparel, leather, footwear Textiles, habillement, cuir et chaussures	100.5	82.9	74.9	55.8	60.2	60.6	65.9	55.2
Chemicals, petroleum, rubber and plastic products Prod. chimiques, pétroliers, caoutch. et plast.	103.0	94.7	97.1	107.8	106.8	102.1	112.6	123.2
Basic metals — Métaux de base	64.4	75.3	70.7	88.1	84.2	92.0	101.2	117.6
Electricity [E] Electricité [E]	123.9	130.1	136.0	139.9	147.8	146.4	165.6	178.1
Korea, Republic of — Corée, République de								
Total industry [CDE] Total, industrie [CDE]	106.2	131.9	154.1	155.0	167.6	176.4	194.5	206.6
Total mining [C] Total, industries extractives [C]	72.7	78.6	77.4	77.3	80.3	79.8	77.4	72.6
Total manufacturing [D] Total, industries manufacturières [D]	105.6	132.0	154.6	154.9	167.5	176.5	195.1	207.1
Food, beverages and tobacco — Aliments, boissons et tabac	95.2	103.1	106.0	111.6	114.5	114.9	117.8	115.2
Textiles, wearing apparel, leather, footwear Textiles, habillement, cuir et chaussures	69.7	74.0	75.1	68.3	65.6	58.2	54.3	50.5
Chemicals, petroleum, rubber and plastic products Prod. chimiques, pétroliers, caoutch. et plast.	115.1	128.0	134.6	136.5	141.2	146.2	152.6	157.0
Basic metals — Métaux de base	98.7	112.7	122.2	124.0	130.1	136.8	143.8	144.3
Metal products — Produits métalliques	119.0	163.2	204.1	207.5	243.3	276.9	339.9	388.5
Electricity and gas [E] Electricité et gaz [E]	119.0	133.7	149.9	160.3	172.4	181.9	192.5	206.1
Kyrgyzstan[10] — Kirghizistan[10]								
Total industry [CDE] Total, industrie [CDE]	...	...	100.0	105.4	93.9	109.9	115.0	101.1
Total mining [C] Total, industries extractives [C]	...	...	100.0	100.2	101.8	102.9	141.8	122.1
Total manufacturing [D] Total, industries manufacturières [D]	...	...	100.0	109.3	97.1	115.7	121.1	102.2
Electricity, gas and water [E] Electricité, gaz et eau [E]	...	...	100.0	92.2	81.6	90.0	91.3	87.1
Malaysia — Malaisie								
Total industry [CDE] Total, industrie [CDE]	114.0	124.3	148.1	142.0	148.4	162.3	180.6	187.9

Country or area and industry [ISIC Rev. 3] Pays ou zone et industrie [CITI Rév. 3]	1998	1999	2000	2001	2002	2003	2004	2005
Total mining [C] Total, industries extractives [C]	109.6	106.1	105.9	108.8	110.7	116.7	123.4	124.0
Total manufacturing [D] Total, industries manufacturières [D]	113.3	127.7	159.8	149.2	156.0	171.5	194.1	204.1
Food, beverages and tobacco — Aliments, boissons et tabac	113.1	127.1	150.9	158.8	166.0	183.9	190.8	203.3
Textiles, wearing apparel, leather, footwear Textiles, habillement, cuir et chaussures	97.8	101.4	112.0	103.9	97.7	94.6	86.0	90.6
Chemicals, petroleum, rubber and plastic products Prod. chimiques, pétroliers, caoutch. et plast.	134.8	152.7	174.4	169.0	171.7	202.5	225.6	247.2
Basic metals — Métaux de base	93.7	134.6	141.6	140.8	144.1	159.7	166.7	157.9
Metal products — Produits métalliques	111.1	128.2	179.4	155.9	167.9	182.4	216.4	222.2
Electricity [E] Electricité [E]	133.2	138.3	146.8	159.4	174.2	186.1	201.5	213.1
Mongolia — Mongolie								
Total industry [CDE] Total, industrie [CDE]	104.7	106.6	110.2	119.2	140.8	147.9	167.2	159.6
Total mining [C] Total, industries extractives [C]	116.5	121.0	128.1	132.9	133.5	132.2	158.1	175.8
Total manufacturing [D] Total, industries manufacturières [D]	73.3	71.1	67.6	82.9	133.6	150.9	162.8	122.9
Food and beverages — Aliments et boissons	69.6	60.7	59.5	71.4	73.3	83.3	85.3	83.4
Textiles, wearing apparel, leather, footwear Textiles, habillement, cuir et chaussures	80.6	88.4	83.0	130.8	335.8	454.7	439.8	178.9
Chemicals and chemical products — Produits chimiques	107.5	112.7	113.1	149.7	144.2	128.9	146.8	90.6
Basic metals — Métaux de base	143.1	145.1	133.3	104.0	202.1	263.1	422.3	579.5
Electricity and gas [E] Electricité et gaz [E]	98.1	101.1	103.6	103.6	105.7	107.5	116.6	121.7
Pakistan[1] — Pakistan[1]								
Total industry [CDE] Total, industrie [CDE]	107.8	108.3	114.2	122.2	133.6	155.1	177.6	...
Total mining [C] Total, industries extractives [C]	101.0	104.1	113.1	112.2	124.1	129.0	140.8	...
Total manufacturing [D] Total, industries manufacturières [D]	109.1	109.1	116.3	123.4	134.3	159.0	183.5	...
Electricity [E] Electricité [E]	100.5	103.9	98.2	117.5	133.0	137.1	149.3	...
Singapore — Singapour								
Total manufacturing [D] Total, industries manufacturières [D]	107.7	122.6	141.3	124.8	135.3	139.4	158.8	173.8
Food, beverages and tobacco — Aliments, boissons et tabac	87.8	92.0	93.4	97.3	94.6	94.3	95.9	102.7
Textiles, wearing apparel, leather, footwear Textiles, habillement, cuir et chaussures	84.4	88.1	101.1	86.3	72.6	70.9	69.1	58.7
Chemicals, petroleum, rubber and plastic products Prod. chimiques, pétroliers, caoutch. et plast.	136.0	159.9	167.9	174.0	227.1	247.2	292.3	315.1
Basic metals — Métaux de base	87.3	92.7	98.4	99.0	101.6	87.3	103.7	121.1
Metal products — Produits métalliques	100.0	114.5	138.0	115.5	120.4	123.2	140.7	156.1
Sri Lanka — Sri Lanka								
Total manufacturing [D] Total, industries manufacturières [D]	97.2	99.4	101.0	104.7	109.2	110.0	113.3	117.4
Food, beverages and tobacco — Aliments, boissons et tabac	94.4	99.5	104.4	107.3	111.8	117.9	122.2	128.3
Textiles, wearing apparel, leather, footwear Textiles, habillement, cuir et chaussures	123.8	131.1	152.0	149.0	145.5	141.7	153.4	160.1
Chemicals, petroleum, rubber and plastic products Prod. chimiques, pétroliers, caoutch. et plast.	101.6	107.9	118.0	121.7	123.6	128.7	135.2	154.0
Basic metals — Métaux de base	97.4	104.2	107.2	108.8	113.3	117.6	127.5	135.5
Metal products — Produits métalliques	128.7	137.5	146.4	150.1	154.9	158.5	162.8	167.2
Syrian Arab Republic — Rép. arabe syrienne								
Total industry [CDE] Total, industrie [CDE]	109.0	109.0	109.0	112.3	118.8	111.2	100.3	...
Total mining [C] Total, industries extractives [C]	102.0	101.0	97.0	93.1	95.1	97.0	98.9	...

Country or area and industry [ISIC Rev. 3] Pays ou zone et industrie [CITI Rév. 3]	1998	1999	2000	2001	2002	2003	2004	2005
Total manufacturing [D] Total, industries manufacturières [D]	110.0	110.0	109.0	105.7	110.1	95.9	107.9	...
Food, beverages and tobacco — Aliments, boissons et tabac	102.1	108.3	107.6	112.4	123.9	119.3	128.1	...
Textiles, wearing apparel, leather, footwear Textiles, habillement, cuir et chaussures	108.3	113.7	126.3	134.9	140.5	132.3	148.0	...
Chemicals, petroleum, rubber and plastic products Prod. chimiques, pétroliers, caoutch. et plast.	109.3	95.1	95.1	112.9	109.0	96.3	111.3	...
Basic metals — Métaux de base	159.0	147.0	138.0	150.4	131.1	127.0	115.9	...
Metal products — Produits métalliques	85.4	93.2	60.6	107.4	90.4	75.8	92.8	...
Electricity and water [E] Electricité et eau [E]	129.0	142.0	155.0	164.3	172.1	181.4	196.9	...
Tajikistan — Tadjikistan								
Total industry [CDE] Total, industrie [CDE]	81.4	86.0	95.3	109.3	118.6	132.6	148.8	160.5
Total mining [C] Total, industries extractives [C]	131.3	131.3	125.0	129.7	137.5	154.7	153.1	154.7
Total manufacturing [D] Total, industries manufacturières [D]	68.3	78.0	85.4	100.0	112.2	122.0	143.9	151.2
Electricity, gas and water [E] Electricité, gaz et eau [E]	112.6	126.3	112.6	116.8	126.3	134.7	131.6	133.7
Thailand — Thaïlande								
Total manufacturing [D] Total, industries manufacturières [D]	96.5	108.6	111.9	113.5	123.3	138.4	149.8	155.5
Turkey — Turquie								
Total industry [CDE] Total, industrie [CDE]	118.6	114.3	121.2	110.7	121.1	131.8	144.5	152.4
Total mining [C] Total, industries extractives [C]	121.7	109.6	106.6	97.9	89.9	86.9	90.4	102.8
Total manufacturing [D] Total, industries manufacturières [D]	118.9	113.9	121.3	109.7	121.7	133.0	146.8	153.9
Food, beverages and tobacco — Aliments, boissons et tabac	120.4	119.2	124.3	122.3	126.3	133.5	129.4	138.0
Textiles, wearing apparel, leather, footwear Textiles, habillement, cuir et chaussures	111.6	105.0	114.2	108.4	118.9	121.1	121.8	106.7
Chemicals, petroleum, rubber and plastic products Prod. chimiques, pétroliers, caoutch. et plast.	120.4	118.3	123.1	116.2	130.5	142.0	155.8	168.2
Basic metals — Métaux de base	118.7	116.5	120.9	114.9	126.4	141.4	157.9	163.2
Metal products — Produits métalliques	138.5	127.6	148.2	115.0	144.3	173.3	227.7	246.9
Electricity, gas and water [E] Electricité, gaz et eau [E]	128.7	135.0	144.9	142.3	150.0	162.7	173.8	187.0
Europe · Europe								
Albania — Albanie								
Total industry [CDE] Total, industrie [CDE]	82.5	59.7	121.3	91.3	107.8	122.6	125.7	...
Total mining [C] Total, industries extractives [C]	56.2	41.4	36.4	32.1	33.4	60.0	52.2	...
Total manufacturing [D] Total, industries manufacturières [D]	68.5	77.7	116.0	77.6	88.0	95.2	107.0	...
Electricity, gas and water [E] Electricité, gaz et eau [E]	114.6	121.5	104.5	81.5	107.4	121.7	107.0	...
Austria — Autriche								
Total industry [CDE] Total, industrie [CDE]	116.2	123.2	134.1	138.1	139.2	142.1	151.0	157.3
Total mining [C] Total, industries extractives [C]	103.9	107.4	112.3	109.6	113.1	112.5	106.2	104.4
Total manufacturing [D] Total, industries manufacturières [D]	117.8	124.9	137.3	139.9	139.9	143.2	153.6	160.0
Food, beverages and tobacco — Aliments, boissons et tabac	113.2	117.1	121.2	123.0	126.6	126.8	128.3	131.4
Textiles, wearing apparel, leather, footwear Textiles, habillement, cuir et chaussures	97.5	90.8	88.9	87.0	86.2	84.6	77.2	73.4
Chemicals, petroleum, rubber and plastic products Prod. chimiques, pétroliers, caoutch. et plast.	112.1	116.8	126.6	131.7	127.3	131.4	137.6	147.3

Country or area and industry [ISIC Rev. 3] Pays ou zone et industrie [CITI Rév. 3]	1998	1999	2000	2001	2002	2003	2004	2005
Basic metals — Métaux de base	114.6	113.9	126.5	134.3	135.6	136.4	148.4	154.6
Metal products — Produits métalliques	128.4	142.3	162.2	164.7	166.4	170.3	190.0	202.2
Electricity, gas and water [E] Electricité, gaz et eau [E]	106.6	112.9	114.6	128.9	137.2	138.1	138.6	145.7
Belarus — Bélarus								
Total industry [CDE] Total, industrie [CDE]	137.5	152.0	163.8	173.7	181.6	194.6	225.7	249.5
Total mining [C] Total, industries extractives [C]	118.6	123.9	117.5	130.7	134.8	147.5	160.9	173.6
Total manufacturing [D] Total, industries manufacturières [D]	139.3	154.2	167.0	176.4	184.3	197.2	229.3	253.4
Electricity [E] Electricité [E]	96.2	101.4	98.7	97.6	100.6	101.5	114.3	113.5
Belgium — Belgique								
Total industry [CDE] Total, industrie [CDE]	108.9	110.1	115.5	115.0	116.7	117.5	121.5	121.0
Total mining [C] Total, industries extractives [C]	116.6	125.2	138.1	139.5	182.2	173.9	175.9	186.7
Total manufacturing [D] Total, industries manufacturières [D]	108.4	109.7	116.2	116.1	117.1	117.7	122.7	120.3
Food, beverages and tobacco — Aliments, boissons et tabac	107.3	103.0	107.3	111.3	117.3	121.2	127.2	129.4
Textiles, wearing apparel, leather, footwear Textiles, habillement, cuir et chaussures	91.0	85.2	87.0	83.2	80.4	77.5	79.4	75.3
Chemicals, petroleum, rubber and plastic products Prod. chimiques, pétroliers, caoutch. et plast.	115.1	122.5	134.9	131.8	140.3	148.3	156.7	150.8
Basic metals — Métaux de base	101.2	101.5	106.9	94.7	95.5	97.9	89.6	74.4
Metal products — Produits métalliques	111.8	112.3	119.2	122.1	116.8	112.8	120.8	122.6
Electricity, gas and water [E] Electricité, gaz et eau [E]	112.7	112.8	109.8	106.9	109.6	112.4	110.1	121.8
Bulgaria — Bulgarie								
Total industry [CDE] Total, industrie [CDE]	78.5	72.2	78.2	79.9	83.6	95.4	111.7	119.1
Total mining [C] Total, industries extractives [C]	90.9	78.6	80.7	73.7	73.3	78.4	94.7	95.1
Total manufacturing [D] Total, industries manufacturières [D]	74.8	69.7	74.7	75.7	81.3	96.6	117.1	126.5
Food, beverages and tobacco — Aliments, boissons et tabac	78.2	73.8	73.3	71.1	71.9	85.4	99.3	104.5
Textiles, wearing apparel, leather, footwear Textiles, habillement, cuir et chaussures	87.9	75.2	85.5	94.1	115.7	149.3	170.9	168.5
Chemicals, petroleum, rubber and plastic products Prod. chimiques, pétroliers, caoutch. et plast.	61.9	61.7	69.7	70.7	67.7	79.8	83.8	92.0
Basic metals — Métaux de base	82.7	69.6	80.9	67.7	72.9	91.3	154.9	166.6
Metal products — Produits métalliques	84.0	71.4	72.3	76.5	87.9	98.6	122.0	142.5
Electricity, gas and water [E] Electricité, gaz et eau [E]	109.2	95.0	112.3	121.7	120.0	123.4	127.0	131.6
Croatia — Croatie								
Total industry [CDE] Total, industrie [CDE]	114.2	112.5	114.4	121.3	127.9	133.1	138.0	145.0
Total mining [C] Total, industries extractives [C]	94.2	96.0	97.8	99.7	116.7	119.4	115.4	112.0
Total manufacturing [D] Total, industries manufacturières [D]	108.6	105.4	108.5	115.4	120.5	126.7	131.8	140.5
Food, beverages and tobacco — Aliments, boissons et tabac	99.1	94.1	94.3	100.5	106.1	111.5	114.7	120.9
Textiles, wearing apparel, leather, footwear Textiles, habillement, cuir et chaussures	88.3	79.4	78.4	82.1	74.4	70.7	60.3	56.4
Chemicals, petroleum, rubber and plastic products Prod. chimiques, pétroliers, caoutch. et plast.	88.8	91.5	96.7	92.4	96.8	95.2	99.1	97.8
Basic metals — Métaux de base	133.3	115.6	120.6	125.7	113.3	119.1	149.5	156.5
Metal products — Produits métalliques	118.4	120.4	121.1	137.0	143.6	153.8	165.4	184.6
Electricity, gas and water [E] Electricité, gaz et eau [E]	169.3	181.0	172.4	180.7	183.8	189.8	197.8	195.7

Country or area and industry [ISIC Rev. 3] Pays ou zone et industrie [CITI Rév. 3]	1998	1999	2000	2001	2002	2003	2004	2005
Czech Republic — République tchèque								
Total industry [CDE] Total, industrie [CDE]	108.2	104.7	105.7	112.7	114.9	121.2	132.8	141.6
Total mining [C] Total, industries extractives [C]	92.8	81.6	88.2	88.9	89.7	90.0	89.4	89.9
Total manufacturing [D] Total, industries manufacturières [D]	110.9	107.9	108.2	116.2	118.6	125.0	138.4	148.9
Food, beverages and tobacco — Aliments, boissons et tabac	107.8	107.2	103.4	105.3	107.2	107.3	105.7	102.7
Textiles, wearing apparel, leather, footwear Textiles, habillement, cuir et chaussures	92.0	81.1	90.4	91.8	85.0	84.1	83.9	82.1
Chemicals, petroleum, rubber and plastic products Prod. chimiques, pétroliers, caoutch. et plast.	107.1	105.1	101.5	111.8	114.8	121.5	133.0	145.8
Basic metals — Métaux de base	86.2	69.0	58.7	59.7	57.7	65.0	70.8	66.1
Metal products — Produits métalliques	139.9	145.9	157.1	170.5	179.4	192.1	225.4	248.6
Electricity, gas and water [E] Electricité, gaz et eau [E]	99.4	95.9	102.1	103.8	103.9	113.1	114.2	112.8
Denmark — Danemark								
Total industry [CD] Total, industrie [CD]	109.4	109.6	115.5	117.2	119.2	118.0	118.6	121.1
Total mining [C] Total, industries extractives [C]	93.0	93.5	93.8	92.3	97.6	95.8	100.7	105.0
Total manufacturing [D] Total, industries manufacturières [D]	109.5	109.7	115.6	117.9	119.1	118.5	117.9	120.0
Food, beverages and tobacco — Aliments, boissons et tabac	98.3	101.6	103.3	103.3	111.0	117.9	114.4	113.3
Textiles, wearing apparel, leather, footwear Textiles, habillement, cuir et chaussures	105.1	101.1	103.2	93.4	88.2	83.9	70.2	68.1
Chemicals, petroleum, rubber and plastic products Prod. chimiques, pétroliers, caoutch. et plast.	116.1	130.7	141.7	152.3	155.4	150.9	139.4	154.2
Basic metals — Métaux de base	107.0	98.0	120.3	109.1	82.6	88.3	81.6	79.9
Metal products — Produits métalliques	112.8	109.3	116.1	121.4	123.3	121.2	123.0	122.9
Estonia — Estonie								
Total industry [CDE] Total, industrie [CDE]	122.7	118.6	135.9	148.0	160.1	177.6	196.2	214.0
Total mining [C] Total, industries extractives [C]	100.7	87.0	91.7	95.0	109.7	115.4	105.2	111.9
Total manufacturing [D] Total, industries manufacturières [D]	127.9	124.7	145.3	160.2	174.1	192.9	216.3	238.5
Food, beverages and tobacco — Aliments, boissons et tabac	103.3	83.1	89.0	97.7	99.6	102.1	107.4	114.1
Textiles, wearing apparel, leather, footwear Textiles, habillement, cuir et chaussures	134.0	135.6	160.6	179.4	193.2	205.3	199.7	185.3
Chemicals, rubber and plastic prod. Prod. chimiques, caoutchouc et plastiques	123.7	115.7	133.7	161.6	179.5	224.4	247.3	265.1
Basic metals — Métaux de base	167.2	162.5	181.2	277.7	360.7	621.6	486.1	397.8
Metal products — Produits métalliques	142.0	149.4	188.3	203.8	236.2	275.8	342.0	406.1
Electricity and gas [E] Electricité et gaz [E]	99.3	93.9	94.3	95.5	96.0	109.7	112.0	111.3
Finland — Finlande								
Total industry [CDE] Total, industrie [CDE]	122.3	129.3	144.5	144.7	147.7	149.4	157.5	153.6
Total mining [C] Total, industries extractives [C]	92.7	128.1	99.4	120.0	131.1	131.7	115.5	148.5
Total manufacturing [D] Total, industries manufacturières [D]	123.5	130.9	147.9	147.2	150.1	150.7	159.9	157.2
Food, beverages and tobacco — Aliments, boissons et tabac	106.8	110.7	109.3	113.4	116.4	118.7	119.9	118.6
Textiles, wearing apparel, leather, footwear Textiles, habillement, cuir et chaussures	100.5	100.4	98.3	100.2	98.1	90.0	88.1	83.4
Chemicals, petroleum, rubber and plastic products Prod. chimiques, pétroliers, caoutch. et plast.	114.5	117.2	127.7	127.1	125.9	125.8	130.3	132.2
Basic metals — Métaux de base	118.2	122.5	129.4	129.0	130.0	133.4	139.1	131.4
Metal products — Produits métalliques	140.1	154.2	191.3	194.0	198.1	197.0	217.5	218.1

Country or area and industry [ISIC Rev. 3] Pays ou zone et industrie [CITI Rév. 3]	1998	1999	2000	2001	2002	2003	2004	2005
Electricity, gas and water [E] Electricité, gaz et eau [E]	110.2	109.9	110.9	117.1	118.6	131.7	133.4	112.0
France — France								
Total industry [CDE] Total, industrie [CDE]	107.9	110.5	114.9	116.4	114.9	114.5	117.2	117.4
Total mining [C] Total, industries extractives [C]	86.9	86.8	88.4	87.4	83.0	82.0	81.3	79.8
Total manufacturing [D] Total, industries manufacturières [D]	109.0	111.5	116.3	117.4	115.8	114.9	117.8	117.9
Food, beverages and tobacco — Aliments, boissons et tabac	105.0	106.7	104.6	105.4	108.3	107.6	107.6	108.0
Textiles, wearing apparel, leather, footwear Textiles, habillement, cuir et chaussures	82.7	74.1	66.9	62.6	55.2	49.1	45.1	40.1
Chemicals, petroleum, rubber and plastic products Prod. chimiques, pétroliers, caoutch. et plast.	113.3	115.1	121.4	123.8	123.6	126.8	130.9	132.6
Basic metals — Métaux de base	106.5	104.0	111.4	108.9	106.6	103.2	105.8	101.3
Metal products — Produits métalliques	115.9	122.2	131.6	134.5	132.7	130.9	136.4	136.7
Electricity, gas and water [E] Electricité, gaz et eau [E]	103.6	105.6	108.6	112.1	112.1	115.2	117.3	117.4
Germany — Allemagne								
Total industry [CDE] Total, industrie [CDE]	107.2	108.4	114.5	114.8	113.5	114.0	117.4	121.4
Total mining [C] Total, industries extractives [C]	85.8	85.5	79.6	74.2	73.1	72.5	70.3	69.2
Total manufacturing [D] Total, industries manufacturières [D]	108.0	109.3	116.3	116.9	115.5	115.7	119.4	123.8
Food, beverages and tobacco — Aliments, boissons et tabac	103.3	106.3	108.8	108.2	108.8	108.6	109.4	114.0
Textiles, wearing apparel, leather, footwear Textiles, habillement, cuir et chaussures	88.8	81.7	79.9	76.5	70.6	65.7	63.5	60.3
Chemicals, petroleum, rubber and plastic products Prod. chimiques, pétroliers, caoutch. et plast.	108.9	111.9	115.7	113.7	117.1	117.8	121.0	125.6
Basic metals — Métaux de base	105.2	101.3	109.6	110.9	111.6	109.5	113.7	114.7
Metal products — Produits métalliques	114.1	115.9	127.8	131.0	129.0	130.3	136.1	143.5
Electricity and gas [E] Electricité et gaz [E]	104.7	105.1	106.5	104.6	104.9	108.7	111.4	111.5
Greece — Grèce								
Total industry [CDE] Total, industrie [CDE]	112.0	114.2	122.5	120.3	121.3	121.6	123.1	121.8
Total mining [C] Total, industries extractives [C]	102.6	96.4	109.3	111.9	122.7	116.4	116.5	110.3
Total manufacturing [D] Total, industries manufacturières [D]	110.2	109.2	114.8	111.9	111.8	111.4	112.6	111.8
Food, beverages and tobacco — Aliments, boissons et tabac	111.8	111.6	113.5	115.4	116.8	114.2	121.0	119.3
Textiles, wearing apparel, leather, footwear Textiles, habillement, cuir et chaussures	91.4	85.9	86.6	80.7	77.0	75.1	69.4	58.5
Chemicals, petroleum, rubber and plastic products Prod. chimiques, pétroliers, caoutch. et plast.	124.8	121.6	130.9	132.2	136.4	137.8	140.2	141.1
Basic metals — Métaux de base	98.3	109.7	125.5	129.7	138.3	136.7	143.8	145.9
Metal products — Produits métalliques	108.0	110.4	119.1	106.9	101.8	104.0	106.2	106.8
Electricity and gas [E] Electricité et gaz [E]	120.0	135.1	151.0	149.6	152.2	163.2	165.5	167.0
Hungary — Hongrie								
Total industry [CDE] Total, industrie [CDE]	129.0	142.7	168.7	175.2	181.0	192.9	207.3	222.6
Total mining [C] Total, industries extractives [C]	74.7	75.1	68.2	79.4	71.9	69.4	76.3	73.6
Total manufacturing [D] Total, industries manufacturières [D]	137.7	154.6	186.5	194.4	201.3	215.4	233.7	252.2
Food, beverages and tobacco — Aliments, boissons et tabac	93.1	95.3	101.6	100.8	102.7	101.8	98.9	95.1
Textiles, wearing apparel, leather, footwear Textiles, habillement, cuir et chaussures	112.4	121.6	133.8	136.7	130.0	117.9	111.4	101.2

Country or area and industry [ISIC Rev. 3] Pays ou zone et industrie [CITI Rév. 3]	1998	1999	2000	2001	2002	2003	2004	2005
Chemicals, petroleum, rubber and plastic products Prod. chimiques, pétroliers, caoutch. et plast.	105.9	100.2	107.6	109.8	114.4	116.3	124.1	132.8
Basic metals — Métaux de base	118.8	113.5	132.2	127.8	133.2	144.0	154.2	149.2
Metal products — Produits métalliques	216.4	297.8	402.2	407.5	421.9	499.8	582.2	669.8
Electricity and gas [E] Electricité et gaz [E]	106.0	104.5	101.7	102.2	106.1	110.5	109.6	111.3
Ireland — Irlande								
Total industry [CDE] Total, industrie [CDE]	152.2	174.6	201.6	222.0	237.9	249.0	249.8	257.3
Total mining [C] Total, industries extractives [C]	78.0	92.9	114.7	114.6	108.9	132.7	129.8	129.4
Total manufacturing [D] Total, industries manufacturières [D]	156.8	180.4	208.8	230.5	247.8	259.1	259.5	267.6
Food, beverages and tobacco — Aliments, boissons et tabac	109.0	114.4	120.4	128.3	133.3	138.4	145.7	147.7
Textiles, wearing apparel, leather, footwear Textiles, habillement, cuir et chaussures	102.1	90.1	73.6	77.4	55.2	48.1	46.4	39.2
Chemicals, rubber and plastic prod. Prod. chimiques, caoutchouc et plastiques	218.7	273.0	310.4	378.5	469.0	488.5	443.8	446.0
Basic metals — Métaux de base	90.4	91.5	94.2	84.3	83.0	79.4	75.3	85.9
Metal products — Produits métalliques	143.8	161.6	213.3	224.4	208.5	235.8	255.7	273.2
Electricity, gas and water [E] Electricité, gaz et eau [E]	113.0	122.6	129.0	137.4	141.9	146.1	152.0	154.6
Italy — Italie								
Total industry [CDE] Total, industrie [CDE]	104.3	104.4	107.7	107.1	105.3	104.3	104.9	103.1
Total mining [C] Total, industries extractives [C]	107.9	107.8	98.4	90.8	106.2	108.2	106.0	114.1
Total manufacturing [D] Total, industries manufacturières [D]	103.9	103.6	106.7	106.1	103.7	101.9	102.3	99.8
Food, beverages and tobacco — Aliments, boissons et tabac	104.4	107.6	109.9	113.9	114.9	117.3	116.0	116.9
Textiles, wearing apparel, leather, footwear Textiles, habillement, cuir et chaussures	99.9	95.2	95.6	95.3	88.5	85.3	82.0	75.6
Chemicals, petroleum, rubber and plastic products Prod. chimiques, pétroliers, caoutch. et plast.	106.8	106.3	108.4	106.5	107.4	106.4	108.0	106.4
Basic metals — Métaux de base	101.8	94.1	100.8	96.8	95.7	97.0	101.4	101.8
Metal products — Produits métalliques	104.0	102.5	106.5	105.0	101.3	98.2	98.3	95.5
Electricity and gas [E] Electricité et gaz [E]	107.3	111.4	118.3	119.0	120.7	126.8	131.3	134.2
Latvia — Lettonie								
Total industry [CDE] Total, industrie [CDE]	123.8	101.7	104.9	112.1	118.6	126.4	134.0	141.5
Total mining [C] Total, industries extractives [C]	117.2	123.9	134.9	141.4	154.2	162.4	180.2	226.2
Total manufacturing [D] Total, industries manufacturières [D]	130.2	103.6	108.4	116.5	123.8	133.5	141.8	151.0
Food, beverages and tobacco — Aliments, boissons et tabac	124.0	102.0	100.6	107.0	112.7	119.4	126.9	133.2
Textiles, wearing apparel, leather, footwear Textiles, habillement, cuir et chaussures	140.8	121.3	133.1	137.9	136.8	132.3	132.2	141.6
Chemicals, rubber and plastic prod. Prod. chimiques, caoutchouc et plastiques	105.5	56.5	48.7	54.7	63.2	60.3	71.3	82.5
Basic metals — Métaux de base	237.6	325.9	325.8	379.9	373.4	456.4	493.6	468.8
Metal products — Produits métalliques	91.7	72.9	91.3	94.5	102.7	117.3	125.9	135.5
Electricity, gas and water [E] Electricité, gaz et eau [E]	98.5	92.5	89.8	94.6	98.8	101.6	106.7	109.8
Lithuania — Lituanie								
Total industry [CDE] Total, industrie [CDE]	117.8	104.6	110.1	127.7	131.6	152.8	169.4	181.4
Total mining [C] Total, industries extractives [C]	185.7	177.1	198.1	263.1	250.8	271.8	251.2	231.4
Total manufacturing [D] Total, industries manufacturières [D]	115.4	102.8	111.9	129.6	133.3	152.1	170.1	184.7

Country or area and industry [ISIC Rev. 3] Pays ou zone et industrie [CITI Rév. 3]	1998	1999	2000	2001	2002	2003	2004	2005
Food, beverages and tobacco — Aliments, boissons et tabac	107.1	97.6	103.6	106.1	103.9	113.0	117.6	129.9
Textiles, wearing apparel, leather, footwear Textiles, habillement, cuir et chaussures	109.9	111.9	121.3	132.1	131.0	130.1	126.2	120.2
Chemicals, petroleum, rubber and plastic products Prod. chimiques, pétroliers, caoutch. et plast.	137.5	134.2	143.0	143.6	169.2	185.3	195.4	223.8
Basic metals — Métaux de base	79.3	172.2	255.8	265.3	211.0	155.5	121.0	150.7
Metal products — Produits métalliques	114.4	117.3	134.5	153.2	180.9	231.6	272.7	300.4
Electricity, gas and water [E] Electricité, gaz et eau [E]	99.9	80.7	68.7	79.1	83.3	108.1	116.0	115.9
Luxembourg — Luxembourg								
Total industry [CDE] Total, industrie [CDE]	114.5	116.3	122.1	126.4	129.5	134.2	139.4	139.7
Total mining [C] Total, industries extractives [C]	100.2	107.8	108.8	109.7	99.7	88.7	86.8	85.8
Total manufacturing [D] Total, industries manufacturières [D]	115.7	117.7	123.6	126.7	128.8	134.2	140.2	142.6
Food and beverages — Aliments et boissons	101.2	105.6	106.6	121.7	124.1	121.2	126.5	133.9
Textiles, wearing apparel, leather, footwear Textiles, habillement, cuir et chaussures	98.8	91.6	98.4	100.5	102.5	106.8	107.0	112.4
Chemicals, rubber and plastic prod. Prod. chimiques, caoutchouc et plastiques	129.6	119.5	128.3	137.9	149.1	159.1	165.3	170.7
Basic metals — Métaux de base	90.1	114.2	120.6	118.9	115.4	118.7	123.1	111.7
Metal products — Produits métalliques	121.6	122.0	122.5	117.6	116.4	120.1	125.0	133.3
Electricity and gas [E] Electricité et gaz [E]	102.0	99.8	106.9	116.3	123.8	128.2	129.8	128.4
Malta — Malte								
Total industry [CDE] Total, industrie [CDE]	97.8	98.5	111.8	102.7	...	...	...	...
Total mining [C] Total, industries extractives [C]	112.9	113.8	152.5	155.5	...	...	...	...
Total manufacturing [D] Total, industries manufacturières [D]	95.2	96.2	110.1	100.0	...	...	...	...
Food, beverages and tobacco — Aliments, boissons et tabac	109.6	112.6	115.9	114.2	...	...	...	...
Textiles, wearing apparel, leather, footwear Textiles, habillement, cuir et chaussures	111.8	113.4	113.3	117.1	...	...	...	...
Chemicals, petroleum, rubber and plastic products Prod. chimiques, pétroliers, caoutch. et plast.	104.4	105.4	91.5	81.9	...	...	...	...
Metal products — Produits métalliques	92.8	93.7	104.4	96.9	...	...	...	...
Electricity and water [E] Electricité et eau [E]	105.9	106.8	110.8	114.1	...	...	...	...
Netherlands — Pays-Bas								
Total industry [CDE] Total, industrie [CDE]	105.2	106.5	110.0	110.5	111.7	110.1	112.9	111.6
Total mining [C] Total, industries extractives [C]	103.1	99.5	97.2	103.6	103.4	100.2	111.1	100.9
Total manufacturing [D] Total, industries manufacturières [D]	106.7	109.2	113.8	112.8	113.4	112.2	114.0	114.2
Food, beverages and tobacco — Aliments, boissons et tabac	102.3	104.6	106.5	105.4	109.0	108.5	109.3	111.4
Textiles, wearing apparel, leather, footwear Textiles, habillement, cuir et chaussures	103.9	105.3	112.6	105.8	101.7	99.4	97.2	93.0
Chemicals, petroleum, rubber and plastic products Prod. chimiques, pétroliers, caoutch. et plast.	99.5	104.4	110.7	114.1	124.6	124.6	124.6	125.0
Basic metals — Métaux de base	107.8	108.0	110.0	109.0	112.0	116.0	126.8	127.0
Metal products — Produits métalliques	110.5	111.5	119.4	118.3	109.4	108.2	112.6	110.7
Electricity, gas and water [E] Electricité, gaz et eau [E]	98.8	96.7	98.5	100.5	112.5	110.8	108.3	108.2
Norway — Norvège								
Total industry [CDE] Total, industrie [CDE]	107.8	107.5	110.7	109.3	110.2	105.7	107.8	107.3
Total mining [C][11] Total, industries extractives [C][11]	109.2	109.8	115.7	119.3	117.6	115.7	113.7	110.5

Country or area and industry [ISIC Rev. 3] Pays ou zone et industrie [CITI Rév. 3]	1998	1999	2000	2001	2002	2003	2004	2005
Total manufacturing [D] Total, industries manufacturières [D]	108.8	106.2	103.0	102.0	101.1	96.7	98.2	101.1
Food, beverages and tobacco — Aliments, boissons et tabac	101.5	98.1	96.2	95.3	93.7	89.9	90.0	87.4
Textiles, wearing apparel, leather, footwear Textiles, habillement, cuir et chaussures	94.6	82.3	75.2	71.5	65.5	56.3	54.1	54.5
Chemicals, petroleum, rubber and plastic products Prod. chimiques, pétroliers, caoutch. et plast.	105.3	105.4	103.6	103.6	102.4	102.4	104.7	108.4
Basic metals — Métaux de base	111.7	115.2	116.3	111.3	109.1	109.5	120.6	119.5
Metal products — Produits métalliques	116.7	114.5	108.4	108.7	111.0	103.7	103.8	110.0
Electricity and gas [E] Electricité et gaz [E]	94.9	99.4	115.7	98.5	105.2	86.8	87.9	110.3
Poland — Pologne								
Total industry [CDE] Total, industrie [CDE]	127.4	133.5	143.5	144.1	146.1	158.9	179.1	186.4
Total mining [C] Total, industries extractives [C]	86.6	83.2	82.1	77.9	75.5	74.1	76.4	74.2
Total manufacturing [D] Total, industries manufacturières [D]	134.9	142.4	153.7	153.5	156.3	172.8	198.0	207.0
Food, beverages and tobacco — Aliments, boissons et tabac	127.0	129.0	130.1	134.0	138.6	146.0	154.7	162.2
Textiles, wearing apparel, leather, footwear Textiles, habillement, cuir et chaussures	120.0	115.9	114.5	110.3	109.4	108.4	108.1	99.7
Chemicals, petroleum, rubber and plastic products Prod. chimiques, pétroliers, caoutch. et plast.	124.9	132.8	147.1	153.2	163.0	186.8	208.0	218.6
Basic metals — Métaux de base	107.2	97.2	106.5	89.6	85.8	89.3	107.3	100.2
Metal products — Produits métalliques	152.3	163.8	180.1	181.2	187.2	215.9	268.8	295.6
Electricity, gas and water [E] Electricité, gaz et eau [E]	104.7	107.1	116.9	126.4	126.1	126.7	128.1	132.0
Portugal — Portugal								
Total industry [CDE] Total, industrie [CDE]	114.0	117.6	118.1	121.6	121.2	121.3	118.1	118.5
Total mining [C] Total, industries extractives [C]	105.2	102.2	103.8	105.8	100.2	90.7	94.6	92.5
Total manufacturing [D] Total, industries manufacturières [D]	112.8	114.4	114.8	117.3	117.8	117.2	116.4	114.6
Food, beverages and tobacco — Aliments, boissons et tabac	109.3	113.5	116.8	119.3	122.7	122.1	125.2	125.1
Textiles, wearing apparel, leather, footwear Textiles, habillement, cuir et chaussures	91.4	86.2	80.4	81.1	77.1	71.2	66.2	60.1
Chemicals, petroleum, rubber and plastic products Prod. chimiques, pétroliers, caoutch. et plast.	110.3	115.0	114.2	113.5	120.1	122.9	123.5	128.4
Basic metals — Métaux de base	112.5	126.3	124.1	114.6	115.5	114.2	117.3	112.7
Metal products — Produits métalliques	130.7	134.8	136.2	141.8	141.4	146.4	146.5	149.2
Electricity and gas [E] Electricité et gaz [E]	124.3	144.3	145.6	158.7	150.4	158.6	132.8	151.6
Republic of Moldova — République de Moldova								
Total industry [CDE] Total, industrie [CDE]	79.5	70.3	75.7	86.1	95.4	110.3	119.3	...
Total mining [C] Total, industries extractives [C]	75.9	65.4	63.9	69.7	86.5	109.1	134.8	...
Total manufacturing [D] Total, industries manufacturières [D]	74.3	65.3	76.9	88.5	100.3	118.3	129.3	...
Electricity, gas and water [E] Electricité, gaz et eau [E]	94.6	81.4	57.8	63.0	61.8	63.5	63.5	...
Romania — Roumanie								
Total industry [CDE] Total, industrie [CDE]	81.9	77.7	83.2	90.4	94.3	97.5	101.8	103.9
Total mining [C] Total, industries extractives [C]	81.6	76.1	79.8	84.3	79.8	79.6	80.8	80.5
Total manufacturing [D] Total, industries manufacturières [D]	82.5	78.5	85.1	93.9	99.8	103.7	109.1	112.1
Food, beverages and tobacco — Aliments, boissons et tabac	85.0	85.9	97.2	117.4	130.7	137.3	130.2	134.4

Country or area and industry [ISIC Rev. 3] Pays ou zone et industrie [CITI Rév. 3]	1998	1999	2000	2001	2002	2003	2004	2005
Textiles, wearing apparel, leather, footwear Textiles, habillement, cuir et chaussures	71.8	73.8	82.5	91.3	95.1	105.0	102.1	88.3
Chemicals, petroleum, rubber and plastic products Prod. chimiques, pétroliers, caoutch. et plast.	64.7	59.1	66.9	67.6	72.8	77.0	92.0	95.4
Basic metals — Métaux de base	92.4	63.9	79.9	90.7	110.4	89.4	100.9	103.2
Metal products — Produits métalliques	97.0	92.2	84.2	88.4	90.4	97.4	106.0	116.9
Electricity, gas and water [E] Electricité, gaz et eau [E]	77.8	72.9	72.7	70.9	68.5	69.6	67.2	66.4
Russian Federation — Fédération de Russie								
Total industry [CDE] Total, industrie [CDE]	88.8	96.7	105.2	108.3	111.7	121.6	131.7	137.0
Total mining [C] Total, industries extractives [C]	94.9	98.7	105.0	111.3	118.8	129.1	137.9	139.7
Total manufacturing [D] Total, industries manufacturières [D]	85.9	96.9	107.5	109.6	110.8	122.2	135.0	142.7
Food, beverages and tobacco — Aliments, boissons et tabac	90.2	100.8	104.9	113.6	121.9	131.1	136.2	142.2
Textiles, wearing apparel, leather, footwear Textiles, habillement, cuir et chaussures	71.2	82.6	101.1	109.7	109.2	112.3	108.7	107.1
Chemicals, petroleum, rubber and plastic products Prod. chimiques, pétroliers, caoutch. et plast.	87.9	104.7	117.6	119.0	120.8	126.1	134.0	139.0
Basic metals — Métaux de base	94.6	103.2	119.0	121.2	127.1	136.3	141.0	144.0
Metal products — Produits métalliques	79.8	91.7	106.7	108.0	101.0	124.3	146.3	156.2
Electricity and gas [E] Electricité et gaz [E]	93.3	92.2	95.9	97.2	101.9	105.3	106.7	107.9
Serbia and Montenegro — Serbie-et-Monténégro								
Total industry [CDE] Total, industrie [CDE]	121.2	91.7	102.1	102.3	104.2	101.4	109.1	109.6
Total mining [C] Total, industries extractives [C]	105.4	86.0	93.8	81.9	83.6	84.6	83.6	85.3
Total manufacturing [D] Total, industries manufacturières [D]	133.4	94.7	108.4	109.3	112.6	107.5	118.3	117.3
Food, beverages and tobacco — Aliments, boissons et tabac	113.5	109.5	110.5	107.5	116.3	113.8	117.8	123.4
Textiles, wearing apparel, leather, footwear Textiles, habillement, cuir et chaussures	127.2	90.3	106.4	108.0	86.6	61.3	58.6	52.6
Chemicals, petroleum, rubber and plastic products Prod. chimiques, pétroliers, caoutch. et plast.	226.0	124.6	141.3	164.2	170.4	184.8	213.4	225.2
Basic metals — Métaux de base	192.6	105.2	142.2	138.3	146.9	149.7	195.9	225.7
Metal products — Produits métalliques	134.4	94.7	114.8	101.5	106.7	96.3	108.9	102.3
Electricity, gas and water [E] Electricité, gaz et eau [E]	109.3	103.1	104.6	105.3	103.1	106.5	108.2	113.8
Slovakia — Slovaquie								
Total industry [CDE] Total, industrie [CDE]	108.6	106.3	115.2	123.2	131.0	137.7	143.0	148.6
Total mining [C] Total, industries extractives [C]	104.7	103.7	101.5	88.2	113.5	107.1	95.4	92.1
Total manufacturing [D] Total, industries manufacturières [D]	110.4	106.6	116.5	128.2	138.8	149.3	155.9	164.1
Electricity, gas and water [E] Electricité, gaz et eau [E]	95.6	98.4	105.0	102.9	96.9	92.1	95.7	92.7
Slovenia — Slovénie								
Total industry [CDE] Total, industrie [CDE]	105.8	105.2	111.8	115.1	117.9	119.6	126.2	130.3
Total mining [C] Total, industries extractives [C]	102.0	97.8	95.3	87.7	94.5	99.9	93.0	99.3
Total manufacturing [D] Total, industries manufacturières [D]	105.4	105.3	112.7	115.9	118.1	120.1	125.8	130.4
Food, beverages and tobacco — Aliments, boissons et tabac	101.8	100.1	106.3	108.8	107.2	108.4	96.8	95.3
Textiles, wearing apparel, leather, footwear Textiles, habillement, cuir et chaussures	94.8	84.8	87.9	81.9	70.1	62.1	54.2	48.9
Chemicals, petroleum, rubber and plastic products Prod. chimiques, pétroliers, caoutch. et plast.	109.4	110.0	121.3	128.3	133.0	145.4	166.5	177.8

Country or area and industry [ISIC Rev. 3] Pays ou zone et industrie [CITI Rév. 3]	1998	1999	2000	2001	2002	2003	2004	2005
Basic metals — Métaux de base	81.6	92.7	103.8	108.4	111.5	119.1	109.9	113.3
Metal products — Produits métalliques	102.2	105.4	114.7	123.5	130.5	135.4	156.4	168.4
Electricity [E] Electricité [E]	112.7	108.1	109.8	120.0	126.6	122.2	145.9	143.8
Spain — Espagne								
Total industry [CDE] Total, industrie [CDE]	111.9	114.8	119.3	117.9	118.0	119.9	122.1	122.2
Total mining [C] Total, industries extractives [C]	92.0	90.1	91.1	88.2	87.7	87.7	83.7	80.3
Total manufacturing [D] Total, industries manufacturières [D]	113.2	115.8	119.7	117.3	117.8	119.6	121.0	120.6
Food, beverages and tobacco — Aliments, boissons et tabac	109.1	109.3	108.3	109.5	113.7	116.3	118.1	119.9
Textiles, wearing apparel, leather, footwear Textiles, habillement, cuir et chaussures	101.5	99.4	97.6	94.4	85.6	79.4	73.8	65.3
Chemicals, petroleum, rubber and plastic products Prod. chimiques, pétroliers, caoutch. et plast.	112.6	118.7	119.7	119.7	125.1	130.0	129.8	129.5
Basic metals — Métaux de base	108.5	109.5	124.7	120.2	127.9	129.4	137.4	134.4
Metal products — Produits métalliques	121.0	122.7	128.8	123.8	119.5	121.3	123.9	122.5
Electricity and gas [E] Electricité et gaz [E]	108.4	115.1	124.9	130.3	130.3	134.0	143.4	149.3
Sweden — Suède								
Total industry [CDE] Total, industrie [CDE]	110.3	113.4	119.9	118.6	118.6	120.1	126.5	129.1
Total mining [C] Total, industries extractives [C]	94.5	96.4	97.8	96.2	99.4	96.2	105.7	112.7
Total manufacturing [D] Total, industries manufacturières [D]	111.1	114.6	121.8	120.5	121.7	124.6	130.2	132.5
Food, beverages and tobacco — Aliments, boissons et tabac	105.1	104.7	103.2	106.4	103.6	99.1	100.1	100.3
Chemicals, petroleum, rubber and plastic products Prod. chimiques, pétroliers, caoutch. et plast.	113.0	117.2	125.7	133.7	140.5	151.2	160.3	160.4
Basic metals — Métaux de base	105.5	105.1	110.6	120.8	126.2	124.4	132.1	127.4
Metal products — Produits métalliques	117.0	124.0	136.1	131.0	126.0	130.0	142.2	150.5
Electricity, gas and water [E] Electricité, gaz et eau [E]	106.2	105.2	106.0	104.5	94.8	87.7	97.8	101.8
Switzerland — Suisse								
Total industry [CDE] Total, industrie [CDE]	108.4	112.2	121.7	120.8	114.6	114.6	119.7	122.9
Total mining [C] Total, industries extractives [C]	87.9	93.4	94.2	94.7	93.3	92.6	96.5	91.5
Total manufacturing [D] Total, industries manufacturières [D]	109.1	112.7	123.2	121.8	115.4	115.3	120.8	124.7
Food, beverages and tobacco — Aliments, boissons et tabac	88.2	86.8	88.5	85.8	90.6	90.1	91.2	95.2
Textiles and wearing apparel — Textiles et habillement	93.1	87.5	87.7	79.7	74.4	70.2	77.0	79.8
Chemicals and chemical products — Produits chimiques	135.8	152.0	163.0	172.0	181.7	197.3	206.4	224.0
Basic metals and metal products Métaux de base et produits métalliques	108.6	108.8	123.9	123.5	108.6	104.5	105.8	105.0
Electricity, gas and water [E] Electricité, gaz et eau [E]	102.4	108.1	107.6	112.2	107.6	109.8	109.3	106.7
TFYR of Macedonia — L'ex-R.y. Macédoine								
Total industry [CDE] Total, industrie [CDE]	109.5	106.7	110.4	99.2	93.9	98.3	96.1	102.9
Ukraine — Ukraine								
Total industry [CDE] Total, industrie [CDE]	91.6	95.9	109.0	123.1	131.2	152.2	170.1	173.7
Total mining [C] Total, industries extractives [C]	95.3	98.3	104.6	108.1	110.6	116.7	121.5	...
Total manufacturing [D] Total, industries manufacturières [D]	93.7	97.1	113.2	132.7	144.5	170.8	195.7	...
Electricity, gas and water [E] Electricité, gaz et eau [E]	90.6	88.3	89.2	91.2	92.5	94.9	93.9	95.1

Country or area and industry [ISIC Rev. 3] Pays ou zone et industrie [CITI Rév. 3]	1998	1999	2000	2001	2002	2003	2004	2005
United Kingdom — Royaume-Uni								
Total industry [CDE] Total, industrie [CDE]	103.0	105.3	107.2	105.7	103.6	103.3	104.1	102.3
Total mining [C] Total, industries extractives [C]	104.2	108.6	105.1	99.3	99.7	94.6	87.1	79.8
Total manufacturing [D] Total, industries manufacturières [D]	102.9	104.1	106.6	105.1	102.5	102.7	104.7	103.6
Food, beverages and tobacco — Aliments, boissons et tabac	102.3	102.1	101.2	102.6	104.7	104.7	106.3	106.9
Textiles, wearing apparel, leather, footwear Textiles, habillement, cuir et chaussures	89.4	83.2	80.3	71.5	66.0	64.6	58.1	56.6
Chemicals, petroleum, rubber and plastic products Prod. chimiques, pétroliers, caoutch. et plast.	102.2	103.4	107.4	110.2	109.1	109.3	111.9	112.1
Basic metals — Métaux de base	101.2	97.4	94.0	91.9	82.3	82.6	84.8	82.8
Metal products — Produits métalliques	108.9	112.8	119.3	115.2	106.9	106.5	109.1	107.9
Electricity, gas and water [E] Electricité, gaz et eau [E]	108.8	112.9	116.3	120.1	120.6	122.5	123.9	123.5
Oceania · Océanie								
Australia[2] — Australie[2]								
Total industry [CDE] Total, industrie [CDE]	108.2	109.9	112.4	116.3	117.8	120.5	120.2	120.8
Total mining [C] Total, industries extractives [C]	113.3	114.3	122.5	130.6	130.4	129.1	124.9	129.2
Total manufacturing [D] Total, industries manufacturières [D]	106.9	109.2	110.1	112.6	115.0	119.3	120.5	118.9
Food, beverages and tobacco — Aliments, boissons et tabac	112.5	116.4	118.1	123.3	122.8	123.9	123.7	125.2
Textiles, wearing apparel, leather, footwear Textiles, habillement, cuir et chaussures	95.1	94.7	91.3	84.9	74.4	68.5	63.4	51.5
Chemicals, petroleum, rubber and plastic products Prod. chimiques, pétroliers, caoutch. et plast.	110.5	112.1	115.8	118.5	119.7	126.6	120.9	120.9
Basic metals and metal products Métaux de base et produits métalliques	108.4	110.2	107.8	110.3	113.9	120.2	123.8	122.8
Electricity, gas and water [E] Electricité, gaz et eau [E]	104.7	106.5	108.6	110.3	109.5	110.5	111.4	112.2
Fiji — Fidji								
Total industry [CDE] Total, industrie [CDE]	119.2	129.7	122.8	131.4	133.6	134.1	149.5	127.8
Total mining [C] Total, industries extractives [C]	113.3	134.5	116.3	117.1	113.6	106.9	122.7	88.5
Total manufacturing [D] Total, industries manufacturières [D]	121.6	130.6	123.1	139.2	138.8	136.3	152.9	123.8
Food, beverages and tobacco — Aliments, boissons et tabac	89.1	96.7	88.6	97.5	105.5	112.0	120.1	125.2
Textiles and wearing apparel — Textiles et habillement	220.9	240.6	227.3	297.6	261.3	234.4	290.5	130.7
Chemicals and chemical products — Produits chimiques	124.7	109.2	95.0	92.3	110.4	92.1	106.4	113.9
Electricity and water [E] Electricité et eau [E]	114.5	125.9	123.9	114.6	123.2	136.0	147.5	149.8
New Zealand[12] — Nouvelle-Zélande[12]								
Total industry [CDE][13] Total, industrie [CDE][13]	103.7	101.0	104.8	107.3	108.4	115.3	115.5	117.1
Total mining [C] Total, industries extractives [C]	114.1	112.1	116.8	118.6	120.0	123.4	113.9	111.0
Total manufacturing [D] Total, industries manufacturières [D]	102.8	99.2	104.1	106.8	108.5	115.8	117.4	119.3
Food, beverages and tobacco — Aliments, boissons et tabac	108.6	104.8	106.7	109.1	111.1	123.7	125.0	123.8
Textiles, wearing apparel, leather, footwear Textiles, habillement, cuir et chaussures	95.4	93.1	96.8	85.6	88.4	90.7	86.2	89.7
Chemicals, petroleum, rubber and plastic products Prod. chimiques, pétroliers, caoutch. et plast.	95.8	93.1	96.0	102.1	98.8	102.1	92.9	97.4
Basic metals and metal products Métaux de base et produits métalliques	104.4	101.6	108.2	114.9	120.1	125.2	133.5	135.6
Electricity, gas and water [E] Electricité, gaz et eau [E]	98.6	101.3	96.9	98.1	95.2	102.7	103.7	108.5

Source

United Nations Statistics Division, New York, the index numbers of industrial production database.

Notes

1 Twelve months beginning 1 July of the year stated.
2 Twelve months ending 30 June of the year stated.
3 Calculated by the Statistics Division of the United Nations from component national indices.
4 Excluding coal mining and crude petroleum.
5 Excluding petroleum refineries.
6 Twelve months ending 30 September of the year stated.
7 Including construction.
8 Index base: 1997=100.
9 Twelve months beginning 1 April of the year stated.
10 Index base: 2000=100.
11 Excluding gas and oil extraction.
12 Twelve months ending 31 March of the year stated.
13 Including forestry and fishing.

Source

Organisation des Nations Unies, Division de statistique, New York, la base de données pour les indices de la production industrielle.

Notes

1 Période de 12 mois commençant le 1er juillet de l'année indiquée.
2 Période de 12 mois finissant le 30 juin de l'année indiquée.
3 Calculé par la Division de Statistiques de l'Organisation des Nations Unies à partir d'indices nationaux plus détaillés.
4 Non compris l'extraction du charbon et de pétrole brut.
5 Non compris les raffineries de pétrole.
6 Période de 12 mois finissant le 30 septembre de l'année indiquée.
7 Y compris la construction.
8 Indice base: 1997=100.
9 Période de 12 mois commençant le 1er avril de l'année indiquée.
10 Indice base: 2000=100.
11 Non compris l'extraction de gaz et de pétrole brut.
12 Période de 12 mois finissant le 31 mars de l'année indiquée.
13 Y compris l'exploitation forestière et la pêche.

Technical notes: tables 16-22

Detailed internationally comparable data on national accounts are compiled and published annually by the Statistics Division, Department of Economic and Social Affairs of the United Nations Secretariat. Data for national accounts aggregates for countries or areas are based on the concepts and definitions contained in *A System of National Accounts* (1968 SNA) and in *System of National Accounts 1993* (1993 SNA). A summary of the conceptual framework, classifications and definitions of transactions is found in the annual United Nations publication, *National Accounts Statistics: Main Aggregates and Detailed Tables*, which presents, in the form of analytical tables, a summary of selected principal national accounts aggregates based on official detailed national accounts data of over 200 countries and areas. Every effort has been made to present the estimates of the various countries or areas in a form designed to facilitate international comparability. The data for some countries or areas has been compiled according to the 1968 SNA. Data for those countries or areas which have started to follow the concepts and definitions of the 1993 SNA is indicated with a footnote. To the extent possible, any other differences in concept, scope, coverage and classification are footnoted as well. Detailed footnotes identifying these differences are also available in the annual national accounts publication mentioned above. Such differences should be taken into account in order to avoid misleading comparisons among countries or areas.

Table 16 shows gross domestic product (GDP) and GDP per capita in US dollars at current prices, GDP at constant 1990 prices and the corresponding real rates of growth. The table is designed to facilitate international comparisons of levels of income generated in production. In order to present comparable coverage for as many countries as possible, the official GDP national currency data are supplemented by estimates prepared by the Statistics Division, based on a variety of data derived from national and international sources. The conversion rates used to translate national currency data into US dollars are the period averages of market exchange rates (MERs) for members of the International Monetary Fund (IMF). These rates, which are published in the *International Financial Statistics* , are communicated to the IMF by national central banks and consist of three types: (a) market rates, determined largely by market forces; (b) official rates, determined by government authorities; and (c) principal rates for countries maintaining multiple exchange rate arrangements. Market rates always take priority and official rates are used only when a free market rate is not available.

For non-members of the IMF, averages of the United Nations operational rates, used for accounting purposes in United Nations transactions with member countries, are applied. These are based on official, commercial and/or tourist rates of exchange.

Notes techniques : tableaux 16 à 22

La Division de statistique du Département des affaires économiques et sociales du Secrétariat de l'Organisation des Nations Unies établit et publie chaque année des données détaillées, comparables au plan international, sur les comptes nationaux. Les données relatives aux agrégats des différents pays et territoires sont établies en fonction des concepts et des définitions du *Système de comptabilité nationale* (SCN de 1968) et du *Système de comptabilité nationale 1993* (SCN de 1993). On trouvera un résumé de l'appareil conceptuel, des classifications et des définitions des opérations dans «*National Accounts Statistics: Main Aggregates and Detailed Tables*», publication annuelle des Nations Unies, qui présente, sous forme de tableaux analytiques, un choix d'agrégats essentiels de comptabilité nationale, issus des comptes nationaux détaillés de plus que 200 pays et territoires. On n'a rien négligé pour présenter les chiffres des différents pays et territoires sous une forme facilitant les comparaisons internationales. Pour plusiers pays, les chiffres ont été établis selon le SCN de 1968. Les données des pays et territoires qui ont commencé à appliquer les concepts et les définitions du SCN de 1993 sont signalés par une note. Dans la mesure du possible, on signale également au moyen de notes les cas où les concepts, la portée, la couverture et la classification ne seraient pas les mêmes. Il y a en outre des notes détaillées explicitant ces différences dans la publication annuelle mentionnée plus haut. Il y a lieu de tenir compte de ces différences pour éviter de tenter des comparaisons qui donneraient matière à confusion.

Le *tableau 16* fait apparaître le produit intérieur brut (PIB) total et par habitant, exprimé en dollars des États-Unis aux prix courants et à prix constants (base 1990), ainsi que les taux de croissance correspondants. Le tableau est conçu pour faciliter les comparaisons internationales du revenu issu de la production. Afin que la couverture soit comparable pour le plus grand nombre possible de pays, la Division de statistique s'appuie non seulement sur les chiffres officiels du PIB exprimé dans la monnaie nationale, mais aussi sur diverses données provenant de sources nationales et internationales. Les taux de conversion utilisés pour exprimer les données nationales en dollars des États-Unis sont, pour les membres du Fonds monétaire international (FMI), les moyennes pour la période considérée des taux de change du marché. Ces derniers, publiés dans *Statistiques financières internationales*, sont communiqués au FMI par les banques centrales des pays et reposent sur trois types de taux : a) taux du marché, déterminés dans une large mesure par les facteurs du marché; b) taux officiels, déterminés par les pouvoirs publics; c) taux principaux, pour les pays pratiquant différents arrangements en matière de taux de change. On donne toujours la priorité aux taux du marché, n'utilisant les taux officiels que lorsqu'on n'a pas de taux du marché libre.

It should be noted that there are practical constraints in the use of MERs for conversion purposes. Their use may result in excessive fluctuations or distortions in the dollar income levels of a number of countries, particularly in those with multiple exchange rates, those coping with inordinate levels of inflation or countries experiencing misalignments caused by market fluctuations. Caution is therefore urged when making inter-country comparisons of incomes as expressed in US dollars.

Alternative methods of making international comparisons have been developed in recent years. One is the Purchasing Power Parities (PPPs) which have been developed as part of the International Comparison Programme; another is the World Bank Atlas method of conversion based on the average of the exchange rates of the current year and the two immediately preceding years that have been adjusted for differences in inflation rates between individual countries and the average of G-5 countries (Germany, France, Japan, the United Kingdom, and the United States). The Statistics Division of the United Nations has developed the Price-Adjusted Rates of Exchange method (PARE) which, like the Atlas method, is designed to adjust exchange rates that do not adequately reflect relative movements of domestic and international inflation. PARE is mainly applied to countries with fixed exchange rate regimes and countries going through a period of high inflation (e.g. transition countries from 1990-1995).

The GDP at constant price series, based primarily on data officially provided by countries or areas and partly on estimates made by the Statistics Division, is transformed into index numbers and rebased to 1990=100. The resulting data are then converted into US dollars at the rate prevailing in the base year 1990. The growth rates are based on the estimates of GDP at constant 1990 prices. The growth rate of the year in question is obtained by dividing the GDP of that year by the GDP of the preceding year.

Table 17 features the percentage distribution of GDP at current prices by expenditure breakdown. It shows the portions of GDP spent on consumption by the household sector (including the non-profit institutions serving households) and the government, the portions spent on gross fixed capital formation, on changes in inventories, and on exports of goods and services, deducting imports of goods and services. The percentages are derived from official data reported to the United Nations by the countries and published in the annual national accounts publication.

Table 18 shows the percentage distribution of value added originating from the various industry components of the *International Standard Industrial Classification of All Economic Activities, Revision 3* (ISIC Rev. 3). This table reflects the economic structure of production in the different countries or areas. The percentages are based on official gross value added

Pour les pays qui ne sont pas membres du FMI, on utilise les moyennes des taux de change opérationnels de l'ONU (qui servent à des fins comptables pour les opérations de l'ONU avec les pays qui en sont membres). Ces taux reposent sur les taux de change officiels, les taux du commerce et/ou les taux touristiques.

Il faut noter que l'utilisation des taux de change du marché pour la conversion des données se heurte à des obstacles pratiques. On risque, ce faisant, d'aboutir à des fluctuations excessives ou à des distorsions du revenu en dollars de certains pays, surtout dans le cas des pays qui pratiquent plusieurs taux de change et de ceux qui connaissent des taux d'inflation exceptionnels ou des décalages provenant des fluctuations du marché. Les comparaisons de revenu entre pays sont donc sujettes à caution lorsqu'on se fonde sur le revenu exprimé en dollars des États-Unis.

D'autres méthodes ont été élaborées ces dernières années pour les comparaisons internationales. L'une, celle de la parité de pouvoir d'achat (PPA), procède du Programme de comparaison internationale ; une autre méthode de conversion, celle de l'Atlas de la Banque mondiale, est basée sur la moyenne des taux de change de l'année en cours et des deux années immédiatement précédentes, ajustés en fonction des différences d'inflation entre les pays considérés et la moyenne des pays du G-5 (Allemagne, États-Unis, France, Japon, et Royaume-Uni). La Division de statistique de l'ONU a mis au point la méthode des Taux de Change Corrigés des Prix (TCCP) qui, comme celle de l'Atlas, est conçue pour corriger les taux de change qui ne rendent pas convenablement compte de l'évolution relative de l'inflation dans un pays par rapport à l'inflation à l'échelon international. Le TCCP sert surtout pour les pays à taux de change fixe et ceux qui connaissent une période de forte inflation (par ex. les pays en transition entre 1990 et 1995).

La série de statistiques du PIB à prix constants est fondée principalement sur des données officiellement communiquées par les pays, et en partie sur des estimations de la Division de statistique; les données permettent de calculer des indices, la base 100 correspondant à 1990. Les chiffres ainsi obtenus sont alors convertis en dollars des États-Unis au taux de change de l'année de base (1990). Les taux de croissance sont calculés à partir des estimations du PIB aux prix constants de 1990. Le taux de croissance de l'année considérée est obtenu en divisant le PIB de l'année par celui de l'année précédente.

Le *tableau 17* montre la répartition (en pourcentage) du PIB aux prix courants par catégorie de dépense. Il indique la part du PIB consacrée aux dépenses de consommation du secteur des ménages (y compris les institutions sans but lucratif au service des ménages) et des administrations publiques et celle qui est consacrée à l'investissement fixe brut, celle qui

at basic current prices broken down by the kind of economic activity: agriculture, hunting, forestry and fishing (categories A+B); mining and quarrying (C); manufacturing (D); electricity, gas and water supply (E); construction (F); wholesale and retail trade, repair of motor vehicles, motorcycles and personal and household goods, restaurants and hotels (G+H); transport, storage and communication (I) and "other activities", comprised of financial intermediation (J), real estate, renting and business activities (K), public administration and defence, compulsory social security (L), education (M), health and social work (N), other community, social and personal service activities (O) and private households with employed persons (P).

Table 19 presents the relationships among the principal national accounting aggregates, namely: gross domestic product (GDP), gross national income (GNI), gross national disposable income (GNDI) and gross savings. GNI is the term used in the 1993 SNA instead of the term Gross National Product (GNP) which was used in the 1968 SNA. The ratio of each aggregate to GDP is derived cumulatively by adding net primary income (or net factor income) from the rest of the world (GNI), adding net current transfers from the rest of the world (GNDI), and deducting final consumption to arrive at gross saving.

Table 20 presents the distribution of government final consumption expenditure by function at current prices. The breakdown by function includes: general public services; defence; public order and safety; economic affairs; environmental protection; housing and community amenities; health; recreation, culture and religion; education; and social protection. The government expenditure is equal to the service produced by general government for its own use. These services are not sold; they are valued in the GDP at their cost to the government.

Table 21 shows the distribution of household final consumption expenditure in the domestic market by purpose at current prices. The percentage shares include: food, beverages, tobacco and narcotics; clothing and footwear; housing, water, electricity, gas and other fuels; furnishings, household equipment and routine maintenance of the house; health; transport and communication; recreation and culture; education; restaurants and hotels; and miscellaneous goods and services.

Table 22: The national indices in this table are shown for the categories "Mining and Quarrying", "Manufacturing" and "Electricity, gas and water". These categories are classified according to Tabulation Categories C, D and E of the ISIC Revision 3 at the 2-digit level. Major deviations from ISIC in the scope of the indices for the above categories are indicated by footnotes to the table.

The category "Total industry" covers Mining, Manufacturing and Electricity, gas and water. The indices for "Total indus-

correspond aux variations de stocks et celle qui correspond aux exportations de biens et services, déduction faite des importations de biens et services. Ces pourcentages sont calculés à partir des chiffres officiels communiqués à l'ONU par les pays, publiés dans l'ouvrage annuel.

Le *tableau 18* montre la répartition (en pourcentage) de la valeur ajoutée par branche d'activité, selon le classement retenu dans la *Classification internationale type, par industrie, de toutes les branches d'activité économique, Révision 3* (CITI Révision 3). Il rend donc compte de la structure économique de la production dans chaque pays. Les pourcentages sont établis à partir des chiffres officiels de valeur ajoutée brute aux prix de base courants, répartis selon les différentes catégories d'activité économique: agriculture, chasse, sylviculture et pêche (catégories A + B); activités extractives (C); activités de fabrication (D); production et distribution d'électricité, de gaz et d'eau (E); construction (F); commerce de gros et de détail, réparation de véhicules automobiles, de motocycles et de biens personnels et domestiques, hôtels et restaurants (G + H); transports, entreposage et communications (I) et « autres activités », y compris intermédiation financière (J), immobilier, locations et activités de services aux entreprises (K), administration publique et défense, sécurité sociale obligatoire (L), éducation (M), santé et action sociale (N), autres activités de services collectifs, sociaux et personnels (O), et ménages privés employant du personnel domestique (P).

Le *tableau 19* montre les rapports entre les principaux agrégats de la comptabilité nationale, à savoir le produit intérieur brut (PIB), le revenu national brut (RNB), le revenu national brut disponible et l'épargne brute. Le revenu national brut est l'agrégat qui remplace dans le SCN de 1993 le produit national brut, utilisé dans le SCN de 1968. Chacun d'entre eux est obtenu par rapport au PIB, en ajoutant les revenus primaires nets (ou revenus nets de facteurs) engendrés dans le reste du monde, pour obtenir le revenu national brut; en ajoutant les transferts courants nets reçus de non-résidents, pour obtenir le revenu national disponible; en soustrayant la consommation finale pour obtenir l'épargne brute.

Le *tableau 20* donne la répartition des dépenses de consommation finale des administrations publiques, par fonction, aux prix courants. La répartition par fonction est la suivante: services généraux des administrations publiques; défense; ordre et sécurité publiques; affaires économiques; protection de l'environnement; logements et équipements collectifs; santé; loisirs, culture et culte; enseignement ; protection sociale. Les dépenses des administrations sont considérées comme égales aux services produits par l'administration pour son propre usage. Ces services ne sont pas vendus et ils sont évalués, dans le PIB, à leur coût pour l'administration.

Le *tableau 21* donne la répartition des dépenses de consommation finale des ménages sur le marché intérieur par fonction

try", however, are the combination of the components shown and share all deviations from ISIC as footnoted for the component series.

The weights used in the calculation of the indices for a particular country are the value added contribution to the gross domestic product (GDP) of the given industry during the base year (value added = output - intermediate consumption). These value added contributions are measured at factor cost. Ideally, every five years the base year is changed, the corresponding base weights are updated and the indices of subsequent years are rebased. Currently, the national indices have been rebased to 1995=100.

aux prix courants. La répartition en pourcentage distingue les rubriques suivantes: alimentation, boissons, tabac et stupéfiants; articles d'habillement et chaussures; logement, eau, gaz, électricité et autres combustibles; meubles, articles de ménage et entretien courant de l'habitation; santé; transports et communication; loisirs et culture; enseignement; restaurants et hôtels; et autres fonctions, y compris les biens et services divers.

Tableau 22: Les indices nationaux de ce tableau sont donnés pour les catégories « Industries extractives et carrières », « Industries manufacturières » et « Électricité, gaz et eau ». Les catégories correspondent à celles des catégories C, D et E de la Classification internationale type, par industrie, de toutes les branches d'activité économique (CITI Révision 3) au niveau des classes à deux chiffres. Tous les indices pour lesquels les catégories s'écartent sensiblement de celles de la CITI sont signalés en note au tableau.

La catégorie « Ensemble de l'industrie » comprend les Industries extractives et carrières, les Industries manufacturières et l'Électricité, gaz et eau. Les indices pour « Ensemble de l'industrie », toutefois, combinent les composantes indiquées et présentent tous les écarts par rapport à la CITI que signalent les notes concernant les séries des composantes.

Les coefficients de pondération utilisés pour le calcul des indices d'un pays donné correspondent à la part de la valeur ajoutée de la branche considérée dans le produit intérieur brut (PIB) pendant l'année de référence (valeur ajoutée = production - consommation intermédiaire). Cette part de la valeur ajoutée est mesurée au coût des facteurs. En principe, l'année de référence change tous les cinq ans, les coefficients de pondération correspondants sont actualisés et les indices des années suivantes sont calculés sur une nouvelle base. À l'heure actuelle, la nouvelle base des indices est 1995=100.

Rates of discount of central banks

Per cent per annum, end of period

Taux d'escompte des banques centrales

Pour cent par année, fin de la période

Country or area — Pays ou zone	1997	1998	1999	2000	2001	2002	2003	2004	2005	2006
Albania[1] — Albanie[1]	32.00	23.44	18.00	10.82	7.00	8.50	6.50	5.25	5.00	5.50
Algeria — Algérie	11.00	9.50	8.50	6.00	6.00	5.50	4.50	4.00	4.00	4.00
Angola — Angola	48.00	58.00	120.00	150.00	150.00	150.00	150.00	95.00	95.00	14.00
Anguilla — Anguilla	8.00	8.00	8.00	8.00	7.00	7.00	6.50	6.50	6.50	6.50
Antigua and Barbuda — Antigua-et-Barbuda	8.00	8.00	8.00	8.00	7.00	7.00	6.50	6.50	6.50	6.50
Armenia — Arménie	65.10	...	...	...	...	...	...	...	...	...
Aruba[1] — Aruba[1]	9.50	9.50	6.50	6.50	6.50	6.50	5.00	5.00	5.00	5.00
Austria[2] — Autriche[2]	2.50	2.50	...	...	...	...	...	...	...	...
Azerbaijan[3] — Azerbaïdjan[3]	12.00	14.00	10.00	10.00	10.00	7.00	7.00	7.00	9.00	9.50
Bahamas[1] — Bahamas[1]	6.50	6.50	5.75	5.75	5.75	5.75	5.75	5.75	5.25	5.25
Bangladesh — Bangladesh	8.00	8.00	7.00	7.00	6.00	6.00	5.00	5.00	5.00	5.00
Barbados[1] — Barbade[1]	9.00	9.00	10.00	10.00	7.50	7.50	7.50	7.50	10.00	12.00
Belarus[3] — Bélarus[3]	8.90	9.60	23.40	#80.00	48.00	38.00	28.00	17.00	11.00	10.00
Belgium[2] — Belgique[2]	2.75	2.75	...	...	...	...	...	...	...	...
Belize[4] — Belize[4]	12.00	12.00	12.00	12.00	12.00	12.00	12.00	12.00	12.00	12.00
Benin — Bénin	6.00	6.00	6.00	6.00	6.00	6.00	4.50	4.00	4.00	4.25
Bolivia — Bolivie	13.25	14.10	12.50	10.00	8.50	12.50	7.50	6.00	5.25	5.25
Botswana[4] — Botswana[4]	12.00	12.75	13.75	14.25	14.25	15.25	14.25	14.25	14.50	15.00
Brazil — Brésil	45.09	39.41	21.37	#18.52	21.43	30.42	23.92	24.55	25.34	19.98
Bulgaria[1] — Bulgarie[1]	#6.65	5.08	4.46	4.63	4.65	3.31	2.83	2.37	#2.05	3.26
Burkina Faso — Burkina Faso	6.00	6.00	6.00	6.00	6.00	6.00	4.50	4.00	4.00	4.25
Burundi[5] — Burundi[5]	12.00	12.00	12.00	14.00	14.00	15.50	14.50	14.50	14.50	11.07
Cameroon — Cameroun	7.50	7.00	7.30	7.00	6.50	6.30	6.00	6.00	5.50	5.25
Canada[1] — Canada[1]	4.50	5.25	5.00	6.00	2.50	3.00	3.00	2.75	3.50	4.50
Cape Verde — Cap-Vert	...	...	...	...	11.50	10.00	8.50	8.50	7.50	8.50
Central African Rep. — Rép. centrafricaine	7.50	7.00	7.60	7.00	6.50	6.30	6.00	6.00	5.50	5.25
Chad — Tchad	7.50	7.00	7.60	7.00	6.50	6.30	6.00	6.00	5.50	5.25
Chile — Chili	7.96	9.12	7.44	8.73	6.50	3.00	2.45	2.25	4.50	5.25
China[1] — Chine[1]	8.55	4.59	3.24	3.24	3.24	2.70	2.70	3.33	3.33	3.33
China, Hong Kong SAR — Chine, Hong Kong RAS	7.00	6.25	7.00	8.00	3.25	2.75	2.50	3.75	5.75	6.75
Colombia — Colombie	31.32	42.28	23.05	18.28	13.25	10.00	12.00	11.25	10.75	10.75
Comoros — Comores	...	...	#6.36	5.63	5.89	4.79	3.82	3.55	3.59	4.34
Congo — Congo	7.50	7.00	7.60	7.00	6.50	6.30	6.00	6.00	5.50	5.25
Costa Rica[6] — Costa Rica[6]	31.00	37.00	34.00	31.50	28.75	31.25	26.00	26.00	27.00	24.75
Côte d'Ivoire — Côte d'Ivoire	6.00	6.00	6.00	6.00	6.00	6.00	4.50	4.00	4.00	4.25
Croatia — Croatie	5.90	5.90	7.90	5.90	5.90	4.50	4.50	4.50	4.50	4.50
Cyprus — Chypre	7.00	7.00	7.00	7.00	5.50	5.00	4.50	5.50	4.25	4.50
Czech Republic[1] — République tchèque[1]	14.75	9.50	5.25	5.25	4.50	2.75	2.00	2.50	2.00	2.50
Dem. Rep. of the Congo — Rép. dém. du Congo	13.00	22.00	120.00	120.00	140.00	24.00	8.00	...	...	...
Denmark — Danemark	3.50	3.50	3.00	4.75	3.25	2.86	2.00	2.00	2.25	3.50
Dominica — Dominique	8.00	8.00	8.00	8.00	7.00	7.00	6.50	6.50	6.50	6.50
Ecuador — Equateur	37.46	61.84	64.40	#13.16	16.44	14.55	11.19	9.86	9.61	9.22
Egypt — Egypte	12.25	12.00	12.00	12.00	11.00	10.00	10.00	10.00	10.00	9.00
Equatorial Guinea — Guinée équatoriale	7.50	7.00	7.60	7.00	6.50	6.30	6.00	6.00	5.50	5.25
Euro Area[7,8] — Zone euro[7,8]	...	...	4.00	5.75	4.25	3.75	3.00	3.00	3.25	4.50
Fiji[1] — Fidji[1]	1.88	2.50	2.50	8.00	1.75	1.75	1.75	2.25	2.75	5.25
Finland[1,2] — Finlande[1,2]	4.00	3.50	...	...	...	...	...	2.25	...	...
Gabon — Gabon	7.50	7.00	7.60	7.00	6.50	6.30	6.00	6.00	5.50	5.25
Gambia — Gambie	14.00	12.00	10.50	10.00	13.00	18.00	29.00	28.00	14.00	9.00

Rates of discount of central banks—Per cent per annum, end of period (*continued*)
Taux d'escompte des banques centrales—Pour cent par année, fin de la période (*suite*)

Country or area — Pays ou zone	1997	1998	1999	2000	2001	2002	2003	2004	2005	2006
Germany[2] — Allemagne[2]	2.50	2.50	...	...	...	...	...	...	...	...
Ghana — Ghana	45.00	37.00	27.00	27.00	27.00	24.50	21.50	18.50	15.50	12.50
Greece[1,2] — Grèce[1,2]	14.50	...	#11.81	8.10	...	...	...	...	...	...
Grenada — Grenade	8.00	8.00	8.00	8.00	7.00	7.00	6.50	6.50	6.50	6.50
Guinea[3] — Guinée[3]	15.00	...	...	11.50	16.25	16.25	16.25	16.25	22.25	...
Guinea-Bissau — Guinée-Bissau	6.00	6.00	6.00	6.00	6.00	6.00	4.50	4.00	4.00	4.25
Guyana — Guyana	11.00	11.25	13.25	11.75	8.75	6.25	5.50	6.00	6.00	6.75
Hungary — Hongrie	20.50	17.00	14.50	11.00	9.75	8.50	12.50	9.50	6.00	8.00
Iceland — Islande	6.55	#8.50	10.00	12.40	12.00	8.20	7.70	10.25	...	...
India[1] — Inde[1]	9.00	9.00	8.00	8.00	6.50	6.25	6.00	6.00	6.00	6.00
Indonesia — Indonésie	20.00	38.44	12.51	14.53	17.62	12.93	8.31	7.43	12.75	9.75
Iran (Islamic Rep. of) — Iran (Rép. islamique d')	...	...	...	...	...	...	11.68	...	...	...
Ireland[2,9] — Irlande[2,9]	6.75	4.06	...	...	...	...	...	...	...	...
Israel — Israël	13.72	13.47	11.20	8.21	5.67	9.18	5.20	3.90	4.44	...
Italy[2] — Italie[2]	5.50	3.00	...	...	...	...	...	...	...	...
Japan — Japon	0.50	0.50	0.50	0.50	0.10	0.10	0.10	0.10	0.10	0.40
Jordan — Jordanie	7.75	9.00	8.00	6.50	5.00	4.50	2.50	3.75	6.50	7.50
Kazakhstan[3] — Kazakhstan[3]	18.50	25.00	18.00	14.00	9.00	7.50	7.00	7.00	8.00	9.00
Kenya — Kenya	32.27	17.07	26.46	...	...	...	...	...	...	...
Korea, Republic of — Corée, République de	5.00	3.00	3.00	3.00	2.50	2.50	2.50	2.00	2.00	2.75
Kuwait — Koweït	7.50	7.00	6.75	7.25	4.25	3.25	3.25	4.75	6.00	6.25
Lao People's Dem. Rep.[1] — Rép. dém. pop. lao[1]	...	35.00	34.89	35.17	35.00	20.00	20.00	20.00	20.00	20.00
Latvia — Lettonie	4.00	4.00	4.00	3.50	3.50	3.00	3.00	4.00	4.00	5.00
Lebanon — Liban	30.00	30.00	25.00	20.00	20.00	20.00	20.00	20.00	12.00	12.00
Lesotho — Lesotho	15.60	19.50	19.00	15.00	13.00	16.19	15.00	13.00	13.00	10.76
Libyan Arab Jamah. — Jamah. arabe libyenne	...	3.00	5.00	5.00	5.00	5.00	5.00	4.00	4.00	4.00
Madagascar — Madagascar	...	...	15.00	...	...	...	...	...	...	...
Malawi — Malawi	23.00	43.00	47.00	50.23	46.80	40.00	35.00	25.00	25.00	20.00
Maldives — Maldives	...	...	...	...	18.00	18.54	19.00	18.25	18.00	18.00
Mali[1] — Mali[1]	6.00	6.00	6.00	6.00	6.00	6.00	4.50	4.00	4.00	4.25
Malta — Malte	5.50	5.50	4.75	4.75	4.25	3.75	#3.00	3.00	3.25	3.75
Mauritius — Maurice	10.46	17.19	...	...	...	...	...	...	...	...
Mongolia[1] — Mongolie[1]	45.50	23.30	11.40	8.65	8.60	9.90	11.50	15.75	4.40	6.42
Montserrat — Montserrat	8.00	8.00	8.00	8.00	7.00	7.00	6.50	6.50	6.50	6.50
Morocco — Maroc	...	6.04	5.42	5.00	4.71	3.79	3.25	3.25	3.25	3.25
Mozambique — Mozambique	12.95	9.95	9.95	9.95	9.95	9.95	9.95	9.95	9.95	9.95
Myanmar[1] — Myanmar[1]	15.00	15.00	12.00	10.00	10.00	10.00	10.00	10.00	10.00	...
Namibia[10] — Namibie[10]	16.00	18.75	11.50	11.25	9.25	12.75	7.75	7.50	7.00	9.00
Nepal[1] — Népal[1]	9.00	9.00	9.00	7.50	6.50	5.50	5.50	5.50	6.00	...
Netherlands Antilles — Antilles néerlandaises	6.00	6.00	6.00	6.00	6.00	6.00	...	...	...	...
New Zealand — Nouvelle-Zélande	9.70	5.60	5.00	6.50	4.75	5.75	5.00	6.50	7.25	7.25
Niger — Niger	6.00	6.00	6.00	6.00	6.00	6.00	4.50	4.00	4.00	4.25
Nigeria — Nigéria	13.50	13.50	18.00	14.00	20.50	16.50	15.00	15.00	13.00	...
Norway — Norvège	5.50	10.00	7.50	9.00	8.50	8.50	4.25	3.75	4.25	5.50
Pakistan — Pakistan	18.00	16.50	13.00	13.00	10.00	7.50	7.50	7.50	9.00	9.50
Papua New Guinea — Papouasie-Nvl-Guinée	9.49	17.07	16.66	9.79	11.73	11.71	#15.50	12.67	9.67	8.13
Paraguay — Paraguay	20.00	20.00	20.00	20.00	20.00	20.00	20.00	20.00	20.00	20.00
Peru — Pérou	15.94	18.72	17.80	14.00	5.00	4.50	3.25	3.75	4.00	5.25
Philippines — Philippines	14.64	12.40	7.89	13.81	8.30	4.19	5.53	8.36	5.70	5.04
Poland — Pologne	24.50	18.25	19.00	21.50	14.00	7.75	5.75	7.00	4.50	4.00
Portugal[2] — Portugal[2]	5.31	3.00	...	...	...	...	...	...	...	...
Russian Federation[3] — Fédération de Russie[3]	28.00	60.00	55.00	25.00	25.00	21.00	16.00	13.00	12.00	11.00
Rwanda — Rwanda	10.75	11.38	11.19	11.69	13.00	13.00	14.50	14.50	12.50	...

23 Rates of discount of central banks — Per cent per annum, end of period (*continued*)
Taux d'escompte des banques centrales — Pour cent par année, fin de la période (*suite*)

Country or area — Pays ou zone	1997	1998	1999	2000	2001	2002	2003	2004	2005	2006
Saint Kitts and Nevis — Saint-Kitts-et-Nevis	8.00	8.00	8.00	8.00	7.00	7.00	6.50	6.50	6.50	6.50
Saint Lucia — Sainte-Lucie	8.00	8.00	8.00	8.00	7.00	7.00	6.50	6.50	6.50	6.50
St. Vincent-Grenadines — St. Vincent-Grenadines	8.00	8.00	8.00	8.00	7.00	7.00	6.50	6.50	6.50	6.50
Sao Tome and Principe — Sao Tomé-et-Principe	55.00	29.50	17.00	17.00	15.50	15.50	14.50	14.50	18.20	28.00
Senegal — Sénégal	6.00	6.00	6.00	6.00	6.00	6.00	4.50	4.00	4.00	4.25
Serbia[1] — Serbie[1]	...	...	...	...	18.67	9.72	10.63	#17.21	19.16	15.35
Seychelles — Seychelles	11.00	5.50	5.50	5.50	5.50	5.50	4.67	3.51	3.87	4.44
Slovakia — Slovaquie	8.80	8.80	8.80	8.80	#7.75	6.50	6.00	4.00	3.00	4.75
Slovenia[1] — Slovénie[1]	11.00	11.00	9.00	11.00	12.00	10.50	7.25	5.00	5.00	4.50
South Africa — Afrique du Sud	16.00	#19.32	12.00	12.00	9.50	13.50	8.00	7.50	7.00	9.00
Spain[1,2] — Espagne[1,2]	4.75	3.00	...	...	...	...	...	...	...	...
Sri Lanka[5] — Sri Lanka[5]	17.00	17.00	16.00	25.00	...	18.00	15.00	15.00	15.00	...
Swaziland — Swaziland	15.75	18.00	12.00	11.00	9.50	13.50	8.00	7.50	7.00	9.00
Sweden[1] — Suède[1]	2.50	2.00	1.50	2.00	2.00	#4.50	3.00	2.00	1.50	...
Switzerland — Suisse	1.00	1.00	0.50	#3.20	1.59	0.50	0.11	0.54	0.73	1.90
Syrian Arab Republic — Rép. arabe syrienne	5.00	5.00	5.00	5.00	5.00	5.00	...	...	...	...
Tajikistan[3] — Tadjikistan[3]	76.00	36.40	20.10	20.60	20.00	#24.75	#15.00	10.00	9.00	12.00
Thailand — Thaïlande	12.50	12.50	4.00	4.00	3.75	3.25	2.75	3.50	5.50	6.50
TFYR of Macedonia[1] — L'ex-R.y. Macédoine[1]	8.90	8.90	8.90	7.90	10.70	10.70	6.50	6.50	6.50	6.50
Togo — Togo	6.00	6.00	6.00	6.00	6.00	6.00	4.50	4.00	4.00	4.25
Trinidad and Tobago[1] — Trinité-et-Tobago[1]	13.00	13.00	13.00	13.00	13.00	7.25	7.00	7.00	8.00	...
Turkey — Turquie	67.00	67.00	60.00	60.00	60.00	55.00	43.00	38.00	23.00	27.00
Uganda[1] — Ouganda[1]	14.08	9.10	15.75	18.86	8.88	13.08	25.62	16.15	14.36	16.30
Ukraine[3] — Ukraine[3]	35.00	60.00	45.00	27.00	12.50	7.00	7.00	9.00	9.50	8.50
United Rep. of Tanzania — Rép.-Unie de Tanzanie	16.20	17.60	20.20	10.70	8.70	9.18	12.34	14.42	19.33	20.07
United States — Etats-Unis	5.00	4.50	5.00	6.00	1.33	0.75	#2.00	3.15	5.16	6.25
Uruguay[11] — Uruguay[11]	95.50	73.70	66.39	57.26	71.66	316.01	46.27	10.00	10.00	10.00
Vanuatu — Vanuatu	...	7.00	7.00	7.00	6.50	6.50	6.50	6.50	6.25	6.00
Venezuela (Boliv. Rep. of) — Venezuela (Rép. bolivar. du)	45.00	60.00	38.00	38.00	37.00	40.00	28.50	28.50	28.50	28.50
Viet Nam[3] — Viet Nam[3]	10.80	12.00	6.00	6.00	4.80	4.80	5.00	5.00	5.00	5.00
Yemen — Yémen	15.00	19.95	18.53	15.89	15.16	13.13	...	...	...	...
Zambia — Zambie	17.70	...	32.93	25.67	40.10	27.87	14.35	16.68	14.81	8.79
Zimbabwe[1] — Zimbabwe[1]	31.50	#39.50	74.41	57.84	57.20	29.65	300.00	110.00	540.00	500.00

Source

International Monetary Fund (IMF), Washington, D.C., "International Financial Statistics," May 2007 and the IMF database.

Notes

1. Central Bank rate.
2. Beginning 1999, see Euro Area. For Greece, beginning 2001, see Euro Area.
3. Refinance rate.
4. Lending rate.
5. Advance rate.
6. Discount rate: commercial.
7. Marginal lending facility rate.
8. "Euro Area" is an official descriptor for the European Economic and Monetary Union (EMU). The participating member states of the EMU are Austria, Belgium, Finland, France, Germany, Greece (beginning 2001), Ireland, Italy, Luxembourg, Netherlands, Portugal, and Spain.
9. Short-term facility rate.
10. Bank of Namibia overdraft rate.
11. Domestic currency.

Source

Fonds monétaire international (FMI), Washington, D.C.,"Statistiques Financières Internationales," mai 2007 et la base de données du FMI.

Notes

1. Taux de la Banque centrale.
2. À compter de 1999, voir zone euro. Pour la Grèce, à compter de 2001, voir zone euro.
3. Taux de refinancement.
4. Taux prêteur.
5. Avances ordinaires à l'état.
6. Taux de l'escompte : effet de commerce.
7. Taux de facilité de prêt marginal.
8. L'expression "zone euro" est un intitulé officiel pour l'Union économique et monétaire (UEM) européenne. L'UEM est composée des pays membres suivants : Allemagne, Autriche, Belgique, Espagne, Finlande, France, Grèce (à partir de 2001), Irlande, Italie, Luxembourg, Pays-Bas et Portugal.
9. Taux de facilité à court terme.
10. Taux de découvert à la « Bank of Namibia ».
11. Monnaie locale.

24 Short-term interest rates

Treasury bill and money market rates: per cent per annum

Taux d'intérêt à court terme

Taux des bons du Trésor et du marché monétaire : pour cent par année

Country or area — Pays ou zone	1997	1998	1999	2000	2001	2002	2003	2004	2005	2006
Albania — Albanie										
Treasury bill — Bons du trésor	32.59	27.49	17.54	10.80	7.72	9.49	8.81	6.79	5.52	...
Algeria — Algérie										
Money market — Marché monétaire	13.00	10.00	9.99	6.45	2.84	3.13	1.91	1.09	2.01	2.34
Treasury bill — Bons du trésor	...	#9.96	10.05	7.95	5.69	1.80	1.25	0.15	1.30	1.65
Anguilla — Anguilla										
Money market — Marché monétaire	5.25	5.25	5.25	5.25	#5.64	6.32	6.07	4.67	4.01	4.76
Antigua and Barbuda — Antigua-et-Barbuda										
Money market — Marché monétaire	5.25	5.25	5.25	5.25	#5.64	6.32	6.07	4.67	4.01	4.78
Treasury bill — Bons du trésor	7.00	7.00	7.00	7.00	7.00	7.00	7.00	7.00	7.00	6.52
Argentina — Argentine										
Money market — Marché monétaire	6.63	6.81	6.99	8.15	24.90	41.35	3.74	1.96	4.11	7.20
Money market B[1] — Marché monétaire B[1]	6.39	6.55	6.07	7.53	12.76	13.01	1.64	2.03	2.86	3.32
Armenia — Arménie										
Money market — Marché monétaire	36.41	27.84	23.65	18.63	19.40	12.29	7.51	4.18	3.17	4.34
Treasury bill — Bons du trésor	57.54	46.99	55.10	24.40	#20.59	14.75	11.91	5.27	4.05	4.87
Australia — Australie										
Money market — Marché monétaire	5.50	4.99	#4.78	5.90	5.06	4.55	4.81	5.25	5.46	5.81
Treasury bill A[2] — Bons du trésor A[2]	5.29	4.84	4.76	5.98	4.80	...	...	...	...	...
Austria[3] — Autriche[3]										
Money market — Marché monétaire	3.27	3.36	...	...	...	...	...	...	...	...
Azerbaijan — Azerbaïdjan										
Treasury bill — Bons du trésor	12.23	14.10	18.31	16.73	16.51	14.12	8.00	4.62	7.52	10.04
Bahamas — Bahamas										
Treasury bill — Bons du trésor	4.35	3.84	1.97	1.03	1.94	2.50	1.78	0.56	0.14	0.87
Bahrain — Bahreïn										
Money market B[4] — Marché monétaire B[4]	...	5.69	5.58	6.89	3.85	2.02	1.24	1.74	3.64	...
Treasury bill — Bons du trésor	5.68	5.53	5.46	6.56	3.78	1.75	1.13	1.56	...	5.04
Barbados — Barbade										
Treasury bill — Bons du trésor	3.61	5.61	5.83	5.29	3.14	2.10	1.41	1.20	4.62	5.96
Belgium — Belgique										
Money market B[3,5] — Marché monétaire B[3,5]	3.46	3.58	...	...	...	...	...	...	...	...
Treasury bill — Bons du trésor	3.38	3.51	2.72	4.02	4.16	3.17	2.23	1.97	2.02	2.73
Belize[6] — Belize[6]										
Treasury bill B — Bons du trésor B	3.51	3.83	5.91	5.91	5.91	4.59	3.22	3.22	3.22	3.22
Benin[7] — Bénin[7]										
Money market A — Marché monétaire A	4.95	4.95	4.95	4.95	4.95	4.95	4.95	4.95	4.95	4.95
Bolivia — Bolivie										
Money market — Marché monétaire	13.97	12.57	13.49	7.40	6.99	8.41	4.07	4.05	3.53	3.80
Money market B[1] — Marché monétaire B[1]	7.85	9.26	8.29	5.68	3.57	2.96	2.12	3.02	3.37	4.62
Treasury bill — Bons du trésor	13.65	12.33	14.07	10.99	11.48	12.41	9.92	7.41	4.96	4.56
Treasury bill B[1] — Bons du trésor B[1]	7.15	7.48	7.84	7.02	4.19	3.56	2.53	3.34	2.85	3.68
Brazil — Brésil										
Money market — Marché monétaire	25.00	29.50	26.26	17.59	17.47	19.11	23.37	16.24	19.12	15.28
Treasury bill — Bons du trésor	24.79	28.57	26.39	18.51	20.06	19.43	22.11	17.14	18.76	14.38
Treasury bill B[1] — Bons du trésor B[1]	11.60	15.04	...	...	11.46	...	...	...	...	...

Short-term interest rates — Treasury bill and money market rates: per cent per annum (*continued*)
Taux d'intérêt à court terme — Taux des bons du Trésor et du marché monétaire : pour cent par année (*suite*)

Country or area — Pays ou zone	1997	1998	1999	2000	2001	2002	2003	2004	2005	2006
Bulgaria — Bulgarie										
Money market B[4] — Marché monétaire B[4]	66.43	2.48	2.93	3.02	3.74	2.47	1.95	1.95	#2.02	2.79
Treasury bill — Bons du trésor	78.35	6.02	5.43	4.21	4.57	4.29	2.81	2.64	...	...
Burkina Faso[7] — Burkina Faso[7]										
Money market A — Marché monétaire A	4.95	4.95	4.95	4.95	4.95	4.95	4.95	4.95	4.95	4.95
Canada — Canada										
Money market A[8] — Marché monétaire A[8]	3.26	4.87	4.74	5.52	4.11	2.45	2.93	2.25	2.66	4.02
Treasury bill — Bons du trésor	3.26	4.73	4.72	5.49	3.77	2.59	2.87	2.22	2.73	4.03
Cape Verde — Cap-Vert										
Treasury bill — Bons du trésor	...	7.26	6.22	7.84	9.48	7.93	5.79	6.23	4.19	2.64
Chile — Chili										
Money market — Marché monétaire	...	...	...	10.09	6.81	4.08	2.72	1.88	3.48	5.02
China, Hong Kong SAR — Chine, Hong Kong RAS										
Money market — Marché monétaire	4.50	5.50	5.75	7.13	2.69	1.50	0.07	0.13	4.25	3.94
Treasury bill — Bons du trésor	7.50	5.04	4.94	5.69	1.69	1.35	-0.08	0.07	3.65	3.29
China, Macao SAR[4] — Chine, Macao RAS[4]										
Money market B — Marché monétaire B	7.54	5.41	5.70	6.29	2.11	1.48	0.11	0.27	4.09	3.91
Colombia[4] — Colombie[4]										
Money market B — Marché monétaire B	23.83	35.00	18.81	10.87	10.43	6.06	6.95	7.01	6.18	6.49
Côte d'Ivoire[7] — Côte d'Ivoire[7]										
Money market A — Marché monétaire A	4.95	4.95	4.95	4.95	4.95	4.95	4.95	4.95	4.95	4.95
Croatia — Croatie										
Money market — Marché monétaire	9.71	11.16	10.21	6.78	3.42	1.75	3.31	5.11	3.10	2.06
Cyprus — Chypre										
Money market — Marché monétaire	4.82	4.80	5.15	5.96	4.93	3.42	3.35	4.01	3.27	2.90
Treasury bill — Bons du trésor	5.38	5.59	5.59	6.01	...	...	3.56	...	...	...
Czech Republic — République tchèque										
Money market — Marché monétaire	17.50	10.08	5.58	5.42	4.69	2.63	2.08	2.56	2.17	2.55
Treasury bill — Bons du trésor	11.21	10.51	5.71	5.37	5.06	2.72	2.04	2.57	1.96	2.51
Denmark[5] — Danemark[5]										
Money market B — Marché monétaire B	3.71	4.27	3.37	4.98	...	3.56	2.38	2.16	2.20	3.18
Dominica — Dominique										
Money market — Marché monétaire	5.25	5.25	5.25	5.25	#5.64	6.32	6.07	4.67	4.01	4.76
Treasury bill — Bons du trésor	6.40	6.40	6.40	6.40	6.40	6.40	6.40	6.40	6.40	6.40
Dominican Republic — Rép. dominicaine										
Money market — Marché monétaire	13.01	16.68	15.30	18.28	13.47	14.50	24.24	36.76	12.57	10.60
Egypt — Egypte										
Treasury bill — Bons du trésor	8.80	8.80	9.00	9.10	7.20	5.50	6.90	9.90	8.57	9.53
El Salvador — El Salvador										
Money market — Marché monétaire	10.43	9.43	10.68	6.93	5.28	4.40	3.86	4.36	5.18	6.00
Estonia — Estonie										
Money market — Marché monétaire	6.45	11.66	5.39	#5.68	5.31	3.88	2.92	2.50	2.38	3.16
Ethiopia — Ethiopie										
Treasury bill — Bons du trésor	3.97	3.48	3.65	2.74	3.06	1.30	#1.31	0.56	0.25	0.08
Euro Area[9] — Zone euro[9]										
Money market A — Marché monétaire A	4.38	3.96	2.97	4.39	4.26	3.32	2.34	2.11	2.19	3.08
Fiji — Fidji										
Money market A[10] — Marché monétaire A[10]	1.91	1.27	1.27	2.58	0.79	0.92	0.86	0.90	1.28	4.78
Treasury bill — Bons du trésor	2.60	2.00	2.00	3.63	1.51	1.66	1.06	1.56	1.94	7.45

Country or area — Pays ou zone	1997	1998	1999	2000	2001	2002	2003	2004	2005	2006
Finland[11] — Finlande[11]										
Money market B — Marché monétaire B	3.23	3.57	2.96	4.39	4.26	3.32	2.33	2.11	2.18	3.08
France — France										
Money market B[3,5] — Marché monétaire B[3,5]	3.24	3.39	...	...	...	...	...	...	...	...
Treasury bill — Bons du trésor	3.35	3.45	2.72	4.23	4.26	3.28	2.27	...	...	...
Treasury bill A[12] — Bons du trésor A[12]	3.35	3.45	2.72	4.23	4.26	3.28	2.27	...	...	...
Georgia — Géorgie										
Money market — Marché monétaire	23.89	42.62	31.26	16.77	17.54	27.69	16.88	11.87	7.71	9.46
Treasury bill — Bons du trésor	...	...	...	...	29.93	43.42	44.26	19.16	...	...
Germany — Allemagne										
Money market B[5] — Marché monétaire B[5]	3.18	3.41	2.73	4.11	4.37	3.28	2.32	2.05	2.09	2.84
Treasury bill — Bons du trésor	3.32	3.42	2.88	4.32	3.66	2.97	1.98	2.00	2.03	3.08
Ghana — Ghana										
Money market — Marché monétaire	...	...	...	...	...	...	24.71	15.73	14.70	10.57
Treasury bill B[13] — Bons du trésor B[13]	42.77	34.33	26.37	36.28	40.96	25.11	27.25	16.57	14.89	9.95
Greece — Grèce										
Money market A[3,14] — Marché monétaire A[3,14]	12.80	13.99	...	...	...	...	...	...	...	...
Treasury bill A — Bons du trésor A	11.38	10.30	8.30	#6.22	4.08	3.50	2.34	2.27	2.33	3.44
Grenada — Grenade										
Money market — Marché monétaire	5.25	5.25	5.25	5.25	#5.64	6.32	6.07	4.67	4.01	4.78
Treasury bill — Bons du trésor	6.50	6.50	6.50	6.50	#7.00	7.00	6.50	5.50	5.50	6.25
Guatemala — Guatemala										
Money market — Marché monétaire	7.77	6.62	9.23	9.33	10.58	9.11	6.65	6.16	6.54	6.56
Guinea-Bissau — Guinée-Bissau										
Money market — Marché monétaire	4.95	4.95	4.95	4.95	4.95	4.95	4.95	4.95	4.95	4.95
Guyana — Guyana										
Treasury bill — Bons du trésor	8.91	8.33	11.31	9.88	7.78	4.94	3.04	3.62	3.79	3.95
Haiti — Haïti										
Treasury bill — Bons du trésor	14.13	16.21	7.71	12.33	13.53	7.56	20.50	12.24	8.29	...
Hungary — Hongrie										
Treasury bill — Bons du trésor	20.13	17.83	14.68	11.03	10.79	8.91	8.22	11.32	6.95	6.87
Iceland — Islande										
Money market — Marché monétaire	7.38	8.12	9.24	11.61	14.51	11.21	5.14	6.22	...	...
Treasury bill B[15] — Bons du trésor B[15]	7.04	7.40	8.61	11.12	11.03	8.01	4.93	6.04	...	...
India[5] — Inde[5]										
Money market B — Marché monétaire B	5.29	...	...	...	...	...	...	...	...	...
Indonesia[5] — Indonésie[5]										
Money market B — Marché monétaire B	27.82	62.79	23.58	10.32	15.03	13.54	7.76	5.38	6.78	9.18
Ireland — Irlande										
Money market A[16] — Marché monétaire A[16]	6.43	3.23	3.14	4.84	3.31	2.88	2.08	2.13	2.40	...
Treasury bill — Bons du trésor	6.03	5.37	...	...	...	...	...	...	...	...
Israel — Israël										
Treasury bill — Bons du trésor	13.39	11.33	11.41	8.81	6.50	7.38	7.00	4.78	4.34	...
Italy — Italie										
Money market — Marché monétaire	6.88	4.99	2.95	4.39	4.26	3.32	2.33	2.10	2.18	3.09
Treasury bill — Bons du trésor	6.33	4.59	3.01	4.53	4.05	3.26	2.19	2.08	2.17	3.18
Jamaica — Jamaïque										
Money market — Marché monétaire	...	24.44	21.50	19.90	19.10	15.09	25.53	12.79	10.96	9.37
Treasury bill — Bons du trésor	21.14	25.65	20.75	18.24	16.71	15.54	25.94	15.47	13.39	12.79

Short-term interest rates—Treasury bill and money market rates: per cent per annum (*continued*)

Taux d'intérêt à court terme—Taux des bons du Trésor et du marché monétaire : pour cent par année (*suite*)

Country or area — Pays ou zone	1997	1998	1999	2000	2001	2002	2003	2004	2005	2006
Japan[5] — Japon[5]										
Money market B — Marché monétaire B	0.48	0.37	0.06	0.11	0.06	0.01	^0.00	^0.00	^0.00	0.12
Jordan — Jordanie										
Money market — Marché monétaire	...	...	5.19	5.28	4.63	3.49	2.58	2.18	3.59	5.55
Kazakhstan — Kazakhstan										
Treasury bill — Bons du trésor	15.15	23.59	15.63	6.59	5.28	5.20	5.86	3.28	3.28	3.28
Kenya — Kenya										
Treasury bill — Bons du trésor	22.87	22.83	13.87	12.05	12.60	8.95	3.51	3.17	8.43	6.73
Korea, Republic of — Corée, République de										
Money market — Marché monétaire	13.24	14.98	5.01	5.16	4.69	4.21	4.00	3.65	3.33	4.19
Money market B[17] — Marché monétaire B[17]	13.39	15.10	8.86	9.35	7.05	6.56	5.43	4.73	4.68	5.17
Kuwait — Koweït										
Money market A[18] — Marché monétaire A[18]	7.05	7.24	6.32	6.82	4.62	2.99	2.47	2.14	2.83	5.62
Treasury bill A[19] — Bons du trésor A[19]	6.98	...	...	...	...	...	...	...	...	...
Kyrgyzstan — Kirghizistan										
Money market — Marché monétaire	...	43.98	43.71	24.26	11.92	...	...	...	3.24	2.83
Treasury bill — Bons du trésor	35.83	43.67	47.19	32.26	19.08	10.15	7.21	4.94	4.40	4.75
Lao People's Dem. Rep. — Rép. dém. pop. lao										
Treasury bill — Bons du trésor	...	23.66	30.00	29.94	22.70	21.41	24.87	20.37	18.61	17.92
Latvia — Lettonie										
Money market — Marché monétaire	3.76	4.42	4.72	2.97	5.23	3.01	2.86	3.25	2.49	3.24
Treasury bill — Bons du trésor	4.73	5.27	6.23	#4.85	5.63	3.52	3.24	...	...	...
Lebanon — Liban										
Treasury bill — Bons du trésor	13.42	12.70	11.57	11.18	11.18	10.90	...	5.25	5.22	5.22
Lesotho — Lesotho										
Treasury bill — Bons du trésor	14.83	15.47	12.45	9.06	9.49	11.34	11.96	8.52	7.23	6.87
Libyan Arab Jamah.[20] — Jamah. arabe libyenne[20]										
Money market B — Marché monétaire B	...	4.00	4.00	4.00	4.00	4.00	4.00	4.00	...	...
Lithuania — Lituanie										
Money market — Marché monétaire	9.55	#6.12	6.26	3.60	3.37	2.21	1.79	1.53	1.97	2.76
Money market B[1] — Marché monétaire B[1]	...	5.52	5.05	6.10	4.03	1.92	1.72	1.73	2.59	3.06
Treasury bill — Bons du trésor	8.64	10.69	11.14	#9.27	5.68	3.72	2.61	...	...	...
Luxembourg[3,4] — Luxembourg[3,4]										
Money market B — Marché monétaire B	3.36	3.48	...	...	...	...	...	...	...	...
Madagascar — Madagascar										
Money market — Marché monétaire	...	12.00	17.25	16.00	9.00	9.00	10.50	16.50	16.50	14.50
Treasury bill — Bons du trésor	...	...	...	...	10.28	...	11.94	12.95	18.84	21.16
Malawi — Malawi										
Treasury bill — Bons du trésor	18.31	32.98	42.85	39.52	42.41	41.75	39.32	28.58	24.36	19.27
Malaysia — Malaisie										
Money market A[21] — Marché monétaire A[21]	7.61	8.46	3.38	2.66	2.79	2.73	2.74	2.70	2.72	3.38
Treasury bill A[12] — Bons du trésor A[12]	6.41	6.86	3.53	2.86	2.79	2.73	2.79	2.40	2.48	3.23
Maldives[5] — Maldives[5]										
Money market B — Marché monétaire B	6.80	6.80	6.80	6.80	...	...	...	...	...	...
Mali[7] — Mali[7]										
Money market A — Marché monétaire A	4.95	4.95	4.95	4.95	4.95	4.95	4.95	4.95	4.95	4.95
Malta[12] — Malte[12]										
Treasury bill A — Bons du trésor A	5.08	5.41	5.15	4.89	4.93	4.03	3.29	2.94	3.18	3.49

Short-term interest rates—Treasury bill and money market rates: per cent per annum (*continued*)
Taux d'intérêt à court terme—Taux des bons du Trésor et du marché monétaire : pour cent par année (*suite*)

Country or area — Pays ou zone	1997	1998	1999	2000	2001	2002	2003	2004	2005	2006
Mauritius — Maurice										
Money market — Marché monétaire	9.43	8.99	10.01	7.66	7.25	6.20	3.22	1.33	2.45	5.59
Mexico — Mexique										
Money market B[22] — Marché monétaire B[22]	21.91	26.89	24.10	16.96	12.89	8.17	6.83	7.15	9.59	7.51
Treasury bill — Bons du trésor	19.80	24.76	21.41	15.24	11.31	7.09	6.23	6.82	9.20	7.19
Montserrat — Montserrat										
Money market — Marché monétaire	5.25	5.25	5.25	5.25	#5.64	6.32	6.07	4.67	4.01	4.76
Morocco — Maroc										
Money market — Marché monétaire	7.89	6.30	5.64	5.41	4.44	2.99	3.22	2.39	2.78	2.58
Mozambique — Mozambique										
Money market — Marché monétaire	...	...	9.92	16.12	#25.00	20.40	13.34	9.87	6.35	15.25
Treasury bill — Bons du trésor	...	...	...	16.97	24.77	29.55	15.31	12.37	9.10	15.04
Namibia — Namibie										
Money market — Marché monétaire	15.41	17.14	13.17	9.19	9.53	10.46	10.03	6.93	6.87	7.12
Treasury bill — Bons du trésor	15.69	17.24	13.28	10.26	9.29	11.00	10.51	7.78	7.09	7.26
Nepal — Népal										
Treasury bill — Bons du trésor	2.52	3.70	4.30	5.30	5.00	3.80	3.85	2.40	2.20	...
Netherlands[3,5] — Pays-Bas[3,5]										
Money market B — Marché monétaire B	3.07	3.21	...	...	...	...	...	...	...	...
Netherlands Antilles[12] — Antilles néerlandaises[12]										
Treasury bill A — Bons du trésor A	5.77	5.82	6.15	6.15	6.15	4.96	2.80	3.86	3.52	4.87
New Zealand — Nouvelle-Zélande										
Money market — Marché monétaire	7.38	6.86	4.33	6.12	5.76	5.40	5.33	5.77	6.76	7.26
Treasury bill A[23] — Bons du trésor A[23]	7.53	7.10	4.58	6.39	5.56	5.52	5.21	5.85	6.53	7.05
Niger[7] — Niger[7]										
Money market A — Marché monétaire A	4.95	4.95	4.95	4.95	4.95	4.95	4.95	4.95	4.95	4.95
Nigeria — Nigéria										
Treasury bill — Bons du trésor	12.00	12.26	17.82	15.50	17.50	19.03	14.79	14.34	7.63	...
Norway[5] — Norvège[5]										
Money market B — Marché monétaire B	3.77	6.03	6.87	6.72	7.38	7.05	4.45	2.17	2.26	3.12
Pakistan — Pakistan										
Money market B[5] — Marché monétaire B[5]	12.10	10.76	9.04	8.57	8.49	5.53	2.14	2.70	6.83	8.89
Treasury bill A[24] — Bons du trésor A[24]	#15.74	...	...	8.38	10.71	6.08	1.87	2.49	7.18	8.54
Panama — Panama										
Money market — Marché monétaire	...	...	...	...	...	2.22	1.50	1.90	3.13	5.06
Papua New Guinea — Papouasie-Nvl-Guinée										
Money market B — Marché monétaire B	...	...	...	9.54	11.05	9.11	13.58	7.79	4.36	3.29
Treasury bill A[25] — Bons du trésor A[25]	9.94	21.18	22.70	17.00	12.36	10.93	18.69	8.85	3.81	3.50
Paraguay — Paraguay										
Money market — Marché monétaire	12.48	20.74	17.26	10.70	13.45	13.19	13.02	1.33	2.29	8.33
Peru[4] — Pérou[4]										
Money market — Marché monétaire	12.80	12.94	16.91	11.41	3.15	3.80	2.51	3.00	3.34	4.51
Money market B — Marché monétaire B	7.48	11.20	6.60	8.40	2.07	2.22	1.09	2.19	4.19	5.37
Philippines — Philippines										
Money market — Marché monétaire	16.16	13.90	10.16	10.84	9.75	7.15	6.97	7.05	7.31	7.84
Treasury bill A[26] — Bons du trésor A[26]	12.89	15.00	10.00	9.91	9.73	5.49	5.87	7.32	6.13	5.29
Poland — Pologne										
Money market — Marché monétaire	22.43	20.59	13.58	18.16	16.23	9.39	5.76	6.03	5.34	4.10
Treasury bill — Bons du trésor	21.58	19.09	13.14	16.62	...	...	...	...	...	4.20

Country or area — Pays ou zone	1997	1998	1999	2000	2001	2002	2003	2004	2005	2006
Portugal — Portugal										
Money market A[3,27] — Marché monétaire A[3,27]	5.78	4.34	2.71	...	...	...	...	...	...	...
Treasury bill — Bons du trésor	4.43	...	...	...	...	...	...	...	...	...
Republic of Moldova — République de Moldova										
Money market — Marché monétaire	28.10	30.91	32.60	20.77	11.04	5.13	11.51	13.19	5.87	9.50
Money market B[1] — Marché monétaire B[1]	...	...	11.88	6.86	9.06	4.80	2.51	0.78	2.49	4.13
Treasury bill — Bons du trésor	23.63	30.54	28.49	22.20	14.24	5.89	15.08	11.89	3.70	7.30
Romania[26] — Roumanie[26]										
Treasury bill A — Bons du trésor A	85.72	63.99	74.21	51.86	42.18	27.03	...	...	...	...
Russian Federation — Fédération de Russie										
Money market — Marché monétaire	20.97	50.56	14.79	7.14	10.10	8.19	3.77	3.33	2.68	3.43
Treasury bill — Bons du trésor	23.43	...	...	12.12	12.45	12.72	5.35	...	...	...
Saint Kitts and Nevis — Saint-Kitts-et-Nevis										
Money market — Marché monétaire	5.25	5.25	5.25	5.25	#5.64	6.32	6.07	4.67	4.01	4.78
Treasury bill — Bons du trésor	6.50	6.50	6.50	6.50	7.50	7.50	7.17	7.00	7.00	7.00
Saint Lucia — Sainte-Lucie										
Money market — Marché monétaire	5.25	5.25	5.25	5.25	#5.64	6.32	6.07	4.67	4.01	4.78
Treasury bill — Bons du trésor	6.02	6.02	6.02	6.02	5.84	5.84	5.44	#5.50	4.48	5.17
St. Vincent-Grenadines — St. Vincent-Grenadines										
Money market — Marché monétaire	5.25	5.25	5.25	5.25	#5.64	6.32	6.07	4.67	4.01	4.76
Treasury bill — Bons du trésor	6.50	6.50	6.50	6.50	7.00	7.00	5.73	4.60	4.85	5.62
Senegal — Sénégal										
Money market — Marché monétaire	4.95	4.95	4.95	4.95	4.95	4.95	4.95	4.95	4.95	4.95
Serbia — Serbie										
Money market — Marché monétaire	...	...	...	...	31.91	15.48	12.69	12.86	20.51	16.51
Treasury bill — Bons du trésor	...	...	...	...	...	...	20.02	21.17	14.58	10.24
Seychelles — Seychelles										
Treasury bill — Bons du trésor	10.50	8.13	5.00	5.00	5.00	5.00	4.61	3.17	3.34	3.70
Sierra Leone — Sierra Leone										
Treasury bill — Bons du trésor	12.71	22.10	32.42	26.22	13.74	15.15	15.68	26.14	22.98	17.71
Singapore — Singapour										
Money market A[14] — Marché monétaire A[14]	4.35	5.00	2.04	2.57	1.99	0.96	0.74	1.04	2.28	3.46
Treasury bill — Bons du trésor	2.32	2.12	1.12	2.18	1.69	0.81	0.64	0.96	2.04	2.95
Slovakia — Slovaquie										
Money market — Marché monétaire	...	...	...	8.08	7.76	6.33	6.08	3.82	3.02	4.83
Slovenia — Slovénie										
Money market — Marché monétaire	9.71	7.45	6.87	6.95	6.90	4.93	5.59	4.40	3.73	3.38
Treasury bill — Bons du trésor	...	...	8.63	10.94	10.88	8.73	6.53	4.17	3.66	3.30
Solomon Islands[12] — Iles Salomon[12]										
Treasury bill A — Bons du trésor A	12.88	6.00	6.00	7.05	8.23	6.87	5.85	6.00	4.53	...
South Africa — Afrique du Sud										
Money market — Marché monétaire	15.59	17.11	13.06	9.54	#8.49	11.11	10.93	7.15	6.62	7.23
Treasury bill — Bons du trésor	15.26	16.53	12.85	10.11	9.68	11.16	10.67	7.53	6.91	7.34
Spain — Espagne										
Money market B[5] — Marché monétaire B[5]	5.49	4.34	2.72	4.11	4.36	3.28	2.31	2.04	2.09	2.83
Treasury bill — Bons du trésor	5.02	3.79	3.01	4.61	3.92	3.34	2.21	2.17	2.19	3.26
Sri Lanka — Sri Lanka										
Money market B[28] — Marché monétaire B[28]	18.42	15.74	16.69	17.30	21.24	12.33	9.68	8.87	10.15	...
Treasury bill — Bons du trésor	...	12.59	12.51	14.02	17.57	12.47	8.09	7.71	9.03	...

Short-term interest rates—Treasury bill and money market rates: per cent per annum (*continued*)

Taux d'intérêt à court terme—Taux des bons du Trésor et du marché monétaire : pour cent par année (*suite*)

Country or area—Pays ou zone	1997	1998	1999	2000	2001	2002	2003	2004	2005	2006
Swaziland—Swaziland										
Money market—Marché monétaire	10.35	10.63	8.86	5.54	5.06	7.31	6.98	4.12	3.47	4.40
Treasury bill—Bons du trésor	14.37	13.09	11.19	8.30	7.16	8.59	10.61	7.94	7.08	7.54
Sweden—Suède										
Money market B[5]—Marché monétaire B[5]	4.21	4.24	3.14	3.81	4.09	4.19	3.29	...	...	...
Treasury bill A[29]—Bons du trésor A[29]	4.11	4.19	3.12	3.95	4.00	4.07	3.03	2.11	1.72	...
Switzerland—Suisse										
Money market—Marché monétaire	1.35	1.22	0.93	#3.50	1.65	0.44	0.09	0.55	0.63	1.94
Treasury bill—Bons du trésor	1.45	1.32	1.17	2.93	2.68	0.94	0.16	0.37	0.71	1.36
Thailand—Thaïlande										
Money market—Marché monétaire	14.59	13.02	1.77	1.95	2.00	1.76	1.31	1.23	2.62	4.64
Togo[7]—Togo[7]										
Money market A—Marché monétaire A	4.95	4.95	4.95	4.95	4.95	4.95	4.95	4.95	4.95	4.95
Trinidad and Tobago—Trinité-et-Tobago										
Treasury bill—Bons du trésor	9.83	11.93	10.40	10.56	8.55	4.83	4.71	4.77	4.86	...
Tunisia—Tunisie										
Money market—Marché monétaire	6.88	6.89	5.99	5.88	6.04	5.93	5.14	5.00	5.00	5.07
Turkey—Turquie										
Money market B[4]—Marché monétaire B[4]	70.32	74.60	73.53	56.72	91.95	49.51	36.16	21.42	14.73	15.59
Treasury bill—Bons du trésor	...	...	...	25.18	85.33	59.50	34.90	22.08	...	...
Uganda[26]—Ouganda[26]										
Treasury bill A—Bons du trésor A	10.59	7.77	7.43	13.19	11.00	5.85	16.87	9.02	8.50	8.12
Ukraine—Ukraine										
Money market—Marché monétaire	22.05	40.41	44.98	18.34	16.57	5.50	7.90	6.34	4.16	3.58
Money market B[1]—Marché monétaire B[1]	...	10.61	5.44	6.27	5.87	3.14	3.61	2.15	2.85	4.13
United Kingdom—Royaume-Uni										
Money market A[30]—Marché monétaire A[30]	6.61	7.21	5.20	5.77	5.08	3.89	3.59	4.29	4.70	4.77
Treasury bill—Bons du trésor	6.48	6.82	5.04	5.80	4.77	3.86	3.55	4.43	4.55	4.65
Treasury bill B[31]—Bons du trésor B[31]	6.62	7.23	5.14	5.83	4.79	3.96	3.55	4.44	4.59	4.67
United Rep. of Tanzania—Rép.-Unie de Tanzanie										
Treasury bill—Bons du trésor	9.59	11.83	10.05	9.78	4.14	3.55	6.26	8.35	10.67	11.64
United States—Etats-Unis										
Money market A[32]—Marché monétaire A[32]	5.57	5.34	5.18	6.31	3.61	1.69	1.11	1.49	3.38	5.03
Money market B[33]—Marché monétaire B[33]	5.46	5.35	4.97	6.24	3.89	1.67	1.13	1.35	3.21	4.96
Treasury bill—Bons du trésor	5.07	4.82	4.66	5.84	3.45	1.61	1.01	1.37	3.15	4.72
Treasury bill A[12]—Bons du trésor A[12]	5.20	4.90	4.77	6.00	3.48	1.63	1.02	1.39	3.21	4.85
Uruguay—Uruguay										
Money market—Marché monétaire	23.43	20.48	13.96	14.82	22.10	86.10	20.76	3.57	1.25	1.60
Treasury bill—Bons du trésor	23.18	...	...	...	...	...	32.53	14.75	4.14	4.54
Treasury bill B[1]—Bons du trésor B[1]	5.18	...	...	...	...	...	...	...	...	...
Vanuatu[34]—Vanuatu[34]										
Money market B—Marché monétaire B	6.00	8.65	6.99	5.58	5.50	5.50	5.50	5.50	5.50	5.50
Venezuela (Bolivarian Republic of)—Venezuela (République bolivarienne du)										
Money market—Marché monétaire	12.47	18.58	7.48	8.14	13.33	28.87	13.23	4.38	2.62	5.26
Viet Nam—Viet Nam										
Treasury bill—Bons du trésor	...	...	...	5.42	5.49	5.92	5.83	...	6.13	4.73
Yemen—Yémen										
Treasury bill—Bons du trésor	15.97	12.53	20.57	14.16	13.25	11.55	12.92	13.84	14.89	15.65

Short-term interest rates—Treasury bill and money market rates: per cent per annum (*continued*)
Taux d'intérêt à court terme—Taux des bons du Trésor et du marché monétaire : pour cent par année (*suite*)

Country or area—Pays ou zone	1997	1998	1999	2000	2001	2002	2003	2004	2005	2006
Zambia—Zambie										
Treasury bill—Bons du trésor	29.48	24.94	36.19	31.37	44.28	34.54	29.97	12.60	16.32	10.37
Zimbabwe—Zimbabwe										
Money market A[9]—Marché monétaire A[9]	25.15	37.22	53.13	64.98	21.52	32.35	110.05	129.58	...	...
Treasury bill—Bons du trésor	22.07	32.78	50.48	64.78	17.60	28.51	52.72	125.68	185.11	322.36

Source

International Monetary Fund (IMF), Washington, D.C., "International Financial Statistics", May 2007 and the IMF database.

Notes

+ The naming conventions for money market rates and treasury bill yields sometimes vary among countries. In this table, three money market and treasury bill descriptions are used: (i) "Money market"/"Treasury bill", (ii) "Money market A"/"Treasury bill A" and (iii) "Money market B"/ "Treasury bill B". These distinctions are shown for those countries for which more than one type of money market rate or treasury bill yield is differentiated by the International Monetary Fund in "International Financial Statistics". In general, "Money market A" and "Treasury bill A" refer to those interest rates or yields whose durations have been specified (e.g. overnight, one month, 91 days, etc.) and "Money market B" and "Treasury bill B" refer to all others containing specific descriptors such as "call money rate", "foreign currency", "interbank", "discounted rate", etc.

1 Foreign currency.
2 13 weeks.
3 Beginning 1999, see Euro Area. For Greece, beginning 2001, see Euro Area.
4 Interbank.
5 Call money rate.
6 Discount rate.
7 Overnight advances.
8 Overnight rate.
9 Interbank rate (3-month maturity).
10 Overnight interbank.
11 Average cost of Central Bank debt.
12 3 months.
13 Discounted.
14 3-month interbank rate.
15 Yield.
16 1-month fixed rate.
17 Corporate bond rate.
18 Interbank deposit rate (3 months).
19 Central Bank bill rate.
20 Interbank call loans (maximum rate).
21 Interbank overnight.
22 Bankers' acceptances.
23 New issue rate: 3-month treasury bills.
24 6 months.
25 182 days.
26 91 days.
27 Up-to-5-days interbank deposit.
28 Interbank call loans.
29 3-month discount notes.
30 Overnight interbank minimum.
31 Bond equivalent.
32 Commercial paper (3 months).
33 Federal funds rate.
34 Interbank borrowing rate.

Source

Fonds monétaire international (FMI), Washington, D.C.,"Statistiques Financières Internationales", mai 2007 et la base de données du FMI.

Notes

+ La manière dont par convention on dénomme les taux du marché monétaire et le rendement des bons du Trésor peut varier selon les pays. Dans le tableau, on utilise trois termes pour le marché monétaire et les bons du Trésor : i) « Marché monétaire »/ « Bons du Trésor », ii) « Marché monétaire A »/ « Bons du Trésor A », iii) « Marché monétaire B »/ « Bons du Trésor B ». Ces distinctions apparaissent pour les pays où le Fonds monétaire international (FMI) distingue dans Statistiques financières internationales plus d'un type de taux du marché monétaire ou de rendement de bons du Trésor. En général, « Marché monétaire A » et « Bons du Trésor A » désignent les taux d'intérêt ou les rendements dont la durée a été précisée (au jour le jour, à un mois, à 91 jours, etc.), « Marché monétaire B » et « Bons du Trésor B » désignant tous les autres assortis de descripteurs précis tels que taux de l'argent au jour le jour, en devises, interbancaire, taux escompté, etc.

1 Devises.
2 Treize semaines.
3 À compter de 1999, voir zone euro. Pour la Grèce, à compter de 2001, voir zone euro.
4 Interbancaire.
5 Taux de l'argent au jour le jour.
6 Taux de l'escompte.
7 Taux des avances à un jour.
8 Taux à un jour.
9 Taux interbancaire (maturité à 3 mois).
10 Taux interbancaire à un jour.
11 Coût moyen de la dette à la Banque centrale.
12 Trois mois.
13 Taux actualisé.
14 Taux interbancaire à trois mois.
15 Rendement.
16 Taux forfaitaire à un mois.
17 Taux des obligations de société.
18 Taux des dépôts interbancaires (à trois mois).
19 Taux d'escompte de la Banque Centrale (a trois mois).
20 Prêts interbancaires remboursables sur demande (taux maximum).
21 Taux interbancaire au jour le jour.
22 Traite bancaire.
23 Taux des émissions nouvelles : bons du Trésor à trois mois.
24 Six mois.
25 Cent quatre-vingt-deux jours.
26 Quatre-vingt-onze jours.
27 Dépôts interbancaires jusqu'à cinq jours.
28 Prêts interbancaires remboursables sur demande.
29 Billets à escompte à trois mois.
30 Taux minimum des prêts interbancaires à un jour.
31 Équivalant à obligation.
32 Effet de commerce (à trois mois).
33 Taux des fonds du système fédéral.
34 Taux des prêts interbancaires.

Technical notes: tables 23 and 24

Detailed information and current figures relating to tables 23 and 24 are contained in *International Financial Statistics*, published by the International Monetary Fund (see also www.imf.org) and in the United Nations *Monthly Bulletin of Statistics*.

Table 23: The discount rates shown represent the rates at which the central bank lends or discounts eligible paper for deposit money banks, typically shown on an end-of-period basis.

Table 24: The rates shown represent short-term treasury bill rates and money market rates. The treasury bill rate is the rate at which short-term securities are issued or traded in the market. The money market rate is the rate on short-term lending between financial institutions.

The naming conventions for money market rates and treasury bill yields sometimes vary among countries. In table 24, three money market and treasury bill descriptions are used: (i) "Money market"/"Treasury bill", (ii) "Money market A"/"Treasury bill A" and (iii) "Money market B"/"Treasury bill B". These distinctions are shown for those countries for which more than one type of money market rate or treasury bill yield is differentiated by the International Monetary Fund in *International Financial Statistics*. In this table, "Money market A" and "Treasury bill A" generally refer to those interest rates or yields whose durations have been specified (e.g. overnight, one month, 91 days, etc.) and "Money market B" and "Treasury bill B" refer to all others containing specific descriptors such as "call money rate", "foreign currency", "interbank", "discounted rate", etc.

Notes techniques : tableaux 23 et 24

Les informations détaillées et les chiffres courants concernant les tableaux 23 et 24 figurent dans les *Statistiques financières internationales* publiées par le Fonds monétaire international (voir aussi www.imf.org) et dans le *Bulletin mensuel de statistique* des Nations Unies.

Tableau 23: Les taux d'escomptes indiqués représentent les taux que la banque centrale applique à ses prêts ou auquel elle réescompte les effets escomptables des banques créatrices de monnaie (généralement, taux de fin de période).

Tableau 24: Les taux indiqués représentent le taux des bons du Trésor et le taux du marché monétaire à court terme. Le taux des bons du Trésor est le taux auquel les effets à court terme sont émis ou négociés sur le marché. Le taux du marché monétaire est le taux prêteur à court terme entre institutions financières.

La manière dont par convention on dénomme les taux du marché monétaire et le rendement des bons du Trésor peut varier selon les pays. Dans le tableau 24, on utilise trois termes pour le marché monétaire et les bons du Trésor : i) « Marché monétaire »/ « Bons du Trésor », ii) « Marché monétaire A »/ « Bons du Trésor A », iii) « Marché monétaire B »/ « Bons du Trésor B ». Ces distinctions apparaissent pour les pays où le Fonds monétaire international distingue dans *Statistiques financières internationales* plus d'un type de taux du marché monétaire ou de rendement de bons du Trésor. En général, dans ce tableau, « Marché monétaire A » et « Bons du Trésor A » désignent les taux d'intérêt ou les rendements dont la durée a été précisée (au jour le jour, à un mois, à 91 jours, etc.), « Marché monétaire B » et « Bons du Trésor B » désignant tous les autres assortis de descripteurs précis tels que taux de l'argent au jour le jour, en devises, interbancaire, taux escompté, etc.

25

Unemployment

Number (thousands) and percentage unemployed, by sex

Chômage

Nombre (milliers) et pourcentage des chômeurs, par sexe

Country or area, source§ — Pays ou zone, source§	1998	1999	2000	2001	2002	2003	2004	2005
Afghanistan[1] — Afghanistan[1]								
MF [BA]	...	...	...	...	...	...	...	363.8
M [BA]	...	...	...	...	...	...	...	172.7
F [BA]	...	...	...	...	...	...	...	191.1
%MF [BA]	...	...	...	...	...	...	...	8.5
%M [BA]	...	...	...	...	...	...	...	7.6
%F [BA]	...	...	...	...	...	...	...	9.5
Albania — Albanie								
MF [A][1,2]	...	...	...	305.5	...	...	...	...
M [A][1,2]	...	...	...	150.1	...	...	...	...
F [A][1,2]	...	...	...	155.4	...	...	...	...
MF [BA][1]	...	...	...	...	...	166.0	157.0	...
M [BA][1]	...	...	...	...	...	88.0	82.0	...
F [BA][1]	...	...	...	...	...	78.0	75.0	...
%MF [BA][1]	...	...	...	...	...	15.2	14.4	...
%M [BA][1]	...	...	...	...	...	13.2	12.4	...
%F [BA][1]	...	...	...	...	...	18.3	17.5	...
MF [FB]	235.0	239.8	215.1	180.5	172.4	163.0	157.0	...
M [FB]	127.0	130.0	113.0	96.0	91.0	86.0	82.0	...
F [FB]	108.0	109.8	102.1	84.5	81.4	77.0	75.0	...
%MF [FB]	17.7	18.4	16.8	16.4	15.8	15.0	14.4	...
%M [FB]	15.8	16.4	14.9	14.2	13.6	12.9	12.4	...
%F [FB]	20.9	21.4	19.3	19.9	19.1	18.2	17.5	...
Algeria[1,3] — Algérie[1,3]								
MF [BA]	...	...	...	2 339.4	...	2 078.3	1 671.5	...
M [BA]	...	...	...	1 934.9	...	1 759.9	1 370.4	...
F [BA]	...	...	...	404.5	...	318.3	301.1	...
%MF [BA]	...	...	...	27.3	...	23.7	17.7	...
%M [BA]	...	...	...	26.6	...	23.4	17.5	...
%F [BA]	...	...	...	31.4	...	25.4	18.1	...
Anguilla[1] — Anguilla[1]								
MF [A][4]	...	...	...	0.4	...	...	...	...
M [A][4]	...	...	...	0.2	...	...	...	...
F [A][4]	...	...	...	0.2	...	...	...	...
%MF [A][4]	...	...	...	6.7	...	...	...	...
%M [A][4]	...	...	...	6.5	...	...	...	...
%F [A][4]	...	...	...	7.0	...	...	...	...
MF [BA]	...	0.6[5]	...	...	0.5[6]	...	...	...
M [BA]	...	0.2[5]	...	...	0.2[6]	...	...	...
F [BA]	...	0.4[5]	...	...	0.3[6]	...	...	...
%MF [BA]	...	8.3[5]	...	...	7.8[6]	...	...	...
%M [BA]	...	4.6[5]	...	...	6.3[6]	...	...	...
%F [BA]	...	12.1[5]	...	...	9.5[6]	...	...	...
Argentina[7] — Argentine[7]								
MF [BA]	1 203.1[8,9]	1 359.6[8,9]	1 460.9[8,9]	1 709.8[8,9]	1 955.8[8,9]	1 633.0[10]	1 361.6[10]	1 141.5[10]
M [BA]	673.0[8,9]	764.9[8,9]	809.9[8,9]	1 021.9[8,9]	1 175.2[8,9]	824.8[10]	687.6[10]	561.7[10]
F [BA]	530.1[8,9]	594.7[8,9]	651.0[8,9]	688.4[8,9]	780.6[8,9]	808.2[10]	673.9[10]	579.8[10]
%MF [BA]	12.8[8,9]	14.1[8,9]	15.0[8,9]	17.4[8,9]	19.6[8,9]	15.4[10]	12.6[10]	10.6[10]
%M [BA]	11.9[8,9]	13.3[8,9]	14.1[8,9]	17.4[8,9]	20.2[8,9]	13.8[10]	11.2[10]	9.2[10]
%F [BA]	14.2[8,9]	15.2[8,9]	16.4[8,9]	17.2[8,9]	18.8[8,9]	17.5[10]	14.5[10]	12.4[10]
Armenia[11,12] — Arménie[11,12]								
MF [FB]	133.8	175.0	153.9	138.4	127.3	118.6	108.6	89.0
M [FB]	40.9	62.3	54.4	47.1	85.7	37.0	32.3	26.0

Country or area, source§ — Pays ou zone, source§	1998	1999	2000	2001	2002	2003	2004	2005
F [FB]	92.8	112.7	99.5	91.3	41.6	81.6	76.3	63.0
%MF [FB]	9.4	11.2	11.7	10.4	10.8	10.1	9.6	8.1
%M [FB]	5.6	7.6	8.0	6.9	7.2	5.9	5.7	4.6
%F [FB]	13.3	15.0	15.7	14.1	14.5	14.4	13.8	12.0
Australia[1,13] — Australie[1,13]								
MF [BA]	728.1	654.9	607.5	667.1	636.9	607.4	570.6	535.0
M [BA]	428.1	379.5	347.7	383.8	363.5	330.0	308.8	286.8
F [BA]	300.0	275.4	259.8	283.3	273.4	277.3	261.7	248.2
%MF [BA]	7.8	7.0	6.4	6.9	6.4	6.0	5.6	5.1
%M [BA]	8.1	7.2	6.5	7.1	6.6	5.9	5.5	5.0
%F [BA]	7.5	6.8	6.2	6.6	6.2	6.2	5.7	5.3
Austria[1] — Autriche[1]								
MF [BA]	165.0[14,15]	146.7[14,15]	138.8[14,15]	142.5[14,15]	161.0[14,15]	168.8[15]	194.6	207.7
M [BA]	88.4[14,15]	81.7[14,15]	73.8[14,15]	77.0[14,15]	91.7[14,15]	94.7[15]	98.0	107.8
F [BA]	76.6[14,15]	65.0[14,15]	65.0[14,15]	65.5[14,15]	69.3[14,15]	74.3[15]	96.6	100.0
%MF [BA]	4.2[14,15]	3.8[14,15]	3.6[14,15]	3.6[14,15]	4.0[14,15]	4.3[15]	4.9	...
%M [BA]	4.0[14,15]	3.7[14,15]	3.3[14,15]	3.5[14,15]	4.1[14,15]	4.3[15]	4.5	...
%F [BA]	4.6[14,15]	3.9[14,15]	3.8[14,15]	3.8[14,15]	3.9[14,15]	4.2[15]	5.4	...
MF [FB]	237.8	221.7	194.3	203.9	232.4	240.1	243.9	252.7
M [FB]	129.4	121.5	107.5	115.3	134.4	139.7	140.3	144.2
F [FB]	108.4	100.2	86.8	88.6	98.0	100.4	103.6	108.4
%MF [FB]	7.2	6.7	5.8	6.1	6.9	7.0	7.1	7.2
%M [FB]	6.9	6.5	5.8	6.2	7.2	7.5	7.5	7.6
%F [FB]	7.5	6.9	5.9	5.9	6.4	6.5	6.6	6.8
Azerbaijan — Azerbaïdjan								
MF [BA][1]	...	...	...	...	...	...	...	368.8
M [BA][1]	...	...	...	...	...	...	...	172.7
F [BA][1]	...	...	...	...	...	...	...	191.1
%MF [BA][1]	...	...	...	...	...	...	...	8.5
%M [BA][1]	...	...	...	...	...	...	...	7.6
%F [BA][1]	...	...	...	...	...	...	...	9.5
MF [FB][12]	42.3	45.2	43.7	48.4	51.0	54.4	55.9	56.3
M [FB][12]	18.2	19.6	19.3	21.8	23.1	25.3	26.7	27.3
F [FB][12]	24.1	25.6	24.5	26.6	27.9	29.1	29.3	29.1
%MF [FB][12]	1.1	1.2	1.2	1.3	1.3	1.4	1.4	1.4
%M [FB][12]	0.9	1.0	1.0	1.1	1.2	1.3	1.3	1.3
%F [FB][12]	1.4	1.4	1.4	1.5	1.5	1.6	1.6	1.6
Bahamas[1,16] — Bahamas[1,16]								
MF [BA]	12.1	12.3	...	11.3	15.3	18.8	18.0	18.2
M [BA]	4.5	5.0	...	5.7	7.6	8.8	8.5	8.4
F [BA]	7.6	7.3	...	5.6	7.7	10.1	9.5	9.8
%MF [BA]	7.8	7.8	...	6.9	9.1	10.8	10.2	10.2
%M [BA]	5.7	6.0	...	7.1	9.1	10.8	9.4	9.2
%F [BA]	9.8	9.7	...	6.8	8.8	10.0	11.0	11.2
Bahrain[1,17] — Bahreïn[1,17]								
MF [A]	...	...	...	16.1	...	...	...	...
M [A]	...	...	...	9.4	...	...	...	...
F [A]	...	...	...	6.7	...	...	...	...
MF [FB][18]	4.1	3.8	6.2	...	8.7	11.8	6.3	6.4
M [FB][18]	2.7	2.6	4.2	...	4.4	6.0	3.1	2.9
F [FB][18]	1.4	1.1	2.0	...	4.4	5.7	3.2	3.5
Bangladesh[1,19] — Bangladesh[1,19]								
MF [BA]	...	...	1 750.0	...	...	2 002.0	...	...
M [BA]	...	...	1 083.0	...	...	1 500.0	...	...
F [BA]	...	...	666.0	...	...	502.0	...	...
%MF [BA]	...	...	3.3	...	...	4.3	...	...
%M [BA]	...	...	3.2	...	...	4.2	...	...
%F [BA]	...	...	3.3	...	...	4.9	...	...

Unemployment—Number (thousands) and percentage unemployed, by sex (*continued*)
Chômage—Nombre (milliers) et pourcentage des chômeurs, par sexe (*suite*)

Country or area, source§ — Pays ou zone, source§	1998	1999	2000	2001	2002	2003	2004	2005
Barbados[1] — Barbade[1]								
MF [BA]	16.8	14.4	13.3	14.3	14.8	16.0	14.3	...
M [BA]	6.0	5.6	5.5	6.0	6.4	7.1	6.7	...
F [BA]	10.9	8.8	7.9	8.3	8.4	8.9	7.5	...
%MF [BA]	12.5	10.5	9.4	9.9	10.3	11.0	9.8	...
%M [BA]	8.4	7.7	7.5	8.0	8.2	9.6	9.0	...
%F [BA]	16.4	13.3	11.5	11.9	12.4	12.6	10.6	...
Belarus[12,20] — Bélarus[12,20]								
MF [FB]	105.9	95.4	95.8	102.9	130.5	136.1	83.0	67.9
M [FB]	35.3	34.2	37.6	40.9	47.8	46.1	25.5	21.1
F [FB]	70.6	61.2	58.2	62.0	82.7	90.0	57.5	46.8
%MF [FB]	2.3	2.1	2.1	2.3	3.0	3.1	1.9	1.5
%M [FB]	1.6	1.6	1.7	1.9	2.3	1.2	...	...
%F [FB]	3.0	2.6	2.4	2.6	3.5	3.9	...	...
Belgium — Belgique								
MF [BA][1]	384.0[16]	375.2	308.5	286.4	332.1	364.3	380.3	390.3
M [BA][1]	179.3[16]	179.4	144.6	147.9	168.1	193.0	191.4	196.0
F [BA][1]	204.7[16]	195.8	163.9	138.4	164.0	171.3	188.9	194.3
%MF [BA][1]	9.1[16]	8.6	7.0	6.6	7.5	8.2	8.5	8.4
%M [BA][1]	7.3[16]	7.2	5.8	6.0	6.7	7.7	7.6	7.6
%F [BA][1]	11.4[16]	10.4	8.7	7.5	8.7	8.9	9.6	9.5
MF [FB][21]	541.0	507.5	474.4	469.7	491.5	538.1	...	...
M [FB][21]	237.4	224.7	208.7	210.8	228.1	253.1	...	...
F [FB][21]	303.6	282.9	265.8	258.9	263.4	285.1	...	...
%MF [FB][21]	12.4	11.6	10.9	10.8	11.2	12.3	...	...
%M [FB][21]	9.7	9.2	8.6	8.7	9.4	10.4	...	...
%F [FB][21]	15.9	14.7	13.8	13.4	13.6	14.7	...	...
Belize[16,22] — Belize[16,22]								
MF [BA]	12.3	11.5	...	8.6	9.5	...	...	12.2
M [BA]	5.9	5.3	...	3.6	4.7	...	...	5.2
F [BA]	6.3	6.1	...	5.0	4.7	...	...	7.0
%MF [BA]	14.3	12.8	...	9.1	10.0	...	...	11.0
%M [BA]	10.6	9.0	...	5.8	7.5	...	...	7.4
%F [BA]	21.3	20.3	...	15.4	15.3	...	...	17.2
Bolivia[8,23] — Bolivie[8,23]								
MF [BA]	...	164.5	183.2	214.9	221.6	...	...	...
M [BA]	...	76.9	83.3	99.4	97.4	...	...	...
F [BA]	...	87.6	99.9	115.5	124.2	...	...	...
%MF [BA]	...	4.3	4.8	5.2	5.5	...	...	...
%M [BA]	...	3.7	3.9	4.5	4.3	...	...	...
%F [BA]	...	5.1	5.9	6.2	6.9	...	...	...
Botswana[24] — Botswana[24]								
MF [A][25]	...	...	...	109.5	...	...	...	...
M [A][25]	...	...	...	51.9	...	...	...	...
F [A][25]	...	...	...	57.6	...	...	...	...
%MF [A][25]	...	...	...	19.6	...	...	...	...
%M [A][25]	...	...	...	16.4	...	...	...	...
%F [A][25]	...	...	...	23.9	...	...	...	...
MF [BA]	115.7	...	90.7	114.9[26]	...	144.5	...	...
M [BA]	56.7	...	46.3	53.6[26]	...	66.9	...	...
F [BA]	59.0	...	44.5	61.2[26]	...	77.6	...	...
%MF [BA]	20.8	...	15.8	19.6[26]	...	23.8	...	...
%M [BA]	18.6	...	14.7	16.4[26]	...	21.4	...	...
%F [BA]	23.6	...	17.2	23.9[26]	...	26.3	...	...
Brazil[3,8,27] — Brésil[3,8,27]								
MF [BA]	6 922.6	7 639.1	...	7 853.4	7 958.5	8 640.0	8 263.8	...
M [BA]	3 301.1	3 667.9	...	3 674.9	3 685.1	3 972.8	3 590.7	...
F [BA]	3 621.5	3 971.2	...	4 178.5	4 273.3	4 667.1	4 673.1	...

Country or area, source§ — Pays ou zone, source§	1998	1999	2000	2001	2002	2003	2004	2005
%MF [BA]	9.0	9.6	...	9.4	9.2	9.7	8.9	...
%M [BA]	7.2	7.9	...	7.5	7.4	7.8	6.8	...
%F [BA]	11.6	12.1	...	11.9	11.6	12.3	11.7	...
Brunei Darussalam[18] — Brunéi Darussalam[18]								
MF [FB]	6.5	5.2	7.0	8.6	5.6	7.1	...	...
M [FB]	2.6	2.1	2.7	3.3	2.1	3.1	...	...
F [FB]	3.8	3.1	4.3	5.3	3.4	4.0	...	...
Bulgaria — Bulgarie								
MF [BA][1]	438.8[29]	486.7[29]	559.0[29]	661.1[29]	599.2[29]	449.1	399.8	334.2
M [BA][1]	240.8[29]	258.6[29]	306.3[29]	363.2[29]	328.7[29]	246.1	221.6	182.5
F [BA][1]	198.0[29]	228.1[29]	252.6[29]	297.8[29]	270.4[29]	203.0	178.2	151.6
%MF [BA][1]	12.2[29]	14.1[29]	16.3[29]	19.4[29]	17.6[29]	13.7	12.0	10.1
%M [BA][1]	12.6[29]	14.0[29]	16.7[29]	20.2[29]	18.3[29]	14.1	12.5	10.3
%F [BA][1]	11.8[29]	14.1[29]	15.9[29]	18.4[29]	16.9[29]	13.2	11.5	9.8
MF [FB][12,28]	465.2	610.6	682.8	662.3	602.5	500.7	450.6[30]	397.3
M [FB][12,28]	211.1	284.5	323.4	321.1	281.1	227.1	201.6[30]	171.8
F [FB][12,28]	254.1	326.1	359.4	341.2	321.5	273.6	249.0[30]	225.5
%MF [FB][12,28]	12.2	16.0	17.9	17.3	16.3	13.5	12.2[30]	10.7
Burkina Faso[18,31] — Burkina Faso[18,31]								
MF [FB]	9.4	7.5	6.6	...	...	...	...	...
M [FB]	7.8	6.2	5.4	...	...	...	...	...
F [FB]	1.6	1.4	1.2	...	...	...	...	...
Burundi[18,32] — Burundi[18,32]								
MF [FB]	2.8	0.7	...	...	...	...	...	...
%MF [FB]	...	14.0	...	...	...	...	...	...
%M [FB]	...	15.0	...	...	...	...	...	...
%F [FB]	...	13.2	...	...	...	...	...	...
Cambodia[33] — Cambodge[33]								
MF [BA]	...	...	133.6[8]	115.8[8]	...	...	503.4[34]	...
M [BA]	...	...	55.0[8]	44.9[8]	...	...	259.5[34]	...
F [BA]	...	...	78.6[8]	71.0[8]	...	...	243.9[34]	...
%MF [BA][8]	...	...	2.5	1.8	...	...	...	...
%M [BA][8]	...	...	2.1	1.5	...	...	...	...
%F [BA][8]	...	...	2.8	2.2	...	...	...	...
Cameroon[1] — Cameroun[1]								
MF [B]	...	...	...	468.0	...	...	...	...
M [B]	...	...	...	263.0	...	...	...	...
F [B]	...	...	...	205.0	...	...	...	...
%MF [B]	...	...	...	7.5	...	...	...	...
%M [B]	...	...	...	8.2	...	...	...	...
%F [B]	...	...	...	6.7	...	...	...	...
Canada[1,35] — Canada[1,35]								
MF [BA]	1 277.6	1 185.2	1 083.5	1 164.1	1 272.2	1 288.9	1 233.7	1 172.8
M [BA]	715.4	662.7	596.0	655.3	725.6	722.4	684.8	649.0
F [BA]	562.2	522.5	487.6	508.7	546.6	566.5	548.9	523.8
%MF [BA]	8.4	7.6	6.8	7.2	7.7	7.6	7.2	6.8
%M [BA]	8.6	7.8	7.0	7.5	8.1	8.0	7.5	7.0
%F [BA]	8.1	7.3	6.7	6.9	7.1	7.2	6.8	6.5
Chile[1,36] — Chili[1,36]								
MF [BA]	419.2	529.1	489.4	469.4	468.7	453.1	494.7	440.4
M [BA]	271.1	322.9	312.5	302.6	298.5	279.2	280.8	248.2
F [BA]	148.1	206.2	176.9	166.9	170.2	173.9	213.9	192.2
%MF [BA]	7.2	8.9	8.3	7.9	7.8	7.4	7.8	6.9
%M [BA]	7.0	8.2	8.0	7.6	7.5	6.9	6.9	6.1
%F [BA]	7.6	10.3	9.0	8.4	8.5	8.3	9.5	8.5
China[1,12,37,38] — Chine[1,12,37,38]								
MF [E]	5 710.0	5 750.0	5 950.0	6 810.0	7 700.0	8 000.0	8 270.0	8 390.0
M [E]	2 705.0	...	...	...	...	...	...	...

Country or area, source§ — Pays ou zone, source§	1998	1999	2000	2001	2002	2003	2004	2005
F [E]	3 005.0	...	...	...	...	...	...	...
%MF [E]	3.1	3.1	3.1	3.6	4.0	4.3	4.2	4.2
China, Hong Kong SAR[1,39,40] — Chine, Hong Kong RAS[1,39,40]								
MF [BA]	154.1	207.5	166.9	174.6	253.8	275.1	239.4	197.3
M [BA]	101.2	140.6	109.6	118.2	163.7	179.9	151.6	127.1
F [BA]	52.9	66.9	57.3	56.4	90.0	95.2	87.8	70.2
%MF [BA]	4.7	6.2	4.9	5.1	7.3	7.9	6.8	5.6
%M [BA]	5.2	7.2	5.6	6.0	8.4	9.2	7.8	6.5
%F [BA]	4.0	4.9	4.1	3.9	5.9	6.2	5.6	4.4
China, Macao SAR[22] — Chine, Macao RAS[22]								
MF [BA]	9.5	13.2	14.2	13.9	13.4	12.9	11.0	10.2
M [BA]	6.4	9.1	9.8	9.4	8.9	8.2	6.7	5.7
F [BA]	3.1	4.2	4.4	4.4	4.4	4.7	4.3	4.5
%MF [BA]	4.6	6.3	6.8	6.4	6.3	6.0	4.8	4.1
%M [BA]	5.7	8.0	8.6	8.1	7.9	7.1	5.5	4.4
%F [BA]	3.3	4.4	4.6	4.4	4.5	4.7	4.0	3.8
Colombia[41] — Colombie[41]								
MF [BA]	998.3[42]	1 415.4[42]	1 526.0[42]	2 846.0[8,43]	3 084.4[8,43]	2 878.1[8,43]	2 766.7[8,43]	2 406.0[8,43]
M [BA]	457.2[42]	649.8[42]	660.2[42]	1 303.5[8,43]	1 440.7[8,43]	1 274.0[8,43]	1 243.1[8,43]	1 066.0[8,43]
F [BA]	541.1[42]	765.6[42]	865.8[42]	1 542.5[8,43]	1 643.8[8,43]	1 604.1[8,43]	1 523.6[8,43]	1 340.0[8,43]
%MF [BA]	15.0[42]	20.1[42]	20.5[42]	14.7[8,43]	15.7[8,43]	14.2[8,43]	13.6[8,43]	11.8[8,43]
%M [BA]	12.5[42]	17.2[42]	16.9[42]	11.6[8,43]	12.7[8,43]	11.0[8,43]	10.6[8,43]	9.0[8,43]
%F [BA]	18.0[42]	23.3[42]	24.5[42]	19.1[8,43]	19.7[8,43]	18.5[8,43]	17.7[8,43]	15.6[8,43]
Costa Rica[24,44] — Costa Rica[24,44]								
MF [BA]	76.5	83.3	71.9	100.4	108.5	117.2	114.9	126.2
M [BA]	40.6	45.6	41.2	55.8	61.6	66.0	62.5	60.2
F [BA]	36.0	37.7	30.8	44.6	46.9	51.2	52.4	66.0
%MF [BA]	5.6	6.0	5.2	6.1	6.4	6.7	6.5	6.6
%M [BA]	4.4	4.9	4.4	5.2	5.6	5.8	5.4	5.0
%F [BA]	8.0	8.2	6.9	7.6	7.9	8.2	8.5	9.6
Croatia — Croatie								
MF [BA][1,45]	198.5	234.0	297.2	276.2	265.8	255.7	249.7	229.1
M [BA][1,45]	100.9	117.4	149.8	134.8	129.7	127.7	120.0	114.4
F [BA][1,45]	97.5	116.6	147.4	141.4	136.0	128.1	129.7	114.7
%MF [BA][1,45]	11.8	13.5	16.1	15.8	14.8	14.3	13.8	12.7
%M [BA][1,45]	11.4	12.8	15.0	14.2	13.4	13.1	12.0	11.7
%F [BA][1,45]	12.1	14.5	17.3	17.9	16.6	15.7	15.7	14.0
MF [FB]	288.0	322.0	358.0	380.0	390.0	330.0	318.0	...
M [FB]	139.0	153.0	169.0	177.0	177.0	140.0	133.0	...
F [FB]	149.0	169.0	189.0	203.0	213.0	190.0	185.0	...
%MF [FB]	17.2	19.1	21.1	22.0	22.3	19.2	...	...
%M [FB]	15.6	17.2	19.0	19.5	19.3	15.5	...	...
%F [FB]	19.0	21.2	23.4	24.7	25.6	23.2	...	...
Cuba[46,47] — Cuba[46,47]								
MF [BA]	284.9	290.9	252.3	191.6	156.1	109.7	87.7	...
M [BA]	128.0	126.1	111.8	93.8	76.9	51.3	49.7	...
F [BA]	156.9	164.8	140.5	97.8	79.2	58.4	38.0	...
%MF [BA]	6.2	6.3	5.4	4.1	3.3	2.3	1.9	...
%M [BA]	4.4	4.3	3.8	3.1	2.6	1.7	1.7	...
%F [BA]	9.4	9.6	8.3	5.8	4.6	3.4	2.2	...
Cyprus[1,48] — Chypre[1,48]								
MF [BA]	...	16.9	14.5	12.8	10.8	14.1	16.7	19.5
M [BA]	...	7.7	5.5	4.8	4.7	7.1	7.0	9.0
F [BA]	...	9.1	8.9	8.1	6.0	7.0	9.7	10.4
%MF [BA]	...	5.7	4.9	4.0	3.3	4.1	4.7	5.3
%M [BA]	...	4.3	3.2	2.6	2.6	3.8	3.5	4.4
%F [BA]	...	7.9	7.4	5.7	4.2	4.6	6.2	6.5

Country or area, source§ — Pays ou zone, source§	1998	1999	2000	2001	2002	2003	2004	2005
MF [FB]	10.4	11.4	10.9	9.5	10.6	12.0	12.7	13.2
M [FB]	5.4	5.6	5.3	4.5	4.7	5.1	5.4	5.8
F [FB]	5.0	5.8	5.7	5.0	5.9	6.8	7.2	7.3
%MF [FB]	3.3	3.6	3.4	2.9	3.2	3.5	3.6	3.7
%M [FB]	2.8	2.9	2.7	2.3	2.3	2.5	2.6	2.9
%F [FB]	4.2	4.8	4.4	3.8	4.3	5.0	5.1	4.7
Czech Republic — République tchèque								
MF [BA][1]	336.0	454.0	455.0	418.0	374.0	399.0	426.0	410.0
M [BA][1]	146.0	211.0	212.0	193.0	169.0	175.0	201.0	187.0
F [BA][1]	190.0	243.0	243.0	225.0	205.0	224.0	225.0	223.0
%MF [BA][1]	6.5	8.7	8.8	8.1	7.3	7.8	8.3	7.9
%M [BA][1]	5.0	7.3	7.3	6.8	5.9	6.1	7.0	6.5
%F [BA][1]	8.3	10.5	10.6	9.9	9.0	9.9	9.9	9.8
MF [FB][12]	387.0	488.0	457.0	462.0	514.0	542.0	542.0	...
M [FB][12]	182.0	240.0	227.0	230.0	257.0	270.0	266.0	...
F [FB][12]	205.0	248.0	230.0	232.0	257.0	272.0	276.0	...
%MF [FB][12]	7.5	9.4	8.8	8.9	9.8	10.3	9.5	...
%M [FB][12]	6.3	8.2	7.8	7.9	8.7	9.2	8.3	...
%F [FB][12]	9.0	10.8	10.0	10.1	11.2	11.8	10.9	...
Denmark — Danemark								
MF [BA][49]	155.3	158.0	131.1	137.0	134.0	157.6	162.6	143.3
M [BA][49]	68.5	71.0	61.2	66.0	66.0	75.7	79.9	69.4
F [BA][49]	86.9	87.0	69.8	71.0	68.0	81.8	82.7	73.9
%MF [BA][49]	5.5	5.5	4.6	4.8	4.7	5.5	5.6	5.0
%M [BA][49]	4.5	4.8	4.0	4.4	4.4	5.0	5.2	4.6
%F [BA][49]	6.6	6.5	5.2	5.3	5.1	6.2	6.1	5.5
MF [FB][50]	182.7	158.2	150.5	145.1	144.7	170.6	176.4	157.4
M [FB][50]	81.0	72.8	68.5	66.5	68.8	83.3	84.6	72.9
F [FB][50]	101.8	85.4	82.0	78.6	75.9	87.3	91.8	84.5
%MF [FB][50]	6.6	5.7	5.4	5.2	5.2	6.2	6.4	5.7
%M [FB][50]	5.5	4.9	4.6	4.5	4.7	5.7	5.8	5.0
%F [FB][50]	7.8	6.5	6.0	5.9	5.8	6.6	7.0	6.5
Dominica[1] — Dominique[1]								
MF [BA]	...	5.2	...	3.1	...	...	...	...
M [BA]	...	2.6	...	2.0	...	...	...	...
F [BA]	...	2.6	...	1.0	...	...	...	...
%MF [BA]	...	15.7	...	11.0	...	...	...	...
%M [BA]	...	13.1	...	11.9	...	...	...	...
%F [BA]	...	19.4	...	9.5	...	...	...	...
Dominican Republic[8] — Rép. dominicaine[8]								
MF [BA]	486.1	477.9	491.4	556.3	596.3	619.7	723.7	715.8
M [BA]	201.7	175.8	174.7	208.0	215.5	243.0	252.5	269.6
F [BA]	284.3	302.1	316.8	348.2	380.8	376.8	471.2	446.3
%MF [BA]	14.4	13.8	13.9	15.6	16.1	16.7	18.4	17.9
%M [BA]	9.3	7.8	7.9	9.3	9.4	10.6	10.5	11.3
%F [BA]	23.8	24.9	23.8	26.0	26.6	26.6	30.7	28.8
Ecuador[8,51] — Equateur[8,51]								
MF [BA]	409.3[33]	543.5[33]	333.1[33]	450.9[6]	352.9[33]	461.1[33]	362.1[33]	333.6[33]
M [BA]	175.5[33]	239.5[33]	138.3[33]	169.0[6]	136.2[33]	215.0[33]	160.7[33]	143.3[33]
F [BA]	233.8[33]	304.0[33]	194.8[33]	282.0[6]	216.7[33]	246.1[33]	201.4[33]	190.3[33]
%MF [BA]	11.5[33]	14.0[33]	9.0[33]	11.0[6]	9.3[33]	11.5[33]	8.6[33]	7.9[33]
%M [BA]	8.4[33]	10.8[33]	6.2[33]	7.1[6]	6.0[33]	9.1[33]	6.6[33]	5.8[33]
%F [BA]	16.0[33]	19.6[33]	13.1[33]	16.2[6]	14.0[33]	15.0[33]	11.4[33]	10.8[33]
Egypt[52,53] — Egypte[52,53]								
MF [BA]	1 447.5	1 480.5	1 698.0	1 783.0	2 020.6	2 240.7	...	...
M [BA]	703.0	726.2	743.5	851.8	983.2	1 186.7	...	...
F [BA]	744.5	754.3	954.5	931.2	1 037.4	1 054.0	...	...
%MF [BA]	8.2	8.1	9.0	9.2	10.2	11.0	...	...

Country or area, source§ — Pays ou zone, source§	1998	1999	2000	2001	2002	2003	2004	2005
%M [BA]	5.1	5.1	5.1	5.6	6.3	7.5	...	...
%F [BA]	19.9	19.4	22.7	22.6	23.9	23.3	...	...
El Salvador[8,47] — El Salvador[8,47]								
MF [BA]	175.7	170.2	173.7	183.5	160.2	187.2	183.9	...
M [BA]	119.9	125.2	136.8	128.8	123.6	148.6	142.7	...
F [BA]	55.8	45.0	36.9	54.7	36.6	38.6	41.1	...
%MF [BA]	7.3	7.0	7.0	7.0	6.2	6.9	6.8	...
%M [BA]	8.2	8.5	9.1	8.1	8.1	9.2	8.7	...
%F [BA]	6.0	4.6	3.6	5.2	3.5	3.7	3.8	...
Estonia — Estonie								
MF [BA][54]	66.1[56]	80.5[56]	89.9	83.1	67.2	66.2	63.6	52.2
M [BA][54]	37.4[56]	45.7[56]	49.5	43.7	36.1	34.2	34.7	28.9
F [BA][54]	28.7[56]	34.8[56]	40.5	39.3	31.0	32.0	28.9	23.3
%MF [BA][54]	9.8[56]	12.2[56]	13.6	12.6	10.3	10.0	9.7	7.9
%M [BA][54]	10.8[56]	13.4[56]	14.5	12.9	10.8	10.2	10.4	8.8
%F [BA][54]	8.8[56]	10.9[56]	12.6	12.2	9.7	9.9	8.9	7.1
MF [FB][55]	18.8	44.0	46.3	54.1	48.2	43.3	...	...
%MF [FB][55]	2.2	5.1	5.3	6.5	5.9	5.3	...	...
Ethiopia — Ethiopie								
MF [BA][8]	...	...	...	...	...	...	845.9[57]	1 653.7[45]
M [BA][8]	...	...	...	...	...	...	304.5[57]	427.9[45]
F [BA][8]	...	...	...	...	...	...	541.4[57]	1 225.8[45]
%MF [BA][8]	...	...	...	...	...	...	22.9[57]	5.0[45]
%M [BA][8]	...	...	...	...	...	...	15.8[57]	2.5[45]
%F [BA][8]	...	...	...	...	...	...	30.6[57]	7.8[45]
MF [FB][19]	29.5	25.7	...	...	...	...	...	...
M [FB][19]	16.6	14.3	...	...	...	...	...	...
F [FB][19]	12.9	11.4	...	...	...	...	...	...
Finland[58] — Finlande[58]								
MF [BA][54]	285.0	261.0	253.0	238.0	237.0	235.0	229.0	220.0
M [BA][54]	143.0	130.0	122.0	117.0	123.0	124.0	118.0	111.0
F [BA][54]	142.0	131.0	131.0	121.0	114.0	111.0	111.0	109.0
%MF [BA][54]	11.3	10.1	9.7	9.1	9.1	9.0	8.8	8.3
%M [BA][54]	10.7	9.6	8.9	8.6	9.1	9.2	8.7	8.1
%F [BA][54]	11.9	10.7	10.6	9.7	9.1	8.9	8.9	8.6
MF [FB][1,59]	362.0	337.0	321.0	302.0	294.0	288.0	288.0	275.0
M [FB][1,59]	183.0	169.0	162.0	153.0	154.0	153.0	152.0	144.0
F [FB][1,59]	179.0	168.0	159.0	149.0	140.0	135.0	136.0	131.0
France — France								
MF [BA][1]	3 006.6[61]	3 014.3[17]	2 590.2[61]	2 285.0[61]	2 341.0[61]	2 655.9	2 727.2	...
M [BA][1]	1 411.0[61]	1 424.6[17]	1 185.0[61]	1 004.0[61]	1 122.5[61]	1 283.4	1 326.5	...
F [BA][1]	1 595.6[61]	1 589.7[17]	1 405.1[61]	1 281.0[61]	1 218.5[61]	1 372.5	1 400.8	...
%MF [BA][1]	11.8[61]	11.7[17]	10.0[61]	8.8[61]	8.9[61]	9.7	9.9	...
%M [BA][1]	10.2[61]	10.2[17]	8.5[61]	7.1[61]	7.9[61]	8.7	9.0	...
%F [BA][1]	13.8[61]	13.6[17]	11.9[61]	10.7[61]	10.1[61]	10.9	11.1	...
MF [E][1]	2 993.4	2 844.3	2 516.6	2 324.8	2 441.3	2 655.8	2 727.2	...
M [E][1]	1 403.9	1 329.2	1 140.7	1 050.0	1 169.4	1 283.3	1 326.5	...
F [E][1]	1 589.5	1 515.8	1 375.9	1 274.8	1 271.8	1 372.5	1 400.8	...
%MF [E][1]	11.5	10.8	9.5	8.7	9.0	9.7	10.0	...
%M [E][1]	9.9	9.3	7.9	7.3	8.0	8.8	9.1	...
%F [E][1]	13.5	12.7	11.4	10.4	10.2	10.8	11.0	...
MF [FB][55,60]	2 981.5	2 792.0	2 354.5	2 117.0	2 254.9	2 390.4	2 439.9	...
M [FB][55,60]	1 466.4	1 368.0	1 137.3	1 035.6	1 154.8	1 247.5	1 266.0	...
F [FB][55,60]	1 515.1	1 423.9	1 217.2	1 081.4	1 100.1	1 142.9	1 173.9	...
French Guiana[1,29] — Guyane française[1,29]								
MF [BA]	16.2	15.5	15.2	15.0	13.5	14.1	15.2	15.9
M [BA]	9.1	7.8	7.3	7.4	6.4	6.6	7.3	7.9
F [BA]	7.1	7.7	7.9	7.6	7.1	7.5	8.0	8.0

Country or area, source§ — Pays ou zone, source§	1998	1999	2000	2001	2002	2003	2004	2005
%MF [BA]	26.5	26.6	25.8	26.3	23.4	24.5	26.3	26.5
%M [BA]	23.9	22.8	21.2	23.0	19.8	20.5	22.6	23.8
%F [BA]	30.7	32.1	32.2	30.5	27.8	29.6	30.8	29.7
French Polynesia[18,22] — Polynésie française[18,22]								
MF [FB]	3.8	...	...	...	...	...	...	...
Georgia — Géorgie								
MF [BA][1]	294.7	277.5	212.2	235.6	265.0	235.9	257.6	279.3
M [BA][1]	161.8	160.1	116.7	126.9	155.5	124.2	143.2	159.2
F [BA][1]	132.9	117.4	95.5	108.7	109.5	111.7	114.4	120.1
%MF [BA][1]	14.5	13.8	10.8	11.0	12.3	11.5	12.6	13.8
%M [BA][1]	15.4	15.3	11.1	11.6	13.7	11.5	13.4	14.8
%F [BA][1]	13.9	12.2	10.5	10.7	10.7	11.5	11.8	12.6
MF [FB][12]	85.5	92.2	101.0	97.8	21.9[62]	42.9	46.6	34.2
M [FB][12]	45.5	38.9	46.5	40.1	12.1[62]	23.2	24.1	17.1
F [FB][12]	40.0	53.3	54.1	57.7	9.8[62]	19.7	22.5	17.1
%MF [FB][12]	4.2	5.0	3.5	5.5	1.2[62]	...	...	...
Germany — Allemagne								
MF [BA][1]	3 849.0[16]	3 503.0[16]	3 127.0[4]	3 150.0[16]	3 486.0[16]	4 023.0[4]	4 388.0[45]	4 583.0[45,62]
M [BA][1]	2 074.0[16]	1 905.0[16]	1 691.0[4]	1 754.0[16]	1 982.0[16]	2 316.0[4]	2 551.0[45]	2 574.0[45,62]
F [BA][1]	1 775.0[16]	1 598.0[16]	1 436.0[4]	1 396.0[16]	1 504.0[16]	1 707.0[4]	1 836.0[45]	2 009.0[45,62]
%MF [BA][1]	9.7[16]	8.8[16]	7.9[4]	7.9[16]	8.7[16]	10.0[4]	11.0[45]	11.1[45,62]
%M [BA][1]	9.2[16]	8.4[16]	7.6[4]	7.8[16]	8.9[16]	10.4[4]	11.5[45]	11.3[45,62]
%F [BA][1]	10.4[16]	9.2[16]	8.3[4]	7.9[16]	8.5[16]	9.5[4]	10.3[45]	10.9[45,62]
MF [FB][53]	3 965.0	3 943.0	3 685.0	3 743.0	3 942.0	4 207.0	4 381.0[3]	4 861.0
M [FB][53]	2 046.8	2 013.0	1 899.0	1 961.0	2 133.0	2 296.0	2 449.0[3]	2 606.0
F [FB][53]	1 918.6	1 930.0	1 786.0	1 782.0	1 809.0	1 911.0	1 932.0[3]	2 255.0
%MF [FB][53]	11.4	11.2	10.0	10.0	10.9	11.7	11.7[3]	13.0
%M [FB][53]	10.7	10.5	9.6	9.9	11.4	11.6	12.5[3]	13.4
%F [FB][53]	12.2	12.0	10.4	10.1	10.3	11.7	10.8[3]	12.7
Gibraltar[63] — Gibraltar[63]								
MF [FB]	0.5	0.4	0.4	0.4	0.5	0.5	0.4	0.5
M [FB]	0.3	0.3	0.3	0.2	0.3	0.3	0.3	0.3
F [FB]	0.2	0.1	0.1	0.2	0.2	0.2	0.2	0.2
Greece[1,56] — Grèce[1,56]								
MF [BA]	489.4	543.3	519.3	478.4	462.1	441.8	492.7	466.7
M [BA]	196.2	212.8	207.2	191.4	180.5	170.8	181.7	166.8
F [BA]	293.2	330.5	312.1	287.0	281.6	271.0	311.0	299.9
%MF [BA]	10.8	11.9	11.2	10.4	9.9	9.3	10.2	9.6
%M [BA]	7.1	7.7	7.4	6.9	6.4	6.0	6.3	5.8
%F [BA]	16.7	18.2	17.0	15.9	15.2	14.3	15.9	15.2
Greenland[1,64] — Groenland[1,64]								
MF [E]	2.9	2.3	2.8	2.5	2.3	2.7	2.8	2.5
M [E]	1.7	1.4	1.6	1.5	1.3	1.6	1.7	1.5
F [E]	1.2	0.9	1.3	1.0	1.0	1.1	1.2	1.1
%MF [E]	11.6	9.0	11.0	9.5	8.8	10.3	10.4	9.3
%M [E]	13.4	10.6	12.0	11.3	9.8	11.9	12.0	10.4
%F [E]	9.7	7.4	10.0	7.7	7.8	8.6	8.8	8.0
Guadeloupe[1,29] — Guadeloupe[1,29]								
MF [BA]	55.9	55.0	49.4	43.7	41.5	44.0	40.3	42.0
M [BA]	24.5	22.3	21.7	19.1	19.0	20.9	17.5	18.1
F [BA]	31.4	32.7	27.7	24.6	22.5	23.1	22.8	23.9
%MF [BA]	30.7	29.8	25.7	27.6	25.7	26.9	24.7	26.0
%M [BA]	25.3	23.2	21.2	23.4	22.6	24.6	21.0	22.0
%F [BA]	36.8	37.1	30.8	32.0	29.1	29.4	28.5	30.1
Guatemala[8] — Guatemala[8]								
MF [BA]	...	79.8	64.9	62.2	154.3	172.2	...	...
M [BA]	...	59.2	40.3	34.4	77.1	79.4	...	...
F [BA]	...	20.6	24.6	27.8	77.2	92.8	...	...

Country or area, source§ — Pays ou zone, source§	1998	1999	2000	2001	2002	2003	2004	2005
%MF [BA]	...	1.9	1.4	1.3	3.1	3.4	...	...
%M [BA]	...	2.2	1.4	1.3	2.5	2.5	...	...
%F [BA]	...	1.4	1.5	1.4	4.3	4.9	...	...
Honduras[8] — Honduras[8]								
MF [BA]	87.7[61]	89.3[61]	...	103.4[5]	93.7[5]	130.3[5]	153.2[4]	107.8[61]
M [BA]	55.5[61]	56.7[61]	...	62.0[5]	...	...	81.0[4]	55.2[61]
F [BA]	32.2[61]	32.6[61]	...	41.4[5]	...	...	72.2[4]	52.6[61]
%MF [BA]	3.9[61]	3.7[61]	...	4.2[5]	3.8[5]	5.1[5]	5.9[4]	4.1[61]
%M [BA]	3.8[61]	3.7[61]	...	4.0[5]	...	...	4.7[4]	3.1[61]
%F [BA]	4.2[61]	3.8[61]	...	4.8[5]	...	...	8.3[4]	6.1[61]
Hungary — Hongrie								
MF [BA][54]	313.0	284.7	262.5	232.9	238.8[65]	244.5	252.9	303.9
M [BA][54]	189.2	170.7	159.5	142.7	138.0[65]	138.5	136.8	159.1
F [BA][54]	123.8	114.0	103.0	90.2	100.8[65]	106.0	116.1	144.8
%MF [BA][54]	7.8	7.0	6.4	5.7	5.8[65]	5.7	6.1	7.2
%M [BA][54]	8.5	7.5	7.0	6.3	6.1[65]	6.1	6.1	7.0
%F [BA][54]	7.0	6.3	5.6	5.0	5.4[65]	5.3	6.1	7.5
MF [FB][12]	404.1	404.5	372.4	342.8	344.9	359.9	400.6	410.6
M [FB][12]	222.7	220.1	202.2	188.7	186.8	189.4	209.6	213.7
F [FB][12]	181.3	184.4	170.2	154.1	158.1	170.5	191.0	197.0
%MF [FB][12]	9.6	9.6	...	...	...	8.4	...	...
%M [FB][12]	...	...	...	...	...	7.9	...	...
%F [FB][12]	...	...	...	...	...	8.9	...	...
Iceland — Islande								
MF [BA][66,67]	4.2	3.1	3.7	3.7	5.3	5.5	5.0	4.3
M [BA][66,67]	1.8	1.2	1.5	1.8	3.1	3.0	2.5	2.3
F [BA][66,67]	2.4	1.9	2.2	1.9	2.2	2.3	2.0	2.0
%MF [BA][66,67]	2.7	2.0	2.3	2.3	3.3	3.4	3.1	2.6
%M [BA][66,67]	2.3	1.5	1.8	2.0	3.6	3.6	2.9	2.6
%F [BA][66,67]	3.3	2.6	2.9	2.5	2.9	3.0	2.7	2.6
MF [FB][55]	3.8	2.6	1.9	2.0	3.6	4.9	...	...
M [FB][55]	1.4	1.0	0.7	0.8	1.8	2.5	...	...
F [FB][55]	2.4	1.6	1.1	1.2	1.8	2.4	...	...
%MF [FB][55]	2.8	1.9	1.3	1.4	2.5	3.4	...	...
%M [FB][55]	1.8	1.2	0.9	1.0	2.1	3.0	...	...
%F [FB][55]	4.0	2.7	1.9	1.9	3.0	3.9	...	...
India — Inde								
MF [BA]	12 541.7[2]	...	16 634.0[17]	...	...	...	...	...
M [BA]	9 489.4[2]	...	11 837.5[17]	...	...	...	...	...
F [BA]	3 052.3[2]	...	4 796.5[17]	...	...	...	...	...
%MF [BA]	3.6[2]	...	4.3[17]	...	...	...	...	...
%M [BA]	3.5[2]	...	4.3[17]	...	...	...	...	...
%F [BA]	3.8[2]	...	4.3[17]	...	...	...	...	...
MF [FB][12,18,22]	40 090.0	40 371.0	41 344.0	41 996.0	41 171.0	41 389.0	40 458.0	39 348.0
M [FB][12,18,22]	30 563.0	30 438.0	30 887.0	31 111.0	30 521.0	30 636.0	29 746.0	28 742.0
F [FB][12,18,22]	9 526.0	9 933.0	10 457.0	10 885.0	10 650.0	10 752.0	10 712.0	10 606.0
Indonesia[1] — Indonésie[1]								
MF [BA][68]	5 062.5	6 030.3	5 813.2	8 005.0	9 132.1	9 531.1	10 251.4	10 854.3
M [BA][68]	2 862.2	...	...	4 032.4	4 727.8	4 928.3	5 345.7	5 483.3
F [BA][68]	2 200.3	...	...	3 972.6	4 404.3	4 602.8	4 905.7	5 371.0
%MF [BA][68]	5.5	6.4	6.1	8.1	9.1	9.5	9.9	13.5
%M [BA][68]	...	...	...	...	...	8.1	8.1	11.5
%F [BA][68]	...	...	...	...	...	12.9	12.9	17.2
MF [FB]	...	1 191.8	...	...	...	...	...	...
Iran (Islamic Rep. of)[8] — Iran (Rép. islamique d')[8]								
MF [BA]	...	...	...	...	...	...	...	2 556.0
M [BA]	...	...	...	...	...	...	...	1 780.0
F [BA]	...	...	...	...	...	...	...	776.0

Country or area, source§ — Pays ou zone, source§	1998	1999	2000	2001	2002	2003	2004	2005
%MF [BA]	...	...	...	...	12.8	...	10.3	11.5
%M [BA]	...	...	...	...	11.2	...	9.8	10.0
%F [BA]	...	...	...	...	22.4	...	17.8	17.0
Iraq[1] — Iraq[1]								
%MF [BA]	...	...	...	...	...	28.1	26.8	...
%M [BA]	...	...	...	...	...	30.2	29.4	...
%F [BA]	...	...	...	...	...	16.0	15.0	...
Ireland — Irlande								
MF [BA][1,69]	126.6	96.9	74.9	65.4	77.2	82.1	84.2	85.6
M [BA][1,69]	78.8	59.4	44.9	39.8	48.8	51.7	54.4	53.2
F [BA][1,69]	47.8	37.5	30.0	25.6	28.3	30.4	29.8	32.4
%MF [BA][1,69]	7.8	5.7	4.3	3.7	4.2	4.4	4.4	4.2
%M [BA][1,69]	8.1	5.9	4.3	3.8	4.6	4.7	4.9	4.6
%F [BA][1,69]	7.4	5.5	4.2	3.5	3.7	3.9	3.7	3.8
MF [FB][55]	227.1	193.2	155.4	142.3	162.5	172.4	166.0	153.3
M [FB][55]	135.7	111.6	88.7	83.0	96.3	100.2	96.1	91.0
F [FB][55]	91.4	81.6	66.7	59.3	66.2	72.2	70.0	62.3
%MF [FB][55]	7.4	5.5	4.1	3.9	4.4	4.6	4.4	4.2
Isle of Man — Ile de Man								
MF [A][1,2]	...	...	...	0.6	...	...	...	...
M [A][1,2]	...	...	...	0.4	...	...	...	...
F [A][1,2]	...	...	...	0.3	...	...	...	...
%MF [A][1,2]	...	...	...	1.6	...	...	...	...
%M [A][1,2]	...	...	...	1.7	...	...	...	...
%F [A][1,2]	...	...	...	1.5	...	...	...	...
MF [FB]	0.4	0.3	0.2	0.2	0.2	0.3	0.4	0.6
M [FB]	0.3	0.2	0.2	0.1	0.1	0.2	0.3	0.4
F [FB]	0.1	0.1	0.1	0.1	0.1	0.1	0.1	0.2
%MF [FB][70]	...	0.8	0.6	0.5	0.5	0.8	1.0	1.4
%M [FB][70]	...	1.0	0.8	0.6	0.7	1.0	1.3	1.8
%F [FB][70]	...	0.5	0.4	0.3	0.4	0.5	0.6	0.9
Israel[1,71] — Israël[1,71]								
MF [BA]	193.4	208.5	213.8	233.9[72]	262.4	279.9	277.7	246.4
M [BA]	100.4	108.8	111.7	120.9[72]	138.4	142.8	136.5	124.9
F [BA]	93.0	99.7	102.1	113.0[72]	124.0	137.1	141.2	121.5
%MF [BA]	8.5	8.9	8.8	9.4[72]	10.3	10.7	10.4	9.0
%M [BA]	8.0	8.5	8.4	8.9[72]	10.1	10.2	9.5	8.5
%F [BA]	9.2	9.4	9.2	9.9[72]	10.6	11.3	11.4	9.5
Italy[1] — Italie[1]								
MF [BA]	2 745.0	2 669.0	2 495.0	2 267.0	2 163.0	2 096.0	...	1 888.6[62]
M [BA]	1 313.0	1 266.0	1 179.0	1 066.0	1 016.0	996.0	...	902.4[62]
F [BA]	1 431.0	1 404.0	1 316.0	1 201.0	1 147.0	1 100.0	...	986.2[62]
%MF [BA]	11.7	11.4	10.5	9.5	9.0	8.7	...	7.7[62]
%M [BA]	9.1	8.8	8.1	7.3	6.9	6.7	...	6.1[62]
%F [BA]	16.0	15.7	14.5	13.0	12.2	11.6	...	10.1[62]
Jamaica[22] — Jamaïque[22]								
MF [BA]	175.0	175.2	171.8	165.4[73]	171.8	128.9	136.8	130.3
M [BA]	61.4	61.4	62.5	63.4[73]	65.7	47.6	54.0	48.6
F [BA]	113.5	113.8	109.2	102.1[73]	106.1	81.3	82.8	81.7
%MF [BA]	15.5	15.7	15.5	15.0[73]	14.3	10.9	11.4	10.9
%M [BA]	10.0	10.0	10.2	10.3[73]	9.9	7.2	8.1	7.4
%F [BA]	22.1	22.4	22.3	21.0[73]	19.8	15.6	15.7	15.3
Japan[1] — Japon[1]								
MF [BA]	2 790.0[74]	3 170.0[74]	3 190.0[74]	3 400.0[74]	3 590.0	3 500.0	3 130.0	2 940.0
M [BA]	1 680.0[74]	1 940.0[74]	1 960.0[74]	2 090.0[74]	2 190.0	2 150.0	1 920.0	1 780.0
F [BA]	1 110.0[74]	1 230.0[74]	1 230.0[74]	1 310.0[74]	1 400.0	1 350.0	1 210.0	1 160.0
%MF [BA]	4.1[74]	4.7[74]	4.7[74]	5.0[74]	5.4	5.3	4.7	4.4

Country or area, source§ — Pays ou zone, source§	1998	1999	2000	2001	2002	2003	2004	2005
%M [BA]	4.2[74]	4.8[74]	4.9[74]	5.2[74]	5.5	5.5	4.9	4.6
%F [BA]	4.0[74]	4.5[74]	4.5[74]	4.7[74]	5.1	4.9	4.4	4.2
Kazakhstan — Kazakhstan								
MF [BA][1]	...	...	...	780.3	690.7	672.1	658.8	...
M [BA][1]	...	...	...	338.0	283.8	281.4	281.1	...
F [BA][1]	...	...	...	442.3	406.9	390.7	377.7	...
%MF [BA][1]	...	...	...	10.4	9.3	8.8	8.4	...
%M [BA][1]	...	...	...	8.9	7.5	7.2	7.0	...
%F [BA][1]	...	...	...	12.0	11.2	10.4	9.8	...
MF [E]	925.8	950.0	906.4	...	...	...	...	...
%MF [E]	13.1	13.5	12.8	...	...	...	...	...
MF [FB][75]	251.9	251.4	231.4	216.1	193.7	142.8	117.7	...
M [FB][75]	95.5	102.0	...	...	...	...	...	...
F [FB][75]	156.4	149.4	...	...	...	...	...	...
%MF [FB][75]	3.7	3.9	3.7	2.9	2.6	1.8	1.5	...
%M [FB][75]	2.6	...	...	...	...	...	...	...
%F [FB][75]	5.0	...	...	...	...	...	...	...
Kenya[1,25] — Kenya[1,25]								
MF [A]	...	1 275.8	...	...	...	...	...	...
Korea, Republic of[1] — Corée, République de[1]								
MF [BA]	1 461.0	1 353.0	979.0[76]	899.0	752.0	818.0	860.0	887.0
M [BA]	983.0	911.0	647.0[76]	591.0	491.0	508.0	534.0	553.0
F [BA]	478.0	442.0	332.0[76]	308.0	261.0	309.7	325.9	334.0
%MF [BA]	6.8	6.3	4.4[76]	4.0	3.3	3.6	3.7	3.7
%M [BA]	7.6	7.1	5.0[76]	4.5	3.7	3.8	3.9	4.0
%F [BA]	5.6	5.1	3.6[76]	3.3	2.8	3.3	3.4	3.4
Kuwait[12] — Koweït[12]								
MF [FD]	8.7	8.9	9.3	9.5	15.1	...	...	...
M [FD]	7.1	7.3	7.5	7.6	9.4	...	...	...
F [FD]	1.5	1.7	1.8	1.9	5.6	...	...	...
%MF [FD]	0.7	0.7	0.8	0.8	1.1	...	...	...
%M [FD]	0.8	0.8	0.8	0.8	1.0	...	...	...
%F [FD]	0.5	0.6	0.7	0.6	1.7	...	...	...
Kyrgyzstan — Kirghizistan								
MF [BA][1,23]	...	...	...	...	265.5	212.3	185.7	...
M [BA][1,23]	...	...	...	...	132.6	113.1	98.8	...
F [BA][1,23]	...	...	...	...	132.9	99.2	86.9	...
%MF [BA][1,23]	...	...	...	...	12.5	9.9	8.5	...
%M [BA][1,23]	...	...	...	...	11.2	9.4	8.0	...
%F [BA][1,23]	...	...	...	...	14.3	10.5	9.3	...
MF [FB]	55.9	54.7	58.3	60.5	60.2	57.4	58.2	68.0
M [FB]	22.6	24.2	27.1	28.0	27.6	26.5	26.8	32.2
F [FB]	33.3	30.6	31.2	32.5	32.6	30.9	31.4	35.8
Lao People's Dem. Rep.[1,17] — Rép. dém. pop. lao[1,17]								
MF [A]	...	...	...	...	...	...	...	37.5
M [A]	...	...	...	...	...	...	...	18.6
F [A]	...	...	...	...	...	...	...	18.9
Latvia — Lettonie								
MF [BA]	162.4[1]	161.4[1]	158.7[1]	144.7[1]	134.5[54]	119.2[54]	118.6[54]	99.1[54]
M [BA]	86.4[1]	88.7[1]	87.0[1]	81.9[1]	74.9[54]	61.7[54]	61.7[54]	52.8[54]
F [BA]	76.0[1]	72.7[1]	71.7[1]	62.7[1]	59.6[54]	57.5[54]	56.9[54]	46.2[54]
%MF [BA]	14.1[1]	14.3[1]	14.4[1]	13.1[1]	12.0[54]	10.6[54]	10.4[54]	8.7[54]
%M [BA]	14.4[1]	15.0[1]	15.4[1]	14.4[1]	12.9[54]	10.7[54]	10.6[54]	9.0[54]
%F [BA]	13.8[1]	13.5[1]	13.5[1]	11.7[1]	11.0[54]	10.5[54]	10.3[54]	8.4[54]
MF [FB][75,77]	111.4	109.5	93.3	91.6	89.7	90.6	90.8	78.5
M [FB][75,77]	46.2	46.7	39.5	39.1	37.0	37.6	37.3	31.5
F [FB][75,77]	65.2	62.8	53.8	52.6	52.7	53.0	53.5	47.0

Country or area, source§ — Pays ou zone, source§	1998	1999	2000	2001	2002	2003	2004	2005
%MF [FB][75,77]	9.2	9.1	7.8	7.7	8.5	8.6	8.5	7.4
%M [FB][75,77]	7.5	7.6	6.5	6.4	6.7	6.8	...	...
%F [FB][75,77]	11.0	10.7	9.2	9.0	10.5	10.6	...	...
Liechtenstein — Liechtenstein								
MF [E]	0.5	0.3	0.3	0.4	0.4	0.7	0.7	...
Lithuania — Lituanie								
MF [BA][1]	226.7	249.0	273.7	284.0	224.4	203.9	184.4	132.9
M [BA][1]	130.9	140.5	158.5	165.6	121.1	105.4	90.6	67.1
F [BA][1]	95.8	108.5	115.2	118.4	103.3	98.4	93.8	65.8
%MF [BA][1]	13.2	14.6	16.4	17.4	13.8	12.4	11.4	8.3
%M [BA][1]	14.7	16.2	18.8	19.9	14.6	12.7	11.0	8.2
%F [BA][1]	11.6	13.0	13.9	14.7	12.9	12.2	11.8	8.3
MF [FB][75,78]	122.8	177.4	225.9	224.0	191.2	158.8	126.4	87.2
M [FB][75,78]	61.7	94.6	123.1	117.7	95.1	73.7	53.8	33.9
F [FB][75,78]	61.1	82.8	102.8	106.3	96.1	85.1	72.6	53.3
%MF [FB][75,78]	6.5	10.0	12.6	12.9	10.9	9.8	7.8	5.4
%M [FB][75,78]	6.5	10.6	13.5	13.5	10.8	9.0	6.5	4.1
%F [FB][75,78]	7.0	9.3	11.6	12.2	11.0	10.5	9.1	6.8
Luxembourg[79] — Luxembourg[79]								
MF [FB]	5.5	5.4	5.0	4.9	5.8	7.6	8.7	9.8
M [FB]	2.9	2.8	2.6	2.6	3.2	4.1	4.7	5.4
F [FB]	2.6	2.5	2.3	2.3	2.7	3.5	4.0	4.4
%MF [FB]	3.1	2.9	2.7	2.7	3.0	3.8	4.2	4.7
Madagascar[80] — Madagascar[80]								
MF [BA][81]	...	...	...	...	...	383.0	...	...
M [BA][81]	...	...	...	...	...	149.8	...	...
F [BA][81]	...	...	...	...	...	233.2	...	...
%MF [BA]	...	...	...	...	...	4.5	...	...
%M [BA]	...	...	...	...	...	3.5	...	...
%F [BA]	...	...	...	...	...	5.6	...	...
Malaysia — Malaisie								
MF [BA][53]	284.0	313.7	286.9	342.4	343.6	369.8	...	...
M [BA][53]	185.3	212.3	182.7	212.3	210.5	235.8	...	...
F [BA][53]	98.7	101.4	104.2	130.1	133.1	134.0	...	...
%MF [BA][53]	3.2	3.4	3.0	3.5	3.5	3.6	...	...
%M [BA][53]	3.1	3.5	3.0	3.4	3.3	3.6	...	...
%F [BA][53]	3.3	3.3	3.1	3.8	3.8	3.6	...	...
MF [FB][1,18]	33.4	31.8	34.3	33.5	37.2	34.8	...	...
Maldives[24,47] — Maldives[24,47]								
MF [A]	...	...	1.7	...	...	...	...	...
M [A]	...	...	0.9	...	...	...	...	...
F [A]	...	...	0.8	...	...	...	...	...
Mali[1] — Mali[1]								
MF [BA]	...	...	...	...	...	...	227.5	...
M [BA]	...	...	...	...	...	...	107.0	...
F [BA]	...	...	...	...	...	...	120.5	...
%MF [BA]	...	...	...	...	...	...	8.8	...
%M [BA]	...	...	...	...	...	...	7.2	...
%F [BA]	...	...	...	...	...	...	10.9	...
Malta[12] — Malte[12]								
MF [BA][1]	...	...	10.3	10.1	11.0	12.1	11.5	12.0
M [BA][1]	...	...	7.3	6.8	7.2	7.8	7.1	7.3
F [BA][1]	...	...	3.0	3.2	3.8	4.3	4.4	4.8
%MF [BA][1]	...	...	6.7	6.4	7.0	7.6	7.2	7.5
%M [BA][1]	...	...	6.8	6.2	6.6	7.1	6.4	6.6
%F [BA][1]	...	...	6.4	7.0	7.7	8.7	9.0	9.4
MF [FB][82]	7.4	7.7	6.6	6.8	6.8	8.2[62]	8.1	...
M [FB][82]	6.4	6.6	5.7	5.6	5.6	6.6[62]	6.5	...

Country or area, source§ — Pays ou zone, source§	1998	1999	2000	2001	2002	2003	2004	2005
F [FB][82]	1.0	1.1	0.9	1.1	1.2	1.6[62]	1.6	...
%MF [FB][82]	5.1	5.3	4.5	4.7	4.7	5.7[62]	5.4	...
%M [FB][82]	6.1	6.3	5.4	5.4	5.4	6.4[62]	6.1	...
%F [FB][82]	2.5	2.6	2.2	2.7	2.9	3.8[62]	3.8	...
Marshall Islands — Iles Marshall								
MF [A][1]	...	4.5	...	...	...	...	...	...
M [A][1]	...	2.7	...	...	...	...	...	...
F [A][1]	...	1.9	...	...	...	...	...	...
%MF [A][1]	...	30.9	...	...	...	...	...	...
%M [A][1]	...	27.6	...	...	...	...	...	...
%F [A][1]	...	37.3	...	...	...	...	...	...
MF [BA][55]	...	...	...	...	...	...	...	0.6
M [BA][55]	...	...	...	...	...	...	...	0.4
F [BA][55]	...	...	...	...	...	...	...	0.3
%MF [BA][55]	...	...	...	...	...	...	...	25.4
%M [BA][55]	...	...	...	...	...	...	...	25.8
%F [BA][55]	...	...	...	...	...	...	...	25.0
Martinique[1,29] — Martinique[1,29]								
MF [BA]	48.5	46.9	44.1	39.8	35.8[62]	36.1	35.9	34.8
M [BA]	22.6	20.9	18.9	16.3	15.4[62]	16.1	15.9	16.2
F [BA]	25.9	26.0	25.2	23.6	20.4[62]	20.1	20.0	18.6
%MF [BA]	29.3	28.1	26.3	24.7	22.3[62]	22.3	22.4	21.7
%M [BA]	26.3	24.5	22.1	20.1	19.2[62]	19.9	19.9	20.1
%F [BA]	32.4	32.0	30.8	29.3	25.4[62]	24.6	24.7	20.1
Mauritius — Maurice								
MF [BA][1]	...	...	...	...	...	...	45.1	52.1
M [BA][1]	...	...	...	...	...	...	20.3	20.3
F [BA][1]	...	...	...	...	...	...	24.8	31.8
%MF [BA][1]	...	...	...	...	...	...	8.5	9.6
%M [BA][1]	...	...	...	...	...	...	5.8	5.8
%F [BA][1]	...	...	...	...	...	...	13.5	16.5
MF [E]	34.4	39.0	45.0	47.7	50.8	54.4	...	...
M [E]	20.4	23.8	28.5	30.5	29.6	31.7	...	...
F [E]	14.0	15.2	16.5	17.2	21.2	22.7	...	...
%MF [E]	6.9	7.7	8.8	9.1	9.7	10.2	...	...
%M [E]	6.1	7.0	8.3	8.8	8.5	9.0	...	...
%F [E]	8.5	9.0	9.6	9.8	12.0	12.6	...	...
MF [FB][1,83]	10.7	12.1	18.0	21.6	22.0	23.4	22.0	33.6
M [FB][1,83]	4.6	5.3	8.6	10.5	10.1	10.1	10.5	15.4
F [FB][1,83]	6.1	6.8	9.5	11.1	11.9	13.3	11.4	18.2
Mexico[22,56] — Mexique[22,56]								
MF [BA]	1 381.7	962.9	1 003.0	1 001.0	1 152.4	1 204.1	1 555.5	1 497.8
M [BA]	729.2	497.3	561.9	553.4	660.6	692.5	837.6	930.2
F [BA]	652.5	465.6	441.1	447.6	491.8	511.5	717.9	567.6
%MF [BA]	3.6	2.5	2.6	2.5	2.9	3.0	3.7	3.5
%M [BA]	2.9	2.0	2.2	2.2	2.5	2.6	3.1	3.4
%F [BA]	5.0	3.5	3.3	3.3	3.5	3.6	4.7	3.6
Mongolia[12,55] — Mongolie[12,55]								
MF [E]	49.8	39.8	38.6	40.3	30.9	33.3	35.6	32.9
M [E]	23.8	18.1	17.8	18.5	14.1	15.3	15.9	14.6
F [E]	26.0	21.6	20.7	21.9	16.8	18.1	19.6	18.3
%MF [E]	5.9	4.7	4.6	4.6	3.5	3.5	3.6	3.3
%M [E]	5.4	4.1	4.1	4.2	3.4	3.2	3.3	3.0
%F [E]	6.4	5.3	5.0	5.1	3.8	3.8	3.9	3.6
Morocco[1] — Maroc[1]								
MF [BA]	...	1 432.2	1 394.3	1 275.0	1 202.7	1 299.0	1 192.5	1 226.4
M [BA]	...	1 044.8	1 035.5	952.0	878.4	922.4	851.2	877.6

Country or area, source[§] — Pays ou zone, source[§]	1998	1999	2000	2001	2002	2003	2004	2005
F [BA]	...	387.9	358.7	323.0	324.3	376.6	341.4	348.8
%MF [BA]	...	13.9	13.6	12.5	11.6	11.9	10.8	11.0
%M [BA]	...	14.2	13.8	12.5	11.6	11.5	10.6	10.8
%F [BA]	...	13.3	13.0	12.5	12.5	13.0	11.4	11.5
Myanmar[84] — Myanmar[84]								
MF [FB]	451.5	425.3	382.1	398.4	435.7	326.5	291.3	189.7
Namibia[85] — Namibie[85]								
MF [BA]	...	...	220.6	...	...	...	...	...
M [BA]	...	...	89.4	...	...	...	...	...
F [BA]	...	...	131.3	...	...	...	...	...
%MF [BA]	...	...	33.8	...	...	...	...	...
%M [BA]	...	...	28.3	...	...	...	...	...
%F [BA]	...	...	39.0	...	...	...	...	...
Nepal[1] — Népal[1]								
MF [BA]	...	178.0	...	...	...	...	...	...
M [BA]	...	98.0	...	...	...	...	...	...
F [BA]	...	80.0	...	...	...	...	...	...
%MF [BA]	...	1.8	...	...	...	...	...	...
%M [BA]	...	2.0	...	...	...	...	...	...
%F [BA]	...	1.7	...	...	...	...	...	...
Netherlands — Pays-Bas								
MF [BA][53]	337.0	277.0	231.0[62]	221.0	259.0	357.0	419.0	430.0
M [BA][53]	155.0	124.0	105.0[62]	102.0	130.0	193.0	228.0	221.0
F [BA][53]	181.0	153.0	126.0[62]	120.0	129.0	164.0	191.0	209.0
%MF [BA][53]	4.4	3.5	2.9[62]	2.8	3.2	4.4	5.1	5.2
%M [BA][53]	3.5	2.8	2.3[62]	3.2	2.9	4.2	5.0	4.9
%F [BA][53]	5.5	4.5	3.6[62]	3.4	3.6	4.5	5.2	5.6
MF [FB][79,86]	286.0	221.5	187.0	146.0	170.0	255.0	...	...
M [FB][79,86]	156.0	115.0	98.0	77.0	91.0	144.0	...	...
F [FB][79,86]	132.0	106.0	90.0	69.0	79.0	111.0	...	...
%MF [FB][79]	4.1	3.2	2.6	2.0	2.3	3.4	...	...
%M [FB][79]	3.7	2.7	2.3	1.8	2.1	3.3	...	...
%F [FB][79]	4.8	3.7	3.1	2.4	2.6	3.5	...	...
Netherlands Antilles[1] — Antilles néerlandaises[1]								
MF [BA][87]	10.5[62]	...	8.5[88]	...	9.1[88]	9.3[88]	...	...
M [BA][87]	4.7[62]	...	3.7[88]	...	4.1[88]	4.0[88]	...	...
F [BA][87]	5.8[62]	...	4.8[88]	...	4.9[88]	5.3[88]	...	...
%MF [BA]	16.6[62]	...	14.2[88]	15.8[88]	15.6[88]	15.1[88]	...	...
%M [BA]	13.7[62]	...	12.0[88]	...	...	...	...	...
%F [BA]	19.2[62]	...	16.2[88]	...	...	...	...	...
New Caledonia[55] — Nouvelle-Calédonie[55]								
MF [FB]	8.3	8.8	9.4	9.9	10.5	10.2	...	...
M [FB]	...	3.9	4.2	4.4	4.8	4.6	...	...
F [FB]	...	4.9	5.2	5.4	5.7	5.6	...	...
New Zealand — Nouvelle-Zélande								
MF [BA][1]	139.1	127.8	113.4	102.3	102.5	93.9	82.0	79.3
M [BA][1]	77.4	72.4	63.4	56.2	54.6	48.0	39.5	39.5
F [BA][1]	61.8	55.4	50.0	46.1	47.9	45.9	42.4	39.8
%MF [BA][1]	7.5	6.8	6.0	5.3	5.2	4.7	3.9	3.7
%M [BA][1]	7.6	7.0	6.1	5.4	5.1	4.4	3.5	3.4
%F [BA][1]	7.4	6.5	5.8	5.3	5.3	5.0	4.4	4.0
MF [FB][89,90]	193.9	221.4	226.9	192.2	168.3	...	...	...
M [FB][89,90]	...	127.2	120.3	103.5	89.1	...	...	...
F [FB][89,90]	...	94.1	106.6	88.7	79.2	...	...	...
Nicaragua[8] — Nicaragua[8]								
MF [E]	215.5	185.1	178.0	122.5	135.3	...	...	...
M [E]	142.9	122.8	118.0	77.3	84.0	...	...	...
F [E]	72.6	62.3	60.0	45.2	51.3	...	...	...

Country or area, source§ — Pays ou zone, source§	1998	1999	2000	2001	2002	2003	2004	2005
%MF [E]	13.3	10.9	9.8	11.3	12.2	...	...	...
%M [E]	8.8	...	...	...	...	...	...	...
%F [E]	14.5	...	...	...	...	...	...	...
Norway — Norvège								
MF [BA][66]	74.0	75.0	81.0	84.0	92.0	107.0	106.0	111.0
M [BA][66]	40.0	42.0	46.0	46.0	52.0	62.0	62.0	61.0
F [BA][66]	34.0	33.0	35.0	38.0	40.0	45.0	45.0	49.0
%MF [BA][66]	3.2	3.2	3.4	3.6	3.9	4.5	4.5	4.6
%M [BA][66]	3.2	3.4	3.6	3.7	4.1	4.9	4.9	4.8
%F [BA][66]	3.3	3.0	3.2	3.4	3.6	4.0	4.0	4.4
MF [FB][55]	56.0	59.6[62]	62.6	62.7	75.2	92.6	91.6	83.5
M [FB][55]	29.8	33.5[62]	36.3	35.7	42.6	54.0	52.2	45.7
F [FB][55]	26.2	26.0[62]	26.4	27.0	32.6	38.6	39.4	37.8
%MF [FB][55]	2.4	2.6[62]	2.7	2.7	3.2	3.9	3.9	3.5
%M [FB][55]	...	...	...	...	...	4.3	4.1	3.6
%F [FB][55]	...	...	...	...	...	3.5	3.5	3.4
Occupied Palestinian Terr.[91] — Terr. palestinien occupé[91]								
MF [BA]	92.0[1]	79.0[1]	98.8[1]	170.5[8]	217.5[8]	194.3[8]	212.2[8]	...
M [BA]	79.2[1]	66.1[1]	85.4[1]	158.0[8]	201.5[8]	172.2[8]	185.8[8]	...
F [BA]	12.8[1]	12.9[1]	13.4[1]	12.5[8]	16.0[8]	22.1[8]	26.4[8]	...
%MF [BA]	14.4[1]	11.8[1]	14.1[1]	25.2[8]	31.2[8]	25.4[8]	26.7[8]	...
%M [BA]	14.4[1]	11.6[1]	14.4[1]	26.9[8]	33.5[8]	26.7[8]	28.0[8]	...
%F [BA]	15.2[1]	13.0[1]	12.3[1]	14.0[8]	17.0[8]	18.4[8]	20.0[8]	...
Pakistan — Pakistan								
MF [BA][6,8]	2 279.0	2 334.0	3 127.0	3 181.0	3 506.0	3 594.0	3 499.0	3 566.0
M [BA][6,8]	1 386.0	1 419.0	2 046.0	2 082.0	2 381.0	2 441.0	2 461.0	2 508.0
F [BA][6,8]	893.0	915.0	1 081.0	1 099.0	1 125.0	1 153.0	1 038.0	1 058.0
%MF [BA][6,8]	5.9	5.9	7.8	7.8	8.3	8.3	7.7	7.7
%M [BA][6,8]	4.2	4.2	6.1	6.1	6.7	6.7	6.6	6.6
%F [BA][6,8]	15.0	15.0	17.3	17.3	16.5	16.5	12.8	12.8
MF [FB][18,92]	212.0	217.0	469.0	477.0	493.0	505.0	576.0	587.0
M [FB][18,92]	186.0	190.0	421.0	428.0	442.0	453.0	477.0	486.0
F [FB][18,92]	26.0	27.0	48.0	49.0	51.0	52.0	99.0	101.0
Panama[1,93] — Panama[1,93]								
MF [BA]	147.1	128.0	147.0	169.7	172.4	170.4	159.9	136.8
M [BA]	69.5	62.1	77.7	92.0	86.5	82.9	76.3	66.7
F [BA]	77.6	65.9	69.3	77.8	85.9	87.3	83.6	70.2
%MF [BA]	13.6	11.8	13.5	14.7	14.1	13.6	12.4	10.3
%M [BA]	10.0	8.9	11.1	12.2	11.2	10.5	9.4	8.1
%F [BA]	19.9	16.9	18.0	19.3	19.2	18.8	17.3	14.0
Papua New Guinea[6,8] — Papouasie-Nvl-Guinée[6,8]								
MF [A]	...	...	68.6	...	...	...	...	...
M [A]	...	...	53.7	...	...	...	...	...
F [A]	...	...	15.0	...	...	...	...	...
%MF [A]	...	...	2.8	...	...	...	...	...
%M [A]	...	...	4.3	...	...	...	...	...
%F [A]	...	...	1.3	...	...	...	...	...
Paraguay[8] — Paraguay[8]								
MF [BA]	...	...	198.7[94]	...	272.6	206.0	...	...
M [BA]	...	...	108.5[94]	...	141.9	105.6	...	...
F [BA]	...	...	89.9[94]	...	130.9	100.4	...	...
%MF [BA]	...	6.8	7.6[94]	...	10.8	8.1	...	...
%M [BA]	...	...	6.8[94]	...	9.0	6.7	...	...
%F [BA]	...	...	8.9[94]	...	13.6	10.1	...	...
Peru[22] — Pérou[22]								
MF [BA]	582.5[95]	624.9[95]	566.5[95]	651.5[95]	359.0[96]	386.0[6,96]	394.4[25,96]	437.1[5,96]
M [BA]	274.4[95]	322.8[95]	318.8[95]	327.5[95]	173.4[96]	187.9[6,96]	207.0[25,96]	209.9[5,96]

Country or area, source§ — Pays ou zone, source§	1998	1999	2000	2001	2002	2003	2004	2005
F [BA]	308.1[95]	302.2[95]	247.7[95]	324.0[95]	185.7[96]	198.1[6,96]	187.4[25,96]	227.2[5,96]
%MF [BA]	7.8[95]	8.0[95]	7.4[95]	7.9[95]	9.7[96]	10.3[6,96]	10.5[25,96]	11.4[5,96]
%M [BA]	6.5[95]	7.5[95]	7.3[95]	7.2[95]	8.3[96]	9.0[6,96]	9.4[25,96]	9.6[5,96]
%F [BA]	9.3[95]	8.6[95]	7.5[95]	8.7[95]	11.6[96]	11.9[6,96]	12.0[25,96]	13.7[5,96]
Philippines[1,87] — Philippines[1,87]								
MF [BA]	3 016.0	2 931.0	3 133.0	3 269.0	3 423.0	3 567.0	3 888.0	2 619.0[62]
M [BA]	1 857.0	1 835.0	1 978.0	1 912.0	2 076.0	2 183.0	2 312.0	1 617.0[62]
F [BA]	1 159.0	1 096.0	1 156.0	1 356.0	1 346.0	1 384.0	1 576.0	1 002.0[62]
%MF [BA]	9.6	9.6	10.1	9.8	10.2	10.2	10.9	7.4[62]
%M [BA]	9.5	9.7	10.3	9.4	10.1	10.1	10.4	7.4[62]
%F [BA]	9.8	9.3	9.9	10.3	10.2	10.3	11.7	7.3[62]
Poland — Pologne								
MF [BA]	1 808.0[1]	2 391.0[1,98]	2 785.0[1]	3 170.0[54]	3 431.0[54]	3 329.0[54]	3 230.0[54]	3 045.0[54]
M [BA]	843.0[1]	1 147.0[1,98]	1 344.0[1]	1 583.0[54]	1 779.0[54]	1 741.0[54]	1 681.0[54]	1 553.0[54]
F [BA]	965.0[1]	1 244.0[1,98]	1 440.0[1]	1 587.0[54]	1 652.0[54]	1 588.0[54]	1 550.0[54]	1 493.0[54]
%MF [BA]	10.5[1]	13.9[1,98]	16.1[1]	18.2[54]	19.9[54]	19.6[54]	19.0[54]	17.7[54]
%M [BA]	9.1[1]	12.4[1,98]	14.4[1]	16.9[54]	19.1[54]	19.0[54]	18.2[54]	16.6[54]
%F [BA]	12.3[1]	15.8[1,98]	18.1[1]	19.8[54]	20.9[54]	20.4[54]	19.9[54]	19.1[54]
MF [FB][75,97]	1 831.4	2 349.8	2 702.6	3 115.1	3 217.0[62]	3 175.7	2 999.6	2 773.0
M [FB][75,97]	760.1	1 042.5	1 211.0	1 473.0	1 571.2[62]	1 541.0	1 431.1	1 286.6
F [FB][75,97]	1 071.3	1 307.3	1 491.6	1 642.1	1 645.8[62]	1 634.7	1 568.5	1 486.4
%MF [FB][75,97]	10.4	13.1	15.1	17.5	20.0[62]	20.0	19.1	17.6
Portugal — Portugal								
MF [BA][1]	251.9	225.8	205.5	213.5	270.5	342.3	365.0	422.3
M [BA][1]	110.6	108.9	89.3	91.6	121.4	160.9	172.9	198.1
F [BA][1]	141.3	116.9	116.2	122.0	149.1	181.4	192.2	224.1
%MF [BA][1]	4.9	4.4	3.9	4.0	5.0	6.3	6.7	7.6
%M [BA][1]	3.9	3.9	3.1	3.2	4.1	5.5	5.8	6.7
%F [BA][1]	6.2	5.0	4.9	5.0	6.0	7.2	7.6	8.7
MF [FB]	400.6	356.8	327.4	324.7	344.6	427.3	...	...
M [FB]	165.3	144.9	128.7	127.0	139.6	182.3	...	...
F [FB]	235.4	211.9	198.8	197.7	205.3	245.0	...	...
Puerto Rico[55,59] — Porto Rico[55,59]								
MF [BA]	175.0	152.0	131.0	145.0	163.0	164.0	145.0	160.0
M [BA]	112.0	101.0	90.0	97.0	101.0	99.0	92.0	97.0
F [BA]	63.0	51.0	42.0	48.0	62.0	65.0	53.0	63.0
%MF [BA]	13.3	11.8	10.1	11.4	12.3	12.0	10.6	11.3
%M [BA]	14.4	13.2	11.8	13.0	13.2	12.8	11.8	12.2
%F [BA]	11.8	9.6	7.7	9.1	10.9	10.9	9.0	10.2
Qatar[1,45] — Qatar[1,45]								
MF [BA]	...	...	...	12.6	...	...	...	...
M [BA]	...	...	...	6.1	...	...	...	...
F [BA]	...	...	...	6.5	...	...	...	...
%MF [BA]	...	...	...	3.9	...	...	...	...
%M [BA]	...	...	...	2.3	...	...	...	...
%F [BA]	...	...	...	12.6	...	...	...	...
Republic of Moldova — République de Moldova								
MF [BA][1]	...	187.2	140.1	117.7	110.0	117.1	116.5	103.7
M [BA][1]	...	113.6	80.6	70.1	64.4	69.9	70.1	59.8
F [BA][1]	...	73.6	59.5	47.6	45.4	47.2	46.4	43.9
%MF [BA][1]	...	11.1	8.5	7.3	6.8	7.9	8.1	7.3
%M [BA][1]	...	13.3	9.7	8.7	8.1	9.6	10.0	8.7
%F [BA][1]	...	8.9	7.2	5.9	5.5	6.4	6.3	6.0
MF [FB][12]	32.0	34.9	28.9	27.6	24.0	19.7	21.0	21.7
M [FB][12]	13.0	13.3	11.9	13.6	11.7	10.3	11.7	11.3
F [FB][12]	19.0	21.6	17.0	14.0	12.3	9.4	9.3	10.4
%MF [FB][12]	1.9	2.1	2.3	2.2	2.1	2.0	2.0	2.0

Country or area, source§ — Pays ou zone, source§	1998	1999	2000	2001	2002	2003	2004	2005
Réunion[1] — Réunion[1]								
MF [A][45]	...	124.2	...	...	...	...	...	...
M [A][45]	...	63.5	...	...	...	...	...	...
F [A][45]	...	60.7	...	...	...	...	...	...
MF [BA][56]	101.2	101.6	103.8	98.4	92.8	99.5	102.5	98.4
M [BA][56]	53.8	54.7	54.4	51.3	47.5	53.4	55.3	50.4
F [BA][56]	47.3	46.9	49.4	47.1	45.2	46.1	47.2	48.0
%MF [BA][56]	37.7	37.7	36.5	33.3	31.0	32.9	33.5	31.9
%M [BA][56]	35.3	36.3	34.4	30.9	28.5	31.4	31.8	28.8
%F [BA][56]	40.9	39.5	39.1	36.4	34.2	34.8	35.8	35.8
Romania — Roumanie								
MF [BA][1]	732.4	789.9	821.2	750.0	845.3[99]	691.8	799.5	704.5
M [BA][1]	410.3	462.5	481.6	436.1	494.1[99]	408.0	490.8	420.3
F [BA][1]	322.1	327.4	339.6	313.9	351.2[99]	283.7	308.7	284.1
%MF [BA][1]	6.3	6.8	7.1	6.6	8.4[99]	7.0	8.0	7.2
%M [BA][1]	6.5	7.4	7.7	7.1	8.9[99]	7.5	9.0	7.7
%F [BA][1]	6.1	6.2	6.4	5.9	7.7[99]	6.4	6.9	6.4
MF [FB][12]	1 025.1	1 130.3	1 007.1	826.9	760.6	658.9	557.9	...
M [FB][12]	539.9	600.2	535.5	445.8	421.1	372.6	323.3	...
F [FB][12]	485.2	530.1	471.6	381.1	339.5	286.3	234.6	...
%MF [FB][12]	10.4	11.8	10.5	8.8	8.4	7.4	6.2	...
%M [FB][12]	10.4	12.1	10.8	9.2	8.9	7.8	6.8	...
%F [FB][12]	10.4	11.6	10.1	8.4	7.8	6.6	5.6	...
Russian Federation — Fédération de Russie								
MF [BA][87,100]	8 876.0	9 323.0	7 138.0	6 303.0	6 153.0	5 716.0	5 775.0	...
M [BA][87,100]	4 787.0	4 966.0	3 781.0	3 411.0	3 322.0	3 064.0	2 902.0	...
F [BA][87,100]	4 090.0	4 293.0	3 357.0	2 892.0	2 831.0	2 652.0	2 872.0	...
%MF [BA][87,100]	13.3	12.6	9.8	8.9	7.9	8.0	7.8	...
%M [BA][87,100]	13.6	12.8	10.2	9.3	7.9	8.3	7.6	...
%F [BA][87,100]	13.0	12.3	9.4	8.5	7.9	7.8	8.0	...
MF [FB][12]	1 929.0	1 263.4	1 037.0	1 122.7	1 309.4	1 600.0	...	...
M [FB][12]	682.0	383.0	322.2	359.5	412.8	...	...	...
F [FB][12]	1 247.0	880.0	714.8	763.2	896.6	...	...	...
%MF [FB][12]	13.3	...	...	...	...	...	...	...
Saint Helena — Sainte-Hélène								
MF [A][45,85]	0.4	...	...	...	...	...	...	...
M [A][45,85]	0.3	...	...	...	...	...	...	...
F [A][45,85]	0.2	...	...	...	...	...	...	...
MF [FB]	0.5	0.4	0.3	...	...	...	...	...
M [FB]	0.3	0.3	0.2	...	...	...	...	...
F [FB]	0.1	0.1	0.1	...	...	...	...	...
Saint Lucia[1] — Sainte-Lucie[1]								
MF [BA]	15.5	13.2	12.5	...	...	...	...	...
M [BA]	7.1	6.1	5.1	...	...	...	...	...
F [BA]	8.5	7.2	7.5	...	...	...	...	...
%MF [BA]	21.6	18.1	16.4	...	...	...	...	...
%M [BA]	18.0	16.0	12.6	...	...	...	...	...
%F [BA]	26.0	20.3	20.7	...	...	...	...	...
San Marino[1,47] — Saint-Marin[1,47]								
MF [E]	0.6	0.4	0.4	0.5	0.7	0.6	0.6	...
M [E]	0.1	0.1	0.1	0.2	0.2	0.2	0.1	...
F [E]	0.4	0.3	0.3	0.4	0.5	0.5	0.4	...
%MF [E]	4.1	3.0	2.8	2.6	3.6	3.1	2.8	...
%M [E]	1.8	1.6	1.7	1.4	1.6	1.5	1.1	...
%F [E]	6.9	4.6	4.1	4.3	6.3	5.5	5.2	...
Saudi Arabia[1] — Arabie saoudite[1]								
MF [BA]	...	254.1	273.6	281.2	326.6	...	...	...
M [BA]	...	183.8	194.3	202.6	225.0	...	...	...

Country or area, source§ — Pays ou zone, source§	1998	1999	2000	2001	2002	2003	2004	2005
F [BA]	...	70.3	79.3	78.6	103.7	...	...	...
%MF [BA]	...	4.3	4.6	4.6	5.2	...	...	...
%M [BA]	...	3.7	3.8	3.9	4.2	...	...	...
%F [BA]	...	8.1	9.3	9.1	11.5	...	...	...
Serbia and Montenegro — Serbie-et-Monténégro								
MF [BA][1,87]	617.0	528.0[102]	480.5[102]	490.2[102]	517.3[102]	562.4[102]	...	...
M [BA][1,87]	303.4	248.9[102]	223.6[102]	242.5[102]	261.5[102]	306.4[102]	...	...
F [BA][1,87]	313.6	279.0[102]	257.0[102]	247.7[102]	255.8[102]	256.0[102]	...	...
%MF [BA][1,87]	13.7	13.7[102]	12.6[102]	12.8[102]	13.8[102]	15.2[102]	...	...
%M [BA][1,87]	11.8	11.7[102]	10.6[102]	11.1[102]	12.4[102]	14.4[102]	...	...
%F [BA][1,87]	16.1	16.2[102]	15.2[102]	15.0[102]	15.8[102]	16.4[102]	...	...
MF [FB][18]	837.6[101]	811.1[102]	805.8[102]	850.0[102]	923.2[102]	1 019.0[102]	...	...
M [FB][18]	364.5[101]	349.3[102]	346.0[102]	369.6[102]	408.7[102]	461.2[102]	...	...
F [FB][18]	473.1[101]	461.8[102]	459.8[102]	480.4[102]	514.5[102]	557.8[102]	...	...
%MF [FB][18]	18.6[101]	21.1[102]	21.2[102]	22.3[102]	24.7[102]	27.6[102]	...	...
%M [FB][18]	14.2[101]	16.4[102]	20.5[102]	22.6[102]	...	...	...	...
%F [FB][18]	24.3[101]	26.8[102]	21.8[102]	22.1[102]	...	...	...	...
Seychelles[1,25] — Seychelles[1,25]								
MF [A]	...	...	...	...	4.3	...	...	...
Singapore — Singapour								
MF [A][1,103]	...	...	97.5	...	...	...	...	100.5[105]
M [A][1,103]	...	...	53.5	...	...	...	...	51.3[105]
F [A][1,103]	...	...	44.0	...	...	...	...	49.2[105]
MF [BA][1,103]	62.1	90.1	...	72.9	111.2	116.4	116.4	...
M [BA][1,103]	35.5	51.4	...	41.7	65.0	65.6	64.6	...
F [BA][1,103]	26.6	38.7	...	31.2	46.2	50.8	51.9	...
%MF [BA][1,103]	3.2	4.6	...	3.4	5.2	5.4	5.3	...
%M [BA][1,103]	3.2	4.5	...	3.5	5.4	5.5	5.4	...
%F [BA][1,103]	3.3	4.6	...	3.4	5.0	5.3	5.3	...
MF [FB][22]	4.4	5.9	4.2	6.4	11.6	13.9	49.6[104]	43.8
M [FB][22]	2.3	3.2	2.3	3.2	5.6	6.8	25.3[104]	22.0
F [FB][22]	2.1	2.7	1.8	3.2	6.0	7.1	24.3[104]	21.8
Slovakia — Slovaquie								
MF [BA][1,106]	317.1	416.8	485.2	508.0	486.9	459.2	481.0	427.5
M [BA][1,106]	167.5	226.6	265.5	282.5	263.9	246.5	250.0	223.6
F [BA][1,106]	149.6	190.2	219.7	225.5	223.0	212.7	231.0	203.8
%MF [BA][1,106]	12.5	16.2	18.6	19.2	18.5	17.4	18.1	16.2
%M [BA][1,106]	11.9	16.0	18.6	19.5	18.4	17.2	17.3	15.3
%F [BA][1,106]	13.2	16.4	18.6	18.8	18.7	17.7	19.1	17.2
MF [FB]	379.5	485.2	517.9	520.6	513.2	443.4	409.0	340.4
M [FB]	193.0	265.8	283.7	284.7	280.8	240.0	211.0	167.9
F [FB]	186.5	219.4	234.2	235.9	232.4	203.4	198.0	172.5
%MF [FB]	13.7	17.3	18.2	18.3	17.8	15.2	14.3	11.6
%M [FB]	13.3	17.9	18.8	18.9	19.0	15.3	13.7	10.8
%F [FB]	14.1	16.6	17.6	17.5	16.5	15.0	14.9	12.7
Slovenia[1] — Slovénie[1]								
MF [BA][56]	75.0	71.0	69.0	57.0	58.0	63.0	61.0	58.0
M [BA][56]	40.0	37.0	36.0	29.0	30.0	32.0	31.0	30.0
F [BA][56]	35.0	34.0	33.0	28.0	28.0	31.0	30.0	28.0
%MF [BA][56]	7.7	7.4	7.2	5.9	5.9	6.6	6.1	5.8
%M [BA][56]	7.6	7.2	7.0	5.6	5.7	6.1	5.7	5.5
%F [BA][56]	7.7	7.6	7.4	6.3	6.3	7.1	6.4	6.1
MF [FB]	126.1	119.0	106.6	101.9	102.6	97.7	92.8	...
M [FB]	63.2	58.8	52.5	50.2	50.1	46.1	43.6	...
F [FB]	62.9	60.2	54.1	51.7	52.1	51.6	49.3	...
%MF [FB]	14.5	13.6	12.2	11.6	11.6	11.2	10.6	...
%M [FB]	13.4	12.4	11.1	10.4	10.4	9.7	9.1	...
%F [FB]	15.7	15.0	13.5	12.9	13.1	13.0	12.4	...

Country or area, source§ — Pays ou zone, source§	1998	1999	2000	2001	2002	2003	2004	2005
South Africa[63] — Afrique du Sud[63]								
MF [BA]	...	3 158.0[107]	4 208.0[108]	4 383.0[108]	4 788.0[108]	4 910.0[109]	4 271.5[109]	4 385.0[109]
M [BA]	...	1 480.0[107]	2 015.0[108]	2 114.0[108]	2 252.0[108]	2 328.0[109]	2 055.0[109]	2 027.0[109]
F [BA]	...	1 677.0[107]	2 194.0[108]	2 268.0[108]	2 535.0[108]	2 581.0[109]	2 216.5[109]	2 357.0[109]
%MF [BA]	...	23.3[107]	26.3[108]	28.0[108]	30.0[108]	28.2[109]	27.1[109]	26.6[109]
%M [BA]	...	19.8[107]	24.1[108]	25.5[108]	26.7[108]	25.3[109]	23.5[109]	27.1[109]
%F [BA]	...	27.8[107]	28.7[108]	30.7[108]	33.6[108]	31.5[109]	31.6[109]	27.0[109]
Spain — Espagne								
MF [BA][55]	3 176.8	2 722.2	2 496.4	1 904.4[62]	2 155.3	2 242.2	2 213.6	1 912.5[62]
M [BA][55]	1 417.7	1 158.3	1 037.4	828.1[62]	929.3	976.4	970.8	862.9[62]
F [BA][55]	1 759.1	1 563.9	1 458.9	1 076.3[62]	1 226.0	1 265.8	1 242.8	1 049.6[62]
%MF [BA][55]	18.6	15.6	13.9	10.6[62]	11.5	11.5	11.0	9.2[62]
%M [BA][55]	13.6	10.9	9.6	7.5[62]	8.2	8.4	8.2	7.0[62]
%F [BA][55]	26.5	22.9	20.4	15.2[62]	16.4	16.0	15.0	12.2[62]
MF [FB][79]	2 359.4	2 085.2	1 963.5	1 930.2[62]	2 049.6	2 096.9	2 113.7	2 069.9[62]
M [FB][79]	1 031.5	871.3	789.7	771.5[62]	836.7	851.1	854.3	818.0[62]
F [FB][79]	1 327.9	1 213.9	1 173.8	1 158.7[62]	1 212.9	1 245.8	1 259.4	1 251.8[62]
Sri Lanka[1,110] — Sri Lanka[1,110]								
MF [BA]	611.3	612.7[43]	546.1	565.9	632.8	700.4[111]	679.1[43]	623.3[25]
M [BA]	277.5	330.7[43]	290.2	309.5	305.8	323.8[111]	318.5[43]	301.6[25]
F [BA]	333.8	282.0[43]	255.9	256.4	327.0	376.6[111]	360.6[43]	321.7[25]
%MF [BA]	10.6	9.1[43]	8.0	7.7	8.7	9.2[111]	8.5[43]	7.7[25]
%M [BA]	7.1	7.4[43]	6.4	5.8	6.5	6.4[111]	6.0[43]	5.5[25]
%F [BA]	16.2	12.6[43]	11.1	11.7	12.8	14.6[111]	13.5[43]	11.9[25]
Suriname[1] — Suriname[1]								
MF [BA]	10.5	11.8	...	...	...	...	...	...
M [BA]	4.6	5.4	...	...	...	...	...	...
F [BA]	5.8	6.5	...	...	...	...	...	...
%MF [BA]	10.6	14.0	...	...	...	...	...	...
%M [BA]	7.2	10.0	...	...	...	...	...	...
%F [BA]	17.0	20.0	...	...	...	...	...	...
Sweden — Suède								
MF [BA][79]	276.0	241.0	203.0	175.0	176.0	217.0	246.0	270.0[62]
M [BA][79]	154.0	133.0	114.0	99.0	101.0	123.0	137.0	148.0[62]
F [BA][79]	122.0	107.0	89.0	76.0	76.0	94.0	109.0	123.0[62]
%MF [BA][79]	6.5	5.6	4.7	4.0	4.0	4.9	5.5	6.0[62]
%M [BA][79]	6.9	5.9	5.0	4.3	4.4	5.3	5.9	6.2[62]
%F [BA][79]	6.0	5.2	4.3	3.6	3.6	4.4	5.1	5.7[62]
MF [FB][1]	285.6	276.7	231.2	193.0	185.8	223.0	239.2	241.4
M [FB][1]	156.3	151.7	126.9	107.2	105.4	127.4	135.1	132.0
F [FB][1]	129.3	125.0	104.3	85.8	80.4	95.6	104.1	109.4
%MF [FB][1]	6.7	6.4	5.3	4.4	4.2	4.9	5.5	5.3
%M [FB][1]	7.0	6.7	5.6	4.7	4.6	5.3	5.9	...
%F [FB][1]	6.4	6.1	5.0	4.1	3.8	4.4	5.1	...
Switzerland[1] — Suisse[1]								
MF [BA][56]	141.8	121.6	105.9	100.6	119.0	170.0	178.0	185.0
M [BA][56]	70.0	59.2	51.0	37.9	62.0	86.0	89.0	88.0
F [BA][56]	71.8	62.4	54.9	62.6	57.0	84.0	89.0	97.0
%MF [BA][56]	3.6	3.1	2.7	2.5	2.9	4.1	4.3	4.4
%M [BA][56]	3.2	2.7	2.3	1.7	2.8	3.8	3.9	3.9
%F [BA][56]	4.1	3.5	3.1	3.5	3.1	4.5	4.7	5.1
MF [FB]	139.7	98.6	72.0	67.2	100.5	145.7	153.1	148.5
M [FB]	77.1	52.6	37.8	35.4	55.9	81.7	83.6	78.8
F [FB]	62.6	46.0	34.2	31.8	44.6	64.0	69.5	69.7
%MF [FB]	3.9	2.7	1.8	1.7	2.5	3.7[112]	3.9[112]	3.8[112]
%M [FB]	3.5	2.4	1.7	1.6	2.5	3.7[112]	3.8[112]	3.6[112]
%F [FB]	4.4	3.3	2.0	1.8	2.6	3.7[112]	4.0[112]	4.0[112]

Country or area, source§ — Pays ou zone, source§	1998	1999	2000	2001	2002	2003	2004	2005
Syrian Arab Republic[1] — Rép. arabe syrienne[1]								
MF [BA]	...	...	...	613.4	637.8	...	...	...
M [BA]	...	...	...	348.4	355.8	...	...	...
F [BA]	...	...	...	265.0	282.0	...	...	...
%MF [BA]	...	...	...	11.2	11.7	...	...	...
%M [BA]	...	...	...	8.0	8.3	...	...	...
%F [BA]	...	...	...	23.9	24.1	...	...	...
Thailand[43] — Thaïlande[43]								
MF [BA]	1 137.9[113]	985.7[113]	812.6[113]	896.3[1]	616.3[1]	543.7[1]	548.9[1]	495.8[1]
M [BA]	625.2[113]	546.4[113]	454.5[113]	511.2[1]	372.1[1]	314.7[1]	324.2[1]	289.9[1]
F [BA]	512.7[113]	439.3[113]	358.0[113]	385.1[1]	244.2[1]	229.0[1]	224.7[1]	206.0[1]
%MF [BA]	3.4[113]	3.0[113]	2.4[113]	2.6[1]	1.8[1]	1.5[1]	1.5[1]	1.4[1]
%M [BA]	3.4[113]	3.0[113]	2.4[113]	2.7[1]	2.0[1]	1.6[1]	1.6[1]	1.5[1]
%F [BA]	3.4[113]	3.0[113]	2.3[113]	2.5[1]	1.6[1]	1.4[1]	1.4[1]	1.2[1]
TFYR of Macedonia — L'ex-R.y. Macédoine								
MF [BA][1]	...	...	...	263.2[16]	263.5[16]	315.9[16]	309.3	323.9
M [BA][1]	...	...	...	149.4[16]	159.1[16]	191.9[16]	186.2	191.1
F [BA][1]	...	...	...	113.8[16]	104.3[16]	124.0[16]	123.1	132.8
%MF [BA][1]	...	...	...	30.5[16]	31.9[16]	36.7[16]	37.2	37.3
%M [BA][1]	...	...	...	29.5[16]	31.7[16]	37.0[16]	36.7	36.5
%F [BA][1]	...	...	...	32.0[16]	32.3[16]	36.3[16]	37.8	38.4
MF [FB][18]	...	...	366.2	360.3	374.1	390.4	391.1	360.0
M [FB][18]	...	...	...	...	...	222.4	224.6	208.4
F [FB][18]	...	...	...	...	...	167.9	166.5	151.6
%MF [FB][18]	46.6	51.5	53.7	...	...	...	...	...
Trinidad and Tobago[1,114] — Trinité-et-Tobago[1,114]								
MF [BA]	79.4	74.0	69.6	62.4	61.1	...	...	...
M [BA]	39.0	37.9	36.1	30.7	27.9	...	...	...
F [BA]	40.4	36.1	33.5	31.7	33.2	...	...	...
%MF [BA]	14.2	13.1	12.2	10.8	10.4	...	...	...
%M [BA]	11.3	10.9	10.2	8.6	7.8	...	...	...
%F [BA]	18.9	16.8	15.2	14.4	14.5	...	...	...
Tunisia — Tunisie								
MF [BA][1]	...	472.5[115]	475.1[115]	469.2[115]	485.5[115]	473.4[115]	473.9	486.4
M [BA][1]	...	345.1[115]	347.4[115]	341.4[115]	351.6[115]	334.7[115]	322.7	328.8
F [BA][1]	...	127.5[115]	127.7[115]	127.8[115]	133.9[115]	138.6[115]	151.2	157.6
%MF [BA][1]	...	16.0[115]	15.7[115]	15.1[115]	15.3[115]	14.5[115]	14.2	14.2
%M [BA][1]	...	15.6[115]	15.3[115]	14.5[115]	14.9[115]	13.9[115]	13.2	13.1
%F [BA][1]	...	17.2[115]	16.9[115]	16.2[115]	16.3[115]	16.2[115]	17.1	17.3
MF [FB][18,84,115]	...	...	77.0	71.9	73.5	77.9	...	...
M [FB][18,84,115]	...	...	42.7	40.5	40.5	41.6	...	...
F [FB][18,84,115]	...	...	34.3	31.5	33.1	36.2	...	...
Turkey — Turquie								
MF [BA]	1 528.0[24]	1 774.0[24]	1 497.0[1,76]	1 967.0[1]	2 464.0[1]	2 493.0[1]	2 498.0[1]	2 519.0[1]
M [BA]	1 107.0[24]	1 275.0[24]	1 111.0[1,76]	1 485.0[1]	1 826.0[1]	1 830.0[1]	1 878.0[1]	1 867.0[1]
F [BA]	421.0[24]	499.0[24]	387.0[1,76]	482.0[1]	638.0[1]	663.0[1]	620.0[1]	652.0[1]
%MF [BA]	6.8[24]	7.7[24]	6.5[1,76]	8.4[1]	10.3[1]	10.5[1]	10.3[1]	10.3[1]
%M [BA]	6.8[24]	7.7[24]	6.6[1,76]	8.7[1]	10.7[1]	10.7[1]	10.5[1]	10.3[1]
%F [BA]	6.9[24]	7.5[24]	6.3[1,76]	7.5[1]	9.4[1]	10.1[1]	9.7[1]	10.3[1]
MF [FB][12,22]	465.2	487.5	730.5	718.7	464.3	587.4	811.9	...
M [FB][12,22]	386.0	413.8	591.9	582.9	379.8	469.4	611.3	...
F [FB][12,22]	79.2	73.7	138.6	135.8	84.5	118.0	200.6	...
Uganda[8,116] — Ouganda[8,116]								
MF [BA]	...	...	...	...	...	346.0	...	...
M [BA]	...	...	...	...	...	128.0	...	...
F [BA]	...	...	...	...	...	218.0	...	...

Country or area, source§ — Pays ou zone, source§	1998	1999	2000	2001	2002	2003	2004	2005
%MF [BA]	...	...	...	...	...	3.2	...	...
%M [BA]	...	...	...	...	...	2.5	...	...
%F [BA]	...	...	...	...	...	3.9	...	...
Ukraine — Ukraine								
MF [BA][117]	2 937.1[23]	2 614.3[65]	2 655.8	2 455.0	2 140.7	2 008.0	1 906.7	1 600.8
M [BA][117]	1 515.1[23]	1 346.5[65]	1 357.4	1 263.0	1 106.5	1 055.7	1 001.6	862.5
F [BA][117]	1 422.0[23]	1 267.8[65]	1 298.4	1 192.0	1 034.2	952.3	905.1	738.3
%MF [BA][117]	11.3[23]	11.6[65]	11.6	10.9	9.6	9.1	8.6	7.2
%M [BA][117]	11.9[23]	11.8[65]	11.6	11.0	9.8	9.4	8.9	7.5
%F [BA][117]	10.8[23]	11.3[65]	11.6	10.8	9.5	8.7	8.3	6.8
MF [FB][20,75]	1 003.2	1 174.5	1 155.2	1 008.1	1 034.2	988.9	981.8	881.5
M [FB][20,75]	382.8	444.9	424.8	362.5	369.2	361.3	361.9	345.9
F [FB][20,75]	620.4	729.6	730.4	645.6	665.0	627.6	619.9	535.6
%MF [FB][20,75]	4.3	5.5	5.5	4.8	5.0	4.8	4.8	4.3
%M [FB][20,75]	3.2	4.0	3.8	3.3	3.4	3.4	3.4	3.2
%F [FB][20,75]	5.5	7.3	7.2	6.4	6.7	6.3	6.3	5.6
United Arab Emirates — Emirats arabes unis								
MF [E]	...	...	41.0	...	...	...	...	...
M [E]	...	...	34.7	...	...	...	...	...
F [E]	...	...	6.3	...	...	...	...	...
%MF [E]	...	...	2.3	...	...	...	...	...
%M [E]	...	...	2.2	...	...	...	...	...
%F [E]	...	...	2.6	...	...	...	...	...
United Kingdom — Royaume-Uni								
MF [BA][55,69]	1 776.4	1 751.7	1 619.1	1 412.9	1 519.4	1 414.0	1 361.0	1 351.6
M [BA][55,69]	1 097.8	1 095.2	991.5	864.1	933.5	866.2	788.1	793.3
F [BA][55,69]	678.6	656.5	627.6	548.8	585.9	547.8	572.9	558.3
%MF [BA][55,69]	6.1	6.0	5.5	4.8	5.1	4.8	4.6	5.0
%M [BA][55,69]	6.8	6.7	6.1	5.3	5.6	5.5	5.0	5.0
%F [BA][55,69]	5.3	5.1	4.8	4.2	4.4	4.1	4.2	4.0
MF [FA][59,118,119]	1 362.4	1 263.1	1 102.3	983.0	958.8	945.9	...	...
M [FA][59,118,119]	1 037.7	963.5	839.6	746.8	723.8	707.6	...	...
F [FA][59,119,120,121]	324.7	299.5	262.6	236.2	235.0	238.5	...	...
%MF [FA][59,118,119]	4.7	4.3	3.8	3.3	3.2	3.1	...	...
%M [FA][59,118,119]	6.5	6.0	5.2	4.6	4.4	4.3	...	...
%F [FA][59,119,120,121]	2.5	2.3	2.0	1.7	1.7	1.7	...	...
United Rep. of Tanzania[8,122] — Rép.-Unie de Tanzanie[8,122]								
MF [BA]	...	...	...	912.8	...	...	...	...
M [BA]	...	...	...	388.4	...	...	...	...
F [BA]	...	...	...	524.4	...	...	...	...
%MF [BA]	...	...	...	5.1	...	...	...	...
%M [BA]	...	...	...	4.4	...	...	...	...
%F [BA]	...	...	...	5.8	...	...	...	...
United States[55,123] — Etats-Unis[55,123]								
MF [BA]	6 210.0	5 880.0	5 655.0	6 742.0	8 378.0	8 774.0	8 149.0	7 591.0
M [BA]	3 266.0	3 066.0	2 954.0	3 663.0	4 597.0	4 906.0	4 456.0	4 059.0
F [BA]	2 944.0	2 814.0	2 701.0	3 079.0	3 781.0	3 868.0	3 694.0	3 531.0
%MF [BA]	4.5	4.2	4.0	4.8	5.8	6.0	5.5	5.1
%M [BA]	4.4	4.1	3.9	4.8	5.9	6.3	5.6	5.1
%F [BA]	4.6	4.3	4.1	4.7	5.6	5.7	5.4	5.1
Uruguay[22,51] — Uruguay[22,51]								
MF [BA]	123.8	137.7	167.7	193.2	211.3	208.5	...	154.9
M [BA]	53.7	59.4	74.7	80.4	93.3	92.2	...	65.4
F [BA]	70.1	78.3	93.0	112.8	118.0	116.2	...	89.5
%MF [BA]	10.1	11.3	13.6	15.3	17.0	16.9	...	12.2
%M [BA]	7.8	8.7	10.9	11.5	13.5	13.5	...	9.5
%F [BA]	13.0	14.6	17.0	19.7	21.2	20.8	...	15.3

Country or area, source§ — Pays ou zone, source§	1998	1999	2000	2001	2002	2003	2004	2005
Venezuela (Bolivarian Republic of)[1] — Venezuela (République bolivarienne du)[1]								
MF [BA]	1 092.6	1 525.5	1 423.5	1 435.8	1 822.6	...	...	...
M [BA]	616.4	877.8	867.7	827.1	998.6	...	...	...
F [BA]	476.2	647.8	555.8	608.7	824.0	...	...	...
%MF [BA]	11.2	14.9	13.9	13.2	15.8	...	...	...
%M [BA]	9.9	13.6	13.4	12.4	14.3	...	...	...
%F [BA]	13.4	17.1	14.8	14.6	18.1	...	...	...
Viet Nam[1,44] — Viet Nam[1,44]								
MF [BA]	866.2	908.9	885.7	1 107.4	871.0	949.0	926.4	...
M [BA]	456.1	438.6	468.0	457.9	398.0	402.4	409.8	...
F [BA]	410.1	470.3	417.7	649.6	473.0	546.6	516.6	...
%MF [BA]	2.3	2.3	2.3	2.8	2.1	2.3	2.1	...
%M [BA]	2.4	2.3	2.4	2.3	1.9	1.9	1.9	...
%F [BA]	2.2	2.4	2.1	3.3	2.3	2.6	2.4	...
Yemen[1] — Yémen[1]								
MF [BA]	...	469.0	...	...	...	...	...	...
M [BA]	...	389.6	...	...	...	...	...	...
F [BA]	...	79.4	...	...	...	...	...	...
%MF [BA]	...	11.5	...	...	...	...	...	...
%M [BA]	...	12.5	...	...	...	...	...	...
%F [BA]	...	8.2	...	...	...	...	...	...
Zambia[24] — Zambie[24]								
MF [B]	508.0	...	...	...	...	...	...	...
M [B]	281.0	...	...	...	...	...	...	...
F [B]	227.0	...	...	...	...	...	...	...
%MF [B]	12.0	...	...	...	...	...	...	...
%M [B]	13.0	...	...	...	...	...	...	...
%F [B]	12.0	...	...	...	...	...	...	...
Zimbabwe[24] — Zimbabwe[24]								
MF [BA]	...	297.8	...	...	...	...	...	...
M [BA]	...	187.1	...	...	...	...	...	...
F [BA]	...	110.7	...	...	...	...	...	...
%MF [BA]	...	6.0	...	...	...	...	...	...
%M [BA]	...	7.3	...	...	...	...	...	...
%F [BA]	...	4.6	...	...	...	...	...	...

Source

International Labour Office (ILO), Geneva, the ILO labour statistics database.

Notes

§ Data sources:
A: Population census.
B: Household surveys.
BA: Labour force sample surveys.
E: Official estimates.
FA: Insurance records.
FB: Employment office records.
FD: Administration reports.

1 Persons aged 15 years and over.
2 April.
3 September of each year.
4 May.
5 September.
6 July.
7 28 urban agglomerations.
8 Persons aged 10 years and over.
9 May and October.

Source

Bureau international du Travail (BIT), Genève, la base de données du BIT.

Notes

§ Sources de données :
A: Recensement de la population.
B: Enquêtes auprès des ménages.
BA: Enquêtes par sondage sur la main-d'œuvre.
E: Evaluations officielles.
FA: Fichiers des assurances.
FB: Fichiers des bureaux de placement.
FD: Rapports administratifs.

1 Personnes âgées de 15 ans et plus.
2 Avril.
3 Septembre de chaque année.
4 Mai.
5 Septembre.
6 Juillet.
7 28 agglomérations urbaines.
8 Personnes âgées de 10 ans et plus.
9 Mai et octobre.

10 Second semester.
11 Persons aged 16 to 63 years.
12 December of each year.
13 Beginning 1995, estimates based on 1996 census benchmarks.
14 Prior to 2003: May and November of each year.
15 Prior to 2004: including conscripts.
16 April of each year.
17 January.
18 Work applicants.
19 Year ending in June of the year indicated.
20 Men aged 16 to 59 years; women aged 16 to 54 years.
21 Beginning April 1985, excluding some elderly unemployed no longer applicants for work.
22 Persons aged 14 years and over.
23 November.
24 Persons aged 12 years and over.
25 August.
26 Population census; August.
27 Excluding rural population of Rondônia, Acre, Amazonas, Roraima, Pará and Amapá.
28 Men aged 16 to 60 years; women aged 16 to 55 years. After 1999, age limits vary according to the year.
29 June of each year.
30 Men aged 16 to 62.5 years; women aged 16 to 57 years. After 1999, age limits vary according to the year.
31 Four employment offices.
32 Bujumbura.
33 November of each year.
34 Persons aged 7 years and over.
35 Excluding residents of the Territories and indigenous persons living on reserves.
36 Fourth quarter of each year.
37 For statistical purposes, the data for China do not include those for the Hong Kong Special Administrative Region (Hong Kong SAR), Macao Special Administrative Region (Macao SAR) and Taiwan Province of China.
38 Unemployed in urban areas.
39 Excluding marine, military and institutional populations.
40 Excluding unpaid family workers who worked for one hour or more.
41 Beginning 1991: estimates based on the 1993 Census results.
42 Prior to 2001: 7 main cities; Sep. of each year. Persons aged 12 years and over.
43 Third quarter.
44 July of each year.
45 March.
46 Men aged 17 to 60 years; women aged 17 to 55years.
47 December.
48 The data relate to the government-controlled areas.
49 Persons aged 15 to 66 years.
50 Persons aged 16 to 66 years.
51 Urban areas.
52 May and November of each year.
53 Persons aged 15 to 64 years.
54 Persons aged 15 to 74 years.
55 Persons aged 16 years and over.
56 Second quarter of each year.
57 Urban areas, April.
58 Excluding elderly unemployment pensioners no longer seeking work.

10 Second semestre.
11 Personnes âgées de 16 à 63 ans.
12 Décembre de chaque année.
13 A partir de 1995, estimations basées sur les données de calage du recensement de 1996.
14 Avant 2003: mai et novembre de chaque année.
15 Avant 2004: y compris les conscrits.
16 Avril de chaque année.
17 Janvier.
18 Demandeurs d'emploi.
19 Année se terminant en juin de l'année indiquée.
20 Hommes âgés de 16 à 59 ans; femmes âgées de 16 à 54 ans.
21 A partir d'avril 1985 : non compris certains chômeurs âgés devenus non demandeurs d'emploi.
22 Personnes âgées de 14 ans et plus.
23 Novembre.
24 Personnes âgées de 12 ans et plus.
25 Août.
26 Recensement de population; août.
27 Non compris la population rurale de Rondônia, Acre, Amazonas, Roraima, Pará et Amapá.
28 Hommes âgés de 16 à 60 ans; femmes âgées de 16 à 55 ans. Après 1999, les limites d'âge varient selon l'année.
29 Juin de chaque année.
30 Hommes âges de 16 à 62,5 ans; femmes âgées de 16 à 57 ans. Après 1999, les limites d'âge varient selon l'année.
31 Quatre bureaux de placement.
32 Bujumbura.
33 Novembre de chaque année.
34 Personnes âgées de 7 ans et plus.
35 Non compris les habitants des Territoires et les populations indigènes vivant dans les réserves.
36 Quatrième trimestre de chaque année.
37 Pour la présentation des statistiques, les données pour la Chine ne comprennent pas la Région Administrative Spéciale de Hong Kong (Hong Kong RAS), la Région Administrative Spéciale de Macao (Macao RAS) et la province de Taiwan.
38 Chômeurs dans les régions urbaines.
39 A l'exclusion des populations marines, militaires et institutionnelles.
40 Non compris les travailleurs familiaux non rémunérés ayant travaillé une heure ou plus.
41 A partir de 1991: estimations basées sur les résultats du Recensement de 1993.
42 Avant 2001: 7 villes principales; sept. de chaque année. Personnes âgées de 10 ans et plus.
43 Troisième trimestre.
44 Juillet de chaque année.
45 Mars.
46 Hommes âgés de 17 à 60 ans; femmes âgées de 17 à 55 ans.
47 Décembre.
48 Les données se réfèrent aux régions sous contrôle gouvernemental.
49 Personnes âgées de 15 à 66 ans.
50 Personnes âgées de 16 à 66 ans.
51 Régions urbaines.
52 Mai et novembre de chaque année.
53 Personnes âgées de 15 à 64 ans.
54 Personnes âgées de 15 à 74 ans.
55 Personnes âgées de 16 ans et plus.
56 Deuxième trimestre de chaque année.
57 Régions urbaines, avril.
58 Non compris chômeurs âgés devenus non demandeurs d'emploi.

59 Excluding persons temporarily laid off.
60 Beginning October 1982, series revised on the basis of new administrative procedures adopted in 1986.
61 March of each year.
62 Methodology revised; data not strictly comparable.
63 Persons aged 15 to 65 years.
64 January of each year.
65 Estimates based on the 2001 Population Census results.
66 Persons aged 16 to 74 years.
67 April and November of each year.
68 May of each year.
69 March to May of each year.
70 Beginning 1991: rates calculated on basis of 1991 Census.
71 Beginning 1998: methodology revised.
72 Data based on revised weighting groups.
73 First and second quarters.
74 Prior to 2002: as from the Special Survey of the Labour Force Survey, february of each year.
75 31 December of each year.
76 Estimates based on the 2000 Population Census results.
77 Age limits vary according to the year.
78 Men aged 16 to 61 years; women aged 16-57 years.
79 Persons aged 16 to 64 years.
80 Persons aged 6 years and over.
81 Totals include persons still attending school (incl. full-time tertiary students).
82 Persons aged 16 to 61 years.
83 Excluding Rodrigues.
84 Persons aged 18 years and over.
85 Persons aged 15 to 69 years.
86 Beginning 1983, persons seeking work for 20 hours or more a week.
87 October of each year.
88 Curaçao.
89 Including students seeking vacation work.
90 Persons aged 15 to 60 years.
91 West Bank and Gaza.
92 Persons aged 18 to 60 years.
93 August of each year.
94 Year beginning in September of year indicated.
95 Prior to 2002: urban areas; third quarter.
96 Metropolitan Lima.
97 Men aged 18 to 64 years; women aged 18 to 59 years (with the exception of juvenile graduates).
98 First and fourth quarters.
99 Estimates based on the 2002 Population Census results.
100 Persons aged 15 to 72 years.
101 Including Kosovo and Metohia.
102 Excluding Kosovo and Metohia.
103 June.
104 Methodology revised.
105 General Household Survey.
106 Excluding persons on child-care leave.
107 October.
108 February and September.
109 March and Sep. of each year

59 Non compris les personnes temporairement mises à pied.
60 A partir d'octobre, série révisée sur la base de nouvelles procédures administratives adoptées en 1986.
61 Mars de chaque année.
62 Méthodologie révisée; les données ne sont pas strictement comparables.
63 Personnes âgées de 15 à 65 ans.
64 Janvier de chaque année.
65 Estimations basées sur les résultats du Recensement de la population de 2001.
66 Personnes âgées de 16 à 74 ans.
67 Avril et novembre de chaque année.
68 Mai de chaque année.
69 Mars-mai de chaque année.
70 A partir de 1991: taux calculés sur la base du Recensement de 1991.
71 A partir de 1998: méthodologie révisée.
72 Données basées sur des groupes de pondération révisés.
73 Premier et deuxième trimestres.
74 Avant 2002: Enquête spécial sur la main-d'oeuvre, février de chaque année.
75 31 décembre de chaque année.
76 Estimations basées sur les résultats du recensement de la population de 2000.
77 Les limites d'âge varient selon l'année.
78 Hommes âgés de 16 à 61 ans; femmes âgées de 16 à 57 ans.
79 Personnes âgées de 16 à 64 ans.
80 Personnes âgées de 6 ans et plus.
81 Les totaux incluent les personnes encore en cours d'études (y compris les étudiants à plein temps de l'enseignement supérieur).
82 Personnes âgées de 16 à 61 ans.
83 Non compris Rodrigues.
84 Personnes âgées de 18 ans et plus.
85 Personnes âgées de 15 à 69 ans.
86 A partir de 1983, personnes en quête de travail pour 20 heures ou plus par semaine.
87 Octobre de chaque année.
88 Curaçao.
89 Y compris les étudiants qui cherchent un emploi pendant les vacances.
90 Personnes âgées de 15 à 60 ans.
91 Cisjordanie et Gaza.
92 Personnes âgées de 18 à 60 ans.
93 Août de chaque année.
94 Année commençant en septembre del'année indiquée.
95 Avant 2002: régions urbaines; troisième trimestre.
96 Lima métropolitaine.
97 Hommes âgés de 18 à 64 ans; femmes âgées de 18 à 59 ans (à l'exception des jeunes diplômés).
98 Première et quatrième trimestres.
99 Estimations basées sur les résultats du Recensement de la population de 2002
100 Personnes âgées de 15 à 72 ans.
101 Y compris Kosovo et Metohia.
102 Non compris Kosovo et Metohia.
103 Juin.
104 Méthodologie révisée.
105 Enquête générale auprès des ménages.
106 Non compris les personnes en congé parental.
107 Octobre.
108 Février et septembre.
109 Mars et sept. de chaque année.

110 Excluding Northern province.
111 First quarter of each year.
112 Beginning 2003, rates calculated on basis of 2000 Census.
113 Persons aged 13 years and over.
114 Beginning 1987, excluding unemployed not previously employed.
115 1999-2003: figures revised on the basis of the 2004 census results.
116 Year ending in April of the year indicated.
117 Persons aged 15-70 years.
118 Beginning April 1983: excl. some categories of men aged 60 and over. Beginning February 1986: data not strictly comparable as a result of changes in compilation date. Beginning Sep. 1988: excl. most under 18-year-olds. Beginning Sept. 1989: excl. some men formerly employed in the coalmining industry.
119 Claimants at unemployment benefits offices.
120 Beginning February 1986: data not strictly comparable as a result of changes in compilation date.
121 Beginning September 1988: excluding most under 18-years-old.
122 Year ending in March of the year indicated.
123 Beginning 1990, estimates based on 1990 census benchmarks.

110 Non compris la province du Nord.
111 Le primer trimestre de chaque année.
112 A partir de 2003, taux calculés sur la base du Recensement de 2000.
113 Personnes âgées de 13 ans et plus.
114 A partir de 1987, non compris les chômeurs n'ayant jamais travaillé.
115 1999-2003: données révisées sur la base des résultats du Recensement de 2004.
116 Année se terminant en avril de l'année indiquée.
117 Personnes âgées de 15 à 70 ans.
118 A partir d'avril 1983: non compris certaines catégories d'hommes âgés de 60 ans et plus. A partir de février 1986: données non strictement comparables en raison d'un changement de date de traitement. A partir de sept. 1988: non compris la plupart des moins de 18 ans. Dès sept 1989: non compris certains hommes ayant précédemment travaillé dans l'industrie charbonnière.
119 Demandeurs auprès des bureaux de prestations de chômage.
120 A partir de février 1986: données non strictement comparables en raison d'un changement de date de traitement.
121 A compter de septembre 1988 non compris la plupart des moins de 18 ans.
122 Année se terminant en mars de l'année indiquée.
123 A partir de 1990, estimations basées sur les données de calage du recensement de 1990.

26 Employment by economic activity

Total employment and persons employed by ISIC Rev. 3 categories (thousands)

Emploi par activité économique

Emploi total et personnes employées par branches de CITI Rév. 3 (milliers)

Country or area Pays ou zone	Year Année	Sex Sexe	Total employment Emploi total	ISIC Rev. 3 Tabulation categories + / CITI Rév. 3 Catégories de classement + Categ. A Catég. A	 Categ. B Catég. B	 Categ. C Catég. C	 Categ. D Catég. D	 Categ. E Catég. E	 Categ. F Catég. F	 Categ. G Catég. G
Albania Albanie	2003	MF	926.0	...	...	6.0	46.0	15.0	57.0	68.0
	2004	MF	931.0	...	...	6.0	56.0	13.0	52.0	64.0
	2005	MF	931.0	...	...	6.0	56.0	12.0	52.0	64.0
Algeria[1,2] Algérie[1,2]	2001	M	5 345.2	1 132.4	69.4	111.0	406.8	99.1	643.8	761.6
	2001	F	883.6	109.1	1.2	8.5	225.0	10.8	6.2	27.3
	2003	M	5 751.0	1 303.1	5.8	78.7	406.3	93.4	790.4	853.7
	2003	F	933.0	101.5	1.3	4.2	210.3	11.1	9.5	27.2
Anguilla[1,3] Anguilla[1,3]	1999	M	3.3[6]	0.1	...	...	0.2	0.1	0.8[6]	0.2
	1999	F	2.9[6]	...	^0.0	...	0.1	0.1	^0.0	0.3
	2001[4]	M	3.0	^0.0	0.1	^0.0	0.1	0.1	0.8	0.3
	2001[4]	F	2.6	^0.0	^0.0	^0.0	0.1	^0.0	^0.0	0.3
	2002[5]	M	3.0	...	...	...	...	...	...	...
	2002[5]	F	2.5	...	...	...	...	...	...	...
Antigua and Barbuda[1,4] Antigua-et-Barbuda[1,4]	2001	M	18.2	0.5	0.3	0.1	0.9	0.4	3.0	2.3
	2001	F	18.0	0.2	^0.0	^0.0	0.6	0.1	0.1	2.6
Argentina[7,8,9] Argentine[7,8,9]	2003	M	5 150.9	81.3	5.2	25.6	828.8	34.9	616.9	1 180.2
	2003	F	3 805.3	36.8	0.9	2.7	402.1	12.3	16.0	650.6
	2004	M	5 446.9	65.7	8.4	30.6	925.4	33.8	717.8	1 230.0
	2004	F	3 968.0	32.0	2.9	2.6	435.0	10.2	14.0	715.7
	2005	M	5 557.3	74.5	6.4	23.2	947.2	44.0	801.1	1 227.0
	2005	F	4 081.4	25.3	1.0	7.7	412.5	5.0	21.9	724.8
Armenia[10] Arménie[10]	2003	M	1 107.6	508.9	0.1	8.2	114.5	23.3	37.2	102.0
	2004	M	1 081.7	507.0	0.1	6.9	111.5	21.2	33.3	103.2
	2005	M	1 105.3	...	...	...	...	...	...	...
Aruba[1] Aruba[1]	1994	M	21.0	^0.0	^0.0	^0.0	1.8	0.5	3.6	3.0
	1994	F	14.9	^0.0	...	...	0.4	0.1	0.3	3.2
	1997	M	23.5	0.1	...	...	2.1	0.7	3.2	3.6
	1997	F	18.0	^0.0	...	...	0.5	0.1	0.2	3.7
Australia[1,10] Australie[1,10]	2003	M	5 227.3	246.1	15.3	67.4	786.3	60.2	660.3	1 011.2
	2003	F	4 232.0	108.7	2.6	8.0	295.9	15.1	95.1	886.9
	2004	M	5 338.0	235.5	11.2	70.0	798.9	61.3	706.7	1 010.1
	2004	F	4 298.3	113.4	2.8	9.0	289.6	12.8	95.8	881.3
	2005	M	5 486.4	240.9	10.6	82.2	786.2	65.2	746.3	1 023.1
	2005	F	4 470.9	108.8	2.6	9.8	283.5	16.7	110.4	930.2
Austria[1,11] Autriche[1,11]	2003	M	2 101.8	111.8	0.7	5.3	546.0	30.5	311.8	257.9
	2003	F	1 696.6	98.3	0.1	0.8	188.3	4.4	26.8	336.7
	2004	M	2 061.5	98.9	...	7.6	513.3	23.8	268.9	276.4
	2004	F	1 682.5	88.5	...	1.0	182.3	4.3	35.1	316.4
	2005	M	2 095.2	114.2	0.1	7.4	520.2	25.5	277.0	267.7
	2005	F	1 728.1	96.1	0.0	1.2	179.8	5.8	36.6	325.9
Azerbaijan Azerbaïdjan	2003	M	1 959.7	799.8	2.4	33.5	74.6	29.4	160.8	233.4
	2003	F	1 787.3	697.2	0.4	8.8	95.3	10.4	19.2	384.9
	2004	M	1 995.8	814.3	2.0	33.9	75.8	29.9	163.7	237.5
	2004	F	1 813.3	688.4	1.3	8.0	105.4	9.9	26.9	393.2
	2005	M	2 017.4	827.0	2.1	34.2	76.3	30.1	165.4	238.4
	2005	F	1 832.8	683.0	1.7	8.0	112.4	9.6	29.0	400.4

Employment by economic activity— Total employment and persons employed by ISIC Rev. 3 categories (thousands) (*continued*)
Emploi par activité économique— Emploi total et personnes employées par branches de CITI Rév. 3 (milliers) (*suite*)

ISIC Rev. 3 Tabulation categories + CITI Rév. 3 Catégories de classement +										
Categ. H Catég. H	Categ. I Catég. I	Categ. J Catég. J	Categ. K Catég. K	Categ. L Catég.L	Categ. M Catég. M	Categ. N Catég. N	Categ. O Catég. O	Categ. P Catég. P	Categ. Q Catég. Q	Country or area Pays ou zone
16.0	32.0	72.0	...	...	49.0	27.0	...	...	...	Albania
17.0	20.0	81.0	...	...	48.0	27.0	...	...	...	Albanie
15.0	19.0	90.0	...	...	47.0	24.0	...	...	...	
78.4	322.5	55.0	50.5	926.3	403.4	128.6	126.7	23.4	6.3	Algeria[1,2]
4.2	17.4	13.1	9.5	81.9	206.9	88.5	60.0	12.2	1.9	Algérie[1,2]
97.6	384.5	49.5	53.6	958.6	400.3	143.2	124.0	4.6	2.4	
4.9	20.9	18.1	14.4	112.6	227.5	101.9	59.4	7.6	0.5	
0.6[6]	0.4	0.1	...	0.3	0.1	...	^0.0	0.1	...	Anguilla[1,3]
0.8[6]	0.1	0.3	...	0.3	0.4	...	0.1	0.2	...	Anguilla[1,3]
0.6	0.3	0.1	0.2	0.3	0.1	^0.0	0.1	^0.0	...	
1.0	0.1	0.1	0.1	0.4	0.2	0.1	0.1	0.1	...	
...	...	...	...	...	...	...	...	...	...	
...	...	...	...	...	...	...	...	...	...	
2.0	1.8	0.3	0.8	2.1	0.4	0.3	1.2	0.2	0.3	Antigua and Barbuda[1,4]
3.0	1.0	0.7	0.7	2.3	1.3	1.4	1.5	1.1	0.2	Antigua-et-Barbuda[1,4]
149.9	510.0	92.8	445.4	486.0	155.2	188.9	264.4	45.1	2.0	Argentina[7,8,9]
96.3	78.8	56.0	210.9	304.7	593.7	460.2	230.2	631.4	2.4	Argentine[7,8,9]
167.6	561.5	92.0	436.2	466.2	154.9	196.6	287.6	53.1	...	
153.5	86.4	51.8	240.2	306.7	557.4	455.9	242.3	649.3	...	
171.2	548.3	93.0	459.4	429.7	174.6	173.8	311.2	56.4	2.1	
144.3	100.6	69.8	283.3	299.0	561.8	454.5	269.7	684.6	1.4	
4.8	41.8	5.0	19.4	27.7	111.7	60.3	42.7	...	...	Armenia[10]
3.9	46.5	5.6	18.3	29.1	100.5	49.8	44.8	...	...	Arménie[10]
...	...	...	...	...	...	...	...	...	...	
3.2	2.3	0.4	1.1	2.6	0.5	0.4	1.6	0.1	^0.0	Aruba[1]
3.1	0.8	1.0	0.9	1.3	0.8	1.2	0.8	1.2	^0.0	Aruba[1]
3.7	2.3	0.5	1.9	2.7	0.5	0.4	1.7	^0.0	...	
3.4	1.0	1.0	1.4	1.6	0.8	1.6	1.4	1.3	^0.0	
196.8	441.0	156.7	627.7	311.9	219.6	203.1	219.3	0.3	0.7	Australia[1,10]
268.1	158.6	190.7	511.4	240.1	462.1	728.5	255.2	2.9	0.5	Australie[1,10]
213.8	450.1	159.6	633.4	312.4	223.8	213.6	224.2	0.4	0.3	
271.9	167.0	187.5	501.9	254.5	468.8	767.6	264.1	2.2	0.6	
216.5	469.3	167.1	662.2	325.7	222.2	220.7	231.3	0.2	0.5	
283.1	171.0	205.1	537.1	257.6	472.1	792.1	282.7	0.3	0.5	
75.8	179.5	63.8	156.6	146.6	64.3	75.0	73.9	0.4	1.9	Austria[1,11]
141.9	58.7	68.0	151.5	90.6	166.4	252.8	95.5	13.2	2.6	Autriche[1,11]
83.4	181.0	68.1	162.7	146.6	64.5	76.1	84.7	1.0	4.5	
143.6	57.3	72.1	164.5	107.5	145.7	249.7	102.6	8.2	3.6	
90.8	179.3	71.1	167.4	136.8	67.7	88.4	77.1	0.4	4.2	
153.4	62.0	72.4	166.7	101.9	154.3	261.3	98.4	9.2	4.0	
7.8	129.3	8.1	58.8	170.5	102.0	68.6	80.3	...	0.4	Azerbaijan
4.0	49.2	4.9	38.7	94.5	228.0	105.2	46.5	...	0.1	Azerbaïdjan
8.0	131.7	8.0	59.9	173.6	103.8	71.4	81.8	...	0.5	
4.4	58.8	5.1	40.1	96.1	227.0	103.2	45.5	...	0.0	
8.1	132.2	8.1	60.5	175.5	104.0	72.3	82.7	...	0.5	
6.1	59.3	5.1	40.1	95.0	231.3	104.9	46.8	...	0.1	

26 Employment by economic activity — Total employment and persons employed by ISIC Rev. 3 categories (thousands) (*continued*)

Emploi par activité économique — Emploi total et personnes employées par branches de CITI Rév. 3 (milliers) (*suite*)

Country or area Pays ou zone	Year Année	Sex Sexe	Total employment Emploi total	ISIC Rev. 3 Tabulation categories + CITI Rév. 3 Catégories de classement + Categ. A Catég. A	Categ. B Catég. B	Categ. C Catég. C	Categ. D Catég. D	Categ. E Catég. E	Categ. F Catég. F	Categ. G Catég. G
Bahamas[1,10,12] Bahamas[1,10,12]	2003	M	79.1	4.2	...	1.5	4.0	...	14.7	12.1
	2003	F	75.8	0.5	...	0.7	2.7	...	0.8	11.8
	2004	M	81.7	6.7	...	1.9	3.8	...	15.8	13.[illegible]
	2004	F	76.6	0.3	...	0.7	2.4	...	0.9	13.9
	2005	M	82.8	5.3	...	1.6	4.8	...	18.1	11.2
	2005	F	77.7	0.3	...	0.4	2.8	...	0.8	12.7
Bangladesh[1,13] Bangladesh[1,13]	2003	M	34 478.0	16 132.0	1 027.0	80.0	2 637.0	90.0	1 445.0	5 894.[illegible]
	2003	F	9 844.0	5 754.0	17.0	1.0	1 706.0	8.0	97.0	214.[illegible]
Belgium[1,14] Belgique[1,14]	2003	M	2 317.0	50.2	0.4	5.4	535.8	25.9	241.7	296.4
	2003	F	1 753.4	21.2	0.2	0.4	178.5	6.2	17.5	263.9
	2004	M	2 354.3	57.3	0.6	6.1	545.7	26.3	252.8	301.5
	2004	F	1 784.9	24.2	...	0.7	172.8	6.0	19.8	263.8
	2005	M	2 386.8	57.8	...	7.8	548.5	25.8	253.8	295.8
	2005	F	1 848.5	27.0	...	...	178.5	6.8	23.0	272.3
Belize[10,12,15] Belize[10,12,15]	1998	M	50.1	...	...	0.3	5.3	1.0	4.2	7.8
	1998	F	23.3	...	...	...	2.3	0.2	0.1	5.1
	1999	M	53.7	...	...	0.3	4.7	0.9	4.4	7.4
	1999	F	24.1	...	...	^0.0	2.6	0.1	0.1	4.9
	2005	M	64.9	16.7	1.5	0.2	6.4	0.8	6.7	10.3
	2005	F	33.7	0.8	0.3	^0.0	3.2	0.2	0.2	6.6
Bolivia[7,11,16] Bolivie[7,11,16]	2000	M	1 167.7	71.7	...	30.1	203.9	14.5	210.5	209.0
	2000	F	923.5	31.0	...	5.3	116.2	1.4	8.4	327.1
	2001	M	1 162.9	...	...	...	...	...	...	...
	2001	F	993.4	...	...	...	...	...	...	...
	2002	M	1 166.5	...	...	...	...	...	...	...
	2002	F	952.0	...	...	...	...	...	...	...
Botswana[10,17] Botswana[10,17]	1998	M	248.9	65.1	...	11.6	22.5	2.7	29.6	21.2
	1998	F	192.2	24.8	...	1.4	24.6	0.3	3.8	27.5
	2000	M	269.4	58.9	...	10.0	19.8	2.0	39.0	25.3
	2000	F	214.0	36.4	...	1.2	22.8	0.2	5.9	38.3
	2003	M	245.4	70.1	...	11.3	18.3	3.5	35.7	20.9
	2003	F	217.0	28.0	...	2.5	26.2	0.9	6.2	40.7
Brazil[2,7,18] Brésil[2,7,18]	2002	M	46 334.2	10 601.2	291.0	235.6	6 763.9	259.3	5 468.3	8 533.2
	2002	F	32 624.6	5 351.3	33.0	18.9	3 914.2	54.4	147.8	5 019.9
	2003	M	46 935.1	10 928.6	298.9	284.8	6 839.5	273.1	5 097.7	8 923.8
	2003	F	33 228.4	5 296.6	44.0	28.2	4 037.9	59.3	122.1	5 291.9
	2004	M	49 242.0	11 714.7	348.3	303.1	7 370.0	299.6	5 220.1	9 043.9
	2004	F	35 354.3	5 615.3	55.6	22.4	4 353.6	54.0	134.2	5 609.3
Brunei Darussalam[1,19] Brunéi Darussalam[1,19]	2001	M	85.8	1.3	0.5	3.2	7.8	2.2	11.4	8.5
	2001	F	60.4	0.2	^0.0	0.8	4.7	0.4	0.9	4.4
Bulgaria[1] Bulgarie[1]	2003	M	1 500.0	184.5	...	33.8	331.9	46.6	136.5	213.1
	2003	F	1 334.0	101.3	...	7.7	344.7	13.4	14.9	210.5
	2004	M	1 550.7	181.1	...	32.1	343.9	47.8	153.7	216.3
	2004	F	1 371.5	101.0	...	6.8	353.3	14.7	16.0	219.3
	2005	M	1 591.4	170.6	...	31.2	364.8	47.9	175.3	219.7
	2005	F	1 388.7	94.8	...	5.6	363.9	16.1	15.2	227.4
Cambodia[7,20] Cambodge[7,20]	2000	MF	5 275.2	...	...	...	...	...	...	...
	2001	MF	6 243.3	...	...	...	...	...	...	...
	2004	MF	6 560.6	2 577.6	31.5	3.9	218.3	0.2	8.9	404.8

Employment by economic activity—Total employment and persons employed by ISIC Rev. 3 categories (thousands) (*continued*)
Emploi par activité économique—Emploi total et personnes employées par branches de CITI Rév. 3 (milliers) (*suite*)

ISIC Rev. 3 Tabulation categories + CITI Rév. 3 Catégories de classement +										
Categ. H Catég. H	Categ. I Catég. I	Categ. J Catég. J	Categ. K Catég. K	Categ. L Catég.L	Categ. M Catég. M	Categ. N Catég. N	Categ. O Catég. O	Categ. P Catég. P	Categ. Q Catég. Q	Country or area Pays ou zone
12.0	7.9	5.7	...	16.8	...	...	...	...	...	Bahamas[1,10,12]
15.9	3.9	9.9	...	29.5	...	...	...	...	...	Bahamas[1,10,12]
9.2	6.8	6.9	...	17.6	...	...	...	...	...	
14.6	3.6	10.7	...	29.5	...	...	...	...	...	
11.4	7.2	6.3	...	16.4	...	...	...	...	...	
17.7	3.5	9.9	...	29.6	...	...	...	...	...	
530.0	2 989.0	204.0	186.0	903.0	867.0	357.0	1 136.0	...	...	Bangladesh[1,13]
33.0	25.0	19.0	7.0	85.0	318.0	146.0	1 413.0	...	...	Bangladesh[1,13]
66.3	248.4	85.2	221.8	220.7	115.9	123.1	73.5	1.6	4.7	Belgium[1,14]
66.6	63.3	69.3	160.6	176.3	235.1	395.6	86.9	7.9	3.9	Belgique[1,14]
66.9	245.7	80.2	217.2	230.2	121.1	116.5	76.9	2.1	7.3	
65.2	67.6	72.1	161.5	189.2	250.2	392.1	82.6	11.2	6.0	
74.0	236.8	88.3	214.8	236.5	128.3	120.0	79.0	4.0	16.5	
70.0	76.5	73.5	154.0	183.0	261.0	397.0	91.0	18.0	15.0	
2.3	3.3	0.6	1.0	3.4	1.9	...	1.3	0.4	0.2	Belize[10,12,15]
3.0	0.5	0.6	0.4	1.5	4.6	...	1.4	2.3	0.1	Belize[10,12,15]
2.5	3.7	0.8	1.2	3.4	2.3	...	1.7	0.5	0.1	
3.3	0.5	0.7	0.3	1.6	4.7	...	1.5	2.4	0.1	
3.2	5.4	0.6	1.5	4.6	2.1	0.7	2.2	1.5	0.3	
5.5	0.9	1.0	0.6	2.2	4.1	2.0	1.7	4.3	0.3	
29.9	131.0	13.5	71.4	54.6	56.6	21.1	47.2	5.2	1.0	Bolivia[7,11,16]
94.5	13.4	6.4	24.5	18.1	76.2	27.7	51.6	121.6	1.8	Bolivie[7,11,16]
...	...	...	...	...	...	...	...	...	...	
...	...	...	...	...	...	...	...	...	...	
...	...	...	...	...	...	...	...	...	...	
...	...	...	...	...	...	...	...	...	...	
3.0	8.4	1.9	7.9	43.5	16.4	4.3	1.8	4.9	0.3	Botswana[10,17]
8.2	2.3	2.3	3.2	26.3	28.8	9.1	1.7	24.2	0.2	Botswana[10,17]
2.4	10.8	2.0	11.7	47.6	18.3	4.4	11.0	2.8	0.2	
7.4	3.0	2.3	6.1	25.7	24.3	7.8	11.0	18.4	0.1	
3.8	9.4	1.5	9.2	36.2	14.2	4.5	4.0	2.4	0.2	
10.9	3.2	3.4	5.1	31.0	24.5	9.5	5.5	19.2	...	
1 500.9	3 290.9	523.2	2 831.5	2 503.8	921.6	652.2	1 342.0	433.3	3.0	Brazil[2,7,18]
1 430.8	401.3	459.4	1 430.0	1 366.9	3 382.3	2 106.6	1 806.5	5 676.8	2.1	Brésil[2,7,18]
1 458.7	3 301.2	540.5	2 986.3	2 518.8	932.7	688.5	1 282.2	402.7	1.7	
1 434.1	423.4	484.7	1 507.8	1 471.2	3 421.1	2 129.1	1 699.8	5 751.9	2.3	
1 518.4	3 428.3	523.7	3 066.8	2 636.9	990.4	686.4	1 449.6	432.4	2.0	
1 504.6	465.9	476.0	1 652.9	1 566.9	3 578.8	2 153.8	2 048.7	6 040.1	2.1	
3.8	3.4	5.1	...	38.7	...	...	...	...	...	Brunei Darussalam[1,19]
3.3	1.4	3.1	...	41.1	...	...	...	...	...	Brunéi Darussalam[1,19]
49.1	156.4	10.8	64.8	139.8	47.1	36.5	48.0	...	...	Bulgaria[1]
79.3	58.4	19.9	50.8	90.4	163.5	118.8	59.6	...	...	Bulgarie[1]
55.6	155.5	11.0	74.9	135.5	46.5	36.2	59.3	...	...	
85.0	56.1	23.4	57.4	85.3	163.9	120.8	67.9	...	...	
59.1	157.8	14.3	80.2	130.8	43.2	36.2	58.9	...	...	
91.1	56.1	23.5	61.4	83.3	164.0	123.4	61.9	...	...	
...	...	...	...	...	...	...	...	...	...	Cambodia[7,20]
...	...	...	...	...	...	...	...	...	...	Cambodge[7,20]
25.1	5.2	3.0	4.8	17.5	33.1	11.9	42.7	14.5	3.0	

26 Employment by economic activity—Total employment and persons employed by ISIC Rev. 3 categories (thousands) (*continued*)

Emploi par activité économique—Emploi total et personnes employées par branches de CITI Rév. 3 (milliers) (*suite*)

Country or area / Pays ou zone	Year / Année	Sex / Sexe	Total employment / Emploi total	ISIC Rev. 3 Tabulation categories + / CITI Rév. 3 Catégories de classement + Categ. A / Catég. A	Categ. B / Catég. B	Categ. C / Catég. C	Categ. D / Catég. D	Categ. E / Catég. E	Categ. F / Catég. F	Categ. G / Catég. G
Canada[1,21,22] / Canada[1,21,22]	2003	M	8 344.3	296.3	24.9	148.1	1 619.7	101.9	806.2	1 485.6
	2003	F	7 320.7	105.8	4.4	29.9	663.8	28.5	93.5	1 234.5
	2004	M	8 479.6	286.8	25.0	155.4	1 643.8	97.4	836.8	1 516.1
	2004	F	7 470.1	105.7	5.0	32.0	653.2	35.7	107.5	1 255.4
	2005	M	8 594.7	295.7	26.1	175.5	1 581.2	93.2	905.4	1 533.4
	2005	F	7 575.0	112.9	4.8	35.2	626.2	32.1	107.0	1 306.4
China, Macao SAR[10,15] / Chine, Macao RAS[10,15]	2003	M	107.0	...	0.3	...	11.6	1.0	14.7	17.3
	2003	F	95.6	0.1	0.1	...	25.5	0.3	1.6	15.5
	2004	M	114.9	0.1	0.3	...	11.4	0.9	16.2	18.6
	2004	F	103.1	0.1	0.1	...	24.5	0.2	2.0	16.6
	2005	M	124.5	...	0.2	...	11.9	1.1	20.7	18.7
	2005	F	113.3	0.1	0.1	...	23.5	0.2	2.5	16.9
Colombia[7,10,23] / Colombie[7,10,23]	2003	M	10 405.0	3 181.1	...	169.7	1 150.2	52.5	745.6	2 334.0
	2003	F	7 078.6	512.6	...	46.7	1 056.0	12.6	22.3	2 101.0
	2004	M	10 547.1	3 096.2	...	176.0	1 239.2	57.8	750.8	2 354.2
	2004	F	7 106.4	481.5	...	21.4	1 182.2	13.6	28.3	2 020.9
	2005	M	10 878.0	3 459.0	...	171.7	1 239.0	...	833.4	2 282.0
	2005	F	7 339.0	614.9	...	43.3	1 112.0	...	25.6	2 149.0
Costa Rica[10,17,24] / Costa Rica[10,17,24]	2003	M	1 069.0	217.1	7.9	2.0	153.3	17.9	108.3	211.8
	2003	F	571.4	22.7	0.7	0.3	76.7	4.2	1.4	110.6
	2004	M	1 093.6	215.6	7.2	2.9	162.1	19.8	105.0	218.7
	2004	F	560.3	21.7	0.8	0.7	66.8	3.8	2.3	111.3
	2005	M	1 153.9	231.3	8.9	3.2	170.4	17.8	113.0	215.2
	2005	F	623.0	29.2	0.6	0.8	72.3	2.7	2.8	117.0
Croatia[1,11,25] / Croatie[1,11,25]	2003	M	850.5	133.7	4.1	8.7	181.3	22.0	115.4	104.2
	2003	F	685.9	120.4	0.5	1.7	111.7	6.1	9.7	108.5
	2004	M	866.4	130.4	4.1	8.3	189.3	21.9	116.9	101.4
	2004	F	696.4	121.1	0.9	0.5	111.5	6.9	10.5	114.4
	2005	M	867.0	134.7	3.9	8.3	174.6	22.2	117.2	105.4
	2005	F	705.9	132.7	0.7	0.8	109.4	6.6	11.0	114.1
Cyprus[1,11,26] / Chypre[1,11,26]	2003	M	181.6	10.9	0.3	0.4	22.4	3.2	32.4	32.7
	2003	F	145.5	5.7	...	0.1	13.5	0.4	2.5	27.0
	2004	M	190.8	10.5	0.4	0.5	24.4	3.0	37.3	34.5
	2004	F	147.2	5.4	...	...	13.2	0.6	2.0	26.8
	2005	M	197.3	10.8	0.5	0.7	27.2	2.2	37.7	34.2
	2005	F	150.7	5.3	...	0.1	12.8	0.5	2.5	26.0
Czech Republic[1] / République tchèque[1]	2003	M	2 686.0	147.0	...	47.0	798.0	61.0	405.0	302.0
	2003	F	2 047.0	66.0	...	7.0	496.0	16.0	33.0	326.0
	2004	M	2 663.0	140.0	...	52.0	786.0	61.0	402.0	308.0
	2004	F	2 044.0	62.0	...	7.0	488.0	15.0	34.0	323.0
	2005	M	2 706.0	131.0	...	44.0	813.0	60.0	420.0	292.0
	2005	F	2 059.0	58.0	...	6.0	484.0	17.0	39.0	323.0
Denmark[27] / Danemark[27]	2003	M	1 447.8	59.1	4.6	4.9	307.8	12.1	165.3	224.6
	2003	F	1 244.6	18.0	^0.0	0.8	133.1	2.3	14.7	171.2
	2004	M	1 451.6	61.8	3.3	4.0	302.7	12.8	168.7	233.5
	2004	F	1 268.5	19.3	0.2	0.3	131.8	3.2	15.8	172.8
	2005	M	1 456.1	60.3	...	...	305.6	11.5	174.3	230.0
	2005	F	1 276.6	20.2	0.0	...	136.8	3.7	18.2	170.8

Employment by economic activity—Total employment and persons employed by ISIC Rev. 3 categories (thousands) (*continued*)
Emploi par activité économique—Emploi total et personnes employées par branches de CITI Rév. 3 (milliers) (*suite*)

ISIC Rev. 3 Tabulation categories + CITI Rév. 3 Catégories de classement +										
Categ. H Catég. H	Categ. I Catég. I	Categ. J Catég. J	Categ. K Catég. K	Categ. L Catég.L	Categ. M Catég. M	Categ. N Catég. N	Categ. O Catég. O	Categ. P Catég. P	Categ. Q Catég. Q	Country or area Pays ou zone
408.8	784.5	234.8	1 026.5	422.5	367.5	299.6	311.4	4.8	0.0	Canada[1,21,22]
597.9	355.3	410.8	853.2	395.9	661.9	1 383.7	430.5	70.5	1.9	Canada[1,21,22]
400.0	794.2	244.2	1 058.9	426.3	355.2	317.9	317.3	3.7	0.0	
606.8	369.5	434.1	859.5	401.7	683.2	1 418.8	439.7	61.9	0.0	
402.4	792.2	254.4	1 100.3	425.8	379.4	310.1	313.9	4.7	0.8	
602.1	361.6	452.6	891.5	404.8	726.7	1 424.5	427.8	57.2	1.7	
11.5	10.4	2.6	7.6	12.3	3.1	1.5	12.6	0.2	0.1	China, Macao SAR[10,15]
10.6	3.8	3.6	4.2	5.5	6.6	3.2	10.9	4.1	...	Chine, Macao RAS[10,15]
11.8	11.1	2.6	8.1	12.4	3.3	1.5	16.1	0.4	...	
12.1	3.8	3.6	4.5	5.5	7.1	3.5	14.8	4.6	...	
11.4	11.1	2.7	9.1	12.6	2.9	1.4	20.3	0.3	0.1	
13.5	3.8	3.8	5.3	6.2	7.4	3.9	20.0	6.0	0.1	
...	1 070.1	96.4	456.5	1 148.3	...	...	...	...	...	Colombia[7,10,23]
...	131.1	113.7	288.8	2 790.8	...	...	...	...	...	Colombie[7,10,23]
...	1 117.6	111.7	480.6	1 160.3	...	...	...	...	...	
...	175.7	115.9	297.8	2 767.2	...	...	...	...	...	
...	1 013.0	113.0	530.9	1 235.0	...	...	...	...	...	
...	188.3	126.5	304.1	2 775.0	...	...	...	...	...	
38.9	82.6	21.2	66.6	47.5	28.2	17.5	34.8	6.9	1.7	Costa Rica[10,17,24]
51.0	11.5	14.4	34.7	28.8	70.2	31.8	37.3	72.4	0.6	Costa Rica[10,17,24]
41.6	84.9	24.2	70.6	47.6	27.4	20.0	29.8	9.3	2.2	
49.8	11.3	12.5	31.4	30.9	68.6	31.3	33.1	81.5	1.7	
41.9	97.8	22.7	73.0	53.2	29.7	25.9	33.9	10.1	0.6	
56.2	14.1	13.5	30.0	28.2	74.4	36.8	31.0	111.1	1.5	
37.2	79.2	9.4	32.6	57.8	18.4	18.0	25.7	1.6	...	Croatia[1,11,25]
47.4	22.1	23.0	31.4	38.7	64.7	69.5	27.2	2.8	...	Croatie[1,11,25]
39.5	82.5	9.2	36.7	57.3	23.1	18.6	25.7	0.2	...	
46.7	20.8	21.3	26.5	44.6	67.5	68.7	31.4	3.1	...	
38.1	81.9	9.8	41.7	58.1	20.5	19.7	30.0	0.3	...	
45.4	21.2	18.6	33.9	42.3	67.0	64.9	32.4	4.3	...	
12.9	11.0	6.8	11.4	15.3	6.8	4.1	9.3	0.1	1.5	Cyprus[1,11,26]
15.9	6.3	9.7	11.1	9.1	14.5	10.2	7.9	10.8	0.8	Chypre[1,11,26]
13.3	12.4	6.8	11.6	15.9	6.4	4.2	7.9	0.3	1.5	
16.7	5.8	9.0	10.9	7.6	15.1	10.9	9.0	13.4	0.7	
12.3	12.6	9.2	11.6	17.9	5.6	4.2	8.5	0.4	1.9	
14.9	5.9	9.0	13.0	8.4	17.1	10.7	9.7	13.8	1.1	
76.0	248.0	34.0	156.0	193.0	69.0	64.0	83.0	1.0	...	Czech Republic[1]
95.0	110.0	62.0	129.0	139.0	219.0	242.0	102.0	4.0	1.0	République tchèque[1]
82.0	246.0	33.0	159.0	180.0	64.0	62.0	88.0	...	...	
93.0	118.0	61.0	122.0	143.0	215.0	262.0	97.0	3.0	1.0	
84.0	250.0	38.0	163.0	179.0	71.0	68.0	93.0	1.0	0.0	
97.0	110.0	59.0	126.0	155.0	226.0	260.0	97.0	3.0	1.0	
29.9	134.4	41.2	147.1	80.9	83.2	79.9	68.6	0.3	1.0	Denmark[27]
36.5	54.0	40.6	101.6	76.9	125.3	397.8	67.4	1.5	1.3	Danemark[27]
28.7	127.7	42.1	146.5	83.4	85.1	80.6	68.4	0.1	0.5	
40.2	57.8	39.2	101.6	80.3	127.9	399.9	72.0	3.1	1.1	
29.8	125.6	41.6	148.0	81.8	89.5	81.2	68.2	...	...	
39.9	49.8	47.3	105.4	85.0	126.7	393.6	73.4	...	...	

Employment by economic activity—Total employment and persons employed by ISIC Rev. 3 categories (thousands) (*continu*

Emploi par activité économique—Emploi total et personnes employées par branches de CITI Rév. 3 (milliers) (*suite*)

Country or area / Pays ou zone	Year / Année	Sex / Sexe	Total employment / Emploi total	ISIC Rev. 3 Tabulation categories + / CITI Rév. 3 Catégories de classement + — Categ. A / Catég. A	Categ. B / Catég. B	Categ. C / Catég. C	Categ. D / Catég. D	Categ. E / Catég. E	Categ. F / Catég. F	Categ. / Catég.
Dominican Republic[7] Rép. dominicaine[7]	2003	M	2 069.5	408.2	...	7.3	310.9	21.2	213.7	425
	2003	F	1 029.0	17.8	...	...	145.1	5.2	6.5	216
	2004	M	2 146.4	455.7	...	4.8	345.5	20.1	205.4	431
	2004	F	1 063.5	20.6	...	0.1	148.6	6.6	7.8	220
	2005	M	2 173.4	446.9	...	5.8	335.5	17.2	206.9	460
	2005	F	1 103.0	30.9	...	0.1	151.2	9.0	6.4	247
Ecuador[7,28,29] Equateur[7,28,29]	2003	M	2 138.4	...	...	...	...	...	...	.
	2003	F	1 392.8	...	...	...	...	...	...	.
	2004	M	2 288.5	247.5	34.2	14.6	335.6	17.3	239.9	589.
	2004	F	1 570.1	73.3	3.3	1.5	203.4	5.6	8.8	506
	2005	M	2 327.8	218.7	38.4	10.6	361.4	15.4	249.4	597.
	2005	F	1 564.0	54.8	12.7	0.1	175.7	3.4	9.4	501.
Egypt[10,30,31] Egypte[10,30,31]	2001	M	14 361.1	3 883.6	108.8	58.1	1 835.6	194.8	1 323.2	1 903
	2001	F	3 195.6	1 017.9	0.3	1.4	279.4	15.4	25.2	222.
	2002	M	14 550.7	3 888.2	112.2	41.3	1 786.5	220.1	1 279.7	2 050.
	2002	F	3 305.5	912.2	1.2	3.2	284.2	21.7	35.4	252
	2003	M	14 651.7	3 898.4	159.3	30.0	1 810.7	208.6	1 313.1	1 941.
	2003	F	3 466.9	1 351.7	1.9	2.0	166.2	20.1	27.9	219.
El Salvador[7,32] El Salvador[7,32]	2002	M	1 404.4	432.7	14.7	3.4	203.4	9.2	131.2	267.
	2002	F	1 008.4	25.7	1.2	0.1	230.7	1.5	5.1	421.
	2003	M	1 467.6	393.1	25.8	2.1	221.8	5.5	159.2	286.
	2003	F	1 052.4	37.3	3.2	0.1	226.0	0.8	3.4	438.
	2004	M	1 494.0	433.0	15.4	1.7	206.2	9.0	157.8	302.
	2004	F	1 032.4	32.7	2.0	0.1	217.2	1.3	4.9	436.
Estonia[11,33] Estonie[11,33]	2003	M	302.5	23.3	2.2	5.0	73.6	8.0	39.9	32.
	2003	F	291.8	11.1	0.1	0.7	60.6	2.2	3.0	48.
	2004	M	299.1	21.1	3.1	6.5	75.1	8.5	42.1	33
	2004	F	296.4	10.3	0.5	1.5	65.8	3.5	4.7	46.
	2005	M	300.5	19.0	2.5	5.4	73.2	9.4	44.2	33.
	2005	F	306.9	10.4	0.3	0.5	66.2	3.1	4.5	47.
Ethiopia[7,10,25] Ethiopie[7,10,25]	1999	M	14 117.8	...	...	...	...	...	...	.
	1999	F	10 778.8	...	...	...	...	...	...	..
	2004[34]	M	1 625.6	168.3	...	9.2	236.9	21.6	141.2	325.
	2004[34]	F	1 228.8	56.8	...	0.8	207.6	7.3	17.6	297.
	2005	M	16 860.3	14 209.4	...	51.4	444.0	25.2	349.9	652.
	2005	F	14 574.8	10 998.8	...	30.6	1 085.3	7.7	95.7	984.
Finland[33] Finlande[33]	2003	M	1 247.0	81.0	1.0	5.0	317.0	15.0	140.0	146.
	2003	F	1 138.0	38.0	...	...	127.0	5.0	11.0	141.
	2004	M	1 250.0	81.0	1.0	5.0	309.0	15.0	138.0	150.
	2004	F	1 137.0	33.0	1.0	...	126.0	4.0	11.0	143.
	2005	M	1 263.0	81.0	1.0	5.0	310.0	14.0	147.0	153.
	2005	F	1 158.0	33.0	1.0	1.0	127.0	5.0	11.0	147.
France[1] France[1]	2002[35]	M	13 103.0	...	...	...	...	...	...	..
	2002[35]	F	10 839.0	...	...	...	...	...	...	..
	2003	M	13 460.5	725.3	15.2	27.2	3 022.7	175.4	1 498.1	1 760.
	2003	F	11 170.5	323.5	2.7	7.6	1 206.7	48.5	154.9	1 532.
	2004	M	13 444.6	663.8	12.1	31.8	2 950.1	182.1	1 511.0	1 789.
	2004	F	11 275.6	316.2	1.9	4.4	1 218.0	37.5	142.6	1 562.

Employment by economic activity—Total employment and persons employed by ISIC Rev. 3 categories (thousands) *(continued)*
Emploi par activité économique—Emploi total et personnes employées par branches de CITI Rév. 3 (milliers) *(suite)*

ISIC Rev. 3 Tabulation categories + CITI Rév. 3 Catégories de classement +										
Categ. H Catég. H	Categ. I Catég. I	Categ. J Catég. J	Categ. K Catég. K	Categ. L Catég.L	Categ. M Catég. M	Categ. N Catég. N	Categ. O Catég. O	Categ. P Catég. P	Categ. Q Catég. Q	Country or area Pays ou zone
86.1	217.9	31.4	250.6	97.3	…	…	…	…	…	Dominican Republic[7] Rép. dominicaine[7]
83.8	21.5	32.3	460.1	40.5	…	…	…	…	…	
90.2	205.8	28.9	263.4	94.8	…	…	…	…	…	
89.6	27.0	26.8	469.8	45.9	…	…	…	…	…	
88.4	215.5	34.5	258.9	103.6	…	…	…	…	…	
103.2	23.0	27.8	460.1	43.9	…	…	…	…	…	
…	…	…	…	…	…	…	…	…	…	Ecuador[7,28,29] Equateur[7,28,29]
…	…	…	…	…	…	…	…	…	…	
62.2	233.9	26.3	138.0	124.9	100.6	47.4	68.5	7.0	1.2	
108.9	30.9	22.8	51.8	49.0	162.4	90.4	107.6	143.4	0.2	
71.0	244.6	26.2	144.1	125.6	91.7	46.9	65.0	20.9	0.4	
119.8	35.5	25.7	55.6	42.6	167.2	85.1	93.7	180.8	0.3	
271.4	1 078.7	152.6	299.5	1 495.6	1 107.5	297.2	315.8	33.2	…	Egypt[10,30,31] Egypte[10,30,31]
53.3	63.5	46.8	38.4	391.2	712.3	269.3	38.1	19.6	…	
287.2	1 060.2	160.5	287.9	1 523.2	1 178.3	301.1	337.0	35.5	…	
50.1	72.7	59.0	54.5	422.3	784.4	293.4	42.5	16.4	…	
276.5	1 093.5	152.0	298.2	1 579.7	1 190.4	293.6	376.7	28.4	…	
14.8	51.8	47.9	49.0	445.4	778.7	252.0	32.1	5.4	…	
…	94.3	62.6	…	71.9	36.5	58.0	…	9.6	…	El Salvador[7,32] El Salvador[7,32]
…	9.1	35.4	…	28.7	58.0	97.4	…	93.6	…	
…	102.1	73.3	…	75.2	32.1	76.9	…	13.4	…	
…	11.6	36.3	…	28.5	52.5	109.8	…	104.2	…	
…	112.6	75.2	…	73.3	30.2	65.5	…	10.5	…	
…	13.2	27.9	…	25.1	56.8	106.2	…	108.2	…	
3.6	36.7	2.6	27.4	19.0	10.7	5.6	12.1	…	…	Estonia[11,33] Estonie[11,33]
13.8	19.5	5.0	17.0	15.5	46.1	30.8	18.3	…	…	
4.3	35.3	2.2	22.6	18.4	10.4	5.6	10.7	…	…	
11.9	16.2	5.7	16.9	18.5	44.1	32.0	18.2	…	…	
4.7	38.7	1.2	27.3	17.5	9.1	4.9	10.3	…	…	
17.3	15.8	5.7	19.2	19.6	45.8	30.2	20.7	…	…	
…	…	…	…	…	…	…	…	…	…	Ethiopia[7,10,25] Ethiopie[7,10,25]
…	…	…	…	…	…	…	…	…	…	
53.4	108.7	16.4	34.4	139.3	137.7	…	197.9	22.4	12.4	
202.2	10.7	5.2	11.5	61.6	95.5	…	57.9	192.2	3.4	
96.8	132.0	21.6	36.1	242.0	178.2	45.6	303.5	23.1	42.7	
672.3	14.5	16.3	16.2	125.9	104.5	32.5	135.2	225.5	25.1	
20.0	128.0	13.0	148.0	76.0	56.0	41.0	53.0	1.0	…	Finland[33] Finlande[33]
56.0	45.0	36.0	115.0	62.0	111.0	305.0	78.0	4.0	…	
20.0	127.0	15.0	151.0	76.0	56.0	44.0	55.0	2.0	1.0	
54.0	45.0	35.0	115.0	62.0	115.0	308.0	79.0	3.0	…	
22.0	127.0	15.0	151.0	72.0	58.0	44.0	58.0	4.0	1.0	
55.0	45.0	32.0	124.0	59.0	111.0	322.0	78.0	4.0	0.0	
…	…	…	…	…	…	…	…	…	…	France[1] France[1]
…	…	…	…	…	…	…	…	…	…	
418.4	1 104.3	325.7	1 354.5	1 155.2	580.0	639.0	451.7	133.3	6.4	
382.0	474.8	389.0	1 080.2	1 141.7	1 123.6	2 165.4	566.2	507.0	6.9	
435.5	1 109.2	298.6	1 397.1	1 199.1	581.1	657.9	451.0	123.0	6.1	
388.9	483.8	378.2	1 083.1	1 100.2	1 124.0	2 260.7	604.9	521.0	8.8	

Country or area Pays ou zone	Year Année	Sex Sexe	Total employment Emploi total	ISIC Rev. 3 Tabulation categories + CITI Rév. 3 Catégories de classement + Categ. A Catég. A	Categ. B Catég. B	Categ. C Catég. C	Categ. D Catég. D	Categ. E Catég. E	Categ. F Catég. F	Categ Catég
Georgia[1] Géorgie[1]	2003	M	957.5	508.3	0.5	2.3	57.8	15.7	39.7	112
	2003	F	857.0	486.6	0.2	0.5	31.0	4.1	0.4	86
	2004	M	926.5	478.2	0.4	3.7	60.6	17.1	41.3	108
	2004	F	856.8	483.7	...	0.2	30.1	3.6	0.7	88
	2005	M	915.2	473.5	0.0	5.2	60.1	18.1	42.4	107
	2005	F	829.4	474.3	0.0	0.6	29.7	5.3	0.7	80
Germany[1] Allemagne[1]	2003[4]	M	19 996.0	588.0	4.0	115.0	5 919.0	227.0	2 273.0	2 327
	2003[4]	F	16 176.0	302.0	1.0	13.0	2 324.0	60.0	334.0	2 742
	2004[25]	M	19 681.0	554.0	3.0	109.0	5 851.0	233.0	2 119.0	2 338
	2004[25]	F	15 978.0	272.0	2.0	11.0	2 284.0	63.0	316.0	2 673
	2005[25,36]	M	20 135.0	578.0	5.0	111.0	5 785.0	246.0	2 090.0	2 528
	2005[25,36]	F	16 432.0	283.0	2.0	12.0	2 247.0	69.0	310.0	2 729
Greece[1,11,37] Grèce[1,11,37]	2003	M	2 666.1	370.7	11.1	12.0	402.5	35.5	336.3	445
	2003	F	1 620.5	271.9	1.8	0.6	162.5	6.8	9.6	291
	2004	M	2 680.2	302.0	10.5	14.0	412.1	30.6	343.2	447
	2004	F	1 650.3	231.5	1.6	0.7	157.6	8.5	6.9	300
	2005	M	2 705.8	299.1	12.6	16.7	407.6	30.9	360.7	466
	2005	F	1 676.2	231.3	1.6	1.1	152.7	6.8	6.6	316
Guyana Guyana	1997	M	160.8	48.7	5.1	5.2	19.0	1.5	12.4	25
	1997	F	79.6	11.8	1.2	2.1	8.9	1.0	4.2	17
Hungary[11,33] Hongrie[11,33]	2003	M	2 126.5	166.6	...	11.0	547.3	50.2	275.1	267
	2003	F	1 795.4	48.6	...	1.8	378.2	18.0	24.3	285
	2004	M	2 117.3	158.0	...	11.3	536.1	46.2	284.3	266
	2004	F	1 783.1	46.9	...	2.9	357.8	17.5	24.4	279
	2005	M	2 116.1	145.4	...	12.6	530.7	47.9	293.9	267
	2005	F	1 785.4	48.6	...	2.3	338.7	16.7	21.2	318
Iceland[10,38,39] Islande[10,38,39]	2003	M	81.5	3.8	4.8	...	14.3	1.0	10.3	11
	2003	F	73.3	2.0	...	...	6.8	0.8	0.8	9
	2004	M	82.3	3.3	4.3	...	14.3	1.3	11.0	11
	2004	F	72.8	2.0	0.5	...	7.3	0.3	0.5	8
	2005	M	85.0	3.5	4.5	...	14.0	1.0	11.5	13
	2005	F	75.0	2.0	0.5	...	6.8	0.8	0.5	9
Iran (Islamic Rep. of) Iran (Rép. islamique d')	1996	M	12 806.2	3 024.4	38.4	115.2	1 968.8	145.2	1 634.7	1 804
	1996	F	1 765.4	294.2	0.3	4.7	583.2	5.4	15.8	38
	2005[7]	M	15 959.0	3 565.0	66.0	115.0	2 586.0	181.0	2 043.0	2 647
	2005[7]	F	3 801.0	1 298.0	1.0	7.0	1 046.0	8.0	17.0	169
Ireland[1,40] Irlande[1,40]	2003	M	1 040.9	100.6	2.3	6.4	200.1	10.8	181.9	127
	2003	F	752.5	13.4	0.3	0.3	86.7	1.8	9.4	124
	2004	M	1 065.0	103.0	2.6	6.3	192.0	10.7	196.0	131
	2004	F	771.0	11.0	...	0.6	88.3	2.8	10.3	129
	2005	M	1 110.1	100.7	2.0	8.0	187.8	10.1	230.2	133
	2005	F	819.1	11.0	...	0.9	84.4	3.0	12.2	133
Isle of Man[1] Ile de Man[1]	1991	M	18.3	...	...	...	...	...	...	...
	1991	F	13.6	...	...	...	...	...	...	...
	1996	M	18.7	...	...	...	...	...	...	...
	1996	F	14.9	...	...	...	...	...	...	...
	2001	M	21.3	0.4	^0.0	0.1	2.4	0.4	2.4	2
	2001	F	17.8	0.1	^0.0	^0.0	0.7	0.1	0.2	2

Employment by economic activity—Total employment and persons employed by ISIC Rev. 3 categories (thousands) (*continued*)
Emploi par activité économique—Emploi total et personnes employées par branches de CITI Rév. 3 (milliers) (*suite*)

ISIC Rev. 3 Tabulation categories + CITI Rév. 3 Catégories de classement +										
Categ. H Catég. H	Categ. I Catég. I	Categ. J Catég. J	Categ. K Catég. K	Categ. L Catég.L	Categ. M Catég. M	Categ. N Catég. N	Categ. O Catég. O	Categ. P Catég. P	Categ. Q Catég. Q	Country or area Pays ou zone
6.8	65.4	4.8	19.0	63.5	27.5	8.0	22.2	1.0	2.4	Georgia[1] Géorgie[1]
9.8	11.5	5.0	13.3	27.9	108.1	41.0	23.0	6.8	1.1	
7.6	61.6	5.0	15.8	60.6	26.6	12.6	22.0	0.7	3.1	
11.1	12.7	7.8	12.6	26.1	107.4	42.1	20.7	7.7	1.3	
7.6	57.9	7.2	15.8	56.1	29.6	12.0	18.1	0.6	2.9	
8.7	11.3	6.1	10.1	25.7	101.2	46.0	20.1	8.6	0.4	
518.0	1 419.0	666.0	1 692.0	1 701.0	679.0	1 001.0	845.0	8.0	17.0	Germany[1] Allemagne[1]
709.0	582.0	686.0	1 529.0	1 272.0	1 354.0	3 029.0	1 098.0	130.0	11.0	
518.0	1 411.0	643.0	1 730.0	1 642.0	675.0	1 009.0	820.0	8.0	18.0	
688.0	560.0	654.0	1 546.0	1 254.0	1 358.0	3 055.0	1 091.0	144.0	8.0	
554.0	1 405.0	657.0	1 869.0	1 622.0	688.0	1 015.0	947.0	13.0	21.0	
742.0	544.0	649.0	1 653.0	1 257.0	1 412.0	3 135.0	1 206.0	166.0	13.0	
162.3	222.0	53.8	131.6	219.3	101.7	73.4	84.7	3.0	0.3	Greece[1,11,37] Grèce[1,11,37]
135.6	41.0	56.3	113.3	105.1	184.2	114.7	71.4	53.9	0.1	
149.3	220.2	56.7	155.5	244.3	124.9	82.4	82.0	4.4	0.4	
130.3	52.2	55.7	127.5	111.7	193.3	136.6	73.1	61.4	1.0	
167.6	219.5	56.9	153.3	232.3	122.5	78.5	78.5	2.6	0.6	
136.6	48.3	56.1	136.1	111.4	189.8	141.7	75.1	65.0	0.0	
0.5	15.1	2.2	4.6	8.5	2.7	1.4	2.8	4.2	...	Guyana Guyana
1.1	5.0	2.1	3.8	6.7	4.0	1.6	2.0	4.0	0.3	
59.7	219.5	22.6	143.6	151.5	71.4	62.5	77.1	0.1	0.7	Hungary[11,33] Hongrie[11,33]
79.7	83.7	50.2	122.3	143.9	257.6	204.7	95.4	1.0	0.5	
62.6	215.5	25.7	149.2	151.0	72.0	61.3	77.2	0.2	0.5	
86.2	80.6	54.5	123.3	147.8	261.0	208.1	91.2	1.3	0.2	
70.8	212.5	26.6	152.8	146.3	72.7	58.4	76.9	0.3	1.1	
83.5	72.9	53.7	123.0	151.6	250.7	204.3	97.5	1.8	0.2	
2.0	6.3	2.0	8.8	4.0	4.0	3.5	5.0	...	...	Iceland[10,38,39] Islande[10,38,39]
3.3	3.5	4.5	5.5	4.0	8.0	21.0	5.0	...	...	
2.3	7.3	2.0	8.3	3.3	3.8	3.5	5.0	...	...	
3.0	3.8	4.8	6.3	4.3	7.8	19.5	5.5	...	...	
2.5	7.5	2.0	9.0	3.5	3.5	3.8	5.0	...	...	
3.0	4.3	4.3	6.0	3.5	8.3	20.5	5.0	...	...	
82.3	955.3	139.3	137.0	1 519.4	581.6	184.2	183.2	57.0	0.7	Iran (Islamic Rep. of) Iran (Rép. islamique d')
2.5	17.5	13.6	12.1	98.7	459.5	118.9	41.2	4.9	0.2	
163.0	1 703.0	214.0	336.0	1 156.0	658.0	242.0	267.0	7.0	7.0	
11.0	37.0	34.0	61.0	103.0	643.0	200.0	144.0	20.0	1.0	
48.4	85.0	31.1	85.1	51.3	34.6	33.7	36.9	0.8	0.4	Ireland[1,40] Irlande[1,40]
66.0	27.0	42.1	68.8	41.0	81.4	136.2	42.6	7.7	0.3	
49.4	87.2	35.1	85.8	48.8	33.2	33.8	43.5	0.9	...	
58.4	26.0	47.6	68.5	40.7	84.7	143.0	50.2	5.5	...	
45.7	91.1	36.3	93.2	48.8	35.8	33.5	43.8	0.8	0.3	
65.3	27.1	48.6	79.0	49.4	87.3	154.5	51.3	6.4	0.4	
...	...	...	...	...	...	...	...	...	...	Isle of Man[1] Ile de Man[1]
...	...	...	...	...	...	...	...	...	...	
...	...	...	...	...	...	...	...	...	...	
...	...	...	...	...	...	...	...	...	...	
1.0	2.0	3.3	1.6	1.7	0.9	0.7	2.0	^0.0	...	
1.0	0.9	4.1	1.4	1.1	1.8	2.5	1.5	0.1	...	

Country or area Pays ou zone	Year Année	Sex Sexe	Total employment Emploi total	ISIC Rev. 3 Tabulation categories + / CITI Rév. 3 Catégories de classement + Categ. A Catég. A	Categ. B Catég. B	Categ. C Catég. C	Categ. D Catég. D	Categ. E Catég. E	Categ. F Catég. F	Categ. Catég.
Israel[1,10] Israël[1,10]	2003	M	1 257.6	34.7	...	273.9	...	15.1	119.3	185.
	2003	F	1 072.6	8.7	...	103.5	...	3.2	10.6	130
	2004	M	1 300.3	39.8	...	277.9	...	15.4	117.9	195
	2004	F	1 100.5	9.2	...	108.6	...	3.9	10.8	129
	2005	M	1 339.9	40.9	...	282.6	...	16.8	117.3	197.
	2005	F	1 153.7	9.1	...	109.0	...	4.5	9.8	140
Italy[1] Italie[1]	2002	M	13 685.0	710.0	36.0	51.0	3 453.0	139.0	1 634.0	2 119
	2002	F	8 236.0	347.0	2.0	12.0	1 509.0	20.0	113.0	1 336
	2003	M	13 769.0	710.0	34.0	51.0	3 475.0	138.0	1 694.0	2 136
	2003	F	8 365.0	328.0	3.0	8.0	1 515.0	22.0	115.0	1 395.
	2005[36]	M	13 795.9	628.2	30.7	35.7	3 417.7	141.3	1 805.7	2 061.
	2005[36]	F	8 825.0	285.9	2.5	4.4	1 406.8	21.6	106.8	1 355.
Japan[1] Japon[1]	2003	M	37 190.0	1 470.0	200.0	40.0	8 040.0	270.0	5 150.0	6 220
	2003	F	25 970.0	1 190.0	70.0	10.0	4 040.0	50.0	890.0	5 760
	2004	M	37 130.0	1 480.0	160.0	30.0	7 900.0	270.0	4 980.0	6 150
	2004	F	26 160.0	1 170.0	50.0	10.0	3 870.0	40.0	860.0	5 750.
	2005	M	37 230.0	1 460.0	170.0	30.0	7 920.0	310.0	4 870.0	6 090.
	2005	F	26 330.0	1 130.0	60.0	10.0	3 770.0	40.0	810.0	5 770.
Kazakhstan[1] Kazakhstan[1]	2002	M	3 486.4	1 250.9	12.1	131.0	322.9	107.3	218.4	415
	2002	F	3 222.5	1 115.8	1.4	36.3	180.8	45.7	50.0	591
	2003	M	3 618.3	1 302.9	14.6	141.4	316.3	121.8	262.5	409
	2003	F	3 366.9	1 144.0	1.2	40.3	190.0	45.3	66.9	605.
	2004	M	3 718.5	1 283.1	15.8	146.1	330.8	110.1	302.7	422.
	2004	F	3 463.3	1 104.8	2.3	39.9	189.0	53.7	78.0	636.
Korea, Republic of[1,10] Corée, République de[1,10]	2003	M	13 031.0	976.0	50.0	16.0	2 730.0	64.0	1 668.0	2 039
	2003	F	9 108.0	901.0	23.0	1.0	1 475.0	12.0	148.0	1 832
	2004	M	13 193.0	911.0	48.0	15.0	2 797.0	59.0	1 658.0	2 010
	2004	F	9 364.0	838.0	28.0	1.0	1 493.0	13.0	162.0	1 795.
	2005	M	13 330.1	920.3	45.1	15.9	2 820.7	58.3	1 656.4	1 993.
	2005	F	9 526.0	826.7	23.4	1.2	1 413.4	12.8	158.0	1 754.
Kyrgyzstan[1,29] Kirghizistan[1,29]	2002	M	1 051.4	518.0	1.5	7.1	76.3	23.2	56.1	119.
	2002	F	798.7	388.4	0.3	0.7	48.4	6.1	4.2	100
	2003	M	1 083.8	470.0	0.3	11.1	72.9	27.3	94.5	132
	2003	F	846.7	364.1	0.3	1.4	67.2	7.7	7.7	125
	2004	M	1 140.7	445.4	0.2	12.1	79.0	30.0	136.1	144
	2004	F	850.5	328.5	0.5	1.4	74.4	9.1	7.9	137.
Latvia[11,33] Lettonie[11,33]	2003	M	516.6	86.3	...	...	99.3	16.6	65.6	57
	2003	F	490.2	48.7	...	...	74.3	4.9	8.8	94
	2004	M	521.8	83.3	...	...	89.9	18.3	77.2	56
	2004	F	495.9	49.2	...	...	73.6	7.2	9.6	94
	2005	M	534.1	81.5	...	...	88.0	16.4	82.2	59
	2005	F	501.8	40.8	...	...	66.1	6.7	8.3	97
Lithuania[1,11] Lituanie[1,11]	2003	M	726.2	152.4	1.4	3.9	129.8	20.5	96.2	103
	2003	F	711.8	103.1	0.1	1.2	134.7	7.3	10.9	111
	2004	M	733.8	131.6	1.8	3.2	129.7	23.1	106.2	112
	2004	F	702.5	94.0	0.2	1.2	125.2	6.4	9.9	116
	2005	M	750.9	122.6	2.2	2.3	134.6	20.8	120.5	111
	2005	F	723.0	81.6	0.6	0.9	131.8	5.7	12.0	122
Luxembourg[41] Luxembourg[41]	2003	MF	291.8	3.9	...	0.3	32.5	1.6	28.5	40
	2004	MF	298.4	3.8	...	0.3	32.4	1.6	29.1	41
	2005	MF	307.1	3.8	...	...	...	...	30.1	.
Madagascar[10,11,42] Madagascar[10,11,42]	2003	M	4 135.7	3 110.1	61.8	4.5	227.0	18.1	54.6	167
	2003	F	3 962.8	3 118.4	25.8	9.7	222.3	0.5	6.0	252

ISIC Rev. 3 Tabulation categories + CITI Rév. 3 Catégories de classement +										
Categ. H Catég. H	Categ. I Catég. I	Categ. J Catég. J	Categ. K Catég. K	Categ. L Catég.L	Categ. M Catég. M	Categ. N Catég. N	Categ. O Catég. O	Categ. P Catég. P	Categ. Q Catég. Q	Country or area Pays ou zone
53.5	108.7	31.9	173.0	67.3	70.5	58.8	53.8	3.5	1.1	Israel[1,10]
40.0	41.3	46.1	128.3	53.0	224.5	191.5	57.6	29.9	0.7	Israël[1,10]
59.1	109.0	30.4	190.4	62.6	70.9	60.5	55.5	2.7	1.3	
44.3	45.1	48.7	129.7	48.9	232.5	194.7	54.0	35.7	0.7	
69.5	115.9	34.3	196.4	64.6	70.1	59.1	60.9	2.4	1.3	
45.6	46.7	47.8	138.9	51.3	244.0	206.5	55.9	38.0	0.7	
480.0	919.0	410.0	942.0	1 316.0	424.0	516.0	490.0	37.0	9.0	Italy[1]
427.0	248.0	254.0	733.0	666.0	1 107.0	812.0	480.0	162.0	7.0	Italie[1]
500.0	908.0	413.0	973.0	1 281.0	410.0	502.0	494.0	39.0	10.0	
453.0	255.0	251.0	755.0	654.0	1 122.0	829.0	490.0	163.0	7.0	
533.4	959.9	379.1	1 299.0	1 025.3	394.4	528.9	503.6	40.9	11.1	
526.3	279.3	261.1	1 077.2	472.3	1 146.6	1 020.5	589.2	262.6	6.4	
1 420.0	3 250.0	810.0	3 960.0	1 790.0	1 320.0	1 160.0	1 740.0	...	...	Japan[1]
2 090.0	720.0	800.0	2 490.0	470.0	1 480.0	3 860.0	1 790.0	...	...	Japon[1]
1 400.0	3 200.0	780.0	4 210.0	1 850.0	1 330.0	1 230.0	1 760.0	...	...	
2 070.0	740.0	810.0	2 670.0	480.0	1 510.0	4 080.0	1 780.0	...	...	
1 410.0	3 080.0	790.0	4 490.0	1 800.0	1 290.0	1 300.0	1 770.0	...	...	
2 020.0	750.0	790.0	2 800.0	490.0	1 570.0	4 240.0	1 780.0	...	...	
15.9	364.2	19.5	131.4	158.7	160.1	61.8	90.0	26.5	0.3	Kazakhstan[1]
40.6	139.5	30.6	72.0	121.7	428.9	230.8	96.3	40.3	...	Kazakhstan[1]
18.4	384.2	18.9	113.9	189.0	163.2	59.9	89.5	11.8	0.1	
51.7	119.7	34.6	93.2	129.2	467.9	239.9	106.9	30.7	0.2	
22.2	389.9	24.0	120.4	192.2	179.1	65.1	94.4	20.4	...	
59.8	129.8	36.7	113.2	142.5	487.1	253.6	106.9	29.0	0.5	
632.0	1 167.0	366.0	1 200.0	568.0	528.0	154.0	853.0	4.0	16.0	Korea, Republic of[1,10]
1 349.0	167.0	385.0	527.0	188.0	956.0	385.0	566.0	188.0	7.0	Corée, République de[1,10]
636.0	1 193.0	364.0	1 324.0	554.0	515.0	174.0	914.0	4.0	18.0	
1 421.0	183.0	374.0	590.0	213.0	991.0	419.0	713.0	121.0	7.0	
638.6	1 227.8	369.5	1 360.5	552.2	522.1	171.1	956.0	4.1	17.7	
1 419.3	200.8	376.2	676.9	238.8	1 045.9	475.9	770.6	125.7	6.4	
11.2	75.0	3.9	18.9	62.0	37.7	19.9	20.5	1.0	...	Kyrgyzstan[1,29]
14.2	15.5	3.9	11.0	20.2	106.7	58.1	16.3	4.3[20]	0.1	Kirghizistan[1,29]
11.3	82.2	4.7	17.6	70.4	46.1	18.3	18.4	6.2	0.3	
22.8	15.3	5.3	10.8	20.8	110.3	62.6	20.1	4.0	0.5	
14.2	95.8	3.7	25.1	64.2	44.2	19.9	20.4	6.2	0.1	
30.2	17.1	4.8	13.4	27.6	117.6	54.0	21.2	4.8	0.3	
4.9	65.5	6.1	25.1	35.3	15.0	8.0	24.6	...	...	Latvia[11,33]
19.7	29.0	9.6	16.9	32.0	63.7	51.1	32.3	...	...	Lettonie[11,33]
7.5	68.7	8.4	21.3	39.8	14.2	7.3	25.0	...	...	
18.1	27.2	10.0	18.9	33.3	68.7	47.1	34.8	...	...	
7.3	66.0	7.6	24.9	44.7	17.3	8.8	25.3	...	...	
20.4	28.5	12.5	24.3	37.1	73.2	49.1	32.3	...	...	
5.5	69.8	5.9	26.8	45.1	27.9	14.2	21.1	2.7	...	Lithuania[1,11]
23.9	22.4	10.9	26.7	29.8	106.9	84.6	33.5	4.0	...	Lituanie[1,11]
6.4	70.2	4.6	30.5	45.3	30.7	15.9	19.5	3.0	0.1	
26.3	23.7	10.4	25.4	32.6	110.3	82.5	36.3	2.1	0.1	
7.1	68.5	4.4	34.2	45.1	35.3	17.2	21.6	3.0	0.2	
26.0	25.4	11.9	28.1	36.6	112.7	81.3	42.1	4.1	...	
13.5	22.5	32.7	49.1	15.4	13.6	20.4	9.9	7.0	...	Luxembourg[41]
13.8	22.5	32.8	51.0	16.2	14.0	21.6	10.2	7.5	...	Luxembourg[41]
...	...	...	...	...	...	...	...	...	...	
21.0	108.1	4.4	...	144.3	33.1	8.8	172.3	...	...	Madagascar[10,11,42]
26.7	9.1	1.3	...	61.3	33.1	5.6	190.2	...	...	Madagascar[10,11,42]

Country or area Pays ou zone	Year Année	Sex Sexe	Total employment Emploi total	ISIC Rev. 3 Tabulation categories + / CITI Rév. 3 Catégories de classement + Categ. A Catég. A	Categ. B Catég. B	Categ. C Catég. C	Categ. D Catég. D	Categ. E Catég. E	Categ. F Catég. F	Categ. G Catég. G
Malaysia[10,30] Malaisie[10,30]	2001	M	6 055.9	895.1	123.6	22.9	1 276.3	49.4	769.1	982.8
	2001	F	3 301.1	393.1	4.1	3.8	907.8	7.9	60.7	475.2
	2002	M	6 141.8	924.9	104.0	24.9	1 215.5	44.5	839.8	1 000.4
	2002	F	3 400.8	391.9	3.7	2.6	853.4	6.1	65.3	496.6
	2003	M	6 323.6	915.1	103.1	26.7	1 255.9	48.7	876.5	1 050.0
	2003	F	3 546.1	386.1	3.9	2.9	875.1	9.0	66.0	542.2
Maldives[11,17] Maldives[11,17]	1995	M	48.9	0.9	12.3	0.4	4.5	0.7	2.8	4.5
	1995	F	18.1	1.4	0.2	^0.0	7.6	0.1	^0.0	0.8
	2000	M	57.4[32]	1.1	9.2[32]	0.4	4.3[32]	1.0[32]	3.6[32]	4.8[32]
	2000	F	28.9[32]	1.4[32]	0.1	^0.0	6.8	0.1	0.1	1.0[32]
Mali[1] Mali[1]	2004	M	1 388.3	657.7	33.3	8.4	136.1	5.1	97.5	266.1
	2004	F	982.5	291.7	2.0	3.0	136.4	0.0	4.7	402.1
Malta[1,43] Malte[1,43]	2003	M	101.2	2.3	...	...	20.6	3.8	10.8	14.3
	2003	F	45.8	0.2	...	...	7.5	0.3	0.4	7.8
	2004	M	103.8	2.4	...	0.7	21.7	2.9	10.4	16.5
	2004	F	44.8	0.3	...	^0.0	7.4	0.3	0.3	5.7
	2005	M	102.8	2.3	0.5	...	21.3	2.5	12.0	14.3
	2005	F	46.0	...	0.3	...	7.3	0.3	0.3	6.5
Mauritius Maurice	2003	M	332.4	36.3	...	0.2	68.5	2.8	47.4	47.3
	2003	F	168.0	13.2	...	0.1	63.5	0.2	0.6	24.0
	2004	M	336.9	35.9	...	0.2	67.7	2.8	48.5	49.3
	2004	F	167.6	13.1	...	0.1	57.5	0.2	0.6	25.5
	2005	M	338.2	34.7	...	0.2	65.7	2.8	49.0	49.5
	2005	F	168.8	14.3	...	0.1	52.5	0.2	0.7	25.5
Mexico[15,37] Mexique[15,37]	2003	M	25 923.4	5 608.9	160.7	120.3	4 299.6	183.8	2 588.6	5 635.8
	2003	F	13 576.5	710.3	14.6	13.7	2 557.6	33.3	54.8	3 604.9
	2004	M	26 418.3	5 628.0	145.3	149.5	4 504.1	199.0	2 503.2	5 800.7
	2004	F	14 557.2	823.9	9.0	16.8	2 681.6	39.9	85.5	3 987.8
	2005	M	26 213.2	5 339.7	149.5	170.5	4 291.0	159.8	3 144.3	5 328.8
	2005	F	15 107.6	744.2	16.4	24.7	2 710.1	28.2	111.3	4 116.1
Mongolia[43,44] Mongolie[43,44]	2003	M	468.8	205.3	...	21.9	24.7	14.3	20.2	60.0
	2003	F	457.7	182.2	...	10.0	30.2	8.4	14.9	69.7
	2004	M	467.1	200.2	...	23.3	26.6	14.6	22.3	53.7
	2004	F	483.4	181.6	...	10.2	30.7	8.8	16.9	80.0
	2005	M	479.4	206.3	...	26.1	21.9	15.9	26.5	59.3
	2005	F	488.9	179.9	...	13.7	23.7	12.6	22.4	82.5
Morocco[1] Maroc[1]	2003	M	7 074.8	2 775.1	...	52.4	732.7	36.1	644.2	1 132.1
	2003	F	2 528.0	1 436.9	...	2.1	459.7	2.8	6.3	96.4
	2004	M	7 155.0	2 887.3	...	39.4	740.5	27.9	656.8	1 519.5
	2004	F	2 666.9	1 610.3	...	1.2	437.5	3.3	5.2	136.3
	2005	M	7 240.7	2 864.4	...	41.1	739.5	29.0	699.4	1 476.7
	2005	F	2 672.6	1 640.8	...	0.7	414.4	2.8	6.0	137.4
Namibia[45] Namibie[45]	2000	M	226.8	69.8	4.7	3.2	11.4	3.7	20.7	17.2
	2000	F	205.0	56.7	3.1	0.7	11.5	0.5	1.0	21.7
Nepal[1] Népal[1]	1999	M	4 736.0	3 164.0	12.0	6.0	366.0	24.0	292.0	283.0
	1999	F	4 727.0	4 026.0	1.0	2.0	186.0	2.0	52.0	125.0
Netherlands[1] Pays-Bas[1]	2003	M	4 370.0	...	...	7.0	792.0	28.0	424.0	666.0
	2003	F	3 460.0	...	...	1.0	243.0	4.0	36.0	566.0
	2004	M	4 305.0	...	...	7.0	810.0	33.0	423.0	571.0
	2004	F	3 477.0	...	...	1.0	241.0	9.0	39.0	537.0
	2005	M	4 270.0	...	...	6.0	787.0	32.0	439.0	590.0
	2005	F	3 514.0	...	...	2.0	235.0	12.0	44.0	544.0

Employment by economic activity—Total employment and persons employed by ISIC Rev. 3 categories (thousands) (*continued*)
Emploi par activité économique—Emploi total et personnes employées par branches de CITI Rév. 3 (milliers) (*suite*)

ISIC Rev. 3 Tabulation categories + CITI Rév. 3 Catégories de classement +										
Categ. H Catég. H	Categ. I Catég. I	Categ. J Catég. J	Categ. K Catég. K	Categ. L Catég.L	Categ. M Catég. M	Categ. N Catég. N	Categ. O Catég. O	Categ. P Catég. P	Categ. Q Catég. Q	Country or area Pays ou zone
312.1	403.0	119.2	212.3	505.7	201.7	54.7	113.6	13.9	0.6	Malaysia[10,30]
273.0	65.2	106.2	136.7	158.9	306.9	118.6	76.8	206.0	0.5	Malaisie[10,30]
317.9	427.6	122.6	239.7	487.1	198.5	63.3	113.9	16.2	1.1	
298.2	69.2	117.8	157.4	176.5	310.2	126.0	78.6	246.5	0.9	
339.5	410.3	118.7	249.4	491.1	229.8	69.3	120.9	16.5	2.2	
304.7	71.3	104.7	154.8	175.4	364.5	148.0	95.2	241.6	1.0	
6.9	5.8	1.4	...	7.2	...	...	...	...	...	Maldives[11,17]
0.3	0.6	0.7	...	5.7	...	...	...	...	...	Maldives[11,17]
9.2[32]	7.2[32]	1.1[32]	...	9.7[32]	...	...	...	...	...	
0.5[32]	0.7[32]	0.6[32]	...	8.4	...	...	...	...	...	
1.4	51.8	4.4	3.5	33.3	35.6	11.4	23.8	18.8	...	Mali[1]
6.3	3.5	0.0	0.6	6.6	18.3	9.5	11.5	85.1	0.9	Mali[1]
7.4	8.7	2.7	5.2	9.9	4.1	5.1	4.8	...	...	Malta[1,43]
4.4	2.6	2.6	2.1	3.3	6.8	5.4	1.7	...	...	Malte[1,43]
7.8	8.8	2.6	5.5	10.5	4.5	5.5	3.4	...	...	
4.5	2.4	1.8	2.4	3.6	8.0	5.6	2.1	...	...	
7.8	9.0	3.0	5.5	10.0	4.3	5.0	3.3	...	...	
4.5	2.5	3.0	2.0	2.8	7.0	6.3	3.3	...	...	
19.6	31.0	4.5	11.7	30.8	11.9	7.3	13.1	...	...	Mauritius
7.8	3.9	3.3	4.9	8.4	13.2	6.7	18.2	...	...	Maurice
20.4	31.7	4.5	12.3	30.6	12.1	7.5	13.4	...	...	
8.0	4.2	3.4	5.8	8.4	14.1	7.0	19.7	...	...	
21.9	31.8	4.8	13.8	30.7	12.2	7.5	13.6	...	...	
9.0	4.2	4.0	5.8	8.7	15.5	8.7	19.6	...	...	
952.9	1 686.7	158.0	882.4	1 243.6	832.3	397.6	821.5	241.0	0.0	Mexico[15,37]
1 180.3	152.3	127.2	440.4	581.1	1 207.2	722.4	545.5	1 599.1	0.0	Mexique[15,37]
1 001.4	1 682.1	163.1	974.9	1 206.5	896.3	402.9	828.3	206.5	0.8	
1 292.0	165.8	122.2	474.2	601.5	1 285.7	814.9	552.0	1 568.8	2.0	
1 048.6	1 704.7	158.7	1 186.5	1 231.8	854.8	382.6	737.9	170.0	2.3	
1 401.8	167.1	149.6	652.7	664.9	1 340.1	762.1	584.8	1 574.5	1.4	
8.1	22.6	5.4	5.3	27.0	20.3	12.0	18.5	3.2	...	Mongolia[43,44]
15.2	16.9	7.2	4.0	17.8	35.0	24.8	18.5	2.9	...	Mongolie[43,44]
10.0	24.8	6.2	5.4	26.1	20.3	13.6	16.9	3.1	...	
18.4	17.6	9.7	5.8	20.1	37.5	25.8	17.6	2.9	...	
10.3	26.0	6.3	4.3	26.1	20.4	12.6	13.7	3.7	...	
19.2	16.4	9.8	4.7	20.6	38.4	26.9	13.0	5.0	...	
151.1	321.1	81.5	...	397.7	745.2	...	...	...	...	Morocco[1]
30.7	21.6	41.9	...	88.0	339.8	...	...	...	...	Maroc[1]
...	323.9	77.5	...	919.1	...	...	...	...	...	
...	23.5	38.5	...	409.8	...	...	...	...	...	
...	350.1	91.2	...	902.1	...	...	...	...	...	
...	30.2	39.1	...	399.3	...	...	...	...	...	
3.0	12.2	2.5	17.9	15.4	11.7	3.0	24.3	4.8	0.2	Namibia[45]
4.7	2.1	2.4	21.4	9.0	18.8	10.1	22.0	17.5	0.2	Namibie[45]
63.0	130.0	17.0	25.0	64.0	126.0	26.0	51.0	80.0	6.0	Nepal[1]
52.0	6.0	2.0	6.0	6.0	37.0	7.0	6.0	209.0	1.0	Népal[1]
140.0	336.0	152.0	595.0	339.0	214.0	222.0	160.0	...	...	Netherlands[1]
157.0	128.0	121.0	401.0	197.0	296.0	952.0	197.0	3.0	...	Pays-Bas[1]
146.0	363.0	145.0	531.0	341.0	201.0	211.0	137.0	...	...	
165.0	123.0	112.0	364.0	205.0	311.0	939.0	169.0	3.0	...	
150.0	350.0	140.0	545.0	330.0	203.0	227.0	128.0	...	...	
157.0	135.0	120.0	367.0	208.0	315.0	980.0	179.0	3.0	...	

26 Employment by economic activity—Total employment and persons employed by ISIC Rev. 3 categories (thousands) (*continued*)
Emploi par activité économique—Emploi total et personnes employées par branches de CITI Rév. 3 (milliers) (*suite*)

Country or area / Pays ou zone	Year / Année	Sex / Sexe	Total employment / Emploi total	ISIC Rev. 3 Tabulation categories + / CITI Rév. 3 Catégories de classement + Categ. A / Catég. A	Categ. B / Catég. B	Categ. C / Catég. C	Categ. D / Catég. D	Categ. E / Catég. E	Categ. F / Catég. F	Categ. G / Catég. G
Netherlands Antilles[1,46]	1997	M	30.5	0.5	...	^0.0	4.3	0.8	4.3	5.3
Antilles néerlandaises[1,46]	1997	F	25.8	0.1	...	^0.0	1.0	0.1	0.3	5.4
	1998	M	29.5	0.5	...	^0.0	4.0	0.8	3.9	5.1
	1998	F	24.7	^0.0	...	^0.0	0.9	0.1	0.3	5.1
	2000	M	27.3[47]	0.5[47]	...	0.1	3.6[47]	0.8[47]	3.4[47]	4.7[47]
	2000	F	24.9[47]	^0.0	...	^0.0	1.0[47]	0.1	0.3	5.2[47]
New Caledonia[15]	1996	M	39.6	3.6	...	1.8	4.1	0.6	6.4	5.0
Nouvelle-Calédonie[15]	1996	F	24.8	1.0	...	0.1	1.4	0.1	0.5	3.4
New Zealand[1,10]	2003	M	1 045.1[48]	105.8[48]	3.3[48]	2.7[48]	199.5[48]	6.4[48]	123.6[48]	187.4[48]
Nouvelle-Zélande[1,10]	2003	F	875.9	47.0[48]	0.6[48]	0.5[48]	79.2[48]	2.1[48]	15.0[48]	160.3[48]
	2004	M	1 094.8	100.9	2.7	3.6	207.2	7.3	135.7	196.8
	2004	F	922.3	47.6	0.5	0.3	84.9	2.2	16.6	162.4
	2005	M	1 118.4	97.9	2.1	3.5	203.8	5.7	143.4	195.6
	2005	F	954.5	47.3	0.6	0.5	78.7	2.4	18.2	167.6
Norway[39]	2003	M	1 198.0	48.0	15.0	27.0	206.0	14.0	146.0	177.0
Norvège[39]	2003	F	1 071.0	19.0	1.0	6.0	71.0	3.0	13.0	160.0
	2004	M	1 201.0	46.0	15.0	27.0	195.0	12.0	149.0	181.0
	2004	F	1 074.0	17.0	1.0	6.0	68.0	4.0	11.0	164.0
	2005	M	1 211.0	45.0	13.0	29.0	198.0	13.0	149.0	184.0
	2005	F	1 078.0	16.0	1.0	7.0	67.0	3.0	10.0	166.0
Occupied Palestinian Terr.[1]	2002	M	398.8	47.1	0.3	1.6	53.5	0.9	51.9	81.3
Terr. palestinien occupé[1]	2002	F	77.9	23.3	...	...	6.3	0.1	0.2	5.5
	2003	M	467.4	55.4	0.3	1.3	62.0	1.0	74.0	96.4
	2003	F	97.2	32.7	...	...	7.4	0.1	0.1	7.7
	2004	M	473.8	56.4	0.3	1.7	63.1	2.0	67.3	94.9
	2004	F	104.7	35.3	...	...	8.4	^0.0	0.2	7.4
Oman[1,10,49]	1993	M	232.5[50]	13.9[50]	8.6[50]	8.0[50]	3.6[50]	1.0[50]	4.7[50]	11.3[5]
Oman[1,10,49]	1993	F	18.9[50]	0.9[50]	^0.0	0.4	1.0[50]	^0.0	0.1	0.6[5]
	1996	M	226.8	9.3	7.8	7.4	3.5	0.3	6.3	13.5
	1996	F	25.4	1.2	0.1	0.2	1.3	^0.0	0.2	1.7
	2000	M	243.1	8.9	7.2	7.8	9.4	1.1	7.8	14.2
	2000	F	38.6	2.0	^0.0	0.7	4.5	^0.0	0.2	2.4
Panama[1,51]	2003	M	703.3	165.9	9.0	1.0	68.4	7.6	76.6	119.1
Panama[1,51]	2003	F	377.2	13.3	0.7	^0.0	28.2	1.2	3.1	75.2
	2004	M	734.3	161.0	8.8	0.7	67.7	7.5	88.8	130.2
	2004	F	400.4	11.3	0.7	...	32.7	0.9	1.8	77.1
	2005	M	755.7	158.5	9.1	1.0	69.4	6.5	87.8	138.3
	2005	F	432.6	18.3	0.5	^0.0	34.9	1.3	3.3	88.6
Peru[11,15,52]	2003[5]	M	1 899.0	13.7	7.2	4.4	307.6	16.1	201.9	442.0
Pérou[11,15,52]	2003	F	1 462.4[5]	3.7[5]	...	1.6[5]	157.7[5]	0.3	2.6[5]	498.1
	2004[19]	M	1 997.5	17.2	4.7	4.7	379.3	9.0	196.0	486.4
	2004	F	1 369.4[19]	5.1[19]	...	0.9[19]	150.4[19]	0.4	2.0[19]	490.6
	2005[6]	M	1 965.9	18.4	3.7	8.7	430.5	3.4	173.5	462.8
	2005	F	1 434.4[6]	2.4[6]	...	...	188.7[6]	0.2	3.7[6]	476.5
Philippines[1,10,46]	2003	M	19 498.0	7 423.0	1 295.0	95.0	1 674.0	92.0	1 655.0	2 245.0
Philippines[1,10,46]	2003	F	12 055.0	2 917.0	105.0	6.0	1 371.0	21.0	33.0	3 417.0
	2004	M	19 836.0	7 572.0	1 279.0	87.0	1 684.0	96.0	1 616.0	2 319.0
	2004	F	11 905.0	2 849.0	86.0	9.0	1 335.0	25.0	27.0	3 469.0
	2005	M	20 205.0	7 720.0	1 304.0	100.0	1 640.0	87.0	1 581.0	2 507.0
	2005	F	12 670.0	3 044.0	103.0	17.0	1 403.0	22.0	35.0	3 708.0

Employment by economic activity—Total employment and persons employed by ISIC Rev. 3 categories (thousands) (*continued*)

Emploi par activité économique—Emploi total et personnes employées par branches de CITI Rév. 3 (milliers) (*suite*)

ISIC Rev. 3 Tabulation categories + CITI Rév. 3 Catégories de classement +										
Categ. H Catég. H	Categ. I Catég. I	Categ. J Catég. J	Categ. K Catég. K	Categ. L Catég. L	Categ. M Catég. M	Categ. N Catég. N	Categ. O Catég. O	Categ. P Catég. P	Categ. Q Catég. Q	Country or area Pays ou zone
1.6	2.9	1.4	2.4	3.6	0.9	0.9	1.3	0.1	0.1	Netherlands Antilles[1,46]
2.4	1.3	2.3	1.4	2.2	1.9	3.4	2.0	2.0	0.1	Antilles néerlandaises[1,46]
1.7	2.7	1.4	2.5	3.4	1.0	0.9	1.4	0.1	0.1	
2.1	1.4	2.3	1.5	2.0	1.9	3.4	1.9	1.7	0.1	
1.7[47]	2.5[47]	1.3[47]	2.4[47]	3.0[47]	1.0[47]	0.8[47]	1.3[47]	0.1	0.1	
1.9[47]	1.5[47]	2.2[47]	1.6[47]	1.9[47]	1.9[47]	3.5[47]	2.0[47]	1.7[47]	0.1	
1.2	2.7	0.6	2.1	6.3	2.8	1.1	0.5	0.3	0.5	New Caledonia[15]
1.7	1.0	0.9	1.2	3.3	3.8	2.3	0.4	3.1	0.4	Nouvelle-Calédonie[15]
35.9[48]	77.7[48]	23.5[48]	108.8[48]	55.1[48]	44.7[48]	28.5[48]	40.1[48]	0.3	...	New Zealand[1,10]
58.9	33.3[48]	30.6[48]	88.1[48]	55.5[48]	106.6[48]	144.9[48]	49.8[48]	2.3[48]	...	Nouvelle-Zélande[1,10]
33.6	82.6	25.4	122.3	55.6	45.5	32.8	40.6	0.2	...	
60.7	35.9	35.2	95.8	58.6	115.5	147.5	54.3	2.4	...	
36.5	82.6	28.6	130.7	63.3	47.5	31.1	42.9	0.2	...	
63.1	36.2	37.2	104.2	63.5	115.6	156.0	58.8	2.3	...	
25.0	109.0	24.0	138.0	83.0	66.0	76.0	43.0	...	...	Norway[39]
45.0	40.0	23.0	86.0	66.0	120.0	364.0	49.0	2.0	...	Norvège[39]
28.0	109.0	25.0	140.0	80.0	68.0	80.0	43.0	...	...	
42.0	40.0	23.0	83.0	64.0	127.0	369.0	53.0	2.0	...	
27.0	113.0	26.0	146.0	77.0	65.0	83.0	41.0	0.0	...	
44.0	39.0	24.0	84.0	62.0	125.0	375.0	54.0	2.0	...	
8.7	26.2	3.3	6.8	61.2	27.4	12.8	11.3	0.1	3.7	Occupied Palestinian Terr.[1]
0.1	0.3	1.1	1.2	5.3	24.0	7.3	1.8	0.3	1.1	Terr. palestinien occupé[1]
9.1	32.1	3.1	7.3	62.6	30.6	14.4	12.5	0.1	4.9	
0.3	0.5	0.8	1.7	5.4	27.7	7.7	3.6	0.3	1.2	
10.4	30.6	3.4	7.3	72.0	31.6	15.2	12.0	0.1	5.5	
0.2	0.7	1.1	2.1	6.1	29.3	8.6	3.4	0.2	1.8	
0.9[50]	11.3[50]	3.6[50]	1.0[50]	135.7[50]	10.9[50]	4.8[50]	9.1[50]	0.2	0.2	Oman[1,10,49]
0.1	0.4	1.4[50]	0.1	4.1[50]	7.0[50]	2.3[50]	0.2	^0.0	^0.0	Oman[1,10,49]
0.6	14.6	4.9	2.7	141.3	9.6	3.3	0.9	^0.0	0.1	
0.2	0.3	1.9	0.7	6.6	8.3	2.4	0.1	...	^0.0	
2.3	19.5	4.7	1.9	133.6	17.8	5.2	1.2	^0.0	^0.0	
0.2	0.8	1.4	1.1	3.3	16.0	5.4	0.2	...	0.1	
24.2	75.4	8.4	28.5	43.0	19.3	14.7	35.0	7.0	0.5	Panama[1,51]
29.1	10.5	13.2	16.1	30.8	44.9	23.2	30.3	56.9	0.5	Panama[1,51]
26.7	76.4	9.1	32.1	42.8	21.9	14.9	37.1	8.0	0.7	
34.5	13.0	15.9	22.0	30.9	44.8	28.3	25.1	61.3	0.1	
28.5	79.5	9.5	39.0	40.3	21.8	15.2	42.1	9.0	0.1	
41.1	11.7	14.8	22.7	29.0	43.1	32.4	29.5	61.0	0.4	
74.5	322.1	23.4	155.3	90.8	97.3	31.1	101.2	9.3	...	Peru[11,15,52]
145.9[5]	26.3[5]	22.7[5]	61.7[5]	38.0[5]	161.6[5]	60.3[5]	101.5[5]	180.4[5]	...	Pérou[11,15,52]
77.6	321.1	17.9	127.6	127.2	86.7	25.4	109.2	7.1	...	
135.4[19]	23.2[19]	15.3[19]	52.5[19]	43.8[19]	117.1[19]	60.5[19]	95.3[19]	177.0[19]	...	
68.1	303.2	21.9	167.3	106.8	83.8	33.1	73.9	6.7	...	
150.0[6]	33.7[6]	20.1[6]	75.8[6]	48.8[6]	139.5[6]	62.8[6]	83.1[6]	149.0[6]	...	
345.0	2 243.0	146.0	493.0	875.0	220.0	87.0	414.0	195.0	1.0	Philippines[1,10,46]
448.0	109.0	183.0	223.0	507.0	695.0	283.0	437.0	1 300.0	1.0	Philippines[1,10,46]
361.0	2 319.0	132.0	481.0	907.0	241.0	99.0	423.0	220.0	1.0	
437.0	126.0	166.0	221.0	543.0	717.0	262.0	386.0	1 245.0	...	
396.0	2 334.0	140.0	495.0	933.0	251.0	102.0	384.0	230.0	2.0	
475.0	136.0	197.0	241.0	562.0	739.0	260.0	397.0	1 332.0	1.0	

Employment by economic activity—Total employment and persons employed by ISIC Rev. 3 categories (thousands) (*continued*)
Emploi par activité économique—Emploi total et personnes employées par branches de CITI Rév. 3 (milliers) (*suite*)

Country or area Pays ou zone	Year Année	Sex Sexe	Total employment Emploi total	ISIC Rev. 3 Tabulation categories + CITI Rév. 3 Catégories de classement + Categ. A Catég. A	Categ. B Catég. B	Categ. C Catég. C	Categ. D Catég. D	Categ. E Catég. E	Categ. F Catég. F	Categ. G Catég. G
Poland[1,53] Pologne[1,53]	2003	M	7 432.0	1 413.0	9.0	219.0	1 670.0	202.0	736.0	936.0
	2003	F	6 185.0	1 085.0	2.0	28.0	923.0	48.0	67.0	1 026.0
	2004	M	7 566.0	1 400.0	10.0	199.0	1 795.0	179.0	735.0	950.0
	2004	F	6 230.0	1 072.0	2.0	28.0	945.0	43.0	54.0	1 047.0
	2005	M	7 809.0	1 391.0	11.0	201.0	1 882.0	181.0	784.0	961.0
	2005	F	6 307.0	1 048.0	...	25.0	949.0	47.0	59.0	1 059.0
Portugal[1] Portugal[1]	2003	M	2 796.8	311.4	17.4	12.8	574.1	30.6	557.3	437.6
	2003	F	2 330.9	312.2	1.1[54]	1.5[54]	444.7	5.5	26.3	337.2
	2004	M	2 788.8	302.1	18.8	13.3	574.7	26.3	521.9	437.6
	2004	F	2 338.6	294.6	2.6[54]	1.3[54]	427.5	4.9	26.2	344.4
	2005	M	2 765.4	285.4	16.5	17.9	561.5	20.4	528.7	435.0
	2005	F	2 357.2	302.2	2.2[54]	1.2[54]	407.1	4.4	25.3	337.9
Qatar[1,55] Qatar[1,55]	1997	M	242.4	9.0	1.3	9.0	24.0	3.2	55.9	30.1
	1997	F	37.7	^0.0	...	0.4	0.1	^0.0	0.2	0.6
	2004	M	373.1	10.2	1.8	16.9	39.7	4.2	116.6	52.3
	2004	F	64.5	^0.0	^0.0	1.1	0.4	0.1	0.4	2.1
Republic of Moldova[1] République de Moldova[1]	2003	M	661.3	291.8	1.4	1.1	67.6	20.0	46.0	67.2
	2003	F	695.2	289.8	0.2	0.3	69.1	6.4	7.2	91.0
	2004	M	631.5	257.6	1.0	0.7	68.4	19.1	46.1	66.3
	2004	F	684.6	274.3	...	0.1	67.0	6.5	5.9	93.3
	2005	M	629.7	257.6	1.4	1.5	65.3	19.5	45.4	69.0
	2005	F	689.0	277.3	0.1	0.3	66.5	6.3	6.2	90.9
Romania[1] Roumanie[1]	2003	M	5 056.7	1 731.3	6.0	120.2	1 061.5	148.3	382.9	404.6
	2003	F	4 165.8	1 554.5	0.6	18.0	937.5	38.8	43.1	456.8
	2004	M	4 980.0	1 543.1	2.3	115.0	1 072.4	147.7	430.9	430.1
	2004	F	4 177.6	1 349.7	1.0	19.5	978.9	44.1	47.6	513.3
	2005	M	5 011.2	1 572.9	...	101.3	1 044.6	145.9	459.5	444.3
	2005	F	4 135.4	1 366.5	...	17.9	915.1	44.4	47.1	523.4
Russian Federation[56,57] Fédération de Russie[56,57]	2003	M	33 827.0	4 381.0	163.0	959.0	7 269.0	1 407.0	3 269.0	3 857.0
	2003	F	32 605.0	2 654.0	32.0	288.0	5 551.0	625.0	820.0	5 832.0
	2004	M	34 181.0	4 056.0	168.0	938.0	7 165.0	1 401.0	3 335.0	4 049.0
	2004	F	33 094.0	2 572.0	37.0	274.0	5 510.0	599.0	792.0	6 082.0
	2005	M	34 549.0	4 106.0	138.0	966.0	7 129.0	1 361.0	3 708.0	4 057.0
	2005	F	33 620.0	2 664.0	28.0	270.0	5 406.0	599.0	867.0	6 326.0
Saint Helena[25,45] Sainte-Hélène[25,45]	1998	M	1.1	0.2	^0.0	...	0.1	^0.0	0.3	0.1
	1998	F	0.9	^0.0	...	...	^0.0	^0.0	^0.0	0.2
Saint Lucia[1] Sainte-Lucie[1]	1998	M	32.3	8.3	0.8	...	2.5	0.6	4.1	4.1
	1998	F	24.1	4.0	^0.0	...	3.0	0.2	0.2	5.3
	1999	M	31.8	7.8	0.6	...	2.3	0.4	5.0	4.2
	1999	F	28.0	4.5	...	...	3.3	0.1	0.4	6.3
	2000	M	35.0	8.3	0.8	...	2.6	0.6	5.6	4.3
	2000	F	28.4	4.0	^0.0	...	3.6	0.1	0.4	7.0
San Marino[1,32] Saint-Marin[1,32]	2002	M	11.5	0.1	...	...	4.5	...	1.5	1.5
	2002	F	7.8	^0.0	...	...	1.7	...	0.1	1.[illegible]
	2003	M	11.5	0.1	...	...	4.5	...	1.6	1.5
	2003	F	7.9	^0.0	...	...	1.8	...	0.1	1.[illegible]
	2004	M	11.8	0.1	...	...	4.6	...	1.6	1.[illegible]
	2004	F	8.1	^0.0	...	...	1.8	...	0.1	1.[illegible]

Employment by economic activity—Total employment and persons employed by ISIC Rev. 3 categories (thousands) (*continued*)
Emploi par activité économique—Emploi total et personnes employées par branches de CITI Rév. 3 (milliers) (*suite*)

ISIC Rev. 3 Tabulation categories + CITI Rév. 3 Catégories de classement +										
Categ. H Catég. H	Categ. I Catég. I	Categ. J Catég. J	Categ. K Catég. K	Categ. L Catég.L	Categ. M Catég. M	Categ. N Catég. N	Categ. O Catég. O	Categ. P Catég. P	Categ. Q Catég. Q	Country or area Pays ou zone
72.0	612.0	84.0	417.0	433.0	232.0	170.0	226.0	1.0	...	Poland[1,53] Pologne[1,53]
157.0	211.0	197.0	276.0	420.0	846.0	668.0	223.0	7.0	...	
81.0	621.0	84.0	468.0	436.0	238.0	160.0	205.0	...	...	
155.0	211.0	187.0	331.0	429.0	822.0	664.0	231.0	15.0	...	
87.0	658.0	94.0	485.0	451.0	251.0	158.0	213.0	...	...	
161.0	205.0	200.0	337.0	442.0	852.0	662.0	246.0	11.0	...	
101.7	168.7	52.8	126.3	215.6	67.3	46.9	70.5	2.6	...	Portugal[1] Portugal[1]
157.8	45.0	34.1	135.8	123.5	219.3	245.3	85.4	155.5	...	
106.3	164.8	60.8	153.0	207.1	75.2	52.7	71.2	2.1	1.2[54]	
159.2	49.7	35.9	139.2	129.3	231.4	260.3	86.0	145.2	1.0[54]	
108.7	163.9	55.3	150.5	214.9	75.4	60.0	68.2	1.7	1.3[54]	
167.1	56.8	39.9	133.2	132.6	239.5	266.9	90.3	149.2	1.3[54]	
5.8	9.1	2.7	4.3	47.7	5.7	2.6	7.3	24.0	0.5	Qatar[1,55] Qatar[1,55]
0.2	0.5	0.4	0.3	2.2	8.2	2.9	0.3	21.1	0.1	
9.7	13.1	3.5	11.2	47.3	7.5	5.4	9.0	23.9	1.0	
0.6	2.2	1.3	0.7	6.2	12.4	6.2	1.2	29.4	0.2	
4.4	52.7	4.2	15.8	41.7	23.8	13.1	9.5	0.7	0.1	Republic of Moldova[1] République de Moldova[1]
13.1	15.1	6.2	10.0	23.9	85.7	55.7	17.4	3.7	0.4	
4.0	56.9	4.5	16.0	40.2	22.7	14.9	12.1	0.9	0.1	
15.1	16.5	9.1	12.9	23.9	85.2	53.8	18.2	2.4	0.3	
4.9	52.4	4.3	16.4	39.0	22.7	14.2	14.7	0.8	0.4	
18.1	18.6	9.1	12.2	22.6	85.6	55.2	17.4	2.5	0.1	
48.2	350.5	28.8	92.5	368.2	115.0	75.6	123.2	...	...	Romania[1] Roumanie[1]
71.2	110.9	54.1	57.4	161.7	291.0	274.7	95.6	...	...	
49.4	339.5	29.1	140.7	370.1	107.5	77.6	124.8	...	...	
98.5	114.6	57.1	90.9	168.1	295.3	284.1	114.9	...	...	
52.2	341.9	30.2	139.2	349.9	110.4	80.8	135.0	...	...	
98.6	108.0	55.3	92.5	170.2	302.4	272.8	120.5	...	...	
267.0	4 179.0	270.0	2 072.0	2 967.0	1 176.0	883.0	702.0	2.0	3.0	Russian Federation[56,57] Fédération de Russie[56,57]
999.0	1 793.0	541.0	1 719.0	1 709.0	4 842.0	3 793.0	1 396.0	9.0	2.0	
270.0	4 412.0	290.0	2 343.0	2 967.0	1 215.0	893.0	679.0	...	...	
953.0	1 849.0	628.0	1 776.0	1 734.0	4 926.0	3 941.0	1 421.0	...	1.0	
293.0	4 321.0	347.0	2 265.0	3 023.0	1 243.0	845.0	739.0	4.0	3.0	
1 004.0	1 928.0	615.0	1 774.0	1 792.0	4 960.0	3 856.0	1 507.0	22.0	1.0	
^0.0	0.1	^0.0	^0.0	0.1	^0.0	^0.0	^0.0	^0.0	^0.0	Saint Helena[25,45] Sainte-Hélène[25,45]
^0.0	0.1	^0.0	^0.0	0.2	0.1	0.1	0.1	^0.0	^0.0	
2.8	3.2	0.5	0.7	3.6	0.2	0.1	0.4	0.4	...	Saint Lucia[1] Sainte-Lucie[1]
2.5	0.9	0.8	0.5	4.3	0.4	0.3	0.7	1.2	...	
2.5	3.3	0.3	0.8	3.3	0.1	0.1	0.6	0.3	...	
3.2	0.9	0.8	0.8	4.5	0.6	0.3	0.9	1.4	...	
3.0	3.3	0.3	0.8	3.2	0.4	0.2	0.7	0.4	...	
3.5	0.8	0.7	0.5	4.3	0.8	0.4	0.8	1.1	...	
0.1	0.3	0.4	...	0.8	^0.0	0.3	2.1	...	...	San Marino[1,32] Saint-Marin[1,32]
0.2	0.2	0.3	...	1.4	^0.0	0.8	1.5	...	...	
...	0.3	0.4	...	0.8	^0.0	0.3	2.1	...	...	
...	0.2	0.3	...	1.4	^0.0	0.8	1.6	...	...	
...	0.3	0.4	...	0.7	^0.0	0.3	2.2	...	...	
...	0.2	0.3	...	1.4	^0.0	0.7	1.7	...	...	

Country or area Pays ou zone	Year Année	Sex Sexe	Total employment Emploi total	ISIC Rev. 3 Tabulation categories + / CITI Rév. 3 Catégories de classement + Categ. A Catég. A	Categ. B Catég. B	Categ. C Catég. C	Categ. D Catég. D	Categ. E Catég. E	Categ. F Catég. F	Categ. G Catég. G
Saudi Arabia[1]	2000	M	4 943.5	323.7	7.9	98.1	434.0	75.5	515.5	896.4
Arabie saoudite[1]	2000	F	769.8	17.8	...	3.8	6.6	0.5	0.4	5.1
	2001	M	5 027.7	334.2	9.1	87.1	460.3	77.3	585.0	832.6
	2001	F	780.9	6.1	...	0.8	7.5	...	0.3	4.6
	2002	M	5 115.8	258.6	12.2	94.6	439.4	65.6	629.3	856.4
	2002	F	797.2	4.9	...	0.8	8.9	...	0.2	5.3
Singapore[1,58]	2002	M	1 137.1	5.1	...	1.0	229.7	7.0	102.1	173.8
Singapour[1,58]	2002	F	880.3	0.9	...	...	137.9	1.9	17.0	130.6
	2003	M	1 122.6	4.0	...	...	228.3	7.0	94.5	166.8
	2003	F	911.1	1.0	...	...	136.4	3.0	20.0	129.7
	2004	M	1 137.7	4.4	...	0.4	221.2	8.1	97.6	180.4
	2004	F	929.2	1.4	...	0.2	135.5	1.6	17.1	139.3
Slovakia[1,11,59]	2003	M	1 177.1	90.6	...	17.3	340.0	37.0	180.8	113.9
Slovaquie[1,11,59]	2003	F	987.5	34.7	...	1.5	230.0	8.4	14.2	156.1
	2004	M	1 193.7	82.4	...	13.3	352.1	34.8	191.4	112.3
	2004	F	976.7	27.5	...	1.1	230.5	9.6	14.0	147.9
	2005	M	1 233.0	79.2	...	13.4	366.2	34.6	196.9	119.7
	2005	F	983.1	25.9	...	1.4	225.7	8.1	12.9	149.8
Slovenia[1,37]	2003	M	488.0	41.0	...	5.0	165.0	7.0	47.0	55.0
Slovénie[1,37]	2003	F	409.0	34.0	...	1.0	99.0	1.0	5.0	63.0
	2004	M	511.0	49.0	...	5.0	168.0	9.0	50.0	56.0
	2004	F	434.0	42.0	...	1.0	103.0	1.0	5.0	64.0
	2005	M	512.0	44.0	...	5.0	174.0	8.0	55.0	51.0
	2005	F	435.0	39.0	...	...	104.0	2.0	4.0	60.0
South Africa[2,60]	2001	M	6 049.0	727.0	...	470.0	1 004.0	80.0	534.0	1 186.0
Afrique du Sud[2,60]	2001	F	4 783.0	324.0	...	17.0	602.0	15.0	60.0	1 212.0
	2002	M	6 184.0	860.0	...	477.0	1 043.0	62.0	515.0	1 069.0
	2002	F	4 841.0	487.0	...	22.0	588.0	18.0	54.0	1 108.0
	2003	M	6 436.0	811.0	...	478.0	1 050.0	67.0	550.0	1 209.0
	2003	F	5 187.0	386.0	...	25.0	584.0	19.0	76.0	1 242.0
Spain[44,61]	2003	M	10 652.9	683.9	40.7	58.7	2 284.2	83.3	1 990.5	1 460.1
Espagne[44,61]	2003	F	6 643.1	258.9	7.4	4.9	753.4	16.3	111.2	1 238.7
	2004	M	10 934.3	684.9	43.7	53.4	2 282.8	84.2	2 134.3	1 493.0
	2004	F	7 036.5	252.7	7.6	6.2	764.8	19.5	118.9	1 324.5
	2005[36]	M	11 388.8	686.3	44.9	53.4	2 327.8	85.7	2 230.1	1 523.4
	2005[36]	F	7 584.4	254.3	15.2	6.9	785.2	20.9	127.1	1 363.5
Sri Lanka[1,62]	2002	MF	6 662.8	2 341.8	...	164.0	1 125.2	...	297.1	839.7
Sri Lanka[1,62]	2003	MF	6 942.8	2 380.9	...	120.1	1 106.9	...	397.2	882.9
Sweden[63]	2003	M	2 191.0	68.0	2.0	6.0	514.0	20.0	221.0	298.0
Suède[63]	2003	F	2 043.0	19.0	...	1.0	175.0	7.0	18.0	229.0
	2004	M	2 186.0	70.0	1.0	5.0	506.0	19.0	224.0	304.0
	2004	F	2 027.0	19.0	...	1.0	173.0	7.0	18.0	225.0
	2005[36]	M	2 225.0	65.0	2.0	6.0	489.0	19.0	236.0	306.0
	2005[36]	F	2 038.0	19.0	0.0	1.0	163.0	8.0	17.0	229.0
Switzerland[1,37,64]	2003	M	2 177.0	109.0	...	481.0	...	...	218.0	288.0
Suisse[1,37,64]	2003	F	1 786.0	58.0	...	178.0	...	...	29.0	288.0
	2004	M	2 173.0	102.0	...	463.0	...	...	226.0	287.0
	2004	F	1 786.0	51.0	...	179.0	...	...	28.0	289.0
	2005	M	2 172.0	103.0	...	469.0	...	...	235.0	268.0
	2005	F	1 801.0	51.0	...	176.0	...	...	27.0	297.0
Tajikistan	1995	M	1 853.0	1 095.0	...	...	183.0	24.0	81.0	87.0
Tadjikistan	1996	M	1 731.0	1 026.0	...	...	181.0	21.0	68.0	69.0
	1997	M	1 143.4	527.6	...	...	136.5	18.0	44.3	40.2

26 **Employment by economic activity**—Total employment and persons employed by ISIC Rev. 3 categories (thousands) (*continued*)
Emploi par activité économique—Emploi total et personnes employées par branches de CITI Rév. 3 (milliers) (*suite*)

ISIC Rev. 3 Tabulation categories + CITI Rév. 3 Catégories de classement +										
Categ. H Catég. H	Categ. I Catég. I	Categ. J Catég. J	Categ. K Catég. K	Categ. L Catég.L	Categ. M Catég. M	Categ. N Catég. N	Categ. O Catég. O	Categ. P Catég. P	Categ. Q Catég. Q	Country or area Pays ou zone
163.7	242.3	41.5	138.8	1 098.7	399.7	168.6	130.6	201.6	5.3	Saudi Arabia[1]
0.9	...	1.0	0.6	17.5	313.2	49.0	2.8	349.4	...	Arabie saoudite[1]
154.2	242.1	56.8	144.3	1 139.0	411.1	187.9	100.2	191.7	5.8	
0.4	5.8	1.7	...	18.6	308.9	90.2	1.7	329.6	1.0	
166.8	258.9	48.5	142.4	1 195.2	419.2	172.6	112.5	235.6	8.0	
3.5	6.4	1.3	0.9	17.6	332.3	51.4	3.0	360.3	0.4	
62.6	165.3	44.7	132.7	108.6	50.1	...	53.3	...	1.2	Singapore[1,58]
62.7	53.5	63.2	104.7	26.8	116.1	...	163.9	...	1.1	Singapour[1,58]
63.9	160.5	42.5	136.7	115.0	53.0	...	48.0	...	1.0	
64.5	55.6	62.2	106.2	33.0	121.0	...	179.0	...	1.0	
63.0	155.8	44.2	145.2	117.2	51.7	...	47.5	...	1.2	
66.3	56.7	63.1	108.8	29.9	125.7	...	182.5	...	1.0	
34.3	107.1	13.4	64.6	78.0	30.3	31.5	36.5	0.4	0.4	Slovakia[1,11,59]
45.2	42.3	30.2	44.1	81.7	128.5	121.3	40.5	7.6	0.5	Slovaquie[1,11,59]
31.6	103.1	15.1	70.4	78.9	34.9	28.3	41.7	0.8	0.2	
52.7	37.5	30.8	50.0	72.8	126.1	126.1	42.2	6.5	0.2	
32.0	106.1	16.6	78.7	77.6	38.6	27.7	43.4	0.5	0.2	
58.3	41.2	31.5	50.6	77.0	125.1	122.4	44.9	7.0	0.1	
15.0	47.0	7.0	29.0	23.0	15.0	9.0	18.0	...	...	Slovenia[1,37]
21.0	12.0	15.0	24.0	26.0	47.0	38.0	20.0	...	...	Slovénie[1,37]
15.0	44.0	7.0	31.0	27.0	16.0	8.0	21.0	...	...	
23.0	13.0	15.0	27.0	29.0	49.0	40.0	19.0	...	...	
16.0	40.0	9.0	34.0	30.0	16.0	8.0	18.0	...	...	
25.0	13.0	14.0	28.0	29.0	53.0	43.0	19.0	...	...	
...	448.0	547.0	...	15.0	...	...	878.0	150.0	...	South Africa[2,60]
...	94.0	428.0	...	8.0	...	...	1 110.0	905.0	...	Afrique du Sud[2,60]
...	442.0	600.0	...	28.0	...	...	891.0	186.0	...	
...	108.0	419.0	...	17.0	...	...	1 153.0	855.0	...	
...	442.0	628.0	...	11.0	...	...	988.0	194.0	...	
...	121.0	451.0	...	8.0	...	...	1 277.0	991.0	...	
563.3	832.6	252.1	721.3	680.7	344.3	259.6	344.9	52.0	0.6	Spain[44,61]
573.5	218.1	145.5	697.3	409.2	613.1	738.5	365.6	490.6	0.9	Espagne[44,61]
591.0	834.5	244.4	776.8	685.6	350.7	263.8	352.7	54.6	0.7	
609.5	229.7	156.6	768.7	439.9	659.2	765.6	375.4	536.8	1.0	
605.2	864.6	249.9	847.4	736.7	384.1	297.1	387.1	61.9	3.1	
685.9	252.6	207.4	831.0	460.1	706.4	837.5	406.6	620.9	3.0	
133.4	282.2	153.5	...	553.7	215.8	70.2	104.2	89.2	...	Sri Lanka[1,62]
104.8	375.7	216.8	...	560.4	253.6	82.1	122.5	85.6	...	Sri Lanka[1,62]
52.0	197.0	39.0	331.0	116.0	118.0	107.0	99.0	...	...	Sweden[63]
67.0	78.0	51.0	217.0	127.0	354.0	579.0	120.0	...	...	Suède[63]
56.0	191.0	38.0	327.0	115.0	119.0	110.0	98.0	...	...	
69.0	75.0	49.0	218.0	131.0	353.0	572.0	116.0	...	...	
54.0	199.0	35.0	357.0	110.0	119.0	119.0	105.0	...	...	
63.0	70.0	46.0	225.0	128.0	353.0	588.0	123.0	...	...	
60.0	167.0	131.0	271.0	130.0	113.0	111.0	95.0	...	...	Switzerland[1,37,64]
85.0	75.0	100.0	177.0	88.0	177.0	351.0	174.0	...	...	Suisse[1,37,64]
61.0	159.0	132.0	286.0	127.0	111.0	112.0	103.0	...	...	
88.0	66.0	91.0	175.0	88.0	191.0	363.0	173.0	...	...	
60.0	156.0	130.0	287.0	127.0	118.0	111.0	106.0	...	...	
87.0	70.0	89.0	166.0	94.0	195.0	370.0	176.0	...	...	
...	58.0	...	...	...	168.0	88.0	...	...	...	Tajikistan
...	58.0	...	...	...	161.0	84.0	...	...	...	Tadjikistan
...	50.9	...	...	...	160.0	82.3	...	...	...	

Employment by economic activity—Total employment and persons employed by ISIC Rev. 3 categories (thousands) *(continued)*
Emploi par activité économique—Emploi total et personnes employées par branches de CITI Rév. 3 (milliers) *(suite)*

Country or area / Pays ou zone	Year / Année	Sex / Sexe	Total employment / Emploi total	Categ. A / Catég. A	Categ. B / Catég. B	Categ. C / Catég. C	Categ. D / Catég. D	Categ. E / Catég. E	Categ. F / Catég. F	Categ. G / Catég. G
				ISIC Rev. 3 Tabulation categories + / CITI Rév. 3 Catégories de classement +						
Thailand[1,10,23] Thaïlande[1,10,23]	2003	M	19 081.5	8 597.8	336.2	30.3	2 415.8	89.8	1 383.4	2 654.5
	2003	F	15 595.6	6 548.3	79.2	9.3	2 670.5	15.4	230.7	2 402.7
	2004	M	19 698.8	8 341.0	313.9	26.1	2 550.2	87.2	1 594.8	2 868.9
	2004	F	16 012.8	6 378.4	82.1	9.1	2 763.1	11.5	283.3	2 582.7
	2005	M	19 470.3	8 250.9	348.7	30.2	2 507.3	88.9	1 578.3	2 759.0
	2005	F	16 832.1	6 756.9	92.2	9.9	2 842.9	18.0	274.8	2 538.0
TFYR of Macedonia[1] L'ex-R.y. Macédoine[1]	2003	M	327.3	71.6	0.2	2.1	70.3	13.1	32.5	36.1
	2003	F	217.8	48.3	...	0.4	61.0	2.1	3.4	26.4
	2004	M	320.6[65]	57.4[65]	0.4	2.5[65]	62.2[65]	13.6[65]	32.5[65]	43.1[65]
	2004	F	202.4[65]	30.3[65]	0.1	0.3	54.1[65]	2.1[65]	4.0[65]	31.1[65]
	2005	M	332.2	65.4	0.3	3.3	62.2	14.6	32.1	43.6
	2005	F	213.1	40.8	0.1	0.2	57.8	2.4	3.2	31.1
Turkey[1,10] Turquie[1,10]	2003	M	15 256.0	3 706.0	12.0	80.0	2 910.0	93.0	936.0	2 806.0
	2003	F	5 891.0	3 447.0	1.0	3.0	753.0	6.0	29.0	399.0
	2004	M	16 023.0	4 075.0	26.0	103.0	3 022.0	77.0	1 004.0	2 895.0
	2004	F	5 768.0	3 298.0	1.0	2.0	779.0	5.0	25.0	413.0
	2005	M	16 346.0	...	...	116.0	3 262.0	74.0	1 143.0	3 130.0
	2005	F	5 700.0	...	...	3.0	822.0	5.0	28.0	481.0
Ukraine Ukraine	2003	MF	20 163.3	4 105.7	...	4 123.2	...	...	833.5	3 752.4
	2004	MF	20 295.7	3 998.3	...	4 077.1	...	...	907.5	3 971.2
	2005	MF	20 680.0	4 005.5	...	4 072.4	...	...	941.5	4 175.2
United Arab Emirates Emirats arabes unis	1995[50]	M	1 159.7	96.7	8.1	29.4	125.2	13.0	252.2	173.1
	1995	F	152.1[50]	0.1	^0.0	0.9[50]	18.4[50]	0.1	1.6[50]	10.0[50]
	2000	M	1 553.0	129.5	10.8	39.4	167.7	17.4	337.8	231.9
	2000	F	226.0	0.1	^0.0	1.3	27.3	0.1	2.3	14.8
United Kingdom[44,66] Royaume-Uni[44,66]	2003	M	14 973.4	258.8	13.5	93.5	3 042.4	132.5	1 882.9	2 128.4
	2003	F	12 847.4	74.5	0.8	9.9	1 056.8	50.3	198.8	2 207.2
	2004	M	15 037.7	266.6	12.2	75.8	2 816.5	128.6	1 948.8	2 167.6
	2004	F	12 970.7	76.5	0.9	10.2	959.1	50.9	218.1	2 170.8
	2005	M	15 061.4	276.8	10.1	89.0	2 777.7	128.0	1 971.2	2 144.2
	2005	F	13 104.2	95.0	1.7	13.8	945.3	48.3	230.5	2 156.8
United States[10,44] Etats-Unis[10,44]	2003	M	73 322.0	1 695.0	...	452.0	11 734.0	913.0	9 164.0	11 434.0
	2003	F	64 404.0	580.0	...	73.0	5 168.0	280.0	975.0	9 272.0
	2004	M	74 524.0	1 687.0	...	483.0	11 485.0	892.0	9 727.0	11 580.0
	2004	F	64 728.0	546.0	...	55.0	4 998.0	276.0	1 041.0	9 289.0
	2005	M	75 973.0	1 654.0	...	545.0	11 370.0	926.0	10 118.0	11 896.0
	2005	F	65 757.0	544.0	...	80.0	4 882.0	250.0	1 079.0	9 508.0
Uruguay[11,15,28] Uruguay[11,15,28]	2002	M	597.9	38.0	...	1.1	102.2	...	75.8	141.6
	2002	F	440.4	5.7	...	0.2	52.0	...	1.6	87.3
	2003	M	589.7	39.3	...	1.1	98.9	...	68.2	140.9
	2003	F	442.3	7.5	...	0.2	52.2	...	1.3	84.5
	2005	M	620.1	...	44.3	...	107.2	...	73.2	152.2
	2005	F	494.4	...	7.4	...	62.0	...	1.5	103.0
Viet Nam[1,24] Viet Nam[1,24]	2002	M	20 355.6	11 460.7	948.6	156.5	1 972.1	97.8	1 357.3	1 521.5
	2002	F	19 806.7	12 184.7	323.3	87.8	2 078.8	20.3	133.6	2 785.0
	2003	M	20 959.2	11 072.5	1 023.1	194.7	2 203.6	103.9	1 631.8	1 673.1
	2003	F	20 216.5	12 164.2	311.3	127.4	2 308.0	24.3	164.7	2 834.2
	2004	M	21 649.3	11 041.3	1 059.3	182.7	2 429.1	117.6	1 774.1	1 778.0
	2004	F	20 666.3	12 027.3	369.9	112.2	2 520.8	24.1	182.5	2 918.0
Yemen[1] Yémen[1]	1999	M	2 731.6	1 146.4	31.4	16.7	112.5	11.0	236.9	382.3
	1999	F	890.1	781.3	...	1.0	23.0	0.8	1.3	11.9

26 Employment by economic activity — Total employment and persons employed by ISIC Rev. 3 categories (thousands) *(continued)*
Emploi par activité économique — Emploi total et personnes employées par branches de CITI Rév. 3 (milliers) *(suite)*

ISIC Rev. 3 Tabulation categories + CITI Rév. 3 Catégories de classement +										
Categ. H Catég. H	Categ. I Catég. I	Categ. J Catég. J	Categ. K Catég. K	Categ. L Catég.L	Categ. M Catég. M	Categ. N Catég. N	Categ. O Catég. O	Categ. P Catég. P	Categ. Q Catég. Q	Country or area Pays ou zone
757.9	849.2	141.2	332.9	602.8	426.2	144.8	269.8	37.3	0.3	Thailand[1,10,23]
1 345.4	138.3	138.1	234.5	300.0	530.9	373.2	351.3	217.5	0.6	Thaïlande[1,10,23]
781.7	914.7	145.7	385.9	679.4	469.0	159.8	334.7	31.0	0.3	
1 424.7	152.8	157.7	247.8	335.6	613.5	375.2	378.0	208.0	0.6	
759.8	900.8	162.1	377.5	726.3	469.2	155.9	298.5	29.8	0.3	
1 540.3	175.0	177.6	274.2	369.4	653.2	455.2	420.3	211.7	1.9	
8.5	25.5	2.5	6.3	24.1	13.2	8.1	12.5	...	0.7	TFYR of Macedonia[1]
4.3	5.2	4.6	4.5	10.6	18.8	22.1	5.3	...	0.8	L'ex-R.y. Macédoine[1]
8.8[65]	26.0[65]	2.9[65]	7.7[65]	28.0[65]	13.7[65]	7.9[65]	13.0[65]	...	0.7[65]	
3.9[65]	4.8[65]	4.8[65]	5.8[65]	11.7[65]	19.9[65]	22.0[65]	6.6[65]	0.2	0.9[65]	
9.1	28.2	2.2	9.0	27.4	13.6	8.5	12.2	^0.0	0.4	
4.5	4.5	4.1	5.8	10.9	18.0	22.8	6.0	0.4	0.6	
773.0	959.0	151.0	394.0	1 022.0	544.0	267.0	536.0	64.0	1.0	Turkey[1,10]
75.0	63.0	78.0	115.0	155.0	323.0	255.0	81.0	110.0	1.0	Turquie[1,10]
782.0	1 038.0	153.0	416.0	1 122.0	512.0	237.0	496.0	62.0	3.0	
90.0	62.0	84.0	132.0	129.0	306.0	232.0	87.0	120.0	2.0	
835.0	1 060.0	156.0	481.0	1 109.0	556.0	256.0	618.0	...	...	
102.0	71.0	81.0	153.0	136.0	349.0	275.0	...	...	...	
...	1 361.4	190.3	914.8	1 170.6	1 637.2	1 366.5	707.7	...	...	Ukraine
...	1 374.9	216.1	919.9	1 050.2	1 648.7	1 348.9	782.9	...	...	Ukraine
...	1 400.5	247.9	966.6	1 028.9	1 668.2	1 356.6	816.7	...	...	
42.2	89.6	13.8	30.6	168.3	24.2	12.7	38.1	40.7	1.0	United Arab Emirates
3.6[50]	4.2[50]	3.0[50]	3.0[50]	6.7[50]	25.0[50]	10.9[50]	1.8[50]	62.5[50]	0.2	Emirats arabes unis
56.5	119.9	18.4	40.9	225.4	32.4	17.0	51.1	54.5	1.3	
5.4	6.3	4.4	4.4	10.0	37.2	16.2	2.7	92.8	0.4	
508.3	1 458.8	593.9	1 782.0	973.3	652.4	627.5	739.2	45.1	9.2	United Kingdom[44,66]
683.3	477.4	637.4	1 302.0	931.2	1 726.2	2 575.8	797.5	95.2	5.6	Royaume-Uni[44,66]
537.9	1 450.8	576.0	1 848.4	978.5	714.4	660.8	738.5	58.2	9.0	
694.8	452.8	605.0	1 309.4	940.9	1 838.9	2 693.9	821.1	98.0	4.5	
534.9	1 465.8	576.1	1 852.2	980.8	686.4	727.6	749.0	45.8	4.9	
671.8	466.4	602.6	1 365.1	1 007.6	1 863.0	2 727.9	804.7	72.1	3.1	
4 232.0	4 335.0	2 773.0	9 454.0	3 343.0	3 608.0	3 383.0	6 809.0	...	...	United States[10,44]
4 788.0	1 422.0	4 061.0	7 339.0	2 899.0	8 218.0	13 050.0	6 279.0	...	...	Etats-Unis[10,44]
4 323.0	4 449.0	2 791.0	9 673.0	3 458.0	3 752.0	3 470.0	6 752.0	...	...	
4 807.0	1 395.0	4 149.0	7 463.0	2 908.0	8 306.0	13 191.0	6 304.0	...	...	
4 348.0	4 707.0	2 920.0	9 804.0	3 558.0	3 804.0	3 500.0	6 823.0	...	...	
4 958.0	1 477.0	4 115.0	7 657.0	2 971.0	8 459.0	13 410.0	6 365.0	...	...	
...	53.1	56.6	...	59.7	13.7	20.6	28.2	7.3	...	Uruguay[11,15,28]
...	9.3	39.9	...	27.1	48.5	56.1	23.9	88.7	...	Uruguay[11,15,28]
...	51.9	54.2	...	61.5	14.3	19.2	30.4	9.3	...	
...	9.3	36.7	...	29.6	47.3	57.5	24.3	91.6	...	
...	49.1	64.0	...	56.4	14.4	19.6	32.3	7.4	...	
...	12.4	40.0	...	29.7	53.3	61.5	32.0	91.6	...	
145.3	1 117.4	59.0	113.8	432.4	318.7	115.6	468.7	69.2	0.9	Viet Nam[1,24]
375.7	149.9	71.0	70.6	157.6	739.9	163.3	343.3	121.0	1.1	Viet Nam[1,24]
195.3	1 150.5	74.0	144.4	457.5	335.1	135.1	480.2	84.1	0.4	
447.9	146.8	74.5	74.2	162.6	762.9	171.0	308.6	132.9	1.0	
176.1	1 128.2	80.8	142.6	516.0	359.6	140.1	624.6	97.4	1.8	
418.9	164.7	78.2	76.6	182.8	825.4	187.9	431.8	143.7	1.4	
42.0	121.0	9.3	18.0	347.7	171.0	31.8	49.1	304.0	0.3	Yemen[1]
0.9	1.5	1.7	0.9	10.3	38.1	10.6	4.0	2.2	0.3	Yémen[1]

26 **Employment by economic activity**—Total employment and persons employed by ISIC Rev. 3 categories (thousands) (*continued*)

Emploi par activité économique—Emploi total et personnes employées par branches de CITI Rév. 3 (milliers) (*suite*)

Source

International Labour Office (ILO), Geneva, the ILO labour statistics database and the "Yearbook of Labour Statistics 2005".

Notes

+ Tabulation categories of ISIC Rev. 3 :
A Agriculture, hunting and forestry.
B Fishing.
C Mining and quarrying.
D Manufacturing.
E Electricity, gas and water supply.
F Construction.
G Wholesale and retail trade, repair of motor vehicles, motor cycles and personal and household goods.
H Hotels and restaurants.
I Transport, storage and communications.
J Financial intermediation.
K Real estate, renting and business activities.
L Public administration and defence; compulsory social security.
M Education.
N Health and social work.
O Other community, social and personal service activities.
P Private households with employed persons.
Q Extra-territorial organizations and bodies.
1 Persons aged 15 years and over.
2 September of each year.
3 Civilian labour force employed.
4 May.
5 July.
6 September.
7 Persons aged 10 years and over.
8 Second semester.
9 28 urban agglomerations.
10 Excluding armed forces.
11 Excluding conscripts.
12 April of each year.
13 Year ending in June of the year indicated.
14 Including professional army; excluding compulsory military service.
15 Persons aged 14 years and over.
16 Urban areas, Nov.
17 Persons aged 12 years and over.
18 Excluding rural population of Rondônia, Acre, Amazonas, Roraima, Pará and Amapá.
19 August.
20 November.
21 Excluding full-time members of the armed forces.
22 Excluding residents of the Territories and indigenous persons living on reserves.
23 Third quarter.
24 July of each year.
25 March.
26 Government-controlled area.
27 Persons aged 15 to 66 years.
28 Urban areas.
29 November of each year.
30 Persons aged 15 to 64 years.
31 May and November of each year.
32 December.
33 Persons aged 15 to 74 years.

Source

Bureau international du travail (BIT), Genève, la base de données du BIT et "l'Annuaire des statistiques du travail 2005".

Notes

+ Catégories de classement de la CITI Rév. 3 :
A Agriculture, chasse et sylvculture.
B Pêche.
C Activitiés extractives.
D Activitiés du fabrication.
E Production et distribution d'électricité, de gaz etd'eau.
F Construction.
G Commerce de gros et de détail; réparation de véhicules automobiles, de motorcycles et de biens personneles et domestiques.
H Hôtels et restaurants.
I Transports, entreposage et communications.
J Intermédiation financière.
K Immobilier, locations et activitiés de services aux enterprises.
L Administration publique et défense; sécurité sociale obligatoire.
M Education.
N Santé et action sociale.
O Autres activités de services collectifs, sociaux et personnels.
P Ménages privés employant du personnel domestique.
Q Organisations et organismes extraterritoriaux.
1 Personnes âgées de 15 ans et plus.
2 Septembre de chaque année.
3 Main-d'oeuvre civile occupée.
4 Mai.
5 Juillet.
6 Septembre.
7 Personnes âgées de 10 ans et plus.
8 Second semestre.
9 28 agglomérations urbaines.
10 Non compris les militaires.
11 Non compris les conscrits.
12 Avril de chaque année.
13 Année se terminant en juin de l'année indiquée.
14 Y compris les militaires de carrière; non compris les militaires du contingent.
15 Personnes âgées de 14 ans et plus.
16 Régions urbaines, nov.
17 Personnes âgées de 12 ans et plus.
18 Non compris la population rurale de Rondônia, Acre, Amazonas, Roraima, Pará et Amapá.
19 Août.
20 Novembre.
21 Non compris les membres à temps complet des forces armées.
22 Non compris les habitants des Territoires et les populations indigènes vivant dans les réserves.
23 Troisième trimestre.
24 Juillet de chaque année.
25 Mars.
26 Région sous contrôle gouvernemental.
27 Personnes âgées de 15 à 66 ans.
28 Régions urbaines.
29 Novembre de chaque année.
30 Personnes âgées de 15 à 64 ans.
31 Mai et novembre de chaque année.
32 Décembre.
33 Personnes âgées de 15 à 74 ans.

34 Urban areas, April.
35 Prior to 2003: March of each year.
36 Methodology revised; data not strictly comparable.
37 Second quarter of each year.
38 April and November of each year.
39 Persons aged 16 to 74 years.
40 March - May of each year.
41 Including the armed forces.
42 Persons aged 6 years and over.
43 December of each year.
44 Persons aged 16 years and over.
45 Persons aged 15 to 69 years.
46 October of each year.
47 Curaçao.
48 Classification revised; data not strictly comparable.
49 Omanis.
50 Population census.
51 August of each year.
52 Metropolitan Lima.
53 Excluding regular military living in barracks and conscripts.
54 Data not reliable; coefficient of variation greater than 20%.
55 March of each year.
56 Persons aged 15 to 72 years.
57 Figures for 1998 - 2005 revised on the basis of the 2002 census results.
58 June.
59 Excluding persons on child-care leave.
60 Persons aged 15 to 65 years.
61 Excluding compulsory military service.
62 First quarter of each year.
63 Persons aged 16 to 64 years.
64 Excluding armed forces and seasonal / border workers.
65 Prior to 2004: April of each year.
66 March - May.

34 Régions urbaines, avril.
35 Avant 2003: mars de chaque année.
36 Méthodologie révisée; les données ne sont pas strictement comparables.
37 Deuxième trimestre de chaque année.
38 Avril et novembre de chaque année.
39 Personnes âgées de 16 à 74 ans.
40 Mars - mai de chaque année.
41 Y compris les forces armées.
42 Personnes âgées de 6 ans et plus.
43 Décembre de chaque année.
44 Personnes âgées de 16 ans et plus.
45 Personnes âgées de 15 à 69 ans.
46 Octobre de chaque année.
47 Curaçao.
48 Classification révisée; données non strictement comparables.
49 Omanais.
50 Recensement de population.
51 Août de chaque année.
52 Lima métropolitaine.
53 Non compris les militaires de carrière vivant dans des casernes et les conscrits.
54 Données non fiables; coefficient de variation supérieur à 20%.
55 Mars de chaque année.
56 Personnes âgées de 15 à 72 ans.
57 Données 1998 - 2005 révisées sur la base des résultats du Recensement de 2002.
58 Juin.
59 Non compris les personnes en congé parental.
60 Personnes âgées de 15 à 65 ans.
61 Non compris les militaires du contingent.
62 Le premier trimestre de chaque année.
63 Personnes âgées de 16 à 64 ans.
64 Non compris les forces armées et les travailleurs saisonniers et frontaliers.
65 Avant 2004: Avril de chaque année.
66 Mars - mai.

Technical notes: tables 25 and 26

Detailed data on labour force and related topics are published in the ILO *Yearbook of Labour Statistics* and on the ILO web site http://laborsta.ilo.org. The series shown in the *Statistical Yearbook* give an overall picture of the availability and disposition of labour resources and, in conjunction with other macroeconomic indicators, can be useful for an overall assessment of economic performance. The ILO *Yearbook of Labour Statistics* provides a comprehensive description of the methodology underlying the labour series. Brief definitions of the major categories of labour statistics are given below.

"Employment" is defined to include persons above a specified age who, during a specified period of time, were in one of the following categories:

(a) "Paid employment", comprising persons who perform some work for pay or profit during the reference period or persons with a job but not at work due to temporary absence, such as vacation, strike, education leave;

(b) "Self-employment", comprising employers, own-account workers, members of producers' cooperatives, persons engaged in production of goods and services for own consumption and unpaid family workers;

(c) Members of the armed forces, students, homemakers and others mainly engaged in non-economic activities during the reference period who, at the same time, were in paid employment or self-employment are considered as employed on the same basis as other categories.

"Unemployment" is defined to include persons above a certain age and who, during a specified period of time were:

(a) "Without work", i.e. were not in paid employment or self-employment;

(b) "Currently available for work", i.e. were available for paid employment or self-employment during the reference period; and

(c) "Seeking work", i.e. had taken specific steps in a specified period to find paid employment or self-employment.

Persons not considered to be unemployed include:

(a) Persons intending to establish their own business or farm, but who had not yet arranged to do so and who were not seeking work for pay or profit;

(b) Former unpaid family workers not at work and not seeking work for pay or profit.

For various reasons, national definitions of employment and unemployment often differ from the recommended inter-

Notes techniques : tableaux 25 et 26

Des données détaillées sur la main-d'œuvre et des sujets connexes sont publiées dans l'*Annuaire des Statistiques du Travail* du BIT et sur le site Web du BIT http://laborsta.ilo.org. Les séries indiquées dans l'*Annuaire des Statistiques* donnent un tableau d'ensemble des disponibilités de main-d'œuvre et de l'emploi de ces ressources et, combinées à d'autres indicateurs économiques, elles peuvent être utiles pour une évaluation générale de la performance économique. L'*Annuaire des statistiques du Travail* du BIT donne une description complète de la méthodologie employée pour établir les séries sur la main-d'œuvre. On trouvera ci-dessous quelques brèves définitions des grandes catégories de statistiques du travail.

Le terme "Emploi" désigne les personnes dépassant un âge déterminé qui, au cours d'une période donnée, se trouvaient dans l'une des catégories suivantes:

(a) La catégorie "emploi rémunéré", composée des personnes faisant un certain travail en échange d'une rémunération ou d'un profit pendant la période de référence, ou les personnes ayant un emploi, mais qui ne travaillaient pas en raison d'une absence temporaire (vacances, grève, congé d'études);

(b) La catégorie "emploi indépendant" regroupe les employeurs, les travailleurs indépendants, les membres de coopératives de producteurs et les personnes s'adonnant à la production de biens et de services pour leur propre consommation et la main -d'œuvre familiale non rémunérée;

(c) Les membres des forces armées, les étudiants, les aides familiales et autres personnes qui s'adonnaient essentiellement à des activités non économiques pendant la période de référence et qui, en même temps, avaient un emploi rémunéré ou indépendant, sont considérés comme employés au même titre que les personnes des autres catégories.

Par "chômeurs", on entend les personnes dépassant un âge déterminé et qui, pendant une période donnée, étaient:

(a) "sans emploi", c'est-à-dire sans emploi rémunéré ou indépendant;

(b) "disponibles", c'est-à-dire qui pouvaient être engagées pour un emploi rémunéré ou pouvaient s'adonner à un emploi indépendant au cours de la période de référence; et

(c) "à la recherche d'un emploi", c'est-à-dire qui avaient pris des mesures précises à un certain moment pour trouver un emploi rémunéré ou un emploi indépendant.

Ne sont pas considérés comme chômeurs:

national standard definitions and thereby limit international comparability. Inter-country comparisons are also complicated by a variety of types of data collection systems used to obtain information on employed and unemployed persons.

Table 25 presents absolute figures on the distribution of employed persons by economic activity, according to ISIC 3. The column for total employment includes economic activities not adequately defined and that are not accounted for in the other categories. Data are arranged as far as possible according to the major divisions of economic activity of the *International Standard Industrial Classification of All Economic Activities*.

Table 26: Figures are presented in absolute numbers and in percentages. Data are normally annual averages of monthly, quarterly or semi-annual data.

The series generally represent the total number of persons wholly unemployed or temporarily laid-off. Percentage figures, where given, are calculated by comparing the number of unemployed to the total members of that group of the labour force on which the unemployment data are based.

(a) Les personnes qui, pendant la période de référence, avaient l'intention de créer leur propre entreprise ou exploitation agricole, mais n'avaient pas encore pris les dispositions nécessaires à cet effet et qui n'étaient pas à la recherche d'un emploi en vue d'une rémunération ou d'un profit;

(b) Les anciens travailleurs familiaux non rémunérés qui n'avaient pas d'emploi et n'étaient pas à la recherche d'un emploi en vue d'une rémunération ou d'un profit.

Pour diverses raisons, les définitions nationales de l'emploi et du chômage diffèrent souvent des définitions internationales types recommandées, limitant ainsi les possibilités de comparaison entre pays. Ces comparaisons se trouvent en outre compliquées par la diversité des systèmes de collecte de données utilisés pour recueillir des informations sur les personnes employées et les chômeurs.

Le *tableau 25* présente les effectifs de personnes employées par activité économique, classés en fonction de la Révision 3. L'emploi total inclut les personnes employées à des activités économiques mal définies et qui ne sont pas classées ailleurs. Les données sont ventilées autant que possible selon les branches d'activité économique de la *Classification internationale type, par industrie, de toutes les activités économiques*.

Tableau 26: Les chiffres sont présentés en valeur absolue et en pourcentage. Les données sont normalement des moyennes annuelles des données mensuelles, trimestrielles ou semestrielles.

Les séries représentent généralement le nombre total des chômeurs complets ou des personnes temporairement mises à pied. Les données en pourcentage, lorsqu'elles figurent dans le tableau, sont calculées en comparant le nombre de chômeurs au nombre total des personnes du groupe de main-d'œuvre sur lequel sont basées les données relatives au chômage.

Wages in manufacturing

By hour, day, week or month

Salaires dans les industries manufacturières

Par heure, jour, semaine ou mois

Country or area § Pays ou zone §	1998	1999	2000	2001	2002	2003	2004	2005
Albania[1,2] (lek) — Albanie[1,2] (lek)								
MF(I) - month mois	9 674.0	10 734.0	11 708.0	14 056.0	14 334.0	16 572.0	17 559.0	...
Anguilla (EC dollar) — Anguilla (dollar des Carraïbes orientales)								
MF(I) - month mois	...	...	1 494.7	...	...	...	...	...
Argentina[3,4] (Argentine peso) — Argentine[3,4] (peso argentin)								
MF(II) - hour heure	4.1	4.2	4.2	4.3	...	...	...	...
Armenia (dram) — Arménie (dram)								
MF(I) - month mois	21 278.0	24 515.0	29 307.0	35 848.0	40 362.0	53 048.0	60 727.0	...
Australia[5,6] (Australian dollar) — Australie[5,6] (dollar australien)								
MF(I) - hour heure	17.4	...	18.2	...	20.5	...	22.8	...
M(I) - hour heure	18.0	...	19.1	...	20.8	...	23.4	...
F(I)- hour heure	15.2	...	16.8	...	18.5	...	19.9	...
Austria[7] (Austrian schilling, euro) — Autriche[7] (schilling autrichien, euro)								
MF(I) - month mois	28 455.0	29 136.0	2 417.0	2 501.0	2 543.0	2 611.0	...	...
M(I) - month mois	31 471.0	32 195.0	2 738.0	2 837.0	2 868.0	2 938.0	...	...
F(I) - month mois	21 480.0	22 009.0	1 662.0	1 716.0	1 755.0	1 795.0	...	...
MF(II) - month mois	25 471.0	26 104.0	1 973.0	2 046.0	2 047.0	2 093.0	...	...
M(II) - month mois	27 972.0	28 646.0	2 186.0	2 271.0	2 257.0	2 303.0	...	...
F(II) - month mois	18 248.0	18 702.0	1 353.0	1 394.0	1 412.0	1 444.0	...	...
MF(V) - month mois	33 829.0	34 547.0	3 191.0	3 273.0	3 358.0	3 436.0	...	...
M(V) - month mois	39 050.0	39 793.0	3 879.0	3 979.0	4 054.0	4 132.0	...	...
F(V) - month mois	25 396.0	25 981.0	2 032.0	2 090.0	2 141.0	2 198.0	...	...
Azerbaijan (manat) — Azerbaïdjan (manat)								
MF(I) - month mois	202 082.6	244 087.1	284 272.3	303 163.6	348 815.6	445 436.5	491 330.2	115.3[8]
Bahrain[9,10] (Bahrain dinar) — Bahreïn[9,10] (dinar de Bahreïn)								
MF(I) - month mois	257.0	227.0	231.0	215.0	228.0	230.0	234.0	228.0
M(I) - month mois	276.0	250.0	255.0	241.0	252.0	250.0	249.0	239.0
F(I) - month mois	125.0	109.0	107.0	100.0	111.0	125.0	138.0	145.0
Belgium[11] (Belgian franc, euro) — Belgique[11] (franc belge, euro)								
MF(I) - hour heure	...	13.1	13.5	14.0	14.4	15.1	15.7	...
M(I) - hour heure	...	13.6	14.0	14.5	14.9	15.5	16.2	...
F(I)- hour heure	...	10.9	11.4	12.1	12.3	12.8	13.7	...
MF(I) - month mois[12]	...	2 189.0	2 261.0	...	2 535.0	2 632.0	...	...
M(I) - month mois[12]	...	2 284.0	...	...	...	...	...	...
F(I) - month mois[12]	...	1 843.0	...	...	...	...	...	...
MF(II) - hour heure[13,14]	417.6	...	...	...	...	...	...	...
M(II) - hour heure[13,14]	436.1	...	...	...	...	...	...	...
F(II) - hour heure[13,14]	345.5	...	...	...	...	...	...	...
MF(V) - hour heure	...	17.0	...	...	...	...	...	...
M(V) - hour heure	...	19.0	...	...	...	...	...	...
F(V) - hour heure	...	14.0	...	...	...	...	...	...
MF(V) - month mois	112 682.0[13,14]	2 864.0	...	...	...	...	...	...
M(V) - month mois	122 031.0[13,14]	3 095.0	...	...	...	...	...	...
F(V) - month mois	87 869.0[13,14]	2 193.0	...	...	...	...	...	...
Bolivia[15] (boliviano) — Bolivie[15] (boliviano)								
MF(II) - month mois	972.0	1 055.0	1 120.0[16]	...	...	...	...	...
Botswana[17] (pula) — Botswana[17] (pula)								
MF(I) - month mois	...	...	...	...	...	...	1 175.0[19]	1 219.0[18]
M(I) - month mois	821.0[18]	...	...	...	...	...	1 492.0[19]	1 608.0[18]
F(I) - month mois	447.0[18]	...	...	...	...	...	877.0[19]	720.0[18]

Country or area § Pays ou zone §	1998	1999	2000	2001	2002	2003	2004	2005
Brazil[20] (real) — Brésil[20] (real)								
MF(I) - month mois	717.4	752.2	763.1	844.6	901.9	...	...	...
M(I) - month mois	800.6	844.5	854.2	946.9	1 009.8	...	...	...
F(I) - month mois	487.8	505.5	524.0	576.5	618.6	...	...	...
Bulgaria[21] (lev) — Bulgarie[21] (lev)								
MF(I) - month mois	194 612.0	203.0[22]	219.0	227.0	236.0	246.0	262.0	291.0
M(I) - month mois	224 492.0	232.0[22]	257.0	271.0	284.0	293.0	311.0	...
F(I) - month mois	163 045.0	172.0[22]	181.0	185.0	192.0	203.0	216.0	...
Cambodia[9] (riel) — Cambodge[9] (riel)								
MF(II) - month mois	243 000.0	...	...	243 000.0	...	...	...	...
Canada[23] (Canadian dollar) — Canada[23] (dollar canadien)								
MF(I) - week semaine	770.9	782.4	796.9	808.1	830.1	842.4	859.0	...
MF(II) - hour heure[24]	17.6	17.8	18.3	18.6	19.1	19.7	20.2	20.6
Chile[25,26] (Chilean peso) — Chili[25,26] (peso chilien)								
MF(I) - month mois	200 773.0	203 540.0	208 257.0	213 394.0	218 740.0	221 860.0	229 575.0	242 160.0
China[27] (yuan) — Chine[27] (yuan)								
MF(I) - month mois	588.7	649.5	729.2	814.5	916.8	1 041.3	1 169.4	...
China, Hong Kong SAR (Hong Kong dollar) — Chine, Hong Kong RAS (dollar de Hong Kong)								
MF(I) - month mois[28,29]	...	...	...	...	...	10 000.0	9 500.0	9 500.0
M(I) - month mois[28,29]	...	...	...	...	...	...	...	9 000.0
F(I) - month mois[28,29]	...	...	...	...	...	...	...	7 000.0
MF(II) - day jour	335.3	334.7	335.4	342.6	326.1	322.2	324.3	279.0
M(II) - day jour	430.6	422.6	428.8	428.5	419.2	406.1	380.4	282.4
F(II) - day jour	262.9	268.9	278.1	280.6	268.2	262.7	280.0	273.8
MF(V) - month mois	11 711.6	11 853.0	11 869.7	12 133.1	11 950.7	11 508.8	11 498.1	11 622.0
M(V) - month mois	12 555.7	12 893.2	12 697.1	12 929.7	12 810.2	12 082.7	11 880.7	12 248.6
F(V) - month mois	10 915.9	10 846.7	11 101.4	11 395.0	11 123.2	11 021.1	11 139.3	11 015.0
China, Macao SAR (Macao pataca) — Chine, Macao RAS (pataca de Macao)								
MF(I) - month mois[30]	...	...	4 044.0	4 102.0	3 970.0	4 010.0	4 178.0	4 390.0
M(I) - month mois[30]	...	...	5 411.0	5 382.0	5 250.0	5 335.0	5 750.0	5 961.0
F(I) - month mois[30]	...	...	3 606.0	3 683.0	3 575.0	3 584.0	3 689.0	3 860.0
MF(VI) - month mois[28]	3 080.0	2 921.0	2 960.0	2 760.0	2 766.0	2 840.0	2 992.0	3 118.0
M(VI) - month mois[28]	4 762.0	4 738.0	4 690.0	4 525.0	4 479.0	4 380.0	4 846.0	4 781.0
F(VI) - month mois[28]	2 656.0	2 510.0	2 613.0	2 431.0	2 435.0	2 544.0	2 656.0	2 800.0
Colombia (Colombian peso) — Colombie (peso colombien)								
MF(I) - month mois	441 965.0[19,32]	455 252.0[19,32]	...	...	353 590.0[31,33]	442 510.0[31]	468 406.0[31]	506 020.0[31]
M(I) - month mois[31]	...	...	...	...	457 189.0[33]	531 791.0	557 571.0	605 537.0
F(I) - month mois[31]	...	...	...	...	258 415.0[33]	347 588.0	365 782.0	394 964.0
MF(VI) - month mois[19,32]	446 445.0	427 313.0	420 734.0	...	...	...	...	...
Costa Rica[34] (Costa Rican colón) — Costa Rica[34] (colón costa-ricien)								
MF(I) - hour heure	...	...	...	...	...	...	...	953.0
M(I) - hour heure	...	...	...	...	...	...	...	1 006.1
F(I)- hour heure	...	...	...	...	...	...	...	793.6
MF(I) - month mois	85 899.0	97 774.5	108 777.0	128 207.0	...	...	...	393 518.0
M(I) - month mois	91 493.0	106 594.0	115 642.0	135 707.0	...	...	...	410 986.0
F(I) - month mois	73 122.0	77 969.3	93 773.0	112 596.0	...	...	...	335 824.0
Croatia[35] (kuna) — Croatie[35] (kuna)								
MF(I) - month mois	3 681.0	3 869.0	4 100.0	4 465.0	4 794.0	4 952.0	5 189.0	...
M(I) - month mois	...	...	...	...	...	5 412.0	5 680.0	...
F(I) - month mois	...	...	...	...	...	4 196.0	4 359.0	...
Cuba[36] (Cuban peso) — Cuba[36] (peso cubain)								
MF(I) - month mois	203.0	233.0	249.0[37]	259.0	267.0	276.0	285.0	...
Cyprus[11,25,38] (Cyprus pound) — Chypre[11,25,38] (livre chypriote)								
MF(I) - hour heure	3.7	3.9	4.0	4.3	4.5	4.6	4.8	4.9
M(I) - hour heure	4.5	4.7	4.8	4.9	5.2	5.4	5.7	5.8

Country or area § Pays ou zone §	1998	1999	2000	2001	2002	2003	2004	2005
F(I)- hour heure	2.7	2.8	2.9	3.2	3.2	3.4	3.5	3.6
MF(II) - hour heure	3.3	3.4	3.5	3.7	3.9	4.1	4.2	4.3
M(II) - hour heure	4.0	4.1	4.2	4.3	4.6	4.8	5.0	5.1
F(II) - hour heure	2.5	2.6	2.7	2.8	2.7	2.9	2.9	3.0
MF(II) - week semaine	130.9	139.2	141.9	152.4	157.3	165.7	169.4	171.8
M(II) - week semaine	166.5	185.9	172.5	176.6	186.3	194.9	203.3	202.9
F(II) - week semaine	96.4	100.2	107.2	109.0	105.5	113.5	108.8	115.6
MF(V) - month mois	741.0	776.0	806.0	814.5	842.0	876.6	928.4	936.8
M(V) - month mois	884.0	919.0	954.0	967.2	1 005.7	1 038.9	1 108.2	1 105.0
F(V) - month mois	509.0	545.0	556.0	593.2	604.3	641.1	667.5	692.9
Czech Republic[39] (Czech koruna) — République tchèque[39] (couronne tchèque)								
MF(I) - month mois	11 513.0	12 271.0	13 188.0	14 130.0	14 897.0	15 842.0	17 035.0[14]	...
MF(II) - hour heure	66.5	...	...	...	...	...	...	...
MF(II) - month mois	9 757.0	10 294.0	11 005.0	11 769.0	12 324.0	13 049.0	14 095.0	14 662.0
M(II) - month mois	11 057.0	11 666.0	12 792.0	13 629.0	14 272.0	15 112.0	16 323.0	16 980.0
F(II) - month mois	7 557.0	7 973.0	8 308.0	8 912.0	9 332.0	9 881.0	10 674.0	11 103.0
Denmark[9,40] (Danish krone) — Danemark[9,40] (couronne danoise)								
MF(I) - hour heure	174.6	182.3	188.6	199.1	207.0	215.3	217.2	...
M(I) - hour heure	183.3	192.2	197.6	207.7	215.3	223.8	226.1	...
F(I)- hour heure	154.8	160.3	166.7	178.8	186.8	194.5	196.8	...
Dominican Republic (Dominican peso) — Rép. dominicaine (peso dominicain)								
MF(I) - hour heure	19.9	27.1	24.1	28.2	29.4	32.7	50.8	...
Ecuador (sucre, US dollar) — Equateur (sucre, dollar des Etats-Unis)								
MF(I) - month mois	3 252.0[41,42]	4 158.3[41,42]	159.6[41]	257.2	294.3	338.2	370.6	...
MF(II) - hour heure	6 119.0[41]	8 556.2[41]	0.8[41]	1.3	...	...	...	...
Egypt[10,11] (Egyptian pound) — Egypte[10,11] (livre égyptienne)								
MF(II) - week semaine	107.0	121.0	125.0	136.0	147.0	150.0	...	...
M(II) - week semaine	112.0	125.0	131.0	142.0	154.0	157.0	...	...
F(II) - week semaine	77.0	94.0	87.0	97.0	104.0	104.0	...	...
El Salvador (El Salvadoran colón, US dollar) — El Salvador (cólon salvadorien, dollar des Etats-Unis)								
MF(I) - month mois	1 993.4	1 746.6	1 790.0	1 750.4	208.7[44]	209.6	211.3	...
M(I) - month mois	2 348.5	2 157.8	2 241.1	2 117.4	253.8[44]	249.6	261.8	...
F(I) - month mois	1 646.0	1 337.1	1 370.4	1 370.5	167.7[44]	171.2	162.5	...
MF(II) - hour heure[43]	10.3	10.7	10.1	...	1.2[44]	1.3	1.4	1.5
M(II) - hour heure[43]	12.0	12.1	11.4	10.3	1.3[44]	1.5	1.7	1.5
F(II) - hour heure[43]	9.0	9.2	9.0	9.5	1.1[44]	1.2	1.2	1.2
Estonia (Estonian kroon) — Estonie (couronne estonienne)								
MF(I) - month mois	4 243.0[45]	4 374.0[45]	4 844.0[45]	5 337.0[45]	5 884.0[45]	6 403.0	7 012.0	...
Fiji[46] (Fiji dollar) — Fidji[46] (dollar des Fidji)								
MF(II) - day jour	14.5	15.2	...	...	...	...	...	...
Finland[12] (Finnish markka, euro) — Finlande[12] (markka finlandais, euro)								
MF(I) - month mois	12 054.0[47]	12 510.0[47]	13 124.0[47]	2 275.0	2 357.0	2 463.0[48]	2 564.0	...
M(I) - month mois	12 880.0[47]	13 305.0[47]	13 939.0[47]	2 402.0	2 475.0	2 581.0[48]	2 685.0	...
F(I) - month mois	10 237.0[47]	10 683.0[47]	11 239.0[47]	1 969.0	2 063.0	2 160.0[48]	2 252.0	...
France (French franc, euro) — France (franc français, euro)								
MF(I) - hour heure[49]	13.1	13.4	14.1	14.7	15.3	15.9	16.4	...
M(I) - hour heure[49]	14.0	14.3	15.0	15.6	16.2	16.8	17.3	...
F(I)- hour heure[49]	10.9	11.2	11.8	12.4	13.0	13.5	14.0	...
MF(I) - month mois[50]	...	1 459.4	1 477.0	1 506.9	1 562.7	...	...	...
M(I) - month mois[50]	...	1 573.8	1 591.0	1 618.5	1 668.8	...	...	...
F(I) - month mois[50]	...	1 191.8	1 205.9	1 241.7	1 307.9	...	...	...
MF(II) - month mois[51]	10 230.0	...	...	...	...	...	...	...
M(II) - month mois[51]	11 680.0	...	...	...	...	...	...	...
F(II) - month mois[51]	9 920.0	...	...	...	...	...	...	...

Country or area § Pays ou zone §	1998	1999	2000	2001	2002	2003	2004	2005
French Guiana (French franc, euro) — Guyane française (franc français, euro)								
MF(I) - hour heure	70.0	70.7	11.2[52]	11.8	...	...	...	...
M(I) - hour heure	74.0	74.5	11.9[52]	12.5	...	...	...	...
French Polynesia (CFP franc) — Polynésie française (franc CFP)								
M(I) - month mois	186 911.0	187 996.0	196 279.0	202 046.0	205 866.0	213 876.0	...	...
F(I) - month mois	153 351.0	160 946.0	165 206.0	176 580.0	177 719.0	186 653.0	...	...
Gambia[53,54] (dalasi) — Gambie[53,54] (dalasi)								
MF(I) - month mois	969.7	...	...	...	...	...	...	...
Georgia (lari) — Géorgie (lari)								
MF(I) - month mois	68.9	87.4	99.3	120.8	143.4	152.5	183.9	212.1
M(I) - month mois	...	101.1	111.2	141.5	165.1	174.9	210.2	243.5
F(I) - month mois	...	63.3	69.3	82.7	101.6	108.4	132.2	147.7
Germany (deutsche mark, euro) — Allemagne (deutsche mark, euro)								
MF(II) - hour heure	26.8[55]	27.5[55]	27.8[55]	14.4	14.7	15.1	15.4	15.6
M(II) - hour heure	28.0[55]	28.8[55]	29.1[55]	15.1	15.4	15.7	16.0	16.2
F(II) - hour heure	20.8[55]	21.4[55]	21.4[55]	11.1	11.4	11.6	11.9	12.0
Gibraltar[11,58] (Gibraltar pound) — Gibraltar[11,58] (livre de Gibraltar)								
MF(II) - hour heure	6.6	6.8	6.4	6.6	7.0	7.2	8.0	8.4
M(II) - hour heure	6.8	7.0	6.6	6.7	7.2	7.2	8.1	8.6
F(II) - hour heure	4.9	5.3	5.3	5.7	5.7	5.9	6.0	6.9
MF(II) - week semaine	339.3	320.0	291.6	299.5	311.3	323.8	400.6	419.1
M(II) - week semaine	358.9	332.6	299.8	306.4	339.5	333.2	414.3	433.3
F(II) - week semaine	192.9	210.4	213.8	233.9	237.1	235.5	249.7	260.0
Greece[10] (drachma, euro) — Grèce[10] (drachma, euro)								
MF(II) - hour heure[59]	1 539.8	...	...	...	...	...	...	...
M(II) - hour heure[59]	1 653.0	...	...	...	...	...	...	...
F(II) - hour heure[59]	1 355.8	...	...	...	...	...	...	...
MF(II) - month mois	...	...	1 020.0	...	1 140.0	...	...	...
MF(V) - month mois[59]	423 142.0	...	...	...	...	...	...	...
M(V) - month mois[59]	456 488.0	...	...	...	...	...	...	...
F(V) - month mois[59]	323 153.0	...	...	...	...	...	...	...
Guadeloupe (French franc, euro) — Guadeloupe (franc français, euro)								
MF(I) - hour heure	62.1	62.7	9.8[52]	10.3	...	...	...	...
M(I) - hour heure	65.2	66.0	10.4[52]	10.8	...	...	...	...
F(I)- hour heure	58.2	58.7	9.2[52]	9.7	...	...	...	...
Guam[9,20] (US dollar) — Guam[9,20] (dollar des Etats-Unis)								
MF(II) - hour heure	...	...	14.0	11.6	13.1	12.2	12.5	12.3
Guatemala (quetzal) — Guatemala (quetzal)								
MF(I) - month mois	1 541.0	1 602.3	1 655.3	1 732.3	1 837.3	...	...	...
Hungary[12] (forint) — Hongrie[12] (forint)								
MF(I) - month mois	68 872.0[60]	76 099.0[61]	88 551.0[61]	101 700.0[61]	114 297.0[61]	124 770.0[61]	136 992.0[61]	146 232.0[61]
M(I) - month mois	79 892.0[60]	86 866.0[61]	100 351.0[61]	115 830.0[61]	127 916.0[61]	140 244.0[61]	153 396.0[61]	...
F(I) - month mois	54 985.0[60]	61 898.0[61]	72 962.0[61]	82 761.0[61]	94 882.0[61]	102 585.0[61]	112 946.0[61]	...
Iceland[33] (Icelandic króna) — Islande[33] (couronne islandaise)								
MF(I) - hour heure[62]	828.0	864.0	945.0	1 049.0	1 108.0	1 173.0	1 234.0	...
M(I) - hour heure[62]	902.0	957.0	1 044.0	1 153.0	1 216.0	1 295.0	1 353.0	...
F(I)- hour heure[62]	730.0	760.0	814.0	905.0	968.0	1 003.0	1 079.0	...
MF(I) - month mois[63]	128 300.0[64]	136 200.0	149 200.0	166 400.0	176 800.0	186 100.0	194 900.0	...
M(I) - month mois[63]	139 900.0[64]	150 800.0	164 600.0	182 600.0	194 000.0	206 000.0	214 000.0	...
F(I) - month mois[63]	114 600.0[64]	121 300.0	129 900.0	145 700.0	156 600.0	161 200.0	173 200.0	...
India * (Indian rupee) — Inde * (roupie indienne)								
MF(II) - month mois	1 211.1	1 548.5	1 280.8	1 893.2	1 158.6	1 066.0	...	...
Indonesia[20,42,65] (Indonesian rupiah) — Indonésie[20,42,65] (roupie indonésien)								
MF(II) - week semaine	64.2	75.3	98.0	129.2	...	...	...	...

Country or area § / Pays ou zone §	1998	1999	2000	2001	2002	2003	2004	2005
Iran (Islamic Rep. of) (Iranian rial) — Iran (Rép. islamique d') (rial iranien)								
MF(I) - month mois	567 630.0	698 899.0	867 526.0	1 014 285.0	1 189 654.0	...	...	...
M(I) - month mois	575 371.0	709 212.0	880 779.0	1 029 232.0	1 198 461.0	...	...	...
F(I) - month mois	455 132.0	554 231.0	685 514.0	828 265.0	1 078 610.0	...	...	...
Ireland[10] (euro) — Irlande[10] (euro)								
MF(I) - week semaine	434.1	462.3	498.2	543.9	569.8	603.5	633.6	...
MF(II) - hour heure	9.3	9.8	10.4	11.5	12.3	12.9	13.5	13.9
M(II) - hour heure	10.2	10.7	11.4	12.4	13.3	13.8	14.4	14.8
F(II) - hour heure	7.6	8.0	8.6	9.4	10.1	10.7	11.1	11.6
MF(II) - week semaine[66]	...	396.6	423.2	457.0	483.0	511.8	534.2	557.6
M(II) - week semaine[66]	...	453.0	477.7	512.4	538.4	564.9	588.9	609.9
F(II) - week semaine[66]	...	298.2	324.7	347.3	365.2	393.8	406.8	430.2
Isle of Man[46] (pound sterling) — Ile de Man[46] (livre sterling)								
MF(I) - hour heure	7.8	9.1	8.5	9.0	10.3	9.7	10.4	10.6
M(I) - hour heure	9.0	9.5	9.2	9.2	10.9	11.0	10.3	10.9
F(I)- hour heure	5.7	7.5	6.8	8.5	7.7	7.5	10.7	9.2
MF(I) - week semaine	313.3	377.1	366.9	361.4	392.0	409.6	412.4	441.0
M(I) - week semaine	366.0	408.9	407.3	381.5	417.3	504.5	455.4	468.0
F(I) - week semaine	209.6	241.1	258.2	278.3	292.8	253.9	265.2	325.0
Israel (new sheqel) — Israël (nouveau sheqel)								
MF(I) - hour heure	39.0	42.0	44.0	...	...	...	...	...
MF(I) - month mois[67]	7 418.0[68]	8 227.0[68]	8 665.0[68]	9 088.0[69]	9 179.0[69]	9 218.0[69]	9 477.0[69,70]	9 848.0[69]
Italy (Italian lira, euro) — Italie (lire italienne, euro)								
MF(II) - hour heure	108.6[71]	110.9[71]	113.1[72]	101.4[72]	104.2[72]	106.9[72]	110.0[72]	113.0[72]
MF(V) - hour heure	109.6[71]	112.1[71]	114.4[72]	101.6[72]	104.5[72]	107.2[72]	110.7[72]	113.5[72]
Jamaica (Jamaican dollar) — Jamaïque (dollar jamaïcain)								
MF(I) - week semaine	4 302.2	5 549.4	5 208.8	5 725.2	6 092.9	...	...	...
Japan[73,74] (yen) — Japon[73,74] (yen)								
MF(I) - month mois	289 600.0	291 100.0	293 100.0	297 500.0	296 400.0	296 500.0	293 100.0	292 100.0
M(I) - month mois	327 900.0	327 700.0	328 100.0	331 400.0	328 300.0	327 800.0	323 100.0	323 800.0
F(I) - month mois	187 300.0	189 000.0	190 700.0	195 000.0	195 600.0	195 800.0	194 100.0	190 900.0
Jersey[46,75,76] (pound) — Jersey[46,75,76] (livre)								
MF(I) - week semaine	390.0	400.0	420.0	450.0	460.0	480.0	500.0	530.0
Jordan[11] (Jordan dinar) — Jordanie[11] (dinar jordanien)								
MF(I) - day jour	5.9[77]	5.5	...	...	...	...	...	...
M(I) - day jour	6.2[77]	5.8	...	...	...	...	...	...
F(I) - day jour	3.7[77]	4.0	...	...	...	...	...	...
MF(I) - month mois	198.5	172.0	189.0	185.0	186.7	...	...	...
M(I) - month mois	210.6	180.0	198.0	195.0	196.0	...	...	...
F(I) - month mois	122.2	123.0	131.0	126.0	129.3	...	...	...
Kazakhstan (tenge) — Kazakhstan (tenge)								
MF(I) - month mois	11 357.0	13 821.0	17 717.0	19 982.0	22 130.0	24 823.0	30 234.0	...
M(I) - month mois	12 246.0	14 991.0	19 510.0	22 184.0	24 479.0	27 515.0	33 542.0	...
F(I) - month mois	9 641.0	11 433.0	13 981.0	15 597.0	17 433.0	19 382.0	23 433.0	...
Korea, Republic of[25,42,78] (Korean won) — Corée, République de[25,42,78] (won coréen)								
MF(I) - month mois	1 284.5	1 475.5	1 601.5	1 702.4	1 907.0	2 074.0	2 279.7	2 458.0
M(I) - month mois	1 467.3	1 686.3	1 826.0	1 936.0	2 177.0	2 369.7	2 599.8	2 798.6
F(I) - month mois	820.1	933.1	1 055.8	1 121.3	1 211.0	1 320.0	1 419.7	1 556.1
Kuwait (Kuwaiti dinar) — Koweït (dinar koweïtien)								
MF(I) - hour heure	1.2	1.2	1.4	...	...	...	...	...
Kyrgyzstan (Kyrgyz som) — Kirghizistan (som kirghize)								
MF(I) - month mois	1 405.8	1 962.3	2 020.1	2 390.6	2 834.0	3 182.6	3 758.6	4 229.6

Country or area § Pays ou zone §	1998	1999	2000	2001	2002	2003	2004	2005
Latvia[79] (lats) — Lettonie[79] (lats)								
MF(I) - month mois	128.3	129.0	135.1	140.3	145.5	159.3	176.4	200.3
M(I) - month mois	136.1	137.5	146.0	150.9	157.3	172.8	192.1	217.9
F(I) - month mois	119.2	118.5	122.9	127.1	131.1	142.0	155.9	177.3
Lithuania (litas) — Lituanie (litas)								
MF(I) - hour heure[80,81]	5.9[82]	6.2[82]	6.2	6.3	6.5	6.6	6.9	7.6
M(I) - hour heure[80,81]	6.6[82]	6.9[82]	6.9	7.1	7.2	7.5	7.7	8.6
F(I)- hour heure[80,81]	5.1[82]	5.4[82]	5.5	5.5	5.7	5.8	5.9	6.5
MF(I) - month mois[80,81]	911.0	963.0	955.0	963.0	982.0	1 016.0[14]	1 085.0	1 204.0
M(I) - month mois[12,26]	1 089.0	...	...	...	...	...	...	...
F(I) - month mois[12,26]	847.0	...	...	...	...	...	...	...
Luxembourg[11] (Luxembourg franc, euro) — Luxembourg[11] (franc luxembourgeois, euro)								
MF(II) - hour heure	470.0[83]	12.2	12.5	12.6	13.1	13.5	14.2	14.7
M(II) - hour heure	490.0[83]	12.7	13.1	13.1	13.6	14.0	14.7	15.2
F(II) - hour heure	337.0[83]	8.7	9.4	9.5	9.8	10.2	10.6	11.1
MF(V) - month mois	144 697.0[83]	3 680.0	3 995.0	3 816.0	3 941.0	4 090.0	4 189.0	4 334.0
M(V) - month mois	155 036.0[83]	3 944.0	3 995.0	4 104.0	4 251.0	4 412.0	4 510.0	4 663.0
F(V) - month mois	98 614.0[83]	2 535.0	2 621.0	2 710.0	2 782.0	2 911.0	3 030.0	3 185.0
Malaysia (ringgit) — Malaisie (ringgit)								
MF(I) - month mois	...	...	1 387.8	1 530.7	...	...	...	...
Malta[20,84] (Maltese lira) — Malte[20,84] (lire maltaise)								
MF(VI) - hour heure	...	...	2.1	2.2	2.3	2.3	2.4	...
M(VI)- hour heure	...	...	2.2	2.3	2.4	2.4	2.4	...
F(VI) - hour heure	...	...	1.8	1.9	2.1	2.2	2.2	...
Mauritius[85] (Mauritian rupee) — Maurice[85] (roupie mauricienne)								
MF(I) - month mois[10]	...	5 142.0	5 544.0	5 856.0	6 155.0	6 668.0	7 299.0	7 798.0
MF(II) - day jour[86]	161.4	166.0	174.3	...	...	...	...	...
MF(V) - month mois[10]	6 912.0	7 034.0	7 638.0	...	...	...	...	...
Mexico (Mexican peso) — Mexique (peso mexicain)								
MF(I) - day jour	92.0	108.7	125.6	143.6	...	...	...	...
MF(I) - hour heure	10.8	12.3	15.3	17.8	18.0	19.4	...	...
M(I) - hour heure	11.8	13.5	16.7	19.3	19.8	21.2	...	...
F(I)- hour heure	8.7	9.9	12.3	14.7	14.4	15.7	...	...
MF(I) - month mois *[87]	2 106.5	2 406.2	2 952.4	3 403.0	3 558.8	3 756.6	3 885.3	...
M(I) - month mois *[87]	2 325.9	2 664.1	3 298.6	3 790.6	3 993.2	4 174.3	4 272.0	...
F(I) - month mois *[87]	1 635.7	1 862.1	2 277.0	2 654.1	2 718.1	2 917.4	3 113.7	...
MF(II) - hour heure	14.8	17.8	20.8	23.5	25.2	26.9	...	...
Mongolia[42] (togrog) — Mongolie[42] (togrog)								
MF(I) - month mois	...	...	66.0[64]	...	68.7	82.7	92.8	100.5
M(I) - month mois	...	...	60.0[64]	65.9	69.3	86.9	98.1	114.9
F(I) - month mois	...	...	70.0[64]	64.8	68.2	75.6	89.1	88.9
Myanmar[88,89] (kyat) — Myanmar[88,89] (kyat)								
M(I) - month mois	1 054.3	1 066.0	...	...	...	...	...	...
F(I) - month mois	1 010.6	1 190.9	...	...	...	...	...	...
M(II) - hour heure	...	...	13.5	19.0	20.8	22.8	29.9	31.9
F(II) - hour heure	...	...	20.8	17.5	19.6	20.3	27.2	28.4
Nepal[84,90,91] (Nepalese rupee) — Népal[84,90,91] (roupie népalaise)								
MF(I) - month mois	...	2 567.0	...	...	...	...	...	...
M(I) - month mois	...	2 867.0	...	...	...	...	...	...
F(I) - month mois	...	1 292.0	...	...	...	...	...	...

Country or area § Pays ou zone §	1998	1999	2000	2001	2002	2003	2004	2005
Netherlands (Netherlands guilder, euro) — Pays-Bas (florin néerlandais, euro)								
MF(I) - hour heure	32.0[94,95]	33.3[94,95]	34.4[94,95]	16.5[20,93]	17.1[20,93]	17.8[20,93]	18.2[20,93]	...
M(I) - hour heure	33.4[94,95]	34.7[94,95]	35.8[94,95]	17.2[20,93]	17.8[20,93]	18.5[20,93]	18.9[20,93]	...
F(I)- hour heure	25.7[94,95]	26.9[94,95]	28.0[94,95]	13.5[20,93]	14.1[20,93]	14.7[20,93]	15.4[20,93]	...
MF(I) - month mois[20,92,93]	4 614.0[95]	4 797.0[95]	4 958.0[95]	2 392.0	2 487.0	2 572.0	2 637.0	...
M(I) - month mois[20,92,93]	4 750.0[95]	4 932.0[95]	5 099.0[95]	2 458.0	2 549.0	2 634.0	2 692.0	...
F(I) - month mois[20,92,93]	3 684.0[95]	3 870.0[95]	4 001.0[95]	1 944.0	2 039.0	2 123.0	2 221.0	...
Netherlands Antilles[96] (Netherlands Antillean guilder) — Antilles néerlandaises[96] (florin des Antilles néerlandaises)								
MF(I) - month mois	2 462.0	...	2 565.0	...	...	...	...	...
New Caledonia (CFP franc) — Nouvelle-Calédonie (franc CFP)								
MF(I) - month mois	...	255 118.0	...	...	...	...	...	...
M(I) - month mois	...	275 779.0	...	...	...	...	...	...
F(I) - month mois	...	224 335.0	...	...	...	...	...	...
New Zealand[76,97,98] (New Zealand dollar) — Nouvelle-Zélande[76,97,98] (dollar néo-zélandais)								
MF(I) - hour heure	16.0	16.5	17.0	17.4	18.0	18.8	19.3	19.6
M(I) - hour heure	16.9	17.4	17.9	18.3	18.9	19.8	20.2	20.5
F(I)- hour heure	13.4	13.9	14.5	14.8	15.3	15.9	16.6	16.8
Nicaragua (córdoba) — Nicaragua (córdoba)								
MF(I) - hour heure	...	...	...	...	...	13.5	13.5	...
MF(I) - month mois	...	...	...	...	...	3 279.0	3 283.0	...
Norway (Norwegian krone) — Norvège (couronne norvégienne)								
MF(I) - month mois[11,12,99,100]	21 417.0[102]	22 441.0[102]	23 388.0[102]	24 426.0	25 991.0	26 944.0	27 920.0	28 922.0
M(I) - month mois[11,12,99]	...	...	...	...	...	27 625.0	28 588.0	29 533.0
F(I) - month mois[11,12,99]	...	...	...	...	...	24 260.0	25 290.0	26 423.0
MF(II) - hour heure[14,38,101]	125.5	...	...	...	...	...	...	...
M(II) - hour heure[14,38,101]	128.3	...	...	...	...	...	...	...
F(II) - hour heure[14,38,101]	112.4	...	...	...	...	...	...	...
Occupied Palestinian Terr.[84,103,104] (new shekel) — Terr. palestinien occupé[84,103,104] (nouveau shekel)								
MF(I) - day jour	57.3	65.4	68.8	68.0	70.1	68.5	66.8	...
M(I) - day jour	61.1	69.3	73.2	73.5	74.7	71.7	70.9	...
F(I) - day jour	32.6	32.4	36.0	35.2	36.8	41.6	30.8	...
Pakistan (Pakistan rupee) — Pakistan (roupie pakistanaise)								
MF(I) - month mois	3 706.0	2 865.8	2 981.0	3 002.2	4 113.7	...	...	...
Panama[28] (balboa) — Panama[28] (balboa)								
MF(I) - month mois[85]	247.0	250.9	...	...	...	...	...	...
M(I) - month mois[85]	249.8	259.0	...	...	...	...	...	...
F(I) - month mois[85]	238.5	241.3	...	...	...	...	...	...
MF(VI) - hour heure[84,105]	...	...	...	...	1.8	1.7	1.9	2.2
M(VI)- hour heure[84,105]	...	...	...	...	1.8	1.7	1.9	2.1
F(VI) - hour heure[84,105]	...	...	...	...	1.9	1.8	2.1	2.7
Paraguay (guaraní) — Paraguay (guaraní)								
MF(I) - month mois	...	...	813 765.0	639 988.0	739 738.0	816 428.0	...	...
M(I) - month mois	...	...	995 539.0	746 213.0	880 891.0	966 821.0	...	...
F(I) - month mois	...	...	402 798.0	408 608.0	453 064.0	514 766.0	...	...
Peru[106] (new sol) — Pérou[106] (nouveau sol)								
MF(II) - day jour	24.9	25.6	27.2	27.1[107]	28.1[108]	27.2[109]	28.0[109]	29.8[109]
MF(V) - month mois	2 067.0	2 155.6	2 315.7	2 286.8[107]	2 430.2[108]	2 356.1[109]	2 460.0[109]	2 418.2[109]
Philippines (Philippine peso) — Philippines (peso philippin)								
MF(I) - day jour[11]	...	...	...	230.7	234.3	237.7	236.7	...
M(I) - day jour[11]	...	...	...	241.1	244.4	249.3	239.8	...
F(I) - day jour[11]	...	...	...	216.6	207.6	221.2	232.1	...
MF(I) - month mois[110,111]	7 734.0	8 347.0	...	9 936.0	...	11 166.0	...	...
M(I) - month mois[110,111]	8 522.0	9 453.0	...	...	...	...	...	...
F(I) - month mois[110,111]	6 810.0	7 168.0	...	...	...	...	...	...

Country or area § Pays ou zone §	1998	1999	2000	2001	2002	2003	2004	2005
Poland[101,112] (zloty) — Pologne[101,112] (zloty)								
MF(I) - month mois	1 203.9	1 660.9	1 827.6	1 938.9	2 000.0	2 058.7	2 140.7	...
Portugal[113] (Portuguese escudo, euro) — Portugal[113] (escudo portugais, euro)								
MF(I) - month mois	...	...	126 923.0	133 939.0	705.0	775.0	806.0	837.0
M(I) - month mois	...	...	151 422.0	159 822.0	840.0	905.0	934.0	966.0
F(I) - month mois	...	...	98 574.0	103 835.0	547.0	596.0	622.0	649.0
MF(II) - hour heure	703.0	718.0	620.0	673.0	3.8	3.7	3.8	3.9
M(II) - hour heure	832.0	856.0	731.0	784.0	4.3	4.2	4.4	4.5
F(II) - hour heure	545.0	554.0	500.0	536.0	2.9	2.9	3.0	3.0
Puerto Rico (US dollar) — Porto Rico (dollar des Etats-Unis)								
MF(II) - hour heure	8.4	8.9	9.4	9.8	10.3	10.5	10.8	...
Qatar (Qatar riyal) — Qatar (riyal qatarien)								
MF(I) - month mois	...	...	...	...	...	...	...	3 394.0
M(I) - month mois	...	...	...	...	...	...	...	3 343.0
F(I) - month mois	...	...	...	...	...	...	...	5 384.0
MF(VI) - month mois[26,84]	...	...	...	1 546.0	...	...	...	...
M(VI) - month mois[26,84]	...	...	...	1 543.0	...	...	...	...
F(VI) - month mois[26,84]	...	...	...	2 987.0	...	...	...	...
Republic of Moldova[39] (Moldovan leu) — République de Moldova[39] (leu moldove)								
MF(I) - month mois	399.0	492.6	677.7	813.1	971.8	1 216.1	1 417.8	1 651.6
Romania (Romanian leu) — Roumanie (leu roumain)								
MF(I) - month mois	1 198 560.0	1 712 748.0	2 535 223.0	3 734 701.0	4 632 583.0	5 804 147.0	7 196 971.0	...
M(I) - month mois	...	...	...	...	...	6 662 800.0	8 167 249.0	...
F(I) - month mois	...	...	...	...	...	4 915 058.0	6 203 325.0	...
Russian Federation[114] (ruble) — Fédération de Russie[114] (ruble)								
MF(I) - month mois	1 026.0	1 580.0	2 371.0	...	4 439.0	5 603.0	...	8 504.0
Saint Helena[115] (pound sterling) — Sainte-Hélène[115] (livre sterling)								
MF(I) - month mois	246.8	237.5	263.1	263.4	296.8	...	...	...
M(I) - month mois	276.1	251.8	272.5	272.9	317.1	...	...	...
F(I) - month mois	129.9	195.3	222.4	229.0	229.5	...	...	...
Saint Lucia[116] (EC dollar) — Sainte-Lucie[116] (dollar des Caraïbes orientales)								
M(II) - hour heure	...	...	5.3	6.3	5.3	...	...	...
F(II) - hour heure	...	...	4.4	4.1	4.5	...	...	...
M(V) - hour heure	...	...	10.8	10.0	21.5	...	...	...
F(V) - hour heure	...	...	8.2	10.2	14.9	...	...	...
M(V) - month mois	...	...	1 477.3	1 588.0	2 435.1	...	...	...
F(V) - month mois	...	...	1 919.8	1 656.3	2 901.7	...	...	...
Saint Vincent-Grenadines (EC dollar) — Saint Vincent-Grenadines (dollar des Caraïbes orientales)								
MF(I) - day jour	25.0	25.8	25.8	26.5	26.5	...	...	...
San Marino (Italian lira, euro) — Saint-Marin (lire italienne, euro)								
MF(I) - day jour[117]	149 357.0	157 158.0	...	...	...	...	...	...
MF(I) - month mois	...	...	...	3 289 004.2[118]	1 868.2	1 922.1	1 900.0	...
Serbia and Montenegro[119] (Yugoslav dinar) — Serbie-et-Monténégro[119] (dinar yougoslave)								
MF(I) - month mois	823.0[120]	1 053.0[120]	2 230.0[120]	4 786.0[120]	11 065.0	12 996.0[121]	16 065.0[121]	20 366.0[121]
Seychelles[122] (Seychelles rupee) — Seychelles[122] (roupie seychelloises)								
MF(I) - month mois	2 853.0	2 962.0	3 067.0	3 235.0	3 300.0	2 986.0	3 042.0	3 314.0
Singapore (Singapore dollar) — Singapour (dollar singapourien)								
MF(I) - month mois	2 716.0[123]	2 803.0	3 036.0	3 117.0	3 154.0	3 265.0	3 350.0	3 495.0
M(I) - month mois	3 311.0[123]	3 384.0	3 653.0	3 752.0	3 762.0	3 881.0	3 969.0	4 111.0
F(I) - month mois	1 916.0[123]	2 007.0	2 181.0	2 226.0	2 283.0	2 374.0	2 442.0	2 563.0
Slovakia[124] (Slovak koruna) — Slovaquie[124] (couronne slovaque)								
MF(I) - month mois	9 980.0	10 758.0	11 722.0	12 908.0	13 837.0	14 873.0	16 378.0	17 604.0
Slovenia (tolar) — Slovénie (tolar)								
MF(I) - month mois	132 080.0	144 110.0	161 296.0	178 596.0	196 220.0	211 060.0	226 029.0	238 985.0[125]

Country or area § Pays ou zone §	1998	1999	2000	2001	2002	2003	2004	2005
South Africa[126] (rand) — Afrique du Sud[126] (rand)								
MF(I) - month mois	3 803.0	4 018.0	4 323.0	4 701.0	5 197.0[14]	...	...	...
Spain (peseta, euro) — Espagne (peseta, euro)								
MF(I) - hour heure	1 429.0[127]	1 463.0[127]	1 499.0[14]	10.5[128]	11.0[128]	11.5[128]	12.0[128]	12.4[128]
Sri Lanka[89] (Sri Lanka rupee) — Sri Lanka[89] (roupie sri-lankaise)								
MF(II) - day jour	174.2	199.2	222.5	230.7	273.1	306.3	309.0	336.5
M(II) - day jour	175.6	203.9	222.6	233.1	278.1	311.2	312.1	338.1
F(II) - day jour	145.7	165.8	185.6	201.3	235.1	253.0	270.0	327.9
MF(II) - hour heure	20.3	22.0	24.9	27.1	31.9	33.2	35.5	36.9
M(II) - hour heure	20.8	22.3	25.3	27.5	32.1	33.6	35.8	37.1
F(II) - hour heure	16.4	18.1	20.4	22.6	28.0	28.9	31.2	35.1
Sweden[129,130] (Swedish krona) — Suède[129,130] (couronne suédoise)								
MF(II) - hour heure	105.1	106.9	111.3	114.9[131]	118.2[131]	122.0[131]	126.1[131]	129.9[131]
M(II) - hour heure	107.0	108.7	113.3	116.9[131]	120.2[131]	124.1[131]	128.4[131]	132.2[131]
F(II) - hour heure	97.6	99.6	103.4	106.6[131]	109.4[131]	112.9[131]	116.8[131]	119.9[131]
Switzerland[132] (Swiss franc) — Suisse[132] (franc suisse)								
MF(I) - month mois	5 717.0	...	5 862.0	...	6 155.0	...	6 349.0	...
M(I) - month mois	6 128.0	...	6 296.0	...	6 552.0	...	6 726.0	...
F(I) - month mois	4 413.0	...	4 550.0	...	4 926.0	...	5 162.0	...
Thailand[85,133] (baht) — Thaïlande[85,133] (baht)								
MF(II) - month mois	6 389.0[134]	5 907.0[134]	5 839.0	6 064.6	6 795.3	6 432.2	...	...
M(II) - month mois	...	...	6 612.0	7 112.7	7 449.2	7 344.8	...	...
F(II) - month mois	...	...	5 052.0	5 122.4	6 143.7	5 538.8	...	...
TFYR of Macedonia[104] (TFYR Macedonian denar) — L'ex-R.y. Macédoine[104] (denar de l'ex-R.Y. Macédoine)								
MF(I) - month mois	...	...	...	...	9 944.0	10 028.0	10 486.0	10 298.0
Trinidad and Tobago (Trinidad and Tobago dollar) — Trinité-et-Tobago (dollar de la Trinité-et-Tobago)								
MF(I) - week semaine	908.7	938.8	1 170.1	1 161.2	1 161.6	...	...	...
Turkey[10] (new Turkish Lira) — Turquie[10] (nouveau livre turque)								
MF(I) - day jour[42]	5 859.0	10 477.2	16 225.0	21 882.0	...	...	...	...
MF(I) - hour heure[135,136]	781.6	1 397.0	2 163.3	2 917.6	...	...	...	...
MF(I) - month mois[136,137]	140 683.6	251 453.0	389 395.8	525 175.7	...	...	...	...
Ukraine (hryvnia) — Ukraine (hryvnia)								
MF(I) - month mois	157.4	188.0	289.0	395.3	441.3	552.9	700.0	905.1
M(I) - month mois	...	...	...	...	509.0	640.8	809.0	1 042.3
F(I) - month mois	...	...	...	...	358.9	443.5	562.9	727.0
United Kingdom[138,139] (pound sterling) — Royaume-Uni[138,139] (livre sterling)								
MF(I) - hour heure	8.0	8.4	8.9	9.3	9.8	10.2	10.5	...
M(I) - hour heure	8.7	9.1	9.6	9.9	10.4	10.8	11.0	...
F(I)- hour heure	6.3	6.5	7.1	7.6	8.2	8.7	9.1	...
MF(I) - week semaine	346.0	356.0	380.0	395.0	410.0	430.0	438.0	...
M(I) - week semaine	375.0	386.0	406.0	421.0	435.0	454.0	462.0	...
F(I) - week semaine	249.0	261.0	286.0	302.0	320.0	343.0	346.0	...
United States (US dollar) — Etats-Unis (dollar des Etats-Unis)								
MF(II) - hour heure[140,141]	13.5	13.9	14.3	14.8	15.3	15.7	16.2	16.6
MF(II) - week semaine[142]	562.5	579.6	567.8	603.6	625.8[14]	...	...	...
Uruguay[54] (Uruguayan peso) — Uruguay[54] (peso uruguayen)								
MF(I) - month mois	...	...	6 855.0	6 856.0	...	...	...	...
Uzbekistan (Uzbek sum) — Ouzbékistan (sum ouzbek)								
MF(I) - month mois	5 424.0	8 823.0	...	...	...	...	...	...
Zimbabwe (Zimbabwe dollar) — Zimbabwe (dollar zimbabwéen)								
MF(I) - hour heure	20.5	29.4	45.9	80.2	144.0	...	...	...
MF(I) - month mois	3 276.8	4 700.4	7 351.1	12 823.7	...	...	...	...

Source

International Labour Office (ILO), Geneva, the ILO labour statistics database and the "Yearbook of Labour Statistics 2005".

Notes

§ I. Employees.
II. Wage earners.
III. Skilled wage earners.
IV. Unskilled wage earners.
V. Salaried employees.
VI. Total employment.

Data are classified according to ISIC Rev. 3 except for the following countries whose data are classified according to Rev.2:

Albania: prior to 1992; Anguilla: prior to 1996; Argentina: prior to 1995; Australia: prior to 1996; Austria: prior to 1995; Azerbaijan: prior to 1997; Belgium: prior to 1995; Bolivia: prior to 1996; Botswana: prior to 1998; Brazil: prior to 1994; British Virgin Islands: prior to 1998; Bulgaria: prior to 1996; Canada: prior to 1993; China: prior to 1995; China, Macao SAR: prior to 1998; Colombia: prior to 2001; Costa Rica: prior to 1999; Croatia: prior to 1996; Cyprus: prior to 1998; Denmark: prior to 1993; Ecuador: prior to 1995; Egypt: prior to 1996; El Salvador: prior to 1997; Finland: prior to 1995; France: prior to 1997; Gambia: prior to 1988; Germany: prior to 1996; Gibraltar: prior to 1998; Hungary: prior to 1992; Ireland: prior to 1999; Isle of Man: prior to 1995; Israel: prior to 1994; Italy: prior to 1996; Jordan: prior to 1994; Kazakhstan: prior to 1993; Korea, Republic of: prior to 1993; Luxembourg: prior to 1995; Mauritius: prior to 1999; Mexico: prior to 1995; Netherlands Antilles: prior to 1989; Netherlands: prior to 1994; New Zealand: prior to 1998; Norway: prior to 1997; Panama: prior to 1996; Paraguay: prior to 2000; Peru: prior to 1995; Philippines: prior to 1996; Poland: prior to 1993; Portugal: prior to 1998; Republic of Moldova: prior to 1996; Romania: prior to 1994; Russian Federation: prior to 1997; San Marino: prior to 2000; Seychelles: prior to 1986; Singapore: prior to 1998; Slovakia: prior to 1990; Slovenia: prior to 1994; Spain: prior to 1996; Sweden: prior to 1993; Switzerland: prior to 1994; Thailand: prior to 2001; Turkey: prior to 1993; Ukraine: prior to 2002; United States: prior to 1993; Uruguay: prior to 2000; Yugoslavia: prior to 1990.

1 Including mining and quarrying.
2 State sector.
3 Local units with 10 or more workers.
4 Production and related workers.
5 Full-time adult non-managerial employees.
6 May of each year.
7 Prior to 2000: ATS; 1 Euro = 13.7603 ATS.
8 New denomination of AZM; 1 AZN=5000 AZM.
9 Private sector.
10 Establishments with 10 or more persons employed.
11 October of each year.
12 Full-time employees.
13 Prior to 1999: BEF; 1 Euro=40.3399 BEF.
14 Series discontinued.
15 Main cities, except Pando.
16 September.
17 Citizens only.
18 March.
19 September of each year.
20 December of each year.
21 Employees under labour contract.
22 New denomination: 1 new lev = 1,000 old leva.
23 Including overtime.
24 Employees paid by the hour.

Source

Bureau international du Travail (BIT), Genève, la base de données du BIT et " Annuaire des statistiques du travail 2005".

Notes

§ I. Salariés.
II. Ouvriers.
III. Ouvriers qualifiés.
IV. Ouvriers non qualifiés.
V. Employés.
VI. Emploi total.

Les données sont classifiées selon la CITI-Rév. 3 à l'exception des données des pays suivants qui sont classifiées selon la CITI-Rév. 2:

Albanie: avant 1992; Allemagne: avant 1996; Anguilla: avant 1996; Antilles néerlandaises: avant 1989; Argentine: avant 1995; Australie: avant 1996; Autriche: avant 1995; Azerbaïdjan: avant 1997; Belgium: avant 1995; Bolivie: avant 1996; Botswana: avant 1998; Brésil: avant 1994; Bulgarie: avant 1996; Canada: avant 1993; Chine: avant 1995; Chine, Macao RAS: avant 1998; Chypre: avant 1998; Colombie: avant 2001; Corée, République de: avant 1993; Costa Rica: avant 1999; Croatie: avant 1996; Danemark: avant 1993; Egypte: avant 1996; El Salvador: avant 1997; Equateur: avant 1995; Espagne: avant 1996; Etats-Unis: avant 1993; Fédération de Russie: avant 1997; Finlande: avant 1995; France: avant 1997; Gambie: avant 1988; Gibraltar: avant 1998; Hongrie: avant 1992; Ile de Man: avant 1995; Iles Vierges britanniques: avant 1998; Irlande: avant 1999; Israël: avant 1994; Italie: avant 1996; Jordanie: avant 1994; Kazakhstan: avant 1993; Luxembourg: avant 1995; Maurice: avant 1999; Mexique: avant 1995; Norvège: avant 1997; Nouvelle-Zélande: avant 1998; Panama: avant 1996; Paraguay: avant 2000; Pays-Bas: avant 1994; Pérou: avant 1995; Philippines: avant 1996; Pologne: avant 1993; Portugal: avant 1998; République de Moldova: avant 1996; Roumanie: avant 1994; Saint-Marin: avant 2000; Seychelles: avant 1986; Singapour: avant 1998; Slovaquie: avant 1990; Slovénie: avant 1994; Suède: avant 1993; Suisse: avant 1994; Thaïlande: avant 2001; Turquie: avant 1993; Ukraine: avant 2002; Uruguay: avant 2000; Yougoslavie: avant 1990.

1 Y compris les industries extractives.
2 Secteur d'Etat.
3 Unités locales occupant 10 ouvriers et plus.
4 Ouvriers à la production et assimilés.
5 Salariés adultes à plein temps, non compris les cadres dirigeants.
6 Mai de chaque année.
7 Avant 2000: ATS; 1 Euro = 13,7603 ATS.
8 Nouvelle dénomination de l'AZM; 1 AZN = 5000 AZM.
9 Secteur privé.
10 Etablissements occupant 10 personnes et plus.
11 Octobre de chaque année.
12 Salariés à plein temps.
13 Avant 1999: BEF; 1 Euro=40.3399 BEF.
14 Série arrêtée.
15 Villes principales, sauf Pando.
16 Septembre.
17 Nationaux seulement.
18 Mars.
19 Septembre de chaque année.
20 Décembre de chaque année.
21 Salariés sous contrat de travail.
22 Nouvelle dénomination: 1 nouveau lev = 1,000 anciens leva.
23 Y compris les heures supplémentaires.
24 Salariés rémunérés à l'heure.

25 Including family allowances and the value of payments in kind.
26 April of each year.
27 State-owned units, urban collective-owned units and other ownership units.
28 Median.
29 Including outworkers.
30 Third quarter of each year.
31 Fourth quarter. Persons aged 10 years and over. Excl. armed forces.
32 Seven main cities.
33 Methodology revised.
34 Usual hours; main occupation; July of each year.
35 Excluding employees in craft and trade.
36 State sector (civilian).
37 Including employment-related allowances received from the State.
38 Adults.
39 Enterprises with 20 or more employees.
40 Excluding young people aged less than 18 years and trainees.
41 Prior to March 2000: sucres; 25,000 sucres =1 US dollar.
42 Figures in thousands.
43 Urban areas.
44 Prior to 2002: colones; 8.75 colones=1 US dollar.
45 Enterprises with 50 or more employees, state-owned and municipal enterprises, institutions and organisations.
46 June of each year.
47 Prior to 2001: FIM; 1 Euro = 5.94573 FIM.
48 From 2003: excl. seasonal and end-of-year bonuses.
49 Including managerial staff and intermediary occupations.
50 Net earnings.
51 Prior to 1999: FRF; 1 Euro=6.55957 FRF.
52 As from 2000: Euros; 1 Euro=6.55957 FRF. Including the overseas departments of France (DOM).
53 Survey results influenced by a low response rate.
54 Establishments with 5 or more persons employed.
55 Prior to 2001: DEM; 1 Euro = 1.95583 DEM.
56 Including family allowances paid directly by the employers.
57 Prior to 1999: DEM; 1 Euro=1.95583 DEM.
58 Excluding part-time workers and juveniles.
59 Prior to 1999: GRD; 1 Euro = 340.750 GRD.
60 Prior to 1999: enterprises with more than 20 employees.
61 Enterprises with 5 or more employees.
62 Adult employees; excluding irregular bonuses and the value of payments in kind.
63 Adult employees; excluding overtime payments and payments in kind.
64 Fourth quarter.
65 Production workers.
66 Including juveniles.
67 Including payments subject to income tax.
68 Including workers from the Judea, Samaria and Gaza areas.
69 Israeli workers only.
70 From 2004: new sample; data not strictly comparable.
71 Index of hourly wage rates (Dec. 1995 = 100); prior to 1996: 1990 = 100.
72 Index of hourly wage rates (December 2000 = 100).
73 Regular scheduled cash earnings.
74 Private sector; establishments with 10 or more regular employees; June of each year .

25 Y compris les allocations familiales et la valeur des paiements en nature.
26 Avril de chaque année.
27 Unités d'Etat, unités collectives urbaines et autres.
28 Médiane.
29 Y compris les travailleurs externes.
30 Troisième trimestre de chaque année.
31 Quatrième trimestre. Personnes âgées de 10 ans et plus. Non compris les forces armées.
32 Sept villes principales.
33 Méthodologie révisée.
34 Heures habituelles; occupation principale; juillet de chaque année.
35 Non compris les salariés dans l'artisanat et dans le commerce.
36 Secteur d'Etat (civils).
37 Y compris les allocations en espèces liées à l'emploi et reçues de l'Etat.
38 Adultes.
39 Entreprises occupant 20 salariés et plus.
40 Non compris les jeunes gens âgés de moins de 18 ans et les apprentis.
41 Avant mars 2000: sucres; 25 000 sucres = 1 dollar EU.
42 Données en milliers.
43 Régions urbaines.
44 Avant 2002: colones; 8.75 colones=1 dollar EU.
45 Entreprises occupant 50 salariés et plus, entreprises d'Etat et municipales, institutions et organisations.
46 Juin de chaque année.
47 Avant 2001: FIM; 1 Euro = 5.94573 FIM.
48 A partir de 2003: non compris les primes saisonnières et de fin d'année.
49 Y compris les cadres et les professions intermédiaires.
50 Gains nets.
51 Avant 1999: FRF; 1 Euro=6,55957 FRF.
52 A partir de 2000: Euros; 1 Euro=6,55957 FRF.Y compris les départements d'outre-mer (DOM).
53 Résultats de l'enquête influencés par un taux de réponse faible.
54 Entreprises occupant 5 salariés et plus.
55 Avant 2001: DEM; 1.Euro = 1.95583 DEM.
56 Y compris les allocations familiales payées directement par l'employeur.
57 Avant 1999: DEM; 1 Euro=1.95583 DEM.
58 Non compris les travailleurs à temps partiel et les jeunes.
59 Avant 1999: GRD; 1 Euro=340.750 GRD.
60 Avant 1999: entreprises occupant moins de 20 salariés.
61 Entreprises occupant 5 salariés et plus.
62 Salariés adultes; non compris les prestations versées irrégulièrement et la valeur des paiements en nature.
63 Salariés adultes; non compris la rémunération des heures supplémentaires et la valeur des paiements en nature.
64 Quatrième trimestre.
65 Travailleurs à la production.
66 Y compris les jeunes gens.
67 Y compris les versements soumis à l'impôt sur le revenu.
68 Y compris les travailleurs des régions de Judée, Samarie et Gaza.
69 Travailleurs israéliens seulement.
70 A partir de 2004: nouvel échantillon; données non strictement comparables.
71 Indice des taux de salaires horaires (déc. 1995 = 100); avant 1996: 1990 = 100.
72 Indice des taux de salaires horaires (décembre 2000 = 100).
73 Gains en espèce tarifés réguliers.
74 Secteur privé; établissements occupant 10 salariés stables ou plus; juin de chaque années.

75 Approximate levels since survey aims at measuring changes; excl. bonuses.
76 Full-time equivalent employees.
77 Prior to 1999: establishments with 5 or more persons employed.
78 Establishments with 10 or more regular employees.
79 Beginning 1997: first quarter of each year.
80 Excluding individual unincorporated enterprises.
81 All employees converted into full-time units.
82 April.
83 Prior to 1999: LUF; 1 Euro = 40.3399 LUF.
84 Persons aged 15 years and over.
85 March of each year.
86 Wage-earners on daily rates of pay.
87 Persons aged 14 years and over.
88 Regular employees.
89 March and Sep. of each year
90 12 months ending in May of year indicated; main occupation.
91 Fluctuations in wages due to small sample size.
92 Full-time employees only.
93 Excluding overtime payments.
94 Dec. of each year. Excl. overtime payments.
95 Prior to 2001: NLG; 1 Euro = 2.20371 NLG.
96 Curaçao.
97 Establishments with the equivalent of more than 0.5 full-time paid employees.
98 February of each year.
99 Only remuneration in cash; excl. overtime payments.
100 Ships, oil platforms and modules.
101 Including the value of payments in kind.
102 Prior to 2001: Establishments affiliated to the Confederation of Norwegian Business and Industry.
103 West Bank and Gaza.
104 Net earnings.
105 August.
106 Prior to 1996, Lima; June. Beginning 1996, urban areas; annual averages.
107 Average of the first three quarters.
108 Metropolitan Lima.
109 Second quarter.
110 Computed on the basis of annual wages.
111 Establishments with 20 or more persons employed.
112 Economic units with 10 or more persons employed; prior to 1999, economic units with more than 5 persons employed.
113 Prior to 2002: PTE; 1 Euro= 200.482 PTE.
114 New denomination: 1 new rouble = 1,000 old roubles.
115 Year ending in March of the year indicated.
116 Unweighted survey results.
117 Prior to 2000: ITL; 1 Euro=1936.27 ITL.
118 Prior to 2002: ITL; 1 Euro=1936.27 ITL.
119 As from 1999: excluding Kosovo and Metohia.
120 Prior to 2002: excl. private sector; net earnings.
121 Excluding Montenegro.
122 Beginning 1988: earnings are exempted from income tax.
123 Methodology revised; data not strictly comparable.
124 Excluding enterprises with less than 20 employees.
125 Beginning 2005, methodology revised: excl. family allowances and the value of payments in kind.
126 Including employers' non-statutory contributions to certain funds.

75 Niveaux approximatifs étant donné que l'enquête vise à mesurer l'évolution; non compris les primes.
76 Salariés en équivalents à plein temps.
77 Avant 1999: établissements occupant 5 personnes et plus.
78 Etablissements occupant 10 salariés stables ou plus.
79 A partir de 1997 : le primer trimestre de chaque année.
80 Non compris les entreprises individuelles non constituées en société.
81 Ensemble des salariés convertis en unités à plein temps.
82 Avril.
83 Avant 1999: LUF; 1 Euro=40.3399 LUF.
84 Personnes âgées de 15 ans et plus.
85 Mars de chaque année.
86 Ouvriers rémunérés sur la base de taux de salaire journaliers.
87 Personnes âgées de 14 ans et plus.
88 Salariés stables.
89 Mars et sept. de chaque année.
90 12 mois se terminant en mai de l'année indiquée; occupation principale.
91 Fluctuations des salaires dues à la faible taille de l'échantillon.
92 Salariés à plein temps seulement.
93 Non compris la rémunération des heures supplémentaires.
94 Déc. de chaque année. Non compris la rémunération des heures supplémentaires.
95 Avant 2001: NGL; 1 Euro = 2.20371 NLG.
96 Curaçao.
97 Etablissements occupant plus de l'équivalent de 0.5 salarié à plein temps.
98 Février de chaque année.
99 Seulement rémunération en espèces; non compris les paiements pour heures supplémentaires.
100 Bateaux, plateformes de pétrole et modules.
101 Y compris la valeur des paiements en nature.
102 Avant 2001: Etablissements affiliés à la "Confederation of Norwegian Business and Industry".
103 Cisjordanie et Gaza.
104 Gains nets.
105 Août.
106 Avant 1996, Lima; juin. A partir de 1996, zones urbaines; moyennes annuelles.
107 Moyenne des trois premiers trimestres.
108 Lima métropolitaine.
109 Deuxième trimestre.
110 Calculés sur la base de salaires annuels.
111 Entreprises occupant 20 salariés et plus.
112 Unités économiques occupant 10 travailleurs et plus; avant 1999, unités économiques occupant plus de 5 personnes.
113 Avant 2002: PTE: 1 Euro= 200,482 PTE.
114 Nouvelle dénomination: 1 nouveau rouble = 1,000 anciens roubles.
115 Année se terminant en mars de l'année indiquée.
116 Résultats d'enquête non pondérés.
117 Avant 2000: ITL; 1 Euro=1936,27 ITL.
118 Avant 2002: ITL; 1 Euro=1936,27 ITL.
119 A partir de 1999: non compris Kosovo et Metohia.
120 Avant 2002: non compris le secteur privé; gains nets.
121 Non compris Monténégro.
122 A partir de 1988: les gains sont exempts de l'impôt sur le revenu.
123 Méthodologie révisée; les données ne sont pas strictement comparables.
124 Non compris les entreprises occupant moins de 20 salariés.
125 A partir de 2005, méthodologie révisée: non compris les allocations familiales et la valeur des paiements en nature.
126 Y compris les cotisations des employeurs à certains fonds privés.

127 Prior to 2001: ESP; 1 Euro = 166.386 ESP.
128 Including overtime payments and irregular gratuities.
129 Including holidays and sick-leave payments and the value of payments in kind.
130 Adults; prior to 1998: 2nd quarter of each year; 1998-2000: Sept-Oct. of each year.
131 Private sector; Sep. of each year.
132 Standardised monthly earnings (40 hours x 4 1/3 weeks).
133 Average wage rates for normal/usual hours of work.
134 Excluding public enterprises.
135 Excluding overtime payments and irregular bonuses and allowances.
136 Figures in thousands; Jan - June.
137 Including overtime payments and irregular bonuses and allowances.
138 Average: spring of each year.
139 Full-time employees; labour force sample survey.
140 National classification not strictly compatible with ISIC.
141 Private sector; production workers.
142 Private sector: production and construction workers and non-supervisory employees.

127 Avant 2001: ESP; 1 Euro = 166,386 ESP.
128 Y compris la rémunération des heures supplémentaires et les prestations versées irrégulièrement.
129 Y compris les paiements pour les vacances, congés de maladie et la valeur des paiements en nature .
130 Adultes; avant 1998: 2ème trimestre de chaque année; 1998-2000: sept.-oct. de chaque année.
131 Secteur privé; sept. de chaque année.
132 Gains mensuels standardisés (40 heures x 4 1/3 semaines).
133 Taux de salaire moyens pour la durée normale/usuelle du travail.
134 Non compris les entreprises publiques.
135 Non compris la rémunération des heures supplémentaires et les prestations versées irrégulièrement.
136 Chiffres en milliers; jan - juin.
137 Y compris la rémunération des heures supplémentaires et les prestations versées irrégulièrement.
138 Moyenne: printemps de chaque année.
139 Salariés à plein temps, enquête par sondage sur la main d'œuvre.
140 Classification nationale non strictement compatible avec la CITI.
141 Secteur privé. Travailleurs à la production.
142 Secteur privé: ouvriers à la production, travailleurs à la construction et salariés sans activité de surveillance.

28

Producer price indices
Index base: 2000 = 100

Indices des prix à la production
Indices base: 2000 = 100

Country or area	1999	2000	2001	2002	2003	2004	2005	Pays ou zone
Argentina								Argentine
Domestic supply[1,2]	96	100	98	173	204	219	238	Offre intérieure[1,2]
Domestic production	96	100	98	168	200	216	235	Production intérieure
Agricultural products[2]	103	100	98	244	236	250	224	Produits agricoles[2]
Industrial products[2,3]	99	100	98	160	190	205	222	Produits industriels[2,3]
Imported goods[3]	100	100	97	253	258	265	271	Produits importés[3]
Australia[4,5]								Australie[4,5]
Domestic supply	96	100	102	103	105	107	110	Offre intérieure
Domestic production	97	100	102	104	106	113	118	Production intérieure
Agricultural products	96	100	118	123	123	...	130	Produits agricoles
Industrial products[2,3,6]	96	100	103	...	104	108	114	Produits industriels[2,3,6]
Imported goods	92	100	...	101	93	88	89	Produits importés
Raw materials	93	100	102	101	101	104	110	Matières premières
Intermediate goods	94	100	101	102	102	104	109	Produits intermédiaires
Consumer goods	96	100	102	105	104	103	106	Biens de consommation
Capital goods	96	100	102	105	106	109	114	Biens d'équipement
Austria								Autriche
Domestic supply[2,7]	96	100	102	101	103	108	110	Offre intérieure[2,7]
Agricultural products	98	100	104	102	108	109	102	Produits agricoles
Intermediate goods	...	100	101	100	102	113	116	Produits intermédiaires
Consumer goods[2]	97	100	102	103	105	106	109	Biens de consommation[2]
Capital goods[2]	102	100	100	100	100	100	99	Biens d'équipement[2]
Bangladesh[5]								Bangladesh[5]
Domestic supply[2,7]	102	100	100	102	108	112	...	Offre intérieure[2,7]
Agricultural products[2,8]	103	100	99	102	108	112	...	Produits agricoles[2,8]
Industrial products[2,3,8]	93	100	101	105	107	110	...	Produits industriels[2,3,8]
Raw materials	102	100	101	103	113	107	...	Matières premières
Belarus[9]								Bélarus[9]
Industrial products	...	...	...	1 729 746	2 376 575	2 949 064	3 304 167	Produits industriels
Consumer goods	311 826	...	...	2 066 288	2 525 710	3 066 546	3 386 018	Biens de consommation
Capital goods	231 992	...	...	1 633 020	2 351 105	2 950 505	3 331 424	Biens d'équipement
Belgium								Belgique
Domestic production[10]	...	100	...	102	103	107	110	Production intérieure[10]
Agricultural products[2]	97	100	104	...	...	...	...	Produits agricoles[2]
Industrial products	92	100	100	101	100	107	107	Produits industriels
Intermediate goods	87	100	101	101	102	108	112	Produits intermédiaires
Consumer goods	97	100	98	98	95	94	96	Biens de consommation
Capital goods	100	100	100	100	100	102	104	Biens d'équipement
Bolivia								Bolivie
Industrial products	95	100	102	104	107	...	...	Produits industriels
Raw materials	106	100	107	108	117	...	...	Matières premières
Consumer goods	93	100	101	103	106	...	...	Biens de consommation
Capital goods	98	100	103	109	110	...	...	Biens d'équipement
Botswana								Botswana
Domestic supply	95	100	105	112	123	133	...	Offre intérieure
Brazil								Brésil
Domestic supply[11]	85	100	113	130	164	185	195	Offre intérieure[11]
Agricultural products[11]	82	100	117	142	186	197	192	Produits agricoles[11]
Industrial products[11]	86	100	111	127	161	180	196	Produits industriels[11]
Raw materials[11]	85	100	113	133	169	191	192	Matières premières[11]
Consumer goods[11]	84	100	109	130	165	176	184	Biens de consommation[11]
Capital goods	90	100	109	121	147	172	190	Biens d'équipement
Bulgaria								Bulgarie
Domestic supply	85	100	104	105	110	117	...	Offre intérieure

Country or area	1999	2000	2001	2002	2003	2004	2005	Pays ou zone
Canada								Canada
Agricultural products[2]	97	100	107	111	108	105	102	Produits agricoles[2]
Industrial products[2,3]	93	...	98	98	97	100	101	Produits industriels[2,3]
Raw materials[12]	82	100	99	98	100	112	126	Matières premières[12]
Intermediate goods	...	...	95	94	94	99	102	Produits intermédiaires
Chile								Chili
Domestic supply	90	100	108	115	123	126	133	Offre intérieure
Domestic production	90	100	106	112	120	126	135	Production intérieure
Agricultural products	92	100	99	113	113	120	129	Produits agricoles
Industrial products[7]	90	100	107	112	121	125	133	Produits industriels[7]
Imported goods	91	100	114	124	131	125	126	Produits importés
China, Hong Kong SAR								Chine, Hong Kong RAS
Industrial products	100	100	98	93	95	98	98	Produits industriels
Colombia[13]								Colombie[13]
Domestic supply[2]	84	100	107	117	124	129	132	Offre intérieure[2]
Domestic production	85	100	108	115	123	131	135	Production intérieure
Agricultural products	87	100	108	117	120	128	135	Produits agricoles
Industrial products	83	100	107	116	124	129	130	Produits industriels
Imported goods	80	100	105	121	127	124	122	Produits importés
Raw materials	83	100	107	116	127	139	138	Matières premières
Intermediate goods	83	100	106	116	124	131	134	Produits intermédiaires
Capital goods	82	100	106	122	126	122	121	Biens d'équipement
Croatia								Croatie
Agricultural products	97	100	108	92	91	95	95	Produits agricoles
Industrial products	91	100	104	95	95	98	101	Produits industriels
Consumer goods	99	100	100	101	104	102	106	Biens de consommation
Capital goods	95	100	98	96	93	92	93	Biens d'équipement
Cyprus[14]								Chypre[14]
Industrial products	94	100	102	105	108	117	121	Produits industriels
Czech Republic								République tchèque
Agricultural products	92	100	108	98	96	103	94	Produits agricoles
Industrial products	95	100	103	102	102	108	111	Produits industriels
Denmark								Danemark
Domestic supply[2,11]	94	100	102	102	102	105	109	Offre intérieure[2,11]
Domestic production[2,11]	95	100	103	103	105	109	113	Production intérieure[2,11]
Imported goods[11]	93	100	101	100	99	100	104	Produits importés[11]
Raw materials	78	100	99	94	94	106	128	Matières premières
Consumer goods	98	100	103	104	105	107	109	Biens de consommation
Ecuador								Equateur
Domestic supply	38	100	100	103	113	125	143	Offre intérieure
Domestic production	46	100	117	110	127	134	140	Production intérieure
Agricultural products	...	100	117	121	100	120	121	Produits agricoles
Egypt								Egypte
Domestic supply[5,7]	102	100	98	103	119	139	168	Offre intérieure[5,7]
Agricultural products	...	100	...	...	...	...	148	Produits agricoles
Raw materials[5]	102	100	98	108	134	162	...	Matières premières[5]
Intermediate goods[5]	101	100	98	103	118	143	...	Produits intermédiaires[5]
Consumer goods	...	100	107	...	...	132	...	Biens de consommation
Capital goods[5]	101	100	99	103	110	146	...	Biens d'équipement[5]
El Salvador								El Salvador
Domestic supply[15]	97	100	...	...	...	...	...	Offre intérieure[15]
Domestic production	99	100	...	...	...	...	...	Production intérieure
Imported goods	97	100	...	...	...	...	...	Produits importés
Finland								Finlande
Domestic supply	92	100	100	99	98	100	104	Offre intérieure
Domestic production	94	100	102	101	101	101	104	Production intérieure
Industrial products	...	100	...	96	95	96	98	Produits industriels
Imported goods	89	100	97	94	94	97	103	Produits importés

Country or area	1999	2000	2001	2002	2003	2004	2005	Pays ou zone
Raw materials	90	100	98	99	96	99	102	Matières premières
Consumer goods[16]	99	100	102	93	98	96	94	Biens de consommation[16]
Capital goods	97	100	101	94	90	89	89	Biens d'équipement
France								**France**
Agricultural products	98	100	103	...	...	...	...	Produits agricoles
Intermediate goods	96	100	102	101	101	104	107	Produits intermédiaires
Consumer goods	...	100	...	...	101	101	101	Biens de consommation
Capital goods	...	100	...	...	101	101	102	Biens d'équipement
Germany								**Allemagne**
Domestic supply	97	100	104	104	103	104	...	Offre intérieure
Agricultural products	94	100	104	98	98	99	102	Produits agricoles
Industrial products	99	100	106	106	104	106	...	Produits industriels
Imported goods	90	100	101	98	96	97	...	Produits importés
Intermediate goods	...	100	111	111	100	102	...	Produits intermédiaires
Consumer goods	...	100	106	106	104	104	...	Biens de consommation
Capital goods	...	100	92	93	102	102	...	Biens d'équipement
Greece								**Grèce**
Domestic supply[17,18]	94	100	103	105	107	111	116	Offre intérieure[17,18]
Domestic production[17,18]	95	100	104	106	109	112	119	Production intérieure[17,18]
Agricultural products[17,19]	98	100	110	122	133	...	...	Produits agricoles[17,19]
Industrial products[17,18]	95	100	103	105	108	112	115	Produits industriels[17,18]
Imported goods[17,18]	94	100	101	102	102	107	111	Produits importés[17,18]
Intermediate goods	...	100	105	105	106	109	112	Produits intermédiaires
Consumer goods	...	100	105	108	111	116	118	Biens de consommation
Capital goods	...	100	101	102	103	107	109	Biens d'équipement
Guatemala								**Guatemala**
Domestic supply	91	100	105	109	114	120	125	Offre intérieure
Domestic production	91	100	107	112	115	121	125	Production intérieure
Agricultural products	91	100	108	109	112	112	112	Produits agricoles
Industrial products	90	100	106	...	117	127	136	Produits industriels
Imported goods	91	100	103	106	112	118	124	Produits importés
India[20]								**Inde[20]**
Domestic supply	97	100	105	107	113	120	...	Offre intérieure
Agricultural products	95	100	97	102	108	99	...	Produits agricoles
Industrial products[3]	100	100	102	111	109	117	...	Produits industriels[3]
Raw materials[21]	98	100	100	97	110	119	...	Matières premières[21]
Indonesia								**Indonésie**
Domestic supply[18]	88	100	114	117	120	130	151	Offre intérieure[18]
Domestic production	80	100	116	126	130	135	151	Production intérieure
Agricultural products	88	100	124	134	134	138	148	Produits agricoles
Industrial products[3]	95	100	111	122	127	133	152	Produits industriels[3]
Imported goods[18]	93	100	112	111	109	120	137	Produits importés[18]
Raw materials	78	100	110	110	116	137	175	Matières premières
Intermediate goods	91	100	114	119	119	130	151	Produits intermédiaires
Consumer goods	90	100	119	126	126	129	140	Biens de consommation
Capital goods	99	100	108	107	107	112	121	Biens d'équipement
Iran (Islamic Rep. of)[2,8]								**Iran (Rép. islamique d')[2,8]**
Domestic supply	85	100	110	119	128	149	166	Offre intérieure
Domestic production	86	100	...	...	...	...	...	Production intérieure
Agricultural products	87	100	108	122	135	158	176	Produits agricoles
Industrial products	75	100	93	97	100	119	127	Produits industriels
Imported goods	85	100	149	...	...	...	...	Produits importés
Raw materials	83	100	112	118	128	164	182	Matières premières
Ireland								**Irlande**
Domestic supply[2,22]	94	100	100	103	98	98	...	Offre intérieure[2,22]
Agricultural products[2,22]	93	100	105	100	91	102	103	Produits agricoles[2,22]
Industrial products[2,3,22]	95	100	102	101	92	...	...	Produits industriels[2,3,22]
Capital goods[8]	96	100	98	92	80	...	...	Biens d'équipement[8]

Country or area	1999	2000	2001	2002	2003	2004	2005	Pays ou zone
Israel[18]								Israël[18]
Industrial products	98	100	101	105	108	113	118	Produits industriels
Italy								Italie
Domestic supply[2,18]	94	100	102	102	105	107	111	Offre intérieure[2,18]
Intermediate goods	91	100	102	100	103	108	111	Produits intermédiaires
Consumer goods	98	100	102	104	107	108	108	Biens de consommation
Capital goods	99	100	101	102	103	105	107	Biens d'équipement
Japan								Japon
Domestic supply[2]	99	100	100	99	96	97	100	Offre intérieure[2]
Domestic production	100	100	99	98	98	96	98	Production intérieure
Agricultural products[8]	103	100	101	100	98	102	100	Produits agricoles[8]
Industrial products[8]	100	100	99	98	95	96	98	Produits industriels[8]
Imported goods	91	100	96	94	93	104	118	Produits importés
Raw materials	88	100	104	104	108	117	144	Matières premières
Intermediate goods	99	100	100	99	97	99	103	Produits intermédiaires
Consumer goods	101	100	100	99	95	95	95	Biens de consommation
Capital goods	102	100	99	97	89	87	85	Biens d'équipement
Jordan								Jordanie
Domestic supply[2]	104	100	99	97	98	106	114	Offre intérieure[2]
Agricultural products	...	100	100	98	99	112	124	Produits agricoles
Intermediate goods	...	100	94	92	92	98	103	Produits intermédiaires
Consumer goods	...	100	97	97	98	98	100	Biens de consommation
Korea, Republic of								Corée, République de
Domestic supply	98	100	100	99	101	108	110	Offre intérieure
Agricultural products[8,23]	104	100	104	106	113	127	122	Produits agricoles[8,23]
Industrial products	98	100	98	96	98	105	109	Produits industriels
Raw materials	81	100	102	104	110	132	156	Matières premières
Intermediate goods	96	100	100	96	98	107	108	Produits intermédiaires
Consumer goods	100	100	101	100	102	105	106	Biens de consommation
Capital goods	103	100	99	95	94	96	94	Biens d'équipement
Kuwait								Koweït
Domestic supply	100	100	102	105	107	108	...	Offre intérieure
Domestic production	100	100	100	102	102	102	...	Production intérieure
Agricultural products	97	100	96	102	106	116	...	Produits agricoles
Industrial products	100	100	102	105	107	107	...	Produits industriels
Imported goods	99	100	102	106	109	109	...	Produits importés
Raw materials	99	100	105	108	...	...	...	Matières premières
Intermediate goods	102	100	100	104	...	...	...	Produits intermédiaires
Consumer goods	99	100	100	103	...	...	...	Biens de consommation
Capital goods	100	100	106	115	...	...	...	Biens d'équipement
Latvia								Lettonie
Domestic supply	99	100	102	103	106	115	124	Offre intérieure
Lithuania								Lituanie
Domestic supply	84	100	98	93	92	100	113	Offre intérieure
Luxembourg								Luxembourg
Industrial products	96	100	101	100	100	109	117	Produits industriels
Imported goods	94	100	103	104	107	116	120	Produits importés
Intermediate goods	94	100	99	97	98	111	122	Produits intermédiaires
Consumer goods[16]	99	100	109	111	105	105	106	Biens de consommation[16]
Capital goods	97	100	102	104	105	109	109	Biens d'équipement
Malaysia								Malaisie
Domestic supply	97	100	95	99	105	114	122	Offre intérieure
Domestic production	97	100	94	99	106	117	126	Production intérieure
Imported goods	99	100	100	99	100	102	103	Produits importés
Mexico								Mexique
Domestic supply[7,24]	346	100	106	110	119	126	132	Offre intérieure[7,24]
Agricultural products	332	100	110	115	128	136	149	Produits agricoles
Industrial products	343	100	104	107	116	120	124	Produits industriels

Country or area	1999	2000	2001	2002	2003	2004	2005	Pays ou zone
Raw materials	89	100	...	103	116	...	...	Matières premières
Consumer goods[8,24]	346	100	106	118	120	124	131	Biens de consommation[8,24]
Capital goods[7,8,24]	326	100	105	108	117	130	133	Biens d'équipement[7,8,24]
Morocco								Maroc
Domestic supply[25]	134	...	...	...	...	...	...	Offre intérieure[25]
Agricultural products	96	100	99	102	97	97	98	Produits agricoles
Industrial products	96	100	98	97	98	103	113	Produits industriels
Netherlands								Pays-Bas
Agricultural products[26,27]	93	100	105	103	105	...	...	Produits agricoles[26,27]
Industrial products	93	100	92	92	93	96	...	Produits industriels
Imported goods	80	100	74	72	72	78	...	Produits importés
Raw materials	84	100	82	80	80	86	...	Matières premières
Intermediate goods	90	100	91	92	92	96	...	Produits intermédiaires
Consumer goods	91	100	90	90	92	94	...	Biens de consommation
Capital goods	99	100	95	97	99	100	...	Biens d'équipement
New Zealand								Nouvelle-Zélande
Agricultural products[2]	89	100	124	123	112	113	114	Produits agricoles[2]
Industrial products[2,28]	93	100	105	105	103	106	110	Produits industriels[2,28]
Intermediate goods[29]	94	100	107	107	106	108	113	Produits intermédiaires[29]
Norway								Norvège
Domestic supply	96	100	105	105	106	107	107	Offre intérieure
Domestic production	...	100	105	106	106	107	107	Production intérieure
Industrial products	96	100	102	101	102	105	109	Produits industriels
Imported goods	95	100	106	...	...	...	...	Produits importés
Raw materials	93	100	99	88	89	98	99	Matières premières
Intermediate goods	97	100	101	99	99	104	106	Produits intermédiaires
Consumer goods	98	100	104	104	104	106	108	Biens de consommation
Capital goods	99	100	102	104	97	108	110	Biens d'équipement
Occupied Palestinian Terr.								Terr. palestinien occupé
Domestic supply[30]	...	...	...	129	131	135	139	Offre intérieure[30]
Domestic production[31]	...	...	4 236	4 169	4 019	...	...	Production intérieure[31]
Agricultural products[30]	...	...	...	138	137	137	...	Produits agricoles[30]
Imported goods[30]	...	...	...	129	136	136	...	Produits importés[30]
Oman[32]								Oman[32]
Domestic supply	...	100	104	102	104	107	...	Offre intérieure
Pakistan[5]								Pakistan[5]
Domestic supply[2,7]	96	100	102	108	113	120	131	Offre intérieure[2,7]
Agricultural products	98	100	102	106	108	119	130	Produits agricoles
Industrial products	98	100	102	104	109	113	114	Produits industriels
Raw materials	104	100	101	116	125	122	115	Matières premières
Panama								Panama
Domestic supply	92	100	97	94	95	100	105	Offre intérieure
Peru								Pérou
Domestic supply	96	100	101	100	102	109	110	Offre intérieure
Domestic production	96	100	101	100	102	107	110	Production intérieure
Agricultural products[33]	105	100	104	97	97	107	109	Produits agricoles[33]
Industrial products[3,8]	94	100	102	101	103	108	111	Produits industriels[3,8]
Imported goods	94	100	101	100	103	108	109	Produits importés
Philippines[34]								Philippines[34]
Domestic supply	98	100	102	106	109	137	149	Offre intérieure
Portugal								Portugal
Domestic supply	86	100	101	92	104	106	...	Offre intérieure
Intermediate goods	95	100	101	98	101	103	...	Produits intermédiaires
Consumer goods	97	100	104	102	106	106	...	Biens de consommation
Capital goods	...	100	102	102	103	105	...	Biens d'équipement
Romania								Roumanie
Industrial products	65	100	141	176	213	242	267	Produits industriels

Country or area	1999	2000	2001	2002	2003	2004	2005	Pays ou zone
Russian Federation								Fédération de Russie
Agricultural products	…	…	…	100	107	138	…	Produits agricoles
Industrial products	…	…	…	100	107	150	156	Produits industriels
Serbia and Montenegro								Serbie-et-Monténégro
Domestic supply[35]	135	…	…	109	105	124	…	Offre intérieure[35]
Agricultural products	39	100	170	…	…	…	…	Produits agricoles
Industrial products	48	100	185	…	…	…	…	Produits industriels
Consumer goods	54	100	201	…	…	…	…	Biens de consommation
Capital goods	44	100	143	…	…	…	…	Biens d'équipement
Singapore								Singapour
Domestic supply[7]	91	100	98	97	99	102	112	Offre intérieure[7]
Domestic production[2,3]	94	100	98	101	97	96	101	Production intérieure[2,3]
Imported goods	92	100	100	100	100	99	104	Produits importés
Slovakia[36]								Slovaquie[36]
Agricultural products	…	100	…	…	95	103	102	Produits agricoles
Industrial products	…	100	…	…	…	110	115	Produits industriels
Slovenia								Slovénie
Agricultural products[37]	124	…	…	…	…	…	…	Produits agricoles[37]
Industrial products	93	100	109	115	118	123	126	Produits industriels
Intermediate goods	…	100	109	114	116	123	127	Produits intermédiaires
Consumer goods	94	100	110	118	123	126	129	Biens de consommation
Capital goods	96	100	104	107	106	108	112	Biens d'équipement
South Africa								Afrique du Sud
Domestic supply[38]	91	100	108	124	126	127	131	Offre intérieure[38]
Domestic production[38]	93	100	108	122	127	130	134	Production intérieure[38]
Agricultural products	96	100	113	140	132	131	124	Produits agricoles
Industrial products[3]	93	100	108	122	125	128	132	Produits industriels[3]
Imported goods	87	100	110	127	122	117	121	Produits importés
Spain								Espagne
Domestic supply[18]	95	100	102	102	104	107	113	Offre intérieure[18]
Intermediate goods	…	100	101	102	102	107	111	Produits intermédiaires
Consumer goods	99	100	104	106	108	111	114	Biens de consommation
Capital goods	99	100	101	103	104	106	108	Biens d'équipement
Sri Lanka								Sri Lanka
Domestic supply	93	100	…	…	…	…	…	Offre intérieure
Domestic production	91	100	…	…	…	…	…	Production intérieure
Imported goods	85	100	…	…	…	…	…	Produits importés
Consumer goods	101	100	…	…	…	…	…	Biens de consommation
Capital goods	104	100	…	…	…	…	…	Biens d'équipement
Sweden[18,39]								Suède[18,39]
Domestic supply[2]	95	100	103	104	103	105	111	Offre intérieure[2]
Domestic production[2]	96	100	103	103	103	106	109	Production intérieure[2]
Imported goods	93	100	105	105	102	105	113	Produits importés
Switzerland								Suisse
Domestic supply[2,7]	97	100	100	99	102	104	…	Offre intérieure[2,7]
Domestic production[2,7]	99	100	101	100	104	107	…	Production intérieure[2,7]
Agricultural products[2]	95	100	110	92	122	119	…	Produits agricoles[2]
Industrial products	101	100	99	100	103	105	…	Produits industriels
Imported goods[7]	94	100	98	96	98	100	…	Produits importés[7]
Raw materials	93	100	89	…	…	…	…	Matières premières
Intermediate goods	…	100	101	99	105	109	…	Produits intermédiaires
Consumer goods	99	100	102	…	…	…	…	Biens de consommation
Capital goods	…	100	101	102	102	102	…	Biens d'équipement
Syrian Arab Republic								Rép. arabe syrienne
Domestic supply	105	100	96	101	…	…	…	Offre intérieure
Agricultural products[25]	141	…	…	…	…	…	…	Produits agricoles[25]
Raw materials	104	100	99	100	…	…	104	Matières premières
Intermediate goods	94	100	…	…	…	…	85	Produits intermédiaires
Consumer goods[25]	149	100	…	…	…	…	102	Biens de consommation[25]

Country or area	1999	2000	2001	2002	2003	2004	2005	Pays ou zone
Thailand								Thaïlande
Domestic supply[2,11]	88	100	93	94	108	116	126	Offre intérieure[2,11]
Agricultural products	102	100	105	116	128	147	176	Produits agricoles
Industrial products[3]	96	100	102	103	106	111	119	Produits industriels[3]
Raw materials	99	100	108	111	120	133	154	Matières premières
Intermediate goods	101	100	101	101	108	119	128	Produits intermédiaires
Consumer goods	98	100	105	110	116	125	143	Biens de consommation
Capital goods	97	100	103	106	106	108	117	Biens d'équipement
TFYR of Macedonia								L'ex-R.y. Macédoine
Domestic supply	92	100	...	...	...	...	...	Offre intérieure
Agricultural products	103	100	...	...	...	...	...	Produits agricoles
Industrial products	92	100	...	...	...	...	...	Produits industriels
Consumer goods	98	100	...	...	...	...	...	Biens de consommation
Capital goods	99	100	...	...	...	...	...	Biens d'équipement
Trinidad and Tobago								Trinité-et-Tobago
Domestic supply[25]	126	126	128	129	130	...	...	Offre intérieure[25]
Industrial products	99	100	101	101	103	...	...	Produits industriels
Tunisia								Tunisie
Agricultural products	97	100	102	107	111	116	...	Produits agricoles
Industrial products	99	100	103	105	108	111	114	Produits industriels
Turkey								Turquie
Domestic supply[2,18,40]	66	100	162	243	305	368	366	Offre intérieure[2,18,40]
Agricultural products	72	100	142	223	298	338	...	Produits agricoles
Industrial products	64	100	167	247	306	340	...	Produits industriels
United Kingdom								Royaume-Uni
Domestic supply	99	100	100	100	101	104	107	Offre intérieure
Domestic production	98	100	100	100	102	104	107	Production intérieure
Agricultural products	102	100	107	100	110	178	171	Produits agricoles
Industrial products[3]	99	100	100	101	101	102	105	Produits industriels[3]
Imported goods	89	100	98	94	96	95	102	Produits importés
Raw materials	93	100	100	96	96	99	111	Matières premières
Intermediate goods	96	100	100	97	100	107	124	Produits intermédiaires
Consumer goods	99	100	102	103	104	106	108	Biens de consommation
Capital goods	101	100	99	99	96	94	100	Biens d'équipement
United States								Etats-Unis
Domestic supply[2]	95	100	101	99	104	110	119	Offre intérieure[2]
Agricultural products[2]	99	100	104	99	112	125	119	Produits agricoles[2]
Industrial products[2,41]	94	100	101	98	103	109	119	Produits industriels[2,41]
Raw materials	82	100	99	90	113	132	151	Matières premières
Intermediate goods	95	100	100	99	104	110	119	Produits intermédiaires
Consumer goods	95	100	102	101	105	110	116	Biens de consommation
Capital goods	99	100	101	100	101	102	104	Biens d'équipement
Uruguay[42]								Uruguay[42]
Domestic supply[2,7]	94	100	...	...	...	...	...	Offre intérieure[2,7]
Domestic production	94	100	107	141	195	...	...	Production intérieure
Agricultural products	93	100	110	166	250	...	...	Produits agricoles
Industrial products[7]	94	100	106	132	177	...	...	Produits industriels[7]
Imported goods	88	100	...	...	...	...	...	Produits importés
Venezuela (Bolivarian Rep. of)								Venezuela (Rép. bolivarienne du)
Domestic supply[7]	88	100	115	...	253	...	...	Offre intérieure[7]
Domestic production[7]	86	100	115	...	237	...	...	Production intérieure[7]
Agricultural products[7]	61	100	141	...	159	...	...	Produits agricoles[7]
Industrial products[7]	88	100	112	...	191	...	...	Produits industriels[7]
Imported goods[7]	91	100	108	...	294	...	...	Produits importés[7]
Raw materials	85	100	123	...	...	...	...	Matières premières
Zimbabwe[25]								Zimbabwe[25]
Domestic supply	1 048	...	...	...	...	...	...	Offre intérieure
Domestic production	1 048	...	...	...	...	...	...	Production intérieure

Source

United Nations Statistics Division, New York, price statistics database.

Notes

1 Domestic agricultural products only.
2 Including exported products.
3 Manufacturing industry only.
4 Including service industries.
5 Annual average refers to average of 12 months ending June.
6 Prices relate only to products for sale or transfer to other sectors or for use as capital equipment.
7 Excluding mining and quarrying.
8 Including imported products.
9 Index base: 1993=100.
10 Excluding construction.
11 Agricultural products and products of manufacturing industry.
12 Valued at purchasers' values.
13 Annual average refers to average of 12 months ending May.
14 For government-controlled areas.
15 San Salvador.
16 Durable goods only.
17 Finished products only.
18 Excluding electricity, gas and water.
19 Including mining and quarrying.
20 Annual average refers to average of 12 months ending March.
21 Primary articles include food, non-food articles and minerals.
22 Excluding Value Added Tax.
23 Including marine foods.
24 Mexico City.
25 Index base: 1990=100.
26 Excluding forestry, fishing and hunting.
27 Crop growing production only, excluding livestock production.
28 Including all outputs of manufacturing.
29 Including all industrial inputs.
30 Index base: 1996=100.
31 Index base: 1997=100.
32 Muscat.
33 Excluding fishing.
34 Metro Manila.
35 Index base: 1998=100.
36 Prices of producers are surveyed without value added tax and without excise taxes.
37 Index base: 1995=100.
38 Excluding gold mining.
39 Excluding agriculture.
40 Excluding industrial finished goods.
41 Excluding foods and feeds production.
42 Montevideo.

Source

Organisation des Nations Unies, Division de statistique, New York, la base de données pour les statistiques des prix.

Notes

1 Produits agricoles intérieurs seulement.
2 Y compris les produits exportés.
3 Industries manufacturières seulement.
4 Y compris industries de service.
5 La moyenne annuelle est la moyenne de douze mois finissant en juin.
6 Uniquement les prix des produits destinés à être vendus ou transférés à d'autres secteurs ou à être utilisés comme biens d'équipement.
7 Non compris les industries extractives.
8 Y compris les produits importés.
9 Indice base: 1993=100.
10 Non compris construction.
11 Produits agricoles et produits des industries manufacturières.
12 A la valeur d'acquisition.
13 La moyenne annuelle est la moyenne de 12 mois finissant en mai.
14 Pour les zones contrôlées par le Gouvernement.
15 San Salvador.
16 Biens durables seulement.
17 Produits finis uniquement.
18 Non compris l'électricité, le gaz et l'eau.
19 Y compris les industries extractives.
20 La moyenne annuelle est la moyenne de douze mois finissant en mars.
21 Les articles primaires comprennent des articles des produits alimentaires, non- alimentaires et des minéraux.
22 Non compris taxe sur la valeur ajoutée.
23 Y compris l'alimentation marine.
24 Mexico.
25 Indice base: 1990=100.
26 Non compris sylviculture, pêche et chasse.
27 Cultures uniquement, non compris les produits de l'élevage.
28 Y compris toute la production du secteur manufacturière.
29 Tous les intrants industriels.
30 Indices base: 1996=100.
31 Indice base: 1997=100.
32 Muscat.
33 Non compris la pêche.
34 L'agglomération de Manille.
35 Indice base : 1998=100.
36 Les enquêtes sur le prix à la production ne prennent pas en considération les taxes à la valeur ajoutée et excise.
37 Indice base: 1995=100.
38 Non compris l'extraction de l'or.
39 Non compris l'agriculture.
40 Non compris les produits finis industriels.
41 Non compris les produits alimentaires et d'affouragement.
42 Montevideo.

Consumer price indices
General and food (Index base: 2000 = 100)

Indices des prix à la consommation
Généraux et alimentation (Indices base : 2000 = 100)

Country or area	1998	1999	2000	2001	2002	2003	2004	2005	Pays ou zone
Albania									Albanie
General	99.6	100.0	100.0[2]	103.1	108.4	110.8	114.0	116.7	Généraux
Food	...	...	100.0[3]	103.7	110.2	115.0	114.9	114.3	Alimentation
Food (1992 =100)[1]	433.2	431.9	...	...	...	...	...	...	Alimentation (1992 =100)[1]
Algeria									Algérie
General	98.6	100.6	100.0	103.5	105.8	109.5	114.5	116.7	Généraux
Food	101.2	102.2	100.0	104.4	106.2	111.0	116.4	116.7	Alimentation
American Samoa									Samoa américaines
General[4]	97.2[2]	98.1	100.0	101.3	103.4	108.5	116.1	122.1	Généraux[4]
Food	101.3[2]	100.5	100.0	101.6	103.1	109.8	123.5	130.4	Alimentation
Angola[5]									Angola[5]
General	6.8	23.5	100.0	252.6	527.6[2]	1 045.8	1 501.2	1 846.0	Généraux
Food	6.7	25.7	100.0	251.1	508.6[2]	...	...	...	Alimentation
Anguilla									Anguilla
General (2001 =100)	91.9	92.5	...	100.0[6]	100.5	103.8	108.3	113.5	Généraux (2001 =100)
Food (2001 =100)	96.9	98.9	...	100.0[6]	100.5	98.0	102.1	105.4	Alimentation (2001 =100)
Antigua and Barbuda									Antigua-et-Barbuda
General	98.2	99.3	100.0	101.5	...	...	...	...	Généraux
Food	95.3	98.2	100.0	103.6	...	...	...	...	Alimentation
Argentina[5,7]									Argentine[5,7]
General	102.1	101.0	100.0[2]	98.9	124.5	141.3	147.5	161.7	Généraux
Food	106.6	102.7	100.0[2]	98.1	132.0	157.3	165.1	183.3	Alimentation
Armenia									Arménie
General	100.2	100.8	100.0	103.1	104.3[2]	109.2	116.3	117.0	Généraux
Food	112.6	106.3	100.0	104.7	107.0[2]	114.4	125.8	126.8	Alimentation
Aruba									Aruba
General	94.0	96.1	100.0	102.9[2]	106.3	110.2	113.0	116.8	Généraux
Food	96.2	98.2	100.0	103.3[2]	106.7	110.1	114.4	...	Alimentation
Australia									Australie
General	94.3	95.7	100.0	104.4	107.6	110.5	113.1	116.1	Généraux
Food	94.4	97.6	100.0	106.6	110.4	114.4	117.1	120.0	Alimentation
Austria									Autriche
General	97.2	97.7	100.0[2]	102.7	104.5	105.9	108.1	110.6	Généraux
Food	99.0	99.0	100.0[2]	103.3	105.2	107.3	109.5	111.0	Alimentation
Azerbaijan									Azerbaïdjan
General	107.4	98.2	100.0	101.6	104.4	106.7	113.9	124.7	Généraux
Food[8]	109.8	97.7	100.0	102.7	106.5	109.9	120.9	134.1	Alimentation[8]
Bahamas									Bahamas
General	97.2	98.4	100.0	102.1	104.2	107.4	108.6	110.8	Généraux
Food	98.2	98.4	100.0	102.1	104.1	104.7	107.8	111.2	Alimentation
Bahrain									Bahreïn
General	102.1	100.7	100.0	98.8	98.3	100.0	102.3	...	Généraux
Food	102.3	101.3	100.0	98.6	97.6	96.2	98.3	...	Alimentation
Bangladesh[9]									Bangladesh[9]
General	92.2	97.9	100.0	101.5	105.4	111.5[2]	118.4	126.7	Généraux
Food	90.7	98.0	100.0	100.8	103.4	110.1[2]	118.3	127.8	Alimentation
Barbados									Barbade
General	96.1	97.6	100.0	102.6[2]	103.0	104.6	106.1	112.5	Généraux
Food	95.2	97.5	100.0	105.3[2]	107.1	110.1	115.0	123.1	Alimentation
Belarus									Bélarus
General	9.5	37.2	100.0	161.1	229.8	295.0	348.3	384.3	Généraux
Food	9.2	37.8	100.0	156.8	217.9	267.6	320.1	358.2	Alimentation

Country or area	1998	1999	2000	2001	2002	2003	2004	2005	Pays ou zone
Belgium									Belgique
General	96.4	97.5	100.0	102.5	104.2	105.8	108.0	111.0[2]	Généraux
Food	98.9	99.1	100.0	104.2	106.5	108.7	110.4	112.5	Alimentation
Belize									Belize
General	100.6	99.4	100.0	101.2	103.4	106.1	109.3	113.3	Généraux
Food[8]	101.1	99.4	100.0	100.5	101.6	104.2	106.9	111.8	Alimentation[8]
Benin[5]									Bénin[5]
General	95.6	95.9	100.0	103.9	106.5	108.1	109.0	114.9	Généraux
Food[1]	99.2	98.8	100.0	102.3	108.0	105.5	104.7	114.4	Alimentation[1]
Bermuda									Bermudes
General	95.1	97.4	100.0	102.9	105.3	108.6	112.5	116.0	Généraux
Food	95.8	97.8	100.0	102.0	103.5	105.6	108.2	111.4	Alimentation
Bhutan									Bhoutan
General	90.0	96.1	100.0	103.4	106.0	107.6	110.9[2]	116.8	Généraux
Food[8]	93.6	99.1	100.0	101.5	103.6	104.5	102.9[2]	108.8	Alimentation[8]
Bolivia[10]									Bolivie[10]
General	93.6	95.6	100.0	101.6	102.5	106.0	110.7	116.6	Généraux
Food	99.5	97.9	100.0	100.6	99.7	103.2	109.3	115.7	Alimentation
Botswana									Botswana
General	85.5	92.2	100.0	106.6	115.1	125.8	134.4	146.1	Généraux
Food	89.4	95.5	100.0	102.6	112.2	125.0	130.9	137.9	Alimentation
Brazil									Brésil
General	89.1	93.4	100.0	106.8	115.9	132.9	141.7	151.4	Généraux
Food	92.0	95.1	100.0	106.7	117.0	140.8	146.5	151.0	Alimentation
British Virgin Islands									Iles Vierges britanniques
General	95.1	97.3	100.0	103.1	103.5	107.2	108.3	110.4	Généraux
Food	98.9	99.7	100.0	104.3	105.3	107.1	108.4	112.1	Alimentation
Brunei Darussalam									Brunéi Darussalam
General	98.9	98.8	100.0	100.6	98.3[2]	98.6	99.5	100.5	Généraux
Food	100.2	100.0	100.0	100.5	100.9[2]	100.0	101.7	102.2	Alimentation
Bulgaria									Bulgarie
General	88.4	90.7	100.0	107.4	113.6	116.3	123.4	129.6	Généraux
Food	2 962.4	90.7[11]	100.0	106.5	106.5	105.4	112.5	117.0	Alimentation
Burkina Faso[5]									Burkina Faso[5]
General	101.4[2]	100.3	100.0	104.9	107.3	109.5	109.0	116.0	Généraux
Food	113.1[2]	106.1	100.0	108.8	112.2	110.3	104.9	120.2	Alimentation
Burundi[5]									Burundi[5]
General	77.0	79.6	100.0	108.1	106.7	118.1	...	...	Généraux
Food	76.4	77.2	100.0	100.6	95.5	107.5	...	...	Alimentation
Cambodia[5]									Cambodge[5]
General	96.9	100.8	100.0	99.4[2]	102.7	103.9	107.9	114.1	Généraux
Food[12]	96.2	103.5	100.0	98.0[2]	99.7	101.2	107.6	116.6	Alimentation[12]
Cameroon									Cameroun
General	97.0	98.8	100.0	104.4	107.4	108.1[13]	108.4	110.5	Généraux
Food	96.8	97.8	100.0	107.0	112.1	111.4[13]	109.2	110.4	Alimentation
Canada									Canada
General	95.7	97.4	100.0	102.6	104.9	107.8	109.8	112.2	Généraux
Food	97.4	98.7	100.0	104.5	107.2	109.1	111.3	114.1	Alimentation
Cape Verde									Cap-Vert
General	98.3	102.5	100.0	99.6	105.4	106.5	104.5	104.9	Généraux
Food	98.3	101.8	100.0	105.3	...	...	...	...	Alimentation
Cayman Islands									Iles Caïmanes
General	91.1	97.4	100.0	101.2	103.6	104.3	108.9	116.5	Généraux
Food	96.5	98.4	100.0	103.5	105.7	109.2	113.9	117.0	Alimentation
Central African Rep.[5]									Rép. centrafricaine[5]
General[4]	99.4	97.1	100.0	103.7	105.2	110.9	108.6	111.7	Généraux[4]
Food	99.4	96.3	100.0	104.7	106.8	112.4	107.2	110.9	Alimentation

Consumer price indices—General and food (Index base: 2000 = 100) *(continued)*

Indices des prix à la consommation—Généraux et alimentation (Indices base : 2000 = 100) *(suite)*

Country or area	1998	1999	2000	2001	2002	2003	2004	2005	Pays ou zone
Chad[5]									Tchad[5]
General	105.6	96.7	100.0	112.4	117.5	116.4[14]	116.6[2]	125.7	Généraux
Food	106.0	92.9	100.0	119.3	125.8[2]	122.6	116.0	129.2	Alimentation
Chile[5]									Chili[5]
General	93.2[2]	96.3	100.0	103.6	106.2	109.1	110.3	113.7	Généraux
Food	98.3[2]	98.6	100.0	100.8	102.9	105.8	104.4	107.5	Alimentation
China									Chine
General	101.3	99.9	100.0	100.7	99.9	101.1	...	...	Généraux
Food	107.2	102.7	100.0	100.0	99.4	102.8	...	...	Alimentation
China, Hong Kong SAR									Chine, Hong Kong RAS
General	108.1	103.8	100.0[15]	98.4	95.4	93.0	92.6	93.6[2]	Généraux
Food	104.1	102.2	100.0[15]	99.2	97.1	95.7	96.7	98.4[2]	Alimentation
China, Macao SAR									Chine, Macao RAS
General	157.9	101.6[16]	100.0[2]	98.0	95.4	93.9	94.9	99.0	Généraux
Food	106.2	101.5	100.0[2]	98.6	96.5	95.3	97.4	101.3	Alimentation
Colombia[17]									Colombie[17]
General	82.1[2]	91.3	100.0	108.7	116.5	125.0	132.5	139.6	Généraux
Food	86.9[2]	91.7	100.0	108.7	118.4	127.2	134.6	143.1	Alimentation
Congo[5]									Congo[5]
General	96.9	100.9	100.0	100.1	104.4	103.8	106.4	109.6	Généraux
Food	100.7	105.5	100.0	98.3	102.9	96.9	90.8	...	Alimentation
Cook Islands[5]									Iles Cook[5]
General	95.7[2]	96.9	100.0	108.7	112.3	114.6	115.6	118.5	Généraux
Food[18]	96.3[2]	96.8	100.0	109.3	116.9	119.9	120.9	122.4	Alimentation[18]
Costa Rica[19]									Costa Rica[19]
General	81.9	90.1	100.0	111.3	121.5	132.9	149.3	169.9	Généraux
Food[8]	83.0	91.1	100.0	110.8	121.8	133.3	151.6	176.5	Alimentation[8]
Côte d'Ivoire[5]									Côte d'Ivoire[5]
General	96.8	97.5	100.0	104.4	107.6	111.1	112.7	117.1	Généraux
Food[1]	104.7	100.0	100.0	105.7	111.6	116.1	111.6	114.3	Alimentation[1]
Croatia									Croatie
General	91.7	95.0	100.0	104.5[2]	106.3	108.2	110.4	114.0	Généraux
Food	99.2	99.6	100.0	102.1[2]	102.3	104.0	105.5	110.4	Alimentation
Cyprus									Chypre
General	94.5[2]	96.0	100.0	102.0	104.8	109.2	111.7	114.5	Généraux
Food	144.5	94.8[20]	100.0	104.1	108.9	114.4	119.0	120.9	Alimentation
Czech Republic									République tchèque
General	94.3	96.2	100.0[2]	104.7	106.6	106.6	109.7	111.7	Généraux
Food[21]	100.7	98.2	100.0[2]	104.3	104.4	104.0	109.0	110.3	Alimentation[21]
Denmark									Danemark
General	94.8	97.1	100.0[2]	102.4	104.8	107.0	108.3	110.2	Généraux
Food	97.0	97.7	100.0[2]	103.9	106.1	107.7	106.6	107.3	Alimentation
Dominica[22]									Dominique[22]
General (2001 =100)	98.0	99.2	...	100.0[6]	100.2	...	...	...	Généraux (2001 =100)
Food (2001 =100)	100.0	100.3	...	100.0[6]	101.5	...	...	...	Alimentation (2001 =100)
Dominican Republic[23]									Rép. dominicaine[23]
General	87.2[2]	92.8	100.0	108.9	114.6	146.0	221.2	230.4	Généraux
Food[1]	94.5	99.6	100.0	106.1	110.7	140.1	237.0	233.2	Alimentation[1]
Ecuador									Equateur
General	33.5	51.0	100.0	137.7	154.9	167.2	171.7	175.9[2]	Généraux
Food[24]	32.9	45.3	100.0	131.2	141.7	145.8	146.9	...	Alimentation[24]
Egypt									Egypte
General	92.5	97.4[2]	100.0	102.2	105.0	109.5	127.4[2]	133.7	Généraux
Food[25]	91.5	97.6[2]	100.0	101.1	105.3	112.3	100.0[26]	105.1	Alimentation[25]
El Salvador[10]									El Salvador[10]
General	97.4	97.8	100.0	103.8	105.7	107.9	112.7	118.0	Généraux
Food	101.2	99.7	100.0	104.6	106.6	108.6	115.5	122.6	Alimentation

Country or area	1998	1999	2000	2001	2002	2003	2004	2005	Pays ou zone
Equatorial Guinea[5]									Guinée équatoriale[5]
General	...	...	100.0	108.8	117.0	125.5	130.9	...	Généraux
Food	177.2	178.2	100.0[11]	111.5	122.2	130.0	135.7	...	Alimentation
Estonia									Estonie
General	93.1	96.2	100.0	105.8	109.5	111.0	114.4	119.0	Généraux
Food[27]	101.5	97.6	100.0	108.3	111.6	109.6	114.2	118.3	Alimentation[27]
Ethiopia[28]									Ethiopie[28]
General	94.5	98.2	100.0	94.5[2]	93.7	100.7	105.8	...	Généraux
Food	92.5	101.1	100.0	87.6[2]	85.7	98.8	102.4	...	Alimentation
Faeroe Islands									Iles Féroé
General	91.3	96.1	100.0	104.9	105.2[2]	106.5	107.2	109.3	Généraux
Food	89.3	97.5	100.0	106.2	108.9[2]	109.5	109.9	111.1	Alimentation
Falkland Is. (Malvinas)[5]									Iles Falkland (Malvinas)[5]
General	92.1	96.0[2]	100.0	101.4	102.0	103.2	...	...	Généraux
Fiji									Fidji
General	97.0	98.9	100.0	104.3	105.0	109.5	112.5	115.1	Généraux
Food[29]	101.5	103.3	100.0	104.1	104.6	111.0	115.2	117.1	Alimentation[29]
Finland									Finlande
General	95.6	96.7	100.0[2]	102.6	104.2	105.1	105.3	106.2	Généraux
Food	99.3	99.0	100.0[2]	104.4	107.4	108.1	108.9	109.2	Alimentation
France									France
General	97.9[2]	98.3	100.0	101.7	103.6	105.8	108.0	109.9	Généraux
Food	97.4[2]	98.0	100.0	105.1	107.8	110.2	110.9	111.0	Alimentation
French Guiana									Guyane française
General	98.4[2]	98.6	100.0	101.6	103.2	105.2	106.4	108.2	Généraux
Food	99.4[2]	98.5	100.0	102.7	105.3	109.3	109.8	110.5	Alimentation
French Polynesia									Polynésie française
General	98.2	99.0	100.0	101.0	103.9	104.3[2]	104.8	105.8	Généraux
Food	99.2	99.2	100.0	102.2	107.4	108.2[2]	110.6	113.2	Alimentation
Gabon[5]									Gabon[5]
General	100.2	99.5	100.0	102.1	102.3	104.4	104.9	104.9	Généraux
Food	100.1	99.5	100.0	105.0	105.2	107.1	105.1	105.5	Alimentation
Gambia[5]									Gambie[5]
General	95.5	99.2	100.0	104.5	113.5	132.8	151.7	...	Généraux
Food	95.9	99.8	100.0	99.3	117.2	141.2	164.0	...	Alimentation
Georgia[30]									Géorgie[30]
General	80.7	96.1	100.0	104.7	110.5	115.8	122.4	132.5	Généraux
Food[8]	83.3	98.7	100.0	106.6	114.6	122.7	132.2	149.6	Alimentation[8]
Germany									Allemagne
General	97.6	98.1	100.0[2]	102.0	103.4	104.5	106.2	108.3	Généraux
Food	101.8	100.5	100.0[2]	104.5	105.3	105.2	104.8	105.3	Alimentation
Ghana									Ghana
General	71.1[2]	79.9	100.0	132.9	151.8	193.3	217.7	250.7	Généraux
Food	82.3[2]	89.4	100.0	123.2	145.6	181.6	211.8	244.7	Alimentation
Gibraltar									Gibraltar
General	98.1	98.9[2]	100.0	101.8	102.5	105.2	107.6	110.9	Généraux
Food	97.7	99.2[2]	100.0	103.5	107.2	111.3	115.1	117.4	Alimentation
Greece									Grèce
General	94.4	96.9[2]	100.0	103.4	107.1	110.9	114.1	118.2[2]	Généraux
Food	95.9	98.1[2]	100.0	105.1	110.7	116.2	116.8	117.5[2]	Alimentation
Greenland									Groenland
General	97.6	98.3	100.0	103.1	107.2	109.0	112.0	113.3	Généraux
Food[31]	96.4	97.3	100.0	103.4	107.6	109.8	111.4	114.5	Alimentation[31]
Grenada									Grenade
General	97.4	97.9	100.0	103.2[2]	104.3	106.6	109.0	...	Généraux
Food	99.1	99.2	100.0	101.8[32]	101.4	102.1	105.4	...	Alimentation
Guadeloupe									Guadeloupe
General	99.6[2]	100.0	100.0	102.6	105.0	107.1	108.6	112.1	Généraux
Food	101.7[2]	101.2	100.0	105.3	108.0	111.7	113.1	116.1	Alimentation

Consumer price indices — General and food (Index base: 2000 = 100) (*continued*)
Indices des prix à la consommation — Généraux et alimentation (Indices base : 2000 = 100) (*suite*)

Country or area	1998	1999	2000	2001	2002	2003	2004	2005	Pays ou zone
Guam									Guam
General	96.1	95.8	100.0	98.8	99.3	100.8	108.0	116.3	Généraux
Food	95.1	94.6	100.0	106.1	112.8	119.1	130.0	141.1	Alimentation
Guatemala[5]									Guatemala[5]
General	89.7	94.4	100.0	107.3[2]	116.0	122.5	131.8	143.8	Généraux
Food	93.8	95.8	100.0	110.0[2]	121.5	128.5	141.8	160.5	Alimentation
Guinea[5]									Guinée[5]
General	89.5	93.5	100.0	105.4	108.4	122.4	141.1[2]	185.3	Généraux
Food	91.2	96.2	100.0	...	114.4[33]	138.8	168.3	230.6	Alimentation
Guinea-Bissau[28]									Guinée-Bissau[28]
General (2003 =100)	...	...	...	...	...	100.0	100.9	104.3	Généraux (2003 =100)
Food (2003 =100)[1]	95.2	93.2	...	...	...	100.0[34]	101.1	104.8	Alimentation (2003 =100)[1]
Guyana[5]									Guyana[5]
General	87.7	94.3	100.0	102.7	108.2	114.6	120.0	128.3	Généraux
Food[8]	88.3	96.0	100.0	100.6	104.5	108.5	113.3	121.7	Alimentation[8]
Haiti[7]									Haïti[7]
General	80.8	87.8	100.0	114.0	125.3	174.5	214.3	249.8[2]	Généraux
Food[1]	89.4	91.1	100.0	115.5	127.4	174.2	223.2	...	Alimentation[1]
Honduras									Honduras
General	84.5	94.3	100.0[2]	109.6	118.0	127.1	137.5	149.5	Généraux
Food	88.3	95.2	100.0[2]	108.7	112.8	117.0	124.9	137.5	Alimentation
Hungary									Hongrie
General	82.8	91.1	100.0	109.2	115.0	120.3	128.5	133.1	Généraux
Food	89.0	91.6	100.0	113.8	119.9	123.2	131.2	134.5	Alimentation
Iceland[35]									Islande[35]
General	92.1	95.2	100.0	106.7	111.8	114.2	117.8	122.6	Généraux
Food	93.0	96.2	100.0	107.4	111.1	108.4	109.7	106.7	Alimentation
India[36]									Inde[36]
General	91.8	96.2	100.0	103.9	108.2	112.5	116.6	121.5	Généraux
Food	96.7	98.2	100.0	102.2	104.9	108.4	111.5	115.0	Alimentation
Indonesia									Indonésie
General	80.0[2]	96.4[37]	100.0[37]	111.5[37]	124.7[37]	133.0[37]	141.3[2,37]	156.0[37]	Généraux
Food	84.0[2]	105.0[37]	100.0[37]	108.5[37]	120.2[37]	121.2[37]	128.3[2,37]	140.3[37]	Alimentation
Iran (Islamic Rep. of)									Iran (Rép. islamique d')
General	73.4	88.8[2]	100.0	111.4	129.0	149.2	165.6	187.8	Généraux
Food[8]	73.9	91.8[2]	100.0	107.3	128.2	143.7	162.3	183.5	Alimentation[8]
Ireland									Irlande
General	93.1	94.7	100.0	104.8[2]	109.7	113.5	116.0	118.8	Généraux
Food	93.3	96.4	100.0	107.0[2]	110.7	112.3	111.9	111.2	Alimentation
Isle of Man									Ile de Man
General	95.4	97.3	100.0[2]	101.7	104.1	107.3	112.8	117.5	Généraux
Food	93.6	97.0	100.0[2]	104.9	113.0	119.6	126.3	131.0	Alimentation
Israel									Israël
General	94.0[2]	98.9	100.0[2]	101.1	106.9[2]	107.7	107.2	108.6	Généraux
Food	91.3[2]	97.7	100.0[2]	102.5	105.4[2]	108.4	108.0	109.9	Alimentation
Italy									Italie
General[38]	95.9	97.5	100.0	102.8	105.4	108.2	110.5	112.4	Généraux[38]
Food	98.1	98.4[39]	100.0	104.1	107.9	111.3	113.7	113.7	Alimentation
Jamaica									Jamaïque
General	87.3	92.4	100.0	107.0	114.6	126.4	143.6	165.5	Généraux
Food	91.4	93.5	100.0	103.4	109.7	120.2	136.5	161.4	Alimentation
Japan									Japon
General	101.0	100.7	100.0[2]	99.3	98.4	98.1	98.1	97.8	Généraux
Food	102.5	102.0	100.0[2]	99.4	98.6	98.4	99.3	98.4	Alimentation
Jordan									Jordanie
General	98.8	99.3	100.0	101.8	103.6[2]	105.3	108.9	112.7	Généraux
Food	101.6	100.7	100.0	100.3	100.5[2]	103.1	107.8	113.4	Alimentation

Consumer price indices — General and food (Index base: 2000 = 100) (*continued*)
Indices des prix à la consommation — Généraux et alimentation (Indices base : 2000 = 100) (*suite*)

Country or area	1998	1999	2000	2001	2002	2003	2004	2005	Pays ou zone
Kazakhstan									Kazakhstan
General	81.6	88.4	100.0	108.4	114.7	122.1	130.5	140.3	Généraux
Food[1]	80.3	86.2	100.0	111.5	119.0	127.3	137.1	148.2	Alimentation[1]
Kenya[5,17]									Kenya[5,17]
General	92.0	94.5	100.0[2]	103.6	105.3	116.7	133.5	149.1	Généraux
Food	95.2	96.8	100.0[2]	102.4	103.9	120.9	143.8	164.9	Alimentation
Kiribati[5]									Kiribati[5]
General	97.9	99.6	100.0	106.0	109.4	111.4	110.3	110.0	Généraux
Food	...	...	100.0[2]	106.1	109.7	112.8	112.8	112.7	Alimentation
Korea, Republic of									Corée, République de
General	97.0	97.8	100.0[2]	104.1	106.9	110.7	114.7	117.8	Généraux
Food	96.5	99.2	100.0[2]	103.5	107.7	112.4	119.5	122.8	Alimentation
Kuwait									Koweït
General	95.4	98.2	100.0[2]	101.8	102.3	103.2	104.5	108.8	Généraux
Food	94.7	99.1	99.8[2]	100.4	101.1	106.6	110.0	119.4	Alimentation
Kyrgyzstan									Kirghizistan
General	62.0	84.2	100.0	106.9	109.1	112.5	117.1	122.2	Généraux
Food	59.9	84.4	100.0	105.7	105.9	108.9	112.4	118.4	Alimentation
Lao People's Dem. Rep.									Rép. dém. pop. lao
General	35.6	81.2	100.0	107.8	119.3	137.8	152.2	...	Généraux
Food (1996 =100)[40]	241.7	529.0	...	...	...	...	...	...	Alimentation (1996 =100)[40]
Latvia									Lettonie
General	95.2	97.4	100.0[2]	102.5	104.5	107.5	114.2	121.9	Généraux
Food	100.4	99.4	100.0[2]	104.8	108.4	111.2	119.5	130.5[41]	Alimentation
Lebanon[5]									Liban[5]
General	...	...	100.0[11]	97.0	95.3	...	...	...	Généraux
Lesotho									Lesotho
General[4]	86.7	94.2	100.0	106.9	120.1	129.0	135.5	...	Généraux[4]
Food	88.9	95.6	100.0	106.5	134.9	142.4	148.1	...	Alimentation
Lithuania									Lituanie
General	98.3	99.1	100.0[2]	101.3	101.6	100.4	101.6	104.3	Généraux
Food	106.7	102.5	100.0[2]	103.5	102.8	99.0	101.2	105.3	Alimentation
Luxembourg									Luxembourg
General	96.0	96.9	100.0	102.7	104.8	106.9	109.3	112.0[2]	Généraux
Food[27]	96.8	98.0	100.0	104.8	108.9	111.0	113.0	114.9[2]	Alimentation[27]
Madagascar									Madagascar
General	...	...	100.0	107.4	125.1	123.0	140.0	152.6	Généraux
Food	...	...	100.0	101.9	117.2	112.9	...	...	Alimentation
Malawi									Malawi
General	53.3	77.2	100.0[2]	122.7	140.8	154.3	172.0	198.5	Généraux
Food	58.4	83.5	100.0[2]	117.6	136.4	143.6	154.4	181.0	Alimentation
Malaysia									Malaisie
General	95.9	98.5	100.0[2]	101.4	103.2	104.4	105.9	109.1[2]	Généraux
Food	93.8	98.1	100.0[2]	100.7	101.4	102.7	105.0	108.8[2]	Alimentation
Maldives[5]									Maldives[5]
General	98.3	101.2	100.0	100.7	101.6	98.7	105.0	108.5	Généraux
Food[1]	100.8	105.0	100.0	102.1	105.7	99.3	115.2	117.6	Alimentation[1]
Mali[5]									Mali[5]
General	101.9[2]	100.7	100.0	105.1	110.4	109.1	105.6	112.4	Généraux
Food[42]	108.8[11]	104.7	100.0	108.1	115.8	111.1	103.3	115.1	Alimentation[42]
Malta									Malte
General	95.6	97.6	100.0	102.9	105.2	105.7[2]	108.7	111.9	Généraux
Food	97.6	98.5	100.0	106.0	107.4	109.2[2]	109.5	111.4	Alimentation
Marshall Islands[5]									Iles Marshall[5]
General	96.8	98.4	100.0	101.8	103.0	100.1	102.3	106.9	Généraux
Food	99.3	100.2	100.0	100.3	102.7	102.5	106.0	106.3	Alimentation
Martinique									Martinique
General	98.6[2]	99.0	100.0	102.1	104.2	106.4	108.6	111.2	Généraux
Food	100.3	100.2[43]	100.0	103.8	108.8	112.5	114.6	118.2	Alimentation

Country or area	1998	1999	2000	2001	2002	2003	2004	2005	Pays ou zone
Mauritania									Mauritanie
General	93.1	96.9	100.0	104.7	108.9	114.4	124.2[2]	139.3	Généraux
Food	92.9	96.3	100.0	106.5	111.3	117.9[44]	131.2[2]	149.3	Alimentation
Mauritius									Maurice
General	89.8	96.0	100.0	105.4	112.2[2]	116.5	122.1	128.1	Généraux
Food	92.8	98.7	100.0	104.1	112.2[2]	115.4	122.3	129.5	Alimentation
Mexico									Mexique
General	78.3	91.3	100.0	106.4	111.7[2]	116.8	122.3	127.2	Généraux
Food[1]	81.2	94.1	100.0	105.4	109.6[2]	115.1	122.9	129.4	Alimentation[1]
Mongolia[28]									Mongolie[28]
General	83.3	89.6	100.0	106.3[2]	107.3	112.8	122.1	137.6	Généraux
Food[1]	84.0	87.0[2]	100.0	101.5	98.5	105.5	118.5	139.4	Alimentation[1]
Morocco									Maroc
General	97.5	98.2	100.0	100.6	103.4	104.6	106.2	107.3	Généraux
Food[8]	99.4	98.5	100.0	99.0	103.2	104.6	106.2	106.5	Alimentation[8]
Mozambique[5]									Mozambique[5]
General	86.3	88.7	100.0	109.1	127.4	144.5	162.7	173.2[2]	Généraux
Food	94.6	89.4	100.0	108.0	126.4	147.9	...	...	Alimentation
Myanmar									Myanmar
General	82.6	100.1	100.0	121.1	190.2	259.8	271.6	297.1	Généraux
Food	84.1	102.6	100.0	119.5	201.2	274.3	277.5	303.2	Alimentation
Namibia									Namibie
General	84.3	91.5	100.0	109.3	121.7	130.4	135.5		Généraux
General (2002 =100)	...	...	...	...	100.0	107.2	111.6	114.1	Généraux (2002 =100)
Food	88.6	93.5	100.0	111.5	133.2	144.1	147.1	...	Alimentation
Food (2002 =100)	...	...	...	...	100.0	109.5	110.4	112.0	Alimentation (2002 =100)
Nepal									Népal
General	91.4	97.7	100.0	102.7	105.9	112.0	115.2	...	Généraux
Food	95.4	102.8	100.0	101.4	104.4	110.1	112.9	...	Alimentation
Netherlands									Pays-Bas
General	95.4	97.5	100.0[2]	104.2	107.6	109.9	111.2	113.1	Généraux
Food	97.9	99.2	100.0[2]	107.0	110.9	111.7	107.8	106.5	Alimentation
Netherlands Antilles[5]									Antilles néerlandaises[5]
General	94.1	94.5	100.0	101.8	102.1	104.3	105.7	109.3	Généraux
Food	92.2	94.1	100.0	103.4	107.3	109.5	114.7	123.3	Alimentation
New Caledonia[5]									Nouvelle-Calédonie[5]
General	98.3	98.5	100.0	102.3	104.1	105.4	106.3	107.6	Généraux
Food	98.5	99.4	100.0	102.6	105.0	107.0	108.3	109.7	Alimentation
New Zealand									Nouvelle-Zélande
General	97.6[2]	97.5	100.0	102.6	105.4	107.2	109.7	113.0	Généraux
Food	97.7[2]	98.7	100.0	106.0	109.4	109.4	110.3	113.1	Alimentation
Nicaragua[5]									Nicaragua[5]
General	80.6	89.7	100.0	107.4[2]	111.6	117.4	127.3	...	Généraux
General (1999 =100)	...	100.0	...	113.5	117.7	124.0	134.5	147.4	Généraux (1999 =100)
Food	90.3	95.2	100.0	108.6[2]	111.8	116.0	127.6	...	Alimentation
Food (1999 =100)	...	100.0	...	112.1	115.7	120.7	133.6	149.0	Alimentation (1999 =100)
Niger[5]									Niger[5]
General[4]	99.5[2]	97.2	100.0	104.0	106.7	105.1	105.2	113.5	Généraux[4]
Food[8]	102.4[2]	97.0	100.0	107.2	112.0	106.7	105.1	120.7	Alimentation[8]
Nigeria									Nigéria
General	87.7	93.5	100.0	118.9	134.2	153.1[2]	...	...	Généraux
Food	96.7	97.6	100.0	128.0	144.8	153.8[2]	...	...	Alimentation
Niue									Nioué
General	95.7	96.6	100.0	106.8	109.7	112.3[2]	116.6[46]	117.0	Généraux
Food	94.5	94.9	100.0	111.2	115.1	118.3[2]	121.2[46]	122.0	Alimentation
Norfolk Island									Ile Norfolk
General	93.5	96.4	100.0	103.1	...	109.1	...	...	Généraux
Food	95.6	97.2	100.0	104.5	...	...	...	...	Alimentation

Country or area	1998	1999	2000	2001	2002	2003	2004	2005	Pays ou zone
Northern Mariana Islands[5]									Iles Mariannes du Nord[5]
General	96.7	98.0	100.0	99.2	99.4	98.4[2]	99.3	...	Généraux
Food	101.9	100.6	100.0	96.6	93.0	90.7[2]	94.9	...	Alimentation
Norway									Norvège
General	94.8[2]	97.0	100.0	103.0	104.4	106.9	107.4	109.1	Généraux
Food	95.4[47]	98.2	100.0	98.1	96.5	99.7	101.5	103.1	Alimentation
Occupied Palestinian Terr.									Terr. palestinien occupé
General	92.2	97.3	100.0	101.2	107.0	111.7	115.1	...	Généraux
Food	94.0	98.4	100.0	99.5	102.1	106.8	109.1	...	Alimentation
Oman[5]									Oman[5]
General	100.7	101.2	100.0	99.0	98.3	97.9	98.3	100.3[2]	Généraux
Food[8]	101.5	101.3	100.0	99.4	98.3	98.2	98.5	102.7[2]	Alimentation[8]
Pakistan									Pakistan
General	92.0	95.8	100.0	103.2	107.4[2]	110.5	118.7	129.5	Généraux
Food	93.3	96.9	100.0	101.8	105.9[2]	108.6	120.2	132.1	Alimentation
Panama[10]									Panama[10]
General	97.3	98.5	100.0	100.3	101.3	102.7	...	...	Généraux
General (2003 =100)	...	...	...	...	...	100.0	100.4	103.3	Généraux (2003 =100)
Food	99.4	99.3	100.0	99.6	98.9	100.2	...	...	Alimentation
Food (2003 =100)	...	...	...	...	...	100.0	101.3	105.6	Alimentation (2003 =100)
Papua New Guinea									Papouasie-Nvl-Guinée
General	75.3	86.5	100.0	109.3	122.2	140.2	...	...	Généraux
Food	75.3	88.0	100.0	109.6	128.3	145.3	...	...	Alimentation
Paraguay[5]									Paraguay[5]
General	86.0	91.8	100.0	107.3	118.5	135.4	141.3	149.5	Généraux
Food	89.5	92.3	100.0	103.8	114.4	139.3	149.8	156.2	Alimentation
Peru[5,7]									Pérou[5,7]
General	93.2	96.4	100.0	102.0	102.2[2]	104.5	108.3	110.1	Généraux
Food	99.5	99.3	100.0	100.5	100.2[2]	101.0	106.6	107.6	Alimentation
Philippines									Philippines
General	89.8	95.9	100.0[2]	106.8	110.1	113.9	120.6	129.8	Généraux
Food[1]	93.1	98.0	100.0[2]	104.7	107.1	109.4	116.3	123.8	Alimentation[1]
Poland									Pologne
General	84.7[11]	90.9	100.0	105.5	107.5	108.4	112.2	114.6	Généraux
Food[24]	89.5[11]	91.2	100.0	105.1	104.6	103.0	108.6	110.6	Alimentation[24]
Portugal									Portugal
General[4]	95.0	97.2	100.0	104.4	108.1[2]	111.6	114.2	116.7	Généraux[4]
Food[48]	95.9	97.9	100.0	106.5	108.1[2]	110.9	112.1	111.3	Alimentation[48]
Puerto Rico									Porto Rico
General	88.9	94.0	100.0	107.0	113.6	122.5	137.1	156.1	Généraux
Food	83.1	91.7	100.0	114.1	127.8	145.8	176.3	212.1	Alimentation
Qatar									Qatar
General	96.3	98.4	100.0[2]	101.5	101.6	104.0	111.0	120.9	Généraux
Food[8]	99.6	99.6	100.0[2]	99.8	101.1	100.7	104.4	107.7	Alimentation[8]
Republic of Moldova									République de Moldova
General	54.7	76.2	100.0	109.8	115.6	129.2	145.3	162.7	Généraux
Food	55.2	73.3	100.0	110.7	115.5	131.2	147.9	168.0	Alimentation
Réunion									Réunion
General	97.3[2]	98.2	100.0	102.3	105.1	106.3	108.1	110.4	Généraux
Food	100.2[2]	99.3	100.0	101.5	108.3	107.5	107.5	108.8	Alimentation
Romania									Roumanie
General	47.1	68.7	100.0	134.5	164.8	189.9	212.5	231.7	Généraux
Food	54.4	69.6	100.0	135.7	160.5	184.1	201.5	213.8	Alimentation
Russian Federation									Fédération de Russie
General	44.6[2]	82.8	100.0	121.5[2]	140.6	159.9	177.3	199.7	Généraux
Food	43.3[2]	85.1	100.0	121.7[2]	136.5	151.8	167.4	190.3	Alimentation
Rwanda[5]									Rwanda[5]
General	98.6	96.2	100.0	103.4	105.4	113.2[2]	126.7	138.3	Généraux
Food	116.2	99.1	100.0	106.0	104.7	119.2[2]	141.7	...	Alimentation

Consumer price indices — General and food (Index base: 2000 = 100) (*continued*)

Indices des prix à la consommation — Généraux et alimentation (Indices base : 2000 = 100) (*suite*)

Country or area	1998	1999	2000	2001	2002	2003	2004	2005	Pays ou zone
Saint Helena									Sainte-Hélène
General (2002 =100)	96.6	98.6	...	...	100.0[49]	100.0	108.8	112.9	Généraux (2002 =100)
Food (2002 =100)	98.2	99.4	...	...	100.0[49]	103.8	112.9	116.1	Alimentation (2002 =100)
Saint Kitts and Nevis[5]									Saint-Kitts-et-Nevis[5]
General	94.8	97.9	...	...	...	...	...	...	Généraux
Food	97.3	97.7	...	...	...	...	...	...	Alimentation
Saint Lucia									Sainte-Lucie
General	93.2	96.4	100.0	105.2	105.0	106.0	107.6	111.8	Généraux
Food	96.0	98.8	100.0	103.2	101.9	104.1	104.9	112.4	Alimentation
Saint Pierre and Miquelon									Saint-Pierre-et-Miquelon
General	91.3	92.2	100.0	102.3	102.5	104.8	106.9	114.0	Généraux
Food	93.5	94.5	100.0	103.5	106.1	106.7	104.9	109.7	Alimentation
Saint Vincent-Grenadines[5]									Saint Vincent-Grenadines[5]
General	98.8	99.8	100.0	100.8[2]	101.5	101.8	104.8	108.7	Généraux
Food	100.6	101.1	100.0	101.0[2]	101.6	100.9	105.6	111.3	Alimentation
Samoa									Samoa
General[4]	98.6	98.9[2]	100.0	103.7	112.2	112.3	130.5[2]	133.0	Généraux[4]
Food	101.1	100.1[2]	100.0	105.1	117.3	115.1	146.2[2]	146.7	Alimentation
San Marino									Saint-Marin
General (2003 =100)	93.8	96.8	...	...	...	100.0[34]	101.4	...	Généraux (2003 =100)
Food (2003 =100)	96.8	98.9	...	...	...	100.0[34]	103.3	...	Alimentation (2003 =100)
Saudi Arabia[50,51]									Arabie saoudite[50,51]
General	102.0	100.6	100.0	99.2	98.6	97.3	99.5[2]	100.2	Généraux
Food[8]	103.6	100.9	100.0	100.6	100.0	96.9	104.4[2]	107.5	Alimentation[8]
Senegal[5]									Sénégal[5]
General	98.5[2]	99.3	100.0	103.0	105.4	105.3	105.9	107.7	Généraux
Food[8]	100.8[52]	101.1	100.0	104.9	110.1	109.4	110.3	114.5	Alimentation[8]
Serbia and Montenegro									Serbie-et-Monténégro
General	37.2	53.9	100.0	189.2	220.4	241.2	267.2	...	Généraux
Food	33.6	48.7	100.0	188.2	200.4	202.0	224.5	...	Alimentation
Seychelles									Seychelles
General	88.6	94.2	100.0	106.0[2]	106.3	109.8	114.0	...	Généraux
Food	99.5	98.6	100.0	104.9[2]	105.6	108.3	109.2	...	Alimentation
Sierra Leone[5]									Sierra Leone[5]
General	75.3	100.9	100.0	102.2	98.8	106.3	121.4	136.0	Généraux
Food	74.8	100.4	100.0	105.2	104.4	112.2	...	...	Alimentation
Singapore									Singapour
General	98.6[2]	98.7	100.0	101.0	100.6	101.1	102.8[2]	103.2	Généraux
Food	98.5[2]	99.4	100.0	100.5	100.5	101.1	103.2[2]	104.6	Alimentation
Slovakia									Slovaquie
General	80.8	89.3	100.0	107.1[2]	110.7	120.2	129.2	132.8	Généraux
Food	92.5	95.0	100.0	105.8[2]	107.4	111.0	116.4	114.7	Alimentation
Slovenia[10]									Slovénie[10]
General	86.5	91.8	100.0	108.4	116.5	123.0	127.4	130.6	Généraux
Food	91.2	94.8	100.0	109.0	117.5	123.1	124.2	...	Alimentation
Solomon Islands[5]									Iles Salomon[5]
General	86.5	93.6	100.0	107.8	119.5	129.4	138.7	149.3	Généraux
Food	83.7	93.1	100.0	108.9	122.1	125.0	136.8	145.1	Alimentation
South Africa									Afrique du Sud
General	90.3	95.0	100.0[2]	105.7	115.4	122.1	123.8	128.0	Généraux
Food	88.5	92.8	100.0[2]	105.4	122.0	131.9	134.9	137.9	Alimentation
Spain[22]									Espagne[22]
General (2001 =100)	94.5	96.7	...	100.0[6]	103.5	106.7	109.9	113.6	Généraux (2001 =100)
Food (2001 =100)	96.8	98.0	...	100.0[6]	104.7	109.0	113.2	116.3	Alimentation (2001 =100)
Sri Lanka[5]									Sri Lanka[5]
General	90.0	94.2	100.0	114.2	125.1	133.0	143.0	159.7	Généraux
Food	92.1	95.7	100.0	115.2	127.5	134.9	145.5	163.0	Alimentation

29 Consumer price indices — General and food (Index base: 2000 = 100) (*continued*)

Indices des prix à la consommation — Généraux et alimentation (Indices base : 2000 = 100) (*suite*)

Country or area	1998	1999	2000	2001	2002	2003	2004	2005	Pays ou zone
Suriname[22,28]									Suriname[22,28]
General (2001 =100)	22.8	45.3	77.4[53]	100.0[2]	115.9	...	156.9[54]	171.4	Généraux (2001 =100)
Food (2001 =100)	25.5	48.6	80.5[53]	100.0[2]	118.1	...	157.8[54]	174.3	Alimentation (2001 =100)
Swaziland									Swaziland
General	85.9	91.0	100.0	107.7	120.3	129.1	133.5	139.9	Généraux
Food	89.3	93.7	100.0	106.5	129.8	145.7	155.7	169.2	Alimentation
Sweden									Suède
General	98.7	99.1	100.0	102.4	104.6	106.6	107.0	107.5	Généraux
Food	98.5	100.0	100.0	102.9	106.2	106.6	106.1	105.4	Alimentation
Switzerland									Suisse
General	97.7	98.5	100.0[2]	101.0	101.7	102.3	103.1	104.4	Généraux
Food	98.6	98.5	100.0[2]	102.1	104.5	105.9	106.5	105.8	Alimentation
Syrian Arab Republic									Rép. arabe syrienne
General	102.8	100.8	100.0	100.4	101.4	109.3[2]	114.1	122.6	Généraux
Food	106.3	102.1	100.0	100.2	99.6	107.3[2]	112.8	122.4	Alimentation
Tajikistan									Tadjikistan
General	64.0	80.7	...	...	...	...	...	...	Généraux
Thailand									Thaïlande
General	98.2	98.5	100.0[2]	101.6	102.3	104.1	107.0[2]	111.8	Généraux
Food	102.0	101.1	100.0[2]	100.7	101.0	104.7	109.4[2]	114.9	Alimentation
TFYR of Macedonia									L'ex-R.y. Macédoine
General	95.2	94.5	100.0	105.5	107.4	108.7	108.3	108.8	Généraux
Food	102.0	100.4	100.0	106.9	108.8	107.3	104.0	102.7	Alimentation
Togo[5]									Togo[5]
General	98.2[2]	98.2	100.0	103.9	107.1	106.0	106.5	113.7	Généraux
Food[1]	109.0[55]	103.5	100.0	105.2	109.3	103.1	101.9	113.0	Alimentation[1]
Tonga									Tonga
General[4]	90.1	93.7	100.0	108.3	119.6[2]	133.5	148.1	160.4	Généraux[4]
Food	94.5	99.7	100.0	111.8	130.6[2]	143.1	156.1	165.5	Alimentation
Trinidad and Tobago									Trinité-et-Tobago
General	93.4	96.6	100.0	105.6	110.0	114.2[2]	118.3	126.5	Généraux
Food	85.0	92.4	100.0	114.0	125.6	142.9[2]	161.1	198.1	Alimentation
Tunisia									Tunisie
General	94.6	97.1	100.0[2]	102.0	104.8	107.6	111.5	113.8	Généraux
Food	93.5	95.6	100.0[2]	102.0	106.1	109.7	115.1	115.2	Alimentation
Turkey									Turquie
General	39.2	64.6	100.0	154.4	223.8	280.4	310.1	329.5[2]	Généraux
Food	44.9	66.8	100.0	150.3	225.3	290.0	316.1	112.1[56]	Alimentation
Tuvalu[5]									Tuvalu[5]
General	93.1	96.3	100.0	101.5	106.7[2]	110.2	113.3	117.0	Généraux
Food	95.2	99.0	100.0	105.3	109.4[2]	117.4	120.8	127.4	Alimentation
Uganda									Ouganda
General	91.5	96.8	100.0	101.9	101.6	110.5	114.5	124.1	Généraux
Food	92.7	99.0	100.0	96.6	92.5	106.7	111.4	126.1	Alimentation
Ukraine									Ukraine
General	63.6	78.0	100.0	112.0	112.8	118.7	129.4	146.9	Généraux
Food[1]	58.2	74.4	100.0	114.4	114.4	121.5	135.1	157.5	Alimentation[1]
United Arab Emirates									Emirats arabes unis
General	96.6	98.6	100.0[2]	102.8	105.8	109.1	114.6	121.7	Généraux
Food[57]	97.0	99.5	100.0[2]	101.0	102.4	104.7	112.0	117.0	Alimentation[57]
United Kingdom									Royaume-Uni
General	95.7	97.1	100.0	101.8	103.5	106.5	109.6	112.7	Généraux
Food	100.0	100.3	100.0	103.3	104.0	105.4	106.0	107.3	Alimentation
United States[58]									Etats-Unis[58]
General	94.7	96.8	100.0	102.9	104.5	106.9	109.7	113.4	Généraux
Food	95.8	97.8	100.0	103.2	105.0	107.3	111.0	113.7	Alimentation
Uruguay[5]									Uruguay[5]
General	90.3	95.5	100.0	104.4	118.9	142.0	155.0	162.3	Généraux
Food	91.3	94.7	100.0	103.1	117.2	142.5	159.2	165.7	Alimentation

Consumer price indices — General and food (Index base: 2000 = 100) (*continued*)
Indices des prix à la consommation — Généraux et alimentation (Indices base : 2000 = 100) (*suite*)

Country or area	1998	1999	2000	2001	2002	2003	2004	2005	Pays ou zone
Vanuatu									Vanuatu
General	95.6	97.6[2]	100.0	103.6	105.7	108.8	110.4	111.7	Généraux
Food	96.6	98.0[2]	100.0	102.2	102.7	105.0	108.6	108.0	Alimentation
Venezuela (Bolivarian Rep. of)[5]									Venezuela (Rép. bolivarienne du)[5]
General	69.6	86.0	100.0[2]	112.5	137.8	180.6	219.9	254.9	Généraux
Food	79.8	93.3	100.0[2]	116.2	149.0	205.2	274.6	332.5	Alimentation
Viet Nam									Viet Nam
General	97.5	101.6	100.0	99.7	103.7	107.0	115.0	...	Généraux
Food[1]	99.8	104.0	100.0	98.6	106.1	108.7	119.8	...	Alimentation[1]
Yemen									Yémen
General	88.0	95.6	100.0	111.9	125.6	139.2	156.6	174.5	Généraux
Food	86.1	95.0	100.0	115.7	121.2	141.4	168.3	199.9	Alimentation
Zambia									Zambie
General	62.6	79.3	100.0	121.4	148.4	180.1	212.5	251.4	Généraux
Food[1]	66.6	81.6	100.0	118.9	151.1	184.5	...	...	Alimentation[1]
Zimbabwe									Zimbabwe
General	40.5	64.2	100.0	176.7	424.3	2 255.8	8 625.7	34 688.3[2]	Généraux
Food	40.0	67.1	100.0	164.1	407.7	2 238.4	8 792.0	42 868.1[2]	Alimentation

Source

International Labour Office (ILO), Geneva, the ILO labour statistics database and the "Yearbook of Labour Statistics 2005".

Notes

1 Including alcoholic beverages and tobacco.
2 Series linked to former series.
3 Series (base 2000=100) replacing former series; prior to 2000: including alcoholic beverages and tobacco.
4 Excluding rent.
5 Data refer to the index of the capital city.
6 Series (base 2001 = 100) replacing former series.
7 Metropolitan area.
8 Including tobacco.
9 Government officials.
10 Urban areas.
11 Series (base 2000=100) replacing former series.
12 Beginning 1997, including tobacco.
13 Prior to December 2003: Douala and Yaoundé only.
14 January-October.
15 Series replacing former series.
16 Series (base 2000=100) replacing former series; prior to 1999: excluding rent.
17 Low-income group.
18 Excluding beverages.
19 Central area.
20 Series (base 2000=100) replacing former series; prior to 1999: including alcoholic beverages and tobacco.
21 Including tobacco, beverages and public catering.
22 Index base: 2001=100.
23 Including direct taxes.
24 Including alcoholic beverages.
25 Index base: 2004=100.
26 Series (base 2004=100) replacing former series; prior to 2004: incl. tobacco.
27 Excluding alcoholic beverages and tobacco.
28 December of each year.
29 Excluding beverages and tobacco.
30 Five cities.
31 Prior to 1996: including tobacco.

Source

Bureau international du Travail (BIT), Genève, la base de données du BIT et "l'Annuaire des statistiques du travail 2005".

Notes

1 Y compris les boissons alcoolisées et le tabac.
2 Série enchaînée à la précédente.
3 Série (base 2000=100) remplaçant la précédente; avant 2000: y compris les boissons alcoolisées et le tabac.
4 Non compris le groupe "Loyer".
5 Les données se réfèrent à l'indice de la ville principale.
6 Série (base 2001 = 100) remplaçant la précédente.
7 Région métropolitaine.
8 Y compris le tabac.
9 Fonctionnaires.
10 Régions urbaines.
11 Série (base 2000=100) remplaçant la précédente.
12 A partir 1997, y compris le tabac.
13 Avant déc. 2003: Douala et Yaoundé seulement.
14 Janvier-octobre.
15 Série remplaçant la précédente.
16 Série (base 2000=100) remplaçant la précédente; avant 1999 : non compris le groupe "Loyer".
17 Familles à revenu modique.
18 Non compris les boissons.
19 Région centrale.
20 Série (base 2000=100) remplaçant la précédente; avant 1999 : y compris les boissons alcoolisées et le tabac.
21 Y compris le tabac, les boissons et la restauration.
22 Indice base : 2001=100.
23 Y compris les impôts directs.
24 Y compris les boissons alcoolisées.
25 Indice base : 2004=100.
26 Série (base 2004=100) remplaçant la précédente; avant 2004: y compris le tabac.
27 Non compris les boissons alcoolisées et le tabac.
28 Décembre de chaque année.
29 Non compris les boissons et le tabac.
30 Cinq villes.
31 Avant 1996: y compris le tabac.

32 Series (base 2000=100) replacing former series; prior to 2001: incl. alcoholic beverages and tobacco.
33 July-December; series linked to former series.
34 Series (base 2003=100) replacing former series.
35 Annual averages are based on the months Feb.-Dec. and the mean of January both years.
36 Industrial workers.
37 Since November 1999: excluding Dili.
38 Excluding tobacco.
39 Prior to 1999: including alcoholic beverages.
40 Index base: 1996=100.
41 Series replacing former series; prior to 2005: including alcoholic beverages and tobacco.
42 Beginning January 1998, including alcoholic beverages and tobacco.
43 Series replacing former series; prior to 1999: including tobacco.
44 January-November.
45 Index base: 2002=100.
46 Average of the last three quarters.
47 Series (base 2000=100) replacing former series; prior to 1998: Food only.
48 Excluding alcoholic beverages.
49 Series (base 2002=100) replacing former series.
50 Middle-income group.
51 All cities.
52 Series linked to former series; prior 1998: excluding tobacco.
53 April-December.
54 March-December.
55 Series (base 2000=100) replacing former series; as from 1998: incl. beverages and tobacco.
56 Series (base 2003 = 100) replacing former series; prior to 2005 incl. alcoholic beverages and tobacco.
57 Including beverages and tobacco.
58 All urban consumers.

32 Série (base 2000=100) remplaçant la précédente; avant 2001 : y compris les boissons alcoolisées et le tabac.
33 Juillet-décembre; série enchaînée à la précédente.
34 Série (base 2003=100) remplaçant la précédente.
35 Les moyennes annuelles sont basées sur les mois de fév.-déc. et la moyenne de janvier des deux années.
36 Travailleurs de l'industrie.
37 A partir de novembre 1999: non compris Dili.
38 Non compris le tabac.
39 Avant 1999 : y compris les boissons alcooliques.
40 Indices base: 1996=100.
41 Série remplaçant la précédente; avant 2005: y compris les boissons alcoolisées et le tabac.
42 A partir de janvier, y compris les boissons alcoolisées et le tabac.
43 Série remplaçant la précédente; avant 1999: y compris le tabac.
44 Janvier-novembre.
45 Indice base : 2002=100.
46 Moyenne des trois derniers trimestres.
47 Série (base 2000=100) remplaçant la précédente; avant 1998: alimentation seulement.
48 Non compris les boissons alcooliques.
49 Série (base 2002=100) remplaçant la précédente.
50 Familles à revenu moyen.
51 Ensemble des villes.
52 Série enchaînée à la précédente; avant 1998 : non compris le tabac.
53 Avril-décembre.
54 Mars-décembre.
55 Série (base 2000 = 100) remplaçant la précédente; à partir 1998: y compris les boissons et le tabac.
56 Série (base 2003=100) remplaçant la précédente; avant 2005 y compris les boissons alcoolisées et le tabac.
57 Y compris les boissons et le tabac.
58 Tous les consommateurs urbains.

Technical notes: tables 27-29

Table 27: The series generally relate to the average earnings per worker in manufacturing industries, according to the *International Standard Industrial Classification of All Economic Activities* (ISIC) Revision 2 or Revision 3. The data are published in the ILO *Yearbook of Labour Statistics* and on the ILO web site http://laborsta.ilo.org and generally cover all employees (i.e. wage earners and salaried employees) of both sexes, irrespective of age. Data which refer exclusively to wage earners (i.e. manual or production workers), salaried employees (i.e. non-manual workers), or to total employment are also shown when available. Earnings generally include bonuses, cost of living allowances, taxes, social insurance contributions payable by the employed person and, in some cases, payments in kind, and normally exclude social insurance contributions payable by the employers, family allowances and other social security benefits. The time of year to which the figures refer is not the same for all countries. In some cases, the series may show wage rates instead of earnings; this is indicated in footnotes.

Table 28: The producer price index (PPI) can be generally described as an index for measuring the average change in the prices of goods and services either as they leave the place of production or as they enter the production process. As such, producer price indices can represent input prices (at purchasers' prices) and output prices (at basic or producer prices) with different levels of aggregation.

The industrial coverage of the PPI can vary across countries. Normally, the PPIs refer to indices related to the agricultural, mining, manufacturing, transport and telecommunications, and public utilities sectors. Many countries are progressively developing service industry PPIs for incorporation within their larger PPI frameworks. PPI prices should be actual transaction prices recorded at the time the transaction occurs (i.e. when ownership changes).

PPIs can be calculated in a number of different combinations. In this publication, the PPIs are classified according to the following scheme:

(a) Components of supply
Domestic supply
Domestic production for domestic market
Agricultural products
Industrial products
Imported goods

(b) Stage of processing
Raw materials
Intermediate goods

(c) End-use
Consumer goods
Capital goods

Notes techniques : tableaux 27 à 29

Tableau 27: Les séries se rapportent généralement aux gains moyens des salariés des industries manufacturières (activités de fabrication), suivant la *Classification internationale type, par industrie, de toutes les branches d'activité économique* (CITI, Rev. 2 ou Rev.3). Les données sont publiées dans *l'Annuaire des statistiques du travail* du BIT et sur le site Web du BIT http://laborsta.ilo.org et généralement portent sur l'ensemble des salariés (qu'ils perçoivent un salaire ou un traitement au mois) des deux sexes, indépendamment de leur âge. Les données qui portent exclusivement sur les salariés horaires (ouvriers, travailleurs manuels), sur les employés percevant un traitement (travailleurs autres que manuels, cadres), ou sur l'emploi total sont aussi présentées si elles sont disponibles. Les gains comprennent en général les primes, les indemnités pour coût de la vie, les impôts, les cotisations de sécurité sociale à la charge de l'employé, et dans certains cas des paiements en nature, mais ne comprennent pas en règle générale la part patronale des cotisations d'assurance sociale, les allocations familiales et les autres prestations de sécurité sociale. La période de l'année visée par les données n'est pas la même pour tous les pays. Dans certains cas, les séries présentent les taux horaires et non pas les gains, ce présente qui est alors signalé en note.

Tableau 28: L'indice des prix à la production peut être caractérisé de manière générale comme un indice permettant de mesurer le changement moyen des prix des biens et des services soit au moment où ils quittent le lieu de production soit au moment où ils arrivent au processus de production. Les indices des prix à la production peuvent donc représenter les prix des intrants (aux prix d'acquisition) et les prix à la sortie de fabrique (aux prix de base, ou prix à la production), les agrégats étant de différents niveaux.

Les branches d'activité couvertes par l'indice des prix à la production peuvent n'être pas les mêmes d'un pays à l'autre. Normalement, l'indice concerne l'agriculture, les industries extractives, les industries manufacturières, les transports et télécommunications et les services publics de distribution. Nombre de pays mettent peu à peu au point des indices des prix à la production pour les services, de manière à pouvoir les intégrer à leurs indices des prix à la production plus généraux. Les prix servant pour ces indices doivent être des prix effectifs de transaction enregistrés au moment où s'effectue la transaction (au moment où le propriétaire change).

Les indices des prix à la production peuvent se calculer selon plusieurs combinaisons différentes. Dans la présente publication, on les classe de la manière ci-après:

(a) Eléments de l'offre
Offre intérieure
Production nationale pour le marché intérieur

Though a few countries are still compiling the wholesale price index (WPI), which is the precedent of the PPI, the WPI has been replaced in most countries by the PPI because of the broader coverage provided by the PPI in terms of products and industries and the conceptual concordance between the PPI and the System of National Accounts. The WPI would normally cover the price of products as they flow from the wholesaler to the retailer and is an index for measuring the price level changes in markets other than retail.

For a more detailed explanation about the PPI, please refer to the *Producer Price Index Manual: Theory and Practice* published by the International Monetary Fund in 2004.

Table 29: Unless otherwise stated, the consumer price index covers all the main classes of expenditure on all items and on food. Monthly data for many of these series may be found in the United Nations *Monthly Bulletin of Statistics*.

Produits agricoles
Produits industriels
Produits importés

(b) Stade de la transformation
Matières premières
Produits intermédiaires

(c) Utilisation finale
Biens de consommation
Biens d'équipement

Même s'il y a encore quelques pays qui compilent l'indice des prix de gros, qui est l'ancêtre de l'indice des prix à la production, la plupart l'ont remplacé par ce dernier, qui offre une couverture plus large de produits et de branches d'activité, et coïncide dans ses concepts avec le Système de comptabilité nationale. L'indice des prix de gros suivait normalement le prix des produits à mesure qu'ils passaient du grossiste au détaillant il permet de mesurer les changements du niveau des prix sur les marchés autres que le marché de détail.

Pour un complément de détails sur l'indice des prix à la production, on se reportera au «*Producer Price Index Manual, Theory and Practice*» publié par le Fonds monétaire international en 2004.

Tableau 29: Sauf indication contraire, les indices des prix à la consommation donnés englobent tous les groupes principaux de dépenses pour l'ensemble des prix et alimentation. Les données mensuelles pour plusieurs de ces séries figurent dans le *Bulletin mensuel de statistique*.

30

Agricultural production
Index base: 1999-01 = 100

Production agricole
Indices base : 1999-01 = 100

Region, country or area — Région, pays ou zone	Agriculture — Agriculture					Food — Produits alimentaires				
	2001	2002	2003	2004	2005	2001	2002	2003	2004	2005
World — Monde	**101.6**	**103.2**	**106.3**	**110.7**	**111.3**	**101.6**	**103.4**	**106.5**	**110.5**	**111.1**
Africa — Afrique	**101.5**	**103.2**	**107.7**	**109.2**	**110.2**	**101.4**	**103.5**	**108.5**	**109.6**	**110.6**
Algeria — Algérie	103.6	104.9	123.8	122.1	122.2	103.6	104.9	124.1	122.3	122.4
Angola — Angola	112.3	122.8	129.2	126.5	145.5	112.5	123.4	129.9	127.1	146.6
Benin — Bénin	102.1	112.7	114.4	119.9	121.0	102.2	109.8	116.1	122.5	123.9
Botswana — Botswana	109.2	106.2	105.4	106.2	106.6	109.3	106.3	105.5	106.4	106.7
Burkina Faso — Burkina Faso	112.7	116.5	126.8	120.0	119.0	114.7	113.1	124.5	110.6	109.5
Burundi — Burundi	103.8	108.7	106.8	106.1	102.1	104.5	107.2	107.4	104.4	104.4
Cameroon — Cameroun	101.8	104.1	106.1	107.3	108.5	101.9	105.5	108.2	108.6	108.1
Cape Verde — Cap-Vert	97.0	91.4	94.1	91.4	91.7	97.0	91.4	94.1	91.4	91.7
Central African Rep. — Rép. centrafricaine	105.0	105.0	102.4	105.3	107.5	105.0	106.4	106.2	109.4	111.7
Chad — Tchad	108.5	107.2	110.1	110.2	110.8	109.0	107.4	114.5	108.9	109.7
Comoros — Comores	101.9	100.7	104.7	104.3	104.3	101.9	100.7	104.8	104.3	104.3
Congo — Congo	101.1	105.0	107.5	109.0	110.4	101.1	104.9	107.3	108.9	110.3
Côte d'Ivoire — Côte d'Ivoire	96.5	96.8	97.2	98.2	97.9	99.6	99.4	100.8	102.1	101.8
Dem. Rep. of the Congo — Rép. dém. du Congo	98.2	96.5	97.2	96.7	96.8	98.5	96.8	97.5	97.0	97.1
Djibouti — Djibouti	104.2	121.8	119.5	131.1	131.4	104.2	121.8	119.5	131.1	131.4
Egypt — Egypte	100.2	104.6	110.0	114.4	116.8	99.4	104.5	111.2	114.5	117.0
Equatorial Guinea — Guinée équatoriale	99.7	94.6	95.6	94.4	94.4	98.1	92.2	93.4	95.1	95.1
Eritrea — Erythrée	96.3	75.4	86.3	85.4	100.3	96.2	75.2	86.2	85.3	100.3
Ethiopia — Ethiopie	107.9	110.7	107.6	112.2	113.9	108.2	111.4	108.2	112.1	113.1
Gabon — Gabon	100.3	101.3	101.6	101.3	101.3	100.3	101.3	101.6	101.4	101.4
Gambia — Gambie	109.2	66.0	83.3	103.8	104.0	109.2	65.9	83.1	103.7	103.9
Ghana — Ghana	102.3	112.7	115.8	120.6	117.0	102.6	113.2	116.2	121.0	117.4
Guinea — Guinée	102.7	105.3	109.4	112.0	113.0	103.2	107.2	111.6	114.5	115.5
Guinea-Bissau — Guinée-Bissau	103.8	101.8	100.5	106.0	110.7	103.7	101.6	100.3	105.9	110.7
Kenya — Kenya	103.0	105.3	108.6	104.8	105.7	102.7	105.4	108.8	104.7	105.5
Lesotho — Lesotho	104.3	98.5	97.3	105.7	105.7	104.3	98.3	97.1	105.9	105.9
Liberia — Libéria	100.6	98.1	98.5	104.0	104.4	99.8	95.8	96.1	101.1	101.7
Libyan Arab Jamah. — Jamah. arabe libyenne	94.5	98.8	103.7	102.3	102.3	94.3	98.8	103.8	102.1	102.1
Madagascar — Madagascar	99.5	96.6	98.6	106.9	107.0	99.5	97.3	98.7	107.5	107.6
Malawi — Malawi	106.0	80.2	88.5	99.7	100.4	108.8	79.2	89.0	101.1	101.8
Mali — Mali	106.5	102.5	118.0	115.1	120.2	100.6	102.7	112.3	111.1	117.3
Mauritania — Mauritanie	100.6	106.0	108.8	108.2	105.6	100.6	106.0	108.8	108.2	105.6
Mauritius — Maurice	116.8	101.9	106.2	104.8	104.8	117.1	102.1	106.6	105.1	105.1
Morocco — Maroc	104.3	111.8	130.8	132.2	118.9	104.3	111.9	131.4	132.8	119.2
Mozambique — Mozambique	99.2	98.5	104.1	108.9	106.7	98.1	97.3	102.7	107.8	105.5
Namibia — Namibie	105.8	113.3	127.5	131.4	136.6	105.8	113.1	127.7	131.7	137.0
Niger — Niger	108.3	107.3	111.8	102.0	101.7	108.9	107.8	112.3	102.4	102.1
Nigeria — Nigéria	99.3	101.5	103.1	106.1	106.1	99.3	101.5	103.1	106.1	106.1
Réunion — Réunion	99.3	95.6	98.8	100.7	101.5	99.3	95.5	98.7	100.7	101.6
Rwanda — Rwanda	99.6	124.6	113.9	113.4	120.8	99.2	125.3	114.7	113.7	121.2
Sao Tome and Principe — Sao Tomé-et-Principe	102.2	103.4	108.1	109.3	108.6	102.2	103.5	108.2	109.4	108.7
Senegal — Sénégal	96.8	60.5	86.2	87.5	99.8	95.9	59.2	84.1	85.4	97.9
Seychelles — Seychelles	98.4	98.8	89.2	100.0	100.0	98.5	99.0	88.2	100.5	100.5
Sierra Leone — Sierra Leone	103.9	109.0	114.9	114.3	114.3	103.8	109.1	115.0	114.3	114.4
Somalia — Somalie	99.3	102.2	104.3	105.4	105.5	99.3	102.1	104.3	105.4	105.5
South Africa — Afrique du Sud	99.9	105.6	105.2	107.1	110.9	99.9	106.4	105.9	107.7	112.0
Sudan — Soudan	106.6	102.6	112.2	107.0	116.7	106.2	102.7	112.4	106.3	116.0
Swaziland — Swaziland	95.4	100.5	103.1	103.1	103.6	96.7	102.9	105.6	105.7	106.2
Togo — Togo	98.5	109.2	109.4	112.5	116.9	96.8	104.0	104.7	106.7	112.2
Tunisia — Tunisie	87.1	84.0	129.5	110.5	109.9	86.9	83.8	129.9	110.7	109.9
Uganda — Ouganda	104.2	108.5	105.3	109.2	109.6	104.5	108.3	105.7	109.1	109.5
United Rep. of Tanzania — Rép.-Unie de Tanzanie	102.9	104.5	103.7	109.3	110.1	101.9	104.9	104.4	107.5	108.2

Region, country or area — Région, pays ou zone	Agriculture — Agriculture 2001	2002	2003	2004	2005	Food — Produits alimentaires 2001	2002	2003	2004	2005
Zambia — Zambie	93.9	94.3	102.5	105.7	97.8	96.0	96.2	105.7	109.2	100.5
Zimbabwe — Zimbabwe	99.9	81.4	79.1	72.7	74.2	100.3	82.4	90.0	85.1	87.1
America, North — Amérique du Nord	**98.8**	**97.6**	**100.8**	**107.4**	**106.7**	**98.4**	**97.8**	**101.0**	**106.9**	**106.0**
Antigua and Barbuda — Antigua-et-Barbuda	102.6	104.1	106.5	108.1	108.1	102.6	104.1	106.4	108.0	108.0
Bahamas — Bahamas	92.5	91.8	100.9	104.2	104.2	92.5	91.8	100.9	104.2	104.2
Barbados — Barbade	97.1	93.6	94.0	98.0	105.4	97.1	93.6	94.0	98.0	105.4
Belize — Belize	105.6	101.7	102.7	117.7	117.1	105.5	101.6	102.7	117.7	117.1
Bermuda — Bermudes	103.3	98.6	98.6	92.8	92.9	103.3	98.6	98.6	92.8	92.9
British Virgin Islands — Iles Vierges britanniques	100.0	100.0	100.1	100.1	100.1	100.0	100.0	100.1	100.1	100.1
Canada — Canada	92.3	87.0	95.8	107.4	106.9	92.3	87.0	95.9	108.0	106.9
Cayman Islands — Iles Caïmanes	100.0	100.0	100.0	100.0	100.0	100.0	100.0	100.0	100.0	100.0
Costa Rica — Costa Rica	100.7	97.6	99.5	100.1	107.7	100.9	98.1	100.6	101.7	110.0
Cuba — Cuba	104.4	107.0	108.2	111.4	103.1	104.6	107.1	109.0	111.9	103.1
Dominica — Dominique	95.1	93.3	90.9	98.7	98.7	95.0	93.2	90.7	98.6	98.6
Dominican Republic — Rép. dominicaine	105.2	108.5	108.6	109.6	109.8	105.7	108.8	109.2	110.1	109.6
El Salvador — El Salvador	97.5	98.2	96.5	98.6	97.0	99.4	103.0	101.0	104.8	102.9
Greenland — Groenland	100.2	99.8	99.7	99.4	99.4	100.2	100.3	100.1	99.6	99.6
Grenada — Grenade	91.3	102.4	98.7	100.0	100.0	91.3	102.4	98.7	100.0	100.0
Guadeloupe — Guadeloupe	102.3	104.5	102.7	102.7	102.7	102.4	104.5	102.7	102.7	102.7
Guatemala — Guatemala	102.0	102.7	103.1	100.8	101.4	103.0	106.4	105.8	104.4	105.1
Haiti — Haïti	99.2	101.6	103.3	100.5	100.5	99.3	101.7	103.4	100.6	100.6
Honduras — Honduras	104.4	132.1	141.7	141.1	151.0	103.1	139.5	150.7	149.0	160.3
Jamaica — Jamaïque	101.8	97.0	97.3	99.0	98.0	101.8	97.0	97.2	99.0	97.9
Martinique — Martinique	94.4	101.7	97.1	99.1	99.1	94.4	101.7	97.1	99.1	99.1
Mexico — Mexique	103.3	102.2	105.5	108.9	109.4	103.5	102.9	106.2	109.3	109.8
Montserrat — Montserrat	100.0	100.0	100.0	100.0	100.0	100.0	100.0	100.0	100.0	100.0
Netherlands Antilles — Antilles néerlandaises	101.3	110.2	...	...	...	101.3	110.2	...	...	...
Nicaragua — Nicaragua	103.5	105.7	118.2	116.1	125.7	105.6	108.6	119.6	120.5	127.4
Panama — Panama	101.6	101.8	99.8	102.0	104.1	101.2	101.9	100.0	102.5	104.5
Puerto Rico — Porto Rico	100.1	98.8	97.2	98.9	98.9	99.9	98.9	96.4	98.2	98.2
Saint Kitts and Nevis — Saint-Kitts-et-Nevis	98.9	97.4	99.1	99.8	59.5	98.9	97.4	99.1	99.8	59.5
Saint Lucia — Sainte-Lucie	87.3	83.7	89.0	79.2	74.6	87.3	83.7	89.0	79.2	74.6
Saint Pierre and Miquelon — Saint-Pierre-et-Miquelon	109.1	112.1	101.0	102.5	102.5	109.1	112.1	101.0	102.5	102.5
St. Vincent-Grenadines — St. Vincent-Grenadines	102.9	107.0	107.8	101.7	107.1	103.0	107.1	107.9	101.7	107.2
Trinidad and Tobago — Trinité-et-Tobago	104.6	129.6	117.9	104.3	108.2	104.6	129.8	117.7	104.5	108.1
United States — Etats-Unis	99.6	98.8	101.4	107.4	106.6	99.2	99.1	101.6	106.8	105.9
United States Virgin Is. — Iles Vierges américaines	100.0	99.4	99.4	99.4	99.4	100.0	99.4	99.4	99.4	99.4
America, South — Amérique du Sud	**103.1**	**107.0**	**112.6**	**117.5**	**120.2**	**102.9**	**106.7**	**113.0**	**116.7**	**119.6**
Argentina — Argentine	99.6	97.9	103.7	103.7	113.2	99.6	98.4	104.2	104.0	113.5
Bolivia — Bolivie	101.9	109.1	115.8	115.9	116.2	101.3	108.8	115.8	116.0	116.3
Brazil — Brésil	104.8	112.3	119.2	126.8	126.6	104.5	111.4	119.7	125.1	125.4
Chile — Chili	106.0	105.9	108.5	112.5	120.0	106.1	106.1	108.8	112.7	120.4
Colombia — Colombie	102.9	105.0	108.0	114.3	115.0	102.6	104.6	107.7	114.2	114.9
Ecuador — Equateur	103.8	101.7	103.8	110.2	113.0	103.4	103.4	105.6	112.1	114.5
Falkland Is. (Malvinas) — Iles Falkland (Malvinas)	99.4	122.9	99.5	99.5	99.5	96.5	96.7	96.7	96.7	96.7
French Guiana — Guyane française	107.9	96.8	98.5	98.4	98.4	107.9	96.8	98.5	98.4	98.4
Guyana — Guyana	99.1	95.3	106.1	105.6	105.6	99.1	95.3	106.1	105.6	105.6
Paraguay — Paraguay	104.1	98.8	111.3	109.7	107.8	103.0	101.9	113.8	107.7	108.7
Peru — Pérou	102.9	108.6	110.9	110.0	115.0	103.1	109.2	111.7	110.5	115.6
Suriname — Suriname	103.0	89.6	96.5	105.4	105.4	103.0	89.6	96.5	105.4	105.4
Uruguay — Uruguay	88.2	92.0	97.6	115.3	119.4	87.7	93.1	99.4	117.9	122.2
Venezuela (Boli. Rep. of) — Venezuela (Rép. boliv. du)	104.7	102.6	95.3	92.6	94.3	104.8	102.9	95.6	92.8	94.4
Asia — Asie	**102.7**	**105.2**	**109.6**	**113.5**	**115.3**	**102.7**	**105.4**	**109.8**	**113.2**	**115.2**
Afghanistan — Afghanistan	90.1	111.4	112.8	119.8	112.1	90.1	112.2	114.1	121.3	113.4
Armenia — Arménie	103.0	108.2	115.2	136.3	130.7	103.3	108.6	116.3	137.8	132.3
Azerbaijan — Azerbaïdjan	107.5	112.0	118.3	118.6	129.4	108.8	115.2	120.4	120.3	129.7
Bahrain — Bahreïn	115.1	126.9	121.9	129.0	140.0	115.1	126.9	121.9	129.0	140.0
Bangladesh — Bangladesh	100.8	103.1	106.9	104.9	110.3	100.5	103.1	107.0	105.0	110.5

Region, country or area — Région, pays ou zone	Agriculture — Agriculture					Food — Produits alimentaires				
	2001	2002	2003	2004	2005	2001	2002	2003	2004	2005
Bhutan — Bhoutan	93.9	93.2	97.7	102.2	102.2	93.8	93.1	97.7	102.3	102.2
Brunei Darussalam — Brunéi Darussalam	114.2	105.1	105.3	138.6	142.8	114.3	105.1	105.3	138.8	143.0
Cambodia — Cambodge	103.2	98.8	116.6	108.0	110.1	103.6	99.3	117.2	109.4	111.5
China[1] — Chine[1]	103.8	109.01	112.2	118.5	121.6	103.5	109.1	112.6	118.2	...
Cyprus — Chypre	99.5	102.9	105.2	106.9	105.4	99.5	102.9	105.1	106.8	105.4
Georgia — Géorgie	98.6	93.0	105.9	99.2	101.1	100.5	94.3	108.0	101.0	103.0
India — Inde	102.0	96.4	105.6	106.2	106.3	102.4	96.6	105.2	105.4	105.6
Indonesia — Indonésie	102.4	109.9	116.5	122.1	123.0	102.3	108.9	115.6	122.5	123.0
Iran (Islamic Rep. of) — Iran (Rép. islamique d')	102.3	110.3	110.6	112.8	114.2	102.6	110.9	111.2	113.6	114.9
Iraq — Iraq	108.7	129.8	105.7	114.0	117.7	108.9	130.6	106.0	114.4	118.2
Israel — Israël	100.8	106.9	108.0	114.5	117.1	100.7	107.2	108.5	114.4	117.7
Japan — Japon	98.6	99.2	95.3	96.2	97.1	98.6	99.3	95.3	96.2	97.1
Jordan — Jordanie	99.7	137.6	117.5	134.1	119.6	100.0	137.1	117.4	134.5	119.7
Kazakhstan — Kazakhstan	108.2	110.1	109.1	106.9	112.2	107.8	110.4	107.8	105.3	111.6
Korea, Dem. P. R. — Corée, R. p. dém. de	105.9	108.2	110.1	110.9	112.7	106.2	108.5	110.6	111.3	113.1
Korea, Republic of — Corée, République de	100.7	94.0	91.2	97.6	95.4	100.9	94.3	91.7	98.2	96.0
Kuwait — Koweït	116.3	102.5	121.1	133.5	134.0	116.4	102.6	121.3	133.7	134.2
Kyrgyzstan — Kirghizistan	104.9	99.1	102.5	104.4	100.9	105.7	101.0	104.3	105.2	101.3
Lao People's Dem. Rep. — Rép. dém. pop. lao	106.2	115.1	110.7	115.8	114.3	107.0	116.9	113.6	117.4	115.3
Lebanon — Liban	93.7	100.6	99.2	101.0	102.5	93.3	101.1	99.7	101.2	102.2
Malaysia — Malaisie	104.8	106.3	113.5	119.9	126.5	105.0	106.4	113.4	118.6	125.8
Maldives — Maldives	103.8	113.5	131.6	113.8	91.9	103.8	113.5	131.6	113.8	91.9
Mongolia — Mongolie	84.2	76.5	65.1	77.1	73.7	83.6	76.2	64.6	77.3	73.8
Myanmar — Myanmar	108.1	111.0	118.7	122.0	124.1	108.2	111.3	119.5	122.8	124.9
Nepal — Népal	103.4	106.6	111.9	112.0	113.3	103.3	106.6	111.8	111.8	113.2
Occupied Palestinian Terr. — Terr. palestinien occupé	105.4	107.7	110.0	108.0	113.6	105.4	107.7	110.0	107.9	113.5
Oman — Oman	101.7	93.1	84.3	95.4	95.5	101.7	93.1	84.1	95.3	95.4
Pakistan — Pakistan	99.0	100.5	104.2	111.9	113.0	99.2	101.3	105.7	109.7	113.0
Philippines — Philippines	104.2	109.2	111.6	116.9	114.1	104.2	109.4	111.8	117.3	114.4
Qatar — Qatar	79.4	111.0	102.5	112.4	114.2	79.4	111.0	102.5	112.4	114.2
Saudi Arabia — Arabie saoudite	116.3	113.9	117.7	114.6	114.1	116.4	114.0	117.8	114.7	114.1
Singapore — Singapour	73.2	95.8	108.7	126.9	124.2	73.2	95.8	108.7	126.9	124.2
Sri Lanka — Sri Lanka	98.8	101.0	103.5	99.5	106.4	98.7	100.3	104.0	98.5	107.0
Syrian Arab Republic — Rép. arabe syrienne	107.1	118.5	116.7	118.9	117.5	108.0	125.5	121.4	121.9	120.2
Tajikistan — Tadjikistan	112.3	128.8	136.6	150.2	150.1	106.8	123.4	133.1	151.3	152.9
Thailand — Thaïlande	104.2	104.8	110.5	104.8	105.3	103.9	104.5	110.0	103.1	103.6
Timor-Leste — Timor-Leste	101.2	108.7	108.1	113.3	113.3	99.7	109.0	108.3	114.5	114.5
Turkey — Turquie	96.3	102.0	103.5	104.4	105.0	96.2	101.8	103.9	104.5	106.1
Turkmenistan — Turkménistan	101.0	103.8	118.0	120.1	119.4	106.8	116.6	127.5	128.2	127.1
United Arab Emirates — Emirats arabes unis	62.3	63.7	57.4	61.0	61.4	62.3	63.5	57.4	60.9	61.4
Uzbekistan — Ouzbékistan	101.4	105.4	107.2	113.6	114.9	101.8	107.5	112.6	114.0	112.1
Viet Nam — Viet Nam	104.5	112.3	117.3	123.6	126.6	103.9	112.8	117.5	123.9	125.8
Yemen — Yémen	107.1	106.3	105.6	106.4	107.5	107.1	106.3	105.4	106.2	107.3
Europe — Europe	**99.8**	**101.5**	**98.3**	**104.6**	**101.1**	**99.8**	**101.6**	**98.4**	**104.8**	**101.2**
Albania — Albanie	102.6	103.2	106.4	110.9	106.9	103.3	104.2	107.9	112.0	108.0
Austria — Autriche	100.0	99.0	96.3	101.1	100.4	100.0	99.0	96.3	101.1	100.4
Belarus — Bélarus	102.8	103.6	101.1	113.1	119.9	102.8	103.7	100.9	112.6	119.5
Belgium — Belgique	95.2	102.8	101.0	104.0	97.3	95.5	102.4	100.2	103.4	96.7
Bosnia and Herzegovina — Bosnie-Herzégovine	96.6	104.1	96.1	115.7	110.5	96.5	103.7	96.2	115.6	110.3
Bulgaria — Bulgarie	100.0	103.9	94.6	108.0	93.0	98.8	102.5	92.9	106.2	91.3
Croatia — Croatie	99.0	113.3	87.8	92.0	93.6	98.9	113.4	87.6	91.8	93.3
Czech Republic — République tchèque	101.5	96.4	88.4	106.2	96.7	101.5	96.4	88.5	106.2	96.8
Denmark — Danemark	100.5	99.7	100.5	101.0	101.1	100.6	99.7	100.6	101.0	101.1
Estonia — Estonie	97.3	99.0	104.1	104.0	106.3	97.3	98.9	104.1	104.0	106.3
Faeroe Islands — Iles Féroé	58.8	66.1	30.3	59.4	59.4	58.8	66.1	30.3	59.4	59.4
Finland — Finlande	101.7	104.8	101.4	104.8	109.4	101.7	104.8	101.4	104.8	109.4
France — France	95.4	102.1	94.8	101.6	97.7	95.3	102.1	94.8	101.6	97.6
Germany — Allemagne	99.5	96.6	92.6	102.9	98.0	99.6	96.7	92.7	103.0	98.0
Greece — Grèce	99.9	92.7	83.8	90.8	94.1	99.1	93.1	83.8	91.5	95.5

Agricultural production — Index base: 1999-01 = 100 (*continued*)
Production agricole — Indices base : 1999-01 = 100 (*suite*)

Region, country or area — Région, pays ou zone	Agriculture — Agriculture					Food — Produits alimentaires				
	2001	2002	2003	2004	2005	2001	2002	2003	2004	2005
Hungary — Hongrie	111.8	96.9	94.4	110.2	107.5	111.9	96.9	94.4	110.2	107.4
Iceland — Islande	100.9	103.3	104.1	105.0	102.6	100.6	104.5	105.3	105.9	103.5
Ireland — Irlande	98.1	94.9	96.1	99.8	97.4	98.1	94.9	96.1	99.8	97.3
Italy — Italie	97.7	94.6	91.2	100.1	97.2	97.6	94.6	91.1	100.3	97.3
Latvia — Lettonie	98.9	107.6	108.6	109.0	124.4	99.0	107.6	108.7	109.0	124.5
Liechtenstein — Liechtenstein	100.0	100.0	100.0	100.0	100.0	100.0	100.0	100.0	100.0	100.0
Lithuania — Lituanie	91.0	105.7	116.4	116.1	108.5	91.1	105.7	116.2	116.1	108.6
Luxembourg — Luxembourg	88.7	101.3	96.9	99.6	96.5	88.7	101.3	96.9	99.6	96.5
Malta — Malte	97.6	97.8	95.8	99.8	99.9	97.6	97.8	95.8	99.8	99.9
Netherlands — Pays-Bas	94.5	96.1	91.7	96.8	93.3	94.5	96.1	91.6	96.8	93.3
Norway — Norvège	96.8	96.6	100.3	103.2	103.0	96.8	96.5	100.3	103.2	103.0
Poland — Pologne	102.3	101.9	103.6	109.3	101.6	102.4	102.0	103.8	109.4	101.7
Portugal — Portugal	95.2	100.8	94.9	101.8	100.4	95.2	100.9	94.9	101.9	100.5
Republic of Moldova — République de Moldova	103.7	111.5	105.6	109.0	112.4	104.8	113.7	108.4	111.8	114.9
Romania — Roumanie	107.8	101.3	107.5	127.9	107.1	107.9	101.3	107.8	128.3	107.4
Russian Federation — Fédération de Russie	104.2	113.3	106.0	110.1	112.4	104.2	113.3	105.9	110.1	112.4
Serbia and Montenegro — Serbie-et-Monténégro	98.7	103.4	101.1	112.3	108.6	98.6	103.2	101.2	112.5	108.7
Slovakia — Slovaquie	100.9	102.9	94.0	110.3	109.6	100.9	102.9	94.0	110.4	109.7
Slovenia — Slovénie	98.3	105.9	102.0	105.1	104.3	98.3	105.9	102.0	105.1	104.3
Spain — Espagne	102.3	102.3	112.4	106.2	95.1	102.4	102.4	112.8	106.6	95.3
Sweden — Suède	99.8	100.9	99.7	100.8	99.9	99.9	101.0	99.8	100.8	99.9
Switzerland — Suisse	99.0	101.0	97.9	101.6	99.8	99.0	101.0	97.9	101.6	99.8
TFYR of Macedonia — L'ex-R.y. Macédoine	93.1	84.3	94.6	104.9	105.1	93.1	83.8	95.3	106.4	104.1
Ukraine — Ukraine	107.9	111.0	98.1	113.3	113.7	107.9	111.0	98.1	113.3	113.7
United Kingdom — Royaume-Uni	92.1	99.5	97.4	98.0	96.9	92.2	99.7	97.5	98.1	97.0
Oceania — Océanie	**102.3**	**89.9**	**100.0**	**99.2**	**101.1**	**103.0**	**91.6**	**103.2**	**101.0**	**103.4**
American Samoa — Samoa américaines	100.0	100.0	100.0	100.0	100.0	100.0	100.0	100.0	100.0	100.0
Australia — Australie	101.7	83.3	95.8	92.9	95.9	102.4	85.0	99.7	94.4	98.3
Cook Islands — Iles Cook	94.8	78.2	60.9	51.7	51.8	94.8	78.2	60.9	51.8	51.9
Fiji — Fidji	95.8	99.1	92.6	95.3	95.7	95.7	99.2	92.5	95.5	95.8
French Polynesia — Polynésie française	102.4	109.5	111.6	109.3	110.3	102.4	109.5	111.6	109.3	110.3
Guam — Guam	100.1	103.9	103.7	107.0	107.0	100.1	103.9	103.7	107.0	107.0
Kiribati — Kiribati	98.9	100.5	101.0	107.0	107.2	98.9	100.5	101.0	107.0	107.2
Marshall Islands — Iles Marshall	92.8	92.8	92.8	92.8	92.8	92.8	92.8	92.8	92.8	92.8
Micronesia (Fed. States of) — Micronésie (Etats féd. de)	100.0	100.2	100.1	100.1	100.1	100.0	100.2	100.1	100.1	100.1
Nauru — Nauru	100.0	100.1	100.2	100.1	100.1	100.0	100.1	100.2	100.1	100.1
New Caledonia — Nouvelle-Calédonie	100.2	100.9	101.3	103.7	103.7	100.1	101.0	101.4	103.7	103.7
New Zealand — Nouvelle-Zélande	104.7	106.2	111.6	116.1	115.0	105.3	107.1	112.9	117.9	116.6
Niue — Nioué	100.7	100.5	100.5	100.5	101.1	100.7	100.5	100.5	100.5	101.1
Papua New Guinea — Papouasie-Nvl-Guinée	99.7	103.3	105.0	106.5	108.2	100.6	104.2	105.9	107.7	109.7
Samoa — Samoa	102.0	101.6	103.3	103.2	103.2	102.0	101.7	103.3	103.3	103.3
Solomon Islands — Iles Salomon	101.4	102.2	104.3	112.7	118.7	101.4	102.2	104.3	112.7	118.7
Tokelau — Tokélaou	100.0	100.0	100.0	100.0	100.0	100.0	100.0	100.0	100.0	100.0
Tonga — Tonga	99.9	103.5	102.2	102.3	102.3	99.9	103.5	102.2	102.3	102.3
Tuvalu — Tuvalu	102.7	104.8	108.4	111.1	111.1	102.7	104.8	108.4	111.1	111.1
Vanuatu — Vanuatu	99.0	89.8	94.0	109.4	110.1	99.0	89.9	94.0	109.4	110.1
Wallis and Futuna Islands — Iles Wallis et Futuna	100.0	100.0	100.0	100.0	100.0	100.0	100.0	100.0	100.0	100.0

Source

Food and Agriculture Organization of the United Nations (FAO), Rome, FAOSTAT data, last accessed October 2006, http://faostat.fao.org.

Source

Organisation des Nations Unies pour l'alimentation et l'agriculture (FAO), Rome, données FAOSTAT, dernier accès octobre 2006, http://faostat.fao.org.

Notes

1 For statistical purposes, the data for China do not include those for the Hong Kong Special Administrative Region (Hong Kong SAR) and Macao Special Administrative Region (Macao SAR).

Notes

1 Pour la présentation des statistiques, les données pour la Chine ne comprennent pas la Région Administrative Spéciale de Hong Kong (Hong Kong RAS) et la Région Administrative Spéciale de Macao (Macao RAS).

31

Cereals
Production: thousand metric tons

Céréales
Production : milliers de tonnes

Region, country or area Région, pays ou zone	1996	1997	1998	1999	2000	2001	2002	2003	2004	2005
World Monde	**2 071 714**	**2 095 156**	**2 083 055**	**2 085 281**	**2 060 184**	**2 107 344**	**2 028 019**	**2 089 643**	**2 281 556**	**2 264 590**
Africa Afrique	**124 570**	**109 978**	**114 553**	**113 574**	**111 773**	**115 701**	**117 201**	**131 576**	**130 540**	**140 034**
Algeria Algérie	4 902	870	3 026	2 021	935	2 659	1 953	4 266	4 033	3 528
Angola Angola	519	448	610	541	510	586	717	717	668	871
Benin Bénin	714	877	867	974	993	943	926	1 043	1 109	1 152
Botswana Botswana	114	45	16	21	25	24	35	37	45	45
Burkina Faso Burkina Faso	2 482	2 014	2 657	2 700	2 286	3 109	3 119	3 564	2 902	3 650
Burundi Burundi	273	305	261	265	245	273	282	279	280	274
Cameroon Cameroun	1 296	1 267	1 412	1 185	1 275	1 356	1 499	1 584	1 684	1 660
Cape Verde Cap-Vert	10	5	5	36	24	20	5	12	10	4
Central African Rep. Rép. centrafricaine	126	138	148	161	166	183	193	201	192	192
Chad Tchad	878	986	1 312	1 231	930	1 321	1 212	1 618	1 213	1 853
Comoros Comores	21	21	21	21	21	21	21	21	21	21
Congo Congo	10	10	11	7	8	8	8	10	10	10
Côte d'Ivoire Côte d'Ivoire	1 310	1 405	1 377	1 278	1 314	1 332	1 349	1 368	2 005	1 545
Dem. Rep. of the Congo Rép. dém. du Congo	1 557	1 532	1 621	1 593	1 572	1 546	1 520	1 521	1 522	1 526
Egypt Egypte	16 542	18 071	17 964	19 401	20 106	18 561	20 194	20 682	20 823	23 040
Eritrea Erythrée	83	95	458	319	121	183	52	99	80	152
Ethiopia Ethiopie	9 390	9 485	7 210	8 393	8 020	9 586	9 004	9 536	10 680	12 800
Gabon Gabon	29	25	27	28	27	26	25	32	32	32
Gambia Gambie	104	101	107	151	176	200	139	205	224	206
Ghana Ghana	1 770	1 669	1 788	1 686	1 711	1 627	2 155	2 041	1 943	1 943
Guinea Guinée	876	927	982	1 042	973	1 031	1 094	1 161	1 142	1 142
Guinea-Bissau Guinée-Bissau	175	140	139	145	178	162	151	121	171	213
Kenya Kenya	2 669	2 700	2 927	2 802	2 591	3 369	3 046	3 352	3 199	3 585
Lesotho Lesotho	257	206	169	174	179	242	195	110	103	95
Liberia Libéria	94	168	209	196	183	145	110	100	110	110

Region, country or area Région, pays ou zone	1996	1997	1998	1999	2000	2001	2002	2003	2004	2005
Libyan Arab Jamah. Jamah. arabe libyenne	160	206	213	213	217	218	212	212	213	233
Madagascar Madagascar	2 685	2 742	2 610	2 756	2 660	2 853	2 787	3 129	3 391	3 851
Malawi Malawi	1 943	1 349	1 904	2 636	2 631	1 742	1 711	2 142	1 843	1 363
Mali Mali	2 219	2 138	2 548	2 894	2 310	2 584	2 532	3 402	2 845	3 399
Mauritania Mauritanie	234	154	189	194	180	124	113	155	120	201
Mauritius Maurice	^0	^0	^0	^0	1	^0	^0	^0	^0	^0
Morocco Maroc	10 104	4 098	6 632	3 846	2 002	4 607	5 293	7 973	8 603	4 265
Mozambique Mozambique	1 379	1 531	1 688	1 912	1 587	1 585	1 662	1 813	2 007	1 922
Namibia Namibie	89	185	70	74	121	107	100	107	107	109
Niger Niger	2 232	1 719	2 973	2 853	2 127	3 161	3 231	3 580	2 732	3 669
Nigeria Nigéria	21 665	21 853	22 040	22 405	21 370	20 090	21 373	22 736	24 321	26 031
Réunion Réunion	16	17	17	17	17	17	17	17	17	17
Rwanda Rwanda	183	223	194	179	240	285	308	298	319	413
Sao Tome and Principe Sao Tomé-et-Principe	5	4	1	1	2	3	3	3	3	3
Senegal Sénégal	976	781	717	1 131	1 026	1 023	785	1 452	1 054	1 433
Sierra Leone Sierra Leone	444	467	373	280	222	261	304	309	309	309
Somalia Somalie	281	305	201	298	392	429	442	403	366	369
South Africa Afrique du Sud	13 666	13 246	10 221	10 065	14 528	10 706	13 046	11 821	12 131	14 172
Sudan Soudan	5 202	4 209	5 583	3 066	3 259	5 339	3 714	6 373	3 502	5 515
Swaziland Swaziland	121	139	119	125	114	84	69	70	69	76
Togo Togo	687	748	624	759	737	715	804	816	787	767
Tunisia Tunisie	2 894	1 081	1 697	1 837	1 118	1 391	550	2 318	2 162	2 134
Uganda Ouganda	1 588	1 625	2 085	2 178	2 112	2 309	2 368	2 508	2 274	2 459
United Rep. of Tanzania Rép.-Unie de Tanzanie	4 873	3 727	3 854	4 485	4 646	4 912	5 271	3 757	4 947	5 425
Zambia Zambie	1 573	1 137	798	1 003	1 050	750	745	1 244	1 377	1 067
Zimbabwe Zimbabwe	3 147	2 785	1 879	1 997	2 538	1 897	756	1 259	837	1 187
America, North Amérique du Nord	**429 347**	**419 748**	**434 836**	**422 669**	**427 662**	**405 518**	**368 434**	**436 169**	**479 849**	**453 227**
Barbados Barbade	1	1	1	^0	^0	^0	^0	^0	^0	^0
Belize Belize	56	60	52	62	48	57	57	56	49	51

Region, country or area Région, pays ou zone	1996	1997	1998	1999	2000	2001	2002	2003	2004	2005
Canada Canada	58 494	49 557	50 993	54 078	51 038	43 391	36 303	50 174	52 684	53 086
Costa Rica Costa Rica	266	282	263	292	285	229	201	198	210	196
Cuba Cuba	718	818	619	797	826	900	1 001	1 076	889	732
Dominican Republic Rép. dominicaine	535	564	530	605	610	771	766	656	620	631
El Salvador El Salvador	867	773	783	857	779	760	814	791	822	895
Guatemala Guatemala	1 140	954	1 164	1 134	1 161	1 199	1 155	1 147	1 172	1 172
Haiti Haïti	412	490	403	475	431	363	374	398	367	367
Honduras Honduras	784	757	590	562	607	603	579	594	502	531
Jamaica Jamaïque	4	3	2	2	2	2	2	1	1	1
Mexico Mexique	29 311	28 062	29 123	27 419	27 991	31 057	28 770	31 384	32 311	27 733
Nicaragua Nicaragua	674	608	618	559	765	755	911	972	773	947
Panama Panama	316	269	233	265	303	342	371	409	341	334
Puerto Rico Porto Rico	1	1	1	1	^0	^0	^0	^0	^0	^0
St. Vincent-Grenadines St. Vincent-Grenadines	1	1	2	1	1	1	1	1	1	1
Trinidad and Tobago Trinité-et-Tobago	23	12	12	7	7	5	7	6	5	6
United States Etats-Unis	335 744	336 536	349 445	335 553	342 809	325 082	297 121	348 304	389 101	366 542
America, South Amérique du Sud	**93 330**	**99 127**	**96 004**	**100 768**	**104 168**	**113 507**	**102 898**	**124 666**	**125 074**	**119 104**
Argentina Argentine	30 700	35 907	37 808	35 036	38 749	35 772	31 631	33 990	35 750	38 554
Bolivia Bolivie	1 139	920	1 146	1 128	1 256	1 280	1 257	1 460	1 296	1 622
Brazil Brésil	44 962	44 876	40 743	47 431	45 897	57 117	50 879	67 453	63 951	55 689
Chile Chili	2 578	3 077	3 098	2 168	2 590	3 116	3 380	3 693	3 956	3 936
Colombia Colombie	3 177	3 207	2 893	3 411	3 765	3 827	3 794	4 729	5 085	4 687
Ecuador Equateur	1 947	1 815	1 485	1 847	1 909	1 644	1 940	2 113	2 704	2 410
French Guiana Guyane française	31	31	25	20	20	32	22	23	26	18
Guyana Guyana	547	576	526	565	453	498	446	506	506	506
Paraguay Paraguay	1 210	1 450	1 156	1 156	1 003	1 455	1 371	1 643	1 979	1 579
Peru Pérou	2 338	2 584	2 840	3 397	3 556	3 741	3 845	3 920	3 438	4 132
Suriname Suriname	229	213	189	180	164	191	157	194	195	195
Uruguay Uruguay	2 222	2 057	1 961	2 194	1 860	1 718	1 606	1 827	2 523	2 192

Region, country or area / Région, pays ou zone	1996	1997	1998	1999	2000	2001	2002	2003	2004	2005
Venezuela (Bolivarian Rep. of) / Venezuela (Rép. Bolivar. du)	2 250	2 413	2 134	2 234	2 948	3 117	2 569	3 116	3 664	3 584
Asia / Asie	**996 933**	**992 855**	**1 016 742**	**1 036 017**	**996 262**	**1 001 369**	**982 904**	**999 134**	**1 040 523**	**1 083 615**
Afghanistan / Afghanistan	3 242	3 683	3 876	3 257	1 940	2 108	3 737	4 207	3 232	5 407
Armenia / Arménie	313	254	323	297	221	364	412	310	452	392
Azerbaijan / Azerbaïdjan	1 000	1 120	918	1 069	1 496	1 956	2 133	1 993	2 087	2 056
Bangladesh / Bangladesh	29 620	29 674	31 578	36 403	39 503	38 029	39 341	40 018	37 759	41 155
Bhutan / Bhoutan	164	173	173	157	107	115	93	108	158	127
Brunei Darussalam / Brunéi Darussalam	^0	^0	^0	^0	^0	^0	^0	1	1	1
Cambodia / Cambodge	3 469	3 457	3 558	4 136	4 183	4 285	3 971	5 026	4 427	6 234
China[1] / Chine[1]	453 665	445 931	458 396	455 193	407 336	398 395	399 998	376 123	413 164	429 374
Cyprus / Chypre	141	48	66	127	48	127	142	165	111	61
Georgia / Géorgie	630	892	589	771	418	704	662	742	663	680
India / Inde	218 750	223 232	226 877	236 206	234 866	242 964	206 570	235 856	232 560	242 284
Indonesia / Indonésie	60 409	58 148	59 406	60 070	61 575	59 808	61 144	63 024	65 314	65 998
Iran (Islamic Rep. of) / Iran (Rép. islamique d')	16 083	15 823	18 979	14 186	12 874	14 945	19 861	20 939	21 510	22 410
Iraq / Iraq	3 005	2 216	2 432	1 605	904	1 819	4 125	3 516	3 308	3 701
Israel / Israël	264	187	249	123	183	242	271	306	273	297
Japan / Japon	13 668	13 320	11 934	12 283	12 796	12 255	12 184	10 824	11 994	12 434
Jordan / Jordanie	97	96	76	27	57	48	115	80	53	102
Kazakhstan / Kazakhstan	11 210	12 359	6 380	14 248	11 539	15 866	15 929	14 739	12 334	13 737
Korea, Dem. P. R. / Corée, R. p. dém. de	2 596	2 867	4 420	3 837	2 945	3 880	4 211	4 393	4 485	5 031
Korea, Republic of / Corée, République de	7 617	7 676	7 132	7 458	7 501	7 860	7 083	6 355	7 323	6 776
Kuwait / Koweït	3	2	3	3	3	3	5	3	3	3
Kyrgyzstan / Kirghizistan	1 325	1 610	1 608	1 618	1 550	1 795	1 712	1 634	1 709	1 622
Lao People's Dem. Rep. / Rép. dém. pop. lao	1 492	1 738	1 784	2 199	2 319	2 447	2 541	2 518	2 733	2 941
Lebanon / Liban	94	90	103	93	123	153	140	146	165	145
Malaysia / Malaisie	2 273	2 168	1 994	2 094	2 206	2 162	2 267	2 329	2 336	2 315
Mongolia / Mongolie	220	240	195	170	142	142	126	165	139	75
Myanmar / Myanmar	18 204	17 217	17 636	20 774	21 964	22 717	22 695	24 165	25 842	26 621

Region, country or area Région, pays ou zone	1996	1997	1998	1999	2000	2001	2002	2003	2004	2005
Nepal Népal	6 378	6 350	6 390	6 930	7 116	7 120	7 215	7 684	7 581	7 687
Occupied Palestinian Terr. Terr. palestinien occupé	51	43	52	14	68	40	77	68	62	72
Oman Oman	6	6	5	5	6	6	6	6	6	6
Pakistan Pakistan	25 395	25 260	27 985	27 756	30 461	27 048	27 173	28 964	30 311	33 508
Philippines Philippines	15 629	15 600	12 377	16 371	16 901	17 480	17 590	18 116	19 910	19 857
Qatar Qatar	5	6	6	7	7	7	7	7	5	8
Saudi Arabia Arabie saoudite	1 932	2 339	2 202	2 454	2 167	2 592	2 853	2 949	3 189	2 999
Sri Lanka Sri Lanka	2 099	2 269	2 731	2 894	2 896	2 728	2 890	3 106	2 668	3 295
Syrian Arab Republic Rép. arabe syrienne	5 990	4 322	5 270	3 301	3 511	6 919	5 930	6 223	5 249	5 630
Tajikistan Tadjikistan	548	559	491	465	545	478	688	866	860	914
Thailand Thaïlande	27 144	27 635	28 265	28 661	30 523	31 211	30 512	33 623	33 624	33 464
Timor-Leste Timor-Leste	159	137	96	149	139	123	147	136	156	145
Turkey Turquie	29 344	29 761	33 187	28 886	32 249	29 571	30 831	30 807	34 050	34 570
Turkmenistan Turkménistan	545	759	1 278	1 567	1 751	1 832	2 461	2 667	2 785	3 035
United Arab Emirates Emirats arabes unis	1	^0	^0	^0	^0	^0	^0	^0	^0	^0
Uzbekistan Ouzbékistan	3 558	3 768	4 132	4 311	3 914	4 056	5 535	6 106	5 860	6 402
Viet Nam Viet Nam	27 933	29 175	30 758	33 149	34 537	34 272	36 960	37 707	39 581	39 549
Yemen Yémen	660	646	833	694	672	700	560	418	490	496
Europe Europe	**390 953**	**441 198**	**386 692**	**375 975**	**384 980**	**431 395**	**436 580**	**355 529**	**470 104**	**427 818**
Albania Albanie	504	602	606	498	566	503	519	489	499	511
Austria Autriche	4 494	5 009	4 776	4 809	4 494	4 830	4 461	4 264	5 315	4 898
Belarus Bélarus	5 482	5 924	4 497	3 413	4 565	4 871	5 710	5 117	6 590	6 089
Belgium Belgique	…	…	…	…	2 513	2 359	2 639	2 561	2 932	2 787
Belgium-Luxembourg Belgique-Luxembourg	2 571	2 393	2 601	2 449	…	…	…	…	…	…
Bosnia and Herzegovina Bosnie-Herzégovine	841	1 242	1 327	1 369	930	1 138	1 308	793	1 439	1 329
Bulgaria Bulgarie	3 404	6 188	5 378	5 221	4 389	6 076	6 770	3 814	7 463	5 839
Croatia Croatie	2 762	3 179	3 210	2 883	2 770	3 396	3 722	2 355	3 268	3 028
Czech Republic République tchèque	6 654	6 995	6 676	6 935	6 460	7 347	6 780	5 770	8 792	7 668
Denmark Danemark	9 218	9 529	9 334	8 774	9 413	9 423	8 804	9 051	8 963	9 283
Estonia Estonie	629	651	576	402	697	558	525	506	608	760

Region, country or area Région, pays ou zone	1996	1997	1998	1999	2000	2001	2002	2003	2004	2005
Finland Finlande	3 711	3 812	2 780	2 882	4 103	3 671	3 938	3 791	3 619	4 058
France France	62 599	63 432	68 664	64 342	65 698	60 237	69 657	54 940	70 523	64 224
Germany Allemagne	42 136	45 486	44 575	44 461	45 271	49 686	43 391	39 426	51 097	45 980
Greece Grèce	4 894	4 970	4 611	4 576	4 968	4 939	4 827	4 710	5 088	5 099
Hungary Hongrie	11 344	14 139	13 038	11 392	10 036	15 046	11 703	8 770	16 779	16 212
Ireland Irlande	2 142	1 944	1 866	2 011	2 174	2 166	1 964	2 147	2 501	1 934
Italy Italie	20 900	19 917	20 731	21 068	20 661	19 933	21 248	17 864	23 294	21 505
Latvia Lettonie	964	1 040	964	783	924	928	1 029	932	1 060	1 314
Lithuania Lituanie	2 615	2 945	2 717	2 048	2 657	2 344	2 531	2 632	2 859	2 811
Luxembourg Luxembourg	...	...	...	...	153	144	169	164	179	161
Malta Malte	7	11	11	11	12	12	12	12	12	12
Netherlands Pays-Bas	1 659	1 450	1 497	1 368	1 732	1 672	1 740	1 820	1 822	1 775
Norway Norvège	1 345	1 288	1 358	1 218	1 300	1 220	1 143	1 287	1 442	1 379
Poland Pologne	25 298	25 399	27 159	25 750	22 341	26 960	26 877	23 391	29 635	26 928
Portugal Portugal	1 673	1 559	1 622	1 678	1 608	1 298	1 497	1 186	1 363	790
Republic of Moldova République de Moldova	1 976	3 487	2 428	2 142	1 905	2 550	2 539	1 583	2 944	2 771
Romania Roumanie	14 200	22 107	15 453	17 037	10 499	18 900	14 357	12 966	24 402	19 350
Russian Federation Fédération de Russie	67 589	86 801	46 937	53 845	64 326	83 398	84 859	65 562	76 231	76 564
Serbia and Montenegro Serbie-et-Monténégro	7 294	10 355	8 668	8 615	5 391	9 040	8 327	5 541	9 893	9 534
Slovakia Slovaquie	3 322	3 741	3 485	2 829	2 202	3 413	3 194	2 490	3 794	3 585
Slovenia Slovénie	488	545	559	480	497	499	614	402	586	579
Spain Espagne	22 366	19 324	22 557	17 988	24 556	18 050	21 710	21 412	24 809	13 999
Sweden Suède	5 954	5 986	5 618	4 931	5 604	5 382	5 398	5 290	5 508	5 051
Switzerland Suisse	1 348	1 223	1 263	1 055	1 206	1 094	1 101	847	1 089	1 057
TFYR of Macedonia L'ex-R.y. Macédoine	546	610	660	638	563	475	556	472	682	645
Ukraine Ukraine	23 448	34 393	25 724	23 950	23 807	38 879	37 994	19 662	40 997	37 258
United Kingdom Royaume-Uni	24 576	23 523	22 768	22 125	23 989	18 959	22 966	21 511	22 027	21 052
Oceania Océanie	**36 581**	**32 249**	**34 229**	**36 278**	**35 337**	**39 854**	**20 002**	**42 569**	**35 466**	**40 793**
Australia Australie	35 646	31 237	33 339	35 369	34 447	38 877	19 029	41 631	34 564	39 862
Fiji Fidji	19	19	6	18	14	16	14	17	16	17

Region, country or area Région, pays ou zone	1996	1997	1998	1999	2000	2001	2002	2003	2004	2005
New Caledonia Nouvelle-Calédonie	2	2	2	2	5	5	4	6	4	4
New Zealand Nouvelle-Zélande	904	980	869	873	854	938	936	899	866	894
Papua New Guinea Papouasie-Nvl-Guinée	9	10	10	11	11	13	13	10	11	11
Solomon Islands Iles Salomon	0	0	1	5	5	5	5	5	6	6
Vanuatu Vanuatu	1	1	1	1	1	1	1	1	1	1

Source

Food and Agriculture Organization of the United Nations (FAO), Rome, FAOSTAT data, last accessed June 2007.

Notes

1 For statistical purposes, the data for China do not include those for the Hong Kong Special Administrative Region (Hong Kong SAR) and Macao Special Administrative Region (Macao SAR).

Source

Organisation des Nations Unies pour l'alimentation et l'agriculture (FAO), Rome, données FAOSTAT, dernier accès juin 2007.

Notes

1 Pour la présentation des statistiques, les données pour la Chine ne comprennent pas la Région Administrative Spéciale de Hong Kong (Hong Kong RAS) et la Région Administrative Spéciale de Macao (Macao RAS).

32

Roundwood

Production (solid volume of roundwood without bark): million cubic metres

Bois rond

Production (volume solide de bois rond sans écorce) : millions de mètres cubes

Region, country or area — Région, pays ou zone	1996	1997	1998	1999	2000	2001	2002	2003	2004	2005
World — Monde	3 234.2	3 304.7	3 224.3	3 292.9	3 358.2	3 270.7	3 298.7	3 367.9	3 423.0	3 502.7
Africa — Afrique	**576.3**	**582.8**	**585.0**	**588.8**	**593.9**	**590.0**	**598.1**	**608.7**	**616.8**	**632.7**
Algeria — Algérie	7.0	7.2	7.3	7.4	7.2	7.4	7.5	7.5	7.7	7.7
Angola — Angola	3.8	3.9	4.0	4.2	4.3	4.3	4.4	4.5	4.6	4.7
Benin — Bénin	6.2	6.2	6.2	6.2	6.2	0.5	0.5	0.5	0.5	6.4
Botswana — Botswana	0.7	0.7	0.7	0.7	0.7	0.7	0.7	0.8	0.8	0.8
Burkina Faso — Burkina Faso	11.0	11.1	11.3	7.8	8.0	8.0	7.2	7.3	9.2	13.1
Burundi — Burundi	7.1	7.4	7.7	5.6	5.8	8.3	8.4	8.6	8.7	8.9
Cameroon — Cameroun	12.6	12.2	11.1	10.9	11.0	10.5	10.6	11.0	11.2	11.3
Central African Rep. — Rép. centrafricaine	3.2	3.4	3.5	2.9	3.0	3.0	2.9	2.8	2.8	2.8
Chad — Tchad	6.0	6.2	6.3	6.5	6.6	6.8	6.9	7.0	7.1	7.2
Congo — Congo	2.2	2.7	2.7	2.4	2.4	2.4	2.4	2.1	2.3	2.3
Côte d'Ivoire — Côte d'Ivoire	11.7	11.6	11.8	11.7	11.9	11.2	10.7	10.2	10.3	10.0
Dem. Rep. of the Congo — Rép. dém. du Congo	63.7	64.9	66.0	67.3	68.6	69.7	70.9	72.2	73.4	74.7
Egypt — Egypte	15.8	16.0	16.1	16.3	16.4	16.6	16.8	16.9	17.1	17.2
Equatorial Guinea — Guinée équatoriale	0.9	1.2	0.9	1.2	1.1	1.1	1.0	0.9	0.9	0.9
Eritrea — Erythrée	1.9	2.0	2.1	2.2	2.2	2.3	1.3	1.3	2.4	2.4
Ethiopia — Ethiopie	83.7	85.5	86.5	88.2	89.9	91.3	92.7	94.5	96.0	97.4
Gabon — Gabon	2.9	3.3	3.3	2.8	3.1	3.1	2.2	4.6	4.6	3.7
Gambia — Gambie	0.6	0.6	0.6	0.6	0.7	0.7	0.7	0.7	0.8	0.8
Ghana — Ghana	21.9	22.0	21.9	21.8	21.7	21.9	21.8	22.1	22.0	22.0
Guinea — Guinée	12.7	8.7	8.7	12.2	12.1	12.1	12.2	12.2	12.3	12.3
Guinea-Bissau — Guinée-Bissau	0.6	0.6	0.6	0.6	0.6	0.6	0.6	0.6	0.6	0.6
Kenya — Kenya	21.0	21.3	21.3	21.5	21.6	21.7	21.8	21.9	22.2	22.4
Lesotho — Lesotho	1.5	1.6	1.6	2.0	2.0	2.0	2.0	2.0	2.0	2.1
Liberia — Libéria	3.1	3.5	4.1	4.5	5.8	6.1	6.7	6.3	6.0	6.1
Libyan Arab Jamah. — Jamah. arabe libyenne	0.6	0.7	0.7	0.7	0.7	0.7	0.7	0.7	0.7	0.7
Madagascar — Madagascar	10.1	9.2	9.2	9.5	9.8	10.0	10.3	10.7	11.0	11.2
Malawi — Malawi	5.3	5.3	5.4	5.4	5.5	5.5	5.5	5.6	5.6	5.7
Mali — Mali	4.9	5.0	5.0	5.1	5.1	5.2	5.3	5.3	5.4	5.4
Mauritania — Mauritanie	1.3	1.3	1.4	1.4	1.4	1.5	1.5	1.5	1.6	1.6
Morocco — Maroc	1.5	0.8	1.7	1.1	1.1	1.0	0.9	0.9	0.9	1.0
Mozambique — Mozambique	17.9	18.0	18.0	18.0	18.0	18.0	18.0	18.0	18.0	18.0
Niger — Niger	7.4	7.6	7.8	8.0	8.2	3.3	8.6	8.8	9.0	9.2
Nigeria — Nigéria	66.2	67.7	67.8	68.3	68.8	69.1	69.5	69.9	70.3	70.7
Rwanda — Rwanda	5.8	7.4	7.5	7.8	5.4	5.5	5.5	5.5	5.5	5.5
Senegal — Sénégal	5.7	5.8	5.8	5.9	5.9	5.9	6.0	6.0	6.0	6.1
Sierra Leone — Sierra Leone	4.7	5.1	5.2	5.3	5.5	5.5	5.5	5.5	5.5	5.5
Somalia — Somalie	8.0	8.3	8.6	9.0	9.3	9.6	9.9	10.3	10.6	10.9
South Africa[1] — Afrique du Sud[1]	32.4	33.2	30.6	30.6	30.6	30.6	30.6	33.2	33.3	33.1
Sudan — Soudan	18.4	18.4	18.6	18.7	18.9	19.0	19.2	19.4	19.7	19.9
Swaziland — Swaziland	1.5	1.5	0.9	0.9	0.9	0.9	0.9	0.9	0.9	0.9
Togo — Togo	5.5	5.6	5.7	5.7	5.8	5.8	5.8	5.9	4.7	5.9
Tunisia — Tunisie	2.2	2.3	2.3	2.3	2.3	2.3	2.3	2.3	2.3	2.4
Uganda — Ouganda	35.4	36.0	36.4	36.9	37.3	37.8	38.3	38.9	39.4	40.0
United Rep. of Tanzania — Rép.-Unie de Tanzanie	22.8	22.9	23.0	23.1	23.1	23.3	23.4	23.6	23.8	24.0
Zambia — Zambie	8.1	8.0	8.0	8.1	8.1	8.1	8.1	8.1	8.1	8.1
Zimbabwe — Zimbabwe	8.6	8.9	9.0	9.3	9.1	9.1	9.1	9.1	9.1	9.1
Northern America — Amérique septentrionale	**680.3**	**677.1**	**671.0**	**663.2**	**668.4**	**635.0**	**644.6**	**638.6**	**670.1**	**671.2**
Canada — Canada	189.8	191.2	176.9	193.9	201.8	185.9	196.6	190.1	208.4	199.3
United States — Etats-Unis	490.6	485.9	494.0	469.3	466.5	449.1	448.0	448.5	461.7	471.9
Latin Amer. and the Carib. — Amér. latine et Caraïb.	**396.0**	**396.9**	**399.2**	**418.4**	**425.0**	**412.7**	**421.0**	**450.0**	**446.3**	**462.2**
Argentina — Argentine	11.4	6.9	5.7	10.6	10.0	9.3	9.3	13.7	14.9	14.9
Bahamas — Bahamas	0.1	0.1	0.0	0.0	0.0	0.0	0.0	0.0	0.0	0.0

Region, country or area — Région, pays ou zone	1996	1997	1998	1999	2000	2001	2002	2003	2004	2005
Belize — Belize	0.2	0.2	0.2	0.2	0.2	0.2	0.2	0.2	0.2	0.2
Bolivia — Bolivie	2.9	3.0	2.9	2.6	2.6	2.7	2.7	2.9	3.0	3.1
Brazil — Brésil	212.3	213.5	213.7	231.6	235.4	223.6	231.0	256.1	243.4	255.9
Chile — Chili	29.8	30.0	31.7	34.0	36.6	37.8	37.8	37.0	42.6	46.1
Colombia — Colombie	9.5	9.6	10.1	10.6	13.1	12.5	11.6	12.0	10.5	9.7
Costa Rica — Costa Rica	5.2	5.2	5.2	5.2	5.2	5.2	5.2	5.1	4.5	4.6
Cuba — Cuba	3.5	3.5	3.5	1.6	1.8	1.7	2.8	2.6	2.5	2.6
Dominican Republic — Rép. dominicaine	0.6	0.6	0.6	0.6	0.6	0.6	0.6	0.6	0.6	0.6
Ecuador — Equateur	11.3	12.1	11.5	5.5	5.7	6.1	6.2	6.3	6.6	6.7
El Salvador — El Salvador	4.3	5.2	5.1	5.2	5.2	5.2	5.2	4.8	4.9	4.9
French Guiana — Guyane française	0.1	0.1	0.1	0.1	0.1	0.1	0.1	0.1	0.2	0.2
Guatemala — Guatemala	13.5	13.8	14.1	14.7	15.0	15.3	15.7	15.9	16.3	16.7
Guyana — Guyana	1.4	1.5	1.3	1.3	1.2	1.2	1.2	1.2	1.3	1.3
Haiti — Haïti	2.2	2.2	2.2	2.2	2.2	2.2	2.2	2.2	2.2	2.2
Honduras — Honduras	9.3	9.4	9.5	9.6	9.5	9.6	9.7	9.5	9.6	9.6
Jamaica — Jamaïque	0.8	0.8	0.8	0.9	0.9	0.9	0.9	0.9	0.9	0.8
Mexico — Mexique	43.3	44.3	45.0	45.4	45.7	45.2	44.0	44.4	45.2	44.6
Nicaragua — Nicaragua	5.9	5.8	5.9	5.9	6.0	5.9	6.0	6.0	6.0	6.0
Panama — Panama	1.4	1.4	1.3	1.3	1.3	1.3	1.3	1.3	1.3	1.3
Paraguay — Paraguay	9.3	9.4	9.5	9.6	9.6	9.7	9.8	9.9	10.0	10.1
Peru — Pérou	7.9	8.4	9.2	9.2	9.3	8.6	8.8	8.4	8.9	9.1
Suriname — Suriname	0.3	0.2	0.2	0.1	0.2	0.2	0.2	0.2	0.2	0.2
Trinidad and Tobago — Trinité-et-Tobago	0.1	0.1	0.1	0.1	0.1	0.1	0.1	0.1	0.1	0.1
Uruguay — Uruguay	4.7	5.0	5.2	5.1	2.9	3.0	3.4	3.7	5.1	5.7
Venezuela (Boliv. Rep. of) — Venezuela (Rép. boliv. du)	4.6	4.7	4.6	5.3	4.7	4.6	5.1	4.8	5.3	4.9
Asia — Asie	**1 066.5**	**1 071.7**	**1 044.4**	**1 036.4**	**1 019.8**	**1 007.9**	**999.8**	**1 003.3**	**1 010.7**	**1 017.0**
Afghanistan — Afghanistan	2.7	2.8	2.9	3.0	3.0	3.1	3.1	3.1	3.2	3.2
Armenia — Arménie	0.0	0.1	0.0	0.0	0.1	0.0	0.1	0.1	0.1	0.0
Bangladesh — Bangladesh	28.5	28.5	28.5	28.5	28.5	28.4	28.0	28.0	28.0	27.9
Bhutan — Bhoutan	4.0	4.0	4.1	4.3	4.4	4.4	4.5	4.5	4.6	4.7
Brunei Darussalam — Brunéi Darussalam	0.2	0.2	0.2	0.2	0.2	0.2	0.2	0.2	0.2	0.2
Cambodia — Cambodge	11.9	11.8	11.6	11.2	10.3	10.0	9.9	9.7	9.5	9.3
China[2,3] — Chine[2,3]	310.8	309.1	296.5	289.4	285.4	282.9	282.1	284.1	284.1	284.1
China, Hong Kong SAR — Chine, Hong Kong RAS	0.1	0.1	0.1	0.1	0.1	0.1	0.1	0.1	0.1	0.1
Georgia — Géorgie	0.0	0.0	0.0	0.0	0.0	0.3	0.4	0.4	0.5	0.6
India — Inde	296.8	296.5	296.3	296.6	296.1	296.7	319.4	321.0	326.6	328.7
Indonesia — Indonésie	143.1	139.1	135.6	130.2	122.5	112.2	115.6	112.0	109.1	106.2
Iran (Islamic Rep. of) — Iran (Rép. islamique d')	1.4	1.5	1.3	1.1	1.1	1.3	0.7	0.9	0.8	0.8
Iraq — Iraq	0.1	0.2	0.2	0.1	0.1	0.1	0.1	0.1	0.1	0.1
Israel — Israël	0.1	0.1	0.1	0.1	0.1	0.0	0.0	0.0	0.0	0.0
Japan — Japon	23.2	22.3	19.6	19.0	18.1	15.9	15.2	15.3	15.7	16.3
Jordan — Jordanie	0.2	0.1	0.2	0.2	0.2	0.2	0.2	0.2	0.3	0.3
Kazakhstan — Kazakhstan	0.3	0.3	0.0	0.5	0.6	0.7	0.5	0.3	0.3	0.3
Korea, Dem. P. R. — Corée, R. p. dém. de	6.1	6.5	6.9	6.9	7.0	7.1	7.1	7.2	7.2	7.3
Korea, Republic of — Corée, République de	3.6	3.5	3.9	4.1	4.0	4.0	4.1	4.1	4.7	4.9
Lao People's Dem. Rep. — Rép. dém. pop. lao	6.5	6.5	6.4	6.7	6.4	6.5	6.3	6.3	6.3	6.3
Lebanon — Liban	0.1	0.1	0.1	0.0	0.0	0.1	0.1	0.1	0.1	0.1
Malaysia — Malaisie	35.1	36.0	26.4	26.6	18.4	19.4	21.1	24.7	27.5	28.2
Mongolia — Mongolie	0.6	0.6	0.6	0.6	0.6	0.6	0.6	0.6	0.6	0.6
Myanmar — Myanmar	21.5	34.8	34.3	37.6	38.1	39.4	38.9	42.2	41.8	42.5
Nepal — Népal	13.1	13.2	13.9	13.9	14.0	14.0	14.0	14.0	14.0	14.0
Pakistan — Pakistan	29.0	30.9	31.8	33.1	33.6	33.2	27.7	28.0	28.7	29.3
Philippines — Philippines	40.3	41.0	42.0	43.0	44.0	44.4	16.0	16.0	16.1	15.8
Sri Lanka — Sri Lanka	10.4	6.8	6.6	6.6	6.6	6.5	6.5	6.4	6.3	6.3
Syrian Arab Republic — Rép. arabe syrienne	0.1	0.1	0.1	0.1	0.1	0.1	0.1	0.1	0.1	0.1
Thailand — Thaïlande	23.4	23.4	23.4	23.4	26.8	27.5	28.1	28.8	28.7	28.6
Turkey — Turquie	19.4	18.1	17.7	16.6	15.9	15.3	16.1	15.8	16.5	16.2
Viet Nam — Viet Nam	31.6	31.3	31.0	30.2	30.9	30.8	30.7	26.4	26.5	31.6

Region, country or area — Région, pays ou zone	1996	1997	1998	1999	2000	2001	2002	2003	2004	2005
Yemen — Yémen	0.3	0.3	0.3	0.3	0.3	0.3	0.3	0.3	0.4	0.4
Europe — Europe	**463.8**	**523.6**	**472.4**	**531.7**	**592.2**	**564.6**	**578.4**	**607.7**	**620.3**	**661.2**
Albania — Albanie	0.4	0.4	0.0	0.2	0.4	0.3	0.3	0.3	0.3	0.3
Austria — Autriche	15.6	15.3	14.0	14.1	13.3	13.5	14.8	17.1	16.5	16.5
Belarus — Bélarus	15.7	17.6	5.9	6.6	6.1	6.5	6.9	7.5	7.5	7.5
Belgium — Belgique	...	...	...	4.8	4.5	4.2	4.5	4.8	4.9	5.0
Belgium-Luxembourg — Belgique-Luxembourg	4.0	4.0	4.8	...	...	...	...	...	...	...
Bosnia and Herzegovina — Bosnie-Herzégovine	0.0	4.0	4.1	4.1	4.3	3.8	4.2	4.1	4.0	3.8
Bulgaria — Bulgarie	3.2	3.0	3.2	4.4	4.8	4.0	4.8	4.8	6.0	5.9
Croatia — Croatie	2.5	3.1	3.4	3.5	3.7	3.5	3.6	3.8	3.8	4.0
Czech Republic — République tchèque	12.6	13.5	14.0	14.2	14.4	14.4	14.5	15.1	15.6	15.5
Denmark — Danemark	2.3	2.1	1.6	1.6	3.0	1.6	1.4	1.6	1.5	2.3
Estonia — Estonie	3.9	5.4	6.1	6.7	8.9	10.2	10.5	10.5	6.8	6.8
Finland — Finlande	46.6	51.3	53.7	53.6	54.3	52.2	53.0	53.8	53.8	51.6
France — France	40.4	41.1	35.5	36.0	45.8	39.8	35.4	32.8	33.6	34.4
Germany — Allemagne	37.0	38.2	39.1	37.6	53.7	39.5	42.4	51.2	54.5	56.9
Greece — Grèce	2.0	1.7	1.7	2.2	2.2	1.9	1.6	1.7	1.7	1.5
Hungary — Hongrie	3.7	4.2	4.2	5.2	5.9	5.8	5.8	5.8	5.7	5.9
Ireland — Irlande	2.3	2.2	2.3	2.6	2.7	2.5	2.6	2.7	2.6	2.6
Italy — Italie	9.1	9.1	9.6	11.1	9.3	8.1	7.5	8.2	8.7	8.0
Latvia — Lettonie	8.1	8.7	10.0	14.0	14.3	12.8	13.5	12.9	12.8	12.8
Lithuania — Lituanie	5.5	5.1	4.9	4.9	5.5	5.7	6.1	6.3	6.1	6.0
Luxembourg — Luxembourg	...	...	...	0.3	0.3	0.3	0.3	0.3	0.3	0.3
Netherlands — Pays-Bas	1.0	1.1	1.0	1.0	1.0	0.9	0.8	1.0	1.0	1.1
Norway — Norvège	8.4	8.3	8.2	8.4	8.2	9.0	8.7	8.3	8.8	9.7
Poland — Pologne	20.3	21.7	23.1	24.3	26.0	25.0	27.1	30.8	32.7	31.9
Portugal — Portugal	9.0	9.0	8.5	9.0	10.8	8.9	8.7	9.7	10.9	11.1
Republic of Moldova — République de Moldova	0.4	0.4	0.4	0.0	0.1	0.1	0.1	0.1	0.1	0.1
Romania — Roumanie	12.3	13.5	11.6	12.7	13.1	12.4	15.2	15.4	15.8	14.5
Russian Federation — Fédération de Russie	96.8	134.7	95.0	143.6	158.1	164.7	165.0	174.0	178.4	186.5
Serbia and Montenegro — Serbie-et-Monténégro	3.1	2.8	2.7	2.5	3.4	2.5	2.9	3.2	3.5	3.2
Slovakia — Slovaquie	5.5	4.9	5.5	5.8	6.2	5.8	5.8	6.4	7.2	9.3
Slovenia — Slovénie	2.0	2.2	2.1	2.1	2.3	2.3	2.3	2.6	2.6	2.7
Spain — Espagne	15.6	15.6	14.9	14.8	14.3	15.1	15.8	16.1	16.3	15.5
Sweden — Suède	56.3	60.2	60.6	58.7	63.3	63.2	66.6	67.1	67.3	98.7
Switzerland — Suisse	4.1	4.5	4.3	4.7	9.2	5.7	4.6	5.1	5.1	5.0
TFYR of Macedonia — L'ex-R.y. Macédoine	0.8	0.8	0.7	0.8	1.1	0.7	0.7	0.8	0.8	0.8
Ukraine — Ukraine	6.3	6.1	8.5	7.9	9.9	9.9	12.3	13.8	14.9	14.6
United Kingdom — Royaume-Uni	7.1	7.5	7.3	7.5	7.8	7.9	7.8	8.1	8.3	8.6
Oceania — Océanie	**51.2**	**52.7**	**52.3**	**54.5**	**59.0**	**60.4**	**56.8**	**59.6**	**58.8**	**58.4**
Australia — Australie	24.4	25.2	26.8	26.6	30.4	31.1	26.2	29.8	30.4	30.5
Fiji — Fidji	0.6	0.5	0.5	0.5	0.5	0.5	0.4	0.4	0.5	0.5
New Zealand — Nouvelle-Zélande	16.4	17.1	15.3	17.7	19.3	20.7	22.1	21.2	19.8	19.1
Papua New Guinea — Papouasie-Nvl-Guinée	8.8	8.8	8.6	8.6	7.7	7.2	7.2	7.2	7.2	7.2
Samoa — Samoa	0.1	0.1	0.1	0.1	0.1	0.1	0.1	0.1	0.1	0.1
Solomon Islands — Iles Salomon	0.9	0.9	0.9	0.9	0.9	0.7	0.7	0.7	0.7	0.7
Vanuatu — Vanuatu	0.1	0.1	0.1	0.1	0.1	0.1	0.1	0.1	0.1	0.1

Source

Food and Agriculture Organization of the United Nations (FAO), Rome, FAOSTAT database, last accessed June 2007.

Notes

1 Data include those for Namibia.
2 For statistical purposes, the data for China do not include those for the Hong Kong Special Administrative Region (Hong Kong SAR) and Macao Special Administrative Region (Macao SAR).
3 Data include those for Taiwan Province of China.

Source

Organisation des Nations Unies pour l'alimentation et l'agriculture (FAO), Rome, la base de données de la FAOSTAT, dernier accès juin 2007.

Notes

1 Les données comprennent les chiffres pour la Namibie.
2 Pour la présentation des statistiques, les données pour la Chine ne comprennent pas la Région Administrative Spéciale de Hong Kong (Hong Kong RAS) et la Région Administrative Spéciale de Macao (Macao RAS).
3 Les données comprennent les chiffres pour la province de Taiwan.

33 Fish production

Capture and aquaculture: metric tons

Production halieutique

Capture et aquaculture : tonnes

Country or area — Pays ou zone	Capture production — Captures					Aquaculture production — Production de l'aquaculture				
	2001	2002	2003	2004	2005	2001	2002	2003	2004	2005
Afghanistan[1] Afghanistan[1]	800	900	900	1 000	1 000	...	...	...	...	...
Albania Albanie	3 310	3 655	2 800[1]	3 563	3 802	286	860	1 473	1 569	1 473
Algeria Algérie	133 623	134 320	141 528	113 462	126 259	454	476	417[1]	586[1]	368
American Samoa Samoa américaines	3 649	6 971	4 984	4 043	3 943	...	...	...	...	...
Angola Angola	254 519	254 807	211 539	240 005	240 000[1]	...	...	...	...	...
Anguilla Anguilla	250[1]	250[1]	250[1]	250	250	...	...	...	...	...
Antigua and Barbuda Antigua-et-Barbuda	1 824	2 374	2 587	2 527	2 999	...	...	...	...	...
Argentina Argentine	949 302	958 644	915 994	946 123	931 472	1 340	1 457	1 647	1 848	2 430
Armenia Arménie	866	465	569	218	220[1]	1 331	1 020	1 064	813	813[1]
Aruba Aruba	163	163[1]	160[1]	162	162[1]	...	...	...	...	...
Australia Australie	191 372	197 183	215 253	229 729	245 935	35 403	38 569	44 183	49 095	47 087
Austria Autriche	362	350	372	400	370	2 393	2 333	2 233	2 267	2 420
Azerbaijan Azerbaïdjan	10 893	11 334	6 694	9 281	9 001	170	168	243	15	15[1]
Bahamas Bahamas	9 290	12 192	12 611	11 347	11 347[1]	13	25[1]	42	10	10[1]
Bahrain Bahreïn	11 230	11 204	13 638	14 334	11 854	0	3	4	8	3
Bangladesh Bangladesh	1 068 417	1 103 855	1 141 241	1 187 274	1 333 866	712 640	786 604	856 956	914 752	882 091
Barbados Barbade	2 676	2 500	2 502[1]	2 000[1]	1 869	...	...	...	...	...
Belarus Bélarus	943	5 877	6 925	890	900[1]	4 666	6 523	5 393	4 150	4 150[1]
Belgium Belgique	30 209	29 028	26 831	26 735	24 567	1 630	1 600	1 010[1]	1 200[1]	1 200[1]
Belize Belize	25 637	54 653	6 620	4 115	3 915	4 460	4 400	10 160	11 428	10 633
Benin Bénin	38 415	40 663	41 648	39 988	38 035	...	7	7[1]	7	372
Bermuda Bermudes	310	394	352	379	406	...	...	...	...	...
Bhutan[1] Bhoutan[1]	300	300	300	300	300	30	...	...	...	...
Bolivia Bolivie	5 940	6 300[1]	6 599	6 746	6 660	320	418	375	450	430
Bosnia and Herzegovina Bosnie-Herzégovine	2 000[1]	2 000[1]	2 000[1]	2 000[1]	2 000[1]	...	4 685	6 635	6 394	7 070
Botswana Botswana	118	139	122	161	132	...	...	...	...	...
Brazil Brésil	730 378	755 582	712 144	746 217	750 283	203 710	242 590	277 640	269 699	257 783
British Indian Ocean Terr. Terr. brit. de l'océan Indien	0	0	0	28	0	...	...	...	...	...

Country or area — Pays ou zone	Capture production — Captures 2001	2002	2003	2004	2005	Aquaculture production — Production de l'aquaculture 2001	2002	2003	2004	2005
British Virgin Islands Iles Vierges britanniques	837	1 062	2 771	1 262	1 300[1]	...	...	...	...	...
Brunei Darussalam Brunéi Darussalam	1 597	2 058	2 226	2 428	2 400[1]	99	157	160	708	708[1]
Bulgaria Bulgarie	6 520	15 008	12 035	8 252	5 434	2 935	2 308	4 465	2 489	3 145
Burkina Faso Burkina Faso	8 500	8 500	9 000	9 000[1]	9 000	5	5	5	5[1]	6[1]
Burundi Burundi	8 964	11 000[1]	14 697	13 855	14 000[1]	100[1]	150[1]	200	200	200[1]
Cambodia Cambodge	428 200	406 182	364 357	305 817	384 000	14 000	14 600	18 500	20 675	26 000
Cameroon Cameroun	121 031	130 135	117 801	129 000[1]	142 345	150[1]	330	320	330[1]	337
Canada Canada	1 041 101	1 062 866	1 110 547	1 176 212	1 080 982	153 046	170 746	150 624	145 018	154 083
Cape Verde Cap-Vert	8 890	8 145	8 721	8 446	7 742	...	...	...	...	...
Cayman Islands Iles Caïmanes	125	125	125	125	125	...	...	...	...	...
Central African Rep.[1] Rép. centrafricaine[1]	15 000	15 000	15 000	15 000	15 000	125	...	...	...	...
Chad[1] Tchad[1]	80 000	75 000	70 000	70 000	70 000	...	...	...	...	...
Channel Islands Iles Anglo-Normandes	3 927	3 449	3 526	3 201	3 505	487	580	684	775	650
Chile Chili	3 797 352	4 272 317	3 612 912	4 918 683	4 330 325	566 096	545 655	563 435	665 421	698 214
China[2] Chine[2]	16 529 389	16 553 144	16 755 653	16 892 793	17 053 191	26 050 101	27 767 251	28 883 642	30 612 602	32 414 084
China, Hong Kong SAR Chine, Hong Kong RAS	173 972	169 790	157 444	167 544	161 964	5 627	4 302	4 857	4 615	4 130
China, Macao SAR[1] Chine, Macao RAS[1]	1 500	1 500	1 500	1 500	1 500	...	...	...	...	...
Colombia Colombie	146 042	124 722	129 792	111 860	121 000[1]	57 660[1]	57 160[1]	60 895	60 072	60 072[1]
Comoros Comores	12 180	13 102	14 115	14 935	15 070	...	...	...	...	...
Congo Congo	48 830	51 927	54 659	54 234	58 368	64	68	69	72	80
Cook Islands Iles Cook	600[1]	1 678[1]	2 611[1]	3 280	3 737	0	0	0	0	0
Costa Rica Costa Rica	34 816	33 020	29 397	20 850	22 340	10 520	17 892	20 546	24 708	24 038
Côte d'Ivoire Côte d'Ivoire	73 556	79 689[1]	68 903	54 398	55 000[1]	1 025	806	866	866	866[1]
Croatia Croatie	18 489	21 230	19 946	30 164	34 669	10 166	8 416	7 605	13 224	13 782
Cuba Cuba	56 152	33 838	41 666	37 274	29 710	25 569	27 044	26 897	27 842	22 635
Cyprus Chypre	81 058	1 968	1 791	1 567	1 916	1 883	1 862	1 821	2 425	2 333
Czech Republic République tchèque	4 646	4 983	5 127	4 528	4 242	20 098	19 210	19 670	19 384	20 455
Dem. Rep. of the Congo Rép. dém. du Congo	214 600[1]	220 000[1]	220 000[1]	220 000[1]	220 000[1]	2 744	2 965	2 965[1]	2 965[1]	2 965[1]
Denmark Danemark	1 510 694	1 442 348	1 036 154	1 089 854	910 613	41 573	32 026	37 772	42 814	39 012
Djibouti Djibouti	260	260	260[1]	260[1]	260[1]	...	...	...	...	...

Country or area — Pays ou zone	Capture production — Captures 2001	2002	2003	2004	2005	Aquaculture production — Production de l'aquaculture 2001	2002	2003	2004	2005
Dominica Dominique	1 200[1]	1 270	950[1]	700[1]	579	7[1]	3	3[1]	3[1]	...
Dominican Republic Rép. dominicaine	13 217	17 261	18 097	14 223	11 106	2 647	3 554	1 944[1]	2 000[1]	980
Ecuador Equateur	586 563	318 642	397 864	336 832	407 723	52 428[1]	62 735[1]	74 500[1]	77 300[1]	78 300[1]
Egypt Egypte	428 651	425 170	430 809	393 494	349 553	342 864	376 296	445 181	471 535	539 748
El Salvador El Salvador	19 010	34 455	35 410	42 415	41 114	395	781	1 131	2 219	2 203
Equatorial Guinea[1] Guinée équatoriale[1]	3 500	3 500	3 500	3 500	3 500	...	...	...	...	...
Eritrea Erythrée	8 820	7 832	6 689	7 404	4 027	...	...	...	...	...
Estonia Estonie	105 167	101 453	79 082	87 906	98 772	467	257	372	252	555
Ethiopia Ethiopie	15 390	12 300	9 213	10 005	9 450	0	0	0	0	0
Faeroe Islands Iles Féroé	515 909	525 991	620 991	599 386	565 260	49 167	56 102	62 746	46 077	23 455
Falkland Is. (Malvinas) Iles Falkland (Malvinas)	68 332	53 261	74 898	55 369	84 546	0	0	0	21	2
Fiji Fidji	42 972	38 800	34 685	46 635	40 000[1]	1 717	401	144	99	99[1]
Finland Finlande	150 056	142 301	121 954	135 427	131 741	15 739	15 132	12 558	12 821	14 355
France France	615 834	631 615	638 393	599 540	574 358	251 620	251 970	239 814	260 655	258 435
French Guiana Guyane française	4 599[1]	4 782[1]	5 565[1]	5 514[1]	5 265[1]	37	38	37	37	37
French Polynesia Polynésie française	15 404	15 543	14 099[1]	12 198[1]	12 152	66	65	65[1]	67	67
Gabon Gabon	42 871	41 571	45 279	45 958	43 863	102	83	80	80	78
Gambia Gambie	34 527	45 769	36 864	31 423	32 000[1]	...	...	...	...	...
Georgia Géorgie	1 636	1 811	3 306	2 951	3 000[1]	80	52	56	72	72[1]
Germany Allemagne	211 282	224 452	260 867	262 103	285 668	53 409	49 852	74 280	57 233	44 685
Ghana Ghana	447 181	371 178	390 756	399 370	392 274	6 000	6 000[1]	938	950	1 154
Greece Grèce	94 190	96 343	93 383	93 886	92 738	97 512	87 928	101 434	97 143	106 208
Greenland Groenland	158 485	195 624	175 321	216 302	216 302[1]	...	...	...	...	...
Grenada Grenade	2 250	2 171	2 544	2 039	2 050[1]	0	...	...	...	...
Guadeloupe Guadeloupe	10 100	10 100	10 100	10 100	10 100	14	23	31	31	31
Guam Guam	278	231	162	180	162	232[1]	233[1]	...	...	...
Guatemala Guatemala	30 524[1]	25 062	26 146	13 277[1]	12 248	5 100[1]	7 978[1]	6 346[1]	4 508[1]	4 508[1]
Guinea Guinée	105 402	92 755	120 242	93 947	96 571[1]	0	...	...	...	...
Guinea-Bissau[1] Guinée-Bissau[1]	6 848	7 324	6 153	6 200	6 200	...	...	...	...	...
Guyana Guyana	53 405	48 017	59 694	56 719	53 372	608	608[1]	608[1]	608[1]	608

	Capture production — Captures					Aquaculture production — Production de l'aquaculture				
Country or area — Pays ou zone	2001	2002	2003	2004	2005	2001	2002	2003	2004	2005
Haiti Haïti	6 800[1]	7 300[1]	7 800[1]	8 300	8 300[1]	...	...	...	...	...
Honduras Honduras	18 159[1]	10 086[1]	10 516[1]	14 940[1]	19 200[1]	12 130	14 557	20 035	22 520	29 380
Hungary Hongrie	6 638	6 750	6 536	7 242	7 609	13 056	11 574	11 870	12 744	13 661
Iceland Islande	1 980 715	2 129 705	1 980 530	1 728 101	1 661 031	4 371	3 585	6 214	8 868	8 256
India Inde	3 777 092	3 736 603	3 712 149	3 391 009	3 481 136	2 119 839	2 187 189	2 312 971	2 794 636	2 837 751
Indonesia Indonésie	4 242 270	4 322 764	4 627 149	4 642 379	4 381 260	864 276	914 071	996 659	1 045 051	1 197 109
Iran (Islamic Rep. of) Iran (Rép. islamique d')	351 140	324 853	350 122	369 990	410 558	62 550	76 817	91 714	104 330	117 354
Iraq Iraq	33 300	26 000	17 200	14 687	20 100	2 000[1]	2 000[1]	2 000[1]	12 196	12 870
Ireland Irlande	356 430	282 352	266 218	280 620	262 532	60 940	62 568	62 516	58 359	60 050
Isle of Man Ile de Man	3 112	3 127	2 984	2 627	2 627[1]	...	...	...	...	...
Israel Israël	5 024	5 043	4 055	3 340	4 151	21 318	22 256	20 776	22 303	22 404
Italy Italie	310 397	269 846	295 694	287 084	298 373	218 269	183 962	191 662	117 786	180 943
Jamaica Jamaïque	12 294	7 797	8 702	13 471	13 096	4 512[1]	6 150	2 969	4 495	5 670
Japan Japon	4 703 146	4 360 667[1]	4 670 452	4 311 848	4 072 895[1]	799 946	826 715	823 873	776 421	746 221
Jordan Jordanie	520	526	481	494	510	540	515	650	487	561
Kazakhstan Kazakhstan	21 654	24 910	25 371	33 896	31 000[1]	417	778	820	589	589[1]
Kenya Kenya	164 151	144 512	120 051	126 867	148 124	1 009	798	1 012	1 035	1 047
Kiribati Kiribati	32 447	31 639	31 542	31 600[1]	34 000[1]	18	14	9	9[1]	12
Korea, Dem. P. R. Corée, R. p. dém. de	206 500	205 000[1]	205 000[1]	205 000[1]	205 000[1]	63 700[1]	63 700[1]	63 700[1]	63 700[1]	63 700[1]
Korea, Republic of Corée, République de	1 990 720	1 671 421	1 642 905	1 575 335	1 639 069	294 484	296 783	387 791	405 748	436 232
Kuwait Koweït	5 846	5 360	4 059	4 833	4 895	195	195[1]	366	375[1]	327
Kyrgyzstan Kirghizistan	57	48	14	7	7[1]	144	94	12	20	20[1]
Lao People's Dem. Rep. Rép. dém. pop. lao	31 000[1]	33 440	29 800	29 800[1]	29 800[1]	50 000	59 716	64 900	64 900	78 000
Latvia Lettonie	128 176	113 677	114 543	125 391	150 618	463	430	637	545	542
Lebanon Liban	3 670	3 970	3 898	3 866	3 798	300	790	790	790	803
Lesotho Lesotho	24	40	42	45	45	8	8[1]	4	2	1
Liberia Libéria	11 286	11 000[1]	10 700[1]	10 359	10 000[1]	14	14[1]	14[1]	...	...
Libyan Arab Jamah. Jamah. arabe libyenne	46 239	46 666	46 666[1]	46 073[1]	46 073[1]	100[1]	0	58[1]	266[1]	266[1]
Lithuania Lituanie	150 831	150 146	157 205	161 988	139 785	2 001	1 750	2 356	2 697	2 013
Madagascar Madagascar	135 583	141 284	140 838	146 751	136 400	7 749	9 713	9 507	8 743	8 500[1]

Country or area — Pays ou zone	Capture production — Captures 2001	2002	2003	2004	2005	Aquaculture production — Production de l'aquaculture 2001	2002	2003	2004	2005
Malawi Malawi	40 619	41 329	53 543	56 463	58 783	568	642	666	733	812
Malaysia Malaisie	1 234 733	1 275 555	1 287 084	1 335 764	1 214 183	158 158	165 119	167 160	171 270	175 834
Maldives Maldives	127 184	163 388	155 415	158 576	185 980	...	...	...	...	...
Mali Mali	100 000[1]	100 000[1]	100 000[1]	100 000[1]	100 000[1]	500[1]	1 008	1 008[1]	1 008[1]	1 008[1]
Malta Malte	895	1 074	1 132	1 134	1 435	1 235	1 116	887	868	736
Marshall Islands Iles Marshall	36 274	39 452	38 375	47 116	56 664	...	...	...	...	...
Martinique Martinique	6 200	6 200[1]	6 200	6 200	5 500	51	80	100	92	92
Mauritania Mauritanie	135 142[1]	149 131[1]	141 898[1]	199 380	247 577	...	...	...	...	...
Mauritius Maurice	10 986	10 706	11 136	10 227	10 048	59	56	33	350	400
Mayotte Mayotte	10 052	4 754	3 464	2 306	2 214	3[1]	...	...	170	164
Mexico Mexique	1 398 592	1 450 719	1 357 191	1 258 973	1 304 830	76 075	73 675	84 475	104 354	117 514
Micronesia (Fed. States of) Micronésie (Etats féd. de)	19 197[1]	23 258[1]	32 379[1]	29 234	29 336	0	0	0	0	0
Monaco[1] Monaco[1]	3	3	3	3	2	...	...	...	...	...
Mongolia Mongolie	290	263	382	305	366	...	...	...	...	...
Montserrat Montserrat	50[1]	46	50[1]	50[1]	50[1]	...	...	...	...	...
Morocco Maroc	1 083 953	894 977	885 131	894 610	932 704	1 403	1 670	1 538	1 718	2 257
Mozambique Mozambique	30 074	36 462	43 933[1]	44 683[1]	42 473	0	677	409	446	1 222
Myanmar Myanmar	1 187 880	1 284 340	1 343 860	1 586 660	1 742 956	121 266	190 120	252 010	400 360	474 510
Namibia Namibie	547 498	624 599	636 227	570 708	552 695	50[1]	50	50[1]	50[1]	50[1]
Nauru Nauru	61[1]	22	44	18	39	...	...	...	...	...
Nepal Népal	16 700	17 900	18 888	19 947	19 983	16 570	17 100	17 680	20 000	22 480
Netherlands Pays-Bas	518 163	464 036	526 281	521 636	549 208	57 064	54 442	66 565	75 725	68 175
Netherlands Antilles[1] Antilles néerlandaises[1]	22 805	12 901	20 149	15 765	2 422	5	...	...	...	...
New Caledonia Nouvelle-Calédonie	3 309	3 417[1]	3 513	3 771	3 315	1 893	1 918	1 784	2 290	2 533
New Zealand Nouvelle-Zélande	569 762	588 688	550 937	545 947	535 394	76 024	86 583	84 642	92 219	105 301
Nicaragua Nicaragua	19 528	16 421	15 326	19 297	30 914	5 750	6 089	7 005	7 880	9 983
Niger Niger	20 800	23 560	55 860	51 466	50 018	21	40	40	40	40
Nigeria Nigéria	452 146	481 056	475 162	465 251	523 182	24 398	30 663	30 677	43 950	56 355
Niue[1] Nioué[1]	200	200	200	200	200	...	...	...	...	...
Northern Mariana Islands Iles Mariannes du Nord	197	198	173	170	196	...	...	...	...	...

	Capture production — Captures					Aquaculture production — Production de l'aquaculture				
Country or area — Pays ou zone	2001	2002	2003	2004	2005	2001	2002	2003	2004	2005
Norway Norvège	2 686 944	2 740 344	2 548 975	2 524 464	2 392 934	510 748	551 297	584 423	636 802	656 636
Occupied Palestinian Terr. Terr. palestinien occupé	1 950	2 379	1 508	2 951	1 805	…	…	…	…	…
Oman Oman	129 907	142 670	138 481	165 082	150 571	0	0	352	503	173
Pakistan Pakistan	543 166	532 134	491 834	479 785	434 473	57 632	66 970	73 047	76 653	80 622
Palau Palaos	1 084	1 027	1 047	1 079	932	2	4	4	5	5
Panama Panama	265 500[1]	229 736	215 398	203 243	214 737	3 127	3 638	6 228	7 048	8 019
Papua New Guinea Papouasie-Nvl-Guinée	120 027[1]	151 825[1]	186 740[1]	229 742[1]	250 280[1]	15	15[1]	15[1]	…	…
Paraguay[1] Paraguay[1]	25 000	24 000	23 000	22 000	21 000	570	1 000	1 300	2 100	2 100
Peru Pérou	7 986 218	8 765 183	6 086 059	9 604 528	9 388 662	7 628	11 614	13 768	22 259	27 468
Philippines Philippines	1 949 076	2 030 622	2 166 324	2 216 037	2 246 352	434 661	443 537	459 615	512 220	557 251
Pitcairn[1] Pitcairn[1]	5	5	5	3	3	…	…	…	…	…
Poland Pologne	225 064	223 440	180 399	192 108	156 247	35 460	32 709	34 526	35 258	36 607
Portugal Portugal	193 266	202 853	212 073	221 316	211 757	8 209	8 288	8 033	6 700	6 485
Puerto Rico Porto Rico	3 794	2 529	2 919	2 428	2 551	414	442	269	417	417[1]
Qatar Qatar	8 864	7 155	11 295	11 134	13 935	1	0	0	0	11
Republic of Moldova République de Moldova	387	565	343	487	531	1 189	1 765	2 638	4 470	4 470[1]
Réunion Réunion	3 889	2 872	2 903	3 373	4 596	130	110	121	107	161
Romania Roumanie	7 637	6 989	9 890	5 095	6 068	10 818	9 248	9 042	8 137	7 284
Russian Federation Fédération de Russie	3 628 422	3 232 282	3 281 448	2 941 533	3 190 946	89 945	101 330	108 684	109 802	114 752
Rwanda Rwanda	6 828	7 000[1]	7 400	7 826	7 800[1]	435	612[1]	1 027	386	386[1]
Saint Helena Sainte-Hélène	866	598	985	1 061	1 130	…	…	…	…	…
Saint Kitts and Nevis Saint-Kitts-et-Nevis	555	355	400[1]	484	450[1]	…	…	…	…	…
Saint Lucia Sainte-Lucie	1 983	1 637	1 462	1 508	1 409	1	2	2[1]	1	1
Saint Pierre and Miquelon Saint-Pierre-et-Miquelon	4 206	3 889	3 975	4 311	3 084	…	…	…	…	…
Saint Vincent-Grenadines Saint Vincent-Grenadines	52 485	44 529	4 782	8 625	2 745	…	…	…	…	…
Samoa Samoa	11 800[1]	9 900[1]	6 600[1]	4 719	4 501[1]	0	0	0	…	…
Sao Tome and Principe Sao Tomé-et-Principe	3 400[1]	3 300[1]	3 283	4 141	3 600[1]	…	…	…	…	…
Saudi Arabia Arabie saoudite	55 331	57 211	55 440	55 418	60 403	8 218	6 744	11 824	11 172	14 375
Senegal Sénégal	433 202	405 824	478 484	445 263	405 070	105	109	98	204	193
Serbia and Montenegro Serbie-et-Monténégro	1 091	1 585	1 798	2 388	2 468[1]	3 536	3 326	3 194	4 616	4 554

Fish production — Capture and aquaculture: metric tons *(continued)*
Production halieutique — Capture et aquaculture : tonnes *(suite)*

Country or area — Pays ou zone	Capture production — Captures 2001	2002	2003	2004	2005	Aquaculture production — Production de l'aquaculture 2001	2002	2003	2004	2005
Seychelles Seychelles	53 534	63 209	85 784	100 435	106 555	282	234	1 084	1 175	772
Sierra Leone Sierra Leone	75 210	82 990	96 926	134 440	145 993	30[1]	...	...	...	...
Singapore Singapour	3 342	2 769	2 085	2 173	1 920	4 443	5 027	5 024	5 406	5 917
Slovakia Slovaquie	1 531	1 746	1 646	1 603	1 693	999	829	881	1 180	955
Slovenia Slovénie	1 827	1 686	1 281	1 022	1 223	1 262	1 289	1 353	1 571	1 536
Solomon Islands[1] Iles Salomon[1]	23 626	25 886	36 873	34 191	28 520	15	...	...	...	...
Somalia[1] Somalie[1]	27 500	29 000	30 000	30 000	30 000	...	...	...	...	...
South Africa Afrique du Sud	750 501	766 937	822 937	888 065	817 608	4 177	4 505	4 896	3 167	3 142
Spain Espagne	1 092 828	892 549	896 442	804 697	848 803	312 647	259 186	272 778	298 855	221 927
Sri Lanka Sri Lanka	281 150	300 240	281 500	283 770	161 960	3 610	2 651	3 462	2 513	1 724
Sudan Soudan	58 000	57 000	59 000	57 000	62 000	1 000	1 600	1 600[1]	1 600[1]	1 600[1]
Suriname Suriname	24 865	25 242[1]	28 180	45 081	39 949	422	422	260	288	242
Swaziland[1] Swaziland[1]	70	70	70	70	70	72	...	...	...	...
Sweden Suède	311 817	294 964	286 875	269 922	256 359	6 773	5 618	6 334	5 989	5 880
Switzerland Suisse	1 715	1 544	1 815	1 602	1 475	1 135	1 135	1 100	1 205	1 214
Syrian Arab Republic Rép. arabe syrienne	8 291	9 178	8 911	8 528	8 447	5 880	5 988	7 217	8 682	8 533
Tajikistan Tadjikistan	137	181	158	184	184[1]	99	143	167	26	26[1]
Thailand Thaïlande	2 833 977	2 842 428	2 849 724	2 839 612	2 599 387	814 121	954 696	1 064 409	1 259 983	1 144 011
TFYR of Macedonia L'ex-R.y. Macédoine	128	148	162	213	246	1 053	883	910	959	868
Timor-Leste Timor-Leste	356	350[1]	350[1]	350[1]	350[1]	...	...	...	...	...
Togo Togo	23 163	20 946	27 485	28 013	27 732	120	1 025	1 221	1 525[1]	1 535
Tokelau[1] Tokélaou[1]	200	200	200	200	200	...	...	...	...	...
Tonga Tonga	4 673	4 791	4 435	1 645	1 900[1]	20	17	22	3	1
Trinidad and Tobago Trinité-et-Tobago	11 918	14 088	9 915	10 034	13 414	7	7[1]	7[1]	...	...
Tunisia Tunisie	98 490	96 685	90 226	111 531	109 117	1 868	1 975	2 130	2 524	2 665
Turkey Turquie	527 733	566 682	507 772	550 482	426 496	67 244	61 165	79 943	94 010	119 177
Turkmenistan Turkménistan	12 749	12 812	14 543	14 992	15 000[1]	43	38	24	16	16[1]
Turks and Caicos Islands Iles Turques et Caïques	6 419	5 767	5 100	5 677	5 491	20[1]	30	25	4	4
Tuvalu Tuvalu	500[1]	600[1]	1 500	2 400	2 560	...	...	5	1	1
Uganda Ouganda	220 726	221 898	241 810	371 789	416 758	2 360	4 915	5 500	5 539	10 817

Fish production — Capture and aquaculture: metric tons (*continued*)
Production halieutique — Capture et aquaculture : tonnes (*suite*)

	Capture production — Captures					Aquaculture production — Production de l'aquaculture				
Country or area — Pays ou zone	2001	2002	2003	2004	2005	2001	2002	2003	2004	2005
Ukraine Ukraine	360 914	265 600	222 349	202 673	244 943	31 037	30 819	25 616	26 223	28 745
United Arab Emirates Emirats arabes unis	112 561	97 574	95 150	90 000[1]	90 000[1]	0	0	2 300	570[1]	570[1]
United Kingdom Royaume-Uni	741 042	689 891	635 486	652 846	669 458	170 516	179 036	181 838	207 203	172 813
United Rep. of Tanzania Rép.-Unie de Tanzanie	335 900	323 530	351 125	347 795	347 800[1]	300	630	2	11	11[1]
United States Etats-Unis	4 944 336	4 937 305	4 938 956	4 959 826	4 888 621	479 254	497 346	544 329	606 549	471 958
United States Virgin Is. Iles Vierges américaines	1 200[1]	1 300[1]	1 492	1 522	1 269	0	0	0	0	0
Uruguay Uruguay	105 137	108 765	117 269	122 986	125 906	17	17	24	21	47
Uzbekistan Ouzbékistan	2 341	1 564	1 349	1 230	1 625[1]	3 988	3 824	3 118	3 093	3 800[1]
Vanuatu Vanuatu	36 038[1]	44 306[1]	57 707	121 219	151 079	...	...	...	1	1
Venezuela (Bolivarian Rep. of) Venezuela (Rép. bolivar. du)	408 655	509 663	520 773	487 000[1]	470 000[1]	16 622	17 860	19 821	22 210	22 210[1]
Viet Nam Viet Nam	1 724 758	1 802 598	1 856 105	1 879 488	1 929 900	588 098[1]	703 041[1]	937 502	1 198 617	1 437 300
Wallis and Futuna Islands Iles Wallis et Futuna	300[1]	300[1]	300	300[1]	300[1]	...	...	...	...	...
Yemen Yémen	142 198	179 584	228 116	256 300	263 000	...	...	...	...	...
Zambia Zambie	65 000[1]	65 000[1]	65 000[1]	65 000[1]	65 000[1]	4 520[1]	4 630[1]	4 501	5 125	5 125[1]
Zimbabwe Zimbabwe	13 000[1]	13 000[1]	13 000[1]	13 000[1]	13 000[1]	2 285	2 213	2 600	2 955	2 452

Source

Food and Agriculture Organization of the United Nations (FAO), Rome, FISHSTAT database.

Notes

1 FAO estimate.

2 For statistical purposes, the data for China do not include those for the Hong Kong Special Administrative Region (Hong Kong SAR), Macao Special Administrative Region (Macao SAR) and Taiwan Province of China.

Source

Organisation des Nations Unies pour l'alimentation et l'agriculture (FAO), Rome, les données des pêches de FISHSTAT.

Notes

1 Estimation de la FAO.

2 Pour la présentation des statistiques, les données pour la Chine ne comprennent pas la Région Administrative Spéciale de Hong Kong (Hong Kong RAS), la Région Administrative Spéciale de Macao (Macao RAS) et la province de Taiwan.

34 Livestock

Stocks: thousand head

Cheptel

Effectifs : milliers de têtes

Region, country or area	1998	1999	2000	2001	2002	2003	2004	2005	Région, pays ou zone
World									**Monde**
Asses, mules or hinnies	**53 754**	**54 123**	**54 069**	**54 152**	**54 186**	**53 030**	**52 628**	**52 159**	**Ânes, mules ou mulets**
Buffaloes	**160 488**	**161 889**	**163 484**	**165 441**	**167 568**	**170 259**	**171 949**	**173 858**	**Buffles**
Cattle	**1 309 796**	**1 313 115**	**1 315 612**	**1 322 015**	**1 336 887**	**1 351 879**	**1 364 364**	**1 376 824**	**Bovins**
Goats	**695 513**	**708 907**	**722 358**	**736 576**	**752 674**	**773 809**	**795 893**	**816 308**	**Caprins**
Horses	**56 818**	**56 869**	**56 749**	**56 588**	**55 995**	**56 508**	**57 274**	**58 108**	**Chevaux**
Pigs	**868 748**	**891 862**	**896 511**	**913 145**	**928 958**	**942 485**	**944 605**	**962 686**	**Porcins**
Sheep	**1 046 024**	**1 052 666**	**1 053 948**	**1 034 429**	**1 029 588**	**1 034 910**	**1 063 705**	**1 084 979**	**Ovins**
Africa									**Afrique**
Asses, mules or hinnies	**14 387**	**14 410**	**14 518**	**14 895**	**15 497**	**15 388**	**15 567**	**15 669**	**Ânes, mules ou mulets**
Buffaloes	**3 149**	**3 330**	**3 379**	**3 532**	**3 550**	**3 777**	**3 845**	**3 920**	**Buffles**
Cattle	**217 715**	**226 912**	**225 958**	**229 576**	**236 114**	**237 574**	**239 278**	**243 715**	**Bovins**
Goats	**205 841**	**209 647**	**213 739**	**219 814**	**224 274**	**228 531**	**233 742**	**235 432**	**Caprins**
Horses	**3 264**	**3 276**	**3 253**	**3 441**	**3 669**	**3 614**	**3 685**	**3 744**	**Chevaux**
Pigs	**19 374**	**19 306**	**20 446**	**21 754**	**22 377**	**23 005**	**23 180**	**24 038**	**Porcins**
Sheep	**230 339**	**236 480**	**237 458**	**242 156**	**245 406**	**247 903**	**254 454**	**254 847**	**Ovins**
Algeria									Algérie
Asses, mules or hinnies	232	220	220	213	215	215	201	201	Ânes, mules ou mulets
Cattle	1 317	1 580	1 595	1 613	1 572	1 561	1 614	1 586	Bovins
Goats	3 257	3 062	3 027	3 129	3 281	3 325	3 451	3 590	Caprins
Horses	46	46	44	44	46	48	45	43	Chevaux
Pigs[1]	6	6	6	6	6	6	6	6	Porcins[1]
Sheep	17 949	17 988	17 616	17 299	17 588	17 503	18 293	18 909	Ovins
Angola									Angola
Asses, mules or hinnies	5[1]	5[1]	5[1]	5[1]	5[1]	5[1]	5[1]	5	Ânes, mules ou mulets
Cattle	3 898[2]	3 900[2]	4 042[2]	4 100[1]	4 150[1]	4 150[1]	4 150[1]	4 150	Bovins
Goats	1 861[2]	2 000[2]	2 150[2]	2 150[1]	2 050[1]	2 050[1]	2 050[1]	2 050	Caprins
Horses	1[1]	1[1]	1[1]	1[1]	1[1]	1[1]	1[1]	1	Chevaux
Pigs	810[1]	800[1]	800[1]	800[1]	780[1]	780[1]	780[1]	780	Porcins
Sheep	305[2]	336[2]	350[2]	350[1]	340[1]	340[1]	340[1]	340	Ovins
Benin									Bénin
Asses, mules or hinnies	1[1]	1[1]	1	1[1]	1[1]	1[1]	1[1]	1[1]	Ânes, mules ou mulets
Cattle	1 371	1 438	1 487	1 584	1 635	1 689	1 745	1 800[1]	Bovins
Goats	1 114	1 176	1 234	1 250[1]	1 270[1]	1 300[1]	1 350[1]	1 380[1]	Caprins
Horses	1[1]	0	1	1[1]	1[1]	1[1]	1[1]	1[1]	Chevaux
Pigs	264	195	297	277	286	297	309	322[1]	Porcins
Sheep	620	654	672	655[1]	670[1]	670[1]	700[1]	750[1]	Ovins
Botswana									Botswana
Asses, mules or hinnies[1]	323	328	333	333	333	333	333	333	Ânes, mules ou mulets[1]
Cattle	2 345	2 581	2 500[1]	2 500[1]	3 060	3 100[1]	3 100[1]	3 100[1]	Bovins
Goats	2 199	2 000[1]	1 900[1]	1 887	1 683	1 700[1]	1 850[1]	1 950[1]	Caprins
Horses[1]	32	33	33	33	33	33	33	33	Chevaux[1]
Pigs[1]	2	5	6	8	8	8	8	8	Porcins[1]
Sheep	393	369	370[1]	306	273	300[1]	300[1]	300[1]	Ovins
Burkina Faso									Burkina Faso
Asses, mules or hinnies	682[1]	724[1]	767[1]	814[1]	863[1]	915	970[1]	1 028[1]	Ânes, mules ou mulets
Cattle	5 820[1]	6 092[1]	6 376[1]	6 674[1]	6 985[1]	7 312	7 653[1]	8 010[1]	Bovins
Goats	8 532[1]	8 813[1]	9 104[1]	9 405[1]	9 715[1]	10 036	10 367[1]	10 709[1]	Caprins
Horses	30[1]	31[1]	32[1]	34[1]	35[1]	36	37[1]	39[1]	Chevaux
Pigs	1 171[1]	1 288[1]	1 417[1]	1 559[1]	1 715[1]	1 887	2 076[1]	2 284[1]	Porcins
Sheep	5 993[1]	6 129[1]	6 267[1]	6 409[1]	6 554[1]	6 703	6 854[1]	7 009[1]	Ovins

Region, country or area	1998	1999	2000	2001	2002	2003	2004	2005	Région, pays ou zone
Burundi									Burundi
Cattle	346	329	320[1]	315[1]	324	355	374	396	Bovins
Goats	659	850[1]	750[1]	750[1]	750[1]	750[1]	750[1]	750	Caprins
Pigs	73	61	70[1]	70[1]	70[1]	70[1]	70[1]	70	Porcins
Sheep	200[1]	200[1]	215[1]	230[1]	230	240	236	243	Ovins
Cameroon									Cameroun
Asses, mules or hinnies[1]	37	37	38	38	39	39	40	40	Ânes, mules ou mulets[1]
Cattle	4 846	5 500	5 882	5 800[1]	5 600[2]	5 800[1]	5 900[1]	6 000[2]	Bovins
Goats	3 750[1]	3 800	4 410	4 400[1]	4 400[1]	4 400[1]	4 400[1]	4 400[1]	Caprins
Horses[1]	16	17	17	17	17	17	17	17	Chevaux[1]
Pigs	1 200	1 000	1 346	1 350[1]	1 350[1]	1 350[1]	1 350[1]	1 350[1]	Porcins
Sheep	3 550[1]	3 650[1]	3 753	3 800[1]	3 800[1]	3 800[1]	3 800[1]	3 800[1]	Ovins
Cape Verde									Cap-Vert
Asses, mules or hinnies[1]	15	15	15	16	16	16	16	16	Ânes, mules ou mulets[1]
Cattle	22[1]	22	22	22[1]	22[1]	22	23[1]	23[1]	Bovins
Goats	115[1]	112	110	110[1]	112[1]	112	113[1]	113[1]	Caprins
Horses[1]	^0	^0	^0	^0	^0	^0	1	1	Chevaux[1]
Pigs[1]	185	200	186	200	200	200	205	205	Porcins[1]
Sheep	10[1]	9	8	8[1]	9[1]	9	10[1]	10[1]	Ovins
Central African Rep.									Rép. centrafricaine
Cattle	2 992	3 060	3 128	3 200	3 273	3 347	3 423[2]	3 423[1]	Bovins
Goats	2 339	2 472	2 614	2 763	2 921	3 087	3 087[1]	3 087[1]	Caprins
Pigs	622	649	678	707	738	771	805[2]	805[1]	Porcins
Sheep	207	211	222	234	246	259	259[1]	259[1]	Ovins
Chad									Tchad
Asses, mules or hinnies	352	350	357	364	372[1]	380[1]	388[1]	388[1]	Ânes, mules ou mulets
Cattle	5 582	5 712	5 852	5 992	6 128[2]	6 268[2]	6 400[1]	6 540[1]	Bovins
Goats	4 939	5 058	5 179	5 304	5 463[2]	5 588[2]	5 717[1]	5 843[1]	Caprins
Horses	208	198	202	255[2]	261[2]	267[2]	273[1]	275[1]	Chevaux
Pigs	20[2]	21[2]	22[2]	22[1]	24[1]	24[1]	25[1]	25[1]	Porcins
Sheep	2 264	2 318	2 374	2 431	2 454[2]	2 511[2]	2 569[1]	2 628[1]	Ovins
Comoros									Comores
Asses, mules or hinnies[1]	5	5	5	5	5	5	5	5	Ânes, mules ou mulets[1]
Cattle	50[2]	50	51[1]	53[1]	55	46[1]	45[1]	45[1]	Bovins
Goats	141[2]	170	113	113	115[1]	115[1]	115[1]	115[1]	Caprins
Sheep	19[2]	20	21[1]	21[1]	21[1]	21[1]	21[1]	21[1]	Ovins
Congo									Congo
Cattle	72	83	87	90	93[1]	100[1]	110[1]	115[1]	Bovins
Goats[1]	280	280	280	280	294	294	294	295	Caprins[1]
Pigs	44[1]	45[1]	46[1]	46[1]	46	46[1]	46[1]	47[1]	Porcins
Sheep	114	115[1]	96	96[1]	98[1]	98[1]	98[1]	99[1]	Ovins
Côte d'Ivoire									Côte d'Ivoire
Cattle	1 346	1 377	1 409	1 442	1 456	1 460[1]	1 500[1]	1 500[1]	Bovins
Goats	1 079	1 111	1 134	1 162	1 191	1 192[1]	1 192[1]	1 192[1]	Caprins
Pigs	278	327	336	346	350	336	343	345[1]	Porcins
Sheep	1 381	1 416	1 451	1 487	1 522	1 523[1]	1 523[1]	1 523[1]	Ovins
Dem. Rep. of the Congo									Rép. dém. du Congo
Cattle	881	853	822	793	761	760	758	757	Bovins
Goats	4 675	4 197	4 131	4 067	4 004	4 010	4 016	4 022	Caprins
Pigs	1 154	1 100	1 049	1 000	953	955	957	959	Porcins
Sheep	954	939	925	911	897	898	899	900	Ovins
Djibouti									Djibouti
Asses, mules or hinnies[1]	9	9	9	9	9	9	9	9	Ânes, mules ou mulets[1]
Cattle	280[1]	297	297	297	297	297[1]	297[1]	297[1]	Bovins
Goats	510	511	511	512	512	512[1]	512[1]	512[1]	Caprins
Sheep	462	466	466	466	466	466[1]	466[1]	466[1]	Ovins

Region, country or area	1998	1999	2000	2001	2002	2003	2004	2005	Région, pays ou zone
Egypt									Egypte
Asses, mules or hinnies[1]	2 996	3 001	3 051	3 051	3 071	3 071	3 071	3 071	Ânes, mules ou mulets[1]
Buffaloes	3 149	3 330	3 379	3 532	3 550[1]	3 777	3 845	3 920[1]	Buffles
Cattle	3 217	3 418	3 530	3 801	4 000[1]	4 227	4 369	4 500[1]	Bovins
Goats	3 261	3 308	3 425	3 497[2]	3 582[2]	3 811	3 889	3 960[1]	Caprins
Horses	45[1]	48	45	53	62[2]	62[1]	62[1]	62[1]	Chevaux
Pigs	29[1]	29	30	30	30[1]	31[1]	31[1]	30[1]	Porcins
Sheep	4 352	4 391	4 469	4 671	5 105[2]	4 939	5 043	5 150[1]	Ovins
Equatorial Guinea[1]									Guinée équatoriale[1]
Cattle	5	5	5	5	5	5	5	5	Bovins
Goats	9	9	9	9	9	9	9	9	Caprins
Pigs	6	6	6	6	6	6	6	6	Porcins
Sheep	37	37	37	38	38	38	38	38	Ovins
Eritrea									Erythrée
Cattle	2 026[2]	2 100[1]	2 150[1]	1 950[1]	1 900[1]	1 927[1]	1 930[1]	1 950[1]	Bovins
Goats[1]	1 650	1 700	1 700	1 700	1 700	1 700	1 700	1 700	Caprins[1]
Sheep	2 129[2]	2 000[1]	2 150[1]	2 150[1]	2 000[1]	2 100[1]	2 100[1]	2 100[1]	Ovins
Ethiopia									Ethiopie
Asses, mules or hinnies	3 432	3 336	3 281	3 670	4 251	4 130[1]	4 091	4 125[1]	Ânes, mules ou mulets
Cattle	35 372	35 095	33 075	35 383	40 639	39 000[1]	38 103	38 500[1]	Bovins
Goats	10 460	9 544	8 598	9 621	9 622[1]	9 623[1]	9 626[1]	9 626[1]	Caprins
Horses	1 231	1 207	1 144	1 254	1 483	1 450[1]	1 447	1 500[1]	Chevaux
Pigs[1]	24	25	25	26	26	28	28	29	Porcins[1]
Sheep	13 428	12 235	10 951	11 438	14 322	15 000[1]	16 576	17 000[1]	Ovins
Gabon									Gabon
Cattle	34[1]	35[1]	36[1]	36[1]	36[1]	35[1]	35[1]	35	Bovins
Goats	89[1]	90[1]	91[1]	90[1]	90[1]	90[1]	90[1]	90	Caprins
Pigs	211[1]	212[1]	213[1]	213[1]	212[1]	212[1]	212[1]	212	Porcins
Sheep	191[1]	195[1]	198[1]	198[1]	195[1]	195[1]	195[1]	195	Ovins
Gambia									Gambie
Asses, mules or hinnies	38	33	35[1]	35[1]	35[1]	35[1]	35[1]	35[1]	Ânes, mules ou mulets
Cattle	359	361	364	323	327	327[1]	328[1]	330[1]	Bovins
Goats	154	150	145	228	262	262[1]	265[1]	270[1]	Caprins
Horses	17	22	17[1]	17[1]	17[1]	17[1]	17[1]	17[1]	Chevaux
Pigs	14[1]	14[1]	14[1]	8	17	18[1]	18[1]	19[1]	Porcins
Sheep	117	111	106	129	146	146[1]	147[1]	148[1]	Ovins
Ghana									Ghana
Asses, mules or hinnies	14[1]	14[1]	14[1]	14[1]	13	14[1]	14[1]	14[1]	Ânes, mules ou mulets
Cattle	1 273	1 288	1 302	1 315	1 330	1 344	1 365[1]	1 385[1]	Bovins
Goats	2 739	2 931	3 077	3 199	3 230	3 560	3 596[1]	3 632[1]	Caprins
Horses	3[1]	3[1]	3[1]	3[1]	3	3[1]	3[1]	3[1]	Chevaux
Pigs	352	332	324	312	310	303	300	305[1]	Porcins
Sheep	2 516	2 658	2 743	2 771	2 922	3 015	3 112[1]	3 211[1]	Ovins
Guinea									Guinée
Asses, mules or hinnies[1]	2	2	2	2	2	2	2	2	Ânes, mules ou mulets[1]
Cattle	2 563	2 697	2 876	3 034	3 200	3 376	3 561	3 756	Bovins
Goats	879	935	1 008	1 076	1 148	1 226	1 308	1 396	Caprins
Horses[1]	3	3	3	3	3	3	3	3	Chevaux[1]
Pigs	52	54	59	62	65	68	71	75	Porcins
Sheep	737	785	846	902	963	1 027	1 096	1 169	Ovins
Guinea-Bissau									Guinée-Bissau
Asses, mules or hinnies[1]	5	5	5	5	5	5	5	5	Ânes, mules ou mulets[1]
Cattle	487	500	512	515[1]	515[1]	520[1]	520[1]	530[1]	Bovins
Goats[1]	315	325	325	325	325	330	330	335	Caprins[1]
Horses[1]	2	2	2	2	2	2	2	2	Chevaux[1]
Pigs[1]	340	345	345	350	350	360	360	370	Porcins[1]
Sheep[1]	280	285	280	285	285	290	290	300	Ovins[1]

Region, country or area	1998	1999	2000	2001	2002	2003	2004	2005	Région, pays ou zone
Kenya									Kenya
Cattle	11 687	12 788	11 706	11 745	11 993	12 531	13 022	13 019	Bovins
Goats	9 674	10 967	9 923	10 980	11 226	11 946	13 391	13 883	Caprins
Horses	2[1]	2[1]	2[1]	2[1]	2[1]	2[1]	2[1]	2	Chevaux
Pigs	358	317	420	333	336	415	380	320	Porcins
Sheep	7 044	8 521	7 856	8 238	8 208	8 195	10 299	10 034	Ovins
Lesotho									Lesotho
Asses, mules or hinnies	151[1]	153[1]	155[1]	155[1]	155	76	155[1]	155	Ânes, mules ou mulets
Cattle	496	571	…	…	704	645	…	…	Bovins
Goats	546	730	…	…	800	790	…	…	Caprins
Horses	95[1]	98[1]	100[1]	100[1]	81	38	100[1]	100	Chevaux
Pigs	60[1]	63[1]	65[1]	65[1]	103	79	65[1]	65[1]	Porcins
Sheep	696	936	…	…	1 053	1 031	…	…	Ovins
Liberia[1]									Libéria[1]
Cattle	36	36	36	36	36	36	36	36	Bovins
Goats	220	220	220	220	220	220	220	220	Caprins
Pigs	120	120	130	130	130	130	130	130	Porcins
Sheep	210	210	210	210	210	210	210	210	Ovins
Libyan Arab Jamah.									Jamah. arabe libyenne
Asses, mules or hinnies[1]	28	29	30	30	30	30	30	30	Ânes, mules ou mulets[1]
Cattle	140[1]	138	130	130	130[1]	130[1]	130[1]	130[1]	Bovins
Goats	1 250	1 250	1 263[2]	1 263[2]	1 265[1]	1 265[1]	1 265[1]	1 265[1]	Caprins
Horses	40[1]	40	45[2]	45[2]	45[2]	45[1]	45[1]	45[1]	Chevaux
Sheep	6 000	5 150	4 124	4 500	4 500	4 500[1]	4 500[1]	4 500[1]	Ovins
Madagascar									Madagascar
Cattle	10 342	10 353	10 364	8 800[1]	7 877	8 020	8 105	9 687	Bovins
Goats	1 250[1]	1 200[1]	1 033	1 180	1 220	1 252	1 249	1 200	Caprins
Horses	0[1]	0[1]	0[1]	0[1]	0[1]	0[1]	0[1]	0	Chevaux
Pigs	1 650[1]	1 500[1]	1 450[1]	1 600[1]	1 600[1]	1 600[1]	1 600[1]	1 600	Porcins
Sheep	640[1]	590[1]	584	633	655	843	650[1]	703	Ovins
Malawi									Malawi
Asses, mules or hinnies	2[1]	2[1]	2[1]	2[1]	2[1]	2[1]	2[1]	2	Ânes, mules ou mulets
Cattle	715	712	764	749	750[1]	750[1]	765	750[1]	Bovins
Goats	1 598	1 427	1 689	1 670	1 700[1]	1 700[1]	1 900	1 900[1]	Caprins
Pigs	427	444	468	436	456	456[1]	456[1]	456	Porcins
Sheep	103	103	112	115	115[1]	115[1]	115[1]	115	Ovins
Mali									Mali
Asses, mules or hinnies	666	680	680[1]	680[1]	700[1]	700[1]	720[1]	720[1]	Ânes, mules ou mulets
Cattle	6 240	6 428	6 620	6 692	7 099	7 312	7 500	7 682	Bovins
Goats	8 932	9 379	9 849	9 903[2]	10 398[2]	11 464[2]	12 036[2]	12 000	Caprins
Horses	150	165	165[1]	165[1]	170[1]	170[1]	172[1]	172[1]	Chevaux
Pigs	65	66	66	67	67	68	68	69	Porcins
Sheep	6 292	6 607	6 200[1]	6 882[2]	7 226[2]	7 967[2]	8 364[2]	8 403	Ovins
Mauritania									Mauritanie
Asses, mules or hinnies[1]	156	157	157	158	158	158	158	158	Ânes, mules ou mulets[1]
Cattle	1 394	1 475	1 520	1 565	1 564	1 600[1]	1 600[1]	1 692	Bovins
Goats	4 555[2]	4 868	5 087	5 316	5 555	5 600[1]	5 600[1]	5 600[1]	Caprins
Horses	20[1]	21[2]	20[2]	20[2]	20[1]	20[1]	20[1]	20[1]	Chevaux
Sheep	6 835[2]	7 689	8 035	8 396	8 774	8 800[1]	8 850[1]	8 850[1]	Ovins
Mauritius									Maurice
Cattle[1]	22	25	27	28	28	28	28	28	Bovins[1]
Goats	92[1]	93[1]	94[1]	95[1]	93[1]	93[1]	93[1]	93	Caprins
Pigs	12[1]	11[1]	13[1]	14[1]	12[1]	13	13[1]	13	Porcins
Sheep	13[1]	14[1]	10[1]	12[1]	12[1]	12[1]	12[1]	12	Ovins

Region, country or area	1998	1999	2000	2001	2002	2003	2004	2005	Région, pays ou zone
Morocco									Maroc
Asses, mules or hinnies	1 504	1 527	1 610	1 516	1 493	1 509	1 510[1]	1 510[1]	Ânes, mules ou mulets
Cattle	2 569	2 566	2 675	2 647	2 670	2 689	2 729	2 729[1]	Bovins
Goats	4 959	4 704	4 931	5 133	5 090	5 208	5 359	5 359[1]	Caprins
Horses	147	149	152	154	148	155	155[1]	155[1]	Chevaux
Pigs	8	8[1]	8[1]	8[1]	8[1]	8[1]	8[1]	8[1]	Porcins
Sheep	14 784	16 576	17 300	17 172	16 336	16 743	17 026	17 026[1]	Ovins
Mozambique									Mozambique
Asses, mules or hinnies[1]	22	23	23	23	23	23	23	23	Ânes, mules ou mulets[1]
Cattle	1 300[1]	1 310[1]	1 320[1]	1 320[1]	1 320[1]	1 320[1]	1 320[1]	1 320	Bovins
Goats	388[1]	390[1]	392[1]	392[1]	392[1]	392[1]	392[1]	392	Caprins
Pigs	176[1]	178[1]	180[1]	180[1]	180[1]	180[1]	180[1]	180	Porcins
Sheep	123[1]	124[1]	125[1]	125[1]	125[1]	125[1]	125[1]	125	Ovins
Namibia									Namibie
Asses, mules or hinnies[1]	157	181	174	176	126	137	142	147	Ânes, mules ou mulets[1]
Cattle	2 192	2 294	2 505	2 509	2 336	2 700[1]	2 900[1]	3 134	Bovins
Goats	1 710	1 690	1 850	1 769	2 083	2 100[1]	2 050[1]	2 043	Caprins
Horses	53	66	62	53	48	48[1]	48[1]	47	Chevaux
Pigs	15	19	23	22	24[1]	28[1]	28[1]	28[1]	Porcins
Sheep	2 086	2 174	2 446	2 370	2 877	2 800[1]	2 700[1]	2 664	Ovins
Niger									Niger
Asses, mules or hinnies	562	570[1]	570[1]	580[1]	580[1]	580[1]	580[1]	580[1]	Ânes, mules ou mulets
Cattle	2 131	2 174	2 217	2 260[1]	2 260[1]	2 260[1]	2 260[1]	2 260[1]	Bovins
Goats	6 307[2]	6 560	6 724	6 900[1]	6 900[1]	6 900[1]	6 900[1]	6 900[1]	Caprins
Horses	102[2]	103[1]	104[1]	105[1]	105[1]	106[1]	106[1]	106[1]	Chevaux
Pigs[1]	39	39	39	39	40	40	40	40	Porcins[1]
Sheep	4 140[2]	4 266	4 392	4 500[1]	4 500[1]	4 500[1]	4 500[1]	4 500[1]	Ovins
Nigeria									Nigéria
Asses, mules or hinnies	1 000[1]	1 000[1]	1 000[1]	1 000[1]	1 000[1]	1 000[1]	1 050[1]	1 050	Ânes, mules ou mulets
Cattle	15 088	15 103	15 118	15 133	15 149	15 164	15 700	15 875	Bovins
Goats[1]	25 500	26 000	26 500	26 500	27 000	27 000	28 000	28 000	Caprins[1]
Horses	204[1]	204[1]	204[1]	205[1]	205[1]	205[1]	206[1]	206	Chevaux
Pigs	4 667	4 853	5 048	5 875	6 112	6 356	6 611[1]	6 650[1]	Porcins
Sheep[1]	20 000	20 500	21 000	21 500	22 000	22 500	23 000	23 000	Ovins[1]
Réunion									Réunion
Cattle	27[1]	27	28	30	31	32	34	34[1]	Bovins
Goats	38[1]	37	38	37	37	37	36	36[1]	Caprins
Pigs	82[1]	77	77	78	79	83	88	89[1]	Porcins
Sheep	2[1]	2	2	2	2	1	1	1[1]	Ovins
Rwanda									Rwanda
Cattle	657	749	732	816	815	992	1 004	1 004	Bovins
Goats	629	704	757	757	920	941	1 264	1 340	Caprins
Pigs	121	160	177	186	208	212	327	347	Porcins
Sheep	192	278	254	278	301	372	470	464	Ovins
Saint Helena									Sainte-Hélène
Cattle	1	1	1	1	1	1	1	1	Bovins
Goats	1	1	1	1	1	1[1]	1[1]	1[1]	Caprins
Pigs	1	1	1	1	1	1[1]	1[1]	1[1]	Porcins
Sheep	1	1	1	1	1[1]	1[1]	1[1]	1[1]	Ovins
Sao Tome and Principe[1]									Sao Tomé-et-Principe[1]
Cattle	4	4	4	4	4	5	5	5	Bovins
Goats	5	5	5	5	5	5	5	5	Caprins
Pigs	2	2	2	2	2	3	3	3	Porcins
Sheep	3	3	3	3	3	3	3	3	Ovins

Region, country or area	1998	1999	2000	2001	2002	2003	2004	2005	Région, pays ou zone
Senegal									Sénégal
Asses, mules or hinnies	376	377	399	407	400	400	412	416	Ânes, mules ou mulets
Cattle	2 912	2 927	2 986	3 061	2 997	3 018	3 039	3 070	Bovins
Goats	3 703	3 833	3 879	3 995	3 900	3 969	4 025	4 105	Caprins
Horses	445	446	471	492	496	500	504	509	Chevaux
Pigs	214	240	269	280	291	303	300	306	Porcins
Sheep	4 345	4 497	4 542	4 678	4 540	4 614	4 739	4 872	Ovins
Seychelles									Seychelles
Cattle[1]	2	2	2	2	2	1	1	1	Bovins[1]
Goats	5[1]	5[1]	5[1]	5[1]	5[1]	5[1]	5[1]	5	Caprins
Pigs	18[1]	18[1]	18[1]	18[1]	19[1]	19[1]	19[1]	19	Porcins
Sierra Leone									Sierra Leone
Cattle[1]	410	420	420	400	400	400	400	400	Bovins[1]
Goats[1]	195	200	220	220	220	220	220	220	Caprins[1]
Pigs	50[1]	52	52[1]	55[1]	52	52[1]	52[1]	52[1]	Porcins
Sheep[1]	358	365	365	370	370	375	375	375	Ovins[1]
Somalia									Somalie
Asses, mules or hinnies[1]	37	37	39	40	40	41	41	41	Ânes, mules ou mulets[1]
Cattle	5 300[1]	5 132	5 139	5 256	5 319[2]	5 350[1]	5 350[1]	5 350[1]	Bovins
Goats[1]	12 500	12 000	12 300	12 700	12 750	12 800	12 800	12 700	Caprins[1]
Horses[1]	1	1	1	1	1	1	1	1	Chevaux[1]
Pigs[1]	4	4	4	4	4	4	4	4	Porcins[1]
Sheep	13 500[1]	13 537	13 808	14 084	14 324[2]	14 350[1]	14 500[1]	13 100[1]	Ovins
South Africa									Afrique du Sud
Asses, mules or hinnies	224[1]	224[1]	164[1]	164[1]	164[1]	164[1]	164[1]	164	Ânes, mules ou mulets
Cattle	13 700	13 800	13 600	13 500	13 635	13 538	13 512	13 764	Bovins
Goats	6 558	6 457	6 706	6 550[1]	6 452	6 358	6 372	6 407	Caprins
Horses	260[1]	258[1]	270[2]	270[1]	270[1]	270[1]	270[1]	270[1]	Chevaux
Pigs	1 641	1 531	1 556	1 592	1 663	1 662	1 651	1 648	Porcins
Sheep	29 345	28 680	28 551	28 800[1]	26 000[1]	25 820	25 360[1]	25 316	Ovins
Sudan									Soudan
Asses, mules or hinnies[1]	721	731	741	751	751	751	751	751	Ânes, mules ou mulets[1]
Cattle	34 584	35 825	37 093	38 325	38 183	38 325[1]	38 325[1]	38 325[1]	Bovins
Goats	36 498	37 346	38 548	39 952	41 485	42 000[1]	42 000[1]	42 000[1]	Caprins
Horses[1]	25	26	26	26	26	26	26	26	Chevaux[1]
Sheep	42 363	44 802	46 095	47 043	48 136	48 000[1]	48 000[1]	48 000[1]	Ovins
Swaziland									Swaziland
Asses, mules or hinnies[1]	15	15	15	15	15	15	15	15	Ânes, mules ou mulets[1]
Cattle	623	614	588[2]	506	522[2]	520[1]	580[1]	580[1]	Bovins
Goats	354	333	422	422[1]	350[1]	274[2]	274[1]	274[1]	Caprins
Horses[1]	1	1	1	1	1	1	1	1	Chevaux[1]
Pigs	30[1]	31[1]	30	30[1]	30[1]	30[1]	30[1]	30[1]	Porcins
Sheep	23	22	27	27[1]	27[1]	35[1]	27[1]	27[1]	Ovins
Togo									Togo
Asses, mules or hinnies[1]	3	3	3	3	3	3	3	3	Ânes, mules ou mulets[1]
Cattle	273	275	277	278[1]	279[1]	279[1]	279[1]	280[1]	Bovins
Goats	1 292	1 357	1 425	1 450[1]	1 460[1]	1 470[1]	1 480[1]	1 480[1]	Caprins
Horses[1]	2	2	2	2	2	2	2	2	Chevaux[1]
Pigs	278	284	289	295[1]	300[1]	310[1]	320[1]	320[1]	Porcins
Sheep	1 274	1 415	1 570	1 600[1]	1 700[1]	1 800[1]	1 850[1]	1 850[1]	Ovins
Tunisia									Tunisie
Asses, mules or hinnies[1]	311	311	311	311	311	311	311	311	Ânes, mules ou mulets[1]
Cattle	723	749	767	763	753	679	657	686	Bovins
Goats	1 232	1 315	1 448	1 450	1 449	1 379	1 412	1 427	Caprins
Horses	56[1]	57	57	57	57[1]	57[1]	57[1]	57[1]	Chevaux
Pigs[1]	6	6	6	6	6	6	6	6	Porcins[1]
Sheep	6 544	6 576	6 926	6 861	6 833	6 613	6 949	7 213	Ovins

Region, country or area	1998	1999	2000	2001	2002	2003	2004	2005	Région, pays ou zone
Uganda									Ouganda
Asses, mules or hinnies	18[1]	18[1]	18[1]	18[1]	18[1]	18[1]	18[1]	18	Ânes, mules ou mulets
Cattle	5 651	5 820	5 966	6 144	6 328	6 519	6 567	6 770	Bovins
Goats	5 999	6 180	6 396	6 620	6 852	7 092	7 566	7 800	Caprins
Pigs	1 475	1 520	1 573	1 644	1 710	1 778	1 940	2 000	Porcins
Sheep	1 014	1 044	1 081	1 180	1 141	1 175	1 552	1 600	Ovins
United Rep. of Tanzania									Rép.-Unie de Tanzanie
Asses, mules or hinnies[1]	178	179	180	182	182	182	182	182	Ânes, mules ou mulets[1]
Cattle	13 796	17 251	16 713	17 037	17 367	17 704	17 472	17 719	Bovins
Goats	11 035	11 643	11 889	12 102	12 324	12 556	12 550[1]	12 550[1]	Caprins
Pigs	410[1]	446	450[1]	455[1]	458	455	455[1]	455[1]	Porcins
Sheep	3 550	3 489	3 501	3 508	3 514	3 521	3 521[1]	3 521[1]	Ovins
Zambia									Zambie
Asses, mules or hinnies	2[1]	2[1]	2[1]	2[1]	2[1]	2[1]	2[1]	2	Ânes, mules ou mulets
Cattle	2 747	2 905	2 621	2 600[1]	2 600[1]	2 600[1]	2 600[1]	2 600[1]	Bovins
Goats	890[2]	1 069[2]	1 249[2]	1 270[1]	1 270[1]	1 270[1]	1 270[1]	1 270	Caprins
Pigs	320[2]	324[2]	309	340[1]	340[1]	340[1]	340[1]	340	Porcins
Sheep	99[2]	120[2]	140[2]	150[1]	150[1]	150[1]	150[1]	150[1]	Ovins
Zimbabwe									Zimbabwe
Asses, mules or hinnies[1]	106	107	108	109	111	113	113	113	Ânes, mules ou mulets[1]
Cattle	5 450	6 069	5 700[1]	5 752	5 600[1]	5 400[1]	5 400[1]	5 400[1]	Bovins
Goats	2 750	2 910	2 950[1]	2 968	2 950[1]	2 970[1]	2 970[1]	2 970[1]	Caprins
Horses[1]	25	26	26	27	27	28	28	28	Chevaux[1]
Pigs	270	279	450[1]	604	605[1]	620[1]	620[1]	610[1]	Porcins
Sheep	520	640	630[1]	600	600[1]	610[1]	610[1]	610[1]	Ovins
America, North									**Amérique du Nord**
Asses, mules or hinnies	**7 500**	**7 514**	**7 521**	**7 539**	**7 541**	**7 548**	**7 527**	**7 527**	**Ânes, mules ou mulets**
Buffaloes	**5**	**5**	**5**	**6**	**6**	**6**	**6**	**6**	**Buffles**
Cattle	**164 674**	**162 574**	**161 857**	**161 874**	**162 643**	**162 175**	**161 722**	**163 794**	**Bovins**
Goats	**13 624**	**14 474**	**14 729**	**14 894**	**15 556**	**15 503**	**15 411**	**15 495**	**Caprins**
Horses	**14 078**	**14 010**	**14 083**	**14 380**	**14 894**	**15 911**	**16 932**	**18 144**	**Chevaux**
Pigs	**94 177**	**95 994**	**94 069**	**95 127**	**94 285**	**94 159**	**95 720**	**95 471**	**Porcins**
Sheep	**16 757**	**16 712**	**17 145**	**17 309**	**17 381**	**17 433**	**17 333**	**17 031**	**Ovins**
Antigua and Barbuda									Antigua-et-Barbuda
Asses, mules or hinnies	1[1]	1[1]	1[1]	1[1]	2[1]	2[1]	2[1]	2	Ânes, mules ou mulets
Cattle	14[1]	14[1]	13	14[1]	14[1]	14[1]	14[1]	14[1]	Bovins
Goats	30[1]	32[1]	34	35[1]	35[1]	36[1]	36[1]	36	Caprins
Pigs[1]	4	5	3	3	3	3	3	3	Porcins[1]
Sheep	17[1]	17[1]	18	18[1]	19[1]	19[1]	19[1]	19	Ovins
Bahamas									Bahamas
Cattle	1[1]	1	1	1	1[1]	1[1]	1[1]	1[1]	Bovins
Goats	16[1]	14	14	14	14[1]	14[1]	15[1]	15	Caprins
Pigs	5[1]	6	5	5	5[1]	5[1]	5[1]	5[1]	Porcins
Sheep	6[1]	6	6	6	6[1]	6[1]	7[1]	7	Ovins
Barbados									Barbade
Asses, mules or hinnies	4[1]	4[1]	4[1]	4[1]	4[1]	4[1]	4[1]	4	Ânes, mules ou mulets
Cattle	21[1]	21[1]	25[1]	15[1]	14[1]	14	8[1]	10[1]	Bovins
Goats[1]	5	4	5	5	5	5	5	5	Caprins[1]
Horses	1[1]	1[1]	1[1]	1[1]	1[1]	1[1]	1[1]	1	Chevaux
Pigs[1]	21	20	17	16	13	16	19	19	Porcins[1]
Sheep[1]	18	6	6	4	8	10	11	11	Ovins[1]
Belize									Belize
Asses, mules or hinnies	4[1]	4[1]	4[1]	4[1]	5[1]	5[1]	5[1]	5	Ânes, mules ou mulets
Cattle	52[1]	58[1]	53[1]	58	57	58	58	58[1]	Bovins
Goats	1[1]	^0[1]	^0[1]	^0[1]	^0[1]	^0	^0[1]	^0[1]	Caprins
Horses	5[1]	5[1]	5[1]	5[1]	5[1]	5[1]	5[1]	5	Chevaux
Pigs	22	24[1]	24[1]	28	23	21	21	21	Porcins
Sheep	4[1]	4[1]	4[1]	4	6	6	6	6[1]	Ovins

Region, country or area	1998	1999	2000	2001	2002	2003	2004	2005	Région, pays ou zone
Bermuda									Bermudes
Cattle[1]	1	1	1	1	1	1	1	1	Bovins[1]
Horses	1[1]	1[1]	1[1]	1[1]	1[1]	1[1]	1	1	Chevaux
Pigs[1]	1	1	1	1	1	1	1	1	Porcins[1]
British Virgin Islands[1]									Iles Vierges britanniques[1]
Cattle	2	2	2	2	2	2	2	2	Bovins
Goats	10	10	10	10	10	10	10	10	Caprins
Pigs	2	2	2	2	2	2	2	2	Porcins
Sheep	6	6	6	6	6	6	6	6	Ovins
Canada									Canada
Asses, mules or hinnies[1]	4	4	4	4	4	4	4	4	Ânes, mules ou mulets[1]
Cattle	13 360	13 211	13 201	13 608	13 762	13 488	14 653	15 063	Bovins
Goats[1]	29	30	30	30	30	30	30	30	Caprins[1]
Horses[1]	380	380	385	385	385	385	385	385	Chevaux[1]
Pigs	11 985	12 429	12 904	13 576	14 367	14 672	14 623	14 675	Porcins
Sheep	662	717	793	948	994	976	997	980	Ovins
Cayman Islands									Iles Caïmanes
Cattle[1]	1	1	1	1	1	1	1	1	Bovins[1]
Costa Rica									Costa Rica
Asses, mules or hinnies	13[1]	13[1]	13[1]	13[1]	13[1]	13[1]	13	13	Ânes, mules ou mulets
Cattle	1 527[2]	1 428	1 358	1 289	1 220	1 150	1 081	1 000[1]	Bovins
Goats	2[1]	2[1]	3[1]	3[1]	4[1]	5[1]	5	5	Caprins
Horses	115[1]	115[1]	115[1]	115[1]	115[1]	115[1]	115	115	Chevaux
Pigs[1]	360	260	275	300	310	315	550	550	Porcins[1]
Sheep	3[1]	3[1]	3[1]	3[1]	3[1]	3[1]	3	3	Ovins
Cuba									Cuba
Asses, mules or hinnies	30	31	30	31	31	31	31	30	Ânes, mules ou mulets
Cattle	4 644	4 406	4 110	4 038	3 972	4 025	3 943	3 950	Bovins
Goats	384	493	715	759	866	951	1 047	1 040	Caprins
Horses	434	430	415	431	438	452	464	470	Chevaux
Pigs	1 422	1 699	1 633	1 313	1 554	1 684	1 593	1 626	Porcins
Sheep	1 563	2 045	2 572	2 524	2 614	2 580	2 410	2 361	Ovins
Dominica									Dominique
Cattle[1]	13	13	13	13	13	13	13	13	Bovins[1]
Goats	10[1]	10[1]	10[1]	10[1]	10[1]	10[1]	10[1]	10	Caprins
Pigs	5[1]	5[1]	5[1]	5[1]	5[1]	5[1]	5[1]	5	Porcins
Sheep	8[1]	8[1]	8[1]	8[1]	8[1]	8[1]	8[1]	8	Ovins
Dominican Republic									Rép. dominicaine
Asses, mules or hinnies	280[1]	283[1]	283[1]	290[1]	290[1]	291[1]	291[1]	291	Ânes, mules ou mulets
Cattle	2 528	1 954	2 018	2 107	2 160	2 160[1]	2 165	2 200[1]	Bovins
Goats	300[1]	163	178	187	188	189[1]	189[1]	190[1]	Caprins
Horses	330[1]	330[1]	330[1]	340[1]	342[1]	343[1]	343[1]	343	Chevaux
Pigs	960	540	539	566	577[1]	578[1]	578[1]	580[1]	Porcins
Sheep	135	105	105	106	121	122[1]	123[1]	123[1]	Ovins
El Salvador									El Salvador
Asses, mules or hinnies	27[1]	27[1]	27[1]	27[1]	27[1]	27[1]	27[1]	27	Ânes, mules ou mulets
Cattle	1 038	1 141	1 050	1 216	1 400[1]	1 249	1 259	1 257	Bovins
Goats	15[1]	14[1]	13[1]	12[1]	11	11[1]	11[1]	11	Caprins
Horses	96[1]	96[1]	96[1]	96[1]	96[1]	96[1]	96[1]	96	Chevaux
Pigs	175	248	186	150	153	337	355	356	Porcins
Sheep	5[1]	5[1]	5[1]	5[1]	5[1]	5[1]	5[1]	5	Ovins
Greenland									Groenland
Sheep	22[1]	22[1]	20	20	19	19	19[1]	19[1]	Ovins

34 Livestock — Stocks: thousand head (*continued*)
Cheptel — Effectifs : milliers de têtes (*suite*)

Region, country or area	1998	1999	2000	2001	2002	2003	2004	2005	Région, pays ou zone
Grenada									Grenade
Asses, mules or hinnies	1[1]	1[1]	1[1]	1[1]	1[1]	1[1]	1[1]	1	Ânes, mules ou mulets
Cattle[1]	4	4	4	4	4	4	4	4	Bovins[1]
Goats	7[1]	7[1]	7[1]	7[1]	7[1]	7[1]	7[1]	7	Caprins
Pigs[1]	5	6	3	3	3	3	3	3	Porcins[1]
Sheep	13[1]	13[1]	13[1]	13[1]	13[1]	13[1]	13[1]	13	Ovins
Guadeloupe									Guadeloupe
Cattle	85	65	65	63	89[2]	77[2]	73[2]	74[1]	Bovins
Goats	29	28	34	47	48	48[2]	48[2]	...	Caprins
Horses[1]	1	1	1	1	1	1	1	1	Chevaux[1]
Pigs	20	29	26	29	33[2]	31[2]	24[2]	30[1]	Porcins
Sheep	3	3	4	4	3[2]	3[2]	3[2]	...	Ovins
Guatemala									Guatemala
Asses, mules or hinnies	48[1]	48[1]	48[1]	48[1]	49[1]	49[1]	49	49	Ânes, mules ou mulets
Cattle	2 330[2]	2 500[1]	2 500[1]	2 500[1]	2 540[1]	2 540[1]	2 540[1]	2 540[1]	Bovins
Goats	110	111	111	112[1]	112[1]	112[1]	112[1]	112	Caprins
Horses	118[1]	119[1]	120[1]	120[1]	122[1]	124[1]	124[1]	124	Chevaux
Pigs	760	683[1]	750[1]	210[1]	212[1]	212[1]	212[1]	212[1]	Porcins
Sheep	400[1]	325[1]	240	245	250[1]	260[1]	260[1]	260[1]	Ovins
Haiti									Haïti
Asses, mules or hinnies	290[1]	290[1]	297[1]	297[1]	297[1]	303[1]	280[1]	280	Ânes, mules ou mulets
Cattle	1 300	1 300[1]	1 430	1 440[1]	1 450[1]	1 455[1]	1 456[1]	1 456	Bovins
Goats	1 618[2]	1 619[1]	1 942	1 942[1]	1 943[1]	1 944[1]	1 900[1]	1 900	Caprins
Horses	490[1]	490[1]	500[1]	501[1]	501[1]	501[1]	500[1]	500	Chevaux
Pigs	800	800[1]	1 000	1 001[1]	1 001[1]	1 002[1]	1 000[1]	1 000	Porcins
Sheep	138	138[1]	152	152[1]	153[1]	154[1]	154[1]	154	Ovins
Honduras									Honduras
Asses, mules or hinnies	92[1]	92[1]	93[1]	93[1]	93[1]	93[1]	93	93	Ânes, mules ou mulets
Cattle	1 945[2]	1 715	1 780	1 875[2]	2 050	2 403	2 451	2 500	Bovins
Goats	29[1]	30[1]	31[1]	32[1]	25	25	24	24	Caprins
Horses	177[1]	178[1]	179[1]	180[1]	180[1]	181[1]	181[1]	181	Chevaux
Pigs	455[1]	473	470	538[2]	538	478	483	490	Porcins
Sheep	14[1]	14[1]	14[1]	14[1]	14	15	15	15	Ovins
Jamaica									Jamaïque
Asses, mules or hinnies	33[1]	33[1]	33[1]	33[1]	33[1]	33	33	33	Ânes, mules ou mulets
Cattle[1]	400	400	400	400	400	430	430	430	Bovins[1]
Goats	440[1]	440[1]	440[1]	440[1]	440[1]	440[1]	440[1]	440	Caprins
Horses	4[1]	4[1]	4[1]	4[1]	4[1]	4	4	4	Chevaux
Pigs	180[1]	180[1]	180[1]	100[1]	85[1]	85[1]	85[1]	85	Porcins
Sheep	2[1]	1[1]	1[1]	1[1]	1[1]	1[1]	1[1]	1	Ovins
Martinique									Martinique
Cattle	25	25[1]	28	28	24	25[1]	25[1]	25[1]	Bovins
Goats	17[1]	17[1]	14	14	13	14[1]	14[1]	14[1]	Caprins
Horses	2[1]	2[1]	1	1	1	1[1]	1[1]	1[1]	Chevaux
Pigs	34[1]	35[1]	26	26	20	20[1]	20[1]	20[1]	Porcins
Sheep	36[1]	34[1]	20	20	18	18[1]	18[1]	18[1]	Ovins
Mexico									Mexique
Asses, mules or hinnies	6 520[1]	6 530[1]	6 530[1]	6 540[1]	6 540[1]	6 540[1]	6 540[1]	6 540	Ânes, mules ou mulets
Cattle	31 060	30 193	30 524	30 621	31 390	31 477	31 248	31 800[1]	Bovins
Goats	9 040	9 068	8 704	8 702	9 130	8 992	8 853	8 992	Caprins
Horses	6 250[1]	6 250[1]	6 250[1]	6 255[1]	6 255[1]	6 260[1]	6 260[1]	6 260	Chevaux
Pigs	14 972	15 748	16 088	17 584	15 123	14 625	15 177	14 625	Porcins
Sheep	5 804	5 949	6 046	6 165	6 417	6 820	7 083	6 820	Ovins
Montserrat									Montserrat
Cattle[1]	10	10	10	10	10	10	10	10	Bovins[1]
Goats	7[1]	7[1]	7[1]	7[1]	7[1]	7[1]	7	7	Caprins
Pigs	1[1]	1[1]	1[1]	1[1]	1[1]	1[1]	1[1]	1	Porcins
Sheep	5[1]	5[1]	5[1]	5[1]	5[1]	5[1]	5	5	Ovins

Region, country or area	1998	1999	2000	2001	2002	2003	2004	2005	Région, pays ou zone
Netherlands Antilles									Antilles néerlandaises
Asses, mules or hinnies	3[1]	3[1]	3[1]	3[1]	3[1]	3[1]	3[1]	3	Ânes, mules ou mulets
Cattle[1]	1	1	^0	^0	1	^0	1	1	Bovins[1]
Goats	13[1]	10[1]	14[1]	13[1]	13[1]	14[1]	14[1]	14	Caprins
Pigs	2[1]	2[1]	2[1]	2[1]	2[1]	2[1]	3[1]	3	Porcins
Sheep	7[1]	7[1]	8[1]	9[1]	9[1]	9[1]	9[1]	9	Ovins
Nicaragua									Nicaragua
Asses, mules or hinnies	54[1]	54[1]	54[1]	55[1]	55[1]	56[1]	57[1]	57	Ânes, mules ou mulets
Cattle	2 735[1]	3 186	3 275	3 300	3 350	3 500	3 400[2]	3 500[1]	Bovins
Goats[1]	6	6	7	7	7	7	7	7	Caprins[1]
Horses[1]	245	245	246	248	250	260	265	268	Chevaux[1]
Pigs[1]	400	109	112	114	118	121	122	123	Porcins[1]
Sheep[1]	4	4	4	4	4	4	4	5	Ovins[1]
Panama									Panama
Asses, mules or hinnies	4[1]	4[1]	4[1]	4[1]	4[1]	4[1]	4[1]	4	Ânes, mules ou mulets
Cattle	1 382	1 360	1 342	1 533	1 533	1 498	1 550[1]	1 600[1]	Bovins
Goats	5[1]	5[1]	5	5	6	6[1]	6[1]	6[1]	Caprins
Horses[1]	165	166	166	168	170	175	178	180	Chevaux[1]
Pigs	252	278	278	235[1]	240[1]	265[1]	270[1]	272[1]	Porcins
Puerto Rico									Porto Rico
Asses, mules or hinnies[1]	5	5	5	5	5	5	5	5	Ânes, mules ou mulets[1]
Cattle	387	384	392	396	400	421	388	377	Bovins
Goats	9	9[1]	9[1]	9[1]	9[1]	5	3	3	Caprins
Horses	25[1]	25[1]	26[1]	26[1]	26[1]	4	5	6	Chevaux
Pigs	115	140	131	112	102	50	50	49	Porcins
Sheep	16	16[1]	16[1]	16[1]	16[1]	6	5	6	Ovins
Saint Kitts and Nevis									Saint-Kitts-et-Nevis
Cattle	4[1]	4[1]	4	4[1]	4[1]	4[1]	4[1]	5	Bovins
Goats	14[1]	14[1]	14	14[1]	14[1]	14[1]	14[1]	16	Caprins
Pigs	3[1]	3	5	4[1]	4[1]	4[1]	4[1]	2[1]	Porcins
Sheep	12[1]	13[1]	14	14[1]	14[1]	14[1]	14[1]	13	Ovins
Saint Lucia									Sainte-Lucie
Asses, mules or hinnies	2[1]	2[1]	2[1]	2[1]	2[1]	2[1]	2[1]	2	Ânes, mules ou mulets
Cattle[1]	12	12	12	12	12	12	12	12	Bovins[1]
Goats	10[1]	10[1]	10[1]	10[1]	10	10[1]	10[1]	10	Caprins
Horses	1[1]	1[1]	1[1]	1[1]	1[1]	1[1]	1[1]	1	Chevaux
Pigs	15[1]	15[1]	15[1]	15[1]	15	15[1]	15[1]	15[1]	Porcins
Sheep	13[1]	13[1]	13[1]	13[1]	13	13[1]	13[1]	13	Ovins
Saint Pierre and Miquelon									Saint-Pierre-et-Miquelon
Sheep	^0[1]	^0[1]	1	1	^0	^0	^0[1]	^0[1]	Ovins
Saint Vincent-Grenadines									Saint Vincent-Grenadines
Asses, mules or hinnies	1[1]	1[1]	1[1]	1[1]	1[1]	1[1]	1[1]	1	Ânes, mules ou mulets
Cattle	6[1]	6[1]	6[1]	6[1]	6[1]	5	5[1]	5[1]	Bovins
Goats	6[1]	6[1]	6[1]	6[1]	6[1]	7	7[1]	7[1]	Caprins
Pigs	9[1]	9[1]	10[1]	10[1]	10[1]	9	9[1]	9	Porcins
Sheep	13[1]	13[1]	13[1]	13[1]	13[1]	12	12[1]	12	Ovins
Trinidad and Tobago									Trinité-et-Tobago
Asses, mules or hinnies	4[1]	4[1]	4[1]	4[1]	4[1]	4[1]	4[1]	4	Ânes, mules ou mulets
Buffaloes	5[1]	5[1]	5[1]	6[1]	6[1]	6[1]	6[1]	6	Buffles
Cattle	34[1]	35[1]	30[1]	30[1]	32[1]	29	29	29[1]	Bovins
Goats[1]	58	58	58	58	59	59	59	59	Caprins[1]
Horses[1]	1	1	1	1	1	1	1	1	Chevaux[1]
Pigs	34[1]	36[1]	36[1]	41[1]	42[1]	41	43[1]	43[1]	Porcins
Sheep[1]	2	2	1	3	4	3	3	3	Ovins[1]

Region, country or area	1998*	1999	2000	2001	2002	2003	2004	2005	Région, pays ou zone
United States									Etats-Unis
Asses, mules or hinnies[1]	80	80	80	80	80	80	80	80	Ânes, mules ou mulets[1]
Cattle	99 744	99 115	98 198	97 277	96 723	96 100	94 888	95 848	Bovins
Goats	1 400	2 250[1]	2 300[1]	2 400[1]	2 530	2 530[1]	2 525[1]	2 523	Caprins
Horses	5 237[2]	5 170	5 240	5 500	6 000	7 000	8 000	9 200	Chevaux
Pigs	61 158	62 206	59 342	59 138	59 722	59 554	60 444	60 645	Porcins
Sheep	7 825	7 215	7 032	6 965	6 623	6 321	6 105	6 135	Ovins
United States Virgin Is.									Iles Vierges américaines
Cattle	8	8	8	8	8[1]	8[1]	8[1]	8[1]	Bovins
Goats[1]	4	4	4	4	4	4	4	4	Caprins[1]
Pigs[1]	3	3	3	3	3	3	3	3	Porcins[1]
Sheep[1]	3	3	3	3	3	3	3	3	Ovins[1]
America, South									**Amérique du Sud**
Asses, mules or hinnies	**6 574**	**6 667**	**6 724**	**6 758**	**6 767**	**6 075**	**6 013**	**5 765**	**Ânes, mules ou mulets**
Buffaloes	**1 018**	**1 069**	**1 103**	**1 119**	**1 115**	**1 149**	**1 134**	**1 095**	**Buffles**
Cattle	**292 161**	**293 878**	**298 637**	**306 033**	**314 760**	**330 036**	**339 349**	**343 156**	**Bovins**
Goats	**18 544**	**19 090**	**19 994**	**19 986**	**20 395**	**22 810**	**23 912**	**24 942**	**Caprins**
Horses	**15 128**	**15 464**	**15 542**	**15 650**	**15 548**	**15 470**	**15 446**	**15 339**	**Chevaux**
Pigs	**50 010**	**47 534**	**48 510**	**49 968**	**49 544**	**50 562**	**51 773**	**52 304**	**Porcins**
Sheep	**75 785**	**75 617**	**75 334**	**73 692**	**70 643**	**69 368**	**69 741**	**70 376**	**Ovins**
Argentina									Argentine
Asses, mules or hinnies	265[1]	275[1]	275[1]	275[1]	275[1]	283[1]	283[1]	283	Ânes, mules ou mulets
Cattle	48 049	49 057	48 674	48 851	48 100	50 869[2]	50 768[2]	50 768[1]	Bovins
Goats	3 400[1]	3 403	3 490	3 387	4 000	4 200[1]	4 200[1]	4 200[1]	Caprins
Horses	3 300[1]	3 600[1]	3 600[1]	3 600[1]	3 650[1]	3 655[1]	3 655[1]	3 655	Chevaux
Pigs[1]	3 500	1 725	1 750	1 700	1 600	1 500	1 490	1 490	Porcins[1]
Sheep	13 500[1]	13 703	13 562	13 500[1]	12 400	12 450[1]	12 450[1]	12 450[1]	Ovins
Bolivia									Bolivie
Asses, mules or hinnies	712[1]	712[1]	712[1]	712[1]	714[1]	717[1]	717	717	Ânes, mules ou mulets
Cattle	6 387	6 556	6 725	6 457	6 576	6 680	6 822	6 822	Bovins
Goats	1 496	1 500	1 500[1]	1 500[1]	1 501[1]	1 501[1]	1 501	1 501	Caprins
Horses	322[1]	322[1]	322[1]	322[1]	323[1]	323[1]	323	323	Chevaux
Pigs	2 637	2 715	2 793	2 851	2 851	2 925	2 984	2 984	Porcins
Sheep	8 409	8 575	8 752	8 902	8 902	8 596	8 550[1]	8 550	Ovins
Brazil									Brésil
Asses, mules or hinnies	2 525	2 572	2 590	2 585	2 556	2 554	2 555	2 380[1]	Ânes, mules ou mulets
Buffaloes	1 017	1 068	1 103	1 119	1 115	1 149	1 134	1 095[1]	Buffles
Cattle	163 154	164 621	169 876	176 389	185 347	195 552	204 513	207 000[1]	Bovins
Goats	8 164	8 623	9 347	9 537	9 429	9 582	10 047	10 700[1]	Caprins
Horses	5 867	5 831	5 832	5 801	5 774	5 828	5 787	5 700[1]	Chevaux
Pigs	30 007	30 839	31 562	32 605	32 013	32 305	33 085	33 200[1]	Porcins
Sheep	14 268	14 400	14 785	14 639	14 287	14 557	15 058	15 200[1]	Ovins
Chile									Chili
Asses, mules or hinnies[1]	38	37	37	38	39	40	40	41	Ânes, mules ou mulets[1]
Cattle	4 160	4 134	4 068	3 980[2]	3 927[2]	3 932[2]	3 989[2]	4 200[1]	Bovins
Goats[1]	740	700	740	705	735	715	725	735	Caprins[1]
Horses[1]	600	610	620	650	660	650	660	670	Chevaux[1]
Pigs	1 962	2 221	2 465	2 750[1]	3 100[1]	3 250[1]	3 215[1]	3 450[1]	Porcins
Sheep	3 754	4 116	4 144	4 090[1]	4 050[1]	3 750[1]	3 680[1]	3 400[1]	Ovins
Colombia									Colombie
Asses, mules or hinnies	1 300[1]	1 310[1]	1 318[1]	1 325[1]	1 333[1]	728	658	571	Ânes, mules ou mulets
Cattle	25 764	24 363	24 364	24 510	24 765	24 799	24 922	25 699	Bovins
Goats	1 050	1 115	1 185	1 136	1 105	3 200	3 771	4 105	Caprins
Horses	2 450[1]	2 500[1]	2 550[1]	2 600[1]	2 650[1]	2 592	2 591	2 554	Chevaux
Pigs	1 450[1]	1 000[1]	990[1]	970[1]	1 100[1]	1 500	1 892	1 724	Porcins
Sheep	1 994	2 196	2 288	2 256	2 045	2 500	2 831	3 333	Ovins

Region, country or area	1998	1999	2000	2001	2002	2003	2004	2005	Région, pays ou zone
Ecuador									Equateur
Asses, mules or hinnies	425[1]	426[1]	427[1]	428[1]	435[1]	306	298	295	Ânes, mules ou mulets
Cattle	5 076	5 106	4 486	4 657	4 486	4 985	5 082	4 971	Bovins
Goats	280	277	280	273	205	141	135	144	Caprins
Horses	520[1]	521[1]	523[1]	525[1]	528[1]	400	411	411	Chevaux
Pigs	2 708	1 205[1]	1 185[1]	1 402[1]	1 527	1 410	1 282	1 281	Porcins
Sheep	2 081	2 150[1]	2 196	2 249	2 381	1 014	1 047	1 053	Ovins
Falkland Is. (Malvinas)									Iles Falkland (Malvinas)
Cattle	4	4[1]	4[1]	4[1]	4[1]	4[1]	4[1]	4[1]	Bovins
Horses	1	1	1	1	1	1	1	1	Chevaux
Sheep	708	700[1]	710[1]	690[1]	690[1]	690[1]	690	690	Ovins
French Guiana									Guyane française
Cattle	9	9[1]	9[1]	9[1]	9[1]	9[1]	9[1]	9[1]	Bovins
Goats[1]	1	1	1	1	1	1	1	1	Caprins[1]
Pigs	10	10[1]	11[1]	11[1]	11[1]	11[1]	11[1]	11[1]	Porcins
Sheep[1]	3	3	3	3	3	3	3	3	Ovins[1]
Guyana									Guyana
Asses, mules or hinnies	1[1]	1[1]	1[1]	1[1]	1[1]	1[1]	1[1]	1	Ânes, mules ou mulets
Cattle[1]	120	110	120	120	100	110	110	110	Bovins[1]
Goats	79[1]	79[1]	79[1]	79[1]	79[1]	79[1]	79[1]	79	Caprins
Horses	2[1]	2[1]	2[1]	2[1]	2[1]	2[1]	2[1]	2	Chevaux
Pigs[1]	9	9	9	9	9	12	12	13	Porcins[1]
Sheep	130[1]	130[1]	130[1]	130[1]	130[1]	130[1]	130[1]	130	Ovins
Paraguay									Paraguay
Asses, mules or hinnies	46[1]	46[1]	46[1]	47[1]	48[1]	50[1]	50[1]	50	Ânes, mules ou mulets
Cattle	9 833[2]	9 647	9 737	9 889	9 260	10 128	9 622	9 622[1]	Bovins
Goats	131[2]	122	123	124	125	106	159	155[1]	Caprins
Horses	400[1]	400[1]	400[1]	358	358[1]	360[1]	360[1]	360	Chevaux
Pigs	2 000[1]	1 850[1]	1 800[1]	1 804	1 365	1 474	1 507	1 600[1]	Porcins
Sheep	395	398	402	406	410	423	525	500[1]	Ovins
Peru									Pérou
Asses, mules or hinnies[1]	744	770	800	830	850	880	895	910	Ânes, mules ou mulets[1]
Cattle	4 657	4 903	4 927	4 962	4 990	5 133	5 181	5 241	Bovins
Goats	2 019	2 068	2 023	1 998	1 942	1 984	1 959	1 957	Caprins
Horses[1]	665	675	690	700	710	720	725	730	Chevaux[1]
Pigs	2 531	2 788	2 819	2 781	2 849	2 992	3 004	3 005	Porcins
Sheep	13 566	14 297	14 686	14 253	14 025	14 752	14 735	14 822	Ovins
Suriname									Suriname
Buffaloes	1	1	^0	^0	^0[1]	^0[1]	^0[1]	^0[1]	Buffles
Cattle	111	120	130	135	136[1]	137[1]	137[1]	137[1]	Bovins
Goats	7	8	7	7	7	6	7[1]	7	Caprins
Pigs	20	20	22	23	25	23	25[1]	25[1]	Porcins
Sheep	7	8	7	8	8[1]	8[1]	8[1]	8[1]	Ovins
Uruguay									Uruguay
Asses, mules or hinnies	5[1]	5[1]	5[1]	5[1]	5[1]	5[1]	5[1]	5	Ânes, mules ou mulets
Cattle	10 297	10 389	10 353	10 595	11 268	11 708	11 958	11 956	Bovins
Goats	15[1]	15[1]	15[1]	15[1]	15[1]	16[1]	16[1]	16	Caprins
Horses	500[1]	500[1]	501[1]	590[1]	390[1]	437	429	432	Chevaux
Pigs	330[1]	360[1]	294	282[1]	270	240	220	257	Porcins
Sheep	16 495	14 491	13 198	12 083	10 801	9 975	9 508	9 712	Ovins
Venezuela (Bolivarian Rep. of)									Venezuela (Rép. bolivar. du)
Asses, mules or hinnies[1]	512	512	512	512	512	512	512	512	Ânes, mules ou mulets[1]
Cattle	14 540	14 859	15 164	15 474	15 791	15 989	16 232	16 615	Bovins
Goats	1 161	1 181	1 205	1 225	1 251	1 280	1 311	1 342	Caprins
Horses[1]	500	500	500	500	500	500	500	500	Chevaux[1]
Pigs	2 845	2 792	2 810	2 780	2 825	2 922	3 047	3 264	Porcins
Sheep	475	451	471	485	512	520	528	525	Ovins

Region, country or area	1998	1999	2000	2001	2002	2003	2004	2005	Région, pays ou zone
Asia									**Asie**
Asses, mules or hinnies	**24 190**	**24 435**	**24 240**	**23 933**	**23 373**	**23 044**	**22 605**	**22 180**	**Ânes, mules ou mulets**
Buffaloes	**156 103**	**157 229**	**158 756**	**160 524**	**162 647**	**165 038**	**166 684**	**168 563**	**Buffles**
Cattle	**442 999**	**443 027**	**444 837**	**443 516**	**444 441**	**446 576**	**451 964**	**457 583**	**Bovins**
Goats	**437 445**	**445 890**	**454 260**	**462 443**	**472 924**	**487 067**	**503 317**	**521 310**	**Caprins**
Horses	**16 595**	**16 678**	**16 645**	**15 956**	**14 995**	**14 629**	**14 412**	**14 252**	**Chevaux**
Pigs	**498 704**	**519 034**	**528 034**	**548 544**	**562 331**	**571 756**	**576 929**	**594 861**	**Porcins**
Sheep	**401 586**	**408 405**	**414 420**	**410 538**	**413 598**	**424 113**	**443 453**	**463 778**	**Ovins**
Afghanistan									Afghanistan
Asses, mules or hinnies[1]	888	950	950	950	950	950	950	950	Ânes, mules ou mulets[1]
Cattle	3 008	3 478	2 900[1]	2 500[1]	3 500[1]	3 700[2]	3 700[1]	3 700[1]	Bovins
Goats	6 599	7 373	7 300[1]	6 200[1]	7 500[1]	7 300	7 300[1]	7 300[1]	Caprins
Horses	100[1]	104	104[1]	104[1]	104[1]	104[1]	104[1]	104[1]	Chevaux
Sheep	16 252	17 690	15 000[1]	13 000[1]	11 000[1]	8 800	8 800[1]	8 800[1]	Ovins
Armenia									Arménie
Asses, mules or hinnies	3[1]	3[1]	2[1]	3[1]	3[1]	3[1]	7	7	Ânes, mules ou mulets
Cattle	466	469	479	497	514	536	566	573	Bovins
Goats	26[2]	38[2]	43[2]	43	46	50	48	47	Caprins
Horses	13	12	12	11	12	12	13	12	Chevaux
Pigs	57	86	71	69	98	111	85	89	Porcins
Sheep	520[2]	508[2]	506[2]	497	546	553	580	557	Ovins
Azerbaijan									Azerbaïdjan
Asses, mules or hinnies	31	33	36	38	39	40	42	45	Ânes, mules ou mulets
Buffaloes	293	292	297	299	304	306	307	309	Buffles
Cattle	1 550	1 621	1 664	1 723	1 794	1 872	1 934	2 007	Bovins
Goats	371	409	494	533	556	594	604	601	Caprins
Horses	53	56	61	64	66	68	69	71	Chevaux
Pigs	21	26	20	19	17	20	20	23	Porcins
Sheep	4 896	5 103	5 280	5 553	6 003	6 392	6 676	6 887	Ovins
Bahrain									Bahreïn
Cattle	13	13[1]	11	10	15	11[1]	9	9[1]	Bovins
Goats	16	17[1]	19[1]	18[1]	23[1]	24[1]	25	26[1]	Caprins
Sheep	17	20[1]	23[1]	27[1]	30[1]	35[1]	39	40[1]	Ovins
Bangladesh									Bangladesh
Buffaloes	820	828[1]	830[1]	850[1]	850[1]	850[1]	850[1]	850[1]	Buffles
Cattle	23 400	23 652[1]	23 900[1]	24 100[1]	24 300[1]	24 500[1]	24 500[1]	24 500[1]	Bovins
Goats	33 500	33 800[1]	34 100[1]	34 400[1]	36 900[1]	36 900[1]	36 900[1]	36 900[1]	Caprins
Sheep	1 110	1 121[1]	1 132[1]	1 143[1]	1 194[1]	1 260[1]	1 260[1]	1 260[1]	Ovins
Bhutan									Bhoutan
Asses, mules or hinnies	28	28	28	28	28	28[1]	28[1]	27[1]	Ânes, mules ou mulets
Buffaloes	3[1]	2[1]	2[1]	2[1]	2	2[1]	2[1]	2[1]	Buffles
Cattle	354[1]	384	355	355[1]	355	372	372[1]	372[1]	Bovins
Goats	36[1]	36	31	38[1]	31	30[1]	30[1]	30[1]	Caprins
Horses	32[1]	31	28	28[1]	29[1]	28	28[1]	28[1]	Chevaux
Pigs	52[1]	52	41	41[1]	41	41	41[1]	41[1]	Porcins
Sheep	32[1]	25	23	26[1]	23	21[1]	20[1]	20[1]	Ovins
Brunei Darussalam									Brunéi Darussalam
Buffaloes	6	6	5	6	6	6	5	5[1]	Buffles
Cattle	2	2	2	2	1	1	1	1[1]	Bovins
Goats	4	4	3	2	3	3	2	3[1]	Caprins
Pigs[1]	1	1	1	1	1	1	2	2	Porcins[1]
Sheep[1]	3	2	2	3	1	2	3	3	Ovins[1]
Cambodia									Cambodge
Buffaloes	694	654	694	626	626	660	651	650[1]	Buffles
Cattle	2 680	2 826	2 993	2 869	2 924	2 985	3 040	3 100[1]	Bovins
Horses	23[1]	25[1]	26[1]	27[1]	27[1]	28[1]	28[1]	28	Chevaux
Pigs	2 339	2 189	1 934	2 115	2 105	2 304	2 429	2 500[1]	Porcins

Region, country or area	1998	1999	2000	2001	2002	2003	2004	2005	Région, pays ou zone
China[3]									Chine[3]
Asses, mules or hinnies	14 334	14 297	14 021	13 757	13 177	12 693	12 164	11 659	Ânes, mules ou mulets
Buffaloes	22 554	22 674	22 595	22 765	22 690	22 729	22 287	22 745[2]	Buffles
Cattle	99 370	101 847	104 554	106 060	105 709	108 274	112 537	115 230[2]	Bovins
Goats	135 116	141 956	148 401	157 362	161 477	172 921	183 363	195 759	Caprins
Horses	8 914	8 983	8 916	8 768	8 262	8 090	7 902	7 641	Chevaux
Pigs	408 425	429 202	437 541	454 410	464 695	469 809	472 896	488 810	Porcins
Sheep	120 956	127 352	131 095	133 160	135 893	143 793	157 330	170 882	Ovins
Cyprus									Chypre
Asses, mules or hinnies[1]	7	7	7	7	7	7	7	7	Ânes, mules ou mulets[1]
Cattle	62	56	54	54	54	59	61	58	Bovins
Goats	302	322	346	379	427	408	378	329	Caprins
Horses[1]	1	1	1	1	1	1	1	1	Chevaux[1]
Pigs	415	431	419	408	451	488	471	428	Porcins
Sheep	250	240	233	246	297	265	279	269	Ovins
Georgia									Géorgie
Asses, mules or hinnies	10[1]	12[1]	12[1]	11	10[1]	10[1]	10[1]	10[1]	Ânes, mules ou mulets
Buffaloes	33	33	35	33	36	37	33	33	Buffles
Cattle	1 027	1 051	1 122	1 177	1 180	1 216	1 243	1 251	Bovins
Goats	59	65	80	81	92	88	93	116	Caprins
Horses	30	34	35	39	39	43	43	44	Chevaux
Pigs	330	366	411	443	445	446	474	484	Porcins
Sheep	525	522	553	547	568	611	629	689	Ovins
India									Inde
Asses, mules or hinnies[1]	1 050	1 050	1 050	1 050	1 050	1 050	1 050	1 050	Ânes, mules ou mulets[1]
Buffaloes	91 034[2]	92 150[2]	93 266[2]	94 382[2]	95 498[2]	96 616	97 700[1]	98 000[1]	Buffles
Cattle	196 966[2]	195 050[2]	193 134[2]	191 218[2]	189 302[2]	187 382	185 500[1]	185 000[1]	Bovins
Goats	122 300[2]	121 800[2]	121 400[2]	120 900[2]	120 500[2]	120 097	120 000[1]	120 000[1]	Caprins
Horses	800[2]	800[2]	800[2]	800[2]	800[2]	788	800[1]	800[1]	Chevaux
Pigs	13 400[2]	13 600[2]	13 700[2]	13 900[2]	14 000[2]	14 142	14 300[1]	14 300[1]	Porcins
Sheep	58 200[2]	58 900[2]	59 600[2]	60 400[2]	61 100[2]	61 789	62 500[1]	62 500[1]	Ovins
Indonesia									Indonésie
Buffaloes	2 829	2 504	2 405	2 333	2 403	2 459	2 403	2 428	Buffles
Cattle	11 634	11 276	11 362	10 562	11 656	10 878	11 108	11 500[1]	Bovins
Goats	13 560	12 701	12 566	12 464	12 549	12 722	12 781	13 182	Caprins
Horses	566	484	412	422	419	413	397	405	Chevaux
Pigs	7 798	7 042	5 357	5 369	5 927	6 151	5 980	6 267	Porcins
Sheep	7 144	7 226	7 427	7 401	7 641	7 811	8 075	8 307	Ovins
Iran (Islamic Rep. of)									Iran (Rép. islamique d')
Asses, mules or hinnies	1 537[2]	1 727[2]	1 775[1]	1 775[1]	1 775[1]	1 775[1]	1 775[1]	1 775[1]	Ânes, mules ou mulets
Buffaloes	474	474	491	507	524	540[1]	560[1]	550[1]	Buffles
Cattle	8 785	8 047	8 270	8 500	8 738	8 900[1]	9 150[1]	8 800[1]	Bovins
Goats	25 757	25 757	25 757	25 757	25 757	26 000	26 300[1]	26 500[1]	Caprins
Horses[1]	130	120	150	150	150	150	140	140	Chevaux[1]
Sheep	53 245	53 900	53 900	53 900	53 900	53 900[1]	54 000[1]	54 000[1]	Ovins
Iraq									Iraq
Asses, mules or hinnies	398[1]	386[1]	391[1]	391	391	391[1]	391[1]	391[1]	Ânes, mules ou mulets
Buffaloes	80[1]	90[1]	115	120	120	120[1]	120[1]	120[1]	Buffles
Cattle	1 320[2]	1 325[2]	1 350[2]	1 458	1 500	1 500[1]	1 500[1]	1 500[1]	Bovins
Goats	1 450[1]	1 400[1]	1 300	743	1 500	1 650[1]	1 650[1]	1 650[1]	Caprins
Horses	48[1]	46[1]	48	48	48[1]	48[1]	48[1]	48[1]	Chevaux
Sheep	6 900[2]	6 000[2]	6 900	6 045	6 100[1]	6 200[1]	6 200[1]	6 200[1]	Ovins
Israel									Israël
Asses, mules or hinnies[1]	7	7	7	7	7	7	7	7	Ânes, mules ou mulets[1]
Cattle	388	395	395	390	355	360	350	357	Bovins
Goats	74	75	62	68	70	75	75	83	Caprins
Horses[1]	4	4	4	4	4	4	4	4	Chevaux[1]
Pigs	163[1]	122[1]	141[1]	155[1]	195[1]	180	190	205	Porcins
Sheep	350	350	380	389	390	400	420	435	Ovins

Region, country or area	1998	1999	2000	2001	2002	2003	2004	2005	Région, pays ou zone
Japan									Japon
Cattle	4 708	4 658	4 588	4 531	4 564	4 524	4 478	4 402	Bovins
Goats[1]	29	33	35	35	35	34	34	34	Caprins[1]
Horses	26[1]	25[1]	25[1]	21[1]	25	25[1]	25[1]	25[1]	Chevaux
Pigs	9 904	9 879	9 806	9 788	9 612	9 725	9 724	9 600	Porcins
Sheep[1]	13	12	10	10	11	11	11	11	Ovins[1]
Jordan									Jordanie
Asses, mules or hinnies	21[1]	21[1]	21[1]	21[1]	21[1]	21[1]	21[1]	21	Ânes, mules ou mulets
Cattle	61	65	65	65	68	66	69	69	Bovins
Goats	650	631	461	426	557	547	501	516	Caprins
Horses[1]	4	4	4	4	4	4	4	4	Chevaux[1]
Sheep	1 935	1 581	1 934	1 484	1 458	1 476	1 529	1 890	Ovins
Kazakhstan									Kazakhstan
Asses, mules or hinnies[1]	29	29	30	30	30	30	30	30	Ânes, mules ou mulets[1]
Buffaloes[1]	9	9	9	9	9	9	9	9	Buffles[1]
Cattle	4 307	3 958	3 998	4 107	4 294	4 560	4 871	5 181	Bovins
Goats	691	835	931	1 042	1 271	1 486	1 827	1 995	Caprins
Horses	1 083	986	970	976	990	1 019	1 064	1 120	Chevaux
Pigs	879	892	984	1 076	1 124	1 230	1 369	1 292	Porcins
Sheep	9 693	8 691	8 725	8 939	9 208	9 788	10 420	11 287	Ovins
Korea, Dem. P. R.									Corée, R. p. dém. de
Cattle	565	577	579	570	575	576	566	578[1]	Bovins
Goats	1 508	1 900	2 276	2 566	2 693	2 717	2 736	2 750[1]	Caprins
Horses	44[1]	45[1]	46[1]	47[1]	48[1]	48	48	48	Chevaux
Pigs	2 475	2 970	3 120	3 137	3 152	3 178	3 194	3 200[1]	Porcins
Sheep	165	185	185	189	170	171	171	172[1]	Ovins
Korea, Republic of									Corée, République de
Cattle	2 922	2 487	2 134	1 954	1 954	1 999	2 163	2 298[2]	Bovins
Goats	539	462	445	440	444	483	527	570[1]	Caprins
Horses	8	8	11	13	14	16	16	16	Chevaux
Pigs	7 544	7 864	8 214	8 720	8 974	9 231	8 908	8 962	Porcins
Sheep	1	1	1	1	1	1	1	1[1]	Ovins
Kuwait									Koweït
Cattle	18	20	21	20	25	27	28[1]	28[1]	Bovins
Goats	130	159	153	130	147	152	150[1]	150[1]	Caprins
Horses	1[1]	1[1]	1[1]	1[1]	1[1]	1[1]	1[1]	1	Chevaux
Sheep	421	476	616	630	800	850[1]	900[1]	900[1]	Ovins
Kyrgyzstan									Kirghizistan
Asses, mules or hinnies	41[1]	44[1]	45[1]	46[1]	46[1]	38	49	44	Ânes, mules ou mulets
Cattle	885	911	932	947	970	988	1 004	1 035	Bovins
Goats	380[2]	502	543	601	640	661	770	808	Caprins
Horses	325	335	350	354	354	361	341	347	Chevaux
Pigs	93	105	105	101	87	87	83	83	Porcins
Sheep	3 425[2]	3 309	3 264	3 198	3 104	3 104	2 884	2 965	Ovins
Lao People's Dem. Rep.									Rép. dém. pop. lao
Buffaloes	1 093	1 008	1 028	1 051	1 089	1 111	1 112	1 097	Buffles
Cattle	1 127	1 000	1 100	1 217	1 208	1 244	1 249	1 272	Bovins
Goats	122	112	121	124	128	137	141	143[1]	Caprins
Horses	27[1]	28[1]	29[1]	29[1]	30[1]	31[1]	31[1]	31	Chevaux
Pigs	1 432	1 320	1 425	1 426	1 416	1 655	1 728	1 827	Porcins
Lebanon									Liban
Asses, mules or hinnies[1]	30	31	31	31	31	31	31	31	Ânes, mules ou mulets[1]
Cattle	72	76	77	78	88	86	80	90[1]	Bovins
Goats	466	436	417	399	409	428	432	430[1]	Caprins
Horses[1]	6	6	6	6	6	6	6	6	Chevaux[1]
Pigs	34	28	26	23	21	14	15[1]	15[1]	Porcins
Sheep	350	378	354	329	298	303	305	340[1]	Ovins

Region, country or area	1998	1999	2000	2001	2002	2003	2004	2005	Région, pays ou zone
Malaysia									Malaisie
Buffaloes	160	150	142	140[1]	131	133	138	137	Buffles
Cattle	714	715	734	742	748	753	787	801	Bovins
Goats	236	238	238	247	233	247	264	271	Caprins
Horses[1]	5	5	4	4	5	7	7	7	Chevaux[1]
Pigs	2 934	1 955	1 808	1 973	2 047	2 071	2 111	2 168	Porcins
Sheep	166	152	157	129	126	115	115	109	Ovins
Mongolia									Mongolie
Asses, mules or hinnies	2	1	1	1[1]	1[1]	1[1]	1[1]	1[1]	Ânes, mules ou mulets
Cattle	3 613	3 726	3 825	3 098	2 070	2 054	1 793	1 842	Bovins
Goats	10 265	11 062	11 034	10 270	9 591	8 858	10 653	12 238	Caprins
Horses	2 893	3 059	3 164	2 661	2 192	1 989	1 969	2 005	Chevaux
Pigs	21	22	15	15	7[1]	6[1]	6[1]	6[1]	Porcins
Sheep	14 166	14 694	15 191	13 876	11 937	11 797	10 756	11 686	Ovins
Myanmar									Myanmar
Asses, mules or hinnies	8[1]	8[1]	8[1]	8[1]	8	8	8	8	Ânes, mules ou mulets
Buffaloes	2 337	2 391	2 441	2 502	2 552	2 603	2 650[1]	2 700	Buffles
Cattle	10 493	10 740	10 982	11 243	11 551	11 728	11 939	12 500	Bovins
Goats	1 319	1 353	1 392	1 439	1 542	1 722[2]	1 756[2]	1 900	Caprins
Horses	120[1]	120[1]	120[1]	120[1]	120	120	120	120	Chevaux
Pigs	3 501	3 715	3 974	4 261	4 499	4 840	5 217	5 700	Porcins
Sheep	369	379	390	403	432	482[2]	492[2]	500	Ovins
Nepal									Népal
Buffaloes	3 419	3 471	3 526	3 624	3 701	3 840	3 953	4 081	Buffles
Cattle	7 049	7 031	7 023	6 983	6 979	6 954	6 966	6 994	Bovins
Goats	6 080	6 205	6 325	6 478	6 607	6 792	6 980	7 154	Caprins
Pigs	766	825	878	913	934	932	935	948	Porcins
Sheep	869	855	852	850	840	828	824	817	Ovins
Occupied Palestinian Terr.									Terr. palestinien occupé
Cattle	22	24	24	27	30	33	32	34[1]	Bovins
Goats	252	295	309	314	355	392	399	400[1]	Caprins
Sheep	538	504	566	616	758	829	812	800[1]	Ovins
Oman									Oman
Asses, mules or hinnies	28[1]	28[1]	29[1]	29	29[1]	29[1]	29[1]	29[1]	Ânes, mules ou mulets
Cattle	271	285	299	314	320	326	330[1]	335[1]	Bovins
Goats	940	959	979	998	1 018	1 039	1 050[1]	1 070[1]	Caprins
Sheep	312	327	344	354	361	368	370[1]	375[1]	Ovins
Pakistan									Pakistan
Asses, mules or hinnies	3 834	3 913	3 997	4 083	4 168	4 258	4 353	4 450	Ânes, mules ou mulets
Buffaloes	21 422	22 032	22 669	23 335	24 030	24 800	25 500	26 300	Buffles
Cattle	21 192	21 592	22 004	22 424	22 858	23 303	23 800	24 200	Bovins
Goats	44 183	45 775	47 426	49 140	50 917	52 763	54 700	56 700	Caprins
Horses	327	325	323	321	318	317	315	313	Chevaux
Sheep	23 800	23 938	24 084	24 236	24 398	24 566	24 700	24 900	Ovins
Philippines									Philippines
Buffaloes	3 013	3 006	3 024	3 066	3 122	3 180	3 270	3 327	Buffles
Cattle	2 395	2 426	2 479	2 496	2 548	2 585	2 560	2 489	Bovins
Goats[1]	6 000	6 125	6 245	6 197	6 250	6 300	6 300	6 500	Caprins[1]
Horses	230[1]	230[1]	230[1]	230[1]	230[1]	230[1]	230[1]	230	Chevaux
Pigs	10 210	10 397	10 713	11 063	11 653	12 364	12 562	12 140	Porcins
Sheep[1]	30	30	30	30	30	30	30	30	Ovins[1]
Qatar									Qatar
Cattle	14	15	15	10	10	10	10	11[1]	Bovins
Goats	175	177	178	140	141	144	146	150[1]	Caprins
Horses	4[1]	4[1]	3	1	2	2	2	2[1]	Chevaux
Sheep	206	212	215	150	153	156	159	200[1]	Ovins

Region, country or area	1998	1999	2000	2001	2002	2003	2004	2005	Région, pays ou zone
Saudi Arabia									Arabie saoudite
Asses, mules or hinnies	100	98	98	98	100[1]	100[1]	100[1]	100[1]	Ânes, mules ou mulets
Cattle	294	281	291	306	322	332	342	350[1]	Bovins
Goats	3 690	2 368	2 462	2 194	2 214	2 200[1]	2 200[1]	2 200[1]	Caprins
Horses	3	3	3	3	3	3[1]	3[1]	3[1]	Chevaux
Sheep	7 422	7 563	7 934	7 006	7 010	7 000[1]	7 000[1]	7 000[1]	Ovins
Singapore[1]									Singapour[1]
Goats	1	1	1	1	1	1	1	1	Caprins
Pigs	180	250	100	100	250	250	250	250	Porcins
Sri Lanka									Sri Lanka
Buffaloes	316	320	305	290	282	280	302	308	Buffles
Cattle	1 178	1 192	1 148	1 153	1 113	1 139	1 161	1 185	Bovins
Goats	519	514	495	493	351[2]	415	405	405	Caprins
Horses	2[1]	2[1]	2[1]	2[1]	2[1]	2[1]	2[1]	2	Chevaux
Pigs	76	74	71	68	82	68	72	85	Porcins
Sheep	12	12	11	12	9[2]	9	11	10	Ovins
Syrian Arab Republic									Rép. arabe syrienne
Asses, mules or hinnies	244	233	229	177	137	137[1]	123	118	Ânes, mules ou mulets
Buffaloes	1	3	3	2	3	3[1]	4	4	Buffles
Cattle	932	978	984	837	867	937	1 024	1 083	Bovins
Goats	1 101	1 046	1 050	979	932	1 017	1 130	1 296	Caprins
Horses	26	27	27	18	17	17[1]	15	15	Chevaux
Pigs	1[1]	1[1]	0	0	0	0	0	0	Porcins
Sheep	15 425	13 998	13 505	12 362	13 497	15 293	17 565	19 651	Ovins
Tajikistan									Tadjikistan
Asses, mules or hinnies	90	106	110	117	123	138	147	156	Ânes, mules ou mulets
Cattle	1 050	1 037	1 037	1 062	1 091	1 136	1 219	1 303	Bovins
Goats	668	701	706	744	779	842	920	975	Caprins
Horses	66	67	72	72	71	73	74	77	Chevaux
Pigs	1	1	1	1	1	1	1	1	Porcins
Sheep	1 554	1 494	1 472	1 478	1 490	1 591	1 672	1 782	Ovins
Thailand									Thaïlande
Buffaloes	2 286	1 912	1 712	1 524	1 613	1 690	1 738	1 771	Buffles
Cattle	5 159	4 756	4 602	4 640	4 820	5 048	5 297	5 610	Bovins
Goats	131	133	144	189	178	214	250	270[1]	Caprins
Horses	11	7	9	8	8	7	3	5[1]	Chevaux
Pigs	7 082	6 370	6 558	6 689	6 879	7 064	7 254	7 534	Porcins
Sheep	40	39	37	43	39	43	48	50[1]	Ovins
Timor-Leste									Timor-Leste
Buffaloes	81	90[1]	100[1]	104	105[1]	107[1]	108[1]	110[1]	Buffles
Cattle	161	97	120[1]	166	168[1]	170[1]	170[1]	171[1]	Bovins
Goats	218	189[2]	75[1]	79	80[1]	80[1]	80[1]	80	Caprins
Horses	34	38[1]	42[1]	45	48[1]	48	48	48	Chevaux
Pigs	309	239	290[1]	339	340[1]	340[1]	346[1]	346[1]	Porcins
Sheep	34	34[1]	20[1]	24	24[1]	25[1]	25	25	Ovins
Turkey									Turquie
Asses, mules or hinnies	782	736	680	588	559	512	490	452	Ânes, mules ou mulets
Buffaloes	194	176	165	146	138	121	113	104	Buffles
Cattle	11 185	11 031	11 054	10 761	10 548	9 804	9 788	10 069	Bovins
Goats	8 376	8 057	7 774	7 201	7 022	6 780	6 772	6 609	Caprins
Horses	345	330	309	271	271	249	227	212	Chevaux
Pigs	5	5	3	3	3	4	7	4	Porcins
Sheep	30 238	29 435	30 256	28 492	26 972	25 174	25 432	25 201	Ovins
Turkmenistan									Turkménistan
Asses, mules or hinnies[1]	25	25	24	25	25	25	25	25	Ânes, mules ou mulets[1]
Cattle	1 100[1]	1 250[1]	1 400[1]	1 600	1 750[1]	1 900	2 000	2 025	Bovins
Goats	400[1]	450[1]	500[1]	570[2]	650[1]	730[2]	750[2]	822[2]	Caprins
Horses[1]	16	16	16	17	17	16	16	16	Chevaux[1]
Pigs	55[1]	40[1]	35[1]	30	30[1]	30	30	30[1]	Porcins
Sheep	6 000[1]	6 800[1]	7 500[1]	8 230[2]	10 350[1]	12 570[2]	13 150[2]	14 267[2]	Ovins

34 Livestock — Stocks: thousand head (*continued*)
Cheptel — Effectifs : milliers de têtes (*suite*)

Region, country or area	1998	1999	2000	2001	2002	2003	2004	2005	Région, pays ou zone
United Arab Emirates									Emirats arabes unis
Cattle	85	91	96	102	107	113	115[1]	115[1]	Bovins
Goats	1 128	1 207	1 279	1 355	1 430	1 495	1 500[1]	1 520[1]	Caprins
Sheep	437	467	495	525	554	583	590[1]	580[1]	Ovins
Uzbekistan									Ouzbékistan
Asses, mules or hinnies	165[1]	165[1]	160[1]	165[1]	160[1]	262	269	289	Ânes, mules ou mulets
Cattle	5 200	5 225	5 268	5 344	5 478	5 879	6 243	6 571	Bovins
Goats	894[2]	884[2]	886[2]	830[2]	923[2]	1 421	1 690	1 797	Caprins
Horses	150[1]	155[1]	155[1]	150[1]	145[1]	148	152	158	Chevaux
Pigs	70	80	80	89	75	90	87	87	Porcins
Sheep	7 706[2]	7 840[2]	8 000[2]	8 100[2]	8 311[2]	8 507	8 890	9 555	Ovins
Viet Nam									Viet Nam
Buffaloes	2 951	2 956	2 897	2 808	2 814	2 835	2 870	2 922	Buffles
Cattle	3 987	4 064	4 128	3 900	4 063	4 394	4 908	5 541[2]	Bovins
Goats	514	471	544	572	622	780	1 020	1 314	Caprins
Horses	123	150	127	113	111	113	113	110	Chevaux
Pigs	18 132	18 886	20 194	21 800	23 170	24 885	26 144	27 435	Porcins
Yemen									Yémen
Asses, mules or hinnies[1]	500	500	500	500	500	500	500	500	Ânes, mules ou mulets[1]
Cattle	1 210	1 228	1 283	1 342	1 355	1 358	1 398	...	Bovins
Goats	6 653	6 840	6 918	7 246	7 318	7 311	7 668	...	Caprins
Horses	3[1]	3[1]	3	3	3	3[1]	3[1]	3[1]	Chevaux
Sheep	5 836	6 016	6 193	6 483	6 548	6 589	7 755	...	Ovins
Europe									**Europe**
Asses, mules or hinnies	**1 095**	**1 088**	**1 057**	**1 017**	**999**	**967**	**907**	**1 009**	**Ânes, mules ou mulets**
Buffaloes	**212**	**256**	**241**	**260**	**249**	**289**	**280**	**274**	**Buffles**
Cattle	**155 757**	**150 615**	**146 959**	**143 248**	**140 673**	**138 457**	**134 245**	**130 441**	**Bovins**
Goats	**19 310**	**19 095**	**18 884**	**18 669**	**18 657**	**19 009**	**18 439**	**18 140**	**Caprins**
Horses	**7 381**	**7 075**	**6 857**	**6 788**	**6 516**	**6 507**	**6 420**	**6 247**	**Chevaux**
Pigs	**201 136**	**204 734**	**200 321**	**192 217**	**194 606**	**197 445**	**191 642**	**190 657**	**Porcins**
Sheep	**159 649**	**154 300**	**148 762**	**139 807**	**136 806**	**137 273**	**138 151**	**137 876**	**Ovins**
Albania									Albanie
Asses, mules or hinnies	130[2]	142[2]	141[2]	127[2]	116[2]	107[2]	127[1]	127[1]	Ânes, mules ou mulets
Cattle	705	720	728	708	690	684	654	655	Bovins
Goats	1 051	1 120	1 106	1 027	929	1 015	944	941	Caprins
Horses	61	63	63	67	65	63	58	53	Chevaux
Pigs	83	81	103	106	114	132	143	147	Porcins
Sheep	1 872	1 941	1 939	1 906	1 844	1 903	1 794	1 760	Ovins
Austria									Autriche
Cattle	2 198	2 172[2]	2 172	2 155	2 118	2 067	2 052	2 051	Bovins
Goats	58	54	72	70	59	58	55	56	Caprins
Horses	74	75	82	63[1]	60[1]	85[1]	80	85[1]	Chevaux
Pigs	3 680	3 810	3 431	3 427	3 440	3 306	3 245	3 125	Porcins
Sheep	384	361	352	358	320	304	326	327	Ovins
Belarus									Bélarus
Asses, mules or hinnies[1]	9	9	8	9	9	9	9	9	Ânes, mules ou mulets[1]
Cattle	4 801	4 686	4 326	4 221	4 085	4 005	3 924	3 963	Bovins
Goats	59	56	58	65	66	64	63	66	Caprins
Horses	233	229	221	217	209	202	192	181	Chevaux
Pigs	3 686	3 698	3 566	3 431	3 373	3 329	3 287	3 407	Porcins
Sheep	127	106	92	89	83	73	63	59	Ovins
Belgium									Belgique
Cattle	...	...	3 042	3 038	2 891	2 778	2 739	2 695	Bovins
Goats	...	...	16	21	25	26	26	26	Caprins
Horses	...	...	31[1]	31	31	33	32	34	Chevaux
Pigs	...	...	7 369	6 834	6 735	6 539	6 355	6 332	Porcins
Sheep	...	...	126	156	146	146	151	155	Ovins

Region, country or area	1998	1999	2000	2001	2002	2003	2004	2005	Région, pays ou zone
Belgium-Luxembourg									**Belgique-Luxembourg**
Cattle	3 184	3 395	…	…	…	…	…	…	Bovins
Goats	11	13	…	…	…	…	…	…	Caprins
Horses[1]	62	60	…	…	…	…	…	…	Chevaux[1]
Pigs	7 436	7 632	…	…	…	…	…	…	Porcins
Sheep[2]	155	158	…	…	…	…	…	…	Ovins[2]
Bosnia and Herzegovina									**Bosnie-Herzégovine**
Buffaloes[1]	5	7	8	13	13	13	13	13	Buffles[1]
Cattle	426[2]	443[2]	462[2]	440[1]	440[1]	440[1]	453	460	Bovins
Goats	…	…	…	…	…	…	72	73	Caprins
Horses	19	20[1]	18[2]	18[1]	20[1]	24[1]	28	27	Chevaux
Pigs	373[2]	350[1]	355[1]	330[1]	450[1]	500[1]	595	653	Porcins
Sheep	581[2]	633[2]	662[2]	640[1]	750[1]	800[1]	893	903	Ovins
Bulgaria									**Bulgarie**
Asses, mules or hinnies	242	237	223	210	212[1]	215[1]	144	215[1]	Ânes, mules ou mulets
Buffaloes	11	10	9	8	7	7	8	8	Buffles
Cattle	612	671	682	640	634	691	728	672	Bovins
Goats	966	1 048	1 046	970	675	754	725	718	Caprins
Horses	126	133	141	140	151	151[1]	126	150[1]	Chevaux
Pigs	1 480	1 722	1 512	1 144	785	996	1 032	931	Porcins
Sheep	2 848	2 774	2 549	2 286	1 571	1 728	1 599	1 693	Ovins
Croatia									**Croatie**
Asses, mules or hinnies	4[1]	4	4	4[1]	4[1]	4[1]	4[1]	4[1]	Ânes, mules ou mulets
Cattle	443	439	427	438	417	444	466	471	Bovins
Goats	84	79	79	93	97	86	126	120[1]	Caprins
Horses	16	13	11	10	8	9	10	11	Chevaux
Pigs	1 166	1 362	1 233	1 234	1 286	1 347	1 489	1 205	Porcins
Sheep	427	489	529	540	580	587	722	796	Ovins
Czech Republic									**République tchèque**
Cattle	1 701	1 657	1 574	1 582	1 520	1 474	1 428	1 397	Bovins
Goats	35	34	32	28	14	13	12	13	Caprins
Horses	20	23	24	26	21	20	20	21	Chevaux
Pigs	4 013	4 001	3 688	3 594	3 441	3 363	3 127	2 877	Porcins
Sheep	94	86	84	90	96	103	116	140	Ovins
Denmark									**Danemark**
Cattle	1 977	1 887	1 868	1 907	1 796	1 724	1 646	1 544	Bovins
Horses	38	40	40	43	38	43	39	47	Chevaux
Pigs	12 095	11 626	11 922	12 608	12 732	12 949	13 233	13 466	Porcins
Sheep	156	143	145	152	131	144	141	161	Ovins
Estonia									**Estonie**
Cattle	326	308	267	253	261	254	257	250	Bovins
Goats	2	2	3	3	4	4	4	3	Caprins
Horses	4	4	4	4	6	5	6	5	Chevaux
Pigs	306	326	286	300	345	341	345	340	Porcins
Sheep	34	29	28	29	29	30	31	39	Ovins
Faeroe Islands									**Iles Féroé**
Cattle	2	2	2	2	2	2	2	2	Bovins
Sheep[1]	68	68	68	68	68	68	68	68	Ovins[1]
Finland									**Finlande**
Cattle	1 117	1 087	1 057	1 037	1 025	1 000	969	959	Bovins
Goats	7	8	9	7	7	7	7	7	Caprins
Horses	56	56	58	59	59	60	61	64	Chevaux
Pigs	1 401	1 351	1 296	1 261	1 315	1 375	1 365	1 401	Porcins
Sheep	128	107	100	96	96	98	109	90	Ovins
France									**France**
Asses, mules or hinnies	31[1]	30[1]	31[1]	31[1]	30[1]	30[1]	32[2]	32[2]	Ânes, mules ou mulets
Cattle	20 023	20 265	20 310	20 462	20 116	19 597	19 320	19 383	Bovins
Goats	1 200	1 199	1 211	1 231	1 232	1 223	1 206	1 213	Caprins
Horses	347	348	349	343	345	350	344	351	Chevaux
Pigs	14 501	14 682	14 930	15 382	15 327	15 139	15 004	15 020	Porcins
Sheep	10 316	10 240	9 578	9 443	9 336	9 256	9 151	9 185	Ovins

Region, country or area	1998	1999	2000	2001	2002	2003	2004	2005	Région, pays ou zone
Germany									Allemagne
Cattle	15 227	14 942	14 658	14 568	14 227	13 644	13 196	13 035	Bovins
Goats	115	125	135	140	160	165	170	170	Caprins
Horses	600	524	476	491	506	525	525[1]	500	Chevaux
Pigs	24 795	26 294	26 001	25 767	25 958	26 334	25 659	26 858	Porcins
Sheep	2 870	2 724	2 743	2 771	2 722	2 697	2 714	2 642	Ovins
Greece									Grèce
Asses, mules or hinnies	115	107	101	96	97[1]	79	73	96[1]	Ânes, mules ou mulets
Buffaloes	1	1	1	1	1	1	1	...	Buffles
Cattle	580	583	602	613	559	573	603	600[1]	Bovins
Goats	5 600	5 615	5 614	5 641	5 669	5 619	5 509	5 400[1]	Caprins
Horses	32	31	30	29	29[1]	28	27	29[1]	Chevaux
Pigs	998	999	973	964	940	934	940	1 000[1]	Porcins
Sheep	8 884	8 930	8 951	8 993	9 058	9 000	8 827	9 000[1]	Ovins
Hungary									Hongrie
Asses, mules or hinnies[1]	4	4	4	4	4	4	4	4	Ânes, mules ou mulets[1]
Cattle	871	873	857	805	783	770	739	723	Bovins
Goats	129	149	189	103	90	87	85	74	Caprins
Horses	72	70	70	74	65	63	62	67	Chevaux
Pigs	4 931	5 479	5 335	4 834	4 822	5 082	4 913	4 059	Porcins
Sheep	858	909	934	1 129	1 136	1 103	1 296	1 397	Ovins
Iceland									Islande
Cattle	76	75	72	70	67	66	65	63	Bovins
Goats	^0	1	^0	^0	^0	^0	^0	^0	Caprins
Horses	78	77	74	74	71	71	72	75	Chevaux
Pigs	43[1]	44[1]	44[1]	44[1]	37	44	36	41	Porcins
Sheep	490	491	466	474	469	463	455	452	Ovins
Ireland									Irlande
Asses, mules or hinnies	8[2]	7[2]	5[2]	5[2]	5[2]	6[2]	6[2]	7[1]	Ânes, mules ou mulets
Cattle	6 882	6 952	7 037	7 050	6 992	6 999	7 016	6 888	Bovins
Goats	15	14	8	8	8	8	8	8[1]	Caprins
Horses	73	76	70	71	73	70	73	70[1]	Chevaux
Pigs	1 717	1 801	1 763	1 732	1 763	1 713	1 646	1 681	Porcins
Sheep	5 577	5 559	5 319	5 056	4 807	4 829	4 850	4 557	Ovins
Italy									Italie
Asses, mules or hinnies	34[1]	33[1]	33[1]	33[1]	33[1]	33[1]	29[2]	33[1]	Ânes, mules ou mulets
Buffaloes	162	200	182	194	185	222	210	205	Buffles
Cattle	7 166	7 129	7 162	6 739	6 510	6 505	6 305	6 255	Bovins
Goats	1 347	1 331	1 397	924	1 025	961	978	945	Caprins
Horses	290[1]	288[1]	280[1]	285[1]	285[1]	290[1]	278	300[1]	Chevaux
Pigs	8 281	8 323	8 415	8 877	9 166	9 157	8 972	9 200	Porcins
Sheep	10 894	10 894	11 017	8 311	8 138	7 951	8 106	7 954	Ovins
Latvia									Lettonie
Cattle	477	434	378	367	385	388	379	371	Bovins
Goats	9	10	8	10	12	13	15	15	Caprins
Horses	23	19	19	20	20	19	15	16	Chevaux
Pigs	430	421	394	394	429	453	444	436	Porcins
Sheep	29	27	29	29	29	32	39	39	Ovins
Liechtenstein									Liechtenstein
Cattle	6	6	6	6	6	6	6	6	Bovins
Pigs	3	3	3	3	3	3	3	3	Porcins
Sheep	3	3	3	3	3	3	3	3	Ovins
Lithuania									Lituanie
Cattle	1 016	923	898	748	752	779	812	792	Bovins
Goats	19	24	25	23	24	22	27	27	Caprins
Horses	79	74	75	68	65	61	64	64	Chevaux
Pigs	1 200	1 159	936	868	1 011	1 061	1 057	1 073	Porcins
Sheep	24	16	14	12	12	14	17	22	Ovins

Region, country or area	1998	1999	2000	2001	2002	2003	2004	2005	Région, pays ou zone
Luxembourg									Luxembourg
Cattle	...	...	205	205	197	190	187	185	Bovins
Goats	...	...	1	1	1	2	2	2	Caprins
Horses	...	...	3	3	3	3	4	4	Chevaux
Pigs	...	...	80	79	80	84	85	90	Porcins
Sheep	...	...	8	8	9	9	10	10	Ovins
Malta									Malte
Asses, mules or hinnies[1]	1	1	1	1	1	1	1	1	Ânes, mules ou mulets[1]
Cattle	19[1]	20[1]	19	19	19	18	19[2]	18[1]	Bovins
Goats	8[1]	7[1]	5	5	5	5	5[1]	5[1]	Caprins
Horses[1]	1	1	1	1	1	1	1	1	Chevaux[1]
Pigs	70[1]	70[1]	80	80	78	73	77[2]	73[1]	Porcins
Sheep	16[1]	16[1]	12[1]	13	12	15	14[2]	15[1]	Ovins
Netherlands									Pays-Bas
Cattle	4 283	4 206	4 070	4 047	3 858	3 759	3 767	3 799	Bovins
Goats	132	153	179	221	255	274	282	282[1]	Caprins
Horses	114	115	118	120	121	126	129	129[1]	Chevaux
Pigs	13 446	13 567	13 118	13 073	11 648	11 169	11 153	11 312	Porcins
Sheep	1 394	1 401	1 308	1 296	1 186	1 185	1 236	1 363	Ovins
Norway									Norvège
Cattle	1 036	1 033	988	979	951	939	931	920	Bovins
Goats	62	60[2]	69	67	65	65	65	65[1]	Caprins
Horses	26	27	28	29	30	28	28[1]	28[1]	Chevaux
Pigs	689	439	392	443	453	497	505	515	Porcins
Sheep	2 399	2 294	2 353	2 453	2 424	2 422	2 416	2 417	Ovins
Poland									Pologne
Cattle	6 955	6 555	6 083	5 734	5 533	5 489	5 353	5 483	Bovins
Goats	...	...	...	...	...	192	176	141	Caprins
Horses	561	551	550	546	330	333	330	312	Chevaux
Pigs	19 168	18 538	17 122	17 106	18 707	18 605	16 988	18 112	Porcins
Sheep	453	392	362	343	345	338	318	316	Ovins
Portugal									Portugal
Asses, mules or hinnies[1]	190	185	180	175	175	165	165	165	Ânes, mules ou mulets[1]
Cattle	1 386	1 409	1 421	1 414	1 404	1 395	1 389	1 443	Bovins
Goats	785	750	630	623	561	538	502	547	Caprins
Horses[1]	24	19	17	17	17	17	17	17	Chevaux[1]
Pigs	2 385	2 350	2 350	2 338	2 389	2 344	2 249	2 348	Porcins
Sheep[1]	5 800	5 850	5 584	5 578	5 478	5 500	5 500	5 500	Ovins[1]
Republic of Moldova									République de Moldova
Asses, mules or hinnies[1]	2	2	2	2	2	2	2	2	Ânes, mules ou mulets[1]
Cattle	551	452	423	394	405	410	373	331	Bovins
Goats	94	94	100	109	112	126	121	119	Caprins
Horses	61	64	67	71	77	78	78	73	Chevaux
Pigs	798	807	683	447	449	508	446	398	Porcins
Sheep	1 115	1 026	930	830	835	830	817	823	Ovins
Romania									Roumanie
Asses, mules or hinnies[1]	31	31	30	31	28	28	28	29	Ânes, mules ou mulets[1]
Cattle	3 235	3 143	3 051	2 870	2 800	2 878	2 897	2 808	Bovins
Goats	610	585	558	538	525	633	678	661	Caprins
Horses	822	839	858	865	860	879	897	840	Chevaux
Pigs	7 097	7 194	5 848	4 797	4 447	5 058	5 145	6 495	Porcins
Sheep	8 938	8 409	8 121	7 657	7 251	7 312	7 447	7 425	Ovins
Russian Federation									Fédération de Russie
Asses, mules or hinnies[1]	25	25	22	20	19	18	17	16	Ânes, mules ou mulets[1]
Buffaloes	17	16	17[1]	17	14	16	18	17	Buffles
Cattle	31 520	28 481	28 032	27 294	27 107	26 524	24 935	22 988	Bovins
Goats	2 291	2 144	2 148	2 212	2 292	2 322	2 361	2 277	Caprins
Horses	2 013	1 801	1 683	1 619	1 578	1 499	1 499	1 409	Chevaux
Pigs	17 348	17 248	18 271	15 708	16 047	17 337	15 980	13 413	Porcins
Sheep	16 483	13 413	12 603	12 561	13 035	13 729	14 669	15 494	Ovins

Region, country or area	1998	1999	2000	2001	2002	2003	2004	2005	Région, pays ou zone
Serbia and Montenegro									Serbie-et-Monténégro
Buffaloes	16	21	23	26	29	29[1]	29[1]	29[1]	Buffles
Cattle	1 878	1 812	1 427	1 341	1 306	1 294	1 276	1 096	Bovins
Goats	312	326	241	237	226	224	195	139	Caprins
Horses	86	76	49	41	39	34	35	34	Chevaux
Pigs	4 150	4 372	4 087	3 634	3 608	3 656	3 463	3 212	Porcins
Sheep	2 402	2 195	1 917	1 783	1 691	1 756	1 838	1 609	Ovins
Slovakia									Slovaquie
Cattle	803	705	664	645	608	593	540	528	Bovins
Goats	27	39	51	51	40	39	39	40	Caprins
Horses	10	10	9	10	8	8	8	8	Chevaux
Pigs	1 810	1 593	1 562	1 488	1 517	1 443	1 149	1 108	Porcins
Sheep	417	326	337	358	316	326	321	320	Ovins
Slovenia									Slovénie
Cattle	446	453	471	494	477	473	450	451	Bovins
Goats	15	17	15	22	20	22	23	22[1]	Caprins
Horses	10	12	14	15	17	17	18[2]	20	Chevaux
Pigs	578	592	558	604	600	656	621	534	Porcins
Sheep	72	73	73	96	94	107	106	94[1]	Ovins
Spain									Espagne
Asses, mules or hinnies	257	257	257[1]	255[1]	250[1]	250[1]	250[1]	252[1]	Ânes, mules ou mulets
Cattle	5 884	5 965	6 217	6 411	6 478	6 548	6 653	6 464	Bovins
Goats	3 007	2 779	2 627	2 876	3 047	3 164	2 833	2 905	Caprins
Horses	248	248	248	238	238[1]	238[1]	238[1]	240[1]	Chevaux
Pigs	19 397	21 668	22 418	22 149	23 518	24 056	24 895	24 884	Porcins
Sheep	24 857	24 190	23 965	24 400	23 813	23 486	22 910	22 749	Ovins
Sweden									Suède
Cattle	1 739	1 713	1 684	1 652	1 638	1 607	1 628	1 619	Bovins
Horses	80[1]	80	89	86[1]	85[1]	96	96	96[1]	Chevaux
Pigs	2 286	2 115	1 918	1 891	1 882	1 903	1 818	1 823	Porcins
Sheep	421	437	432	452	427	448	466	479	Ovins
Switzerland									Suisse
Asses, mules or hinnies	2[1]	2[1]	4	4	4	5	5	6	Ânes, mules ou mulets
Cattle	1 641	1 609	1 588	1 611	1 594	1 565	1 570	1 545	Bovins
Goats	60	62	63	63	66	67	71	74	Caprins
Horses	46	49	50	50	51	53	54	55	Chevaux
Pigs	1 487	1 452	1 498	1 548	1 557	1 529	1 538	1 610	Porcins
Sheep	422	424	421	420	430	445	441	446	Ovins
TFYR of Macedonia									L'ex-R.y. Macédoine
Buffaloes	1	1	1	1[1]	1	1	1	1[1]	Buffles
Cattle	289	267	270	265[2]	259	260	255	248	Bovins
Horses	60	60	57	57[1]	57[1]	57[1]	57[1]	57[1]	Chevaux
Pigs	184	197	226	204	196	179	158	156	Porcins
Sheep	1 631	1 315	1 289	1 251	1 234	1 239	1 432	1 244	Ovins
Ukraine									Ukraine
Asses, mules or hinnies	13[1]	12[1]	12[2]	12[1]	11[1]	12[1]	12[1]	12[1]	Ânes, mules ou mulets
Cattle	12 759	11 722	10 627	9 424	9 421	9 108	7 712	6 903	Bovins
Goats	822	828	825	912	998	1 034	965	894	Caprins
Horses	737	721	698	701	693	684	637	591	Chevaux
Pigs	9 479	10 083	10 073	7 652	8 370	9 204	7 322	6 466	Porcins
Sheep	1 540	1 198	1 060	963	967	950	893	875	Ovins
United Kingdom									Royaume-Uni
Cattle	11 519	11 423	11 133	10 600	10 343	10 517	10 551	10 378	Bovins
Goats	77	80	77	76	75	93	89	92	Caprins
Horses[1]	178	180	182	184	184	184	184	184	Chevaux[1]
Pigs	8 146	7 284	6 482	5 845	5 588	5 047	5 161	4 851	Porcins
Sheep	44 471	44 656	42 264	36 716	35 834	35 846	35 848	35 253	Ovins

Region, country or area	1998	1999	2000	2001	2002	2003	2004	2005	Région, pays ou zone
Oceania									**Océanie**
Asses, mules or hinnies	**9**	**9**	**9**	**9**	**9**	**9**	**9**	**9**	**Ânes, mules ou mulets**
Cattle	**36 490**	**36 109**	**37 364**	**37 768**	**38 256**	**37 062**	**37 805**	**38 136**	**Bovins**
Goats	**749**	**711**	**751**	**770**	**868**	**889**	**1 072**	**941**	**Caprins**
Horses	**372**	**366**	**370**	**373**	**372**	**377**	**379**	**381**	**Chevaux**
Pigs	**5 348**	**5 260**	**5 131**	**5 535**	**5 814**	**5 557**	**5 360**	**5 355**	**Porcins**
Sheep	**161 907**	**161 152**	**160 828**	**150 926**	**145 754**	**138 820**	**140 573**	**141 068**	**Ovins**
American Samoa									Samoa américaines
Pigs	11[1]	11[1]	11[1]	11[1]	11[1]	11[1]	11[1]	11	Porcins
Australia									Australie
Asses, mules or hinnies	2[1]	2[1]	2[1]	2[1]	2[1]	2	2	2	Ânes, mules ou mulets
Cattle	26 852	26 578	27 588	27 721	27 870	26 664	27 465	27 782	Bovins
Goats	220	220[1]	260[1]	295[1]	400[1]	420[1]	595	461	Caprins
Horses	220[1]	220[1]	220[1]	220[1]	220[1]	220[1]	219	221	Chevaux
Pigs	2 768	2 626	2 511	2 748	2 940	2 658	2 548	2 538	Porcins
Sheep	117 491	115 456	118 552	110 900	106 166	99 252	101 287	101 125	Ovins
Cook Islands									Iles Cook
Goats	3	3	3	2[1]	2[1]	1	1[1]	1[1]	Caprins
Pigs	40	40	40	40	40	30	32[1]	32[1]	Porcins
Fiji									Fidji
Cattle	345	330[1]	335[1]	340[1]	320[1]	310[1]	310[1]	310[1]	Bovins
Goats	235[1]	237	241	246	250[1]	250[1]	260[1]	260[1]	Caprins
Horses	44[1]	44[1]	44[1]	44[1]	44[1]	44[1]	44[1]	44	Chevaux
Pigs	112	146	135	137	138[1]	139[1]	139[1]	140[1]	Porcins
Sheep[1]	7	7	7	7	6	6	5	5	Ovins[1]
French Polynesia									Polynésie française
Cattle[1]	9	9	11	11	11	12	11	12	Bovins[1]
Goats[1]	16	17	17	17	17	17	17	17	Caprins[1]
Horses	2[1]	2[1]	2[1]	2[1]	2[1]	2[1]	2[1]	2	Chevaux
Pigs[1]	31	34	35	33	30	28	28	27	Porcins[1]
Guam									Guam
Goats	1[1]	1[1]	1[1]	1[1]	1	1	1	1	Caprins
Pigs[1]	4	5	5	5	5	5	5	5	Porcins[1]
Kiribati									Kiribati
Pigs	10[1]	10	11[1]	11[1]	12[1]	12[1]	12[1]	12[1]	Porcins
Micronesia (Fed. States of)									Micronésie (Etats féd. de)
Cattle	14[1]	14[1]	14[1]	14[1]	14[1]	14[1]	14[1]	14	Bovins
Goats[1]	4	4	4	4	4	4	4	4	Caprins[1]
Pigs[1]	32	32	32	32	32	32	32	32	Porcins[1]
Nauru									Nauru
Pigs	3[1]	3[1]	3[1]	3[1]	3[1]	3[1]	3[1]	3	Porcins
New Caledonia									Nouvelle-Calédonie
Cattle	110[1]	110[1]	110[1]	110[1]	111	111[1]	111[1]	111[1]	Bovins
Goats	10[1]	10[1]	10[1]	9[1]	8	8[1]	8[1]	8[1]	Caprins
Horses[1]	12	12	12	12	12	12	12	12	Chevaux[1]
Pigs	27[1]	27[1]	26[1]	26[1]	25	26[1]	26[1]	26[1]	Porcins
Sheep	3[1]	3[1]	3[1]	3[1]	2	2[1]	2[1]	2[1]	Ovins
New Zealand									Nouvelle-Zélande
Cattle	8 873	8 778	9 015	9 281	9 637	9 656	9 599	9 609	Bovins
Goats	228	186	183	163	153	155	153	155[1]	Caprins
Horses	75[1]	70[1]	73[1]	77	76	80	83[1]	83	Chevaux
Pigs	351	369	369	354	342	377	389	341	Porcins
Sheep	44 400	45 680	42 260	40 010	39 572	39 552	39 271	39 928	Ovins
Niue									Nioué
Pigs[1]	2	2	2	2	2	2	2	2	Porcins[1]

34 Livestock — Stocks: thousand head (*continued*)
Cheptel — Effectifs : milliers de têtes (*suite*)

Region, country or area	1998	1999	2000	2001	2002	2003	2004	2005	Région, pays ou zone
Papua New Guinea									Papouasie-Nvl-Guinée
Cattle	86[2]	87[2]	87[2]	88[2]	89[2]	90[1]	91[1]	92[1]	Bovins
Goats	2[2]	2[2]	2[2]	2[2]	2[2]	3[1]	3[1]	3[1]	Caprins
Horses	2[2]	2[2]	2[2]	2[2]	2[2]	2[1]	2[1]	2	Chevaux
Pigs	1 550[2]	1 550[2]	1 550[2]	1 700[2]	1 800[2]	1 800[2]	1 700[1]	1 750[1]	Porcins
Sheep	6[2]	6[2]	6[2]	6[2]	7[2]	7[1]	7[1]	8[1]	Ovins
Samoa									Samoa
Asses, mules or hinnies[1]	7	7	7	7	7	7	7	7	Ânes, mules ou mulets[1]
Cattle	27[1]	28	28[2]	28[1]	28[1]	28[1]	29[1]	29[1]	Bovins
Horses	2[1]	2	2[1]	2[1]	2[1]	2[1]	2[1]	2[1]	Chevaux
Pigs	170[1]	167	170[1]	201	201[1]	201[1]	201[1]	201[1]	Porcins
Solomon Islands[1]									Iles Salomon[1]
Cattle	13	13	13	13	13	13	14	14	Bovins
Pigs	57	58	50	51	51	51	52	53	Porcins
Tokelau									Tokélaou
Pigs	1[1]	1[1]	1[1]	1[1]	1[1]	1[1]	1[1]	1	Porcins
Tonga									Tonga
Cattle	10[1]	10	11[1]	11[1]	11[1]	11[1]	11[1]	11[1]	Bovins
Goats	12[1]	12[2]	13[1]	13[1]	13[1]	13[1]	13[1]	13[1]	Caprins
Horses[1]	11	11	11	11	11	11	11	11	Chevaux[1]
Pigs[1]	81	81	81	81	81	81	81	81	Porcins[1]
Tuvalu									Tuvalu
Pigs	13[1]	13[1]	13[1]	13[1]	14[1]	14[1]	14[1]	14	Porcins
Vanuatu[1]									Vanuatu[1]
Cattle	151	151	151	151	151	152	150	152	Bovins
Goats	12	12	12	12	12	12	12	12	Caprins
Horses	3	3	3	3	3	3	3	3	Chevaux
Pigs	62	62	62	62	62	62	62	62	Porcins
Wallis and Futuna Islands									Iles Wallis et Futuna
Goats[1]	7	7	7	7	7	7	7	7	Caprins[1]
Pigs[1]	25	25	25	25	25	25	25	25	Porcins[1]

Source

Food and Agriculture Organization of the United Nations (FAO), Rome, FAOSTAT data, last accessed February 2007.

Notes

1 FAO estimate.
2 International reliable sources (USDA, WTO, World Bank, IMF).
3 For statistical purposes, the data for China do not include those for the Hong Kong Special Administrative Region (Hong Kong SAR) and Macao Special Administrative Region (Macao SAR).

Source

Organisation des Nations Unies pour l'alimentation et l'agriculture (FAO), Rome, données FAOSTAT, dernier accès février 2007.

Notes

1 Estimation de la FAO.
2 Sources internationales fiables (Département of Agriculture des États-Unis, OMC, Banque mondiale, FMI).
3 Pour la présentation des statistiques, les données pour la Chine ne comprennent pas la Région Administrative Spéciale de Hong Kong (Hong Kong RAS) et la Région Administrative Spéciale de Macao (Macao RAS).

35

Fertilizers

Nitrogen, phosphate and potash: thousand metric tons of plant nutrients

Engrais

Azote, phosphates et potasse : milliers de tonnes d'éléments fertilisants

Country/area and type of fertilizer	Production - Production				Consumption - Consommation				Pays/zone et type d'engrais
	2002	2003	2004	2005	2002	2003	2004	2005	
Albania									**Albanie**
Nitrogen	...	...	...	...	30.9	29.1	31.1	33.8	Azote
Phosphate	...	...	...	...	18.4	20.0	22.2	23.0	Phosphates
Potash	...	...	...	...	0.2	0.1	0.3	0.7	Potasse
Algeria									**Algérie**
Nitrogen	72.6	99.7	153.8	113.2	28.0	17.1	89.4	66.4	Azote
Phosphate	23.0	6.0	53.6	20.4	23.5	6.4	43.0	15.6	Phosphates
Potash	0.0	0.0	0.0	0.0	21.3	21.6	23.6	25.4	Potasse
Angola									**Angola**
Nitrogen	...	...	...	...	2.8	1.8	7.2	3.7	Azote
Phosphate	...	...	...	...	1.0	1.5	3.6	1.5	Phosphates
Potash	...	...	...	...	1.4	2.7	4.0	2.3	Potasse
Argentina									**Argentine**
Nitrogen	523.7	607.5	665.2	659.7	534.6	740.7	864.7	790.3	Azote
Phosphate	...	...	...	...	286.6	420.8	595.2	561.4	Phosphates
Potash	...	...	...	...	21.2	38.8	33.2	43.9	Potasse
Armenia									**Arménie**
Nitrogen	3.0	...	...	...	15.7	10.5	12.5	10.3	Azote
Phosphate	...	...	...	...	^0.0	^0.0	1.2	^0.0	Phosphates
Potash	...	...	...	...	0.0	^0.0	^0.0	^0.0	Potasse
Australia*									**Australie***
Nitrogen	354.5	371.4	400.3	408.0	972.3	932.9	1 056.5	952.2	Azote
Phosphate	637.3	647.2	659.1	617.3	1 077.4	1 019.5	1 116.3	1 041.1	Phosphates
Potash	...	...	...	...	215.6	220.7	258.8	222.1	Potasse
Austria									**Autriche**
Nitrogen	243.0	290.4	266.6	266.6	171.0	182.5	194.0	198.0	Azote
Phosphate	82.6	82.6	82.6	82.6	77.5	63.6	61.1	62.6	Phosphates
Potash	...	...	...	...	75.6	75.8	60.4	62.8	Potasse
Azerbaijan									**Azerbaïdjan**
Nitrogen	...	...	...	...	15.8	15.3	22.6	20.8	Azote
Phosphate	...	...	...	...	1.6	0.3	0.5	7.3	Phosphates
Potash	...	...	...	...	1.9	1.2	2.2	3.9	Potasse
Bangladesh									**Bangladesh**
Nitrogen	1 155.4	1 140.4	1 040.2	1 018.2	1 079.1	1 097.3	1 160.0	1 196.1	Azote
Phosphate	129.0	110.7	86.8	111.8	321.8	319.1	336.9	370.9	Phosphates
Potash	0.0	0.0	0.0	0.0	156.0	162.1	167.0	190.3	Potasse
Barbados									**Barbade**
Nitrogen	...	...	...	...	0.6	0.7	2.8	1.2	Azote
Phosphate	...	...	...	...	0.1	0.4	^0.0	0.1	Phosphates
Potash	...	...	...	...	^0.0	^0.0	^0.0	0.1	Potasse
Belarus									**Bélarus**
Nitrogen	644.4	635.9	665.0	681.0	281.6	320.6	422.5	461.2	Azote
Phosphate	74.0	86.2	114.3	134.7	69.8	70.0	107.1	141.2	Phosphates
Potash	3 811.9	4 276.3	4 712.1	4 885.9	492.2	478.2	492.1	626.5	Potasse
Belize									**Belize**
Nitrogen	...	...	...	...	1.9	20.7	9.0	4.1	Azote
Phosphate	...	...	...	...	2.3	4.6	15.9	1.5	Phosphates
Potash	...	...	...	...	...	1.4	5.0	^0.0	Potasse
Benin									**Bénin**
Nitrogen	...	...	...	...	23.6	1.3	0.1	^0.0	Azote
Phosphate	...	...	...	...	10.4	0.4	0.0	0.0	Phosphates
Potash	...	...	...	...	7.8	0.4	0.0	^0.0	Potasse

Country/area and type of fertilizer	Production - Production				Consumption - Consommation				Pays/zone et type d'engrais
	2002	2003	2004	2005	2002	2003	2004	2005	
Bolivia									Bolivie
Nitrogen	...	...	...	...	6.0	6.2	7.3	12.3	Azote
Phosphate	...	...	...	...	6.5	5.1	5.6	7.8	Phosphates
Potash	...	...	...	...	0.8	1.6	6.3	4.7	Potasse
Bosnia and Herzegovina									Bosnie-Herzégovine
Nitrogen	...	...	...	...	18.6	10.8	33.7	36.1	Azote
Phosphate	...	...	...	...	7.0	3.5	13.1	11.7	Phosphates
Potash	...	...	...	...	7.0	3.7	13.3	11.9	Potasse
Brazil									Brésil
Nitrogen	899.3	849.6	848.2	914.3	1 778.5	2 338.5	2 201.0	2 070.5	Azote
Phosphate	1 410.6	1 735.5	1 821.7	1 636.9	2 258.6	3 101.8	3 414.0	2 513.6	Phosphates
Potash	363.8	377.3	371.5	371.7	2 981.4	3 899.3	4 236.6	3 472.5	Potasse
Bulgaria									Bulgarie
Nitrogen	*270.4	*281.1	*345.5	*383.5	283.6	308.5	372.0	417.7	Azote
Phosphate	120.3	*129.0	*123.6	*134.8	90.6	133.6	125.5	137.6	Phosphates
Potash	0.0	0.0	0.0	0.0	7.5	3.0	3.9	6.3	Potasse
Burkina Faso									Burkina Faso
Nitrogen	...	...	...	...	2.0	22.1	24.5	22.6	Azote
Phosphate	...	...	...	...	0.0	0.1	0.2	20.6	Phosphates
Potash	...	...	...	...	0.0	0.4	0.4	17.9	Potasse
Burundi									Burundi
Nitrogen	0.0	0.0	0.0	0.0	0.5	0.3	0.4	1.1	Azote
Phosphate	0.0	0.0	0.0	0.0	0.8	0.0	0.6	2.3	Phosphates
Potash	0.0	0.0	0.0	0.0	^0.0	^0.0	^0.0	^0.0	Potasse
Cambodia									Cambodge
Nitrogen	...	...	...	...	7.8	5.2	7.5	...	Azote
Phosphate	...	...	...	...	12.8	8.2	11.7	...	Phosphates
Potash	...	...	...	...	1.0	0.9	0.7	0.0	Potasse
Cameroon									Cameroun
Nitrogen	0.0	0.0	0.0	0.0	13.1	20.3	35.9	22.8	Azote
Phosphate	0.0	0.0	0.0	0.0	8.6	11.7	15.7	5.9	Phosphates
Potash	0.0	0.0	0.0	0.0	13.1	14.0	24.1	18.2	Potasse
Canada									Canada
Nitrogen	*3 087.6	*2 905.0	*3 048.1	3 109.0	*1 643.0	*1 649.9	*1 539.5	1 776.7	Azote
Phosphate	*291.8	*337.4	*331.8	278.0	*656.3	*685.8	*610.3	693.1	Phosphates
Potash	*8 134.4	*9 543.8	*10 317.2	8 073.1	*335.9	*349.8	*331.6	328.6	Potasse
Chile									Chili
Nitrogen	115.0	167.6	164.9	162.1	246.3	221.1	339.2	297.4	Azote
Phosphate	...	...	...	...	155.7	186.4	175.1	160.9	Phosphates
Potash	409.0	391.0	387.1	387.9	105.8	87.7	122.1	130.4	Potasse
China									Chine
Nitrogen	27 608.8	28 862.9	30 020.7	30 401.6	29 040.1	28 639.2	28 781.9	30 173.0	Azote
Phosphate	7 791.3	8 848.1	9 542.1	10 439.6	10 036.5	9 773.9	10 148.6	10 880.0	Phosphates
Potash	754.0	878.0	1 200.0	2 148.0	5 109.4	4 943.6	5 837.8	7 813.2	Potasse
Colombia									Colombie
Nitrogen	*84.2	*90.4	*66.4	*65.9	356.7	369.7	351.9	333.0	Azote
Phosphate	*5.4	*10.7	*10.7	*10.7	118.3	123.6	128.2	69.9	Phosphates
Potash	...	...	...	...	208.3	242.0	238.2	63.9	Potasse
Costa Rica									Costa Rica
Nitrogen	...	...	...	...	37.3	65.2	72.9	104.3	Azote
Phosphate	...	...	...	...	23.1	31.6	23.1	17.9	Phosphates
Potash	...	...	...	...	47.0	81.1	68.9	110.5	Potasse
Côte d'Ivoire									Côte d'Ivoire
Nitrogen	...	...	...	...	30.0	20.0	40.6	16.2	Azote
Phosphate	...	...	...	...	27.3	32.8	8.5	10.7	Phosphates
Potash	...	...	...	...	29.6	29.4	27.2	22.9	Potasse

Fertilizers—Nitrogen, phosphate and potash: thousand metric tons of plant nutrients (*continued*)
Engrais—Azote, phosphates et potasse : milliers de tonnes d'éléments fertilisants (*suite*)

Country/area and type of fertilizer	Production - Production				Consumption - Consommation				Pays/zone et type d'engrais
	2002	2003	2004	2005	2002	2003	2004	2005	
Croatia									Croatie
Nitrogen	262.0	216.0	254.9	254.1	129.8	61.1	68.1	57.1	Azote
Phosphate	50.0	50.0	60.0	60.0	39.9	44.0	39.1	24.8	Phosphates
Potash	...	...	...	...	50.8	65.6	70.4	55.8	Potasse
Cuba									Cuba
Nitrogen	2.4	3.8	6.4	3.9	61.8	18.6	29.3	23.3	Azote
Phosphate	1.1	0.9	0.8	1.1	18.1	10.4	5.6	12.9	Phosphates
Potash	1.1	0.9	0.8	1.1	51.6	21.4	17.2	33.6	Potasse
Cyprus									Chypre
Nitrogen	0.0	0.0	0.0	0.0	10.4	11.1	9.5	8.1	Azote
Phosphate	0.0	0.0	0.0	0.0	6.7	6.9	5.9	4.5	Phosphates
Potash	0.0	0.0	0.0	0.0	2.8	3.5	4.0	4.3	Potasse
Czech Republic									République tchèque
Nitrogen	274.2	291.3	304.9	305.2	320.3	289.5	297.0	342.1	Azote
Phosphate	11.6	15.5	23.2	23.2	47.9	52.3	71.2	62.0	Phosphates
Potash	0.0	0.0	0.0	0.0	46.2	46.8	65.1	60.6	Potasse
Denmark									Danemark
Nitrogen	116.2	148.5	92.8	0.0	158.4	218.1	212.5	115.2	Azote
Phosphate	15.0	15.0	7.5	0.0	5.4	15.8	34.3	7.5	Phosphates
Potash	0.0	0.0	0.0	0.0	58.3	75.1	97.1	11.3	Potasse
Ecuador									Equateur
Nitrogen	...	...	...	...	132.3	119.9	135.6	116.3	Azote
Phosphate	...	...	...	...	36.7	33.9	43.4	38.6	Phosphates
Potash	...	...	...	...	58.9	50.0	98.8	40.6	Potasse
Egypt									Egypte
Nitrogen	1 557.5	1 558.8	1 584.4	1 568.1	1 070.0	1 598.4	1 656.3	1 915.0	Azote
Phosphate	187.0	200.0	309.4	310.1	142.2	178.4	235.2	258.2	Phosphates
Potash	...	...	5.4	4.5	57.7	47.5	39.3	26.0	Potasse
El Salvador									El Salvador
Nitrogen	...	...	...	...	32.1	35.1	44.8	33.8	Azote
Phosphate	...	...	...	...	14.2	10.1	11.2	17.9	Phosphates
Potash	...	...	...	...	0.0[1]	5.9	0.0[1]	20.3	Potasse
Eritrea									Erythrée
Nitrogen	...	...	...	...	2.8	0.7	^0.0	1.4	Azote
Phosphate	...	...	...	...	0.7	0.1	0.0	...	Phosphates
Potash	...	...	...	...	...	0.1	0.0	...	Potasse
Estonia									Estonie
Nitrogen	24.3	34.0	59.3	96.1	38.9	90.4	100.5	87.4	Azote
Phosphate	...	...	...	...	160.1	145.6	145.9	182.0	Phosphates
Potash	...	...	...	...	9.3	8.5	22.3	18.3	Potasse
Ethiopia									Ethiopie
Nitrogen	...	...	...	...	97.6	34.1	14.8	10.2	Azote
Phosphate	...	...	...	...	70.0	28.2	3.2	23.9	Phosphates
Potash	...	...	...	...	0.0	0.0	0.0	0.0	Potasse
Fiji									Fidji
Nitrogen	...	...	...	...	9.4	3.2	7.7	6.6	Azote
Phosphate	...	...	...	...	2.7	0.1	^0.0	^0.0	Phosphates
Potash	...	...	...	...	0.1	^0.0	^0.0	^0.0	Potasse
Finland									Finlande
Nitrogen	274.0	278.7	278.7	291.8	179.0	163.9	173.9	192.5	Azote
Phosphate	96.0	76.8	76.8	73.0	48.2	22.2	40.5	29.8	Phosphates
Potash	0.0	0.0	0.0	0.0	73.0	76.0	80.4	77.9	Potasse
France									France
Nitrogen	1 000.0	1 228.4	1 083.7	1 131.1	2 203.2	2 375.4	2 373.0	2 320.1	Azote
Phosphate	157.3	154.1	225.8	188.6	713.3	746.0	768.8	627.2	Phosphates
Potash	130.0	0.0	0.0	0.0	965.1	978.4	979.9	812.6	Potasse

Fertilizers—Nitrogen, phosphate and potash: thousand metric tons of plant nutrients (*continued*)
Engrais—Azote, phosphates et potasse : milliers de tonnes d'éléments fertilisants (*suite*)

Country/area and type of fertilizer	Production - Production				Consumption - Consommation				Pays/zone et type d'engrais
	2002	2003	2004	2005	2002	2003	2004	2005	
Gabon									Gabon
Nitrogen	...	...	...	...	0.6	0.2	0.7	0.1	Azote
Phosphate	...	...	...	...	0.2	0.1	0.3	^0.0	Phosphates
Potash	...	...	...	...	1.1	0.8	0.7	0.7	Potasse
Georgia									Géorgie
Nitrogen	83.0	90.0	130.0	115.3	21.4	24.2	20.5	27.7	Azote
Phosphate	...	...	...	...	2.6	0.4	0.6	1.6	Phosphates
Potash	...	...	...	...	2.4	...	0.7	1.0	Potasse
Germany									Allemagne
Nitrogen	1 256.3	1 121.0	1 160.6	1 254.3	1 787.8	1 827.8	1 778.4	1 785.0	Azote
Phosphate	60.0	60.0	60.0	60.0	327.4	409.4	359.2	314.5	Phosphates
Potash	3 201.2	3 261.5	3 345.2	3 246.6	479.7	486.5	478.4	426.1	Potasse
Ghana									Ghana
Nitrogen	...	...	...	...	15.8	6.6	7.9	15.9	Azote
Phosphate	...	...	...	...	2.3	8.1	13.9	6.0	Phosphates
Potash	...	...	...	...	2.3	3.8	7.4	9.6	Potasse
Greece									Grèce
Nitrogen	215.0	209.6	167.3	166.1	272.0	284.7	281.6	276.0	Azote
Phosphate	91.0	83.7	83.7	83.7	120.5	109.0	115.7	108.8	Phosphates
Potash	0.0	0.0	0.0	0.0	32.4	45.9	82.3	49.1	Potasse
Guatemala									Guatemala
Nitrogen	...	...	...	...	84.2	118.1	119.5	131.5	Azote
Phosphate	...	...	...	...	46.2	46.7	52.8	60.4	Phosphates
Potash	...	...	...	...	11.9	12.8	6.8	6.7	Potasse
Guinea									Guinée
Nitrogen	...	...	...	...	1.8	1.7	2.5	2.4	Azote
Phosphate	...	...	...	...	0.3	0.2	0.8	0.5	Phosphates
Potash	...	...	...	...	0.3	0.1	0.8	0.5	Potasse
Guyana									Guyana
Nitrogen	...	...	...	...	13.6	9.6	19.1	6.2	Azote
Phosphate	...	...	...	...	1.3	0.7	0.5	1.6	Phosphates
Potash	...	...	...	...	^0.0	^0.0	0.5	^0.0	Potasse
Honduras									Honduras
Nitrogen	...	...	...	...	0.6	51.7	42.3	44.7	Azote
Phosphate	...	...	...	...	^0.0	6.3	8.8	14.7	Phosphates
Potash	...	...	...	...	0.0[1]	0.7	2.3	3.0	Potasse
Hungary									Hongrie
Nitrogen	210.1	205.3	266.1	311.3	372.6	306.7	373.0	367.8	Azote
Phosphate	22.3	0.0	0.0	0.0	100.3	91.4	109.2	94.2	Phosphates
Potash	0.0	0.0	0.0	0.0	89.9	93.8	109.5	105.4	Potasse
Iceland									Islande
Nitrogen	...	...	...	...	7.7	7.2	10.3	7.2	Azote
Phosphate	...	...	...	...	4.8	3.4	8.7	5.0	Phosphates
Potash	...	...	...	...	3.6	2.6	6.0	5.5	Potasse
India									Inde
Nitrogen	10 391.7	10 468.7	11 205.6	11 218.2	10 517.0	10 641.1	11 609.9	12 597.9	Azote
Phosphate	3 802.1	3 541.9	3 945.6	4 092.6	4 029.4	3 905.4	4 238.9	5 226.4	Phosphates
Potash	0.0	0.0	0.0	0.0	1 568.4	1 546.3	2 054.7	2 764.0	Potasse
Indonesia									Indonésie
Nitrogen	2 867.9	2 670.0	2 640.6	2 698.7	2 533.1	2 232.1	2 580.5	2 529.2	Azote
Phosphate	215.9	249.8	261.8	292.2	327.3	321.6	421.6	419.7	Phosphates
Potash	0.0	0.0	0.0	0.0	304.7	330.4	671.2	493.9	Potasse
Iran (Islamic Rep. of)									Iran (Rép. islamique d')
Nitrogen	768.1	764.3	721.5	652.2	840.3	851.7	0.0[1]	905.0	Azote
Phosphate	146.7	153.6	139.0	182.8	200.4	184.9	207.0	240.0	Phosphates
Potash	...	...	...	...	94.1	101.5	198.6	115.1	Potasse

Country/area and type of fertilizer	Production - Production				Consumption - Consommation				Pays/zone et type d'engrais
	2002	2003	2004	2005	2002	2003	2004	2005	
Ireland									Irlande
Nitrogen	208.0	0.0	0.0	0.0	358.5	353.1	331.0	346.5	Azote
Phosphate	...	...	...	...	118.0	112.0	102.8	77.5	Phosphates
Potash	...	...	...	...	73.4	70.6	100.9	137.3	Potasse
Israel									Israël
Nitrogen	84.6	86.3	91.6	86.7	32.8	39.1	35.8	38.3	Azote
Phosphate	267.0	365.0	348.9	424.3	0.0[1]	89.6	33.4	80.6	Phosphates
Potash	1 918.0	1 958.3	2 136.5	2 260.4	532.4	858.6	210.9	577.8	Potasse
Italy									Italie
Nitrogen	400.2	474.6	463.7	413.2	728.5	773.4	742.4	616.8	Azote
Phosphate	50.0	50.0	50.0	50.0	457.3	457.3	409.6	312.5	Phosphates
Potash	0.0	0.0	0.0	0.0	384.6	374.8	344.8	285.7	Potasse
Jamaica									Jamaïque
Nitrogen	...	...	...	...	8.2	0.3	9.8	1.7	Azote
Phosphate	...	...	...	...	4.2	0.2	6.2	0.0[1]	Phosphates
Potash	...	...	...	...	0.4	0.3	0.4	3.7	Potasse
Japan									Japon
Nitrogen	854.5	795.7	791.7	766.5	556.6	567.9	547.0	547.2	Azote
Phosphate	337.9	326.3	312.4	305.3	661.2	*629.9	647.9	629.4	Phosphates
Potash*	0.0	0.0	0.0	0.0	516.2	534.5	516.2	...	Potasse*
Jordan									Jordanie
Nitrogen	103.0	90.5	118.4	118.3	88.8	56.3	21.5	21.9	Azote
Phosphate	263.1	231.4	302.7	302.2	199.2	105.8	38.8	43.0	Phosphates
Potash	1 173.6	1 176.0	1 157.4	1 097.4	22.2	0.0[1]	39.2	80.2	Potasse
Kazakhstan									Kazakhstan
Nitrogen	16.4	20.9	38.0	20.5	66.4	70.2	70.5	68.6	Azote
Phosphate	78.0	112.5	120.0	81.1	54.0	62.5	107.2	72.4	Phosphates
Potash	...	...	...	...	2.9	1.9	2.8	2.8	Potasse
Kenya									Kenya
Nitrogen	...	...	...	...	62.7	118.5	74.6	38.9	Azote
Phosphate	...	...	...	...	75.5	293.8	103.7	44.2	Phosphates
Potash	...	...	...	...	0.0[1]	0.0[1]	4.6	10.5	Potasse
Korea, Republic of									Corée, République de
Nitrogen	224.7	206.0	252.8	183.0	363.4	358.9	394.3	354.2	Azote
Phosphate	323.1	292.3	324.6	271.3	146.3	143.5	157.0	162.3	Phosphates
Potash	0.0	0.0	0.0	0.0	180.1	175.9	196.0	205.9	Potasse
Kuwait									Koweït
Nitrogen	255.3	350.5	336.7	374.4	21.2	...	0.0[1]	47.8	Azote
Potash	...	...	...	...	0.0	0.0	0.0	0.0	Potasse
Kyrgyzstan									Kirghizistan
Nitrogen	...	...	...	...	9.2	14.7	16.3	28.6	Azote
Phosphate	...	...	...	...	0.2	0.1	0.2	^0.0	Phosphates
Potash^	...	...	...	...	0.0	0.0	0.0	0.0	Potasse^
Latvia									Lettonie
Nitrogen	0.0	0.0	0.0	0.0	36.0	59.2	62.3	45.9	Azote
Phosphate	0.0	0.0	0.0	0.0	4.5	11.8	17.0	16.4	Phosphates
Potash	0.0	0.0	0.0	0.0	8.6	17.2	19.8	16.7	Potasse
Lebanon									Liban
Nitrogen	...	...	...	...	19.7	23.6	23.8	15.8	Azote
Phosphate	89.5	82.5	120.9	116.8	18.8	0.0[1]	0.0[1]	0.0[1]	Phosphates
Potash	...	...	...	...	8.1	8.2	9.5	9.4	Potasse
Libyan Arab Jamah.									Jamah. arabe libyenne
Nitrogen	388.7	379.5	381.3	384.1	76.1	32.4	47.1	75.6	Azote
Phosphate	...	...	...	...	39.2	21.6	36.8	36.8	Phosphates
Potash	...	...	...	...	5.0	6.1	6.5	5.1	Potasse

Fertilizers—Nitrogen, phosphate and potash: thousand metric tons of plant nutrients (*continued*)
Engrais—Azote, phosphates et potasse : milliers de tonnes d'éléments fertilisants (*suite*)

Country/area and type of fertilizer	Production - Production				Consumption - Consommation				Pays/zone et type d'engrais
	2002	2003	2004	2005	2002	2003	2004	2005	
Lithuania									Lituanie
Nitrogen	506.6	548.3	569.8	663.2	13.7	38.7	50.4	0.0[1]	Azote
Phosphate	343.7	381.9	392.7	400.1	67.4	67.3	94.1	121.1	Phosphates
Potash	41.8	45.9	48.7	42.3	99.5	118.7	136.3	107.3	Potasse
Luxembourg									Luxembourg
Nitrogen	0.0	0.0	0.0	0.0	26.1	26.6	24.6	22.4	Azote
Phosphate	0.0	0.0	0.0	0.0	4.9	3.5	4.2	3.9	Phosphates
Potash	0.0	0.0	0.0	0.0	5.1	4.7	3.4	3.1	Potasse
Madagascar									Madagascar
Nitrogen	...	...	...	...	2.6	4.1	2.7	7.2	Azote
Phosphate	...	...	...	...	1.8	0.9	1.9	4.3	Phosphates
Potash	...	...	...	...	1.8	1.3	1.9	4.3	Potasse
Malawi									Malawi
Nitrogen	...	...	...	...	34.1	39.5	25.9	56.5	Azote
Phosphate	...	...	...	...	7.1	7.3	7.1	18.7	Phosphates
Potash	...	...	...	...	7.2	5.0	4.0	16.6	Potasse
Malaysia									Malaisie
Nitrogen	584.8	582.0	481.0	542.7	462.4	474.1	829.1	696.7	Azote
Phosphate	*91.8	91.3	74.5	85.2	123.8	113.0	82.7	132.6	Phosphates
Potash	...	...	...	...	603.7	737.4	855.4	688.4	Potasse
Malta									Malte
Nitrogen	...	...	...	...	0.6	0.5	0.7	0.5	Azote
Phosphate	...	...	...	...	0.2	0.2	0.3	0.1	Phosphates
Potash	...	...	...	...	0.2	0.2	0.3	0.1	Potasse
Mauritius									Maurice
Nitrogen	15.3	8.6	2.6	0.0	12.7	6.9	2.2	9.7	Azote
Phosphate	...	0.0	0.0	0.0	0.7	7.1	0.9	5.3	Phosphates
Potash	...	0.0	0.0	0.0	8.6	15.5	10.6	10.7	Potasse
Mexico									Mexique
Nitrogen	379.2	370.5	310.5	246.8	1 184.4	1 206.1	1 169.8	1 098.8	Azote
Phosphate	98.4	99.0	99.1	83.4	466.3	481.8	496.3	447.0	Phosphates
Potash	0.0	0.0	0.0	0.0	202.9	182.0	243.3	185.0	Potasse
Mongolia									Mongolie
Nitrogen	...	...	...	...	4.4	3.7	5.5	4.0	Azote
Phosphate	...	...	...	...	0.0	0.0	^0.0	0.1	Phosphates
Potash	...	...	...	...	0.0	^0.0	^0.0	0.1	Potasse
Morocco									Maroc
Nitrogen	338.7	308.0	329.2	264.1	248.2	207.5	263.6	184.7	Azote
Phosphate	1 148.3	1 118.4	1 057.2	1 042.1	233.2	219.5	256.2	126.7	Phosphates
Potash	0.0	0.0	0.0	0.0	69.5	73.8	68.4	49.6	Potasse
Mozambique									Mozambique
Nitrogen	...	...	...	...	17.7	25.0	16.3	6.4	Azote
Phosphate	...	...	...	...	2.0	6.5	4.2	0.4	Phosphates
Potash	...	...	...	...	6.9	3.9	3.9	0.3	Potasse
Myanmar									Myanmar
Nitrogen	5.1	7.9	6.6	2.1	3.1	8.6	6.6	2.1	Azote
Phosphate	...	...	...	...	4.6	4.4	^0.0	^0.0	Phosphates
Potash	...	...	...	...	8.4	9.0	1.1	...	Potasse
Namibia									Namibie
Nitrogen	...	...	...	...	2.9	0.8	1.9	1.0	Azote
Phosphate	...	...	...	...	0.1	0.2	0.3	0.3	Phosphates
Potash	...	...	...	...	0.1	0.1	0.3	0.2	Potasse
Nepal									Népal
Nitrogen	0.0	0.0	0.0	0.0	37.3	17.8	15.1	8.0	Azote
Phosphate	0.0	0.0	0.0	0.0	18.3	17.8	11.2	9.8	Phosphates
Potash	0.0	0.0	0.0	0.0	0.0	1.4	1.4	4.9	Potasse

Country/area and type of fertilizer	Production - Production				Consumption - Consommation				Pays/zone et type d'engrais
	2002	2003	2004	2005	2002	2003	2004	2005	
Netherlands									Pays-Bas
Nitrogen	1 427.1	1 584.7	1 534.7	1 508.6	206.3	289.8	274.1	265.4	Azote
Phosphate	*138.5	*141.4	*142.2	*109.5	92.3	53.8	56.9	177.5	Phosphates
Potash	0.0	0.0	0.0	0.0	355.0	200.6	149.0	122.9	Potasse
New Zealand									Nouvelle-Zélande
Nitrogen	114.0	120.0	121.0	116.3	308.1	346.9	388.2	423.2	Azote
Phosphate	286.8	297.0	328.0	339.2	402.4	441.4	486.9	472.8	Phosphates
Potash	0.0	0.0	0.0	0.0	163.7	157.5	158.6	157.9	Potasse
Nicaragua									Nicaragua
Nitrogen	0.0	0.0	0.0	0.0	35.2	36.7	33.4	36.2	Azote
Phosphate	0.0	0.0	0.0	0.0	14.4	20.1	15.8	11.1	Phosphates
Potash	0.0	0.0	0.0	0.0	6.3	7.8	13.3	8.8	Potasse
Niger									Niger
Nitrogen	...	...	...	...	6.5	4.3	2.4	3.0	Azote
Phosphate	...	...	...	...	1.8	2.1	2.1	1.3	Phosphates
Potash	...	...	...	...	0.2	0.0	0.6	0.3	Potasse
Nigeria									Nigéria
Nitrogen	...	...	...	...	94.4	137.6	101.0	115.0	Azote
Phosphate	...	...	...	...	41.4	49.4	14.0	58.9	Phosphates
Potash	...	...	...	...	30.4	42.7	37.1	41.3	Potasse
Norway									Norvège
Nitrogen	329.5	357.0	367.7	326.0	101.3	104.2	105.1	106.9	Azote
Phosphate	254.8	266.2	286.5	255.8	12.6	12.6	12.8	12.7	Phosphates
Potash	0.0	0.0	0.0	0.0	45.1	46.3	46.3	45.9	Potasse
Pakistan									Pakistan
Nitrogen	2 192.0	2 273.0	2 244.6	2 475.9	2 385.0	2 479.1	2 502.6	3 073.7	Azote
Phosphate	111.0	254.0	348.0	323.4	647.4	785.9	719.0	955.7	Phosphates
Potash	12.0	13.0	...	15.2	10.7	59.5	...	40.0	Potasse
Panama									Panama
Nitrogen	0.0	0.0	0.0	0.0	15.2	17.6	15.2	15.6	Azote
Phosphate	0.0	0.0	0.0	0.0	4.1	5.3	2.4	1.6	Phosphates
Potash	0.0	0.0	0.0	0.0	2.8	4.5	5.5	1.6	Potasse
Paraguay									Paraguay
Nitrogen	...	...	...	...	34.9	41.7	50.7	41.9	Azote
Phosphate	...	...	...	...	68.4	94.6	113.8	103.9	Phosphates
Potash	...	...	...	...	49.8	81.0	99.8	81.8	Potasse
Peru									Pérou
Nitrogen	...	...	...	...	210.6	204.1	210.9	180.4	Azote
Phosphate	0.6	0.6	0.5	0.4	50.3	62.7	72.6	65.9	Phosphates
Potash	...	...	...	...	45.7	48.9	47.1	55.9	Potasse
Philippines									Philippines
Nitrogen	207.8	160.0	155.5	136.5	445.2	612.9	679.4	561.6	Azote
Phosphate	193.7	159.7	155.9	132.4	227.1	241.3	178.7	161.3	Phosphates
Potash	...	...	...	...	49.9	84.1	90.8	89.8	Potasse
Poland									Pologne
Nitrogen	1 035.1	1 128.5	1 166.7	1 218.9	906.0	625.0	871.4	747.0	Azote
Phosphate	441.1	455.2	493.0	435.3	326.8	312.1	405.5	327.7	Phosphates
Potash	0.0	0.0	0.0	0.0	417.9	454.5	618.7	480.3	Potasse
Portugal									Portugal
Nitrogen	123.4	126.9	122.0	104.6	196.2	177.1	180.7	117.6	Azote
Phosphate	48.0	48.0	48.0	48.0	78.4	71.9	60.7	62.0	Phosphates
Potash	0.0	0.0	0.0	0.0	48.9	42.6	45.1	36.2	Potasse
Republic of Moldova									Rép. de Moldova
Nitrogen	...	...	...	...	21.3	12.7	21.3	21.6	Azote
Phosphate	...	...	...	...	0.8	1.7	2.2	4.0	Phosphates
Potash	...	...	...	...	0.5	0.9	1.2	1.9	Potasse

35 Fertilizers — Nitrogen, phosphate and potash: thousand metric tons of plant nutrients (*continued*)

Engrais — Azote, phosphates et potasse : milliers de tonnes d'éléments fertilisants (*suite*)

Country/area and type of fertilizer	Production - Production 2002	2003	2004	2005	Consumption - Consommation 2002	2003	2004	2005	Pays/zone et type d'engrais
Romania									Roumanie
Nitrogen	806.1	1 035.0	772.3	1 194.1	239.1	252.1	270.1	299.2	Azote
Phosphate	67.8	...	0.1	...	73.0	95.1	94.1	138.1	Phosphates
Potash	...	...	...	...	14.1	15.1	15.8	24.1	Potasse
Russian Federation									Fédération de Russie
Nitrogen	4 749.0	4 623.6	5 209.1	5 398.9	654.2	512.8	774.5	791.7	Azote
Phosphate	*2 438.7	*2 620.2	*2 821.4	*2 702.6	313.2	296.0	333.9	523.6	Phosphates
Potash	4 445.3	4 797.2	5 657.0	6 322.9	705.9	467.5	676.0	625.2	Potasse
Saudi Arabia									Arabie saoudite
Nitrogen	1 290.0	1 299.7	1 250.3	1 368.5	98.2	250.3	230.7	182.8	Azote
Phosphate	124.0	152.8	116.0	135.4	104.5	164.7	130.5	136.9	Phosphates
Potash	0.0	0.0	0.0	0.0	0.6	14.1	6.3	9.0	Potasse
Senegal									Sénégal
Nitrogen	*15.0	*25.0	*31.2	*10.0	19.4	14.2	44.8	35.3	Azote
Phosphate	*31.8	*40.5	*40.0	*20.0	9.3	12.1	15.0	14.6	Phosphates
Potash	0.0	*0.0	*0.0	*0.0	7.3	7.5	8.3	15.0	Potasse
Slovakia									Slovaquie
Nitrogen	213.8	257.0	297.1	289.4	61.6	100.6	73.0	120.4	Azote
Phosphate	...	...	...	...	22.7	16.8	22.3	18.7	Phosphates
Potash	...	...	...	...	21.9	15.8	19.9	17.4	Potasse
Slovenia									Slovénie
Nitrogen	0.4	0.3	0.4	^0.0	32.2	29.2	29.5	29.2	Azote
Phosphate	^0.0	^0.0	^0.0	^0.0	17.6	15.3	15.6	14.7	Phosphates
Potash	^0.0	0.0	^0.0	^0.0	26.0	22.8	23.1	21.5	Potasse
South Africa									Afrique du Sud
Nitrogen	298.4	310.0	259.2	281.5	338.5	521.4	412.5	393.5	Azote
Phosphate	280.0	364.0	336.0	313.5	157.2	171.9	287.6	212.3	Phosphates
Potash	...	...	...	...	152.9	107.3	138.2	60.1	Potasse
Spain									Espagne
Nitrogen	772.1	791.5	714.8	748.0	976.6	1 132.6	1 013.2	871.8	Azote
Phosphate	382.4	387.6	366.8	343.0	562.8	589.0	550.4	485.4	Phosphates
Potash	407.2	505.1	553.2	494.6	473.1	485.1	503.9	405.2	Potasse
Sri Lanka									Sri Lanka
Nitrogen	...	...	...	...	188.3	150.7	163.2	182.8	Azote
Phosphate	10.5	10.5	10.7	11.0	35.2	37.6	34.8	36.1	Phosphates
Potash	...	...	...	...	61.6	61.2	60.8	62.4	Potasse
Sudan									Soudan
Nitrogen	0.0	0.0	0.0	0.0	54.4	57.5	74.6	39.7	Azote
Phosphate	0.0	0.0	0.0	0.0	2.9	5.6	8.4	10.3	Phosphates
Potash	0.0	0.0	0.0	0.0	0.0	0.0	0.0	0.2	Potasse
Suriname									Suriname
Nitrogen	...	...	...	...	4.1	5.8	6.3	2.7	Azote
Phosphate	...	...	...	...	0.2	0.4	0.4	0.2	Phosphates
Potash	...	...	...	...	0.1	0.1	0.2	0.2	Potasse
Sweden									Suède
Nitrogen	62.9	57.1	59.2	53.2	167.4	213.2	171.9	153.9	Azote
Phosphate	24.0	24.0	24.0	24.0	38.0	48.1	61.7	52.1	Phosphates
Potash	...	...	...	...	44.2	53.4	54.9	34.2	Potasse
Switzerland									Suisse
Nitrogen	...	...	...	...	40.5	40.8	52.2	51.3	Azote
Phosphate	...	...	...	...	15.9	15.6	11.7	13.4	Phosphates
Potash	...	...	...	...	23.7	20.1	25.6	26.8	Potasse
Syrian Arab Republic									Rép. arabe syrienne
Nitrogen	154.5	131.9	112.5	129.2	221.6	220.5	288.1	295.7	Azote
Phosphate	85.1	107.6	103.6	127.8	91.5	115.5	112.4	182.4	Phosphates
Potash	...	...	...	...	0.8	5.9	2.2	1.9	Potasse

Country/area and type of fertilizer	Production - Production 2002	2003	2004	2005	Consumption - Consommation 2002	2003	2004	2005	Pays/zone et type d'engrais
Thailand									Thaïlande
Nitrogen	108.0	109.0	130.9	111.0	1 018.8	1 253.6	1 153.1	1 045.1	Azote
Phosphate	80.0	51.4	57.2	57.2	408.2	562.0	469.0	322.0	Phosphates
Potash	...	...	...	...	273.8	452.0	386.5	356.9	Potasse
TFYR of Macedonia									L'ex-R.y. Macédoine
Nitrogen	...	...	...	...	9.0	9.3	6.0	8.4	Azote
Phosphate	...	...	...	...	0.0[1]	1.4	1.2	2.5	Phosphates
Potash	...	...	...	...	6.4	2.5	0.8	1.9	Potasse
Togo									Togo
Nitrogen	...	...	...	...	4.9	6.2	4.2	7.0	Azote
Phosphate	...	...	...	...	3.7	5.7	1.8	6.7	Phosphates
Potash	...	...	...	...	3.7	5.7	1.8	6.7	Potasse
Trinidad and Tobago									Trinité-et-Tobago
Nitrogen	310.2	297.8	285.0	344.0	22.6	59.9	23.6	65.8	Azote
Phosphate	...	...	...	...	0.5	0.2	^0.0	0.1	Phosphates
Potash	...	...	...	...	0.7	1.1	0.5	1.0	Potasse
Tunisia									Tunisie
Nitrogen	273.7	287.0	285.0	251.7	37.5	52.6	59.8	70.6	Azote
Phosphate	968.3	1 009.7	1 014.2	916.0	24.8	39.2	43.6	103.9	Phosphates
Potash	...	...	...	...	7.6	9.5	1.3	1.3	Potasse
Turkey*									Turquie*
Nitrogen	651.7	561.9	515.7	528.7	1 267.1	1 358.4	1 351.0	1 381.8	Azote
Phosphate	311.2	367.0	222.2	243.9	339.5	548.3	415.4	519.1	Phosphates
Potash	0.0	0.0	0.0	0.0	84.7	108.5	127.2	130.3	Potasse
Uganda									Ouganda
Nitrogen	...	...	...	...	3.7	4.3	4.0	2.6	Azote
Phosphate	...	...	...	...	2.1	3.0	3.3	2.0	Phosphates
Potash	...	...	...	...	1.7	2.0	1.5	1.2	Potasse
Ukraine									Ukraine
Nitrogen	2 239.3	2 393.8	2 316.7	2 534.5	443.5	329.2	351.7	457.1	Azote
Phosphate	...	...	...	...	33.1	43.1	19.0	21.1	Phosphates
Potash	...	1.0	1.7	...	42.4	76.2	104.0	126.2	Potasse
United Kingdom									Royaume-Uni
Nitrogen	679.4	668.3	653.4	660.4	1 182.6	1 102.2	1 138.2	1 066.5	Azote
Phosphate	197.5	183.5	168.6	164.5	272.7	269.0	273.4	245.1	Phosphates
Potash	783.8	835.7	792.7	655.8	390.7	373.8	379.5	348.8	Potasse
United Rep. of Tanzania									Rép.-Unie de Tanzanie
Nitrogen	...	...	...	...	23.4	35.4	31.8	67.8	Azote
Phosphate	...	...	...	...	3.4	5.0	13.8	19.8	Phosphates
Potash	...	...	...	...	3.6	3.2	7.7	7.8	Potasse
United States									Etats-Unis
Nitrogen[2]	9 386.5	8 691.0	9 016.8	7 652.5	10 969.9	11 818.7	11 191.6	10 926.1	Azote[2]
Phosphate	10 391.9	10 641.4	10 535.2	9 804.0	3 892.3	4 376.8	4 207.6	4 063.0	Phosphates
Potash	822.8	793.8	887.2	801.7	4 491.0	5 007.8	4 693.3	4 284.6	Potasse
Uruguay									Uruguay
Nitrogen	...	...	...	...	26.0	52.4	73.4	66.8	Azote
Phosphate	12.0	12.0	12.0	12.0	57.9	83.6	109.1	113.6	Phosphates
Potash	...	...	...	...	0.4	4.0	8.3	5.4	Potasse
Venezuela (Bolivarian Rep. of)									Venezuela (Rép. bolivar. du)
Nitrogen	539.5	542.2	715.7	705.0	258.3	327.1	263.2	282.0	Azote
Phosphate	36.0	30.0	35.0	40.0	43.1	45.0	139.3	79.6	Phosphates
Potash	0.0	...	...	...	59.5	67.0	100.6	77.1	Potasse
Viet Nam									Viet Nam
Nitrogen	49.2	*68.1	*218.5	*424.1	1 150.3	1 231.5	1 299.3	1 098.8	Azote
Phosphate	*189.3	*206.3	*223.1	*249.0	511.5	591.3	543.7	530.1	Phosphates
Potash	...	...	...	...	351.0	430.0	464.5	356.0	Potasse

Fertilizers—Nitrogen, phosphate and potash: thousand metric tons of plant nutrients (*continued*)

Engrais—Azote, phosphates et potasse : milliers de tonnes d'éléments fertilisants (*suite*)

Country/area and type of fertilizer	Production - Production				Consumption - Consommation				Pays/zone et type d'engrais
	2002	2003	2004	2005	2002	2003	2004	2005	
Yemen									Yémen
Nitrogen	...	...	...	...	11.3	4.9	1.9	2.0	Azote
Phosphate	...	...	...	...	...	0.1	0.6	0.5	Phosphates
Potash	...	...	...	...	0.3	0.7	0.7	0.3	Potasse
Zimbabwe									Zimbabwe
Nitrogen	61.1	55.4	46.7	41.5	70.7	65.7	53.3	58.3	Azote
Phosphate	38.3	27.2	17.1	17.1	48.1	34.9	22.3	27.5	Phosphates
Potash	...	...	...	...	11.5	10.6	9.0	23.2	Potasse

Source

Food and Agriculture Organization of the United Nations (FAO), Rome, FAOSTAT data, last accessed July 2007.

Notes

1 Apparent consumption has been set to zero due to utilization from stockpiles.

2 There might be double counting of ammonia.

Source

Organisation des Nations Unies pour l'alimentation et l'agriculture (FAO), Rome, données FAOSTAT, dernier accès juillet 2007.

Notes

1 La consommation apparente a été mise à zéro en raison de l'utilisation des réserves.

2 Il peut y avoir double comptage de l'ammoniaque.

Technical notes: tables 30-35

The series shown on agriculture and fishing have been furnished by the Food and Agriculture Organization of the United Nations (FAO). They refer mainly to the long-term trends in the growth of agricultural output and the food supply, the output of principal agricultural commodities and fish production.

Agricultural production is defined to include all crops and livestock products except those used for seed and fodder and other intermediate uses in agriculture; for example deductions are made for eggs used for hatching. Intermediate input of seeds and fodder and similar items refer to both domestically produced and imported commodities. For further details, reference may be made to *FAO Statistical Yearbook*. FAO data are also available through the Internet at http://faostat.fao.org.

Table 30: "Agriculture" relates to the production of all crops and livestock products. The "Food Index" includes those commodities which are considered edible and contain nutrients.

The index numbers of agricultural output and food production are calculated by the Laspeyres formula with the base year period 1999-2001. The latter is provided in order to diminish the impact of annual fluctuations in agricultural output during base years on the indices for the period. Production quantities of each commodity are weighted by 1999-2001 average national producer prices and summed for each year. The index numbers are based on production data for a calendar year. These may differ in some instances from those actually produced and published by the individual countries themselves due to variations in concepts, coverage, weights and methods of calculation. Efforts have been made to estimate these methodological differences to achieve a better international comparability of data.

Detailed data on agricultural production are published by FAO in its *Statistical Yearbook*.

Table 31: The data on the production of cereals relate to crops harvested for dry grain only. Cereals harvested for hay, green feed or used for grazing are excluded.

Table 32: The data on roundwood refer to wood in the rough, wood in its natural state as felled or otherwise harvested, with or without bark, round, split, roughly squared or in other form (i.e. roots, stumps, burls, etc.). It may also be impregnated (e.g. telegraph poles) or roughly shaped or pointed. It comprises all wood obtained from removals, i.e. the quantities removed from forests and from trees outside the forest, including wood recovered from natural, felling and logging losses during the period—calendar year or forest year.

Table 33: The data cover (i) capture production from marine and inland fisheries and (ii) aquaculture, and are expressed in terms of live weight. They include fish, crustaceans and molluscs but exclude sponges, corals, pearls, seaweed, crocodiles, and aquatic mammals (such as whales and dolphins).

Notes techniques : tableaux 30 à 35

Les séries présentées sur l'agriculture et la pêche ont été fournies par l'Organisation des Nations Unies pour l'alimentation et l'agriculture (FAO) et portent principalement sur les tendances à long terme de la croissance de la production agricole et des approvisionnements alimentaires, et sur la production des principales denrées agricoles et la production halieutique.

La production agricole se définit comme comprenant l'ensemble des produits agricoles et des produits de l'élevage à l'exception de ceux utilisés comme semences et comme aliments pour les animaux, et pour les autres utilisations intermédiaires en agriculture; par exemple, on déduit les œufs utilisés pour la reproduction. L'apport intermédiaire de semences et d'aliments pour les animaux et d'autres éléments similaires se rapportent à la fois à des produits locaux et importés. Pour tous détails complémentaires, on se reportera à l'*Annuaire statistique de la FAO*. Des statistiques peuvent également être consultées sur le site Web de la FAO http://faostat.fao.org.

Tableau 30: "L'agriculture" se rapporte à la production de tous les produits de l'agriculture et de l'élevage. "L'indice des produits alimentaires" comprend les produits considérés comme comestibles et qui contiennent des éléments nutritifs.

Les indices de la production agricole et de la production alimentaire sont calculés selon la formule de Laspeyres avec les années 1999-2001 pour période de base. Le choix d'une période de plusieurs années permet de diminuer l'incidence des fluctuations annuelles de la production agricole pendant les années de base sur les indices pour cette période. Les quantités produites de chaque denrée sont pondérées par les prix nationaux moyens à la production de 1999-2001, et additionnées pour chaque année. Les indices sont fondés sur les données de production d'une année civile. Ils peuvent différer dans certains cas des indices effectivement établis et publiés par les pays eux-mêmes par suite de différences dans les concepts, la couverture, les pondérations et les méthodes de calcul. On s'est efforcé d'estimer ces différences méthodologiques afin de rendre les données plus facilement comparables à l'échelle internationale.

Des chiffres détaillés de production sont publiés dans l'*Annuaire statistique de la FAO*.

Tableau 31: Les données sur la production de céréales se rapportent uniquement aux céréales récoltées pour le grain sec; celles cultivées pour le foin, le fourrage vert ou le pâturage en sont exclues.

Tableau 32: Les données sur le bois rond se réfèrent au bois brut, bois à l'état naturel, tel qu'il a été abattu ou récolté autrement, avec ou sans écorce, fendu, grossièrement équarri ou sous une autre forme (par exemple, racines, souches, loupes, etc.). Il peut être également imprégné (par exemple, dans le cas des poteaux télégraphiques) et dégrossi ou taillé en pointe.

The flag of the vessel is considered as the paramount indication of the nationality of the catch. Marine fisheries data include landings by domestic craft in foreign ports and exclude landings by foreign craft in domestic ports.

To separate aquaculture from capture fisheries production, at least two criteria must apply i.e., the human intervention in one or more of the phases of the growth cycle, and individual, corporate or state ownership of the organism reared and harvested.

Data on aquaculture production are published in the *FAO Yearbook of Fishery Statistics, Aquaculture Production*; capture production statistics are published in the *FAO Yearbook of Fishery Statistics, Capture Production.*

Table 34: The data refer to livestock numbers grouped into twelve-month periods ending 30 September of the year stated and cover all domestic animals irrespective of their age and place or purpose of their breeding.

Table 35: The data generally refer to the fertilizer year 1 July-30 June.

Nitrogenous fertilizers: data refer to the nitrogen content of commercial inorganic fertilizers.

Phosphate fertilizers: data refer to commercial phosphoric acid (P_2O_5) of super phosphates, ammonium phosphate and basic slag.

Potash fertilizers: data refer to K_2O content of commercial potash, muriate, nitrate and sulphate of potash, manure salts, kainit and nitrate of soda potash.

Cette catégorie comprend tous les bois provenant des quantités enlevées en forêt ou provenant des arbres poussant hors forêt, y compris le volume récupéré sur les déchets naturels et les déchets d'abattage et de transport pendant la période envisagée (année civile ou forestière).

Tableau 33: Les données ont trait (i) à la pêche maritime et intérieure et (ii) à l'aquaculture, et sont exprimées en poids vif. Elles comprennent poissons, crustacés et mollusques, mais excluent éponges, coraux, perles, algues, crocodiles et les mammifères aquatiques (baleines, dauphins, etc.).

Le pavillon du navire est considéré comme la principale indication de la nationalité de la prise. Les données de pêche maritime comprennent les quantités débarquées par des bateaux nationaux dans des ports étrangers et excluent les quantités débarquées par des bateaux étrangers dans des ports nationaux.

Pour séparer la production d'aquaculture de la pêche de capture, au moins deux critères doivent se vérifier, c'est-à-dire l'intervention humaine dans une ou plusieurs des phases du cycle de croissance, et l'appartenance de l'organisme élevé et récolté à une personne physique, à une personne morale ou à l'état.

Les données sur la production de l'aquaculture sont publiées dans *l'Annuaire statistique des pêches, production de l'aquaculture*; celles sur les captures sont publiées dans *l'Annuaire statistique des pêches, captures.*

Tableau 34: Les statistiques sur les effectifs du cheptel sont groupées en périodes de 12 mois se terminant le 30 septembre de l'année indiquée et s'entendent de tous les animaux domestiques, quel que soit leur âge, leur emplacement ou le but de leur élevage.

Tableau 35: Les données sur les engrais se rapportent en général à une période d'un an comptée du 1er juillet au 30 juin.

Engrais azotés : les données se rapportent à la teneur en azote des engrais commerciaux inorganiques.

Engrais phosphatés : les données se rapportent à l'acide phosphorique (P_2O_5) et englobent la teneur en (P_2O_5) des superphosphates, du phosphate d'ammonium et des scories de déphosphoration.

Engrais potassiques : les données se rapportent à la teneur en K_2O des produits potassiques commerciaux, muriate, nitrate et sulfate de potasse, sels d'engrais, kainite et nitrate de soude potassique.

36

Sugar

Production and consumption: thousand metric tons; consumption per capita: kilograms

Sucre

Production et consommation : milliers de tonnes ; consommation per habitant : kilogrammes

Country or area	1999	2000	2001	2002	2003	2004	2005	Pays ou zone
World								**Monde**
Production	**134 964**	**130 004**	**130 644**	**142 067**	**148 117**	**147 243**	**141 314**	**Production**
Consumption	**126 606**	**127 337**	**131 687**	**137 659**	**141 347**	**146 685**	**147 405**	**Consommation**
Consumption per cap. (kg.)	**21**	**21**	**22**	**22**	**23**	**23**	**23**	**Consom. par hab.(kg.)**
Afghanistan								**Afghanistan**
Consumption*	60	60	60	70	90	120	140	Consommation*
Consumption per cap. (kg.)	3	3	3	3	4	5	6	Consom. par hab.(kg.)
Albania								**Albanie**
Production*	3	3	3	3	3	3	3	Production*
Consumption*	65	68	68	75	85	88	90	Consommation*
Consumption per cap. (kg.)	21	19	22	24	27	28	29	Consom. par hab.(kg.)
Algeria								**Algérie**
Consumption*	900	935	965	1 040	1 100	1 135	1 185	Consommation*
Consumption per cap. (kg.)	30	31	31	33	35	35	36	Consom. par hab.(kg.)
Angola								**Angola**
Production*	32	...	...	...	...	...	...	Production*
Consumption*	120	130	155	185	195	205	225	Consommation*
Consumption per cap. (kg.)	10	10	11	13	13	13	13	Consom. par hab.(kg.)
Argentina								**Argentine**
Production	*1 882	*1 580	*1 630	*1 680	1 952	1 857	2 165	Production
Consumption	*1 450	*1 485	*1 520	*1 515	1 515	1 574	1 654	Consommation
Consumption per cap. (kg.)	40	41	41	40	40	41	42	Consom. par hab.(kg.)
Armenia								**Arménie**
Production	...	...	...	...	...	...	2	Production
Consumption	*70	*72	*73	*74	87	*87	*95	Consommation
Consumption per cap. (kg.)	18	19	19	23	27	27	30	Consom. par hab.(kg.)
Australia								**Australie**
Production	5 514	4 417	4 768	5 614	5 315	5 530	5 393	Production
Consumption	*1 005	1 049	1 068	1 100	1 089	1 043	1 034	Consommation
Consumption per cap. (kg.)	53	55	55	56	55	52	51	Consom. par hab.(kg.)
Azerbaijan								**Azerbaïdjan**
Production	...	...	...	...	...	...	2	Production
Consumption*	160	160	160	165	175	180	185	Consommation*
Consumption per cap. (kg.)	20	20	20	20	21	22	22	Consom. par hab.(kg.)
Bahamas								**Bahamas**
Consumption	10	11	8	9	11	12	13	Consommation
Consumption per cap. (kg.)	33	35	27	32	34	36	38	Consom. par hab.(kg.)
Bangladesh								**Bangladesh**
Production	*162	*110	109	229	*166	*125	*120	Production
Consumption*	440	500	550	635	695	790	880	Consommation*
Consumption per cap. (kg.)	3	4	4	5	5	6	6	Consom. par hab.(kg.)
Barbados								**Barbade**
Production	53	58	*50	*45	*36	*35	*40	Production
Consumption*	15	15	15	15	15	15	15	Consommation*
Consumption per cap. (kg.)	56	56	56	56	56	56	56	Consom. par hab.(kg.)
Belarus								**Bélarus**
Production	151	186	196	162	*255	*340	*435	Production
Consumption	*357	380	422	410	*410	*415	*420	Consommation
Consumption per cap. (kg.)	35	38	42	41	42	42	43	Consom. par hab.(kg.)
Belize								**Belize**
Production	124	128	114	119	111	125	102	Production
Consumption	15	15	12[1]	12	12	12	12	Consommation
Consumption per cap. (kg.)	61	58	46	44	44	42	42	Consom. par hab.(kg.)
Benin								**Bénin**
Production*	4	5	5	5	4	4	5	Production*
Consumption	*45	*46	22	*28	*35	*36	*37	Consommation
Consumption per cap. (kg.)	8	8	3	4	5	5	5	Consom. par hab.(kg.)

Country or area	1999	2000	2001	2002	2003	2004	2005	Pays ou zone
Bermuda								**Bermudes**
Consumption	1	2	2	2	2	2	2	Consommation
Consumption per cap. (kg.)	17	25	25	25	25	25	25	Consom. par hab.(kg.)
Bolivia								**Bolivie**
Production	293	311	390	426	387	464	*400	Production
Consumption	290	*293	*295	*300	*305	*310	*320	Consommation
Consumption per cap. (kg.)	35	35	34	34	34	34	34	Consom. par hab.(kg.)
Bosnia and Herzegovina								**Bosnie-Herzégovine**
Consumption*	80	90	110	120	130	130	135	Consommation*
Consumption per cap. (kg.)	21	24	29	31	34	34	35	Consom. par hab.(kg.)
Botswana								**Botswana**
Consumption	45	46	46	47	48	48	50	Consommation
Consumption per cap. (kg.)	28	28	27	27	27	27	28	Consom. par hab.(kg.)
Brazil								**Brésil**
Production	20 646	16 464	20 336	23 567	25 730	27 290	28 135	Production
Consumption	*9 500	*9 725	*9 800	10 520	10 217	10 857	10 950	Consommation
Consumption per cap. (kg.)	57	58	57	60	58	59	59	Consom. par hab.(kg.)
Brunei Darussalam								**Brunéi Darussalam**
Consumption	5	6	10	10	11	11	11	Consommation
Consumption per cap. (kg.)	16	19	30	29	31	31	30	Consom. par hab.(kg.)
Bulgaria								**Bulgarie**
Production*	2	2	3	3	3	3	5	Production*
Consumption*	225	230	240	255	265	270	275	Consommation*
Consumption per cap. (kg.)	28	28	30	33	34	35	36	Consom. par hab.(kg.)
Burkina Faso								**Burkina Faso**
Production	30	*30	*35	*40	*40	*40	*40	Production
Consumption*	45	50	55	60	65	65	75	Consommation*
Consumption per cap. (kg.)	4	4	5	6	6	5	6	Consom. par hab.(kg.)
Burundi								**Burundi**
Production	23	24	20	20	22	22	23	Production
Consumption	23	24	23	25	26	27	29	Consommation
Consumption per cap. (kg.)	4	4	4	3	3	4	7	Consom. par hab.(kg.)
Cambodia								**Cambodge**
Consumption*	75	85	90	115	120	130	170	Consommation*
Consumption per cap. (kg.)	6	7	7	9	9	10	13	Consom. par hab.(kg.)
Cameroon								**Cameroun**
Production	*52	41	94	104	120	*125	119	Production
Consumption	*95	*95	112	145	145	*150	92	Consommation
Consumption per cap. (kg.)	7	6	8	10	10	10	6	Consom. par hab.(kg.)
Canada								**Canada**
Production*	118	123	95	64	85	115	105	Production*
Consumption*	1 200	1 235	1 240	1 255	1 400	1 425	1 425	Consommation*
Consumption per cap. (kg.)	39	40	40	40	44	45	44	Consom. par hab.(kg.)
Cape Verde								**Cap-Vert**
Consumption*	13	13	15	16	17	17	17	Consommation*
Consumption per cap. (kg.)	30	31	34	36	37	36	35	Consom. par hab.(kg.)
Central African Rep.								**Rép. centrafricaine**
Consumption*	4	4	4	5	6	9	11	Consommation*
Consumption per cap. (kg.)	1	1	1	1	2	2	3	Consom. par hab.(kg.)
Chad								**Tchad**
Production*	32	32	32	32	33	30	35	Production*
Consumption*	55	57	57	65	75	80	85	Consommation*
Consumption per cap. (kg.)	7	7	7	15	8	8	9	Consom. par hab.(kg.)
Chile								**Chili**
Production	487	457	*430	576	374	401	386	Production
Consumption	729	683	*685	*685	*685	673	682	Consommation
Consumption per cap. (kg.)	49	45	44	46	45	44	44	Consom. par hab.(kg.)
China[2]								**Chine**[2]
Production	8 527	7 616	7 161	9 805	11 433	10 912	*9 785	Production
Consumption	*8 300	*8 500	*8 900	*9 975	11 065	11 613	*11 785	Consommation
Consumption per cap. (kg.)	7	7	7	8	9	9	9	Consom. par hab.(kg.)

Country or area	1999	2000	2001	2002	2003	2004	2005	Pays ou zone
China, Hong Kong SAR								**Chine, Hong Kong RAS**
Consumption*	180	181	185	180	185	185	185	Consommation*
Consumption per cap. (kg.)	27	27	28	27	27	27	27	Consom. par hab.(kg.)
China, Macao SAR								**Chine, Macao RAS**
Consumption	7	7	7	8	8	8	8	Consommation
Consumption per cap. (kg.)	16	17	17	17	20	21	17	Consom. par hab.(kg.)
Colombia								**Colombie**
Production	2 241	2 391	2 260	2 523	2 646	2 740	2 683	Production
Consumption	1 281[3]	1 343[3]	1 309[3]	1 356[3]	1 348	1 521	1 512	Consommation
Consumption per cap. (kg.)	31	32	30	31	30	34	33	Consom. par hab.(kg.)
Comoros								**Comores**
Consumption	5	6	8	9	9	9	9	Consommation
Consumption per cap. (kg.)	7	8	11	11	11	11	12	Consom. par hab.(kg.)
Congo								**Congo**
Production	*35	*40	*45	33	*45	*55	63	Production
Consumption	*30	*35	*45	32	*50	*55	76	Consommation
Consumption per cap. (kg.)	11	12	15	10	15	16	25	Consom. par hab.(kg.)
Costa Rica								**Costa Rica**
Production	*378	338	358	*360	*358	*405	398	Production
Consumption	*210	208	*210	*225	*230	*230	225	Consommation
Consumption per cap. (kg.)	62	60	54	56	56	54	53	Consom. par hab.(kg.)
Côte d'Ivoire								**Côte d'Ivoire**
Production	152	189	*155	*170	*145	*120	*145	Production
Consumption*	170	180	190	200	205	210	215	Consommation*
Consumption per cap. (kg.)	11	11	11	12	11	11	11	Consom. par hab.(kg.)
Croatia								**Croatie**
Production	114	57	131	160	116	173	204	Production
Consumption*	175	175	175	180	185	190	200	Consommation*
Consumption per cap. (kg.)	39	40	40	41	42	43	45	Consom. par hab.(kg.)
Cuba								**Cuba**
Production	3 875	4 057	3 748	3 522	2 278	*2 600	*1 300	Production
Consumption	711	705	698	698	682	*700	*700	Consommation
Consumption per cap. (kg.)	64	63	62	62	60	62	63	Consom. par hab.(kg.)
Cyprus								**Chypre**
Consumption	*30	*31	32	*33	*36	...	...	Consommation
Consumption per cap. (kg.)	40	41	42	47	47	...	...	Consom. par hab.(kg.)
Czech Republic								**République tchèque**
Production	420	434	484	523	522	...	...	Production
Consumption	*450	440	*450	*475	399	...	...	Consommation
Consumption per cap. (kg.)	44	43	44	47	39	...	...	Consom. par hab.(kg.)
Dem. Rep. of the Congo								**Rép. dém. du Congo**
Production*	65	75	60	65	65	60	60	Production*
Consumption*	75	75	75	85	85	90	95	Consommation*
Consumption per cap. (kg.)	2	2	1	2	2	2	2	Consom. par hab.(kg.)
Djibouti								**Djibouti**
Consumption	12	13	13	13	14	15	16	Consommation
Consumption per cap. (kg.)	14	15	15	15	16	17	18	Consom. par hab.(kg.)
Dominican Republic								**Rép. dominicaine**
Production	421	438	491	516	525	*530	*475	Production
Consumption	*350	298	352	366	322	*360	*370	Consommation
Consumption per cap. (kg.)	42	35	41	45	37	41	41	Consom. par hab.(kg.)
Ecuador								**Equateur**
Production	601	*500	*495	*475	*505	*490	*470	Production
Consumption*	425	440	465	480	485	485	488	Consommation*
Consumption per cap. (kg.)	35	36	37	38	38	37	37	Consom. par hab.(kg.)
Egypt								**Egypte**
Production	*1 269	*1 450	*1 585	*1 490	*1 425	1 489	*1 625	Production
Consumption*	2 150	2 250	2 325	2 400	2 500	2 600	2 675	Consommation*
Consumption per cap. (kg.)	34	35	36	36	37	37	36	Consom. par hab.(kg.)
El Salvador								**El Salvador**
Production	585	562	527	476	530	555	633	Production
Consumption	234	236	244	217	209	212	225	Consommation
Consumption per cap. (kg.)	38	38	38	33	33	33	35	Consom. par hab.(kg.)

Country or area	1999	2000	2001	2002	2003	2004	2005	Pays ou zone
Eritrea								**Erythrée**
Consumption	8	8	8	9	15	16	20	Consommation
Consumption per cap. (kg.)	2	2	2	2	4	4	5	Consom. par hab.(kg.)
Estonia								**Estonie**
Consumption*	65	70	73	73	80	...	...	Consommation*
Consumption per cap. (kg.)	46	49	53	49	60	...	...	Consom. par hab.(kg.)
Ethiopia								**Ethiopie**
Production	235	251	*305	287	*295	*325	*345	Production
Consumption	199	246	*240	211	*260	*295	*305	Consommation
Consumption per cap. (kg.)	3	4	4	3	4	4	4	Consom. par hab.(kg.)
EU-25[4]								**UE-25**[4]
Production	18 731	17 854	15 500	18 268	16 578	21 843	21 698	Production
Consumption	15 007	14 112	13 588	14 370	14 137	17 691	16 765	Consommation
Consumption per cap. (kg.)	40	37	36	38	37	39	37	Consom. par hab.(kg.)
Fiji								**Fidji**
Production	377	353	327	334	330	330	306	Production
Consumption	38	41	45[5]	53	55	58[5]	55	Consommation
Consumption per cap. (kg.)	47	51	56	64	66	69	66	Consom. par hab.(kg.)
Gabon								**Gabon**
Production	*16	*17	*18	*18	25	*19	*21	Production
Consumption*	18	19	19	20	21	21	21	Consommation*
Consumption per cap. (kg.)	15	15	15	16	16	16	15	Consom. par hab.(kg.)
Gambia								**Gambie**
Consumption*	50	58	60	65	70	70	70	Consommation*
Consumption per cap. (kg.)	36	41	42	41	47	47	54	Consom. par hab.(kg.)
Georgia								**Géorgie**
Consumption*	105	108	110	120	125	135	135	Consommation*
Consumption per cap. (kg.)	24	24	25	28	29	31	32	Consom. par hab.(kg.)
Ghana								**Ghana**
Consumption*	145	150	155	170	185	200	205	Consommation*
Consumption per cap. (kg.)	7	8	8	9	9	10	10	Consom. par hab.(kg.)
Gibraltar								**Gibraltar**
Consumption	3	3	2	2	2	2	2	Consommation
Consumption per cap. (kg.)	83	83	73	55	60	67	53	Consom. par hab.(kg.)
Guatemala								**Guatemala**
Production	1 687	1 675	1 661	1 910	1 801	2 092	2 015	Production
Consumption	460	468	496	534	585	585	657	Consommation
Consumption per cap. (kg.)	42	41	43	45	48	47	52	Consom. par hab.(kg.)
Guinea								**Guinée**
Production*	25	25	25	25	26	26	25	Production*
Consumption*	85	90	95	100	110	110	120	Consommation*
Consumption per cap. (kg.)	11	11	12	12	13	12	13	Consom. par hab.(kg.)
Guinea-Bissau								**Guinée-Bissau**
Consumption	5	7	7	7	8	9	14	Consommation
Consumption per cap. (kg.)	4	6	6	6	6	7	11	Consom. par hab.(kg.)
Guyana								**Guyana**
Production	336	273	284	331	*302	*320	246	Production
Consumption	25	24	24	24	*25	*26	22	Consommation
Consumption per cap. (kg.)	32	31	35	31	33	35	31	Consom. par hab.(kg.)
Haiti								**Haïti**
Production*	5	5	5	5	...	...	...	Production*
Consumption*	160	165	165	170	175	175	205	Consommation*
Consumption per cap. (kg.)	21	21	20	21	21	20	23	Consom. par hab.(kg.)
Honduras								**Honduras**
Production	190	*320	316	*320	300	357	*360	Production
Consumption	235	236	237	*240	249	250	*250	Consommation
Consumption per cap. (kg.)	37	37	39	33	36	36	35	Consom. par hab.(kg.)
Hungary								**Hongrie**
Production[6]	446	309	434	347	257	...	...	Production[6]
Consumption[6]	399	367	317	313	282	...	...	Consommation[6]
Consumption per cap. (kg.)	40	37	31	31	28	...	...	Consom. par hab.(kg.)

Country or area	1999	2000	2001	2002	2003	2004	2005	Pays ou zone
Iceland								**Islande**
Consumption*	12	13	12	12	12	12	11	Consommation*
Consumption per cap. (kg.)	43	46	41	41	41	41	38	Consom. par hab.(kg.)
India								**Inde**
Production	17 406	20 247	19 906	19 525	21 702	14 432	15 216	Production
Consumption	16 278	16 546	17 274	17 857	18 625	19 858	20 110	Consommation
Consumption per cap. (kg.)	17	17	17	17	18	19	20	Consom. par hab.(kg.)
Indonesia								**Indonésie**
Production*	1 490	1 685	1 850	2 150	1 780	2 225	2 435	Production*
Consumption*	3 000	3 375	3 500	3 675	3 800	3 915	4 052	Consommation*
Consumption per cap. (kg.)	15	16	17	17	18	18	18	Consom. par hab.(kg.)
Iran (Islamic Rep. of)								**Iran (Rép. islamique d')**
Production*	940	920	900	995	1 270	1 310	1 300	Production*
Consumption*	1 900	1 960	1 965	1 975	2 025	2 060	2 110	Consommation*
Consumption per cap. (kg.)	30	31	30	30	31	31	31	Consom. par hab.(kg.)
Iraq								**Iraq**
Consumption*	400	405	425	500	650	675	675	Consommation*
Consumption per cap. (kg.)	17	17	18	20	26	26	25	Consom. par hab.(kg.)
Israel								**Israël**
Consumption*	370	380	400	410	425	440	455	Consommation*
Consumption per cap. (kg.)	60	60	62	62	64	65	66	Consom. par hab.(kg.)
Jamaica								**Jamaïque**
Production	212	210	205	175	154	181	126	Production
Consumption	98	129	136	126	129	111	123	Consommation
Consumption per cap. (kg.)	38	50	52	48	49	42	46	Consom. par hab.(kg.)
Japan								**Japon**
Production	913	842	823	901	934	976	965	Production
Consumption	2 541	2 413	2 339	2 433	2 415	2 403	2 397	Consommation
Consumption per cap. (kg.)	20	19	18	19	19	19	19	Consom. par hab.(kg.)
Jordan								**Jordanie**
Consumption	*180	*185	*190	*200	216	*235	*255	Consommation
Consumption per cap. (kg.)	36	37	36	37	40	44	47	Consom. par hab.(kg.)
Kazakhstan								**Kazakhstan**
Production	*25	*30	*25	46	62	40	*22	Production
Consumption*	303	312	365	438	442	450	455	Consommation*
Consumption per cap. (kg.)	20	21	25	30	30	30	30	Consom. par hab.(kg.)
Kenya								**Kenya**
Production	512	437	377	537	448	562	532	Production
Consumption	662	663	*625	652	692	728	756	Consommation
Consumption per cap. (kg.)	23	22	20	21	21	22	23	Consom. par hab.(kg.)
Korea, Dem. P. R.								**Corée, R. p. dém. de**
Consumption*	60	65	70	70	75	85	95	Consommation*
Consumption per cap. (kg.)	3	3	3	3	3	4	4	Consom. par hab.(kg.)
Korea, Republic of								**Corée, République de**
Consumption[7]	966	1 012	1 086	1 129	1 134	1 171	1 257	Consommation[7]
Consumption per cap. (kg.)	21	21	23	24	24	24	26	Consom. par hab.(kg.)
Kuwait								**Koweït**
Consumption*	70	73	75	80	80	85	90	Consommation*
Consumption per cap. (kg.)	33	33	33	35	34	36	37	Consom. par hab.(kg.)
Kyrgyzstan								**Kirghizistan**
Production	45	57	29	41	75	88	45	Production
Consumption*	100	110	110	115	120	120	120	Consommation*
Consumption per cap. (kg.)	21	22	22	23	24	24	23	Consom. par hab.(kg.)
Lao People's Dem. Rep.								**Rép. dém. pop. lao**
Consumption*	20	21	25	30	30	35	45	Consommation*
Consumption per cap. (kg.)	4	4	5	6	5	6	8	Consom. par hab.(kg.)
Latvia								**Lettonie**
Production[6]	72	68	56	77	75	...	...	Production[6]
Consumption[6]	82	78	*78	*78	73	...	...	Consommation[6]
Consumption per cap. (kg.)	34	32	33	33	31	...	...	Consom. par hab.(kg.)
Lebanon								**Liban**
Production	40	34	...	...	...	...	4	Production
Consumption	*130	122	*135	*140	*145	*150	151	Consommation
Consumption per cap. (kg.)	38	35	38	36	39	43	42	Consom. par hab.(kg.)

Country or area	1999	2000	2001	2002	2003	2004	2005	Pays ou zone
Liberia								**Libéria**
Consumption	8	10	9	10	10	10	15	Consommation
Consumption per cap. (kg.)	3	3	3	3	3	3	3	Consom. par hab.(kg.)
Libyan Arab Jamah.								**Jamah. arabe libyenne**
Consumption*	220	225	230	240	250	260	270	Consommation*
Consumption per cap. (kg.)	44	44	43	45	46	47	48	Consom. par hab.(kg.)
Lithuania								**Lituanie**
Production[6]	121	137	118	150	143	...	...	Production[6]
Consumption[6]	*110	95	111	89	89	...	...	Consommation[6]
Consumption per cap. (kg.)	30	26	32	26	26	...	...	Consom. par hab.(kg.)
Madagascar								**Madagascar**
Production	*85	*70	*50	32	27	26	27	Production
Consumption	*95	*98	*98	104	117	129	132	Consommation
Consumption per cap. (kg.)	6	6	6	7	7	8	8	Consom. par hab.(kg.)
Malawi								**Malawi**
Production	187	209	*205	261	*257	*255	*265	Production
Consumption	137	127	*140	*145	*150	*155	*160	Consommation
Consumption per cap. (kg.)	14	12	13	13	13	13	13	Consom. par hab.(kg.)
Malaysia								**Malaisie**
Production*	107	108	105	110	80	80	80	Production*
Consumption*	1 040	1 045	1 050	1 090	1 175	1 215	1 225	Consommation*
Consumption per cap. (kg.)	48	45	44	44	47	48	47	Consom. par hab.(kg.)
Maldives								**Maldives**
Consumption	5	6	5	5	5	5	6	Consommation
Consumption per cap. (kg.)	18	22	16	18	17	17	19	Consom. par hab.(kg.)
Mali								**Mali**
Production*	31	32	32	32	34	35	35	Production*
Consumption*	75	80	80	90	95	95	100	Consommation*
Consumption per cap. (kg.)	8	8	8	8	9	8	9	Consom. par hab.(kg.)
Malta								**Malte**
Consumption*[6]	22	23	23	23	25	...	...	Consommation*[6]
Consumption per cap. (kg.)	56	58	59	59	63	...	...	Consom. par hab.(kg.)
Mauritania								**Mauritanie**
Consumption*	125	130	135	135	140	140	145	Consommation*
Consumption per cap. (kg.)	49	49	50	48	49	48	49	Consom. par hab.(kg.)
Mauritius								**Maurice**
Production	396	604	685	553	538	606	524	Production
Consumption	42	42	44	43	41	42	39	Consommation
Consumption per cap. (kg.)	36	35	36	35	34	34	32	Consom. par hab.(kg.)
Mexico								**Mexique**
Production	5 030	4 816	5 614	5 073	5 442	5 672	5 619	Production
Consumption	4 400	4 619	4 857	5 069	5 328	5 300	4 877	Consommation
Consumption per cap. (kg.)	45	46	48	49	52	50	47	Consom. par hab.(kg.)
Mongolia								**Mongolie**
Consumption	10	20	20	21	22	23	25	Consommation
Consumption per cap. (kg.)	4	8	8	9	9	9	10	Consom. par hab.(kg.)
Morocco								**Maroc**
Production	522	556	*530	*505	*505	*540	513	Production
Consumption	1 018	1 034	*1 050	*1 100	1 057	*1 150	1 163	Consommation
Consumption per cap. (kg.)	36	36	36	37	35	38	38	Consom. par hab.(kg.)
Mozambique								**Mozambique**
Production	46	*45	*60	*170	*225	205	265	Production
Consumption	*70	*90	*95	*110	*120	134	135	Consommation
Consumption per cap. (kg.)	4	5	5	5	7	7	7	Consom. par hab.(kg.)
Myanmar								**Myanmar**
Production	43	75	*125	*125	*135	*150	*150	Production
Consumption	69	*85	*90	*120	*135	*150	*155	Consommation
Consumption per cap. (kg.)	2	2	2	2	3	3	3	Consom. par hab.(kg.)
Namibia								**Namibie**
Consumption*	45	46	47	48	50	55	55	Consommation*
Consumption per cap. (kg.)	25	25	26	26	28	30	30	Consom. par hab.(kg.)

Country or area	1999	2000	2001	2002	2003	2004	2005	Pays ou zone
Nepal								**Népal**
Production*	150	110	65	110	125	140	130	Production*
Consumption*	110	115	120	125	125	130	135	Consommation*
Consumption per cap. (kg.)	5	5	5	5	5	5	5	Consom. par hab.(kg.)
Netherlands Antilles								**Antilles néerlandaises**
Consumption*	20	21	22	25	25	25	26	Consommation*
Consumption per cap. (kg.)	105	117	129	147	139	131	129	Consom. par hab.(kg.)
New Zealand								**Nouvelle-Zélande**
Consumption	198	212	*215	*220	*225	*230	*235	Consommation
Consumption per cap. (kg.)	52	55	55	56	56	57	57	Consom. par hab.(kg.)
Nicaragua								**Nicaragua**
Production	351	398	*390	*370	333	*440	*470	Production
Consumption	179	157	*160	*175	*190	*200	*205	Consommation
Consumption per cap. (kg.)	36	31	31	31	35	37	37	Consom. par hab.(kg.)
Niger								**Niger**
Production*	10	10	10	10	15	10	10	Production*
Consumption*	50	55	55	65	70	70	75	Consommation*
Consumption per cap. (kg.)	5	5	5	5	6	5	6	Consom. par hab.(kg.)
Nigeria								**Nigéria**
Production	*17	36	7	7	...	...	...	Production
Consumption	*700	*760	975	1 317	1 046	1 222	1 236	Consommation
Consumption per cap. (kg.)	6	7	8	11	8	9	10	Consom. par hab.(kg.)
Norway								**Norvège**
Consumption*	185	185	184	182	180	180	178	Consommation*
Consumption per cap. (kg.)	42	41	41	40	40	40	39	Consom. par hab.(kg.)
Pakistan								**Pakistan**
Production	3 709	2 053	2 720	3 334	4 063	4 481	2 839	Production
Consumption	*3 196	*3 295	*3 390	*3 490	3 875	4 004	4 075	Consommation
Consumption per cap. (kg.)	24	24	24	24	26	27	27	Consom. par hab.(kg.)
Panama								**Panama**
Production	183	161	146	152	147	157	157	Production
Consumption*	85	95	105	110	113	115	117	Consommation*
Consumption per cap. (kg.)	30	33	36	36	38	36	35	Consom. par hab.(kg.)
Papua New Guinea								**Papouasie-Nvl-Guinée**
Production	47	41	45	53	50	46	44	Production
Consumption	38	35	35	37	35	35	35	Consommation
Consumption per cap. (kg.)	8	7	7	8	7	6	6	Consom. par hab.(kg.)
Paraguay								**Paraguay**
Production*	112	90	95	115	116	115	117	Production*
Consumption*	108	108	110	110	115	115	120	Consommation*
Consumption per cap. (kg.)	20	20	20	19	19	19	20	Consom. par hab.(kg.)
Peru								**Pérou**
Production	*655	*725	*755	*850	*970	813	695	Production
Consumption	*900	*925	*950	*975	*995	967	896	Consommation
Consumption per cap. (kg.)	36	36	36	36	36	35	32	Consom. par hab.(kg.)
Philippines								**Philippines**
Production	1 913	1 826	1 895	1 988	2 245	2 423	2 184	Production
Consumption	1 854	2 052	1 974	2 059	2 117	2 102	2 037	Consommation
Consumption per cap. (kg.)	25	28	26	26	26	25	24	Consom. par hab.(kg.)
Poland								**Pologne**
Production[6]	1 968	2 104	1 626	2 038	1 912	...	...	Production[6]
Consumption*[6]	1 720	1 730	1 740	1 745	1 760	...	...	Consommation*[6]
Consumption per cap. (kg.)	45	45	45	45	46	...	...	Consom. par hab.(kg.)
Republic of Moldova								**République de Moldova**
Production	108	102	130	*125	107	111	133	Production
Consumption	*125	*105	*105	*110	*115	106	*125	Consommation
Consumption per cap. (kg.)	34	29	29	26	32	29	30	Consom. par hab.(kg.)
Romania								**Roumanie**
Production	86	54	71	75	57	*55	67	Production
Consumption*	530	550	565	570	590	584	595	Consommation*
Consumption per cap. (kg.)	24	25	25	26	27	27	28	Consom. par hab.(kg.)

Sugar — Production and consumption: thousand metric tons; consumption per capita: kilograms (*continued*)
Sucre — Production et consommation : milliers de tonnes ; consommation par habitant : kilogrammes (*suite*)

Country or area	1999	2000	2001	2002	2003	2004	2005	Pays ou zone
Russian Federation								**Fédération de Russie**
Production	1 651	1 705	1 757	1 757	1 892	2 496	2 719	Production
Consumption	5 565	5 707	5 848	6 673	*6 850	*6 700	*6 600	Consommation
Consumption per cap. (kg.)	38	39	41	47	47	46	46	Consom. par hab.(kg.)
Rwanda								**Rwanda**
Consumption*	3	3	10	11	11	11	14	Consommation*
Consumption per cap. (kg.)	0	0	1	1	1	1	2	Consom. par hab.(kg.)
Saint Kitts and Nevis								**Saint-Kitts-et-Nevis**
Production*	20	20	20	20	22	20	20	Production*
Consumption*	2	3	3	3	4	5	6	Consommation*
Consumption per cap. (kg.)	50	63	50	50	51	49	46	Consom. par hab.(kg.)
Samoa								**Samoa**
Production	2	2	2	2	2	2	2	Production
Consumption	2	2	2	3	4	4	4	Consommation
Consumption per cap. (kg.)	8	8	8	12	15	15	15	Consom. par hab.(kg.)
Saudi Arabia								**Arabie saoudite**
Consumption*	570	595	620	650	690	720	760	Consommation*
Consumption per cap. (kg.)	29	29	30	30	31	32	33	Consom. par hab.(kg.)
Senegal								**Sénégal**
Production*	95	90	95	95	90	90	90	Production*
Consumption*	170	165	170	175	175	180	185	Consommation*
Consumption per cap. (kg.)	19	18	18	18	17	17	17	Consom. par hab.(kg.)
Serbia and Montenegro								**Serbie-et-Monténégro**
Production	248	*170	209	*230	*270	*335	*415	Production
Consumption*	300	275	300	300	310	315	325	Consommation*
Consumption per cap. (kg.)	28	26	28	37	38	39	40	Consom. par hab.(kg.)
Sierra Leone								**Sierra Leone**
Production*	7	7	7	7	5	6	6	Production*
Consumption*	15	20	20	21	22	25	26	Consommation*
Consumption per cap. (kg.)	3	4	4	4	4	5	5	Consom. par hab.(kg.)
Singapore								**Singapour**
Consumption*	280	285	300	305	310	310	315	Consommation*
Consumption per cap. (kg.)	71	71	73	73	74	73	73	Consom. par hab.(kg.)
Slovakia								**Slovaquie**
Production[6]	213	140	173	197	171	...	...	Production[6]
Consumption[6]	*225	*230	*235	*240	206	...	...	Consommation[6]
Consumption per cap. (kg.)	42	43	44	45	38	...	...	Consom. par hab.(kg.)
Slovenia								**Slovénie**
Production[6]	*60	44	*50	*44	*55	...	...	Production[6]
Consumption*[6]	95	105	90	90	100	...	...	Consommation*[6]
Consumption per cap. (kg.)	48	53	45	45	50	...	...	Consom. par hab.(kg.)
Somalia								**Somalie**
Production*	20	15	20	20	20	20	15	Production*
Consumption*	170	180	185	190	200	200	205	Consommation*
Consumption per cap. (kg.)	20	21	20	19	20	20	20	Consom. par hab.(kg.)
South Africa								**Afrique du Sud**
Production	2 547	2 691	2 311	2 767	2 418	2 234	2 507	Production
Consumption	1 386	1 453	1 341	1 478	1 436	1 484	1 565	Consommation
Consumption per cap. (kg.)	32	33	30	33	32	32	33	Consom. par hab.(kg.)
Sri Lanka								**Sri Lanka**
Production*	19	15	20	20	21	60	60	Production*
Consumption*	550	560	575	600	620	640	655	Consommation*
Consumption per cap. (kg.)	29	29	31	32	32	33	33	Consom. par hab.(kg.)
Sudan								**Soudan**
Production	635	680	719	744	686	789	728	Production
Consumption	*450	430	523	568	568	624	877	Consommation
Consumption per cap. (kg.)	15	14	17	18	17	19	22	Consom. par hab.(kg.)
Suriname								**Suriname**
Production*	7	10	10	10	5	5	5	Production*
Consumption*	18	19	19	20	20	20	21	Consommation*
Consumption per cap. (kg.)	42	45	46	39	42	41	42	Consom. par hab.(kg.)

Sugar — Production and consumption: thousand metric tons; consumption per capita: kilograms (*continued*)
Sucre — Production et consommation : milliers de tonnes ; consommation par habitant : kilogrammes (*suite*)

Country or area	1999	2000	2001	2002	2003	2004	2005	Pays ou zone
Swaziland								**Swaziland**
Production	571	553	567	675	616	594	653	Production
Consumption	103	105	107	107	109	112	*114	Consommation
Consumption per cap. (kg.)	113	113	107	112	99	98	97	Consom. par hab.(kg.)
Switzerland								**Suisse**
Production	177	*231	*187	222	185	*225	221	Production
Consumption	328	*375	*385	393	463	*475	526	Consommation
Consumption per cap. (kg.)	46	52	53	54	63	64	70	Consom. par hab.(kg.)
Syrian Arab Republic								**Rép. arabe syrienne**
Production	100	118	121	*120	*120	*105	*110	Production
Consumption*	720	730	745	760	775	790	800	Consommation*
Consumption per cap. (kg.)	45	45	45	44	44	44	44	Consom. par hab.(kg.)
Tajikistan								**Tadjikistan**
Consumption*	60	60	60	70	80	85	105	Consommation*
Consumption per cap. (kg.)	10	10	10	11	12	13	15	Consom. par hab.(kg.)
Thailand								**Thaïlande**
Production	5 456	6 157	5 370	6 438	7 737	7 462	4 589	Production
Consumption	1 776	1 816	1 955	1 978	2 073	2 303	2 352	Consommation
Consumption per cap. (kg.)	29	29	31	31	33	36	36	Consom. par hab.(kg.)
TFYR of Macedonia								**L'ex-R.y. Macédoine**
Production	7	13	6	*10	16	16	16	Production
Consumption*	55	60	60	65	65	70	70	Consommation*
Consumption per cap. (kg.)	27	30	30	32	32	35	34	Consom. par hab.(kg.)
Togo								**Togo**
Consumption*	45	45	45	45	48	50	60	Consommation*
Consumption per cap. (kg.)	10	10	10	9	10	10	11	Consom. par hab.(kg.)
Trinidad and Tobago								**Trinité-et-Tobago**
Production	92	115	89	104	67	43	33	Production
Consumption	70	78	79	70	70	*75	*75	Consommation
Consumption per cap. (kg.)	55	60	62	54	55	59	58	Consom. par hab.(kg.)
Tunisia								**Tunisie**
Production	9	2	...	...	...	...	...	Production
Consumption	292	294	309	319	*330	335	332	Consommation
Consumption per cap. (kg.)	31	31	32	33	33	34	33	Consom. par hab.(kg.)
Turkey								**Turquie**
Production	2 491	2 273	2 360	2 128	2 136	2 053	2 171	Production
Consumption	1 836	*1 925	1 973	1 782	1 725	1 894	1 978	Consommation
Consumption per cap. (kg.)	29	29	29	26	24	27	27	Consom. par hab.(kg.)
Turkmenistan								**Turkménistan**
Production	...	...	...	...	1	*2	*3	Production
Consumption*	70	70	70	70	75	75	80	Consommation*
Consumption per cap. (kg.)	15	15	15	15	15	14	14	Consom. par hab.(kg.)
Uganda								**Ouganda**
Production*	137	130	140	160	180	190	195	Production*
Consumption*	150	155	160	180	195	210	225	Consommation*
Consumption per cap. (kg.)	7	7	7	8	9	9	10	Consom. par hab.(kg.)
Ukraine								**Ukraine**
Production	1 640	1 686	1 802	*1 545	1 690	*1 945	*2 060	Production
Consumption*	1 800	1 875	2 005	2 100	2 300	2 300	2 350	Consommation*
Consumption per cap. (kg.)	36	38	41	43	48	49	50	Consom. par hab.(kg.)
United Rep. of Tanzania								**Rép.-Unie de Tanzanie**
Production	114	*130	*115	187	218	211	278	Production
Consumption	*200	*208	*200	165	218	221	268	Consommation
Consumption per cap. (kg.)	6	6	6	5	6	6	7	Consom. par hab.(kg.)
United States								**Etats-Unis**
Production	*8 243	8 080	7 774	6 805	7 964	7 647	6 784	Production
Consumption	9 067	9 051	9 139[8]	9 079	8 844	8 994	9 248	Consommation
Consumption per cap. (kg.)	33	32	32	32	30	31	31	Consom. par hab.(kg.)
Uruguay								**Uruguay**
Production*	9	8	7	7	6	7	6	Production*
Consumption	101	*102	*105	*110	*115	*120	*125	Consommation
Consumption per cap. (kg.)	31	31	32	33	35	36	38	Consom. par hab.(kg.)

Country or area	1999	2000	2001	2002	2003	2004	2005	Pays ou zone
Uzbekistan								**Ouzbékistan**
Production	*20	11	*7	*7	...	...	...	Production
Consumption*	435	450	475	490	495	495	505	Consommation*
Consumption per cap. (kg.)	18	18	19	19	20	20	21	Consom. par hab.(kg.)
Venezuela (Bolivarian Rep. of)								**Venezuela (Rép. bolivar. du)**
Production	*535	*645	*585	*550	*510	694	*690	Production
Consumption	*870	*893	*910	*925	*930	1 020	*1 050	Consommation
Consumption per cap. (kg.)	36	37	37	37	36	39	40	Consom. par hab.(kg.)
Viet Nam								**Viet Nam**
Production	*878	1 155	*850	*890	*975	*1 070	875	Production
Consumption	*750	*810	*875	*950	*1 005	*1 035	906	Consommation
Consumption per cap. (kg.)	10	10	11	12	13	13	11	Consom. par hab.(kg.)
Yemen								**Yémen**
Consumption*	390	410	425	445	470	480	495	Consommation*
Consumption per cap. (kg.)	22	23	23	23	24	23	23	Consom. par hab.(kg.)
Zambia								**Zambie**
Production	*210	*190	199	233	230	245	248	Production
Consumption	*115	*145	102	116	104	115	95	Consommation
Consumption per cap. (kg.)	11	14	11	11	9	10	9	Consom. par hab.(kg.)
Zimbabwe								**Zimbabwe**
Production	583	571	548	565	482	456	430	Production
Consumption	376	374	305	335	315	311	295	Consommation
Consumption per cap. (kg.)	29	30	24	27	25	27	25	Consom. par hab.(kg.)

Source

International Sugar Organization (ISO), London, the ISO database and the "Sugar Yearbook 2005".

Notes

1 Including store losses of 1,159 tons and accidental losses of 129 tons.

2 For statistical purposes, the data for China do not include those for the Hong Kong Special Administrative Region (Hong Kong SAR), Macao Special Administrative Region (Macao SAR) and Taiwan Province of China.

3 Including non-human consumption: 1983-6,710 tons; 1984-19,797 tons; 1985-79,908 tons; 1986-98,608 tons; 1987-147,262 tons; 1988-122,058 tons; 1989-52,230 tons; 1991-13,541 tons; 1994-12,178 tons; 1995-10,211 tons; 1996-14,648 tons; 1997-13,893 tons; 1998-17,082 tons; 1999-42,635 tons; 2000-31,836 tons; 2001-13,534 tons; 2002-16,750 tons.

4 For member states of this grouping, see Annex I – Other groupings.

5 Including 11,572 tons sold to other Pacific Island nations in 1994; 12,520 tons in 1995; 14,154 tons in 1996; 13,109 tons in 1997; 6,444 tons in 2001 and 10,686 tons in 2004.

6 Beginning 2004, data for Cyprus, Czech Republic, Estonia, Hungary, Latvia, Lithuania, Malta, Poland, Slovakia, Slovenia are incorporated in the European Union data.

7 Including sugar used for the production of mono-sodium glutamate and llysin: 1987-44,600 tons; 1988-92,200 tons; 1989-94,500 tons; 1990-89,400 tons; 1991-77,300 tons; 1992-75,800 tons; 1993-89,800 tons; 1994-170,384 tons; 1995-200,863 tons; 1996-257,700 tons; 1997-257,310 tons; 1998-258,247 tons; 1999-152,739 tons; 2000-159,027 tons; 2001-210,498 tons; 2002-197,939 tons; 2003-226,191 tons; 2004-235,773 tons; 2005-300,000 (estimated).

8 Including 19,780 tons used for livestock feed.

Source

Organisation internationale du sucre (OIS), Londres, la base de données de l'OIS et "l'Annuaire du sucre 2005".

Notes

1 Y compris des pertes de 1 159 tonnes au cours du stockage et des pertes accidentelles de 129 tonnes.

2 Pour la présentation des statistiques, les données pour la Chine ne comprennent pas la Région Administrative Spéciale de Hong Kong (Hong Kong RAS), la Région Administrative Spéciale de Macao (Macao RAS) et la province de Taiwan.

3 Dont consommation non humaine : 1983-6701 tonnes; 1984-19797 tonnes; 1985-79908 tonnes; 1986-98608 tonnes; 1987-147262 tonnes; 1988-122058 tonnes; 1989-52230 tonnes; 1991-13541 tonnes; 1994-12178 tonnes; 1995-10211 tonnes; 1996-14648 tonnes; 1997-13893 tonnes; 1998-17082 tonnes; 1999-42635 tonnes; 2000-31836 tonnes; 2001-13534 tonnes; 2002-16750 tonnes.

4 Pour les Etats membres de ce groupements, voir annexe I – Autres groupements.

5 Y compris 11572 tonnes vendues aux autres îles pacifiques en 1994; 12520 tonnes en 1995; 14154 tonnes en 1996; 13109 tonnes en 1997; et 6444 tonnes en 2001 et 10686 tonnes in 2004.

6 A partir de 2004, les données pour Chypre, République tchèque, Estonie, Hongrie, Lettonie, Lituanie, Malta, Pologne, Slovaquie, Slovénie sont inclus dans la Union européen.

7 Y compris la sucre utilisée pour la production du glutamate monosodium et lysine: 1987-44600 tonnes ; 1988-92200 tonnes; 1989-94500 tonnes; 1990-89400 tonnes; 1991-77300 tonnes ; 1992-75800 tonnes; 1993-89800 tonnes; 1994-170384 tonnes; 1995-200863 tonnes; 1996-257700 tonnes; 1997-257310 tonnes; 1998-258247 tonnes; 1999-152739 tonnes; 2000-159027 tonnes; 2001-210498 tonnes; 2002-197939 tonnes; 2003-226191 tonnes; 2004-235773 tonnes; 2005-300000 (estimation).

8 Y compris 19 780 tonnes utilisées pour les aliments du bétail.

37

Meat
Production: thousand metric tons

Viande
Production : milliers de tonnes

Region, country or area	1998	1999	2000	2001	2002	2003	2004	2005	Région, pays ou zone
World									**Monde**
Buffalo	**2 880**	**2 966**	**2 994**	**2 953**	**3 018**	**2 951**	**3 065**	**3 117**	**Buffle**
Cattle	**55 304**	**56 351**	**56 919**	**56 088**	**57 855**	**58 474**	**59 749**	**60 129**	**Bovine**
Goat	**3 495**	**3 585**	**3 732**	**3 843**	**4 023**	**4 251**	**4 364**	**4 562**	**Chèvre**
Pig	**88 434**	**89 282**	**90 097**	**92 082**	**95 220**	**98 028**	**100 105**	**102 770**	**Porc**
Sheep	**7 317**	**7 384**	**7 592**	**7 611**	**7 669**	**7 848**	**8 185**	**8 433**	**Mouton**
Africa									**Afrique**
Buffalo	**266**	**277**	**288**	**189**	**203**	**229**	**269**	**270**	**Buffle**
Cattle	**3 706**	**3 800**	**3 989**	**3 927**	**4 131**	**4 234**	**4 327**	**4 436**	**Bovine**
Goat	**768**	**775**	**783**	**797**	**824**	**835**	**843**	**847**	**Chèvre**
Pig	**684**	**697**	**703**	**759**	**771**	**782**	**807**	**804**	**Porc**
Sheep	**1 036**	**1 051**	**1 067**	**1 103**	**1 096**	**1 116**	**1 117**	**1 124**	**Mouton**
Algeria									Algérie
Cattle	103	117	133	105	116[1]	121	125[2]	125[1]	Bovine
Goat	12	12	12	12	12	12	12	12	Chèvre
Sheep	167	163	164	165[1]	165[1]	165[1]	165[1]	165[1]	Mouton
Angola									Angola
Cattle	85[1]	85[1]	85[1]	85[1]	85[1]	85[1]	85[1]	85	Bovine
Goat	8	9	10	10	9	9	9	9	Chèvre
Pig	29[1]	29[1]	29[1]	29[1]	28[1]	28[1]	28[1]	28	Porc
Sheep	1	1	1	1	1	1	1	1	Mouton
Benin									Bénin
Cattle	20	19	18	19	20	20	21	22	Bovine
Goat	4	4	4	4	4	4	5	5	Chèvre
Pig	3	2	4	3	4	4	4	4	Porc
Sheep	2	2	3	3	3	3	3	3	Mouton
Botswana									Botswana
Cattle	37	27	29	34	31	27	31	31	Bovine
Goat	6	6	5	5	5	5	5	5	Chèvre
Pig	1	^0	1	^0	^0	^0	^0	^0	Porc
Sheep	2	2	2	2	2	2	2	2	Mouton
Burkina Faso									Burkina Faso
Cattle	77	80	84	88	92	96	101	106	Bovine
Goat	22	23	24	24	25	26	27	28	Chèvre
Pig	17	18	20	22	25	27	30	33	Porc
Sheep	14	14	15	15	15	16	16	16	Mouton
Burundi									Burundi
Cattle	10	9	9	9	9	6	5	6	Bovine
Goat	3	3	3	3	3	3	3	3	Chèvre
Pig	4	4	4	4	4	4	4	4	Porc
Sheep	1	1	1	1	1	1	1	1	Mouton
Cameroon									Cameroun
Cattle	77[1]	91[2]	93[2]	95[2]	90[1]	90[1]	93[1]	94[1]	Bovine
Goat	14	14	16	16	16	16	16	16	Chèvre
Pig	14	12	16	16	16	16	16	16	Porc
Sheep	15	16	16	16	16	16	16	16	Mouton
Cape Verde									Cap-Vert
Cattle	1	^0	^0	1[1]	^0	^0	^0	^0	Bovine
Pig	6	7[1]	7	7[1]	7[1]	7[1]	7[1]	7[1]	Porc
Central African Rep.									Rép. centrafricaine
Cattle	51[2]	51[2]	67	67	69	71[1]	74[2]	74[1]	Bovine
Goat	8[1]	8[1]	10[2]	10[1]	11	12[1]	12[1]	12[1]	Chèvre
Pig	12[1]	12[1]	12[2]	13[1]	13	13	14[2]	14[1]	Porc
Sheep	1	1	1	1	1	2	2	2	Mouton

Region, country or area	1998	1999	2000	2001	2002	2003	2004	2005	Région, pays ou zone
Chad									Tchad
Cattle	80	78	74	77	76	78	80	82	Bovine
Goat	18	18	19	20	20	21	21	22	Chèvre
Sheep	11	11	12	12	13	13	13	14	Mouton
Comoros									Comores
Cattle	1	1	1	1	1	1	1	1	Bovine
Goat	^0	1	^0	^0	^0	^0	^0	^0	Chèvre
Congo									Congo
Cattle	1	2	2	2	2	2	2	2	Bovine
Goat	1	1	1	1	1	1	1	1	Chèvre
Pig	2	2	2	2	2	2	2	2	Porc
Côte d'Ivoire									Côte d'Ivoire
Cattle	52	47	48	46	53	51	52	52	Bovine
Goat	5[2]	5[2]	5[2]	5[1]	4	4	4	4	Chèvre
Pig	11	13	13[2]	14	14	12	12	12	Porc
Sheep	7[2]	6[2]	5	5	5	5	5	5	Mouton
Dem. Rep. of the Congo									Rép. dém. du Congo
Cattle	14	14	14	13	12	12	12	12	Bovine
Goat	22	19	19	19	18	18	18	18	Chèvre
Pig	29	27	26	25	24	24	24	24	Porc
Sheep	3	3	3	3	3	3	3	3	Mouton
Djibouti									Djibouti
Cattle	4	4	6	6	6	6	6	6	Bovine
Goat	2	2	2	2	2	2	2	2	Chèvre
Sheep	2	2	2	2	2	2	2	2	Mouton
Egypt									Egypte
Buffalo	266	277	288	189	203	229	269	270[1]	Buffle
Cattle	252	233	256[2]	247[2]	252	287	325	320[1]	Bovine
Goat	30	30	25[1]	25[1]	26	21	17	18[1]	Chèvre
Pig	3[1]	3	3[2]	3[2]	3[1]	2	2	2	Porc
Sheep	65	50[1]	50	53	52	50	40	43[1]	Mouton
Eritrea									Erythrée[1]
Cattle	16	16	16	15	14	17	17	17	Bovine
Goat	5	6	6	6	6	6	6	6	Chèvre
Sheep	6	6	6	6	6	7	7	6	Mouton
Ethiopia									Ethiopie
Cattle	274	290	294[1]	304[1]	353[1]	338[1]	331[1]	336[1]	Bovine
Goat	28[1]	27[1]	26[1]	29[1]	29[1]	29[1]	29[1]	29	Chèvre
Pig1	1	1	1	1	1	2	2	2	Porc[1]
Sheep[1]	36	36	36	38	48	50	55	57	Mouton[1]
Gabon									Gabon
Cattle	1	1	1	1	1	1	1	1	Bovine
Pig	3	3	3	3	3	3	3	3	Porc
Sheep	1	1	1	1	1	1	1	1	Mouton
Gambia									Gambie
Cattle	3	3	3	3	3	3	3	3	Bovine
Goat	^0	^0	^0	1	1	1	1	1	Chèvre
Ghana									Ghana
Cattle	21	21	24	24	24	24	25	25	Bovine
Goat	7	7	10	11	11	12	12	12	Chèvre
Pig	11	10	11	11	10	10	11	10	Porc
Sheep	7	7	9	10	10	10	11	11	Mouton
Guinea									Guinée
Cattle	29	30	32	33	34	34	35	37	Bovine
Goat	4	4	4	5	5	5	6	6	Chèvre
Pig	2	2	2	2	2	2	2	2	Porc
Sheep	3	3	3	4	4	4	4	5	Mouton

Region, country or area	1998	1999	2000	2001	2002	2003	2004	2005	Région, pays ou zone
Guinea-Bissau									Guinée-Bissau
Cattle	4	4	5	5	5	5	5	5	Bovine
Goat	1	1	1	1	1	1	1	1	Chèvre
Pig	10	11	11	11	11	11	11	12	Porc
Sheep	1	1	1	1	1	1	1	1	Mouton
Kenya									Kenya
Cattle	270	279	257	282	319	343	350	396	Bovine
Goat	30	34	31	31	43	39	39	39	Chèvre
Pig	11	11	11	15	11	15	15	13	Porc
Sheep	22	28	27	34	39	36	36	37	Mouton
Lesotho									Lesotho
Buffalo[1]	...	...	9	8	6	5	...	3	Buffle[1]
Cattle	10	9	...	...	...	...	...	...	Bovine
Goat	1	...	...	...	...	...	...	...	Chèvre
Pig	3	3	3	3	3	3	3	3	Porc
Sheep	3	3	...	...	...	...	...	...	Mouton
Liberia									Libéria
Cattle	1	1	1	1	1	1	1	1	Bovine
Goat	1	1	1	1	1	1	1	1	Chèvre
Pig	4	4	4	4	4	4	4	4	Porc
Sheep	1	1	1	1	1	1	1	1	Mouton
Libyan Arab Jamah.									Jamah. arabe libyenne
Cattle[1]	44	16	8	6	6	6	6	6	Bovine[1]
Goat	6[1]	6[1]	6[1]	6	6	6	6	6	Chèvre
Sheep	39[1]	34[1]	27[1]	32[1]	27[1]	27	27	27	Mouton
Madagascar									Madagascar
Cattle	148	148	148	119	112	115	147	147	Bovine
Goat	6	6	5	6	6	6	6	6	Chèvre
Pig	72	65	63	70	70	70	70	70	Porc
Sheep	2	2	2	2	2	3	2	2	Mouton
Malawi									Malawi
Cattle	14	15	16	16	16	16	16	16	Bovine
Goat	6	5	6	6	6	6	7	7	Chèvre
Pig	19	20	22	20	21	21	21	21	Porc
Mali									Mali
Cattle	91	89	76	85	103	113	98	98	Bovine
Goat	32	35	36	39	42	46	48	49	Chèvre
Pig	2	2	2	2	2	2	2	2	Porc
Sheep	26	25	26	29	31	34	36	36	Mouton
Mauritania									Mauritanie
Cattle[1]	14	14	21	22	22	23	23	23	Bovine[1]
Goat	11	12	12	13	14	14	14	14	Chèvre
Sheep	19	21	22	23	24	24	25	25	Mouton
Mauritius									Maurice
Cattle	3	3	3	2	2	3	2	2	Bovine
Pig	1	1	1	1	1	1	1	1	Porc
Morocco									Maroc
Cattle	120	135	140	159	170	150	148	148[1]	Bovine
Goat	22	20	22	21	20[1]	21[1]	21[1]	21[1]	Chèvre
Pig	1	1	1[2]	1[1]	1[1]	1[1]	1[1]	1[1]	Porc
Sheep	115	126	125	125	110	105	103	103[1]	Mouton
Mozambique									Mozambique
Cattle	38	38	38	38	38	38	38	38	Bovine
Goat	2	2	2	2	2	2	2	2	Chèvre
Pig	13	13	13	13	13	13	13	13	Porc
Sheep	1	1	1	1	1	1	1	1	Mouton

Region, country or area	1998	1999	2000	2001	2002	2003	2004	2005	Région, pays ou zone
Namibia									Namibie
Cattle	38	45	64	58	61	78	82	89	Bovine
Goat	4	5	5	4	5	5	5	5	Chèvre
Pig1	1	1	1	1	1	1	1	1	Porc[1]
Sheep	2	4	5	8	13	12	12	11	Mouton
Niger									Niger
Cattle	39[1]	40[1]	41[2]	42[2]	35[1]	37[1]	37[1]	37[1]	Bovine
Goat	23	25	25	25	22	25	25	25	Chèvre
Pig	1	1	1	1	1	1	1	1	Porc
Sheep	14	15	15	16	13	15	15	15	Mouton
Nigeria									Nigéria
Cattle	297	298	279[1]	279[1]	280[1]	280[1]	280[1]	280	Bovine
Goat	133	137	139	140	142	142	147	147	Chèvre
Pig	144	153	158	185	193	200	208	208	Porc
Sheep	89	91	95	94	97	99	101	101	Mouton
Réunion									Réunion
Cattle	2	2	2	2	2[1]	2[1]	2[1]	2[1]	Bovine
Pig	11	12	12	12	12[1]	13[1]	14[1]	14[1]	Porc
Rwanda									Rwanda
Cattle	16	18	17	19	20	24	23	23	Bovine
Goat	2	2	3	3	3	3	4	5	Chèvre
Pig	2	3	3	3	4	4	6	6	Porc
Sheep	1	1	1	1	1	1	1	1	Mouton
Senegal									Sénégal
Cattle	42	45	46	48	45	43	43	46	Bovine
Goat	10	9	10	9	9	9	10	10	Chèvre
Pig	5	7	9	9	11	10	9	10	Porc
Sheep	15	14	13	16	15	15	15	16	Mouton
Seychelles									Seychelles
Pig	1	1	1	1	1	1	1	1	Porc
Sierra Leone									Sierra Leone
Cattle	6	7	5	5	5	5	5	5	Bovine
Pig	2	2	2	2	2	2	2	2	Porc
Sheep	1	1	1	1	1	1	1	1	Mouton
Somalia									Somalie
Cattle	62	58	62	63	62	66	66	66	Bovine
Goat	36	38	33	33	39	42	42	42	Chèvre
Sheep	39	30	35	47	40	48	48	48	Mouton
South Africa									Afrique du Sud
Cattle	496	513	622	525	574	610	632	672	Bovine
Goat[1]	37	36	36	36	36	36	36	37	Chèvre[1]
Pig	119	123	104	111	111	134	145	140[1]	Porc
Sheep	91	112	118	104	105	120	120	122	Mouton
Sudan									Soudan
Cattle[1]	265	276	296	320	325	325	325	325	Bovine[1]
Goat	123	114	118	122[1]	126[1]	126[1]	126[1]	126[1]	Chèvre
Sheep[1]	141	142	143	150	144	144	144	144	Mouton[1]
Swaziland									Swaziland
Cattle	14[1]	14[1]	18	8	13	13[1]	13[1]	13[1]	Bovine
Goat	2	2	3	3	2	2	2	2	Chèvre
Pig	1	1	1	1	1	1	1	1	Porc
Sheep	^0	1	^0	^0	^0	^0	^0	^0	Mouton
Togo									Togo
Cattle	5	5	5	6	6	6	6	6	Bovine
Goat	3	3	4	4	4	4	4	4	Chèvre
Pig	4	4	4	5	5	5	5	5	Porc
Sheep	3	3	3	4	4	4	4	4	Mouton

Region, country or area	1998	1999	2000	2001	2002	2003	2004	2005	Région, pays ou zone
Tunisia									Tunisie
Cattle	53	58	60	60	64	58	53	55[1]	Bovine
Goat	9	10	9	9	10	9	9	10[1]	Chèvre
Sheep	50	53	54	56	58	51	52	55[1]	Mouton
Uganda									Ouganda
Cattle	93[1]	96[1]	97[1]	101[1]	106	110[1]	106[1]	106[1]	Bovine
Goat	23[1]	24[1]	25[1]	25[1]	25[1]	29[1]	29[1]	29	Chèvre
Pig	73[1]	75[1]	77[1]	81[1]	84[1]	60[1]	60[1]	60	Porc
Sheep[1]	5	5	5	6	6	8	8	6	Mouton[1]
United Rep. of Tanzania									Rép.-Unie de Tanzanie
Cattle[1]	198	215	225	230	246	246	246	246	Bovine[1]
Goat	27	29	29	30	31	31	31	31	Chèvre
Pig	11	12	13	13	13	13	13	13	Porc
Sheep	11	11	10	10	10	10	10	10	Mouton
Zambia									Zambie
Cattle	41	47	41	41	41	41[1]	41[1]	41[1]	Bovine
Goat	3	4	5	5	5	5	5	5	Chèvre
Pig	10	11	10	11	11	11	11	11	Porc
Sheep	^0	^0	1	1	1	1	1	1	Mouton
Zimbabwe									Zimbabwe
Cattle	74	95	101	101[1]	99[1]	97[1]	97[1]	97[1]	Bovine
Goat	12	13	13	13	13	13	13	13	Chèvre
Pig	13	13	20	27	27	28	28	28	Porc
Sheep	^0	1	1	1	1	1	1	1	Mouton
America, North									**Amérique du Nord**
Cattle	**14 936**	**15 356**	**15 552**	**15 259**	**15 755**	**15 296**	**14 877**	**14 980**	**Bovine**
Goat	**49**	**48**	**51**	**52**	**55**	**56**	**55**	**56**	**Chèvre**
Pig	**11 275**	**11 633**	**11 580**	**11 781**	**12 175**	**12 297**	**12 640**	**12 744**	**Porc**
Sheep	**163**	**162**	**162**	**162**	**165**	**161**	**161**	**162**	**Mouton**
Antigua and Barbuda									Antigua-et-Barbuda
Cattle	^0	^0	^0	1[1]	1[1]	1[1]	1[1]	1[1]	Bovine
Barbados									Barbade
Cattle	1	1	1	^0	^0	^0	^0	^0	Bovine
Pig	3	2	2	2	1	2	2	2[1]	Porc
Belize									Belize
Cattle	1	1	1	1	2	2	3	2[1]	Bovine
Pig	1	1	1	1	1	1	1	1	Porc
Canada									Canada
Cattle	1 182	1 264	1 263	1 262	1 294	1 190	1 496	1 523	Bovine
Pig	1 392	1 566	1 640	1 731	1 858	1 882	1 936	1 914	Porc
Sheep	10	11	13	14	15	16	18	17	Mouton
Costa Rica									Costa Rica
Cattle	82	84	82	74	68	74	69	65[1]	Bovine
Pig	25	29	31	36	36	36	38	39	Porc
Cuba									Cuba
Cattle	74	76	76	75	66	56	55	60	Bovine
Goat	1[1]	1	2	2	2	3	3	3	Chèvre
Pig	81	99	94	76	90	94	98	97	Porc
Sheep	4[1]	5	6[1]	6	7	7	7	7	Mouton
Dominica									Dominique
Cattle	1	1	1	1	1	1	1	1	Bovine
Dominican Republic									Rép. dominicaine
Cattle	80	66	69	71	72	75[1]	79[1]	78[1]	Bovine
Goat	1	1	1	1	1	1	1	1	Chèvre
Pig	64	58	61	63	64	65[1]	65[1]	66[1]	Porc
El Salvador									El Salvador
Cattle	34	34	35	35	40	29	26	27	Bovine
Pig	10	14	11	9	9	8	8	11	Porc

Region, country or area	1998	1999	2000	2001	2002	2003	2004	2005	Région, pays ou zone
Guadeloupe									Guadeloupe
Cattle	3	3	3[1]	3[1]	3[1]	3[1]	3[1]	3[1]	Bovine
Pig	1[1]	1[1]	1[1]	1[1]	1	1[1]	1[1]	1[1]	Porc
Guatemala									Guatemala
Cattle	54	62	62[1]	62[1]	63[1]	63[1]	63[1]	63[1]	Bovine
Pig	28	24	25[1]	25[1]	26[1]	26[1]	26[1]	26	Porc
Sheep	2	2	1	1	1	1	1	1	Mouton
Haiti									Haïti
Cattle	31	31[1]	40	41[1]	42[1]	43[1]	43[1]	43	Bovine
Goat	5[2]	5[1]	6	7[1]	7[1]	7[1]	6[1]	6	Chèvre
Pig	27	27[1]	28	31[1]	33[1]	33[1]	33[1]	33	Porc
Sheep	1[2]	1[1]	1	1[1]	1[1]	1[1]	1[1]	1	Mouton
Honduras									Honduras
Cattle	57	55	55	55	54	61	64	73	Bovine
Pig	9	9	10	10	9	8	9	9	Porc
Jamaica									Jamaïque
Cattle	12	15	14	13	14	15[1]	15[1]	15[1]	Bovine
Goat	2[1]	2[1]	2[1]	2[1]	2[1]	2[1]	2[1]	2	Chèvre
Pig	6	7	7	6	5	5[1]	5[1]	5	Porc
Martinique									Martinique
Cattle	2	2	2	2	2	2[1]	2[1]	2[1]	Bovine
Pig	2	2	2	2	2	2[1]	2[1]	2[1]	Porc
Mexico									Mexique
Cattle	1 380	1 400	1 409	1 445	1 468	1 504	1 543	1 557	Bovine
Goat	38	37	39	39	42	42	42	42	Chèvre
Pig	961	994	1 030	1 058	1 070	1 035	1 058	1 103	Porc
Sheep	30	31	33	36	38	42	42	46	Mouton
Montserrat									Montserrat
Cattle	1	1	1	1	1	1	1	1	Bovine
Nicaragua									Nicaragua
Cattle	46	46[1]	53[1]	54	60	66	75	74	Bovine
Pig	6	6	6	6	6	6	7	7	Porc
Panama									Panama
Cattle	76	71	70	67	65	61	64	63[1]	Bovine
Pig	19	21	22	18	18	20	21	21[1]	Porc
Puerto Rico									Porto Rico
Cattle	14[1]	18	15	13	11	10	13	10	Bovine
Pig	14[1]	9	9	10	9	9	12	11	Porc
Saint Lucia									Sainte-Lucie
Cattle	1	1	1	1	1	1	1	1	Bovine
Pig	1	1	1	1	1	1	1	1	Porc
Saint Vincent-Grenadines									Saint Vincent-Grenadines
Pig	1	1	1	1	1	1	1	1	Porc
Trinidad and Tobago									Trinité-et-Tobago
Cattle	1	1	1	1	1	1	1[1]	1[1]	Bovine
Pig	2	2	2	2	3	3	3[1]	3[1]	Porc
United States									Etats-Unis
Cattle	11 803	12 123	12 298	11 982	12 427	12 039	11 261	11 317	Bovine
Pig	8 623	8 758	8 597	8 691	8 929	9 056	9 312	9 392	Porc
Sheep	114	113	106	101	101[2]	92[2]	90[2]	88	Mouton
United States Virgin Is.									Iles Vierges américaines
Cattle[1]	1	1	1	1	1	1	1	1	Bovine[1]
America, South									**Amérique du Sud**
Cattle	**10 816**	**11 628**	**11 863**	**11 630**	**12 050**	**12 310**	**13 339**	**13 453**	**Bovine**
Goat	**76**	**79**	**82**	**78**	**80**	**81**	**82**	**83**	**Chèvre**
Pig	**3 403**	**3 493**	**3 706**	**3 808**	**3 967**	**4 276**	**4 402**	**4 427**	**Porc**
Sheep	**242**	**248**	**254**	**255**	**230**	**229**	**239**	**251**	**Mouton**

Region, country or area	1998	1999	2000	2001	2002	2003	2004	2005	Région, pays ou zone
Argentina									Argentine
Cattle	2 469	2 720	2 718	2 461	2 493	2 658	3 024	2 980	Bovine
Goat	9	9	9	9	9[1]	10[1]	10[1]	10[1]	Chèvre
Pig	184	215	214	198	165	150	150[1]	150[1]	Porc
Sheep	48[2]	45[2]	50[1]	50[1]	50[1]	52[1]	52[1]	52[1]	Mouton
Bolivia									Bolivie
Cattle	155	155	160	161	165	168	172	172	Bovine
Goat	6	6	6	6	6	6	6	6	Chèvre
Pig	72	74	76	97	101	104	108	108	Porc
Sheep	15	15	16	16	17	18	18	18	Mouton
Brazil									Brésil
Cattle	5 794	6 413	6 579	6 824	7 139	7 230	7 774	7 774[1]	Bovine
Goat[1]	34	38	39	39	40	41	41	41	Chèvre[1]
Pig	2 400[1]	2 400[1]	2 600[1]	2 637	2 798	3 059	3 110	3 110[1]	Porc
Sheep[1]	68	71	72	72	69	68	76	76	Mouton[1]
Chile									Chili
Cattle	256	226	226	218	200	192	208	216	Bovine
Goat	5	5	5	5	5	5	5	5	Chèvre
Pig	235	244	261	303	351	365	373	411	Porc
Sheep	11	13	11	11	10	10	10	9	Mouton
Colombia									Colombie
Cattle	766	716	745	700[1]	675[1]	642	717	792	Bovine
Goat	6	6	7[1]	6[1]	6[1]	7[1]	7[1]	7[1]	Chèvre
Pig	75	107	105	98	109	124	130	128	Porc
Sheep	6[1]	6	7[2]	7[1]	6[1]	7[1]	7[1]	7[1]	Mouton
Ecuador									Equateur
Cattle	158	164	174	189	188	203	206	207	Bovine
Goat	1	1	1[1]	1	1	1	1	1	Chèvre
Pig	100	110	108	128	140	148	157	165	Porc
Sheep	10[2]	10[1]	10[1]	10[1]	10	10	11	11	Mouton
Falkland Is. (Malvinas)									Iles Falkland (Malvinas)
Sheep	1	1	1	1	1	1	1	1	Mouton
French Guiana									Guyane française
Pig	1	1	1	1	1	1[1]	1[1]	1[1]	Porc
Guyana									Guyana
Cattle	2	2	2	2[2]	2[1]	2[1]	2[1]	2[1]	Bovine
Pig1	1	1	1	1	1	1	1	1	Porc[1]
Sheep	1	1	1	1	1	1	1	1	Mouton
Paraguay									Paraguay
Cattle	231[2]	246[2]	239	200	205	215	215	215[1]	Bovine
Goat	1	1	1	1	1	1	1	1	Chèvre
Pig	119	120	114	117	78	93	156	105	Porc
Sheep	3	3	2	2	3[1]	3[1]	3[1]	3[1]	Mouton
Peru									Pérou
Cattle	124	134	136	138	142	138	146	153	Bovine
Goat	6	7	7	6	6	6	7	7	Chèvre
Pig	71	66	72	85	85	93	98	103	Porc
Sheep	23	30	31	32	32	32	34	34	Mouton
Suriname									Suriname
Cattle	2	2	2	2	2	2[1]	2[1]	2[1]	Bovine
Pig	1	1	1	1	1	1[1]	1[1]	1[1]	Porc
Uruguay									Uruguay
Cattle	450	458	453	317[2]	412	424	496	516[2]	Bovine
Pig	26	27	26	23	20	17	15	19	Porc
Sheep	55[2]	51[2]	51[2]	51[1]	31	27	27	37[2]	Mouton
Venezuela (Bolivarian Rep. of)									Venezuela (Rép. bolivarienne du)
Cattle	408	391	429	418	429	435	376	425	Bovine
Goat	7	5	7	4	5	5	5	6	Chèvre
Pig	118	128	126	119	119	120	101	126	Porc
Sheep	2	3	2	2	2	2	2	3	Mouton

Region, country or area	1998	1999	2000	2001	2002	2003	2004	2005	Région, pays ou zone
Asia									**Asie**
Buffalo	**2 612**	**2 687**	**2 704**	**2 763**	**2 813**	**2 720**	**2 794**	**2 840**	**Buffle**
Cattle	**10 658**	**10 849**	**11 163**	**11 082**	**11 651**	**12 227**	**12 890**	**13 306**	**Bovine**
Goat	**2 459**	**2 540**	**2 679**	**2 782**	**2 926**	**3 138**	**3 245**	**3 438**	**Chèvre**
Pig	**46 791**	**46 787**	**48 238**	**50 269**	**52 239**	**54 511**	**56 676**	**59 709**	**Porc**
Sheep	**3 247**	**3 338**	**3 482**	**3 540**	**3 717**	**3 937**	**4 296**	**4 511**	**Mouton**
Afghanistan									Afghanistan
Cattle	171[2]	149[2]	126[2]	108[2]	150[2]	144[1]	144[1]	144[1]	Bovine
Goat	38	34	33	27	39	33	33	33	Chèvre
Sheep	129[2]	141[1]	120[1]	104[1]	88[1]	72[1]	72[1]	72	Mouton
Armenia									Arménie
Cattle	35	32	31	29	30	30	33	34	Bovine
Pig	7	8	9	9	10	12	9	9	Porc
Sheep	5	5	8	7	6	6	7	8	Mouton
Azerbaijan									Azerbaïdjan
Cattle	50	52	56	57	63	67	69	71	Bovine
Pig	1	2	1	1	1	1	2	2	Porc
Sheep	32	35	35	37	38	39	41	42	Mouton
Bahrain									Bahreïn
Cattle	1	1	1	1	1	1	1	1	Bovine
Goat	1	1	^0	5	6	5	6	6	Chèvre
Sheep	5	8	7	3	1	2	2	2	Mouton
Bangladesh									Bangladesh
Buffalo	4	4[2]	4[2]	4[2]	4[2]	4[1]	4[1]	4[1]	Buffle
Cattle	161	171[2]	173[2]	174[2]	178[2]	180[1]	180[1]	180	Bovine
Goat	126	127[2]	129[2]	129[2]	137[2]	137[1]	137[1]	137[1]	Chèvre
Sheep	3	3[2]	3[2]	3[2]	3[2]	3[1]	3[1]	3[1]	Mouton
Bhutan									Bhoutan
Cattle	5	6	5	5	5	5	5	5	Bovine
Pig	1	1	1	1	1	1	1	1	Porc
Brunei Darussalam									Brunéi Darussalam
Buffalo	^0	^0	^0	^0	1	1	^0	^0	Buffle
Cattle	1	5	3	3	3	3	3	3	Bovine
Cambodia									Cambodge
Buffalo	10	9	10	9	9	10	13	14	Buffle
Cattle	42	42	57	58	53	54	54	60	Bovine
Pig	100	103	105	108	110	120	123	128	Porc
China[4,5]									Chine[4,5]
Buffalo	339[2]	367[2]	361[2]	379[2]	387[2]	305[2]	330[2]	346	Buffle
Cattle	4 486[2]	4 711[2]	4 991[2]	5 131[2]	5 480[2]	6 019[2]	6 449[2]	6 790	Bovine
Goat[2]	1 111	1 182	1 304	1 390	1 490	1 683	1 756	1 927	Chèvre[2]
Pig	39 900	39 900	41 406	42 982	44 358	46 233	48 118	51 201	Porc
Sheep	1 239[2]	1 335[2]	1 440[2]	1 540[2]	1 680[2]	1 892[2]	2 240[2]	2 431	Mouton
Cyprus[6]									Chypre[6]
Cattle	4	4	4	4	4	4[1]	4[1]	...	Bovine
Goat	5	6	6	7	8	8[1]	8[1]	8[1]	Chèvre
Pig	47	49	52	51	52	53[1]	54[1]	54[1]	Porc
Sheep	5	4	4	4	5	5[1]	5[1]	5[1]	Mouton
Georgia									Géorgie
Cattle	43	41	48	47	49	50	50	49	Bovine
Pig	42	41	37	35	36	37	35	33	Porc
Sheep	8	7	9	8	8	8	9	10	Mouton
India									Inde
Buffalo	1 382	1 399	1 416	1 433	1 450	1 467	1 483	1 488	Buffle
Cattle	1 401	1 421	1 442	1 452	1 463	1 473	1 483	1 494	Bovine
Goat	462	466	467	469	470	473	475	475	Chèvre
Pig	466	473	476	483	487	490	497	497	Porc
Sheep	226	228	229	230	233	236	239	239	Mouton

Region, country or area	1998	1999	2000	2001	2002	2003	2004	2005	Région, pays ou zone
Indonesia									Indonésie
Buffalo	46	48	46	44	42	41	40	41	Buffle
Cattle	343	309	340	339	330	370	448	464	Bovine
Goat	48	45	45	49	58	64	57	59	Chèvre
Pig	622	550	413	463	512	528	567	578	Porc
Sheep	34	32	33	45	69	81	66	66	Mouton
Iran (Islamic Rep. of)									Iran (Rép. islamique d')
Buffalo	11	11	12	12	13	13	13	12	Buffle
Cattle	324	286	269	274	284	312[1]	320[1]	320[1]	Bovine
Goat	109	104	110	111	105	105[1]	105[1]	105[1]	Chèvre
Sheep	309	293	326	333	345	346[1]	348[1]	389[1]	Mouton
Iraq									Iraq
Buffalo[1]	3	3	4	4	4	4	4	4	Buffle[1]
Cattle[1]	45	45	46	49	50	50	50	50	Bovine[1]
Goat[1]	8	8	7	4	8	8	8	8	Chèvre[1]
Sheep	20	20	24	21	20	20	20	20	Mouton
Israel[7]									Israël[7]
Cattle	44	46	64	62	80	91	83	90	Bovine
Goat	2[1]	2	2	2	2	2	3	3	Chèvre
Pig	12	9	15	16	16	17	18	19	Porc
Sheep	5[2]	5[2]	5[2]	5[2]	5[1]	5[1]	5[1]	5[1]	Mouton
Japan									Japon
Cattle	529	540	530	459	537	496	514	499	Bovine
Pig	1 291	1 277	1 256	1 232	1 246	1 274	1 263	1 245	Porc
Jordan									Jordanie
Cattle	3	4	3	4	3	4	4	7	Bovine
Goat	4	3	2	2	1	2[1]	2[1]	2[1]	Chèvre
Sheep	7[2]	4	5	5	4	4[1]	4[1]	4[1]	Mouton
Kazakhstan									Kazakhstan
Cattle	348	344	306	288	296	312	330	345[2]	Bovine
Goat	5	4[2]	4[2]	5[2]	7	7[2]	8[2]	8[2]	Chèvre
Pig	79	98	133	181	187	185	199	207[2]	Porc
Sheep	114	95[2]	91	92	94	96	102	110[2]	Mouton
Korea, Dem. P. R.									Corée, R. p. dém. de
Cattle	20	20	20	21	22	22	21	22	Bovine
Goat	7	9	10	11	11	11	11	11	Chèvre
Pig	112	134	140	145	163	163	165	168	Porc
Sheep	1	1	1	1	1	1	1	1	Mouton
Korea, Republic of									Corée, République de
Cattle	376	342	306	233	211	188	195[2]	195	Bovine
Goat	3	3	3	3	3	3	3	3	Chèvre
Pig	939	996	916	928	1 005	1 149[2]	1 100[2]	1 036[2]	Porc
Kuwait									Koweït
Cattle[1]	2	2	2	2	2	2	2	2	Bovine[1]
Goat	^0	1	1	^0	1	1	1	1	Chèvre
Sheep[1]	38	34	34	31	37	31	30	30	Mouton[1]
Kyrgyzstan									Kirghizistan
Cattle	95	95	101	100	105	94	95	91	Bovine
Goat	3	3	4	7	7	7	7	7	Chèvre
Pig	30	29	24	26	23	22	25	19	Porc
Sheep	41[2]	43	39	37	37	37	38	39	Mouton
Lao People's Dem. Rep.									Rép. dém. pop. lao
Buffalo	16	19	17	17	17	18	19	19	Buffle
Cattle	15	19	16	17	20	22	22[1]	23[1]	Bovine
Goat	^0	^0	^0	^0	^0	1	^0	1	Chèvre
Pig	31	32	28	32	32	36	27	28	Porc

Region, country or area	1998	1999	2000	2001	2002	2003	2004	2005	Région, pays ou zone
Lebanon									Liban
Cattle	31	51	58	43	55	53	53	53	Bovine
Goat	3	3	3	3	3	3	3	3	Chèvre
Pig	3	2	2	2	2	1	1	1	Porc
Sheep	5	6	6	17	14	14	15	15	Mouton
Malaysia									Malaisie
Buffalo	4	3	3	3	4	4	5	5	Buffle
Cattle	18	18	15	16	18	20	21	21	Bovine
Goat	1	1	1	1	1	1	1	1	Chèvre
Pig	260	159	160	185	193	198	203	206	Porc
Mongolia									Mongolie
Cattle	99	105	113	67	61	44	52	47[1]	Bovine
Goat	30	32	30	28	20[2]	19[2]	33[2]	35[1]	Chèvre
Pig	^0	^0	1	1	^0	^0	^0	^0	Porc
Sheep	90	97	90	77	75[2]	62[2]	65[2]	67[1]	Mouton
Myanmar									Myanmar
Buffalo	20	20	20	21	22	22	23	23	Buffle
Cattle	101	101	102	104	108	97	114	114	Bovine
Goat	7	7	7	7	8	9[1]	9[1]	9[1]	Chèvre
Pig	91	107	113	121	123	132	143	143	Porc
Sheep	2	2	2	2	2	2[1]	2[1]	2[1]	Mouton
Nepal									Népal
Buffalo	117	120	122	125	128	131	134	139	Buffle
Cattle	48	48	48	47	47	48	48	49	Bovine
Goat	36	36	37	38	39	40	41	42	Chèvre
Pig	13	14	15	15	16	16	15	16	Porc
Sheep	3	3	3	3	3	3	3	3	Mouton
Occupied Palestinian Terr.									Terr. palestinien occupé
Cattle	12	12	14	11	8	7	6	7	Bovine
Goat	3	3	4	3	4	5	4	4	Chèvre
Sheep	7	7	7	5	10	13	12	10	Mouton
Oman									Oman
Cattle	4	5	4	4	4	4	4	4	Bovine
Goat	4	4	5	6	8	10	14	14	Chèvre
Sheep	13	13	13	13	13	12	11	11	Mouton
Pakistan									Pakistan
Buffalo	441	454	466	480	494	508	524	540	Buffle
Cattle	405	413	420	423	431	445	455	475	Bovine
Goat	289	300	310	321	333	345	357	370	Chèvre
Sheep	156	156	157	159	159	161	161	162	Mouton
Philippines									Philippines
Buffalo	56	69	72	72	76	76	80	79[2]	Buffle
Cattle	156	190	190	183	183	181	179	175[2]	Bovine
Goat	31[2]	33	34	33	34	33	34[2]	35[1]	Chèvre
Pig	933	973	1 008	1 064	1 332	1 346	1 376	1 100	Porc
Qatar									Qatar
Cattle	^0	^0	1	^0	^0	^0	^0	^0	Bovine
Goat	1	1	1	1	1	1	1	1	Chèvre
Sheep	7	5	6	8	8	7	6	6	Mouton
Saudi Arabia									Arabie saoudite
Cattle	21[2]	21[2]	22[2]	22[2]	22[2]	22[2]	23[1]	23	Bovine
Goat	20	21	22[2]	22[2]	22[2]	23[1]	23[1]	23[1]	Chèvre
Sheep	69[2]	77[2]	76[2]	76[2]	76[2]	76[1]	76[1]	76[1]	Mouton
Singapore									Singapour
Pig	84	31[1]	21[1]	23	21	19	20	0	Porc

Region, country or area	1998	1999	2000	2001	2002	2003	2004	2005	Région, pays ou zone
Sri Lanka									Sri Lanka
Buffalo	4	4	4	3	3	3	4	4	Buffle
Cattle	25	24	29	27	28	29	28	29	Bovine
Goat	2	2	2	2	2	1	1	1	Chèvre
Pig	2	2	2	2	2	2	2	2	Porc
Syrian Arab Republic									Rép. arabe syrienne
Cattle	43	47	47	42	47	47	47[1]	55	Bovine
Goat	6	5	5	5	5	5[1]	5[1]	5[1]	Chèvre
Sheep	154	177	184	169	184[1]	207[1]	207[1]	180	Mouton
Tajikistan									Tadjikistan
Cattle	15	15[2]	12[2]	15[2]	19[2]	23[2]	25[2]	24[2]	Bovine
Sheep	13	13[2]	16[2]	13[2]	14[2]	19[2]	21[2]	19[2]	Mouton
Thailand									Thaïlande
Buffalo	69	60	52	58	58	59	60	62	Buffle
Cattle	183	170	171	176	183	190	115	115[1]	Bovine
Goat	1	1	1	1	1	1	1	1	Chèvre
Pig	469	454	475	632	645	661	677	683	Porc
Timor-Leste									Timor-Leste
Buffalo	^0	1	1	1	1	1	1	1	Buffle
Cattle	2	1	1	1	1	1	1	1	Bovine
Goat	1	1	^0	^0	^0	^0	^0	^0	Chèvre
Pig	9	6	6	8	8	8	10	10	Porc
Turkey									Turquie
Buffalo	5	5	4	2	2	2	2	2	Buffle
Cattle	359	350	355	332	328	290	365	322	Bovine
Goat	57[2]	55[2]	53[1]	48[1]	47[1]	45[1]	45[1]	45[1]	Chèvre
Sheep	317[2]	313[2]	321[1]	303[1]	286[1]	267[1]	273[1]	272[1]	Mouton
Turkmenistan									Turkménistan
Cattle	61	63	72[2]	84[1]	92[2]	101[2]	106[1]	100[1]	Bovine
Goat	3[2]	3[2]	5[2]	5[1]	6[2]	6[2]	7[1]	7[1]	Chèvre
Pig	1	1	1[2]	^0[2]	^0[2]	^0[2]	^0[1]	^0[1]	Porc
Sheep	58[2]	60[2]	66[2]	75[1]	83[2]	90[2]	95[1]	90[1]	Mouton
United Arab Emirates									Emirats arabes unis
Cattle	8	21	15	8	9	10	10	10	Bovine
Goat	7	8	8	9	11	10	14	15	Chèvre
Sheep	24	18	16	14	17	14	14	14	Mouton
Uzbekistan									Ouzbékistan
Cattle	400	371[2]	390[2]	404[2]	425	456	494	518	Bovine
Pig	15	20[2]	15[2]	11[2]	4	11	14	16	Porc
Sheep	82	73[2]	79[2]	75[2]	71	74	70	74	Mouton
Viet Nam									Viet Nam
Buffalo	84	90	92	97	99	53	57	60	Buffle
Cattle	79	89	92	98	102	108	120	153	Bovine
Goat	5	5	5	5	5	6	8	9	Chèvre
Pig	1 228	1 318	1 409	1 515	1 654	1 795	2 012	2 288	Porc
Yemen									Yémen
Cattle	45	47	52	56	59	60	65	…	Bovine
Goat[1]	22	22	23	24	25	26	26	26	Chèvre[1]
Sheep[1]	23	24	24	25	27	29	34	35	Mouton[1]
Europe									**Europe**
Buffalo	**2**	**2**	**3**	**2**	**2**	**2**	**3**	**6**	**Buffle**
Cattle	**12 575**	**12 124**	**11 772**	**11 458**	**11 642**	**11 653**	**11 552**	**11 119**	**Bovine**
Goat	**131**	**131**	**124**	**120**	**121**	**125**	**120**	**120**	**Chèvre**
Pig	**25 786**	**26 184**	**25 381**	**24 969**	**25 538**	**25 606**	**25 039**	**24 562**	**Porc**
Sheep	**1 468**	**1 439**	**1 415**	**1 275**	**1 296**	**1 262**	**1 294**	**1 302**	**Mouton**
Albania									Albanie
Cattle	32[2]	34[2]	36[2]	35[2]	38[2]	40	40[2]	41	Bovine
Goat	6[2]	6[2]	7	7	7	7	8[2]	7[1]	Chèvre
Pig	7[2]	6[2]	8[2]	8[2]	9[2]	9[2]	10[2]	11	Porc
Sheep	11[2]	12[2]	12[2]	12[1]	12	12	14[2]	13	Mouton

Region, country or area	1998	1999	2000	2001	2002	2003	2004	2005	Région, pays ou zone
Austria									Autriche
Cattle	197	203	203	215	212	208	206	204	Bovine
Goat	1	1	1	1	1	1	1	1	Chèvre
Pig	661[2]	684[2]	620[2]	614[2]	653[2]	518	515	510	Porc
Sheep	7	6	7	7	7	7	7	7	Mouton
Belarus									Bélarus
Cattle	271	262	213	231	227	211	224	256	Bovine
Pig	320	311	302	303	301	301	299	321	Porc
Sheep	3	3	3	3	2	2	2	1	Mouton
Belgium									Belgique
Cattle	...	...	275	285	305	275	281	289	Bovine
Pig	...	...	1 042	1 062	1 041	1 026	1 057	1 008	Porc
Sheep	...	...	4	5	3	3	4	2	Mouton
Belgium-Luxembourg									Belgique-Luxembourg
Cattle	303	281	...	...	...	...	...	...	Bovine
Pig	1 085	1 005	...	...	...	...	...	...	Porc
Sheep	4	5	...	...	...	...	...	...	Mouton
Bosnia and Herzegovina									Bosnie-Herzégovine
Cattle	12	12[1]	13[2]	13[2]	14[1]	15[1]	19	24	Bovine
Pig1	12	12	11	11	10	8	8	8	Porc[1]
Sheep	3[1]	3[1]	3	3[1]	2[1]	2[1]	2	2	Mouton
Bulgaria									Bulgarie
Buffalo	1[1]	1[1]	1[1]	1[1]	^0	^0	^0	^0	Buffle
Cattle	55[2]	61[2]	60[2]	69[2]	24	29	31	30	Bovine
Goat	7[2]	8[2]	8[2]	7[2]	5	7	6	7	Chèvre
Pig	248	267	243	237	245[1]	71	78	75	Porc
Sheep	46[2]	50[2]	51[2]	44[2]	47[2]	13	14	18	Mouton
Croatia									Croatie
Cattle	26	28	28	26	27	28	32	25[2]	Bovine
Pig	60[2]	64	64[2]	64[2]	65[2]	62[2]	61[2]	49[1]	Porc
Sheep	2[2]	4	2	2	2	3	2	3[2]	Mouton
Czech Republic									République tchèque
Cattle	134	121	108	109	106	104	97	87	Bovine
Pig	476	452	417	415	416	411	388	352	Porc
Sheep	3	3	1	1	1	1	1	1	Mouton
Denmark									Danemark
Cattle	162	157	154	153	154	147	150	150[1]	Bovine
Pig	1 629	1 642	1 625	1 716	1 759	1 762	1 810	1 800[1]	Porc
Sheep	2	1	1	2	1	2	2	2[1]	Mouton
Estonia									Estonie
Cattle	19	22	15	14	17	13	15	13	Bovine
Pig	32	31	30	34	40	40	41	40	Porc
Faeroe Islands									Iles Féroé
Sheep	1	1	1	1	1	1	1	1	Mouton
Finland									Finlande
Cattle	94	90	91	90	91	96	93	87	Bovine
Pig	185	182	173	174	184	193	198	204	Porc
Sheep	1	1	1	1	1	1	1	1	Mouton
France									France
Cattle	1 632	1 609	1 528	1 566	1 640	1 632	1 565	1 529[2]	Bovine
Goat	9	6	7	7	7	7	6[2]	7[2]	Chèvre
Pig	2 328	2 353	2 312	2 315	2 346	2 339	2 293	2 257[2]	Porc
Sheep	135	132	133	134	128	129	122[2]	123[2]	Mouton
Germany									Allemagne
Cattle	1 367	1 374	1 304	1 362	1 316	1 226	1 258	1 167	Bovine
Pig	3 834	4 103	3 982	4 074	4 110	4 239	4 323	4 500	Porc
Sheep	44	44	48	46	44	46	48	49	Mouton

Region, country or area	1998	1999	2000	2001	2002	2003	2004	2005	Région, pays ou zone
Greece									Grèce
Cattle	73	67	63	60	62	62	75	75[1]	Bovine
Goat	55	56	44	43	45	47	44	43[1]	Chèvre
Pig	134	138	141	137	110	111	135	135[1]	Porc
Sheep	90	90	81	79	82	80[1]	81[1]	81[1]	Mouton
Hungary									Hongrie
Cattle	47	51	67	52	48	61	53	46[2]	Bovine
Pig	570	626	613	556	580	510	487	456	Porc
Sheep	3	4	4	3	3[1]	1	1	1	Mouton
Iceland									Islande
Cattle	3	4	4	4	4	4	4	4	Bovine
Pig	4	5	5	5	6	6	6	5	Porc
Sheep	8	9	10	9	9	9	9	9	Mouton
Ireland									Irlande
Cattle	594	644	577	579	540	568	564	546	Bovine
Pig	242	250	230	241	231	217	208[2]	208[1]	Porc
Sheep	86	90	83	78	67	63[2]	72[2]	70[1]	Mouton
Italy									Italie
Buffalo	1	1	1	1	2	1	3	6	Buffle
Cattle	1 111	1 164	1 152	1 133	1 134	1 127	1 145	1 102	Bovine
Goat	3	4	4	4	4	3	3	3	Chèvre
Pig	1 412	1 472	1 479	1 510	1 536	1 590	1 590	1 515	Porc
Sheep	70	70	65	62	58	58	59	59	Mouton
Latvia									Lettonie
Cattle	26	23	22	19	16	21	22	20	Bovine
Pig	36	35	32	32	36	37	37	38	Porc
Lithuania									Lituanie
Cattle	81	77	75	47	45	43	48	47	Bovine
Goat	...	...	...	...	...	1	^0	1	Chèvre
Pig	96	91	85	72	95	91	97	106	Porc
Sheep	1	1	1	1	1	^0	^0	^0	Mouton
Luxembourg									Luxembourg
Cattle	...	...	17	11	19	17	16	17	Bovine
Pig	...	...	13	11	11	12	11	13	Porc
Malta									Malte
Cattle	2	2	2	2	2	1	1	1[1]	Bovine
Pig	10	10	9	10	10	10	8[2]	8[1]	Porc
Netherlands									Pays-Bas
Cattle	535	508	471	372	384	365	386	395	Bovine
Goat	^0	1[2]	^0	^0	^0	^0	^0	^0	Chèvre
Pig	1 725	1 711	1 623	1 432	1 377	1 253	1 289	1 306	Porc
Sheep	17	18	18	18	17	15	16	16[1]	Mouton
Norway									Norvège
Cattle	91	96	91	86	85	85	86	84	Bovine
Pig	106	109	103	109	104	106	114	117	Porc
Sheep	23	23	23	24	25	25	26	25	Mouton
Poland									Pologne
Cattle	430	385	349	316	281	317	311	310	Bovine
Pig	2 026	2 043	1 923	1 849	2 023	2 190	1 956	1 956	Porc
Sheep	1	2	1	1	1	1	2	1	Mouton
Portugal									Portugal
Cattle	96	97	100	95	106	105	118	118	Bovine
Goat	3	3	2	2	2	2	2	1[2]	Chèvre
Pig	332	346	329	317	330	329	315	327	Porc
Sheep	23	22	24	22	24	22	22	22[2]	Mouton
Republic of Moldova									République de Moldova
Cattle	24	21	18	16	16	16	23[2]	24[2]	Bovine
Pig	58	61	50	44	45	43	38[2]	39[2]	Porc
Sheep	4	4	3	3	3	3	3[2]	3[2]	Mouton

Region, country or area	1998	1999	2000	2001	2002	2003	2004	2005	Région, pays ou zone
Romania									Roumanie
Cattle	150	153	162	145	156	185	162	161	Bovine
Goat	3	4	4	4	3	5	6	5	Chèvre
Pig	617	595	502	460	476	533	374	398	Porc
Sheep	53	54	49	48	51	62	67	53	Mouton
Russian Federation									Fédération de Russie
Cattle	2 247	1 868	1 894	1 873	1 957	1 990	1 951	1 793	Bovine
Goat	22	20	20	20	20	19	18	18	Chèvre
Pig	1 505	1 485	1 569	1 498	1 583	1 706	1 643	1 520	Porc
Sheep	156	124	119	114	115	114	125	134	Mouton
Serbia and Montenegro									Serbie-et-Monténégro
Cattle[2]	216	185	194	165	166	164	161	156	Bovine[2]
Goat	1	1	1	1	1	1	1	1	Chèvre
Pig [2]	625	653	635	565	617	574	539	562	Porc[2]
Sheep	29	22	23	22	19	21	20	21	Mouton
Slovakia									Slovaquie
Cattle	59	50	48	38	42	33	33	26	Bovine
Pig	227	220	164	153	154	183	167	140	Porc
Sheep	2	1	2	2	2	2	2	2[1]	Mouton
Slovenia									Slovénie
Cattle	48	48	43	49	43	52	47	46[2]	Bovine
Pig	65	71	60	66	62	64	71	70[2]	Porc
Sheep	1	1	1	1	1	1	1[1]	1[1]	Mouton
Spain									Espagne
Cattle	651	661	651	651	679	706	714	714	Bovine
Goat	16	17	16	15	15	14	13	17	Chèvre
Pig	2 744	2 893	2 905	2 989	3 070	3 190	3 076	3 101	Porc
Sheep	233	221	232	236	237	236	231	224	Mouton
Sweden									Suède
Cattle	143	145	150	143	147	140	142	136	Bovine
Pig	330	325	277	276	284	288	295	275	Porc
Sheep	3	4	4	4	4	4	4	4	Mouton
Switzerland									Suisse
Cattle	147	146	128	138	140	137	134	132	Bovine
Goat	1	1	1	^0	^0	^0	^0	1	Chèvre
Pig	232	226	225	234	236	230	227	236	Porc
Sheep	6	6	6	6	6	6	7	6	Mouton
TFYR of Macedonia									L'ex-R.y. Macédoine
Cattle	6	7	6	7[2]	7	9	9	8	Bovine
Pig	9	9	9	8	11	10	9	9	Porc
Sheep	6	4	5[1]	6[1]	5	6	7	7	Mouton
Ukraine									Ukraine
Cattle	793	791	754	646	704	723	618	562	Bovine
Goat	4	4	8	7	9	9	8	8	Chèvre
Pig	668	656	676	591	599	631	559	494	Porc
Sheep	17	15	9	8	8	8	8[2]	8	Mouton
United Kingdom									Royaume-Uni
Cattle	699	679	705	645	694	699	719	762	Bovine
Pig	1 135	1 042	899	777	774	716	708	706	Porc
Sheep	375	392	383	267	307	303	312	331	Mouton
Oceania									**Océanie**
Buffalo^	**0**	**0**	**0**	**0**	**0**	**0**	**0**	**0**	**Buffle^**
Cattle	**2 611**	**2 593**	**2 581**	**2 731**	**2 625**	**2 754**	**2 764**	**2 835**	**Bovine**
Goat	**11**	**11**	**13**	**13**	**16**	**17**	**19**	**19**	**Chèvre**
Pig	**495**	**488**	**489**	**496**	**530**	**556**	**542**	**525**	**Porc**
Sheep	**1 161**	**1 145**	**1 213**	**1 277**	**1 165**	**1 143**	**1 079**	**1 083**	**Mouton**

Region, country or area	1998	1999	2000	2001	2002	2003	2004	2005	Région, pays ou zone
Australia[8]									Australie[8]
Cattle	1 955	2 011	1 988	2 119	2 028	2 073	2 033	2 162	Bovine
Goat	8	8	11	11	14	14	17	17	Chèvre
Pig	369	362	364	365	396	420	406	388	Porc
Sheep	616	628	680	715	644	597	561	595	Mouton
Cook Islands									Iles Cook
Pig	1	1	1	1	1	1	1	1	Porc
Fiji									Fidji
Cattle	9	9	9	9	9	8	8	8	Bovine
Goat	1[1]	1[1]	1	1	1	1	1	1	Chèvre
Pig	3	4	4	4	4	4	4	4	Porc
French Polynesia									Polynésie française
Pig	1	1	1	1	1	1	1	1[1]	Porc
Kiribati									Kiribati
Pig	1	1	1	1	1	1	1	1	Porc
Micronesia (Fed. States of)									Micronésie (Etats féd. de)
Pig	1	1	1	1	1	1	1	1	Porc
New Caledonia									Nouvelle-Calédonie
Cattle	4	4	4	4	4	4	4[1]	4[1]	Bovine
Pig	1	1	1	1[1]	1[1]	1[1]	1[1]	1[1]	Porc
New Zealand									Nouvelle-Zélande
Cattle	634	561	572	590	576	660	710	652	Bovine
Goat	2	2	1	2	1	1	2	1[1]	Chèvre
Pig	50	49	47	47	47	48	52	50	Porc
Sheep	545	517	533	562	521	546	518	488	Mouton
Papua New Guinea									Papouasie-Nvl-Guinée
Cattle	3	3	3	3	3	3	3	3	Bovine
Pig	58	58	58	64	68	68	64	66	Porc
Samoa									Samoa
Cattle[1]	1	1	1	1	1	1	1	1	Bovine[1]
Pig	3[1]	3[1]	4[1]	4	4[1]	4[1]	4[1]	4	Porc
Solomon Islands									Iles Salomon
Cattle	1	1	1	1	1	1	1	1	Bovine
Pig	2	2	2	2	2	2	2	2	Porc
Tonga									Tonga
Pig	1	1	1	1	1	1	1	1	Porc
Vanuatu									Vanuatu
Cattle	4	4	4	3	3	3	3	3	Bovine
Pig	3	3	3	3	3	3	3	3	Porc

Source

Food and Agriculture Organization of the United Nations (FAO), Rome, FAOSTAT data, last accessed June 2007.

Notes

1 FAO estimate.
2 International reliable sources (USDA, WTO, World Bank, IMF).
3 Including Anguilla.
4 Data include those for Taiwan Province of China.
5 For statistical purposes, the data for China do not include those for the Hong Kong Special Administrative Region (Hong Kong SAR) and Macao Special Administrative Region (Macao SAR).
6 The data relate to the government-controlled areas.
7 Data refer to fiscal years ending 30 September.
8 Data refer to fiscal years ending 30 June.

Source

Organisation des Nations Unies pour l'alimentation et l'agriculture (FAO), Rome, données FAOSTAT, dernier accès juin 2007.

Notes

1 Estimation de la FAO.
2 Sources internationales fiables (Département de l'Agriculture des États-Unis, OMC, Banque Mondiale, FMI).
3 Y compris Anguilla.
4 Les données comprennent les chiffres pour la province de Taiwan.
5 Pour la présentation des statistiques, les données pour la Chine ne comprennent pas la Région Administrative Spéciale de Hong Kong (Hong Kong RAS) et la Région Administrative Spéciale de Macao (Macao RAS).
6 Les données se réfèrent aux régions sous contrôle gouvernemental.
7 Les données se réfèrent aux exercices budgétaires finissant le 30 septembre.
8 Les données se réfèrent aux exercices budgétaires finissant le 30 juin.

38

Beer
Production: thousand hectoliters

Bière
Production : milliers d'hectolitres

Country or area Pays ou zone	1995	1996	1997	1998	1999	2000	2001	2002	2003	2004
Albania Albanie	89	9	151	93	87	86	117	150	144	296
Algeria Algérie	402	377	370	382	383	453	435	283	186	...
Angola[1] Angola[1]	280	797	1 150	1 288	1 609	...	...	...	...	...
Argentina Argentine	10 913	11 615	12 687	12 395	12 448	12 685	12 390	11 990	12 950	...
Armenia Arménie	53	29	50	133	84	79	100	71	73	88
Australia[2] Australie[2]	17 880	17 430	17 350	17 570	17 380	17 680	17 450	17 440	17 270	17 360
Austria Autriche	9 767	9 445	9 303	8 837	8 884	8 725	8 528	8 745	8 980	...
Azerbaijan Azerbaïdjan	22	13	16	12	69	71	117	125	133	180
Barbados Barbade	74	76	75	87	76	69	67	68	69	...
Belarus Bélarus	1 518	2 013	2 413	2 604	2 728	2 371	2 174	2 026	2 056	2 272
Belgium Belgique	15 110	14 648	14 758	14 763	15 094[3]	15 509[3]	15 068[3]	15 063[3]	15 924[3]	...
Belize Belize	49	41	37	42	66	92	...	...	...	...
Benin[4] Bénin[4]	330	349	364	329	347	...	...	...	...	...
Bolivia Bolivie	175	160	187	186	166	...	...	...	...	...
Bosnia and Herzegovina Bosnie-Herzégovine	...	537	745	844	975	676[5]	480[5]	652[5]	#1 316	...
Botswana Botswana	1 366	1 351	1 005	1 019	1 591	1 976	1 692	1 396	1 198	...
Brazil Brésil	67 284	63 559	66 582	66 453	62 491	87 882	91 372	79 883	76 921	...
Bulgaria Bulgarie	4 331	4 402	3 031	3 765	3 890	3 977	4 097	3 888	4 355	3 997
Burkina Faso[4] Burkina Faso[4]	372	435	460	501	516	...	...	...	...	...
Burundi Burundi	1 404	1 228	1 161	1 036	1 084	892	702	752	876	...
Cameroon Cameroun	2 933	3 124[4]	3 124	3 370	3 373	3 340	3 740	4 196	4 597	...
Canada Canada	22 966	21 303	21 816	24 352	24 605	24 515	25 551	25 368	19 299	...
Central African Rep. Rép. centrafricaine	269	175[4]	209[4]	219[4]	243[4]	...	...	...	...	...
Chad Tchad	95	134[4]	123[4]	...	...	...	...	...	...	...
Chile Chili	3 551	3 459	3 640	3 666	3 343	3 221	3 374	3 401	3 490	...

Country or area Pays ou zone	1995	1996	1997	1998	1999	2000	2001	2002	2003	2004
China[6] Chine[6]	128 406	137 664	154 610	162 693	...	...	...	...	...	...
China, Hong Kong SAR Chine, Hong Kong RAS	983	897	894	...	...	...	...	...	...	...
Colombia Colombie	20 525	...	18 290	16 461	14 213	...	...	...	...	...
Congo Congo	505	510	342	494	480	526	623	661	658	674
Croatia Croatie	3 166	3 292	3 607	3 759	3 663	3 847	3 799	3 624	3 679	3 606
Cuba Cuba	1 328	1 504	1 639	1 759	2 009	2 136	2 197	2 331	2 313	2 221
Cyprus Chypre	352	331	333	365	405	409	404	383	367	371
Czech Republic République tchèque	17 687	18 057	18 558	18 290	17 945	17 796	17 734	17 987	18 216	18 596
Denmark Danemark	9 903	9 591	9 181	8 044	8 205	7 455	7 233	8 202	8 352	8 550
Dominica Dominique	3	14	11	11	8	11	9	10	...	...
Dominican Republic Rép. dominicaine	2 082	...	2 593	2 993	3 484	3 666	3 176	3 554	...	...
Ecuador Equateur	3 201	2 163	238	633	555	353	...	...	...	...
Egypt Egypte	360	380	...	...	352	261	122	...	...	...
Estonia Estonie	492	459	543	744	957	950	1 015	1 044	1 040	119
Ethiopia Ethiopie	724[7]	876[7]	843[7]	831[7]	921[7]	1 111[7]	1 605[7]	1 812	2 123	...
Fiji Fidji	150	170	170	170	185	179	184	199	150	...
Finland Finlande	4 702	4 980	4 840	4 341	4 733	4 574	4 650	4 777	4 606	4 948
France France	18 311	17 140	17 010	16 551	16 623	15 993	15 716	15 344	15 437	...
Gabon Gabon	816	...	801	847	778	812	867	792	754	...
Georgia Géorgie	65	48	79	97	126	234	257	273	284	476
Germany Allemagne	111 875	108 938	108 729	106 993	107 479	106 877	106 372	102 133	98 933	97 748
Greece Grèce	4 040	3 769	3 797	4 139	4 342	4 423	4 494	4 548	4 090	3 890
Guatemala Guatemala	1 471	1 655	1 303	1 363	1 443	1 406	...	...	...	...
Guyana Guyana	97	112	129	131	129	118	81	...	...	...
Hungary Hongrie	7 697	7 270	6 973	7 163	6 996	7 194	7 142	7 237	7 255	6 467
Iceland Islande	52	63	64	71	77	88	123	103	108	...
India Inde	3 700[8]	4 255[8]	4 331[8]	4 332[8]	3 632[8]	3 025	2 352	2 696	3 609	...

Country or area Pays ou zone	1995	1996	1997	1998	1999	2000	2001	2002	2003	2004
Indonesia Indonésie	1 136	...	531	502	401	...	437	237	...	...
Iran (Islamic Rep. of)[9] Iran (Rép. islamique d')[9]	...	...	130	155	127	145	...	...	...	...
Ireland Irlande	9 255	10 765	12 095	12 584	...	...	...	...	...	...
Italy Italie	10 616	9 559	10 379	11 073	11 123	11 173	11 375	11 208	13 994	13 692
Jamaica Jamaïque	662	690	674	670	656	697	784	774	585	...
Japan[10] Japon[10]	70 568	67 439	66 971	63 297	58 573	55 081	51 855	46 215	41 323	37 833
Kazakhstan Kazakhstan	812	636	693	850	824	1 357	1 732	2 020	2 348	2 780
Kenya Kenya	3 474	2 759	2 704	2 630	1 885	2 029	1 843	1 919	2 223	2 375
Korea, Republic of Corée, République de	17 554	17 210	16 907	14 080	14 866	16 544	17 765	18 224	17 863	18 033
Kyrgyzstan Kirghizistan	121	143	145	129	122	124	87	71	77	116
Lao People's Dem. Rep. Rép. dém. pop. lao	151	...	...	...	...	...	...	...	...	...
Lithuania Lituanie	1 093	1 139	1 406	1 557	1 852	2 065	2 174	2 683	2 520	2 782
Luxembourg Luxembourg	518	483	481	469	450	438	397	386	391	...
Madagascar Madagascar	246	347	234	297	446	467	502	439	...	92
Malawi Malawi	289	277	780	678	684	739	1 033	...	...	...
Mali Mali	52	60	...	...	...	...	...	...	...	...
Mauritius Maurice	309	312	340	376	358	375	386	376	401	...
Mexico Mexique	44 205	48 111	51 315	54 569	57 905	59 851	61 632	63 530	65 462	67 575
Mozambique Mozambique	244	374	631	75	95	989	982	779	1 044	1 025
Nepal[11] Népal[11]	168	183	215	139	188	217	233	...	...	...
Netherlands Pays-Bas	22 380[12,13]	22 670[12,13]	23 780[12,13]	23 040[12,13]	23 799[12,13]	24 956[12,13]	24 605[13]	24 774[13]	25 699	...
New Zealand Nouvelle-Zélande	3 488[13]	3 435[13]	3 214	3 206	3 148	2 980	3 070	3 093	3 127	2 902
Niger Niger	...	78	72	70	69	72	68	65	...	...
Nigeria Nigéria	1 461	...	...	...	...	...	...	...	...	...
Norway Norvège	2 255	...	2 396	1 833	2 651	...	2 462	2 377	...	2 352
Panama Panama	1 274	1 229	1 335	1 448	1 461	1 399	...	...	...	...
Peru Pérou	7 615	7 473	7 650	6 557	6 168	5 706	5 296	6 170	6 483	6 733

38 Beer — Production: thousand hectolitres (*continued*)
Bière — Production : milliers d'hectolitres (*suite*)

Country or area Pays ou zone	1995	1996	1997	1998	1999	2000	2001	2002	2003	2004
Poland Pologne	15 205	16 667	19 281	21 017	23 360	#24 739	15 069	26 715	28 412	29 794
Portugal Portugal	6 895	6 619	6 494	6 617	6 641	6 718	6 509	6 689	7 110	7 712
Puerto Rico Porto Rico	397	360	317	263	259	...	...	...	...	...
Republic of Moldova[14] République de Moldova[14]	276	226	238	278	202	249	318	438	566	653
Romania Roumanie	8 768	8 118	7 651	9 989	11 133	12 664	12 087	11 513	13 087	14 159
Russian Federation Fédération de Russie	21 335	20 832	26 103	33 631	44 484	51 563	63 780	70 266	75 540	83 787
Saint Kitts and Nevis Saint-Kitts-et-Nevis	17	20	19	20	20	20	20	20	...	...
Serbia and Montenegro Serbie-et-Monténégro	5 611	5 987	6 106	6 630	#6 786	6 734	6 063	5 764	6 049	...
Seychelles Seychelles	58	63	71	72	68	70	72	76	65	...
Slovakia Slovaquie	4 369	4 666	5 577	4 478	4 473	4 491	422	475	468	388
Slovenia Slovénie	2 104	2 133	...	1 976	2 084	2 463	2 449	...	...	...
Spain Espagne	25 396	24 520	24 786	22 428	26 007	26 388	26 802	28 631	31 028	31 467
Suriname Suriname	65	72	...	...	...	...	...	...	...	...
Sweden Suède	5 471	5 320	5 129	4 763	4 718	4 686	4 522	4 527	4 255	3 870
Switzerland[13] Suisse[13]	3 672	...	...	...	...	...	...	...	...	...
Syrian Arab Republic Rép. arabe syrienne	102	102	97	97	121	91	100	104	100	109
Tajikistan Tadjikistan	47	6	6	9	7	4	8	9	9	11
Thailand Thaïlande	6 473	7 591	8 742	9 770	10 422	11 650	12 380	12 750	16 020	16 320
TFYR of Macedonia L'ex-R.y. Macédoine	620	622	600	578	652	661	618	657	680	716
Trinidad and Tobago Trinité-et-Tobago	428	419	407	517	522	625	...	...	...	...
Tunisia Tunisie	659	662	780	813	912	1 066	1 087	1 100	997	...
Turkey Turquie	6 946	7 381	7 656	7 130	7 188	7 649	7 441	7 845	8 363	8 812
Turkmenistan Turkménistan	113	17	44	29	37	52	79	84	...	...
Uganda Ouganda	512	642	896	1 105	1 178	1 261	1 079	989	...	...
Ukraine Ukraine	7 102	6 025	6 125	6 842	8 407	10 765	13 059	15 000	17 012	19 373
United Kingdom Royaume-Uni	6 537	6 312	6 482	6 092	6 251	5 421	5703	6065	6425	7362
United Rep. of Tanzania Rép.-Unie de Tanzanie	893[15]	1 251[15]	1 483[15]	1 707[15]	1 674	1 830	1 756	1 759	1 941	2 026[15]

Country or area Pays ou zone	1995	1996	1997	1998	1999	2000	2001	2002	2003	2004
United States[16] Etats-Unis[16]	...	233 485	...	...	...	...	...	...	...	...
Uruguay Uruguay	998	913	939	860	741	706	629	507	415	...
Uzbekistan Ouzbékistan	724	677	619	569[17]	422[17]	609[17]	...	...	...	...
Viet Nam Viet Nam	4 650	5 334	5 811	6 700	6 898	7 791	8 712	9 398	11 189	13 428

Source

United Nations Statistics Division, New York, the industrial commodity statistics database and the "Industrial Commodity Statistics Yearbook 2004".

Notes

1 Source: Economist Intelligence Unit (London).
2 Excluding light beer containing less than 1.15% by volume of alcohol.
3 Incomplete coverage.
4 Source: Afristat: Sub-Saharan African Observatory of Economics and Statistics (Bamako, Mali).
5 Excluding the Federation of Bosnia and Herzegovina.
6 Original data in metric tons.
7 Twelve months ending 7 July of the year stated.
8 Production by large- and medium-scale establishments only.
9 Production by establishments employing 10 or more persons.
10 Twelve months beginning 1 April of the year stated.
11 Twelve months beginning 16 July of the year stated.
12 Production by establishments employing 20 or more persons.
13 Sales.
14 Excluding the Transnistria region.
15 Tanganyika only.
16 Twelve months ending 30 September of the year stated.
17 Source: "Statistical Yearbook for Asia and the Pacific", United Nations Economic and Social Commission for Asia and the Pacific (Bangkok).

Source

Organisation des Nations Unies, Division de statistique, New York, la base de données pour les statistiques industrielles par produit et "l'Annuaire de statistiques industrielles par produit 2004".

Notes

1 Source: "Economist Intelligence Unit" (London).
2 Non compris la bière légère contenant moins de 1.15 p. 100 en volume d'alcool.
3 Couverture incomplète.
4 Source : Afristat : Observatoire Economique et Statistique d'Afrique Subsaharienne (Bamako, Mali).
5 Non compris la Fédération de Bosnie et Herzégovine.
6 Données d'origine exprimées en tonnes.
7 Période de 12 mois finissant le 7 juillet de l'année indiquée.
8 Production des grandes et moyennes entreprises seulement.
9 Production des établissements occupant 10 personnes ou plus.
10 Période de 12 mois commençant le 1er avril de l'année indiquée.
11 Période de 12 mois commençant le 16 juillet de l'année indiquée.
12 Production des établissements occupant 20 personnes ou plus.
13 Ventes.
14 Non compris la région de Transnistria.
15 Tanganyika seulement.
16 Période de 12 mois finissant le 30 septembre de l'année indiquée.
17 Source : "Annuaire des Statistiques de l'Asie et Pacifique", Conseil Economique et Social des Nations Unies pour l'Asie et le Pacifique (Bangkok).

39

Cigarettes
Production: millions

Cigarettes
Production : millions

Country or area Pays ou zone	1995	1996	1997	1998	1999	2000	2001	2002	2003	2004
Albania Albanie	685[1]	483[1]	414[1]	764[1]	647[1]	372[1]	126[1]	50	15	...
Andorra Andorre	...	...	...	1	1	1	1	1	2	2
Argentina Argentine	1 963	1 971	1 940	1 967	1 996	1 843	1 739	1 812	1 990	1 890
Armenia Arménie	1 043	...	815	2 489	3 132	2 109	1 623	2 815	3 222	2 720
Austria Autriche	16 297	...	...	...	...	...	...	...	...	...
Azerbaijan Azerbaïdjan	1 926	766	827	241	416	2 363	6 808	6 296	6 611	3 671
Bangladesh[2] Bangladesh[2]	17 379	16 222	18 601	19 889	19 558	19 732	20 120	20 384	22 499	...
Barbados Barbade	65	...	...	...	...	...	...	...	...	...
Belarus Bélarus	6 228	6 267	6 787	7 296	9 259	10 356	11 182	10 524	10 442	12 627
Belgium Belgique	18 826	17 471	18 061	17 519	14 713[3]	...	...	...	...	...
Belize Belize	95	79	88	94	91	84	...	...	...	...
Bolivia Bolivie	1 583	1 490	1 484	1 538	1 404	...	...	...	...	...
Bosnia and Herzegovina Bosnie-Herzégovine	...	3 198	3 886	4 830	5 974	491[4]	690[4]	662[4]	#5 062	...
Brazil Brésil	...	...	...	...	...	17 860	15 820	100 193	21 099	...
Bulgaria Bulgarie	74 603	57 238	43 315	33 181	25 715	26 681	26 659	23 227	25 914	24 462
Burundi Burundi	523	450	377	317	353	286	293	312	354	...
Cameroon Cameroun	...	...	2 704	3 084	3 249	2 984	2 814	2 785	1 903	...
Canada Canada	50 775	49 362	47 263	48 854	47 224	46 068	44 403	37 127	...	...
Central African Rep. Rép. centrafricaine	30	...	...	...	...	...	...	...	...	...
Chad Tchad	569	714[5]	786[5]	...	...	...	...	...	...	...
Chile Chili	10 891	11 569	12 522	12 904	13 271	13 796	13 305	13 839	13 776	...
China[6] Chine[6]	35	34	34	34	33	34	34	35	36	...
China, Hong Kong SAR[7] Chine, Hong Kong RAS[7]	22 767	21 386	20 929	13 470	...	...	...	...	...	...
China, Macao SAR[1,8] Chine, Macao RAS[1,8]	450	450	...	...	...	...	...	...	...	...
Colombia Colombie	10 491	...	11 662	12 472	15 182	...	...	...	...	...

39 Cigarettes — Production: millions (*continued*)
Cigarettes — Production : millions (*suite*)

Country or area Pays ou zone	1995	1996	1997	1998	1999	2000	2001	2002	2003	2004
Congo Congo	600	776	380	0	0	0	102	662	748	750
Costa Rica[1,8] Costa Rica[1,8]	16	16	...	...	...	...	...	...	...	...
Croatia Croatie	12 110	11 548	11 416	11 987	12 785	13 692	14 738	15 047	15 613	14 256
Cuba Cuba	13	11	11	12	13	12	12	13	14	13
Cyprus Chypre	2 528	2 728	3 662	4 362	4 783	4 980	3 803	2 534	2 661	3 709
Denmark Danemark	11 902	11 804	12 262	12 392	11 749	11 413	11 089	12 039	12 898	13 458
Dominican Republic Rép. dominicaine	4 092	4 192	3 972	4 098	4 005	3 898	3 338	3 509	...	...
Ecuador Equateur	1 734	1 745	1 678	1 997	2 178	2 773	...	...	2 975	...
Egypt Egypte	42 469	46 000	50 000	52 000	52 336	56 614	61 000	62 018	63 396	...
El Salvador El Salvador	1 701	1 756	...	...	...	...	...	...	...	...
Estonia Estonie	1 864	954	...	...	...	...	...	...	...	...
Ethiopia Ethiopie	1 583[9]	1 862[9]	2 024[9]	2 029[9]	1 829[9]	1 931[9]	1 904[9]	1 511	1 511	...
Fiji Fidji	437	439	450	410	446	396	442	479	418	...
Finland Finlande	6 542	5 910	6 790	4 062	4 877	3 981	3 999	4 130	3 946	868
France France	46 361	46 931	44 646	43 304	42 405	42 398	39 000	39 600	36 900	...
Gabon Gabon	297	...	331	463	670	859	880	860	...	...
Georgia Géorgie	1 840	1 183	917	601	132	296	1 615	1 894	2 972	2 808
Germany Allemagne	201 070	193 279	181 747	181 904	204 631	206 770	213 793	212 500	205 237	208 347
Ghana Ghana	...	...	1 747	1 399	1 158	1 166	1 481	1 800	...	...
Greece Grèce	38 491	36 478	29 529	31 705	31 535	34 256	25 516	28 091	26 249	28 048
Guatemala Guatemala	2 616	1 725	2 198	4 184	4 376	4 262	...	...	...	...
Guyana Guyana	318	400	221	...	...	...	...	...	...	...
Honduras Honduras	...	...	...	3 814	4 586	5 655	5 984	6 010	...	...
Hungary Hongrie	25 709	27 594	26 057	26 849	22 985	21 608	20 787	21 748	20 181	12 119
India Inde	69 589[10]	73 841[10]	83 162[10]	79 313[10]	82 504[10]	82 504[10]	60 577[11]	54 991[11]	49 769[11]	...
Iran (Islamic Rep. of) Iran (Rép. islamique d')	9 787[12]	11 860[12]	10 304[12]	14 335	20 081	13 800	13 363	12 700	12 200	18 700
Iraq Iraq	...	...	...	...	...	...	...	...	...	812

Country or area / Pays ou zone	1995	1996	1997	1998	1999	2000	2001	2002	2003	2004
Ireland / Irlande	7 500[1,8]	4 976	4 605	6 452	6 176	6 461	6 807	6 599	...	...
Israel[1] / Israël[1]	4 933	4 793	...	...	...	...	...	...	...	...
Italy / Italie	50 247[1]	51 489[1]	51 894[1]	50 785	45 159	43 694[1]	45 368[1]	37 342	40 350	...
Jamaica / Jamaïque	1 216	1 219	1 175	1 160	1 073	995	1 027	1 049	889	...
Japan[13] / Japon[13]	334 700	348 300	328 000	336 600	332 200	324 500	313 900	...	...	...
Jordan / Jordanie	3 675	4 738	1 853[14]	1 144[14]	*1 602[14]	*1 300[14]	...	...	...	...
Kazakhstan / Kazakhstan	12 080	19 121	24 109	21 747	18 773	19 293	21 395	23 453	25 715	28 038
Kenya / Kenya	8	8	9	8	7	6	6	5	5	5
Korea, Republic of / Corée, République de	87 959	94 709	96 725	101 011	95 995	94 531	94 116	94 433	123 166	133 206
Kyrgyzstan / Kirghizistan	1 332	975	716	862	2 103	3 169	3 013	2 927	3 102	3 170
Lao People's Dem. Rep. / Rép. dém. pop. lao	1 062	...	856[13]	1 104[13]	...	...	...	...	...	...
Latvia / Lettonie	2 101	1 876	1 775	2 018	1 909	...	...	...	...	...
Lebanon[1] / Liban[1]	#535	539	793	672	945	1 009	...	...	...	...
Lithuania / Lituanie	4 876	4 538	5 755	7 427	8 217	7 207	...	...	...	...
Madagascar / Madagascar	2 354[1]	2 957[1]	2 826[1]	3 303[1]	...	...	...	...	...	8
Malawi / Malawi	1 160	975	731	501	...	...	...	...	...	...
Malaysia / Malaisie	15 918[1]	16 896[1]	20 236[1]	18 410[1]	15 504[1]	27 271[1]	25 618	23 079	23 971	...
Mali / Mali	22	21	16[5]	10[5]	10[5]	...	...	...	...	...
Mauritius / Maurice	1 215	1 193	1 144	1 034	979	1 049	861	928	938	...
Mexico / Mexique	37 575	38 331	38 786	44 917	45 373	44 400	44 904	43 834	41 856	40 752
Mozambique / Mozambique	106	250	250	950	1 084	1 417	1 359	1 255	1 390	...
Myanmar[15] / Myanmar[15]	752	1 727	1 991	2 040	2 270	2 559	2 650	2 657	2 806	3 183
Nepal[16] / Népal[16]	7 430	8 067	7 944	8 127	7 315	6 584	6 979	...	...	...
Netherlands[17,18] / Pays-Bas[17,18]	97 727	...	...	...	...	...	...	...	...	...
New Zealand / Nouvelle-Zélande	3 338[18]	3 660[18]	3 234	3 086	2 949	2 916	2 396	2 509	2 176	2 122
Nicaragua / Nicaragua	...	...	1 580	1 789	780[19]	...	...	...	...	...
Nigeria / Nigéria	256	...	...	...	...	...	...	...	...	...

Country or area Pays ou zone	1995	1996	1997	1998	1999	2000	2001	2002	2003	2004
Pakistan[2] Pakistan[2]	32 747	45 506	46 101	48 215	51 579	46 976	58 259	55 318	49 365	55 399
Panama Panama	1 136	663	752	...	...	...	...	...	...	...
Peru Pérou	3 041	3 358	3 029	3 115	3 581	3 605	3 310	3 766	2 707	2 168
Philippines[1,8] Philippines[1,8]	7 440	7 440	...	...	...	...	...	...	...	...
Poland Pologne	100 627	95 293	95 798	96 741	95 056	#78 792	82 421	78 746	78 792	83 376
Portugal Portugal	13 102	12 743	14 606	15 889	18 189	20 561	23 376	25 581	24 950	26 415
Republic of Moldova[20] République de Moldova[20]	7 108	9 657	9 539	7 512	8 731	9 262	9 421	6 310	7 126	7 050
Romania Roumanie	14 747[21]	16 536[21]	25 943[21]	...	...	...	...	38 033	37 808	28 677
Russian Federation Fédération de Russie	99 500	112 000	140 000	196 000	266 000	334 000	356 000	383 000	376 000	377 000
Serbia and Montenegro Serbie-et-Monténégro	12 686	13 176	10 988	14 597	#13 126	14 451	13 968	15 388	...	...
Seychelles Seychelles	56	62	70	61	60	40	36	24	50	...
Spain Espagne	78 676	77 675	77 315	81 940	74 873	74 799	...	...	...	48 651
Sri Lanka Sri Lanka	5 822	6 160	5 712	5 797	5 333	4 889	*4 973	...	...	...
Suriname Suriname	472	483	...	...	...	...	...	...	...	...
Sweden Suède	7 193	7 251	6 291	5 692	6 060	5 958	5 959	...	...	...
Switzerland Suisse	41 976	42 955	37 638	34 453	32 139	34 299	33 565	37 160	38 140	39 059
Syrian Arab Republic[1] Rép. arabe syrienne[1]	9 699	8 528	10 137	10 398	10 991	11 097	12 007	12 863	13 412	...
Tajikistan Tadjikistan	964	604	153	191	209	667	1 155	585	468	727
Thailand Thaïlande	43 020	48 173	43 387	34 585	31 146	30 732	29 807	30 772	31 908	34 761
TFYR of Macedonia L'ex-R.y. Macédoine	...	...	...	...	...	...	7 766	6 567	5 120	5 654
Trinidad and Tobago Trinité-et-Tobago	920	1 102	1 386	1 680	1 945	2 050	...	...	...	...
Tunisia Tunisie	7 421	7 159	7 735	9 813	11 066	12 231	12 354	13 230	13 227	...
Turkey Turquie	80 700[1]	73 787[1]	74 984[1]	81 616[1]	75 135[1]	76 613[1]	77 160	131 561	111 881	103 371
Uganda Ouganda	1 576	1 702	1 846	1 866	1 602	1 344	1 220	1 092	...	...
Ukraine Ukraine	48 033	44 900	54 488	59 275	54 052	58 774	69 731	81 088	96 776	108 946
United Kingdom Royaume-Uni	152 269	168 514	167 670	152 998	143 794	139 125	109 025	124 896	89 639	85 691
United Rep. of Tanzania Rép.-Unie de Tanzanie	3 699	3 733	4 710	4 012	3 371	3 745	3 491	3 778	3 920	4 308[22]

Country or area Pays ou zone	1995	1996	1997	1998	1999	2000	2001	2002	2003	2004
United States Etats-Unis	746 500	754 500	719 600	679 700	611 929	...	...	...	...	...
Uruguay Uruguay	3 561	6 018	6 872	10 187	11 161	10 894	9 616	8 449	5 718	...
Uzbekistan Ouzbékistan	2 742	5 172	8 521	7 582[13]	10 668[13]	7 766[13]	...	...	...	...
Viet Nam Viet Nam	2 147	2 160	2 123	2 196	2 147	2 836	3 075	3 375	3 871	4 192
Yemen Yémen	6 540	6 740	6 800	5 980	5 760	4 780	6 020	5 780	5 960	...

Source

United Nations Statistics Division, New York, the industrial statistics database and the "Industrial Commodity Statistics Yearbook 2004".

Notes

1 Original data in units of weight. Computed on the basis of one million cigarettes per ton.
2 Twelve months ending 30 June of the year stated.
3 Incomplete coverage.
4 Excluding the Federation of Bosnia and Herzegovina.
5 Source: Afristat: Sub-Saharan African Observatory of Economics and Statistics (Bamako, Mali).
6 For statistical purposes, the data for China do not include those for the Hong Kong Special Administrative Region (Hong Kong SAR) and Macao Special Administrative Region (Macao SAR).
7 Including cigarillos.
8 Source: Food and Agriculture Organization of the United Nations (Rome).
9 Twelve months ending 7 July of the year stated.
10 Production by large- and medium-scale establishments only.
11 Production by establishments employing 50 or more persons.
12 Production by establishments employing 10 or more persons.
13 Source: "Statistical Yearbook for Asia and the Pacific", United Nations Economic and Social Commission for Asia and the Pacific (Bangkok).
14 Source: "Bulletin of Industrial Statistics for the Arab Countries", United Nations Economic and Social Commission for Western Asia (Beirut).
15 Government production only.
16 Twelve months beginning 16 July of the year stated.
17 Production by establishments employing 20 or more persons.
18 Sales.
19 Beginning August 1999, national production discontinued.
20 Excluding the Transnistria region.
21 Including cigars.
22 Tanganyika only.

Source

Organisation des Nations Unies, Division de statistique, New York, la base de données pour les statistiques industrielles et "l'Annuaire de statistiques industrielles par produit 2004".

Notes

1 Données d'origine exprimées en poids. Calcul sur la base d'un million cigarettes par tonne.
2 Période de 12 mois finissant le 30 juin de l'année indiquée.
3 Couverture incomplète.
4 Non compris la Fédération de Bosnie et Herzégovine.
5 Source : Afristat : Observatoire Economique et Statistique d'Afrique Subsaharienne (Bamako, Mali).
6 Pour la présentation des statistiques, les données pour la Chine ne comprennent pas la Région Administrative Spéciale de Hong Kong (Hong Kong RAS) et la Région Administrative Spéciale de Macao (Macao RAS).
7 Y compris les cigarillos.
8 Source: Organisation des Nations Unies pour l'alimentation et l'agriculture (Rome).
9 Période de 12 mois finissant le 7 juillet de l'année indiquée.
10 Production des grandes et moyennes entreprises seulement.
11 Production des établissements occupant 50 personnes ou plus.
12 Production des établissements occupant 10 personnes ou plus.
13 Source : "Annuaire des Statistiques de l'Asie et Pacifique", Conseil Economique et Social des Nations Unies pour l'Asie et le Pacifique (Bangkok).
14 Source: "Bulletin of Industrial Statistics for the Arab Countries", Commission économique et sociale pour l'Asie occidentale (Beyrouth).
15 Production de l'Etat seulement.
16 Période de 12 mois commençant le 16 juillet de l'année indiquée.
17 Production des établissements occupant 20 personnes ou plus.
18 Ventes.
19 A partir d'août 1999, la production nationale a été discontinuée.
20 Non compris la région de Transnistria.
21 Y compris les cigares.
22 Tanganyika seulement.

40

Sawnwood

Production (sawn): thousand cubic metres

Sciages

Production (sciés) : milliers de mètres cubes

Region, country or area — Région, pays ou zone	1996	1997	1998	1999	2000	2001	2002	2003	2004	2005
World Monde	**387 084**	**393 783**	**378 638**	**389 041**	**386 014**	**379 549**	**394 240**	**400 302**	**419 979**	**428 459**
Africa Afrique	**7 867**	**7 505**	**7 423**	**7 415**	**8 320**	**7 921**	**7 490**	**8 474**	**9 486**	**9 278**
Algeria — Algérie	13	13	13	13	13	13	13	13	13	13
Angola — Angola	5	5	5	5	5	5	5	5	5	5
Benin — Bénin	11	12	13	13	13	32	46	31	31	31
Burkina Faso — Burkina Faso	1	2	1	1	1	1	2	2	1	1
Burundi — Burundi	33	33	33	80	83	83	83	83	83	83
Cameroon — Cameroun	685	560	588	600	1 154	800	652	658	702	702
Central African Rep. — Rép. centrafricaine	61	72	91	79	102	150	97	69	69	69
Chad — Tchad	2	2	2	2	2	2	2	2	2	2
Congo — Congo	59	64	73	74	93	126	170	168	200	209
Côte d'Ivoire — Côte d'Ivoire	596	613	623	611	603	630	620	503	503	363
Dem. Rep. of the Congo — Rép. dém. du Congo	85	90	80	70	40	10	35	15	15	15
Egypt — Egypte	0	0	3	4	4	2	3	3	2	2
Equatorial Guinea — Guinée équatoriale	4	4	4	4	4	4	4	4	4	4
Ethiopia — Ethiopie	33	60	60	60	60	60	14	18	18	18
Gabon — Gabon	50	30	60	98	88	112	176	231	133	232
Gambia — Gambie	1	1	1	1	1	1	1	1	1	1
Ghana — Ghana	604	575	590	454	475	480	461	496	480	460
Guinea — Guinée	85	25	26	26	26	26	26	26	26	26
Guinea-Bissau — Guinée-Bissau	16	16	16	16	16	16	16	16	16	16
Kenya — Kenya	185	185	185	185	185	84	78	78	78	78
Liberia — Libéria	90	90	6	4	10	20	30	25	20	20
Libyan Arab Jamah. — Jamah. arabe libyenne	31	31	31	31	31	31	31	31	31	31
Madagascar — Madagascar	84	84	84	102	485	400	95	493	893	893
Malawi — Malawi	45	45	45	45	45	45	45	45	45	45
Mali — Mali	13	13	13	13	13	13	13	13	13	13
Mauritius — Maurice	3	3	5	5	3	3	3	3	3	3
Morocco — Maroc	83	83	83	83	83	83	83	83	83	83
Mozambique — Mozambique	42	33	28	28	28	28	28	28	32	38
Niger — Niger	4	4	4	4	4	4	4	4	4	4
Nigeria — Nigéria	2 178	2 000	2 000	2 000	2 000	2 000	2 000	2 000	2 000	2 000
Réunion — Réunion	2	2	2	2	2	2	2	2	2	2
Rwanda — Rwanda	59	74	76	79	79	79	79	79	79	79
Sao Tome and Principe — Sao Tomé-et-Principe	5	5	5	5	5	5	5	5	5	5
Senegal — Sénégal	23	23	23	23	23	23	23	23	23	23
Sierra Leone — Sierra Leone	5	5	5	5	5	5	5	5	5	5
Somalia — Somalie	14	14	14	14	14	14	14	14	14	14
South Africa[1] — Afrique du Sud[1]	1 574	1 574	1 498	1 498	1 498	1 498	1 498	2 171	2 824	2 660
Sudan — Soudan	45	45	51	51	51	51	51	51	51	51
Swaziland — Swaziland	100	102	102	102	102	102	102	102	102	102
Togo — Togo	15	17	18	21	19	15	13	13	13	14
Tunisia — Tunisie	20	20	20	20	20	20	20	20	20	20

Sawnwood — Production (sawn): thousand cubic metres (*continued*)
Sciages — Production (sciés) : milliers de mètres cubes (*suite*)

Region, country or area — Région, pays ou zone	1996	1997	1998	1999	2000	2001	2002	2003	2004	2005
Uganda — Ouganda	215	229	245	264	264	264	264	264	264	264
United Rep. of Tanzania — Rép.-Unie de Tanzanie	24	24	24	24	24	24	24	24	24	24
Zambia — Zambie	245	157	157	157	157	157	157	157	157	157
Zimbabwe — Zimbabwe	418	465	416	438	386	397	397	397	397	397
Northern America Amérique septentrionale	**133 227**	**136 570**	**136 176**	**143 026**	**141 541**	**139 723**	**147 124**	**143 051**	**154 019**	**155 805**
Canada — Canada	47 025	47 665	47 185	50 412	50 465	53 708	58 481	56 892	60 952	60 187
United States — Etats-Unis	86 202	88 906	88 991	92 615	91 076	86 015	88 643	86 159	93 067	95 619
Latin America and the Caribbean Amér. latine et Caraïbes	**34 254**	**35 129**	**35 935**	**36 621**	**36 653**	**38 169**	**39 249**	**39 961**	**41 623**	**41 707**
Argentina — Argentine	1 711	1 170	1 377	1 408	821	2 130	2 130	1 388	1 562	1 562
Bahamas — Bahamas	1	1	1	1	1	1	1	1	1	1
Belize — Belize	35	35	35	35	35	35	35	35	35	35
Bolivia — Bolivie	181	180	515	244	239	308	299	347	402	408
Brazil — Brésil	18 830	19 310	19 520	20 530	21 600	21 950	22 488	23 090	23 480	23 557
Chile — Chili	4 140	4 661	4 551	5 254	5 698	5 872	6 439	7 004	8 015	8 298
Colombia — Colombie	1 134	1 085	910	730	587	539	527	599	622	407
Costa Rica — Costa Rica	780	780	780	780	812	812	812	812	426	488
Cuba — Cuba	130	130	130	146	179	190	147	181	189	220
Dominica — Dominique	0	0	0	0	0	0	0	47	66	66
Ecuador — Equateur	1 886	2 075	2 079	1 455	715	794	750	750	755	755
El Salvador — El Salvador	70	58	58	58	58	58	68	68	16	16
French Guiana — Guyane française	15	15	15	15	15	15	15	15	15	15
Guadeloupe — Guadeloupe	1	1	1	1	1	1	1	1	1	1
Guatemala — Guatemala	355	355	308	235	340	340	340	366	366	366
Guyana — Guyana	97	57	50	50	29	30	31	38	36	36
Haiti — Haïti	14	14	14	14	14	14	14	14	14	14
Honduras — Honduras	322	379	369	419	442	419	470	421	454	400
Jamaica — Jamaïque	64	65	66	66	66	66	66	66	66	66
Martinique — Martinique	1	1	1	1	1	1	1	1	1	1
Mexico — Mexique	2 543	2 961	3 260	3 110	3 110	2 829	2 691	2 740	2 962	2 674
Nicaragua — Nicaragua	160	148	148	148	148	65	45	45	67	54
Panama — Panama	19	17	8	46	48	42	24	27	30	30
Paraguay — Paraguay	500	550	550	550	550	550	550	550	550	550
Peru — Pérou	693	482	590	835	646	506	626	528	671	743
Suriname — Suriname	40	41	41	28	60	56	47	56	58	72
Trinidad and Tobago — Trinité-et-Tobago	29	38	27	18	32	41	43	39	32	41
Uruguay — Uruguay	269	269	269	269	203	203	224	230	252	268
Venezuela (Boliv. Rep. of) — Venezuela (Rép. boliv. du)	233	250	261	174	202	301	364	501	479	562
Asia Asie	**92 203**	**90 189**	**72 096**	**71 670**	**61 939**	**59 654**	**63 778**	**68 373**	**67 959**	**69 421**
Afghanistan — Afghanistan	400	400	400	400	400	400	400	400	400	400
Armenia — Arménie	0	0	0	0	4	4	4	3	2	2
Azerbaijan — Azerbaïdjan	0	0	0	0	1	^0	^0	^0	^0	^0
Bangladesh — Bangladesh	70	70	70	70	70	70	255	388	388	388
Bhutan — Bhoutan	18	18	18	22	31	31	31	31	31	31
Brunei Darussalam — Brunéi Darussalam	90	90	90	90	90	90	90	90	90	90
Cambodia — Cambodge	100	71	40	26	20	5	10	4	4	4
China[2,3] — Chine[2,3]	26 552	20 124	17 875	15 859	6 434	7 638	8 520	11 300	11 300	11 300

Region, country or area — Région, pays ou zone	1996	1997	1998	1999	2000	2001	2002	2003	2004	2005
China, Hong Kong SAR — Chine, Hong Kong RAS	441	441	441	441	441	441	441	441	441	441
Cyprus — Chypre	16	14	11	12	9	9	7	6	5	4
Georgia — Géorgie	5	5	5	10	10	44	59	71	69	69
India — Inde	10 624	18 520	8 400	8 400	7 900	7 900	10 990	11 880	13 661	14 789
Indonesia — Indonésie	7 338	7 238	7 125	6 625	6 500	6 750	6 230	7 620	4 330	4 330
Iran (Islamic Rep. of) — Iran (Rép. islamique d')	144	141	129	96	106	106	170	79	68	62
Iraq — Iraq	8	8	12	12	12	12	12	12	12	12
Japan — Japon	23 844	21 709	18 625	17 952	17 094	15 485	14 402	13 929	13 603	12 825
Kazakhstan — Kazakhstan	0	0	182	183	244	224	232	265	265	265
Korea, Dem. P. R. — Corée, R. p. dém. de	280	280	280	280	280	280	280	280	280	280
Korea, Republic of — Corée, République de	4 291	4 759	2 240	4 300	4 544	4 420	4 410	4 380	4 366	4 366
Kyrgyzstan — Kirghizistan	0	2	23	23	6	6	6	15	22	22
Lao People's Dem. Rep. — Rép. dém. pop. lao	429	498	389	439	200	185	192	125	125	130
Lebanon — Liban	9	9	9	9	9	9	9	9	9	9
Malaysia — Malaisie	8 382	7 326	5 091	5 237	5 590	4 696	4 643	4 769	4 934	5 173
Mongolia — Mongolie	170	200	300	300	300	300	300	300	300	300
Myanmar — Myanmar	351	372	299	298	545	671	1 012	1 001	1 056	1 530
Nepal — Népal	620	620	630	630	630	630	630	630	630	630
Pakistan — Pakistan	1 280	1 024	1 051	1 075	1 087	1 180	1 180	1 180	1 260	1 296
Philippines — Philippines	313	351	222	288	151	199	163	246	339	263
Singapore — Singapour	25	25	25	25	25	25	25	25	25	25
Sri Lanka — Sri Lanka	5	5	5	5	29	61	61	61	61	61
Syrian Arab Republic — Rép. arabe syrienne	9	9	9	9	9	9	9	9	9	9
Thailand — Thaïlande	307	426	103	178	220	233	288	288	288	288
Turkey — Turquie	4 268	3 833	4 891	5 039	5 528	5 036	5 579	5 615	6 215	6 445
Viet Nam — Viet Nam	1 398	1 184	2 705	2 937	2 950	2 036	2 667	2 450	2 900	3 110
Europe Europe	**112 606**	**117 378**	**119 718**	**122 822**	**129 501**	**126 558**	**127 959**	**132 213**	**138 211**	**143 031**
Albania — Albanie	5	5	28	35	90	197	97	97	97	97
Austria — Autriche	8 200	8 450	8 737	9 628	10 390	10 227	10 415	10 473	11 133	11 074
Belarus — Bélarus	1 545	1 545	2 131	2 175	1 808	2 058	2 182	2 304	2 304	2 304
Belgium — Belgique	…	…	…	1 056	1 150	1 275	1 175	1 215	1 235	1 285
Belgium-Luxembourg — Belgique-Luxembourg	1 100	1 150	1 267	…	…	…	…	…	…	…
Bosnia and Herzegovina — Bosnie-Herzégovine	20	320	330	330	320	310	738	888	1 319	1 319
Bulgaria — Bulgarie	253	253	253	325	312	332	332	332	569	569
Croatia — Croatie	598	644	676	685	642	574	640	585	582	624
Czech Republic — République tchèque	3 405	3 393	3 427	3 584	4 106	3 889	3 800	3 805	3 940	4 003
Denmark — Danemark	583	583	238	344	364	283	244	248	196	196
Estonia — Estonie	400	729	850	1 200	1 436	1 623	1 825	1 954	2 029	2 200
Finland — Finlande	9 780	11 430	12 300	12 768	13 420	12 770	13 390	13 745	13 544	12 269
France — France	9 600	9 607	10 220	10 236	10 536	10 518	9 815	9 539	9 774	9 950
Germany — Allemagne	14 267	14 730	14 972	16 096	16 340	16 131	17 119	17 596	19 538	22 121
Greece — Grèce	337	130	137	140	123	123	196	191	191	191
Hungary — Hongrie	285	317	298	308	291	264	293	299	205	215
Ireland — Irlande	687	642	675	811	888	925	818	1 005	939	894
Italy — Italie	1 650	1 751	1 600	1 630	1 630	1 600	1 605	1 590	1 580	1 590
Latvia — Lettonie	1 614	2 700	3 200	3 640	3 900	3 840	3 947	3 951	3 988	4 227
Lithuania — Lituanie	1 450	1 250	1 150	1 150	1 300	1 200	1 300	1 400	1 450	1 500
Luxembourg — Luxembourg	…	…	…	133	133	133	133	133	133	133

Sawnwood — Production (sawn): thousand cubic metres (*continued*)
Sciages — Production (sciés) : milliers de mètres cubes (*suite*)

Region, country or area — Région, pays ou zone	1996	1997	1998	1999	2000	2001	2002	2003	2004	2005
Netherlands — Pays-Bas	359	401	349	362	390	268	258	269	273	279
Norway — Norvège	2 420	2 520	2 525	2 336	2 280	2 253	2 225	2 186	2 230	2 331
Poland — Pologne	3 747	4 214	4 320	4 137	4 262	3 083	3 180	3 360	3 743	3 930
Portugal — Portugal	1 731	1 731	1 490	1 430	1 427	1 492	1 298	1 383	1 060	1 010
Republic of Moldova — République de Moldova	29	30	30	6	5	5	5	5	5	5
Romania — Roumanie	1 693	1 861	2 200	2 818	3 396	3 059	3 696	4 246	4 588	4 321
Russian Federation — Fédération de Russie	21 913	20 600	19 580	19 100	20 000	19 600	19 240	20 155	21 355	22 500
Serbia and Montenegro — Serbie-et-Monténégro	378	391	438	364	504	391	432	514	575	497
Slovakia — Slovaquie	629	767	1 265	1 265	1 265	1 265	1 265	1 651	1 837	2 621
Slovenia — Slovénie	496	510	664	455	439	460	506	511	461	461
Spain — Espagne	3 080	3 080	3 178	3 178	3 760	4 275	3 524	3 630	3 730	3 660
Sweden — Suède	14 370	15 669	15 124	14 858	16 176	15 988	16 172	16 800	16 900	18 000
Switzerland — Suisse	1 355	1 280	1 400	1 525	1 625	1 400	1 392	1 345	1 505	1 591
TFYR of Macedonia — L'ex-R.y. Macédoine	40	34	27	37	36	23	20	21	28	18
Ukraine — Ukraine	2 296	2 306	2 258	2 141	2 127	1 995	1 950	2 019	2 392	2 184
United Kingdom — Royaume-Uni	2 291	2 356	2 382	2 537	2 630	2 728	2 731	2 768	2 783	2 862
Oceania Océanie	**6 927**	**7 013**	**7 291**	**7 486**	**8 061**	**7 524**	**8 640**	**8 231**	**8 680**	**9 218**
Australia — Australie	3 530	3 481	3 711	3 673	3 983	3 525	4 119	3 732	4 023	4 718
Fiji — Fidji	102	133	131	64	72	72	84	84	112	125
New Caledonia — Nouvelle-Calédonie	3	3	3	3	3	3	3	3	3	3
New Zealand — Nouvelle-Zélande	3 032	3 136	3 178	3 653	3 910	3 821	4 301	4 289	4 419	4 249
Papua New Guinea — Papouasie-Nvl-Guinée	218	218	218	40	40	40	70	60	60	60
Samoa — Samoa	21	21	21	21	21	21	21	21	21	21
Solomon Islands — Iles Salomon	12	12	12	12	12	12	12	12	12	12
Tonga — Tonga	1	1	2	2	2	2	2	2	2	2
Vanuatu — Vanuatu	7	7	15	18	18	28	28	28	28	28

Source

Food and Agriculture Organization of the United Nations (FAO), Rome, FAOSTAT database, last accessed June 2007.

Notes

1 Data include those for Namibia.
2 For statistical purposes, the data for China do not include those for the Hong Kong Special Administrative Region (Hong Kong SAR) and Macao Special Administrative Region (Macao SAR).
3 Data include those for Taiwan Province of China.

Source

Organisation des Nations Unies pour l'alimentation et l'agriculture (FAO), Rome, la base de données de la FAOSTAT, dernier accès juin 2007.

Notes

1 Les données comprennent les chiffres pour la Namibie.
2 Pour la présentation des statistiques, les données pour la Chine ne comprennent pas la Région Administrative Spéciale de Hong Kong (Hong Kong RAS) et la Région Administrative Spéciale de Macao (Macao RAS).
3 Les données comprennent les chiffres pour la province de Taiwan.

41

Paper and paperboard

Production: thousand metric tons

Papiers et cartons

Production : milliers de tonnes

Region, country or area — Région, pays ou zone	1996	1997	1998	1999	2000	2001	2002	2003	2004	2005
World Monde	**284 302**	**301 316**	**301 671**	**316 403**	**324 582**	**322 039**	**331 534**	**341 087**	**354 832**	**354 091**
Africa Afrique	**2 634**	**2 885**	**3 027**	**3 761**	**3 961**	**4 479**	**4 546**	**4 687**	**4 900**	**4 900**
Algeria — Algérie	56	65	94	26	41	41	41	41	41	41
Cameroon — Cameroun	5	0	0	0	0	0	0	0	0	0
Dem. Rep. of the Congo — Rép. dém. du Congo	3	3	3	3	3	3	3	3	3	3
Egypt — Egypte	221	282	343	343	440	460	460	460	460	460
Ethiopia — Ethiopie	8	10	6	10	12	12	11	14	16	16
Kenya — Kenya	129	129	129	129	129	67	80	100	165	165
Libyan Arab Jamah. — Jamah. arabe libyenne	6	6	6	6	6	6	6	6	6	6
Madagascar — Madagascar	3	4	13	7	11	10	9	10	10	10
Morocco — Maroc	106	107	110	109	109	129	129	129	129	129
Mozambique — Mozambique	1	0	0	0	0	0	0	0	0	0
Nigeria — Nigéria	21	19	19	19	19	19	19	19	19	19
South Africa[1] — Afrique du Sud[1]	1 871	2 047	2 105	2 900	2 982	3 523	3 579	3 645	3 774	3 774
Sudan — Soudan	3	3	3	3	3	3	3	3	3	3
Tunisia — Tunisie	90	97	88	94	94	94	94	109	121	121
Uganda — Ouganda	3	3	3	3	3	3	3	3	3	3
United Rep. of Tanzania — Rép.-Unie de Tanzanie	25	25	25	25	25	25	25	25	25	25
Zambia — Zambie	2	4	4	4	4	4	4	4	4	4
Zimbabwe — Zimbabwe	81	81	76	80	80	80	80	117	121	121
Northern America Amérique septentrionale	**102 460**	**107 480**	**105 326**	**108 950**	**107 173**	**101 083**	**102 105**	**100 832**	**102 683**	**101 110**
Canada — Canada	18 414	18 969	18 875	20 280	20 921	19 834	20 226	20 120	20 599	19 673
United States — Etats-Unis	84 046	88 511	86 451	88 670	86 252	81 249	81 879	80 712	82 084	81 437
Latin America and the Caribbean Amérique latine et Caraïbes	**12 610**	**13 762**	**13 624**	**13 837**	**14 498**	**15 703**	**15 772**	**16 601**	**18 007**	**18 193**
Argentina — Argentine	991	1 133	978	1 012	1 270	1 338	1 417	1 444	1 644	1 656
Barbados — Barbade	0	0	0	0	0	0	0	0	0	2
Bolivia — Bolivie	2	2	2	0	0	0	0	0	0	0
Brazil — Brésil	5 885	6 475	6 524	6 255	6 473	7 354	7 354	7 811	8 221	8 221
Chile — Chili	680	614	598	824	861	876	1 016	1 098	1 168	1 210
Colombia — Colombie	693	704	712	733	771	771	847	864	899	919
Costa Rica — Costa Rica	20	20	20	20	20	20	20	20	20	20
Cuba — Cuba	57	57	57	57	57	57	25	33	27	30
Dominican Republic — Rép. dominicaine	21	21	130	130	130	130	130	130	130	130
Ecuador — Equateur	86	91	91	91	91	91	94	101	100	100
El Salvador — El Salvador	56	56	56	56	56	56	56	56	56	56
Guatemala — Guatemala	31	31	31	31	31	31	31	31	31	31
Honduras — Honduras	103	88	95	95	95	95	95	95	95	95
Mexico — Mexique	3 047	3 491	3 673	3 784	3 865	4 056	3 987	4 149	4 689	4 841
Panama — Panama	28	28	0	0	0	0	0	0	0	0
Paraguay — Paraguay	13	13	13	13	13	13	13	13	13	13
Peru — Pérou	140	140	63	63	83	86	88	91	91	91

Region, country or area — Région, pays ou zone	1996	1997	1998	1999	2000	2001	2002	2003	2004	2005
Uruguay — Uruguay	86	90	88	92	88	88	89	89	100	98
Venezuela (Boliv. Rep. of) — Venezuela (Rép. boliv. du)	671	708	493	581	594	641	510	576	723	680
Asia Asie	**81 636**	**85 108**	**85 484**	**91 734**	**95 061**	**97 993**	**103 426**	**110 142**	**115 293**	**115 157**
Armenia — Arménie	0	0	0	0	20	1	2	2	2	2
Azerbaijan — Azerbaïdjan	0	0	0	0	28	146	144	148	148	148
Bahrain — Bahreïn	0	0	0	0	0	0	0	15	15	15
Bangladesh — Bangladesh	90	70	46	46	46	46	46	83	58	58
China[2,3] — Chine[2,3]	26 380	27 230	27 800	29 608	30 900	33 400	37 800	43 000	48 934	48 934
China, Hong Kong SAR — Chine, Hong Kong RAS	280	180	180	180	190	180	180	180	180	180
India — Inde	3 025	2 922	3 320	3 845	3 794	4 094	4 105	4 075	4 434	4 183
Indonesia — Indonésie	4 121	4 822	5 487	6 978	6 977	6 995	6 995	7 040	7 223	7 223
Iran (Islamic Rep. of) — Iran (Rép. islamique d')	205	205	20	25	46	46	415	411	411	411
Iraq — Iraq	18	18	20	20	30	33	33	27	33	33
Israel — Israël	275	275	242	275	275	275	275	275	275	275
Japan — Japon	30 014	31 014	29 886	30 631	31 828	30 717	30 686	30 457	29 253	29 295
Jordan — Jordanie	31	32	32	32	19	27	25	54	54	54
Kazakhstan — Kazakhstan	0	0	0	3	24	47	64	58	58	58
Korea, Dem. P. R. — Corée, R. p. dém. de	80	80	80	80	80	80	80	80	80	80
Korea, Republic of — Corée, République de	7 681	8 334	7 750	8 875	9 308	9 332	9 812	10 148	10 511	10 549
Kuwait — Koweït	0	0	0	0	42	42	42	56	56	56
Kyrgyzstan — Kirghizistan	0	0	0	0	2	7	16	3	2	2
Lebanon — Liban	42	42	42	42	64	66	66	100	103	103
Malaysia — Malaisie	674	711	761	859	791	851	851	983	946	954
Myanmar — Myanmar	15	39	41	37	39	42	49	45	43	45
Nepal — Népal	13	13	13	13	13	13	13	13	13	13
Pakistan — Pakistan	447	500	527	574	592	1 165	1 165	1 165	986	1 010
Philippines — Philippines	613	613	987	1 010	1 107	1 056	1 056	1 091	1 097	1 097
Saudi Arabia — Arabie saoudite	0	0	0	0	50	70	70	214	279	279
Singapore — Singapour	87	87	87	87	87	87	87	87	87	87
Sri Lanka — Sri Lanka	25	25	25	25	24	25	25	25	25	25
Syrian Arab Republic — Rép. arabe syrienne	1	1	1	1	11	15	15	62	75	75
Thailand — Thaïlande	2 036	2 271	2 367	2 434	2 312	2 445	2 444	3 420	3 431	3 431
Turkey — Turquie	1 105	1 246	1 357	1 349	1 567	1 513	1 643	1 609	1 153	1 153
United Arab Emirates — Emirats arabes unis	0	0	0	0	55	58	58	78	81	81
Uzbekistan — Ouzbékistan	0	0	0	0	8	8	9	11	11	11
Viet Nam — Viet Nam	125	125	190	356	384	762	807	779	888	888
Europe Europe	**81 777**	**88 774**	**90 825**	**94 740**	**100 175**	**99 266**	**102 166**	**104 921**	**109 930**	**110 532**
Albania — Albanie	44	44	44	1	3	3	3	3	3	3
Austria — Autriche	3 653	3 816	4 009	4 142	4 386	4 250	4 419	4 565	4 852	4 950
Belarus — Bélarus	131	131	195	208	236	224	216	279	279	279
Belgium — Belgique	...	...	...	1 727	1 727	1 662	1 704	1 919	1 957	1 897
Belgium-Luxembourg — Belgique-Luxembourg	1 432	1 432	1 831	...	...	...	...	...	...	...
Bosnia and Herzegovina — Bosnie-Herzégovine	0	0	0	0	0	0	0	60	81	81
Bulgaria — Bulgarie	150	150	153	126	136	171	171	171	326	326
Croatia — Croatie	304	393	403	417	406	451	467	463	464	592

Paper and paperboard — Production: thousand metric tons (*continued*)
Papiers et cartons — Production : milliers de tonnes (*suite*)

Region, country or area — Région, pays ou zone	1996	1997	1998	1999	2000	2001	2002	2003	2004	2005
Czech Republic — République tchèque	714	772	768	770	804	864	870	920	934	969
Denmark — Danemark	345	391	393	397	263	389	384	388	402	423
Estonia — Estonie	53	35	43	48	54	70	75	64	66	68
Finland — Finlande	10 442	12 149	12 703	12 947	13 509	12 502	12 789	13 058	14 036	12 391
France — France	8 556	9 143	9 161	9 603	10 006	9 625	9 809	9 939	10 255	10 332
Germany — Allemagne	14 733	15 930	16 311	16 742	18 182	17 879	18 526	19 310	20 391	21 679
Greece — Grèce	750	478	622	545	496	495	493	493	533	533
Hungary — Hongrie	363	820	434	473	506	495	517	546	579	571
Ireland — Irlande	0	0	42	42	43	43	44	45	45	45
Italy — Italie	6 954	8 032	8 254	8 568	9 129	8 926	9 317	9 491	9 667	9 999
Latvia — Lettonie	8	16	18	19	16	24	33	38	38	39
Lithuania — Lituanie	31	25	37	37	53	68	78	92	99	113
Netherlands — Pays-Bas	2 987	3 159	3 180	3 256	3 332	3 174	3 346	3 339	3 459	3 471
Norway — Norvège	2 096	2 129	2 260	2 241	2 300	2 220	2 114	2 186	2 294	2 223
Poland — Pologne	1 528	1 660	1 718	1 839	1 934	2 086	2 342	2 461	2 635	2 732
Portugal — Portugal	1 026	1 080	1 136	1 163	1 290	1 419	1 537	1 530	1 664	1 577
Romania — Roumanie	332	324	301	289	340	395	370	443	454	371
Russian Federation — Fédération de Russie	3 224	3 339	3 595	4 535	5 310	5 625	5 978	6 377	6 830	7 024
Serbia and Montenegro — Serbie-et-Monténégro	249	300	326	230	180	241	254	148	159	229
Slovakia — Slovaquie	467	526	597	803	925	988	710	674	798	858
Slovenia — Slovénie	456	430	491	417	411	633	704	511	558	558
Spain — Espagne	3 768	3 968	3 545	4 435	4 765	5 131	5 365	5 437	5 526	5 697
Sweden — Suède	9 018	9 756	9 879	10 071	10 786	10 534	10 724	11 062	11 589	11 736
Switzerland — Suisse	1 461	1 583	1 592	1 748	1 616	1 750	1 805	1 818	1 777	1 751
TFYR of Macedonia — L'ex-R.y. Macédoine	21	21	15	14	17	15	19	18	16	20
Ukraine — Ukraine	293	264	293	311	411	480	532	618	723	760
United Kingdom — Royaume-Uni	6 189	6 479	6 477	6 576	6 605	6 434	6 452	6 455	6 442	6 235
Oceania Océanie	**3 185**	**3 308**	**3 385**	**3 381**	**3 713**	**3 515**	**3 519**	**3 904**	**4 018**	**4 199**
Australia — Australie	2 320	2 418	2 541	2 564	2 836	2 672	2 645	3 090	3 097	3 244
New Zealand — Nouvelle-Zélande	865	890	844	817	877	843	874	814	921	955

Source

Food and Agriculture Organization of the United Nations (FAO), Rome, FAOSTAT database, last accessed June 2007.

Notes

1 Data include those for Namibia.
2 For statistical purposes, the data for China do not include those for the Hong Kong Special Administrative Region (Hong Kong SAR) and Macao Special Administrative Region (Macao SAR).
3 Data include those for Taiwan Province of China.

Source

Organisation des Nations Unies pour l'alimentation et l'agriculture (FAO), Rome, la base de données de la FAOSTAT, dernier accès juin 2007.

Notes

1 Les données comprennent les chiffres pour la Namibie.
2 Pour la présentation des statistiques, les données pour la Chine ne comprennent pas la Région Administrative Spéciale de Hong Kong (Hong Kong RAS) et la Région Administrative Spéciale de Macao (Macao RAS).
3 Les données comprennent les chiffres pour la province de Taiwan.

42

Cement
Production: thousand metric tons

Ciment
Production : milliers de tonnes

Country or area — Pays ou zone	1995	1996	1997	1998	1999	2000	2001	2002	2003	2004
Afghanistan — Afghanistan	115[1]	116[1]	116[1]	116[1]	116[1]	25[1]	16[1]	27[1]	24	70[2]
Albania — Albanie	200[1]	150[1]	100[1]	84[1]	107[1]	180[1]	30[1]	50[1]	578	530
Algeria — Algérie	6 783[1]	7 470[1]	7 146[1]	7 836[1]	7 685[1]	8 700[1]	8 710[1]	9 277[1]	8 192	9 000[2]
Angola[2] — Angola[2]	*200	*270	301	*350	207	201	*200	*250	250	250
Argentina — Argentine	5 477	5 117	6 769	7 092	7 187	6 121	5 545	3 910	5 218	6 254
Armenia — Arménie	228	281	293	314	287	219	275	355	384	501
Australia — Australie	7 124	6 397	6 701	7 236	7 704	7 937	6 821	7 236	7 517	9 214
Austria — Autriche	3 843[2]	3 900	3 852	...	...	3 776[2]	3 863[2]	3 800[2]	3 800[2]	3 800[2]
Azerbaijan[1] — Azerbaïdjan[1]	196	223	303	201	171	251	523	848	1 008	1 428
Bahrain — Bahreïn	...	192[1]	172[1]	230[1]	156[1]	89[1]	89[1]	67[1]	70[2]	75[2]
Bangladesh[1] — Bangladesh[1]	316	420	610	468	1 514	1 868	2 340	2 514	1 776	1 872
Barbados — Barbade	76	108	176	257	257	268	250	298	325	330[2]
Belarus — Bélarus	1 235	1 467	1 876	2 035	1 998	1 847	1 803	2 171	2 472	2 731
Belgium — Belgique	7 501	6 996	6 996	6 852	7 463	7 150[2]	*7 500[2]	*8 000[2]	8 000[2]	8 000[2]
Benin — Bénin	380[1]	411[1]	442[1]	520[1]	520[1]	250[1]	250[1]	250[1]	*250[2]	250[2]
Bhutan[2] — Bhoutan[2]	*140	*160	*160	*150	*150	*150	*160	*160	*160	170
Bolivia — Bolivie	690	709	762	938	1 234	1 072	983	1 010[2]	1 138[2]	1 276[2]
Bosnia and Herzegovina — Bosnie-Herzégovine	...	200	414	563	683	164[3]	145[3]	213[3]	#891	1 045[2]
Brazil — Brésil	28 256	34 559	37 995	39 942	40 248	37 562	38 302	37 462	...	38 000[2]
Brunei Darussalam — Brunéi Darussalam	...	...	...	...	222	241[1]	234[1]	220[1]	235[2]	240[2]
Bulgaria — Bulgarie	2 070	2 137	1 654	1 723	2 047	2 207	2 061	2 141	2 398	2 043
Burkina Faso — Burkina Faso	...	...	50[2]	50[2]	50[2]	50[1]	50[1]	50[1]	*30[2]	30[2]
Cambodia[2] — Cambodge[2]	...	...	...	150	...	...	...	...	...	...
Cameroon — Cameroun	522[1]	600[1]	633[1]	740[1]	852[1]	1 570[1]	980[1]	950[1]	949	930[2]
Canada — Canada	10 440	11 587	11 736[4]	12 168	12 643	12 753	12 793	13 081	13 424[2]	14 017[2]
Chile — Chili	3 304	3 627	3 718	3 890	2 508	2 686	3 145	3 462[2]	3 622[2]	3 798[2]
China — Chine	475 606	491 189	511 738	536 000	573 000	597 000	661 040	725 000	862 081	966 820
China, Hong Kong SAR — Chine, Hong Kong RAS	1 913	2 027	1 925	1 539	1 387	1 284	1 279	1 206	1 189	1 250[2]
Colombia — Colombie	9 908	...	10 878	8 673	6 677	7 131	6 776	6 633	7 300[2]	8 000[2]
Congo — Congo	98	43	20	0	0	0	...	...	...	...
Costa Rica[2] — Costa Rica[2]	865	830	940	1 085	1 100	1 050	1 200	1 200	1 320	1 300
Côte d'Ivoire — Côte d'Ivoire	1 100[1]	1 000[1]	1 100[1]	650[1]	650[1]	650[1]	650[1]	650[1]	650[2]	650[2]
Croatia — Croatie	1 708	1 842	2 134	3 873	2 712	2 852	3 246	3 378	3 571	3 514
Cuba — Cuba	1 456[5]	1 438	1 701	1 724	1 797	1 643	1 335	1 336	1 357	1 409
Cyprus — Chypre	1 024	1 021	910	1 207	1 157	1 398	1 367	1 445	1 638	1 688
Czech Republic — République tchèque	4 831	5 016	4 874	4 599	4 241	4 093	3 591	3 249	3 502	3 829
Dem. Rep. of the Congo[2] — Rép. dém. du Congo[2]	235	241	125	134	159	161	192	*190	190	...
Denmark — Danemark	2 584	2 628	2 544	2 548	2 422	2 536	2 576	2 545	2 580	2 892
Dominican Republic — Rép. dominicaine	1 450	1 642	1 822	1 872	2 295	2 505	2 746	3 050	2 907[2]	2 636[2]
Ecuador — Equateur	2 549	2 601	2 900[2]	2 539	2 262	2 800[2]	2 947	3 113	3 100[2]	3 100[2]
Egypt — Egypte	14 237[1]	15 569[1]	15 569[1]	15 569[1]	11 933[1]	25 101[1]	26 811[1]	23 000[1]	16 281	28 000[2]
El Salvador — El Salvador	914[5]	996	1 667	1 073	1 031[2]	1 064[2]	1 174[2]	1 318[2]	1 390[2]	1 400[2]
Eritrea[2] — Erythrée[2]	...	...	60	50	*45	*45	*45	*45	*45	45
Estonia — Estonie	418	388	422	321	358	329	405	466	506	614

Country or area — Pays ou zone	1995	1996	1997	1998	1999	2000	2001	2002	2003	2004
Ethiopia — Ethiopie	609[6]	672[6]	775[6]	783[6]	767[6]	816[6]	819	919	890	1 300[2]
Fiji — Fidji	91	84	96	89	99	87	99	102	100	100[2]
Finland — Finlande	907	975	1 152	1 232	1 310	1 422	1 325	1 198	1 493	1 691
France — France	19 724	18 337	18 309	19 434	20 302	20 000[2]	20 652	20 244	20 544	...
French Guiana[2] — Guyane française[2]	...	...	51	88	*88	*88	*58	*62	*62	62
Gabon — Gabon	154[1]	180[1]	200[1]	198[1]	162[1]	166[1]	240[1]	257[1]	261	350[2]
Georgia — Géorgie	59	85	94	199	341	348	335	347	345	442
Germany — Allemagne	38 858	37 006	37 210	38 464	39 970	38 088	33 689	32 012	32 349[2]	31 954[2]
Ghana — Ghana	*1 300[2]	*1 500[2]	1 446	1 573	1 851	1 673	1 490	1 414	1 900[2]	2 000[2]
Greece — Grèce	10 914	13 391	13 660	14 207	13 624	14 147	15 563	15 500[2]	18 742[7]	15 000[2]
Guadeloupe * — Guadeloupe *	230	230[2]	230[2]	230[2]	230[2]	230[2]	230[2]	230[2]	230[2]	230[2]
Guatemala — Guatemala	1 257	1 173	1 480	1 496	2 120	2 039	1 976	2 068	1 900[2]	1 900[2]
Guinea — Guinée	...	...	260[1]	277[1]	297[1]	300[1]	300[1]	300[1]	360[2]	360[2]
Haiti[2] — Haïti[2]	...	...	...	...	...	...	204	290	200	300
Honduras — Honduras	995[5]	952[2]	*1 041[2]	896[2]	980[2]	1 284[2]	*1 321[2]	*1 360[2]	1 400[2]	1 400[2]
Hungary — Hongrie	2 875	2 747	2 811	2 999	2 980	3 326	3 452	3 510	3 575	3 363
Iceland — Islande	82	90	110	118	131	144	125	83	85	140[2]
India — Inde	67 722	73 261	82 873	87 646	100 230	99 227	106 491	111 778	117 035	125 000[2]
Indonesia[1] — Indonésie[1]	23 136	24 648	20 702	22 344	22 806	27 789	18 629	33 000	40 476	32 448
Iran (Islamic Rep. of) — Iran (Rép. islamique d')	16 904[1]	17 703[1]	18 349[1]	20 049[1]	22 219[1]	23 276[1]	24 755[1]	30 000[1]	30 000[2]	30 000[2]
Iraq — Iraq	2 108[1]	2 100[1]	2 500[1]	2 000[1]	2 000[1]	2 000[1]	2 000[1]	2 000[1]	*1 000[2]	*3 000[2]
Ireland — Irlande	1 830	2 042	2 247	2 395	2 616	2 784	2 779	2 693	3 065	3 348
Israel — Israël	6 204	6 723	5 916	6 476[2]	6 354[2]	*5 703[2]	*4 700[2]	*4 584[2]	*4 632[2]	*4 494[2]
Italy — Italie	33 716	33 327	33 718	35 512	36 827	39 588	40 494	42 050	37 021	37 843
Jamaica — Jamaïque	518	559	588	558	504[5]	521[5]	596	622	608	808
Japan — Japon	90 474	94 492	91 938	81 328	80 120	81 097	76 550	...	...	...
Jordan[1] — Jordanie[1]	3 415	3 512	3 250	2 650	2 688	2 640	3 149	3 557	3 516	4 068
Kazakhstan[1] — Kazakhstan[1]	1 772	1 115	657	622	838	1 175	2 029	2 128	2 580	3 660
Kenya — Kenya	1 566	1 570	1 580	1 453	1 389	1 348	1 319	1 537	1 659	1 873
Korea, Dem. P. R.[2] — Corée, R. p. dém. de[2]	*17 000	*17 000	7 000	7 000	*4 000	*4 600	*5 160	*5 320	*5 540	5 500
Korea, Republic of — Corée, République de	56 101	58 434	60 317	46 791	48 579	51 417	53 062	56 823	60 725	56 955
Kuwait[1] — Koweït[1]	1 363	1 070	1 370	2 310	947	1 187	921	1 584	1 863	1 710
Kyrgyzstan — Kirghizistan	310[1]	546[1]	658[1]	709[1]	386[1]	453[1]	469[1]	533[1]	757	876[1]
Lao People's Dem. Rep. — Rép. dém. pop. lao	59	78[2]	84[2]	80[2]	*80[2]	*92[2]	*92[2]	*240[2]	*250[2]	*250[2]
Latvia — Lettonie	204	325	246	366	...	...	...	...	...	...
Lebanon — Liban	3 470[1]	3 430[1]	3 126[1]	3 316[1]	2 714[1]	2 808[1]	2 890[1]	2 852[1]	2 900[2]	2 900[2]
Liberia*[2] — Libéria*[2]	5	15	7	10	15	71	63	54	30	30
Libyan Arab Jamah.[1] — Jamah. arabe libyenne[1]	3 000	3 000	3 000	3 000	3 000	3 000	3 000	3 000	3 500	3 600
Lithuania — Lituanie	649	656	710	781	668	559	541	601	599	753
Luxembourg — Luxembourg	714	667	683	699	742	749	725	729	709	750[2]
Madagascar — Madagascar	38	44	36	44	46[2]	48[2]	51	34	33[2]	23
Malawi — Malawi	124	88	70	83	104	156[2]	111	174[2]	190[2]	190[2]
Malaysia[1] — Malaisie[1]	10 713	12 349	12 668	10 379	10 104	11 445	13 820	14 336	17 244	17 328
Mali — Mali	13[1]	21[1]	10[1]	10[1]	10[1]	10[1]	18[8]	...	...	...
Martinique * — Martinique *	225	220[2]	220[2]	220[2]	220[2]	255[2]	255[2]	221[2]	225[2]	225[2]
Mauritania — Mauritanie	120[1]	120[1]	125[1]	50[1]	50[1]	156[1]	181[1]	174[1]	*200[2]	*200[2]
Mexico — Mexique	25 122	28 047	29 526	30 728	31 802	33 228	32 134	33 372	33 594	34 992
Mongolia — Mongolie	109	106	*112[2]	109	104	92	68	148	162	62

42 Cement — Production: thousand metric tons (*continued*)
Ciment — Production : milliers de tonnes (*suite*)

Country or area — Pays ou zone	1995	1996	1997	1998	1999	2000	2001	2002	2003	2004
Morocco[1] — Maroc[1]	6 399	6 588	7 236	7 155	7 194	7 497	8 058	8 057	9 276	9 828
Mozambique — Mozambique	146[1]	179[1]	217[1]	264[1]	266[1]	348[1]	421[1]	274[1]	582	484
Myanmar[9] — Myanmar[9]	525	513	524	371	343	400	384	462	581	527
Nepal — Népal	327[10]	309[10]	227[10]	139[10]	191[10]	206[10]	387	*290[2]	*295[2]	*285[2]
Netherlands — Pays-Bas	3 180[2]	3 140[2]	3 230	3 200	3 200	3 200	*3 450[2]	*3 400[2]	*3 400[2]	*3 400[2]
New Caledonia — Nouvelle-Calédonie	99	89	84	89	93	91	100	100	100[2]	100[2]
New Zealand[2] — Nouvelle-Zélande[2]	950	974	976	950	*1 030	1 070	1 080	1 090	1 100	1 110
Nicaragua — Nicaragua	324[2]	360[2]	361	412	536	568	588	549[2]	590[2]	590[2]
Niger — Niger	31[1]	30[1]	30[1]	30[1]	30[1]	40[1]	40[1]	55[1]	40[2]	40[2]
Nigeria — Nigéria	1 573[1]	2 545[1]	2 520[1]	2 700[1]	2 500[1]	2 500[1]	3 000[1]	3 000[1]	*2 100[2]	2 300[2]
Norway — Norvège	1 613	1 690	1 724[2]	1 676[2]	1 827[2]	1 851[2]	*1 870[2]	…	…	…
Oman — Oman	1 280[1]	1 206[1]	1 233[1]	1 217[1]	1 990[1]	1 815[1]	1 370[1]	1 400[1]	2 100[2]	2 500[2]
Pakistan — Pakistan	7 913	9 567	9 536	9 364	9 635	9 314[1]	9 674[1]	9 935[1]	11 316[1]	14 712[1]
Panama — Panama	658[5]	651	752	814	976	849[5]	*760[2]	*760[2]	*770[2]	*770[2]
Paraguay — Paraguay	624	627	603	586	556	516	505	447	505	660[2]
Peru — Pérou	3 645	3 678	4 092	4 069	3 327	3 658	3 589	4 115	4 203	4 602
Philippines — Philippines	10 566	12 429[2]	14 681	12 888	12 557	11 959	11 378	11 396	10 000[2]	…
Poland — Pologne	13 914	13 959	15 003	14 970	15 555	#14 943	12 090	11 213	11 624	12 148
Portugal — Portugal	7 965	8 536	9 445	9 845	10 057	10 293	10 168	9 728	8 598	8 839
Puerto Rico — Porto Rico	1 398	1 508	1 586	1 646	1 757	…	…	…	…	…
Qatar — Qatar	475[1]	486[1]	584[1]	857[1]	959[1]	1 029[1]	1 209[1]	1 346[1]	1 340[1]	1 400[2]
Republic of Moldova[11] — République de Moldova[11]	49	40	122	74	50	222	158	279	255	440
Réunion — Réunion	313	229	200	342	263	258	*380[2]	*380[2]	*380[2]	*380[2]
Romania — Roumanie	6 842	6 956	6 553	7 300	6 252	8 411	5 668	5 767	5 879	6 211
Russian Federation — Fédération de Russie	36 466	27 791	26 688	25 974	28 529	32 389	35 271	37 705	40 998	45 615
Rwanda — Rwanda	36	42	61	60	66	71[2]	91[2]	101[2]	105[2]	104[2]
Saudi Arabia — Arabie saoudite	15 773[1]	16 437[1]	15 448[1]	15 776[1]	16 381[1]	18 296[1]	20 963[1]	21 000[1]	23 000[2]	23 200[2]
Senegal — Sénégal	694[1]	810[1]	854[1]	847[1]	1 030[1]	1 000[1]	1 000[1]	1 000[1]	1 694[8]	2 150[2]
Serbia and Montenegro — Serbie-et-Monténégro	1 696	2 212	2 011	2 253	#1 575	2 117	2 418	2 396	2 075	2 240[2]
Sierra Leone — Sierra Leone	…	…	…	100[2]	45[2]	100[1]	100[1]	100[1]	170[2]	170[2]
Singapore[2] — Singapour[2]	*3 200	*3 300	*3 300	2 340	1 660	1 150	*600	*200	150	150
Slovakia — Slovaquie	2 981	4 234	5 856	3 066	3 084	3 045	3 011	3 121	3 115	3 031
South Africa — Afrique du Sud	7 437	7 664	7 891	7 676	8 211	8 715	8 036[2]	8 525[2]	8 883[2]	12 348[2]
Spain — Espagne	27 220	26 339	27 860	27 943[2]	…	…	…	…	…	…
Sri Lanka — Sri Lanka	956	670	966	2 151	2 354	2 432	2 123	973	1 163	1 400[2]
Sudan — Soudan	350[1]	380[1]	276[1]	198[1]	231[1]	146[1]	190[1]	190[1]	272[2]	280[2]
Suriname — Suriname	50[1]	50[1]	65[1]	65[1]	65[1]	60[1]	65[1]	65[1]	*65[2]	*65[2]
Sweden — Suède	2 550	2 503	2 320	2 373	2 293	2 613	2 644	2 765	2 841	2 731
Switzerland — Suisse	4 024[2]	3 638[2]	3 568[2]	*3 600[2]	3 548[2]	3 771[2]	3 950[2]	*4 000[2]	3 800[2]	3 955
Syrian Arab Republic — Rép. arabe syrienne	4 804[1]	4 817[1]	4 838[1]	5 016[1]	5 134[1]	4 631[1]	5 428[1]	5 399[1]	5 220[1]	5 098
Tajikistan[1] — Tadjikistan[1]	78	57	36	18	33	55	69	89	168	192
Thailand — Thaïlande	34 051	38 749	37 136	22 722	25 354	25 499	27 913	31 679	32 530	35 626
TFYR of Macedonia — L'ex-R.y. Macédoine	523	490	610	461	563	801	630	778	832	812
Togo — Togo	350[1]	413[1]	421[1]	500[1]	600[1]	700[1]	800[1]	800[1]	*800[2]	…
Trinidad and Tobago — Trinité-et-Tobago	559	617	677	700	740	743	697	744	750[2]	…
Tunisia[1] — Tunisie[1]	4 998	4 566	4 378	4 588	4 860	5 647	5 721	6 020	6 480	6 192
Turkey — Turquie	33 084[1]	35 090[1]	36 035	38 175	34 215	36 238	30 111	32 546	35 264	38 594
Turkmenistan — Turkménistan	437[1]	438[1]	601[1]	750[1]	780[1]	420[1]	448[1]	486[1]	200	450[2]

42 Cement — Production: thousand metric tons (*continued*)
Ciment — Production : milliers de tonnes (*suite*)

Country or area — Pays ou zone	1995	1996	1997	1998	1999	2000	2001	2002	2003	2004
Uganda — Ouganda	84[1]	195[1]	290[1]	321[1]	347[1]	367[1]	431[1]	506[1]	507[2]	520[2]
Ukraine — Ukraine	3 902	3 339	3 535	3 358	3 387	3 631	4 367	4 456	4 962	5 243
United Arab Emirates — Emirats arabes unis	6 000[1]	6 000[1]	6 330[1]	7 066[1]	7 069[1]	6 100[1]	6 100[1]	6 500[1]	*8 000[2]	*8 000[2]
United Kingdom — Royaume-Uni	13 374	13 530	14 307	14 764	14 544	12 452[2]	11 854[2]	*11 089[2]	11 215[2]	11 250[2]
United Rep. of Tanzania — Rép.-Unie de Tanzanie	739	726	621	778[2]	833	833	901[12]	1 026	1 187[12]	1 281[12]
United States[13] — Etats-Unis[13]	76 906	79 266	82 582	83 931	85 952	87 546	88 900	89 732	92 843	97 434
Uruguay — Uruguay	593	631	818	940	839	688	1 015[2]	442[14]	489[14]	658[14]
Uzbekistan — Ouzbékistan	3 419[1]	3 277[1]	3 286[1]	3 400[1]	3 300[1]	3 284[1]	3 722[1]	4 000[1]	*4 000[2]	*4 000[2]
Venezuela (Boliv. Rep. of) — Venezuela (Rép. bolivar. du)	*6 900	7 556[2]	8 145[2]	8 202[2]	*8 500[2]	*8 600[2]	*8 700[2]	*7 000[2]	*7 700[2]	*9 000[2]
Viet Nam — Viet Nam	5 828	6 585	8 019	9 738	10 489	13 298	16 073	21 121	24 127	26 153
Yemen — Yémen	1 100[1]	1 028[1]	1 038[1]	1 195[1]	1 454[1]	1 406[1]	1 449[1]	1 582[1]	1 541	1 546[2]
Zambia — Zambie	312[2]	348[2]	384[2]	351[2]	300[2]	335	309	343	424	480[2]
Zimbabwe — Zimbabwe	948	996	954	1 115	1 105	1 000	549	*600[2]	*400[2]	*400[2]

Source

United Nations Statistics Division, New York, the industrial statistics database and the "Industrial Commodity Statistics Yearbook 2004".

Notes

1. Source: Organisation of the Islamic Conference (Jeddah, Saudi Arabia).
2. Source: U. S. Geological Survey (Washington, D. C.).
3. Excluding the Federation of Bosnia and Herzegovina.
4. Shipments.
5. Source: United Nations Economic Commission for Latin America and the Caribbean (Santiago).
6. Twelve months ending 7 July of the year stated.
7. Incomplete coverage.
8. Source: Afristat: Sub-Saharan African Observatory of Economics and Statistics (Bamako, Mali).
9. Government production only.
10. Twelve months beginning 16 July of the year stated.
11. Excluding the Transnistria region.
12. Tanganyika only.
13. Excluding Puerto Rico.
14. Portland cement only.

Source

Organisation des Nations Unies, Division de statistique, New York, la base de données pour les statistiques industrielles et "l'Annuaire de statistiques industrielles par produit 2004".

Notes

1. Source: Organisation de la Conférence islamique (Jeddah, Arabie saoudite).
2. Source: "U. S. Geological Survey" (Washington, D. C.).
3. Non compris la Fédération de Bosnie et Herzégovine.
4. Expéditions.
5. Source: Commission économique des Nations Unies pour l'Amérique Latine et des Caraïbes (Santiago).
6. Période de 12 mois finissant le 7 juillet de l'année indiquée.
7. Couverture incomplète.
8. Source: "Afristat: Sub-Saharan African Observatory of Economics and Statistics (Bamako, Mali)".
9. Production de l'Etat seulement.
10. Période de 12 mois commençant le 16 juillet de l'année indiquée.
11. Non compris la région de Transnistria.
12. Tanganyika seulement.
13. Non compris Puerto Rico.
13. Ciment Portland uniquement.

Aluminium, unwrought

Total production: thousand metric tons

Aluminium non travaillé

Production totale : milliers de tonnes

Country or area — Pays ou zone	1995	1996	1997	1998	1999	2000	2001	2002	2003	2004
Argentina — Argentine	183	185	187	187	206	261	248	269	272	272
Australia[1] — Australie[1]	1 285	1 331	1 395	1 589	1 686	...	...	...	...	...
Austria — Autriche	94[2]	98	119[2]	126	143[2]	158[2]	158[2]	...	...	...
Azerbaijan[3] — Azerbaïdjan[3]	...	...	...	...	...	...	...	...	19	30
Bahrain — Bahreïn	449	456	490[3]	501[3]	502	512	523[3]	519[3]	532[3]	530[3]
Bosnia and Herzegovina — Bosnie-Herzégovine	...	...	...	32	57	95[3]	96[3]	103[3]	113	115[3]
Brazil — Brésil	1 305[2]	1 343[2]	1 369[2]	1 388[2]	1 440[3]	1 035	951	1 449	1 195	1 457[3]
Bulgaria — Bulgarie	...	...	...	...	...	1	...	...	...	...
Cameroon — Cameroun	71	82[4]	98	89	93	100	181	72	79	77[3]
Canada — Canada	2 269[2]	2 384[2]	2 433[2]	2 485[2]	2 502	2 373[3]	2 583[3]	2 709[3]	2 792[3]	2 592[3]
China[5] — Chine[5]	1 870	1 896	2 180	2 362	2 809	2 989	3 576	4 511	5 866	6 690
Colombia^ — Colombie^	0	...	...	...	...	...	...	...	...	...
Croatia — Croatie	31	33	18	16	14	14	15	15	0	...
Czech Republic[3] — République tchèque[3]	...	45	45	45	40	40	...	...	...	...
Egypt — Egypte	136[6]	150[6]	119[6]	187[6]	193[3]	189[3]	191[3]	195[3]	195[3]	215[3]
Finland — Finlande	5	5	2	2	...	...	...	...	...	...
France* — France*	364	380	635	663	694	701	713	713	685	...
Germany — Allemagne	430	358	349	375	395	404	404	410	438	...
Ghana — Ghana	135[2]	137[2]	152	56	114	156	162	133	...	...
Greece — Grèce	132	141	132	161	161	168[3]	166[3]	165[3]	166[7]	165[3]
Hungary — Hongrie	35	94	98	92	89	89[3]	110[3]	...	...	...
Iceland — Islande	100	102	123	160	161	167	169	194	286	271[3]
India — Inde	518	516	539	542[3]	614[3]	644[3]	624[3]	671[3]	799[3]	862[3]
Indonesia — Indonésie	228[2]	223[2]	219[2]	133[2]	112[2,8]	160[3]	180[3]	*160[3]	200[3]	230[3]
Iran (Islamic Rep. of) — Iran (Rép. islamique d')	145[2]	104[2]	125[2]	137[2]	164[2]	146[3]	160[3]	169[3]	170[3]	170[3]
Italy — Italie	590	561	631	690	689	757	766	782	#74	76
Japan — Japon	1 227[9]	1 238[9]	1 330[9]	1 207[9]	1 158[9]	1 214[9]	1 171	...	...	...
Kazakhstan^ — Kazakhstan^	...	...	...	...	...	...	...	0	0	...
Korea, Republic of — Corée, République de	...	...	...	...	...	312	325	357	356	454
Mozambique — Mozambique	...	...	...	...	...	54[3]	266[3]	273[3]	409	548
Netherlands — Pays-Bas	408	377[3]	382	366	391	405	294[3]	284[3]	278[3]	326[3]
New Zealand — Nouvelle-Zélande	281[2]	293[2]	318[2]	389[2]	348[3]	328[3]	322[3]	335[3]	340[3]	350[3]
Norway — Norvège	*919	*923	977[2]	1 058[2]	1 199[3]	1 280[3]	1 291[3]	...	...	...
Poland — Pologne	56	52	54	54	51	#12	12	14	15	14
Romania[9,10] — Roumanie[9,10]	144	145	164	175	174	181	183	190	205	...
Russian Federation[3] — Fédération de Russie[3]	2 724	2 874	2 906	3 005	3 146	3 245	3 300	3 347	3 478	3 593
Serbia and Montenegro — Serbie-et-Monténégro	17	37	67	61	#73	88	100	112	117	115[3]
Slovakia — Slovaquie	25	311	110[2]	121	109	110	...	...	...	...
South Africa[3] — Afrique du Sud[3]	229	570	673	677	689	673	662	707	738	863
Spain — Espagne	469[2]	515[2]	533[2]	570[2]	588[2]	366[3]	376[3]	380[3]	389[3]	...
Suriname — Suriname	28	29	29	28	7	...	...	2	...	...
Sweden — Suède	118[3]	28	34	31	36	35	35	29	28	0
Switzerland — Suisse	26[2]	33[2]	35[2]	47[2]	41[2]	36[3]	36[3]	40[3]	44[3]	45[3]
Tajikistan — Tadjikistan	237	198	189	196	229	269[3]	289[3]	306[3]	319[3]	358[3]

43 Aluminium, unwrought — Total production : thousand metric tons (*continued*)
Aluminium non travaillé — Production totale : milliers de tonnes (*suite*)

Country or area — Pays ou zone	1995	1996	1997	1998	1999	2000	2001	2002	2003	2004
TFYR of Macedonia — L'ex-R.y. Macédoine	5	5	5	7	6	4	3	5	5	...
Turkey — Turquie	62	62	62	62	62	62	62	63	63	60[3]
Ukraine[3] — Ukraine[3]	*138	*130	101	178	226	104	106	112	114	113
United Arab Emirates[3] — Emirats arabes unis[3]	...	...	...	...	...	^0	1	1	1	1
United Kingdom — Royaume-Uni	468[9]	501[9]	114	494[3]	547[3]	305[3]	341[3]	344[3]	343[3]	360[3]
United States — Etats-Unis	3 375	3 577	3 603	3 713	3 779	3 668	2 637	2 707	2 703	2 516
Venezuela (Bolivarian Rep. of) Venezuela (Rép. bolivarienne du)	654[2]	656[2]	668[2]	617[2]	595[2]	571[3]	571[3]	605[3]	601[3]	624[3]

Source

United Nations Statistics Division, New York, the industrial statistics database and the "Industrial Commodity Statistics Yearbook 2004".

Notes

1 Twelve months ending 30 June of the year stated.
2 Source: World Metal Statistics (London).
3 Source: U. S. Geological Survey (Washington, D. C.).
4 Source: "African Statistical Yearbook", Economic Commission for Africa (Addis Ababa).
5 For statistical purposes, the data for China do not include those for the Hong Kong Special Administrative Region (Hong Kong SAR), Macao Special Administrative Region (Macao SAR) and Taiwan Province of China.
6 Including aluminium plates, shapes and bars.
7 Incomplete coverage.
8 Primary metal production only.
9 Including alloys.
10 Including pure content of virgin alloys.

Source

Organisation des Nations Unies, Division de statistique, New York, la base de données pour les statistiques industrielles et "l'Annuaire de statistiques industrielles par produit 2004".

Notes

1 Période de 12 mois finissant le 30 juin de l'année indiquée.
2 Source: "World Metal Statistics" (Londres).
3 Source: "U. S. Geological Survey" (Washington, D. C.).
4 Source : "Annuaire des Statistiques de l'Afrique", Conseil Economique pour l'Afrique (Addis Ababa).
5 Pour la présentation des statistiques, les données pour la Chine ne comprennent pas la Région Administrative Spéciale de Hong Kong (Hong Kong RAS), la Région Administrative Spéciale de Macao (Macao RAS) et la province de Taiwan.
6 Y compris les tôles, les profilés et les barres d'aluminium.
7 Couverture incomplète.
8 Production du métal de première fusion seulement.
9 Y compris les alliages.
10 Y compris la teneur pure des alliages de première fusion.

44

Radio receivers

Production: thousands

Récepteurs de radio

Production : milliers

Country or area — Pays ou zone	1995	1996	1997	1998	1999	2000	2001	2002	2003	2004
Bangladesh — Bangladesh	4	11	20	10	13	13	14	10	13	...
Belarus — Bélarus	277	138	170	114	195	101	56	47	31	21
Brazil — Brésil	4 729	2 941	4 211	2 753	2 039	2 958	3 456	1 364	2 481	...
Bulgaria — Bulgarie	2	0	...	...	...	...	...	...	...	...
China, Hong Kong SAR — Chine, Hong Kong RAS	1 698	...	...	...	...	...	...	...	...	...
Cuba — Cuba	23	14	30	17	12	11	11	10	6	66
Denmark — Danemark	92	99	91	91	90	86	100	84	68	64
Finland — Finlande	82	...	...	...	...	...	...	...	...	...
France — France	...	...	3 853	4 586	2 961	3 195	3 508	3 357	3 498	...
Germany — Allemagne	3 182	3 342	3 632	3 884	4 021	4 025	4 746	...	...	...
Hungary — Hongrie	103	310	528	2 328	2 412	2 320	3 459	2 917	2 991	2 840
India — Inde	116	47	33	2	0	0	0	0	0	...
Indonesia[1] — Indonésie[1]	3 805	...	4 177	...	4 937	...	...	...	...	...
Iran (Islamic Rep. of)[2] — Iran (Rép. islamique d')[2]	45	56	76	127	114	139	129	275	...	...
Ireland — Irlande	0	0	0	0	2	77	105	134	174	1 490
Japan — Japon	7 181	2 638	2 434	2 623	2 678	2 384	1 972	#2 496	2 892	2 324
Kazakhstan — Kazakhstan	12	3	3	3	0	0	0	...	...	...
Korea, Republic of — Corée, République de	1 123	1 088	855	556	801	1 420	1 692	1 234	318	31
Kyrgyzstan — Kirghizistan	...	864	...	...	...	...	...	...	...	...
Latvia — Lettonie	9	10	10	2	2	...	...	...	...	...
Malaysia — Malaisie	38 767	29 431	33 491	30 265	32 957	36 348	28 839	21 735	27 634	...
Mexico — Mexique	341	379	537	731	913	1 087	946	1 544	1 580	1 310
Poland — Pologne	225	206	143	154	132	#109	13	11	28	34
Portugal — Portugal	...	4 372	4 552	6 102	6 965	8 046	8 652	8 470	7 310	7 805
Republic of Moldova[3] — République de Moldova[3]	16	67	94	51	10	18	3	5	3	6
Romania — Roumanie	29[1]	76[1]	28[1]	10[1]	0[1]	0	0	4	0	...
Russian Federation — Fédération de Russie	988	477	342	235	332	390	281	253	278	194
Serbia and Montenegro — Serbie-et-Monténégro	0	1	0	0	#0	0	0	...	...	...
Spain — Espagne	54	82	313	508	357	57	85	52	47	71
Sweden — Suède	...	...	2	3	3	3	2	...	...	...
Ukraine — Ukraine	125	47	25	10	27	36	26	33	21	106
United Kingdom — Royaume-Uni	1 480	1 531	2 062	...	...	505	...	...	...	...
United Rep. of Tanzania — Rép.-Unie de Tanzanie	76	54	56	15[4]	...	...	...	...	...	...
Viet Nam — Viet Nam	111	94	145	205	140	145	71	67	24	24

Source

United Nations Statistics Division, New York, the industrial statistics database and the "Industrial Commodity Statistics Yearbook 2004".

Source

Organisation des Nations Unies, Division de statistique, New York, la base de données pour les statistiques industrielles et "l'Annuaire de statistiques industrielles par produit 2004"

Notes

1 Including radios with tape recording units.
2 Production by establishments employing 10 or more persons.
3 Excluding the Transnistria region.
4 Tanganyika only.

Notes

1 Y compris les récepteurs de radio avec appareil enregistreur à bande magnétique incorporés.
2 Production des établissements occupant 10 personnes ou plus.
3 Non compris la région de Transnistria.
4 Tanganyika seulement.

Refrigerators for household use

Production: thousands

Réfrigérateurs à usage domestique

Production : milliers

Country or area — Pays ou zone	1995	1996	1997	1998	1999	2000	2001	2002	2003	2004
Algeria — Algérie	131	137	175	215	181	117	64	153	150	...
Argentina — Argentine	49	45	401	424	354	325	246	162	...	...
Australia — Australie	423	403	398	441	427	...	...	...	...	...
Azerbaijan — Azerbaïdjan	25	7	0	3	1	1	2	4	5	10
Belarus — Bélarus	746	754	795	802	802	812	830	856	886	953
Brazil — Brésil	3 242	3 776	3 592	3 034	2 796	...	...	...	...	...
Bulgaria — Bulgarie	49	36	21	...	...	...	...	...	...	...
Chile — Chili	272	213	268	229	242	271	280	230	232	...
China[1] — Chine[1]	9 185	9 797	10 444	10 600	12 100	12 790	13 513	15 989	22 426	30 076
Colombia — Colombie	465	...	...	...	...	...	...	...	...	...
Cuba — Cuba	...	...	...	6	10	9	9	10	8	7
Denmark — Danemark	1 141	941	1 091	1 046	1 061	1 008	863	805	798	667
Ecuador — Equateur	156	17	133	88	38	55	...	...	142	...
Egypt — Egypte	236	250	...	...	527	191	451	640	808	...
Finland — Finlande	104	68	102	107	...	...	...	0	...	...
France — France	...	...	490	640	509	555	542	528	544	...
Germany — Allemagne	...	...	...	...	...	...	...	2 354	2 107	2 061
Greece[2,3] — Grèce[2,3]	...	...	...	...	...	...	...	...	381	...
Hungary — Hongrie	714	736	835	708	849	995	1 058	1 866	1 883	1 625
India — Inde	1 913	1 705	1 600	1 902	2 012	2 009	2 469	2 735	3 715	...
Indonesia — Indonésie	291	...	573	417	240	774	...	...	...	...
Iran (Islamic Rep. of) — Iran (Rép. islamique d')	575[4]	756[4]	786[4]	1 200	1 236	973	917	978	946	799
Ireland — Irlande	41	24	160	0	15	0	10	10	11	12
Italy — Italie	5 908	5 402	5 562	6 280	6 582	6 987	6 936	7 088	7 197	7 201
Japan — Japon	5 013	5 163	5 369	4 851	4 543	4 224	3 875	3 317	2 859	...
Kazakhstan — Kazakhstan	...	...	...	...	...	2	...	...	...	...
Korea, Republic of — Corée, République de	3 975	4 292	4 257	3 790	4 735	6 304	6 448	8 254	7 267	7 122
Kyrgyzstan — Kirghizistan	1	0	0	...	...	...	...	...	...	...
Lithuania — Lituanie	187	138	88	116	118	101	94	111	98	107
Malaysia — Malaisie	295	257	249	206	194	215	186	172	187	...
Mexico — Mexique	1 256	1 448	1 943	1 986	2 083	2 049	2 071	2 222	2 162	2 291
Nigeria — Nigéria	19	...	...	...	...	...	...	...	...	...
Peru — Pérou	161	81	101	118	42	51	*68	64	*46	...
Poland — Pologne	585	584	705	714	726	#172	152	101	215	273
Portugal — Portugal	239	265	333	403	430	424	417	440	452	399
Republic of Moldova[5] — Rép. de Moldova[5]	24	1	2	0	...	...	...	...	...	...
Romania — Roumanie	435[3]	446[3]	429[3]	366[3]	323[3]	341[3]	313[3]	212	319	260
Russian Federation — Fédération de Russie	1 789	1 064	1 186	1 043	1 173	1 327	1 719	1 938	2 218	2 589
Serbia and Monteneg. — Serbie-et-Monténég.	50	51	81	48	#5	20	0	10	...	...
Slovakia — Slovaquie	330	393	258	228	206	177	53	...	...	...
South Africa — Afrique du Sud	365[6]	411[6]	388	399	440	508	662	702	711	...
Spain — Espagne	1 269	1 260	1 960	2 415	2 107	2 153	...	...	...	...
Sweden — Suède	610	377	428	368	549	575	593	627	655	639

45 Refrigerators for household use — Production: thousands (*continued*)
Réfrigérateurs à usage domestique — Production : milliers (*suite*)

Country or area — Pays ou zone	1995	1996	1997	1998	1999	2000	2001	2002	2003	2004
Syrian Arab Republic — Rép. arabe syrienne	156	155	138	137	120	96	110	113	...	...
Tajikistan — Tadjikistan	^0	1	2	1	2	2	2	1	1	2
Thailand — Thaïlande	...	2 246	2 384	1 631[7]	...	...	...	...	...	...
TFYR of Macedonia — L'ex-R.y. Macédoine	51	20	12	*4	0	0	9	1	0	0
Trinidad and Tobago — Trinité-et-Tobago	1	0	...	...	...	...	...	...	...	...
Turkey — Turquie	1 680	1 612	1 945	1 993	2 083	2 405	2 245	3 017	4 011	4 867
Ukraine — Ukraine	562	431	382	390	409	451	509	583	340	313
United Kingdom — Royaume-Uni	756[8]	749[8]	746[8]	662[8]	620[8]	581[8]	565[8]	476[8]	745	317[8]
United States[9,10] — Etats-Unis[9,10]	11 005	11 132	12 092	11 279	11 716	12 355	11 776	11 145	11 639	...
Uzbekistan — Ouzbékistan	19	13	13	16[11]	2[11]	1[11]	...	...	...	...
Viet Nam — Viet Nam	...	...	...	...	...	175	223	342	479	622

Source

United Nations Statistics Division, New York, the industrial statistics database and the "Industrial Commodity Statistics Yearbook 2004".

Notes

1 For statistical purposes, the data for China do not include those for the Hong Kong Special Administrative Region (Hong Kong SAR), Macao Special Administrative Region (Macao SAR) and Taiwan Province of China.
2 Incomplete coverage.
3 Including freezers.
4 Production by establishments employing 10 or more persons.
5 Excluding the Transnistria region.
6 Including deep freezers and deep freeze-refrigerator combinations.
7 Beginning 1999, series discontinued.
8 Excluding chest freezers of a capacity <= 800 litres.
9 Shipments.
10 Electric domestic refrigerators only.
11 Source: "Statistical Yearbook for Asia and the Pacific", United Nations Economic and Social Commission for Asia and the Pacific (Bangkok).

Source

Organisation des Nations Unies, Division de statistique, New York, la base de données pour les statistiques industrielles et "l'Annuaire de statistiques industrielles par produit 2004".

Notes

1 Pour la présentation des statistiques, les données pour la Chine ne comprennent pas la Région Administrative Spéciale de Hong Kong (Hong Kong RAS), la Région Administrative Spéciale de Macao (Macao RAS) et la province de Taiwan.
2 Couverture incomplète.
3 Y compris les congélateurs.
4 Production des établissements occupant 10 personnes ou plus.
5 Non compris la région de Transnistria.
6 Y compris congélateurs-conservateurs et congélateurs combinés avec un réfrigérateur.
7 A partir de 1999, les séries ont été discontinuées.
8 Non compris congélateurs-conservateurs de type coffre, à capacité <= 800 litres.
9 Expéditions.
10 Réfrigérateurs électriques de ménage seulement.
11 Source : "Annuaire des Statistiques de l'Asie et Pacifique", Conseil Economique et Social des Nations Unies pour l'Asie et le Pacifique (Bangkok).

Technical notes: tables 36-45

Industrial activity includes mining and quarrying, manufacturing and the production of electricity, gas and water. These activities correspond to the major divisions 2, 3 and 4 respectively of the *International Standard Industrial Classification of All Economic Activities*.

Many of the tables are based primarily on data compiled for the United Nations *Industrial Commodity Statistics Yearbook*. Data taken from alternate sources are footnoted.

The methods used by countries for the computation of industrial output are, as a rule, consistent with those described in the United Nations *International Recommendations for Industrial Statistics* and provide a satisfactory basis for comparative analysis. In some cases, however, the definitions and procedures underlying computations of output differ from approved guidelines. The differences, where known, are indicated in the footnotes to each table.

Table 36: The statistics on sugar were obtained from the database and the *Sugar Yearbook* of the International Sugar Organization. The data shown cover the production and consumption of centrifugal sugar from both beet and cane, and refer to calendar years.

The consumption data relate to the apparent consumption of centrifugal sugar in the country concerned, including sugar used for the manufacture of sugar-containing products whether exported or not and sugar used for purposes other than human consumption as food. Unless otherwise specified, the statistics are expressed in terms of raw value (i.e. sugar polarizing at 96 degrees). The world total also includes data for countries not shown separately whose sugar consumption was less than 10,000 metric tons.

Table 37: The data refer to meat from animals slaughtered within the national boundaries irrespective of the origin of the animals. Production figures of cattle, buffalo, pig (including bacon and ham), sheep and goat meat are in terms of carcass weight, excluding edible offal, tallow and lard. All data refer to total meat production, i.e. from both commercial and farm slaughter.

Table 38: The data refer to beer made from malt, including ale, stout, and porter.

Table 39 presents data on cigarettes only, unless otherwise indicated.

Table 40: The data refer to the aggregate of sawnwood and sleepers, coniferous or non-coniferous. The data cover wood planed, unplaned, grooved, tongued and the like, sawn lengthwise or produced by a profile-chipping process, and planed wood which may also be finger-jointed, tongued or grooved, chamfered, rabbeted, V-jointed, beaded and so on. Wood flooring is excluded. Sleepers may be sawn or hewn.

Notes techniques : tableaux 36 à 45

L'activité industrielle comprend les industries extractives (mines et carrières), les industries manufacturières et la production d'électricité, de gaz et d'eau. Ces activités correspondent aux grandes divisions 2, 3 et 4, respectivement, de la *Classification internationale type par industrie de toutes les branches d'activité économique*.

Un grand nombre de ces tableaux sont établis principalement sur la base de données compilée pour l'*Annuaire de statistiques industrielles par produit* des Nations Unies. Les données tirées d'autres sources sont signalées par une note.

En règle générale, les méthodes employées par les pays pour le calcul de leur production industrielle sont conformes à celles dans *Recommandations internationales concernant les statistiques industrielles* des Nations Unies et offrent une base satisfaisante pour une analyse comparative. Toutefois, dans certains cas, les définitions des méthodes sur lesquelles reposent les calculs de la production diffèrent des directives approuvées. Lorsqu'elles sont connues, les différences sont indiquées par une note.

Tableau 36: Les données sur le sucre proviennent de la base de données et de l'*Annuaire du sucre* de l'Organisation internationale du sucre. Les données présentées portent sur la production et la consommation de sucre centrifugé à partir de la betterave et de la canne à sucre, et se rapportent à des années civiles.

Les données de la consommation se rapportent à la consommation apparente de sucre centrifugé dans le pays en question, y compris le sucre utilisé pour la fabrication de produits à base de sucre, exportés ou non, et le sucre utilisé à d'autres fins que pour la consommation alimentaire humaine. Sauf indication contraire, les statistiques sont exprimées en valeur brute (sucre polarisant à 96 degrés). Le total mondial compris également les données relatives aux pays où la consommation de sucre est inférieure à 10.000 tonnes.

Le *tableau 37* indique la production de viande provenant des animaux abattus à l'intérieur des frontières nationales, quelle que soient leurs origines. Les chiffres de production de viande bovine, de buffle, de porc (y compris le bacon et le jambon), de mouton et de chèvre se rapportent à la production en poids de carcasses et ne comprennent pas le saindoux, le suif et les abats comestibles. Toutes les données se rapportent à la production totale de viande, c'est-à-dire à la fois aux animaux abattus à des fins commerciales et des animaux sacrifiés à la ferme.

Tableau 38: Les données se rapportent à la bière produite à partir du malte, y compris ale, stout et porter (bière anglaise, blonde et brune).

Le *tableau 39* se rapporte seulement aux cigarettes, sauf indication contraire.

Table 41 presents statistics on the production of all paper and paper board. The data cover newsprint, printing and writing paper, construction paper and paperboard, household and sanitary paper, special thin paper, wrapping and packaging paper and paperboard.

Table 42: Statistics on all hydraulic cements used for construction (Portland, metallurgic, aluminous, natural, and so on) are shown.

Table 43: The data refer to unwrought aluminium obtained by electrolytic reduction of alumina (primary) and re-melting metal waste or scrap (secondary).

Table 44: The data on radio receivers include complete receiving sets, irrespective of frequencies covered, made for home, automobile and general use, including battery sets. Radio-gramophone combinations are included.

Table 49: The data refer to refrigerators of the compression type or of the absorption type, of the sizes commonly used in private households. Insulated cabinets to contain an active refrigerating element (block ice) but no machine are excluded.

Tableau 40: Les données font référence à un agrégat des sciages de bois de conifères et de non-conifères et des traverses de chemins de fer. Elles comprennent les bois rabotés, non rabotés, rainés, languetés, etc. sciés en long ou obtenus à l'aide d'un procédé de profilage par enlèvement de copeaux et les bois rabotés qui peuvent être également à joints digitiformes languetés ou rainés, chanfreinés, à feuillures, à joints en V, à rebords, etc. Cette rubrique ne comprend pas les éléments de parquet en bois. Les traverses de chemin de fer comprennent les traverses sciées ou équarries à la hache.

Le *tableau 41* présente les statistiques sur la production de tout papier et carton. Les données comprennent le papier journal, les papiers d'impression et d'écriture, les papiers et cartons de construction, les papiers de ménage et les papiers hygiéniques, les papiers minces spéciaux, les papiers d'empaquetage et d'emballage et carton.

Tableau 42: Les données sur tous les ciments hydrauliques utilisés dans la construction (portland métallurgique, alumineux, naturel, etc.) sont présentées.

Tableau 43: Les données se rapportent à la production d'aluminium non travaillé obtenue par réduction électrolytique de l'alumine (formes primaires) et par refonte de déchets et débris de métal (formes secondaires).

Tableau 44: Les données sur les récepteurs de radio comprennent les récepteurs complets, d'appartement, d'automobiles et d'usage général, y compris les postes à piles quelles que soient les longueurs d'ondes captées. Cette rubrique comprend les récepteurs avec phonographes ou tourne-disques incorporés.

Tableau 49: Les données se rapportent aux appareils frigorifiques du type à compression ou à absorption de la taille des appareils communément utilisés dans les ménages. Cette rubrique ne comprend pas les glacières conçues pour contenir un élément frigorifique actif (glace en bloc) mais non pour contenir équipement frigorifique.

Railway traffic

Passenger-kilometres and freight net ton-kilometres: millions

Trafic ferroviaire

Voyageurs-kilomètres et tonnes-kilomètres nettes de fret: millions

Country or area — Pays ou zone	1996	1997	1998	1999	2000	2001	2002	2003	2004	2005
Albania — Albanie										
Passenger-kilometres Voyageurs-kilomètres	168	95	116	121	183	138	123	105	...	...
Freight net ton-kilometres Tonnes-kilomètres nettes de fret	42	23	25	26	28	19	20	31	...	...
Algeria — Algérie										
Passenger-kilometres Voyageurs-kilomètres	1 826	1 360	1 163	1 069	1 142	981	...	...	...	...
Freight net ton-kilometres Tonnes-kilomètres nettes de fret	2 194	2 892	2 174	2 033	1 980	1 990	...	...	...	...
Argentina — Argentine										
Passenger-kilometres[1] Voyageurs-kilomètres[1]	8 524	9 324	9 652	9 102	8 939	7 975	6 586	...	...	...
Freight net ton-kilometres Tonnes-kilomètres nettes de fret	8 505	9 835	9 852	9 101	8 696	8 989	9 444	...	...	...
Armenia — Arménie										
Passenger-kilometres Voyageurs-kilomètres	84	84	52	46	47	48	48	41	30	27
Freight net ton-kilometres Tonnes-kilomètres nettes de fret	351	381	419	323	354	344	452	529	678	654
Austria — Autriche										
Passenger-kilometres Voyageurs-kilomètres	9 689	8 140	7 971	7 997	8 206	8 240	8 300	8 249	8 704	9 061
Freight net ton-kilometres Tonnes-kilomètres nettes de fret	13 909	14 791	15 348	15 556	17 110	17 387	17 627	17 836	18 760	18 957
Azerbaijan — Azerbaïdjan										
Passenger-kilometres Voyageurs-kilomètres	558	489	533	422	493	537	584	654	789	878
Freight net ton-kilometres Tonnes-kilomètres nettes de fret	2 778	3 515	4 702	5 052	5 770	6 141	6 980	7 719	7 536	9 628
Bangladesh[2] — Bangladesh[2]										
Passenger-kilometres Voyageurs-kilomètres	3 333	3 754	3 855	...	...	...	...	...	...	...
Freight net ton-kilometres Tonnes-kilomètres nettes de fret	689	782	804	...	...	...	...	...	...	...
Belarus[3] — Bélarus[3]										
Passenger-kilometres Voyageurs-kilomètres	11 657	12 909	13 268	16 874	17 722	15 264	14 349	13 308	13 893	10 351
Freight net ton-kilometres Tonnes-kilomètres nettes de fret	26 018	30 636	30 370	30 529	31 425	29 727	34 169	38 402	40 331	43 559
Belgium — Belgique										
Passenger-kilometres Voyageurs-kilomètres	6 788	6 984	7 097	7 354	7 755	8 036	8 260	8 265	8 676	9 150
Freight net ton-kilometres Tonnes-kilomètres nettes de fret	7 244	7 465	7 600	7 392	7 674	7 080	7 297	7 293	7 691	8 130
Benin — Bénin										
Passenger-kilometres Voyageurs-kilomètres	117	121	119	121	121	101	...	...	...	...
Freight net ton-kilometres Tonnes-kilomètres nettes de fret	178	218	221	215	314	316	482	...	...	...
Bolivia — Bolivie										
Passenger-kilometres Voyageurs-kilomètres	197	225	270	271	259	267	280	283	286	...
Freight net ton-kilometres Tonnes-kilomètres nettes de fret	780	839	908	832	856	750	873	901	1 058	...

Railway traffic — Passenger-kilometres and freight net ton-kilometres: millions (*continued*)
Trafic ferroviaire — Voyageurs-kilomètres et tonnes-kilomètres nettes de fret: millions (*suite*)

Country or area — Pays ou zone	1996	1997	1998	1999	2000	2001	2002	2003	2004	2005
Botswana — Botswana										
Passenger-kilometres Voyageurs-kilomètres	81	82	71	75	...	...	...	...	...	...
Freight net ton-kilometres Tonnes-kilomètres nettes de fret	668	1 049	1 278	1 037	874	704	714	637	...	...
Brazil — Brésil										
Passenger-kilometres[4] Voyageurs-kilomètres[4]	9 048	7 876	7 224	6 528	5 852	...	...	...	...	...
Freight net ton-kilometres[5] Tonnes-kilomètres nettes de fret[5]	128 976	138 724	142 446	140 957	154 870	162 235	170 177	182 644	205 711	...
Bulgaria — Bulgarie										
Passenger-kilometres Voyageurs-kilomètres	5 065	5 886	4 740	3 819	3 472	2 990	2 598	2 517	2 404	2 389
Freight net ton-kilometres[6] Tonnes-kilomètres nettes de fret[6]	7 549	7 444	6 152	5 297	5 538	4 904	4 627	5 274	5 211	5 163
Cambodia — Cambodge										
Passenger-kilometres Voyageurs-kilomètres	22	51	44	50	15	...	...	...	...	...
Freight net ton-kilometres Tonnes-kilomètres nettes de fret	4	37	76	76	91	...	...	...	...	...
Cameroon — Cameroun										
Passenger-kilometres Voyageurs-kilomètres	306[7]	283[7]	292[7]	311[7]	711[7]	303[7]	308	322	...	...
Freight net ton-kilometres Tonnes-kilomètres nettes de fret	869[7]	850[7]	888[7]	916[7]	1 063[7]	1 159[7]	1 179	1 090	...	...
Canada — Canada										
Passenger-kilometres Voyageurs-kilomètres	1 519	1 515	1 458	1 593	1 533	1 553	1 597	1 434	1 414	...
Freight net ton-kilometres Tonnes-kilomètres nettes de fret	282 489	306 943	299 508	298 836	321 894	321 291	318 315	318 345	336 482	...
Chile — Chili										
Passenger-kilometres Voyageurs-kilomètres	644	552	519	638	737	871	770	829	820	753
Freight net ton-kilometres Tonnes-kilomètres nettes de fret	2 366	2 330	2 650	2 896	3 135	3 318	3 338	3 575	3 898	3 848
China[8,9] — Chine[8,9]										
Passenger-kilometres Voyageurs-kilomètres	334 759	358 486	377 342	413 593	453 260	476 682	496 938	478 861	571 217	606 196
Freight net ton-kilometres Tonnes-kilomètres nettes de fret	1 310 616	1 326 988	1 256 008	1 291 033	1 377 049	1 469 414	1 565 842	1 724 665	1 928 884	2 072 602
China, Hong Kong SAR[10] — Chine, Hong Kong RAS[10]										
Passenger-kilometres Voyageurs-kilomètres	3 914	4 172	4 252	4 321	4 533	4 559	4 618	4 256	4 485	4 731
Freight net ton-kilometres Tonnes-kilomètres nettes de fret	30	24	15	15	15	12	13	11	9	7
Colombia — Colombie										
Passenger-kilometres Voyageurs-kilomètres	257	232	204	160	50	55	37	17	25	...
Congo — Congo										
Passenger-kilometres Voyageurs-kilomètres	360	235	242	8	84	171	76	57	135	167
Freight net ton-kilometres Tonnes-kilomètres nettes de fret	289	139	135	16	85	228	307	250	232	264
Croatia — Croatie										
Passenger-kilometres[11] Voyageurs-kilomètres[11]	1 205	1 158	1 092	1 137	1 252	1 241	1 195	1 163	1 213	1 266
Freight net ton-kilometres Tonnes-kilomètres nettes de fret	1 717	1 715[12]	1 831[12]	1 685[12]	1 788[12]	2 074[12]	2 206[12]	2 487[12]	2 493[12]	2 835[12]

Country or area — Pays ou zone	1996	1997	1998	1999	2000	2001	2002	2003	2004	2005
Cuba — Cuba										
Passenger-kilometres Voyageurs-kilomètres	2 156	1 962	1 750	1 499	1 737	1 758	1 681	2 046	1 760	1 514
Freight net ton-kilometres Tonnes-kilomètres nettes de fret	871	859	822	806	808	842	811	792	704	770
Czech Republic — République tchèque										
Passenger-kilometres Voyageurs-kilomètres	8 111	7 721	7 018	6 954	7 300	7 299	6 597	6 518	6 590	6 667
Freight net ton-kilometres[13] Tonnes-kilomètres nettes de fret[13]	22 338	21 010	18 709	16 713	17 496	16 882	15 810	15 862	15 092	14 866
Denmark — Danemark										
Passenger-kilometres Voyageurs-kilomètres	4 621	4 978	5 163	5 113	5 327	5 521	5 541	5 620	5 741	5 764
Freight net ton-kilometres[14] Tonnes-kilomètres nettes de fret[14]	1 757	1 983	2 058	1 938	2 025	1 961	1 906	1 985	2 147	1 967
Ecuador — Equateur										
Passenger-kilometres Voyageurs-kilomètres	51	47	44	5	5	32	33	4	2	...
Freight net ton-kilometres Tonnes-kilomètres nettes de fret	1	...	14	...	...	...	...	...	...	...
Egypt[15] — Egypte[15]										
Passenger-kilometres Voyageurs-kilomètres	55 888	60 617	64 077	68 423	57 859	38 106	39 083	46 185	52 682	55 187
Freight net ton-kilometres Tonnes-kilomètres nettes de fret	4 117	3 969	4 012	3 464	4 184	4 138	4 188	4 104	4 663	4 064
El Salvador — El Salvador										
Passenger-kilometres Voyageurs-kilomètres	7	7	6	8	10	11	...	...	...	...
Freight net ton-kilometres Tonnes-kilomètres nettes de fret	17	17	24	19	13	8	...	...	...	...
Estonia — Estonie										
Passenger-kilometres Voyageurs-kilomètres	309	261	236	238	263	183	177	182	193	248
Freight net ton-kilometres Tonnes-kilomètres nettes de fret	4 198	5 141	6 079	7 295	8 102	8 557	9 697	9 670	10 488	10 639
Ethiopia[16,17] — Ethiopie[16,17]										
Passenger-kilometres Voyageurs-kilomètres	218	206	151	150	152	173	123	82	...	...
Freight net ton-kilometres Tonnes-kilomètres nettes de fret	104	106	90	116	116	80	85	97	...	...
Finland — Finlande										
Passenger-kilometres Voyageurs-kilomètres	3 254	3 376	3 377	3 415	3 405	3 282	3 318	3 338	3 352	3 478
Freight net ton-kilometres[18] Tonnes-kilomètres nettes de fret[18]	8 806	9 856	9 885	9 753	10 107	9 857	9 664	10 047	10 105	9 706
France — France										
Passenger-kilometres Voyageurs-kilomètres	59 770	61 830	64 460	66 590	69 870	71 550	73 530	72 200	74 300	...
Freight net ton-kilometres[19] Tonnes-kilomètres nettes de fret[19]	50 500	54 820	55 090	54 350	55 450	50 400	50 040	47 000	45 000	...
Georgia — Géorgie										
Passenger-kilometres Voyageurs-kilomètres	380	294	397	355	453	401	401	387	614	...
Freight net ton-kilometres Tonnes-kilomètres nettes de fret	1 141	2 006	2 574	3 160	3 912	4 481	5 075	5 539	4 856	...
Germany — Allemagne										
Passenger-kilometres Voyageurs-kilomètres	75 975	73 917	72 389	73 587	75 111	75 314	70 819	70 784	72 565	74 946
Freight net ton-kilometres[20] Tonnes-kilomètres nettes de fret[20]	70 000	73 900	74 200	71 900	77 500	76 165	76 283	79 841	86 409	95 421

Country or area — Pays ou zone	1996	1997	1998	1999	2000	2001	2002	2003	2004	2005
Ghana — Ghana										
Passenger-kilometres Voyageurs-kilomètres	211	177	192	129	83	53	61	86	80	...
Freight net ton-kilometres Tonnes-kilomètres nettes de fret	151	148	138	151	165	220	244	242	216	...
Greece — Grèce										
Passenger-kilometres Voyageurs-kilomètres	1 752	1 783	1 552	1 453	1 629	1 783	1 836	1 574	1 669	1 854
Freight net ton-kilometres[21] Tonnes-kilomètres nettes de fret[21]	350	330	322	347	427	380	397	457	592	614
Guatemala — Guatemala										
Freight net ton-kilometres Tonnes-kilomètres nettes de fret	836	...	...	...	...	...	...	...	...	...
Hungary — Hongrie										
Passenger-kilometres Voyageurs-kilomètres	8 582	8 669	8 884	9 514	9 693	10 005	10 531	10 286	10 544	9 880
Freight net ton-kilometres Tonnes-kilomètres nettes de fret	7 634	8 149	8 150	7 734	8 095	7 731	7 752	8 109	8 749	9 090
India[22] — Inde[22]										
Passenger-kilometres Voyageurs-kilomètres	357 013	379 897	403 884	430 666	457 022	490 912	515 044	541 208	575 702	615 634
Freight net ton-kilometres Tonnes-kilomètres nettes de fret	277 567	284 249	281 513	305 201	312 371	333 228	353 194	381 241	407 398	439 596
Indonesia — Indonésie										
Passenger-kilometres Voyageurs-kilomètres	15 223	15 518	16 970	18 610	19 228	18 270	16 330	15 031	13 991	...
Freight net ton-kilometres Tonnes-kilomètres nettes de fret	4 700	5 030	4 963	5 035	5 009	4 859	4 450	4 356	4 580	...
Iran (Islamic Rep. of) — Iran (Rép. islamique d')										
Passenger-kilometres Voyageurs-kilomètres	7 044	6 103	5 631	6 451	7 119	8 043	8 582	9 314	10 012	11 149
Freight net ton-kilometres Tonnes-kilomètres nettes de fret	13 638	14 400	12 638	14 082	14 179	14 613	15 842	18 048	18 182	19 127
Iraq — Iraq										
Passenger-kilometres Voyageurs-kilomètres	1 169	1 200	825	503	381	460	573	154	21	2
Freight net ton-kilometres Tonnes-kilomètres nettes de fret	908	942	750	821	746	933	1 684	435	160	73
Ireland — Irlande										
Passenger-kilometres Voyageurs-kilomètres	1 295	1 388	1 421	1 458	1 389	1 515	1 628	1 601	1 582	1 781
Freight net ton-kilometres Tonnes-kilomètres nettes de fret	570	522	466	526	491	516	426	398	399	303
Israel — Israël										
Passenger-kilometres Voyageurs-kilomètres	294	346	383	529	781	961	1 116	1 278	1 423	1 618
Freight net ton-kilometres Tonnes-kilomètres nettes de fret	1 152	992	1 049	1 128	1 173	1 098	1 102	1 112	1 173	1 149
Italy — Italie										
Passenger-kilometres Voyageurs-kilomètres	44 782	43 591	41 392	43 424	47 133	46 752	45 957	45 222	49 254	50 088
Freight net ton-kilometres[23] Tonnes-kilomètres nettes de fret[23]	23 314	25 228	24 704	23 781	25 839	24 352	23 060	22 457	22 183	22 760
Japan — Japon										
Passenger-kilometres Voyageurs-kilomètres	400 712	301 510	391 073	384 943	384 906	385 403	382 892	382 035	385 282	359 806
Freight net ton-kilometres Tonnes-kilomètres nettes de fret	24 991	18 661	23 136	22 676	22 131	22 363	21 984	22 549	22 643	22 722

Country or area — Pays ou zone	1996	1997	1998	1999	2000	2001	2002	2003	2004	2005
Jordan — Jordanie										
Passenger-kilometres Voyageurs-kilomètres	1	2	2	2	2	4	3	1	1	...
Freight net ton-kilometres Tonnes-kilomètres nettes de fret	735	625	596	585	671	371	531	497	563	...
Kazakhstan — Kazakhstan										
Passenger-kilometres Voyageurs-kilomètres	14 188	12 802	10 668	8 859	10 215	10 384	10 449	10 686	11 849	12 136
Freight net ton-kilometres Tonnes-kilomètres nettes de fret	112 688	106 425	103 045	91 700	124 983	135 653	133 088	147 672	163 455	171 855
Kenya — Kenya										
Passenger-kilometres Voyageurs-kilomètres	385	393	432	306	302	216	306	295	279	489
Freight net ton-kilometres Tonnes-kilomètres nettes de fret	1 338	1 068	1 111	1 492	1 557	1 603	1 638	1 789	1 454	1 358
Korea, Republic of — Corée, République de										
Passenger-kilometres Voyageurs-kilomètres	29 580	30 073	28 576	28 606	28 527	28 882	27 492	27 228	28 459	31 004
Freight net ton-kilometres Tonnes-kilomètres nettes de fret	12 947	12 710	10 372	10 072	10 803	10 492	10 784	11 057	10 641	...
Kyrgyzstan — Kirghizistan										
Passenger-kilometres Voyageurs-kilomètres	92	93	59	31	44	50	43	50	45	46
Freight net ton-kilometres Tonnes-kilomètres nettes de fret	481	472	466	354	338	332	395	562	715	662
Latvia — Lettonie										
Passenger-kilometres Voyageurs-kilomètres	1 149	1 154	1 059	984	715	706	744	762	811	894
Freight net ton-kilometres Tonnes-kilomètres nettes de fret	12 412[14]	13 970[14]	12 995[14]	12 210[14]	13 310[14]	14 179[14]	15 020[14]	17 955[14]	18 618	19 779
Lithuania — Lituanie										
Passenger-kilometres Voyageurs-kilomètres	954	842	800	745	611	533	498	432	443	428
Freight net ton-kilometres[24] Tonnes-kilomètres nettes de fret[24]	8 103	8 622	8 265	7 849	8 918	7 741	9 767	11 457	11 637	12 457
Luxembourg — Luxembourg										
Passenger-kilometres Voyageurs-kilomètres	284	295	300	310	332	346	268	262	266	272
Freight net ton-kilometres Tonnes-kilomètres nettes de fret	570	610	622	656	678	628	612	560	593	414
Madagascar — Madagascar										
Passenger-kilometres Voyageurs-kilomètres	...	81	35	28	19	...	...	...	...	...
Freight net ton-kilometres[6,20] Tonnes-kilomètres nettes de fret[6,20]	...	81	71	44	26	...	...	...	...	...
Malawi[22] — Malawi[22]										
Passenger-kilometres Voyageurs-kilomètres	26	17	21	19	25	22	42	30	30	...
Freight net ton-kilometres Tonnes-kilomètres nettes de fret	57	46	55	62	80	66	64	18	26	...
Malaysia — Malaisie										
Passenger-kilometres Voyageurs-kilomètres	1 385	1 508	1 411	1 333	1 241	1 199	1 138	1 031	1 152	...
Freight net ton-kilometres Tonnes-kilomètres nettes de fret	1 398	1 338	993	909	918	1 095	1 073	887	1 017	...
Mali — Mali										
Passenger-kilometres Voyageurs-kilomètres	181	223	218	211	201	208	196	0	0	0
Freight net ton-kilometres Tonnes-kilomètres nettes de fret	261	258	268	242	193	180	188	356	383	334

Country or area — Pays ou zone	1996	1997	1998	1999	2000	2001	2002	2003	2004	2005
Mexico — Mexique										
Passenger-kilometres Voyageurs-kilomètres	1 799	1 508	460	254	82	67	69	78	74	73
Freight net ton-kilometres Tonnes-kilomètres nettes de fret	41 723	42 442	46 873	47 273	48 333	46 615	51 616	54 132	54 387	54 054
Mongolia — Mongolie										
Passenger-kilometres Voyageurs-kilomètres	733	951	981	1 010	1 067	1 062	1 067	1 039	1 219	1 234
Freight net ton-kilometres Tonnes-kilomètres nettes de fret	2 529	2 254	2 815	3 492	4 283	5 288	6 461	7 253	8 878	9 948
Morocco — Maroc										
Passenger-kilometres Voyageurs-kilomètres	1 776	1 856	1 875	1 880	1 956	2 019	2 145	2 374	2 645	2 987
Freight net ton-kilometres Tonnes-kilomètres nettes de fret	4 757	4 835	4 827	4 795	4 650	4 699	4 974	5 146	5 563	5 918
Mozambique — Mozambique										
Passenger-kilometres Voyageurs-kilomètres	358	387	155	145	130	142	138	82	106	...
Freight net ton-kilometres Tonnes-kilomètres nettes de fret	983	896	765	737	605	778	808	778	794	...
Myanmar — Myanmar										
Passenger-kilometres Voyageurs-kilomètres	4 294	3 784	3 948	4 112	4 451	4 447	4 804	4 284	4 164	...
Freight net ton-kilometres[6] Tonnes-kilomètres nettes de fret[6]	748	674	988	1 049	1 222	1 218	1 196	1 016	886	...
Netherlands — Pays-Bas										
Passenger-kilometres Voyageurs-kilomètres	14 131	14 485	14 879	14 330	14 666	14 392	14 288	13 848	14 079	14 730
Freight net ton-kilometres Tonnes-kilomètres nettes de fret	3 163	3 435	3 793	3 988	4 522	4 293	4 323	4 962	5 225	5 028
New Zealand[15] — Nouvelle-Zélande[15]										
Freight net ton-kilometres Tonnes-kilomètres nettes de fret	3 260	3 505	3 547	3 636	4 040	...	...	...	...	...
Nigeria — Nigéria										
Passenger-kilometres Voyageurs-kilomètres	170	179	...	...	...	...	...	...	...	...
Freight net ton-kilometres Tonnes-kilomètres nettes de fret	114	120	...	...	...	...	...	...	...	...
Norway — Norvège										
Passenger-kilometres Voyageurs-kilomètres	2 449	2 561	2 652	2 733	2 707	2 594	2 543	2 474	2 657	2 715
Freight net ton-kilometres Tonnes-kilomètres nettes de fret	2 804	2 975	2 948	2 894	2 955	2 887	3 019	2 627	2 845	3 149
Pakistan[2] — Pakistan[2]										
Passenger-kilometres Voyageurs-kilomètres	19 114	18 771	18 979	18 761	19 292	20 004	19 793	20 346	22 987	23 609
Freight net ton-kilometres Tonnes-kilomètres nettes de fret	4 538	4 444	3 939	3 612	3 799	4 681	4 594	4 568	4 789	5 011
Panama — Panama										
Passenger-kilometres Voyageurs-kilomètres	122[25]	9[27]	...	...	...	24 576[27]	35 693[26]	52 324[28]	53 377[28]	44 734[28]
Freight net ton-kilometres Tonnes-kilomètres nettes de fret	710[26]	306[26,27]	...	...	...	4 896[26,27]	20 665[26]	41 863[28]	52 946[28]	138 104[28]
Paraguay — Paraguay										
Freight net ton-kilometres Tonnes-kilomètres nettes de fret	3	2	1	1	...	...	1	...	...	...
Peru[6] — Pérou[6]										
Passenger-kilometres Voyageurs-kilomètres	222	206	180	69	107	124	99	103	119	126
Freight net ton-kilometres Tonnes-kilomètres nettes de fret	878	839	890	677	874	1 154	1 112	1 117	1 147	1 115

Country or area — Pays ou zone	1996	1997	1998	1999	2000	2001	2002	2003	2004	2005
Philippines — Philippines										
Passenger-kilometres Voyageurs-kilomètres	69	175	181	171	123	110	93	86	84	20
Freight net ton-kilometres Tonnes-kilomètres nettes de fret	0	0	0	…	49	67	63	…	…	…
Poland — Pologne										
Passenger-kilometres Voyageurs-kilomètres	26 569	25 806	25 664	26 198	24 093	22 469	20 809	19 638	18 690	18 155
Freight net ton-kilometres Tonnes-kilomètres nettes de fret	68 332	68 651	61 760	55 471	54 448	47 913	47 756	49 584	52 332	49 972
Portugal — Portugal										
Passenger-kilometres Voyageurs-kilomètres	4 503[29]	4 563[29]	4 602[29]	4 380	3 834	3 898	3 926	3 585	3 693	3 753
Freight net ton-kilometres Tonnes-kilomètres nettes de fret	2 178[29]	2 632[29]	2 340[29]	2 562	2 569	2 498	2 583	2 443	2 589	2 826
Republic of Moldova[3] — République de Moldova[3]										
Passenger-kilometres Voyageurs-kilomètres	882	789	656	343	315	325	355	352	346	355
Freight net ton-kilometres Tonnes-kilomètres nettes de fret	2 897	2 937	2 575	1 191	1 513	1 980	2 748	3 019	3 006	3 053
Romania[30] — Roumanie[30]										
Passenger-kilometres Voyageurs-kilomètres	18 356	15 795	13 422	12 304	11 632	10 966	8 502	8 529	8 638	7 985
Freight net ton-kilometres Tonnes-kilomètres nettes de fret	24 254	22 111	16 619	14 679	16 354	16 102	15 218	15 039	17 022	16 582
Russian Federation — Fédération de Russie										
Passenger-kilometres Voyageurs-kilomètres	181 200	170 300	152 900	141 000	167 100	157 900	152 900	157 600	164 300	172 200
Freight net ton-kilometres Tonnes-kilomètres nettes de fret	1 131 000	1 100 000	1 020 000	1 205 000	1 373 000	1 434 000	1 510 000	1 669 000	1 802 000	1 858 000
Saudi Arabia — Arabie saoudite										
Passenger-kilometres Voyageurs-kilomètres	170	192	222	224	270	285	236	232	301	…
Freight net ton-kilometres Tonnes-kilomètres nettes de fret	691	726	856	938	849	802	688	778	892	…
Senegal — Sénégal										
Passenger-kilometres Voyageurs-kilomètres	103	78	63	71	74	88	105	129	122[31]	…
Freight net ton-kilometres Tonnes-kilomètres nettes de fret	474	446	435	401	361	321	345	375	358[31]	…
Serbia and Montenegro — Serbie-et-Monténégro										
Passenger-kilometres Voyageurs-kilomètres	1 830	1 744	1 622	860	1 436	1 262	1 141	970	962	…
Freight net ton-kilometres[6] Tonnes-kilomètres nettes de fret[6]	2 062	2 432	2 793	1 267	1 969	2 042	2 328	2 646	3 258	…
Slovakia — Slovaquie										
Passenger-kilometres Voyageurs-kilomètres	3 769	3 057	3 092	2 968	2 870	2 805	2 682	2 316	2 228	2 182
Freight net ton-kilometres Tonnes-kilomètres nettes de fret	12 017	12 373	11 753	9 859	11 234	10 929	10 383	10 113	9 702	9 463
Slovenia — Slovénie										
Passenger-kilometres Voyageurs-kilomètres	613	616	645	623	705	715	749	777	764	777
Freight net ton-kilometres[32] Tonnes-kilomètres nettes de fret[32]	2 550	2 852	2 859	2 784	2 857	2 837	3 018	3 274	3 149	3 245
South Africa[33,34] — Afrique du Sud[33,34]										
Passenger-kilometres Voyageurs-kilomètres	1 198	1 393	1 775	1 794	3 930	…	…	…	…	…
Freight net ton-kilometres Tonnes-kilomètres nettes de fret	99 818	99 773	103 866	102 777	106 786	…	…	…	…	…

Country or area—Pays ou zone	1996	1997	1998	1999	2000	2001	2002	2003	2004	2005
Spain—Espagne										
Passenger-kilometres Voyageurs-kilomètres	16 637	17 883	18 875	18 143[35]	19 958[36]	20 649[36]	21 019[36]	20 874[36]	20 578[36]	...
Freight net ton-kilometres[6] Tonnes-kilomètres nettes de fret[6]	10 219	11 488	11 801	11 489[35]	12 071[36]	12 217[36]	12 146[36]	12 299[36]	11 963[36]	...
Sri Lanka[37]—Sri Lanka[37]										
Passenger-kilometres Voyageurs-kilomètres	3 103	3 146	3 073	3 104	3 208	3 979	4 079	4 627	4 684	...
Freight net ton-kilometres Tonnes-kilomètres nettes de fret	107	98	105	103	88	109	131	129	134	...
Swaziland—Swaziland										
Freight net ton-kilometres Tonnes-kilomètres nettes de fret	684	670	653	677	753	746	728	726	710	...
Sweden—Suède										
Passenger-kilometres Voyageurs-kilomètres	6 953[38]	7 022[38]	7 230[38]	7 701[38]	8 243	8 732	8 874	8 834	8 658	8 900
Freight net ton-kilometres Tonnes-kilomètres nettes de fret	18 846	19 181	19 163	19 090	20 088	19 547	19 197	20 170	20 856	21 783
Switzerland—Suisse										
Passenger-kilometres Voyageurs-kilomètres	11 890	12 051	12 148	12 501	12 620	13 301	14 147	14 509	14 914	...
Freight net ton-kilometres Tonnes-kilomètres nettes de fret	7 210	7 868	8 351	8 763	9 937	10 091	9 639	9 534	10 245	...
Syrian Arab Republic—Rép. arabe syrienne										
Passenger-kilometres Voyageurs-kilomètres	454	294	182	187	197	307	384	525	692	607
Freight net ton-kilometres Tonnes-kilomètres nettes de fret	1 864	1 472	1 430	1 577	1 568	1 492	1 814	1 885	1 923	2 256
Tajikistan—Tadjikistan										
Passenger-kilometres Voyageurs-kilomètres	95	129	121	61	73	32	42	50	50	46
Freight net ton-kilometres Tonnes-kilomètres nettes de fret	1 719	1 384	1 458	1 282	1 326	1 248	1 086	1 086	1 118	1 066
Thailand[37]—Thaïlande[37]										
Passenger-kilometres Voyageurs-kilomètres	12 205	11 804	10 947	9 894	9 935	10 321	10 378	10 251	9 332	...
Freight net ton-kilometres Tonnes-kilomètres nettes de fret	3 286	3 410	2 874	2 929	3 384	3 724	3 898	3 976	4 085	...
TFYR of Macedonia—L'ex-R.y. Macédoine										
Passenger-kilometres Voyageurs-kilomètres	120	141	150	150	176	133	98	92	94	94
Freight net ton-kilometres Tonnes-kilomètres nettes de fret	271	279	408	380	527	462	334	373	426	530
Tunisia—Tunisie										
Passenger-kilometres[39] Voyageurs-kilomètres[39]	988	1 094	1 133	1 196	1 258	1 285	1 265	1 239	1 294	1 317
Freight net ton-kilometres[6,40] Tonnes-kilomètres nettes de fret[6,40]	2 329	2 338	2 349	2 365	2 274	2 279	2 250	2 173	2 081	2 068
Turkey—Turquie										
Passenger-kilometres Voyageurs-kilomètres	5 229	5 840	6 161	6 146	5 833	5 568	5 204	5 878	5 237	5 036
Freight net ton-kilometres Tonnes-kilomètres nettes de fret	9 018	9 717	8 466	8 446	9 895	7 562	7 224	8 669	9 417	9 152
Uganda—Ouganda										
Passenger-kilometres Voyageurs-kilomètres	25	5[41]	...	...	...	...	...	...	...	...
Freight net ton-kilometres Tonnes-kilomètres nettes de fret	184	144	148	200	219	217	217	212	229	...

Railway traffic — Passenger-kilometres and freight net ton-kilometres: millions (*continued*)
Trafic ferroviaire — Voyageurs-kilomètres et tonnes-kilomètres nettes de fret: millions (*suite*)

Country or area — Pays ou zone	1996	1997	1998	1999	2000	2001	2002	2003	2004	2005
Ukraine — Ukraine										
Passenger-kilometres Voyageurs-kilomètres	59 080	54 540	49 938	47 600	51 767	49 661	50 544	52 558	51 726	52 655
Freight net ton-kilometres Tonnes-kilomètres nettes de fret	160 384	160 433	158 693	156 336	172 840	177 465	193 141	225 287	233 987	223 980
United Kingdom[22,42] — Royaume-Uni[22,42]										
Passenger-kilometres Voyageurs-kilomètres	32 135	34 950	36 270	38 500	38 200	39 100	39 700	40 900	41 762	43 211
Freight net ton-kilometres Tonnes-kilomètres nettes de fret	15 144	16 949	17 369	18 200	18 100	19 400	18 500	18 900	20 600	22 100
United States — Etats-Unis										
Passenger-kilometres[43] Voyageurs-kilomètres[43]	8 127	8 317	8 539	8 581	8 852	8 950	8 594	9 141	8 869	...
Freight net ton-kilometres Tonnes-kilomètres nettes de fret	1 984 654[44]	1 974 337[44]	2 015 138[44]	2 098 066[44]	2 145 632[44]	2 188 827[44]	2 205 716[44]	2 270 741[44]	...	...
Uruguay — Uruguay										
Passenger-kilometres Voyageurs-kilomètres	...	17	14	10	9	9	8	11	11	12
Freight net ton-kilometres Tonnes-kilomètres nettes de fret	182	204	244	272	239	209	178	188	297	331
Uzbekistan — Ouzbékistan										
Passenger-kilometres Voyageurs-kilomètres	2	2	2	2	2	2	2	2	2	...
Freight net ton-kilometres Tonnes-kilomètres nettes de fret	20	17	16	14	15	16	18	19	18	...
Venezuela (Bolivarian Rep. of) — Venezuela (Rép. bolivarienne du)										
Passenger-kilometres Voyageurs-kilomètres	15	...	...	...	...	...	...	...	...	...
Freight net ton-kilometres Tonnes-kilomètres nettes de fret	45	54	79	54	59	81	32	12	22	...
Viet Nam — Viet Nam										
Passenger-kilometres Voyageurs-kilomètres	2 261	2 476	2 542	2 722	3 200	3 426	3 697	4 069	4 376	...
Freight net ton-kilometres Tonnes-kilomètres nettes de fret	1 684	1 533	1 369	1 446	1 955	2 054	2 392	2 725	2 745	...
Yemen — Yémen										
Passenger-kilometres Voyageurs-kilomètres	2 260	2 492	...	...	...	...	...	...	...	...
Zambia — Zambie										
Passenger-kilometres Voyageurs-kilomètres	749	755	586	...	...	...	...	...	...	...
Freight net ton-kilometres Tonnes-kilomètres nettes de fret	666	758	702	...	...	...	...	...	...	...
Zimbabwe[15,45] — Zimbabwe[15,45]										
Freight net ton-kilometres Tonnes-kilomètres nettes de fret	4 990	5 115	9 122	4 375	3 326	3 100	4 088	...	...	...

Source

United Nations Statistics Division, New York, transport statistics database.

Source

Organisation des Nations Unies, Division de statistique, New York, la base de données pour les statistiques des transports.

Notes

1 Including urban transport only.
2 Data refer to fiscal years beginning 1 July.
3 Including passengers carried without revenues.
4 Including service traffic, animals, baggage and parcels.
5 Including urban Railway traffic.
6 Including service traffic.

Notes

1 Les chemins de fer urbains seulement.
2 Les données se réfèrent aux exercices budgétaires commençant le 1er juillet.
3 Y compris passagers transportés gratuitement.
4 Y compris le trafic de service, les animaux, les bagages et les colis.
5 Y compris le trafic de chemins-de-fer urbain.
6 Y compris le trafic de service.

7 From 1996 to 2001, annual data cover 12 months ending June.
8 For statistical purposes, the data for China do not include those for the Hong Kong Special Administrative Region (Hong Kong SAR), Macao Special Administrative Region (Macao SAR) and Taiwan Province of China.
9 May include service traffic.
10 Kowloon - Canton Railway only.
11 Beginning 1993, railway transport of passengers includes urban transport of passengers.
12 Excluding privately-owned wagons.
13 Including only state-owned railways.
14 Including passengers' baggage and parcel post.
15 Data refer to fiscal years ending 30 June.
16 Including traffic of the Djibouti portion of the Djibouti-Addis Ababa line.
17 Data refer to fiscal years beginning 7 July.
18 Beginning 1995, wagon loads traffic only.
19 Including passengers' baggage.
20 Including service traffic and baggage.
21 Including military and government traffic.
22 Data refer to fiscal years beginning 1 April.
23 Excluding livestock.
24 Prior to 1994, data refer to operated ton-kilometres which is the weight in tons of freight carried multiplied by the distance in kilometres actually run; beginning 1994, data refer to net ton-kilometres which is the weight in tons of freight carried multiplied by distance in kilometres for which payments were made.
25 Panama Railway and National Railway of Chiriquí.
26 Panama Railway only.
27 Beginning August 1997, railway operations closed. Beginning July 2001, Panama Railway resumed operations.
28 In kilometres.
29 Excluding river traffic of the railway company.
30 Including military and government personnel.
31 National estimation.
32 Prior to 2004, data are based on goods movements (origin/destination of goods irrespective of modes of transport). Since 2004 data are based on journeys (place of loading/unloading from rail vehicle).
33 Beginning 1988, excluding Namibia.
34 Data refer to fiscal years ending 31 March.
35 RENFE only.
36 RENFE and narrow-gauge trains.
37 Data refer to fiscal years ending 30 September.
38 Including Swedish State Railways and MTAB.
39 Including military traffic.
40 Ordinary goods only.
41 Beginning late 1997, passenger services suspended.
42 Excluding Northern Ireland.
43 Including National Passenger Railroad Corporation (Amtrak) only.
44 Class I railways only.
45 Including traffic in Botswana.

7 Pour la période de 1996 à 2001, les données annuelles se réfèrent aux douze mois finissant en juin.
8 Pour la présentation des statistiques, les données pour la Chine ne comprennent pas la Région Administrative Spéciale de Hong Kong (Hong Kong RAS), la Région Administrative Spéciale de Macao (Macao RAS) et la province de Taiwan.
9 Le trafic de service peut être compris.
10 Chemin de fer de Kowloon-Canton seulement.
11 A compter de l'année 1993 y compris le transport urbain de passagers.
12 Non compris wagons privés.
13 Y compris chemins-de-fer de l'état seulement.
14 Y compris les bagages des voyageurs et les colis postaux.
15 Les données se réfèrent aux exercices budgétaires finissant le 30 juin.
16 Y compris le trafic de la ligne Djibouti-Addis Abeba en Djibouti.
17 Les données se réfèrent aux exercices budgétaires commençant le 7 juillet.
18 A compter de 1995, y compris trafic de charge de wagon seulement.
19 Y compris les bagages des voyageurs.
20 Y compris les transports pour les besoins du service et les bagages.
21 Y compris le trafic militaire et de l'Etat.
22 Les données se réfèrent aux exercices budgétaires commençant le 1er avril.
23 Non compris le bétail.
24 Avant 1994, les données se réfèrent aux tonnes-kilomètres transportées, c'est-à-dire le produit du poids et de la distance effectivement parcourue. A partir de l'année 1994, l'unité utilisée est la tonne-kilomètre nette, c'est-à-dire le produit du poids et de la distance pour lequel un paiement a été effectué.
25 Chemin de fer de Panama et chemin de fer national de Chiriqui.
26 Chemin de fer de Panama seulement.
27 A cessé de fonctionner en août 1997. A compter de juillet 2001, le Chemin de fer de Panama a recommencé des opérations.
28 En kilomètres.
29 Non compris le trafic fluvial de la compagnie des chemins de fer.
30 Y compris les militaires et les fonctionnaires.
31 Estimation nationale.
32 Avant 2004, les données sont basées sur le mouvement des marchandises (origine/destination quel que soit le mode de transport). À partir de 2004, les données sont basées sur les trajets (lieu de chargement/de déchargement des wagons).
33 A partir de 1988, non compris la Namibie.
34 Les données se réfèrent aux exercices budgétaires finissant le 31 mars.
35 RENFE seulement.
36 Réseau national des chemins de fer espagnols et chemins de fer à voie étroite.
37 Les données se réfèrent aux exercices budgétaires finissant le 30 septembre.
38 Y compris chemins-de-fer de l'état y MTAB.
39 Y compris le trafic militaire.
40 Petite vitesse seulement.
41 A compter de l'année de 1997, transport passager interrompu.
42 Non compris l'Irlande du Nord.
43 Y compris "National Passenger Railroad Corporation" (Amtrak) seulement.
44 Réseaux de catégorie 1 seulement.
45 Y compris le trafic en Botswana.

Motor vehicles in use

Passenger cars and commercial vehicles: thousands

Véhicules automobiles en circulation

Voitures de tourisme et véhicules utilitaires : milliers

Country or area — Pays ou zone	1996	1997	1998	1999	2000	2001	2002	2003	2004	2005
Afghanistan — Afghanistan										
Passenger cars — Voitures de tourisme	...	...	...	...	...	...	29.0	40.0	40.0	41.0
Commercial vehicles — Véhicules utilitaires	...	...	...	...	...	...	51.0	76.0	83.0	100.0
Albania — Albanie										
Passenger cars — Voitures de tourisme	67.2	76.8	90.7	99.0	114.5	133.5	148.5	174.7	...	...
Commercial vehicles — Véhicules utilitaires	30.6	33.2	37.1	40.9	43.0	73.0	73.0	88.8	...	...
Algeria — Algérie										
Passenger cars — Voitures de tourisme	1 588.0	1 615.1	1 634.4	1 676.8	1 692.1	1 708.4	1 739.3	1 775.3	1 834.9	1 905.9
Commercial vehicles — Véhicules utilitaires	958.1	952.7	963.9	986.7	995.7	1 002.3	1 009.8	1 021.6	1 039.0	1 068.5
American Samoa — Samoa américaines										
Passenger cars — Voitures de tourisme	5.4	5.3	5.7	6.2	7.3	7.2	6.7	6.7	6.5	6.6
Commercial vehicles — Véhicules utilitaires	0.5	0.5	0.7	0.7	0.7	0.7	0.7	0.6	0.6	0.5
Andorra — Andorre										
Passenger cars — Voitures de tourisme	35.4	36.6	38.2	40.2	41.8	42.6	43.9	45.8	47.6	49.6
Commercial vehicles — Véhicules utilitaires	4.2	4.3	4.5	4.8	4.8	4.9	4.9	5.1	5.3	5.5
Antigua and Barbuda[1] — Antigua-et-Barbuda[1]										
Passenger cars — Voitures de tourisme	21.6	23.7	24.0	...	...	...	...	...	...	...
Argentina — Argentine										
Passenger cars — Voitures de tourisme	4 783.9	4 904.3	5 047.8	5 056.0	5 386.0	5 418.0	5 349.0	4 668.0	4 926.0	5 230.0
Commercial vehicles — Véhicules utilitaires	1 287.0	1 372.0	1 496.0	1 550.0	1 566.0	1 529.0	1 488.0	1 198.0	1 684.0	1 775.0
Australia[2] — Australie[2]										
Passenger cars — Voitures de tourisme	9 021.5	9 239.5	9 526.7	9 686.2	...	9 835.9	10 101.4	10 366.0	10 629.0	10 896.0
Commercial vehicles — Véhicules utilitaires	2 075.6	2 111.7	2 177.5	2 214.9	...	2 236.4	2 349.5	2 381.0	2 467.0	2 561.0
Austria[3] — Autriche[3]										
Passenger cars — Voitures de tourisme	3 690.7	3 782.5	3 887.2	4 009.6	4 097.1	4 182.0	3 987.1	4 054.3	4 109.0	4 157.0
Commercial vehicles — Véhicules utilitaires	317.0	325.0	336.0	346.0	355.0	360.0	348.0	353.0	362.0	367.0
Azerbaijan — Azerbaïdjan										
Passenger cars — Voitures de tourisme	273.7	271.3	281.3	311.6	332.1	343.0	350.6	400.0	439.0	479.0
Commercial vehicles — Véhicules utilitaires	122.9	115.6	117.6	113.0	101.4	100.5	101.4	104.9	110.1	126.4
Bahrain — Bahreïn										
Passenger cars — Voitures de tourisme	140.0	147.9	160.2	169.6	175.7	187.0	...	...	...	...
Commercial vehicles — Véhicules utilitaires	31.5	32.8	34.5	35.7	36.8	38.4	...	...	...	...
Bangladesh — Bangladesh										
Passenger cars — Voitures de tourisme	55.8	61.2	65.0	...	...	...	...	...	...	...
Commercial vehicles — Véhicules utilitaires	126.8	138.1	145.9	...	...	...	...	...	...	...
Barbados — Barbade										
Passenger cars[4] — Voitures de tourisme[4]	49.8	53.6	57.5	62.1	...	...	...	...	...	...
Commercial vehicles[5] — Véhicules utilitaires[5]	6.9	7.9	8.6	9.4	...	...	...	...	...	...
Belarus — Bélarus										
Passenger cars — Voitures de tourisme	1 035.8	1 132.8	1 279.2	1 351.1	1 421.9	1 467.6	1 552.4	1 656.2	1 708.0	1 771.0
Belgium — Belgique										
Passenger cars — Voitures de tourisme	4 336.1	4 412.1	4 488.5	4 580.0	4 675.1	4 736.6	4 784.1	4 821.0	4 874.0	4 919.0
Commercial vehicles — Véhicules utilitaires	471.8	491.3	510.1	539.0	563.2	587.3	602.1	603.0	626.0	652.0
Belize[6,7] — Belize[6,7]										
Passenger cars — Voitures de tourisme	17.0	19.1	19.3	24.2	26.1	28.8	32.6	...	...	...
Commercial vehicles — Véhicules utilitaires	3.1	3.6	3.7	6.5	6.4	7.6	7.8	...	...	...
Bermuda — Bermudes										
Passenger cars — Voitures de tourisme	21.2	21.6	22.0	22.6	20.0	20.3	20.8	21.0	22.0[8]	22.0[8]
Commercial vehicles — Véhicules utilitaires	4.2	4.2	4.5	4.4	4.6	4.8	4.8	4.7	5.0[9]	5.0[9]

Country or area — Pays ou zone	1996	1997	1998	1999	2000	2001	2002	2003	2004	2005
Bolivia — Bolivie										
Passenger cars — Voitures de tourisme	220.3	234.1	178.3	166.0	234.0	244.0	249.0	264.0	294.0	...
Commercial vehicles — Véhicules utilitaires	119.8	124.8	110.4	99.0	139.0	146.0	150.0	158.0	174.0	...
Botswana — Botswana										
Passenger cars — Voitures de tourisme	26.7	28.2	37.0	44.5	48.0	54.0	60.0	65.0	74.0	83.0
Commercial vehicles — Véhicules utilitaires	48.1	52.3	58.7	67.9	85.0	91.0	97.0	102.0	108.0	111.0
British Virgin Islands — Iles Vierges britanniques										
Passenger cars — Voitures de tourisme	5.6	5.8	5.9	6.0	6.1	7.1	7.4	8.1	9.1	...
Commercial vehicles — Véhicules utilitaires	1.3	1.4	1.4	1.5	1.5	1.6	1.8	1.6	2.2	...
Brunei Darussalam — Brunéi Darussalam										
Passenger cars — Voitures de tourisme	150.0	163.0	170.6	176.3	182.7	189.1	200.1	211.8	225.2	240.0
Commercial vehicles — Véhicules utilitaires	17.3	18.3	18.6	19.1	19.3	19.7	20.3	20.8	21.3	22.1
Bulgaria — Bulgarie										
Passenger cars — Voitures de tourisme	1 707.0	1 730.5	1 809.4	1 908.4	1 992.8	2 085.7	2 174.1	2 309.3	2 438.0	2 538.0
Commercial vehicles — Véhicules utilitaires	270.7	273.2	283.8	293.5	301.7	312.5	323.0	337.2	354.0	371.0
Cambodia — Cambodge										
Passenger cars — Voitures de tourisme	6.3	8.4	8.0	8.5	8.3	...	...	...	...	...
Commercial vehicles — Véhicules utilitaires	1.4	1.8	1.6	1.5	3.1	...	...	...	...	...
Cameroon — Cameroun										
Passenger cars — Voitures de tourisme	100.9	102.2	105.8	110.7	115.9	134.5	151.9	173.1	...	...
Commercial vehicles — Véhicules utilitaires	40.6	41.6	43.2	45.3	47.4	51.1	37.4	57.4	...	...
Canada[3] — Canada[3]										
Passenger cars — Voitures de tourisme	13 251.1	13 486.9	13 887.3	16 538.0	16 861.0	17 054.8	17 543.6	17 756.0	17 920.0	18 124.0
Commercial vehicles — Véhicules utilitaires	3 476.2	3 526.9	3 625.8	649.1[10]	668.0[10]	654.5[10]	644.3[10]	660.4[10]	675.0[10]	708.0[10]
Cape Verde — Cap-Vert										
Passenger cars — Voitures de tourisme	9.3	10.3	11.4	13.5	...	...	...	...	...	...
Commercial vehicles — Véhicules utilitaires	2.2	2.5	2.8	3.1	...	...	...	...	...	...
Cayman Islands — Iles Caïmanes										
Passenger cars — Voitures de tourisme	14.9	16.0	15.8	17.9	19.8	20.3	22.6	...	19.6	23.7
Commercial vehicles — Véhicules utilitaires	3.4	3.7	3.5	4.0	4.3	4.4	4.8	...	5.9	6.3
Central African Rep. — Rép. centrafricaine										
Passenger cars — Voitures de tourisme	...	...	...	...	...	...	0.8	0.7	0.8	0.8
Commercial vehicles — Véhicules utilitaires	...	...	...	...	...	...	0.6	0.4	0.5	0.7
Chile — Chili										
Passenger cars — Voitures de tourisme	1 121.2	1 175.8	1 236.9	1 323.8	1 320.5	1 351.9	1 373.1	1 402.8	1 489.0	1 595.0
Commercial vehicles[11] — Véhicules utilitaires[11]	585.7[12]	635.2[12]	672.2[12]	708.5[12]	701.3	712.9	734.0	737.6	756.0	789.0
China[13] — Chine[13]										
Passenger cars[14] — Voitures de tourisme[14]	4 880.2	5 805.6	6 548.3	7 402.3	8 537.3	9 939.6	12 023.7	14 788.1	17 359.1	21 324.6
Commercial vehicles[15] — Véhicules utilitaires[15]	5 750.3	6 012.3	6 278.9	6 769.5	7 163.2	7 652.4	8 122.2	8 535.1	8 930.0	9 555.5
China, Hong Kong SAR — Chine, Hong Kong RAS										
Passenger cars — Voitures de tourisme	311.0	333.0	336.0	340.0	350.0	359.0	359.0	357.0	363.0	369.0
Commercial vehicles — Véhicules utilitaires	134.0	136.0	134.0	133.0	134.0	133.0	131.0	130.0	131.0	131.0
China, Macao SAR[11] — Chine, Macao RAS[11]										
Passenger cars — Voitures de tourisme	39.0	43.0	46.0	48.0	49.0	50.0	53.0	57.0	61.0	66.0
Commercial vehicles — Véhicules utilitaires	6.0	7.0	7.0	7.0	7.0	7.0	7.0	7.0	7.0	8.0
Costa Rica — Costa Rica										
Passenger cars — Voitures de tourisme	272.9[3]	294.1	316.8	326.5	342.0	354.4	367.8	581.0	621.0	669.0
Commercial vehicles — Véhicules utilitaires	151.1[3]	153.1	164.8	169.8	177.9	184.3	191.3	195.0	199.0	199.0
Croatia — Croatie										
Passenger cars — Voitures de tourisme	835.7	932.3	1 000.0	1 063.5	1 124.8	1 195.5	1 244.3	1 293.4	1 338.0	1 385.0
Commercial vehicles — Véhicules utilitaires	99.5	114.5	120.6	123.4	127.2	134.3	143.5	153.1	160.0	168.0[16]
Cuba[17] — Cuba[17]										
Commercial vehicles — Véhicules utilitaires	16.0	17.0	18.0	20.0	23.0	23.0	23.0	24.0	24.0	...

Country or area — Pays ou zone	1996	1997	1998	1999	2000	2001	2002	2003	2004	2005
Cyprus — Chypre										
Passenger cars — Voitures de tourisme	226.8	235.0	249.2	257.0	267.6	280.1	287.6	302.5	336.0	355.0
Commercial vehicles — Véhicules utilitaires	108.0	109.7	113.6	115.8	119.6	123.2	123.3	125.7	125.0	126.0
Czech Republic[18] — République tchèque[18]										
Passenger cars — Voitures de tourisme	3 192.5[20]	3 391.5[20]	3 493.0[20]	3 439.7[20]	3 438.9[20]	3 529.8	3 647.1	3 706.0	3 815.5	3 958.7
Commercial vehicles[19] — Véhicules utilitaires[19]	281.1[21]	305.1[21]	320.6[21]	329.9[21]	339.3[21]	364.1	397.6	414.0	444.7	488.4
Denmark[3,22] — Danemark[3,22]										
Passenger cars — Voitures de tourisme	1 739.0	1 783.0	1 817.0	1 844.0	1 854.0	1 873.0	1 888.0	1 895.0	1 916.0	1 965.0
Commercial vehicles — Véhicules utilitaires	354.0	360.0	372.0	387.0	399.0	406.0	416.0	427.0	450.0	484.0
Dominica — Dominique										
Passenger cars — Voitures de tourisme	7.9	8.3	8.7	6.0	7.0	7.0	8.0	8.0	9.0	10.0
Commercial vehicles — Véhicules utilitaires	3.3	3.3	3.4	4.0	5.0	6.0	6.0	7.0	7.0	8.0
Dominican Republic — Rép. dominicaine										
Passenger cars — Voitures de tourisme	271.0	331.0	385.0	446.0	456.0	561.0	615.0	638.0	662.0	721.0
Commercial vehicles — Véhicules utilitaires	165.0[23]	202.0[23]	237.0[23]	247.0	283.0	285.0	309.0	320.0	329.0	351.0
Ecuador — Equateur										
Passenger cars — Voitures de tourisme	268.0	277.0	301.0	322.0	336.0	326.0	358.0	394.0	411.0	...
Commercial vehicles — Véhicules utilitaires	248.0	256.0	258.0	272.0	281.0	268.0	278.0	297.0	306.0	...
Egypt — Egypte										
Passenger cars — Voitures de tourisme	1 372.0	1 439.0	1 525.0	1 616.0	1 700.0	1 767.0	1 847.0	1 881.0	1 960.0	2 081.0
Commercial vehicles — Véhicules utilitaires	484.0	508.0	539.0	577.0	600.0	624.0	650.0	686.0	715.0	741.0
El Salvador — El Salvador										
Passenger cars — Voitures de tourisme	121.8	129.8	136.6	142.2	148.0	...	...	...	...	...
Commercial vehicles — Véhicules utilitaires	218.6	227.3	235.4	243.0	250.8	...	...	...	...	...
Estonia — Estonie										
Passenger cars — Voitures de tourisme	406.6	427.7	451.0	458.7	463.9	407.3	400.7	434.0	471.0	494.0
Commercial vehicles — Véhicules utilitaires	78.0	83.1	86.9	87.2	88.2	86.0	86.0	89.0	91.0	91.0
Ethiopia[2] — Ethiopie[2]										
Passenger cars — Voitures de tourisme	62.4	66.2	68.9	71.0	73.1	76.0	81.2	...	...	...
Commercial vehicles — Véhicules utilitaires	29.0	30.3	34.0	34.6	39.4	43.7	44.5	...	...	...
Fiji — Fidji										
Passenger cars[24] — Voitures de tourisme[24]	51.7	53.4	54.7	58.0	60.6	66.1	70.2	75.3	80.7	86.6
Commercial vehicles[25] — Véhicules utilitaires[25]	48.5	49.5	50.0	51.3	52.3	53.2	54.4	55.6	57.2	59.1
Finland — Finlande										
Passenger cars — Voitures de tourisme	1 942.8	1 948.1	2 021.1	2 082.6	2 134.7	2 160.6	2 194.7	2 274.6	2 346.7	2 430.3
Commercial vehicles[26] — Véhicules utilitaires[26]	266.9	275.4	289.7	303.2	314.2	322.3	329.7	337.5	365.9	374.6
France — France										
Passenger cars — Voitures de tourisme	25 500.0	26 090.0	26 810.0	27 480.0	28 060.0	28 700.0	29 160.0	29 560.0	29 700.0	...
Commercial vehicles[27] — Véhicules utilitaires[27]	5 437.0	5 561.0	5 680.0	5 790.0	5 933.0	6 083.0	6 178.0	6 424.0	...	...
Georgia — Géorgie										
Passenger cars — Voitures de tourisme	323.6	265.6	260.4	247.9	244.8	247.8	252.0	255.2	...	...
Commercial vehicles — Véhicules utilitaires	90.7	79.6	71.0	68.9	66.8	69.6	69.6	68.6	...	...
Germany[28] — Allemagne[28]										
Passenger cars — Voitures de tourisme	40 987.5	41 372.0	41 673.8	42 323.7	42 839.9	43 772.2	44 383.3	44 657.3	45 022.9	45 375.5
Commercial vehicles — Véhicules utilitaires	3 272.0	3 294.0	3 333.0	3 422.0	...	3 567.0	3 596.0	3 551.0	3 505.0	3 484.0
Gibraltar — Gibraltar										
Passenger cars — Voitures de tourisme	19.0	19.0	20.0	22.4	25.5	27.2	13.0[29]	13.0[29]	14.0[29]	15.0[29]
Commercial vehicles — Véhicules utilitaires	2.0	2.0	2.0	1.8	2.0	3.0	1.0[29]	2.0[29]	3.0[29]	2.0[29]
Greece — Grèce										
Passenger cars — Voitures de tourisme	2 339.4	2 500.1	2 675.7	2 928.9	3 195.1	3 423.7	3 646.1	3 839.5	4 074.0	4 303.0
Commercial vehicles — Véhicules utilitaires	939.9	977.5	1 013.7	1 050.8	1 084.5	1 112.9	1 136.4	1 158.2	1 186.0	1 213.0
Greenland[3] — Groenland[3]										
Passenger cars — Voitures de tourisme	2.6	1.8	2.0	2.4	1.9	2.5	2.5	3.0	3.0	3.0
Commercial vehicles — Véhicules utilitaires	1.2	1.5	1.4	1.5	0.9	1.7	1.8	2.0	2.0	2.0

Country or area—Pays ou zone	1996	1997	1998	1999	2000	2001	2002	2003	2004	2005
Grenada—Grenade										
Passenger cars[30]—Voitures de tourisme[30]	9.7	10.7	12.0	13.3	14.6	15.8	...	...	...	...
Commercial vehicles—Véhicules utilitaires	2.4	2.7	3.1	3.6	3.9	4.2	...	...	...	...
Guam—Guam										
Passenger cars—Voitures de tourisme	79.1	67.8	69.0	66.4	64.5	45.5	52.7	...	...	...
Commercial vehicles—Véhicules utilitaires	33.8	28.9	28.9	27.4	26.6	19.3	21.9	...	...	...
Guatemala—Guatemala										
Passenger cars[1]—Voitures de tourisme[1]	...	...	373.2	553.3	1 026.7	1 101.6	1 143.2	1 217.3	1 328.1	...
Commercial vehicles—Véhicules utilitaires	...	...	21.2	...	...	...	...	...	...	...
Haiti—Haïti										
Passenger cars—Voitures de tourisme	59.0	...	...	93.0	...	...	...	...	...	...
Commercial vehicles—Véhicules utilitaires	35.0	...	...	61.6	...	...	...	...	...	...
Honduras—Honduras										
Passenger cars—Voitures de tourisme	46.3	50.3	73.1	46.0	...	...	...	...	...	...
Commercial vehicles—Véhicules utilitaires	48.6	49.1	53.9	39.3	...	...	...	...	...	...
Hungary—Hongrie										
Passenger cars—Voitures de tourisme	2 264.2	2 297.1	2 218.0	2 255.5	2 364.7	2 482.8	2 629.5	2 777.2	2 828.0	2 889.0
Commercial vehicles—Véhicules utilitaires	351.3	360.9	355.4	363.0	384.3	398.3	399.3	409.9	412.0	427.0
Iceland—Islande										
Passenger cars—Voitures de tourisme	124.9	132.5	140.4	151.4	158.9	159.9	161.7	166.9	175.0	187.0
Commercial vehicles[31]—Véhicules utilitaires[31]	16.6	17.5	18.1	19.4	21.1	21.7	22.0	22.9	25.0	27.0
India—Inde										
Passenger cars—Voitures de tourisme	4 204.0	4 672.0	5 138.0	5 556.0	6 143.0	7 058.0	7 613.0	8 619.0	...	...
Commercial vehicles[32]—Véhicules utilitaires[32]	6 330.0	6 931.0	7 588.0	7 991.0	8 596.0	9 377.0	9 730.0	10 889.0	...	...
Indonesia—Indonésie										
Passenger cars—Voitures de tourisme	2 409.1	2 639.5	2 772.5	2 897.8	3 038.9	3 189.0	3 403.4	3 885.2	4 464.3	5 494.0
Commercial vehicles—Véhicules utilitaires	2 030.2	2 160.0	2 220.5	2 273.2	2 373.4	2 482.4	2 579.6	2 845.0	3 300.0	4 106.0
Iraq[33]—Iraq[33]										
Passenger cars—Voitures de tourisme	729.0	722.0	736.0	753.0	745.0	818.0	827.0	...	...	...
Commercial vehicles—Véhicules utilitaires	347.0	324.0	349.0	342.0	357.0	312.0	311.0	...	...	...
Ireland[34]—Irlande[34]										
Passenger cars[35,36]—Voitures de tourisme[35,36]	1 067.8	1 145.9	1 209.2	1 283.4	1 333.9	1 402.3	1 467.0	1 528.0	1 605.0	1 685.0
Commercial vehicles—Véhicules utilitaires	155.9[23]	168.2[23]	181.0[23]	199.0[23]	217.3[23]	231.7[23]	245.0[23]	264.0[23]	282.0[23]	300.0[37]
Israel—Israël										
Passenger cars—Voitures de tourisme	1 195.1	1 252.0	1 298.0	1 341.3	1 422.0	1 485.9	1 522.1	1 545.4	1 593.0	1 652.0
Commercial vehicles—Véhicules utilitaires	279.0	292.0	297.9	308.8	328.0	345.2	354.9	356.6	363.7	370.8
Italy—Italie										
Passenger cars—Voitures de tourisme	29 911.0	30 155.0	31 056.0	32 038.0	32 583.8	33 239.0	33 706.0	34 310.0	33 973.0	34 667.0
Commercial vehicles—Véhicules utilitaires	3 171.9	3 275.2	3 411.6	3 563.0	3 741.8	3 927.0	4 158.6	4 359.6	4 455.0	4 636.0
Japan[38]—Japon[38]										
Passenger cars[39]—Voitures de tourisme[39]	46 869.0	48 611.0	49 896.0	51 165.0	52 738.0	53 541.2	54 540.5	55 213.0	55 995.0	57 091.0
Commercial vehicles—Véhicules utilitaires	20 334.0	19 859.0	19 821.0	18 869.0	18 463.6	18 103.6	17 716.3	17 314.6	17 014.0	16 968.0
Jordan[3]—Jordanie[3]										
Passenger cars—Voitures de tourisme	193.0	191.0	202.0	213.0	255.8	290.0	357.0	365.0	396.0	...
Commercial vehicles—Véhicules utilitaires	87.0	95.0	101.0	94.0	103.0	112.0	146.0	163.0	176.0	...
Kazakhstan—Kazakhstan										
Passenger cars—Voitures de tourisme	997.5	973.3	971.2	987.7	1 000.3	1 057.8	1 062.6	1 149.0	1 204.0	1 405.0
Commercial vehicles[40]—Véhicules utilitaires[40]	360.4	315.3	277.1	257.4	256.6	268.5	280.3	300.0	305.0	368.0
Kenya[3,41]—Kenya[3,41]										
Passenger cars—Voitures de tourisme	202.7	211.9	225.1	238.9	244.8	255.4	270.0	283.0	308.0	324.0
Commercial vehicles—Véhicules utilitaires	187.7	196.1	239.4	249.8	256.2	263.7	273.0	285.0	299.0	309.0
Korea, Republic of[42]—Corée, République de[42]										
Passenger cars—Voitures de tourisme	6 893.6	7 586.5	7 580.9	7 837.2	8 083.9	8 889.3	9 737.4	10 278.9	10 621.0	...

47 Motor vehicles in use — Passenger cars and commercial vehicles: thousands (*continued*)
Véhicules automobiles en circulation — Voitures de tourisme et véhicules utilitaires : milliers (*suite*)

Country or area — Pays ou zone	1996	1997	1998	1999	2000	2001	2002	2003	2004	2005
Commercial vehicles — Véhicules utilitaires	2 625.6	2 791.2	2 854.0	3 291.3	3 938.2	3 985.4	4 169.7	4 263.0	4 267.0	...
Kuwait — Koweït										
Passenger cars — Voitures de tourisme	701.2	540.0	585.0	624.0	667.0	715.0	756.0	781.0	849.0	919.0
Commercial vehicles — Véhicules utilitaires	160.0	115.0	124.0	130.0	112.0	136.0	160.0	174.0	194.0	215.0
Kyrgyzstan — Kirghizistan										
Passenger cars — Voitures de tourisme	172.4	176.1	187.7	187.3	189.8	189.8	188.7	189.0	196.0	201.0
Latvia — Lettonie										
Passenger cars — Voitures de tourisme	379.9	431.8	482.7	525.6	556.8	586.2	619.1	648.9	686.0	742.0
Commercial vehicles — Véhicules utilitaires	90.2	95.4	96.5	101.8	108.6	111.0	113.9	115.6	118.0	124.0
Lebanon — Liban										
Passenger cars — Voitures de tourisme	1 250.5	1 299.4[33]	1 335.7[33]	1 370.6[33]	1 370.8[33]	1 370.9[33]	...	...	...	...
Commercial vehicles — Véhicules utilitaires	87.4	92.1[33]	95.4[33]	98.2[33]	100.2[33]	102.4[33]	...	...	...	...
Libyan Arab Jamah. — Jamah. arabe libyenne										
Passenger cars — Voitures de tourisme	796.3	859.0	...	...	549.6[43]	552.7[43]	...	...	...	...
Commercial vehicles — Véhicules utilitaires	357.5	362.4	...	...	177.4[43]	195.5[43]	...	...	...	...
Lithuania — Lituanie										
Passenger cars — Voitures de tourisme	785.1	882.1	980.9	1 089.3	1 172.4	1 133.5	1 180.9	1 256.9	1 316.0	1 455.0
Commercial vehicles — Véhicules utilitaires	104.8	108.6	114.6	112.2	113.7	115.6	120.9	126.1	130.0	137.0
Luxembourg — Luxembourg										
Passenger cars — Voitures de tourisme	231.7	236.8	244.1	253.4	272.1	280.7	287.2	293.4	300.0	304.0
Commercial vehicles — Véhicules utilitaires	25.5	26.2	27.3	28.8	34.0	36.0	37.0	39.0	39.0	41.0
Malawi[3] — Malawi[3]										
Passenger cars — Voitures de tourisme	1.6	2.0	...	...	...	...	...	2.0	2.0	...
Commercial vehicles — Véhicules utilitaires	1.9	3.0	...	...	...	...	...	2.0	3.0	...
Malaysia[44] — Malaisie[44]										
Passenger cars — Voitures de tourisme	325.7	379.5	163.8	300.4	350.4	400.4	423.3	431.5	482.0	...
Commercial vehicles[26] — Véhicules utilitaires[26]	102.7	96.5	19.0	28.6	36.8	40.1	42.8	48.0	53.0	...
Maldives — Maldives										
Passenger cars — Voitures de tourisme	0.4	0.7	1.5	1.5	1.8	1.7	1.8	2.7	3.4	4.2
Commercial vehicles — Véhicules utilitaires	0.1	0.1	0.2	0.2	0.2	0.1	0.1	0.2	0.3	0.3
Mali — Mali										
Passenger cars — Voitures de tourisme	26.0	29.0	30.0	42.0	46.0	51.0	54.0	58.0	66.0	72.0
Commercial vehicles — Véhicules utilitaires	19.0	19.0	...	...	...	...	35.0	35.0	38.0	47.0
Malta — Malte										
Passenger cars — Voitures de tourisme	166.2	183.8	191.8	201.8	210.9	219.0	227.2	235.9	...	...
Commercial vehicles — Véhicules utilitaires	39.4	47.4	49.5	51.2	51.4	52.6	53.3	54.6	...	...
Mauritius — Maurice										
Passenger cars — Voitures de tourisme	68.1	73.4	78.5	83.0	87.5	92.7	98.9	105.3	115.0	124.0
Commercial vehicles — Véhicules utilitaires	25.3	26.6	29.1	31.7	34.2	36.5	38.0	39.3	40.0	41.0
Mexico[3] — Mexique[3]										
Passenger cars — Voitures de tourisme	7 831.0	8 403.0	9 086.0	9 583.0	10 176.0	11 352.0	12 255.0	12 742.0	13 388.0	14 662.0
Commercial vehicles — Véhicules utilitaires	3 743.0	4 004.0	4 255.0	4 540.0	5 142.0	5 668.0	6 160.0	6 625.0	2 972.0	7 384.0
Morocco — Maroc										
Passenger cars — Voitures de tourisme	1 018.1	1 060.3	1 108.7	1 161.9	1 211.1	1 253.0	1 295.5	1 334.0	...	...
Commercial vehicles[11] — Véhicules utilitaires[11]	351.6	365.7	382.0	400.3	415.7	431.0	444.0	457.0	...	...
Mozambique — Mozambique										
Passenger cars[45] — Voitures de tourisme[45]	36.0	45.0	35.0	...	...	...	...	99.0	112.0	...
Commercial vehicles[46] — Véhicules utilitaires[46]	10.0	9.0	13.0	...	...	...	...	35.0	40.0	...
Myanmar[3] — Myanmar[3]										
Passenger cars — Voitures de tourisme	171.3	177.9	177.6	171.1	173.9	175.4	178.0	183.0	188.0	...
Commercial vehicles — Véhicules utilitaires	68.3	74.8	75.9	83.4	90.4	98.9	113.0	121.0	131.0	...
Nepal — Népal										
Passenger cars — Voitures de tourisme	39.8	42.8	46.9	49.4	47.5	59.1	63.5	...	...	...

Country or area — Pays ou zone	1996	1997	1998	1999	2000	2001	2002	2003	2004	2005
Commercial vehicles — Véhicules utilitaires	131.8	147.9	164.2	185.8	51.6	66.0	72.7	...	...	...
Netherlands[3,47] — Pays-Bas[3,47]										
Passenger cars — Voitures de tourisme	5 664.0	5 810.0	5 931.0	6 120.0	6 343.0	6 539.0	6 711.0	6 855.0	6 908.0	6 992.0
Commercial vehicles — Véhicules utilitaires	666.0	695.0	738.0	806.0	884.0	950.0	997.0	1 039.0	1 070.0	1 098.0
New Caledonia — Nouvelle-Calédonie										
Passenger cars — Voitures de tourisme	55.1	57.9	76.4[1]	80.3[1]	87.0[1]	89.2[1]	92.6[1]	96.3[1]	102.0	107.0
New Zealand[48] — Nouvelle-Zélande[48]										
Passenger cars — Voitures de tourisme	1 655.8	1 697.2	1 768.2	1 855.8	1 905.6	1 936.8	1 988.9	2 041.7	2 148.0	2 217.0
Commercial vehicles — Véhicules utilitaires	403.1	407.8	422.6	433.6	438.1	436.3	443.0	451.8	472.0	490.0
Nicaragua — Nicaragua										
Passenger cars — Voitures de tourisme	50.7	57.6	62.9	67.9	73.0	82.2	...	...	...	...
Commercial vehicles — Véhicules utilitaires	63.8	72.8	81.7	91.1	98.1	107.7	...	...	...	...
Niger — Niger										
Passenger cars — Voitures de tourisme	2.7	2.1	2.7	3.9	3.7	4.7	5.3	5.3	9.3	...
Commercial vehicles — Véhicules utilitaires	0.6	0.7	0.8	1.0	1.2	1.3	1.5	1.9	3.8	...
Nigeria[49] — Nigéria[49]										
Passenger cars — Voitures de tourisme	40.7	52.3	...	...	...	...	...	...	...	...
Commercial vehicles — Véhicules utilitaires	10.5	13.5	...	...	...	...	...	...	...	...
Norway[3] — Norvège[3]										
Passenger cars — Voitures de tourisme	1 661.2	1 758.0	1 786.0	1 813.6	1 851.9	1 872.9	1 899.7	1 933.6	1 978.0	2 029.0
Commercial vehicles[50] — Véhicules utilitaires[50]	392.1	412.2	427.0	440.0	451.0	462.2	464.8	470.3	480.0	494.0
Oman — Oman										
Passenger cars[51] — Voitures de tourisme[51]	216.2	245.1	279.1	310.4	344.0	359.2	390.0	324.0	...	...
Commercial vehicles[15] — Véhicules utilitaires[15]	92.0	101.2	110.7	117.6	124.6	132.9	140.2	109.1	...	...
Pakistan[2,3] — Pakistan[2,3]										
Passenger cars — Voitures de tourisme	816.0	863.0	930.0	1 004.0	1 066.0	1 131.0	1 171.0	1 263.0	1 353.0	1 462.0
Commercial vehicles — Véhicules utilitaires	334.0	352.0	379.0	406.0	435.0	463.0	489.0	548.0	601.0	663.0
Panama — Panama										
Passenger cars — Voitures de tourisme	188.3	198.7	212.6	222.4	223.1	219.4	225.0	234.0	245.0	251.0
Commercial vehicles — Véhicules utilitaires	60.5	64.2	68.4	71.9	74.4	70.3	74.0	75.0	80.0	79.0
Paraguay — Paraguay										
Passenger cars — Voitures de tourisme	305.5	272.1	357.7	401.7	415.8	...	...	326.0[52]	337.7	361.4
Commercial vehicles — Véhicules utilitaires	42.0	36.9	48.0	53.6	56.4	...	...	54.3[52]	57.6	62.4
Peru — Pérou										
Passenger cars — Voitures de tourisme	557.0	595.8	645.9	684.5	716.9	750.6	834.2	906.6	...	...
Commercial vehicles — Véhicules utilitaires	379.5	389.9	409.8	429.7	446.0	458.4	508.0	555.3	...	...
Philippines — Philippines										
Passenger cars — Voitures de tourisme	1 803.7	1 934.7	1 993.2	2 084.7	2 156.1	2 218.6	2 401.9	2 425.1	2 581.9	2 575.7
Commercial vehicles — Véhicules utilitaires	249.7	274.8	263.1	276.6	282.3	285.3	291.7	287.0	302.0	297.8
Poland — Pologne										
Passenger cars — Voitures de tourisme	8 054.4	8 533.5	8 890.8	9 282.8	9 991.3	10 503.1	11 028.9	11 243.8	11 975.0	...
Commercial vehicles — Véhicules utilitaires	1 517.6	1 569.9	1 644.4	1 762.9	1 962.7	2 062.9	2 247.3	2 396.0	2 476.0	...
Portugal[53] — Portugal[53]										
Passenger cars[54] — Voitures de tourisme[54]	4 002.6[41]	4 272.5[41]	4 587.3[41]	4 931.7[41]	5 260.3	5 537.1	5 787.7	5 995.0	...	...
Commercial vehicles — Véhicules utilitaires	1 292.2[41]	1 383.9[41]	1 492.4[41]	1 600.1[41]	1 727.9	1 828.1	1 908.9	1 973.4	...	...
Puerto Rico[2] — Porto Rico[2]										
Passenger cars — Voitures de tourisme	1 738.3	1 852.7	1 974.5	2 057.7	2 046.9	2 075.5	2 058.6	2 079.3	2 211.0	2 208.0
Commercial vehicles — Véhicules utilitaires	70.2	73.6	79.7	85.9	85.5	118.3	88.7	89.7	78.0	80.0
Qatar — Qatar										
Passenger cars — Voitures de tourisme	...	...	...	188.3	199.5	213.3	230.2	242.3	267.8	...
Commercial vehicles — Véhicules utilitaires	...	...	...	88.9	92.9	98.1	109.7	114.2	122.3	...
Republic of Moldova[55] — République de Moldova[55]										
Passenger cars — Voitures de tourisme	174.0	206.0	223.0	232.0	238.0	257.0	269.0	266.0	274.0	293.0

47 Motor vehicles in use — Passenger cars and commercial vehicles: thousands (*continued*)

Véhicules automobiles en circulation — Voitures de tourisme et véhicules utilitaires : milliers (*suite*)

Country or area — Pays ou zone	1996	1997	1998	1999	2000	2001	2002	2003	2004	2005
Commercial vehicles[56] — Véhicules utilitaires[56]	12.0	10.0	9.0	8.0	7.0	6.0	6.0	5.0	5.0	5.0
Réunion — Réunion										
Passenger cars — Voitures de tourisme	150.6	159.3	167.9	180.6	247.8	258.4	271.1	280.8	309.0	339.0
Commercial vehicles — Véhicules utilitaires	52.0	52.0	49.0	52.0	54.0	51.0	53.0	52.0	57.0	64.0
Romania — Roumanie										
Passenger cars — Voitures de tourisme	2 392.0	2 447.0[57]	2 595.0[57]	2 702.0[57]	2 778.0[57]	2 881.0[57]	2 973.0	3 088.0	3 225.0	3 364.0
Commercial vehicles — Véhicules utilitaires	409.0	430.0[57]	446.0[57]	458.0[57]	468.0[57]	479.0[57]	488.0	505.0	526.0	533.0
Russian Federation[58] — Fédération de Russie[58]										
Passenger cars — Voitures de tourisme	15 464.3	17 631.6	18 819.6	19 624.4	20 246.9	21 152.1	22 342.3	23 271.4	24 091.3	25 461.3
Commercial vehicles — Véhicules utilitaires	3 041.2	4 277.6	4 260.0	4 082.7	4 122.0	4 217.7	4 331.1	4 363.3	4 470.1	4 564.3
Saint Kitts and Nevis — Saint-Kitts-et-Nevis										
Passenger cars — Voitures de tourisme	5.5	6.3	6.3	7.7	8.0	8.0	9.0	9.0	9.0	...
Commercial vehicles — Véhicules utilitaires	2.5	2.4	2.9	3.9	4.0	3.0	3.0	3.0	3.0	...
Saint Lucia — Sainte-Lucie										
Passenger cars — Voitures de tourisme	13.5	17.0	19.4	21.4	23.0	24.8	23.8	...	...	...
Commercial vehicles — Véhicules utilitaires	10.8	8.1	8.4	8.8	9.0	9.2	9.8	...	...	...
Saint Vincent-Grenadines — Saint Vincent-Grenadines										
Passenger cars — Voitures de tourisme	6.1	7.4	8.0	8.7	9.1	9.9	11.0	12.0	13.0	14.0
Commercial vehicles — Véhicules utilitaires	3.2	3.8	4.1	3.9	4.0	4.0	5.0	5.0	5.0	5.0
Samoa — Samoa										
Passenger cars — Voitures de tourisme	6.2	6.0	5.0	8.3	5.2	5.6	5.3	6.9	8.9	9.6
Commercial vehicles — Véhicules utilitaires	0.7	0.6	0.4	0.7	1.2	1.1	1.2	1.3	1.3	1.2
Saudi Arabia[1,59] — Arabie saoudite[1,59]										
Passenger cars — Voitures de tourisme	6 333.9	6 580.0	7 046.2	7 553.9	8 049.1	8 467.0	9 009.1	9 484.9	9 946.6	...
Senegal — Sénégal										
Passenger cars — Voitures de tourisme	112.0	118.0	132.0	150.0	169.0	193.0	126.0[60]	166.0[60]	147.0[60]	...
Commercial vehicles — Véhicules utilitaires	51.0	54.0	59.0	65.0	71.0	79.0	39.0[60]	53.0[60]	46.0[60]	...
Serbia and Montenegro — Serbie-et-Monténégro										
Passenger cars — Voitures de tourisme	...	...	...	1 667.9	1 392.6	1 481.4	1 446.6	1 494.5	1 554.1	...
Commercial vehicles[61] — Véhicules utilitaires[61]	...	...	...	150.5	132.9	140.2	139.2	146.0	158.4	...
Seychelles — Seychelles										
Passenger cars — Voitures de tourisme	6.2	6.7	6.5	6.4	5.9	5.4	5.9	6.2	...	...
Commercial vehicles — Véhicules utilitaires	2.0	2.1	2.2	2.2	2.3	2.2	2.4	2.4	...	...
Sierra Leone — Sierra Leone										
Passenger cars — Voitures de tourisme	...	...	...	...	...	...	2.8	3.6	3.9	7.7
Commercial vehicles — Véhicules utilitaires	...	...	...	...	...	...	5.7	7.1	7.6	7.7
Singapore — Singapour										
Passenger cars — Voitures de tourisme	384.5	396.4	395.2	403.2	413.5	426.4	425.7	427.1	439.9	463.0
Commercial vehicles — Véhicules utilitaires	142.7	144.8	142.6	141.3	137.2	139.9	138.6	137.7	139.6	141.4
Slovakia — Slovaquie										
Passenger cars — Voitures de tourisme	1 058.4	1 135.9	1 196.1	1 236.4	1 274.2	1 292.8	1 326.9	1 356.2	1 197.0	1 304.0
Commercial vehicles — Véhicules utilitaires	127.2	135.0	144.4	149.4	153.2	161.5	171.3	183.0	175.0	197.0
Slovenia — Slovénie										
Passenger cars — Voitures de tourisme	740.9	778.3	813.4	848.3	868.3	884.2	896.7	913.7	936.3	971.1
Commercial vehicles — Véhicules utilitaires	42.6	44.9	46.4	48.5	50.8	52.6	54.3	56.1	59.1	62.7
Spain — Espagne										
Passenger cars — Voitures de tourisme	14 753.8	15 297.4	16 050.1	16 847.4	17 449.2	18 150.8	18 732.6	18 688.0	19 542.0	20 250.0
Commercial vehicles — Véhicules utilitaires	3 200.3	3 360.1	3 561.5	3 788.7	3 977.9	4 161.1	4 315.8	4 419.0	4 660.0	4 908.0
Sri Lanka[3] — Sri Lanka[3]										
Passenger cars — Voitures de tourisme	246.5	261.6	284.3	309.5	335.0[62]	353.7[62]	386.6	443.9	507.0	...
Commercial vehicles — Véhicules utilitaires	191.5	199.2	211.2	227.1	238.3	245.7	255.3	268.4	280.0	...
Suriname — Suriname										
Passenger cars — Voitures de tourisme	46.0	50.0	55.0	60.0	61.0	55.0	64.0	71.0	76.0	...

Country or area — Pays ou zone	1996	1997	1998	1999	2000	2001	2002	2003	2004	2005
Commercial vehicles — Véhicules utilitaires	19.5	20.5	21.1	22.5	23.5	21.7	26.4	29.3	30.0	...
Swaziland[7] — Swaziland[7]										
Passenger cars — Voitures de tourisme	29.0	39.9	33.9	35.8	37.9	39.9	41.5	46.4	49.7	54.9
Commercial vehicles — Véhicules utilitaires	37.3	40.2	42.5	45.1	47.6	49.9	51.8	56.2	60.3	66.1
Sweden — Suède										
Passenger cars — Voitures de tourisme	3 655.0	3 703.0	3 792.0	3 890.2	3 999.0	4 019.0	4 043.0	4 075.4	4 113.0	4 154.0
Commercial vehicles — Véhicules utilitaires	326.5	336.1	352.9	369.2	388.6	409.9	422.9	435.3	453.0	475.0
Switzerland[34] — Suisse[34]										
Passenger cars — Voitures de tourisme	3 268.1	3 323.4	3 383.2	3 467.3	3 545.2	3 629.7	3 701.1	3 753.9	3 811.4	3 863.8
Commercial vehicles — Véhicules utilitaires	300.7	302.7	306.4	313.6	318.8	326.6	332.5	335.9	342.9	353.1
Syrian Arab Republic — Rép. arabe syrienne										
Passenger cars — Voitures de tourisme	173.6	175.9	179.0	180.7	181.7	193.5	227.6	253.0	281.0	333.0
Commercial vehicles — Véhicules utilitaires	251.4	269.1	282.6	313.5	345.6	348.7	367.1	382.0	394.0	442.0
Tajikistan — Tadjikistan										
Passenger cars — Voitures de tourisme	151.5	154.1	146.6	141.7	117.1	...	...	...	...	...
Commercial vehicles — Véhicules utilitaires	9.6	10.2	13.3	16.4	16.8	...	...	...	...	...
Thailand — Thaïlande										
Passenger cars[63] — Voitures de tourisme[63]	2 098.6	2 350.4	2 529.2	2 650.5	2 665.4	2 864.0	3 259.5	3 398.8	2 993.0	3 943.0
Commercial vehicles[64] — Véhicules utilitaires[64]	3 149.3	3 534.9	3 746.7	4 065.3	4 220.1	4 373.4	4 579.7	4 678.7	4 366.0	5 732.0
TFYR of Macedonia — L'ex-R.y. Macédoine										
Passenger cars — Voitures de tourisme	284.0	289.0	289.0	290.0	300.0	309.6	307.6	300.0	249.0	253.0
Commercial vehicles — Véhicules utilitaires	29.0	29.6	29.9	30.1	31.8	33.9	33.0	32.0	28.0	28.0
Tonga — Tonga										
Passenger cars — Voitures de tourisme	9.0	9.0	10.0	11.0	5.0	5.0	6.0	7.0	...	...
Commercial vehicles — Véhicules utilitaires	10.0	9.0	9.0	10.0	4.0	4.0	6.0	7.0	...	...
Trinidad and Tobago — Trinité-et-Tobago										
Passenger cars — Voitures de tourisme	180.2	194.3	213.4	229.4	249.0	261.0	275.0	286.0	302.0	320.0
Commercial vehicles — Véhicules utilitaires	44.9	47.7	51.1	53.9	57.0	59.0	61.0	64.0	67.0	71.0
Tunisia — Tunisie										
Passenger cars — Voitures de tourisme	379.2	415.2	445.6	482.2	516.5	552.9	...	...	...	...
Commercial vehicles[65] — Véhicules utilitaires[65]	201.5	217.1	233.0	250.3	265.7	281.5	...	...	...	...
Turkey — Turquie										
Passenger cars[66] — Voitures de tourisme[66]	3 274.1	3 570.1	3 838.3	4 072.3	4 422.2	4 534.8	4 600.1	4 700.3	5 400.0	5 773.0
Commercial vehicles[31] — Véhicules utilitaires[31]	1 083.9	1 215.7	1 353.6	1 443.2	1 583.7	1 629.9	1 679.1	1 794.1	2 374.0	2 654.0
Uganda — Ouganda										
Passenger cars — Voitures de tourisme	...	...	...	...	49.0	53.0	54.0	57.0	58.0	65.0
Commercial vehicles — Véhicules utilitaires	...	...	...	...	74.0	80.0	82.0	88.0	98.0	104.0
Ukraine — Ukraine										
Passenger cars — Voitures de tourisme	4 872.3	5 024.0	5 127.3	5 210.8	5 250.1	5 312.6	5 400.0[67]	5 524.0[67]	5 446.0[67]	5 539.0[67]
Commercial vehicles — Véhicules utilitaires	925.0	918.0	900.0	880.0	838.0	809.0	938.0[67]	940.0[67]	917.0[67]	889.0[67]
United Kingdom[68] — Royaume-Uni[68]										
Passenger cars — Voitures de tourisme	22 819.0	23 450.0	23 922.0	24 628.0	25 067.0	25 816.0	26 493.0	26 992.0	27 806.0	28 326.0
Commercial vehicles — Véhicules utilitaires	3 035.0	3 104.0	3 167.0	3 333.0	3 388.0	3 497.0	3 552.0	3 707.0	3 916.0	4 053.0
United States — Etats-Unis										
Passenger cars[69] — Voitures de tourisme[69]	198 662.0	199 973.0	203 168.7	207 788.4	212 706.4	221 821.1	220 932.0	222 701.4	...	...
Commercial vehicles — Véhicules utilitaires	7 707.4	7 780.8	8 447.8	8 520.2	8 768.8	8 607.2	8 687.9	8 688.6	...	...
Uruguay — Uruguay										
Passenger cars — Voitures de tourisme	485.1	516.9	578.3	662.3	669.7	652.0	622.0	526.0	529.0	471.0
Commercial vehicles — Véhicules utilitaires	48.4	50.3	53.9	57.8	58.0	30.0	50.0	57.0	58.0	61.0
Viet Nam[70] — Viet Nam[70]										
Commercial vehicles — Véhicules utilitaires	42.0	42.0	49.0	58.0	69.9	88.2	88.7	212.9	205.9	...
Yemen — Yémen										
Passenger cars — Voitures de tourisme	259.4	327.1	380.6	301.2[33]	323.1[33]	346.6[33]	...	...	...	...

47 Motor vehicles in use — Passenger cars and commercial vehicles: thousands *(continued)*
Véhicules automobiles en circulation — Voitures de tourisme et véhicules utilitaires : milliers *(suite)*

Country or area — Pays ou zone	1996	1997	1998	1999	2000	2001	2002	2003	2004	2005
Commercial vehicles — Véhicules utilitaires	345.3	413.1	422.1	534.0[33]	560.3[33]	587.9[33]	...	...	...	...
Zambia — Zambie										
Passenger cars — Voitures de tourisme	3.7	...	...	...	...	...	...	...	...	...
Commercial vehicles — Véhicules utilitaires	3.9	...	...	...	...	...	...	...	...	...
Zimbabwe — Zimbabwe										
Passenger cars — Voitures de tourisme	422.4	464.7	521.0	534.6	544.5	556.0	571.0	585.0	598.0	...
Commercial vehicles — Véhicules utilitaires	42.2	46.4	54.3	58.5	67.7	81.0	84.0	100.0	103.0	...

Source

United Nations Statistics Division, New York, transport statistics database.

Notes

1. Including commercial vehicles.
2. Data refer to fiscal years beginning 1 July.
3. Including vehicles operated by police or other governmental security organizations.
4. Including buses and coaches.
5. Including pick-ups.
6. Number of licensed vehicles.
7. Excluding government vehicles.
8. Including private cars.
9. Includes Buses, Taxis & Limousines; Trucks & Tank Wagons; General Haulage; Construction Vehicles; Forces Vehicles; and Tractors & Trailers.
10. Including only vehicles (trucks) weighing 4,500 kilograms to 14,999 kilograms and vehicles (tractor-trailers and Class A trucks) weighing 15,000 kilograms or more.
11. Including special-purpose vehicles.
12. Including mini-buses.
13. For statistical purposes, the data for China do not include those for the Hong Kong Special Administrative Region (Hong Kong SAR) and Macao Special Administrative Region (Macao SAR).
14. Including vehicles seating more than nine persons.
15. Trucks only.
16. Work vehicles are included.
17. Including specialized enterprises only.
18. Beginning 1996, methodological change in calculation.
19. Including special-purpose commercial vehicles and farm tractors.
20. Including vans.
21. Excluding vans.
22. Excluding Faeroe Islands.
23. Including large public service excavators and trench diggers.
24. Including private and government cars, rental and hired cars.
25. Including pick-ups, ambulances, light and heavy fire engines and all other vehicles such as trailers, cranes, loaders, forklifts, etc.
26. Excluding tractors.
27. Including only trailers and semi-trailer combinations less than 10 years old.
28. Beginning 2001, data refer to fiscal years ending 1 January. For all previous years data refer to fiscal years ending 1 July.

Source

Organisation des Nations Unies, Division de statistique, New York, la base de données pour les statistiques des transports.

Notes

1. Y compris véhicules utilitaires.
2. Les données se réfèrent aux exercices budgétaires commençant le 1er juillet.
3. Y compris véhicules de la police ou d'autres services gouvernementaux d'ordre public.
4. Y compris autobus et autocars.
5. Y compris fourgonnettes.
6. Nombre de véhicules automobiles licensés.
7. Non compris les véhicules des administrations publiques.
8. Y compris les voitures particulières.
9. Y compris autocars, taxis et véhicules de louage; camions et camions-citernes; véhicules de transports généraux ; engins de chantier; véhicules de transport de troupes; tracteurs et remorques.
10. Y compris seulement véhicules (camions) pesant de 4,500 kilogrammes à 14,999 kilogrammes et véhicules (semi-remorques et camions de Classe A) pesant 15,000 kilogrammes ou plus.
11. Y compris véhicules à usages spéciaux.
12. Y compris minibuses.
13. Pour la présentation des statistiques, les données pour la Chine ne comprennent pas la Région Administrative Spéciale de Hong Kong (Hong Kong RAS) et la Région Administrative Spéciale de Macao (Macao RAS).
14. Y compris véhicules dont le nombre de places assises est supérieur à neuf.
15. Camions seulement.
16. Y compris les véhicules de travail.
17. Ne comprend que les entreprises spécialisées.
18. Changement de méthode de calcul introduit en 1996.
19. Y compris véhicules utilitaires à usages spéciaux et tracteurs agricoles.
20. Y compris fourgons.
21. Non compris fourgons.
22. Non compris les Iles Féroés.
23. Y compris les grosses excavatrices et machines d'excavation de tranchées de travaux publics.
24. Y compris les voitures particulières et celles des administrations publiques, les voitures de location et de louage.
25. Y compris les fourgonnettes, les ambulances, les voitures de pompiers légères pompiers légères et lourdes, et tous autres véhicules tels que remorques, grues, chargeuses, chariots élévateurs à fourches, etc.
26. Non compris tracteurs.
27. Y compris les légères remorques et semi-remorques de moins de 10 ans seulement.
28. A compter de l'année 2001, les données se réfèrent aux exercices budgétaires finissant le 1er janvier. Pour toutes les années antérieures, les données se réfèrent aux exercices budgétaires finissant le 1er juillet.

29 Beginning 2002, data refer to motor vehicles with renewed licenses.
30 Including "other, not specified", registered motor vehicles.
31 Excluding tractors and semi-trailer combinations.
32 Including goods vehicles, tractors, trailers, three-wheeled passengers and goods vehicles and other miscellaneous vehicles which are not separately classified.
33 Source: United Nations Economic and Social Commission for Western Asia (ESCWA).
34 Data refer to fiscal years ending 30 September.
35 Including school buses.
36 Including mini-buses equipped for transport of nine to fifteen passengers.
37 Excluding jeeps.
38 Excluding small vehicles.
39 Including cars with a seating capacity of up to 10 persons.
40 Including lorries (trucks), buses and semi-trailer combinations.
41 Including vehicles no longer in circulation.
42 Number of registered motor vehicles.
43 Excluding government passenger-cars.
44 Registration of new motor vehicles only.
45 Light vehicles carrying passengers and goods.
46 Heavy vehicles carrying passengers and goods.
47 Excluding diplomatic corps vehicles.
48 Data refer to fiscal years ending 31 March.
49 Newly registered.
50 Including hearses (Norway: registered before 1981).
51 Excluding taxis.
52 Data as of November 2003.
53 Excluding Madeira and Azores.
54 Including light miscellaneous vehicles.
55 Excluding data from the left side of River Nistru and municipality Bender.
56 For the period 1980-1994, including motor vehicles for general use owned by Ministry of Transport. Beginning 1995, including motor vehicles owned by enterprises with main activity as road transport enterprises.
57 The series was revised by the Ministry of Administration and Interior.
58 Beginning 1997, data provided by State Inspection for security of road traffic of the Russian Federation Ministry of Internal Affairs.
59 Including motorcycles.
60 Including registration of new motor vehicles.
61 Excluding semi-trailers.
62 Including three-wheelers.
63 Including micro-buses and passenger pick-ups.
64 Including pick-ups, taxis, cars for hire, small rural buses.
65 Including trailers.
66 Including vehicles seating not more than eight persons, including the driver.
67 As of 1 August.
68 Figures prior to 1992 were derived from vehicle taxation class; beginning 1992, figures derived from vehicle body type.
69 Including motorcycles (prior to 1993 only), mini-vans, sport-utility vehicles and pick-up trucks.

29 À partir de 2002, les données concernent les véhicules à moteur dont l'immatriculation a été renouvelée.
30 Y compris "autres, non-spécifiés", véhicules automobiles enregistrés.
31 Non compris ensembles tracteur-remorque et semi-remorque.
32 Y compris véhicules de transport de marchandises, camions-remorques, remorques, véhicules à trois roues (passagers et marchandises) et autres véhicules divers qui ne font pas l'objet d'une catégorie séparée.
33 Source : Commission économique et sociale pour l'Asie occidentale (CESAO).
34 Les données se réfèrent aux exercices budgétaires finissant le 30 septembre.
35 Y compris l'autobus de l'école.
36 Y compris mini-buses ayant une capacité de neuf à quinze passagers.
37 Non compris jeeps.
38 Non compris les petits véhicules.
39 Y compris véhicules comptant jusqu'à 10 places.
40 Y compris les camions, les autocars et les semi-remorques.
41 Y compris véhicules retirés de la circulation.
42 Nombre de véhicules automobiles enregistrés.
43 Non compris les voitures de tourisme du gouvernement.
44 Immatriculation de véhicules automobiles neufs seulement.
45 Véhicules légers (passagers et marchandises).
46 Véhicules lourds (passagers et marchandises).
47 Non compris véhicules des diplomates.
48 Les données se réfèrent aux exercices budgétaires finissant le 31 mars.
49 Enregistrés récemment.
50 Y compris corbillards (Norvège : enregistrés avant 1981).
51 Non compris taxis.
52 Données telles qu'en novembre 2003.
53 Non compris Madère et Azores.
54 Y compris les véhicules légers divers.
55 Non comprises les données concernant la rive gauche du Dniestr et la municipalité de Bender.
56 Pour la période 1980 - 1994, y compris les véhicules à moteur d'usage général appartenant au Ministère des transports. A partir de 1995, y compris les véhicules pour les entreprises de transport.
57 La série a été révisée par le Ministère de l'administration et de l'intérieur.
58 A partir de 1997, données fournies par l'Inspectorat d'Etat pour la sécurité routière du Ministère de l'Intérieur de la Fédération de Russie.
59 Y compris motocyclettes.
60 Y compris immatriculation de automobiles véhicules neufs.
61 Non compris semi-remorques.
62 Y compris véhicules à trois roues.
63 Y compris les microbus et les camionnettes de transport de passagers.
64 Y compris les camionnettes, les taxis, les voitures de louage, les petits autobus ruraux.
65 Y compris remorques.
66 Y compris véhicules dont le nombre de places assises (y compris celle du conducteur) n'est pas supérieur à huit.
67 Dès le 1er août.
68 Les chiffres antérieurs à 1992 ont été calculés selon les catégories fiscales de véhicules; à partir de 1992, ils ont été calculés selon les types de carrosserie.
69 Y compris motocyclettes (antérieur à 1993 seulement), fourgonnettes, véhicules de la classe quatre-x-quatre et camionnettes légères.

International maritime transport

Vessels entered and cleared: thousand net registered tons

Transports maritimes internationaux

Navires entrés et sortis : milliers de tonneaux de jauge nette

Country or area — Pays ou zone	1996	1997	1998	1999	2000	2001	2002	2003	2004	2005
Albania — Albanie										
Vessels entered — Navires entrés	1 218	1 053	1 419	1 115	2 212	2 558	2 673	2 876	...	...
Vessels cleared — Navires sortis	213	123	61	29	72	69	64	208	...	...
Algeria[1] — Algérie[1]										
Vessels entered — Navires entrés	93 913	103 201	106 256	113 681	117 918	118 994	130 950	140 059	114 105	151 003
Vessels cleared — Navires sortis	93 676	103 187	106 036	113 627	117 937	119 074	130 706	139 954	113 364	150 798
American Samoa[2] — Samoa américaines[2]										
Vessels entered — Navires entrés	452	725	589	884	791	892	1 000	1 000	953	890
Vessels cleared — Navires sortis	452	725	589	884	799	855	874	997	971	908
Antigua and Barbuda — Antigua-et-Barbuda										
Vessels entered — Navires entrés	57 386	94 907	...	...	...	...	...	...	...	...
Vessels cleared — Navires sortis	544 328	667 126	...	...	...	...	...	...	...	...
Australia[6] — Australie[6]										
Vessels entered — Navires entrés	...	125 809	158 849	177 127	186 434	180 107	163 358[3]	175 655[3]	203 673	...
Vessels cleared — Navires sortis	...	125 667	158 828	177 199	185 920	179 319	163 334[3]	175 129[3]	204 215	...
Azerbaijan — Azerbaïdjan										
Vessels entered — Navires entrés	...	...	...	...	...	...	...	...	...	1 627
Vessels cleared — Navires sortis	...	...	...	...	...	...	...	...	...	1 578
Bahrain — Bahreïn										
Vessels entered — Navires entrés	2	2	...	...	...	...	...	...	...	...
Bangladesh[4] — Bangladesh[4]										
Vessels entered — Navires entrés	5 928	5 488	5 794	6 509	...	...	...	...	...	...
Vessels cleared — Navires sortis	3 136	2 866	2 556	2 949	...	...	...	...	...	...
Barbados — Barbade										
Vessels entered — Navires entrés	14 002	15 146	16 893	14 470	15 875	...	...	...	...	...
Belgium — Belgique										
Vessels entered — Navires entrés	297 664	337 862	367 684	386 211	415 640	436 927	447 106	427 037	451 641	477 864
Vessels cleared — Navires sortis	297 610	333 694	360 987	375 519	404 159	422 703	439 861	414 680	444 956	431 998
Benin — Bénin										
Vessels entered — Navires entrés	1 321	1 296	1 289	1 095	1 184	1 260	1 307	1 539	...	...
Vessels cleared — Navires sortis	...	5 377	5 961	...	...	7 992	8 569	8 450	...	...
Brazil — Brésil										
Vessels entered — Navires entrés	82 593	86 720	92 822	78 774	84 423	88 562	...	...	...	...
Vessels cleared — Navires sortis	192 889	209 331	216 273	217 810	237 170	258 962	...	...	...	...
Brunei Darussalam — Brunéi Darussalam										
Vessels entered — Navires entrés	...	...	...	...	...	...	1 735	...	...	...
Vessels cleared — Navires sortis	...	...	...	...	...	...	1 732	...	...	...
Cambodia[5] — Cambodge[5]										
Vessels entered — Navires entrés	726	715	781	1 056	1 313	...	...	...	...	...
Vessels cleared — Navires sortis	145	293	319	191	179	...	...	...	...	...
Cameroon[6,7] — Cameroun[6,7]										
Vessels entered — Navires entrés	1 157	1 159	1 154	1 234	1 215	1 273	1 278	...	...	...
Canada[8] — Canada[8]										
Vessels entered — Navires entrés	66 166	74 422	81 539	82 976	90 925	92 790	91 899	93 612	90 984	...
Vessels cleared — Navires sortis	117 452	124 999	120 349	122 282	128 549	121 712	120 212	126 234	124 221	...

Country or area — Pays ou zone	1996	1997	1998	1999	2000	2001	2002	2003	2004	2005
Cape Verde — Cap-Vert										
Vessels entered — Navires entrés	3 601	3 590	4 296	...	...	...	...	...	...	...
China, Hong Kong SAR — Chine, Hong Kong RAS										
Vessels entered — Navires entrés	229 444	250 303	261 694	267 255	300 606	340 027	372 415	388 224	399 031	424 703
Vessels cleared — Navires sortis	229 474	250 399	261 552	267 419	300 522	340 163	372 574	386 292	399 025	424 477
China, Macao SAR[6] — Chine, Macao RAS[6]										
Vessels cleared — Navires sortis	...	...	...	...	10 736[1,9]	1 975	2 820	2 451	2 364	...
Colombia — Colombie										
Vessels entered — Navires entrés	11 268	12 814	15 003	12 902	13 400	14 148	14 555	15 431	16 269	...
Vessels cleared — Navires sortis	45 576	43 530	61 327	67 280	66 878	66 669	63 132	70 787	79 539	...
Congo — Congo										
Vessels entered — Navires entrés	7 645	...	8 045	8 507	8 529	8 522	9 432	10 886	12 003	12 811
Vessels cleared — Navires sortis	1 878	...	1 732	1 706	1 781	1 921	2 015	2 150	2 219	2 390
Costa Rica — Costa Rica										
Vessels entered — Navires entrés	4 135	3 555	4 024	2 168	2 019	1 923	2 101	2 167	2 167	2 012
Vessels cleared — Navires sortis	2 992	2 941	3 405	2 168	2 019	1 923	2 101	2 167	2 167	2 012
Croatia — Croatie										
Vessels entered — Navires entrés	13 587[1]	16 131[1]	16 410[1]	14 685[1]	13 925	22 425	24 436	31 024	42 929	47 050
Vessels cleared — Navires sortis	10 393[1]	11 502[1]	11 912[1]	11 374[1]	12 686	20 560	20 577	26 457	39 508	42 830
Cuba[10] — Cuba[10]										
Vessels entered — Navires entrés	...	...	1 348	2 696	3 840	4 716	2 505	1 399	1 100	...
Vessels cleared — Navires sortis	...	...	1 371	766	657	512	268	317	174	...
Cyprus — Chypre										
Vessels entered — Navires entrés	19 033	16 478	15 955	18 001	20 571	20 310	19 969	19 169	18 359	20 960
Dominica — Dominique										
Vessels entered — Navires entrés	...	...	...	1 596	1 539	1 415	1 618	1 704	1 630	1 302
Vessels cleared — Navires sortis	...	...	...	1 596	1 539	1 415	1 618	1 704	1 630	1 302
Dominican Republic — Rép. dominicaine										
Vessels entered — Navires entrés	9 238	10 113	10 719	13 603	14 245	14 013	14 560	14 256	12 730	13 135
Vessels cleared — Navires sortis	1 341	1 822	1 673	1 609	2 170	2 507	1 749	1 957	2 144	2 912
Ecuador — Equateur										
Vessels entered — Navires entrés	3 283	3 263	3 158	2 019	4 711	3 064	5 408	8 948	12 721	...
Vessels cleared — Navires sortis	17 450	18 277	16 937	18 051	16 779	18 761	18 755	37 147	46 981	...
Egypt — Egypte										
Vessels entered — Navires entrés	47 824	48 866	40 834	36 333	69 801	73 888	78 484	41 028	50 930	...
Vessels cleared — Navires sortis	43 386	40 924	33 711	32 186	54 142	63 741	61 339	19 923	32 017	...
El Salvador — El Salvador										
Vessels entered — Navires entrés	3 345	5 633	7 969	3 374	12 986	9 312	13 820	6 983	...	...
Vessels cleared — Navires sortis	822	550	490	566	1 431	1 560	3 833	694	...	...
Estonia[1] — Estonie[1]										
Vessels entered — Navires entrés	...	...	...	...	112 455	115 405	134 467	146 239	155 726	...
Vessels cleared — Navires sortis	...	...	...	...	112 541	115 294	134 728	146 059	156 066	...
Fiji — Fidji										
Vessels entered — Navires entrés	4 070	...	...	...	...	...	...	...	...	...
Finland[6] — Finlande[6]										
Vessels entered — Navires entrés	131 338	144 923	148 690	153 149	155 556	157 730	166 143	175 237	195 107	200 403
Vessels cleared — Navires sortis	135 651	148 366	150 969	154 700	152 070	157 639	166 291	174 836	195 180	200 206
France[11,12] — France[11,12]										
Vessels entered — Navires entrés	2 202 359	2 235 239	2 164 285	2 080 509	2 120 282	2 252 518	2 438 562	...	...	...

Country or area — Pays ou zone	1996	1997	1998	1999	2000	2001	2002	2003	2004	2005
Germany — Allemagne										
Vessels entered — Navires entrés	251 500	260 553	263 470	271 978	816 843[1]	808 574[1]	818 784[1]	852 224[1]	934 671[1]	918 038[1]
Vessels cleared — Navires sortis	229 959	235 110	237 071	249 225	770 241[1]	774 443[1]	785 265[1]	824 651[1]	918 568[1]	880 784[1]
Gibraltar — Gibraltar										
Vessels entered — Navires entrés	222	190	156	161	208	180	155	133	45	74
Greece — Grèce										
Vessels entered — Navires entrés	38 549	38 704	43 786	44 662	45 072	45 973	50 861	51 893	51 938	50 616
Vessels cleared — Navires sortis	21 356	19 359	21 865	22 302	22 526	23 970	21 806	26 025	24 448	24 602
Guatemala — Guatemala										
Vessels entered — Navires entrés	3 680	4 505	5 950	5 986	6 246	6 095	5 855	6 627	9 534	...
Vessels cleared — Navires sortis	3 275	3 815	4 565	4 362	4 714	4 633	4 135	5 020	5 211	...
Haiti[13] — Haïti[13]										
Vessels entered — Navires entrés	1 680	1 304	...	...	...	...	...	...	...	...
India[14,15] — Inde[14,15]										
Vessels entered — Navires entrés	48 358	47 055	48 512	60 850	55 466	55 982	47 582	59 011	68 111	...
Vessels cleared — Navires sortis	44 494	45 819	39 031	41 187	38 043	41 716	44 244	50 744	88 733	...
Indonesia — Indonésie										
Vessels entered — Navires entrés	259 096	286 314	246 838	252 893	303 587	331 164	361 246	223 169	246 091	273 722
Vessels cleared — Navires sortis	75 055	97 885	82 711	73 938	79 813	83 115	86 554	70 525	82 250	84 769
Iran (Islamic Rep. of) — Iran (Rép. islamique d')										
Vessels entered — Navires entrés	17 155	27 756	46 937	62 828	65 008	67 199	70 956	78 253	87 134	99 689
Ireland[6] — Irlande[6]										
Vessels entered — Navires entrés	54 602	165 925[1]	176 228[1]	190 818[1]	196 713[1]	210 882[1]	216 460[1]	218 429[1]	218 355[1]	219 926[1]
Vessels cleared — Navires sortis	16 787	16 463	16 669	17 645	17 954	17 234	16 863	17 183	16 323	16 431
Italy — Italie										
Vessels entered — Navires entrés	190 910	226 977	250 830	277 384	211 242	222 594	264 678	288 050	278 306	284 399
Vessels cleared — Navires sortis	160 757	132 532	152 655	167 550	137 864	149 902	187 194	200 772	191 187	200 200
Jamaica — Jamaïque										
Vessels entered — Navires entrés	12 339	12 815	...	...	...	...	...	...	...	...
Vessels cleared — Navires sortis	6 043	6 457	6 553	...	...	...	...	...	...	...
Japan[6] — Japon[6]										
Vessels entered — Navires entrés	422 256	438 111	425 193	446 482	461 903	459 840	461 420	491 619	494 187	508 773
Jordan — Jordanie										
Vessels entered — Navires entrés	2 265	2 572	2 190	2 351	2 505	2 673	2 789	2 694	2 888	...
Vessels cleared — Navires sortis	470	423	418	...	...	...	...	...	...	...
Kenya[6,7] — Kenya[6,7]										
Vessels entered — Navires entrés	8 694	8 442	8 561	8 188	9 126	10 600	10 564	11 931	12 920	13 312
Korea, Republic of — Corée, République de										
Vessels entered — Navires entrés	537 163	578 373	586 629	691 166	755 225	770 284	819 677	858 660	922 142	...
Vessels cleared — Navires sortis	542 600	584 164	595 072	693 598	737 999	776 250	828 211	864 522	932 277	...
Kuwait — Koweït										
Vessels entered — Navires entrés	9 676	9 171	9 357	10 698	10 842	10 870	12 121	13 283	14 610	14 416
Vessels cleared — Navires sortis	1 223	1 285	1 178	1 201	1 071	1 071	1 178	1 262	1 279	1 352
Latvia[1] — Lettonie[1]										
Vessels entered — Navires entrés	...	...	...	...	...	...	...	...	19 001	21 645
Vessels cleared — Navires sortis	...	...	...	...	...	...	...	...	54 737	57 626
Libyan Arab Jamah. — Jamah. arabe libyenne										
Vessels entered — Navires entrés	5 638	5 980	6 245	5 304	2 721	2 538	...	...	...	...
Vessels cleared — Navires sortis	624	647	739	815	1 009	949	...	...	...	...

48 International maritime transport — Vessels entered and cleared: thousand net registered tons (*continued*)
Transports maritimes internationaux — Navires entrés et sortis : milliers de tonneaux de jauge nette (*suite*)

Country or area — Pays ou zone	1996	1997	1998	1999	2000	2001	2002	2003	2004	2005
Lithuania[1] — Lituanie[1]										
Vessels entered — Navires entrés	32 187[6]	34 259[6]	35 680[6]	32 438[6]	37 138[6]	34 310[6]	38 532[6]	42 844[6]	23 517	26 091
Vessels cleared — Navires sortis	31 383[6]	34 161[6]	35 658[6]	32 419[6]	37 044[6]	33 932[6]	38 269[6]	42 712[6]	35 753	38 472
Madagascar[6] — Madagascar[6]										
Vessels entered — Navires entrés	...	4 169	3 920	2 629	4 842	...	...	...	...	...
Malaysia — Malaisie										
Vessels entered — Navires entrés	154 191	164 525	160 663	183 262	198 380	221 752	242 116	257 997	270 874	...
Vessels cleared — Navires sortis	146 827	154 832	155 237	172 876	191 771	214 133	230 724	249 729	265 917	...
Malta — Malte										
Vessels entered — Navires entrés	9 830	11 597	13 738	16 725	17 299	23 829	25 136	24 415	...	...
Vessels cleared — Navires sortis	3 779	4 976	2 493	5 084	7 528	23 752	25 161	24 393	...	...
Mauritius[6] — Maurice[6]										
Vessels entered — Navires entrés	4 999	5 485	5 925	6 725	6 387	7 026	8 595	8 399	7 800	6 786
Vessels cleared — Navires sortis	5 140	5 263	5 924	6 129	6 087	6 482	7 871	8 843	8 662	6 713
Mexico — Mexique										
Vessels entered — Navires entrés	27 533	33 317	43 185	44 814	51 814	50 380	54 427	53 360	52 628	60 527
Vessels cleared — Navires sortis	117 598	125 571	125 682	119 284	124 880	129 020	132 158	140 293	141 988	144 652
Morocco[1,16] — Maroc[1,16]										
Vessels entered — Navires entrés	164 961	196 619	219 617	266 956	263 637	271 696	304 024	300 535	345 052	337 084
Myanmar — Myanmar										
Vessels entered — Navires entrés	2 806	1 868	3 458	4 014	5 458	5 863	3 367	3 157	2 652	...
Vessels cleared — Navires sortis	1 962	1 689	1 783	3 651	3 206	999	797	1 059	762	...
Netherlands[1] — Pays-Bas[1]										
Vessels entered — Navires entrés	441 281	456 522	472 977	497 120	535 817	548 745	563 688	589 756	626 583	623 591
Vessels cleared — Navires sortis	291 089	290 813	301 559	342 349	367 279	381 292	398 345	415 743	436 038	432 192
Nigeria — Nigéria										
Vessels entered — Navires entrés	2 043	2 464	...	...	...	...	...	...	...	...
Vessels cleared — Navires sortis	2 104	2 510	...	...	...	...	...	...	...	...
Norway[17] — Norvège[17]										
Vessels entered — Navires entrés	147 192	148 060	148 764	155 805	...	...	...	...	121 342	140 109
Vessels cleared — Navires sortis	...	...	...	...	...	...	...	...	160 317	173 121
Oman — Oman										
Vessels entered — Navires entrés	2 155	2 226	2 102	2 087	2 142	2 457	2 688	2 667	...	...
Vessels cleared — Navires sortis	5 529	6 781	7 147	7 008	...	...	...	...	...	...
Pakistan[4] — Pakistan[4]										
Vessels entered — Navires entrés	22 632	26 915	26 502	26 702	27 005	26 453	27 262	30 485	32 468	41 189
Vessels cleared — Navires sortis	7 728	5 748	6 983	7 296	7 500	9 173	11 861	18 483	18 798	23 917
Panama — Panama										
Vessels entered — Navires entrés	3 262	4 431	9 879	12 008	13 301	13 765	11 459	13 837	18 626	19 019
Vessels cleared — Navires sortis	2 367	2 927	6 453	7 298	7 369	9 694	9 735	11 969	17 441	18 855
Peru — Pérou										
Vessels entered — Navires entrés	7 515	6 701	7 675	6 948	6 901	7 150	8 260	9 403	...	...
Vessels cleared — Navires sortis	4 731	6 082	4 668	5 696	6 499	6 637	6 112	6 535	...	...
Poland — Pologne										
Vessels entered — Navires entrés	20 997	24 280	25 549	24 161	26 176	26 568	25 976	29 063	30 237	...
Vessels cleared — Navires sortis	25 566	28 877	30 065	30 062	32 225	31 730	32 802	39 658	37 963	...
Portugal — Portugal										
Vessels entered — Navires entrés	...	...	...	84 077	85 423[1,18]	82 659[1,18]	85 423[1,18]	89 025[1,18]	93 005[1]	102 256[1]
Vessels cleared — Navires sortis	...	...	...	84 666	85 348[1,18]	82 537[1,18]	85 560[1,18]	89 627[1,18]	94 223[1]	102 320[1]

Country or area—Pays ou zone	1996	1997	1998	1999	2000	2001	2002	2003	2004	2005
Réunion[16]—Réunion[16]										
Vessels entered—Navires entrés	2 595	2 755	3 065	3 059	3 266	3 364	3 195	3 435	3 891	3 765
Russian Federation[6]—Fédération de Russie[6]										
Vessels entered—Navires entrés	...	...	67 110	82 544	76 376	83 581	117 306	107 786	...	...
Vessels cleared—Navires sortis	...	...	68 830	82 939	76 369	81 830	100 620	106 937	...	...
Saint Lucia—Sainte-Lucie										
Vessels entered—Navires entrés	5 317	6 803	...	...	...	...	...	...	...	...
Saint Vincent-Grenadines—Saint Vincent-Grenadines										
Vessels entered—Navires entrés	1 204	1 253	1 274	1 478	1 543	1 275	1 507	1 561	1 641	1 675
Vessels cleared—Navires sortis	1 204	1 253	1 274	1 478	1 543	1 275	1 507	1 561	1 641	1 675
Samoa—Samoa										
Vessels entered—Navires entrés	544	662	685	827	763	769	848	844	809	823
Senegal—Sénégal										
Vessels entered—Navires entrés	2 542	2 460	2 467	2 511	2 205	2 235	2 360	2 097	2 085	...
Vessels cleared—Navires sortis	2 542	2 460	2 467	2 511	2 213	2 235	2 360	2 019	2 067	...
Serbia and Montenegro—Serbie-et-Monténégro										
Vessels entered—Navires entrés	1 960	1 828	1 589	1 859	2 057	2 165	1 780	3 282	...	...
Vessels cleared—Navires sortis	1 155	1 360	1 091	1 091	1 368	1 148	1 373	2 922	...	...
Seychelles—Seychelles										
Vessels entered—Navires entrés	872	1 059	1 099	1 139	1 105	1 023	1 276	1 332	...	...
Singapore—Singapour										
Vessels entered—Navires entrés	117 723	130 333	140 922	141 523	145 383	146 265	142 745	...	...	...
Vessels cleared—Navires sortis	117 662	130 237	140 838	141 745	145 415	146 322	142 765	...	...	...
Slovenia—Slovénie										
Vessels entered—Navires entrés	5 067	5 960	6 686	7 762	6 605	6 444	6 825	7 943	8 947	9 271
Vessels cleared—Navires sortis	2 251	3 254	3 652	4 394	3 969	3 986	4 430	4 865	5 149	5 650
South Africa[1]—Afrique du Sud[1]										
Vessels entered—Navires entrés	14 075	14 383	13 559	12 695	12 041	12 763	13 593	14 311	13 284	13 927
Vessels cleared—Navires sortis	586 492	629 033	631 059	606 231	577 520	634 997	688 975	706 199	...	...
Spain—Espagne										
Vessels entered—Navires entrés	149 874	152 951	170 817	184 362	194 911	198 696	212 985	218 507	...	...
Vessels cleared—Navires sortis	51 657	54 243	56 449	56 817	59 247	59 297	61 510	67 404	...	...
Sri Lanka—Sri Lanka										
Vessels entered—Navires entrés	29 882	33 188	36 011	37 399	37 418	34 690	39 336	41 831	40 894	...
Suriname—Suriname										
Vessels entered—Navires entrés	1 270	1 307	1 411	1 344	1 120	1 212	1 185	1 317	1 518	...
Vessels cleared—Navires sortis	2 018	2 135	2 206	2 391	2 186	2 306	2 138	2 174	2 142	...
Sweden[1]—Suède[1]										
Vessels entered—Navires entrés	88 828	95 655	101 977	158 718[19]	935 481[20]	925 202[20]	953 350[20]	960 929[20]	1 000 644[20,21]	...
Vessels cleared—Navires sortis	79 888	82 877	84 722	143 200[19]	917 926[20]	910 735[20]	937 947[20]	947 954[20]	990 452[20,21]	...
Syrian Arab Republic[6]—Rép. arabe syrienne[6]										
Vessels entered[7]—Navires entrés[7]	2 901	2 640	2 622	2 928	2 798	2 827	2 979	3 012	3 711	4 397
Vessels cleared—Navires sortis	2 792	2 573	2 562	2 845	2 696	2 791	2 900	2 928	3 524	3 927
Thailand—Thaïlande										
Vessels entered—Navires entrés	93 033	84 052	62 339	71 094	68 079	...	...	...	...	...
Vessels cleared—Navires sortis	22 231	23 757	24 920	31 125	33 154	...	...	...	...	...
Tunisia[1]—Tunisie[1]										
Vessels entered—Navires entrés	38 513	42 749	43 546	52 441	56 632	58 610	65 153	67 273	71 713	77 249
Vessels cleared—Navires sortis	38 541	42 561	43 513	52 464	56 551	58 595	65 108	67 178	71 737	77 255

International maritime transport—Vessels entered and cleared: thousand net registered tons (*continued*)
Transports maritimes internationaux—Navires entrés et sortis : milliers de tonneaux de jauge nette (*suite*)

Country or area—Pays ou zone	1996	1997	1998	1999	2000	2001	2002	2003	2004	2005
Turkey—Turquie										
Vessels entered—Navires entrés	59 861	78 474	142 303[1]	136 456[1]	152 191[1]	125 997[1]	...	...	...	...
Vessels cleared—Navires sortis	58 766	77 952	89 712[1]	88 761[1]	92 406[1]	96 867[1]	...	...	...	...
Ukraine—Ukraine										
Vessels entered—Navires entrés	3 287	3 108	4 843	5 085	6 840	7 404	7 605	10 955	11 675	13 331
Vessels cleared—Navires sortis	21 550	28 765	36 027	44 030	42 704	49 310	62 197	56 171	65 436	70 698
United States[8,22]—Etats-Unis[8,22]										
Vessels entered—Navires entrés	371 107	410 157	431 565	440 341	464 358	451 929	488 385	524 327	538 513	...
Vessels cleared—Navires sortis	305 250	318 435	327 092	302 344	332 445	310 973	341 558	342 707	347 086	...
Uruguay—Uruguay										
Vessels entered—Navires entrés	5 505	5 844	5 262	4 386	5 257	5 196	5 132	4 806	5 067	4 867
Vessels cleared—Navires sortis	24 975	26 844	24 499	21 596	19 587	19 820	21 203	22 325	22 262	24 063
Yemen—Yémen										
Vessels entered—Navires entrés	10 477	10 268	11 210	12 085	12 898	13 846	14 575	16 182	15 395	...
Vessels cleared—Navires sortis	4 562	5 958	9 851	10 724	11 658	11 668	10 758	10 794	...	...

Source

United Nations Statistics Division, New York, transport statistics database.

Notes

1 Gross registered tons.
2 Data refer to fiscal years ending 30 September.
3 Incomplete coverage.
4 Data refer to fiscal years beginning 1 July.
5 Sihanoukville Port and Phnom Penh Port.
6 Including vessels in ballast.
7 All entrances counted.
8 Including Great Lakes international traffic (Canada: also St. Lawrence).
9 Including passenger vessels entered from and departed for Mainland China and Hong Kong SAR.
10 Cuban vessels only.
11 Taxable volume in thousands of cubic metres.
12 Including national maritime transport.
13 Port-au-Prince.
14 Data refer to fiscal years beginning 1 April.
15 Excluding minor and intermediate ports.
16 Including vessels cleared.
17 Gross tonnage for a sample of Norwegian ports.
18 Excluding the Azores.
19 Break in series. Beginning this year, data are based on a survey of all ports in Sweden.
20 Including all passenger vessels and ferries.
21 Beginning 2004, including cruise passenger vessels.
22 Excluding traffic with United States Virgin Islands.

Source

Organisation des Nations Unies, Division de statistique, New York, la base de données pour les statistiques des transports.

Notes

1 Tonneaux de jauge brute.
2 Les données se réfèrent aux exercices budgétaires finissant le 30 septembre.
3 Couverture incomplète.
4 Les données se réfèrent aux exercices budgétaires commençant le 1er juillet.
5 Port de Sihanoukville et Port de Phnom Penh.
6 Y compris navires sur lest.
7 Toutes entrées comprises.
8 Y compris trafic international des Grands Lacs (Canada: et du St. Laurent).
9 Y compris les navires à passagers en provenance de Chine continentale et de la RAS de Hong Kong, ou en partance pour ces deux destinations.
10 Navires de Cuba seulement.
11 Volume taxable en milliers de mètres cubes.
12 Y compris transports maritimes nationaux.
13 Port-au-Prince.
14 Les données se réfèrent aux exercices budgétaires commençant le 1er avril.
15 Non compris les ports petits et moyens.
16 Y compris navires sortis.
17 Tonnage brute pour un échantillon de ports norvégiens.
18 Non compris les Açores.
19 Discontinuité dans la série. A compter de cette année, les données sont basées sur une enquête menée auprès de tous les ports de Suède.
20 Y compris tous les navires à passagers et les transbordeurs.
21 A compter de 2004, y compris navires de croisière.
22 Non compris le trafic avec les Iles Vierges américaines.

Civil aviation: scheduled airline traffic

Passengers carried (thousands); kilometres (millions)

Aviation civile : trafic régulier des lignes aériennes

Passagers transportés (milliers) ; kilomètres (millions)

Country or area and traffic	Total traffic (domestic and international) Trafic total (intérieur et international) 2001	2002	2003	2004	International traffic Trafic international 2001	2002	2003	2004	Pays ou zone et trafic
Albania									Albanie
Kilometres flown	2	2	2	3	2	2	2	3	Kilomètres parcourus
Passengers carried	146	138	159	180	146	138	159	180	Passagers transportés
Passenger-kilometres	93	96	121	136	93	96	121	136	Passagers-kilomètres
Total tonne-kilometres	8	9	11	12	8	9	11	12	Tonnes-kilomètres totales
Algeria									Algérie
Kilometres flown	42	42	41	44	25	27	27	30	Kilomètres parcourus
Passengers carried	3 419	3 002	3 293	3 236	2 076	1 876	2 019	1 913	Passagers transportés
Passenger-kilometres	3 501	3 257	3 415	3 353	2 722	2 605	2 672	2 652	Passagers-kilomètres
Total tonne-kilometres	338	313	328	323	264	251	258	258	Tonnes-kilomètres totales
Angola									Angola
Kilometres flown	5	5	5	6	3	3	4	4	Kilomètres parcourus
Passengers carried	193	190	198	222	101	101	99	113	Passagers transportés
Passenger-kilometres	465	470	479	548	413	417	417	479	Passagers-kilomètres
Total tonne-kilometres	92	92	98	111	87	87	92	105	Tonnes-kilomètres totales
Antigua and Barbuda									Antigua-et-Barbuda
Kilometres flown	12	11	12	5	12	11	12	5	Kilomètres parcourus
Passengers carried	1 369	1 287	1 428	714	1 369	1 287	1 428	714	Passagers transportés
Passenger-kilometres	304	301	325	114	304	301	325	114	Passagers-kilomètres
Total tonne-kilometres	30	30	32	10	30	30	32	10	Tonnes-kilomètres totales
Argentina									Argentine
Kilometres flown	107	102	104	111	28	38	48	50	Kilomètres parcourus
Passengers carried	5 809	5 257	5 946	6 795	1 032	1 248	1 709	1 872	Passagers transportés
Passenger-kilometres	8 330	9 844	12 381	14 450	3 580	5 568	7 764	9 036	Passagers-kilomètres
Total tonne-kilometres	883	956	1 218	1 413	445	556	787	918	Tonnes-kilomètres totales
Armenia									Arménie
Kilometres flown	9	8	8	12	9	8	8	12	Kilomètres parcourus
Passengers carried	369	408	370	510	369	408	370	510	Passagers transportés
Passenger-kilometres	706	747	716	974	706	747	716	974	Passagers-kilomètres
Total tonne-kilometres	81	73	70	97	81	73	70	97	Tonnes-kilomètres totales
Australia									Australie
Kilometres flown	556	640	482	547	238	212	204	235	Kilomètres parcourus
Passengers carried	33 477	39 022	36 400	41 597	8 530	7 961	7 452	8 464	Passagers transportés
Passenger-kilometres	84 931	86 138	83 886	94 811	54 549	52 583	49 244	54 712	Passagers-kilomètres
Total tonne-kilometres	10 050	9 726	9 524	11 075	7 008	6 694	6 212	7 273	Tonnes-kilomètres totales
Austria									Autriche
Kilometres flown	134	130	130	149	130	126	126	145	Kilomètres parcourus
Passengers carried	6 550	7 070	6 903	7 619	6 188	6 646	6 461	7 166	Passagers transportés
Passenger-kilometres	13 875	13 794	14 558	17 530	13 770	13 682	14 440	17 407	Passagers-kilomètres
Total tonne-kilometres	1 786	1 859	1 983	2 366	1 776	1 847	1 971	2 353	Tonnes-kilomètres totales
Azerbaijan									Azerbaïdjan
Kilometres flown	10	11	12	14	8	8	9	11	Kilomètres parcourus
Passengers carried	544	575	684	1 007	147	171	245	501	Passagers transportés
Passenger-kilometres	511	579	751	1 276	282	347	497	983	Passagers-kilomètres
Total tonne-kilometres	112	128	135	149	89	105	111	121	Tonnes-kilomètres totales
Bahamas									Bahamas
Kilometres flown	7	6	6	7	4	4	4	3	Kilomètres parcourus
Passengers carried	1 626	1 543	1 601	900	975	886	984	398	Passagers transportés
Passenger-kilometres	391	369	388	219	286	266	287	129	Passagers-kilomètres
Total tonne-kilometres	48	47	48	20	35	33	35	12	Tonnes-kilomètres totales

Country or area and traffic	Total traffic (domestic and international) Trafic total (intérieur et international) 2001	2002	2003	2004	International traffic Trafic international 2001	2002	2003	2004	Pays ou zone et trafic
Bahrain[1]									Bahreïn[1]
Kilometres flown	28	27	40	50	28	27	40	50	Kilomètres parcourus
Passengers carried	1 250	1 256	1 850	2 285	1 250	1 256	1 850	2 285	Passagers transportés
Passenger-kilometres	3 076	2 944	4 494	5 954	3 076	2 944	4 494	5 954	Passagers-kilomètres
Total tonne-kilometres	525	523	769	981	525	523	769	981	Tonnes-kilomètres totales
Bangladesh									Bangladesh
Kilometres flown	27	27	29	30	26	26	27	29	Kilomètres parcourus
Passengers carried	1 450	1 536	1 579	1 650	1 110	1 172	1 205	1 324	Passagers transportés
Passenger-kilometres	4 395	4 580	4 662	5 042	4 323	4 503	4 583	4 972	Passagers-kilomètres
Total tonne-kilometres	599	684	704	747	593	677	697	740	Tonnes-kilomètres totales
Belarus									Bélarus
Kilometres flown	7	7	7	7	7	7	7	7	Kilomètres parcourus
Passengers carried	222	205	234	274	222	203	232	274	Passagers transportés
Passenger-kilometres	339	308	338	399	339	308	337	399	Passagers-kilomètres
Total tonne-kilometres	33	30	32	38	33	29	32	38	Tonnes-kilomètres totales
Belgium									Belgique
Kilometres flown	186	115	103	125	186	115	103	125	Kilomètres parcourus
Passengers carried	8 489	2 342	2 904	3 265	8 489	2 342	2 904	3 265	Passagers transportés
Passenger-kilometres	15 320	2 606	3 958	4 738	15 320	2 606	3 958	4 738	Passagers-kilomètres
Total tonne-kilometres	2 356	890	961	1 130	2 356	890	961	1 130	Tonnes-kilomètres totales
Benin[2]									Bénin[2]
Kilometres flown	1	...	...	...	1	...	...	...	Kilomètres parcourus
Passengers carried	46	...	...	...	46	...	...	...	Passagers transportés
Passenger-kilometres	130	...	...	...	130	...	...	...	Passagers-kilomètres
Total tonne-kilometres	19	...	...	...	19	...	...	...	Tonnes-kilomètres totales
Bhutan									Bhoutan
Kilometres flown	1	2	2	2	1	2	2	2	Kilomètres parcourus
Passengers carried	35	41	36	45	35	41	36	45	Passagers transportés
Passenger-kilometres	47	61	56	69	47	61	56	69	Passagers-kilomètres
Total tonne-kilometres	4	6	5	6	4	6	5	6	Tonnes-kilomètres totales
Bolivia									Bolivie
Kilometres flown	18	18	22	22	13	12	14	15	Kilomètres parcourus
Passengers carried	1 557	1 509	1 771	1 844	550	446	568	586	Passagers transportés
Passenger-kilometres	1 567	1 432	1 744	1 787	1 201	982	1 311	1 341	Passagers-kilomètres
Total tonne-kilometres	159	148	187	186	124	106	145	145	Tonnes-kilomètres totales
Bosnia and Herzegovina									Bosnie-Herzégovine
Kilometres flown	1	1	1	...	1	1	1	...	Kilomètres parcourus
Passengers carried	65	66	73	...	65	66	73	...	Passagers transportés
Passenger-kilometres	44	43	47	...	44	43	47	...	Passagers-kilomètres
Total tonne-kilometres	6	5	6	...	6	5	6	...	Tonnes-kilomètres totales
Botswana									Botswana
Kilometres flown	3	3	3	3	2	2	2	2	Kilomètres parcourus
Passengers carried	170	179	189	213	123	124	131	149	Passagers transportés
Passenger-kilometres	77	80	83	95	55	54	55	63	Passagers-kilomètres
Total tonne-kilometres	7	8	8	9	5	5	5	6	Tonnes-kilomètres totales
Brazil									Brésil
Kilometres flown	547	529	443	441	155	137	123	129	Kilomètres parcourus
Passengers carried	34 286	35 890	32 293	35 264	3 819	3 387	3 448	3 727	Passagers transportés
Passenger-kilometres	46 603	46 092	44 192	47 462	21 502	20 761	20 252	21 286	Passagers-kilomètres
Total tonne-kilometres	5 726	5 763	5 447	5 844	3 050	2 950	2 875	3 013	Tonnes-kilomètres totales
Brunei Darussalam									Brunéi Darussalam
Kilometres flown	26	27	28	30	26	27	28	30	Kilomètres parcourus
Passengers carried	1 008	1 036	956	1 080	1 008	1 036	956	1 080	Passagers transportés
Passenger-kilometres	3 624	3 715	3 591	3 852	3 624	3 715	3 591	3 852	Passagers-kilomètres
Total tonne-kilometres	458	496	473	478	458	496	473	478	Tonnes-kilomètres totales

Country or area and traffic	Total traffic (domestic and international) Trafic total (intérieur et international)				International traffic Trafic international				Pays ou zone et trafic
	2001	2002	2003	2004	2001	2002	2003	2004	
Bulgaria									Bulgarie
Kilometres flown	6	1	7	11	5	1	7	10	Kilomètres parcourus
Passengers carried	234	63	311	476	185	38	270	431	Passagers transportés
Passenger-kilometres	362	57	457	747	342	47	442	731	Passagers-kilomètres
Total tonne-kilometres	31	5	42	71	29	4	41	69	Tonnes-kilomètres totales
Burkina Faso[2]									Burkina Faso[2]
Kilometres flown	2	1	1	1	2	1	1	1	Kilomètres parcourus
Passengers carried	100	53	54	61	83	37	36	41	Passagers transportés
Passenger-kilometres	158	29	29	33	154	24	24	28	Passagers-kilomètres
Total tonne-kilometres	22	3	3	3	21	2	2	3	Tonnes-kilomètres totales
Cambodia									Cambodge
Kilometres flown	...	2	2	2	...	1	1	1	Kilomètres parcourus
Passengers carried	...	125	165	162	...	13	70	74	Passagers transportés
Passenger-kilometres	...	61	106	98	...	14	82	77	Passagers-kilomètres
Total tonne-kilometres	...	9	12	12	...	5	11	10	Tonnes-kilomètres totales
Cameroon									Cameroun
Kilometres flown	5	11	9	11	4	9	8	9	Kilomètres parcourus
Passengers carried	247	322	315	356	157	235	225	257	Passagers transportés
Passenger-kilometres	489	646	629	720	423	585	562	646	Passagers-kilomètres
Total tonne-kilometres	91	79	77	88	84	73	70	81	Tonnes-kilomètres totales
Canada									Canada
Kilometres flown	567	885	870	936	357	387	338	373	Kilomètres parcourus
Passengers carried	24 204	36 202	36 264	40 701	12 135	13 370	12 191	12 936	Passagers transportés
Passenger-kilometres	68 804	80 426	76 328	87 025	46 436	49 540	45 875	51 151	Passagers-kilomètres
Total tonne-kilometres	7 979	9 942	8 816	9 886	5 624	6 422	5 406	5 978	Tonnes-kilomètres totales
Cape Verde									Cap-Vert
Kilometres flown	4	4	5	9	3	3	3	7	Kilomètres parcourus
Passengers carried	243	237	253	560	87	87	86	224	Passagers transportés
Passenger-kilometres	276	279	285	804	240	242	242	725	Passagers-kilomètres
Total tonne-kilometres	27	26	27	74	23	23	23	66	Tonnes-kilomètres totales
Central African Rep.[2]									Rép. centrafricaine[2]
Kilometres flown	1	...	...	...	1	...	...	...	Kilomètres parcourus
Passengers carried	46	...	...	...	46	...	...	...	Passagers transportés
Passenger-kilometres	130	...	...	...	130	...	...	...	Passagers-kilomètres
Total tonne-kilometres	19	...	...	...	19	...	...	...	Tonnes-kilomètres totales
Chad[2]									Tchad[2]
Kilometres flown	1	...	...	...	1	...	...	...	Kilomètres parcourus
Passengers carried	46	...	...	...	46	...	...	...	Passagers transportés
Passenger-kilometres	130	...	...	...	130	...	...	...	Passagers-kilomètres
Total tonne-kilometres	19	...	...	...	19	...	...	...	Tonnes-kilomètres totales
Chile									Chili
Kilometres flown	110	108	107	110	73	70	71	72	Kilomètres parcourus
Passengers carried	5 316	4 987	5 247	5 464	2 200	2 120	2 387	2 479	Passagers transportés
Passenger-kilometres	11 520	11 094	12 187	12 874	8 308	8 110	9 140	9 648	Passagers-kilomètres
Total tonne-kilometres	2 329	2 110	2 237	2 260	1 981	1 785	1 913	1 922	Tonnes-kilomètres totales
China[3]									Chine[3]
Kilometres flown	1 017	1 149	1 195	1 542	165	199	209	287	Kilomètres parcourus
Passengers carried	72 661	83 672	86 041	119 789	6 604	8 050	6 641	10 553	Passagers transportés
Passenger-kilometres	105 870	123 908	124 591	176 268	23 699	28 821	24 346	39 179	Passagers-kilomètres
Total tonne-kilometres	13 802	16 200	17 641	22 912	4 529	5 400	6 246	7 679	Tonnes-kilomètres totales
China, Hong Kong SAR									Chine, Hong Kong RAS
Kilometres flown	251	231	272	338	251	231	272	338	Kilomètres parcourus
Passengers carried	14 064	15 636	13 025	17 893	14 064	15 636	13 025	17 893	Passagers transportés
Passenger-kilometres	48 268	53 148	46 402	62 094	48 268	53 148	46 402	62 094	Passagers-kilomètres
Total tonne-kilometres	9 693	10 821	10 278	12 939	9 693	10 821	10 278	12 939	Tonnes-kilomètres totales

Country or area and traffic	Total traffic (domestic and international) Trafic total (intérieur et international) 2001	2002	2003	2004	International traffic Trafic international 2001	2002	2003	2004	Pays ou zone et trafic
China, Macao SAR									Chine, Macao RAS
Kilometres flown	16	18	15	23	16	18	15	23	Kilomètres parcourus
Passengers carried	1 706	1 728	1 212	1 800	1 706	1 728	1 212	1 800	Passagers transportés
Passenger-kilometres	1 908	2 056	1 566	2 127	1 908	2 056	1 566	2 127	Passagers-kilomètres
Total tonne-kilometres	213	236	198	320	213	236	198	320	Tonnes-kilomètres totales
Colombia									Colombie
Kilometres flown	122	114	110	118	65	57	54	69	Kilomètres parcourus
Passengers carried	9 604	9 425	8 665	8 829	2 090	1 842	1 714	1 781	Passagers transportés
Passenger-kilometres	8 657	8 271	8 299	9 045	5 082	4 272	4 210	4 382	Passagers-kilomètres
Total tonne-kilometres	1 386	1 281	1 390	1 926	1 031	871	953	1 442	Tonnes-kilomètres totales
Congo[2]									Congo[2]
Kilometres flown	3	1	1	...	2	0	0	...	Kilomètres parcourus
Passengers carried	95	47	52	...	49	2	2	...	Passagers transportés
Passenger-kilometres	157	27	31	...	134	4	4	...	Passagers-kilomètres
Total tonne-kilometres	22	3	3	...	19	0	0	...	Tonnes-kilomètres totales
Costa Rica									Costa Rica
Kilometres flown	24	22	20	24	22	18	16	19	Kilomètres parcourus
Passengers carried	738	680	750	901	631	512	584	706	Passagers transportés
Passenger-kilometres	2 152	1 784	1 671	2 173	2 143	1 766	1 654	2 152	Passagers-kilomètres
Total tonne-kilometres	179	107	122	157	178	105	120	155	Tonnes-kilomètres totales
Côte d'Ivoire[2]									Côte d'Ivoire[2]
Kilometres flown	1	...	...	...	1	...	...	...	Kilomètres parcourus
Passengers carried	46	...	...	...	46	...	...	...	Passagers transportés
Passenger-kilometres	130	...	...	...	130	...	...	...	Passagers-kilomètres
Total tonne-kilometres	19	...	...	...	19	...	...	...	Tonnes-kilomètres totales
Croatia									Croatie
Kilometres flown	11	11	12	12	9	10	10	10	Kilomètres parcourus
Passengers carried	1 063	1 127	1 267	1 336	688	736	795	866	Passagers transportés
Passenger-kilometres	736	783	869	941	622	665	726	796	Passagers-kilomètres
Total tonne-kilometres	70	74	81	88	59	63	68	74	Tonnes-kilomètres totales
Cuba									Cuba
Kilometres flown	19	15	19	21	17	12	16	18	Kilomètres parcourus
Passengers carried	882	589	664	743	567	339	429	480	Passagers transportés
Passenger-kilometres	3 171	1 887	2 036	2 241	3 019	1 795	1 945	2 140	Passagers-kilomètres
Total tonne-kilometres	361	223	224	246	340	210	211	232	Tonnes-kilomètres totales
Cyprus									Chypre
Kilometres flown	22	25	30	32	22	25	30	32	Kilomètres parcourus
Passengers carried	1 503	1 705	1 883	2 013	1 503	1 705	1 883	2 013	Passagers transportés
Passenger-kilometres	3 012	3 436	3 935	4 230	3 012	3 436	3 935	4 230	Passagers-kilomètres
Total tonne-kilometres	314	355	408	442	314	355	408	442	Tonnes-kilomètres totales
Czech Republic									République tchèque
Kilometres flown	42	44	53	67	41	44	52	66	Kilomètres parcourus
Passengers carried	2 566	2 809	3 391	4 219	2 523	2 760	3 339	4 157	Passagers transportés
Passenger-kilometres	3 576	3 855	4 938	5 988	3 564	3 842	4 923	5 970	Passagers-kilomètres
Total tonne-kilometres	351	378	485	584	350	377	483	582	Tonnes-kilomètres totales
Denmark[4]									Danemark[4]
Kilometres flown	92	81	78	82	83	72	73	78	Kilomètres parcourus
Passengers carried	6 382	6 322	5 886	5 923	4 845	5 013	4 855	5 088	Passagers transportés
Passenger-kilometres	6 952	7 453	7 202	7 857	6 380	6 956	6 968	7 685	Passagers-kilomètres
Total tonne-kilometres	876	925	885	952	814	870	863	935	Tonnes-kilomètres totales
Ecuador									Equateur
Kilometres flown	8	7	9	11	3	2	0	0	Kilomètres parcourus
Passengers carried	1 285	1 184	1 521	1 828	87	61	16	13	Passagers transportés
Passenger-kilometres	715	626	674	788	188	112	9	3	Passagers-kilomètres
Total tonne-kilometres	70	64	64	75	21	13	1	0	Tonnes-kilomètres totales

Civil aviation: scheduled airline traffic—Passengers carried (thousands); kilometres (millions) (*continued*)
Aviation civile : trafic régulier des lignes aériennes—Passagers transportés (milliers) ; kilomètres (millions) (*suite*)

Country or area and traffic	Total traffic (domestic and international) Trafic total (intérieur et international)				International traffic Trafic international				Pays ou zone et trafic
	2001	2002	2003	2004	2001	2002	2003	2004	
Egypt									Egypte
Kilometres flown	64	64	63	69	59	59	58	63	Kilomètres parcourus
Passengers carried	4 389	4 527	4 181	4 621	2 981	3 141	2 916	3 260	Passagers transportés
Passenger-kilometres	8 893	9 000	8 103	8 918	8 241	8 357	7 517	8 298	Passagers-kilomètres
Total tonne-kilometres	1 051	1 068	975	1 053	991	1 009	921	997	Tonnes-kilomètres totales
El Salvador									El Salvador
Kilometres flown	26	26	34	40	26	26	34	40	Kilomètres parcourus
Passengers carried	1 692	1 804	2 271	2 391	1 692	1 804	2 182	2 391	Passagers transportés
Passenger-kilometres	2 907	3 300	3 644	4 236	2 907	3 300	3 616	4 236	Passagers-kilomètres
Total tonne-kilometres	308	309	339	407	308	309	336	407	Tonnes-kilomètres totales
Estonia									Estonie
Kilometres flown	6	6	7	8	6	6	7	8	Kilomètres parcourus
Passengers carried	277	304	395	510	275	298	389	510	Passagers transportés
Passenger-kilometres	246	283	415	547	246	280	413	547	Passagers-kilomètres
Total tonne-kilometres	24	27	39	51	24	27	39	51	Tonnes-kilomètres totales
Ethiopia									Ethiopie
Kilometres flown	32	34	35	42	28	31	32	38	Kilomètres parcourus
Passengers carried	1 028	1 103	1 147	1 403	754	831	881	1 110	Passagers transportés
Passenger-kilometres	2 953	3 287	3 573	4 394	2 835	3 170	3 460	4 270	Passagers-kilomètres
Total tonne-kilometres	402	442	484	595	392	432	474	584	Tonnes-kilomètres totales
Fiji									Fidji
Kilometres flown	23	20	21	22	14	16	17	18	Kilomètres parcourus
Passengers carried	613	715	766	837	407	450	516	587	Passagers transportés
Passenger-kilometres	2 391	2 906	2 233	2 430	2 355	2 872	2 190	2 389	Passagers-kilomètres
Total tonne-kilometres	306	368	298	318	302	365	294	314	Tonnes-kilomètres totales
Finland									Finlande
Kilometres flown	95	91	97	108	74	73	80	92	Kilomètres parcourus
Passengers carried	6 698	6 416	6 184	7 049	3 960	4 012	3 971	4 796	Passagers transportés
Passenger-kilometres	8 195	8 807	9 056	11 142	6 923	7 649	7 981	10 009	Passagers-kilomètres
Total tonne-kilometres	920	1 025	1 086	1 342	808	924	991	1 242	Tonnes-kilomètres totales
France[5]									France[5]
Kilometres flown	888	856	860	867	630	602	620	663	Kilomètres parcourus
Passengers carried	49 008	47 834	47 641	46 507	23 549	23 894	23 904	24 863	Passagers transportés
Passenger-kilometres	112 308	114 698	112 260	116 850	75 804	79 164	79 027	86 476	Passagers-kilomètres
Total tonne-kilometres	15 126	15 507	15 293	16 147	11 593	12 049	12 029	13 158	Tonnes-kilomètres totales
Gabon									Gabon
Kilometres flown	7	7	8	9	5	5	5	6	Kilomètres parcourus
Passengers carried	374	366	386	431	173	173	170	194	Passagers transportés
Passenger-kilometres	637	643	655	750	565	571	571	656	Passagers-kilomètres
Total tonne-kilometres	107	106	112	128	100	100	104	119	Tonnes-kilomètres totales
Georgia									Géorgie
Kilometres flown	4	4	6	7	4	4	6	7	Kilomètres parcourus
Passengers carried	111	112	180	229	111	112	180	229	Passagers transportés
Passenger-kilometres	235	230	384	473	235	230	384	473	Passagers-kilomètres
Total tonne-kilometres	23	23	37	46	23	23	37	46	Tonnes-kilomètres totales
Germany									Allemagne
Kilometres flown	861	927	1 070	1 198	738	801	952	1 082	Kilomètres parcourus
Passengers carried	56 389	61 890	72 693	82 100	37 251	42 818	53 645	63 493	Passagers transportés
Passenger-kilometres	111 303	124 246	149 672	170 628	103 102	116 020	141 313	162 427	Passagers-kilomètres
Total tonne-kilometres	18 004	19 425	21 937	24 736	17 161	18 594	21 097	23 911	Tonnes-kilomètres totales
Ghana									Ghana
Kilometres flown	18	12	12	5	18	12	12	5	Kilomètres parcourus
Passengers carried	301	256	241	96	301	256	241	96	Passagers transportés
Passenger-kilometres	1 233	912	906	363	1 233	912	906	363	Passagers-kilomètres
Total tonne-kilometres	157	107	101	41	157	107	101	41	Tonnes-kilomètres totales

Country or area and traffic	Total traffic (domestic and international) Trafic total (intérieur et international) 2001	2002	2003	2004	International traffic Trafic international 2001	2002	2003	2004	Pays ou zone et trafic
Greece									Grèce
Kilometres flown	95	82	80	96	68	58	55	67	Kilomètres parcourus
Passengers carried	8 430	7 579	7 657	9 277	3 320	3 015	2 855	3 587	Passagers transportés
Passenger-kilometres	9 801	8 587	7 650	9 166	8 212	7 194	6 177	7 421	Passagers-kilomètres
Total tonne-kilometres	1 029	891	785	927	879	760	640	759	Tonnes-kilomètres totales
Guyana									Guyana
Kilometres flown	1	...	...	...	1	...	...	...	Kilomètres parcourus
Passengers carried	48	...	...	...	48	...	...	...	Passagers transportés
Passenger-kilometres	175	...	...	...	175	...	...	...	Passagers-kilomètres
Total tonne-kilometres	17	...	...	...	17	...	...	...	Tonnes-kilomètres totales
Hungary									Hongrie
Kilometres flown	39	39	46	52	39	39	46	52	Kilomètres parcourus
Passengers carried	2 075	2 134	2 362	2 546	2 075	2 134	2 362	2 546	Passagers transportés
Passenger-kilometres	3 146	3 116	3 130	3 510	3 146	3 116	3 130	3 510	Passagers-kilomètres
Total tonne-kilometres	324	312	314	344	324	312	314	344	Tonnes-kilomètres totales
Iceland									Islande
Kilometres flown	32	26	25	29	32	26	25	29	Kilomètres parcourus
Passengers carried	1 358	1 199	1 134	1 333	1 358	1 199	1 134	1 333	Passagers transportés
Passenger-kilometres	3 714	3 188	2 998	3 635	3 714	3 188	2 998	3 635	Passagers-kilomètres
Total tonne-kilometres	475	413	378	481	475	413	378	481	Tonnes-kilomètres totales
India									Inde
Kilometres flown	221	244	277	327	78	81	94	115	Kilomètres parcourus
Passengers carried	17 419	17 633	19 455	23 934	4 291	4 049	4 348	5 250	Passagers transportés
Passenger-kilometres	25 708	27 478	31 196	38 888	13 888	15 052	17 221	21 617	Passagers-kilomètres
Total tonne-kilometres	2 854	3 035	3 410	4 238	1 682	1 797	2 011	2 497	Tonnes-kilomètres totales
Indonesia									Indonésie
Kilometres flown	150	159	211	263	50	62	40	55	Kilomètres parcourus
Passengers carried	10 397	12 113	20 358	26 781	2 217	2 513	1 984	2 823	Passagers transportés
Passenger-kilometres	16 169	18 419	21 274	28 447	9 793	10 298	6 487	8 800	Passagers-kilomètres
Total tonne-kilometres	1 978	1 879	2 164	2 963	1 269	1 093	776	1 080	Tonnes-kilomètres totales
Iran (Islamic Rep. of)									Iran (Rép. islamique d')
Kilometres flown	73	75	89	91	30	28	34	37	Kilomètres parcourus
Passengers carried	9 533	9 892	11 664	11 878	1 916	1 942	2 282	2 554	Passagers transportés
Passenger-kilometres	8 793	8 616	10 231	11 657	3 439	3 022	3 761	4 925	Passagers-kilomètres
Total tonne-kilometres	854	835	1 002	1 136	370	329	401	509	Tonnes-kilomètres totales
Ireland									Irlande
Kilometres flown	119	138	197	236	118	138	197	236	Kilomètres parcourus
Passengers carried	15 451	19 729	28 923	34 749	15 093	19 630	28 890	34 749	Passagers transportés
Passenger-kilometres	13 917	18 575	27 441	34 597	13 871	18 552	27 433	34 597	Passagers-kilomètres
Total tonne-kilometres	1 458	1 756	2 573	3 216	1 454	1 754	2 572	3 216	Tonnes-kilomètres totales
Israel									Israël
Kilometres flown	83	90	89	99	74	81	83	93	Kilomètres parcourus
Passengers carried	3 989	3 708	3 678	4 969	2 695	2 482	2 581	3 970	Passagers transportés
Passenger-kilometres	13 514	12 234	12 465	14 674	13 146	11 862	12 157	14 381	Passagers-kilomètres
Total tonne-kilometres	2 083	2 437	2 535	2 695	2 050	2 404	2 507	2 669	Tonnes-kilomètres totales
Italy									Italie
Kilometres flown	393	351	398	407	270	235	265	284	Kilomètres parcourus
Passengers carried	31 031	28 245	36 077	35 922	12 153	10 989	13 613	14 729	Passagers transportés
Passenger-kilometres	40 950	34 328	40 823	43 237	30 706	24 735	28 559	32 136	Passagers-kilomètres
Total tonne-kilometres	5 568	4 798	5 343	5 626	4 574	3 859	4 171	4 572	Tonnes-kilomètres totales
Jamaica									Jamaïque
Kilometres flown	46	41	48	53	46	41	48	53	Kilomètres parcourus
Passengers carried	1 946	2 016	1 838	2 008	1 946	2 016	1 838	2 008	Passagers transportés
Passenger-kilometres	4 412	4 912	5 005	5 060	4 412	4 912	5 005	5 060	Passagers-kilomètres
Total tonne-kilometres	471	589	484	499	471	589	484	499	Tonnes-kilomètres totales

Country or area and traffic	Total traffic (domestic and international) Trafic total (intérieur et international)				International traffic Trafic international				Pays ou zone et trafic
	2001	2002	2003	2004	2001	2002	2003	2004	
Japan									**Japon**
Kilometres flown	853	853	834	838	447	443	420	432	Kilomètres parcourus
Passengers carried	107 823	109 038	103 650	101 741	18 487	18 839	14 411	16 259	Passagers transportés
Passenger-kilometres	162 290	164 134	146 856	151 810	90 194	90 595	73 610	81 674	Passagers-kilomètres
Total tonne-kilometres	21 717	22 470	21 071	22 027	15 426	16 075	14 643	15 803	Tonnes-kilomètres totales
Jordan									**Jordanie**
Kilometres flown	36	37	36	42	36	37	36	42	Kilomètres parcourus
Passengers carried	1 178	1 300	1 353	1 660	1 178	1 300	1 353	1 660	Passagers transportés
Passenger-kilometres	3 848	4 146	4 498	5 327	3 848	4 146	4 498	5 327	Passagers-kilomètres
Total tonne-kilometres	530	577	602	740	530	577	602	740	Tonnes-kilomètres totales
Kazakhstan									**Kazakhstan**
Kilometres flown	16	25	31	22	10	13	17	13	Kilomètres parcourus
Passengers carried	501	757	1 010	835	247	305	405	308	Passagers transportés
Passenger-kilometres	1 268	1 730	2 149	1 898	945	1 141	1 404	1 197	Passagers-kilomètres
Total tonne-kilometres	137	184	222	185	105	127	151	118	Tonnes-kilomètres totales
Kenya									**Kenya**
Kilometres flown	32	36	41	43	27	31	35	40	Kilomètres parcourus
Passengers carried	1 418	1 600	1 732	2 005	990	1 148	1 250	1 513	Passagers transportés
Passenger-kilometres	3 706	3 939	4 245	5 310	3 522	3 754	4 050	5 105	Passagers-kilomètres
Total tonne-kilometres	427	465	527	674	410	448	509	655	Tonnes-kilomètres totales
Korea, Dem. P. R.									**Corée, R. p. dém. de**
Kilometres flown	1	1	1	1	1	1	1	1	Kilomètres parcourus
Passengers carried	79	84	75	94	79	84	75	94	Passagers transportés
Passenger-kilometres	33	35	32	39	33	35	32	39	Passagers-kilomètres
Total tonne-kilometres	5	5	5	6	5	5	5	6	Tonnes-kilomètres totales
Korea, Republic of									**Corée, République de**
Kilometres flown	361	400	370	407	304	343	311	355	Kilomètres parcourus
Passengers carried	33 710	34 832	33 373	34 511	12 215	14 077	13 051	15 917	Passagers transportés
Passenger-kilometres	60 143	65 852	57 624	67 131	52 403	58 249	50 104	60 103	Passagers-kilomètres
Total tonne-kilometres	12 265	13 875	12 134	14 140	11 503	13 123	11 402	13 443	Tonnes-kilomètres totales
Kuwait									**Koweït**
Kilometres flown	37	41	39	44	37	41	39	44	Kilomètres parcourus
Passengers carried	2 085	2 299	2 186	2 496	2 085	2 299	2 186	2 496	Passagers transportés
Passenger-kilometres	6 010	6 706	6 311	7 285	6 010	6 706	6 311	7 285	Passagers-kilomètres
Total tonne-kilometres	777	867	795	892	777	867	795	892	Tonnes-kilomètres totales
Kyrgyzstan									**Kirghizistan**
Kilometres flown	6	5	6	6	5	4	5	5	Kilomètres parcourus
Passengers carried	192	174	206	246	102	85	103	125	Passagers transportés
Passenger-kilometres	363	315	372	418	326	280	332	370	Passagers-kilomètres
Total tonne-kilometres	39	35	39	40	35	32	35	36	Tonnes-kilomètres totales
Lao People's Dem. Rep.									**Rép. dém. pop. lao**
Kilometres flown	2	2	3	3	1	1	1	1	Kilomètres parcourus
Passengers carried	211	220	219	272	61	65	58	72	Passagers transportés
Passenger-kilometres	86	91	90	113	38	40	37	45	Passagers-kilomètres
Total tonne-kilometres	9	9	9	12	4	5	4	5	Tonnes-kilomètres totales
Latvia									**Lettonie**
Kilometres flown	6	6	7	13	6	6	7	13	Kilomètres parcourus
Passengers carried	255	265	340	594	255	265	340	594	Passagers transportés
Passenger-kilometres	180	184	245	581	180	184	245	581	Passagers-kilomètres
Total tonne-kilometres	17	18	23	53	17	18	23	53	Tonnes-kilomètres totales
Lebanon									**Liban**
Kilometres flown	20	20	20	22	20	20	20	22	Kilomètres parcourus
Passengers carried	816	874	935	1 087	816	874	935	1 087	Passagers transportés
Passenger-kilometres	1 658	1 749	1 905	2 197	1 658	1 749	1 905	2 197	Passagers-kilomètres
Total tonne-kilometres	229	244	253	292	229	244	253	292	Tonnes-kilomètres totales

Country or area and traffic	Total traffic (domestic and international) Trafic total (intérieur et international) 2001	2002	2003	2004	International traffic Trafic international 2001	2002	2003	2004	Pays ou zone et trafic
Libyan Arab Jamah.									Jamah. arabe libyenne
Kilometres flown	4	4	8	9	...	...	4	5	Kilomètres parcourus
Passengers carried	583	559	742	850	...	...	115	161	Passagers transportés
Passenger-kilometres	409	409	825	985	...	...	346	454	Passagers-kilomètres
Total tonne-kilometres	33	33	69	82	...	...	31	41	Tonnes-kilomètres totales
Lithuania									Lituanie
Kilometres flown	10	10	10	12	10	10	10	12	Kilomètres parcourus
Passengers carried	304	304	329	448	304	303	329	447	Passagers transportés
Passenger-kilometres	347	355	395	557	347	355	395	557	Passagers-kilomètres
Total tonne-kilometres	33	34	37	52	33	34	37	52	Tonnes-kilomètres totales
Luxembourg									Luxembourg
Kilometres flown	66	70	74	78	66	70	74	78	Kilomètres parcourus
Passengers carried	886	823	854	856	886	823	854	856	Passagers transportés
Passenger-kilometres	586	437	548	573	586	437	548	573	Passagers-kilomètres
Total tonne-kilometres	3 821	4 197	4 397	4 722	3 821	4 197	4 397	4 722	Tonnes-kilomètres totales
Madagascar									Madagascar
Kilometres flown	12	5	9	11	7	2	4	6	Kilomètres parcourus
Passengers carried	566	391	452	514	146	241	140	167	Passagers transportés
Passenger-kilometres	835	319	715	911	654	266	562	736	Passagers-kilomètres
Total tonne-kilometres	103	48	74	95	86	42	60	78	Tonnes-kilomètres totales
Malawi									Malawi
Kilometres flown	3	3	4	5	2	2	2	3	Kilomètres parcourus
Passengers carried	113	105	109	122	66	67	68	78	Passagers transportés
Passenger-kilometres	221	140	147	167	148	80	86	99	Passagers-kilomètres
Total tonne-kilometres	23	14	16	18	16	8	11	12	Tonnes-kilomètres totales
Malaysia									Malaisie
Kilometres flown	217	232	247	278	169	176	179	207	Kilomètres parcourus
Passengers carried	16 107	16 275	16 710	19 227	7 197	7 527	6 949	8 369	Passagers transportés
Passenger-kilometres	35 658	36 923	38 415	44 642	31 011	32 191	32 309	37 823	Passagers-kilomètres
Total tonne-kilometres	5 233	5 345	5 689	6 672	4 807	4 920	5 126	6 047	Tonnes-kilomètres totales
Maldives									Maldives
Kilometres flown	7	1	2	2	4	...	...	...	Kilomètres parcourus
Passengers carried	367	58	60	76	226	...	...	...	Passagers transportés
Passenger-kilometres	447	26	28	35	385	...	...	...	Passagers-kilomètres
Total tonne-kilometres	56	2	3	3	49	...	...	...	Tonnes-kilomètres totales
Mali[2]									Mali[2]
Kilometres flown	1	...	...	...	1	...	...	...	Kilomètres parcourus
Passengers carried	46	...	...	...	46	...	...	...	Passagers transportés
Passenger-kilometres	130	...	...	...	130	...	...	...	Passagers-kilomètres
Total tonne-kilometres	19	...	...	...	19	...	...	...	Tonnes-kilomètres totales
Malta									Malte
Kilometres flown	25	22	22	22	25	22	22	22	Kilomètres parcourus
Passengers carried	1 340	1 399	1 309	1 365	1 340	1 399	1 309	1 365	Passagers transportés
Passenger-kilometres	2 359	2 305	2 174	2 282	2 359	2 305	2 174	2 282	Passagers-kilomètres
Total tonne-kilometres	227	221	209	212	227	221	209	212	Tonnes-kilomètres totales
Marshall Islands									Iles Marshall
Kilometres flown	1	1	1	1	0	0	0	0	Kilomètres parcourus
Passengers carried	19	25	27	29	1	1	1	1	Passagers transportés
Passenger-kilometres	25	32	36	38	2	2	1	1	Passagers-kilomètres
Total tonne-kilometres	2	3	4	4	0	0	0	0	Tonnes-kilomètres totales
Mauritania[2]									Mauritanie[2]
Kilometres flown	2	1	1	1	2	0	0	0	Kilomètres parcourus
Passengers carried	156	106	116	128	61	15	14	17	Passagers transportés
Passenger-kilometres	174	45	49	56	147	17	17	19	Passagers-kilomètres
Total tonne-kilometres	23	4	5	5	21	2	2	2	Tonnes-kilomètres totales

	Total traffic (domestic and international) Trafic total (intérieur et international)				International traffic Trafic international				
Country or area and traffic	2001	2002	2003	2004	2001	2002	2003	2004	Pays ou zone et trafic
Mauritius									Maurice
Kilometres flown	30	30	33	44	29	29	32	43	Kilomètres parcourus
Passengers carried	1 002	1 006	1 043	1 089	913	909	929	991	Passagers transportés
Passenger-kilometres	5 194	5 084	5 243	5 739	5 140	5 026	5 175	5 680	Passagers-kilomètres
Total tonne-kilometres	669	667	687	739	664	661	680	733	Tonnes-kilomètres totales
Mexico									Mexique
Kilometres flown	363	337	344	366	157	144	149	163	Kilomètres parcourus
Passengers carried	20 173	19 619	19 642	21 168	5 743	5 312	5 383	6 071	Passagers transportés
Passenger-kilometres	29 621	28 264	28 927	31 924	14 511	13 347	13 517	15 499	Passagers-kilomètres
Total tonne-kilometres	3 029	3 216	3 300	3 645	1 606	1 689	1 739	1 979	Tonnes-kilomètres totales
Monaco									Monaco
Kilometres flown	1	1	1	1	1	1	1	1	Kilomètres parcourus
Passengers carried	78	104	95	84	78	104	95	84	Passagers transportés
Passenger-kilometres	2	7	6	4	2	7	6	4	Passagers-kilomètres
Total tonne-kilometres	0	1	1	0	0	1	1	0	Tonnes-kilomètres totales
Mongolia									Mongolie
Kilometres flown	6	7	9	9	4	5	5	5	Kilomètres parcourus
Passengers carried	255	270	289	310	136	153	139	162	Passagers transportés
Passenger-kilometres	574	661	691	735	470	560	552	611	Passagers-kilomètres
Total tonne-kilometres	52	69	71	74	43	59	58	63	Tonnes-kilomètres totales
Morocco									Maroc
Kilometres flown	63	58	59	70	59	55	56	67	Kilomètres parcourus
Passengers carried	3 681	3 146	2 638	3 004	2 766	2 501	2 049	2 363	Passagers transportés
Passenger-kilometres	7 112	6 045	4 905	5 551	6 820	5 834	4 710	5 341	Passagers-kilomètres
Total tonne-kilometres	715	626	528	642	687	605	507	617	Tonnes-kilomètres totales
Mozambique									Mozambique
Kilometres flown	7	7	6	7	3	3	3	3	Kilomètres parcourus
Passengers carried	264	282	281	294	85	98	103	100	Passagers transportés
Passenger-kilometres	353	397	405	372	169	201	214	133	Passagers-kilomètres
Total tonne-kilometres	39	43	43	37	20	23	23	14	Tonnes-kilomètres totales
Myanmar									Myanmar
Kilometres flown	...	15	16	19	...	11	11	13	Kilomètres parcourus
Passengers carried	...	1 186	1 117	1 392	...	776	691	863	Passagers transportés
Passenger-kilometres	...	1 154	1 083	1 339	...	932	848	1 043	Passagers-kilomètres
Total tonne-kilometres	...	106	100	122	...	85	78	94	Tonnes-kilomètres totales
Namibia									Namibie
Kilometres flown	9	9	11	11	6	6	8	8	Kilomètres parcourus
Passengers carried	215	222	266	283	179	179	222	235	Passagers transportés
Passenger-kilometres	754	760	930	913	734	734	904	885	Passagers-kilomètres
Total tonne-kilometres	151	98	139	147	149	95	136	144	Tonnes-kilomètres totales
Nauru									Nauru
Kilometres flown	3	3	3	3	3	3	3	3	Kilomètres parcourus
Passengers carried	164	175	156	195	164	175	156	195	Passagers transportés
Passenger-kilometres	287	302	275	338	287	302	275	338	Passagers-kilomètres
Total tonne-kilometres	29	30	28	34	29	30	28	34	Tonnes-kilomètres totales
Nepal									Népal
Kilometres flown	9	10	8	9	8	9	6	8	Kilomètres parcourus
Passengers carried	641	681	356	445	517	553	279	349	Passagers transportés
Passenger-kilometres	1 153	1 211	663	816	1 135	1 191	652	802	Passagers-kilomètres
Total tonne-kilometres	119	127	64	77	117	125	63	76	Tonnes-kilomètres totales
Netherlands[6]									Pays-Bas[6]
Kilometres flown	425	424	429	460	424	423	428	459	Kilomètres parcourus
Passengers carried	19 261	22 119	22 590	24 627	19 128	22 000	22 482	24 526	Passagers transportés
Passenger-kilometres	68 793	68 979	68 688	75 706	68 775	68 962	68 673	75 692	Passagers-kilomètres
Total tonne-kilometres	11 154	11 244	11 331	12 487	11 152	11 243	11 329	12 486	Tonnes-kilomètres totales

49 Civil aviation: scheduled airline traffic — Passengers carried (thousands); kilometres (millions) (*continued*)
Aviation civile : trafic régulier des lignes aériennes — Passagers transportés (milliers) ; kilomètres (millions) (*suite*)

	Total traffic (domestic and international) Trafic total (intérieur et international)				International traffic Trafic international				
Country or area and traffic	2001	2002	2003	2004	2001	2002	2003	2004	Pays ou zone et trafic
New Zealand									Nouvelle-Zélande
Kilometres flown	190	180	164	176	101	96	109	116	Kilomètres parcourus
Passengers carried	11 467	11 285	10 334	11 305	3 443	3 746	4 042	4 338	Passagers transportés
Passenger-kilometres	23 069	23 323	23 280	24 710	19 414	19 802	20 440	21 536	Passagers-kilomètres
Total tonne-kilometres	2 846	2 787	3 203	3 307	2 453	2 463	2 902	2 970	Tonnes-kilomètres totales
Niger[2]									Niger[2]
Kilometres flown	1	...	...	...	1	...	...	...	Kilomètres parcourus
Passengers carried	46	...	...	...	46	...	...	...	Passagers transportés
Passenger-kilometres	130	...	...	...	130	...	...	...	Passagers-kilomètres
Total tonne-kilometres	19	...	...	...	19	...	...	...	Tonnes-kilomètres totales
Nigeria									Nigéria
Kilometres flown	4	6	12	12	1	1	4	5	Kilomètres parcourus
Passengers carried	529	512	520	540	33	41	51	51	Passagers transportés
Passenger-kilometres	402	522	638	683	25	27	15	10	Passagers-kilomètres
Total tonne-kilometres	37	57	61	64	3	3	2	2	Tonnes-kilomètres totales
Norway[4]									Norvège[4]
Kilometres flown	149	129	127	128	74	64	66	68	Kilomètres parcourus
Passengers carried	14 556	13 699	12 806	12 277	4 659	4 474	4 407	4 410	Passagers transportés
Passenger-kilometres	10 461	10 546	10 506	10 321	6 140	6 444	6 726	6 958	Passagers-kilomètres
Total tonne-kilometres	1 224	1 231	1 211	1 199	793	822	834	864	Tonnes-kilomètres totales
Oman[1]									Oman[1]
Kilometres flown	33	32	45	52	31	31	43	50	Kilomètres parcourus
Passengers carried	1 980	2 104	2 777	3 267	1 817	1 931	2 617	3 094	Passagers transportés
Passenger-kilometres	4 026	4 133	5 899	7 455	3 889	3 989	5 765	7 313	Passagers-kilomètres
Total tonne-kilometres	518	485	746	945	502	468	731	931	Tonnes-kilomètres totales
Pakistan									Pakistan
Kilometres flown	71	61	68	79	54	47	52	63	Kilomètres parcourus
Passengers carried	6 012	4 141	4 522	5 097	2 690	2 205	2 433	2 985	Passagers transportés
Passenger-kilometres	11 649	10 680	11 880	13 459	9 854	9 089	10 154	11 713	Passagers-kilomètres
Total tonne-kilometres	1 438	1 322	1 432	1 629	1 241	1 141	1 239	1 433	Tonnes-kilomètres totales
Panama									Panama
Kilometres flown	40	38	43	46	40	38	43	46	Kilomètres parcourus
Passengers carried	1 115	1 048	1 313	1 501	1 115	1 048	1 313	1 501	Passagers transportés
Passenger-kilometres	3 004	2 974	3 529	4 100	3 004	2 974	3 529	4 100	Passagers-kilomètres
Total tonne-kilometres	317	317	375	442	317	317	375	442	Tonnes-kilomètres totales
Papua New Guinea									Papouasie-Nvl-Guinée
Kilometres flown	17	18	11	12	6	6	5	5	Kilomètres parcourus
Passengers carried	1 188	1 235	691	763	276	296	127	146	Passagers transportés
Passenger-kilometres	1 110	1 175	576	667	628	660	334	389	Passagers-kilomètres
Total tonne-kilometres	124	133	76	84	77	82	50	57	Tonnes-kilomètres totales
Paraguay									Paraguay
Kilometres flown	6	6	6	7	5	5	5	7	Kilomètres parcourus
Passengers carried	281	269	299	373	266	254	288	366	Passagers transportés
Passenger-kilometres	294	279	320	433	290	274	318	431	Passagers-kilomètres
Total tonne-kilometres	26	25	29	39	26	25	29	39	Tonnes-kilomètres totales
Peru									Pérou
Kilometres flown	38	38	44	50	21	22	29	31	Kilomètres parcourus
Passengers carried	1 844	2 092	2 226	3 225	442	500	547	741	Passagers transportés
Passenger-kilometres	2 627	2 340	2 796	3 901	1 605	1 279	1 727	2 296	Passagers-kilomètres
Total tonne-kilometres	357	317	382	594	254	208	265	417	Tonnes-kilomètres totales
Philippines									Philippines
Kilometres flown	69	79	75	82	52	53	53	57	Kilomètres parcourus
Passengers carried	5 652	6 449	6 435	7 388	2 501	2 547	2 416	2 765	Passagers transportés
Passenger-kilometres	13 454	14 216	13 904	15 739	11 483	11 753	11 387	12 845	Passagers-kilomètres
Total tonne-kilometres	1 666	1 755	1 729	1 929	1 457	1 497	1 468	1 630	Tonnes-kilomètres totales

Civil aviation: scheduled airline traffic — Passengers carried (thousands); kilometres (millions) (*continued*)
Aviation civile : trafic régulier des lignes aériennes — Passagers transportés (milliers) ; kilomètres (millions) (*suite*)

Country or area and traffic	Total traffic (domestic and international) Trafic total (intérieur et international) 2001	2002	2003	2004	International traffic Trafic international 2001	2002	2003	2004	Pays ou zone et trafic
Poland									Pologne
Kilometres flown	70	66	68	73	64	59	61	66	Kilomètres parcourus
Passengers carried	2 670	2 846	3 252	3 493	2 078	2 196	2 495	2 678	Passagers transportés
Passenger-kilometres	4 915	5 111	5 434	5 861	4 739	4 921	5 213	5 622	Passagers-kilomètres
Total tonne-kilometres	562	581	608	654	547	565	589	634	Tonnes-kilomètres totales
Portugal									Portugal
Kilometres flown	112	117	128	149	94	100	110	124	Kilomètres parcourus
Passengers carried	6 650	6 796	7 590	9 052	4 003	4 403	4 994	5 756	Passagers transportés
Passenger-kilometres	11 182	12 109	13 562	16 093	9 540	10 674	11 904	13 634	Passagers-kilomètres
Total tonne-kilometres	1 236	1 314	1 455	1 723	1 071	1 169	1 289	1 467	Tonnes-kilomètres totales
Qatar[1]									Qatar[1]
Kilometres flown	50	65	59	87	50	65	59	87	Kilomètres parcourus
Passengers carried	2 778	3 571	3 184	4 453	2 778	3 571	3 184	4 453	Passagers transportés
Passenger-kilometres	6 510	8 608	8 003	12 172	6 510	8 608	8 003	12 172	Passagers-kilomètres
Total tonne-kilometres	876	1 095	1 003	1 579	876	1 095	1 003	1 579	Tonnes-kilomètres totales
Republic of Moldova									République de Moldova
Kilometres flown	5	5	5	6	5	5	5	6	Kilomètres parcourus
Passengers carried	120	129	179	201	120	129	179	201	Passagers transportés
Passenger-kilometres	146	161	223	257	146	161	223	257	Passagers-kilomètres
Total tonne-kilometres	14	15	22	26	14	15	22	26	Tonnes-kilomètres totales
Romania									Roumanie
Kilometres flown	26	21	26	28	24	19	24	26	Kilomètres parcourus
Passengers carried	1 139	959	1 255	1 338	1 036	858	1 034	1 150	Passagers transportés
Passenger-kilometres	1 856	1 593	1 696	1 532	1 816	1 555	1 634	1 463	Passagers-kilomètres
Total tonne-kilometres	178	153	160	144	175	150	155	137	Tonnes-kilomètres totales
Russian Federation									Fédération de Russie
Kilometres flown	568	653	602	694	198	196	199	250	Kilomètres parcourus
Passengers carried	20 301	20 892	22 723	25 949	6 688	6 667	6 972	8 404	Passagers transportés
Passenger-kilometres	48 321	49 890	53 894	62 010	19 638	19 552	20 478	25 151	Passagers-kilomètres
Total tonne-kilometres	5 292	5 580	6 018	7 064	2 305	2 395	2 513	3 224	Tonnes-kilomètres totales
Samoa									Samoa
Kilometres flown	2	2	4	5	1	1	3	4	Kilomètres parcourus
Passengers carried	173	182	198	247	90	97	121	151	Passagers transportés
Passenger-kilometres	291	306	279	343	281	295	270	332	Passagers-kilomètres
Total tonne-kilometres	29	31	27	32	28	29	26	31	Tonnes-kilomètres totales
Sao Tome and Principe									Sao Tomé-et-Principe
Kilometres flown	0	0	0	1	0	0	0	0	Kilomètres parcourus
Passengers carried	35	34	36	40	21	21	21	24	Passagers transportés
Passenger-kilometres	14	14	15	17	7	7	7	8	Passagers-kilomètres
Total tonne-kilometres	1	1	1	2	1	1	1	1	Tonnes-kilomètres totales
Saudi Arabia									Arabie saoudite
Kilometres flown	126	124	125	135	73	71	72	81	Kilomètres parcourus
Passengers carried	12 836	13 564	13 822	14 943	4 218	4 622	4 801	5 251	Passagers transportés
Passenger-kilometres	20 217	20 804	20 801	22 557	13 495	13 818	13 693	14 897	Passagers-kilomètres
Total tonne-kilometres	2 633	2 748	2 739	3 000	1 945	2 031	2 014	2 229	Tonnes-kilomètres totales
Senegal[2]									Sénégal[2]
Kilometres flown	4	7	6	8	4	7	6	8	Kilomètres parcourus
Passengers carried	176	231	130	416	145	199	96	379	Passagers transportés
Passenger-kilometres	319	572	388	767	304	554	378	756	Passagers-kilomètres
Total tonne-kilometres	116	20	35	69	109	18	34	68	Tonnes-kilomètres totales
Serbia and Montenegro									Serbie-et-Monténégro
Kilometres flown	13	17	18	20	11	14	16	17	Kilomètres parcourus
Passengers carried	1 117	1 185	1 298	1 414	615	767	871	943	Passagers transportés
Passenger-kilometres	897	1 081	1 199	1 286	750	949	1 061	1 137	Passagers-kilomètres
Total tonne-kilometres	85	98	156	122	72	87	137	108	Tonnes-kilomètres totales

Country or area and traffic	Total traffic (domestic and international) Trafic total (intérieur et international) 2001	2002	2003	2004	International traffic Trafic international 2001	2002	2003	2004	Pays ou zone et trafic
Seychelles									Seychelles
Kilometres flown	9	12	12	14	9	11	11	13	Kilomètres parcourus
Passengers carried	420	518	413	462	153	250	187	213	Passagers transportés
Passenger-kilometres	925	1 397	986	1 134	917	1 387	976	1 123	Passagers-kilomètres
Total tonne-kilometres	101	153	114	131	100	152	113	130	Tonnes-kilomètres totales
Sierra Leone									Sierra Leone
Kilometres flown	1	1	1	1	1	1	1	1	Kilomètres parcourus
Passengers carried	14	14	14	16	14	14	14	16	Passagers transportés
Passenger-kilometres	73	74	74	85	73	74	74	85	Passagers-kilomètres
Total tonne-kilometres	13	13	13	15	13	13	13	15	Tonnes-kilomètres totales
Singapore									Singapour
Kilometres flown	350	361	341	397	350	361	341	397	Kilomètres parcourus
Passengers carried	16 374	17 257	14 737	16 996	16 374	17 257	14 737	16 996	Passagers transportés
Passenger-kilometres	70 232	75 620	65 387	79 085	70 232	75 620	65 387	79 085	Passagers-kilomètres
Total tonne-kilometres	12 595	14 140	13 062	14 206	12 595	14 140	13 062	14 206	Tonnes-kilomètres totales
Slovakia									Slovaquie
Kilometres flown	2	3	5	12	1	2	4	11	Kilomètres parcourus
Passengers carried	43	83	190	636	34	53	159	601	Passagers transportés
Passenger-kilometres	85	94	220	848	82	85	211	837	Passagers-kilomètres
Total tonne-kilometres	11	9	20	65	11	8	19	64	Tonnes-kilomètres totales
Slovenia									Slovénie
Kilometres flown	11	12	13	14	11	12	13	14	Kilomètres parcourus
Passengers carried	690	721	758	765	690	721	758	765	Passagers transportés
Passenger-kilometres	657	678	700	711	657	678	700	711	Passagers-kilomètres
Total tonne-kilometres	63	66	67	67	63	66	67	67	Tonnes-kilomètres totales
Solomon Islands									Iles Salomon
Kilometres flown	4	4	2	3	1	1	1	1	Kilomètres parcourus
Passengers carried	81	85	68	85	18	19	23	28	Passagers transportés
Passenger-kilometres	52	55	59	73	37	39	47	58	Passagers-kilomètres
Total tonne-kilometres	6	6	6	7	4	5	5	6	Tonnes-kilomètres totales
South Africa									Afrique du Sud
Kilometres flown	167	170	188	194	92	94	104	109	Kilomètres parcourus
Passengers carried	7 948	8 167	9 160	9 879	2 693	2 834	2 996	3 156	Passagers transportés
Passenger-kilometres	22 061	22 914	24 666	26 048	17 192	17 953	18 852	19 684	Passagers-kilomètres
Total tonne-kilometres	2 746	2 853	3 125	3 270	2 225	2 330	2 505	2 618	Tonnes-kilomètres totales
Spain									Espagne
Kilometres flown	460	442	473	520	268	261	279	308	Kilomètres parcourus
Passengers carried	41 470	40 381	42 507	45 540	12 807	12 858	13 515	14 704	Passagers transportés
Passenger-kilometres	55 324	54 044	57 594	64 141	37 295	36 511	38 723	43 509	Passagers-kilomètres
Total tonne-kilometres	5 897	5 715	6 096	6 859	4 173	4 040	4 268	4 858	Tonnes-kilomètres totales
Sri Lanka									Sri Lanka
Kilometres flown	34	29	34	43	34	29	34	43	Kilomètres parcourus
Passengers carried	1 719	1 741	1 958	2 413	1 719	1 741	1 958	2 413	Passagers transportés
Passenger-kilometres	6 641	6 327	6 910	8 310	6 641	6 327	6 910	8 310	Passagers-kilomètres
Total tonne-kilometres	822	778	864	1 068	822	778	864	1 068	Tonnes-kilomètres totales
Sudan									Soudan
Kilometres flown	6	6	7	8	5	5	5	6	Kilomètres parcourus
Passengers carried	415	409	420	473	270	270	264	301	Passagers transportés
Passenger-kilometres	761	767	786	898	652	659	659	758	Passagers-kilomètres
Total tonne-kilometres	98	98	103	116	85	85	88	100	Tonnes-kilomètres totales
Suriname									Suriname
Kilometres flown	5	5	5	5	5	5	4	5	Kilomètres parcourus
Passengers carried	203	191	258	289	198	186	253	283	Passagers transportés
Passenger-kilometres	898	889	1 470	1 616	896	887	1 469	1 616	Passagers-kilomètres
Total tonne-kilometres	103	101	183	201	103	101	183	201	Tonnes-kilomètres totales

Country or area and traffic	Total traffic (domestic and international) Trafic total (intérieur et international) 2001	2002	2003	2004	International traffic Trafic international 2001	2002	2003	2004	Pays ou zone et trafic
Sweden[4]									Suède[4]
Kilometres flown	167	130	129	133	96	81	86	89	Kilomètres parcourus
Passengers carried	13 123	12 421	11 873	11 624	5 811	5 958	5 900	5 976	Passagers transportés
Passenger-kilometres	11 277	11 663	11 638	11 976	7 879	8 643	8 846	9 304	Passagers-kilomètres
Total tonne-kilometres	1 384	1 427	1 410	1 452	1 059	1 137	1 142	1 197	Tonnes-kilomètres totales
Switzerland									Suisse
Kilometres flown	304	256	218	172	299	252	216	170	Kilomètres parcourus
Passengers carried	16 915	13 292	10 118	9 287	15 567	12 311	9 642	8 624	Passagers transportés
Passenger-kilometres	33 470	26 704	23 295	20 602	33 211	26 501	23 186	20 456	Passagers-kilomètres
Total tonne-kilometres	4 970	3 720	3 617	2 986	4 945	3 699	3 605	2 971	Tonnes-kilomètres totales
Syrian Arab Republic									Rép. arabe syrienne
Kilometres flown	15	16	9	11	14	15	9	11	Kilomètres parcourus
Passengers carried	761	824	940	1 170	647	705	908	1 135	Passagers transportés
Passenger-kilometres	1 465	1 609	1 744	2 212	1 422	1 565	1 727	2 193	Passagers-kilomètres
Total tonne-kilometres	153	169	173	219	149	165	171	217	Tonnes-kilomètres totales
Tajikistan									Tadjikistan
Kilometres flown	6	9	10	11	5	8	8	9	Kilomètres parcourus
Passengers carried	274	397	413	498	202	316	291	342	Passagers transportés
Passenger-kilometres	573	864	854	1 000	542	829	803	937	Passagers-kilomètres
Total tonne-kilometres	54	82	84	96	51	79	79	90	Tonnes-kilomètres totales
Thailand									Thaïlande
Kilometres flown	182	194	204	223	158	173	175	193	Kilomètres parcourus
Passengers carried	17 662	18 112	17 892	20 343	11 343	12 537	11 774	13 671	Passagers transportés
Passenger-kilometres	44 142	48 337	45 449	51 564	40 584	45 084	41 910	47 699	Passagers-kilomètres
Total tonne-kilometres	5 702	6 241	5 920	6 579	5 345	5 913	5 579	6 209	Tonnes-kilomètres totales
TFYR of Macedonia									L'ex-R.y. Macédoine
Kilometres flown	5	3	3	3	5	3	3	3	Kilomètres parcourus
Passengers carried	315	166	201	211	315	166	201	211	Passagers transportés
Passenger-kilometres	377	236	280	276	377	236	280	276	Passagers-kilomètres
Total tonne-kilometres	36	21	25	25	36	21	25	25	Tonnes-kilomètres totales
Togo[2]									Togo[2]
Kilometres flown	1	...	...	...	1	...	...	...	Kilomètres parcourus
Passengers carried	46	...	...	...	46	...	...	...	Passagers transportés
Passenger-kilometres	130	...	...	...	130	...	...	...	Passagers-kilomètres
Total tonne-kilometres	19	...	...	...	19	...	...	...	Tonnes-kilomètres totales
Tonga									Tonga
Kilometres flown	1	1	1	1	...	...	...	...	Kilomètres parcourus
Passengers carried	57	58	61	75	...	...	...	...	Passagers transportés
Passenger-kilometres	13	14	15	19	...	...	...	...	Passagers-kilomètres
Total tonne-kilometres	1	1	1	2	...	...	...	...	Tonnes-kilomètres totales
Trinidad and Tobago									Trinité-et-Tobago
Kilometres flown	29	28	31	28	29	28	31	28	Kilomètres parcourus
Passengers carried	1 388	1 269	1 084	1 132	1 079	1 164	972	1 088	Passagers transportés
Passenger-kilometres	2 723	2 875	2 671	3 013	2 697	2 866	2 662	3 009	Passagers-kilomètres
Total tonne-kilometres	288	295	276	314	285	294	275	314	Tonnes-kilomètres totales
Tunisia									Tunisie
Kilometres flown	26	24	25	28	26	24	25	28	Kilomètres parcourus
Passengers carried	1 926	1 789	1 720	1 940	1 926	1 789	1 720	1 940	Passagers transportés
Passenger-kilometres	2 696	2 511	2 459	2 853	2 696	2 511	2 459	2 853	Passagers-kilomètres
Total tonne-kilometres	283	266	261	299	283	266	261	299	Tonnes-kilomètres totales
Turkey									Turquie
Kilometres flown	143	140	142	161	108	108	111	119	Kilomètres parcourus
Passengers carried	10 604	10 640	10 745	14 276	4 990	5 276	5 239	6 094	Passagers transportés
Passenger-kilometres	16 058	16 818	16 451	20 500	12 907	13 822	13 343	15 422	Passagers-kilomètres
Total tonne-kilometres	1 996	2 117	2 071	2 448	1 679	1 813	1 756	1 959	Tonnes-kilomètres totales

Country or area and traffic	Total traffic (domestic and international) Trafic total (intérieur et international) 2001	2002	2003	2004	International traffic Trafic international 2001	2002	2003	2004	Pays ou zone et trafic
Turkmenistan									Turkménistan
Kilometres flown	22	22	22	17	11	11	12	11	Kilomètres parcourus
Passengers carried	1 407	1 407	1 412	1 612	345	345	307	436	Passagers transportés
Passenger-kilometres	1 608	1 608	1 538	1 916	1 104	1 104	1 005	1 363	Passagers-kilomètres
Total tonne-kilometres	156	156	150	182	110	110	102	131	Tonnes-kilomètres totales
Uganda									Ouganda
Kilometres flown	2	2	2	3	2	2	2	3	Kilomètres parcourus
Passengers carried	41	41	40	46	41	41	40	46	Passagers transportés
Passenger-kilometres	235	237	237	272	235	237	237	272	Passagers-kilomètres
Total tonne-kilometres	42	42	44	50	42	42	44	50	Tonnes-kilomètres totales
Ukraine									Ukraine
Kilometres flown	30	32	38	54	26	27	30	44	Kilomètres parcourus
Passengers carried	986	1 120	1 476	2 200	816	882	1 054	1 610	Passagers transportés
Passenger-kilometres	1 418	1 578	2 351	3 826	1 322	1 443	2 115	3 282	Passagers-kilomètres
Total tonne-kilometres	149	156	231	372	140	144	211	325	Tonnes-kilomètres totales
United Arab Emirates[1]									Emirats arabes unis[1]
Kilometres flown	136	159	207	277	136	159	207	277	Kilomètres parcourus
Passengers carried	7 676	9 667	11 610	14 314	7 676	9 667	11 610	14 314	Passagers transportés
Passenger-kilometres	26 202	33 125	41 504	54 703	26 202	33 125	41 504	54 703	Passagers-kilomètres
Total tonne-kilometres	4 148	5 261	6 760	8 979	4 148	5 261	6 760	8 979	Tonnes-kilomètres totales
United Kingdom[7]									Royaume-Uni[7]
Kilometres flown	1 049	1 048	1 087	1 205	921	925	965	1 066	Kilomètres parcourus
Passengers carried	70 021	72 381	76 389	86 055	51 703	52 802	55 604	63 515	Passagers transportés
Passenger-kilometres	158 717	156 594	166 518	182 736	151 059	148 305	157 503	173 205	Passagers-kilomètres
Total tonne-kilometres	19 914	20 041	20 689	22 260	19 257	19 335	19 942	21 474	Tonnes-kilomètres totales
United Rep. of Tanzania									Rép.-Unie de Tanzanie
Kilometres flown	4	3	4	5	3	2	3	3	Kilomètres parcourus
Passengers carried	175	134	150	243	77	67	61	82	Passagers transportés
Passenger-kilometres	181	136	151	216	134	93	102	135	Passagers-kilomètres
Total tonne-kilometres	21	14	16	22	15	9	10	14	Tonnes-kilomètres totales
United States[8]									Etats-Unis[8]
Kilometres flown	10 268	9 946	10 526	11 634	2 057	1 901	1 937	2 161	Kilomètres parcourus
Passengers carried	618 149	595 561	615 944	676 655	63 793	63 008	61 639	70 458	Passagers transportés
Passenger-kilometres	1 040 472	1 014 132	1 035 277	1 160 236	284 299	270 076	261 070	303 202	Passagers-kilomètres
Total tonne-kilometres	124 982	125 555	130 979	144 508	44 999	44 496	42 991	48 560	Tonnes-kilomètres totales
Uruguay									Uruguay
Kilometres flown	7	7	8	9	7	7	8	9	Kilomètres parcourus
Passengers carried	559	525	464	564	559	525	464	564	Passagers transportés
Passenger-kilometres	582	577	1 029	1 076	582	577	1 029	1 076	Passagers-kilomètres
Total tonne-kilometres	65	64	118	101	65	64	118	101	Tonnes-kilomètres totales
Uzbekistan									Ouzbékistan
Kilometres flown	57	39	40	44	45	32	33	37	Kilomètres parcourus
Passengers carried	2 256	1 451	1 466	1 588	1 379	1 036	1 048	1 183	Passagers transportés
Passenger-kilometres	5 268	3 835	3 889	4 454	4 806	3 600	3 646	4 215	Passagers-kilomètres
Total tonne-kilometres	580	417	424	486	538	396	401	464	Tonnes-kilomètres totales
Vanuatu									Vanuatu
Kilometres flown	3	3	3	3	3	3	3	3	Kilomètres parcourus
Passengers carried	97	104	83	104	97	104	83	104	Passagers transportés
Passenger-kilometres	212	223	176	217	212	223	176	217	Passagers-kilomètres
Total tonne-kilometres	21	23	18	21	21	23	18	21	Tonnes-kilomètres totales
Venezuela (Bolivarian Rep. of)									Venezuela (Rép. bolivar. du)
Kilometres flown	80	79	50	57	24	28	17	21	Kilomètres parcourus
Passengers carried	6 334	6 369	3 887	4 944	1 534	1 361	726	1 018	Passagers transportés
Passenger-kilometres	3 681	4 103	2 048	2 469	1 781	2 162	841	991	Passagers-kilomètres
Total tonne-kilometres	364	405	187	218	190	227	78	88	Tonnes-kilomètres totales

49 Civil aviation: scheduled airline traffic—Passengers carried (thousands); kilometres (millions) (*continued*)
Aviation civile : trafic régulier des lignes aériennes—Passagers transportés (milliers) ; kilomètres (millions) (*suite*)

Country or area and traffic	Total traffic (domestic and international) Trafic total (intérieur et international) 2001	2002	2003	2004	International traffic Trafic international 2001	2002	2003	2004	Pays ou zone et trafic
Viet Nam									Viet Nam
Kilometres flown	40	50	48	60	27	34	32	43	Kilomètres parcourus
Passengers carried	3 427	4 082	3 969	5 050	1 472	1 790	1 644	2 298	Passagers transportés
Passenger-kilometres	5 621	6 676	6 246	8 518	4 083	4 895	4 459	6 428	Passagers-kilomètres
Total tonne-kilometres	645	756	726	983	479	562	523	745	Tonnes-kilomètres totales
Yemen									Yémen
Kilometres flown	18	16	18	22	17	15	17	21	Kilomètres parcourus
Passengers carried	841	869	844	1 022	601	632	622	778	Passagers transportés
Passenger-kilometres	1 580	1 598	1 956	2 473	1 497	1 518	1 876	2 382	Passagers-kilomètres
Total tonne-kilometres	174	180	225	282	166	172	217	274	Tonnes-kilomètres totales
Zambia									Zambie
Kilometres flown	2	2	2	2	0	0	1	1	Kilomètres parcourus
Passengers carried	49	47	45	50	12	12	17	19	Passagers transportés
Passenger-kilometres	16	16	14	16	5	5	6	7	Passagers-kilomètres
Total tonne-kilometres	1	1	1	1	0	0	1	1	Tonnes-kilomètres totales
Zimbabwe									Zimbabwe
Kilometres flown	15	8	6	6	14	7	5	6	Kilomètres parcourus
Passengers carried	308	251	201	225	188	155	102	116	Passagers transportés
Passenger-kilometres	723	674	437	500	674	635	391	450	Passagers-kilomètres
Total tonne-kilometres	224	87	58	67	219	83	54	62	Tonnes-kilomètres totales

Source

International Civil Aviation Organization (ICAO), Montreal, the ICAO Integrated Statistical Database (ISDB).

Notes

1 Includes apportionment (1/4) of the traffic of Gulf Air, a multinational airline with headquarters in Bahrain and operated by four Gulf States.

2 Includes apportionment (1/10) of the traffic of Air Afrique, a multinational airline with headquarters in Côte d'Ivoire and operated by 10 African states until 1991. From 1992 includes apportionment (1/11) of the traffic of Air Afrique and operated by 11 African states.

3 For statistical purposes, the data for China do not include those for the Hong Kong Special Administrative Region (Hong Kong SAR), Macao Special Administrative Region (Macao SAR) and Taiwan Province of China.

4 Includes the apportionment of international operations performed by Scandinavian Airlines System (SAS): Denmark (2/7), Norway (2/7) and Sweden (3/7).

5 Includes data for airlines based in the territories and dependencies of France.

6 Includes data for airlines based in the territories and dependencies of the Netherlands.

7 Includes data for airlines based in the territories and dependencies of the United Kingdom (2001 and 2002).

8 Includes data for airlines based in the territories and dependencies of the United States.

Source

Organisation de l'aviation civile internationale (OACI), Montréal, la base de données statistiques intégrée (ISDB).

Notes

1 Ces chiffres comprennent une partie du trafic (1/4) assurée par Gulf Air, compagnie aérienne multinationale dont le siège est situé en Bahreïn et est exploitée conjointement par 4 Etats Gulf.

2 Ces chiffres comprennent une partie du trafic (1/10) assurée par Air Afrique, compagnie aérienne multinationale dont le siège est situé en Côte d'Ivoire et est exploitée conjointement par 10 Etats Africains jusqu'à 1991. A partir de 1992 ces chiffres comprennent une partie du trafic (1/11) assurée par Air Afrique et exploitée conjointement par 11 Etats Africains.

3 Pour la présentation des statistiques, les données pour la Chine ne comprennent pas la Région Administrative Spéciale de Hong Kong (Hong Kong RAS), la Région Administrative Spéciale de Macao (Macao RAS) et la province de Taiwan.

4 Y compris une partie des vols internationaux effectués par le SAS; Danemark (2/7), Norvège (2/7) et Suède (3/7).

5 Y compris les données relatives aux compagnies aériennes ayant des bases d'opérations dans les territoires et dépendances de France.

6 Y compris les données relatives aux compagnies aériennes ayant des bases d'opérations dans les territoires et dépendances des Pays-Bas.

7 Y compris les données relatives aux compagnies aériennes ayant des bases d'opération dans les territoires et dépendances du Royaume-Uni (2001 et 2002).

8 Y compris les données relatives aux compagnies aériennes ayant des bases d'opérations dans les territoires et dépendances des Etats-Unis.

Technical notes: tables 46-49

Table 46: Data refer to domestic and international traffic on all railway lines within each country shown, except railways entirely within an urban unit, and plantation, industrial mining, funicular and cable railways. The figures relating to passenger-kilometres include all passengers except military, government and railway personnel when carried without revenue. Those relating to ton-kilometres are freight net ton-kilometres and include both fast and ordinary goods services but exclude service traffic, mail, baggage and non-revenue governmental stores.

Table 47: Passenger cars include vehicles seating not more than nine persons (including the driver), such as taxis, jeeps and station wagons. Commercial vehicles include: vans, lorries (trucks), buses, tractor and semi-trailer combinations but exclude trailers and farm tractors. Special purpose vehicles such as two- or three-wheeled cycles and motorcycles, trams, trolley-buses, ambulances, hearses and military vehicles operated by police or other governmental security organizations are excluded.

Table 48: The figures for vessels entered and cleared, unless otherwise stated, represent the sum of the net registered tonnage of sea-going foreign and domestic merchant vessels (power and sailing) entered with cargo from or cleared with cargo to a foreign port and refer to only one entrance or clearance for each foreign voyage. Net registered tonnage refers to the internal capacity of a vessel measured in units of 100 cubic feet less the space occupied by boilers, engines, shaft alleys, chain lockers, officers' and crew quarters and other spaces not available for carrying passengers or freight. Where possible, the data exclude vessels "in ballast", i.e. entering without unloading or clearing without loading goods.

Table 49: Data for total traffic cover both domestic and international scheduled services operated by airlines registered in each country. Scheduled services include supplementary services occasioned by overflow traffic on regularly scheduled trips and preparatory flights for newly scheduled services. The data are prepared by the International Civil Aviation Organization (see also www.icao.int).

The following terms have been used in the table:

- Kilometres flown refers to aircraft kilometres performed, which is the sum of the products obtained by multiplying the number of revenue flight stages flown by the corresponding stage distance.
- Passengers carried - the number of passengers carried is obtained by counting each passenger on a particular flight (with one flight number) once only and not repeatedly on each individual stage of that flight, with a single exception that a passenger flying on both the international and do-

Notes techniques : tableaux 46 à 49

Tableau 46: Les données se rapportent au trafic intérieur et international de toutes les lignes de chemins de fer du pays indiqué, à l'exception des lignes situées entièrement à l'intérieur d'une agglomération urbaine ou desservant une plantation ou un complexe industriel minier, des funiculaires et des téléfériques. Les chiffres relatifs aux voyageurs-kilomètres se rapportent à tous les voyageurs sauf les militaires, les fonctionnaires et le personnel des chemins de fer, qui sont transportés gratuitement. Les chiffres relatifs aux tonnes-kilomètres se rapportent aux tonnes-kilomètres nettes de fret et comprennent les services rapides et ordinaires de transport de marchandises, à l'exception des transports pour les besoins du service, du courrier, des bagages et des marchandises transportées gratuitement pour les besoins de l'Etat.

Tableau 47: Les voitures de tourisme comprennent les véhicules automobiles dont le nombre de places assises (y compris celle du conducteur) est inférieur ou égal à neuf, tels que les taxis, jeeps et breaks. Les véhicules utilitaires comprennent les fourgons, camions, autobus et autocars, les ensembles tracteurs-remorques et semi-remorques, mais ne comprennent pas les remorques et les tracteurs agricoles. Les véhicules à usage spécial, tels que les cycles à deux ou trois roues et motocyclettes, les tramways, les trolleybus, les ambulances, les corbillards, les véhicules militaires utilisés par la police ou par d'autres services publics de sécurité ne sont pas compris dans ces chiffres.

Tableau 48: Sauf indication contraire, les données relatives aux navires entrés et sortis représentent la jauge nette totale des navires marchands de haute mer (à moteur ou à voile) nationaux ou étrangers, qui entrent ou sortent chargés, en provenance ou à destination d'un port étranger. On ne compte qu'une seule entrée et une seule sortie pour chaque voyage international. Le tonnage enregistré net concerne la capacité intérieure d'un navire, mesurée en unités de 100 pieds cubes, moins l'espace occupé par les chaudières, les moteurs, les tunnels d'arbre, les soutes aux chaînes, les emménagements des officiers et des marins, et les autres espaces qui ne sont pas disponibles pour le transport de passagers ou de fret. Dans la mesure du possible, le tableau exclut les navires sur lest (c'est-à-dire les navires entrant sans décharger ou sortant sans avoir chargé).

Tableau 49: Les données relatives au trafic total se rapportent aux services réguliers, intérieurs ou internationaux des compagnies de transport aérien enregistrées dans chaque pays. Les services réguliers comprennent aussi les vols supplémentaires nécessités par un surcroît d'activité des services réguliers et les vols préparatoires en vue de nouveaux services réguliers. Les données sont préparées par l'Organisation de l'aviation civile internationale (voir aussi www.icao.int).

Les termes ci-après ont été utilisés dans le tableau:

mestic stages of the same flight should be counted as both a domestic and an international passenger.

- Passenger-kilometres performed - a passenger-kilometre is performed when a passenger is carried one kilometre. Calculation of passenger-kilometres equals the sum of the products obtained by multiplying the number of revenue passengers carried on each flight stage by the stage distance. The resultant figure is equal to the number of kilometres travelled by all passengers.
- Tonne-kilometres performed - a metric tonne of revenue load carried one kilometre. Tonne-kilometres performed equals the sum of the product obtained by multiplying the number of total tonnes of revenue load (passengers, freight and mail) carried on each flight stage by the stage distance. See http://www.icaodata.com/Terms.aspx for more information.

- Kilomètres parcourus – le nombre de kilomètres parcourus équivaut à la somme des produits du nombre de vols payants effectués sur chaque étape par la longueur de l'étape.
- Passagers transportés – pour calculer le nombre de passagers transportés, on compte chaque passager d'un vol donné (correspondant à un numéro de vol) une seule fois et non pour chacune des étapes de ce vol; toutefois, les passagers qui voyagent sur une étape internationale et sur une étape intérieure d'un même vol doivent être comptés à la fois comme passagers d'un vol intérieur et comme passagers d'un vol international.
- Passager-kilomètre réalisé – un passager-kilomètre est réalisé lorsqu'un passager est transporté sur une distance d'un kilomètre. Le nombre de passagers-kilomètres réalisés équivaut à la somme des produits du nombre de passagers payants transportés sur chaque étape par la longueur de l'étape. Le total obtenu est égal au nombre de kilomètres parcourus par l'ensemble des passagers.
- Tonnes-kilomètres réalisées – la tonne-kilomètre est une unité de mesure qui correspond au déplacement d'une tonne métrique de charge payante sur un kilomètre. Les tonnes-kilomètres réalisées sont la somme des produits du nombre de tonnes de charge payante (passagers, fret, envois postaux) transportées sur chaque étape par la longueur de l'étape. Pour plus de détails, voir http://www.icaodata.com/Terms.aspx.

Production, trade and consumption of commercial energy

Thousand metric tons of oil equivalent and kilograms per capita

Production, commerce et consommation d'énergie commerciale

Milliers de tonnes d'équivalent pétrole et kilogrammes par habitant

Region, country or area	Year Année	Primary energy production – Production d'énergie primaire: Total Totale	Solids Solides	Liquids Liquides	Gas Gaz	Electricity Electricité	Changes in stocks Variations des stocks	Imports Importations	Exports Exportations
World	**2001**	**8 840 425**	**2 261 788**	**3 762 810**	**2 355 050**	**460 777**	**66 749**	**3 769 815**	**3 763 075**
	2002	**8 898 696**	**2 286 135**	**3 711 561**	**2 429 897**	**471 103**	**10 703**	**3 817 511**	**3 760 929**
	2003	**9 270 367**	**2 440 337**	**3 868 171**	**2 491 562**	**470 296**	**13 635**	**3 979 729**	**3 962 615**
	2004	**9 693 989**	**2 630 696**	**4 015 758**	**2 551 949**	**495 586**	**21 476**	**4 260 226**	**4 241 058**
Africa	**2001**	**674 540**	**126 992**	**420 460**	**119 292**	**7 795**	**1 166**	**83 197**	**446 866**
	2002	**678 236**	**125 065**	**415 578**	**128 902**	**8 691**	**125**	**85 356**	**442 121**
	2003	**714 629**	**129 579**	**441 351**	**135 209**	**8 489**	**807**	**85 358**	**472 162**
	2004	**751 813**	**131 753**	**468 548**	**142 512**	**9 000**	**-1 219**	**90 831**	**500 402**
Algeria	2001	168 238	...	94 944	73 289	6	-478	779	123 897
	2002	176 262	...	99 499	76 759	5	68	1 062	129 014
	2003	183 893	...	106 283	77 587	23	-42	972	136 335
	2004	188 399	...	111 558	76 819	22	*102	1 235	141 768
Angola	2001	37 037	...	36 469	*481	87	124	448	34 794
	2002	44 706	...	44 045	563	98	-80	423	42 522
	2003	43 843	...	43 083	*653	107	-166	588	41 676
	2004	50 274	...	49 443	681	151	780	856	47 554
Benin	2001	35	...	35	...	0	17	823	238
	2002	40	...	40	...	0	19	998	299
	2003	20	...	20	...	0	11	1 133	344
	2004	*20	...	*20	...	0	21	1 296	456
Burkina Faso	2001	5	...	...	...	5	...	*347	0
	2002	6	...	...	...	6	...	*359	0
	2003	8	...	...	...	8	...	*364	0
	2004	9	...	...	...	9	...	*364	0
Burundi	2001	12	2	...	...	10	2	*87	...
	2002	13	2	...	...	11	0	*93	...
	2003	*13	2	...	...	*11	0	*86	...
	2004	*13	2	...	...	*11	0	*84	...
Cameroon	2001	7 324	...	7 025	...	299	-13	15	5 99[illegible]
	2002	6 713	...	6 439	...	274	-64	98	5 51[illegible]
	2003	7 038	...	6 735	...	303	-156	89	5 51[illegible]
	2004	6 974	...	6 637	...	337	3	33	5 47[illegible]
Cape Verde	2001	1	...	...	...	1	...	*76	...
	2002	0	...	...	...	0	...	*85	...
	2003	0	...	...	...	0	...	*89	...
	2004	1	...	...	...	1	...	*98	...
Central African Rep.	*2001	7	...	...	...	7	2	111	...
	2002	*7	...	...	...	*7	0	*111	...
	2003	*7	...	...	...	*7	0	*105	...
	2004	*7	...	...	...	*7	0	*105	...
Chad*	2001	...	...	...	...	...	...	60	...
	2002	...	...	...	...	...	...	59	...
	2003	...	...	...	...	...	...	58	...
	2004	...	...	...	...	...	...	61	...
Comoros*	2001	0	...	...	...	0	...	27	...
	2002	0	...	...	...	0	...	27	...
	2003	0	...	...	...	0	...	30	...
	2004	0	...	...	...	0	...	30	...
Congo	2001	12 895	0	12 749	116	29	...	26	12 48[illegible]
	2002	12 404	0	12 251	118	34	...	31	12 05[illegible]
	2003	11 322	0	11 177	*116	29	...	31	10 8[illegible]
	2004	11 360	0	11 209	*116	34	...	81	11 1[illegible]

0 Production, trade and consumption of commercial energy — Thousand metric tons of oil equivalent and kilograms per capita (*continued*)

Production, commerce et consommation d'énergie commerciale — Milliers de tonnes d'équivalent pétrole et kilogrammes par habitant (*suite*)

Bunkers - Soutes			Consumption - Consommation							
Air Avion	Sea Maritime	Unallocated Nondistribué	Per capita Par habitant	Total Totale	Solids Solides	Liquids Liquides	Gas Gaz	Electricity Electricité	Year Année	Région, pays ou zone
108 713	**140 648**	**248 407**	**1 322**	**8 282 648**	**2 276 747**	**3 213 417**	**2 330 768**	**461 716**	**2001**	**Monde**
110 729	**144 751**	**197 996**	**1 339**	**8 491 098**	**2 331 600**	**3 250 154**	**2 436 870**	**472 475**	**2002**	
112 082	**144 810**	**273 681**	**1 365**	**8 743 273**	**2 502 646**	**3 273 756**	**2 496 258**	**470 613**	**2003**	
121 792	**157 851**	**274 361**	**1 408**	**9 137 677**	**2 700 142**	**3 397 340**	**2 544 627**	**495 569**	**2004**	
4 690	**7 419**	**20 807**	**342**	**276 789**	**96 059**	**114 661**	**57 869**	**8 200**	**2001**	**Afrique**
4 538	**6 517**	**19 777**	**351**	**290 514**	**92 953**	**121 705**	**66 886**	**8 970**	**2002**	
4 488	**7 482**	**20 079**	**348**	**294 970**	**96 731**	**122 113**	**67 610**	**8 516**	**2003**	
4 480	**6 483**	**18 623**	**360**	**313 875**	**103 909**	**131 325**	**69 586**	**9 054**	**2004**	
*312	192	5 256	1 211	39 840	572	19 339	19 921	7	2001	Algérie
*319	243	4 726	1 276	42 954	714	20 557	21 680	3	2002	
*273	217	5 378	1 241	42 705	761	20 543	21 377	24	2003	
219	332	3 588	1 240	43 626	524	23 071	20 008	23	2004	
501	...	219	174	1 847	...	1 279	*481	87	2001	Angola
431	...	210	188	2 045	...	1 384	563	98	2002	
301	...	213	215	2 407	...	1 647	*653	107	2003	
343	...	-258	238	2 711	...	1 880	681	151	2004	
21	...	0	85	583	...	543	...	39	2001	Bénin
24	...	0	99	696	...	650	...	46	2002	
26	...	0	107	772	...	728	...	44	2003	
25	...	*0	100	814	...	764	...	50	2004	
...	...	...	*29	*352	0	*347	...	5	2001	Burkina Faso
...	...	...	*29	*365	0	*359	...	6	2002	
...	...	...	*29	*372	0	*364	...	8	2003	
...	...	...	*28	*373	0	*364	...	9	2004	
*9	...	...	*13	*88	2	*73	...	13	2001	Burundi
*9	...	...	*14	*97	2	*80	...	14	2002	
*9	...	...	*12	*90	2	*74	...	*14	2003	
*9	...	...	*12	*88	2	*72	...	*14	2004	
62	20	82	79	1 198	...	899	...	299	2001	Cameroun
71	18	64	78	1 205	...	931	...	274	2002	
71	14	433	79	1 249	...	945	...	303	2003	
71	15	158	80	1 281	...	944	...	337	2004	
...	*6	...	*175	*71	0	*70	...	1	2001	Cap-Vert
...	*6	...	*193	*79	0	*78	...	0	2002	
...	*6	...	*202	*83	0	*83	...	0	2003	
...	*7	...	*219	*91	0	*90	...	1	2004	
20	...	...	24	97	...	89	...	7	*2001	Rép. centrafricaine
*20	...	...	*24	*99	...	*91	...	*7	2002	
*21	...	...	*22	*92	...	*84	...	*7	2003	
*21	...	...	*22	*92	...	*84	...	*7	2004	
19	...	...	5	41	...	41	...	...	2001	Tchad*
19	...	...	5	40	...	40	...	...	2002	
19	...	...	4	39	...	39	...	...	2003	
19	...	...	4	42	...	42	...	...	2004	
...	...	...	45	27	...	27	...	0	2001	Comores*
...	...	...	44	27	...	27	...	0	2002	
...	...	...	47	30	...	30	...	0	2003	
...	...	...	46	30	...	30	...	0	2004	
...	...	24	126	410	0	238	116	55	2001	Congo
...	...	13	111	371	0	187	118	65	2002	
...	...	46	127	432	0	256	*116	60	2003	
...	...	-164	137	480	0	295	*116	69	2004	

50 Production, trade and consumption of commercial energy—Thousand metric tons of oil equivalent and kilograms per capita *(continued)*

Production, commerce et consommation d'énergie commerciale—Milliers de tonnes d'équivalent pétrole et kilogrammes par habitant *(suite)*

Region, country or area	Year Année	Primary energy production – Production d'énergie primaire Total Totale	Solids Solides	Liquids Liquides	Gas Gaz	Electricity Electricité	Changes in stocks Variations des stocks	Imports Importations	Exports Exportations
Côte d'Ivoire	2001	1 731	...	302	1 274	155	...	3 046	2 246
	2002	2 196	...	749	1 298	149	...	3 209	2 348
	2003	2 353	...	1 055	1 141	158	...	2 989	2 816
	2004	2 292	...	1 302	840	150	...	3 872	3 897
Dem. Rep. of the Congo	2001	1 800	69	1 225	...	506	...	500	1 338
	2002	1 743	71	1 151	...	521	...	505	1 267
	2003	1 693	73	1 083	...	536	...	513	1 202
	2004	1 696	76	1 033	...	587	...	689	1 163
Djibouti*	2001	...	...	...	...	...	...	563	...
	2002	...	...	...	...	...	...	573	...
	2003	...	...	...	...	...	...	582	...
	2004	...	...	...	...	...	...	582	...
Egypt	2001	61 468	34	39 787	20 456	1 191	1 440	4 141	11 044
	2002	66 456	26	39 989	25 122	1 319	187	2 873	9 896
	2003	70 207	26	40 699	28 399	1 082	*454	2 590	11 061
	2004	71 456	23	39 575	30 725	1 132	*-398	3 901	10 588
Equatorial Guinea	2001	10 440	...	10 440	*0	*0	...	*54	*10 440
	2002	12 040	...	11 597	*443	*0	...	*56	11 597
	2003	10 748	...	10 299	448	*0	...	*55	10 299
	2004	7 901	...	7 453	*447	*0	...	*48	7 098
Eritrea	2001	0	...	...	...	0	13	234	0
	2002	0	...	...	...	0	-22	191	0
	2003	0	...	...	...	0	21	258	0
	2004	0	...	...	...	0	-22	234	3
Ethiopia	2001	155	...	...	...	155	-234	1 910	...
	2002	175	...	...	...	175	-241	1 959	...
	2003	197	...	...	...	197	-272	2 046	...
	2004	217	...	...	...	217	-397	2 127	...
Gabon	2001	15 161	...	14 995	91	75	-104	174	14 388
	2002	14 156	...	13 975	102	79	-163	71	13 421
	2003	11 239	...	11 056	106	77	-163	116	10 703
	2004	10 930	...	10 736	117	77	-155	88	10 350
Gambia*	2001	...	...	...	...	...	...	96	2
	2002	...	...	...	...	...	...	97	2
	2003	...	...	...	...	...	...	97	2
	2004	...	...	...	...	...	...	98	2
Ghana	2001	568	...	...	...	568	0	2 451	376
	2002	433	...	...	...	433	-6	2 600	345
	2003	334	...	...	...	334	-6	2 607	224
	2004	454	...	...	...	454	0	2 491	278
Guinea*	2001	37	...	...	...	37	...	398	...
	2002	38	...	...	...	38	...	400	...
	2003	38	...	...	...	38	...	405	...
	2004	38	...	...	...	38	...	405	...
Guinea-Bissau*	2001	...	...	...	...	...	...	97	...
	2002	...	...	...	...	...	...	100	...
	2003	...	...	...	...	...	...	100	...
	2004	...	...	...	...	...	...	100	...
Kenya	2001	248	...	...	...	248	...	3 555	569
	2002	301	...	...	...	301	...	2 901	404
	2003	348	...	...	...	348	...	2 992	32[illegible]
	2004	336	...	...	...	336	...	3 667	424

50 Production, trade and consumption of commercial energy—Thousand metric tons of oil equivalent and kilograms per capita (*continued*)

Production, commerce et consommation d'énergie commerciale—Milliers de tonnes d'équivalent pétrole et kilogrammes par habitant (*suite*)

Bunkers - Soutes			Consumption - Consommation							
Air Avion	Sea Maritime	Unallocated Nondistribué	Per capita Par habitant	Total Totale	Solids Solides	Liquids Liquides	Gas Gaz	Electricity Electricité	Year Année	Région, pays ou zone
107	93	-239	151	2 570	...	1 240	1 274	55	2001	Côte d'Ivoire
*96	91	207	154	2 663	...	1 350	1 298	14	2002	
*108	91	281	116	2 046	...	862	1 141	43	2003	
92	91	287	101	1 797	...	928	840	29	2004	
*96	2	0	16	864	218	247	...	398	2001	Rép. dém. du Congo
*96	2	0	16	883	225	247	...	410	2002	
*97	2	0	16	904	232	249	...	422	2003	
121	2	0	19	1 099	251	385	...	463	2004	
70	363	...	185	129	...	129	...	...	2001	Djibouti*
75	378	...	165	119	...	119	...	...	2002	
80	380	...	163	122	...	122	...	...	2003	
80	380	...	158	122	...	122	...	...	2004	
491	2 643	4 908	697	45 084	824	22 629	20 456	1 176	2001	Egypte
480	1 963	4 372	795	52 431	647	25 386	25 122	1 276	2002	
490	2 737	4 569	795	53 486	476	24 336	27 667	1 007	2003	
712	1 843	4 843	842	57 769	893	28 423	27 381	1 072	2004	
...	...	0	*112	*54	...	*54	*0	*0	2001	Guinée équatoriale
...	...	0	*1 007	*499	...	*56	*443	*0	2002	
...	...	0	994	504	...	*55	448	*0	2003	
...	...	355	*957	*496	...	*48	*447	*0	2004	
11	8	...	55	202	...	202	...	0	2001	Erythrée
8	0	...	53	205	...	205	...	0	2002	
11	1	...	55	224	...	224	...	0	2003	
11	0	...	57	242	...	242	...	0	2004	
97	...	752	22	1 451	...	1 296	...	155	2001	Ethiopie
92	...	756	23	1 527	...	1 353	...	175	2002	
89	...	*760	24	1 666	...	1 469	...	197	2003	
100	...	*764	27	1 877	...	1 659	...	217	2004	
*72	144	256	456	578	...	412	91	75	2001	Gabon
*79	144	146	462	600	...	418	102	79	2002	
*72	145	-12	458	609	...	426	106	77	2003	
*60	149	1	450	613	...	419	117	77	2004	
...	...	...	66	94	...	94	...	...	2001	Gambie*
...	...	...	65	95	...	95	...	...	2002	
...	...	...	63	95	...	95	...	...	2003	
...	...	...	62	96	...	96	...	...	2004	
91	...	450	105	2 102	...	1 521	...	582	2001	Ghana
94	...	496	102	2 104	...	1 625	...	479	2002	
140	...	611	94	1 972	...	1 631	...	341	2003	
115	...	120	112	2 433	...	1 960	...	472	2004	
22	...	...	47	413	...	376	...	37	2001	Guinée*
22	...	...	47	415	...	378	...	38	2002	
22	...	...	47	421	...	383	...	38	2003	
22	...	...	46	421	...	383	...	38	2004	
10	...	...	66	86	...	86	...	...	2001	Guinée-Bissau*
10	...	...	67	90	...	90	...	...	2002	
10	...	...	66	90	...	90	...	...	2003	
10	...	...	65	90	...	90	...	...	2004	
...	84	285	92	2 865	47	2 555	...	263	2001	Kenya
...	84	-81	89	2 795	70	2 405	...	320	2002	
...	13	48	90	2 957	65	2 529	...	363	2003	
...	37	361	95	3 181	76	2 762	...	343	2004	

50 Production, trade and consumption of commercial energy—Thousand metric tons of oil equivalent and kilograms per capita (*continued*)

Production, commerce et consommation d'énergie commerciale—Milliers de tonnes d'équivalent pétrole et kilogrammes par habitant (*suite*)

Region, country or area	Year Année	Primary energy production – Production d'énergie primaire: Total Totale	Solids Solides	Liquids Liquides	Gas Gaz	Electricity Electricité	Changes in stocks Variations des stocks	Imports Importations	Exports Exportations
Liberia*	2001	...	...	...	...	...	...	159	
	2002	...	...	...	...	...	...	163	
	2003	...	...	...	...	...	...	166	
	2004	...	...	...	...	...	...	166	
Libyan Arab Jamah.	2001	72 445	...	66 836	5 609	...	...	...	53 7[illegible]
	2002	68 428	...	62 791	5 636	...	...	...	49 4[illegible]
	2003	76 752	...	70 943	5 809	...	...	...	57 3[illegible]
	2004	83 943	...	77 590	6 353	...	...	...	64 3[illegible]
Madagascar	2001	46	...	...	...	46	...	799	*[illegible]
	2002	46	...	...	...	46	...	802	*[illegible]
	2003	52	...	...	...	52	...	*805	*[illegible]
	2004	55	...	...	...	55	...	*808	*[illegible]
Malawi	2001	*129	34	...	...	*95	*-2	264	
	2002	*139	42	...	...	*97	0	272	
	2003	*148	46	...	...	*101	0	271	
	2004	*158	*49	...	...	*109	0	*284	*[illegible]
Mali	*2001	20	...	...	...	20	...	201	
	*2002	20	...	...	...	20	...	203	
	2003	*20	...	...	...	*20	...	201	
	2004	*21	...	...	...	*21	...	*210	
Mauritania	*2001	3	...	...	...	3	...	859	
	2002	*3	...	...	...	*3	...	844	
	*2003	3	...	...	...	3	...	849	
	*2004	3	...	...	...	3	...	853	
Mauritius	2001	6	...	...	...	6	6	1 219	
	2002	*7	...	...	...	*7	*-44	1 154	
	2003	10	...	...	...	10	-30	1 185	
	2004	10	...	...	...	10	14	1 260	
Morocco	2001	146	1	10	42	93	336	12 728	1 2[illegible]
	2002	143	0	13	40	90	-84	11 898	7[illegible]
	2003	192	0	10	39	143	93	11 404	2[illegible]
	2004	212	0	11	47	154	-194	12 723	7[illegible]
Mozambique	2001	778	20	...	1	757	27	793	6[illegible]
	2002	1 123	31	...	2	1 090	10	930	9[illegible]
	2003	937	26	...	2	909	30	1 006	7[illegible]
	2004	2 280	27	...	1 249	1 004	-20	1 377	2 0[illegible]
Niger*	2001	123	123	...	...	...	...	275	
	2002	125	125	...	...	...	...	281	
	2003	125	125	...	...	...	...	281	
	2004	125	125	...	...	...	...	282	
Nigeria	2001	131 386	2	116 979	13 887	518	698	3 558	115 5[illegible]
	2002	118 155	30	102 525	14 881	718	-159	4 756	101 0[illegible]
	2003	136 383	16	117 964	17 729	674	-396	7 501	124 3[illegible]
	2004	150 196	2	128 734	20 866	594	224	7 680	136 2[illegible]
Réunion	2001	48	...	...	...	48	...	769	
	2002	*49	...	...	...	*49	...	768	
	2003	*50	...	...	...	*50	...	*774	
	2004	*50	...	...	...	*50	...	*783	
Rwanda	2001	*14	...	...	*0	*14	...	*200	
	2002	*15	...	...	*0	*14	...	*207	
	2003	*15	...	...	*0	*14	...	*207	
	2004	*15	...	...	*0	*14	...	*195	

Production, trade and consumption of commercial energy—Thousand metric tons of oil equivalent and kilograms per capita *(continued)*

Production, commerce et consommation d'énergie commerciale—Milliers de tonnes d'équivalent pétrole et kilogrammes par habitant *(suite)*

Bunkers - Soutes			Consumption - Consommation							
Air Avion	Sea Maritime	Unallocated Nondistribué	Per capita Par habitant	Total Totale	Solids Solides	Liquids Liquides	Gas Gaz	Electricity Electricité	Year Année	Région, pays ou zone
3	12	...	52	143	...	143	...	...	2001	Libéria*
3	13	...	52	146	...	146	...	...	2002	
3	13	...	53	149	...	149	...	...	2003	
3	13	...	53	149	...	149	...	...	2004	
221	89	2 524	2 707	15 815	...	10 923	4 892	...	2001	Jamah. arabe libyenne
218	89	2 496	2 690	16 198	...	11 133	5 064	...	2002	
213	89	2 451	2 674	16 637	...	11 509	5 128	...	2003	
215	89	2 481	2 616	16 794	...	11 439	5 355	...	2004	
2	*17	146	*41	*660	*7	*608	...	46	2001	Madagascar
2	*17	143	*41	*667	*7	*614	...	46	2002	
*2	*17	*142	*40	*676	*7	*617	...	52	2003	
*2	*17	*145	*38	*679	*7	*617	...	55	2004	
...	...	...	36	390	56	240	...	*94	2001	Malawi
...	...	...	36	399	51	251	...	*96	2002	
...	...	...	35	407	37	270	...	*101	2003	
...	...	...	*34	*431	*40	*283	...	*109	2004	
18	...	...	20	203	...	183	...	20	*2001	Mali
18	...	...	19	206	...	185	...	20	*2002	
20	...	...	19	201	...	181	...	*20	2003	
21	...	...	*19	*210	...	*189	...	*21	2004	
18	32	...	295	812	4	805	...	3	*2001	Mauritanie
*18	*32	...	282	797	*4	790	...	*3	2002	
18	32	...	275	802	5	794	...	3	*2003	
18	35	...	269	804	5	796	...	3	*2004	
78	203	...	787	937	209	722	...	6	2001	Maurice
96	*169	...	783	940	*219	714	...	*7	2002	
92	135	...	825	998	221	766	...	10	2003	
91	146	...	835	1 019	202	806	...	10	2004	
287	13	1 038	342	9 980	3 571	6 142	42	225	2001	Maroc
291	13	1 011	340	10 087	3 682	6 156	40	208	2002	
301	13	669	340	10 223	3 423	6 496	39	264	2003	
331	*13	1 006	360	11 000	3 830	6 823	47	300	2004	
35	3	...	47	847	0	404	1	442	2001	Mozambique
32	5	...	57	1 061	6	416	2	637	2002	
22	38	...	59	1 101	15	441	2	642	2003	
36	43	...	80	1 563	16	638	3	906	2004	
23	...	...	35	376	123	234	...	18	2001	Niger*
24	...	...	34	381	125	238	...	18	2002	
24	...	...	33	381	125	238	...	18	2003	
25	...	...	32	382	125	238	...	19	2004	
432	435	1 028	143	16 798	*5	10 570	5 704	518	2001	Nigéria
388	427	1 004	167	20 194	33	11 864	7 578	718	2002	
400	574	700	146	18 206	18	10 767	6 747	674	2003	
197	523	719	155	19 963	4	10 354	9 011	594	2004	
...	82	...	1 005	736	...	688	...	48	2001	Réunion
...	80	...	992	738	...	689	...	*49	2002	
...	81	...	*985	*743	...	*694	...	*50	2003	
...	83	...	*980	*751	...	*701	...	*50	2004	
*10	...	...	*24	*204	...	*179	*0	*25	2001	Rwanda
*12	...	...	*24	*208	...	*180	*0	28	2002	
*12	...	...	*23	*209	...	*182	*0	*27	2003	
*12	...	...	*22	*197	...	*173	*0	*24	2004	

50 Production, trade and consumption of commercial energy—Thousand metric tons of oil equivalent and kilograms per capit (*continued*)

Production, commerce et consommation d'énergie commerciale—Milliers de tonnes d'équivalent pétrole et kilogrammes p habitant (*suite*)

Region, country or area	Year Année	Primary energy production – Production d'énergie primaire Total Totale	Solids Solides	Liquids Liquides	Gas Gaz	Electricity Electricité	Changes in stocks Variations des stocks	Imports Importations	Expor Exportatio
Saint Helena	2001	...	...	...	...	...	...	4	.
	2002	...	...	...	...	...	...	4	.
	2003	...	...	...	...	...	...	*4	.
	2004	...	...	...	...	...	...	3	.
Sao Tome and Principe*	2001	1	...	...	...	1	...	31	.
	2002	1	...	...	...	1	...	31	.
	2003	1	...	...	...	1	...	31	.
	2004	1	...	...	...	1	...	31	.
Senegal	2001	1	...	...	1	0	49	1 566	4
	2002	19	...	...	3	17	0	1 527	7
	2003	39	...	...	10	29	70	1 711	19
	2004	37	...	...	12	25	-94	1 809	18
Seychelles	2001	...	...	...	...	...	...	323	.
	2002	...	...	...	...	...	...	282	.
	*2003	...	...	...	...	...	...	287	.
	*2004	...	...	...	...	...	...	287	.
Sierra Leone	2001	...	...	...	...	...	...	*355	*
	2002	...	...	...	...	...	...	*365	*
	2003	...	...	...	...	...	...	*368	1
	2004	...	...	...	...	...	...	*481	2
South Africa[1]	2001	132 006	123 711	4 885	2 018	1 392	-1 058	29 653	45 34
	2002	130 407	121 896	4 960	2 001	1 551	528	32 380	47 49
	2003	133 925	126 682	4 492	1 199	1 552	1 178	29 562	43 49
	2004	137 277	128 889	4 840	1 843	1 706	-1 286	28 668	40 59
Sudan	2001	10 500	...	10 394	...	106	277	353	8 31
	2002	12 146	...	12 035	...	111	131	309	9 48
	2003	13 350	...	13 250	...	100	135	350	10 46
	2004	15 091	...	15 000	...	91	116	385	11 82
Togo	2001	8	...	...	...	8	-66	341	.
	2002	15	...	...	...	15	0	416	.
	2003	21	...	...	...	21	0	701	.
	2004	14	...	...	...	14	0	752	.
Tunisia	2001	5 421	...	3 386	2 028	7	212	5 377	3 84
	2002	5 461	...	3 519	1 934	8	116	5 435	3 96
	2003	5 188	...	3 202	1 969	17	113	5 409	3 57
	2004	5 702	...	3 408	2 276	17	21	5 959	3 94
Uganda	2001	143	...	...	...	143	...	471	*1
	2002	144	...	...	...	144	...	483	*1
	*2003	144	...	...	...	144	...	488	1
	2004	*163	...	...	...	*163	...	518	*1
United Rep. of Tanzania	2001	276	55	...	0	221	...	911	.
	2002	289	55	...	0	234	...	1 046	.
	2003	258	38	...	0	219	...	1 118	.
	2004	367	45	...	119	203	...	1 209	.
Western Sahara*	2001	...	...	...	...	...	...	85	.
	2002	...	...	...	...	...	...	85	.
	2003	...	...	...	...	...	...	85	..
	2004	...	...	...	...	...	...	85	..
Zambia	2001	799	120	...	...	679	45	572	10
	2002	821	124	...	...	697	52	597	7
	2003	840	130	...	...	710	56	627	5
	2004	865	137	...	...	727	56	657	3

50 **Production, trade and consumption of commercial energy**—Thousand metric tons of oil equivalent and kilograms per capita (*continued*)

Production, commerce et consommation d'énergie commerciale—Milliers de tonnes d'équivalent pétrole et kilogrammes par habitant (*suite*)

Bunkers - Soutes			Consumption - Consommation							
Air Avion	Sea Maritime	Unallocated Nondistribué	Per capita Par habitant	Total Totale	Solids Solides	Liquids Liquides	Gas Gaz	Electricity Electricité	Year Année	Région, pays ou zone
...	...	...	566	4	0	4	...	...	2001	Sainte-Hélène
...	...	...	562	4	0	4	...	...	2002	
...	...	...	*558	*4	0	*4	...	...	2003	
...	...	...	415	3	0	3	...	...	2004	
...	...	...	191	32	...	31	...	1	2001	Sao Tomé-et-Principe*
...	...	...	186	32	...	31	...	1	2002	
...	...	...	179	32	...	31	...	1	2003	
...	...	...	174	32	...	31	...	1	2004	
226	75	55	105	1 114	...	1 114	1	0	2001	Sénégal
186	75	3	112	1 214	...	1 194	3	17	2002	
*209	85	5	107	1 191	...	1 152	10	29	2003	
276	83	26	120	1 369	...	1 331	12	25	2004	
31	*81	...	2 609	211	...	211	...	...	2001	Seychelles
*24	*78	...	2 222	180	...	180	...	...	2002	
26	80	...	2 230	181	...	181	...	...	*2003	
26	80	...	2 230	181	...	181	...	...	*2004	
*47	*87	*63	*34	*154	0	*154	...	...	2001	Sierra Leone
*52	*88	*67	*32	*152	0	*152	...	...	2002	
*52	*88	*69	*27	*143	0	*143	...	...	2003	
54	*71	*84	44	252	0	252	...	...	2004	
901	2 704	3 759	2 156	110 011	87 555	18 643	2 018	1 795	2001	Afrique du Sud[1]
894	2 470	3 878	2 100	107 528	84 464	19 072	2 001	1 992	2002	
878	2 601	3 521	2 180	111 814	88 925	20 039	1 199	1 651	2003	
772	2 390	3 814	2 328	119 657	95 549	20 567	1 843	1 698	2004	
124	8	81	65	2 051	...	1 945	...	106	2001	Soudan
130	8	153	79	2 551	...	2 440	...	111	2002	
136	8	93	87	2 868	...	2 768	...	100	2003	
142	8	212	95	3 178	...	3 087	...	91	2004	
18	...	...	82	397	...	354	...	43	2001	Togo
24	...	...	82	407	...	364	...	43	2002	
74	...	...	127	648	...	598	...	50	2003	
87	...	...	113	679	...	635	...	44	2004	
...	0	83	689	6 662	67	3 715	2 872	8	2001	Tunisie
...	0	77	689	6 735	57	3 803	2 871	3	2002	
...	0	61	694	6 852	16	3 844	2 976	15	2003	
...	11	36	770	7 650	0	4 030	3 606	15	2004	
...	...	...	25	600	...	471	...	129	2001	Ouganda
...	...	...	25	612	...	483	...	129	2002	
...	...	...	24	617	...	488	...	129	*2003	
...	...	...	24	666	...	518	...	*148	2004	
65	23	0	32	1 099	55	823	0	221	2001	Rép.-Unie de Tanzanie
69	23	0	36	1 243	55	954	0	234	2002	
74	23	0	36	1 279	38	1 021	0	219	2003	
79	23	0	39	1 473	45	1 097	119	212	2004	
6	...	...	314	79	...	79	...	...	2001	Sahara occidental*
6	...	...	308	79	...	79	...	...	2002	
6	...	...	301	79	...	79	...	...	2003	
6	...	...	294	79	...	79	...	...	2004	
45	...	37	108	1 143	79	476	...	588	2001	Zambie
46	...	38	112	1 203	80	493	...	630	2002	
49	...	41	118	1 267	85	516	...	667	2003	
51	...	43	117	1 338	90	540	...	708	2004	

50 Production, trade and consumption of commercial energy—Thousand metric tons of oil equivalent and kilograms per capit (*continued*)

Production, commerce et consommation d'énergie commerciale—Milliers de tonnes d'équivalent pétrole et kilogrammes p habitant (*suite*)

Region, country or area	Year Année	Primary energy production – Production d'énergie primaire Total Totale	Solids Solides	Liquids Liquides	Gas Gaz	Electricity Electricité	Changes in stocks Variations des stocks	Imports Importations	Expor Exportatio
Zimbabwe	2001	3 078	2 820	...	...	258	-128	1 314	14
	2002	2 992	2 663	...	...	329	-124	1 240	14
	2003	2 876	2 415	...	...	461	-125	1 074	14
	2004	2 853	2 379	...	...	475	11	822	14
America, North	**2001**	**2 095 993**	**519 145**	**719 520**	**728 416**	**128 912**	**66 501**	**862 400**	**413 53**
	2002	**2 099 269**	**498 017**	**727 060**	**735 919**	**138 273**	**-20 616**	**842 863**	**418 57**
	2003	**2 082 350**	**481 383**	**738 323**	**725 882**	**136 762**	**-6 251**	**891 600**	**437 81**
	2004	**2 094 218**	**500 585**	**734 668**	**718 209**	**140 756**	**-3**	**948 384**	**455 44**
Antigua and Barbuda*	2001	...	...	...	...	...	...	171	
	2002	...	...	...	...	...	...	180	
	2003	...	...	...	...	...	...	190	
	2004	...	...	...	...	...	...	196	
Aruba	2001	120	...	120	...	...	...	*636	.
	2002	120	...	120	...	...	...	*652	.
	2003	120	...	120	...	...	...	*661	.
	2004	120	...	120	...	...	...	*661	.
Bahamas	*2001	...	...	...	...	...	2	2 915	2 09
	*2002	...	...	...	...	...	3	3 064	2 10
	*2003	...	...	...	...	...	50	3 163	2 20
	2004	...	...	...	...	...	0	*3 209	*2 24
Barbados	2001	93	...	63	30	...	-16	323	6
	2002	107	...	80	27	...	0	337	8
	2003	98	...	74	24	...	0	324	7
	2004	107	...	84	23	...	0	351	8
Belize	2001	8	...	...	...	8	...	272	.
	*2002	8	...	...	...	8	...	286	.
	*2003	9	...	...	...	9	...	300	.
	*2004	9	...	...	...	9	...	305	.
Bermuda*	2001	...	...	...	...	...	...	184	.
	2002	...	...	...	...	...	...	198	.
	2003	...	...	...	...	...	...	196	.
	2004	...	...	...	...	...	...	203	.
British Virgin Islands*	2001	...	...	...	...	...	...	20	.
	2002	...	...	...	...	...	...	23	.
	2003	...	...	...	...	...	...	26	.
	2004	...	...	...	...	...	...	29	.
Canada	2001	376 541	35 759	136 265	169 219	35 298	-2 572	71 970	207 89
	2002	382 997	32 919	143 013	170 380	36 686	-3 403	69 278	207 44
	2003	384 517	30 390	150 627	167 960	35 540	-4 339	76 138	203 65
	2004	393 509	32 622	156 203	167 463	37 221	-7 315	78 305	213 85
Cayman Islands*	2001	...	...	...	...	...	...	113	.
	2002	...	...	...	...	...	...	117	.
	2003	...	...	...	...	...	...	123	.
	2004	...	...	...	...	...	...	126	.
Costa Rica	2001	587	...	...	...	587	0	1 884	18
	2002	629	...	...	...	629	87	2 049	22
	2003	615	...	...	...	615	-4	2 104	10
	2004	668	...	...	...	668	-3	2 030	19
Cuba	2001	3 479	...	2 918	555	6	236	5 300	.
	2002	4 213	...	3 659	545	9	*-170	4 367	.
	2003	4 335	...	3 711	613	11	157	4 404	.
	2004	3 948	...	3 284	656	8	*134	5 257	.

Production, trade and consumption of commercial energy—Thousand metric tons of oil equivalent and kilograms per capita (*continued*)

Production, commerce et consommation d'énergie commerciale—Milliers de tonnes d'équivalent pétrole et kilogrammes par habitant (*suite*)

Bunkers - Soutes		Consumption - Consommation								
Air Avion	Sea Maritime	Unallocated Nondistribué	Per capita Par habitant	Total Totale	Solids Solides	Liquids Liquides	Gas Gaz	Electricity Electricité	Year Année	Région, pays ou zone
89	...	...	362	4 287	2 664	1 016	...	607	2001	Zimbabwe
62	...	...	348	4 149	2 511	964	...	674	2002	
35	...	...	324	3 895	2 280	881	...	735	2003	
7	...	...	272	3 513	2 251	612	...	650	2004	
21 695	**24 640**	**17 793**	**4 907**	**2 414 232**	**479 328**	**1 103 797**	**702 278**	**128 830**	**2001**	**Amérique du Nord**
21 137	**28 089**	**2 302**	**4 999**	**2 492 640**	**484 740**	**1 115 925**	**753 444**	**138 531**	**2002**	
20 609	**23 835**	**19 395**	**4 921**	**2 478 545**	**488 603**	**1 128 608**	**724 677**	**136 657**	**2003**	
20 989	**29 334**	**17 465**	**4 942**	**2 519 370**	**497 307**	**1 161 956**	**719 362**	**140 744**	**2004**	
45	...	...	1 760	118	...	118	...	...	2001	Antigua-et-Barbuda*
50	...	...	1 852	124	...	124	...	...	2002	
48	...	...	1 959	133	...	133	...	...	2003	
50	...	...	2 024	138	...	138	...	...	2004	
*70	...	*445	*3 445	*241	...	*241	...	...	2001	Aruba
*73	...	*450	*3 527	*248	...	*248	...	...	2002	
*75	...	*455	*3 538	*251	...	*251	...	...	2003	
*75	...	*455	*3 519	*251	...	*251	...	...	2004	
37	184	...	2 032	595	1	594	...	...	*2001	Bahamas
40	229	...	2 332	688	1	686	...	...	*2002	
43	244	...	2 084	619	2	617	...	...	*2003	
*44	*254	...	*2 217	*664	*2	*662	...	...	2004	
...	...	-2	1 385	371	...	341	30	...	2001	Barbade
...	...	-1	1 357	365	...	338	27	...	2002	
...	...	-1	1 293	349	...	325	24	...	2003	
...	...	-1	1 383	375	...	352	23	...	2004	
17	*12	...	980	252	...	241	...	11	2001	Belize
19	12	...	994	263	...	253	...	11	*2002	
22	12	...	1 028	275	...	264	...	11	*2003	
23	12	...	1 018	279	...	268	...	11	*2004	
17	3	...	2 659	165	...	165	...	...	2001	Bermudes*
19	3	...	2 842	176	...	176	...	...	2002	
17	3	...	2 842	176	...	176	...	...	2003	
18	3	...	2 811	183	...	183	...	...	2004	
...	...	...	979	20	...	20	...	...	2001	Iles Vierges britanniques*
...	...	...	1 079	23	...	23	...	...	2002	
...	...	...	1 171	26	...	26	...	...	2003	
...	...	...	1 311	29	...	29	...	...	2004	
1 053	1 173	-8 446	8 040	249 407	27 300	108 932	79 866	33 309	2001	Canada
907	882	-10 118	8 181	256 559	26 127	113 970	81 498	34 963	2002	
699	507	-8 415	8 482	268 547	26 284	118 720	88 587	34 956	2003	
885	617	-8 896	8 535	272 668	25 689	123 922	86 735	36 321	2004	
19	...	...	2 303	94	...	94	...	...	2001	Iles Caïmanes*
21	...	...	2 413	97	...	97	...	...	2002	
22	...	...	2 422	102	...	102	...	...	2003	
23	...	...	2 407	104	...	104	...	...	2004	
...	...	46	559	2 241	0	1 676	...	565	2001	Costa Rica
...	...	74	559	2 287	18	1 677	...	593	2002	
...	...	148	593	2 472	49	1 815	...	608	2003	
...	...	233	536	2 276	39	1 589	...	648	2004	
187	95	210	716	8 051	9	7 481	555	6	2001	Cuba
202	68	325	723	8 155	9	7 592	545	9	2002	
221	67	820	661	7 475	9	6 841	613	11	2003	
223	72	351	743	8 425	9	7 752	656	8	2004	

50 Production, trade and consumption of commercial energy—Thousand metric tons of oil equivalent and kilograms per capita (*continued*)

Production, commerce et consommation d'énergie commerciale—Milliers de tonnes d'équivalent pétrole et kilogrammes par habitant (*suite*)

Region, country or area	Year Année	Primary energy production – Production d'énergie primaire Total Totale	Solids Solides	Liquids Liquides	Gas Gaz	Electricity Electricité	Changes in stocks Variations des stocks	Imports Importations	Exports Exportations
Dominica	2001	2	...	...	...	2	...	38	...
	2002	3	...	...	...	3	...	35	...
	2003	2	...	...	...	2	...	38	...
	2004	3	...	...	...	3	...	36	...
Dominican Republic	2001	48	...	...	...	48	0	6 289	...
	2002	75	...	...	...	75	0	6 641	...
	2003	143	...	...	...	143	0	6 479	...
	2004	170	...	...	...	170	36	6 066	...
El Salvador	2001	183	...	...	...	183	-21	2 204	320
	2002	183	...	...	...	183	17	2 235	318
	2003	209	...	...	...	209	44	2 239	188
	2004	200	...	...	...	200	39	2 284	274
Greenland	2001	...	...	...	...	...	...	*194	*7
	2002	...	...	...	...	...	...	*195	*7
	2003	...	...	...	...	...	...	*196	*7
	2004	...	...	...	...	...	...	197	*7
Grenada	2001	...	...	...	...	...	1	83	...
	2002	...	...	...	...	...	0	81	...
	2003	...	...	...	...	...	0	83	...
	2004	...	...	...	...	...	0	82	...
Guadeloupe*	2001	...	...	...	...	...	...	601	...
	2002	...	...	...	...	...	...	624	...
	2003	...	...	...	...	...	...	635	...
	2004	...	...	...	...	...	...	642	...
Guatemala	2001	1 315	...	1 149	...	166	-82	3 195	1 090
	2002	1 490	...	1 344	...	146	0	3 402	1 297
	2003	1 560	...	1 347	...	213	0	3 350	1 384
	2004	1 216	...	1 007	...	209	26	3 846	993
Haiti	2001	*24	...	...	...	*24	...	533	...
	2002	*21	...	...	...	*21	...	549	...
	2003	*23	...	...	...	*23	...	538	...
	2004	*24	...	...	...	*24	...	561	...
Honduras	2001	204	...	...	...	204	162	1 866	[illegible]
	2002	211	...	...	...	211	242	2 052	[illegible]
	2003	187	...	...	...	187	243	2 204	18
	2004	202	...	...	...	202	5	2 278	2
Jamaica	2001	5	...	...	...	5	0	3 657	8
	2002	8	...	...	...	8	-116	3 486	10
	2003	13	...	...	...	13	35	3 802	12
	2004	14	...	...	...	14	12	3 738	12
Martinique	2001	...	...	...	...	...	...	*898	*21
	2002	...	...	...	...	...	...	*961	*22
	2003	...	...	...	...	...	...	*666	*22
	*2004	...	...	...	...	...	...	674	22
Mexico	2001	218 600	3 524	176 292	35 100	3 684	48	21 824	96 76
	2002	221 836	3 343	179 047	35 994	3 452	442	22 659	101 94
	2003	233 827	2 944	190 001	37 726	3 157	-949	22 525	109 39
	2004	237 911	3 044	191 899	39 440	3 528	1 643	24 544	109 24
Montserrat*	2001	...	...	...	...	...	...	18	...
	2002	...	...	...	...	...	...	20	...
	2003	...	...	...	...	...	...	22	...
	2004	...	...	...	...	...	...	22	...

50 Production, trade and consumption of commercial energy—Thousand metric tons of oil equivalent and kilograms per capita *(continued)*

Production, commerce et consommation d'énergie commerciale—Milliers de tonnes d'équivalent pétrole et kilogrammes par habitant *(suite)*

Bunkers - Soutes			Consumption - Consommation							
Air Avion	Sea Maritime	Unallocated Nondistribué	Per capita Par habitant	Total Totale	Solids Solides	Liquids Liquides	Gas Gaz	Electricity Electricité	Year Année	Région, pays ou zone
...	...	...	573	41	...	38	...	2	2001	Dominique
...	...	...	545	38	...	35	...	3	2002	
...	...	...	582	41	...	38	...	2	2003	
...	...	...	558	39	...	36	...	3	2004	
76	...	604	663	5 656	142	5 466	0	48	2001	Rép. dominicaine
80	...	487	709	6 149	163	5 911	0	75	2002	
92	...	630	669	5 900	740	5 012	4	143	2003	
*93	...	112	669	5 995	544	5 276	5	170	2004	
72	...	80	303	1 935	1	1 725	...	210	2001	El Salvador
66	...	44	303	1 973	1	1 756	...	216	2002	
70	...	32	319	2 114	0	1 878	...	236	2003	
77	...	-32	315	2 127	0	1 894	...	233	2004	
...	...	...	*3 308	*186	0	*186	...	...	2001	Groenland
...	...	...	*3 324	*187	0	*187	...	...	2002	
...	...	...	*3 342	*188	0	*188	...	...	2003	
...	...	...	3 360	189	0	189	...	...	2004	
*7	...	...	793	75	...	75	...	...	2001	Grenade
*7	...	...	782	73	...	73	...	...	2002	
*8	...	...	930	75	...	75	...	...	2003	
*8	...	...	925	74	...	74	...	...	2004	
95	...	...	1 170	506	...	506	...	...	2001	Guadeloupe*
102	...	...	1 195	522	...	522	...	...	2002	
103	...	...	1 210	531	...	531	...	...	2003	
103	...	...	1 211	538	...	538	...	...	2004	
46	122	179	270	3 155	140	2 870	...	145	2001	Guatemala
37	122	109	277	3 327	273	2 941	...	113	2002	
41	122	0	278	3 363	258	2 926	...	179	2003	
44	122	280	290	3 597	323	3 102	...	173	2004	
35	...	...	61	522	...	498	...	*24	2001	Haïti
35	...	...	62	535	...	514	...	*21	2002	
27	...	...	60	533	...	511	...	*23	2003	
24	...	...	62	561	...	537	...	*24	2004	
23	...	...	283	1 884	86	1 567	...	231	2001	Honduras
24	...	...	293	1 998	99	1 652	...	247	2002	
26	...	...	301	2 104	118	1 770	...	215	2003	
*29	...	...	337	2 419	122	2 064	...	233	2004	
161	30	216	1 220	3 170	37	3 128	...	5	2001	Jamaïque
195	30	35	1 237	3 243	62	3 173	...	8	2002	
195	30	24	1 283	3 400	59	3 328	...	13	2003	
*186	*25	57	1 252	3 350	46	3 290	...	14	2004	
21	*40	*51	*1 370	*573	...	*573	...	...	2001	Martinique
22	*44	*74	*1 410	*596	...	*596	...	...	2002	
22	*44	*-224	*1 406	*599	...	*599	...	...	2003	
23	45	-235	1 434	616	...	616	...	...	*2004	
2 641	1 107	7 243	1 321	132 621	5 032	85 562	38 338	3 689	2001	Mexique
2 571	796	6 105	1 302	132 636	5 158	81 412	42 597	3 469	2002	
2 593	815	7 001	1 331	137 503	5 638	82 139	46 643	3 082	2003	
2 491	773	5 315	1 365	142 992	5 070	85 907	48 570	3 445	2004	
...	1	...	2 067	17	...	17	...	...	2001	Montserrat*
...	1	...	2 325	19	...	19	...	...	2002	
...	1	...	2 296	21	...	21	...	...	2003	
...	1	...	2 235	21	...	21	...	...	2004	

50 Production, trade and consumption of commercial energy — Thousand metric tons of oil equivalent and kilograms per cap *(continued)*

Production, commerce et consommation d'énergie commerciale — Milliers de tonnes d'équivalent pétrole et kilogrammes habitant *(suite)*

Region, country or area	Year Année	Primary energy production – Production d'énergie primaire Total Totale	Solids Solides	Liquids Liquides	Gas Gaz	Electricity Electricité	Changes in stocks Variations des stocks	Imports Importations	Expo[rts] Exportati[ons]
Netherlands Antilles	2001	...	...	...	...	...	...	15 271	9
	2002	...	...	...	...	...	...	13 679	8 3
	2003	...	...	...	...	...	...	13 260	8 0
	2004	...	...	...	...	...	...	13 827	8 0
Nicaragua	2001	35	...	...	...	35	26	1 330	
	2002	32	...	...	...	32	-35	1 279	
	2003	49	...	...	...	49	37	1 378	
	2004	50	...	...	...	50	-35	1 370	
Panama	2001	215	...	...	...	215	79	2 915	6
	2002	292	...	...	...	292	-155	2 143	4
	2003	243	...	...	...	243	-20	2 054	2
	2004	325	...	...	...	325	-608	1 350	2
Puerto Rico	2001	18	...	...	...	18	...	587	
	2002	19	...	...	...	19	...	587	
	2003	22	...	...	...	22	...	689	
	2004	12	...	...	...	12	...	634	
Saint Kitts and Nevis*	2001	...	...	...	...	...	...	34	
	2002	...	...	...	...	...	...	38	
	2003	...	...	...	...	...	...	42	
	2004	...	...	...	...	...	...	42	
Saint Lucia	2001	...	...	...	...	...	...	119	
	2002	...	...	...	...	...	...	97	
	2003	...	...	...	...	...	...	118	
	2004	...	...	...	...	...	...	123	
Saint Pierre and Miquelon	2001	...	...	...	...	...	...	*22	
	*2002	...	...	...	...	...	...	24	
	*2003	...	...	...	...	...	...	28	
	*2004	...	...	...	...	...	...	27	
Saint Vincent-Grenadines	2001	2	...	...	...	2	...	59	
	2002	2	...	...	...	2	...	62	
	*2003	3	...	...	...	3	...	65	
	*2004	3	...	...	...	3	...	67	
Trinidad and Tobago	2001	20 191	...	7 099	13 092	...	215	5 017	12 9
	2002	23 440	...	8 186	15 254	...	290	4 728	14 7
	2003	31 831	...	8 620	23 210	...	324	4 702	22 4
	2004	30 798	...	6 336	24 462	...	290	3 449	21 4
United States	2001	1 474 322	479 861	395 614	510 421	88 425	68 423	711 859	81 4
	2002	1 463 580	461 755	391 610	513 719	96 495	-17 818	696 737	81 1
	2003	1 424 545	448 050	383 823	496 347	96 325	-1 829	738 859	89 7
	2004	1 424 929	464 919	375 735	486 164	98 110	5 773	791 853	98 3
America, South	**2001**	**521 974**	**38 257**	**351 518**	**87 239**	**44 960**	**1 750**	**85 179**	**255 8**
	2002	**508 196**	**37 834**	**337 895**	**85 658**	**46 809**	**13 140**	**83 078**	**241 9**
	2003	**509 848**	**41 177**	**330 949**	**88 746**	**48 975**	**5 442**	**80 880**	**239 5**
	2004	**541 292**	**43 782**	**348 692**	**98 286**	**50 534**	**-353**	**90 335**	**264 0**
Argentina	2001	83 174	120	42 043	37 215	3 797	-9	2 802	27 5
	2002	79 835	57	40 439	35 747	3 593	179	2 142	26 1
	2003	83 044	53	39 678	39 747	3 567	-38	1 707	25 1
	2004	85 978	30	39 157	43 483	3 307	-115	2 299	22 8
Bolivia	2001	6 411	...	1 939	4 289	183	-192	354	3 8
	2002	7 337	...	1 925	5 223	189	-268	300	4 9
	2003	8 279	...	1 978	6 108	193	11	329	4 2
	2004	10 617	...	1 939	8 494	185	0	193	7 9

50 Production, trade and consumption of commercial energy — Thousand metric tons of oil equivalent and kilograms per capita *(continued)*

Production, commerce et consommation d'énergie commerciale — Milliers de tonnes d'équivalent pétrole et kilogrammes par habitant *(suite)*

Bunkers - Soutes			Consumption - Consommation							
Air Avion	Sea Maritime	Unallocated Nondistribué	Per capita Par habitant	Total Totale	Solids Solides	Liquids Liquides	Gas Gaz	Electricity Electricité	Year Année	Région, pays ou zone
71	1 709	2 064	9 259	1 611	...	1 611	...	...	2001	Antilles néerlandaises
75	1 704	1 690	10 583	1 841	...	1 841	...	...	2002	
80	1 712	1 877	8 736	1 564	...	1 564	...	...	2003	
84	1 720	1 680	10 320	2 250	...	2 250	...	...	2004	
25	...	66	236	1 230	...	1 193	...	36	2001	Nicaragua
15	...	68	234	1 251	...	1 218	...	33	2002	
12	...	73	244	1 287	...	1 239	...	48	2003	
11	...	52	253	1 360	...	1 310	...	50	2004	
5	...	242	714	2 145	44	1 892	...	208	2001	Panama
2	...	113	651	1 993	31	1 671	...	291	2002	
2	...	0	676	2 106	0	1 878	...	228	2003	
0	...	0	650	2 063	1	1 748	...	314	2004	
...	...	...	158	605	...	...	587	18	2001	Porto Rico
...	...	...	157	606	...	...	587	19	2002	
...	...	...	183	712	...	...	689	22	2003	
...	...	...	166	646	...	...	634	12	2004	
...	...	...	869	34	...	34	...	...	2001	Saint-Kitts-et-Nevis*
...	...	...	974	38	...	38	...	...	2002	
...	...	...	1 080	42	...	42	...	...	2003	
...	...	...	1 080	42	...	42	...	...	2004	
...	...	...	752	119	...	119	...	...	2001	Sainte-Lucie
...	...	...	608	97	...	97	...	...	2002	
...	...	...	732	118	...	118	...	...	2003	
...	...	...	749	123	...	123	...	...	2004	
...	4	...	*2 625	*18	...	*18	...	...	2001	Saint-Pierre-et-Miquelon
...	5	...	2 770	19	...	19	...	...	*2002	
...	6	...	3 065	21	...	21	...	...	*2003	
...	6	...	2 920	20	...	20	...	...	*2004	
...	...	...	528	61	...	59	...	2	2001	Saint Vincent-Grenadines
...	...	...	555	64	...	62	...	2	2002	
...	...	...	578	68	...	65	...	3	*2003	
...	...	...	595	70	...	67	...	3	*2004	
61	339	394	8 689	11 295	...	1 271	10 024	...	2001	Trinité-et-Tobago
8	668	676	9 001	11 755	...	1 257	10 498	...	2002	
8	744	543	9 581	12 476	...	1 380	11 096	...	2003	
6	898	-1 397	9 929	12 973	...	1 322	11 651	...	2004	
16 910	19 820	14 401	6 971	1 985 218	446 536	875 484	572 878	90 319	2001	Etats-Unis
16 566	23 525	2 170	7 125	2 054 694	452 799	885 747	617 691	98 457	2002	
16 183	19 528	16 433	6 958	2 023 356	455 445	894 014	577 019	96 877	2003	
16 469	24 786	19 491	6 980	2 051 914	465 462	916 281	571 088	99 082	2004	
1 915	**5 633**	**18 586**	**917**	**323 380**	**22 216**	**169 684**	**86 599**	**44 881**	**2001**	**Amérique du Sud**
1 898	**5 749**	**8 621**	**894**	**319 956**	**21 050**	**166 954**	**85 276**	**46 676**	**2002**	
2 118	**5 538**	**17 362**	**884**	**320 705**	**22 027**	**161 067**	**88 784**	**48 827**	**2003**	
2 763	**5 886**	**17 397**	**929**	**341 907**	**22 996**	**171 143**	**97 226**	**50 543**	**2004**	
...	570	3 444	1 451	54 404	340	18 649	31 467	3 947	2001	Argentine
...	502	3 336	1 365	51 787	290	16 992	30 404	4 102	2002	
...	588	3 162	1 476	55 890	524	17 708	33 658	4 000	2003	
...	542	5 019	1 568	59 931	463	19 792	36 070	3 606	2004	
...	...	421	311	2 651	...	1 755	712	184	2001	Bolivie
...	...	457	287	2 502	...	1 603	708	190	2002	
...	...	335	439	3 964	...	1 670	2 101	194	2003	
...	...	-324	350	3 231	...	1 505	1 541	185	2004	

50 Production, trade and consumption of commercial energy—Thousand metric tons of oil equivalent and kilograms per capita (*continued*)

Production, commerce et consommation d'énergie commerciale—Milliers de tonnes d'équivalent pétrole et kilogrammes par habitant (*suite*)

Region, country or area	Year Année	Primary energy production – Production d'énergie primaire Total Totale	Solids Solides	Liquids Liquides	Gas Gaz	Electricity Electricité	Changes in stocks Variations des stocks	Imports Importations	Exports Exportations
Brazil	2001	109 933	4 175	74 649	6 847	24 261	-3 557	51 733	12 907
	2002	121 521	3 798	83 147	8 787	25 789	-2 126	49 382	19 902
	2003	127 292	3 429	86 941	9 495	27 427	624	44 696	20 787
	2004	129 451	3 985	86 852	10 032	28 582	-876	51 508	22 419
Chile	2001	4 728	403	508	1 953	1 864	303	18 381	681
	2002	4 774	303	476	2 001	1 994	384	19 021	784
	2003	4 540	403	433	1 760	1 944	388	20 351	1 219
	2004	4 143	132	432	*1 750	1 829	964	22 528	998
Colombia	2001	68 726	28 237	31 317	6 438	2 734	232	478	45 108
	2002	67 826	28 502	29 971	6 432	2 921	3 065	479	41 419
	2003	70 010	32 517	28 223	6 157	3 114	616	334	45 393
	2004	71 559	34 900	26 877	*6 481	*3 301	8	319	48 347
Ecuador	2001	22 036	...	21 195	233	608	457	1 403	14 817
	2002	21 426	...	20 543	236	647	718	1 695	14 067
	2003	22 504	...	21 499	388	617	1 133	1 530	14 911
	2004	28 430	...	27 386	407	637	305	2 108	20 335
Falkland Is. (Malvinas)*	2001	3	3	...	...	...	...	10	...
	2002	3	3	...	...	...	...	10	...
	2003	3	3	...	...	...	...	11	...
	2004	3	3	...	...	...	...	11	...
French Guiana	*2001	...	...	...	...	...	...	320	...
	2002	...	...	...	...	...	...	325	...
	*2003	...	...	...	...	...	...	326	...
	*2004	...	...	...	...	...	...	326	...
Guyana	2001	...	...	...	...	...	0	516	..
	2002	...	...	...	...	...	-1	524	..
	2003	...	...	...	...	...	0	508	..
	2004	...	...	...	...	...	0	492	..
Paraguay	2001	3 896	...	0	...	3 896	20	1 192	3 36
	2002	4 145	...	0	...	4 145	11	1 259	3 59
	2003	4 451	...	0	...	4 451	-71	1 226	3 88
	2004	4 464	...	0	...	4 464	-11	1 292	3 86
Peru	2001	7 638	12	5 401	709	1 515	48	5 662	3 07
	2002	7 731	15	5 415	749	1 551	662	6 091	3 26
	2003	7 736	10	5 327	805	1 594	1 030	7 004	3 80
	2004	8 097	11	5 235	*1 165	1 687	-432	6 272	3 06
Suriname	2001	758	...	643	...	115	...	230	13
	2002	731	...	615	...	116	...	248	13
	2003	705	...	588	...	117	...	268	12
	2004	730	...	612	...	118	...	272	14
Uruguay	2001	791	...	...	...	791	-22	2 098	21
	2002	820	...	...	...	820	-241	1 601	25
	2003	733	...	...	...	733	130	2 029	24
	2004	411	...	...	...	411	76	2 716	39
Venezuela (Bolivarian Rep. of)	2001	213 881	5 306	173 823	29 554	5 198	4 468	0	144 13
	2002	192 047	5 155	155 363	26 483	5 045	10 757	0	127 37
	2003	180 550	4 762	146 281	24 288	5 219	1 618	561	119 73
	2004	197 409	4 721	160 202	26 473	6 013	-271	0	133 65
Asia	**2001**	**3 260 032**	**1 048 245**	**1 557 184**	**555 138**	**99 465**	**-4 204**	**1 261 086**	**1 440 06**
	2002	**3 284 596**	**1 096 594**	**1 493 483**	**594 004**	**100 514**	**6 302**	**1 305 924**	**1 383 73**
	2003	**3 577 698**	**1 249 318**	**1 596 696**	**630 643**	**101 042**	**6 445**	**1 365 715**	**1 492 81**
	2004	**3 867 965**	**1 413 205**	**1 679 509**	**661 751**	**113 501**	**10 716**	**1 512 575**	**1 617 91**

0

Production, trade and consumption of commercial energy—Thousand metric tons of oil equivalent and kilograms per capita *(continued)*

Production, commerce et consommation d'énergie commerciale—Milliers de tonnes d'équivalent pétrole et kilogrammes par habitant *(suite)*

Bunkers - Soutes			Consumption - Consommation							
Air Avion	Sea Maritime	Unallocated Nondistribué	Per capita Par habitant	Total Totale	Solids Solides	Liquids Liquides	Gas Gaz	Electricity Electricité	Year Année	Région, pays ou zone
585	3 335	9 206	801	139 190	15 876	84 689	11 110	27 515	2001	Brésil
722	3 661	8 721	794	140 023	14 776	82 560	13 753	28 934	2002	
1 100	3 219	6 960	778	139 299	15 322	79 185	14 171	30 621	2003	
1 090	3 348	6 641	817	148 337	15 950	83 079	17 512	31 796	2004	
57	243	576	1 380	21 249	2 860	10 181	6 345	1 864	2001	Chili
2	194	897	1 381	21 534	2 907	10 144	6 490	1 994	2002	
6	372	585	1 401	22 321	2 864	10 186	7 159	2 111	2003	
4	479	-95	1 511	24 322	3 888	10 968	7 474	1 992	2004	
625	231	2 082	486	20 926	2 723	9 045	6 438	2 720	2001	Colombie
629	232	1 708	485	21 253	2 445	9 508	6 432	2 868	2002	
589	249	2 308	475	21 188	2 746	9 268	6 157	3 018	2003	
587	303	1 486	467	21 147	1 941	9 565	*6 481	*3 160	2004	
...	257	691	560	7 217	...	6 374	233	610	2001	Equateur
...	266	750	558	7 321	...	6 434	236	652	2002	
...	258	649	551	7 083	...	5 981	388	714	2003	
...	226	2 557	546	7 116	...	5 930	407	779	2004	
...	...	...	4 386	13	3	10	...	...	2001	Iles Falkland (Malvinas)*
...	...	...	4 386	13	3	10	...	...	2002	
...	...	...	4 725	14	3	11	...	...	2003	
...	...	...	4 725	14	3	11	...	...	2004	
4	...	...	1 857	316	...	316	...	...	*2001	Guyane française
*4	...	...	1 837	322	...	322	...	...	2002	
4	...	...	1 779	322	...	322	...	...	*2003	
4	...	...	1 683	322	...	322	...	...	*2004	
13	...	...	659	503	...	503	...	...	2001	Guyana
12	...	...	670	512	...	512	...	...	2002	
12	...	...	648	496	...	496	...	...	2003	
12	...	...	626	479	...	479	...	...	2004	
7	...	0	301	1 697	...	1 165	...	531	2001	Paraguay
20	...	1	307	1 775	...	1 222	...	554	2002	
26	...	1	310	1 836	...	1 269	...	567	2003	
18	...	2	310	1 879	...	1 283	...	595	2004	
358	...	-294	384	10 114	366	7 524	709	1 515	2001	Pérou
201	...	-686	388	10 376	610	7 465	749	1 551	2002	
139	...	-894	393	10 658	525	7 734	805	1 594	2003	
443	...	-10	410	11 302	750	7 701	*1 165	1 687	2004	
...	...	197	1 557	652	...	538	...	115	2001	Suriname
...	...	161	1 630	686	...	570	...	116	2002	
...	...	137	1 671	707	...	590	...	117	2003	
...	...	144	1 631	716	...	598	...	118	2004	
...	343	141	658	2 211	1	1 495	31	683	2001	Uruguay
...	325	70	595	2 013	1	1 319	21	671	2002	
...	336	47	587	2 001	1	1 268	59	673	2003	
...	340	45	663	2 275	1	1 560	103	611	2004	
265	654	2 123	2 515	62 237	47	27 439	29 554	5 198	2001	Venezuela (Rép. Bolivar. du)
307	569	-6 795	2 372	59 838	17	28 293	26 483	5 045	2002	
241	517	4 071	2 136	54 926	41	25 378	24 288	5 219	2003	
606	649	1 931	2 329	60 836	0	28 350	26 473	6 013	2004	
27 761	**54 713**	**171 909**	**760**	**2 830 875**	**1 170 878**	**1 015 616**	**544 027**	**100 354**	**2001**	**Asie**
31 201	**55 218**	**153 543**	**785**	**2 960 521**	**1 228 612**	**1 040 500**	**590 023**	**101 386**	**2002**	
31 358	**58 435**	**190 648**	**831**	**3 163 716**	**1 375 605**	**1 059 888**	**626 955**	**101 268**	**2003**	
36 745	**63 293**	**195 282**	**898**	**3 456 588**	**1 558 697**	**1 131 144**	**653 242**	**113 506**	**2004**	

50 Production, trade and consumption of commercial energy — Thousand metric tons of oil equivalent and kilograms per capi (*continued*)

Production, commerce et consommation d'énergie commerciale — Milliers de tonnes d'équivalent pétrole et kilogrammes p habitant (*suite*)

Region, country or area	Year Année	Primary energy production – Production d'énergie primaire Total Totale	Solids Solides	Liquids Liquides	Gas Gaz	Electricity Electricité	Changes in stocks Variations des stocks	Imports Importations	Expo Exportati
Afghanistan	2001	*145	18	...	*102	*25	*10	*128	
	2002	69	15	...	7	48	0	*98	
	2003	85	24	...	6	54	0	*100	
	2004	75	24	...	3	48	0	197	
Armenia	2001	254	...	...	...	254	...	1 645	
	2002	339	...	...	...	339	...	1 322	
	2003	342	...	...	...	342	...	1 470	
	2004	361	...	...	...	361	...	1 586	
Azerbaijan	2001	20 015	...	14 919	4 984	112	114	3 164	10 6
	2002	20 150	...	15 344	4 632	174	-101	3 775	11 5
	2003	20 221	...	15 391	4 618	212	-3	3 886	10 9
	2004	20 457	...	15 565	4 655	237	42	4 861	11 4
Bahrain	2001	15 306	...	9 504	5 802	...	-366	2 883	9 7
	2002	15 720	...	9 611	6 108	...	-549	3 174	9 9
	2003	16 098	...	9 798	6 300	...	-603	3 283	10 3
	2004	16 333	...	9 781	6 552	...	-315	3 326	9 9
Bangladesh	2001	9 364	...	100	9 178	85	30	4 216	
	2002	9 840	...	93	9 655	92	21	4 208	
	2003	10 591	...	108	10 386	97	-133	4 227	
	2004	11 374	...	97	11 171	105	-56	4 269	
Bhutan*	2001	198	35	...	...	163	...	87	1
	2002	200	36	...	...	163	...	85	1
	2003	198	35	...	...	163	...	85	1
	2004	204	36	...	...	168	...	89	1
Brunei Darussalam	2001	20 745	...	10 101	10 644	...	30	1	18 5
	2002	21 299	...	10 611	10 688	...	-30	9	19 0
	2003	22 540	...	11 016	11 524	...	-17	0	20 0
	2004	22 366	...	10 965	11 401	...	35	0	19 5
Cambodia*	2001	3	...	...	...	3	...	178	
	2002	3	...	...	...	3	...	182	
	2003	3	...	...	...	3	...	178	
	2004	3	...	...	...	3	...	178	
China[2]	2001	913 984	689 809	163 959	34 858	25 357	78	91 538	75 6
	2002	958 234	726 772	167 000	37 540	26 922	5 104	104 577	72 8
	2003	1 098 103	860 139	169 600	40 246	28 119	4 786	128 182	80 8
	2004	1 242 421	995 163	175 873	36 897	34 488	7 666	179 041	72 5
China, Hong Kong SAR	2001	...	...	...	...	...	694	21 439	1 5
	2002	...	...	...	...	...	35	22 067	1 3
	2003	...	...	...	...	...	-71	22 558	1 4
	2004	...	...	...	...	...	-34	25 501	1 6
China, Macao SAR	2001	...	...	...	...	...	23	597	
	2002	...	...	...	...	...	-8	613	
	2003	...	...	...	...	...	-3	626	
	2004	...	...	...	...	...	18	760	
Cyprus	2001	...	...	...	...	...	-65	2 493	
	2002	...	...	...	...	...	65	2 570	
	2003	...	...	...	...	...	-67	2 654	
	2004	...	...	...	...	...	-37	2 389	
Georgia	2001	613	1	99	37	477	-25	1 514	1
	2002	675	4	74	16	582	-43	1 346	1
	2003	723	5	140	17	561	-23	1 500	1
	2004	634	5	98	11	520	0	1 700	1

Production, trade and consumption of commercial energy—Thousand metric tons of oil equivalent and kilograms per capita (*continued*)

Production, commerce et consommation d'énergie commerciale—Milliers de tonnes d'équivalent pétrole et kilogrammes par habitant (*suite*)

Bunkers - Soutes			Consumption - Consommation							
Air Avion	Sea Maritime	Unallocated Nondistribué	Per capita Par habitant	Total Totale	Solids Solides	Liquids Liquides	Gas Gaz	Electricity Electricité	Year Année	Région, pays ou zone
*5	...	...	*12	*257	18	*104	*102	*34	2001	Afghanistan
*5	...	...	*8	*162	15	*84	7	56	2002	
*8	...	...	8	177	24	*83	6	63	2003	
0	...	...	12	272	24	188	3	57	2004	
60	...	25	526	1 753	0	263	1 268	222	2001	Arménie
60	...	0	465	1 544	13	271	953	308	2002	
27	...	0	457	1 735	19	316	1 081	318	2003	
39	...	0	598	1 809	0	311	1 201	296	2004	
222	...	563	1 432	11 592	...	3 375	8 047	170	2001	Azerbaïdjan
271	...	636	1 423	11 575	...	3 207	8 070	298	2002	
338	...	342	1 534	12 451	...	3 824	8 280	347	2003	
343	...	299	1 593	13 229	...	3 833	9 042	354	2004	
353	...	1 653	10 354	6 782	...	980	5 802	...	2001	Bahreïn
426	...	2 012	10 442	7 017	...	909	6 108	...	2002	
477	...	1 891	10 540	7 273	...	972	6 300	...	2003	
521	...	1 925	10 736	7 601	...	1 049	6 552	...	2004	
202	36	496	91	12 815	350	3 202	9 178	85	2001	Bangladesh
209	36	403	93	13 379	350	3 282	9 655	92	2002	
234	36	474	105	14 207	350	3 374	10 386	97	2003	
242	36	426	108	14 994	350	3 367	11 171	105	2004	
...	...	...	68	140	45	50	...	44	2001	Bhoutan*
...	...	...	66	138	43	52	...	42	2002	
...	...	...	63	134	42	49	...	42	2003	
...	...	...	65	141	45	53	...	43	2004	
...	...	-240	7 089	2 375	...	965	1 410	...	2001	Brunéi Darussalam
...	...	-351	7 690	2 622	...	1 239	1 383	...	2002	
...	...	-417	8 456	2 934	...	1 526	1 409	...	2003	
...	...	-510	8 962	3 280	...	1 706	1 574	...	2004	
...	...	...	14	180	...	178	...	3	2001	Cambodge*
...	...	...	14	185	...	182	...	3	2002	
...	...	...	14	181	...	178	...	3	2003	
...	...	...	13	181	...	178	...	3	2004	
*351	3 935	50 461	685	875 056	641 067	176 746	32 608	24 635	2001	Chine[2]
390	3 935	57 858	718	922 713	677 435	183 591	35 402	26 285	2002	
339	2 503	64 698	831	1 073 096	805 891	200 849	38 871	27 486	2003	
129	289	80 617	970	1 260 182	950 010	241 481	34 725	33 966	2004	
3 039	3 777	...	1 848	12 425	3 994	5 425	2 252	754	2001	Chine, Hong Kong RAS
3 923	4 997	...	1 741	11 776	4 479	4 470	2 139	688	2002	
3 547	5 411	...	1 791	12 198	5 743	4 445	1 376	635	2003	
4 004	7 724	...	1 772	12 147	5 244	4 335	1 987	580	2004	
...	...	...	1 315	574	...	558	...	17	2001	Chine, Macao RAS
...	...	...	1 406	621	...	604	...	17	2002	
...	...	...	1 404	630	...	614	...	15	2003	
...	...	...	1 594	742	...	729	...	13	2004	
337	191	34	2 858	1 995	40	1 955	...	...	2001	Chypre
304	138	44	2 861	2 020	41	1 979	...	...	2002	
330	124	36	3 120	2 231	40	2 191	...	...	2003	
304	55	6	2 822	2 061	42	2 018	...	...	2004	
10	...	13	378	1 975	14	559	903	499	2001	Géorgie
13	...	14	372	1 925	14	535	755	621	2002	
13	...	54	401	2 054	30	527	857	640	2003	
38	...	21	417	2 169	8	527	1 004	630	2004	

50 Production, trade and consumption of commercial energy—Thousand metric tons of oil equivalent and kilograms per capit (*continued*)

Production, commerce et consommation d'énergie commerciale—Milliers de tonnes d'équivalent pétrole et kilogrammes p habitant (*suite*)

Region, country or area	Year Année	Primary energy production – Production d'énergie primaire: Total Totale	Solids Solides	Liquids Liquides	Gas Gaz	Electricity Electricité	Changes in stocks Variations des stocks	Imports Importations	Expo Exportatio
India	2001	261 530	195 848	36 351	21 155	8 176	-1 839	96 586	7 7
	2002	271 548	203 948	37 306	22 884	7 410	734	102 761	8 3
	2003	285 766	215 981	37 199	24 270	8 316	978	107 267	12 9
	2004	300 205	228 921	38 059	24 075	9 152	1 625	119 151	14 9
Indonesia	2001	220 915	64 753	86 999	67 952	1 210	-1 433	25 086	151 2
	2002	230 648	72 142	83 996	73 209	1 302	-1 304	27 839	149 3
	2003	238 989	76 525	85 016	76 241	1 206	303	26 537	154 5
	2004	234 670	83 790	81 804	67 767	1 310	0	34 812	164 3
Iran (Islamic Rep. of)	2001	251 321	848	192 711	57 327	435	232	7 337	136 2
	2002	249 842	877	183 275	64 995	695	-138	8 687	144 4
	2003	282 949	862	208 257	72 876	954	-132	10 575	162 8
	2004	283 254	872	205 084	76 384	914	0	13 010	154 0
Iraq	2001	119 382	...	116 824	2 505	53	0	16	91 0
	2002	101 972	...	99 829	2 088	56	0	0	72 0
	2003	67 081	...	65 628	1 416	37	0	393	41 7
	2004	101 482	...	99 016	2 423	42	459	4 473	76 1
Israel	2001	105	91	4	9	1	155	22 659	2 8
	2002	117	101	5	8	3	-429	22 964	2 7
	2003	110	96	3	8	3	-361	23 818	3 0
	2004	1 142	97	2	1 041	2	-263	24 009	3 5
Japan	2001	43 801	1 860	595	5 476	35 870	-2 930	410 963	5 2
	2002	39 825	0	608	5 637	33 580	-1 408	420 060	4 8
	2003	35 871	0	670	5 259	29 943	-389	429 912	4 8
	2004	38 953	0	293	5 123	33 537	-931	437 082	5 0
Jordan	2001	235	...	2	229	4	97	4 874	
	2002	222	...	2	215	5	1	5 056	
	2003	250	...	2	244	*5	-23	5 241	
	2004	254	...	1	248	5	112	5 306	
Kazakhstan	2001	89 580	37 206	40 411	11 268	695	43	8 379	51 8
	2002	97 222	35 625	47 682	13 151	764	41	12 504	62 0
	2003	107 317	39 172	51 933	15 470	742	39	12 569	68 9
	2004	121 026	39 548	60 185	20 601	693	17	16 983	82 0
Korea, Dem. P. R.	2001	20 205	19 293	...	...	911	106	1 497	2
	2002	19 204	18 291	...	...	913	106	1 487	2
	2003	19 633	18 625	...	...	1 008	103	1 490	2
	2004	20 118	19 043	...	...	1 075	104	1 472	2
Korea, Republic of	2001	11 716	1 717	...	...	9 999	2 224	192 740	32 8
	2002	12 190	1 493	0	...	10 698	3 119	189 415	25 1
	2003	13 226	1 484	0	...	11 742	5 490	191 176	22 8
	2004	13 209	1 436	0	...	11 774	2 241	199 490	25 8
Kuwait	2001	114 578	...	106 271	8 307	...	0	261	82 6
	2002	108 201	...	100 751	7 450	...	0	483	76 6
	2003	123 567	...	114 887	8 680	...	0	589	86 3
	2004	135 111	...	126 071	9 040	...	...	118	95 8
Kyrgyzstan	2001	1 323	147	76	31	1 069	-56	1 074	2
	2002	1 174	143	76	28	928	-28	1 590	2
	2003	1 336	123	69	25	1 118	-23	1 646	3
	2004	1 449	135	74	27	1 212	-10	1 791	4
Lao People's Dem. Rep.*	2001	300	196	...	...	104	...	143	6
	2002	307	199	...	...	107	...	144	6
	2003	307	199	...	...	107	...	144	6
	2004	310	203	...	...	107	...	149	6

50 Production, trade and consumption of commercial energy — Thousand metric tons of oil equivalent and kilograms per capita (*continued*)

Production, commerce et consommation d'énergie commerciale — Milliers de tonnes d'équivalent pétrole et kilogrammes par habitant (*suite*)

Bunkers - Soutes			Consumption - Consommation							
Air Avion	Sea Maritime	Unallocated Nondistribué	Per capita Par habitant	Total Totale	Solids Solides	Liquids Liquides	Gas Gaz	Electricity Electricité	Year Année	Région, pays ou zone
2 344	88	27 761	312	321 985	212 398	80 140	21 155	8 292	2001	Inde
2 329	39	33 319	314	329 546	220 028	79 108	22 884	7 526	2002	
2 470	31	33 312	321	343 309	230 306	80 272	24 270	8 461	2003	
*2 765	53	35 083	338	364 924	246 275	85 277	24 075	9 298	2004	
507	77	-2 868	472	98 430	18 091	50 984	28 145	1 210	2001	Indonésie
863	72	-2 433	529	111 988	21 013	51 586	38 087	1 302	2002	
1 035	293	3 369	494	105 998	14 272	50 998	39 521	1 206	2003	
1 321	352	1 787	467	101 645	9 958	59 488	30 889	1 310	2004	
905	639	-4 531	1 939	125 143	1 258	62 242	61 235	409	2001	Iran (Rép. islamique d')
*803	606	-26 929	2 131	139 693	1 330	68 894	68 758	711	2002	
*774	585	-20 271	2 253	149 735	1 287	72 391	75 054	1 003	2003	
812	619	-14 919	2 323	155 665	1 195	74 694	78 833	942	2004	
527	...	1 157	1 074	26 657	...	24 099	2 505	53	2001	Iraq
516	...	3 678	1 006	25 709	...	23 566	2 088	56	2002	
418	...	3 268	837	22 052	...	20 599	1 416	37	2003	
1 200	...	1 375	988	26 821	...	24 242	2 423	156	2004	
4	177	-568	3 098	20 162	8 132	12 141	9	-119	2001	Israël
4	269	-304	3 130	20 752	8 828	12 033	8	-117	2002	
*4	272	57	3 092	20 864	8 963	12 017	8	-124	2003	
*4	229	637	3 050	20 954	9 110	10 927	1 041	-123	2004	
6 115	4 442	16 204	3 348	425 643	108 499	204 551	76 724	35 870	2001	Japon
6 938	4 659	12 643	3 392	432 166	112 019	209 848	76 719	33 580	2002	
6 720	5 120	19 025	3 376	430 463	115 283	203 711	81 525	29 943	2003	
6 951	5 360	17 776	3 460	441 823	126 150	201 825	80 312	33 537	2004	
221	2	111	903	4 678	...	4 422	229	26	2001	Jordanie
223	0	91	931	4 963	...	4 716	215	32	2002	
184	0	91	956	5 239	...	4 963	244	32	2003	
300	12	304	857	4 831	...	4 507	248	75	2004	
...	...	1 417	3 009	44 632	25 478	8 210	10 095	849	2001	Kazakhstan
...	...	1 135	3 132	46 541	26 563	8 035	11 045	898	2002	
...	...	468	3 379	50 380	28 934	7 515	13 316	615	2003	
...	...	1 649	3 621	54 296	28 650	9 787	15 352	506	2004	
...	...	16	954	21 369	19 339	1 119	...	911	2001	Corée, R. p. dém. de
...	...	16	903	20 359	18 323	1 122	...	913	2002	
...	...	15	918	20 795	18 662	1 125	...	1 008	2003	
...	...	13	937	21 263	19 086	1 102	...	1 075	2004	
654	6 147	19 204	3 028	143 349	47 175	66 211	19 964	9 999	2001	Corée, République de
922	5 863	17 565	3 128	149 020	49 651	66 368	22 304	10 698	2002	
1 201	6 543	17 590	3 140	150 774	50 373	65 268	23 390	11 742	2003	
1 311	7 205	21 028	3 225	155 075	53 726	61 978	27 598	11 774	2004	
403	414	8 157	10 200	23 206	...	14 898	8 307	...	2001	Koweït
465	538	8 573	9 917	22 431	...	14 981	7 450	...	2002	
717	556	10 350	11 551	26 163	...	17 483	8 680	...	2003	
784	567	9 766	10 559	28 246	...	19 206	9 040	...	2004	
...	...	-2	452	2 238	290	386	651	910	2001	Kirghizistan
...	...	2	511	2 554	491	368	826	869	2002	
...	...	5	535	2 697	588	448	681	980	2003	
...	...	2	547	2 783	555	559	744	926	2004	
...	...	...	70	380	196	127	...	56	2001	Rép. dém. pop. lao*
...	...	...	70	386	199	126	...	60	2002	
...	...	...	68	387	199	125	...	62	2003	
...	...	...	65	395	203	131	...	62	2004	

50 Production, trade and consumption of commercial energy — Thousand metric tons of oil equivalent and kilograms per capit[illegible] (*continued*)

Production, commerce et consommation d'énergie commerciale — Milliers de tonnes d'équivalent pétrole et kilogrammes p[illegible] habitant (*suite*)

Region, country or area	Year Année	Primary energy production – Production d'énergie primaire Total Totale	Solids Solides	Liquids Liquides	Gas Gaz	Electricity Electricité	Changes in stocks Variations des stocks	Imports Importations	Expo[illegible] Exportatio[illegible]
Lebanon	2001	*72	...	...	...	*72	-36	5 096	[illegible]
	2002	106	...	...	...	106	-15	5 007	[illegible]
	2003	69	...	...	...	69	0	5 769	[illegible]
	2004	*96	...	...	...	*96	0	5 024	[illegible]
Malaysia	2001	*77 583	344	35 296	*41 390	553	-488	18 819	42 9[illegible]
	2002	*80 916	223	37 546	*42 691	456	733	17 877	43 5[illegible]
	2003	*84 384	107	39 102	*44 681	494	-587	20 089	45 8[illegible]
	2004	90 405	268	37 548	52 089	501	-897	25 672	49 1[illegible]
Maldives	2001	...	...	...	...	...	...	246	*[illegible]
	2002	...	...	...	...	...	...	307	*[illegible]
	2003	...	...	...	...	...	...	273	*[illegible]
	2004	...	...	...	...	...	...	313	*[illegible]
Mongolia	2001	1 626	1 626	...	...	...	...	525	
	2002	1 742	1 742	...	...	...	...	496	
	2003	1 742	1 742	...	...	...	...	542	1[illegible]
	2004	2 111	2 111	...	...	...	...	595	3[illegible]
Myanmar	2001	7 070	412	674	5 828	157	14	1 147	5 1[illegible]
	2002	7 461	344	883	6 042	192	-272	962	5 2[illegible]
	2003	9 116	609	983	7 330	193	-92	922	6 3[illegible]
	2004	9 443	631	1 018	7 594	200	-95	954	6 5[illegible]
Nepal	2001	166	7	...	...	159	...	1 069	[illegible]
	2002	191	8	...	...	182	...	866	[illegible]
	2003	202	8	...	...	195	...	932	[illegible]
	2004	209	8	...	...	201	...	965	[illegible]
Occupied Palestinian Terr.	2001	...	...	...	...	...	0	382	
	2002	...	...	...	...	...	0	388	
	2003	...	...	...	...	...	0	379	
	2004	...	...	...	...	...	*-1	390	
Oman	2001	61 517	...	47 833	13 685	...	-1 012	401	53 7[illegible]
	2002	60 002	...	44 940	15 062	...	-1 286	385	50 1[illegible]
	2003	57 595	...	41 078	16 517	...	-1 562	299	47 5[illegible]
	2004	56 115	...	39 249	16 866	...	*-747	422	46 3[illegible]
Pakistan	2001	25 197	1 464	2 966	19 117	1 650	-75	17 085	4[illegible]
	2002	26 655	1 574	3 273	19 983	1 826	-31	16 609	2[illegible]
	2003	28 379	1 566	3 309	21 432	2 071	-219	13 100	4[illegible]
	2004	34 762	2 169	3 415	26 730	2 448	-68	16 338	3[illegible]
Philippines	2001	2 280	581	63	126	1 510	-518	23 413	5[illegible]
	2002	4 135	786	277	1 585	1 487	*-411	22 055	9[illegible]
	2003	4 827	869	20	2 416	1 523	116	21 629	8[illegible]
	2004	5 127	1 173	19	2 311	1 624	-253	21 615	6[illegible]
Qatar	2001	65 344	...	39 080	26 264	...	-573	...	48 1[illegible]
	2002	69 057	...	40 215	28 842	...	1 866	...	48 1[illegible]
	2003	71 131	...	40 987	30 144	...	2 598	...	49 4[illegible]
	2004	81 622	...	43 266	38 357	...	496	...	58 9[illegible]
Saudi Arabia	2001	478 769	...	428 730	50 039	...	-54	604	348 8[illegible]
	2002	444 495	...	391 072	53 422	...	1 514	1 036	305 7[illegible]
	2003	519 227	...	463 251	55 976	...	264	122	372 5[illegible]
	2004	554 465	...	493 251	61 214	...	*150	0	*406 9[illegible]
Singapore	2001	...	...	...	...	...	1 728	84 119	35 5[illegible]
	2002	...	...	...	...	...	85	86 039	38 4[illegible]
	2003	...	...	...	...	...	-3 077	84 525	41 8[illegible]
	2004	...	...	...	...	...	-1 256	96 971	46 2[illegible]

50

Production, trade and consumption of commercial energy—Thousand metric tons of oil equivalent and kilograms per capita (*continued*)

Production, commerce et consommation d'énergie commerciale—Milliers de tonnes d'équivalent pétrole et kilogrammes par habitant (*suite*)

Bunkers - Soutes			Consumption - Consommation							
Air Avion	Sea Maritime	Unallocated Nondistribué	Per capita Par habitant	Total Totale	Solids Solides	Liquids Liquides	Gas Gaz	Electricity Electricité	Year Année	Région, pays ou zone
132	15	...	1 430	5 057	141	4 736	...	180	2001	Liban
129	15	...	1 386	4 985	141	4 692	...	152	2002	
*129	0	...	1 531	5 708	141	5 499	...	69	2003	
131	15	...	1 286	4 975	140	4 720	...	*115	2004	
1 763	153	5 142	*2 109	*46 883	2 909	19 832	*23 588	553	2001	Malaisie
1 786	90	4 404	2 127	48 211	3 676	20 277	*23 803	456	2002	
1 853	71	7 556	2 154	49 750	5 336	19 592	*24 328	494	2003	
2 073	85	6 152	2 531	59 537	9 293	21 786	28 002	456	2004	
...	...	...	647	179	...	179	...	...	2001	Maldives
...	...	...	806	226	...	226	...	...	2002	
...	...	...	675	195	...	195	...	...	2003	
...	...	...	809	240	...	240	...	...	2004	
...	...	...	880	2 150	1 633	501	...	15	2001	Mongolie
...	...	...	904	2 236	1 742	482	...	13	2002	
...	...	...	841	2 183	1 642	527	...	14	2003	
...	...	...	853	2 345	1 751	580	...	14	2004	
69	3	306	56	2 715	49	1 428	1 080	157	2001	Myanmar
72	2	449	60	2 954	52	1 593	1 117	192	2002	
82	3	126	72	3 562	97	1 787	1 484	193	2003	
85	3	130	74	3 688	100	1 850	1 538	200	2004	
38	...	...	50	1 184	344	673	...	167	2001	Népal
43	...	...	41	997	160	659	...	179	2002	
40	...	...	44	1 077	204	683	...	190	2003	
41	...	...	42	1 114	211	707	...	196	2004	
...	...	...	116	380	1	200	...	179	2001	Terr. palestinien occupé
...	...	...	114	388	3	187	...	198	2002	
...	...	...	108	379	0	180	...	199	2003	
...	...	...	104	391	*1	224	...	166	2004	
261	50	6	3 588	8 892	...	3 001	5 891	...	2001	Oman
369	34	56	4 358	11 060	...	3 616	7 445	...	2002	
369	1	219	4 872	11 357	...	3 313	8 044	...	2003	
*200	1	-118	4 784	10 831	...	3 357	7 474	...	2004	
784	16	945	284	40 180	2 122	17 290	19 117	1 650	2001	Pakistan
873	12	1 080	284	41 089	2 323	16 958	19 983	1 826	2002	
804	44	1 185	264	39 259	2 659	13 096	21 432	2 071	2003	
908	63	1 315	319	48 580	4 460	14 935	26 737	2 448	2004	
596	217	1 800	296	23 027	5 927	15 464	126	1 510	2001	Philippines
610	226	463	306	24 340	5 698	15 570	1 585	1 487	2002	
588	185	984	294	23 703	5 411	14 353	2 416	1 523	2003	
*619	139	867	303	24 758	6 093	14 730	2 311	1 624	2004	
...	...	34	30 645	17 743	...	5 795	11 948	...	2001	Qatar
...	...	-29	30 778	19 021	...	6 887	12 134	...	2002	
...	...	-51	30 034	19 101	...	6 635	12 467	...	2003	
...	...	-47	33 324	22 227	...	6 502	15 725	...	2004	
2 498	2 151	8 011	5 623	117 945	...	67 906	50 039	...	2001	Arabie saoudite
2 545	2 200	9 632	5 765	123 897	...	70 474	53 422	...	2002	
2 593	2 216	11 238	5 926	130 494	...	74 518	55 976	...	2003	
2 808	*2 314	5 786	6 020	136 503	...	75 289	61 214	...	2004	
*1 281	20 219	10 487	3 580	14 848	0	12 864	1 985	...	2001	Singapour
*1 238	19 965	11 960	3 444	14 316	0	11 094	3 221	...	2002	
*1 259	20 662	8 762	3 456	15 099	0	10 116	4 983	...	2003	
*1 290	23 395	12 490	3 482	14 762	6	8 881	5 875	...	2004	

50 Production, trade and consumption of commercial energy — Thousand metric tons of oil equivalent and kilograms per capit[illegible] *(continued)*

Production, commerce et consommation d'énergie commerciale — Milliers de tonnes d'équivalent pétrole et kilogrammes p[illegible] habitant *(suite)*

		Primary energy production – Production d'énergie primaire					Changes in stocks		
Region, country or area	Year Année	Total Totale	Solids Solides	Liquids Liquides	Gas Gaz	Electricity Electricité	Variations des stocks	Imports Importations	Expo[illegible] Exportatio[illegible]
Sri Lanka	2001	268	...	...	...	268	-45	3 565	
	2002	232	...	...	...	232	76	3 895	
	2003	285	...	...	...	285	-114	3 496	
	2004	255	...	...	...	255	-2	4 086	[illegible]
Syrian Arab Republic	2001	34 421	...	29 094	*5 034	293	0	4 589	20 8[illegible]
	2002	37 710	...	31 286	*6 123	301	0	1 714	20 0[illegible]
	2003	34 533	...	28 124	*6 168	241	*11	1 350	16 9[illegible]
	2004	30 177	...	23 419	6 393	365	-20	1 625	12 0[illegible]
Tajikistan	2001	1 274	12	18	36	1 208	...	2 145	3[illegible]
	2002	1 355	27	16	27	1 285	...	2 256	3[illegible]
	2003	1 460	26	18	30	1 386	...	2 153	3[illegible]
	2004	1 528	29	18	30	1 451	...	2 242	4[illegible]
Thailand	2001	33 304	8 630	7 730	16 402	542	-334	45 859	7 4[illegible]
	2002	34 946	8 623	8 574	17 106	643	-1 363	48 059	8 0[illegible]
	2003	35 923	8 289	10 113	16 893	628	-936	52 192	7 8[illegible]
	2004	36 439	8 824	10 348	16 747	520	-981	58 712	8 5[illegible]
Timor-Leste*	2001	...	...	...	...	...	...	...	[illegible]
	2002	7 317	...	7 317	...	...	...	53	7 2[illegible]
	2003	7 317	...	7 317	...	...	...	53	7 2[illegible]
	2004	7 367	...	7 367	...	...	...	58	7 2[illegible]
Turkey	2001	18 424	13 541	2 520	285	2 078	-223	50 107	1 4[illegible]
	2002	17 503	11 827	2 420	346	2 909	-222	55 546	2 2[illegible]
	2003	16 544	10 630	2 351	512	3 051	437	62 760	3 7[illegible]
	2004	17 000	10 144	2 251	629	3 975	-453	65 413	4 5[illegible]
Turkmenistan	2001	55 105	...	8 681	46 425	0	...	87	38 2[illegible]
	2002	58 499	...	10 174	48 325	0	...	87	40 5[illegible]
	2003	63 928	...	10 390	53 538	0	...	87	45 3[illegible]
	2004	63 513	...	10 120	53 393	0	...	87	46 7[illegible]
United Arab Emirates	2001	166 074	...	129 390	36 684	...	0	8 287	109 2[illegible]
	2002	153 484	...	113 044	40 440	...	0	7 997	101 6[illegible]
	2003	175 349	...	133 595	41 754	...	0	10 581	111 3[illegible]
	2004	179 471	...	136 785	42 686	...	0	12 221	126 1[illegible]
Uzbekistan	2001	60 680	731	7 480	51 958	512	17	1 164	6 6[illegible]
	2002	60 900	665	7 352	52 339	545	16	990	5 4[illegible]
	2003	60 842	511	7 868	51 918	546	12	991	4 6[illegible]
	2004	62 217	727	7 533	53 393	564	17	1 025	4 0[illegible]
Viet Nam	2001	29 126	9 073	17 184	1 246	1 622	-210	9 126	20 5[illegible]
	2002	32 490	11 130	17 167	2 571	1 622	0	10 111	21 4[illegible]
	2003	33 521	11 690	17 131	3 009	1 690	0	10 437	21 5[illegible]
	2004	45 408	17 850	20 844	5 127	1 587	700	11 526	27 0[illegible]
Yemen	2001	21 484	...	21 484	...	...	63	1 551	17 1[illegible]
	2002	21 618	...	21 618	...	...	420	2 007	17 4[illegible]
	2003	21 300	...	21 300	...	...	567	2 425	17 0[illegible]
	2004	20 050	...	20 050	...	...	908	2 738	15 3[illegible]
Europe	**2001**	**2 035 124**	**359 615**	**672 966**	**826 621**	**175 921**	**-3 997**	**1 442 707**	**1 044 0[illegible]**
	2002	**2 072 777**	**353 275**	**700 679**	**846 004**	**172 819**	**10 118**	**1 463 684**	**1 105 6[illegible]**
	2003	**2 132 967**	**363 136**	**726 782**	**871 925**	**171 124**	**7 317**	**1 519 348**	**1 152 4[illegible]**
	2004	**2 178 756**	**358 023**	**751 446**	**891 718**	**177 569**	**11 197**	**1 580 807**	**1 230 9[illegible]**
Albania	2001	629	5	311	8	306	...	877	
	2002	726	18	393	13	302	...	988	1[illegible]
	2003	851	19	375	13	444	...	935	[illegible]
	2004	931	26	420	15	470	...	1 029	[illegible]

Production, trade and consumption of commercial energy—Thousand metric tons of oil equivalent and kilograms per capita (*continued*)

Production, commerce et consommation d'énergie commerciale—Milliers de tonnes d'équivalent pétrole et kilogrammes par habitant (*suite*)

Bunkers - Soutes			Consumption - Consommation							
Air Avion	Sea Maritime	Unallocated Nondistribué	Per capita Par habitant	Total Totale	Solids Solides	Liquids Liquides	Gas Gaz	Electricity Electricité	Year Année	Région, pays ou zone
68	154	135	188	3 521	1	3 253	...	268	2001	Sri Lanka
100	145	124	194	3 683	1	3 450	...	232	2002	
115	114	131	185	3 536	68	3 183	...	285	2003	
132	119	118	203	3 937	67	3 615	...	255	2004	
95	...	1 232	1 005	16 803	3	11 474	*5 034	293	2001	Rép. arabe syrienne
*109	...	1 571	1 031	17 679	2	11 253	*6 123	301	2002	
*100	...	1 794	967	16 995	6	10 580	*6 168	241	2003	
120	...	1 654	1 001	18 005	3	11 244	6 393	365	2004	
5	...	13	497	3 047	58	1 117	549	1 324	2001	Tadjikistan
4	...	12	515	3 258	73	1 135	698	1 352	2002	
4	...	15	512	3 195	72	1 226	511	1 387	2003	
4	...	15	520	3 343	75	1 319	525	1 424	2004	
...	...	4 358	1 079	67 706	12 744	32 149	22 046	767	2001	Thaïlande
...	...	5 225	1 119	71 053	12 768	33 852	23 571	862	2002	
...	...	7 384	1 174	73 796	13 281	35 800	23 899	815	2003	
...	...	6 759	1 268	80 809	14 859	40 882	24 289	779	2004	
...	...	...	...	...	...	...	...	...	2001	Timor-Leste*
...	...	75	56	53	...	53	...	...	2002	
...	...	75	54	53	...	53	...	...	2003	
...	...	76	57	58	...	58	...	...	2004	
521	237	4 025	912	62 521	20 354	24 876	14 858	2 434	2001	Turquie
867	537	3 301	952	66 315	20 518	26 245	16 373	3 181	2002	
904	626	3 063	1 005	70 545	22 127	25 629	19 690	3 100	2003	
974	1 008	3 462	1 031	72 907	22 646	25 556	20 788	3 917	2004	
...	...	354	3 639	16 607	...	3 937	12 760	-90	2001	Turkménistan
...	...	512	3 774	17 475	...	4 125	13 441	-91	2002	
...	...	167	3 939	18 503	...	4 333	14 262	-92	2003	
...	...	25	3 536	16 853	...	4 235	12 760	-142	2004	
987	8 926	10 692	12 762	44 515	...	14 784	29 731	...	2001	Emirats arabes unis
1 271	8 253	1 210	13 087	49 130	...	15 320	33 811	...	2002	
1 302	9 876	8 855	13 513	54 537	...	19 482	35 055	...	2003	
3 524	11 072	-7 776	13 438	58 699	...	22 581	36 118	...	2004	
...	...	-2 033	2 293	57 247	713	9 222	46 758	555	2001	Ouzbékistan
...	...	-2 001	2 303	58 412	649	9 076	48 149	537	2002	
...	...	-2 277	2 277	59 406	498	9 828	48 542	538	2003	
...	...	-1 957	2 332	61 129	710	9 191	50 673	556	2004	
148	...	-2	225	17 785	6 280	8 637	1 246	1 622	2001	Viet Nam
172	...	-3	263	20 945	6 896	9 856	2 571	1 622	2002	
159	...	-3	273	22 231	7 280	10 251	3 009	1 690	2003	
266	...	-3	352	28 952	10 430	11 808	5 127	1 587	2004	
112	85	1 177	244	4 407	...	4 407	...	...	2001	Yémen
105	117	790	254	4 753	...	4 753	...	...	2002	
94	126	678	268	5 194	...	5 194	...	...	2003	
105	126	869	261	5 431	...	5 431	...	...	2004	
49 256	**47 128**	**26 961**	**2 701**	**2 314 438**	**465 593**	**761 683**	**911 435**	**175 726**	**2001**	**Europe**
49 116	**48 037**	**16 305**	**2 695**	**2 307 196**	**461 010**	**761 566**	**911 705**	**172 915**	**2002**	
50 473	**48 453**	**28 280**	**2 763**	**2 365 380**	**476 829**	**757 867**	**959 243**	**171 441**	**2003**	
53 581	**51 700**	**27 342**	**2 770**	**2 384 755**	**473 443**	**757 797**	**976 020**	**177 496**	**2004**	
44	...	91	391	1 365	22	879	8	456	2001	Albanie
44	...	131	407	1 429	22	912	13	483	2002	
48	...	155	431	1 519	21	961	13	523	2003	
59	...	155	551	1 718	28	1 187	15	487	2004	

50 Production, trade and consumption of commercial energy — Thousand metric tons of oil equivalent and kilograms per capita (*continued*)

Production, commerce et consommation d'énergie commerciale — Milliers de tonnes d'équivalent pétrole et kilogrammes par habitant (*suite*)

Region, country or area	Year Année	Primary energy production – Production d'énergie primaire: Total Totale	Solids Solides	Liquids Liquides	Gas Gaz	Electricity Electricité	Changes in stocks Variations des stocks	Imports Importations	Exports Exportations
Austria	2001	6 603	314	1 033	1 643	3 612	-1 018	23 262	2 987
	2002	6 846	368	1 065	1 784	3 630	-105	24 458	2 975
	2003	6 388	300	1 036	1 985	3 067	-68	26 829	3 265
	2004	6 442	61	1 085	1 865	3 431	235	27 555	3 766
Belarus	2001	2 543	453	1 852	235	3	-17	29 282	6 654
	2002	2 576	501	1 846	227	2	155	31 962	8 887
	2003	2 467	410	1 820	234	2	-190	33 858	9 878
	2004	2 498	453	1 804	237	3	203	37 874	12 693
Belgium	2001	4 261	131	...	...	4 130	768	74 098	22 038
	2002	4 309	104	...	...	4 205	-763	73 157	23 344
	2003	4 272	78	...	...	4 195	51	77 240	23 220
	2004	4 219	0	...	...	4 219	115	79 216	25 017
Bosnia and Herzegovina	2001	2 889	2 451	...	...	438	-365	1 255	202
	2002	3 246	2 793	...	...	453	133	1 303	183
	2003	3 019	2 555	...	...	465	-126	1 437	272
	2004	3 181	2 674	...	...	507	-117	1 539	265
Bulgaria	2001	6 370	4 432	35	35	1 868	-188	11 903	2 761
	2002	6 369	4 326	37	34	1 971	479	11 441	2 357
	2003	6 343	4 513	30	31	1 770	-332	11 508	2 089
	2004	6 421	4 345	30	311	1 735	461	12 340	2 899
Croatia	2001	3 811	...	1 420	1 825	566	-118	6 155	1 673
	2002	3 773	...	1 382	1 924	467	377	7 023	1 672
	2003	3 729	...	1 317	1 987	424	-142	7 171	1 842
	2004	3 860	...	1 258	1 995	606	-6	7 676	2 216
Czech Republic	2001	25 904	24 105	183	135	1 480	-365	19 372	7 603
	2002	25 339	23 090	265	127	1 856	30	19 708	7 654
	2003	25 861	23 019	317	146	2 379	111	19 978	7 759
	2004	26 595	23 624	306	180	2 485	462	19 736	7 303
Denmark	2001	25 709	0	16 904	8 433	373	-85	12 782	20 161
	2002	27 039	0	18 169	8 448	422	-651	12 195	21 960
	2003	26 656	0	18 173	8 003	480	-129	14 355	21 743
	2004	29 269	...	19 262	9 438	569	133	14 549	24 324
Estonia	2001	2 748	2 747	...	...	1	-125	2 022	150
	2002	2 951	2 950	...	...	1	27	1 826	177
	2003	3 441	3 439	...	...	2	40	1 975	253
	2004	3 220	3 217	...	...	3	-112	2 291	250
Faeroe Islands	2001	7	0	...	...	7	...	*215	...
	2002	8	0	...	...	8	...	*217	...
	2003	8	0	...	...	8	...	*219	...
	2004	8	0	...	...	8	...	*219	...
Finland	2001	4 546	1 446	...	...	3 100	-115	23 590	4 77[illegible]
	2002	5 060	2 211	...	...	2 849	-1 014	24 146	5 21[illegible]
	2003	4 637	1 850	...	...	2 787	498	28 305	5 68[illegible]
	2004	4 070	810	...	...	3 260	-1 539	26 656	5 75[illegible]
France[3]	2001	48 082	1 656	1 712	1 677	43 037	-1 512	162 590	22 97[illegible]
	2002	47 805	1 307	1 595	1 611	43 292	2 193	163 114	22 70[illegible]
	2003	47 886	1 454	1 471	1 424	43 538	-481	167 386	26 24[illegible]
	2004	47 450	566	1 436	1 231	44 217	-579	172 294	27 79[illegible]
Germany	2001	95 690	56 497	3 509	17 702	17 982	-4 002	241 620	27 27[illegible]
	2002	96 477	56 891	3 872	17 764	17 949	-3 196	235 891	27 83[illegible]
	2003	95 787	56 034	4 120	17 689	17 944	-1 598	240 728	28 31[illegible]
	2004	95 786	56 882	3 522	16 379	19 003	1 332	251 586	34 69[illegible]

50 **Production, trade and consumption of commercial energy**—Thousand metric tons of oil equivalent and kilograms per capita (*continued*)

Production, commerce et consommation d'énergie commerciale—Milliers de tonnes d'équivalent pétrole et kilogrammes par habitant (*suite*)

Bunkers - Soutes			Consumption - Consommation							
Air Avion	Sea Maritime	Unallocated Nondistribué	Per capita Par habitant	Total Totale	Solids Solides	Liquids Liquides	Gas Gaz	Electricity Electricité	Year Année	Région, pays ou zone
533	...	819	3 309	26 544	3 754	11 483	7 676	3 631	2001	Autriche
499	...	984	3 352	26 950	3 806	11 690	7 763	3 690	2002	
428	...	1 096	3 533	28 497	4 141	12 412	8 394	3 550	2003	
502	...	1 110	3 487	28 384	3 852	12 369	8 467	3 696	2004	
...	...	2 327	2 292	22 862	754	5 335	16 059	714	2001	Bélarus
...	...	2 833	2 283	22 663	673	5 074	16 350	566	2002	
...	...	3 444	2 349	23 193	647	4 938	17 018	590	2003	
...	...	3 040	2 487	24 436	553	5 130	18 469	283	2004	
1 122	5 385	2 630	4 523	46 417	7 942	18 918	14 644	4 913	2001	Belgique
1 241	7 035	3 352	4 196	43 257	6 726	16 808	14 864	4 858	2002	
1 478	7 098	4 369	4 374	45 296	6 263	18 285	16 002	4 746	2003	
1 360	7 978	3 846	4 340	45 119	6 079	17 963	16 189	4 887	2004	
...	...	...	1 137	4 307	2 816	877	270	344	2001	Bosnie-Herzégovine
...	...	...	1 106	4 233	2 660	936	280	357	2002	
...	...	...	1 125	4 310	2 681	972	292	366	2003	
...	...	...	1 170	4 572	2 791	1 112	341	328	2004	
104	97	542	1 890	14 957	7 103	3 539	3 043	1 273	2001	Bulgarie
125	107	777	1 775	13 966	6 413	3 451	2 671	1 430	2002	
160	139	1 065	1 883	14 730	7 209	3 445	2 778	1 298	2003	
154	117	527	1 872	14 603	6 976	3 628	2 770	1 230	2004	
21	29	248	1 828	8 112	529	4 174	2 572	838	2001	Croatie
20	24	145	1 927	8 560	654	4 502	2 634	770	2002	
24	22	-110	2 086	9 264	764	5 123	2 618	759	2003	
29	24	331	2 013	8 941	816	4 473	2 731	922	2004	
163	...	1 363	3 557	36 512	20 568	6 359	8 925	660	2001	République tchèque
168	...	1 650	3 482	35 545	19 807	6 236	8 624	877	2002	
203	...	1 647	3 540	36 120	20 070	6 351	8 714	985	2003	
291	...	1 773	3 575	36 503	19 964	6 752	8 653	1 133	2004	
800	1 141	-4	3 081	16 478	4 131	6 878	5 146	323	2001	Danemark
692	941	-100	3 054	16 392	4 080	6 927	5 141	244	2002	
719	991	106	3 327	17 580	5 618	7 038	5 179	-255	2003	
818	806	-90	3 303	17 828	5 185	7 173	5 149	322	2004	
17	102	...	3 384	4 626	3 073	817	789	-53	2001	Estonie
20	120	...	3 258	4 434	3 010	821	662	-59	2002	
19	114	...	3 680	4 990	3 537	859	756	-161	2003	
28	153	...	3 843	5 192	3 598	885	861	-152	2004	
...	...	...	*4 816	*222	0	*215	...	7	2001	Iles Féroé
...	...	...	*4 880	*224	0	*217	...	8	2002	
...	...	...	*4 924	*226	0	*219	...	8	2003	
...	...	...	*4 854	*226	0	*219	...	8	2004	
355	582	-1 919	4 708	24 458	6 226	10 157	4 119	3 956	2001	Finlande
351	655	-1 440	4 886	25 437	6 706	10 763	4 093	3 875	2002	
362	650	-1 360	5 193	27 109	8 398	10 969	4 538	3 205	2003	
418	524	-1 988	5 280	27 561	7 701	11 758	4 424	3 678	2004	
4 643	2 720	8 464	2 905	173 380	12 845	81 659	41 720	37 156	2001	France[3]
4 805	2 646	8 272	2 840	170 304	13 912	78 074	41 649	36 669	2002	
5 079	2 852	9 855	2 852	171 722	14 805	75 332	43 758	37 827	2003	
5 427	3 211	9 666	2 811	174 227	14 837	75 863	44 644	38 883	2004	
6 925	2 239	5 810	3 636	299 059	85 200	111 573	83 990	18 296	2001	Allemagne
6 869	2 396	6 616	3 540	291 849	83 131	105 941	83 967	18 809	2002	
6 975	2 641	6 467	3 559	293 719	83 430	104 373	88 009	17 907	2003	
7 596	2 704	6 292	3 571	294 756	86 613	101 887	87 479	18 778	2004	

50 Production, trade and consumption of commercial energy—Thousand metric tons of oil equivalent and kilograms per capita (*continued*)

Production, commerce et consommation d'énergie commerciale—Milliers de tonnes d'équivalent pétrole et kilogrammes par habitant (*suite*)

Region, country or area	Year Année	Primary energy production – Production d'énergie primaire Total Totale	Solids Solides	Liquids Liquides	Gas Gaz	Electricity Electricité	Changes in stocks Variations des stocks	Imports Importations	Exports Exportations
Gibraltar	2001	...	...	...	...	...	...	1 187	...
	2002	...	...	...	...	...	...	1 208	...
	2003	...	...	...	...	...	...	1 239	...
	2004	...	...	...	...	...	...	1 278	...
Greece	2001	9 232	8 691	193	45	304	-123	26 497	3 205
	2002	9 828	9 231	191	47	359	1 009	27 733	3 710
	2003	9 671	8 947	138	34	551	-883	28 920	5 299
	2004	9 891	9 175	134	32	549	1 009	30 704	5 044
Hungary	2001	8 451	2 869	1 578	2 773	1 231	-789	17 094	2 571
	2002	8 491	2 686	1 950	2 638	1 217	126	18 536	2 991
	2003	8 225	2 743	1 959	2 561	962	466	20 167	2 800
	2004	7 953	2 318	1 942	2 650	1 043	6	19 634	2 606
Iceland	2001	690	...	...	...	690	-3	922	...
	2002	723	...	...	...	723	-24	947	...
	2003	730	...	...	...	730	-52	921	...
	2004	741	...	...	...	741	31	1 047	...
Ireland	2001	1 840	966	...	732	142	178	15 386	1 338
	2002	1 535	636	...	753	146	-165	15 521	1 481
	2003	1 950	1 220	...	604	126	271	15 346	1 599
	2004	1 885	974	...	765	146	446	15 225	1 242
Italy[4]	2001	23 787	88	4 099	13 870	5 730	-2 736	172 249	19 968
	2002	24 136	103	5 535	13 307	5 191	3 496	178 139	19 247
	2003	22 757	157	5 570	12 635	4 394	-2 274	184 480	21 546
	2004	22 222	62	5 445	11 795	4 920	105	188 826	22 767
Latvia	2001	260	16	...	...	244	-221	2 799	40
	2002	245	32	...	...	213	-178	2 788	44
	2003	201	2	...	...	199	79	3 215	9
	2004	274	3	...	...	272	236	3 862	39
Lithuania	2001	1 569	8	471	53	1 037	-177	9 711	5 65
	2002	1 788	11	434	60	1 283	-146	9 476	5 45
	2003	1 862	10	382	53	1 416	128	10 599	6 24
	2004	1 743	11	303	49	1 380	168	12 434	7 74
Luxembourg	2001	78	...	...	...	78	-29	3 856	9
	2002	88	...	...	...	88	16	4 323	26
	2003	81	...	...	...	81	6	4 509	25
	2004	78	...	...	...	78	-13	5 006	28
Malta	2001	...	...	...	...	...	...	755	...
	2002	...	...	...	...	...	...	801	...
	2003	...	...	...	...	...	...	909	...
	2004	...	...	...	...	...	...	925	...
Netherlands	2001	64 662	...	2 334	61 904	424	228	134 518	103 78
	2002	63 875	...	3 141	60 305	429	-900	132 497	102 28
	2003	61 618	...	3 137	58 013	468	-235	129 156	98 28
	2004	71 881	...	2 953	68 428	500	432	130 684	107 46
Norway[5]	2001	223 275	1 200	157 551	54 301	10 223	-2 056	5 855	209 17
	2002	229 999	1 431	151 681	65 716	11 170	303	5 086	215 31
	2003	231 743	1 976	147 011	73 604	9 152	1 071	5 871	214 94
	2004	234 210	1 949	144 627	78 215	9 419	-396	6 087	219 39
Poland	2001	76 499	71 488	767	3 880	364	-643	30 937	19 40
	2002	76 084	71 049	728	3 966	341	1 091	31 781	19 38
	2003	76 233	71 132	794	4 013	294	260	32 287	18 18
	2004	75 844	70 253	900	4 362	330	341	34 187	18 26

0

Production, trade and consumption of commercial energy—Thousand metric tons of oil equivalent and kilograms per capita (*continued*)

Production, commerce et consommation d'énergie commerciale—Milliers de tonnes d'équivalent pétrole et kilogrammes par habitant (*suite*)

Bunkers - Soutes			Consumption - Consommation							
Air Avion	Sea Maritime	Unallocated Nondistribué	Per capita Par habitant	Total Totale	Solids Solides	Liquids Liquides	Gas Gaz	Electricity Electricité	Year Année	Région, pays ou zone
4	1 070	...	4 060	114	...	114	...	...	2001	Gibraltar
4	1 088	...	4 132	116	...	116	...	...	2002	
4	1 115	...	4 277	120	...	120	...	...	2003	
4	1 150	...	4 422	124	...	124	...	...	2004	
760	3 528	-993	2 685	29 351	9 604	17 358	1 870	519	2001	Grèce
760	3 158	-1 462	2 765	30 385	9 612	18 164	2 001	608	2002	
785	3 237	-1 263	2 851	31 417	9 700	18 734	2 251	731	2003	
809	3 263	-699	2 823	31 168	9 762	18 138	2 476	792	2004	
221	...	860	2 224	22 682	3 516	5 762	11 901	1 503	2001	Hongrie
208	...	141	2 315	23 559	3 429	6 537	12 012	1 582	2002	
204	...	585	2 400	24 337	3 520	6 051	13 207	1 559	2003	
220	...	737	2 374	24 018	3 249	6 070	13 014	1 685	2004	
115	47	110	4 750	1 344	92	562	...	690	2001	Islande
101	67	120	4 900	1 406	96	587	...	723	2002	
103	68	120	4 887	1 412	91	591	...	730	2003	
119	71	126	4 918	1 441	103	597	...	741	2004	
703	163	-46	3 892	14 890	3 038	7 749	3 982	121	2001	Irlande
746	150	3	3 805	14 841	2 937	7 627	4 087	189	2002	
731	172	62	3 648	14 461	2 802	7 375	4 058	226	2003	
691	151	6	3 618	14 573	2 501	7 741	4 050	280	2004	
3 409	2 834	-2 635	3 027	175 196	13 529	87 223	64 555	9 890	2001	Italie[4]
3 199	3 002	-3 149	3 045	176 480	14 008	88 813	64 118	9 542	2002	
3 598	3 234	-495	3 130	181 627	15 272	86 888	70 690	8 776	2003	
3 568	3 381	1 315	3 108	179 911	17 190	80 522	73 354	8 844	2004	
27	198	0	1 275	3 015	102	1 096	1 411	406	2001	Lettonie
28	194	0	1 255	2 945	75	1 021	1 435	415	2002	
40	190	0	1 329	3 098	63	1 112	1 497	426	2003	
48	205	3	1 402	3 252	51	1 269	1 480	452	2004	
10	102	-90	1 659	5 783	98	2 564	2 425	696	2001	Lituanie
12	112	101	1 648	5 729	165	2 359	2 480	725	2002	
22	111	140	1 678	5 812	211	2 138	2 694	769	2003	
34	112	207	1 714	5 907	206	2 262	2 678	761	2004	
348	...	...	8 017	3 519	110	2 074	772	563	2001	Luxembourg
377	...	...	8 443	3 749	93	2 103	1 170	383	2002	
392	...	...	8 793	3 939	78	2 279	1 182	400	2003	
427	...	...	9 711	4 386	94	2 591	1 333	368	2004	
59	23	...	1 723	674	...	674	...	...	2001	Malte
90	23	...	1 742	688	...	688	...	...	2002	
79	23	...	2 031	806	...	806	...	...	2003	
101	23	...	2 004	801	...	801	...	...	2004	
3 205	14 768	-9 069	5 396	86 266	7 812	37 047	39 497	1 910	2001	Pays-Bas
3 342	14 709	-16 800	5 820	93 738	8 305	43 770	39 824	1 837	2002	
3 288	13 774	-16 387	5 684	92 046	8 535	41 585	39 998	1 929	2003	
3 518	14 965	-14 635	5 586	90 817	8 333	39 762	40 828	1 895	2004	
362	816	-6 759	6 127	27 590	944	10 091	6 025	10 530	2001	Norvège[5]
399	670	-11 768	6 668	30 165	813	14 459	4 558	10 335	2002	
210	567	-13 042	7 439	33 861	789	17 349	5 894	9 829	2003	
242	520	-13 364	7 406	33 900	921	17 649	4 929	10 402	2004	
275	265	1 476	2 242	86 654	57 751	17 588	11 530	-215	2001	Pologne
270	275	2 550	2 182	84 296	56 480	16 845	11 237	-267	2002	
292	290	1 742	2 296	87 754	57 998	17 823	12 512	-580	2003	
286	258	1 921	2 329	88 961	57 023	19 208	13 199	-469	2004	

50 Production, trade and consumption of commercial energy — Thousand metric tons of oil equivalent and kilograms per cap *(continued)*

Production, commerce et consommation d'énergie commerciale — Milliers de tonnes d'équivalent pétrole et kilogrammes habitant (*suite*)

Region, country or area	Year Année	Primary energy production – Production d'énergie primaire Total Totale	Solids Solides	Liquids Liquides	Gas Gaz	Electricity Electricité	Changes in stocks Variations des stocks	Imports Importations	Exp Exportati
Portugal	2001	1 267	...	...	...	1 267	252	22 752	1
	2002	750	...	...	...	750	-501	23 281	1
	2003	1 431	...	...	...	1 431	449	23 415	1
	2004	950	...	...	...	950	-413	23 948	1
Republic of Moldova	2001	6	...	...	...	6	17	3 353	
	2002	10	...	...	...	10	-15	3 143	
	2003	6	...	...	...	6	54	3 492	
	2004	5	...	...	...	5	-9	3 562	
Romania	2001	25 774	5 788	6 256	11 978	1 751	295	12 827	2
	2002	24 993	5 268	6 093	11 779	1 854	259	14 085	4
	2003	24 783	5 724	5 909	11 587	1 562	-249	14 001	3
	2004	24 654	5 502	5 724	11 531	1 897	1 010	16 383	4
Russian Federation	2001	998 275	103 614	346 527	521 232	26 903	6 683	22 373	403
	2002	1 037 102	99 717	377 885	533 190	26 310	8 008	22 428	445
	2003	1 109 168	107 591	419 326	555 733	26 517	12 165	25 533	493
	2004	1 160 610	109 516	457 060	566 269	27 764	6 775	22 063	544
Serbia and Montenegro	2001	10 235	7 760	899	505	1 071	...	4 163	[illegible]
	2002	10 431	8 204	812	405	1 010	...	5 134	[illegible]
	2003	10 561	8 613	773	328	847	...	5 422	[illegible]
	2004	10 730	8 767	652	285	1 025	...	6 108	[illegible]
Slovakia	2001	3 192	1 003	111	167	1 911	-430	15 917	4
	2002	3 281	997	108	161	2 015	117	16 477	4
	2003	3 028	907	84	185	1 852	-137	16 472	4
	2004	2 948	864	42	215	1 826	474	17 314	4
Slovenia	2001	1 683	899	0	6	778	-212	4 214	[illegible]
	2002	1 793	1 019	1	5	768	-58	4 332	[illegible]
	2003	1 774	1 050	0	5	719	10	4 596	[illegible]
	2004	1 872	1 045	0	5	822	30	4 798	[illegible]
Spain	2001	18 233	7 539	338	523	9 833	-453	105 743	5
	2002	16 581	7 189	390	519	8 483	2 066	114 506	4
	2003	17 589	6 811	424	219	10 137	-82	116 812	5 5
	2004	17 126	6 632	374	344	9 776	-782	125 425	7
Sweden	2001	13 305	263	0	...	13 042	533	29 893	11
	2002	11 949	332	0	...	11 618	-1 676	29 396	9 9
	2003	10 808	345	0	...	10 464	1 035	32 574	10 4
	2004	12 319	369	40	...	11 910	-470	31 712	12 1
Switzerland[6]	2001	6 004	...	0	28	5 976	-180	18 651	3 5
	2002	5 544	...	0	26	5 518	40	18 315	3 3
	2003	5 562	...	0	27	5 535	-160	18 164	3 4
	2004	5 398	...	0	28	5 370	15	18 044	2 9
TFYR of Macedonia	2001	2 238	2 185	...	...	54	-44	1 224	[illegible]
	2002	2 108	2 043	...	...	65	182	1 349	[illegible]
	2003	2 108	1 989	...	...	118	-37	1 331	[illegible]
	2004	2 080	1 953	...	...	127	4	1 314	[illegible]
Ukraine	2001	60 244	31 765	3 789	17 090	7 600	0	72 614	9 9
	2002	59 478	30 699	3 820	17 409	7 550	0	77 280	13 5
	2003	62 962	33 210	4 059	17 885	7 809	0	87 417	17 0
	2004	61 447	30 850	3 003	19 087	8 507	308	87 354	18 1
United Kingdom	2001	254 534	19 238	121 094	105 841	8 362	3 055	98 192	116 7
	2002	249 441	18 068	119 285	103 787	8 301	-598	97 694	121 5
	2003	236 771	17 038	108 558	102 926	8 249	-2 203	100 578	111 1
	2004	217 947	15 121	99 123	96 006	7 697	1 303	118 321	101 4

Production, trade and consumption of commercial energy—Thousand metric tons of oil equivalent and kilograms per capita (*continued*)

Production, commerce et consommation d'énergie commerciale—Milliers de tonnes d'équivalent pétrole et kilogrammes par habitant (*suite*)

Bunkers - Soutes			Consumption - Consommation							
Air Avion	Sea Maritime	Unallocated Nondistribué	Per capita Par habitant	Total Totale	Solids Solides	Liquids Liquides	Gas Gaz	Electricity Electricité	Year Année	Région, pays ou zone
591	482	1 366	1 952	20 038	3 176	13 069	2 506	1 288	2001	Portugal
598	491	1 035	2 052	21 191	3 585	13 661	3 033	913	2002	
635	589	1 247	1 955	20 351	3 381	12 370	2 929	1 671	2003	
695	670	1 102	2 018	21 140	3 420	12 542	3 670	1 507	2004	
18	...	...	916	3 325	69	481	2 586	189	2001	République de Moldova
19	...	...	869	3 149	73	549	2 293	234	2002	
12	...	...	946	3 420	89	597	2 431	302	2003	
*11	...	...	836	3 527	83	641	2 545	258	2004	
113	...	1 111	1 541	34 104	7 487	10 334	14 644	1 639	2001	Roumanie
97	...	616	1 539	33 543	7 800	8 992	15 143	1 608	2002	
118	...	401	1 596	34 681	8 111	8 821	16 366	1 383	2003	
137	...	1 535	1 553	33 722	8 125	8 316	15 486	1 795	2004	
9 251	...	12 906	4 066	588 240	90 600	110 624	361 477	25 539	2001	Fédération de Russie
9 599	...	10 458	4 068	585 612	90 497	108 077	361 841	25 197	2002	
9 754	...	13 497	4 226	605 357	91 177	108 146	380 667	25 367	2003	
9 897	...	12 465	4 232	608 820	88 262	108 270	385 179	27 109	2004	
48	...	496	1 236	13 418	7 938	2 139	1 923	1 418	2001	Serbie-et-Monténégro
59	...	463	1 338	14 490	8 543	2 617	1 934	1 396	2002	
64	...	593	1 379	14 925	8 949	2 867	2 022	1 087	2003	
47	...	752	1 451	15 707	9 296	3 227	2 182	1 001	2004	
...	...	190	2 845	15 302	4 033	2 821	6 854	1 594	2001	Slovaquie
...	...	457	2 800	15 061	3 882	3 002	6 519	1 658	2002	
...	...	405	2 797	15 047	4 201	2 890	6 299	1 658	2003	
...	...	124	2 784	14 977	4 113	3 089	6 109	1 666	2004	
27	...	0	2 765	5 503	1 587	2 345	945	626	2001	Slovénie
28	...	0	2 817	5 616	1 739	2 296	911	671	2002	
26	...	0	2 877	5 739	1 684	2 314	1 007	733	2003	
20	...	0	2 931	5 851	1 712	2 386	999	755	2004	
2 773	6 877	6 743	2 547	102 844	19 351	55 141	18 222	10 129	2001	Espagne
2 667	7 020	6 500	2 641	107 906	22 161	55 969	20 835	8 941	2002	
2 798	7 150	7 699	2 678	111 267	20 379	56 917	23 726	10 245	2003	
3 103	7 376	7 884	2 730	117 946	21 887	58 575	27 969	9 516	2004	
712	1 417	1 346	3 168	28 139	2 712	12 040	973	12 415	2001	Suède
527	1 225	2 293	3 254	28 988	2 799	13 120	990	12 078	2002	
513	1 645	2 332	3 061	27 367	2 645	12 168	987	11 567	2003	
628	1 937	2 076	3 093	27 758	2 908	12 139	983	11 729	2004	
1 500	12	-55	2 736	19 877	148	11 837	2 814	5 078	2001	Suisse[6]
1 330	8	5	2 608	19 106	137	11 076	2 762	5 131	2002	
1 210	10	27	2 612	19 176	143	10 846	2 920	5 268	2003	
1 155	9	7	2 589	19 293	134	10 838	3 012	5 309	2004	
23	...	7	1 594	3 244	2 336	737	80	91	2001	L'ex-R.y. Macédoine
39	...	8	1 494	3 034	2 000	819	83	133	2002	
7	...	6	1 542	3 126	2 043	809	74	200	2003	
6	...	12	1 558	3 162	2 046	823	65	229	2004	
317	...	103	2 498	122 485	33 192	12 749	69 207	7 337	2001	Ukraine
302	...	1 666	2 504	121 209	32 546	13 048	68 332	7 282	2002	
372	...	3 439	2 718	129 473	37 119	12 629	72 340	7 385	2003	
372	...	1 956	2 698	128 006	33 083	13 681	73 192	8 049	2004	
9 659	2 231	-476	3 701	221 541	41 406	74 602	96 277	9 256	2001	Royaume-Uni
9 479	1 923	-151	3 635	214 953	37 634	72 899	95 395	9 025	2002	
9 720	1 770	439	3 649	216 486	40 264	72 363	95 424	8 435	2003	
10 759	2 092	-851	3 711	221 522	39 947	76 136	97 097	8 341	2004	

50 Production, trade and consumption of commercial energy—Thousand metric tons of oil equivalent and kilograms per cap (*continued*)

Production, commerce et consommation d'énergie commerciale—Milliers de tonnes d'équivalent pétrole et kilogrammes habitant (*suite*)

Region, country or area	Year Année	Primary energy production – Production d'énergie primaire Total Totale	Solids Solides	Liquids Liquides	Gas Gaz	Electricity Electricité	Changes in stocks Variations des stocks	Imports Importations	Expo Exportati
Oceania	**2001**	**252 763**	**169 534**	**41 162**	**38 344**	**3 724**	**5 534**	**35 247**	**162 6**
	2002	**255 622**	**175 350**	**36 866**	**39 410**	**3 996**	**1 634**	**36 606**	**168 8**
	2003	**252 874**	**175 745**	**34 070**	**39 157**	**3 904**	**-125**	**36 828**	**167 8**
	2004	**259 945**	**183 349**	**32 897**	**39 473**	**4 226**	**1 138**	**37 292**	**172 2**
Australia	2001	237 424	167 832	35 779	32 353	1 461	5 907	26 821	156 [illegible]
	2002	240 766	173 380	32 264	33 711	1 410	1 675	27 597	163 6
	2003	239 903	173 536	30 120	34 790	1 458	115	27 344	162 9
	2004	247 454	181 098	29 321	35 557	1 478	794	27 428	168 [illegible]
Cook Islands*	2001	...	...	...	...	...	...	19	
	2002	...	...	...	...	...	...	19	
	2003	...	...	...	...	...	...	21	
	2004	...	...	...	...	...	...	21	
Fiji	2001	*36	...	...	...	*36	...	603	*[illegible]
	*2002	36	...	...	...	36	...	594	[illegible]
	*2003	37	...	...	...	37	...	564	[illegible]
	*2004	37	...	...	...	37	...	528	[illegible]
French Polynesia	2001	9	...	...	...	9	...	226	
	2002	8	...	...	...	8	...	276	
	2003	8	...	...	...	8	...	*272	
	*2004	8	...	...	...	8	...	274	
Kiribati	2001	...	...	...	...	...	...	10	
	*2002	...	...	...	...	...	...	10	
	*2003	...	...	...	...	...	...	10	
	*2004	...	...	...	...	...	...	10	
Nauru*	2001	...	...	...	...	...	...	52	
	2002	...	...	...	...	...	...	52	
	2003	...	...	...	...	...	...	53	
	2004	...	...	...	...	...	...	53	
New Caledonia	2001	32	...	...	...	32	...	588	
	2002	28	...	...	...	28	...	755	
	2003	28	...	...	...	28	...	868	
	2004	29	...	...	...	29	...	808	
New Zealand	2001	*11 731	1 702	2 016	*5 912	2 101	-374	5 949	2 3
	2002	11 868	1 970	1 849	*5 620	2 429	-41	6 323	2 4
	2003	10 215	2 209	1 431	*4 287	2 289	-240	6 686	2 2
	2004	9 978	2 251	1 302	*3 837	2 589	345	7 168	1 9
Niue*	2001	...	...	...	...	...	...	1	
	2002	...	...	...	...	...	...	1	
	2003	...	...	...	...	...	...	1	
	2004	...	...	...	...	...	...	1	
Palau*	2001	2	...	...	...	2	...	91	
	2002	2	...	...	...	2	...	91	
	2003	2	...	...	...	2	...	96	
	2004	2	...	...	...	2	...	96	
Papua New Guinea	2001	3 525	...	3 367	*79	79	...	*713	*3 2
	2002	2 911	...	2 753	*79	*79	...	*713	*2 6
	2003	2 678	...	2 519	*80	*79	...	*733	2 4
	2004	2 433	...	2 274	*80	*80	...	*723	*2 2
Samoa*	2001	3	...	...	...	3	...	48	
	2002	3	...	...	...	3	...	48	
	2003	3	...	...	...	3	...	50	
	2004	3	...	...	...	3	...	51	

50 **Production, trade and consumption of commercial energy**—Thousand metric tons of oil equivalent and kilograms per capita (*continued*)

Production, commerce et consommation d'énergie commerciale—Milliers de tonnes d'équivalent pétrole et kilogrammes par habitant (*suite*)

Bunkers - Soutes			Consumption - Consommation							
Air Avion	Sea Maritime	Unallocated Nondistribué	Per capita Par habitant	Total Totale	Solids Solides	Liquids Liquides	Gas Gaz	Electricity Electricité	Year Année	Région, pays ou zone
3 396	**1 117**	**-7 649**	**3 994**	**122 932**	**42 673**	**47 976**	**28 560**	**3 724**	**2001**	**Océanie**
2 839	**1 141**	**-2 552**	**3 848**	**120 270**	**43 234**	**43 505**	**29 536**	**3 996**	**2002**	
3 038	**1 068**	**-2 083**	**3 751**	**119 956**	**42 852**	**44 213**	**28 988**	**3 904**	**2003**	
3 232	**1 157**	**-1 747**	**3 727**	**121 182**	**43 790**	**43 976**	**29 190**	**4 226**	**2004**	
2 604	788	-7 532	5 446	105 585	41 645	39 910	22 569	1 461	2001	Australie
2 061	733	-2 344	5 217	102 574	42 229	35 097	23 837	1 410	2002	
2 246	733	-1 966	5 176	103 125	41 460	35 587	24 621	1 458	2003	
2 266	842	-1 514	5 169	104 476	42 418	35 306	25 274	1 478	2004	
9	...	...	486	9	...	9	...	...	2001	Iles Cook*
9	...	...	462	9	...	9	...	...	2002	
10	...	...	488	10	...	10	...	...	2003	
10	...	...	484	10	...	10	...	...	2004	
*98	*41	...	462	390	*10	343	...	*36	2001	Fidji
90	41	...	456	390	10	343	...	36	*2002	
68	36	...	448	389	10	342	...	37	*2003	
45	36	...	426	375	9	329	...	37	*2004	
*6	*38	...	805	191	...	182	...	9	2001	Polynésie française
*6	*38	...	992	239	...	231	...	8	2002	
*6	*36	...	*971	*237	...	*229	...	8	2003	
6	46	...	864	230	...	222	...	8	*2004	
*1	...	...	109	9	...	9	...	...	2001	Kiribati
1	...	...	106	9	...	9	...	...	*2002	
1	...	...	100	9	...	9	...	...	*2003	
1	...	...	92	9	...	9	...	...	*2004	
7	...	...	3 722	45	...	45	...	...	2001	Nauru*
7	...	...	3 649	45	...	45	...	...	2002	
7	...	...	3 658	46	...	46	...	...	2003	
7	...	...	3 590	46	...	46	...	...	2004	
...	...	...	2 796	598	181	385	...	32	2001	Nouvelle-Calédonie
...	...	...	3 493	758	193	537	...	28	2002	
...	...	...	3 800	866	219	619	...	28	2003	
...	...	...	3 500	808	197	582	...	29	2004	
620	247	-182	3 875	14 980	835	6 132	*5 912	2 101	2001	Nouvelle-Zélande
615	326	-252	3 865	15 121	800	6 272	*5 620	2 429	2002	
648	259	-153	3 495	14 118	1 162	6 381	*4 287	2 289	2003	
846	231	-265	3 448	14 082	1 165	6 491	*3 836	2 589	2004	
...	...	...	507	1	...	1	...	...	2001	Nioué*
...	...	...	507	1	...	1	...	...	2002	
...	...	...	507	1	...	1	...	...	2003	
...	...	...	507	1	...	1	...	...	2004	
14	...	...	3 956	79	...	77	...	2	2001	Palaos*
14	...	...	3 956	79	...	77	...	2	2002	
15	...	...	4 110	82	...	80	...	2	2003	
15	...	...	4 106	82	...	80	...	2	2004	
*31	*3	65	*177	*872	*1	*713	*79	79	2001	Papouasie-Nvl-Guinée
*31	*3	44	*173	*872	*1	*713	*79	*79	2002	
*31	*3	36	*168	*892	*1	*732	*80	*79	2003	
*31	*3	31	*163	*881	*1	*721	*80	*80	2004	
...	...	...	324	51	...	48	...	3	2001	Samoa*
...	...	...	322	51	...	48	...	3	2002	
...	...	...	309	54	...	50	...	3	2003	
...	...	...	304	54	...	51	...	3	2004	

50 Production, trade and consumption of commercial energy—Thousand metric tons of oil equivalent and kilograms per capita (*continued*)

Production, commerce et consommation d'énergie commerciale—Milliers de tonnes d'équivalent pétrole et kilogrammes par habitant (*suite*)

Region, country or area	Year Année	Primary energy production – Production d'énergie primaire: Total Totale	Solids Solides	Liquids Liquides	Gas Gaz	Electricity Electricité	Changes in stocks Variations des stocks	Imports Importations	Exports Exportations
Solomon Islands*	2001	...	...	...	...	...	...	59	...
	2002	...	...	...	...	...	...	59	...
	2003	...	...	...	...	...	...	61	...
	2004	...	...	...	...	...	...	61	...
Tonga	2001	...	...	...	...	...	...	37	...
	2002	...	...	...	...	...	...	*37	...
	2003	...	...	...	...	...	...	*39	...
	2004	...	...	...	...	...	...	*40	...
Vanuatu	2001	...	...	...	...	...	...	*29	...
	2002	...	...	...	...	...	...	*29	...
	2003	...	...	...	...	...	...	*30	...
	2004	...	...	...	...	...	...	*30	...

Source

United Nations Statistics Division, New York, the energy statistics database, last accessed January 2007.

Notes

1 Refers to the Southern African Customs Union.
2 For statistical purposes, the data for China do not include those for the Hong Kong Special Administrative Region (Hong Kong SAR), Macao Special Administrative Region (Macao SAR) and Taiwan Province of China.
3 Including Monaco.
4 Including San Marino.
5 Including Svalbard and Jan Mayen Islands.
6 Including Liechtenstein.

Source

Organisation des Nations Unies, Division de statistique, New York, la bas de données pour les statistiques énergétiques, dernier accès janvier 2007.

Notes

1 Se réfèrent à l'Union douanière d'afrique australe.
2 Pour la présentation des statistiques, les données pour la Chine ne comprennent pas la Région Administrative Spéciale de Hong Kong (Hong Kong RAS), la Région Administrative Spéciale de Macao (Macao RAS) et la province de Taiwan.
3 Y compris Monaco.
4 Y compris Saint-Marin.
5 Y compris îles Svalbard et Jan Mayen.
6 Y compris Liechtenstein.

50 Production, trade and consumption of commercial energy—Thousand metric tons of oil equivalent and kilograms per capita (*continued*)

Production, commerce et consommation d'énergie commerciale—Milliers de tonnes d'équivalent pétrole et kilogrammes par habitant (*suite*)

Bunkers - Soutes			Consumption - Consommation							
Air Avion	Sea Maritime	Unallocated Nondistribué	Per capita Par habitant	Total Totale	Solids Solides	Liquids Liquides	Gas Gaz	Electricity Electricité	Year Année	Région, pays ou zone
3	...	...	117	56	...	56	...	...	2001	Iles Salomon*
3	...	...	114	56	...	56	...	...	2002	
3	...	...	115	58	...	58	...	...	2003	
3	...	...	111	58	...	58	...	...	2004	
1	...	...	357	36	0	36	...	...	2001	Tonga
*1	...	...	*357	*36	0	*36	...	...	2002	
*1	...	...	*377	*38	0	*38	...	...	2003	
*1	...	...	*355	*39	0	*39	...	...	2004	
...	...	...	*142	*29	0	*29	...	...	2001	Vanuatu
...	...	...	*138	*29	0	*29	...	...	2002	
...	...	...	*140	*30	0	*30	...	...	2003	
...	...	...	*139	*30	0	*30	...	...	2004	

51 Energy production

Production d'énergie

Region, country or area / Région, pays ou zone	Year / Année	Hard coal and lignite / Houille et lignite	Crude petroleum and NGL / Pétrole brut et GNL	Motor gasoline / Essence auto	Jet fuel / Carbu-réacteurs	Gas-diesel oil / Gazole/carburant diesel	Residual fuel oil / Mazout résiduel	Liquefied petroleum gas / Gaz de pétrole liquéfiés	Natural gas (terajoules) / Gaz naturel (térajoules)	Electricity (million kWh) / Electricité (millions de kWh)
		Thousand metric tons — Milliers de tonnes								
World Monde	**2001**	**4 803 346**	**3 724 618**	**846 795**	**208 168**	**1 041 985**	**603 764**	**235 710**	**98 583 440**	**15 566 563**
	2002	**4 854 330**	**3 672 348**	**871 252**	**206 350**	**1 039 571**	**593 930**	**239 519**	**101 716 809**	**16 182 943**
	2003	**5 178 195**	**3 826 831**	**878 167**	**205 835**	**1 078 777**	**594 203**	**244 346**	**104 298 102**	**16 765 899**
	2004	**5 547 198**	**3 988 537**	**893 228**	**218 475**	**1 123 187**	**599 902**	**251 772**	**106 824 364**	**17 535 781**
Africa Afrique	**2001**	**229 560[1]**	**415 482**	**24 174**	**7 752**	**35 957**	**35 203**	**12 205**	**4 994 533**	**450 480**
	2002	**226 088[1]**	**410 674**	**24 227**	**7 933**	**36 340**	**36 920**	**13 124**	**5 396 878**	**483 124**
	2003	**244 106[1]**	**436 841**	**23 002**	**7 897**	**35 392**	**33 970**	**12 726**	**5 660 937**	**508 615**
	2004	**248 218[1]**	**463 560**	**21 945**	**7 954**	**36 153**	**33 885**	**12 298**	**5 966 704**	**538 820**
Algeria Algérie	2001	...	90 947	2 058	1 452	6 441	5 755	9 047	3 068 448	26 624
	2002	...	95 534	1 939	1 393	6 044	5 833	9 956	3 213 741	27 647
	2003	...	102 501	1 893	1 315	6 186	6 093	9 756	3 248 416	29 571
	2004	...	107 144	1 925	986	6 340	5 560	9 223	3 216 262	31 250
Angola Angola	2001	...	36 469[2]	107	331	641	553	31	*20 140	1 638
	2002	...	44 045[2]	105	350	669	591	39	23 560	1 765
	2003	...	43 083[2]	108	352	683	609	40	*27 360	1 995
	2004	...	49 443[2]	96	302	669	604	28	28 500	2 504
Benin Bénin	2001	...	35[2]	...	...	...	...	...	...	66
	2002	...	40[2]	...	...	...	...	...	...	63
	2003	...	20[2]	...	...	...	...	...	...	80
	2004	...	*20[2]	...	...	...	...	...	...	81
Burkina Faso Burkina Faso	2001	...	...	...	...	...	...	...	...	330
	2002	...	...	...	...	...	...	...	...	340
	2003	...	...	...	...	...	...	...	...	360
	2004	...	...	...	...	...	...	...	...	400
Burundi Burundi	2001	...	...	...	...	...	...	...	...	117
	2002	...	...	...	...	...	...	...	...	129
	*2003	...	...	...	...	...	...	...	...	132
	*2004	...	...	...	...	...	...	...	...	135
Cameroon Cameroun	2001	...	7 025[2]	331	60	422	358	28	...	3 541
	2002	...	6 439[2]	232	69	370	317	18	...	3 300
	2003	...	6 735[2]	290	69	446	327	21	...	3 684
	2004	...	6 637[2]	402	69	607	388	28	...	4 110
Cape Verde Cap-Vert	2001	...	...	...	...	...	...	...	...	165
	2002	...	...	...	...	...	...	...	...	182
	2003	...	...	...	...	...	...	...	...	200
	2004	...	...	...	...	...	...	...	...	220
Central African Rep.* Rép. centrafricaine*	2001	...	...	...	...	...	...	...	...	108
	2002	...	...	...	...	...	...	...	...	108
	2003	...	...	...	...	...	...	...	...	110
	2004	...	...	...	...	...	...	...	...	110
Chad* Tchad*	2001	...	...	...	...	...	...	...	...	98
	2002	...	...	...	...	...	...	...	...	98
	2003	...	...	...	...	...	...	...	...	99
	2004	...	...	...	...	...	...	...	...	99
Comoros* Comores*	2001	...	...	...	...	...	...	...	...	19
	2002	...	...	...	...	...	...	...	...	19
	2003	...	...	...	...	...	...	...	...	20
	2004	...	...	...	...	...	...	...	...	20

Region, country or area Région, pays ou zone	Year Année	Hard coal and lignite Houille et lignite	Crude petroleum and NGL Pétrole brut et GNL	Motor gasoline Essence auto	Jet fuel Carbu-réacteurs	Gas-diesel oil Gazole/carburant diesel	Residual fuel oil Mazout résiduel	Liquefied petroleum gas Gaz de pétrole liquéfiés	Natural gas (terajoules) Gaz naturel (térajoules)	Electricity (million kWh) Electricité (millions de kWh)
		Thousand metric tons — Milliers de tonnes								
Congo Congo	2001	...	12 703	56	56	107	267	3	4 877	340
	2002	...	12 209	41	43	75	228	2	4 940	397
	2003	...	11 142	53	38	119	287	4	*4 865	343
	2004	...	11 595	49	47	120	295	5	*4 865	399
Côte d'Ivoire Côte d'Ivoire	2001	...	302[2]	480	103	1 128	414	71	53 350	4 903
	2002	...	749[2]	487	92	1 084	337	69	54 353	5 308
	2003	...	1 055[2]	359	104	745	318	49	47 770	5 093
	2004	...	1 302[2]	589	88	1 313	209	80	35 157	5 411
Dem. Rep. of the Congo Rép. dém. du Congo	2001	99[1]	1 225[2]	...	...	...	...	...	...	5 898
	2002	102[1]	1 151[2]	...	...	...	...	...	...	6 075
	2003	105[1]	1 083[2]	...	...	...	...	...	...	6 258
	2004	108[1]	1 033[2]	...	...	...	...	...	...	6 852
Djibouti Djibouti	2001	...	...	...	...	...	...	...	...	180
	2002	...	...	...	...	...	...	...	...	190
	2003	...	...	...	...	...	...	...	...	200
	2004	...	...	...	...	...	...	...	...	200
Egypt Egypte	2001	48[1]	39 343	5 613	1 331	6 635	10 589	1 737	856 436	76 808
	2002	37[1]	39 611	6 046	1 693	7 702	10 003	1 728	1 051 806	85 946
	2003	37[1]	*40 477	*6 306	1 469	8 235	10 532	1 739	1 189 024	*91 932
	2004	33[1]	*39 232	*5 000	2 080	7 922	11 273	1 724	1 286 413	*101 299
Equatorial Guinea Guinée équatoriale	2001	...	10 440[2]	...	...	...	...	...	*0	*23
	2002	...	11 597[2]	...	...	...	...	...	*18 537	*26
	2003	...	10 299[2]	...	...	...	...	...	18 773	*26
	2004	...	7 453[2]	...	...	...	...	...	*18 730	*27
Eritrea Erythrée	2001	...	...	...	...	...	...	...	...	232
	2002	...	...	...	...	...	...	...	...	258
	2003	...	...	...	...	...	...	...	...	276
	2004	...	...	...	...	...	...	...	...	283
Ethiopia Ethiopie	2001	...	...	...	...	...	...	3	...	1 821
	2002	...	...	...	...	...	...	3	...	2 050
	2003	...	...	...	...	...	...	*3	...	2 309
	2004	...	...	...	...	...	...	*3	...	2 547
Gabon Gabon	2001	...	14 995[2]	54	42	173	220	7	3 796	1 530
	2002	...	13 975[2]	64	58	219	254	10	4 271	1 581
	2003	...	11 056[2]	69	54	210	302	9	4 421	1 636
	2004	...	10 736[2]	68	45	228	324	9	4 912	1 537
Gambia Gambie	2001	...	...	...	...	...	...	...	...	135
	2002	...	...	...	...	...	...	...	...	151
	*2003	...	...	...	...	...	...	...	...	151
	*2004	...	...	...	...	...	...	...	...	151
Ghana Ghana	2001	...	...	286	64	353	261	7	...	7 864
	2002	...	...	346	82	447	196	24	...	7 301
	2003	...	...	382	91	493	216	26	...	5 908
	2004	...	...	553	107	568	199	66	...	6 044
Guinea* Guinée*	2001	...	...	...	...	...	...	...	...	796
	2002	...	...	...	...	...	...	...	...	798
	2003	...	...	...	...	...	...	...	...	801
	2004	...	...	...	...	...	...	...	...	801
Guinea-Bissau* Guinée-Bissau*	2001	...	...	...	...	...	...	...	...	60
	2002	...	...	...	...	...	...	...	...	60
	2003	...	...	...	...	...	...	...	...	61
	2004	...	...	...	...	...	...	...	...	61

Region, country or area Région, pays ou zone	Year Année	Hard coal and lignite Houille et lignite	Crude petroleum and NGL Pétrole brut et GNL	Motor gasoline Essence auto	Jet fuel Carbu-réacteurs	Gas-diesel oil Gazole/carburant diesel	Residual fuel oil Mazout résiduel	Liquefied petroleum gas Gaz de pétrole liquéfiés	Natural gas (terajoules) Gaz naturel (térajoules)	Electricity (million kWh) Electricité (millions de kWh)
		Thousand metric tons — Milliers de tonnes								
Kenya Kenya	2001	...	...	273	224	436	535	28	...	4 611
	2002	...	...	253	191	405	533	24	...	4 849
	2003	...	...	263	204	411	524	24	...	5 185
	2004	...	...	275	212	387	620	27	...	5 568
Liberia Libéria	2001	...	...	...	...	...	...	...	...	320
	2002	...	...	...	...	...	...	...	...	320
	2003	...	...	...	...	...	...	...	...	320
	2004	...	...	...	...	...	...	...	...	330
Libyan Arab Jamah. Jamah. arabe libyenne	2001	...	66 681	2 059	1 546	4 916	4 731	320	234 839	16 111
	2002	...	62 629	2 020	1 525	4 843	4 659	315	235 980	17 351
	2003	...	70 781	1 972	1 491	4 737	4 556	310	243 200	18 943
	2004	...	77 420	1 991	1 504	4 782	4 597	310	266 001	20 202
Madagascar Madagascar	2001	...	...	*112	*1	*55	*77	*6	...	790
	2002	...	...	*112	*1	*57	*77	*6	...	790
	2003	...	...	*113	*1	*57	*77	*6	...	900
	2004	...	...	*113	*1	*57	*77	*6	...	990
Malawi Malawi	2001	48[1]	...	...	...	...	...	...	...	*1 103
	2002	60[1]	...	...	...	...	...	...	...	*1 129
	2003	66[1]	...	...	...	...	...	...	...	*1 177
	*2004	70[1]	...	...	...	...	...	...	...	1 270
Mali* Mali*	2001	...	...	...	...	...	...	...	...	415
	2002	...	...	...	...	...	...	...	...	417
	2003	...	...	...	...	...	...	...	...	449
	2004	...	...	...	...	...	...	...	...	455
Mauritania* Mauritanie*	2001	...	...	...	...	...	...	...	...	232
	2002	...	...	...	...	...	...	...	...	234
	2003	...	...	...	...	...	...	...	...	238
	2004	...	...	...	...	...	...	...	...	240
Mauritius Maurice	2001	...	...	...	...	...	...	...	...	1 910
	*2002	...	...	...	...	...	...	...	...	1 949
	2003	...	...	...	...	...	...	...	...	2 082
	2004	...	...	...	...	...	...	...	...	2 165
Morocco Maroc	2001	2[1]	10[2]	343	271	2 415	2 401	234	1 749	15 615
	2002	0	13[2]	377	137	2 323	1 999	232	1 693	16 680
	2003	0	10[2]	132	108	1 535	1 747	67	1 633	18 109
	2004	0	11[2]	257	174	2 254	2 264	104	1 977	18 241
Mozambique Mozambique	2001	28[1]	...	...	...	...	...	...	47	8 849
	2002	44[1]	...	...	...	...	...	...	92	12 713
	2003	37[1]	...	...	...	...	...	...	96	10 602
	2004	38[1]	...	...	...	...	...	...	52 312	11 714
Niger* Niger*	2001	176[1]	...	...	...	...	...	...	...	240
	2002	178[1]	...	...	...	...	...	...	...	243
	2003	178[1]	...	...	...	...	...	...	...	245
	2004	178[1]	...	...	...	...	...	...	...	247
Nigeria Nigéria	2001	3[1]	116 665	2 596	417	2 522	2 716	89	581 413	15 453
	2002	43[1]	102 189	2 603	374	2 484	2 593	81	623 048	21 544
	2003	23[1]	117 666	1 036	386	1 418	1 838	17	742 296	20 183
	2004	3[1]	128 308	534	189	1 179	1 866	17	873 602	20 224
Réunion* Réunion*	2001	...	...	...	...	...	...	...	...	1 579
	2002	...	...	...	...	...	...	...	...	1 613
	2003	...	...	...	...	...	...	...	...	1 618
	2004	...	...	...	...	...	...	...	...	1 620

Region, country or area Région, pays ou zone	Year Année	Hard coal and lignite Houille et lignite	Crude petroleum and NGL Pétrole brut et GNL	Motor gasoline Essence auto	Jet fuel Carbu-réacteurs	Gas-diesel oil Gazole/carburant diesel	Residual fuel oil Mazout résiduel	Liquefied petroleum gas Gaz de pétrole liquéfiés	Natural gas (terajoules) Gaz naturel (térajoules)	Electricity (million kWh) Electricité (millions de kWh)
		Thousand metric tons — Milliers de tonnes								
Rwanda* Rwanda*	2001	...	...	...	...	...	...	...	13	169
	2002	...	...	...	...	...	...	...	13	172
	2003	...	...	...	...	...	...	...	13	172
	2004	...	...	...	...	...	...	...	7	173
Saint Helena Sainte-Hélène	2001	...	...	...	...	...	...	...	...	7
	2002	...	...	...	...	...	...	...	...	7
	*2003	...	...	...	...	...	...	...	...	7
	2004	...	...	...	...	...	...	...	...	8
Sao Tome and Principe* Sao Tomé-et-Principe*	2001	...	...	...	...	...	...	...	...	18
	2002	...	...	...	...	...	...	...	...	18
	2003	...	...	...	...	...	...	...	...	18
	2004	...	...	...	...	...	...	...	...	18
Senegal Sénégal	2001	...	...	111	56	392	231	7	25	1 904
	2002	...	...	140	72	375	255	9	114	2 046
	2003	...	...	151	126	463	316	12	423	2 155
	2004	...	...	148	132	471	327	10	506	2 351
Seychelles Seychelles	2001	...	...	...	...	...	...	...	...	210
	2002	...	...	...	...	...	...	...	...	219
	*2003	...	...	...	...	...	...	...	...	220
	*2004	...	...	...	...	...	...	...	...	220
Sierra Leone* Sierra Leone*	2001	...	...	30	18	74	55	...	...	250
	2002	...	...	31	20	74	55	...	...	257
	2003	...	...	31	20	74	55	...	...	259
	2004	...	...	32	21	60	55	...	...	85
Somalia* Somalie*	2001	...	...	...	...	...	...	...	...	282
	2002	...	...	...	...	...	...	...	...	282
	2003	...	...	...	...	...	...	...	...	284
	2004	...	...	...	...	...	...	...	...	286
South Africa[3] Afrique du Sud[3]	2001	224 845[1]	4 865	8 478	1 639	7 634	5 131	324	84 478	213 131
	2002	221 531[1]	4 941	8 085	1 637	7 383	8 026	316	83 764	220 688
	2003	239 934[1]	4 483	8 360	1 874	7 593	5 162	307	50 218	237 127
	2004	244 092[1]	4 825	8 343	1 778	7 141	4 192	305	77 172	247 777
Sudan Soudan	2001	...	10 394[2]	842	115	965	249	215	...	2 560
	2002	...	12 035[2]	985	169	1 123	290	241	...	2 897
	2003	...	13 250[2]	1 111	170	1 273	328	284	...	3 354
	2004	...	15 000[2]	1 228	192	1 400	361	300	...	3 883
Togo Togo	2001	...	...	...	...	...	...	...	...	167
	2002	...	...	...	...	...	...	...	...	234
	2003	...	...	...	...	...	...	...	...	291
	2004	...	...	...	...	...	...	...	...	262
Tunisia Tunisie	2001	...	3 383	252	...	467	596	45	84 922	10 854
	2002	...	3 517	261	...	469	604	48	80 966	11 281
	2003	...	3 200	263	...	506	609	49	82 428	11 829
	2004	...	3 401	224	...	432	595	50	95 312	13 067
Uganda Ouganda	2001	...	...	...	...	...	...	...	...	1 668
	2002	...	...	...	...	...	...	...	...	1 674
	*2003	...	...	...	...	...	...	...	...	1 675
	*2004	...	...	...	...	...	...	...	...	1 896
United Rep. of Tanzania Rép.-Unie de Tanzanie	2001	78[1]	...	...	...	...	...	...	0	2 806
	2002	79[1]	...	...	...	...	...	...	0	2 896
	2003	55[1]	...	...	...	...	...	...	0	2 741
	2004	65[1]	...	...	...	...	...	...	4 975	2 478

Region, country or area / Région, pays ou zone	Year / Année	Hard coal and lignite / Houille et lignite	Crude petroleum and NGL / Pétrole brut et GNL	Motor gasoline / Essence auto	Jet fuel / Carbu-réacteurs	Gas-diesel oil / Gazole/carburant diesel	Residual fuel oil / Mazout résiduel	Liquefied petroleum gas / Gaz de pétrole liquéfiés	Natural gas (terajoules) / Gaz naturel (térajoules)	Electricity (million kWh) / Electricité (millions de kWh)
		Thousand metric tons — Milliers de tonnes								
Western Sahara / Sahara occidental	2001	...	...	...	...	...	...	...	...	80
	2002	...	...	...	...	...	...	...	...	90
	2003	...	...	...	...	...	...	...	...	90
	2004	...	...	...	...	...	...	...	...	90
Zambia / Zambie	2001	204[1]	...	93	26	181	64	3	...	7 943
	2002	210[1]	...	100	27	194	70	3	...	8 152
	2003	221[1]	...	110	25	208	74	3	...	8 308
	2004	233[1]	...	118	27	223	79	3	...	8 512
Zimbabwe / Zimbabwe	2001	4 029[1]	...	...	...	...	...	...	...	7 906
	2002	3 804[1]	...	...	...	...	...	...	...	8 587
	2003	3 450[1]	...	...	...	...	...	...	...	8 789
	2004	3 398[1]	...	...	...	...	...	...	...	9 908
America, North / Amérique du Nord	**2001**	**1 103 117**	**703 814**	**398 468**	**80 677**	**234 982**	**88 748**	**88 947**	**30 497 324**	**4 762 333**
	2002	**1 070 209**	**710 330**	**411 756**	**79 439**	**228 623**	**80 042**	**85 870**	**30 811 452**	**4 969 711**
	2003	**1 044 040**	**720 377**	**415 129**	**78 665**	**239 857**	**80 644**	**84 294**	**30 391 212**	**4 997 792**
	2004	**1 084 758**	**716 667**	**408 921**	**82 426**	**247 131**	**79 372**	**84 281**	**30 069 994**	**5 109 021**
Anguilla / Anguilla	2001	...	...	...	...	...	...	...	...	54
	2002	...	...	...	...	...	...	...	...	55
	2003	...	...	...	...	...	...	...	...	58
	2004	...	...	...	...	...	...	...	...	62
Antigua and Barbuda* / Antigua-et-Barbuda*	2001	...	...	...	...	...	...	...	...	100
	2002	...	...	...	...	...	...	...	...	105
	2003	...	...	...	...	...	...	...	...	109
	2004	...	...	...	...	...	...	...	...	109
Aruba / Aruba	2001	...	120[2]	...	...	...	...	...	...	808
	2002	...	120[2]	...	...	...	...	...	...	810
	2003	...	120[2]	...	...	...	...	...	...	816
	2004	...	120[2]	...	...	...	...	...	...	816
Bahamas / Bahamas	2001	...	...	...	...	...	...	...	...	1 770
	2002	...	...	...	...	...	...	...	...	1 886
	2003	...	...	...	...	...	...	...	...	1 990
	*2004	...	...	...	...	...	...	...	...	2 087
Barbados / Barbade	2001	...	63[2]	...	...	...	...	2	1 257	827
	2002	...	80[2]	...	...	...	...	1	1 139	859
	2003	...	74[2]	...	...	...	...	1	1 020	871
	2004	...	84[2]	...	...	...	...	1	973	895
Belize / Belize	2001	...	...	...	...	...	...	...	...	147
	*2002	...	...	...	...	...	...	...	...	159
	*2003	...	...	...	...	...	...	...	...	169
	*2004	...	...	...	...	...	...	...	...	169
Bermuda / Bermudes	2001	...	...	...	...	...	...	...	...	615
	2002	...	...	...	...	...	...	...	...	644
	2003	...	...	...	...	...	...	...	...	664
	*2004	...	...	...	...	...	...	...	...	661
British Virgin Islands / Iles Vierges britanniques	*2001	...	...	...	...	...	...	...	...	45
	2002	...	...	...	...	...	...	...	...	40
	*2003	...	...	...	...	...	...	...	...	45
	*2004	...	...	...	...	...	...	...	...	45
Canada / Canada	2001	70 355	132 647	32 222	4 242	28 722	7 319	22 986	7 084 850	589 757
	2002	66 508	139 107	33 737	3 938	29 253	6 879	22 059	7 133 466	601 135
	2003	62 163	146 760	33 689	4 200	31 136	7 989	21 892	7 032 164	589 967
	2004	65 997	152 169	33 024	4 597	31 590	8 724	22 264	7 011 348	598 514

Region, country or area Région, pays ou zone	Year Année	Hard coal and lignite Houille et lignite	Crude petroleum and NGL Pétrole brut et GNL	Motor gasoline Essence auto	Jet fuel Carbu-réacteurs	Gas-diesel oil Gazole/carburant diesel	Residual fuel oil Mazout résiduel	Liquefied petroleum gas Gaz de pétrole liquéfiés	Natural gas (terajoules) Gaz naturel (térajoules)	Electricity (million kWh) Electricité (millions de kWh)
		Thousand metric tons — Milliers de tonnes								
Cayman Islands Iles Caïmanes	*2001	...	...	...	...	...	...	...	...	330
	2002	...	...	...	...	...	...	...	...	410
	2003	...	...	...	...	...	...	...	...	414
	*2004	...	...	...	...	...	...	...	...	420
Costa Rica Costa Rica	2001	...	...	...	...	86	154	0	...	6 941
	2002	...	...	...	...	143	240	2	...	7 485
	2003	...	...	...	...	173	224	2	...	7 566
	2004	...	...	...	...	162	127	2	...	8 210
Cuba Cuba	2001	...	2 886[2]	406	...	464	903	89	23 217	15 300
	2002	...	3 628[2]	319	...	292	774	66	22 827	15 699
	2003	...	3 680[2]	412	...	444	1 024	93	25 675	15 811
	2004	...	3 253[2]	331	...	385	858	63	27 470	15 652
Dominica Dominique	2001	...	...	...	...	...	...	...	...	81
	2002	...	...	...	...	...	...	...	...	80
	2003	...	...	...	...	...	...	...	...	79
	2004	...	...	...	...	...	...	...	...	79
Dominican Republic Rép. dominicaine	2001	...	...	233	44	327	450	38	...	10 308
	2002	...	...	268	61	395	486	38	...	11 510
	2003	...	...	284	54	411	449	42	...	13 489
	2004	...	...	445	*55	430	843	33	...	13 759
El Salvador El Salvador	2001	...	...	121	40	157	591	15	...	3 908
	2002	...	...	127	39	151	526	14	...	4 100
	2003	...	...	135	45	195	485	12	...	4 128
	2004	...	...	143	*52	199	543	14	...	4 564
Greenland* Groenland*	2001	...	...	...	...	...	...	...	...	264
	2002	...	...	...	...	...	...	...	...	266
	2003	...	...	...	...	...	...	...	...	268
	2004	...	...	...	...	...	...	...	...	270
Grenada Grenade	2001	...	...	...	...	...	...	...	...	146
	2002	...	...	...	...	...	...	...	...	153
	2003	...	...	...	...	...	...	...	...	153
	2004	...	...	...	...	...	...	...	...	157
Guadeloupe Guadeloupe	*2001	...	...	...	...	...	...	...	...	1 225
	2002	...	...	...	...	...	...	...	...	1 160
	2003	...	...	...	...	...	...	...	...	1 165
	*2004	...	...	...	...	...	...	...	...	1 165
Guatemala Guatemala	2001	...	1 149[2]	147	16	268	290	8	...	5 856
	2002	...	1 344[2]	111	13	203	211	6	...	6 191
	2003	...	1 347[2]	0	0	0	0	0	...	6 561
	2004	...	1 007[2]	0	0	20	0	0	...	7 009
Haiti Haïti	2001	...	...	...	...	...	...	...	...	594
	2002	...	...	...	...	...	...	...	...	547
	2003	...	...	...	...	...	...	...	...	535
	2004	...	...	...	...	...	...	...	...	547
Honduras Honduras	2001	...	...	...	...	...	...	...	...	3 917
	2002	...	...	...	...	...	...	...	...	4 165
	2003	...	...	...	...	...	...	...	...	4 530
	2004	...	...	...	...	...	...	...	...	4 877
Jamaica Jamaïque	2001	...	...	129	68	173	435	10	...	6 656
	2002	...	...	150	89	242	591	14	...	6 934
	2003	...	...	111	62	158	495	7	...	7 146
	2004	...	...	95	63	129	370	9	...	7 217

Region, country or area / Région, pays ou zone	Year / Année	Hard coal and lignite / Houille et lignite	Crude petroleum and NGL / Pétrole brut et GNL	Motor gasoline / Essence auto	Jet fuel / Carbu-réacteurs	Gas-diesel oil / Gazole/ carburant diesel	Residual fuel oil / Mazout résiduel	Liquefied petroleum gas / Gaz de pétrole liquéfiés	Natural gas (terajoules) / Gaz naturel (térajoules)	Electricity (million kWh) / Electricité (millions de kWh)
		Thousand metric tons — Milliers de tonnes								
Martinique Martinique	*2001	...	...	158	...	163	280	24	...	1 120
	2002	...	...	*160	...	*176	*300	*26	...	1 180
	*2003	...	...	161	...	177	300	26	...	1 185
	*2004	...	...	163	...	178	310	27	...	1 190
Mexico Mexique	2001	11 345	175 282	16 289	2 586	13 891	24 814	870	1 469 563	209 159
	2002	10 984	178 085	16 654	2 584	13 165	25 599	982	1 506 981	214 628
	2003	9 599	189 016	18 587	2 717	15 182	22 581	1 059	1 579 524	217 867
	2004	9 882	190 897	19 855	2 770	16 057	21 089	1 056	1 651 290	224 077
Montserrat Montserrat	2001	...	...	...	...	...	...	...	...	12
	2002	...	...	...	...	...	...	...	...	20
	2003	...	...	...	...	...	...	...	...	21
	2004	...	...	...	...	...	...	...	...	21
Netherlands Antilles Antilles néerlandaises	2001	...	...	1 777	884	2 392	5 558	118	...	1 095
	2002	...	...	1 644	710	2 058	4 629	119	...	1 088
	2003	...	...	1 701	770	2 129	4 230	125	...	1 079
	2004	...	...	1 716	790	2 202	4 188	118	...	1 065
Nicaragua Nicaragua	2001	...	...	104	26	239	477	19	...	2 473
	2002	...	...	102	15	199	409	17	...	2 655
	2003	...	...	101	13	193	401	20	...	2 707
	2004	...	...	98	11	215	432	16	...	2 822
Panama Panama	2001	...	...	281	...	702	902	32	...	5 124
	2002	...	...	156	...	289	344	40	...	5 293
	2003	...	...	0	...	0	0	0	...	5 576
	2004	...	...	0	...	0	0	0	...	5 860
Puerto Rico Porto Rico	2001	...	...	...	...	...	...	...	...	21 390
	2002	...	...	...	...	...	...	...	...	22 340
	2003	...	...	...	...	...	...	...	...	23 280
	2004	...	...	...	...	...	...	...	...	24 130
Saint Kitts and Nevis Saint-Kitts-et-Nevis	*2001	...	...	...	...	...	...	...	...	100
	2002	...	...	...	...	...	...	...	...	110
	2003	...	...	...	...	...	...	...	...	127
	*2004	...	...	...	...	...	...	...	...	130
Saint Lucia Sainte-Lucie	2001	...	...	...	...	...	...	...	...	287
	2002	...	...	...	...	...	...	...	...	288
	2003	...	...	...	...	...	...	...	...	299
	2004	...	...	...	...	...	...	...	...	309
Saint Pierre and Miquelon* Saint-Pierre-et-Miquelon*	2001	...	...	...	...	...	...	...	...	43
	2002	...	...	...	...	...	...	...	...	50
	2003	...	...	...	...	...	...	...	...	52
	2004	...	...	...	...	...	...	...	...	52
St. Vincent-Grenadines St. Vincent-Grenadines	2001	...	...	...	...	...	...	...	...	107
	2002	...	...	...	...	...	...	...	...	108
	*2003	...	...	...	...	...	...	...	...	110
	*2004	...	...	...	...	...	...	...	...	110
Trinidad and Tobago Trinité-et-Tobago	2001	...	7 007	1 314	675	1 643	3 534	553	548 129	5 644
	2002	...	8 082	1 313	665	1 546	3 175	639	638 636	5 644
	2003	...	8 497	1 216	685	1 522	3 247	726	971 764	6 437
	2004	...	7 890	1 096	615	1 421	2 971	699	1 024 185	6 430
Turks and Caicos Islands Iles Turques et Caïques	2001	...	...	...	...	...	...	...	...	10
	2002	...	...	...	...	...	...	...	...	10
	2003	...	...	...	...	...	...	...	...	10
	2004	...	...	...	...	...	...	...	...	10

Region, country or area / Région, pays ou zone	Year / Année	Hard coal and lignite / Houille et lignite	Crude petroleum and NGL / Pétrole brut et GNL	Motor gasoline / Essence auto	Jet fuel / Carbu-réacteurs	Gas-diesel oil / Gazole/ carburant diesel	Residual fuel oil / Mazout résiduel	Liquefied petroleum gas / Gaz de pétrole liquéfiés	Natural gas (terajoules) / Gaz naturel (térajoules)	Electricity (million kWh) / Electricité (millions de kWh)
		Thousand metric tons — Milliers de tonnes								
United States / Etats-Unis	2001	1 021 417	384 660	345 287	72 096	185 755	43 041	64 183	21 370 308	3 865 090
	2002	992 717	379 884	357 015	71 325	180 511	35 879	61 847	21 508 403	4 050 864
	2003	972 278	370 883	358 732	70 119	188 137	39 219	60 289	20 781 065	4 081 468
	2004	1 008 879	361 247	351 954	73 473	194 143	38 916	*59 978	20 354 728	4 174 481
United States Virgin Is.* / Iles Vierges américaines*	2001	...	...	...	...	...	...	...	...	1 030
	2002	...	...	...	...	...	...	...	...	1 040
	2003	...	...	...	...	...	...	...	...	1 040
	2004	...	...	...	...	...	...	...	...	1 050
America, South / Amérique du Sud	**2001**	**57 478[1]**	**344 696**	**45 112**	**10 958**	**64 686**	**47 354**	**15 293**	**3 652 513**	**689 758**
	2002	**56 915[1]**	**330 630**	**44 062**	**10 720**	**63 362**	**45 025**	**14 811**	**3 586 321**	**707 585**
	2003	**62 158[1]**	**323 587**	**39 344**	**9 820**	**66 836**	**43 043**	**16 131**	**3 715 622**	**745 497**
	2004	**66 102[1]**	**339 738**	**43 773**	**10 659**	**71 769**	**46 352**	**16 427**	**4 115 018**	**791 790**
Argentina / Argentine	2001	204[1]	42 602	4 569	1 344	10 317	2 361	3 620	1 558 100	90 324
	2002	97[1]	41 312	4 884	1 305	9 402	1 803	3 450	1 496 647	85 055
	2003	89[1]	41 128	4 636	1 135	9 957	1 946	4 143	1 664 109	92 609
	2004	51[1]	38 892	4 018	1 209	10 590	2 368	4 431	1 820 534	100 260
Bolivia / Bolivie	2001	...	1 912	405	110	409	1	351	179 577	3 981
	2002	...	1 799	406	117	442	4	253	218 691	4 188
	2003	...	1 956	406	121	482	0	301	255 726	4 269
	2004	...	2 193	455	122	622	0	322	355 620	4 542
Brazil / Brésil	2001	5 654[1]	68 381	14 380	3 011	27 788	17 797	4 602	286 688	328 509
	2002	5 144[1]	76 311	13 894	2 938	27 994	16 925	4 745	367 896	345 671
	2003	4 646[1]	79 081	13 477	3 073	30 608	15 779	4 934	397 527	364 339
	2004	5 406[1]	78 846	13 738	3 357	34 079	16 074	5 144	420 030	387 451
Chile / Chili	2001	576[1]	489	2 035	693	3 797	1 574	557	81 777	43 918
	2002	433[1]	457	2 110	606	3 793	1 368	417	83 772	45 483
	2003	576[1]	414	2 265	574	3 865	1 814	533	73 681	48 780
	2004	188[1]	413	2 383	650	3 693	2 294	681	*73 280	51 984
Colombia / Colombie	2001	43 441[1]	31 305	5 092	1 028	3 312	2 986	773	269 559	43 684
	2002	43 850[1]	29 959	4 676	1 031	3 275	3 136	737	269 287	45 242
	2003	50 025[1]	28 200	4 756	1 254	3 308	2 932	868	257 762	47 682
	2004	53 693[1]	26 865	4 963	861	3 689	3 330	654	*271 346	*50 291
Ecuador / Equateur	2001	...	21 188	1 557	223	1 803	3 786	207	9 760	11 050
	2002	...	20 537	1 506	260	1 822	3 544	177	9 869	11 888
	2003	...	21 493	1 516	239	1 600	3 646	231	16 234	11 546
	2004	...	27 386[2]	895	279	1 621	3 657	141	17 056	12 585
Falkland Is. (Malvinas)* / Iles Falkland (Malvinas)*	2001	...	...	...	...	...	...	...	...	16
	2002	...	...	...	...	...	...	...	...	16
	2003	...	...	...	...	...	...	...	...	16
	2004	...	...	...	...	...	...	...	...	16
French Guiana / Guyane française	2001	...	...	...	...	...	...	...	...	430
	2002	...	...	...	...	...	...	...	...	450
	2003	...	...	...	...	...	...	...	...	440
	2004	...	...	...	...	...	...	...	...	430
Guyana / Guyana	2001	...	...	...	...	...	...	...	...	919
	2002	...	...	...	...	...	...	...	...	914
	2003	...	...	...	...	...	...	...	...	820
	2004	...	...	...	...	...	...	...	...	835
Paraguay / Paraguay	2001	...	...	13	...	52	32	...	...	45 308
	2002	...	...	11	...	48	34	...	...	48 203
	2003	...	...	10	...	42	30	...	...	51 762
	2004	...	...	8	...	33	20	...	...	51 921

Region, country or area / Région, pays ou zone	Year / Année	Hard coal and lignite / Houille et lignite	Crude petroleum and NGL / Pétrole brut et GNL	Motor gasoline / Essence auto	Jet fuel / Carbu-réacteurs	Gas-diesel oil / Gazole/ carburant diesel	Residual fuel oil / Mazout résiduel	Liquefied petroleum gas / Gaz de pétrole liquéfiés	Natural gas (terajoules) / Gaz naturel (térajoules)	Electricity (million kWh) / Electricité (millions de kWh)
		Thousand metric tons — Milliers de tonnes								
Peru / Pérou	2001	18[1]	5 374	1 527	340	1 779	3 327	310	29 696	20 785
	2002	22[1]	5 385	1 491	353	1 897	3 195	321	31 377	21 981
	2003	15[1]	5 298	1 559	195	1 932	3 304	319	33 696	22 925
	2004	16[1]	5 188	1 284	418	1 916	3 268	412	*48 761	25 547
Suriname / Suriname	2001	...	643[2]	...	...	39	314	...	...	1 467
	2002	...	615[2]	...	...	40	334	...	...	1 482
	2003	...	588[2]	...	...	39	333	...	...	1 496
	2004	...	612[2]	...	...	39	335	...	...	1 509
Uruguay / Uruguay	2001	...	...	288	54	574	506	88	...	9 250
	2002	...	...	216	40	422	392	63	...	9 605
	2003	...	...	321	24	592	448	66	...	8 578
	2004	...	...	520	44	772	519	86	...	5 936
Venezuela (Bolivar. Rep.of) / Venezuela (Rép. Boliv. du)	2001	7 585[1]	172 802	15 247	4 155	14 816	14 669	4 785	1 237 356	90 117
	2002	7 369[1]	154 255	14 868	4 070	14 226	14 290	4 648	1 108 782	87 406
	2003	6 807[1]	145 429	10 398	3 205	14 411	12 812	4 737	1 016 887	90 235
	2004	6 748[1]	159 344	15 509	3 719	14 715	14 486	4 555	1 108 392	98 482
Asia / Asie	**2001**	**2 058 718**	**1 543 915**	**176 853**	**54 492**	**368 687**	**243 859**	**81 342**	**23 242 524**	**4 938 454**
	2002	**2 144 616**	**1 474 876**	**184 014**	**55 931**	**369 836**	**242 572**	**86 053**	**24 869 774**	**5 266 279**
	2003	**2 442 948**	**1 575 608**	**192 756**	**57 021**	**386 968**	**248 883**	**89 909**	**26 403 777**	**5 647 260**
	2004	**2 760 811**	**1 671 195**	**203 723**	**63 545**	**414 278**	**246 408**	**96 190**	**27 706 190**	**6 112 695**
Afghanistan / Afghanistan	2001	26[1]	...	...	...	...	...	...	*4 250	*395
	2002	21[1]	...	...	...	...	...	...	285	696
	2003	35[1]	...	...	...	...	...	...	242	826
	2004	34[1]	...	...	...	...	...	...	119	779
Armenia / Arménie	2001	...	...	...	...	...	...	...	...	5 745
	2002	...	...	...	...	...	...	...	...	5 519
	2003	...	...	...	...	...	...	...	...	5 501
	2004	...	...	...	...	...	...	...	...	6 030
Azerbaijan / Azerbaïdjan	2001	...	14 909	598	543	1 562	2 648	88	208 670	18 969
	2002	...	15 334	610	507	1 593	2 569	94	193 928	19 543
	2003	...	15 381	720	654	1 641	2 470	148	193 326	21 285
	2004	...	15 549	852	647	1 789	2 141	182	194 905	21 643
Bahrain / Bahreïn	2001	...	9 472	844	1 943	4 341	2 581	213	242 921	6 779
	2002	...	9 582	746	1 980	4 233	2 835	210	255 748	7 278
	2003	...	9 769	810	1 866	4 295	3 008	201	263 779	7 768
	2004	...	9 752	755	2 178	4 500	2 734	204	274 330	8 448
Bangladesh / Bangladesh	2001	...	93[4]	133	4	274	61	20	384 256	17 392
	2002	...	86[4]	129	3	260	49	21	404 256	18 665
	2003	...	100[4]	150	2	303	58	20	434 849	19 712
	2004	...	90[4]	136	2	274	52	20	467 723	21 466
Bhutan* / Bhoutan*	2001	50[1]	...	...	...	...	...	...	...	1 896
	2002	52[1]	...	...	...	...	...	...	...	1 898
	2003	50[1]	...	...	...	...	...	...	...	1 900
	2004	51[1]	...	...	...	...	...	...	...	1 952
Brunei Darussalam / Brunéi Darussalam	2001	...	10 049	193	74	154	75	13	445 654	2 910
	2002	...	10 548	198	79	153	70	14	447 477	3 036
	2003	...	10 938	202	82	165	77	14	482 490	3 169
	2004	...	10 872	201	80	172	89	15	477 318	3 236
Cambodia* / Cambodge*	2001	...	...	...	...	...	...	...	...	104
	2002	...	...	...	...	...	...	...	...	129
	2003	...	...	...	...	...	...	...	...	130
	2004	...	...	...	...	...	...	...	...	130

Region, country or area Région, pays ou zone	Year Année	Hard coal and lignite Houille et lignite	Crude petroleum and NGL Pétrole brut et GNL	Motor gasoline Essence auto	Jet fuel Carbu-réacteurs	Gas-diesel oil Gazole/carburant diesel	Residual fuel oil Mazout résiduel	Liquefied petroleum gas Gaz de pétrole liquéfiés	Natural gas (terajoules) Gaz naturel (térajoules)	Electricity (million kWh) Electricité (millions de kWh)
		Thousand metric tons — Milliers de tonnes								
China[5] Chine[5]	2001	1 381 000[1]	163 959[2]	41 550	...	74 856	18 644	9 523	1 459 431	1 471 657
	2002	1 455 000[1]	167 000[2]	43 208	...	77 061	18 455	10 368	1 571 720	1 640 481
	2003	1 722 000[1]	169 600[2]	47 909	...	85 328	20 048	12 117	1 685 000	1 907 380
	2004	1 992 324[1]	175 873[2]	52 236	...	98 436	20 293	14 170	1 544 800	2 193 736
China, Hong Kong SAR Chine, Hong Kong RAS	2001	...	...	...	...	...	...	...	...	32 429
	2002	...	...	...	...	...	...	...	...	34 312
	2003	...	...	...	...	...	...	...	...	35 506
	2004	...	...	...	...	...	...	...	...	37 129
China, Macao SAR Chine, Macao RAS	2001	...	...	...	...	...	...	...	...	1 604
	2002	...	...	...	...	...	...	...	...	1 702
	2003	...	...	...	...	...	...	...	...	1 796
	2004	...	...	...	...	...	...	...	...	1 973
Cyprus Chypre	2001	...	...	150	13	390	482	31	...	3 551
	2002	...	...	154	8	362	423	33	...	3 785
	2003	...	...	146	0	327	362	28	...	4 044
	2004	...	...	40	0	88	112	9	...	4 176
Georgia Géorgie	2001	1[1]	99[2]	...	...	2	10	...	1 537	6 937
	2002	6[1]	74[2]	...	...	2	12	...	650	7 257
	2003	8[1]	140[2]	...	...	2	13	...	712	7 116
	2004	8[1]	98[2]	...	...	2	14	...	461	6 924
India Inde	2001	352 601	36 029	9 232	2 610	39 785	12 187	6 646	885 699	*578 452
	2002	367 290	36 981	10 133	2 702	39 490	12 246	7 181	958 122	596 543
	2003	389 204	36 891	10 906	4 180	41 966	12 768	7 551	1 016 146	633 275
	2004	412 952	37 766	11 062	4 890	46 244	14 542	7 841	1 007 951	665 873
Indonesia Indonésie	2001	92 505[1]	85 026	7 617	1 127	14 075	12 009	2 190	2 845 020	95 097
	2002	103 060[1]	81 906	8 344	1 216	13 724	11 951	1 819	3 065 116	*113 245
	2003	109 321[1]	82 945	8 306	1 186	14 432	11 755	2 007	3 192 073	101 381
	2004	119 700[1]	*79 803	9 398	1 486	14 623	10 995	2 514	2 837 254	*103 536
Iran (Islamic Rep. of) Iran (Rép. islamique d')	2001	1 212[1]	*189 956	8 788	972	22 244	21 120	3 297	2 400 165	130 029
	2002	1 253[1]	176 221	10 374	860	22 572	27 620	3 455	2 721 192	140 759
	2003	1 232[1]	197 497	10 606	941	22 958	26 127	3 750	3 051 153	152 569
	2004	1 246[1]	206 775	10 836	795	23 771	25 840	4 146	3 198 059	164 481
Iraq Iraq	2001	...	117 464	3 551	657	7 158	8 423	1 551	104 880	33 366
	2002	...	100 469	3 460	640	6 884	8 221	1 546	87 400	34 978
	2003	...	65 949	3 097	573	6 610	7 404	848	59 280	29 455
	2004	...	98 951	3 278	607	4 906	8 257	938	101 455	33 410
Israel Israël	2001	415[6]	4[2]	1 983	...	3 140	3 572	521	365	43 838
	2002	458[6]	5[2]	2 211	...	2 838	3 368	482	335	45 393
	2003	437[6]	3[2]	2 231	...	2 977	3 440	474	321	47 236
	2004	439[6]	2[2]	2 467	...	2 750	3 168	532	43 585	49 025
Japan Japon	2001	3 208[1]	572	42 836	8 149	58 969	31 325	5 016	229 287	1 044 930
	2002	0	582	42 599	8 188	57 948	32 943	4 902	236 027	1 064 101
	2003	0	642	43 073	7 671	57 402	34 037	4 525	220 188	1 051 104
	2004	0	663	42 647	7 902	57 059	31 004	4 448	214 508	1 080 124
Jordan Jordanie	2001	...	2[2]	641	212	1 001	1 383	138	9 586	7 544
	2002	...	2[2]	657	216	1 113	1 289	136	9 000	8 127
	2003	...	2[2]	667	178	1 160	1 251	134	10 200	8 041
	2004	...	1[2]	579	291	1 187	1 402	116	10 400	8 967
Kazakhstan Kazakhstan	2001	84 402	40 091	1 582	46	2 245	2 737	891	471 773	55 350
	2002	80 906	47 269	1 691	38	2 304	2 797	1 046	550 604	58 331
	2003	89 176	51 451	1 562	309	2 128	2 584	966	647 698	63 819
	2004	89 945	59 485	1 928	294	2 888	2 708	1 303	862 531	66 942

Region, country or area / Région, pays ou zone	Year / Année	Hard coal and lignite / Houille et lignite	Crude petroleum and NGL / Pétrole brut et GNL	Motor gasoline / Essence auto	Jet fuel / Carbu-réacteurs	Gas-diesel oil / Gazole/carburant diesel	Residual fuel oil / Mazout résiduel	Liquefied petroleum gas / Gaz de pétrole liquéfiés	Natural gas (terajoules) / Gaz naturel (térajoules)	Electricity (million kWh) / Electricité (millions de kWh)
		Thousand metric tons — Milliers de tonnes								
Korea, Dem. P. R. / Corée, R. p. dém. de	2001	30 536	...	188	...	207	119	...	...	20 200
	2002	28 950	...	189	...	207	119	...	...	19 777
	2003	29 479	...	185	...	201	116	...	...	21 035
	2004	30 140	...	188	...	203	117	...	...	21 974
Korea, Republic of / Corée, République de	2001	3 817[1]	...	9 001	8 398	30 275	34 085	3 379	...	313 983
	2002	3 318[1]	...	9 052	8 717	28 732	28 569	3 477	...	336 258
	2003	3 298[1]	...	8 594	7 087	28 033	30 816	3 273	...	352 381
	2004	3 191[1]	...	8 882	9 864	29 383	30 509	3 312	...	370 718
Kuwait / Koweït	2001	...	105 710	1 494	1 936	10 562	6 047	4 047	347 806	34 829
	2002	...	100 219	1 380	1 703	11 285	7 446	3 744	311 914	36 892
	2003	...	114 291	1 350	1 867	12 043	9 741	4 191	363 426	39 802
	2004	...	125 858	1 914	2 258	12 038	9 589	4 598	378 504	41 256
Kyrgyzstan / Kirghizistan	2001	475	76[2]	48	...	43	40	...	1 288	13 667
	2002	459	76[2]	40	...	27	43	...	1 171	11 922
	2003	416	69[2]	27	...	22	39	...	1 054	14 025
	2004	461	74[2]	19	...	27	42	...	1 132	15 145
Lao People's Dem. Rep.* / Rép. dém. pop. lao*	2001	280[1]	...	...	...	...	...	...	...	1 250
	2002	285[1]	...	...	...	...	...	...	...	1 290
	2003	285[1]	...	...	...	...	...	...	...	1 295
	2004	290[1]	...	...	...	...	...	...	...	1 295
Lebanon / Liban	*2001	...	...	...	...	...	...	...	...	9 750
	2002	...	...	...	...	...	...	...	...	9 660
	2003	...	...	...	...	...	...	...	...	10 547
	2004	...	...	...	...	...	...	...	...	10 192
Malaysia / Malaisie	2001	491[1]	35 200	4 400	2 861	8 331	2 288	2 007	*1 732 929	71 384
	2002	318[1]	37 436	4 245	2 489	8 271	2 351	2 206	*1 787 405	74 196
	2003	153[1]	39 044	4 363	2 293	8 922	1 777	1 582	*1 870 708	78 427
	2004	382[1]	37 237	4 496	2 608	9 463	1 828	1 303	2 180 862	82 282
Maldives / Maldives	2001	...	...	...	...	...	...	...	...	116
	2002	...	...	...	...	...	...	...	...	126
	2003	...	...	...	...	...	...	...	...	141
	2004	...	...	...	...	...	...	...	...	160
Mongolia / Mongolie	2001	5 305	...	...	...	...	...	...	...	3 017
	2002	5 668	...	...	...	...	...	...	...	3 112
	2003	5 666	...	...	...	...	...	...	...	3 138
	2004	6 865	...	...	...	...	...	...	...	3 303
Myanmar / Myanmar	2001	642	672	233	67	366	114	15	244 015	4 689
	2002	558	881	277	71	430	115	15	252 967	5 864
	2003	978	982	361	77	294	75	11	306 893	6 213
	2004	1 013	1 017	374	80	305	78	11	317 937	6 437
Nepal / Népal	2001	10[1]	...	...	...	...	...	...	...	1 867
	2002	12[1]	...	...	...	...	...	...	...	2 123
	2003	11[1]	...	...	...	...	...	...	...	2 267
	2004	11[1]	...	...	...	...	...	...	...	2 345
Oman / Oman	2001	...	47 815	496	187	713	1 809	*99	572 951	9 737
	2002	...	44 921	705	252	889	2 257	*122	630 632	10 331
	2003	...	41 058	642	217	878	2 259	119	691 553	10 714
	2004	...	39 226	593	178	864	2 121	119	706 149	11 499
Pakistan / Pakistan	2001	3 095[1]	2 956	1 183	771	2 476	3 152	314	800 401	68 117
	2002	3 328[1]	3 261	1 316	857	2 766	3 063	348	836 631	72 406
	2003	3 312[1]	3 297	1 075	997	2 937	3 058	355	897 330	75 682
	2004	4 587[1]	3 402	1 326	1 185	3 603	3 132	389	1 119 118	85 699

Region, country or area Région, pays ou zone	Year Année	Hard coal and lignite Houille et lignite	Crude petroleum and NGL Pétrole brut et GNL	Motor gasoline Essence auto	Jet fuel Carbu-réacteurs	Gas-diesel oil Gazole/carburant diesel	Residual fuel oil Mazout résiduel	Liquefied petroleum gas Gaz de pétrole liquéfiés	Natural gas (terajoules) Gaz naturel (térajoules)	Electricity (million kWh) Electricité (millions de kWh)
		Thousand metric tons — Milliers de tonnes								
Philippines Philippines	2001	1 230	63[2]	2 196	613	4 563	4 656	511	5 283	47 059
	2002	1 665	277[2]	2 072	641	4 008	5 169	462	66 367	48 484
	2003	1 840	20[2]	1 844	634	3 851	3 899	397	101 146	52 897
	2004	2 485	19[2]	1 501	590	3 004	3 537	263	96 743	55 957
Qatar Qatar	2001	...	38 547	580	488	513	674	2 237	1 099 633	9 951
	2002	...	39 708	1 319	831	889	755	2 526	1 207 536	10 940
	2003	...	40 443	1 815	921	965	429	2 436	1 262 086	12 012
	2004	...	42 724	1 711	956	979	619	2 385	1 605 919	13 233
Saudi Arabia Arabie saoudite	2001	...	426 117	11 586	4 148	25 980	25 455	24 807	2 095 045	133 674
	2002	...	388 305	11 190	4 100	25 832	23 676	25 650	2 236 692	141 736
	2003	...	460 010	12 591	4 519	28 899	25 432	27 974	2 343 609	153 000
	2004	...	489 153	13 598	4 923	31 144	25 944	29 719	2 562 899	156 506
Singapore Singapour	2001	...	...	3 855	5 967	10 815	7 337	857	...	33 089
	2002	...	...	3 632	5 361	10 775	6 614	818	...	34 664
	2003	...	...	3 350	6 735	9 938	6 400	870	...	35 331
	2004	...	...	3 948	6 481	11 711	7 042	872	...	36 810
Sri Lanka Sri Lanka	2001	...	...	189	89	627	714	15	...	6 625
	2002	...	...	226	72	717	800	18	...	6 951
	2003	...	...	196	96	622	745	15	...	7 711
	2004	...	...	203	126	693	855	15	...	8 158
Syrian Arab Republic Rép. arabe syrienne	2001	...	29 084	1 339	193	4 130	5 466	300	*210 743	26 712
	2002	...	31 276	1 386	*222	4 035	5 126	293	*256 360	28 013
	2003	...	28 115	1 262	*204	3 906	4 793	286	*258 245	29 534
	2004	...	*23 410	1 338	245	4 123	4 536	286	267 670	32 077
Tajikistan Tadjikistan	2001	30	18[2]	...	...	...	...	...	1 506	14 382
	2002	56	16[2]	...	...	...	...	...	1 130	15 302
	2003	46	18[2]	...	...	...	...	...	1 246	16 509
	2004	51	18[2]	...	...	...	...	...	1 250	17 277
Thailand Thaïlande	2001	19 617[6]	7 389	5 791	3 179	13 856	6 290	3 348	686 719	108 420
	2002	19 602[6]	8 222	5 745	3 579	14 473	5 867	3 286	716 194	115 513
	2003	18 843[6]	9 721	6 012	3 253	15 608	5 947	3 446	707 276	*116 984
	2004	20 060[6]	9 903	6 674	3 774	17 511	6 335	3 917	701 157	125 727
Timor-Leste* Timor-Leste*	2001	...	...	...	...	...	...	...	...	...
	2002	...	6 789	...	...	...	...	2 193	...	300
	2003	...	6 789	...	...	...	...	2 193	...	300
	2004	...	6 835	...	...	...	...	2 200	...	300
Turkey Turquie	2001	62 097	2 520[2]	2 968	1 199	7 340	8 456	712	11 950	122 725
	2002	53 984	2 420[2]	3 718	1 606	7 720	7 970	741	14 477	129 400
	2003	48 563	2 351[2]	3 837	1 682	8 087	8 038	758	21 448	140 581
	2004	46 377	2 251[2]	3 479	1 767	7 665	7 845	762	26 350	150 698
Turkmenistan Turkménistan	2001	...	8 632	1 283	236	2 547	1 586	...	1 943 706	10 610
	2002	...	10 117	1 292	270	2 360	1 640	...	2 023 273	10 700
	2003	...	10 332	1 361	270	2 478	1 831	...	2 241 513	10 800
	2004	...	10 063	1 265	296	2 511	1 745	...	2 235 451	11 470
United Arab Emirates Emirats arabes unis	2001	...	125 534	1 271	4 838	4 995	1 985	7 057	1 535 886	43 172
	2002	...	109 062	1 335	5 390	5 157	1 704	7 146	1 693 142	46 856
	2003	...	131 769	1 288	5 459	5 107	1 173	7 403	1 748 141	49 450
	2004	...	136 157	1 746	5 400	6 371	1 291	7 671	1 787 162	52 417
Uzbekistan Ouzbékistan	2001	2 711[6]	7 221	1 687	288	1 826	1 700	42	2 175 359	47 502
	2002	2 467[6]	7 088	1 603	274	1 735	1 675	43	2 191 336	49 310
	2003	1 895[6]	7 608	1 842	314	1 993	1 925	44	2 173 692	49 400
	2004	2 699[6]	7 325	1 736	296	1 879	1 814	40	2 235 451	51 030

Region, country or area Région, pays ou zone	Year Année	Hard coal and lignite Houille et lignite	Crude petroleum and NGL Pétrole brut et GNL	Motor gasoline Essence auto	Jet fuel Carbu-réacteurs	Gas-diesel oil Gazole/ carburant diesel	Residual fuel oil Mazout résiduel	Liquefied petroleum gas Gaz de pétrole liquéfiés	Natural gas (terajoules) Gaz naturel (térajoules)	Electricity (million kWh) Electricité (millions de kWh)
		Thousand metric tons — Milliers de tonnes								
Viet Nam Viet Nam	2001	12 962[1]	17 151	...	...	...	...	264	52 168	30 791
	2002	15 900[1]	17 125	...	...	...	...	349	107 642	35 796
	2003	16 700[1]	17 092	...	...	...	...	307	125 993	*40 925
	2004	25 500[1]	20 804	...	...	...	...	335	214 663	46 029
Yemen Yémen	2001	...	21 449	903	345	968	630	64	...	3 643
	2002	...	21 572	967	339	844	532	95	...	3 769
	2003	...	21 251	1 059	388	819	586	87	...	4 094
	2004	...	19 999	1 138	317	883	268	89	...	4 337
Europe Europe	**2001**	**1 021 384**	**676 891**	**188 379**	**48 816**	**324 613**	**186 383**	**34 555**	**34 588 450**	**4 462 310**
	2002	**1 010 202**	**709 590**	**192 404**	**47 168**	**328 240**	**187 248**	**37 949**	**35 399 638**	**4 481 846**
	2003	**1 036 549**	**736 724**	**193 308**	**47 501**	**336 247**	**185 993**	**39 436**	**36 484 965**	**4 590 389**
	2004	**1 027 691**	**763 792**	**199 785**	**49 006**	**340 476**	**192 465**	**41 098**	**37 311 026**	**4 693 878**
Albania Albanie	2001	21[6]	311[2]	35	9	64	42	1	327	3 692
	2002	77[6]	393[2]	21	1	85	80	0	544	3 686
	2003	81[6]	375[2]	6	1	95	45	0	544	5 230
	2004	109[6]	420[2]	35	16	73	67	1	636	5 559
Austria Autriche	2001	1 206[6]	1 012	1 922	513	3 959	1 047	0	68 413	62 344
	2002	1 412[6]	1 040	1 927	484	3 984	1 012	23	74 295	62 488
	2003	1 152[6]	1 011	1 811	446	3 849	1 062	50	82 603	60 100
	2004	235[6]	1 061	1 738	455	3 529	1 032	57	77 550	64 125
Belarus Bélarus	2001	...	1 852[2]	1 824	...	3 879	4 408	184	9 849	25 042
	2002	...	1 846[2]	1 756	...	4 606	5 099	194	9 501	26 455
	2003	...	1 820[2]	1 895	...	4 913	4 790	216	9 810	26 627
	2004	...	1 804[2]	2 842	...	5 845	5 501	418	9 942	31 211
Belgium Belgique	2001	218[1]	...	5 493	1 913	12 777	7 015	647	...	79 821
	2002	173[1]	...	5 775	2 067	12 464	7 603	656	...	82 069
	2003	129[1]	...	5 865	2 048	13 013	8 689	627	...	84 630
	2004	0	...	5 789	2 143	12 327	8 380	511	...	85 643
Bosnia and Herzegovina Bosnie-Herzégovine	2001	7 863[6]	...	...	...	...	...	...	...	10 327
	2002	8 961[6]	...	...	...	...	...	...	...	10 785
	2003	8 196[6]	...	...	...	...	...	...	...	11 250
	2004	8 578[6]	...	...	...	...	...	...	...	12 599
Bulgaria Bulgarie	2001	26 647	35[2]	1 151	154	1 978	1 095	120	853	43 969
	2002	26 053	37[2]	1 030	123	1 817	1 203	97	752	42 679
	2003	27 335	30[2]	967	144	1 878	718	85	597	42 600
	2004	26 485	30[2]	1 401	142	1 912	958	103	12 432	41 621
Croatia Croatie	2001	...	1 392	1 210	72	1 650	1 021	406	76 395	12 175
	2002	...	1 355	1 209	68	1 640	1 062	432	80 572	12 286
	2003	...	1 291	1 261	75	1 873	1 036	437	83 205	12 690
	2004	...	1 178	1 226	91	1 741	1 012	377	83 528	13 295
Czech Republic République tchèque	2001	66 106	183[2]	1 104	168	2 250	773	190	5 671	74 647
	2002	63 356	265[2]	1 246	160	2 412	376	157	5 338	76 348
	2003	63 906	317[2]	1 322	140	2 590	445	168	6 098	83 227
	2004	64 076	306[2]	1 289	147	2 673	394	181	7 555	84 333
Denmark Danemark	2001	...	16 887[2]	2 239	543	3 220	1 567	167	353 062	37 769
	2002	...	18 143[2]	2 074	529	3 258	1 574	163	353 693	39 317
	2003	...	18 143[2]	2 082	611	3 451	1 519	168	335 062	46 264
	2004	...	19 262[2]	1 986	606	3 329	1 557	164	395 033	40 477
Estonia Estonie	2001	11 838[6]	...	...	...	...	...	...	...	8 484
	2002	12 400[6]	...	...	...	...	...	...	...	8 520
	2003	14 892[6]	...	...	...	...	...	...	...	10 159
	2004	13 993[6]	...	...	...	...	...	...	...	10 128

Region, country or area Région, pays ou zone	Year Année	Hard coal and lignite Houille et lignite	Crude petroleum and NGL Pétrole brut et GNL	Motor gasoline Essence auto	Jet fuel Carbu-réacteurs	Gas-diesel oil Gazole/ carburant diesel	Residual fuel oil Mazout résiduel	Liquefied petroleum gas Gaz de pétrole liquéfiés	Natural gas (terajoules) Gaz naturel (térajoules)	Electricity (million kWh) Electricité (millions de kWh)
		Thousand metric tons — Milliers de tonnes								
Faeroe Islands Iles Féroé	2001	...	...	...	...	...	...	...	...	200
	2002	...	...	...	...	...	...	...	...	240
	2003	...	...	...	...	...	...	...	...	270
	2004	...	...	...	...	...	...	...	...	290
Finland Finlande	2001	...	...	3 785	441	5 058	1 306	150	...	74 453
	2002	...	...	4 350	659	5 128	1 403	227	...	74 901
	2003	...	...	4 304	614	5 038	1 267	273	...	84 230
	2004	...	...	4 321	714	5 078	1 445	267	...	85 817
France[7] France[7]	2001	2 671	1 632	18 151	6 051	34 936	11 291	2 955	70 222	548 704
	2002	2 068	1 519	16 920	5 238	33 110	10 626	2 524	67 438	559 186
	2003	2 243	1 405	16 804	5 169	34 979	10 919	2 917	59 621	566 949
	2004	872[1]	1 364	16 878	5 616	34 421	11 887	2 830	51 530	572 241
Germany Allemagne	2001	206 033	3 278[2]	26 021	4 195	46 943	13 192	3 020	741 143	586 340
	2002	210 987	3 509[2]	25 970	4 157	47 455	12 183	2 956	743 728	571 645
	2003	207 838	3 690[2]	26 449	4 194	48 638	12 232	3 056	740 615	599 470
	2004	211 077	3 463[2]	26 467	4 424	49 551	14 013	2 918	685 342	616 785
Gibraltar Gibraltar	2001	...	...	...	...	...	...	...	...	126
	2002	...	...	...	...	...	...	...	...	129
	2003	...	...	...	...	...	...	...	...	134
	2004	...	...	...	...	...	...	...	...	136
Greece Grèce	2001	66 344[6]	191	3 770	1 791	5 452	7 361	762	1 870	53 704
	2002	70 468[6]	189	3 802	1 705	5 624	7 188	694	1 973	54 608
	2003	68 299[6]	137	3 653	1 630	6 053	7 456	672	1 442	58 478
	2004	70 041[6]	133	3 629	1 720	5 369	7 095	598	1 337	59 344
Hungary Hongrie	2001	13 914[6]	1 540	1 401	176	2 547	1 291	278	115 224	36 414
	2002	13 027[6]	1 884	1 573	183	3 096	358	392	109 582	36 156
	2003	13 301[6]	1 898	1 477	202	3 124	367	392	106 329	34 145
	2004	11 242[6]	1 878	1 465	239	2 989	313	408	110 100	33 708
Iceland Islande	2001	...	...	...	...	...	...	...	...	8 033
	2002	...	...	...	...	...	...	...	...	8 416
	2003	...	...	...	...	...	...	...	...	8 500
	2004	...	...	...	...	...	...	...	...	8 623
Ireland Irlande	2001	...	...	669	...	1 173	1 132	59	30 639	24 982
	2002	...	...	660	...	955	1 047	60	31 519	25 170
	2003	...	...	639	...	988	1 005	59	25 293	25 235
	2004	...	...	552	...	964	966	53	32 025	25 627
Italy[8] Italie[8]	2001	139[1]	4 097	20 956	3 736	37 076	19 295	2 694	580 723	279 009
	2002	163[1]	5 535[2]	20 804	4 023	38 993	17 190	2 472	557 137	*285 276
	2003	250[1]	5 570[2]	20 699	4 187	38 389	18 018	2 610	529 017	293 884
	2004	98[1]	5 445[2]	20 662	3 787	39 536	17 543	2 613	493 813	303 347
Latvia Lettonie	2001	...	...	...	...	...	...	...	...	4 281
	2002	...	...	...	...	...	...	...	...	3 977
	2003	...	...	...	...	...	...	...	...	3 979
	2004	...	...	...	...	...	...	...	...	4 683
Lithuania Lituanie	2001	...	471[2]	1 889	669	2 021	1 161	450	...	14 737
	2002	...	434[2]	1 719	655	1 850	1 229	455	...	17 721
	2003	...	382[2]	1 882	695	2 064	1 381	435	...	19 488
	2004	...	302[2]	2 331	850	2 523	1 674	525	...	19 274
Luxembourg Luxembourg	2001	...	...	...	...	...	...	...	...	1 186
	2002	...	...	...	...	...	...	...	...	3 675
	2003	...	...	...	...	...	...	...	...	3 620
	2004	...	...	...	...	...	...	...	...	4 136

Region, country or area Région, pays ou zone	Year Année	Hard coal and lignite Houille et lignite	Crude petroleum and NGL Pétrole brut et GNL	Motor gasoline Essence auto	Jet fuel Carbu-réacteurs	Gas-diesel oil Gazole/carburant diesel	Residual fuel oil Mazout résiduel	Liquefied petroleum gas Gaz de pétrole liquéfiés	Natural gas (terajoules) Gaz naturel (térajoules)	Electricity (million kWh) Electricité (millions de kWh)
		Thousand metric tons — Milliers de tonnes								
Malta Malte	2001	...	...	...	...	...	...	...	...	1 943
	2002	...	...	...	...	...	...	...	...	2 052
	2003	...	...	...	...	...	...	...	...	2 236
	2004	...	...	...	...	...	...	...	...	2 216
Netherlands Pays-Bas	2001	...	2 263	14 423	6 655	22 167	10 730	3 974	2 591 786	93 781
	2002	...	3 074	15 767	6 174	19 583	12 654	4 664	2 524 867	96 066
	2003	...	3 076	15 730	6 669	20 787	12 333	4 780	2 428 905	96 763
	2004	...	2 891	15 539	6 935	20 234	13 073	5 070	2 864 924	100 770
Norway[9] Norvège[9]	2001	1 788[1]	163 696	3 287	654	6 478	1 647	1 444	2 273 483	119 727
	2002	2 132[1]	163 017	2 920	582	6 010	1 503	5 609	2 751 407	130 705
	2003	2 944[1]	159 431	3 546	415	6 635	1 702	6 167	3 081 659	107 405
	2004	2 904[1]	157 879	3 261	423	6 241	1 845	6 423	3 274 692	110 598
Poland Pologne	2001	163 544	767[2]	4 242	623	7 141	3 424	254	162 449	145 616
	2002	161 915	728[2]	3 932	575	6 314	3 325	255	166 037	144 126
	2003	163 794	765[2]	3 871	647	6 722	3 253	269	167 997	151 631
	2004	162 428	886[2]	3 978	679	7 371	2 754	259	182 618	154 159
Portugal Portugal	2001	...	...	2 615	618	4 533	2 703	371	...	46 509
	2002	...	...	2 518	511	4 827	2 358	341	...	46 107
	2003	...	...	2 732	703	4 955	2 388	379	...	46 852
	2004	...	...	2 551	779	4 703	2 969	365	...	45 105
Republic of Moldova République de Moldova	*2001	...	...	...	...	...	...	...	...	3 585
	*2002	...	...	...	...	...	...	...	...	3 233
	*2003	...	...	...	...	...	...	...	...	3 413
	2004	...	...	...	...	...	...	...	...	3 617
Romania Roumanie	2001	33 289	6 238	2 731	185	4 199	1 797	325	501 496	53 866
	2002	30 414	6 072	3 569	105	4 689	1 700	344	493 064	54 735
	2003	33 063	5 890	3 295	158	3 988	1 562	327	485 135	55 140
	2004	31 792[6]	5 705	3 419	177	4 170	1 559	366	482 759	56 503
Russian Federation Fédération de Russie	2001	251 438	345 841	27 610	8 966	50 161	55 575	7 903	21 807 667	891 284
	2002	240 980	377 173	28 992	9 303	52 724	58 896	7 610	22 308 334	891 285
	2003	260 379	418 582	29 315	9 453	53 930	56 377	8 571	23 252 111	916 286
	2004	262 344	456 253	30 505	9 592	55 389	58 330	8 760	23 693 333	931 865
Serbia and Montenegro Serbie-et-Monténégro	2001	36 370	899[2]	488	64	847	691	80	21 153	*34 980
	2002	38 440	812[2]	672	78	1 123	839	87	16 946	*34 910
	2003	40 348	773[2]	617	85	1 254	919	79	13 723	*35 216
	2004	41 157	652[2]	821	56	1 315	853	95	11 951	38 489
Slovakia Slovaquie	2001	3 424[6]	106	1 438	48	2 406	718	238	7 009	32 046
	2002	3 404[6]	103	1 555	42	2 341	620	191	6 754	32 427
	2003	3 097[6]	80	1 597	63	2 351	635	184	7 745	31 179
	2004	2 952[6]	42	1 670	61	2 598	585	206	6 603	30 567
Slovenia Slovénie	2001	4 133[6]	0	...	...	...	...	...	244	14 466
	2002	4 686[6]	1[2]	...	...	...	...	...	222	14 690
	2003	4 830[6]	0	...	...	...	...	...	199	14 019
	2004	4 809[6]	0	...	...	...	...	...	201	15 279
Spain Espagne	2001	22 678	338[2]	9 272	3 745	20 177	11 784	1 574	21 904	236 043
	2002	22 034	316[2]	8 871	3 567	20 820	12 122	1 561	21 718	244 963
	2003	20 562	322[2]	9 047	3 061	21 631	10 130	1 211	9 149	260 727
	2004	20 487	255[2]	10 434	2 713	21 563	9 125	1 058	14 398	280 007
Sweden Suède	2001	...	...	4 020	143	7 677	5 919	279	...	161 616
	2002	...	...	3 987	57	6 964	5 069	272	...	146 733
	2003	...	...	4 309	109	6 942	5 170	360	...	135 435
	2004	...	...	4 506	208	7 238	5 450	423	...	151 727

Region, country or area / Région, pays ou zone	Year / Année	Hard coal and lignite / Houille et lignite	Crude petroleum and NGL / Pétrole brut et GNL	Motor gasoline / Essence auto	Jet fuel / Carbu-réacteurs	Gas-diesel oil / Gazole/ carburant diesel	Residual fuel oil / Mazout résiduel	Liquefied petroleum gas / Gaz de pétrole liquéfiés	Natural gas (terajoules) / Gaz naturel (térajoules)	Electricity (million kWh) / Electricité (millions de kWh)
		Thousand metric tons — Milliers de tonnes								
Switzerland[10] Suisse[10]	2001	...	...	1 154	407	2 025	775	183	...	72 124
	2002	...	...	1 175	406	2 011	743	209	...	66 893
	2003	...	...	1 072	344	1 893	759	178	...	67 166
	2004	...	...	1 362	350	2 148	701	196	...	65 299
TFYR of Macedonia L'ex-R.y. Macédoine	2001	8 106[6]	...	104	7	224	282	11	...	6 361
	2002	7 580[6]	...	78	11	172	254	9	...	6 090
	2003	7 382[6]	...	126	0	322	343	21	...	6 737
	2004	7 245[6]	...	146	0	359	282	20	...	6 665
Ukraine Ukraine	2001	61 684	3 703	3 920	360	4 799	5 429	503	715 529	172 972
	2002	59 483	3 732	4 588	340	5 792	7 381	627	728 882	173 734
	2003	64 249	3 967	4 308	361	6 323	7 956	738	748 794	180 354
	2004	59 670	4 314	4 393	468	6 448	8 114	753	799 130	182 157
United Kingdom Royaume-Uni	2001	31 930[1]	120 159	21 455	5 910	26 796	11 912	5 333	4 431 339	384 952
	2002	29 989[1]	118 413	22 944	5 365	28 393	10 551	4 668	4 345 335	387 364
	2003	28 279[1]	107 769	22 627	5 277	27 579	11 517	4 007	4 309 312	398 671
	2004	25 097[1]	98 269	24 589	5 615	28 839	12 988	5 080	4 019 594	395 853
Oceania Océanie	**2001**	**333 089**	**39 821**	**13 809**	**5 473**	**13 060**	**2 217**	**3 368**	**1 608 096**	**263 229**
	2002	**346 300**	**36 249**	**14 789**	**5 159**	**13 170**	**2 123**	**1 712**	**1 652 746**	**274 398**
	2003	**348 393**	**33 693**	**14 628**	**4 931**	**13 478**	**1 669**	**1 850**	**1 641 590**	**276 345**
	2004	**359 617**	**33 585**	**15 080**	**4 885**	**13 381**	**1 421**	**1 479**	**1 655 432**	**289 576**
American Samoa Samoa américaines	2001	...	...	...	...	...	...	...	...	171
	2002	...	...	...	...	...	...	...	...	179
	2003	...	...	...	...	...	...	...	...	188
	2004	...	...	...	...	...	...	...	...	188
Australia Australie	2001	329 177	35 310	12 309	4 639	11 120	1 886	3 149	1 354 543	216 845
	2002	341 841	31 884	13 259	4 271	11 091	1 696	1 506	1 411 424	226 320
	2003	343 213	29 863	13 108	4 080	11 430	1 310	1 694	1 456 588	228 045
	2004	354 461	29 812	13 453	3 937	11 590	1 071	1 312	1 488 699	239 497
Cook Islands Iles Cook	2001	...	...	...	...	...	...	...	...	26
	2002	...	...	...	...	...	...	...	...	28
	2003	...	...	...	...	...	...	...	...	29
	2004	...	...	...	...	...	...	...	...	30
Fiji* Fidji*	2001	...	...	...	...	...	...	...	...	520
	2002	...	...	...	...	...	...	...	...	520
	2003	...	...	...	...	...	...	...	...	526
	2004	...	...	...	...	...	...	...	...	540
French Polynesia Polynésie française	2001	...	...	...	...	...	...	...	...	496
	2002	...	...	...	...	...	...	...	...	507
	2003	...	...	...	...	...	...	...	...	479
	*2004	...	...	...	...	...	...	...	...	485
Guam Guam	2001	...	...	...	...	...	...	...	...	1 736
	2002	...	...	...	...	...	...	...	...	1 603
	2003	...	...	...	...	...	...	...	...	1 457
	2004	...	...	...	...	...	...	...	...	1 589
Kiribati Kiribati	2001	...	...	...	...	...	...	...	...	10
	2002	...	...	...	...	...	...	...	...	10
	2003	...	...	...	...	...	...	...	...	10
	2004	...	...	...	...	...	...	...	...	10
Nauru* Nauru*	2001	...	...	...	...	...	...	...	...	30
	2002	...	...	...	...	...	...	...	...	30
	2003	...	...	...	...	...	...	...	...	32
	2004	...	...	...	...	...	...	...	...	32

Region, country or area / Région, pays ou zone	Year / Année	Hard coal and lignite / Houille et lignite	Crude petroleum and NGL / Pétrole brut et GNL	Motor gasoline / Essence auto	Jet fuel / Carbu-réacteurs	Gas-diesel oil / Gazole/carburant diesel	Residual fuel oil / Mazout résiduel	Liquefied petroleum gas / Gaz de pétrole liquéfiés	Natural gas (terajoules) / Gaz naturel (térajoules)	Electricity (million kWh) / Electricité (millions de kWh)
		Thousand metric tons — Milliers de tonnes								
New Caledonia / Nouvelle-Calédonie	2001	...	...	...	...	...	...	...	...	1 729
	2002	...	...	...	...	...	...	...	...	1 749
	2003	...	...	...	...	...	...	...	...	1 758
	2004	...	...	...	...	...	...	...	...	1 678
New Zealand / Nouvelle-Zélande	2001	3 912	1 979	1 500	815	1 910	331	219	*247 524	38 749
	2002	4 459	1 813	1 530	869	2 049	427	206	*235 294	40 346
	2003	5 180	1 403	1 520	832	2 018	359	156	*179 476	40 441
	2004	5 156	1 273	1 627	930	1 763	350	167	*160 633	41 813
Niue* / Nioué*	2001	...	...	...	...	...	...	...	...	3
	2002	...	...	...	...	...	...	...	...	3
	2003	...	...	...	...	...	...	...	...	3
	2004	...	...	...	...	...	...	...	...	3
Palau / Palaos	2001	...	...	...	...	...	...	...	...	128
	2002	...	...	...	...	...	...	...	...	127
	2003	...	...	...	...	...	...	...	...	128
	*2004	...	...	...	...	...	...	...	...	128
Papua New Guinea / Papouasie-Nvl-Guinée	2001	...	2 532[2]	...	*19	*30	...	...	6 029	2 570
	2002	...	2 552[2]	...	*19	*30	...	...	6 028	2 760
	2003	...	2 427[2]	...	*19	*30	...	...	5 526	3 030
	*2004	...	2 500[2]	...	18	28	...	...	6 100	3 360
Samoa* / Samoa*	2001	...	...	...	...	...	...	...	...	105
	2002	...	...	...	...	...	...	...	...	105
	2003	...	...	...	...	...	...	...	...	106
	2004	...	...	...	...	...	...	...	...	110
Solomon Islands* / Iles Salomon*	2001	...	...	...	...	...	...	...	...	32
	2002	...	...	...	...	...	...	...	...	32
	2003	...	...	...	...	...	...	...	...	33
	2004	...	...	...	...	...	...	...	...	33
Tonga* / Tonga*	2001	...	...	...	...	...	...	...	...	36
	2002	...	...	...	...	...	...	...	...	36
	2003	...	...	...	...	...	...	...	...	36
	2004	...	...	...	...	...	...	...	...	36
Vanuatu* / Vanuatu*	2001	...	...	...	...	...	...	...	...	43
	2002	...	...	...	...	...	...	...	...	43
	2003	...	...	...	...	...	...	...	...	44
	2004	...	...	...	...	...	...	...	...	44

Source

United Nations Statistics Division, New York, the energy statistics database, last accessed January 2007.

Notes

1 Hard coal only.
2 Crude petroleum only.
3 Refers to the Southern African Customs Union.
4 Natural gas liquids only.
5 For statistical purposes, the data for China do not include those for the Hong Kong Special Administrative Region (Hong Kong SAR), Macao Special Administrative Region (Macao SAR) and Taiwan Province of China.
6 Lignite only.
7 Including Monaco.
8 Including San Marino.
9 Including Svalbard and Jan Mayen Islands.
10 Including Liechtenstein.

Source

Organisation des Nations Unies, Division de statistique, New York, la base de données pour les statistiques énergétiques, dernier accès janvier 2007.

Notes

1 Houille seulement.
2 Pétrole brut seulement.
3 Se réfèrent à l'Union douanière d'afrique australe.
4 Liquides de gaz naturel seulement.
5 Pour la présentation des statistiques, les données pour la Chine ne comprennent pas la Région Administrative Spéciale de Hong Kong (Hong Kong RAS), la Région Administrative Spéciale de Macao (Macao RAS) et la province de Taiwan.
6 Lignite seulement.
7 Y compris Monaco.
8 Y compris Saint-Marin.
9 Y compris îles Svalbard et Jan Mayen.
10 Y compris Liechtenstein.

Technical notes: tables 50 and 51

Tables 50: Data are presented in metric tons of oil equivalent (TOE), to which the individual energy commodities are converted in the interests of international uniformity and comparability.

To convert from original units to TOE, the data in original units (metric tons, terajoules, kilowatt hours, cubic metres) are multiplied by conversion factors. For a list of the relevant conversion factors and a detailed description of methods, see the United Nations *Energy Statistics Yearbook* and related methodological publications.

Included in the production of commercial primary energy for *solids* are hard coal, lignite, peat and oil shale; *liquids* are comprised of crude petroleum and natural gas liquids; *gas* comprises natural gas; and *electricity* is comprised of primary electricity generation from hydro, nuclear, geothermal, wind, tide, wave and solar sources.

In general, data on stocks refer to changes in stocks of producers, importers and/or industrial consumers at the beginning and end of each year.

International trade of energy commodities is based on the "general trade" system, that is, all goods entering and leaving the national boundary of a country are recorded as imports and exports.

Sea/air bunkers refer to the amounts of fuels delivered to ocean-going ships or aircraft of all flags engaged in international traffic. Consumption by ships engaged in transport in inland and coastal waters, or by aircraft engaged in domestic flights, is not included.

Data on consumption refer to "apparent consumption" and are derived from the formula "production + imports – exports – bunkers +/– stock changes". Accordingly, the series on apparent consumption may in some cases represent only an indication of the magnitude of actual gross inland availability.

Included in the consumption of commercial energy for *solids* are consumption of primary forms of solid fuels, net imports and changes in stocks of secondary fuels; *liquids* are comprised of consumption of energy petroleum products including feedstocks, natural gasoline, condensate, refinery gas and input of crude petroleum to thermal power plants; *gases* include the consumption of natural gas, net imports and changes in stocks of gasworks and coke-oven gas; and *electricity* is comprised of production of primary electricity and net imports of electricity.

Table 51: The definitions of the energy commodities are as follows:

- Hard coal: Coal that has a high degree of coalification with a gross calorific value above 23,865 KJ/kg (5,700

Notes techniques : tableaux 50 et 51

Tableau 50 : Les données relatives aux divers produits énergétiques ont été converties en tonnes d'équivalent pétrole (TEP), dans un souci d'uniformité et pour permettre les comparaisons entre la production de différents pays.

Pour passer des unités de mesure d'origine à l'unité commune, les données en unités d'origine (tonnes, terajoules, kilowatt-heures, mètres cubes) sont multipliées par des facteurs de conversion. Pour une liste des facteurs de conversion appropriée et pour des descriptions détaillées des méthodes appliquées, se reporter à *l'Annuaire des statistiques de l'énergie* des Nations Unies et aux publications méthodologiques apparentées.

Sont compris dans la production d'énergie primaire commerciale: pour *les solides*, la houille, le lignite, la tourbe et le schiste bitumineux; pour *les* liquides, le pétrole brut et les liquides de gaz naturel; pour *les gaz*, le gaz naturel; pour *l'électricité*, l'électricité primaire de source hydraulique, nucléaire, géothermique, éolienne, marémotrice, des vagues et solaire.

En général, les variations des stocks se rapportent aux différences entre les stocks des producteurs, des importateurs ou des consommateurs industriels au début et à la fin de chaque année.

Le commerce international des produits énergétiques est fondé sur le système du "commerce général", c'est-à-dire que tous les biens entrant sur le territoire national d'un pays ou en sortant sont respectivement enregistrés comme importations et exportations.

Les soutes maritimes/aériens se rapportent aux quantités de combustibles livrées aux navires de mer et aéronefs assurant des liaisons commerciales internationales, quel que soit leur pavillon. La consommation des navires effectuant des opérations de transport sur les voies navigables intérieures ou dans les eaux côtières n'est pas incluse, tout comme celle des aéronefs effectuant des vols intérieurs.

Les données sur la consommation se rapportent à la "consommation apparente" et sont obtenues par la formule "production + importations – exportations – soutes +/– variations des stocks". En conséquence, les séries relatives à la consommation apparente peuvent occasionnellement ne donner qu'une indication de l'ordre de grandeur des disponibilités intérieures brutes réelles.

Sont compris dans la consommation d'énergie commerciale: pour *les solides*, la consommation de combustibles solides primaires, les importations nettes et les variations de stocks de combustibles solides secondaires; pour *les liquides*, la consommation de produits pétroliers énergétiques y compris les charges d'alimentation des usines de traitement, l'essence naturelle, le condensat et le gaz de raffinerie ainsi que le pétrole brut consommé dans les centrales thermiques pour

kcal/kg) on an ash-free but moist basis, and a mean random reflectance of vitrinite of at least 0.6. Slurries, middlings and other low-grade coal products, which cannot be classified according to the type of coal from which they are obtained, are included under hard coal.

- Lignite: Non-agglomerating coal with a low degree of coalification which retained the anatomical structure of the vegetable matter from which it was formed. Its gross calorific value is less than 17,435 KJ/kg (4,165 kcal/kg), and it contains greater than 31 per cent volatile matter on a dry mineral matter free basis.
- Crude petroleum: A mineral oil consisting of a mixture of hydrocarbons of natural origin, yellow to black in color, of variable density and viscosity. Data in this category also includes lease or field condensate (separator liquids) which is recovered from gaseous hydrocarbons in lease separation facilities, as well as synthetic crude oil, mineral oils extracted from bituminous minerals such as shales and bituminous sand, and oils from coal liquefaction.
- Natural gas liquids (NGL): Liquid or liquefied hydrocarbons produced in the manufacture, purification and stabilization of natural gas. NGLs include, but are not limited to, ethane, propane, butane, pentane, natural gasoline, and plant condensate.
- Motor gasoline: Light hydrocarbon oil for use in internal combustion engines such as motor vehicles, excluding aircraft. It distills between 35°C and 200°C, and is treated to reach a sufficiently high octane number of generally between 80 and 100 RON. Treatment may be by reforming, blending with an aromatic fraction, or the addition of benzole or other additives (such as tetraethyl lead).
- Jet fuel: Consists of gasoline-type jet fuel and kerosene-type jet fuel. Gasoline-type jet fuel: All light hydrocarbon oils for use in aviation gas-turbine engines. It distills between 100°C and 250°C with at least 20% of volume distilling at 143°C. It is obtained by blending kerosene and gasoline or naphtha in such a way that the aromatic content does not exceed 25% in volume. Additives are included to reduce the freezing point to -58°C or lower, and to keep the Reid vapour pressure between 0.14 and 0.21 kg/cm^2.
- Kerosene-type jet fuel: Medium oil for use in aviation gas-turbine engines with the same distillation characteristics and flash point as kerosene, with a maximum aromatic content of 20% in volume. It is treated to give a kinematic viscosity of less than 15 cSt at -34°C and a freezing point below -50°C.
- Gas-diesel oil (distillate fuel oil): Heavy oils distilling between 200°C and 380°C, but distilling less than 65%

la production d'électricité; pour *les gaz*, la consommation de gaz naturel, les importations nettes et les variations de stocks de gaz d'usines à gaz et de gaz de cokerie; pour *l'électricité*, la production d'électricité primaire et les importations nettes d'électricité.

Tableau 51: Les définitions des produits énergétiques sont données ci-après :

- Houille: Charbon à haut degré de houillification et à pouvoir calorifique brut supérieur à 23 865 kJ/kg (5 700 kcal/kg), valeur mesurée pour un combustible exempt de cendres, mais humide et ayant un indice moyen de réflectance de la vitrinite au moins égal à 0,6. Les schlamms, les mixtes et autres produits du charbon de faible qualité qui ne peuvent être classés en fonction du type de charbon dont ils sont dérivés, sont inclus dans cette rubrique.
- Lignite: Le charbon non agglutinant d'un faible degré de houillification qui a gardé la structure anatomique des végétaux dont il est issu. Son pouvoir calorifique supérieur est inférieur à 17 435 kJ/kg (4 165 kcal/kg) et il contient plus de 31% de matières volatiles sur produit sec exempt de matières minérales.
- Pétrole brut: Huile minérale constituée d'un mélange d'hydrocarbures d'origine naturelle, de couleur variant du jaune au noir, d'une densité et d'une viscosité variable. Figurent également dans cette rubrique les condensats directement récupérés sur les sites d'exploitation des hydrocarbures gazeux (dans les installations prévues pour la séparation des phases liquide et gazeuse), le pétrole brut synthétique, les huiles minérales brutes extraites des roches bitumineuses telles que schistes, sables asphaltiques et les huiles issues de la liquéfaction du charbon.
- Liquides de gaz naturel (LGN): Hydrocarbures liquides ou liquéfiés produits lors de la fabrication, de la purification et de la stabilisation du gaz naturel. Les liquides de gaz naturel comprennent l'éthane, le propane, le butane, le pentane, l'essence naturelle et les condensats d'usine, sans que la liste soit limitative.
- Essence auto : Hydrocarbure léger utilisé dans les moteurs à combustion interne, tels que ceux des véhicules à moteur, à l'exception des aéronefs. Sa température de distillation se situe entre 35°C et 200°C et il est traité de façon à atteindre un indice d'octane suffisamment élevé, généralement entre 80 et 100 IOR. Le traitement peut consister en reformage, mélange avec une fraction aromatique, ou adjonction de benzol ou d'autres additifs (tels que du plomb tétraéthyle).
- Carburéacteurs: Comprennent les carburéacteurs du type essence et les carburéacteurs du type kérosène. Carburéacteurs du type essence: Comprennent tous

in volume at 250°C, including losses, and 85% or more at 350°C. Its flash point is always above 50°C and its specific gravity is higher than 0.82. Heavy oils obtained by blending are grouped together with gas oils on the condition that their kinematic viscosity does not exceed 27.5 cSt at 38°C. Also included are middle distillates intended for the petrochemical industry. Gas-diesel oils are used as a fuel for internal combustion in diesel engines, as a burner fuel in heating installations, such as furnaces, and for enriching water gas to increase its luminosity. Other names for this product are diesel fuel, diesel oil and gas oil.

- Residual fuel oil: A heavy oil that makes up the distillation residue. It comprises all fuels (including those obtained by blending) with a kinematic viscosity above 27.5 cSt at 38°C. Its flash point is always above 50°C and its specific gravity is higher than 0.90. It is commonly used by ships and industrial large-scale heating installations as a fuel in furnaces or boilers.
- Liquefied petroleum gas (LPG): Hydrocarbons which are gaseous under conditions of normal temperature and pressure but are liquefied by compression or cooling to facilitate storage, handling and transportation. It comprises propane, butane, or a combination of the two. Also included is ethane from petroleum refineries or natural gas producers' separation and stabilization plants.
- Natural gas: Gases consisting mainly of methane occurring naturally in underground deposits. It includes both non-associated gas (originating from fields producing only hydrocarbons in gaseous form) and associated gas (originating from fields producing both liquid and gaseous hydrocarbons), as well as methane recovered from coal mines and sewage gas. Production of natural gas refers to dry marketable production, measured after purification and extraction of natural gas liquids and sulphur. Extraction losses and the amounts that have been reinjected, flared, and vented are excluded from the data on production.
- Electricity production refers to gross production, which includes the consumption by station auxiliaries and any losses in the transformers that are considered integral parts of the station. Included also is total electric energy produced by pumping installations without deduction of electric energy absorbed by pumping.

les hydrocarbures légers utilisés dans les turboréacteurs d'aviation. Leur température de distillation se situe entre 100°C et 250°C et donne au moins 20% en volume de distillat à 143°C. Ils sont obtenus par mélange de pétrole lampant et d'essence ou de naphta de façon que la teneur en composés aromatiques ne dépasse pas 25% en volume. Des additifs y sont ajoutés afin d'abaisser le point de congélation à -58°C ou au-dessous, et de maintenir la tension de vapeur Reid entre 0,14 et 0,21 kg/cm^2.

- Carburéacteurs du type kerosene: Huiles moyennement visqueuses utilisées dans les turboréacteurs d'aviation, ayant les mêmes caractéristiques de distillation et le même point d'éclair que le pétrole lampant et une teneur en composés aromatiques ne dépassant pas 20% en volume. Elles sont traitées de façon à atteindre une viscosité cinématique de moins de 15 cSt à -34°C et un point de congélation inférieur à -50°C.
- Gazole/carburant diesel (mazout distillé):Huiles lourdes dont la température de distillation se situe entre 200°C et 380°C, mais qui donnent moins de 65% en volume de distillat à 250°C (y compris les pertes) et 85% ou davantage à 350°C. Leur point d'éclair est toujours supérieur à 50°C et leur densité supérieure à 0,82. Les huiles lourdes obtenues par mélange sont classées dans la même catégorie que les gazoles à condition que leur viscosité cinématique ne dépasse pas 27,5 cSt à 38°C. Sont compris dans cette rubrique les distillats moyens destinés à l'industrie pétrochimique. Les gazoles servent de carburant pour la combustion interne dans les moteurs diesel, de combustible dans les installations de chauffage telles que les chaudières, et d'additifs destinés à augmenter la luminosité de la flamme du gaz à l'eau. Ce produit est aussi connu sous les appellations de gazole ou gasoil et carburant ou combustible diesel.
- Gaz de pétrole liquéfiés (GPL): Hydrocarbures qui sont à l'état gazeux dans des conditions de température et de pression normales mais sont liquéfiés par compression ou refroidissement pour en faciliter l'entreposage, la manipulation et le transport. Dans cette rubrique figurent le propane et le butane ou un mélange de ces deux hydrocarbures. Est également inclus l'éthane produit dans les raffineries ou dans les installations de séparation et de stabilisation des producteurs de gaz naturel.
- Gaz naturel: gaz constitué essentiellement de méthane, extraits de gisements naturels souterrains. Il peut s'agir aussi bien de gaz non associé (provenant de gisements qui produisent uniquement des hydrocarbures gazeux) que de gaz associé (provenant de gisements qui produisent à la fois des hydrocarbures liquides et gazeux) ou de

méthane récupéré dans les mines de charbon et le gaz de gadoues. La production de gaz naturel se rapporte à la production de gaz commercialisable sec, mesurée après purification et extraction des condensats de gaz naturel et du soufre. Les quantités réinjectées, brûlées à la torchère ou éventées et les pertes d'extraction sont exclues des données sur la production.

- La production d'électricité se rapporte à la production brute, qui comprend la consommation des équipements auxiliaires des centrales et les pertes au niveau des transformateurs considérés comme faisant partie intégrante de ces centrales, ainsi que la quantité totale d'énergie électrique produite par les installations de pompage sans déductions de l'énergie électrique absorbée par ces dernières.

52 Land

Thousand hectares

Terres

En milliers d'hectares

Country or area — Pays ou zone	Latest available year / Dernière année disponible	Area — Superficie: Land area / Superficie des terres	Area — Superficie: Arable land / Terres arables	Area — Superficie: Permanent crops / Cultures permanentes	2005: Forest cover / Superficie forestière	Net change — Variation nette: From 1990 - de 1990: Arable land / Terres arables	Net change — Variation nette: From 1990 - de 1990: Permanent crops / Cultures permanentes	Net change — Variation nette: 1990 - 2005: Forest cover / Superficie forestière
Africa — Afrique								
Algeria — Algérie	2003	238 174	7 545[1]	670[1]	2 277	464	116	487
Angola — Angola	2003	124 670	3 300[1]	290[1]	59 104	400	-210	-1 872
Benin — Bénin	2003	11 062	2 650[1]	267[1]	2 351	1 035	162	-971
Botswana — Botswana	2003	56 673	377[1]	3[1]	11 943	-41	0	-1 775
British Indian Ocean Terr. — Terr. brit. de l'océan Indien	2003	8	...	...	3	...	...	0
Burkina Faso — Burkina Faso	2003	27 360	4 840[1]	60[1]	6 794	1 320	5	-360
Burundi — Burundi	2003	2 568	990[1]	365[1]	152	60	5	-137
Cameroon — Cameroun	2003	46 540	5 960[1]	1 200[1]	21 245	20	-30	-3 300
Cape Verde — Cap-Vert	2003	403	46[1]	3[1]	84	5	1	26
Central African Rep. — Rép. centrafricaine	2003	62 298	1 930[1]	94[1]	22 755	10	8	-448
Chad — Tchad	2003	125 920	3 600[1]	30[1]	11 921	327	3	-1 189
Comoros — Comores	2003	223	80[1]	52[1]	5	2	17	-7
Congo — Congo	2003	34 150	495[1]	52[1]	22 471	16	10	-255
Côte d'Ivoire — Côte d'Ivoire	2003	31 800	3 300[1]	3 600[1]	10 405	870	100	183
Dem. Rep. of the Congo — Rép. dém. du Congo	2003	226 705	6 700[1]	1 100[1]	133 610	30	-90	-6 921
Djibouti — Djibouti	2003	2 318	1[1]	...	6	0	...	0
Egypt — Egypte	2005	99 545	3 000[1]	520[1]	67	716	156	23
Equatorial Guinea — Guinée équatoriale	2003	2 805	130[1]	100[1]	1 632	0	0	-228
Eritrea — Erythrée	2003	10 100	562[1]	3[1]	1 554	...	...	-67
Ethiopia — Ethiopie	2003	100 000	11 056[1]	713[1]	13 000	...	...	-2 114
Gabon — Gabon	2003	25 767	325[1]	170[1]	21 775	30	8	-152
Gambia — Gambie	2003	1 000	315[1]	5[1]	471	133	0	29
Ghana — Ghana	2003	22 754	4 185[1]	2 200[1]	5 517	1 485	700	-1 931
Guinea — Guinée	2003	24 572	1 100[1]	650[1]	6 724	372	150	-684
Guinea-Bissau — Guinée-Bissau	2003	2 812	300[1]	250[1]	2 072	0	133	-144
Kenya — Kenya	2003	56 914	4 650[1]	562[1]	3 522	450	62	-186
Lesotho — Lesotho	2003	3 035	330[1]	4[1]	8	13	0	3
Liberia — Libéria	2003	9 632	382[1]	220[1]	3 154	-18	5	-904
Libyan Arab Jamah. — Jamah. arabe libyenne	2003	175 954	1 815[1]	335[1]	217	10	-15	0
Madagascar — Madagascar	2003	58 154	2 950[1]	600[1]	12 838	230	-5	-854
Malawi — Malawi	2003	9 408	2 450[1]	140[1]	3 402	635	25	-494
Mali — Mali	2005	122 019	4 800[1]	40[1]	12 572	2 747	0	-1 500
Mauritania — Mauritanie	2003	102 522	488[1]	12[1]	267	88	6	-148
Mauritius — Maurice	2005	203	100[1]	6[1]	37	0	0	-2
Mayotte — Mayotte	2005	...	...	...	5	...	...	-1
Morocco — Maroc	2003	44 630	8 484	892	4 364	-223	156	75
Mozambique — Mozambique	2003	78 409	4 350[1]	230[1]	19 262	900	0	-750
Namibia — Namibie	2003	82 329	815[1]	5[1]	7 661	155	3	-1 101
Niger — Niger	2003	126 670	14 483[1]	17[1]	1 266	3 447	6	-679
Nigeria — Nigéria	2003	91 077	30 500[1]	2 900[1]	11 089	961	365	-6 145
Réunion — Réunion	2003	250	35	4	84	-12	-1	-3
Rwanda — Rwanda	2003	2 467	1 200[1]	270[1]	480	320	-35	162
Saint Helena — Sainte-Hélène	2003	31	4[1]	...	2	2	...	0
Sao Tome and Principe — Sao Tomé-et-Principe	2003	96	8[1]	47[1]	27	6	8	0

		Area — Superficie			2005	Net change — Variation nette: From 1990 - de 1990		1990 - 2005
Country or area — Pays ou zone	Latest available year / Dernière année disponible	Land area / Superficie des terres	Arable land / Terres arables	Permanent crops / Cultures permanentes	Forest cover / Superficie forestière	Arable land / Terres arables	Permanent crops / Cultures permanentes	Forest cover / Superficie forestière
Senegal — Sénégal	2003	19 253	2 460[1]	47[1]	8 673	135	22	-675
Seychelles — Seychelles	2003	46	1[1]	6[1]	40	0	1	0
Sierra Leone — Sierra Leone	2003	7 162	570[1]	75[1]	2 754	84	21	-290
Somalia — Somalie	2003	62 734	1 045[1]	26[1]	7 131	23	6	-1 151
South Africa — Afrique du Sud	2003	121 447	14 753	959	9 203	1 313	99	0
Sudan — Soudan	2003	237 600	17 000[1]	420[1]	67 546	4 000	185	-8 835
Swaziland — Swaziland	2003	1 720	178[1]	14[1]	541	-2	2	69
Togo — Togo	2003	5 439	2 510[1]	120[1]	386	410	30	-299
Tunisia — Tunisie	2003	15 536	2 790	2 140	1 056	-119	198	413
Uganda — Ouganda	2003	19 710	5 200[1]	2 150[1]	3 627	200	300	-1 297
United Rep. of Tanzania — Rép.-Unie de Tanzanie	2003	88 359	4 000[1]	1 100[1]	35 257	500	200	-6 184
Western Sahara — Sahara occidental	2003	26 600	5[1]	...	1 011	1	...	0
Zambia — Zambie	2003	74 339	5 260[1]	29[1]	42 452	11	10	-6 672
Zimbabwe — Zimbabwe	2003	38 685	3 220[1]	130[1]	17 540	330	10	-4 694
America, North — Amérique du Nord								
Antigua and Barbuda — Antigua-et-Barbuda	2003	44	8[1]	2[1]	9	0	0	0
Aruba — Aruba	2003	19	2[1]	...	...	0	...	...
Bahamas — Bahamas	2003	1 001	8[1]	4[1]	515	0	2	0
Barbados — Barbade	2003	43	16[1]	1[1]	2	0	0	0
Belize — Belize	2003	2 281	70[1]	32[1]	1 653	18	7	0
Bermuda — Bermudes	2003	5	1[1]	...	1	0	...	0
British Virgin Islands — Iles Vierges britanniques	2003	15	3[1]	1[1]	4	0	0	0
Canada — Canada	2003	909 351	45 660[1]	6 455[1]	310 134	156	94	0
Cayman Islands — Iles Caïmanes	2003	26	1[1]	...	12	0	...	0
Costa Rica — Costa Rica	2003	5 106	225[1]	300[1]	2 391	-35	50	-173
Cuba — Cuba	2003	10 982	3 063[1]	725[1]	2 713	32	-85	655
Dominica — Dominique	2003	75	5[1]	16[1]	46	0	5	-4
Dominican Republic — Rép. dominicaine	2003	4 838	1 096[1]	500[1]	1 376	46	50	0
El Salvador — El Salvador	2003	2 072	660[1]	250[1]	298	110	-10	-77
Grenada — Grenade	2003	34	2[1]	10[1]	4	0	0	0
Guadeloupe — Guadeloupe	2003	169	20	5	80	-1	-3	-4
Guatemala — Guatemala	2003	10 843	1 440[1]	610[1]	3 938	140	125	-810
Haiti — Haïti	2003	2 756	780[1]	320[1]	105	0	0	-11
Honduras — Honduras	2003	11 189	1 068[1]	360[1]	4 648	-394	2	-2 737
Jamaica — Jamaïque	2003	1 083	174[1]	110[1]	339	55	10	-6
Martinique — Martinique	2003	106	10	11	46	0	1	0
Mexico — Mexique	2003	190 869	24 800[1]	2 500[1]	64 238	800	600	-4 778
Montserrat — Montserrat	2003	10	2[1]	...	4	0	...	0
Netherlands Antilles — Antilles néerlandaises	2003	80	8[1]	...	1	0	...	0
Nicaragua — Nicaragua	2003	12 140	1 925[1]	236[1]	5 189	625	41	-1 349
Panama — Panama	2003	7 443	548[1]	147[1]	4 294	49	-8	-82
Puerto Rico — Porto Rico	2005	887	71[1]	42[1]	408	6	-8	4
Saint Kitts and Nevis — Saint-Kitts-et-Nevis	2003	36	7[1]	1[1]	5	-1	-1	0
Saint Lucia — Sainte-Lucie	2003	61	4[1]	14[1]	17	-1	1	0
Saint Pierre and Miquelon — Saint-Pierre-et-Miquelon	2003	23	3[1]	...	3	0	...	0
Saint Vincent-Grenadines — Saint Vincent-Grenadines	2003	39	7[1]	7[1]	11	2	0	2
Trinidad and Tobago — Trinité-et-Tobago	2003	513	75[1]	47[1]	226	1	1	-9
Turks and Caicos Islands — Iles Turques et Caïques	2003	43	1[1]	...	34	0	...	0
United States — Etats-Unis	2005	916 192	174 448[1]	2 730	303 089	-11 228	630	4 441
United States Virgin Is. — Iles Vierges américaines	2003	35	2[1]	1[1]	10	-2	0	-2

Country or area — Pays ou zone	Latest available year / Dernière année disponible	Area — Superficie: Land area / Superficie des terres	Area — Superficie: Arable land / Terres arables	Area — Superficie: Permanent crops / Cultures permanentes	2005: Forest cover / Superficie forestière	Net change — Variation nette: From 1990 – de 1990: Arable land / Terres arables	Net change — Variation nette: From 1990 – de 1990: Permanent crops / Cultures permanentes	Net change — Variation nette: 1990 – 2005: Forest cover / Superficie forestière
America, South — Amérique du Sud								
Argentina — Argentine	2003	273 669	27 900[1]	1 000[1]	33 021	1 500	-20	-2 241
Bolivia — Bolivie	2003	108 438	3 050[1]	206[1]	58 740	950	51	-4 055
Brazil — Brésil	2003	845 942[1]	59 000[1]	7 600[1]	477 698	8 319	873	-42 329
Chile — Chili	2003	74 880	1 982[1]	325[1]	16 121	-820	78	858
Colombia — Colombie	2005	110 950	2 004[1]	1 609[1]	60 728	-1 300	-86	-711
Ecuador — Equateur	2005	27 684	1 348[1]	1 214	10 853	-256	-107	-2 964
Falkland Is. (Malvinas) — Iles Falkland (Malvinas)	2003	1 217	...	...	0	...	...	0
French Guiana — Guyane française	2003	8 815	12[1]	4[1]	8 063	2	2	-28
Guyana — Guyana	2003	19 685	480[1]	30[1]	15 104	0	8	0
Paraguay — Paraguay	2003	39 730	3 040[1]	96[1]	18 475	930	7	-2 682
Peru — Pérou	2003	128 000	3 700[1]	610[1]	68 742	200	190	-1 414
Suriname — Suriname	2003	15 600	58[1]	10[1]	14 776	1	-1	0
Uruguay — Uruguay	2003	17 502	1 370[1]	42[1]	1 506	110	-3	601
Venezuela (Boliv. Rep. of) — Venezuela (Rép. boliv. du)	2003	88 205	2 600[1]	800[1]	47 713	-232	22	-4 313
Asia — Asie								
Afghanistan — Afghanistan	2003	65 209	7 910[1]	138	867	0	8	-442
Armenia — Arménie	2005	2 820	495	60	283	...	...	-63
Azerbaijan — Azerbaïdjan	2005	8 266	1 843	221	936	...	...	0
Bahrain — Bahreïn	2005	71	2	4	...	0	2	...
Bangladesh — Bangladesh	2005	13 017	7 955	460	871	-1 182	160	-11
Bhutan — Bhoutan	2005	4 700	159[1]	18	3 195	46	-1	160
Brunei Darussalam — Brunéi Darussalam	2005	527	14	5	278	11	1	-35
Cambodia — Cambodge	2005	17 652	3 700	156	10 447	5	46	-2 499
China — Chine	2005	929 100	142 688[1]	12 800[1]	197 290	19 688	5 300	40 149
China, Hong Kong SAR — Chine, Hong Kong RAS	2005	105	5	1[1]	...	-1	0	...
China, Macao SAR — Chine, Macao RAS	2005	2	...	...	...	...	...	...
Cyprus — Chypre	2005	924	100	39	174	-6	-12	13
Georgia — Géorgie	2005	6 949	802	264	2 760	...	...	0
India — Inde	2005	297 319	159 650[1]	10 000	67 701	-3 138	3 350	3 762
Indonesia — Indonésie	2005	181 157	23 000	13 600	88 495	2 747	1 880	-28 072
Iran (Islamic Rep. of) — Iran (Rép. islamique d')	2005	163 620	16 100	1 500	11 075	910	190	0
Iraq — Iraq	2003	43 737	5 750[1]	269[1]	822	450	-21	18
Israel — Israël	2005	2 164	317[1]	75[1]	171	-26	-13	17
Japan — Japon	2005	36 450	4 360	332	24 868	-408	-143	-82
Jordan — Jordanie	2005	8 824	184	86	83	5	16	0
Kazakhstan — Kazakhstan	2005	269 970	22 364[1]	136	3 337	...	...	-85
Korea, Dem. P. R. — Corée, R. p. dém. de	2005	12 041	2 800	200	6 187	512	20	-2 014
Korea, Republic of — Corée, République de	2005	9 873	1 635[1]	200	6 265	-318	44	-106
Kuwait — Koweït	2005	1 782	15[1]	3	6	11	2	3
Kyrgyzstan — Kirghizistan	2005	19 180	1 284	72	869	...	...	33
Lao People's Dem. Rep. — Rép. dém. pop. lao	2005	23 080	1 000	81	16 142	201	20	-1 172
Lebanon — Liban	2003	1 023	170[1]	143[1]	136	-13	21	15
Malaysia — Malaisie	2003	32 855	1 800[1]	5 785[1]	20 890	100	537	-1 486
Maldives — Maldives	2003	30	4[1]	9[1]	1	0	5	0
Mongolia — Mongolie	2003	156 650	1 198[1]	2[1]	10 252	-172	1	-1 240
Myanmar — Myanmar	2003	65 755	10 093	888	32 222	526	386	-6 997
Nepal — Népal	2005	14 300	2 357	130[1]	3 636	70	64	-1 181
Occupied Palestinian Terr. — Terr. palestinien occupé	2005	602	107	115	9	-4	0	0
Oman — Oman	2003	30 950	37[1]	43[1]	2	2	-2	0

Country or area — Pays ou zone	Latest available year / Dernière année disponible	Area — Superficie: Land area / Superficie des terres	Area — Superficie: Arable land / Terres arables	Area — Superficie: Permanent crops / Cultures permanentes	2005: Forest cover / Superficie forestière	Net change — Variation nette: From 1990 – de 1990: Arable land / Terres arables	Net change — Variation nette: From 1990 – de 1990: Permanent crops / Cultures permanentes	Net change — Variation nette: 1990 – 2005: Forest cover / Superficie forestière
Pakistan — Pakistan	2005	77 088	21 275[1]	795	1 902	791	339	-625
Philippines — Philippines	2003	29 817	5 700[1]	5 000[1]	7 162	220	600	-3 412
Qatar — Qatar	2005	1 100	18[1]	3	...	8	2	...
Saudi Arabia — Arabie saoudite	2003	214 969	3 600[1]	198	2 728	210	107	0
Singapore — Singapour	2005	68	0[1]	0[1]	2	-1	-1	0
Sri Lanka — Sri Lanka	2003	6 463	916[1]	1 000[1]	1 933	41	-25	-417
Syrian Arab Republic — Rép. arabe syrienne	2005	18 378	4 873	869	461	-12	128	89
Tajikistan — Tadjikistan	2003	13 996	930[1]	127[1]	410	...	...	2
Thailand — Thaïlande	2003	51 089	14 133[1]	3 554	14 520	-3 361	445	-1 445
Timor-Leste — Timor-Leste	2003	1 487	122[1]	68[1]	798	12	10	-168
Turkey — Turquie	2005	76 963	23 830	2 776	10 175	-817	-254	495
Turkmenistan — Turkménistan	2003	46 993	2 200[1]	66[1]	4 127	...	...	0
United Arab Emirates — Emirats arabes unis	2003	8 360	64	190	312	29	170	67
Uzbekistan — Ouzbékistan	2003	42 540	4 700[1]	340[1]	3 295	...	...	250
Viet Nam — Viet Nam	2005	31 007	6 600	2 350	12 931	1 261	1 305	3 568
Yemen — Yémen	2003	52 797	1 537[1]	132	549	14	29	0
Europe — Europe								
Albania — Albanie	2005	2 740	578	122	794	-1	-3	5
Andorra — Andorre	2005	47	1	...	16	0	...	0
Austria — Autriche	2005	8 245	1 387	66	3 862	-39	-13	86
Belarus — Bélarus	2005	20 748	5 455[1]	116	7 894	...	...	518
Belgium — Belgique	2005	3 023	844	23	667	...	...	-10
Bosnia and Herzegovina — Bosnie-Herzégovine	2005	5 120	1 000	97	2 185	...	...	-25
Bulgaria — Bulgarie	2005	10 864	3 173	201	3 625	-683	-99	298
Channel Islands — Iles Anglo-Normandes	2005	...	...	...	1	...	...	0
Croatia — Croatie	2005	5 592	1 110	116	2 135	...	...	19
Czech Republic — République tchèque	2005	7 726	3 047	238	2 648	...	...	18
Denmark — Danemark	2005	4 243	2 237	7	500	-324	-3	55
Estonia — Estonie	2005	4 239	591	12	2 284	...	...	121
Faeroe Islands — Iles Féroé	2003	140	3[1]	...	...	...	...	...
Finland — Finlande	2005	30 459	2 234	6	22 500	-35	0	306
France — France	2005	55 010	18 507	1 128	15 554	508	-63	1 016
Germany — Allemagne	2005	34 877	11 903	198	11 076	-68	-245	335
Gibraltar — Gibraltar	2005	1	...	...	0	...	...	0
Greece — Grèce	2005	12 890	2 627	1 132	3 752	-272	64	453
Holy See — Saint-Siège	2005	...	...	...	0	...	...	0
Hungary — Hongrie	2005	8 961	4 600	207	1 976	-454	-27	175
Iceland — Islande	2005	10 025	7	...	46	0	...	21
Ireland — Irlande	2005	6 889	1 215	2	669	174	-1	228
Isle of Man — Ile de Man	2005	...	...	...	3	...	...	0
Italy — Italie	2005	29 411	7 744	2 539[1]	9 979	-1 268	-421	1 596
Latvia — Lettonie	2005	6 229	1 092	13	2 941	...	...	166
Liechtenstein — Liechtenstein	2005	16[1]	4[1]	...	7	0	...	1
Lithuania — Lituanie	2005	6 268	1 906	40	2 099	...	...	154
Luxembourg — Luxembourg	2005	259	60	2	87	...	...	1
Malta — Malte	2005	32	9	1	...	-3	0	...
Monaco — Monaco	2005	...	...	...	0	...	...	0
Netherlands — Pays-Bas	2005	3 388	908	33	365	29	3	20
Norway — Norvège	2005	30 428	859	...	9 387	-5	...	257
Poland — Pologne	2005	30 633	12 141	378	9 192	-2 247	33	311

Country or area — Pays ou zone	Latest available year / Dernière année disponible	Area — Superficie			2005	Net change — Variation nette		
						From 1990 - de 1990		1990 - 2005
		Land area / Superficie des terres	Arable land / Terres arables	Permanent crops / Cultures permanentes	Forest cover / Superficie forestière	Arable land / Terres arables	Permanent crops / Cultures permanentes	Forest cover / Superficie forestière
Portugal — Portugal	2005	9 150	1 534[1]	774[1]	3 783	-810	-7	684
Republic of Moldova — République de Moldova	2005	3 287	1 848	298	329	...	...	10
Romania — Roumanie	2005	22 998	9 288[1]	540	6 370	-162	-51	-1
Russian Federation — Fédération de Russie	2005	1 638 139	121 781	1 800	808 790	...	...	-160
San Marino — Saint-Marin	2003	6	1[1]	...	...	0	...	...
Serbia and Montenegro — Serbie-et-Monténégro	2005	10 200	3 505[1]	317[1]	2 694	...	...	135
Slovakia — Slovaquie	2005	4 810	1 391	26	1 929	...	...	7
Slovenia — Slovénie	2005	2 014	176	27	1 264	...	...	76
Spain — Espagne	2005	49 919	13 700	4 930	17 915	-1 635	93	4 436
Sweden — Suède	2005	41 033	2 703	3	27 528	-142	-1	161
Switzerland — Suisse	2005	4 000	410	24	1 221	19	3	66
TFYR of Macedonia — L'ex-R.y. Macédoine	2005	2 543	566	46	906	...	...	0
Ukraine — Ukraine	2005	57 938	32 452	901	9 575	...	...	301
United Kingdom — Royaume-Uni	2005	24 193	5 729	47	2 845	-891	-19	234
Oceania — Océanie								
American Samoa — Samoa américaines	2003	20	2[1]	3[1]	18	0	1	0
Australia — Australie	2005	768 230	49 402[1]	340[1]	163 678	1 502	159	-4 226
Christmas Is. — Ile Christmas	2003	13	...	...	...	...	...	...
Cocos (Keeling) Islands — Iles des Cocos (Keeling)	2003	1	...	...	...	...	...	...
Cook Islands — Iles Cook	2003	24	4[1]	2[1]	16	2	-2	1
Fiji — Fidji	2003	1 827	200[1]	85[1]	1 000	40	5	21
French Polynesia — Polynésie française	2003	366	3[1]	22[1]	105	1	1	0
Guam — Guam	2003	55	2[1]	10[1]	26	0	0	0
Kiribati — Kiribati	2003	73	2[1]	35[1]	2	0	-2	0
Marshall Islands — Iles Marshall	2005	18	2	8	...	...	...	...
Micronesia (Fed. States of) — Micronésie (Etats féd. de)	2003	70	4[1]	32[1]	63	...	...	0
Nauru — Nauru	2003	2	...	...	0	...	...	0
New Caledonia — Nouvelle-Calédonie	2003	1 828	6[1]	4[1]	717	-3	-2	0
New Zealand — Nouvelle-Zélande	2003	26 799	1 500[1]	1 872[1]	8 309	-1 011	518	589
Niue — Nioué	2003	26	3[1]	4[1]	14	0	1	-3
Norfolk Island — Ile Norfolk	2003	4	...	...	...	...	...	...
Northern Mariana Islands — Iles Mariannes du Nord	2003	46	6[1]	2[1]	33	...	...	-2
Palau — Palaos	2003	46	4[1]	2[1]	40	-18	-38	2
Papua New Guinea — Papouasie-Nvl-Guinée	2003	45 286	225[1]	650[1]	29 437	33	70	-2 086
Pitcairn — Pitcairn	2005	...	...	...	4	...	...	0
Samoa — Samoa	2003	283	60[1]	69[1]	171	5	2	41
Solomon Islands — Iles Salomon	2003	2 799	18[1]	59[1]	2 172	1	7	-596
Tokelau — Tokélaou	2003	1	...	...	0	...	...	0
Tonga — Tonga	2003	72	15[1]	11[1]	4	-1	-1	0
Tuvalu — Tuvalu	2003	3	...	2[1]	1	...	0	0
Vanuatu — Vanuatu	2003	1 219	20[1]	85[1]	440	0	0	0
Wallis and Futuna Islands — Iles Wallis et Futuna	2003	14	1[1]	5[1]	5	0	0	-1

Source

Food and Agriculture Organization of the United Nations (FAO), Rome, FAOSTAT data, last accessed January 2007, and FAO Forestry website: FRA 2005 Global Tables.

Notes

1 FAO estimate.

Source

Organisation des Nations Unies pour l'alimentation et l'agriculture (FAO), Rome, données FAOSTAT, dernier accès janvier 2007, et le site web du Département des forêts de la FAO: Tableaux mondiaux de FRA 2005.

Notes

1 Estimation de la FAO.

53

CO_2 emission estimates

From fossil fuel combustion, cement production and gas flared (thousand metric tons of carbon dioxide)

Estimation des émissions de CO_2

Dues à la combustion de combustibles fossiles, à la production de ciment et au gaz brûlés à la torchère (milliers de tonnes de dioxyde de carbone)

Country or area — Pays ou zone	1995	1996	1997	1998	1999	2000	2001	2002	2003	2004
Afghanistan Afghanistan	1 239	1 177	1 096	1 038	821	770	634	352	389	693
Albania Albanie	1 873	1 826	1 437	1 577	2 130	2 141	2 302	2 552	3 032	3 674
Algeria Algérie	94 671	96 548	87 950	107 118	190 152	195 695	191 398	196 084	193 602	194 001
Angola Angola	11 303	9 987	6 306	5 763	6 588	6 603	7 296	7 828	8 850	7 897
Antigua and Barbuda Antigua-et-Barbuda	323	323	337	334	348	352	352	370	400	414
Argentina Argentine	119 352	126 886	131 502	133 181	141 119	136 807	127 752	120 602	130 120	141 786
Armenia Arménie	3 410	2 563	3 237	3 362	3 014	3 465	3 538	2 988	3 428	3 648
Aruba Aruba	1 800	1 833	1 873	1 694	1 708	2 090	2 097	2 134	2 156	2 156
Australia[1] Australie[1]	306 736	314 207	321 840	335 784	345 030	351 951	359 603	364 728	372 879	381 803
Austria[1] Autriche[1]	63 655	67 321	67 146	66 828	65 435	66 178	70 171	71 935	77 553	77 077
Azerbaijan Azerbaïdjan	33 334	31 028	29 466	30 969	33 216	30 236	28 186	28 278	29 591	31 365
Bahamas Bahamas	1 730	1 730	1 741	1 793	1 796	1 796	1 796	2 082	1 870	2 009
Bahrain Bahreïn	15 849	15 596	17 316	18 438	18 009	18 661	13 928	15 695	16 465	16 949
Bangladesh Bangladesh	22 599	23 812	24 832	23 959	25 158	28 051	32 564	33 774	35 585	37 165
Barbados Barbade	829	851	898	1 144	1 210	1 184	1 214	1 225	1 188	1 269
Belarus[1] Bélarus[1]	56 233	57 078	59 245	56 761	54 044	51 911	50 988	51 231	51 396	54 920
Belgium[1] Belgique[1]	123 632	127 762	122 272	127 933	122 911	123 986	124 110	123 311	126 974	126 907
Belize Belize	378	308	389	370	601	689	711	744	781	792
Benin Bénin	1 327	1 265	1 217	1 214	1 566	1 617	1 738	2 053	2 280	2 387
Bermuda Bermudes	455	462	462	462	495	495	495	528	528	550
Bhutan Bhoutan	253	301	392	389	385	396	403	400	385	414
Bolivia Bolivie	8 121	8 733	9 840	10 324	9 455	8 231	7 351	6 878	9 954	6 973
Bosnia and Herzegovina Bosnie-Herzégovine	4 044	5 272	12 652	16 531	19 226	23 054	14 676	14 361	14 562	15 596
Botswana Botswana	3 512	3 113	3 201	3 817	3 527	4 275	4 242	4 418	4 044	4 301
Brazil Brésil	258 913	285 464	298 105	312 008	316 627	323 626	332 154	325 404	313 196	331 795
British Virgin Islands Iles Vierges britanniques	51	59	59	59	59	59	59	66	77	84
Brunei Darussalam Brunéi Darussalam	5 210	5 147	5 496	5 598	6 526	8 524	6 944	7 446	8 055	8 810
Bulgaria[1] Bulgarie[1]	64 744	63 449	61 665	54 419	50 736	50 176	51 851	49 083	53 795	53 096

53 CO_2 emission estimates — From fossil fuel combustion, cement production and gas flared (thousand metric tons of carbon dioxide) (*continued*)

Estimation des émissions de CO_2 — Dues à la combustion de combustibles fossiles, à la production de ciment et au gaz brûlés à la torchère (milliers de tonnes de dioxyde de carbone) (*suite*)

Country or area — Pays ou zone	1995	1996	1997	1998	1999	2000	2001	2002	2003	2004
Burkina Faso Burkina Faso	972	983	994	1 012	1 089	1 063	1 052	1 082	1 096	1 096
Burundi Burundi	216	224	227	227	231	249	227	249	227	220
Cambodia Cambodge	550	601	587	587	524	532	535	546	535	535
Cameroon Cameroun	4 169	4 590	3 208	3 208	3 080	3 432	3 424	3 421	4 616	3 839
Canada[1] Canada[1]	493 437	506 379	518 578	526 876	542 321	566 257	559 937	567 463	593 063	593 093
Cape Verde Cap-Vert	114	139	143	154	172	180	209	235	249	275
Cayman Islands Iles Caïmanes	286	282	282	282	279	282	282	290	304	312
Central African Rep. Rép. centrafricaine	235	235	246	249	264	268	268	275	253	253
Chad Tchad	95	103	114	114	121	125	121	121	117	125
Chile Chili	44 795	51 266	58 935	58 415	63 368	59 617	55 328	57 352	57 641	62 418
China[2] Chine[2]	3 199 588	3 341 668	3 290 413	3 108 881	3 257 076	3 339 321	3 421 560	3 628 030	4 251 393	5 010 170
China, Hong Kong SAR Chine, Hong Kong RAS	29 884	27 501	28 861	37 304	40 857	38 459	36 692	35 365	38 500	37 411
China, Macao SAR Chine, Macao RAS	1 232	1 408	1 489	1 558	1 518	1 631	1 694	1 837	1 862	2 207
Colombia Colombie	59 067	60 816	64 823	65 920	56 512	57 711	55 782	54 954	57 366	53 634
Comoros Comores	66	66	66	70	81	84	81	81	88	88
Congo Congo	1 547	1 701	2 335	2 412	2 489	2 401	3 124	2 841	2 885	3 542
Cook Islands Iles Cook	22	22	22	22	29	29	29	29	29	29
Costa Rica Costa Rica	4 861	4 733	4 968	5 323	5 518	5 532	5 624	5 668	6 475	6 405
Côte d'Ivoire Côte d'Ivoire	6 871	8 117	7 904	2 951	7 127	5 400	5 254	6 878	5 459	5 162
Croatia[1] Croatie[1]	16 250	16 941	18 024	18 915	19 702	19 417	20 434	21 498	22 883	22 551
Cuba Cuba	25 374	26 650	24 311	23 988	25 085	25 206	24 260	25 228	24 282	25 818
Cyprus Chypre	5 133	5 276	5 422	5 936	6 013	6 427	6 442	6 533	7 285	6 750
Czech Republic[1] République tchèque[1]	132 125	133 863	138 389	129 188	122 099	129 017	129 033	124 040	128 075	127 297
Dem. Rep. of the Congo Rép. dém. du Congo	2 552	2 570	2 497	2 533	2 247	1 646	1 566	1 591	1 624	2 104
Denmark[1] Danemark[1]	61 514	75 109	65 598	61 569	58 762	54 428	56 077	55 630	60 879	55 395
Djibouti Djibouti	370	367	367	367	385	385	389	359	367	367
Dominica Dominique	81	73	81	77	81	103	114	103	114	106
Dominican Republic Rép. dominicaine	16 084	17 543	18 236	18 680	18 870	20 113	20 231	21 495	21 264	19 640
Ecuador Equateur	22 680	24 201	18 540	22 639	21 620	21 345	23 981	24 593	23 222	29 268

53 CO_2 emission estimates — From fossil fuel combustion, cement production and gas flared (thousand metric tons of carbon dioxide) (*continued*)

Estimation des émissions de CO_2 — Dues à la combustion de combustibles fossiles, à la production de ciment et au gaz brûlés à la torchère (milliers de tonnes de dioxyde de carbone) (*suite*)

Country or area — Pays ou zone	1995	1996	1997	1998	1999	2000	2001	2002	2003	2004
Egypt Egypte	95 085	102 036	107 822	121 559	124 577	138 725	127 785	143 524	143 956	158 237
El Salvador El Salvador	5 287	4 894	5 756	5 793	5 697	5 741	5 947	6 027	6 379	6 167
Equatorial Guinea Guinée équatoriale	125	132	143	147	242	260	257	4 363	4 359	5 426
Eritrea Erythrée	293	348	524	590	620	609	634	642	700	755
Estonia[1] Estonie[1]	19 315	20 264	20 225	18 318	16 771	16 849	17 083	17 312	19 106	19 232
Ethiopia Ethiopie	2 134	3 725	4 275	5 023	5 070	5 818	6 647	6 830	7 303	7 981
Faeroe Islands Iles Féroé	620	631	634	642	649	649	649	653	660	660
Falkland Is. (Malvinas) Iles Falkland (Malvinas)	40	44	48	37	37	37	44	44	44	44
Fiji Fidji	891	924	759	730	832	858	1 115	1 115	1 111	1 071
Finland[1] Finlande[1]	58 105	63 916	62 609	59 233	58 845	57 113	62 563	65 043	73 099	69 115
France[1,3] France[1,3]	392 983	406 683	400 834	421 272	411 141	405 647	409 263	404 705	412 091	417 353
Gabon Gabon	3 725	3 619	3 696	1 613	1 430	1 470	1 932	1 635	1 181	1 371
Gambia Gambie	216	216	216	235	253	271	279	282	282	286
Georgia Géorgie	2 284	4 007	4 282	4 957	4 348	4 535	3 751	3 380	3 751	3 912
Germany[1] Allemagne[1]	920 155	943 608	914 700	906 672	881 685	886 258	899 301	886 480	892 545	885 854
Ghana Ghana	5 327	5 646	6 280	6 306	6 456	6 196	6 827	7 355	7 736	7 190
Gibraltar Gibraltar	301	180	84	312	323	334	345	348	363	374
Greece[1] Grèce[1]	87 426	89 623	94 361	98 966	98 141	103 963	106 210	105 905	109 914	110 280
Greenland Groenland	502	517	521	528	539	557	561	565	568	572
Grenada Grenade	172	176	205	191	205	205	220	216	220	216
Guadeloupe Guadeloupe	1 507	1 514	1 536	1 525	1 587	1 631	1 650	1 683	1 712	1 734
Guatemala Guatemala	7 164	6 651	7 597	8 751	8 927	10 196	10 552	10 999	10 651	12 220
Guinea Guinée	1 206	1 228	1 236	1 239	1 276	1 280	1 294	1 324	1 338	1 338
Guinea-Bissau Guinée-Bissau	231	231	235	231	249	253	260	271	271	271
Guyana Guyana	1 474	1 518	1 595	1 653	1 650	1 580	1 518	1 547	1 500	1 445
Haiti Haïti	942	1 093	1 423	1 232	1 331	1 368	1 591	1 686	1 675	1 756
Honduras Honduras	3 879	3 963	4 158	4 649	4 741	5 030	5 712	6 038	6 493	7 615
Hungary[1] Hongrie[1]	61 655	63 029	61 305	60 578	60 499	58 735	60 260	58 623	61 686	59 994
Iceland[1] Islande[1]	2 216	2 307	2 411	2 399	2 573	2 582	2 592	2 683	2 626	2 283

53 CO_2 emission estimates — From fossil fuel combustion, cement production and gas flared (thousand metric tons of carbon dioxide) (*continued*)

Estimation des émissions de CO_2 — Dues à la combustion de combustibles fossiles, à la production de ciment et au gaz brûlés à la torchère (milliers de tonnes de dioxyde de carbone) (*suite*)

Country or area — Pays ou zone	1995	1996	1997	1998	1999	2000	2001	2002	2003	2004
India Inde	915 521	998 808	1 041 774	1 070 158	1 139 531	1 155 043	1 180 964	1 226 459	1 263 723	1 342 962
Indonesia Indonésie	303 025	352 326	362 899	291 279	332 473	365 631	360 509	415 335	408 222	378 250
Iran (Islamic Rep. of) Iran (Rép. islamique d')	268 471	298 769	312 862	307 880	328 103	350 614	365 345	377 326	403 643	433 571
Iraq Iraq	74 000	67 984	66 774	70 767	70 734	72 867	84 981	90 766	75 481	81 652
Ireland[1] Irlande[1]	34 783	36 081	38 504	40 306	42 136	44 241	46 704	45 701	44 519	45 266
Israel Israël	51 882	51 984	60 358	59 306	58 422	64 164	64 197	68 336	70 224	71 247
Italy[1] Italie[1]	445 384	438 843	443 056	454 031	459 051	463 311	469 062	470 821	486 126	489 590
Jamaica Jamaïque	9 701	10 192	10 629	9 727	9 767	10 317	10 625	10 306	10 728	10 592
Japan[1] Japon[1]	1 226 390	1 239 310	1 234 781	1 198 578	1 233 716	1 254 619	1 239 275	1 276 772	1 284 376	1 285 814
Jordan Jordanie	13 591	14 185	14 416	14 544	14 570	15 523	15 501	16 366	17 100	16 465
Kazakhstan Kazakhstan	173 584	144 561	135 234	128 877	124 698	139 810	157 074	165 474	178 658	200 278
Kenya Kenya	7 490	9 261	8 267	10 035	10 170	10 416	9 371	7 967	8 839	10 588
Kiribati Kiribati	22	37	29	33	29	33	29	29	29	29
Korea, Dem. P. R. Corée, R. p. dém. de	259 298	256 632	234 642	64 915	71 382	76 948	79 903	76 116	77 523	79 111
Korea, Republic of Corée, République de	373 818	408 163	424 123	363 680	395 617	430 564	438 311	446 494	454 234	465 643
Kuwait Koweït	54 455	51 211	74 535	78 268	81 105	82 612	79 731	77 846	91 983	99 364
Kyrgyzstan Kirghizistan	4 627	5 796	5 620	5 987	4 682	4 645	3 850	4 953	5 378	5 727
Lao People's Dem. Rep. Rép. dém. pop. lao	315	528	719	818	887	1 012	1 166	1 250	1 254	1 280
Latvia[1] Lettonie[1]	8 802	9 081	8 535	8 157	7 550	6 907	7 410	7 331	7 477	7 485
Lebanon Liban	13 620	13 796	15 644	15 996	16 597	15 351	16 260	16 099	18 610	16 264
Liberia Libéria	323	337	348	385	400	429	462	466	462	469
Libyan Arab Jamah. Jamah. arabe libyenne	43 735	40 237	48 560	53 590	52 600	55 159	56 655	58 008	59 280	59 914
Liechtenstein[1] Liechtenstein[1]	...	...	...	...	...	...	...	...	240	239
Lithuania[1] Lituanie[1]	...	...	...	15 663	...	...	13 326	12 704	12 287	13 350
Luxembourg[1] Luxembourg[1]	9 276	9 390	8 681	7 705	8 437	8 952	9 227	10 226	10 702	11 997
Madagascar Madagascar	1 261	1 360	1 646	1 734	1 921	2 269	2 313	2 317	2 511	2 731
Malawi Malawi	711	697	744	777	1 082	1 012	1 008	1 016	946	1 045
Malaysia Malaisie	119 524	122 842	124 914	113 941	107 987	126 472	135 880	141 386	156 521	177 584
Maldives Maldives	275	319	367	334	466	499	539	682	587	726

53 CO_2 emission estimates — From fossil fuel combustion, cement production and gas flared (thousand metric tons of carbon dioxide) (*continued*)

Estimation des émissions de CO_2 — Dues à la combustion de combustibles fossiles, à la production de ciment et au gaz brûlés à la torchère (milliers de tonnes de dioxyde de carbone) (*suite*)

Country or area — Pays ou zone	1995	1996	1997	1998	1999	2000	2001	2002	2003	2004
Mali Mali	466	488	524	517	539	543	546	554	539	565
Malta Malte	2 948	3 131	3 336	2 104	2 302	2 104	2 060	2 108	2 464	2 453
Mauritania Mauritanie	2 944	2 940	2 933	2 438	2 475	2 482	2 530	2 486	2 500	2 555
Mauritius Maurice	1 829	1 950	1 998	2 196	2 467	2 768	2 966	2 981	3 146	3 197
Mexico Mexique	405 234	407 778	422 645	426 227	416 922	418 968	430 190	419 001	435 140	438 021
Monaco[1] Monaco[1]	112	116	116	114	115	113	114	112	107	100
Mongolia Mongolie	7 919	8 040	7 710	7 703	7 553	7 501	7 883	8 286	8 033	8 553
Montserrat Montserrat	44	40	48	51	48	48	48	55	62	62
Morocco Maroc	30 349	31 185	31 853	31 963	32 861	34 261	37 994	38 474	37 931	41 169
Mozambique Mozambique	1 111	1 041	1 126	1 118	1 173	1 335	1 346	1 419	1 569	2 167
Myanmar Myanmar	6 926	7 193	7 413	8 025	8 781	9 114	7 795	8 876	9 459	9 760
Namibia Namibie	1 690	1 829	1 851	1 950	1 741	1 749	2 068	2 126	2 328	2 471
Nauru Nauru	139	139	139	139	136	136	139	139	143	143
Nepal Népal	2 038	2 486	2 783	2 251	3 223	3 230	3 454	2 713	2 951	3 043
Netherlands[1] Pays-Bas[1]	170 625	177 709	171 126	173 239	167 725	169 577	175 163	174 910	178 528	180 944
Netherlands Antilles Antilles néerlandaises	5 312	4 949	7 362	3 391	3 230	3 289	3 329	3 391	4 055	4 088
New Caledonia Nouvelle-Calédonie	1 716	1 752	1 811	1 793	2 020	2 266	1 906	2 423	2 775	2 577
New Zealand[1] Nouvelle-Zélande[1]	27 201	28 222	30 414	29 107	30 561	31 037	33 042	33 030	34 681	34 039
Nicaragua Nicaragua	2 838	2 926	3 135	3 421	3 626	3 769	3 978	3 930	3 817	4 007
Niger Niger	1 133	1 137	1 140	1 137	1 166	1 184	1 195	1 214	1 214	1 214
Nigeria Nigéria	44 142	49 583	51 911	51 046	54 778	89 644	94 971	110 443	104 797	114 025
Niue Nioué	4	4	4	4	4	4	4	4	4	4
Norway[1] Norvège[1]	37 774	40 771	40 958	41 055	41 916	41 531	42 917	42 036	43 550	43 982
Occupied Palestinian Terr. Terr. palestinien occupé	...	...	414	609	660	799	579	546	517	649
Oman Oman	15 879	15 222	15 593	16 667	20 813	22 056	24 601	30 925	32 095	30 899
Pakistan Pakistan	84 533	94 165	94 418	97 475	100 401	106 087	106 579	108 210	101 626	125 669
Panama Panama	3 472	4 880	5 958	5 958	5 635	5 756	7 003	5 837	6 046	5 661
Papua New Guinea Papouasie-Nvl-Guinée	2 409	2 409	2 453	2 346	2 691	2 559	2 533	2 467	2 500	2 449
Paraguay Paraguay	3 963	3 754	4 191	4 502	4 502	3 688	3 824	3 993	4 139	4 180

53

CO_2 emission estimates — From fossil fuel combustion, cement production and gas flared (thousand metric tons of carbon dioxide) (*continued*)

Estimation des émissions de CO_2 — Dues à la combustion de combustibles fossiles, à la production de ciment et au gaz brûlés à la torchère (milliers de tonnes de dioxyde de carbone) (*suite*)

Country or area — Pays ou zone	1995	1996	1997	1998	1999	2000	2001	2002	2003	2004
Peru Pérou	23 508	23 849	26 419	26 632	28 703	27 856	26 929	26 573	26 793	31 493
Philippines Philippines	62 833	65 813	77 201	75 811	72 952	77 993	76 651	78 059	76 611	80 512
Poland[1] Pologne[1]	348 172	372 530	361 626	337 448	329 697	314 812	317 844	308 277	319 082	316 700
Portugal[1] Portugal[1]	53 131	50 258	53 543	58 234	64 894	63 762	65 018	69 250	64 600	65 705
Qatar Qatar	31 746	32 894	37 506	33 766	32 923	36 388	42 569	46 206	46 213	52 904
Republic of Moldova République de Moldova	11 186	11 519	10 790	9 628	6 537	6 599	7 124	6 786	7 252	7 685
Réunion Réunion	1 925	2 020	2 126	2 288	2 134	2 236	2 236	2 240	2 255	2 277
Romania[1] Roumanie[1]	132 826	138 256	123 435	109 622	92 811	95 621	100 380	107 626	113 050	116 361
Russian Federation[1] Fédération de Russie[1]	1 728 177	1 687 126	1 617 195	1 562 005	1 558 608	1 556 492	1 583 130	1 565 952	1 619 711	1 617 937
Rwanda Rwanda	491	510	532	535	565	572	587	594	601	572
Saint Helena Sainte-Hélène	11	15	15	18	22	11	11	11	11	11
Saint Kitts and Nevis Saint-Kitts-et-Nevis	95	103	103	103	103	103	103	114	125	125
Saint Lucia Sainte-Lucie	312	326	312	297	337	352	352	290	352	367
Saint Pierre and Miquelon Saint-Pierre-et-Miquelon	70	70	48	55	55	55	55	59	66	62
Saint Vincent-Grenadines Saint Vincent-Grenadines	128	132	132	161	165	154	176	183	194	198
Samoa Samoa	132	132	132	132	139	139	143	143	150	150
Sao Tome and Principe Sao Tomé-et-Principe	77	77	77	81	88	88	92	92	92	92
Saudi Arabia Arabie saoudite	244 321	272 929	235 071	221 029	232 153	272 031	285 072	298 439	305 595	308 393
Senegal Sénégal	3 468	3 714	3 241	3 402	3 670	3 945	4 172	4 345	4 385	4 993
Serbia and Montenegro Serbie-et-Monténégro	40 047	46 081	49 190	51 819	36 674	40 839	43 702	47 255	49 931	53 322
Seychelles Seychelles	191	198	414	440	513	565	642	543	546	546
Sierra Leone Sierra Leone	506	543	554	528	510	535	601	623	616	994
Singapore Singapour	46 840	53 718	62 147	56 274	55 929	56 516	56 552	55 533	47 838	52 252
Slovakia[1] Slovaquie[1]	43 841	44 389	44 662	43 649	42 630	40 924	43 896	41 945	42 362	42 498
Slovenia[1] Slovénie[1]	14 908	15 666	15 978	15 722	15 088	15 177	16 145	16 212	16 012	16 464
Solomon Islands Iles Salomon	161	161	161	161	161	161	169	169	176	176
Somalia Somalie	11	...	...	...	...	...	...	...	...	...
South Africa Afrique du Sud	377 425	380 677	392 585	392 241	392 882	397 091	399 969	389 905	406 480	437 032
Spain[1] Espagne[1]	255 724	242 993	262 655	270 747	296 302	307 673	311 552	330 551	333 837	354 562

CO_2 emission estimates—From fossil fuel combustion, cement production and gas flared (thousand metric tons of carbon dioxide) (*continued*)

Estimation des émissions de CO_2—Dues à la combustion de combustibles fossiles, à la production de ciment et au gaz brûlés à la torchère (milliers de tonnes de dioxyde de carbone) (*suite*)

Country or area — Pays ou zone	1995	1996	1997	1998	1999	2000	2001	2002	2003	2004
Sri Lanka Sri Lanka	5 796	6 973	7 560	7 740	8 520	10 189	10 185	10 783	10 291	11 534
Sudan Soudan	4 242	3 890	5 342	4 627	5 092	5 532	6 368	8 117	8 997	10 372
Suriname Suriname	2 156	2 104	2 115	2 137	2 152	2 126	2 266	2 251	2 240	2 284
Swaziland Swaziland	455	341	400	532	796	1 005	983	968	957	957
Sweden[1] Suède[1]	58 206	61 713	57 127	57 624	54 771	53 503	54 245	55 401	56 469	55 360
Switzerland[1] Suisse[1]	43 336	44 056	43 408	44 627	44 844	43 918	44 697	43 798	44 894	45 317
Syrian Arab Republic Rép. arabe syrienne	43 383	43 823	40 329	47 486	49 055	48 461	47 343	49 916	48 659	68 420
Tajikistan Tadjikistan	5 169	5 782	5 089	5 122	5 114	3 996	4 341	4 766	4 682	5 004
Thailand Thaïlande	181 411	202 654	210 005	186 320	196 901	201 502	217 036	230 583	246 114	268 082
TFYR of Macedonia L'ex-R.y. Macédoine	10 691	11 739	10 632	12 047	11 186	11 406	11 384	10 383	10 423	10 420
Timor-Leste Timor-Leste	...	...	...	...	...	...	...	161	161	176
Togo Togo	895	1 001	935	1 093	1 474	1 628	1 459	1 489	2 196	2 310
Tonga Tonga	110	110	114	110	128	121	106	106	114	117
Trinidad and Tobago Trinité-et-Tobago	20 249	20 923	18 518	21 257	25 536	27 812	28 586	30 892	32 384	32 557
Tunisia Tunisie	15 721	16 850	16 935	17 998	18 097	19 721	20 520	20 791	20 887	22 885
Turkey[1] Turquie[1]	171 854	190 668	203 723	202 713	201 712	223 806	207 379	216 433	230 987	241 884
Turkmenistan Turkménistan	35 369	32 300	31 130	27 640	36 784	37 323	41 554	44 296	45 616	41 726
Uganda Ouganda	953	1 052	1 137	1 335	1 390	1 525	1 620	1 694	1 712	1 826
Ukraine[1] Ukraine[1]	393 514	357 853	344 604	308 191	309 291	296 534	298 875	301 293	320 543	316 942
United Arab Emirates Emirats arabes unis	73 564	43 519	44 707	126 780	114 491	159 461	148 037	127 594	183 083	149 188
United Kingdom[1] Royaume-Uni[1]	549 820	571 661	549 072	551 368	542 290	548 045	563 371	547 341	558 938	562 359
United Rep. of Tanzania Rép.-Unie de Tanzanie	3 545	3 461	2 882	2 555	2 541	2 651	3 131	3 589	3 806	4 352
United States[1,3] Etats-Unis[1,3]	5 325 290	5 508 728	5 580 868	5 620 176	5 695 039	5 864 465	5 795 192	5 815 889	5 877 677	5 987 984
Uruguay Uruguay	4 524	5 246	5 265	5 213	6 167	4 909	4 660	4 418	4 458	5 477
Uzbekistan Ouzbékistan	106 153	109 402	109 831	127 312	127 843	129 013	129 808	132 298	133 684	137 907
Vanuatu Vanuatu	66	84	84	81	81	81	84	84	88	88
Venezuela (Bolivarian Rep. of) Venezuela (Rép. bolivarienne du)	164 686	173 609	170 178	178 757	178 731	162 061	166 471	139 990	155 571	172 623
Viet Nam Viet Nam	29 840	35 284	45 653	47 823	48 586	53 858	60 853	72 127	77 161	98 663
Western Sahara Sahara occidental	209	213	220	224	235	238	238	238	238	238

53 **CO_2 emission estimates**—From fossil fuel combustion, cement production and gas flared (thousand metric tons of carbon dioxide) (*continued*)

Estimation des émissions de CO_2—Dues à la combustion de combustibles fossiles, à la production de ciment et au gaz brûlés à la torchère (milliers de tonnes de dioxyde de carbone) (*suite*)

Country or area — Pays ou zone	1995	1996	1997	1998	1999	2000	2001	2002	2003	2004
Yemen Yémen	12 165	15 923	16 608	13 364	14 991	15 871	17 620	18 075	19 013	21 114
Zambia Zambie	2 170	1 870	2 390	2 313	1 807	1 818	1 906	1 969	2 123	2 288
Zimbabwe Zimbabwe	16 066	15 890	15 219	15 087	16 806	14 812	13 536	12 700	11 475	10 559

Source

Carbon Dioxide Information Analysis Center (CDIAC) of the Oak Ridge National Laboratory, Oak Ridge, Tennessee, U.S.A., database on national CO_2 emission estimates from fossil fuel burning, cement production and gas flaring and the Secretariat of the United Nations Framework Convention on Climate Change (UNFCCC), Bonn, Secretariat of the UNFCCC database.

The majority of the data have been taken from the CDIAC database; all other data have been taken from the UNFCCC database and are footnoted accordingly.

Notes

1 Source: Secretariat of the UNFCCC.
2 For statistical purposes, the data for China do not include those for the Hong Kong Special Administrative Region (Hong Kong SAR), Macao Special Administrative Region (Macao SAR) and Taiwan Province of China.
3 Including territories.

Source

"Carbon Dioxide Information Analysis Center (CDIAC) of the Oak Ridge National Laboratory, Oak Ridge, Tennessee, U.S.A., database on national CO_2 emission estimates from fossil fuel burning, cement production and gas flaring" et la Secrétariat de la convention-cadre concernant les changements climatiques (CCCC) des Nations Unies, Bonn, la base de données du Secrétariat de la CCCC.

La majorité des données proviennent de la base de données du CDIAC ; les autres, qui proviennent de la base de données du Secrétariat de la CCCC, sont signalées par une note.

Notes

1 Source : Secrétariat de la CCCC des Nations Unies.
2 Pour la présentation des statistiques, les données pour la Chine ne comprennent pas la Région Administrative Spéciale de Hong Kong (Hong Kong RAS), la Région Administrative Spéciale de Macao (Macao RAS) et la province de Taiwan.
3 Y compris les territoires.

54 Ozone-depleting chlorofluorocarbons (CFCs)

Consumption: ozone-depleting potential (ODP) metric tons

Chlorofluorocarbones (CFC) qui appauvrissent la couche d'ozone

Consommation : tonnes de potentiel de destruction de l'ozone (PDO)

Country or area — Pays ou zone	1996	1997	1998	1999	2000	2001	2002	2003	2004	2005
Afghanistan — Afghanistan	380.0	380.0	...	...	...	...	...	...	177.9	141.2
Albania — Albanie	40.1	41.9	46.5	53.1	61.9	68.8	49.9	35.0	36.6	14.3
Algeria — Algérie	2 292.2	1 774.2	1 549.2	1 502.2	1 474.6	1 021.8	1 761.8	1 761.8	1 045.0	859.0
Angola — Angola	114.8	114.8	115.9	...	107.0	114.8	105.0	104.2	75.6	52.0
Antigua and Barbuda — Antigua-et-Barbuda	10.3	10.3	26.5	-2.0[1]	5.0	3.1	3.7	1.5	1.9	1.1
Argentina — Argentine	4 202.1	3 523.7	3 546.3	4 316.3	2 396.7	3 293.1	2 139.2	2 255.2	2 211.6	1 675.5
Armenia — Arménie	196.5	191.2	185.9	9.0	25.0	162.7	172.7	172.7	110.7	84.0
Australia — Australie	234.2	183.9	195.1	274.1	6.5	6.0	9.8	1.1	-61.8[1]	-51.4[1]
Azerbaijan — Azerbaïdjan	456.5	201.2	152.2	99.9	87.8	52.0	12.0	10.2	15.1	21.9
Bahamas — Bahamas	72.0	52.7	54.6	53.8	65.9	63.0	55.4	29.6	18.8	13.0
Bahrain — Bahreïn	137.2	147.2	149.5	129.0	113.1	106.0	94.6	85.8	64.8	58.7
Bangladesh — Bangladesh	628.3	832.2	830.4	800.6	805.0	807.9	328.0	333.0	294.9	263.0
Barbados — Barbade	22.4	17.2	22.5	16.5	8.1	12.5	9.5	8.6	14.1	6.7
Belarus — Bélarus	523.5	371.8	256.2	193.7	0.0	0.0	0.0	0.0	0.0	0.0
Belize — Belize	24.7	26.1	25.0	25.1	15.5	28.0	21.7	15.1	12.2	9.6
Benin — Bénin	58.4	59.6	54.2	56.6	54.6	54.0	35.5	17.3	11.5	10.0
Bhutan — Bhoutan	0.2	0.2	0.0	0.0	0.0	...	...	...	0.1	0.1
Bolivia — Bolivie	87.1	58.4	74.1	72.2	78.8	76.7	65.5	32.1	42.4	26.7
Bosnia and Herzegovina — Bosnie-Herzégovine	20.6	49.0	45.1	151.0	175.9	199.7	243.6	230.0	187.9	50.8
Botswana — Botswana	5.4	6.8	2.6	2.6	2.5	4.0	3.6	5.1	2.7	1.9
Brazil — Brésil	10 872.0	9 809.7	9 542.9	11 612.0	9 275.1	6 230.9	3 000.6	3 224.3	1 870.5	967.2
Brunei Darussalam — Brunéi Darussalam	80.1	90.0	63.5	36.7	46.6	31.4	43.4	32.3	60.2	39.0
Bulgaria — Bulgarie	4.0	0.0	0.0	0.0	0.0	0.0	0.0	0.0	0.0	0.0
Burkina Faso — Burkina Faso	37.6	37.6	37.0	30.6	25.4	19.6	16.3	13.2	10.5	7.4
Burundi — Burundi	58.8	61.9	64.5	59.6	53.8	46.5	19.1	9.2	3.9	3.5
Cambodia — Cambodge	94.2	94.2	94.2	94.2	94.2	94.2	94.2	86.7	70.4	44.5
Cameroon — Cameroun	280.4	259.5	311.8	361.5	368.7	364.1	226.0	220.5	148.5	120.0
Canada — Canada	128.8	136.2	42.2	-4.8[1]	10.1	0.1	-12.6[1]	-0.2[1]	0.0	0.0
Cape Verde — Cap-Vert	2.3	2.2	2.1	2.0	1.9	1.9	1.8	1.8	1.5	0.9
Central African Rep. — Rép. centrafricaine	6.4	0.0	7.0	1.4	4.3	4.0	4.4	4.1	3.9	2.6
Chad — Tchad	34.6	36.3	38.1	37.5	36.5	31.6	27.1	22.8	14.2	11.3
Chile — Chili	878.2	674.5	737.9	657.5	576.0	470.2	370.2	424.5	230.8	221.5
China[2] — Chine[2]	47 089.0	51 076.4	55 414.2	42 983.4	39 123.6	33 922.6	30 621.2	22 808.8	17 902.5	13 123.8
Colombia — Colombie	2 301.8	2 166.4	1 224.0	985.5	1 149.3	1 164.8	907.0	1 058.1	898.5	556.9
Comoros — Comores	2.3	2.9	3.6	2.5	2.7	1.9	1.8	1.2	1.1	0.9
Congo — Congo	12.8	9.2	6.6	9.3	11.4	2.5	5.5	7.0	4.7	3.7
Cook Islands — Iles Cook	1.7	1.2	0.5	0.0	0.0	...	...	0.0	0.0	0.0
Costa Rica — Costa Rica	497.2	94.8	-204.2[1]	152.3	105.9	144.6	137.4	142.5	111.5	96.1
Côte d'Ivoire — Côte d'Ivoire	383.9	144.4	267.8	166.2	206.4	148.0	106.5	93.4	79.4	70.1
Croatia — Croatie	184.1	280.4	85.7	141.5	171.2	113.8	140.1	88.7	78.2	43.5
Cuba — Cuba	663.8	665.4	531.4	571.4	533.7	504.0	488.8	481.0	445.1	208.6
Cyprus — Chypre	141.0	143.0	81.0	114.9	165.0	137.6	131.8	62.5	...	...
Czech Republic — République tchèque	49.6	11.6	7.9	11.2	5.1	2.9	3.7	-4.4[1]	...	...
Dem. Rep. of the Congo — Rép. dém. du Congo	735.0	469.0	688.5	368.1	386.6	639.4	569.4	566.9	329.1	268.7
Djibouti — Djibouti	21.5	18.9	20.6	20.6	20.7	18.0	15.8	12.1	8.8	7.1

Ozone-depleting chlorofluorocarbons (CFCs) — Consumption: ozone-depleting potential (ODP) metric tons (*continued*)

Chlorofluorocarbones (CFC) qui appauvrissent la couche d'ozone — Consommation : tonnes de potentiel de destruction de l'ozone (PDO) (*suite*)

Country or area — Pays ou zone	1996	1997	1998	1999	2000	2001	2002	2003	2004	2005
Dominica — Dominique	1.7	1.7	2.1	1.1	2.1	1.6	3.0	1.4	1.0	1.4
Dominican Republic — Rép. dominicaine	558.7	426.8	311.4	752.1	401.9	485.8	329.8	266.5	310.4	204.3
Ecuador — Equateur	269.2	320.4	271.7	153.0	230.5	207.0	229.6	256.3	147.4	132.5
Egypt — Egypte	1 732.0	1 632.0	1 540.0	1 373.6	1 267.0	1 334.8	1 294.0	1 102.2	1 047.6	821.2
El Salvador — El Salvador	312.1	277.8	194.6	109.5	99.1	116.9	101.6	97.5	75.6	119.2
Eritrea — Erythrée	34.3	40.3	25.5	25.2	48.8	...	...	...	...	30.2
Estonia — Estonie	-442.2[1]	45.2	69.8	56.3	15.7	-0.4[1]	0.0	0.0	...	...
Ethiopia — Ethiopie	33.8	35.1	38.2	39.2	39.2	34.6	30.0	28.0	16.0	15.0
Fiji — Fidji	26.7	13.7	13.1	9.4	0.0	0.0	0.0	0.0	0.0	0.0
Gabon — Gabon	11.5	12.0	12.0	7.8	13.7	6.4	5.0	5.0	4.5	2.1
Gambia — Gambie	20.6	28.0	10.9	6.9	6.1	5.8	4.7	5.1	0.2	0.7
Georgia — Géorgie	23.5	30.9	26.0	21.5	21.5	18.8	15.5	12.6	8.6	8.2
Ghana — Ghana	14.2	48.7	50.3	46.8	47.0	35.6	21.2	32.0	35.6	17.5
Grenada — Grenade	4.9	6.5	3.8	2.9	2.9	1.3	2.1	2.1	1.9	0.6
Guatemala — Guatemala	235.6	207.3	188.7	191.1	187.9	265.0	239.6	147.1	65.4	57.5
Guinea — Guinée	44.0	45.9	41.8	39.9	37.5	35.4	31.3	25.9	16.7	9.3
Guinea-Bissau — Guinée-Bissau	26.3	26.8	27.1	26.0	26.0	26.9	27.2	29.4	25.2	12.5
Guyana — Guyana	41.0	27.8	29.2	39.9	24.4	19.8	14.3	10.4	11.9	23.5
Haiti — Haïti	169.0	169.0	...	...	169.0	169.0	181.2	115.9	132.5	81.4
Honduras — Honduras	523.3	354.1	157.4	334.8	172.3	121.6	131.2	219.1	167.8	122.6
Hungary — Hongrie	0.0	3.9	1.3	0.6	0.5	0.0	0.3	-1.3[1]	...	...
Iceland — Islande	0.0	0.0	0.0	0.0	0.0	0.0	0.0	0.0	0.0	0.0
India — Inde	6 937.4	6 703.3	5 264.7	4 142.9	5 614.3	4 514.3	3 917.7	2 631.5	2 241.6	1 957.8
Indonesia — Indonésie	9 012.0	7 634.8	6 182.8	5 865.8	5 411.1	5 003.3	5 506.3	4 829.3	3 925.5	2 385.3
Iran (Islamic Rep. of) — Iran (Rép. islamique d')	3 692.0	5 883.0	5 571.0	4 399.0	4 156.5	4 204.8	4 437.8	4 088.8	3 471.9	2 221.0
Israel — Israël	7.0	0.0	0.0	0.0	0.0	0.0	0.0	0.0	0.0	0.0
Jamaica — Jamaïque	91.1	106.6	199.0	210.4	59.8	48.6	31.7	16.2	16.0	5.0
Japan — Japon	-614.4[1]	-113.0[1]	-208.0[1]	23.2	-24.2[1]	-5.5[1]	19.5	4.0	0.0	0.0
Jordan — Jordanie	627.4	857.4	647.2	398.0	354.0	321.0	90.0	74.4	58.4	59.6
Kazakhstan — Kazakhstan	825.6	668.8	1 025.5	730.0	523.9	290.0	112.0	30.4	11.2	0.0
Kenya — Kenya	166.8	250.6	245.3	241.1	203.3	168.6	152.3	168.6	131.7	160.6
Kiribati — Kiribati	0.7	0.6	0.5	0.0	0.0	0.0	0.0	0.0	0.0	0.0
Korea, Dem. P. R. — Corée, R. p. dém. de	267.0	233.0	112.0	106.0	77.0	320.8	299.0	587.4	7.3	91.8
Korea, Republic of — Corée, République de	8 220.2	9 220.2	5 298.8	7 402.6	7 395.4	6 802.2	6 646.6	5 171.6	5 012.2	2 730.0
Kuwait — Koweït	471.9	484.8	399.2	450.0	419.9	354.2	349.0	247.4	233.0	152.7
Kyrgyzstan — Kirghizistan	67.4	69.6	56.8	52.4	53.5	53.0	38.0	33.0	22.9	8.1
Lao People's Dem. Rep. — Rép. dém. pop. lao	43.3	43.3	43.3	44.1	44.6	41.2	42.3	35.3	23.1	19.5
Latvia — Lettonie	307.0	23.0	25.3	21.6	35.2	0.0	0.0	0.0	...	...
Lebanon — Liban	735.3	621.3	475.3	463.4	527.9	533.4	491.7	480.2	347.0	287.3
Lesotho — Lesotho	5.9	3.5	3.4	2.8	2.4	1.8	1.6	1.4	1.2	0.0
Liberia — Libéria	67.4	55.7	31.1	18.2	41.4	25.1	32.8	26.3	14.2	5.0
Libyan Arab Jamah. — Jamah. arabe libyenne	729.8	647.5	659.8	894.0	985.4	985.4	985.4	704.1	459.0	252.0
Liechtenstein — Liechtenstein	0.0	0.0	-0.1[1]	0.0	0.0	0.0	0.0	0.0	-0.1[1]	0.0
Lithuania — Lituanie	288.7	99.9	103.8	85.3	36.5	0.0	0.0	0.0	...	...
Madagascar — Madagascar	20.5	103.6	23.9	26.3	12.4	9.9	7.8	7.2	7.1	7.0
Malawi — Malawi	55.9	55.6	56.9	50.4	21.5	19.0	19.0	18.7	11.4	5.6
Malaysia — Malaisie	3 038.2	3 348.4	2 333.7	2 010.1	1 979.8	1 946.9	1 605.5	1 174.4	1 128.5	668.3

Country or area — Pays ou zone	1996	1997	1998	1999	2000	2001	2002	2003	2004	2005
Maldives — Maldives	0.0	7.8	0.9	1.5	4.6	14.0	2.8	0.0	0.0	0.0
Mali — Mali	109.3	111.1	113.1	37.1	29.2	27.0	26.0	26.0	25.0	25.0
Malta — Malte	70.2	60.1	106.6	97.2	67.6	63.1	10.3	14.0	...	...
Marshall Islands — Iles Marshall	1.1	1.1	0.6	1.1	0.5	0.2	0.2	0.2	0.0	0.0
Mauritania — Mauritanie	7.8	16.0	14.7	13.4	14.2	15.0	14.7	14.3	7.1	6.1
Mauritius — Maurice	36.2	27.3	39.0	18.6	19.1	14.5	7.3	4.0	3.4	-0.1[1]
Mexico — Mexique	4 858.8	4 157.2	3 482.9	2 837.9	3 059.5	2 223.9	1 946.7	1 983.2	3 208.4	1 604.0
Micronesia (Fed. States of) — Micronésie (Etats féd. de)	1.1	1.2	1.2	1.2	1.0	1.1	1.9	1.7	1.5	0.4
Monaco — Monaco	0.0	0.0	0.0	0.0	0.0	0.0	0.0	0.0	0.0	0.0
Mongolia — Mongolie	12.2	12.5	13.2	12.4	11.2	9.3	6.9	5.7	4.1	3.7
Morocco — Maroc	814.0	886.0	923.6	870.6	564.0	435.2	668.6	474.8	329.0	38.7
Mozambique — Mozambique	21.7	12.7	3.2	13.8	9.9	8.4	9.9	1.7	1.6	1.2
Myanmar — Myanmar	58.6	54.8	52.3	30.7	26.3	39.4	43.5	51.6	29.6	14.8
Namibia — Namibie	19.3	19.3	16.4	16.8	22.1	24.0	20.0	17.2	7.7	0.0
Nauru — Nauru	0.5	0.5	0.5	0.4	0.4	0.4	0.0	0.0	0.0	0.0
Nepal — Népal	27.0	29.0	32.9	25.0	94.0	0.0	0.0	0.0	0.0	0.0
New Zealand — Nouvelle-Zélande	1.6	0.0	0.0	0.0	-2.6[1]	0.0	-4.7[1]	0.0	-1.1[1]	0.0
Nicaragua — Nicaragua	82.7	55.7	37.3	52.6	44.4	35.2	54.9	29.9	48.4	36.0
Niger — Niger	18.1	59.4	60.7	58.3	39.9	29.1	26.6	24.5	23.0	15.1
Nigeria — Nigéria	4 548.1	4 866.2	4 761.5	4 286.2	4 094.8	3 665.5	3 286.7	2 662.4	2 116.1	466.1
Niue — Nioué	0.1	0.0	0.0	0.0	0.0	...	...	0.0	0.0	0.0
Norway — Norvège	2.8	2.6	-16.4[1]	-60.2[1]	-39.8[1]	-48.1[1]	-73.5[1]	-65.5[1]	-54.6[1]	-21.8[1]
Oman — Oman	264.9	250.5	261.1	259.6	282.1	207.3	179.5	134.5	98.7	54.3
Pakistan — Pakistan	1 670.8	1 263.8	1 196.0	1 421.8	1 945.3	1 666.3	1 647.0	1 124.0	805.0	453.0
Palau — Palaos	1.1	2.1	2.1	0.4	0.6	0.6	0.1	1.0	0.9	0.2
Panama — Panama	354.8	357.9	346.0	301.1	249.9	180.4	195.3	168.5	134.7	92.8
Papua New Guinea — Papouasie-Nvl-Guinée	62.7	36.4	45.2	35.5	47.9	15.0	34.6	22.7	17.2	15.1
Paraguay — Paraguay	180.4	240.1	113.4	345.3	153.5	116.0	96.9	91.8	141.0	250.7
Peru — Pérou	243.0	258.8	326.7	295.6	347.0	189.0	196.5	178.4	145.7	127.7
Philippines — Philippines	3 039.0	2 746.8	2 130.2	2 087.6	2 905.2	2 049.4	1 644.5	1 422.4	1 389.8	1 014.2
Poland — Pologne	549.4	308.3	314.1	187.0	174.8	179.0	201.5	126.3	...	...
Qatar — Qatar	102.4	111.0	120.8	89.0	85.8	85.4	86.7	95.1	63.7	37.0
Republic of Moldova — République de Moldova	51.5	83.1	40.5	11.1	31.7	23.5	29.6	18.9	20.0	14.4
Romania — Roumanie	762.8	720.5	582.0	338.1	360.6	185.7	359.4	362.1	116.7	180.2
Russian Federation — Fédération de Russie	12 345.3	10 986.2	11 821.1	14 824.4	23 820.8	0.0	0.0	258.0	373.6	349.0
Rwanda — Rwanda	30.2	34.4	37.7	30.1	30.1	30.1	30.1	30.1	27.1	12.3
Saint Kitts and Nevis — Saint-Kitts-et-Nevis	3.4	3.6	1.6	2.6	7.0	6.6	5.3	2.8	3.3	1.5
Saint Lucia — Sainte-Lucie	8.3	8.5	6.3	3.2	4.2	4.1	7.6	2.5	0.8	1.5
Saint Vincent-Grenadines — Saint Vincent-Grenadines	0.8	2.2	2.3	10.0	6.0	6.9	6.0	3.1	2.1	1.0
Samoa — Samoa	4.5	4.5	2.6	6.1	0.6	2.0	2.2	0.0	0.0	0.0
Sao Tome and Principe — Sao Tomé-et-Principe	4.2	5.2	3.8	3.4	3.9	4.1	4.3	4.6	4.0	2.3
Saudi Arabia — Arabie saoudite	1 668.2	1 899.0	1 921.8	1 710.4	1 593.6	1 593.0	1 531.0	1 300.0	1 150.0	...
Senegal — Sénégal	178.4	138.1	128.5	121.1	116.5	98.0	71.9	51.0	40.0	30.0
Serbia and Montenegro — Serbie-et-Monténégro	895.6	832.5	519.4	548.6	309.7	263.3	371.7	412.0	282.8	52.1
Seychelles — Seychelles	2.2	2.5	2.0	1.1	0.8	0.7	1.5	0.6	0.0	0.0
Sierra Leone — Sierra Leone	86.7	81.9	81.0	75.9	75.9	92.9	80.8	66.3	64.5	26.2
Singapore — Singapour	36.8	-178.9[1]	16.7	24.1	21.7	21.6	0.9	11.1	6.6	-0.7[1]

Ozone-depleting chlorofluorocarbons (CFCs)—Consumption: ozone-depleting potential (ODP) metric tons (*continued*)
Chlorofluorocarbones (CFC) qui appauvrissent la couche d'ozone—Consommation : tonnes de potentiel de destruction de l'ozone (PDO) (*suite*)

Country or area — Pays ou zone	1996	1997	1998	1999	2000	2001	2002	2003	2004	2005
Slovakia — Slovaquie	0.0	1.2	1.4	1.4	1.7	3.3	0.8	0.6	...	...
Slovenia — Slovénie	1.2	0.4	0.1	0.1	0.3	2.6	0.4	0.6	...	...
Solomon Islands — Iles Salomon	2.0	2.3	0.8	6.2	0.3	0.6	0.5	0.8	1.1	0.9
Somalia — Somalie	241.3	241.7	246.9	48.6	65.6	86.9	98.5	108.2	97.2	...
South Africa — Afrique du Sud	0.0	98.3	155.1	117.3	80.5	16.0	86.6	60.8	61.8	30.0
Sri Lanka — Sri Lanka	497.8	318.5	250.4	216.4	220.3	190.4	185.0	179.9	155.7	149.2
Sudan — Soudan	429.5	306.0	294.5	294.5	291.5	266.0	253.0	216.0	203.0	185.0
Suriname — Suriname	41.0	42.0	42.0	43.0	44.0	46.0	46.0	12.3	9.2	7.5
Swaziland — Swaziland	22.1	16.3	2.2	2.1	0.1	1.3	1.2	1.9	3.1	1.5
Switzerland[1] — Suisse[1]	-43.3	-40.9	-28.1	-4.5	-5.8	-1.6	-3.4	-9.1	-19.0	-30.0
Syrian Arab Republic — Rép. arabe syrienne	2 260.0	2 043.7	1 245.6	1 280.7	1 174.7	1 392.2	1 201.6	1 124.6	928.3	869.7
Tajikistan — Tadjikistan	34.9	48.2	56.3	50.7	28.0	28.3	11.8	4.7	0.0	0.0
Thailand — Thaïlande	5 550.2	4 448.0	3 783.0	3 610.6	3 568.3	3 375.1	2 177.3	1 857.0	1 358.3	1 259.9
TFYR of Macedonia — L'ex-R.y. Macédoine	514.0	487.1	62.8	191.9	49.5	46.7	34.1	49.3	8.8	11.8
Togo — Togo	33.7	35.2	36.7	41.7	37.5	34.7	35.3	33.7	26.4	18.6
Tonga — Tonga	0.9	1.2	0.0	83.4	0.5	0.7	0.8	0.3	0.0	0.0
Trinidad and Tobago — Trinité-et-Tobago	114.1	134.6	155.6	81.7	101.3	79.2	63.6	62.5	35.0	18.3
Tunisia — Tunisie	882.0	970.2	790.6	566.0	555.0	570.0	465.8	362.5	271.0	205.0
Turkey — Turquie	3 758.8	3 869.6	3 985.0	1 791.1	820.2	731.2	698.9	440.9	257.6	132.8
Turkmenistan — Turkménistan	29.6	26.4	25.3	18.6	21.0	57.7	10.5	43.4	58.4	17.9
Tuvalu — Tuvalu	0.4	0.3	0.3	0.2	0.0	0.0	0.0	0.0	0.0	0.0
Uganda — Ouganda	12.8	13.9	11.4	12.2	12.7	13.4	12.7	4.1	0.2	0.2
Ukraine — Ukraine	1 401.0	1 404.7	1 100.7	951.2	838.7	1 076.5	119.7	77.8	80.0	53.1
United Arab Emirates — Emirats arabes unis	511.2	562.8	737.4	529.2	476.2	423.4	370.4	317.5	291.0	264.6
United Rep. of Tanzania — Rép.-Unie de Tanzanie	293.6	187.7	131.5	88.9	215.5	131.2	71.5	148.2	98.8	98.9
United States — Etats-Unis	1 331.0	742.5	2 706.0	2 903.8	2 613.0	2 805.2	1 357.2	1 605.2	1 153.6	1 496.6
Uruguay — Uruguay	172.1	193.1	194.0	111.4	106.8	102.3	75.2	111.4	90.9	97.6
Uzbekistan — Ouzbékistan	260.3	53.0	119.8	52.8	41.7	15.3	0.0	0.0	0.0	0.0
Vanuatu — Vanuatu	0.0	0.0	0.0	0.0	0.0	0.0	0.0	0.0	0.0	0.0
Venezuela (Boliv. Rep. of) — Venezuela (Rép. boliv. du)	3 040.9	3 703.9	3 213.9	1 922.1	2 705.9	2 546.2	1 552.8	1 313.5	2 944.6	1 841.8
Viet Nam — Viet Nam	520.0	500.0	392.0	293.9	220.0	243.0	235.5	243.7	241.0	234.8
Yemen — Yémen	1 673.7	1 364.4	1 060.8	1 040.7	1 045.0	1 023.4	959.9	758.6	746.4	710.5
Zambia — Zambie	30.4	28.7	26.7	24.3	23.3	11.8	10.6	10.4	10.0	9.5
Zimbabwe — Zimbabwe	456.6	435.4	390.2	229.1	145.0	259.4	129.1	117.5	112.9	49.0

Source

United Nations Environment Programme (UNEP), Ozone Secretariat (Nairobi).

Notes

1 Negative numbers can occur when destruction and/or exports exceed production plus imports, implying that the destruction and/or exports are from stockpiles.

2 Data include those for Taiwan Province of China.

Source

Secrétariat de l'ozone du programme des Nations Unies pour l'environnement (PNUE) (Nairobi).

Notes

1 Il peut y avoir des chiffres négatifs, lorsque les quantités exportées, ajoutées aux quantités détruites, sont supérieures aux quantités effectivement produites ajoutées aux quantités importées, ce qui est le cas par exemple lorsque les exportations proviennent des stocks reportés d'un exercice précédent.

2 Les données comprennent les chiffres pour la province de Taiwan.

55 Threatened species

Number by taxonomic group

Espèces menacées

Nombre par groupe taxonomique

Country or area — Pays ou zone	Year Année	Mammals Mammifères	Birds Oiseaux	Reptiles Reptiles	Amphibians Amphibiens	Fishes Poissons	Molluscs Mollusques	Invertebrates Invertébrés	Plants Plantes	Total
Afghanistan Afghanistan	2002	13	11	1	1	0	0	1	1	28
	2004	12	17	1	1	0	0	1	1	33
	2006	16	18	1	1	0	0	1	1	38
Albania Albanie	2002	3	3	4	0	7	0	4	0	21
	2004	1	9	4	2	17	0	4	0	37
	2006	2	9	4	2	22	0	4	0	43
Algeria Algérie	2002	13	6	2	0	1	0	11	2	35
	2004	12	11	2	1	10	0	12	2	50
	2006	15	13	7	3	18	0	14	3	73
American Samoa Samoa américaines	2002	3	2	2	0	0	5	0	1	13
	2004	3	9	2	0	4	5	0	1	24
	2006	3	11	2	0	5	5	0	1	27
Andorra Andorre	2002	3	0	0	0	0	1	3	0	7
	2004	1	0	0	0	0	1	3	0	5
	2006	2	0	1	0	1	1	3	0	8
Angola Angola	2002	19	15	4	0	0	5	1	19	63
	2004	11	20	4	0	9	5	1	26	76
	2006	14	21	5	0	16	5	1	26	88
Anguilla Anguilla	2002	0	0	4	0	0	0	0	3	7
	2004	0	0	4	0	11	0	0	3	18
	2006	1	0	4	0	12	0	0	3	20
Antigua and Barbuda Antigua-et-Barbuda	2002	0	1	5	0	0	0	0	4	10
	2004	0	2	5	0	11	0	0	4	22
	2006	1	1	5	0	12	0	0	4	23
Argentina Argentine	2002	34	39	5	5	2	0	11	42	138
	2004	32	55	5	30	12	0	10	42	186
	2006	32	57	5	33	22	0	10	44	203
Armenia Arménie	2002	11	4	5	0	1	0	7	1	29
	2004	9	12	5	0	1	0	7	1	35
	2006	11	12	5	0	1	0	6	1	36
Aruba Aruba	2002	1	0	3	0	0	0	1	0	5
	2004	1	1	3	0	12	0	1	0	18
	2006	2	2	3	0	13	0	1	0	21
Australia Australie	2002	63	37	38	35	44	175	107	38	537
	2004	63	60	38	47	74	176	107	56	621
	2006	64	65	39	47	85	176	107	56	639
Austria Autriche	2002	7	3	0	0	7	22	22	3	64
	2004	5	8	0	0	7	22	22	3	67
	2006	6	12	1	0	7	22	21	4	73
Azerbaijan Azerbaïdjan	2002	13	8	5	0	5	0	6	0	37
	2004	11	11	5	0	5	0	6	0	38
	2006	11	13	5	0	5	0	5	0	39
Bahamas Bahamas	2002	5	4	6	0	4	0	1	4	24
	2004	5	10	6	0	15	0	1	5	42
	2006	5	10	7	0	17	0	1	5	45
Bahrain Bahreïn	2002	1	6	0	0	1	0	0	0	8
	2004	1	7	4	0	6	0	0	0	18
	2006	2	7	4	0	6	0	0	0	19
Bangladesh Bangladesh	2002	23	23	20	0	0	0	0	12	78
	2004	22	23	20	0	8	0	0	12	85
	2006	31	32	21	2	13	0	0	12	111

Country or area — Pays ou zone	Year Année	Mammals Mammifères	Birds Oiseaux	Reptiles Reptiles	Amphibians Amphibiens	Fishes Poissons	Molluscs Mollusques	Invertebrates Invertébrés	Plants Plantes	Total
Barbados Barbade	2002	0	1	3	0	1	0	0	2	7
	2004	0	3	4	0	11	0	0	2	20
	2006	1	3	4	0	12	0	0	2	22
Belarus Bélarus	2002	7	3	0	0	0	0	5	0	15
	2004	6	4	0	0	0	0	8	0	18
	2006	6	5	0	0	0	0	8	0	19
Belgium Belgique	2002	11	2	0	0	0	4	7	0	24
	2004	9	10	0	0	6	4	7	0	36
	2006	9	12	0	0	8	4	8	0	41
Belize Belize	2002	4	2	4	0	6	0	1	28	45
	2004	5	3	4	6	18	0	1	30	67
	2006	5	3	5	6	19	0	1	30	69
Benin Bénin	2002	8	2	1	0	0	0	0	11	22
	2004	6	2	1	0	8	0	0	14	31
	2006	12	2	5	0	12	0	0	14	45
Bermuda Bermudes	2002	2	2	2	0	2	0	25	4	37
	2004	2	3	2	0	11	0	25	4	47
	2006	2	3	2	0	13	0	25	4	49
Bhutan Bhoutan	2002	22	12	0	0	0	0	1	7	42
	2004	21	18	0	1	0	0	1	7	48
	2006	25	18	1	2	0	0	1	7	54
Bolivia Bolivie	2002	24	28	2	1	0	0	1	70	126
	2004	26	30	2	21	0	0	1	70	150
	2006	24	32	3	23	0	0	1	71	154
Bosnia and Herzegovina Bosnie-Herzégovine	2002	10	3	1	1	6	0	10	1	32
	2004	8	8	1	1	11	0	10	1	40
	2006	8	9	2	1	25	0	10	1	56
Botswana Botswana	2002	6	7	0	0	0	0	0	0	13
	2004	6	9	0	0	0	0	0	0	15
	2006	8	9	0	0	0	0	0	0	17
Brazil Brésil	2002	81	114	22	6	17	21	13	381	655
	2004	74	120	22	24	42	21	13	381	697
	2006	73	124	22	28	58	21	13	382	721
British Indian Ocean Terr. Terr. brit. de l'océan Indien	2002	0	0	2	0	0	0	0	1	3
	2004	0	0	2	0	4	0	0	1	7
	2006	0	0	2	0	5	0	0	1	8
British Virgin Islands Iles Vierges britanniques	2002	0	2	6	1	0	0	0	4	13
	2004	0	2	6	2	10	0	0	10	30
	2006	1	1	6	2	11	0	0	10	31
Brunei Darussalam Brunéi Darussalam	2002	11	14	3	0	2	0	0	99	129
	2004	11	25	4	3	6	0	0	99	148
	2006	15	25	5	15	7	0	0	101	168
Bulgaria Bulgarie	2002	14	10	2	0	10	0	7	0	43
	2004	12	11	2	0	10	0	9	0	44
	2006	13	12	2	0	12	0	8	0	47
Burkina Faso Burkina Faso	2002	7	2	1	0	0	0	0	2	12
	2004	6	2	1	0	0	0	0	2	11
	2006	9	3	1	0	0	0	0	2	15
Burundi Burundi	2002	6	7	0	0	0	0	3	2	18
	2004	7	9	0	6	0	1	3	2	28
	2006	12	11	0	6	18	1	4	2	54
Cambodia Cambodge	2002	24	19	10	0	7	0	0	29	89
	2004	23	24	10	3	12	0	0	31	103
	2006	29	25	15	6	15	0	0	32	122
Cameroon Cameroun	2002	40	15	1	1	27	1	3	155	243
	2004	42	18	1	50	35	1	3	334	484
	2006	43	18	4	53	39	1	1	355	514

Country or area — Pays ou zone	Year Année	Mammals Mammifères	Birds Oiseaux	Reptiles Reptiles	Amphibians Amphibiens	Fishes Poissons	Molluscs Mollusques	Invertebrates Invertébrés	Plants Plantes	Total
Canada Canada	2002	14	8	2	1	16	0	10	1	52
	2004	16	19	2	1	24	1	10	1	74
	2006	18	21	3	1	26	2	10	1	82
Cape Verde Cap-Vert	2002	3	2	0	0	1	0	0	2	8
	2004	3	4	0	0	14	0	0	2	23
	2006	3	5	3	0	15	0	0	2	28
Cayman Islands Iles Caïmanes	2002	0	1	2	0	0	1	0	2	6
	2004	0	3	3	0	10	1	0	2	19
	2006	0	3	6	0	11	1	0	2	23
Central African Rep. Rép. centrafricaine	2002	14	3	1	0	0	0	0	10	28
	2004	11	3	1	0	0	0	0	15	30
	2006	12	3	1	0	0	0	0	15	31
Chad Tchad	2002	17	5	1	0	0	1	0	2	26
	2004	12	5	1	0	0	1	0	2	21
	2006	14	5	1	0	0	1	0	2	23
Chile Chili	2002	21	22	0	3	4	0	0	40	90
	2004	22	32	0	20	9	0	0	40	123
	2006	22	35	1	21	12	0	2	39	132
China[1] Chine[1]	2002	79	74	31	1	32	1	3	168	389
	2004	80	82	31	86	47	1	3	443	773
	2006	84	88	34	91	59	1	5	442	804
China, Hong Kong SAR Chine, Hong Kong RAS	2002	1	11	1	0	2	1	0	4	20
	2004	1	20	1	3	7	1	0	6	39
	2006	1	20	1	3	9	1	2	6	43
China, Macao SAR Chine, Macao RAS	2002	0	1	0	0	0	0	0	0	1
	2004	0	2	0	0	3	0	0	0	5
Christmas Is. Ile Christmas	2002	0	5	2	0	0	0	0	1	8
	2004	0	5	3	0	4	0	0	1	13
	2006	0	5	3	0	5	0	0	1	14
Cocos (Keeling) Islands Iles des Cocos (Keeling)	2002	0	0	0	0	1	0	0	0	1
	2004	0	1	1	0	3	0	0	0	5
	2006	0	1	1	0	4	1	0	0	7
Colombia Colombie	2002	41	78	14	0	8	0	0	213	354
	2004	39	86	15	208	23	0	0	222	593
	2006	38	88	16	217	28	0	2	225	614
Comoros Comores	2002	2	9	2	0	1	0	4	5	23
	2004	2	10	2	0	4	0	4	5	27
	2006	3	10	2	0	5	0	4	5	29
Congo Congo	2002	15	3	1	0	1	1	0	33	54
	2004	14	4	1	0	10	1	0	35	65
	2006	14	4	2	0	12	1	4	36	73
Cook Islands Iles Cook	2002	1	7	2	0	0	0	0	1	11
	2004	1	15	2	0	4	0	0	1	23
	2006	1	15	2	0	6	0	0	1	25
Costa Rica Costa Rica	2002	14	13	7	1	1	0	9	110	155
	2004	13	18	8	60	13	0	9	110	231
	2006	11	19	8	64	15	0	12	111	240
Côte d'Ivoire Côte d'Ivoire	2002	19	12	2	1	0	1	0	101	136
	2004	23	11	2	14	11	1	0	105	167
	2006	25	11	5	15	15	1	0	109	181
Croatia Croatie	2002	9	4	1	1	22	0	11	0	48
	2004	7	9	1	2	27	0	11	0	57
	2006	7	11	2	2	40	0	13	0	75
Cuba Cuba	2002	11	18	7	0	6	0	3	160	205
	2004	11	18	7	47	23	0	3	163	272
	2006	11	18	7	47	26	0	5	163	277

Country or area — Pays ou zone	Year Année	Mammals Mammifères	Birds Oiseaux	Reptiles Reptiles	Amphibians Amphibiens	Fishes Poissons	Molluscs Mollusques	Invertebrates Invertébrés	Plants Plantes	Total
Cyprus Chypre	2002	3	3	3	0	1	0	0	1	11
	2004	3	11	3	0	7	0	0	1	25
	2006	4	12	4	0	9	0	0	7	36
Czech Republic République tchèque	2002	8	2	0	0	7	2	17	4	40
	2004	6	9	0	0	7	2	17	4	45
	2006	7	11	0	0	10	2	16	4	50
Dem. Rep. of the Congo Rép. dém. du Congo	2002	40	28	2	0	1	41	4	55	171
	2004	29	30	2	13	10	14	8	65	171
	2006	29	30	4	13	24	14	13	66	193
Denmark Danemark	2002	5	1	0	0	0	1	10	3	20
	2004	4	10	0	0	7	1	10	3	35
	2006	4	12	0	0	10	1	10	3	40
Djibouti Djibouti	2002	4	5	0	0	1	0	0	2	12
	2004	4	6	0	0	9	0	0	2	21
	2006	7	6	2	0	12	0	0	2	29
Dominica Dominique	2002	1	3	4	0	0	0	0	11	19
	2004	1	4	4	2	11	0	0	11	33
	2006	2	5	4	2	13	0	0	11	37
Dominican Republic Rép. dominicaine	2002	5	15	10	1	0	0	2	29	62
	2004	5	16	10	31	10	0	2	30	104
	2006	5	14	10	31	12	0	6	30	108
Ecuador Equateur	2002	33	62	10	0	3	23	0	197	328
	2004	34	69	10	163	12	48	0	1 815	2 151
	2006	34	76	11	165	14	48	0	1 832	2 180
Egypt Egypte	2002	13	7	6	0	0	0	1	2	29
	2004	6	17	6	0	14	0	1	2	46
	2006	14	18	11	0	17	0	1	2	63
El Salvador El Salvador	2002	2	0	4	0	2	0	1	23	32
	2004	2	3	5	8	5	0	1	25	49
	2006	4	4	7	11	7	0	0	26	59
Equatorial Guinea Guinée équatoriale	2002	16	5	2	1	0	0	2	23	49
	2004	17	6	2	5	8	0	2	61	101
	2006	18	5	3	5	10	0	0	63	104
Eritrea Erythrée	2002	12	7	6	0	0	0	0	3	28
	2004	9	7	6	0	9	0	0	3	34
	2006	13	8	6	0	12	0	0	3	42
Estonia Estonie	2002	4	3	0	0	0	0	4	0	11
	2004	4	3	0	0	1	0	4	0	12
	2006	5	4	0	0	2	0	4	0	15
Ethiopia Ethiopie	2002	35	16	1	0	0	3	1	22	78
	2004	35	20	1	9	0	3	3	22	93
	2006	40	21	1	9	3	3	12	22	111
Faeroe Islands Iles Féroé	2002	3	0	0	0	0	0	0	0	3
	2004	4	0	0	0	7	0	0	0	11
	2006	4	0	0	0	8	0	0	0	12
Falkland Is. (Malvinas) Iles Falkland (Malvinas)	2002	4	6	0	0	0	0	0	0	10
	2004	4	16	0	0	1	0	0	5	26
	2006	4	18	0	0	2	0	0	5	29
Fiji Fidji	2002	5	12	6	1	1	2	0	65	92
	2004	5	13	6	1	8	2	0	66	101
	2006	5	12	6	1	9	3	0	66	102
Finland Finlande	2002	5	3	0	0	0	1	9	1	19
	2004	3	10	0	0	1	1	9	1	25
	2006	4	11	0	0	3	1	9	1	29
France France	2002	18	5	3	2	5	34	31	2	100
	2004	16	15	3	3	16	34	31	2	120
	2006	16	17	5	2	23	34	29	7	133

Country or area — Pays ou zone	Year Année	Mammals Mammifères	Birds Oiseaux	Reptiles Reptiles	Amphibians Amphibiens	Fishes Poissons	Molluscs Mollusques	Invertebrates Invertébrés	Plants Plantes	Total
French Guiana Guyane française	2002	10	0	7	0	0	0	0	16	33
	2004	10	0	7	3	13	0	0	16	49
	2006	9	0	7	3	18	0	0	16	53
French Polynesia Polynésie française	2002	3	23	1	0	5	29	0	47	108
	2004	3	33	1	0	9	29	0	47	122
	2006	3	35	2	0	10	30	0	47	127
Gabon Gabon	2002	15	5	1	0	1	0	1	71	94
	2004	11	5	1	2	12	0	1	107	139
	2006	13	5	4	4	16	0	0	108	150
Gambia Gambie	2002	3	2	1	0	1	0	0	3	10
	2004	3	2	1	0	11	0	0	4	21
	2006	10	2	2	0	14	0	0	4	32
Georgia Géorgie	2002	13	3	7	1	6	0	10	0	40
	2004	11	8	7	1	6	0	10	0	43
	2006	13	10	7	1	9	0	9	0	49
Germany Allemagne	2002	11	5	0	0	6	9	22	12	65
	2004	9	14	0	0	12	9	22	12	78
	2006	10	16	0	0	15	9	21	12	83
Ghana Ghana	2002	14	8	2	0	0	0	0	115	139
	2004	15	8	2	10	8	0	0	117	160
	2006	18	9	5	10	13	0	0	117	172
Gibraltar Gibraltar	2002	0	1	0	0	0	2	0	0	3
	2004	1	5	0	0	10	2	0	0	18
	2006	1	5	0	0	10	2	0	0	18
Greece Grèce	2002	13	7	6	1	20	1	10	2	60
	2004	11	14	6	4	27	1	10	2	75
	2006	12	15	5	5	49	1	13	11	111
Greenland Groenland	2002	7	0	0	0	0	0	0	1	8
	2004	7	0	0	0	4	0	0	1	12
	2006	8	3	0	0	6	0	0	1	18
Grenada Grenade	2002	0	1	4	0	1	0	0	3	9
	2004	1	2	4	1	12	0	0	3	23
	2006	1	3	4	1	13	0	0	3	25
Guadeloupe Guadeloupe	2002	5	1	5	0	0	1	0	7	19
	2004	5	2	5	2	11	1	0	7	33
	2006	6	4	6	3	12	1	0	7	39
Guam Guam	2002	2	2	2	0	1	5	0	3	15
	2004	2	6	2	0	6	5	0	3	24
	2006	2	11	2	0	7	6	0	4	32
Guatemala Guatemala	2002	6	6	8	0	3	2	6	77	108
	2004	7	10	10	74	14	2	6	85	208
	2006	9	11	11	79	16	2	5	86	219
Guinea Guinée	2002	12	10	1	1	0	0	3	21	48
	2004	18	10	1	5	8	0	3	22	67
	2006	22	10	3	8	15	0	3	22	83
Guinea-Bissau Guinée-Bissau	2002	3	0	1	0	1	0	1	4	10
	2004	5	1	1	0	10	0	1	4	22
	2006	9	1	3	0	15	0	0	4	32
Guyana Guyana	2002	11	2	6	0	0	0	1	23	43
	2004	13	3	6	6	13	0	1	23	65
	2006	11	3	6	9	18	0	1	23	71
Haiti Haïti	2002	4	14	8	1	2	0	2	27	58
	2004	4	15	9	46	12	0	2	28	116
	2006	4	13	9	47	13	0	4	29	119
Honduras Honduras	2002	10	5	6	0	1	0	2	108	132
	2004	10	6	10	53	14	0	2	111	206
	2006	9	6	11	59	16	0	1	110	212

Country or area — Pays ou zone	Year Année	Mammals Mammifères	Birds Oiseaux	Reptiles Reptiles	Amphibians Amphibiens	Fishes Poissons	Molluscs Mollusques	Invertebrates Invertébrés	Plants Plantes	Total
Hungary Hongrie	2002	9	8	1	0	8	1	24	1	52
	2004	7	9	1	0	8	1	24	1	51
	2006	9	12	1	0	10	1	26	1	60
Iceland Islande	2002	6	0	0	0	0	0	0	0	6
	2004	7	0	0	0	8	0	0	0	15
	2006	8	2	0	0	10	0	0	0	20
India Inde	2002	88	72	25	3	9	2	21	244	464
	2004	85	79	25	66	28	2	21	246	552
	2006	89	82	26	68	35	2	20	247	569
Indonesia Indonésie	2002	147	114	28	0	68	3	28	384	772
	2004	146	121	28	33	91	3	28	383	833
	2006	146	121	28	39	105	3	28	387	857
Iran (Islamic Rep. of) Iran (Rép. islamique d')	2002	22	13	8	2	7	0	3	1	56
	2004	21	18	8	4	14	0	3	1	69
	2006	25	19	9	4	15	0	5	1	78
Iraq Iraq	2002	11	11	2	0	2	0	2	0	28
	2004	9	18	2	1	3	0	2	0	35
	2006	12	18	2	2	5	0	2	0	41
Ireland Irlande	2002	5	1	0	0	0	1	1	1	9
	2004	4	8	0	0	6	1	2	1	22
	2006	4	9	0	0	7	1	2	1	24
Israel Israël	2002	14	12	4	0	1	5	5	0	41
	2004	13	18	4	0	12	5	5	0	57
	2006	16	21	10	0	24	5	6	0	82
Italy Italie	2002	14	5	4	4	9	16	41	3	96
	2004	12	15	4	5	17	16	42	3	114
	2006	12	16	5	6	30	16	42	20	147
Jamaica Jamaïque	2002	5	12	8	4	1	0	5	206	241
	2004	5	12	8	17	12	0	5	208	267
	2006	5	12	9	17	13	0	5	208	269
Japan Japon	2002	37	34	11	10	13	25	20	11	161
	2004	37	53	11	20	27	25	20	12	205
	2006	38	56	11	20	35	25	18	12	215
Jordan Jordanie	2002	10	8	1	0	0	0	3	0	22
	2004	7	14	1	0	5	0	3	0	30
	2006	12	15	5	0	12	0	3	0	47
Kazakhstan Kazakhstan	2002	16	15	2	1	7	0	4	1	46
	2004	15	23	2	1	7	0	4	1	53
Kenya Kenya	2002	51	24	5	0	18	12	3	98	211
	2004	33	28	5	4	29	16	11	103	229
	2006	32	27	5	6	68	16	16	104	274
Kiribati Kiribati	2002	0	4	1	0	0	1	0	0	6
	2004	0	5	1	0	4	1	0	0	11
	2006	0	6	2	0	4	1	0	0	13
Korea, Dem. P. R. Corée, R. p. dém. de	2002	13	19	0	0	0	0	1	3	36
	2004	12	22	0	1	5	0	1	3	44
	2006	13	23	0	1	8	0	2	3	50
Korea, Republic of Corée, République de	2002	13	25	0	0	0	0	1	0	39
	2004	12	34	0	1	7	0	1	0	55
	2006	12	35	0	1	10	0	2	0	60
Kuwait Koweït	2002	1	7	1	0	0	0	0	0	9
	2004	1	12	1	0	6	0	0	0	20
	2006	5	12	2	0	9	0	0	0	28
Kyrgyzstan Kirghizistan	2002	7	4	2	0	0	0	3	1	17
	2004	6	4	2	0	0	0	3	1	16
	2006	9	6	2	0	0	0	3	1	21

Country or area — Pays ou zone	Year Année	Mammals Mammifères	Birds Oiseaux	Reptiles Reptiles	Amphibians Amphibiens	Fishes Poissons	Molluscs Mollusques	Invertebrates Invertébrés	Plants Plantes	Total
Lao People's Dem. Rep. Rép. dém. pop. lao	2002	31	20	12	0	6	0	0	18	87
	2004	30	21	11	4	6	0	0	19	91
	2006	35	24	12	9	6	0	0	20	106
Latvia Lettonie	2002	4	3	0	0	1	0	8	0	16
	2004	4	8	0	0	3	0	8	0	23
	2006	5	9	0	0	4	0	9	0	27
Lebanon Liban	2002	5	7	1	0	0	0	1	0	14
	2004	5	10	1	0	9	0	1	0	26
	2006	9	10	7	0	10	0	3	0	39
Lesotho Lesotho	2002	3	7	0	0	1	0	1	1	13
	2004	3	7	0	0	1	0	1	1	13
	2006	3	7	0	2	1	0	1	1	15
Liberia Libéria	2002	17	11	2	0	0	1	1	46	78
	2004	20	11	2	4	8	1	2	46	94
	2006	21	11	4	11	14	1	1	46	109
Libyan Arab Jamah. Jamah. arabe libyenne	2002	8	1	3	0	0	0	0	1	13
	2004	5	7	3	0	9	0	0	1	25
	2006	9	8	5	0	8	0	0	1	31
Liechtenstein Liechtenstein	2002	2	1	0	0	0	0	5	0	8
	2004	2	1	0	0	0	0	5	0	8
	2006	2	1	0	0	0	0	4	0	7
Lithuania Lituanie	2002	5	4	0	0	1	0	5	0	15
	2004	5	4	0	0	3	0	5	0	17
	2006	6	5	0	0	4	0	6	0	21
Luxembourg Luxembourg	2002	3	1	0	0	0	2	2	0	8
	2004	3	3	0	0	0	2	2	0	10
	2006	3	3	0	0	0	2	2	0	10
Madagascar Madagascar	2002	50	27	18	2	14	24	8	162	305
	2004	49	34	18	55	66	24	8	276	530
	2006	48	36	18	55	72	24	8	277	538
Malawi Malawi	2002	8	11	0	0	0	8	0	13	40
	2004	7	13	0	5	0	9	2	14	50
	2006	7	13	0	5	102	9	7	14	157
Malaysia Malaisie	2002	50	37	21	0	20	1	2	681	812
	2004	50	40	21	45	34	17	2	683	892
	2006	51	43	22	47	45	19	2	688	917
Maldives Maldives	2002	0	1	2	0	0	0	0	0	3
	2004	0	2	2	0	8	0	0	0	12
	2006	1	2	2	0	10	0	0	0	15
Mali Mali	2002	13	4	1	0	1	0	0	6	25
	2004	12	5	1	0	1	0	0	6	25
	2006	15	7	1	0	1	0	0	6	30
Malta Malte	2002	2	1	0	0	2	3	0	0	8
	2004	1	10	0	0	11	3	0	0	25
	2006	1	10	0	0	11	3	0	3	28
Marshall Islands Iles Marshall	2002	1	1	2	0	0	1	0	0	5
	2004	1	2	2	0	7	1	0	0	13
	2006	1	2	2	0	8	1	0	0	14
Martinique Martinique	2002	0	2	5	0	0	1	0	8	16
	2004	0	3	5	1	11	1	0	8	29
	2006	1	4	5	2	12	1	0	8	33
Mauritania Mauritanie	2002	10	2	2	0	0	0	0	0	14
	2004	7	5	2	0	11	0	1	0	26
	2006	12	6	3	0	17	0	1	0	39
Mauritius Maurice	2002	3	9	4	0	1	27	5	87	136
	2004	3	13	5	0	7	27	5	87	147
	2006	4	17	7	0	9	27	5	88	157

Country or area — Pays ou zone	Year Année	Mammals Mammifères	Birds Oiseaux	Reptiles Reptiles	Amphibians Amphibiens	Fishes Poissons	Molluscs Mollusques	Invertebrates Invertébrés	Plants Plantes	Total
Mayotte Mayotte	2002	0	3	2	0	0	0	1	0	6
	2004	0	3	2	0	1	0	1	0	7
	2006	1	4	2	0	1	0	1	0	9
Mexico Mexique	2002	70	39	18	4	88	4	36	221	480
	2004	72	57	21	190	106	5	36	261	748
	2006	74	62	21	204	109	5	35	261	771
Micronesia (Fed. States of) Micronésie (Etats féd. de)	2002	6	5	2	0	1	4	0	4	22
	2004	6	8	2	0	6	4	0	4	30
	2006	5	8	2	0	8	4	0	6	33
Monaco Monaco	2004	0	0	0	0	9	0	0	0	9
	2006	0	0	0	0	6	0	0	0	6
Mongolia Mongolie	2002	14	16	0	0	1	0	3	0	34
	2004	13	22	0	0	1	0	3	0	39
	2006	14	22	0	0	1	0	3	0	40
Montserrat Montserrat	2002	1	2	3	0	0	0	0	3	9
	2004	1	2	3	1	11	0	0	3	21
	2006	2	2	5	1	12	0	0	3	25
Morocco Maroc	2002	16	9	2	0	1	0	7	2	37
	2004	12	13	2	2	11	0	8	2	50
	2006	17	14	10	2	25	0	9	2	79
Mozambique Mozambique	2002	14	16	5	0	4	6	1	36	82
	2004	12	23	5	3	21	4	1	46	115
	2006	15	24	5	7	39	4	2	47	143
Myanmar Myanmar	2002	39	35	20	0	1	1	1	37	134
	2004	39	41	20	0	7	1	1	38	147
	2006	40	49	26	7	15	1	1	38	177
Namibia Namibie	2002	15	11	3	1	3	1	0	5	39
	2004	10	18	4	1	11	1	0	24	69
	2006	10	22	5	2	16	1	1	24	81
Nauru Nauru	2002	0	2	0	0	0	0	0	0	2
	2004	0	2	0	0	3	0	0	0	5
	2006	0	2	0	0	5	0	0	0	7
Nepal Népal	2002	31	25	5	0	0	0	1	6	68
	2004	29	31	6	3	0	0	1	7	77
	2006	32	34	9	3	0	0	0	7	85
Netherlands Pays-Bas	2002	10	4	0	0	2	1	6	0	23
	2004	9	11	0	0	7	1	6	0	34
	2006	10	13	0	0	9	1	6	0	39
Netherlands Antilles Antilles néerlandaises	2002	3	1	6	0	0	0	0	2	12
	2004	3	4	6	0	13	0	0	2	28
	2006	2	4	6	0	13	0	0	2	27
New Caledonia Nouvelle-Calédonie	2002	6	10	2	0	1	10	1	214	244
	2004	6	16	2	0	10	10	1	217	262
	2006	6	16	3	0	12	11	1	217	266
New Zealand Nouvelle-Zélande	2002	8	63	11	1	8	5	8	21	125
	2004	8	74	12	4	16	5	9	21	149
	2006	8	80	12	4	16	5	9	21	155
Nicaragua Nicaragua	2002	6	5	7	0	1	2	0	39	60
	2004	6	8	8	10	17	2	0	39	90
	2006	6	8	8	10	19	2	3	39	95
Niger Niger	2002	11	3	0	0	0	0	1	2	17
	2004	10	2	0	0	0	0	1	2	15
	2006	13	2	1	0	2	0	1	2	21
Nigeria Nigéria	2002	27	9	2	0	2	0	1	119	160
	2004	25	9	2	13	12	0	1	170	232
	2006	30	10	5	19	16	0	1	172	253

Country or area — Pays ou zone	Year Année	Mammals Mammifères	Birds Oiseaux	Reptiles Reptiles	Amphibians Amphibiens	Fishes Poissons	Molluscs Mollusques	Invertebrates Invertébrés	Plants Plantes	Total
Niue Nioué	2002	0	1	1	0	0	0	0	0	2
	2004	0	8	1	0	3	0	0	0	12
	2006	0	8	1	0	4	0	0	0	13
Norfolk Island Ile Norfolk	2002	0	7	2	0	0	12	0	1	22
	2004	0	17	2	0	2	12	0	1	34
	2006	0	19	2	0	2	12	0	1	36
Northern Mariana Islands Iles Mariannes du Nord	2002	2	8	2	0	0	2	0	4	18
	2004	2	13	2	0	5	2	0	4	28
	2006	2	13	2	0	6	4	0	5	32
Norway Norvège	2002	10	2	0	0	0	1	8	2	23
	2004	9	6	0	0	7	1	8	2	33
	2006	10	7	0	0	9	1	8	2	37
Occupied Palestinian Terr. Terr. palestinien occupé	2002	1	1	0	0	0	0	0	0	2
	2004	0	4	0	0	0	0	0	0	4
	2006	0	4	4	0	0	0	1	0	9
Oman Oman	2002	9	10	4	0	4	0	1	6	34
	2004	12	14	4	0	18	0	1	6	55
	2006	13	14	4	0	21	0	4	6	62
Pakistan Pakistan	2002	19	17	9	0	3	0	0	2	50
	2004	17	30	9	0	14	0	0	2	72
	2006	23	32	9	0	20	0	0	2	86
Palau Palaos	2002	3	2	2	0	0	5	0	3	15
	2004	3	2	2	0	6	5	0	3	21
	2006	3	2	2	0	7	5	0	4	23
Panama Panama	2002	20	16	7	0	5	0	2	192	242
	2004	17	20	7	52	17	0	2	195	310
	2006	18	20	7	60	19	0	2	196	322
Papua New Guinea Papouasie-Nvl-Guinée	2002	58	32	9	0	13	2	10	142	266
	2004	58	33	9	10	31	2	10	142	295
	2006	58	32	10	10	37	2	10	142	301
Paraguay Paraguay	2002	10	26	2	0	0	0	0	10	48
	2004	11	27	2	0	0	0	0	10	50
	2006	9	29	2	2	0	0	0	12	54
Peru Pérou	2002	49	76	6	1	1	0	2	269	404
	2004	46	94	6	78	8	0	2	274	508
	2006	46	98	8	86	8	0	2	276	524
Philippines Philippines	2002	50	67	8	23	31	3	16	193	391
	2004	50	70	8	48	49	3	16	212	456
	2006	51	74	9	48	58	3	17	215	475
Pitcairn Pitcairn	2002	0	8	0	0	0	5	0	7	20
	2004	0	11	1	0	3	5	0	7	27
	2006	0	11	1	0	4	5	0	7	28
Poland Pologne	2002	15	4	0	0	1	1	14	4	39
	2004	12	12	0	0	3	1	14	4	46
	2006	13	14	0	0	4	1	15	4	51
Portugal Portugal	2002	17	7	0	1	9	67	15	15	131
	2004	15	15	1	0	20	67	15	15	148
	2006	15	16	3	0	36	67	15	15	167
Puerto Rico Porto Rico	2002	2	8	8	3	0	0	1	48	70
	2004	2	12	8	13	9	0	1	52	97
	2006	2	13	8	13	11	0	1	54	102
Qatar Qatar	2002	0	6	1	0	0	0	0	0	7
	2004	0	7	1	0	4	0	0	0	12
	2006	1	7	2	0	6	0	0	0	16
Republic of Moldova République de Moldova	2002	6	5	1	0	9	0	5	0	26
	2004	4	8	1	0	9	0	5	0	27
	2006	5	8	1	0	9	0	4	0	27

Country or area — Pays ou zone	Year Année	Mammals Mammifères	Birds Oiseaux	Reptiles Reptiles	Amphibians Amphibiens	Fishes Poissons	Molluscs Mollusques	Invertebrates Invertébrés	Plants Plantes	Total
Réunion Réunion	2002	3	5	2	0	1	14	2	14	41
	2004	3	8	2	0	5	14	2	14	48
	2006	4	10	2	0	5	14	2	16	53
Romania Roumanie	2002	17	8	2	0	10	0	22	1	60
	2004	15	13	2	0	10	0	22	1	63
	2006	15	14	2	0	13	0	22	1	67
Russian Federation Fédération de Russie	2002	45	38	6	0	13	1	29	7	139
	2004	43	47	6	0	18	1	29	7	151
	2006	44	53	6	0	22	1	28	7	161
Rwanda Rwanda	2002	9	9	0	0	0	0	2	3	23
	2004	13	9	0	8	0	0	4	3	37
	2006	17	12	0	8	9	0	5	3	54
Saint Helena Sainte-Hélène	2002	1	13	1	0	7	0	2	9	33
	2004	1	20	1	0	10	0	2	26	60
	2006	1	20	1	0	11	0	2	26	61
Saint Kitts and Nevis Saint-Kitts-et-Nevis	2002	0	1	3	0	1	0	0	2	7
	2004	1	2	3	0	11	0	0	2	19
	2006	1	1	5	1	12	0	0	2	22
Saint Lucia Sainte-Lucie	2002	1	5	6	0	0	0	0	6	18
	2004	2	5	6	0	10	0	0	6	29
	2006	2	5	6	0	11	0	0	6	30
Saint Pierre and Miquelon Saint-Pierre-et-Miquelon	2002	0	1	0	0	0	0	0	0	1
	2004	0	1	0	0	1	0	0	0	2
	2006	0	0	0	0	1	0	0	0	1
St. Vincent-Grenadines St. Vincent-Grenadines	2002	2	2	4	0	0	0	0	4	12
	2004	2	2	4	1	11	0	0	4	24
	2006	3	3	4	1	12	0	0	4	27
Samoa Samoa	2002	3	7	1	0	0	1	0	2	14
	2004	3	7	1	0	4	1	0	2	18
	2006	3	8	2	0	5	1	0	2	21
San Marino — Saint-Marin	2002	2	0	0	0	0	0	0	0	2
Sao Tome and Principe Sao Tomé-et-Principe	2002	3	9	1	0	0	1	1	27	42
	2004	3	10	1	3	7	1	1	35	61
Saudi Arabia Arabie saoudite	2002	8	15	2	0	1	0	1	3	30
	2004	9	17	2	0	9	0	1	3	41
	2006	12	18	2	0	13	0	2	3	50
Senegal Sénégal	2002	12	4	6	0	1	0	0	7	30
	2004	11	5	6	0	18	0	0	7	47
	2006	15	6	7	0	23	0	0	7	58
Serbia and Montenegro Serbie-et-Monténégro	2002	12	5	1	0	10	0	19	1	48
	2004	10	10	1	1	20	0	19	1	62
Seychelles Seychelles	2002	4	10	4	4	0	1	2	43	68
	2004	3	13	3	6	10	2	2	45	84
	2006	4	13	10	6	12	2	3	45	95
Sierra Leone Sierra Leone	2002	12	10	3	0	0	0	4	43	72
	2004	12	10	3	2	8	0	4	47	86
	2006	15	10	3	2	12	0	2	47	91
Singapore Singapour	2002	3	7	3	0	5	0	1	54	73
	2004	3	10	4	0	13	0	1	54	85
	2006	5	14	5	0	20	0	1	55	100
Slovakia Slovaquie	2002	9	4	1	0	8	6	13	2	43
	2004	7	11	1	0	8	6	13	2	48
	2006	8	13	1	0	9	6	13	2	52
Slovenia Slovénie	2002	9	1	0	1	8	0	42	0	61
	2004	7	7	0	2	16	0	42	0	74
	2006	7	8	1	2	21	0	42	0	81

Country or area — Pays ou zone	Year Année	Mammals Mammifères	Birds Oiseaux	Reptiles Reptiles	Amphibians Amphibiens	Fishes Poissons	Molluscs Mollusques	Invertebrates Invertébrés	Plants Plantes	Total
Solomon Islands Iles Salomon	2002	20	23	4	0	2	2	4	16	71
	2004	20	21	4	2	5	2	4	16	74
	2006	20	20	4	2	7	2	4	16	75
Somalia Somalie	2002	19	10	2	0	3	1	0	17	52
	2004	15	13	2	0	16	1	0	17	64
	2006	15	13	3	0	21	1	1	17	71
South Africa Afrique du Sud	2002	42	28	19	9	29	10	102	45	284
	2004	29	36	20	21	49	18	109	75	357
	2006	28	38	20	21	58	18	123	73	379
Spain Espagne	2002	24	7	7	3	11	27	35	14	128
	2004	20	20	8	4	24	27	36	14	153
	2006	20	21	18	6	44	27	35	48	219
Sri Lanka Sri Lanka	2002	22	14	8	0	11	0	2	280	337
	2004	21	16	8	44	23	0	2	280	394
	2006	21	17	8	52	29	0	52	280	459
Sudan Soudan	2002	23	6	2	0	0	0	1	17	49
	2004	16	10	2	0	8	0	2	17	55
	2006	19	11	3	0	11	0	2	17	63
Suriname Suriname	2002	12	1	6	0	0	0	0	27	46
	2004	12	0	6	2	12	0	0	27	59
	2006	11	0	6	2	19	0	0	27	65
Svalbard and Jan Mayen Is. Svalbard et îles Jan Mayen	2002	5	0	0	0	0	0	0	0	5
	2004	5	2	0	0	2	0	0	0	9
	2006	6	3	0	0	2	0	0	0	11
Swaziland Swaziland	2002	4	5	0	0	0	0	0	3	12
	2004	6	6	0	0	0	0	0	11	23
	2006	8	8	0	1	0	0	0	11	28
Sweden Suède	2002	7	2	0	0	0	1	12	3	25
	2004	5	9	0	0	6	1	12	3	36
	2006	5	11	0	0	9	1	12	3	41
Switzerland Suisse	2002	5	2	0	0	4	0	30	2	43
	2004	4	8	0	1	4	0	30	2	49
	2006	4	9	0	1	8	0	29	3	54
Syrian Arab Republic Rép. arabe syrienne	2002	4	8	3	0	0	0	3	0	18
	2004	3	11	3	0	9	0	3	0	29
	2006	10	14	7	0	22	0	5	0	58
Tajikistan Tadjikistan	2002	9	7	1	0	3	0	2	2	24
	2004	7	9	1	0	3	0	2	2	24
	2006	10	10	1	0	5	0	2	2	30
Thailand Thaïlande	2002	37	37	18	0	22	1	0	78	193
	2004	36	42	19	3	36	1	0	84	221
	2006	38	49	22	3	49	1	0	88	250
TFYR of Macedonia L'ex-R.y. Macédoine	2002	11	3	2	0	4	0	5	0	25
	2004	9	9	2	0	4	0	5	0	29
	2006	9	11	2	0	8	0	5	0	35
Timor-Leste Timor-Leste	2002	0	6	0	0	0	0	0	0	6
	2004	0	7	1	0	3	0	0	0	11
Togo Togo	2002	9	0	2	0	0	0	0	9	20
	2004	7	2	2	3	8	0	0	10	32
	2006	12	2	4	3	12	0	0	10	43
Tokelau Tokélaou	2002	0	1	2	0	0	0	0	0	3
	2004	0	1	2	0	3	0	0	0	6
	2006	0	1	2	0	4	0	0	0	7
Tonga Tonga	2002	2	3	2	0	1	2	0	2	12
	2004	2	3	2	0	4	2	0	3	16
	2006	2	4	3	0	5	2	0	3	19

Country or area — Pays ou zone	Year Année	Mammals Mammifères	Birds Oiseaux	Reptiles Reptiles	Amphibians Amphibiens	Fishes Poissons	Molluscs Mollusques	Invertebrates Invertébrés	Plants Plantes	Total
Trinidad and Tobago Trinité-et-Tobago	2002	1	1	5	0	0	0	0	1	8
	2004	1	2	5	9	15	0	0	1	33
	2006	1	4	5	9	18	0	0	1	38
Tunisia Tunisie	2002	11	5	3	0	0	0	5	0	24
	2004	10	9	3	0	9	0	5	0	36
	2006	15	9	4	2	14	0	7	0	51
Turkey Turquie	2002	17	11	12	3	22	0	13	3	81
	2004	15	14	12	5	30	0	13	3	92
	2006	18	16	13	10	52	0	11	3	123
Turkmenistan Turkménistan	2002	13	6	2	0	7	0	5	0	33
	2004	12	13	2	0	8	0	5	0	40
	2006	16	14	1	0	9	0	5	0	45
Turks and Caicos Islands Iles Turques et Caïques	2002	0	3	5	0	0	0	0	2	10
	2004	0	3	5	0	10	0	0	2	20
	2006	1	2	5	0	11	0	0	2	21
Tuvalu Tuvalu	2002	0	1	1	0	0	1	0	0	3
	2004	0	1	1	0	5	1	0	0	8
	2006	0	1	2	0	6	2	0	0	11
Uganda Ouganda	2002	20	13	0	0	27	7	3	33	103
	2004	29	15	0	6	27	10	9	38	134
	2006	28	15	1	10	49	10	17	40	170
Ukraine Ukraine	2002	16	8	2	0	11	0	14	1	52
	2004	14	13	2	0	11	0	14	1	55
	2006	17	13	2	0	14	0	14	1	61
United Arab Emirates Emirats arabes unis	2002	3	8	1	0	1	0	0	0	13
	2004	5	11	1	0	6	0	0	0	23
	2006	7	12	2	0	8	0	2	0	31
United Kingdom Royaume-Uni	2002	12	2	0	0	3	2	9	13	41
	2004	10	10	0	0	12	2	8	13	55
	2006	10	13	0	0	14	2	8	13	60
United Rep. of Tanzania Rép.-Unie de Tanzanie	2002	42	33	5	0	17	41	6	235	379
	2004	34	37	5	40	28	17	16	239	416
	2006	35	39	5	41	130	17	25	241	533
United States Etats-Unis	2002	37	55	27	25	130	256	301	169	1 000
	2004	40	71	27	50	154	261	300	240	1 143
	2006	41	79	27	53	159	273	303	243	1 178
United States Virgin Is. Iles Vierges américaines	2002	1	2	5	0	0	0	0	7	15
	2004	1	5	5	1	10	0	0	9	31
	2006	2	5	5	2	10	0	0	11	35
Uruguay Uruguay	2002	6	11	3	0	2	0	1	1	24
	2004	6	24	3	4	11	0	1	1	50
	2006	7	26	3	4	22	0	1	1	64
Uzbekistan Ouzbékistan	2002	9	9	2	0	4	0	1	1	26
	2004	7	16	2	0	4	0	1	1	31
	2006	10	16	2	0	5	0	1	1	35
Vanuatu Vanuatu	2002	5	7	2	0	0	0	0	9	23
	2004	5	7	2	0	5	0	0	10	29
	2006	5	8	2	0	7	2	0	10	34
Venezuela (Bolivarian Rep. of) Venezuela (Rép. bolivar. du)	2002	26	24	13	0	7	0	1	67	138
	2004	26	25	13	68	19	0	1	67	219
	2006	26	25	13	71	26	0	3	69	233
Viet Nam Viet Nam	2002	40	37	24	1	9	0	0	126	237
	2004	41	41	24	15	23	0	0	145	289
	2006	45	42	27	18	30	0	0	148	310
Wallis and Futuna Islands Iles Wallis et Futuna	2002	0	1	0	0	0	0	0	1	2
	2004	0	9	0	0	3	0	0	1	13
	2006	0	9	1	0	3	0	0	1	14

Threatened species — Number by taxonomic group (*continued*)
Espèces menacées — Nombre par groupe taxonomique (*suite*)

Country or area — Pays ou zone	Year Année	Mammals Mammifères	Birds Oiseaux	Reptiles Reptiles	Amphibians Amphibiens	Fishes Poissons	Molluscs Mollusques	Invertebrates Invertébrés	Plants Plantes	Total
Western Sahara Sahara occidental	2002	3	0	0	0	0	0	0	0	3
	2004	4	3	0	0	11	0	1	0	19
	2006	9	4	2	0	14	0	1	0	30
Yemen Yémen	2002	5	12	2	0	0	2	0	52	73
	2004	6	14	2	1	11	2	0	159	195
	2006	9	14	2	1	13	2	4	159	204
Zambia Zambie	2002	11	11	0	0	0	4	2	8	36
	2004	11	12	0	1	0	4	3	8	39
	2006	12	12	0	1	6	4	3	8	46
Zimbabwe Zimbabwe	2002	11	10	0	0	0	0	2	14	37
	2004	8	10	0	6	0	0	2	17	43
	2006	10	11	0	6	0	0	5	18	50

Source

The World Conservation Union (IUCN) / Species Survival Commission (SSC), Gland, Switzerland and Cambridge, United Kingdom, "IUCN Red List of Threatened Species", 2002, 2004 and 2006.

Notes

1 For statistical purposes, the data for China do not include those for the Hong Kong Special Administrative Region (Hong Kong SAR), Macao Special Administrative Region (Macao SAR) and Taiwan Province of China.

Source

Union mondiale pour la nature (UICN) / Commission de la sauvergarde des espèces, Gland, Suisse, et Cambridge, Royaume-Uni, "La liste rouge des espèces menacées de l'UICN", 2002, 2004 et 2006.

Notes

1 Pour la présentation des statistiques, les données pour la Chine ne comprennent pas la Région Administrative Spéciale de Hong Kong (Hong Kong RAS), la Région Administrative Spéciale de Macao (Macao RAS) et la province de Taiwan.

Technical notes: tables 52-55

Table 52: The data on land are compiled by the Food and Agriculture Organization of the United Nations (FAO). The protected areas data are taken from the United Nations Environment Programme (UNEP) World Conservation Monitoring Centre.

FAO's definitions of the land categories are as follows:

- *Land area*: Total area excluding area under inland water bodies. The definition of inland water bodies generally includes major rivers and lakes.
- *Arable land*: Land under temporary crops (double-cropped areas are counted only once); temporary meadows for mowing or pasture; land under market and kitchen gardens; and land temporarily fallow (less than five years). Abandoned land resulting from shifting cultivation is not included in this category. Data for "arable land" are not meant to indicate the amount of land that is potentially cultivable.
- *Permanent crops*: Land cultivated with crops that occupy the land for long periods and need not be replanted after each harvest, such as cocoa, coffee and rubber. This category includes land under flowering shrubs, fruit trees, nut trees and vines, but excludes land under trees grown for wood or timber.
- *Forest:* In the *Global Forest Resources Assessment 2005* the following definition is used for forest. Forest includes natural forests and forest plantations and is used to refer to land with a tree crown cover (or equivalent stocking level) of more than 10 per cent and area of more than 0.5 hectares. The trees should be able to reach a minimum height of 5 metres at maturity *in situ*. Forest may consist either of closed forest formations where trees of various storeys and undergrowth cover a high proportion of the ground; or open forest formations with a continuous vegetation cover in which the tree crown cover exceeds 10 per cent. Young natural stands and all plantations established for forestry purposes that have yet to reach a crown density of 10 per cent or tree height of 5 metres are included under forest, as are areas normally forming part of the forest area that are temporarily unstocked as a result of human intervention or natural causes but that are expected to revert to forest.

Table 53: The sources of the data presented on the emissions of carbon dioxide (CO_2) are the Carbon Dioxide Information Analysis Center (CDIAC) of the Oak Ridge National Laboratory in the USA and the Secretariat of the United Nations Framework Convention on Climate Change (UNFCCC). The majority of the data have been taken from the CDIAC database. The data taken from the UNFCCC database are footnoted accordingly.

Notes techniques : tableaux 52 à 55

Tableau 52: Les données relatives aux terres sont compilées par l'Organisation des Nations Unies pour l'alimentation et l'agriculture (FAO). Les données relatives aux aires protégées viennent du Centre mondial de surveillance pour la conservation du Programme des Nations Unies pour l'environnement (PNUE).

Les définitions de la FAO en ce qui concerne les terres sont les suivantes:

- *Superficie totale des terres*: Superficie totale, à l'exception des eaux intérieures. Les eaux intérieures désignent généralement les principaux fleuves et lacs.
- *Terres arables*: Terres affectées aux cultures temporaires (les terres sur lesquelles est pratiquée la double culture ne sont comptabilisées qu'une fois), prairies temporaires à faucher ou à pâturer, jardins maraîchers ou potagers et terres en jachère temporaire (moins de cinq ans). Cette définition ne comprend pas les terres abandonnées du fait de la culture itinérante. Les données relatives aux terres arables ne peuvent être utilisées pour calculer la superficie des terres aptes à l'agriculture.
- *Cultures permanentes*: Superficie des terres avec des cultures qui occupent la terre pour de longues périodes et qui ne nécessitent pas d'être replantées après chaque récolte, comme le cacao, le café et le caoutchouc. Cette catégorie comprend les terres plantées d'arbustes à fleurs, d'arbres fruitiers, d'arbres à noix et de vignes, mais ne comprend pas les terres plantées d'arbres destinés à la coupe.
- *Superficie forestière:* Dans *l'Évaluation des ressources forestières mondiales 2005*, la FAO a défini les forêts comme suit : les forêts, qui comprennent les forêts naturelles et les plantations forestières, sont des terres où le couvert arboré (ou la densité de peuplement équivalente) est supérieur à 10 % et représente une superficie de plus de 0,5 hectares. Les arbres doivent être susceptibles d'atteindre sur place, à leur maturité, une hauteur de 5 mètres minimum. Il peut s'agir de forêts denses, où les arbres de différente hauteur et le sous-bois couvrent une proportion importante du sol, ou de forêts claires, avec un couvert végétal continu, où le couvert arboré est supérieur à 10 %. Les jeunes peuplements naturels et toutes les plantations d'exploitation forestière n'ayant pas encore atteint une densité de couvert arboré de 10 % ou une hauteur de 5 mètres sont inclus dans les forêts, de même que les aires formant naturellement partie de la superficie forestière mais temporairement déboisées du fait d'une intervention de l'homme ou de causes naturelles, mais devant redevenir boisées.

Tableau 53: Les données sur les émissions de dioxyde de carbone (CO_2) proviennent du « Carbon Dioxide

The CDIAC estimates of CO_2 emissions are derived primarily from United Nations energy statistics on the consumption of liquid and solid fuels and gas consumption and flaring, and from cement production estimates from the Bureau of Mines of the U.S. Department of Interior. The emissions presented in the table are in units of 1,000 metric tons of carbon dioxide (CO_2); to convert CO_2 into carbon, divide the data by 3.66406. Full details of the procedures for calculating emissions are given in *Global, Regional, and National Annual C02 Emissions Estimates from Fossil Fuel Burning, Hydraulic Cement Production, and Gas Flaring* and in the CDIAC web site (see http://cdiac.esd.ornl.gov). Relative to other industrial sources for which CO_2 emissions are estimated, statistics on gas flaring activities are sparse and sporadic. In countries where gas flaring activities account for a considerable proportion of the total CO_2 emissions, the sporadic nature of gas flaring statistics may produce spurious or misleading trends in national CO_2 emissions over the period covered by the table.

The UNFCCC data in the table are indicated by a footnote, and cover countries parties to Annex I of the United Nations Framework Convention on Climate Change.

Table 54: Chlorofluorocarbons (CFCs) are synthetic compounds formerly used as refrigerants and aerosol propellants and known to be harmful to the ozone layer of the atmosphere. In the Montreal Protocol on Substances that Deplete the Ozone Layer, CFCs to be measured are found in vehicle air conditioning units, domestic and commercial refrigeration and air conditioning/heat pump equipment, aerosol products, portable fire extinguishers, insulation boards, panels and pipe covers, and pre-polymers.

The Parties to the Montreal Protocol on Substances that Deplete the Ozone Layer report data on CFCs to the Ozone Secretariat of the United Nations Environment Programme. The data on CFCs are shown in ozone depleting potential (ODP) tons that are calculated by multiplying the quantities in metric tons reported by the Parties, by the ODP of that substance, and added together.

Consumption is defined as production plus imports, minus exports of controlled substances. Feedstocks are exempt and are therefore subtracted from the imports and/or production. Similarly, the destroyed amounts are also subtracted. Negative numbers can occur when destruction and/or exports exceed production plus imports, implying that the destruction and/or exports are from stockpiles.

Table 55: Data on the number of threatened species in each group of animals and plants are compiled by the World Conservation Union (IUCN)/Species Survival Commission (SSC) and published in the IUCN *Red List of Threatened Species*.

Information Analysis Center » (CDIAC) du « Oak Ridge National Laboratory » (États-Unis) et du Secrétariat de la convention-cadre concernant les changements climatiques (CCCC) des Nations Unies. La majorité des données proviennent de la base de données du CDIAC. Les données qui proviennent du Secrétariat de la CCCC sont signalées par une note.

Les estimations du Carbon Dioxide Information Analysis Center sont obtenues essentiellement à partir des statistiques de l'énergie des Nations Unies relatives à la consommation de combustibles liquides et solides, à la production et à la consommation de gaz de torche, et des chiffres de production de ciment du « Bureau of Mines » du « Department of Interior » des États-Unis. Les émissions sont indiquées en milliers de tonnes de dioxyde de carbone (à diviser par 3.66406 pour avoir les chiffres de carbone). On peut voir dans le détail les méthodes utilisées pour calculer les émissions dans «*Global, Regional, and National Annual C02 Emissions Estimates from Fossil Fuel Burning, Hydraulic Cement Production, and Gas Flaring*» et sur le site Web du Carbon Dioxide Information Analysis Center (voir http://cdiac.esd.ornl.gov). Par rapport à d'autres sources industrielles pour lesquelles on calcule les émissions de CO_2, les statistiques sur la production de gaz de torche sont rares et sporadiques. Dans les pays où cette production représente une proportion considérable de l'ensemble des émissions de dioxyde de carbone, on peut voir apparaître de ce fait des chiffres parasites ou trompeurs pour ce qui est des tendances des émissions nationales de dioxyde de carbone durant la période visée par le tableau.

Les données provenant du secrétariat de la Convention-cadre sont signalées par une note, et couvrent les pays qui sont parties à l'Annexe 1 de la Convention-cadre des Nations Unies sur les changements climatiques.

Tableau 54: Les chlorofluorocarbones (CFC) sont des substances de synthèse utilisées comme réfrigérants et propulseurs d'aérosols, dont on sait qu'elles appauvrissent la couche d'ozone. Aux termes du Protocole de Montréal relatif à des substances qui appauvrissent la couche d'ozone, la production de certains CFC doit être mesurée : ils sont utilisés dans les climatiseurs de véhicules, le matériel domestique et commercial de réfrigération et de climatisation (pompes à chaleur), les produits sous forme d'aérosols, les extincteurs d'incendie portables, les planches, panneaux et gaines isolants, et les prépolymères.

Les Parties au Protocole de Montréal communiquent leurs données concernant les CFC au secrétariat de l'ozone du Programme des Nations Unies pour l'environnement. Les données sur les CFC, indiquées en tonnes de potentiel de destruction de l'ozone (PDO), sont calculées en multipliant

The list provides a catalogue of those species that are considered globally threatened. The categories used in the Red List are as follows: Extinct, Extinct in the Wild, Critically Endangered, Endangered, Vulnerable, Near Threatened and Data Deficient.

le nombre de tonnes signalé par les Parties par le potentiel de destruction coefficient de la substance considérée, et en faisant la somme de ces PDO.

La consommation est définie comme production de substances contrôlées, plus les importations, moins les exportations. Les produits intermédiaires de l'industrie sont exemptés, et on les soustrait donc des importations et/ou de la production. De même, on soustrait aussi les quantités détruites. On peut obtenir des quantités négatives, lorsque les quantités détruites et/ou exportées sont supérieures à la somme production + importations, ce qui signifie que les quantités détruites ou exportées ont été prélevées sur les stocks accumulés.

Tableau 55: Les données relatives aux espèces menacées pour chaque groupe d'animaux et de plantes, réunies par la Commission de la sauvegarde des espèces de l'Union mondiale pour la nature (UICN), sont publiées dans la *Liste rouge des espèces menacées* de l'UICN.

Cette liste répertorie les espèces animales considérées comme menacées à l'échelle mondiale, réparties entre les catégories ci-après : éteintes, éteintes à l'état sauvage, gravement menacées d'extinction, menacées d'extinction, vulnérables, quasi menacées, et catégorie à données insuffisantes.

Human resources in research and development (R & D)
Full-time equivalent (FTE)

Personnel employé dans la recherche et le développement (R–D)
Equivalent temps plein (ETP)

Country or area Pays ou zone	Year Année	Total R & D personnel Total du personnel de R-D	Researchers Chercheurs		Technicians and equivalent staff Techniciens et personnel assimilé		Other supporting staff Autre personnel de soutien
			Total M & W Total H & F	Women Femmes	Total M & W Total H & F	Women Femmes	Total M & W Total H & F
Algeria[1] — Algérie[1]	2005	7 331	5 593	2 043	1 134	...	604
American Samoa[1,2] — Samoa américaines[1,2]	2002	5	5	...	...	...	...
Argentina[3] Argentine[3]	1999	36 939	26 004	...	10 935[4]	...	...
	2000	37 515	26 420	20 233[2]	11 095[4]	...	...
	2001	37 444	25 656	19 945[2]	11 788[4]	...	...
	2002	37 413	26 083	20 888[2]	11 330[4]	...	...
	2003	39 393	27 367	22 068[2]	12 026[4]	...	...
	2004	42 454	29 471	23 487[2]	12 983[4]	...	...
Armenia[1,2] Arménie[1,2]	1999	6 528	4 443	...	413	...	1 672
	2000	7 309	4 971	2 565	373	...	1 965
	2001	6 965	5 087	2 175	415	...	1 463
	2002	6 737	4 927	2 314	451	...	1 359
	2003	6 277	4 667	2 138	313	...	1 297
	2004	6 685	4 788	2 235	423	...	1 474
	2005	6 892	5 056	2 329	345	...	1 491
Australia[5] Australie[5]	2000	95 621	66 001	...	...	...	...
	2002	107 209	73 173	...	...	...	...
	2004	119 384	81 740	...	...	...	...
Austria Autriche	2002	38 893[5]	24 124[5]	3 811[7]	10 194[5]	2 683[7]	4 575[5]
	2004	42 891[5]	25 955[5]	4 740[7]	12 067[5]	2 901[7]	4 869[5]
	2005[6]	46 612	28 207	...	...	...	...
Azerbaijan[2] Azerbaïdjan[2]	1999	15 678	10 161	4 883	1 349	...	4 168
	2000	15 809	10 168	4 971	1 478	...	4 163
	2001	15 929	10 139	5 069	1 552	...	4 238
	2002	16 019	10 195	5 236	1 609	...	4 215
	2003	17 190	10 830	5 541	1 825	...	4 535
	2004	17 712	11 531	6 110	1 749	...	4 432
	2005	18 164	11 603	6 056	1 825	...	4 736
Belarus[2] Bélarus[2]	1999	27 982	18 817	8 851	2 452	...	6 713
	2000	29 032	19 707	9 099	2 574	...	6 751
	2001	28 186	19 133	8 648	2 332	...	6 721
	2002	26 871	18 557	8 361	2 050	...	6 264
	2003	26 038	17 702	7 785	2 337	...	5 999
	2004	24 946	17 034	7 556	2 068	...	5 844
	2005	26 142	18 267	7 897	2 112	...	5 763
Belgium Belgique	1999[5]	49 466	29 732	...	10 890	...	8 844
	2000	53 391[5]	30 540[5]	7 786[7]	14 428[5]	4 263[7]	8 424[5]
	2001	55 949[5]	32 237[5]	8 254[7]	15 038[5]	4 497[7]	8 675[5]
	2002	52 054[5]	30 668[5]	8 316[7]	15 358[7]	4 498[7]	6 028[7]
	2003	52 256[5]	30 917[5]	8 585[7]	15 293[7]	4 572[7]	6 046[7]
	*2004[7]	52 911	31 465	...	...	...	...
	*2005[7]	54 128	31 953	...	...	...	...
Bolivia[3] Bolivie[3]	1999	810	600	429[2]	180	...	30
	2000	820	600	419[2]	170	...	50
	#2001	1 200	1 050	495[2]	50	...	100
	2002	1 190	1 040	...	50	...	100
Botswana[1,2] — Botswana[1,2]	2005	2 140	1 728	529	...	412	...

Human resources in research and development (R & D) — Full-time equivalent (FTE) (*continued*)

Personnel employé dans la recherche et le développement (R–D) — Equivalent temps plein (ETP) (*suite*)

Country or area Pays ou zone	Year Année	Total R & D personnel Total du personnel de R - D	Researchers Chercheurs: Total M & W Total H & F	Researchers Chercheurs: Women Femmes	Technicians and equivalent staff Techniciens et personnel assimilé: Total M & W Total H & F	Technicians and equivalent staff Techniciens et personnel assimilé: Women Femmes	Other supporting staff Autre personnel de soutien: Total M & W Total H & F
Brazil[3] Brésil[3]	2000	119 279	64 002	48 679[2]	55 277[4]	...	...
	2001	122 044	67 785	52 326[2]	54 259[4]	...	...
	2002	125 092	71 859	56 235[2]	53 233[4]	...	...
	2003	142 229	79 301	62 677[2]	62 928[4]	...	...
	2004	157 595	84 979	67 616[2]	72 616[4]	...	...
Brunei Darussalam Brunéi Darussalam	2002	140	99	79[2]	...	...	...
	2003	140	98	78[2]	...	...	...
Bulgaria[7] Bulgarie[7]	1999	16 087	10 580	4 656	3 829	2 578	1 678
	2000	15 259	9 479	4 354	3 833	2 441	1 947
	2001	14 949	9 217	4 247	3 786	2 355	1 946
	2002	15 029	9 223	4 353	3 713	2 374	2 093
	2003	15 453	9 589	4 535	3 735	2 294	2 129
	2004	15 647	9 827	4 642	3 721	2 236	2 099
	2005	15 853	10 053	...	...	...	...
Burkina Faso[1] Burkina Faso[1]	2001	820	232	...	242	...	346
	2002	828	236	34	244	...	348
	2003	888	251	32[8]	260	...	377
	2004	890	293	34[9]	227	...	370
	2005	888	247	32	225	...	416
Cambodia[1,6] — Cambodge[1,6]	2002	494	223	50	170	...	102
Cameroon[1] — Cameroun[1]	2005	...	462	88	...	...	...
Canada Canada	1999[5]	153 197	98 813	...	34 017	...	20 367
	2000[5]	167 861	108 492	...	38 070	...	21 299
	*2001[5,6]	178 980	114 957	...	40 371	...	23 652
	*2002[5,6]	177 120	112 624	...	40 382	...	24 114
	2003[10]	189 520	118 860	...	44 330	...	26 330
	2004[10]	199 060	125 330	...	46 890	...	26 840
Cape Verde[1] Cap-Vert[1]	2001	130	45	...	14	...	71
	2002	151	60	56[2]	15	...	76
Chile[3] Chili[3]	1999	10 774	6 157	...	4 617[4]	...	...
	2000	11 073	6 328	...	4 745[4]	...	...
	2001	11 173	6 446	...	4 727[4]	...	...
	2002	...	6 942	2 785[2]	...	...	...
	#2003	20 104	12 322	5 168[2]	4 723	...	3 059
	2004	21 691	13 427	5 503[2]	4 865	...	3 399
China[5,11] Chine[5,11]	1999[9]	821 700	531 100	...	...	...	...
	#2000	922 131	695 062	...	...	...	...
	2001	956 482	742 726	...	...	...	...
	2002	1 035 197	810 525	...	...	...	...
	2003	1 094 831	862 108	...	...	...	...
	2004	1 152 617	926 252	...	...	...	...
China, Hong Kong SAR Chine, Hong Kong RAS	1999	10 118	7 922	...	1 302	...	896
	2000	9 802	7 728	...	1 374	...	699
	2001	11 041	9 149	...	1 162	...	730
	2002	12 890	10 639	...	1 532	...	719
	2003	16 864	13 497	...	2 138	...	1 228
	2004	18 846	14 594	...	2 904	...	1 348
China, Macao SAR[1,6] Chine, Macao RAS[1,6]	2001	196	114	20	74	...	8
	2002	196	105	16	81	...	10
	2003	249	147	27	94	...	8
	2004	349	244	48	97	...	8
	2005	409	298	62	102	...	9

Country or area Pays ou zone	Year Année	Total R & D personnel Total du personnel de R - D	Researchers Chercheurs		Technicians and equivalent staff Techniciens et personnel assimilé		Other supporting staff Autre personnel de soutien
			Total M & W Total H & F	Women Femmes	Total M & W Total H & F	Women Femmes	Total M & W Total H & F
Colombia[3] Colombie[3]	1999	5 925	4 065	2 193[2]	1 860[4]	...	...
	2000	6 262	4 240	2 335[2]	2 022[4]	...	...
	2001	#4 383	#3 136	2 473[2]	#1 247[4]	...	...
	2002	5 534	3 539	2 846[2]	1 995[4]	...	...
	#2003	8 216	4 829	4 038[2]	3 387[4]	...	...
	2004	9 918	5 632	4 780[2]	4 286[4]	...	...
Congo[1] Congo[1]	1999	227	110	15	114	22	3
	2000	217	102	13	111	22	4
Costa Rica[2,3] Costa Rica[2,3]	1999	...	1 412	...	...	...	...
	2003	...	1 171	480	...	...	...
	2004	...	1 078	445	...	...	...
Croatia Croatie	1999	8 827	5 523	2 426	1 615	954	1 689
	2000	10 399	6 772	2 929	1 750	...	1 877
	2001	10 043	6 656	2 964	1 676	...	1 711
	2002	12 960	8 572	3 651	1 981	...	2 407
	2003[7]	9 148	5 861	2 799	2 056	1 086[7]	1 231
	2004[7]	11 162	7 140	3 256	2 573	1 046	1 449
Cuba[2,3] Cuba[2,3]	1999	29 063	5 468[9]	...	23 595[4]	...	...
	2000	29 568	5 378[9]	...	24 190[4]	...	...
	2001	32 721	5 849[9]	...	26 872[4]	...	...
	2002	34 326	6 057[9]	...	28 269[4]	...	...
	2003	33 855	5 075[9]	...	28 780[4]	...	...
	2004	34 094	5 115[9]	...	28 979[4]	...	...
Cyprus[7] Chypre[7]	1999	681	278	81	197	71	205
	2000	680	303	91	195	68	181
	2001	690	333	105	186	65	169
	2002	822	435	137	206	80	181
	2003	922	490	157	239	87	194
	2004	1 017	583	197	243	95	191
	*2005	1 075	630	...	...	...	...
Czech Republic République tchèque	1999[5]	24 106	13 535	...	7 403	...	3 168
	2000	24 198[5]	13 852[5]	3 551[7]	7 319[5]	3 038[7]	3 027[5]
	2001	26 107[5]	14 987[5]	3 853[7]	8 109[5]	3 447[7]	3 011[5]
	2002	26 032[5]	14 974[5]	3 917[7]	8 090[5]	3 216[7]	2 968[5]
	2003	27 957[5]	15 809[5]	4 121[7]	9 001[5]	3 347[7]	3 147[5]
	2004	28 765[5]	16 300[5]	4 052[7]	9 445[5]	3 407[7]	3 020[5]
	2005	#43 370[5]	#24 169[5]	6 349[7]	13 773[5]	5 153[7]	5 429[5]
Dem. Rep. of the Congo[1,2] Rép. dém. du Congo[1,2]	2004	31 923	9 072	...	1 444	...	21 407
	2005	33 478	10 411	...	1 510	...	21 557
Denmark Danemark	1999	36 452[5]	18 945[5,12]	4 986[7]	...	...	...
	2000[5]	37 693	...	...	...	...	...
	2001	39 893[5]	19 453[5,12,13]	5 559[7]	...	...	...
	2002	42 406[5]	#25 546[5]	#6 930[7]	...	...	...
	2003	41 607[5]	24 882[5]	6 925[7]	...	...	...
	2004[5]	42 687	26 167	...	...	...	...
	*2005	43 545[5]	28 187[7]	...	...	...	...
Ecuador[3] Equateur[3]	#2001	1 164[2]	514	157[2]	516[2,4]	...	...
	2002	1 271[2]	550	160[2]	575[2,4]	...	...
	2003	1 555[2]	645	241[2]	710[2,4]	...	...
El Salvador[2,3] El Salvador[2,3]	1999	...	487	88	...	...	...
	2003	...	252	78	...	...	...
	2004	...	258	80	...	...	...

Country or area Pays ou zone	Year Année	Total R & D personnel Total du personnel de R-D	Researchers / Chercheurs: Total M & W Total H & F	Researchers / Chercheurs: Women Femmes	Technicians and equivalent staff / Techniciens et personnel assimilé: Total M & W Total H & F	Technicians and equivalent staff / Techniciens et personnel assimilé: Women Femmes	Other supporting staff / Autre personnel de soutien: Total M & W Total H & F
Estonia[7] Estonie[7]	1999	4 545	3 002	1 252	750	529	793
	2000	3 710	2 666	1 109	530	368	514
	2001	3 745	2 681	1 125	472	296	592
	2002	4 129	3 059	1 262	524	317	546
	2003	4 144	3 017	1 273	573	362	554
	2004	4 735	3 369	1 390	654	370	712
	*2005	4 363	3 331	…	…	…	…
Ethiopia[1] — Ethiopie[1]	2005	5 112	1 608	111	779	…	2 725
Finland[5] Finlande[5]	1999	50 604	32 676[12]	12 355[2]	…	…	…
	2000	52 604	34 847[12]	12 904[2]	…	…	…
	2001	53 424	36 889[12]	13 814[2]	…	…	…
	2002	55 044	38 632[12]	15 025[2]	…	…	…
	2003	57 196	41 724[12]	15 931[2]	…	…	…
	2004	58 281	#41 004	#14 834[2,12]	…	…	…
	2005	57 471	39 582	…	…	…	…
France[5] France[5]	1999	314 452	160 424	…	…	…	…
	2000	#327 466	#172 070	58 124[2,9]	…	…	…
	2001	333 518	177 372	59 630[2,9]	…	…	…
	2002	343 718	186 420	#64 333[2]	…	…	…
	2003	346 078	192 790	66 713[2]	…	…	…
	2004	352 485	200 064	68 818[2]	…	…	…
Gabon[1,2] — Gabon[1,2]	2004	188	80	25	68	…	40
Gambia[1] Gambie[1]	2001	77	40	…	25	…	12
	2002	77	40	…	25	…	12
	2003	81	44	…	25	…	12
	2004	82	44	3	28	…	10
	2005	84	46	4	28	…	10
Georgia[2] Géorgie[2]	1999	15 138	12 786	…	2 352	…	…
	2000	12 726	11 071	…	1 655	…	…
	2001	15 100	12 400	6 400	1 180	…	1 520
	2002	16 031	11 997	6 165	1 246	…	2 788
	2003	17 819	11 572	5 809	1 895	…	4 352
	2004	16 698	10 910	5 664	2 262	…	3 526
	2005	13 415	8 112	4 275	1 810	…	3 493
Germany Allemagne	1999	479 599[5]	254 691[5]	36 616[7]	126 420[7]	78 836[7]	…
	2000[5]	484 734	257 874[6]	…	…	…	…
	2001	480 606[5]	264 385[5]	42 588[7]	…	…	…
	2002[5]	480 004	265 812[6]	…	…	…	…
	2003	472 533[5]	268 942[5]	43 422[7]	89 957[5]	…	113 634[5]
	2004	470 971[5]	270 749[5]	…	87 302[7]	…	112 920[7]
	2005[5,6]	469 500	268 100	…	…	…	…
Greece Grèce	1999	26 382[5]	14 748[5]	…	5 839[5]	5 673[2]	5 796[5]
	2001	30 226[5]	14 371[5]	4 710[7]	9 636[5]	5 796[2]	6 219[5]
	2003	31 849[5]	15 631[5]	5 198[7]	9 207[7]	5 724[2,7]	7 011[7]
	*2005[5]	34 004	17 024	…	…	…	…
Greenland Groenland	2001[6]	35	30	10	5[4]	…	…
	2002	34	30	9	3[4]	…	…
	2003[6]	41	37	12	5[4]	…	…
	2004	48	40	11	8[4]	…	…
Guinea[1,2] — Guinée[1,2]	2000	3 711	2 117	122	768	…	826

Country or area Pays ou zone	Year Année	Total R & D personnel Total du personnel de R - D	Researchers / Chercheurs Total M & W Total H & F	Researchers / Chercheurs Women Femmes	Technicians and equivalent staff / Techniciens et personnel assimilé Total M & W Total H & F	Technicians and equivalent staff / Techniciens et personnel assimilé Women Femmes	Other supporting staff / Autre personnel de soutien Total M & W Total H & F
Honduras[2,3] Honduras[2,3]	2000	2 167	479	160	1 688[4]	712[4]	...
	2001	2 262	525	164	1 737[4]	677[4]	...
	2002	2 321	516	149	1 805[4]	830[4]	...
	2003	2 280	539	143	1 741[4]	731[4]	...
Hungary[5,14] Hongrie[5,14]	1999	21 329	12 579	7 554[2]	5 037	...	3 713
	2000	23 534	14 406	9 537[2]	5 166	...	3 962
	2001	22 942	14 666	9 363[2]	4 752	...	3 524
	2002	23 703	14 965	10 039[2]	4 936	...	3 802
	2003	23 311	15 180	10 647[2]	4 641	...	3 490
	2004	22 826	14 904	10 484[2]	*4 713	...	*3 209
	2005	23 239	15 878	10 731[2]	...	...	...
Iceland Islande	1999	2 390[5]	1 578[5]	501[7]	461[5]	169[5]	352[5]
	2000[6,7]	2 646	...	...	...	...	...
	2001	2 901[5]	1 859[5,13]	641[7]	587[7,13]	269[7]	463[7,13]
	2002[5,6]	2 797	...	...	...	...	...
	2003	2 940[5]	1 917[5]	690[7]	594[5]	248[7]	429[5]
	2004[7]	3 050	1 987	...	...	...	...
India — Inde	1999	318 443	115 936	13 912	90 045	...	112 462
Indonesia Indonésie	2000	56 356	44 984	...	...	...	...
	2001	51 544	42 722	...	...	...	...
Iran (Islamic Rep. of)[2] — Iran (Rép. islamique d')[2]	2004	91 584	51 899	10 300	22 186	...	17 499
Ireland Irlande	1999[5,6]	11 929	7 877	...	...	...	...
	2000[5,6]	12 762	8 516	...	2 598	...	1 648
	2001[5]	13 317	8 949	...	2 347	...	2 021
	2002	13 582[5,6]	9 376[5,6]	2 602[7]	2 369[5,6]	586[7]	1 837[5,6]
	2003	14 450[5]	10 039[5]	2 883[7]	2 511[5]	633[7]	1 900[5]
	2004[5]	*15 713	*10 910	...	2 667[6]	...	2 136[6]
	*2005[5,6]	16 168	11 151	...	...	...	...
Italy[5] Italie[5]	1999	142 506	65 098[13]	26 450[2]	77 620[13]	...	...
	2000	150 066	66 110	27 908[2]	...	...	...
	2001	153 905	66 702	28 176[2]	...	...	...
	2002	164 023	71 242	31 220[2]	...	...	...
	2003	161 828	70 332	31 483[2]	...	...	...
	2004	164 026	72 012	33 064[2]	...	...	...
Japan[5] Japon[5]	1999	919 132	658 910	...	84 527	...	175 695
	2000	896 847	647 572	...	78 951	...	170 324
	2001	892 057	675 898	85 207[2]	68 754	22 433[2]	147 405
	2002	#857 300	#646 547	88 674[2]	67 040	22 964[2]	143 713
	2003	882 414	675 330	96 133[2]	67 389	24 650[2]	139 695
	2004	896 211	677 206	98 690[2]	...	...	...
Jordan[2] — Jordanie[2]	2003	42 153	15 891	3 385	19 322	2 073	6 940
Kazakhstan Kazakhstan	1999	13 850	9 624	4 678	1 179	...	3 047
	2000	12 829	9 009	4 544	1 183	...	2 637
	#2001	15 339[15]	9 223	4 624	1 140	...	4 976[15]
	2002	15 998[15]	9 366	4 558	1 364	...	5 268[15]
	2003	16 578[15]	9 899	4 809	1 300	...	5 379[15]
	2004	16 715[15]	10 382	5 017	1 102	...	5 231[15]
	2005	18 912[15]	11 910	6 013	1 270	...	5 732[15]

Country or area Pays ou zone	Year Année	Total R & D personnel Total du personnel de R - D	Researchers / Chercheurs Total M & W Total H & F	Researchers / Chercheurs Women Femmes	Technicians and equivalent staff / Techniciens et personnel assimilé Total M & W Total H & F	Technicians and equivalent staff / Techniciens et personnel assimilé Women Femmes	Other supporting staff / Autre personnel de soutien Total M & W Total H & F
Korea, Republic of[1,5] Corée, République de[1,5]	1999	137 874	100 210	13 009[2]	26 160	...	11 504
	2000	138 077	108 370	16 385[2]	21 202	...	8 505
	2001	165 715	136 337	19 930[2]	21 314	...	8 064
	2002	172 270	141 917	22 057[2]	23 428	...	6 925
	2003	186 214	151 254	22 613[2]	26 926	18 158[2]	8 034
	2004	194 055	156 220	25 198[2]	...	...	...
	2005	215 345	179 812	30 174[2]	...	...	...
Kuwait[1] Koweït[1]	#2001	403	160[2]	37[2]	184	...	59
	2002	402	163[2]	37[2]	201	...	38
	2003	427	203[2]	48[2]	224	...	...
	2004	458	195[2]	43[2]	235	...	28
	2005	489	200[2]	42[2]	254	...	35
Kyrgyzstan[2] Kirghizistan[2]	1999	3 088	2 284	1 114	205	...	599
	2000	2 886	2 121	1 028	194	...	571
	2001	2 958	2 099	1 001	248	...	611
	2002	2 922	2 065	1 019	257	...	600
	2003	2 699	1 979	990	229	...	491
	2004	2 844	2 019	971	307	...	518
	2005	2 911	2 187	977	226	...	498
Latvia Lettonie	1999	4 301	2 626	1 277	726	419[7]	949
	#2000	5 449	3 814	1 881	635	371[7]	1 000
	2001	5 476	3 497	1 927	809	536[7]	1 170
	2002	5 294	3 451	1 835	660	367[7]	1 183
	2003[7]	4 858	3 203	1 707	742	416	913
	2004[7]	5 103	3 324	1 806	802	456	977
	2005[7]	5 483	3 282	1 636	1 062	554	1 139
Lesotho[1,2]—Lesotho[1,2]	2002	196	81	31[9]	47	...	68
Lithuania[7] Lituanie[7]	1999	12 794	8 539	...	1 983	...	2 272
	2000	11 791	7 777	3 388	1 774	1 156	2 240
	2001	11 949	8 075	3 766	1 725	1 215	2 149
	2002	9 531	6 326	2 989	1 490	1 058	1 715
	2003	9 648	6 606	3 196	1 476	1 029	1 566
	2004	10 557	7 356	3 481	1 531	992	1 670
	2005	11 002	7 637	3 706	1 436	939	1 929
Luxembourg Luxembourg	2000	3 663[5]	1 646[5]	...	#1 673[7]	...	...
	2003	4 010[5]	1 949[5]	322[7]	1 685[5,6]	...	376[5,6]
	2004[5]	4 318	2 031	...	...	...	...
	*2005	4 360[5]	2 091[5]	...	1 694[7]	...	575[7]
Madagascar[1] Madagascar[1]	1999	1 114	227	...	862	...	25
	2000	985	240	...	730	...	15
	#2001	1 741	822	253	243	...	676
	2002	1 712	788	241	245	...	679
	2003	1 696	814	259	188	...	694
	2004	1 705	847	410	175	...	683
	2005	1 477	806	246	119	...	552
Malaysia Malaisie	2000	10 060	6 423	2 045	921	...	2 716
	2002	10 731	7 157	2 451	1 379	...	2 195
	2004	17 887	12 669	4 701	1 598	...	3 619
Malta[7] Malte[7]	2002	475	272	...	45	...	158
	2003	413	276	...	...	...	...
	#2004	717	436	109	147	17	134
	*2005	701	442	121	144	16	114

Country or area Pays ou zone	Year Année	Total R & D personnel Total du personnel de R - D	Researchers / Chercheurs Total M & W Total H & F	Researchers / Chercheurs Women Femmes	Technicians and equivalent staff / Techniciens et personnel assimilé Total M & W Total H & F	Technicians and equivalent staff / Techniciens et personnel assimilé Women Femmes	Other supporting staff / Autre personnel de soutien Total M & W Total H & F
Mexico[5] Mexique[5]	1999	39 736[6]	21 879[6,13]	…	9 525[10,13]	…	8 442[10,13]
	2001	43 455	23 390[10,13]	…	9 268[10,13]	…	8 735[10,13]
	2003	60 039	33 484	14 073[2,6]	15 304[10,13]	…	11 013[10,13]
Monaco[1,2] Monaco[1,2]	2004	18	9	4	6	…	3
	2005	18	10	5	5	…	3
Mongolia[1,2] Mongolie[1,2]	1999	1 955	1 794	…	…	…	161
	2000	2 113	1 631	…	294	150	188
	#2001	2 752	2 087	901	215	…	450
	2002	2 879	1 973	923	177	…	729
	2003	2 638	1 995	909	154	…	489
	2004	2 642	1 991	907	146	…	505
	2005	2 283	1 731	819	81	…	471
Morocco[2] Maroc[2]	1999	…	24 713[1]	5 009[9]	…	…	…
	2000	…	24 760[1]	4 957[9]	…	…	…
	2001	…	24 719[1]	5 061[9]	…	…	…
	2002	…	25 790[1]	5 133[9]	…	…	…
	2003	…	23 559[1]	6 049[9]	…	…	…
	2004	…	24 483[1]	6 872	…	…	…
	2005	…	24 835[1]	6 580	…	…	…
Mozambique[1,2] — Mozambique[1,2]	2002	2 467[9]	468	…	1 999[4,9]	…	…
Myanmar[1] Myanmar[1]	1999	#2 797	510	…	#2 238	…	49
	2001	4 373	574	…	3 754	…	46
	2002	7 418	837	…	6 499	…	82
Nepal — Népal	2002	6 500	1 500	450[2]	3 500	…	1 500
Netherlands Pays-Bas	1999	86 774[5]	40 390[5]	…	22 397[7]	…	23 985[7]
	2000[5]	87 999	42 088	…	24 347	…	21 563
	2001[5]	89 206	45 517	…	22 264	…	21 428
	2002	87 423[5]	#38 159[5]	…	28 026[7]	…	21 240[7]
	2003	85 986[5]	37 282[5]	7 852[2]	28 508[7]	7 767[2,6,7]	20 195[7]
	*2004[5]	91 594	…	…	…	…	…
New Zealand[5] Nouvelle-Zélande[5]	1999	13 085	8 768	…	2 568	…	1 750
	#2001	17 768	13 133	8 657[2]	2 784	1 617[2]	1 851
	2003	21 410	15 568	…	3 285	…	2 556
Nicaragua[2,3] Nicaragua[2,3]	2002	456	256	96[9]	200[4]	…	…
	2004	371	326	…	#45	15[4]	…
Niger[1] Niger[1]	2001	611	109	…	122	…	380
	2002	594	104	…	118	…	372
	2003	569	100	…	115	…	354
	2004	599	106	…	133	…	360
	2005	595	101	…	137	…	357
Nigeria[1,2] Nigéria[1,2]	2001	45 096	18 867	3 578	7 889	…	18 340
	2002	45 798	18 426	3 359	7 945	…	19 427
	2003	50 534	22 046	4 110	7 843	…	20 645
	2004	…	23 871	4 132	8 215	…	…
	2005	59 242	27 482	4 624	8 958	…	22 803
Norway[5] Norvège[5]	1999	25 400	18 295[12]	8 615[2,12]	…	…	…
	2001	27 068	20 048	9 883[2,12]	…	…	…
	2002	27 335	…	…	…	…	…
	2003	29 014	20 989	10 505[2]	…	…	…
	2004	29 745	21 161	…	…	…	…
	2005	30 557	21 851	…	…	…	…
Pakistan — Pakistan	2005	53 159	12 689	2 053	6 471	…	33 999

Country or area Pays ou zone	Year Année	Total R & D personnel Total du personnel de R - D	Researchers / Chercheurs Total M & W Total H & F	Researchers / Chercheurs Women Femmes	Technicians and equivalent staff / Techniciens et personnel assimilé Total M & W Total H & F	Technicians and equivalent staff / Techniciens et personnel assimilé Women Femmes	Other supporting staff / Autre personnel de soutien Total M & W Total H & F
Panama[3] Panama[3]	#1999	962	288	…	674[4]	257[2,4]	…
	2000	964	286	…	678[4]	273[2,4,8]	…
	2001	894	276	…	618[4]	231[2,4]	…
	2002	1 469	297	…	1 172[4]	442[2,4]	…
	2003	1 512	304	…	1 208[4]	477[2,4]	…
	#2004	…	…	…	…	130	630[2]
Paraguay[3] Paraguay[3]	2001	1 149	481	294[2]	669[4]	471[2,4]	…
	2002	1 106	455	398[2]	651[4]	515[2,4]	…
	2003	1 114	458	406[2]	656[4]	504[2,4]	…
	2004	1 204	495	444[2]	709[4]	525[2,4]	…
Peru[2,3] — Pérou[2,3]	2004	8 434	4 965	…	1 757	…	1 712
Philippines[2] Philippines[2]	2002	9 325	7 203	3 893	956	…	1 166
	2003	13 488	8 866	4 674	1 245	…	3 377
Poland Pologne	1999[5]	82 368	56 433	…	15 362	…	10 573
	2000[5]	78 925	55 174	33 572[2]	13 648	10 578[2]	10 103
	2001	77 232[5]	56 148[5]	…	12 364[7]	…	8 720[7]
	2002[5]	76 214	56 725	…	11 435	…	8 054
	2003	77 040[5]	58 595[5]	21 947[7]	10 881[5]	8 430[2,7]	7 564[5]
	2004	78 362[5]	60 944[5]	22 684[7]	10 044[7]	7 844[2,7]	7 374[5]
	2005	76 761[5]	62 162[5]	…	8 947[7]	…	5 652[5]
Portugal Portugal	1999[5]	20 806	15 752	12 255[2]	2 479	…	2 576
	2000[6]	21 888[5]	16 738[5]	7 437[7]	2 676[5]	…	2 473[5]
	2001	22 970[5]	17 725[5]	7 940[7]	2 874[5]	1 056[7]	2 371[5]
	2002[6]	24 250[5]	18 984[5]	8 538[7]	3 031[5]	1 164[7]	2 235[5]
	2003	25 529[5]	20 242[5]	9 136[7]	3 189[5]	1 272[7]	2 098[5]
	*2004[6]	25 590	20 623	…	…	…	…
	*2005	25 651	21 003	…	…	…	…
Republic of Moldova[2] République de Moldova[2]	1999	2 479	722	208	1 005	…	752
	2000	2 395	737	212	967	…	691
	2001	2 262	738	222	888	…	636
	2002	2 201	729	221	855	…	617
Romania Roumanie	1999	44 091[5]	23 473[5]	10 335[7]	8 843[7]	5 155[7]	11 775[7]
	2000	33 892[5]	20 476[5]	8 785[7]	6 482[7]	3 853[7]	6 934[7]
	2001	32 639[5]	19 726[5]	8 551[7]	5 952[7]	3 447[7]	6 961[7]
	2002	32 799[5]	20 286[5]	9 181[7]	6 436[7]	3 540[7]	6 077[7]
	2003	33 077[5]	20 965[5]	9 340[7]	5 434[7]	3 174[7]	6 678[7]
	2004	33 361[5]	21 257[5]	9 480[7]	5 525[7]	3 199[7]	6 579[7]
Russian Federation Fédération de Russie	1999	989 291[5]	497 030[5]	186 264[2,5,9]	80 498[7]	…	411 763[7]
	2000	1 007 257[5]	506 420[5]	187 792[2,5,9]	83 490[7]	…	417 348[7]
	2001	1 008 091[5]	505 778[5]	185 609[2,5,9]	83 914[7]	…	418 399[7]
	2002	986 854[5]	491 944[5]	179 120[2,5,9]	83 413[7]	…	411 497[7]
	2003	973 382[5]	487 477[5]	177 538[2,5,9]	80 514[7]	…	405 391[7]
	2004	951 569[5]	477 647[5]	172 177[2,5,9]	79 560[7]	…	394 362[7]
	2005[5]	919 716	464 577	165 993[2,9]	…	…	…
Saint Helena[1] Sainte-Hélène[1]	1999	40	4	1	38	13	…
	2000	33	2	…	8	4	23
Saint Lucia[2] — Sainte-Lucie[2]	1999	311	74	10[9]	237	…	…
Saint Vincent-Grenadines[2] Saint Vincent-Grenadines[2]	2001	129	20	…	109	…	…
	2002	131	21	…	110	…	…
Saudi Arabia[1,2] Arabie saoudite[1,2]	1999	3 515	1 218	216	1 353	…	944
	2000	3 601	1 218	220	1 427	…	956
	2001	3 708	1 239	225[9]	1 498	…	971
	2002	4 182	1 513	263	1 674	…	995

Country or area / Pays ou zone	Year / Année	Total R & D personnel / Total du personnel de R - D	Researchers / Chercheurs: Total M & W / Total H & F	Researchers / Chercheurs: Women / Femmes	Technicians and equivalent staff / Techniciens et personnel assimilé: Total M & W / Total H & F	Technicians and equivalent staff / Techniciens et personnel assimilé: Women / Femmes	Other supporting staff / Autre personnel de soutien: Total M & W / Total H & F
Senegal[1,2] — Sénégal[1,2]	2005	4 200	2 349	...	1 751	...	100
Serbia and Montenegro[1,2,16] Serbie-et-Monténégro[1,2,16]	1999	24 198	12 163	4 755	5 651	...	6 384
	2000	23 117	11 969	4 815	5 448	...	5 700
	2001	19 415	10 071	4 246	4 518	...	4 826
	2002	21 291	10 855	4 663	4 631	...	5 805
	2003	22 054	11 353	4 968	4 732	...	5 969
	2004	22 485	11 637	5 071	4 844	...	6 004
	2005	22 641	11 551	5 050	4 894	...	6 196
Seychelles[1] — Seychelles[1]	2005	180	13	4	53	...	114
Singapore Singapour	1999	15 097	12 598	...	1 450	...	1 049
	2000	19 365	16 633	...	1 360	...	1 372
	2001	19 453	16 741	...	1 435	...	1 277
	2002	21 871	18 120	5 517[2]	1 586	...	2 165
	2003	23 514	20 024	5 938[2]	...	...	...
	2004	25 492	21 359	6 506[2]	...	...	...
	2005	28 586	23 789	7 346[2]	...	...	...
Slovakia Slovaquie	1999	14 849[5]	9 204[5]	3 516[7]	3 858[5]	2 198[7]	1 787[5]
	2000	15 221[5]	9 955[5]	3 867[7]	3 597[5]	1 979[7]	1 669[5]
	2001	14 422[5]	9 585[5]	3 817[7]	3 323[5]	1 798[7]	1 514[5]
	2002	13 631[5]	9 181[5]	3 749[7]	3 032[5]	1 586[7]	1 418[5]
	2003	13 354[5]	9 627[5]	3 946[7]	2 483[5]	1 433[7]	1 244[5]
	2004	14 329[5]	10 718[5]	4 427[7]	2 402[5]	1 331[7]	1 209[5]
	2005	14 404[5]	10 921[5]	4 484[7]	2 245[7]	1 218[7]	1 238[7]
Slovenia Slovénie	1999	8 495[5]	4 427[5]	1 487[7]	3 088[7]	758[7]	980[7]
	2000	8 568[5]	4 336[5]	1 525[7]	3 213[7]	773[7]	1 019[7]
	2001	8 608[5]	4 498[5]	1 547[7]	3 146[7]	1 256[7]	964[7]
	2002	8 615[5]	4 642[5]	1 606[7]	3 140[7]	1 199[7]	833[7]
	2003	6 805[5]	3 775[5]	1 202[7]	2 281[7]	838[7]	749[7]
	2004	7 132[5]	4 030[5]	1 288[7]	2 323[7]	882[7]	779[7]
	2005	*7 021[5]	*3 834[5]	*1 288[7]	2 487[7]	*929[7]	*700[7]
South Africa Afrique du Sud	2001	21 195	14 182	5 112	3 374	...	3 639
	2003	25 190	14 131	5 365	5 143	...	5 916
	2004	29 696	17 915	6 852	5 176	...	6 606
Spain Espagne	1999	102 237[5]	61 568[5]	19 989[7]	23 593[5]	6 483[7]	17 076[5]
	2000[5]	120 618	76 670	...	25 622	...	18 326
	2001	125 750[5]	80 081[5]	28 208[7]	28 460[5]	7 437[7]	17 209[5]
	2002	134 258[5]	83 318[5]	29 767[7]	30 376[5]	9 561[7]	20 564[5]
	2003	151 487[5]	92 523[5]	33 985[7]	36 278[5]	11 381[7]	22 687[5]
	2004	161 933[5]	100 994[5]	37 580[7]	37 871[7]	12 578[7]	23 068[7]
	*2005[5,6]	173 804	109 753	...	...	...	...
Sri Lanka Sri Lanka	2000[1]	...	2 537	1 294[2,9]	1 551[2]	...	...
	#2004	5 475	2 679	861	1 474	...	1 322
Sudan[2] Soudan[2]	1999	14 923	7 300	1 554	2 947	...	4 676
	2000	15 333	7 500	1 644	3 028	...	4 805
	2001	16 050	7 850	1 664	3 170	...	5 030
	2002	18 604	9 100	2 754	3 674	...	5 830
	2003	18 808	9 200	2 784	3 714	...	5 894
	2004	19 772	9 340	2 830	4 641	...	5 791
	2005	23 726	11 208	...	5 569	...	6 949
Sweden Suède	1999[5]	66 674	39 921	...	...	...	...
	2001[5]	72 190	45 995	...	...	...	...
	2003	72 978[5]	47 836[5]	7 841[7]	...	...	...
	2005[5]	77 925	54 041	...	...	...	...

Country or area Pays ou zone	Year Année	Total R & D personnel Total du personnel de R-D	Researchers / Chercheurs: Total M & W Total H & F	Researchers / Chercheurs: Women Femmes	Technicians and equivalent staff / Techniciens et personnel assimilé: Total M & W Total H & F	Technicians and equivalent staff / Techniciens et personnel assimilé: Women Femmes	Other supporting staff / Autre personnel de soutien: Total M & W Total H & F
Switzerland Suisse	2000	52 285[5]	26 105[5]	8 985[2,5]	16 580[7]	3 885[2,7]	9 600[7]
	2004	52 250[5]	25 400[5]	11 555[2,5]	17 130[7]	3 590[2,7]	9 720[7]
Tajikistan[2] Tadjikistan[2]	2001	2 799	1 845	908	391	...	563
	2002	2 628	1 752	701	312	...	564
	2003	2 425	1 544	438	270	...	611
	2004	2 487	1 548	407	247	...	692
	2005	3 220	1 993	...	324	...	903
Thailand Thaïlande	1999	20 048	10 418	...	5 281	...	4 349
	2001	32 011	17 710	...	7 110	...	7 191
	2003	42 379	18 114	13 607[2]	13 139	...	11 126
TFYR of Macedonia L'ex-R.y. Macédoine	1999	929	781	330	58	...	90
	2000	924	754	335	70	...	100
	2001	#1 630	#1 240	596	#199	...	#191
	2002	1 518	1 164	571	140	...	214
	2003	1 464	1 118	557	137	...	209
	2004	1 447	1 069	538	195	...	183
	2005	1 434	1 113	576	168	...	153
Trinidad and Tobago[2,3] Trinité-et-Tobago[2,3]	2000	1 589	447	153	1 142	445	...
	2001	...	509	192	...	...	...
	2003	...	518	208	...	...	...
	2004	#908	550	213	#358	#132	...
Tunisia Tunisie	1999	8 589	6 911[15]	...	326[1]	...	1 352
	2000	9 229	7 516[15]	...	341[1]	...	1 372
	2001	10 090	8 515[15]	...	294[1]	...	1 281
	2002	11 510	9 910[15]	...	329[1]	...	1 271
	2003	12 857	11 265[15]	5 471[15]	357[1]	...	1 235
	2004	14 556	12 950[15]	6 145[15]	379[1]	...	1 227
	2005	16 289	14 650[15]	6 995[15]	413[1]	...	1 226
Turkey[5] Turquie[5]	1999	24 267[9]	20 065	...	2 371[9]	776[2]	1 831[9]
	2000	27 003[9]	23 083	...	2 361[9]	901[2]	1 559[9]
	2001	27 698[9]	22 702	...	2 560[9]	688[2]	2 436[9]
	2002	28 964[9]	23 995	...	2 567[9]	672[2]	2 402[9]
	2003	38 308[9]	32 660	...	...	...	...
	2004	39 960[9]	33 876	...	...	...	...
Uganda[2] Ouganda[2]	1999	1 102	503	189	309	...	290
	2000	1 187	549	206	330	...	308
	2001	1 278	568	213	366	...	344
	2002	1 370	630	236	384	...	356
	2003	1 468	675	253	411	...	382
	2004	1 573	724	272	440	...	409
	2005	1 686	776	291	472	...	438
Ukraine[2] Ukraine[2]	1999	166 551	94 726	...	31 273	...	40 552
	2000	156 372	89 192	...	31 536	...	35 644
	2001	147 116	86 366	36 164	26 975	...	33 775
	2002	142 763	85 211	36 557	22 236	...	35 316
	2003	139 470	83 890	36 174	20 951	...	34 629
	2004	140 284	85 742	37 634	20 861	...	33 681
	2005	137 564	85 246	37 586	20 266	...	32 052
United States[5] Etats-Unis[5]	1999	...	1 260 920	...	...	...	...
	2000[17]	...	1 289 262	...	...	...	...
	2001[17]	...	1 320 096	...	...	...	...
	2002[17]	...	1 334 628	...	...	...	...

56 Human resources in research and development (R & D)—Full-time equivalent (FTE) (*continued*)
Personnel employé dans la recherche et le développement (R–D)—Equivalent temps plein (ETP) (*suite*)

Country or area Pays ou zone	Year Année	Total R & D personnel Total du personnel de R - D	Researchers / Chercheurs: Total M & W Total H & F	Researchers / Chercheurs: Women Femmes	Technicians and equivalent staff / Techniciens et personnel assimilé: Total M & W Total H & F	Technicians and equivalent staff / Techniciens et personnel assimilé: Women Femmes	Other supporting staff / Autre personnel de soutien: Total M & W Total H & F
United States Virgin Is.[1] Iles Vierges américaines[1]	1999	31	9	...	6	...	16
	2000	33	11	2	6	...	16
	#2001	36	6	...	15	...	15
	2002	36	6	...	15	...	15
	2003	37	6	...	15	...	16
	2004	38	7	...	15	...	16
	2005	39	8	...	15	...	16
Uruguay[3] Uruguay[3]	1999	792	724	...	68[4]	...	...
	2000	1 097	922	...	175[4]	...	...
	2002	1 412	1 242	...	170[4]	...	...
Venezuela (Bolivarian Rep. of)[2,3] Venezuela (Rép. bolivarienne du)[2,3]	1999	...	4 435	...	...	...	...
	2000	...	4 688	1 969	...	...	...
	2001	...	4 756	1 998	...	...	...
	2002	...	5 580	2 541	...	...	...
	2003	...	6 100	2 818	...	...	...
	2004	...	7 164	3 295	...	...	...
Viet Nam—Viet Nam	2002	11 356	9 328	...	...	...	...
Zambia[2] Zambie[2]	2002	1 084	268	31[9]	276	...	540
	2003	1 141	288	36[9]	295	...	558
	2004	1 307	356	79[9]	376	...	575
	2005	3 285	792	116[9]	1 240	...	1 253

Source

United Nations Educational, Scientific and Cultural Organization (UNESCO) Institute for Statistics, Montreal, the UNESCO Institute of Statistics database.

Notes

1 Partial data.
2 Head count instead of Full-time equivalent.
3 Source : "Red Ibero Americana de Indicadores de Ciencia y Tecnologia (RICYT)".
4 Includes other supporting staff.
5 Source: OECD.
6 National estimation.
7 Source: EUROSTAT.
8 UIS estimation.
9 Underestimated or based on underestimated data.
10 Source: National statistical publication(s).
11 For statistical purposes, the data for China do not include those for the Hong Kong Special Administrative Region (Hong Kong SAR) and Macao Special Administrative Region (Macao SAR).
12 University graduates instead of researchers.
13 The sum of the breakdown does not add to the total.
14 Defence excluded (all or mostly).
15 Overestimated or based on overestimated data.
16 Data exclude Montenegro and Kosovo.
17 OECD estimation.

Source

L'Institut de statistique de l'Organisation des Nations Unies pour l'éducation, la science et la culture (UNESCO), Montréal, la base de données de l'Institut de statistique de l'UNESCO.

Notes

1 Données partielles.
2 Personnes physiques au lieu d'Equivalents temps plein.
3 Source : "Red IberoAmericana de Indicadores de Ciencia y Tecnologia (RICYT)".
4 Y compris autre personnel de soutien.
5 Source : OCDE.
6 Estimation nationale.
7 Source: EUROSTAT.
8 Estimation de l'ISU.
9 Sous-estimé ou basé sur des données sous-estimées.
10 Source: Publications des statistiques nationales.
11 Pour la présentation des statistiques, les données pour la Chine ne comprennent pas la Région Administrative Spéciale de Hong Kong (Hong Kong RAS) et la Région Administrative Spéciale de Macao (Macao RAS).
12 Diplômes universitaires au lieu de chercheurs.
13 La somme de toutes les valeurs diffère du total.
14 A l'exclusion de la défense (en totalité ou en grande partie).
15 Surestimé ou fondé sur des données surestimées.
16 Les données excluent celles de Monténégro et Kosovo.
17 Estimation de l'OCDE.

57

Gross domestic expenditure on R & D by source of funds

National currency and percentage distribution

Dépenses intérieures brutes de recherche et développement par source de financement

Monnaie nationale et répartition en pourcentage

Country or area (monetary unit) / Pays ou zone (unité monétaire)	Year / Année	Gross domestic expenditure on R&D (000) / Dépenses int. brutes de R-D (000)	Source of funds (%) / Source de financement (%)					
			Business enterprises / Entreprises	Government / Etat	Higher education / Enseignement supérieur	Private non-profit / Institut. privées sans but lucratif	Funds from abroad / Fonds de l'étranger	Not distributed / Non répartis
Algeria (Algerian dinar)[1] / Algérie (dinar algérien)[1]	2002	16 571 247	...	...	...	...	...	...
	2003	10 306 455	...	...	...	...	...	...
	2004	10 058 086	...	...	...	...	...	...
American Samoa (US dollar)[1] / Samoa américaines (dollar des Etats-Unis)[1]	2001	1 117	...	...	...	...	...	...
Argentina (Argentine peso)[2] / Argentine (peso argentin)[2]	2002	1 215 500	22.5	41.8	32.2	2.2	1.2	0.0
	2003	1 541 700	26.1	44.2	25.9	2.3	1.4	0.0
	2004	1 958 700	30.7	43.0	23.5	1.7	1.1	0.0
Armenia (dram)[1] / Arménie (dram)[1]	2003	3 894 500	...	48.7	...	...	11.7	39.6
	2004	4 045 100	...	51.8	...	...	9.2	39.0
	2005	4 814 400	...	53.8	...	...	5.7	40.5
Australia (Australian dollar)[3] / Australie (dollar australien)[3]	2000	10 417 100	46.3	45.5	4.7	...	3.5	...
	2002	13 211 600	50.7[4]	41.2[4]	1.9	...	3.6[4]	2.7
	2004	15 772 900	51.6[4]	39.8[4]	2.1	...	3.6[4]	2.8
Austria (euro)[3] / Autriche (euro)[3]	2004	5 249 550	47.2	32.6	0.9	...	19.4	...
	2005	5 784 150[5]	45.7[5]	36.4[5]	0.3	...	17.6[5]	...
	2006	6 240 300[5]	45.8[5]	36.9[5]	0.3	...	17.0[5]	...
Azerbaijan (manat) / Azerbaïdjan (manat)	2003	23 223[6]	24.7	71.4	0.0	3.8	0.0	0.0
	2004	25 446[6]	23.0	74.4	0.0	1.3	1.3	0.0
	2005	27 542[6]	18.7	77.5	0.0	1.3	2.4	0.0
Belarus (Belarussian rouble) / Bélarus (rouble bélarussien)	2003	223 582 700	21.1	69.1	2.4	0.0	7.5	0.0
	2004	313 745 800	20.3	69.7	2.4	0.0	7.6	0.0
	2005	441 491 000	21.2	71.9	0.7	0.0	6.3	0.0
Belgium (euro) / Belgique (euro)	2003	5 177 440[3]	60.3[3]	23.6[3]	2.7[7]	0.5[7]	12.9[3]	0.0[3]
	2004[3]	5 349 610	...	...	...	...	...	...
	2005[3]	5 427 720	...	...	...	...	...	...
Bermuda (Bermuda dollar) / Bermudes (dollar des Bermudes)	1997	1 726	...	...	...	...	...	...
Bolivia (boliviano)[2] / Bolivie (boliviano)[2]	2000	149 261	22.0	22.0	32.0	15.0	9.0	0.0
	2001	157 920	18.0	21.0	33.0	17.0	11.0	0.0
	2002	156 801	16.0	20.0	31.0	19.0	14.0	0.0
Botswana (pula)[8] / Botswana (pula)[8]	2005	205 567	...	...	...	...	...	...
Brazil (real)[2] / Brésil (real)[2]	2002	13 412 000	40.3	57.9	1.8	...	...	...
	2003	15 042 200	39.2	58.7	2.1	...	...	...
	2004	16 116 800	39.9	57.9	2.2	...	...	...
Brunei Darussalam (Brunei dollar)[9] / Brunéi Darussalam (dollar du Brunéi)[9]	2002	1 666	...	...	...	...	...	...
	2003	2 104	...	...	...	...	...	...
Bulgaria (lev)[7] / Bulgarie (lev)[7]	2003	173 010	26.8	66.9	0.4	0.2	5.8	0.0
	2004	194 000	28.2	65.8	0.3	0.2	5.5	0.0
	2005	208 142	...	...	...	...	...	...
Burkina Faso (CFA franc)[1] / Burkina Faso (franc CFA)[1]	2003	6 628 789	...	100.0	...	...	...	...
	2004	6 185 018	...	100.0	...	...	...	...
	2005	4 914 954	...	100.0	...	...	...	...
Cambodia (riel)[1,5] / Cambodge (riel)[1,5]	2002	8 357 010	...	17.9	0.0	43.0	28.4	10.6
Canada (Canadian dollar)[3] / Canada (dollar canadien)[3]	2004	26 003 000	49.0	23.4[10]	15.9[10]	2.8[10]	9.0	0.0
	*2005	27 174 000	47.9	23.9[10]	16.6[10]	2.9[10]	8.7	0.0
	*2006	28 357 000	46.7	24.2[10]	17.4[10]	3.1[10]	8.5	0.0

57 Gross domestic expenditure on R & D by source of funds—National currency and percentage distribution (*continued*)

Dépenses intérieures brutes de recherche et développement par source de financement—Monnaie nationale et répartition en pourcentage (*suite*)

Country or area (monetary unit) Pays ou zone (unité monétaire)	Year Année	Gross domestic expenditure on R&D (000) Dépenses int. brutes de R-D (000)	Source of funds (%) / Source de financement (%) Business enterprises Entreprises	Govern-ment Etat	Higher education Enseigne-ment supérieur	Private non-profit Institut. privées sans but lucratif	Funds from abroad Fonds de l'étranger	Not distributed Non répartis
Chile (Chilean peso)[2] Chili (peso chilien)[2]	2002	#315 638 375	#33.2	#54.6	0.4	#0.3	#11.3	0.0
	2003	341 665 097	43.6	43.2	0.8	0.4	12.0	0.0
	2004	393 616 720	45.8	44.4	0.8	0.3	8.7	0.0
China (yuan)[3,11] Chine (yuan)[3,11]	2003	153 963 000	60.1	29.9	...	...	2.0	8.0
	2004	196 633 000	65.7	26.6	...	...	1.3	6.4
	2005	244 997 300	67.0	26.3	...	...	0.9	5.8
China, Hong Kong SAR (Hong Kong dollar) Chine, Hong Kong RAS (dollar de Hong Kong)	2002	7 543 600	35.3	62.8	0.2	...	1.7	...
	2003	8 548 800	42.6	55.0	0.3	...	2.1	...
	2004	9 505 200	47.8	47.0	0.1	...	5.1	...
China, Macao SAR (Macao pataca)[1,5] Chine, Macao RAS (pataca de Macao)[1,5]	2003	41 303	...	...	...	...	...	...
	2004	45 629	...	...	...	...	...	...
	2005	97 850	...	...	...	...	...	...
Colombia (Colombian peso)[2] Colombie (peso colombien)[2]	1999	302 038 500	45.0	24.0	29.0	2.0	...	...
	2000	306 385 210	48.4	16.6	33.6	1.4	...	...
	2001	313 720 990	46.9	13.2	38.3	1.7	...	...
Costa Rica (Costa Rican colón)[2] Costa Rica (colón costa-ricien)[2]	2000	19 033 194	...	...	...	...	...	...
	2003	24 918 750	...	...	...	...	...	...
	2004	30 390 300	...	...	...	...	...	...
Croatia (kuna)[7] Croatie (kuna)[7]	2002	2 006 000	45.7	46.4	6.4	...	1.5	...
	2003	2 209 000	42.1	55.9	...	...	2.2	...
	2004	2 586 000	43.0	46.6	7.9	...	2.6	...
Cuba (Cuban peso)[2] Cuba (peso cubain)[2]	2002	189 600	35.0	60.0	...	...	5.0	...
	2003	209 100	35.0	60.0	...	...	5.0	...
	2004	230 100	35.0	60.0	...	...	5.0	...
Cyprus (Cyprus pound)[7] Chypre (livre chypriote)[7]	2003	23 933	19.9	60.1	3.8	2.3	13.9	0.0
	2004	27 220	18.9	63.7	4.3	1.6	11.5	0.0
	2005	31 400	...	...	...	...	...	...
Czech Republic (Czech koruna) République tchèque (couronne tchèque)	2003	32 246 600[3]	51.5[3]	41.8[3]	1.2[7]	1.0[7]	4.6[3]	0.0[3]
	2004	35 083 040[3]	52.8[3]	41.9[3]	1.5[7]	0.1[7]	3.7[3]	0.0[3]
	2005	42 198 420[3]	54.1[3]	40.9[3]	1.1[7]	0.0[7]	4.0[3]	0.0[3]
Dem. Rep. of the Congo (Congo franc)[1] Rép. dém. du Congo (franc congolais)[1]	2004	11 014 833[8]	...	100.0	...	...	...	...
	2005	16 116 424[8]	...	100.0	...	...	...	...
Denmark (Danish krone)[3] Danemark (couronne danoise)[3]	2003	36 074 810	59.9	27.1	2.7[12]	0.0[13]	10.3	0.0
	2004	36 451 400	...	...	...	...	...	...
	2005	37 980 100	...	...	...	...	...	...
Ecuador (sucre)[2] Equateur (sucre)[2]	#2001	12 600	...	...	...	...	...	...
	2002	15 800	...	...	...	...	...	...
	2003	18 600	...	...	...	...	...	...
Egypt (Egyptian pound)[1] Egypte (livre égyptienne)[1]	1998	572 200	...	...	...	...	...	...
	1999	573 700	...	...	...	...	...	...
	2000	654 600	...	...	...	...	...	...
El Salvador (El Salvadoran colón)[2] El Salvador (cólon salvadorien)[2]	1998	84 437	1.2	51.9	13.2	10.4	23.4	0.0
Estonia (Estonian kroon)[7] Estonie (couronne estonienne)[7]	2003	1 046 200	33.0	48.6	2.9	0.4	15.2	0.0
	2004	1 294 000	36.5	44.1	1.7	0.6	17.0	0.0
	*2005	1 628 800	...	...	...	...	...	...
Ethiopia (Ethiopian birr)[1] Ethiopie (birr éthiopien)[1]	2005	192 227	...	69.2	...	0.1	30.8	...
Finland (euro) Finlande (euro)	2004	5 253 420[3]	69.3[3]	26.3[3]	0.2[7]	1.0[7]	3.2[3]	0.0[3]
	2005[3]	5 473 700	...	...	...	...	...	...
	2006[3,5]	5 736 300	...	...	...	...	...	...
France (euro) France (euro)	2003	34 569 100[3]	50.8[3]	39.0[3]	0.9[7]	0.9[7]	8.4[3]	0.0[3]
	2004	35 534 090[3]	51.7[3]	37.6[3]	1.0[7]	0.9[7]	8.8[3]	0.0[3]
	2005[5]	36 395 830	...	...	...	...	...	...

57 Gross domestic expenditure on R & D by source of funds—National currency and percentage distribution *(continued)*

Dépenses intérieures brutes de recherche et développement par source de financement—Monnaie nationale et répartition en pourcentage *(suite)*

Country or area (monetary unit) Pays ou zone (unité monétaire)	Year Année	Gross domestic expenditure on R&D (000) Dépenses int. brutes de R-D (000)	Source of funds (%) / Source de financement (%) Business enterprises Entreprises	Government Etat	Higher education Enseignement supérieur	Private non-profit Institut. privées sans but lucratif	Funds from abroad Fonds de l'étranger	Not distributed Non répartis
Georgia (lari) Géorgie (lari)	2003	18 635	...	...	...	...	...	...
	2004	23 991	...	...	...	...	...	...
	2005	20 520	...	...	...	...	...	...
Germany (euro)[3] Allemagne (euro)[3]	2003	54 538 500	66.3	31.2	0.3[12]	0.0[13]	2.3	0.0
	2004	55 214 900	66.8	30.4	0.4[12]	0.0[13]	2.5	0.0
	2005[5]	56 356 000	...	...	...	...	...	...
Greece (euro) Grèce (euro)	2003	977 780[3]	28.2[3]	46.4[3]	2.6[7]	1.2[7]	21.6[3]	0.0[3]
	*2004[3]	1 021 470	...	...	...	...	...	...
	*2005[3]	1 112 100	...	...	...	...	...	...
Greenland (Danish Kroner) Groenland (couronne danoise)	2002	54 345	...	...	...	...	...	...
	2003[5]	52 169	...	...	...	...	...	...
	2004	70 543	...	...	...	...	...	...
Guam (US dollar)[1] Guam (dollar des Etats-Unis)[1]	2001	3 813	...	...	...	...	...	...
Honduras (lempira)[2] Honduras (lempira)[2]	2001	45 400	...	...	...	...	...	...
	2002	54 000	...	...	...	...	...	...
	2003	60 200	...	...	...	...	...	...
Hungary (forint)[3,14] Hongrie (forint)[3,14]	2003	175 772 900	30.7	58.0	0.4	...	10.7	0.2
	2004	181 525 400	37.1	51.8	0.6	...	10.4	0.1
	2005	207 764 000	39.4	49.4	0.3	...	10.7	0.2
Iceland (Icelandic króna) Islande (couronne islandaise)	2002[3,5]	24 097 030	...	...	...	...	...	...
	2003[3]	23 720 000	43.9	40.1	1.5	...	14.5	...
	2004[7]	25 862 000	...	...	...	...	...	...
India (Indian rupee) Inde (roupie indienne)	2003	180 001 600	20.3[12]	75.6	4.2	0.0[13]	...	...
	2004	197 269 900[5]	20.0[5,12]	75.4[5]	4.5[5]	0.0[13]	...	...
	2005	216 395 800[5]	19.8[5,12]	75.3[5]	4.9[5]	0.0[13]	...	...
Indonesia (Indonesian rupiah) Indonésie (roupie indonésien)	2000	940 776 000[1]	25.7[1]	72.7	1.1[12]	0.0[13]	...	0.5
	2001	783 045 000[1]	14.7[1]	84.5	0.2[12]	0.0[13]	...	0.7
Iran (Islamic Rep. of) (Iranian rial) Iran (Rép. islamique d') (rial iranien)	2002	5 072 849 732	18.6	74.7	6.7	...	...	...
	2003	7 483 899 781	16.5	75.8	7.7	...	...	...
	2004	8 259 299 100	19.6	69.0	11.4	...	...	...
Ireland (euro)[3] Irlande (euro)[3]	2003[5]	1 607 400	59.5	30.4	1.6	...	8.5	...
	*2004	1 780 400	57.2	32.2	1.7	...	8.9	...
	*2005[5]	2 020 100	58.7	32.9	1.7	...	6.6	...
Israel (new sheqel)*[3,14] Israël (nouveau sheqel)*[3,14]	2003	23 393 000	...	...	...	...	...	...
	2004	24 273 000	...	...	...	...	...	...
	2005	27 405 000	...	...	...	...	...	...
Italy (euro)[3] Italie (euro)[3]	2002	14 599 500	...	...	...	...	...	...
	2003	14 769 000	...	...	...	...	...	...
	2004	15 253 000	...	...	...	...	...	...
Jamaica (Jamaican dollar)[2] Jamaïque (dollar jamaïcain)[2]	2001	207 700	...	...	...	...	...	...
	2002	286 800	...	...	...	...	...	...
Japan (yen) Japon (yen)	2002	15 551 513 000[3]	74.1[3]	18.4[15]	6.5[5,7]	1.1[7]	0.4[3]	0.0[3]
	2003	15 683 403 000[3]	74.7[3]	18.0[15]	6.3[5,7]	1.2[7]	0.3[3]	0.0[3]
	2004	15 782 743 000[3]	74.8[3]	18.1[15]	6.8[5,12]	0.0[3,13]	0.3[3]	0.0[3]
Jordan (Jordan dinar) Jordanie (dinar jordanien)	2002	22 888	...	...	...	...	...	...
Kazakhstan (tenge) Kazakhstan (tenge)	2003	11 643 480	38.6	41.9	...	...	5.6	13.9
	2004	14 579 835	29.0	50.0	...	...	2.4	18.7
	2005	21 527 364	26.4	51.2	...	...	1.5	20.9
Korea, Republic of (Korean won)[1,3] Corée, République de (won coréen)[1,3]	2003	19 068 682 000	74.0	23.9	1.7	...	0.4	...
	2004	22 185 343 340	75.0	23.1	1.4	...	0.5	...
	2005	24 155 413 600	75.0	23.0	1.3	...	0.7	...

57 Gross domestic expenditure on R & D by source of funds—National currency and percentage distribution (*continued*)

Dépenses intérieures brutes de recherche et développement par source de financement—Monnaie nationale et répartition en pourcentage (*suite*)

Country or area (monetary unit) / Pays ou zone (unité monétaire)	Year / Année	Gross domestic expenditure on R&D (000) / Dépenses int. brutes de R-D (000)	Source of funds (%) / Source de financement (%)					
			Business enterprises / Entreprises	Government / Etat	Higher education / Enseignement supérieur	Private non-profit / Institut. privées sans but lucratif	Funds from abroad / Fonds de l'étranger	Not distributed / Non répartis
Kuwait (Kuwaiti dinar)[1] Koweït (dinar koweïtien)[1]	2000	14 512	20.9	79.1	...	...	...	...
	2001	19 136	20.1	79.9	...	...	...	...
	2002	20 864	20.0	80.0	...	...	...	...
Kyrgyzstan (Kyrgyz som) Kirghizistan (som kirghize)	2003	186 800	53.7	45.1	0.1	0.0	1.1	0.0
	2004	188 000	45.9	53.4	0.0	0.0	0.7	0.0
	2005	200 400	36.4	63.6	0.0	0.0	0.0	0.0
Latvia (lats)[7] Lettonie (lats)[7]	2003	24 167	33.2	46.4	...	...	20.4	...
	2004	31 068	46.3	31.2	...	...	22.5	...
	2005	50 609	34.3	46.0	1.2	...	18.5	...
Lesotho (loti)[1] Lesotho (loti)[1]	2002	3 422	...	...	...	...	...	...
	2003	3 762	...	...	...	...	...	...
	2004	5 400	...	...	...	...	...	...
Lithuania (litas)[7] Lituanie (litas)[7]	2003	381 800	16.7	64.6	4.8	0.1	13.8	0.0
	2004	472 700	19.9	63.1	6.0	0.3	10.7	0.0
	2005	542 000	20.8	62.7	5.7	0.2	10.5	0.0
Luxembourg (euro)[3] Luxembourg (euro)[3]	2003	425 800	80.4	11.2	0.2[12]	0.0	8.3	0.0
	2004	447 700	...	...	...	...	...	...
	*2005	458 000	...	...	...	...	...	...
Madagascar (Malagasy ariary)[1] Madagascar (ariary malgache)[1]	2003	20 962 077[6]	...	...	70.6	...	29.4	...
	2004	16 469 769[6]	...	...	73.8	...	26.2	...
	2005	15 942 004	...	...	89.1	...	10.9	...
Malaysia (ringgit) Malaisie (ringgit)	2000	1 671 500	...	...	...	...	...	...
	2002	2 500 600	51.5	32.1	4.9	0.0	11.5	0.0
	2004	2 843 800	71.2	21.5	6.9	0.0	0.4	0.0
Malta (Maltese lira)[7] Malte (lire maltaise)[7]	2003	4 881	...	...	...	...	...	...
	#2004	11 800	...	...	...	...	...	...
	*2005	11 807	...	...	...	...	...	...
Mauritius (Mauritian rupee)[1] Maurice (roupie mauricienne)[1]	2003	529 139	...	100.0	...	...	...	...
	2004	666 071	...	100.0	...	...	...	...
	2005	690 030	...	100.0	...	...	...	...
Mexico (Mexican peso) Mexique (peso mexicain)	2002[3]	27 337 140	34.7	55.5	8.2[2]	0.8[2]	0.8	0.0
	2003[3]	29 931 530	34.7	56.1	7.7[2]	0.8[2]	0.8	0.0
	2004	31 484 400	35.6	54.3	8.1[2]	1.2[2]	0.8	0.0
Monaco (euro)[1] Monaco (euro)[1]	2005	1 291	...	...	...	...	...	...
Mongolia (togrog)[1] Mongolie (togrog)[1]	2003	4 605 600	4.8	90.5	2.2	...	0.9	1.6
	2004	6 322 500	7.4	87.0	2.1	...	2.3	1.3
	2005	7 231 100	10.4	77.8	0.8	...	4.4	6.5
Morocco (Moroccan dirham) Maroc (dirham marocain)	2001	2 706 510	...	...	...	...	...	...
	2002	2 447 850	21.6	37.1	41.2	...	...	...
	2003	3 144 000	12.3	40.3	47.4	...	...	...
Mozambique (metical)[1,8] Mozambique (metical)[1,8]	2002	501 580 800	...	34.7	...	...	65.3	...
Myanmar (kyat)[1,9] Myanmar (kyat)[1,9]	2000	2 886 055	...	...	...	...	...	...
	2001	2 535 022	...	...	...	...	...	...
	2002	9 122 008	...	...	...	...	...	...
Netherlands (euro) Pays-Bas (euro)	2002	8 018 200[3]	50.0[3]	37.1[3]	0.1[7]	1.1[7]	11.7[3]	0.0[3]
	2003	8 376 000[3]	51.1[3]	36.2[3]	0.1[7]	1.3[7]	11.3[3]	0.0[3]
	2004[3]	8 723 000	...	...	...	...	...	...
New Zealand (New Zealand dollar)[3] Nouvelle-Zélande (dollar néo-zélandais)[3]	1999	1 091 380	34.1	50.6	11.0	...	4.3	...
	#2001	1 416 200	37.8[4]	47.1[4]	10.0[4]	...	6.7[4]	...
	2003	1 593 100	38.5	45.1	9.6	...	6.8	...

Gross domestic expenditure on R & D by source of funds — National currency and percentage distribution (*continued*)

Dépenses intérieures brutes de recherche et développement par source de financement — Monnaie nationale et répartition en pourcentage (*suite*)

Country or area (monetary unit) Pays ou zone (unité monétaire)	Year Année	Gross domestic expenditure on R&D (000) Dépenses int. brutes de R-D (000)	Source of funds (%) / Source de financement (%) Business enterprises Entreprises	Govern-ment Etat	Higher education Enseigne-ment supérieur	Private non-profit Institut. privées sans but lucratif	Funds from abroad Fonds de l'étranger	Not distributed Non répartis
Nicaragua (córdoba)[2] Nicaragua (córdoba)[2]	1997	27 000	...	...	...	...	...	...
	2002	26 000	...	...	...	...	...	...
Norway (Norwegian krone) Norvège (couronne norvégienne)	2003	27 301 700[3]	49.2[3]	41.9[3]	0.6[7]	0.8[7]	7.4[3]	0.0[3]
	2004[3]	27 765 700	...	...	...	...	...	...
	2005[3]	28 821 300	...	...	...	...	...	...
Pakistan (Pakistan rupee) Pakistan (roupie pakistanaise)	2001	7 017 890[1,5]	...	100.0	...	...	...	...
	2002	9 785 470[1,5]	...	100.0	...	...	...	...
	2005	28 397 000	...	87.0	11.9	...	0.3	0.8
Panama (balboa)[2] Panama (balboa)[2]	2002	44 466	0.6	26.2	2.1	0.2	70.8	0.0
	2003	43 970	0.6	25.5	1.8	1.0	71.0	0.0
	2004	33 950	0.1	35.0	2.6	2.5	59.8	0.0
Paraguay (guaraní)[2] Paraguay (guaraní)[2]	2002	30 821 390	0.0	63.2	12.7	2.3	21.8	0.0
	2003	30 316 461	0.0	63.2	12.7	2.3	21.8	0.0
	2004	34 878 381	0.0	63.1	12.7	2.3	21.9	0.0
Peru (new sol)[2] Pérou (nouveau sol)[2]	2002	204 530	...	...	...	...	...	...
	2003	220 950	...	...	...	...	...	...
	2004	355 071	...	...	...	...	...	...
Philippines (Philippine peso) Philippines (peso philippin)	2002	5 770 000	68.6	19.1	5.9	0.2	5.5	0.7
	2003	5 910 000	68.0	21.9	4.8	0.4	3.8	1.1
Poland (zloty) Pologne (zloty)	2003	4 558 300[3]	27.0[3]	66.0[3]	2.1[7]	0.3[7]	4.6[3]	0.0[3]
	2004	5 155 400[3]	26.9[3]	65.2[3]	2.4[7]	0.3[7]	5.2[3]	0.0[3]
	2005	5 574 600[3]	30.3[3]	60.7[3]	2.9[7]	0.3[7]	5.7[3]	0.0[3]
Portugal (euro) Portugal (euro)	2003	1 019 580[3]	31.7[3]	60.1[3]	1.3[7]	1.9[7]	5.0[3]	0.0[3]
	*2004[3]	1 104 150	...	...	...	...	...	...
	*2005[3]	1 188 720	...	...	...	...	...	...
Republic of Moldova (Moldovan leu) République de Moldova (leu moldove)	1996	68 069	...	...	...	...	...	...
	1997	71 941	51.4	47.8	0.2	...	0.6	...
Romania (Romanian leu)[3] Roumanie (leu roumain)[3]	2002	574 390[6]	41.6	48.4	3.0	0.0	7.1	0.0
	2003	762 060[6]	45.4	47.6	1.5	0.0	5.5	0.0
	2004	952 870[6]	44.0	49.0	1.5	0.0	5.5	0.0
Russian Federation (ruble) Fédération de Russie (ruble)	2003	169 862 370[3]	30.8[3]	59.6[3]	0.5[3,7]	0.2[7]	9.0[3]	0.0[3]
	2004	196 039 900[3]	31.4[3]	60.6[3]	0.4[3,7]	0.1[7]	7.6[3]	0.0[3]
	2005[3]	230 785 200	30.0	62.0	0.5[12]	0.0[13]	7.6	0.0
Saint Helena (pound sterling)[1] Sainte-Hélène (livre sterling)[1]	1998	30 082	...	...	...	...	...	...
	1999	40 390	...	...	...	...	...	...
	2000	51 156	...	...	...	...	...	...
Saint Lucia (EC dollar)[8] Sainte-Lucie (dollar des Caraïbes orientales)[8]	1998	13 597	...	...	...	...	...	...
	1999	6 814	...	...	...	...	...	...
Saint Vincent-Grenadines (EC dollar) Saint Vincent-Grenadines (dollar des Caraïbes orientales)	2001	500	...	...	...	...	...	...
	2002	1 500	...	...	...	...	...	...
Senegal (CFA franc)[1] Sénégal (franc CFA)[1]	2005	4 090 000[5]	...	100.0	...	...	...	...
Serbia and Montenegro (Yugoslav dinar)[1,16] Serbie-et-Monténégro (dinar yougoslave)[1,16]	2003	14 710 671	...	...	...	...	...	...
	2004	19 466 276	...	...	...	...	...	...
	2005	24 637 550	...	...	...	...	...	...
Seychelles (Seychelles rupee)[1] Seychelles (roupie seychelloises)[1]	2003	15 696	...	97.5	...	0.7	1.8	...
	2004	15 999	...	97.5	...	0.8	1.8	...
	2005	15 271	...	97.1	...	0.7	2.2	...
Singapore (Singapore dollar)[3] Singapour (dollar singapourien)[3]	2003	3 424 470	51.6	41.8	0.4	...	6.2	...
	2004	4 061 900	55.3	37.9	1.0	...	5.8	...
	2005	4 582 210	58.8	36.4	0.5	...	4.4	...

57 Gross domestic expenditure on R & D by source of funds—National currency and percentage distribution (*continued*)
Dépenses intérieures brutes de recherche et développement par source de financement—Monnaie nationale et répartition en pourcentage (*suite*)

Country or area (monetary unit) Pays ou zone (unité monétaire)	Year Année	Gross domestic expenditure on R&D (000) Dépenses int. brutes de R-D (000)	Source of funds (%) / Source de financement (%): Business enterprises Entreprises	Govern-ment Etat	Higher education Enseigne-ment supérieur	Private non-profit Institut. privées sans but lucratif	Funds from abroad Fonds de l'étranger	Not distributed Non répartis
Slovakia (Slovak koruna) Slovaquie (couronne slovaque)	2003	7 016 000[3]	45.1[3]	50.8[3]	0.3[7]	0.4[7]	3.3[3]	0.0[3]
	2004	6 965 000[3]	38.3[3]	57.1[3]	0.3[7]	0.0[7]	4.3[3]	0.0[3]
	2005	7 503 000[3]	36.6[3]	57.0[3]	0.3[7]	0.0[7]	6.0[3]	0.0[3]
Slovenia (tolar) Slovénie (tolar)	2003	76 596 700[3]	52.2[3]	37.5[3]	0.4[7]	0.1[7]	9.9[3]	0.0[3]
	2004	90 722 700[3]	58.5[3]	30.0[3]	0.3[7]	0.1[7]	11.1[3]	0.0[3]
	2005	*81 054 200[3]	65.3[3]	27.2[3]	0.7[7]	0.0[7]	6.8[3]	0.0[3]
South Africa (rand) Afrique du Sud (rand)	2001	7 488 074	53.3	35.2	0.0	5.4	6.1	0.0
	2003	10 082 559	52.1	27.9	3.5	5.5	10.9	0.0
	2004	12 009 981	44.5	23.7	9.2	6.8	15.8	0.0
Spain (euro) Espagne (euro)	2003	8 213 040[3]	48.4[3]	40.1[3]	5.4[7]	0.4[7]	5.7[3]	0.0[3]
	2004	8 945 760[3]	48.0[3]	41.0[3]	4.1[7]	0.7[7]	6.2[3]	0.0[3]
	*2005[3,5]	10 099 800	…	…	…	…	…	…
Sri Lanka (Sri Lanka rupee) Sri Lanka (roupie sri-lankaise)	1996	1 410 000	1.7	52.8	21.2	…	24.4	…
	#2000[1]	1 810 000	7.7	51.7	18.5	0.0	4.5	17.5
	#2004	3 807 500	0.6	67.5	…	0.0	22.6	9.3
Sudan (Sudanese dinar) Soudan (dinar soudanaise)	2002	15 400 000	…	…	…	…	…	…
	2003	15 650 000	…	…	…	…	…	…
	2004	16 373 000	…	…	…	…	…	…
Sweden (Swedish krona)[3] Suède (couronne suédoise)[3]	2001	97 276 600[17]	71.6	21.3	3.8[12]	0.0[13]	3.4	0.1
	2003	97 100 000[17]	65.0	23.5	0.4[7]	3.9[7]	7.3	0.0
	2005[17]	103 113 000	…	…	…	…	…	…
Switzerland (Swiss franc) Suisse (franc suisse)	1996	9 990 000[3]	67.5[3]	26.9[3]	1.3[7]	1.2[7]	3.1[3]	0.0[3]
	2000	10 675 000[3]	69.1[3]	23.2[3]	2.1[7]	1.4[7]	4.3[3]	0.0[3]
	2004	13 100 000[3]	69.7[3]	22.7[3]	1.5[7]	0.8[7]	5.2[3]	0.0[3]
Tajikistan (somoni) Tadjikistan (somoni)	2003	3 278	7.9	65.1	…	…	…	27.0
	2004	4 130	4.8	64.7	0.1	…	…	30.4
	2005	6 862	2.2	91.9	0.3	…	…	5.5
Thailand (baht) Thaïlande (baht)	2002	13 302 039[5]	36.8	…	…	…	…	63.2
	2003	15 499 201	41.8	38.6	15.1	0.6	2.6	1.3
	2004	16 571 000	35.5	…	…	…	…	64.5
TFYR of Macedonia (TFYR Macedonian denar) L'ex-R.y. Macédoine (denar de l'ex-R.Y. Macédoine)	2003	565 984	…	…	…	…	…	…
	2004	652 470	…	…	…	…	…	…
	2005	704 036	…	…	…	…	…	…
Trinidad and Tobago (Trinidad and Tobago dollar)[2] Trinité-et-Tobago (dollar de la Trinité-et-Tobago)[2]	2002	76 000	…	…	…	…	…	…
	2003	81 900	…	…	…	…	…	…
	2004	95 700	…	…	…	…	…	…
Tunisia (Tunisian dinar) Tunisie (dinar tunisien)	2003	234 000	9.6	47.0	34.2	0.0	7.5	1.7
	2004	350 000	12.6	35.4	28.0	0.0	9.4	14.6
	2005[5]	384 000	14.1	45.1	30.5	0.0	10.4	0.0
Turkey (new Turkish Lira) Turquie (nouveau livre turque)	2002	1 843 290[3,6]	41.3[3]	50.6[3]	…	6.9[7]	1.3[3]	…
	2003[3]	2 197 090[6]	36.2	57.0	5.2	…	1.6	…
	2004[3]	2 897 520[6]	37.9	57.0	4.8	…	0.4	…
Uganda (Uganda shilling) Ouganda (shilling ougandais)	2003	123 872 000[8]	2.0[5]	7.0[5]	0.6[5]	0.3[5]	90.1[5]	0.0
	2004	152 982 000[8]	2.0[5]	7.0[5]	0.6[5]	0.3[5]	90.1[5]	0.0
	2005	188 933 000[8]	2.0[5]	7.0[5]	0.6[5]	0.3[5]	90.1[5]	0.0
Ukraine (hryvnia) Ukraine (hryvnia)	2003	2 972 301	35.6[9]	37.5[9]	0.1[9]	0.3[9]	24.3[9]	2.2[9]
	2004	3 732 459	32.9[9]	42.3[9]	0.2[9]	0.4[9]	21.4[9]	2.9[9]
	2005	4 551 153	32.3[9]	40.1[9]	0.1[9]	0.4[9]	24.4[9]	2.8[9]
United Kingdom (pound sterling) Royaume-Uni (livre sterling)	2002	19 175 800[3]	43.6[3]	28.8[3]	1.0[7]	5.0[7]	21.6[3]	0.0[3]
	2003	19 831 000[3]	42.3[3]	31.6[3]	1.0[7]	4.7[7]	20.4[3]	0.0[3]
	2004[3]	20 331 000	44.2	32.8	1.1	4.7	17.3	0.0

57 Gross domestic expenditure on R & D by source of funds — National currency and percentage distribution (*continued*)

Dépenses intérieures brutes de recherche et développement par source de financement — Monnaie nationale et répartition en pourcentage (*suite*)

Country or area (monetary unit) Pays ou zone (unité monétaire)	Year Année	Gross domestic expenditure on R&D (000) Dépenses int. brutes de R-D (000)	Source of funds (%) Source de financement (%)					
			Business enterprises Entreprises	Government Etat	Higher education Enseignement supérieur	Private non-profit Institut. privées sans but lucratif	Funds from abroad Fonds de l'étranger	Not distributed Non répartis
United States (US dollar)[3] Etats-Unis (dollar des Etats-Unis)[3]	2002	276 260 200[18]	65.4[18,19]	29.2[18]	2.6[7]	2.7[7]	...	...
	*2003	292 437 410[18]	63.8[18,19]	30.8[18]	2.8[7]	2.9[7]	...	...
	*2004	312 535 430[18]	63.7[18,19]	31.0[18]	...	...	...	5.4
United States Virgin Is. (US dollar)[1] Iles Vierges américaines (dollar des Etats-Unis)[1]	2003	2 623	...	81.0	18.6	0.4	...	...
	2004	4 562	...	91.2	8.8	...	...	...
	2005	1 523	...	76.1	23.9	...	...	...
Uruguay (Uruguayan peso)[2] Uruguay (peso uruguayen)[2]	1999	609 655	35.6	9.4	47.1	...	7.9	...
	2000	577 855	39.3	20.3	35.7	...	4.8	...
	2002	688 900	46.7	17.1	31.4	0.1	4.7	0.0
Venezuela (Bolivarian Rep. of) (bolívar)[2] Venezuela (Rép. bolivarienne du) (bolívar)[2]	2002	431 199 400[8]	22.9	59.1	18.0	...	...	...
	2003	390 550 100[8]	#1.0	#71.6	#27.4	...	...	...
	2004	525 755 900[8]	14.3	62.3	23.4	...	...	...
Viet Nam (dong) Viet Nam (dong)	2002	1 032 560 900	18.1	74.1	0.7[12]	0.0[13]	6.3	0.8
Zambia (Zambia kwacha)[1] Zambie (kwacha zambie)[1]	2003	1 965 987	...	...	...	...	...	...
	2004	6 607 523	...	...	...	...	...	...
	2005	9 272 025	...	...	...	...	...	...

Source

United Nations Educational, Scientific and Cultural Organization (UNESCO) Institute for Statistics, Montreal, the UNESCO Institute of Statistics database.

Notes

1. Partial data.
2. Source : "Red Ibero Americana de Indicadores de Ciencia y Tecnologia (RICYT)".
3. Source: OECD.
4. The sum of the breakdown does not add to the total.
5. National estimation.
6. Data have been converted from the former national currency using the appropriate irrevocable conversion rate.
7. Source: EUROSTAT.
8. Overestimated or based on overestimated data.
9. UIS estimation.
10. Source: National statistical publication(s).
11. For statistical purposes, the data for China do not include those for the Hong Kong Special Administrative Region (Hong Kong SAR) and Macao Special Administrative Region (Macao SAR).
12. Includes private non-profit institutions.
13. Included elsewhere.
14. Defence excluded (all or mostly).
15. OECD estimation.
16. Data exclude Montenegro and Kosovo.
17. Underestimated or based on underestimated data.
18. Excludes most or all capital expenditure.
19. Including funds from abroad.

Source

L'Institut de statistique de l'Organisation des Nations Unies pour l'éducation, la science et la culture (UNESCO), Montréal, la base de données de l'Institut de statistique de l'UNESCO.

Notes

1. Données partielles.
2. Source : "Red IberoAmericana de Indicadores de Ciencia y Tecnologia (RICYT)".
3. Source : OCDE.
4. La somme de toutes les valeurs diffère du total.
5. Estimation nationale.
6. Les données ont été converties à partir de l'ancienne monnaie nationale et du taux de conversion irrévocable approprié.
7. Source: EUROSTAT.
8. Surestimé ou fondé sur des données surestimées.
9. Estimation de l'ISU.
10. Source: Publications des statistiques nationales.
11. Pour la présentation des statistiques, les données pour la Chine ne comprennent pas la Région Administrative Spéciale de Hong Kong (Hong Kong RAS) et la Région Administrative Spéciale de Macao (Macao RAS).
12. Y compris institutions privées sans but lucratif.
13. Inclus ailleurs.
14. A l'exclusion de la défense (en totalité ou en grande partie).
15. Estimation de l'OCDE.
16. Les données excluent celles de Monténégro et Kosovo.
17. Sous-estimé ou basé sur des données sous-estimées.
18. A l'exclusion des dépenses d'équipement (en totalité ou en grande partie).
19. Y compris les fonds étrangers.

Technical notes: tables 56 and 57

Research and experimental development (R&D) is defined as any creative work undertaken on a systematic basis in order to increase the stock of knowledge, including knowledge of man, culture and society, and the use of this stock of knowledge to devise new applications.

Table 56: The data presented on human resources in research and development (R&D) are compiled by the UNESCO Institute for Statistics. Data for certain countries are provided to UNESCO by OECD, EUROSTAT and the Network on Science and Technology Indicators (RICYT).

The definitions and classifications applied by UNESCO in the table are based on those set out in the *Recommendation concerning the International Standardization of Statistics on Science and Technology* (UNESCO, 1978) and in the *Frascati Manual* (OECD, 2002).

The three categories of personnel shown are defined as follows:

- *Researchers* are professionals engaged in the conception or creation of new knowledge, products, processes, methods and systems, and in the planning and management of R&D projects. Postgraduate students engaged in R&D are considered as researchers.
- *Technicians and equivalent staff* comprise persons whose main tasks require technical knowledge and experience in one or more fields of engineering, physical and life sciences, or social sciences and humanities. They participate in R&D by performing scientific and technical tasks involving the application of concepts and operational methods, normally under the supervision of researchers. As distinguished from technicians participating in the R&D under the supervision of researchers in engineering, physical and life sciences, equivalent staff perform the corresponding R&D tasks in the social sciences and humanities.
- *Other supporting staff* includes skilled and unskilled craftsmen, secretarial and clerical staff participating in or directly associated with R&D projects. Included in this category are all managers and administrators dealing mainly with financial and personnel matters and general administration, insofar as their activities are a direct service to R&D.

Headcount data reflect the total number of persons employed in R&D, independently from their dedication. Full-time equivalent may be thought of as one person-year. Thus, a person who normally spends 30% of his/her time on R&D and the rest on other activities (such as teaching, university administration and student counselling) should be considered as 0.3 FTE. Similarly, if a full-time R&D worker is employed at an R&D unit for only six months, this results in an FTE of 0.5.

Notes techniques : tableaux 56 et 57

La recherche et le développement expérimental (R-D) englobe tous les travaux de création entrepris de façon systématique en vue d'accroître la somme des connaissances, y compris la connaissance de l'homme, de la culture et de la société, ainsi que l'utilisation de cette somme de connaissances pour de nouvelles applications.

Tableau 56: Les données présentées sur le personnel employé dans la recherche et le développement (R-D) sont compilées par l'Institut de statistique de l'UNESCO. Les données de certains pays ont été fournies à l'UNESCO par l'OCDE, EUROSTAT et «la Red de Indicadores de Ciencia y Technología (RICYT)».

Les définitions et classifications appliquées par l'UNESCO sont basées sur la Recommandation concernant la normalisation internationale des statistiques relatives à la science et à la technologie (UNESCO, 1978) et sur le Manuel de Frascati (OCDE, 2002).

Les trois catégories du personnel présentées sont définies comme suivant:

- *Les chercheurs* sont des spécialistes travaillant à la conception ou à la création de connaissances, de produits, de procédés, de méthodes et de systèmes, et dans la planification et la gestion de projets de R-D. Les étudiants diplômés ayant des activités de R-D sont considérés comme des chercheurs.
- *Techniciens et personnel assimilé* comprend des personnes dont les tâches principales requièrent des connaissances et une expérience technique dans un ou plusieurs domaines de l'ingénierie, des sciences physiques et de la vie ou des sciences sociales et humaines. Ils participent à la R-D en exécutant des tâches scientifiques et techniques faisant intervenir l'application de principes et de méthodes opérationnelles, généralement sous le contrôle de chercheurs. Pour se distinguer des techniciens qui participent à la R-D sous le contrôle de chercheurs dans les domaines de l'ingénierie, des sciences physiques et de la vie, le personnel assimilé effectue des travaux correspondants dans les sciences sociales et humaines.
- *Autre personnel de soutien* comprend les travailleurs, qualifiés ou non, et le personnel de secrétariat et de bureau qui participent à l'exécution des projets de R-D ou qui sont directement associés à l'exécution de tels projets. Sont inclus dans cette catégorie les gérants et administrateurs qui s'occupent principalement de problèmes financiers, le personnel et l'administration en général, dans la mesure où leurs activités ont une relation directe avec la R-D.

Personnes physiques est le nombre total de personnes qui sont principalement ou partiellement affectées à la R-D. Ce

More information can be found on the UNESCO Institute for Statistics web site www.uis.unesco.org.

Table 57: The data presented on gross domestic expenditure on research and development are compiled by the UNESCO Institute for Statistics. Data for certain countries are provided to UNESCO by OECD, EUROSTAT and the Network on Science and Technology Indicators (RICYT).

Gross domestic expenditure on R&D (GERD) is total intramural expenditure on R&D performed on the national territory during a given period. It includes R&D performed within a country and funded from abroad but excludes payments made abroad for R&D.

The sources of funds for GERD are classified according to the following five categories:

- *Business enterprise funds* include funds allocated to R&D by all firms, organizations and institutions whose primary activity is the market production of goods and services (other than the higher education sector) for sale to the general public at an economically significant price, and those private non-profit institutes mainly serving these firms, organizations and institutions.
- *Government funds* refer to funds allocated to R&D by the central (federal), state or local government authorities. These include all departments, offices and other bodies which furnish, but normally do not sell to the community, those common services, other than higher education, which cannot be conveniently and economically provided, as well as those that administer the state and the economic and social policy of the community. Public enterprises funds are included in the business enterprise funds sector. Government funds also include private non-profit institutes controlled and mainly financed by government.
- *Higher education funds* include funds allocated to R&D by institutions of higher education comprising all universities, colleges of technology, other institutes of post-secondary education, and all research institutes, experimental stations and clinics operating under the direct control of or administered by or associated with higher educational establishments.
- *Private non-profit funds* are funds allocated to R&D by non-market, private non-profit institutions serving the general public, as well as by private individuals and households.
- *Funds from abroad* refer to funds allocated to R&D by institutions and individuals located outside the political frontiers of a country except for vehicles, ships, aircraft and space satellites operated by domestic organizations and testing grounds acquired by such organizations, and by all international organizations (except business enterprises) including their facilities and operations within the country's borders.

dénombrement inclut les employés à 'temps plein' et les employés à 'temps partiel'. Équivalent temps plein (ETP) peut être considéré comme une année-personne. Ainsi, une personne qui consacre 30% de son temps en R&D et le reste à d'autres activités (enseignement, administration universitaire ou direction d'étudiants) compte pour 0.3 ETP en R&D. De façon analogue, si un employé travaille à temps plein dans un centre de R&D pendant six mois seulement, il compte pour 0.5 ETP.

Pour tout renseignement complémentaire, voir le site Web de l'Institut de statistique de l'UNESCO www.uis.unesco.org.

Tableau 57: Les données présentées sur les dépenses intérieures brutes de recherche et développement sont compilées par l'Institut de statistique de l'UNESCO. Les données de certains pays ont été fournies à l'UNESCO par l'OCDE, EUROSTAT et «la Red de Indicadores de Ciencia y Technología (RICYT)».

La dépense intérieure brute de R-D (DIRD) est la dépense totale intra-muros afférente aux travaux de R-D exécutés sur le territoire national pendant une période donnée. Elle comprend la R-D exécutée sur le territoire national et financée par l'étranger mais ne tient pas compte des paiements effectués à l'étranger pour des travaux de R-D.

Les sources de financement pour la DIRD sont classées selon les cinq catégories suivantes:

- *Les fonds des entreprises* incluent les fonds alloués à la R-D par toutes les firmes, organismes et institutions dont l'activité première est la production marchande de biens ou de services (autres que dans le secteur d'enseignement supérieur) en vue de leur vente au public, à un prix qui correspond à la réalité économique, et les institutions privées sans but lucratif principalement au service de ces entreprises, organismes et institutions.
- *Les fonds de l'Etat* sont les fonds fournis à la R-D par le gouvernement central (fédéral), d'état ou par les autorités locales. Ceci inclut tous les ministères, bureaux et autres organismes qui fournissent, sans normalement les vendre, des services collectifs autres que d'enseignement supérieur, qu'il n'est pas possible d'assurer de façon pratique et économique par d'autres moyens et qui, de surcroît, administrent les affaires publiques et appliquent la politique économique et sociale de la collectivité. Les fonds des entreprises publiques sont compris dans ceux du secteur des entreprises. Les fonds de l'Etat incluent également les institutions privées sans but lucratif contrôlées et principalement financées par l'Etat.
- *Les fonds de l'enseignement supérieur* inclut les fonds fournis à la R-D par les établissements d'enseignement supérieur tels que toutes les universités, grandes écoles, instituts de technologie et autres établissements post-secondaires, ainsi que tous les instituts de recherche, les stations d'es-

The absolute figures for R&D expenditure should not be compared country by country. Such comparisons would require the conversion of national currencies into a common currency by means of special R&D exchange rates. Official exchange rates do not always reflect the real costs of R&D activities and comparisons are based on such rates can result in misleading conclusions, although they can be used to indicate a gross order of magnitude.

More information can be found on the UNESCO Institute for Statistics web site www.uis.unesco.org.

sais et les cliniques qui travaillent sous le contrôle direct des établissements d'enseignement supérieur ou qui sont administrés par ces derniers ou leur sont associés.

- *Les fonds d'institutions privées sans but lucratif* sont les fonds destinés à la R-D par les institutions privées sans but lucratif non marchandes au service du public, ainsi que par les simples particuliers ou les ménages.
- *Les fonds étrangers* concernent les fonds destinés à la R-D par les institutions et les individus se trouvant en dehors des frontières politiques d'un pays, à l'exception des véhicules, navires, avions et satellites utilisés par des institutions nationales, ainsi que des terrains d'essai acquis par ces institutions, et par toutes les organisations internationales (à l'exception des entreprises), y compris leurs installations et leurs activités à l'intérieur des frontières d'un pays.

Il faut éviter de comparer les chiffres absolus concernant les dépenses de R-D d'un pays à l'autre. On ne pourrait procéder à des comparaisons détaillées qu'en convertissant en une même monnaie les sommes libellées en monnaie nationale au moyen de taux de change spécialement applicables aux activités de R-D. Les taux de change officiels ne reflètent pas toujours le coût réel des activités de R-D, et les comparaisons établies sur la base de ces taux peuvent conduire à des conclusions trompeuses; toutefois, elles peuvent être utilisées pour donner une idée de l'ordre de grandeur.

Pour tout renseignement complémentaire, voir le site Web de l'Institut de statistique de l'UNESCO www.uis.unesco.org.

Part Four

International economic relations

Chapter XVI International merchandise trade (tables 58-60)

Chapter XVII International tourism (tables 61-63)

Chapter XVIII Balance of payments (table 64)

Chapter XIX International finance (tables 65 and 66)

Chapter XX Development assistance (tables 67-69)

Part Four of the *Yearbook* presents statistics on international economic relations in areas of international merchandise trade, international tourism, balance of payments and assistance to developing countries. The series cover all countries or areas of the world for which data have been made available.

Quatrième partie

Relations économiques internationales

Chapitre XVI Commerce international des marchandises (tableaux 58 à 60)

Chapitre XVII Tourisme international (tableaux 61 à 63)

Chapitre XVIII Balance des paiements (tableau 64)

Chapitre XIX Finances internationales (tableaux 65 et 66)

Chapitre XX Aide au développement (tableaux 67 à 69)

La quatrième partie de l'*Annuaire* présente des statistiques sur les relations économiques internationales dans les domaines du commerce international des marchandises, du tourisme international, de la balance des paiements et de l'assistance aux pays en développement. Les séries couvrent tous les pays ou les zones du monde pour lesquels des données sont disponibles.

Total imports and exports

Imports c.i.f., exports f.o.b. and balance, value in million US dollars

Importations et exportations totales

Importations c.a.f., exportations f.o.b. et balance, valeur en millions de dollars E.U.

Region, country or area&	Sys.t	1999	2000	2001	2002	2003	2004	2005	Région, pays ou zone&
World									**Monde**
Imports		**5 458 744**	**6 155 738**	**5 935 208**	**6 149 371**	**7 166 739**	**8 744 818**	**9 905 011**	**Importations**
Exports		**5 353 458**	**5 983 103**	**5 752 323**	**6 025 725**	**7 005 620**	**8 515 138**	**9 667 598**	**Exportations**
Balance		**-105 286**	**-172 635**	**-182 885**	**-123 646**	**-161 119**	**-229 680**	**-237 414**	**Balance**
Developed economies[1,2]									**Economies développées[1,2]**
Imports		**3 979 609**	**4 379 017**	**4 213 952**	**4 336 231**	**5 033 241**	**5 994 197**	**6 645 526**	**Importations**
Exports		**3 756 025**	**4 012 321**	**3 897 400**	**4 033 866**	**4 642 448**	**5 466 695**	**5 924 751**	**Exportations**
Balance		**-223 585**	**-366 696**	**-316 552**	**-302 365**	**-390 794**	**-527 502**	**-720 775**	**Balance**
Asia and the Pacific - Developed economies									**Asie et Pacifique - Economies dévelop.**
Imports		**376 016**	**447 181**	**406 269**	**399 695**	**457 240**	**541 373**	**599 179**	**Importations**
Exports		**468 737**	**538 650**	**460 616**	**470 894**	**526 583**	**626 710**	**655 223**	**Exportations**
Balance		**92 720**	**91 469**	**54 348**	**71 199**	**69 343**	**85 337**	**56 043**	**Balance**
Australia									Australie
Imports	G	69 158	71 537	63 890	72 693	89 089	109 383	125 283	Importations
Exports	G	56 080	63 878	63 389	65 036	71 551	86 420	105 833	Exportations
Balance		-13 078	-7 659	-501	-7 657	-17 539	-22 962	-19 449	Balance
Japan									Japon
Imports	G	310 039	379 491	349 189	337 209	383 085	454 592	514 988	Importations
Exports	G	417 659	479 227	403 616	416 730	471 999	565 743	594 986	Exportations
Balance		107 620	99 736	54 427	79 520	88 914	111 150	79 998	Balance
New Zealand									Nouvelle-Zélande
Imports	G	14 299	13 905	13 308	15 046	18 559	23 195	26 234	Importations
Exports	G	12 477	13 297	13 730	14 382	16 527	20 344	21 729	Exportations
Balance		-1 821	-608	422	-664	-2 033	-2 850	-4 505	Balance
Europe - Developed economies[3]									**Europe - Economies dévelop.[3]**
Imports		**2 394 327**	**2 516 836**	**2 485 626**	**2 592 441**	**3 121 025**	**3 760 844**	**4 111 844**	**Importations**
Exports		**2 418 758**	**2 498 950**	**2 527 434**	**2 696 323**	**3 206 440**	**3 824 788**	**4 125 392**	**Exportations**
Balance		**24 431**	**-17 886**	**41 807**	**103 882**	**85 415**	**63 944**	**13 548**	**Balance**
Andorra									Andorre
Imports	S	...	...	...	...	...	1 767	1 781	Importations
Exports	S	...	...	...	...	...	123	141	Exportations
Balance		...	...	...	...	...	-1 644	-1 641	Balance
Austria									Autriche
Imports	S	69 557	68 986	70 492	72 796	91 595	113 344	119 965	Importations
Exports	S	64 126	64 167	66 492	73 113	89 257	111 720	117 740	Exportations
Balance		-5 431	-4 819	-3 999	316	-2 339	-1 623	-2 225	Balance
Belgium[4]									Belgique[4]
Imports	S	164 610	176 992	178 715	198 125	234 947	285 596	318 768	Importations
Exports	S	178 976	187 876	190 361	215 877	255 598	306 816	335 868	Exportations
Balance		14 366	10 884	11 646	17 752	20 650	21 220	17 100	Balance
Croatia									Croatie
Imports	G	7 799	7 887	9 147	10 722	14 209	16 589	18 560	Importations
Exports	G	4 303	4 432	4 666	4 904	6 187	8 024	8 773	Exportations
Balance		-3 496	-3 455	-4 481	-5 818	-8 022	-8 565	-9 788	Balance
Czech Republic[5]									République tchèque[5]
Imports	S	28 087	32 180	36 473	40 736	51 245	68 435	76 347	Importations
Exports	S	26 245	29 057	33 399	38 488	48 715	67 198	77 988	Exportations
Balance		-1 842	-3 123	-3 075	-2 249	-2 530	-1 237	1 641	Balance
Denmark									Danemark
Imports	S	44 518	44 364	44 132	48 890	56 227	66 845	74 251	Importations
Exports	S	50 398	50 390	51 077	56 308	65 280	75 568	83 569	Exportations
Balance		5 880	6 025	6 945	7 418	9 052	8 723	9 318	Balance

Total imports and exports—Imports c.i.f., exports f.o.b., and balance, value in million US dollars (*continued*)

Importations et exportations totales—Importations c.a.f., exportations f.o.b. et balance, valeur en millions de dollars E.U. (*suite*)

Region, country or area&	Sys.t	1999	2000	2001	2002	2003	2004	2005	Région, pays ou zone&
Estonia[3,6]									Estonie[3,6]
Imports	S	3 427	4 236	4 280	4 810	6 480	8 336	10 111	Importations
Exports	S	2 383	3 166	3 298	3 448	4 539	5 936	7 688	Exportations
Balance		-1 045	-1 070	-982	-1 363	-1 942	-2 400	-2 423	Balance
Faeroe Islands									Iles Féroé
Imports	G	470	532	498	...	...	...	...	Importations
Exports	G	468	472	514	...	...	...	...	Exportations
Balance		-2	-60	16	...	...	...	...	Balance
Finland									Finlande
Imports	G	31 617	33 900	32 114	33 642	41 600	50 677	58 474	Importations
Exports	G	41 841	45 482	42 802	44 671	52 513	60 916	65 240	Exportations
Balance		10 224	11 582	10 688	11 029	10 913	10 239	6 765	Balance
France[7]									France[7]
Imports	S	294 976	310 989	302 016	312 164	370 144	442 605	482 357	Importations
Exports	S	302 482	300 085	297 188	312 011	364 170	424 441	439 032	Exportations
Balance		7 507	-10 904	-4 828	-154	-5 975	-18 164	-43 325	Balance
Germany[8]									Allemagne[8]
Imports	S	473 551	495 450	486 053	490 157	604 729	718 269	777 531	Importations
Exports	S	542 884	550 222	571 460	615 705	751 824	911 859	977 913	Exportations
Balance		69 334	54 772	85 407	125 548	147 095	193 591	200 382	Balance
Gibraltar									Gibraltar
Imports		485	480	435	385	468	535	...	Importations
Exports		120	126	120	148	147	199	...	Exportations
Balance		-365	-354	-315	-236	-320	-336	...	Balance
Greece									Grèce
Imports	S	28 720	29 221	29 928	31 164	44 375	51 559	53 989	Importations
Exports	S	10 475	10 747	9 483	10 315	13 195	14 996	17 017	Exportations
Balance		-18 244	-18 474	-20 444	-20 849	-31 180	-36 564	-36 972	Balance
Greenland									Groenland
Imports	G	409	364	366	398	492	559	...	Importations
Exports	G	276	271	283	323	412	482	...	Exportations
Balance		-134	-93	-83	-76	-81	-77	...	Balance
Hungary[6,9]									Hongrie[6,9]
Imports	S	27 923	31 955	33 724	37 787	47 602	59 636	65 783	Importations
Exports	S	24 950	28 016	30 530	34 512	42 532	54 893	62 179	Exportations
Balance		-2 973	-3 939	-3 195	-3 276	-5 070	-4 744	-3 604	Balance
Iceland									Islande
Imports	G	2 503	2 591	2 253	2 274	2 788	3 551	4 557	Importations
Exports	G	2 005	1 891	2 021	2 227	2 386	2 896	2 947	Exportations
Balance		-498	-700	-232	-47	-403	-654	-1 610	Balance
Ireland									Irlande
Imports	G	47 195	51 444	51 305	51 508	53 315	61 413	69 178	Importations
Exports	G	71 221	77 097	83 020	87 497	92 431	104 204	109 605	Exportations
Balance		24 026	25 653	31 715	35 990	39 117	42 791	40 427	Balance
Italy									Italie
Imports	S	220 327	238 071	236 128	246 613	297 405	355 269	385 521	Importations
Exports	S	235 180	239 934	244 253	254 219	299 468	353 544	373 486	Exportations
Balance		14 852	1 863	8 125	7 606	2 063	-1 726	-12 035	Balance
Latvia[3]									Lettonie[3]
Imports	S	2 945	3 187	3 504	4 053	5 242	7 048	8 592	Importations
Exports	S	1 723	1 867	2 001	2 284	2 893	3 983	5 108	Exportations
Balance		-1 222	-1 320	-1 504	-1 769	-2 350	-3 066	-3 483	Balance
Lithuania[3]									Lituanie[3]
Imports	G	4 627	5 219	6 060	7 524	9 668	12 386	15 510	Importations
Exports	G	2 754	3 548	4 279	5 231	6 970	9 307	11 782	Exportations
Balance		-1 873	-1 671	-1 781	-2 294	-2 698	-3 079	-3 729	Balance

Total imports and exports—Imports c.i.f., exports f.o.b., and balance, value in million US dollars *(continued)*

Importations et exportations totales—Importations c.a.f., exportations f.o.b. et balance, valeur en millions de dollars E.U. *(suite)*

Region, country or area&	Sys.t	1999	2000	2001	2002	2003	2004	2005	Région, pays ou zone&
Luxembourg									Luxembourg
Imports	S	11 045	10 718	11 153	11 602	13 694	16 829	17 565	Importations
Exports	S	7 895	7 950	8 239	8 499	9 980	12 181	12 699	Exportations
Balance		-3 150	-2 768	-2 914	-3 103	-3 714	-4 648	-4 866	Balance
Malta									Malte
Imports	G	2 841	3 400	2 726	2 840	3 399	3 824	3 807	Importations
Exports	G	1 980	2 443	1 958	2 223	2 468	2 628	2 376	Exportations
Balance		-861	-957	-768	-616	-931	-1 196	-1 432	Balance
Netherlands									Pays-Bas
Imports	S	187 468	198 926	195 569	194 130	234 014	284 020	309 797	Importations
Exports	S	200 250	213 425	216 180	219 857	264 849	318 066	349 850	Exportations
Balance		12 783	14 499	20 611	25 727	30 835	34 046	40 053	Balance
Norway									Norvège
Imports	G	34 172	34 351	32 954	34 889	39 284	48 062	54 786	Importations
Exports	G	45 474	60 063	59 193	59 576	67 103	81 709	101 917	Exportations
Balance		11 302	25 712	26 239	24 687	27 818	33 646	47 131	Balance
Poland									Pologne
Imports	S	45 778	48 970	50 378	55 141	68 153	89 094	100 759	Importations
Exports	S	27 323	31 684	36 159	41 032	53 699	74 831	89 214	Exportations
Balance		-18 455	-17 285	-14 219	-14 108	-14 453	-14 264	-11 545	Balance
Portugal									Portugal
Imports	S	39 826	38 192	39 422	38 326	40 843	49 225	53 407	Importations
Exports	S	25 228	23 279	24 449	25 536	30 714	33 023	32 137	Exportations
Balance		-14 599	-14 913	-14 973	-12 791	-10 129	-16 201	-21 270	Balance
Slovakia									Slovaquie
Imports	S	11 688	13 413	15 501	17 460	23 760	30 469	36 168	Importations
Exports	S	10 062	11 889	12 641	14 478	21 966	27 605	31 997	Exportations
Balance		-1 625	-1 524	-2 860	-2 983	-1 794	-2 864	-4 171	Balance
Slovenia									Slovénie
Imports	S	10 083	10 116	10 148	10 933	13 853	17 571	19 626	Importations
Exports	S	8 546	8 732	9 252	10 357	12 767	15 879	17 896	Exportations
Balance		-1 537	-1 384	-895	-576	-1 086	-1 692	-1 730	Balance
Spain									Espagne
Imports	S	144 438	152 901	153 634	163 575	208 553	257 672	287 610	Importations
Exports	S	109 966	113 348	115 175	123 563	156 024	182 156	191 021	Exportations
Balance		-34 473	-39 553	-38 459	-40 012	-52 529	-75 516	-96 589	Balance
Sweden									Suède
Imports	G	68 721	73 331	64 316	67 667	84 197	100 792	111 326	Importations
Exports	G	84 772	87 759	78 173	82 965	102 405	123 306	130 210	Exportations
Balance		16 050	14 428	13 857	15 298	18 208	22 514	18 884	Balance
Switzerland									Suisse
Imports	S	75 440	76 104	77 086	82 387	95 600	110 324	119 784	Importations
Exports	S	76 124	74 867	78 082	87 370	100 744	117 820	126 099	Exportations
Balance		684	-1 237	996	4 983	5 144	7 496	6 314	Balance
United Kingdom									Royaume-Uni
Imports	G	317 963	334 371	320 956	335 458	380 821	451 715	483 064	Importations
Exports	G	268 203	281 525	267 357	276 315	304 268	341 621	371 406	Exportations
Balance		-49 760	-52 846	-53 599	-59 143	-76 553	-110 094	-111 658	Balance
North America - Developed economies									**Amerique du Nord - Economies dévelop.**
Imports		**1 209 266**	**1 415 000**	**1 322 058**	**1 344 096**	**1 454 976**	**1 691 980**	**1 934 503**	**Importations**
Exports		**868 530**	**974 722**	**909 350**	**866 649**	**909 424**	**1 015 197**	**1 144 137**	**Exportations**
Balance		**-340 736**	**-440 278**	**-412 707**	**-477 447**	**-545 552**	**-676 783**	**-790 366**	**Balance**
Bermuda									Bermudes
Imports	G	712	720	721	...	833	...	937	Importations
Exports	G	...	...	...	...	52	...	26	Exportations
Balance		...	...	...	...	-781	...	-911	Balance

Total imports and exports—Imports c.i.f., exports f.o.b., and balance, value in million US dollars (*continued*)
Importations et exportations totales—Importations c.a.f., exportations f.o.b. et balance, valeur en millions de dollars E.U. (*suite*)

Region, country or area&	Sys.t	1999	2000	2001	2002	2003	2004	2005	Région, pays ou zone&
Canada[5]									Canada[5]
Imports	G	214 791	238 812	221 757	221 961	239 083	273 084	323 498	Importations
Exports	G	238 422	276 645	259 857	252 408	272 696	304 456	359 421	Exportations
Balance		23 631	37 833	38 100	30 447	33 613	31 371	35 923	Balance
United States[10]									Etats-Unis[10]
Imports	G	1 059 440	1 259 300	1 179 180	1 200 230	1 303 050	1 525 680	1 732 350	Importations
Exports	G	695 797	781 918	729 100	693 103	724 771	818 520	907 158	Exportations
Balance		-363 643	-477 382	-450 080	-507 127	-578 279	-707 160	-825 192	Balance
South-eastern Europe									**Europe du Sud-Est**
Imports		**25 349**	**29 344**	**33 798**	**38 806**	**50 176**	**65 367**	**79 198**	**Importations**
Exports		**16 257**	**19 353**	**20 679**	**23 930**	**30 313**	**39 681**	**46 969**	**Exportations**
Balance		**-9 091**	**-9 992**	**-13 119**	**-14 876**	**-19 863**	**-25 686**	**-32 228**	**Balance**
Albania									Albanie
Imports	G	1 154	1 090	1 327	1 503	1 864	2 309	2 614	Importations
Exports	G	351	258	307	340	448	605	658	Exportations
Balance		-803	-832	-1 020	-1 164	-1 416	-1 703	-1 956	Balance
Bosnia and Herzegovina									Bosnie-Herzégovine
Imports	S	3 276	3 083	3 342	3 912	4 777	...	...	Importations
Exports	S	749	1 067	1 031	1 015	1 372	...	...	Exportations
Balance		-2 528	-2 017	-2 311	-2 897	-3 405	...	...	Balance
Bulgaria									Bulgarie
Imports	S	5 454	6 505	7 263	7 987	10 887	14 467	18 163	Importations
Exports	S	3 964	4 809	5 115	5 749	7 540	9 931	11 740	Exportations
Balance		-1 490	-1 696	-2 148	-2 238	-3 346	-4 536	-6 423	Balance
Romania									Roumanie
Imports	S	10 392	13 055	15 561	17 862	24 003	32 664	40 463	Importations
Exports	S	8 505	10 367	11 391	13 876	17 619	23 485	27 730	Exportations
Balance		-1 887	-2 688	-4 170	-3 986	-6 384	-9 179	-12 733	Balance
Serbia and Montenegro									Serbie-et-Monténégro
Imports	S	3 296	3 711	4 837	...	...	...	...	Importations
Exports	S	1 498	1 723	1 903	...	...	...	...	Exportations
Balance		-1 798	-1 988	-2 934	...	...	...	...	Balance
TFYR of Macedonia									L'ex-R.y. Macédoine
Imports	S	1 776	2 094	1 694	1 995	2 306	2 932	3 228	Importations
Exports	S	1 191	1 323	1 158	1 116	1 367	1 676	2 041	Exportations
Balance		-585	-771	-536	-880	-939	-1 256	-1 187	Balance
CIS[§3]									**CEI**[§3]
Imports		**61 262**	**70 829**	**82 776**	**89 214**	**113 387**	**149 462**	**186 954**	**Importations**
Exports		**103 640**	**143 503**	**142 673**	**152 848**	**190 863**	**261 414**	**333 656**	**Exportations**
Balance		**42 378**	**72 674**	**59 897**	**63 634**	**77 475**	**111 952**	**146 701**	**Balance**
Asia									**Asia**
Imports		**11 878**	**13 706**	**16 077**	**16 078**	**20 244**	**26 890**	**33 426**	**Importations**
Exports		**12 790**	**18 176**	**18 559**	**19 663**	**23 590**	**32 589**	**41 536**	**Exportations**
Balance		**912**	**4 469**	**2 482**	**3 585**	**3 346**	**5 699**	**8 110**	**Balance**
Armenia									Arménie
Imports	S	800	882	874	987	1 280	1 351	1 768	Importations
Exports	S	232	294	343	505	686	715	950	Exportations
Balance		-568	-588	-532	-482	-594	-636	-818	Balance
Azerbaijan									Azerbaïdjan
Imports	G	1 036	1 172	1 431	1 666	2 626	3 516	4 211	Importations
Exports	G	930	1 745	2 314	2 167	2 590	3 615	4 347	Exportations
Balance		-106	573	883	502	-36	99	136	Balance
Georgia									Géorgie
Imports	G	585	709	752	796	1 141	1 851	2 492	Importations
Exports	G	241	323	317	347	463	656	868	Exportations
Balance		-343	-386	-436	-449	-679	-1 195	-1 623	Balance

Region, country or area&	Sys.t	1999	2000	2001	2002	2003	2004	2005	Région, pays ou zone&
Kazakhstan									Kazakhstan
Imports	G	3 655	5 040	6 446	6 584	8 409	12 781	17 353	Importations
Exports	G	5 872	8 812	8 639	9 670	12 927	20 093	27 849	Exportations
Balance		2 217	3 772	2 193	3 086	4 518	7 312	10 497	Balance
Kyrgyzstan									Kirghizistan
Imports	S	600	554	467	587	717	941	1 102	Importations
Exports	S	454	505	476	486	582	719	672	Exportations
Balance		-146	-50	9	-101	-135	-222	-430	Balance
Tajikistan									Tadjikistan
Imports	G	664	675	688	721	881	...	...	Importations
Exports	G	689	784	652	737	797	...	...	Exportations
Balance		25	109	-36	17	-84	...	...	Balance
Turkmenistan									Turkménistan
Imports	G	...	...	...	2 119	2 512	...	...	Importations
Exports	G	...	...	...	2 856	2 632	...	...	Exportations
Balance		...	...	...	736	120	...	...	Balance
Uzbekistan									Ouzbékistan
Imports	G	3 111	2 947	3 137	2 712	...	...	...	Importations
Exports	G	3 236	3 265	3 265	2 988	...	...	...	Exportations
Balance		125	317	128	276	...	...	...	Balance
Europe									**Europe**
Imports		**49 384**	**57 122**	**66 699**	**73 136**	**93 143**	**122 572**	**153 529**	**Importations**
Exports		**90 850**	**125 327**	**124 114**	**133 185**	**167 273**	**228 825**	**292 120**	**Exportations**
Balance		**41 466**	**68 205**	**57 415**	**60 049**	**74 130**	**106 253**	**138 591**	**Balance**
Belarus									Bélarus
Imports	G	6 674	8 646	8 286	9 092	11 558	16 491	16 708	Importations
Exports	G	5 909	7 326	7 451	8 021	9 946	13 774	15 979	Exportations
Balance		-765	-1 320	-836	-1 071	-1 612	-2 717	-729	Balance
Republic of Moldova									République de Moldova
Imports	G	586	776	893	1 039	1 403	1 773	2 293	Importations
Exports	G	474	472	568	644	789	980	1 091	Exportations
Balance		-112	-305	-325	-395	-614	-793	-1 202	Balance
Russian Federation									Fédération de Russie
Imports	G	30 278	33 880	41 883	46 177	57 347	75 569	98 688	Importations
Exports	G	72 885	103 093	99 969	106 712	133 656	181 663	241 118	Exportations
Balance		42 607	69 213	58 086	60 535	76 309	106 093	142 429	Balance
Ukraine									Ukraine
Imports	G	11 846	13 956	15 775	16 977	23 020	28 997	36 136	Importations
Exports	G	11 582	14 573	16 265	17 957	23 067	32 666	34 228	Exportations
Balance		-264	617	490	980	47	3 669	-1 908	Balance
Northern Africa									**Afrique du Nord**
Imports		**47 523**	**46 790**	**47 433**	**50 144**	**52 776**	**67 659**	**80 167**	**Importations**
Exports		**37 043**	**52 419**	**47 732**	**47 902**	**60 615**	**78 936**	**106 003**	**Exportations**
Balance		**-10 480**	**5 629**	**298**	**-2 241**	**7 839**	**11 277**	**25 836**	**Balance**
Algeria									Algérie
Imports	S	9 161	9 169	9 941	11 969	12 392	18 166	20 039	Importations
Exports	S	12 530	22 030	19 139	18 801	23 206	31 300	44 389	Exportations
Balance		3 369	12 861	9 198	6 832	10 814	13 133	24 350	Balance
Egypt[11]									Egypte[11]
Imports	S	16 022	14 010	12 756	12 552	11 170	12 859	19 851	Importations
Exports	S	3 559	4 691	4 128	4 708	6 327	7 530	10 672	Exportations
Balance		-12 463	-9 319	-8 628	-7 844	-4 842	-5 329	-9 179	Balance
Libyan Arab Jamah.									Jamah. arabe libyenne
Imports	G	4 158	3 704	4 363	4 412	4 312	6 333	7 175	Importations
Exports	G	7 941	12 626	10 902	9 880	14 541	20 837	30 322	Exportations
Balance		3 783	8 922	6 538	5 468	10 230	14 503	23 148	Balance

Region, country or area&	Sys.†	1999	2000	2001	2002	2003	2004	2005	Région, pays ou zone&
Morocco									Maroc
Imports	S	9 925	11 534	11 038	11 864	14 250	17 807	20 341	Importations
Exports	S	7 367	7 423	7 144	7 849	8 778	9 917	10 549	Exportations
Balance		-2 558	-4 111	-3 893	-4 014	-5 472	-7 890	-9 792	Balance
Tunisia									Tunisie
Imports	G	8 475	8 567	9 529	9 526	10 910	12 818	13 177	Importations
Exports	G	5 872	5 850	6 621	6 871	8 027	9 685	10 494	Exportations
Balance		-2 603	-2 717	-2 908	-2 655	-2 883	-3 133	-2 683	Balance
Sub-Saharan Africa									**Afrique subsaharienne**
Imports		**78 598**	**81 087**	**85 319**	**83 895**	**109 068**	**135 567**	**159 344**	**Importations**
Exports		**78 042**	**92 541**	**88 009**	**90 822**	**110 580**	**145 840**	**181 043**	**Exportations**
Balance		**-557**	**11 454**	**2 691**	**6 927**	**1 512**	**10 273**	**21 699**	**Balance**
Angola[5]									Angola[5]
Imports	S	3 109	3 040	3 179	3 760	5 480	5 832	8 150	Importations
Exports	S	5 157	7 921	6 534	8 328	9 508	12 975	23 670	Exportations
Balance		2 048	4 881	3 355	4 568	4 028	7 143	15 520	Balance
Benin									Bénin
Imports	S	749	567	623	725	892	894	895	Importations
Exports	S	422	392	372	450	555	667	288	Exportations
Balance		-327	-174	-251	-275	-337	-227	-607	Balance
Botswana									Botswana
Imports	G	2 197	2 469	1 825	1 667	2 590	3 458	4 016	Importations
Exports	G	2 645	2 681	2 366	2 259	3 018	3 596	4 315	Exportations
Balance		447	213	541	592	428	138	299	Balance
Burkina Faso									Burkina Faso
Imports	G	568	654	509	553	688	945	1 287	Importations
Exports	G	216	241	227	247	319	480	600	Exportations
Balance		-353	-413	-282	-306	-368	-465	-687	Balance
Burundi									Burundi
Imports	S	118	148	139	129	157	176	266	Importations
Exports	S	54	50	39	30	38	47	98	Exportations
Balance		-64	-98	-101	-99	-119	-129	-168	Balance
Cameroon									Cameroun
Imports	S	1 314	1 483	1 849	1 876	2 032	2 411	2 441	Importations
Exports	S	1 595	1 823	1 746	1 814	2 260	2 482	2 480	Exportations
Balance		281	341	-104	-62	228	71	38	Balance
Cape Verde									Cap-Vert
Imports	G	262	237	234	276	351	387	438	Importations
Exports	G	11	11	10	11	13	15	18	Exportations
Balance		-251	-227	-224	-266	-338	-372	-421	Balance
Central African Rep.									Rép. centrafricaine
Imports	S	131	117	107	121	130	151	165	Importations
Exports	S	146	160	142	147	122	125	139	Exportations
Balance		15	44	35	27	-8	-26	-26	Balance
Chad									Tchad
Imports	S	317	319	680	1 638	788	750	854	Importations
Exports	S	244	184	189	184	599	2 256	3 245	Exportations
Balance		-73	-135	-491	-1 454	-189	1 506	2 391	Balance
Congo									Congo
Imports	S	844	735	1 103	1 096	1 348	1 765	2 035	Importations
Exports	S	1 555	2 477	2 052	2 294	2 693	3 451	4 979	Exportations
Balance		711	1 742	950	1 197	1 345	1 686	2 944	Balance
Côte d'Ivoire									Côte d'Ivoire
Imports	S	3 252	2 783	2 420	2 462	3 237	4 176	4 686	Importations
Exports	S	4 667	3 885	3 955	5 279	5 803	6 938	7 176	Exportations
Balance		1 415	1 102	1 535	2 817	2 566	2 761	2 490	Balance

Total imports and exports—Imports c.i.f., exports f.o.b., and balance, value in million US dollars (*continued*)
Importations et exportations totales—Importations c.a.f., exportations f.o.b. et balance, valeur en millions de dollars E.U. (*suite*)

Region, country or area&	Sys.t	1999	2000	2001	2002	2003	2004	2005	Région, pays ou zone&
Dem. Rep. of the Congo									Rép. dém. du Congo
Imports	S	568	697	807	1 081	1 594	1 986	2 270	Importations
Exports	S	809	824	901	1 132	1 374	1 850	2 190	Exportations
Balance		241	126	94	51	-220	-137	-80	Balance
Djibouti									Djibouti
Imports	G	153	...	...	...	...	...	...	Importations
Exports	G	12	...	...	...	...	...	...	Exportations
Balance		-140	...	...	...	...	...	...	Balance
Equatorial Guinea									Guinée équatoriale
Imports	G	424	451	812	508	1 225	1 536	2 049	Importations
Exports	G	708	1 097	1 831	2 121	2 803	4 684	6 948	Exportations
Balance		284	646	1 020	1 613	1 578	3 147	4 899	Balance
Eritrea									Erythrée
Imports	G	382	...	...	...	...	...	...	Importations
Exports	G	20	...	...	...	...	...	...	Exportations
Balance		-362	...	...	...	...	...	...	Balance
Ethiopia									Ethiopie
Imports	G	1 538	1 261	1 807	1 622	2 119	3 087	4 127	Importations
Exports	G	469	486	456	480	496	678	883	Exportations
Balance		-1 069	-775	-1 351	-1 142	-1 623	-2 409	-3 244	Balance
Gabon									Gabon
Imports	S	841	996	858	955	1 036	1 277	1 401	Importations
Exports	S	2 392	2 605	2 519	2 413	2 827	3 492	4 653	Exportations
Balance		1 552	1 610	1 661	1 458	1 791	2 215	3 252	Balance
Gambia									Gambie
Imports	G	192	187	134	146	156	229	237	Importations
Exports	G	12	15	10	12	8	10	9	Exportations
Balance		-180	-172	-124	-134	-149	-219	-228	Balance
Ghana									Ghana
Imports	G	3 505	2 973	...	...	...	...	...	Importations
Exports	G	1 935	1 317	...	...	...	...	...	Exportations
Balance		-1 570	-1 656	...	...	...	...	...	Balance
Guinea-Bissau									Guinée-Bissau
Imports	G	50	59	62	59	66	96	119	Importations
Exports	G	51	62	62	54	65	87	80	Exportations
Balance		1	4	1	-5	-1	-9	-39	Balance
Kenya									Kenya
Imports	G	2 833	3 105	3 189	3 245	3 725	4 553	6 149	Importations
Exports	G	1 747	1 734	1 943	2 116	2 411	2 684	3 293	Exportations
Balance		-1 086	-1 372	-1 246	-1 129	-1 314	-1 869	-2 856	Balance
Lesotho									Lesotho
Imports	G	866	809	748	814	1 121	1 437	1 408	Importations
Exports	G	172	221	278	376	485	713	675	Exportations
Balance		-694	-589	-470	-438	-636	-723	-733	Balance
Madagascar									Madagascar
Imports	S	731	999	956	605	1 115	1 411	1 531	Importations
Exports	S	574	828	932	490	863	935	733	Exportations
Balance		-158	-171	-24	-115	-252	-476	-798	Balance
Malawi									Malawi
Imports	G	673	533	563	695	786	933	1 095	Importations
Exports	G	453	379	449	407	525	483	496	Exportations
Balance		-221	-153	-113	-288	-261	-449	-599	Balance
Mali									Mali
Imports	S	824	807	989	929	1 248	1 327	1 269	Importations
Exports	S	571	552	724	874	928	1 024	1 136	Exportations
Balance		-253	-255	-265	-54	-320	-302	-133	Balance

Total imports and exports—Imports c.i.f., exports f.o.b., and balance, value in million US dollars (*continued*)
Importations et exportations totales—Importations c.a.f., exportations f.o.b. et balance, valeur en millions de dollars E.U. (*suite*)

Region, country or area&	Sys.†	1999	2000	2001	2002	2003	2004	2005	Région, pays ou zone&
Mauritius									Maurice
Imports	G	2 248	2 091	1 987	2 159	2 364	2 771	3 160	Importations
Exports	G	1 588	1 551	1 628	1 801	1 899	1 993	2 144	Exportations
Balance		-659	-540	-359	-358	-465	-778	-1 016	Balance
Mozambique									Mozambique
Imports	S	1 139	1 158	1 063	1 640	1 753	1 970	2 420	Importations
Exports	S	263	364	703	810	1 045	1 504	1 790	Exportations
Balance		-876	-794	-360	-830	-708	-466	-630	Balance
Namibia									Namibie
Imports	G	1 609	1 539	1 542	1 484	1 999	2 432	2 440	Importations
Exports	G	1 233	1 317	1 180	1 077	1 267	1 835	1 987	Exportations
Balance		-376	-222	-362	-407	-732	-598	-453	Balance
Niger									Niger
Imports	S	410	395	411	470	624	789	919	Importations
Exports	S	288	284	273	279	351	381	411	Exportations
Balance		-122	-111	-139	-191	-272	-408	-507	Balance
Nigeria									Nigéria
Imports	G	8 588	8 721	11 586	7 547	10 853	14 164	15 200	Importations
Exports	G	13 856	20 975	17 261	15 107	19 887	31 148	42 277	Exportations
Balance		5 268	12 254	5 675	7 560	9 033	16 984	27 077	Balance
Rwanda									Rwanda
Imports	G	250	211	250	203	245	284	432	Importations
Exports	G	60	52	85	56	58	98	125	Exportations
Balance		-190	-159	-165	-147	-187	-186	-306	Balance
Senegal									Sénégal
Imports	G	1 561	1 518	1 727	2 038	2 395	2 844	3 326	Importations
Exports	G	1 025	919	1 002	1 070	1 259	1 464	1 598	Exportations
Balance		-536	-598	-726	-968	-1 136	-1 379	-1 728	Balance
Seychelles									Seychelles
Imports	G	434	343	478	421	412	497	676	Importations
Exports	G	145	193	217	227	273	199	212	Exportations
Balance		-289	-150	-262	-194	-139	-297	-464	Balance
Sierra Leone									Sierra Leone
Imports	S	80	149	182	264	303	286	345	Importations
Exports	S	6	13	29	49	92	139	159	Exportations
Balance		-74	-136	-153	-216	-211	-148	-186	Balance
South Africa[12,13]									Afrique du Sud[12,13]
Imports	G	26 697	29 700	28 264	29 281	41 120	53 518	62 325	Importations
Exports	G	26 708	29 987	29 283	29 733	36 503	46 148	51 640	Exportations
Balance		11	287	1 019	452	-4 617	-7 370	-10 685	Balance
Sudan[14]									Soudan[14]
Imports	G	1 415	1 553	2 301	2 446	2 882	4 075	6 757	Importations
Exports	G	780	1 807	1 699	1 949	2 542	3 778	4 824	Exportations
Balance		-635	254	-602	-497	-340	-297	-1 933	Balance
Swaziland									Swaziland
Imports	G	1 068	1 039	1 116	946	1 523	1 926	2 232	Importations
Exports	G	937	903	1 048	1 038	1 644	1 951	2 138	Exportations
Balance		-131	-137	-68	93	121	25	-95	Balance
Togo									Togo
Imports	S	486	485	516	579	844	558	593	Importations
Exports	S	388	361	357	427	616	367	359	Exportations
Balance		-98	-124	-159	-152	-228	-191	-234	Balance
Uganda									Ouganda
Imports	G	1 342	1 512	1 594	1 112	1 251	1 463	1 895	Importations
Exports	G	517	469	457	442	563	605	821	Exportations
Balance		-825	-1 043	-1 138	-670	-688	-858	-1 075	Balance

Region, country or area&	Sys.t	1999	2000	2001	2002	2003	2004	2005	Région, pays ou zone&
United Rep. of Tanzania									Rép.-Unie de Tanzanie
Imports	G	1 550	1 523	1 715	1 661	2 129	2 509	2 668	Importations
Exports	G	543	663	777	902	1 129	1 335	1 479	Exportations
Balance		-1 007	-860	-937	-758	-1 000	-1 174	-1 190	Balance
Zambia									Zambie
Imports	S	823	997	1 309	1 284	1 576	2 018	2 741	Importations
Exports	S	1 068	681	993	961	981	1 462	1 692	Exportations
Balance		245	-316	-316	-323	-595	-556	-1 049	Balance
Zimbabwe									Zimbabwe
Imports	G	2 125	1 864	1 715	1 752	1 710	2 203	2 750	Importations
Exports	G	1 888	1 925	1 206	1 397	1 400	1 520	1 490	Exportations
Balance		-238	61	-509	-354	-310	-683	-1 260	Balance
Latin America and the Carib.									**Amér. latine et Caraïbes**
Imports		**322 973**	**373 794**	**365 507**	**341 602**	**353 255**	**431 717**	**507 156**	**Importations**
Exports		**293 956**	**352 004**	**337 787**	**341 835**	**372 426**	**458 173**	**553 336**	**Exportations**
Balance		**-29 017**	**-21 790**	**-27 720**	**234**	**19 171**	**26 455**	**46 181**	**Balance**
Caribbean									**Caraïbes**
Imports		**22 526**	**25 162**	**25 258**	**25 949**	**26 533**	**29 192**	**33 231**	**Importations**
Exports		**8 818**	**10 393**	**10 281**	**9 926**	**11 759**	**13 843**	**16 563**	**Exportations**
Balance		**-13 709**	**-14 769**	**-14 976**	**-16 024**	**-14 774**	**-15 349**	**-16 668**	**Balance**
Anguilla									Anguilla
Imports	S	92	95	78	70	77	102	130	Importations
Exports	S	3	4	3	4	4	6	15	Exportations
Balance		-89	-90	-75	-66	-73	-97	-115	Balance
Antigua and Barbuda									Antigua-et-Barbuda
Imports	G	414	402	377	400	422	451	610	Importations
Exports	G	38	50	39	39	45	47	57	Exportations
Balance		-376	-352	-338	-361	-377	-404	-553	Balance
Aruba									Aruba
Imports	S	782	835	841	841	848	875	1 031	Importations
Exports	S	29	173	149	128	83	80	107	Exportations
Balance		-753	-662	-693	-713	-764	-796	-925	Balance
Bahamas[15]									Bahamas[15]
Imports	G	1 757	2 074	1 912	1 728	1 762	1 586	...	Importations
Exports	G	462	576	423	446	425	357	...	Exportations
Balance		-1 295	-1 498	-1 489	-1 282	-1 337	-1 228	...	Balance
Barbados									Barbade
Imports	G	1 108	1 156	1 087	1 039	1 133	1 413	1 604	Importations
Exports	G	264	272	259	242	250	278	359	Exportations
Balance		-844	-884	-827	-798	-883	-1 135	-1 245	Balance
Cuba									Cuba
Imports	S	...	...	...	...	4 613	5 549	...	Importations
Exports	S	...	...	...	...	1 672	2 181	...	Exportations
Balance		...	...	...	...	-2 941	-3 369	...	Balance
Dominica									Dominique
Imports	S	138	148	131	116	128	145	164	Importations
Exports	S	56	54	44	43	40	40	41	Exportations
Balance		-83	-95	-88	-74	-88	-105	-123	Balance
Dominican Republic[5,16]									Rép. dominicaine[5,16]
Imports	G	5 207	6 416	5 937	6 037	5 266	5 368	7 207	Importations
Exports	G	805	966	805	834	1 041	1 251	1 398	Exportations
Balance		-4 402	-5 450	-5 132	-5 204	-4 225	-4 117	-5 809	Balance
Grenada									Grenade
Imports	S	214	248	219	213	257	278	...	Importations
Exports	S	47	71	60	58	42	30	...	Exportations
Balance		-166	-177	-160	-154	-215	-248	...	Balance

Total imports and exports—Imports c.i.f., exports f.o.b., and balance, value in million US dollars (*continued*)
Importations et exportations totales—Importations c.a.f., exportations f.o.b. et balance, valeur en millions de dollars E.U. (*suite*)

Region, country or area&	Sys.t	1999	2000	2001	2002	2003	2004	2005	Région, pays ou zone&
Haiti									Haïti
Imports	G	1 035	1 040	1 017	1 122	1 187	1 317	1 449	Importations
Exports	G	338	313	275	279	346	394	470	Exportations
Balance		-697	-727	-742	-842	-841	-923	-979	Balance
Jamaica									Jamaïque
Imports	G	2 899	3 302	3 361	3 533	3 633	3 772	4 458	Importations
Exports	G	1 241	1 295	1 220	1 123	1 177	1 390	1 499	Exportations
Balance		-1 658	-2 007	-2 140	-2 410	-2 457	-2 382	-2 959	Balance
Saint Kitts and Nevis									Saint-Kitts-et-Nevis
Imports	S	153	196	189	201	205	203	270	Importations
Exports	S	28	33	31	27	48	47	50	Exportations
Balance		-125	-163	-158	-174	-157	-156	-220	Balance
Saint Lucia									Sainte-Lucie
Imports	S	355	355	355	309	403	459	550	Importations
Exports	S	59	47	51	49	85	...	...	Exportations
Balance		-296	-308	-304	-260	-318	...	...	Balance
Saint Vincent-Grenadines									Saint Vincent-Grenadines
Imports	S	201	163	172	179	201	226	240	Importations
Exports	S	49	47	41	39	38	33	40	Exportations
Balance		-152	-116	-130	-139	-163	-192	-200	Balance
Trinidad and Tobago									Trinité-et-Tobago
Imports	S	2 740	3 308	3 576	3 644	3 892	4 858	5 050	Importations
Exports	S	2 803	4 274	4 275	3 883	5 178	6 374	8 476	Exportations
Balance		63	966	698	239	1 286	1 516	3 426	Balance
Latin America									**Amérique latine**
Imports		**300 446**	**348 632**	**340 250**	**315 652**	**326 721**	**402 525**	**473 925**	**Importations**
Exports		**285 138**	**341 611**	**327 506**	**331 910**	**360 667**	**444 330**	**536 774**	**Exportations**
Balance		**-15 308**	**-7 021**	**-12 744**	**16 257**	**33 945**	**41 804**	**62 849**	**Balance**
Argentina									Argentine
Imports	S	25 508	25 280	20 320	8 990	13 834	22 445	28 691	Importations
Exports	S	23 309	26 341	26 543	25 650	29 566	34 576	40 106	Exportations
Balance		-2 200	1 061	6 223	16 660	15 732	12 131	11 415	Balance
Belize									Belize
Imports	G	370	524	517	525	552	514	593	Importations
Exports	G	186	210	163	158	191	205	207	Exportations
Balance		-184	-314	-354	-366	-361	-309	-386	Balance
Bolivia									Bolivie
Imports	G	1 755	1 830	1 708	1 770	1 616	1 844	2 341	Importations
Exports	G	1 051	1 230	1 285	1 299	1 598	2 146	2 671	Exportations
Balance		-704	-600	-423	-471	-18	302	329	Balance
Brazil									Brésil
Imports	G	51 909	59 053	58 640	49 716	50 859	66 410	77 625	Importations
Exports	G	48 011	55 086	58 223	60 362	73 084	96 475	118 308	Exportations
Balance		-3 897	-3 967	-418	10 646	22 225	30 065	40 683	Balance
Chile									Chili
Imports	S	15 987	18 507	17 429	17 092	19 389	24 918	32 637	Importations
Exports	S	17 162	19 210	18 272	18 180	21 664	32 215	40 574	Exportations
Balance		1 175	703	843	1 088	2 276	7 298	7 937	Balance
Colombia									Colombie
Imports	G	10 659	11 539	12 834	12 711	13 889	16 746	21 204	Importations
Exports	G	11 575	13 043	12 290	11 911	13 080	16 224	21 146	Exportations
Balance		917	1 505	-544	-800	-809	-522	-59	Balance
Costa Rica									Costa Rica
Imports	S	6 355	6 389	6 569	7 188	7 663	8 268	9 812	Importations
Exports	S	6 662	5 850	5 021	5 264	6 102	6 301	7 026	Exportations
Balance		308	-539	-1 547	-1 924	-1 561	-1 967	-2 786	Balance

Region, country or area&	Sys.t	1999	2000	2001	2002	2003	2004	2005	Région, pays ou zone&
Ecuador									Equateur
Imports	G	3 017	3 721	5 363	6 431	6 703	8 226	10 287	Importations
Exports	G	4 451	4 927	4 678	5 042	6 223	7 753	10 100	Exportations
Balance		1 434	1 206	-685	-1 390	-480	-473	-187	Balance
El Salvador									El Salvador
Imports	S	3 140	3 795	3 866	3 902	4 375	4 871	5 362	Importations
Exports	S	1 177	1 332	1 213	1 238	1 255	1 381	1 572	Exportations
Balance		-1 963	-2 463	-2 653	-2 664	-3 120	-3 489	-3 790	Balance
Guatemala									Guatemala
Imports	S	4 560	5 171	5 606	6 304	6 722	7 812	8 810	Importations
Exports	S	2 494	2 711	2 464	2 473	2 632	2 939	3 477	Exportations
Balance		-2 066	-2 460	-3 143	-3 831	-4 090	-4 873	-5 333	Balance
Guyana									Guyana
Imports	S	548	582	583	576	576	652	790	Importations
Exports	S	523	502	490	496	513	593	553	Exportations
Balance		-25	-80	-93	-81	-63	-59	-237	Balance
Honduras									Honduras
Imports	S	2 676	2 855	2 942	2 981	3 276	3 916	4 613	Importations
Exports	S	1 164	1 380	1 324	1 321	1 321	1 537	1 679	Exportations
Balance		-1 512	-1 475	-1 617	-1 660	-1 954	-2 379	-2 934	Balance
Mexico[5,17]									Mexique[5,17]
Imports	G	141 975	174 500	168 276	168 679	170 490	197 347	221 414	Importations
Exports	G	136 391	166 367	158 547	160 682	165 396	189 083	213 891	Exportations
Balance		-5 584	-8 133	-9 729	-7 997	-5 094	-8 264	-7 523	Balance
Nicaragua									Nicaragua
Imports	G	1 861	1 805	1 775	1 754	1 879	2 212	2 595	Importations
Exports	G	546	643	589	561	605	756	858	Exportations
Balance		-1 315	-1 163	-1 186	-1 193	-1 275	-1 457	-1 737	Balance
Panama[18]									Panama[18]
Imports	S	3 516	3 379	2 964	2 982	3 086	3 594	4 180	Importations
Exports	S	822	859	911	846	864	944	1 018	Exportations
Balance		-2 694	-2 519	-2 053	-2 136	-2 222	-2 651	-3 162	Balance
Paraguay									Paraguay
Imports	S	1 906	2 193	2 182	1 672	2 065	3 097	2 880	Importations
Exports	S	741	869	990	951	1 242	1 627	1 688	Exportations
Balance		-1 165	-1 324	-1 192	-721	-824	-1 470	-1 192	Balance
Peru[5]									Pérou[5]
Imports	S	6 793	7 407	7 273	7 440	8 244	9 812	12 084	Importations
Exports	S	6 088	6 955	7 026	7 714	9 091	12 617	16 587	Exportations
Balance		-706	-452	-248	274	846	2 805	4 503	Balance
Suriname									Suriname
Imports	G	616	574	136	137	176	217	281	Importations
Exports	G	506	560	201	157	187	232	266	Exportations
Balance		-110	-14	64	20	11	15	-15	Balance
Uruguay									Uruguay
Imports	G	3 357	3 466	3 061	1 964	2 190	3 114	3 879	Importations
Exports	G	2 237	2 295	2 060	1 861	2 206	2 931	3 405	Exportations
Balance		-1 120	-1 171	-1 000	-103	16	-183	-474	Balance
Venezuela (Bolivarian Rep. of)									Venezuela (Rép. bolivar. du)
Imports	G	14 064	16 213	18 323	12 963	9 256	16 679	24 027	Importations
Exports	G	20 190	31 413	25 353	25 890	23 990	33 994	51 859	Exportations
Balance		6 126	15 200	7 030	12 927	14 734	17 315	27 832	Balance
Eastern Asia									**Asie orientale**
Imports		**424 747**	**559 236**	**522 820**	**583 412**	**740 940**	**978 656**	**1 128 323**	**Importations**
Exports		**482 613**	**591 842**	**558 102**	**633 487**	**788 880**	**1 032 705**	**1 256 278**	**Exportations**
Balance		**57 866**	**32 606**	**35 282**	**50 075**	**47 941**	**54 049**	**127 954**	**Balance**

Region, country or area[&]	Sys.[t]	1999	2000	2001	2002	2003	2004	2005	Région, pays ou zone[&]
China[19]									Chine[19]
Imports	S	165 699	225 094	243 553	295 170	412 760	561 229	659 953	Importations
Exports	S	194 931	249 203	266 098	325 596	438 228	593 326	761 953	Exportations
Balance		29 232	24 109	22 545	30 426	25 468	32 097	102 000	Balance
China, Hong Kong SAR									Chine, Hong Kong RAS
Imports	G	179 520	212 805	201 076	207 644	231 896	271 074	299 533	Importations
Exports	G	173 885	201 860	189 894	200 092	223 762	259 260	289 337	Exportations
Balance		-5 635	-10 945	-11 182	-7 552	-8 134	-11 814	-10 196	Balance
China, Macao SAR									Chine, Macao RAS
Imports	G	2 040	2 255	2 386	2 530	2 755	3 478	3 913	Importations
Exports	G	2 200	2 539	2 300	2 356	2 581	2 812	2 476	Exportations
Balance		160	284	-87	-174	-174	-666	-1 438	Balance
Korea, Republic of									Corée, République de
Imports	G	119 752	160 481	141 098	152 126	178 827	224 463	261 238	Importations
Exports	G	143 685	172 267	150 439	162 470	193 817	253 845	284 419	Exportations
Balance		23 933	11 786	9 341	10 344	14 990	29 382	23 181	Balance
Mongolia									Mongolie
Imports	G	513	615	638	691	801	1 021	1 184	Importations
Exports	G	454	536	521	524	616	870	1 065	Exportations
Balance		-59	-79	-116	-167	-185	-151	-119	Balance
Southern Asia									**Asie australe**
Imports		**85 380**	**94 593**	**96 152**	**107 240**	**133 879**	**176 926**	**231 817**	**Importations**
Exports		**74 325**	**90 958**	**86 989**	**98 493**	**116 168**	**147 337**	**188 807**	**Exportations**
Balance		**-11 055**	**-3 635**	**-9 163**	**-8 747**	**-17 711**	**-29 589**	**-43 010**	**Balance**
Afghanistan									Afghanistan
Imports	G	...	1 176	1 696	2 452	2 101	2 177	...	Importations
Exports	G	...	137	68	100	144	314	...	Exportations
Balance		...	-1 039	-1 628	-2 352	-1 957	-1 863	...	Balance
Bangladesh									Bangladesh
Imports	G	7 685	8 358	8 349	7 913	9 516	12 611	12 881	Importations
Exports	G	3 919	4 787	4 826	4 566	5 263	6 615	7 233	Exportations
Balance		-3 766	-3 572	-3 523	-3 348	-4 253	-5 996	-5 648	Balance
Bhutan									Bhoutan
Imports	G	182	175	191	196	249	411	...	Importations
Exports	G	116	103	106	113	133	182	...	Exportations
Balance		-66	-73	-85	-84	-116	-229	...	Balance
India[20]									Inde[20]
Imports	G	46 971	51 563	50 391	56 496	72 559	98 155	138 095	Importations
Exports	G	35 666	42 378	43 352	50 353	58 964	75 877	99 452	Exportations
Balance		-11 305	-9 185	-7 038	-6 143	-13 595	-22 278	-38 643	Balance
Iran (Islamic Rep. of)[21,22]									Iran (Rép. islamique d')[21,22]
Imports	S	12 683	14 347	17 627	21 180	27 676	35 207	41 561	Importations
Exports	S	21 030	28 345	23 904	28 237	33 991	44 403	58 400	Exportations
Balance		8 347	13 998	6 277	7 057	6 315	9 196	16 840	Balance
Maldives									Maldives
Imports	G	402	389	393	392	471	642	745	Importations
Exports	G	64	76	76	90	113	122	103	Exportations
Balance		-338	-313	-317	-301	-358	-519	-641	Balance
Nepal									Népal
Imports	G	1 422	1 573	1 475	1 419	1 754	1 870	1 860	Importations
Exports	G	602	804	738	567	662	756	829	Exportations
Balance		-820	-768	-737	-851	-1 092	-1 114	-1 031	Balance
Pakistan									Pakistan
Imports	G	10 216	10 864	10 192	11 227	13 038	17 949	25 356	Importations
Exports	G	8 431	9 028	9 238	9 908	11 930	13 379	16 050	Exportations
Balance		-1 786	-1 836	-953	-1 319	-1 107	-4 570	-9 306	Balance
Sri Lanka									Sri Lanka
Imports	G	5 870	6 281	5 973	6 105	6 672	7 973	8 833	Importations
Exports	G	4 594	5 433	4 815	4 699	5 125	5 757	6 347	Exportations
Balance		-1 276	-848	-1 158	-1 406	-1 547	-2 216	-2 487	Balance

Total imports and exports—Imports c.i.f., exports f.o.b., and balance, value in million US dollars *(continued)*
Importations et exportations totales—Importations c.a.f., exportations f.o.b. et balance, valeur en millions de dollars E.U. *(suite)*

Region, country or area&	Sys.†	1999	2000	2001	2002	2003	2004	2005	Région, pays ou zone&
South-eastern Asia									**Asie du Sud-Est**
Imports		**253 901**	**312 916**	**286 728**	**299 868**	**321 976**	**413 305**	**480 446**	**Importations**
Exports		**306 236**	**364 527**	**327 625**	**346 274**	**377 041**	**473 030**	**539 322**	**Exportations**
Balance		**52 335**	**51 611**	**40 897**	**46 406**	**55 065**	**59 725**	**58 876**	**Balance**
Brunei Darussalam									Brunéi Darussalam
Imports	S	1 342	1 098	1 148	1 003	1 244	1 298	...	Importations
Exports	S	2 579	3 877	3 401	3 742	4 144	4 606	...	Exportations
Balance		1 237	2 778	2 253	2 739	2 901	3 308	...	Balance
Cambodia									Cambodge
Imports	S	1 243	1 424	1 456	1 675	1 732	2 075	1 268	Importations
Exports	S	1 040	1 123	1 296	1 489	1 771	2 188	1 369	Exportations
Balance		-203	-302	-160	-186	38	113	100	Balance
Indonesia									Indonésie
Imports	S	33 321	43 594	37 534	38 310	42 246	54 874	69 498	Importations
Exports	S	51 243	65 405	57 360	59 166	64 108	72 168	86 227	Exportations
Balance		17 922	21 811	19 826	20 856	21 862	17 294	16 729	Balance
Lao People's Dem. Rep.									Rép. dém. pop. lao
Imports	S	525	535	528	431	524	506	809	Importations
Exports	S	311	330	331	298	378	361	506	Exportations
Balance		-214	-205	-197	-133	-146	-145	-303	Balance
Malaysia									Malaisie
Imports	G	65 385	81 963	73 867	79 868	81 949	105 299	114 410	Importations
Exports	G	84 617	98 230	88 006	93 264	99 370	125 745	140 871	Exportations
Balance		19 231	16 266	14 139	13 396	17 421	20 446	26 460	Balance
Myanmar									Myanmar
Imports	G	2 323	2 401	2 877	2 348	2 092	2 196	1 927	Importations
Exports	G	1 136	1 647	2 382	3 046	2 485	2 380	3 813	Exportations
Balance		-1 187	-755	-496	698	392	184	1 887	Balance
Philippines									Philippines
Imports	G	32 569	36 887	34 944	37 202	39 502	42 345	46 963	Importations
Exports	G	36 577	39 794	32 664	36 510	36 231	39 680	39 879	Exportations
Balance		4 008	2 907	-2 280	-692	-3 271	-2 664	-7 084	Balance
Singapore									Singapour
Imports	G	111 062	134 546	116 004	116 441	127 935	173 582	200 050	Importations
Exports	G	114 682	137 806	121 755	125 177	144 183	198 633	229 652	Exportations
Balance		3 620	3 259	5 752	8 736	16 248	25 051	29 602	Balance
Thailand									Thaïlande
Imports	S	50 350	61 923	61 961	64 645	75 824	94 410	118 158	Importations
Exports	S	58 473	68 963	64 919	68 108	80 324	96 248	110 178	Exportations
Balance		8 123	7 039	2 959	3 463	4 499	1 839	-7 980	Balance
Viet Nam									Viet Nam
Imports	G	11 742	15 638	15 999	19 000	24 863	31 091	36 476	Importations
Exports	G	11 540	14 449	15 100	16 530	20 176	25 625	31 625	Exportations
Balance		-202	-1 189	-899	-2 470	-4 687	-5 466	-4 851	Balance
Western Asia									**Asie occidentale**
Imports		**172 088**	**200 704**	**193 302**	**210 812**	**247 283**	**321 538**	**394 666**	**Importations**
Exports		**200 466**	**258 587**	**240 840**	**251 751**	**310 660**	**404 999**	**530 259**	**Exportations**
Balance		**28 377**	**57 883**	**47 538**	**40 939**	**63 377**	**83 460**	**135 593**	**Balance**
Bahrain									Bahreïn
Imports	G	3 698	4 634	4 306	5 012	5 657	6 485	7 946	Importations
Exports	G	4 363	6 195	5 577	5 794	6 632	7 519	10 024	Exportations
Balance		665	1 561	1 271	782	974	1 034	2 078	Balance
Cyprus[23]									Chypre[23]
Imports	G	3 618	3 846	3 922	3 863	4 288	5 659	6 282	Importations
Exports	G	995	951	976	770	834	1 081	1 303	Exportations
Balance		-2 623	-2 895	-2 946	-3 094	-3 455	-4 577	-4 979	Balance
Israel[24]									Israël[24]
Imports	S	33 166	37 686	35 449	35 517	36 303	42 864	47 142	Importations
Exports	S	25 794	31 404	29 081	29 347	31 784	38 618	42 659	Exportations
Balance		-7 371	-6 282	-6 368	-6 170	-4 519	-4 245	-4 483	Balance

Region, country or area&	Sys.†	1999	2000	2001	2002	2003	2004	2005	Région, pays ou zone&
Jordan									Jordanie
Imports	G	3 717	4 597	4 871	5 076	5 743	8 128	10 506	Importations
Exports	G	1 832	1 899	2 294	2 770	3 082	3 922	4 302	Exportations
Balance		-1 885	-2 698	-2 577	-2 306	-2 662	-4 206	-6 204	Balance
Kuwait									Koweït
Imports	S	7 617	7 157	7 869	9 008	10 993	12 630	17 488	Importations
Exports	S	12 164	19 436	16 203	15 369	20 678	28 599	44 869	Exportations
Balance		4 547	12 279	8 334	6 361	9 685	15 968	27 381	Balance
Lebanon									Liban
Imports	G	6 207	6 230	7 293	6 447	7 171	9 400	9 359	Importations
Exports	G	677	715	890	1 046	1 524	1 748	1 837	Exportations
Balance		-5 530	-5 515	-6 404	-5 401	-5 646	-7 652	-7 522	Balance
Occupied Palestinian Terr.									Terr. palestinien occupé
Imports	S	...	2 383	...	1 516	...	2 373	...	Importations
Exports	S	...	401	273	241	...	322	...	Exportations
Balance		...	-1 982	...	-1 275	...	-2 052	...	Balance
Oman									Oman
Imports	G	4 674	5 040	5 798	6 005	6 572	8 865	8 827	Importations
Exports	G	7 238	11 319	11 074	11 172	11 669	13 341	18 692	Exportations
Balance		2 564	6 279	5 276	5 166	5 096	4 476	9 865	Balance
Qatar									Qatar
Imports	S	2 500	3 252	3 758	4 052	4 897	6 005	10 061	Importations
Exports	S	7 212	11 594	10 706	10 771	13 193	18 451	25 339	Exportations
Balance		4 713	8 342	6 948	6 719	8 295	12 447	15 278	Balance
Saudi Arabia									Arabie saoudite
Imports	S	27 973	30 197	31 181	32 293	36 915	44 744	59 458	Importations
Exports	S	50 693	77 480	67 973	72 453	93 245	125 997	...	Exportations
Balance		22 720	47 283	36 792	40 160	56 331	81 253	...	Balance
Syrian Arab Republic									Rép. arabe syrienne
Imports	S	3 832	4 055	4 757	5 097	5 120	7 070	...	Importations
Exports	S	3 464	4 674	5 254	6 831	5 731	5 384	...	Exportations
Balance		-368	620	497	1 734	611	-1 686	...	Balance
Turkey									Turquie
Imports	S	40 671	54 503	41 399	49 663	65 637	96 368	115 682	Importations
Exports	S	26 587	27 775	31 334	34 561	46 576	61 683	71 928	Exportations
Balance		-14 084	-26 728	-10 065	-15 101	-19 061	-34 685	-43 753	Balance
United Arab Emirates									Emirats arabes unis
Imports	G	33 231	35 009	37 293	42 652	52 074	61 588	76 984	Importations
Exports	G	43 307	49 878	48 773	52 163	67 135	82 750	112 537	Exportations
Balance		10 076	14 869	11 480	9 511	15 061	21 163	35 553	Balance
Yemen									Yémen
Imports	S	2 033	2 326	2 472	2 783	3 680	...	...	Importations
Exports	S	2 437	4 078	3 372	3 273	3 733	...	...	Exportations
Balance		404	1 751	900	490	53	...	...	Balance
Oceania									**Océanie**
Imports		**7 314**	**7 428**	**7 421**	**8 147**	**10 758**	**10 424**	**11 413**	**Importations**
Exports		**4 856**	**5 050**	**4 487**	**4 516**	**5 626**	**6 329**	**7 174**	**Exportations**
Balance		**-2 458**	**-2 378**	**-2 934**	**-3 631**	**-5 131**	**-4 094**	**-4 239**	**Balance**
American Samoa[25]									Samoa américaines[25]
Imports	S	453	506	516	499	624	604	...	Importations
Exports	S	345	346	318	388	460	446	...	Exportations
Balance		-108	-160	-198	-111	-164	-158	...	Balance
Cook Islands									Iles Cook
Imports	G	41	50	47	47	71	76	81	Importations
Exports	G	4	9	7	5	9	7	5	Exportations
Balance		-38	-41	-40	-42	-62	-69	-76	Balance

Total imports and exports—Imports c.i.f., exports f.o.b., and balance, value in million US dollars (*continued*)
Importations et exportations totales—Importations c.a.f., exportations f.o.b. et balance, valeur en millions de dollars E.U. (*suite*)

Region, country or area[&]	Sys.[t]	1999	2000	2001	2002	2003	2004	2005	Région, pays ou zone[&]
Fiji									Fidji
Imports	G	903	826	794	898	1 171	1 274	1 607	Importations
Exports	G	609	479	442	549	678	679	722	Exportations
Balance		-293	-347	-352	-349	-492	-595	-886	Balance
French Polynesia									Polynésie française
Imports	S	887	931	1 016	1 267	1 561	1 469	1 702	Importations
Exports	S	229	197	175	169	151	183	210	Exportations
Balance		-658	-733	-840	-1 098	-1 410	-1 286	-1 492	Balance
Kiribati[5]									Kiribati[5]
Imports	G	41	39	41	...	...	...	...	Importations
Exports	G	9	6	5	...	...	...	...	Exportations
Balance		-32	-33	-36	...	...	...	...	Balance
Marshall Islands									Iles Marshall
Imports	G	...	68	...	...	...	...	...	Importations
Exports	G	8	7	...	...	...	...	...	Exportations
Balance		...	-61	...	...	...	...	...	Balance
Micronesia (Fed. States of)[5]									Micronésie (Etats féd. de)[5]
Imports	S	12	...	...	...	...	...	...	Importations
New Caledonia									Nouvelle-Calédonie
Imports	S	1 006	924	932	1 008	2 596	1 635	1 774	Importations
Exports	S	467	606	453	476	784	1 012	1 119	Exportations
Balance		-539	-318	-479	-533	-1 811	-622	-655	Balance
Palau									Palaos
Imports	S	78	123	...	...	...	...	...	Importations
Exports	S	11	...	...	...	...	...	...	Exportations
Balance		-67	...	...	...	...	...	...	Balance
Papua New Guinea									Papouasie-Nvl-Guinée
Imports	G	1 194	1 151	1 071	1 235	1 368	1 680	1 729	Importations
Exports	G	1 880	2 095	1 805	1 641	2 206	2 558	3 200	Exportations
Balance		686	944	734	406	838	878	1 472	Balance
Samoa									Samoa
Imports	S	115	106	120	127	128	155	187	Importations
Exports	S	20	14	16	14	15	11	12	Exportations
Balance		-95	-92	-104	-114	-113	-145	-175	Balance
Solomon Islands									Iles Salomon
Imports	S	109	98	80	65	68	85	144	Importations
Exports	S	123	65	46	57	74	97	102	Exportations
Balance		14	-33	-34	-7	7	12	-41	Balance
Tonga									Tonga
Imports	G	73	69	72	89	94	105	110	Importations
Exports	G	13	9	7	14	18	15	13	Exportations
Balance		-60	-60	-66	-75	-76	-90	-97	Balance
Vanuatu									Vanuatu
Imports	G	98	87	86	90	105	128	140	Importations
Exports	G	26	26	19	19	27	37	40	Exportations
Balance		-72	-60	-67	-71	-78	-91	-100	Balance
Non Petrol. Exports[26]									Pétrole non Compris[26]
Exports		73 025	102 397	100 182	92 853	86 061	79 766	73 931	Exportations
Additional country groupings									**Groupements supplémentaires de pays**
ANCOM[§]									ANCOM[§]
Imports		36 241	40 636	45 442	41 255	39 652	53 231	69 837	Importations
Exports		43 309	57 495	50 573	51 795	53 926	72 656	102 256	Exportations
Balance		7 067	16 859	5 131	10 540	14 273	19 426	32 419	Balance
APEC[§]									CEAP[§]
Imports		2 452 862	2 962 074	2 765 369	2 859 268	3 222 681	3 924 010	4 501 456	Importations
Exports		2 355 757	2 761 942	2 535 107	2 605 038	2 926 363	3 557 661	4 104 722	Exportations
Balance		-97 104	-200 132	-230 262	-254 230	-296 317	-366 350	-396 735	Balance

58 **Total imports and exports**—Imports c.i.f., exports f.o.b., and balance, value in million US dollars (*continued*)

Importations et exportations totales—Importations c.a.f., exportations f.o.b. et balance, valeur en millions de dollars E.U. (*suite*)

Region, country or area&	Sys.t	1999	2000	2001	2002	2003	2004	2005	Région, pays ou zone&
CARICOM§									CARICOM§
Imports		12 096	13 421	13 024	13 091	13 936	15 471	17 382	Importations
Exports		6 128	7 633	6 944	6 387	7 951	9 431	11 830	Exportations
Balance		-5 968	-5 788	-6 080	-6 704	-5 985	-6 041	-5 551	Balance
COMESA§									COMESA§
Imports		37 205	35 145	35 855	35 396	39 936	48 307	65 894	Importations
Exports		20 771	25 449	23 513	26 014	31 409	39 746	56 104	Exportations
Balance		-16 435	-9 697	-12 342	-9 382	-8 526	-8 561	-9 789	Balance
LDC§									PMA§
Imports		39 098	41 509	45 655	47 969	57 283	68 175	75 666	Importations
Exports		26 035	33 154	33 778	37 046	43 421	57 025	72 325	Exportations
Balance		-13 063	-8 355	-11 877	-10 923	-13 862	-11 150	-3 341	Balance
MERCOSUR§									MERCOSUR§
Imports		82 680	89 992	84 203	62 342	68 948	95 066	113 075	Importations
Exports		74 298	84 591	87 816	88 823	106 097	135 608	163 507	Exportations
Balance		-8 382	-5 401	3 613	26 481	37 149	40 542	50 432	Balance
NAFTA§									ALENA§
Imports		1 350 497	1 588 750	1 489 591	1 511 990	1 624 557	1 888 306	2 154 784	Importations
Exports		1 004 901	1 141 068	1 067 883	1 027 313	1 074 797	1 204 253	1 357 993	Exportations
Balance		-345 596	-447 682	-421 709	-484 677	-549 760	-684 053	-796 792	Balance
OECD§									OCDE§
Imports		4 247 314	4 730 763	4 525 142	4 661 727	5 390 052	6 440 297	7 160 601	Importations
Exports		4 040 244	4 352 942	4 210 490	4 361 131	5 009 793	5 922 245	6 437 425	Exportations
Balance		-207 071	-377 821	-314 652	-300 596	-380 259	-518 051	-723 175	Balance
OPEC§									OPEP§
Imports		155 287	174 700	185 059	190 176	216 559	280 509	354 344	Importations
Exports		256 708	353 519	308 562	316 989	383 050	505 664	684 118	Exportations
Balance		101 421	178 819	123 503	126 814	166 491	225 155	329 774	Balance
EU25									UE25
Imports		2 275 006	2 396 877	2 365 295	2 463 127	2 969 767	3 583 710	3 915 529	Importations
Exports		2 290 314	2 357 138	2 382 849	2 541 433	3 028 976	3 613 180	3 884 063	Exportations
Balance		15 308	-39 739	17 553	78 306	59 209	29 470	-31 466	Balance
Extra-EU25,27									Extra-UE25 27
Imports		794 370	916 360	880 948	889 542	1 063 891	1 283 863	1 467 448	Importations
Exports		732 804	788 642	801 722	854 112	999 614	1 205 484	1 331 212	Exportations
Balance		-61 566	-127 718	-79 227	-35 430	-64 277	-78 379	-136 235	Balance

Source

United Nations Statistics Division, New York, trade statistics database.

Notes

& The regional totals for imports and exports have been adjusted to exclude the re-exports of countries or areas comprising each region.

§ For member states of this grouping, see Annex I – Other groupings. The totals have been calculated for all periods shown according to the current composition.

t Systems of trade: Two systems of recording trade, the General trade system (G) and the Special trade system (S), are in common use. They differ mainly in the way warehoused and re-exported goods are recorded. See the Technical notes for an explanation of the trade systems.

1 This classification is intended for statistical convenience and does not, necessarily, express a judgement about the stage reached by a particular country in the development process.

2 Developed economies of the Asia-Pacific region, Europe, and North America.

Source

Organisation des Nations Unies, Division de statistique, New York, la base de données pour les statistiques du commerce extérieur.

Notes

& Les totaux régionaux pour importations et exportations ont été ajustés pour exclure les re-exportations des pays ou zones qui comprennent la région.

§ Pour les Etats membres de ce groupements, voir annexe I – Autres groupements. Les totales ont été calculés pour toutes les périodes données suivant la composition présente.

t Systèmes de commerce : Deux systèmes d'enregistrement du commerce sont couramment utilisés, le Commerce général (G) et le Commerce spécial (S). Ils ne diffèrent que par la façon dont sont enregistées les merchandises entreposées et les merchandises réexportées. Voir les Notes techniques pour une explication des Systèmes de commerce.

1 Cette classification est utilisée pour plus de commodité dans la présentation des statistique et n'implique pas nécessairement un jugement quant au stage de développement auquel est parvenu un pays donné.

2 Économies développées de la région Asie-Pacifique, de l'Europe, et de l'Amérique de Nord.

3 Prior to 1992 Estonia, Latvia, and Lithuania were included in the region CIS as members of the former USSR, and hence not included in the region Developed countries - Europe.
4 Economic Union of Belgium and Luxembourg. Intertrade between the two countries is excluded. Beginning January 1997, data refer to Belgium only and include trade between Belgium and Luxembourg.
5 Imports FOB.
6 Beginning January 1994, foreign trade statistics exclude re-exports.
7 Beginning 1997, trade data for France include the import and export values of French Guiana, Guadeloupe, Martinique, and Réunion.
8 Prior to January 1991, excludes trade conducted in accordance with the supplementary protocol to the treaty on the basis of relations between the Federal Republic of Germany and the former German Democratic Republic.
9 Prior to 1996 data exclude customs free zones, repairs on goods, and operational leasing.
10 Including the trade of the U.S. Virgin Islands and Puerto Rico but excluding shipments of merchandise between the United States and its other possessions (Guam, American Samoa, etc.). Data include imports and exports of non-monetary gold.
11 Imports exclude petroleum imported without stated value. Exports cover domestic exports.
12 Exports include gold.
13 Beginning in January 1998, foreign trade data refer to South Africa only, excluding intra-trade of the Southern African Common Customs Area. Prior to January 1998, trade data refer to the Southern African Common Customs Area, which includes Botswana, Lesotho, Namibia, South Africa and Swaziland.
14 Year ending June 30 through 1994. Year ending December 31 thereafter.
15 Beginning 1990, trade statistics exclude certain oil and chemical products.
16 Export and import values exclude trade in the processing zone.
17 Trade data include maquiladoras and exclude goods from customs-bonded warehouses. Total exports include revaluation and exports of silver.
18 Exports include re-exports and petroleum products.
19 For statistical purposes, the data for China do not include those for the Hong Kong Special Administrative Region (Hong Kong SAR), Macao Special Administrative Region (Macao SAR) and Taiwan Province of China.
20 Excluding military goods, fissionable materials, bunkers, ships, and aircraft.
21 Year ending 20 March of the years stated.
22 Data include oil and gas. Data on the value and volume of oil exports and on the value of total exports are rough estimates based on information published in various petroleum industry journals.
23 Data refer to government controlled areas.
24 Imports and exports net of returned goods. The figures also exclude Judea and Samaria and the Gaza area.
25 Year ending 30 September.
26 Data refer to total exports less petroleum exports of Asia Middle East countries where petroleum, in this case, is the sum of SITC groups 333, 334 and 335.
27 Excluding intra-EU trade.

3 Avant 1992, l'Estonie, Lettonie et Lituanie étaient inclus dans la région CEI comme membres de l'ancienne URSS, et puis n'étaient pas inclus dans la région Pays développés - Europe.
4 L'Union économique belgo-luxembourgeoise. Non compris le commerce entre ces pays. A partir de janvier 1997, les données se rapportent à Belgique seulement et recouvrent les échanges entre la Belgique et le Luxembourg
5 Importations FOB.
6 A partir de janvier 1994, les statistiques du commerce extérieur non compris les réexportations.
7 A compter de 1997, les valeurs de commerce pour la France comprennent les valeurs des importations et des exportations de la Guyane française, la Guadeloupe, la Martinique, et la Réunion.
8 Avant janvier 1991, non compris le commerce effectué en accord avec le protocole additionnel au traité définissant la base des relations entre la République Fédérale d'Allemagne et l'ancienne République Démocratique Allemande.
9 Avant 1996 les données excluent des zones franches, des réparations sur des marchandises, et le crédit-bail opérationnel.
10 Y compris le commerce des Iles Vierges américaines et de Porto Rico mais non compris les échanges de marchandise, entre les Etats-Unis et leurs autres possessions (Guam, Samoa americaines, etc.). Les données comprennent les importations et exportations d'or non-monétaire.
11 Non compris le petrole brute dont la valeur des importations ne sont pas stipulée. Les exportations sont les exportations d'intérieur.
12 Les exportations comprennent l'or.
13 A compter de janvier 1998, les données sur le commerce extérieur ne se rapportent qu'à l'Afrique du Sud. et ne tiennent pas compte des échanges commerciaux entre les pays de l'Union douanière de l'Afrique du Sud. qui incluait l'Afrique du Sud, Botswana, Lesotho, Namibie, et Swaziland.
14 Année finissant juin 30 à 1994. Année finissant décembre 31 ensuite.
15 A compter de 1990, les statistiques commerciales font exclusion de certains produits pétroliers et chimiques.
16 Les valeurs à l'exportation et à l'importation excluent le commerce de la zone de transformation.
17 Les statistiques du commerce extérieur comprennent maquiladoras et ne comprennent pas les marchandises provenant des entrepôts en douane. Les exportations comprennent la réevaluation et les données sur les exportations d'argent.
18 Exportations comprennent re-exportations et produits pétroliers.
19 Pour la présentation des statistiques, les données pour la Chine ne comprennent pas la Région Administrative Spéciale de Hong Kong (Hong Kong RAS), la Région Administrative Spéciale de Macao (Macao RAS) et la province de Taiwan.
20 A l'exclusion des marchandises militaires, des matières fissibles, des soutes, des bateaux, et de l'avion.
21 Année finissant le 20 mars de l'année indiquée.
22 Les données comprennent le pétrole et le gaz. La valeur des exportations de pétrole et des exportations totales sont des évaluations grossières basées sur l'information pubilée à divers journaux d'industrie de pétrole.
23 Les données se rapportent aux zones contrôlées par le Gouvernement.
24 Importations et exportations nets, ne comprennant pas les marchandises retournées. Sont également exclues les données de la Judée et de Samaria et ainsi que la zone de Gaza.
25 Année finissant le 30 septembre.
26 Les données se rapportent aux exportations totales moins les exportations pétrolières de moyen-orient d'Asie. Dans ce cas, le pétrole est la somme des groupes CTCI 333, 334 et 335.
27 Non compris le commerce de l'intra-UE.

# Total imports and exports: index numbers
2000 = 100

# Importations et exportations totales : indices
2000 = 100

Country or area	1996	1997	1998	1999	2001	2002	2003	2004	2005	Pays ou zone
Argentina										Argentine
Imports: volume	82	108	117	101	83	38	58	87	108	Imp. : volume
Imports: unit value	115	112	106	100	97	94	94	101	105	Imp. : valeur unitaire
Exports: volume	77	88	98	97	104	105	110	118	134	Exp. : volume
Exports: unit value	118	114	102	91	97	93	102	111	113	Exp. : valeur unitaire
Terms of trade	103	102	97	91	99	99	108	110	107	Termes de l'échange
Purchasing power of exports	79	90	94	89	104	104	120	129	144	Pouvoir d'achat des export.
Australia										Australie
Imports: volume	69	77	84	92	96	108	120	137	...	Imp. : volume
Imports: unit value[1]	117	111	102	102	94	95	104	111	117	Imp. : valeur unitaire[1]
Exports: volume	77	87	87	91	103	104	102	106	...	Exp. : volume
Exports: unit value[1]	118	114	101	96	98	100	111	129	153	Exp. : valeur unitaire[1]
Terms of trade	101	103	100	94	104	106	106	116	131	Termes de l'échange
Purchasing power of exports	77	90	86	86	107	110	108	123	...	Pouvoir d'achat des export.
Austria										Autriche
Imports: volume	58	73	84	92	106	103	111	132	...	Imp. : volume
Imports: unit value	163	134	124	115	97	100	114	125	...	Imp. : valeur unitaire
Exports: volume	55	72	82	100	109	113	119	139	...	Exp. : volume
Exports: unit value	166	135	126	105	95	101	114	126	...	Exp. : valeur unitaire
Terms of trade	102	101	102	91	98	101	100	101	...	Termes de l'échange
Purchasing power of exports	56	72	83	91	107	114	119	140	...	Pouvoir d'achat des export.
Belgium[2]										Belgique[2]
Imports: volume	82	85	91	91	101	109	111	118	126	Imp. : volume
Imports: unit value	119	110	106	102	100	103	120	136	143	Imp. : valeur unitaire
Exports: volume	78	84	88	91	102	111	113	121	126	Exp. : volume
Exports: unit value	123	112	111	105	99	104	121	135	142	Exp. : valeur unitaire
Terms of trade	103	102	104	102	100	101	100	99	99	Termes de l'échange
Purchasing power of exports	81	86	92	93	102	112	113	120	125	Pouvoir d'achat des export.
Bolivia										Bolivie
Exports: volume	96	101	96	88	107	129	145	173	194	Exp. : volume
Exports: unit value	126	90	79	78	92	81	90	122	142	Exp. : valeur unitaire
Brazil										Brésil
Imports: volume	97	94	98	92	100	97	100	111	101	Imp. : volume
Imports: unit value	99	125	105	96	100	87	86	102	131	Imp. : valeur unitaire
Exports: volume	81	85	94	93	111	121	131	154	162	Exp. : volume
Exports: unit value	106	113	100	94	95	91	101	114	132	Exp. : valeur unitaire
Terms of trade	108	90	95	98	95	105	117	112	101	Termes de l'échange
Purchasing power of exports	88	77	89	91	106	126	154	172	164	Pouvoir d'achat des export.
Bulgaria										Bulgarie
Imports: unit value	...	...	...	...	96	98	112	130	140	Imp. : valeur unitaire
Exports: unit value	...	...	...	...	95	95	114	133	142	Exp. : valeur unitaire
Terms of trade	...	...	...	...	99	98	102	102	102	Termes de l'échange
Canada										Canada
Imports: volume[3]	67	79	86	96	94	96	100	109	119	Imp. : volume[3]
Imports: unit value[3]	102	101	94	96	99	98	102	108	116	Imp. : valeur unitaire[3]
Exports: volume	70	76	82	91	96	97	95	102	105	Exp. : volume
Exports: unit value	100	98	97	106	98	93	104	115	129	Exp. : valeur unitaire
Terms of trade	98	97	103	110	99	95	102	106	111	Termes de l'échange
Purchasing power of exports	69	73	85	101	95	92	97	108	117	Pouvoir d'achat des export.

Country or area	1996	1997	1998	1999	2001	2002	2003	2004	2005	Pays ou zone
China, Hong Kong SAR										Chine, Hong Kong RAS
Imports: volume	85	91	85	85	98	106	119	136	148	Imp. : volume
Imports: unit value	110	107	102	100	97	93	93	96	98	Imp. : valeur unitaire
Exports: volume	81	86	82	85	97	105	120	138	154	Exp. : volume
Exports: unit value	110	108	104	101	98	95	94	95	96	Exp. : valeur unitaire
Terms of trade	100	100	102	101	101	102	101	99	98	Termes de l'échange
Purchasing power of exports	81	86	84	86	98	107	121	137	150	Pouvoir d'achat des export.
Colombia										Colombie
Imports: unit value	122	120	110	103	98	95	95	103	114	Imp. : valeur unitaire
Exports: unit value	104	115	103	96	89	84	87	96	111	Exp. : valeur unitaire
Terms of trade	85	96	93	93	91	89	92	93	97	Termes de l'échange
Czech Republic										République tchèque
Imports: unit value[3]	122	110	105	100	101	107	123	138	148	Imp. : valeur unitaire[3]
Exports: unit value	123	111	114	105	102	111	130	148	155	Exp. : valeur unitaire
Terms of trade	101	101	108	105	101	104	105	107	105	Termes de l'échange
Denmark										Danemark
Imports: volume	82	88	93	93	102	108	106	113	122	Imp. : volume
Imports: unit value	126	114	113	108	98	102	119	133	138	Imp. : valeur unitaire
Exports: volume	80	84	86	92	103	109	107	110	116	Exp. : volume
Exports: unit value	129	115	112	108	99	103	122	136	143	Exp. : valeur unitaire
Terms of trade	102	101	99	100	101	101	102	102	104	Termes de l'échange
Purchasing power of exports	81	85	85	92	104	110	109	113	121	Pouvoir d'achat des export.
Dominica										Dominique
Imports: volume	95	90	94	97	98	82	...	...	...	Imp. : volume
Imports: unit value	96	97	116	95	95	91	...	...	...	Imp. : valeur unitaire
Exports: volume	105	101	94	92	78	72	...	...	...	Exp. : volume
Exports: unit value	104	134	113	113	101	101	...	...	...	Exp. : valeur unitaire
Terms of trade	108	137	98	119	106	111	...	...	...	Termes de l'échange
Purchasing power of exports	113	139	91	110	82	80	...	...	...	Pouvoir d'achat des export.
Ecuador										Equateur
Imports: volume	96	133	166	96	119	148	161	168	204	Imp. : volume
Exports: volume	102	102	96	93	101	99	107	133	117	Exp. : volume
Exports: unit value	88	85	64	77	88	94	107	118	150	Exp. : valeur unitaire
Estonia										Estonie
Imports: unit value	...	...	113	109	98	103	121	135	140	Imp. : valeur unitaire
Exports: unit value	120	111	113	107	129	136	173	194	199	Exp. : valeur unitaire
Terms of trade	...	...	99	98	132	132	143	144	143	Termes de l'échange
Finland										Finlande
Imports: volume	81	88	95	96	97	104	103	108	114	Imp. : volume
Imports: unit value	115	105	102	101	98	97	115	131	146	Imp. : valeur unitaire
Exports: volume	75	85	89	92	99	104	106	112	111	Exp. : volume
Exports: unit value	118	106	105	102	96	94	107	117	127	Exp. : valeur unitaire
Terms of trade	102	101	103	101	97	97	93	89	87	Termes de l'échange
Purchasing power of exports	77	85	92	93	97	101	98	99	96	Pouvoir d'achat des export.
France[4]										France[4]
Imports: volume	63	71	79	87	116	112	112	125	136	Imp. : volume
Imports: unit value	143	125	118	109	95	95	114	122	122	Imp. : valeur unitaire
Exports: volume	65	75	83	89	119	112	110	118	125	Exp. : volume
Exports: unit value	150	129	124	114	97	98	118	127	126	Exp. : valeur unitaire
Terms of trade	105	103	104	105	102	103	104	104	104	Termes de l'échange
Purchasing power of exports	68	77	86	93	121	116	114	123	130	Pouvoir d'achat des export.
Germany[5,6]										Allemagne[5,6]
Imports: volume	71	77	85	89	101	100	110	121	126	Imp. : volume
Imports: unit value	129	115	111	104	97	98	111	121	123	Imp. : valeur unitaire
Exports: volume	69	77	83	87	103	104	115	129	136	Exp. : volume
Exports: unit value	138	121	118	111	99	102	119	129	130	Exp. : valeur unitaire
Terms of trade	107	105	107	107	102	104	107	107	105	Termes de l'échange
Purchasing power of exports	74	81	89	93	105	109	123	139	143	Pouvoir d'achat des export.

Country or area	1996	1997	1998	1999	2001	2002	2003	2004	2005	Pays ou zone
Greece										Grèce
Imports: volume	69	70	85	90	...	...	...	...	...	Imp. : volume
Imports: unit value[1]	135	122	119	115	100	106	127	144	158	Imp. : valeur unitaire[1]
Exports: volume	72	80	90	96	...	...	...	...	...	Exp. : volume
Exports: unit value[1]	129	117	111	107	98	104	124	143	149	Exp. : valeur unitaire[1]
Terms of trade	95	96	93	93	98	98	98	99	95	Termes de l'échange
Purchasing power of exports	68	77	84	90	...	...	...	...	...	Pouvoir d'achat des export.
Honduras										Honduras
Exports: volume	80	60	77	70	104	105	95	111	...	Exp. : volume
Exports: unit value	117	133	134	101	96	91	79	98	137	Exp. : valeur unitaire
Hungary[7,8]										Hongrie[7,8]
Imports: volume	46	58	72	83	104	109	120	139	147	Imp. : volume
Imports: unit value	123	114	111	106	101	107	123	135	138	Imp. : valeur unitaire
Exports: volume	45	58	71	82	108	114	125	147	164	Exp. : volume
Exports: unit value	125	117	116	108	101	107	122	134	134	Exp. : valeur unitaire
Terms of trade	102	103	104	103	100	100	100	99	97	Termes de l'échange
Purchasing power of exports	45	60	74	84	107	114	124	146	159	Pouvoir d'achat des export.
Iceland										Islande
Imports: volume	70	74	92	96	90	...	...	...	...	Imp. : volume
Imports: unit value	113	105	104	101	97	...	...	...	...	Imp. : valeur unitaire
Exports: volume	94	96	93	100	107	...	...	...	...	Exp. : volume
Exports: unit value	106	102	110	106	99	...	...	...	...	Exp. : valeur unitaire
Terms of trade	94	97	105	104	102	...	...	...	...	Termes de l'échange
Purchasing power of exports	88	92	97	104	109	...	...	...	...	Pouvoir d'achat des export.
India[9]										Inde[9]
Imports: volume	73	81	92	101	105	115	139	151	...	Imp. : volume
Imports: unit value	104	103	91	96	96	104	108	139	...	Imp. : valeur unitaire
Exports: volume	72	68	70	81	104	126	134	152	...	Exp. : volume
Exports: unit value	103	117	107	101	94	92	104	116	...	Exp. : valeur unitaire
Terms of trade	99	114	117	105	98	89	96	84	...	Termes de l'échange
Purchasing power of exports	71	77	82	85	102	112	129	127	...	Pouvoir d'achat des export.
Indonesia										Indonésie
Exports: volume	86	110	102	84	121	100	97	101	64	Exp. : volume
Exports: unit value	109	104	81	65	90	96	103	120	81	Exp. : valeur unitaire
Ireland										Irlande
Imports: volume	58	67	79	86	99	97	90	98	112	Imp. : volume
Imports: unit value	119	114	109	107	100	101	112	120	121	Imp. : valeur unitaire
Exports: volume	50	58	72	84	105	104	99	110	113	Exp. : volume
Exports: unit value	119	114	110	110	99	104	115	116	119	Exp. : valeur unitaire
Terms of trade	100	100	101	103	98	102	103	97	99	Termes de l'échange
Purchasing power of exports	50	58	73	86	103	107	103	107	111	Pouvoir d'achat des export.
Israel										Israël
Imports: volume	76	77	77	88	93	93	92	103	105	Imp. : volume
Imports: unit value	111	106	100	97	99	99	104	112	120	Imp. : valeur unitaire
Exports: volume	63	69	74	80	96	97	101	116	119	Exp. : volume
Exports: unit value	103	102	99	100	96	96	100	106	114	Exp. : valeur unitaire
Terms of trade	93	96	99	103	98	98	96	95	95	Termes de l'échange
Purchasing power of exports	58	67	73	82	94	95	97	110	113	Pouvoir d'achat des export.
Italy										Italie
Imports: volume	76	83	90	93	99	99	100	103	102	Imp. : volume
Imports: unit value	115	106	103	99	100	105	125	144	157	Imp. : valeur unitaire
Exports: volume	92	94	94	92	101	99	96	99	97	Exp. : volume
Exports: unit value	115	108	109	107	101	108	130	149	159	Exp. : valeur unitaire
Terms of trade	100	101	107	108	101	103	104	103	101	Termes de l'échange
Purchasing power of exports	92	95	100	99	102	101	100	102	98	Pouvoir d'achat des export.

Country or area	1996	1997	1998	1999	2001	2002	2003	2004	2005	Pays ou zone
Japan										Japon
Imports: volume	85	87	82	90	99	100	107	115	118	Imp. : volume
Imports: unit value	108	103	90	91	87	86	91	101	112	Imp. : valeur unitaire
Exports: volume	81	91	90	91	90	97	102	113	114	Exp. : volume
Exports: unit value	106	97	91	95	94	89	96	104	109	Exp. : valeur unitaire
Terms of trade	98	94	101	105	107	104	105	103	98	Termes de l'échange
Purchasing power of exports	80	85	90	96	97	101	108	116	111	Pouvoir d'achat des export.
Jordan										Jordanie
Imports: volume	92	90	85	84	103	104	109	136	155	Imp. : volume
Imports: unit value	103	101	100	97	102	105	115	130	148	Imp. : valeur unitaire
Exports: volume	82	88	90	93	123	142	152	190	182	Exp. : volume
Exports: unit value	117	114	107	105	101	102	102	114	131	Exp. : valeur unitaire
Terms of trade	113	113	107	107	99	97	88	87	88	Termes de l'échange
Purchasing power of exports	93	99	97	100	122	137	135	166	161	Pouvoir d'achat des export.
Kenya										Kenya
Imports: volume	89	95	96	87	...	...	...	...	...	Imp. : volume
Imports: unit value	101	107	105	98	...	...	...	...	...	Imp. : valeur unitaire
Exports: unit value	112	128	125	101	...	...	...	...	...	Exp. : valeur unitaire
Terms of trade	110	120	119	103	...	...	...	...	...	Termes de l'échange
Korea, Republic of										Corée, République de
Imports: volume	85	87	65	84	98	110	118	132	140	Imp. : volume
Imports: unit value	112	107	88	87	91	88	96	107	117	Imp. : valeur unitaire
Exports: volume	54	62	74	83	101	114	133	163	178	Exp. : volume
Exports: unit value	141	131	103	100	87	83	85	92	93	Exp. : valeur unitaire
Terms of trade	125	122	117	114	95	95	89	85	79	Termes de l'échange
Purchasing power of exports	68	76	86	95	96	108	119	139	141	Pouvoir d'achat des export.
Latvia										Lettonie
Imports: unit value	...	...	102	97	98	106	122	140	150	Imp. : valeur unitaire
Exports: unit value	114	110	108	105	99	104	121	145	153	Exp. : valeur unitaire
Terms of trade	...	...	106	108	101	98	99	104	102	Termes de l'échange
Libyan Arab Jamah.										Jamah. arabe libyenne
Imports: volume	185	208	156	147	173	214	...	...	...	Imp. : volume
Imports: unit value	97	93	96	115	83	48	...	...	...	Imp. : valeur unitaire
Exports: volume	123	129	94	108	110	95	...	...	...	Exp. : volume
Exports: unit value	75	64	53	72	87	88	...	...	...	Exp. : valeur unitaire
Terms of trade	77	69	55	63	104	185	...	...	...	Termes de l'échange
Purchasing power of exports	95	89	52	68	115	175	...	...	...	Pouvoir d'achat des export.
Lithuania										Lituanie
Imports: volume	...	...	...	...	120	143	155	182	209	Imp. : volume
Imports: unit value	106	105	99	95	97	101	117	127	138	Imp. : valeur unitaire
Exports: volume	...	...	...	...	125	145	161	185	214	Exp. : volume
Exports: unit value	101	103	97	94	97	101	120	137	151	Exp. : valeur unitaire
Terms of trade	95	97	98	99	101	100	102	108	109	Termes de l'échange
Purchasing power of exports	...	...	...	...	126	146	164	199	233	Pouvoir d'achat des export.
Malaysia										Malaisie
Imports: volume	...	...	...	...	92	97	...	...	...	Imp. : volume
Imports: unit value	...	...	...	...	98	99	...	...	...	Imp. : valeur unitaire
Exports: volume	...	...	...	...	96	102	...	...	...	Exp. : volume
Exports: unit value	...	...	...	...	94	93	...	...	...	Exp. : valeur unitaire
Terms of trade	...	...	...	...	96	94	...	...	...	Termes de l'échange
Purchasing power of exports	...	...	...	...	92	96	...	...	...	Pouvoir d'achat des export.
Mauritius										Maurice
Imports: volume	...	...	99	107	98	103	100	105	110	Imp. : volume
Exports: volume	...	...	95	98	116	121	112	108	119	Exp. : volume

Country or area	1996	1997	1998	1999	2001	2002	2003	2004	2005	Pays ou zone
Mexico										Mexique
Imports: unit value	98	99	98	97	101	100	103	108	114	Imp. : valeur unitaire
Exports: unit value	96	95	90	93	98	100	105	117	127	Exp. : valeur unitaire
Terms of trade	98	96	91	96	97	100	102	108	112	Termes de l'échange
Morocco										Maroc
Imports: volume	61	66	82	89	98	105	114	126	...	Imp. : volume
Imports: unit value	142	126	109	107	97	98	109	121	...	Imp. : valeur unitaire
Exports: volume	105	106	104	102	102	107	102	103	...	Exp. : volume
Exports: unit value	128	118	115	110	94	99	116	127	...	Exp. : valeur unitaire
Terms of trade	90	94	105	103	97	101	106	104	...	Termes de l'échange
Purchasing power of exports	95	100	109	105	99	107	109	108	...	Pouvoir d'achat des export.
Netherlands										Pays-Bas
Imports: volume	76	81	89	96	97	95	98	106	115	Imp. : volume
Imports: unit value	123	113	108	103	101	101	118	131	133	Imp. : valeur unitaire
Exports: volume	75	82	88	92	102	103	106	116	122	Exp. : volume
Exports: unit value	124	114	109	101	100	100	116	127	133	Exp. : valeur unitaire
Terms of trade	101	101	101	98	99	98	99	96	100	Termes de l'échange
Purchasing power of exports	76	83	88	90	100	101	104	112	122	Pouvoir d'achat des export.
New Zealand										Nouvelle-Zélande
Imports: volume	85	88	91	103	102	111	124	142	151	Imp. : volume
Imports: unit value	125	118	99	100	94	98	109	118	125	Imp. : valeur unitaire
Exports: volume	88	93	92	95	103	109	112	119	118	Exp. : volume
Exports: unit value	125	117	99	99	101	99	111	129	138	Exp. : valeur unitaire
Terms of trade	100	99	99	99	107	102	102	109	111	Termes de l'échange
Purchasing power of exports	88	92	92	93	110	111	115	130	130	Pouvoir d'achat des export.
Norway[10]										Norvège[10]
Imports: volume[11]	76	83	94	94	101	103	106	118	129	Imp. : volume[11]
Imports: unit value[11]	141	127	118	109	98	104	116	127	133	Imp. : valeur unitaire[11]
Exports: volume[11]	88	93	93	95	105	107	107	108	108	Exp. : volume[11]
Exports: unit value[11]	93	86	71	78	93	94	104	127	161	Exp. : valeur unitaire[11]
Terms of trade	66	68	61	71	95	91	90	100	122	Termes de l'échange
Purchasing power of exports	58	63	56	68	99	97	97	109	131	Pouvoir d'achat des export.
Pakistan										Pakistan
Imports: volume	92	94	90	101	112	123	123	142	165	Imp. : volume
Imports: unit value	96	97	86	93	94	95	109	122	138	Imp. : valeur unitaire
Exports: volume	87	82	79	89	102	109	110	103	126	Exp. : volume
Exports: unit value	115	115	118	109	94	90	96	103	103	Exp. : valeur unitaire
Terms of trade	120	118	137	118	100	95	89	85	75	Termes de l'échange
Purchasing power of exports	105	97	109	105	102	104	98	87	95	Pouvoir d'achat des export.
Panama[12]										Panama[12]
Exports: volume	...	...	143	105	...	81	84	83	...	Exp. : volume
Papua New Guinea										Papouasie-Nvl-Guinée
Exports: unit value	95	98	80	79	90	85	101	126	...	Exp. : valeur unitaire
Peru										Pérou
Exports: volume	86	91	78	88	114	126	122	135	150	Exp. : volume
Exports: unit value	87	90	70	75	84	87	97	100	170	Exp. : valeur unitaire
Philippines										Philippines
Imports: volume	98	106	85	95	114	116	116	137	...	Imp. : volume
Imports: unit value[1]	180	162	121	118	80	84	83	81	...	Imp. : valeur unitaire[1]
Exports: volume	62	74	80	87	89	105	98	107	...	Exp. : volume
Exports: unit value[1]	146	134	105	121	84	77	79	77	...	Exp. : valeur unitaire[1]
Terms of trade	82	83	87	103	104	91	96	95	...	Termes de l'échange
Purchasing power of exports	51	61	70	89	92	96	94	102	...	Pouvoir d'achat des export.

Country or area	1996	1997	1998	1999	2001	2002	2003	2004	2005	Pays ou zone
Poland										Pologne
Imports: volume	62	75	90	94	103	111	120	141	152	Imp. : volume
Imports: unit value[1]	121	114	111	103	100	101	116	131	141	Imp. : valeur unitaire[1]
Exports: volume	63	72	76	81	112	121	144	170	189	Exp. : volume
Exports: unit value[1]	122	113	115	108	102	107	118	139	150	Exp. : valeur unitaire[1]
Terms of trade	101	99	103	105	102	105	102	107	107	Termes de l'échange
Purchasing power of exports	63	71	79	85	114	127	146	181	202	Pouvoir d'achat des export.
Portugal										Portugal
Imports: volume	...	...	...	...	97	94	94	...	...	Imp. : volume
Imports: unit value[1]	130	115	110	106	89	91	110	...	...	Imp. : valeur unitaire[1]
Exports: volume	...	...	...	...	95	95	97	...	...	Exp. : volume
Exports: unit value[1]	131	119	116	109	93	96	112	...	...	Exp. : valeur unitaire[1]
Terms of trade	101	104	106	103	105	106	102	...	...	Termes de l'échange
Purchasing power of exports	...	...	...	...	99	101	99	...	...	Pouvoir d'achat des export.
Republic of Moldova										République de Moldova
Imports: volume	...	...	...	...	118	139	180	...	...	Imp. : volume
Imports: unit value	...	...	...	...	97	92	95	...	...	Imp. : valeur unitaire
Exports: volume	...	...	...	...	122	142	170	...	...	Exp. : volume
Exports: unit value	...	...	...	...	93	87	88	...	...	Exp. : valeur unitaire
Terms of trade	...	...	...	...	96	95	93	...	...	Termes de l'échange
Purchasing power of exports	...	...	...	...	117	134	158	...	...	Pouvoir d'achat des export.
Romania										Roumanie
Imports: volume	...	...	...	...	124	143	169	207	244	Imp. : volume
Imports: unit value	144	133	117	105	96	96	106	106	112	Imp. : valeur unitaire
Exports: volume	...	...	...	...	112	132	144	166	179	Exp. : volume
Exports: unit value	126	118	109	102	98	102	119	125	137	Exp. : valeur unitaire
Terms of trade	88	89	93	97	102	106	112	118	122	Termes de l'échange
Purchasing power of exports	...	...	...	...	114	139	161	195	218	Pouvoir d'achat des export.
Russian Federation										Fédération de Russie
Imports: volume	...	...	...	...	123	136	168	222	288	Imp. : volume
Exports: volume	...	...	...	...	99	105	133	180	240	Exp. : volume
Seychelles										Seychelles
Imports: volume	77	68	83	105	...	...	...	...	...	Imp. : volume
Imports: unit value	144	146	136	120	...	...	...	...	...	Imp. : valeur unitaire
Exports: volume	38	51	51	78	...	...	...	...	...	Exp. : volume
Exports: unit value	88	110	143	114	...	...	...	...	...	Exp. : valeur unitaire
Terms of trade	61	75	105	94	...	...	...	...	...	Termes de l'échange
Purchasing power of exports	23	38	54	73	...	...	...	...	...	Pouvoir d'achat des export.
Singapore										Singapour
Imports: volume	85	92	83	88	89	96	...	...	...	Imp. : volume
Imports: unit value[1]	114	107	93	93	97	96	99	104	111	Imp. : valeur unitaire[1]
Exports: volume	76	81	82	86	95	100	116	155	173	Exp. : volume
Exports: unit value[1]	120	112	97	96	93	91	90	93	96	Exp. : valeur unitaire[1]
Terms of trade	105	105	104	103	96	94	91	89	87	Termes de l'échange
Purchasing power of exports	79	85	86	89	91	95	106	139	151	Pouvoir d'achat des export.
Slovakia										Slovaquie
Imports: unit value	...	...	...	...	...	106	129	147	...	Imp. : valeur unitaire
Exports: unit value	...	...	...	...	...	105	139	174	...	Exp. : valeur unitaire
Terms of trade	...	...	...	...	...	99	108	118	...	Termes de l'échange
Slovenia										Slovénie
Imports: volume	...	...	88	96	101	105	111	...	...	Imp. : volume
Imports: unit value	...	...	113	104	100	104	124	...	...	Imp. : valeur unitaire
Exports: volume	...	...	86	89	105	110	115	...	...	Exp. : volume
Exports: unit value	...	...	119	109	100	106	126	...	...	Exp. : valeur unitaire
Terms of trade	...	...	105	105	100	102	102	...	...	Termes de l'échange
Purchasing power of exports	...	...	90	94	105	112	117	...	...	Pouvoir d'achat des export.

Country or area	1996	1997	1998	1999	2001	2002	2003	2004	2005	Pays ou zone
South Africa[10,13]										Afrique du Sud[10,13]
Imports: volume	94	99	101	93	100	105	115	131	144	Imp. : volume
Imports: unit value	107	107	99	98	94	93	116	136	144	Imp. : valeur unitaire
Exports: volume	83	88	90	91	102	102	103	105	112	Exp. : volume
Exports: unit value	114	113	104	100	96	96	123	148	156	Exp. : valeur unitaire
Terms of trade	106	106	105	102	101	104	107	109	109	Termes de l'échange
Purchasing power of exports	89	93	94	92	103	106	109	114	122	Pouvoir d'achat des export.
Spain										Espagne
Imports: volume	...	...	...	92	104	109	117	129	...	Imp. : volume
Imports: unit value[1]	125	112	108	102	96	99	116	131	138	Imp. : valeur unitaire[1]
Exports: volume	...	...	...	89	104	107	114	120	...	Exp. : volume
Exports: unit value[1]	131	117	115	109	98	102	121	134	140	Exp. : valeur unitaire[1]
Terms of trade	105	105	107	106	101	103	104	102	102	Termes de l'échange
Purchasing power of exports	...	...	...	94	106	111	118	123	...	Pouvoir d'achat des export.
Sri Lanka										Sri Lanka
Imports: volume	73	82	89	90	91	101	111	122	126	Imp. : volume
Imports: unit value	...	...	...	...	98	90	...	...	...	Imp. : valeur unitaire
Exports: volume	74	82	81	84	92	93	98	106	113	Exp. : volume
Exports: unit value	102	105	110	101	97	91	97	101	104	Exp. : valeur unitaire
Terms of trade	...	...	...	...	98	101	...	...	...	Termes de l'échange
Purchasing power of exports	...	...	...	...	90	94	...	...	...	Pouvoir d'achat des export.
Sweden										Suède
Imports: volume	71	78	86	89	95	94	100	108	116	Imp. : volume
Imports: unit value[1]	122	110	104	103	93	99	117	132	139	Imp. : valeur unitaire[1]
Exports: volume	70	78	85	90	98	101	106	117	122	Exp. : volume
Exports: unit value[1]	132	117	112	106	90	94	111	121	124	Exp. : valeur unitaire[1]
Terms of trade	108	107	107	104	97	95	95	92	90	Termes de l'échange
Purchasing power of exports	76	83	91	93	96	96	101	108	109	Pouvoir d'achat des export.
Switzerland										Suisse
Imports: volume	76	80	87	93	101	99	100	104	106	Imp. : volume
Imports: unit value	129	116	112	107	100	105	121	135	143	Imp. : valeur unitaire
Exports: volume	81	87	91	93	103	105	105	111	115	Exp. : volume
Exports: unit value	126	111	110	109	101	107	124	137	141	Exp. : valeur unitaire
Terms of trade	97	96	99	103	101	102	102	102	99	Termes de l'échange
Purchasing power of exports	79	83	90	95	104	106	107	113	114	Pouvoir d'achat des export.
Thailand										Thaïlande
Imports: volume	102	91	67	82	89	100	112	124	135	Imp. : volume
Imports: unit value	111	109	98	95	109	102	107	121	140	Imp. : valeur unitaire
Exports: volume	63	68	73	82	92	101	109	119	124	Exp. : volume
Exports: unit value	127	122	107	102	102	97	105	118	130	Exp. : valeur unitaire
Terms of trade	114	112	109	107	93	95	99	98	93	Termes de l'échange
Purchasing power of exports	72	76	80	88	85	96	108	116	115	Pouvoir d'achat des export.
Turkey										Turquie
Imports: volume	63	78	76	75	75	91	121	153	172	Imp. : volume
Imports: unit value	116	106	101	96	100	98	106	120	128	Imp. : valeur unitaire
Exports: volume	70	79	87	90	122	142	173	199	219	Exp. : volume
Exports: unit value	123	117	112	104	97	96	105	122	129	Exp. : valeur unitaire
Terms of trade	106	111	111	109	98	97	99	102	101	Termes de l'échange
Purchasing power of exports	74	88	96	98	119	137	171	203	222	Pouvoir d'achat des export.
United Kingdom										Royaume-Uni
Imports: volume	72	79	86	91	105	110	112	120	128	Imp. : volume
Imports: unit value[1]	114	112	106	104	94	96	104	116	120	Imp. : valeur unitaire[1]
Exports: volume	79	85	86	89	102	101	101	102	111	Exp. : volume
Exports: unit value[1]	116	115	111	106	94	98	108	122	125	Exp. : valeur unitaire[1]
Terms of trade	101	103	104	102	99	102	104	105	105	Termes de l'échange
Purchasing power of exports	80	88	90	91	101	103	105	108	117	Pouvoir d'achat des export.

Total imports and exports: index numbers—2000 = 100 (*continued*)
Importations et exportations totales : indices—2000 = 100 (*suite*)

Country or area	1996	1997	1998	1999	2001	2002	2003	2004	2005	Pays ou zone
United States[14]										Etats-Unis[14]
Imports: volume	64	72	81	90	97	101	107	118	125	Imp. : volume
Imports: unit value[1]	102	99	93	94	96	94	97	102	110	Imp. : valeur unitaire[1]
Exports: volume[15]	77	86	88	90	94	90	93	101	109	Exp. : volume[15]
Exports: unit value[1,15]	104	103	100	98	99	98	100	104	107	Exp. : valeur unitaire[1,15]
Terms of trade	103	104	107	105	103	104	103	101	97	Termes de l'échange
Purchasing power of exports	79	89	94	95	97	94	96	102	105	Pouvoir d'achat des export.
Uruguay										Uruguay
Imports: unit value	112	108	101	96	94	87	...	...	...	Imp. : valeur unitaire
Exports: unit value	122	119	118	101	98	93	...	...	...	Exp. : valeur unitaire
Terms of trade	109	110	117	106	104	106	...	...	...	Termes de l'échange
Venezuela (Bolivarian Rep. of)[1]										Venezuela (Rép. bolivarienne du)[1]
Imports: unit value	99	98	102	102	105	105	112	123	126	Imp. : valeur unitaire

Source

United Nations Statistics Division, New York, trade statistics database.

Notes

1 Price index numbers.
2 Prior to 1997, the data refer to the Economic Union of Belgium and Luxembourg and intertrade between the two countries is excluded. Beginning January 1997, data refer to Belgium only and include trade between Belgium and Luxembourg.
3 Imports FOB.
4 Beginning 1997, trade data for France include the import and export values of French Guiana, Guadeloupe, Martinique, and Réunion.
5 Prior to 1991, data refer to the Federal Republic of Germany.
6 Prior to January 1991, excluding trade conducted in accordance with the supplementary protocol to the treaty on the basis of relations between the Federal Republic of Germany and the former German Democratic Republic.
7 Beginning 1989, data exclude re-exports.
8 Prior to 1996 data exclude customs free zones, repairs on goods, and operational leasing.
9 Excluding military goods, fissionable materials, bunkers, ships, and aircraft.
10 Exports include gold.
11 Index numbers exclude ships.
12 Exports include re-exports and petroleum products.
13 Beginning in January 1998, foreign trade data refer to South Africa only, excluding intra-trade of the Southern African Common Customs Area. Prior to January 1998, trade data refer to the Southern African Common Customs Area, which includes Botswana, Lesotho, Namibia, South Africa and Swaziland.
14 Including the trade of the U.S. Virgin Islands and Puerto Rico but excluding shipments of merchandise between the United States and its other possessions (Guam, American Samoa, etc.). Data include imports and exports of non-monetary gold.
15 Excluding military goods.

Source

Organisation des Nations Unies, Division de statistique, New York, la base de données pour les statistiques du commerce extérieur.

Notes

1 Indices de prix.
2 Avant 1997, les données se rapportent à l'Union économique belgo-luxembourgeoise et ne comprennent pas le commerce entre ces pays. A partir de janvier 1997, les données se rapportent à Belgique seulement et recouvrent les échanges entre la Belgique et le Luxembourg.
3 Importations FOB.
4 A compter de 1997, les valeurs de commerce pour la France comprennent les valeurs des importations et des exportations de la Guyane française, la Guadeloupe, la Martinique, et la Réunion.
5 Avant 1991, les données se rapportent à la République Fédérale d'Allemagne.
6 Avant janvier 1991, non compris le commerce effectué en accord avec le protocole additionnel au traité définissant la base des relations entre la République Fédérale d'Allemagne et l'ancienne République Démocratique Allemande.
7 A compter 1989, les données non compris les réexportations.
8 Avant 1996 les données excluent des zones franches, des réparations sur des marchandises, et le crédit-bail opérationnel.
9 A l'exclusion des marchandises militaires, des matières fissibles, des soutes, des bateaux, et de l'avion.
10 Les exportations comprennent l'or.
11 Non compris les navires.
12 Exportations comprennent re-exportations et produits pétroliers.
13 A compter de janvier 1998, les données sur le commerce extérieur ne se rapportent qu'à l'Afrique du Sud. et ne tiennent pas compte des échanges commerciaux entre les pays de l'Union douanière de l'Afrique du Sud, qui incluait l'Afrique du Sud, Botswana, Lesotho, Namibie, et Swaziland.
14 Y compris le commerce des Iles Vierges américaines et de Porto Rico mais non compris les échanges de marchandise, entre les Etats-Unis et leurs autres possessions (Guam, Samoa americaihes, etc.). Les données comprennent les importations et exportations d'or non-monétaire.
15 Non compris les importations des biens militaires.

Manufactured goods exports

Unit value and volume indices: 2000 = 100; value: thousand million US dollars

Exportations des produits manufacturés

Indices de valeur unitaire et de volume : 2000 = 100; valeur : milliards de dollars des E.U.

Region, country or area — Région, pays ou zone	1995	1996	1997	1998	1999	2001	2002	2003	2004	2005
Total — Total										
Unit value indices, US $[1] Indices de valeur unitaire, $ des E.U.[1]	**122**	**118**	**110**	**108**	**103**	**98**	**98**	**104**	**111**	**...**
Unit value indices, SDRs Indices de valeur unitaire, DTS	**106**	**107**	**105**	**106**	**99**	**102**	**99**	**99**	**98**	**...**
Volume indices[1] Indices de volume[1]	**66**	**71**	**80**	**82**	**89**	**101**	**103**	**112**	**116**	**...**
Value, thousand million US $[1] Valeur, millards de $ des E.U.[1]	**3 744.7**	**3 871.7**	**4 064.2**	**4 094.8**	**4 194.4**	**4 548.0**	**4 649.3**	**5 355.5**	**5 938.1**	**...**
Developed economies — Économies développées										
Unit value indices, US $ Indices de valeur unitaire, $ des E.U.	123	119	111	110	105	98	99	108	117	120
Unit value indices, SDRs Indices de valeur unitaire, DTS	107	108	106	107	101	102	100	102	103	107
Volume indices Indices de volume	71	75	83	85	90	103	102	106	116	120
Value, thousand million US $ Valeur, millards de $ des E.U.	2 775.1	2 846.2	2 955.5	2 983.8	3 021.0	3 215.3	3 197.1	3 652.7	4 305.8	4 578.1
Americas — Amériques										
Unit value indices, US $ Indices de valeur unitaire, $ des E.U.	**100**	**99**	**101**	**100**	**99**	**99**	**100**	**103**	**106**	**108**
Volume indices Indices de volume	**73**	**78**	**87**	**89**	**93**	**103**	**90**	**90**	**100**	**106**
Value, thousand million US $ Valeur, millards de $ des E.U.	**557.0**	**593.7**	**667.7**	**675.6**	**703.7**	**781.4**	**685.2**	**704.0**	**803.0**	**872.0**
Canada — Canada										
Unit value indices, US $ Indices de valeur unitaire, $ des E.U.	104	105	106	101	99	97	96	103	112	119
Unit value indices, national currency Indices de val. unitaire, monnaie nationale	96	97	99	101	99	102	102	98	98	97
Volume indices Indices de volume	74	76	80	88	99	104	103	101	107	110
Value, thousand million US $ Valeur, millards de $ des E.U.	128.2	134.0	142.9	148.7	165.6	168.8	166.5	173.6	200.0	219.0
United States — Etats-Unis										
Unit value indices, US $[2] Indices de valeur unitaire, $ des E.U.[2]	98	98	99	100	99	100	102	103	104	104
Unit value indices, national currency[2] Indices de val. unitaire, monnaie nationale[2]	98	98	99	100	99	100	102	103	104	104
Volume indices Indices de volume	73	79	89	89	91	103	86	87	97	105
Value, thousand million US $ Valeur, millards de $ des E.U.	428.8	459.7	524.8	527.0	538.1	612.6	518.8	530.4	603.0	653.1
Europe — Europe										
Unit value indices, US $ Indices de valeur unitaire, $ des E.U.	**135**	**131**	**117**	**117**	**110**	**99**	**100**	**112**	**122**	**125**
Volume indices Indices de volume	**68**	**73**	**82**	**84**	**89**	**106**	**108**	**113**	**124**	**128**
Value, thousand million US $ Valeur, millards de $ des E.U.	**1 741.8**	**1 802.2**	**1 826.5**	**1 884.5**	**1 856.3**	**1 986.4**	**2 052.1**	**2 426.2**	**2 877.4**	**3 055.7**
Austria — Autriche										
Unit value indices, US $[3] Indices de valeur unitaire, $ des E.U.[3]	205	185	152	141	118	94	100	...	...	...
Unit value indices, national currency[3] Indices de val. unitaire, monnaie nationale[3]	138	131	125	117	102	98	98	...	...	...

Manufactured goods exports — Unit value and volume indices: 2000 = 100; value: thousand million US dollars (*continued*)
Exportations des produits manufacturés — Indices de valeur unitaire et de volume : 2000 = 100; valeur : milliards de dollars des E.U. (*suite*)

Region, country or area — Région, pays ou zone	1995	1996	1997	1998	1999	2001	2002	2003	2004	2005
Volume indices Indices de volume	50	57	70	74	86	124	118	...	...	...
Value, thousand million US $ Valeur, millards de $ des E.U.	51.4	52.3	53.1	51.7	50.4	58.3	59.0	76.8	96.7	100.2
Belgium — Belgique										
Unit value indices, US $[4] Indices de valeur unitaire, $ des E.U.[4]	132	127	115	114	108	99	106	125	141	148
Unit value indices, national currency Indices de val. unitaire, monnaie nationale	89	90	94	95	94	102	103	103	105	110
Volume indices Indices de volume	76	79	84	87	92	100	100	100	106	107
Value, thousand million US $ Valeur, millards de $ des E.U.	133.6	132.4	127.0	132.2	131.8	131.6	139.5	166.3	198.7	209.9
Denmark — Danemark										
Unit value indices, US $ Indices de valeur unitaire, $ des E.U.	134	130	118	116	112	100	103	122	136	138
Unit value indices, national currency Indices de val. unitaire, monnaie nationale	93	93	96	96	97	102	100	101	101	102
Volume indices Indices de volume	69	71	81	84	95	105	114	119	119	129
Value, thousand million US $ Valeur, millards de $ des E.U.	29.4	29.2	30.2	31.2	33.8	33.5	37.2	46.4	51.4	56.6
Finland — Finlande										
Unit value indices, US $ Indices de valeur unitaire, $ des E.U.	128	121	109	107	104	95	100	117	120	131
Unit value indices, national currency Indices de val. unitaire, monnaie nationale	87	86	88	89	90	98	98	96	89	97
Volume indices Indices de volume	68	72	81	89	89	103	98	98	109	108
Value, thousand million US $ Valeur, millards de $ des E.U.	34.7	34.8	35.1	38.0	36.7	38.9	38.9	45.4	51.8	56.1
France — France										
Unit value indices, US $ Indices de valeur unitaire, $ des E.U.	139	135	120	120	113	98	84	101	111	111
Unit value indices, national currency Indices de val. unitaire, monnaie nationale	97	97	98	100	98	101	83	83	82	82
Volume indices Indices de volume	64	68	76	82	86	119	120	118	127	132
Value, thousand million US $ Valeur, millards de $ des E.U.	222.9	229.4	225.8	244.3	242.5	290.2	251.9	298.5	351.8	365.3
Germany — Allemagne										
Unit value indices, US $ Indices de valeur unitaire, $ des E.U.	150	140	121	124	111	99	104	118	128	...
Unit value indices, national currency Indices de val. unitaire, monnaie nationale	101	99	99	103	97	102	102	96	95	...
Volume indices Indices de volume	63	68	79	80	86	105	107	114	128	...
Value, thousand million US $ Valeur, millards de $ des E.U.	455.8	459.7	455.3	477.9	461.1	499.2	534.8	644.3	790.3	...
Greece — Grèce										
Unit value indices, US $ Indices de valeur unitaire, $ des E.U.	149	143	122	113	107	...	...	...	...	...
Unit value indices, national currency Indices de val. unitaire, monnaie nationale	95	94	91	91	90	...	...	...	...	...
Volume indices Indices de volume	66	73	84	93	86	...	...	...	...	...
Value, thousand million US $ Valeur, millards de $ des E.U.	6.0	6.3	6.2	6.3	5.6	6.0	5.7	8.7	8.5	...
Iceland — Islande										
Unit value indices, US $[4] Indices de valeur unitaire, $ des E.U.[4]	128	118	113	100	...	...	...	...	...	...

Manufactured goods exports—Unit value and volume indices: 2000 = 100; value: thousand million US dollars (*continued*)

Exportations des produits manufacturés—Indices de valeur unitaire et de volume : 2000 = 100; valeur : milliards de dollars des E.U. (*suite*)

Region, country or area — Région, pays ou zone	1995	1996	1997	1998	1999	2001	2002	2003	2004	2005
Volume indices Indices de volume	52	56	64	72	...	...	...	...	...	...
Value, thousand million US \$ Valeur, millards de \$ des E.U.	0.4	0.4	0.4	0.4	0.6	0.7	0.7	0.8	1.0	1.1
Ireland — Irlande										
Unit value indices, US \$[4] Indices de valeur unitaire, \$ des E.U.[4]	125	124	104	96	...	...	...	...	...	...
Volume indices Indices de volume	38	46	63	86	...	...	...	...	...	...
Value, thousand million US \$ Valeur, millards de \$ des E.U.	31.2	37.0	42.8	53.6	59.6	75.1	77.7	79.4	88.7	94.0
Italy — Italie										
Unit value indices, US \$[4] Indices de valeur unitaire, \$ des E.U.[4]	120	123	112	119	113	100	...	104	...	118
Volume indices Indices de volume	82	87	90	87	86	105	...	119	...	128
Value, thousand million US \$ Valeur, millards de \$ des E.U.	209.0	226.9	215.0	219.7	206.7	223.2	226.1	262.5	309.7	320.2
Netherlands — Pays-Bas										
Unit value indices, US \$[5] Indices de valeur unitaire, \$ des E.U.[5]	141	132	117	115	109	104	104	120	130	139
Unit value indices, national currency[5] Indices de val. unitaire, monnaie nationale[5]	94	93	96	95	95	107	102	98	97	103
Volume indices Indices de volume	64	68	89	83	88	115	117	122	135	136
Value, thousand million US \$ Valeur, millards de \$ des E.U.	113.9	114.0	133.5	121.7	122.2	152.8	154.6	186.1	224.7	240.4
Norway — Norvège										
Unit value indices, US \$ Indices de valeur unitaire, \$ des E.U.	135	127	116	112	106	97	100	110	126	131
Unit value indices, national currency Indices de val. unitaire, monnaie nationale	97	93	93	96	94	99	91	89	96	96
Volume indices Indices de volume	65	68	88	95	96	92	110	110	112	119
Value, thousand million US \$ Valeur, millards de \$ des E.U.	14.5	14.4	17.0	17.7	16.8	14.8	18.3	20.3	23.5	25.9
Portugal — Portugal										
Unit value indices, US \$[4] Indices de valeur unitaire, \$ des E.U.[4]	137	129	116	113	108	99	...	...	...	...
Volume indices Indices de volume	68	73	80	89	94	103	...	...	...	...
Value, thousand million US \$ Valeur, millards de \$ des E.U.	19.5	19.9	19.5	21.1	21.3	21.4	23.1	27.5	30.5	28.8
Spain — Espagne										
Unit value indices, US \$[4] Indices de valeur unitaire, \$ des E.U.[4]	132	132	117	115	...	...	...	...	...	...
Volume indices Indices de volume	60	68	79	84	...	...	...	...	...	...
Value, thousand million US \$ Valeur, millards de \$ des E.U.	71.4	80.5	82.3	86.3	88.7	91.4	99.0	124.0	142.8	150.1
Sweden — Suède										
Unit value indices, US \$ Indices de valeur unitaire, \$ des E.U.	131	132	117	112	106	...	...	...	...	...
Unit value indices, national currency Indices de val. unitaire, monnaie nationale	102	97	97	97	96	...	...	...	...	...
Volume indices Indices de volume	77	76	91	91	100	...	...	...	...	...
Value, thousand million US \$ Valeur, millards de \$ des E.U.	67.4	67.7	71.4	68.7	71.1	58.7	66.9	82.4	101.0	111.0
Switzerland — Suisse										
Unit value indices, US \$[4] Indices de valeur unitaire, \$ des E.U.[4]	128	126	112	111	109	104	109	...	...	...

Manufactured goods exports—Unit value and volume indices: 2000 = 100; value: thousand million US dollars *(continued)*

Exportations des produits manufacturés—Indices de valeur unitaire et de volume : 2000 = 100; valeur : milliards de dollars des E.U. *(suite)*

Region, country or area—Région, pays ou zone	1995	1996	1997	1998	1999	2001	2002	2003	2004	2005
Volume indices Indices de volume	78	78	83	87	94	97	99	...	...	...
Value, thousand million US $ Valeur, millards de $ des E.U.	77.8	77.5	72.9	75.7	80.0	78.8	84.5	96.8	113.7	...
United Kingdom—Royaume-Uni										
Unit value indices, US $ Indices de valeur unitaire, $ des E.U.	116	115	115	114	108	95	98	108	120	120
Unit value indices, national currency Indices de val. unitaire, monnaie nationale	111	111	106	104	101	99	99	100	99	100
Volume indices Indices de volume	75	82	89	89	90	96	102	103	104	111
Value, thousand million US $ Valeur, millards de $ des E.U.	201.3	218.4	237.7	236.4	225.6	210.2	232.6	258.1	290.2	310.5
Other developed economies—Autres économies développées										
Unit value indices, US $ Indices de valeur unitaire, $ des E.U.	**118**	**110**	**104**	**99**	**98**	**94**	**91**	**97**	**107**	**113**
Volume indices Indices de volume	**77**	**78**	**85**	**82**	**90**	**91**	**96**	**103**	**111**	**110**
Value, thousand million US $ Valeur, millards de $ des E.U.	**476.2**	**450.4**	**461.3**	**423.7**	**461.0**	**447.5**	**459.8**	**522.5**	**625.4**	**650.4**
Australia—Australie										
Unit value indices, US $ Indices de valeur unitaire, $ des E.U.	121	117	112	98	97	93	92	101	133	151
Unit value indices, national currency Indices de val. unitaire, monnaie nationale	94	87	87	90	87	104	97	89	104	114
Volume indices Indices de volume	61	79	86	83	91	99	104	103	88	88
Value, thousand million US $ Valeur, millards de $ des E.U.	15.6	19.8	20.4	17.3	18.7	19.5	20.2	22.0	25.0	28.2
Israel—Israël										
Unit value indices, US $ Indices de valeur unitaire, $ des E.U.	77	77	75	77	83	98	95	95	99	109
Volume indices Indices de volume	75	82	94	95	98	95	98	105	124	125
Value, thousand million US $ Valeur, millards de $ des E.U.	17.1	18.8	20.8	21.7	24.2	27.6	27.5	29.5	36.5	40.5
Japan—Japon										
Unit value indices, US $ Indices de valeur unitaire, $ des E.U.	119	110	104	100	98	94	92	97	107	112
Unit value indices, national currency Indices de val. unitaire, monnaie nationale	103	111	117	121	104	110	106	105	107	114
Volume indices Indices de volume	79	79	85	81	89	89	94	100	110	109
Value, thousand million US $ Valeur, millards de $ des E.U.	425.8	393.6	402.1	369.6	397.5	378.0	391.8	443.3	534.1	553.7
New Zealand—Nouvelle-Zélande										
Unit value indices, US $ Indices de valeur unitaire, $ des E.U.	134	131	122	101	96	98	99	112	125	136
Unit value indices, national currency Indices de val. unitaire, monnaie nationale	93	86	84	85	83	105	97	88	86	88
Volume indices Indices de volume	70	73	80	92	99	108	105	109	116	115
Value, thousand million US $ Valeur, millards de $ des E.U.	4.4	4.5	4.6	4.3	4.5	5.0	4.9	5.7	6.8	7.3
South Africa—Afrique du Sud										
Unit value indices, US $ Indices de valeur unitaire, $ des E.U.	190	165	...	...	...	...	...	...	...	...
Unit value indices, national currency Indices de val. unitaire, monnaie nationale	99	102	...	...	...	...	...	...	...	...
Volume indices Indices de volume	46	55	...	...	...	...	...	...	...	...

Manufactured goods exports—Unit value and volume indices: 2000 = 100; value: thousand million US dollars (*continued*)
Exportations des produits manufacturés—Indices de valeur unitaire et de volume : 2000 = 100; valeur : milliards de dollars des E.U. (*suite*)

Region, country or area — Région, pays ou zone	1995	1996	1997	1998	1999	2001	2002	2003	2004	2005
Value, thousand million US $ Valeur, milliards de $ des E.U.	13.4	13.8	13.3	10.8	16.1	17.5	15.3	22.0	...	...
Developing economies — Économies en développment										
Unit value indices, US $ Indices de valeur unitaire, $ des E.U.	**120**	**114**	**108**	**104**	**97**	**98**	**96**	**97**	**98**	...
Unit value indices, SDRs Indices de valeur unitaire, DTS	**104**	**104**	**103**	**101**	**93**	**102**	**98**	**92**	**87**	...
Volume indices Indices de volume	**57**	**64**	**73**	**76**	**86**	**96**	**107**	**124**	**118**	...
Value, thousand million US $ Valeur, millards de $ des E.U.	**969.6**	**1 025.5**	**1 108.7**	**1 111.0**	**1 173.3**	**1 332.7**	**1 452.2**	**1 702.8**	**1 632.3**	...
China, Hong Kong SAR — Chine, Hong Kong RAS										
Unit value indices, US $ Indices de valeur unitaire, $ des E.U.	111	111	107	104	102	95	93	93	94	96
Unit value indices, national currency Indices de val. unitaire, monnaie nationale	110	110	106	103	101	96	93	93	94	96
Volume indices Indices de volume	113	104	107	100	93	88	93	70	71	75
Value, thousand million US $ Valeur, millards de $ des E.U.	28.2	25.8	25.7	23.3	21.2	18.9	19.4	14.7	15.1	16.3
India — Inde										
Unit value indices, US $ Indices de valeur unitaire, $ des E.U.	117	94	113	107	121	92	99	...	...	...
Unit value indices, national currency Indices de val. unitaire, monnaie nationale	84	74	92	98	116	95	107	...	...	...
Volume indices Indices de volume	57	74	65	67	69	105	115	...	...	...
Value, thousand million US $ Valeur, millards de $ des E.U.	23.3	24.3	26.0	25.3	29.3	33.6	39.9	48.8	...	...
Korea, Republic of — Corée, République de										
Unit value indices, US $ Indices de valeur unitaire, $ des E.U.	136	125	115	101	96	92	82	83	92	96
Unit value indices, national currency Indices de val. unitaire, monnaie nationale	93	89	95	125	101	105	91	87	93	87
Volume indices Indices de volume	54	59	66	73	87	95	97	118	145	175
Value, thousand million US $ Valeur, millards de $ des E.U.	115.5	116.0	120.0	116.3	130.6	137.3	125.4	153.0	207.9	262.8
Pakistan — Pakistan										
Unit value indices, US $ Indices de valeur unitaire, $ des E.U.	113	111	117	115	106	100	96	101	108	...
Unit value indices, national currency Indices de val. unitaire, monnaie nationale	68	76	91	99	100	117	109	111	119	...
Volume indices Indices de volume	77	90	82	79	90	101	113	140	137	...
Value, thousand million US $ Valeur, millards de $ des E.U.	6.7	7.8	7.4	7.1	7.4	7.8	8.4	10.9	11.4	...
Singapore — Singapour										
Unit value indices, US $ Indices de valeur unitaire, $ des E.U.	127	123	116	105	101	98	100	99	98	...
Volume indices Indices de volume	67	72	77	75	82	89	90	104	129	...
Value, thousand million US $ Valeur, millards de $ des E.U.	101.0	106.0	106.6	94.2	99.7	103.7	106.7	122.8	151.7	...
Turkey — Turquie										
Unit value indices, US $[6] Indices de valeur unitaire, $ des E.U.[6]	139	127	116	109	105	99	96	108	124	130
Volume indices Indices de volume	52	60	76	85	89	115	139	165	192	207
Value, thousand million US $ Valeur, millards de $ des E.U.	16.3	17.3	20.0	21.0	21.2	26.0	30.3	40.4	54.2	61.0

60 Manufactured goods exports — Unit value and volume indices: 2000 = 100; value: thousand million US dollars (*continued*)
Exportations des produits manufacturés — Indices de valeur unitaire et de volume : 2000 = 100; valeur : milliards de dollars des E.U. (*suite*)

Source

United Nations Statistics Division, New York, trade statistics database.

Notes

1 Excludes trade of the countries of Eastern Europe and the former USSR.
2 Beginning 1989, derived from price indices; national unit value index is discontinued.
3 Series linked at 1988 and 1995 by a factor calculated by the United Nations Statistics Division.
4 Beginning 1981, indices are calculated by the United Nations Statistics Division; for Netherlands beginning 1988, for Belgium 1988 to 1992 and for Switzerland 1988 to 1995.
5 Derived from sub-indices using current weights; for Netherlands 1989 to 1996.
6 Industrial products.

Source

Organisation des Nations Unies, Division de statistique, New York, la base de données pour les statistiques du commerce extérieur.

Notes

1 Non compris le commerce des pays de l'Europe de l'Est et l'ex-URSS.
2 A partir de 1989, calculés à partir des indices des prix; l'indice de la valeur unitaire nationale est discontinué.
3 Les séries sont enchainées à 1988 et 1995 par un facteur calculé par la Division de Statistique des Nations Unies.
4 A partir de 1981, les indices sont calculés par la Division de statistique des Nations Unies; pour la Pays-Bas 1988, pour la Belgique 1988-1992 et pour la Suisse 1988 to 1995.
5 Calculés à partir de sous-indices à coefficients de pondération correspondant à la période en cours; pour les Pays-Bas de 1989 à 1996.
6 Produits industriels.

Technical notes: tables 58-60

Tables 58-60: Current data (annual, monthly and/or quarterly) for most of the series are published regularly by the Statistics Division in the United Nations *Monthly Bulletin of Statistics*. More detailed descriptions of the tables and notes on methodology appear in the United Nations publications *International Trade Statistics: Concepts and Definitions* and the *International Trade Statistics Yearbook*. More detailed data including series for individual countries showing the value in national currencies for imports and exports and notes on these series can be found in the *International Trade Statistics Yearbook* and in the *Monthly Bulletin of Statistics*.

Data are obtained from national published sources, from data supplied by the governments for dissemination in United Nations publications and from publications of other United Nations agencies.

Territory

The statistics reported by each country refer to its customs area, which in most cases coincides with its geographical area.

Systems of trade

Two systems of recording trade are in common use, differing mainly in the way warehoused and re-exported goods are recorded:

(a) Special trade (S): special imports are the combined total of imports for direct domestic consumption (including transformation and repair) and withdrawals from bonded warehouses or free zones for domestic consumption. Special exports comprise exports of national merchandise, namely, goods wholly or partly produced or manufactured in the country, together with exports of nationalized goods. (Nationalized goods are goods which, having been included in special imports, are then exported without transformation);

(b) General trade (G): general imports are the combined total of imports for direct domestic consumption and imports into bonded warehouses or free zones. General exports are the combined total of national exports and re-exports. Re-exports, in the general trade system, consist of the outward movement of nationalized goods plus goods which; after importation, move outward from bonded warehouses or free zones without having been transformed.

Valuation

Goods are, in general, valued according to the transaction value. In the case of imports, the transaction value is the value at which the goods were purchased by the importer plus the

Notes techniques : tableaux 58 à 60

Tableaux 58-60: La Division de statistique des Nations Unies publie régulièrement dans le *Bulletin mensuel de statistique* des données courantes (annuelles, mensuelles et/ou trimestrielles) pour la plupart des séries de ces tableaux. Des descriptions plus détaillées des tableaux et des notes méthodologiques figurent dans les publications des Nations Unies *Statistiques du commerce international, Concepts et définitions* et l'*Annuaire statistique du Commerce international*. Des données plus détaillées, comprenant des séries indiquant la valeur en monnaie nationale des importations et des exportations des divers pays et les notes accompagnant ces séries figurent dans l'*Annuaire statistique du Commerce international* et dans le *Bulletin mensuel de statistique*.

Les données proviennent de publications nationales et des informations fournies par les gouvernements pour les publications des Nations Unies ainsi que de publications d'autres institutions des Nations Unies.

Territoire

Les statistiques fournies par chaque pays se rapportent au territoire douanier de ce pays. Le plus souvent, ce territoire coïncide avec l'étendue géographique du pays.

Systèmes de commerce

Deux systèmes d'enregistrement du commerce sont couramment utilisés, et ne diffèrent que par la façon dont sont enregistrées les marchandises entreposées et les marchandises réexportées:

(a) Commerce spécial (S): les importations spéciales représentent le total combiné des importations destinées directement à la consommation intérieure (transformations et réparations comprises) et les marchandises retirées des entrepôts douaniers ou des zones franches pour la consommation intérieure. Les exportations spéciales comprennent les exportations de marchandises nationales, c'est-à-dire des biens produits ou fabriqués en totalité ou en partie dans le pays, ainsi que les exportations de biens nationalisés. (Les biens nationalisés sont des biens qui, ayant été inclus dans les importations spéciales, sont ensuite réexportés tels quels).

(b) Commerce général (G): les importations générales sont le total combiné des importations destinées directement à la consommation intérieure et des importations placées en entrepôt douanier ou destinées aux zones franches. Les exportations générales sont le total combiné des exportations de biens nationaux et

cost of transportation and insurance to the frontier of the importing country (c.i.f. valuation). In the case of exports, the transaction value is the value at which the goods were sold by the exporter, including the cost of transportation and insurance to bring the goods onto the transporting vehicle at the frontier of the exporting country (f.o.b. valuation).

Currency conversion

Conversion of values from national currencies into United States dollars is done by means of external trade conversion factors which are generally weighted averages of exchange rates, the weight being the corresponding monthly or quarterly value of imports or exports.

Coverage

The statistics relate to merchandise trade. Merchandise trade is defined to include, as far as possible, all goods which add to or subtract from the material resources of a country as a result of their movement into or out of the country. Thus, ordinary commercial transactions, government trade (including foreign aid, war reparations and trade in military goods), postal trade and all kinds of silver (except silver coins after their issue), are included in the statistics. Since their movement affects monetary rather than material resources, monetary gold, together with currency and titles of ownership after their issue into circulation, are excluded.

Commodity classification

The commodity classification of trade is in accordance with the United Nations *Standard International Trade Classification* (SITC).

World and regional totals

The regional, economic and world totals have been adjusted: (a) to include estimates for countries or areas for which full data are not available; (b) to include insurance and freight for imports valued f.o.b.; (c) to include countries or areas not listed separately; (d) to approximate special trade; (e) to approximate calendar years; and (f) where possible, to eliminate incomparabilities owing to geographical changes, by adjusting the figures for periods before the change to be comparable to those for periods after the change.

Volume and unit value index numbers

These index numbers show the changes in the volume of imports or exports (volume index) and the average price of imports or exports (unit value index).

des réexportations. Ces dernières, dans le système du commerce général, comprennent les exportations de biens nationalisés et de biens qui, après avoir été importés, sortent des entrepôts de douane ou des zones franches sans avoir été transformés.

Evaluation

En général, les marchandises sont évaluées à la valeur de la transaction. Dans le cas des importations, cette valeur est celle à laquelle les marchandises ont été achetées par l'importateur plus le coût de leur transport et de leur assurance jusqu'à la frontière du pays importateur (valeur c.a.f.). Dans le cas des exportations, la valeur de la transaction est celle à laquelle les marchandises ont été vendues par l'exportateur, y compris le coût de transport et d'assurance des marchandises jusqu'à leur chargement sur le véhicule de transport à la frontière du pays exportateur (valeur f.à.b.).

Conversion des monnaies

La conversion en dollars des Etats-Unis de valeurs exprimées en monnaie nationale se fait par application de coefficients de conversion du commerce extérieur, qui sont généralement les moyennes pondérées des taux de change, le poids étant la valeur mensuelle ou trimestrielle correspondante des importations ou des exportations.

Couverture

Les statistiques se rapportent au commerce des marchandises. Le commerce des marchandises se définit comme comprenant, dans toute la mesure du possible, toutes les marchandises que l'ajoute ou retranche aux ressources matérielles d'un pays suite à leur importation ou à leur exportation par ce pays. Ainsi, les transactions commerciales ordinaires, le commerce pour le compte de l'Etat (y compris l'aide extérieure, les réparations pour dommages de guerre et le commerce des fournitures militaires), le commerce par voie postale et les transactions de toutes sortes sur l'argent (à l'exception des transactions sur les pièces d'argent après leur émission) sont inclus dans ces statistiques. La monnaie or ainsi que la monnaie et les titres de propriété après leur mise en circulation sont exclus, car leurs mouvements influent sur les ressources monétaires plutôt que sur les ressources matérielles.

Classification par marchandise

La classification par marchandise du commerce extérieur est celle adoptée dans la *Classification type pour le commerce international* des Nations Unies (CTCI).

Description of tables

Table 58: World imports and exports are the sum of imports and exports of Developed economies, Developing economies and other. The regional totals for imports and exports and have been adjusted to exclude the re-exports of countries or areas comprising each region. Estimates for certain countries or areas not shown separately as well as for those shown separately but for which no data are yet available are included in the regional and world totals. Export and import values in terms of U.S. dollars are derived by the United Nations Statistics Division from data published in national publications, from data in the replies to the *Monthly Bulletin of Statistics* questionnaires and from data published by the International Monetary Fund (IMF) in the publication *International Financial Statistics*.

Table 59: These index numbers show the changes in the volume (quantum index) and the average price (unit value index) of total imports and exports. The terms of trade figures are calculated by dividing export unit value indices by the corresponding import unit value indices. The product of the net terms of trade and the volume index of exports is called the index of the purchasing power of exports. The footnotes to countries appearing in table 58 also apply to the index numbers in this table.

Table 60: Manufactured goods are defined here to comprise sections 5 through 8 of the Standard International Trade Classification (SITC). These sections are: chemicals and related products, manufactured goods classified chiefly by material, machinery and transport equipment and miscellaneous manufactured articles. The economic and geographic groupings in this table are in accordance with those of table 58, although table 58 includes more detailed geographical sub-groups which make up the groupings "other developed economies" and "developing economies" of this table.

The unit value indices are obtained from national sources, except those of a few countries which the United Nations Statistics Division compiles using their quantity and value figures. For countries that do not compile indices for manufactured goods exports conforming to the above definition, sub-indices are aggregated to approximate an index of SITC sections 5-8. Unit value indices obtained from national indices are rebased, where necessary, so that 2000=100. Indices in national currency are converted into US dollars using conversion factors obtained by dividing the weighted average exchange rate of a given currency in the current period by the weighted average exchange rate in the base period. All aggregate unit value indices are current period weighted.

The indices in Special Drawing Rights (SDRs) are calculated by multiplying the equivalent aggregate indices in United

Totaux mondiaux et régionaux

Les totaux économiques, régionaux et mondiaux ont été ajustés de manière: (a) à inclure les estimations pour les pays ou régions pour lesquels on ne disposait pas de données complètes; (b) à inclure l'assurance et le fret dans la valeur f.o.b. des importations; (c) à inclure les pays ou régions non indiqués séparément; (d) à donner une approximation du commerce spécial; (e) à les ramener à des années civiles; et (f) à éliminer, dans la mesure du possible, les données non comparables par suite de changements géographiques, en ajustant les chiffres correspondant aux périodes avant le changement de manière à les rendre comparables à ceux des périodes après le changement.

Indices de volume et de valeur unitaire

Ces indices indiquent les variations du volume des importations ou des exportations (indice de volume) et du prix moyen des importations ou des exportations (indice de valeur unitaire).

Description des tableaux

Tableau 58: Les importations et les exportations totales pour le monde se composent des importations et exportations des Economies développées, des Economies en développement et des autres. Les totaux régionaux pour importations et exportations ont été ajustés pour exclure les re-exportations des pays ou zones que comprennent une région donnée. Les totaux régionaux et mondiaux comprennent des estimations pour certains pays ou zones ne figurant pas séparément mais pour lesquels les données ne sont pas encore disponibles. Les valeurs en dollars des E.U. des exportations et des importations ont été obtenues par la Division de statistique des Nations Unies à partir des réponses aux questionnaires du *Bulletin Mensuel de Statistique*, des données publiées par le Fonds Monétaire International dans la publication *Statistiques financières internationales*.

Tableau 59: Ces indices indiquent les variations du volume (indice de quantum) et du prix moyen (indice de valeur unitaire) des importations et des exportations totales. Les chiffres relatifs aux termes de l'échange se calculent en divisant les indices de valeur unitaire des exportations par les indices correspondants de valeur unitaire des importations. Le produit de la valeur nette des termes de l'échange et de l'indice du volume des exportations est appelé indice du pouvoir d'achat des exportations. Les notes figurant au bas du tableau 58 concernant certains pays s'appliquent également aux indices du présent tableau.

Tableau 60: Les produits manufacturés se définissent comme correspondant aux sections 5 à 8 de la Classification type

States dollars by conversion factors obtained by dividing the SDR/US$ exchange rate in the current period by the rate in the base period.

The volume indices are derived from the value data and the unit value indices. All aggregate volume indices are base period weighted.

pour le commerce international (CTCI). Ces sections sont: produits chimiques et produits liés connexes, biens manufacturés classés principalement par matière première, machines et équipements de transport et articles divers manufacturés. Les groupements économiques et géographiques de ce tableau sont conformes à ceux du tableau 58; toutefois, le tableau 58 comprend des subdivisions géographiques plus détaillées qui composent les groupements "autres économies développées" et "économies en développement" du présent tableau.

Les indices de valeur unitaire sont obtenus de sources nationales, à l'exception de ceux de certains pays que la Division de statistique des Nations Unies compile en utilisant les chiffres de ces pays relatifs aux quantités et aux valeurs. Pour les pays qui n'établissent pas d'indices conformes à la définition ci-dessus pour leurs exportations de produits manufacturés, on fait la synthèse de sous-indices de manière à établir un indice proche de celui des sections 5 à 8 de la CTCI. Le cas échéant, les indices de valeur unitaire obtenus à partir des indices nationaux sont ajustés sur la base 2000=100. On convertit les indices en monnaie nationale en indices en dollars des Etats-Unis en utilisant des facteurs de conversion obtenus en divisant la moyenne pondérée des taux de change d'une monnaie donnée pendant la période courante par la moyenne pondérée des taux de change de la période de base. Tous les indices globaux de valeur unitaire sont pondérés pour la période courante.

On calcule les indices en droits de tirages spéciaux (DTS) en multipliant les indices globaux équivalents en dollars des Etats-Unis par les facteurs de conversion obtenus en divisant le taux de change DTS/dollars E.U. de la période courante par le taux correspondant de la période de base.

On détermine les indices de volume à partir des données de valeur et des indices de valeur unitaire. Tous les indices globaux de volume sont pondérés par rapport à la période de base.

Tourist/visitor arrivals by region of origin

Arrivées de touristes/visiteurs par région de provenance

Country or area of destination and region of origin&	Series Série	2001	2002	2003	2004	2005	Pays ou zone de destination et région de provenance&
Albania	VFN						Albanie
Total		342 908	469 691	557 210	645 409	747 837	Total
Africa		66	75	233	174	174	Afrique
Americas		13 596	15 790	18 895	25 519	34 816	Amériques
Europe		320 477	439 151	531 927	609 821	703 205	Europe
Asia, East/S.East/Oceania		2 035	2 901	3 805	4 288	5 444	Asie, Est/S.-Est/Océanie
Southern Asia		309	351	424	410	354	Asie du Sud
Western Asia		1 074	752	896	775	837	Asie occidentale
Region not specified		5 351	10 671	1 030	4 422	3 007	Région non spécifiée
Algeria	VFN						Algérie
Total[1]		901 446	988 060	1 166 287	1 233 719	1 443 090	Total[1]
Africa		62 661	72 041	111 941	131 066	161 182	Afrique
Americas		3 220	4 626	4 949	6 830	8 117	Amériques
Europe		107 162	140 844	157 093	198 230	227 618	Europe
Asia, East/S.East/Oceania		5 373	9 491	8 260	9 401	15 157	Asie, Est/S.-Est/Océanie
Western Asia		17 843	24 143	22 671	23 035	29 132	Asie occidentale
Region not specified		705 187	736 915	861 373	865 157	1 001 884	Région non spécifiée
American Samoa	TFN						Samoa américaines
Total		36 009	...	...	...	24 496	Total
Africa		10	...	...	...	11	Afrique
Americas		7 339	...	...	...	6 899	Amériques
Europe		493	...	...	...	382	Europe
Asia, East/S.East/Oceania		28 084	...	...	...	16 933	Asie, Est/S.-Est/Océanie
Southern Asia		23	...	...	...	37	Asie du Sud
Western Asia		10	...	...	...	8	Asie occidentale
Region not specified		50	...	...	...	226	Région non spécifiée
Andorra	TFR						Andorre
Total		3 516 261	3 387 586	3 137 738	2 791 116	2 418 409	Total
Europe		3 516 261	3 387 586	3 137 738	2 791 116	2 418 409	Europe
Angola	TFR						Angola
Total		67 379	90 532	106 625	194 329	209 956	Total
Africa		14 580	16 618	30 915	41 873	43 138	Afrique
Americas		9 192	15 044	14 770	34 045	36 140	Amériques
Europe		38 176	52 169	55 190	101 180	110 025	Europe
Asia, East/S.East/Oceania		4 391	4 746	5 396	16 061	15 358	Asie, Est/S.-Est/Océanie
Southern Asia		661	828	...	...	2 144	Asie du Sud
Western Asia		379	1 127	354	1 170	3 151	Asie occidentale
Anguilla	TFR						Anguilla
Total[2]		47 965	43 969	46 915	53 987	62 084	Total[2]
Americas		38 726	37 479	39 295	44 799	52 054	Amériques
Europe		8 027	5 415	6 308	7 667	8 113	Europe
Region not specified		1 212	1 075	1 312	1 521	1 917	Région non spécifiée
Antigua and Barbuda	TFR						Antigua-et-Barbuda
Total[2,3]		193 176	198 185	224 032	245 456	238 804	Total[2,3]
Americas		107 275	108 235	112 809	129 316	124 404	Amériques
Western Asia		78 115	81 907	98 665	113 033	105 735	Asie occidentale
Region not specified		7 786	8 043	12 558	3 107	8 665	Région non spécifiée
Argentina	TFN						Argentine
Total[2]		2 620 464	2 820 039	2 995 271	*3 456 526	*3 895 396	Total[2]
Americas		2 157 191	2 419 591	2 424 735	2 721 888	3 052 035	Amériques
Europe		370 933	323 729	455 998	546 184	633 536	Europe
Region not specified		92 340	76 719	114 538	188 454	209 825	Région non spécifiée

Country or area of destination and region of origin&	Series Série	2001	2002	2003	2004	2005	Pays ou zone de destination et région de provenance&
Armenia	TFR						Arménie
Total		123 262	162 089	206 094	262 959	318 563	Total
Africa		62	89	133	184	335	Afrique
Americas		41 408	46 088	58 258	75 496	85 994	Amériques
Europe		47 896	79 761	98 884	127 242	160 479	Europe
Asia, East/S.East/Oceania		2 762	3 369	5 669	9 355	13 592	Asie, Est/S.-Est/Océanie
Southern Asia		18 350	19 090	23 995	27 551	29 981	Asie du Sud
Western Asia		12 784	13 692	19 155	23 131	28 182	Asie occidentale
Aruba	TFR						Aruba
Total		691 419	642 627	641 906	728 157	732 514	Total
Americas		642 995	595 350	584 651	665 489	666 454	Amériques
Europe		44 961	43 970	54 711	60 428	63 181	Europe
Asia, East/S.East/Oceania		169	209	162	211	191	Asie, Est/S.-Est/Océanie
Region not specified		3 294	3 098	2 382	2 029	2 688	Région non spécifiée
Australia	VFR						Australie
Total[4]		4 855 669	4 841 152	4 745 855	5 214 981	5 496 988	Total[4]
Africa		73 453	68 244	69 535	67 711	70 876	Afrique
Americas		577 450	556 186	537 494	561 454	584 194	Amériques
Europe		1 196 661	1 198 361	1 228 033	1 261 477	1 329 439	Europe
Asia, East/S.East/Oceania		2 893 463	2 924 158	2 811 834	3 205 477	3 373 876	Asie, Est/S.-Est/Océanie
Southern Asia		65 967	60 687	63 264	75 233	89 356	Asie du Sud
Western Asia		34 724	30 962	34 432	43 484	49 147	Asie occidentale
Region not specified		13 951	2 554	1 263	145	100	Région non spécifiée
Austria	TCER						Autriche
Total[5]		18 180 079	18 610 925	19 077 630	19 372 816	19 952 350	Total[5]
Africa		35 737	25 779	27 206	32 114	42 259	Afrique
Americas		787 930	646 863	599 474	673 695	691 644	Amériques
Europe		16 474 203	16 983 956	17 386 722	17 445 939	18 030 663	Europe
Asia, East/S.East/Oceania		576 226	593 583	618 852	755 406	792 197	Asie, Est/S.-Est/Océanie
Southern Asia		32 159	39 011	29 619	39 882	39 204	Asie du Sud
Western Asia		33 320	28 524	37 667	43 202	67 833	Asie occidentale
Region not specified		240 504	293 209	378 090	382 578	288 550	Région non spécifiée
Azerbaijan	TFR						Azerbaïdjan
Total		766 992	834 351	1 013 811	1 348 655	1 177 277	Total
Africa		...	108	320	661	544	Afrique
Americas		...	6 532	7 951	12 358	11 272	Amériques
Europe		272 273	581 633	746 916	1 050 943	945 662	Europe
Asia, East/S.East/Oceania		...	2 748	4 271	6 051	6 825	Asie, Est/S.-Est/Océanie
Southern Asia		321 882	241 352	252 669	275 147	211 032	Asie du Sud
Western Asia		...	1 978	1 684	2 143	1 942	Asie occidentale
Region not specified		172 837	...	...	1 352	...	Région non spécifiée
Bahamas	TFR						Bahamas
Total		1 537 780	1 513 151	1 510 169	1 561 312	1 608 153	Total
Africa		469	1 166	1 409	1 427	1 261	Afrique
Americas		1 417 578	1 406 458	1 392 578	1 455 375	1 484 921	Amériques
Europe		94 897	80 140	93 714	84 121	85 857	Europe
Asia, East/S.East/Oceania		11 350	8 080	6 285	6 890	7 178	Asie, Est/S.-Est/Océanie
Southern Asia		291	377	381	347	285	Asie du Sud
Western Asia		548	347	346	616	283	Asie occidentale
Region not specified		12 647	16 583	15 456	12 536	28 368	Région non spécifiée
Bahrain	VFN						Bahreïn
Total[2]		4 387 930	4 830 943	4 844 497	5 667 331	6 313 232	Total[2]
Africa		38 907	46 663	59 989	76 325	82 121	Afrique
Americas		139 550	177 089	192 206	200 481	189 778	Amériques
Europe		235 484	256 437	260 698	333 920	357 623	Europe
Asia, East/S.East/Oceania		135 121	187 058	211 749	267 978	287 257	Asie, Est/S.-Est/Océanie
Southern Asia		391 812	521 796	561 050	648 003	720 007	Asie du Sud
Western Asia		3 447 056	3 641 900	3 558 805	4 140 624	4 676 446	Asie occidentale

Country or area of destination and region of origin&	Series Série	2001	2002	2003	2004	2005	Pays ou zone de destination et région de provenance&
Bangladesh	TFN						Bangladesh
Total		207 199	207 246	244 509	271 270	207 662	Total
Africa		1 561	1 297	2 012	2 147	1 730	Afrique
Americas		19 230	17 538	30 795	37 404	18 673	Amériques
Europe		50 184	46 641	63 749	77 307	48 961	Europe
Asia, East/S.East/Oceania		37 937	41 019	42 824	51 230	35 887	Asie, Est/S.-Est/Océanie
Southern Asia		94 382	97 623	102 503	99 939	99 458	Asie du Sud
Western Asia		3 811	3 128	2 626	3 243	2 861	Asie occidentale
Region not specified		94	...	...	...	92	Région non spécifiée
Barbados	TFR						Barbade
Total		507 078	497 899	531 211	551 502	547 534	Total
Africa		852	626	668	753	1 117	Afrique
Americas		256 125	275 144	291 623	301 268	311 222	Amériques
Europe		247 165	219 006	233 791	245 919	230 167	Europe
Asia, East/S.East/Oceania		2 021	2 103	4 027	2 679	2 710	Asie, Est/S.-Est/Océanie
Southern Asia		454	503	466	627	756	Asie du Sud
Western Asia		160	101	160	145	154	Asie occidentale
Region not specified		301	416	476	111	1 408	Région non spécifiée
Belarus	TFN						Bélarus
Total[6]		61 358	63 336	64 190	67 297	90 588	Total[6]
Africa		67	58	65	47	399	Afrique
Americas		4 883	2 999	3 522	5 892	4 663	Amériques
Europe		55 007	56 833	57 916	58 524	82 247	Europe
Asia, East/S.East/Oceania		791	2 766	1 833	2 150	1 860	Asie, Est/S.-Est/Océanie
Southern Asia		278	279	472	269	594	Asie du Sud
Western Asia		332	401	382	415	825	Asie occidentale
Belgium	TCER						Belgique
Total[7]		6 451 513	6 719 653	6 689 998	6 709 740	6 747 123	Total[7]
Africa		64 293	60 026	62 755	60 872	62 455	Afrique
Americas		427 918	399 576	368 814	382 249	390 160	Amériques
Europe		5 592 062	5 798 298	5 846 966	5 800 440	5 835 628	Europe
Asia, East/S.East/Oceania		267 755	347 725	294 364	318 231	298 360	Asie, Est/S.-Est/Océanie
Southern Asia		26 644	38 542	32 362	33 152	34 844	Asie du Sud
Western Asia		19 140	17 724	17 502	17 664	19 793	Asie occidentale
Region not specified		53 701	57 762	67 235	97 132	105 883	Région non spécifiée
Belize	TFN						Belize
Total[1]		195 956	199 521	220 574	230 835	236 573	Total[1]
Africa		271	374	337	349	...	Afrique
Americas		148 981	154 321	174 784	185 254	179 357	Amériques
Europe		29 736	29 115	33 530	32 768	33 466	Europe
Asia, East/S.East/Oceania		3 524	3 411	3 754	4 285	...	Asie, Est/S.-Est/Océanie
Western Asia		445	405	370	481	...	Asie occidentale
Region not specified		12 999	11 895	7 799	7 698	23 750	Région non spécifiée
Benin	TFR						Bénin
Total		87 555	72 288	175 000[8]	173 500[8]	176 000[8]	Total
Africa		49 619	49 387	148 646	147 536	140 185	Afrique
Americas		602	1 281	471	360	500	Amériques
Europe		36 226	21 090	25 403	25 157	31 500	Europe
Asia, East/S.East/Oceania		498	220	225	261	321	Asie, Est/S.-Est/Océanie
Southern Asia		262	115	137	125	2 956	Asie du Sud
Western Asia		151	185	112	61	518	Asie occidentale
Region not specified		197	10	6	...	20	Région non spécifiée
Bermuda	TFR						Bermudes
Total[3]		278 153	284 024	256 579	271 620	269 591	Total[3]
Americas		241 268	243 793	222 396	235 546	232 661	Amériques
Europe		28 508	30 669	25 938	25 873	26 678	Europe
Asia, East/S.East/Oceania		868	861	503	834	639	Asie, Est/S.-Est/Océanie
Region not specified		7 509	8 701	7 742	9 367	9 613	Région non spécifiée

Country or area of destination and region of origin&	Series Série	2001	2002	2003	2004	2005	Pays ou zone de destination et région de provenance&
Bhutan	TFN						Bhoutan
Total		6 393	5 599	6 261	9 249	13 626	Total
Africa		27	17	14	14	...	Afrique
Americas		2 367	2 142	2 025	3 601	5 113	Amériques
Europe		2 530	2 020	2 764	3 899	5 439	Europe
Asia, East/S.East/Oceania		1 368	1 306	1 413	1 676	2 769	Asie, Est/S.-Est/Océanie
Southern Asia		14	16	13	15	...	Asie du Sud
Region not specified		87	98	32	44	305	Région non spécifiée
Bolivia	THSN						Bolivie
Total[9]		378 551	380 202	367 036	390 888	413 267	Total[9]
Africa		862	977	1 117	1 278	1 661	Afrique
Americas		215 131	216 960	209 715	227 280	250 107	Amériques
Europe		145 969	145 972	140 913	143 413	141 621	Europe
Asia, East/S.East/Oceania		16 589	16 293	15 291	18 917	19 878	Asie, Est/S.-Est/Océanie
Bonaire	TFR						Bonaire
Total		50 395	52 085	62 179	63 156	62 550	Total
Americas		33 816	33 548	32 771	34 576	32 244	Amériques
Europe		16 326	18 152	29 079	27 973	30 066	Europe
Asia, East/S.East/Oceania		31	...	...	...	...	Asie, Est/S.-Est/Océanie
Region not specified		222	385	329	607	240	Région non spécifiée
Bosnia and Herzegovina	TCER						Bosnie-Herzégovine
Total		138 528	159 763	165 465	190 300	217 273	Total
Americas		8 365	8 286	7 339	8 442	8 030	Amériques
Europe		125 189	145 883	152 246	176 588	203 564	Europe
Asia, East/S.East/Oceania		1 131	1 496	1 870	2 177	2 355	Asie, Est/S.-Est/Océanie
Southern Asia		367	122	189	116	265	Asie du Sud
Western Asia		193	93	94	132	46	Asie occidentale
Region not specified		3 283	3 883	3 727	2 845	3 013	Région non spécifiée
Botswana	TFR						Botswana
Total		1 193 378	1 273 784	1 405 535	1 522 807	...	Total
Africa		1 018 701	1 095 572	1 235 404	1 353 125	...	Afrique
Americas		25 059	19 014	18 025	21 023	...	Amériques
Europe		55 036	56 917	55 054	58 432	...	Europe
Asia, East/S.East/Oceania		11 679	11 972	12 442	11 848	...	Asie, Est/S.-Est/Océanie
Southern Asia		2 718	4 542	1 889	2 223	...	Asie du Sud
Western Asia		...	20	...	...	...	Asie occidentale
Region not specified		80 185	85 747	82 721	76 156	...	Région non spécifiée
Brazil	TFR						Brésil
Total		4 772 575	3 784 898	4 132 847	4 793 703	5 358 170	Total
Africa		36 352	40 259	52 489	64 678	75 676	Afrique
Americas		3 131 693	2 205 618	2 396 832	2 703 442	2 998 060	Amériques
Europe		1 445 576	1 414 962	1 543 559	1 860 259	2 097 357	Europe
Asia, East/S.East/Oceania		127 394	108 201	128 640	155 605	177 381	Asie, Est/S.-Est/Océanie
Western Asia		11 326	7 118	5 595	6 064	7 002	Asie occidentale
Region not specified		20 234	8 740	5 732	3 655	2 694	Région non spécifiée
British Virgin Islands	TFR						Iles Vierges britanniques
Total		295 625	281 696	317 758	...	...	Total
Americas		258 994	250 013	261 201	...	...	Amériques
Europe		33 270	28 511	49 952	...	...	Europe
Region not specified		3 361	3 172	6 605	...	...	Région non spécifiée
Brunei Darussalam	VFN						Brunéi Darussalam
Total		840 272	...	...	...	815 054	Total
Americas		6 408	...	...	...	3 530	Amériques
Europe		30 494	...	...	...	14 428	Europe
Asia, East/S.East/Oceania		786 143	...	...	...	791 190	Asie, Est/S.-Est/Océanie
Southern Asia		14 949	...	...	...	5 211	Asie du Sud
Western Asia		2 278	...	...	...	695	Asie occidentale

Country or area of destination and region of origin&	Series Série	2001	2002	2003	2004	2005	Pays ou zone de destination et région de provenance&
Bulgaria	VFR						Bulgarie
Total[10,11]		5 103 797	5 562 917	6 240 932	6 981 597	7 282 455	Total[10,11]
Africa		2 984	3 778	3 848	2 937	2 774	Afrique
Americas		52 124	46 934	54 701	67 605	76 514	Amériques
Europe		4 950 963	5 426 164	6 088 039	6 806 650	7 087 954	Europe
Asia, East/S.East/Oceania		23 873	21 957	26 521	32 067	35 127	Asie, Est/S.-Est/Océanie
Southern Asia		12 916	9 498	11 613	12 199	11 396	Asie du Sud
Western Asia		14 811	14 144	15 132	16 124	17 569	Asie occidentale
Region not specified		46 126	40 442	41 078	44 015	51 121	Région non spécifiée
Burkina Faso	THSN						Burkina Faso
Total[1]		128 449	150 204	163 123	222 201	244 728	Total[1]
Africa		50 241	55 144	65 459	96 385	100 674	Afrique
Americas		8 041	9 840	10 025	12 991	14 724	Amériques
Europe		62 870	73 076	76 743	99 742	113 496	Europe
Asia, East/S.East/Oceania		2 695	3 760	3 271	4 550	6 582	Asie, Est/S.-Est/Océanie
Western Asia		593	876	1 447	1 982	2 220	Asie occidentale
Region not specified		4 009	7 508	6 178	6 551	7 032	Région non spécifiée
Burundi	TFN						Burundi
Total[12]		36 000	74 406	74 116	133 228	148 418	Total[12]
Africa		17 000	24 802	24 706	1 333	49 473	Afrique
Americas		2 000	2 090	2 308	5 908	9 956	Amériques
Europe		14 000	6 156	7 620	29 409	29 486	Europe
Asia, East/S.East/Oceania		3 000	1 054	1 162	4 528	4 023	Asie, Est/S.-Est/Océanie
Region not specified		...	40 304	38 320	92 050	55 480	Région non spécifiée
Cambodia	TFR						Cambodge
Total		408 377[13]	786 526	701 014	1 055 202[14]	1 421 615[15]	Total
Americas		43 905	113 144	88 662	122 169	152 328	Amériques
Europe		66 088	218 950	183 353	242 811	310 006	Europe
Asia, East/S.East/Oceania		158 407	409 489	412 245	589 230	786 506	Asie, Est/S.-Est/Océanie
Southern Asia		4 691	4 459	5 286	7 132	7 516	Asie du Sud
Region not specified		135 286	40 484	11 468	93 860	165 259	Région non spécifiée
Cameroon	THSN						Cameroun
Total		220 578	226 019	...	189 856	176 372	Total
Africa		100 282	104 695	...	80 013	88 739	Afrique
Americas		12 611	13 506	...	11 593	10 002	Amériques
Europe		99 624	98 570	...	83 272	68 058	Europe
Asia, East/S.East/Oceania		4 168	4 882	...	4 248	4 580	Asie, Est/S.-Est/Océanie
Western Asia		1 087	1 153	...	4 583	2 007	Asie occidentale
Region not specified		2 806	3 213	...	6 147	2 986	Région non spécifiée
Canada	TFR						Canada
Total[16]		19 679 392	20 056 988	17 534 298	19 095 342	*18 770 444	Total[16]
Africa		61 264	54 111	52 437	58 210	61 842	Afrique
Americas		15 973 802	16 576 444	14 588 791	15 468 775	14 867 460	Amériques
Europe		2 323 626	2 095 148	1 872 693	2 202 397	2 397 323	Europe
Asia, East/S.East/Oceania		1 195 365	1 209 706	900 328	1 221 981	1 282 007	Asie, Est/S.-Est/Océanie
Southern Asia		78 435	79 073	79 792	96 342	109 681	Asie du Sud
Western Asia		46 900	42 506	40 257	47 637	52 131	Asie occidentale
Cape Verde	THSR						Cap-Vert
Total		134 169	125 852	150 048	157 052	197 844	Total
Africa		3 392	10 003	5 225	10 034	9 432	Afrique
Americas		2 382	1 665	1 740	1 472	2 102	Amériques
Europe		121 508	105 790	134 749	136 304	173 318	Europe
Region not specified		6 887	8 394	8 334	9 242	12 992	Région non spécifiée
Cayman Islands	TFR						Iles Caïmanes
Total[3]		334 071	302 797	293 513	259 929	167 802	Total[3]
Africa		400	353	373	321	325	Afrique
Americas		310 175	281 796	272 381	242 012	152 735	Amériques

Country or area of destination and region of origin&	Series Série	2001	2002	2003	2004	2005	Pays ou zone de destination et région de provenance&
Europe		21 428	18 705	19 001	15 938	13 221	Europe
Asia, East/S.East/Oceania		1 514	1 382	1 201	1 216	1 129	Asie, Est/S.-Est/Océanie
Southern Asia		233	238	274	176	97	Asie du Sud
Western Asia		84	100	65	72	24	Asie occidentale
Region not specified		237	223	218	194	271	Région non spécifiée
Central African Rep.	TFN						Rép. centrafricaine
Total[3]		9 873	2 910	5 687	8 156	11 969	Total[3]
Africa		4 970	1 455	3 111	3 501	6 156	Afrique
Americas		697	176	374	449	639	Amériques
Europe		3 454	1 025	1 881	3 674	4 349	Europe
Asia, East/S.East/Oceania		449	170	288	317	373	Asie, Est/S.-Est/Océanie
Western Asia		51	15	18	192	397	Asie occidentale
Region not specified		252	69	15	23	55	Région non spécifiée
Chad	THSN						Tchad
Total		56 850	32 334	20 974	25 899	29 356	Total
Africa		16 911	7 514	5 141	5 855	6 695	Afrique
Americas		5 122	6 485	4 368	5 609	5 976	Amériques
Europe		31 889	15 225	10 029	12 690	14 805	Europe
Asia, East/S.East/Oceania		1 623	1 000	297	398	550	Asie, Est/S.-Est/Océanie
Western Asia		924	2 110	1 139	1 347	1 330	Asie occidentale
Region not specified		381	…	…	…	…	Région non spécifiée
Chile	TFN						Chili
Total		1 723 107	1 412 315	1 613 523	1 785 024	2 027 082	Total
Africa		2 495	2 476	2 872	3 653	3 544	Afrique
Americas		1 429 293	1 119 232	1 242 956	1 360 342	1 553 381	Amériques
Europe		249 985	245 494	309 008	344 774	384 886	Europe
Asia, East/S.East/Oceania		37 155	40 786	54 476	69 883	74 927	Asie, Est/S.-Est/Océanie
Southern Asia		1 807	1 697	2 039	3 605	4 257	Asie du Sud
Western Asia		721	728	637	812	682	Asie occidentale
Region not specified		1 651	1 902	1 535	1 955	5 405	Région non spécifiée
China[17]	VFN						Chine[17]
Total		89 012 924	97 908 252	91 662 082	109 038 218	120 292 255	Total
Africa		62 827	84 541	91 949	154 223	210 533	Afrique
Americas		1 278 383	1 509 574	1 132 937	1 789 500	2 145 758	Amériques
Europe		2 732 112	3 007 483	2 789 888	4 096 999	5 165 588	Europe
Asia, East/S.East/Oceania		84 610 214	92 865 905	87 214 341	102 393 763	112 053 459	Asie, Est/S.-Est/Océanie
Southern Asia		277 288	380 512	383 121	514 163	599 435	Asie du Sud
Western Asia		37 202	52 122	46 856	84 376	110 966	Asie occidentale
Region not specified		14 898	8 115	2 990	5 194	6 516	Région non spécifiée
China, Hong Kong SAR	TFR						Chine, Hong Kong RAS
Total		8 878 200	10 688 700	9 676 300	13 655 100	14 773 200	Total
Africa		55 700	63 600	68 100	91 100	116 600	Afrique
Americas		1 050 500	1 094 900	713 400	1 091 600	1 196 700	Amériques
Europe		824 200	855 000	588 000	888 700	1 083 900	Europe
Asia, East/S.East/Oceania		6 769 200	8 486 600	8 154 000	11 368 600	12 124 500	Asie, Est/S.-Est/Océanie
Southern Asia		125 800	131 400	113 700	159 500	180 500	Asie du Sud
Western Asia		52 800	57 200	39 100	55 600	71 000	Asie occidentale
China, Hong Kong SAR	VFR						Chine, Hong Kong RAS
Total		13 725 332	16 566 382	15 536 839	21 810 630	23 359 417	Total
Africa		77 079	91 670	98 862	146 130	206 487	Afrique
Americas		1 258 567	1 346 840	925 907	1 399 572	1 565 350	Amériques
Europe		1 063 767	1 135 044	822 146	1 201 751	1 471 602	Europe
Asia, East/S.East/Oceania		11 046 891	13 654 656	13 410 004	18 705 602	19 706 889	Asie, Est/S.-Est/Océanie
Southern Asia		249 204	302 794	255 104	326 183	363 080	Asie du Sud
Western Asia		29 824	35 378	24 816	31 392	45 951	Asie occidentale
Region not specified		…	…	…	…	58	Région non spécifiée

Country or area of destination and region of origin&	Series Série	2001	2002	2003	2004	2005	Pays ou zone de destination et région de provenance&
China, Macao SAR	VFN						Chine, Macao RAS
Total[18]		10 278 973	11 530 841	11 887 876	16 672 556	18 711 187	Total[18]
Africa		4 092	4 407	4 657	5 897	7 941	Afrique
Americas		118 817	128 219	95 502	147 953	182 830	Amériques
Europe		130 265	127 614	94 078	128 887	161 204	Europe
Asia, East/S.East/Oceania		10 005 009	11 249 556	11 673 256	16 361 807	18 321 056	Asie, Est/S.-Est/Océanie
Southern Asia		17 731	17 719	17 324	23 771	32 335	Asie du Sud
Western Asia		938	899	1 147	1 843	2 601	Asie occidentale
Region not specified		2 121	2 427	1 912	2 398	3 220	Région non spécifiée
Colombia	VFN						Colombie
Total[19]		615 623	566 761	624 909	790 940	*933 243	Total[19]
Africa		991	970	886	929	1 312	Afrique
Americas		468 908	428 403	485 259	618 262	730 925	Amériques
Europe		129 475	117 500	125 073	155 651	182 822	Europe
Asia, East/S.East/Oceania		12 015	11 854	11 271	13 294	15 395	Asie, Est/S.-Est/Océanie
Southern Asia		1 320	1 226	1 119	1 404	1 618	Asie du Sud
Western Asia		1 769	1 062	1 004	1 399	1 167	Asie occidentale
Region not specified		1 145	5 746	297	1	4	Région non spécifiée
Comoros	TFN						Comores
Total[3]		19 356	18 936	14 229	17 603	...	Total[3]
Africa		11 820	8 715	5 590	6 344	...	Afrique
Americas		167	60	26	162	...	Amériques
Europe		6 932	9 490	8 003	10 562	...	Europe
Asia, East/S.East/Oceania		102	64	610	165	...	Asie, Est/S.-Est/Océanie
Region not specified		335	607	...	370	...	Région non spécifiée
Congo	THSR						Congo
Total		27 363	21 611	...	...	...	Total
Africa		11 750	11 006	...	...	...	Afrique
Americas		874	694	...	...	...	Amériques
Europe		12 029	8 752	...	...	...	Europe
Region not specified		2 710	1 159	...	...	...	Région non spécifiée
Cook Islands	TFR						Iles Cook
Total[20]		74 575	72 781	78 328	83 333	88 397	Total[20]
Americas		13 413	11 505	11 390	8 445	6 475	Amériques
Europe		22 816	19 630	21 559	20 410	18 171	Europe
Asia, East/S.East/Oceania		38 061	41 277	45 008	53 962	63 276	Asie, Est/S.-Est/Océanie
Region not specified		285	369	371	516	475	Région non spécifiée
Costa Rica	TFN						Costa Rica
Total		1 131 406	1 113 359	1 238 692	1 452 926	1 679 051	Total
Africa		837	900	1 048	1 194	1 164	Afrique
Americas		952 087	927 509	1 017 831	1 213 784	1 411 640	Amériques
Europe		156 571	164 263	198 242	215 072	241 751	Europe
Asia, East/S.East/Oceania		14 648	16 140	16 403	16 043	23 687	Asie, Est/S.-Est/Océanie
Region not specified		7 263	4 547	5 168	6 833	809	Région non spécifiée
Croatia	TCER						Croatie
Total[21]		6 544 217	6 944 345	7 408 590	7 911 874	8 466 886	Total[21]
Americas		67 316	74 938	84 470	119 485	140 031	Amériques
Europe		6 428 582	6 806 518	7 244 346	7 692 506	8 192 055	Europe
Asia, East/S.East/Oceania		26 675	36 068	43 173	58 370	83 273	Asie, Est/S.-Est/Océanie
Region not specified		21 644	26 821	36 601	41 513	51 527	Région non spécifiée
Cuba	VFR						Cuba
Total		1 774 541	1 686 162	1 905 682	2 048 572	2 319 334	Total
Africa		6 565	5 641	6 679	5 868	6 619	Afrique
Americas		834 660	787 729	916 818	1 025 756	1 215 857	Amériques
Europe		898 110	859 129	942 052	976 727	1 047 669	Europe
Asia, East/S.East/Oceania		28 586	27 354	32 463	33 861	41 858	Asie, Est/S.-Est/Océanie
Southern Asia		4 273	4 096	5 559	4 176	5 149	Asie du Sud

Country or area of destination and region of origin&	Series Série	2001	2002	2003	2004	2005	Pays ou zone de destination et région de provenance&
Western Asia		1 866	1 737	1 514	1 517	1 622	Asie occidentale
Region not specified		481	476	597	667	560	Région non spécifiée
Curaçao	TFR						Curaçao
Total[3]		204 603	217 963	221 395	223 439	222 099	Total[3]
Americas		124 616	141 006	125 794	128 873	123 391	Amériques
Europe		73 190	70 390	91 384	89 752	94 957	Europe
Region not specified		6 797	6 567	4 217	4 814	3 751	Région non spécifiée
Cyprus	TFR						Chypre
Total		2 696 732	2 418 238	2 303 247	2 349 012	2 470 063	Total
Africa		7 696	7 267	7 241	5 296	7 577	Afrique
Americas		30 186	26 734	23 246	22 924	28 991	Amériques
Europe		2 591 565	2 323 568	2 207 434	2 263 145	2 375 332	Europe
Asia, East/S.East/Oceania		13 695	11 697	12 266	13 042	14 951	Asie, Est/S.-Est/Océanie
Southern Asia		7 652	3 383	3 130	1 992	2 777	Asie du Sud
Western Asia		45 261	45 170	49 413	41 379	40 233	Asie occidentale
Region not specified		677	419	517	1 234	202	Région non spécifiée
Czech Republic	TCEN						République tchèque
Total		5 405 239	4 742 773	5 075 756	6 061 225	6 336 128	Total
Africa		15 794	12 842	14 097	15 394	18 539	Afrique
Americas		296 706	238 767	282 239	380 056	400 840	Amériques
Europe		4 849 479	4 248 907	4 528 009	5 314 123	5 495 760	Europe
Asia, East/S.East/Oceania		243 260	242 257	251 411	351 652	420 989	Asie, Est/S.-Est/Océanie
Dem. Rep. of the Congo	TFN						Rép. dém. du Congo
Total		54 813	28 179[3]	35 141[3]	36 238[3]	*61 007	Total
Africa		37 793	9 088	20 380	14 531	36 489	Afrique
Americas		2 746	3 678	2 568	4 592	3 824	Amériques
Europe		10 682	11 273	9 037	13 117	14 751	Europe
Asia, East/S.East/Oceania		3 592	4 140	3 156	3 998	5 943	Asie, Est/S.-Est/Océanie
Denmark	TCER						Danemark
Total		3 683 977	3 435 563	3 473 808	4 421 442[22]	4 698 668	Total
Americas		89 383	79 513	78 382	126 276	147 289	Amériques
Europe		3 455 308	3 220 983	3 253 489	4 065 043	4 357 752	Europe
Asia, East/S.East/Oceania		46 455	49 299	46 850	82 957	110 098	Asie, Est/S.-Est/Océanie
Region not specified		92 831	85 768	95 087	147 166	83 529	Région non spécifiée
Dominica	TFR						Dominique
Total		66 393	69 193	73 190	80 087	79 257	Total
Americas		54 471	58 153	61 536	69 115	68 164	Amériques
Europe		10 825	10 131	10 772	10 208	10 258	Europe
Asia, East/S.East/Oceania		498	455	486	387	529	Asie, Est/S.-Est/Océanie
Region not specified		599	454	396	377	306	Région non spécifiée
Dominican Republic	TFR						Rép. dominicaine
Total[1,3]		2 868 915[23]	2 793 209[23]	3 268 182[23]	3 443 205[23]	*3 690 692	Total[1,3]
Americas		1 238 611	1 260 558	1 493 912	1 591 605	1 711 341	Amériques
Europe		1 141 968	1 030 981	1 249 200	1 269 571	1 370 366	Europe
Asia, East/S.East/Oceania		1 809	1 294	1 588	1 665	2 071	Asie, Est/S.-Est/Océanie
Southern Asia		...	...	...	...	337	Asie du Sud
Region not specified		486 527	500 376	523 482	580 364	606 577	Région non spécifiée
Ecuador	VFN						Equateur
Total[2]		640 561	682 962	760 776	818 927	860 784	Total[2]
Africa		1 588	2 107	1 720	2 191	2 269	Afrique
Americas		510 714	549 927	617 088	662 019	682 835	Amériques
Europe		112 390	113 435	124 137	133 495	151 957	Europe
Asia, East/S.East/Oceania		15 863	17 493	17 831	21 195	23 718	Asie, Est/S.-Est/Océanie
Region not specified		6	...	...	27	5	Région non spécifiée
Egypt	VFN						Egypte
Total[2]		4 648 485	5 191 678	6 044 160	8 103 609	8 607 807	Total[2]
Africa		145 554	161 497	183 035	244 662	263 847	Afrique

Country or area of destination and region of origin&	Series Série	2001	2002	2003	2004	2005	Pays ou zone de destination et région de provenance&
Americas		251 462	171 458	187 828	257 418	297 675	Amériques
Europe		3 132 459	3 583 791	4 203 687	5 919 575	6 047 194	Europe
Asia, East/S.East/Oceania		209 888	213 771	226 756	296 189	411 048	Asie, Est/S.-Est/Océanie
Southern Asia		39 536	46 110	51 042	63 310	73 000	Asie du Sud
Western Asia		867 911	1 012 613	1 188 994	1 317 883	1 511 285	Asie occidentale
Region not specified		1 675	2 438	2 818	4 572	3 758	Région non spécifiée
El Salvador	TFN						El Salvador
Total		734 627	950 597	857 378	966 416	1 154 386	Total
Africa		...	...	424	582	628	Afrique
Americas		659 611	872 588	812 192	923 127	1 112 319	Amériques
Europe		21 731	26 523	34 782	33 053	31 488	Europe
Asia, East/S.East/Oceania		3 239	3 726	8 898	9 654	9 951	Asie, Est/S.-Est/Océanie
Region not specified		50 046	47 760	1 082	...	...	Région non spécifiée
Eritrea	VFN						Erythrée
Total[1]		113 024	100 828	80 029	87 298	83 307	Total[1]
Africa		7 092	8 185	3 147	4 503	3 182	Afrique
Americas		2 829	2 094	2 321	2 559	2 263	Amériques
Europe		9 734	8 378	8 367	10 142	8 364	Europe
Asia, East/S.East/Oceania		2 568	1 700	1 953	2 484	2 267	Asie, Est/S.-Est/Océanie
Southern Asia		2 231	2 549	2 580	2 420	2 985	Asie du Sud
Western Asia		4 021	3 565	2 857	4 196	3 862	Asie occidentale
Region not specified		84 549	74 357	58 804	60 994	60 384	Région non spécifiée
Estonia	TCER						Estonie
Total		984 550	1 003 383	1 112 746	1 374 414	1 453 013	Total
Africa		...	...	542	641	1 033	Afrique
Americas		16 878	15 601	14 823	23 448	24 040	Amériques
Europe		948 540	967 167	1 080 977	1 333 979	1 410 660	Europe
Asia, East/S.East/Oceania		6 907	6 587	10 663	13 456	15 124	Asie, Est/S.-Est/Océanie
Region not specified		12 225	14 028	5 741	2 890	2 156	Région non spécifiée
Estonia	THSR						Estonie
Total		847 812	936 737	1 008 631	1 300 070	1 358 089	Total
Americas		15 861	15 117	12 574	20 114	20 837	Amériques
Europe		814 124	901 265	980 537	1 263 489	1 320 886	Europe
Asia, East/S.East/Oceania		6 754	6 820	6 389	7 105	7 726	Asie, Est/S.-Est/Océanie
Region not specified		11 073	13 535	9 131	9 362	8 640	Région non spécifiée
Estonia	VFR						Estonie
Total		3 230 323	3 253 012	3 377 837[24]	...	...	Total
Americas		106 769	77 932	92 505	...	...	Amériques
Europe		3 093 211	3 153 624	3 244 469	...	...	Europe
Asia, East/S.East/Oceania		14 886	14 348	17 817	...	...	Asie, Est/S.-Est/Océanie
Region not specified		15 457	7 108	23 046	...	...	Région non spécifiée
Ethiopia	TFN						Ethiopie
Total[12,25]		148 438	156 327	179 910	184 079	227 398	Total[12,25]
Africa		61 234	59 640	82 152	65 744	85 501	Afrique
Americas		14 514	19 433	27 456	33 895	41 380	Amériques
Europe		32 540	34 280	43 647	47 955	57 103	Europe
Asia, East/S.East/Oceania		7 478	7 916	7 645	9 825	12 188	Asie, Est/S.-Est/Océanie
Southern Asia		3 244	3 778	3 602	4 641	7 125	Asie du Sud
Western Asia		9 908	9 189	14 366	20 618	22 162	Asie occidentale
Region not specified		19 520	22 091	1 042	1 401	1 939	Région non spécifiée
Fiji	TFR						Fidji
Total[2]		348 014	397 859	430 800	502 765	549 911	Total[2]
Americas		68 263	68 617	69 313	77 605	85 536	Amériques
Europe		51 425	65 047	71 641	71 372	78 507	Europe
Asia, East/S.East/Oceania		226 190	261 690	288 321	351 819	383 691	Asie, Est/S.-Est/Océanie
Region not specified		2 136	2 505	1 525	1 969	2 177	Région non spécifiée

Country or area of destination and region of origin&	Series Série	2001	2002	2003	2004	2005	Pays ou zone de destination et région de provenance&
Finland	TCER						Finlande
Total		1 999 300	2 042 540	2 047 444	2 083 487[26]	2 080 194	Total
Africa		4 603	3 646	3 370	3 185	4 123	Afrique
Americas		119 946	108 446	102 034	111 245	105 992	Amériques
Europe		1 615 004	1 659 534	1 683 624	1 698 936	1 712 228	Europe
Asia, East/S.East/Oceania		142 083	157 635	146 652	167 808	158 128	Asie, Est/S.-Est/Océanie
Southern Asia		5 849	5 285	5 361	5 965	7 445	Asie du Sud
Western Asia		3 408	3 857	3 463	3 168	3 613	Asie occidentale
Region not specified		108 407	104 137	102 940	93 180	88 665	Région non spécifiée
France	TFR						France
Total		75 202 000	77 012 000	75 048 000	75 121 000	*76 001 000	Total
Africa		921 000	924 000	889 000	895 000	910 000	Afrique
Americas		5 291 000	4 639 000	3 954 000	4 206 000	4 651 000	Amériques
Europe		66 491 000	69 078 000	68 072 000	67 711 000	67 629 000	Europe
Asia, East/S.East/Oceania		2 114 000	2 080 000	1 890 000	2 058 000	2 501 000	Asie, Est/S.-Est/Océanie
Western Asia		325 000	249 000	210 000	237 000	268 000	Asie occidentale
Region not specified		60 000	42 000	33 000	14 000	42 000	Région non spécifiée
French Guiana	TFR						Guyane française
Total		...	65 000	...	...	...	Total
Americas		...	17 550	...	...	...	Amériques
Europe		...	44 850	...	...	...	Europe
Region not specified		...	2 600	...	...	...	Région non spécifiée
French Polynesia	TFR						Polynésie française
Total[2,3]		227 547	188 998	212 692	211 828	208 045	Total[2,3]
Africa		280	253	294	257	235	Afrique
Americas		106 875	72 468	89 454	86 032	80 067	Amériques
Europe		83 556	76 100	80 182	79 944	81 643	Europe
Asia, East/S.East/Oceania		36 386	39 697	42 235	45 083	45 655	Asie, Est/S.-Est/Océanie
Southern Asia		43	46	62	75	69	Asie du Sud
Western Asia		191	182	163	172	165	Asie occidentale
Region not specified		216	252	302	265	211	Région non spécifiée
Gabon	TFN						Gabon
Total[27]		169 191	208 348	222 257	...	...	Total[27]
Africa		42 433	52 408	55 487	...	...	Afrique
Americas		2 700	...	...	...	...	Amériques
Europe		118 631	...	...	...	...	Europe
Asia, East/S.East/Oceania		1 330	...	...	...	...	Asie, Est/S.-Est/Océanie
Western Asia		2 987	...	...	...	...	Asie occidentale
Region not specified		1 110	155 940	166 770	...	...	Région non spécifiée
Gambia	TFN						Gambie
Total[28]		57 231	81 005	73 485	90 095	...	Total[28]
Africa		409	726	4 542	1 330	...	Afrique
Americas		821	1 075	643	3 248	...	Amériques
Europe		54 468	77 155	63 625	81 955	...	Europe
Region not specified		1 533	2 049	4 675	3 562	...	Région non spécifiée
Georgia	TFR						Géorgie
Total		302 215	298 469	313 442	368 312	560 021	Total
Africa		707	586	306	788	431	Afrique
Americas		7 315	8 156	8 731	11 209	14 842	Amériques
Europe		281 691	275 332	288 648	342 596	533 129	Europe
Asia, East/S.East/Oceania		5 161	6 865	6 756	4 952	3 244	Asie, Est/S.-Est/Océanie
Southern Asia		5 274	5 822	6 683	6 635	6 641	Asie du Sud
Western Asia		1 254	1 250	1 835	1 563	973	Asie occidentale
Region not specified		813	458	483	569	761	Région non spécifiée
Germany	TCER						Allemagne
Total		17 861 293	17 969 396	18 399 093	20 136 979	21 500 067	Total
Africa		147 387	143 714	143 156	146 454	144 391	Afrique

Country or area of destination and region of origin&	Series Série	2001	2002	2003	2004	2005	Pays ou zone de destination et région de provenance&
Americas		2 334 247	2 150 961	2 048 770	2 337 209	2 397 527	Amériques
Europe		13 093 176	13 288 813	13 877 895	14 918 028	16 099 891	Europe
Asia, East/S.East/Oceania		1 651 279	1 715 992	1 605 064	1 931 265	2 000 752	Asie, Est/S.-Est/Océanie
Western Asia		116 740	128 054	142 732	160 110	185 497	Asie occidentale
Region not specified		518 464	541 862	581 476	643 913	672 009	Région non spécifiée
Ghana	TFN						Ghana
Total[1]		438 828	482 637	530 827	583 819	428 533	Total[1]
Africa		149 305	164 210	180 609	198 638	172 913	Afrique
Americas		36 855	40 534	44 581	49 031	62 572	Amériques
Europe		108 782	119 642	131 587	144 724	100 509	Europe
Asia, East/S.East/Oceania		21 106	23 214	25 532	28 081	16 812	Asie, Est/S.-Est/Océanie
Western Asia		3 329	3 661	4 026	4 428	10 632	Asie occidentale
Region not specified		119 451	131 376	144 492	158 917	65 095	Région non spécifiée
Greece	TFN						Grèce
Total[29]		14 057 331	14 179 999	13 969 393	13 312 629	14 276 465	Total[29]
Africa		24 421	22 265	19 184	23 073	22 961	Afrique
Americas		231 675	217 369	219 391	236 274	297 189	Amériques
Europe		13 482 856	13 630 328	13 459 272	12 766 224	13 593 248	Europe
Asia, East/S.East/Oceania		243 122	242 040	212 791	226 973	287 353	Asie, Est/S.-Est/Océanie
Southern Asia		4 424	4 252	3 919	4 828	3 657	Asie du Sud
Western Asia		70 833	63 745	54 836	55 257	72 057	Asie occidentale
Grenada	TFN						Grenade
Total[1]		123 351	132 416	142 355	133 865	98 548	Total[1]
Africa		632	494	522	562	325	Afrique
Americas		66 036	76 572	80 126	77 126	58 629	Amériques
Europe		40 170	38 976	43 167	36 222	22 423	Europe
Asia, East/S.East/Oceania		1 279	980	1 062	722	1 054	Asie, Est/S.-Est/Océanie
Western Asia		166	115	109	132	121	Asie occidentale
Region not specified		15 068	15 279	17 369	19 101	15 996	Région non spécifiée
Guadeloupe	THSR						Guadeloupe
Total		379 000[30]	...	438 819[30]	455 981[30]	371 985[31]	Total
Americas		13 000	...	...	...	...	Amériques
Europe		361 000	...	386 737	406 204	369 800	Europe
Region not specified		5 000	...	52 082	49 777	2 185	Région non spécifiée
Guam	TFR						Guam
Total[20]		1 159 071	1 058 704	909 506	1 159 881	1 227 587	Total[20]
Americas		42 545	42 975	41 160	46 754	46 362	Amériques
Europe		1 312	1 436	...	1 511	1 750	Europe
Asia, East/S.East/Oceania		1 077 140	984 373	808 623	1 068 997	1 133 807	Asie, Est/S.-Est/Océanie
Region not specified		38 074	29 920	59 723	42 619	45 668	Région non spécifiée
Guatemala	TFN						Guatemala
Total		835 492	884 190	880 223	1 181 526	1 315 646	Total
Americas		676 176	712 261	703 841	1 006 614	1 148 318	Amériques
Europe		134 869	144 846	150 920	149 871	139 996	Europe
Asia, East/S.East/Oceania		22 490	24 370	21 999	23 167	24 921	Asie, Est/S.-Est/Océanie
Western Asia		418	590	603	365	1 182	Asie occidentale
Region not specified		1 539	2 123	2 860	1 509	1 229	Région non spécifiée
Guinea	TFN						Guinée
Total		37 677	42 507	43 966[32]	44 622	45 330[32]	Total
Africa		17 851	21 868	15 771	13 330	15 427	Afrique
Americas		3 557	3 430	3 546	4 378	4 589	Amériques
Europe		12 928	11 646	15 162	15 500	15 312	Europe
Asia, East/S.East/Oceania		1 703	2 447	1 940	2 454	2 607	Asie, Est/S.-Est/Océanie
Southern Asia		552	794	732	985	1 334	Asie du Sud
Western Asia		726	1 705	1 042	566	653	Asie occidentale
Region not specified		360	617	5 773	7 409	5 408	Région non spécifiée

Country or area of destination and region of origin&	Series Série	2001	2002	2003	2004	2005	Pays ou zone de destination et région de provenance&
Guinea	TFR						Guinée
Total[32]		...	...	43 966	42 041	45 334	Total[32]
Africa		...	...	19 227	17 915	17 008	Afrique
Americas		...	...	4 064	4 377	5 336	Amériques
Europe		...	...	17 114	15 564	18 007	Europe
Asia, East/S.East/Oceania		...	...	1 833	2 160	2 545	Asie, Est/S.-Est/Océanie
Southern Asia		...	...	641	985	1 251	Asie du Sud
Western Asia		...	...	938	1 040	628	Asie occidentale
Region not specified		...	...	149	...	559	Région non spécifiée
Guinea-Bissau	TFN						Guinée-Bissau
Total[3]		7 754	...	...	...	4 978[33]	Total[3]
Africa		2 052	...	...	...	1 224	Afrique
Americas		433	...	...	...	451	Amériques
Europe		3 824	...	...	...	3 123	Europe
Asia, East/S.East/Oceania		159	...	...	...	102	Asie, Est/S.-Est/Océanie
Southern Asia		103	...	...	...	66	Asie du Sud
Western Asia		169	...	...	...	12	Asie occidentale
Region not specified		1 014	...	...	...	...	Région non spécifiée
Guyana	TFR						Guyana
Total		99 317	104 341[34]	100 911[34]	121 989[34]	116 596[34]	Total
Americas		88 861	94 620	91 022	111 078	105 468	Amériques
Europe		8 689	8 190	8 136	9 056	8 704	Europe
Region not specified		1 767	1 531	1 753	1 855	2 424	Région non spécifiée
Haiti	TFR						Haïti
Total		141 632	140 112	136 031	96 439	112 267	Total
Americas		129 041	126 683	125 214	90 615	103 595	Amériques
Europe		11 132	11 312	7 659	4 246	6 720	Europe
Region not specified		1 459	2 117	3 158	1 578	1 952	Région non spécifiée
Honduras	TFN						Honduras
Total		517 914	549 500	610 535	640 981	673 035	Total
Africa		242	297	206	251	231	Afrique
Americas		460 223	493 330	557 262	584 831	610 179	Amériques
Europe		50 242	48 681	45 152	47 504	53 482	Europe
Asia, East/S.East/Oceania		6 662	6 727	7 115	7 542	8 437	Asie, Est/S.-Est/Océanie
Southern Asia		173	209	260	278	321	Asie du Sud
Western Asia		136	96	102	109	90	Asie occidentale
Region not specified		236	160	438	466	295	Région non spécifiée
Hungary	TCEN						Hongrie
Total[35]		3 070 261	3 013 116	2 948 224	3 269 868	3 446 362	Total[35]
Africa		7 122	5 739	5 756	12 379	10 310	Afrique
Americas		181 147	169 967	173 862	202 180	218 304	Amériques
Europe		2 730 416	2 688 940	2 626 677	2 860 588	2 985 842	Europe
Asia, East/S.East/Oceania		92 817	82 781	77 189	104 805	132 564	Asie, Est/S.-Est/Océanie
Region not specified		58 759	65 689	64 740	89 916	99 342	Région non spécifiée
Hungary	VFN						Hongrie
Total[36]		30 679 480	31 739 243	31 412 483	36 635 132	38 554 561	Total[36]
Africa		12 972	11 026	14 300	15 833	13 502	Afrique
Americas		451 043	427 547	385 191	515 112	490 440	Amériques
Europe		29 978 851	31 081 931	30 817 730	35 781 644	37 744 758	Europe
Asia, East/S.East/Oceania		194 379	183 789	167 361	247 520	272 207	Asie, Est/S.-Est/Océanie
Southern Asia		16 553	9 899	10 858	15 641	15 179	Asie du Sud
Western Asia		12 364	8 775	8 478	26 037	9 538	Asie occidentale
Region not specified		13 318	16 276	8 565	33 345	8 937	Région non spécifiée
Iceland	TCEN						Islande
Total		672 156	704 633	771 323	836 230	871 401	Total
Africa		...	...	...	...	1 104	Afrique
Americas		74 398	69 342	72 174	74 857	84 839	Amériques

Country or area of destination and region of origin&	Series Série	2001	2002	2003	2004	2005	Pays ou zone de destination et région de provenance&
Europe		553 309	593 315	642 762	706 580	714 982	Europe
Asia, East/S.East/Oceania		6 734	7 048	9 013	10 520	29 723	Asie, Est/S.-Est/Océanie
Region not specified		37 715	34 928	47 374	44 273	40 753	Région non spécifiée
India	TFN						Inde
Total[2]		2 537 282	2 384 364	2 726 214	3 457 477	3 918 610	Total[2]
Africa		86 718	80 317	89 201	111 711	130 753	Afrique
Americas		439 672	459 462	540 128	690 169	804 394	Amériques
Europe		890 359	796 613	942 061	1 257 239	1 434 983	Europe
Asia, East/S.East/Oceania		336 543	327 976	393 281	511 681	584 753	Asie, Est/S.-Est/Océanie
Southern Asia		672 133	630 653	666 889	790 698	841 969	Asie du Sud
Western Asia		67 380	66 051	68 917	80 073	86 450	Asie occidentale
Region not specified		44 477	23 292	25 737	15 906	35 308	Région non spécifiée
Indonesia	TFR						Indonésie
Total		5 153 620	5 033 400	4 467 021	5 321 165	5 002 101	Total
Africa		40 282	36 503	30 244	35 507	27 450	Afrique
Americas		243 097	222 052	175 546	209 779	209 511	Amériques
Europe		861 970	808 067	605 904	720 706	798 408	Europe
Asia, East/S.East/Oceania		3 920 183	3 877 195	3 575 842	4 265 551	3 837 107	Asie, Est/S.-Est/Océanie
Southern Asia		51 223	51 596	48 114	53 839	69 024	Asie du Sud
Western Asia		36 865	37 987	31 371	35 783	60 601	Asie occidentale
Iraq	VFN						Iraq
Total		126 654	…	…	…	…	Total
Africa		127	…	…	…	…	Afrique
Americas		32	…	…	…	…	Amériques
Europe		501	…	…	…	…	Europe
Asia, East/S.East/Oceania		110	…	…	…	…	Asie, Est/S.-Est/Océanie
Southern Asia		124 434	…	…	…	…	Asie du Sud
Western Asia		20	…	…	…	…	Asie occidentale
Region not specified		1 430	…	…	…	…	Région non spécifiée
Ireland	TFR						Irlande
Total		6 353 000	6 477 000	6 764 000	6 953 000	7 334 000	Total
Africa		32 000	29 000	32 000	42 000	39 000	Afrique
Americas		915 000	860 000	913 000	975 000	956 000	Amériques
Europe		5 189 000	5 387 000	5 623 000	5 677 000	6 113 000	Europe
Asia, East/S.East/Oceania		217 000	201 000	196 000	259 000	226 000	Asie, Est/S.-Est/Océanie
Israel	TFR						Israël
Total[2]		1 195 689	861 859	1 063 381	1 505 606	1 902 787	Total[2]
Africa		35 597	29 323	29 547	40 122	41 450	Afrique
Americas		350 484	260 912	347 622	486 508	602 573	Amériques
Europe		703 607	484 353	598 231	857 133	1 107 142	Europe
Asia, East/S.East/Oceania		53 231	35 885	42 384	65 953	87 572	Asie, Est/S.-Est/Océanie
Southern Asia		14 262	10 745	10 172	15 155	22 911	Asie du Sud
Western Asia		30 842	28 356	23 159	28 561	29 946	Asie occidentale
Region not specified		7 666	12 285	12 266	12 174	11 193	Région non spécifiée
Italy	TFN						Italie
Total[37]		39 562 697	39 798 969	39 604 118	37 070 775	36 512 500	Total[37]
Africa		192 538	179 251	122 472	205 617	250 705	Afrique
Americas		2 158 479	2 064 520	1 680 228	2 988 244	3 250 284	Amériques
Europe		35 839 204	36 001 041	36 583 819	32 521 819	31 571 338	Europe
Asia, East/S.East/Oceania		1 199 891	1 382 734	1 074 563	1 088 281	1 111 603	Asie, Est/S.-Est/Océanie
Southern Asia		75 108	89 329	67 001	135 290	115 193	Asie du Sud
Western Asia		97 477	82 093	76 035	129 760	212 716	Asie occidentale
Region not specified		…	1	…	1 764	661	Région non spécifiée
Jamaica	TFR						Jamaïque
Total[3,12]		1 276 516	1 266 366	1 350 285	1 414 786	1 478 663	Total[3,12]
Africa		1 271	1 131	1 084	1 139	889	Afrique
Americas		1 083 499	1 076 044	1 119 679	1 161 840	1 233 846	Amériques

Country or area of destination and region of origin&	Series Série	2001	2002	2003	2004	2005	Pays ou zone de destination et région de provenance&
Europe		181 891	179 902	219 406	242 904	234 952	Europe
Asia, East/S.East/Oceania		8 725	8 292	9 051	7 971	8 129	Asie, Est/S.-Est/Océanie
Southern Asia		731	530	643	554	464	Asie du Sud
Western Asia		334	392	363	350	347	Asie occidentale
Region not specified		65	75	59	28	36	Région non spécifiée
Japan	TFN						Japon
Total[2]		4 771 555	5 238 963	5 211 725	6 137 905	6 727 926	Total[2]
Africa		14 640	16 698	16 434	16 946	20 583	Afrique
Americas		866 137	927 598	824 345	951 074	1 032 140	Amériques
Europe		630 128	688 250	665 187	744 142	817 092	Europe
Asia, East/S.East/Oceania		3 189 259	3 528 489	3 625 013	4 337 788	4 761 395	Asie, Est/S.-Est/Océanie
Southern Asia		66 120	72 580	76 217	83 856	92 676	Asie du Sud
Western Asia		3 062	3 394	3 166	3 285	3 072	Asie occidentale
Region not specified		2 209	1 954	1 363	814	968	Région non spécifiée
Jordan	TFN						Jordanie
Total[1]		1 671 510	2 384 472	2 353 087	2 852 803	2 986 589	Total[1]
Africa		17 497	19 582	17 537	19 938	30 234	Afrique
Americas		51 768	51 908	64 545	93 477	111 975	Amériques
Europe		285 113	313 467	314 858	374 428	391 846	Europe
Asia, East/S.East/Oceania		29 309	43 251	43 883	60 121	64 191	Asie, Est/S.-Est/Océanie
Southern Asia		16 782	36 421	27 034	37 885	42 947	Asie du Sud
Western Asia		897 296	1 497 960	1 464 910	1 780 755	1 828 735	Asie occidentale
Region not specified		373 745	421 883	420 320	486 199	516 661	Région non spécifiée
Kazakhstan	VFR						Kazakhstan
Total		2 692 590	3 677 921	3 236 788	4 291 040	4 364 949	Total
Africa		1 687	1 159	1 064	1 506	1 703	Afrique
Americas		19 134	24 699	23 203	32 345	30 768	Amériques
Europe		2 585 032	3 569 412	3 114 377	4 125 909	4 194 081	Europe
Asia, East/S.East/Oceania		68 649	65 929	72 359	96 660	113 842	Asie, Est/S.-Est/Océanie
Southern Asia		10 049	12 437	17 733	20 849	19 036	Asie du Sud
Western Asia		2 234	3 330	2 917	1 984	2 276	Asie occidentale
Region not specified		5 805	955	5 135	11 787	3 243	Région non spécifiée
Kenya	VFR						Kenya
Total[38]		995 066	1 001 297	1 146 099	...	...	Total[38]
Africa		270 734	272 429	311 819	...	...	Afrique
Americas		84 555	85 083	97 389	...	...	Amériques
Europe		571 615	575 197	658 384	...	...	Europe
Asia, East/S.East/Oceania		44 003	44 278	50 681	...	...	Asie, Est/S.-Est/Océanie
Southern Asia		23 858	24 007	27 479	...	...	Asie du Sud
Region not specified		301	303	347	...	...	Région non spécifiée
Kiribati	TFN						Kiribati
Total[3]		4 581[39]	4 935[39]	4 905[39]	3 616[40]	3 037[40]	Total[3]
Americas		908	1 112	786	123	300	Amériques
Europe		457	504	388	387	133	Europe
Asia, East/S.East/Oceania		2 536	2 722	2 875	2 463	2 185	Asie, Est/S.-Est/Océanie
Region not specified		680	597	856	643	419	Région non spécifiée
Korea, Republic of	VFN						Corée, République de
Total[41]		5 147 204	5 347 468	4 753 604	5 818 138	6 022 752	Total[41]
Africa		15 511	16 322	14 834	14 649	14 464	Afrique
Americas		506 787	556 440	505 067	610 562	640 050	Amériques
Europe		454 777	536 261	514 403	531 257	540 694	Europe
Asia, East/S.East/Oceania		3 787 356	3 829 548	3 334 633	4 252 976	4 441 757	Asie, Est/S.-Est/Océanie
Southern Asia		88 338	81 648	86 000	95 398	92 189	Asie du Sud
Western Asia		7 850	10 715	8 045	11 155	13 050	Asie occidentale
Region not specified		286 585	316 534	290 622	302 141	280 548	Région non spécifiée

Country or area of destination and region of origin&	Series Série	2001	2002	2003	2004	2005	Pays ou zone de destination et région de provenance&
Kuwait	VFN						Koweït
Total		2 071 616	2 315 568	2 602 300	3 056 093	...	Total
Africa		18 495	24 407	26 167	29 144	...	Afrique
Americas		39 261	50 267	103 447	115 260	...	Amériques
Europe		69 166	80 650	94 168	125 509	...	Europe
Asia, East/S.East/Oceania		99 139	117 923	124 868	158 006	...	Asie, Est/S.-Est/Océanie
Southern Asia		577 813	648 075	745 679	855 730	...	Asie du Sud
Western Asia		1 264 107	1 391 296	1 505 733	1 769 220	...	Asie occidentale
Region not specified		3 635	2 950	2 238	3 224	...	Région non spécifiée
Kyrgyzstan	TFR						Kirghizistan
Total		98 558	139 589	341 990[42]	398 078[42]	315 290[42]	Total
Americas		4 388	11 936	12 744	12 266	13 023	Amériques
Europe		44 733	88 148	269 575	356 982	273 696	Europe
Asia, East/S.East/Oceania		8 384	11 333	14 005	16 766	22 099	Asie, Est/S.-Est/Océanie
Southern Asia		1 588	3 400	5 395	5 864	6 364	Asie du Sud
Western Asia		73	45	...	...	80	Asie occidentale
Region not specified		39 392	24 727	40 271	6 200	28	Région non spécifiée
Lao People's Dem. Rep.	VFN						Rép. dém. pop. lao
Total		673 823	735 662	636 361	894 806	1 095 315	Total
Americas		34 370	46 704	39 453	47 153	60 061	Amériques
Europe		84 153	107 439	97 314	116 180	134 472	Europe
Asia, East/S.East/Oceania		549 112	575 268	495 253	728 262	897 177	Asie, Est/S.-Est/Océanie
Southern Asia		4 137	3 763	2 932	1 845	2 096	Asie du Sud
Region not specified		2 051	2 488	1 409	1 366	1 509	Région non spécifiée
Latvia	TCER						Lettonie
Total		322 916	360 927	414 924	545 366	730 146	Total
Africa		86	87	151	83	71	Afrique
Americas		13 427	15 014	14 128	21 091	20 423	Amériques
Europe		297 865	332 107	386 070	500 979	680 362	Europe
Asia, East/S.East/Oceania		7 782	7 611	7 603	9 511	9 941	Asie, Est/S.-Est/Océanie
Southern Asia		278	403	294	308	570	Asie du Sud
Western Asia		94	158	131	196	524	Asie occidentale
Region not specified		3 384	5 547	6 547	13 198	18 255	Région non spécifiée
Lebanon	TFN						Liban
Total[43]		837 072	956 464	1 015 793	1 278 469	1 139 524	Total[43]
Africa		29 995	37 240	39 453	45 095	31 073	Afrique
Americas		101 199	108 329	120 239	152 175	136 904	Amériques
Europe		237 411	250 817	267 077	337 337	316 561	Europe
Asia, East/S.East/Oceania		54 266	60 543	65 581	92 285	87 813	Asie, Est/S.-Est/Océanie
Southern Asia		82 183	95 647	102 035	128 120	129 315	Asie du Sud
Western Asia		329 945	403 000	421 148	520 230	436 549	Asie occidentale
Region not specified		2 073	888	260	3 227	1 309	Région non spécifiée
Lesotho	VFR						Lesotho
Total		294 644	287 280	329 301	303 530[8]	303 578[8]	Total
Africa		285 804	278 662	302 924	290 295	289 342	Afrique
Americas		885	861	2 842	1 375	1 490	Amériques
Europe		5 893	5 746	12 569	7 568	7 930	Europe
Asia, East/S.East/Oceania		2 062	2 011	4 009	2 551	2 657	Asie, Est/S.-Est/Océanie
Region not specified		...	...	6 957	1 741	2 159	Région non spécifiée
Libyan Arab Jamah.	VFN						Jamah. arabe libyenne
Total *[44]		952 934	857 952	957 896	999 343	...	Total *[44]
Africa		514 887	438 881	457 721	482 704	...	Afrique
Americas		677	1 943	1 926	2 201	...	Amériques
Europe		39 857	36 418	42 056	45 657	...	Europe
Asia, East/S.East/Oceania		5 646	6 611	6 601	6 942	...	Asie, Est/S.-Est/Océanie
Southern Asia		4 065	4 325	4 031	3 704	...	Asie du Sud
Western Asia		387 802	369 774	445 561	458 124	...	Asie occidentale
Region not specified		...	...	...	11	...	Région non spécifiée

Country or area of destination and region of origin&	Series Série	2001	2002	2003	2004	2005	Pays ou zone de destination et région de provenance&
Liechtenstein	THSR						Liechtenstein
Total		56 475	48 727	49 002	48 501	49 767	Total
Africa		193	223	214	198	170	Afrique
Americas		3 667	2 852	2 414	2 739	2 888	Amériques
Europe		51 018	43 990	44 740	43 836	44 944	Europe
Asia, East/S.East/Oceania		1 597	1 662	1 634	1 728	1 635	Asie, Est/S.-Est/Océanie
Southern Asia		...	...	...	...	47	Asie du Sud
Region not specified		...	...	...	...	83	Région non spécifiée
Lithuania	TCER						Lituanie
Total		353 889	393 126	438 299	590 043	681 487	Total
Africa		290	271	400	525	1 159	Afrique
Americas		15 256	15 673	16 324	22 385	23 626	Amériques
Europe		321 788	357 990	400 338	538 078	621 649	Europe
Asia, East/S.East/Oceania		10 649	9 808	11 003	15 472	15 032	Asie, Est/S.-Est/Océanie
Region not specified		5 906	9 384	10 234	13 583	20 021	Région non spécifiée
Luxembourg	TCER						Luxembourg
Total		836 122	884 674	867 048	877 712	912 641	Total
Americas		36 048	33 136	28 562	29 777	32 247	Amériques
Europe		769 416	809 403	801 138	806 575	840 107	Europe
Region not specified		30 658	42 135	37 348	41 360	40 287	Région non spécifiée
Madagascar	TFN						Madagascar
Total[3]		170 208	61 674	139 000	228 785	277 422	Total[3]
Africa		31 488	6 218	17 000	39 302	52 277	Afrique
Americas		6 808	1 880	4 000	9 180	13 853	Amériques
Europe		119 144	43 172	100 000	175 727	202 530	Europe
Asia, East/S.East/Oceania		3 404	617	2 000	3 432	6 404	Asie, Est/S.-Est/Océanie
Region not specified		9 364	9 787	16 000	1 144	2 358	Région non spécifiée
Malawi	TFR						Malawi
Total[36]		266 339	382 647	424 000	427 360	437 718	Total[36]
Africa		203 358	299 973	320 360	335 651	336 856	Afrique
Americas		11 809	15 251	18 070	20 828	18 725	Amériques
Europe		43 070	55 222	67 500	48 929	60 437	Europe
Asia, East/S.East/Oceania		...	5 542	9 940	11 313	8 698	Asie, Est/S.-Est/Océanie
Southern Asia		...	1 659	3 620	6 815	9 549	Asie du Sud
Region not specified		8 102	5 000	4 510	3 824	3 453	Région non spécifiée
Malaysia	TFR						Malaisie
Total[45]		12 775 073	13 292 010	10 576 915	15 703 406	16 431 055	Total[45]
Africa		161 926	148 102	133 762	136 587	128 208	Afrique
Americas		321 841	283 216	270 157	271 901	274 915	Amériques
Europe		703 724	636 972	456 351	540 306	618 188	Europe
Asia, East/S.East/Oceania		10 832 535	11 456 003	9 073 882	13 983 381	14 685 975	Asie, Est/S.-Est/Océanie
Southern Asia		212 083	244 351	209 120	248 673	321 246	Asie du Sud
Western Asia		107 775	126 239	78 324	124 331	145 861	Asie occidentale
Region not specified		435 189	397 127	355 319	398 227	256 662	Région non spécifiée
Maldives	TFN						Maldives
Total[3]		460 984	484 680	563 593	616 716	395 320	Total[3]
Africa		2 060	3 002	3 984	5 325	3 460	Afrique
Americas		6 814	7 487	7 660	9 385	7 238	Amériques
Europe		364 105	373 428	443 093	475 707	306 856	Europe
Asia, East/S.East/Oceania		68 967	77 289	83 640	99 735	55 985	Asie, Est/S.-Est/Océanie
Southern Asia		17 007	20 533	21 580	22 047	19 377	Asie du Sud
Western Asia		2 031	2 941	3 636	4 517	2 404	Asie occidentale
Mali	THSN						Mali
Total		88 639	95 851	110 365	112 654	142 814	Total
Africa		19 241	21 165	27 816	29 256	35 985	Afrique
Americas		8 393	9 232	9 393	12 494	13 287	Amériques
Europe		50 694	55 763	62 744	64 252	80 968	Europe

Country or area of destination and region of origin&	Series Série	2001	2002	2003	2004	2005	Pays ou zone de destination et région de provenance&
Asia, East/S.East/Oceania		1 081	1 189	1 200	3 117	2 090	Asie, Est/S.-Est/Océanie
Western Asia		2 445	2 567	2 712	1 524	1 064	Asie occidentale
Region not specified		6 785	5 935	6 500	2 011	9 420	Région non spécifiée
Malta	TFN						Malte
Total		1 180 145	1 133 814	1 126 601	1 156 028[46]	1 171 344[46]	Total
Africa		8 694	9 086	...	...	...	Afrique
Americas		27 945	27 005	20 657	18 720	18 136	Amériques
Europe		1 079 862	1 039 904	939 793	982 623	990 018	Europe
Asia, East/S.East/Oceania		22 246	25 020	...	...	...	Asie, Est/S.-Est/Océanie
Southern Asia		1 613	1 549	...	...	...	Asie du Sud
Western Asia		33 771	25 484	20 218	12 831	10 663	Asie occidentale
Region not specified		6 014	5 766	145 933	141 854	152 527	Région non spécifiée
Marshall Islands	TFR						Iles Marshall
Total		5 444[3]	6 002[3]	7 195[3]	9 007[20]	9 173[20]	Total
Americas		1 994	2 156	2 189	2 099	1 721	Amériques
Europe		115	147	196	160	160	Europe
Asia, East/S.East/Oceania		3 073	3 397	4 422	4 466	5 577	Asie, Est/S.-Est/Océanie
Region not specified		262	302	388	2 282	1 715	Région non spécifiée
Martinique	TFR						Martinique
Total		460 382	446 689	453 159	470 890	484 127	Total
Americas		54 744	70 378	71 559	73 011	81 247	Amériques
Europe		403 316	371 978	379 922	396 138	399 083	Europe
Region not specified		2 322	4 333	1 678	1 741	3 797	Région non spécifiée
Mauritius	TFR						Maurice
Total		660 318	681 648	702 018	718 861	761 063	Total
Africa		168 319	172 351	173 996	175 295	184 821	Afrique
Americas		8 055	7 451	8 106	8 380	8 791	Amériques
Europe		437 615	451 791	465 620	477 347	503 037	Europe
Asia, East/S.East/Oceania		24 534	24 694	21 934	27 026	28 924	Asie, Est/S.-Est/Océanie
Southern Asia		20 946	22 869	27 277	26 558	31 087	Asie du Sud
Western Asia		729	2 287	4 800	3 883	3 737	Asie occidentale
Region not specified		120	205	285	372	666	Région non spécifiée
Mexico	TFR						Mexique
Total[12]		19 810 459	19 666 677	18 665 384	20 617 746	*21 914 917	Total[12]
Americas		19 172 090	19 133 397	18 155 315	19 705 636	20 691 415	Amériques
Europe		362 480	479 174	443 366	...	...	Europe
Region not specified		275 889	54 106	66 703	912 110	1 223 502	Région non spécifiée
Micronesia (Fed. States of)	TFR						Micronésie (Etats féd. de)
Total[47]		15 253	19 056	18 211	19 260	18 958	Total[47]
Americas		7 074	8 439	7 671	7 744	7 955	Amériques
Europe		1 205	1 483	1 568	1 408	2 019	Europe
Asia, East/S.East/Oceania		6 890	9 044	8 884	9 982	8 895	Asie, Est/S.-Est/Océanie
Region not specified		84	90	88	126	89	Région non spécifiée
Monaco	THSN						Monaco
Total		269 925	262 520	234 638	250 159	285 675	Total
Africa		2 372	2 440	2 228	2 230	2 601	Afrique
Americas		37 342	32 499	23 660	25 132	28 626	Amériques
Europe		206 791	205 062	186 972	190 326	214 131	Europe
Asia, East/S.East/Oceania		13 481	12 143	9 781	12 653	11 746	Asie, Est/S.-Est/Océanie
Western Asia		3 322	4 024	3 320	3 367	3 190	Asie occidentale
Region not specified		6 617	6 352	8 677	16 451	25 381	Région non spécifiée
Mongolia	TFN						Mongolie
Total		165 899	228 719	201 153	300 537	337 790	Total
Africa		180	143	209	263	297	Afrique
Americas		6 296	7 973	6 863	12 198	12 913	Amériques
Europe		79 368	97 674	72 345	98 592	100 123	Europe
Asia, East/S.East/Oceania		79 492	122 106	120 691	188 250	223 411	Asie, Est/S.-Est/Océanie

Country or area of destination and region of origin&	Series Série	2001	2002	2003	2004	2005	Pays ou zone de destination et région de provenance&
Southern Asia		462	655	803	966	792	Asie du Sud
Western Asia		93	155	229	249	232	Asie occidentale
Region not specified		8	13	13	19	22	Région non spécifiée
Montserrat	TFR						Montserrat
Total		9 822	9 836	8 390	10 138	9 690	Total
Americas		7 189	7 014	5 932	6 822	6 448	Amériques
Europe		2 540	2 759	2 414	3 197	3 196	Europe
Region not specified		93	63	44	119	46	Région non spécifiée
Morocco	TFN						Maroc
Total[1]		4 379 990	4 453 259	4 761 271	5 476 712	5 843 360	Total[1]
Africa		96 694	91 698	103 194	123 070	143 855	Afrique
Americas		149 103	119 229	107 877	127 974	140 194	Amériques
Europe		1 864 450	1 868 540	1 880 177	2 309 477	2 607 239	Europe
Asia, East/S.East/Oceania		43 459	44 242	41 651	48 874	51 745	Asie, Est/S.-Est/Océanie
Southern Asia		5 548	6 053	5 383	6 486	7 723	Asie du Sud
Western Asia		85 391	85 996	78 639	84 298	91 029	Asie occidentale
Region not specified		2 135 345	2 237 501	2 544 350	2 776 533	2 801 575	Région non spécifiée
Mozambique	VFR						Mozambique
Total		404 093	942 885	726 099	711 060	954 433	Total
Africa		367 593	848 259	591 647	623 240	851 999	Afrique
Americas		...	10 401	5 035	5 647	12 399	Amériques
Europe		36 500	53 691	42 698	56 508	47 999	Europe
Asia, East/S.East/Oceania		...	5 721	...	...	8 036	Asie, Est/S.-Est/Océanie
Region not specified		...	24 813	86 719	25 665	34 000	Région non spécifiée
Myanmar	TFN						Myanmar
Total[48]		204 862	217 212	205 610	241 938	232 218	Total[48]
Africa		312	430	390	395	488	Afrique
Americas		16 671	17 824	16 426	20 451	20 701	Amériques
Europe		57 490	65 477	60 364	65 411	67 933	Europe
Asia, East/S.East/Oceania		122 327	124 280	115 614	141 683	129 922	Asie, Est/S.-Est/Océanie
Southern Asia		6 646	7 179	11 668	12 167	11 254	Asie du Sud
Western Asia		1 416	2 022	1 148	1 831	1 920	Asie occidentale
Namibia	TFR						Namibie
Total		670 497	757 201	695 221	...	777 890	Total
Africa		536 203	591 612	525 885	...	601 737	Afrique
Americas		9 056	9 625	11 775	...	14 685	Amériques
Europe		112 182	140 781	141 834	...	146 362	Europe
Asia, East/S.East/Oceania		...	3 430	4 280	...	4 607	Asie, Est/S.-Est/Océanie
Region not specified		13 056	11 753	11 447	...	10 499	Région non spécifiée
Nepal	TFR						Népal
Total		361 237	275 468	338 132	385 297	375 398	Total
Africa		2 038	1 117	1 501	1 346	1 285	Afrique
Americas		42 751	25 110	25 156	29 791	26 385	Amériques
Europe		142 483	97 026	111 822	131 999	112 341	Europe
Asia, East/S.East/Oceania		88 005	67 985	91 582	96 565	92 733	Asie, Est/S.-Est/Océanie
Southern Asia		85 960	84 230	108 071	124 804	139 288	Asie du Sud
Region not specified		...	...	...	792	3 366	Région non spécifiée
Netherlands	TCER						Pays-Bas
Total		9 499 800	9 595 300	9 180 600	9 646 500	10 011 900	Total
Africa		140 500	172 800	130 600	117 300	101 100	Afrique
Americas		1 202 900	1 099 700	996 100	1 131 500	1 222 200	Amériques
Europe		7 478 800	7 591 600	7 431 800	7 644 000	7 939 900	Europe
Asia, East/S.East/Oceania		677 600	731 200	622 100	753 700	748 700	Asie, Est/S.-Est/Océanie
New Caledonia	TFR						Nouvelle-Calédonie
Total[12]		100 515	103 933	101 983	99 515	100 651	Total[12]
Africa		592	520	489	615	637	Afrique
Americas		1 870	2 141	1 753	1 676	1 785	Amériques

Country or area of destination and region of origin&	Series Série	2001	2002	2003	2004	2005	Pays ou zone de destination et région de provenance&
Europe		27 652	32 683	32 492	29 992	30 268	Europe
Asia, East/S.East/Oceania		69 980	67 998	65 382	65 892	67 753	Asie, Est/S.-Est/Océanie
Region not specified		421	591	1 867	1 340	208	Région non spécifiée
New Zealand	VFR						Nouvelle-Zélande
Total[49]		1 909 381	2 045 064	2 104 420	2 334 153	2 365 529	Total[49]
Africa		21 331	20 679	19 395	18 673	19 709	Afrique
Americas		240 296	261 273	266 245	275 699	275 616	Amériques
Europe		387 222	423 200	460 938	488 674	521 267	Europe
Asia, East/S.East/Oceania		1 158 944	1 240 381	1 271 657	1 468 307	1 484 424	Asie, Est/S.-Est/Océanie
Southern Asia		14 988	19 410	17 028	17 830	19 833	Asie du Sud
Western Asia		5 474	5 922	7 048	8 122	8 871	Asie occidentale
Region not specified		81 126	74 199	62 109	56 848	35 809	Région non spécifiée
Nicaragua	TFN						Nicaragua
Total		482 869[2]	471 622[2]	525 775[2]	614 782	712 444[1]	Total
Africa		560	287	378	515	621	Afrique
Americas		432 474	417 226	464 176	552 846	619 305	Amériques
Europe		40 153	44 730	49 147	52 564	58 964	Europe
Asia, East/S.East/Oceania		8 940	8 732	10 674	8 326	11 235	Asie, Est/S.-Est/Océanie
Southern Asia		590	549	1 254	437	1 522	Asie du Sud
Western Asia		131	64	89	76	82	Asie occidentale
Region not specified		21	34	57	18	20 715	Région non spécifiée
Niger	TFN						Niger
Total		52 463	39 337	55 344	57 000	63 451	Total
Africa		34 964	26 198	37 000	38 000	37 926	Afrique
Americas		2 165	1 574	2 000	2 500	3 150	Amériques
Europe		13 500	10 110	14 344	14 500	18 388	Europe
Asia, East/S.East/Oceania		1 327	983	1 400	1 500	2 835	Asie, Est/S.-Est/Océanie
Region not specified		507	472	600	500	1 152	Région non spécifiée
Nigeria	VFN						Nigéria
Total		1 752 948	2 045 543	2 253 115	2 646 411	2 778 365	Total
Africa		1 234 733	1 450 814	1 554 308	1 825 312	1 916 246	Afrique
Americas		68 435	80 412	94 486	111 020	116 563	Amériques
Europe		270 056	317 317	372 846	438 093	459 985	Europe
Asia, East/S.East/Oceania		108 097	110 832	130 228	153 020	160 666	Asie, Est/S.-Est/Océanie
Southern Asia		36 335	44 701	52 523	61 714	64 796	Asie du Sud
Western Asia		29 414	34 560	40 608	47 714	50 095	Asie occidentale
Region not specified		5 878	6 907	8 116	9 538	10 014	Région non spécifiée
Niue	TFR						Nioué
Total[3,50]		1 446	2 084	2 706	2 550	2 793	Total[3,50]
Americas		189	252	178	138	181	Amériques
Europe		178	275	235	168	295	Europe
Asia, East/S.East/Oceania		1 075	1 387	2 247	2 217	2 272	Asie, Est/S.-Est/Océanie
Region not specified		4	170	46	27	45	Région non spécifiée
Northern Mariana Islands	VFN						Iles Mariannes du Nord
Total		444 284	475 547	459 458	535 873	506 846	Total
Americas		35 460	36 451	34 670	37 334	37 989	Amériques
Europe		566	598	439	666	1 300	Europe
Asia, East/S.East/Oceania		407 104	437 322	422 811	494 826	465 360	Asie, Est/S.-Est/Océanie
Region not specified		1 154	1 176	1 538	3 047	2 197	Région non spécifiée
Norway	TFN						Norvège
Total[51]		3 073 000	3 111 000	3 269 000	3 628 000	3 859 000	Total[51]
Americas		141 000	126 000	144 000	176 000	155 000	Amériques
Europe		2 817 000	2 865 000	3 009 000	3 307 000	3 521 000	Europe
Asia, East/S.East/Oceania		...	35 000	35 000	35 000	41 000	Asie, Est/S.-Est/Océanie
Region not specified		115 000	85 000	81 000	110 000	142 000	Région non spécifiée
Occupied Palestinian Terr.	THSN						Terr. palestinien occupé
Total		42 776	33 424	36 722	56 011	88 360	Total
Africa		459	1 209	604	641	971	Afrique

Country or area of destination and region of origin&	Series Série	2001	2002	2003	2004	2005	Pays ou zone de destination et région de provenance&
Americas		7 659	6 480	6 407	10 649	13 735	Amériques
Europe		23 539	18 352	23 701	35 210	55 324	Europe
Asia, East/S.East/Oceania		9 816	6 487	4 872	8 399	16 490	Asie, Est/S.-Est/Océanie
Western Asia		1 303	896	1 138	1 112	1 840	Asie occidentale
Occupied Palestinian Terr.	VFR						Terr. palestinien occupé
Total[52]		81 472	9 453	46 356	...	...	Total[52]
Africa		1 682	88	337	...	...	Afrique
Americas		23 377	1 402	5 836	...	...	Amériques
Europe		24 571	4 656	18 569	...	...	Europe
Asia, East/S.East/Oceania		7 286	1 073	8 111	...	...	Asie, Est/S.-Est/Océanie
Southern Asia		1 742	113	561	...	...	Asie du Sud
Western Asia		58	...	...	...	...	Asie occidentale
Region not specified		22 756	2 121	12 942	...	...	Région non spécifiée
Oman	THSN						Oman
Total		647 320	643 326	629 525	908 466	1 114 498	Total
Africa		20 191	17 277	19 035	28 266	18 307	Afrique
Americas		48 574	36 022	36 356	40 154	34 137	Amériques
Europe		197 279	197 015	163 855	280 727	336 757	Europe
Asia, East/S.East/Oceania		36 913	66 416	51 026	54 971	69 310	Asie, Est/S.-Est/Océanie
Southern Asia		77 033	85 238	101 971	130 565	127 104	Asie du Sud
Western Asia		154 554	192 817	204 586	249 285	198 577	Asie occidentale
Region not specified		112 776	48 541	52 696	124 498	330 306	Région non spécifiée
Pakistan	TFN						Pakistan
Total		499 719	498 059	500 918	647 993	798 260	Total
Africa		14 877	11 620	11 721	12 521	14 691	Afrique
Americas		82 159	87 884	85 910	103 104	146 548	Amériques
Europe		205 140	215 280	192 854	280 877	356 804	Europe
Asia, East/S.East/Oceania		42 711	43 920	43 521	59 503	83 607	Asie, Est/S.-Est/Océanie
Southern Asia		123 957	116 449	146 655	160 345	158 549	Asie du Sud
Western Asia		30 466	22 329	19 593	28 365	31 920	Asie occidentale
Region not specified		409	577	664	3 278	6 141	Région non spécifiée
Palau	TFR						Palaos
Total[53]		54 111	58 560	68 296	94 894	86 126	Total[53]
Americas		5 375	4 774	4 511	6 507	5 910	Amériques
Europe		930	834	818	1 837	2 390	Europe
Asia, East/S.East/Oceania		46 191	51 504	61 400	84 449	75 503	Asie, Est/S.-Est/Océanie
Region not specified		1 615	1 448	1 567	2 101	2 323	Région non spécifiée
Panama	VFR						Panama
Total[54]		410 605	426 154	468 686	*498 415	*576 050	Total[54]
Africa		412	334	354	335	390	Afrique
Americas		367 028	375 518	410 957	438 872	507 185	Amériques
Europe		31 876	38 417	43 355	45 254	52 339	Europe
Asia, East/S.East/Oceania		11 194	11 864	13 968	13 919	16 095	Asie, Est/S.-Est/Océanie
Western Asia		95	21	52	35	41	Asie occidentale
Papua New Guinea	TFR						Papouasie-Nvl-Guinée
Total		54 235	53 761	56 282	59 013	69 251	Total
Africa		244	271	193	241	353	Afrique
Americas		6 142	6 990	5 215	5 440	6 491	Amériques
Europe		5 161	4 733	4 218	4 739	4 155	Europe
Asia, East/S.East/Oceania		40 148	39 316	45 999	47 963	57 516	Asie, Est/S.-Est/Océanie
Southern Asia		2 540	2 451	657	630	736	Asie du Sud
Paraguay	TFN						Paraguay
Total[4,55]		278 672	250 423	268 175	309 287	340 845	Total[4,55]
Africa		139	161	185	211	253	Afrique
Americas		260 112	231 727	248 364	284 325	311 628	Amériques
Europe		15 411	13 915	15 375	19 788	23 201	Europe
Asia, East/S.East/Oceania		3 010	4 620	4 251	4 718	5 466	Asie, Est/S.-Est/Océanie

Country or area of destination and region of origin&	Series Série	2001	2002	2003	2004	2005	Pays ou zone de destination et région de provenance&
Southern Asia		...	...	...	148	200	Asie du Sud
Western Asia		...	...	...	96	97	Asie occidentale
Region not specified		...	...	...	1	...	Région non spécifiée
Peru	TFN						Pérou
Total		900 514	997 628[56]	1 069 517	1 276 610[57]	1 486 005[57]	Total
Africa		1 796	1 889	2 127	2 727	3 464	Afrique
Americas		533 730	713 555	762 290	924 656	1 060 708	Amériques
Europe		221 151	236 157	252 435	284 723	344 832	Europe
Asia, East/S.East/Oceania		38 420	44 454	49 918	62 275	74 040	Asie, Est/S.-Est/Océanie
Southern Asia		1 107	1 320	1 294	1 357	1 976	Asie du Sud
Western Asia		146	119	117	129	198	Asie occidentale
Region not specified		104 164	134	1 336	743	787	Région non spécifiée
Philippines	TFR						Philippines
Total[1]		1 796 893	1 932 677	1 907 226	2 291 352	2 623 084	Total[1]
Africa		1 685	1 465	1 442	1 700	2 294	Afrique
Americas		451 008	453 667	444 264	545 867	604 793	Amériques
Europe		201 815	183 910	177 338	212 305	246 449	Europe
Asia, East/S.East/Oceania		985 941	1 154 439	1 128 540	1 359 256	1 565 359	Asie, Est/S.-Est/Océanie
Southern Asia		22 193	20 822	21 543	24 997	28 485	Asie du Sud
Western Asia		16 073	18 500	16 736	20 683	24 532	Asie occidentale
Region not specified		118 178	99 874	117 363	126 544	151 172	Région non spécifiée
Poland	TCER						Pologne
Total		3 151 513	3 145 439	3 331 870	3 934 064	4 310 401	Total
Africa		3 788	5 051	6 009	5 483	5 637	Afrique
Americas		201 289	189 177	182 309	232 723	242 264	Amériques
Europe		2 791 284	2 818 036	3 022 645	3 521 865	3 882 651	Europe
Asia, East/S.East/Oceania		64 127	64 206	66 951	98 239	110 944	Asie, Est/S.-Est/Océanie
Southern Asia		6 550	6 238	4 843	8 659	8 293	Asie du Sud
Western Asia		3 189	2 621	3 780	4 403	3 648	Asie occidentale
Region not specified		81 286	60 110	45 333	62 692	56 964	Région non spécifiée
Poland	VFN						Pologne
Total		61 431 266	50 734 623	52 129 778	61 917 759	64 606 085	Total
Africa		9 497	8 699	9 538	11 114	13 217	Afrique
Americas		306 871	272 329	294 313	345 181	439 417	Amériques
Europe		60 981 868	50 315 365	51 691 151	61 385 787	63 926 773	Europe
Asia, East/S.East/Oceania		85 061	87 430	88 693	123 114	163 414	Asie, Est/S.-Est/Océanie
Southern Asia		8 554	8 875	9 483	11 710	13 219	Asie du Sud
Western Asia		6 414	6 277	6 065	6 471	7 636	Asie occidentale
Region not specified		33 001	35 648	30 535	34 382	42 409	Région non spécifiée
Portugal	TCER						Portugal
Total[58]		5 391 886	5 444 072	5 301 778	5 514 268	5 675 805	Total[58]
Africa		42 641	42 960	42 758	45 827	46 424	Afrique
Americas		536 373	496 163	448 955	478 555	510 966	Amériques
Europe		4 675 170	4 738 548	4 660 911	4 786 057	4 930 205	Europe
Asia, East/S.East/Oceania		127 461	155 682	138 217	190 924	175 644	Asie, Est/S.-Est/Océanie
Southern Asia		6 003	6 895	7 237	8 247	8 163	Asie du Sud
Western Asia		4 238	3 824	3 700	4 658	4 403	Asie occidentale
Portugal	TFR						Portugal
Total[2,58]		12 167 200	11 644 231	11 707 228	11 616 899	...	Total[2,58]
Americas		536 248	463 847	480 544	494 343	...	Amériques
Europe		11 281 780	10 849 103	10 887 861	10 754 110	...	Europe
Asia, East/S.East/Oceania		40 053	43 964	40 055	44 019	...	Asie, Est/S.-Est/Océanie
Region not specified		309 119	287 317	298 768	324 427	...	Région non spécifiée
Puerto Rico	TFR						Porto Rico
Total[59]		3 551 200	3 087 100	3 238 300	3 541 000	3 685 900	Total[59]
Americas		2 635 000	2 230 400	2 470 500	2 754 400	2 847 400	Amériques
Region not specified		916 200	856 700	767 800	786 600	838 500	Région non spécifiée

Country or area of destination and region of origin&	Series Série	2001	2002	2003	2004	2005	Pays ou zone de destination et région de provenance&
Qatar	THSR						Qatar
Total[60]		375 954	586 645	556 965	732 454	912 997	Total[60]
Europe		56 426	102 983	88 620	195 732	233 315	Europe
Asia, East/S.East/Oceania		59 755	107 832	127 348	145 974	159 279	Asie, Est/S.-Est/Océanie
Western Asia		231 456	312 063	282 538	295 335	364 977	Asie occidentale
Region not specified		28 317	63 767	58 459	95 413	155 426	Région non spécifiée
Republic of Moldova	VFN						République de Moldova
Total[61]		15 690	20 161	23 598	26 045	25 073	Total[61]
Africa		27	40	45	71	15	Afrique
Americas		1 148	1 788	2 556	2 564	3 161	Amériques
Europe		14 028	17 631	20 152	22 686	21 223	Europe
Asia, East/S.East/Oceania		377	411	295	307	277	Asie, Est/S.-Est/Océanie
Southern Asia		30	10	25	25	35	Asie du Sud
Western Asia		80	281	525	392	362	Asie occidentale
Réunion	TFR						Réunion
Total		424 000	426 000	432 000	430 000	409 000	Total
Africa		45 805	30 625	27 367	26 222	24 800	Afrique
Europe		347 215	356 828	366 725	370 474	344 100	Europe
Region not specified		30 980	38 547	37 908	33 304	40 100	Région non spécifiée
Romania	VFR						Roumanie
Total		4 938 375	4 793 722	5 594 828	6 600 115	5 839 374	Total
Africa		4 735	4 984	5 461	6 585	6 992	Afrique
Americas		96 012	102 481	115 373	139 463	154 244	Amériques
Europe		4 757 141	4 603 867	5 391 609	6 360 587	5 580 091	Europe
Asia, East/S.East/Oceania		36 393	41 703	41 610	49 309	57 028	Asie, Est/S.-Est/Océanie
Southern Asia		13 971	12 423	12 856	15 344	15 566	Asie du Sud
Western Asia		28 181	27 105	26 867	27 760	24 090	Asie occidentale
Region not specified		1 942	1 159	1 052	1 067	1 363	Région non spécifiée
Russian Federation	VFN						Fédération de Russie
Total		21 594 788	23 308 711	22 521 059	22 064 213	22 200 649	Total
Africa		34 463	31 473	28 985	29 217	26 909	Afrique
Americas		305 601	342 594	420 857	477 338	457 301	Amériques
Europe		19 704 037	21 097 290	20 236 821	19 607 077	19 690 628	Europe
Asia, East/S.East/Oceania		868 636	1 150 430	1 106 605	1 313 669	1 315 480	Asie, Est/S.-Est/Océanie
Southern Asia		48 236	57 708	58 804	62 927	68 421	Asie du Sud
Western Asia		24 341	28 312	31 792	31 765	33 405	Asie occidentale
Region not specified		609 474	600 904	637 195	542 220	608 505	Région non spécifiée
Rwanda	TFR						Rwanda
Total[62]		113 185	...	...	...	...	Total[62]
Africa		99 928	...	...	...	...	Afrique
Americas		2 785	...	...	...	...	Amériques
Europe		8 395	...	...	...	...	Europe
Asia, East/S.East/Oceania		699	...	...	...	...	Asie, Est/S.-Est/Océanie
Southern Asia		1 045	...	...	...	...	Asie du Sud
Western Asia		333	...	...	...	...	Asie occidentale
Saba	TFR						Saba
Total		9 005	10 778	10 260	11 012	11 462	Total
Americas		4 378	4 380	4 106	4 764	4 933	Amériques
Europe		4 012	4 565	4 732	5 043	5 484	Europe
Region not specified		615	1 833	1 422	1 205	1 045	Région non spécifiée
Saint Eustatius	TFR						Saint-Eustache
Total[63]		9 597	9 781	10 451	11 056	10 355	Total[63]
Americas		3 447	3 403	3 483	3 732	3 457	Amériques
Europe		4 499	4 600	5 272	5 505	5 400	Europe
Region not specified		1 651	1 778	1 696	1 819	1 498	Région non spécifiée
Saint Kitts and Nevis	TFR						Saint-Kitts-et-Nevis
Total[3]		70 565	67 531	...	...	...	Total[3]
Americas		59 285	60 023	...	...	...	Amériques

Country or area of destination and region of origin&	Series Série	2001	2002	2003	2004	2005	Pays ou zone de destination et région de provenance&
Europe		8 726	5 464	...	...	...	Europe
Region not specified		2 554	2 044	...	...	...	Région non spécifiée
Saint Lucia	TFR						Sainte-Lucie
Total[2]		250 132	253 463	276 948	298 431	*317 939	Total[2]
Americas		165 239	175 390	183 349	197 433	214 621	Amériques
Europe		82 672	76 199	90 193	96 793	101 790	Europe
Asia, East/S.East/Oceania		205	278	373	282	260	Asie, Est/S.-Est/Océanie
Region not specified		2 016	1 596	3 033	3 923	1 268	Région non spécifiée
Saint Maarten	TFN						Saint-Martin
Total[64]		402 649	380 801	427 587	475 032	462 492	Total[64]
Americas		269 613	259 506	301 018	338 241	328 532	Amériques
Europe		97 449	87 147	88 259	96 404	92 413	Europe
Region not specified		35 587	34 148	38 310	40 387	41 547	Région non spécifiée
St. Vincent-Grenadines	TFR						St. Vincent-Grenadines
Total[3]		70 686	77 631	78 535	86 722	95 506	Total[3]
Americas		50 572	58 465	60 315	66 871	74 173	Amériques
Europe		18 850	17 997	17 201	18 652	19 928	Europe
Region not specified		1 264	1 169	1 019	1 199	1 405	Région non spécifiée
Samoa	TFR						Samoa
Total		88 263	88 971	92 486	98 155	101 807	Total
Americas		8 837	9 095	8 959	8 311	9 682	Amériques
Europe		5 797	4 762	5 136	4 756	4 632	Europe
Asia, East/S.East/Oceania		73 403	74 833	78 155	84 882	87 217	Asie, Est/S.-Est/Océanie
Region not specified		226	281	236	206	276	Région non spécifiée
San Marino	VFN						Saint-Marin
Total[65]		3 035 650	3 102 453	2 882 207	2 812 488	2 107 092[22]	Total[65]
Africa		...	...	...	...	111	Afrique
Americas		...	...	...	...	17 479	Amériques
Europe		...	...	...	...	2 035 386	Europe
Asia, East/S.East/Oceania		...	...	...	...	53 328	Asie, Est/S.-Est/Océanie
Southern Asia		...	...	...	...	436	Asie du Sud
Western Asia		...	...	...	...	270	Asie occidentale
Region not specified		3 035 650	3 102 453	2 882 207	2 812 488	82	Région non spécifiée
Sao Tome and Principe	TFN						Sao Tomé-et-Principe
Total		7 460	9 189	9 609	10 705	10 518	Total
Africa		1 384	1 798	2 120	2 205	2 014	Afrique
Americas		...	...	269	298	222	Amériques
Europe		4 238	2 360	6 258	6 312	7 684	Europe
Region not specified		1 838	5 031	962	1 890	598	Région non spécifiée
Saudi Arabia	TFN						Arabie saoudite
Total		6 726 620	7 511 299	7 332 233	8 599 430	8 036 613	Total
Africa		535 099	606 791	525 045	675 441	436 292	Afrique
Americas		47 109	51 981	46 496	53 190	70 196	Amériques
Europe		304 894	338 580	334 159	424 297	340 310	Europe
Asia, East/S.East/Oceania		595 847	660 329	612 340	752 905	439 021	Asie, Est/S.-Est/Océanie
Southern Asia		1 371 162	1 618 928	1 868 897	1 932 990	1 142 202	Asie du Sud
Western Asia		3 853 143	4 212 598	3 923 873	4 752 257	5 607 356	Asie occidentale
Region not specified		19 366	22 092	21 423	8 350	1 236	Région non spécifiée
Senegal	THSN						Sénégal
Total		396 254	426 825	353 539	363 490	386 564	Total
Africa		77 623	86 037	85 664	89 660	87 565	Afrique
Americas		10 683	9 536	10 025	12 431	13 989	Amériques
Europe		301 087	322 631	252 568	242 944	274 439	Europe
Asia, East/S.East/Oceania		2 208	1 864	2 273	3 705	3 837	Asie, Est/S.-Est/Océanie
Western Asia		915	994	1 253	1 672	1 467	Asie occidentale
Region not specified		3 738	5 763	1 756	13 078	5 267	Région non spécifiée

Country or area of destination and region of origin&	Series Série	2001	2002	2003	2004	2005	Pays ou zone de destination et région de provenance&
Senegal	TFN						Sénégal
Total		...	...	...	666 616	769 489	Total
Africa		...	...	...	209 226	265 113	Afrique
Americas		...	...	...	24 686	26 274	Amériques
Europe		...	...	...	348 852	392 767	Europe
Region not specified		...	...	...	83 852	85 335	Région non spécifiée
Serbia and Montenegro	TCEN						Serbie-et-Monténégro
Total		351 333	448 223	481 070	579 886	724 684	Total
Americas		10 555	14 593	16 812	16 837	20 091	Amériques
Europe		327 263	418 676	449 932	545 288	683 031	Europe
Asia, East/S.East/Oceania		3 089	3 442	4 156	5 631	6 722	Asie, Est/S.-Est/Océanie
Region not specified		10 426	11 512	10 170	12 130	14 840	Région non spécifiée
Seychelles	TFR						Seychelles
Total		129 762	132 246	122 038	120 765	128 654	Total
Africa		13 821	13 819	13 578	12 598	12 478	Afrique
Americas		6 854	3 670	3 477	4 030	3 867	Amériques
Europe		103 270	108 246	99 961	98 654	103 581	Europe
Asia, East/S.East/Oceania		2 624	2 678	1 977	2 135	2 647	Asie, Est/S.-Est/Océanie
Southern Asia		1 690	1 810	1 275	1 437	1 623	Asie du Sud
Western Asia		1 503	2 023	1 770	1 911	4 458	Asie occidentale
Sierra Leone	TFR						Sierra Leone
Total[3]		24 067	28 463	38 107	43 560	40 023	Total[3]
Africa		11 427	13 519	23 341	24 446	21 798	Afrique
Americas		3 211	3 785	4 699	4 790	4 713	Amériques
Europe		6 250	7 403	6 460	9 476	9 879	Europe
Asia, East/S.East/Oceania		1 812	2 134	1 995	2 257	2 343	Asie, Est/S.-Est/Océanie
Western Asia		1 367	1 622	1 612	2 591	1 290	Asie occidentale
Singapore	VFR						Singapour
Total[66]		7 522 163	7 567 110	6 127 288	8 328 658	8 943 029	Total[66]
Africa		81 150	70 117	55 997	70 626	78 803	Afrique
Americas		433 552	416 375	314 728	422 167	470 493	Amériques
Europe		1 124 435	1 112 156	885 146	1 081 336	1 136 024	Europe
Asia, East/S.East/Oceania		5 297 821	5 426 216	4 426 234	6 072 654	6 445 012	Asie, Est/S.-Est/Océanie
Southern Asia		508 302	490 262	415 151	626 153	751 437	Asie du Sud
Western Asia		71 516	46 770	29 844	55 449	56 165	Asie occidentale
Region not specified		5 387	5 214	188	273	5 095	Région non spécifiée
Slovakia	TCEN						Slovaquie
Total		1 219 099	1 398 740	1 386 791	1 401 189	1 514 980	Total
Africa		3 131	2 960	2 581	2 482	2 252	Afrique
Americas		35 922	33 352	33 981	38 712	42 100	Amériques
Europe		1 147 970	1 326 492	1 316 120	1 316 705	1 412 628	Europe
Asia, East/S.East/Oceania		30 089	34 130	32 258	42 249	55 992	Asie, Est/S.-Est/Océanie
Southern Asia		1 515	1 437	1 305	384	603	Asie du Sud
Western Asia		334	224	241	314	328	Asie occidentale
Region not specified		138	145	305	343	1 077	Région non spécifiée
Slovenia	TCEN						Slovénie
Total		1 218 721	1 302 019	1 373 137	1 498 843	1 544 786	Total
Americas		33 344	36 232	35 945	45 880	48 436	Amériques
Europe		1 159 864	1 235 856	1 307 775	1 410 662	1 452 584	Europe
Asia, East/S.East/Oceania		15 065	17 430	17 141	24 237	28 396	Asie, Est/S.-Est/Océanie
Region not specified		10 448	12 501	12 276	18 064	15 370	Région non spécifiée
Solomon Islands	TFR						Iles Salomon
Total		...	...	6 595	...	9 400[67]	Total
Americas		...	...	600	...	642	Amériques
Europe		...	...	464	...	545	Europe
Asia, East/S.East/Oceania		...	...	5 406	...	8 128	Asie, Est/S.-Est/Océanie
Region not specified		...	...	125	...	85	Région non spécifiée

Country or area of destination and region of origin&	Series Série	2001	2002	2003	2004	2005	Pays ou zone de destination et région de provenance&
South Africa	TFR						Afrique du Sud
Total[68]		5 787 368	6 429 583	6 504 890	6 677 844	7 368 742	Total[68]
Africa		4 130 975	4 452 762	4 450 212	4 638 371	5 370 137	Afrique
Americas		241 991	254 586	262 496	290 625	322 099	Amériques
Europe		1 028 236	1 274 365	1 338 976	1 306 389	1 328 521	Europe
Asia, East/S.East/Oceania		193 955	229 128	224 610	238 829	238 885	Asie, Est/S.-Est/Océanie
Southern Asia		28 012	34 062	41 018	36 172	36 045	Asie du Sud
Western Asia		13 062	14 955	15 048	16 037	17 194	Asie occidentale
Region not specified		151 137	169 725	172 530	151 421	55 861	Région non spécifiée
Spain	TFR						Espagne
Total		50 093 557	52 326 766	50 853 822	52 429 836	55 913 780	Total
Americas		2 174 344	2 079 643	1 893 950	2 079 065	2 232 851	Amériques
Europe		46 827 387	49 303 582	47 835 345	49 238 605	52 189 873	Europe
Asia, East/S.East/Oceania		265 047	240 637	237 392	150 583	181 050	Asie, Est/S.-Est/Océanie
Region not specified		826 779	702 904	887 135	961 583	1 310 006	Région non spécifiée
Sri Lanka	TFR						Sri Lanka
Total[2]		336 794	393 171	500 642	566 202	549 308	Total[2]
Africa		952	1 611	1 991	1 855	2 340	Afrique
Americas		16 412	20 421	25 744	30 500	47 162	Amériques
Europe		211 049	208 374	265 802	298 776	236 481	Europe
Asia, East/S.East/Oceania		49 079	66 084	84 145	91 076	100 774	Asie, Est/S.-Est/Océanie
Southern Asia		53 758	90 189	116 171	133 532	152 315	Asie du Sud
Western Asia		5 544	6 492	6 789	10 463	10 236	Asie occidentale
Sudan	TFN						Soudan
Total		50 000	51 580	52 291	60 577	245 798[12]	Total
Africa		7 000	7 000	7 000	9 000	58 991	Afrique
Americas		4 000	...	...	...	20 751	Amériques
Europe		11 000	12 000	14 000	17 000	55 796	Europe
Asia, East/S.East/Oceania		10 000	13 000	14 000	17 000	109 380	Asie, Est/S.-Est/Océanie
Southern Asia		5 000	...	...	...	...	Asie du Sud
Western Asia		13 000	...	...	...	...	Asie occidentale
Region not specified		...	19 580	17 291	17 577	880	Région non spécifiée
Suriname	TFR						Suriname
Total		...	...	...	137 808	160 022	Total
Africa		...	...	...	...	279	Afrique
Americas		...	...	...	44 802	56 338	Amériques
Europe		...	...	...	86 913	99 265	Europe
Asia, East/S.East/Oceania		...	...	...	...	3 247	Asie, Est/S.-Est/Océanie
Southern Asia		...	...	...	...	498	Asie du Sud
Region not specified		...	...	...	6 093	395	Région non spécifiée
Suriname	TFN						Suriname
Total[69]		54 341	60 223	82 298	74 887	...	Total[69]
Africa		31	32	187	177	...	Afrique
Americas		3 362	4 307	6 903	7 986	...	Amériques
Europe		49 475	54 477	74 153	64 011	...	Europe
Asia, East/S.East/Oceania		1 375	1 306	998	2 522	...	Asie, Est/S.-Est/Océanie
Southern Asia		98	68	55	165	...	Asie du Sud
Region not specified		...	33	2	26	...	Région non spécifiée
Swaziland	THSR						Swaziland
Total[60]		283 177	255 927	218 813	352 040	311 656	Total[60]
Africa		145 169	173 420	110 054	151 879	134 456	Afrique
Americas		20 217	10 380	11 092	4 968	4 398	Amériques
Europe		84 988	40 483	87 999	110 709	98 009	Europe
Asia, East/S.East/Oceania		5 676	5 244	2 343	3 485	3 085	Asie, Est/S.-Est/Océanie
Region not specified		27 127	26 400	7 325	80 999	71 708	Région non spécifiée
Sweden	TFR						Suède
Total[70]		7 431 000	7 459 000	7 627 000	...	...	Total[70]
Africa		37 000	42 000	46 000	...	...	Afrique

Country or area of destination and region of origin[&]	Series Série	2001	2002	2003	2004	2005	Pays ou zone de destination et région de provenance[&]
Americas		546 000	413 000	467 000	...	...	Amériques
Europe		6 437 000	6 656 000	6 696 000	...	...	Europe
Asia, East/S.East/Oceania		411 000	348 000	380 000	...	...	Asie, Est/S.-Est/Océanie
Region not specified		...	...	38 000	...	...	Région non spécifiée
Switzerland	THSN						Suisse
Total		7 454 855[71]	6 867 696[71]	6 530 108[71]	...	7 228 851[72]	Total
Africa		79 164	74 195	72 786	...	78 143	Afrique
Americas		1 026 667	871 279	757 015	...	829 551	Amériques
Europe		5 277 161	4 906 368	4 821 157	...	5 304 949	Europe
Asia, East/S.East/Oceania		937 554	865 244	727 005	...	846 703	Asie, Est/S.-Est/Océanie
Southern Asia		72 291	80 430	84 685	...	93 472	Asie du Sud
Western Asia		62 018	70 180	67 460	...	76 033	Asie occidentale
Syrian Arab Republic	TCEN						Rép. arabe syrienne
Total[73,74]		...	1 657 779	2 084 956	3 029 964	3 367 935	Total[73,74]
Africa		...	63 008	73 487	89 664	92 585	Afrique
Americas		...	16 577	43 901	57 032	57 795	Amériques
Europe		...	113 436	204 445	313 956	430 120	Europe
Asia, East/S.East/Oceania		...	6 228	25 897	36 852	35 088	Asie, Est/S.-Est/Océanie
Southern Asia		...	293 628	228 357	217 947	268 952	Asie du Sud
Western Asia		...	1 055 832	1 470 289	2 259 703	2 416 358	Asie occidentale
Region not specified		...	109 070	38 580	54 810	67 037	Région non spécifiée
Syrian Arab Republic	VFN						Rép. arabe syrienne
Total[2,73]		3 326 610	4 272 911	4 388 119	6 153 653	5 837 980	Total[2,73]
Africa		71 383	71 089	73 487	89 664	92 585	Afrique
Americas		43 415	44 588	43 901	58 032	57 795	Amériques
Europe		471 541	645 942	651 800	933 239	946 853	Europe
Asia, East/S.East/Oceania		23 178	27 767	25 897	36 852	35 088	Asie, Est/S.-Est/Océanie
Southern Asia		237 188	340 457	228 357	217 947	268 952	Asie du Sud
Western Asia		2 425 119	3 093 856	3 325 490	4 760 773	4 369 669	Asie occidentale
Region not specified		54 786	49 212	39 187	57 146	67 038	Région non spécifiée
Tajikistan	VFR						Tadjikistan
Total		5 200	...	...	...	...	Total
Americas		887	...	...	...	...	Amériques
Europe		3 300	...	...	...	...	Europe
Asia, East/S.East/Oceania		467	...	...	...	...	Asie, Est/S.-Est/Océanie
Southern Asia		512	...	...	...	...	Asie du Sud
Western Asia		34	...	...	...	...	Asie occidentale
Thailand	TFR						Thaïlande
Total[1]		10 132 509	10 872 976	10 082 109	11 737 413	11 567 341	Total[1]
Africa		90 963	89 153	67 121	82 711	72 875	Afrique
Americas		604 059	640 142	576 587	692 792	739 703	Amériques
Europe		2 395 796	2 549 488	2 320 807	2 706 062	2 778 693	Europe
Asia, East/S.East/Oceania		6 491 782	6 955 363	6 510 375	7 500 966	7 194 866	Asie, Est/S.-Est/Océanie
Southern Asia		350 043	413 741	411 224	495 473	552 081	Asie du Sud
Western Asia		129 307	151 180	118 339	172 699	178 718	Asie occidentale
Region not specified		70 559	73 909	77 656	86 710	50 405	Région non spécifiée
TFYR of Macedonia	TCEN						L'ex-R.y. Macédoine
Total		98 946	122 861	157 692	165 306	197 216	Total
Americas		7 846	7 773	8 373	8 362	8 439	Amériques
Europe		87 396	110 878	143 387	151 215	182 534	Europe
Asia, East/S.East/Oceania		1 082	1 566	2 362	2 143	2 747	Asie, Est/S.-Est/Océanie
Region not specified		2 622	2 644	3 570	3 586	3 496	Région non spécifiée
Togo	THSN						Togo
Total		56 629	57 539	60 592	82 686	80 763	Total
Africa		33 554	28 636	31 334	43 842	45 967	Afrique
Americas		2 343	1 975	1 785	2 738	2 633	Amériques
Europe		17 680	24 097	24 484	30 018	27 092	Europe
Asia, East/S.East/Oceania		1 311	1 125	1 452	3 492	2 627	Asie, Est/S.-Est/Océanie

Country or area of destination and region of origin&	Series Série	2001	2002	2003	2004	2005	Pays ou zone de destination et région de provenance&
Western Asia		1 619	1 680	1 495	2 500	2 371	Asie occidentale
Region not specified		122	26	42	96	73	Région non spécifiée
Tonga	TFR						Tonga
Total[3]		32 386	36 588	40 110	41 208	41 862	Total[3]
Africa		55	92	...	...	...	Afrique
Americas		6 706	7 860	7 930	8 202	8 147	Amériques
Europe		4 601	4 082	4 131	3 408	2 908	Europe
Asia, East/S.East/Oceania		20 920	24 477	27 932	28 972	30 424	Asie, Est/S.-Est/Océanie
Southern Asia		104	77	...	...	...	Asie du Sud
Region not specified		...	...	117	626	383	Région non spécifiée
Trinidad and Tobago	TFR						Trinité-et-Tobago
Total[3]		383 101	384 212	409 069	442 596	463 191	Total[3]
Africa		935	997	935	1 017	1 299	Afrique
Americas		285 882	308 018	324 175	347 181	365 311	Amériques
Europe		89 002	71 133	79 236	89 512	91 424	Europe
Asia, East/S.East/Oceania		3 874	2 670	3 313	2 925	3 046	Asie, Est/S.-Est/Océanie
Southern Asia		1 492	1 164	1 136	1 411	1 632	Asie du Sud
Western Asia		262	219	239	221	338	Asie occidentale
Region not specified		1 654	11	35	329	141	Région non spécifiée
Tunisia	TFN						Tunisie
Total[2]		5 387 300	5 063 538	5 114 304	5 997 929	6 378 435	Total[2]
Africa		676 236	786 053	872 251	984 538	993 378	Afrique
Americas		28 486	21 920	23 217	30 347	35 202	Amériques
Europe		3 609 526	2 918 526	2 840 307	3 482 052	3 869 035	Europe
Asia, East/S.East/Oceania		7 804	7 167	9 389	10 784	13 710	Asie, Est/S.-Est/Océanie
Western Asia		1 046 184	1 310 607	1 355 878	1 471 752	1 440 387	Asie occidentale
Region not specified		19 064	19 265	13 262	18 456	26 723	Région non spécifiée
Turkey	TFN						Turquie
Total		10 782 673	12 789 827	13 340 956	16 826 062	20 272 877	Total
Africa		118 870	130 758	119 122	131 148	154 489	Afrique
Americas		326 732	253 804	213 136	282 586	390 884	Amériques
Europe		9 473 313	11 359 447	11 871 694	14 946 162	17 663 077	Europe
Asia, East/S.East/Oceania		247 202	280 607	241 996	288 326	421 643	Asie, Est/S.-Est/Océanie
Southern Asia		342 218	450 787	522 054	660 787	994 620	Asie du Sud
Western Asia		262 894	303 860	359 281	498 095	625 686	Asie occidentale
Region not specified		11 444	10 564	13 673	18 958	22 478	Région non spécifiée
Turkmenistan	TFN						Turkménistan
Total		5 244	10 791	8 214	14 799	11 611	Total
Africa		...	...	...	...	1	Afrique
Americas		388	249	207	374	384	Amériques
Europe		2 848	2 344	1 855	3 915	3 284	Europe
Asia, East/S.East/Oceania		682	545	466	1 053	753	Asie, Est/S.-Est/Océanie
Southern Asia		1 310	7 631	5 649	9 425	7 185	Asie du Sud
Western Asia		16	22	37	32	4	Asie occidentale
Turks and Caicos Islands	TFR						Iles Turques et Caïques
Total		165 920	154 961	...	...	...	Total
Americas		148 025	140 349	...	...	...	Amériques
Europe		11 086	10 634	...	...	...	Europe
Asia, East/S.East/Oceania		57	35	...	...	...	Asie, Est/S.-Est/Océanie
Region not specified		6 752	3 943	...	...	...	Région non spécifiée
Tuvalu	TFN						Tuvalu
Total		1 140	1 313	1 377	1 290	1 085	Total
Americas		65	92	130	79	101	Amériques
Europe		102	108	97	108	104	Europe
Asia, East/S.East/Oceania		957	1 075	1 101	1 043	828	Asie, Est/S.-Est/Océanie
Region not specified		16	38	49	60	52	Région non spécifiée
Uganda	TFR						Ouganda
Total		205 287	254 212	304 656	512 379	467 728	Total

Country or area of destination and region of origin&	Series Série	2001	2002	2003	2004	2005	Pays ou zone de destination et région de provenance&
Africa		149 907	192 278	233 043	405 706	337 188	Afrique
Americas		12 922	14 785	16 409	23 438	28 557	Amériques
Europe		30 395	33 850	39 207	48 847	62 312	Europe
Asia, East/S.East/Oceania		4 757	4 188	4 845	8 150	10 046	Asie, Est/S.-Est/Océanie
Southern Asia		5 514	6 439	7 647	12 139	13 879	Asie du Sud
Western Asia		1 792	1 836	1 976	3 133	2 731	Asie occidentale
Region not specified		...	836	1 529	10 966	13 015	Région non spécifiée
Ukraine	TFR						Ukraine
Total		9 174 165	10 516 665	12 513 883	...	...	Total
Africa		5 227	4 748	12 367	...	...	Afrique
Americas		64 096	52 632	83 451	...	...	Amériques
Europe		9 061 051	10 408 714	12 345 396	...	...	Europe
Asia, East/S.East/Oceania		17 107	21 900	26 362	...	...	Asie, Est/S.-Est/Océanie
Southern Asia		7 453	9 866	13 978	...	...	Asie du Sud
Western Asia		13 399	14 777	18 720	...	...	Asie occidentale
Region not specified		5 832	4 028	13 609	...	...	Région non spécifiée
United Arab Emirates	THSN						Emirats arabes unis
Total[75]		4 133 531	5 445 367	5 871 023	...	...	Total[75]
Africa		218 162	310 722	306 872	...	...	Afrique
Americas		149 802	238 749	254 362	...	...	Amériques
Europe		1 115 373	1 468 015	1 584 792	...	...	Europe
Asia, East/S.East/Oceania		284 878	395 061	427 506	...	...	Asie, Est/S.-Est/Océanie
Southern Asia		590 378	807 094	921 698	...	...	Asie du Sud
Western Asia		1 220 738	1 556 533	1 583 258	...	...	Asie occidentale
Region not specified		554 200	669 193	792 535	...	...	Région non spécifiée
United Kingdom	VFR						Royaume-Uni
Total		22 835 000	24 181 000	24 715 000	27 754 000	29 970 000	Total
Africa		630 000	631 000	569 000	639 000	654 000	Afrique
Americas		4 582 000	4 619 000	4 326 000	4 692 000	4 597 000	Amériques
Europe		15 060 000	16 409 000	17 371 000	19 582 000	21 742 000	Europe
Asia, East/S.East/Oceania		1 834 000	1 854 000	1 809 000	2 086 000	2 190 000	Asie, Est/S.-Est/Océanie
Southern Asia		326 000	308 000	294 000	371 000	407 000	Asie du Sud
Western Asia		403 000	360 000	346 000	384 000	380 000	Asie occidentale
United Rep. of Tanzania	VFR						Rép.-Unie de Tanzanie
Total		525 122	575 296	576 198	582 807	612 754	Total
Africa		213 013	249 601	267 940	256 455	275 718	Afrique
Americas		45 544	59 077	49 781	53 437	61 604	Amériques
Europe		162 225	191 982	191 025	221 865	220 255	Europe
Asia, East/S.East/Oceania		46 605	30 087	27 208	22 928	24 714	Asie, Est/S.-Est/Océanie
Southern Asia		28 060	27 867	26 502	16 528	19 935	Asie du Sud
Western Asia		29 675	16 682	13 742	11 594	10 528	Asie occidentale
United States	TFR						Etats-Unis
Total		46 906 868	43 580 707	41 218 213	46 086 257	49 205 528	Total
Africa		286 783	241 011	236 067	240 488	251 654	Afrique
Americas		29 577 703	28 035 856	26 368 298	29 195 830	31 178 408	Amériques
Europe		9 906 957	8 964 202	8 981 711	10 055 657	10 701 847	Europe
Asia, East/S.East/Oceania		6 535 276	5 888 710	5 192 366	6 086 708	6 518 211	Asie, Est/S.-Est/Océanie
Southern Asia		362 792	324 315	329 660	370 315	411 277	Asie du Sud
Western Asia		237 357	126 613	110 111	137 259	144 131	Asie occidentale
United States Virgin Is.	THSN						Iles Vierges américaines
Total		597 437	585 684	623 394	603 944	609 754	Total
Africa		170	828	134	289	162	Afrique
Americas		540 598	494 324	531 270	560 581	561 091	Amériques
Europe		8 708	6 144	7 747	15 819	18 911	Europe
Asia, East/S.East/Oceania		389	333	363	379	501	Asie, Est/S.-Est/Océanie
Region not specified		47 572	84 055	83 880	26 876	29 089	Région non spécifiée
Uruguay	VFN						Uruguay
Total[1]		2 136 446	1 353 872	1 508 055	1 870 858	1 917 049	Total[1]

Country or area of destination and region of origin&	Series Série	2001	2002	2003	2004	2005	Pays ou zone de destination et région de provenance&
Americas		1 708 380	1 030 738	1 159 580	1 457 944	1 497 756	Amériques
Europe		70 009	56 159	73 230	97 223	119 553	Europe
Asia, East/S.East/Oceania		5 531	5 618	6 230	7 221	11 686	Asie, Est/S.-Est/Océanie
Western Asia		2 627	170	131	489	182	Asie occidentale
Region not specified		349 899	261 187	268 884	307 981	287 872	Région non spécifiée
Uzbekistan	TFR						Ouzbékistan
Total		344 900	331 500	231 000	261 600	...	Total
Africa		1 000	1 000	1 000	1 000	...	Afrique
Americas		10 000	4 100	2 000	12 000	...	Amériques
Europe		109 000	99 800	51 000	68 600	...	Europe
Asia, East/S.East/Oceania		192 900	195 100	145 000	140 000	...	Asie, Est/S.-Est/Océanie
Southern Asia		8 000	8 000	8 000	10 000	...	Asie du Sud
Western Asia		24 000	23 500	24 000	30 000	...	Asie occidentale
Vanuatu	TFR						Vanuatu
Total		53 300	49 461	50 400	61 454	62 082	Total
Americas		1 413	1 438	1 625	1 954	1 625	Amériques
Europe		2 683	2 948	3 003	3 388	3 503	Europe
Asia, East/S.East/Oceania		48 234	44 256	44 876	55 027	55 853	Asie, Est/S.-Est/Océanie
Region not specified		970	819	896	1 085	1 101	Région non spécifiée
Venezuela (Bolivarian Rep. of)	TFN						Venezuela (Rép. bolivar. du)
Total		584 399	431 677	336 974	486 401	706 103	Total
Africa		819	518	438	640	918	Afrique
Americas		280 101	185 276	154 334	217 699	307 932	Amériques
Europe		290 914	237 250	175 159	258 178	382 708	Europe
Asia, East/S.East/Oceania		6 835	3 756	3 201	4 475	6 284	Asie, Est/S.-Est/Océanie
Southern Asia		468	302	270	344	494	Asie du Sud
Western Asia		643	432	371	492	706	Asie occidentale
Region not specified		4 619	4 143	3 201	4 573	7 061	Région non spécifiée
Viet Nam	VFR						Viet Nam
Total[12]		2 330 050	2 627 988	2 428 735	2 927 873	3 467 757	Total[12]
Americas		266 433	303 519	258 991	326 286	396 997	Amériques
Europe		307 722	343 360	293 636	354 735	425 774	Europe
Asia, East/S.East/Oceania		1 484 799	1 694 624	1 669 541	2 008 366	2 365 222	Asie, Est/S.-Est/Océanie
Southern Asia		8 086	...	...	...	...	Asie du Sud
Region not specified		263 010	286 485	206 567	238 486	279 764	Région non spécifiée
Yemen	THSN						Yémen
Total		75 579	98 020	154 667	273 732	336 070	Total
Africa		4 867	3 045	8 627	10 853	12 628	Afrique
Americas		2 879	4 429	12 932	17 988	18 253	Amériques
Europe		26 920	15 828	13 033	28 608	26 456	Europe
Asia, East/S.East/Oceania		6 209	11 303	16 666	40 604	39 032	Asie, Est/S.-Est/Océanie
Western Asia		34 704	63 415	103 409	175 679	239 701	Asie occidentale
Zambia	TFR						Zambie
Total		*491 991	*565 073	412 675	515 000	668 862	Total
Africa		316 736	363 783	298 485	366 918	461 000	Afrique
Americas		29 546	33 935	22 667	29 053	37 580	Amériques
Europe		113 375	130 218	71 363	91 863	121 712	Europe
Asia, East/S.East/Oceania		29 803	34 230	17 297	23 107	39 912	Asie, Est/S.-Est/Océanie
Southern Asia		2 531	2 907	2 863	4 059	8 658	Asie du Sud
Zimbabwe	VFR						Zimbabwe
Total		2 217 429	2 041 202	2 256 205	1 854 488	1 558 501	Total
Africa		1 737 186	1 760 097	1 942 052	1 523 090	1 356 384	Afrique
Americas		111 727	65 194	61 181	75 161	43 976	Amériques
Europe		265 236	149 995	169 938	155 767	112 608	Europe
Asia, East/S.East/Oceania		103 280	65 916	68 414	90 405	38 767	Asie, Est/S.-Est/Océanie
Southern Asia		...	...	12 411	6 316	4 777	Asie du Sud
Western Asia		...	...	2 209	3 749	1 989	Asie occidentale

Source

World Tourism Organization (UNWTO), Madrid, UNWTO statistics database and the "Yearbook of Tourism Statistics", 2006 edition.

Notes

& For a listing of the Member States of the regions of origin, see Annex I, with the following exceptions:

Africa includes the countries and territories listed under Africa in Annex I but excludes Egypt, Guinea-Bissau, Liberia, Libyan Arab Jamahiriya, and Western Sahara.

Americas is as shown in Annex I, but excludes Falkland Islands (Malvinas), Greenland and Saint Pierre and Miquelon.

Europe is as shown in Annex I, but excludes Channel Islands, Faeroe Islands, Holy See, Isle of Man and Svalbard and Jan Mayen Islands. The Europe group also includes Armenia, Azerbaijan, Cyprus, Israel, Kazahkstan, Kyrgyzstan, Tajikistan, Turkey, Turkmenistan and Uzbekistan.

Asia, East and South East/Oceania includes the countries and territories listed under Eastern Asia and South-eastern Asia in Annex I (except for Timor-Leste), and under Oceania except for Christmas Island, Cocos Island, Norfolk Island, Nauru, Wake Island, Johnston Island, Midway Islands, Pitcairn, Tokelau and Wallis and Futuna Islands. The Asia, East and South East/Oceania group also includes Taiwan Province of China.

Southern Asia is as shown in Annex I under South-central Asia, but excludes Kazakhstan, Kyrgyzstan, Tajikistan, Turkmenistan and Uzbekistan.

Western Asia is as shown in Annex I but excludes Armenia, Azerbaijan, Cyprus, Georgia, Israel, Occupied Palestinian Territory, and Turkey. The Western Asia group also includes Egypt and the Libyan Arab Jamahiriya.

TFN: Arrivals of non-resident tourists at national borders (excluding same-day visitors), by nationality.
TFR: Arrivals of non-resident tourists at national borders (excluding same- day visitors), by country of residence.
TCEN: Arrivals of non-resident tourists in all types of accommodation establishments, by nationality.
TCER: Arrivals of non-resident tourists in all types of accommodation establishments, by country of residence.
THSN: Arrivals of non-resident tourists in hotels and similar establishments, by nationality.
THSR: Arrivals of non-resident tourists in hotels and similar establishments, by country of residence.
VFN: Arrivals of non-resident visitors at national borders (including tourists and same-day visitors), by nationality.
VFR: Arrivals of non-resident visitors at national borders (including tourists and same-day visitors), by country of residence.

Footnotes on the totals also apply to the other regions.

1 Arrivals of nationals residing abroad are included in the total and are all accounted for in "region not specified" only.

2 Excluding nationals of the country residing abroad.

3 Air arrivals.

4 Excluding nationals residing abroad and crew members.

5 Including private accommodation.

6 Organized tourism.

7 Hotels establishments, campings, holiday centres, holiday villages and specific categories of accommodation.

Source

Organisation mondiale du tourisme (OMT), Madrid, la base de données de l'OMT, et "l'Annuaire des statistiques du tourisme", 2006 édition.

Notes

& On se reportera à l'Annexe I pour les États Membres classés dans les différentes régions de provenance, avec les exceptions ci-après ;

Afrique – Comprend les États et territoires énumérés à l'Annexe I, sauf l'Égypte, la Guinée-Bissau, le Libéria, la Jamahiriya arabe libyenne, et le Sahara occidental.

Amériques – Comprend les États et territoires énumérés à l'Annexe I, sauf les îles Falkland (Malvinas), le Groënland, et Saint-Pierre-et-Miquelon.

Europe – Comprend les États et territoires énumérés à l'Annexe I, sauf les îles Anglo-normandes, les îles Féroé, l'île de Man, le Saint-Siège et les îles Svalbard et Jan Mayen. Le Groupe comprend en revanche l'Arménie, l'Azerbaïdjan, Chypre, Israël, le Kazakhstan, le Kirghizistan, la Turquie, le Tadjikistan, le Turkménistan, et l'Ouzbékistan.

L'Asie de l'Est et du Sud-Est/Océanie – Comprend les États et territoires énumérés à l'Annexe I dans les Groupes Asie de l'Est et Asie de Sud-Est sauf le Timor-Leste, et les États et territoires énumérés dans le Groupe Océanie sauf les îles Christmas, les îles Cocos, l'île Johnston, les îles Midway, Nauru, l'îles Norfolk, Pitcairn, Tokélou, l'île Wake et Wallis-et-Futuna. Le Groupe Asie de l'Est et du Sud-Est/Océanie comprend en revanche la Province chinoise de Taiwan.

Asie du Sud – Comprend les États et territoires énumérés à l'Annexe I, sauf le Kazakhstan, le Kirghizistan, l'Ouzbékistan, le Tadjikistan et le Turkménistan.

Asie occidentale – Comprend les États et territoires énumérés à l'Annexe I, sauf l'Arménie, l'Azerbaïdjan, Chypre, la Géorgie, Israël, le territoire Palestinien Occupé et la Turquie. Le Groupe comprend en revanche l'Égypte et la Jamahiriya arabe libyenne.

TFN : Arrivées de touristes non résidents aux frontières nationales (a l'exclusion de visiteurs de la journée), par nationalité.
TFR : Arrivées de touristes non résidents aux frontières nationales (a l'exclusion de visiteurs de la journée), par pays de résidence.
TCEN : Arrivées de touristes non résidents dans tous les types d'établissements d'hébergement, par nationalité.
TCER : Arrivées de touristes non résidents dans tous les types d'établissements d'hébergement, par pays de résidence.
THSN : Arrivées de touristes non résidents dans les hôtels et établissements assimilés, par nationalité.
THSR : Arrivées de touristes non résidents dans les hôtels et établissements assimilés, par pays de résidence.
VFN : Arrivées de visiteurs non résidents aux frontières nationales (y compris touristes et visiteurs de la journée), par nationalité.
VFR : Arrivées de visiteurs non résidents aux frontières nationales (y compris touristes et visiteurs de la journée), par pays de résidence.

Les notes de pied en les totales se réfèrent aussi aux autres régions.

1 Les arrivées de nationaux résidant à l'étranger sont comprises dans le total, et sont toutes comptabilisées uniquement dans la catégorie Région non spécifiée.

2 A l'exclusion des nationaux du pays résidant à l'étranger.

3 Arrivées par voie aérienne.

4 A l'exclusion des nationaux du pays résidant à l'étranger et des membres des équipages.

5 Y compris hébergement privé.

6 Tourisme organisé.

7 Établissements hôteliers, terrains de camping, centres de vacances, villages de vacances et catégories spécifiques d'hébergement.

8 Estimates.

9 International tourist arrivals in hotels of regional capitals.

10 Including transit visitors.

11 Excluding children without own passports.

12 Arrivals of nationals residing abroad are included in the total and are also accounted for in the individual regions.

13 Air arrivals at Pochentong and Siem Reap Airports. "Region not specified" 1998 to 2001: including arrivals at Siem Reap Airport by direct-flights; 2000: 87,012; 2001: 133,688.

14 Arrivals in the Phreah Vihear Province are included in the total and are all accounted for in "Region not specified": 2004 - 67,843.

15 Arrivals in the Phreah Vihear Province are included in the total and are all accounted for in "region not specified": 88,615.

16 Different types of methodological changes that affect the estimates for 2000 and 2001 for expenditures and characteristics of International Tourists to Canada, have been introduced in 2002. Therefore, Statistics Canada advises not to compare the estimates for 2000 and 2001 with the years prior because of these methodological changes for the non-count estimates (one of the reasons ALS numbers are not provided).

17 For statistical purposes, the data for China do not include those for the Hong Kong Special Administrative Region (Hong Kong SAR), Macao Special Administrative Region (Macao SAR) and Taiwan Province of China.

18 Including arrivals by sea, land and by air.

19 Source: "Departamento Administrativo de Seguridad (DAS)".

20 Air and sea arrivals.

21 Including arrivals in ports of nautical tourism.

22 New methodology.

23 Excluding the passengers at Herrera airport.

24 Starting from 2004, border statistics are not collected any more.

25 Arrivals through all ports of entry.

26 Due to a change in the methodology, data are not comparable to previous years.

27 Arrivals of non-resident tourists at Libreville airport.

28 Charter tourists only.

29 Information based on administrative data.

30 Estimates for continental Guadeloupe (without Saint-Martin and Saint-Barthelemy).

31 Data based on a survey conducted at Guadeloupe airport.

32 Air arrivals at Conakry airport.

33 Arrivals at "Osvaldo Vieira" Airport.

34 Arrivals to Timehri airport only.

35 Collective accommodation establishments.

36 Departures.

37 Excluding seasonal and border workers.

38 Excluding nationals of the country residing abroad. All data are estimates, projected using 1989 market shares. Source: Economic survey various years.

39 Tarawa and Christmas Island.

40 Tarawa only.

41 Including nationals residing abroad and crew members.

42 New data source: Department of Customs Control.

43 Excluding Syrian nationals, Palestinians and students.

8 Estimations.

9 Arrivées de touristes internationaux dans les hôtels des capitales de département.

10 Y compris les visiteurs en transit.

11 A l'exclusion d'enfants sans passeports personnels.

12 Les arrivées de nationaux résidant à l'étranger sont comprises dans le total, et comptabilisées aussi dans chacune des régions.

13 Arrivées par voie aérienne aux aéroports de Pochentong et de Siem Reap. "Région non spécifiée" 1998 à 2001: y compris les arrivées à l'aéroport de Siem Reap en vols directs; 2000: 87 012; 2001: 133 688.

14 Les arrivées dans la province de Phreah Vihear sont comprises dans le total, et sont toutes prises en compte dans "Région non spécifiée" : 2004 – 67 843.

15 Les arrivées dans la province de Phreah Vihear sont comprises dans le total, et sont toutes prises en compte dans "Région non spécifiée": 88.615.

16 En 2002, il a été adopté différents types de changements méthodologiques qui ont eu des effets sur les estimations des dépenses et des caractéristiques des touristes internationaux ayant visité le Canada en 2000 et 2001. Pour 2000 et 2001, Statistique Canada conseille par conséquent de ne pas comparer les estimations ne reposant pas sur des comptages aux données des années précédentes (c'est une des raisons pour lesquelles les données DMS ne sont pas fournies).

17 Pour la présentation des statistiques, les données pour la Chine ne comprennent pas la Région Administrative Spéciale de Hong Kong (Hong Kong RAS), la Région Administrative Spéciale de Macao (Macao RAS) et la province de Taiwan.

18 Y compris les arrivées par mer, terre et air.

19 Source: "Departamento Administrativo de Seguridad (DAS)".

20 Arrivées par voie aérienne et maritime.

21 Y compris les arrivées dans des ports à tourisme nautique.

22 Nouvelle méthodologie.

23 A l'exclusion des passagers à l'aéroport de Herrera.

24 À partir de 2004, les statistiques de frontière ne sont plus collectées.

25 Arrivées à travers tous les ports d'entrée.

26 Dû à un changement dans la méthodologie, l'information n'est pas comparable à celle des années précédentes.

27 Arrivées de touristes non résidents à l'aéroport de Libreville.

28 Arrivées en vols à la demande seulement.

29 Information tirée de données administratives.

30 Estimations pour la Guadeloupe continentale (sans Saint-Martin et Saint-Barthélemy).

31 Données tirées d'une enquête réalisée à l'aéroport de Guadeloupe.

32 Arrivées par voie aérienne à l'aéroport de Conakry.

33 Arrivées à l'aéroport "Osvaldo Vieira".

34 Arrivées à l'aéroport de Timehri seulement.

35 Etablissements d'hébergement collectif.

36 Départs.

37 A l'exclusion des travailleurs saisoniers et frontaliers.

38 A l'exclusion des nationaux du pays résidant à l'étranger. Toutes les données représentent des estimations, dont la projection a été faite sur la base des taux de marché de l'année 1989. Source: Enquête économique de diverses années.

39 Tarawa et Ile Christmas.

40 Tarawa uniquement.

41 Y compris les nationaux résidant à l'étranger et membres des équipages.

42 Nouvelle source d'information: Département du Contrôle douanier.

43 A l'exclusion des ressortissants syriens, palestiniens et sous-études.

44 Travellers.

45 Including Singapore residents crossing the frontier by road through Johore Causeway.

46 Departures by air and by sea.

47 Arrivals in the States of Kosrae, Chuuk, Pohnpei and Yap.

48 Including tourist arrivals through border entry points to Yangon.

49 Data regarding to short term movements are compiled from a random sample of passenger declarations. Arrivals of nationals residing abroad are included in the total and are also accounted for in the individual regions. Source: Statistics New Zealand, External Migration.

50 Including Niuans residing usually in New Zealand.

51 Figures are based on "The Guest survey" carried out by "Institute of Transport Economics".

52 Arrivals to the West Bank only; excluding Jerusalem and the Gaza Strip due to the lack of control on the borders of these regions.

53 Air arrivals (Palau International Airport).

54 Total number of visitors broken down by permanent residence who arrived in Panama at Tocumen International Airport.

55 E/D cards in the "Silvio Petirossi" airport and passenger counts at the national border crossings - National Police and SENATUR.

56 From 2002, new estimated series including tourists with identity document other than a passport.

57 Preliminary estimates.

58 Including arrivals from abroad to insular possessions of Madeira and the Azores.

59 Arrivals by air. Fiscal year July to June. Source: "Junta de Planificación de Puerto Rico".

60 Arrivals in hotels only.

61 Visitors who enjoyed the services of the economic agents officially registered under tourism activity and accommodation (excluding the regions of the left bank of the Dniestr and the municipality of Bender).

62 January-November.

63 Excluding Netherlands Antillean residents.

64 Arrivals at Princess Juliana International airport. Including visitors to St. Maarten (the French side of the island).

65 Including Italian visitors.

66 Excluding Malaysian citizens arriving by land.

67 Without 1st quarter.

68 Excluding arrivals by work and contract workers.

69 Arrivals at Zanderij Airport.

70 Data according to IBIS-Survey (Incoming Visitors to Sweden) during the years 2001 to 2003, (no data collected before 2001 or after 2003). Source: Swedish Tourist Authority and Statistics Sweden.

71 Hotels, motels and inns.

72 Hotels and health establishments.

73 Data source: The survey of Incoming Tourism in 2002 and 2004.

74 Excluding private accommodation.

75 Domestic tourism and arrivals of nationals residing abroad are included in the total and are all accounted for in "Region not specified" only.

44 Voyaeurs.

45 Y compris les résidents de Singapour traversant la frontière par voie terrestre à travers le Johore Causeway.

46 Départs par voies aérienne et maritime.

47 Arrivées dans les États de Kosrae, Chuuk, Pohnpei et Yap.

48 Comprenant les arrivées de touristes aux postes-frontières de Yangon.

49 Les données relatives aux mouvements de courte durée sont obtenues à partir d'un échantillon aléatoire de déclarations des passagers. Les arrivées de nationaux résidant à l'étranger sont comprises dans le total, et comptabilisées aussi dans chacune des régions. Source : Statistiques de la Nouvelle Zélande, Immigration.

50 Y compris les nationaux de Niue résidant habituellement en Nouvelle-Zélande.

51 Les chiffres se fondent sur "l'enquête auprès de la clientèle" de l'Institut d'économie des transports.

52 Uniquement arrivées en Cisjordanie; Jérusalem et la bande de Gaza sont exclus en raison du manque de contrôle aux frontières dans ces zones.

53 Arrivées par voie aérienne (Aéroport international de Palau).

54 Nombre total de visiteurs arrivées au Panama par l'aéroport international de Tocúmen.

55 Cartes d'embarquement et de débarquement à l'aéroport Silvio Petirossi et comptages des passagers lors du franchissement des frontières nationales – Police Nationale et SENATUR.

56 À partir de 2002, nouvelle série estimée comprenant les touristes avec une pièce d'identité autre qu'un passeport.

57 Estimations préliminaires.

58 Y compris les arrivées en provenance de l'étranger aux possessions insulaires de Madère et des Açores.

59 Arrivées par voie aérienne. Année fiscale de juillet à juin. Source: "Junta de Planificación de Puerto Rico".

60 Arrivées dans les hôtels uniquement.

61 Visiteurs qui ont bénéficié des services des agents économiques officiellement enregistrés avec le type d'activité tourisme et des unités d'hébergement qui leur appartiennent (à l'exception des régions de la partie gauche du Dniestr et de la municipalité de Bender).

62 Janvier-novembre.

63 A l'exclusion des résidents des Antilles Néerlandaises.

64 Arrivées à l'aéroport international "Princess Juliana". Y compris les visiteurs à Saint-Martin (partie française de l'île).

65 Y compris les visiteurs italiens.

66 Non compris les arrivées de malaysiens par voie terrestre.

67 À l'exclusion du 1er trimestre.

68 À l'exclusion des arrivées par travail et les travailleurs contractuels.

69 Arrivées à l'aéroport de Zanderij.

70 Données reposant sur l'enquête IBIS (auprès des visiteurs du tourisme récepteur) portant sur les années 2001 à 2003 (aucune donnée n'a été collectée avant 2001 ni après 2003). Source: "Swedish Tourist Authority" et "Statistics Sweden".

71 Hôtels, motels et auberges.

72 Hôtels et établissements de cure.

73 Source des données: enquête du tourisme récepteur en 2002 et 2004.

74 À l'exclusion de l'hébergement chez des particuliers.

75 Les touristes nationaux et les arrivées de nationaux résidant à l'étranger sont compris dans le total, et sont tous pris en compte uniquement dans "Région non spécifiée" seulement.

Tourist/visitor arrivals and tourism expenditure

Arrivées de touristes/visiteurs et dépenses touristiques

Country or area Pays ou zone	Number of tourist/visitor arrivals (thousands) Nombre d'arrivées de touristes/visiteurs (milliers) 2001	2002	2003	2004	2005	Tourism expenditure (million US dollars)[t] Dépenses touristiques (millions de dollars E.U.)[t] 2001	2002	2003	2004	2005
Albania Albanie	34[1]	36[1]	41[1]	42[1]	46[1]	451	492	537	756	880
Algeria Algérie	901[2,3]	988[2,3]	1 166[2,3]	1 234[2,3]	1 443[2,3]	100[4]	110[4]	112[4]	178[4]	184[4]
American Samoa[5] Samoa américaines[5]	36	...	...	...	24	...	...	...	...	...
Andorra[5] Andorre[5]	3 516	3 387	3 138	2 791	2 418	...	...	...	...	...
Angola Angola	67[5]	91[5]	107[5]	194[5]	210[5]	36	51	63	82	103
Anguilla Anguilla	48[5,6]	44[5,6]	47[5,6]	54[5,6]	62[5,6]	62[7]	57[7]	60[7]	69[7]	86[7]
Antigua and Barbuda Antigua-et-Barbuda	215[5,6]	218[5,6]	239[5,6]	268[5,6]	261[5,6]	272[7]	274[7]	300[7]	338[7]	327[7]
Argentina Argentine	2 620[5]	2 820[5]	2 995[5]	*3 457[5,8]	*3 895[5,8]	2 756	1 716	2 306	2 662	3 241
Armenia Arménie	123[5]	162[5]	206[5]	263[5]	319[5]	81	82	90	103	161
Aruba Aruba	691[5]	643[5]	642[5]	728[5]	733[5]	825	831	858	1 052[7]	1 096[7]
Australia Australie	4 435[5,9]	4 420[5,9]	4 354[5,9]	4 774[5,9]	5 020[5,9]	12 376	13 030	15 510	18 908	20 637
Austria Autriche	18 180[10]	18 611[10]	19 078[10]	19 373[10]	19 952[10]	12 033	13 046	16 342	18 385	19 310
Azerbaijan Azerbaïdjan	767[5]	834[5]	1 014[5]	1 349[5]	1 177[5]	57	63	70	79	100
Bahamas Bahamas	1 538[5]	1 513[5]	1 510[5]	1 561[5]	1 608[5]	1 665	1 773	1 770	1 897	2 079
Bahrain Bahreïn	2 789[5]	3 167[5]	2 955[5]	3 514[5]	3 914[5]	886	986	1 206	1 504	1 603
Bangladesh Bangladesh	207[5]	207[5]	245[5]	271[5]	208[5]	48[7]	59	59	76	78
Barbados Barbade	507[5]	498[5]	531[5]	552[5]	548[5]	706	666	767	785	905
Belarus Bélarus	61[5,11]	63[5,11]	64[5,11]	67[5,11]	91[5,11]	273	295	339	362	346
Belgium Belgique	6 452[10]	6 720[10]	6 690[10]	6 710[10]	6 747[10]	8 304	7 598	8 848	10 091	10 879
Belize Belize	196[5]	200[5]	221[5]	231[5]	237[5]	111[7]	122[7]	150[7]	168[7]	204[7]
Benin Bénin	88[5]	72[5]	175[5,12]	174[5,12]	176[5,12]	86	95	108	122	...
Bermuda Bermudes	278[5,9]	284[5,9]	257[5,9]	272[5,9]	270[5,9]	351[4]	378[4]	342[4]	354[4]	393[4]
Bhutan Bhoutan	6[5]	6[5]	6[5]	9[5]	14[5]	9[4]	8[4]	8[4]	13[4]	19[4]
Bolivia Bolivie	316[5]	334[5]	420[5]	478[5]	504[5]	119	144	244	283	346
Bonaire Bonaire	50[5]	52[5]	62[5]	63[5]	63[5]	64[7,13]	65[7,13]	84[7,13]	84[7,13]	85[7,13]
Bosnia and Herzegovina Bosnie-Herzégovine	139[10]	160[10]	165[10]	190[10]	217[10]	279	307	404	543	604
Botswana Botswana	1 193[5]	1 274[5]	1 406[5]	1 523[5]	1 675[5]	235	324	459	550	563

Country or area Pays ou zone	Number of tourist/visitor arrivals (thousands) Nombre d'arrivées de touristes/visiteurs (milliers)					Tourism expenditure (million US dollars)[t] Dépenses touristiques (millions de dollars E.U.)[t]				
	2001	2002	2003	2004	2005	2001	2002	2003	2004	2005
Brazil Brésil	4 773[5]	3 785[5]	4 133[5]	4 794[5]	5 358[5]	1 845	2 142	2 673	3 389	4 169
British Virgin Islands Iles Vierges britanniques	296[5]	282[5]	318[5]	304[5]	337[5]	401[4]	345[4]	342[4]	393[4]	437[4]
Brunei Darussalam[3] Brunéi Darussalam[3]	840	...	...	...	815	...	...	...	...	...
Bulgaria Bulgarie	3 186[5,14]	3 433[5,14]	4 048[5,14]	4 630[5,14]	4 837[5,14]	1 262	1 392	2 051	2 797	3 026
Burkina Faso Burkina Faso	128[15]	150[15]	163[15]	222[15]	245[15]	25	...	...	...	...
Burundi Burundi	36[2,5]	74[2,5]	74[2,5]	133[2,5]	148[2,5]	1	2	1	2	2
Cambodia Cambodge	605[5]	787[5]	701[5]	1 055[5]	1 422[5]	429	509	441	674	927
Cameroon Cameroun	221[15]	226[15]	...	190[15]	176[15]	182	124	162	...	...
Canada Canada	19 679[5,16]	20 057[5,16]	17 534[5,16]	19 095[5,16]	18 770[5,16]	12 680	12 744	12 236	14 953	15 830
Cape Verde Cap-Vert	134[15]	126[15]	150[15]	157[15]	198[15]	77	101	137	164	177
Cayman Islands Iles Caïmanes	334[5,9]	303[5,9]	294[5,9]	260[5,9]	168[5,9]	585[4]	607[4]	518[4]	519[4]	353[4]
Central African Rep. Rép. centrafricaine	10[5,17]	3[5,17]	6[5,17]	8[5,17]	12[5,17]	5[18]	3[18]	4[4,18]	4[4,18]	...
Chad Tchad	57[15]	32[15]	21[15]	26[15]	29[15]	23[18]	25[18]	...	...	...
Chile Chili	1 723[5]	1 412[5]	1 614[5]	1 785[5]	2 027[5]	1 184	1 221	1 310	1 626	1 779
China[19] Chine[19]	33 167[5]	36 803[5]	32 970[5]	41 761[5]	46 809[5]	19 006	21 742	18 708	27 755	31 842
China, Hong Kong SAR Chine, Hong Kong RAS	8 878[5]	10 689[5]	9 676[5]	13 655[5]	14 773[5]	7 924[20]	9 850[20]	9 020[20]	11 893[20]	13 586[20]
China, Macao SAR Chine, Macao RAS	5 842[5,12]	6 565[5,12]	6 309[5,12]	8 324[5,12]	9 014[5,12]	3 745[20]	4 440[20]	5 303[20]	7 344[20]	7 757[20]
Colombia Colombie	616[3]	567[3]	625[3]	791[3]	933[3]	1 483	1 237	1 191	1 366	1 570
Comoros Comores	19[5,9]	19[5,9]	14[5,9]	18[5,9]	20[5,9]	9[4]	10[4]	11[4]	13[4]	14[4]
Congo Congo	27[15]	22[15]	...	...	...	23	26	30	23	34[7]
Cook Islands Iles Cook	75[5]	73[5]	78[5]	83[5]	88[5]	38[4]	46[4]	69[4]	72[4]	92[4]
Costa Rica Costa Rica	1 131[5]	1 113[5]	1 239[5]	1 453[5]	1 679[5]	1 339	1 292	1 424	1 586	1 804
Côte d'Ivoire Côte d'Ivoire	...	...	...	...	...	58	56	76	91	83[7]
Croatia Croatie	6 544[10]	6 944[10]	7 409[10]	7 912[10]	8 467[10]	3 463	3 953	6 514	6 945	7 625
Cuba Cuba	1 736[5,9]	1 656[5,9]	1 847[5,9]	2 017[5,9]	2 261[5,9]	1 692[4]	1 633[4]	1 846[4]	1 915[4]	1 920[4]
Curaçao Curaçao	205[5,9]	218[5,9]	221[5,9]	223[5,9]	222[5,9]	271[4]	290[4]	286[4]	296[4]	284[4]
Cyprus Chypre	2 697[5]	2 418[5]	2 303[5]	2 349[5]	2 470[5]	2 203	2 146	2 325	2 550	2 644
Czech Republic République tchèque	5 405[10]	4 743[10]	5 076[10]	6 061[10]	6 336[10]	3 106[7]	3 376	4 069	4 960	5 580
Dem. Rep. of the Congo[5] Rép. dém. du Congo[5]	55	28[9]	35[9]	36[9]	61[9]	...	...	...	...	...

Country or area Pays ou zone	Number of tourist/visitor arrivals (thousands) Nombre d'arrivées de touristes/visiteurs (milliers)					Tourism expenditure (million US dollars)[t] Dépenses touristiques (millions de dollars E.U.)[t]				
	2001	2002	2003	2004	2005	2001	2002	2003	2004	2005
Denmark Danemark	3 684[10]	3 436[10]	3 474[10]	4 421[21]	4 699[21]	4 003[7]	4 750[7]	5 258[7]	5 671[7]	4 493[7]
Djibouti Djibouti	22[15]	23[15]	23[15]	26[15]	30[15]	...	...	7[7,22]	7[7,22]	7[7,22]
Dominica Dominique	66[5]	69[5]	73[5]	80[5]	79[5]	46[7]	46[7]	52[7]	61[7]	56[7]
Dominican Republic Rép. dominicaine	2 882[5,23]	2 811[5,23]	3 282[5,23]	3 450[5,23]	3 691[5,23]	2 798[7]	2 730[7]	3 128[7]	3 152[7]	3 508[7]
Ecuador Equateur	641[3,6]	683[3,6]	761[3,6]	819[3,6]	861[3,6]	438	449	408	464	488
Egypt Egypte	4 357[5]	4 906[5]	5 746[5]	7 795[5]	8 244[5]	4 119	4 133	4 704	6 328	7 206
El Salvador El Salvador	735[5,6]	951[5,6]	857[5,6]	966[5,6]	1 154[5,6]	452	521	664	736	838
Equatorial Guinea[18] Guinée équatoriale[18]	...	...	...	...	...	14	...	...	...	...
Eritrea Erythrée	113[2,3]	101[2,3]	80[2,3]	87[2,3]	83[2,3]	74[4]	73[4]	74[4]	73[4]	66[4]
Estonia Estonie	1 320[5,24]	1 362[5,24]	1 462[5,24]	1 750[5,25]	1 900[5,25]	661	737	883	1 111	1 207
Ethiopia Ethiopie	148[5,26]	156[5,26]	180[5,26]	184[5,26]	227[5,26]	218	261	336	458	533
Fiji Fidji	348[5,6]	398[5,6]	431[5,6]	503[5,6]	550[5,6]	197[4,7]	254[4,7]	487[4]	581[4]	670[4]
Finland Finlande	2 826[5]	2 875[5]	2 601[5]	2 840[5]	3 140[5]	2 066	2 242	2 677	2 976	3 055
France France	75 202[5,27]	77 012[5,27]	75 048[5,27]	75 121[5,27]	76 001[5,27]	30 363[7]	32 437[7]	36 617[7]	40 693[7]	42 167[7]
French Guiana Guyane française	65[5]	65[5]	...	...	95[5,28]	42[4]	45[4]	...	...	45[4]
French Polynesia Polynésie française	228[5,6]	189[5,6]	213[5,6]	212[5,6]	208[5,6]	...	471	651	737	779
Gabon Gabon	169[5,29]	208[5,29]	222[5,29]	...	...	46	77	84	74	...
Gambia Gambie	57[5,30]	81[5,30]	73[5,30]	90[5,30]	111[5,30]	...	...	58	51	57
Georgia Géorgie	302[5]	298[5]	313[5]	368[5]	560[5]	136	144	172	209	288
Germany Allemagne	17 861[10]	17 969[10]	18 399[10]	20 137[10]	21 500[10]	24 175	26 690	30 154	35 616	38 381
Ghana Ghana	439[2,5]	483[2,5]	531[2,5]	584[2,5]	429[2,5]	374	383	441	495	827
Greece Grèce	14 057[5,31]	14 180[5,31]	13 969[5,31]	13 313[5,31]	14 276[5,31]	9 216	10 005	10 842	12 809	13 697
Grenada Grenade	123[5]	132[5]	142[5]	134[5]	99[5]	83[7]	91[7]	104[7]	83[7]	71[7]
Guadeloupe Guadeloupe	521[32]	...	439[32,33]	456[32,33]	456[32,34]	...	...	...	...	246[4]
Guam[5] Guam[5]	1 159	1 059	910	1 160	1 228	...	...	...	...	...
Guatemala Guatemala	835[5]	884[5]	880[5]	1 182[5]	1 316[5]	588	647	646	806	883
Guinea Guinée	38[5]	43[5]	44[5,35]	45[5]	45[5,35]	22	43[7,20]	32	30[7,20]	...
Guinea-Bissau Guinée-Bissau	8[5,9]	...	...	...	5[5,9]	3[7]	2[7]	3	2	...
Guyana Guyana	99[5]	104[5,36]	101[5,36]	122[5,36]	117[5,36]	65	53	28	29	37

Country or area / Pays ou zone	Number of tourist/visitor arrivals (thousands) / Nombre d'arrivées de touristes/visiteurs (milliers)					Tourism expenditure (million US dollars)[t] / Dépenses touristiques (millions de dollars E.U.)[t]				
	2001	2002	2003	2004	2005	2001	2002	2003	2004	2005
Haiti / Haïti	142	140	136	96	112	105[7]	112[7]	93[7]	87[7]	110[7]
Honduras / Honduras	518[5]	550[5]	611[5]	641[5]	673[5]	260	305	358	435	476
Hungary / Hongrie	3 070[10]	3 013[10]	2 948[10]	3 270[10]	3 446[10]	4 191	3 774	4 119	4 129	4 581
Iceland / Islande	672[10]	705[10]	771[10]	836[10]	871[10]	383	415	486	558	631
India / Inde	2 537[5,6]	2 384[5,6]	2 726[5,6]	3 457[5,6]	3 919[5,6]	3 497	3 476	4 128	…	…
Indonesia / Indonésie	5 153[5]	5 033[5]	4 467[5]	5 321[5]	5 002[5]	5 277[7]	5 797	4 461	5 226	5 092
Iran (Islamic Rep. of) / Iran (Rép. islamique d')	1 402[5]	1 585[5]	1 546[5]	1 659[5]	…	1 122[37]	1 607[37]	1 266[37]	1 305[37]	1 329[37]
Iraq / Iraq	127	…	…	…	…	15[7,38]	45[7,38]	…	…	…
Ireland / Irlande	6 353[5,39]	6 476[5,39]	6 764[5,39]	6 953[5,39]	7 333[5,39]	3 789	4 229	5 206	6 075	6 722
Israel / Israël	1 196[5,6]	862[5,6]	1 063[5,6]	1 506[5,6]	1 903[5,6]	2 769	2 325	2 401	2 813	3 414
Italy / Italie	39 563[5,40]	39 799[5,40]	39 604[5,40]	37 071[5,40]	36 513[5,40]	26 916	28 192	32 592	37 872	38 264
Jamaica / Jamaïque	1 277[5,41]	1 266[5,41]	1 350[5,41]	1 415[5,41]	1 479[5,41]	1 494	1 482	1 621	1 733	1 783
Japan / Japon	4 772[5,6]	5 239[5,6]	5 212[5,6]	6 138[5,6]	6 728[5,6]	5 750	6 069	11 475	14 343	15 555
Jordan / Jordanie	1 672[2,5]	2 384[2,5]	2 353[2,5]	2 853[2,5]	2 987[2,5]	884	1 254	1 266	1 621	1 759
Kazakhstan / Kazakhstan	1 845[5]	2 832[5]	2 410[5]	3 073[5]	3 143[5]	502	680	638	803	809
Kenya / Kenya	828[5]	825[5]	927[5]	1 193[5]	1 536[5]	536	513	619	799	969
Kiribati / Kiribati	5[5,42]	5[5,42]	5[5,42]	4[5,43]	3[5,43]	3[4]	…	…	…	…
Korea, Republic of / Corée, République de	5 147[3,44]	5 347[3,44]	4 753[3,44]	5 818[3,44]	6 023[3,44]	7 919	7 621	7 005	8 226	8 148
Kuwait / Koweït	2 072[3]	2 316[3]	2 602[3]	3 056[3]	…	285	322	330	413	408
Kyrgyzstan / Kirghizistan	99[5]	140[5]	342[5,45]	398[5,45]	315[5,45]	32	53	65	97	94
Lao People's Dem. Rep. / Rép. dém. pop. lao	173[5]	215[5]	196[5]	407[5]	672[5]	104[7]	113[4,7]	87[4,7]	119[4,7]	146[4,7]
Latvia / Lettonie	591[5,46]	848[5,46]	971[5,46]	1 079[5,46]	1 116[5,46]	154	200	271	343	446
Lebanon / Liban	837[5,47]	956[5,47]	1 016[5,47]	1 278[5,47]	1 140[5,47]	837[4,48]	4 284[7]	6 782	5 931	5 869
Lesotho / Lesotho	295[3]	287[3]	329[3]	304[3]	304[3]	23[7]	20[7]	28[7]	34[7]	30[7]
Libyan Arab Jamah. / Jamah. arabe libyenne	169[5]	135[5]	142[5]	149[5]	…	90	202	243	261	301
Liechtenstein[15] / Liechtenstein[15]	56	49	49	49	50	…	…	…	…	…
Lithuania / Lituanie	1 271[5]	1 428[5]	1 491[5]	1 800[5]	2 000[5]	425	556	700	834	975
Luxembourg / Luxembourg	836[10]	885[10]	867[10]	878[10]	913[10]	1 780[7]	2 547	3 149	3 883	…
Madagascar / Madagascar	170[5,9]	62[5,9]	139[5,9]	229[5,9]	277[5,9]	149	62	69	84	98

Country or area Pays ou zone	Number of tourist/visitor arrivals (thousands) Nombre d'arrivées de touristes/visiteurs (milliers)					Tourism expenditure (million US dollars)[t] Dépenses touristiques (millions de dollars E.U.)[t]				
	2001	2002	2003	2004	2005	2001	2002	2003	2004	2005
Malawi Malawi	266[5,49]	383[5,49]	424[5,49]	427[5,49]	438[5,49]	40	39[50]	35[50]	36[50]	36[50]
Malaysia Malaisie	12 775[5,51]	13 292[5,51]	10 577[5,51]	15 703[5,51]	16 431[5,51]	7 627	8 084	6 799	9 181	10 389
Maldives Maldives	461[5,9]	485[5,9]	564[5,9]	617[5,9]	395[5,9]	327[7]	337[7]	402[7]	471[7]	287[7]
Mali Mali	89[9,15]	96[9,15]	110[9,15]	113[9,15]	143[9,15]	91	105	136	142	149
Malta Malte	1 180[5]	1 134[5]	1 127[5]	1 156[5,52]	1 171[5,52]	704	757	869	953	923
Marshall Islands Iles Marshall	5[5,9]	6[5,9]	7[5,9]	9[5,53]	9[5,53]	4[4]	4[4]	...	...	...
Martinique Martinique	460[5]	447[5]	453[5]	471[5]	484[5]	245[4]	237[4]	247[4]	291[4]	280[4]
Mauritius Maurice	660[5]	682[5]	702[5]	719[5]	761[5]	820	829	960	1 156	1 189
Mexico Mexique	19 810[2,5]	19 667[2,5]	18 665[2,5]	20 618[2,5]	21 915[2,5]	9 190	9 547	10 058	11 609	12 801
Micronesia (Fed. States of) Micronésie (Etats féd. de)	15[5,54]	19[5,54]	18[5,54]	19[5,54]	19[5,54]	15[4]	17[4]	17[4]	17[4]	17[4]
Monaco[15] Monaco[15]	270	263	235	250	286	...	...	...	...	...
Mongolia Mongolie	166[5,55]	229[5,55]	201[5,55]	301[5,55]	338[5,55]	49	143	154	205	223
Montserrat Montserrat	10[5]	10[5]	8[5]	10[5]	10[5]	8[7]	9[7]	7[7]	9[7]	9[7]
Morocco Maroc	4 380[2,5]	4 453[2,5]	4 761[2,5]	5 477[2,5]	5 843[2,5]	2 966	3 157	3 802	4 541	5 426
Mozambique Mozambique	323[5]	541[5]	441[5]	470[5]	578[5]	64[7]	65	106	96	138
Myanmar Myanmar	205[5,56]	217[5,56]	206[5,56]	242[5,56]	232[5,56]	132	136	70	98	...
Namibia Namibie	670[5]	757[5]	695[5]	...	778[5]	264	251	383	426	348[7]
Nepal Népal	361[5,57]	275[5,57]	338[5,57]	385[5,57]	375[5,57]	191	135	233	260	160
Netherlands Pays-Bas	9 500[10]	9 595[10]	9 181[10]	9 646[10]	10 012[10]	11 147	11 745	9 164[7]	10 311[7]	10 383[7]
New Caledonia Nouvelle-Calédonie	101[2,5]	104[2,5]	102[2,5]	100[2,5]	101[2,5]	94[4,7]	156[7]	196[7]	241[7]	253[7]
New Zealand Nouvelle-Zélande	1 909[3]	2 045[3]	2 104[3]	2 334[3]	2 365[3]	2 350[7]	3 077[7]	4 030[7]	4 771[7]	4 984[7]
Nicaragua Nicaragua	483[5]	472[5]	526[5]	615[5]	712[5]	138	138	164	196	211
Niger Niger	52[5]	39[5]	55[5]	57[5]	63[5]	30[7]	20[7]	29	32	34[4,7]
Nigeria Nigéria	850[5]	887[5]	924[5]	962[5]	1 010[5]	168	256	58	49	46
Niue Nioué	1[5,58]	2[5,58]	3[5,58]	3[5,58]	3[5,58]	...	...	...	...	1[4]
Northern Mariana Islands[5,9] Iles Mariannes du Nord[5,9]	438	466	452	525	498	...	...	...	...	...
Norway Norvège	3 073[5,59]	3 111[5,59]	3 269[5,59]	3 628[5,59]	3 859[5,59]	2 380	2 581	2 989	3 455	3 884
Occupied Palestinian Terr. Terr. palestinien occupé	43[15]	33[15]	37[15]	56[15]	88[15]	35[7,60]	33[7,60]	107[7,60]	56[7,60]	...
Oman Oman	829[5,61]	817[5,61]	1 039[5,61]	1 195[5,61]	...	539	539	546	604	679

Country or area Pays ou zone	Number of tourist/visitor arrivals (thousands) Nombre d'arrivées de touristes/visiteurs (milliers)					Tourism expenditure (million US dollars)[t] Dépenses touristiques (millions de dollars E.U.)[t]				
	2001	2002	2003	2004	2005	2001	2002	2003	2004	2005
Pakistan Pakistan	500[5]	498[5]	501[5]	648[5]	798[5]	533	562	620	765	827
Palau Palaos	54[5,62]	59[5,62]	68[5,62]	95[5,62]	86[5,62]	59[4]	47[4]	76[4]	97[4]	...
Panama Panama	519[5]	534[5]	566[5]	621[5]	702[5]	665	710	804	903	1 108
Papua New Guinea Papouasie-Nvl-Guinée	54[5]	54[5]	56[5]	59[5]	69[5]	5[7]	3[7]	4[7]	6	4
Paraguay Paraguay	279[5,63]	250[5,63]	268[5,63]	309[5,63]	341[5,63]	91	76	81	87	96
Peru Pérou	901[5,64]	998[5,64]	1 070[5,64]	1 277[5,64]	1 486[5,64]	763	863	1 001	1 169	1 371
Philippines Philippines	1 797[2,5]	1 933[2,5]	1 907[2,5]	2 291[2,5]	2 623[2,5]	2 011	2 018	1 821	2 390	2 620
Poland Pologne	15 000[5]	13 980[5]	13 720[5]	14 290[5]	15 200[5]	5 121	4 971	4 733	6 499	7 127
Portugal Portugal	12 167[5,65]	11 644[5,65]	11 707[5,65]	11 617[5,65]	...	6 236	6 595	7 607	8 991	9 222
Puerto Rico Porto Rico	3 551[5,66]	3 087[5,66]	3 238[5,66]	3 541[5,66]	3 686[5,66]	2 728[4,67]	2 486[4,67]	2 677[4,67]	3 024[4,67]	3 239[4,67]
Qatar Qatar	376[15,33]	587[15,33]	557[15,33]	732[15,33]	913[15,33]	272[7,68]	285[7,68]	369[7,68]	498[7,68]	760[7,68]
Republic of Moldova République de Moldova	16[5,69]	18[5,69]	21[5,69]	24[5,69]	23[5,69]	58	72	83	134	163
Réunion Réunion	424[5]	426[5]	432[5]	430[5]	409[5]	281[4]	329[4]	413[4]	448[4]	384[4]
Romania Roumanie	4 938[3]	4 794[3]	5 595[3]	6 600[3]	5 839[3]	419	400	523	607	1 310
Russian Federation Fédération de Russie	19 457[5]	21 279[5]	20 443[5]	19 892[5]	19 940[5]	4 726	5 429	5 879	6 958	7 402
Rwanda Rwanda	113[5,70]	...	...	...	...	29	31[7]	30[7]	44[7]	49[7]
Saba[5] Saba[5]	9	11	10	11	11	...	...	...	...	...
Saint Eustatius[5,71] Saint-Eustache[5,71]	10	10	10	11	10	...	...	...	...	...
Saint Kitts and Nevis Saint-Kitts-et-Nevis	71[5,9]	69[5,9]	91[5,9]	118[5,9]	127[5,9]	62[7]	57[7]	75[7]	103[7]	107[7]
Saint Lucia Sainte-Lucie	250[5,6]	253[5,6]	277[5,6]	298[5,6]	318[5,6]	233[7]	210[7]	282[7]	326[7]	345[7]
Saint Maarten Saint-Martin	403[5,72]	381[5,72]	428[5,72]	475[5,72]	462[5,72]	484[73]	489[73]	538[73]	613[73]	619[73]
Saint Vincent-Grenadines Saint Vincent-Grenadines	71[5,9]	78[5,9]	79[5,9]	87[5,9]	96[5,9]	89[7]	91[7]	91[7]	96[7]	105[7]
Samoa Samoa	88[5]	89[5]	92[5]	98[5]	102[5]	39[4,7]	45[4,7]	54[4,7]	71	78
San Marino[15,74] Saint-Marin[15,74]	49	46	41	42	50	...	...	...	...	...
Sao Tome and Principe Sao Tomé-et-Principe	8[5]	9[5]	10[5]	11[5]	11[5]	10[7]	10[7]	...	...	...
Saudi Arabia Arabie saoudite	6 727[5]	7 511[5]	7 332[5]	8 599[5]	8 037[5]	...	...	3 418[4]	6 486[4]	5 181[4]
Senegal Sénégal	396[15]	427[15]	354[15]	363[15]	387[15]	175	210	269	287	...
Serbia and Montenegro Serbie-et-Monténégro	351[10]	448[10]	481[10]	580[10]	725[10]	54[4,7]	97[4,7]	201[4,7]	...	...
Seychelles Seychelles	130[5]	132[5]	122[5]	121[5]	129[5]	221	247	259	256	269

Tourist/visitor arrivals and tourism expenditure (*continued*)
Arrivées de touristes/visiteurs et dépenses touristiques (*suite*)

Country or area Pays ou zone	Number of tourist/visitor arrivals (thousands) Nombre d'arrivées de touristes/visiteurs (milliers)					Tourism expenditure (million US dollars)[t] Dépenses touristiques (millions de dollars E.U.)[t]				
	2001	2002	2003	2004	2005	2001	2002	2003	2004	2005
Sierra Leone Sierra Leone	24[5,9]	28[5,9]	38[5,9]	44[5,9]	40[5,9]	14[7]	38[7]	60[7]	58[7]	64[7]
Singapore Singapour	5 857[5]	5 855[5]	4 703[5]	6 553[5]	7 080[5]	4 619[7]	4 428[7]	3 783[7]	5 224[7]	5 736[7]
Slovakia Slovaquie	1 219[10]	1 399[10]	1 387[10]	1 401[10]	1 515[10]	649[4]	742	876	932[4]	1 210[4,7]
Slovenia Slovénie	1 219[10]	1 302[10]	1 373[10]	1 499[10]	1 555[10]	1 059	1 152	1 427	1 726	1 894
Solomon Islands Iles Salomon	...	...	7[5]	...	9[5,75]	5[7,76]	1[7,76]	2[7,76]	4[7,76]	2[7,76]
South Africa Afrique du Sud	5 787[5,77]	6 430[5,77]	6 505[5,77]	6 678[5,77]	7 369[5,77]	3 256	3 696	6 533	7 380	8 448
Spain Espagne	50 094[5]	52 327[5]	50 854[5]	52 430[5]	55 914[5]	33 829	35 469	43 863	49 996	52 960
Sri Lanka Sri Lanka	337[5,6]	393[5,6]	501[5,6]	566[5,6]	549[5,6]	347	594	709	808	729
Sudan Soudan	50[5]	52[5]	52[5]	61[5]	246[2,5]	3[7]	108[7]	18[7]	21[7]	89[7]
Suriname Suriname	54[5,78]	60[5,78]	82[5,78]	138[5]	160[5]	26	17	18	52	96
Swaziland Swaziland	283[15,33]	256[15,33]	461[15]	459[15]	839[15]	32	68	113	54	69
Sweden Suède	7 431[5,79]	7 458[5,79]	7 627[5,79]	...	...	5 200	5 671	6 548	7 649	8 584
Switzerland Suisse	7 455[15]	6 868[15]	6 530[15]	...	7 229[15]	10 013	9 742	11 048	12 351	12 961
Syrian Arab Republic Rép. arabe syrienne	1 801[5]	2 186[5]	2 085[5]	3 033[5]	3 368[5]	1 150[7]	970[7]	877	1 888	2 283
Tajikistan Tadjikistan	4[5]	...	...	...	...	...	5	7	9	10
Thailand Thaïlande	10 133[2,5]	10 873[2,5]	10 082[2,5]	11 737[2,5]	11 567[2,5]	9 380	10 388	10 456	13 054	12 629
TFYR of Macedonia L'ex-R.y. Macédoine	99[10]	123[10]	158[10]	165[10]	197[10]	49	55	65	77	92
Togo Togo	57[15]	58[15]	61[15]	83[15]	81[15]	14	16	26	25	...
Tonga Tonga	32[5,9]	37[5,9]	40[5,9]	41[5,9]	42[5,9]	7[7,80]	8[7,80]	14[7,80]	15[7,80]	11[7,80]
Trinidad and Tobago Trinité-et-Tobago	383[5,9]	384[5,9]	409[5,9]	443[5,9]	463[5,9]	361	402	437	568	661[4]
Tunisia Tunisie	5 387[5,6]	5 064[5,6]	5 114[5,6]	5 998[5,6]	6 378[5,6]	2 061	1 832	1 935	2 432	2 782
Turkey Turquie	10 783[5]	12 790[5]	13 341[5]	16 826[5]	20 273[5]	10 067[81]	11 901[81]	13 203[7,82]	15 888[7,82]	18 152[7,82]
Turkmenistan[5] Turkménistan[5]	5	11	8	15	12	...	...	...	...	...
Turks and Caicos Islands Iles Turques et Caïques	166[5]	155[5]	164[5]	173[5]	200[5]	311[4]	292[4]	...	...	...
Tuvalu[5] Tuvalu[5]	1	1	1	1	1	...	...	...	...	...
Uganda Ouganda	205[5]	254[5]	305[5]	512[5]	468[5]	187	195	185	257	357
Ukraine Ukraine	9 174[5]	10 517[5]	12 514[5]	15 629[5]	...	759	1 001	1 204	2 931	3 542
United Arab Emirates Emirats arabes unis	4 134[15,83]	5 445[15,83]	5 871[15,83]	...	...	1 200[4]	1 332[4]	1 439[4]	1 594[4]	2 200[4]
United Kingdom Royaume-Uni	22 835[3]	24 180[3]	24 715[3]	27 755[3]	29 971[3]	26 137	27 819	30 736	37 166	39 573

Country or area Pays ou zone	Number of tourist/visitor arrivals (thousands) Nombre d'arrivées de touristes/visiteurs (milliers)					Tourism expenditure (million US dollars)[t] Dépenses touristiques (millions de dollars E.U.)[t]				
	2001	2002	2003	2004	2005	2001	2002	2003	2004	2005
United Rep. of Tanzania Rép.-Unie de Tanzanie	501[5]	550[5]	552[5]	566[5]	590[5]	626	639	654	762	836
United States Etats-Unis	46 907[5,84]	43 581[5,84]	41 218[5,84]	46 086[5,84]	49 206[5,84]	106 705	101 798	98 998	112 941	122 944
United States Virgin Is. Iles Vierges américaines	527[5]	520[5]	538[5]	544[5]	575[5]	1 234[4]	1 195[4]	1 257[4]	1 356[4]	1 493[4]
Uruguay Uruguay	1 892[5]	1 258[5]	1 420[5]	1 756[5]	1 808[5]	700	409	419	591	690
Uzbekistan Ouzbékistan	345[5]	332[5]	231[5]	262[5]	...	72[4]	68[4]	48[4]	57[4]	...
Vanuatu Vanuatu	53[5]	49[5]	50[5]	61[5]	62[5]	58	62	71	82	93
Venezuela (Bolivarian Rep. of) Venezuela (Rép. bolivar. du)	584[5]	432[5]	337[5]	486[5]	706[5]	677	484	378	531	713
Viet Nam Viet Nam	2 330[3]	2 628[3]	2 429[3]	2 928[3]	3 468[3]	...	...	1 400[4]	1 700[4]	1 880[4]
Yemen Yémen	76[15]	98[15]	155[15]	274[15]	336[15]	38[7]	38[7]	139[7]	139[7]	181[7]
Zambia Zambie	492[5]	565[5]	413[5]	515[5]	669[5]	117[4]	134[4]	149[4]	161[4]	164[4]
Zimbabwe Zimbabwe	2 217[3]	2 041[3]	2 256[3]	1 854[3]	1 559[3]	81[4]	76[4]	61[4]	194[4]	99[4]

Source

World Tourism Organization (UNWTO), Madrid, the UNWTO Statistics Database.

Notes

t The majority of the data have been provided to the UNWTO by the International Monetary Fund (IMF). Exceptions are footnoted.

1 Arrivals of non-resident tourists in hotels only.
2 Including nationals of the country residing abroad.
3 Arrivals of non-resident visitors at national borders.
4 Figures provided by the country to the World Tourism Organisation (UNWTO).
5 Arrivals of non-resident tourists at national borders.
6 Excluding nationals of the country residing abroad.
7 Excluding passenger transport.
8 Starting 2004, as a result of the importance of the "Survey on International Tourism", the estimates of the series of the "Travel" item of the Balance of Payments were modified. For this reason, the data are not rigorously comparable with those of previous years.
9 Air arrivals.
10 Arrivals of non-resident tourists in all types of tourism accommodation establishments.
11 Organized tourism.
12 Country estimates.
13 Source: Central Bank of the Netherlands Antilles.
14 Excluding children without own passports.
15 Arrivals of non-resident tourists in hotels and similar establishments.

Source

Organisation mondiale du tourisme (OMT), Madrid, la base de données de l'OMT.

Notes

t La majorité des données sont celles que le Fonds monétaire international (FMI) a fournis à l'Organisation mondiale du tourisme (OMT). Les exceptions sont signalées par une note.
1 Arrivées de touristes non résidents dans les hôtels seulement.
2 Y compris les nationaux du pays résidant à l'étranger.
3 Arrivées de visiteurs non résidents aux frontières nationales.
4 Les chiffres de dépense sont ceux que le pays a fournis à l'Organisation mondiale du tourisme (OMT).
5 Arrivées de touristes non résidents aux frontières nationales.
6 A l'exclusion des nationaux du pays résidant à l'étranger.
7 Non compris le transport de passagers.
8 À partir de 2004, vu l'importance de l'« Enquête sur le tourisme international », des modifications ont été apportées aux estimations de la série du poste « Voyages » de la balance des paiements. C'est la raison pour laquelle les données ne sont pas rigoureusement comparables avec celles des années précédentes.
9 Arrivées par voie aérienne.
10 Arrivées de touristes non résidents dans tous les types d'établissements d'hébergement touristique.
11 Tourisme organisé.
12 Estimations du pays.
13 Source: "Central Bank of the Netherlands Antilles".
14 A l'exclusion d'enfants sans passeports personnels.
15 Arrivées de touristes non résidents dans les hôtels et établissements assimilés.

16 Different types of methodological changes that affect the estimates for 2000 and 2001 for expenditures and characteristics of International Tourists to Canada, have been introduced in 2002. Therefore, Statistics Canada advises not to compare the estimates for 2000 and 2001 with the years prior because of these methodological changes for the non-count estimates (one of the reasons ALS numbers are not provided).
17 Arrivals by air to Bangui only.
18 Source: "Banque des Etats de l'Afrique Centrale (B.E.A.C.)".
19 For statistical purposes, the data for China do not include those for the Hong Kong Special Administrative Region (Hong Kong SAR), Macao Special Administrative Region (Macao SAR) and Taiwan Province of China.
20 The expenditure figures used were the ones provided by the country to UNWTO, as this data series is more complete than that provided by the International Monetary Fund (IMF).
21 Arrivals of non-resident tourists in all types of accommodation establishments. New methodology.
22 Source: "Banque centrale de Djibouti".
23 Air arrivals. Including nationals residing abroad.
24 Starting from 2004, border statistics are not collected any more.
25 Calculated on the basis of accommodation statistics and "Foreign Visitor Survey" carried out by the Statistical Office of Estonia. Starting from 2004, border statistics are not collected any more.
26 Arrivals through all ports of entry. Including nationals residing abroad.
27 Estimates based on the 1996 survey at national borders. Data revised from 1996.
28 2005 survey at Cayenne-Rochambeau airport on departure.
29 Arrivals of non-resident tourists at Libreville airport.
30 Charter tourists only.
31 Data based on surveys.
32 Arrivals of non-resident tourists in all types of accommodation establishments. Air arrivals. Excluding the north islands (Saint Martin and Saint Barthelemy).
33 Arrivals in hotels only.
34 Data based on a survey conducted at Guadeloupe airport.
35 Air arrivals at Conakry airport.
36 Arrivals to Timehri airport only.
37 Source: Central Bank of Islamic Republic of Iran.
38 Source: Central Bank of Iraq.
39 Including tourists from Northern Ireland.
40 Excluding seasonal and border workers.
41 Including nationals residing abroad; E/D cards. Air arrivals.
42 Air arrivals. Tarawa and Christmas Island.
43 Air arrivals. Tarawa only.
44 Including nationals residing abroad and crew members.
45 New data source: Department of Customs Control.
46 Departures. Survey of persons crossing the state border.
47 Excluding Syrian nationals.
48 Due to the lack of data on international tourism receipts concerning statistics on inbound tourism, the Department of "Internet and Statistics Service of the Ministry of Tourism" considers that a tourist spends an average of US$ 1,000.
49 Departures.

16 En 2002, il a été adopté différents types de changements méthodologiques qui ont eu des effets sur les estimations des dépenses et des caractéristiques des touristes internationaux ayant visité le Canada en 2000 et 2001. Pour 2000 et 2001, Statistique Canada conseille par conséquent de ne pas comparer les estimations ne reposant pas sur des comptages aux données des années précédentes (c'est une des raisons pour lesquelles les données DMS ne sont pas fournies).
17 Arrivées par voie aérienne à Bangui uniquement.
18 Source: Banque des Etats de l'Afrique Centrale (B.E.A.C.).
19 Pour la présentation des statistiques, les données pour la Chine ne comprennent pas la Région Administrative Spéciale de Hong Kong (Hong Kong RAS), la Région Administrative Spéciale de Macao (Macao RAS) et la province de Taiwan.
20 Les données de dépense sont celles que le pays a fournies à l'OMT car il s'agit d'une série plus complète que celle obtenue du Fonds monétaire international (FMI).
21 Arrivées de touristes non résidents dans tous les types d'établissements d'hébergement. Nouvelle méthodologie.
22 Source: Banque centrale de Djibouti.
23 Arrivées par voie aérienne. Y compris les nationaux résidant à l'étranger.
24 À partir de 2004, les statistiques de frontière ne sont plus collectées.
25 Calculé sur la base des statistiques d'hébergement et de la "Foreign Visitor Survey" menée par la "Statistical Office of Estonia". À partir de 2004, les statistiques de frontière ne sont plus collectées.
26 Arrivées à travers tous les ports d'entrée. Y compris les nationaux résidant à l'étranger.
27 Estimation à partir de l'enquête aux frontières 1996. Données révisées depuis 1996.
28 Enquête 2005 au départ de l'aéroport de Cayenne-Rochambeau.
29 Arrivées de touristes non résidents à l'aéroport de Libreville.
30 Arrivées en vols à la demande seulement.
31 Données obtenues au moyen d'enquêtes.
32 Arrivées de touristes non résidents dans tous les types d'établissements d'hébergement. Arrivées par voie aérienne. À l'exclusion des îles du nord (Saint Martin et Saint Barthélemy).
33 Arrivées dans les hôtels uniquement.
34 Données tirées d'une enquête réalisée à l'aéroport de Guadeloupe.
35 Arrivées par voie aérienne à l'aéroport de Conakry.
36 Arrivées à l'aéroport de Timehri seulement.
37 Source: "Central Bank of Islamic Republic of Iran".
38 Source: "Central Bank of Iraq".
39 Y compris touristes de l'Irlande du Nord.
40 A l'exclusion des travailleurs saisoniers et frontaliers.
41 Y compris les nationaux résidant à l'étranger; cartes d'embarquement. Arrivées par voie aérienne.
42 Arrivées par voie aérienne. Tarawa et Ile Christmas.
43 Arrivées par voie aérienne. Tarawa uniquement.
44 Y compris les nationaux résidant à l'étranger et membres des équipages.
45 Nouvelle source d'information: Département du Contrôle douanier.
46 Départs. Enquête auprès des personnes qui traversent les frontières du pays.
47 A l'exclusion des ressortissants syriens.
48 Du fait d'un manque de données sur les recettes du tourisme international concernant les statistiques sur le tourisme récepteur, le Département « Internet et Service Statistique du Ministère du Tourisme » considère qu'un touriste dépense en moyenne 1.000$EU.
49 Départs.

50 Source: Reserve Bank of Malawi.
51 Including Singapore residents crossing the frontier by road through Johore Causeway.
52 Departures by air and by sea.
53 Air and sea arrivals.
54 Arrivals in the States of Kosrae, Chuuk, Pohnpei and Yap.
55 Excluding diplomats and foreign residents in Mongolia.
56 Including tourist arrivals through border entry points to Yangon.
57 Including arrivals from India.
58 Arrivals by air, including Niueans residing usually in New Zealand.
59 Figures are based on "The Guest survey" carried out by "Institute of Transport Economics".
60 West Bank and Gaza.
61 Inbound Tourism Survey.
62 Air arrivals (Palau International Airport).
63 Excluding nationals residing abroad and crew members. E/D cards in the "Silvio Petirossi" airport and passenger counts at the national border crossings - National Police and SENATUR.
64 From 2002, new estimated series including tourists with identity document other than a passport.
65 Including arrivals from abroad to insular possessions of Madeira and the Azores. Excluding nationals residing abroad. Due to a change in the methodology, data are not available from 2005.
66 Arrivals by air. Fiscal year July to June. Source: "Junta de Planificación de Puerto Rico".
67 Fiscal years (July-June).
68 Source: Qatar Central Bank.
69 Visitors who enjoyed the services of the economic agents officially registered under tourism activity and accommodation (excluding the regions of the left bank of the Dniestr and the municipality of Bender).
70 January-November.
71 Excluding Netherlands Antillean residents.
72 Including air arrivals to Saint-Martin (the French side of the island).
73 Including the estimates for Saba and Saint Eustatius. Excluding passenger transport. Source: Central Bank of the Netherlands Antilles.
74 Including Italian visitors.
75 Without 1st quarter.
76 Source: Central Bank of Solomon Islands.
77 Excluding arrivals by work and contract workers.
78 Arrivals at Zanderij Airport.
79 Data according to IBIS-Survey (Incoming Visitors to Sweden) during the years 2001 to 2003, (no data collected before 2001 or after 2003). Source: Swedish Tourist Authority and Statistics Sweden.
80 Source: National Reserve Bank of Tonga.
81 Country data. Including expenditure of the nationals residing abroad. Excluding passenger transport.
82 Including expenditure of the nationals residing abroad.
83 Including nationals residing abroad. Arrivals in hotels only. Including domestic tourism.
84 Including Mexicans staying one or more nights in the United States.

50 Source: "Reserve Bank of Malawi".
51 Y compris les résidents de Singapour traversant la frontière par voie terrestre à travers le Johore Causeway.
52 Départs par voies aérienne et maritime.
53 Arrivées par voie aérienne et maritime.
54 Arrivées dans les États de Kosrae, Chuuk, Pohnpei et Yap.
55 Sont exclus les diplomates et les étrangers qui résident en Mongolie.
56 Comprenant les arrivées de touristes aux postes-frontières de Yangon.
57 Y compris les arrivées à Inde.
58 Arrivées par voie aérienne et y compris les nationaux de Niue résidant habituellement en Nouvelle-Zélande.
59 Les chiffres se fondent sur "l'enquête auprès de la clientèle" de l'Institut d'économie des transports.
60 Cisjordanie et Gaza.
61 Enquête du tourisme récepteur.
62 Arrivées par voie aérienne (Aéroport international de Palau).
63 À l'exclusion des nationaux résidant à l'étranger et membres des équipages. Cartes d'embarquement et de débarquement à l'aéroport Silvio Petirossi et comptages des passagers lors du franchissement des frontières nationales – Police nationale et SENATUR.
64 À partir de 2002, nouvelle série estimée comprenant les touristes avec une pièce d'identité autre qu'un passeport.
65 Y compris les arrivées en provenance de l'étranger aux possessions insulaires de Madère et des Açores. A l'exclusion des nationaux résidant à l'étranger. La méthodologie a été modifiée et pour cela, à partir de 2005 les données ne sont pas disponibles.
66 Arrivées par voie aérienne. Année fiscale de juillet à juin. Source: "Junta de Planificación de Puerto Rico".
67 Années fiscales (juillet-juin).
68 Source: "Qatar Central Bank".
69 Visiteurs qui ont bénéficié des services des agents économiques officiellement enregistrés avec le type d'activité tourisme et des unités d'hébergement qui leur appartiennent (à l'exception des régions de la partie gauche du Dniestr et de la municipalité de Bender).
70 Janvier-novembre.
71 A l'exclusion des résidents des Antilles Néerlandaises.
72 Y compris les arrivées par voie aérienne à Saint-Martin (côté français de l'île).
73 Y compris estimations pour Saba et Saint-Eustache. Non compris le transport de passagers. Source: "Central Bank of the Netherlands Antilles".
74 Y compris les visiteurs italiens.
75 À l'exclusion du 1er trimestre.
76 Source: "Central Bank of Solomon Islands".
77 À l'exclusion des arrivées par travail et les travailleurs contractuels.
78 Arrivées à l'aéroport de Zanderij.
79 Données reposant sur l'enquête IBIS (auprès des visiteurs du tourisme récepteur) portant sur les années 2001 à 2003 (aucune donnée n'a été collectée avant 2001 ni après 2003). Source: "Swedish Tourist Authority" et "Statistics Sweden".
80 Source: "National Reserve Bank of Tonga".
81 Données du pays. Y compris les dépenses des nationaux résidant à l'étranger. Non compris le transport de passagers.
82 Y compris dépenses des nationaux résidant à l'étranger.
83 Y compris les nationaux résidant à l'étranger. Arrivées dans les hôtels seulement. Y compris le tourisme interne.
84 Incluyant Mexicains passant 1 nuit ou plus aux EU.

Tourism expenditure in other countries

Total, travel and passenger transport: million US dollars

Dépenses touristiques dans d'autres pays

Total, voyage et transport de passagers : millions de dollars E.U.

Country or area	2001	2002	2003	2004	2005	Pays ou zone
Albania						Albanie
Total	269	387	507	668	808	Total
Travel	257	366	489	641	786	Voyage
Passenger transport	12	21	18	27	22	Transport de passagers
Algeria[1]						Algérie[1]
Total	194	248	255	394	370	Total
Angola						Angola
Total	80	53	49	86	135	Total
Travel	66	19	12	39	74	Voyage
Passenger transport	14	34	37	47	61	Transport de passagers
Anguilla						Anguilla
Travel	9	8	9	9	10	Voyage
Antigua and Barbuda						Antigua-et-Barbuda
Travel	32	33	35	37	40	Voyage
Argentina						Argentine
Total	4 888	2 744	2 997	3 204	3 572	Total
Travel	3 893	2 328	2 511	2 604	2 817	Voyage
Passenger transport	995	416	486	600	755	Transport de passagers
Armenia						Arménie
Total	59	85	97	102	146	Total
Travel	40	54	67	65	117	Voyage
Passenger transport	19	31	30	37	29	Transport de passagers
Aruba						Aruba
Total	156	173	213	253	268	Total
Travel	135	160	189	223	241	Voyage
Passenger transport	21	13	24	30	27	Transport de passagers
Australia						Australie
Total	8 070	8 513	10 085	13 884	15 076	Total
Travel	5 877	6 091	7 295	10 290	11 282	Voyage
Passenger transport	2 193	2 422	2 790	3 594	3 794	Transport de passagers
Austria						Autriche
Total	9 787	10 301	12 894	13 411	12 755	Total
Travel	8 956	9 460	11 757	11 834	10 994	Voyage
Passenger transport	831	841	1 137	1 577	1 761	Transport de passagers
Azerbaijan						Azerbaïdjan
Total	119	111	120	140	188	Total
Travel	109	106	111	126	164	Voyage
Passenger transport	10	5	9	14	24	Transport de passagers
Bahamas						Bahamas
Total	342	338	404	469	528	Total
Travel	256	244	305	316	344	Voyage
Passenger transport	86	94	99	153	184	Transport de passagers
Bahrain						Bahreïn
Total	423	550	492	528	574	Total
Travel	250	380	372	387	414	Voyage
Passenger transport	173	170	120	141	160	Transport de passagers
Bangladesh						Bangladesh
Total	341	309	389	442	371	Total
Travel	165	113	165	161	132	Voyage
Passenger transport	176	196	224	281	239	Transport de passagers
Barbados						Barbade
Total	149	146	154	163	153	Total
Travel	101	99	105	108	96	Voyage
Passenger transport	48	47	49	55	57	Transport de passagers

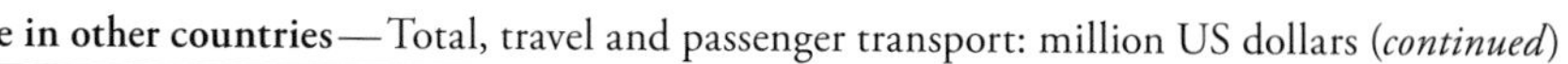

63 Tourism expenditure in other countries — Total, travel and passenger transport: million US dollars (*continued*)
Dépenses touristiques dans d'autres pays — Total, voyage et transport de passagers : millions de dollars E.U. (*suite*)

Country or area	2001	2002	2003	2004	2005	Pays ou zone
Belarus						Bélarus
Total	533	593	510	588	672	Total
Travel	501	559	473	538	604	Voyage
Passenger transport	32	34	37	50	68	Transport de passagers
Belgium						Belgique
Total	10 878	11 270	13 402	15 456	16 636	Total
Travel	9 776[2]	10 185	12 210	13 956	14 814	Voyage
Passenger transport	1 102	1 085	1 192	1 500	1 822	Transport de passagers
Belize						Belize
Total	45	48	50	47	45	Total
Travel	42	44	46	43	42	Voyage
Passenger transport	3	4	4	4	3	Transport de passagers
Benin						Bénin
Total	48	49	53	59	...	Total
Travel	17	20	21	29	...	Voyage
Passenger transport	31	29	32	30	...	Transport de passagers
Bermuda[1]						Bermudes[1]
Total	...	243	248	276	294	Total
Bolivia						Bolivie
Total	114	114	198	232	258	Total
Travel	83	80	139	164	186	Voyage
Passenger transport	31	34	59	68	72	Transport de passagers
Bonaire[3]						Bonaire[3]
Travel	2	2	3	6	5	Voyage
Bosnia and Herzegovina						Bosnie-Herzégovine
Total	96	112	145	162	160	Total
Travel	74	85	106	117	123	Voyage
Passenger transport	22	27	39	45	37	Transport de passagers
Botswana						Botswana
Total	215	197	235	280	301	Total
Travel	204	184	230	276	282	Voyage
Passenger transport	11	13	5	4	19	Transport de passagers
Brazil						Brésil
Total	3 765	2 929	2 874	3 752	5 905	Total
Travel	3 199	2 396	2 261	2 871	4 720	Voyage
Passenger transport	566	533	613	881	1 185	Transport de passagers
Bulgaria						Bulgarie
Total	836	1 018	1 467	1 893	1 836	Total
Travel	589	717	1 033	1 333	1 293	Voyage
Passenger transport	247	301	434	560	543	Transport de passagers
Burkina Faso						Burkina Faso
Total	35	...	...	...	...	Total
Travel	22	...	...	...	...	Voyage
Passenger transport	13	...	...	...	...	Transport de passagers
Burundi						Burundi
Total	...	...	...	30	62	Total
Travel	12	14	15	24	60	Voyage
Passenger transport	...	...	...	6	2	Transport de passagers
Cambodia						Cambodge
Total	59	64	60	80	138	Total
Travel	37	38	36	48	97	Voyage
Passenger transport	22	26	24	32	41	Transport de passagers
Cameroon						Cameroun
Total	199	205	294	...	...	Total
Travel	160	171	212	...	...	Voyage
Passenger transport	39	34	82	...	...	Transport de passagers

Tourism expenditure in other countries — Total, travel and passenger transport: million US dollars (*continued*)

Dépenses touristiques dans d'autres pays — Total, voyage et transport de passagers : millions de dollars E.U. (*suite*)

Country or area	2001	2002	2003	2004	2005	Pays ou zone
Canada						Canada
Total	14 635	14 257	16 309	19 657	23 061	Total
Travel	11 961	11 722	13 337	15 914	18 341	Voyage
Passenger transport	2 674	2 535	2 972	3 743	4 720	Transport de passagers
Cape Verde						Cap-Vert
Total	55	63	89	91	82	Total
Travel	47	56	71	78	67	Voyage
Passenger transport	8	7	18	13	15	Transport de passagers
Central African Rep.[4]						Rép. centrafricaine[4]
Total	29	29	31[1]	32[1]	...	Total
Chad[4]						Tchad[4]
Total	56	80	...	...	...	Total
Chile						Chili
Total	939	932	1 109	1 250	1 381	Total
Travel	708	673	850	977	1 057	Voyage
Passenger transport	231	259	259	273	324	Transport de passagers
China[5]						Chine[5]
Total	14 992	16 759	16 716	21 360	24 715	Total
Travel	13 909	15 398	15 187	19 149	21 759	Voyage
Passenger transport	1 083	1 361	1 529	2 211	2 956	Transport de passagers
China, Hong Kong SAR[6]						Chine, Hong Kong RAS[6]
Travel	12 317	12 418	11 447	13 270	13 307	Voyage
Colombia						Colombie
Total	1 556	1 355	1 349	1 466	1 562	Total
Travel	1 164	1 075	1 062	1 108	1 127	Voyage
Passenger transport	392	280	287	358	435	Transport de passagers
Congo						Congo
Total	82	85	118	176	...	Total
Travel	65	70	78	103	103	Voyage
Passenger transport	17	15	40	73	...	Transport de passagers
Costa Rica						Costa Rica
Total	434	430	434	481	556	Total
Travel	364	345	353	406	470	Voyage
Passenger transport	70	85	81	75	86	Transport de passagers
Côte d'Ivoire						Côte d'Ivoire
Total	289	490	551	572	...	Total
Travel	187	358	387	382	346	Voyage
Passenger transport	102	132	164	190	...	Transport de passagers
Croatia						Croatie
Total	677	852	709	881	786	Total
Travel	606	781	672	848	754	Voyage
Passenger transport	71	71	37	33	32	Transport de passagers
Cyprus						Chypre
Total	568	588	700	906	1 001	Total
Travel	428	516	611	810	932	Voyage
Passenger transport	140	72	89	96	69	Transport de passagers
Czech Republic						République tchèque
Total	...	1 797	2 177	2 660	2 605	Total
Travel	1 386	1 597	1 934	2 280	2 405	Voyage
Passenger transport	...	200	243	380	200	Transport de passagers
Denmark						Danemark
Travel	4 861	5 828	6 658	7 269	5 690	Voyage
Djibouti[7]						Djibouti[7]
Travel	...	...	3	3	3	Voyage
Dominica						Dominique
Travel	9	9	9	9	10	Voyage

63 Tourism expenditure in other countries — Total, travel and passenger transport: million US dollars (*continued*)
Dépenses touristiques dans d'autres pays — Total, voyage et transport de passagers : millions de dollars E.U. (*suite*)

Country or area	2001	2002	2003	2004	2005	Pays ou zone
Dominican Republic						Rép. dominicaine
Total	425	429	408	448	494	Total
Travel	291	295	272	310	352	Voyage
Passenger transport	134	134	136	138	142	Transport de passagers
Ecuador						Equateur
Total	465	507	500	577	616	Total
Travel	340	364	354	391	401	Voyage
Passenger transport	125	143	146	186	215	Transport de passagers
Egypt						Egypte
Total	1 248	1 309	1 465	1 543	1 932	Total
Travel	1 132	1 266	1 321	1 257	1 629	Voyage
Passenger transport	116	43	144	286	303	Transport de passagers
El Salvador						El Salvador
Total	247	266	311	383	430	Total
Travel	195	191	230	302	347	Voyage
Passenger transport	52	75	81	81	83	Transport de passagers
Equatorial Guinea[4]						Guinée équatoriale[4]
Total	30	...	...	...	...	Total
Estonia						Estonie
Total	253	305	404	481	538	Total
Travel	192	231	319	400	448	Voyage
Passenger transport	61	74	85	81	90	Transport de passagers
Ethiopia						Ethiopie
Total	50	56	63	59	...	Total
Travel	44	45	50	58	77	Voyage
Passenger transport	6	11	13	1	...	Transport de passagers
Fiji[1]						Fidji[1]
Total	...	...	87	118	131	Total
Travel	65	55	69	94	106	Voyage
Passenger transport	...	...	18	24	25	Transport de passagers
Finland						Finlande
Total	2 442	2 437	2 956	3 381	3 529	Total
Travel	1 852	2 006	2 435	2 820	2 968	Voyage
Passenger transport	590	431	521	561	561	Transport de passagers
France						France
Travel	18 109	19 518	23 396	28 544	31 180	Voyage
French Polynesia						Polynésie française
Total	...	264	335	425	421	Total
Travel	...	180	236	311	303	Voyage
Passenger transport	...	84	99	114	118	Transport de passagers
Gabon						Gabon
Total	256	237	239	275	...	Total
Travel	225	197	194	214	...	Voyage
Passenger transport	31	40	45	61	...	Transport de passagers
Gambia						Gambie
Total	...	...	8	6	7	Total
Travel	...	...	4	4	5	Voyage
Passenger transport	...	...	4	2	2	Transport de passagers
Georgia						Géorgie
Total	136	189	170	196	238	Total
Travel	107	149	130	147	169	Voyage
Passenger transport	29	40	40	49	69	Transport de passagers
Germany						Allemagne
Total	56 709	59 486	72 597	79 216	80 276	Total
Travel	51 810	52 660	64 628	70 614	72 488	Voyage
Passenger transport	4 899	6 826	7 969	8 602	7 788	Transport de passagers

Tourism expenditure in other countries — Total, travel and passenger transport: million US dollars *(continued)*
Dépenses touristiques dans d'autres pays — Total, voyage et transport de passagers : millions de dollars E.U. *(suite)*

Country or area	2001	2002	2003	2004	2005	Pays ou zone
Ghana						Ghana
Total	165	184	216	270	472	Total
Travel	105	119	138	186	303	Voyage
Passenger transport	60	65	78	84	169	Transport de passagers
Greece						Grèce
Total	4 189	2 453	2 439	2 880	3 046	Total
Travel	4 177	2 436	2 431	2 872	3 039	Voyage
Passenger transport	12	17	8	8	7	Transport de passagers
Grenada						Grenade
Travel	8	8	8	9	11	Voyage
Guatemala						Guatemala
Total	267	329	373	456	500	Total
Travel	226	276	312	391	444	Voyage
Passenger transport	41	53	61	65	56	Transport de passagers
Guinea						Guinée
Total	26	38	36	29	...	Total
Travel	18	31	26	25	...	Voyage
Passenger transport	8	7	10	4	...	Transport de passagers
Guinea-Bissau						Guinée-Bissau
Total	6	10	21	22	...	Total
Travel	3	5	13	13	...	Voyage
Passenger transport	3	5	8	9	...	Transport de passagers
Guyana						Guyana
Total	62	44	30	35	45	Total
Travel	55	38	26	30	40	Voyage
Passenger transport	7	6	4	5	5	Transport de passagers
Haiti						Haïti
Total	168	174	196	206	173	Total
Travel	18	18	42	72	54	Voyage
Passenger transport	150	156	154	134	119	Transport de passagers
Honduras						Honduras
Total	203	215	258	291	315	Total
Travel	128	149	200	228	248	Voyage
Passenger transport	75	66	58	63	67	Transport de passagers
Hungary						Hongrie
Total	1 887	2 209	2 700	2 909	3 037	Total
Travel	1 808	2 133	2 594	2 848	2 925	Voyage
Passenger transport	79	76	106	61	112	Transport de passagers
Iceland						Islande
Total	...	372	522	695	986	Total
Travel	372	370	521	693	975	Voyage
Passenger transport	...	2	1	2	11	Transport de passagers
India						Inde
Total	5 099	4 990	4 758	...	...	Total
Travel	3 006	2 988	3 510	...	...	Voyage
Passenger transport	2 093	2 002	1 248	...	...	Transport de passagers
Indonesia						Indonésie
Total	...	5 042	4 427	4 569	4 741	Total
Travel	3 406	3 289	3 082	3 507	3 584	Voyage
Passenger transport	...	1 753	1 345	1 062	1 157	Transport de passagers
Iran (Islamic Rep. of)[8]						Iran (Rép. islamique d')[8]
Total	714	3 990	4 120	4 402	4 810	Total
Travel	708	3 750	3 842	4 093	4 380	Voyage
Passenger transport	6	240	278	309	430	Transport de passagers
Iraq[9]						Iraq[9]
Travel	31	26	...	...	...	Voyage

Tourism expenditure in other countries—Total, travel and passenger transport: million US dollars (*continued*)
Dépenses touristiques dans d'autres pays—Total, voyage et transport de passagers : millions de dollars E.U. (*suite*)

Country or area	2001	2002	2003	2004	2005	Pays ou zone
Ireland						Irlande
Total	2 956	3 835	4 832	5 291	6 168	Total
Travel	2 858	3 755	4 736	5 177	6 056	Voyage
Passenger transport	98	80	96	114	112	Transport de passagers
Israel						Israël
Total	3 887	3 323	3 342	3 663	3 780	Total
Travel	2 945	2 543	2 550	2 796	2 895	Voyage
Passenger transport	942	780	792	867	885	Transport de passagers
Italy						Italie
Total	16 997	19 636	23 731	24 062	26 459	Total
Travel	14 795	16 924	20 589	20 460	22 371	Voyage
Passenger transport	2 202	2 712	3 142	3 602	4 088	Transport de passagers
Jamaica						Jamaïque
Total	227	274	269	318	291	Total
Travel	206	258	252	286	250	Voyage
Passenger transport	21	16	17	32	41	Transport de passagers
Japan						Japon
Total	35 526	34 977	36 505	48 175	48 102	Total
Travel	26 531	26 656	28 958	38 252	37 565	Voyage
Passenger transport	8 995	8 321	7 547	9 923	10 537	Transport de passagers
Jordan						Jordanie
Total	421	505	503	585	653	Total
Travel	378	453	452	524	585	Voyage
Passenger transport	43	52	51	61	68	Transport de passagers
Kazakhstan						Kazakhstan
Total	761	863	783	997	940	Total
Travel	673	757	669	844	753	Voyage
Passenger transport	88	106	114	153	187	Transport de passagers
Kenya						Kenya
Total	183	...	...	...	...	Total
Travel	143	126	127	108	124	Voyage
Passenger transport	40	...	...	...	...	Transport de passagers
Korea, Republic of						Corée, République de
Total	8 349	11 440	11 063	13 507	16 831	Total
Travel	7 617	10 465	10 103	12 350	15 314	Voyage
Passenger transport	732	975	960	1 157	1 517	Transport de passagers
Kuwait						Koweït
Total	3 207	3 413	3 751	4 149	4 743	Total
Travel	2 842	3 021	3 348	3 701	4 277	Voyage
Passenger transport	365	392	403	448	466	Transport de passagers
Kyrgyzstan						Kirghizistan
Total	21	18	25	60	71	Total
Travel	12	10	17	50	58	Voyage
Passenger transport	9	8	8	10	13	Transport de passagers
Latvia						Lettonie
Total	255	267	365	429	655	Total
Travel	223	230	328	378	584	Voyage
Passenger transport	32	37	37	51	71	Transport de passagers
Lebanon						Liban
Total	...	...	3 319	3 719	3 535	Total
Travel	...	2 683	2 943	3 170	2 878	Voyage
Passenger transport	...	...	376	549	657	Transport de passagers
Lesotho						Lesotho
Total	12	16	30	37	36	Total
Travel	9	14	26	30	27	Voyage
Passenger transport	3	2	4	7	9	Transport de passagers

Tourism expenditure in other countries—Total, travel and passenger transport: million US dollars (*continued*)
Dépenses touristiques dans d'autres pays—Total, voyage et transport de passagers : millions de dollars E.U. (*suite*)

Country or area	2001	2002	2003	2004	2005	Pays ou zone
Libyan Arab Jamah.						Jamah. arabe libyenne
Total	572	654	689	789	920	Total
Travel	445	586	557	603	680	Voyage
Passenger transport	127	68	132	186	240	Transport de passagers
Lithuania						Lituanie
Total	227	334	476	643	757	Total
Travel	219	326	471	636	744	Voyage
Passenger transport	8	8	5	7	13	Transport de passagers
Luxembourg						Luxembourg
Total	...	1 963	2 445	2 950	...	Total
Travel	1 464	1 942	2 423	2 911	2 976	Voyage
Passenger transport	...	21	22	39	...	Transport de passagers
Madagascar						Madagascar
Total	179	109	39	41	27	Total
Travel	130	91	37	35	25	Voyage
Passenger transport	49	18	2	6	2	Transport de passagers
Malawi						Malawi
Total	53	76[10]	61[10]	62[10]	58[10]	Total
Travel	41	69[10]	48[10]	50[10]	47[10]	Voyage
Passenger transport	12	7[10]	13[10]	12[10]	11[10]	Transport de passagers
Malaysia						Malaisie
Total	3 391	3 330	3 401	3 737	4 339	Total
Travel	2 614	2 618	2 846	3 093	3 711	Voyage
Passenger transport	777	712	555	644	628	Transport de passagers
Maldives						Maldives
Total	59	60	60	75	94	Total
Travel	45	46	46	56	70	Voyage
Passenger transport	14	14	14	19	24	Transport de passagers
Mali						Mali
Total	65	62	94	125	133	Total
Travel	36	36	48	66	77	Voyage
Passenger transport	29	26	46	59	56	Transport de passagers
Malta						Malte
Total	204	180	238	292	308	Total
Travel	180	154	215	256	268	Voyage
Passenger transport	24	26	23	36	40	Transport de passagers
Mauritius						Maurice
Total	216	224	236	277	295	Total
Travel	198	204	216	255	275	Voyage
Passenger transport	18	20	20	22	20	Transport de passagers
Mexico						Mexique
Total	6 685	7 087	7 252	8 034	8 951	Total
Travel	5 702	6 060	6 253	6 959	7 600	Voyage
Passenger transport	983	1 027	999	1 075	1 351	Transport de passagers
Micronesia (Fed. States of)[1]						Micronésie (Etats féd. de)[1]
Total	5	5	6	5	6	Total
Mongolia						Mongolie
Total	59	125	144	207	222	Total
Travel	55	119	138	193	205	Voyage
Passenger transport	4	6	6	14	17	Transport de passagers
Montserrat						Montserrat
Travel	2	2	2	2	3	Voyage
Morocco						Maroc
Total	589	670	845	913	999	Total
Travel	389	444	548	575	612	Voyage
Passenger transport	200	226	297	338	387	Transport de passagers

Country or area	2001	2002	2003	2004	2005	Pays ou zone
Mozambique						Mozambique
Total	132	115	141	140	187	Total
Travel	114	113	140	134	176	Voyage
Passenger transport	18	2	1	6	11	Transport de passagers
Myanmar						Myanmar
Total	32	34	36	32	...	Total
Travel	27	29	32	29	...	Voyage
Passenger transport	5	5	4	3	...	Transport de passagers
Namibia						Namibie
Travel	71	55	74	122	108	Voyage
Nepal						Népal
Total	128	108	119	205	221	Total
Travel	80	69	81	154	163	Voyage
Passenger transport	48	39	38	51	58	Transport de passagers
Netherlands						Pays-Bas
Total	13 061	14 201	...	...	...	Total
Travel	11 994	12 976	14 593	16 346	16 082	Voyage
Passenger transport	1 067	1 225	...	...	...	Transport de passagers
New Caledonia						Nouvelle-Calédonie
Travel	...	104	128	167	171	Voyage
New Zealand						Nouvelle-Zélande
Travel	1 255	1 386	1 649	2 217	2 657	Voyage
Nicaragua						Nicaragua
Total	128	125	139	154	161	Total
Travel	76	69	75	89	90	Voyage
Passenger transport	52	56	64	65	71	Transport de passagers
Niger						Niger
Total	33	29	39	42	55[2]	Total
Travel	26	17	22	22	32[2]	Voyage
Passenger transport	7	12	17	20	23[2]	Transport de passagers
Nigeria						Nigéria
Total	858	910	2 076	1 469	1 385	Total
Travel	831	881	1 795	1 161	1 109	Voyage
Passenger transport	27	29	281	308	276	Transport de passagers
Norway						Norvège
Total	4 671	5 542	6 992	8 788	...	Total
Travel	4 363	5 121	6 619	8 383	9 753	Voyage
Passenger transport	308	421	373	405	...	Transport de passagers
Occupied Palestinian Terr.[11]						Terr. palestinien occupé[11]
Travel	424	388	317	286	...	Voyage
Oman						Oman
Total	703	702	752	796	838	Total
Travel	518	530	578	616	643	Voyage
Passenger transport	185	172	174	180	195	Transport de passagers
Pakistan						Pakistan
Total	555	491	1 163	1 612	1 748	Total
Travel	252	255	925	1 268	1 275	Voyage
Passenger transport	303	236	238	344	473	Transport de passagers
Palau[1]						Palaos[1]
Total	2	2	2	2	...	Total
Panama						Panama
Total	227	252	267	294	388	Total
Travel	174	179	208	239	271	Voyage
Passenger transport	53	73	59	55	117	Transport de passagers
Papua New Guinea						Papouasie-Nvl-Guinée
Total	...	...	...	72	56	Total
Travel	38	60	52	71	56	Voyage
Passenger transport	...	...	...	1	1	Transport de passagers

Tourism expenditure in other countries — Total, travel and passenger transport: million US dollars *(continued)*
Dépenses touristiques dans d'autres pays — Total, voyage et transport de passagers : millions de dollars E.U. *(suite)*

Country or area	2001	2002	2003	2004	2005	Pays ou zone
Paraguay						Paraguay
Total	130	118	115	121	129	Total
Travel	72	65	67	71	79	Voyage
Passenger transport	58	53	48	50	50	Transport de passagers
Peru						Pérou
Total	774	780	794	821	900	Total
Travel	546	580	598	620	680	Voyage
Passenger transport	228	200	196	201	220	Transport de passagers
Philippines						Philippines
Total	1 918	1 874	1 649	1 526	1 547	Total
Travel	1 711	1 626	1 413	1 275	1 279	Voyage
Passenger transport	207	248	236	251	268	Transport de passagers
Poland						Pologne
Total	3 594	3 364	3 002	4 157	4 686	Total
Travel	3 495	3 202	2 801	3 841	4 341	Voyage
Passenger transport	99	162	201	316	345	Transport de passagers
Portugal						Portugal
Total	2 606	2 632	2 982	3 368	3 763	Total
Travel	2 114	2 125	2 409	2 762	3 073	Voyage
Passenger transport	492	507	573	606	690	Transport de passagers
Puerto Rico[12]						Porto Rico[12]
Total	1 456	1 319	1 420	1 584	1 663	Total
Travel	1 004	928	985	1 085	1 143	Voyage
Passenger transport	452	391	435	499	520	Transport de passagers
Qatar[13]						Qatar[13]
Travel	366	423	471	691	1 759	Voyage
Republic of Moldova						République de Moldova
Total	90	109	124	157	197	Total
Travel	75	95	105	135	167	Voyage
Passenger transport	15	14	19	22	30	Transport de passagers
Romania						Roumanie
Total	475	448	572	672	1 022	Total
Travel	449	396	479	539	878	Voyage
Passenger transport	26	52	93	133	144	Transport de passagers
Russian Federation						Fédération de Russie
Total	9 760	11 713	13 427	16 527	18 795	Total
Travel	9 285	11 284	12 880	15 730	17 804	Voyage
Passenger transport	475	429	547	797	991	Transport de passagers
Rwanda						Rwanda
Total	33	...	...	...	...	Total
Travel	20	24	26	31	37	Voyage
Passenger transport	13	...	...	...	...	Transport de passagers
Saint Kitts and Nevis						Saint-Kitts-et-Nevis
Travel	8	8	8	10	11	Voyage
Saint Lucia						Sainte-Lucie
Travel	32	34	36	37	40	Voyage
Saint Maarten[3,14]						Saint-Martin[3,14]
Travel	137	140	143	88	104	Voyage
St. Vincent-Grenadines						St. Vincent-Grenadines
Travel	12	10	13	14	14	Voyage
Samoa						Samoa
Total	...	...	...	12	13	Total
Travel	...	...	...	5	9	Voyage
Passenger transport	...	...	...	7	4	Transport de passagers
Sao Tome and Principe						Sao Tomé-et-Principe
Total	2	2	...	...	...	Total
Travel	1	1	...	...	...	Voyage
Passenger transport	1	1	...	...	...	Transport de passagers

63 Tourism expenditure in other countries — Total, travel and passenger transport: million US dollars (*continued*)
Dépenses touristiques dans d'autres pays — Total, voyage et transport de passagers : millions de dollars E.U. (*suite*)

Country or area	2001	2002	2003	2004	2005	Pays ou zone
Saudi Arabia[1]						Arabie saoudite[1]
Total	...	7 370	4 165	5 038	4 764	Total
Senegal						Sénégal
Total	112	112	129	138	...	Total
Travel	43	43	55	57	...	Voyage
Passenger transport	69	69	74	81	...	Transport de passagers
Seychelles						Seychelles
Total	41	53	54	53	59	Total
Travel	23	33	36	34	39	Voyage
Passenger transport	18	20	18	19	20	Transport de passagers
Sierra Leone						Sierra Leone
Total	42	39	38	30	34	Total
Travel	42	39	37	30	32	Voyage
Passenger transport	^0	^0	1	^0	2	Transport de passagers
Singapore						Singapour
Travel	6 621	8 157	7 991	9 585	9 853	Voyage
Slovakia						Slovaquie
Total	340[2]	506	662	903[2]	...	Total
Travel	289[2]	442	573	745[2]	846[2]	Voyage
Passenger transport	51[2]	64	89	158[2]	...	Transport de passagers
Slovenia						Slovénie
Total	560	647	806	937	1 019	Total
Travel	528	608	753	868	950	Voyage
Passenger transport	32	39	53	69	69	Transport de passagers
Solomon Islands[15]						Iles Salomon[15]
Travel	7	6	4	9	5	Voyage
South Africa						Afrique du Sud
Total	2 366	2 251	3 654	4 238	4 813	Total
Travel	1 878	1 811	2 889	3 157	3 374	Voyage
Passenger transport	488	440	765	1 081	1 439	Transport de passagers
Spain						Espagne
Total	8 466	9 366	11 330	14 864	18 440	Total
Travel	6 529	7 295	9 071	12 153	15 046	Voyage
Passenger transport	1 937	2 071	2 259	2 711	3 394	Transport de passagers
Sri Lanka						Sri Lanka
Total	404	438	462	499	553	Total
Travel	251	263	279	296	315	Voyage
Passenger transport	153	175	183	203	238	Transport de passagers
Sudan						Soudan
Travel	74	91	119	176	668	Voyage
Suriname						Suriname
Total	62	54	68	85	94	Total
Travel	23	10	6	14	17	Voyage
Passenger transport	39	44	62	71	77	Transport de passagers
Swaziland						Swaziland
Total	48	40	44	22	23	Total
Travel	47	39	43	16	15	Voyage
Passenger transport	1	1	1	6	8	Transport de passagers
Sweden						Suède
Total	7 916	8 221	9 375	10 984	11 847	Total
Travel	6 921	7 301	8 296	10 130	10 776	Voyage
Passenger transport	995	920	1 079	854	1 071	Transport de passagers
Switzerland						Suisse
Total	8 179	8 347	9 194	10 599	11 060	Total
Travel	6 235	6 674	7 463	8 779	9 262	Voyage
Passenger transport	1 944	1 673	1 731	1 820	1 798	Transport de passagers

Tourism expenditure in other countries—Total, travel and passenger transport: million US dollars (*continued*)
Dépenses touristiques dans d'autres pays—Total, voyage et transport de passagers : millions de dollars E.U. (*suite*)

Country or area	2001	2002	2003	2004	2005	Pays ou zone
Syrian Arab Republic						Rép. arabe syrienne
Total	...	...	734	698	593	Total
Travel	670	760	700	650	550	Voyage
Passenger transport	...	...	34	48	43	Transport de passagers
Tajikistan						Tadjikistan
Travel	...	2	2	3	4	Voyage
Thailand						Thaïlande
Total	3 334	3 888	3 539	5 343	5 790	Total
Travel	2 924	3 303	2 921	4 514	4 995	Voyage
Passenger transport	410	585	618	829	795	Transport de passagers
TFYR of Macedonia						L'ex-R.y. Macédoine
Total	60	61	71	83	94	Total
Travel	39	45	48	54	60	Voyage
Passenger transport	21	16	23	29	34	Transport de passagers
Togo						Togo
Total	20	26	37	38	...	Total
Travel	5	5	7	8	...	Voyage
Passenger transport	15	21	30	30	...	Transport de passagers
Tonga						Tonga
Travel	3	3	...	...	...	Voyage
Trinidad and Tobago						Trinité-et-Tobago
Total	172	208	143	141	288[2]	Total
Travel	151	186	107	96	222[2]	Voyage
Passenger transport	21	22	36	45	66[2]	Transport de passagers
Tunisia						Tunisie
Total	322	303	355	427	443	Total
Travel	273	260	300	340	365	Voyage
Passenger transport	49	43	55	87	78	Transport de passagers
Turkey						Turquie
Travel	1 738	1 881	2 113	2 524	2 872	Voyage
Uganda						Ouganda
Total	...	...	...	136	137	Total
Travel	...	...	...	133	133	Voyage
Passenger transport	...	...	...	3	4	Transport de passagers
Ukraine						Ukraine
Total	676	794	953	2 660	3 078	Total
Travel	566	657	789	2 463	2 805	Voyage
Passenger transport	110	137	164	197	273	Transport de passagers
United Arab Emirates[1]						Emirats arabes unis[1]
Total	3 321	3 654	3 959	4 475	5 300	Total
United Kingdom						Royaume-Uni
Total	46 411	51 125	58 627	69 463	73 786	Total
Travel	37 931	41 744	47 853	56 444	59 593	Voyage
Passenger transport	8 480	9 381	10 774	13 019	14 193	Transport de passagers
United Rep. of Tanzania						Rép.-Unie de Tanzanie
Total	363	362	375	470	577	Total
Travel	327	338	353	445	554	Voyage
Passenger transport	36	24	22	25	23	Transport de passagers
United States						Etats-Unis
Total	85 453	81 707	81 889	93 386	99 624	Total
Travel	62 820	61 738	60 932	69 663	73 558	Voyage
Passenger transport	22 633	19 969	20 957	23 723	26 066	Transport de passagers
Uruguay						Uruguay
Total	333	243	236	267	328	Total
Travel	252	178	169	194	252	Voyage
Passenger transport	81	65	67	73	76	Transport de passagers

Tourism expenditure in other countries—Total, travel and passenger transport: million US dollars (*continued*)
Dépenses touristiques dans d'autres pays—Total, voyage et transport de passagers : millions de dollars E.U. (*suite*)

Country or area	2001	2002	2003	2004	2005	Pays ou zone
Vanuatu						Vanuatu
Total	...	11	14	15	13	Total
Travel	8	9	12	13	11	Voyage
Passenger transport	...	2	2	2	2	Transport de passagers
Venezuela (Bolivarian Rep. of)						Venezuela (Rép. bolivar. du)
Total	1 718	1 546	1 311	1 603	1 837	Total
Travel	1 108	981	859	1 076	1 281	Voyage
Passenger transport	610	565	452	527	556	Transport de passagers
Yemen						Yémen
Total	136	135	134	183	224	Total
Travel	79	78	77	126	167	Voyage
Passenger transport	57	57	57	57	57	Transport de passagers
Zambia[1]						Zambie[1]
Travel	57	67	77	89	94	Voyage

Source

World Tourism Organization (UNWTO), Madrid, UNWTO statistics database and the "Yearbook of Tourism Statistics", 2006 edition. The majority of the data have been provided to the UNWTO by the International Monetary Fund (IMF). Exceptions are footnoted.

Notes

1 Figures provided by the country to the World Tourism Organisation (UNWTO).
2 Country data.
3 Source: Central Bank of the Netherlands Antilles.
4 Source: "Banque des Etats de l'Afrique Centrale (B.E.A.C.)".
5 For statistical purposes, the data for China do not include those for the Hong Kong Special Administrative Region (Hong Kong SAR), Macao Special Administrative Region (Macao SAR) and Taiwan Province of China.
6 Source: Census and Statistics Department.
7 Source: "Banque centrale de Djibouti".
8 Source: Central Bank of Islamic Republic of Iran.
9 Source: Central Bank of Iraq.
10 Source: Reserve Bank of Malawi.
11 West Bank and Gaza.
12 Fiscal years (July-June). The expenditure figures are those provided by the country to UNWTO, which do not appear in the International Monetary Fund data.
13 Source: Qatar Central Bank.
14 Including the estimates for Saba and Saint Eustatius. Excluding passenger transport.
15 Source: Central Bank of Solomon Islands.

Source

Organisation mondiale du tourisme (OMT), Madrid, la base de données de l'OMT, et "l'Annuaire des statistiques du tourisme", 2006 édition. La majorité des données sont celles que le Fonds monétaire international (FMI) a fournis à l'Organisation mondiale du tourisme (OMT). Les exceptions sont signalées par une note.

Notes

1 Les chiffres de dépense sont ceux que le pays a fournis à l'Organisation mondiale du tourisme (OMT).
2 Données du pays.
3 Source: "Central Bank of the Netherlands Antilles".
4 Source: Banque des Etats de l'Afrique Centrale (B.E.A.C.).
5 Pour la présentation des statistiques, les données pour la Chine ne comprennent pas la Région Administrative Spéciale de Hong Kong (Hong Kong RAS), la Région Administrative Spéciale de Macao (Macao RAS) et la province de Taiwan.
6 Source: "Census and Statistics Department".
7 Source: Banque centrale de Djibouti.
8 Source: "Central Bank of Islamic Republic of Iran".
9 Source: "Central Bank of Iraq".
10 Source: "Reserve Bank of Malawi".
11 Cisjordanie et Gaza.
12 Années fiscales (juillet-juin). Les chiffres de dépense sont ceux que le pays a fournis à l'OMT mais ils ne figurent pas dans les données du Fonds monétaire international.
13 Source: "Qatar Central Bank".
14 Y compris estimations pour Saba et Saint-Eustache. Non compris le Transport de passagers.
15 Source: "Central Bank of Solomon Islands".

Technical notes: tables 61-63

The data on international tourism have been supplied by the United Nations World Tourism Organization (UNWTO) from detailed tourism information published in the *Compendium of Tourism Statistics* and in the *Tourism Factbook* online available from http://www.unwto.org/statistics/index.htm.

For statistical purposes, the term "international visitor" describes "any person who travels to a country other than that in which he/she has his/her usual residence but outside his/her usual environment for a period not exceeding 12 months and whose main purpose of visit is other than the exercise of an activity remunerated from within the country visited".

International visitors include: (a) *tourists* (overnight visitors): "visitors who stay at least one night in a collective or private accommodation in the country visited"; and (b) *same-day visitors*: "visitors who do not spend the night in a collective or private accommodation in the country visited". The figures do not include immigrants, residents in a frontier zone, persons domiciled in one country or area and working in an adjoining country or area, members of the armed forces and diplomats and consular representatives when they travel from their country of origin to the country in which they are stationed and vice-versa. The figures also exclude persons in transit who do not formally enter the country through passport control, such as air transit passengers who remain for a short period in a designated area of the air terminal or ship passengers who are not permitted to disembark. This category includes passengers transferred directly between airports or other terminals. Other passengers in transit through a country are classified as visitors.

Tables 61 and 62: Data on arrivals of non-resident (or international) visitors may be obtained from different sources. In some cases data are obtained from border statistics derived from administrative records (police, immigration, traffic counts and other types of controls), border surveys and registrations at accommodation establishments.

Unless otherwise stated, table 61 shows the number of non-resident tourist/visitor arrivals at national borders classified by their region of origin. Totals correspond to the total number of arrivals from the regions indicated in the table. However, these totals may not correspond to the number of tourist arrivals shown in table 62. The latter excludes same-day visitors except when indicated whereas they may be included in table 61.

When a person visits the same country several times a year, an equal number of arrivals is recorded. Likewise, if a person visits several countries during the course of a single trip, his/her arrival in each country is recorded separately. Consequently, arrivals cannot be assumed to be equal to the number of persons travelling.

Notes techniques : tableaux 61 à 63

Les données sur le tourisme international ont été fournies par l'Organisation mondiale du tourisme (l'OMT) qui publie des renseignements détaillés sur le tourisme dans *le Compendium de statistiques du tourisme* et dans le *Tourism Factbook* en ligne au http://www.unwto.org/statistics/index.htm.

A des fins statistiques, l'expression "visiteur international" désigne "toute personne qui se rend dans un pays autre que celui où elle a son lieu de résidence habituelle, mais différent de son environnement habituel, pour une période de 12 mois au maximum, dans un but principal autre que celui d'y exercer une profession rémunérée".

Entrent dans cette catégorie: (a) *les touristes* (visiteurs passant la nuit), c'est à dire "les visiteurs qui passent une nuit au moins en logement collectif ou privé dans le pays visité"; et (b) *les visiteurs ne restant que la journée*, c'est à dire "les visiteurs qui ne passent pas la nuit en logement collectif ou privé dans le pays visité". Ces chiffres ne comprennent pas les immigrants, les résidents frontaliers, les personnes domiciliées dans une zone ou un pays donné et travaillant dans une zone ou pays limitrophe, les membres des forces armées et les membres des corps diplomatique et consulaire lorsqu'ils se rendent de leur pays d'origine au pays où ils sont en poste, et vice versa. Ne sont pas non plus inclus les voyageurs en transit, qui ne pénètrent pas officiellement dans le pays en faisant contrôler leurs passeports, tels que les passagers d'un vol en escale, qui demeurent pendant un court laps de temps dans une aire distincte de l'aérogare, ou les passagers d'un navire qui ne sont pas autorisés à débarquer. Cette catégorie comprend également les passagers transportés directement d'une aérogare à l'autre ou à un autre terminal. Les autres passagers en transit dans un pays sont classés parmi les visiteurs.

Tableaux 61 et 62: Les données relatives aux arrivées des visiteurs non résidents (ou internationaux) peuvent être obtenues de différentes sources. Dans certains cas, elles proviennent des statistiques des frontières tirées des registres administratifs (contrôles de police, de l'immigration, de la circulation et autres effectués aux frontières nationales), des enquêtes statistiques aux frontières et des enregistrements d'établissements d'hébergement touristique.

Sauf indication contraire, le tableau 61 indique le nombre d'arrivées de touristes/visiteurs non résidents aux frontières nationales par région de provenance. Les totaux correspondent au nombre total d'arrivées de touristes des régions indiquées sur le tableau. Les chiffres totaux peuvent, néanmoins, ne pas coïncider avec le nombre des arrivées de touristes indiqué dans le tableau 62, qui sauf indication contraire ne comprend pas les visiteurs ne restant que la journée, lesquels peuvent au contraire être inclus dans les chiffres du tableau 61.

Expenditure associated with tourism activity of visitors has been traditionally identified with the travel item of the Balance of Payments (BOP): in the case of inbound tourism, those expenditures in the country of reference associated with non-resident visitors are registered as "credits" in the BOP and refer to "travel receipts".

The new conceptual framework approved by the United Nations Statistical Commission in relation to the measurement of tourism macroeconomic activity (the so-called Tourism Satellite Account) considers that "tourism industries and products" includes transport of passengers. Consequently, a better estimate of tourism-related expenditures by resident and non-resident visitors in an international scenario would be, in terms of the BOP, the value of the travel item plus that of the passenger transport item.

Nevertheless, users should be aware that BOP estimates include, in addition to expenditures associated with visitors, those related to other types of individuals.

The data published should allow international comparability and therefore correspond to those published by the International Monetary Fund (and provided by the Central Banks). Exceptions are footnoted.

Table 63: Indicators on expenditure (in other countries) are equivalent to those for inbound tourism but are registered as "debits" in the BOP's *travel* and *passenger transport* items. The data published are also provided by the International Monetary Fund and the same previous warning is applicable.

More detailed tourism information from the United Nations World Tourism Organization is available in the *Compendium of Tourism Statistics* and from http://www.unwto.org/statistics/index.htm; information on the balance of payments is published by the International Monetary Fund in the *Balance of Payments Statistics Yearbook.*

Lorsqu'une personne visite le même pays plusieurs fois dans l'année, il est enregistré un nombre égal d'arrivées. En outre, si une personne visite plusieurs pays au cours d'un seul et même voyage, son arrivée dans chaque pays est enregistrée séparément. Par conséquent, on ne peut pas partir du postulat que les arrivées sont égales au nombre de personnes qui voyagent.

Les dépenses associées à l'activité touristique des visiteurs sont traditionnellement identifiées au poste «Voyages» de la balance des paiements. Dans le cas du tourisme récepteur, ces dépenses associées aux visiteurs non résidents sont enregistrées dans la balance des paiements comme des «crédits» et il s'agit de «recettes au titre des voyages».

Le cadre conceptuel approuvé par la Commission de statistique de l'Organisation des Nations Unies concernant l'évaluation de l'activité touristique à l'échelle macroéconomique (cadre qu'il est convenu d'appeler compte satellite du tourisme) considère que la notion «industries et produits touristiques» englobe le transport de passagers. Par conséquent, une meilleure estimation des dépenses liées au tourisme international que font les visiteurs résidents et non résidents serait, sous l'angle de la balance des paiements, la somme des valeurs des postes «Voyages» et «Transport de passagers».

Néanmoins, les utilisateurs doivent être conscients que les estimations de la balance des paiements comprennent, outre les dépenses associées aux visiteurs, celles liées à d'autres types d'individus.

Les données publiées doivent permettre la comparabilité internationale et donc correspondre à celles publiées par le Fonds monétaire international (FMI) qui viennent des banques centrales. Les exceptions sont signalées par une note de pied.

Tableau 63: Les indicateurs relatifs aux dépenses touristiques dans d'autres pays sont équivalents à ceux du tourisme récepteur mais ils sont enregistrés comme «débits» aux postes «Voyages» et «Transport de passagers» de la balance des paiements. Les données publiées sont également fournies par le FMI. Il y a lieu de faire la même mise en garde que plus haut.

On trouvera plus de renseignements publiés par l'Organisation mondiale du tourisme dans le *Compendium des statistiques du tourisme* et au http://www.unwto.org/statistics/index.htm; des renseignements sur la balance des paiements sont publiés par le Fonds monétaire international dans *Balance of Payments Statistics Yearbook.*

Balance of payments summary

Millions of US dollars

Résumé de la balance des paiements

Millions de dollars des E.U.

Country or area	1999	2000	2001	2002	2003	2004	2005	Pays ou zone
Albania								**Albanie**
Current account	-155	-156	-217	-408	-407	-358	-571	Compte des transactions courantes
Goods: exports f.o.b.	275	256	305	330	447	603	656	Biens : exportations f.à.b.
Goods: imports f.o.b.	-938	-1 070	-1 332	-1 485	-1 783	-2 195	-2 478	Biens : importations f.à.b.
Services: credit	269	448	534	585	720	1 003	1 165	Services : crédit
Services: debit	-163	-429	-444	-590	-803	-1 055	-1 383	Services : débit
Income: credit	86	116	163	148	195	204	227	Revenus : crédit
Income: debit	-10	-9	-14	-21	-24	-28	-53	Revenus : débit
Current transfers, n.i.e.: credit	509	629	648	684	924	1 200	1 519	Transferts courants, n.i.a. : crédit
Current transfers: debit	-183	-96	-77	-59	-82	-91	-225	Transferts courants : débit
Capital account, n.i.e.	23	78	118	121	157	132	123	Compte de capital, n.i.a.
Financial account, n.i.e.	34	188	110	213	201	396	393	Compte financier, n.i.a.
Net errors and omissions	206	10	136	108	147	115	204	Erreurs et omissions nettes
Reserves and related items	-107	-120	-147	-36	-98	-286	-148	Réserves et postes apparentés
Angola								**Angola**
Current account	-1 710	796	-1 431	-150	-720	686	5 138	Compte des transactions courantes
Goods: exports f.o.b.	5 157	7 921	6 534	8 328	9 508	13 475	24 109	Biens : exportations f.à.b.
Goods: imports f.o.b.	-3 109	-3 040	-3 179	-3 760	-5 480	-5 832	-8 353	Biens : importations f.à.b.
Services: credit	153	267	203	207	201	323	177	Services : crédit
Services: debit	-2 595	-2 699	-3 518	-3 322	-3 321	-4 803	-6 791	Services : débit
Income: credit	24	34	23	18	12	33	26	Revenus : crédit
Income: debit	-1 396	-1 715	-1 584	-1 652	-1 739	-2 517	-4 057	Revenus : débit
Current transfers, n.i.e.: credit	154	123	208	142	186	124	173	Transferts courants, n.i.a. : crédit
Current transfers: debit	-99	-96	-118	-110	-87	-118	-146	Transferts courants : débit
Capital account, n.i.e.	7	18	4	...	...	0	0	Compte de capital, n.i.a.
Financial account, n.i.e.	1 740	-446	950	-357	1 371	-623	-3 115	Compte financier, n.i.a.
Net errors and omissions	-79	-51	-309	150	-388	277	-378	Erreurs et omissions nettes
Reserves and related items	43	-318	786	356	-263	-340	-1 645	Réserves et postes apparentés
Anguilla								**Anguilla**
Current account	-51	-61	-40	-36	-44	-48	-53	Compte des transactions courantes
Goods: exports f.o.b.	3	4	4	4	4	6	15	Biens : exportations f.à.b.
Goods: imports f.o.b.	-81	-83	-68	-62	-68	-90	-114	Biens : importations f.à.b.
Services: credit	69	65	70	66	69	78	95	Services : crédit
Services: debit	-38	-41	-39	-39	-44	-47	-52	Services : débit
Income: credit	4	4	2	2	2	8	8	Revenus : crédit
Income: debit	-7	-13	-9	-8	-8	-7	-7	Revenus : débit
Current transfers, n.i.e.: credit	8	11	10	9	10	14	12	Transferts courants, n.i.a. : crédit
Current transfers: debit	-9	-8	-9	-8	-10	-10	-11	Transferts courants : débit
Capital account, n.i.e.	8	10	9	8	8	8	9	Compte de capital, n.i.a.
Financial account, n.i.e.	59	45	20	18	46	42	50	Compte financier, n.i.a.
Net errors and omissions	-14	7	15	12	-3	-2	^0	Erreurs et omissions nettes
Reserves and related items	-2	^0	-4	-2	-7	-1	-5	Réserves et postes apparentés
Antigua and Barbuda								**Antigua-et-Barbuda**
Current account	-57	-67	-65	-109	-102	-83	-136	Compte des transactions courantes
Goods: exports f.o.b.	37	52	41	39	45	55	58	Biens : exportations f.à.b.
Goods: imports f.o.b.	-353	-342	-321	-336	-353	-379	-416	Biens : importations f.à.b.
Services: credit	439	415	401	394	413	468	461	Services : crédit
Services: debit	-177	-156	-170	-171	-182	-190	-205	Services : débit
Income: credit	12	16	19	8	9	12	9	Revenus : crédit
Income: debit	-35	-60	-43	-50	-47	-57	-51	Revenus : débit
Current transfers, n.i.e.: credit	24	18	23	23	29	25	26	Transferts courants, n.i.a. : crédit
Current transfers: debit	-4	-9	-13	-17	-16	-17	-18	Transferts courants : débit
Capital account, n.i.e.	18	39	12	14	10	21	214	Compte de capital, n.i.a.
Financial account, n.i.e.	52	42	60	102	99	63	-58	Compte financier, n.i.a.

Country or area	1999	2000	2001	2002	2003	2004	2005	Pays ou zone
Net errors and omissions	-2	-21	8	1	19	6	-13	Erreurs et omissions nettes
Reserves and related items	-10	6	-16	-8	-26	-6	-7	Réserves et postes apparentés
Argentina								Argentine
Current account	-11 943	-8 981	-3 780	8 720	8 065	3 158	5 395	Compte des transactions courantes
Goods: exports f.o.b.	23 309	26 341	26 543	25 651	29 939	34 576	40 106	Biens : exportations f.à.b.
Goods: imports f.o.b.	-24 103	-23 889	-19 158	-8 473	-13 134	-21 311	-27 302	Biens : importations f.à.b.
Services: credit	4 719	4 936	4 627	3 459	4 427	5 182	6 271	Services : crédit
Services: debit	-8 830	-9 219	-8 490	-4 978	-5 713	-6 634	-7 628	Services : débit
Income: credit	6 075	7 420	5 358	3 022	3 086	3 467	4 100	Revenus : crédit
Income: debit	-13 566	-14 968	-13 085	-10 509	-11 059	-12 705	-10 720	Revenus : débit
Current transfers, n.i.e.: credit	790	792	856	819	943	1 114	1 234	Transferts courants, n.i.a. : crédit
Current transfers: debit	-337	-393	-431	-270	-424	-532	-667	Transferts courants : débit
Capital account, n.i.e.	149	106	157	406	40	47	91	Compte de capital, n.i.a.
Financial account, n.i.e.	14 448	7 853	-14 971	-20 686	-15 861	-10 297	1 461	Compte financier, n.i.a.
Net errors and omissions	-642	-154	-2 810	-1 842	-1 321	98	674	Erreurs et omissions nettes
Reserves and related items	-2 013	1 176	21 405	13 402	9 077	6 993	-7 621	Réserves et postes apparentés
Armenia								Arménie
Current account	-307	-278	-200	-148	-189	-162	-193	Compte des transactions courantes
Goods: exports f.o.b.	247	310	353	514	696	738	1 005	Biens : exportations f.à.b.
Goods: imports f.o.b.	-721	-773	-773	-883	-1 130	-1 196	-1 593	Biens : importations f.à.b.
Services: credit	136	137	187	184	207	247	332	Services : crédit
Services: debit	-198	-193	-204	-225	-276	-317	-391	Services : débit
Income: credit	94	104	104	137	166	311	365	Revenus : crédit
Income: debit	-39	-51	-39	-48	-71	-274	-321	Revenus : débit
Current transfers, n.i.e.: credit	201	209	201	200	245	389	474	Transferts courants, n.i.a. : crédit
Current transfers: debit	-26	-20	-27	-26	-27	-59	-65	Transferts courants : débit
Capital account, n.i.e.	13	28	30	68	90	34	51	Compte de capital, n.i.a.
Financial account, n.i.e.	286	250	175	147	174	161	326	Compte financier, n.i.a.
Net errors and omissions	13	17	11	-4	-2	-1	3	Erreurs et omissions nettes
Reserves and related items	-5	-17	-17	-63	-73	-33	-187	Réserves et postes apparentés
Aruba								Aruba
Current account	-429	211	321	-335	-150	14	-259	Compte des transactions courantes
Goods: exports f.o.b.	1 391	2 526	2 424	1 488	2 052	2 724	3 484	Biens : exportations f.à.b.
Goods: imports f.o.b.	-1 995	-2 583	-2 369	-2 019	-2 396	-2 998	-3 536	Biens : importations f.à.b.
Services: credit	922	1 008	988	997	1 048	1 244	1 304	Services : crédit
Services: debit	-661	-646	-615	-608	-728	-794	-927	Services : débit
Income: credit	40	53	50	34	34	36	40	Revenus : crédit
Income: debit	-77	-73	-98	-159	-76	-96	-496	Revenus : débit
Current transfers, n.i.e.: credit	36	39	42	35	40	43	49	Transferts courants, n.i.a. : crédit
Current transfers: debit	-85	-115	-100	-103	-124	-145	-176	Transferts courants : débit
Capital account, n.i.e.	2	11	-1	21	100	18	18	Compte de capital, n.i.a.
Financial account, n.i.e.	450	-204	-228	339	-5	-38	192	Compte financier, n.i.a.
Net errors and omissions	-20	-33	-9	15	18	7	27	Erreurs et omissions nettes
Reserves and related items	-3	15	-83	-40	36	-2	22	Réserves et postes apparentés
Australia								Australie
Current account	-21 282	-14 763	-7 433	-15 824	-28 645	-38 781	-40 900	Compte des transactions courantes
Goods: exports f.o.b.	56 096	64 004	63 626	65 014	70 517	87 161	107 011	Biens : exportations f.à.b.
Goods: imports f.o.b.	-65 857	-68 866	-61 890	-70 528	-85 862	-105 230	-120 383	Biens : importations f.à.b.
Services: credit	18 898	19 894	18 092	19 594	23 747	28 485	31 047	Services : crédit
Services: debit	-18 777	-18 934	-17 351	-18 388	-21 941	-27 943	-30 505	Services : débit
Income: credit	7 404	8 977	8 200	8 522	10 491	14 307	16 420	Revenus : crédit
Income: debit	-19 019	-19 791	-18 132	-19 974	-25 439	-35 293	-44 129	Revenus : débit
Current transfers, n.i.e.: credit	3 003	2 622	2 242	2 310	2 767	3 145	3 277	Transferts courants, n.i.a. : crédit
Current transfers: debit	-3 032	-2 669	-2 221	-2 373	-2 927	-3 414	-3 638	Transferts courants : débit
Capital account, n.i.e.	819	615	591	443	736	817	963	Compte de capital, n.i.a.
Financial account, n.i.e.	27 613	12 954	8 155	16 249	34 734	38 636	47 421	Compte financier, n.i.a.
Net errors and omissions	-444	-171	-218	-746	53	493	-227	Erreurs et omissions nettes
Reserves and related items	-6 705	1 365	-1 096	-122	-6 877	-1 166	-7 256	Réserves et postes apparentés

Country or area	1999	2000	2001	2002	2003	2004	2005	Pays ou zone
Austria								Autriche
Current account	-6 655	-4 864	-3 636	565	-638	1 382	4 252	Compte des transactions courantes
Goods: exports f.o.b.	64 422	64 684	66 900	73 668	89 622	112 070	117 233	Biens : exportations f.à.b.
Goods: imports f.o.b.	-68 051	-67 421	-68 169	-70 080	-88 480	-109 020	-113 806	Biens : importations f.à.b.
Services: credit	31 306	31 342	33 352	35 386	42 964	49 153	53 921	Services : crédit
Services: debit	-29 422	-29 653	-31 437	-34 996	-41 261	-46 737	-49 107	Services : débit
Income: credit	12 673	11 992	12 031	13 816	16 169	19 891	24 151	Revenus : crédit
Income: debit	-15 552	-14 456	-15 111	-15 406	-17 357	-21 216	-25 488	Revenus : débit
Current transfers, n.i.e.: credit	2 925	2 914	3 267	3 815	4 388	5 314	6 257	Transferts courants, n.i.a. : crédit
Current transfers: debit	-4 956	-4 267	-4 468	-5 639	-6 683	-8 073	-8 908	Transferts courants : débit
Capital account, n.i.e.	-265	-432	-529	-378	8	-341	-237	Compte de capital, n.i.a.
Financial account, n.i.e.	4 789	3 407	1 795	-4 713	-2 483	-2 618	-1 627	Compte financier, n.i.a.
Net errors and omissions	-40	1 143	482	2 803	1 089	-272	-3 138	Erreurs et omissions nettes
Reserves and related items	2 172	746	1 888	1 723	2 023	1 849	750	Réserves et postes apparentés
Azerbaijan								Azerbaïdjan
Current account	-600	-168	-52	-768	-2 021	-2 589	167	Compte des transactions courantes
Goods: exports f.o.b.	1 025	1 858	2 079	2 305	2 625	3 743	7 649	Biens : exportations f.à.b.
Goods: imports f.o.b.	-1 433	-1 539	-1 465	-1 823	-2 723	-3 582	-4 350	Biens : importations f.à.b.
Services: credit	257	260	290	362	432	492	683	Services : crédit
Services: debit	-485	-485	-665	-1 298	-2 047	-2 730	-2 653	Services : débit
Income: credit	11	56	41	37	53	65	202	Revenus : crédit
Income: debit	-56	-391	-409	-422	-495	-766	-1 847	Revenus : débit
Current transfers, n.i.e.: credit	135	135	176	228	225	263	626	Transferts courants, n.i.a. : crédit
Current transfers: debit	-53	-62	-100	-158	-91	-74	-142	Transferts courants : débit
Capital account, n.i.e.	...	...	...	-29	-23	-4	41	Compte de capital, n.i.a.
Financial account, n.i.e.	690	493	126	918	2 280	2 960	78	Compte financier, n.i.a.
Net errors and omissions	42	^0	-1	-87	-112	-50	-126	Erreurs et omissions nettes
Reserves and related items	-133	-326	-73	-34	-124	-317	-161	Réserves et postes apparentés
Bahamas								Bahamas
Current account	-324	-633	-645	-423	-474	-307	-765	Compte des transactions courantes
Goods: exports f.o.b.	407	465	417	422	427	477	549	Biens : exportations f.à.b.
Goods: imports f.o.b.	-1 677	-1 983	-1 804	-1 749	-1 759	-1 907	-2 401	Biens : importations f.à.b.
Services: credit	1 801	1 973	1 804	2 062	2 055	2 244	2 482	Services : crédit
Services: debit	-934	-1 026	-973	-1 016	-1 092	-1 231	-1 373	Services : débit
Income: credit	393	317	185	108	79	80	173	Revenus : crédit
Income: debit	-520	-457	-383	-292	-232	-221	-279	Revenus : débit
Current transfers, n.i.e.: credit	218	88	121	55	60	265	103	Transferts courants, n.i.a. : crédit
Current transfers: debit	-12	-10	-11	-13	-11	-14	-18	Transferts courants : débit
Capital account, n.i.e.	-15	-16	-21	-25	-37	-48	-60	Compte de capital, n.i.a.
Financial account, n.i.e.	616	430	265	405	535	358	490	Compte financier, n.i.a.
Net errors and omissions	-212	158	371	103	85	180	247	Erreurs et omissions nettes
Reserves and related items	-65	61	31	-60	-110	-183	88	Réserves et postes apparentés
Bahrain								Bahreïn
Current account	-37	830	227	-50	201	415	1 575	Compte des transactions courantes
Goods: exports f.o.b.	4 363	6 243	5 657	5 887	6 721	7 621	10 131	Biens : exportations f.à.b.
Goods: imports f.o.b.	-3 468	-4 394	-4 047	-4 697	-5 319	-6 135	-7 606	Biens : importations f.à.b.
Services: credit	859	933	950	1 068	1 260	1 558	1 662	Services : crédit
Services: debit	-700	-738	-748	-927	-886	-933	-977	Services : débit
Income: credit	5 118	6 328	3 794	1 679	1 267	2 544	5 016	Revenus : crédit
Income: debit	-5 389	-6 552	-4 116	-2 204	-1 760	-3 119	-5 428	Revenus : débit
Current transfers, n.i.e.: credit	37	22	23	15	0	0	0	Transferts courants, n.i.a. : crédit
Current transfers: debit	-856	-1 013	-1 287	-872	-1 082	-1 120	-1 223	Transferts courants : débit
Capital account, n.i.e.	100	50	100	102	50	50	50	Compte de capital, n.i.a.
Financial account, n.i.e.	230	-30	-417	-1 234	493	-395	-1 368	Compte financier, n.i.a.
Net errors and omissions	-268	-650	214	1 218	-700	88	37	Erreurs et omissions nettes
Reserves and related items	-25	-200	-123	-35	-44	-158	-294	Réserves et postes apparentés

Country or area	1999	2000	2001	2002	2003	2004	2005	Pays ou zone
Bangladesh								Bangladesh
Current account	-364	-306	-535	739	132	-279	-176	Compte des transactions courantes
Goods: exports f.o.b.	5 458	6 399	6 085	6 102	7 050	8 151	9 302	Biens : exportations f.à.b.
Goods: imports f.o.b.	-7 536	-8 053	-8 133	-7 780	-9 492	-11 157	-12 502	Biens : importations f.à.b.
Services: credit	778	815	752	849	1 012	1 083	1 249	Services : crédit
Services: debit	-1 397	-1 620	-1 522	-1 406	-1 711	-1 931	-2 207	Services : débit
Income: credit	94	78	77	57	57	103	117	Revenus : crédit
Income: debit	-258	-345	-362	-322	-361	-474	-910	Revenus : débit
Current transfers, n.i.e.: credit	2 501	2 426	2 573	3 245	3 586	3 960	4 785	Transferts courants, n.i.a. : crédit
Current transfers: debit	-5	-7	-5	-6	-8	-13	-11	Transferts courants : débit
Capital account, n.i.e.	364	249	235	364	387	142	262	Compte de capital, n.i.a.
Financial account, n.i.e.	-447	-256	262	-256	289	665	142	Compte financier, n.i.a.
Net errors and omissions	258	282	-106	-349	81	-25	-644	Erreurs et omissions nettes
Reserves and related items	189	31	144	-497	-889	-503	416	Réserves et postes apparentés
Barbados								Barbade
Current account	-148	-146	-111	-168	-170	-337	-387	Compte des transactions courantes
Goods: exports f.o.b.	275	286	271	253	264	293	379	Biens : exportations f.à.b.
Goods: imports f.o.b.	-989	-1 030	-952	-955	-1 066	-1 264	-1 464	Biens : importations f.à.b.
Services: credit	1 029	1 090	1 069	1 041	1 165	1 224	1 457	Services : crédit
Services: debit	-458	-487	-499	-491	-519	-556	-680	Services : débit
Income: credit	67	70	73	72	75	75	85	Revenus : crédit
Income: debit	-138	-152	-166	-174	-182	-197	-257	Revenus : débit
Current transfers, n.i.e.: credit	94	109	126	120	127	126	160	Transferts courants, n.i.a. : crédit
Current transfers: debit	-28	-31	-32	-34	-34	-38	-67	Transferts courants : débit
Capital account, n.i.e.	1	2	1	0	0	0	0	Compte de capital, n.i.a.
Financial account, n.i.e.	120	289	285	119	203	135	391	Compte financier, n.i.a.
Net errors and omissions	63	32	47	25	34	45	18	Erreurs et omissions nettes
Reserves and related items	-36	-178	-222	24	-67	157	-22	Réserves et postes apparentés
Belarus								Bélarus
Current account	-194	-338	-411	-326	-434	-1 194	434	Compte des transactions courantes
Goods: exports f.o.b.	5 646	6 640	7 334	7 965	10 076	13 942	16 109	Biens : exportations f.à.b.
Goods: imports f.o.b.	-6 216	-7 525	-8 141	-8 879	-11 324	-16 126	-16 610	Biens : importations f.à.b.
Services: credit	753	1 000	1 143	1 341	1 500	1 747	1 959	Services : crédit
Services: debit	-439	-563	-841	-908	-915	-1 058	-1 250	Services : débit
Income: credit	21	26	27	45	126	158	283	Revenus : crédit
Income: debit	-63	-72	-78	-83	-113	-159	-228	Revenus : débit
Current transfers, n.i.e.: credit	137	177	202	260	292	391	281	Transferts courants, n.i.a. : crédit
Current transfers: debit	-33	-22	-57	-67	-77	-88	-111	Transferts courants : débit
Capital account, n.i.e.	60	69	56	53	69	49	41	Compte de capital, n.i.a.
Financial account, n.i.e.	400	140	265	666	279	1 046	-61	Compte financier, n.i.a.
Net errors and omissions	-246	254	11	-294	-3	274	112	Erreurs et omissions nettes
Reserves and related items	-20	-125	79	-98	90	-175	-525	Réserves et postes apparentés
Belgium								Belgique
Current account	...	...	...	11 611	12 906	12 537	9 328	Compte des transactions courantes
Goods: exports f.o.b.	...	...	...	169 166	204 962	245 426	263 021	Biens : exportations f.à.b.
Goods: imports f.o.b.	...	...	...	-159 648	-194 003	-235 718	-257 136	Biens : importations f.à.b.
Services: credit	...	...	...	37 822	44 708	52 708	55 754	Services : crédit
Services: debit	...	...	...	-35 863	-42 862	-49 023	-51 294	Services : débit
Income: credit	...	...	...	36 372	40 213	48 891	57 954	Revenus : crédit
Income: debit	...	...	...	-31 897	-33 732	-43 269	-52 560	Revenus : débit
Current transfers, n.i.e.: credit	...	...	...	5 275	6 515	7 949	9 253	Transferts courants, n.i.a. : crédit
Current transfers: debit	...	...	...	-9 616	-12 894	-14 427	-15 664	Transferts courants : débit
Capital account, n.i.e.	...	...	...	-585	-1 021	-497	-844	Compte de capital, n.i.a.
Financial account, n.i.e.	...	...	...	-6 483	-12 518	-10 660	-10 652	Compte financier, n.i.a.
Net errors and omissions	...	...	...	-4 579	-1 093	-2 103	-8	Erreurs et omissions nettes
Reserves and related items	...	...	...	35	1 725	723	2 176	Réserves et postes apparentés
Belgium-Luxembourg[1]								Belgique-Luxembourg[1]
Current account	14 086	11 381	9 392	...	...	...	...	Compte des transactions courantes
Goods: exports f.o.b.	161 263	164 677	163 498	...	...	...	...	Biens : exportations f.à.b.

Country or area	1999	2000	2001	2002	2003	2004	2005	Pays ou zone
Goods: imports f.o.b.	-154 237	-162 086	-159 790	...	...	...	...	Biens : importations f.à.b.
Services: credit	45 292	49 789	50 314	...	...	...	...	Services : crédit
Services: debit	-39 167	-41 868	-43 316	...	...	...	...	Services : débit
Income: credit	71 892	75 673	78 906	...	...	...	...	Revenus : crédit
Income: debit	-66 125	-70 625	-75 999	...	...	...	...	Revenus : débit
Current transfers, n.i.e.: credit	7 041	7 014	7 316	...	...	...	...	Transferts courants, n.i.a. : crédit
Current transfers: debit	-11 872	-11 193	-11 535	...	...	...	...	Transferts courants : débit
Capital account, n.i.e.	-54	-213	26	...	...	...	...	Compte de capital, n.i.a.
Financial account, n.i.e.	-13 470	-9 233	-7 978	...	...	...	...	Compte financier, n.i.a.
Net errors and omissions	-2 430	-2 894	3	...	...	...	...	Erreurs et omissions nettes
Reserves and related items	1 867	959	-1 442	...	...	...	...	Réserves et postes apparentés
Belize								Belize
Current account	-73	-162	-191	-165	-180	-152	-159	Compte des transactions courantes
Goods: exports f.o.b.	262	282	269	310	316	307	322	Biens : exportations f.à.b.
Goods: imports f.o.b.	-376	-478	-478	-497	-522	-481	-556	Biens : importations f.à.b.
Services: credit	149	153	166	176	212	235	293	Services : crédit
Services: debit	-105	-123	-121	-130	-139	-146	-158	Services : débit
Income: credit	5	7	9	4	5	4	7	Revenus : crédit
Income: debit	-45	-60	-76	-72	-91	-118	-118	Revenus : débit
Current transfers, n.i.e.: credit	42	61	54	59	59	61	68	Transferts courants, n.i.a. : crédit
Current transfers: debit	-4	-3	-14	-16	-18	-15	-17	Transferts courants : débit
Capital account, n.i.e.	1	-3	6	14	4	10	3	Compte de capital, n.i.a.
Financial account, n.i.e.	96	205	165	151	117	191	174	Compte financier, n.i.a.
Net errors and omissions	1	11	9	-9	47	-81	1	Erreurs et omissions nettes
Reserves and related items	-25	-52	11	8	11	32	-19	Réserves et postes apparentés
Benin								Bénin
Current account	-191	-111	-160	-239	-349	-317	...	Compte des transactions courantes
Goods: exports f.o.b.	421	392	373	448	541	569	...	Biens : exportations f.à.b.
Goods: imports f.o.b.	-635	-516	-553	-679	-819	-842	...	Biens : importations f.à.b.
Services: credit	177	136	147	152	172	216	...	Services : crédit
Services: debit	-215	-192	-192	-209	-254	-287	...	Services : débit
Income: credit	29	31	29	25	26	39	...	Revenus : crédit
Income: debit	-40	-43	-43	-51	-64	-76	...	Revenus : débit
Current transfers, n.i.e.: credit	87	91	87	93	57	73	...	Transferts courants, n.i.a. : crédit
Current transfers: debit	-15	-11	-10	-19	-8	-8	...	Transferts courants : débit
Capital account, n.i.e.	70	73	49	38	34	52	...	Compte de capital, n.i.a.
Financial account, n.i.e.	25	11	36	-61	32	-6	...	Compte financier, n.i.a.
Net errors and omissions	7	7	8	2	182	-38	...	Erreurs et omissions nettes
Reserves and related items	89	20	69	261	100	310	...	Réserves et postes apparentés
Bolivia								Bolivie
Current account	-488	-446	-274	-352	76	337	498	Compte des transactions courantes
Goods: exports f.o.b.	1 051	1 246	1 285	1 299	1 598	2 146	2 671	Biens : exportations f.à.b.
Goods: imports f.o.b.	-1 539	-1 610	-1 580	-1 639	-1 497	-1 725	-2 190	Biens : importations f.à.b.
Services: credit	259	224	236	257	364	416	489	Services : crédit
Services: debit	-450	-468	-399	-433	-551	-607	-683	Services : débit
Income: credit	157	140	121	103	71	76	121	Revenus : crédit
Income: debit	-353	-365	-333	-308	-374	-461	-494	Revenus : débit
Current transfers, n.i.e.: credit	415	420	432	408	511	543	649	Transferts courants, n.i.a. : crédit
Current transfers: debit	-29	-33	-35	-38	-46	-52	-65	Transferts courants : débit
Capital account, n.i.e.	0	0	0	0	0	0	0	Compte de capital, n.i.a.
Financial account, n.i.e.	868	462	441	649	36	361	42	Compte financier, n.i.a.
Net errors and omissions	-353	-55	-203	-640	-174	-625	-122	Erreurs et omissions nettes
Reserves and related items	-27	39	36	343	62	-73	-418	Réserves et postes apparentés
Bosnia and Herzegovina								Bosnie-Herzégovine
Current account	-501	-396	-743	-1 191	-1 631	-1 794	-2 116	Compte des transactions courantes
Goods: exports f.o.b.	832	1 130	1 134	1 110	1 477	2 087	2 590	Biens : exportations f.à.b.
Goods: imports f.o.b.	-4 129	-3 894	-4 092	-4 449	-5 637	-6 656	-7 544	Biens : importations f.à.b.
Services: credit	464	450	497	524	721	864	950	Services : crédit
Services: debit	-285	-263	-269	-305	-384	-432	-459	Services : débit

64 Balance of payments summary—Millions of US dollars (*continued*)
Résumé de la balance des paiements—Millions de dollars des E.U. (*suite*)

Country or area	1999	2000	2001	2002	2003	2004	2005	Pays ou zone
Income: credit	793	667	625	605	654	644	649	Revenus : crédit
Income: debit	-65	-76	-93	-97	-121	-162	-196	Revenus : débit
Current transfers, n.i.e.: credit	1 975	1 667	1 528	1 524	1 781	2 073	2 095	Transferts courants, n.i.a. : crédit
Current transfers: debit	-86	-75	-73	-102	-123	-210	-199	Transferts courants : débit
Capital account, n.i.e.	625	546	400	412	466	432	410	Compte de capital, n.i.a.
Financial account, n.i.e.	-48	84	985	533	1 073	1 416	1 763	Compte financier, n.i.a.
Net errors and omissions	225	-173	110	117	306	399	431	Erreurs et omissions nettes
Reserves and related items	-301	-61	-752	129	-214	-453	-488	Réserves et postes apparentés
Botswana								Botswana
Current account	583	545	618	143	462	287	1 469	Compte des transactions courantes
Goods: exports f.o.b.	2 658	2 675	2 315	2 319	3 024	3 696	4 429	Biens : exportations f.à.b.
Goods: imports f.o.b.	-1 873	-1 773	-1 604	-1 642	-2 127	-2 864	-2 826	Biens : importations f.à.b.
Services: credit	331	325	340	490	643	748	856	Services : crédit
Services: debit	-518	-547	-513	-510	-652	-793	-857	Services : débit
Income: credit	430	378	378	268	383	227	456	Revenus : crédit
Income: debit	-696	-729	-495	-994	-1 098	-1 254	-1 268	Revenus : débit
Current transfers, n.i.e.: credit	474	426	383	400	538	743	896	Transferts courants, n.i.a. : crédit
Current transfers: debit	-223	-209	-185	-188	-248	-217	-218	Transferts courants : débit
Capital account, n.i.e.	21	38	6	16	22	32	31	Compte de capital, n.i.a.
Financial account, n.i.e.	-231	-214	-509	-217	-379	-286	54	Compte financier, n.i.a.
Net errors and omissions	21	-2	56	119	66	-90	-191	Erreurs et omissions nettes
Reserves and related items	-394	-367	-170	-61	-171	57	-1 363	Réserves et postes apparentés
Brazil								Brésil
Current account	-25 400	-24 225	-23 215	-7 637	4 177	11 738	14 199	Compte des transactions courantes
Goods: exports f.o.b.	48 011	55 086	58 223	60 362	73 084	96 475	118 308	Biens : exportations f.à.b.
Goods: imports f.o.b.	-49 272	-55 783	-55 572	-47 241	-48 290	-62 809	-73 551	Biens : importations f.à.b.
Services: credit	7 189	9 498	9 322	9 551	10 447	12 584	16 095	Services : crédit
Services: debit	-14 172	-16 660	-17 081	-14 509	-15 378	-17 260	-24 243	Services : débit
Income: credit	3 936	3 621	3 280	3 295	3 339	3 199	3 194	Revenus : crédit
Income: debit	-22 780	-21 507	-23 023	-21 486	-21 891	-23 719	-29 162	Revenus : débit
Current transfers, n.i.e.: credit	1 969	1 828	1 934	2 627	3 132	3 582	4 050	Transferts courants, n.i.a. : crédit
Current transfers: debit	-281	-307	-296	-237	-265	-314	-493	Transferts courants : débit
Capital account, n.i.e.	339	273	-36	433	498	339	663	Compte de capital, n.i.a.
Financial account, n.i.e.	8 056	29 376	20 331	-3 909	-157	-3 333	13 801	Compte financier, n.i.a.
Net errors and omissions	240	2 557	-498	-154	-933	-2 145	-1 096	Erreurs et omissions nettes
Reserves and related items	16 765	-7 981	3 418	11 266	-3 586	-6 599	-27 566	Réserves et postes apparentés
Bulgaria								Bulgarie
Current account	-652	-703	-805	-319	-1 022	-1 671	-3 244	Compte des transactions courantes
Goods: exports f.o.b.	4 006	4 825	5 113	5 354	7 081	9 931	11 754	Biens : exportations f.à.b.
Goods: imports f.o.b.	-5 087	-6 000	-6 693	-7 013	-9 657	-13 619	-17 204	Biens : importations f.à.b.
Services: credit	1 788	2 175	2 163	2 203	2 961	4 029	4 404	Services : crédit
Services: debit	-1 474	-1 670	-1 910	-1 755	-2 447	-3 238	-3 404	Services : débit
Income: credit	265	321	706	924	1 298	1 539	1 516	Revenus : crédit
Income: debit	-451	-644	-681	-581	-954	-1 236	-1 323	Revenus : débit
Current transfers, n.i.e.: credit	329	355	599	654	865	1 121	1 238	Transferts courants, n.i.a. : crédit
Current transfers: debit	-29	-64	-100	-106	-170	-199	-225	Transferts courants : débit
Capital account, n.i.e.	-2	25	^0	^0	^0	204	256	Compte de capital, n.i.a.
Financial account, n.i.e.	721	781	663	3 513	2 738	3 428	6 387	Compte financier, n.i.a.
Net errors and omissions	30	34	515	-716	-889	371	-772	Erreurs et omissions nettes
Reserves and related items	-96	-137	-373	-2 478	-827	-2 332	-2 627	Réserves et postes apparentés
Burkina Faso								Burkina Faso
Current account	...	-392	-381	...	...	...	...	Compte des transactions courantes
Goods: exports f.o.b.	...	206	223	...	...	...	...	Biens : exportations f.à.b.
Goods: imports f.o.b.	...	-518	-509	...	...	...	...	Biens : importations f.à.b.
Services: credit	...	31	37	...	...	...	...	Services : crédit
Services: debit	...	-140	-141	...	...	...	...	Services : débit
Income: credit	...	14	15	...	...	...	...	Revenus : crédit
Income: debit	...	-34	-40	...	...	...	...	Revenus : débit
Current transfers, n.i.e.: credit	...	88	72	...	...	...	...	Transferts courants, n.i.a. : crédit

Balance of payments summary—Millions of US dollars (*continued*)
Résumé de la balance des paiements—Millions de dollars des E.U. (*suite*)

Country or area	1999	2000	2001	2002	2003	2004	2005	Pays ou zone
Current transfers: debit	...	-39	-38	...	...	...	...	Transferts courants : débit
Capital account, n.i.e.	...	176	165	...	...	...	...	Compte de capital, n.i.a.
Financial account, n.i.e.	...	19	25	...	...	...	...	Compte financier, n.i.a.
Net errors and omissions	...	5	3	...	...	...	...	Erreurs et omissions nettes
Reserves and related items	...	192	187	...	...	...	...	Réserves et postes apparentés
Burundi								Burundi
Current account	-23	-54	-40	-10	-37	-182	-263	Compte des transactions courantes
Goods: exports f.o.b.	55	49	39	31	38	48	57	Biens : exportations f.à.b.
Goods: imports f.o.b.	-97	-108	-108	-105	-130	-163	-241	Biens : importations f.à.b.
Services: credit	4	4	5	8	7	16	35	Services : crédit
Services: debit	-25	-44	-39	-44	-46	-74	-112	Services : débit
Income: credit	2	2	2	1	1	1	3	Revenus : crédit
Income: debit	-11	-14	-16	-13	-19	-20	-21	Revenus : débit
Current transfers, n.i.e.: credit	51	58	80	116	115	13	20	Transferts courants, n.i.a. : crédit
Current transfers: debit	-2	-2	-3	-3	-3	-3	-3	Transferts courants : débit
Capital account, n.i.e.	^0	^0	^0	^0	-1	132	192	Compte de capital, n.i.a.
Financial account, n.i.e.	-7	-7	-4	-41	-50	-40	-15	Compte financier, n.i.a.
Net errors and omissions	-19	-33	-30	3	-13	3	-25	Erreurs et omissions nettes
Reserves and related items	49	95	74	47	101	87	111	Réserves et postes apparentés
Cambodia								Cambodge
Current account	-189	-138	-90	-109	-236	-185	-356	Compte des transactions courantes
Goods: exports f.o.b.	1 130	1 397	1 571	1 770	2 087	2 589	2 910	Biens : exportations f.à.b.
Goods: imports f.o.b.	-1 592	-1 936	-2 094	-2 361	-2 668	-3 269	-3 928	Biens : importations f.à.b.
Services: credit	294	428	525	604	545	801	1 107	Services : crédit
Services: debit	-293	-329	-349	-377	-434	-513	-631	Services : débit
Income: credit	51	67	58	51	44	49	68	Revenus : crédit
Income: debit	-150	-190	-195	-234	-223	-270	-322	Revenus : débit
Current transfers, n.i.e.: credit	378	432	404	448	425	444	461	Transferts courants, n.i.a. : crédit
Current transfers: debit	-8	-7	-8	-9	-12	-15	-21	Transferts courants : débit
Capital account, n.i.e.	11	36	45	8	66	68	95	Compte de capital, n.i.a.
Financial account, n.i.e.	191	184	149	258	233	283	294	Compte financier, n.i.a.
Net errors and omissions	37	16	-30	14	-28	-35	-22	Erreurs et omissions nettes
Reserves and related items	-50	-98	-74	-171	-36	-131	-11	Réserves et postes apparentés
Cameroon								Cameroun
Current account	-509	-249	-376	-445	-675	...	...	Compte des transactions courantes
Goods: exports f.o.b.	1 745	1 986	1 891	1 964	2 448	...	...	Biens : exportations f.à.b.
Goods: imports f.o.b.	-1 334	-1 484	-1 797	-1 812	-2 141	...	...	Biens : importations f.à.b.
Services: credit	434	590	858	939	445	...	...	Services : crédit
Services: debit	-715	-957	-1 082	-1 212	-1 098	...	...	Services : débit
Income: credit	38	26	47	43	50	...	...	Revenus : crédit
Income: debit	-806	-519	-380	-420	-495	...	...	Revenus : débit
Current transfers, n.i.e.: credit	170	173	147	127	205	...	...	Transferts courants, n.i.a. : crédit
Current transfers: debit	-41	-64	-61	-75	-90	...	...	Transferts courants : débit
Capital account, n.i.e.	11	17	56	61	198	...	...	Compte de capital, n.i.a.
Financial account, n.i.e.	-243	-170	142	307	842	...	...	Compte financier, n.i.a.
Net errors and omissions	125	112	-124	-130	105	...	...	Erreurs et omissions nettes
Reserves and related items	617	290	302	207	-470	...	...	Réserves et postes apparentés
Canada								Canada
Current account	1 765	19 622	16 281	12 604	10 315	21 157	26 555	Compte des transactions courantes
Goods: exports f.o.b.	248 494	289 022	271 849	263 908	285 068	330 106	374 308	Biens : exportations f.à.b.
Goods: imports f.o.b.	-220 203	-243 975	-226 132	-227 410	-244 891	-279 880	-320 517	Biens : importations f.à.b.
Services: credit	36 117	40 230	38 804	40 481	43 778	49 111	53 647	Services : crédit
Services: debit	-40 573	-44 118	-43 843	-45 070	-52 227	-58 914	-64 956	Services : débit
Income: credit	22 158	24 746	16 823	19 444	21 216	28 905	39 832	Revenus : crédit
Income: debit	-44 777	-47 036	-42 238	-38 745	-42 380	-47 930	-55 341	Revenus : débit
Current transfers, n.i.e.: credit	3 796	4 122	4 500	4 387	4 815	5 730	6 662	Transferts courants, n.i.a. : crédit
Current transfers: debit	-3 247	-3 368	-3 480	-4 391	-5 063	-5 970	-7 082	Transferts courants : débit
Capital account, n.i.e.	3 400	3 581	3 721	3 145	2 982	3 424	4 881	Compte de capital, n.i.a.
Financial account, n.i.e.	-5 968	-14 500	-11 609	-14 360	-18 010	-31 258	-27 511	Compte financier, n.i.a.

Country or area	1999	2000	2001	2002	2003	2004	2005	Pays ou zone
Net errors and omissions	6 736	-4 984	-6 220	-1 574	1 457	3 842	-2 589	Erreurs et omissions nettes
Reserves and related items	-5 933	-3 720	-2 172	185	3 255	2 836	-1 335	Réserves et postes apparentés
Cape Verde								Cap-Vert
Current account	-74	-58	-56	-72	-77	-58	-34	Compte des transactions courantes
Goods: exports f.o.b.	26	38	37	42	53	58	89	Biens : exportations f.à.b.
Goods: imports f.o.b.	-239	-226	-232	-278	-344	-391	-438	Biens : importations f.à.b.
Services: credit	105	108	130	153	224	242	277	Services : crédit
Services: debit	-116	-100	-119	-142	-203	-199	-208	Services : débit
Income: credit	2	5	8	6	13	19	19	Revenus : crédit
Income: debit	-10	-18	-13	-18	-30	-34	-52	Revenus : débit
Current transfers, n.i.e.: credit	167	146	156	182	229	279	310	Transferts courants, n.i.a. : crédit
Current transfers: debit	-9	-12	-22	-16	-19	-32	-31	Transferts courants : débit
Capital account, n.i.e.	4	11	24	9	21	18	20	Compte de capital, n.i.a.
Financial account, n.i.e.	128	32	39	81	6	68	90	Compte financier, n.i.a.
Net errors and omissions	-9	-12	-24	-8	-5	7	-24	Erreurs et omissions nettes
Reserves and related items	-49	28	17	-10	56	-35	-52	Réserves et postes apparentés
Chile								Chili
Current account	99	-898	-1 100	-580	-779	2 074	1 315	Compte des transactions courantes
Goods: exports f.o.b.	17 162	19 210	18 272	18 180	21 664	32 520	41 297	Biens : exportations f.à.b.
Goods: imports f.o.b.	-14 735	-17 091	-16 428	-15 794	-17 941	-22 935	-30 492	Biens : importations f.à.b.
Services: credit	3 869	4 083	4 138	4 386	5 070	6 034	7 020	Services : crédit
Services: debit	-4 606	-4 802	-4 983	-5 087	-5 688	-6 780	-7 656	Services : débit
Income: credit	912	1 598	1 458	1 114	1 552	1 983	2 452	Revenus : crédit
Income: debit	-3 145	-4 453	-3 985	-3 960	-6 041	-9 820	-13 097	Revenus : débit
Current transfers, n.i.e.: credit	841	765	713	954	901	1 411	2 236	Transferts courants, n.i.a. : crédit
Current transfers: debit	-198	-207	-286	-372	-296	-339	-445	Transferts courants : débit
Capital account, n.i.e.	0	0	0	83	0	5	41	Compte de capital, n.i.a.
Financial account, n.i.e.	237	787	1 362	1 634	1 145	-2 001	1 623	Compte financier, n.i.a.
Net errors and omissions	-1 083	427	-861	-952	-724	-270	-1 268	Erreurs et omissions nettes
Reserves and related items	747	-317	599	-185	357	191	-1 711	Réserves et postes apparentés
China[2]								Chine[2]
Current account	21 115	20 518	17 401	35 422	45 875	68 659	160 818	Compte des transactions courantes
Goods: exports f.o.b.	194 716	249 131	266 075	325 651	438 270	593 393	762 484	Biens : exportations f.à.b.
Goods: imports f.o.b.	-158 734	-214 657	-232 058	-281 484	-393 618	-534 410	-628 295	Biens : importations f.à.b.
Services: credit	26 248	30 431	33 334	39 745	46 734	62 434	74 404	Services : crédit
Services: debit	-31 589	-36 031	-39 267	-46 528	-55 306	-72 133	-83 796	Services : débit
Income: credit	8 330	12 550	9 388	8 344	16 095	20 544	38 959	Revenus : crédit
Income: debit	-22 800	-27 216	-28 563	-23 290	-23 933	-24 067	-28 324	Revenus : débit
Current transfers, n.i.e.: credit	5 368	6 861	9 125	13 795	18 483	24 326	27 735	Transferts courants, n.i.a. : crédit
Current transfers: debit	-424	-550	-633	-811	-848	-1 428	-2 349	Transferts courants : débit
Capital account, n.i.e.	-26	-35	-54	-50	-48	-69	4 102	Compte de capital, n.i.a.
Financial account, n.i.e.	5 204	1 958	34 832	32 341	52 774	110 729	58 862	Compte financier, n.i.a.
Net errors and omissions	-17 641	-11 748	-4 732	7 504	17 985	26 834	-16 441	Erreurs et omissions nettes
Reserves and related items	-8 652	-10 693	-47 447	-75 217	-116 586	-206 153	-207 342	Réserves et postes apparentés
China, Hong Kong SAR								Chine, Hong Kong RAS
Current account	10 248	6 993	9 786	12 412	16 470	15 728	20 233	Compte des transactions courantes
Goods: exports f.o.b.	174 719	202 698	190 926	200 300	224 656	260 263	289 579	Biens : exportations f.à.b.
Goods: imports f.o.b.	-177 878	-210 891	-199 257	-205 353	-230 435	-269 575	-297 206	Biens : importations f.à.b.
Services: credit	35 625	40 430	41 135	44 601	46 555	55 157	63 762	Services : crédit
Services: debit	-23 870	-24 698	-24 899	-25 964	-26 126	-31 138	-33 979	Services : débit
Income: credit	46 809	54 483	48 058	41 511	43 181	52 003	64 806	Revenus : crédit
Income: debit	-43 617	-53 359	-44 398	-40 787	-39 525	-48 997	-64 604	Revenus : débit
Current transfers, n.i.e.: credit	570	538	605	777	529	626	943	Transferts courants, n.i.a. : crédit
Current transfers: debit	-2 109	-2 208	-2 385	-2 673	-2 366	-2 611	-3 067	Transferts courants : débit
Capital account, n.i.e.	-1 780	-1 546	-1 174	-2 011	-1 065	-329	-634	Compte de capital, n.i.a.
Financial account, n.i.e.	1 061	4 165	-6 626	-19 751	-20 953	-20 094	-21 448	Compte financier, n.i.a.
Net errors and omissions	499	431	2 699	6 973	6 542	7 980	3 227	Erreurs et omissions nettes
Reserves and related items	-10 028	-10 044	-4 684	2 377	-994	-3 286	-1 378	Réserves et postes apparentés

Balance of payments summary—Millions of US dollars (*continued*)
Résumé de la balance des paiements—Millions de dollars des E.U. (*suite*)

Country or area	1999	2000	2001	2002	2003	2004	2005	Pays ou zone
China, Macao SAR								Chine, Macao RAS
Current account	...	...	...	2 739	3 179	4 253	3 367	Compte des transactions courantes
Goods: exports f.o.b.	...	...	...	2 358	2 585	2 816	2 478	Biens : exportations f.à.b.
Goods: imports f.o.b.	...	...	...	-3 277	-3 678	-4 658	-5 271	Biens : importations f.à.b.
Services: credit	...	...	...	4 758	5 605	8 063	8 614	Services : crédit
Services: debit	...	...	...	-1 071	-1 175	-1 364	-1 576	Services : débit
Income: credit	...	...	...	449	394	381	801	Revenus : crédit
Income: debit	...	...	...	-468	-547	-959	-1 580	Revenus : débit
Current transfers, n.i.e.: credit	...	...	...	90	103	98	84	Transferts courants, n.i.a. : crédit
Current transfers: debit	...	...	...	-99	-108	-124	-184	Transferts courants : débit
Capital account, n.i.e.	...	...	...	139	88	274	515	Compte de capital, n.i.a.
Financial account, n.i.e.	...	...	...	-1 086	-1 677	-1 535	-417	Compte financier, n.i.a.
Net errors and omissions	...	...	...	-1 499	-1 066	-1 894	-2 230	Erreurs et omissions nettes
Reserves and related items	...	...	...	-293	-524	-1 098	-1 234	Réserves et postes apparentés
Colombia								Colombie
Current account	671	764	-1 089	-1 358	-974	-909	-1 890	Compte des transactions courantes
Goods: exports f.o.b.	12 037	13 722	12 848	12 316	13 812	17 224	21 730	Biens : exportations f.à.b.
Goods: imports f.o.b.	-10 262	-11 090	-12 269	-12 078	-13 258	-15 878	-20 134	Biens : importations f.à.b.
Services: credit	1 940	2 049	2 190	1 867	1 921	2 255	2 664	Services : crédit
Services: debit	-3 144	-3 307	-3 602	-3 302	-3 360	-3 935	-4 766	Services : débit
Income: credit	923	1 054	919	717	553	671	1 074	Revenus : crédit
Income: debit	-2 278	-3 337	-3 529	-3 584	-3 951	-4 970	-6 539	Revenus : débit
Current transfers, n.i.e.: credit	1 703	1 911	2 656	3 010	3 565	3 994	4 342	Transferts courants, n.i.a. : crédit
Current transfers: debit	-248	-238	-302	-304	-256	-270	-260	Transferts courants : débit
Capital account, n.i.e.	0	0	0	0	0	0	0	Compte de capital, n.i.a.
Financial account, n.i.e.	-551	50	2 453	1 305	652	3 134	3 229	Compte financier, n.i.a.
Net errors and omissions	-432	48	-139	192	134	244	387	Erreurs et omissions nettes
Reserves and related items	312	-862	-1 225	-139	188	-2 470	-1 726	Réserves et postes apparentés
Congo								Congo
Current account	-231	648	-28	-34	520	674	903	Compte des transactions courantes
Goods: exports f.o.b.	1 560	2 492	2 055	2 289	2 637	3 433	4 730	Biens : exportations f.à.b.
Goods: imports f.o.b.	-523	-455	-681	-691	-831	-969	-1 356	Biens : importations f.à.b.
Services: credit	146	137	144	165	194	197	235	Services : crédit
Services: debit	-869	-738	-852	-927	-875	-1 016	-1 560	Services : débit
Income: credit	30	14	15	6	10	13	15	Revenus : crédit
Income: debit	-570	-819	-694	-866	-596	-962	-1 138	Revenus : débit
Current transfers, n.i.e.: credit	15	39	18	13	26	34	31	Transferts courants, n.i.a. : crédit
Current transfers: debit	-20	-20	-34	-23	-44	-56	-54	Transferts courants : débit
Capital account, n.i.e.	10	8	13	5	17	13	6	Compte de capital, n.i.a.
Financial account, n.i.e.	-336	-822	-653	-464	-701	-775	-823	Compte financier, n.i.a.
Net errors and omissions	-99	-78	-12	-220	-116	-93	326	Erreurs et omissions nettes
Reserves and related items	656	243	681	713	280	181	-412	Réserves et postes apparentés
Costa Rica								Costa Rica
Current account	-667	-707	-603	-857	-880	-796	-959	Compte des transactions courantes
Goods: exports f.o.b.	6 576	5 813	4 923	5 270	6 163	6 370	7 100	Biens : exportations f.à.b.
Goods: imports f.o.b.	-5 996	-6 024	-5 743	-6 548	-7 252	-7 791	-9 230	Biens : importations f.à.b.
Services: credit	1 666	1 936	1 925	1 868	2 021	2 242	2 616	Services : crédit
Services: debit	-1 195	-1 273	-1 180	-1 183	-1 245	-1 384	-1 499	Services : débit
Income: credit	198	243	193	158	146	144	234	Revenus : crédit
Income: debit	-2 020	-1 495	-872	-598	-922	-589	-449	Revenus : débit
Current transfers, n.i.e.: credit	201	204	266	297	369	371	471	Transferts courants, n.i.a. : crédit
Current transfers: debit	-97	-110	-116	-121	-160	-159	-200	Transferts courants : débit
Capital account, n.i.e.	0	9	18	12	24	11	0	Compte de capital, n.i.a.
Financial account, n.i.e.	683	-35	271	857	595	472	873	Compte financier, n.i.a.
Net errors and omissions	213	391	168	-51	35	64	143	Erreurs et omissions nettes
Reserves and related items	-230	341	146	38	226	249	-57	Réserves et postes apparentés
Côte d'Ivoire								Côte d'Ivoire
Current account	-120	-241	-61	768	294	241	-12	Compte des transactions courantes
Goods: exports f.o.b.	4 662	3 888	3 946	5 275	5 788	6 919	7 488	Biens : exportations f.à.b.

Country or area	1999	2000	2001	2002	2003	2004	2005	Pays ou zone
Goods: imports f.o.b.	-2 766	-2 402	-2 418	-2 456	-3 231	-4 291	-5 094	Biens : importations f.à.b.
Services: credit	586	482	578	585	664	763	801	Services : crédit
Services: debit	-1 459	-1 227	-1 271	-1 545	-1 780	-2 033	-2 080	Services : débit
Income: credit	163	142	137	141	171	190	192	Revenus : crédit
Income: debit	-919	-794	-723	-771	-830	-841	-855	Revenus : débit
Current transfers, n.i.e.: credit	137	79	89	132	196	187	189	Transferts courants, n.i.a. : crédit
Current transfers: debit	-523	-409	-399	-594	-683	-653	-654	Transferts courants : débit
Capital account, n.i.e.	14	8	10	8	14	146	181	Compte de capital, n.i.a.
Financial account, n.i.e.	-581	-363	-66	-1 029	-1 035	-912	-1 052	Compte financier, n.i.a.
Net errors and omissions	-22	-13	31	-26	-888	16	21	Erreurs et omissions nettes
Reserves and related items	708	608	86	278	1 615	508	863	Réserves et postes apparentés
Croatia								**Croatie**
Current account	-1 406	-458	-724	-1 915	-2 132	-1 841	-2 588	Compte des transactions courantes
Goods: exports f.o.b.	4 395	4 567	4 759	5 004	6 308	8 210	8 955	Biens : exportations f.à.b.
Goods: imports f.o.b.	-7 693	-7 770	-8 860	-10 652	-14 216	-16 560	-18 301	Biens : importations f.à.b.
Services: credit	3 724	4 071	4 884	5 582	8 569	9 373	9 921	Services : crédit
Services: debit	-2 098	-1 822	-1 949	-2 414	-2 982	-3 565	-3 400	Services : débit
Income: credit	255	356	425	435	510	814	832	Revenus : crédit
Income: debit	-622	-741	-967	-960	-1 728	-1 598	-2 070	Revenus : débit
Current transfers, n.i.e.: credit	968	1 098	1 193	1 375	1 741	1 974	2 027	Transferts courants, n.i.a. : crédit
Current transfers: debit	-335	-218	-209	-285	-334	-488	-552	Transferts courants : débit
Capital account, n.i.e.	25	21	134	443	84	28	61	Compte de capital, n.i.a.
Financial account, n.i.e.	2 863	1 836	2 206	2 909	4 682	2 973	4 929	Compte financier, n.i.a.
Net errors and omissions	-1 023	-743	-218	-623	-1 233	-1 092	-1 380	Erreurs et omissions nettes
Reserves and related items	-458	-656	-1 398	-815	-1 401	-68	-1 022	Réserves et postes apparentés
Cyprus								**Chypre**
Current account	-170	-488	-322	-379	-292	-827	-929	Compte des transactions courantes
Goods: exports f.o.b.	1 000	951	975	852	925	1 173	1 545	Biens : exportations f.à.b.
Goods: imports f.o.b.	-3 310	-3 557	-3 553	-3 735	-4 108	-5 222	-5 776	Biens : importations f.à.b.
Services: credit	3 947	4 068	4 340	4 531	5 372	6 235	6 478	Services : crédit
Services: debit	-1 560	-1 585	-1 615	-1 742	-2 237	-2 644	-2 700	Services : débit
Income: credit	493	572	559	757	905	1 160	1 615	Revenus : crédit
Income: debit	-845	-1 115	-1 083	-1 158	-1 295	-1 697	-2 184	Revenus : débit
Current transfers, n.i.e.: credit	146	237	147	270	386	585	631	Transferts courants, n.i.a. : crédit
Current transfers: debit	-42	-60	-93	-153	-242	-417	-539	Transferts courants : débit
Capital account, n.i.e.	0	5	6	20	38	134	87	Compte de capital, n.i.a.
Financial account, n.i.e.	845	530	965	826	46	912	1 429	Compte financier, n.i.a.
Net errors and omissions	-36	-55	-38	-77	21	152	116	Erreurs et omissions nettes
Reserves and related items	-639	8	-611	-389	188	-371	-703	Réserves et postes apparentés
Czech Republic								**République tchèque**
Current account	-1 466	-2 690	-3 273	-4 265	-5 785	-6 538	-3 143	Compte des transactions courantes
Goods: exports f.o.b.	26 259	29 019	33 404	38 480	48 705	67 220	77 951	Biens : exportations f.à.b.
Goods: imports f.o.b.	-28 161	-32 115	-36 482	-40 720	-51 224	-68 265	-76 295	Biens : importations f.à.b.
Services: credit	7 048	6 839	7 092	7 083	7 789	9 699	10 800	Services : crédit
Services: debit	-5 850	-5 436	-5 567	-6 439	-7 320	-9 218	-9 954	Services : débit
Income: credit	1 859	1 952	2 233	2 052	2 681	3 398	4 390	Revenus : crédit
Income: debit	-3 209	-3 323	-4 422	-5 632	-6 966	-9 535	-10 874	Revenus : débit
Current transfers, n.i.e.: credit	1 310	948	959	1 465	1 663	1 830	3 129	Transferts courants, n.i.a. : crédit
Current transfers: debit	-722	-575	-489	-553	-1 114	-1 666	-2 291	Transferts courants : débit
Capital account, n.i.e.	-2	-5	-9	-4	-3	-595	202	Compte de capital, n.i.a.
Financial account, n.i.e.	3 080	3 835	4 569	10 621	5 620	7 277	6 379	Compte financier, n.i.a.
Net errors and omissions	27	-296	499	266	611	118	440	Erreurs et omissions nettes
Reserves and related items	-1 639	-844	-1 787	-6 618	-442	-263	-3 879	Réserves et postes apparentés
Denmark								**Danemark**
Current account	3 047	2 262	4 848	3 460	6 963	5 941	9 731	Compte des transactions courantes
Goods: exports f.o.b.	49 787	50 084	50 466	55 473	64 537	75 050	82 660	Biens : exportations f.à.b.
Goods: imports f.o.b.	-43 128	-43 443	-43 048	-47 810	-54 840	-65 524	-75 243	Biens : importations f.à.b.
Services: credit	19 982	23 721	25 134	26 667	31 672	36 304	43 616	Services : crédit
Services: debit	-18 402	-21 063	-22 121	-24 305	-28 254	-33 401	-37 218	Services : débit

Country or area	1999	2000	2001	2002	2003	2004	2005	Pays ou zone
Income: credit	9 090	11 883	10 737	9 265	11 180	12 784	23 538	Revenus : crédit
Income: debit	-11 546	-15 907	-13 748	-12 805	-13 796	-15 114	-23 476	Revenus : débit
Current transfers, n.i.e.: credit	4 239	3 395	3 719	3 466	4 615	5 120	3 845	Transferts courants, n.i.a. : crédit
Current transfers: debit	-6 974	-6 410	-6 291	-6 489	-8 151	-9 279	-7 992	Transferts courants : débit
Capital account, n.i.e.	128	-11	14	152	-7	13	307	Compte de capital, n.i.a.
Financial account, n.i.e.	7 414	-3 311	-5 712	3 819	-5 129	-19 023	-8 750	Compte financier, n.i.a.
Net errors and omissions	-1 024	-4 460	4 167	-1 887	2 846	11 644	-2 794	Erreurs et omissions nettes
Reserves and related items	-9 564	5 521	-3 317	-5 546	-4 674	1 426	1 506	Réserves et postes apparentés
Dominica								Dominique
Current account	-36	-70	-58	-49	-45	-60	-82	Compte des transactions courantes
Goods: exports f.o.b.	56	55	44	44	41	43	42	Biens : exportations f.à.b.
Goods: imports f.o.b.	-122	-130	-116	-102	-105	-128	-146	Biens : importations f.à.b.
Services: credit	101	90	77	80	77	88	84	Services : crédit
Services: debit	-59	-53	-50	-54	-44	-46	-50	Services : débit
Income: credit	5	5	4	3	2	3	3	Revenus : crédit
Income: debit	-30	-44	-26	-28	-27	-35	-31	Revenus : débit
Current transfers, n.i.e.: credit	20	15	16	17	17	22	22	Transferts courants, n.i.a. : crédit
Current transfers: debit	-7	-7	-7	-7	-8	-6	-6	Transferts courants : débit
Capital account, n.i.e.	12	11	18	20	19	27	18	Compte de capital, n.i.a.
Financial account, n.i.e.	38	55	28	18	20	13	60	Compte financier, n.i.a.
Net errors and omissions	-3	-6	7	16	1	12	13	Erreurs et omissions nettes
Reserves and related items	-11	10	5	-6	5	8	-10	Réserves et postes apparentés
Dominican Republic								Rép. dominicaine
Current account	-429	-1 027	-741	-798	1 036	1 047	-500	Compte des transactions courantes
Goods: exports f.o.b.	5 137	5 737	5 276	5 165	5 471	5 936	6 146	Biens : exportations f.à.b.
Goods: imports f.o.b.	-8 041	-9 479	-8 779	-8 838	-7 627	-7 888	-9 876	Biens : importations f.à.b.
Services: credit	2 850	3 228	3 110	3 071	3 469	3 504	3 910	Services : crédit
Services: debit	-1 248	-1 373	-1 284	-1 314	-1 219	-1 213	-1 457	Services : débit
Income: credit	218	300	271	300	341	336	416	Revenus : crédit
Income: debit	-1 193	-1 341	-1 363	-1 452	-1 734	-2 155	-2 373	Revenus : débit
Current transfers, n.i.e.: credit	1 997	2 096	2 232	2 452	2 512	2 701	2 928	Transferts courants, n.i.a. : crédit
Current transfers: debit	-149	-193	-205	-183	-176	-174	-194	Transferts courants : débit
Capital account, n.i.e.	0	0	0	0	0	0	0	Compte de capital, n.i.a.
Financial account, n.i.e.	1 061	1 597	1 707	383	-16	118	1 164	Compte financier, n.i.a.
Net errors and omissions	-480	-618	-452	-139	-1 568	-987	43	Erreurs et omissions nettes
Reserves and related items	-151	48	-515	554	548	-178	-707	Réserves et postes apparentés
Ecuador								Equateur
Current account	918	921	-654	-1 272	-424	-551	-59	Compte des transactions courantes
Goods: exports f.o.b.	4 615	5 137	4 821	5 258	6 446	7 968	10 427	Biens : exportations f.à.b.
Goods: imports f.o.b.	-3 028	-3 743	-5 178	-6 160	-6 366	-7 684	-9 714	Biens : importations f.à.b.
Services: credit	730	849	862	884	881	1 014	1 012	Services : crédit
Services: debit	-1 181	-1 269	-1 434	-1 600	-1 624	-1 968	-2 112	Services : débit
Income: credit	75	70	48	30	27	35	82	Revenus : crédit
Income: debit	-1 383	-1 476	-1 412	-1 335	-1 555	-1 940	-2 021	Revenus : débit
Current transfers, n.i.e.: credit	1 188	1 437	1 686	1 710	1 789	2 043	2 333	Transferts courants, n.i.a. : crédit
Current transfers: debit	-99	-85	-47	-58	-22	-18	-66	Transferts courants : débit
Capital account, n.i.e.	2	-1	15	16	8	8	13	Compte de capital, n.i.a.
Financial account, n.i.e.	-1 344	-6 602	899	1 037	175	347	-131	Compte financier, n.i.a.
Net errors and omissions	-521	-15	-573	-2	312	587	454	Erreurs et omissions nettes
Reserves and related items	944	5 697	313	221	-70	-391	-277	Réserves et postes apparentés
Egypt								Egypte
Current account	-1 635	-971	-388	622	3 743	3 922	2 103	Compte des transactions courantes
Goods: exports f.o.b.	5 237	7 061	7 025	7 118	8 987	12 320	16 073	Biens : exportations f.à.b.
Goods: imports f.o.b.	-15 165	-15 382	-13 960	-12 879	-13 189	-18 895	-23 818	Biens : importations f.à.b.
Services: credit	9 494	9 803	9 042	9 320	11 073	14 197	14 643	Services : crédit
Services: debit	-6 452	-7 513	-7 037	-6 629	-6 474	-8 020	-10 508	Services : débit
Income: credit	1 788	1 871	1 468	698	578	572	1 425	Revenus : crédit
Income: debit	-1 045	-983	-885	-965	-832	-818	-1 460	Revenus : débit
Current transfers, n.i.e.: credit	4 564	4 224	4 056	4 002	3 708	4 615	5 831	Transferts courants, n.i.a. : crédit

Country or area	1999	2000	2001	2002	2003	2004	2005	Pays ou zone
Current transfers: debit	-55	-52	-98	-42	-109	-48	-82	Transferts courants : débit
Capital account, n.i.e.	...	0	...	0	...	...	-40	Compte de capital, n.i.a.
Financial account, n.i.e.	-1 421	-1 646	190	-3 333	-5 725	-4 461	5 591	Compte financier, n.i.a.
Net errors and omissions	-1 558	587	-1 146	1 906	1 575	-45	-2 427	Erreurs et omissions nettes
Reserves and related items	4 614	2 030	1 345	804	407	584	-5 226	Réserves et postes apparentés
El Salvador								El Salvador
Current account	-239	-431	-150	-405	-702	-632	-786	Compte des transactions courantes
Goods: exports f.o.b.	2 534	2 963	2 892	3 020	3 153	3 337	3 432	Biens : exportations f.à.b.
Goods: imports f.o.b.	-3 890	-4 703	-4 824	-4 885	-5 439	-5 999	-6 440	Biens : importations f.à.b.
Services: credit	640	698	704	783	948	1 075	1 141	Services : crédit
Services: debit	-823	-933	-954	-1 023	-1 055	-1 153	-1 213	Services : débit
Income: credit	113	141	169	159	140	144	183	Revenus : crédit
Income: debit	-395	-394	-435	-483	-563	-604	-754	Revenus : débit
Current transfers, n.i.e.: credit	1 591	1 830	2 374	2 111	2 200	2 634	2 932	Transferts courants, n.i.a. : crédit
Current transfers: debit	-9	-33	-75	-88	-86	-67	-67	Transferts courants : débit
Capital account, n.i.e.	79	109	199	209	113	100	136	Compte de capital, n.i.a.
Financial account, n.i.e.	575	288	230	688	1 049	99	723	Compte financier, n.i.a.
Net errors and omissions	-206	-12	-457	-615	-143	380	-131	Erreurs et omissions nettes
Reserves and related items	-208	46	178	124	-316	53	59	Réserves et postes apparentés
Eritrea								Erythrée
Current account	-209	-105	...	...	...	...	...	Compte des transactions courantes
Goods: exports f.o.b.	21	37	...	...	...	...	...	Biens : exportations f.à.b.
Goods: imports f.o.b.	-510	-471	...	...	...	...	...	Biens : importations f.à.b.
Services: credit	48	61	...	...	...	...	...	Services : crédit
Services: debit	-105	-28	...	...	...	...	...	Services : débit
Income: credit	8	9	...	...	...	...	...	Revenus : crédit
Income: debit	-2	-11	...	...	...	...	...	Revenus : débit
Current transfers, n.i.e.: credit	346	306	...	...	...	...	...	Transferts courants, n.i.a. : crédit
Current transfers: debit	-15	-7	...	...	...	...	...	Transferts courants : débit
Capital account, n.i.e.	1	...	...	...	...	...	...	Compte de capital, n.i.a.
Financial account, n.i.e.	196	63	...	...	...	...	...	Compte financier, n.i.a.
Net errors and omissions	13	-23	...	...	...	...	...	Erreurs et omissions nettes
Reserves and related items	-1	64	...	...	...	...	...	Réserves et postes apparentés
Estonia								Estonie
Current account	-295	-299	-325	-779	-1 115	-1 458	-1 445	Compte des transactions courantes
Goods: exports f.o.b.	2 453	3 298	3 367	3 508	4 597	5 983	7 783	Biens : exportations f.à.b.
Goods: imports f.o.b.	-3 331	-4 080	-4 142	-4 626	-6 164	-8 002	-9 628	Biens : importations f.à.b.
Services: credit	1 490	1 486	1 607	1 706	2 224	2 830	3 156	Services : crédit
Services: debit	-918	-886	-963	-1 106	-1 393	-1 756	-2 156	Services : débit
Income: credit	134	119	173	205	249	436	669	Revenus : crédit
Income: debit	-236	-322	-454	-530	-785	-1 073	-1 369	Revenus : débit
Current transfers, n.i.e.: credit	154	115	115	126	266	424	497	Transferts courants, n.i.a. : crédit
Current transfers: debit	-41	-29	-29	-61	-110	-300	-398	Transferts courants : débit
Capital account, n.i.e.	1	26	14	38	50	93	140	Compte de capital, n.i.a.
Financial account, n.i.e.	418	393	269	752	1 275	1 622	1 702	Compte financier, n.i.a.
Net errors and omissions	-5	8	-1	59	-39	14	-11	Erreurs et omissions nettes
Reserves and related items	-119	-128	42	-69	-169	-271	-386	Réserves et postes apparentés
Ethiopia								Ethiopie
Current account	-465	13	-373	-137	-136	-668	-1 568	Compte des transactions courantes
Goods: exports f.o.b.	467	486	456	480	496	678	917	Biens : exportations f.à.b.
Goods: imports f.o.b.	-1 387	-1 131	-1 626	-1 455	-1 895	-2 768	-3 701	Biens : importations f.à.b.
Services: credit	474	506	523	585	762	1 005	1 012	Services : crédit
Services: debit	-466	-490	-524	-580	-709	-958	-1 194	Services : débit
Income: credit	17	16	16	14	19	32	43	Revenus : crédit
Income: debit	-50	-52	-48	-37	-43	-60	-48	Revenus : débit
Current transfers, n.i.e.: credit	501	698	854	876	1 267	1 421	1 426	Transferts courants, n.i.a. : crédit
Current transfers: debit	-20	-20	-24	-21	-33	-17	-24	Transferts courants : débit
Capital account, n.i.e.	2	...	...	...	0	0	0	Compte de capital, n.i.a.
Financial account, n.i.e.	-180	28	-178	-83	247	73	759	Compte financier, n.i.a.

Country or area	1999	2000	2001	2002	2003	2004	2005	Pays ou zone
Net errors and omissions	407	-231	-229	-915	-390	-354	486	Erreurs et omissions nettes
Reserves and related items	236	190	781	1 134	280	949	323	Réserves et postes apparentés
Euro Area								Zone euro
Current account	-25 311	-81 550	#-19 307	51 058	37 032	62 733	-28 061	Compte des transactions courantes
Goods: exports f.o.b.	867 341	907 876	#920 862	997 538	1 171 840	1 402 540	1 516 190	Biens : exportations f.à.b.
Goods: imports f.o.b.	-787 364	-879 079	#-855 641	-875 371	-1 051 220	-1 272 110	-1 448 240	Biens : importations f.à.b.
Services: credit	259 052	259 061	#287 093	313 477	375 550	449 742	493 150	Services : crédit
Services: debit	-278 414	-278 422	#-290 507	-299 913	-353 249	-413 985	-450 308	Services : débit
Income: credit	226 516	257 859	#243 993	232 313	275 511	336 990	399 094	Revenus : crédit
Income: debit	-263 807	-299 287	#-279 688	-270 655	-317 572	-370 704	-453 067	Revenus : débit
Current transfers, n.i.e.: credit	69 751	62 454	#71 214	80 040	92 082	102 145	104 699	Transferts courants, n.i.a. : crédit
Current transfers: debit	-118 386	-112 011	#-116 632	-126 371	-155 908	-171 876	-189 579	Transferts courants : débit
Capital account, n.i.e.	13 547	8 409	#5 619	9 621	14 999	21 789	15 371	Compte de capital, n.i.a.
Financial account, n.i.e.	2 418	14 005	#-41 447	-15 306	-33 434	-29 772	77 797	Compte financier, n.i.a.
Net errors and omissions	-2 230	42 984	#38 686	-42 396	-51 840	-70 446	-89 004	Erreurs et omissions nettes
Reserves and related items	11 576	16 152	#16 449	-2 977	33 243	15 696	23 897	Réserves et postes apparentés
Faeroe Islands								Iles Féroé
Current account	176	99	146	126	-7	...	...	Compte des transactions courantes
Goods: exports f.o.b.	472	477	516	537	594	...	...	Biens : exportations f.à.b.
Goods: imports f.o.b.	-455	-515	-479	-472	-684	...	...	Biens : importations f.à.b.
Services: credit	56	54	57	71	78	...	...	Services : crédit
Services: debit	-95	-97	-105	-132	-147	...	...	Services : débit
Income: credit	114	102	91	92	106	...	...	Revenus : crédit
Income: debit	-79	-67	-76	-73	-76	...	...	Revenus : débit
Current transfers, n.i.e.: credit	166	148	147	109	128	...	...	Transferts courants, n.i.a. : crédit
Current transfers: debit	-3	-2	-4	-7	-6	...	...	Transferts courants : débit
Fiji								Fidji
Current account	13	...	...	...	...	...	...	Compte des transactions courantes
Goods: exports f.o.b.	538	...	...	...	...	...	...	Biens : exportations f.à.b.
Goods: imports f.o.b.	-653	...	...	...	...	...	...	Biens : importations f.à.b.
Services: credit	525	...	...	...	...	...	...	Services : crédit
Services: debit	-390	...	...	...	...	...	...	Services : débit
Income: credit	47	...	...	...	...	...	...	Revenus : crédit
Income: debit	-83	...	...	...	...	...	...	Revenus : débit
Current transfers, n.i.e.: credit	43	...	...	...	...	...	...	Transferts courants, n.i.a. : crédit
Current transfers: debit	-14	...	...	...	...	...	...	Transferts courants : débit
Capital account, n.i.e.	14	...	...	...	...	...	...	Compte de capital, n.i.a.
Financial account, n.i.e.	-104	...	...	...	...	...	...	Compte financier, n.i.a.
Net errors and omissions	33	...	...	...	...	...	...	Erreurs et omissions nettes
Reserves and related items	45	...	...	...	...	...	...	Réserves et postes apparentés
Finland								Finlande
Current account	8 045	10 526	12 077	13 929	10 727	14 826	9 517	Compte des transactions courantes
Goods: exports f.o.b.	41 983	45 703	42 980	44 862	52 740	61 139	65 450	Biens : exportations f.à.b.
Goods: imports f.o.b.	-29 815	-32 019	-30 321	-32 022	-39 792	-48 369	-55 888	Biens : importations f.à.b.
Services: credit	6 522	7 728	9 205	10 441	11 471	15 170	17 007	Services : crédit
Services: debit	-7 615	-8 440	-8 105	-8 073	-10 007	-12 285	-15 203	Services : débit
Income: credit	5 664	7 265	8 568	8 606	9 349	13 128	14 038	Revenus : crédit
Income: debit	-7 712	-8 989	-9 573	-9 210	-11 980	-12 880	-14 316	Revenus : débit
Current transfers, n.i.e.: credit	1 658	1 611	1 562	1 674	1 963	2 040	1 897	Transferts courants, n.i.a. : crédit
Current transfers: debit	-2 640	-2 334	-2 239	-2 350	-3 018	-3 118	-3 469	Transferts courants : débit
Capital account, n.i.e.	49	103	83	125	150	187	174	Compte de capital, n.i.a.
Financial account, n.i.e.	-6 414	-8 841	-10 942	-7 312	-11 978	-11 303	-3 721	Compte financier, n.i.a.
Net errors and omissions	-1 667	-1 438	-808	-6 857	594	-2 804	-6 167	Erreurs et omissions nettes
Reserves and related items	-13	-351	-410	115	508	-907	197	Réserves et postes apparentés
France								France
Current account	41 509	18 581	28 759	10 997	11 803	-6 808	-33 289	Compte des transactions courantes
Goods: exports f.o.b.	299 949	298 198	294 621	307 196	361 913	421 275	439 218	Biens : exportations f.à.b.
Goods: imports f.o.b.	-283 010	-301 817	-291 785	-299 557	-358 487	-429 941	-471 362	Biens : importations f.à.b.
Services: credit	82 085	80 917	82 298	86 130	98 759	109 516	115 986	Services : crédit

Country or area	1999	2000	2001	2002	2003	2004	2005	Pays ou zone
Services: debit	-63 524	-61 044	-56 861	-68 907	-82 863	-98 462	-106 102	Services : débit
Income: credit	71 244	72 392	74 106	58 037	88 728	116 426	135 448	Revenus : crédit
Income: debit	-52 215	-56 809	-59 042	-57 435	-76 801	-103 721	-119 134	Revenus : débit
Current transfers, n.i.e.: credit	18 766	17 872	17 279	19 766	24 050	26 028	26 043	Transferts courants, n.i.a. : crédit
Current transfers: debit	-31 787	-31 127	-31 857	-34 232	-43 495	-47 930	-53 387	Transferts courants : débit
Capital account, n.i.e.	1 424	1 392	-308	-192	-8 231	1 810	661	Compte de capital, n.i.a.
Financial account, n.i.e.	-50 473	-32 549	-33 247	-20 338	13 538	-12 960	-38 490	Compte financier, n.i.a.
Net errors and omissions	6 092	10 143	-770	5 567	-15 835	22 066	62 072	Erreurs et omissions nettes
Reserves and related items	1 448	2 433	5 567	3 965	-1 274	-4 108	9 047	Réserves et postes apparentés
Gabon								Gabon
Current account	390	1 001	517	338	766	924	...	Compte des transactions courantes
Goods: exports f.o.b.	2 499	3 321	2 614	2 556	3 178	4 072	...	Biens : exportations f.à.b.
Goods: imports f.o.b.	-911	-798	-847	-935	-1 043	-1 216	...	Biens : importations f.à.b.
Services: credit	281	178	168	86	172	156	...	Services : crédit
Services: debit	-867	-858	-710	-759	-840	-939	...	Services : débit
Income: credit	84	48	30	18	48	13	...	Revenus : crédit
Income: debit	-653	-827	-659	-496	-570	-978	...	Revenus : débit
Current transfers, n.i.e.: credit	43	16	34	5	7	10	...	Transferts courants, n.i.a. : crédit
Current transfers: debit	-86	-79	-113	-136	-188	-194	...	Transferts courants : débit
Capital account, n.i.e.	5	^0	3	3	43	0	...	Compte de capital, n.i.a.
Financial account, n.i.e.	-757	-568	-674	-437	-650	-499	...	Compte financier, n.i.a.
Net errors and omissions	323	-152	-104	-125	-260	-357	...	Erreurs et omissions nettes
Reserves and related items	38	-280	258	222	101	-68	...	Réserves et postes apparentés
Gambia								Gambie
Current account	...	...	...	...	-2	-44	-50	Compte des transactions courantes
Goods: exports f.o.b.	...	...	...	...	78	109	101	Biens : exportations f.à.b.
Goods: imports f.o.b.	...	...	...	...	-156	-207	-215	Biens : importations f.à.b.
Services: credit	...	...	...	...	84	73	80	Services : crédit
Services: debit	...	...	...	...	-36	-46	-45	Services : débit
Income: credit	...	...	...	...	5	2	3	Revenus : crédit
Income: debit	...	...	...	...	-32	-30	-35	Revenus : débit
Current transfers, n.i.e.: credit	...	...	...	...	89	78	88	Transferts courants, n.i.a. : crédit
Current transfers: debit	...	...	...	...	-33	-24	-26	Transferts courants : débit
Capital account, n.i.e.	...	...	...	...	5	5	1	Compte de capital, n.i.a.
Financial account, n.i.e.	...	...	...	...	-10	47	68	Compte financier, n.i.a.
Net errors and omissions	...	...	...	...	3	-9	-54	Erreurs et omissions nettes
Reserves and related items	...	...	...	...	5	1	36	Réserves et postes apparentés
Georgia								Géorgie
Current account	-198	-269	-212	-234	-383	-423	-752	Compte des transactions courantes
Goods: exports f.o.b.	330	459	496	603	831	1 092	1 472	Biens : exportations f.à.b.
Goods: imports f.o.b.	-863	-971	-1 046	-1 092	-1 469	-2 008	-2 686	Biens : importations f.à.b.
Services: credit	217	206	314	392	443	540	698	Services : crédit
Services: debit	-224	-216	-237	-357	-390	-483	-625	Services : débit
Income: credit	211	179	98	161	177	252	263	Revenus : crédit
Income: debit	-65	-61	-65	-134	-146	-154	-171	Revenus : débit
Current transfers, n.i.e.: credit	229	163	246	222	208	389	351	Transferts courants, n.i.a. : crédit
Current transfers: debit	-33	-28	-18	-29	-36	-51	-54	Transferts courants : débit
Capital account, n.i.e.	-7	-5	-5	18	20	41	59	Compte de capital, n.i.a.
Financial account, n.i.e.	136	93	210	26	319	453	665	Compte financier, n.i.a.
Net errors and omissions	56	187	35	6	-21	2	11	Erreurs et omissions nettes
Reserves and related items	14	-6	-28	184	65	-73	18	Réserves et postes apparentés
Germany								Allemagne
Current account	-26 794	-31 955	482	40 710	46 594	117 929	128 959	Compte des transactions courantes
Goods: exports f.o.b.	537 370	543 285	563 670	609 779	744 806	903 447	978 181	Biens : exportations f.à.b.
Goods: imports f.o.b.	-468 592	-487 821	-476 256	-484 024	-600 061	-718 051	-789 773	Biens : importations f.à.b.
Services: credit	83 923	83 150	88 714	103 144	123 659	145 963	157 576	Services : crédit
Services: debit	-141 001	-137 254	-141 916	-145 158	-172 837	-195 272	-207 218	Services : débit
Income: credit	92 396	106 635	91 209	97 983	118 531	164 443	192 808	Revenus : crédit
Income: debit	-104 549	-114 297	-100 956	-115 005	-135 518	-148 016	-167 120	Revenus : débit

Country or area	1999	2000	2001	2002	2003	2004	2005	Pays ou zone
Current transfers, n.i.e.: credit	17 289	15 348	15 337	15 923	18 983	20 172	22 149	Transferts courants, n.i.a. : crédit
Current transfers: debit	-43 630	-41 002	-39 319	-41 933	-50 970	-54 757	-57 644	Transferts courants : débit
Capital account, n.i.e.	-151	6 188	-327	-225	353	513	-1 691	Compte de capital, n.i.a.
Financial account, n.i.e.	-26 886	28 987	-16 131	-40 754	-71 601	-146 895	-151 168	Compte financier, n.i.a.
Net errors and omissions	39 717	-8 442	10 509	-1 709	23 970	26 646	21 299	Erreurs et omissions nettes
Reserves and related items	14 115	5 222	5 466	1 979	684	1 807	2 601	Réserves et postes apparentés
Ghana								Ghana
Current account	-964	-387	-325	-32	302	-316	-812	Compte des transactions courantes
Goods: exports f.o.b.	2 006	1 936	1 867	2 015	2 562	2 704	2 802	Biens : exportations f.à.b.
Goods: imports f.o.b.	-3 280	-2 767	-2 969	-2 707	-3 233	-4 297	-5 345	Biens : importations f.à.b.
Services: credit	468	504	532	555	630	702	1 066	Services : crédit
Services: debit	-646	-584	-606	-621	-900	-1 058	-1 264	Services : débit
Income: credit	15	16	16	15	21	45	43	Revenus : crédit
Income: debit	-147	-123	-124	-189	-178	-242	-230	Revenus : débit
Current transfers, n.i.e.: credit	638	649	978	912	1 408	1 831	2 125	Transferts courants, n.i.a. : crédit
Current transfers: debit	-18	-18	-19	-12	-9	0	-9	Transferts courants : débit
Capital account, n.i.e.	0	0	0	0	0	0	0	Compte de capital, n.i.a.
Financial account, n.i.e.	746	369	392	-39	340	202	796	Compte financier, n.i.a.
Net errors and omissions	82	-352	-189	57	-139	37	26	Erreurs et omissions nettes
Reserves and related items	136	369	121	14	-504	77	-10	Réserves et postes apparentés
Greece								Grèce
Current account	-7 295	-9 820	-9 400	-9 582	-12 804	-13 476	-17 879	Compte des transactions courantes
Goods: exports f.o.b.	8 545	10 202	10 615	9 865	12 578	15 739	17 631	Biens : exportations f.à.b.
Goods: imports f.o.b.	-26 496	-30 440	-29 702	-31 321	-38 184	-47 360	-51 884	Biens : importations f.à.b.
Services: credit	16 506	19 239	19 456	20 142	24 283	33 085	34 159	Services : crédit
Services: debit	-9 251	-11 286	-11 589	-9 819	-11 250	-14 020	-14 742	Services : débit
Income: credit	2 577	2 807	1 885	1 532	2 911	3 495	4 072	Revenus : crédit
Income: debit	-3 248	-3 692	-3 652	-3 488	-7 414	-8 920	-11 102	Revenus : débit
Current transfers, n.i.e.: credit	4 957	4 116	4 592	5 536	7 202	7 901	8 615	Transferts courants, n.i.a. : crédit
Current transfers: debit	-884	-764	-1 005	-2 029	-2 930	-3 396	-4 628	Transferts courants : débit
Capital account, n.i.e.	2 211	2 112	2 153	1 530	1 411	2 990	2 563	Compte de capital, n.i.a.
Financial account, n.i.e.	7 478	10 830	537	11 578	6 417	6 836	15 633	Compte financier, n.i.a.
Net errors and omissions	42	-550	1 011	-1 663	253	373	-421	Erreurs et omissions nettes
Reserves and related items	-2 435	-2 573	5 699	-1 863	4 723	3 277	104	Réserves et postes apparentés
Grenada								Grenade
Current account	-53	-88	-105	-126	-144	-59	-129	Compte des transactions courantes
Goods: exports f.o.b.	74	83	64	41	46	33	39	Biens : exportations f.à.b.
Goods: imports f.o.b.	-185	-221	-197	-181	-226	-236	-280	Biens : importations f.à.b.
Services: credit	144	153	133	131	134	157	128	Services : crédit
Services: debit	-80	-89	-85	-91	-83	-94	-107	Services : débit
Income: credit	4	5	4	4	4	6	4	Revenus : crédit
Income: debit	-30	-39	-45	-52	-54	-45	-28	Revenus : débit
Current transfers, n.i.e.: credit	27	30	30	32	48	126	119	Transferts courants, n.i.a. : crédit
Current transfers: debit	-8	-10	-9	-10	-12	-5	-5	Transferts courants : débit
Capital account, n.i.e.	31	32	43	32	43	40	44	Compte de capital, n.i.a.
Financial account, n.i.e.	28	64	47	100	90	47	59	Compte financier, n.i.a.
Net errors and omissions	-1	-1	21	24	-6	14	-1	Erreurs et omissions nettes
Reserves and related items	-5	-7	-6	-31	17	-42	27	Réserves et postes apparentés
Guatemala								Guatemala
Current account	-1 026	-1 050	-1 253	-1 235	-1 039	-1 211	-1 387	Compte des transactions courantes
Goods: exports f.o.b.	2 781	3 085	2 860	2 819	3 060	3 368	3 701	Biens : exportations f.à.b.
Goods: imports f.o.b.	-4 226	-4 742	-5 142	-5 791	-6 176	-7 175	-8 070	Biens : importations f.à.b.
Services: credit	700	777	1 045	1 145	1 059	1 178	1 238	Services : crédit
Services: debit	-791	-825	-928	-1 066	-1 126	-1 308	-1 477	Services : débit
Income: credit	76	214	317	161	179	173	249	Revenus : crédit
Income: debit	-281	-424	-402	-479	-497	-492	-585	Revenus : débit
Current transfers, n.i.e.: credit	754	908	1 024	2 078	2 559	3 088	3 605	Transferts courants, n.i.a. : crédit
Current transfers: debit	-40	-43	-28	-101	-97	-43	-47	Transferts courants : débit
Capital account, n.i.e.	68	86	93	124	134	135	125	Compte de capital, n.i.a.

Country or area	1999	2000	2001	2002	2003	2004	2005	Pays ou zone
Financial account, n.i.e.	638	1 521	1 547	1 197	1 516	1 709	1 605	Compte financier, n.i.a.
Net errors and omissions	195	86	87	-65	-61	-25	-88	Erreurs et omissions nettes
Reserves and related items	125	-643	-474	-21	-550	-608	-255	Réserves et postes apparentés
Guinea								Guinée
Current account	-214	-155	-102	-200	-188	-175	...	Compte des transactions courantes
Goods: exports f.o.b.	636	666	731	709	609	726	...	Biens : exportations f.à.b.
Goods: imports f.o.b.	-582	-587	-562	-669	-644	-688	...	Biens : importations f.à.b.
Services: credit	113	68	103	90	134	85	...	Services : crédit
Services: debit	-364	-285	-319	-331	-307	-275	...	Services : débit
Income: credit	25	23	11	6	13	10	...	Revenus : crédit
Income: debit	-107	-101	-114	-52	-124	-37	...	Revenus : débit
Current transfers, n.i.e.: credit	80	89	92	71	195	55	...	Transferts courants, n.i.a. : crédit
Current transfers: debit	-15	-29	-44	-25	-62	-50	...	Transferts courants : débit
Capital account, n.i.e.	0	0	0	92	58	-30	...	Compte de capital, n.i.a.
Financial account, n.i.e.	117	8	-12	-115	59	78	...	Compte financier, n.i.a.
Net errors and omissions	21	84	-2	143	-157	69	...	Erreurs et omissions nettes
Reserves and related items	76	63	117	80	229	59	...	Réserves et postes apparentés
Guinea-Bissau								Guinée-Bissau
Current account	...	...	-27	-9	-7	-13	...	Compte des transactions courantes
Goods: exports f.o.b.	...	...	63	54	65	76	...	Biens : exportations f.à.b.
Goods: imports f.o.b.	...	...	-62	-59	-65	-83	...	Biens : importations f.à.b.
Services: credit	...	...	4	6	6	8	...	Services : crédit
Services: debit	...	...	-30	-27	-36	-44	...	Services : débit
Income: credit	...	...	1	1	2	1	...	Revenus : crédit
Income: debit	...	...	-13	-10	-11	-11	...	Revenus : débit
Current transfers, n.i.e.: credit	...	...	10	30	40	47	...	Transferts courants, n.i.a. : crédit
Current transfers: debit	...	...	^0	-5	-7	-7	...	Transferts courants : débit
Capital account, n.i.e.	...	...	25	39	43	27	...	Compte de capital, n.i.a.
Financial account, n.i.e.	...	...	-17	-21	-13	1	...	Compte financier, n.i.a.
Net errors and omissions	...	...	6	-3	6	-4	...	Erreurs et omissions nettes
Reserves and related items	...	...	13	-6	-29	-11	...	Réserves et postes apparentés
Guyana								Guyana
Current account	-50	-82	-91	-62	-45	-20	-96	Compte des transactions courantes
Goods: exports f.o.b.	522	503	485	490	508	584	546	Biens : exportations f.à.b.
Goods: imports f.o.b.	-519	-550	-541	-514	-525	-592	-720	Biens : importations f.à.b.
Services: credit	147	169	172	172	157	161	147	Services : crédit
Services: debit	-178	-193	-192	-196	-172	-208	-197	Services : débit
Income: credit	11	12	10	8	5	4	3	Revenus : crédit
Income: debit	-72	-70	-69	-63	-60	-43	-42	Revenus : débit
Current transfers, n.i.e.: credit	76	101	98	129	127	194	261	Transferts courants, n.i.a. : crédit
Current transfers: debit	-37	-54	-54	-89	-84	-120	-95	Transferts courants : débit
Capital account, n.i.e.	16	16	32	31	44	46	52	Compte de capital, n.i.a.
Financial account, n.i.e.	53	111	84	54	35	39	127	Compte financier, n.i.a.
Net errors and omissions	3	-4	-45	-2	-19	-42	-99	Erreurs et omissions nettes
Reserves and related items	-22	-40	20	-21	-15	-22	17	Réserves et postes apparentés
Haiti								Haïti
Current account	-60	-114	-132	-88	-45	-54	54	Compte des transactions courantes
Goods: exports f.o.b.	343	332	305	274	333	378	459	Biens : exportations f.à.b.
Goods: imports f.o.b.	-1 018	-1 087	-1 055	-980	-1 116	-1 210	-1 308	Biens : importations f.à.b.
Services: credit	188	172	139	148	136	113	134	Services : crédit
Services: debit	-235	-282	-260	-270	-301	-315	-447	Services : débit
Income: credit	0	0	0	0	0	0	2	Revenus : crédit
Income: debit	-13	-9	-9	-14	-14	-12	-39	Revenus : débit
Current transfers, n.i.e.: credit	674	771	769	776	948	1 032	1 313	Transferts courants, n.i.a. : crédit
Current transfers: debit	0	-11	-19	-22	-31	-39	-59	Transferts courants : débit
Capital account, n.i.e.	0	0	0	0	0	0	0	Compte de capital, n.i.a.
Financial account, n.i.e.	85	-16	82	-17	-76	50	47	Compte financier, n.i.a.
Net errors and omissions	1	73	44	37	123	45	-55	Erreurs et omissions nettes
Reserves and related items	-26	57	5	68	-1	-41	-46	Réserves et postes apparentés

Country or area	1999	2000	2001	2002	2003	2004	2005	Pays ou zone
Honduras								Honduras
Current account	-625	-262	-339	-260	-282	-426	-86	Compte des transactions courantes
Goods: exports f.o.b.	1 756	2 012	1 935	1 977	2 090	2 393	2 648	Biens : exportations f.à.b.
Goods: imports f.o.b.	-2 510	-2 670	-2 769	-2 806	-3 035	-3 677	-4 188	Biens : importations f.à.b.
Services: credit	474	479	487	530	598	719	779	Services : crédit
Services: debit	-502	-597	-627	-617	-673	-757	-848	Services : débit
Income: credit	81	118	92	58	47	51	102	Revenus : crédit
Income: debit	-236	-252	-262	-251	-305	-410	-434	Revenus : débit
Current transfers, n.i.e.: credit	355	718	894	947	1 085	1 369	1 985	Transferts courants, n.i.a. : crédit
Current transfers: debit	-42	-70	-90	-99	-89	-114	-130	Transferts courants : débit
Capital account, n.i.e.	111	30	37	24	22	22	19	Compte de capital, n.i.a.
Financial account, n.i.e.	203	-29	124	161	136	732	-186	Compte financier, n.i.a.
Net errors and omissions	122	104	105	57	-74	46	-89	Erreurs et omissions nettes
Reserves and related items	188	157	74	19	197	-373	342	Réserves et postes apparentés
Hungary								Hongrie
Current account	-3 775	-4 004	-3 205	-4 693	-6 721	-8 561	-7 451	Compte des transactions courantes
Goods: exports f.o.b.	25 608	28 762	31 081	34 792	42 943	55 689	62 245	Biens : exportations f.à.b.
Goods: imports f.o.b.	-27 778	-31 675	-33 318	-36 911	-46 221	-58 695	-64 041	Biens : importations f.à.b.
Services: credit	5 213	5 901	7 029	7 417	9 211	10 890	12 810	Services : crédit
Services: debit	-4 360	-4 775	-5 550	-6 849	-9 150	-10 605	-11 902	Services : débit
Income: credit	902	1 165	1 302	1 236	1 371	1 877	2 187	Revenus : crédit
Income: debit	-3 794	-3 740	-4 152	-4 870	-5 541	-8 013	-8 957	Revenus : débit
Current transfers, n.i.e.: credit	711	674	781	1 070	1 283	1 633	2 592	Transferts courants, n.i.a. : crédit
Current transfers: debit	-278	-316	-377	-579	-616	-1 338	-2 386	Transferts courants : débit
Capital account, n.i.e.	29	270	317	191	-27	328	886	Compte de capital, n.i.a.
Financial account, n.i.e.	6 469	4 960	2 775	2 565	6 858	11 988	13 796	Compte financier, n.i.a.
Net errors and omissions	-389	-174	29	145	226	-1 773	-2 328	Erreurs et omissions nettes
Reserves and related items	-2 335	-1 052	84	1 792	-336	-1 981	-4 904	Réserves et postes apparentés
Iceland								Islande
Current account	-589	-847	-336	145	-534	-1 317	-2 632	Compte des transactions courantes
Goods: exports f.o.b.	2 009	1 902	2 016	2 240	2 386	2 896	3 107	Biens : exportations f.à.b.
Goods: imports f.o.b.	-2 316	-2 376	-2 091	-2 090	-2 596	-3 415	-4 590	Biens : importations f.à.b.
Services: credit	930	1 044	1 086	1 118	1 378	1 623	2 041	Services : crédit
Services: debit	-1 027	-1 164	-1 074	-1 123	-1 503	-1 838	-2 560	Services : débit
Income: credit	129	147	171	305	376	470	1 451	Revenus : crédit
Income: debit	-304	-390	-435	-318	-559	-1 035	-2 055	Revenus : débit
Current transfers, n.i.e.: credit	5	6	8	36	12	10	11	Transferts courants, n.i.a. : crédit
Current transfers: debit	-15	-16	-17	-22	-28	-27	-38	Transferts courants : débit
Capital account, n.i.e.	-1	-3	4	-1	-5	-3	-27	Compte de capital, n.i.a.
Financial account, n.i.e.	864	846	172	-65	444	1 925	2 322	Compte financier, n.i.a.
Net errors and omissions	-189	-70	111	-17	401	-404	408	Erreurs et omissions nettes
Reserves and related items	-86	74	48	-61	-307	-202	-71	Réserves et postes apparentés
India								Inde
Current account	-3 228	-4 601	1 410	7 060	6 853	...	...	Compte des transactions courantes
Goods: exports f.o.b.	36 877	43 247	44 793	51 141	59 338	...	...	Biens : exportations f.à.b.
Goods: imports f.o.b.	-45 556	-53 887	-51 211	-54 700	-68 208	...	...	Biens : importations f.à.b.
Services: credit	14 509	16 684	17 337	19 478	23 397	...	...	Services : crédit
Services: debit	-17 271	-19 187	-20 099	-21 041	-25 710	...	...	Services : débit
Income: credit	1 919	2 521	3 524	3 188	3 779	...	...	Revenus : crédit
Income: debit	-5 629	-7 414	-7 666	-7 097	-8 230	...	...	Revenus : débit
Current transfers, n.i.e.: credit	11 958	13 548	15 140	16 789	22 833	...	...	Transferts courants, n.i.a. : crédit
Current transfers: debit	-35	-114	-407	-698	-345	...	...	Transferts courants : débit
Capital account, n.i.e.	...	716	743	102	3 839	...	...	Compte de capital, n.i.a.
Financial account, n.i.e.	9 579	9 623	7 252	11 882	14 792	...	...	Compte financier, n.i.a.
Net errors and omissions	313	331	-715	-191	183	...	...	Erreurs et omissions nettes
Reserves and related items	-6 664	-6 069	-8 690	-18 853	-25 667	...	...	Réserves et postes apparentés
Indonesia								Indonésie
Current account	5 783	7 992	6 901	7 824	8 107	1 563	929	Compte des transactions courantes
Goods: exports f.o.b.	51 242	65 407	57 365	59 165	64 109	70 767	86 179	Biens : exportations f.à.b.

Country or area	1999	2000	2001	2002	2003	2004	2005	Pays ou zone
Goods: imports f.o.b.	-30 599	-40 365	-34 669	-35 652	-39 546	-50 615	-63 856	Biens : importations f.à.b.
Services: credit	4 599	5 214	5 500	6 663	5 293	12 045	12 926	Services : crédit
Services: debit	-12 376	-15 637	-15 880	-17 045	-17 400	-20 856	-23 728	Services : débit
Income: credit	1 891	2 458	2 004	1 318	1 054	1 995	2 333	Revenus : crédit
Income: debit	-10 887	-10 901	-8 940	-8 365	-7 272	-12 912	-14 182	Revenus : débit
Current transfers, n.i.e.: credit	1 914	1 816	1 520	2 210	2 053	2 433	2 457	Transferts courants, n.i.a. : crédit
Current transfers: debit	0	0	0	-470	-184	-1 294	-1 199	Transferts courants : débit
Capital account, n.i.e.	0	0	0	0	0	0	334	Compte de capital, n.i.a.
Financial account, n.i.e.	-5 944	-7 896	-7 617	-1 103	-949	-2 368	-4 849	Compte financier, n.i.a.
Net errors and omissions	2 077	3 829	701	-1 763	-3 510	-1 393	-2 024	Erreurs et omissions nettes
Reserves and related items	-1 916	-3 926	15	-4 958	-3 647	2 198	5 610	Réserves et postes apparentés
Iran (Islamic Rep. of)								Iran (Rép. islamique d')
Current account	6 555	12 481	...	...	...	...	...	Compte des transactions courantes
Goods: exports f.o.b.	21 030	28 345	...	...	...	...	...	Biens : exportations f.à.b.
Goods: imports f.o.b.	-13 433	-15 207	...	...	...	...	...	Biens : importations f.à.b.
Services: credit	1 216	1 382	...	...	...	...	...	Services : crédit
Services: debit	-2 457	-2 296	...	...	...	...	...	Services : débit
Income: credit	181	404	...	...	...	...	...	Revenus : crédit
Income: debit	-473	-604	...	...	...	...	...	Revenus : débit
Current transfers, n.i.e.: credit	508	539	...	...	...	...	...	Transferts courants, n.i.a. : crédit
Current transfers: debit	-17	-82	...	...	...	...	...	Transferts courants : débit
Capital account, n.i.e.	0	0	...	...	...	...	...	Compte de capital, n.i.a.
Financial account, n.i.e.	-5 894	-10 189	...	...	...	...	...	Compte financier, n.i.a.
Net errors and omissions	-210	-1 209	...	...	...	...	...	Erreurs et omissions nettes
Reserves and related items	-451	-1 083	...	...	...	...	...	Réserves et postes apparentés
Ireland								Irlande
Current account	245	-516	-690	-1 101	89	-1 081	-5 331	Compte des transactions courantes
Goods: exports f.o.b.	67 831	73 530	77 623	84 216	88 590	100 116	104 080	Biens : exportations f.à.b.
Goods: imports f.o.b.	-44 244	-48 520	-50 360	-50 769	-51 709	-61 102	-67 271	Biens : importations f.à.b.
Services: credit	15 688	18 538	23 465	29 901	42 061	52 718	57 287	Services : crédit
Services: debit	-26 534	-31 272	-35 339	-42 829	-54 597	-65 384	-69 810	Services : débit
Income: credit	24 442	27 613	28 850	27 200	34 095	43 457	53 902	Revenus : crédit
Income: debit	-38 191	-41 160	-45 202	-49 515	-58 879	-71 388	-84 209	Revenus : débit
Current transfers, n.i.e.: credit	5 308	4 143	7 400	7 538	7 027	6 626	7 020	Transferts courants, n.i.a. : crédit
Current transfers: debit	-4 055	-3 388	-7 128	-6 842	-6 500	-6 123	-6 330	Transferts courants : débit
Capital account, n.i.e.	593	1 074	635	512	126	368	324	Compte de capital, n.i.a.
Financial account, n.i.e.	-4 185	7 912	16	468	-3 481	3 301	-2 986	Compte financier, n.i.a.
Net errors and omissions	1 373	-8 509	434	-171	1 375	-4 023	6 216	Erreurs et omissions nettes
Reserves and related items	1 974	39	-395	292	1 890	1 435	1 776	Réserves et postes apparentés
Israel								Israël
Current account	-1 464	-1 009	-1 350	-976	1 371	2 926	4 295	Compte des transactions courantes
Goods: exports f.o.b.	25 816	31 188	27 967	27 535	30 187	36 658	40 101	Biens : exportations f.à.b.
Goods: imports f.o.b.	-30 567	-34 728	-31 714	-31 971	-33 294	-39 488	-43 868	Biens : importations f.à.b.
Services: credit	11 956	15 056	12 467	11 797	13 322	15 979	17 504	Services : crédit
Services: debit	-10 263	-11 905	-11 848	-10 904	-11 205	-12 825	-13 711	Services : débit
Income: credit	2 766	3 625	2 728	2 455	2 812	2 992	5 532	Revenus : crédit
Income: debit	-7 445	-10 714	-7 608	-6 674	-6 862	-6 667	-7 234	Revenus : débit
Current transfers, n.i.e.: credit	7 122	7 466	7 791	8 165	7 556	7 358	7 010	Transferts courants, n.i.a. : crédit
Current transfers: debit	-849	-997	-1 133	-1 380	-1 146	-1 081	-1 038	Transferts courants : débit
Capital account, n.i.e.	569	466	721	207	535	667	727	Compte de capital, n.i.a.
Financial account, n.i.e.	3 630	1 189	-350	-3 115	-2 536	-7 331	-7 466	Compte financier, n.i.a.
Net errors and omissions	-2 862	-325	1 367	2 815	435	717	3 735	Erreurs et omissions nettes
Reserves and related items	127	-321	-388	1 068	195	3 020	-1 292	Réserves et postes apparentés
Italy								Italie
Current account	8 111	-5 781	-652	-9 369	-19 407	-15 713	-27 724	Compte des transactions courantes
Goods: exports f.o.b.	235 856	240 473	244 931	252 618	298 118	352 172	372 750	Biens : exportations f.à.b.
Goods: imports f.o.b.	-212 420	-230 925	-229 392	-239 206	-286 641	-341 277	-372 690	Biens : importations f.à.b.
Services: credit	58 788	56 556	57 676	60 439	71 767	84 535	89 960	Services : crédit
Services: debit	-57 707	-55 601	-57 753	-63 166	-74 332	-83 255	-90 605	Services : débit

Country or area	1999	2000	2001	2002	2003	2004	2005	Pays ou zone
Income: credit	46 361	38 671	38 574	43 303	48 780	53 119	61 357	Revenus : crédit
Income: debit	-57 411	-50 680	-48 911	-57 854	-69 003	-71 456	-78 436	Revenus : débit
Current transfers, n.i.e.: credit	16 776	15 797	16 137	20 871	20 650	21 809	24 378	Transferts courants, n.i.a. : crédit
Current transfers: debit	-22 132	-20 073	-21 915	-26 375	-28 745	-31 360	-34 439	Transferts courants : débit
Capital account, n.i.e.	2 964	2 879	846	-80	2 667	2 324	2 195	Compte de capital, n.i.a.
Financial account, n.i.e.	-17 415	7 504	-3 570	11 224	20 437	7 360	23 044	Compte financier, n.i.a.
Net errors and omissions	-1 711	-1 355	2 787	1 395	-2 583	3 185	1 455	Erreurs et omissions nettes
Reserves and related items	8 051	-3 247	588	-3 169	-1 115	2 844	1 030	Réserves et postes apparentés
Jamaica								Jamaïque
Current account	-216	-367	-759	-1 074	-773	-509	-1 079	Compte des transactions courantes
Goods: exports f.o.b.	1 499	1 563	1 454	1 309	1 386	1 602	1 664	Biens : exportations f.à.b.
Goods: imports f.o.b.	-2 686	-3 004	-3 073	-3 180	-3 328	-3 546	-4 246	Biens : importations f.à.b.
Services: credit	1 978	2 026	1 897	1 912	2 138	2 297	2 330	Services : crédit
Services: debit	-1 323	-1 423	-1 514	-1 597	-1 586	-1 725	-1 729	Services : débit
Income: credit	166	193	218	221	218	270	328	Revenus : crédit
Income: debit	-498	-543	-656	-826	-789	-852	-1 004	Revenus : débit
Current transfers, n.i.e.: credit	758	969	1 091	1 338	1 524	1 892	1 935	Transferts courants, n.i.a. : crédit
Current transfers: debit	-111	-149	-177	-251	-334	-446	-357	Transferts courants : débit
Capital account, n.i.e.	-11	2	-22	-17	^0	2	-3	Compte de capital, n.i.a.
Financial account, n.i.e.	95	854	1 661	911	314	1 216	1 265	Compte financier, n.i.a.
Net errors and omissions	-4	30	-14	-61	28	-14	46	Erreurs et omissions nettes
Reserves and related items	136	-518	-865	241	431	-695	-230	Réserves et postes apparentés
Japan								Japon
Current account	114 604	119 660	87 798	112 447	136 216	172 059	165 783	Compte des transactions courantes
Goods: exports f.o.b.	403 694	459 513	383 592	395 581	449 119	538 999	567 572	Biens : exportations f.à.b.
Goods: imports f.o.b.	-280 369	-342 797	-313 378	-301 751	-342 723	-406 866	-473 614	Biens : importations f.à.b.
Services: credit	60 998	69 238	64 516	65 712	77 621	97 611	110 210	Services : crédit
Services: debit	-115 158	-116 864	-108 249	-107 940	-111 528	-135 514	-134 256	Services : débit
Income: credit	92 049	97 199	103 095	91 478	95 211	113 331	141 062	Revenus : crédit
Income: debit	-34 471	-36 799	-33 874	-25 709	-23 971	-27 628	-37 618	Revenus : débit
Current transfers, n.i.e.: credit	6 212	7 380	6 152	10 038	6 508	6 907	9 738	Transferts courants, n.i.a. : crédit
Current transfers: debit	-18 350	-17 211	-14 056	-14 960	-14 020	-14 782	-17 311	Transferts courants : débit
Capital account, n.i.e.	-16 467	-9 259	-2 869	-3 321	-3 998	-4 787	-4 878	Compte de capital, n.i.a.
Financial account, n.i.e.	-38 845	-78 313	-48 160	-63 381	71 924	22 500	-122 682	Compte financier, n.i.a.
Net errors and omissions	16 965	16 866	3 718	388	-16 990	-28 918	-15 898	Erreurs et omissions nettes
Reserves and related items	-76 256	-48 955	-40 487	-46 134	-187 153	-160 854	-22 325	Réserves et postes apparentés
Jordan								Jordanie
Current account	405	59	-4	537	1 179	-18	-2 311	Compte des transactions courantes
Goods: exports f.o.b.	1 832	1 899	2 294	2 770	3 082	3 883	4 301	Biens : exportations f.à.b.
Goods: imports f.o.b.	-3 292	-4 074	-4 301	-4 501	-5 078	-7 261	-9 317	Biens : importations f.à.b.
Services: credit	1 702	1 637	1 483	1 775	1 740	2 057	2 283	Services : crédit
Services: debit	-1 698	-1 722	-1 726	-1 883	-1 889	-2 146	-2 542	Services : débit
Income: credit	468	670	649	484	493	558	758	Revenus : crédit
Income: debit	-480	-535	-461	-372	-374	-326	-383	Revenus : débit
Current transfers, n.i.e.: credit	2 155	2 611	2 366	2 524	3 501	3 562	3 030	Transferts courants, n.i.a. : crédit
Current transfers: debit	-281	-427	-307	-260	-295	-346	-441	Transferts courants : débit
Capital account, n.i.e.	88	65	22	69	94	2	8	Compte de capital, n.i.a.
Financial account, n.i.e.	231	285	-302	485	-187	-278	1 358	Compte financier, n.i.a.
Net errors and omissions	29	284	40	-161	263	472	1 024	Erreurs et omissions nettes
Reserves and related items	-752	-693	244	-930	-1 348	-179	-79	Réserves et postes apparentés
Kazakhstan								Kazakhstan
Current account	-171	366	-1 390	-1 024	-273	335	-724	Compte des transactions courantes
Goods: exports f.o.b.	5 989	9 288	8 928	10 027	13 233	20 603	28 301	Biens : exportations f.à.b.
Goods: imports f.o.b.	-5 645	-7 120	-7 944	-8 040	-9 554	-13 818	-17 979	Biens : importations f.à.b.
Services: credit	933	1 053	1 260	1 540	1 712	2 009	2 248	Services : crédit
Services: debit	-1 104	-1 850	-2 635	-3 538	-3 753	-5 108	-7 524	Services : débit
Income: credit	109	139	225	234	255	423	680	Revenus : crédit
Income: debit	-608	-1 393	-1 462	-1 361	-2 002	-3 286	-6 037	Revenus : débit
Current transfers, n.i.e.: credit	175	352	394	426	279	353	809	Transferts courants, n.i.a. : crédit

Country or area	1999	2000	2001	2002	2003	2004	2005	Pays ou zone
Current transfers: debit	-18	-103	-156	-312	-443	-841	-1 222	Transferts courants : débit
Capital account, n.i.e.	-234	-291	-185	-120	-28	-21	14	Compte de capital, n.i.a.
Financial account, n.i.e.	1 299	1 307	2 614	1 359	2 766	4 701	929	Compte financier, n.i.a.
Net errors and omissions	-642	-813	-654	320	-932	-1 016	-2 163	Erreurs et omissions nettes
Reserves and related items	-253	-570	-385	-535	-1 534	-3 999	1 944	Réserves et postes apparentés
Kenya								Kenya
Current account	-90	-199	-320	-118	146	-353	-495	Compte des transactions courantes
Goods: exports f.o.b.	1 757	1 782	1 891	2 162	2 412	2 721	3 240	Biens : exportations f.à.b.
Goods: imports f.o.b.	-2 732	-3 044	-3 238	-3 159	-3 555	-4 351	-5 408	Biens : importations f.à.b.
Services: credit	935	993	1 120	1 054	1 198	1 557	1 886	Services : crédit
Services: debit	-570	-719	-810	-708	-691	-939	-1 132	Services : débit
Income: credit	32	45	46	35	60	45	73	Revenus : crédit
Income: debit	-191	-178	-168	-179	-148	-172	-182	Revenus : débit
Current transfers, n.i.e.: credit	685	927	854	689	884	828	1 095	Transferts courants, n.i.a. : crédit
Current transfers: debit	-5	-6	-16	-12	-14	-43	-67	Transferts courants : débit
Capital account, n.i.e.	55	50	51	81	163	145	103	Compte de capital, n.i.a.
Financial account, n.i.e.	166	270	148	-174	406	40	511	Compte financier, n.i.a.
Net errors and omissions	-166	-127	131	194	-290	154	-3	Erreurs et omissions nettes
Reserves and related items	34	7	-10	16	-425	13	-117	Réserves et postes apparentés
Korea, Republic of								Corée, République de
Current account	24 522	12 251	8 033	5 394	11 950	28 174	16 559	Compte des transactions courantes
Goods: exports f.o.b.	145 375	176 221	151 478	163 414	197 289	257 710	288 996	Biens : exportations f.à.b.
Goods: imports f.o.b.	-116 912	-159 267	-137 990	-148 637	-175 337	-220 141	-255 523	Biens : importations f.à.b.
Services: credit	26 529	30 534	29 055	28 388	32 957	41 882	45 375	Services : crédit
Services: debit	-27 180	-33 381	-32 927	-36 585	-40 381	-49 928	-58 467	Services : débit
Income: credit	3 245	6 375	6 650	6 900	7 176	9 410	10 244	Revenus : crédit
Income: debit	-8 404	-8 797	-7 848	-6 467	-6 850	-8 328	-11 564	Revenus : débit
Current transfers, n.i.e.: credit	6 421	6 500	6 687	7 314	7 859	9 151	10 124	Transferts courants, n.i.a. : crédit
Current transfers: debit	-4 552	-5 934	-7 072	-8 932	-10 764	-11 583	-12 626	Transferts courants : débit
Capital account, n.i.e.	-389	-615	-731	-1 087	-1 398	-1 753	-2 313	Compte de capital, n.i.a.
Financial account, n.i.e.	12 709	12 725	3 025	7 338	15 308	9 359	2 804	Compte financier, n.i.a.
Net errors and omissions	-3 581	-571	2 951	124	-68	2 895	2 815	Erreurs et omissions nettes
Reserves and related items	-33 260	-23 790	-13 278	-11 769	-25 791	-38 675	-19 864	Réserves et postes apparentés
Kuwait								Koweït
Current account	5 026	14 679	8 322	4 265	9 427	18 163	32 634	Compte des transactions courantes
Goods: exports f.o.b.	12 224	19 478	16 237	15 367	21 795	30 089	46 874	Biens : exportations f.à.b.
Goods: imports f.o.b.	-6 708	-6 451	-7 047	-8 117	-9 880	-11 663	-15 671	Biens : importations f.à.b.
Services: credit	1 541	1 803	1 661	1 647	3 146	3 741	4 700	Services : crédit
Services: debit	-5 134	-4 894	-5 354	-5 837	-6 614	-7 583	-8 842	Services : débit
Income: credit	6 094	7 315	5 427	3 716	3 733	6 584	9 389	Revenus : crédit
Income: debit	-985	-616	-524	-369	-372	-456	-555	Revenus : débit
Current transfers, n.i.e.: credit	99	85	53	50	66	88	67	Transferts courants, n.i.a. : crédit
Current transfers: debit	-2 102	-2 041	-2 132	-2 192	-2 446	-2 638	-3 328	Transferts courants : débit
Capital account, n.i.e.	703	2 217	2 931	1 672	1 431	433	797	Compte de capital, n.i.a.
Financial account, n.i.e.	-5 706	-13 779	-5 623	-5 038	-12 101	-16 830	-28 130	Compte financier, n.i.a.
Net errors and omissions	895	-848	-2 722	-1 869	-582	-1 137	-4 680	Erreurs et omissions nettes
Reserves and related items	-918	-2 268	-2 908	970	1 824	-629	-621	Réserves et postes apparentés
Kyrgyzstan								Kirghizistan
Current account	-252	-123	-52	-79	-104	-101	-228	Compte des transactions courantes
Goods: exports f.o.b.	463	511	480	498	590	733	687	Biens : exportations f.à.b.
Goods: imports f.o.b.	-551	-506	-449	-571	-723	-904	-1 106	Biens : importations f.à.b.
Services: credit	65	62	83	142	158	210	256	Services : crédit
Services: debit	-155	-148	-125	-148	-160	-224	-291	Services : débit
Income: credit	11	17	12	6	5	11	17	Revenus : crédit
Income: debit	-84	-99	-71	-64	-67	-111	-97	Revenus : débit
Current transfers, n.i.e.: credit	1	43	23	61	100	201	345	Transferts courants, n.i.a. : crédit
Current transfers: debit	-1	-2	-4	-3	-7	-18	-38	Transferts courants : débit
Capital account, n.i.e.	-15	-11	-32	-8	-1	-20	-21	Compte de capital, n.i.a.
Financial account, n.i.e.	245	83	46	98	28	169	14	Compte financier, n.i.a.

Country or area	1999	2000	2001	2002	2003	2004	2005	Pays ou zone
Net errors and omissions	-4	18	24	10	123	97	303	Erreurs et omissions nettes
Reserves and related items	26	33	13	-20	-47	-145	-68	Réserves et postes apparentés
Lao People's Dem. Rep.								Rép. dém. pop. lao
Current account	-121	-8	-82	...	...	...	...	Compte des transactions courantes
Goods: exports f.o.b.	338	330	311	...	...	...	...	Biens : exportations f.à.b.
Goods: imports f.o.b.	-528	-535	-528	...	...	...	...	Biens : importations f.à.b.
Services: credit	130	176	166	...	...	...	...	Services : crédit
Services: debit	-52	-43	-32	...	...	...	...	Services : débit
Income: credit	11	7	6	...	...	...	...	Revenus : crédit
Income: debit	-50	-60	-40	...	...	...	...	Revenus : débit
Current transfers, n.i.e.: credit	80	116	34	...	...	...	...	Transferts courants, n.i.a. : crédit
Current transfers: debit	-51	...	...	...	...	...	...	Transferts courants : débit
Capital account, n.i.e.	0	...	...	...	...	...	...	Compte de capital, n.i.a.
Financial account, n.i.e.	-47	126	136	...	...	...	...	Compte financier, n.i.a.
Net errors and omissions	-165	-74	-57	...	...	...	...	Erreurs et omissions nettes
Reserves and related items	333	-43	4	...	...	...	...	Réserves et postes apparentés
Latvia								Lettonie
Current account	-654	-371	-626	-625	-921	-1 774	-2 002	Compte des transactions courantes
Goods: exports f.o.b.	1 889	2 079	2 243	2 545	3 171	4 221	5 361	Biens : exportations f.à.b.
Goods: imports f.o.b.	-2 916	-3 123	-3 578	-4 024	-5 173	-7 002	-8 379	Biens : importations f.à.b.
Services: credit	1 024	1 150	1 179	1 238	1 506	1 780	2 165	Services : crédit
Services: debit	-689	-690	-671	-701	-929	-1 178	-1 557	Services : débit
Income: credit	158	215	278	289	368	500	768	Revenus : crédit
Income: debit	-214	-198	-221	-235	-393	-788	-957	Revenus : débit
Current transfers, n.i.e.: credit	114	406	373	538	924	1 289	1 373	Transferts courants, n.i.a. : crédit
Current transfers: debit	-21	-211	-229	-275	-394	-595	-776	Transferts courants : débit
Capital account, n.i.e.	13	36	41	21	76	144	212	Compte de capital, n.i.a.
Financial account, n.i.e.	768	413	900	687	937	1 962	2 630	Compte financier, n.i.a.
Net errors and omissions	38	-75	^0	-71	-13	71	-317	Erreurs et omissions nettes
Reserves and related items	-165	-3	-314	-12	-79	-403	-524	Réserves et postes apparentés
Lebanon								Liban
Current account	...	...	...	-4 385	-4 997	-4 122	-1 881	Compte des transactions courantes
Goods: exports f.o.b.	...	...	...	1 018	1 733	2 050	2 278	Biens : exportations f.à.b.
Goods: imports f.o.b.	...	...	...	-5 979	-6 528	-8 506	-8 368	Biens : importations f.à.b.
Services: credit	...	...	...	4 429	9 462	9 704	10 758	Services : crédit
Services: debit	...	...	...	-3 367	-6 488	-8 230	-7 854	Services : débit
Income: credit	...	...	...	567	1 487	1 311	2 667	Revenus : crédit
Income: debit	...	...	...	-1 131	-4 992	-2 167	-2 420	Revenus : débit
Current transfers, n.i.e.: credit	...	...	...	2 591	4 079	5 325	4 399	Transferts courants, n.i.a. : crédit
Current transfers: debit	...	...	...	-2 513	-3 751	-3 609	-3 343	Transferts courants : débit
Capital account, n.i.e.	...	...	...	13	29	50	27	Compte de capital, n.i.a.
Financial account, n.i.e.	...	...	...	3 350	3 107	6 429	3 757	Compte financier, n.i.a.
Net errors and omissions	...	...	...	-1 196	-3 175	-1 576	-2 359	Erreurs et omissions nettes
Reserves and related items	...	...	...	2 219	5 036	-782	455	Réserves et postes apparentés
Lesotho								Lesotho
Current account	-221	-151	-95	-143	-135	-76	-44	Compte des transactions courantes
Goods: exports f.o.b.	173	211	279	357	475	707	650	Biens : exportations f.à.b.
Goods: imports f.o.b.	-779	-728	-679	-763	-994	-1 302	-1 260	Biens : importations f.à.b.
Services: credit	44	43	40	35	50	64	55	Services : crédit
Services: debit	-50	-43	-49	-55	-85	-96	-94	Services : débit
Income: credit	325	289	235	207	304	379	370	Revenus : crédit
Income: debit	-81	-63	-57	-45	-54	-76	-65	Revenus : débit
Current transfers, n.i.e.: credit	149	140	137	123	172	251	304	Transferts courants, n.i.a. : crédit
Current transfers: debit	-2	-1	-3	-2	-2	-3	-3	Transferts courants : débit
Capital account, n.i.e.	15	22	17	24	27	33	21	Compte de capital, n.i.a.
Financial account, n.i.e.	136	85	89	89	98	63	48	Compte financier, n.i.a.
Net errors and omissions	29	62	155	-98	-57	-16	15	Erreurs et omissions nettes
Reserves and related items	41	-18	-166	128	66	-5	-40	Réserves et postes apparentés

Country or area	1999	2000	2001	2002	2003	2004	2005	Pays ou zone
Libyan Arab Jamah.								Jamah. arabe libyenne
Current account	2 136	7 740	3 683	117	3 642	3 503	14 945	Compte des transactions courantes
Goods: exports f.o.b.	7 276	13 508	10 985	9 851	14 664	17 425	28 849	Biens : exportations f.à.b.
Goods: imports f.o.b.	-4 302	-4 129	-4 825	-7 408	-7 200	-8 768	-11 174	Biens : importations f.à.b.
Services: credit	59	172	184	401	442	437	534	Services : crédit
Services: debit	-989	-895	-1 034	-1 544	-1 597	-1 914	-2 349	Services : débit
Income: credit	546	723	684	1 249	1 587	1 339	1 837	Revenus : crédit
Income: debit	-235	-1 152	-1 583	-1 653	-2 581	-2 692	-2 118	Revenus : débit
Current transfers, n.i.e.: credit	7	16	20	13	255	254	418	Transferts courants, n.i.a. : crédit
Current transfers: debit	-226	-503	-748	-792	-1 928	-2 578	-1 052	Transferts courants : débit
Capital account, n.i.e.	...	0	0	0	0	0	0	Compte de capital, n.i.a.
Financial account, n.i.e.	-1 045	-149	-977	89	-167	1 047	392	Compte financier, n.i.a.
Net errors and omissions	-403	-1 133	-1 413	72	-459	1 182	74	Erreurs et omissions nettes
Reserves and related items	-688	-6 458	-1 293	-278	-3 016	-5 732	-15 411	Réserves et postes apparentés
Lithuania								Lituanie
Current account	-1 194	-675	-574	-721	-1 278	-1 725	-1 831	Compte des transactions courantes
Goods: exports f.o.b.	3 147	4 050	4 889	6 028	7 658	9 306	11 774	Biens : exportations f.à.b.
Goods: imports f.o.b.	-4 551	-5 154	-5 997	-7 343	-9 362	-11 689	-14 690	Biens : importations f.à.b.
Services: credit	1 092	1 059	1 157	1 464	1 878	2 444	3 104	Services : crédit
Services: debit	-786	-679	-700	-915	-1 264	-1 632	-2 055	Services : débit
Income: credit	115	186	206	192	235	355	448	Revenus : crédit
Income: debit	-373	-379	-385	-375	-717	-967	-1 075	Revenus : débit
Current transfers, n.i.e.: credit	167	247	262	232	302	612	951	Transferts courants, n.i.a. : crédit
Current transfers: debit	-5	-4	-4	-3	-8	-154	-289	Transferts courants : débit
Capital account, n.i.e.	-3	2	1	56	68	287	331	Compte de capital, n.i.a.
Financial account, n.i.e.	1 061	702	778	1 048	1 642	1 141	2 262	Compte financier, n.i.a.
Net errors and omissions	-42	128	154	79	181	192	-49	Erreurs et omissions nettes
Reserves and related items	179	-158	-359	-463	-613	104	-712	Réserves et postes apparentés
Luxembourg								Luxembourg
Current account	1 650	2 562	1 674	2 568	2 345	3 991	4 088	Compte des transactions courantes
Goods: exports f.o.b.	8 565	8 635	8 996	9 535	10 942	13 527	14 545	Biens : exportations f.à.b.
Goods: imports f.o.b.	-11 151	-11 056	-11 395	-11 599	-13 938	-17 079	-18 662	Biens : importations f.à.b.
Services: credit	17 134	20 301	19 945	20 280	25 283	33 684	40 833	Services : crédit
Services: debit	-11 840	-13 581	-13 708	-12 254	-15 377	-20 789	-24 572	Services : débit
Income: credit	47 931	50 400	52 302	49 009	51 205	63 874	75 216	Revenus : crédit
Income: debit	-48 413	-51 678	-53 941	-52 123	-55 220	-68 136	-82 141	Revenus : débit
Current transfers, n.i.e.: credit	2 282	2 750	2 269	3 604	3 782	4 039	4 753	Transferts courants, n.i.a. : crédit
Current transfers: debit	-2 859	-3 211	-2 794	-3 884	-4 332	-5 130	-5 882	Transferts courants : débit
Capital account, n.i.e.	...	...	...	-89	-142	-695	1 305	Compte de capital, n.i.a.
Financial account, n.i.e.	...	...	...	-2 702	-2 086	-3 516	-5 228	Compte financier, n.i.a.
Net errors and omissions	...	...	...	258	-9	228	-214	Erreurs et omissions nettes
Reserves and related items	...	...	...	-35	-108	-8	48	Réserves et postes apparentés
Madagascar								Madagascar
Current account	-252	-283	-170	-528	-458	-541	-626	Compte des transactions courantes
Goods: exports f.o.b.	584	824	928	859	854	990	834	Biens : exportations f.à.b.
Goods: imports f.o.b.	-742	-997	-955	-1 066	-1 111	-1 427	-1 427	Biens : importations f.à.b.
Services: credit	326	364	351	397	322	425	498	Services : crédit
Services: debit	-456	-522	-511	-704	-619	-637	-615	Services : débit
Income: credit	21	22	24	46	16	15	24	Revenus : crédit
Income: debit	-63	-64	-106	-178	-94	-89	-104	Revenus : débit
Current transfers, n.i.e.: credit	111	122	114	156	357	245	208	Transferts courants, n.i.a. : crédit
Current transfers: debit	-32	-31	-15	-36	-183	-62	-45	Transferts courants : débit
Capital account, n.i.e.	129	115	113	102	143	182	192	Compte de capital, n.i.a.
Financial account, n.i.e.	-14	-31	-139	-96	-126	251	-6	Compte financier, n.i.a.
Net errors and omissions	32	39	-57	29	67	-35	91	Erreurs et omissions nettes
Reserves and related items	104	160	253	493	374	143	349	Réserves et postes apparentés
Malawi								Malawi
Current account	-158	-73	-60	-201	...	...	...	Compte des transactions courantes
Goods: exports f.o.b.	448	403	428	422	...	...	...	Biens : exportations f.à.b.

Country or area	1999	2000	2001	2002	2003	2004	2005	Pays ou zone
Goods: imports f.o.b.	-575	-462	-472	-573	...	...	...	Biens : importations f.à.b.
Services: credit	49	34	44	49	...	...	...	Services : crédit
Services: debit	-185	-167	-171	-222	...	...	...	Services : débit
Income: credit	26	33	12	6	...	...	...	Revenus : crédit
Income: debit	-51	-51	-43	-45	...	...	...	Revenus : débit
Current transfers, n.i.e.: credit	138	143	149	170	...	...	...	Transferts courants, n.i.a. : crédit
Current transfers: debit	-8	-8	-6	-9	...	...	...	Transferts courants : débit
Financial account, n.i.e.	220	189	213	134	...	...	...	Compte financier, n.i.a.
Net errors and omissions	-29	-24	-221	157	...	...	...	Erreurs et omissions nettes
Reserves and related items	-33	-91	68	-90	...	...	...	Réserves et postes apparentés
Malaysia								Malaisie
Current account	12 604	8 488	7 287	7 190	13 381	14 872	19 980	Compte des transactions courantes
Goods: exports f.o.b.	84 097	98 429	87 981	93 383	104 999	126 642	141 808	Biens : exportations f.à.b.
Goods: imports f.o.b.	-61 453	-77 602	-69 597	-75 248	-79 289	-99 149	-108 653	Biens : importations f.à.b.
Services: credit	11 919	13 941	14 455	14 878	13 578	16 768	19 576	Services : crédit
Services: debit	-14 735	-16 747	-16 657	-16 448	-17 532	-19 078	-21 956	Services : débit
Income: credit	2 003	1 986	1 847	2 139	3 448	4 216	5 373	Revenus : crédit
Income: debit	-7 499	-9 594	-8 590	-8 734	-9 376	-10 677	-11 691	Revenus : débit
Current transfers, n.i.e.: credit	801	756	537	661	508	447	299	Transferts courants, n.i.a. : crédit
Current transfers: debit	-2 529	-2 680	-2 689	-3 442	-2 955	-4 298	-4 776	Transferts courants : débit
Capital account, n.i.e.	...	...	...	0	0	0	0	Compte de capital, n.i.a.
Financial account, n.i.e.	-6 619	-6 276	-3 892	-3 142	-3 196	3 969	-9 806	Compte financier, n.i.a.
Net errors and omissions	-1 273	-3 221	-2 394	-391	-4	3 034	-6 530	Erreurs et omissions nettes
Reserves and related items	-4 712	1 009	-1 000	-3 657	-10 181	-21 875	-3 644	Réserves et postes apparentés
Maldives								Maldives
Current account	-79	-51	-59	-36	-32	-134	-330	Compte des transactions courantes
Goods: exports f.o.b.	91	109	110	132	152	181	162	Biens : exportations f.à.b.
Goods: imports f.o.b.	-354	-342	-346	-345	-414	-567	-655	Biens : importations f.à.b.
Services: credit	343	348	354	363	432	507	317	Services : crédit
Services: debit	-108	-110	-110	-111	-121	-158	-190	Services : débit
Income: credit	9	10	8	6	6	8	11	Revenus : crédit
Income: debit	-40	-40	-45	-41	-45	-51	-37	Revenus : débit
Current transfers, n.i.e.: credit	20	19	20	11	13	7	61	Transferts courants, n.i.a. : crédit
Current transfers: debit	-40	-46	-50	-50	-55	-61	1	Transferts courants : débit
Capital account, n.i.e.	0	0	0	0	0	0	0	Compte de capital, n.i.a.
Financial account, n.i.e.	76	40	35	74	56	153	261	Compte financier, n.i.a.
Net errors and omissions	11	7	-6	2	2	25	46	Erreurs et omissions nettes
Reserves and related items	-9	4	30	-40	-26	-44	23	Réserves et postes apparentés
Mali								Mali
Current account	-253	-255	-310	-149	-271	-409	-438	Compte des transactions courantes
Goods: exports f.o.b.	571	545	725	875	928	976	1 101	Biens : exportations f.à.b.
Goods: imports f.o.b.	-606	-592	-735	-712	-988	-1 093	-1 245	Biens : importations f.à.b.
Services: credit	110	99	151	169	224	241	274	Services : crédit
Services: debit	-372	-335	-421	-387	-482	-532	-588	Services : débit
Income: credit	31	21	22	36	21	24	68	Revenus : crédit
Income: debit	-101	-119	-188	-276	-181	-219	-275	Revenus : débit
Current transfers, n.i.e.: credit	146	157	161	182	266	251	286	Transferts courants, n.i.a. : crédit
Current transfers: debit	-32	-31	-25	-36	-58	-58	-58	Transferts courants : débit
Capital account, n.i.e.	113	102	107	104	114	151	149	Compte de capital, n.i.a.
Financial account, n.i.e.	117	220	146	189	289	100	298	Compte financier, n.i.a.
Net errors and omissions	9	-5	9	-6	45	-26	7	Erreurs et omissions nettes
Reserves and related items	13	-63	47	-138	-177	184	-16	Réserves et postes apparentés
Malta								Malte
Current account	-134	-480	-150	106	-156	-356	-477	Compte des transactions courantes
Goods: exports f.o.b.	2 017	2 479	2 023	2 342	2 592	2 721	2 556	Biens : exportations f.à.b.
Goods: imports f.o.b.	-2 680	-3 233	-2 575	-2 681	-3 232	-3 599	-3 682	Biens : importations f.à.b.
Services: credit	1 218	1 092	1 099	1 201	1 379	1 574	1 617	Services : crédit
Services: debit	-762	-761	-759	-798	-894	-1 043	-1 164	Services : débit
Income: credit	1 241	917	839	857	905	967	1 201	Revenus : crédit

Country or area	1999	2000	2001	2002	2003	2004	2005	Pays ou zone
Income: debit	-1 201	-1 009	-800	-833	-934	-1 032	-1 360	Revenus : débit
Current transfers, n.i.e.: credit	103	93	201	281	276	348	653	Transferts courants, n.i.a. : crédit
Current transfers: debit	-70	-60	-178	-263	-248	-292	-299	Transferts courants : débit
Capital account, n.i.e.	26	19	1	7	17	83	193	Compte de capital, n.i.a.
Financial account, n.i.e.	435	232	143	231	259	-9	517	Compte financier, n.i.a.
Net errors and omissions	-88	8	261	-56	24	76	-15	Erreurs et omissions nettes
Reserves and related items	-238	222	-255	-288	-144	206	-218	Réserves et postes apparentés
Mauritius								Maurice
Current account	-124	-37	276	249	93	-112	-340	Compte des transactions courantes
Goods: exports f.o.b.	1 589	1 552	1 628	1 801	1 898	1 993	2 144	Biens : exportations f.à.b.
Goods: imports f.o.b.	-2 108	-1 944	-1 846	-2 013	-2 201	-2 573	-2 938	Biens : importations f.à.b.
Services: credit	1 036	1 070	1 222	1 149	1 280	1 456	1 618	Services : crédit
Services: debit	-728	-763	-810	-793	-906	-1 023	-1 216	Services : débit
Income: credit	43	49	75	80	47	52	143	Revenus : crédit
Income: debit	-60	-65	-61	-67	-77	-66	-151	Revenus : débit
Current transfers, n.i.e.: credit	196	168	193	195	163	168	162	Transferts courants, n.i.a. : crédit
Current transfers: debit	-93	-104	-125	-104	-111	-119	-101	Transferts courants : débit
Capital account, n.i.e.	^0	-1	-1	-2	-1	-2	-2	Compte de capital, n.i.a.
Financial account, n.i.e.	181	258	-240	84	90	8	50	Compte financier, n.i.a.
Net errors and omissions	134	10	-86	9	40	78	126	Erreurs et omissions nettes
Reserves and related items	-190	-231	52	-341	-222	27	165	Réserves et postes apparentés
Mexico								Mexique
Current account	-13 956	-18 708	-17 707	-14 125	-8 867	-6 705	-4 913	Compte des transactions courantes
Goods: exports f.o.b.	136 362	166 121	158 780	161 046	164 766	187 999	214 233	Biens : exportations f.à.b.
Goods: imports f.o.b.	-141 975	-174 458	-168 397	-168 679	-170 546	-196 810	-221 820	Biens : importations f.à.b.
Services: credit	11 734	13 756	12 701	12 740	12 617	14 047	16 137	Services : crédit
Services: debit	-14 471	-17 360	-17 194	-17 660	-18 141	-19 779	-21 440	Services : débit
Income: credit	4 475	5 977	5 326	4 051	3 858	5 617	5 867	Revenus : crédit
Income: debit	-16 366	-19 712	-18 237	-15 875	-15 263	-14 807	-18 359	Revenus : débit
Current transfers, n.i.e.: credit	6 313	6 999	9 336	10 287	13 880	17 108	20 526	Transferts courants, n.i.a. : crédit
Current transfers: debit	-27	-30	-22	-35	-37	-80	-57	Transferts courants : débit
Capital account, n.i.e.	0	0	0	0	0	0	0	Compte de capital, n.i.a.
Financial account, n.i.e.	18 125	23 847	26 000	27 018	22 254	11 835	12 692	Compte financier, n.i.a.
Net errors and omissions	80	1 986	-979	-5 534	-3 569	-1 026	-814	Erreurs et omissions nettes
Reserves and related items	-4 250	-7 126	-7 314	-7 359	-9 817	-4 104	-6 965	Réserves et postes apparentés
Mongolia								Mongolie
Current account	-112	-156	-154	-158	-148	-25	...	Compte des transactions courantes
Goods: exports f.o.b.	454	536	523	524	627	872	...	Biens : exportations f.à.b.
Goods: imports f.o.b.	-511	-608	-624	-680	-827	-901	...	Biens : importations f.à.b.
Services: credit	76	78	114	184	208	338	...	Services : crédit
Services: debit	-146	-163	-205	-266	-257	-504	...	Services : débit
Income: credit	7	13	15	14	14	17	...	Revenus : crédit
Income: debit	-7	-20	-17	-19	-25	-28	...	Revenus : débit
Current transfers, n.i.e.: credit	18	25	40	127	167	231	...	Transferts courants, n.i.a. : crédit
Current transfers: debit	-4	-17	0	-42	-55	-50	...	Transferts courants : débit
Capital account, n.i.e.	0	...	0	0	0	0	...	Compte de capital, n.i.a.
Financial account, n.i.e.	70	90	107	157	5	-23	...	Compte financier, n.i.a.
Net errors and omissions	24	-19	-32	14	-6	1	...	Erreurs et omissions nettes
Reserves and related items	19	86	79	-13	149	46	...	Réserves et postes apparentés
Montserrat								Montserrat
Current account	-1	-8	-6	-10	-8	-9	-16	Compte des transactions courantes
Goods: exports f.o.b.	1	1	1	2	2	5	2	Biens : exportations f.à.b.
Goods: imports f.o.b.	-19	-19	-17	-22	-25	-25	-26	Biens : importations f.à.b.
Services: credit	20	16	15	14	12	15	15	Services : crédit
Services: debit	-22	-23	-22	-16	-18	-23	-20	Services : débit
Income: credit	1	1	1	1	1	1	2	Revenus : crédit
Income: debit	-7	-4	-2	-4	-2	-5	-5	Revenus : débit
Current transfers, n.i.e.: credit	26	22	22	21	27	28	22	Transferts courants, n.i.a. : crédit
Current transfers: debit	-3	-3	-4	-5	-5	-5	-6	Transferts courants : débit

Country or area	1999	2000	2001	2002	2003	2004	2005	Pays ou zone
Capital account, n.i.e.	1	4	8	13	14	12	10	Compte de capital, n.i.a.
Financial account, n.i.e.	-6	2	-4	-2	-8	-2	7	Compte financier, n.i.a.
Net errors and omissions	-5	-3	4	1	3	^0	^0	Erreurs et omissions nettes
Reserves and related items	11	4	-2	-2	-1	-1	-1	Réserves et postes apparentés
Morocco								Maroc
Current account	-171	-501	1 606	1 472	1 552	922	1 018	Compte des transactions courantes
Goods: exports f.o.b.	7 509	7 419	7 142	7 839	8 771	9 922	10 690	Biens : exportations f.à.b.
Goods: imports f.o.b.	-9 957	-10 654	-10 164	-10 900	-13 117	-16 408	-18 894	Biens : importations f.à.b.
Services: credit	3 115	3 034	4 029	4 360	5 478	6 710	8 098	Services : crédit
Services: debit	-2 003	-1 892	-2 118	-2 413	-2 861	-3 451	-3 845	Services : débit
Income: credit	187	276	326	377	370	505	689	Revenus : crédit
Income: debit	-1 172	-1 140	-1 159	-1 115	-1 162	-1 176	-1 003	Revenus : débit
Current transfers, n.i.e.: credit	2 246	2 574	3 670	3 441	4 214	4 974	5 441	Transferts courants, n.i.a. : crédit
Current transfers: debit	-96	-118	-120	-115	-141	-154	-158	Transferts courants : débit
Capital account, n.i.e.	-9	-6	-9	-6	-10	-8	-5	Compte de capital, n.i.a.
Financial account, n.i.e.	-13	-774	-966	-1 336	-1 091	102	-155	Compte financier, n.i.a.
Net errors and omissions	123	114	230	-182	-297	-282	-414	Erreurs et omissions nettes
Reserves and related items	69	1 166	-861	52	-154	-733	-445	Réserves et postes apparentés
Mozambique								Mozambique
Current account	-912	-764	-657	-869	-816	-607	-761	Compte des transactions courantes
Goods: exports f.o.b.	284	364	726	810	1 044	1 504	1 745	Biens : exportations f.à.b.
Goods: imports f.o.b.	-1 090	-1 046	-997	-1 476	-1 648	-1 850	-2 242	Biens : importations f.à.b.
Services: credit	295	325	250	339	304	256	342	Services : crédit
Services: debit	-406	-446	-618	-577	-574	-531	-648	Services : débit
Income: credit	58	79	56	52	56	75	99	Revenus : crédit
Income: debit	-215	-271	-291	-655	-221	-374	-459	Revenus : débit
Current transfers, n.i.e.: credit	256	337	255	827	293	371	479	Transferts courants, n.i.a. : crédit
Current transfers: debit	-95	-106	-37	-189	-70	-57	-76	Transferts courants : débit
Capital account, n.i.e.	180	227	257	222	271	578	188	Compte de capital, n.i.a.
Financial account, n.i.e.	404	83	-25	-732	373	-47	95	Compte financier, n.i.a.
Net errors and omissions	2	37	-60	-60	208	216	281	Erreurs et omissions nettes
Reserves and related items	326	416	485	1 439	-35	-141	197	Réserves et postes apparentés
Myanmar								Myanmar
Current account	-285	-212	-154	97	-19	112	...	Compte des transactions courantes
Goods: exports f.o.b.	1 294	1 662	2 522	2 421	2 710	2 927	...	Biens : exportations f.à.b.
Goods: imports f.o.b.	-2 181	-2 165	-2 444	-2 022	-1 912	-1 999	...	Biens : importations f.à.b.
Services: credit	512	478	408	426	249	255	...	Services : crédit
Services: debit	-291	-328	-361	-309	-420	-460	...	Services : débit
Income: credit	52	35	37	37	29	40	...	Revenus : crédit
Income: debit	-55	-169	-549	-620	-771	-786	...	Revenus : débit
Current transfers, n.i.e.: credit	385	290	249	188	118	161	...	Transferts courants, n.i.a. : crédit
Current transfers: debit	^0	-14	-14	-23	-23	-27	...	Transferts courants : débit
Financial account, n.i.e.	251	213	348	-32	137	125	...	Compte financier, n.i.a.
Net errors and omissions	-12	-24	-14	-19	-79	-143	...	Erreurs et omissions nettes
Reserves and related items	46	23	-180	-45	-39	-94	...	Réserves et postes apparentés
Namibia								Namibie
Current account	158	293	58	128	336	573	...	Compte des transactions courantes
Goods: exports f.o.b.	1 197	1 309	1 147	1 072	1 262	1 827	...	Biens : exportations f.à.b.
Goods: imports f.o.b.	-1 401	-1 310	-1 349	-1 283	-1 726	-2 110	...	Biens : importations f.à.b.
Services: credit	324	222	294	283	420	482	...	Services : crédit
Services: debit	-446	-333	-276	-224	-249	-385	...	Services : débit
Income: credit	271	248	200	173	284	368	...	Revenus : crédit
Income: debit	-108	-226	-269	-134	-54	-218	...	Revenus : débit
Current transfers, n.i.e.: credit	380	419	347	270	426	642	...	Transferts courants, n.i.a. : crédit
Current transfers: debit	-58	-37	-36	-30	-27	-35	...	Transferts courants : débit
Capital account, n.i.e.	23	113	96	41	68	77	...	Compte de capital, n.i.a.
Financial account, n.i.e.	-288	-489	-504	-349	-667	-722	...	Compte financier, n.i.a.
Net errors and omissions	-42	-100	-8	-30	-66	-65	...	Erreurs et omissions nettes
Reserves and related items	149	184	359	210	329	137	...	Réserves et postes apparentés

Country or area	1999	2000	2001	2002	2003	2004	2005	Pays ou zone
Nepal								Népal
Current account	-256	-299	-339	56	120	-45	1	Compte des transactions courantes
Goods: exports f.o.b.	612	776	721	632	703	773	903	Biens : exportations f.à.b.
Goods: imports f.o.b.	-1 494	-1 590	-1 486	-1 425	-1 666	-1 908	-2 276	Biens : importations f.à.b.
Services: credit	655	506	413	305	372	461	380	Services : crédit
Services: debit	-212	-200	-215	-237	-266	-385	-435	Services : débit
Income: credit	56	72	70	57	49	63	140	Revenus : crédit
Income: debit	-28	-35	-59	-71	-69	-78	-92	Revenus : débit
Current transfers, n.i.e.: credit	182	189	240	828	1 022	1 092	1 441	Transferts courants, n.i.a. : crédit
Current transfers: debit	-27	-17	-24	-33	-25	-63	-61	Transferts courants : débit
Capital account, n.i.e.	0	0	0	102	25	16	40	Compte de capital, n.i.a.
Financial account, n.i.e.	-25	76	-217	-405	-354	-488	-277	Compte financier, n.i.a.
Net errors and omissions	58	146	257	-67	310	416	139	Erreurs et omissions nettes
Reserves and related items	223	77	300	313	-101	102	96	Réserves et postes apparentés
Netherlands								Pays-Bas
Current account	15 684	7 264	9 810	11 018	29 867	52 108	48 936	Compte des transactions courantes
Goods: exports f.o.b.	195 694	205 271	203 201	209 516	264 966	318 397	347 862	Biens : exportations f.à.b.
Goods: imports f.o.b.	-179 747	-187 471	-184 015	-190 950	-228 447	-276 536	-301 402	Biens : importations f.à.b.
Services: credit	52 023	49 319	51 248	56 138	63 227	73 774	80 087	Services : crédit
Services: debit	-49 458	-51 339	-53 713	-57 204	-63 897	-69 443	-73 308	Services : débit
Income: credit	43 567	45 506	43 458	40 304	59 006	81 323	97 020	Revenus : crédit
Income: debit	-40 040	-47 803	-43 631	-40 245	-57 773	-66 007	-90 827	Revenus : débit
Current transfers, n.i.e.: credit	4 564	4 399	4 475	4 961	8 444	9 770	11 145	Transferts courants, n.i.a. : crédit
Current transfers: debit	-10 918	-10 618	-11 214	-11 501	-15 660	-19 170	-21 642	Transferts courants : débit
Capital account, n.i.e.	-214	-97	-3 200	-545	-3 069	-1 670	-1 835	Compte de capital, n.i.a.
Financial account, n.i.e.	-9 857	-7 604	-3 852	-4 527	-23 964	-52 912	-44 488	Compte financier, n.i.a.
Net errors and omissions	-10 224	657	-3 110	-6 077	-3 272	1 563	-4 403	Erreurs et omissions nettes
Reserves and related items	4 611	-219	351	132	437	911	1 790	Réserves et postes apparentés
Netherlands Antilles								Antilles néerlandaises
Current account	-277	-37	-210	-59	5	-113	-148	Compte des transactions courantes
Goods: exports f.o.b.	467	675	637	577	654	776	971	Biens : exportations f.à.b.
Goods: imports f.o.b.	-1 584	-1 656	-1 747	-1 598	-1 672	-1 956	-2 285	Biens : importations f.à.b.
Services: credit	1 519	1 614	1 651	1 626	1 701	1 799	1 847	Services : crédit
Services: debit	-662	-732	-790	-793	-812	-801	-813	Services : débit
Income: credit	101	126	104	91	90	95	103	Revenus : crédit
Income: debit	-121	-103	-84	-90	-97	-105	-108	Revenus : débit
Current transfers, n.i.e.: credit	180	243	212	361	395	311	401	Transferts courants, n.i.a. : crédit
Current transfers: debit	-176	-204	-193	-233	-254	-233	-265	Transferts courants : débit
Capital account, n.i.e.	108	30	37	28	26	79	96	Compte de capital, n.i.a.
Financial account, n.i.e.	69	-135	298	90	-36	^0	21	Compte financier, n.i.a.
Net errors and omissions	24	13	92	-6	32	42	80	Erreurs et omissions nettes
Reserves and related items	75	130	-218	-52	-27	-8	-49	Réserves et postes apparentés
New Zealand								Nouvelle-Zélande
Current account	-3 515	-2 672	-1 423	-2 453	-3 497	-6 535	-9 622	Compte des transactions courantes
Goods: exports f.o.b.	12 657	13 462	13 871	14 495	16 805	20 466	21 956	Biens : exportations f.à.b.
Goods: imports f.o.b.	-13 028	-12 850	-12 449	-14 351	-17 291	-21 886	-24 683	Biens : importations f.à.b.
Services: credit	4 386	4 408	4 452	5 325	6 733	7 991	8 510	Services : crédit
Services: debit	-4 581	-4 481	-4 327	-4 788	-5 761	-7 250	-8 238	Services : débit
Income: credit	919	693	610	1 138	1 417	1 530	1 451	Revenus : crédit
Income: debit	-4 036	-4 141	-3 734	-4 347	-5 622	-7 587	-9 077	Revenus : débit
Current transfers, n.i.e.: credit	609	634	585	642	856	901	1 243	Transferts courants, n.i.a. : crédit
Current transfers: debit	-440	-398	-433	-567	-635	-699	-784	Transferts courants : débit
Capital account, n.i.e.	-217	-180	480	813	502	156	-197	Compte de capital, n.i.a.
Financial account, n.i.e.	1 974	1 966	1 075	2 386	3 868	8 870	11 185	Compte financier, n.i.a.
Net errors and omissions	1 947	743	-319	340	-91	-1 863	1 043	Erreurs et omissions nettes
Reserves and related items	-188	143	187	-1 086	-783	-629	-2 410	Réserves et postes apparentés
Nicaragua								Nicaragua
Current account	-928	-839	-799	-699	-651	-696	-800	Compte des transactions courantes
Goods: exports f.o.b.	749	881	895	917	1 050	1 365	1 552	Biens : exportations f.à.b.

Country or area	1999	2000	2001	2002	2003	2004	2005	Pays ou zone
Goods: imports f.o.b.	-1 820	-1 802	-1 804	-1 834	-2 021	-2 440	-2 865	Biens : importations f.à.b.
Services: credit	214	221	223	226	258	286	309	Services : crédit
Services: debit	-335	-343	-352	-337	-363	-388	-426	Services : débit
Income: credit	31	31	15	9	7	9	22	Revenus : crédit
Income: debit	-228	-233	-255	-210	-197	-202	-142	Revenus : débit
Current transfers, n.i.e.: credit	460	406	479	531	617	673	750	Transferts courants, n.i.a. : crédit
Current transfers: debit	0	0	0	0	0	0	0	Transferts courants : débit
Capital account, n.i.e.	307	296	298	312	284	307	289	Compte de capital, n.i.a.
Financial account, n.i.e.	526	49	13	189	105	58	223	Compte financier, n.i.a.
Net errors and omissions	-300	37	-4	-203	-207	-70	26	Erreurs et omissions nettes
Reserves and related items	395	456	492	401	470	401	262	Réserves et postes apparentés
Niger								Niger
Current account	-137	-104	-92	-165	-219	-231	...	Compte des transactions courantes
Goods: exports f.o.b.	287	283	272	279	352	437	...	Biens : exportations f.à.b.
Goods: imports f.o.b.	-335	-324	-331	-371	-488	-590	...	Biens : importations f.à.b.
Services: credit	34	38	57	51	63	93	...	Services : crédit
Services: debit	-140	-132	-147	-152	-193	-262	...	Services : débit
Income: credit	14	13	12	13	17	26	...	Revenus : crédit
Income: debit	-33	-30	-27	-37	-43	-39	...	Revenus : débit
Current transfers, n.i.e.: credit	57	64	88	65	83	129	...	Transferts courants, n.i.a. : crédit
Current transfers: debit	-22	-17	-16	-12	-10	-25	...	Transferts courants : débit
Capital account, n.i.e.	62	55	40	92	92	249	...	Compte de capital, n.i.a.
Financial account, n.i.e.	48	98	61	69	97	-173	...	Compte financier, n.i.a.
Net errors and omissions	26	-14	14	-9	-15	116	...	Erreurs et omissions nettes
Reserves and related items	2	-35	-22	12	44	39	...	Réserves et postes apparentés
Nigeria								Nigéria
Current account	506	7 429	2 478	1 083	3 391	16 840	24 202	Compte des transactions courantes
Goods: exports f.o.b.	12 876	19 132	17 992	15 613	23 976	34 766	48 069	Biens : exportations f.à.b.
Goods: imports f.o.b.	-8 588	-8 717	-11 097	-10 876	-16 152	-15 009	-17 288	Biens : importations f.à.b.
Services: credit	980	1 833	1 653	2 524	3 473	3 336	4 164	Services : crédit
Services: debit	-3 476	-3 300	-4 640	-4 922	-5 715	-5 973	-7 321	Services : débit
Income: credit	240	218	199	184	82	157	705	Revenus : crédit
Income: debit	-2 818	-3 365	-2 997	-2 854	-3 325	-2 689	-7 437	Revenus : débit
Current transfers, n.i.e.: credit	1 301	1 637	1 373	1 422	1 063	2 273	3 329	Transferts courants, n.i.a. : crédit
Current transfers: debit	-9	-8	-6	-9	-12	-21	-18	Transferts courants : débit
Capital account, n.i.e.	13	33	0	55	20	36	23	Compte de capital, n.i.a.
Financial account, n.i.e.	-4 002	-6 219	-3 035	-6 609	-10 285	-13 061	-23 586	Compte financier, n.i.a.
Net errors and omissions	-54	1 847	779	782	5 614	4 676	9 758	Erreurs et omissions nettes
Reserves and related items	3 538	-3 089	-223	4 689	1 260	-8 491	-10 397	Réserves et postes apparentés
Norway								Norvège
Current account	8 859	25 079	27 546	24 269	27 698	33 000	46 560	Compte des transactions courantes
Goods: exports f.o.b.	46 136	60 393	59 448	59 555	68 666	83 164	104 179	Biens : exportations f.à.b.
Goods: imports f.o.b.	-35 496	-34 485	-33 046	-35 263	-40 504	-49 035	-54 490	Biens : importations f.à.b.
Services: credit	16 351	17 718	18 355	19 488	21 663	25 263	29 305	Services : crédit
Services: debit	-15 364	-14 991	-15 798	-17 972	-20 569	-24 304	-29 549	Services : débit
Income: credit	5 541	7 546	9 671	10 351	14 077	17 117	18 764	Revenus : crédit
Income: debit	-6 877	-9 851	-9 502	-9 654	-12 712	-16 570	-18 819	Revenus : débit
Current transfers, n.i.e.: credit	1 711	1 657	1 815	1 877	2 049	2 553	2 983	Transferts courants, n.i.a. : crédit
Current transfers: debit	-3 144	-2 908	-3 398	-4 112	-4 972	-5 188	-5 814	Transferts courants : débit
Capital account, n.i.e.	-174	-91	-90	-191	678	-154	-633	Compte de capital, n.i.a.
Financial account, n.i.e.	-1 735	-14 805	-28 720	-10 534	-21 745	-22 300	-33 376	Compte financier, n.i.a.
Net errors and omissions	-966	-6 498	-1 216	-6 814	-6 303	-5 319	-8 040	Erreurs et omissions nettes
Reserves and related items	-5 984	-3 686	2 481	-6 730	-328	-5 227	-4 511	Réserves et postes apparentés
Occupied Palestinian Terr.[3]								Terr. palestinien occupé[3]
Current account	-1 328	-1 012	-735	-457	-998	-1 483	...	Compte des transactions courantes
Goods: exports f.o.b.	603	560	448	365	374	404	...	Biens : exportations f.à.b.
Goods: imports f.o.b.	-3 221	-2 932	-2 111	-1 836	-2 290	-2 770	...	Biens : importations f.à.b.
Services: credit	475	462	178	192	214	181	...	Services : crédit
Services: debit	-520	-566	-702	-651	-516	-490	...	Services : débit

Country or area	1999	2000	2001	2002	2003	2004	2005	Pays ou zone
Income: credit	960	867	504	392	458	459	...	Revenus : crédit
Income: debit	-23	-42	-19	-11	-2	-33	...	Revenus : débit
Current transfers, n.i.e.: credit	572	764	1 068	1 187	917	904	...	Transferts courants, n.i.a. : crédit
Current transfers: debit	-174	-123	-101	-97	-153	-139	...	Transferts courants : débit
Capital account, n.i.e.	282	198	226	301	305	670	...	Compte de capital, n.i.a.
Financial account, n.i.e.	742	875	360	10	895	749	...	Compte financier, n.i.a.
Net errors and omissions	269	29	134	161	-101	92	...	Erreurs et omissions nettes
Reserves and related items	35	-91	16	-15	-100	-27	...	Réserves et postes apparentés
Oman								Oman
Current account	-460	3 129	2 082	1 941	1 483	569	4 717	Compte des transactions courantes
Goods: exports f.o.b.	7 237	11 318	11 074	11 170	11 670	13 381	18 692	Biens : exportations f.à.b.
Goods: imports f.o.b.	-4 299	-4 593	-5 308	-5 633	-6 086	-7 873	-8 029	Biens : importations f.à.b.
Services: credit	413	452	606	606	645	726	822	Services : crédit
Services: debit	-1 714	-1 759	-1 899	-1 880	-2 180	-2 756	-3 052	Services : débit
Income: credit	187	291	307	242	244	260	403	Revenus : crédit
Income: debit	-846	-1 129	-1 165	-962	-1 137	-1 343	-1 862	Revenus : débit
Current transfers, n.i.e.: credit	0	0	0	0	0	0	0	Transferts courants, n.i.a. : crédit
Current transfers: debit	-1 438	-1 451	-1 532	-1 602	-1 672	-1 826	-2 257	Transferts courants : débit
Capital account, n.i.e.	-3	8	-10	5	10	21	-16	Compte de capital, n.i.a.
Financial account, n.i.e.	128	-370	-503	-798	-312	585	-981	Compte financier, n.i.a.
Net errors and omissions	539	-504	-555	-842	-525	-665	-932	Erreurs et omissions nettes
Reserves and related items	-205	-2 263	-1 015	-307	-656	-510	-2 788	Réserves et postes apparentés
Pakistan								Pakistan
Current account	-920	-85	1 878	3 854	3 573	-817	-3 608	Compte des transactions courantes
Goods: exports f.o.b.	7 673	8 739	9 131	9 832	11 869	13 297	15 432	Biens : exportations f.à.b.
Goods: imports f.o.b.	-9 520	-9 896	-9 741	-10 428	-11 978	-16 693	-21 773	Biens : importations f.à.b.
Services: credit	1 373	1 380	1 459	2 429	2 968	2 749	3 678	Services : crédit
Services: debit	-2 146	-2 252	-2 330	-2 241	-3 294	-5 333	-7 510	Services : débit
Income: credit	119	118	113	128	180	221	658	Revenus : crédit
Income: debit	-1 959	-2 336	-2 189	-2 414	-2 404	-2 584	-3 172	Revenus : débit
Current transfers, n.i.e.: credit	3 582	4 200	5 496	6 593	6 300	7 666	9 169	Transferts courants, n.i.a. : crédit
Current transfers: debit	-42	-38	-61	-45	-68	-140	-90	Transferts courants : débit
Capital account, n.i.e.	...	...	...	40	1 138	591	202	Compte de capital, n.i.a.
Financial account, n.i.e.	-2 364	-3 099	-389	-784	-1 751	-1 810	4 079	Compte financier, n.i.a.
Net errors and omissions	768	557	708	974	-52	685	-198	Erreurs et omissions nettes
Reserves and related items	2 516	2 627	-2 197	-4 084	-2 908	1 351	-475	Réserves et postes apparentés
Panama								Panama
Current account	-1 159	-673	-170	-96	-580	-1 061	-782	Compte des transactions courantes
Goods: exports f.o.b.	5 288	5 839	5 992	5 315	5 072	6 078	7 591	Biens : exportations f.à.b.
Goods: imports f.o.b.	-6 628	-6 981	-6 689	-6 350	-6 274	-7 617	-8 907	Biens : importations f.à.b.
Services: credit	1 848	1 994	1 993	2 278	2 510	2 739	3 144	Services : crédit
Services: debit	-1 146	-1 141	-1 103	-1 310	-1 312	-1 460	-1 729	Services : débit
Income: credit	1 501	1 575	1 384	953	793	787	1 060	Revenus : crédit
Income: debit	-2 192	-2 136	-1 974	-1 226	-1 614	-1 808	-2 184	Revenus : débit
Current transfers, n.i.e.: credit	203	209	278	299	311	300	343	Transferts courants, n.i.a. : crédit
Current transfers: debit	-32	-32	-52	-55	-64	-81	-100	Transferts courants : débit
Capital account, n.i.e.	3	2	2	0	0	0	0	Compte de capital, n.i.a.
Financial account, n.i.e.	1 837	332	1 301	194	178	391	1 804	Compte financier, n.i.a.
Net errors and omissions	-490	262	-499	45	133	274	-346	Erreurs et omissions nettes
Reserves and related items	-191	77	-634	-144	269	396	-676	Réserves et postes apparentés
Papua New Guinea								Papouasie-Nvl-Guinée
Current account	95	345	282	-129	-35	-82	423	Compte des transactions courantes
Goods: exports f.o.b.	1 927	2 094	1 813	1 640	2 201	2 555	3 278	Biens : exportations f.à.b.
Goods: imports f.o.b.	-1 071	-999	-932	-1 077	-1 187	-1 459	-1 525	Biens : importations f.à.b.
Services: credit	248	243	285	162	233	203	302	Services : crédit
Services: debit	-728	-772	-662	-678	-868	-998	-1 167	Services : débit
Income: credit	19	32	20	27	16	20	26	Revenus : crédit
Income: debit	-291	-242	-250	-229	-493	-456	-565	Revenus : débit
Current transfers, n.i.e.: credit	60	62	76	86	144	130	167	Transferts courants, n.i.a. : crédit

Country or area	1999	2000	2001	2002	2003	2004	2005	Pays ou zone
Current transfers: debit	-69	-73	-67	-59	-81	-77	-94	Transferts courants : débit
Capital account, n.i.e.	0	0	0	0	0	0	0	Compte de capital, n.i.a.
Financial account, n.i.e.	16	-254	-152	56	-282	-42	-752	Compte financier, n.i.a.
Net errors and omissions	14	13	-2	91	40	26	47	Erreurs et omissions nettes
Reserves and related items	-125	-104	-129	-19	277	98	282	Réserves et postes apparentés
Paraguay								Paraguay
Current account	-165	-163	-266	93	125	138	-22	Compte des transactions courantes
Goods: exports f.o.b.	2 312	2 329	1 890	1 858	2 170	2 863	3 266	Biens : exportations f.à.b.
Goods: imports f.o.b.	-2 753	-2 866	-2 504	-2 138	-2 446	-3 108	-3 758	Biens : importations f.à.b.
Services: credit	575	595	555	568	574	629	661	Services : crédit
Services: debit	-493	-420	-390	-355	-329	-301	-340	Services : débit
Income: credit	213	261	256	196	166	165	193	Revenus : crédit
Income: debit	-195	-238	-240	-153	-175	-304	-268	Revenus : débit
Current transfers, n.i.e.: credit	177	178	168	118	166	196	224	Transferts courants, n.i.a. : crédit
Current transfers: debit	-2	-2	-2	-2	-2	-2	-2	Transferts courants : débit
Capital account, n.i.e.	20	3	15	4	15	16	20	Compte de capital, n.i.a.
Financial account, n.i.e.	89	64	148	41	147	47	60	Compte financier, n.i.a.
Net errors and omissions	-244	-243	53	-263	-54	69	-110	Erreurs et omissions nettes
Reserves and related items	301	339	50	126	-233	-270	52	Réserves et postes apparentés
Peru								Pérou
Current account	-1 464	-1 526	-1 144	-1 063	-935	-11	1 030	Compte des transactions courantes
Goods: exports f.o.b.	6 088	6 955	7 026	7 714	9 091	12 616	17 247	Biens : exportations f.à.b.
Goods: imports f.o.b.	-6 743	-7 366	-7 221	-7 422	-8 255	-9 824	-12 084	Biens : importations f.à.b.
Services: credit	1 594	1 529	1 455	1 530	1 695	1 914	2 179	Services : crédit
Services: debit	-2 256	-2 234	-2 345	-2 471	-2 549	-2 756	-3 092	Services : débit
Income: credit	655	737	670	370	322	332	618	Revenus : crédit
Income: debit	-1 767	-2 146	-1 771	-1 827	-2 466	-3 753	-5 629	Revenus : débit
Current transfers, n.i.e.: credit	992	1 008	1 050	1 052	1 234	1 467	1 797	Transferts courants, n.i.a. : crédit
Current transfers: debit	-27	-9	-8	-8	-6	-6	-6	Transferts courants : débit
Capital account, n.i.e.	-54	-251	-143	-107	-107	-86	-152	Compte de capital, n.i.a.
Financial account, n.i.e.	545	1 015	1 534	1 983	820	2 375	82	Compte financier, n.i.a.
Net errors and omissions	112	631	185	197	783	178	450	Erreurs et omissions nettes
Reserves and related items	862	130	-432	-1 010	-561	-2 456	-1 411	Réserves et postes apparentés
Philippines								Philippines
Current account	-2 874	-2 225	-1 744	-279	288	1 633	2 338	Compte des transactions courantes
Goods: exports f.o.b.	34 243	37 347	31 313	34 403	35 339	38 794	40 231	Biens : exportations f.à.b.
Goods: imports f.o.b.	-40 220	-43 318	-37 578	-39 933	-41 190	-44 478	-47 777	Biens : importations f.à.b.
Services: credit	3 468	3 377	3 072	3 428	3 389	4 043	4 462	Services : crédit
Services: debit	-5 088	-5 247	-5 360	-5 430	-5 352	-5 815	-5 858	Services : débit
Income: credit	2 723	3 336	3 553	3 306	3 330	3 725	3 937	Revenus : crédit
Income: debit	-3 784	-3 363	-3 604	-3 733	-3 614	-3 796	-4 060	Revenus : débit
Current transfers, n.i.e.: credit	5 969	5 909	7 119	7 948	8 626	9 420	11 706	Transferts courants, n.i.a. : crédit
Current transfers: debit	-185	-266	-259	-268	-240	-260	-303	Transferts courants : débit
Capital account, n.i.e.	163	138	62	27	54	17	40	Compte de capital, n.i.a.
Financial account, n.i.e.	4 209	3 234	366	394	481	-1 671	51	Compte financier, n.i.a.
Net errors and omissions	2 269	-1 624	629	33	-902	-282	-789	Erreurs et omissions nettes
Reserves and related items	-3 767	477	687	-175	79	303	-1 640	Réserves et postes apparentés
Poland								Pologne
Current account	-12 487	-9 981	-5 375	-5 009	-4 599	-10 676	-5 105	Compte des transactions courantes
Goods: exports f.o.b.	30 060	35 902	41 663	46 742	61 007	81 862	96 395	Biens : exportations f.à.b.
Goods: imports f.o.b.	-45 132	-48 209	-49 324	-53 991	-66 732	-87 484	-99 161	Biens : importations f.à.b.
Services: credit	8 363	10 398	9 753	10 037	11 174	13 471	16 227	Services : crédit
Services: debit	-6 982	-8 993	-8 966	-9 186	-10 647	-12 457	-14 315	Services : débit
Income: credit	1 837	2 250	2 625	1 948	2 108	2 017	2 513	Revenus : crédit
Income: debit	-2 847	-3 709	-4 015	-3 837	-5 745	-13 536	-13 699	Revenus : débit
Current transfers, n.i.e.: credit	2 898	3 008	3 737	4 181	5 316	8 101	11 036	Transferts courants, n.i.a. : crédit
Current transfers: debit	-684	-628	-848	-903	-1 080	-2 650	-4 101	Transferts courants : débit
Capital account, n.i.e.	55	34	76	-7	-46	1 180	995	Compte de capital, n.i.a.
Financial account, n.i.e.	10 462	10 221	3 173	7 180	8 686	8 418	14 524	Compte financier, n.i.a.

Country or area	1999	2000	2001	2002	2003	2004	2005	Pays ou zone
Net errors and omissions	2 126	350	1 699	-1 516	-2 835	1 879	-2 268	Erreurs et omissions nettes
Reserves and related items	-156	-624	427	-648	-1 206	-801	-8 146	Réserves et postes apparentés
Portugal								Portugal
Current account	-10 414	-11 748	-11 355	-9 947	-9 207	-12 962	-17 007	Compte des transactions courantes
Goods: exports f.o.b.	24 899	24 663	24 456	25 975	32 055	37 128	38 167	Biens : exportations f.à.b.
Goods: imports f.o.b.	-39 326	-39 195	-38 362	-39 286	-46 233	-55 771	-59 022	Biens : importations f.à.b.
Services: credit	9 259	9 016	9 379	10 357	12 354	14 840	15 105	Services : crédit
Services: debit	-7 323	-7 053	-6 826	-7 146	-8 293	-9 688	-10 056	Services : débit
Income: credit	4 261	4 570	5 435	4 722	6 399	7 915	7 703	Revenus : crédit
Income: debit	-6 029	-7 101	-8 787	-7 373	-8 740	-10 856	-11 635	Revenus : débit
Current transfers, n.i.e.: credit	6 079	5 415	5 582	5 445	6 443	7 152	7 038	Transferts courants, n.i.a. : crédit
Current transfers: debit	-2 234	-2 063	-2 233	-2 641	-3 191	-3 680	-4 307	Transferts courants : débit
Capital account, n.i.e.	2 458	1 512	1 069	1 906	3 010	2 808	2 139	Compte de capital, n.i.a.
Financial account, n.i.e.	9 172	10 872	10 758	8 265	558	9 470	14 448	Compte financier, n.i.a.
Net errors and omissions	-1 001	-265	381	794	-816	-1 180	-1 320	Erreurs et omissions nettes
Reserves and related items	-216	-371	-852	-1 017	6 455	1 863	1 741	Réserves et postes apparentés
Republic of Moldova								République de Moldova
Current account	-79	-108	-37	-26	-135	-54	-264	Compte des transactions courantes
Goods: exports f.o.b.	474	477	565	660	805	994	1 105	Biens : exportations f.à.b.
Goods: imports f.o.b.	-611	-770	-880	-1 038	-1 428	-1 748	-2 296	Biens : importations f.à.b.
Services: credit	136	165	171	217	254	355	424	Services : crédit
Services: debit	-178	-202	-209	-257	-300	-376	-447	Services : débit
Income: credit	121	139	174	229	341	490	539	Revenus : crédit
Income: debit	-96	-118	-78	-73	-111	-133	-136	Revenus : débit
Current transfers, n.i.e.: credit	111	214	236	256	333	401	591	Transferts courants, n.i.a. : crédit
Current transfers: debit	-35	-13	-16	-19	-28	-36	-43	Transferts courants : débit
Capital account, n.i.e.	1	-14	-21	-19	-19	-18	-17	Compte de capital, n.i.a.
Financial account, n.i.e.	-35	126	19	20	83	111	206	Compte financier, n.i.a.
Net errors and omissions	-4	-9	16	-19	54	108	186	Erreurs et omissions nettes
Reserves and related items	116	5	23	43	17	-147	-111	Réserves et postes apparentés
Romania								Roumanie
Current account	-1 297	-1 355	-2 229	-1 525	-3 311	-6 382	-8 621	Compte des transactions courantes
Goods: exports f.o.b.	8 503	10 366	11 385	13 876	17 618	23 485	27 730	Biens : exportations f.à.b.
Goods: imports f.o.b.	-9 595	-12 050	-14 354	-16 487	-22 155	-30 150	-37 348	Biens : importations f.à.b.
Services: credit	1 365	1 747	2 032	2 347	3 028	3 614	5 083	Services : crédit
Services: debit	-1 785	-1 993	-2 153	-2 338	-2 958	-3 879	-5 518	Services : débit
Income: credit	152	325	455	413	372	433	1 533	Revenus : crédit
Income: debit	-563	-610	-737	-872	-1 077	-3 582	-4 432	Revenus : débit
Current transfers, n.i.e.: credit	804	1 079	1 417	1 808	2 200	4 188	4 939	Transferts courants, n.i.a. : crédit
Current transfers: debit	-178	-219	-274	-272	-339	-491	-607	Transferts courants : débit
Capital account, n.i.e.	45	36	95	93	213	643	731	Compte de capital, n.i.a.
Financial account, n.i.e.	697	2 102	2 938	4 079	4 400	10 761	14 089	Compte financier, n.i.a.
Net errors and omissions	794	125	731	-856	-289	1 167	612	Erreurs et omissions nettes
Reserves and related items	-239	-908	-1 535	-1 791	-1 013	-6 189	-6 811	Réserves et postes apparentés
Russian Federation								Fédération de Russie
Current account	24 616	46 839	33 935	29 116	35 410	59 003	83 836	Compte des transactions courantes
Goods: exports f.o.b.	75 551	105 033	101 884	107 301	135 929	183 207	243 798	Biens : exportations f.à.b.
Goods: imports f.o.b.	-39 537	-44 862	-53 764	-60 966	-76 070	-97 382	-125 434	Biens : importations f.à.b.
Services: credit	9 067	9 565	11 442	13 611	16 229	20 356	24 593	Services : crédit
Services: debit	-13 351	-16 230	-20 572	-23 497	-27 122	-33 732	-39 435	Services : débit
Income: credit	3 881	4 753	6 800	5 677	11 057	11 998	17 377	Revenus : crédit
Income: debit	-11 597	-11 489	-11 038	-12 260	-24 228	-24 767	-36 225	Revenus : débit
Current transfers, n.i.e.: credit	1 183	807	744	1 352	2 537	3 640	4 689	Transferts courants, n.i.a. : crédit
Current transfers: debit	-582	-738	-1 561	-2 103	-2 922	-4 317	-5 528	Transferts courants : débit
Capital account, n.i.e.	-328	10 676	-9 378	-12 396	-993	-1 624	-12 764	Compte de capital, n.i.a.
Financial account, n.i.e.	-17 008	-33 855	-3 308	1 345	3 558	-4 056	2 649	Compte financier, n.i.a.
Net errors and omissions	-8 984	-9 737	-9 982	-6 502	-9 713	-6 433	-8 753	Erreurs et omissions nettes
Reserves and related items	1 704	-13 923	-11 266	-11 563	-28 262	-46 890	-64 968	Réserves et postes apparentés

Country or area	1999	2000	2001	2002	2003	2004	2005	Pays ou zone
Rwanda								Rwanda
Current account	-141	-94	-102	-126	-121	-198	-84	Compte des transactions courantes
Goods: exports f.o.b.	62	68	93	67	63	98	128	Biens : exportations f.à.b.
Goods: imports f.o.b.	-247	-223	-245	-233	-229	-276	-355	Biens : importations f.à.b.
Services: credit	51	59	66	65	76	103	129	Services : crédit
Services: debit	-193	-200	-189	-202	-204	-240	-304	Services : débit
Income: credit	8	14	14	8	6	6	27	Revenus : crédit
Income: debit	-18	-28	-34	-27	-37	-39	-44	Revenus : débit
Current transfers, n.i.e.: credit	210	233	210	215	223	169	352	Transferts courants, n.i.a. : crédit
Current transfers: debit	-13	-17	-18	-20	-20	-18	-18	Transferts courants : débit
Capital account, n.i.e.	70	62	50	66	41	61	93	Compte de capital, n.i.a.
Financial account, n.i.e.	-33	11	-44	81	-21	-21	-59	Compte financier, n.i.a.
Net errors and omissions	89	21	71	-8	23	-9	26	Erreurs et omissions nettes
Reserves and related items	15	^0	26	-13	78	168	23	Réserves et postes apparentés
Saint Kitts and Nevis								Saint-Kitts-et-Nevis
Current account	-82	-66	-107	-125	-116	-90	-107	Compte des transactions courantes
Goods: exports f.o.b.	45	51	55	63	57	57	58	Biens : exportations f.à.b.
Goods: imports f.o.b.	-135	-173	-167	-178	-176	-175	-194	Biens : importations f.à.b.
Services: credit	101	99	98	90	108	135	143	Services : crédit
Services: debit	-85	-76	-75	-79	-80	-83	-92	Services : débit
Income: credit	6	6	5	6	6	8	8	Revenus : crédit
Income: debit	-35	-36	-39	-44	-49	-50	-49	Revenus : débit
Current transfers, n.i.e.: credit	24	70	27	28	30	31	32	Transferts courants, n.i.a. : crédit
Current transfers: debit	-4	-7	-11	-12	-11	-13	-14	Transferts courants : débit
Capital account, n.i.e.	6	6	11	15	5	5	14	Compte de capital, n.i.a.
Financial account, n.i.e.	95	77	114	116	105	95	67	Compte financier, n.i.a.
Net errors and omissions	-16	-21	-6	2	5	3	18	Erreurs et omissions nettes
Reserves and related items	-3	4	-12	-9	1	-14	7	Réserves et postes apparentés
Saint Lucia								Sainte-Lucie
Current account	-97	-95	-107	-105	-146	-100	-183	Compte des transactions courantes
Goods: exports f.o.b.	61	53	54	69	72	109	69	Biens : exportations f.à.b.
Goods: imports f.o.b.	-312	-312	-272	-272	-355	-369	-414	Biens : importations f.à.b.
Services: credit	306	324	274	250	318	367	390	Services : crédit
Services: debit	-136	-133	-131	-129	-145	-151	-164	Services : débit
Income: credit	2	4	3	4	5	6	2	Revenus : crédit
Income: debit	-41	-48	-49	-39	-55	-77	-81	Revenus : débit
Current transfers, n.i.e.: credit	32	29	29	28	29	30	33	Transferts courants, n.i.a. : crédit
Current transfers: debit	-10	-10	-15	-16	-16	-16	-17	Transferts courants : débit
Capital account, n.i.e.	25	14	25	20	17	3	7	Compte de capital, n.i.a.
Financial account, n.i.e.	66	86	87	89	135	126	180	Compte financier, n.i.a.
Net errors and omissions	9	8	8	2	12	-3	-19	Erreurs et omissions nettes
Reserves and related items	-4	-13	-13	-6	-18	-27	15	Réserves et postes apparentés
Saint Vincent-Grenadines								Saint Vincent-Grenadines
Current account	-73	-24	-38	-42	-79	-103	-110	Compte des transactions courantes
Goods: exports f.o.b.	50	52	43	41	40	39	43	Biens : exportations f.à.b.
Goods: imports f.o.b.	-177	-144	-152	-158	-177	-199	-212	Biens : importations f.à.b.
Services: credit	126	128	133	137	133	145	157	Services : crédit
Services: debit	-66	-56	-58	-57	-65	-73	-82	Services : débit
Income: credit	3	3	2	3	4	5	12	Revenus : crédit
Income: debit	-23	-22	-19	-21	-28	-34	-45	Revenus : débit
Current transfers, n.i.e.: credit	23	25	23	24	24	25	27	Transferts courants, n.i.a. : crédit
Current transfers: debit	-9	-8	-11	-12	-11	-11	-9	Transferts courants : débit
Capital account, n.i.e.	8	6	9	11	14	19	14	Compte de capital, n.i.a.
Financial account, n.i.e.	54	25	49	15	49	82	65	Compte financier, n.i.a.
Net errors and omissions	15	8	-11	9	16	27	27	Erreurs et omissions nettes
Reserves and related items	-4	-14	-9	7	1	-25	4	Réserves et postes apparentés
Samoa								Samoa
Current account	-19	...	...	...	...	-17	-24	Compte des transactions courantes
Goods: exports f.o.b.	18	...	...	...	...	12	12	Biens : exportations f.à.b.

Country or area	1999	2000	2001	2002	2003	2004	2005	Pays ou zone
Goods: imports f.o.b.	-116	...	...	...	...	-155	-187	Biens : importations f.à.b.
Services: credit	61	...	...	...	...	95	112	Services : crédit
Services: debit	-25	...	...	...	...	-42	-53	Services : débit
Income: credit	3	...	...	...	...	4	6	Revenus : crédit
Income: debit	-2	...	...	...	...	-21	-20	Revenus : débit
Current transfers, n.i.e.: credit	45	...	...	...	...	105	114	Transferts courants, n.i.a. : crédit
Current transfers: debit	-3	...	...	...	...	-15	-8	Transferts courants : débit
Capital account, n.i.e.	24	...	...	...	...	44	41	Compte de capital, n.i.a.
Financial account, n.i.e.	-1	...	...	...	...	-7	-10	Compte financier, n.i.a.
Net errors and omissions	2	...	...	...	...	-12	-7	Erreurs et omissions nettes
Reserves and related items	-7	...	...	...	...	-8	1	Réserves et postes apparentés
Sao Tome and Principe								Sao Tomé-et-Principe
Current account	-16	-19	-21	-23	...	...	...	Compte des transactions courantes
Goods: exports f.o.b.	4	3	3	5	...	...	...	Biens : exportations f.à.b.
Goods: imports f.o.b.	-22	-25	-24	-28	...	...	...	Biens : importations f.à.b.
Services: credit	12	14	13	13	...	...	...	Services : crédit
Services: debit	-12	-11	-12	-13	...	...	...	Services : débit
Income: credit	...	...	0	...	...	...	...	Revenus : crédit
Income: debit	-5	-4	-5	-5	...	...	...	Revenus : débit
Current transfers, n.i.e.: credit	6	4	4	5	...	...	...	Transferts courants, n.i.a. : crédit
Current transfers: debit	...	...	0	...	...	...	...	Transferts courants : débit
Capital account, n.i.e.	9	12	15	12	...	...	...	Compte de capital, n.i.a.
Financial account, n.i.e.	4	3	2	4	...	...	...	Compte financier, n.i.a.
Net errors and omissions	^0	-2	3	^0	...	...	...	Erreurs et omissions nettes
Reserves and related items	3	5	1	7	...	...	...	Réserves et postes apparentés
Saudi Arabia								Arabie saoudite
Current account	411	14 317	9 353	11 873	28 048	51 926	87 132	Compte des transactions courantes
Goods: exports f.o.b.	50 689	77 481	67 973	72 464	93 244	125 998	174 635	Biens : exportations f.à.b.
Goods: imports f.o.b.	-25 683	-27 704	-28 607	-29 624	-33 868	-41 050	-51 327	Biens : importations f.à.b.
Services: credit	5 373	4 779	5 008	5 177	5 713	5 852	5 916	Services : crédit
Services: debit	-18 830	-25 228	-19 281	-19 980	-20 857	-25 696	-27 947	Services : débit
Income: credit	5 804	3 345	4 125	3 714	2 977	4 278	4 943	Revenus : crédit
Income: debit	-2 883	-2 865	-4 644	-3 925	-4 277	-3 800	-4 671	Revenus : débit
Current transfers, n.i.e.: credit	0	0	0	0	0	0	0	Transferts courants, n.i.a. : crédit
Current transfers: debit	-14 058	-15 490	-15 220	-15 954	-14 883	-13 655	-14 418	Transferts courants : débit
Capital account, n.i.e.	0	0	0	0	0	0	0	Compte de capital, n.i.a.
Financial account, n.i.e.	2 404	-11 652	-11 262	-9 137	-26 440	-47 428	-87 596	Compte financier, n.i.a.
Net errors and omissions^	0	0	0	0	0	0	0	Erreurs et omissions nettes^
Reserves and related items	-2 815	-2 665	1 909	-2 736	-1 608	-4 498	464	Réserves et postes apparentés
Senegal								Sénégal
Current account	-320	-332	-245	-317	-437	-513	...	Compte des transactions courantes
Goods: exports f.o.b.	1 027	920	1 003	1 067	1 257	1 509	...	Biens : exportations f.à.b.
Goods: imports f.o.b.	-1 373	-1 337	-1 428	-1 604	-2 066	-2 496	...	Biens : importations f.à.b.
Services: credit	416	387	398	456	569	670	...	Services : crédit
Services: debit	-430	-405	-414	-474	-591	-698	...	Services : débit
Income: credit	80	76	62	65	86	95	...	Revenus : crédit
Income: debit	-199	-188	-166	-195	-223	-226	...	Revenus : débit
Current transfers, n.i.e.: credit	225	275	354	414	596	715	...	Transferts courants, n.i.a. : crédit
Current transfers: debit	-66	-61	-53	-46	-65	-83	...	Transferts courants : débit
Capital account, n.i.e.	99	83	146	127	150	750	...	Compte de capital, n.i.a.
Financial account, n.i.e.	-55	27	-103	-88	3	-54	...	Compte financier, n.i.a.
Net errors and omissions	8	-9	8	31	11	16	...	Erreurs et omissions nettes
Reserves and related items	268	231	194	247	273	-199	...	Réserves et postes apparentés
Seychelles								Seychelles
Current account	-127	-54	-158	-108	-12	-64	-179	Compte des transactions courantes
Goods: exports f.o.b.	146	195	216	237	286	301	356	Biens : exportations f.à.b.
Goods: imports f.o.b.	-370	-312	-429	-380	-376	-456	-620	Biens : importations f.à.b.
Services: credit	277	287	294	313	330	327	368	Services : crédit
Services: debit	-156	-190	-216	-217	-220	-216	-255	Services : débit

Country or area	1999	2000	2001	2002	2003	2004	2005	Pays ou zone
Income: credit	8	10	8	7	12	9	10	Revenus : crédit
Income: debit	-32	-43	-37	-75	-55	-43	-54	Revenus : débit
Current transfers, n.i.e.: credit	10	7	8	8	13	17	21	Transferts courants, n.i.a. : crédit
Current transfers: debit	-11	-8	-4	-2	-3	-3	-4	Transferts courants : débit
Capital account, n.i.e.	16	1	9	5	7	1	6	Compte de capital, n.i.a.
Financial account, n.i.e.	14	76	94	131	-31	-30	139	Compte financier, n.i.a.
Net errors and omissions	-2	3	1	-10	-5	1	5	Erreurs et omissions nettes
Reserves and related items	99	-26	54	-17	41	93	29	Réserves et postes apparentés
Sierra Leone								Sierra Leone
Current account	-99	-112	-98	-125	-99	-141	-169	Compte des transactions courantes
Goods: exports f.o.b.	6	13	29	60	111	154	185	Biens : exportations f.à.b.
Goods: imports f.o.b.	-87	-137	-165	-255	-311	-274	-362	Biens : importations f.à.b.
Services: credit	22	42	52	38	66	61	78	Services : crédit
Services: debit	-101	-113	-111	-81	-94	-92	-91	Services : débit
Income: credit	6	7	4	18	2	4	5	Revenus : crédit
Income: debit	-14	-13	-15	-21	-17	-71	-56	Revenus : débit
Current transfers, n.i.e.: credit	69	92	121	119	149	80	74	Transferts courants, n.i.a. : crédit
Current transfers: debit	-1	-5	-13	-4	-5	-3	-2	Transferts courants : débit
Capital account, n.i.e.	0	0	^0	8	16	18	37	Compte de capital, n.i.a.
Financial account, n.i.e.	-27	125	30	19	34	76	38	Compte financier, n.i.a.
Net errors and omissions	111	-3	97	-16	-50	-54	-36	Erreurs et omissions nettes
Reserves and related items	16	-10	-30	114	100	100	130	Réserves et postes apparentés
Singapore								Singapour
Current account	14 361	10 728	11 760	11 918	22 317	26 318	33 212	Compte des transactions courantes
Goods: exports f.o.b.	127 051	153 095	136 609	140 776	161 740	201 026	232 257	Biens : exportations f.à.b.
Goods: imports f.o.b.	-113 124	-139 138	-119 360	-121 958	-132 173	-168 100	-194 367	Biens : importations f.à.b.
Services: credit	24 933	28 171	27 466	29 549	36 263	46 778	51 308	Services : crédit
Services: debit	-25 230	-29 506	-31 790	-33 389	-39 729	-50 006	-54 260	Services : débit
Income: credit	16 227	15 623	13 863	13 554	16 472	19 419	22 976	Revenus : crédit
Income: debit	-14 470	-16 357	-13 856	-15 475	-19 122	-21 648	-23 517	Revenus : débit
Current transfers, n.i.e.: credit	135	128	124	127	131	136	137	Transferts courants, n.i.a. : crédit
Current transfers: debit	-1 161	-1 288	-1 295	-1 267	-1 266	-1 286	-1 321	Transferts courants : débit
Capital account, n.i.e.	-191	-163	-161	-160	-168	-184	-202	Compte de capital, n.i.a.
Financial account, n.i.e.	-12 857	-5 760	-11 738	-10 248	-16 670	-14 355	-19 986	Compte financier, n.i.a.
Net errors and omissions	2 875	1 945	-727	-183	1 196	308	-950	Erreurs et omissions nettes
Reserves and related items	-4 188	-6 751	867	-1 327	-6 675	-12 087	-12 074	Réserves et postes apparentés
Slovakia								Slovaquie
Current account	-1 155	-694	...	-1 955	-282	...	...	Compte des transactions courantes
Goods: exports f.o.b.	10 201	11 896	...	14 460	21 944	...	...	Biens : exportations f.à.b.
Goods: imports f.o.b.	-11 310	-12 791	...	-16 626	-22 593	...	...	Biens : importations f.à.b.
Services: credit	1 899	2 241	...	2 812	3 297	...	...	Services : crédit
Services: debit	-1 844	-1 805	...	-2 351	-3 056	...	...	Services : débit
Income: credit	268	268	...	342	907	...	...	Revenus : crédit
Income: debit	-568	-623	...	-791	-1 026	...	...	Revenus : débit
Current transfers, n.i.e.: credit	466	344	...	480	537	...	...	Transferts courants, n.i.a. : crédit
Current transfers: debit	-268	-224	...	-282	-292	...	...	Transferts courants : débit
Capital account, n.i.e.	158	91	...	110	102	...	...	Compte de capital, n.i.a.
Financial account, n.i.e.	1 789	1 472	...	5 230	1 661	...	...	Compte financier, n.i.a.
Net errors and omissions	-14	51	...	298	27	...	...	Erreurs et omissions nettes
Reserves and related items	-777	-920	...	-3 684	-1 508	...	...	Réserves et postes apparentés
Slovenia								Slovénie
Current account	-697	-548	31	244	-216	-893	-681	Compte des transactions courantes
Goods: exports f.o.b.	8 623	8 808	9 343	10 471	12 916	16 065	18 146	Biens : exportations f.à.b.
Goods: imports f.o.b.	-9 858	-9 947	-9 962	-10 719	-13 539	-17 322	-19 404	Biens : importations f.à.b.
Services: credit	1 877	1 888	1 961	2 316	2 791	3 455	3 976	Services : crédit
Services: debit	-1 522	-1 438	-1 458	-1 732	-2 183	-2 603	-2 915	Services : débit
Income: credit	427	434	463	468	589	667	781	Revenus : crédit
Income: debit	-363	-408	-444	-617	-821	-1 060	-1 143	Revenus : débit
Current transfers, n.i.e.: credit	335	341	390	473	538	698	878	Transferts courants, n.i.a. : crédit

Balance of payments summary—Millions of US dollars (*continued*)
Résumé de la balance des paiements—Millions de dollars des E.U. (*suite*)

Country or area	1999	2000	2001	2002	2003	2004	2005	Pays ou zone
Current transfers: debit	-215	-225	-261	-416	-508	-792	-998	Transferts courants : débit
Capital account, n.i.e.	-1	3	-3	-159	-191	-123	-138	Compte de capital, n.i.a.
Financial account, n.i.e.	576	680	1 204	1 987	567	702	844	Compte financier, n.i.a.
Net errors and omissions	41	42	53	-255	150	17	181	Erreurs et omissions nettes
Reserves and related items	81	-178	-1 285	-1 817	-310	296	-206	Réserves et postes apparentés
Solomon Islands								Iles Salomon
Current account	21	...	...	...	...	...	...	Compte des transactions courantes
Goods: exports f.o.b.	165	...	...	...	...	...	...	Biens : exportations f.à.b.
Goods: imports f.o.b.	-110	...	...	...	...	...	...	Biens : importations f.à.b.
Services: credit	56	...	...	...	...	...	...	Services : crédit
Services: debit	-87	...	...	...	...	...	...	Services : débit
Income: credit	5	...	...	...	...	...	...	Revenus : crédit
Income: debit	-22	...	...	...	...	...	...	Revenus : débit
Current transfers, n.i.e.: credit	42	...	...	...	...	...	...	Transferts courants, n.i.a. : crédit
Current transfers: debit	-26	...	...	...	...	...	...	Transferts courants : débit
Capital account, n.i.e.	9	...	...	...	...	...	...	Compte de capital, n.i.a.
Financial account, n.i.e.	-34	...	...	...	...	...	...	Compte financier, n.i.a.
Net errors and omissions	-2	...	...	...	...	...	...	Erreurs et omissions nettes
Reserves and related items	5	...	...	...	...	...	...	Réserves et postes apparentés
South Africa								Afrique du Sud
Current account	-675	-191	343	884	-1 902	-7 003	-9 142	Compte des transactions courantes
Goods: exports f.o.b.	28 534	31 950	31 064	31 772	38 700	48 237	55 280	Biens : exportations f.à.b.
Goods: imports f.o.b.	-24 526	-27 252	-25 809	-27 016	-35 270	-48 518	-56 484	Biens : importations f.à.b.
Services: credit	5 210	5 046	4 845	4 985	8 298	9 682	11 157	Services : crédit
Services: debit	-5 759	-5 823	-5 232	-5 504	-8 045	-10 328	-12 155	Services : débit
Income: credit	1 791	2 511	2 480	2 179	2 857	3 259	4 640	Revenus : crédit
Income: debit	-5 000	-5 696	-6 267	-4 975	-7 447	-7 576	-9 569	Revenus : débit
Current transfers, n.i.e.: credit	66	106	126	139	252	257	240	Transferts courants, n.i.a. : crédit
Current transfers: debit	-993	-1 033	-865	-695	-1 248	-2 015	-2 251	Transferts courants : débit
Capital account, n.i.e.	-62	-52	-31	-15	44	52	30	Compte de capital, n.i.a.
Financial account, n.i.e.	3 154	73	-1 188	-1 452	-1 961	7 651	11 403	Compte financier, n.i.a.
Net errors and omissions	-500	649	855	260	3 466	5 623	3 474	Erreurs et omissions nettes
Reserves and related items	-1 916	-480	22	322	354	-6 324	-5 766	Réserves et postes apparentés
Spain								Espagne
Current account	-18 080	-23 185	-24 065	-22 239	-30 886	-54 865	-83 388	Compte des transactions courantes
Goods: exports f.o.b.	112 919	115 769	117 522	127 162	158 049	185 209	196 580	Biens : exportations f.à.b.
Goods: imports f.o.b.	-144 732	-152 856	-152 039	-161 794	-203 205	-251 939	-281 784	Biens : importations f.à.b.
Services: credit	52 331	52 453	55 651	60 247	74 308	86 078	94 663	Services : crédit
Services: debit	-31 975	-33 171	-35 182	-38 712	-47 951	-59 188	-67 129	Services : débit
Income: credit	15 263	18 904	20 243	21 536	27 209	33 948	39 445	Revenus : crédit
Income: debit	-24 794	-25 753	-31 509	-33 194	-38 910	-48 986	-60 701	Revenus : débit
Current transfers, n.i.e.: credit	13 204	11 380	12 143	14 575	17 048	20 366	20 194	Transferts courants, n.i.a. : crédit
Current transfers: debit	-10 296	-9 911	-10 893	-12 059	-17 434	-20 353	-24 656	Transferts courants : débit
Capital account, n.i.e.	6 924	4 797	4 811	7 236	9 274	10 450	10 107	Compte de capital, n.i.a.
Financial account, n.i.e.	-10 748	15 261	18 169	17 782	4 353	36 964	73 885	Compte financier, n.i.a.
Net errors and omissions	-892	247	-257	912	1 769	1 039	-2 524	Erreurs et omissions nettes
Reserves and related items	22 795	2 880	1 341	-3 690	15 490	6 412	1 920	Réserves et postes apparentés
Sri Lanka								Sri Lanka
Current account	-561	-1 044	-237	-268	-106	-677	-740	Compte des transactions courantes
Goods: exports f.o.b.	4 596	5 440	4 817	4 699	5 133	5 757	6 347	Biens : exportations f.à.b.
Goods: imports f.o.b.	-5 365	-6 484	-5 377	-5 495	-6 005	-7 200	-7 977	Biens : importations f.à.b.
Services: credit	964	939	1 355	1 268	1 411	1 527	1 540	Services : crédit
Services: debit	-1 414	-1 621	-1 749	-1 584	-1 679	-1 908	-2 089	Services : débit
Income: credit	167	149	108	75	170	157	35	Revenus : crédit
Income: debit	-419	-449	-375	-328	-341	-360	-332	Revenus : débit
Current transfers, n.i.e.: credit	1 078	1 166	1 155	1 287	1 414	1 564	1 968	Transferts courants, n.i.a. : crédit
Current transfers: debit	-168	-183	-172	-190	-209	-214	-233	Transferts courants : débit
Capital account, n.i.e.	80	49	50	65	74	64	250	Compte de capital, n.i.a.
Financial account, n.i.e.	413	447	-136	-196	-219	-133	67	Compte financier, n.i.a.

Country or area	1999	2000	2001	2002	2003	2004	2005	Pays ou zone
Net errors and omissions	-27	186	15	136	-114	-189	-75	Erreurs et omissions nettes
Reserves and related items	95	361	308	262	365	935	498	Réserves et postes apparentés
Sudan								Soudan
Current account	-465	-557	-618	-1 008	-955	-871	-3 013	Compte des transactions courantes
Goods: exports f.o.b.	780	1 807	1 699	1 949	2 542	3 778	4 824	Biens : exportations f.à.b.
Goods: imports f.o.b.	-1 256	-1 366	-1 395	-2 294	-2 536	-3 586	-5 946	Biens : importations f.à.b.
Services: credit	82	27	15	132	36	44	114	Services : crédit
Services: debit	-275	-648	-660	-818	-830	-1 065	-1 844	Services : débit
Income: credit	19	5	18	29	10	22	44	Revenus : crédit
Income: debit	-123	-580	-572	-638	-879	-1 135	-1 406	Revenus : débit
Current transfers, n.i.e.: credit	702	651	730	1 086	1 218	1 580	1 681	Transferts courants, n.i.a. : crédit
Current transfers: debit	-394	-453	-453	-454	-517	-510	-480	Transferts courants : débit
Capital account, n.i.e.	-23	-119	-93	#0	0	0	0	Compte de capital, n.i.a.
Financial account, n.i.e.	435	432	561	761	1 284	1 428	2 885	Compte financier, n.i.a.
Net errors and omissions	148	338	-24	479	-14	212	727	Erreurs et omissions nettes
Reserves and related items	-95	-94	175	-232	-315	-769	-598	Réserves et postes apparentés
Suriname								Suriname
Current account	-29	32	-84	-131	-159	-138	-144	Compte des transactions courantes
Goods: exports f.o.b.	342	399	437	369	488	782	1 212	Biens : exportations f.à.b.
Goods: imports f.o.b.	-298	-246	-297	-322	-458	-740	-1 189	Biens : importations f.à.b.
Services: credit	79	91	59	39	59	141	204	Services : crédit
Services: debit	-151	-216	-174	-166	-195	-271	-352	Services : débit
Income: credit	8	13	5	8	12	16	24	Revenus : crédit
Income: debit	-8	-7	-113	-51	-60	-79	-64	Revenus : débit
Current transfers, n.i.e.: credit	2	1	2	13	25	76	52	Transferts courants, n.i.a. : crédit
Current transfers: debit	-3	-3	-3	-21	-30	-63	-30	Transferts courants : débit
Capital account, n.i.e.	4	2	2	6	9	19	15	Compte de capital, n.i.a.
Financial account, n.i.e.	-22	-139	104	-38	-37	-24	-21	Compte financier, n.i.a.
Net errors and omissions	43	114	56	144	194	218	169	Erreurs et omissions nettes
Reserves and related items	4	-10	-78	19	-7	-76	-20	Réserves et postes apparentés
Swaziland								Swaziland
Current account	-35	-75	-57	58	116	115	46	Compte des transactions courantes
Goods: exports f.o.b.	937	905	1 043	1 029	1 626	1 738	1 828	Biens : exportations f.à.b.
Goods: imports f.o.b.	-1 068	-1 041	-1 124	-939	-1 508	-1 599	-1 755	Biens : importations f.à.b.
Services: credit	69	228	114	102	255	464	282	Services : crédit
Services: debit	-192	-308	-225	-196	-299	-632	-458	Services : débit
Income: credit	164	154	157	144	144	144	132	Revenus : crédit
Income: debit	-76	-119	-54	-146	-147	-125	-113	Revenus : débit
Current transfers, n.i.e.: credit	241	234	230	198	333	367	396	Transferts courants, n.i.a. : crédit
Current transfers: debit	-110	-127	-195	-136	-287	-243	-268	Transferts courants : débit
Capital account, n.i.e.	^0	^0	^0	^0	...	-2	1	Compte de capital, n.i.a.
Financial account, n.i.e.	48	17	-67	-54	-27	-152	80	Compte financier, n.i.a.
Net errors and omissions	13	52	68	-29	-133	20	-130	Erreurs et omissions nettes
Reserves and related items	-26	6	57	26	44	19	2	Réserves et postes apparentés
Sweden								Suède
Current account	5 982	6 617	6 696	12 784	22 844	27 485	23 643	Compte des transactions courantes
Goods: exports f.o.b.	87 568	87 431	76 200	84 172	102 080	125 214	134 904	Biens : exportations f.à.b.
Goods: imports f.o.b.	-71 854	-72 216	-62 368	-67 541	-83 147	-101 799	-115 203	Biens : importations f.à.b.
Services: credit	19 904	20 252	21 997	24 009	30 654	38 719	43 167	Services : crédit
Services: debit	-22 617	-23 440	-23 020	-23 958	-28 771	-33 056	-35 155	Services : débit
Income: credit	19 871	20 074	17 934	18 018	22 934	28 816	35 016	Revenus : crédit
Income: debit	-23 291	-22 137	-20 786	-19 044	-22 638	-25 592	-34 471	Revenus : débit
Current transfers, n.i.e.: credit	2 341	2 602	2 578	3 345	3 577	3 680	4 922	Transferts courants, n.i.a. : crédit
Current transfers: debit	-5 940	-5 950	-5 839	-6 218	-1 845	-8 498	-9 537	Transferts courants : débit
Capital account, n.i.e.	-2 143	384	509	-79	-46	94	309	Compte de capital, n.i.a.
Financial account, n.i.e.	-1 413	-3 297	1 824	-10 704	-20 163	-34 769	-22 226	Compte financier, n.i.a.
Net errors and omissions	-545	-3 534	-10 078	-1 336	-558	6 091	-1 477	Erreurs et omissions nettes
Reserves and related items	-1 881	-170	1 048	-665	-2 076	1 100	-249	Réserves et postes apparentés

Country or area	1999	2000	2001	2002	2003	2004	2005	Pays ou zone
Switzerland								Suisse
Current account	28 578	33 562	22 483	24 919	44 807	56 688	60 973	Compte des transactions courantes
Goods: exports f.o.b.	91 787	94 810	95 897	104 281	118 837	141 874	151 309	Biens : exportations f.à.b.
Goods: imports f.o.b.	-90 937	-92 739	-94 258	-97 577	-111 825	-126 083	-145 422	Biens : importations f.à.b.
Services: credit	29 277	29 884	28 469	30 306	35 237	43 085	47 106	Services : crédit
Services: debit	-15 861	-15 561	-16 460	-17 286	-19 112	-24 401	-26 242	Services : débit
Income: credit	50 081	61 844	53 074	42 150	63 636	72 418	106 711	Revenus : crédit
Income: debit	-30 620	-40 466	-39 001	-31 167	-36 582	-44 260	-63 512	Revenus : débit
Current transfers, n.i.e.: credit	7 539	6 540	9 699	10 599	13 180	14 273	14 926	Transferts courants, n.i.a. : crédit
Current transfers: debit	-12 688	-10 749	-14 938	-16 385	-18 563	-20 218	-23 903	Transferts courants : débit
Capital account, n.i.e.	-515	-3 541	1 523	-1 159	-667	-1 400	-783	Compte de capital, n.i.a.
Financial account, n.i.e.	-33 040	-30 128	-36 926	-23 174	-24 996	-63 083	-91 883	Compte financier, n.i.a.
Net errors and omissions	2 292	-4 107	13 542	1 963	-15 740	9 414	14 002	Erreurs et omissions nettes
Reserves and related items	2 685	4 214	-622	-2 549	-3 405	-1 618	17 691	Réserves et postes apparentés
Syrian Arab Republic								Rép. arabe syrienne
Current account	201	1 061	1 221	1 440	728	-629	-1 065	Compte des transactions courantes
Goods: exports f.o.b.	3 806	5 146	5 706	6 668	5 762	5 260	6 542	Biens : exportations f.à.b.
Goods: imports f.o.b.	-3 590	-3 723	-4 282	-4 458	-4 430	-6 542	-8 482	Biens : importations f.à.b.
Services: credit	1 651	1 699	1 781	1 559	1 331	2 766	3 227	Services : crédit
Services: debit	-1 612	-1 667	-1 694	-1 883	-1 806	-2 058	-2 236	Services : débit
Income: credit	356	345	379	250	282	385	395	Revenus : crédit
Income: debit	-899	-1 224	-1 162	-1 175	-1 139	-1 114	-1 258	Revenus : débit
Current transfers, n.i.e.: credit	491	495	512	499	743	690	763	Transferts courants, n.i.a. : crédit
Current transfers: debit	-2	-10	-19	-20	-15	-16	-16	Transferts courants : débit
Capital account, n.i.e.	80	63	17	20	20	18	18	Compte de capital, n.i.a.
Financial account, n.i.e.	173	-139	-244	-250	-436	-194	151	Compte financier, n.i.a.
Net errors and omissions	-195	-171	26	-160	383	1 018	453	Erreurs et omissions nettes
Reserves and related items	-259	-814	-1 020	-1 050	-695	-213	443	Réserves et postes apparentés
Tajikistan								Tadjikistan
Current account	...	...	...	-15	-5	-57	-19	Compte des transactions courantes
Goods: exports f.o.b.	...	...	...	699	906	1 097	1 108	Biens : exportations f.à.b.
Goods: imports f.o.b.	...	...	...	-823	-1 026	-1 232	-1 431	Biens : importations f.à.b.
Services: credit	...	...	...	69	89	123	146	Services : crédit
Services: debit	...	...	...	-105	-122	-213	-252	Services : débit
Income: credit	...	...	...	1	1	2	10	Revenus : crédit
Income: debit	...	...	...	-42	-71	-59	-50	Revenus : débit
Current transfers, n.i.e.: credit	...	...	...	202	285	348	600	Transferts courants, n.i.a. : crédit
Current transfers: debit	...	...	...	-16	-67	-123	-150	Transferts courants : débit
Capital account, n.i.e.	...	...	...	0	0	0	0	Compte de capital, n.i.a.
Financial account, n.i.e.	...	...	...	72	63	93	101	Compte financier, n.i.a.
Net errors and omissions	...	...	...	-56	-30	-33	-76	Erreurs et omissions nettes
Reserves and related items	...	...	...	-2	-28	-4	-6	Réserves et postes apparentés
Thailand								Thaïlande
Current account	12 428	9 313	5 101	4 691	4 772	2 759	-7 857	Compte des transactions courantes
Goods: exports f.o.b.	56 775	67 894	63 082	66 089	78 083	94 979	109 199	Biens : exportations f.à.b.
Goods: imports f.o.b.	-42 762	-56 193	-54 539	-57 008	-66 909	-84 194	-105 995	Biens : importations f.à.b.
Services: credit	14 635	13 868	13 024	15 391	15 798	19 040	20 163	Services : crédit
Services: debit	-13 583	-15 460	-14 610	-16 720	-18 169	-23 077	-27 120	Services : débit
Income: credit	3 092	4 235	3 917	3 421	3 150	3 244	3 642	Revenus : crédit
Income: debit	-6 083	-5 616	-6 375	-7 084	-8 123	-9 364	-10 750	Revenus : débit
Current transfers, n.i.e.: credit	806	952	990	978	1 326	2 479	3 351	Transferts courants, n.i.a. : crédit
Current transfers: debit	-452	-366	-389	-375	-385	-348	-348	Transferts courants : débit
Financial account, n.i.e.	-11 073	-10 434	-2 498	-540	-4 385	3 661	12 557	Compte financier, n.i.a.
Net errors and omissions	33	-685	-327	1 386	132	-710	717	Erreurs et omissions nettes
Reserves and related items	-1 388	1 806	-2 276	-5 537	-518	-5 710	-5 417	Réserves et postes apparentés
TFYR of Macedonia								L'ex-R.y. Macédoine
Current account	-32	-72	-244	-358	-149	-415	-81	Compte des transactions courantes
Goods: exports f.o.b.	1 190	1 321	1 155	1 112	1 363	1 672	2 040	Biens : exportations f.à.b.
Goods: imports f.o.b.	-1 686	-2 011	-1 682	-1 916	-2 211	-2 784	-3 097	Biens : importations f.à.b.

Country or area	1999	2000	2001	2002	2003	2004	2005	Pays ou zone
Services: credit	273	317	245	253	327	408	472	Services : crédit
Services: debit	-231	-268	-264	-275	-337	-462	-505	Services : débit
Income: credit	24	42	53	51	60	85	98	Revenus : crédit
Income: debit	-67	-87	-93	-81	-92	-124	-153	Revenus : débit
Current transfers, n.i.e.: credit	619	788	726	536	779	837	1 110	Transferts courants, n.i.a. : crédit
Current transfers: debit	-155	-173	-383	-37	-38	-46	-45	Transferts courants : débit
Capital account, n.i.e.	0	^0	1	8	-7	-5	-2	Compte de capital, n.i.a.
Financial account, n.i.e.	14	290	326	257	237	440	507	Compte financier, n.i.a.
Net errors and omissions	160	61	2	-30	-26	8	-13	Erreurs et omissions nettes
Reserves and related items	-142	-279	-86	122	-55	-28	-411	Réserves et postes apparentés
Togo								Togo
Current account	-127	-140	-169	-140	-162	-206	...	Compte des transactions courantes
Goods: exports f.o.b.	391	362	357	424	598	601	...	Biens : exportations f.à.b.
Goods: imports f.o.b.	-489	-485	-516	-576	-755	-853	...	Biens : importations f.à.b.
Services: credit	68	62	72	90	95	150	...	Services : crédit
Services: debit	-131	-118	-130	-148	-204	-239	...	Services : débit
Income: credit	40	33	26	26	27	39	...	Revenus : crédit
Income: debit	-79	-62	-55	-47	-50	-73	...	Revenus : débit
Current transfers, n.i.e.: credit	74	73	88	113	161	207	...	Transferts courants, n.i.a. : crédit
Current transfers: debit	-2	-5	-11	-22	-34	-37	...	Transferts courants : débit
Capital account, n.i.e.	7	9	21	14	21	40	...	Compte de capital, n.i.a.
Financial account, n.i.e.	156	163	151	151	143	292	...	Compte financier, n.i.a.
Net errors and omissions	-4	5	-5	5	-10	14	...	Erreurs et omissions nettes
Reserves and related items	-32	-37	2	-30	9	-141	...	Réserves et postes apparentés
Tonga								Tonga
Current account	...	...	-11	-3	...	...	...	Compte des transactions courantes
Goods: exports f.o.b.	...	...	7	18	...	...	...	Biens : exportations f.à.b.
Goods: imports f.o.b.	...	...	-64	-73	...	...	...	Biens : importations f.à.b.
Services: credit	...	...	20	23	...	...	...	Services : crédit
Services: debit	...	...	-28	-32	...	...	...	Services : débit
Income: credit	...	...	6	7	...	...	...	Revenus : crédit
Income: debit	...	...	-2	-4	...	...	...	Revenus : débit
Current transfers, n.i.e.: credit	...	...	63	75	...	...	...	Transferts courants, n.i.a. : crédit
Current transfers: debit	...	...	-12	-16	...	...	...	Transferts courants : débit
Capital account, n.i.e.	...	...	10	13	...	...	...	Compte de capital, n.i.a.
Financial account, n.i.e.	...	...	1	-3	...	...	...	Compte financier, n.i.a.
Net errors and omissions	...	...	2	^0	...	...	...	Erreurs et omissions nettes
Reserves and related items	...	...	-2	-7	...	...	...	Réserves et postes apparentés
Trinidad and Tobago								Trinité-et-Tobago
Current account	31	544	416	76	985	1 447	...	Compte des transactions courantes
Goods: exports f.o.b.	2 816	4 290	4 304	3 920	5 205	6 403	...	Biens : exportations f.à.b.
Goods: imports f.o.b.	-2 752	-3 322	-3 586	-3 682	-3 912	-4 894	...	Biens : importations f.à.b.
Services: credit	603	554	574	637	685	851	...	Services : crédit
Services: debit	-274	-388	-370	-373	-371	-371	...	Services : débit
Income: credit	68	81	109	64	78	66	...	Revenus : crédit
Income: debit	-468	-709	-648	-544	-759	-664	...	Revenus : débit
Current transfers, n.i.e.: credit	69	64	64	96	101	99	...	Transferts courants, n.i.a. : crédit
Current transfers: debit	-31	-26	-31	-42	-42	-42	...	Transferts courants : débit
Financial account, n.i.e.	38	174	322	397	34	-200	...	Compte financier, n.i.a.
Net errors and omissions	93	-277	-235	-358	-610	-537	...	Erreurs et omissions nettes
Reserves and related items	-162	-441	-502	-116	-409	-710	...	Réserves et postes apparentés
Tunisia								Tunisie
Current account	-442	-821	-840	-746	-730	-551	-303	Compte des transactions courantes
Goods: exports f.o.b.	5 873	5 840	6 628	6 857	8 027	9 679	10 488	Biens : exportations f.à.b.
Goods: imports f.o.b.	-8 015	-8 093	-8 997	-8 981	-10 297	-12 110	-12 456	Biens : importations f.à.b.
Services: credit	2 920	2 767	2 912	2 681	2 937	3 629	4 004	Services : crédit
Services: debit	-1 234	-1 218	-1 425	-1 450	-1 612	-1 986	-2 182	Services : débit
Income: credit	89	94	95	72	81	114	118	Revenus : crédit
Income: debit	-978	-1 036	-1 036	-1 056	-1 174	-1 412	-1 777	Revenus : débit

Country or area	1999	2000	2001	2002	2003	2004	2005	Pays ou zone
Current transfers, n.i.e.: credit	920	854	1 016	1 156	1 343	1 564	1 537	Transferts courants, n.i.a. : crédit
Current transfers: debit	-18	-29	-34	-25	-36	-31	-35	Transferts courants : débit
Capital account, n.i.e.	59	3	53	75	59	108	127	Compte de capital, n.i.a.
Financial account, n.i.e.	1 083	646	1 063	845	1 101	1 439	1 149	Compte financier, n.i.a.
Net errors and omissions	38	-33	13	-35	-47	-18	-37	Erreurs et omissions nettes
Reserves and related items	-738	205	-288	-140	-383	-977	-936	Réserves et postes apparentés
Turkey								Turquie
Current account	-1 341	-9 822	3 392	-1 524	-8 036	-15 604	-23 155	Compte des transactions courantes
Goods: exports f.o.b.	28 842	30 721	34 373	40 124	51 206	67 047	76 949	Biens : exportations f.à.b.
Goods: imports f.o.b.	-39 027	-52 680	-38 106	-47 407	-65 216	-90 925	-109 875	Biens : importations f.à.b.
Services: credit	16 440	19 519	15 230	14 040	18 006	22 947	25 857	Services : crédit
Services: debit	-8 949	-8 153	-6 098	-6 161	-7 502	-10 163	-11 891	Services : débit
Income: credit	2 350	2 836	2 753	2 486	2 246	2 651	3 684	Revenus : crédit
Income: debit	-5 888	-6 839	-7 753	-7 042	-7 803	-8 288	-9 347	Revenus : débit
Current transfers, n.i.e.: credit	5 011	4 866	3 051	2 481	1 088	1 165	1 489	Transferts courants, n.i.a. : crédit
Current transfers: debit	-120	-92	-58	-45	-61	-38	-21	Transferts courants : débit
Capital account, n.i.e.	0	0	0	0	0	0	0	Compte de capital, n.i.a.
Financial account, n.i.e.	4 979	8 584	-14 557	1 194	7 192	17 752	44 116	Compte financier, n.i.a.
Net errors and omissions	1 716	-2 696	-1 723	116	4 931	2 112	2 215	Erreurs et omissions nettes
Reserves and related items	-5 354	3 934	12 888	214	-4 087	-4 260	-23 176	Réserves et postes apparentés
Uganda								Ouganda
Current account	-711	-825	-369	-362	-354	-215	-277	Compte des transactions courantes
Goods: exports f.o.b.	484	450	476	481	563	709	864	Biens : exportations f.à.b.
Goods: imports f.o.b.	-989	-950	-975	-1 052	-1 246	-1 467	-1 784	Biens : importations f.à.b.
Services: credit	196	213	217	225	266	358	508	Services : crédit
Services: debit	-419	-459	-506	-558	-502	-666	-800	Services : débit
Income: credit	35	53	37	24	28	36	50	Revenus : crédit
Income: debit	-163	-166	-203	-148	-171	-206	-209	Revenus : débit
Current transfers, n.i.e.: credit	330	340	889	1 023	923	1 230	1 414	Transferts courants, n.i.a. : crédit
Current transfers: debit	-184	-308	-304	-357	-214	-209	-319	Transferts courants : débit
Capital account, n.i.e.	0	0	0	0	0	0	0	Compte de capital, n.i.a.
Financial account, n.i.e.	253	321	441	178	359	342	343	Compte financier, n.i.a.
Net errors and omissions	2	41	19	9	-8	-4	15	Erreurs et omissions nettes
Reserves and related items	455	464	-91	175	3	-123	-82	Réserves et postes apparentés
Ukraine								Ukraine
Current account	1 658	1 481	1 402	3 174	2 891	6 909	2 531	Compte des transactions courantes
Goods: exports f.o.b.	13 189	15 722	17 091	18 669	23 739	33 432	35 024	Biens : exportations f.à.b.
Goods: imports f.o.b.	-12 945	-14 943	-16 893	-17 959	-23 221	-29 691	-36 159	Biens : importations f.à.b.
Services: credit	3 869	3 800	3 995	4 682	5 214	7 859	9 354	Services : crédit
Services: debit	-2 292	-3 004	-3 580	-3 535	-4 444	-6 622	-7 548	Services : débit
Income: credit	98	143	167	165	254	389	758	Revenus : crédit
Income: debit	-967	-1 085	-834	-769	-835	-1 034	-1 743	Revenus : débit
Current transfers, n.i.e.: credit	754	967	1 516	1 967	2 270	2 671	3 111	Transferts courants, n.i.a. : crédit
Current transfers: debit	-48	-119	-60	-46	-86	-95	-266	Transferts courants : débit
Capital account, n.i.e.	-10	-8	3	17	-17	7	-65	Compte de capital, n.i.a.
Financial account, n.i.e.	-879	-752	-191	-1 065	264	-4 339	8 103	Compte financier, n.i.a.
Net errors and omissions	-953	-148	-221	-895	-965	-54	156	Erreurs et omissions nettes
Reserves and related items	184	-573	-993	-1 231	-2 173	-2 523	-10 725	Réserves et postes apparentés
United Kingdom								Royaume-Uni
Current account	-35 185	-37 357	-31 416	-24 606	-24 468	-35 184	-52 715	Compte des transactions courantes
Goods: exports f.o.b.	268 884	284 378	272 279	279 866	307 799	349 657	384 332	Biens : exportations f.à.b.
Goods: imports f.o.b.	-315 896	-334 228	-331 567	-351 636	-387 254	-461 133	-509 404	Biens : importations f.à.b.
Services: credit	119 068	120 397	120 978	135 308	158 615	197 431	207 882	Services : crédit
Services: debit	-97 054	-99 747	-100 193	-110 023	-127 250	-149 916	-163 589	Services : débit
Income: credit	166 472	204 239	202 931	187 292	205 803	260 540	340 410	Revenus : crédit
Income: debit	-164 464	-197 289	-186 115	-151 837	-165 703	-211 709	-290 214	Revenus : débit
Current transfers, n.i.e.: credit	21 414	16 031	20 794	18 414	19 953	23 663	31 435	Transferts courants, n.i.a. : crédit
Current transfers: debit	-33 609	-31 137	-30 523	-31 991	-36 431	-43 716	-53 569	Transferts courants : débit
Capital account, n.i.e.	1 205	2 569	1 890	1 420	2 425	3 777	2 801	Compte de capital, n.i.a.

Country or area	1999	2000	2001	2002	2003	2004	2005	Pays ou zone
Financial account, n.i.e.	33 731	24 388	20 627	12 053	31 754	10 441	54 818	Compte financier, n.i.a.
Net errors and omissions	-788	15 699	4 442	10 499	-12 303	21 372	-3 171	Erreurs et omissions nettes
Reserves and related items	1 036	-5 300	4 456	635	2 592	-407	-1 732	Réserves et postes apparentés
United Rep. of Tanzania								**Rép.-Unie de Tanzanie**
Current account	-835	-499	-237	22	-111	-246	-536	Compte des transactions courantes
Goods: exports f.o.b.	543	663	851	980	1 216	1 473	1 664	Biens : exportations f.à.b.
Goods: imports f.o.b.	-1 415	-1 368	-1 560	-1 511	-1 933	-2 340	-2 661	Biens : importations f.à.b.
Services: credit	600	627	915	920	948	1 117	1 226	Services : crédit
Services: debit	-795	-682	-650	-633	-726	-965	-1 164	Services : débit
Income: credit	43	50	55	68	87	82	80	Revenus : crédit
Income: debit	-148	-180	-244	-218	-250	-260	-284	Revenus : débit
Current transfers, n.i.e.: credit	446	464	475	478	610	711	678	Transferts courants, n.i.a. : crédit
Current transfers: debit	-109	-73	-80	-61	-63	-65	-75	Transferts courants : débit
Capital account, n.i.e.	348	420	1 004	786	693	460	617	Compte de capital, n.i.a.
Financial account, n.i.e.	565	493	-222	201	344	383	251	Compte financier, n.i.a.
Net errors and omissions	-157	-416	-593	-686	-453	-389	-687	Erreurs et omissions nettes
Reserves and related items	79	1	49	-323	-472	-208	355	Réserves et postes apparentés
United States								**Etats-Unis**
Current account	-299 846	-415 148	-388 958	-472 443	-527 514	-665 288	-791 509	Compte des transactions courantes
Goods: exports f.o.b.	686 271	774 632	721 842	685 933	716 704	811 010	898 457	Biens : exportations f.à.b.
Goods: imports f.o.b.	-1 029 990	-1 224 420	-1 145 930	-1 164 740	-1 260 750	-1 472 960	-1 677 400	Biens : importations f.à.b.
Services: credit	279 610	295 965	283 054	288 788	299 392	340 932	376 788	Services : crédit
Services: debit	-199 204	-223 739	-221 764	-231 049	-250 239	-290 278	-314 575	Services : débit
Income: credit	293 926	350 919	288 252	270 652	303 063	374 912	474 647	Revenus : crédit
Income: debit	-280 036	-329 863	-263 121	-258 440	-266 469	-347 322	-463 353	Revenus : débit
Current transfers, n.i.e.: credit	8 881	10 828	9 011	12 321	14 921	19 371	15 775	Transferts courants, n.i.a. : crédit
Current transfers: debit	-59 308	-69 473	-60 306	-75 908	-84 131	-100 952	-101 847	Transferts courants : débit
Capital account, n.i.e.	-4 937	-1 010	-1 271	-1 470	-3 320	-2 262	-4 351	Compte de capital, n.i.a.
Financial account, n.i.e.	227 399	486 663	405 152	506 849	536 822	579 616	771 354	Compte financier, n.i.a.
Net errors and omissions	68 657	-70 210	-9 996	-29 243	-7 517	85 130	10 406	Erreurs et omissions nettes
Reserves and related items	8 727	-295	-4 927	-3 693	1 529	2 804	14 100	Réserves et postes apparentés
Uruguay								**Uruguay**
Current account	-508	-566	-488	322	-56	3	24	Compte des transactions courantes
Goods: exports f.o.b.	2 291	2 384	2 139	1 922	2 281	3 145	3 774	Biens : exportations f.à.b.
Goods: imports f.o.b.	-3 187	-3 311	-2 915	-1 874	-2 098	-2 992	-3 753	Biens : importations f.à.b.
Services: credit	1 262	1 276	1 123	754	803	1 112	1 311	Services : crédit
Services: debit	-802	-882	-801	-600	-636	-786	-939	Services : débit
Income: credit	736	782	832	453	242	372	563	Revenus : crédit
Income: debit	-879	-842	-895	-405	-730	-960	-1 057	Revenus : débit
Current transfers, n.i.e.: credit	78	48	48	84	95	127	143	Transferts courants, n.i.a. : crédit
Current transfers: debit	-5	-21	-18	-12	-12	-14	-17	Transferts courants : débit
Capital account, n.i.e.	0	0	0	0	0	5	4	Compte de capital, n.i.a.
Financial account, n.i.e.	147	779	457	-1 928	4	-82	924	Compte financier, n.i.a.
Net errors and omissions	251	-47	334	-2 292	1 009	378	-173	Erreurs et omissions nettes
Reserves and related items	110	-166	-304	3 897	-958	-304	-778	Réserves et postes apparentés
Vanuatu								**Vanuatu**
Current account	-33	-14	-15	-39	-47	-62	-83	Compte des transactions courantes
Goods: exports f.o.b.	26	27	20	20	27	38	38	Biens : exportations f.à.b.
Goods: imports f.o.b.	-84	-77	-78	-78	-92	-113	-131	Biens : importations f.à.b.
Services: credit	115	130	119	84	99	101	109	Services : crédit
Services: debit	-72	-70	-73	-51	-61	-66	-73	Services : débit
Income: credit	21	19	17	22	24	27	28	Revenus : crédit
Income: debit	-26	-32	-21	-34	-40	-46	-54	Revenus : débit
Current transfers, n.i.e.: credit	19	27	40	6	5	5	7	Transferts courants, n.i.a. : crédit
Current transfers: debit	-31	-38	-38	-9	-10	-10	-6	Transferts courants : débit
Capital account, n.i.e.	-50	-24	-16	-2	-4	-2	-4	Compte de capital, n.i.a.
Financial account, n.i.e.	56	19	13	27	40	54	57	Compte financier, n.i.a.
Net errors and omissions	4	-1	8	-4	2	6	18	Erreurs et omissions nettes
Reserves and related items	23	19	10	18	9	5	11	Réserves et postes apparentés

Country or area	1999	2000	2001	2002	2003	2004	2005	Pays ou zone
Venezuela (Bolivarian Rep. of)								Venezuela (Rép. bolivarienne du)
Current account	2 112	11 853	1 983	7 599	11 796	15 522	25 533	Compte des transactions courantes
Goods: exports f.o.b.	20 963	33 529	26 667	26 781	27 230	39 668	55 473	Biens : exportations f.à.b.
Goods: imports f.o.b.	-14 492	-16 865	-19 211	-13 360	-10 483	-17 021	-23 693	Biens : importations f.à.b.
Services: credit	1 352	1 182	1 376	1 013	878	1 115	1 356	Services : crédit
Services: debit	-4 191	-4 435	-4 681	-3 922	-3 512	-4 497	-5 222	Services : débit
Income: credit	2 272	3 049	2 603	1 474	1 729	2 052	4 159	Revenus : crédit
Income: debit	-3 725	-4 437	-4 623	-4 230	-4 066	-5 723	-6 441	Revenus : débit
Current transfers, n.i.e.: credit	203	261	356	288	257	227	210	Transferts courants, n.i.a. : crédit
Current transfers: debit	-270	-431	-504	-445	-237	-299	-309	Transferts courants : débit
Capital account, n.i.e.	0	0	0	0	0	0	0	Compte de capital, n.i.a.
Financial account, n.i.e.	-516	-2 969	-211	-9 246	-5 547	-10 861	-16 874	Compte financier, n.i.a.
Net errors and omissions	-538	-2 926	-3 601	-2 781	-795	-2 506	-3 234	Erreurs et omissions nettes
Reserves and related items	-1 058	-5 958	1 829	4 428	-5 454	-2 155	-5 425	Réserves et postes apparentés
Viet Nam								Viet Nam
Current account	1 177	1 106	682	-604	-1 931	-957	217	Compte des transactions courantes
Goods: exports f.o.b.	11 540	14 448	15 027	16 706	20 149	26 485	32 442	Biens : exportations f.à.b.
Goods: imports f.o.b.	-10 568	-14 073	-14 546	-17 760	-22 730	-28 772	-33 280	Biens : importations f.à.b.
Services: credit	2 493	2 702	2 810	2 948	3 272	3 867	4 176	Services : crédit
Services: debit	-3 040	-3 252	-3 382	-3 698	-4 050	-4 739	-5 282	Services : débit
Income: credit	142	331	318	167	125	188	364	Revenus : crédit
Income: debit	-571	-782	-795	-888	-936	-1 079	-1 583	Revenus : débit
Current transfers, n.i.e.: credit	1 181	1 732	1 250	1 921	2 239	3 093	3 380	Transferts courants, n.i.a. : crédit
Current transfers: debit	0	0	0	0	...	...	...	Transferts courants : débit
Capital account, n.i.e.	0	0	0	0	...	...	...	Compte de capital, n.i.a.
Financial account, n.i.e.	1 058	-316	371	2 090	3 279	2 807	2 926	Compte financier, n.i.a.
Net errors and omissions	-925	-680	-847	-1 038	798	-915	-1 059	Erreurs et omissions nettes
Reserves and related items	-1 310	-110	-206	-448	-2 146	-935	-2 084	Réserves et postes apparentés
Yemen								Yémen
Current account	358	1 337	667	538	149	225	1 215	Compte des transactions courantes
Goods: exports f.o.b.	2 478	3 797	3 367	3 621	3 934	4 676	6 380	Biens : exportations f.à.b.
Goods: imports f.o.b.	-2 120	-2 484	-2 600	-2 932	-3 557	-3 859	-4 124	Biens : importations f.à.b.
Services: credit	183	211	166	166	318	370	372	Services : crédit
Services: debit	-719	-809	-848	-935	-1 004	-1 059	-1 161	Services : débit
Income: credit	57	150	179	135	99	104	178	Revenus : crédit
Income: debit	-752	-927	-869	-901	-1 008	-1 450	-1 835	Revenus : débit
Current transfers, n.i.e.: credit	1 262	1 472	1 344	1 457	1 442	1 493	1 458	Transferts courants, n.i.a. : crédit
Current transfers: debit	-31	-72	-71	-73	-75	-49	-53	Transferts courants : débit
Capital account, n.i.e.	2	339	50	0	5	163	202	Compte de capital, n.i.a.
Financial account, n.i.e.	-415	-376	-53	-157	20	-69	-569	Compte financier, n.i.a.
Net errors and omissions	129	295	-110	43	156	53	-414	Erreurs et omissions nettes
Reserves and related items	-74	-1 594	-553	-425	-330	-373	-434	Réserves et postes apparentés
Zambia								Zambie
Current account	-447	-584	...	...	...	...	...	Compte des transactions courantes
Goods: exports f.o.b.	772	757	...	...	...	...	...	Biens : exportations f.à.b.
Goods: imports f.o.b.	-870	-978	...	...	...	...	...	Biens : importations f.à.b.
Services: credit	107	114	...	...	...	...	...	Services : crédit
Services: debit	-306	-340	...	...	...	...	...	Services : débit
Income: credit	44	46	...	...	...	...	...	Revenus : crédit
Income: debit	-178	-166	...	...	...	...	...	Revenus : débit
Current transfers, n.i.e.: credit	0	0	...	...	...	...	...	Transferts courants, n.i.a. : crédit
Current transfers: debit	-16	-18	...	...	...	...	...	Transferts courants : débit
Capital account, n.i.e.	196	153	...	...	...	...	...	Compte de capital, n.i.a.
Financial account, n.i.e.	-174	-274	...	...	...	...	...	Compte financier, n.i.a.
Net errors and omissions	-229	185	...	...	...	...	...	Erreurs et omissions nettes
Reserves and related items	654	520	...	...	...	...	...	Réserves et postes apparentés

Source

International Monetary Fund (IMF), Washington, D.C., "International Financial Statistics," May 2007 and the IMF database.

Notes

1 BLEU trade data refer to the Belgium-Luxembourg Economic Union and exclude transactions between the two countries. Beginning in 1997, trade data are for Belgium only, which includes trade between Belgium and Luxembourg.

2 For statistical purposes, the data for China do not include those for the Hong Kong Special Administrative Region (Hong Kong SAR), Macao Special Administrative Region (Macao SAR) and Taiwan Province of China.

3 West Bank and Gaza.

Source

Fonds monétaire international (FMI), Washington, D.C.,"Statistiques Financières Internationales," mai 2007 et la base de données du FMI.

Notes

1 Les données sur le commerce extérieur se rapportent à l'Union économique belgo-luxembourgeoise (UEBL) et ne couvrent pas les transactions entre les deux pays. A compter de 1997, les données sur le commerce extérieur ne se rapportent qu'à la Belgique, et recouvrent les échanges entre la Belgique et le Luxembourg.

2 Pour la présentation des statistiques, les données pour la Chine ne comprennent pas la Région Administrative Spéciale de Hong Kong (Hong Kong RAS), la Région Administrative Spéciale de Macao (Macao RAS) et la province de Taiwan.

3 Cisjordanie et Gaza.

Technical notes: table 64

A balance of payments can be broadly described as the record of an economy's international economic transactions. It shows (a) transactions in goods, services and income between an economy and the rest of the world, (b) changes of ownership and other changes in that economy's monetary gold, special drawing rights (SDRs) and claims on and liabilities to the rest of the world, and (c) unrequited transfers and counterpart entries needed to balance in the accounting sense any entries for the foregoing transactions and changes which are not mutually offsetting.

The balance of payments data are presented on the basis of the methodology and presentation of the fifth edition of the *Balance of Payments Manual* (BPM5), published by the International Monetary Fund in September 1993. The BPM5 incorporates several major changes to take account of developments in international trade and finance over the years, and to better harmonize the Fund's balance of payments methodology with the methodology of the 1993 *System of National Accounts* (SNA). The Fund's balance of payments has been converted for all periods from the BPM4 basis to the BPM5 basis; thus the time series conform to the BPM5 methodology with no methodological breaks.

The detailed definitions concerning the content of the basic categories of the balance of payments are given in the *Balance of Payments Manual (fifth edition)*.Brief explanatory notes are given below to clarify the scope of the major items.

Goods: exports f.o.b. and *Goods: imports f.o.b.* are both measured on the "free-on-board" (f.o.b.) basis—that is, by the value of the goods at the border of the exporting country; in the case of imports, this excludes the cost of freight and insurance incurred beyond the border of the exporting country.

Services and *income* cover transactions in real resources between residents and non-residents other than those classified as merchandise, including (a) shipment and other transportation services, including freight, insurance and other distributive services in connection with the movement of commodities, (b) travel, i.e. goods and services acquired by non-resident travellers in a given country and similar acquisitions by resident travellers abroad, and (c) investment income which covers income of non-residents from their financial assets invested in the compiling economy (debit) and similar income of residents from their financial assets invested abroad (credit).

Current transfers, n.i.e.: credit comprises all current transfers received by the reporting country, except those made to the country to finance its "overall balance", hence, the label "n.i.e." (not included elsewhere). (Note: some of the capital and financial accounts labelled "n.i.e." denote that *Exceptional financing items* and *Liabilities constituting foreign authorities' reserves* (LCFARs) have been excluded.)

Notes techniques : tableau 64

La balance des paiements peut se définir d'une façon générale comme le relevé des transactions économiques internationales d'une économie. Elle indique (a) les transactions sur biens, services et revenus entre une économie et le reste du monde, (b) les transferts de propriété et autres variations intervenues au niveau des avoirs en or monétaire de cette économie, de ses avoirs en droits de tirages spéciaux (DTS) ainsi que de ses créances financières sur le reste du monde ou de ses engagements financiers envers lui et (c) les "inscriptions de transferts sans contrepartie" et de "contrepartie" destinées à équilibrer, d'un point de vue comptable, les transactions et changements précités qui ne se compensent pas réciproquement.

Les données de la balance des paiements sont présentées conformément à la méthodologie et à la classification recommandées dans la cinquième édition du *Manuel de la balance des paiements*, publiée en septembre 1993 par le Fonds monétaire international. La cinquième édition fait état de plusieurs changements importants qui ont été opérés de manière à rendre compte de l'évolution des finances et des changes internationaux pendant les années et à harmoniser davantage la méthodologie de la balance des paiements du FMI avec celle du *Système de comptabilité nationale* (SCN) de 1993. Les statistiques incluses dans la balance des paiements du FMI ont été converties et sont désormais établies, pour toutes les périodes, sur la base de la cinquième et non plus de la quatrième édition; en conséquence, les séries chronologiques sont conformes aux principes de la cinquième édition, sans rupture due à des différences d'ordre méthodologique.

Les définitions détaillées relatives au contenu des postes fondamentaux de la balance des paiements figurent dans le *Manuel de la balance des paiements (cinquième édition)*. De brèves notes explicatives sont présentées ci-après pour clarifier la portée de ces principales rubriques.

Les Biens: exportations, f.à.b. et *Biens: importations, f.à.b.* sont évalués sur la base f.à.b. (franco à bord) - c'est-à-dire à la frontière du pays exportateur; dans le cas des importations, cette valeur exclut le coût du fret et de l'assurance au-delà de la frontière du pays exportateur.

Services et *revenus*: transactions en ressources effectuées entre résidents et non résidents, autres que celles qui sont considérées comme des marchandises, notamment: (a) expéditions et autres services de transport, y compris le fret, l'assurance et les autres services de distribution liés aux mouvements de marchandises; (b) voyages, à savoir les biens et services acquis par des voyageurs non résidents dans un pays donné et achats similaires faits par des résidents voyageant à l'étranger; et (c) revenus des investissements, qui correspondent aux

Capital account, n.i.e. refers mainly to capital transfers linked to the acquisition of a fixed asset other than transactions relating to debt forgiveness plus the disposal of nonproduced, nonfinancial assets, and to capital transfers linked to the disposal of fixed assets by the donor or to the financing of capital formation by the recipient, plus the acquisition of nonproduced, nonfinancial assets.

Financial account, n.i.e. is the net sum of the balance of direct investment, portfolio investment, and other investment transactions.

Net errors and omissions is a residual category needed to ensure that all debit and credit entries in the balance of payments statement sum to zero and reflects statistical inconsistencies in the recording of the credit and debit entries.

Reserves and related items is the sum of transactions in reserve assets, LCFARs, exceptional financing, and use of Fund credit and loans.

For further information see *International Financial Statistics* and www.imf.org.

revenus que les non résidents tirent de leurs avoirs financiers placés dans l'économie déclarante (débit) et les revenus similaires que les résidents tirent de leurs avoirs financiers placés à l'étranger (crédit).

Les transferts courants, n.i.a: crédit englobent tous les transferts courants reçus par l'économie qui établit sa balance des paiements, à l'exception de ceux qui sont destinés à financer sa "balance globale"—c'est ce qui explique la mention "n.i.a." (non inclus ailleurs). (Note: comptes de capital et d'opérations financières portent la mention "n.i.a.", ce qui signifie que les postes de *Financement exceptionnel* et les *Engagements constituant des réserves pour les autorités étrangères* ont été exclus de ces composantes du compte de capital et d'opérations financières.)

Le Compte de capital, n.i.a retrace principalement les transferts de capital liés à l'acquisition d'un actif fixe autres que les transactions ayant trait à des remises de dettes plus les cessions d'actifs non financiers non produits, et les transferts de capital liés à la cession d'actifs fixes par le donateur ou au financement de la formation de capital par le bénéficiaire, plus les acquisitions d'actifs non financiers non produits.

Le Compte financier, n.i.a est la somme des soldes des investissements directs, des investissements de portefeuille et des autres investissements.

Le poste des *Erreurs et omissions nettes* est une catégorie résiduelle qui est nécessaire pour assurer que la somme de toutes les inscriptions effectuées au débit et au crédit est égal à zéro et qui laisse apparaître les écarts entre les montants portés au débit et ceux qui sont inscrits au crédit.

Le montant de *Réserves et postes apparentés* est égal à la somme de transactions afférentes aux avoirs de réserve, aux engagements constituant des réserves pour les autorités étrangères, au financement exceptionnel et à l'utilisation des crédits et des prêts du FMI.

Pour plus de renseignements, voir *Statistiques financières internationales* et www.imf.org.

Exchange rates

National currency per US dollar

Cours des changes

Valeur du dollar des États-Unis en monnaie nationale

Country or area Pays ou zone	1997	1998	1999	2000	2001	2002	2003	2004	2005	2006
Afghanistan[1,2] (afghani) — Afghanistan[1,2] (afghani)										
End of period Fin de période	3.000	3.000	#46.791	...	47.259	#44.875	#48.865	48.220	50.410	...
Period average Moyenne sur période	3.000	3.000	45.106	61.629	65.690	41.459	48.763	47.845	49.495	...
Albania (lek) — Albanie (lek)										
End of period Fin de période	149.140	140.580	135.120	142.640	136.550	133.740	106.580	92.640	103.580	94.140
Period average Moyenne sur période	148.933	150.633	137.691	143.709	143.485	140.155	121.863	102.780	99.870	98.103
Algeria (Algerian dinar) — Algérie (dinar algérien)										
End of period Fin de période	58.414	60.353	69.314	75.343	77.820	79.723	72.613	72.614	73.380	71.158
Period average Moyenne sur période	57.707	58.739	66.574	75.260	77.215	79.682	77.395	72.061	73.276	72.647
Angola (readjusted kwanza) — Angola (réajusté kwanza)										
End of period Fin de période	0.262	0.697	#5.580	16.818	31.949	58.666	79.082	85.988	80.780	80.264
Period average Moyenne sur période	0.229	0.393	2.791	10.041	22.058	43.530	74.606	83.541	87.159	80.368
Anguilla (EC dollar) — Anguilla (dollar des Caraïbes orientales)										
End of period Fin de période	2.700	2.700	2.700	2.700	2.700	2.700	2.700	2.700	2.700	2.700
Antigua and Barbuda (EC dollar) — Antigua-et-Barbuda (dollar des Caraïbes orientales)										
End of period Fin de période	2.700	2.700	2.700	2.700	2.700	2.700	2.700	2.700	2.700	2.700
Period average Moyenne sur période	2.700	2.700	2.700	2.700	2.700	2.700	2.700	2.700	2.700	2.700
Argentina[3] (Argentine peso) — Argentine[3] (peso argentin)										
End of period Fin de période	1.000	1.000	1.000	1.000	1.000	3.320	2.905	2.959	3.012	3.042
Period average Moyenne sur période	1.000	1.000	1.000	1.000	1.000	3.063	2.901	2.923	2.904	3.054
Armenia (dram) — Arménie (dram)										
End of period Fin de période	494.980	522.030	523.770	552.180	561.810	584.890	566.000	485.840	450.190	363.500
Period average Moyenne sur période	490.847	504.915	535.062	539.526	555.078	573.353	578.763	533.451	457.687	416.040
Aruba (Aruban florin) — Aruba (florin de Aruba)										
End of period Fin de période	1.790	1.790	1.790	1.790	1.790	1.790	1.790	1.790	1.790	1.790
Period average Moyenne sur période	1.790	1.790	1.790	1.790	1.790	1.790	1.790	1.790	1.790	1.790
Australia (Australian dollar) — Australie (dollar australien)										
End of period Fin de période	1.532	1.629	1.530	1.805	1.959	1.766	1.333	1.284	1.363	1.264
Period average Moyenne sur période	1.347	1.592	1.550	1.725	1.933	1.841	1.542	1.360	1.310	1.328
Austria[4] (Austrian schilling, euro) — Autriche[4] (schilling autrichien, euro)										
End of period Fin de période	12.633	11.747	0.995	1.075	1.135	0.954	0.792	0.734	0.848	0.759
Period average Moyenne sur période	12.204	12.379	0.939	1.085	1.118	1.063	0.886	0.805	0.804	0.797
Azerbaijan[5] (manat) — Azerbaïdjan[5] (manat)										
End of period Fin de période	0.778	0.778	0.876	0.913	0.955	0.979	0.985	0.981	0.919	0.871

Country or area Pays ou zone	1997	1998	1999	2000	2001	2002	2003	2004	2005	2006
Period average Moyenne sur période	0.797	0.774	0.824	0.895	0.931	0.972	0.982	0.983	0.945	0.893
Bahamas[1] (Bahamian dollar) — Bahamas[1] (dollar des Bahamas)										
End of period Fin de période	1.000	1.000	1.000	1.000	1.000	1.000	1.000	1.000	1.000	1.000
Period average Moyenne sur période	1.000	1.000	1.000	1.000	1.000	1.000	1.000	1.000	1.000	1.000
Bahrain (Bahrain dinar) — Bahreïn (dinar de Bahreïn)										
End of period Fin de période	0.376	0.376	0.376	0.376	0.376	0.376	0.376	0.376	0.376	0.376
Period average Moyenne sur période	0.376	0.376	0.376	0.376	0.376	0.376	0.376	0.376	0.376	0.376
Bangladesh[1] (taka) — Bangladesh[1] (taka)										
End of period Fin de période	45.450	48.500	51.000	54.000	57.000	57.900	58.782	60.742	66.210	69.065
Period average Moyenne sur période	43.892	46.906	49.085	52.142	55.807	57.888	58.150	59.513	64.328	68.933
Barbados (Barbados dollar) — Barbade (dollar de la Barbade)										
End of period Fin de période	2.000	2.000	2.000	2.000	2.000	2.000	2.000	2.000	2.000	2.000
Period average Moyenne sur période	2.000	2.000	2.000	2.000	2.000	2.000	2.000	2.000	2.000	2.000
Belarus (Belarussian rouble) — Bélarus (rouble bélarussien)										
End of period Fin de période	30.740	106.000	320.000	1 180.000	1 580.000	1 920.000	2 156.000	2 170.000	2 152.000	2 140.000
Period average Moyenne sur période	26.021	46.128	249.295	876.750	1 390.000	1 790.920	2 051.270	2 160.260	2 153.820	2 144.560
Belgium[4] (Belgian franc, euro) — Belgique[4] (franc belge, euro)										
End of period Fin de période	36.920	34.575	0.995	1.075	1.135	0.954	0.792	0.734	0.848	0.759
Period average Moyenne sur période	35.774	36.299	0.939	1.085	1.118	1.063	0.886	0.805	0.804	0.797
Belize (Belize dollar) — Belize (dollar du Belize)										
End of period Fin de période	2.000	2.000	2.000	2.000	2.000	2.000	2.000	2.000	2.000	2.000
Period average Moyenne sur période	2.000	2.000	2.000	2.000	2.000	2.000	2.000	2.000	2.000	2.000
Benin[6] (CFA franc) — Bénin[6] (franc CFA)										
End of period Fin de période	598.810	562.210	#652.953	704.951	744.306	625.495	519.364	481.578	556.037	498.069
Period average Moyenne sur période	583.669	589.952	#615.699	711.976	733.039	696.988	581.200	528.285	527.468	522.890
Bhutan (ngultrum) — Bhoutan (ngultrum)										
End of period Fin de période	39.280	42.480	43.490	46.750	48.180	48.030	45.605	43.585	45.065	44.245
Period average Moyenne sur période	36.313	41.259	43.055	44.942	47.186	48.610	46.583	45.317	44.100	45.307
Bolivia[7] (boliviano) — Bolivie[7] (boliviano)										
End of period Fin de période	5.365	5.645	5.990	6.390	6.820	7.490	7.830	8.050	8.040	7.980
Period average Moyenne sur période	5.254	5.510	5.812	6.184	6.607	7.170	7.659	7.936	8.066	8.012
Bosnia and Herzegovina (convertible marka) — Bosnie-Herzégovine (marka convertible)										
End of period Fin de période	1.792	1.673	1.947	2.102	2.219	1.865	1.549	1.436	1.658	1.485
Period average Moyenne sur période	1.734	1.760	1.836	2.123	2.186	2.078	1.733	1.575	1.573	1.559
Botswana (pula) — Botswana (pula)										
End of period Fin de période	3.810	4.458	4.632	5.362	6.983	5.468	4.443	4.281	5.513	6.031

Exchange rates—National currency per US dollar (*continued*)
Cours des changes—Valeur du dollar des Etats-Unis en monnaie nationale (*suite*)

Country or area Pays ou zone	1997	1998	1999	2000	2001	2002	2003	2004	2005	2006
Period average Moyenne sur période	3.651	4.226	4.624	5.102	5.841	6.328	4.950	4.693	5.110	5.837
Brazil[8] (real) — Brésil[8] (real)										
End of period Fin de période	1.116	1.209	1.789	1.955	2.320	3.533	2.888	2.654	2.340	2.137
Period average Moyenne sur période	1.078	1.161	1.815	1.830	2.358	2.921	3.077	2.925	2.434	2.175
Brunei Darussalam (Brunei dollar) — Brunéi Darussalam (dollar du Brunéi)										
End of period Fin de période	1.676	1.661	1.666	1.732	1.851	1.737	1.701	1.634	1.664	1.534
Period average Moyenne sur période	1.485	1.674	1.695	1.724	1.792	1.791	1.742	1.690	1.664	1.589
Bulgaria (lev) — Bulgarie (lev)										
End of period Fin de période	1.777	1.675	1.947	2.102	2.219	1.885	1.549	1.436	1.658	1.485
Period average Moyenne sur période	1.682	1.760	1.836	2.123	2.185	2.077	1.733	1.575	1.574	1.559
Burkina Faso[6] (CFA franc) — Burkina Faso[6] (franc CFA)										
End of period Fin de période	598.810	562.210	#652.953	704.951	744.306	625.495	519.364	481.578	556.037	498.069
Period average Moyenne sur période	583.669	589.952	#615.699	711.976	733.039	696.988	581.200	528.285	527.468	522.890
Burundi (Burundi franc) — Burundi (franc burundais)										
End of period Fin de période	408.380	505.160	628.580	778.200	864.200	1 071.230	1 093.000	1 109.510	997.780	1 002.470
Period average Moyenne sur période	352.351	447.766	563.563	720.673	830.353	930.749	1 082.620	1 100.910	1 081.580	1 028.430
Cambodia (riel) — Cambodge (riel)										
End of period Fin de période	3 452.000	3 770.000	3 770.000	3 905.000	3 895.000	3 930.000	3 984.000	4 027.000	4 112.000	4 057.000
Period average Moyenne sur période	2 946.250	3 744.420	3 807.830	3 840.750	3 916.330	3 912.080	3 973.330	4 016.250	4 092.500	4 103.250
Cameroon[6] (CFA franc) — Cameroun[6] (franc CFA)										
End of period Fin de période	598.810	562.210	#652.953	704.951	744.306	625.495	519.364	481.578	556.037	498.069
Period average Moyenne sur période	583.669	589.952	#615.699	711.976	733.039	696.988	581.200	528.285	527.468	522.890
Canada (Canadian dollar) — Canada (dollar canadien)										
End of period Fin de période	1.429	1.531	1.443	1.500	1.593	1.580	1.292	1.204	1.165	1.165
Period average Moyenne sur période	1.385	1.484	1.486	1.485	1.549	1.569	1.401	1.301	1.212	1.134
Cape Verde (Cape Verde escudo) — Cap-Vert (escudo du Cap-Vert)										
End of period Fin de période	96.235	94.255	109.765	118.506	125.122	105.149	87.308	80.956	93.473	83.728
Period average Moyenne sur période	93.177	98.158	103.502	119.687	123.228	117.168	97.703	88.808	88.670	87.901
Central African Rep.[6] (CFA franc) — Rép. centrafricaine[6] (franc CFA)										
End of period Fin de période	598.810	562.210	#652.953	704.951	744.306	625.495	519.364	481.578	556.037	498.069
Period average Moyenne sur période	583.669	589.952	#615.699	711.976	733.039	696.988	581.200	528.285	527.468	522.890
Chad[6] (CFA franc) — Tchad[6] (franc CFA)										
End of period Fin de période	598.810	562.210	#652.953	704.951	744.306	625.495	519.364	481.578	556.037	498.069
Period average Moyenne sur période	583.669	589.952	#615.699	711.976	733.039	696.988	581.200	528.285	527.468	522.890
Chile[1] (Chilean peso) — Chili[1] (peso chilien)										
End of period Fin de période	439.810	473.770	530.070	572.680	656.200	712.380	599.420	559.830	514.210	534.430

Country or area Pays ou zone	1997	1998	1999	2000	2001	2002	2003	2004	2005	2006
Period average Moyenne sur période	419.295	460.288	508.777	539.588	634.938	688.936	691.433	609.369	560.090	530.287
China[1] (yuan)—Chine[1] (yuan)										
End of period Fin de période	8.280	8.279	8.280	8.277	8.277	8.277	8.277	8.277	8.070	7.809
Period average Moyenne sur période	8.290	8.279	8.278	8.279	8.277	8.277	8.277	8.277	8.194	7.973
China, Hong Kong SAR (Hong Kong dollar)—Chine, Hong Kong RAS (dollar de Hong Kong)										
End of period Fin de période	7.746	7.746	7.771	7.796	7.797	7.798	7.763	7.774	7.753	7.775
Period average Moyenne sur période	7.742	7.745	7.758	7.791	7.799	7.799	7.787	7.788	7.777	7.768
China, Macao SAR (Macao pataca)—Chine, Macao RAS (pataca de Macao)										
End of period Fin de période	7.982	7.980	8.005	8.034	8.031	8.033	7.997	8.010	7.987	8.006
Period average Moyenne sur période	7.975	7.979	7.992	8.026	8.034	8.033	8.021	8.022	8.011	8.001
Colombia (Colombian peso)—Colombie (peso colombien)										
End of period Fin de période	1 293.580	1 507.520	1 873.770	2 187.020	2 301.330	2 864.790	2 780.820	2 412.100	2 284.220	2 225.440
Period average Moyenne sur période	1 140.960	1 426.040	1 756.230	2 087.900	2 299.630	2 504.240	2 877.650	2 628.610	2 320.830	2 361.140
Comoros[9] (Comorian franc)—Comores[9] (franc comorien)										
End of period Fin de période	449.105	421.655	489.715	528.714	558.230	469.122	389.523	361.183	417.028	373.552
Period average Moyenne sur période	437.747	442.459	461.775	533.982	549.779	522.741	435.900	396.214	395.601	392.168
Congo[6] (CFA franc)—Congo[6] (franc CFA)										
End of period Fin de période	598.810	562.210	#652.953	704.951	744.306	625.495	519.364	481.578	556.037	498.069
Period average Moyenne sur période	583.669	589.952	#615.699	711.976	733.039	696.988	581.200	528.285	527.468	522.890
Costa Rica (Costa Rican colón)—Costa Rica (colón costa-ricien)										
End of period Fin de période	244.290	271.420	298.190	318.020	341.670	378.720	418.530	458.610	496.680	517.895
Period average Moyenne sur période	232.598	257.229	285.685	308.187	328.871	359.818	398.662	437.935	477.787	511.302
Côte d'Ivoire[6] (CFA franc)—Côte d'Ivoire[6] (franc CFA)										
End of period Fin de période	598.810	562.210	#652.953	704.951	744.306	625.495	519.364	481.578	556.037	498.069
Period average Moyenne sur période	583.669	589.952	#615.699	711.976	733.039	696.988	581.200	528.285	527.468	522.890
Croatia (kuna)—Croatie (kuna)										
End of period Fin de période	6.303	6.248	7.648	8.155	8.356	7.146	6.119	5.637	6.234	5.578
Period average Moyenne sur période	6.161	6.363	7.112	8.278	8.342	7.872	6.705	6.034	5.949	5.838
Cyprus (Cyprus pound)—Chypre (livre chypriote)										
End of period Fin de période	0.526	0.498	0.575	0.617	0.650	0.547	0.465	0.425	0.484	0.439
Period average Moyenne sur période	0.514	0.518	0.543	0.622	0.643	0.611	0.517	0.469	0.464	0.459
Czech Republic (Czech koruna)—République tchèque (couronne tchèque)										
End of period Fin de période	34.636	29.855	35.979	37.813	36.259	30.141	25.654	22.365	24.588	20.876
Period average[1] Moyenne sur période[1]	31.698	32.281	34.569	38.598	38.035	32.739	28.209	25.700	23.957	22.596
Dem. Rep. of the Congo[10] (Congo franc)—Rép. dém. du Congo[10] (franc congolais)										
End of period Fin de période	1 060.000	#2.450	4.500	50.000	313.600	382.140	#372.520	444.088	431.279	503.430

Country or area Pays ou zone	1997	1998	1999	2000	2001	2002	2003	2004	2005	2006
Period average Moyenne sur période	1 313.450	1.607	4.018	21.818	206.617	346.485	405.178	395.930	473.908	468.279
Denmark (Danish krone) — Danemark (couronne danoise)										
End of period Fin de période	6.826	6.387	7.399	8.021	8.410	7.082	5.958	5.468	6.324	5.661
Period average Moyenne sur période	6.605	6.701	6.976	8.083	8.323	7.895	6.588	5.991	5.997	5.947
Djibouti (Djibouti franc) — Djibouti (franc djiboutien)										
End of period Fin de période	177.721	177.721	177.721	177.721	177.721	177.721	177.721	177.721	177.721	177.721
Period average Moyenne sur période	177.721	177.721	177.721	177.721	177.721	177.721	177.721	177.721	177.721	177.721
Dominica (EC dollar) — Dominique (dollar des Caraïbes orientales)										
End of period Fin de période	2.700	2.700	2.700	2.700	2.700	2.700	2.700	2.700	2.700	2.700
Period average Moyenne sur période	2.700	2.700	2.700	2.700	2.700	2.700	2.700	2.700	2.700	2.700
Dominican Republic[1] (Dominican peso) — Rép. dominicaine[1] (peso dominicain)										
End of period Fin de période	14.366	15.788	16.039	16.674	17.149	21.194	37.250	31.109	34.879	33.797
Period average Moyenne sur période	14.266	15.267	16.033	16.415	16.952	18.610	30.831	42.120	30.409	33.365
Ecuador[1] (sucre) — Equateur[1] (sucre)										
End of period Fin de période	4 428.000	6 825.000	20 243.000	25 000.000	25 000.000	25 000.000	25 000.000	25 000.000	25 000.000	25 000.000
Period average Moyenne sur période	3 998.270	5 446.570	11 786.800	24 988.400	25 000.000	25 000.000	25 000.000	25 000.000	25 000.000	25 000.000
Egypt[1] (Egyptian pound) — Egypte[1] (livre égyptienne)										
End of period Fin de période	3.388	3.388	3.405	3.690	4.490	4.500	6.153	6.131	5.732	5.704
Period average Moyenne sur période	3.389	3.388	3.395	3.472	3.973	4.500	5.851	6.196	5.779	5.733
El Salvador[1] (El Salvadoran colón) — El Salvador[1] (cólon salvadorien)										
End of period Fin de période	8.755	8.755	8.755	8.755	8.750	8.750	8.750	8.750	8.750	8.750
Period average Moyenne sur période	8.756	8.755	8.755	8.755	8.750	8.750	8.750	8.750	8.750	8.750
Equatorial Guinea[6] (CFA franc) — Guinée équatoriale[6] (franc CFA)										
End of period Fin de période	598.810	562.210	#652.953	704.951	744.306	625.495	519.364	481.578	556.037	498.069
Period average Moyenne sur période	583.669	589.952	#615.699	711.976	733.039	696.988	581.200	528.285	527.468	522.890
Eritrea (nakfa) — Erythrée (nakfa)										
End of period Fin de période	#7.125	7.597	9.600	10.200	13.798	14.309	13.788	13.788	15.375	15.375
Period average Moyenne sur période	#6.837	7.362	8.153	9.625	11.310	13.958	13.878	13.788	15.368	15.375
Estonia (Estonian kroon) — Estonie (couronne estonienne)										
End of period Fin de période	14.336	13.410	15.562	16.820	17.692	14.936	12.410	11.471	13.221	11.882
Period average Moyenne sur période	13.882	14.075	14.678	16.969	17.478	16.612	13.856	12.596	12.584	12.466
Ethiopia (Ethiopian birr) — Ethiopie (birr éthiopien)										
End of period Fin de période	6.864	7.503	8.134	8.314	8.558	8.581	8.621	8.652	8.681	8.776
Period average Moyenne sur période	6.709	7.116	7.942	8.217	8.458	8.568	8.600	8.636	8.666	8.699
Euro Area[11] (euro) — Zone euro[11] (euro)										
End of period Fin de période	...	...	0.995	1.075	1.135	0.954	0.792	0.734	0.848	0.759

Country or area Pays ou zone	1997	1998	1999	2000	2001	2002	2003	2004	2005	2006
Period average Moyenne sur période	...	...	0.939	1.085	1.118	1.063	0.886	0.805	0.804	0.797
Fiji (Fiji dollar) — Fidji (dollar des Fidji)										
End of period Fin de période	1.549	1.986	1.966	2.186	2.309	2.065	1.722	1.645	1.745	1.664
Period average Moyenne sur période	1.444	1.987	1.970	2.129	2.277	2.187	1.896	1.733	1.691	1.731
Finland[4] (Finnish markka, euro) — Finlande[4] (markka finlandais, euro)										
End of period Fin de période	5.421	5.096	0.995	1.075	1.135	0.954	0.792	0.734	0.848	0.759
Period average Moyenne sur période	5.191	5.344	0.939	1.085	1.118	1.063	0.886	0.805	0.804	0.797
France[4] (French franc, euro) — France[4] (franc français, euro)										
End of period Fin de période	5.988	5.622	0.995	1.075	1.135	0.954	0.792	0.734	0.848	0.759
Period average Moyenne sur période	5.837	5.900	0.939	1.085	1.118	1.063	0.886	0.805	0.804	0.797
Gabon[6] (CFA franc) — Gabon[6] (franc CFA)										
End of period Fin de période	598.810	562.210	#652.953	704.951	744.306	625.495	519.364	481.578	556.037	498.069
Period average Moyenne sur période	583.669	589.952	#615.699	711.976	733.039	696.988	581.200	528.285	527.468	522.890
Gambia (dalasi) — Gambie (dalasi)										
End of period Fin de période	10.530	10.991	11.547	14.888	16.932	23.392	30.960	29.674	28.135	28.047
Period average Moyenne sur période	10.200	10.643	11.395	12.788	15.687	19.918	27.306	30.030	28.575	28.066
Georgia (lari) — Géorgie (lari)										
End of period Fin de période	1.304	1.800	1.930	1.975	2.060	2.090	2.075	1.825	1.793	1.714
Period average Moyenne sur période	1.298	1.390	2.025	1.976	2.073	2.196	2.146	1.917	1.813	1.780
Germany[4] (deutsche mark, euro) — Allemagne[4] (deutsche mark, euro)										
End of period Fin de période	1.792	1.673	0.995	1.075	1.135	0.954	0.792	0.734	0.848	0.759
Period average Moyenne sur période	1.734	1.760	0.939	1.085	1.118	1.063	0.886	0.805	0.804	0.797
Ghana[1] (cedi) — Ghana[1] (cedi)										
End of period Fin de période	2 272.730	2 325.580	3 535.140	7 047.650	7 321.940	8 438.820	8 852.320	9 054.260	9 130.820	9 235.300
Period average Moyenne sur période	2 050.170	2 314.150	2 669.300	5 455.060	7 170.760	7 932.700	8 677.370	9 004.630	9 072.540	9 174.380
Greece[4] (drachma, euro) — Grèce[4] (drachma, euro)										
End of period Fin de période	282.610	282.570	328.440	365.620	1.135	0.954	0.792	0.734	0.848	0.759
Period average Moyenne sur période	273.058	295.529	305.647	365.399	1.118	1.063	0.886	0.805	0.804	0.797
Grenada (EC dollar) — Grenade (dollar des Caraïbes orientales)										
End of period Fin de période	2.700	2.700	2.700	2.700	2.700	2.700	2.700	2.700	2.700	2.700
Period average Moyenne sur période	2.700	2.700	2.700	2.700	2.700	2.700	2.700	2.700	2.700	2.700
Guatemala (quetzal) — Guatemala (quetzal)										
End of period Fin de période	6.177	6.848	7.821	7.731	8.001	7.807	8.041	7.748	7.610	7.625
Period average Moyenne sur période	6.065	6.395	7.386	7.763	7.859	7.822	7.941	7.947	7.634	7.603
Guinea (Guinean franc) — Guinée (franc guinéen)										
End of period Fin de période	1 144.950	1 298.030	1 736.000	1 882.270	1 988.330	1 976.000	2 000.000	2 550.000	4 500.000	...

65 Exchange rates — National currency per US dollar (*continued*)
Cours des changes — Valeur du dollar des Etats-Unis en monnaie nationale (*suite*)

Country or area Pays ou zone	1997	1998	1999	2000	2001	2002	2003	2004	2005	2006
Period average Moyenne sur période	1 095.330	1 236.830	1 387.400	1 746.870	1 950.560	1 975.840	1 984.930	2 225.030	3 644.330	...
Guinea-Bissau[12] (CFA franc) — Guinée-Bissau[12] (franc CFA)										
End of period Fin de période	598.810	562.210	652.953	704.951	744.306	625.495	519.364	481.578	556.037	498.069
Period average Moyenne sur période	583.669	589.952	#615.699	711.976	733.039	696.988	581.200	528.285	527.468	522.890
Guyana[1] (Guyana dollar) — Guyana[1] (dollar guyanais)										
End of period Fin de période	144.000	162.250	180.500	184.750	189.500	191.750	194.250	199.750	200.250	201.000
Period average Moyenne sur période	142.401	150.519	177.995	182.430	187.321	190.665	193.878	198.307	199.875	200.188
Haiti[1] (gourde) — Haïti[1] (gourde)										
End of period Fin de période	17.311	16.505	17.965	22.524	26.339	37.609	42.085	37.232	43.000	37.591
Period average Moyenne sur période	16.655	16.766	16.938	21.171	24.429	29.251	42.367	38.352	40.449	40.409
Honduras[1] (lempira) — Honduras[1] (lempira)										
End of period Fin de période	13.094	13.808	14.504	15.141	15.920	16.923	17.748	18.633	18.895	18.895
Period average Moyenne sur période	13.004	13.385	14.213	14.839	15.474	16.433	17.345	18.206	18.832	18.895
Hungary (forint) — Hongrie (forint)										
End of period Fin de période	203.500	219.030	252.520	284.730	279.030	225.160	207.920	180.290	213.580	191.620
Period average Moyenne sur période	186.789	214.402	237.146	282.179	286.490	257.887	224.307	202.746	199.582	210.390
Iceland (Icelandic króna) — Islande (couronne islandaise)										
End of period Fin de période	72.180	69.320	72.550	84.700	102.950	80.580	70.990	61.040	62.980	71.660
Period average Moyenne sur période	70.904	70.958	72.335	78.616	97.425	91.662	76.709	70.192	62.982	70.195
India (Indian rupee) — Inde (roupie indienne)										
End of period Fin de période	39.280	42.480	43.490	46.750	48.180	48.030	45.605	43.585	45.065	44.245
Period average Moyenne sur période	36.313	41.259	43.055	44.942	47.186	48.610	46.583	45.317	44.100	45.307
Indonesia (Indonesian rupiah) — Indonésie (roupie indonésien)										
End of period Fin de période	4 650.000	8 025.000	7 085.000	9 595.000	10 400.000	8 940.000	8 465.000	9 290.000	9 830.000	9 020.000
Period average Moyenne sur période	2 909.380	10 013.600	7 855.150	8 421.780	10 260.900	9 311.190	8 577.130	8 938.850	9 704.740	9 159.320
Iran (Islamic Rep. of) (Iranian rial) — Iran (Rép. islamique d') (rial iranien)										
End of period Fin de période	1 754.260	1 750.930	1 752.290	2 262.930	1 750.950	#7 951.980	8 272.110	8 793.000	9 091.000	9 223.000
Period average Moyenne sur période	1 752.920	1 751.860	1 752.930	1 764.430	1 753.560	#6 906.960	8 193.890	8 613.990	8 963.960	9 170.940
Iraq[1] (Iraqi dinar) — Iraq[1] (dinar iraquien)										
End of period Fin de période	0.310	0.310	0.310	0.310	0.310	0.310	...	1 469.000	1 487.000	...
Period average Moyenne sur période	0.311	0.311	0.311	0.311	0.311	0.311	...	1 453.420	1 472.000	...
Ireland[4] (Irish pound, euro) — Irlande[4] (livre irlandaise, euro)										
End of period Fin de période	0.699	0.672	0.995	1.075	1.135	0.954	0.792	0.734	0.848	0.759
Period average Moyenne sur période	0.660	0.702	0.939	1.085	1.118	1.063	0.886	0.805	0.804	0.797
Israel (new sheqel) — Israël (nouveau sheqel)										
End of period Fin de période	3.536	4.161	4.153	4.041	4.416	4.737	4.379	4.308	4.603	4.225

Exchange rates — National currency per US dollar (*continued*)
Cours des changes — Valeur du dollar des Etats-Unis en monnaie nationale (*suite*)

Country or area Pays ou zone	1997	1998	1999	2000	2001	2002	2003	2004	2005	2006
Period average Moyenne sur période	3.449	3.800	4.140	4.077	4.206	4.738	4.554	4.482	4.488	4.456
Italy[4] (Italian lira, euro) — Italie[4] (lire italienne, euro)										
End of period Fin de période	1 759.190	1 653.100	0.995	1.075	1.135	0.954	0.792	0.734	0.848	0.759
Period average Moyenne sur période	1 703.100	1 736.210	0.939	1.085	1.118	1.063	0.886	0.805	0.804	0.797
Jamaica (Jamaican dollar) — Jamaïque (dollar jamaïcain)										
End of period Fin de période	36.341	37.055	41.291	45.415	47.286	50.762	60.517	61.450	64.381	67.032
Period average Moyenne sur période	35.405	36.550	39.044	42.986	45.996	48.416	57.741	61.197	62.281	65.744
Japan (yen) — Japon (yen)										
End of period Fin de période	129.950	115.600	102.200	114.900	131.800	119.900	107.100	104.120	117.970	118.950
Period average Moyenne sur période	120.991	130.905	113.907	107.765	121.529	125.388	115.933	108.193	110.218	116.299
Jordan (Jordan dinar) — Jordanie (dinar jordanien)										
End of period Fin de période	0.709	0.709	0.709	0.709	0.709	0.709	0.709	0.709	0.709	0.709
Period average Moyenne sur période	0.709	0.709	0.709	0.709	0.709	0.709	0.709	0.709	0.709	0.709
Kazakhstan (tenge) — Kazakhstan (tenge)										
End of period Fin de période	75.550	83.800	138.200	144.500	150.200	154.600	144.220	130.000	133.980	127.000
Period average Moyenne sur période	75.438	78.303	119.523	142.133	146.736	153.279	149.576	136.035	132.880	126.089
Kenya (Kenya shilling) — Kenya (shilling kényen)										
End of period Fin de période	62.678	61.906	72.931	78.036	78.600	77.072	76.139	77.344	72.367	69.397
Period average Moyenne sur période	58.732	60.367	70.326	76.176	78.563	78.749	75.936	79.174	75.554	72.101
Kiribati (Australian dollar) — Kiribati (dollar australien)										
End of period Fin de période	1.532	1.629	1.530	1.805	1.959	1.766	1.333	1.284	1.363	1.264
Period average Moyenne sur période	1.347	1.592	1.550	1.725	1.933	1.841	1.542	1.360	1.310	1.328
Korea, Republic of (Korean won) — Corée, République de (won coréen)										
End of period Fin de période	1 695.000	1 204.000	1 138.000	1 264.500	1 313.500	1 186.200	1 192.600	1 035.100	1 011.600	929.800
Period average Moyenne sur période	951.289	1 401.440	1 188.820	1 130.960	1 290.990	1 251.090	1 191.610	1 145.320	1 024.120	954.791
Kuwait (Kuwaiti dinar) — Koweït (dinar koweïtien)										
End of period Fin de période	0.305	0.302	0.304	0.305	0.308	0.300	0.295	0.295	0.292	0.289
Period average Moyenne sur période	0.303	0.305	0.304	0.307	0.307	0.304	0.298	0.295	0.292	0.290
Kyrgyzstan (Kyrgyz som) — Kirghizistan (som kirghize)										
End of period Fin de période	17.375	29.376	45.429	48.304	47.719	46.095	44.190	41.625	41.301	38.124
Period average Moyenne sur période	17.363	20.838	39.008	47.704	48.378	46.937	43.648	42.650	41.012	40.153
Lao People's Dem. Rep. (kip) — Rép. dém. pop. lao (kip)										
End of period Fin de période	2 634.500	4 274.000	7 600.000	8 218.000	9 490.000	10 680.000	10 467.000	10 376.500	10 743.000	9 745.000
Period average Moyenne sur période	1 259.980	3 298.330	7 102.020	7 887.640	8 954.580	10 056.300	10 569.000	10 585.500	10 655.200	10 159.900
Latvia (lats) — Lettonie (lats)										
End of period Fin de période	0.590	0.569	0.583	0.613	0.638	0.594	0.541	0.516	0.593	0.536

Exchange rates—National currency per US dollar (*continued*)

Cours des changes—Valeur du dollar des Etats-Unis en monnaie nationale (*suite*)

Country or area Pays ou zone	1997	1998	1999	2000	2001	2002	2003	2004	2005	2006
Period average Moyenne sur période	0.581	0.590	0.585	0.607	0.628	0.618	0.572	0.540	0.565	0.560
Lebanon (Lebanese pound)—Liban (livre libanaise)										
End of period Fin de période	1 527.000	1 508.000	1 507.500	1 507.500	1 507.500	1 507.500	1 507.500	1 507.500	1 507.500	1 507.500
Period average Moyenne sur période	1 539.450	1 516.130	1 507.840	1 507.500	1 507.500	1 507.500	1 507.500	1 507.500	1 507.500	1 507.500
Lesotho[1] (loti)—Lesotho[1] (loti)										
End of period Fin de période	4.868	5.860	6.155	7.569	12.127	8.640	6.640	5.630	6.325	6.970
Period average Moyenne sur période	4.608	5.528	6.110	6.940	8.609	10.541	7.565	6.460	6.359	6.772
Liberia[1] (Liberian dollar)—Libéria[1] (dollar libérien)										
End of period Fin de période	1.000	#43.250	39.500	42.750	49.500	65.000	50.500	54.500	56.500	59.500
Period average Moyenne sur période	1.000	#41.508	41.903	40.953	48.583	61.754	59.379	54.906	57.096	58.013
Libyan Arab Jamah. (Libyan dinar)—Jamah. arabe libyenne (dinar libyen)										
End of period Fin de période	0.470	0.450	0.462	0.540	0.650	1.210	1.300	1.244	1.352	1.285
Period average Moyenne sur période	0.461	0.468	0.464	0.512	0.605	1.271	1.293	1.305	1.308	1.314
Lithuania (litas)—Lituanie (litas)										
End of period Fin de période	4.000	4.000	4.000	4.000	4.000	3.311	2.762	2.535	2.910	2.630
Period average Moyenne sur période	4.000	4.000	4.000	4.000	4.000	3.677	3.061	2.781	2.774	2.752
Luxembourg[4] (Luxembourg franc, euro)—Luxembourg[4] (franc luxembourgeois, euro)										
End of period Fin de période	36.920	34.575	0.995	1.075	1.135	0.954	0.792	0.734	0.848	0.759
Period average Moyenne sur période	35.774	36.299	0.939	1.085	1.118	1.063	0.886	0.805	0.804	0.797
Madagascar[13] (Malagasy ariary)—Madagascar[13] (ariary malgache)										
End of period Fin de période	1 056.930	1 080.440	1 308.640	1 310.090	1 326.240	1 286.950	1 219.620	1 869.400	#2 159.820	2 013.950
Period average Moyenne sur période	1 018.180	1 088.280	1 256.760	1 353.500	1 317.700	1 366.390	1 238.330	1 868.860	2 003.030	2 142.300
Malawi (Malawi kwacha)—Malawi (kwacha malawien)										
End of period Fin de période	21.228	43.884	46.438	80.076	67.294	87.139	108.566	108.943	123.781	139.343
Period average Moyenne sur période	16.444	31.073	44.088	59.544	72.197	76.687	97.433	108.898	118.420	136.014
Malaysia (ringgit)—Malaisie (ringgit)										
End of period Fin de période	3.892	3.800	3.800	3.800	3.800	3.800	3.800	3.800	3.780	3.532
Period average Moyenne sur période	2.813	3.924	3.800	3.800	3.800	3.800	3.800	3.800	3.787	3.668
Maldives[14] (rufiyaa)—Maldives[14] (rufiyaa)										
End of period Fin de période	11.770	11.770	11.770	11.770	12.800	12.800	12.800	12.800	12.800	12.800
Period average Moyenne sur période	11.770	11.770	11.770	11.770	12.242	12.800	12.800	12.800	12.800	12.800
Mali[6] (CFA franc)—Mali[6] (franc CFA)										
End of period Fin de période	598.810	562.210	#652.953	704.951	744.306	625.495	519.364	481.578	556.037	498.069
Period average Moyenne sur période	583.669	589.952	#615.699	711.976	733.039	696.988	581.200	528.285	527.468	522.890
Malta (Maltese lira)—Malte (lire maltaise)										
End of period Fin de période	0.391	0.377	0.412	0.438	0.452	0.399	0.343	0.319	0.363	0.326

Country or area Pays ou zone	1997	1998	1999	2000	2001	2002	2003	2004	2005	2006
Period average Moyenne sur période	0.386	0.389	0.399	0.438	0.450	0.434	0.377	0.345	0.346	0.341
Mauritania (ouguiya) — Mauritanie (ouguiya)										
End of period Fin de période	168.350	205.780	225.000	252.300	264.120	268.710	265.600	257.190	270.610	...
Period average Moyenne sur période	151.853	188.476	209.514	238.923	255.629	271.739	263.030	...	265.528	...
Mauritius (Mauritian rupee) — Maurice (roupie mauricienne)										
End of period Fin de période	22.265	24.784	25.468	27.882	30.394	29.197	26.088	28.204	30.667	34.337
Period average Moyenne sur période	21.057	23.993	25.186	26.250	29.129	29.962	27.902	27.499	29.496	31.708
Mexico[1] (Mexican peso) — Mexique[1] (peso mexicain)										
End of period Fin de période	8.083	9.865	9.514	9.572	9.142	10.313	11.236	11.265	10.778	10.881
Period average Moyenne sur période	7.919	9.136	9.560	9.456	9.342	9.656	10.789	11.286	10.898	10.899
Micronesia (Fed. States of) (US dollar) — Micronésie (Etats féd. de) (dollar des Etats-Unis)										
End of period Fin de période	1.000	1.000	1.000	1.000	1.000	1.000	1.000	1.000	1.000	1.000
Period average Moyenne sur période	1.000	1.000	1.000	1.000	1.000	1.000	1.000	1.000	1.000	1.000
Mongolia (togrog) — Mongolie (togrog)										
End of period Fin de période	813.160	902.000	1 072.370	1 097.000	1 102.000	1 125.000	1 168.000	1 209.000	1 221.000	1 165.000
Period average Moyenne sur période	789.993	840.828	1 021.870	1 076.670	1 097.700	1 110.310	1 146.540	1 185.280	1 205.220	1 179.700
Montserrat (EC dollar) — Montserrat (dollar des Caraïbes orientales)										
End of period Fin de période	2.700	2.700	2.700	2.700	2.700	2.700	2.700	2.700	2.700	2.700
Morocco (Moroccan dirham) — Maroc (dirham marocain)										
End of period Fin de période	9.714	9.255	10.087	10.619	11.560	10.167	8.750	8.218	9.249	8.457
Period average Moyenne sur période	9.527	9.604	9.804	10.626	11.303	11.021	9.574	8.868	8.865	8.796
Mozambique[1] (metical) — Mozambique[1] (metical)										
End of period Fin de période	11 543.000	12 366.000	13 300.000	#17 140.500	23 320.400	23 854.300	23 856.700	18 899.300	24 183.000	#25 970.000
Period average Moyenne sur période	11 543.600	11 874.600	12 775.100	15 227.200	20 703.600	23 678.000	23 782.300	22 581.300	23 061.000	25 400.800
Myanmar (kyat) — Myanmar (kyat)										
End of period Fin de période	6.306	6.043	6.199	6.530	6.770	6.258	5.726	5.479	5.953	5.656
Period average Moyenne sur période	6.184	6.274	6.223	6.426	6.684	6.573	6.076	5.746	5.761	5.784
Namibia (Namibia dollar) — Namibie (dollar namibien)										
End of period Fin de période	4.868	5.860	6.155	7.569	12.127	8.640	6.640	5.630	6.325	6.970
Period average Moyenne sur période	4.608	5.528	6.110	6.940	8.609	10.541	7.565	6.460	6.359	6.772
Nepal (Nepalese rupee) — Népal (roupie népalaise)										
End of period Fin de période	63.300	67.675	68.725	74.300	76.475	78.300	74.040	71.800	74.050	71.100
Period average Moyenne sur période	58.010	65.976	68.239	71.094	74.949	77.877	76.141	73.674	71.368	72.756
Netherlands[4] (Netherlands guilder, euro) — Pays-Bas[4] (florin néerlandais, euro)										
End of period Fin de période	2.017	1.889	0.995	1.075	1.135	0.954	0.792	0.734	0.848	0.759
Period average Moyenne sur période	1.951	1.984	0.939	1.085	1.118	1.063	0.886	0.805	0.804	0.797

Country or area Pays ou zone	1997	1998	1999	2000	2001	2002	2003	2004	2005	2006
Netherlands Antilles (Netherlands Antillean guilder) — Antilles néerlandaises (florin des Antilles néerlandaises)										
End of period Fin de période	1.790	1.790	1.790	1.790	1.790	1.790	1.790	1.790	1.790	1.790
Period average Moyenne sur période	1.790	1.790	1.790	1.790	1.790	1.790	1.790	1.790	1.790	1.790
New Zealand (New Zealand dollar) — Nouvelle-Zélande (dollar néo-zélandais)										
End of period Fin de période	1.719	1.898	1.921	2.272	2.407	1.899	1.539	1.392	1.468	1.417
Period average Moyenne sur période	1.512	1.868	1.890	2.201	2.379	2.162	1.722	1.509	1.420	1.542
Nicaragua[1,15] (córdoba) — Nicaragua[1,15] (córdoba)										
End of period Fin de période	9.995	11.194	12.318	13.057	13.841	14.671	15.552	16.329	17.146	18.003
Period average Moyenne sur période	9.448	10.582	11.809	12.684	13.372	14.251	15.105	15.937	16.733	17.570
Niger[6] (CFA franc) — Niger[6] (franc CFA)										
End of period Fin de période	598.810	562.210	#652.953	704.951	744.306	625.495	519.364	481.578	556.037	498.069
Period average Moyenne sur période	583.669	589.952	#615.699	711.976	733.039	696.988	581.200	528.285	527.468	522.890
Nigeria[1] (naira) — Nigéria[1] (naira)										
End of period Fin de période	21.886	#21.886	97.950	109.550	112.950	126.400	136.500	132.350	129.000	...
Period average Moyenne sur période	21.886	#21.886	92.338	101.697	111.231	120.578	129.222	132.888	131.274	...
Norway (Norwegian krone) — Norvège (couronne norvégienne)										
End of period Fin de période	7.316	7.600	8.040	8.849	9.012	6.966	6.680	6.040	6.770	6.260
Period average Moyenne sur période	7.073	7.545	7.799	8.802	8.992	7.984	7.080	6.741	6.443	6.413
Oman (rial Omani) — Oman (rial omani)										
End of period Fin de période	0.385	0.385	0.385	0.385	0.385	0.385	0.385	0.385	0.385	0.385
Period average Moyenne sur période	0.385	0.385	0.385	0.385	0.385	0.385	0.385	0.385	0.385	0.385
Pakistan (Pakistan rupee) — Pakistan (roupie pakistanaise)										
End of period Fin de période	44.050	45.885	#51.785	58.029	60.864	58.534	57.215	59.124	59.830	60.918
Period average Moyenne sur période	41.112	45.047	#49.501	53.648	61.927	59.724	57.752	58.258	59.515	60.271
Panama (balboa) — Panama (balboa)										
End of period Fin de période	1.000	1.000	1.000	1.000	1.000	1.000	1.000	1.000	1.000	1.000
Period average Moyenne sur période	1.000	1.000	1.000	1.000	1.000	1.000	1.000	1.000	1.000	1.000
Papua New Guinea (kina) — Papouasie-Nvl-Guinée (kina)										
End of period Fin de période	1.751	2.096	2.695	3.072	3.762	4.019	3.333	3.125	3.096	3.030
Period average Moyenne sur période	1.438	2.074	2.571	2.782	3.389	3.895	3.564	3.223	3.102	3.057
Paraguay (guaraní) — Paraguay (guaraní)										
End of period Fin de période	2 360.000	2 840.190	3 328.860	3 526.900	4 682.000	7 103.590	6 114.960	6 250.000	6 120.000	5 190.000
Period average Moyenne sur période	2 177.860	2 726.490	3 119.070	3 486.350	4 105.930	5 716.260	6 424.340	5 974.580	6 177.960	5 635.460
Peru[16] (new sol) — Pérou[16] (nouveau sol)										
End of period Fin de période	2.730	3.160	3.510	3.527	3.444	3.514	3.463	3.282	3.430	3.196
Period average Moyenne sur période	2.664	2.930	3.383	3.490	3.507	3.517	3.479	3.413	3.296	3.274

Country or area Pays ou zone	1997	1998	1999	2000	2001	2002	2003	2004	2005	2006
Philippines (Philippine peso) — Philippines (peso philippin)										
End of period Fin de période	39.975	39.059	40.313	49.998	51.404	53.096	55.569	56.267	53.067	49.132
Period average Moyenne sur période	29.471	40.893	39.089	44.192	50.993	51.604	54.203	56.040	55.086	51.314
Poland (zloty) — Pologne (zloty)										
End of period Fin de période	3.518	3.504	4.148	4.143	3.986	3.839	3.741	2.990	3.261	2.911
Period average Moyenne sur période	3.279	3.475	3.967	4.346	4.094	4.080	3.889	3.658	3.236	3.103
Portugal[4] (Portuguese escudo, euro) — Portugal[4] (escudo portugais, euro)										
End of period Fin de période	183.326	171.829	0.995	1.075	1.135	0.954	0.792	0.734	0.848	0.759
Period average Moyenne sur période	175.312	180.104	0.939	1.085	1.118	1.063	0.886	0.805	0.804	0.797
Qatar (Qatar riyal) — Qatar (riyal qatarien)										
End of period Fin de période	3.640	3.640	3.640	3.640	3.640	3.640	3.640	3.640	3.640	3.640
Period average Moyenne sur période	3.640	3.640	3.640	3.640	3.640	3.640	3.640	3.640	3.640	3.640
Republic of Moldova (Moldovan leu) — République de Moldova (leu moldove)										
End of period Fin de période	4.661	8.323	11.590	12.383	13.091	13.822	13.220	12.461	12.832	12.905
Period average Moyenne sur période	4.624	5.371	10.516	12.434	12.865	13.571	13.945	12.330	12.600	13.131
Romania[1,17] (Romanian leu) — Roumanie[1,17] (leu roumain)										
End of period Fin de période	0.802	1.095	1.826	2.593	3.160	3.350	3.260	2.907	#3.108	2.568
Period average Moyenne sur période	0.717	0.888	1.533	2.171	2.906	3.306	3.320	3.264	2.914	2.809
Russian Federation[18] (ruble) — Fédération de Russie[18] (ruble)										
End of period Fin de période	5.960	#20.650	27.000	28.160	30.140	31.784	29.455	27.749	28.783	26.331
Period average Moyenne sur période	5.785	#9.705	24.620	28.129	29.169	31.349	30.692	28.814	28.284	27.191
Rwanda (Rwanda franc) — Rwanda (franc rwandais)										
End of period Fin de période	304.672	320.338	349.530	430.486	457.900	511.854	580.280	566.860	553.719	548.652
Period average Moyenne sur période	301.530	312.314	333.942	389.696	442.992	475.365	537.655	577.449	557.823	551.712
Saint Kitts and Nevis (EC dollar) — Saint-Kitts-et-Nevis (dollar des Caraïbes orientales)										
End of period Fin de période	2.700	2.700	2.700	2.700	2.700	2.700	2.700	2.700	2.700	2.700
Period average Moyenne sur période	2.700	2.700	2.700	2.700	2.700	2.700	2.700	2.700	2.700	2.700
Saint Lucia (EC dollar) — Sainte-Lucie (dollar des Caraïbes orientales)										
End of period Fin de période	2.700	2.700	2.700	2.700	2.700	2.700	2.700	2.700	2.700	2.700
Period average Moyenne sur période	2.700	2.700	2.700	2.700	2.700	2.700	2.700	2.700	2.700	2.700
St. Vincent-Grenadines (EC dollar) — St. Vincent-Grenadines (dollar des Caraïbes orientales)										
End of period Fin de période	2.700	2.700	2.700	2.700	2.700	2.700	2.700	2.700	2.700	2.700
Period average Moyenne sur période	2.700	2.700	2.700	2.700	2.700	2.700	2.700	2.700	2.700	2.700
Samoa (tala) — Samoa (tala)										
End of period Fin de période	2.766	3.010	3.018	3.341	3.551	3.217	2.778	2.673	2.764	2.685
Period average Moyenne sur période	2.559	2.948	3.013	3.286	3.478	3.376	2.973	2.781	2.710	2.779

Country or area Pays ou zone	1997	1998	1999	2000	2001	2002	2003	2004	2005	2006
San Marino[4] (Italian lira, euro) — Saint-Marin[4] (lire italienne, euro)										
End of period Fin de période	1 759.190	1 653.100	0.995	1.075	1.135	0.954	0.792	0.734	0.848	0.759
Period average Moyenne sur période	1 703.100	1 736.210	0.939	1.085	1.118	1.063	0.886	0.805	0.804	0.797
Sao Tome and Principe (dobra) — Sao Tomé-et-Principe (dobra)										
End of period Fin de période	6 969.730	6 885.000	7 300.000	8 610.650	9 019.710	9 191.840	9 455.900	10 104.000	11 929.700	13 073.900
Period average Moyenne sur période	4 552.510	6 883.240	7 118.960	7 978.170	8 842.110	9 088.330	9 347.580	9 902.320	10 558.000	12 445.400
Saudi Arabia (Saudi Arabian riyal) — Arabie saoudite (riyal saoudien)										
End of period Fin de période	3.750	3.750	3.750	3.750	3.750	3.750	3.750	3.750	3.745	3.745
Period average Moyenne sur période	3.750	3.750	3.750	3.750	3.750	3.750	3.750	3.750	3.747	3.745
Senegal[6] (CFA franc) — Sénégal[6] (franc CFA)										
End of period Fin de période	598.810	562.210	#652.953	704.951	744.306	625.495	519.364	481.578	556.037	498.069
Period average Moyenne sur période	583.669	589.952	#615.699	711.976	733.039	696.988	581.200	528.285	527.468	522.890
Serbia (dinar) — Serbie (dinar)										
End of period Fin de période	5.912	10.031	11.662	63.166	67.670	58.985	54.637	57.936	72.219	59.976
Period average Moyenne sur période	5.912	10.031	11.662	63.166	66.914	60.341	55.604	58.572	72.438	59.637
Seychelles (Seychelles rupee) — Seychelles (roupie seychelloises)										
End of period Fin de période	5.125	5.452	5.368	6.269	5.752	5.055	5.500	5.500	5.500	5.796
Period average Moyenne sur période	5.026	5.262	5.343	5.714	5.858	5.480	5.401	5.500	5.500	5.520
Sierra Leone (leone) — Sierra Leone (leone)										
End of period Fin de période	1 333.330	1 590.760	2 276.050	1 666.670	2 161.270	2 191.730	2 562.180	2 860.490	2 932.520	2 973.940
Period average Moyenne sur période	981.482	1 563.620	1 804.200	2 092.120	1 986.150	2 099.030	2 347.940	2 701.300	2 889.590	2 961.910
Singapore (Singapore dollar) — Singapour (dollar singapourien)										
End of period Fin de période	1.676	1.661	1.666	1.732	1.851	1.737	1.701	1.634	1.664	1.534
Period average Moyenne sur période	1.485	1.674	1.695	1.724	1.792	1.791	1.742	1.690	1.664	1.589
Slovakia (Slovak koruna) — Slovaquie (couronne slovaque)										
End of period Fin de période	34.782	36.913	42.266	47.389	48.467	40.036	32.920	28.496	31.948	26.246
Period average[1] Moyenne sur période[1]	33.616	35.233	41.363	46.035	48.355	45.327	36.773	32.257	31.018	29.697
Slovenia (tolar) — Slovénie (tolar)										
End of period Fin de période	169.180	161.200	196.771	227.377	250.946	221.071	189.367	176.243	202.430	181.931
Period average Moyenne sur période	159.688	166.134	181.769	222.656	242.749	240.248	207.114	192.381	192.705	191.028
Solomon Islands (Solomon Islands dollar) — Iles Salomon (dollar des Iles Salomon)										
End of period Fin de période	4.748	4.859	5.076	5.099	5.565	7.457	7.491	7.508	7.576	7.616
Period average Moyenne sur période	3.717	4.816	4.838	5.089	5.278	6.749	7.506	7.485	7.530	7.610
South Africa[1] (rand) — Afrique du Sud[1] (rand)										
End of period Fin de période	4.868	5.860	6.155	7.569	12.127	8.640	6.640	5.630	6.325	6.970
Period average Moyenne sur période	4.608	5.528	6.110	6.940	8.609	10.541	7.565	6.460	6.359	6.772

Country or area Pays ou zone	1997	1998	1999	2000	2001	2002	2003	2004	2005	2006
Spain[4] (peseta, euro) — Espagne[4] (peseta, euro)										
End of period Fin de période	151.702	142.607	0.995	1.075	1.135	0.954	0.792	0.734	0.848	0.759
Period average Moyenne sur période	146.414	149.395	0.939	1.085	1.118	1.063	0.886	0.805	0.804	0.797
Sri Lanka (Sri Lanka rupee) — Sri Lanka (roupie sri-lankaise)										
End of period Fin de période	61.285	68.297	72.170	82.580	93.159	96.725	96.738	104.605	102.117	107.706
Period average Moyenne sur période	58.995	64.450	70.635	77.005	89.383	95.662	96.521	101.194	100.498	103.914
Sudan[1] (Sudanese dinar) — Soudan[1] (dinar soudanaise)										
End of period Fin de période	172.206	237.801	257.700	257.350	261.430	261.680	260.160	250.630	230.540	201.330
Period average Moyenne sur période	157.574	200.802	252.550	257.123	258.702	263.306	260.983	257.905	243.606	217.153
Suriname[19] (Surinamese dollar) — Suriname[19] (dollar surinamais)										
End of period Fin de période	401.000	401.000	987.500	2 178.500	2 178.500	2 515.000	#2 625.000	#2 715.000	2 740.000	2 745.000
Period average Moyenne sur période	401.000	401.000	859.437	1 322.470	2 178.500	2 346.750	#2 601.330	#2 733.580	2 731.670	2 743.750
Swaziland (lilangeni) — Swaziland (lilangeni)										
End of period Fin de période	4.868	5.860	6.155	7.569	12.127	8.640	6.640	5.630	6.325	6.970
Period average Moyenne sur période	4.608	5.528	6.110	6.940	8.609	10.541	7.565	6.460	6.359	6.772
Sweden (Swedish krona) — Suède (couronne suédoise)										
End of period Fin de période	7.877	8.061	8.525	9.535	10.668	8.825	7.189	6.615	7.958	6.864
Period average Moyenne sur période	7.635	7.950	8.262	9.162	10.329	9.737	8.086	7.349	7.473	7.378
Switzerland (Swiss franc) — Suisse (franc suisse)										
End of period Fin de période	1.455	1.377	1.600	1.637	1.677	1.387	1.237	1.132	1.314	1.220
Period average Moyenne sur période	1.451	1.450	1.502	1.689	1.688	1.559	1.347	1.244	1.245	1.254
Syrian Arab Republic[1] (Syrian pound) — Rép. arabe syrienne[1] (livre syrienne)										
End of period Fin de période	11.225	11.225	11.225	11.225	11.225	11.225	11.225	11.225	11.225	11.225
Period average Moyenne sur période	11.225	11.225	11.225	11.225	11.225	11.225	11.225	11.225	11.225	11.225
Tajikistan (somoni) — Tadjikistan (somoni)										
End of period Fin de période	0.747	0.978	1.436	#2.200	2.550	3.000	2.957	3.037	3.199	3.427
Period average Moyenne sur période	0.562	0.777	1.238	#2.076	2.372	2.764	3.061	2.971	3.117	3.298
Thailand (baht) — Thaïlande (baht)										
End of period Fin de période	#47.247	36.691	37.470	43.268	44.222	43.152	39.591	39.061	41.030	36.046
Period average Moyenne sur période	#31.364	41.359	37.814	40.112	44.432	42.960	41.485	40.222	40.220	37.882
TFYR of Macedonia (TFYR Macedonian denar) — L'ex-R.y. Macédoine (denar de l'ex-R.Y. Macédoine)										
End of period Fin de période	55.421	51.836	60.339	66.328	69.172	58.598	49.050	45.068	51.859	46.450
Period average Moyenne sur période	50.004	54.462	56.902	65.904	68.037	64.350	54.322	49.410	49.284	48.802
Togo[6] (CFA franc) — Togo[6] (franc CFA)										
End of period Fin de période	598.810	562.210	#652.953	704.951	744.306	625.495	519.364	481.578	556.037	498.069
Period average Moyenne sur période	583.669	589.952	#615.699	711.976	733.039	696.988	581.200	528.285	527.468	522.890

Country or area Pays ou zone	1997	1998	1999	2000	2001	2002	2003	2004	2005	2006
Tonga (pa'anga) — Tonga (pa'anga)										
End of period Fin de période	1.362	1.616	1.608	1.977	2.207	2.229	2.020	1.912	2.060	...
Period average Moyenne sur période	1.264	1.492	1.599	1.759	2.124	2.195	2.146	1.972	1.943	...
Trinidad and Tobago (Trinidad and Tobago dollar) — Trinité-et-Tobago (dollar de la Trinité-et-Tobago)										
End of period Fin de période	6.300	6.597	6.300	6.300	6.290	6.300	6.300	6.300	6.310	6.295
Period average Moyenne sur période	6.252	6.298	6.299	6.300	6.233	6.249	6.295	6.299	6.300	6.308
Tunisia (Tunisian dinar) — Tunisie (dinar tunisien)										
End of period Fin de période	1.148	1.101	1.253	1.385	1.468	1.334	1.208	1.199	1.363	1.297
Period average Moyenne sur période	1.106	1.139	1.186	1.371	1.439	1.422	1.289	1.246	1.297	1.331
Turkey[20] (new Turkish Lira) — Turquie[20] (nouvelle livre turque)										
End of period Fin de période	0.206	0.315	0.541	0.673	1.450	1.644	1.397	1.340	#1.345	1.409
Period average Moyenne sur période	0.152	0.261	0.419	0.625	1.226	1.507	1.501	1.426	1.344	1.429
Turkmenistan (Turkmen manat) — Turkménistan (manat turkmène)										
End of period Fin de période	4 165.000	5 200.000	5 200.000	5 200.000	5 200.000	...	...	...	...	...
Period average Moyenne sur période	4 143.420	4 890.170	5 200.000	5 200.000	5 200.000	...	...	...	...	...
Uganda[1] (Uganda shilling) — Ouganda[1] (shilling ougandais)										
End of period Fin de période	1 140.110	1 362.690	1 506.040	1 766.680	1 727.400	1 852.570	1 935.320	1 738.590	1 816.860	1 741.440
Period average Moyenne sur période	1 083.010	1 240.310	1 454.830	1 644.480	1 755.660	1 797.550	1 963.720	1 810.300	1 780.670	1 831.450
Ukraine (hryvnia) — Ukraine (hryvnia)										
End of period Fin de période	1.899	3.427	5.216	5.435	5.299	5.332	5.332	5.305	5.050	5.050
Period average Moyenne sur période	1.862	2.450	4.130	5.440	5.372	5.327	5.333	5.319	5.125	5.050
United Arab Emirates (UAE dirham) — Emirats arabes unis (dirham des EAU)										
End of period Fin de période	3.673	3.673	3.673	3.673	3.673	3.673	3.673	3.673	3.673	3.673
Period average Moyenne sur période	3.671	3.673	3.673	3.673	3.673	3.673	3.673	3.673	3.673	3.673
United Kingdom (pound sterling) — Royaume-Uni (livre sterling)										
End of period Fin de période	0.605	0.601	0.619	0.670	0.690	0.620	0.560	0.518	0.581	0.509
Period average Moyenne sur période	0.611	0.604	0.618	0.661	0.695	0.667	0.613	0.546	0.550	0.544
United Rep. of Tanzania (Tanzania shilling) — Rép.-Unie de Tanzanie (shilling tanzanien)										
End of period Fin de période	624.570	681.000	797.330	803.260	916.300	976.300	1 063.620	1 042.960	1 165.510	1 261.640
Period average Moyenne sur période	612.123	664.671	744.759	800.409	876.412	966.583	1 038.420	1 089.330	1 128.930	1 251.900
United States (US dollar) — Etats-Unis (dollar des Etats-Unis)										
End of period Fin de période	1.000	1.000	1.000	1.000	1.000	1.000	1.000	1.000	1.000	1.000
Period average Moyenne sur période	1.000	1.000	1.000	1.000	1.000	1.000	1.000	1.000	1.000	1.000
Uruguay (Uruguayan peso) — Uruguay (peso uruguayen)										
End of period Fin de période	10.040	10.817	11.615	12.515	14.768	27.200	29.300	26.350	24.100	24.400
Period average Moyenne sur période	9.442	10.472	11.339	12.100	13.319	21.257	28.209	28.704	24.479	24.073

Country or area Pays ou zone	1997	1998	1999	2000	2001	2002	2003	2004	2005	2006
Uzbekistan (Uzbek sum)—Ouzbékistan (sum ouzbek)										
End of period Fin de période	...	...	140.000	...	...	...	...	...	...	...
Period average Moyenne sur période	62.917	94.492	124.625	236.608	...	...	...	...	...	...
Vanuatu (vatu)—Vanuatu (vatu)										
End of period Fin de période	124.310	129.780	128.890	142.810	146.740	133.170	111.810	106.530	112.330	106.480
Period average Moyenne sur période	115.873	127.517	129.075	137.643	145.313	139.198	122.189	111.790	109.246	111.224
Venezuela (Bolivarian Republic of) (bolívar)—Venezuela (République bolivarienne du) (bolívar)										
End of period Fin de période	504.250	564.500	648.250	699.750	763.000	1 401.250	1 598.000	1 918.000	2 147.000	2 147.000
Period average Moyenne sur période	488.635	547.556	605.717	679.960	723.666	1 160.950	1 606.960	1 891.330	2 089.750	2 147.000
Viet Nam (dong)—Viet Nam (dong)										
End of period Fin de période	12 292.000	13 890.000	14 028.000	14 514.000	15 084.000	15 403.000	15 646.000	15 777.000	15 916.000	16 054.000
Period average Moyenne sur période	11 683.300	13 268.000	13 943.200	14 167.700	14 725.200	15 279.500	15 509.600	...	15 858.900	15 994.300
Yemen (Yemeni rial)—Yémen (rial yéménite)										
End of period Fin de période	130.460	141.650	159.100	165.590	173.270	179.010	184.310	185.870	195.080	198.500
Period average Moyenne sur période	129.281	135.882	155.718	161.718	168.672	175.625	183.448	184.776	191.509	197.049
Zambia (Zambia kwacha)—Zambie (kwacha zambie)										
End of period Fin de période	1 414.840	2 298.920	2 632.190	4 157.830	3 830.400	4 334.400	4 645.480	4 771.310	3 508.980	4 406.670
Period average Moyenne sur période	1 314.500	1 862.070	2 388.020	3 110.840	3 610.940	4 398.590	4 733.270	4 778.880	4 463.500	3 603.070
Zimbabwe (Zimbabwe dollar)—Zimbabwe (dollar zimbabwéen)										
End of period Fin de période	18.608	37.369	38.139	55.066	55.036	55.036	823.723	5 729.270	77 964.600	...
Period average Moyenne sur période	12.111	23.679	38.301	44.418	55.052	55.036	697.424	5 068.660	22 363.600	...

Source

International Monetary Fund (IMF), Washington, D.C., "International Financial Statistics," May 2007 and the IMF database.

Notes

1 Principal rate.
2 In October 2002, Afghanistan redenominated its currency. One afghani is equal to 1,000 old afghanis.
3 Pesos per million US dollars through 1983, per thousand US dollars through 1988 and per US dollar up to 2001. A unified floating exchange rate regime was introduced on 11 Feb. 2002, with the exchange rate determined by market conditions.
4 Beginning 1999 - euro (Greece, beginning 2001).
5 The manat, which was first introduced on 15 August 1992 and circulated alongside the Russian ruble at a fixed rate of 10 rubles per manat, became the sole legal tender in Azerbaijan on 1 January 1994. On 1 January 2006, the new manat, equivalent to 5,000 old manats, was introduced.
6 Prior to January 1999, the official rate was pegged to the French franc. On 12 January 1994, the CFA franc was devalued to CFAF 100 per French franc from CFAF 50 at which it had been fixed since 1948. From 1 January 1999, the CFAF is pegged to the euro at a rate of CFA francs 655.957 per euro.

Source

Fonds monétaire international (FMI), Washington, D.C.,"Statistiques Financières Internationales," mai 2007 et la base de données du FMI.

Notes

1 Taux principal.
2 L'Afghanistan a changé en octobre 2002 la valeur de sa monnaie : un afghani vaut 1 000 afghanis anciens.
3 Pesos par million de dollars des États-Unis jusqu'en 1983, par millier de dollars des États-Unis jusqu'en 1988 et par dollar des États-Unis apres 2001. Un régime de taux de change flottant unifié a été introduit le 11 février 2002, le taux de change étant déterminé par le marché.
4 A partir de 1999 - euro (Grèce, à partir de 2001).
5 Le manat, introduit d'abord le 15 août 1992 et circulant parallèlement au rouble russe, au taux fixe de 10 roubles pour un manat, est la seule monnaie ayant cours légal en Azerbaïdjan depuis le 1er janvier 1994. Le nouveau manat, valant 5 000 manats anciens, a été introduit le 1er janvier 2006.
6 Avant janvier 1999, le taux officiel était établi par référence au franc français. Le 12 janvier 1994, le franc CFA a été dévalué; son taux par rapport au franc français, auquel il est rattaché depuis 1948, est passé de 50 à 100 francs CFA pour 1 franc français. A compter du 1er janvier 1999, le taux officiel est établi par référence à l'euro à un taux de 655 957 francs CFA pour un euro.

7 Bolivianos per million US dollars through 1983, per thousand US dollars for 1984, and per US dollar thereafter.

8 Reals per trillion US dollars through 1983, per billion US dollars 1984-1988, per million US dollars 1989-1992, and per US dollar thereafter.

9 Prior to January 1999, the official rate was pegged to the French franc Beginning 12 January 1994, the CFA franc was devalued to CFAF 75 per French franc from CFAF 50 at which it had been fixed since 1948. From January 1, 1999, the CFAF is pegged to the euro at a rate of CFA franc 491.9677 per euro.

10 New Zaires per million US dollars through 1990, per thousand US dollars for 1991-1995, and per US dollar thereafter.

11 "Euro Area" is an official descriptor for the European Economic and Monetary Union (EMU). The participating member states of the EMU are Austria, Belgium, Finland, France, Germany, Greece (beginning 2001), Ireland, Italy, Luxembourg, Netherlands, Portugal, and Spain.

12 Prior to January 1999, the official rate was pegged to the French franc at CFAF 100 per French franc. The CFA franc was adopted as national currency as of May 2, 1997. The Guinean peso and the CFA franc were set at PG65 per CFA franc. From January 1, 1999, the CFAF is pegged to the euro at a rate of CFA franc 655.957 per euro.

13 Effective 1 January 2005, Madagascar announced a new currency, the ariary. One ariary is equal to 5 Malagasy francs.

14 Effective 19 October 1994, the official rate of the rufiyaa was pegged to the US dollar at a rate of Rf 11.77 per US dollar. Effective 25 July 2001, the rufiyaa was devalued and fixed at Rf 12.80 per US dollar.

15 Gold córdobas per billion US dollars through 1987, per million US dollars for 1988, per thousand US dollars for 1989-1990 and per US dollar thereafter.

16 New soles per billion US dollars through 1987, per million US dollars for 1988-1989, and per US dollar thereafter.

17 Effective 1 July 2005, Romania redenominated its currency. One new leu is equal to 10,000 old lei.

18 The post-1 January 1998 ruble is equal to 1,000 pre-January 1998 rubles.

19 On 1 January 2004, the Surinamese dollar, equal to 1,000 Surinamese guilders, replaced the guilder as the currency unit.

20 Effective 1 January 2005, Turkey adopted a new currency, the new Turkish lira. One new Turkish lira (yeni Türk lirasi) is equal to 1,000,000 Turkish lira (Türk lirasi).

7 Bolivianos par million de dollars des États-Unis jusqu'en 1983, par millier de dollars des États-Unis en 1984, et par dollar des États-Unis après cette date.

8 Reals par trillion de dollars des États-Unis jusqu'en 1983, par millard de dollars des États-Unis 1984-1988, par million de dollars des États-Unis 1989-1992, et par dollar des État-Unis après cette date.

9 Avant janvier 1999, le taux de change officiel est raccroché au taux de change du franc français. Le 12 janvier 1994, le CFA a été dévalué de 50 par franc français, valeur qu'il avait conservée depuis 1948, à 75 par franc français. A compter du 1er janvier 1999, le taux officiel est établi par référence à l'euro : 491 9677 francs CFA pour un euro.

10 Nouveaux zaïres par million de dollars des États-Unis jusqu'en 1990, par millier de dollars des États-Unis en 1991 et 1995, et par dollar des États-Unis après cette date.

11 L'expression "zone euro" est un intitulé officiel pour l'Union économique et monétaire (UEM) européene. L'UEM est composée des pays membres suivants : Allemagne, Autriche, Belgique, Espagne, Finlande, France, Grèce (à partir de 2001), Irlande, Italie, Luxembourg, Pays-Bas et Portugal.

12 Avant janvier 1999, le taux de change officiel était fixé à 100 francs CFA pour un franc français. Le franc CFA avait été adopté comme monnaie nationale à compter du 2 mai 1997. Le taux de change du peso guinéen par rapport au franc CFA a été établi à 65 pesos guinéens pour 1 franc CFA. A compter du 1er janvier 1999, le taux officiel est établi par référence à l'euro : 655 957 francs CFA pour un euro.

13 À compter du 1er janvier 2005, Madagascar a adopté une nouvelle monnaie, l'ariary, qui vaut 5 francs malgaches.

14 À compter du 19 octobre 1994, le taux de change officiel du rufiyaa est indexé sur le dollar des États-Unis, et établi à 11,77 Rf pour 1 dollar. À compter du 25 juillet 2001, le rufiyaa a été dévalué et le taux de change fixe est de 12,80 Rf pour 1 dollar.

15 Cordobas d'or par milliard de dollars des États-Unis jusqu'en 1987, par million de dollars en 1988, par millier de dollars des États-Unis en 1989-1990 et par dollar des États Unis après cette date.

16 Nouveaux soles par milliard de dollars des États-Unis jusqu'en 1987, par million de dollars des États-Unis en 1988-1989 et par dollar des États-Unis après cette date.

17 À compter du 1er juillet 2005, la Roumanie a changé la valeur de sa monnaie : un nouveau leu vaut 10 000 lei anciens.

18 Le rouble ayant cours après le 1er janvier 1998 vaut 1 000 roubles de la période antérieure à cette date.

19 Le 1er janvier 2004, le dollar de Suriname, égal à 1 000 florins de Suriname, a remplacé le florin comme unité monétaire.

20 À compter du 1er janvier 2005, la Turquie a adopté une nouvelle monnaie, la nouvelle livre turque (yeni Türk lirasi), qui vaut 1 000 000 de livres turques (Türk lirasi).

Total external and public/publicly guaranteed long-term debt of developing countries

Millions of US dollars

A. Total external debt&

Total de la dette extérieure et dette publique extérieure à long terme garantie par l'Etat des pays en développement

Millions de dollars des E.U.

A. Total de la dette extérieure&

Developing economies	1999	2000	2001	2002	2003	2004	2005	Economies en développement
Total long-term debt	**1 925 730**	**1 896 600**	**1 872 230**	**1 933 510**	**2 062 180**	**2 177 970**	**2 147 180**	**Total de la dette à long terme**
Public and publicly guaranteed	1 395 670	1 356 640	1 334 940	1 389 420	1 468 900	1 513 470	1 361 630	Dette publique ou garantie par l'Etat
Official creditors	806 691	780 214	750 229	778 047	818 008	830 873	725 590	Créanciers publics
Multilateral	332 868	332 635	337 902	357 694	380 797	393 456	380 487	Multilatéraux
IBRD	111 005	111 885	112 325	111 117	109 080	106 085	100 127	BIRD
IDA	86 604	86 843	89 220	100 613	113 973	124 347	121 466	IDA
Bilateral	272 758	250 920	237 171	257 782	289 952	296 786	245 974	Bilatéraux
Private creditors	588 978	576 430	584 710	611 368	650 893	682 601	636 044	Créanciers privées
Bonds	339 612	373 105	372 673	397 515	436 718	467 926	428 857	Obligations
Commercial banks	165 865	132 485	146 017	153 556	157 319	163 144	162 688	Banques commerciales
Other private	83 500	70 840	66 019	60 297	56 855	51 531	44 500	Autres institutions privées
Private non-guaranteed	530 058	539 954	537 288	544 092	593 277	664 498	785 545	Dette privée non garantie
Undisbursed debt	**306 869**	**240 444**	**216 125**	**219 358**	**235 836**	**221 565**	**198 326**	**Dette (montants non versés)**
Official creditors	244 764	185 166	172 886	177 583	181 356	180 415	170 100	Créanciers publics
Private creditors	62 104	55 278	43 238	41 774	54 480	41 150	28 226	Créanciers privées
Commitments	**147 465**	**151 531**	**160 818**	**122 317**	**147 740**	**140 811**	**148 878**	**Engagements**
Official creditors	65 918	51 381	66 399	52 927	51 888	51 418	53 264	Créanciers publics
Private creditors	81 547	100 151	94 419	69 390	95 852	89 393	95 614	Créanciers privées
Disbursements	**257 612**	**250 389**	**260 781**	**252 078**	**306 741**	**390 843**	**460 339**	**Versements**
Public and publicly guaranteed	142 148	141 625	136 725	119 297	136 663	151 435	148 261	Dette publique ou garantie par l'Etat
Official creditors	60 539	53 830	51 635	46 003	49 964	47 309	46 813	Créanciers publics
Multilateral	37 113	35 067	34 256	32 035	37 831	34 058	34 906	Mutilatéraux
IBRD	14 061	13 430	12 305	10 288	11 521	10 467	9 624	BIRD
IDA	5 397	5 219	6 091	6 768	6 528	7 699	7 025	IDA
Bilateral	23 426	18 763	17 379	13 968	12 134	13 251	11 907	Bilatéraux
Private creditors	81 608	87 795	85 090	73 294	86 699	104 126	101 448	Créanciers privées
Bonds	51 042	59 191	44 064	39 927	51 138	65 152	64 391	Obligations
Commercial banks	18 588	19 913	34 642	28 522	28 935	34 428	33 083	Banques commerciales
Other private	11 978	8 691	6 385	4 844	6 626	4 546	3 975	Autres institutions privées
Private non-guaranteed	115 464	108 764	124 056	132 781	170 077	239 408	312 078	Dette privée non garantie
Principal repayments	**218 042**	**232 256**	**242 036**	**255 257**	**286 213**	**316 336**	**354 598**	**Remboursements du principal**
Public and publicly guaranteed	107 867	120 835	119 627	123 059	144 701	137 298	156 347	Dette publique ou garantie par l'Etat
Official creditors	44 311	49 066	44 456	54 975	64 195	59 229	77 315	Créanciers publics
Multilateral	18 915	23 175	18 868	30 779	36 271	31 214	27 391	Multilatéraux
IBRD	9 778	9 784	9 765	15 981	17 493	15 240	12 535	BIRD
IDA	869	949	1 085	1 243	1 322	1 546	1 634	IDA
Bilateral	25 396	25 891	25 588	24 197	27 924	28 015	49 924	Bilatéraux
Private creditors	63 557	71 770	75 171	68 083	80 505	78 070	79 032	Créanciers privées
Bonds	23 113	34 997	34 462	28 224	38 571	37 664	46 086	Obligations
Commercial banks	27 003	24 401	27 775	28 140	30 870	31 907	24 077	Banques commerciales
Other private	13 440	12 371	12 934	11 719	11 065	8 499	8 869	Autres institutions privées
Private non-guaranteed	110 174	111 421	122 409	132 198	141 512	179 037	198 251	Dette privée non garantie

Total external and public/publicly guaranteed long-term debt of developing countries—Millions of US dollars (*continued*)

A. Total external debt&

Total de la dette extérieure et dette publique extérieure à long terme garantie par l'Etat de pays en développement—Millions de dollars des E.U. (*suite*)

A. Total de la dette extérieure&

Developing economies	1999	2000	2001	2002	2003	2004	2005	Economies en développement
Net flows	**39 570**	**18 133**	**18 746**	**-3 179**	**20 528**	**74 508**	**105 741**	**Apports nets**
Public and publicly guaranteed	34 280	20 790	17 099	-3 762	-8 037	14 137	-8 086	Dette publique ou garantie par l'Etat
Official creditors	16 228	4 764	7 179	-8 972	-14 231	-11 919	-30 503	Créanciers publics
Multilateral	18 198	11 892	15 388	1 256	1 559	2 844	7 515	Multilatéraux
IBRD	4 283	3 646	2 541	-5 693	-5 972	-4 773	-2 911	BIRD
IDA	4 528	4 271	5 007	5 525	5 205	6 154	5 392	IDA
Bilateral	-1 970	-7 128	-8 209	-10 228	-15 790	-14 764	-38 017	Bilatéraux
Private creditors	18 052	16 026	9 920	5 210	6 194	26 056	22 417	Créanciers privées
Bonds	27 929	24 194	9 602	11 703	12 568	27 488	18 305	Obligations
Commercial banks	-8 415	-4 489	6 867	382	-1 934	2 521	9 006	Banques commerciales
Other private	-1 462	-3 680	-6 549	-6 875	-4 439	-3 953	-4 894	Autres institutions privées
Private non-guaranteed	5 290	-2 657	1 647	583	28 565	60 371	113 827	Dette privée non garantie
Interest payments	**93 921**	**99 522**	**95 239**	**83 025**	**88 116**	**84 977**	**93 816**	**Paiements d'intérets**
Public and publicly guaranteed	61 990	66 721	63 811	57 110	60 462	57 932	64 672	Dette publique ou garantie par l'Etat
Official creditors	26 852	26 993	28 039	24 033	23 705	22 096	24 208	Créanciers publics
Multilateral	14 857	15 574	15 258	13 626	12 163	11 011	10 848	Multilatéraux
IBRD	7 245	7 665	7 456	6 380	5 124	4 141	4 174	BIRD
IDA	588	578	576	695	698	896	898	IDA
Bilateral	11 995	11 419	12 780	10 407	11 542	11 085	13 360	Bilatéraux
Private creditors	35 138	39 728	35 772	33 077	36 757	35 836	40 464	Créanciers privées
Bonds	23 035	26 645	23 339	22 891	26 160	26 880	31 347	Obligations
Commercial banks	7 884	9 364	9 020	7 795	8 175	7 025	7 584	Banques commerciales
Other private	4 219	3 720	3 413	2 391	2 422	1 931	1 533	Autres institutions privées
Private non-guaranteed	31 931	32 801	31 428	25 915	27 653	27 045	29 144	Dette privée non garantie
Net transfers	**-54 351**	**-81 389**	**-76 493**	**-86 205**	**-67 588**	**-10 469**	**11 924**	**Transferts nets**
Public and publicly guaranteed	-27 710	-45 931	-46 712	-60 872	-68 500	-43 795	-72 758	Dette publique ou garantie par l'Etat
Official creditors	-10 623	-22 228	-20 859	-33 005	-37 937	-34 015	-54 710	Créanciers publics
Multilateral	3 341	-3 682	130	-12 370	-10 604	-8 167	-3 333	Multilatéraux
IBRD	-2 962	-4 020	-4 915	-12 073	-11 096	-8 913	-7 084	BIRD
IDA	3 940	3 693	4 430	4 830	4 508	5 258	4 494	IDA
Bilateral	-13 964	-18 546	-20 990	-20 635	-27 333	-25 849	-51 377	Bilatéraux
Private creditors	-17 086	-23 703	-25 853	-27 867	-30 563	-9 779	-18 048	Créanciers privées
Bonds	4 895	-2 450	-13 737	-11 188	-13 592	608	-13 042	Obligations
Commercial banks	-16 299	-13 853	-2 154	-7 413	-10 109	-4 504	1 422	Banques commerciales
Other private	-5 682	-7 400	-9 962	-9 267	-6 862	-5 883	-6 427	Autres institutions privées
Private non-guaranteed	-26 641	-35 458	-29 781	-25 332	912	33 326	84 682	Dette privée non garantie
Total debt service	**311 963**	**331 778**	**337 274**	**338 282**	**374 329**	**401 312**	**448 414**	**Total du service de la dette**
Public and publicly guaranteed	169 857	187 556	183 437	180 169	205 163	195 230	221 019	Dette publique ou garantie par l'Etat
Official creditors	71 163	76 058	72 494	79 008	87 901	81 325	101 523	Créanciers publics
Multilateral	33 772	38 749	34 126	44 404	48 435	42 224	38 239	Multilatéraux
IBRD	17 023	17 450	17 220	22 362	22 617	19 380	16 709	BIRD
IDA	1 457	1 527	1 661	1 938	2 020	2 442	2 531	IDA
Bilateral	37 390	37 309	38 368	34 604	39 466	39 100	63 284	Bilatéraux
Private creditors	98 695	111 498	110 943	101 161	117 262	113 906	119 496	Créanciers publics
Bonds	46 148	61 641	57 801	51 115	64 731	64 545	77 433	Obligations
Commercial banks	34 888	33 765	36 795	35 935	39 044	38 932	31 661	Banques commerciales
Other private	17 659	16 091	16 347	14 111	13 487	10 429	10 402	Autres institutions privées
Private non-guaranteed	142 105	144 222	153 837	158 113	169 166	206 082	227 395	Dette privée non garantie

Total external and public/publicly guaranteed long-term debt of developing countries

Millions of US dollars

B. Public and publicly guaranteed long-term debt

Total de la dette extérieure et dette publique extérieure à long terme garantie par l'Etat des pays en développement

Millions de dollars E.U.

B. Dette publique extérieure à long terme garantie par l'Etat

Country or area — Pays ou zone	1996	1997	1998	1999	2000	2001	2002	2003	2004	2005
Albania Albanie	405.1	412.1	506.1	583.4	921.3	970.9	994.8	1 231.9	1 402.6	1 374.6
Algeria Algérie	31 285.5	28 714.5	28 484.2	25 897.3	23 331.6	20 849.4	21 283.4	21 830.7	20 391.8	15 475.9
Angola Angola	9 377.3	8 681.6	9 099.6	8 713.0	8 084.8	6 982.7	7 530.9	7 620.0	8 109.9	9 427.9
Argentina Argentine	62 226.7	66 888.7	77 147.7	84 444.4	88 122.2	88 441.9	92 904.8	99 894.4	104 111.1	61 951.7
Armenia Arménie	402.7	484.4	568.6	651.4	675.1	715.6	818.5	877.2	960.7	922.5
Azerbaijan Azerbaïdjan	247.9	237.3	314.2	528.4	761.3	805.6	1 065.2	1 307.2	1 405.5	1 344.2
Bangladesh Bangladesh	14 661.0	13 876.7	15 098.7	15 995.2	15 167.7	14 741.0	16 403.5	18 083.0	19 186.4	17 937.7
Barbados Barbade	383.0	366.9	387.8	443.9	548.2	700.7	712.2	721.2	702.5	660.0
Belarus Bélarus	728.9	681.4	796.4	709.1	688.9	664.3	748.6	710.0	743.5	783.2
Belize Belize	250.4	268.1	282.9	341.0	556.6	648.5	779.3	948.4	920.9	969.7
Benin Bénin	1 447.0	1 396.4	1 472.0	1 472.9	1 441.9	1 505.4	1 689.2	1 726.2	1 827.1	1 762.4
Bhutan Bhoutan	112.9	117.6	171.0	181.8	202.2	265.2	376.9	481.5	593.3	636.7
Bolivia Bolivie	4 257.4	4 131.4	4 294.1	4 245.3	4 136.5	3 123.9	3 514.5	4 153.7	4 550.8	4 564.0
Bosnia and Herzegovina Bosnie-Herzégovine	...	...	...	2 244.2	1 959.0	1 781.9	2 035.3	2 321.0	2 690.7	2 559.9
Botswana Botswana	620.5	534.7	524.7	484.5	437.8	378.9	472.4	484.6	488.3	438.1
Brazil Brésil	96 368.1	87 772.7	99 122.0	93 876.0	98 245.7	98 194.1	101 337.0	101 277.0	97 700.5	94 496.6
Bulgaria Bulgarie	8 223.0	7 736.8	7 972.8	7 777.6	7 671.3	7 386.6	7 479.9	7 369.2	6 732.0	4 586.7
Burkina Faso Burkina Faso	1 163.6	1 143.3	1 289.6	1 361.3	1 227.8	1 314.9	1 408.8	1 597.5	1 904.8	1 919.8
Burundi Burundi	1 084.9	1 025.6	1 082.1	1 053.1	1 036.0	985.6	1 104.3	1 251.9	1 324.9	1 227.9
Cambodia Cambodge	2 177.3	2 192.7	2 261.4	2 292.9	2 328.1	2 392.8	2 587.3	2 868.4	3 079.7	3 154.7
Cameroon Cameroun	8 244.8	8 021.8	8 339.7	7 823.5	7 604.2	7 232.5	7 557.6	8 372.4	7 492.2	5 521.3
Cape Verde Cap-Vert	196.0	199.5	240.9	308.0	314.6	341.3	385.0	441.4	463.9	460.6
Central African Rep. Rép. centrafricaine	850.4	801.5	841.0	826.1	795.7	756.8	980.0	900.4	929.5	870.8

Total external and public/publicly guaranteed long-term debt of developing countries—Millions of US dollars (*continued*)

B. Public and publicly guaranteed long term debt

Total de la dette extérieure et dette publique extérieure à long terme garantie par l'Etat de pays en développement—Millions de dollars E.U. (*suite*)

B. Dette publique extérieure à long terme garantie par l'Etat

Country or area — Pays ou zone	1996	1997	1998	1999	2000	2001	2002	2003	2004	2005
Chad Tchad	926.6	928.2	1 001.5	1 054.0	1 031.2	1 023.9	1 190.9	1 461.7	1 582.2	1 537.3
Chile Chili	4 883.3	4 367.1	5 004.8	5 654.6	5 255.2	5 581.2	6 799.5	8 046.3	9 426.0	9 096.4
China Chine	102 260.2	112 821.4	99 424.1	99 217.3	94 860.0	91 775.7	88 613.2	85 329.2	89 773.2	82 853.1
Colombia Colombie	14 850.1	15 432.5	16 745.3	20 216.6	20 799.6	21 773.6	20 668.8	22 783.5	23 771.4	22 491.4
Comoros Comores	214.7	211.9	220.7	214.8	207.9	223.1	245.4	265.3	275.2	259.3
Congo Congo	4 652.3	4 270.4	4 237.2	3 920.4	3 744.1	3 617.6	3 960.7	4 412.5	5 609.2	5 161.4
Costa Rica Costa Rica	2 923.2	2 768.7	3 032.5	3 194.8	3 264.0	3 272.8	3 139.1	3 619.5	3 778.8	3 470.0
Côte d'Ivoire Côte d'Ivoire	11 366.7	10 427.1	10 799.7	9 699.1	9 063.4	8 602.7	9 110.3	9 700.5	9 827.6	9 006.8
Croatia Croatie	3 337.1	4 273.8	4 924.8	5 523.2	6 111.3	6 424.5	7 679.3	10 062.1	11 596.3	9 782.0
Dem. Rep. of the Congo Rép. dém. du Congo	9 275.2	8 628.3	9 214.3	8 262.3	7 880.2	7 586.5	8 845.4	10 161.3	10 125.0	9 411.8
Djibouti Djibouti	279.3	253.0	263.8	248.4	237.9	235.7	305.2	366.5	393.7	389.0
Dominica Dominique	102.1	94.6	98.1	99.0	147.8	193.4	200.4	206.3	224.2	231.5
Dominican Republic Rép. dominicaine	3 523.4	3 461.1	3 482.4	3 584.0	3 311.3	3 790.3	4 029.9	5 080.6	5 815.2	6 092.6
Ecuador Equateur	12 443.8	12 876.2	13 089.1	13 555.8	11 337.3	11 250.0	11 240.1	11 368.3	10 626.6	10 662.0
Egypt Egypte	29 047.5	26 978.8	27 793.9	26 269.5	24 510.0	25 342.0	25 874.9	27 265.8	27 352.7	24 892.3
El Salvador El Salvador	2 316.6	2 396.3	2 441.6	2 647.0	2 771.3	3 249.3	4 710.4	5 210.9	5 382.7	4 759.8
Equatorial Guinea Guinée équatoriale	222.2	208.6	216.5	207.9	198.9	192.1	209.1	227.7	244.4	223.9
Eritrea Erythrée	44.3	75.5	146.1	252.6	298.0	394.8	489.2	605.1	704.0	723.0
Estonia Estonie	216.5	197.5	234.4	205.5	210.5	186.5	481.7	560.1	561.8	434.7
Ethiopia Ethiopie	9 505.1	9 448.7	9 637.1	5 387.0	5 341.0	5 573.3	6 336.7	7 073.5	6 425.0	6 063.3
Fiji Fidji	159.4	172.7	156.2	134.9	114.2	101.3	131.5	195.4	193.4	225.8
Gabon Gabon	3 971.6	3 664.8	3 835.4	3 293.0	3 453.5	3 041.3	3 240.9	3 394.8	3 800.1	3 582.4
Gambia Gambie	411.9	401.2	433.6	431.1	437.9	435.3	507.3	566.6	621.8	626.4
Georgia Géorgie	1 106.3	1 189.5	1 301.0	1 309.1	1 273.9	1 310.6	1 444.9	1 564.0	1 593.1	1 494.4
Ghana Ghana	4 327.5	4 429.2	5 004.0	5 144.2	4 994.4	5 253.5	5 755.7	6 422.5	5 892.6	5 734.4

Total external and public/publicly guaranteed long-term debt of developing countries—Millions of US dollars (*continued*)

B. Public and publicly guaranteed long term debt

Total de la dette extérieure et dette publique extérieure à long terme garantie par l'Etat de pays en développement—Millions de dollars E.U. (*suite*)

B. Dette publique extérieure à long terme garantie par l'Etat

Country or area — Pays ou zone	1996	1997	1998	1999	2000	2001	2002	2003	2004	2005
Grenada Grenade	118.8	107.7	107.2	112.1	179.8	183.9	294.1	300.1	346.7	390.0
Guatemala Guatemala	2 209.2	2 323.9	2 428.6	2 531.9	2 539.7	2 928.4	3 097.7	3 426.6	3 794.5	3 687.8
Guinea Guinée	2 980.6	3 008.7	3 126.4	3 061.0	2 940.4	2 843.8	2 972.5	3 154.0	3 187.7	2 930.5
Guinea-Bissau Guinée-Bissau	856.2	838.4	874.3	834.2	715.5	627.2	662.3	712.5	737.9	671.3
Guyana Guyana	1 351.6	1 328.9	1 197.9	1 129.8	1 123.8	1 095.4	1 145.4	1 217.1	1 141.8	1 020.8
Haiti Haïti	847.8	906.4	986.5	1 045.0	1 043.0	1 031.4	1 066.3	1 208.8	1 225.4	1 276.4
Honduras Honduras	4 026.5	4 058.9	3 949.2	4 121.3	4 210.8	3 860.7	4 061.4	4 426.0	4 832.3	4 151.7
Hungary Hongrie	18 724.5	15 128.7	15 904.3	16 869.4	14 354.5	12 696.5	13 551.3	16 473.4	21 093.4	21 215.9
India Inde	78 045.2	79 398.1	84 611.3	86 410.3	80 050.9	78 818.4	82 256.5	84 640.1	89 004.4	80 280.9
Indonesia Indonésie	60 011.9	55 968.5	67 416.4	73 790.1	69 519.9	68 503.9	71 145.1	74 023.5	71 990.6	72 334.8
Iran (Islamic Rep. of) Iran (Rép. islamique d')	11 710.6	8 285.1	7 712.0	5 731.9	4 706.6	5 291.5	6 604.0	8 933.4	9 984.9	10 492.5
Jamaica Jamaïque	3 192.6	2 774.5	2 975.5	2 883.9	3 759.5	4 308.4	4 598.9	4 568.4	5 241.2	5 507.5
Jordan Jordanie	6 448.1	6 143.4	6 498.3	6 714.2	6 182.8	6 632.3	7 071.7	7 172.6	7 227.2	6 877.7
Kazakhstan Kazakhstan	1 946.5	2 621.6	3 037.8	3 360.1	3 622.5	3 450.2	3 210.4	3 469.4	3 232.9	2 183.9
Kenya Kenya	5 573.7	5 093.1	5 513.2	5 344.1	5 045.5	4 710.7	5 244.7	5 837.1	6 099.1	5 519.9
Kyrgyzstan Kirghizistan	626.3	750.6	933.9	1 134.4	1 220.3	1 256.8	1 397.3	1 584.5	1 742.4	1 670.0
Lao People's Dem. Rep. Rép. dém. pop. lao	2 185.8	2 246.8	2 373.1	2 471.3	2 452.6	2 455.9	2 620.2	1 894.9	2 036.6	1 970.9
Latvia Lettonie	300.4	313.7	404.2	864.8	827.1	978.2	1 123.6	1 238.1	1 580.2	1 318.2
Lebanon Liban	1 933.4	2 349.1	4 047.8	5 332.4	6 579.9	8 957.0	13 833.3	14 784.9	17 455.9	17 912.0
Lesotho Lesotho	663.5	641.9	660.5	661.0	656.7	578.5	631.8	676.0	724.1	646.7
Liberia Libéria	1 110.0	1 061.3	1 092.3	1 062.2	1 040.1	1 011.8	1 064.6	1 126.8	1 176.9	1 114.7
Lithuania Lituanie	736.2	1 053.4	1 220.6	2 122.6	2 194.9	2 368.9	2 484.9	2 120.9	2 514.1	1 510.8
Madagascar Madagascar	3 535.7	3 865.1	4 096.1	4 358.2	4 285.8	3 786.7	4 130.1	4 615.8	3 486.7	3 177.6
Malawi Malawi	2 092.2	2 096.3	2 304.8	2 587.0	2 544.6	2 469.1	2 670.6	2 935.0	3 295.8	3 039.9
Malaysia Malaisie	15 702.0	16 807.5	18 154.5	18 930.1	19 233.7	24 156.3	26 414.7	25 399.6	25 570.3	22 449.3

Total external and public/publicly guaranteed long-term debt of developing countries—Millions of US dollars (*continued*)
B. Public and publicly guaranteed long term debt

Total de la dette extérieure et dette publique extérieure à long terme garantie par l'Etat de pays en développement—Millions de dollars E.U. (*suite*)
B. Dette publique extérieure à long terme garantie par l'Etat

Country or area — Pays ou zone	1996	1997	1998	1999	2000	2001	2002	2003	2004	2005
Maldives Maldives	163.5	164.3	183.4	194.1	184.7	180.7	223.0	258.5	313.0	307.0
Mali Mali	2 762.7	2 701.9	2 833.1	2 813.6	2 671.0	2 642.5	2 517.8	2 910.1	3 136.0	2 842.6
Mauritania Mauritanie	2 169.2	2 077.1	2 048.9	2 147.8	2 028.5	1 914.3	1 916.0	2 054.3	2 059.7	2 043.3
Mauritius Maurice	1 152.5	1 152.5	1 126.1	1 138.2	834.5	767.0	839.6	930.1	861.3	730.9
Mexico Mexique	92 797.6	83 302.2	87 044.7	87 910.7	81 488.2	94 230.4	99 821.0	106 962.9	108 810.5	108 786.0
Mongolia Mongolie	485.8	533.3	650.0	841.1	833.4	823.7	949.0	1 137.5	1 306.6	1 266.7
Morocco Maroc	22 393.3	20 413.9	20 730.7	18 850.9	17 277.9	15 722.6	14 783.9	15 164.3	14 862.9	13 112.8
Mozambique Mozambique	5 357.8	5 211.0	6 030.8	4 880.2	4 742.4	2 586.9	2 901.8	3 206.7	3 596.4	3 727.3
Myanmar Myanmar	4 803.5	5 068.7	5 052.7	5 337.1	5 241.6	5 006.5	5 390.8	5 857.4	5 646.6	5 195.7
Nepal Népal	2 345.7	2 332.3	2 590.6	2 932.9	2 804.9	2 654.3	2 928.5	3 237.2	3 401.2	3 217.5
Nicaragua Nicaragua	5 148.3	5 364.4	5 635.6	5 778.8	5 492.3	5 437.2	5 573.2	5 893.5	4 125.1	4 113.2
Niger Niger	1 315.9	1 308.6	1 440.5	1 454.6	1 462.6	1 412.9	1 596.4	1 880.7	1 783.9	1 770.7
Nigeria Nigéria	25 430.5	22 631.2	23 445.0	22 357.7	30 019.9	29 218.1	28 057.1	31 350.2	32 637.3	20 342.2
Oman Oman	2 645.8	2 567.1	2 235.0	2 595.8	2 970.0	2 687.5	2 048.7	1 558.1	1 207.0	842.4
Pakistan Pakistan	23 621.7	23 973.4	26 140.2	28 134.7	27 173.2	26 436.2	28 015.7	30 768.6	30 889.2	29 489.6
Panama Panama	5 138.4	5 077.2	5 421.0	5 679.5	5 706.5	6 329.1	6 405.6	6 490.0	7 233.8	7 513.9
Papua New Guinea Papouasie-Nvl-Guinée	1 544.9	1 338.4	1 430.0	1 517.1	1 490.3	1 397.0	1 479.3	1 504.5	1 445.1	1 266.4
Paraguay Paraguay	1 415.2	1 463.8	1 590.6	2 074.5	2 059.8	1 981.0	2 045.4	2 200.6	2 431.0	2 263.6
Peru Pérou	20 218.9	19 215.8	19 309.8	19 491.5	19 236.9	18 898.9	20 410.5	22 530.8	24 199.1	22 222.0
Philippines Philippines	27 072.0	26 394.8	29 172.9	34 770.6	33 744.5	29 210.2	32 319.5	36 146.5	35 931.8	35 233.5
Poland Pologne	39 025.0	33 996.7	34 160.6	32 180.3	29 775.3	24 040.9	27 543.7	33 251.0	34 737.8	35 093.9
Republic of Moldova République de Moldova	548.7	795.8	796.5	719.1	852.8	792.0	825.8	848.2	754.3	699.7
Romania Roumanie	5 631.7	6 346.5	6 646.4	5 640.6	6 589.2	7 034.3	9 034.4	11 729.4	13 666.9	13 341.1
Russian Federation Fédération de Russie	101 915.5	106 541.6	121 574.3	121 188.3	111 018.3	103 790.5	96 069.1	99 054.4	102 912.0	75 359.0
Rwanda Rwanda	986.7	995.7	1 122.0	1 163.7	1 148.5	1 164.7	1 306.6	1 418.0	1 545.1	1 419.6

Total external and public/publicly guaranteed long-term debt of developing countries — Millions of US dollars (*continued*)

B. Public and publicly guaranteed long term debt

Total de la dette extérieure et dette publique extérieure à long terme garantie par l'Etat de pays en développement — Millions de dollars E.U. (*suite*)

B. Dette publique extérieure à long terme garantie par l'Etat

Country or area — Pays ou zone	1996	1997	1998	1999	2000	2001	2002	2003	2004	2005
Saint Kitts and Nevis Saint-Kitts-et-Nevis	62.7	112.0	124.4	133.8	152.7	214.7	260.9	314.9	313.5	299.3
Saint Lucia Sainte-Lucie	121.4	119.9	133.6	140.9	167.6	166.0	210.7	235.0	256.6	248.9
St. Vincent-Grenadines St. Vincent-Grenadines	95.3	94.2	109.8	163.2	164.9	163.8	174.1	195.2	223.9	248.3
Samoa Samoa	162.8	148.3	154.3	156.6	147.3	143.3	156.8	177.7	185.7	177.3
Sao Tome and Principe Sao Tomé-et-Principe	225.7	226.0	244.5	294.4	300.4	301.7	317.1	337.4	349.0	326.7
Senegal Sénégal	3 229.3	3 235.4	3 481.9	3 337.2	3 176.3	3 142.6	3 506.3	3 921.4	3 440.4	3 467.4
Serbia and Montenegro Serbie-et-Monténégro	6 526.6	6 108.9	6 461.1	6 194.6	6 177.9	6 177.5	7 814.9	8 475.1	8 519.7	7 972.1
Seychelles Seychelles	175.7	169.3	199.6	210.8	219.5	220.6	283.6	328.5	345.2	401.7
Sierra Leone Sierra Leone	1 046.7	1 023.5	1 093.4	1 066.0	1 005.8	1 120.9	1 260.0	1 417.7	1 509.6	1 420.4
Slovakia Slovaquie	3 962.8	4 449.5	5 417.4	5 957.7	6 304.2	5 531.2	4 295.0	4 507.7	5 162.9	3 340.0
Solomon Islands Iles Salomon	100.5	96.5	113.7	125.3	120.7	130.9	150.2	151.3	155.3	148.1
Somalia Somalie	1 918.2	1 852.5	1 886.4	1 859.4	1 825.1	1 794.7	1 859.9	1 936.1	1 949.0	1 881.5
South Africa Afrique du Sud	10 347.5	11 516.9	10 667.8	8 173.3	9 087.7	7 941.0	9 427.1	9 120.1	9 793.4	11 661.6
Sri Lanka Sri Lanka	7 120.4	7 077.5	8 063.6	8 412.9	7 944.1	7 499.7	8 400.4	9 158.8	9 847.5	9 811.6
Sudan Soudan	9 369.2	8 998.2	9 225.9	8 852.0	10 447.9	10 641.8	10 938.9	11 391.4	11 741.1	11 163.0
Swaziland Swaziland	271.0	283.6	307.1	308.1	286.7	283.2	335.8	386.8	410.9	450.5
Syrian Arab Republic Rép. arabe syrienne	16 762.2	16 326.4	16 352.6	16 142.4	15 929.8	15 809.2	15 848.7	15 847.6	15 742.4	5 640.2
Tajikistan Tadjikistan	656.8	669.0	702.5	741.3	755.1	761.6	901.1	911.8	758.3	785.3
Thailand Thaïlande	16 887.1	22 292.0	28 087.6	31 305.8	29 452.5	26 208.0	22 523.8	17 701.6	15 247.5	13 483.0
TFYR of Macedonia L'ex-R.y. Macédoine	856.3	941.7	1 053.8	1 138.3	1 192.1	1 145.2	1 264.6	1 437.7	1 536.8	1 613.2
Togo Togo	1 310.2	1 214.1	1 325.3	1 286.6	1 227.6	1 191.9	1 323.4	1 484.9	1 608.7	1 468.7
Tonga Tonga	62.5	57.7	64.2	68.7	65.1	62.7	72.6	85.6	87.5	83.2
Trinidad and Tobago Trinité-et-Tobago	1 876.2	1 532.8	1 477.9	1 485.4	1 584.7	1 532.4	1 543.9	1 598.5	1 417.8	1 196.9
Tunisia Tunisie	9 376.8	9 333.2	9 494.3	9 474.5	8 884.3	9 071.0	10 933.5	13 234.5	14 575.0	12 982.3
Turkey Turquie	48 403.8	47 513.3	50 197.3	50 505.7	56 191.4	54 046.8	59 986.6	64 244.3	68 352.4	62 580.4

66 Total external and public/publicly guaranteed long-term debt of developing countries — Millions of US dollars (*continued*)

B. Public and publicly guaranteed long term debt

Total de la dette extérieure et dette publique extérieure à long terme garantie par l'Etat de pays en développement — Millions de dollars E.U. (*suite*)

B. Dette publique extérieure à long terme garantie par l'Etat

Country or area — Pays ou zone	1996	1997	1998	1999	2000	2001	2002	2003	2004	2005
Uganda Ouganda	3 162.0	3 377.0	3 386.4	2 995.3	3 052.4	3 305.9	3 577.8	4 190.4	4 460.8	4 250.3
Ukraine Ukraine	6 647.5	7 015.2	8 971.9	9 590.4	8 141.8	8 098.5	8 272.1	8 890.9	10 589.5	10 458.4
United Rep. of Tanzania Rép.-Unie de Tanzanie	6 104.3	5 775.6	6 086.9	6 316.3	5 732.0	5 276.3	5 719.5	5 722.4	6 226.4	6 183.0
Uruguay Uruguay	4 080.2	4 549.7	5 108.2	5 079.6	5 512.6	6 030.6	6 683.7	7 094.2	7 437.6	7 865.6
Uzbekistan Ouzbékistan	1 980.8	2 107.6	2 660.7	3 565.2	3 763.5	3 905.4	4 005.5	4 149.0	4 117.4	3 638.5
Vanuatu Vanuatu	42.9	39.7	55.2	64.5	73.1	70.2	76.5	82.0	83.6	71.9
Venezuela (Bolivarian Rep. of) Venezuela (Rép. bolivar. du)	27 745.9	27 053.4	28 034.9	27 653.9	27 432.5	24 915.3	23 063.8	24 155.6	24 640.3	29 317.3
Viet Nam Viet Nam	21 962.3	18 982.4	19 873.7	20 479.4	11 586.1	11 436.3	12 178.6	14 363.3	15 613.7	16 512.6
Yemen Yémen	5 622.0	3 433.8	5 231.8	5 372.3	4 059.2	4 276.8	4 497.4	4 744.5	4 799.3	4 717.1
Zambia Zambie	5 369.2	5 251.5	5 326.3	4 505.4	4 443.7	4 826.6	5 264.5	5 582.3	5 871.7	4 084.9
Zimbabwe Zimbabwe	3 317.2	3 066.9	3 191.3	2 982.5	2 774.0	2 678.8	3 020.7	3 388.2	3 558.0	3 221.7

Source

World Bank, Washington, D.C., "Global Development Finance 2006", volumes 1 and 2.

Notes

& The following abbreviations have been used in the table:

IBRD: International Bank for Reconstruction and Development
IDA: International Development Association

Source

Banque mondiale, Washington, D.C., "Global Development Finance 2006 ", volumes 1 et 2.

Notes

& Les abbréviations ci-après ont été utilisées dans le tableau :

BIRD : Banque internationale pour la réconstruction et la développement
IDA : Association internationale de développement

Technical notes: tables 65 and 66

Table 65: Foreign exchange rates are shown in units of national currency per US dollar. The exchange rates are classified into three broad categories, reflecting both the role of the authorities in the determination of the exchange and/or the multiplicity of exchange rates in a country. The *market rate* is used to describe exchange rates determined largely by market forces; the *official rate* is an exchange rate determined by the authorities, sometimes in a flexible manner. For countries maintaining multiple exchange arrangements, the rates are labelled *principal rate*, *secondary rate*, and *tertiary rate*. Unless otherwise stated, the table refers to end of period and period averages of market exchange rates or official exchange rates. For further information see *International Financial Statistics* and www.imf.org.

Table 66: The data on external debt for developing countries were extracted from *Global Development Finance 2006*, published by the World Bank. In this table, developing countries are those in which 2004 GNI per capita was below $10,066.

The World Bank Debtor Reporting System (DRS) maintains statistics on the external debt of developing countries on a loan-by-loan basis. The estimated total external indebtedness of developing countries is a combination of DRS data and other information obtained from creditors through the debt data collection systems of other agencies such as the Bank for International Settlements (BIS) and the Organization for Economic Co-operation and Development (OECD), supplemented by market sources and estimates made by country economists of the World Bank and desk officers of the International Monetary Fund (IMF).

Long-term external debt is defined as debt that has an original or extended maturity of more than one year and that is owed to non-residents and is repayable in foreign currency, goods, or services. Long-term debt has three components: a) public debt, which is an external obligation of a public debtor, including the national government, a political subdivision (or an agency of either), and autonomous public bodies; b) publicly guaranteed debt, which is an external obligation of a private debtor that is guaranteed for repayment by a public entity; and c) private non-guaranteed external debt, which is an external obligation of a private debtor that is not guaranteed for repayment by a public entity. Public and publicly guaranteed long-term debts are aggregated.

All data related to public and publicly guaranteed debt are from debtors except for those on lending by some multilateral agencies, in which case the data are taken from the creditors' records. These creditors include the African Development Bank, the Asian Development Bank, the Central Bank for Economic Integration, the Inter-American Development Bank, the International Bank for Reconstruction and

Notes techniques : tableaux 65 et 66

Tableau 65: Les taux des changes sont exprimés par le nombre d'unités de monnaie nationale pour un dollar des Etats-Unis. Les taux de change sont classés en trois catégories, qui dénotent le rôle des autorités dans l'établissement des taux de change et/ou la multiplicité des taux de change dans un pays. Par *taux du marché*, on entend les taux de change déterminés essentiellement par les forces du marché; le *taux officiel* est un taux de change établi par les autorités, parfois selon des dispositions souples. Pour les pays qui continuent à mettre en œuvre des régimes de taux de change multiples, les taux sont désignés par les appellations suivantes: "taux principal", "taux secondaire" et "taux tertiaire". Sauf indication con-traire, le tableau indique des taux de fin de période et les moyennes sur la période, des taux de change du marché ou des taux de change officiels. Pour plus de renseignements, voir *Statistiques financières internationales* et www.imf.org.

Tableau 66: Les données concernant la dette extérieure des pays en développement sont tirées de «*Global Development Finance 2006*», publié par la Banque. Les pays en développement sont dans ce tableau ceux où le RNB par habitant était en 2004 inférieur à 10 066 dollars.

Le Système de notification de la dette de la Banque mondiale sert à tenir à jour prêt par prêt les statistiques de la dette extérieure des pays en développement. Le total estimatif de la dette extérieure des pays en développement a été calculé en combinant les données du Système de notification avec d'autres informations obtenues auprès des créanciers par le biais des systèmes de collecte de données d'autres organismes, tels que la Banque des règlements internationaux (BRI) et l'Organisation de coopération et développement économiques, ou de sources du marché, et avec des estimations des économistes chargés des pays à la Banque mondiale et au Fonds monétaire international (FMI).

La dette extérieure à long terme s'entend de celle dont la maturité d'origine (ou la maturité après prorogation) est à plus d'un an, contractée auprès de non-résidents et remboursable en devises, en biens ou en services. La dette à long terme comporte trois éléments : a) la dette publique, dette (ou administration relevant de l'un ou de l'autre), et administrations publiques autonomes; b) la dette garantie par une administration publique, obligation extérieure d'un débiteur privé dont le remboursement est garanti par une entité publique; c) la dette extérieure privée non garantie, obligation extérieure d'un débiteur privé dont le remboursement n'est pas garanti par une entité publique. La dette extérieure publique et la dette extérieure garantie à long terme sont agrégées.

Toutes les données concernant la dette publique et la dette garantie par une entité publique proviennent des débiteurs, sauf celles concernant les prêts consentis par certains orga-

Development (IBRD) and the International Development Association (IDA). (The IBRD and IDA are components of the World Bank.)

The data referring to public and publicly guaranteed debt do not include data for (a) transactions with the International Monetary Fund, (b) debt repayable in local currency, (c) direct investment and (d) short-term debt (that is, debt with an original maturity of less than a year).

The data referring to private non-guaranteed debt also exclude the above items but include contractual obligations on loans to direct-investment enterprises by foreign parent companies or their affiliates.

Data are aggregated by type of creditor. The breakdown is as follows:

Official creditors

(a) Loans from international organizations (multilateral loans), excluding loans from funds administered by an international organization on behalf of a single donor government. The latter are classified as loans from governments;

(b) Loans from governments (bilateral loans) and from autonomous public bodies;

Private creditors

(a) Suppliers: Credits from manufacturers, exporters, or other suppliers of goods;

(b) Financial markets: Loans from private banks and other private financial institutions as well as publicly issued and privately placed bonds;

(c) Other: External liabilities on account of nationalized properties and unclassified debts to private creditors.

A distinction is made between the following categories of external public debt:

- Debt outstanding (including undisbursed) is the sum of disbursed and undisbursed debt and represents the total outstanding external obligations of the borrower at year-end;
- Debt outstanding (disbursed only) is total outstanding debt drawn by the borrower at year-end;
- Commitments are the total of loans for which contracts are signed in the year specified;
- Disbursements are drawings on outstanding loan commitments during the year specified;
- Service payments are actual repayments of principal amortization and interest payments made in foreign currencies, goods or services in the year specified;

nismes multilatéraux, pour lesquels les données proviennent des dossiers des créanciers : il s'agit notamment de la Banque africaine de développement, de la Banque asiatique de développement, de la Banque centrale d'intégration économique, de la Banque interaméricaine de développement, de la Banque internationale de reconstruction et de développement (BIRD) et de l'Association internationale de développement (IDA) (la BIRD et l'IDA font partie du groupe de la Banque mondiale).

Les statistiques relatives à la dette publique ou à la dette garantie par l'Etat ne comprennent pas les données concernant: (a) les transactions avec le Fonds monétaire international; (b) la dette remboursable en monnaie nationale; (c) les investissements directs; et (d) la dette à court terme (c'est-à-dire la dette dont l'échéance initiale est inférieure à un an).

Les statistiques relatives à la dette privée non garantie ne comprennent pas non plus les éléments précités, mais comprennent les obligations contractuelles au titre des prêts consentis par des sociétés mères étrangères ou leurs filiales à des entreprises créées dans le cadre d'investissements directs.

Les données sont groupées par type de créancier, comme suit:

Créanciers publics

(a) Les prêts obtenus auprès d'organisations internationales (prêts multilatéraux), à l'exclusion des prêts au titre de fonds administrés par une organisation internationale pour le compte d'un gouvernement donateur précis, qui sont classés comme prêts consentis par des gouvernements;

(b) Les prêts consentis par des gouvernements (prêts bilatéraux) et par des organisations publiques autonomes.

Créanciers privés

(a) Fournisseurs: Crédits consentis par des fabricants exportateurs et autres fournisseurs de biens;

(b) Marchés financiers: prêts consentis par des banques privées et autres institutions financières privées, et émissions publiques d'obligations placées auprès d'investisseurs privés;

(c) Autres créanciers: engagements vis-à-vis de l'extérieur au titre des biens nationalisés et dettes diverses à l'égard de créanciers privés.

On fait une distinction entre les catégories suivantes de dette publique extérieure:

- L'encours de la dette (y compris les fonds non décaissés) est la somme des fonds décaissés et non décaissés et représente le total des obligations extérieures en cours de l'emprunteur à la fin de l'année;

Technical notes: tables 65 and 66 (*continued*)

- Net flows (or net lending) are disbursements minus principal repayments;
- Net transfers are net flows minus interest payments or disbursements minus total debt-service payments.

The countries included in the table are those for which data are sufficiently reliable to provide a meaningful presentation of debt outstanding and future service payments.

Notes techniques : tableaux 65 et 66 (*suite*)

- L'encours de la dette (fonds décaissés seulement) est le montant total des tirages effectués par l'emprunteur sur sa dette en cours à la fin de l'année;
- Les engagements représentent le total des prêts dont les contrats ont été signés au cours de l'année considérée;
- Les décaissements sont les sommes tirées sur l'encours des prêts pendant l'année considérée;
- Les paiements au titre du service de la dette sont les remboursements effectifs du principal et les paiements d'intérêts effectués en devises, biens ou services pendant l'année considérée;
- Les flux nets (ou prêts nets) sont les décaissements moins les remboursements de principal;
- Les transferts nets désignent les flux nets moins les paiements d'intérêts, ou les décaissements moins le total des paiements au titre du service de la dette.

Les pays figurant sur ce tableau sont ceux pour lesquels les données sont suffisamment fiables pour permettre une présentation significative de l'encours de la dette et des paiements futurs au titre du service de la dette.

Disbursements of bilateral and multilateral official development assistance and official aid to individual recipients

Versements d'aide publique au développement et d'aide publique bilatérales et multilatérales aux bénéficiaires

Country or area Pays ou zone	Year Année	Net disbursements (US $) — Versements nets ($E.U.) Bilateral (millions) Bilatérale (millions)	Multilateral[1] (millions) Multilatérale[1] (millions)	Total (millions) Total (millions)	Per capita Par habitant
Developing Countries, total Pays en développement, total	**2001**	**35 123.5**	**15 545.8**	**50 669.3**	...
	2002	**40 752.2**	**16 749.0**	**57 501.2**	...
	2003	**49 755.4**	**17 451.9**	**67 207.2**	...
	2004	**54 282.2**	**21 353.8**	**75 636.0**	...
	2005	**82 133.3**	**21 839.1**	**103 972.4**	...
Afghanistan Afghanistan	2001	322.9	76.3	399.2	18.6
	2002	985.9	290.5	1 276.4	57.5
	2003	1 199.7	362.8	1 562.5	67.6
	2004	1 701.1	418.4	2 119.5	88.0
	2005	2 191.7	536.4	2 728.1	108.8
Albania Albanie	2001	149.8	117.4	267.2	86.6
	2002	177.2	122.6	299.8	96.8
	2003	230.3	109.7	340.0	109.1
	2004	165.0	121.9	286.9	91.5
	2005	190.0	119.7	309.6	98.2
Algeria Algérie	2001	63.4	106.5	170.0	5.5
	2002	122.8	62.9	185.6	5.9
	2003	168.8	68.2	237.0	7.4
	2004	234.7	79.7	314.4	9.7
	2005	289.7	71.4	361.1	11.0
Angola Angola	2001	179.4	104.2	283.6	19.8
	2002	286.4	129.1	415.5	28.2
	2003	372.2	122.3	494.5	32.6
	2004	1 015.7	131.3	1 147.0	73.4
	2005	258.2	183.0	441.2	27.4
Anguilla Anguilla	2001	3.0	0.5	3.5	309.7
	2002	1.8	-1.1	0.7	62.7
	2003	1.8	2.1	3.9	332.5
	2004	1.4	1.3	2.7	223.1
	2005	4.3	-0.3	4.0	327.2
Antigua and Barbuda Antigua-et-Barbuda	2001	6.0	1.8	7.8	99.9
	2002	11.1	4.1	15.2	190.4
	2003	3.0	2.0	5.0	62.2
	2004	1.2	1.4	2.6	31.6
	2005	6.9	0.2	7.1	85.7
Argentina Argentine	2001	10.1	132.4	142.5	3.8
	2002	51.9	-1.5	50.4	1.3
	2003	98.2	2.9	101.1	2.7
	2004	78.5	13.9	92.4	2.4
	2005	77.9	20.0	97.9	2.5
Armenia Arménie	2001	124.2	73.2	197.4	64.4
	2002	171.4	120.8	292.2	95.8
	2003	127.4	120.8	248.2	81.7
	2004	133.1	119.9	253.1	83.6
	2005	148.1	44.2	192.4	63.7
Azerbaijan Azerbaïdjan	2001	148.4	73.0	221.5	27.0
	2002	232.2	104.9	337.0	41.0
	2003	158.5	131.7	290.2	35.1
	2004	92.3	57.5	149.8	18.0
	2005	109.7	84.0	193.7	23.2

Disbursements of bilateral and multilateral official development assistance and official aid to individual recipients (*continued*)
Versements d'aide publique au développement et d'aide publique bilatérales et multilatérales aux bénéficiaires (*suite*)

Country or area Pays ou zone	Year Année	Net disbursements (US $) — Versements nets ($E.U.) Bilateral (millions) Bilatérale (millions)	Multilateral[1] (millions) Multilatérale[1] (millions)	Total (millions) Total (millions)	Per capita Par habitant
Bahrain Bahreïn	2001	1.2	-0.2	1.0	1.5
	2002	1.1	2.6	3.7	5.5
	2003	1.1	-0.1	1.1	1.5
	2004	1.4	-0.8	0.6	0.9
Bangladesh Bangladesh	2001	578.4	432.3	1 010.7	7.1
	2002	520.8	375.9	896.7	6.2
	2003	695.0	687.1	1 382.1	9.4
	2004	632.7	754.2	1 386.9	9.2
	2005	562.9	726.7	1 289.6	8.4
Barbados Barbade	2001	2.8	-4.0	-1.2	-4.1
	2002	2.8	0.4	3.2	11.1
	2003	2.4	17.3	19.7	68.1
	2004	2.6	26.3	28.8	99.0
	2005	6.1	-8.2	-2.1	-7.3
Belarus Bélarus	2005	33.7	9.3	43.0	4.4
Belize Belize	2001	10.2	10.9	21.1	84.1
	2002	9.0	9.3	18.3	71.1
	2003	4.2	7.8	12.0	45.5
	2004	3.8	4.5	8.3	30.9
	2005	7.5	5.4	12.9	46.7
Benin Bénin	2001	144.5	126.4	270.8	36.3
	2002	140.1	73.5	213.5	27.7
	2003	196.1	99.8	295.9	37.2
	2004	210.0	175.0	385.0	46.8
	2005	206.9	142.0	348.9	41.1
Bhutan Bhoutan	2001	42.5	19.3	61.8	107.6
	2002	42.9	31.7	74.5	126.1
	2003	52.1	24.7	76.8	126.3
	2004	53.1	25.5	78.6	126.2
	2005	57.0	32.8	89.8	140.9
Bolivia Bolivie	2001	535.8	197.7	733.4	86.4
	2002	482.2	197.1	679.2	78.4
	2003	552.9	375.5	928.4	105.1
	2004	557.3	211.6	768.9	85.3
	2005	388.3	190.1	578.3	63.0
Bosnia and Herzegovina Bosnie-Herzégovine	2001	376.7	241.9	618.6	160.8
	2002	292.3	250.6	542.9	139.9
	2003	331.2	202.0	533.2	136.8
	2004	298.8	351.4	650.2	166.5
	2005	287.6	236.4	524.1	133.9
Botswana Botswana	2001	24.2	3.2	27.4	15.6
	2002	36.7	2.2	38.9	21.9
	2003	27.4	2.1	29.5	16.4
	2004	31.8	16.9	48.7	26.8
	2005	51.9	19.0	70.9	38.6
Brazil Brésil	2001	156.8	71.0	227.8	1.3
	2002	197.6	3.8	201.4	1.1
	2003	184.3	8.4	192.6	1.1
	2004	147.2	8.4	155.6	0.8
	2005	170.9	19.7	190.6	1.0

Country or area Pays ou zone	Year Année	Net disbursements (US $) — Versements nets ($E.U.)			
		Bilateral (millions) Bilatérale (millions)	Multilateral[1] (millions) Multilatérale[1] (millions)	Total (millions) Total (millions)	Per capita Par habitant
Burkina Faso Burkina Faso	2001	220.9	155.1	376.1	30.7
	2002	229.9	196.3	426.2	33.7
	2003	265.7	238.3	504.0	38.5
	2004	331.4	282.2	613.6	45.4
	2005	338.5	319.3	657.8	47.2
Burundi Burundi	2001	54.7	82.4	137.1	20.0
	2002	84.7	86.8	171.5	24.3
	2003	121.2	106.2	227.4	31.2
	2004	185.8	175.8	361.5	47.8
	2005	180.7	184.1	364.8	46.4
Cambodia Cambodge	2001	264.8	151.9	416.7	32.0
	2002	272.8	188.7	461.4	34.8
	2003	319.2	184.3	503.5	37.3
	2004	297.4	161.3	458.8	33.4
	2005	344.4	175.5	520.0	37.3
Cameroon Cameroun	2001	356.7	131.5	488.2	30.1
	2002	436.2	219.8	655.9	39.4
	2003	755.8	142.9	898.7	52.8
	2004	572.1	199.1	771.2	44.3
	2005	336.0	76.9	412.9	23.2
Cape Verde Cap-Vert	2001	49.0	28.5	77.5	168.1
	2002	43.2	49.9	93.2	197.2
	2003	90.2	53.3	143.5	296.7
	2004	90.8	48.5	139.3	281.3
	2005	104.2	56.4	160.6	316.9
Central African Rep. Rép. centrafricaine	2001	47.9	18.0	65.9	16.8
	2002	39.6	20.1	59.7	14.9
	2003	32.4	18.8	51.2	12.6
	2004	54.8	55.1	109.9	26.7
	2005	62.2	33.0	95.2	22.7
Chad Tchad	2001	72.8	111.8	184.6	21.0
	2002	67.0	159.1	226.2	24.8
	2003	95.5	151.0	246.5	26.0
	2004	163.1	155.1	318.2	32.4
	2005	166.6	213.2	379.8	37.4
Chile Chili	2001	39.6	17.1	56.8	3.6
	2002	-13.8	4.9	-8.9	-0.6
	2003	61.4	16.6	78.0	4.9
	2004	25.9	29.7	55.6	3.4
	2005	75.6	75.0	150.6	9.2
China[2] Chine[2]	2001	1 079.8	343.4	1 423.1	1.1
	2002	1 211.5	227.4	1 438.9	1.1
	2003	1 139.5	174.7	1 314.2	1.0
	2004	1 584.9	63.0	1 647.8	1.3
	2005	1 689.4	39.2	1 728.5	1.3
Colombia Colombie	2001	372.3	7.1	379.4	9.0
	2002	426.1	12.4	438.5	10.2
	2003	767.1	32.8	799.8	18.3
	2004	481.7	36.6	518.3	11.7
	2005	457.9	51.9	509.9	11.3
Comoros Comores	2001	9.6	16.2	25.8	36.0
	2002	11.0	16.6	27.6	37.4
	2003	11.1	13.3	24.4	32.2
	2004	13.9	11.6	25.5	32.8
	2005	17.2	8.1	25.2	31.6

Disbursements of bilateral and multilateral official development assistance and official aid to individual recipients (*continued*)
Versements d'aide publique au développement et d'aide publique bilatérales et multilatérales aux bénéficiaires (*suite*)

Country or area Pays ou zone	Year Année	Net disbursements (US $) — Versements nets ($E.U.) Bilateral (millions) Bilatérale (millions)	Multilateral[1] (millions) Multilatérale[1] (millions)	Total (millions) Total (millions)	Per capita Par habitant
Congo Congo	2001	29.6	44.6	74.2	22.6
	2002	41.4	15.4	56.8	16.9
	2003	33.9	35.0	68.9	20.0
	2004	47.8	67.6	115.4	32.7
	2005	1 359.5	89.3	1 448.8	401.3
Cook Islands Iles Cook	2001	3.9	0.9	4.8	308.3
	2002	3.5	0.3	3.8	249.4
	2003	4.6	1.2	5.8	393.3
	2004	5.9	2.9	8.8	610.6
	2005	7.0	0.8	7.8	554.2
Costa Rica Costa Rica	2001	6.1	-5.0	1.1	0.3
	2002	4.5	-0.2	4.3	1.0
	2003	31.0	-3.7	27.3	6.5
	2004	11.4	2.6	14.0	3.3
	2005	25.0	3.9	28.9	6.7
Côte d'Ivoire Côte d'Ivoire	2001	158.5	9.8	168.4	9.7
	2002	831.1	236.4	1 067.5	60.3
	2003	281.2	-27.7	253.5	14.1
	2004	196.6	-36.9	159.7	8.7
	2005	151.0	-32.4	118.6	6.4
Croatia Croatie	2001	74.4	24.5	98.9	22.0
	2002	82.1	29.8	111.9	24.8
	2003	80.3	37.9	118.2	26.1
	2004	87.4	32.7	120.1	26.4
	2005	61.3	60.8	122.1	26.8
Cuba Cuba	2001	33.7	19.4	53.1	4.8
	2002	49.6	10.8	60.5	5.4
	2003	59.3	15.2	74.5	6.6
	2004	69.8	26.8	96.6	8.6
	2005	68.7	18.9	87.6	7.8
Dem. Rep. of the Congo Rép. dém. du Congo	2001	143.4	99.6	242.9	4.7
	2002	351.0	823.7	1 174.7	21.9
	2003	5 009.5	406.4	5 415.9	98.2
	2004	1 165.0	659.2	1 824.1	32.0
	2005	1 034.3	792.8	1 827.1	31.1
Djibouti Djibouti	2001	28.1	29.7	57.8	77.3
	2002	36.9	38.7	75.6	99.1
	2003	37.0	39.4	76.4	98.3
	2004	39.4	27.2	66.7	84.3
	2005	53.7	23.1	76.8	95.5
Dominica Dominique	2001	5.0	13.9	18.8	275.6
	2002	14.0	15.9	29.9	438.1
	2003	3.4	7.5	10.8	158.9
	2004	10.7	18.3	29.0	425.7
	2005	4.5	10.5	15.0	221.4
Dominican Republic Rép. dominicaine	2001	101.9	4.8	106.6	12.0
	2002	138.2	6.5	144.7	16.0
	2003	60.4	8.2	68.6	7.5
	2004	84.5	-0.1	84.4	9.1
	2005	56.6	19.9	76.5	8.1
Ecuador Equateur	2001	147.6	24.8	172.4	13.8
	2002	205.1	10.0	215.1	17.0
	2003	173.6	1.2	174.9	13.7
	2004	158.5	-0.2	158.3	12.3
	2005	174.8	35.0	209.8	16.1

Country or area Pays ou zone	Year Année	Net disbursements (US $) — Versements nets ($E.U.) Bilateral (millions) Bilatérale (millions)	Multilateral[1] (millions) Multilatérale[1] (millions)	Total (millions) Total (millions)	Per capita Par habitant
Egypt Egypte	2001	1 090.3	104.0	1 194.3	17.6
	2002	1 123.9	82.5	1 206.4	17.5
	2003	775.1	84.1	859.2	12.2
	2004	1 175.6	260.4	1 436.0	20.1
	2005	658.8	237.8	896.5	12.3
El Salvador El Salvador	2001	231.1	5.5	236.6	37.6
	2002	217.9	14.4	232.3	36.3
	2003	170.4	21.1	191.4	29.5
	2004	201.7	14.1	215.9	32.8
	2005	162.4	34.3	196.7	29.5
Equatorial Guinea Guinée équatoriale	2001	13.1	0.6	13.7	31.1
	2002	13.7	6.6	20.2	44.8
	2003	17.6	3.4	21.0	45.4
	2004	23.1	6.4	29.5	62.4
	2005	29.6	9.4	39.0	80.5
Eritrea Erythrée	2001	151.4	126.5	277.9	72.5
	2002	120.7	96.5	217.2	54.3
	2003	185.5	130.7	316.1	75.7
	2004	177.5	90.3	267.8	61.5
	2005	226.4	131.9	358.2	79.1
Ethiopia Ethiopie	2001	367.1	708.7	1 075.8	15.1
	2002	489.2	774.3	1 263.5	17.3
	2003	1 033.3	528.1	1 561.5	20.8
	2004	1 024.7	757.4	1 782.1	23.1
	2005	1 201.7	705.9	1 907.6	24.2
Fiji Fidji	2001	24.0	1.7	25.7	31.8
	2002	31.3	2.5	33.8	41.5
	2003	42.9	7.9	50.8	62.1
	2004	36.4	27.1	63.5	77.2
	2005	38.8	24.8	63.6	76.8
Gabon Gabon	2001	-8.0	16.5	8.5	7.0
	2002	49.5	22.2	71.6	58.3
	2003	-41.2	30.1	-11.1	-8.9
	2004	23.5	16.3	39.9	31.4
	2005	29.8	24.0	53.8	41.7
Gambia Gambie	2001	13.4	37.7	51.1	35.7
	2002	17.5	40.3	57.9	39.2
	2003	19.7	40.0	59.6	39.1
	2004	11.6	53.6	65.2	41.5
	2005	15.0	43.0	58.1	35.9
Georgia Géorgie	2001	151.6	142.0	293.5	62.9
	2002	209.6	92.3	301.9	65.4
	2003	163.9	53.0	216.9	47.5
	2004	209.1	95.4	304.5	67.4
	2005	198.4	102.8	301.2	67.3
Ghana Ghana	2001	386.7	251.3	638.0	30.9
	2002	406.2	238.0	644.2	30.5
	2003	478.8	464.8	943.6	43.7
	2004	896.8	456.3	1 353.0	61.3
	2005	602.7	503.4	1 106.1	49.1
Grenada Grenade	2001	3.3	4.1	7.5	73.6
	2002	2.2	9.1	11.3	110.2
	2003	8.3	3.4	11.7	112.7
	2004	10.5	5.3	15.8	151.1
	2005	20.0	24.8	44.7	424.9

Disbursements of bilateral and multilateral official development assistance and official aid to individual recipients (*continued*)
Versements d'aide publique au développement et d'aide publique bilatérales et multilatérales aux bénéficiaires (*suite*)

Country or area Pays ou zone	Year Année	Net disbursements (US $) — Versements nets ($E.U.)			
		Bilateral (millions) Bilatérale (millions)	Multilateral[1] (millions) Multilatérale[1] (millions)	Total (millions) Total (millions)	Per capita Par habitant
Guatemala Guatemala	2001	201.2	24.8	226.0	19.6
	2002	199.6	48.2	247.8	21.0
	2003	216.0	29.3	245.4	20.3
	2004	203.7	15.5	219.1	17.7
	2005	218.5	33.3	251.8	19.8
Guinea Guinée	2001	122.1	159.6	281.7	33.7
	2002	125.6	117.0	242.5	28.5
	2003	134.6	104.6	239.1	27.6
	2004	178.3	101.9	280.2	31.7
	2005	127.8	54.1	181.9	20.2
Guinea-Bissau Guinée-Bissau	2001	30.4	28.8	59.2	41.9
	2002	25.8	33.5	59.3	40.8
	2003	97.6	47.6	145.2	96.7
	2004	28.6	48.4	77.0	49.7
	2005	39.4	39.6	79.0	49.5
Guyana Guyana	2001	46.0	51.4	97.4	132.5
	2002	34.0	30.6	64.6	87.7
	2003	28.7	57.9	86.5	117.3
	2004	70.3	63.7	134.0	181.3
	2005	38.7	98.0	136.7	184.8
Haiti Haïti	2001	136.0	34.7	170.6	19.6
	2002	125.4	29.9	155.4	17.5
	2003	153.2	59.0	212.2	23.6
	2004	209.1	50.5	259.5	28.4
	2005	354.4	160.5	514.8	55.4
Honduras Honduras	2001	422.3	254.7	677.1	107.1
	2002	297.9	172.5	470.4	73.0
	2003	235.5	155.3	390.8	59.5
	2004	328.4	316.8	645.2	96.3
	2005	456.1	223.0	679.1	99.4
India Inde	2001	904.5	801.3	1 705.8	1.6
	2002	785.3	657.8	1 443.1	1.3
	2003	384.3	541.7	926.1	0.8
	2004	14.6	676.2	690.8	0.6
	2005	846.3	874.6	1 720.8	1.5
Indonesia Indonésie	2001	1 345.2	97.0	1 442.1	6.7
	2002	1 162.0	123.2	1 285.2	5.9
	2003	1 550.7	164.9	1 715.6	7.8
	2004	-146.3	226.8	80.5	0.4
	2005	2 247.2	230.1	2 477.3	11.0
Iran (Islamic Rep. of) Iran (Rép. islamique d')	2001	90.8	22.5	113.4	1.7
	2002	81.5	31.6	113.1	1.7
	2003	102.1	25.8	127.9	1.9
	2004	138.9	32.9	171.8	2.5
	2005	78.2	21.0	99.2	1.4
Iraq Iraq	2001	100.8	20.0	120.8	4.7
	2002	85.1	20.8	105.8	4.0
	2003	2 095.0	70.4	2 165.4	80.5
	2004	4 393.8	142.0	4 535.8	165.2
	2005	21 426.6	53.2	21 479.8	767.2
Jamaica Jamaïque	2001	-1.0	44.2	43.2	16.6
	2002	-3.8	28.3	24.5	9.3
	2003	1.1	2.1	3.1	1.2
	2004	7.8	67.2	75.1	28.2
	2005	11.2	24.3	35.5	13.2

Disbursements of bilateral and multilateral official development assistance and official aid to individual recipients *(continued)*
Versements d'aide publique au développement et d'aide publique bilatérales et multilatérales aux bénéficiaires *(suite)*

Country or area Pays ou zone	Year Année	Net disbursements (US $) — Versements nets ($E.U.) Bilateral (millions) Bilatérale (millions)	Multilateral[1] (millions) Multilatérale[1] (millions)	Total (millions) Total (millions)	Per capita Par habitant
Jordan Jordanie	2001	302.1	133.1	435.1	88.5
	2002	370.9	148.5	519.4	102.7
	2003	1 092.2	134.6	1 226.7	235.6
	2004	433.8	147.2	581.0	108.2
	2005	440.8	145.4	586.2	105.7
Kazakhstan Kazakhstan	2001	122.7	15.9	138.6	9.3
	2002	143.9	18.4	162.3	10.9
	2003	228.0	15.3	243.3	16.2
	2004	203.3	21.7	224.9	14.9
	2005	153.3	21.4	174.7	11.5
Kenya Kenya	2001	270.5	185.7	456.2	14.2
	2002	288.1	93.0	381.1	11.6
	2003	320.3	198.9	519.2	15.4
	2004	470.8	194.5	665.3	19.2
	2005	494.6	259.7	754.3	21.2
Kiribati Kiribati	2001	10.4	2.0	12.4	144.7
	2002	18.7	2.1	20.8	238.8
	2003	12.8	5.5	18.4	206.9
	2004	10.1	6.6	16.7	184.6
	2005	21.3	6.5	27.8	302.2
Korea, Dem. P. R. Corée, R. p. dém. de	2001	52.3	65.0	117.3	5.1
	2002	187.8	75.5	263.4	11.3
	2003	114.8	51.7	166.4	7.1
	2004	137.3	47.5	184.8	7.9
	2005	39.4	41.5	80.9	3.4
Kyrgyzstan Kirghizistan	2001	71.3	112.8	184.1	36.8
	2002	95.2	83.1	178.2	35.2
	2003	112.6	80.8	193.4	37.9
	2004	109.6	114.5	224.0	43.5
	2005	126.4	83.2	209.6	40.3
Lao People's Dem. Rep. Rép. dém. pop. lao	2001	151.0	92.7	243.8	45.9
	2002	177.8	98.5	276.3	51.1
	2003	188.8	109.8	298.6	54.4
	2004	177.8	89.9	267.7	48.0
	2005	159.0	126.3	285.3	50.4
Lebanon Liban	2001	103.7	60.0	163.7	42.8
	2002	102.4	77.6	180.0	46.5
	2003	118.8	111.1	229.9	58.7
	2004	128.5	138.8	267.3	67.4
	2005	129.8	115.0	244.8	61.0
Lesotho Lesotho	2001	29.5	27.9	57.4	30.0
	2002	29.7	47.7	77.5	40.1
	2003	32.9	47.4	80.3	41.2
	2004	35.1	71.8	106.9	54.4
	2005	39.1	29.7	68.8	34.7
Liberia Libéria	2001	15.6	22.8	38.4	12.1
	2002	27.0	24.8	51.8	15.9
	2003	70.3	36.2	106.5	32.4
	2004	163.0	49.9	212.9	63.6
	2005	148.6	87.5	236.1	68.6
Libyan Arab Jamah. Jamah. arabe libyenne	2005	16.8	3.6	20.5	3.5

Country or area Pays ou zone	Year Année	Net disbursements (US $) — Versements nets ($E.U.)			
		Bilateral (millions) Bilatérale (millions)	Multilateral[1] (millions) Multilatérale[1] (millions)	Total (millions) Total (millions)	Per capita Par habitant
Madagascar Madagascar	2001	146.0	228.9	374.9	22.5
	2002	125.9	244.6	370.5	21.6
	2003	224.9	314.9	539.9	30.6
	2004	684.6	564.1	1 248.7	68.9
	2005	500.5	428.7	929.1	49.8
Malawi Malawi	2001	195.8	197.4	393.2	32.9
	2002	224.9	141.6	366.5	29.9
	2003	313.7	201.3	515.0	41.0
	2004	308.2	191.6	499.8	38.8
	2005	322.1	250.8	572.9	43.3
Malaysia Malaisie	2001	24.9	3.2	28.1	1.2
	2002	85.4	1.8	87.2	3.6
	2003	104.5	4.4	108.9	4.4
	2004	287.0	3.2	290.1	11.5
	2005	20.1	7.4	27.4	1.1
Maldives Maldives	2001	15.2	9.8	25.0	90.0
	2002	12.9	15.3	28.2	99.9
	2003	8.7	9.2	17.9	62.5
	2004	8.8	13.5	22.4	77.0
	2005	39.7	22.5	62.1	210.3
Mali Mali	2001	208.5	129.7	338.3	32.8
	2002	256.8	155.4	412.2	38.9
	2003	271.9	272.4	544.3	49.8
	2004	327.5	240.8	568.4	50.5
	2005	378.2	313.1	691.3	59.5
Malta Malte	2001	0.0	3.1	3.1	8.0
	2002	0.2	11.3	11.5	29.2
Marshall Islands Iles Marshall	2001	67.4	6.6	74.0	1 403.0
	2002	55.4	7.0	62.4	1 165.5
	2003	51.5	5.0	56.5	1 036.3
	2004	49.5	1.6	51.1	919.4
	2005	55.8	0.7	56.5	996.1
Mauritania Mauritanie	2001	81.3	187.5	268.8	101.7
	2002	146.6	199.3	345.9	127.1
	2003	136.1	104.9	241.0	86.0
	2004	83.1	96.6	179.7	62.4
	2005	124.5	65.6	190.2	64.2
Mauritius Maurice	2001	8.1	6.1	14.2	11.9
	2002	3.5	19.6	23.1	19.1
	2003	-17.7	2.5	-15.2	-12.4
	2004	14.7	25.4	40.2	32.6
	2005	22.2	9.8	31.9	25.7
Mayotte Mayotte	2001	119.3	0.9	120.2	...
	2002	125.2	-0.3	124.9	...
	2003	166.1	0.0	166.0	...
	2004	208.6	-0.2	208.5	...
	2005	201.9	-0.5	201.3	...
Mexico Mexique	2001	40.7	31.9	72.6	0.7
	2002	92.6	39.8	132.4	1.3
	2003	73.6	24.1	97.7	1.0
	2004	78.9	34.6	113.5	1.1
	2005	160.6	27.5	188.0	1.8

Country or area Pays ou zone	Year Année	Net disbursements (US $) — Versements nets ($E.U.) Bilateral (millions) Bilatérale (millions)	Multilateral[1] (millions) Multilatérale[1] (millions)	Total (millions) Total (millions)	Per capita Par habitant
Micronesia (Fed. States of) Micronésie (Etats féd. de)	2001	134.6	2.9	137.5	1 280.8
	2002	110.1	1.6	111.6	1 034.6
	2003	109.3	3.0	112.4	1 034.3
	2004	85.2	1.1	86.3	788.9
	2005	104.4	1.9	106.4	966.3
Mongolia Mongolie	2001	141.1	64.0	205.1	82.4
	2002	141.3	44.8	186.1	74.1
	2003	148.0	86.6	234.6	92.6
	2004	154.4	95.7	250.1	97.8
	2005	131.9	54.0	185.9	72.0
Montserrat Montserrat	2001	32.7	0.3	33.0	7 120.4
	2002	45.3	-1.8	43.5	9 285.4
	2003	36.3	0.2	36.5	7 312.6
	2004	37.4	7.1	44.5	8 308.7
	2005	27.0	0.9	27.8	4 939.6
Morocco Maroc	2001	342.1	141.5	483.7	16.6
	2002	216.6	135.0	351.6	11.9
	2003	335.7	157.3	492.9	16.5
	2004	393.5	243.8	637.3	21.1
	2005	289.3	308.8	598.1	19.6
Mozambique Mozambique	2001	720.2	206.7	926.9	49.7
	2002	1 661.0	537.4	2 198.4	114.9
	2003	697.1	336.8	1 033.9	52.7
	2004	731.3	510.7	1 242.0	61.9
	2005	770.8	513.3	1 284.1	62.5
Myanmar Myanmar	2001	89.2	36.0	125.1	2.7
	2002	79.1	32.6	111.7	2.4
	2003	83.4	34.9	118.3	2.5
	2004	81.5	39.3	120.8	2.5
	2005	77.8	58.7	136.5	2.8
Namibia Namibie	2001	77.5	30.6	108.1	56.5
	2002	84.8	47.4	132.2	68.1
	2003	110.3	33.5	143.8	73.0
	2004	124.0	33.8	157.8	79.1
	2005	98.8	22.8	121.5	60.2
Nauru Nauru	2001	7.1	0.1	7.2	719.9
	2002	11.6	...	11.6	1 154.6
	2003	16.0	0.1	16.1	1 602.5
	2004	13.6	0.1	13.7	1 355.5
	2005	8.9	0.1	9.0	889.1
Nepal Népal	2001	270.2	114.5	384.8	15.4
	2002	279.4	60.9	340.3	13.3
	2003	320.4	142.1	462.5	17.8
	2004	318.5	106.0	424.5	16.0
	2005	348.7	77.4	426.0	15.7
Nicaragua Nicaragua	2001	714.7	214.8	929.4	179.3
	2002	287.2	227.6	514.8	97.9
	2003	521.8	306.8	828.5	155.6
	2004	856.3	376.9	1 233.2	228.6
	2005	509.5	229.6	739.1	135.3
Niger Niger	2001	113.6	140.7	254.3	22.1
	2002	114.5	179.5	294.0	24.6
	2003	244.5	212.2	456.7	36.9
	2004	305.7	235.4	541.1	42.2
	2005	255.7	259.4	515.0	38.8

Country or area Pays ou zone	Year Année	Net disbursements (US $) — Versements nets ($E.U.) Bilateral (millions) Bilatérale (millions)	Multilateral[1] (millions) Multilatérale[1] (millions)	Total (millions) Total (millions)	Per capita Par habitant
Nigeria Nigéria	2001	107.5	61.6	169.1	1.3
	2002	215.0	80.7	295.7	2.3
	2003	199.8	108.8	308.6	2.3
	2004	314.6	263.9	578.5	4.2
	2005	5 966.3	471.2	6 437.5	45.5
Niue Nioué	2001	3.2	0.1	3.3	1 831.2
	2002	4.2	0.2	4.4	2 508.5
	2003	8.8	0.1	8.9	5 201.6
	2004	13.8	0.2	14.0	8 402.2
	2005	20.1	1.0	21.1	12 922.8
Occupied Palestinian Terr. Terr. palestinien occupé	2001	280.2	342.2	622.4	190.5
	2002	410.2	429.3	839.5	247.8
	2003	490.8	455.4	946.2	269.6
	2004	605.3	481.4	1 086.7	298.9
	2005	569.4	516.0	1 085.3	288.5
Oman Oman	2001	8.1	-0.4	7.7	3.2
	2002	-0.4	0.3	-0.1	0.0
	2003	10.5	1.1	11.5	4.7
	2004	2.0	-0.3	1.7	0.7
	2005	3.9	1.3	5.1	2.0
Pakistan Pakistan	2001	1 110.1	817.4	1 927.4	13.1
	2002	702.5	1 381.4	2 083.9	13.9
	2003	536.3	527.0	1 063.2	7.0
	2004	382.2	1 027.9	1 410.1	9.1
	2005	832.2	699.9	1 532.1	9.7
Palau Palaos	2001	33.9	0.2	34.1	1 742.4
	2002	30.9	0.2	31.1	1 575.6
	2003	25.3	0.1	25.4	1 274.5
	2004	19.4	0.1	19.5	971.9
	2005	23.4	0.1	23.4	1 164.1
Panama Panama	2001	17.1	-0.2	16.9	5.6
	2002	23.3	-2.2	21.1	6.9
	2003	31.3	-3.0	28.3	9.1
	2004	25.3	-1.6	23.7	7.5
	2005	17.3	1.6	18.9	5.8
Papua New Guinea Papouasie-Nvl-Guinée	2001	198.0	1.5	199.5	36.1
	2002	197.1	5.9	203.0	35.9
	2003	218.8	2.1	220.9	38.1
	2004	249.7	19.3	269.1	45.3
	2005	245.3	21.2	266.5	43.9
Paraguay Paraguay	2001	58.3	2.5	60.8	11.1
	2002	50.8	5.1	55.9	10.0
	2003	55.4	-5.7	49.8	8.8
	2004	26.4	-6.0	20.5	3.5
	2005	55.3	-6.7	48.6	8.2
Peru Pérou	2001	425.6	22.3	447.9	17.2
	2002	463.0	23.3	486.2	18.5
	2003	447.7	45.7	493.4	18.5
	2004	439.3	29.4	468.8	17.4
	2005	310.2	82.8	393.0	14.4
Philippines Philippines	2001	501.8	67.1	568.9	7.3
	2002	509.1	34.4	543.6	6.8
	2003	703.8	28.2	732.0	9.0
	2004	433.2	21.7	454.9	5.5
	2005	526.4	27.4	553.8	6.5

Disbursements of bilateral and multilateral official development assistance and official aid to individual recipients *(continued)*
Versements d'aide publique au développement et d'aide publique bilatérales et multilatérales aux bénéficiaires *(suite)*

Country or area Pays ou zone	Year Année	Net disbursements (US $) — Versements nets ($E.U.) Bilateral (millions) Bilatérale (millions)	Multilateral[1] (millions) Multilatérale[1] (millions)	Total (millions) Total (millions)	Per capita Par habitant
Republic of Moldova République de Moldova	2001	78.8	37.6	116.4	28.5
	2002	86.3	50.5	136.9	33.9
	2003	80.4	32.8	113.2	28.5
	2004	76.6	37.0	113.6	28.9
	2005	106.1	77.4	183.5	47.3
Rwanda Rwanda	2001	148.9	149.9	298.8	35.0
	2002	199.1	154.7	353.8	40.4
	2003	213.4	121.4	334.8	37.6
	2004	216.9	271.2	488.1	53.9
	2005	292.0	283.8	575.9	62.4
Saint Helena Sainte-Hélène	2001	14.7	0.4	15.2	2 497.9
	2002	13.4	0.5	13.9	2 255.7
	2003	17.6	0.4	18.0	2 877.3
	2004	26.1	0.2	26.2	4 145.8
	2005	22.5	0.1	22.6	3 524.0
Saint Kitts and Nevis Saint-Kitts-et-Nevis	2001	1.3	7.7	8.9	191.6
	2002	6.1	20.1	26.2	554.0
	2003	-0.3	0.3	0.0	-0.4
	2004	-0.2	0.9	0.8	16.1
	2005	1.6	1.8	3.4	69.2
Saint Lucia Sainte-Lucie	2001	0.8	15.8	16.5	107.0
	2002	12.5	21.2	33.7	215.9
	2003	4.8	10.0	14.8	93.8
	2004	-23.7	2.3	-21.4	-134.2
	2005	6.5	4.5	11.0	68.0
Saint Vincent-Grenadines Saint Vincent-Grenadines	2001	0.7	7.8	8.5	72.7
	2002	1.1	4.3	5.3	45.2
	2003	3.7	2.6	6.3	53.3
	2004	7.3	3.8	11.1	93.4
	2005	5.7	-0.9	4.8	40.5
Samoa Samoa	2001	27.3	15.7	43.0	240.3
	2002	30.8	6.4	37.2	206.4
	2003	27.0	6.0	33.0	181.7
	2004	24.6	6.0	30.6	167.9
	2005	29.9	13.9	43.8	238.4
Sao Tome and Principe Sao Tomé-et-Principe	2001	21.9	16.3	38.2	267.9
	2002	19.2	6.8	26.0	179.0
	2003	25.5	12.2	37.6	254.9
	2004	21.7	11.7	33.4	222.2
	2005	18.4	13.5	31.9	208.7
Saudi Arabia Arabie saoudite	2001	10.5	2.5	13.0	0.6
	2002	13.4	3.0	16.4	0.8
	2003	9.9	1.7	11.6	0.5
	2004	8.5	1.7	10.2	0.4
	2005	13.8	2.0	15.8	0.7
Senegal Sénégal	2001	223.7	189.3	413.0	38.9
	2002	242.8	191.3	434.0	39.9
	2003	314.4	135.8	450.2	40.3
	2004	755.5	298.9	1 054.4	91.9
	2005	440.1	248.8	688.8	58.5
Serbia and Montenegro Serbie-et-Monténégro	2001	631.1	669.4	1 300.6	121.1
	2002	1 921.3	3.4	1 924.7	180.5
	2003	853.0	444.2	1 297.2	122.6
	2004	583.7	564.6	1 148.3	109.2
	2005	808.2	280.9	1 089.1	104.0

Country or area Pays ou zone	Year Année	Net disbursements (US $) — Versements nets ($E.U.) Bilateral (millions) Bilatérale (millions)	Multilateral[1] (millions) Multilatérale[1] (millions)	Total (millions) Total (millions)	Per capita Par habitant
Seychelles Seychelles	2001	8.2	5.2	13.4	163.2
	2002	3.7	4.2	7.9	95.0
	2003	4.9	3.2	8.1	96.6
	2004	6.1	2.9	9.1	106.7
	2005	7.9	10.8	18.7	219.1
Sierra Leone Sierra Leone	2001	166.8	174.3	341.2	72.5
	2002	225.3	124.6	349.9	71.1
	2003	208.3	92.0	300.3	58.2
	2004	162.6	196.4	359.1	66.6
	2005	130.4	212.8	343.3	61.4
Slovenia Slovénie	2001	0.0	125.5	125.5	63.2
	2002	2.4	50.3	52.7	26.5
Solomon Islands Iles Salomon	2001	24.6	34.1	58.7	137.5
	2002	21.3	4.9	26.2	59.8
	2003	56.5	3.7	60.1	133.8
	2004	116.8	4.5	121.3	263.2
	2005	172.3	25.9	198.2	419.5
Somalia Somalie	2001	88.5	44.9	133.4	18.3
	2002	102.4	44.4	146.8	19.6
	2003	113.6	60.1	173.7	22.5
	2004	139.7	60.0	199.7	25.1
	2005	146.1	90.2	236.2	28.8
South Africa Afrique du Sud	2001	313.3	113.5	426.7	9.3
	2002	375.3	128.5	503.8	10.8
	2003	477.3	163.2	640.5	13.6
	2004	459.2	168.4	627.6	13.2
	2005	486.0	213.5	699.5	14.6
Sri Lanka Sri Lanka	2001	279.9	20.0	299.9	15.9
	2002	188.5	135.2	323.6	17.1
	2003	271.0	388.5	659.4	34.8
	2004	337.2	162.0	499.1	26.2
	2005	857.1	284.5	1 141.6	59.7
Sudan Soudan	2001	107.6	63.1	170.8	5.0
	2002	232.3	59.9	292.2	8.4
	2003	332.0	277.8	609.8	17.2
	2004	847.9	118.8	966.7	26.7
	2005	1 472.0	315.2	1 787.2	48.4
Suriname Suriname	2001	20.0	3.2	23.2	52.7
	2002	7.7	3.9	11.6	26.1
	2003	4.0	6.8	10.9	24.3
	2004	15.8	8.1	23.9	53.0
	2005	33.5	10.4	43.9	97.0
Swaziland Swaziland	2001	4.2	21.8	25.9	24.1
	2002	6.6	11.7	18.3	16.8
	2003	12.7	20.3	33.0	29.9
	2004	7.3	14.4	21.7	19.4
	2005	20.2	25.8	46.0	40.9
Syrian Arab Republic Rép. arabe syrienne	2001	92.3	34.3	126.6	7.5
	2002	25.0	47.2	72.2	4.1
	2003	28.8	91.9	120.7	6.7
	2004	15.7	111.3	127.0	6.9
	2005	5.9	74.6	80.5	4.3

Country or area Pays ou zone	Year Année	Net disbursements (US $) — Versements nets ($E.U.)			
		Bilateral (millions) Bilatérale (millions)	Multilateral[1] (millions) Multilatérale[1] (millions)	Total (millions) Total (millions)	Per capita Par habitant
Tajikistan Tadjikistan	2001	63.5	103.7	167.1	26.8
	2002	128.8	38.0	166.8	26.4
	2003	80.3	63.5	143.7	22.5
	2004	91.9	139.1	230.9	35.7
	2005	105.9	129.8	235.7	36.0
Thailand Thaïlande	2001	270.9	15.0	285.9	4.7
	2002	279.6	17.4	296.9	4.8
	2003	-984.4	24.1	-960.3	-15.5
	2004	-23.7	48.1	24.5	0.4
	2005	-219.9	40.3	-179.6	-2.8
TFYR of Macedonia L'ex-R.y. Macédoine	2001	164.2	81.5	245.8	121.9
	2002	179.8	93.0	272.8	134.9
	2003	179.3	85.2	264.5	130.5
	2004	162.2	83.3	245.5	120.9
	2005	167.1	56.1	223.1	109.7
Timor-Leste Timor-Leste	2001	153.9	39.9	193.8	228.4
	2002	187.0	30.7	217.7	243.0
	2003	127.3	27.3	154.6	162.1
	2004	133.2	20.0	153.2	151.1
	2005	160.1	24.3	184.4	172.8
Togo Togo	2001	28.5	11.1	39.6	7.1
	2002	39.2	9.0	48.2	8.4
	2003	46.3	1.9	48.1	8.1
	2004	52.3	16.3	68.7	11.3
	2005	59.4	27.1	86.6	13.9
Tokelau Tokélaou	2001	3.8	0.1	3.9	2 579.8
	2002	4.6	0.2	4.8	3 231.9
	2003	6.2	0.2	6.4	4 430.6
	2004	8.4	0.1	8.4	5 932.4
	2005	15.9	0.1	16.0	11 406.1
Tonga Tonga	2001	20.6	-0.4	20.2	206.0
	2002	16.7	5.5	22.2	225.6
	2003	15.0	10.8	25.8	261.5
	2004	14.9	4.3	19.2	193.8
	2005	24.7	7.0	31.7	319.0
Trinidad and Tobago Trinité-et-Tobago	2001	4.3	-6.1	-1.8	-1.3
	2002	5.7	-14.4	-8.7	-6.7
	2003	5.1	-8.2	-3.1	-2.4
	2004	7.2	-9.3	-2.0	-1.5
	2005	6.1	-8.2	-2.2	-1.6
Tunisia Tunisie	2001	183.7	192.7	376.3	38.9
	2002	144.6	77.3	221.9	22.7
	2003	207.7	94.8	302.5	30.6
	2004	230.8	95.5	326.3	32.6
	2005	269.1	105.2	374.3	37.0
Turkey Turquie	2001	-29.0	142.6	113.6	1.6
	2002	99.0	161.1	260.1	3.7
	2003	19.5	145.9	165.4	2.3
	2004	-16.5	308.3	291.8	4.1
	2005	51.8	410.2	461.9	6.3
Turkmenistan Turkménistan	2001	33.1	7.2	40.3	8.8
	2002	26.0	5.7	31.7	6.9
	2003	16.7	6.7	23.4	5.0
	2004	11.4	7.2	18.5	3.9
	2005	11.8	5.3	17.1	3.5

Disbursements of bilateral and multilateral official development assistance and official aid to individual recipients (*continued*)
Versements d'aide publique au développement et d'aide publique bilatérales et multilatérales aux bénéficiaires (*suite*)

Country or area Pays ou zone	Year Année	Net disbursements (US $) — Versements nets ($E.U.) Bilateral (millions) Bilatérale (millions)	Multilateral[1] (millions) Multilatérale[1] (millions)	Total (millions) Total (millions)	Per capita Par habitant
Turks and Caicos Islands Iles Turques et Caïques	2001	5.1	1.6	6.7	334.5
	2002	2.6	1.5	4.1	193.8
	2003	1.2	1.0	2.2	97.7
	2004	1.2	1.9	3.2	133.8
	2005	3.1	2.1	5.2	212.6
Tuvalu Tuvalu	2001	6.9	2.6	9.5	926.3
	2002	11.2	0.6	11.7	1 137.0
	2003	5.5	0.4	5.8	564.3
	2004	5.4	2.6	8.0	769.5
	2005	5.9	3.1	8.9	856.2
Uganda Ouganda	2001	386.3	402.1	788.4	31.0
	2002	466.1	238.3	704.4	26.8
	2003	587.3	387.6	974.9	35.9
	2004	683.9	512.2	1 196.0	42.7
	2005	704.3	491.8	1 196.1	41.3
Ukraine Ukraine	2005	252.1	116.8	368.9	7.9
United Rep. of Tanzania Rép.-Unie de Tanzanie	2001	943.8	330.2	1 274.0	36.7
	2002	902.8	330.6	1 233.4	34.6
	2003	965.6	738.1	1 703.7	46.6
	2004	1 028.7	729.8	1 758.5	46.9
	2005	871.0	621.8	1 492.9	38.8
Uruguay Uruguay	2001	10.7	3.7	14.4	4.3
	2002	6.8	3.0	9.8	2.9
	2003	7.7	6.2	14.0	4.2
	2004	9.9	11.6	21.5	6.5
	2005	2.8	11.2	14.0	4.2
Uzbekistan Ouzbékistan	2001	106.7	16.7	123.4	4.9
	2002	152.9	20.5	173.4	6.8
	2003	167.5	16.6	184.1	7.1
	2004	205.8	25.4	231.2	8.8
	2005	124.1	31.5	155.6	5.9
Vanuatu Vanuatu	2001	24.1	7.4	31.5	162.4
	2002	22.4	5.1	27.5	138.0
	2003	28.2	4.2	32.4	158.6
	2004	34.6	3.1	37.7	179.7
	2005	33.4	6.1	39.4	183.1
Venezuela (Bolivarian Rep. of) Venezuela (Rép. bolivarienne du)	2001	33.5	10.5	44.0	1.8
	2002	42.0	14.1	56.1	2.2
	2003	64.2	16.1	80.2	3.1
	2004	28.4	15.9	44.2	1.7
	2005	20.8	27.1	47.8	1.8
Viet Nam Viet Nam	2001	819.5	593.2	1 412.7	17.6
	2002	746.0	508.6	1 254.7	15.4
	2003	967.7	785.6	1 753.3	21.2
	2004	1 184.8	617.8	1 802.6	21.5
	2005	1 252.1	634.1	1 886.2	22.2
Wallis and Futuna Islands Iles Wallis et Futuna	2001	50.3	...	50.3	3 366.1
	2002	52.7	0.1	52.7	3 519.1
	2003	53.6	1.9	55.5	3 699.0
	2004	71.5	1.3	72.8	4 843.6
	2005	71.7	0.4	72.0	4 776.8

Disbursements of bilateral and multilateral official development assistance and official aid to individual recipients (*continued*)

Versements d'aide publique au développement et d'aide publique bilatérales et multilatérales aux bénéficiaires (*suite*)

Country or area Pays ou zone	Year Année	Net disbursements (US $) — Versements nets ($E.U.) Bilateral (millions) Bilatérale (millions)	Multilateral[1] (millions) Multilatérale[1] (millions)	Total (millions) Total (millions)	Per capita Par habitant
Yemen Yémen	2001	99.8	240.4	340.2	18.2
	2002	119.4	106.0	225.4	11.7
	2003	126.6	109.3	235.9	11.9
	2004	152.7	100.0	252.7	12.3
	2005	134.7	166.7	301.3	14.3
Zambia Zambie	2001	274.1	73.7	347.8	32.6
	2002	359.5	277.4	636.9	58.6
	2003	591.9	-8.2	583.7	52.7
	2004	745.8	376.8	1 122.6	99.6
	2005	835.9	108.6	944.5	82.3
Zimbabwe Zimbabwe	2001	148.6	16.9	165.5	13.0
	2002	177.8	20.7	198.5	15.4
	2003	160.7	25.3	186.0	14.4
	2004	166.4	19.9	186.3	14.3
	2005	178.8	188.8	367.6	28.0

Source

Organization for Economic Co-operation and Development (OECD), Paris, the OECD Development Assistance Committee database, last accessed January 2007. Per capita calculated by the United Nations Statistics Division from the World Population Prospects: The 2006 Revision, mid-year population data.

Notes

1 As reported by OECD/DAC, covers agencies of the United Nations family, the European Commission, IDA and the concessional lending facilities of regional development banks. Excludes non-concessional flows (i.e., less than 25% grant elements).

2 For statistical purposes, the data for China do not include those for the Hong Kong Special Administrative Region (Hong Kong SAR), Macao Special Administrative Region (Macao SAR) and Taiwan Province of China.

Source

Organisation de coopération et de développement économiques (OCDE), Paris, la base de données du comité d'aide au développement de l'OCDE, dernier accès janvier 2007. Les données par habitant ont été calculées par la Division de statistiques de l'ONU de "World Population Prospects: The 2006 Revision," d'après les données de la population au milieu de l'année.

Notes

1 Communiqué par le Comité d'aide au développement de l'OCDE, comprend les institutions et organismes du système des Nations Unies, la commission européenne, l'Association internationale de développement, et les mécanismes de prêt à des conditions privilégiées des banques régionales de développement. Les apports aux conditions du marché (élément de libéralité inférieur à 25) en sont exclus.

2 Pour la présentation des statistiques, les données pour la Chine ne comprennent pas la Région Administrative Spéciale de Hong Kong (Hong Kong RAS), la Région Administrative Spéciale de Macao (Macao RAS) et la province de Taiwan.

Net official development assistance from DAC countries to developing countries and multilateral organizations

Net disbursements: millions of US dollars and as a percentage of gross national income (GNI)

Aide publique au développement nette des pays du CAD aux pays en développement et aux organisations multilatérales

Versements nets : millions de dollars E.U. et en pourcentage du revenu national brut (RNB)

Country or area Pays ou zone	2000		2001		2002		2003		2004		2005	
	US $ $ E.U. (millions)	As % of GNI En % du RNB	US $ $ E.U. (millions)	As % of GNI En % du RNB	US $ $ E.U. (millions)	As % of GNI En % du RNB	US $ $ E.U. (millions)	As % of GNI En % du RNB	US $ $ E.U. (millions)	As % of GNI En % du RNB	US $ $ E.U. (millions)	As % of GNI En % du RNB
Total Total	53 749	0.22	52 435	0.22	58 292	0.24	69 085	0.25	79 410	0.26	106 777	0.33
Australia Australie	987	0.27	873	0.25	989	0.26	1 219	0.25	1 460	0.25	1 680	0.25
Austria Autriche	440	0.23	633	0.34	520	0.26	505	0.20	678	0.23	1 573	0.52
Belgium Belgique	820	0.36	867	0.37	1 072	0.43	1 853	0.60	1 463	0.41	1 963	0.53
Canada Canada	1 744	0.25	1 533	0.22	2 004	0.28	2 031	0.24	2 599	0.27	3 756	0.34
Denmark Danemark	1 664	1.06	1 634	1.03	1 643	0.96	1 748	0.84	2 037	0.85	2 109	0.81
Finland Finlande	371	0.31	389	0.32	462	0.35	558	0.35	680	0.37	902	0.46
France France	4 105	0.30	4 198	0.31	5 486	0.37	7 253	0.40	8 473	0.41	10 026	0.47
Germany Allemagne	5 030	0.27	4 990	0.27	5 324	0.27	6 784	0.28	7 534	0.28	10 082	0.36
Greece Grèce	226	0.20	202	0.17	276	0.21	362	0.21	321	0.16	384	0.17
Ireland Irlande	234	0.29	287	0.33	398	0.40	504	0.39	607	0.39	719	0.42
Italy Italie	1 376	0.13	1 627	0.15	2 332	0.20	2 433	0.17	2 462	0.15	5 091	0.29
Japan Japon	13 508	0.28	9 847	0.23	9 283	0.23	8 880	0.20	8 922	0.19	13 147	0.28
Luxembourg Luxembourg	123	0.71	139	0.76	147	0.77	194	0.81	236	0.83	256	0.82
Netherlands Pays-Bas	3 135	0.84	3 172	0.82	3 338	0.81	3 972	0.80	4 204	0.73	5 115	0.82
New Zealand Nouvelle-Zélande	113	0.25	112	0.25	122	0.22	165	0.23	212	0.23	274	0.27
Norway Norvège	1 264	0.76	1 346	0.80	1 696	0.89	2 042	0.92	2 199	0.87	2 786	0.94
Portugal Portugal	271	0.26	268	0.25	323	0.27	320	0.22	1 031	0.63	377	0.21
Spain Espagne	1 195	0.22	1 737	0.30	1 712	0.26	1 961	0.23	2 437	0.24	3 018	0.27
Sweden Suède	1 799	0.80	1 666	0.77	2 012	0.84	2 400	0.79	2 722	0.78	3 362	0.94
Switzerland Suisse	890	0.34	908	0.34	939	0.32	1 299	0.39	1 545	0.41	1 767	0.44
United Kingdom Royaume-Uni	4 501	0.32	4 579	0.32	4 924	0.31	6 282	0.34	7 883	0.36	10 767	0.47
United States Etats-Unis	9 955	0.10	11 429	0.11	13 290	0.13	16 320	0.15	19 705	0.17	27 622	0.22

Source

Organisation for Economic Co-operation and Development (OECD), Paris, the OECD Development Assistance Committee database, last accessed January 2007.

Source

Organisation de coopération et de développement économiques (OCDE), Paris, la base de données du Comité d'aide au développement de l'OCDE, dernier accès janvier 2007.

Socio-economic development assistance through the United Nations system

Development grants: thousands of US dollars, 2005

Assistance en matière de développement socioéconomique fournie par le système des Nations Unies

Subventions au développement : en milliers de dollars des E.U., 2005

Region, country or area Région, pays ou zone	UNDP[a] PNUD[a]	UNFPA FNUAP	UNHCR HCR	UNICEF	WFP[b] PAM[b]	Specialized agencies[c] Institutions spécialisées[c]	IFAD FIDA	Total develop. grants Total subventions au développ.
Total Total	**3 652 906**	**388 022**	**1 141 632**	**1 960 434**	**2 892 401**	**3 322 838**	**343 488**	**13 701 722**
Regional programmes Totaux régionnaux	**349 210**	**111 582**	**251 497**	**111 683**	**20 473**	**1 748 351**	**0**	**2 592 796**
Africa Afrique	**3 086**	**10 470**	**16 976**	**15 668**	**4 861**	**352 291**	**0**	**403 352**
Americas Amériques	**1 666**	**5 068**	**3 619**	**8 266**	**538**	**75 260**	**0**	**94 417**
Asia and the Pacific Asie et le Pacifique	**268**	**11 149**	**104**	**15 585**	**15 074**	**139 244**	**0**	**181 424**
Europe Europe	**202**	**1 974**	**782**	**5 406**	**0**	**98 634**	**0**	**106 998**
Western Asia Asie occidentale	**606**	**1 999**	**1 879**	**2 403**	**0**	**548 495**	**0**	**555 383**
Global/Interregional Global/Interrégional	**67 725**	**80 923**	**61 375**	**64 355**	**0**	**522 673**	**0**	**797 051**
Total all countries Total, tous pays	**3 303 696**	**276 440**	**890 136**	**1 848 750**	**2 871 928**	**1 574 487**	**343 488**	**11 108 925**
Afghanistan Afghanistan	347 197	4 884	56 336	50 228	94 040	46 179	0	598 864
Albania Albanie	9 117	397	1 955	3 613	2 103	4 424	2 962	24 571
Algeria Algérie	3 176	736	4 552	1 543	11 330	3 682	1 000	26 020
Angola Angola	30 584	1 920	21 004	32 214	50 777	14 915	3 129	154 544
Antigua and Barbuda Antigua-et-Barbuda	232	0	0	0	0	25	0	257
Argentina Argentine	321 660	452	839	3 625	0	10 628	3 915	341 119
Armenia Arménie	5 704	589	1 847	1 210	2 345	1 524	2 229	15 447
Aruba Aruba	0	0	0	0	0	6	0	6
Australia[1] Australie[1]	0	0	1 006	0	0	25	0	1 031
Austria Autriche	0	0	1 251	0	0	142	0	1 392
Azerbaijan Azerbaïdjan	10 959	664	3 482	3 411	5 548	1 843	3 288	29 195
Bahamas Bahamas	0	0	0	0	0	406	0	406
Bahrain Bahreïn	1 492	0	0	0	0	454	0	1 946
Bangladesh Bangladesh	33 911	5 395	2 878	55 867	35 938	23 782	13 921	171 691
Barbados Barbade	3 287	0	0	0	0	504	0	3 791

Socio-economic development assistance through the United Nations system—Development grants: thousands of US dollars, 2005 (*continued*)

Assistance en matière de développement socioéconomique fournie par le système des Nations Unies—Subventions au développement : en milliers de dollars des E.U., 2005 (*suite*)

Region, country or area Région, pays ou zone	UNDP[a] PNUD[a]	UNFPA FNUAP	UNHCR HCR	UNICEF	WFP[b] PAM[b]	Specialized agencies[c] Institutions spécialisées[c]	IFAD FIDA	Total develop. grants Total subventions au développ.
Belarus Bélarus	7 261	283	913	1 062	0	729	0	10 249
Belgium Belgique	0	0	2 878	0	0	195	0	3 074
Belize Belize	783	0	0	963	0	500	368	2 614
Benin Bénin	9 085	2 646	1 912	8 660	3 067	4 585	7 518	37 473
Bhutan Bhoutan	2 760	2 246	0	2 926	2 287	2 227	1 238	13 685
Bolivia Bolivie	22 516	1 493	0	9 721	4 279	5 982	2 503	46 493
Bosnia and Herzegovina Bosnie-Herzégovine	19 210	337	10 639	4 388	0	4 441	2 147	41 162
Botswana Botswana	4 354	885	2 005	2 218	0	3 523	0	12 985
Brazil Brésil	148 986	1 105	1 848	10 929	0	156 687	2 878	322 432
British Virgin Islands Iles Vierges britanniques	0	0	0	0	0	1	0	1
Brunei Darussalam Brunéi Darussalam	0	0	0	0	0	59	0	59
Bulgaria Bulgarie	28 286	276	1 028	0	0	1 758	0	31 348
Burkina Faso Burkina Faso	22 060	2 674	0	13 778	3 699	10 450	6 931	59 592
Burundi Burundi	28 041	1 089	37 736	18 867	40 818	12 513	3 848	142 913
Cambodia Cambodge	26 529	1 956	1 514	17 352	9 158	15 304	4 449	76 263
Cameroon Cameroun	5 166	2 783	2 318	9 793	2 001	6 203	2 401	30 665
Canada Canada	0	0	1 328	0	0	79	0	1 406
Cape Verde Cap-Vert	1 844	751	0	1 051	557	1 973	442	6 618
Central African Rep. Rép. centrafricaine	17 703	2 322	3 335	7 467	3 702	4 664	0	39 193
Chad Tchad	14 707	2 127	72 036	23 622	50 254	8 173	1 236	172 155
Chile Chili	42 818	208	0	911	0	2 643	0	46 579
China[2] Chine[2]	52 209	4 717	3 798	19 657	9 933	34 924	18 398	143 635
China, Hong Kong SAR Chine, Hong Kong RAS	0	0	0	0	0	38	0	38
China, Macao SAR Chine, Macao RAS	0	0	0	0	0	162	0	162
Colombia Colombie	91 820	1 068	8 725	5 663	11 041	6 557	1 820	126 694
Comoros Comores	3 773	462	0	1 494	0	2 422	65	8 216
Congo Congo	5 439	629	8 182	4 634	3 983	3 148	1 157	27 171

Socio-economic development assistance through the United Nations system — Development grants: thousands of US dollars, 2005 (*continued*)

Assistance en matière de développement socioéconomique fournie par le système des Nations Unies — Subventions au développement : en milliers de dollars des E.U., 2005 (*suite*)

Region, country or area Région, pays ou zone	UNDP[a] PNUD[a]	UNFPA FNUAP	UNHCR HCR	UNICEF	WFP[b] PAM[b]	Specialized agencies[c] Institutions spécialisées[c]	IFAD FIDA	Total develop. grants Total subventions au developp.
Cook Islands Iles Cook	0	0	0	0	0	467	0	467
Costa Rica Costa Rica	2 287	587	1 374	758	0	2 595	730	8 331
Côte d'Ivoire Côte d'Ivoire	20 475	1 572	10 843	18 158	24 306	6 348	1 802	83 504
Croatia Croatie	3 768	0	4 587	637	0	1 480	0	10 471
Cuba Cuba	12 862	658	316	1 720	7 590	2 942	0	26 087
Cyprus Chypre	17 954	0	629	0	0	153	0	18 735
Czech Republic République tchèque	0	0	872	0	0	1 381	0	2 253
Dem. Rep. of the Congo Rép. dém. du Congo	213 943	6 952	32 177	67 468	62 023	22 531	0	405 094
Djibouti Djibouti	2 114	445	3 536	2 753	5 046	2 933	0	16 827
Dominica Dominique	232	0	0	0	0	550	166	948
Dominican Republic Rép. dominicaine	6 400	804	0	3 639	19	4 183	1 151	16 197
Ecuador Equateur	22 999	906	3 380	3 863	204	5 437	0	36 789
Egypt Egypte	45 737	1 828	4 269	15 009	4 452	13 128	10 469	94 891
El Salvador El Salvador	22 446	804	0	3 417	2 107	4 743	6 621	40 139
Equatorial Guinea Guinée équatoriale	2 209	1 576	0	1 481	0	2 308	0	7 574
Eritrea Erythrée	8 994	1 971	10 372	10 785	64 364	5 260	1 420	103 166
Estonia Estonie	0	0	0	0	0	596	0	596
Ethiopia Ethiopie	21 165	4 185	16 059	83 253	336 239	32 550	14 996	508 447
Fiji Fidji	5 496	0	0	0	0	2 669	0	8 165
Finland Finlande	0	0	0	0	0	70	0	70
France France	0	0	2 540	0	0	1 260	0	3 800
French Guiana Guyane française	0	0	0	0	0	54	0	54
French Polynesia Polynésie française	0	0	0	0	0	40	0	40
Gabon Gabon	5 351	142	2 934	1 122	0	2 949	0	12 497
Gambia Gambie	2 273	587	648	1 905	2 148	2 935	1 889	12 385
Georgia Géorgie	12 152	505	4 623	1 840	4 622	1 841	628	26 211
Germany Allemagne	0	0	1 925	0	0	345	0	2 271

Socio-economic development assistance through the United Nations system — Development grants: thousands of US dollars, 2005 (*continued*)

Assistance en matière de développement socioéconomique fournie par le système des Nations Unies — Subventions au développement : en milliers de dollars des E.U., 2005 (*suite*)

Region, country or area Région, pays ou zone	UNDP[a] PNUD[a]	UNFPA FNUAP	UNHCR HCR	UNICEF	WFP[b] PAM[b]	Specialized agencies[c] Institutions spécialisées[c]	IFAD FIDA	Total develop. grants Total subventions au developp.
Ghana Ghana	6 358	3 692	8 446	15 075	4 918	9 292	5 979	53 760
Greece Grèce	0	0	1 429	0	0	572	0	2 001
Grenada Grenade	746	0	0	0	0	2 248	194	3 188
Guatemala Guatemala	61 941	1 503	0	5 789	8 983	14 634	3 412	96 261
Guinea Guinée	4 548	1 378	18 404	9 446	12 455	4 656	1 674	52 561
Guinea-Bissau Guinée-Bissau	9 527	1 038	0	3 446	3 110	2 443	0	19 564
Guyana Guyana	4 202	0	0	2 116	245	1 251	1 424	9 238
Haiti Haïti	33 099	4 158	0	10 712	21 473	7 147	3 432	80 022
Honduras Honduras	133 421	2 702	0	1 966	3 643	5 285	3 126	150 143
Hungary Hongrie	0	0	2 047	0	0	702	0	2 749
India Inde	35 134	13 672	3 332	115 207	12 986	89 017	16 184	285 531
Indonesia Indonésie	71 073	15 735	24 072	121 417	133 775	40 778	1 075	407 925
Iran (Islamic Rep. of) Iran (Rép. islamique d')	7 085	1 515	13 898	12 553	763	11 191	0	47 005
Iraq Iraq	127 450	4 716	25 432	104 933	28 940	151 896	0	443 366
Ireland Irlande	0	0	539	0	0	0	0	539
Israel Israël	0	0	117	0	0	296	0	413
Italy Italie	0	0	1 905	0	0	6 972	0	8 878
Jamaica Jamaïque	1 741	0	0	2 380	0	1 866	0	5 986
Japan Japon	0	0	2 442	0	0	2 680	0	5 123
Jordan Jordanie	9 504	293	4 465	1 259	409	4 575	2 648	23 154
Kazakhstan Kazakhstan	10 050	608	1 291	2 189	0	1 810	0	15 948
Kenya Kenya	21 990	3 767	35 395	14 736	79 968	8 501	5 543	169 901
Kiribati Kiribati	0	0	0	0	0	764	0	764
Korea, Dem. P. R. Corée, R. p. dém. de	3 169	974	0	12 676	55 410	13 871	5 103	91 204
Korea, Republic of Corée, République de	3 239	0	515	0	0	2 411	0	6 165
Kuwait Koweït	0	0	0	650	0	551	0	1 201

Socio-economic development assistance through the United Nations system — Development grants: thousands of US dollars, 2005 (*continued*)

Assistance en matière de développement socioéconomique fournie par le système des Nations Unies — Subventions au développement : en milliers de dollars des E.U., 2005 (*suite*)

Region, country or area Région, pays ou zone	UNDP[a] PNUD[a]	UNFPA FNUAP	UNHCR HCR	UNICEF	WFP[b] PAM[b]	Specialized agencies[c] Institutions spécialisées[c]	IFAD FIDA	Total develop. grants Total subventions au développ.
Kyrgyzstan Kirghizistan	8 372	841	2 213	1 338	4	2 209	480	15 457
Lao People's Dem. Rep. Rép. dém. pop. lao	11 246	1 213	0	6 974	4 664	8 862	4 088	37 047
Latvia Lettonie	1 900	49	0	0	0	791	0	2 740
Lebanon Liban	11 195	613	3 042	1 279	0	4 496	1 344	21 969
Lesotho Lesotho	2 131	133	0	4 021	22 088	3 468	1 696	33 537
Liberia Libéria	44 927	781	46 042	18 166	35 290	7 653	0	152 858
Libyan Arab Jamah. Jamah. arabe libyenne	1 376	0	720	0	2 326	5 818	0	10 240
Lithuania Lituanie	1 198	69	0	0	0	598	0	1 865
Luxembourg Luxembourg	0	0	0	0	0	2	0	2
Madagascar Madagascar	8 005	1 453	0	10 534	6 960	7 804	4 599	39 355
Malawi Malawi	14 494	3 679	2 458	21 716	61 261	6 921	2 050	112 580
Malaysia Malaisie	6 164	480	2 711	1 137	0	1 712	0	12 204
Maldives Maldives	13 215	1 625	0	24 563	4 719	6 478	0	50 601
Mali Mali	7 537	1 650	0	15 605	17 025	6 367	6 650	54 834
Malta Malte	0	0	35	0	0	424	0	459
Marshall Islands Iles Marshall	0	0	0	0	0	243	0	243
Mauritania Mauritanie	5 228	2 205	610	5 462	18 861	6 508	2 198	41 072
Mauritius Maurice	1 282	-11	0	0	0	1 754	1 467	4 492
Mexico Mexique	15 025	2 179	1 607	4 082	0	19 747	2 249	44 889
Micronesia (Fed. States of) Micronésie (Etats féd. de)	0	0	0	0	0	350	0	350
Mongolia Mongolie	4 865	1 049	195	2 822	0	5 222	3 444	17 597
Montserrat Montserrat	60	0	0	0	0	0	0	60
Morocco Maroc	7 284	2 745	485	3 077	16	7 680	6 701	27 987
Mozambique Mozambique	14 565	5 894	2 411	21 398	45 470	10 076	7 988	107 802
Myanmar Myanmar	23 949	4 022	4 341	18 227	9 119	9 719	0	69 378
Namibia Namibie	7 039	701	3 056	3 989	791	4 263	0	19 839

Socio-economic development assistance through the United Nations system — Development grants: thousands of US dollars, 2005 *(continued)*

Assistance en matière de développement socioéconomique fournie par le système des Nations Unies — Subventions au développement : en milliers de dollars des E.U., 2005 *(suite)*

Region, country or area Région, pays ou zone	UNDP[a] PNUD[a]	UNFPA FNUAP	UNHCR HCR	UNICEF	WFP[b] PAM[b]	Specialized agencies[c] Institutions spécialisées[c]	IFAD FIDA	Total develop. grants Total subventions au développ.
Nauru Nauru	0	0	0	0	0	131	0	131
Nepal Népal	15 380	6 548	7 415	16 721	16 909	17 984	2 008	82 965
Netherlands Pays-Bas	0	0	0	0	0	230	0	230
Netherlands Antilles Antilles néerlandaises	0	0	0	0	0	97	0	97
New Caledonia Nouvelle-Calédonie	0	0	0	0	0	22	0	22
New Zealand[1] Nouvelle-Zélande[1]	0	0	0	0	0	16	0	16
Nicaragua Nicaragua	22 652	2 504	0	5 778	9 082	3 711	673	44 400
Niger Niger	7 569	3 291	0	30 218	44 069	23 428	996	109 572
Nigeria Nigéria	34 957	7 929	2 844	59 785	0	64 807	7 037	177 359
Niue Nioué	0	0	0	0	0	677	0	677
Norway Norvège	0	0	0	0	0	781	0	781
Occupied Palestinian Terr.[3] Terr. palestinien occupé[3]	0	0	0	15 118	24 432	1 671	0	41 221
Oman Oman	0	155	0	470	0	2 239	0	2 863
Pakistan Pakistan	32 951	9 542	33 431	82 009	49 776	50 100	9 100	266 909
Palau Palaos	0	0	0	0	0	82	0	82
Panama Panama	79 982	500	846	920	0	21 859	1 994	106 100
Papua New Guinea Papouasie-Nvl-Guinée	3 951	722	456	3 178	0	4 325	0	12 632
Paraguay Paraguay	25 856	819	0	2 139	0	1 098	-78	29 834
Peru Pérou	95 833	22 035	0	6 365	4 309	7 575	4 796	140 913
Philippines Philippines	18 431	5 692	190	8 237	0	10 294	4 316	47 160
Poland Pologne	2 608	74	804	0	0	2 631	0	6 117
Portugal Portugal	0	0	56	0	0	63	0	119
Puerto Rico Porto Rico	0	0	0	0	0	48	0	48
Qatar Qatar	6 004	0	0	0	0	472	0	6 476
Republic of Moldova République de Moldova	6 273	347	631	3 201	0	1 199	1 364	13 016
Réunion Réunion	0	0	0	0	0	76	0	76

Socio-economic development assistance through the United Nations system — Development grants: thousands of US dollars, 2005 (*continued*)

Assistance en matière de développement socioéconomique fournie par le système des Nations Unies — Subventions au développement : en milliers de dollars des E.U., 2005 (*suite*)

Region, country or area Région, pays ou zone	UNDP[a] PNUD[a]	UNFPA FNUAP	UNHCR HCR	UNICEF	WFP[b] PAM[b]	Specialized agencies[c] Institutions spécialisées[c]	IFAD FIDA	Total develop. grants Total subventions au développ.
Romania Roumanie	4 847	573	1 935	2 415	0	2 442	5 891	18 104
Russian Federation Fédération de Russie	30 440	617	15 004	10 761	8 019	12 070	0	76 911
Rwanda Rwanda	8 657	1 864	7 449	7 495	18 768	4 882	7 058	56 174
Saint Helena Sainte-Hélène	0	0	0	0	0	69	0	69
Saint Kitts and Nevis Saint-Kitts-et-Nevis	204	0	0	0	0	37	0	241
Saint Lucia Sainte-Lucie	186	0	0	0	0	274	0	460
Saint Vincent-Grenadines Saint Vincent-Grenadines	225	0	0	0	0	81	0	306
Samoa Samoa	3 373	0	0	0	0	2 087	0	5 460
Sao Tome and Principe Sao Tomé-et-Principe	2 250	381	0	837	768	1 815	652	6 703
Saudi Arabia Arabie saoudite	1 449	0	1 854	0	0	14 480	0	17 783
Senegal Sénégal	8 469	2 418	1 853	7 230	6 221	7 543	13 821	47 555
Serbia and Montenegro Serbie-et-Monténégro	17 478	0	22 712	5 589	0	9 322	0	55 100
Seychelles Seychelles	0	48	0	0	0	1 711	0	1 759
Sierra Leone Sierra Leone	8 392	1 654	22 112	14 782	13 330	6 468	0	66 738
Singapore Singapour	0	0	53	0	0	188	0	240
Slovakia Slovaquie	12 694	0	713	0	0	972	0	14 379
Slovenia Slovénie	0	0	513	0	0	646	0	1 159
Solomon Islands Iles Salomon	0	0	0	0	0	2 635	0	2 635
Somalia Somalie	24 772	329	7 834	37 065	22 761	21 326	0	114 086
South Africa Afrique du Sud	9 329	906	3 055	5 471	480	5 758	0	24 999
Spain Espagne	0	0	1 261	0	0	385	0	1 646
Sri Lanka Sri Lanka	27 987	2 856	17 770	74 196	60 801	28 868	1 558	214 036
Sudan Soudan	44 435	8 092	62 843	154 487	684 970	62 454	6 862	1 024 143
Suriname Suriname	0	0	0	0	0	629	0	629
Swaziland Swaziland	984	517	0	3 668	10 774	2 614	1 577	20 133
Sweden Suède	0	0	1 905	0	0	592	0	2 497

Socio-economic development assistance through the United Nations system — Development grants: thousands of US dollars, 2005 (*continued*)

Assistance en matière de développement socioéconomique fournie par le système des Nations Unies — Subventions au développement : en milliers de dollars des E.U., 2005 (*suite*)

Region, country or area / Région, pays ou zone	UNDP[a] / PNUD[a]	UNFPA / FNUAP	UNHCR / HCR	UNICEF	WFP[b] / PAM[b]	Specialized agencies[c] / Institutions spécialisées[c]	IFAD / FIDA	Total develop. grants / Total subventions au développ.
Switzerland / Suisse	0	0	735	0	0	84	0	819
Syrian Arab Republic / Rép. arabe syrienne	5 130	1 952	1 828	1 207	3 900	4 830	3 754	22 601
Tajikistan / Tadjikistan	15 022	748	1 252	3 582	13 234	3 159	0	36 997
Thailand / Thaïlande	11 599	2 138	8 852	12 530	400	9 905	0	45 424
TFYR of Macedonia / L'ex-R.y. Macédoine	5 255	11	3 477	1 572	0	2 750	3 163	16 229
Timor-Leste / Timor-Leste	15 715	1 485	523	7 259	1 331	2 835	0	29 147
Togo / Togo	10 125	642	0	3 500	289	3 601	0	18 156
Tokelau / Tokélaou	0	0	0	0	0	71	0	71
Tonga / Tonga	0	0	0	0	0	941	0	941
Trinidad and Tobago / Trinité-et-Tobago	6 139	0	0	0	0	1 570	0	7 709
Tunisia / Tunisie	2 886	436	265	954	0	4 983	5 463	14 987
Turkey / Turquie	9 575	1 054	8 000	3 280	0	3 539	1 599	27 046
Turkmenistan / Turkménistan	1 671	507	997	1 076	0	275	0	4 526
Turks and Caicos Islands / Iles Turques et Caïques	0	0	0	0	0	21	0	21
Tuvalu / Tuvalu	0	0	0	0	0	120	0	120
Uganda / Ouganda	7 627	3 801	18 255	35 217	110 744	11 832	7 994	195 470
Ukraine / Ukraine	8 794	650	2 761	2 886	0	3 526	0	18 617
United Arab Emirates / Emirats arabes unis	1 636	0	0	0	0	405	0	2 041
United Kingdom / Royaume-Uni	0	0	1 917	0	0	417	0	2 334
United Rep. of Tanzania / Rép.-Unie de Tanzanie	30 824	5 099	29 458	20 127	43 649	12 291	9 583	151 030
United States / Etats-Unis	0	0	3 297	0	0	133	0	3 430
Uruguay / Uruguay	14 529	450	0	1 039	0	1 811	948	18 776
Uzbekistan / Ouzbékistan	12 080	874	1 216	2 823	0	2 557	0	19 549
Vanuatu / Vanuatu	0	0	0	0	0	1 393	0	1 393
Venezuela (Bolivarian Rep. of) / Venezuela (Rép. bolivar. du)	22 252	822	1 719	1 763	0	7 248	0	33 803
Viet Nam / Viet Nam	13 304	7 596	490	13 262	0	18 496	7 452	60 599

Socio-economic development assistance through the United Nations system—Development grants: thousands of US dollars, 2005 (*continued*)

Assistance en matière de développement socioéconomique fournie par le système des Nations Unies—Subventions au développement : en milliers de dollars des E.U., 2005 (*suite*)

Region, country or area Région, pays ou zone	UNDP[a] PNUD[a]	UNFPA FNUAP	UNHCR HCR	UNICEF	WFP[b] PAM[b]	Specialized agencies[c] Institutions spécialisées[c]	IFAD FIDA	Total develop. grants Total subventions au developp.
Yemen Yémen	12 303	3 642	4 494	19 537	7 514	9 742	5 023	62 255
Zambia Zambie	5 575	1 751	13 184	8 263	52 010	5 922	4 921	91 626
Zimbabwe Zimbabwe	10 804	4 404	1 799	14 087	67 998	9 237	0	108 328
Other countries[4] Autres pays[4]	**15 373**	**2 228**	**0**	**1 040**	**139 734**	**10 029**	**1 500**	**169 904**
Not elsewhere classified[4] Non-classé ailleurs[4]	**275 657**	**0**	**166 761**	**0**	**0**	**11 754**	**0**	**454 172**

Source

United Nations, "Operational activities of the United Nations for international development cooperation, Report of the Secretary-General, Addendum, Comprehensive statistical data on operational activities for development for the year 2005" (A/62/74).
The following abbreviations have been used in the table:
IFAD: International Fund for Agricultural Development
UNDP: United Nations Development Programme
UNFPA: United Nations Population Fund
UNHCR: United Nations High Commissioner for Refugees
UNICEF: United Nations Children's Fund
WFP: World Food Programme.

Notes

a Total of central resources and UNDP-administered funds.
b Includes extra-budgetary expenditures and WFP project expenditures for development activities and emergency operations. Of the latter, most was financed from the International Emergency Food Reserve and the remainder from WFP general resources.
c Total of regular budget and extra-budgetary. Regular budget includes grants financed by specialized agencies and other organizations; the major share of such expenditures is financed by WHO. Extra-budgetary includes grants financed by specialized agencies and other organizations; i.e., from funds not elsewhere specified in the table. Starting in 1998 it includes UNEP extra-budgetary expenditures. Also included are expenditures financed from government "self-supporting" contributions.
1 UNHCR figure for Australia includes expenditures in New Zealand.
2 For statistical purposes, the data for China do not include those for the Hong Kong Special Administrative Region (Hong Kong SAR) and Macao Special Administrative Region (Macao SAR).
3 West Bank and Gaza.
4 Expenditures reported with no further breakdown.

Source

Nations Unies, "Activités opérationnelles du système des Nations Unies au service de la coopération internationale pour le développement, Rapport du Secrétaire général, Additif, Données statistiques globales sur les activités opérationnelles au service du développement pour 2005" (A/62/74).
Les abréviations ci-après ont été utilisées dans le tableau :
FIDA : Fonds international de développement agricole
PNUD : Programme des Nations Unies pour le développement
FNUAP : Fonds des Nations Unies pour la population
HCR : Haut Commissariat des Nations Unies
UNICEF : Fonds des Nations Unies pour l'enfance
PAM : Programme alimentaire mondial.

Notes

a Y compris ressources centrales et fonds gérés.
b Y compris les dépenses extrabudgétaires et celles afférentes aux projets du PAM relatifs aux activités de développement et aux opérations de secours d'urgence. Les dépenses au titre des opérations de secours d'urgence ont été financées pour la plus grande partie au moyen de la réserve alimentaire internationale d'urgence, le reste étant imputé sur les ressources générales du PAM.
c Y compris budget ordinaire et extrabudgétaire. Budget ordinaire compris subventions financées par les institutions spécialisées et autres organisations sur les budgets ordinaires; la plus grande part est financée par l'OMS. Extrabudgétaire compris subventions financées par les institutions spécialisées et autres organisations sur les budgets ordinaires; fonds ne figurant pas ailleurs dans le tableau, y compris les dépenses financées au moyen des contributions "d'auto-assistance" versées par les gouvernements, comme indiqué dans la rubrique explicative, et, à partir de 1998, les dépenses du PNUE financées à l'aide de fonds extrabudgétaires.
1 Les données de l'UNHCR pour Australie compris les dépenses en Nouvelle Zélande.
2 Pour la présentation des statistiques, les données pour la Chine ne comprennent pas la Région Administrative Spéciale de Hong Kong (Hong Kong RAS) et la Région Administrative Spéciale de Macao (Macao RAS).
3 Cisjordanie et Gaza.
4 Dépenses communiquées sans autre ventilation.

Technical notes: tables 67-69

Table 67 presents estimates of flows of financial resources to individual recipients either directly (bilaterally) or through multilateral institutions (multilaterally).

The multilateral institutions include the World Bank Group, regional banks, financial institutions of the European Union and a number of United Nations institutions, programmes and trust funds.

The source of data is the Development Assistance Committee of OECD to which member countries reported data on their flow of resources to developing countries and territories, countries and territories in transition, and multilateral institutions.

Additional information on definitions, methods and sources can be found in OECD's *Geographical Distribution of Financial Flows to Aid Recipients* and www.oecd.org.

Table 68 presents the development assistance expenditures of donor countries. This table includes donors' contributions to multilateral agencies; therefore, the overall totals differ from those in table 67, which include disbursements by multilateral agencies.

Table 69 includes data on expenditures on operational activities for development undertaken by the organizations of the United Nations system. Operational activities encompass, in general, those activities of a development cooperation character that seek to mobilize or increase the potential and capacity of countries to promote economic and social development and welfare, including the transfer of resources to developing countries or regions in a tangible or intangible form.

Expenditures on operational activities for development are financed from contributions from governments and other official and non-official sources to a variety of funding channels in the United Nations system. These include United Nations funds and programmes such as contributions to the United Nations Development Programme, contributions to funds administered by the United Nations Development Programme, and regular (assessed) and other extra budgetary contributions to specialized agencies.

Data are taken from the 2007 report of the Secretary-General to the General Assembly on operational activities for development.

Notes techniques : tableaux 67 à 69

Le *tableau 67* présente les estimations des flux de ressources financières mises à la disposition des pays soit directement (aide bilatérale) soit par l'intermédiaire d'institutions multilatérales (aide multilatérale).

Les institutions multilatérales comprennent le Groupe de la Banque mondiale, les banques régionales, les institutions financières de l'Union européenne et un certain nombre d'institutions, de programmes et de fonds d'affectation spéciale des Nations Unies.

La source de données est le Comité d'aide au développement de l'OCDE, auquel les pays membres ont communiqué des données sur les flux de ressources qu'ils mettent à la disposition des pays et territoires en développement et en transition et des institutions multilatérales.

Pour plus de renseignements sur les définitions, méthodes et sources, se reporter à la publication de l'OCDE, *la Répartition géographique des ressources financières de aux pays bénéficiaires de l'Aide* et www.oecd.org.

Le *tableau 68* présente les dépenses que les pays donateurs consacrent à l'aide publique au développement (APD). Ces chiffres incluent les contributions des donateurs à des agences multilatérales, de sorte que les totaux diffèrent de ceux du tableau 67, qui incluent les dépenses des agences multilatérales.

Le *tableau 69* présente des données sur les dépenses consacrées à des activités opérationnelles pour le développement par les organisations du système des Nations Unies. Par "activités opérationnelles", on entend en général les activités ayant trait à la coopération au développement, qui visent à mobiliser ou à accroître les potentialités et aptitudes que présentent les pays pour promouvoir le développement et le bien-être économiques et sociaux, y compris les transferts de ressources vers les pays ou régions en développement sous forme tangible ou non.

Les dépenses consacrées aux activités opérationnelles pour le développement sont financées au moyen de contributions que les gouvernements et d'autres sources officielles et non officielles apportent à divers organes de financement, tels que fonds et programmes du système des Nations Unies. On peut citer notamment les contributions au Programme des Nations Unies pour le développement, les contributions aux fonds gérés par le Programme des Nations Unies pour le développement, les contributions régulières (budgétaires) et les contributions extrabudgétaires aux institutions spécialisées.

Les données sont extraites du rapport annuel de 2007 du Secrétaire général à la session de l'Assemblée générale sur les activités opérationnelles pour le développement.

Annex I

Country and area nomenclature, regional and other groupings

A. Changes in country or area names

In the periods covered by the statistics in the *Statistical Yearbook*, the following changes in designation have taken place:

Brunei Darussalam was formerly listed as Brunei;

Burkina Faso was formerly listed as Upper Volta;

Cambodia was formerly listed as Democratic Kampuchea;

Cameroon was formerly listed as United Republic of Cameroon;

Côte d'Ivoire was formerly listed as Ivory Coast;

Czech Republic, Slovakia: Since 1 January 1993, data for the Czech Republic and Slovakia, where available, are shown separately under the appropriate country name. For periods prior to 1 January 1993, where no separate data are available for the Czech Republic and Slovakia, unless otherwise indicated, data for the former Czechoslovakia are shown under the country name "former Czechoslovakia";

Democratic Republic of the Congo was formerly listed as Zaire;

Germany: Through the accession of the German Democratic Republic to the Federal Republic of Germany with effect from 3 October 1990, the two German States have united to form one sovereign State. As from the date of unification, the Federal Republic of Germany acts in the United Nations under the designation "Germany". All data shown which pertain to Germany prior to 3 October 1990 are indicated separately for the Federal Republic of Germany and the former German Democratic Republic based on their respective territories at the time indicated;

Hong Kong Special Administrative Region of China: Pursuant to a Joint Declaration signed on 19 December 1984, the United Kingdom restored Hong Kong to the People's Republic of China with effect from 1 July 1997; the People's Republic of China resumed the exercise of sovereignty over the territory with effect from that date;

Macao Special Administrative Region of China: Pursuant to the joint declaration signed on 13 April 1987, Portugal restored Macao to the People's Republic of China with effect from 20 December 1999; the People's Republic of China resumed the exercise of sovereignty over the territory with effect from that date;

Myanmar was formerly listed as Burma;

Palau was formerly listed as Pacific Islands and includes data for Federated States of Micronesia, Marshall Islands and Northern Mariana Islands;

Annexe I

Nomenclature des pays ou zones, groupements régionaux et autres groupements

A. Changements dans le nom des pays ou zones

Au cours des périodes sur lesquelles portent les statistiques, dans l'*Annuaire Statistique* les changements de désignation suivants ont eu lieu:

Le *Brunei Darussalam* apparaissait antérieurement sous le nom de Brunei;

Le *Burkina Faso* apparaissait antérieurement sous le nom de la Haute-Volta;

Le *Cambodge* apparaissait antérieurement sous le nom de la Kampuchéa démocratique;

Le *Cameroun* apparaissait antérieurement sous le nom de République-Unie du Cameroun;

République tchèque, Slovaquie: Depuis le 1er janvier 1993, les données relatives à la République tchèque, et à la Slovaquie, lorsqu'elles sont disponibles, sont présentées séparément sous le nom de chacun des pays. En ce qui concerne la période précédant le 1er janvier 1993, pour laquelle on ne possède pas de données séparées pour les deux Républiques, les données relatives à l'ex-Tchécoslovaquie sont, sauf indication contraire, présentées sous le titre "l'ex-Tchécoslovaquie";

La *République démocratique du Congo* apparaissait antérieurement sous le nom de Zaïre;

Allemagne: En vertu de l'adhésion de la République démocratique allemande à la République fédérale d'Allemagne, prenant effet le 3 octobre 1990, les deux Etats allemands se sont unis pour former un seul Etat souverain. A compter de la date de l'unification, la République fédérale d'Allemagne est désigné à l'ONU sous le nom d'"Allemagne". Toutes les données se rapportant à l'Allemagne avant le 3 octobre figurent dans deux rubriques séparées basées sur les territoires respectifs de la République fédérale d'Allemagne et l'ex-République démocratique allemande selon la période indiquée;

Hong Kong, région administrative spéciale de Chine: Conformément à une Déclaration commune signée le 19 décembre 1984, le Royaume-Uni a rétrocédé Hong Kong à la République populaire de Chine, avec effet au 1er juillet 1997; la souveraineté de la République populaire de Chine s'exerce à nouveau sur le territoire à compter de cette date;

Macao, région administrative spéciale de Chine: Conformément à une Déclaration commune signée le 13 avril 1987, le Portugal a rétrocédé Macao à la République populaire de Chine, avec effet au 20 décembre 1999; la souveraineté de la République populaire de Chine s'exerce à nouveau sur le territoire à compter de cette date;

Saint Kitts and Nevis was formerly listed as Saint Christopher and Nevis;

Serbia, Montenegro: As of 1992, data provided for Yugoslavia refer to the Federal Republic of Yugoslavia which was composed of the two republics of Serbia and Montenegro. On 4 February 2003, the official name of the "Federal Republic of Yugoslavia" was changed to "Serbia and Montenegro". On 3 June 2006, Serbia and Montenegro formally dissolved into two independent countries. When data are available separately for Montenegro and/or Serbia, they are shown under the respective heading.

Timor-Leste: Formerly East Timor;

Former *USSR*: In 1991, the Union of Soviet Socialist Republics formally dissolved into fifteen independent countries (Armenia, Azerbaijan, Belarus, Estonia, Georgia, Kazakhstan, Kyrgyzstan, Latvia, Lithuania, Republic of Moldova, Russian Federation, Tajikistan, Turkmenistan, Ukraine and Uzbekistan). Whenever possible, data are shown for the individual countries. Otherwise, data are shown for the former USSR;

Yemen: On 22 May 1990 Democratic Yemen and Yemen merged to form a single State. Since that date they have been represented as one Member with the name 'Yemen'.

It should be noted that unless otherwise indicated, for statistical purposes, the data for China exclude those for Hong Kong Special Administrative Region of China, Macao Special Administrative Region of China and Taiwan province of China.

B. Regional groupings

The scheme of regional groupings given below presents seven regions based mainly on continents. Five of the seven continental regions are further subdivided into 21 regions that are so drawn as to obtain greater homogeneity in sizes of population, demographic circumstances and accuracy of demographic statistics. This nomenclature is widely used in international statistics and is followed to the greatest extent possible in the present *Yearbook* in order to promote consistency and facilitate comparability and analysis. However, it is by no means universal in international statistical compilation, even at the level of continental regions, and variations in international statistical sources and methods dictate many unavoidable differences in particular fields in the present *Yearbook*. General differences are indicated in the footnotes to the classification presented below. More detailed differences are given in the footnotes and technical notes to individual tables.

Neither is there international standardization in the use of the terms "developed" and "developing" countries, areas or regions. These terms are used in the present publication

Le *Myanmar* apparaissait antérieurement sous le nom de Birmanie;

Les *Palaos* apparaissait antérieurement sous le nom de Iles du Pacifique y compris les données pour les Etats fédérés de Micronésie, les îles Marshall et îles Mariannes du Nord;

Saint-Kitts-Et-Nevis apparaissait antérieurement sous le nom de Saint-Christophe-et-Nevis;

Serbie, Monténégro : Les données fournies pour la Yougoslavie à partir de 1992 se rapportent à la République fédérale de Yougoslavie, qui était composée des deux républiques de la Serbie et du Monténégro. Le 4 février 2003, la «République fédérale de Yougoslavie», ayant changé de nom officiel, est devenu la «Serbie-et-Monténégro». Le 3 juin 2006, la Serbie-et-Monténégro s'est officiellement dissoute pour former deux États indépendants. Lorsque des données sont disponibles séparément pour la Serbie et le Monténégro, elles sont présentées dans leurs catégories respectives.

Timor-Leste: Ex Timor oriental;

L'ex-*URSS*: En 1991, l'Union des républiques socialistes soviétiques s'est séparé en 15 pays distincts (Arménie, Azerbaïdjan, Belarus, Estonie, Géorgie, Kazakhstan, Kirghizistan, Lettonie, Lituanie, République de Moldova, Fédération de Russie, Tadjikistan, Turkménistan, Ukraine, Ouzbékistan). Les données sont présentées pour ces pays pris séparément quand cela est possible. Autrement, les données sont présentées pour l'ex-URSS;

Yémen: Le Yémen et le Yémen démocratique ont fusionné le 22 mai 1990 pour ne plus former qu'un seul Etat, qui est depuis lors représenté comme tel à l'Organisation, sous le nom 'Yémen'.

Il convient de noter que sauf indication contraire, les données statistiques relatives à la Chine ne comprennent pas celles qui concernent la région administrative spéciale de Hong Kong, la région administrative spéciale de Macao et la province chinoise de Taiwan.

B. Groupements régionaux

Le système de groupements régionaux présenté ci-dessous comporte sept régions basées principalement sur les continents. Cinq des sept régions continentales sont elles-mêmes subdivisées, formant ainsi 21 régions délimitées de manière à obtenir une homogénéité accrue dans les effectifs de population, les situations démographiques et la précision des statistiques démographiques. Cette nomenclature est couramment utilisée aux fins des statistiques internationales et a été appliquée autant qu'il a été possible dans le présent *Annuaire* en vue de renforcer la cohérence et de faciliter la comparaison et l'analyse. Son utilisation pour l'établissement des statistiques internationales n'est cependant rien moins qu'universelle, même au niveau des régions continentales,

to refer to regional groupings generally considered as "developed": these are Europe and the former USSR, the United States of America and Canada in Northern America, and Australia, Japan and New Zealand in Asia and Oceania. These designations are intended for statistical convenience and do not necessarily express a judgement about the stage reached by a particular country or area in the development process. Differences from this usage are indicated in the notes to individual tables.

et les variations que présentent les sources et méthodes statistiques internationales entraînent inévitablement de nombreuses différences dans certains domaines de cet *Annuaire*. Les différences d'ordre général sont indiquées dans les notes figurant au bas de la classification présentée ci-dessous. Les différences plus spécifiques sont mentionnées dans les notes techniques et notes de bas de page accompagnant les divers tableaux.

L'application des expressions "développés" et "en développement" aux pays, zones ou régions n'est pas non plus normalisée à l'échelle internationale. Ces expressions sont utilisées dans la présente publication en référence aux groupements régionaux généralement considérés comme "développés", à savoir l'Europe et l'ex-URSS, les Etats-Unis d'Amérique et le Canada en Amérique septentrionale, et l'Australie, le Japon et la Nouvelle-Zélande dans la région de l'Asie et du Pacifique. Ces appellations sont employées pour des raisons de commodité statistique et n'expriment pas nécessairement un jugement sur le stade de développement atteint par tel ou tel pays ou zone. Les cas différant de cet usage sont signalés dans les notes accompagnant les tableaux concernés.

Africa

Sub-Saharan Africa

Eastern Africa

Burundi
Comoros
Djibouti
Eritrea
Ethiopia
Kenya
Madagascar
Malawi
Mauritius
Mozambique
Réunion
Rwanda
Seychelles
Somalia
Uganda
United Republic of Tanzania
Zambia
Zimbabwe

Middle Africa

Angola
Cameroon
Central African Republic
Chad
Congo
Democratic Republic of the Congo
Equatorial Guinea
Gabon
Sao Tome and Principe

Southern Africa

Botswana
Lesotho
Namibia
South Africa
Swaziland

Afrique

Afrique subsaharienne

Afrique orientale

Burundi
Comores
Djibouti
Erythrée
Ethiopie
Kenya
Madagascar
Malawi
Maurice
Mozambique
Ouganda
République-Unie de Tanzanie
Réunion
Rwanda
Seychelles
Somalie
Zambie
Zimbabwe

Afrique centrale

Angola
Cameroun
Congo
Gabon
Guinée équatoriale
République centrafricaine
République démocratique du Congo
Sao Tomé-et-Principe
Tchad

Afrique australe

Afrique du Sud
Botswana
Lesotho
Namibie
Swaziland

Western Africa

Benin
Burkina Faso
Cape Verde
Côte d'Ivoire
Gambia
Ghana
Guinea
Guinea-Bissau
Liberia
Mali
Mauritania
Niger
Nigeria
Saint Helena
Senegal
Sierra Leone
Togo

Northern Africa

Algeria
Egypt
Libyan Arab Jamahiriya
Morocco
Sudan
Tunisia
Western Sahara

Americas

Latin America and the Caribbean

Caribbean

Anguilla
Antigua and Barbuda
Aruba
Bahamas
Barbados
British Virgin Islands
Cayman Islands
Cuba
Dominica
Dominican Republic
Grenada
Guadeloupe
Haiti
Jamaica
Martinique
Montserrat
Netherlands Antilles
Puerto Rico
Saint Kitts and Nevis
Saint Lucia
Saint Vincent and the Grenadines
Trinidad and Tobago
Turks and Caicos Islands
United States Virgin Islands

Central America

Belize
Costa Rica
El Salvador
Guatemala
Honduras
Mexico
Nicaragua
Panama

South America

Argentina
Bolivia
Brazil
Chile
Colombia
Ecuador
Falkland Islands (Malvinas)
French Guiana
Guyana
Paraguay
Peru
Suriname
Uruguay
Venezuela

Northern America[a]

Bermuda
Canada
Greenland
Saint Pierre and Miquelon
United States of America

Afrique occidentale

Bénin
Burkina Faso
Cap-Vert
Côte d'Ivoire
Gambie
Ghana
Guinée
Guinée-Bissau
Libéria
Mali
Mauritanie
Niger
Nigéria
Sainte-Hélène
Sénégal
Sierra Leone
Togo

Afrique septentrionale

Algérie
Egypte
Jamahiriya arabe libyenne
Maroc
Sahara occidental
Soudan
Tunisie

Amériques

Amérique latine et Caraïbes

Caraïbes

Anguilla
Antigua-et-Barbuda
Antilles néerlandaises
Aruba
Bahamas
Barbade
Cuba
Dominique
Grenade
Guadeloupe
Haïti
Iles Caïmanes
Iles Turques et Caïques
Iles Vierges américaines
Iles Vierges britanniques
Jamaïque
Martinique
Montserrat
Porto Rico
République dominicaine
Sainte-Lucie
Saint-Kitts-et-Nevis
Saint-Vincent-et-les Grenadines
Trinité-et-Tobago

Amérique centrale

Belize
Costa Rica
El Salvador
Guatemala
Honduras
Mexique
Nicaragua
Panama

Amérique du Sud

Argentine
Bolivie
Brésil
Chili
Colombie
Equateur
Guyana
Guyane française
Iles Falkland (Malvinas)
Paraguay
Pérou
Suriname
Uruguay
Venezuela

Amérique septentrionale[a]

Bermudes
Canada
Etats-Unis d'Amérique
Groenland
Saint-Pierre-et-Miquelon

Asia

Eastern Asia

China
China, Hong Kong Special Administrative Region
China, Macao Special Administrative Region
Democratic People's Republic of Korea
Japan
Mongolia
Republic of Korea

South-central Asia

Afghanistan
Bangladesh
Bhutan
India
Iran (Islamic Republic of)
Kazakhstan
Kyrgyzstan
Maldives
Nepal
Pakistan
Sri Lanka
Tajikistan
Turkmenistan
Uzbekistan

South-eastern Asia

Brunei Darussalam
Cambodia
Indonesia
Lao People's Democratic Republic
Malaysia
Myanmar
Philippines
Singapore
Thailand
Timor-Leste
Viet Nam

Western Asia

Armenia
Azerbaijan
Bahrain
Cyprus
Georgia
Iraq
Israel
Jordan
Kuwait
Lebanon
Occupied Palestinian Territory
Oman
Qatar
Saudi Arabia
Syrian Arab Republic
Turkey
United Arab Emirates
Yemen

Europe

Eastern Europe

Belarus
Bulgaria
Czech Republic
Hungary
Poland
Republic of Moldova
Romania
Russian Federation
Slovakia
Ukraine

Northern Europe

Channel Islands
Denmark
Estonia
Faeroe Islands
Finland
Iceland
Ireland
Isle of Man
Latvia
Lithuania
Norway
Svalbard and Jan Mayen Islands
Sweden
United Kingdom

Asie

Asie orientale

Chine
Chine, Hong Kong, région administrative spéciale
Chine, Macao, région administrative spéciale
Japon
Mongolie
République de Corée
République populaire démocratique de Corée

Asie centrale et du Sud

Afghanistan
Bangladesh
Bhoutan
Inde
Iran (République islamique d')
Kazakhstan
Kirghizistan
Maldives
Népal
Ouzbékistan
Pakistan
Sri Lanka
Tadjikistan
Turkménistan

Asie du Sud-Est

Brunéi Darussalam
Cambodge
Indonésie
Malaisie
Myanmar
Philippines
République démocratique populaire lao
Singapour
Thaïlande
Timor-Leste
Viet Nam

Asie occidentale

Arabie saoudite
Arménie
Azerbaïdjan
Bahreïn
Chypre
Emirats arabes unis
Géorgie
Iraq
Israël
Jordanie
Koweït
Liban
Oman
Qatar
République arabe syrienne
Territoire palestinien occupé
Turquie
Yémen

Europe

Europe orientale

Bélarus
Bulgarie
Fédération de Russie
Hongrie
Pologne
République de Moldova
République tchèque
Roumanie
Slovaquie
Ukraine

Europe septentrionale

Danemark
Estonie
Finlande
Ile de Man
Iles Anglo-Normandes
Iles Féroé
Iles Svalbard et Jan Mayen
Irlande
Islande
Lettonie
Lituanie
Norvège
Royaume-Uni
Suède

Southern Europe

Albania
Andorra
Bosnia and Herzegovina
Croatia
Gibraltar
Greece
Holy See
Italy
Malta
Portugal
San Marino
Serbia and Montenegro
Slovenia
Spain
The former Yugoslav Republic of Macedonia

Western Europe

Austria
Belgium
France
Germany
Liechtenstein
Luxembourg
Monaco
Netherlands
Switzerland

Oceania

Australia and New Zealand

Australia
New Zealand
Norfolk Island

Melanesia

Fiji
New Caledonia
Papua New Guinea
Solomon Islands
Vanuatu

Micronesia-Polynesia

Micronesia

Guam
Kiribati
Marshall Islands
Micronesia (Federated States of)
Nauru
Northern Mariana Islands
Palau

Polynesia

American Samoa
Cook Islands
French Polynesia
Niue
Pitcairn
Samoa
Tokelau
Tonga
Tuvalu
Wallis and Futuna Islands

C. Other groupings

Following is a list of other groupings and their compositions presented in the *Yearbook*. These groupings are organized mainly around economic and trade interests in regional associations.

Andean Common Market (ANCOM)

Bolivia
Colombia
Ecuador
Peru
Venezuela

Europe méridionale

Albanie
Andorre
Bosnie-Herzégovine
Croatie
Espagne
Ex-République yougoslave de Macédoine
Gibraltar
Grèce
Italie
Malte
Portugal
Saint-Marin
Saint-Siège
Serbie-et-Monténégro
Slovénie

Europe occidentale

Allemagne
Autriche
Belgique
France
Liechtenstein
Luxembourg
Monaco
Pays-Bas
Suisse

Océanie

Australie et Nouvelle-Zélande

Australie
Ile Norfolk
Nouvelle-Zélande

Mélanésie

Fidji
Iles Salomon
Nouvelle-Calédonie
Papouasie-Nouvelle-Guinée
Vanuatu

Micronésie-Polynésie

Micronésie

Guam
Iles Mariannes septentrionales
Iles Marshall
Kiribati
Micronésie (Etats fédérés de)
Nauru
Palaos

Polynésie

Iles Cook
Iles Wallis-et-Futuna
Nioué
Pitcairn
Polynésie française
Samoa
Samoa américaines
Tokélaou
Tonga
Tuvalu

C. Autres groupements

On trouvera ci-après une liste des autres groupements et de leur composition, présentée dans l'*Annuaire*. Ces groupements correspondent essentiellement à des intérêts économiques et commerciaux d'après les associations régionales.

Marché commun andin (ANCOM)

Bolivie
Colombie
Equateur
Pérou
Venezuela

Asia-Pacific Economic Cooperation (APEC)

Australia
Brunei Darussalam
Canada
Chile
China
China, Hong Kong Special Administrative Region
Indonesia
Japan
Malaysia
Mexico
New Zealand
Papua New Guinea
Peru
Philippines
Republic of Korea
Russian Federation
Singapore
Taiwan Province of China
Thailand
United States of America
Viet Nam

Caribbean Community and Common Market (CARICOM)

Antigua and Barbuda
Bahamas (member of the Community only)
Barbados
Belize
Dominica
Grenada
Guyana
Haiti
Jamaica
Montserrat
Saint Kitts and Nevis
Saint Lucia
Saint Vincent and the Grenadines
Suriname
Trinidad and Tobago

Common Market for Eastern and Southern Africa (COMESA)

Angola
Burundi
Comoros
Democratic Republic of the Congo
Djibouti
Egypt
Eritrea
Ethiopia
Kenya
Madagascar
Malawi
Mauritius
Namibia
Rwanda
Seychelles
Sudan
Swaziland
Uganda
Zambia
Zimbabwe

Commonwealth of Independent States (CIS)

Armenia
Azerbaijan
Belarus
Georgia
Kazakhstan
Kyrgyzstan
Republic of Moldova
Russian Federation
Tajikistan
Turkmenistan
Ukraine
Uzbekistan

European Union (EU)

Austria
Belgium
Denmark
Finland
France
Germany
Greece
Ireland
Italy
Luxembourg
Netherlands
Portugal
Spain
Sweden
United Kingdom

Coopération économique Asie-Pacifique (CEAP)

Australie
Brunéi Darussalam
Canada
Chili
Chine
Chine, Hong Kong, région administrative spéciale
Etats-Unis d'Amérique
Fédération de Russie
Indonésie
Japon
Malaisie
Mexique
Nouvelle-Zélande
Papouasie-Nouvelle-Guinée
Pérou
Philippines
Province chinoise de Taiwan
République de Corée
Singapour
Thaïlande
Viet Nam

Communauté des Caraïbes et Marché commun des Caraïbes (CARICOM)

Antigua-et-Barbuda
Bahamas (membre de la communauté seulement)
Barbade
Belize
Dominique
Grenade
Guyana
Haïti
Jamaïque
Montserrat
Sainte-Lucie
Saint-Kitts-et-Nevis
Saint-Vincent-et-les Grenadines
Suriname
Trinité-et-Tobago

Marché commun de l'Afrique de l'Est et de l'Afrique australe (COMESA)

Angola
Burundi
Comores
Djibouti
Egypte
Erythrée
Ethiopie
Kenya
Madagascar
Malawi
Maurice
Namibie
Ouganda
République démocratique du Congo
Rwanda
Seychelles
Soudan
Swaziland
Zambie
Zimbabwe

Communauté d'Etats indépendants (CEI)

Arménie
Azerbaïdjan
Belarus
Fédération de Russie
Géorgie
Kazakhstan
Kirghizistan
Ouzbékistan
République de Moldova
Tadjikistan
Turkménistan
Ukraine

Union européenne (UE)

Allemagne
Autriche
Belgique
Danemark
Espagne
Finlande
France
Grèce
Irlande
Italie
Luxembourg
Pays-Bas
Portugal
Royaume-Uni
Suède

Least developed countries (LDCs)[b]

Afghanistan
Angola
Bangladesh
Benin
Bhutan
Burkina Faso
Burundi
Cambodia
Cape Verde
Central African Republic
Chad
Comoros
Democratic Republic of the Congo
Djibouti
Equatorial Guinea
Eritrea
Ethiopia
Gambia
Guinea
Guinea-Bissau
Haiti
Kiribati
Lao People's Democratic Republic
Lesotho
Liberia
Madagascar
Malawi
Maldives
Mali
Mauritania
Mozambique
Myanmar
Nepal
Niger
Rwanda
Samoa
Sao Tome and Principe
Senegal
Sierra Leone
Solomon Islands
Somalia
Sudan
Togo
Tuvalu
Uganda
United Republic of Tanzania
Vanuatu
Yemen
Zambia

Mercado Común Sudamericano (MERCOSUR)

Argentina
Brazil
Paraguay
Uruguay

North American Free Trade Agreement (NAFTA)

Canada
Mexico
United States of America

Organisation for Economic Cooperation and Development (OECD)

Australia
Austria
Belgium
Canada
Czech Republic
Denmark
Finland
France
Germany
Greece
Hungary
Iceland
Ireland
Italy
Japan
Luxembourg
Mexico
Netherlands
New Zealand
Norway
Poland
Portugal
Republic of Korea
Slovakia
Spain
Sweden
Switzerland
Turkey
United Kingdom
United States of America

Pays les moins avancés (PMA)b

Afghanistan
Angola
Bangladesh
Bénin
Bhoutan
Burkina Faso
Burundi
Cambodge
Cap-Vert
Comores
Djibouti
Erythrée
Ethiopie
Gambie
Guinée
Guinée équatoriale
Guinée-Bissau
Haïti
Iles Salomon
Kiribati
Lesotho
Libéria
Madagascar
Malawi
Maldives
Mali
Mauritanie
Mozambique
Myanmar
Népal
Niger
Ouganda
République centrafricaine
République démocratique du Congo
République démocratique populaire lao
République-Unie de Tanzanie
Rwanda
Samoa
Sao Tomé-et-Principe
Sénégal
Sierra Leone
Somalie
Soudan
Tchad
Togo
Tuvalu
Vanuatu
Yémen
Zambie

Marché commun sud-américain (Mercosur)

Argentine
Brésil
Paraguay
Uruguay

Accord de libre-échange nord-américain (ALENA)

Canada
Etats-Unis d'Amérique
Mexique

Organisation de coopération et de développement économiques (OCDE)

Allemagne
Australie
Autriche
Belgique
Canada
Danemark
Espagne
Etats-Unis d'Amérique
Finlande
France
Grèce
Hongrie
Irlande
Islande
Italie
Japon
Luxembourg
Mexique
Norvège
Nouvelle-Zélande
Pays-Bas
Pologne
Portugal
République de Corée
République tchèque
Royaume-Uni
Slovaquie
Suède
Suisse
Turquie

Organization of Petroleum Exporting Countries (OPEC)

Algeria
Indonesia
Iran (Islamic Republic of)
Iraq
Kuwait
Libyan Arab Jamahiriya
Nigeria
Qatar
Saudi Arabia
United Arab Emirates
Venezuela

Southern African Customs Union (SACU)

Botswana
Lesotho
Namibia
South Africa
Swaziland

Notes

a The continent of North America comprises Northern America, Caribbean and Central America.

b As determined by the General Assembly in its resolution 49/133.

Organisation des pays exportateurs de pétrole (OPEP)

Algérie
Arabie saoudite
Emirats arabes unis
Indonésie
Iran (République islamique d')
Iraq
Jamahiriya arabe libyenne
Koweït
Nigéria
Qatar
Venezuela

Union douanière d'Afrique australe

Afrique du Sud
Botswana
Lesotho
Namibie
Swaziland

Notes

a Le continent de l'Amérique du Nord comprend l'Amérique septentrionale, les Caraïbes et l'Amérique centrale.

b Comme déterminé par l'Assemblée générale dans sa résolution 49/133.

Annex II

Annexe II

Conversion coefficients and factors

The metric system of weights and measures is employed in the *Statistical Yearbook*. In this system, the relationship between units of volume and capacity is: 1 litre = 1 cubic decimetre (dm3) exactly (as decided by the 12th International Conference of Weights and Measures, New Delhi, November 1964).

Section A shows the equivalents of the basic metric, British imperial and United States units of measurements. According to an agreement between the national standards institutions of English-speaking nations, the British and United States units of length, area and volume are now identical, and based on the yard = 0.9144 metre exactly. The weight measures in both systems are based on the pound = 0.45359237 kilogram exactly (Weights and Measures Act 1963 (London), and *Federal Register announcement of 1 July 1959: Refinement of Values for the Yard and Pound* (Washington D.C.)).

Section B shows various derived or conventional conversion coefficients and equivalents.

Section C shows other conversion coefficients or factors which have been utilized in the compilation of certain tables in the *Statistical Yearbook*. Some of these are only of an approximate character and have been employed solely to obtain a reasonable measure of international comparability in the tables.

For a comprehensive survey of international and national systems of weights and measures and of units' weights for a large number of commodities in different countries, see *World Weights and Measures*.

Coefficients et facteurs de conversion

L'*Annuaire statistique* utilise le système métrique pour les poids et mesures. La relation entre unités métriques de volume et de capacité est: 1 litre = 1 décimètre cube (dm3) exactement (comme fut décidé à la Conférence internationale des poids et mesures, New Delhi, novembre 1964).

La section A fournit les équivalents principaux des systèmes de mesure métrique, britannique et américain. Suivant un accord entre les institutions de normalisation nationales des pays de langue anglaise, les mesures britanniques et américaines de longueur, superficie et volume sont désormais identiques, et sont basées sur le yard = 0.9144 mètre exactement. Les mesures de poids se rapportent, dans les deux systèmes, à la livre (pound) = 0.45359237 kilogramme exactement (*Weights and Measures Act 1963* (Londres), et *Federal Register Announcement of 1 July 1959: Refinement of Values for the Yard and Pound* (Washington, D.C.)).

La section B fournit divers coefficients et facteurs de conversion conventionnels ou dérivés.

La section C fournit d'autres coefficients ou facteurs de conversion utilisés dans l'élaboration de certains tableaux de l'*Annuaire statistique*. D'aucuns ne sont que des approximations et n'ont été utilisés que pour obtenir un degré raisonnable de comparabilité sur le plan international.

Pour une étude d'ensemble des systèmes internationaux et nationaux de poids et mesures, et d'unités de poids pour un grand nombre de produits dans différents pays, voir *World Weights and Measures*.

A. Equivalents of metric, British imperial and United States units of measure

A. Equivalents des unités métriques, britanniques et des États-Unis

Metric units Unités métriques	British imperial and US equivalents Equivalents en mesures britanniques et des Etats-Unis		British imperial and US units Unités britanniques et des Etats-Unis	Metric equivalents Equivalents en mesures métriques	
Length — Longueur					
1 centimetre – centimètre (cm)	0.3937008	inch	1 inch	2.540	cm
1 metre – mètre (m)	3.280840	feet	1 foot	30.480	cm
	1.093613	yard	1 yard	0.9144	m
1 kilometre – kilomètre (km)	0.6213712	mile	1 mile	1609.344	m
	0.5399568	international nautical mile	1 international nautical mile	1852.000	m
Area — Superficie					
1 square centimetre – (cm^2)	0.1550003	square inch	1 square inch	6.45160	cm^2
1 square metre – (m^2)	10.763910	square feet	1 square foot	9.290304	dm^2
	1.195990	square yards	1 square yard	0.83612736	m^2
1 hectare – (ha)	2.471054	acres	1 acre	0.4046856	ha
1 square kilometre – (km^2)	0.3861022	square mile	1 square mile	2.589988	km^2
Volume					
1 cubic centimetre – (cm^3)	0.06102374	cubic inch	1 cubic inch	16.38706	cm^3
1 cubic metre – (m^3)	35.31467	cubic feet	1 cubic foot	28.316847	dm^3
	1.307951	cubic yards	1 cubic yard	0.76455486	m^3

Metric units Unités métriques	British imperial and US equivalents Equivalents en mesures britanniques et des Etats-Unis	British imperial and US units Unités britanniques et des Etats-Unis	Metric equivalents Equivalents en mesures métriques
Capacity — Capacité			
1 litre (l)	0.8798766 British imperial quart	1 British imperial quart	1.136523 l
	1.056688 U.S. liquid quart	1 U.S. liquid quart	0.9463529 l
	0.908083 U.S. dry quart	1 U.S. dry quart	1.1012208 l
1 hectolitre (hl)	21.99692 British imperial gallons	1 British imperial gallon	4.546092 l
	26.417200 U.S. gallons	1 U.S. gallon	3.785412 l
	2.749614 British imperial bushels	1 imperial bushel	36.368735 l
	2.837760 U.S. bushels	1 U.S. bushel	35.239067 l
Weight or mass — Poids			
1 kilogram (kg)	35.27396 av. ounce	1 av. ounce	28.349523 g
	32.15075 troy ounces	1 troy ounce	31.10348 g
	2.204623 av. pounds	1 av. pound	453.59237 g
		1 cental (100 lb.)	45.359237 kg
		1 hundredweight (112 lb.)	50.802345 kg
1 ton – tonne (t)	1.1023113 short tons	1 short ton (2 000 lb.)	0.9071847 t
	0.9842065 long tons	1 long ton (2 240 lb.)	1.0160469 t

B. Various conventional or derived coefficients

Railway and air transport

- 1 passenger-mile = 1.609344 passenger kilometre
- 1 short ton-mile = 1.459972 tonne-kilometre
- 1 long ton-mile = 1.635169 tonne kilometre

Ship tonnage

- 1 registered ton (100 cubic feet) = 2.83m3
- 1 British shipping ton (42 cubic feet) = 1.19m3
- 1 U.S. shipping ton (40 cubic feet) = 1.13m3
- 1 deadweight ton (dwt ton = long ton) = 1.016047 metric ton

Electric energy

- 1 Kilowatt (kW) = 1.34102 British horsepower (hp)
- 1.35962 cheval vapeur (cv)

C. Other coefficients or conversion factors employed in *Statistical Yearbook* tables

Roundwood

- Equivalent in solid volume without bark.

Sugar

- 1 metric ton raw sugar = 0.9 metric ton refined sugar
- For the United States and its possessions:
- 1 metric ton refined sugar = 1.07 metric tons raw sugar

B. Divers coefficients conventionnels ou dérivés

Transport ferroviaire et aérien

- 1 voyageur (passager)-kilomètre = 0.621371 passenger-mile
- 1 tonne-kilomètre = 0.684945 short ton-mile
- 0.611558 long ton-mile

Tonnage de navire

- 1 mètre cubique – m3 = 0.353 tonne de jauge
- 0.841 British shipping ton
- 0.885 US shipping ton
- 1 tonne métrique = 0.984 dwt ton

Energie électrique

- 1 British horsepower (hp) = 0.7457 kW
- 1 cheval vapeur (cv) = 0.735499 kW

C. Autres coefficients ou facteurs de conversion utilisés dans les tableaux de l'*Annuaire statistique*

Bois rond

- Equivalences en volume solide sans écorce.

Sucre

- 1 tonne métrique de sucre brut = 0.9 tonne métrique de sucre raffiné
- Pour les États-Unis et leurs possessions:
- 1 tonne métrique de sucre raffiné = 1.07 tonne métrique de sucre brut

Annex III

Tables added and omitted

A. *Tables added*

The present issue of the *Statistical Yearbook* includes the following five tables which were not presented in the previous issue:

- Table 9: Population in urban and rural areas, rates of growth and largest urban agglomeration population;
- Table 26: Employment by economic activity;
- Table 34: Livestock;
- Table 35: Fertilizers;
- Table 55: Threatened species.

B. *Tables omitted*

The following tables which were presented in previous issues are not presented in the present issue. They will be updated in future issues of the *Yearbook* when new data become available:

- Selected indicators of life expectancy, childbearing and mortality;
- Daily newspapers;
- Non-daily newspapers and periodicals;
- Book production: number of titles by the Universal Decimal Classification;
- Cinemas: number, seating capacity and annual attendance;
- Television and radio receivers in use;
- Oil crops;
- Fabrics;
- Leather footwear;
- Sulphuric acid;
- Pig iron and crude steel;
- Passenger cars;
- Washing machines for household use;
- Machine tools;
- Lorries (trucks);
- Water supply and sanitation coverage.

C. *Table discontinued*

- Merchant shipping: fleets.

Annexe III

Tableaux ajoutés et supprimés

A. *Tableaux ajoutés*

Dans ce numéro de l'*Annuaire statistique*, les cinq tableaux suivants qui n'ont pas été présentés dans le numéro antérieur, ont été ajoutés:

- Tableau 9: Population urbaine, population rurale, taux d'accroissement et population de l'agglomération urbaine la plus peuplée;
- Tableau 26 : Emploi par activité économique;
- Tableau 34 : Cheptel;
- Tableau 35 : Engrais;
- Tableau 55 : Espèces menacées.

B. *Tableaux supprimés*

Les tableaux suivants qui ont été repris dans les éditions antérieures n'ont pas été repris dans la présente édition. Ils seront actualisés dans les futures livraisons de l'*Annuaire* à mesure que des données nouvelles deviendront disponibles:

- Choix d'indicateurs de l'espérance de vie, de la maternité et de la mortalité;
- Journaux quotidiens;
- Journaux non quotidiens et périodiques
- Production de livres : nombre de titres classés d'après la Classification Décimale Universelle
- Cinémas : nombre d'établissements, nombre de sièges et fréquentation annuelle
- Récepteurs de télévision et de radiodiffusion sonore en circulation
- Cultures oléagineuses;
- Tissus;
- Chaussures de cuir;
- Acide sulfurique;
- Fonte et acier brut;
- Voitures de tourisme;
- Machines à laver à usage domestique;
- Machines-outils;
- Camions ;
- Accès à l'eau et à l'assainissement.

C. *Tableau discontinué*

- Transports maritimes: flotte marchande.

Statistical sources and references

A. Statistical sources

1. Carbon Dioxide Information Analysis Center, *Global, Regional, and National CO2 Emissions Estimates from Fossil-Fuel Burning, Hydraulic Cement Production, and Gas Flaring* (Oak Ridge, Tennessee, USA); web site http://cdiac.esd.ornl.gov.
2. Food and Agriculture Organization of the United Nations, *FAO Statistical Yearbook* (Rome); web site http://faostat.fao.org.
3. ________, *FAO Yearbook of Fishery Statistics, Aquaculture production* (Rome).
4. ________, *FAO Yearbook of Fishery Statistics, Capture production* (Rome).
5. ________, *Global Forest Resources Assessment 2005* (Rome); web site www.fao.org/forestry/fra2005.
6. International Civil Aviation Organization (Montreal); web site www.icao.int.
7. International Labour Office, *Yearbook of Labour Statistics* (Geneva); web site http://laborsta.ilo.org.
8. International Monetary Fund, *Balance of Payments Statistics Yearbook* (Washington, D.C.); web site www.imf.org.
9. ________, *International Financial Statistics* (Washington, D.C.).
10. International Sugar Organization, *Sugar Yearbook* (London).
11. International Telecommunication Union, *World Telecommunication Development Report* (Geneva); web site www.itu.int.
12. ________, *Yearbook of Statistics, Telecommunication Services, Chronological Time Series* (Geneva).
13. Organisation for Economic Co-operation and Development, *Development Co-operation Report* (Paris); web site www.oecd.org.
14. ________, *Geographical Distribution of Financial Flows to Aid Recipients* (Paris).
15. United Nations, *Demographic Yearbook 2004* (United Nations publication, Sales No. E/F.07.XIII.1).
16. ________, *Energy Statistics Yearbook 2004* (United Nations publication, Sales No. 07XVII.2).
17. ________, *Industrial Commodity Statistics Yearbook 2004* (United Nations publications, Sales No. B.06.XVII.14).
18. ________, *International Trade Statistics Yearbook 2005*, PDF (United Nations publication, Sales No. 07.XVII.7 H P).

Sources statistiques et références

A. Sources statistiques

1. "Carbon Dioxide Information Analysis Center, "*Global, Regional, and National CO2 Emissions Estimates from Fossil-Fuel Burning, Hydraulic Cement Production, and Gas Flaring*" (Oak Ridge, Tennessee, USA); site Web http://cdiac.esd.ornl.gov.
2. Organisation des Nations Unies pour l'alimentation et l'agriculture, *Annuaire Statistique de la FAO* (Rome); site Web http://faostat.fao.org.
3. ________, *Annuaire statistique des pêches, production de l'aquaculture* (Rome).
4. ________, *Annuaire statistique des pêches, captures* (Rome).
5. ________, *Evaluation des ressources forestières mondiales 2005* (Rome); site Web www.fao.org/forestry/fra2005.
6. Organisation de l'aviation civile internationale (Montréal); site Web www.icao.int.
7. Bureau international du Travail, *Annuaire des statistiques du Travail* (Genève); site Web http://laborsta.ilo.org.
8. Fonds monétaire international, "*Balance of Payments Statistics Yearbook*", (Washington, D.C.); site Web www.imf.org.
9. ________, *Statistiques financières internationales*, (Washington, D.C.).
10. Organisation internationale du sucre, *Annuaire du sucre* (Londres).
11. Union internationale des télécommunications, "*World Telecommunication Development Report*" (Genève); site Web www.itu.int.
12. ________, "*Yearbook of Statistics, Telecommunication Services, Chronological Time Series*" (Genève).
13. Organisation de Coopération et de Développement Economiques, *Coopération pour le développement, Rapport* (Paris); site Web www.oecd.org.
14. ________, *Répartition géographique des ressources financières allouées aux pays bénéficiaires de l'aide*, (Paris).
15. Nations Unies, *Annuaire démographique 2004* (publication des Nations Unies, No de vente E/F.07.XIII.1
16. ________, *Annuaire des statistiques de l'énergie 2004* (publication des Nations Unies, No de vente 07XVII.2).
17. ________, *Annuaire des statistiques industrielles par produit 2004* (publications des Nations Unies, No de vente B.06.XVII.14).

19. ________, *Monthly Bulletin of Statistics*, various issues up to March 2007 (United Nations publication, Series Q).
20. ________, *National Accounts Statistics: Main Aggregates and Detailed Tables, 2005* (United Nations publication, Sales No. 06.XVII.11)
21. ________, *Operational activities of the United Nations for international development cooperation, Report of the Secretary-General, Addendum, Comprehensive statistical data on operational activities for development for the year 2005 (A/62/74).*
22. ________, *World Population Prospects: The 2006 Revision* (United Nations publication, forthcoming).
23. ________, *World Urbanization Prospects: The 2005 Revision* (United Nations publication, Sales No. 08.XIII.2).
24. United Nations Educational, Scientific and Cultural Organization Institute for Statistics (Montreal); web site www.uis.unesco.org.
25. World Bank, *Global Development Finance*, vols. I and II, (Washington, D.C.); web site www.worldbank.org.
26. World Conservation Union (IUCN) / Species Survival Commission (SSC), Gland, Switzerland and Cambridge, United Kingdom, "IUCN Red List of Threatened Species", 2002, 2004 and 2006; web site www.iucnredlist.org.
27. World Tourism Organization, *Yearbook of Tourism Statistics, 2006 edition* (Madrid); web site www.world-tourism.org.

B. References

37. International Labour Office, *International Standard Classification of Occupations, Revised Edition 1968* (Geneva, 1969); revised edition, 1988, *ISCO-88* (Geneva, 1990).
38. International Monetary Fund, *Balance of Payments Manual, Fifth Edition* (Washington, D.C., 1993).
39. United Nations, *Classifications of Expenditure According to Purpose: Classification of the Functions of Government (COFOG), Classification of Individual Consumption According to Purpose (COICOP), Classification of the Purposes of Non-Profit Institutions Serving Households (COPNI), Classification of the Outlays of Producers According to Purpose (COPP),* Series M, No. 84 (United Nations publication, Sales No. E.00.XVII.6).
40. ________, *Energy Statistics: Definitions, Units of Measure and Conversion Factors*, Series F, No. 44 (United Nations publication, Sales No. E.86.XVII.21).
41. ________, *Energy Statistics: Manual for Developing Countries*, Series F, No. 56 (United Nations publication, Sales No. E.91.XVII.10).

18. ________, *Annuaire statistique du commerce international 2005*, PDF (publication des Nations Unies, No de vente 07.XVII.7 H P).
19. ________, *Bulletin mensuel de statistique*, différentes éditions, jusqu'à mars 2007 (publication des Nations Unies, Série Q).
20. ________, "*National Accounts Statistics: Main Aggregates and Detailed Tables, 2005*" (publication des Nations Unies, No de vente 06.XVII.11.
21. ________, *Activités opérationnelles du système des Nations Unies au service de la coopération internationale pour le développement, Rapport du Secrétaire général, Additif, Données statistiques globales sur les activités opérationnelles au service du développement pour 2005 (A/62/74).*
22. ________,"*World Population Prospects: The 2006 Revision*" (à venir).
23. ________, *World Urbanization Prospects: The 2005 Revision,* (No de vente 08.XIII.2)
24. Institut de statistique de l'Organisation des Nations Unies pour l'éducation, la science et la culture (Montréal); site Web www.uis.unesco.org.
25. Banque mondiale, "*Global Development Finance*, Vols. I et II," (Washington, D.C.).
26. Union mondiale pour la nature (UICN) / Commission de la sauvegarde des espèces, Gland, Suisse, et Cambridge, Royaume-Uni, "La liste rouge des espèces menacées de l'UICN", 2002, 2004 et 2006 ; site Web www.iucnredlist.org.
27. Organisation mondiale du tourisme, *l'Annuaire des statistiques du tourisme, 2006* (Madrid); site Web www.world-tourism.org.

B. Références

37. Organisation internationale du Travail, *Classification internationale type des professions, édition révisée* 1968 (Genève, 1969); édition révisée 1988, *CITP-88* (Genève, 1990).
38. Fonds monétaire international, *Manuel de la balance des paiements, cinquième édition* (Washington, D.C., 1993).
39. Nations Unies, "*Classifications of Expenditure According to Purpose: Classification of the Functions of Government (COFOG), Classification of Individual Consumption According to Purpose (COICOP), Classification of the Purposes of Non-Profit Institutions Serving Households (COPNI), Classification of the Outlays of Producers According to Purpose (COPP)*", Série M, No 84 (publication des Nations Unies, No de vente E. 00.XVII.6).

42. ________, *Handbook of Vital Statistics Systems and Methods*, vol. I, *Legal, Organization and Technical Aspects*, Series F, No. 35, vol. I (United Nations publication, Sales No. E.91.XVII.5).
43. ________, *Handbook on Social Indicators*, Studies in Methods, Series F, No. 49 (United Nations publication, Sales No. E.89.XVII.6).
44. ________, *International Recommendations for Industrial Statistics*, Series M, No. 48, Rev. 1 (United Nations publication, Sales No. E.83.XVII.8).
45. ________, *International Standard Industrial Classification of All Economic Activities*, Statistical Papers, Series M, No. 4, Rev. 2 (United Nations publication, Sales No. E.68.XVII.8); Rev. 3 (United Nations publication, Sales No. E.90.XVII.11).
46. ________, *International Trade Statistics: Concepts and Definitions*, Series M, No. 52, Rev. 1 (United Nations publication, Sales No. E.82.XVII.14).
47. ________, *Methods Used in Compiling the United Nations Price Indexes for External Trade*, volume 1, Statistical Papers, Series M, No. 82 (United Nations Publication, Sales No. E.87.XVII.4).
48. ________, *Principles and Recommendations for Population and Housing Censuses*, Statistical Papers, Series M, No. 67 (United Nations publication, Sales No. E.80.XVII.8).
49. ________, *Provisional Guidelines on Statistics of International Tourism*, Statistical Papers, Series M, No. 62 (United Nations publication, Sales No. E.78. XVII.6).
50. ________ and World Tourism Organization, *Recommendations on Tourism Statistics*, Statistical Papers, Series M, No. 83 (United Nations publication, Sales No. E.94.XVII.6).
51. ________, *Standard International Trade Classification, Revision 3*, Statistical Papers, Series M, No. 34, Rev. 3 (United Nations publication, Sales No. E.86.XVII.12), *Revision 2*, Series M, No. 34, Rev. 2 (United Nations publication), *Revision*, Series M, No. 34, Revision (United Nations publication, Sales No. E.61.XVII.6).
52. ________, *Supplement to the Statistical Yearbook and the Monthly Bulletin of Statistics, 1977*, Series S and Series Q, Supplement 2 (United Nations publication, Sales No. E.78.XVII.10).
53. ________, *System of National Accounts, Studies in Methods*, Series F, No. 2, Rev. 3 (United Nations publication, Sales No. E.69.XVII.3).
54. ________, *System of National Accounts 1993*, Studies in Methods, Series F, No. 2, Rev. 4 (United Nations publication, Sales No. E.94.XVII.4).

40. ________, *Statistiques de l'énergie: définitions, unités de mesures et facteurs de conversion*, Série F, No 44 (publication des Nations Unies, No de vente F.86.XVII.21).
41. ________, *Statistiques de l'énergie: Manuel pour les pays en développement*, Série F, No 56 (publication des Nations Unies, No de vente F.91.XVII.10).
42. ________, "*Handbook of Vital Statistics System and Methods*, Vol. 1, *Legal, Organization and Technical Aspects*", Série F, No 35, Vol. 1 (publication des Nations Unies, No de vente E.91.XVII.5).
43. ________, *Manuel des indicateurs sociaux*, Série F, No 49 (publication des Nations Unies, No de vente F.89.XVII.6).
44. ________, *Recommandations internationales concernant les statistiques industrielles*, Série M, No 48, Rev. 1 (publication des Nations Unies, No de vente F.83.XVII.8).
45. ________, *Classification internationale type, par industrie, de toutes les branches d'activité économique*, Série M, No 4, Rev. 2 (publication des Nations Unies, No de vente F.68.XVII.8); Rev. 3 (publication des Nations Unies, No de vente F.90.XVII.11).
46. ________, *Statistiques du commerce international: Concepts et définitions*, Série M, No 52, Rev. 1 (publication des Nations Unies, No de vente F.82.XVII.14).
47. ________, *Méthodes utilisées par les Nations Unies pour établir les indices des prix des produits de base entrant dans le commerce international*, Série M, No 82, Vol. 1 (publication des Nations Unies, No de vente F.87.XVII.4).
48. ________, *Principes et recommandations concernant les recensements de la population et de l'habitation*, Série M, No 67 (publication des Nations Unies, No de vente F.80.XVII.8).
49. ________, *Directives provisoires pour l'établissement des statistiques du tourisme international*, Série M, No 62 (publication des Nations Unies, No de vente 78.XVII.6).
50. ________ et l'Organisation mondiale du tourisme, "*Recommendations on Tourism Statistics*, Statistical Papers", Série M, No. 83 (publication des Nations Unies, No. de vente E.94.XVII.6).
51. ________, *Classification type pour le commerce international (troisième version révisée)*, Série M, No 34, Rev. 3 (publication des Nations Unies, No de vente F.86.XVII.12), *Révision 2*, Série M, No 34, Rev. 2 (publication des Nations Unies), *Révision*, Série M, No. 34, Révision (publication des Nations Unies, No de vente F.61.XVII.6).

55. ________, *Towards a System of Social and Demographic Statistics, Studies in Methods*, Series F, No. 18 (United Nations publication, Sales No. E.74.XVII.8).
56. ________, *World Weights and Measures* (United Nations publication, Sales No. E.66.XVII.3).
57. World Health Organization, *Manual of the International Statistical Classification of Diseases, Injuries and Causes of Death*, vol. 1 (Geneva, 1977).
58. World Tourism Organization, *Methodological Supplement to World Travel and Tourism Statistics* (Madrid, 1985).

52. ________, *Supplément à l'Annuaire statistique et au bulletin mensuel de statistique, 1977,* Série S et Série Q, supplément 2 (publication des Nations Unies, No de vente F.78.XVII.10).
53. ________, *Système de comptabilité nationale*, Série F, No 2, Rev. 3 (publication des Nations Unies, No de vente F.69.XVII.3).
54. ________, *Système de comptabilité nationale 1993*, Série F, No 2, Rev. 4 (publication des Nations Unies, No de vente F.94.XVII.4).
55. ________, *Vers un système de statistiques démographiques et sociales, Etudes méthodologiques,* Série F, No 18 (publication des Nations Unies, No. de vente F.74.XVII.8).
56. ________, "*World Weights and Measures*" (publication des Nations Unies, No. de vente E.66.XVII.3).
57. Organisation mondiale de la santé, *Manuel de la classification statistique internationale des maladies, traumatismes et causes de décès*, Vol. 1 (Genève, 1977).
58. Organisation mondiale du tourisme, *Supplément méthodologique aux statistiques des voyages et du tourisme mondiaux* (Madrid, 1985).

Index

Note: References to tables are indicated by **boldface** type. For citations or organizations, *see* Index of Organizations.

D

E

F

L

M

N

O

P

Q

R

U

V

W

Y

Index of organizations

W

كيفية الحصول على منشورات الأمم المتحدة

يمكن الحصول على منشورات الأمم المتحدة من المكتبات ودور التوزيع في جميع أنحاء العالم . استعلم عنها من المكتبة التي تتعامل معها أو اكتب إلى : الأمم المتحدة ، قسم البيع في نيويورك أو في جنيف .

如何购取联合国出版物

联合国出版物在全世界各地的书店和经售处均有发售。请向书店询问或写信到纽约或日内瓦的联合国销售组。

HOW TO OBTAIN UNITED NATIONS PUBLICATIONS

United Nations publications may be obtained from bookstores and distributors throughout the world. Consult your bookstore or write to: United Nations, Sales Section, New York or Geneva.

COMMENT SE PROCURER LES PUBLICATIONS DES NATIONS UNIES

Les publications des Nations Unies sont en vente dans les librairies et les agences dépositaires du monde entier. Informez-vous auprès de votre libraire ou adressez-vous à : Nations Unies, Section des ventes, New York ou Genève.

КАК ПОЛУЧИТЬ ИЗДАНИЯ ОРГАНИЗАЦИИ ОБЪЕДИНЕННЫХ НАЦИЙ

Издания Организации Объединенных Наций можно купить в книжных магазинах и агентствах во всех районах мира. Наводите справки об изданиях в вашем книжном магазине или пишите по адресу: Организация Объединенных Наций, Секция по продаже изданий, Нью-Йорк или Женева.

COMO CONSEGUIR PUBLICACIONES DE LAS NACIONES UNIDAS

Las publicaciones de las Naciones Unidas están en venta en librerías y casas distribuidoras en todas partes del mundo. Consulte a su librero o diríjase a: Naciones Unidas, Sección de Ventas, Nueva York o Ginebra.

Litho in United Nations, New York
07-30953—December 2007—4,460
ISBN 978-92-1-061228-9
ISSN 0082-8459

United Nations publication
Sales No. E/F.07.XVII.1
ST/ESA/STAT/SER.S/27